iGAAP 2009

IFRS Reporting in the UK

Third edition

iGAAP 2009

IFRS Reporting in the UK

Third edition

Principal authors

Phil Barden
(*Team leader*)
Veronica Poole
Norma Hall
Ken Rigelsford
Andrew Spooner

Deloitte & Touche LLP

LexisNexis®

Published by LexisNexis, a Division of Reed Elsevier (UK) Ltd, Halsbury House, 35 Chancery Lane, London, WC2A 1EL, and London House, 20–22 East London Street, Edinburgh EH7 4BQ

ISBN 978 0 7545 3581 2

British Library Cataloguing-in-Publication Data

A catalogue record of this book is available from the British Library.

Typset by Letterpart Ltd, Reigate, Surrey

Printed in the UK by CPI William Clowes Beccles NR34 7TL

Foreword by Ken Wild

Welcome to our third guide to IFRS reporting in the UK

Two years ago, to give us all a bit of a breather, the IASB made a commitment not to require the adoption of any new Standards before 1 January 2009. Nevertheless, the intervening period has seen the issue of a number of Standards, Interpretations and minor amendments, and as we approach 2009, there are more significant changes on the horizon, not least the completion of convergence with US GAAP. In addition, the impact of the credit crunch and a perception in some quarters that accounting standards have aggravated this global crisis mean that our respite seems well and truly over.

In response to the current economic environment, the IASB is accelerating the completion of a number of projects on its agenda, including those relating to off-balance sheet vehicles, fair value in illiquid markets and disclosures about valuations. These projects will lead in turn to revised or new Standards. Hopefully they will also achieve the IASB's aim of reducing complexity, particularly around financial instruments. And there are numerous Standards, Interpretations and amendments with 2009 effective dates already in issue, just waiting for endorsement!

The EU endorsement process continues to be a threat to the goal of a single set of high quality standards used throughout the world. There is now likely to be at least one instance where endorsement will be delayed beyond an Interpretation's effective date. Let's hope this doesn't set a dangerous precedent, which leaves Europe out of kilter with the rest of the global business community.

Across the pond, the SEC has already eliminated the requirement for foreign private issuers using IFRS to reconcile to US GAAP and recently unveiled a roadmap which could see even US companies switching from US GAAP to IFRS by 2014.

IFRS is now used for public reporting purposes in over 100 countries, ranging from Australia to Zimbabwe. Other countries are expected to follow in the next few years, including Chile, Korea, Brazil and Canada. By 2011, a clear majority of the largest global companies could be using IFRS.

But will it be IFRS as we know it? Global convergence will only be successful if it is governed by a coherent set of principles rather than a vast book of rules. However, the convergence of the accounting standards themselves may be relatively easy compared to ensuring that IFRS is interpreted and applied in a globally consistent manner, rather than as a variety of local versions. Only if a common financial reporting language is achieved in practice, will investors and other interested parties be able to examine and compare companies in a transparent and equal way. We hope this book will play its part in achieving that goal. It is a practical guide to tackling the challenges which applying IFRS entails and draws upon the expertise of IFRS specialists from Hong Kong, South Africa, Paris, Copenhagen, Australia, the United States, the UK and beyond. It is no surprise that the book is larger than ever – we have increased our interpretative guidance once again, as our thinking on key issues and complexities has developed.

Ken Wild

Global Leader – International Accounting Standards
Deloitte

Acknowledgements

Our thanks to the members of the UK technical department and the following Deloitte IFRS Centres of Excellence for their assistance in writing, reviewing and otherwise contributing to this book:

Copenhagen	Denmark
Hong Kong	China
Johannesburg	South Africa
London	United Kingdom
Melbourne	Australia
Montreal	Canada
Paris	France
Wilton	United States

Glossary of terms and abbreviations

the 1985 Act	Companies Act 1985, as amended
the 2006 Act	Companies Act 2006, as amended
ABI	Association of British Insurers
AC	Acquiring company
Accounting Regulations	The Large and Medium-sized Companies and Groups (Accounts and Reports) Regulations 2008 (Statutory Instrument 2008 no.410)
the Act	Either the Companies Act 1985 or the Companies Act 2006, as amended, whichever is applicable in the context
the Acts	Both the Companies Act 1985 and the Companies Act 2006, as amended
AFS	Available-for-sale
AGM	Annual general meeting
AIM	Alternative Investment Market
AIM company	A company, any class of whose securities is quoted on the Alternative Investment Market
APB	The UK Auditing Practices Board which issues auditing standards, practice notes and bulletins. Refers to both the 'old APB' which was a committee of the Consultative Committee of Accountancy Bodies and the 'new APB' which is a subsidiary of the FRC
ARC	The Accounting Regulatory Committee which advises the European Commission on endorsement of IFRSs
ARD	Accounting reference date
ARP	Accounting reference period
ASB	The UK Accounting Standards Board, which issues FRSs, FREDs, etc.
BERR	Department for Business, Enterprise & Regulatory Reform
Cadbury Code	Code of Best Practice, issued by the Cadbury Committee (now superseded)
Cadbury Committee	Committee on the Financial Aspects of Corporate Governance

CESR	The Committee of European Securities Regulators
CGU	Cash-generating unit
Combined Code	The corporate governance code issued by the Financial Services Authority. References to the Combined Code are to the 2006 Code unless otherwise stated
Commission	European Commission
DTI	Department of Trade and Industry (now BERR)
DTR	The Disclosure and Transparency Rules of the FSA Handbook
EASDAQ	European Association of Securities Dealers Automated Quotation System
EBT	Employee benefit trust
EC	European Commission
ED	Exposure Draft
EEA	European Economic Area (i.e. the EU plus Norway, Iceland and Liechtenstein)
EFRAG	The European Financial Reporting Advisory Group, a private sector body which makes recommendations to the European Commission's Accounting Regulatory Committee
EPS	Earnings per share
ESOP	Employee share ownership plan
EU	European Union
FASB	Financial Accounting Standards Board (USA)
FIFO	First in, first out
FRAG	Refers to pronouncements of the former Financial Reporting and Auditing Group (of the ICAEW)
FRC	Financial Reporting Council
FRED	Financial Reporting Exposure Draft, issued by the ASB
FRRP	Financial Reporting Review Panel
FRS	Financial Reporting Standard, issued by the ASB
FRSSE	Financial Reporting Standard for Smaller Entities, issued by the ASB
FSA	Financial Services Authority
FTSE 100	Financial Times Stock Exchange top 100 companies (share index)
FVTPL	Fair value through profit or loss

G4 + 1	A group comprising members of the standard–setting bodies of the UK, USA, Australia, Canada and New Zealand. The group was disbanded in February 2001. Representatives of IASC attended as observers.
GAAP	Generally accepted accounting practice
GN	Guidance Note, issued by the Institute and Faculty of Actuaries
Greenbury Committee	Study Group on Directors' Remuneration
Hampel Committee	Committee on Corporate Governance
HMRC	HM Revenue & Customs
HTM	Held-to-maturity
IAS	International Accounting Standard
IASB	International Accounting Standards Board
IASC	International Accounting Standards Committee, predecessor to the IASB
ICAEW	The Institute of Chartered Accountants in England & Wales
ICAS	The Institute of Chartered Accountants of Scotland
ICSA	Institute of Chartered Secretaries and Administrators
IFRIC	International Financial Reporting Interpretations Committee of the IASB (also refers to individual interpretations issued by the IFRIC)
IFRS	International Financial Reporting Standard
IRR	Internal rate of return
ISA	International Standard on Auditing, issued by the International Auditing and Assurance Standards Board
ISA (UK and Ireland)	International Standard on Auditing as amended for use in the UK and Ireland, issued by the Auditing Practices Board
JANE	Joint arrangement that is not an entity
JCE	Jointly controlled entity
JV	Joint venture
LIBOR	London Inter-Bank Offer Rate
LIFFE	London International Financial Futures and Options Exchange
LIFO	Last in, first out

Listed company	A company, any class of whose securities is listed (i.e. admitted to the Official List of the UK Listing Authority)
Listing Rules	The listing rules made by the competent authority (see UK Listing Authority) for the purposes of Part VI of the Financial Services and Markets Act 2000 and published in the book entitled "The Listing Rules" as from time to time amended
LTIP	Long-term incentive plan
NASDAQ	National Association of Securities Dealers Automated Quotation System
NRV	Net realisable value
NI	National insurance
OFR	Operating and financial review
P & L	Profit and loss account
PAYE	Pay as you earn
PFI	Private finance initiative
PLUS-listed company	A company, any class of whose securities is listed on the PLUS-listed market, and which therefore follows the FSA's Listing Rules and Disclosure and Transparency Rules
PLUS-quoted company	A company, any class of whose securities is quoted on the PLUS-quoted market, and which therefore follows the PLUS Rules for Issuers
Review Panel	Financial Reporting Review Panel
RICS	The Royal Institution of Chartered Surveyors
RIE	Recognised investment exchange
ROI	Return on investment
RPI	Retail price index
Rutteman guidance	The guidance on internal financial control, and reporting issued by the Rutteman Working group in 1994 (now superseded by the Turnbull guidance)
SAS	Statement of Auditing Standards, issued by the Auditing Practices Board, now superseded by ISA (UK and Ireland)
SARG	Standards Advice Review Group, established by the European Commission to review endorsement advice from EFRAG
SAYE	Save as you earn
SEC	Securities and Exchange Commission (USA)
SFAS	Statement of Financial Accounting Standards, issued by the FASB

SI	Statutory instrument – the government order which amends or supplements legislation. In the context of this manual, these will normally be amendments to the Companies Acts
SIC	Standing Interpretations Committee, predecessor to IFRIC (also refers to individual interpretations issued by SIC)
Small Companies Accounting Regulations	The Small Companies and Groups (Accounts and Directors' Report) Regulations 2008 (Statutory Instrument 2008 no.409)
Smith guidance	The guidance issued by the FRC on audit committees
SORIE	Statement of Recognised Income and Expense
SORP	Statement of Recommended Practice, which gives recommendations of accounting practices for specialised industries or sectors
SPE	Special purpose entity
SSAP	Statement of Standard Accounting Practice, promulgated by the ASB
TC	Target company
TECH	Technical Release
TSR	Total shareholder return
Turnbull guidance	The final guidance issued by the Turnbull Committee to provide guidance to assist listed companies in implementing the requirements of the Combined Code relating to internal control. Initially issued in September 1999 and revised in October 2005.
UK Listing Authority, UKLA	The FSA acting in its capacity as the competent authority for the purposes of Part VI of the Financial Services and Markets Act 2000
UITF	Urgent Issues Task Force of the ASB
UITF Abstract	Consensus pronouncement issued by the UITF
VAT	Value added tax
WEEE	Waste electrical and electronic equipment
WE&EE Directive	The European Union's Directive on Waste Electrical and Electronic Equipment
WEEE Regulations	The Waste Electrical and Electronic Equipment Regulations 2006, which incorporated the provisions of the WE&EE Directive into UK law

Summary of contents

Table of contents

Introduction

1 Scope and objectives of this manual

The objective of this manual is to introduce and explain the financial reporting requirements that apply to UK companies that are required (or choose) to report under International Financial Reporting Standards (IFRSs). As explained in **section 3** below, IFRSs are defined to include the numbered IFRSs issued by the International Accounting Standards Board (IASB), International Accounting Standards (IASs) originally issued by its predecessor body (as amended) and approved interpretations of these standards. The expression is used in this broad sense in this manual unless the context requires otherwise.

The decision of the European Union (EU) to mandate the use of IFRSs for certain companies led to a huge amount of activity. The International Accounting Standards Board (IASB) undertook an ambitious programme to replace or update existing standards to create a 'stable platform' for 2005; the European Commission (the Commission) reviewed IASB standards and guidance under its endorsement mechanism; and UK legislation was drafted to allow most other companies to adopt IFRSs. Although the first wave of transition to IFRSs is now complete, many practical questions will continue to arise and interpretation of IFRSs will continue to evolve as new issues are identified and solutions developed by those preparing and auditing financial statements. Solutions that do not appear contentious against a UK background may, nevertheless, be challenged by those with a different background. The aim of global consistency is a huge challenge. It must therefore be recognised that the views expressed in this manual remain subject to change.

2 IFRS and UK specific material

The structure of this manual is as follows:

- **chapters 2** to **44** and **appendices 1** and **2** deal with the framework and accounting standards issued by the IASB and interpretations of those standards. Where there are specific UK requirements relating to a topic covered by an international accounting standard, they are dealt with in the same chapter or appendix; and

- **chapters 45** to **52** deal with other requirements that apply to UK companies reporting under IFRSs.

Transitional requirements are discussed for standards that have become effective for periods beginning after 1 January 2007. In addition, where IFRS 1 requires compliance with the transitional requirements in standards, the relevant requirements are explained.

The format of the manual has been devised to give guidance on reporting and accounting matters as clearly as possible. Text is highlighted differently to reflect whether it represents official or interpretative material and whether it is specific to UK companies. Accordingly, in **chapters 2** to **44** and **appendices 1** and **2**:

- requirements drawn from official IASB material are shown in unshaded text;

- interpretative material supplementing the IASB guidance is highlighted by grey shading; and

UK
- *any requirement or other guidance that is specific to UK companies is highlighted in a box denoted by the letters UK in a circle.*

Chapters 45 to **52** are concerned only with requirements specific to UK companies. Accordingly, in those chapters:

- requirements drawn from official material are shown in unshaded text; and

- interpretative material is highlighted by grey shading.

Except where the context requires otherwise, interpretative examples follow the convention often adopted by the IASB of referring to years as 20X1, 20X2 etc. rather than specifying real calendar years. In such examples, although 20X3 follows 20X2, no further significance attaches to the final digit. Thus, subject to context, 20X1 might represent 2009 or any other relevant year.

3 References and abbreviations used

International Financial Reporting Standards are defined in IAS 1 *Presentation of Financial Statements* as Standards and Interpretations adopted by the IASB. They comprise:

- International Financial Reporting Standards;
- International Accounting Standards; and
- Interpretations developed by the International Financial Reporting Interpretations Committee (IFRIC) or the former Standing Interpretations Committee (SIC).

These are referred to collectively in this manual as 'IFRSs'.

EU legislation and the Companies Act both refer to 'international accounting standards' but define them to have this wider meaning, subject to the EU adoption process described at **1.2** in **chapter 1**.

References to International Financial Reporting Standards, International Accounting Standards, IFRIC Interpretations and SIC Interpretations are indicated as follows:

IFRS 2.19	Paragraph 19 of IFRS 2
IAS 19.13	Paragraph 13 of IAS 19
IFRIC 1.2	Paragraph 2 of IFRIC Interpretation 1
SIC-27.3	Paragraph 3 of SIC Interpretation 27

References to material accompanying International Financial Reporting Standards, International Accounting Standards, IFRIC Interpretations and SIC Interpretations are indicated as follows:

IAS 39.AG4	Paragraph AG4 of the application guidance to IAS 39
IFRS 2.B18	Paragraph B18 of appendix B to IFRS 2
IFRIC 13.BC21	Paragraph BC21 of the Basis for Conclusions accompanying IFRIC 13
IFRS 4.IG3	Paragraph IG3 of the guidance on implementing IFRS 4
IAS 32.IE32	Paragraph IE32 of the illustrative examples accompanying IAS 32

This manual deals with the financial reporting requirements of the Companies Act 2006 and also the Companies Act 1985. All references to 'the 2006 Act' are to the UK Companies Act 2006 as amended by statutory instruments issued up to 31 July 2008. All references to 'the 1985 Act' in this manual are to the UK Companies Act 1985 as amended by the Companies Act 1989, other primary legislation and statutory instruments issued up to 31 July 2008. Unless otherwise stated, all references to 'the Act' are to both the 2006 Act and the 1985 Act.

Part 15 of the 2006 Act 'Accounts and reports' and related Regulations came into effect for periods beginning on or after 6 April 2008, except where otherwise stated. They replaced all of the equivalent requirements of the 1985 Act. Most of the requirements are unchanged but there are some significant exceptions. Most of the detailed requirements are now to be found in Regulations rather than in the primary legislation. Unless otherwise stated, all references to 'the Accounting Regulations' are to 'The Large and Medium-sized Companies and Groups (Accounts and Reports) Regulations 2008' which were made on 19 February 2008 (Statutory Instrument 2008 no.410).

References to the requirements of the 2006 and 1985 Acts and of the Accounting Regulations are indicated as follows:

CA 2006 s415(2)	Section 415 subsection (2) of the 2006 Act
CA 1985 s234(2)	Section 234 subsection (2) of the 1985 Act
CA 2006 Sch. 7: 3(1)	Paragraph 3, subparagraph (1) of Schedule 7 to the 2006 Act
CA 1985 Sch. 7: 1(2)	Paragraph 1, subparagraph (2) of Schedule 7 to the 1985 Act
Acc Regs Sch. 7: 2(1)	Paragraph 2, subparagraph (1) of Schedule 7 to the Accounting Regulations

References to UK accounting standards, UITF Abstracts, the Listing Rules issued by the UK Listing Authority, the Disclosure and Transparency Rules of the FSA Handbook, and Technical Releases are indicated as follows:

FRS 7.15	Paragraph 15 of FRS 7
SSAP 20.20	Paragraph 20 of SSAP 20
UITF 26.3	Paragraph 3 of UITF Abstract 26
LR 9.8.4R	Listing Rule 9.8.4
DTR 4.2.3	Disclosure and Transparency Rule 4.2.3
TECH 01/08 2.10	Paragraph 2.10 of Technical Release 01/08

A glossary of abbreviations used in the text is presented at the front of this manual.

4 Contents of this edition

This edition of the manual includes the reporting and accounting requirements contained in:

- the Companies Act 1985, as amended by the Companies Act 1989 and by statutory instruments up to 31 July 2008;
- the Companies Act 2006, as amended by statutory instruments up to 31 July 2008;
- other relevant statutory instruments issued up to 31 July 2008;
- IFRSs 1 to 8;

- IASs 1, 2, 7, 8, 10 to 12, 14, 16 to 21, 23, 24, 27 to 29, 31 to 34 and 36 to 41;
- SIC Interpretations 7, 10, 12, 13, 15, 21, 25, 27, 29, 31 and 32;
- IFRIC Interpretations 1, 2 and 4 to 16; and
- the Listing Rules and Disclosure and Transparency Rules issued by the UK Listing Authority as at 31 July 2008.

4.1 Pension schemes

The accounting requirements for UK pension schemes differ in certain key respects from those for companies. In addition, at the time of writing, it appears unlikely that UK pension schemes will adopt international accounting standards in the near future. Accordingly, this manual does not address the requirements of IAS 26 *Accounting and Reporting by Retirement Benefit Plans*.

4.2 Specialised industries

This manual does not deal with certain requirements and issues that will affect companies in specialised industries, particularly banking, insurance and the extractive industries. In particular:

- the manual does not address the requirements of IAS 30 *Disclosures in the Financial Statements of Banks and Similar Financial Institutions*, which was superseded, for years beginning on or after 1 January 2007, by IFRS 7 *Financial Instruments: Disclosures* which has wider application;
- although **chapters 13** to **22** provide an overview of the requirements of IAS 32 *Financial Instruments: Presentation*, IAS 39 *Financial Instruments: Recognition and Measurement* and IFRS 7 *Financial Instruments: Disclosures*, they do not address some of the more complex issues (particularly in the area of hedging) that may affect banks and similar financial institutions; and
- the manual does not address the requirements of IFRS 6 *Exploration for and Evaluation of Mineral Resources*.

The specialised issues facing insurance companies are beyond the scope of this manual but the requirements of IFRS 4 *Insurance Contracts* are discussed in **chapter 44**. Those requirements are of wider application, because they specify how all entities should determine whether certain arrangements are within the scope of IFRS 4 or of other standards such as IAS 39.

1 UK regulatory background

1 Sources of accounting requirements and guidance

This section of the chapter discusses the sources of accounting requirements for UK companies including standards issued by the IASB, the role of the European Commission in endorsing those standards and additional requirements stemming from UK law. The remainder of the chapter covers:

(a) entities required to use IFRSs for consolidated financial statements (**section 2**);

(b) UK entities permitted to use IFRSs for consolidated and individual financial statements (**section 3**); and

(c) enforcement of accounting requirements (**section 4**).

1.1 International Accounting Standards Board

1.1.1 Introduction

The International Accounting Standards Board (IASB) is an independent body that issues International Financial Reporting Standards (IFRSs). Since it began work in 2001, it has issued a number of new IFRSs. In addition, it has adopted all of the International Accounting Standards (IASs) issued by its predecessor body, the International Accounting Standards Committee (IASC). Most of these have subsequently been amended or superseded. IAS 15 *Information Reflecting the Effects of Changing Prices* was withdrawn.

The International Financial Reporting Interpretations Committee (IFRIC) is a committee that assists the IASB, with the aim of providing timely guidance on newly identified financial reporting issues not specifically addressed in IASB Standards or issues where there may be unsatisfactory or conflicting interpretations. It was established in March 2002, replacing the Standing Interpretations Committee (SIC), its predecessor. Upon its inception, the IASB adopted extant SIC Interpretations, but many have since been amended or superseded by new or revised Standards.

As part of due process, the IASB and IFRIC publish Exposure Drafts and draft Interpretations respectively. Such drafts are issued for comment and their proposals are subject to revision. Accordingly, until the effective date of an IFRS or IFRIC Interpretation, the requirements of any existing Standard or Interpretation remain in force. Changes in accounting policies are considered at **3.2** in **chapter 4**, including issues about early adoption of new standards and the status of proposals in Exposure Drafts when considering such changes.

Further details about the IASB can be found on its website at:

http://www.iasb.org

1.1.2 The 'stable platform' of standards

In July 2006, the IASB announced that it will not require the application of new IFRSs under development or major amendments to existing IFRSs before 1 January 2009. The IASB noted that this will provide four years of stability for those companies that adopted IFRSs in 2005. Companies will, however, be permitted to adopt the new standards on a voluntary basis before their effective dates. Interpretations by IFRIC and minor amendments to correct problems identified in practice are not subject to this delay.

The IASB also announced, at the same time, that it will allow at least one year between the date of publication of a major new standard (or a major change to an existing standard) and the date when implementation is required. This policy will allow time for translations and implementation of new standards into practice and law.

1.1.3 Convergence with US GAAP and the 'roadmap'

After a joint meeting in September 2002, the IASB and the US Financial Accounting Standards Board (FASB) issued their 'Norwalk agreement' in which each acknowledged their commitment to the development of high quality, compatible accounting standards that could be used for both domestic and cross-border financial reporting. At that meeting, the FASB and the IASB pledged to use their best efforts to make their existing standards fully compatible as soon as practicable and to co-ordinate their future work programmes to ensure that once achieved, compatibility is maintained. At subsequent joint meetings, the FASB and the IASB reaffirmed their commitment to the convergence of US Generally Accepted Accounting Principles (US GAAP) and IFRSs. A common set of high quality global standards remains the long-term strategic priority of both the FASB and the IASB.

In February 2006, the IASB and the FASB published 'A roadmap for convergence between IFRSs and US GAAP – 2006/2008'. This set out a series of goals to be achieved by 2008. These goals did not require anything like complete convergence between US GAAP and IFRSs. They envisaged some limited changes to certain standards and the publication of 'due process documents' which may be only discussion papers in some cases. Nevertheless, achievement of these goals was seen as an important factor (but not the only one) in the removal of the requirement for SEC registrants reporting under IFRSs to reconcile to US GAAP.

In November 2007, the Securities and Exchange Commission (SEC) voted to allow foreign private issuers to prepare their financial statements using International Financial Reporting Standards (IFRSs) without reconciling to US GAAP. The new rule is effective for years ending after 15 November 2007.

The SEC voted that, with one exception, a foreign private issuer's financial statements must fully comply with the IASB's version of IFRSs. The exception relates to foreign private issuers that use the version of IFRSs that includes the European Commission's 'carve-out' for IAS 39, Financial Instruments: Recognition and Measurement (see **1.2.4** below). The Commission voted to allow such issuers to prepare their financial statements using that version for a two-year period as long as a reconciliation to the IASB's version of IFRSs is provided. After the two-year period, these issuers will either have to use the IASB's version of IFRSs or provide a reconciliation to US GAAP.

Most of the goals set out in the 2006 Memorandum of Understanding have now been reached so the IASB and FASB met in April 2008 to discuss an updated Work Plan to help direct the work plan of the two boards through to at least 2011. The updated Work Plan was published in June 2008.

Further details about the 'roadmap' and the related projects can be found on the IASB website.

1.2 Role of the European Commission

1.2.1 Introduction

In June 2002, the European Commission adopted a Regulation ('the IAS Regulation') [EC Regulation No.1606/2002] requiring certain companies governed by the law of a member state, for each financial year starting on or after 1 January 2005, to prepare their consolidated financial statements in accordance with 'international accounting standards'. The companies concerned are those with their securities admitted to a 'regulated market' in any member state at the end of the reporting period. The IAS Regulation explains that 'international accounting standards' means International Accounting Standards, International Financial Reporting Standards and related interpretations issued or adopted by the IASB and endorsed by the EU. Accordingly, the European Commission applies an 'endorsement mechanism' to decide whether to endorse each standard by reference to a number of qualitative criteria (understandability, relevance, reliability, comparability, the 'European public good' and the need to give a 'true and fair view'). The endorsement mechanism is described at **1.2.2** below and its implications for annual and interim reporting is discussed at **1.2.6** and **1.2.7**. The application of the requirement for certain companies to prepare their consolidated financial statements in accordance with IFRSs is described more fully in **section 2** below.

1.2.2 The endorsement mechanism

The effect of the IAS Regulation is to give the force of EU law to adopted IFRSs. The European Commission's legal advice was that it would not be possible to delegate the setting of EU law to a private sector body (such as the IASB) that was not democratically accountable. Therefore a mechanism was established to endorse each IFRS for use in the EU.

This process has both a technical level and a political level. The technical merits of each IFRS and IFRIC interpretation are considered by the European Financial Reporting Advisory Group (EFRAG) which is a private sector body. EFRAG makes recommendations to the Accounting Regulatory Committee (ARC). The Chairman of the UK Accounting Standards Board participates in the work of the Technical Expert Group (TEG) of EFRAG, as an observer with full rights to participate in debates. Details of the work of EFRAG can be found on its website at:

http://www.efrag.org

ARC comprises representatives of the member state governments of the EU and advises the Commission. The UK is represented by BERR (previously the DTI). The final decision on endorsement is formally made by the Commission.

In 2006, the Commission set up a Standards Advice Review Group. The role of the group is to advise the Commission, before it takes a decision on endorsement, on whether EFRAG's opinion on endorsement is well-balanced and objective. The group should normally deliver its opinion within three weeks of EFRAG's opinion.

The IAS Regulation states that, for a standard to be adopted, it must first meet the basic requirements of the Fourth and Seventh Company Law Directives, that is to say that its application results in a true and fair view of the financial position and performance of the entity. This appears non-contentious and the IAS Regulation notes that this principle should be considered without implying a strict conformity with each and every provision of those Directives (i.e. Schedules 1, 6 and 10 to the Accounting Regulations made using the powers conferred by the 2006 Act, previously Schedules 4 and 4A to the 1985 Act in the UK). Each standard must also meet the basic criteria as to the quality of information required for financial statements to be useful to users. But perhaps more controversially, each standard must be 'conducive to the European public good' which adds a political dimension to the decision.

Regulations adopting standards and interpretations legally come into force three days after publication in the Official Journal of the EU. The length of the process from publication of a standard or interpretation by the IASB until the publication of the related Regulation in the Official Journal allowing for translation into the official languages of the EU, preparation of the 'effects study', consideration by EFRAG and by ARC, formal adoption by the Commission, consideration by the European Parliament and publication in the Official Journal varies depending on the standard or interpretation. IFRIC 12 has been awaiting EU endorsement for nearly 2 years. Concern had been expressed to the Commission about the time taken by this process and discussions have taken place at the Accounting Regulatory Committee about how the process might be speeded up. However, following an amendment to the process of endorsement in March 2008 it is likely that the time taken to adopt a new or amended IFRS or interpretation for use in Europe will increase. The main changes, compared to the previous regulatory procedure, consist of:

(a) the systematic consultation of both the European Parliament (EP) and the Council of the EU; and

(b) substantially broadened right of oversight of the EP and the Council. Furthermore, the EP and the Council both have a longer, three month oversight period, starting when all linguistic versions of a draft Regulation endorsing IFRS or Interpretation have been submitted to them.

Both the EP and Council may oppose proposals provided by the European Commission (EC) on the following grounds:

(a) the proposal by the EC exceeds the implementing powers provided:

(b) the proposal is not compatible with the aim or the content of the IAS Regulation: or

(c) the proposal does not respect the principles of subsidiarity or proportionality under the Treaty.

In the case of opposition by any of the two parties (EP or Council), the proposal by the EC cannot be adopted.

The Commission has stated that if a standard or interpretation is endorsed and published in the Official Journal after the end of the reporting period but before the date of approval of the financial statements, it can be treated as endorsed for the purposes of those financial statements if application prior to the date of endorsement is permitted by both the Regulation endorsing the document and the related IASB document. This statement was made at the 30 November 2005 meeting of the Accounting Regulatory Committee and can be found at:

http://ec.europa.eu./internal_market/accounting/docs/arc/2005-11-30-extract-summary-record_en.pdf

At its meeting on 30 November 2005, the Accounting Regulatory Committee considered the appropriate formulation for expressing compliance with the IAS Regulation. It concluded that reference should be made to 'IFRSs as adopted by the European Union' although the expression 'IFRSs as adopted for use in the European Union' had previously been commonly used.

1.2.3 Progress with endorsement

The EFRAG website (see **1.2.2** above) contains a summary of the status of the endorsement process including the expected date of endorsement, which is updated regularly. The 1 August 2008 Endorsement Status report on the EFRAG website lists the following standards, amendments to standards and interpretations as issued by the IASB but not yet adopted by the EU:

Standard	**EFRAG expected date of endorsement**
IFRS 3 (revised January 2008) *Business Combinations*	Q1 2009
Interpretations	
IFRIC 12 *Service Concession Arrangements* (November 2006)	Q1 2009
IFRIC 13 *Customer Loyalty Programmes* (June 2007)	End 2008

Standard	EFRAG expected date of endorsement
IFRIC 14 *IAS 19 – The Limit on a Defined Benefit Asset, Minimum Funding Requirements and their Interaction* (July 2007)	End 2008
IFRIC 15 *Agreements for the Construction of Real Estate* (July 2008)	Q1 2009
IFRIC 16 *Hedges of a Net Investment in a Foreign Operation* (July 2008)	Q1 2009
Amendments	
Amendment to IAS 23 Borrowing Costs (March 2007)	End 2008
Amendments to IAS 1 Presentation of Financial Statements (September 2007)	End 2008
Amendment to IFRS 2 Share-based Payment: Vesting Conditions and Cancellations (January 2008)	End 2008
Amendments to IAS 27 Consolidated and Separate Financial Statements (January 2008)	Q1 2009
Amendments to IAS 32 and IAS 1 Puttable financial instruments and obligations arising on liquidation (February 2008)	Q1 2009
Improvements to IFRS (May 2008)	Q1 2009
Amendments to IFRS 1 and IAS 27 Cost of an investment in a subsidiary, jointly controlled entity or associate (May 2008)	Q1 2009
IAS 39 Financial Instruments: Recognition and Measurement: Eligible Hedged Items (July 2008)	To be confirmed

There is a difference, relating to hedge accounting, between the version of IAS 39 *Financial Instruments: Recognition and Measurement* that was endorsed by the EU and the one issued by the IASB. This is known as the IAS 39 'carve out' and is described at **1.2.4** below.

1.2.4 *The IAS 39 'carve out'*

In November 2004, the European Commission endorsed a version of IAS 39 which had certain paragraphs deleted. This is commonly referred to as the IAS 39 'carve out'. The paragraphs related to certain hedge accounting requirements and the so called 'fair value option'. Guidance issued by the Commission in November 2003 appeared to suggest that the Commission had only the power to accept or reject a standard as a whole. However, the Commission subsequently obtained legal advice that it can 'decide on the partial application of a standard where such standard covers several accounting areas which are distinct and separable'. The reasons for this and the implications were set out in an Explanatory Memorandum published by the Commission on 24 September 2004.

In December 2004, the ASB published its own guidance on the application of IAS 39 by entities preparing their financial statements in accordance with EU-adopted IFRSs. This guidance can be found on the ASB's website *www.frc.org.uk/asb* attached to Press Notice PN 262.

In June 2005, the IASB issued the amendment to IAS 39 *The Fair Value Option*, which restricts use of the fair value option for financial assets and financial liabilities. The amendment was adopted by the Commission on 15 November 2005, with adoption being retroactive to 1 January 2005. However, although the carve out for the fair value option has been removed, the carve out for certain hedging requirements is expected to remain until the disagreements on this subject have been resolved.

The differences between the carved out version of IAS 39 and the full version are of most significance for banks and similar financial institutions. Such companies will need to consider these matters carefully and take their own advice. It is possible for any company to comply with both versions of the standard by complying with the hedge accounting requirements in the full version of the standard as issued by the IASB. This is what the ASB recommended UK companies to do.

1.2.5 *The status of standards that have not been endorsed*

A company can voluntarily comply with an IFRS that has not been adopted by the EU provided that it does not conflict with a standard that has been adopted. If a standard is not adopted, it does not appear to be possible under EU law for a member state government or any other body to require compliance with its requirements in annual financial statements. This is because the philosophy behind the IAS Regulation is one of 'maximum harmonisation' to achieve a level playing field for companies throughout Europe. Guidance published by the European Commission in November 2003 explains the issue as follows.

> 'In a principle-based system such as IASs there will always exist transactions or arrangements that are not covered by explicit rules. In such circumstances IASs specifically require management to use its judgement to determine the most appropriate treatment (IAS 1[1997], paragraph 22) [now paragraphs 11 and 12 of IAS 8 as revised in December 2003]. This judgement does not amount to a free choice, as IASs require that it is exercised having regard to the IASB Framework, definitions, other standards and best practice. Consistent with

> the application of adopted IASs further to the IAS Regulation, national law may not, by specifying particular treatments, restrict or hinder this requirement to apply judgement in the manner envisaged.
>
> As the IAS Regulation is directly applicable, member states will ensure that they do not seek to apply to the company any additional elements of national law that are contrary to, conflict with or restrict a company's compliance with adopted IASs, further to the IAS Regulation.'

However, the Commission appears to have now contradicted its own earlier guidance by indicating that a member state could mandate compliance with the full hedging requirements of IAS 39. It is possible that market pressures might encourage many companies to apply a standard that had not been adopted provided that it was not in conflict with an endorsed IFRS.

A number of complex issues may arise from the failure to adopt an IFRS. For example:

- a company that did not comply with an IFRS that had not been endorsed would not be able to make an unqualified statement of compliance with IFRSs. It would therefore appear to be unable to apply IFRS 1 on first time adoption of IFRSs although the Commission's view is that this is possible (see **section 3** in **chapter 5**);
- there may be cross references between standards that make one standard inoperable without the other; and
- it is unclear to what extent the requirements in IAS 8 concerning sources of guidance when a matter is not dealt with in IFRSs would oblige companies to have regard to a standard that had not been endorsed.

It is to be hoped that these problems will be minimised by new standards and interpretations being endorsed by the Commission without undue delay.

1.2.6 *Implications for year-end reporting*

UK companies that prepare their financial statements in accordance with IFRSs are legally required to prepare them in accordance with IFRSs as adopted by the EU. It is currently possible to comply with both IFRSs as adopted by the EU and IFRSs as issued by the IASB and many companies make it clear in their financial statements that they also comply with IFRSs as issued by the IASB.

IOSCO issued a press release in February 2008 (see http://www.iosco.org/news/pdf/IOSCONEWS112.pdf) urging public companies to clarify the accounting standards used in the preparation of their accounts to mitigate the risk of investors assuming all company accounts are generally comparable. Making clear in financial statements that a company's financial statements are in compliance with IFRSs as issued by the IASB, if that is the case, is strongly encouraged as there are advantages from the viewpoint of the capital markets. This is especially true in the case of a Foreign Private Issuer taking advantage of the SEC's recent rule change not to reconcile their IFRS statement to US GAAP. The ability to do this is dependent on the progress of endorsement by the EU which is discussed in **section 1.2.3** above.

1.2.7 Implications for interim reporting

As explained at **1.2.2** above, endorsement is a potentially lengthy process. This is likely to be a particular problem for interim results.

For periods commencing on or after 20 January 2007, listed companies that prepare consolidated financial statements have to prepare their half yearly reports in accordance with IAS 34 *Interim Financial Reporting* as required by the Disclosure and Transparency Rules. IAS 34 adopts a similar approach to the previous Listing Rules in that it requires interim reports to adopt the policies that are expected to be applied in the full year financial statements. The fact that a new standard or an interpretation has not been endorsed by the EU at the date of approval of the interim report does not appear to prevent it being applied in that interim report provided that it is expected to be endorsed by the time that the full year financial statements are approved.

Interim reporting is considered more fully in **chapter 39**.

1.3 Additional UK requirements

Where UK companies are required (or choose) to report under IFRSs, they are still subject to additional UK requirements. In particular:

- although such companies are exempt from most of the Acts' (see **1.3.1** below) financial reporting requirements (see **1.4** below), all other requirements of the Acts continue to apply (e.g. the rules on capital maintenance and distributions continue to apply to shares even if they are presented as liabilities in accordance with IFRSs);
- listed companies (i.e. those companies admitted to the Official List by the Financial Services Authority (FSA)) need to comply with the requirements contained in the 'Listing Rules' issued by the FSA (as

part of the FSA Handbook). Companies with a primary listing on the main market of the London Stock Exchange or PLUS-listed are admitted to the FSA Official List. They are required to make certain corporate governance and other disclosures;

- companies whose shares are dealt in on the Alternative Investment Market (AIM) need to comply with the requirements contained in 'The AIM Rules' issued by the London Stock Exchange; and

- companies which are PLUS-quoted on the primary market operated by PLUS need to comply with the requirements set out in the PLUS Rules for Issuers and Disclosure Standards.

Although AIM companies sometimes choose to comply with certain aspects of the Listing Rules, this is on a voluntary basis. AIM companies are not subject to the periodic financial reporting requirements of the FSA.

For periods beginning on or after 20 January 2007, companies admitted to trading on a regulated market also have to comply with the requirements on periodic financial reporting in chapter 4 of the Disclosure and Transparency Rules (DTR) issued by the FSA. These rules replace some of the Listing Rules for such periods. They are derived from the EU Transparency Obligations Directive and apply to companies whose transferable securities, whether shares or debt, are admitted to trading on a regulated market and whose home state is the United Kingdom e.g. the PLUS-listed market and the main market of the London Stock Exchange. The main impact of these rules on annual financial statements is to shorten the deadline for publication from six months to four months. They require most listed companies to prepare an 'annual management report' although the content is included in the existing content for a directors' report, with one exception relating to disclosures about branches. They also require a 'responsibility statement' made by the persons responsible in the company. The periodic financial reporting rules in the DTR do not apply to AIM companies, nor to those with only debt securities listed on the Professional Securities Market. There are certain other exemptions available.

Statements of Recommended Practice (SORPs) are recommendations on accounting practices for specialised industries or sectors. They supplement UK accounting standards and other requirements in the light of the particular factors appertaining to the given industry or sector. Existing SORPs have been developed within the framework of UK accounting standards and are revised as UK GAAP converges with IFRSs. However,

SORPs have no formal status under IFRSs and to mandate compliance with them would be contrary to EU law (see **1.2.5** above).

Where consolidated financial statements are prepared in accordance with IFRSs, that fact must be stated in the notes to the financial statements. [CA 2006 s406, previously CA 1895 s227B] Similarly, where individual financial statements are prepared in accordance with IFRSs, that fact must be stated in the notes to the financial statements. [CA 2006 s397, previously CA 1985 s226B]

1.3.1 The Companies Act 2006

The Companies Act 2006 received Royal Assent on 8 November 2006. The Act consolidates virtually all of the requirements of the 1985 and 1989 Acts but makes significant changes to those requirements.

Changes to financial reporting requirements are relatively limited. Many of the detailed requirements, for example those that were found in Schedule 4 to the 1985 Act, are contained in secondary legislation 'The Large and Medium-sized Companies and Groups (Accounts and Reports) Regulations 2008' (the Accounting Regulations) which were made on 19 February 2008 (Statutory Instrument 2008 no.410). Companies that qualify as 'small' under the Act can refer to the Small Companies and Groups (Accounts and Directors' Report) Regulations 2008 (the Small Companies Accounting Regulations) (Statutory Instrument 2008 no.409). The financial reporting requirements of the 2006 Act (including the Accounting Regulations and the Small Companies Accounting Regulations) came into force for years beginning on or after 6 April 2008.

References are made to both the 2006 and 1985 Act throughout this manual and any significant changes are explained.

The 2006 Act includes a requirement that the directors of a company must not approve the accounts unless they are satisfied that they give a true and fair view of the assets, liabilities, financial position and profit or loss of the company. In the case of group accounts this requirement applies to the undertakings included in the consolidation as a whole, so far as concerns the members of the company. [CA 2006 s393(1)] This overarching requirement applies irrespective of whether the accounts are prepared under IFRSs or UK GAAP. The 1985 Act contains no explicit requirement for accounts prepared under IFRSs to give a true and fair view although there is a requirement for auditors to report in these terms.

Section 393 was not in the original Companies Bill but was added as the Bill was makings its way through Parliament. The ministerial statement on its introduction was to the effect that the clear primacy of the true and fair concept had become blurred as a result of a combination of UK and EU law provisions. The opportunity was being taken to express the principle more clearly in the legislation.

In May 2008, the FRC published an Opinion by Martin Moore QC on the continued relevance of the true and fair requirement for the preparation and audit of financial statements following the introduction of IFRSs and the enactment of the 2006 Act. The opinion, which is available on the FRC website (www.frc.org.uk), confirms the continuing relevance of earlier legal opinions on the interpretation of the true and fair requirement. One of the significant conclusions in the May 2008 Opinion is that 'the requirement set out in applicable international accounting standards to present fairly is not a different requirement to that of showing a true and fair view but is a different articulation of the same concept'.

There should not be a conflict between the requirement to comply with IFRSs and the requirement to give a true and fair view except in extremely rare circumstances. However, the Opinion notes that the preparation of financial statements is not a mechanical process where compliance with accounting standards will automatically ensure that those statements show a true and fair view, or a fair presentation. For example, additional disclosures might be required to achieve a true and fair view.

1.3.2 *Meaning of 'company'*

Except where it indicates otherwise, when the 2006 Act and 1985 Act refer to a 'company' they mean a company formed and registered under either that Act or (subject to certain exceptions which differ slightly between the 1985 and 2006 Acts) the former Companies Acts. [CA 2006 s1(1) and s1171, previously CA 1985 s735(1)] Some bodies are called companies but do not fall within the Act's definition — for example, open-ended investment companies. Unless the context indicates otherwise, references in this manual to a 'company' have the same meaning as in the Acts and do not encompass those other bodies.

The Acts use the term 'body corporate' to refer more generally to incorporated entities, including those incorporated outside the UK. In this manual the more general term 'entity' is often used. This is to be consistent with the terminology used in IFRSs.

The meaning of 'company' for the purposes of determining which entities are within the scope of the IAS Regulation is considered at **2.1** below.

1.4 UK requirements that do not apply to IFRS adopters

UK companies preparing group financial statements in accordance with IFRSs are not required to comply with Schedule 6 to the Accounting Regulations. The equivalent for those companies required to follow the 1985 Act is Schedule 4A, or, for banking and insurance companies, Schedules 9 and 9A respectively.

Similarly, UK companies preparing individual financial statements in accordance with IFRSs are not required to comply with Schedule 1 to the Accounting Regulations (or, for banking and insurance companies, Schedules 2 and 3 respectively). The equivalent for companies required to comply with the 1985 Act, is Schedule 4, or, for banking and insurance companies, Schedules 9 and 9A respectively.

When preparing group or individual financial statements in accordance with IFRSs, such companies are not required to comply with, or have regard to, standards and other pronouncements issued or adopted by the UK Accounting Standards Board and its Urgent Issues Task Force.

Although the requirements of the Schedules mentioned above do not apply to financial statements prepared under IFRSs, the following financial reporting requirements continue to apply:

- section 494 of the 2006 Act, previously section 390B of the 1985 Act, and related Regulations dealing with disclosure of auditors' remuneration for audit and non-audit services. These requirements are explained at **8.2** in **chapter 3**;
- section 411 of the Companies Act 2006, previously section 231A of the 1985 Act dealing with particulars of staff numbers and costs. These requirements are considered at **8.1** in **chapter 3**;
- schedule 4 of the Accounting Regulations (previously Schedule 5 to the 1985 Act) dealing with disclosures about subsidiaries, associates and certain other investments. These disclosures are dealt with at **7.3** to **7.5** in **chapter 33**;
- schedule 5 of the Accounting Regulations (previously Schedule 6 to the 1985 Act) dealing with directors' remuneration (see **chapter 48**) and
- the requirements of s413 of the 2006 Act (requirement previously within Schedule 6 to the 1985 Act) regarding loans and other transactions with directors and officers (see **chapter 32**);

- sections 415–419 of the Companies Act 2006 and Schedule 7 to the Accounting Regulations (previously sections 234, 234ZZA, 234ZZB and Schedule 7 of the Companies Act 1985) concerning the contents of the directors' report;
- sections 420 and 421 of the Companies Act 2006 and Schedule 8 to the Accounting Regulations (previously section 234B and Schedule 7A to the Companies Act 1985) concerning the contents of the directors' remuneration report;
- the new requirement in s410A of the 2006 Act relating to the disclosure of off balance sheet arrangements which apply for periods commencing on or after 6 April 2008 (see **8.4** in **chapter 3**); and
- the new requirements for disclosure of liability limitation agreements which apply to reports issued on or after 6 April 2008 (see **8.3** in **chapter 3**).

2 Entities required to use IFRSs for consolidated financial statements

The IAS Regulation discussed at **1.2** above requires companies governed by the law of a member state, for each financial year starting on or after 1 January 2005, to prepare their consolidated financial statements in accordance with (endorsed) international accounting standards if, at the balance sheet date, their securities (equity or debt) are admitted to a 'regulated market' of any member state. Various aspects of this requirement are discussed below.

The IAS Regulation permits member states to postpone by two years the application of the Regulation to companies with only debt securities traded on a regulated market. The UK did not take up this option and therefore companies with only debt securities admitted to a regulated market are required to prepare their consolidated financial statements under IFRSs. However, many such companies do not themselves have subsidiaries and therefore do not prepare consolidated financial statements. For example, they may be subsidiaries within a larger group, that have been set up to raise debt finance. The requirements applicable to such companies are considered at **2.5** below.

2.1 Meaning of 'company'

The Regulation applies to 'companies'. Guidance issued by the European Commission in November 2003 (see **2.8** below) explains that companies are defined in the Treaty of Rome which states that:

> 'Companies or firms' means companies or firms constituted under civil or commercial law, including co-operative societies, and other legal persons governed by public or private law, save for those which are non-profit-making.

The guidance goes on to note that this definition is reflected in the scope of each of the Accounting Directives (which have been enacted into UK law in the Companies Act 2006 and Companies Act 1985). Accordingly, in principle, all companies incorporated under the Companies Acts are within the scope of the Regulation unless they are 'non profit making'. But most are not required to adopt IFRSs, for example because they do not have securities admitted to a regulated market.

The Regulation applies to some entities that are not companies incorporated under the Companies Act but are 'companies' under the Treaty of Rome. A DTI (now BERR) Consultation Document issued in March 2004 indicated that these include building societies, friendly societies and industrial and provident societies.

2.2 Meaning of 'regulated market'

There is a definition of 'regulated market' for this purpose in the Markets in Financial Instruments Directive (MiFID). The European Commission website includes a list of regulated markets at:

http://ec.europa.eu/internal_market/securities/isd/mifid_en.htm

which is updated from time to time.

The list of UK regulated markets notified to the Commission under Article 16 of the Investment Services Directive as at 1 March 2008 is as follows:

- London Stock Exchange – Regulated Market;
- ICE Futures Europe;
- The London International Financial Futures and Options Exchange (LIFFE);
- The London Metal Exchange;
- Virt-x Exchange Limited;
- PLUS-listed market; and
- EDX

As explained at **2.6** below, the Alternative Investment Market (AIM) is not a regulated market for this purpose.

PLUS Markets is a new stock exchange in London for small and mid-cap companies. The PLUS-listed and PLUS-quoted markets provide access to both capital and profile for companies and funds. The PLUS-quoted market admits companies in accordance with the PLUS Rules for Issuers and is not a regulated market. Companies which are PLUS-listed are subject to the same reporting requirements as those listed on the main market. For more information on the PLUS market see their website (www.plusmarketsgroup.com).

Some UK incorporated companies have securities that are not traded on a market in the UK but are traded on a market in another EU member state. Such companies should check the status of the market on which they are traded against the complete list.

2.3 Companies required to prepare consolidated financial statements

Guidance issued by the European Commission in November 2003 (see **2.8** below) clarifies that the determination of whether or not a company is required to prepare consolidated financial statements will continue to be made by reference to national law transposed from the Seventh Directive. In the UK context this means the Companies Act 2006 or Companies Act 1985 (as applicable, see **1.3.1** above), as further supplemented by FRS 2 *Accounting for Subsidiary Undertakings*.

However, this distinction is only relevant to the determination of whether consolidated financial statements are required and not to the scope of any consolidation. For example, once it has been established that consolidated financial statements are required, it is not possible to exclude a subsidiary from consolidation based on an exemption in national law where this would not be permitted under IFRSs. This is considered in more detail in the Commission's guidance.

Under the 2006 and 1985 Acts and FRS 2, consolidated financial statements will be required if:

- the company was a parent company (i.e. it had subsidiary undertakings) at its period end; unless
- it is exempt from preparing consolidated financial statements.

If a company disposes of all its subsidiary undertakings during the year, it will not be required to prepare group financial statements as a matter of law. This contrasts with the position under IAS 27 (see **4.1** in **chapter 33**). Such a company will fall outside of the scope of the IAS Regulation even though IAS 27 would require the preparation of consolidated financial statements in these circumstances.

The UK GAAP definition of subsidiary undertaking is considered at **2.3.1** below and the UK GAAP exemptions from preparing consolidated financial statements are considered at **2.3.2** below. In almost all cases it will be immediately apparent either that consolidated financial statements are required or that they are not required, irrespective of whether this is considered under UK GAAP or IFRSs. It is, however, important to understand the distinction explained above which will be relevant in rare cases. The requirement to prepare consolidated financial statements under IFRSs is considered in **chapter 33**.

2.3.1 UK GAAP definition of subsidiary undertaking

The definition of a subsidiary undertaking used under UK GAAP is different from that of a subsidiary included in IAS 27 (see **section 3** in **chapter 33**). Accordingly, it is possible that an undertaking may be a subsidiary undertaking for UK GAAP purposes, even though it would not be a subsidiary under IFRSs or vice versa. But in practice it is unlikely that different conclusions will be reached over whether control exists.

A parent may be required to prepare consolidated financial statements because it has subsidiary undertakings as a matter of law. However, if all of those subsidiary undertakings are not subsidiaries for the purposes of IAS 27, there will be nothing to consolidate under IAS 27.

Under s1162 of the 2006 Act (previously s258 of the 1985 Act) and FRS 2, an undertaking is the parent undertaking of another undertaking (a subsidiary undertaking) if any of the following apply:

- it holds a majority of the voting rights in the undertaking; [CA 2006 s1162(2)(a), previously CA 1985 s258(2)(a)]

- it is a member of the undertaking and has the right to appoint or remove directors holding a majority of the voting rights at meetings of the board on all, or substantially all, matters; [CA 2006 s1162(2)(b) and Sch. 7: 3(1), previously CA 1985 s258(2)(b) and Sch. 10A: 3(1)]

- it has the right to exercise a dominant influence over the undertaking:
  [CA 2006 s1162(2)(c) and Sch. 7: 4(2), previously CA 1985 s258(2)(c) and Sch. 10A: 4(2)]

- by virtue of provisions contained in the undertaking's Articles; or
- by virtue of a control contract. The control contract must be in writing and of a kind authorised by the Articles of the controlled undertaking. It must also be permitted by the law under which that undertaking is established;

- it is a member of the undertaking and controls alone, pursuant to an agreement with other shareholders or members, a majority of the voting rights in the undertaking; [CA 2006 s1162(2)(d), previously CA 1985 s258(2)(d)]
- it has the power to exercise, or actually exercises, dominant influence or control over the undertaking; [CA 2006 s1162(4)(a), previously CA 1985 s258(4)(a)] or
- it and the subsidiary undertaking are managed on a unified basis. [CA 2006 s1162(4)(b), previously CA 1985 s258(4)(b)]

The various expressions used in the above definition are further defined and explained elsewhere in the Acts and in FRS 2.

A parent undertaking is also treated as the parent undertaking of the subsidiary undertakings of its subsidiary undertakings. [CA 2006 s1162(5), previously CA 1985 s258(5)]

For the purpose of the definition above, an undertaking is treated as a member of another undertaking if:

[CA 2006 s1162(3), previously CA 1985 s258(3)]

- any of its subsidiary undertakings is a member of that undertaking; or
- any shares in that other undertaking are held by a person acting on behalf of the undertaking or any of its subsidiary undertakings.

This clause makes it clear that any shares held by another on behalf of the parent are equivalent to direct holdings of the parent in that undertaking.

2.3.2 *UK GAAP exemptions from preparing consolidated financial statements*

Although the 1985 and 2006 Acts offer exemptions from preparing consolidated financial statements for

- certain small groups;

- certain medium sized groups (only if applying the 1985 Act); and
- certain parents included in financial statements of larger groups;

these exemptions are not available to companies with securities listed on a regulated market of an EEA state. Accordingly, they will not be available to companies within the scope of the EU Regulation. The exemptions are described in more detail at **4.2** in **chapter 33**.

Both the Acts and FRS 2 recognise that a parent undertaking is relieved from preparing consolidated financial statements if each of its subsidiary undertakings is individually excluded from consolidation under s405 of the Companies Act 2006 or s229 of the Companies Act 1985. [CA 2006 s402 (previously CA 1985 s229(5)) and FRS 2.21(d)] The circumstances which justify exclusion from consolidation of an individual subsidiary undertaking are as follows:

- immateriality (see **2.3.2.1** below);
- expense or delay (see **2.3.2.2** below);
- severe long-term restrictions (see **2.3.2.3** below); and
- temporary control (see **2.3.2.4** below).

2.3.2.1 Immateriality

Since the definition of a subsidiary undertaking covers all relevant entities irrespective of materiality, the Act includes a specific exclusion for subsidiaries on grounds of immateriality. The Act permits an individual subsidiary to be excluded from consolidation 'if its inclusion is not material for the purpose of giving a true and fair view'. [CA 2006 s405(2), previously CA 1985 s229(2)] However, the Act qualifies this by stating 'but two or more undertakings may be excluded only if they are not material taken together'. Similarly, FRS 2 states that 'the FRS deals only with material items. Thus, this ground for exclusion requires no special mention in the FRS'. [FRS 2.78(a)]

It is clear that under s402 of the Companies Act 2006 (previously s229(5) of the Companies Act 1985) a UK company is exempt from the requirement to prepare consolidated accounts if all of its subsidiaries can be excluded from consolidation on the grounds that they are, in aggregate, immaterial. There has, however, been some inconclusive discussion at the EU Accounting Regulatory Committee about whether this approach correctly reflects the intentions of the Seventh Company Law Directive. Proposals have now been put forward by the European Commission to clarify the Directive in line with the UK position.

2.3.2.2 *Expense or delay*

The Act permits subsidiary undertakings to be excluded from consolidation if the information necessary for preparing consolidated financial statements cannot be obtained without disproportionate expense or undue delay. [CA 2006 s405(3)(b), previously CA 1985 s229(3)(b)]

However, FRS 2 seeks to remove the exclusion completely. The FRS reduces the exclusion to a test of materiality by stating 'neither disproportionate expense nor undue delay in obtaining the information necessary for the preparation of consolidated financial statements can justify excluding from consolidation subsidiary undertakings that are individually or collectively material in the context of the group'. [FRS 2.24]

2.3.2.3 *Severe long-term restrictions*

The Act allows a subsidiary undertaking to be excluded from consolidation where 'severe long-term restrictions substantially hinder the exercise of the rights of the parent company over the assets or management of that undertaking'. [CA 2006 s405(3)(a), previously CA 1985 s229(3)(a)] FRS 2 toughens this from a permissible exclusion to a required exclusion by stating that the subsidiary undertaking *should* be excluded from consolidation. [FRS 2.25(a)] The argument presented is that exclusion from consolidation for this reason is justified only where the effect of the restrictions is to prevent the parent from controlling the subsidiary undertaking.

The rights referred to must be those that result in the undertaking being a subsidiary undertaking (under s1162 of the 2006 Act or s258 of the 1985 Act) and, without which, it would not be a subsidiary undertaking. Since control is most commonly achieved through the exercise of votes in general meeting, restrictions justifying exclusion would normally involve the parent being rendered unable to exercise those votes. Similarly, if the definition of subsidiary undertaking is met by another of the s1162 (of the 2006 Act) or s258 (of the 1985 Act) clauses, e.g. control of votes in the management body, or actual exercise of dominant influence, it would need to be demonstrated that this essential aspect of control had been removed or restricted to the point where control no longer exists. The FRS also states that it is not enough that restrictions are threatened or another party has the power to impose them. It is required that there is a severe and restricting effect in practice. Whereas SSAP 14 required that restrictions be in place 'for the foreseeable future', FRS 2 does not make any equivalent statement. As a minimum, it suggests that there should be an expectation of continuation of restrictions beyond one year.

An example of where the use of this exclusion may be seen is cited by FRS 2, i.e. when a subsidiary is made the subject of a UK insolvency procedure, control may pass to the administrator, administrative receiver or liquidator. A voluntary arrangement does not necessarily lead to loss of control. [FRS 2.78(c)] Similarly, insolvency procedures in overseas jurisdictions may not lead to loss of control.

It should be noted that, though a liquidation implies severe long-term restrictions, a receivership or administration order does not give rise to severe long-term restrictions if the subsidiary is expected to come out of receivership or administration in due course.

Where a subsidiary is made the subject of an insolvency procedure soon after the year end, the issue arises as to whether that subsidiary can be excluded from consolidation. As stated at **2.3** above, the assessment of whether group financial statements are required depends on the situation at the balance sheet date. As the administrator, administrative receiver or liquidator is appointed after the year end, there are no severe long-term restrictions at the balance sheet date and therefore the subsidiary should be included in the group financial statements.

Restrictions on cash flows from a subsidiary undertaking, perhaps because it is located in a foreign jurisdiction, do not normally amount to a severe restriction of rights. The fact that a parent may not be able to remit dividends from the subsidiary or use the funds for other parts of the group outside the country of operation does not by itself indicate that the parent no longer has control over the operating and financial policies of that subsidiary. Indeed, subsidiaries are often set up in the face of such restrictions and are, presumably, expected to be beneficial to the parent.

2.3.2.4 Temporary control

The Act permits exclusion where 'the interest of the parent is held exclusively with a view to subsequent resale'. [CA 2006 s405(3)(c), previously CA 1985 s229(3)(c)] FRS 2 repeats the same exclusion, but requires, rather than permits, such a subsidiary to be excluded. FRS 2 also imposes an additional condition that the subsidiary undertaking must have not previously been consolidated in group financial statements prepared by the parent. [FRS 2.25(b)]

FRS 2 further restricts the use of this exemption by defining an 'interest held exclusively with a view to subsequent resale' as:

[FRS 2.11]

(a) an interest for which a purchaser has been identified or is being sought and which is reasonably expected to be disposed of within approximately one year of its date of acquisition; or

(b) an interest that was acquired as a result of the enforcement of a security, unless the interest has become part of the continuing activities of the group or the holder acts as if it intends the interest to become so.

The first condition above depends both on an immediate intention to sell and the expectation of a sale within approximately one year of acquisition. The inclusion of the words 'approximately one year' means that where at the end of that year disposal has not been completed, it will be acceptable to continue to exclude the subsidiary from consolidation provided that, at the date the financial statements are signed, the terms of the sale have been agreed, the process of disposing of the interest is substantially complete and the disposal is expected to be completed within a few weeks of the anniversary of the acquisition.

The second condition above depends on the method of acquiring the interest, i.e. the enforcement of a security. However, if the group has taken the interest (acquired by enforcing a security) into the continuing activities of the business, or it acts as though it intends to take that interest in, the undertaking should be consolidated.

The condition also applies to transactions that are, in substance, the acquisition of an interest by the enforcement of a security. For instance, an entity may have initially lent money on the security of a property. The borrower subsequently defaults on the loan and enters into a financial restructuring whereby the lender receives a majority of shares in the borrower. The lender should exclude the subsidiary from consolidation on the grounds that in effect it was acquired as a result of the enforcement of a security, unless, of course, the interest has, or is to, become part of the investor's continuing activities.

2.4 Companies choosing to prepare consolidated financial statements

A company otherwise within the scope of the IAS Regulation may not be required, but may nevertheless choose, to prepare consolidated financial statements. In such circumstances, it appears that those consolidated financial statements must be prepared in accordance with international accounting standards. As consolidated financial statements prepared by a listed company they are apparently within the scope of the IAS Regulation, notwithstanding that they are prepared voluntarily. However, it is difficult to envisage the circumstances in which this would arise.

2.5 Listed companies that are not parents

As a matter of law, listed companies that do not have to prepare consolidated financial statements may continue to use UK GAAP in their financial statements. But it is possible that such companies may come under market pressure to report under IFRSs.

In a Consultation Paper issued in October 2003 (CP 203) the FSA invited comments on whether the Listing Rules should require issuers that do not have subsidiaries to prepare their financial statements in accordance with IFRSs. The great majority of quoted 'solo companies' are investment trusts, which prepare their financial statements in accordance with the relevant Statement of Recommended Practice (SORP). The FSA pointed out that if such companies were required to use IFRSs, they would no longer be able to apply the SORP. There is no equivalent standard in the IFRS literature.

Following the outcome of this consultation, the Listing Rules were revised but did not require compliance with IFRSs. Those rules have subsequently been superseded by DTR 4.1.6R which provides that an issuer that is not required to prepare consolidated financial statements must prepare financial statements in accordance with the national law of the EEA State in which the parent company is incorporated. Companies incorporated in the UK therefore have a choice between UK GAAP and IFRSs which are both permitted by law. Some solo companies will decide to adopt IFRSs in any event to be consistent with competitors or because they are finance subsidiaries within larger groups using IFRSs. Most investment trusts continue to report under UK GAAP.

2.6 AIM companies

From 12 October 2004, AIM has operated as an exchange-regulated market, relinquishing its EU 'regulated market' status. This means that AIM companies fall outside the scope of the IAS Regulation.

For periods commencing on or after 1 January 2007, the AIM Rules of the London Stock Exchange require an AIM company incorporated in an EEA country to prepare its financial statements in accordance with IFRSs.

However, where, at the end of the relevant financial year, the company is not a parent company, it may prepare its financial statements either in accordance with IFRSs or in accordance with the accounting and company legislation and regulations that are applicable to the company due to its country of incorporation (i.e. UK GAAP in the case of a UK company).

The intention is to mirror the rules applicable to listed companies (i.e. solo companies are not required to apply IFRSs) but the wording used is slightly different.

> The AIM rules are not clear regarding the situation where a company is a parent company but is exempt from preparing group financial statements on the grounds that all of its subsidiaries are immaterial or subject to severe long-term restrictions. However, in practice companies may ask via their Nomad for a derogation from this requirement and continue to prepare UK GAAP financial statements.

AIM companies which have subsidiaries are effectively obliged by the AIM Rules to elect to prepare 'IAS Group accounts' as a matter of company law (see **3.2** below).

2.7 Unlisted groups with listed subsidiaries

A privately owned group may have raised finance by means of a subsidiary company issuing quoted debt. In these circumstances, the consolidated financial statements of the group are not required to be prepared in accordance with IFRSs. This is because the IAS Regulation applies to *companies* that have *their* securities admitted to trading on a regulated market.

2.8 European Commission guidance

As mentioned above, in November 2003, the European Commission issued guidance relating to certain aspects of the IAS Regulation. It is entitled 'Comments concerning certain Articles of the [IAS Regulation] and the Fourth Council Directive .... and the Seventh Council Directive .... on accounting'. It can be found on the European Commission website at:

http://europa.eu.int/comm/internal_market/accounting/docs/ias/200311-comments/ias-200311-comments_en.pdf

3 UK entities permitted to use IFRSs for consolidated and individual financial statements

The IAS Regulation gives Member States an option to permit or require that:

- the individual company financial statements of listed companies; and
- the consolidated and individual financial statements of unlisted companies

should also be prepared under IFRSs.

This has been implemented in the UK to allow companies, other than charities, to prepare their individual and/or group financial statements in accordance with either UK GAAP or IFRSs, subject to the constraints discussed below. Companies that are charities must continue to prepare their individual and group financial statements in accordance with UK GAAP.

Where companies prepare both individual and group financial statements, the choice between IFRSs and UK GAAP operates separately for each. A company that is required by Article 4 of the IAS Regulation to use IFRSs for its consolidated financial statements still has a free choice of using IFRSs or UK GAAP for its individual financial statements. Similarly, a company outside of the scope of the IAS Regulation that has chosen to use IFRSs for its consolidated financial statements does not have to use IFRSs for its individual financial statements. Although less likely in practice, it would also be possible by law for a parent company to prepare IAS individual financial statements while preparing UK GAAP consolidated financial statements.

The Acts require that consolidated and individual financial statements (when required) are published together. This continues to apply where the consolidated and individual financial statements are prepared using different frameworks. The Acts do not specify whether the financial statements should be presented as separate sections of the report or combined together into a single set of primary statements and notes. In practice, the statements will be clearer if the separate section approach is taken when two frameworks are combined in a single document. The availability of the exemption in s408 of the Companies Act 2006 (previously s230 of the Companies Act 1985) from presenting the profit and loss account of the parent when consolidated financial statements are presented is considered at **3.5** below.

3.1 Individual financial statements

UK companies, other than charities, are permitted to prepare either:

[CA 2006 s395(1), previously CA 1985 s226(2)]

- 'Companies Act individual accounts' (i.e. in accordance with UK GAAP); or
- 'IAS individual accounts' (i.e. in accordance with IFRSs).

Subject to the constraints discussed at **3.3** below, this is a free choice. Once a company has prepared IAS individual accounts it must continue to do so for all future years [CA 2006 s395(3), previously CA 1985 s226(4)] unless there is a 'relevant change of circumstance', namely:

[CA 2006 s395(4) previously CA 1985 s226(5)]

- the company becomes a subsidiary undertaking of another undertaking that does not prepare IAS individual accounts; or
- the company ceases to be a company with securities admitted to trading on a regulated market; or
- a parent undertaking of the company ceases to be a company with securities admitted to trading on a regulated market.

In addition, for companies applying the 2006 Act, a relevant change of circumstance is also the company ceasing to be a subsidiary undertaking.

> The Companies Act 2006 (Amendment) (Accounts and Reports) Regulations 2008 amended s395 of the Companies Act 2006 to fix an anomaly that existed previously. Where a company ceases to be a subsidiary of one company but has not 'become a subsidiary undertaking of another undertaking that does not prepare IAS individual accounts' e.g. because it has been acquired by an individual, the amendment permits this company to revert to preparing UK GAAP financial statements if it so wishes.

The above requirement also applies where a company has in the past prepared IAS individual accounts, has reverted to Companies Act individual accounts (following a relevant change of circumstance), and then prepares IAS individual accounts again. [CA 2006 s395(5), previously CA 1985 s226(6)] In effect (but again subject to the constraints discussed at **3.3** below), there is always freedom to move from Companies Act to IAS individual accounts, but any move in the opposite direction is only possible following a relevant change of circumstance.

The 'relevant changes in circumstance' above make reference to 'securities admitted to trading on a regulated market'. As discussed at **2.2** above AIM is not a regulated market. This means that an entity traded on AIM that adopts IFRSs in accordance with the AIM rules (see **2.6** above) and subsequently ceases to be traded on AIM will not be able to revert back to UK GAAP by claiming there has been a relevant change in circumstance whereby 'the company ceases to be a company with securities admitted to trading on a regulated market'. [CA 2006 s395(4)(b), previously CA 1985 s226(5)(b)] The entity could only revert to UK GAAP if it meets one of the other specified relevant changes in circumstance stated in s395 of the 2006 Act or s226 of the 1985 Act.

If a company that ceases to be an AIM company reverts to UK GAAP when there is no relevant change of circumstance per the Act then its accounts will not be prepared in accordance with the Act.

As explained in **example 3D** in **chapter 5**, a company may be a first-time adopter of IFRSs, for the purposes of applying IFRS 1, on more than one occasion. A company that prepares IAS individual accounts, reverts to Companies Act individual accounts for one or more years and then again prepares IAS individual accounts will be treated as a first-time adopter on that second occasion as if it had never previously reported under IFRSs.

3.2 Group financial statements

UK parent companies, other than charities, are permitted to prepare either:

[CA 2006 s403(2), previously CA 1985 s227(3)]

- 'Companies Act group accounts' (i.e. in accordance with UK GAAP); or
- 'IAS group accounts' (i.e. in accordance with IFRSs).

Again, subject to the constraints discussed at **3.3** below, this is a free choice, but once a parent company has prepared IAS group accounts it must continue to do so for all future years [CA 2006 s403(4) previously CA 1985 s227(5)] unless there is a 'relevant change of circumstance', namely:

[CA 2006 s403(5), previously CA 1985 s227(6)]

- the company becomes a subsidiary undertaking of another undertaking that does not prepare IAS group accounts; or

- the company ceases to be a company with securities admitted to trading on a regulated market; or
- a parent undertaking of the company ceases to be a company with securities admitted to trading on a regulated market.

The 2006 Act introduced the company ceasing to be a subsidiary undertaking as an additional relevant change in circumstance for companies preparing IAS individual accounts (see **3.1** above). This does not extend to companies which have prepared IAS group accounts.

The above requirement also applies where a parent company has in the past prepared IAS group accounts, has reverted to Companies Act group accounts (following a relevant change of circumstance), and then prepares IAS group accounts again. [CA 2006 s403(6), previously CA 1985 s227(7)] In effect (but again subject to the constraints discussed at **3.3** below), there is always freedom to move from Companies Act to IAS group accounts, but any move in the opposite direction is only possible following a relevant change of circumstance. The implications of this for the application of IFRS 1 are described at **3.1** above.

3.3 Consistency of individual financial statements

The Act places constraints on the choice between Companies Act and IAS individual accounts where a UK parent company prepares group accounts. The basic rule is that the individual accounts of:

[CA 2006 s407(1), previously CA 1985 s227C(1)]

- the UK parent company; and
- any subsidiary undertakings preparing accounts in accordance with the Act (e.g. UK subsidiary companies),

must be prepared using the same framework (i.e. either Companies Act or IAS individual accounts, but not a mixture of the two).

There are exceptions to this basic rule:

[CA 2006 s407, previously CA 1985 s227C]

- the requirement for consistency does not apply to charities. Thus, although a company which is a charity must prepare Companies Act individual accounts, this does not prevent its parent or subsidiary undertakings from preparing IAS individual accounts;

- where subsidiary undertakings prepare Companies Act individual accounts, a UK parent may nevertheless prepare IAS individual accounts if it also prepares IAS group accounts. Inconsistency between the parent and subsidiary undertakings is permitted in these circumstances; and

- the individual accounts of the parent and subsidiary undertakings need not be prepared using the same framework to the extent that, in the opinion of the directors, there are good reasons for not doing so.

The second exception was provided so as not to discourage parent companies from using IFRSs for their individual financial statements. This is important because parent companies are required to present their individual and group financial statements within the same annual report. There are obvious advantages of using a consistent financial reporting framework for both. However, there may also be some significant disadvantages including the potential effect on distributable profits and some disclosure requirements that are more onerous than those under UK GAAP.

The exception does not apply to the reverse situation (i.e. when the subsidiaries prepare IAS individual accounts and the parent wants to prepare Companies Act individual accounts) because there would be no similar justification. In very rare circumstances, such an inconsistency might be justified by reference to the third exception for 'good reasons'.

Guidance Notes produced by the DTI (now BERR) in October 2004 indicate that the exception for 'good reasons' is intended 'to provide a degree of flexibility where there are genuine (including cost/benefit) grounds for using different accounting frameworks within a group of companies'. The Guidance Notes list the following examples of 'good reasons':

- a group using IFRSs might acquire a subsidiary undertaking that has not been using IFRSs. In the first year of acquisition, it might not be practical for the newly acquired company to switch to IFRSs immediately;

- a group may contain subsidiary undertakings that are themselves publicly traded, so that market pressures or regulatory requirements to use IFRSs might come into play, without necessarily justifying a switch to IFRSs for the non-publicly traded subsidiaries;

- a subsidiary undertaking (or a parent) may be planning to list, and so might wish to convert to IFRSs in advance, but the rest of group may not intend to list; and

- a group may contain minor or dormant subsidiaries where the costs of changing accounting framework would outweigh the benefits.

The examples given in the Guidance Notes do not appear to be intended to be exhaustive. The Guidance Notes conclude that 'the key point is that the directors of the parent company must be able to justify any inconsistency to shareholders, regulators or other interested parties'.

3.4 Small and medium-sized companies

Certain small and medium-sized companies are entitled to exemptions from some financial reporting and filing requirements. The exemptions available to such companies choosing to prepare their financial statements under IFRSs are limited compared to those preparing Companies Act accounts. The position for such companies is broadly as follows:

- small companies that choose to prepare their financial statements under IFRSs must apply IFRSs in full. There are simplified accounting requirements contained in the Act specifically for companies that qualify as small but they apply only to small companies choosing to prepare Companies Act accounts;
- small companies following IFRSs must also comply with additional Companies Act accounting requirements (see **1.4** above). However, there are certain exemptions from/ simplifications of specific UK disclosure requirements in the financial statements including those relating to staff numbers and costs and directors' remuneration, as set out in s411(1) of the Companies Act 2006 and Schedule 3 to the Small Companies Accounting Regulations (previously s246(3) to the Companies Act 1985) as well as simplified auditors' remuneration disclosures that apply also to small companies preparing financial statements under IFRSs. Where accounts are prepared in accordance with the provisions applicable to companies subject to the small companies regime, disclosure to this effect must be made in a prominent position on the balance sheet; [CA 2006 s414(3), previously CA 1985 s246(8)]
- small companies can prepare either a full directors' report in accordance with the Accounting Regulations [2008 Acc Regs Sch 7, previously CA 1985 Sch 7] or a directors' report prepared in accordance with Schedule 5 of the Small Companies Regulations. [CA 1985 s246(4)] Where a company takes this option it must state that fact. [CA 2006 s419(2), previously CA 1985 s246(8)(b)] Small companies are exempt from disclosing the amount directors recommend should be paid by way of a dividend. [CA 2006 s416(3), previously CA 1985 s246(4)] Under Companies Act 2006, small companies subject to the

small companies' regime are exempt also from including a business review in their directors' report; [CA 2006 s417(1)]

- the limited relaxation of disclosure requirements for medium-sized companies in s445(3) of the 2006 Act (previously s246A of the 1985 Act) is only available to companies that prepare Companies Act accounts with the exception that under the 2006 Act medium-sized companies are exempt from the requirement to disclose information on non-financial KPIs within the directors' report; [CA 2006 s417(7)]

- small companies reporting under IFRSs may continue to file accounts with the Registrar of Companies which may omit the profit and loss account and the directors' report (sometimes referred to as 'filleted accounts') and make use of certain exemptions from UK specific disclosure requirements. Where this option is taken the copy of the balance sheet must contain a statement that the annual report and accounts have been delivered in accordance with the provisions applicable to companies subject to the small companies regime. However, the ability to file an abbreviated balance sheet in accordance with Schedule 4 of the Small Companies Accounting Regulations or Schedule 8A of the 1985 Act is lost and the full IFRS balance sheet and related notes have to be filed. A small company filing 'filleted accounts' under the 1985 Act is required to use a special form of auditors' report but under the 2006 Act the full audit report is required to be filed. As many small companies are exempt from audit, the form of auditors' report will not generally be an issue; and

- under s248 of the 1985 Act, small and medium sized groups that are not ineligible groups are exempt from the requirement to prepare group accounts. For small groups, the exemption continues to be available as a matter of law under the 2006 Act. [CA 2006 s398] Under the 2006 Act there is no equivalent exemption for medium-sized groups. As explained in **chapter 33**, there is no equivalent exemption in IAS 27 and so a small company could not, in practice, use this exemption and claim that the financial statements complied with IFRSs. However, it might be able to claim that its financial statements complied with IFRSs as adopted by the EU for the reasons explained in **chapter 33**.

The thresholds for small and medium-sized company and group exemptions have been raised in the Companies Act 2006. The revised limits are not included in the text of the 2006 Act but have been inserted into s382(3) of the 2006 Act by the Companies Act 2006 (Amendment) (Accounts and Reports) Regulations 2008. The detailed requirements for the exemptions and entitlement to them are beyond the scope of this manual.

3.5 Exemption from presenting parent's profit and loss account

When a parent company that prepares consolidated financial statements prepares its individual financial statements under UK GAAP, it is exempt from the requirement to publish its individual profit and loss account and the related notes. As a matter of law, companies reporting under IFRSs in their individual financial statements can use this exemption. There was initially some uncertainty about whether companies could use this exemption in practice, for example, because they would be unable to make an unqualified statement of compliance with IFRSs. However, the DTI (now BERR) published guidance notes which indicate that, in its view, a company's ability to apply IFRS 1 would not be affected. This is on the basis that section 408 of the 2006 Act, which was previously section 230 of the 1985 Act, is a 'publication exemption' and that the financial statements required to be published are an extract from the full IFRS separate financial statements.

Parent companies have to publish company balance sheets, cash flow statements and any statements of recognised income and expenditure. So it may be simpler to publish the income statement even though it is not required by law. However, many UK companies reporting under IFRSs continue to use the exemption in practice.

4 Enforcement of accounting requirements

4.1 Introduction

Companies incorporated under the Companies Acts are required by the Acts to prepare annual financial statements that comply with the accounting requirements of the Acts, including the requirement to give a true and fair view. Previously under the 1985 Act, companies preparing their financial statements in accordance with IFRSs were outside the scope of this requirement. The Act has been amended such that the requirement for financial statements to give a true and fair view applies equally to Companies Act accounts and IAS accounts under the 2006 Act (see **1.3.1** above).

Prior to the Companies Act 1989, responsibility for 'policing' these requirements rested with BERR (previously the DTI). The 1989 Act introduced new procedures for the revision of defective accounts. These procedures, which are also within the Companies Act 2006, included allowing a person, authorised by the Secretary of State, the power to apply to the court for an order requiring the directors of a company to prepare revised financial statements. The Secretary of State has authorised the Financial

Reporting Review Panel (the Panel) for this purpose. From April 2006 the scope of the Panel's review was extended to include directors' reports issued in respect of financial years beginning on or after 1 April 2006 (which is one year after the requirements for the enhanced business review came into force).

A company that prepares 'IAS group accounts' or 'IAS individual accounts' is under a direct legal obligation to prepare those accounts in accordance with IFRSs as adopted by the EU. This is different from the position under UK GAAP where the obligation to comply with accounting standards is an indirect one which operates through the requirement to give a true and fair view.

4.2 Enforcement by the Secretary of State

Where the Secretary of State believes that a company's annual accounts or directors' report may not comply with the requirements of the Act, he or she may give notice to the directors indicating the matters in question. If, after a specified period (not less than one month), the directors have not given the Secretary of State a satisfactory explanation or have not revised the annual accounts or directors' report so as to comply with the Act, the Secretary of State may apply to the court to order the directors to do so. [CA 2006 s455, previously CA 1985 s245A] If the court orders the preparation of revised accounts, it may give directions with respect to the auditing of the revised annual accounts, the revision of any directors' report, directors' remuneration report or summary financial statement, and the steps required by the directors to bring the making of the court order to the notice of persons likely to rely on the previous financial statements. If the court orders the company to prepare a revised directors'' report it may give directions as to the review of the report by the auditors, the revision of any summary financial statement, and steps required by the directors to bring making of the court order to the notice of persons likely to rely on the previous report. If the court finds that the accounts or report did not comply with the Act, it may order all costs or any part of the costs in connection with the application and the revision of the financial statements to be borne by those directors who had approved the defective financial statements. [CA 2006 s456, previously CA 1985 s245B]

The voluntary revision by directors of defective financial statements is discussed in **chapter 52**.

4.3 Enforcement by the Financial Reporting Review Panel

The Panel's authority extends to all companies that prepare financial statements under the 2006 or 1985 Acts irrespective of whether they are prepared under IFRSs or UK GAAP. In practice, the Panel normally exercises this authority only in connection with the financial statements of public companies and large private companies. The Panel may, however, exercise its authority in connection with the financial statements of other companies when it considers appropriate. The following come within the Panel's remit:

- public limited companies;
- companies within a group headed by a plc;
- any private company not qualifying as small or medium-sized; and
- any private company within a group which does not qualify as small or medium-sized.

The financial statements of those companies outside of the Panel's remit are policed by BERR.

The Panel can ask directors to explain apparent departures from law and accounting requirements. If the Panel is not satisfied by the directors' explanations, it aims to persuade them to adopt a more appropriate treatment. The directors may then voluntarily withdraw the financial statements or directors' report and replace them with revised financial statements or a revised directors' report, that correct the error. Depending on the circumstances, the Panel may accept other forms of remedial action, for example restatement of the comparative figures in the next annual financial statements. Failing voluntary correction, the Panel can exercise its powers to secure the necessary revision of the original financial statements or directors' report through a court order. The Panel maintains a legal costs fund of £2m for this purpose. To date the Panel has been successful in resolving all cases brought to its attention without having to apply for a court order.

The Panel does not offer advice on the application of accounting standards or the requirements of the Companies Act. There is no provision for 'pre-clearance' of accounting treatments with the Panel as happens in some other jurisdictions.

Until comparatively recently, the Panel did not actively monitor the financial statements of those companies within its remit. It responded to complaints from members of the public, referrals from the FSA of companies whose auditors had qualified their reports and unfavourable press comments on companies' financial statements. However, it assumed a pro-active role in response to the 2003 report of the Co-ordinating Group on Audit and Accounting. This group was set up by the Government to consider how the UK should respond to some well publicised corporate failures around that time.

The Panel now considers any matter drawn to its attention from a review of reports selected by the Panel, or by complaints or press comments, including matters drawn to its attention by the FSA and by HMRC. It initially considers whether there is, prima facie, a case to answer. When there is such a case, the Chairman appoints a group to conduct the enquiry. A group is normally made up of five members including either the Chairman or the Deputy Chairman. Other members are chosen from the Panel to provide a balance of experience relevant to the enquiry and to avoid any conflicts of interests. The other members of the Panel are not involved and the group's exchanges with the company are confidential.

The group puts its concerns to the directors and may discuss them in correspondence and at meetings. The Panel encourages directors to consult their auditors, to involve their audit committee and to take any other advice they feel necessary. The process is informal but is intended to combine efficiency with fairness. As defective financial statements could mislead the public, the procedures are intended to allow for speedy rectification. The group aims to reach agreement with the directors of the company by persuasion. If the group is satisfied by the company's explanations, the case is closed and the fact that an enquiry was made remains confidential. Where the directors do agree to take some remedial action the Panel issues a Press Notice. The Panel does not comment on or discuss its conclusions.

The Panel selects accounts for review in a number of ways. First, the Panel discusses with the Financial Services Authority and the Panel's Standing Advisory Group which sectors of the economy are under strain or likely to give rise to difficult accounting issues. Then the Panel chooses a number of sectors and reviews a selection of accounts in each. Next, the Panel is developing its own risk model to identify cases where accounting problems are more likely – cases of poor corporate governance, for example. Then the Panel looks at specific topical accounting issues and last but not least responds to complaints from the public, the press and the City. In all cases the selection is based on the Panel's assessment of the risk of non-compliance and the risk of significant consequences if there is non-compliance.

On 9 November 2007, the Panel announced that its monitoring activity for 2008/9 will focus on the banking, travel and leisure, retail, commercial property and house builders sectors. The selection of companies will be drawn from the full range of companies within the Panel's remit, including large private companies.

The Panel's remit was extended by the Companies (Audit, Investigations and Community Enterprise Act) 2004. The Panel was appointed to keep under review interim reports of UK listed companies. The Panel's remit was also extended to include financial information published by listed issuers that are not governed by the Companies Act, for example non-corporate UK entities with traded securities and certain overseas issuers.

The Panel's remit was also extended to cover directors' reports issued in respect of financial years beginning on or after 1 April 2006 (which is one year after the requirements for the enhanced business review came into force).

In June 2008 the Panel announced its approach to the review of accounts whose audit report is qualified for failure to comply with the 1985 Act. The Panel arranged for notification of qualified audit reports on accounts that fall within its remit. The Panel writes to some of the companies concerned, drawing attention to the directors' responsibilities under the Acts to prepare accounts that comply with the law and accounting standards. The Panel will advise directors that, at this stage it will not be opening an enquiry into the accounts which have caused it to write, but the Panel will review their next set of accounts and will take appropriate action in accordance with its operating procedures if the qualification remains.
The Panel has a clear interest in company accounts which are qualified by their auditors for breach of accounting requirements as it is a strong indicator that the financial statements may not be properly prepared in accordance with the law and give a true and fair view. The FRRP hopes that this approach will encourage directors who presently prepare accounts that do not comply with the law to address the non-compliance so that neither the audit qualification nor an FRRP enquiry is necessary in future.

When UK companies report under IFRSs, enforcement is still a matter of UK company law. The Panel continues to play the role described above. However, there has been much discussion about the need for consistent enforcement of IFRSs within the EU and more widely throughout the world. The Committee of European Securities Regulators (CESR) has published Standard No. 2 *Financial Information – Co-ordination of enforcement activities*. Details of the CESR Standard can be found at:

www.cesr-eu.org

Further details of the Panel's procedures, which were revised on 1 August 2008, may be found on its website:

www.frc.org.uk/frrp.

The Panel's remit was extended by the Companies (Audit, Investigations and Community Enterprise) Act 2004. The Panel was appointed to keep under review interim reports of UK listed companies. The Panel's remit was also extended to include financial information published by listed issuers that are not governed by the Companies Act, for example non-corporate UK entities with traded securities and certain overseas issuers.

The Panel's remit was also extended to cover directors' reports issued in respect of financial years beginning on or after 1 April 2006 (which is one year after the requirements for the enhanced business review came into force).

In June 2008, the Panel announced its approach to the review of accounts whose audit report is qualified for failure to comply with the 1985 Act. The Panel arranged for notification of qualified audit reports on accounts that fall within its remit. The Panel writes to some of the companies concerned, drawing attention to the directors' responsibilities under the Acts to prepare accounts that comply with the law and accounting standards. The Panel will advise directors that at this stage it will not be opening an enquiry into the accounts which have caused it to write, but the Panel will review their next set of accounts and will take appropriate action in accordance with its operating procedures if the qualification remains. The Panel has a clear interest in company accounts which are qualified by their auditors for breach of accounting requirements as it is a strong indicator that the financial statements may not be properly prepared in accordance with the law and give a true and fair view. The FRRP hopes that this approach will encourage directors who presently prepare accounts that do not comply with the law to address the non-compliance so that neither the audit qualification nor an FRRP enquiry is necessary in future.

When UK companies report under IFRS, enforcement is still a matter of UK company law. The Panel continues to play the role described above. However, there has been much discussion about the need for consistent enforcement of IFRSs within the EU and more widely throughout the world. The Committee of European Securities Regulators (CESR) has published Standard No. 2 *Financial Information – Coordination of Enforcement Activities*. Details of the CESR Standard can be found at:

www.cesr-eu.org

Further details of the Panel's procedures, which were revised on 1 August 2008, may be found on its website:

www.frc.org.uk/frrp

2 Framework for the preparation and presentation of financial statements

1 Introduction

The IASB's *Framework for the Preparation and Presentation of Financial Statements* sets out the concepts underlying the preparation and presentation of financial statements for external users. It serves as a guide to the Board in developing accounting standards and as a guide to resolving accounting issues that are not addressed directly in an International Accounting Standard, an International Financial Reporting Standard or an Interpretation.

This chapter discusses the contents of the Framework in the following sections:

Section 2	Purpose and status of the Framework
Section 3	Scope
Section 4	Users and their information needs
Section 5	Responsibility for the preparation of financial statements
Section 6	The objective of financial statements
Section 7	Assumptions underlying the preparation of financial statements
Section 8	Qualitative characteristics of financial statements
Section 9	The elements of financial statements
Section 10	Concepts of capital and capital maintenance
Section 11	Future developments

A comprehensive discussion of each of the topics covered in the Framework is beyond the scope of this text. The following sections therefore provide a very brief summary of the matters discussed therein.

The Framework is, for the most part, fairly similar to its UK equivalent, the ASB's Statement of Principles for Financial Reporting, *and in fact the ASB drew on the Framework when preparing the Statement of Principles.* UK

There are some differences in drafting, for example in the definition of liabilities, but most of the concepts will be familiar.

1.1 Terminology

When the IASB revised IAS 1 *Presentation of Financial Statements* in 2007, it did not amend the terminology used in the Framework. Accordingly, the Framework still refers, for example, to the income statement and balance sheet, rather than to the statements of comprehensive income and financial position.

2 Purpose and status of the Framework

The purposes of the Framework are to:

[FR.1]

- assist the IASB in the development of future IFRSs, and in its review of existing IFRSs;
- assist the IASB in promoting harmonisation of regulations, accounting standards and procedures relating to the presentation of financial statements by providing a basis for reducing the number of alternative accounting treatments permitted by IFRSs;
- assist national standard-setting bodies in developing national standards;
- assist preparers of financial statements in applying IFRSs and in dealing with topics that have yet to form the subject of an IFRS;
- assist auditors in forming an opinion as to whether financial statements conform with IFRSs;
- assist users of financial statements in interpreting the information contained in financial statements prepared in conformity with IFRSs; and
- provide those who are interested in the work of the IASB with information about its approach to the formulation of IFRSs.

The Framework is not itself an International Financial Reporting Standard, and hence it does not define standards for particular measurement or disclosure issues. There may be contradictions between the Framework and individual Standards or Interpretations, which are being addressed by the IASB over time. Where such a conflict arises, the Standard or Interpretation takes precedence. This is a key point in that it clarifies that the principles of the Framework cannot be used to justify a treatment that contravenes an extant IFRS.

Some of the older Standards depart from the Framework, in that they:

- recognise assets or liabilities that do not meet the Framework definitions (for example, actuarial gains and losses deferred under IAS 19 *Employee Benefits* – see **chapter 24**); or
- measure assets or liabilities on bases other than those specified in the Framework (for example, government grants recognised at a nominal amount under IAS 20 *Accounting for Government Grants and Disclosure of Government Assistance* – see **chapter 41**).

As noted above, where there is conflict between a Standard and the Framework, the Standard prevails.

In the absence of a Standard or an Interpretation that specifically applies to a transaction, IAS 8 *Accounting Policies, Changes in Accounting Estimates and Errors* requires that management should use its judgement in developing and applying an accounting policy that results in information that is relevant and reliable. In making that judgement, IAS 8.11 requires management to consider first the requirements and guidance in Standards and Interpretations dealing with similar and related issues, and second the definitions, recognition criteria and measurement concepts for assets, liabilities, income and expenses in the Framework. This elevation of the importance of the Framework was added in the 2003 revisions to IAS 8 (see **section 3.1** of **chapter 4**).

3 Scope

The Framework deals specifically with:

[FR.5]

- the objective of financial statements;
- the qualitative characteristics that determine the usefulness of information in financial statements;

- the definition, recognition and measurement of the elements from which financial statements are constructed; and
- concepts of capital and capital maintenance.

The Framework addresses general purpose financial statements that an entity (including a state-owned business entity) prepares and presents at least annually to meet the common information needs of a wide range of users external to the entity. Therefore, the Framework does not necessarily apply to special purpose financial reports such as reports to tax authorities, reports to governmental regulatory authorities, prospectuses prepared in connection with securities offerings, and reports prepared in connection with business combinations. [FR.6]

4 Users and their information needs

The Framework identifies the following users of financial statements: investors, employees, lenders, suppliers and other trade creditors, customers, governments and their agencies, and the public. [FR.9] All of these categories use financial statements to help them in decision making. Although all of the information needs of these users cannot be met by financial statements, there are needs that are common to all users. The Framework concludes that, as investors are providers of risk capital to the entity, financial statements that meet the needs of investors will generally meet most of the information needs of other users as well. [FR.10]

The Framework notes that financial statements cannot provide all of the information that users may need to make economic decisions. For one thing, financial statements show the financial effects of past events and transactions, whereas the decisions that most users of financial statements have to make relate to the future. Further, financial statements provide only a limited amount of the non-financial information needed by users of financial statements.

5 Responsibility for the preparation of financial statements

The management of the entity has the primary responsibility for the preparation and presentation of the financial statements of the entity. [FR.11]

6 The objective of financial statements

The objective of financial statements is to provide information about the financial position, performance and changes in financial position of an entity that is useful to a wide range of users in making economic decisions. [FR.12]

Financial statements also show the results of the stewardship of management, or the accountability of management for the resources entrusted to it. [FR.14]

6.1 Financial position

The financial position of an entity is affected by the economic resources it controls, its financial structure, its liquidity and solvency, and its capacity to adapt to changes in the environment in which it operates. [FR.16]

Information regarding the financial position of an entity is primarily presented in the balance sheet. [FR.19]

6.2 Performance

Performance includes the ability of an entity to earn a profit on the resources that have been invested in it. Information about the amounts and variability of profits helps in forecasting future cash flows from the entity's existing resources and in forecasting potential additional cash flows from additional resources that might be invested in the entity. [FR.17]

Information about performance is primarily provided in an income statement. [FR.19]

> The Framework preceded the introduction of the Statement of Recognised Income and Expense and, therefore, does not refer to it.

6.3 Changes in financial position

Users of financial statements seek information about changes in financial position arising from the investing, financing and operating activities that an entity has undertaken during the reporting period. This information helps in assessing how well the entity is able to generate cash and cash equivalents and how it uses those cash flows. [FR.18]

The cash flow statement provides this kind of information. [FR.19]

6.4 Notes and supplementary schedules

The financial statements also contain notes and supplementary schedules and other information that:

[FR.21]

- explain items in the balance sheet and income statement;
- disclose the risks and uncertainties affecting the entity;
- explain any resources and obligations not recognised in the balance sheet.

7 Assumptions underlying the preparation of financial statements

The key assumptions underlying the preparation of financial statements are:

[FR.22 & 23]

- the accrual basis of accounting; and
- going concern.

These assumptions are discussed in **chapter 3.**

8 Qualitative characteristics of financial statements

Qualitative characteristics are the attributes that make the information provided in financial statements useful to users. [FR.24] The Framework identifies the four primary qualitative characteristics of financial statements as:

- understandability;
- relevance;
- reliability; and
- comparability.

These characteristics are discussed in sections **8.1** to **8.4**.

In determining the financial information to be reported, preparers of financial statements may need to arrive at a balance between these qualitative characteristics. The relative importance of the characteristics in different circumstances will be a matter of professional judgement.

For example, if there is undue delay in the reporting of information, it may lose relevance. Preparers may need to balance the relative merits of timely reporting and the provision of reliable information. To provide information on a timely basis, it may be necessary to report before all of the aspects of a transaction are known, thus impairing the reliability of the information. Conversely, if reporting is delayed until all of the aspects of the transaction are known, the information may no longer be relevant to the decision-making of users.

A balance also needs to be achieved between the benefit to be derived from the disclosure of information and the cost of its inclusion. The benefits derived from information should exceed the cost of providing it. The achievement of an appropriate balance requires judgement – and the Framework acknowledges that it can be difficult to apply a cost-benefit test in any particular case. Nevertheless, the Framework encourages standard-setters in particular, as well as preparers and users of financial statements, to be aware of this constraint.

The Framework concludes that the application of the principal qualitative characteristics discussed below, and of appropriate accounting standards, normally results in financial statements that show a true and fair view. [FR.46]

8.1 Understandability

The first essential quality of financial information is that it is readily understandable by users. In determining the level of explanation that is required in financial statements, the Framework allows a preparer to assume that the user has a reasonable knowledge of business and economic activities and accounting, and a willingness to study the information with reasonable diligence. Relevant complex information should not be excluded from financial statements merely on the basis that it is too difficult for certain users to understand. [FR.25]

8.2 Relevance

Information is considered to be relevant to the needs of users when it influences the economic decisions of users by helping them to evaluate past, present or future events, or by confirming or correcting their past evaluations. [FR.26]

In determining whether or not information is relevant to the needs of the user, preparers of financial statements will need to take account of the nature and materiality of the information. Information is considered to be material if its omission or misstatement could reasonably be expected to influence the economic decisions of users taken on the basis of the financial statements. Materiality depends on the size of the item or error judged in the particular circumstances of its omission or misstatement. [FR.30]

8.3 Reliability

To be useful, information must be reliable, i.e. it must be free from material error and bias, and it must represent faithfully that which it purports to represent. [FR.31]

There will be circumstances where information is relevant, but it is so unreliable that it is potentially misleading. The Framework cites the example of a claim for damages under a disputed legal action where it may be inappropriate for the entity to recognise the full amount of the claim in the balance sheet, although it may be appropriate to disclose the amount and the circumstances of the claim.

8.3.1 Faithful representation

Most financial information is subject to some risk of not representing faithfully that which it purports to represent. This is because of inherent difficulties either in identifying the transactions or other events to be accounted for, or in devising appropriate measurement bases for such transactions or events. In some cases, the measurement of the financial effects of items may be so uncertain that it is more appropriate to exclude them from the financial statements. In other cases, however, it may be appropriate to recognise them, and to disclose the risk of error surrounding their recognition and measurement. [FR.34]

8.3.2 Substance over form

In order to ensure a faithful representation, transactions and other events should be accounted for and presented in accordance with their substance and economic reality, and not merely their legal form. [FR.35]

For the vast majority of routine transactions, substance and form will be the same, and the application of the principle of substance over form will not alter the established method of accounting. However, there will be transactions where the substance and the legal form differ, or where the substance is not readily apparent. In practice, common features of such transactions often include:

- the deliberate separation of legal title and the underlying benefits (e.g. leases, consignment inventories, factored debts and the use of special purpose entities);

- options granted where the exercise of the option can be considered a virtual certainty (e.g. sale with put and call options to repurchase); and

- a series of transactions designed so that the commercial effect can only be appreciated when the series is taken as a whole (e.g. securitisations, project financing and circular finance structures).

The key to accounting in accordance with the principle of substance over form is to obtain a full understanding of the rationale behind the transaction as a whole, including the role of each party, and the commercial logic for their involvement. This requires:

- a realistic appreciation of why the transaction exists and why each party is involved. In determining the substance of a transaction, all of its aspects and implications should be identified and greater weight given to those more likely to have a commercial effect in practice;

- placing the transaction in context. A group or series of transactions that achieves or is designed to achieve an overall commercial effect should be viewed as a whole;

- an assessment of what has been achieved by the transaction. To determine the substance of a transaction, it is necessary to establish whether it has given rise to new assets or liabilities for the reporting entity or whether it has changed the entity's existing assets or liabilities;

- identification of the risk-takers. Evidence that an entity has rights or other access to benefits (and hence has an asset) is provided if the entity is exposed to the risks inherent in the benefits, taking into account the likelihood of those risks having a commercial effect in practice. Similarly, evidence that an entity has an obligation to transfer benefits (and hence has a liability) is given if there is some circumstance in which the entity is unable to avoid, legally or commercially, an outflow of benefits; and

- a realistic appraisal of conditional events. Where a transaction incorporates one or more options, guarantees or conditional provisions, their commercial effect should be assessed in the context of all of the aspects and implications of the transaction, in order to determine what assets and liabilities exist.

In practice, the following analysis will assist in understanding the commercial effects of the transaction:

- obtain all relevant documentation and agreements, including side letters, that impact the likely course of events. Documents should always be in final form and include monetary details where relevant;
- identify the role played by each party to the transaction (in particular, the equity participants to a transaction) and the reason for their involvement. It is reasonable to suppose that a financial institution will limit its interest to that of financier – any assertion to the contrary should be supported by clear evidence. If a transaction appears to lack logic from the point of view of one or more participants, then it is likely that either all of the relevant parts of the transaction have not been identified, or that the commercial effect of some aspect of the transaction has been incorrectly assessed;
- assess the likely course of action (including options) – place greater emphasis on the probable course of events and, accordingly, little or no emphasis on unlikely events. The consequences of liquidation of one of the parties should only be considered where this is a likely event; and
- test the transaction's responsiveness, and the return for each participant, in the event of marginal changes in variables, such as interest rates, asset values and the timing of events. This provides useful insight into the role of the parties involved, e.g. whether a participant obtains a risk-taker's return, or a financier's return.

8.3.3 *Neutrality*

To be reliable, the information contained in financial statements must be neutral, i.e. it must be free from bias. Financial statements are not neutral if, by the selection or presentation of information, they influence the making of a decision or judgement in order to achieve a predetermined result or outcome. [FR.36]

8.3.4 *Prudence*

Prudence is the inclusion of a degree of caution in the exercise of judgement under conditions of uncertainty, such that assets or income are not overstated, and liabilities or expenses are not understated. [FR.37]

However, the exercise of prudence does not allow, for example, the creation of hidden reserves or excessive provisions, the deliberate understatement of assets or income, or the deliberate overstatement of liabilities or expenses. Such actions would result in financial statements that were not neutral and, therefore, not having the quality of reliability.

8.3.5 *Completeness*

The final aspect of reliability referred to in the Framework is completeness, i.e. in order to be reliable the information in financial statements must be complete within the bounds of materiality and cost. [FR.38] The omission of information can cause the financial statements to be false or misleading, and thus unreliable.

8.4 Comparability

Users of financial statements will wish to identify trends in the financial position of an entity over time, and to compare the financial statements of different entities in order to evaluate their relative financial position, performance and changes in financial position. In order to satisfy the requirements of users, it is therefore necessary that the measurement and presentation of the financial effect of like transactions and other events should be carried out in a consistent manner throughout a reporting entity, and over time for that entity, and in a consistent manner by different entities. [FR.39]

An important implication of this principle is that users of financial information should be informed of the accounting policies used in the preparation of that information, any changes to those accounting policies, and the effects of any such changes. [FR.40]

However, the Framework states that the need for comparability should not be an impediment to improved financial reporting. It is not appropriate for an entity to continue accounting in the same manner for a transaction or other event if the policy adopted does not result in the reporting of relevant and reliable information. It is also inappropriate for an entity to leave its accounting policies unchanged when more relevant and reliable alternatives exist.

9 The elements of financial statements

The Framework provides definitions for the elements of financial statements, as well as principles for the recognition and measurement of those elements.

9.1 Assets

9.1.1 Definition

The Framework defines an asset as a resource controlled by the entity as a result of past events and from which future economic benefits are expected to flow to the entity. [FR.49(a)]

The future economic benefit embodied in an asset is the potential to contribute, directly or indirectly, to the flow of cash and cash equivalents. [FR.53] Such benefits may flow to the entity in a number of ways – e.g. by use in the production process, by exchange for other assets, as settlement of a liability, or by distribution to the owners of the entity.

Many assets have physical form – but that is not essential to the existence of an asset. For example, intangibles such as patents and copyrights are assets if future economic benefits are expected to flow from them to the entity and if they are controlled by the entity.

The entity's control over those future economic benefits will most commonly be evidenced by legal ownership, but that is not essential. For example, property held on lease is an asset if the entity controls the benefits that are expected to flow from it.

The entity will usually have legal rights over an asset – but not necessarily so. For example, know-how obtained from a development activity may meet the definition of an asset when, by keeping the know-how secret, an entity controls the benefits that are expected to flow from it.

The assets of an entity must result from a past transaction or event. Assets are most usually acquired by purchasing or producing them – but this will not always be the case, e.g. where assets are received by way of government grant or contributions from equity participants.

9.1.2 *Recognition*

An asset should be recognised in the balance sheet when:

[FR.89]

- it is probable that the future economic benefits will flow to the entity; and
- the asset has a cost or value that can be measured reliably.

The assessment of the degree of uncertainty attaching to the flow of future economic benefits is made on the basis of the evidence available when the financial statements are prepared. An asset is not recognised in the balance sheet when expenditure has been incurred from which it is considered improbable that economic benefits will flow to the entity beyond the current accounting period. Instead, such a transaction is dealt with as an expense in the income statement.

9.1.3 *Measurement*

The determination of the monetary amount at which an asset is to be recognised in the balance sheet involves the selection of a particular basis of measurement.

The most common bases of measurement for assets are:

[FR.100]

- historical cost – assets are recorded at the amount of cash or cash equivalents paid or the fair value of the consideration given to acquire them at the time of their acquisition;
- current cost – assets are carried at the amount of cash or cash equivalents that would have to be paid if the same or an equivalent asset was acquired currently;
- realisable value – assets are carried at the amount of cash or cash equivalents that could currently be obtained by selling the asset in an orderly disposal; and
- present value – assets are carried at the present discounted value of the future net cash inflows that the item is expected to generate in the normal course of business.

The Framework does not indicate a preference for any of these measurement bases. It points out that the measurement basis most commonly adopted is historical cost – often combined with other bases. For example, inventories are usually carried at the lower of cost and net realisable value.

9.2 Liabilities

9.2.1 Definition

The Framework defines a liability as a present obligation of the entity arising from past events, the settlement of which is expected to result in an outflow from the entity of resources embodying economic benefits. [FR.49(b)]

An essential characteristic of a liability is that the entity has a present obligation. An obligation is a duty or responsibility to act or perform in a certain way. Obligations may be legally enforceable, e.g. a binding contract or a statutory requirement. Obligations also arise, however, from normal business practice, custom and a desire to maintain good business relations or to act in an equitable manner. For example, an entity may decide as a matter of policy to rectify faults in its products after the warranty period has expired, even though it has no legal obligation to do so, with the objective of maintaining its reputation with customers.

The Framework draws a distinction between a present obligation and a future commitment. A decision by management to acquire an asset or to incur expenditure in the future does not, of itself, create a present obligation. An obligation normally arises only when the goods are delivered or an irrevocable agreement is entered into.

The settlement of a liability usually involves the entity giving up resources embodying economic benefits – whether by payment of cash, transfer of other assets, provision of services, replacement of the obligation by another obligation, or conversion of the obligation to equity.

UK *The ASB's* Statement of Principles for Financial Reporting *defines liabilities as obligations of an entity to transfer economic benefits as a result of past transactions or events. There is a subtle difference here between the Framework and the Statement of Principles. The Framework focuses first on whether there is an obligation (which might be to transfer economic benefits or to issue equity) and then on whether a transfer of economic benefits is probable. The Statement of Principles focuses only on whether there is an obligation to transfer economic benefits.*

Thus, based only on these definitions (but see below), an entity with a choice over whether to settle an obligation by transferring cash or equity would hypothetically recognise a liability under the Framework (if cash settlement is probable) but would not have a liability based only on the Statement of Principles.

In practice, both the IASB and the ASB have issued more specific guidance on this particular point (in IAS 32 Financial Instruments: Presentation *and in its UK equivalent FRS 25* Financial Instruments: Presentation *respectively). Thus, although there is a theoretical difference of principle here, it appears unlikely that it will have an impact in practice.*

9.2.2 *Recognition*

A liability should be recognised in the balance sheet when:

[FR.91]

- it is probable that an outflow of resources embodying economic benefits will result from the settlement of a present obligation; and
- the amount at which the settlement will take place can be measured reliably.

In practice, obligations under contracts that are equally proportionately unperformed (e.g. liabilities for inventories ordered but not yet received) are generally not recognised as liabilities in the financial statements (see **chapter 11** for discussion of executory contracts).

9.2.3 *Measurement*

The determination of the monetary amount at which a liability is to be recognised in the balance sheet involves the selection of a particular basis of measurement.

The most common bases of measurement for liabilities are:

[FR.100]

- historical cost – liabilities are recorded at the amount of the proceeds received in exchange for the obligation or at the amounts of cash or cash equivalents expected to be paid to satisfy the liability in the normal course of business;

- current cost – liabilities are carried at the undiscounted amount of cash or cash equivalents that would be required to settle the obligation currently;
- settlement value – liabilities are carried at their settlement values, i.e. at the undiscounted amounts of cash or cash equivalents expected to be paid to satisfy the liabilities in the normal course of business; and
- present value – liabilities are carried at the present discounted value of the future net cash outflows that are expected to be required to settle the liabilities in the normal course of business.

The Framework does not indicate a preference for any of these measurement bases.

9.3 Equity

The Framework defines equity as the residual interest in the assets of the entity after deducting all of its liabilities. [FR.49(c)]

Equity may be sub-classified in the balance sheet. For example, funds contributed by shareholders, retained earnings and capital reserves may be shown separately. Such classifications can be relevant to the decision needs of users of the financial statements when they indicate legal or other restrictions on the ability of the entity to distribute or otherwise apply its equity. They may also reflect the fact that parties with ownership interests in an entity have differing rights in relation to the receipt of dividends and the repayment of capital.

9.4 Income

9.4.1 Definition

Income is defined as increases in economic benefits during the accounting period in the form of inflows or enhancements of assets, or decreases of liabilities, that result in increases in equity, other than those relating to contributions from equity participants. [FR.70(a)]

Income can be subdivided into:

- revenue – which arises in the course of the ordinary activities of the entity and is referred to by a variety of different names including sales, fees, interest, dividends, royalties and rent; and
- gains – which represent other items that meet the definition of income. They include, for example, gains arising on the disposal of

non-current assets, and unrealised gains arising on the revaluation of financial instruments or non-current assets.

9.4.2 *Recognition*

Income is recognised when an increase in future economic benefits related to an increase in an asset or a decrease in a liability has arisen that can be measured reliably. [FR.92] This means that recognition of income occurs simultaneously with the recognition of increases in assets or decreases in liabilities. Generally, such recognition will occur when the movements in assets/liabilities can be measured reliably and have a sufficient degree of certainty.

The amount at which income is recognised will be determined by the movements in assets/liabilities as discussed in the previous sections.

Specific criteria for the recognition of particular types of revenue are set out in IAS 18 *Revenue* (see **chapter 23**).

9.5 Expenses

9.5.1 *Definition*

Expenses are defined as decreases in economic benefits during the accounting period in the form of outflows or depletions of assets, or incurrences of liabilities, that result in decreases in equity, other than those relating to distributions to equity participants. [FR.70(b)]

9.5.2 *Recognition*

Expenses are recognised in the income statement when a decrease in future economic benefits related to a decrease in an asset or an increase in a liability has arisen that can be measured reliably. [FR.94] This means that recognition of expenses occurs simultaneously with the recognition of decreases in assets or increases in liabilities.

The amount at which expenses are recognised will be determined by the movements in assets/liabilities as discussed in the previous sections.

The recognition of expenses in the income statement will be affected by any direct association between the costs incurred and the earning of specific items of income (i.e. matching). However, the application of the matching principle does not allow the recognition of items in the balance sheet that do not meet the definition of assets or liabilities.

When economic benefits are expected to arise over several accounting periods, and the association with income can only be broadly or indirectly determined, expenses are recognised in the income statement on the basis of systematic and rational allocation procedures (e.g. depreciation or amortisation of non-current assets). These allocation procedures are intended to recognise expenses in the accounting periods in which the associated economic benefits are consumed or expire.

An expense is recognised immediately in the income statement in those cases when the expenditure produces no future economic benefits, or when future economic benefits do not qualify, or cease to qualify, for recognition in the balance sheet as an asset.

An expense is also recognised in the income statement when a liability is incurred without the recognition of an asset, e.g. when a liability arises under a product warranty.

9.6 Transactions with equity participants

The definitions of both income and expenses set out in the previous sections exclude contributions from and distributions to equity participants. These exclusions are based on the principle that profit or loss of the entity cannot be created simply by transferring resources to or from the owners of the entity.

10 Concepts of capital and capital maintenance

The Framework identifies two concepts of capital maintenance:

[FR.104]

- financial capital maintenance – under which profit is earned only if the financial (or money) amount of the net assets at the end of the reporting period exceeds the financial (or money) amount of net assets at the beginning of the reporting period, after excluding any distributions to, and contributions from, owners during the period; and
- physical capital maintenance – under which a profit is earned only if the physical productive capacity (or operating capability) of the entity (or the resources or funds needed to achieve that capacity) at the end of the period exceeds the physical productive capacity at the beginning of the period, after excluding any distributions to, and contributions from, owners during the period.

The Framework does not indicate a preference for either of these concepts of capital maintenance.

The selection of a concept of capital maintenance (and of the measurement basis to be used) determines the accounting model used in preparation of the financial statements. The Framework acknowledges that different accounting models exhibit different degrees of relevance and reliability, and that preparers of financial statements should seek a balance between those characteristics.

11 Future developments

At their joint meeting in October 2004, the IASB and the US FASB decided to add to their respective agendas a joint project to develop a common conceptual framework, built on both the existing IASB Framework and the FASB Conceptual Framework, that both Boards would use as a basis for their accounting standards.

The project will be addressed in eight stages:

Phase A: Objective and qualitative characteristics (see **11.1**)

Phase B: Elements: recognition and measurement attributes

Phase C: Initial and subsequent measurement

Phase D: Reporting entity (see **11.2**)

Phase E: Presentation and disclosure

Phase F: Status of the Framework in GAAP hierarchy

Phase G: Applicability to not-for-profit

Phase H: Other issues, if necessary

The Boards' initial focus is on business entities in the private sector. The concepts developed through the project will then be considered for application to financial reporting for other entities, such as not-for-profit-entities and business entities in the public sector.

11.1 Phase A: Objectives and qualitative characteristics

In May 2008, an Exposure Draft of Chapters 1 and 2 of the Conceptual Framework (Objective and Qualitative Characteristics) was published. Comments are invited by 29 September 2008. The draft reflects the boards' updated proposals in the light of comments received on an initial consultation document published in July 2006.

Chapter 1 proposes the following objective of financial reporting:

> 'The objective of general purpose financial reporting is to provide financial information about the reporting entity that is useful to present and potential equity investors, lenders and other creditors in making decisions in their capacity as capital providers. Capital providers are the primary users of financial reporting. To accomplish the objective, financial reports should communicate information about an entity's economic resources, claims on those resources, and the transactions and other events and circumstances that change them. The degree to which that financial information is useful will depend on its qualitative characteristics.'

The reference to 'present and potential' investors is intended to acknowledge that general purpose financial reports are used both for future investment decisions and assessing the stewardship of resources already committed to the entity. The Exposure Draft states that financial reporting should provide information that enables capital providers to assess the entity's ability to generate net cash inflows and management's ability to protect and enhance the capital providers' investments.

The stewardship responsibilities of management are addressed specifically. The Exposure Draft notes that management 'is accountable to the entity's capital providers for the custody and safekeeping of the entity's economic resources and for their efficient and profitable use' and that the entity complies with applicable laws, regulations and contractual requirements. The ability of management to discharge these responsibilities effectively has an effect on the entity's ability to generate net cash inflows in the future, implying that potential investors are also assessing management performance as they make their investment decision.

Chapter 2 considers the qualitative characteristics and constraints of decision-useful financial reporting information. The Boards have refined the approach in the discussion paper, such that there are two 'fundamental qualitative characteristics':

- relevance; and
- faithful representation.

Relevant information is that which has predictive value, confirmatory value or both; in other words it is capable of influencing the decisions of capital providers. The users do not need to use such information, merely to have access to it. Faithful representation implies that decision-useful financial information represents faithfully the economic phenomenon that it purports to represent.

In addition, there are certain characteristics that 'enhance' the decision-usefulness of financial information. These are complementary to the fundamental qualitative characteristics and are: comparability (including consistency), verifiability, timeliness and understandability. The 'enhancing qualitative characteristics' help to distinguish more useful information from less useful information.

There are two pervasive constraints that limit the information provided in useful financial reports:

- materiality; and
- cost.

Information is material if its omission or misstatement could influence the decisions that users make on the basis of an entity's financial information. Materiality is not a matter to be considered by standard-setters but by preparers and their auditors. The benefits of providing financial reporting information should justify the costs of providing that information.

The chapters in this Exposure Draft would add a Preface and replace paragraphs 9 – 22 and 24 – 46 of the current IASB Framework. The remainder of the Framework is unaffected, as it will be amended by subsequent chapters in the conceptual framework project.

11.2 Phase D: Reporting entity

Also in May 2008, a Discussion Paper was published on Phase D: The Reporting Entity. Comments are similarly invited by 29 September 2008. The Discussion Paper sets out the boards' preliminary views on the reporting entity concept and related issues. Although the reporting entity concept determines some important aspects of financial reporting, the boards' existing frameworks do not address it specifically.

In brief, the boards' preliminary views are that:

- a reporting entity is a circumscribed area of business activity of interest to present and potential equity investors, lenders and other capital providers;
- control is the basis for determining the composition of a group reporting entity; and
- consolidated financial statements should be prepared from the perspective of the group reporting entity.

It is proposed that a reporting entity need not be based on a legal structure, but rather on the existence of a circumscribed area of business activity of interest to present and potential equity investors, lenders and other capital providers. A reporting entity could be represented by a subset of a legal entity, such as an unincorporated branch, or it could be represented as the aggregate of two or more entities such as those comprised in consolidated or combined financial statements. While such a broad definition may present some practical difficulties (such as the fact that when a reporting entity is defined as a component of a legal entity, creditors of an entity may have recourse to assets other than those of the 'reporting entity'), it is suggested that these issues could be dealt with at the standards level, for example through requirement of specific disclosure.

11.3 Timetable

Final versions of the chapters from Phase A are expected in the first half of 2009, and an exposure draft on Phase D is planned for the second half of 2009. Discussion papers on phases C and B are planned for the first and second half of 2009 respectively. The timing for the remaining phases has not yet been determined.

3 Presentation of financial statements

1 Introduction

IAS 1 *Presentation of Financial Statements* was published in December 2007 and replaces the previous version of the standard of the same title which was issued in 2003 and subsequently amended. The revised version is mandatory for annual periods beginning on or after 1 January 2009. The Standard was most recently amended by *Improvements to IFRSs* issued in May 2008.

The objective of the Standard is to prescribe the basis for presentation of general purpose financial statements, to ensure comparability both with an entity's financial statements of previous periods and with the financial statements of other entities. The Standard sets out overall requirements for the presentation of financial statements, guidelines for their structure and minimum requirements for their contents. [IAS 1(2007).1, previously IAS 1(2003).1]

The Standard was revised in 2007 as the first phase of the IASB's project on financial statement presentation. The main changes from the 2003 version of IAS 1 are to require:

- presentation of all non-owner changes in equity (i.e. 'comprehensive income') either in one statement of comprehensive income or in two statements (i.e. a separate income statement and a statement of comprehensive income). Components of comprehensive income may not be presented in the statement of changes in equity. Comprehensive income includes profit or loss plus other comprehensive income (e.g. changes in revaluation surplus under IAS 16 and gains and losses arising from retranslation of a foreign operation under IAS 21);
- presentation of a statement of financial position (i.e. a balance sheet – see below) as at the beginning of the earliest comparative period when an accounting policy is applied retrospectively or there is a retrospective restatement;
- disclosure of income tax relating to each component of other comprehensive income; and
- disclosure of reclassification adjustments (i.e. 'recycling') relating to components of other comprehensive income.

The revised Standard also changes the titles of the financial statements. In addition to the new statement of comprehensive income described above, the balance sheet becomes the 'statement of financial position' and the cash flow statement becomes the 'statement of cash flows'. However, the use of these new titles in financial statements is not mandatory.

The revised standard also uses the term 'owners' which it defines to mean holders of instruments classified as equity. [IAS 1(2007).7] The Board decided to adopt the term 'owners' and use it throughout IAS 1 to converge with the US standard SFAS 130 although, in practice, it means the same as 'equity'. [IAS 1(2007).BC38]

This chapter covers both the 2003 and 2007 versions of IAS 1 and explains the changes more fully. It generally uses the new terminology except where the context requires otherwise. In addition to the substantive amendments described above, the 2007 revision restructured the Standard and made numerous changes of wording and paragraph numbering. This chapter includes references for both the 2003 and 2007 versions of the Standard.

UK *The equivalent requirements of UK GAAP are set out in the company law, FRS 3* Reporting Financial Performance *and FRS 18* Accounting Policies. *In general, the requirements of IAS 1 are less prescriptive than those of UK GAAP.*

The new requirement in IAS 1 for a statement of comprehensive income will be familiar to UK companies. The presentation of a statement of recognised gains and losses as a primary statement has been required since 1992. In 2000, the ASB put forward proposals in FRED 22 for a single performance statement but these were not implemented at the time because attention turned to convergence with international standards.

This chapter discusses the requirements of IAS 1 and related UK requirements in the following sections.

Section 2	General requirements
Section 3	Fair presentation and compliance with IFRSs
Section 4	The statement of financial position (i.e. balance sheet)
Section 5	The statement of comprehensive income (including the income statement)
Section 6	The statement of changes in equity
Section 7	The notes

Section 8 UK specific disclosure requirements

Section 9 Future developments

Guidance on Implementing IAS 1, which accompanies but is not part of IAS 1, sets out an illustrative financial statements structure. Guidance on the format and content of financial statements is also available in *iGAAP 2008 Financial statements for UK listed groups.*

2 General requirements

2.1 Introduction

IAS 1 requires particular disclosures in the statement of financial position, statement of comprehensive income, separate income statement (if presented) and the statement of changes in equity. It also requires disclosure of other line items either in those statements or in the notes. Presentation and disclosure requirements for the statement of cash flows are contained in IAS 7 (see **chapter 30**). [IAS 1(2007).47, previously IAS 1(2003).42]

IAS 1 sometimes uses the term 'disclosure' in a broad sense, encompassing items presented in the financial statements. Disclosures are also required by other IFRSs. Unless specified to the contrary in IAS 1 or another IFRS, such disclosures may be made in the financial statements. [IAS 1(2007).48, previously IAS 1(2003).43]

> The intention of this paragraph in IAS 1(2007) is not very clear from its wording. However, the equivalent paragraph in IAS 1(2003) makes the point much more clearly that, unless specified otherwise, disclosures may be made either on the face of statements such as the income statement and balance sheet, or in the notes.

2.2 Scope

The scope of the Standard is all general purpose financial statements prepared and presented in accordance with IFRSs. [IAS 1(2007).2, previously IAS 1(2003).2] The effect of the Standard is, therefore, pervasive and will impact on every set of financial statements prepared under IFRSs.

Other IFRSs set out the recognition, measurement and disclosure requirements for specific transactions and other events. [IAS 1(2007).3, previously IAS 1(2003).1]

IAS 1 does not prescribe a fixed format for the presentation of the statement of comprehensive income, the statement of financial position or the statement of changes in equity. It does, however, set out minimum disclosures in those statements. In addition, it establishes further items that may be presented either in those statements or in the notes.

General purpose financial statements are defined in IAS 1 as 'those intended to meet the needs of users who are not in a position to require an entity to prepare reports tailored to their particular information needs'. References to 'financial statements' in IAS 1 are references to general purpose financial statements. [IAS 1(2007).7, previously IAS 1(2003).3]

IAS 1(2003).3 states that general purpose financial statements include those that are presented separately or within another public document such as an annual report or a prospectus. An amended version of these words referring to 'public documents such as a regulatory filing or report to shareholders' was included in the 2006 exposure draft of the amendments to IAS 1. As explained in IAS 1(2007).BC11-BC13, this explanatory wording was omitted from the revised standard 'because the Board did not intend to extend the definition of general purpose financial statements'. The previous wording was not reinstated but could still be relevant.

The Standard applies equally to all entities, including those that present consolidated financial statements and those that present separate financial statements as defined in IAS 27. [IAS 1(2007).4, previously IAS 1(2003).3]

The requirements of IFRSs apply equally to the financial statements of an individual entity and to consolidated financial statements for a group of entities. But IAS 1 does not preclude the presentation of consolidated financial statements complying with IFRSs and financial statements of the parent entity under national requirements within the same document. The basis of preparation of each should be clearly disclosed. Where parent-only financial statements are prepared under IFRSs, the requirements of IAS 27 apply for those separate financial statements (see **chapter 33**). In practice, the two sets of financial statements should generally be presented as separate sections of the document so as to avoid mixing information prepared under different GAAPs on the same page (e.g. columnar layouts mixing parent-only and consolidated information should be avoided). This would not preclude cross references between the two sections of the document to avoid repetition of information that is the same on both bases.

This is an issue for UK companies because they must continue to present the individual financial statements (subject to a statutory exemption from publication of the income statement) of the parent company. As more fully considered in ***chapter 1****, they generally have a choice between IFRSs and UK GAAP for the parent only financial statements.* UK

The Standard does not apply to the structure and content of condensed interim financial statements prepared in accordance with IAS 34 *Interim Financial Reporting*. But paragraphs 13 to 41 of IAS 1(2003) and paragraphs 15 to 35 of IAS 1(2007) apply to such interim reports. [IAS 1(2007).4, previously IAS 1(2003).3]

The paragraphs referred to in IAS 1(2007) are those dealing with fair presentation and compliance with IFRSs (see **section 3** below), going concern (see **2.4** below), accruals accounting (see **2.5** below), materiality and aggregation (see **2.7** below) and offsetting (see **2.8** below). The paragraphs referred to in IAS 1(2003) additionally refer to those dealing with consistency of presentation (see **2.6** below) and comparative information (see **2.9** below). IAS 1(2007).BC33 explains that the Board decided not to reflect in IAS 34.8 (i.e. minimum components of an interim report) its decision to require the inclusion of a statement of financial position at the beginning of the earliest comparative period in a complete set of financial statements. IAS 34 has a year-to-date approach to interim reporting and does not replicate the requirements of IAS 1 in terms of comparative information.

IAS 1 uses terminology that is suitable for profit-oriented entities, including public sector business entities. The Standard notes that entities with not-for-profit activities in the private sector or public sector seeking to apply it may need to amend the descriptions used for particular line items in the financial statements and for the financial statements themselves. [IAS 1(2007).5, previously IAS 1(2003).5]

Similarly, entities that do not have equity as defined in IAS 32 *Financial Instruments: Presentation* (e.g. some mutual funds) and entities whose share capital is not equity (e.g. some co-operatives) may need to adapt the presentation in the financial statements of members' or unit holders' interests (see **2.1.2** in **chapter 15**). [IAS 1(2007).6, previously IAS 1(2003).6]

2.3 Purpose and content of financial statements

Financial statements are a structured representation of the financial position and financial performance of an entity. The objective of financial statements is to provide information about the financial position, financial performance and cash flows of an entity that is useful to a wide range of users in making economic decisions. Financial statements also show the results of management's stewardship of the resources entrusted to it. IAS 1 explains that to meet this objective, financial statements provide information about an entity's:

- assets;
- liabilities;
- equity;
- income and expenses, including gains and losses;
- contributions by and distributions to owners in their capacity as owners; and
- cash flows.

This information, together with other information in the notes, assists users of financial statements in predicting the entity's future cash flows, including their timing and certainty. [IAS 1(2007).9, previously IAS 1(2003).7]

IAS 1, therefore, specifies that a complete set of financial statements comprises:

[IAS 1(2007).10, previously IAS 1(2003).8]

- a statement of financial position at the end of each period (see **section 4** below);
- a statement of comprehensive income for a period when IAS 1(2007) has been adopted and an income statement for a period when it has not (see **section 5** below);
- a statement of changes in equity for the period, the contents of which will differ according to whether IAS 1(2007) has been adopted (see **section 6** below);
- a statement of cash flows for the period (see **chapter 30**);
- notes, comprising a summary of significant accounting policies and other explanatory information (see **section 7** below); and
- only when IAS 1(2007) is adopted, a statement of financial position as at the beginning of the earliest comparative period when an entity

applies an accounting policy retrospectively or makes a retrospective restatement of items in its financial statements, or when it reclassifies items in its financial statements (see **2.9** below).

> IAS 1(2007).10 specifically permits the use of other titles for the statements. For example, it is possible to continue to use the term 'balance sheet' to describe the statement of financial position.

In a complete set of financial statements, all of the financial statements should be presented with equal prominence. [IAS 1(2007).11]

> This is a new requirement in IAS 1(2007). IAS 1(2007).BC22 explains that the reason for the requirement is that the financial performance of an entity can be assessed only after all aspects of the financial statements are taken into account and understood in their entirety. In practice, the most significant effects of this new requirement are likely to be that:
>
> - where an entity elects to present an income statement together with a separate statement displaying components of other comprehensive income, the second statement must be given equal prominence with the income statement; and
>
> - the statement of changes in equity, showing contributions from and distributions to owners must be presented with equal prominence to the other statements although under IAS 1(2003) these movements can be shown in the notes when a Statement of Recognised Income and Expense is presented.

As explained in **section 5** below, the components of profit or loss may be presented either as part of a single statement of comprehensive income or in a separate income statement. When an income statement is presented, it is required to be displayed immediately before the statement of comprehensive income. [IAS 1(2007).12]

> This requirement would not prevent the statement of comprehensive income being on a separate page from the income statement although it should be on the next page and be given equal prominence.

IAS 1 notes that many entities present, outside of the financial statements, a review by management that describes and explains the main features of the entity's financial performance and financial position together with the principal uncertainties that it faces (generally referred to in international accounting literature as Management Commentary (MC)). Many entities also present, outside the financial statements, other statements, such as environmental reports and corporate governance statements. Reports and statements presented outside the financial statements are outside the scope of IFRSs. [IAS 1(2007).13–14, previously IAS 1(2003).9–10]

Information presented in a Management Commentary, or other statement, may repeat information in the financial statements. All information required under IFRSs should be presented in the notes or elsewhere in the financial statements. Omission of a disclosure in the financial statements because it is in the MC, or other similar statement, is not permitted.

UK

Requirements for narrative reporting in the UK are included in company law and supplemented by the ASB's Statement Operating and Financial Review. *These are considered in* ***chapter 46****.*

2.4 Going concern

2.4.1 General

IAS 1 requires management to make an assessment of the entity's ability to continue as a going concern when preparing financial statements. Financial statements should be prepared on a going concern basis unless management intends either to liquidate the entity or to cease trading, or has no realistic alternative but to do so. [IAS 1(2007).25, previously IAS 1(2003).23]

UK

This is consistent with the requirements of FRS 18 Accounting Policies. *Neither FRS 18 nor IAS 1 provides details of any alternative basis and how it might differ from the going concern basis (see the further discussion at* ***2.4.2*** *below).*

IAS 1 does not explain what it means for an entity to 'continue as a going concern', so it is appropriate to look to the IASB's *Framework*. Paragraph 23 of the *Framework* explains that financial statements 'are normally prepared on the assumption that an entity is a going concern and will continue in operation for the foreseeable future. Hence, it is assumed that the entity has neither the intention nor the need to liquidate or curtail materially the scale of its operations [...]'.

In assessing whether the going concern assumption is appropriate, management takes into account all available information about the future. IAS 1 states that the information should cover at least twelve months from the end of the reporting period but not be limited to that period. The degree of consideration depends on the facts of each case. When an entity has a history of profitable operations and ready access to financial resources, a conclusion that the going concern basis of accounting is appropriate may be reached without detailed analysis. In other cases, management may need to consider a wide range of factors relating to current and expected profitability, debt repayment schedules and potential sources of replacement financing before it can satisfy itself that the going concern basis is appropriate. [IAS 1(2007).26, previously IAS 1(2003).24]

UK

This is again very similar to UK GAAP. FRS 18 does not specify a minimum period that information about the future should cover. But it includes a requirement that where the foreseeable future considered by the directors has been limited to a period of less than one year from the date of approval of the financial statements, that fact should be disclosed. This requirement is consistent with International Standard on Auditing (UK and Ireland) 570. The UK has adopted International Standards on Auditing but with additional UK requirements which include a requirement for auditors to disclose in their report if the period considered is less than twelve months from approval of the financial statements, unless this is clearly disclosed in the financial statements.

The effective minimum period under IAS 1 is, therefore, shorter than that under UK GAAP because it is by reference to the end of the reporting period rather than the date of approval of the financial statements. In practice this should have little practical effect on the work that is required to confirm that the going concern basis is appropriate.

When management is aware, in making its assessment, of material uncertainties related to events or conditions that may cast significant doubt upon the entity's ability to continue as a going concern, those uncertainties should be disclosed. [IAS 1(2007).25, previously IAS 1(2003).23]

It must be emphasised that when an entity prepares financial statements on a going concern basis, this does not imply a level of confidence that the entity will be able to continue as a going concern. Even when an entity is in severe financial difficulties, IAS 1 will *require* the going concern basis to be used unless management either intends to liquidate the entity or cease trading, or has no realistic alternative but to do so. Accordingly, an entity will depart from the going concern basis only when it is, in effect, clear that it is *not* a going concern. Where there is significant uncertainty over whether an entity can continue in operational existence, IAS 1 requires the going concern basis to be used and appropriate disclosures to be provided.

Where there are doubts about an entity's ability to continue trading, the fact that the going concern basis must be used will not obviate the need to consider whether any assets should be written down to recoverable amount and whether provision is required for any unavoidable costs under onerous contracts.

2.4.2 *Departure from the going concern basis*

If financial statements are not prepared on a going concern basis, the financial statements should disclose that fact, together with the basis on which the financial statements are prepared and the reason why the entity is not regarded as a going concern. [IAS 1(2007).25, previously IAS 1(2003).23]

Before considering further the appropriate basis of preparation for the financial statements of an entity that will cease or has ceased trading, it is worth pausing to consider whether statutory financial statements will be required at all. This will depend on the legal and regulatory requirements in the jurisdiction concerned.

UK *In the UK, if a liquidator has been appointed or if the company will be 'struck off' before the filing deadline is reached, the Registrar of Companies will not expect to receive the financial statements and they need not be prepared (see* ***section 6*** *in* ***chapter 45****). In addition, once a company is in liquidation there are generally no directors to sign, or even produce the accounts. If it is concluded that financial statements should be prepared, the appropriate basis of preparation should be subject to careful consideration and consultation.*

It will always be appropriate to consider the need to write down assets for impairment when an entity will cease or has ceased trading. When financial statements are prepared on a going concern basis, assets may be stated at an amount which is greater than their net realisable value provided that it is no greater than their 'value in use' which is defined in IAS 36 as 'the present value of the future cash flows expected to be derived from an asset or cash-generating unit'. However, where a decision has been made to cease trading, there are unlikely to be any material cash flows from the use of the asset other than from its disposal. It is sometimes argued that an impairment should not be provided for where it arises from a decision taken after the reporting period to terminate the business. However, such a decision may well indicate that the asset was impaired at the earlier date. This is because the decision to dispose of the asset suggests that the value to be obtained from its continuing use was no greater than its realisable value. Therefore, irrespective of whether the financial statements are prepared on a going concern basis or on a different basis, consideration should be given to writing down assets to net realisable value.

When financial statements are prepared using a 'break-up basis', it is sometimes argued that the objective of the financial statements changes from reporting financial performance to consideration of whether the assets are sufficient to meet the creditors and quantifying the amount of any surplus that may be available for distribution to the shareholders. On this interpretation of the 'break-up basis', provision would be made for losses subsequent to the end of the reporting period and for the costs of winding up the business irrespective of whether an irrevocable decision to terminate the business had been made at the end of the reporting period. Assets would also be restated to their actual or estimated sale proceeds even if this was different from their market value at the end of the reporting period. However, the preparation of financial statements on this basis is not considered appropriate except perhaps in very rare circumstances. This is because the financial statements should reflect the circumstances existing at the end of the reporting period. For example, if the assets include quoted securities it is difficult to see why these should be recorded at below their market value even if they are sold for a lower amount after the year end. The loss on disposal in the subsequent period reflects the decision to hold them rather than to sell them at the end of the reporting period. For similar reasons, it would not be appropriate to make provision for future losses or liabilities for which there was no commitment at the end of the reporting period.

Therefore, even if an entity has ceased trading, the financial statements should generally be prepared on a basis that is consistent with accounting standards but amended to reflect the fact that the 'going concern' assumption is not appropriate. As explained above, such a basis accommodates writing assets down to their net realisable value. It also accommodates providing for contractual commitments which may have become onerous as a consequence of the decision to cease trading. In many straightforward circumstances, for example where a group entity transfers its assets and liabilities to another group entity at book value, there may be no practical difference between this basis and a 'break-up basis' as described above.

Another issue to consider is whether fixed assets should be reclassified as current assets and long-term liabilities reclassified as current liabilities. As discussed at **3.1.1** in **chapter 29**, assets classified as non-current in accordance with IAS 1 should not be disclosed as current assets unless and until they meet the 'held for sale' criteria in IFRS 5. However, long-term liabilities may have to be reclassified as current liabilities because of breaches of borrowing covenants and similar factors which existed at the end of the reporting period.

Where financial statements are prepared for an entity that will cease or has ceased trading, the financial statements should include an appropriate note about the basis of preparation. An example of such a note is as follows:

> 'As explained in note x, the entity has ceased trading since the end of the reporting period. The financial statements have been prepared on a basis other than that of a going concern which includes, where appropriate, writing down the entity's assets to net realisable value. Provision has also been made for any contractual commitments that have become onerous at the end of the reporting period. The financial statements do not include any provision for the future costs of terminating the business of the entity except to the extent that such costs were committed at the end of the reporting period.'

It would be usual for auditors to draw attention to such a basis of preparation note without modifying their opinion.

Another common situation is where an entity has ceased trading but no material adjustments would be required even if the financial statements were prepared on a break-up basis. For example, this might be the case where the entity has only short-term debtors and creditors which are expected to be settled at their book value following the termination of the business. Another example would be where the business has been transferred to another group entity for consideration equal to the book value of the assets and liabilities. The following is an example of a 'Basis of preparation' note which might be appropriate in such a case.

> 'As explained in note x, the entity transferred its trade, assets and liabilities to a fellow subsidiary on [date] and has ceased

trading. As required by IAS 1 *Presentation of Financial Statements*, management has prepared the financial statements on the basis that the entity is no longer a going concern. No material adjustments arose as a result of ceasing to apply the going concern basis. All assets and liabilities were transferred to the fellow subsidiary at their book value.'

As with the previous example, it would be usual for auditors to draw attention to such a basis of preparation note without modifying their opinion.

2.4.2.1 *Entities becoming dormant*

As explained above, IAS 1 and IAS 10 require a departure from the going concern basis in certain circumstances. Where an entity has ceased to trade during the year, or since the year end, its financial statements should not be prepared on a going concern basis. It will be appropriate instead to use a basis other than that of a going concern.

Where an entity ceases to trade, and management intends to liquidate it, it would seem appropriate for any subsequent accounts also to be prepared on a basis other than that of a going concern.

However, IAS 1 and IAS 10 do not offer any guidance where an entity has ceased to trade, but management intends to keep it in existence (e.g. as a dormant company). To provide clarity to users of the financial statements, a sensible approach would be for the accounts to be prepared on a basis other than that of a going concern until such time as the only figures reported in the current and prior year statements of comprehensive income and financial position relate to that ongoing existence (i.e. any effects of ceasing to trade have been 'washed through'). Thereafter, it seems most helpful for the accounts not to be described as departing from the going concern basis. This is because the accounts will no longer include any items relating to the trade that had ceased, and, therefore, references to such cessation may be confusing. This approach is illustrated in **example 2.4.2.1** below.

Note that, where an entity has been dormant since its establishment, its financial statements will be prepared on a going concern basis unless management intends to liquidate it. This is because it has not ceased to trade.

Example 2.4.2.1

Departure from going concern basis

Company X has a December year end. It ceases trading during 20X1, and finishes disposing of assets during 20X2. By the 20X2 year end, the only items in the statement of financial position are interests in subsidiaries and intragroup debtors and creditors, which are not expected to be settled in the foreseeable future. The directors intend to keep X in existence. The suggested basis of preparation of accounts is as follows:

20X1	a basis other than that of a going concern
20X2	a basis other than that of a going concern (both statements of comprehensive income include effects of ceasing to trade)
20X3	a basis other than that of a going concern (prior year statement of comprehensive income includes effects of ceasing to trade)
20X4	going concern basis (all effects of ceasing to trade have been washed through)

2.5 Accruals basis of accounting

IAS 1 requires financial statements, except for cash flow information, to be prepared using the accruals basis of accounting. Under this basis, items are recognised as assets, liabilities, equity, income and expenses when they satisfy the definitions and recognition criteria for those elements in the IASB's *Framework*. [IAS 1(2007).27–28, previously IAS 1(2003).25–26]

2.6 Consistency of presentation

The presentation and classification of items in the financial statements should be retained from one period to the next unless:

[IAS 1(2007).45, previously IAS 1(2003).27]

- it is apparent, following a significant change in the nature of the entity's operations (e.g. a major acquisition or disposal) or a review of its financial statements, that another presentation or classification would be more appropriate having regard to the criteria for selection and application of accounting policies in IAS 8 *Accounting Policies, Changes in Accounting Estimates and Errors* (see **section 3** in **chapter 4**); or

- an IFRS requires a change in presentation.

The presentation of the financial statements is changed only if the changed presentation provides information that is reliable and is more relevant to users of the financial statements and the revised structure is likely to continue, so that comparability is not impaired. When making such a change of presentation, the comparative information is reclassified in accordance with IAS 1(2003).38–39 or IAS 1(2007).41–42 (see **2.9** below). [IAS 1(2007).46, previously IAS 1(2003).28]

2.7 Materiality and aggregation

Each material class of similar items is presented separately in the financial statements. Items of a dissimilar nature or function are presented separately unless they are immaterial. [IAS 1(2007).29, previously IAS 1(2003).29]

Financial statements result from processing large numbers of transactions or other events that are aggregated into classes according to their nature or function. The final stage in this process is the presentation of condensed and classified data which form line items in the financial statements. If a line item is not individually material, it is aggregated with other items either in those statements or in the notes. An item that is not sufficiently material to warrant separate presentation in those statements may warrant separate presentation in the notes. [IAS 1(2007).30, previously IAS 1(2003).30]

IAS 1 confirms that a specific disclosure requirement in an IFRS need not be satisfied if the information is not material. [IAS 1(2007).31, previously IAS 1(2003).31]

IAS 1(2007) contains the following definition of 'material':

[IAS 1(2007).7, previously IAS 1(2003).11]

> 'Omissions or misstatements of items are material if they could, individually or collectively, influence the economic decisions that users make on the basis of the financial statements. Materiality depends on the size and nature of the omission or misstatement judged in the surrounding circumstances. The size or nature of the item, or a combination of both, could be the determining factor.'

The definition is worded slightly differently from the definition in IAS 1(2003) but there is no substantive difference in meaning.

Assessing whether an omission or misstatement could influence the economic decisions of users, and so be material, requires consideration of the characteristics of those users. The IASB's *Framework* states that 'users are assumed to have a reasonable knowledge of business and economic activities and accounting and a willingness to study the information with reasonable diligence'. The assessment, therefore, needs to take into account how users with such attributes could reasonably be expected to be influenced in making economic decisions. [IAS 1(2007).7, previously IAS 1(2003).12]

2.8 Offsetting

Assets and liabilities, and income and expenses, are not offset unless required or permitted by an IFRS. [IAS 1(2007).32, previously IAS 1(2003).32] This basic principle is supplemented by some further guidance in IAS 1 as described in this section. More detailed requirements concerning offsetting a financial asset and a financial liability are given in IAS 32 (see **chapter 21**).

It is important that assets and liabilities, and income and expenses, are reported separately. Offsetting in the statements of comprehensive income or financial position, except when this reflects the substance of the transactions or other events, detracts from the ability of users both to understand the transactions (or other events or conditions) that have occurred and to assess the entity's future cash flows. Measuring assets net of valuation allowances (e.g. inventories or debtors) is not regarded as offsetting for the purposes of applying IAS 1. [IAS 1(2007).33, previously IAS 1(2003).33]

Example 2.8A

Netting costs and revenues (1)

An entity that sells goods and/or services as a principal to third parties at an amount that equals cost incurred cannot present revenues and expenses net. The practice of selling goods or providing services at cost does not represent a contractual arrangement for reimbursement of the costs of goods and services. Amounts should, therefore, be presented gross.

Example 2.8B

Netting costs and revenues (2)

Company A has signed a contract with an insurance company whereby it receives a commission for every policy it sells on behalf of the insurance company. Company A contracts with individual agents to sell these insurance policies and agrees to split the commission evenly with the agents. Company A provides administrative facilities and office space to the agents. The insurance company is aware of the arrangements between Company A and the agents but pays the full commission to Company A which then pays half the commission to the agent who sold the policy. The amount paid by Company A to the agents cannot be offset against the revenues received from the insurance company. The above facts do not represent an agency arrangement between Company A and the insurance company (see **3.1** in **chapter 23**).

Example 2.8C

Withholding tax

Company A pays a dividend to Company B. Company B receives a net amount as Company A is required to deduct withholding tax on dividends that it pays to the tax authorities on Company B's behalf. Company B cannot present the dividends net. Withholding tax is generally taken to mean tax on dividends (or other income) that has been deducted by the payer (A) of the income and is paid over to the tax authorities on behalf of the recipient (B) of the dividend, so that the recipient receives the net amount. In accordance with IAS 18.7 'revenue is the gross inflow of economic benefits . . .'. Where the withholding tax is tax actually suffered by B, it is appropriate to recognise the incoming dividend at an amount that is gross of the withholding tax and the tax shown as part of the tax charge. Therefore, dividends from investments should be presented on a gross basis. IAS 1(2007).82(d) and IAS 1(2003).81(d) require a specific line item for tax expense. It follows that this line item should include all tax expenses, including withholding taxes suffered.

Example 2.8D

Netting costs and revenues (3)

Company S sells goods to a customer (Company P), and bills the customer amounts for shipping and handling costs. The appropriate classification of amounts billed to a customer for shipping and handling costs will depend on the circumstances and, in particular, whether the amounts billed represent a direct recharge of costs incurred on behalf of the customer by the seller.

Where, in its capacity as principal, Company S bills the customer for shipping and handling costs arising on the transaction, and the goods are derecognised by Company S on the date that the goods are received by Company P, these amounts represent revenues earned for the goods provided and should be classified as revenue.

Alternatively, where Company S has shipped the goods on behalf of Company P (e.g. where Company S is acting as the agent in relation to shipping the goods and the goods are derecognised by the Company S at the point of dispatch), and Company S has incurred shipping and handling charges that are to be recharged to Company P, then netting the amounts recharged against Company S's shipping and handling expense may be a more faithful representation.

IAS 18 *Revenue* (see **chapter 23**) defines revenue and requires it to be measured at the fair value of the consideration received or receivable, taking into account any trade discounts and volume rebates allowed to the entity. Other transactions may be undertaken that do not generate revenue but are incidental to the main revenue-generating activities. The results of such transactions are presented by netting any income and related expenses arising from the same transaction when this reflects the substance of the transactions or other events. For example:

[IAS 1(2007).34, previously IAS 1(2003).34]

- gains and losses on disposal of non-current assets, including investments and operating assets, are reported by deducting from the proceeds of disposal the carrying amount and related selling expenses; and
- expenditure related to a provision that is recognised in accordance with IAS 37 and reimbursed under a contractual arrangement with a third party (e.g. a supplier's warranty agreement) may be netted against the related reimbursement.

Also, gains and losses arising from a group of similar transactions are reported on a net basis. For example, foreign exchange gains and losses, and gains and losses arising on financial instruments held for trading, are presented net although they should be reported separately if material. [IAS 1(2007).35, previously IAS 1(2003).35]

2.9 Comparative information

Except when IFRSs permit or require otherwise, comparative information should be given for the previous period, for all amounts reported in the financial statements. Comparative information is included for narrative and descriptive information when it is relevant to an understanding of the current period's financial statements. [IAS 1(2007).38, previously IAS 1(2003).36]

Additional requirements apply if IAS 1(2007) has been adopted. As a minimum, two statements of financial position and two of each of the other statements and related notes are required. However, when an entity applies an accounting policy retrospectively or makes a retrospective restatement of items in its financial statements or when it reclassifies items in its financial statements, it is required, as a minimum to present three statements of financial position, two of each of the other statements, and related notes. In this case, statements of financial position must be presented at:

[IAS 1(2007).39]

- the end of the current period;

- the end of the previous period (which is the same as the beginning of the current period); and
- the beginning of the earliest comparative period.

The requirement for a statement of financial position at the beginning of the earliest comparative period is a new one in the revised Standard. The exposure draft which preceded the Standard proposed that such an additional statement should always be presented. However, many respondents expressed concern that the proposed requirement would be burdensome. The IASB therefore decided to require only two statements of financial position except 'when an entity applies an accounting policy retrospectively or makes a retrospective restatement of items in its financial statements, or when it reclassifies items in its financial statements' (see IAS 1(2007).BC31-BC32). The reference here is to 'financial statements', rather than statement of financial position, and therefore, given frequent changes to IFRSs over the next few years and the reclassifications required when IAS 1(2007) is adopted, it is likely that companies will choose to present three statements of financial position as a matter of routine.

IAS 1(2007).41 states that when an entity changes the presentation or classification of items in its financial statements, the entity should reclassify comparative amounts and, hence, three statements of financial position are required. However, three statements of financial position are not required for 'recycling' adjustments, as a restatement of comparative amounts is not required for these types of adjustments. For example, under IAS 39, amounts recognised in other comprehensive income relating to available-for-sale financial assets or in a cash flow hedging reserve are 'recycled' to profit or loss on sale of the financial asset or during the period in which the hedged item affects profit or loss.

Narrative information provided in the financial statements for the previous period may continue, in some cases, to be relevant in the current period. IAS 1 gives the example of a legal dispute, the outcome of which was uncertain at the end of the immediately preceding reporting period and is yet to be resolved. Users of the financial statements benefit from the information that the uncertainty existed at the end of the immediately preceding reporting period and the steps that have been taken during the current period to resolve the uncertainty. [IAS 1(2007).40, previously IAS 1(2003).37]

The example given in IAS 1 is not particularly helpful because it suggests that the uncertainty has yet to be resolved and, therefore, it is clear that some disclosure would be required in the current year. A better example might be where the legal claim had been settled in the year. In this case it is likely that some disclosure would be judged relevant to an understanding of the current period's financial statements but the level of detail provided might be less than in the previous year given that the uncertainties have been resolved.

When the presentation or classification of items in the financial statements is amended, comparative amounts are reclassified unless this is impracticable. When comparative amounts are reclassified, disclosure is required of:

[IAS 1(2007).41, previously IAS 1(2003).38]

- the nature of the reclassification;
- the amount of each item or class of items that is reclassified; and
- the reason for the reclassification.

Applying a requirement is impracticable for this purpose 'when the entity cannot apply it after making every reasonable effort to do so'. [IAS 1(2007).7, previously IAS 1(2003).11]

Enhancing the inter-period comparability of information assists users in making economic decisions, especially by allowing the assessment of trends in financial information for predictive purposes. But in some circumstances it is impracticable to reclassify comparative information to achieve comparability. For example, data may not have been collected in the prior period in a way that allows reclassification and it may be impracticable to recreate the information. [IAS 1(2007).43, previously IAS 1(2003).40]

Restatement is not impracticable just because of the cost or effort involved. When revising IAS 1 in 2003, the IASB considered replacing the exemption with one based on 'undue cost or effort'. However, based on comments received on the Exposure Draft, the IASB decided that an exemption based on management's assessment of undue cost or effort was too subjective to be applied consistently by different entities. The IASB decided that balancing costs and benefits was a task for the Board when it sets accounting requirements rather than for entities when they apply those requirements. Therefore, although the Standard does not explicitly say that undue cost or effort does not alone make restatement impracticable, this is the clear intention of the Board and is consistent with the definition of 'impracticable' in IAS 1(2007).7 and IAS 1(2003).11. [IAS 1(2007).BC34-BC36, previously IAS 1(2003).BC38–40]

Entities sometimes change classification or presentation of items in the financial statements to achieve a more appropriate presentation. Where applicable, comparative information should be restated to make it comparable. Whether the comparative information should be headed up (e.g. as 'represented', 'restated' or 'adjusted') depends on the significance of the change, i.e. its impact on either the entity's results or equity. There is no explicit requirement for such headings in IFRSs, although their inclusion is common practice. In each case, it is a matter of judgement and consideration of any local regulatory requirements. Irrespective of the heading, entities should still provide disclosures for the change in presentation or reclassification in accordance with IAS 1(2007).41 and IAS 1(2003).38 as applicable.

When it is impracticable to reclassify comparative amounts, disclosure is required of:

[IAS 1(2007).42, previously IAS 1(2003).39]

- the reason for not reclassifying the amounts; and
- the nature of the adjustments that would have been made if the amounts had been reclassified.

IAS 8 sets out adjustments to comparative information required when an entity changes an accounting policy or corrects an error (see **chapter 4**). [IAS 1(2007).44, previously IAS 1(2003).41]

The reference to the more specific requirements of IAS 8 within IAS 1 appears to envisage that it is possible to have a 'reclassification' that is not a change in accounting policy. No examples are given in IAS 1.

Under UK GAAP, it is clearer that a change of presentation in the financial statements is a change in accounting policy. FRS 18 gives the example of an entity that has previously included certain overheads within cost of sales and now proposes that these overheads will be included in administrative expenses. So, under UK GAAP, reclassifications are regarded as either arising from changes in accounting policies or the correction of fundamental errors. UK

2.10 Identification of financial statements

The financial statements should be identified clearly and distinguished from other information in the same published document. [IAS 1(2007).49, previously IAS 1(2003).44] IFRSs apply only to financial statements. They do not necessarily apply to other information provided in an annual report, a regulatory filing, or other document. Therefore, it is important that users can distinguish information that is prepared using IFRSs from other information that may be useful to users but is not subject to those requirements. [IAS 1(2007).50, previously IAS 1(2003).45]

Information given outside of the financial statements may be subject to separate regulatory requirements. For example, there may be a requirement for such information to be consistent with the financial statements.

IAS 1 requires each financial statement and the notes to be identified clearly. In addition, the following information is required to be 'displayed prominently' and repeated when it is necessary for the information presented to be understandable:

[IAS 1(2007).51, previously IAS 1(2003).46]

- the name of the reporting entity or other means of identification;
- any change in that information from the end of the preceding reporting period;
- whether the financial statements are of an individual entity or a group of entities;
- the date of the end of the reporting period or the period covered by the set of financial statements or notes;
- the presentation currency, as defined in IAS 21; and
- the level of rounding used in presenting amounts in the financial statements.

IAS 1 explains that these requirements are normally met by presenting appropriate headings for pages, statements, notes, columns and the like. Judgement is required in determining the best way of presenting such information. For example, when the financial statements are presented electronically, separate pages are not always used. The items listed above are then presented frequently enough to ensure a proper understanding of the information. [IAS 1(2007).52, previously IAS 1(2003).47]

The words 'frequently enough' were included in IAS 1(2003) but have been omitted from the equivalent paragraph in IAS 1(2007). However, the intention is presumably the same.

Financial statements may be made more understandable by presenting information in thousands or millions of units of the presentation currency. This is acceptable as long as the level of rounding is disclosed and material information is not omitted. [IAS 1(2007).53, previously IAS 1(2003).48]

Different levels of rounding may be appropriate for different disclosures. For example, while it may be appropriate to disclose line items in the statements of financial position and comprehensive income in millions of units of the presentation currency for a very large group, a greater level of detail is likely to be necessary for disclosure of management remuneration and some other related party transactions.

2.11 Frequency of reporting

IAS 1 states that a complete set of financial statements, including comparative information, should be presented at least 'annually'. However, it clearly envisages that the financial statements may cover a period longer or shorter than twelve months.

When the end of the reporting period is changed and the financial statements are presented for a period that is longer or shorter than one year, IAS 1 requires the following disclosures:

[IAS 1(2007).36, previously IAS 1(2003).49]

- the period covered by the financial statements;
- the reason for using a longer or shorter period; and
- the fact that the amounts presented in the financial statements are not entirely comparable.

Financial statements are normally presented covering a one year period. But for practical reasons, some entities prefer to report on a 52/53 week basis (e.g. always to the last Saturday in the month). IAS 1 states that it does not preclude this practice. [IAS 1(2007).37, previously IAS 1(2003).50]

The 2007 revision of IAS 1 has helpfully removed the words 'because the resulting financial statements are unlikely to be materially different from those that would be presented for one year' from this paragraph. This removes any doubt that the practice might be unacceptable in circumstances where there might be a material difference (e.g. a major acquisition or disposal within a few days of the end of the reporting period.

UK

Regulatory requirements in the UK for changes in the reporting periods are considered in ***chapter 45****.*

3 Fair presentation and compliance with IFRSs

Financial statements must not be described as complying with IFRSs unless they comply with all of the requirements of IFRSs. IAS 1 requires an entity whose financial statements comply with IFRSs to make an explicit and unreserved statement of such compliance in the notes. [IAS 1(2007).16, previously IAS 1(2003).14]

An entity cannot claim compliance with IFRSs if it states that it complies with IFRSs except for one or more Standards. Compliance with IFRSs is clearly defined in IAS 1(2003).14 and IAS 1(2007).16 which, taken together with IAS 8.11–12, means that financial statements must:

- comply with IASs and IFRSs;
- comply with all IFRICs and SICs; and
- in the absence of specific guidance in IFRSs:
  - apply by analogy other IFRSs;
  - apply the IASB *Framework*; or
  - apply pronouncements of national standard setters to the extent that these are consistent with other IFRSs, other SICs, other IFRICs and the IASB *Framework*.

Financial statements should not be described as complying with IFRSs unless they comply with all the applicable requirements.

This principle applies to any departure from IFRSs that is necessary to comply with national law. For example, suppose an entity is incorporated in a country where the legislation does not permit unrealised gains to be reported in profit or loss. The entity prepares its financial statements in compliance with IFRSs including recording derivatives at fair value, but, to comply with its national laws, takes the fair value gains directly to equity reserve until the derivative is derecognised. The entity cannot claim compliance with IFRSs. The fact that an entity is prevented by legislation from complying with IFRSs does not change the requirement in IFRSs.

UK

As more fully explained in ***chapter 1****, UK companies adopting IFRSs will not have any such conflict. This is because the EU IAS Regulation overrides national laws. In any event, company law has been amended in accordance with the EU Fair Value Directive and Accounts Modernisation Directive to remove most of the conflicts with IFRSs that might otherwise have arisen. This is to facilitate the convergence of UK GAAP with IFRSs.*

An effect of this requirement is that the financial statements would not comply with IFRSs if they omitted the statement of compliance, even if they were otherwise in full compliance with IFRSs. Although this may at first appear to be a rather technical point, it has implications for the application of IFRS 1. For example, an entity that had prepared financial statements in full compliance with IFRSs, other than including an unqualified statement of compliance, would still be a first-time adopter for the purposes of applying IFRS 1 when it first made such an unqualified statement of compliance (see **chapter 5**).

However, this rule should not be abused to enable an entity to apply IFRS 1 where this would not be appropriate. For example, it would not be acceptable for an IFRS reporter deliberately to omit the statement of compliance (or indeed any other disclosures) in one year with the intention of being able to apply IFRS 1 in the following year.

Financial statements should present fairly the financial position, financial performance and cash flows of an entity. Fair presentation requires the faithful representation of the effects of transactions, other events and conditions in accordance with the definitions and recognition criteria set out in the IASB's *Framework*. The application of IFRSs, with additional disclosure where necessary, is presumed to result in financial statements that achieve a fair presentation. [IAS 1(2007).15, previously IAS 1(2003).13]

In virtually all circumstances, a fair presentation is achieved by compliance with applicable IFRSs. A fair presentation also requires an entity:

[IAS 1(2007).17, previously IAS 1(2003).15]

- to select and apply accounting policies in accordance with IAS 8 which sets out a hierarchy of authoritative guidance that management considers in the absence of an IFRS that specifically applies to the item (see **chapter 4**);
- to present information, including accounting policies, in a manner that provides relevant, reliable, comparable and understandable information; and
- to provide additional disclosures when compliance with the specific requirements in IFRSs is insufficient to enable users to understand the impact of particular transactions, other events or conditions on the entity's financial position or financial performance.

Inappropriate accounting policies are not rectified either by disclosure of the accounting policies used or by notes or explanatory material. [IAS 1(2007).18, previously IAS 1(2003).16]

In extremely rare circumstances, management may conclude that compliance with a requirement in an IFRS would be so misleading that it would conflict with the objective of financial statements set out in the IASB's *Framework*. In such circumstances, IAS 1 requires the entity to depart from that requirement 'if the relevant regulatory framework requires, or otherwise does not prohibit, such a departure'. [IAS 1(2007).19, previously IAS 1(2003).17]

IAS 1(2003).BC9 and IAS 1(2007).BC28 explain that departing from a requirement in a Standard or an Interpretation when considered necessary to achieve a fair presentation would conflict with the regulatory framework in some jurisdictions. But the departure would be required (and not just permitted) by IAS 1 when the relevant conditions were met. Arguably, this is no more of a departure from a Standard than where an exemption is given in specified circumstances. However, the IASB acknowledged these concerns and drafted the Standard to enable entities to comply with the requirements of the Standard when the relevant regulatory framework prohibits departures from accounting standards, while retaining the principle that entities should, to the maximum extent possible, ensure that financial statements provide a fair presentation.

UK

In the UK, company law does not prohibit departures from accounting standards. Although the law is silent on such departures in the context of IFRSs, it is generally accepted that they would not contravene the law provided that the departure was made in accordance with the requirements of a Standard (i.e. IAS 1). Indeed, in the context of UK GAAP, the Companies Acts permit most of their own detailed provisions to be overridden where this is necessary to give a true and fair view. FRS 18 permits departures from the requirements of UK accounting standards on similar grounds. So the concept behind this requirement of IAS 1 is very familiar in the UK.

IAS 1 explains that an item of information would conflict with the objective of financial statements when it does not represent faithfully the transactions, other events and conditions that it either purports to represent or could reasonably be expected to represent and, consequently, it would be likely to influence economic decisions made by users of financial statements. When assessing whether complying with a specific requirement of an IFRS would be so misleading that it would conflict with the objective of financial statements set out in the IASB's *Framework*, management should consider:

[IAS 1(2007).24, previously IAS 1(2003).22]

- why the objective of financial statements is not achieved in the particular circumstances; and
- how the entity's circumstances differ from those of other entities that comply with the requirement. If other entities in similar circumstances comply with the requirement, there is a rebuttable presumption that the entity's compliance with the requirement would not be so misleading that it would conflict with the objective of financial statements set out in the *Framework*.

When a departure is made from a requirement of an IFRS in the circumstances described above, the following disclosures are required:

[IAS 1(2007).20, previously IAS 1(2003).18]

- a statement that the management has concluded that the financial statements present fairly the entity's financial position, financial performance and cash flows;

- a statement that the entity has complied with applicable IFRSs, except that it has departed from a particular requirement to achieve a fair presentation;
- the title of the IFRS from which there has been a departure;
- the nature of the departure, including the treatment that the IFRS would require;
- the reason why that treatment would be so misleading in the circumstances that it would conflict with the objective of financial statements set out in the IASB's *Framework*;
- the treatment adopted; and
- for each period presented, the financial effect of the departure on each item in the financial statements that would have been reported in complying with the requirement.

IAS 1 also requires disclosures to be made when there was a departure from a requirement of a Standard or an Interpretation in a prior period that affects the amounts recognised in the financial statements for the current period. In such cases, the disclosures listed above should be made excluding the first two items. [IAS 1(2007).21–22, previously IAS 1(2003).19–20]

IAS 1 specifies additional disclosures that apply in those extremely rare circumstances in which management concludes that compliance with a requirement in a Standard or an Interpretation would be so misleading that it would conflict with the objective of financial statements set out in the *Framework* but the relevant regulatory framework prohibits departure from the requirement. In this case the entity should, to the maximum extent possible, reduce the perceived misleading aspects of compliance by disclosing:

[IAS 1(2007).23, previously IAS 1(2003).21]

- the title of the IFRS in question;
- the nature of the requirement;
- the reason why management has concluded that complying with that requirement is so misleading in the circumstances that it conflicts with the objectives of financial statements set out in the *Framework*; and
- for each period presented, the adjustments to each item in the financial statements that management has concluded would be necessary to achieve a fair presentation.

These requirements of IAS 1(2003).21 and IAS 1(2007).23 will not be relevant for UK companies, because company law does not prohibit such departures. UK

4 The statement of financial position

IAS 1, as revised in 2007, uses the title 'statement of financial position' in place of ;'balance sheet' although they have the same meaning. The use of the new terminology is not mandatory and it is acceptable to continue to use the title 'balance sheet', or other similar expressions, in financial statements when the revised Standard has been adopted. However, this publication uses the new terminology except where the context requires otherwise.

4.1 Current / non-current distinction

Current and non-current assets, and current and non-current liabilities, are presented as separate classifications in the statement of financial position. Further detailed requirements are set out below. This is subject to an exception when a presentation based on liquidity provides information that is reliable and is more relevant. When this exception applies, all assets and liabilities are presented in order of liquidity. [IAS 1(2007).60, previously IAS 1(2003).51]

IAS 1(2003) refers to items being presented 'broadly' in order of liquidity but this flexibility is omitted from IAS 1(2007).

For some entities (e.g. financial institutions), a presentation of assets and liabilities in increasing or decreasing order of liquidity provides information that is reliable and is more relevant than a current / non-current presentation. This is because the entity does not supply goods or services within a clearly identifiable operating cycle (see below). [IAS 1(2007).63, previously IAS 1(2003).54]

The current / non-current presentation has some similarities with the formats adopted by UK companies reporting under the Companies Acts. However, a UK company adopting IFRSs may have to make some changes to the format of its balance sheet. The term 'non-current assets' is not equivalent to 'fixed assets' because they are defined differently. Consequently, for example, some debtor balances due in more than one year are UK *classified as non-current assets under IFRSs although they are classified as current assets (rather than fixed assets) under UK GAAP.*

Whichever method of presentation is adopted (i.e. current / non-current or liquidity), for each asset and liability line item that combines amounts expected to be recovered or settled:

- no more than twelve months after the reporting period; and
- more than twelve months after the reporting period,

the amount expected to be recovered or settled after more than twelve months should be disclosed. [IAS 1(2007).61, previously IAS 1(2003).52]

This disclosure may be given in the notes and does not have to be in the statement of financial position itself. As explained later in this section, it is possible for current assets and current liabilities to include amounts due after twelve months.

When an entity supplies goods or services within a clearly identifiable operating cycle, separate classification of current and non-current assets and liabilities provides useful information by distinguishing the net assets that are continually circulating as working capital from those used in the entity's long term operations. It also highlights assets that are expected to be realised within the current operating cycle and liabilities that are due for settlement within that same period. [IAS 1(2007).62, previously IAS 1(2003).53]

The operating cycle of an entity is the time between the acquisition of assets for processing and their realisation in cash or cash equivalents. When an entity's normal operating cycle is not clearly identifiable, its duration is assumed to be twelve months. [IAS 1(2007).68, previously IAS 1(2003).59]

The IFRIC was asked to consider whether the guidance in IAS 1 on current assets was applicable only if an entity had a predominant operating cycle. This is particularly relevant to the inventories of conglomerates which, on a narrow reading of the wording, might always have to refer to the twelve-month criteria, rather than the operating cycle criterion. The IFRIC decided not to consider the question further because, in its view, it was clear that the wording in paragraph 57 should be read in both the singular and the plural and that it was the nature of inventories in relation to the operating cycle that was relevant to classification. Furthermore, if inventories of different cycles were held, and it was material to readers' understanding of an entity's financial position, then the general requirements in IAS 1(2003).71or IAS 1(2007).57 required disclosure of further information. This rejection was published in the June 2005 edition of the IFRIC Update.

IAS 1 permits an entity to present some assets and liabilities using a current / non-current classification and others in order of liquidity when this provides information that is reliable and more relevant. [IAS 1(2007).64, previously IAS 1(2003).55]

IAS 1 states that such a mixed basis may be appropriate 'when an entity has diverse operations'. In practice it is likely to be a combination of financial and non-financial operations, rather than just 'diversity', that would make such an approach necessary.

Information about the expected realisation dates of assets and liabilities is useful in assessing liquidity and solvency. IFRS 7 (see **chapter 21**) requires disclosure of the maturity dates of financial assets and financial liabilities. Financial assets include trade and other receivables. Financial liabilities include trade and other payables. Information about the expected date of recovery of non-monetary assets such as inventories and expected date of settlement for liabilities such as provisions is also useful, whether assets and liabilities are classified as current or as non-current. For example, the amount of inventories that is expected to be recovered more than twelve months after the reporting period should be disclosed. [IAS 1(2007).65, previously IAS 1(2003).56]

4.1.1 Employee benefits

Where an entity uses a current/non-current distinction to present the statement of financial position (i.e. rather than a liquidity presentation), it is not required to split post-employment benefits accounted for under IAS 19 between current and non-current either in the statement of financial position or in the notes.

IAS 19 states that the Standard does not specify whether an entity should distinguish current and non-current portions of assets and liabilities arising from post-employment benefits. [IAS 19.118] The Basis for Conclusions of IAS 19 states that the IASB decided not to specify whether an entity should distinguish between the current and non-current portions of such assets and liabilities, because such a distinction may sometimes be arbitrary.

Although IAS 1 has not been modified to reflect this exemption, the more specific references of IAS 19 apply. Similarly, it is not considered that paragraph 52 of IAS 1 requires separate disclosure of the portions of the employment benefit assets and liabilities that are expected to be recovered or settled before and after twelve months from the end of the reporting period, since the concepts of 'recovery' and 'settlement' for such assets and liabilities are unclear.

IAS 19 requires the disclosure of the employer's best estimate of contributions expected to be paid to defined benefit plans during the annual period beginning after the reporting period, as soon as that information can reasonably be determined. [IAS 19.120A]

The exemption in IAS 19.118 applies only to post-employment benefits. There is no exemption from the requirements in IAS 1 for short-term and other long-term employee benefit liabilities such as annual leave, long-term disability leave and long-service leave.

To the extent that employees are entitled to take their annual / long-service leave in the next 12 months, whether they are expected to take it or not, the liability should be classified as 'current'. The entity does not have an unconditional right to defer settlement of the liability for at least 12 months after the end of the reporting period.

To the extent that employees are not entitled to take a portion of their annual / long-service leave during the next 12 months because, for example, additional years of service must first be provided (i.e. the leave has not yet vested), and the employer is not expected to allow such leave to be taken early, that portion should be classified as 'non-current'.

Employees do not have an unconditional right to long-term disability benefits. Those rights arise when employees fall ill. IAS 19.130 requires the measurement for long-term disability benefits to reflect the probability of payment / right arising. Consistent with this is a split between 'current' and 'non-current' based on the expected payment profile at the end of the reporting period.

4.1.2 Derivatives

The presentation of derivatives in the statement of financial position is considered generally in **section 5** of **chapter 16**. Guidance on the presentation of embedded derivatives is set out in **section 13** of **chapter 17**.

4.2 Current assets

An asset is classified as a current asset when it satisfies any of the following criteria:

- it is expected to be realised in the entity's normal operating cycle;
- it is intended for sale or consumption in the entity's normal operating cycle;
- it is held primarily for the purpose of trading;
- it is expected to be realised within twelve months of the reporting period; or
- it is cash or a cash equivalent (as defined in IAS 7 – see **chapter 30**) unless it is restricted from being exchanged or used to settle a liability for at least twelve months after the reporting period.

All other assets are classified as non-current. [IAS 1(2007).66, previously IAS 1(2003).57]

> Where an entity adopts a current / non-current method of presentation for the statement of financial position, immature agricultural produce cannot be presented as a current asset, separate from the agricultural asset to which it is attached. Until harvest, agricultural produce forms part of the total biological asset. This asset should be presented as a single asset in the statement of financial position and classified as either current on non-current in accordance with IAS 1. Long-term biological assets (e.g. fruit trees and vines) would be classified as non-current assets, as the requirements of IAS 1(2003).57 or IAS 1(2007).66 would not be met for the asset as a whole. In all cases, biological assets should be presented as a separate line item in the statement of financial position in accordance with IAS 1(2003).68(f) or IAS 1(2007).54(f) (see **4.4** below).

The Standard uses the term 'non-current' to include tangible, intangible and financial assets of a long-term nature. It does not prohibit the use of alternative descriptions providing the meaning is clear. [IAS 1(2007).67, previously IAS 1(2003).58]

Current assets include assets (e.g. inventories and trade receivables) that are sold, consumed or realised as part of the normal operating cycle even when they are not expected to be realised within twelve months after the reporting period. Current assets also include assets primarily held for the purpose of trading (examples include some financial assets classified as held for trading in accordance with IAS 39) and the current portion of non-current financial assets. [IAS 1(2007).68, previously IAS 1(2003).59]

The previous paragraph reflects the amendment made to IAS 1 by *Improvements to IFRSs* published in May 2008 which clarified that current assets include some, but not necessarily all, financial assets classified as held for trading in accordance with IAS 39. Further background on this amendment in the context of derivatives is given in **section 5** of **chapter 16**.

4.3 Current liabilities

A liability is classified as a current liability when it satisfies any of the following criteria:

- it is expected to be settled in the entity's normal operating cycle;
- it is held primarily for the purposes of trading;
- it is due to be settled within twelve months after the reporting period; or
- the entity does not have an unconditional right to defer settlement of the liability for at least twelve months after the reporting period.

All other liabilities are classified as non-current. [IAS 1(2007).69, previously IAS 1(2003).60]

The reference to 'settlement' includes conversion of a liability into equity. Therefore, the liability component of a convertible instrument that the entity could be required to settle in shares at any time is classified as current. The IASB proposed to amend this requirement as part of the 2007 annual improvements project. As explained at **9.2** below, this amendment has been deferred pending further discussion and therefore the existing requirement to classify such liabilities as current continues to apply.

Example 4.3A

Classification of refundable deposits

A primary school requires a deposit to be paid upon enrolment into the school. Should the student leave the school, this deposit is refundable with one school-term's notice (four months). The majority of students enrol into just one primary school and, having completed the seven-year study period, receive the deposit back at the end of that seven-year period.

The deposits should be classified as current liabilities. Despite the historical evidence that indicates that the majority of the deposits are only repaid after the seven-year period, the deposits are payable on four months notice. IAS 1(2003).60 or IAS 1(2007).69 states that a liability should be classified as current when the entity does not have an unconditional right to defer settlement of the liability for at least twelve months after the reporting period. Therefore, the deposits should be classified as current liabilities.

The following example considers the situation where the amortised cost of a liability at the end of the reporting period exceeds its principal amount, for example due to accrued unpaid interest.

Example 4.3B

Current / non-current presentation of non-derivative financial liabilities

An entity issues a 6 per cent £100 million bond at par on 30 June 20X0. The bond is repayable at par 10 years after issuance on 30 June 20Y0. Interest of £6 million is paid annually. There are no issue costs. The liability is measured at amortised cost using an effective interest rate of 6 per cent. For illustrative purposes only, it is assumed the amortised cost of the bond is £103 million at 31 December 20X0.

How should the entity disclose the carrying amount of the bond in its statement of financial position at 31 December 20X0? Specifically, how is the presentation of the bond in the financial statements affected by IAS 1(2003).62 and IAS 1(2007).71 which refer to the inclusion of the 'current portion of non-current financial liabilities' in current liabilities?

Two methods of classification are acceptable under IFRSs. An entity should adopt one of the following methods as an accounting policy choice and should apply it consistently in accordance with IAS 8.13.

One approach is to present the entire amortised cost carrying amount of £103 million in non-current liabilities. IAS 1(2003).60 and IAS 1(2007).71 support this classification because:

- the liability is not expected to be settled in the entity's normal operating cycle;
- the liability is not held primarily for the purpose of trading;
- the liability is not due until 20Y0 (i.e. the principal is not expected to be settled within 12 months of the end of the reporting period); and
- the entity has the unconditional right to defer settlement of the liability for at least twelve months after the reporting period.

Under this approach, interest on the bond represents servicing of the liability instead of its settlement. Therefore, the amount of interest to be paid within twelve months of the end of the reporting period does not constitute the 'current portion of non-current financial liabilities' described in IAS

1(2003).62 or IAS 1(2007).71. The current portion of the bond would be the portion of its principal amount repayable within twelve months of the reporting period.

The alternative method is to present £3 million separately as a current liability. This is the difference between the amortised cost carrying amount and the par value repayable on maturity. This current liability represents interest accrued at the year-end. The remaining carrying amount of £100 million would be classified as a non-current liability.

Some current liabilities, such as trade payables and some accruals for employee and other operating costs, are part of the working capital used in the entity's normal operating cycle. Such items are classified as current liabilities even if they are due to be settled more than twelve months after the reporting period. The same normal operating cycle applies to the classification of an entity's assets and liabilities. When the normal operating cycle is not clearly identifiable, its duration is assumed to be twelve months. [IAS 1(2007).70, previously IAS 1(2003).61]

Other current liabilities are not settled as part of the normal operating cycle but are due for settlement within twelve months after the reporting period or held primarily for the purpose of trading (examples include some financial liabilities classified as held for trading in accordance with IAS 39, bank overdrafts, the current portion of non-current financial liabilities, dividends payable, income taxes and other non-trade payables). Financial liabilities that provide financing on a long-term basis (i.e. not working capital used in the normal operating cycle) and are not due for settlement within twelve months after the reporting period are non-current liabilities. This is subject to an exception when the entity breaches an undertaking under a long-term loan arrangement (see **4.3.1** below). [IAS 1(2007).71, previously IAS 1(2003).62]

The previous paragraph reflects the amendment made to IAS 1 by *Improvements to IFRSs* published in May 2008 which clarified that current liabilities include some, but not necessarily all, financial liabilities classified as held for trading in accordance with IAS 39. Further background on this amendment in the context of derivatives is given in **section 5** of **chapter 16**.

Financial liabilities are classified as current when they are due to be settled within twelve months after the reporting period even if:

[IAS 1(2007).72, previously IAS 1(2003).63]

- the original term was for a period longer than twelve months; and

- an agreement to refinance, or to reschedule payments, on a long-term basis is completed after the reporting period and before the financial statements are authorised for issue.

If an entity expects, and has the discretion, to refinance or roll over an obligation for at least twelve months after the reporting period under an existing loan facility, it classifies the obligation as non-current. This is so even if it would otherwise be due within a shorter period. But when refinancing or rolling over the obligation is not at the discretion of the entity (e.g. there is no arrangement for refinancing), the potential to refinance is not considered (and the obligation is therefore classified as current). [IAS 1(2007).73, previously IAS 1(2003).64]

IAS 1(2007) uses the expression 'arrangement for refinancing' in place of 'agreement to refinance' but it appears unlikely that any change of substance was intended. Some other references to 'agreements' have been replaced by references to 'arrangements' in the revised Standard.

For loans classified as current liabilities, IAS 1 states that if the following events occur between the end of the reporting period and the date the financial statements are authorised for issue, those events are disclosed as non-adjusting events in accordance with IAS 10:

[IAS 1(2007).76, previously IAS 1(2003).67]

- refinancing on a long-term basis;
- rectification of a breach of a long-term loan arrangement; and
- the granting by the lender of a period of grace to rectify a breach of a long-term loan arrangement ending at least twelve months after the reporting period.

4.3.1 *Breaches of covenants*

When a provision of a long-term loan arrangement is breached on or before the end of the reporting period with the effect that the liability becomes payable on demand, the liability is classified as current. This is so, even if the lender has agreed, after the reporting period and before authorisation of the financial statements for issue, not to demand payment as a consequence of the breach. The liability is classified as current because, at the end of the reporting period, the entity does not have an unconditional right to defer settlement for at least twelve months after that date. [IAS 1(2007).74, previously IAS 1(2003).65]

The liability is classified as non-current if the lender agreed before the end of the reporting period to provide a period of grace ending at least twelve months after the reporting period. That is to say, a period within which the entity can rectify the breach and during which the lender cannot demand immediate repayment. [IAS 1(2007).75, previously IAS 1(2003).66]

This approach is tougher than the 1997 version of IAS 1 which permitted, in some circumstances, a refinancing after the reporting period to be taken into account in assessing whether a liability should be classified as current or non-current. The Board decided that reporting should reflect contractual arrangements in force at the end of the reporting period. Refinancing a liability after the reporting period does not affect the entity's solvency or liquidity at that date. A refinancing after the reporting period is a non-adjusting event in accordance with IAS 10 and should not affect the presentation of the entity's statement of financial position. The reasons for the approach taken in the revised Standard are more fully set out in IAS 1(2003).BC20-BC29 and IAS 1(2007).BC39 – BC48.

4.4 Information to be presented in the statement of financial position

IAS 1(2007) uses the expression 'in the statement of financial position' in place of 'on the face of the balance sheet'. However, it is clearly the intention that these items are shown 'on the face of' the statement itself. Disclosure in the notes would not be adequate to comply with the Standard.

The statement of financial position should include, at a minimum, line items that present the following amounts:

[IAS 1(2007).54, previously IAS 1(2003).68 and IAS 1(2003).68A]

- property, plant and equipment;
- investment property;
- intangible assets;
- financial assets (other than investments accounted for using the equity method, trade and other receivables and cash and cash equivalents, which are presented separately);
- investments accounted for using the equity method;
- biological assets;

- inventories;
- trade and other receivables;
- cash and cash equivalents;
- the total of assets classified as held for sale and assets included in disposal groups classified as held for sale in accordance with IFRS 5 (see **chapter 29**);
- trade and other payables;
- provisions;
- financial liabilities (other than trade and other payables, and provisions, which are presented separately);
- liabilities and assets for current tax, as defined in IAS 12;
- deferred tax liabilities and deferred tax assets, as defined in IAS 12;
- liabilities included in disposal groups classified as held for sale in accordance with IFRS 5 (see **chapter 29**);
- non-controlling interests (see below), presented within equity; and
- issued capital and reserves attributable to owners of the parent.

IAS 27, as amended in 2008, replaces the term 'minority interests' with 'non-controlling interests'. This amendment is effective for periods beginning on or after 1 July 2009. If an entity applies the revised IAS 27 for an earlier period, the amendment to IAS 1 is applied for that earlier period.

Cash and cash equivalents are defined in IAS 7. Cash equivalents are short-term, highly liquid investments that are readily convertible to known amounts of cash and which are subject to an insignificant risk of changes in value. IAS 7.7 states that an investment normally qualifies as a cash equivalent only when it has a short maturity of three months or less from the date of inception. The definition of cash equivalents is discussed further at **4.2** in **chapter 30**.

IAS 7.8 states that bank borrowings are generally considered to be financing activities but then explains that in some countries bank overdrafts which are repayable on demand form an integral part of an entity's cash management. IAS 7 notes that a characteristic of such banking arrangements is that the balance often fluctuates from being positive to overdrawn. In these circumstances, bank overdrafts are included as a component of cash and cash equivalents for the purposes of applying IAS 7 (see **chapter 30**). It might be thought that the guidance in IAS 7 would result in the statement of financial position caption 'cash and cash equivalents' being presented net of such overdrafts. However, this approach should be restricted to the presentation of the statement of cash flows and overdrafts should be netted against positive cash balances only when the offset criteria in IAS 32 are met.

Additional line items, headings and subtotals are presented in the statement of financial position when such presentation is relevant to an understanding of the entity's financial position. [IAS 1(2007).55, previously IAS 1(2003).69]

For example, retirement benefit obligations under a defined benefit pension scheme might be very material and so would be presented separately in the statement of financial position.

When current and non-current assets and current and non-current liabilities are presented as separate classifications in the statement of financial position, deferred tax cannot be classified as a current asset or a current liability. [IAS 1(2007).56, previously IAS 1(2003).70]

The Standard does not prescribe the order or the format in which items are to be presented. The Standard merely provides a list of items (see above) that are sufficiently different in nature or function to warrant separate presentation in the statement of financial position. In addition:

[IAS 1(2007).57, previously IAS 1(2003).71]

- line items are included when the size, nature or function of an item or aggregation of similar items is such that separate presentation is relevant to an understanding of the entity's financial position; and
- the descriptions used and the ordering of items or aggregation of similar items may be amended according to the nature of the entity and its transactions, to provide information that is relevant to an understanding of the entity's financial position. For example, a financial institution may amend the above descriptions to provide information that is relevant to the operations of a financial institution.

The judgement on whether additional items are presented separately is based on an assessment of:

[IAS 1(2007).58, previously IAS 1(2003).72]

- the nature and liquidity of the assets;

- the function of the assets within the entity; and
- the amounts, nature and timing of liabilities.

The use of different measurement bases for different classes of assets suggests that their nature or function differs and, therefore, that they should be presented as separate line items. For example, different classes of property, plant and equipment can be carried at cost or revalued amounts in accordance with IAS 16 *Property, Plant and Equipment*. [IAS 1(2007).59, previously IAS 1(2003).73]

4.5 Information to be presented in the statement of financial position or in the notes

4.5.1 General requirements

Further sub-classifications of the line items presented should be disclosed either in the statement of financial position or in the notes, classified in a manner that is appropriate to the entity's operations. [IAS 1(2007).77, previously IAS 1(2003).74]

The details provided depend on the requirements of IFRSs and on the size, nature and function of the amounts involved. The factors set out in IAS 1(2003).72 and IAS 1(2007).58 (see **4.4** above) are also used to decide on the basis of sub-classifications. IAS 1 gives the following examples:

[IAS 1(2007).78, previously IAS 1(2003).75]

- items of property, plant and equipment are disaggregated into classes in accordance with IAS 16;
- receivables are disaggregated into amounts receivable from trade customers, receivables from related parties, prepayments and other amounts;
- inventories are sub-classified, in accordance with IAS 2, into classifications such as merchandise, production supplies, materials, work in progress and finished goods;
- provisions are disaggregated into provisions for employee benefits and other items; and
- equity capital and reserves are disaggregated into various classes, such as paid-in capital, share premium and reserves.

4.5.2 *Share capital and reserves*

4.5.2.1 *Introduction*

IAS 1 requires several disclosures about share capital and reserves. These are described at **4.5.2.2** and **4.5.2.3** below.

In straightforward cases, these disclosures will be concerned with the amounts included in the statement of financial position caption 'issued capital and reserves attributable to owners (i.e. equity holders) of the parent'. This will not always be the case because amounts that are legally share capital will sometimes be presented, in whole or in part, as liabilities in the statement of financial position in accordance with IAS 32.

It is possible to meet the requirements of IAS 1 by including a single line in the statement of financial position (see above) and providing further details in the notes. It is, however, common for entities to provide greater detail in the statement of financial position. For example, they may show share capital, share premium, retained earnings and several other types of reserves.

UK *This is different from UK GAAP because the statutory formats specify certain items such as share capital and share premium that must be shown on the face of the balance sheet.*

The question then arises of which line items should be reduced by the amounts presented as liabilities.

When the liability recognised is equal to the proceeds of issue of a class of shares, the amounts presented as 'share capital' and 'share premium' may be reduced to exclude those amounts (i.e. so they relate to equity shares only). This is probably the most common approach although showing the amount included in liabilities as a separate deduction is also acceptable. The disclosures required by IAS 1 about share capital can be given in the note dealing with the liability. Alternatively, details about all classes of share capital may be given in a single note but distinguishing separately those classes and amounts that have been presented as liabilities.

The position is more complicated when a class of shares (e.g. redeemable convertible preference shares) is accounted for as a compound financial instrument with an equity component and a liability component. There are several possibilities including:

- the share capital and share premium could be shown at their 'legal' amounts with a separate negative reserve equal to the liability recognised; or
- the share capital and share premium could be shown as those amounts that relate to equity shares with a separate line item such as 'equity component of preference shares'; or
- the deduction for the liability might be made first from the share premium and then from share capital; or
- the deduction for the liability might be made from share capital and share premium in proportion to the allocation of the original proceeds of issue between those captions.

All of these are acceptable provided that adequate explanation is provided. The key point is that the total amount presented as equity is unaffected by these choices.

There are some specific instances where IFRSs requires a separate component of equity to be maintained. For example, IAS 21 requires certain exchange differences to be accumulated in a separate component of equity and IAS 16 requires a surplus on revaluation of an asset to be recognised in other comprehensive income and accumulated in equity under the heading of revaluation surplus. Subject to these (and other) specific requirements, there is some flexibility about whether certain items are accounted for as separate components within equity or are, for example, included within retained earnings.

The following paragraphs taken from the Basis for Conclusion to IAS 19 provide support for the argument that 'retained earnings' need not be the cumulative total of profit or loss less amounts distributed to owners:

> 48W. In IFRSs, the phrase 'retained earnings' is not defined and the IASB has not discussed what it should mean. In particular, retained earnings is not defined as the cumulative total of profit or loss less amounts distributed to owners. As with recycling, practice varies under IFRSs. Some amounts that are recognised outside profit or loss are required to be presented in a separate component of equity, for example exchange gains and losses on

foreign subsidiaries. Other such amounts are not, for example gains and losses on available-for-sale financial assets.

48X. The IASB does not believe that it is appropriate to introduce a definition of retained earnings in the context of these amendments to IAS 19. The proposal in the exposure draft was based on practical considerations. As with recycling, there is no rational basis for transferring actuarial gains and losses from a separate component in equity into retained earnings at a later date. As discussed above, the IASB has added a requirement to disclose the cumulative amount recognised in the statement of recognised income and expense to provide users with further information.

For example, the credit to equity required by IFRS 2 for equity-settled share-based payments may either be credited to a separate reserve or to retained earnings. This issue is considered further at **8.5** in **chapter 25**.

UK

One type of reserve that is often found in the financial statements of UK companies is a 'merger reserve' arising as a result of merger relief or group reconstruction relief under sections 611 and 612 of the 2006 Act (previously sections 131 and 132 of the 1985 Act). These reliefs from crediting certain amounts to the share premium account are, as a matter of law, available to companies reporting under IFRSs.

However, as explained at ***6.1.3*** *in* ***chapter 33****, prior to endorsement of the changes made to IFRS 1 and IAS 27 in May 2008, a UK parent company producing IFRS accounts will not be able to take advantage of section 615 of the 2006 Act (previously section 133 of the 1985 Act) so as to record an investment in a subsidiary at less than the fair value of the consideration paid to acquire that subsidiary. It is therefore necessary to record an amount in equity that is not legally share premium although, in economic terms, it is in the nature of a premium on issue of shares. There is no equivalent requirement in UK GAAP for the separate financial statements of the parent but it has been necessary to make an adjustment to create such a reserve on consolidation (where it is not recognised in the parent's separate financial statements) so as to establish the cost of acquisition in accordance with FRS 6. The only change on transition to IFRSs is, therefore, that this reserve will also arise in the separate financial statements of the parent company.*

The term 'merger reserve' has been widely used in the UK to describe this type of reserve when reporting under UK GAAP and this description is still acceptable when reporting under IFRSs. However, it may be less well understood by users of financial statements outside the UK. An alternative approach is to refer to the reserve as 'other reserves' in the statement of financial position and provide a description of the reserves in the notes along the lines of 'other reserves comprise the non-statutory premium arising on shares issued as consideration for acquisitions of subsidiaries where merger relief under the relevant section of the Companies Act applies'.

4.5.2.2 *Disclosures about share capital*

For each class of share capital, the following should be disclosed, either in the statement of financial position or in the notes:

[IAS 1(2007).79(a), previously IAS 1(2003).76(a)]

- the number of shares authorised;
- the number of shares issued and fully paid;
- the number of shares issued but not fully paid;
- the par value per share, or the fact that the shares have no par value;
- a reconciliation of the number of shares outstanding at the beginning and at the end of the period;
- the rights, preferences and restrictions attaching to that class including restrictions on distributions of dividends and the repayment of capital;
- shares in the entity held by its subsidiaries or associates; and
- shares reserved for issue under options and contracts for the sale of shares, including the terms and amounts.

In accordance with IAS 32, all or part of the amounts recognised for shares in the statement of financial position may be classified as liabilities. The above disclosure requirements apply irrespective of whether the shares are classified as equity or debt or a combination of the two.

It is unclear whether the requirement to disclose 'shares in the entity held by its subsidiaries or associates' refers to the number of shares or the amount of the deduction within equity. In the context of the other disclosures required by this paragraph of IAS 1, it appears to refer to the number of shares. This is consistent with the inclusion of shares held by associates of the entity which would not result in a deduction within equity. However, IAS 32.34 states that 'the amount of treasury shares held is disclosed separately either in the statement of financial position or in the notes, in accordance with IAS 1 *Presentation of Financial Statements*'. This refers to the 'amount' of treasury shares rather than their number but appears to be a reminder of the disclosure requirement in IAS 1 rather than an additional requirement. It is recommended that the number of own shares held and the amount of any deduction for treasury shares within equity are both disclosed where relevant.

UK

These disclosures are similar to, but go beyond, those required under UK company law following the withdrawal of the disclosure requirements in FRS 4 in 2005. It is not legally possible for a UK incorporated company to have shares of no par value.

It is also not usually legally possible in the UK for a subsidiary (as defined by law) to hold shares in its parent but shares are often held through an ESOP trust. Such a trust would generally be included in the consolidated accounts of the parent under IFRSs (see ***section 9*** *of* ***chapter 25****) and so the disclosure requirement would apply to shares held by the trust.*

Some entities such as partnerships or trusts do not have a share capital. In such cases, information equivalent to that described above for share capital should be disclosed, showing changes during the period in each category of equity interest and the rights, preferences and restrictions attaching to each category of equity interest. [IAS 1(2007).80, previously IAS 1(2003).77]

UK

In a UK context, this would also cover, for example, limited liability partnerships and companies limited by guarantee.

Puttable Financial Instruments and Obligations Arising on Liquidation (Amendments to IAS 32 and IAS 1), issued in February 2008, amends paragraph 138 of IAS 1(2007) and inserts new paragraphs 8A, 80A and 136A. The amendments must be applied for annual periods beginning on or after 1 January 2009. Earlier application is permitted. If an entity applies these amendments for an earlier period, it should disclose that fact and apply the related amendments to IAS 32, IAS 39, IFRS 7 and IFRIC 2 at the same time.

The new paragraph 80 requires that, if an entity has reclassified:

- a puttable instrument classified as an equity instrument; or
- an instrument that imposes on the entity an obligation to deliver to another party a pro rata share of the net assets of the entity only on liquidation and classified as an equity instrument,

between financial liabilities and equity, the amount reclassified into and out of each category (financial liabilities or equity), and the timing and reason for that reclassification, should be disclosed. [IAS 1(2007).80A]

The terms used in the two bullet points above have the meaning specified in IAS 32 (as amended).

4.5.2.3 Disclosures about reserves

A description of the nature and purpose of each reserve within equity has to be given, either in the statement of financial position or in the notes. [IAS 1(2007).79(b), previously IAS 1(2003).76(b)]

Whilst IAS 1 requires financial statements to include additional information as to the nature and purpose of each reserve, it does not include any further or more precise guidance about what information is needed.

By allowing this information to be disclosed in the statement of financial position, the IASB has indicated that the required information might be sufficiently disclosed by a precise wording of the name of the reserve. Thus, reserves that are commonly encountered, such as revaluation reserves on property, plant and equipment, share premium account, translation reserves on foreign entities, etc., generally do not need to be explained further in order for investors to understand the nature and purpose of the reserves.

However, if, for example, the entity wishes to designate special reserves within equity, which are not familiar to users of financial statements, supplementary information regarding the purpose of the reserve, and how it will be utilised, is needed.

UK

There is no specific requirement under IFRSs to say whether reserves are distributable or not although this might form part of the description of the nature and purpose of the reserve. Distributable profits are more likely to diverge from retained earnings under IFRSs than under UK GAAP (see ***chapter 49****) and, therefore, this might be seen as useful information for users of the financial statements. Such disclosures would, however, be relevant only to the separate financial statements and not the consolidated financial statements because the latter have no relevance for distributions.*

It may be thought helpful to users of financial statements if there is an indication of which reserves are distributable but, as noted above, there is no legal requirement to do so. In some cases, there may be practical difficulties with providing such an analysis. For example, there may be uncertainties about whether certain profits are realised or unrealised. There is generally no need for directors to form a view on whether profits are realised unless they intend to utilise them to make a distribution.

5 The statement of comprehensive income

IAS 1(2007), which must be adopted for periods beginning on or after 1 January 2009, requires a complete set of financial statements to include a statement of comprehensive income (see **2.3** above). This may be presented as a single statement which presents all items of income and expense recognised in a period. An alternative presentation is also permitted, in which all items of income and expense are recognised in two statements:

[IAS 1(2007).81]

- a statement displaying components of profit or loss (i.e. a separate income statement) (see **5.1** below); and
- a second statement beginning with profit or loss and displaying components of other comprehensive income (i.e. a statement of comprehensive income) (see **5.4** below).

When a separate income statement is presented (i.e. the alternative presentation), it is required to be displayed immediately before the statement of comprehensive income. [IAS 1(2007).12]

This does not appear to prohibit the statement of comprehensive income being on a separate page from the income statement provided that it is on the immediately following page.

IAS 1(2003) includes no requirement for a statement of comprehensive income. It requires items of other comprehensive income to be included in the statement of changes in equity (see **section 6** below).

One method of presenting a statement of changes in equity in accordance with IAS 1(2003) involves the presentation of a Statement of Recognised Income and Expense (SORIE). This statement is similar to the statement of other comprehensive income required by IAS 1(2007). Therefore, entities which have adopted this presentation can continue to use a similar presentation. The main impact of IAS 1(2007) is to prohibit the presentation of a single statement of changes in equity which mixes together items of other comprehensive income with changes of equity arising from transactions with owners in their capacity as owners (e.g. dividends paid).

UK

UK companies have, since 1992, been required to present a second performance statement known as a Statement of Total Recognised Gains and Losses (STRGL). On transition to IFRSs, many of those companies have presented a SORIE under IAS 1(2003) so the impact of IAS 1(2007) will not be significant in this respect.

In December 2000, the ASB published proposals in FRED 22 to amend FRS 3 to require a single performance statement. This proposal was not taken forward at the time because attention turned to convergence with international standards.

5.1 Profit or loss for the period

All items of income or expense recognised in a period are recognised in profit or loss unless an IFRS requires or permits otherwise. [IAS 1(2007).88, previously IAS 1(2003).78)

UK

This is similar to UK GAAP but with a significant difference. Under UK GAAP, FRS 3.13 requires that gains and losses may be excluded from the profit and loss account only if they are specifically permitted or required to be taken directly to reserves by FRS 3 or other accounting standards or, in the absence of a relevant accounting standard, by law. The reference to the law is significant. For companies reporting under UK GAAP, paragraph 12 of Schedule 4 to the Act states that only profits that are realised at the balance sheet date may be included in the profit and loss account (see ***5.3** in **chapter 49*** *for the meaning of realised profits) although there is an exception to this rule when the fair value accounting provisions of the Act are applied. The requirements of Schedule 4 do not apply to UK companies reporting under IFRSs. Therefore, a common difference between UK GAAP and IFRSs is that unrealised gains that are reported in the income statement under IFRSs are usually reported in the Statement of Total Recognised Gains and Losses under UK GAAP.*

Some IFRSs specify circumstances where particular items are recognised outside profit or loss in the current period. IAS 8 deals with two such circumstances which are the correction of errors and changes in accounting policies (see **chapter 4**). Other IFRSs require or permit components of other comprehensive income that meet the *Framework's* definition of income or expense to be excluded from profit or loss. [IAS 1(2007).89, previously IAS 1(2003).79]

Examples of such items include:

- revaluation surpluses under IAS 16 (see **chapter 6**);
- certain gains and losses arising from the translation of the financial statements of a foreign operation under IAS 21 (see **chapter 28**); and
- gains and losses on remeasuring available-for-sale financial assets under IAS 39 (see **chapter 14**).

5.2 Information to be presented in the statement of comprehensive income

5.2.1 Minimum requirements

As a minimum, the statement of comprehensive income includes line items that present the following amounts for the period:

[IAS 1(2007).82, previously IAS 1(2003).81]

- revenue;
- finance costs;
- share of the profit or loss of associates and joint ventures accounted for using the equity method;
- tax expense;
- a single amount comprising the total of:
  - the post-tax profit or loss of discontinued operations; and
  - the post-tax gain or loss recognised on the measurement to fair value less costs to sell, or on the disposal of the assets or disposal groups constituting the discontinued operation;
- profit or loss;
- each component of other comprehensive income, classified by nature (excluding amounts included in the next item below);
- share of other comprehensive income of associates and joint ventures accounted for using the equity method; and
- total comprehensive income.

The last three items are not required by IAS 1(2003) which requires an income statement comprising the first six items. However, details of other comprehensive income components are disclosed in the statement of changes in equity (see **section 6** below).

Total comprehensive income is defined as the change in equity during a period resulting from transactions and other events, other than those changes resulting from transactions with owners in their capacity as owners. Total comprehensive income comprises all components of 'profit or loss' and 'other comprehensive income'. [IAS 1(2007).7]

Although IAS 1 uses the terms 'profit or loss', 'other comprehensive income' and 'total comprehensive income', other terms may be used to describe the totals as long as the meaning is clear. For example, the term 'net income' may be used to describe profit or loss. [IAS 1(2007).8]

IAS 1(2007) permits a separate income statement to be presented including the first six items listed above. Where this presentation is adopted, the disclosures required by IAS 1(2007).83(a) concerning non-controlling interests (see **5.3** below) should be given as part of the income statement. [IAS 1(2007).84]

It is not necessary for there to be a single total for each of these items in the statement of comprehensive income (or income statement). For example, revenue from sale of goods to customers may be presented separately from interest receivable (which falls within the definition of revenue in IAS 18). However, it is necessary to be able to arrive at the total by adding together items that appear in the income statement. This is more fully explained at **5.2.2** below.

5.2.2 *Net finance costs*

At its October 2004 meeting, the IFRIC discussed a potential agenda topic of whether it is acceptable to present a line item for 'net finance costs' in the income statement without showing the finance costs and finance revenue comprising it. IFRIC members noted that paragraph 81 of IAS 1(2003) (see above) requires the face of the income statement to include line items that present, inter alia, amounts for revenue and for finance costs. IFRIC members, therefore, agreed:

- taken together, paragraphs 32 (prohibition on netting off – see **2.8** above) and 81 of IAS 1(2003) preclude presenting 'net finance costs' (or a similar term) in the income statement without showing the finance costs and finance revenues comprising it; but

- this does not preclude presentation of finance revenue followed immediately by finance costs and a sub-total for 'net finance costs' in the income statement, as illustrated below.

	20X1	20X0
	£'000	£'000
Operating profit	126,342	49,774
Investment revenues	3,501	717
Finance costs	(36,187)	(32,165)
Net finance costs	(32,686)	(31,448)
Share of profit of associates	12,763	983
Other gains and losses	(563)	(44)
Profit before tax	105,856	19,265

The IFRIC decided not to develop an Interpretation on this but the above conclusion was set out in the October 2004 edition of *IFRIC Update*.

The conclusion reached by the IFRIC is, in part, due to the fact that the definition of 'revenue' in IAS 18 is broad and includes income of a financial nature as well as income from the sale of goods or the rendering of services. IAS 18 lists 'interest' and 'dividends' as categories of revenue that should be disclosed separately. Before the IFRIC conclusion on net finance costs, there had been some uncertainty over whether paragraph 81 of IAS 1(2003) should be interpreted as requiring a single total for each item listed or whether several 'line items' could be presented to represent a single requirement in paragraph 81 (e.g. revenue). The IFRIC conclusion on net finance costs effectively confirms that it is acceptable to show separate items for revenue from customers and for finance revenue without having to total the two items in the income statement.

UK *This is significantly different from UK GAAP under which many companies have presented net finance costs on the face of the profit and loss account with the analysis between the gross components given in a note.*

5.2.3 *Non-controlling interests*

IAS 27, as amended in 2008, replaces the term 'minority interests' with 'non-controlling interests'. This amendment is effective for periods beginning on or after 1 July 2009. If an entity applies the revised IAS 27 for an earlier period, the amendment to IAS 1 is applied for that earlier period.

IAS 1(2007) requires the following items to be disclosed in the statement of comprehensive income as allocations of profit or loss for the period:

[IAS 1(2007).83]

- profit or loss for the period attributable to:
  - non-controlling interests; and
  - owners of the parent; and
- total comprehensive income for the period attributable to:
  - non-controlling interests; and
  - owners of the parent.

IAS 1(2003) includes a similar requirement that the following items should also be disclosed on the face of the income statement as allocations of profit or loss for the period:

[IAS 1(2003).82]

- profit or loss attributable to non-controlling interests; and
- profit or loss attributable to equity holders of the parent.

IAS 1(2003) does not include any requirement to provide a similar analysis of total comprehensive income although, in effect, a similar requirement is imposed by IAS 1(2003).96 in relation to the statement of changes in equity (see **section 6** below).

The reference to presentation 'as allocations of profit' means that these items are not items of income or expense. IAS 1(2007).BC59 and IAS 1(2003).BC19 explain that this presentation (which was a change from the 1997 version of the Standard) is consistent with IAS 27 *Consolidated and Separate Financial Statements* which requires minority interest (non-controlling interest) to be presented within equity because it does not meet the definition of a liability in the IASB's *Framework*.

The Implementation Guidance on IAS 1(2003) illustrated how this requirement could be met as follows:

Profit for the period	XXX

Attributable to:	
Equity holders of the parent	XXX
Minority interests	XXX
	XXX

A presentation that shows the profit for the period as a sub-total and then deducts non-controlling interests to arrive at the profit attributable to the equity holders of the parent would not be regarded as meeting the requirement of IAS 1.

5.2.4 *Additional items*

Additional line items, headings and sub-totals are presented in the statement of comprehensive income (and any separate income statement) when such a presentation is relevant to an understanding of the entity's financial performance. [IAS 1(2007).85, previously IAS 1(2003).83]

Disclosing the components of financial performance assists users in understanding the financial performance achieved and in making projections of future financial performance. To explain the elements of financial performance, it may be necessary to:

- include additional line items in the statement of comprehensive income (and in any separate income statement);
- amend the descriptions used; and
- amend the ordering of items.

Factors to be considered include materiality and the nature and function of the items of income and expense. For example, a financial institution may amend the descriptions to provide information that is relevant to the operations of such an institution. However, income and expense items are not offset unless the criteria in IAS 1 are met (see **2.8** above). [IAS 1(2007).86, previously IAS 1(2003).84]

5.2.5 *Results of operating activities*

The 1997 version of IAS 1 required the results of operating activities to be disclosed as a line item on the face of the income statement. The IASB decided to omit this requirement, when the Standard was revised in 2003, on the basis that the term was not defined and that it was inappropriate to require disclosure of an undefined item.

However, the IASB recognises that an entity may elect to disclose the results of operating activities, or a similar line item, even though the term is not defined. IAS 1(2007).BC56 and IAS 1(2003).BC13 note that in such cases, it is necessary to ensure the amount disclosed is representative of activities that would normally be considered as 'operating'. In the IASB's view, it would be misleading and would impair the comparability of financial statements if items of an operating nature were excluded from the results of operating activities, even if that had been industry practice. For example, it would be inappropriate to exclude items clearly related to operations (e.g. inventory write-downs and restructuring or relocation expenses) because they occur irregularly or infrequently or are unusual in amount. Similarly, it would be inappropriate to exclude items on the grounds that they do not involve cash flows, such as depreciation and amortisation charges.

The Implementation Guidance to the 1997 version of IAS 1 illustrated 'Profit from operations' as being struck after all income and expenses other than finance costs and income from associates. Where there is investment income, it would be usual to show this below profit from operations. Based on the IASB's views expressed in IAS 1(2007).BC 56 and IAS 1(2003).BC13, it would not be appropriate to exclude items such as restructuring costs. There does however appear to be flexibility to disclose the results of associates either within or below profit from operations (see **5.2.7** below).

Under UK GAAP, FRS 3 effectively requires presentation of a sub-total for operating profit because it specifies various items to be included in that sub-total and various items that must be presented below that sub-total. Many UK companies have continued to present such a sub-total when reporting under IFRSs. Where such a sub-total is reported, it is necessary to consider how to treat any items that would have been reported below operating profit under FRS 3.20. UK

Based on the guidance above, it would seem inappropriate to present the costs of a 'fundamental reorganisation or restructuring' below operating profit under IFRSs even though this is a requirement of FRS 3.

Similarly, since the use of property, plant and equipment is generally part of an entity's operating activities, circumstances in which gains and losses on the sale of property, plant and equipment should be presented outside operating profit seem likely to be extremely rare.

Where profits or losses on the sale or termination of an operation fall within discontinued operations, they will be presented separately in accordance

*with IFRS 5 (see **chapter 29**). In other cases, since they relate to (the cessation of) operating activities they would normally be included within operating profit. However, it may be appropriate to present such gains or losses outside operating profit where they are clearly different in nature from operating activities.*

5.2.6 *Extraordinary items*

IAS 1 states that items of income and expense must not be presented as 'extraordinary items', in the statement of comprehensive income, in any separate income statement, or in the notes. [IAS 1(2007).87, previously IAS 1(2003).85]

This may appear to be a slightly odd requirement in that IAS 1 does not define extraordinary items or say how they might be presented if they were not prohibited. To understand this, it is necessary to be aware that a previous version of IAS 8 included a definition of such items as 'income and expenses that arise from events or transactions that are clearly distinct from the ordinary activities of the enterprise and, therefore, are not expected to recur frequently or regularly'. It required such items to be disclosed on the face of the income statement separately from the profit or loss on ordinary activities (i.e. normally as a single net of tax number after profit from ordinary activities and before net profit). The IASB decided, as part of the revisions of IAS 1 and IAS 8 in 2003, to prohibit the presentation of extraordinary items because they result from the normal business risks faced by an entity and do not warrant presentation in a separate component of the income statement. The reasons are more fully set out in IAS 1(2007).BC60 – 64 and IAS 1(2003).BC14 – 18.

UK *This will be familiar to UK companies because extraordinary items are, for all practical purposes, prohibited by FRS 3.*

5.2.7 *Equity-accounted results of associates and joint ventures*

The share of the profit or loss of associates and joint ventures accounted for using the equity method is one of the line items that is required to be presented in the statement of comprehensive income (and any separate income statement) (see **5.2.1** above).

This item should be presented on an after tax basis. IAS 28.38 requires the equity-accounted share of profits or losses to be 'separately disclosed'. IAS 1 requires the disclosure to be in the statement of comprehensive income (or any separate income statement). The statement of comprehensive income illustrated in the Implementation Guidance accompanying IAS 1 notes that 'this means the share of associates' profit attributable to owners of the associates, i.e. it is after tax and non-controlling interests in the associates'. This precludes separating the equity-accounted earnings of the investment over different line items in the income statement. Also, IAS 28.11 states that 'under the equity method, the investment in an associate is initially recognised at cost and the carrying amount is increased or decreased to recognise the investor's share of the profit or loss of the investee after the date of acquisition'. Therefore, the investment is recognised as one-line item in the statement of financial position. IAS 28.11 continues with 'the investor's share of profit or loss of the investee is recognised in the investor's profit or loss'. Taking these together, it is apparent that the investor's share of profit or loss of the investee should be presented by a one-line item in the statement of comprehensive income (or any separate income statement).

This is different from UK GAAP. FRS 9 requires a single line for the investor's share of the associate's operating results. The investor's share of other items such as finance costs and tax expense are shown either adjacent to, or combined with, the equivalent items for the group. UK

As noted above, the equity-accounted results of associates and jointly controlled entities are presented on an after tax basis. A question therefore arises as to whether the line item should be presented either before or after the tax expense line in the statement of comprehensive income. In the list of items in IAS 1(2007).82 and IAS 1(2003).81, the line item appears above tax expense. The illustrative statement of comprehensive income in the Guidance on Implementing IAS 1 presents the item before tax expense but after all other expenses including finance costs. But there is no requirement in the Standard that the items must appear in any particular order. Therefore, it would be possible to present the share of results of associates and joint ventures below the tax expense line although it must be presented before the 'profit for the period'.

It is also possible to present the item as part of profit from operations, where such a sub-total is presented. Such an approach may be attractive to entities which view these interests as part of their operations.

UK

As noted above, FRS 9 requires a disaggregated presentation of the results of associates. The investor's share of the operating results of its associates is included immediately below the group operating results. Under IFRSs, the single net of tax number could be included in this position, or after finance costs as shown in the illustrative examples in the Guidance on Implementing IAS 1, or below tax expense as discussed above.

5.2.8 *Other presentation issues*

The following sections deal with some other issues about presentation of items in the statement of comprehensive income or income statement.

5.2.8.1 *Presentation of tax-based structuring income*

Bank A may undertake to lend money to Company B. After assessing the credit worthiness of Company B, Bank A concludes that it would charge an interest rate of 12 per cent. The bank structures the loan such that it receives favourable tax deductions and recovers half of the interest that it would have charged Company B from these deductions. Consequently, it charges Company B interest at 6 per cent but requires Company B to sign an agreement that if the tax deductions do not arise, or are less than expected, it will pay the difference as an increased interest charge.

Bank A cannot record interest income at 12 per cent and increase its tax expense accordingly. The substance of the transaction is that the entity has originated a loan which bears interest at a rate of 6 per cent. Interest and tax are separate items and are accounted for separately and recognised in the tax line and interest line of the statement of comprehensive income or any separate income statement.

5.2.8.2 *Investment income as revenue*

IAS 18.7 defines revenue as the gross inflow of economic resources during the period arising from ordinary activities, excluding inflows from equity participants. IAS 1(2007).82 and IAS 1(2003).81 require the disclosure of revenue in the statement of comprehensive income but IAS 1(2007).85 and IAS 1(2003).83 add that additional line items should be added when it is necessary to explain the financial performance of the entity.

Unless investment is one of the principal activities of the entity, in most circumstances, it will be necessary to show investment revenue as a separate line item to explain the entity's financial performance. IAS 1(2007).82 and IAS 1(2003).81 do not preclude showing revenue on two separate lines in this manner (see also **section 5.2.2** above concerning net finance costs).

Note that IAS 18.35(b) requires entities to disclose the amount of each significant category of revenue recognised during the period, including revenue arising from interest and revenue arising from dividends.

5.2.8.3 *Exchange gains and losses*

IAS 21.52 requires an entity to disclose the amount of exchange differences recognised in profit or loss, except for those arising on financial instruments measured at fair value in accordance with IAS 39.

IAS 21 is silent regarding classification in profit or loss of foreign currency exchange gains and losses. Foreign exchange gains and losses should be classified based on the nature of the transactions or events which give rise to those foreign exchange gains or losses. For example, recording foreign currency gains and losses on operational items (trade receivables, payables, etc.) within income from operations, and recording foreign currency exchange gains and losses on issued debt in finance costs (but not in interest payable), may be appropriate.

Classification of foreign exchange gains or losses in the statement of comprehensive income (including any separate income statement) is a matter of accounting policy which must be disclosed and applied consistently year-on-year. In addition, where the impact of foreign exchange gains or losses is material, in accordance with IAS 1(2007).97 and IAS 1(2003).86, their nature and amount should be disclosed separately, either in the statement of comprehensive income (including any separate income statement) or in the notes. Hence, where an entity classifies foreign exchange gains or losses on operating items within income from operations, and the impact of these is material, the entity may elect to present foreign exchange gains and losses on operating items as a separate item within income from operations.

5.2.8.4 *Fair value gains and losses on derivatives that are economic hedges*

The presentation of gains and losses on such derivatives when hedge accounting is not applied is discussed at **5.1** in **chapter 16**.

5.3 Information to be presented in the statement or in the notes

5.3.1 *General requirements*

IAS 1 requires that, when items of income and expense are material, their nature and amount should be disclosed separately. [IAS 1(2007).97, previously IAS 1(2003).86] The Standard lists the following items as examples of circumstances that would give rise to separate disclosure:

[IAS 1(2007).98, previously IAS 1(2003).87]

- write-downs of inventories to net realisable value and reversals of such write-downs;
- write-downs of property, plant and equipment to recoverable amount, and reversals of such write-downs;
- restructuring of activities and reversals of any provisions for such costs;
- disposals of items of property, plant and equipment;
- disposals of investments;
- discontinued operations;
- litigation settlements; and
- other reversals of provisions.

UK

IAS 1 does not use the UK GAAP expression 'exceptional items' but has a similar concept that when items of income or expense are material, their nature and amount should be disclosed separately. The list of examples given in IAS 1 is similar to a list of items that would typically be disclosed as exceptional items under UK GAAP. Disclosure may be made either on the face of the income statement or in the notes, though the requirements at **5.3.2** *below need to be considered if disclosure is to be on the face of the* *statement. There is no equivalent in IAS 1 to the UK GAAP requirement to present certain items below operating profit (see **5.2.5** above).*

5.3.2 *Analysis by nature and function*

An analysis of expenses recognised in profit or loss should be provided using a classification based on either the nature of the expenses (e.g. depreciation, employee costs etc) or their function within the entity (e.g. cost of sales, administrative expenses etc). The choice of classification method should be based on whichever provides information that is reliable and more relevant. [IAS 1(2007).99, previously IAS 1(2003).88] IAS 1 encourages, but does not require, this analysis to be in the statement of comprehensive income (or in any separate income statement). [IAS 1(2007).100, previously IAS 1(2003).89]

UK

This is similar to the choice provided in UK GAAP between Format 1 and Format 2 for the profit and loss account although IFRSs are less prescriptive about the line items to be disclosed.

IAS 1 explains that there are two forms of analysis whereby expenses are sub-classified to highlight components of financial performance that may differ in terms of their frequency, potential for gain or loss and predictability. These are analysis by nature and analysis by function. [IAS 1(2007).101, previously IAS 1(2003).90]

The first method of analysis is by the nature of expenses (e.g. depreciation, purchases of materials, transport costs, employee benefits and advertising costs). This method is simple to apply because no allocation of expenses to functional classifications is necessary. IAS 1 gives the following example of a classification using the nature of expense method. [IAS 1(2007).102, previously IAS 1(2003).91]

Example 5.3.2A

Analysis by nature of expenses

Revenue		X
Other income	X	
Changes in inventories of finished goods and work in progress	X	
Raw materials and consumables used	X	
Employee benefits expense	X	
Depreciation and amortisation expense	X	
Other expenses	X	
Total expenses		(X)
Profit before tax		X

The second method of analysis is by function (e.g. cost of sales, distribution costs and administrative expenses). At a minimum, cost of sales must be disclosed separately from other expenses when expenses are analysed by their function. This method can provide more relevant information to users than classification by nature. But allocating costs to functions may require arbitrary allocations and involve considerable judgement. IAS 1 gives the following example of a classification using the function of expense method. [IAS 1(2007).103, previously IAS 1(2003).92]

Example 5.3.2B

Analysis by function of expense

Revenue	X
Cost of sales	X
Gross profit	X
Other income	X
Distribution costs	X
Administrative expenses	X
Other expenses	X
Profit before tax	X

When an entity chooses to classify expenses by function, it is also required to disclose additional information on the nature of the expenses, including:

[IAS 1(2007).104, previously IAS 1(2003).93]

- depreciation and amortisation expense; and
- employee benefits expense (as defined in IAS 19 *Employee Benefits*).

Example 5.3.2C

Shipping and handling costs

Company A, acting in the capacity of principal, sells goods to a customer. Company A classifies expenses by function in its statement of comprehensive income. Company A may adopt a policy of including shipping and handling costs in cost of sales. This treatment is permitted by IAS 2.38, which states that the circumstances of the entity may warrant the inclusion of distribution costs in cost of sales.

Alternatively, shipping and handling costs may be included in a separate 'distribution costs' classification or, if insignificant, in 'other operating expenses'. The key points are to ensure that:

- the classification is appropriate to the entity's circumstances;
- the classification is consistent from year to year; and

- material items are separately identified, as required by IAS 1(2007).97 and IAS 1(2003).86).

The presentation of shipping and handling costs as a deduction from revenues is not permitted (see **2.8** above).

Where Company A is acting as agent, it may be appropriate to net the shipping costs incurred and the shipping costs recharged (see **2.8** above).

There is a UK requirement to disclose 'staff costs' which applies irrespective of whether the financial statements are prepared under UK GAAP or under IFRSs. Separate totals are required for wages and salaries, social security costs and other pension costs. This requirement is considered at ***8.1.2*** *below.* UK

The choice between the two methods of analysis depends on historical and industry factors and the nature of the entity. Both methods provide an indication of those costs that might vary, directly or indirectly, with the level of sales or production. IAS 1 requires management to select the more relevant and reliable presentation because each method has merit for different types of entities. However, additional disclosure about the nature of the expenses is required when the primary analysis is by function because information on the nature of expenses is useful in predicting future cash flows. [IAS 1(2007).105, previously IAS 1(2003).94]

At its October 2004 meeting, IFRIC discussed a potential agenda topic of whether to tighten the requirement in IAS 1(2003).88 for the presentation of an analysis of expenses by nature or function. The purpose of the clarification would be to enhance comparability by reminding constituents that ad hoc mixing of classifications of expenses by nature and function in an analysis is not permitted.

IFRIC members were advised that there was some evidence that entities classify expenses on a functional basis but exclude certain 'unusual' expenses from the functional classification to which they relate and present these items separately by nature. Examples are inventory write-downs, employee termination benefits and impairments.

The October 2004 edition of *IFRIC Update* records that the IFRIC instructed the staff to write to the IASB to describe the issue and ask whether developing guidance on the application of IAS 1 would fall within the scope of the IASB's project on reporting comprehensive income. The November 2004 edition of *IASB Update* records that the Board decided that amendments to IAS 1 specifying which expenses should be included in particular functional classifications should not be addressed outside its project on reporting comprehensive income (now known as the financial statements presentation project).

However, even in the absence of a formal Interpretation from the IFRIC, the mixing of the two methods of analysis in the way described above should be avoided.

5.3.3 *Dividends*

IAS 1(2007) requires the amount of dividends recognised as distributions to owners during the period, and the related amount per share, to be presented either in the statement of changes in equity or in the notes. [IAS 1(2007).107]

The presentation of such disclosures in the statement of comprehensive income is not permitted if IAS 1(2007) has been adopted. IAS 1(2007).BC75 explains that this is because dividends are distributions to owners in their capacity as owners and the statement of changes in equity presents all owner changes in equity. The Board concluded that an entity should not present dividends in the statement of comprehensive income because that statement presents non-owner changes in equity.

IAS 1(2003) also requires the amount of dividends recognised as distributions to owners during the year, and the related amounts per share, to be disclosed. However, it permits this disclosure to be on the face of the income statement or in the statement of changes in equity or in the notes. [IAS 1(2003).95]

Even before adoption of IAS 1(2007), it is preferable that dividends are presented in the notes rather than in the income statement. This treatment recognises modern thinking that dividends are not part of financial performance or comprehensive income. It also recognises that some users of financial statements may find it confusing that prior year proposed dividends have been deducted from current year profits while current year proposed dividends have been ignored (i.e. dividends are effectively on a paid basis to comply with IAS 10).

UK *There is no requirement in UK GAAP to show dividends per share for unquoted companies. Dividends paid by subsidiaries to parents are often expressed as an aggregate amount (e.g. £5m) without regard to the number of shares that the subsidiary has in issue. The result of dividing the amount of the dividend by the number of shares in issue may result in a meaningless number for dividends per share. But nevertheless, it is a requirement of IAS 1 for the subsidiary to disclose an amount per share for dividends recognised in the period.*

Further disclosures relating to dividends are considered at **7.4.2** below.

5.3.4 *Columnar presentation of the statement of comprehensive income*

There is nothing in IAS 1 to prevent additional information being given in the statement of comprehensive income provided that it is not misleading. This is sometimes done through the use of a columnar layout, where the total column gives the amounts required by IAS 1 and the additional columns provide an analysis of some or all of those amounts between two components. For example, columns may be used to present the results of two business segments in the statement of comprehensive income. They may also be used to separate out certain types of income or expense such as those that require separate disclosure in accordance with IAS 1(2007).97 and IAS 1(2003).86 (see **5.3.1** above).

However, to avoid the risk that the additional information may be misleading, the description of the columns should be unambiguous and as factual as possible. The objective is for the descriptions to be clear enough to be understood by a general reader of the financial statements without further explanation. The use of terms such as 'core performance', 'underlying performance' and 'special items' should be avoided because they may be ambiguous or, in the extreme, misleading. Where necessary, a clear definition should be provided of those items that are included in a separate column.

It is common practice for UK companies reporting under UK GAAP to use columnar presentations for their profit and loss accounts. One example is that investment trusts (see below), and some property investment companies, use columns to distinguish between capital profits and revenue profits. Another common example is the segregation of exceptional items and/or the amortisation of goodwill and intangible assets. UK

Some changes of practice become necessary on transition to IFRSs, for example because 'exceptional items' is not a term used under IFRSs and goodwill is not amortised under IFRSs. However, provided that the columns are accurately described and will not mislead the users of the financial

statements, their use is not prohibited. It has become accepted practice that companies reporting under IFRSs may continue to use the term 'exceptional items' to describe the types of items required to be disclosed by IAS 1(2007).97 and IAS 1(2003).86 provided that the financial statements define the term and that the definition is applied consistently from one period to another.

The Association of Investment Companies (AIC) (which changed its name from the Association of Investment Trust Companies (AITC) in October 2006) published guidance stating that 'following discussions with the International Accounting Standards Board, the AITC believes that .... the retention of the three column approach under IAS will enable an ITC to continue to provide the users of its accounts with relevant information that the AITC considers is essential in assessing the financial performance of the ITC in the reporting period concerned. The AITC therefore recommends that ITCs preparing accounts under IAS should provide Revenue and Capital columns on the face of the income statement in a format similar to that recommended by the SORP'.

5.4 Other comprehensive income

The requirements set out in this section apply only to entities that are applying IAS 1(2007).

Other comprehensive income comprises items of income and expense (including reclassification adjustments) that are not recognised in profit or loss as required or permitted by IFRSs and includes:

[IAS 1(2007).7]

- changes in revaluation surplus (see IAS 16 and IAS 38);
- actuarial gains and losses on defined benefit plans (see IAS 19);
- gains and losses arising from translating the financial statements of a foreign operation (see IAS 21);
- gains and losses on remeasuring available-for-sale financial assets (see IAS 39); and
- the effective portion of gains and losses on hedging instruments in a cash flow hedge (see IAS 39).

The credit made to equity for equity-settled share-based payments, in accordance with IFRS 2, should not be included in other comprehensive income. This is because it arises from a transaction with owners in their capacity as such. The credit represents either the proceeds of the grant of an equity instrument or, where a subsidiary recognises an expense for a grant of its parent's equity instruments, a capital contribution from the parent.

5.4.1 *Income tax*

The amount of income tax relating to each component of other comprehensive income, including reclassification adjustments, should be disclosed either in the statement of comprehensive income or in the notes. [IAS 1(2007).90]

IAS 1(2003) does not include such a requirement. As explained in IAS 1(2007).IN14, the purpose of this new requirement is to provide users with tax information relating to the components of other comprehensive income because they often have tax rates different from those applied to profit or loss. Many respondents to the exposure draft expressed concern about this proposed requirement, observing that it may involve an arbitrary allocation process and that information may not be readily available. However, the Board decided to retain this requirement in the Standard for the reasons explained in IAS 1(2007).BC66–68.

The components of other comprehensive income may be presented either:

[IAS 1(2007).91]

- net of related tax effects; or
- before related tax effects with one amount shown for the aggregate amount of income tax relating to those components.

This permits a choice of presentation in the statement of comprehensive income. As explained in IAS 1(2007).BC65, there are advantages to each method of presentation and the Board decided to permit either to be use. However, where the income tax effects are aggregated into a single item in the statement, it is still necessary to disclose in the notes the amount of tax attributable to each item of other comprehensive income as required by IAS 1(2007).90.

5.4.2 *Reclassification adjustments*

Reclassification adjustments are amounts reclassified to profit or loss in the current period that were recognised in other comprehensive income in the current or previous periods. [IAS 1(2007).7]

Reclassification adjustments arise, for example, on disposal of a foreign operation, on derecognition of available-for-sale financial assets and when a hedged forecast transaction affects profit or loss. [IAS 1(2007).95] Reclassification adjustments do not arise on changes in revaluation surplus recognised in accordance with IAS 16 or IAS 38. They also do not arise on actuarial gains and losses on defined benefit plans recognised in accordance with IAS 19.93A. These components are recognised in other comprehensive income and are not reclassified to profit or loss in subsequent periods. Changes in revaluation surplus may be transferred to retained earnings in subsequent periods as the asset is used or when it is derecognised. Actuarial gains and losses are reported in retained earnings in the period in which they are recognised as other comprehensive income. [IAS 1(2007).96]

IAS 1(2007) requires disclosure of reclassification adjustments relating to components of other comprehensive income. [IAS 1(2007).92] Such reclassification adjustments may be presented in the statement of comprehensive income or in the notes. When reclassification adjustments are presented in the notes, the components of other comprehensive income are stated after any related reclassification adjustments. [IAS 1(2007).94]

This is a new requirement in IAS 1(2007). The reasons for it are explained in IAS 1(2007).BC69–73. In practice, this information has often been given in the past but is not explicitly required by IAS 1(2003).

Other IFRSs specify whether and when amounts previously recognised in other comprehensive income are reclassified to profit or loss (see above). Such reclassifications are referred to in IAS 1(2007) as 'reclassification adjustments'. A reclassification adjustment is included with the related component of other comprehensive income in the period that the adjustment is reclassified to profit or loss. [IAS 1(2007).93]

IAS 1(2007) gives the example of gains realised on the disposal of available-for-sale financial assets that are included in profit or loss of the current period. These amounts may have been recognised in other comprehensive income as unrealised gains in the current or previous periods. Those unrealised gains must be deducted from other comprehensive income in the period in which the realised gains are reclassified to profit or loss to avoid including them twice in total comprehensive income. [IAS 1(2007).93]

UK *IAS 1(2007) uses the terms 'realised' and 'unrealised' here to distinguish the gain on disposal from the gain on remeasurement. However, this will not*

> *necessarily correspond with whether the profits are realised as a matter of UK company law and therefore potentially available for distribution as dividends. Some profits on remeasurement will be 'realised profits' for this purpose (see* ***section 5*** *of* ***chapter 49****).*

6 The statement of changes in equity

IAS 1(2003) and IAS 1(2007) both require the presentation of a statement of changes in equity. However, the requirements for this statement are significantly different in the two versions of the Standard.

Section 6.1 below sets out the requirements for the statement of changes in equity when IAS 1(2007) is applied. In summary, the requirement is for a statement showing a reconciliation between the opening and closing balance on each component of equity. The statement shows only non-owner changes in equity with total comprehensive income shown as a single item.

Section 6.2 below sets out the requirements for the statement of changes in equity when IAS 1(2003) is applied. The requirements are less prescriptive than those in IAS 1(2007) and permit owner changes in equity to be combined with non-owner changes in equity in a single statement in some cases.

6.1 The requirements of IAS 1(2007)

Changes in an entity's equity between the beginning and end of the reporting period reflect the increase or decrease in its net assets during the period. Except for changes resulting from transactions with owners in their capacity as owners (e.g. equity contributions and distributions), the overall change in equity during a period represents the total amount of income and expense, including gains and losses, generated by the entity's activities during that period. [IAS 1(2007).109]

IAS 1(2007) requires the presentation of a statement of changes in equity, showing in the statement:

[IAS 1(2007).106]

- total comprehensive income for the period, showing separately the total amounts attributable to owners of the parent and to non-controlling interests;

- for each component of equity, the effects of retrospective application or retrospective restatement recognised in accordance with IAS 8; and
- for each component of equity, a reconciliation between the carrying amount at the beginning and the end of the period, separately disclosing changes resulting from:
  - profit or loss;
  - each item of other comprehensive income; and
  - transactions with owners in their capacity as owners, showing separately contributions by and distributions to owners and changes in ownership interests in subsidiaries that do not result in a loss of control.

IAS 27, as amended in 2008, amended IAS 1(2007).106. The amended requirements are set out above. This amendment is effective for periods beginning on or after 1 July 2009. If an entity applies the revised IAS 27 for an earlier period, the amendment to IAS 1 is applied for that earlier period. The amendment is applied retrospectively.

The main change of substance made by the amendment is to insert the reference to changes in interests in subsidiaries that do not result in a loss of control. The amended text is also more specific about the need to disclose separately the three types of changes listed.

For the purpose of IAS 1(2007).106, components of equity include, for example, each class of contributed equity, the accumulated balance of each class of other comprehensive income and retained earnings. [IAS 1(2007).108]

The statement must contain a reconciliation of each component of equity. It is not, therefore, possible to present a simple statement showing only the movements on total equity, with details of movements on individual components of equity given in the notes. In fact, there is no explicit requirement in the Standard to provide totals, across all components of equity, for each type of movement. However, this is likely to be helpful in practice. For example, it will eliminate the effects of amounts transferred between different components of equity which have no effect on total equity.

An illustrative statement of changes in equity is provided in the *Guidance on Implementing IAS 1.* This adopts a columnar layout with a column for each component of equity and a total column. This format is not prescribed by the Standard but is likely to be commonly adopted in practice. It might be quite cluttered if there are numerous different components of equity.

Some respondents to the 2006 exposure draft asked the Board to clarify whether the effects of retrospective application or retrospective restatement, as defined in IAS 8, should be regarded as non-owner changes in equity. In IAS 1(2007).BC74 the Board explains that the effects of such restatements are not changes in equity in the period but provide a reconciliation between the previous period's closing balance and the opening balance in the statement of changes in equity.

The amount of dividends recognised as distributions to owners during the period, and the related amount per share, must be shown either in the statement or in the notes (see **5.3.3** above). [IAS 1(2007).107]

It will be necessary to show dividends, at least in aggregate, in the statement because they are one of the owner changes in equity. However, details of individual dividends and the amounts per share will typically be shown in a note, combined with the disclosures about dividends proposed or declared after the reporting period required by IAS 1(2007).137(a) (see **7.4.2** below).

IAS 8 requires retrospective adjustments to effect changes in accounting policies, to the extent practicable, except when the transitional provisions in another IFRS require otherwise. IAS 8 also requires that restatements to correct errors are made retrospectively, to the extent practicable. Retrospective adjustments and retrospective restatements are not changes in equity but they are adjustments to the opening balance of retained earnings, except when an IFRS requires retrospective adjustment to another component of equity. IAS 1(2007).106(b) requires disclosure in the statement of changes in equity of the total adjustment to each component of equity resulting, separately, from changes in accounting policies and from correction of errors. These adjustments are disclosed for each prior period and the beginning of the period. [IAS 1(2007).110]

6.2 The requirements of IAS 1(2003)

IAS 1(2003) requires the financial statements to include a statement showing either all changes in equity, or changes in equity other than those arising from capital transactions with owners and distributions to owners (i.e. transactions with equity holders acting in their capacity as equity holders).

UK

The second approach is similar to the statement of total recognised gains and losses under UK GAAP except that IFRSs require, in most cases, recycling of gains and losses which were taken initially direct to equity.

When the option in IAS 19 to permit immediate recognition of actuarial gains and losses outside of the income statement is used, the actuarial gains and losses should be presented in a statement of changes in equity titled 'Statement of recognised income and expense' that comprises only the items specified in paragraph 96 of IAS 1(2003). In particular, the statement should exclude transactions with equity holders acting in their capacity as equity holders, such as dividends and subscriptions for new share capital (see below).

Changes in equity between two balance sheet dates reflect the increase or decrease in the entity's net assets during the period. Except for changes resulting from transactions with equity holders acting in their capacity as equity holders (and transaction costs directly related to such transactions, e.g. costs incurred in connection with the issuance of shares or tax in excess of the related cumulative remuneration expense relating to share based payments), the overall change in equity during the period represents the total amount of income and expense, including gains and losses, generated by the entity's activities during that period. This is irrespective of whether those items of income and expenses are recognised in profit or loss, or directly as changes in equity. [IAS 1(2003).98] The Standard requires the presentation of a statement of changes in equity that highlights an entity's total income and expenses, including those that are recognised directly in equity. [IAS 1(2003).99]

The credit made to equity for equity-settled share-based payments, in accordance with IFRS 2, should not be included in a statement of recognised income and expense. This is because it arises from a transaction with equity holders in their capacity as such. The credit represents either the proceeds of the grant of an equity instrument or, where a subsidiary recognises an expense for a grant of its parent's equity instruments, a capital contribution from the parent.

The face of the statement of changes in equity should show the following items:

[IAS 1(2003).96.]

- profit or loss for the period;
- each item of income and expense for the period that (as required by other IFRSs) is recognised directly in equity, and a total of such items;
- total income and expense for the period (calculated as the sum of the above two items), showing separately the amounts attributable to equity holders of the parent and to minority interests; and
- for each component of equity, the effects of changes in accounting policies and corrections of errors recognised in accordance with IAS 8.

UK

IAS 1(2003) requires amounts disclosed in the Statement of Changes in Equity to be disclosed gross of minority interests, whereas under UK GAAP, FRS 3 requires items in the STRGL to be disclosed net of minority interests.

IAS 8 requires retrospective adjustments to effect changes in accounting policies, to the extent practicable, except when the transitional provisions in another IFRS require otherwise. IAS 8 also requires that restatements to correct errors are made retrospectively, to the extent practicable. Retrospective adjustments and retrospective restatements are made to the balance of retained earnings, except when an IFRS requires retrospective adjustment to another component of equity. Paragraph 96(d) of IAS 1(2003) (i.e. the last bullet point above) requires disclosure in the statement of changes in equity of the total adjustment to each component of equity resulting, separately, from changes in accounting policies and from correction of errors. These adjustments are disclosed for each prior period and the beginning of the period. [IAS 1(2003).100]

Subject to the restriction noted above when a SORIE is presented, the following items are presented either on the face of the statement or in the notes:

[IAS 1(2003).97]

- the amounts of transactions with equity holders acting in their capacity as equity holders, showing separately distributions to equity holders;
- the balance of retained earnings (i.e. accumulated profit or loss) at the beginning of the period and at the balance sheet date, and changes during the period; and
- a reconciliation between the carrying amounts of each class of contributed equity and each reserve at the beginning and end of the period, separately disclosing each change.

IAS 1(2003) does not require these disclosures to be made in the form of a single statement or a note reconciling the movements in total equity at the beginning of the period to total equity at the balance sheet date. For example, separate notes that reconcile the movement on each reserve or component of equity would meet the requirements of the Standard. But users of the financial statements may find an overall reconciliation helpful, for example, by eliminating the effects of transfers between different reserves that have no effect on total equity.

IAS 1(2003) requires entities to present, as a primary statement, a statement of changes in equity, which either:

- includes all changes in equity (i.e. all items listed in paragraph 96 and 97); or
- includes all changes in equity other than those arising from capital transactions with owners and distributions to owners (i.e. items listed in paragraph 96). If this option is chosen, the statement must be called a 'statement of recognised income and expense', and the 'excluded items' must be shown in an equity reconciliation in the notes to the financial statements.

Where an entity has taken the option in IAS 19 to recognise actuarial gains and losses immediately outside profit or loss, it is only permitted to choose the second option (i.e. the SORIE).

For entities taking the SORIE option, it is acceptable to show the equity reconciliation immediately below the SORIE, providing:

- it is NOT called a 'statement of changes in equity' – a name such as 'reconciliation of movements in equity' is appropriate; and
- it does NOT reproduce the detailed analysis from the SORIE, but instead shows only the totals from the SORIE.

This is because it would be confusing to have a statement described as a statement of changes in equity which did not meet the requirements of IAS 1, for example because it included only some of the items required to be included in such a statement. Furthermore, the

SORIE is itself a statement of changes in equity, and it would be confusing to have two primary statements dealing with changes in equity.

IAS 1 notes that the requirements of paragraphs 96 and 97 may be met in various ways. One example is a columnar layout that reconciles the opening and closing balances of each element of equity. An alternative is to present only the items required by paragraph 96 in the statement of changes in equity (which will then be called 'Statement of recognised income and expense') with the items shown in paragraph 97 shown in the notes. [IAS 1(2003).101] The Guidance on Implementing IAS 1(2003) contains illustrations of both these presentations.

6.2.1 *Classification of recycled amounts in the SORIE*

Gains and losses are sometimes recycled from equity to profit or loss (e.g. relating to available-for-sale investments and cash flow hedges) or from equity to the carrying amount of hedged items (e.g. relating to cash flow hedges). The question arises as to whether these items should be included in the total for 'net income recognised directly in equity' in a SORIE.

There are two alternative presentations, Alt 1 and Alt 2. The first (Alt 1) follows the format in the Guidance on Implementing IAS 1. The second format (Alt 2) segregates items of income and expense that are recognised in equity from 'transfers' (i.e. items transferred from equity when gains or losses are recycled). This format differs from the IASB illustration, and leads to a different total for 'net income recognised in equity'.

The requirement of IAS 1(2003).96(b) to present a total for items of income and expense recognised directly in equity might be seen to support the separation of the transfers. Otherwise, such items are characterised as gains or losses recognised in equity – which may be considered by some as inappropriate. For example, unless the transfers are separately classified, the transfer from equity to profit or loss of a revaluation gain, once an available-for-sale investment is disposed of, is characterised as a loss recognised in equity. However, Alt 1 is equally acceptable and is consistent with the Guidance on Implementing IAS 1.

Note that the illustrations below do not meet all of the IAS 1 disclosure requirements for classification of recycled items in the SORIE.

IAS 1(2007) introduces an explicit requirement to disclose 'reclassification adjustments' (i.e. the 'transfers' mentioned above) separately in the statement of comprehensive income itself or in the notes. However, it is clear from the standard and from the illustrative statement of comprehensive income which accompanies the standard that the reclassification adjustments are part of comprehensive income and that there is no requirement to show them separately on the face of the statement. For example, the illustrative statement includes a single line for 'Cash flow hedges' which is analysed in the notes between gains and losses arising during the year and reclassification adjustments.

Consolidated Statement of Recognised Income and Expense for the year ended 31 December 20X1 (Alt 1)

	Year ended 31/12/X1 £'000	Year ended 31/12/X0 £'000
Gain/(loss) on revaluation of property	64,709	(4,369)
(Deferred tax liability arising) reversal of deferred tax liability on revaluation of land and buildings	(3,692)	320
Cash flow hedges		
Gains taken to equity	1,723	550
Transferred to profit or loss for the year	(995)	(895)
Transferred to initial carrying amount of hedged item	(218)	-
Available-for-sale investments		
Valuation gains taken to equity	251	201
Transferred to profit or loss on sale	(611)	-
Exchange differences on translation of foreign operations	(12,718)	2,706
Net income recognised directly in equity	48,449	(1,487)
Profit for the year	100,366	19,626
Total recognised income and expense for the year	148,815	18,139

Consolidated Statement of Recognised Income and Expense for the year ended 31 December 20X1 (Alt 2)

	Year ended 31/12/X1 £'000	Year ended 31/12/X0 £'000
Gain/(loss) on revaluation of property	64,709	(4,369)
(Deferred tax liability arising) reversal of deferred tax liability on revaluation of land and buildings	(3,692)	320
Gains (losses) on cash flow hedges	1,723	550

Gains (losses) on revaluation of available-for-sale investments	251	201
Exchange differences on translation of foreign operations	(12,718)	2,706
Net income recognised directly in equity	50,273	(592)
Transfers:		
To profit or loss on sale of available-for-sale investments	(611)	-
To profit or loss on cash flow hedges	(995)	(895)
To initial carrying amount of hedged item on cash flow hedges	(218)	-
Profit for the year	100,366	19,626
Total recognised income and expense for the year	148,815	18,139

7 The notes

7.1 Structure

Notes contain information in addition to that presented in the statement of financial position, statement of comprehensive income, separate income statement (if presented), statement of changes in equity and statement of cash flows. Notes provide narrative descriptions or disaggregations of items presented in those statements and information about items that do not qualify for recognition in those statements. [IAS 1(2007).7]

The notes are required to:

[IAS 1(2007).112, previously IAS 1(2003).103]

- present information about the basis of preparation of the financial statements and the specific accounting policies used in accordance with the relevant paragraphs of IAS 1 (see **7.2** below);
- disclose the information required by IFRSs that is not presented elsewhere in the financial statements; and
- provide additional information that is not presented elsewhere in the statements but is relevant to an understanding of any of them.

The notes should, so far as practicable, be presented in a systematic manner. Each item in the statement of financial position, statement of comprehensive income, statement of changes in equity, statement of cash flows and any separate income statement should be cross referenced to any related information in the notes. [IAS 1(2007).113, previously IAS 1(2003).104] The notes are normally presented in the following order, which assists users to understand the financial statements and compare them with financial statements of other entities:

[IAS 1(2007).114, previously IAS 1(2003).105]

- a statement of compliance with IFRSs (see **section 3** above);
- a summary of significant accounting policies applied (see **7.2** below);
- supporting information for items presented in the financial statements in the order in which each statement and each line item is presented; and
- other disclosures including:
  - contingent liabilities (see **chapter 11**) and unrecognised contractual commitments; and
  - non-financial disclosures, for example an entity's financial risk management objectives and policies (see **chapter 21**).

In some circumstances, it may be necessary or desirable to vary the order of specific items within the notes. For example, information on changes in fair value recognised in profit or loss may be combined with information on maturities of financial instruments, although the former disclosures relate to the statement of comprehensive income (or any separate income statement) and the latter relate to the statement of financial position. Nevertheless, a systematic structure for the notes should be retained as far as practicable. [IAS 1(2007).115, previously IAS 1(2003).106]

There is a case for putting all of the disclosures about financial instruments required by IFRS 7 in a single note (or a sequence of notes). This will combine the disclosures about the impact of financial instruments on the statement of financial position and the statement of comprehensive income (and any separate income statement) in one place.

Notes providing information about the basis of preparation of the financial statements and specific accounting policies may be presented as a separate section of the financial statements. [IAS 1(2007).116, previously IAS 1(2003).107]

That is to say, it is possible to present a statement of accounting policies that does not form one of the numbered notes to the financial statements.

7.2 Disclosure of accounting policies

The financial statements should include a summary of significant accounting policies that includes:

[IAS 1(2007).117, previously IAS 1(2003).108]

- the measurement basis (or bases) used in preparing the financial statements; and
- the other accounting policies used that are relevant to an understanding of the financial statements.

7.2.1 Measurement bases

It is important that users of the financial statements are informed about the measurement basis or bases used because the basis will significantly affect their analysis. Examples of measurement bases are historical cost, current cost, net realisable value, fair value or recoverable amount. When more than one measurement basis is used in the financial statements, for example when particular classes of assets are revalued, it is sufficient to provide an indication of the categories of assets and liabilities to which each measurement basis is applied. [IAS 1(2007).118, previously IAS 1(2003).109]

7.2.2 Accounting policies

In deciding whether a particular accounting policy should be disclosed, management considers whether disclosure would assist users in understanding how transactions, other events and conditions are reflected in the reported financial performance and position. Disclosure of particular accounting policies is especially useful to users when those policies are selected from alternatives allowed in IFRSs. For example, a venturer in a jointly controlled entity would disclose whether the interest was accounted for using proportionate consolidation or the equity method. Some IFRSs that permit a choice of policies contain specific disclosure requirements about those choices. For example, IAS 16 requires disclosure of the measurement bases used for classes of property, plant and equipment. [IAS 1(2007).119, previously IAS 1(2003).110]

Each entity considers the nature of its operations and the policies that the users of its financial statements would expect to be disclosed for that type of entity. For example, an entity that is subject to income taxes would be expected to disclose its policies for accounting for taxes, including those for deferred tax. Similarly, an entity with significant foreign operations or transactions in foreign currencies should disclose its policies for the recognition of foreign exchange gains and losses. [IAS 1(2007).120, previously IAS 1(2003).111]

An accounting policy may be significant because of the nature of an entity's operations even if amounts for current or prior periods are not material. It is also appropriate to disclose each significant policy that is not specifically required by IFRSs but is selected and applied in accordance with IAS 8. [IAS 1(2007).121, previously IAS 1(2003).112]

Although IAS 1 highlights the particular importance of the disclosure of policies where there is a choice under the relevant IFRSs, it is clear that significant policies should be disclosed even if there is no choice. This is required by the Standard and is useful for users of the financial statements who may not be familiar with all of the requirements of the applicable Standards.

UK

In the UK, the Financial Reporting Review Panel has expressed concern about the inclusion of accounting policies that are irrelevant to a company's circumstances. For example, they may have been copied from another company or from model financial statements without being appropriately tailored to the reporting company's circumstances. However, care must be taken to distinguish this situation from the one described above where a policy is significant because of the nature of the entity's operations even though the amounts involved may be immaterial in the current and prior year.

7.2.3 Judgements that management has made

The summary of significant accounting policies or other notes should disclose the judgements management has made, in the process of applying the entity's accounting policies, that have the most significant effect on the amounts recognised in the financial statements. This requirement excludes judgements involving estimations which are subject to a separate disclosure requirement (see **7.3** below). [IAS 1(2007).122, previously IAS 1(2003).113]

In the process of applying the entity's accounting policies, management makes various judgements, apart from those involving estimations, that can significantly affect the amounts recognised in the financial statements. Examples given in IAS 1 are:

[IAS 1(2007).123, previously IAS 1(2003).114]

- whether financial assets are held-to-maturity investments;
- when substantially all the significant risks and rewards of ownership of financial assets and lease assets are transferred to other entities;
- whether, in substance, particular sales of goods are financing arrangements and, therefore, do not give rise to revenue; and
- whether the substance of the relationship between the entity and a special purpose entity indicates that the special purpose entity is controlled by the entity.

In some instances, similar disclosures are specifically required by other IFRSs. For example, IAS 27 requires disclosure of the reasons why an ownership interest does not constitute control even though more than half the voting rights are held. IAS 40 requires, when classification is difficult, disclosure of the criteria developed to distinguish investment property from owner-occupied property and property held for sale in the ordinary course of business. [IAS 1(2007).124, previously IAS 1(2003).115]

As explained in IAS 1(2007).BC77–78 and IAS 1(2003).BC30–31, this was a new disclosure requirement in the 2003 revised version of the Standard. The examples were added in response to comments received on the Exposure Draft to make the purpose of the requirement clearer. Disclosure of the most important judgements will help users of financial statements to understand how accounting policies have been applied and to make comparisons between entities. Accordingly, such disclosures will be most useful when they avoid 'boilerplate' and explain clearly the most important judgements made.

There is no equivalent requirement under UK GAAP in FRS 18. UK

7.3 Key sources of estimation uncertainty

When there are uncertainties that have a significant risk of causing material adjustment to the carrying amount of assets and liabilities within the next financial year, the notes should disclose:

[IAS 1(2007).125, previously IAS 1(2003).116]

- information about the assumptions concerning the future; and
- other major sources of estimation uncertainty at the end of the reporting period.

In respect of those assets and liabilities, the notes should include details of:

[IAS 1(2007).125, previously IAS 1(2003).116]

- their nature; and
- their carrying amount at the end of the reporting period.

These disclosures are separate from those about judgements made by management in the process of applying accounting policies (see **7.2.3** above).

Determining the carrying amount of some assets and liabilities requires estimation of the effects of uncertain future events. For example, in the absence of recently observed market prices, future-oriented estimates are necessary to measure:

- the recoverable amount of classes of property, plant and equipment;
- the effect of technological obsolescence on inventories;
- provisions subject to the future outcome of litigation in progress; and
- long-term employee benefit liabilities such as pension obligations.

These estimates involve assumptions about such items as the risk adjustment to cash flows or discount rates, future changes in salaries and future changes in prices affecting other costs. [IAS 1(2007).126, previously IAS 1(2003).117]

The assumptions and other sources of estimation uncertainty to be disclosed relate to the estimates that require management's most difficult, subjective or complex judgements. Those judgements become more subjective and complex as the number of variables and assumptions affecting the possible future resolution increases. The potential for a consequential material adjustment to the carrying amount of assets and liabilities normally increases accordingly. [IAS 1(2007).127, previously IAS 1(2003).118]

These disclosures are not required for assets or liabilities that are measured at fair value based on recently observed market prices. This is so even if there is a significant risk that their carrying amounts might change materially within the next financial year. This is because these changes would not arise from assumptions or other sources of estimation uncertainty at the end of the reporting period. [IAS 1(2007).128, previously IAS 1(2003).119]

These disclosures should be presented in a manner that helps users of the financial statements to understand the judgements management makes about the future and about other key sources of estimation uncertainty. The nature and extent of the information to be disclosed will vary according to the nature of the assumptions and the other circumstances. Examples in IAS 1 of the types of disclosures to be made are:

[IAS 1(2007).129, previously IAS 1(2003).120]

- the nature of the assumption or other estimation uncertainty;
- the sensitivity of the carrying amounts to the methods, assumptions and estimates underlying their calculation, including the reasons for the sensitivity;
- the expected resolution of an uncertainty and the range of reasonably possible outcomes within the next financial year in respect of the carrying amounts of the assets and liabilities affected; and
- an explanation of changes made to past assumptions concerning those assets and liabilities, if the uncertainty remains unresolved.

However, the Standard confirms that it is not necessary to disclose budget information or forecasts in making these disclosures. [IAS 1(2007).130, previously IAS 1(2003).121]

It may be impracticable to disclose the extent of the possible effects of an assumption or another key source of estimation uncertainty at the end of the reporting period. In this case, the entity discloses that it is reasonably possible, based on existing knowledge, that outcomes within the next financial year that are different from assumptions could require a material adjustment to the carrying amount of the affected asset or liability. In all cases, the nature and the carrying amount of the specific asset or liability (or class of assets or liabilities) is disclosed. [IAS 1(2007).131, previously IAS 1(2003).122]

The disclosures of particular judgements that management made in the process of applying the entity's accounting policies (see **7.2.3** above) do not relate to the disclosures of sources of estimation uncertainty described in this section. [IAS 1(2007).132, previously IAS 1(2003).123]

Some other IFRSs include specific requirements for disclosures that would otherwise be required by IAS 1. The following examples are given in IAS 1:

[IAS 1(2007).133, previously IAS 1(2003).124]

- IAS 37 requires disclosures, in specified circumstances, of major assumptions concerning future events affecting classes of provisions;

- IFRS 7 requires disclosure of significant assumptions used in estimating fair values of financial assets and financial liabilities that are carried at fair value; and
- IAS 16 requires disclosure of significant assumptions used in estimating fair values of revalued items of property, plant and equipment.

As explained in IAS 1(2007).BC79–84 and IAS 1(2003).BC32–37 this was a new disclosure requirement in the 2003 revised version of IAS 1. It is noteworthy that IAS 1(2007).BC81 and IAS 1(2003).BC34 state that these disclosures would be made 'in respect of relatively few assets and liabilities (or classes of them)' because they relate only to the most difficult, subjective or complex judgements.

It is also important to understand that the scope of the disclosure is limited to items that have a significant risk of causing material adjustment to the carrying amount of assets or liabilities 'within the next financial year'. IAS 1(2007).BC84 and IAS 1(2003).BC37 explain that the longer the future period to which the disclosures relate, the greater the range of items that would qualify for disclosure and the less specific those disclosures could be made. Therefore, the IASB decided to limit the scope of the requirement in this way, noting that a period longer than the next financial year might obscure the most relevant information with other disclosures.

7.4 Other disclosures

7.4.1 Details about the entity

The following should be disclosed in the financial statements, unless disclosed elsewhere in information published with the financial statements:

[IAS 1(2007).138, previously IAS 1(2003).126]

- the domicile and legal form of the entity;
- its country of incorporation;
- the address of its registered office (or principal place of business, if different);
- a description of the nature of the entity's operations and its principal activities;
- the name of the parent and the ultimate parent of the group; and

- if the entity is a limited life entity, information about the length of is life.

The last requirement about limited life entities was inserted by the *Puttable Instruments* amendment explained at **7.4.5** below.

UK

Several of these requirements are not found in UK GAAP but, in practice, the information will be given or be self evident.

It is unclear what is intended by the requirement to disclose the entity's 'domicile' and this term is not defined in the Standard. Its normal dictionary definition is 'home' or 'place of permanent residence'. In practice this is likely to be the same as the country of incorporation or the principal place of business.

7.4.2 *Dividends*

IAS 1 requires disclosure in the notes of:

[IAS 1(2007).137, previously IAS 1(2003).125]

- the amount of dividends proposed or declared before the financial statements were authorised for issue but not recognised as a distribution to owners;
- the related amount per share; and
- the amount of any cumulative preference dividends not recognised.

These disclosures are in addition to the disclosure required for the amount of dividends recognised as distributions to owners during the period and the related amount per share (see **5.3.3** above).

UK

Under UK GAAP, there is a requirement to disclose in the notes (if not disclosed on the face of the profit and loss account):

- *the aggregate amount of dividends paid in the financial year (other than those for which a liability existed at the immediately preceding balance sheet date;*
- *the aggregate amount of dividends that the company is liable to pay at the balance sheet date); and*
- *the aggregate amount of dividends that are proposed before the date of approval of the accounts, and not otherwise disclosed under the above requirements.*

> *This is similar to the requirements under IAS 1 although worded differently.*
>
> *As considered at* **5.3.3** *above, there is no requirement for unlisted companies to disclose dividends per share under UK GAAP.*

7.4.3 Disclosures about service concession arrangements

SIC-29 *Service Concession Arrangements: Disclosures* specifies certain disclosures that are required for such arrangements to meet the requirements of IAS 1(2007).112(c) and IAS 1(2003).103(c) (see **7.1** above). These paragraphs require disclosures to provide additional information that is not presented in the primary financial statements but is relevant to an understanding of them.

IFRIC 12 made the following consequential amendments to SIC-29:

- the title was amended to 'Service Concession Arrangements: Disclosures';
- references to 'Concession Operator' were changed to 'operator' and references to 'Concession Provider' were changed to 'grantor';
- an additional requirement was added to disclose 'how the service arrangement has been classified'; and
- an additional requirement was added to require an operator to disclose the amount of revenue and profits or losses recognised in the period on exchanging construction services for a financial asset or an intangible asset.

Examples of service concession arrangements given in SIC-29 are water treatment and supply facilities, motorways, car parks, tunnels, bridges, airports and telecommunications networks. SIC-29 also explains that outsourcing the operation of an entity's internal services (e.g. employee restaurant, building maintenance, accounting or IT functions) are not service concession arrangements. [SIC-29.1]

Certain aspects and disclosures relating to some service concession arrangements are addressed in other Standards. For example, IAS 16 would apply to property, plant and equipment used in a service concession arrangement. However, SIC-29 points out that service concession arrangements may involve executory contracts that are not addressed in IFRSs, unless the contracts are onerous, in which case IAS 37 applies. SIC-29, therefore, addresses additional disclosures that are relevant to service concession arrangements. [SIC-29.5]

All aspects of service concession arrangements should be considered in determining the appropriate disclosure in the notes. An operator and a grantor should disclose the following in each period:

[SIC-29.6]

- a description of the arrangement;
- significant terms of the arrangement that may affect the amount, timing and certainty of future cash flows (e.g. the period of the concession, re-pricing dates and the basis upon which re-pricing or re-negotiation is determined);
- the nature and extent (e.g. quantity, time period or amount as appropriate) of:
  - rights to use specified assets;
  - obligations to provide or rights to expect provision of services;
  - obligations to acquire or build items of property, plant and equipment;
  - obligations to deliver or rights to receive specified assets at the end of the concession period;
  - renewal and termination options; and
  - other rights and obligations (e.g. major overhauls);
- changes in the arrangement occurring during the period; and
- how the service arrangement has been classified.

In addition, an operator discloses the amount of revenue and profits or losses recognised in the period on exchanging construction services for a financial asset or an intangible asset. [SIC-29.6A]

These disclosures are required to be provided individually for each service concession arrangement or in aggregate for each class of service concession arrangements. For this purpose, a class is a grouping of service concession arrangements involving services of a similar nature. For example, arrangements for water treatment services could be treated as a class. [SIC-29.7]

The accounting for service concession arrangements is dealt with by IFRIC 12 (see **section 10** of **chapter 40**).

7.4.4 Capital disclosures

IAS 1(2003) was amended in 2005 to introduce disclosures about capital with effect for periods beginning on or after 1 January 2007. The principle is that an entity should disclose information that enables users of its financial statements to evaluate the entity's objectives, policies and processes for managing capital. [IAS 1(2007).134, previously IAS 1(2003).124A]

To comply with this principle, the Standard requires an entity to disclose the following:

.[IAS 1(2007).135, previously IAS 1(2003).124B]

- qualitative information about its objectives, policies and processes for managing capital, including but not limited to:
  - a description of what it manages as capital;
  - when an entity is subject to externally imposed capital requirements, the nature of those requirements and how those requirements are incorporated into the management of capital; and
  - how it is meeting its objectives for managing capital;
- summary quantitative data about what it manages as capital. Some entities regard some financial liabilities (e.g. some forms of subordinated debt) as part of capital. Other entities regard capital as excluding some components of equity (e.g. components arising from cash flow hedges);
- any changes in the foregoing from the previous period;
- whether, during the period, it has complied with any externally imposed capital requirements to which it is subject; and
- when the entity has not complied with the externally imposed capital requirements to which it is subject, the consequences of such non-compliance.

The Standard requires these disclosures to be based on the information provided internally to the entity's key management personnel.

An entity may manage capital in a number of ways and be subject to a number of different capital requirements. A conglomerate may include entities that undertake banking activities and insurance activities. Those entities may operate in several jurisdictions. When an aggregate disclosure of capital requirements and how capital is managed would not provide useful information or distorts a financial statement user's understanding of an entity's capital resources, the entity should disclose separate information for each capital requirement to which it is subject. [IAS 1(2007).136, previously IAS 1(2003).124C]

7.4.5 *Puttable financial instruments classified as equity*

Puttable Financial Instruments and Obligations Arising on Liquidation (*Amendments to IAS 32 and IAS 1*), issued in February 2008, amends paragraph 138 of IAS 1(2007) and inserts new paragraphs 8A, 80A and 136A. The amendments must be applied for annual periods beginning on or after 1 January 2009. Earlier application is permitted. If an entity applies these amendments for an earlier period, it should disclose that fact and apply the related amendments to IAS 32, IAS 39, IFRS 7 and IFRIC 2 at the same time.

The new paragraph 136A requires the following disclosures about puttable financial instruments classified as equity instruments:

[IAS 1(2007).136A]

- summary quantitative data about the amount classified as equity;
- the entity's objectives, policies and processes for managing its obligation to repurchase or redeem the instruments when required to do so by the instrument holders, including any change from the previous period;
- the expected cash outflow on redemption or repurchase of that class of financial instruments; and
- information about how the expected cash outflow on redemption or repurchase was determined.

Puttable financial instruments have the same meaning as in IAS 32 (as amended). [IAS 1(2007).8A]

8 UK specific disclosure requirements

As explained in ***chapter 1****, UK disclosure requirements relating to the form and content of financial statements do not generally apply when the financial statements are prepared under IFRSs. However, certain requirements continue to apply. This section deals with the requirements for the disclosure of employee information, auditors' remuneration, liability limitation agreements and off balance sheet arrangements.* UK

8.1 Employee information

UK

The requirements of the 2006 Act about disclosure of employee numbers and costs are the same as those in the 1985 Act except that the opportunity has been taken to correct an error that was introduced into the 1985 Act in 2005. Consequently, companies applying the 2006 Act will no longer have to make these disclosures in relation to the parent company's individual accounts when they prepare consolidated accounts and make the disclosures in relation to the group.

These requirements do not apply to a company that is subject to the small companies regime.

8.1.1 *Number of employees*

UK

The total average number of employees in the financial year and a division of this total by categories determined by the directors, having regard to the manner in which the company's activities are organised, should be disclosed. [CA 2006 s411(1) and (2), previously CA 1985 s231A(1) and (5)]

The average number of employees is derived by dividing the sum of the number of employees employed under contracts of service in each month (whether throughout the month or not) by the number of months in the financial year. [CA 2006 s411(3) and(4), previously s231A(2) and (3)]

This requirement applies in relation to group accounts as if the undertakings included in the consolidation were a single company. [CA 2006 s411(7), previously CA 1985 s231A(6)]

Under the 2006 Act, the individual profit and loss account of the company need not contain the information about employee numbers and costs required by s411 when the company prepares group accounts in accordance with the Act and the notes to the company's individual balance sheet shows the company's profit or loss for the financial year determined in accordance with the Act. [CA 2006 s408(2)]

The term 'under contracts of service' is not defined, but does not appear to be restricted to those employees who have a written service contract. It seems appropriate that all employees, other than occasional casual workers, should be presumed as being employed under contracts of service. However, a director who acts purely in a non-executive capacity is not employed under a contract of service for this purpose. It should be noted that employees to be included are not restricted to those who are employed in the UK.

Some companies may have no (or few) employees of their own and rely on sub-contractors or employees of another group company. In such cases the 'employees' are not employed under contracts of service with the company because their contracts are with another company. These 'employees' should be excluded for the purposes of the statutory disclosures but it may be helpful to provide additional information about the number and cost of persons employed under sub-contract arrangements.

The directors have considerable flexibility as to how they divide employees into categories, e.g. by function (production, selling and distribution, administration), by activity (drilling and exploration, chemicals, textiles), by job description (managers and supervisors, factory workers, clerical staff, salesmen, researchers).

8.1.2 *Staff costs*

The 1985 Act and the 2006 Act both require disclosure of the following costs in respect of all employees who are taken into account in determining the number of employees in **8.1.1** *above:* UK

[CA 2006 s411(5), previously CA 1985 s231A(4)]

- *wages and salaries paid and payable;*
- *social security costs incurred by the company;*
- *other pension costs.*

The expressions 'pension costs' and 'social security costs' are defined in legislation for this purpose.

Pension costs include any costs incurred by the company in respect of:

[CA 2006 s411(6), previously CA 1985 s231A(7)]

- *any pension scheme established for the purposes of providing pensions for persons currently or formerly employed by the company;*
- *any sums set aside for future payment of pensions directly by the company to current or former employees; and*
- *any pensions paid directly to such persons without having first been set aside.*

Social security costs means any contributions by the company to any state social security or pension scheme, fund or arrangement. [CA 2006 s411(6), previously CA 1985 s231A(7)]

As considered at **5.3.2** *above, there is a requirement in IAS 1(2007).104 and IAS 1(2003).93 to disclose a total for 'employee benefits expense'. For this purpose, employee benefits are defined, as in IAS 19, as all forms of consideration given by an entity in exchange for services rendered by employees. It is likely that this total required by IAS 1 will generally correspond to the total of the staff cost disclosures set out above.*

Social security contributions are specifically mentioned as being included in short-term employee benefits in IAS 19.4.

Wages and salaries should include bonuses and other incentive payments, whether payable under contract or not, and the emoluments of directors (other than non-executive directors). Redundancy payments should be excluded, as they do not constitute wages or salaries, but they should be disclosed separately if the amount is material.

The costs of post-employment benefits other than pensions, if material, could be included as a separate category.

The charge to the profit and loss account under IFRS 2 Share-based Payment should be included in 'wages and salaries' or, if material, shown separately. Any provision for National Insurance on share option gains (see **section 10** *of* **chapter 25***) should be included under 'social security costs'.*

Under IAS 19, the amount charged to the profit and loss account under a defined contribution scheme is the contributions payable to the scheme for the accounting period. This amount will be included in 'other pension costs' for the statutory disclosure of staff costs.

The position for a defined benefit scheme is not entirely clear. Under IAS 19, charges and credits may arise within operating charges, within financing items and within the statement of total recognised income and expense (or other comprehensive income when IAS 1(2007) is adopted). It is suggested that, for the purposes of the staff costs disclosure, only those items included within operating costs should be included under 'other pension costs', and there should also be a statement that items reported elsewhere (mainly interest cost, expected return on assets and actuarial gains and losses) are excluded.

8.2 Auditors' remuneration

For periods beginning on or after 6 April 2008, the Companies (Disclosure of Auditor Remuneration) Regulations 2005 (SI 2005/2417) are superseded by the Companies (Disclosure of Auditor Remuneration and Liability Limitation Agreements) Regulations 2008 (SI 2008/489). The 2008 Regulations reproduce the requirements of the 2005 Regulations with only very minor changes of substance. The only changes of significance are: UK

- *the 2008 Regulations (as for the 2006 Act itself) apply to companies incorporated in the United Kingdom rather than in Great Britain. Therefore, unlike the 2005 Regulations, they apply to companies incorporated in Northern Ireland;*
- *in relation to the types of 'other services' to be disclosed separately, the 2005 Regulations stated that, where a service could fall within more than one type, it should be treated as falling within the first mentioned. This requirement has been deleted, providing slightly greater flexibility in some cases;*
- *the 2008 Regulations include a very limited exemption from disclosure of certain fees for 'other services' receivable by a 'distant associate' of the auditors. This new exemption is explained at* **8.2.5.4** *below, for completeness, but will be relevant only in very rare circumstances; and*
- *the Secretary of State (or a body to which he has delegated this function) may require the auditors of a medium-sized company to give him limited information about other fees paid to them if the company does not voluntarily disclose that information. This implements a new EU requirement but does not affect the disclosures to be made by medium-sized companies in their financial statements (i.e. they continue to benefit from an exemption from disclosure of 'other services').*

The disclosure requirements apply to services supplied by auditors and their 'associates'. The definition of 'associates' is explained at **8.2.2.1** *below and is not changed in substance by the 2008 Regulations.*

8.2.1 *Introduction*

In 2005, Regulations were issued requiring companies to provide more detail about the types of services that they and their 'associates' purchase from their auditors and 'associates' of their auditors. The intention was to give shareholders and others information on which to make a judgement about whether the provision of non-audit services is a threat to the auditors' UK *objectivity or independence and to enable users of accounts to make meaningful comparisons across companies. The requirements formed part of the UK Government's policy response to Enron and other US accounting scandals as recommended by the Coordinating Group on Audit and Accounting Issues (CGAA) in its final report. They complemented other developments such as Ethical Standard 5* Non-audit services provided to audited entities *issued by the UK Auditing Practices Board. They also anticipated new European requirements for disclosure of fees for non-audit services which are required under the Statutory Audit Directive.*

The detailed legal requirements are set out in the 2008 Regulations which supersede the 2005 Regulations for periods beginning on or after 6 April 2008. The Regulations address all of the requirements for disclosure of auditors' remuneration and not just those on the disclosure of remuneration for non-audit work. They apply irrespective of whether the accounts are prepared under IFRSs or UK GAAP.

The Regulations apply to companies incorporated under the Companies Act 2006 and its predecessor Acts. They also apply to entities that have to comply with the requirements of the Act because of other legislation, unless specifically exempted. Examples include

- *limited liability partnerships (for periods beginning on or after 1 October 2008);*
- *qualifying partnerships under the Partnership and Unlimited Companies (Accounts) Regulations 1993 (SI 1993/1820) or the Partnerships (Accounts) Regulations 2008 (2008/569); and*
- *overseas companies that choose to have an audit under section 700 of the 1985 Act as modified by the Oversea Companies (Accounts) (Modifications and Exemptions) Order 1990 (SI 1990/440). Section 700 of the 1985 Act will be superseded by Part 34 of the 2006 Act but not until 1 October 2009.*

The 2005 Regulations apply only to companies incorporated in Great Britain and do not extend to companies incorporated in Northern Ireland. No equivalent Regulations were issued in 2005 for Northern Ireland and therefore the previous disclosure requirements continued to apply to companies incorporated there. The 2008 Regulations apply to companies incorporated in the United Kingdom which includes Northern Ireland.

The Regulations require 'other services' to be analysed into ten specified categories. They also contain definitions of 'associates' for both a company and a company's auditors.

The Regulations were drawn up in the light of, but differ in detail from, the disclosure requirements of the EU Statutory Audit Directive. The Government believes that compliance with the Regulations will ensure compliance with the Directive. The Regulations require more extensive disclosures than the Directive although it is not clear that the information required by the Directive can in all cases be derived from the disclosures made under the Regulations.

The ICAEW developed guidance on the application of the 2005 Regulations. This was published in October 2006 as TECH 06/06 Disclosure of auditor remuneration *and subsequently revised in July 2007. The guidance aims to ensure that directors and auditors understand the nature and purpose of the requirements and, in particular, the basis for deciding into which categories and sub-categories a service provided by the auditors falls.*

This section sets out the requirements of the Regulations as supplemented by TECH 06/06 as revised in July 2007. It also refers, where relevant, to the changes made by the 2008 Regulations (which are very limited). The section is divided into the following sub-sections:

- *definitions* (**8.2.2**);
- *general requirements (i.e. those applying to audit services and other services)* (**8.2.3**);
- *disclosure of remuneration for audit services* (**8.2.4**);
- *disclosure of remuneration for other services* (**8.2.5**);
- *presentation of information* (**8.2.6**)*; and*
- *other matters* (**8.2.7**).

8.2.2 *Definitions*

This section explains certain defined terms that are used in the Regulations. UK

8.2.2.1 *Associates of a company's auditors*

As more fully explained in **8.2.5** *below, in the case of 'other services' the Regulations require disclosure of remuneration receivable by the company's auditors and any person who was, at any time during the period to which the accounts relate, an associate of the company's auditors. Schedule 1 to the Regulations defines the associates of a company's auditors.* UK

Schedule 1 to the 2008 Regulations also defines a 'distant associate' which is relevant for the disclosure exemption described at **8.2.5.4** *below.*

The definition of associate is comprehensive and designed to capture a wide range of individuals and organisations connected with the auditors. It includes but is not limited to entities controlled by the company's auditors and entities able to exert control over the company's auditors. For example, it includes entities that are associated through the use of a common name or through the sharing of significant professional resources. Associates of a company's auditors include bodies corporate and partnerships outside the United Kingdom [TECH 06/06 8.1]

As explained below, some relationships are caught even where the degree of influence may be insignificant.

Each of the following are to be regarded as an associate of the company's auditors:

[2008 Regulations Sch 1(1), previously 2005 Regulations Sch 1(1)]

(1) *any person controlled by the company's auditors or by any associate of the company's auditors (whether alone or through two or more persons acting together to secure or exercise control), but only if that control does not arise solely by virtue of the company's auditors or any associate of the company's auditors acting:*

(*a*) *as an insolvency practitioner in relation to any person. For this purpose 'acting as an insolvency practitioner' should be construed in accordance with section 388 of the Insolvency Act 1986;*

(*b*) *in the capacity of a receiver, or a receiver or manager, of the property of a company or other body corporate. For this purpose, this expression includes a receiver, or, as the case may be, a receiver or manager, of part only of that property; or*

(*c*) *as a judicial factor on the estate of any person;*

(2) *any person who, or group of persons acting together which, has control of the company's auditors;*

(3) *any person using a trading name which is the same as or similar to a trading name used by the company's auditors, but only if the company's auditors use that trading name with the intention of creating the impression of a connection between them and that other person; and*

(4) *any person who is party to an arrangement with the company's auditors, with or without any other person, under which costs, profits, quality control, business strategy or significant professional resources are shared.*

The last part of this definition appears to cover a wide variety of possible arrangements. The definition of an auditor's associates is derived from but expands on the definition of a 'network' set out in the May 2002 EC Recommendation Statutory Auditors' Independence in the EU: A Set of Fundamental Principles. This states that network 'includes the Audit Firm which performs the statutory audit, together with its affiliates and any other entity controlled by the audit firm or under common control, ownership or management or otherwise affiliated or associated with the audit firm through the use of a common name or through the sharing of significant common professional services.' This affiliation or association need not be one that could be perceived by an outsider. If the intention of the Regulations is to capture something that should be considered as part of the auditor's network despite the lack of a common name, then an agreement with another party to share costs or profits on a particular engagement would not appear to make the other party necessarily an associate of the auditor. [TECH 06/06 8.3]

The Regulations include some further specific provisions where the company's auditors are a partnership. For this purpose a partnership includes a Limited Liability Partnership (LLP). It also includes a partnership constituted under the law of a country or territory outside the United Kingdom. References in the Regulations to 'partner' includes a member of an LLP. [2008 Regulations Sch 1(5), previously 2005 Regulations Sch 1(4)]

Where the company's auditors are a partnership, each of the following, in addition to those relationships described above, are regarded as their associates:

[2008 Regulations Sch 1(2), previously 2005 Regulations Sch 1(2)]

(1) *any other partnership which has a partner in common with the company's auditors;*

(2) *any partner in the company's auditors;*

(3) *any body corporate which is in the same group as a body corporate which is a partner in the company's auditors or in a partnership which has a partner in common with the company's auditors; and*

(4) *any body corporate of which a partner in the company's auditors is a director.*

This definition takes no account of the degree of control or influence involved. A single partner in common will make one firm an associate of another even if both firms have several hundred partners and the individual holds no managerial role within either firm.

The final part of the definition may cause particular difficulties. If a partner in an audit firm is also a director (e.g. non executive) of a company that supplies services to a client of the audit firm, payments for the supply of those services are required to be included within the appropriate category of 'other services'. These services need not be of a professional nature and could, for example, be cleaning services in which case they would be included in Category 10. [TECH 06/06 8.2]

However, under the 2008 Regulations, such services may be covered by the de minimis exemption for services provided by distant associates (see **8.2.5.4** *below)*

The supply of goods is not covered by the Regulations and would not have to be disclosed.

The directors of the company are responsible for ensuring the company's compliance with the Regulations but they will not know who is associated with the auditors. Accordingly, auditors will need to establish procedures to identify all such entities and make the details available to their clients (see **8.2.7.1** *below).*

The Regulations also include some further specific provisions where the company's auditors are a body corporate other than one which is a partnership for the purposes of the Regulations.

The term 'body corporate' is broader than 'company' as used in company law. For example, it includes a company incorporated outside the United Kingdom. Although an LLP is a body corporate, the Regulations specifically provide for it to be subject to the rules on partnerships rather than those for bodies corporate.

Where a company's auditors are a body corporate (other than one which is also a partnership as defined above), each of the following are regarded as their associates:

[2008 Regulations Sch 1(3), previously 2005 Regulations Sch 1(3)]

(1) *any other body corporate which has a director in common with the company's auditors;*

(2) *any director of the company's auditors;*

(3) *any body corporate which is in the same group as a body corporate which is a director of, or has a director in common with, the company's auditors;*

(4) *any partnership in which a director of the company's auditors is a partner;*

(5) *any body corporate which is in the same group as the company's auditors; and*

(6) *any partnership in which any such body corporate which is in the same group as the company's auditors is a partner.*

For the purposes of the Regulations, including the interpretation of the definitions considered above:

[2008 Regulations Sch 1(5), previously 2005 Regulations Sch 1(4)]

(1) *a person able, directly or indirectly, to control or materially to influence the operating and financial policies of another person is construed as having control of that person; and*

(2) *a body corporate is in the same group as another body corporate if it is a parent or subsidiary of that body corporate, or a subsidiary of a parent of that body corporate.*

As noted above, the 2008 Regulations include a definition of a 'distant associate' of a company's auditors. Distant associates are a sub-set of associates and are defined in the Regulations by reference to a list of numbered sub-paragraphs within the definition of associates. This is not reproduced here because of its limited relevance but includes, where the auditors are a partnership or an LLP, any body corporate of which a partner in the company's auditors is a director.

8.2.2.2 Associates of a company

For the purposes of the Regulations, references to an associate of the company are references to: UK

[2008 Regulations Reg 3(2)(c), previously 2005 Regulations Reg 2(2)(b)]

(1) *any subsidiary of that company, other than a subsidiary in respect of which severe long-term restrictions substantially hinder the exercise of the rights of the company over the assets and management of the subsidiary; and*

(2) *any scheme which is an associated pension scheme in relation to the company (see 8.2.2.3 below).*

In both cases this includes those outside the United Kingdom. [TECH 06/06 12.1]

The terminology used in the Regulations is potentially confusing because it uses the term 'associates' to mean subsidiaries. A company's 'associates' as defined in accounting standards are not 'associates' for the purposes of the Regulations and fees paid by such entities will not be included in the required disclosures for the investing company. Similarly, joint ventures or jointly controlled entities, as defined in accounting standards, will not be included for the purposes of the disclosures. [TECH 06/06 13.1]

However, where any work performed by the company's auditors on such entities goes towards supporting an opinion on the group accounts, this will be part of the group audit and will fall to be included in the group audit fee disclosure. [TECH 06/06 13.1]

Additional voluntary disclosures of the audit fee of an 'associate' or 'joint venture' might be considered good practice if such interests are particularly material. [TECH 06/06 13.1]

8.2.2.3 *Associated pension scheme*

UK *An associated pension scheme means, for a company, a scheme for the provision of benefits for or in respect of directors or employees (or former directors or employees) of the company or any subsidiary of the company, where:*

[2008 Regulations Reg 3(1), previously 2005 Regulations Reg 2(1)]

(1) *the benefits consist of or include any pension, lump sum, gratuity or other like benefit given or to be given on retirement or on death or in anticipation of retirement or, in connection with past service, after retirement or death; and*

(2) *either:*

(i) *a majority of the trustees are appointed by (or by a person acting on behalf of) the company or a subsidiary of the company; or*

(ii) *the company, or a subsidiary of the company, exercises a dominant influence over the appointment of the auditors (if any) of the scheme.*

The requirements apply equally to overseas pension schemes (e.g. the pension schemes of overseas subsidiaries) and UK pension schemes. The definition includes both final salary and money purchase schemes. Industry-wide schemes are not thought likely to fall within this definition. [TECH 06/06 15.1]

It is important to note that (2)(ii) of the above definition is a test about influence over the appointment of auditors and does not refer to the way in which the company and the pension scheme trustees interact after the appointment. [TECH 06/06 15.2]

Under the Pensions Act 1995, the scheme auditors must be appointed by the trustees. In considering whether a scheme is an associated scheme for the purposes of the Regulations, the company will need to understand the process adopted by the trustees in making the appointment of the scheme auditors and to assess the level of influence over that process exercised by the company or any of its subsidiaries. It might be helpful for the directors to consider the definition of 'actual exercise of dominant influence' given in FRS 2 Accounting for subsidiary undertakings *which is as follows:*

'The actual exercise of dominant influence is the exercise of an influence that achieves the result that the operating and financial policies of the undertaking influenced are set in accordance with the wishes of the holder of the influence and for the holder's benefit whether or not those wishes are explicit. The actual exercise of dominant influence is identified by its effect in practice rather than by the way in which it is exercised.' [TECH 06/06 15.3]

8.2.2.4 Small and medium-sized companies

Small and medium-sized companies are subject to significantly less onerous requirements under the Regulations. For the purpose of the 2005 Regulations, a company is small or medium-sized in relation to a financial year if it qualifies as small or medium-sized in relation to that year by virtue of s247 of the 1985 Act and is entitled to the exemptions mentioned in s246 or 246A (as the case may be) of that Act in its accounts for that year. [2005 Regulations Reg 2(2)(a)] UK

Under the 2008 Regulations, a company is small in relation to a financial year if the small companies regime as defined in section 381 of the 2006 Act applies to that financial year. A company is medium-sized in relation to a financial year if it qualifies as medium-sized in relation to that year under section 465 of the 2006 Act and is not excluded from being medium-sized under section 567(1) of that Act. [2008 Regulations Reg 3(2)]

In practice, the test is the same as the one that determines whether the company is entitled to file abbreviated accounts. [TECH 06/06 9.1]

In addition to meeting the size criteria, it is important to consider whether the company might be ineligible for the exemptions because it falls within one of the ineligible categories.

8.2.2.5 Parent and subsidiary

UK

In the 2005 Regulations, the terms 'parent' and 'subsidiary' are defined to mean respectively a parent undertaking and a subsidiary undertaking as defined in s258 of the 1985 Act which is a body corporate. The terms 'parent company' and 'subsidiary company' are defined to mean respectively a parent and a subsidiary which is a company. [2005 Regulations Reg 2(1)]

In the 2008 Regulations, 'parent' means a parent undertaking as defined in section 1162 of the 2006 Act which is a body corporate. A 'parent company' is a parent which is a company. A 'subsidiary' means a subsidiary undertaking (as defined in section 1162 of the 2006 Act) which is a body corporate. A 'subsidiary company' is a subsidiary which is a company. [2008 Regulations Reg 3(1)]

The term 'body corporate' is explained at **8.2.2.1** *above.*

8.2.3 General requirements

8.2.3.1 Expenses and benefits in kind

UK

Remuneration includes payments in respect of expenses and benefits in kind. [2008 Regulations Reg 3(1), previously 2005 Regulations Reg 2(1)]

Where remuneration includes benefits in kind, its nature and estimated money value must be disclosed in the notes. [2008 Regulations Reg 4(2) and Reg 5(2), previously 2005 Regulations Reg 3(2) and Reg 4(2)]

8.2.3.2 More than one auditor

UK

Where more than one person has been appointed as a company's auditor during the period to which the accounts relate, separate disclosure is required in respect of the remuneration of each such person. [2008 Regulations Reg 4(3) and Reg 5(5), previously 2005 Regulations Reg 3(3) and Reg 4(5)] This would, for example, apply where there had been a change of auditors. [TECH 06/06 20.1]

Although the Regulations refer to a person appointed as a company's auditor 'during' the period, if a replacement auditor is actually appointed after the year end to conduct the audit of the year that has now passed, the fee receivable by the replacement auditor in respect of the year in question should be disclosed separately from fees received or receivable (if any) in respect of the year by the auditor who served during that year. [TECH 06/06 21.1]

Where joint auditors are appointed, remuneration receivable by each joint auditor should be disclosed separately. [TECH 06/06 22.1]

8.2.3.3 VAT

The amounts disclosed should exclude VAT, whether or not it is recoverable. This is because the focus of the Regulations is on what is receivable by the auditors rather than the cost to the company. [TECH 06/06 49.1] UK

8.2.4 Disclosure of remuneration for the audit

The notes to the annual accounts are required to disclose the amount of any remuneration receivable by the company's auditors for the auditing of the accounts. This requirement applies to all companies irrespective of whether they qualify as small or medium-sized. [2008 Regulations Reg 4(1) and Reg 5(1)(a), previously 2005 Regulations Reg 3(1) and Reg 4(1)(a)] UK

8.2.4.1 Amounts to be included

The audit fee includes all remuneration receivable for work carried out as part of the audit of the accounts of the company. It includes, for example, the fee for reporting on directors' remuneration for quoted companies. It also includes fees for work carried out to satisfy the auditors' responsibilities under law and auditing standards in relation to material accompanying the accounts such as the directors' report and any corporate governance statements. [TECH 06/06 18.1] UK

Work may be undertaken within the audit firm as part of the audit by non-audit professionals. For example, they may be involved in reviewing specialist work such as tax computations, actuarial valuations and property valuations. Such work is regarded as 'audit assist' and the fee for such work is included in the audit fee for disclosure purposes. Where tax work, for example, is carried out for a single fee covering both compliance and audit assist work, then the fee should be apportioned between the two types of service. [TECH 06/06 14.1]

A single fee may be agreed (and a single engagement letter be in place) for the audit and for the provision of other services (e.g. the review of interim financial information). Where this is the case, the auditors should provide a reasonable breakdown of the total fee into the different services. [TECH 06/06 30.1]

The fee disclosed for the audit of the accounts is conventionally the fee for the year on which the auditors are reporting. This is confirmed in the Regulations which requires the fee to be disclosed for 'the auditing of the accounts'. This is not a time-sensitive phrase, but rather calls for disclosure of the fee for a particular audit regardless of the year in which the work is performed or the fee is expensed. However, this is not intended to suggest that any necessary adjustment for over- and under-accruals of previous year audit fees may not be included within the audit fees for the current year. It may be helpful to disclose the effect of such adjustments when the amount is material to the fee disclosed or to the trend in disclosed audit fees. [TECH 06/06 18.5]

If the audit fee charged in the year includes an amount for work carried out in the previous year by the previous auditor (e.g. the fee was under-accrued), this amount should be disclosed separately as required by the Regulations. There is no explicit requirement for separate disclosure where there has been no change of auditors. [TECH 06/06 18.6]

8.2.4.2 Groups

UK

When consolidated accounts are presented as part of the annual accounts, the audit fee to be disclosed is that for the group. There is no requirement to disclose separately the fee for auditing the individual accounts of the parent company. This will be included in the amount disclosed for the group. This is because the Regulations requires disclosure of the fees for auditing the 'annual accounts' which is a term defined in section 471 of the 2006 Act and section 262(1) of the 1985 Act to include the individual accounts and, where required, the group accounts. [TECH 06/06 18.2]

The parent company's auditors may invoice a single fee to the parent company for the audit of the entire group. The Regulations require disclosure of the audit fee regardless of who has borne it. The appropriate fee should therefore be allocated to each UK subsidiary for disclosure purposes in its annual accounts. In the group accounts, the fee for the audit of the group accounts should exclude amounts that are not in respect of the audit of the consolidated accounts (i.e. in respect of the audit of the annual accounts of subsidiaries). Where the parent itself recharges fees around group companies, this will often be an appropriate basis for disclosure. [TECH 06/06 25.1]

Where a group audit fee is charged to the parent company and not subsequently recharged to the subsidiaries, it was regarded as acceptable, under the requirements which applied prior to the 2005 Regulations, for the subsidiaries to disclose no audit fees and to explain that the cost had been borne by the parent. This approach is no longer acceptable because the focus of the current requirements is on the amount receivable by the auditors for the audit of the company, irrespective of who has paid the fees. It is therefore necessary to apportion the group audit fee between the companies in the group for the purposes of disclosure even if the cost has not been recharged. A reasonable approximation is acceptable and this should not involve a great deal of work. [TECH 06/06 25.2]

In the context of a group audit, work will often be performed on a subsidiary's accounts by both a head office audit team and a subsidiary audit team from the parent company's auditors. For the purposes of disclosure, it will generally be reasonable to allocate the fee for all such work performed by the head office team to the group audit fee, and the fee for all such work performed by the subsidiary audit team to the subsidiary's statutory audit fee, which will fall to be included in Category 1 under 'Other services' in the group's disclosure (see **8.2.5.3** *below) and as the subsidiary's audit fee in its own individual accounts. [TECH 06/06 18.3]*

Where a subsidiary has been invoiced separately (i.e. where the parent has not been invoiced with a single fee for the entire group – see above), the fee will generally relate to all the work performed at that subsidiary (including work common to both the consolidation pack and the local statutory accounts, work relating solely to the local statutory accounts and work relating solely to the audit of the consolidation pack). It will generally be reasonable to show the combined amount as being the subsidiary's audit fee for the purposes of disclosure in the subsidiary's own annual accounts and to be included in Category 1 under 'Other services' in the group's disclosures (see paragraph **8.2.5.3** *below). [TECH 06/06 18.4]*

However, in those cases where the fee for the work relating solely to the audit of the consolidation pack is clearly identifiable, its classification should be considered separately from that of the remaining subsidiary audit fee. This amount will be disclosed differently in the group accounts depending on whether the subsidiary's auditor is the parent company auditor or an associate of the parent company auditor. [TECH 06/06 18.4A]

In the group accounts, if the subsidiary is audited by the parent company auditor, any clearly identifiable element of the subsidiary fee relating solely to the audit of the subsidiary's consolidation pack would be disclosed within the group audit fee because it relates to the audit of the parent company's annual accounts. If the subsidiary is audited by an associate of the parent company auditor, the element of the subsidiary fee relating solely to the consolidation pack cannot be included in the audit fee in the group accounts because the services have not been supplied by the parent company auditor (see **8.2.5.3** *below). It will therefore be included in Category 1 in the group accounts (see below). [TECH 06/06 18.4B]*

In the accounts of the subsidiary, any such clearly identifiable element of the subsidiary fee relating solely to the consolidation pack will be disclosed within Category 2 in the subsidiary's accounts. This is because the services are supplied pursuant to legislation (i.e. the legislation that requires the parent company to prepare group accounts). They cannot be included in Category 1 because the parent company is not an associate of its subsidiary (see **8.2.5.2** *below). In practice, the subsidiary will often be exempt from making disclosures about 'other services' (see* **8.2.5.1** *below). [TECH 06/06 18.4C]*

In group accounts, the audit fee disclosed is the fee receivable by the auditor of the parent company for auditing the accounts of that company including its work on the consolidated accounts. This includes the fee for work performed by the parent company's auditors on consolidation returns although it will generally exclude the amount for work on those returns performed by a subsidiary's audit team (see above). Fees receivable by the parent company's auditors for the statutory audit of subsidiaries, separate from their audit of the group accounts, should not be included here but instead included within the first category of 'other services' (see above and **8.2.5.3** *below). [TECH 06/06 23.1]*

The amounts included under this heading are fees receivable by the parent company's auditors only and do not include amounts receivable by associates of the parent company's auditors. Therefore, fees for audit-related work performed pursuant to legislation by associates of the parent company's auditors, whether in relation to consolidation returns or local legislative requirements, are always disclosed within the first category under 'other services' (see **8.2.5.3** *below). The Regulations are unclear about the treatment of fees paid to an associate of the auditors for work on the audit of the company itself (e.g. a branch). This is considered below.[TECH 06/06 23.2]*

If the audit of a subsidiary is performed by another firm that is not an associate of the parent company's auditors, this does not mean that the group has joint auditors. Fees paid by subsidiaries to the unassociated firm (sometimes referred to as 'secondary auditors') are not disclosable in the group accounts, although voluntary disclosure is not prohibited. [TECH 06/06 24.1]

Examples of the fees for work of the parent company's auditor that will be included in or excluded from the fees for auditing the accounts are as follows:

[TECH 06/06 23.3]

- *Included – Fees for the work of the parent company's auditors on the parent company's processes to derive its consolidated accounts from the consolidation returns received from the undertakings included in the consolidation.*
- *Excluded – Fees for work carried out by the parent company's auditors under the terms of engagement with another undertaking included in the consolidation, on the audit of the accounts of that undertaking pursuant to legislation in relation to those accounts. Instead these fees are included within Category 1 under 'Other services'.*
- *Excluded – Fees for work carried out by an associate of the auditors, for example by a foreign associate that is the auditor of an undertaking included in the consolidation, on the audit of the accounts of that other undertaking. In this case, the remuneration is included within Category 1 under 'Other services'.*

There is likely to be a significant variation in the way that different groups analyse the total cost of auditing the group between audit fees and Category 1 of 'Other services'. This will, in part, depend on the legal structure but will also be a matter of judgement about how fees are allocated. A group which has most of its operating subsidiaries in jurisdictions where there is no statutory audit requirement will disclose most of the cost of auditing the group as a whole as audit fees where the fees are paid to the parent company auditor. Conversely, a UK based group where all of the subsidiaries are subject to statutory audit requirements will disclose most of the cost of auditing the group as a whole as Category 1 of 'Other services' if the approach suggested above is applied. Consequently, the total of the two amounts is likely to be of interest to users of the financial statements. Companies may consider presenting a sub-total of the two separate amounts that are required by law (see ***8.2.6.8*** *below).[TECH 06/06 23.4]*

The Regulations are unclear about the treatment of fees paid to an associate of the auditor for the audit of a branch of the company. This might arise in the case of an overseas branch. It appears to conflict with the Regulations to include amounts paid to an associate of the auditor in the audit fee. However, putting the fees into Category 1 of 'Other services' does not appear to be correct either because the fees relate to the audit of the company and not to its associates. A literal interpretation of the Regulations suggests that such fees should be included in Category 2 because the services are supplied pursuant to legislation. However, the associate may be acting as the auditor's agent and, where this is the case, inclusion in the audit fee would be appropriate. [TECH 06/06 18.8]

8.2.4.3 Small and medium-sized companies

UK

In the accounts required to be sent to members under section 423 of the 2006 Act or section 238 of the 1985 Act, small and medium-sized companies are required to disclose only the fee receivable by the auditors (including any benefits in kind) for the audit itself. This is the case whether those accounts are just individual or also group accounts.

If a small company prepares abbreviated accounts for filing with the Registrar of Companies, the abbreviated accounts need not include disclosure of auditors' remuneration. [TECH 06/06 10.1]

If a medium-sized company prepares abbreviated accounts, there is no exemption from disclosure of auditors' remuneration for audit services in those abbreviated accounts.

8.2.4.4 IFRS transition fees

UK

In most cases, the work performed by the auditors on IFRS transition would be necessary to enable them to give their opinion on the first IFRS financial statements, including the reconciliations required by IFRS 1. Where this is so, the fees are for the audit of the accounts and should be disclosed as audit fees. This is so even if they are billed separately. It is also the case where a separate report is provided on the transition work unless this significantly increased the scope of the auditors' work. [TECH 06/06 48.1]

Where the work performed by the auditors goes significantly beyond what would be required of them as auditors to give their opinion on the financial statements, the fees will be included in Category 10 'All other services'. As explained at **8.2.5.3** *below, Category 10 includes advice on accounting matters where this is unrelated to the auditing of the accounts. [TECH 06/06 48.2]*

The IFRS transition work may be done at the same time as the auditors' review of the company's first IFRS interim report. However, it will generally be disclosed as relating to the audit rather than the interim review because it would have been required irrespective of whether an interim review was performed. The 2005 Regulations provide that where a service could fall within more than one category, it is treated as falling within the one highest on the list. This requirement is omitted from the 2008 Regulations. [TECH 06/06 48.3]

8.2.5 *Disclosure of remuneration for other services*

8.2.5.1 Companies required to make disclosures

The notes to the annual accounts of a company that is not small or medium-sized are required to disclose the remuneration receivable by: UK

(1) *the company's auditors; or*

(2) *any person who was, at any time during the period to which the accounts relate, an associate of the company's auditors,*

for the supply of other services (i.e. other than auditing the accounts of the company) to the company or any of its associates. [2008 Regulations Reg 5(1)(b), previously 2005 Regulations Reg 4(1)(b)]

Under the 2008 Regulations, this is subject to a very limited exception for some fees receivable by 'distant associates' of the company's auditors (see **8.2.5.4** *below)*

The disclosure requirement is subject to an exemption for the individual accounts of certain parents and subsidiaries. The notes to the individual accounts of:

(1) *a parent company which is required to prepare and does prepare group accounts in accordance with the 1985 Act or the 2006 Act; and*

(2) *a subsidiary company where its parent is required to prepare and does prepare group accounts in accordance with the 1985 Act or the 2006 Act and the company is included in the consolidation,*

need not disclose information about other services if the group accounts are required by the Regulations to give the disclosures for the group and the individual accounts state that the group accounts are so required. [2008 Regulations Reg 6(2) and (3), previously 2005 Regulations Reg 5(2)]

The fee for auditing the individual accounts of each company in a group must be disclosed in that company's accounts (other than the parent itself – see **8.2.4.2***). However, it is not necessary to disclose in the individual accounts of a parent, or of a consolidated subsidiary, amounts receivable by the company's auditors or their associates in respect of 'other services', where the information is required to be given in the group accounts required to be prepared in accordance with the 1985 Act or the 2006 Act (whether under UK GAAP or IFRSs) and the individual accounts state that the group accounts are required to give that information. [TECH 06/06 26.1]*

This is a very useful exemption which will be available to most large UK parent companies and their subsidiaries. Small and medium-sized companies do not have to make disclosures about 'other services' and therefore do not need to rely on this exemption. There are two important conditions which must be met for the exemption to apply:

- *the parent company must be required to prepare group accounts. This is discussed further below but the key point is that it may not be sufficient that group accounts are actually prepared in practice; they must be required; and*
- *a statement must be included in the individual accounts of the parent and subsidiaries using the exemption to the effect that the group accounts are required to disclose the information. Suggested wording is illustrated at* **8.2.6.8** *below.*

If a subsidiary's accounts are approved before those of the parent, there can be no absolute certainty that the parent will prepare consolidated accounts and make the disclosures required by the Regulations. It may be reasonable, in some cases, for the subsidiary to assume that the parent will meet its legal obligations in due course and so the exemption from the Regulations should be available. This might be so, for example, where the parent is a UK listed company. However, the subsidiary's directors should in all cases make such enquiries as they consider necessary to establish that the exemption will be available. If they are in any doubt, the exemption should not be used. The UK parent company may be entitled to an exemption from preparing consolidated accounts under s228 or s228A of the 1985 Act or s400 or 401 of the 2006 Act. Where this is the case, the subsidiary should establish whether or not the parent intends to use the exemption and consider the risk that any such decision might subsequently be reversed. [TECH 06/06 26.5]

As explained above, the exemption under the Regulations applies only where the group accounts upon which the exemption depends are prepared as a requirement of the Acts. Therefore a company that is a subsidiary of a foreign immediate or ultimate parent and either has no subsidiaries or takes exemption from preparing group accounts under s228 or s228A of the 1985 Act or s400 or s401 of the 2006 Act, is not eligible for the exemption in Regulation 5(2)(b) of the 2005 Regulations or in Regulation 6(2)(b) of the 2008 Regulations. It must therefore disclose in its individual accounts fees for other services and thus has to give the full disclosures, including in respect of services to its (unconsolidated) associates, if relevant. This is because the foreign parent's group accounts will not be prepared in accordance with the 1985 Act or the 2006 Act. A consolidated UK subsidiary is eligible for the exemption even if its auditor is different from that of its parent. [TECH 06/06 26.2]

The exemption under the Regulations is available only where the parent company is 'required to prepare' group accounts in accordance with the Act. This could be read as implying that the exemption is not available where the parent company is entitled to one of the exemptions under s228 or s228A of the 1985 Act or s400 or s401 of the 2006 Act but chooses voluntarily to prepare group accounts. This is not so provided that the group accounts are deemed to be required as described in the next paragraph below. The exemption from disclosing 'other services' in the individual accounts will be available provided that group accounts are actually prepared and make the disclosures required by the Regulations, and that the individual accounts include the exemption statement that is a requirements for the exemption. [TECH 06/06 26.3]

An intermediate parent company is exempt under s228 or s228A of the 1985 Act and s400 and s401 of the 2006 Act from the requirement to prepare group accounts if, inter alia, it discloses in its individual accounts that it is taking advantage of that exemption. If it elects to prepare group accounts as part of its annual accounts and it does not make that disclosure it will therefore be preparing group accounts because it is required to do so, and not 'voluntarily' so far as the Act is concerned. The company and its consolidated subsidiaries will thus be eligible to take advantage in their individual accounts of the exemption from disclosing non-audit services. [TECH 06/06 26.4]

The exemptions considered above are for the individual accounts of a parent and its subsidiaries. There is no exemption in relation to any group accounts. Therefore an intermediate holding company which is a subsidiary of another UK company but prepares group accounts (e.g. because it has listed debt or because it falls into the circumstances discussed above) has no exemption from the disclosure in its group accounts of 'other services'. This is so even though its parent prepares group accounts and makes disclosures in accordance with the Regulations. [TECH 06/06 26.6]

Section 230 of the 1985 Act and s408 of the 2006 Act do not permit details of a company's audit fee and fees for other services to be excluded when advantage is taken of the exemption from publishing in its annual accounts the company's individual profit and loss account. The disclosures on audit fees and fees for other services are required specifically by the Regulations, rather than generally as a note to the profit and loss account/income statement. However, if a company is required to prepare group accounts as part of its annual accounts, then it will be exempt from providing information about the fees for its individual accounts anyway (provided that it makes the necessary exemption statement), as discussed at **8.2.4.2** *above. [TECH 06/06 27.1]*

8.2.5.2 *Amounts to be disclosed*

UK

Separate disclosure is required for each type of service specified in Schedule 2 to the Regulations but not for each service falling within a type of service (see **8.2.5.3** *below). [2008 Regulations Reg 5(3), previously 2005 Regulations Reg 4(3)]*

Separate disclosure is also required in respect of services supplied to the company and its subsidiaries on the one hand and to associated pension schemes on the other (see **8.2.6.4** *below). [2008 Regulations Reg 5(4), previously 2005 Regulations Reg 4(4)]*

In the case of group accounts, the disclosure of other services is made as if the undertakings included in the consolidation were a single company, except where the group qualifies as small or medium-sized under s249 of the 1985 Act or s383 or s466 of the 2006 Act and is not an ineligible group under s248(2) of the 1985 Act or s384(2) or s467(2) of the 2006 Act. [2008 Regulations Reg 6(1), previously 2005 Regulations Reg 5(1)]

The stipulation to apply Regulation 4(1)(b) of the 2005 Regulations and Regulation 5(1)(b) of the 2008 Regulations as if the undertakings included in the consolidation were a single company has the following effect. If, under EU-adopted IFRSs, the consolidation includes an undertaking that is not a subsidiary undertaking as a matter of law, then the parent company's disclosure of the group's fees for other services will include services provided to that undertaking because it is included in the consolidation. [TECH 06/06 28.1]

The fact that the undertakings included in the consolidation are treated as a single company does not mean that fees other than those paid to the parent company's auditors and their associates are included in the disclosure (i.e. fees paid to any 'secondary auditors' are excluded). [TECH 06/06 28.2]

As explained at **8.2.4.1** *above, the fee disclosed for the audit of the annual accounts is conventionally the fee for the year on which the auditor is reporting. The same approach should be used for any fees for auditing the company's associates (which will be included in Category 1 of 'Other services') and for regulatory filings that relate to the signing of an audit opinion (which will be included in Category 2 of 'Other services'). Other fees which are unrelated to the audit for a particular year should be calculated on an accruals basis (i.e. for work carried out in the period). The amount disclosed should be the amount charged to income or capitalised within assets (e.g. fees relating to due diligence work) or included within issue costs of debt or equity during the company's reporting period. [TECH 06/06 29.5]*

The Regulations require disclosure of 'any remuneration receivable by the company's auditors or [their associates] for the supply of other services to the company or its associates'. The associates of a company are defined in the Regulations as being most subsidiaries (see **8.2.2.2** *above) and all associated pension schemes but do not include parent companies. Therefore fees for services that are supplied by a company's auditor (or its associates) to its parent company do not have to be disclosed in the subsidiary's accounts. [TECH 06/06 29.6]*

For example, consider a company that is a subsidiary of a foreign parent. Its auditor may provide services which do not relate to the statutory audit of the company but are necessary for the consolidated accounts of the foreign parent. For example, they might relate to the audit of a consolidation return under US GAAP. In this case, whether the services have been supplied to the parent or the subsidiary will depend on the facts. In some cases it will be clear that the services were supplied to the foreign parent although the work may physically have been carried out at the premises of the UK subsidiary company. Where this is the case, the fees for these services will not be included in the amounts disclosed by the subsidiary for 'other services'. Factors to consider when determining which company the services have been supplied to include the addressee of the engagement letter and any reports. The identity of the company which paid the fees may be a relevant factor where the other evidence is unclear or conflicting about the identity of the company to which the services were supplied. But payment of fees is not itself the basis for disclosure where the services have clearly been supplied to another company. However, where such services have been supplied to the subsidiary they will fall within category 2 (see **8.2.4.2** *above). [TECH 06/06 29.7]*

A single fee may be agreed (and a single engagement letter be in place) for the audit and for the provision of other services (e.g. the review of interim financial information). Where this is the case, the auditors should provide a reasonable breakdown of the total fee into the different services. [TECH 06/06 30.1]

8.2.5.3 The categories of other services

UK *Schedule 2 to the Regulations specifies the types of service in respect of which disclosure is required for 'other services'. The 2005 Regulations state that where a service could fall within more than one type, the schedule specifies that it must be treated as falling within the first mentioned but this requirement is omitted from the 2008 Regulations. The specified types of services are:*

(1) *the auditing of accounts of associates of the company pursuant to legislation (including that of countries and territories outside Great Britain). The 2008 Regulations specify 'outside the United Kingdom' but this does not change the substance of the requirement which is to include services supplied pursuant to legislation anywhere in the world;*

(2) *other services supplied pursuant to such legislation;*

(3) *other services relating to taxation;*

(4) *services relating to information technology;*

(5) *internal audit services;*

(6) *valuation and actuarial services;*

(7) *services relating to litigation;*

(8) *services relating to recruitment and remuneration;*

(9) *services relating to corporate finance transactions entered into or proposed to be entered into by or on behalf of the company or any of its associates; and*

(10) *all other services.*

The aggregate amount receivable by the auditors and their associates for each of the types of service set out above must be disclosed by companies other than those that qualify as small or medium-sized. The ten types of services are listed moving broadly from services where no conflict of interest is likely to arise to ones that might be thought to warrant more scrutiny. An exception to this principle is the last category 'all other services'. This is the default category for all non-specified services and thus could contain a wide variety of services. [TECH 06/06 29.1]

The Regulations require disclosure only of fees for services and therefore no disclosure is required of fees for any supply of goods that the auditors or their associates might make. However, the definition of remuneration in Regulation 2 includes payments in respect of expenses and benefits in kind. [TECH 06/06 29.4]

The specified categories are not consistent with those required by the US Securities and Exchange Commission. SEC registrants will be required to comply with two similar but separate requirements. Disclosures presented in accordance with SEC requirements will not fulfil the UK statutory disclosure requirements. Disclosures presented in accordance with UK statutory requirements will not fulfil SEC requirements. The DTI (now BERR) has acknowledged that this is the case in the Explanatory Memorandum issued with the 2005 Regulations. [TECH 06/06 32.1]

CATEGORY 1: AUDITING ACCOUNTS OF ASSOCIATES PURSUANT TO LEGISLATION

Category 1 comprises 'the auditing of accounts of associates of the company pursuant to legislation (including that of countries and territories outside Great Britain / the United Kingdom)'. It includes fees receivable by the auditors and their associates for auditing the accounts of subsidiaries and associated pension schemes (both inside and outside Great Britain / the United Kingdom). The reference to legislation includes the requirement to prepare consolidated accounts for the parent, as well as the statutory audit of subsidiaries. The reference to 'accounts' is not limited to statutory accounts and may include consolidation returns. However, fees receivable by the parent company's auditors for work on the consolidated accounts, including the head office audit team's review of consolidation returns of subsidiaries, will be included in the amount disclosed as the group audit fee (see ***8.2.4*** *above). [TECH 06/06 37.1]* UK

Fees receivable by the parent company's auditors for the statutory audit of subsidiaries, separate from their audit of the group accounts, should be disclosed in the group accounts in Category 1. [TECH 06/06 37.2]

Fees receivable by associates of the parent company's auditors can never be included in audit fees in the group accounts (see ***8.2.4*** *above). Therefore, audit-related fees for work performed by associates of the parent company's auditors, whether in relation to consolidation returns or local legislative requirements, are always disclosed within Category 1. [TECH 06/06 37.3]*

An audit that is not carried out pursuant to legislation would fall within Category 5 'Internal audit services' or Category 10 'All other services'. The

latter should be rare. Inclusion within Category 10 would arise only if the audit was not necessary for the purposes of the consolidation and was not required by local legislative requirements. [TECH 06/06 37.4]

A subsidiary will usually be exempt in its individual accounts from disclosing fees paid for 'other services' (see **8.2.5.1** *above). However, where this is not the case, in a GB/UK subsidiary's accounts, any separately identifiable fee paid to the subsidiary's auditors for the audit of that subsidiary's consolidation return, to the extent that the work was not necessary for the audit of the subsidiary's own accounts, is disclosed under the appropriate category (see* **8.2.4.2** *above) unless the services have been supplied to the parent in which case no disclosure will be required in the subsidiary's accounts (see* **8.2.5.2**). *The fee for this work may be material and separately identifiable if, for example, the consolidation return and the subsidiary's own accounts are prepared using different accounting frameworks. Another example would be the audit of information at the subsidiary in support of hedge documentation prepared at group level in accordance with IAS 39 / FRS 26* Financial instruments: Recognition and Measurement *for the purposes of achieving hedge accounting in the group accounts but that was not relevant for the subsidiary as it may not have hedged the exposure or may have hedged in a different manner for the purposes of its own accounts. [TECH 06/06 37.5]*

CATEGORY 2: *OTHER SERVICES SUPPLIED PURSUANT TO SUCH LEGISLATION*

UK

Category 2 comprises services in relation to other statutory and regulatory filings or engagements of the audit client and all its associates that are carried out by the auditors or their associates. This would include, for example:

[TECH 06/06 38.1]

- *regulatory reporting where it is specified that certain letters or reports must be obtained under the Listing Rules;*
- *statutory or regulatory reporting on internal controls, even though such reports do not typically include the term 'audit';*
- *certain reports relating to government grants (where they are required pursuant to legislation);*
- *reports under s108 of the 1985 Act or s1150 of the 2006 Act 'Non-cash consideration to be valued before allotment';*

- *reports under s109 of the 1985 Act or s600 of the 2006 Act 'Transfer to public company of non-cash asset in initial period';*
- *reports under s173 of the 1985 Act or s714 of the 2006 Act 'Purchase of own shares out of capital';*
- *reports under section 156 of the 1985 Act (there is no equivalent provision in the 2006 Act) in relation to financial assistance by a company for the acquisition of its own shares in so far as the fee relates to work undertaken to meet the statutory requirements. Fees for non-statutory aspects of the work (e.g. verifying a statement by the directors that the transaction does not breach legal requirements) are included in Category 10;*
- *elements of reports under section 404 of the US Public Company Accounting Reform and Investor Protection Act of 2002 (Sarbanes-Oxley) (see below); and*
- *reports on form 20-F for SEC registrants to the extent of any additional work beyond that required for the statutory audit of the consolidated accounts. Work common to the statutory accounts and the form 20-F should be included within the audit fee for disclosure purposes.*

Only those fees that relate to carrying out work to meet the statutory or regulatory requirements should be included in Category 2. [TECH 06/06 38.1]

The services included in Category 2 are not restricted to those which are required by legislation to be performed by the company's auditors. It is sufficient that the services are themselves required to be performed by legislation without specifying who should perform them. [TECH 06/06 38.2]

When performing an audit, an approach may be taken whereby work performed on internal controls forms an integral part of the audit procedures for the UK statutory audit and is also sufficient for the signing of the section 404 report. Consequently, in this case, the fees for work on internal controls will be included in the audit fee disclosure. However, to the extent that there is additional cost in preparing the section 404 report itself, that cost falls within Category 2. If there is additional work performed on internal controls to give the section 404 report that would not be required for the UK statutory audit (e.g. controls are tested that are not relied upon for the UK statutory audit), any additional fee relating to this work also falls within Category 2. [TECH 06/06 38.3]

In the group financial statements, only the fees relating to work performed on internal controls within the parent company and over the consolidation process should be included in the group audit fee. To the extent that work is performed as part of the audit on the internal controls of a subsidiary, these fees form part of the fee for auditing the subsidiary. As such, from a group perspective, they will fall to be included in Category 1. However, if the work on the internal controls of the subsidiary is only carried out for the purposes of the section 404 report, the fees will fall to be disclosed within Category 2. [TECH 06/06 38.4]

There is no statutory requirement in the UK for a review of the half-yearly report by a company's auditors. Where a review is performed, it is conducted in accordance with APB Bulletin 1999/4 Review of interim financial information. Such a review is referred to in the Listing Rules and the Disclosure and Transparency Rules as a review by auditors. Where such a review is carried out by a listed company's auditors and where a report is published, the fee should be included in Category 2 because the Rules are established under the authority of the Financial Services and Markets Act. [TECH 06/06 39.1]

Where a review of interim financial information is performed by a company's auditors other than as required by legislation (e.g. for an AIM company), the fees receivable by the auditors for that review will be included in Category 10 'All other services'. [TECH 06/06 39.2]

CATEGORY 3: OTHER SERVICES RELATING TO TAXATION

UK

Fees for both tax compliance services and tax advisory services are included within Category 3. They do not need to be disclosed separately but some companies may wish to do so. Fees for work carried out as part of the audit of the accounts (e.g. auditing tax provisions) are included as part of the amount receivable for auditing the accounts of the company (or of its associates, as appropriate, in which case the fees would be included in Category 1). [TECH 06/06 40.1]

CATEGORY 4: SERVICES RELATING TO INFORMATION TECHNOLOGY

UK

This category is self explanatory. TECH 06/06 provides no additional guidance.

CATEGORY 5: INTERNAL AUDIT SERVICES

UK

According to Ethical Standards, an audit firm may provide internal audit services, provided it does not place significant reliance on that work when carrying out the external audit and carrying out the work would not involve undertaking part of the role of management, and subject to safeguards. [TECH 06/06 41.1]

CATEGORY 6: VALUATION AND ACTUARIAL SERVICES

Ethical Standards preclude an audit firm from carrying out a valuation if it would both involve a significant degree of subjective judgement and have a material effect on the accounts. Actuarial valuation services are subject to the same general principles. Where audit-assist work is undertaken by specialists on valuations undertaken by others, this should be included in the audit fee for disclosure purposes. [TECH 06/06 42.1] UK

Ethical Standard 5 explicitly permits an auditor to provide valuation reports under sections 108 and 109 of the Companies Act 1985 but these will be disclosed within Category 2 because the services are supplied pursuant to legislation (see above). As explained above, under the 2005 Regulations, a service is treated as falling within the category highest on the list where it could fall into more than one category. [TECH 06/06 42.2]

CATEGORY 7: SERVICES RELATING TO LITIGATION

This category is self explanatory. TECH 06/06 provides no additional guidance. UK

CATEGORY 8: SERVICES RELATING TO RECRUITMENT AND REMUNERATION

This category is self explanatory. TECH 06/06 provides no additional guidance. UK

CATEGORY 9: CORPORATE FINANCE SERVICES

Category 9 comprises 'services relating to corporate finance transactions entered into or proposed to be entered into by or on behalf of the company or any of its associates'. It will include fees related to work such as acquisition due diligence and long-form reports, irrespective of whether the company is the vendor or purchaser. However, if the work is required by legislation (e.g. it is required by the Listing Rules or the Prospectus Rules which are UK *established under the authority of the Financial Services and Markets Act 2000), it will be included within Category 2 which is higher on the list. This does not strictly apply under the 2008 Regulations but is nevertheless likely to be the most appropriate treatment. [TECH 06/06 43.1]*

CATEGORY 10: ALL OTHER SERVICES

UK *The following are examples of services that do not fall within categories higher on the list and which therefore fall within 'All other services':*

- *advice on accounting matters where this is unrelated to the auditing of the accounts. This could include fees for IFRS transition work where this goes significantly beyond what would be required to give an opinion on the financial statements (see* **8.2.4.4** *above);*
- *provision of accounting services to a listed company in an emergency (as permitted by paragraph 121 of Ethical Standard 5);*
- *non-regulatory reporting on internal controls and corporate governance matters;*
- *environmental audits, corporate social responsibility reports and similar services;*
- *secondments of the auditors' staff to the audit client (as permitted by paragraph 33 of Ethical Standard 2);*
- *some services provided by a company of which a partner in the audit firm is a director;*
- *the audit of a subsidiary that is not necessary for the purposes of the consolidation and is not required by local legislative requirements (see Category 1 above); and*
- *an interim review that is not required by law, for example in the case of an AIM company (see Category 2 above).*

This is not intended to be an exhaustive list.

While it is not necessary to show individual amounts for the different services within Category 10, or indeed any other category, narrative explanation of the nature of the services included in this category may be helpful to users of the accounts. This may be particularly useful where there are no amounts, or only immaterial amounts, disclosed in the earlier categories (e.g. such that the largest single amount is described as 'other') or where the category includes a mixture of assurance and advisory services. [TECH 06/06 44.1]

8.2.5.4 *The exemption for 'distant associates'*

UK

The 2008 Regulations introduce an new exemption from disclosure of certain fees for services supplied by a 'distant associate' of a company's auditors. However, the exemption is available only if:

- *the associate meets the definition of a 'distant associate' (see* **8.2.2.1** *above);*
- *the services fall within 'All other services' (i.e. they are* ***not*** *any of the nine specified categories described at* **8.2.5.3**, *for example services relating to taxation etc); and*
- *the fees in question do not exceed £10,000 or a lower limit is some cases (see below).*

All three conditions must be met.

This exemption was included in the 2008 Regulations in response to concern that the definition of associates of the auditors was too broad and included entities which would not ordinarily be thought of as connected with the auditors (see **8.2.2.1** *above). However, rather than narrowing the definition of associates, the Government agreed to this limited disclosure exemption which adds to the complexity of the Regulations. The limited exemption from disclosure is as follows.*

Disclosure is not required of remuneration receivable for the supply of services falling within paragraph 10 of Schedule 2 to the 2008 Regulations (i.e. 'all other services') supplied by a distant associate of the company's auditors where the total remuneration receivable for all of those services supplied by that associate does not exceed either:

- *£10,000, or*
- *1% of the total audit remuneration received by the company's auditor in the most recent financial year of the auditor which ended no later than the end of the financial year of the company to which the accounts relate.*

For this purpose 'financial year of the auditor' means:

- *the period of not more than 18 months in respect of which the auditors' profit and loss account is required to be made up (whether by law or by or in accordance with the auditor's constitution (if any)), or*
- *failing any such requirement, the period of 12 months beginning with 1 April.*

Also, 'total audit remuneration received' means the total remuneration received for the auditing pursuant to legislation (including that of countries and territories outside the United Kingdom) of any accounts of any person.

8.2.6 Presentation of information

8.2.6.1 Location of disclosures

UK *The Regulations require the information to be disclosed in the notes to the annual accounts. The DTI (now BERR) has advised that the alternative of a cross reference to information given elsewhere within the annual report will not be sufficient. [TECH 04/06 5.1]*

Although it is unclear why a very specific cross reference, for which there are precedents, would be unacceptable in this case, the disclosures should nevertheless be made in the notes to the accounts. If auditors' remuneration is also discussed in an audit committee report or other corporate governance statement, a specific cross reference may be made from that material to the information about auditors' remuneration given in the notes to the accounts.

8.2.6.2 Comparative information

UK *The Regulations are silent on the matter of comparative figures. However, the information is required to be given in the notes to the accounts and so the general requirements for comparatives in IAS 1 Presentation of Financial Statements apply. [TECH 06/06 6.1]*

8.2.6.3 Totals and sub-totals

UK *There is no requirement to disclose an aggregated total of fees for 'other services' but this is permitted. [TECH 06/06 36.1]*

Sub-totals are not required but they are permitted. Companies may wish to sub-total the fees for the audit of the accounts of the company itself together with fees for the audits of accounts of subsidiaries which are required to be disclosed within the relevant category within 'other services'. [TECH 06/06 19.1]

Companies may wish to provide a total of the amounts for 'other services'. This is permitted. However, it should be remembered that 'other services' may include amounts for auditing the accounts of subsidiaries and for work done by associates of the parent company's auditors on auditing the consolidation (e.g. auditing consolidation returns). These amounts would conventionally be thought of as 'audit fees' and so a straight comparison of the amounts disclosed for 'audit' and 'other services' may give a misleading impression of the amount of non-audit work being performed by the company's auditors and their associates. The illustrative disclosures at ***8.2.6.8*** *below offer a possible solution.*

8.2.6.4 *Associated pension schemes*

UK

The Regulations require disclosure of fees receivable by a company's auditors and their associates from the company's associated pension schemes for services supplied to those schemes. This applies irrespective of whether or not the company's auditors or any of their associates are the auditors of the pension scheme. [TECH 06/06 16.1]

The same information must be disclosed for associated pension schemes as is required for the company or group (i.e. using the same categories of other services). The information must be disclosed separately from the information for the company and/or group. [TECH 06/06 16.2]

This might be achieved, for example, by the use of a columnar layout with separate columns for the group and for associated pension schemes. However, where the range of services supplied to the pension scheme is limited, it may be more appropriate to provide the amounts and descriptions of services supplied to associated pension schemes in the form of a separate narrative paragraph.

8.2.6.5 *Analysis of other services*

UK

The ten types of service specified do not have to be disclosed in the order in which they are listed in the Schedule. However, this order should generally be followed in the interests of consistency. [TECH 06/06 33.1]

Sub-analysis of the individual categories is not required. This may, however, be desirable in some instances. For example, companies may wish to distinguish between tax compliance work and tax advisory work. [TECH 06/06 34.1]

8.2.6.6 *Nil and immaterial amounts*

UK

It is not necessary to disclose nil amounts. Therefore captions for which there are no amounts in the current year or the prior year may be omitted. There is no explicit exemption from disclosing immaterial amounts. [TECH 06/06 35.1]

Information in the notes to the financial statements is often reported in thousands or even millions of units of the presentation currency. IAS 1(2007).53 and IAS 1(2003).48 confirm that this is acceptable so long as the level of rounding in presentation is disclosed (i.e. it is clear that the amounts are, for example, thousands of pounds) and material information is not omitted. The same approach appears to be acceptable for the disclosure of auditors' remuneration based on past practice.

8.2.6.7 *Narrative disclosures*

UK

There is no requirement in the Regulations for any description of the services provided beyond the specified categories of 'other services'.

Listed companies may need to make some narrative disclosure under the Combined Code to explain how the auditors' objectivity and independence is safeguarded where the auditor provides non-audit services. This would usually be in the corporate governance statement or audit committee report rather than in the notes to the accounts. [TECH 06/06 47.1]

8.2.6.8 *Illustrative disclosures*

UK

TECH 06/06 includes an example of disclosures as an appendix. This example is based on specific facts and circumstances and is helpful in understanding how fees should be allocated between the audit of the accounts of the company and the various specified categories of other services. However, it does not fulfil the need for 'model' disclosures meeting the requirements of the Regulations because it assumes that there are no services supplied under the majority of the categories.

The following example illustrates a possible format for disclosures in accordance with the Regulations. It illustrates the inclusion of a sub-total for total audit fees which is not required by the Regulations but may be helpful for users of the accounts as discussed at **8.2.6.3** *above.*

UK

Example 8.2.6.8

Illustrative disclosures

	20X1 £'000	20X0 £'000
Fees payable to the company's auditors for the audit of the company's annual accounts	X	X
Fees payable to the company's auditors and their associates for other services to the group	X	X
The audit of the company's subsidiaries pursuant to legislation	X	X
Total audit fees	X	X
Other services pursuant to legislation	X	X
Tax services	X	X
Information technology services	X	X
Internal audit services	X	X
Valuation and actuarial services	X	X
Litigation services	X	X
Recruitment and remuneration services	X	X
Corporate finance services	X	X
Other services	X	X
Total non-audit fees	X	X
Fees payable to the company's auditors and their associates in respect of associated pension schemes		
Audit	X	X
[Specify categories of other services]	X	X
	X	X

Fees payable to [Name of auditors] and their associates for non-audit services to the company are not required to be disclosed because the consolidated financial statements are required to disclose such fees on a consolidated basis.

UK

The footnote is required to qualify for the exemption from disclosing the amounts attributable to the company as well as those for the group. In the case of a subsidiary making use of the exemption, the following wording may be used for the footnote:

> *'Fees payable to [Name of auditors] and their associates for non-audit services to the company are not required to be disclosed because the consolidated financial statements of the parent company are required to disclose such fees on a consolidated basis.'*
>
> *This example assumes that all group companies are audited by the parent company's auditors and their associates. As explained in* **8.2.4.2** *above, fees payable to other firms for the audit of subsidiaries or branches are not included in the amounts to be disclosed in accordance with the Regulations. However, where such fees are material, additional voluntary disclosures might be considered to enable the total cost of auditing the group to be understood by users of the financial statements.*

8.2.7 *Other matters*

8.2.7.1 *Duty of auditors to supply information*

UK

> *The auditors of a company are required to supply the directors of the company with such information as is necessary to enable the disclosures of 'other services' to be made. [2008 Regulations Reg 7, previously 2005 Regulations Reg 6]*
>
> *The directors of the company are responsible for ensuring the company's compliance with the Regulations. They will generally be able to do this from information available within the accounting records of the company and its associates that are subsidiaries. [TECH 06/06 7.1]*
>
> *As noted above, the Regulations require the auditor to supply the directors of the company with such information as is necessary to enable the disclosure required by the Regulations to be made. Generally, it should be sufficient to supply the directors with a list of the auditor's associates. Some auditors may wish, as a matter of client service, to go further than required by law and supply their clients with the relevant amounts of fees for disclosure purposes. This information will generally be readily available as a result of the need to comply with Ethical Standards. This would also potentially remove the need to supply clients with a list of the firm's associates. However, auditors will need to bear in mind the self review threat that will arise when this approach is taken. [TECH 06/06 7.2]*
>
> *The directors will generally need to contact the trustees of associated pension schemes to obtain the necessary information in respect of those schemes. Under normal circumstances, the list of the auditor's associates should be sufficient to enable the directors to obtain the information from the trustees. However, if the trustees refuse to provide the information to the*

directors, the auditor is required by the Regulation to supply the directors with the necessary information regarding services by it and its associates to the company's associated pension schemes, even though the pension schemes are not legally part of the group. The ICAEW has been advised by the DTI (now BERR) that this specific statutory obligation overrides any general legal or contractual duty of confidentiality owed by the auditor to its pension scheme client. [TECH 06/06 7.3]

8.2.7.2 *Failure to make the required disclosures*

Under the 2005 Regulations, sections 233(5) and 245 to 245C of the 1985 Act apply in relation to a failure to make the disclosures required by the Regulations as they apply in relation to a failure to comply with the requirements of the Act. [2005 Regulations Reg 7] There is no equivalent explicit provision in the 2008 Regulations but non-compliance with the Regulations would nevertheless amount to non-compliance with the Act. UK

In practice this means that the penalties imposed on directors, and the provisions about revision of defective accounts, apply to any failure to make appropriate disclosures about auditors' remuneration in the same way that they apply to any other failure to meet the applicable requirements of the Act.

8.2.7.3 *Amounts receivable by auditors from third parties*

Fees may be payable by third parties to a company's auditors for work carried out by them under separate engagements unrelated to the audit and under instructions from a third party but nevertheless in relation to a mutual client. Examples include litigation support work where the auditors may report directly to the solicitors, and credit investigation reports where the report may be made to the bank. In each case, the fees may be payable by the third party but the service is provided to the audit client. Since the substance of the service is that it has been rendered to the audit client, the fee should be subject to disclosure. Such fees should be disclosed in the appropriate category or categories. In these examples, they would fall within Category 7 'Services relating to litigation' and Category 10 'All other services', respectively. [TECH 06/06 45.1] UK

The key point is that disclosure does not depend on which company pays the fees but on which company the services are supplied to. These will often be the same but this will not always be the case. [TECH 06/06 45.2]

For example, banks sometimes require their customers to appoint accountants to prepare reports as a condition of continued lending. The bank's customer will normally pay the fees. The accountants appointed may coincidentally be the auditors of the bank. It would be unusual for the bank to require the work to be performed by their auditors although they may appear on a shortlist of approved firms. In many cases it will be clear that the services are being supplied to the bank's customer rather than to the bank itself. In fact, if the accountants were also the auditors of the bank's customer, it would be expected that the fees would be disclosed as 'other services' in that company's accounts. Consequently, it would not be expected that the amounts would also be disclosed as 'other services' in the bank's accounts. In each case it will be necessary to consider the particular arrangements and form a view on whether the services are being supplied to the bank or to the bank's customer. [TECH 06/06 45.3]

8.2.7.4 Relationship with ethical standards

UK

In addition to legislative measures for disclosure, auditors are bound by the Auditing Practices Board's Ethical Standards. In particular, Ethical Standard 5 Non-audit services provided to audited entities *imposes certain constraints and safeguards in relation to the provision of non-audit services. Ethical Standard 5 includes a definition of non-audit services which excludes services performed that legislation or regulation specify can be performed by the auditors. Therefore some services that are not non-audit services for the purposes of Ethical Standard 5 will be disclosed as 'other services' under the Regulations. [TECH 06/06 0.8]*

8.3 Liability limitation agreements

UK

From 6 April 2008, companies may enter into liability limitation agreements with their auditors, subject to the provisions of the Act. Few such agreements have been entered into initially pending the development of guidance by the Financial Reporting Council (FRC). This guidance was issued in final form on 30 June 2008 and it is to be expected that such agreements will now become more common. The guidance, which can be downloaded from the FRC website at www.frc.org.uk:

- *explains what is and is not allowed under the 2006 Act;*
- *sets out some of the factors that will be relevant when assessing the case for an agreement;*
- *explains what matters should be covered in an agreement and provides specimen clauses for inclusion; and*

- *explains the process to be followed for obtaining shareholder approval and provides specimen wording for inclusion in resolutions and the notice of the general meeting.*

A company that enters into such an agreement must make disclosures about the agreement in its accounts. These requirements are included in the Companies (Disclosure of Auditor Remuneration and Liability Limitation Agreements) Regulations 2008 (SI 2008/489) and are set out below. They apply with effect from 6 April 2008 rather than for periods beginning on or after that date. Therefore, these disclosures may be required for a period when the accounts are still drawn up in accordance with the 1985 Act.

A company which has entered into a liability limitation agreement with its auditors must disclose:

- *its principal terms; and*

- *the date of the resolution approving the agreement or the agreement's principal terms or, in the case of a private company, the date of the resolution waiving the need for such approval, in a note to the company's annual accounts.*

The annual accounts in which these disclosure must be made are those for the financial year to which the agreement relates unless the agreement was entered into too late for it to be reasonably practicable for the disclosure to be made in those accounts.

If the agreement was entered into too late for it to be reasonably practicable for the required disclosure to be made in the accounts for the financial year to which the agreement relates, the disclosure are made in a note to the company's next following annual accounts.

For this purpose, the 'principal terms' of an agreement are defined in s536(4) of the 2006 Act as terms specifying, or relevant to the determination of:

- *the kind (or kinds) of acts or omissions covered;*

- *the financial year to which the agreement relates; or*

- *the limit to which the auditor's liability is subject.*

8.4 Disclosure of off balance sheet arrangements

UK

This new disclosure requirement applies to companies reporting under IFRSs and under UK GAAP. It does not apply to companies that are subject to the small companies regime. The requirement is in s410A of the 2006 Act, which was inserted by SI 2008/393.

If in any financial year:

- *the company is, or has been, party to arrangements that are not reflected in its balance sheet, and*
- *at the balance sheet date the risks or benefits arising from those arrangements are material,*

the following information must be given in notes to the company's annual accounts.

The information required is:

- *the nature and business purpose of the arrangements, and*
- *the financial impact of the arrangements on the company.*

The information need only be given to the extent necessary for enabling the financial position of the company to be assessed.

If the company qualifies as medium-sized in relation to the financial year, it need not disclose the financial impact of the arrangements on the company but must still disclose the nature and purpose of the arrangements.

The requirement applies in relation to group accounts as if the undertakings included in the consolidation were a single company.

Recital (9) to EU Directive 2006/46/EC which introduces the requirement into the Fourth Directive explains it in the following way:

'Such off-balance-sheet arrangements could be any transactions or agreements which companies may have with entities, even unincorporated ones, that are not included in the balance sheet. Such off-balance-sheet arrangements may be associated with the creation or use of one or more Special Purpose Entities (SPEs) and offshore activities designed to address, inter alia, economic, legal, tax or accounting objectives. Examples of such off-balance-sheet arrangements include risk and benefit-sharing arrangements or obligations arising from a contract such as debt factoring, combined sale and repurchase agreements, consignment stock arrangements, take or pay arrangements, securitisation arranged through separate

companies and unincorporated entities, pledged assets, operating leasing arrangements, outsourcing and the like. Appropriate disclosure of the material risks and benefits of such arrangements that are not included in the balance sheet should be set out in the notes to the accounts or the consolidated accounts.'

This explanation is not formally part of the requirements of the Directive but could potentially be taken into account by a court when interpreting its requirements.

The new requirement must be seen in the context of the EU Accounting Directives which set a minimum standard for accounting and disclosure throughout Europe. UK GAAP and IFRSs go well beyond the minimum requirements of the directives in ensuring that assets and liabilities are not inappropriately excluded from the balance sheet. They also impose disclosure requirements on some types of arrangements which are not included in the balance sheet, such as operating leases and contingent liabilities. IAS 1 includes a requirement to disclose key judgements made by management (see **7.2.3** *above) which might include, for example, a decision about whether or not to consolidate an SPE. Therefore, compliance with accounting standards should usually be sufficient to ensure compliance with the law.*

9 Future developments

9.1 Financial statements presentation

Phase A of the financial statements presentation project concluded with the publication of the revised IAS 1 in December 2007. The requirements of the revised standard, which are mandatory for periods beginning on or after 1 January 2009, are addressed in the body of this chapter.

Phase B of the project will address more fundamental issues, including:

- consistent principles for aggregating information in each financial statement;
- the totals and subtotals that should be reported in each financial statement;
- whether components of other recognised income and expense should be reclassified to profit or loss and, if so, the characteristics of the transactions and events that should be reclassified and when reclassification should be made; and
- whether the direct or the indirect method of presenting operating cash flows provides more useful information.

A Discussion Paper dealing with these issues is expected during 2008.

9.2 Annual improvements project

The IASB's 2007 annual improvements project proposed three amendments to IAS 1.

The amendment relating to the current / non-current classification of derivatives was issued in May 2008 and is addressed at **4.2** and **4.3** above. The amendment is effective for periods beginning on or after 1 January 2009 with early application permitted.

UK

Although the amendment has not yet been adopted by the EU, it is a clarification and does not conflict with IAS 1(2003) or IAS 1(2007) and may therefore be applied by UK companies.

The proposed amendment relating to the current / non-current classification of convertible instruments has been deferred pending further discussion of the comments received. IAS 1 requires a liability to be classified as current if the entity does not have an unconditional right to defer settlement for at least twelve months from the end of the reporting period. The *Framework* states that settlement includes conversion of a liability into equity. Consequently, the liability component of a convertible instrument that the entity could be required to settle in shares at any time would be classified as current. The Board proposed to limit the requirement for an entity to have an unconditional right to defer settlement to settlement by transfer of cash or other assets.

The proposed amendment relating to the statement of compliance with IFRSs has been deferred pending further discussion of the comments received. The Board proposed to insert, into IAS 1, disclosure requirements for entities that refer to IFRSs in describing the basis on which their financial statements are prepared but are not able to make an explicit and unreserved statement of compliance with IFRSs. Such an entity would be required to make disclosures about how its financial statements would have been different if prepared in full compliance with IFRSs.

UK

*As explained in **chapter 1**, UK companies are required by law to comply with IFRSs as adopted by the EU but are normally able, at present, to also confirm compliance with IFRSs as issued by the IASB. The proposed amendment to IAS 1 would therefore not affect UK companies at present but might do so in future if the EU fails to adopt new or revised standards issued by the IASB.*

4 Accounting policies, changes in accounting estimates and errors

1 Introduction

IAS 8 *Accounting Policies, Changes in Accounting Estimates and Errors* was published in 2003, superseding IAS 8 *Net Profit or Loss for the Period, Fundamental Errors and Changes in Accounting Policies*, revised in 1993. The revised Standard was developed as part of the IASB's Improvements to International Accounting Standards project. The Standard also replaced SIC-2 *Consistency – Capitalisation of Borrowing Costs* and SIC-18 *Consistency -Alternative Method*. The revised Standard applied for annual periods beginning on or after 1 January 2005. It was most recently amended when *Improvements to IFRSs* was issued in May 2008.

The objective of IAS 8 is to prescribe the criteria for selecting and changing accounting policies. IAS 1 *Presentation of Financial Statements* (see **chapter 3**) sets out the disclosure requirements for accounting policies (excepting changes in accounting policies). IAS 8 deals with the accounting and disclosure requirements regarding changes in accounting policies, changes in accounting estimates and the correction of errors. The revised Standard removed the concept of a 'fundamental error' and instead includes all material prior period errors within its scope.

> *Under UK GAAP, the equivalent material is to be found mainly in FRS 18 Accounting Policies. FRS 3* Reporting Financial Performance *deals with the requirements for prior period adjustments for changes of accounting policies and correction of fundamental errors. Probably the most significant difference between these standards and IAS 8 is that the latter requires all material errors to be corrected by retrospective restatement whereas UK GAAP requires this treatment only for fundamental errors (i.e. consistent with the previous requirements of IAS 8). IAS 8 also requires some additional disclosures that are not found in UK GAAP.* (UK)

This chapter discusses the requirements of IAS 8 in the following sections:

Section 2 Definitions

Section 3 Accounting policies

Section 4 Changes in accounting estimates

Section 5 Errors

Section 6 Impracticability in respect of retrospective application and retrospective restatement

IAS 8 states that the tax effects of corrections of prior period errors and of retrospective adjustments made to apply changes in accounting policies are accounted for and disclosed in accordance with IAS 12 *Income Taxes*. [IAS 8.4] This is unhelpful because, although IAS 12.58 requires current and deferred tax to be reported in profit or loss except in certain specified circumstances, that Standard does not contain any explicit requirements in respect of prior period errors and retrospective adjustments. The paragraph is presumably intended to mean that IAS 12 is applied to the restated pre-tax amounts to establish the amount of any current and deferred tax assets or liabilities. IAS 12 is considered in **chapter 12**. The disclosure requirements in IAS 8 which refer to the line items affected would include the current and deferred tax items where applicable.

2 Definitions

IAS 8.5 contains definitions of certain terms used in the Standard. This section sets out some of these definitions with further explanations where necessary.

2.1 Accounting policies

Accounting policies are defined as the specific principles, bases, conventions, rules and practices applied by an entity in preparing and presenting financial statements.

This definition is fundamental to the sections of IAS 8 which deal with the selection of accounting policies (see **3.1** below) and changes in accounting policies (see **3.2** below). In particular, it is necessary to distinguish between changes in accounting policies and changes in accounting estimates (see **2.2** below).

UK

Under UK GAAP, FRS 18 has a broadly consistent but longer definition of accounting policies.

2.2 Changes in accounting estimates

A change in an accounting estimate is an adjustment of the carrying amount of an asset or a liability, or the amount of the periodic consumption of an asset, that results from the assessment of the present status of, and expected future benefits and obligations associated with, assets and liabilities. Changes in accounting estimates result from new information or new developments and, accordingly, are not corrections of errors. [IAS 8.5]

The identification, recognition and disclosure of changes in accounting estimates are considered in **section 4** below.

2.3 International Financial Reporting Standards (IFRSs)

IFRSs are the Standards and Interpretations adopted by the IASB. They set out accounting policies that the IASB has concluded, if adopted, will result in the presentation of relevant and reliable information in financial statements. IFRSs comprise:

- International Financial Reporting Standards;
- International Accounting Standards; and
- Interpretations developed by the International Financial Reporting Interpretations Committee (IFRIC) or the former Standing Interpretations Committee (SIC).

IFRSs are accompanied by guidance to assist entities applying their requirements. All such guidance states whether it is an integral part of IFRSs. Guidance that is an integral part of IFRSs is mandatory. Guidance that is not an integral part of IFRSs does not contain requirements for financial statements. [IAS 8.9]

The previous paragraph is based on IAS 8.9 as amended in May 2008 by *Improvements to IFRSs*. The purpose of the amendment (and related amendments to IAS 8.7 and IAS 8.11) was to clarify that Implementation Guidance published with IFRSs does not form part of those IFRSs and therefore is not mandatory. The amendment proposed in the October 2007 Exposure Draft made a clear distinction between Implementation Guidance which is not mandatory and Application Guidance which is mandatory. The final amendment is written in more general terms but has a similar effect.

Although Implementation Guidance does not contain mandatory requirements, it is nevertheless indicative of the way in which the IASB believes the Standard should be implemented. Paragraph 7 of IAS 8, before the amendment referred to above, required any relevant

Implementation Guidance to be 'considered' when applying an IFRS. Departures from such Guidance should therefore be made only after careful consideration and when they can be demonstrated to be fully justified.

IFRIC agenda decisions do not form part of IFRSs. However, the agenda decisions can be considered when selecting a suitable accounting policy for a transaction not specifically addressed by a Standard or Interpretation (see **3.1** below).

2.4 Material omissions or misstatements

Omissions or misstatements are material if they could, individually or collectively, influence the economic decisions that users make on the basis of the financial statements. Materiality has both quantitative and qualitative aspects which should be judged in the context of the surrounding circumstances. Either the size or the nature, or a combination of both, could be the determining factor in deciding whether an item is material.

When assessing whether an omission or misstatement is material (i.e. whether it could influence economic decisions of users of the financial statements), consideration must be given to the characteristics of the users. As stated in the *Framework for the Preparation and Presentation of Financial Statements*, users are assumed to have 'a reasonable knowledge of business and economic activities and accounting and a willingness to study the information with reasonable diligence'. [IAS 8.6] Thus, IFRSs do not contain any quantitative thresholds for defining materiality.

The definition of material omissions or misstatements is relevant to the determination of whether prior period errors (see **2.5** below) are material. This, in turn, determines whether retrospective restatement is required when such errors have arisen in a prior period (see **section 5** below).

2.5 Prior period errors

Prior period errors are omissions from, and misstatements in, the entity's financial statements for one or more prior periods resulting from a failure to use, or misuse of, reliable information that:

- was available when financial statements for those periods were authorised for issue; and

- could reasonably be expected to have been obtained and taken into account in the preparation and presentation of those financial statements.

Examples of such errors may include mathematical mistakes, mistakes in applying accounting policies, oversights or misinterpretations of facts, and fraud.

> *As explained at* ***5.2*** *below, IAS 8 requires all material prior period errors to be corrected by retrospective restatement unless this is impracticable. This contrasts with the UK GAAP treatment under which only 'fundamental errors' are corrected in this way.* UK

2.6 Retrospective application and restatement

Retrospective application of a change in accounting policy involves the application of the new accounting policy to transactions, other events and conditions as if that policy had always been applied.

Retrospective restatement is the correction of the recognition, measurement and disclosure of elements of the financial statements as if a prior period error had never happened.

2.7 Prospective application

Prospective application of a change in accounting policy involves the application of the new accounting policy to transactions, other events and conditions that occur after the date on which the policy changes.

Prospective recognition of a change in accounting estimate means that the effect of the change in estimate is recognised in the current and future periods affected by the change. The change is applied to transactions, other events and conditions from the date of the change in estimate.

2.8 Impracticable

If an entity has made every reasonable effort to apply a requirement, but cannot apply it, then applying that requirement is deemed impracticable. Retrospective application of a change in accounting policy, or retrospective restatement to correct an error is impracticable if:

- the effects of the retrospective application or retrospective restatement cannot be determined;

- assumptions are required about what management's intent would have been in that period; or
- significant estimates of amounts are required, and it is impossible to distinguish objectively, from other information, information about those estimates that:
  - provides evidence of circumstances that existed on the date(s) as at which those amounts are to be recognised, measured or disclosed; and
  - would have been available when the financial statements for that prior period were authorised for issue.

For some types of estimates (e.g. an estimate of fair value not based on an observable price or observable inputs), it is impracticable to distinguish these types of information. When retrospective application or retrospective restatement would require making a significant estimate for which it is impossible to distinguish these two types of information, it is impracticable to apply the new accounting policy or correct the prior period error retrospectively. [IAS 8.52]

This definition is relevant to exemptions from the general rule of retrospective application for changes in accounting policies (see **3.2** below) and the correction of material prior period errors (see **5.2** below). Impracticability in respect of retrospective application and retrospective restatement are considered further in **section 6** below.

3 Accounting policies

3.1 Selection of accounting policies

When an IFRS specifically applies to a transaction, other event or condition, the accounting policy or policies applied to that item are determined by applying the IFRS. [IAS 8.7]

The previous paragraph is based on IAS 8.7 as amended in May 2008 by *Improvements to IFRSs*. The purpose of the amendment (and related amendments to IAS 8.9 and IAS 8.11) was to clarify that Implementation Guidance published with IFRSs does not form part of those IFRSs and, therefore, is not mandatory. The words 'and considering any relevant Implementation Guidance issued by the IASB with the IFRS' were deleted from the end of IAS 8.7. However, as explained at **2.3** above, departures from any such Guidance should be made only after careful consideration and when they can be demonstrated to be fully justified.

It is not necessary to apply these policies if the effect of applying them is immaterial. But this does not mean that immaterial departures from IFRSs can be made, or left uncorrected, in order to achieve a particular presentation of an entity's financial position, performance or cash flows. [IAS 8.8]

This is similar to UK GAAP in that the Foreword to accounting standards *states that those standards need not be applied to immaterial items. But the explicit requirement about the correction of intentional misstatements will be new to UK entities reporting under IFRSs.* UK

In practice, an entity will sometimes wish to consider applying the requirements of IFRSs even where the effect is immaterial. This is in part because materiality is subject to judgement based on both quantitative and qualitative factors, but also because items that are not material in the current period may become material in a subsequent period.

If there is no IFRS that specifically applies to the transaction, event or condition under consideration, judgement is required by management in developing and applying an accounting policy that results in information that is:

[IAS 8.10]

- relevant to the economic decision-making needs of users; and
- reliable, in that the financial statements:
  - represent faithfully the financial position, financial performance and cash flows of the entity;
  - reflect the economic substance of transactions, other events and conditions, and not merely the legal form;
  - are neutral, i.e. free from bias;
  - are prudent; and
  - are complete in all material respects.

When selecting an appropriate accounting policy, IAS 8 requires it to be both neutral and prudent. These two characteristics can sometimes be viewed as being in tension with one another. The IASB's

Framework provides useful insights on how these two characteristics reconcile with each other by explaining that neutrality means that preparation of financial statements should not involve any deliberate or predetermined action in order to achieve a certain outcome.

Prudence is simply the exercise of caution when making judgements for various uncertainties in order to avoid overstatement of assets or income and understatement of liabilities or expenses. The *Framework* explains that 'the exercise of prudence does not allow . . . the creation of hidden reserves or excessive provisions, the deliberate understatement of assets or income, or the deliberate overstatement of liabilities or expenses, because the financial statements would not be neutral and, therefore, not have the quality of reliability'. [FR.37]

UK

FRS 18 states that the objectives against which an entity should judge the appropriateness of accounting policies to its particular circumstances are: relevance; reliability; comparability; and understandability. This differs slightly to the guidance of IAS 8 which puts emphasis on relevance and reliability.

In practical terms, in forming a judgement about a suitable accounting policy, management should refer to, and consider the applicability of, the following sources in descending order:

[IAS 8.11]

- requirements in IFRSs dealing with similar and related issues; and
- the definitions, recognition criteria and measurement concepts for assets, liabilities, income and expenses in the *Framework*.

This paragraph of IAS 8 was amended in May 2008 by *Improvements to IFRSs* to delete the reference to 'Guidance' for the reasons that are explained above.

IFRIC agenda decisions form an important source of guidance although they do not form part of IFRSs. Relevant agenda decisions should be carefully considered as indicative (but not definitive) guidance when selecting a suitable accounting policy for a transaction not specifically addressed by a Standard or Interpretation.

The most recent pronouncements of other standard-setting bodies that use a similar conceptual framework to develop accounting standards, accounting literature and accepted industry practices may also be considered, providing they do not conflict with the above sources. [IAS 8.12]

There is no similar specific statement in UK GAAP allowing entities to consider pronouncements of other standard-setting bodies when selecting a suitable accounting policy. In practice preparers of financial statements have sometimes looked to international standards and to US GAAP in the absence of relevant UK requirements.

UK

A more interesting issue concerns the extent to which UK entities reporting under IFRSs should continue to apply UK GAAP requirements when these do not conflict with IFRSs. Given that UK GAAP is based on a conceptual framework that is similar to the IASB's Framework, *it is likely that UK GAAP may provide helpful guidance in some instances. This would, however, be appropriate only where the relevant UK standard was consistent with the IASB* Framework.

Accounting policies should be applied consistently for similar transactions, other events and conditions, unless an IFRS specifically requires or permits categorisation of items for which different policies may be appropriate. If this is the case, an appropriate accounting policy should be selected and applied consistently to each category. [IAS 8.13]

IAS 27 requires that consistent accounting policies are applied within a group for the purposes of consolidated financial statements. [IAS 27(2008).24 & 25, previously IAS 27(2003).28 & 29] There is no such requirement for the individual financial statements of a parent and its subsidiaries.

In practice, most subsidiaries will choose to apply accounting policies that are applied by their parent because this will simplify the consolidation process. Also, the factors that determine the most appropriate policy for the group will often also determine that the same policy is the most appropriate for the subsidiary.

3.2 Changes in accounting policies

An accounting policy can be changed only if the change:

[IAS 8.14]

- is required by an IFRS; or
- results in the financial statements providing reliable and more relevant information about the effects of transactions, other events or conditions on the entity's financial position, financial performance or cash flows.

It is important that changes in accounting policies are only made if one of the above criteria is met; otherwise comparability over time within the financial statements will be lost. [IAS 8.15]

One consequence of this is that if a policy is changed in one year, it is unlikely to be justifiable to change it back to the original policy in a subsequent year. For example, an entity that used the 'corridor' under IAS 19 and then changed to a policy of immediate recognition of actuarial gains and losses in other comprehensive income would find it difficult to justify changing back again in a subsequent period. Similarly, it would be difficult to justify the adoption of a policy that would have to be changed again in a subsequent year because of a new Standard or an Interpretation that had been issued but was not yet effective at the date of the first change.

UK *Under UK GAAP, the Companies Act specifies that accounting policies should be applied consistently within the same accounts and from one financial year to the next, unless there are special reasons for departing from the principle. FRS 18 requires accounting policies to be reviewed regularly and changed whenever a new policy is judged more appropriate than the existing policy. However, FRS 18 notes that frequent changes to accounting policies will not enhance comparability over the longer term, and that accounting policies should not be changed unless the benefit to users outweighs the corresponding disadvantages. The Standard also notes that consistency is not an end in itself and it should not therefore impede the introduction of improved accounting practices that result in overall benefit to users. In practice the approach under IFRSs is similar to UK GAAP although the words are different.*

Example 3.2A

Early adoption of a new IFRS

Company M's reporting period ended on 31 December 20X1 and it has applied IFRSs for several years. On 15 January 20X2, a new final Standard was issued by the IASB that encourages early adoption. Company M will not issue its 20X1 financial statements until 1 March 20X2.

Can Company M apply this new final Standard issued after the reporting period, but prior to the issue of financial statements, to its 20X1 fiscal year?

Yes. Since the new final Standard allows for early adoption, Company M has the option to adopt the new final Standard in periods where financial statements have not yet been issued. If the new final Standard does not allow for early adoption, early application is not permitted.

Company M may not adopt exposure drafts or other guidance that has not been issued in its final form by the date of issue of its financial statements where this would conflict with the requirements of current IFRSs.

IAS 8.20 specifically provides that early application of an IFRS is not a voluntary change in accounting policy. Therefore, any specific transitional provisions in the new Standard should be applied for Company M's 20X1 fiscal year. If the new Standard does not include any specific transitional provisions relating to the change in accounting policy, the change should be applied retrospectively.

If the entity decides not to adopt the Standard in advance of its effective date, the requirements of IAS 8.30 apply (see **3.4.3** below).

UK

Under UK GAAP, FRS 18 notes that an entity may take account of a Financial Reporting Exposure Draft (FRED) in judging which accounting policies are most appropriate to its particular circumstances. But the standard is clear that an entity is not free to adopt an accounting policy based on a FRED unless the policy is consistent with the requirements of existing accounting standards and UITF Abstracts. Furthermore, the standard points out that there may be changes between a FRED and the ensuing standard and highlights the risk that this might lead to an entity having to make two successive changes in accounting policy. There is no equivalent guidance in IAS 8 but there is no reason why a similar approach would not be appropriate under IFRSs.

A UK company may be unable to adopt a new IFRS until it has been adopted for use in the EU where it would conflict with an existing IFRS (see ***1.2*** *in* ***chapter 1****). This may, in practice, prevent early adoption in some cases.*

Example 3.2B

Voluntary change in accounting policy for joint ventures

An entity is a first-time adopter in 20X1. In the 20X1 financial statements, the entity adopts an accounting policy of proportionate consolidation for its jointly controlled entities. In 20X3, the entity determines that the equity method would provide a reliable and more relevant presentation because most other entities in its business sector adopt the equity method. Therefore, it decides to make a voluntary change in its accounting policy.

As this is a voluntary change in accounting policy, the new accounting policy should be applied retrospectively for all jointly controlled entities (see **8.1** in **chapter 36**).

It should be noted that the application of an accounting policy to a transaction, other event or condition that differs in substance from those previously occurring in an entity does not qualify as a change in accounting policy. Equally, the application of a new accounting policy to a transaction, event or condition that had not previously occurred in an entity (or was previously immaterial) does not qualify as a change in accounting policy. [IAS 8.16]

Example 3.2C

Change in use of property

An entity owns an office building that has been classified as property, plant and equipment and accounted for under IAS 16 using the cost model. During the current year, management vacated the property and leased it out to a third party. The entity's accounting policy for its investment property under IAS 40 is to use the fair value model.

This change in use of the building does not result in a change of accounting policy. The entity's policies for each type of property remain unchanged but the property in question is accounted for as an investment property from the date when its use changed. No retrospective restatement is required in this situation.

IAS 8 states that the initial application of a policy to revalue assets in accordance with IAS 16 *Property, Plant and Equipment* or IAS 38 *Intangible Assets* is a change in accounting policy to be dealt with as a revaluation in accordance with those Standards rather than in accordance with IAS 8. IAS 8 also states that its requirements in paragraphs 19 to 31 do not apply to such changes in accounting policy. [IAS 8.17–18]

There is no further guidance in IAS 16 or IAS 38 on how such a change in accounting policy should be recognised or disclosed, but Example 3 in the Guidance on Implementing IAS 8 (see **3.3.1** below) notes that a change from the cost model to the revaluation model is required to be accounted for prospectively.

3.2.1 *Applying changes in accounting policies*

When an entity initially applies an IFRS, the change is accounted for in accordance with the specific transitional provisions of that IFRS. If the IFRS does not contain transitional provisions, the change is applied retrospectively. [IAS 8.19] Early application of a Standard does not constitute a voluntary change in accounting policy. [IAS 8.20]

If an entity changes an accounting policy voluntarily, the change is applied retrospectively. [IAS 8.19]

Example 3.2.1

Voluntary change in accounting policy and restatement of comparative figures

An entity adopts a voluntary change in accounting policy. Under national law it is a requirement to reconcile changes to the closing balance at the end of the immediate past year. Is this acceptable under IAS 8.19?

According to IAS 8.22, the change in accounting policy should be adjusted against the opening balance of each affected component of equity for the earliest period presented and the other comparative amounts. The reconciliation required by national law is also effectively required by IAS 8.29(c).

As noted in **section 3.1**, in the absence of an IFRS that applies to a specific transaction, other event or condition, the pronouncements of standard setters using a similar conceptual framework may be considered in selecting an appropriate accounting policy. If, following an amendment of such a pronouncement, an entity chooses to change an accounting policy, this change is accounted for, and disclosed as a voluntary change in accounting policy in accordance with IAS 8. [IAS 8.21] In other words, the entity may not apply any transitional provisions in the pronouncement of the other standard setter.

3.3 Retrospective application

Except when the impracticability exception discussed at **3.3.1** below applies, if retrospective application of an accounting policy is required by the criteria in **3.2.1** above, it is accounted for as follows:

[IAS 8.22]

- the opening balance of each affected component of equity for the earliest prior period presented is adjusted as if the new accounting policy had always been applied; and
- the other comparative amounts disclosed for each prior period presented are adjusted as if the new accounting policy had always been applied.

The adjustment made to the affected component of equity in the opening statement of financial position is the amount relating to periods before those presented in the financial statements and is usually made to retained earnings, but may be made to another component of equity, e.g. to comply with an IFRS. [IAS 8.26]

UK

Paragraph 26 of the standard also notes that any other information about prior periods, such as historical summaries of financial data, is also adjusted as far back as is practicable. However, in the UK, historical summaries do not usually form part of the financial statements and are therefore outside of the scope of this requirement. If the earlier periods in such summaries have not been restated, this should be made clear.

The following example is taken from the Implementation Guidance at IAS 8.IG 2.1–2.8. The example will cease to be applicable when the revised version of IAS 23 (see **chapter 27**) is adopted (and has been withdrawn as a consequential amendment arising from that revised Standard). It nevertheless provides a useful example of the principles involved even though the particular change of policy that is illustrated will no longer be possible.

Example 3.3

Change in accounting policy with retrospective application

[IAS 8 Implementation Guidance Example 2]

During 20X2, Gamma Co changed its accounting policy for the treatment of borrowing costs that are directly attributable to the acquisition of a hydro-electric power station under construction for use by Gamma. In previous periods, Gamma had capitalised such costs. Gamma has now decided to treat these costs as an expense, rather than capitalise them. Management judges that the new policy is preferable because it results in a more transparent treatment of finance costs and is consistent with local industry practice, making Gamma's financial statements more comparable.

Gamma capitalised borrowing costs incurred of CU2,600 during 20X1 and CU5,200 in periods before 20X1. All borrowing costs incurred in previous years in respect of the acquisition of the power station were capitalised.

Gamma's accounting records for 20X2 show profit before interest and income taxes of CU30,000; interest expense of CU3,000 (which relates only to 20X2); and income taxes of CU8,100. Gamma has not yet recognised any depreciation on the power station because it is not yet in use.

In 20X1, Gamma reported:

	CU
Profit before interest and income taxes	18,000
Interest expense	-
Profit before income taxes	18,000
Income taxes	(5,400)
Profit	12,600

20X1 opening retained earnings was CU20,000 and closing retained earnings was CU32,600. Gamma's tax rate was 30 per cent for 20X2, 20X1 and prior periods.

Gamma had CU10,000 of share capital throughout, and no other components of equity except for retained earnings. Its shares are not publicly traded and it does not disclose earnings per share.

Gamma Co
Extract from the income statement

	20X2	(restated) 20X1
	CU	CU
Profit before interest and income taxes	30,000	8,000
Interest expense	(3,000)	(2,600)
Profit before income taxes	27,000	15,400
Income taxes	(8,100)	(4,620)
Profit	18,900	10,780

Gamma Co
Statement of changes in equity

	Share capital	(restated) Retained earnings	Total
	CU	CU	CU
Balance at 31 December 20X0 as previously reported	10,000	20,000	30,000
Change in accounting policy for the capitalisation of interest (net of income taxes of CU1,560) (Note 1)	-	(3,640)	(3,640)
Balance as at 31 December 20X0 as restated	10,000	16,360	26,360
Profit for the year ended 31 December 20X1 (restated)	-	10,780	10,780
Balance at 31 December 20X1	10,000	27,140	37,140
Profit for the year ended 31 December 20X2	-	18,900	18,900
Balance at 31 December 20X2	10,000	46,040	56,040

Extracts from the Notes

During 20X2, Gamma changed its accounting policy for the treatment of borrowing costs related to a hydro-electric power station under construction for use by Gamma. Previously, Gamma capitalised such costs. They are now written off as expenses as incurred. Management judges that this policy provides reliable and more relevant information because it results in a more transparent treatment of finance costs and is consistent with local industry practice, making Gamma's financial statements more comparable. This change in accounting policy has been accounted for retrospectively, and the comparative statements for 20X1 have been restated. The effect of the change on 20X1 is tabulated below. Opening retained earnings for 20X1 have been reduced by CU3,640, which is the amount of the adjustment relating to periods prior to 20X1.

Effect on 20X1	**CU**
(Increase) in interest expense	(2,600)
Decrease in income tax expense	780
(Decrease) in profit	(1,820)
Effect on periods prior to 20X1	
(Decrease) in profit (CU5,200 interest expense less tax of CU1,560)	(3,640)
(Decrease) in assets in the course of construction and in retained earnings at 31 December 20X1	(5,460)

3.3.1 Limitations on retrospective application

When retrospective application of a change in accounting policy is required by paragraph 19 of IAS 8, the change is applied retrospectively except to the extent that it is impracticable to determine either the period-specific effects or the cumulative effect of the change. [IAS 8.23] The definition of 'impracticable' is considered at **2.8** above and further guidance is provided in **section 6** below.

The impracticability exemption applies both to voluntary changes in accounting policies and to those made in accordance with the transitional provisions made in a new or revised IFRS. This is a change from the previous version of IAS 8 which limited the exemption to voluntary changes in accounting policies. The IASB reconsidered this and decided that the need for the exemption applies equally to all changes in accounting policy. [IAS 8.BC29]

When it is impracticable to determine the period-specific effects of changing an accounting policy on comparative information for one or more prior periods presented, the new accounting policy is applied to the carrying amounts of assets and liabilities as at the beginning of the earliest period for which retrospective application is practicable. This may be the current period. Corresponding adjustments are made to the opening balance of each affected component of equity for that period. [IAS 8.24]

When a new policy is applied retrospectively, it is applied to comparative periods as far back as is practicable. Retrospective application to a prior period is not practicable unless it is practicable to determine the cumulative effect on the amounts in both the opening and closing statements of financial position for that period. [IAS 8.26]

When it is impracticable to determine the cumulative effect, at the beginning of the current period, of applying a new accounting policy to all prior periods, the comparative information is adjusted to apply the new accounting policy prospectively from the earliest date practicable. [IAS 8.25] That is to say the new policy is applied prospectively from the start of the earliest period practicable. The portion of the cumulative adjustment to assets, liabilities and equity arising before that date is therefore disregarded. Changing an accounting policy is permitted even if it is impracticable to apply the policy prospectively for any prior period. [IAS 8.27]

The following example is taken from the Implementation Guidance at IAS 8.IG 3.1–3.4.

Example 3.3.1

Prospective application of a change in accounting policy when retrospective application is not practicable

[IAS 8 Implementation Guidance Example 3]

During 20X2, Delta Co changed its accounting policy for depreciating property, plant and equipment, so as to apply much more fully a components approach, whilst at the same time adopting the revaluation model.

In years before 20X2, Delta's asset records were not sufficiently detailed to apply a components approach fully. At the end of 20X1, management commissioned an engineering survey, which provided information on the components held and their fair values, useful lives, estimated residual values and depreciable amounts at the beginning of 20X2. However, the survey did not provide a sufficient basis for reliably estimating the cost of those components that had not previously been accounted for separately, and the existing records before the survey did not permit this information to be reconstructed.

Delta's management considered how to account for each of the two aspects of the accounting change. They determined that it was not practicable to account for the change to a fuller components approach retrospectively, or to account for that change prospectively from any earlier date than the start of 20X2. Also, the change from a cost model to a revaluation model is required to be accounted for prospectively. Therefore, management concluded that it should apply Delta's new policy prospectively from the start of 20X2.

Additional information:

Delta's tax rate is 30 per cent.

	CU
Property, plant and equipment at the end of 20X1:	
Cost	25,000
Depreciation	(14,000)
Net book value	11,000
Prospective depreciation expense for 20X2 (old basis)	1,500
Some results of the engineering survey:	
Valuation	17,000
Estimated residual value	3,000
Average remaining asset life (years)	7

Depreciation expense on existing property, plant and equipment for 20X2 (new basis)	2,000

Extract from the notes

From the start of 20X2, Delta changed its accounting policy for depreciating property, plant and equipment, so as to apply much more fully a components approach, whilst at the same time adopting the revaluation model. Management takes the view that this policy provides reliable and more relevant information because it deals more accurately with the components of property, plant and equipment and is based on up-to-date values. The policy has been applied prospectively from the start of 20X2 because it was not practicable to estimate the effects of applying the policy either retrospectively, or prospectively from any earlier date. Accordingly, the adoption of the new policy has no effect on prior years. The effect on the current year is to increase the carrying amount of property, plant and equipment at the start of the year by CU6,000; increase the opening deferred tax provision by CU1,800; create a revaluation reserve at the start of the year of CU4,200; increase depreciation expense by CU500; and reduce tax expense by CU150.

3.4 Disclosure

3.4.1 Initial application of an IFRS

The requirements in this section apply on the initial application of an IFRS. They do not apply on first-time adoption of IFRSs in which case the disclosure requirements in IFRS 1 apply instead. But they do apply to early adoption of a new Standard which is not regarded as a voluntary change of policy for the purposes of IAS 8.

If the initial application of an IFRS:

- has an effect on the current period or any prior period; or
- would have such an effect except that it is impracticable to determine the amount of any adjustment; or
- may have an effect on future periods,

the following should be disclosed:

- the title of the IFRS;
- when applicable, that the change in accounting policy is made in accordance with its transitional provisions;
- the nature of the change in accounting policy;
- when applicable, a description of the transitional provisions;

- when applicable, the transitional provisions that might have an effect on future periods;
- for the current period and each prior period presented, to the extent practicable, the amount of the adjustment:
    - for each financial statement line item affected; and
    - if IAS 33 *Earning per Share* applies to the entity, for basic and diluted earnings per share;
- the amount of the adjustment relating to periods before those presented, to the extent practicable; and
- if retrospective application is impracticable for a particular prior period, or for periods before those presented, the circumstances that led to the existence of that condition and a description of how and from when the change in accounting policy has been applied.

Financial statements of subsequent periods need not repeat these disclosures. [IAS 8.28]

When adopting a new Standard or Interpretation with specific transitional provisions, the entity should still follow the disclosure requirements of IAS 8.28 to the extent that the transitional provisions do not override those requirements or make them inapplicable. For example, if a new Standard requires prospective application only, the disclosures concerning the amount of the adjustments and line items affected in prior periods will not be relevant.

These requirements are similar to those in FRS 18 although more detailed and extensive. The requirements to make the disclosures when the initial application of an IFRS 'may have an effect on future periods' will be new to UK companies adopting IFRSs for the first time and could easily be overlooked when there is no effect on the current or prior periods. UK

3.4.2 *Voluntary change in accounting policy*

Early adoption of a new IFRS is not a voluntary change in accounting policy for the purposes of IAS 8. [IAS 8.20] Therefore, the requirements at **3.4.1** apply to such changes instead of the requirements in this section.

When a voluntary change in accounting policy:

- has an effect on the current period or any prior period; or

- would have such an effect except that it is impracticable to determine the amount of any adjustment; or
- may have an effect on future periods,

the following should be disclosed:

- the nature of the change in accounting policy;
- the reasons why applying the new accounting policy provides reliable and more relevant information;
- for the current period and each prior period presented, to the extent practicable, the amount of the adjustment:
  - for each financial statement line item affected; and
  - if IAS 33 applies to the entity, for basic and diluted earnings per share;
- the amount of the adjustment relating to periods before those presented, to the extent practicable; and
- if retrospective application is impracticable for a particular prior period, or for periods before those presented, the circumstances that led to the existence of that condition and a description of how and from when the change in accounting policy has been applied.

Financial statements of subsequent periods need not repeat these disclosures. [IAS 8.29]

3.4.3 *Lack of implementation of a new Standard that is not yet effective*

When an entity has not applied a new Standard or an Interpretation that has been issued but is not yet effective, the following is disclosed by the entity:

[IAS 8.30]

- this fact; and
- known or reasonably estimable information relevant to assessing the possible impact that application of the new IFRS will have on the entity's financial statements in the period of initial application.

Example 3.4.3

Disclosure of the impact of IFRSs issued after the end of the reporting period

Does the disclosure requirement of IAS 8.30 apply to IFRSs issued before the date of issue of the financial statements, or only to IFRSs issued before the end of the reporting period?

Disclosure should be made in terms of IAS 8.30 in respect of all Standards or Interpretations issued before the date of issue of the financial statements.

UK

Although it has been regarded as good practice to make disclosures along these lines in the Operating and Financial Review, there is no requirement equivalent to this in UK GAAP. The extent to which it will be practicable to assess the impact of a new standard is likely to be influenced by the time interval between its publication and the approval of the relevant financial statements.

In complying with the general requirement of paragraph 30 of IAS 8, an entity should consider disclosing:

[IAS 8.31]

- the title of the new IFRS;
- the nature of the impending change or changes in accounting policy;
- the date by which application of the IFRS is required;
- the date as at which it plans to apply the IFRS initially; and
- either:
  - a discussion of the impact that initial application of the IFRS is expected to have on the entity's financial statements; or
  - if that impact is not known or reasonably estimable, a statement to that effect.

It is clear from BC31 in the Basis for Conclusions to IAS 8 that the matters listed in paragraph 31 of the Standard are not intended to be mandatory disclosure requirements. They are instead matters to be considered in applying paragraph 30. In particular, BC31 notes that the disclosure requirements are not intended to be more onerous than those of US GAAP. BC 31 also explains that the requirements in paragraph 30 were changed from the Exposure Draft to clarify that an entity need disclose information only if it is known or reasonably estimable.

The question arises of whether it is necessary for the financial statements to list every new or amended IFRS that has been issued but is not yet effective, even if it is expected to have no material effect on the reporting entity. The best approach is to provide a complete list because this clearly meets the requirements of the Standard and reduces the possibility that some new pronouncements will be overlooked.

However, a briefer disclosure may be acceptable in some cases. For example, it may be acceptable to not mention a pronouncement that plainly does not affect the reporting entity because of its scope. Another factor to consider is that where a new pronouncement has no material effect, it may be possible to adopt it early and so exclude it from the disclosures required by IAS 8.30.

Where a complete list is not provided, it may be wise to include a statement to the effect that the impact of all other IFRSs not yet adopted is not expected to be material.

This information should be given for pronouncements that have been issued by the date of approval of the financial statements. It will be helpful if the relevant note to the financial statements either specifies the date at which the details are given or refers explicitly to them being as at the date of authorisation of the financial statements.

UK

As explained in ***chapter 1****, new and amended IFRSs have to be adopted by the EU. Until adoption is effective, the new or amended requirements cannot be applied by UK entities to the extent that they are inconsistent with existing IFRSs. Therefore, at any time, there may be IFRSs that have been issued by the IASB but which UK entities are not free to adopt early.*

Within the context of EU-adopted IFRSs, it is possible to read IAS 8.30 as referring only to those IFRSs which have been adopted by the EU. However, it is preferable, for completeness, to list all of the IFRSs issued by the IASB which have not been adopted by the entity. Additional explanation could be provided to identify those that have not been adopted by the EU, although this should not usually be necessary. In any event, many UK companies claim compliance with IFRSs as issued by the IASB as well as compliance with EU-adopted IFRSs and therefore have to give the complete list.

4 Changes in accounting estimates

4.1 Identification of accounting estimates

The definition of changes in accounting estimates is set out at **2.2** above.

Accounting estimates arise from inherent uncertainties in business activities which mean that many items in financial statements cannot be measured with precision but can only be estimated. Estimates are formed using judgements based on the latest available, reliable information. Common examples of estimates in the financial statements include:

[IAS 8.32]

- allowances for bad debts;
- allowances for stock obsolescence;
- the fair value of financial assets or financial liabilities;
- the useful lives of, or the expected pattern of consumption of the future economic benefits embodied in, depreciable assets; and
- warranty obligations.

The use of reasonable estimates is essential in the preparation of financial statements. A revision of an estimate may be required if the circumstances on which the estimate was based change, or if new information or experience is gained. The revision of an estimate does not relate to prior periods and is not equivalent to the correction of an error. [IAS 8.34]

> *This treatment of a revision of an estimate is the same as the treatment under UK GAAP.*

UK

It should be noted that a change in the measurement basis applied to an item in the financial statements constitutes a change in accounting policy, not a change in accounting estimate. In cases where it is difficult to distinguish between a change in an accounting policy and a change in an accounting estimate, the change is treated as a change in an accounting estimate. [IAS 8.35]

> *There is no such default provision in UK GAAP favouring one treatment when it is difficult to distinguish between a change of policy and a change of estimate. But FRS 18 includes a lot of material on the distinction between accounting policies and estimation techniques which is not found in IAS 8.*

UK

4.2 Recognition of changes in accounting estimates

The effect of a change in an accounting estimate is recognised prospectively by including it in profit or loss in:

[IAS 8.36–38]

- the period of the change, if the change affects that period only (e.g. revision of a bad debts estimate); or
- the period of the change and future periods, if the change affects both (e.g. revision of the useful economic life of a depreciable asset).

Example 4.2

Change in estimate of a provision for a lawsuit

Should a change in the estimate of the outcome of a pending lawsuit be charged to the statement of comprehensive income in the year of the change?

Yes. Even though the original estimate of the outcome might have been made several years ago, and the case may continue for a considerable period of time, a change in the estimate of the outcome should be charged to the statement of comprehensive income in the period (year) of the change.

However, to the extent that a change in an accounting estimate gives rise to changes in assets and liabilities, or relates to an item of equity, it shall be recognised by adjusting the carrying amount of the related asset, liability or equity item in the period of the change. [IAS 8.37]

In other words, a change in accounting estimate need not be reported in profit or loss where it is appropriately reflected in the carrying value of other assets or liabilities, or taken directly to equity, in accordance with the requirements of other IFRSs.

When a change in an accounting estimate is recognised in profit or loss, the change should be recognised in the same line item as the underlying item. For example, if the best estimate of a provision for a legal claim is reduced downwards, the credit in profit or loss should be included within the expense heading where the original expense was recognised. This ensures that the cumulative amount charged under that heading is correct. If this causes a material distortion of the expense heading in question, additional disclosure may be required in accordance with IAS 1(2007).98 or IAS 1(2003).87 as appropriate (see **5.3.1** in **chapter 3**).

4.3 Disclosure

An entity discloses the nature and amount of a change in an accounting estimate that has an effect in the current period or is expected to have an effect in future periods. The disclosure of the effect on future periods need not be disclosed when it is impracticable to estimate that effect. [IAS 8.39]

If the amount of the effect in future periods is not disclosed because estimating it is impracticable, the entity should disclose this fact. [IAS 8.40]

UK

There is no direct equivalent of this requirement in UK GAAP. However, company law requires disclosure of the effect of any amounts relating to any preceding financial year included in any item in the profit and loss account. Also, where a change in an accounting estimate is material, it may fall within the definition of an exceptional item. The specific disclosure requirement in IAS 8 will lead to more frequent disclosure of the effect of changes of estimates than under UK GAAP.

5 Errors

5.1 Material errors

Financial statements do not comply with IFRSs if they contain either:

- material errors; or
- immaterial errors made intentionally in order to achieve a particular presentation of an entity's financial position, financial performance or cash flows.

The definition of 'material' for this purpose is considered at **2.4** above.

Errors can occur in respect of the recognition, measurement, presentation or disclosure of elements of the financial statements. [IAS 8.41]

Errors are distinguished from changes in accounting estimates because accounting estimates, by their very nature, are items which may need revision as additional information becomes known. For example, the gain or loss recognised on the outcome of a contingency is not the correction of an error. [IAS 8.48]

Although, in principle, the distinction between errors and corrections of estimates is clear, it may sometimes be difficult in practice to establish what information was available, or should have been available, at the time when an estimate was made.

5.2 Correction of errors

If a current period error is discovered before the financial statements are authorised for issue, it is corrected in that period. However, if a material error remains undetected until a subsequent period, the prior period error is corrected retrospectively in the first set of financial statements authorised for issue after its discovery. [IAS 8.41]

Except where it is impracticable to do so (see below), material prior period errors are corrected by:

[IAS 8.42]

- restating the comparative amounts for the prior period(s) presented in which the error occurred; or
- if the error occurred before the earliest prior period presented, restating the opening balances of assets, liabilities and equity for the earliest prior period presented.

The correction of the prior period error is excluded from the profit or loss in the period of discovery. [IAS 8.46]

The Standard does not differentiate between fundamental errors and other material prior period errors because the Board concluded that the definition of 'fundamental errors' in the previous version was difficult to interpret consistently as the main feature of the definition – that the error causes the financial statement of one of more prior periods no longer to be considered to have been reliable – was also a feature of all material prior period errors. [IAS 8.BC12]

UK

This is a significant difference from the requirements of UK GAAP. Under UK GAAP, a prior period adjustment is made only for a change in accounting policy, or for a fundamental error. A fundamental error is defined by FRS 3 as an error of such significance as to destroy the true and fair view and hence the validity of the financial statements. IAS 8 states prior period adjustments are made for material errors, i.e. the error does not need to be fundamental.

IAS 8 refers to the correction of material prior period errors by retrospective restatement but does not say that *only* material errors may be corrected in this way. It is silent on the correction of immaterial errors which is consistent with the fact that IFRSs do not apply to immaterial items. Nevertheless, the explicit reference to 'material' in IAS 8.42 suggests that only material errors should be corrected in this way. This is the way in which the requirement is normally interpreted.

A prior period error is corrected by retrospective restatement, except to the extent that it is impracticable to determine either:

[IAS 8.43]

- the period-specific effects; or
- the cumulative effect of the error.

The definition of 'impracticable' is considered at **2.8** above and further guidance is provided in **section 6** below.

If it is impracticable to determine the period-specific effects of an error on comparative information for one or more prior periods presented, the opening balances of assets, liabilities and equity are restated for the earliest period for which retrospective restatement is practicable. This may be the current period. [IAS 8.44]

If it is impracticable to determine the cumulative effect on all prior periods of a prior period error at the beginning of the current period, the comparative information is restated to correct the error prospectively from the earliest date practicable. [IAS 8.45] The entity therefore disregards the portion of the cumulative restatement of assets, liabilities and equity arising before that date. [IAS 8.47]

Paragraph 46 of the standard also notes that any other information about prior periods, such as historical summaries of financial data, is also adjusted as far back as is practicable. However, in the UK, historical summaries do not usually form part of the financial statements and are therefore outside of the scope of this requirement. If the earlier periods in such summaries have not been restated, this should be made clear. UK

5.3 Disclosure of prior period errors

When a material prior period error is corrected in accordance with IAS 8, the following should be disclosed:

- the nature of the prior period error;
- for each prior period presented, to the extent practicable, the amount of the correction:

  - for each financial statement line item affected; and
  - if IAS 33 applies to the entity, for basic and diluted earnings per share;
- the amount of the correction at the beginning of the earliest prior period presented; and
- if retrospective restatement is impracticable for a particular prior period, the circumstances that led to the existence of that condition and a description of how and from when the error has been corrected.

Financial statements of subsequent periods need not repeat these disclosures. [IAS 8.49]

6 Impracticability in respect of retrospective application and retrospective restatement

6.1 Obstacles faced in retrospective application and restatement

Impracticable is defined in **section 2.8**. It may be impracticable to adjust comparative information for one or more prior periods to achieve comparability with the current period. This may be the case because data was not collected in the prior period(s) in a way that allows either retrospective application of a new accounting policy, or retrospective restatement to correct a prior period error, and it may be impracticable to recreate the information. [IAS 8.50]

Restatement is not impracticable just because of the cost or effort involved. When revising IAS 8 in 2003, the IASB considered replacing the exemption with one based on 'undue cost or effort'. However, based on comments received on the Exposure Draft, the IASB decided that an exemption based on management's assessment of undue cost or effort was too subjective to be applied consistently by different entities. The IASB decided that balancing costs and benefits was a task for the Board when it sets accounting requirements rather than for entities when they apply those requirements. The Standard does not explicitly state that undue cost or effort in itself will not make restatement impracticable. But this is the clear intention of the Board and is consistent with the definition in the Standard. [IAS 8.BC24]

6.1.1 *Estimates*

It is often necessary to make estimates in applying an accounting policy to elements of financial statements recognised or disclosed in respect of transactions, other events or conditions. Estimation is inherently subjective, and estimates may be developed after the reporting period.

Furthermore, developing estimates is potentially more difficult when retrospectively applying an accounting policy or making a retrospective restatement to correct a prior period error, because of the longer period of time that might have passed since the affected transaction, other event or condition occurred. However, the objective of estimates relating to prior periods remains the same as for estimates made in the current period, i.e. for the estimate to reflect the circumstances that existed *when the transaction, other event or condition occurred.* [IAS 8.51]

As explained at **2.8** above, it may sometimes be impracticable to distinguish information that:

- provides evidence of circumstances that existed on the date(s) as at which the transaction, other event or condition occurred; and
- would have been available when the financial statements for that period were authorised for issue,

from other information. [IAS 8.52]

Nevertheless, IAS 8 notes that the fact that significant estimates are frequently required when amending comparative information presented for prior periods does not prevent reliable adjustment or correction of the comparative information. [IAS 8.53]

6.2 Hindsight

Hindsight should not be used when applying a new accounting policy to, or correcting amounts for, a prior period, either in making assumptions about what management's intentions would have been in a prior period or estimating the amounts recognised, measured or disclosed in a prior period.

For example, when an entity corrects a prior period error in measuring financial assets previously classified as held-to-maturity investments in accordance with IAS 39 *Financial Instruments: Recognition and Measurement*, it does not change their basis of measurement for that period if management decided later not to hold them to maturity.

A second example given in IAS 8 is that of an entity's calculation of its liability for employees' accumulated sick leave in accordance with IAS 19 *Employee Benefits*. When correcting a prior period error in relation to this calculation, the entity disregards information about an unusually severe influenza season during the next period that became available after the financial statements for the prior period were authorised for issue. [IAS 8.53]

5 First-time adoption of IFRSs

1 Introduction

IFRS 1 was published in June 2003 and has subsequently been amended numerous times as a consequence of other new and amended standards. As part of its annual improvements project, the IASB published proposals to restructure IFRS 1. The main change proposed is to remove some transitional provisions relating to particular IFRSs from the main body of the IFRS to appendices. The restructuring will not alter the technical content of IFRS 1. However, some transitional provisions will be removed as they are no longer relevant.

This chapter does not address the restructured Standard which had not been published in final form at the time of writing. However, some of the provisions of IFRS 1 that are no longer relevant have been omitted from the chapter or mentioned only briefly.

The objective of IFRS 1 is to ensure that an entity's first-time IFRS financial statements (and interim financial reports for part of the period covered by those financial statements) contain high quality information that:

[IFRS 1.1]

- is transparent for users and comparable over all periods presented;
- provides a suitable starting point for accounting under IFRSs; and
- can be generated at a cost that does not exceed the benefits to users.

This chapter discusses the requirements of IFRS 1 in the following sections:

Section 2	Definitions
Section 3	Scope
Section 4	Opening IFRS statement of financial position
Section 5	Accounting policies
Section 6	Exemptions from other IFRSs
Section 7	Exceptions to retrospective application of other IFRSs

Section 8 Presentation and disclosure

Section 9 Effective date

Section 10 Future developments

The requirements of IFRS 1 for financial instruments are set out in **chapter 22** and not repeated in this chapter.

The Standard should be applied by an entity in its first IFRS financial statements. It should also be applied in each interim financial report, if any, that an entity presents under IAS 34 *Interim Financial Reporting* for part of the period covered by its first IFRS financial statements. [IFRS 1.2]

IFRS 1 applies when an entity adopts IFRSs for the first time by an explicit and unreserved statement of compliance with IFRSs. [IFRS 1.IN1] This is considered in detail in **section 3** below.

UK

UK listed companies will generally have made such a statement for the first time for the first reporting period beginning on or after 1 January 2005. Other UK companies may make such a statement at a later date when they choose, or are required, to report under IFRSs. For example, AIM companies are required by the AIM Rules to use IFRSs for their consolidated financial statements for periods beginning on or after 1 January 2007.

IFRS 1 generally requires an entity to comply with each IFRS effective at the end of the reporting period for its first IFRS financial statements. In the opening IFRS statement of financial position (at the beginning of the earliest period for which an entity presents full comparative information under IFRSs) an entity should:

[IFRS 1.10]

- recognise all assets and liabilities whose recognition is required by IFRSs;
- not recognise items as assets or liabilities if IFRSs do not permit such recognition;
- reclassify items that it recognised under previous GAAP as one type of asset, liability or component of equity, but are a different asset, liability or component of equity under IFRSs; and
- apply IFRSs in measuring all recognised assets and liabilities.

These requirements are dealt with in **sections 4** and **5** below.

IFRS 1 grants limited exemptions from these requirements in specified areas where the cost of complying with them would be likely to exceed the benefits to users of financial statements (see **section 6** below). The IFRS also prohibits retrospective application of IFRSs in some areas, particularly where retrospective application would require judgements by management about past conditions after the outcome of a particular transaction is already known (see **section 7** below). [IFRS 1.IN4]

IFRS 1 also requires disclosures that explain how the transition from previous GAAP to IFRSs affected the entity's reported financial position, financial performance and cash flows (see **section 8** below). [IFRS 1.IN5]

IFRS 1 has been amended by the many subsequent IFRSs and amendments to IFRSs. References in this chapter are to IFRS 1 as amended, except where the context requires otherwise.

The IASB has published Implementation Guidance which accompanies, but is not part of, IFRS 1. This chapter follows the structure of IFRS 1 but incorporates the material in the Implementation Guidance, where relevant, under the appropriate headings.

2 Definitions

Appendix A to IFRS 1, which is an integral part of the IFRS, contains defined terms that are used in the Standard. This section sets out those definitions with additional explanation as necessary.

2.1 Date of transition to IFRSs

The date of transition to IFRSs is defined as:

> 'The beginning of the earliest period for which an entity presents full comparative information under IFRSs in its first IFRS financial statements.' [IFRS 1(Appendix A)]

The date is of particular significance because it is the date at which an entity prepares its opening IFRS statement of financial position (see **section 4** below).

> The reference to 'full comparative information under IFRSs' in the definition is significant. An entity with a December year end could therefore treat 1 January 20X2 as its date of transition to IFRSs while presenting 'additional' 20X1 comparatives under local GAAP.

Complications arise when there is a change to the end of the reporting period. For example, suppose that an entity changes the end of its reporting period to 31 December 20X2 when the end of its most recent reporting period was 31 March 20X2. The entity will adopt IFRSs for the first time in its 31 December 20X3 financial statements and present one comparable period. Although it might be thought that the entity's date of transition is 1 April 20X2, IFRS 1 is not completely clear on this point.

IFRS 1 states that to comply with IAS 1 'an entity's first IFRS financial statements should include at least one year of comparative information under IFRSs' (emphasis added). IAS 1 requires that comparative information for the previous period should be presented. Furthermore, IAS 1 does not require the comparable period to be one year when there is a change in the reporting period. The Basis for Conclusions to IFRS 1 discusses the IASB's reasons for not requiring an additional comparative period to that required by IAS 1. IFRS 1.BC86 states that the IASB did not intend to 'require a first-time adopter to present more comparative information than IAS 1 requires, because such a requirement would impose costs out of proportion to the benefits to users'. Given the reference to the requirements of IAS 1 in IFRS 1, it was not the intent of the IASB to impose requirements in excess of those of IAS 1 through using the term 'one year' in paragraph 36 of IFRS 1. Therefore, the entity can use 1 April 20X2 as its date of transition. However, it does have the option under IAS 1 to restate the comparable period by using 1 January 20X2 as its date of transition. This restatement may be required by certain regulatory regimes.

UK *For a UK company, restating the length of the comparative period would be inconsistent with the requirements of company law.*

2.2 Deemed cost

Deemed cost is defined as:

[IFRS 1(Appendix A)]

> 'An amount used as a surrogate for cost or depreciated cost at a given date. Subsequent depreciation or amortisation assumes that the entity had initially recognised the asset or liability at the given date and that its cost was equal to the deemed cost'.

The use of fair value or a previous revaluation as deemed cost on transition to IFRSs is considered at **6.2** below.

2.3 Fair value

Fair value is defined as:

[IFRS 1(Appendix A)]

> 'The amount for which an asset could be exchanged, or a liability settled, between knowledgeable, willing parties in an arm's length transaction.'

2.4 First IFRS financial statements

The first IFRS financial statements are:

[IFRS 1(Appendix A)]

> 'The first annual financial statements in which an entity adopts International Financial Reporting Standards (IFRSs), by an explicit and unreserved statement of compliance with IFRSs.'

The meaning of an 'explicit and unreserved statement of compliance with IFRSs' is considered in **section 3** below.

2.5 First IFRS reporting period

The first IFRS reporting period is:

[IFRS 1(Appendix A)]

> 'The latest reporting period covered by an entity's first IFRS financial statements.'

> This definition is as amended by IAS 1(2007) although the amendment did not change the substance of the definition.

2.6 First-time adopter

A first-time adopter is:

[IFRS 1(Appendix A)]

> 'An entity that presents its first IFRS financial statements.'

2.7 International Financial Reporting Standards (IFRSs)

International Financial reporting Standards are defined as:

[IFRS 1(Appendix A)]

> 'Standards and Interpretations adopted by the International Accounting Standards Board (IASB). They comprise:
>
> - International Financial Reporting Standards;
> - International Accounting Standards; and
> - Interpretations developed by the International Financial Reporting Interpretations Committee (IFRIC) or the former Standing Interpretations Committee (SIC).'

2.8 Opening IFRS statement of financial position

An opening IFRS statement of financial position is:

[IFRS 1(Appendix A)]

> 'An entity's statement of financial position at the date of transition to IFRSs.'

The above definition is as amended by IAS 1(2007). Prior to the amendment, IFRS 1 included a definition of an entity's opening IFRS balance sheet which was similar, although it clarified that the opening IFRS balance sheet might be 'published or unpublished'. This is not relevant to entities applying IAS 1(2007). The requirement to present three statements of financial position will ensure that the statement at the date of transition to IFRSs will always be published.

2.9 Previous GAAP

Previous GAAP is:

[IFRS 1(Appendix A)]

> 'The basis of accounting that a first-time adopter used immediately before adopting IFRSs.'

An entity may have previously prepared two complete sets of financial statements under different GAAPs. For example, a UK company may have prepared its statutory financial statements under

UK GAAP and, in addition, prepared a complete set of US GAAP financial statements because it has a listing in the US.

In such cases, it is for management to determine, in accordance with its regulatory environment, whether to transition from the statutory financial statements (under local GAAP) or from the other set of financial statements it has presented. The determination of which GAAP is previous GAAP is subject to the following:

- an entity cannot have more than one set of IFRS financial statements. Therefore, it must have only one starting point for transition to IFRSs (albeit that it may choose to reconcile between this starting point and another previously used accounting framework);
- under IFRSs, management has a free choice in identifying its previous GAAP. However, such a free choice may be eliminated by the regulatory regimes within which it operates; and
- the choice of previous GAAP must be a reasonable one (i.e. previous financial statements prepared for a specific purpose with limited circulation would not be an appropriate starting point when compared with the financial statements prepared for circulation to the entity's main user groups).

2.10 Reporting date

Prior to its amendment by IAS 1(2007), IFRS 1 defined the reporting date as:

[IFRS 1(Appendix A)]

> 'The end of the latest period covered by financial statements or by an interim financial report.'

This definition is no longer relevant as a consequence of the amendment to the definition of the 'first IFRS reporting period' which no longer includes this expression (see **2.5** above).

IAS 1(2007) replaced all references to 'reporting date' in IFRSs with references to 'end of the reporting period'.

3 Scope

An entity should apply IFRS 1 in:

[IFRS 1.2]

- its first IFRS financial statements; and
- each interim financial report, if any, that it presents under IAS 34 *Interim Financial Reporting* for part of the period covered by its first IFRS financial statements.

UK

> *The Disclosure and Transparency Rules require UK listed companies which prepare consolidated accounts to prepare their interim reports in accordance with IAS 34 for annual periods beginning on or after 20 January 2007. AIM companies are not covered by these requirements.*

An entity's first IFRS financial statements are the first annual financial statements in which the entity adopts IFRSs, by an explicit and unreserved statement, in those financial statements, of compliance with IFRSs. [IFRS 1.3]

IFRS 1 indicates that financial statements under IFRSs are an entity's first IFRS financial statements if, for example, the entity presented its most recent previous financial statements:

[IFRS 1.3(a)]

- under national requirements that are not consistent with IFRSs in all respects;
- in conformity with IFRSs in all respects, except that the financial statements did not contain an explicit and unreserved statement that they complied with IFRSs;
- containing an explicit statement of compliance with some, but not all, IFRSs;
- under national requirements inconsistent with IFRSs, using some individual IFRSs to account for items for which national requirements did not exist; or
- under national requirements, with a reconciliation of some amounts to the amounts determined under IFRSs.

Further examples given in IFRS 1 of when financial statements under IFRSs are an entity's first IFRS financial statements are when the entity:

[IFRS 1.3(b) – (d)]

- prepared financial statements under IFRSs for internal use only, without making them available to the entity's owners or any other external users;
- prepared a reporting package under IFRSs for consolidation purposes without preparing a complete set of financial statements as defined in IAS 1; or
- did not present financial statements for previous periods.

IFRS 1 also gives examples of when it does not apply. These are when an entity:

[IFRS 1.4]

- stops presenting financial statements under national requirements, having previously presented them as well as another set of financial statements that contained an explicit and unreserved statement of compliance with IFRSs;
- presented financial statements in the previous year under national requirements and those financial statements contained an explicit and unreserved statement of compliance with IFRSs; or
- presented financial statements in the previous year that contained an explicit and unreserved statement of compliance with IFRSs, even if the auditors qualified their audit report on those financial statements.

Some commentators on ED 1 suggested that the test imposed in the ED was too rigid and that an entity should not be regarded as a first-time adopter if its previous financial statements contained a statement of compliance with IFRSs except for some specified and explicit departures. This argument might be particularly strong where the departures related to disclosure only. But the IASB considered this and noted that to implement such an approach, it would be necessary to establish how many departures are needed, and how serious they must be, before an entity would conclude that it had not adopted IFRSs. Therefore, the IASB decided that the Standard should contain a simple test that gives an unambiguous answer. [IFRS 1.BC5]

IFRS 1 does not apply to changes in accounting policies made by an entity that already applies IFRSs. Such changes are subject to the requirements of IAS 8 (see **chapter 4**) and specific transitional requirements in other IFRSs. [IFRS 1.5]

The following examples illustrate some of these scenarios.

Example 3A

Compliance with all IFRSs

Company A issued financial statements stating compliance with all IFRSs, and with an unqualified audit opinion, in 20X1. In 20X2, Company A's auditors note that certain disclosure requirements of IAS 1 were omitted, in error, from the 20X1 financial statements. Is Company A within the scope of IFRS 1?

No. While Company A should not have claimed unreserved compliance with IFRSs for its 20X1 financial statements, these financial statements have already been considered IFRS compliant and relied upon as such. Therefore, any errors are accounted for in accordance with IAS 8.

Example 3B

Reserved compliance

An entity explicitly stated its reserved compliance with all IFRSs in its most recent previous financial statements. Is the entity a first-time adopter?

The entity becomes a first-time adopter when its financial statements first contain an explicit and unreserved statement of compliance with IFRSs. The following would not be considered unreserved statements of compliance:

- compliant with local GAAP, which is consistent with or similar to IFRSs; or
- compliant with IFRSs, except certain IFRSs.

Example 3C

External users

Is an entity a first-time adopter if it prepares a supplementary set of its most recent previous financial statements stating compliance with IFRSs, but only distributes these financial statements to a select group of users, such as a financial institution?

No. If financial statements stating compliance with IFRSs have been issued externally, regardless of the extent of distribution, those financial statements prevent the entity from being regarded as a first-time adopter. The same would apply if the entity prepared a separate set of IFRS financial statements for a commercial transaction that was issued to counterparties.

Example 3D

Compliant with IFRSs in previous years but not the most recent one

Company B issued financial statements in 20X1 and 20X2 with an unreserved statement of compliance with IFRSs. In 20X3, Company B only issued financial statements compliant with local GAAP. Is Company B a first-time adopter in 20X4?

Yes. IFRS 1 requires that an entity's most recent previous financial statements be in compliance with IFRSs. The movement from IFRSs to local GAAP is seen as a departure from reporting under IFRSs, that would change the carrying amounts of assets and liabilities. Therefore, the provisions of IFRS 1 must be applied to the first subsequent financial statements stating compliance with IFRSs, even if this adoption is not 'first-time'.

UK

Most of the circumstances described above will not be relevant to UK companies. Where a UK company adopts IFRSs for its financial statements, those financial statements will normally contain an explicit and unreserved statement of compliance with IFRSs and no such statement will have been made previously. Therefore, they will be its first IFRS financial statements and IFRS 1 will apply.

Some UK companies will have previously prepared financial statements under IFRSs for internal use only, without making them available to the company's owners or any other external users. More commonly, they may have prepared a reporting package under IFRSs for consolidation purposes without preparing a complete set of financial statements as defined in IAS 1. These circumstances will not prevent the company being a first-time adopter and IFRS 1 will apply.

In very rare cases, a UK company might have prepared and made available to external parties a supplementary set of financial statements including an explicit and unreserved statement of compliance with IFRSs. Such a company would not be a first-time adopter and could not apply IFRS 1 when adopting IFRSs for statutory reporting purposes. As explained in **example 3C** *above, this would apply regardless of the extent of distribution of those financial statements.*

If a UK company departed from a requirement of an IFRS in its first IFRS financial statements, it would not be able to make an unreserved statement of compliance with IFRSs. It would therefore not be within the scope of IFRS 1. The implication of this is that it would not be able to use any of the exemptions in IFRS 1 and would have to prepare the financial statements as if it had always reported under IFRSs taking into account previous versions of standards and their transitional provisions. However, a qualified audit report which referred to non-compliance with IFRSs would not prevent a company applying IFRS 1 provided that the directors had made an explicit and unreserved statement of compliance with IFRSs. That is to say that if there is a disagreement between the directors and the auditors about the application or interpretation of a standard, it is the view of the directors that prevails for the purposes of applying IFRS 1.

A specific issue may arise in the UK through the use of the EU-endorsed version of IAS 39. A company that had complied with the EU-endorsed version of the standard but not with the 'full' version issued by the IASB would not be able to make an unreserved statement of compliance with IFRSs. The European Commission has issued a statement that contains the following comment on this issue:

> *'IFRS 1, which was adopted under Commission Regulation No 707/2004, requires in principle companies to comply with each IAS/IFRS at the reporting date for its first IFRS financial statements, but grants limited exemptions in specified areas. This standard is therefore of major importance for the great majority of listed European companies which do not yet report according to IAS/IFRS before 2005.* ***Those companies which apply IAS 39 — as endorsed with the two carve outs under the present Regulation — can still make use of the exemptions under IFRS 1*** *[emphasis added] because the reasoning is exactly the same: IFRS 1 should help "first time adopters" since the costs for complying with full IAS/IFRS will outweigh the benefits for the users of financial statements of such companies. As the two carve outs under IAS 39 are as limited as possible in substance and in time and the issues are likely to be resolved during 2005, it would be disproportionate in terms of costs for companies to take away the advantages granted under IFRS 1 whilst not offering any advantages to users of financial statements. Recital 12 [to the Regulation endorsing IAS 39] expressly confirms this.'*

This is of less relevance now than when it was issued because the IASB amended IAS 39 in respect of the 'fair value option'. The amended version of IAS 39 was subsequently adopted by the EU so that one of the 'carve-outs' has fallen away. The second 'carve-out', which relates to hedge accounting, still exists but has been used by very few UK companies. Nevertheless, this guidance may have continuing relevance if other differences develop between IFRSs as adopted by the EU and those issued by the IASB.

In December 2004 the UK ASB issued guidance on the application of IAS 39 by entities preparing their financial statements in accordance with EU-adopted IFRSs. This guidance refers to uncertainties concerning the status of the above statement made by the European Commission. It concludes, however, that an entity can avoid these uncertainties by complying from the outset with both the original and endorsed versions of the standard and states that the ASB's advice to entities is to do that.

4 Opening IFRS statement of financial position

An entity should prepare and present an opening IFRS statement of financial position (see **2.8** above) at the date of transition to IFRSs (see **2.1** above). This is the starting point for its accounting under IFRSs. [IFRS 1.6]

For entities that are not applying IAS 1(2007), there is no requirement to publish the opening IFRS balance sheet in the first IFRS financial statements. [IFRS 1.6]

IAS 1(2007) amended IFRS 1 to delete the reference to there being no requirement to publish the opening IFRS balance sheet. This is a consequence of the amendment made to IAS 1 to require a third statement of financial position, at the beginning of the earliest comparative period, when an entity applies an accounting policy retrospectively or makes a retrospective restatement or reclassification.

Although, for those entities not applying IAS 1(2007), there is no requirement to publish the opening IFRS balance sheet, IFRS 1 requires a reconciliation of reported equity under previous GAAP to equity under IFRSs at the date of transition (see **8.2.1** below). If this reconciliation is presented along the lines illustrated in the IFRS 1 Implementation Guidance (IG Example 11), the effect will be to present the opening IFRS balance sheet alongside the previous GAAP balance sheet using a columnar layout. But there are other ways of meeting the reconciliation requirement, for example by simply presenting a list of reconciling items between equity under previous GAAP and equity under IFRSs.

5 Accounting policies

5.1 General

IFRS 1 requires an entity to use the same accounting policies in its opening IFRS statement of financial position and throughout all periods presented in its first IFRS financial statements. Those accounting policies must comply with each IFRS effective at the end of its first IFRS reporting period, subject to exemptions and exceptions that are explained in **section 6** and **section 7** below. [IFRS 1.7]

An entity may not therefore apply different versions of IFRSs that were effective at earlier dates. However, new IFRSs that are not yet mandatory may be applied if they permit early adoption. [IFRS 1.8]

The transitional provisions in other IFRSs apply to changes in accounting policies made by entities that already use IFRSs. They do not apply to a first-time adopter's transition to IFRSs except in certain specified circumstances that are explained in **section 6** and **section 7** below. [IFRS 1.9]

For example, an entity with a 31 March year end prepares its first IFRS financial statements at 31 March 20X3. It presents a single year of comparative figures. The entity's date of transition to IFRSs is therefore 1 April 20X1.

The entity applies all of those IFRSs that are effective for years beginning on or before 1 April 20X2 (i.e. those that are effective at the end of its reporting period) and ignores any transitional provisions in those IFRSs except where IFRS 1 specifies that they should be applied. Those IFRSs should be applied in preparing the opening statement of financial position at 1 April 20X1, the comparative statement of financial position at 31 March 20X2 and the statement of financial position at 31 March 20X3 in accordance with IFRSs. The entity is permitted but not required to apply any new IFRSs that have been issued but are not mandatory at the end of the reporting period provided that the IFRSs in question permit early adoption.

Subject to the exemptions and exceptions described in **sections 6** and **7** below, an entity should, in its opening IFRS statement of financial position:

[IFRS 1.10]

- recognise all assets and liabilities whose recognition is required by IFRSs;
- not recognise items as assets or liabilities if IFRSs do not permit such recognition;
- reclassify items that it recognised under previous GAAP as one type of asset, liability or component of equity, but are a different type of asset, liability or component of equity under IFRSs; and
- apply IFRSs in measuring all recognised assets and liabilities.

The adjustments arising from this restatement of the opening statement of financial position from previous GAAP to IFRSs should be recognised as an adjustment to retained earnings or, if appropriate, another category of equity, at the date of transition to IFRSs. [IFRS 1.11]

The following sections deal only with those IASs and IFRSs where IFRS 1, or its Implementation Guidance, has specific requirements or guidance.

5.2 IAS 12 *Income Taxes*

Under IAS 12, the measurement of current and deferred tax reflects tax rates and tax laws that have been enacted or substantively enacted by the end of the reporting period. The effect of changes in tax rates and tax laws are accounted for when those changes are enacted or substantively enacted. [IFRS 1.IG6]

This is similar to UK GAAP under FRS 16 and FRS 19. Therefore, although the amount of deferred tax provided may be different under IFRSs, any changes to tax rates and tax laws should be reflected in the same period as would have been required under UK GAAP. UK

IAS 12 *Income Taxes* should be applied to temporary differences between the carrying amount of the assets and liabilities in the opening IFRS statement of financial position and their tax bases. [IFRS 1.IG5]

IAS 12 provides an exemption from recognising deferred tax when the initial recognition is not the result of a business combination and affects neither accounting profit nor taxable profit. The requirement to recognise deferred taxes on transition to IFRSs does not eliminate the initial recognition exemption in IAS 12. In restating deferred taxes under IAS12, an entity identifies whether a temporary difference arose on the initial recognition of the asset or liability. In such cases, the requirements of paragraphs 15 and 24 of IAS 12 still apply and no deferred tax is provided. In all other cases, the requirements of IFRS 1 to recognise deferred tax should be applied.

The following examples illustrate the application of this requirement. Further examples concerning deferred tax on business combinations before the date of transition to IFRSs are provided at **6.1.12** below.

Example 5.2A

Deferred tax when valuation used as deemed cost

Entity G is adopting IFRSs for the first time. The entity has previously purchased land for £100. Under its previous GAAP the entity revalued the land to £120, but did not recognise any deferred tax in respect of this revaluation. The entity decides to get a valuation of the land at transition date and uses this value, £150, as the deemed cost in accordance with IFRS 1.16. Part of the purchase price (£10) is disallowable as a deduction by the local taxation authorities, and accordingly the asset has a tax base at the date of purchase and the date of transition of £90. The tax rate in the local jurisdiction is 30 per cent. The initial recognition exemption applies to the disallowable expenditure of £10. There is no temporary difference between the remainder of the initial cost and the tax base (both £90). On the date of transition Entity G will recognise a deferred tax liability of £15 [(150 – 100)*30%] being the deferred tax in respect of the difference between deemed cost and initial cost (£50).

Example 5.2B

Deferred tax on intangible asset recognised on transition

Entity X recognised, on application of IFRS 1, an intangible asset relating to development expenditure which was not acquired in a business combination. The expenditure had, under previous GAAP, been expensed for accounting purposes, but did not affect taxable profits at the time of the transaction (50 per cent was allowed for tax purposes over a period of five years). Had the intangible asset been recognised under IFRSs from the outset, a temporary difference would have arisen initially, and the transaction (restated to comply with IFRSs) would have affected neither taxable nor accounting profits at that date. In these circumstances, the exemption in IAS 12.15 applies, and Entity X is not required to recognise deferred tax in relation to this temporary difference.

Entity X may still, however, be required to account for any temporary differences which have subsequently arisen (between initial transaction date and the date of transition to IFRSs) as a result of differences between accounting amortisation and the tax write off period.

Example 5.2C

Deferred tax asset not recognised under previous GAAP

Company X (X) is a first-time adopter in 20X4. Under local GAAP, deferred taxes were provided based on timing differences. In 20X1, by means of an internal group re-organisation that had no effect for financial reporting purposes, X created, in the books of a subsidiary, an asset for tax purposes that will be deductible in the tax return over three years. This asset is not recognised for financial reporting purposes, and does not meet any asset recognition criteria under IFRSs. Hence, the asset will not be recognised on first-time adoption.

In its first IFRS consolidated financial statements, X should recognise a deferred tax asset at the date of transition to IFRSs for the net carrying amount of the tax asset that arose in 20X1. A temporary difference exists and a deferred tax asset should be recognised in the group's consolidated financial statements. The initial charge is an adjustment on first-time adoption of IFRSs and so will be recognised in retained earnings. Subsequent changes in the amount of the deferred tax asset will be taken to profit or loss.

IAS 12 *Income Taxes* paragraphs 9 and 17 provide examples of one type of temporary difference (i.e. 'timing differences'). However, IAS 12 is, overall, driven by a statement of financial position approach, irrespective of whether an expense or income has previously been recognised in the statement of comprehensive income (or any separate income statement presented in accordance with IAS 1(2007).81(b)), such that the comparison should follow a statement of financial position analysis of the tax consequences on settlement (i.e. deferred tax is recognised on the difference between the tax base and the carrying amount for accounting purposes). If a tax base of an asset exists for tax purposes and no asset exists for accounting purposes, the carrying amount of that asset or liability should be deemed to be zero.

5.3 IAS 16 *Property, Plant and Equipment*

If an entity's depreciation methods and rates under previous GAAP are acceptable under IFRSs, it accounts for any change in estimated useful life or depreciation pattern prospectively from when it makes that change in estimate. This is consistent with the requirements of IFRS 1 on changes of estimates and with paragraph 61 of IAS 16. [IFRS 1.IG7]

UK

This will generally not be a significant issue for UK companies because the depreciation requirements of IAS 16 are similar to those of FRS 15.

*However, there are some differences which might arise including the possibly more widespread use of component depreciation (see below) under IFRSs and the different basis for measuring residual values under IFRSs (see 7.2 in **chapter 6**).*

Depreciation methods and rates under previous GAAP may differ from those that would be acceptable under IFRSs. For example, they may have been adopted solely for tax purposes. In such cases, where the effect is material, the accumulated depreciation is adjusted retrospectively in the opening IFRS statement of financial position so that it complies with IFRSs. [IFRS 1.IG7]

IAS 16 requires each part of an item of property, plant and equipment with a cost that is significant in relation to the total cost of the item to be depreciated separately. But IAS 16 does not prescribe the unit of measure for recognition of an asset (i.e. what constitutes an item of property, plant and equipment). Thus, judgement is required in applying the recognition criteria to an entity's specific circumstances. [IFRS 1.IG12]

UK

Under UK GAAP, FRS 15 has a similar concept of component depreciation although it is differently expressed from the requirements of IAS 16. UK companies moving to IFRSs should consider whether their existing policies in this respect meet the requirements of IAS 16.

The construction or commissioning of an asset results in some cases in an obligation for an entity to dismantle or remove the asset and restore the site on which the asset stands. In this case IAS 37 should be applied in recognising and measuring any resulting provision. IAS 16 is then applied to determine the resulting amount included in the cost of the asset, before depreciation and impairment losses. The Implementation Guidance to IFRS 1 notes that items such as depreciation and impairment losses cause differences between the carrying amount of the provision and the amount included in the carrying amount of the asset. Changes in such liabilities are accounted for in accordance with IFRIC 1 *Changes to Existing Decommissioning, Restoration and Similar Liabilities*. However, paragraph 25E of IFRS 1, as inserted by IFRIC 1, provides an exemption for changes that occurred before the date of transition to IFRSs, and prescribes an alternative treatment where the exemption is used (see **6.8** below) [IFRS 1.IG13]

The use of fair value or previous revaluations as deemed cost on first-time adoption of IFRSs is considered at **6.2** below.

5.4 IAS 17 *Leases*

A first-time adopter may apply the transitional provisions of IFRIC 4 *Determining whether an Arrangement contains a Lease* (see **6.9** below). With this exception, no special exemptions for leases are available to a first-time adopter under IFRS 1. Accordingly, a first-time adopter must apply IAS 17 in full in its first IFRS financial statements, both in respect of the current period and any comparative periods.

The optional exemption in IFRS 1 that permits a first-time adopter to measure items of property, plant and equipment at fair value (see **6.2** below) applies to items capitalised in the financial statements under a finance lease. A first-time adopter may therefore measure these items at fair value at the date of transition. The finance lease liability is recognised at the net present value of the lease payments.

There are no explicit exemptions or exceptions in IFRS 1 from retrospective application of IAS 17. A first-time adopter is therefore required to recognise all assets held under finance leases at the date of transition. If they were not previously recognised, this involves determining the fair value of the assets at the inception of the lease (or the present value of the minimum lease payments, if lower) depreciated to the date of transition and the finance lease liability amortised at the rate implicit in the lease. It may be difficult and even impracticable to determine the fair value, at the inception of the lease, of the asset acquired in the lease. However, the entity may elect to measure the asset capitalised under a finance lease at fair value at the date of transition to IFRSs in accordance with the optional exemption in IFRS 1.

At the date of transition to IFRSs, a lessee or lessor classifies leases as operating leases or finance leases on the basis of circumstances existing at the inception of the lease (see paragraph 13 of IAS 17). The lessee and lessor may agree to change the provisions of the lease in a manner that would have resulted in a different classification had the changed terms been in effect at the inception of the lease. If so, the revised agreement is considered as a new agreement over its term, but changes in estimates (e.g. of the economic life or residual value of the leased property) or changes of circumstances (e.g. default by the lessee) do not give rise to a new classification of the lease. [IFRS 1.IG14]

When IAS 17 was revised in 1997, the net cash investment method for recognising finance income of lessors was eliminated. IAS 17 permits finance lessors to eliminate this method prospectively. However, the transitional provisions of IAS 17 do not apply to an entity's opening IFRS statement of financial position (see **5.1** above). Therefore a finance lessor measures finance lease receivables in its opening IFRS statement of financial position as if the net cash investment method had never been permitted. [IFRS 1.IG15]

This point is of particular relevance to UK companies because SSAP 21 requires the use of the net cash investment method which is not permitted under the current version of IAS 17. Finance lessors will therefore have to remeasure their finance lease receivables in the opening IFRS statement of financial position unless it is clear that the effect cannot be material. UK

SIC-15 *Operating Leases – Incentives* applies to lease terms beginning on or after 1 January 1999. However, a first-time adopter must apply SIC-15 to all leases irrespective of whether they started before or after that date. [IFRS 1.IG16]

5.5 IAS 18 *Revenue*

Amounts may have been received that do not yet qualify for recognition as revenue under IAS 18 *Revenue*. An entity should recognise the amount received as a liability in its opening IFRS statement of financial position and measure the liability at the amount received. [IFRS 1.IG17]

5.6 IAS 19 *Employee Benefits*

The actuarial assumptions used at the date of transition to IFRSs should be consistent with the actuarial assumptions made for the same date under previous GAAP (after adjustments to reflect any differences in accounting policies) unless there is objective evidence that those assumptions were in error. The impact of any later revisions to those assumptions is an actuarial gain or loss of the period in which the entity makes the revisions. [IFRS 1.IG19]

It may be necessary to make actuarial assumptions at the date of transition to IFRSs that were not necessary under previous GAAP. Any such assumptions should not reflect conditions that arose after the date of transition to IFRSs. In particular, discount rates and the fair value of plan assets at the date of transition to IFRSs reflect market conditions at that date. Similarly, actuarial assumptions at the date of transition to IFRSs about future employee turnover rates should not reflect a significant increase in estimated employee turnover rates as a result of a curtailment of the pension plan that occurred after the date of transition to IFRSs. [IFRS 1.IG20]

An entity's first IFRS financial statements will usually reflect measurements of employee benefit obligations at three dates (the end of the reporting period, the date of the comparative statement of financial position and the date of transition to IFRSs). IAS 19 encourages the involvement of a qualified actuary in the measurement of all material post-employment benefit obligations. However, the IFRS 1 Implementation Guidance notes that, to minimise cost, an entity may request a qualified actuary to carry out a detailed actuarial valuation at one or two dates and roll the valuation(s) forward or back to other dates. Any such roll forward or roll back should reflect any material transactions and other material events (including changes in market prices and interest rates) between those dates. [IFRS 1.IG21]

UK

IAS 19 is consistent with FRS 17 in most respects other than the recognition of actuarial gains and losses. Following the amendment to IAS 19 in December 2004, that standard now provides an optional treatment for actuarial gains and losses that is broadly consistent with UK GAAP. Both standards require the use of the projected unit method of actuarial valuation and require liabilities to be discounted using a high quality corporate bond rate.

One difference between IAS 19 and FRS 17 was that the former requires investments to be valued at bid prices whereas the latter required them to be valued at mid market prices. However, FRS 17 has been amended in this respect to converge with IAS 19 for periods beginning on or after 6 April 2007. Subject to this, UK companies adopting IFRSs should find that the estimates made for the purposes of FRS 17 should normally be suitable for use under IAS 19. The guidance in IFRS 1.IG21 about rolling valuations back or forward is therefore unlikely to be relevant to a UK company.

The election available to a first-time adopter to recognise all cumulative actuarial gains and losses at the date of transition to IFRSs is considered in **6.3** below.

5.7 IAS 29 *Financial Reporting in Hyperinflationary Economies*

IAS 21 should be complied with to determine the reporting entity's functional currency and presentation currency. IAS 29 should be applied to any periods during which the economy of the functional or presentation currency was hyperinflationary. [IFRS 1.IG32]

An entity may elect to use the fair value of an item of property, plant and equipment at the date of transition to IFRSs as its deemed cost at that date. In this case it should give the disclosures required by paragraph 44 of IFRS 1 (see **8.2.2** below). [IFRS 1.IG33]

If the entity elects to use the exemptions in paragraphs 16 to 19 of IFRS 1 (i.e. fair value or revaluation as deemed cost – see **6.2** below) it should apply IAS 29 to periods after the date for which the revalued amount or fair value was determined. [IFRS 1.IG34]

Example 5.7

Restatement of share capital for first-time adopters

Country A's economy was hyperinflationary until 31 December 20X1. An entity operating in Country A with CUR as its functional currency is a first-time adopter of IFRSs with a transition date of 1 January 20X9. The entity was established and its share capital was contributed by shareholders before 31 December 20X1. The entity applies the IFRS 1.13 fair value as deemed cost exemption for property, plant and equipment, and does not have any other non-monetary assets or liabilities acquired or originated prior to 31 December 20X1.

The entity should inflate its historical cost amount of share capital in its first IFRS financial statements. Unless there is a specific exemption, IFRS 1 requires retrospective application of the Standards effective at the end of the reporting period of the entity's first IFRS financial statements. Therefore, IAS 29 should be applied to the period during which CUR was a hyperinflationary currency. Components of equity, such as share capital, should therefore be restated in accordance with IAS 29.24 from the transaction date to the end of the period of hyperinflation. The entity should restate from the transaction date to 31 December 20X1. There is no exemption from restatement of the share capital, or other components of equity except retained earnings which are derived from all other amounts in the restated statement of financial position.

5.8 IAS 36 *Impairment of Assets*

IAS 36 should be applied:

- to determine whether any impairment loss exists at the date of transition to IFRSs;
- to measure any impairment loss that exists at that date; and
- to reverse any impairment loss that no longer exists at that date.

The first IFRS financial statements should include the disclosures that IAS 36 would have required if the impairment losses, or reversals, had been recognised in the period beginning with the date of transition to IFRSs. [IFRS 1.IG39]

The estimates used to determine whether an impairment loss is recognised and to measure any such impairment loss at the date of transition to IFRSs should be consistent with estimates made for the same date under previous GAAP, after making adjustments to reflect differences in accounting policies. This applies unless there is objective evidence that those assumptions were in error. The impact of any later revisions to those estimates should be reported as an event of the period in which the revisions are made. [IFRS 1.IG40]

In assessing the need to recognise an impairment loss and in measuring any such impairment loss at the date of transition to IFRSs, it may be necessary to make estimates that were not necessary under previous

GAAP. Such estimates and assumptions should not reflect conditions that arose after the date of transition to IFRSs. [IFRS 1.IG41]

The transitional provisions of IAS 36 do not apply to the opening IFRS statement of financial position. [IFRS 1.IG42]

IAS 36 requires the reversal of impairment losses in some cases. If the opening IFRS statement of financial position reflects impairment losses, any later reversal of those losses should be reflected in profit or loss except when IAS 36 requires them to be treated as a revaluation. This applies to both impairment losses recognised under previous GAAP and to additional impairment losses recognised on transition to IFRSs. [IFRS 1.IG43]

For UK companies, the requirements of IAS 36 are similar to those of FRS 11. Therefore, adjustments to impairment losses on transition to IFRSs should not generally be necessary. UK

5.9 IAS 37 *Provisions, Contingent Liabilities and Contingent Assets*

The estimates used to determine whether a provision is recognised and to measure any such provision at the date of transition to IFRSs should be consistent with estimates made for the same date under previous GAAP, after making adjustments to reflect differences in accounting policies. This applies unless there is objective evidence that those assumptions were in error. The impact of any later revisions to those estimates should be reported as an event of the period in which the revisions are made. [IFRS 1.IG40]

In assessing the need to recognise a provision and in measuring any such provision at the date of transition to IFRSs, it may be necessary to make estimates that were not necessary under previous GAAP. Such estimates and assumptions should not reflect conditions that arose after the date of transition to IFRSs. [IFRS 1.IG41]

The transitional provisions of IAS 37 do not apply to the opening IFRS statement of financial position. [IFRS 1.IG41]

For UK companies, the requirements of IAS 37 are similar to those of FRS 12. Therefore, adjustments to provisions on transition to IFRSs should not generally be necessary. UK

5.10 IAS 38 *Intangible Assets*

The opening IFRS statement of financial position should:

[IFRS 1.IG44]

- exclude all intangible assets and other intangible items that do not meet the criteria for recognition in IAS 38 at the date of transition to IFRSs; and
- include all intangible assets that meet the recognition criteria in IAS 38 at the date of transition to IFRSs except as described below.

The exception in the second case is for intangible assets acquired in a business combination that were not recognised in the acquirer's consolidated statement of financial position under previous GAAP and also would not qualify for recognition under IAS 38 in the separate statement of financial position of the acquiree (see **6.1** below). [IFRS 1.IG44]

The criteria in IAS 38 require an entity to recognise an intangible asset if, and only if:

- it is probable that the future economic benefits that are attributable to the asset will flow to the entity; and
- the cost of the asset can be measured reliably.

IAS 38 supplements these criteria with further, more specific criteria for internally generated intangibles. [IFRS 1.IG45]

Under IAS 38, the costs of creating internally generated intangible assets are capitalised prospectively from the date when the recognition criteria are met. IAS 38 does not permit the use of hindsight to conclude retrospectively that the recognition criteria were met. So even if it is possible to conclude retrospectively that a future inflow of economic benefits is probable and the costs can be reconstructed reliably, IAS 38 does not permit the capitalisation of costs incurred before the date when the entity both:

[IFRS 1.IG46]

- concludes, based on an assessment made and documented at the date of that conclusion, that it is probable that future economic benefits from the asset will flow to the entity; and
- has a reliable system for accumulating the costs of internally generated intangible assets when, or shortly after, they are incurred.

If an internally generated intangible asset qualifies for recognition at the date of transition to IFRSs, the asset should be recognised in the opening IFRS statement of financial position even if the related expenditure had been recognised as an expense under previous GAAP. If the asset does not qualify for recognition under IAS 38 until a later date, its cost is the sum of the expenditure incurred from that date. [IFRS 1.IG47]

For example, Company A adopts IFRSs with a date of transition of 1 January 20X4. At that date, certain internal development projects were determined to be in the development phase in accordance with IAS 38. Is Company A required to recognise an asset for the development costs that would have been recognised under IAS 38 had the entity reported under IFRSs prior to the date of transition?

If Company A can reliably measure the development costs incurred, then recognition of the asset is required. However, IFRS 1 recognises that in many cases where prior cost data was not reliably segregated between research and development, the measurement of the development costs may not be reliable and should not be required. If measurement can be determined reliably from the date the recognition criteria were met, then restatement of the asset would be as if IAS 38 had been applied. That is, only costs incurred during the development phase should be capitalised in the opening IFRS statement of financial position at 1 January 20X4.

The guidance in IFRS 1.IG46 has the effect of prohibiting recognition of an asset for development costs incurred before the date on which the entity concluded, based on an assessment made and documented at the date of that conclusion, that it was probable that future economic benefits from the asset would flow to the entity. In most cases where an entity had a policy of writing off development costs as incurred under previous GAAP, no such assessment would have been made at the time. No asset would therefore be recognised for development costs in the opening IFRS statement of financial position. But in some cases, development costs may have been recorded and controlled through a system that involved such an assessment being made for commercial rather than financial reporting reasons. Such an assessment may, depending on the facts, constitute an appropriate basis for recognising an asset for development costs on transition to IFRSs.

The criteria described above for recognition of intangible assets under IAS 38 also apply to intangible assets acquired separately. Documentation prepared at the time to support the decision to acquire an asset will usually contain an assessment of the future economic benefits. Also, the cost of separately acquired intangible assets can usually be measured reliably. [IFRS 1.IG48]

UK

UK GAAP prohibits the capitalisation of internally generated intangible assets other than in the case of development costs, which are subject to SSAP 13, and in very rare cases when the asset has a readily ascertainable market value. Therefore it should be rare for intangible assets to have been capitalised under UK GAAP that would not meet the recognition criteria in IAS 38.

Some intangible assets that were not recognised under UK GAAP would meet the criteria for recognition under IAS 38.

One specific instance where adjustments may be required is development costs. IAS 38 and SSAP 13 contain broadly similar criteria for the recognition of development costs. But when the criteria are met, IAS 38 requires the costs to be capitalised whereas SSAP 13 permits an alternative policy of writing off such costs. Most UK companies choose to write off development costs as incurred which is permitted by SSAP 13. UK companies will have to consider whether they incur development costs and, if so, assess whether or not they would meet the criteria for recognition in IAS 38. However, for the reasons explained above, it will often not be appropriate to recognise development costs as an asset in the opening IFRS statement of financial position, even where they will be recognised in respect of costs incurred after the date of transition.

If the amortisation methods and rates used under previous GAAP would be acceptable under IFRSs, the accumulated amortisation should not be restated in the opening IFRS statement of financial position. Any change in estimated useful life or amortisation pattern should be accounted for prospectively from the period when the change of estimate is made. But in some cases the amortisation methods and rates under previous GAAP might not be acceptable under IFRSs, for example because they were adopted solely for tax purposes. In such cases, where the effect is material, the accumulated amortisation in the opening IFRS statement of financial position should be adjusted retrospectively so that it complies with IFRSs. [IFRS 1.IG51]

UK

For UK companies, it is likely that the amortisation methods and rates adopted under UK GAAP will generally be acceptable under IAS 38. FRS 10 and IAS 38 share the principle of amortisation over the estimate of an asset's economic useful life.

Example 5.10

Indefinite-life intangible asset amortised under previous GAAP

A first-time adopter has an intangible asset. Under previous GAAP, the intangible was being amortised over 20 years. Previous GAAP required that all intangible assets be amortised and did not have the concept of indefinite-life intangible assets. On first-time adoption of IFRSs, the asset is deemed to have an indefinite useful life.

The entity should treat the change of classification to indefinite life as a change in accounting policy. As discussed in IFRS 1.IG51, the entity's previous amortisation method under previous GAAP is not acceptable under IFRSs. Therefore, the change from finite to indefinite life is a change in accounting policy that should be accounted for retrospectively in accordance with IFRS 1.

The transitional provisions in IAS 38.130, which state that a change in life from a finite to an indefinite useful life should be accounted for as a change in an accounting estimate, do not apply to first-time adopters. The entity must retrospectively restate the intangible as an indefinite-life asset, subject to mandatory annual impairment tests.

5.11 IAS 40 *Investment Property*

If the fair value model in IAS 40 is adopted, investment property should be measured at fair value at the date of transition to IFRSs. The transitional requirements in IAS 40 do not apply. [IFRS 1.IG61]

If the cost model in IAS 40 is adopted, the requirements of IFRS 1 and related Implementation Guidance for property, plant and equipment should be applied (see **5.3** above). [IFRS 1.IG62]

Many UK companies with investment property elect to use the fair value model because they have become accustomed to obtaining annual valuations under SSAP 19 and their shareholders will expect to see this information. Even if the cost model is used under IAS 40, disclosure of fair value is generally required by way of note. The requirement under the IAS 40 fair value model to report gains and losses in the profit and loss account is likely to be a significant factor when UK companies decide which model to use. UK

6 Optional exemptions from IFRSs

A first-time adopter may elect to use one or more of the following exemptions:

- business combinations (see **6.1** below);
- fair value or revaluation as deemed cost (see **6.2** below);
- employee benefits (see **6.3** below);
- cumulative translation differences (see **6.4** below);
- compound financial instruments (see **chapter 22**);
- assets and liabilities of subsidiaries, associates and joint ventures (see **6.5** below);
- designation of previously recognised financial instruments (see **chapter 22**);
- share-based payment transactions (see **6.6** below);
- insurance contracts (see **6.7** below);
- decommissioning liabilities included in the cost of property, plant and equipment (see **6.8** below);
- leases (see **6.9** below);
- fair value measurement of financial assets or financial liabilities at initial recognition (see **chapter 22**);
- borrowing costs (see **6.10** below);
- service concession arrangements (see **6.11** below); and
- investments in subsidiaries, associates and jointly controlled entities (see **6.12** below). [IFRS 1.13]

ED 1 proposed that a first-time adopter should use either all the exemptions or none of them. However, the IASB reconsidered this approach in the light of comments received and grouped the exceptions to retrospective application into two groups. The first group consists of optional exemptions which may be selected independently of each other. These are dealt with in this section. Entities adopting IFRSs will therefore need to decide in each case the advantages and disadvantages of using these exemptions.

The second group consists of mandatory exceptions where full retrospective application is prohibited. These are considered in **section 7** below and are in respect of some aspects of derecognition, hedge accounting, estimates, assets classified as held for sale and discontinued operations. [IFRS 1.BC28 & 29]

When more than one voluntary exemption affects an account balance, more than one exemption can be applied. The decision to apply individual voluntary exemptions is independent. There is no requirement to use a particular voluntary exemption as the result of choosing another voluntary exemption.

For example, an entity might not restate a business combination prior to the date of transition so that the deemed cost of property, plant and equipment is the carrying amount under previous GAAP immediately after the business combination. The entity can override this deemed cost with a later deemed cost, such as fair value at the date of transition.

IFRS 1 states that the exemptions should not be applied by analogy to other items. [IFRS 1.13]

For example, a first-time adopter cannot use fair value or the carrying amount of an item as deemed cost except as specifically set out below. The Standard specifies limited circumstances where retrospective restatement in accordance with IFRSs does not apply. Unless the amount is immaterial, in all other circumstances, IFRSs should be applied retrospectively.

Some of the exemptions discussed below refer to fair value. In determining fair values for the purposes of applying IFRS 1, the definition of fair value in Appendix A (see **2.3** above) is applied together with any more specific guidance in other IFRSs on the determination of fair values for the asset or liability in question. Fair values should reflect conditions that existed at the date for which they were determined. [IFRS 1.14]

The previous paragraph is based on IFRS 1 as amended by IFRS 3(2008). However, before that amendment, the requirement was similar, in substance, but referred specifically to the fact that IFRS 3 explains how to determine the fair values of acquired assets and liabilities in a business combination.

Example 6.5.5 considers how to apply the IFRS 1 exemptions in consolidated financial statements that include equity accounting for associates. It would apply equally to accounting for jointly controlled entities.

6.1 Business combinations

Any business combinations after the date of transition to IFRSs will be dealt with in accordance with IFRS 3. For business combinations that were recognised before the date of transition to IFRSs, the requirements of Appendix B to IFRS 1 are applied. These are considered in this section.

IFRS 3 was revised in January 2008. The revised standard comes into effect for business combinations for which the acquisition date is on or after the beginning of the first annual reporting period beginning on or after 1 January 2009. Earlier application is permitted. The requirements of IFRS 1 set out in this section are, in general, applicable regardless of whether IFRS 3(2004) or IFRS 3(2008) is being applied. IFRS 3(2008) made a few amendments to Appendix B of IFRS 1 and these changes are highlighted below.

UK *UK companies will not be able to apply IFRS 3(2008) until it has been adopted by the EU.*

The Implementation Guidance to IFRS 1 on business combinations comprises Examples IG2 to IG7. In general, these Examples deal with situations which are unlikely to arise in the UK (because the relevant UK standards and IFRSs are similar) or are straightforward numerical examples which demonstrate application of the relevant requirements.

6.1.1 Scope and consistent use of the exemption

A first-time adopter may elect not to apply IFRS 3 retrospectively to business combinations that occurred before the date of transition to IFRSs. However, if any business combination is restated to comply with IFRS 3, all later business combinations have to be restated.

If IFRS 3(2008) is being applied, IAS 27 (as amended in 2008) must also be applied from the same date. For example, if a first-time adopter elects to restate a business combination that occurred on 1 September 2007, it has to restate all business combinations that occurred between that date and the date of transition to IFRSs. It also has to apply the revised version of IAS 27 from 1 September 2007.

If, instead, IFRS 3(2004) is being applied, IAS 36 (as revised in 2004) and IAS 38 (as revised in 2004) must also be applied from the same date. For example, if a first-time adopter elects to restate a business combination that occurred on 1 September 2007, it has to restate all business combinations that occurred between that date and the date of transition to IFRSs. It also has to apply the revised versions of IAS 36 and IAS 38 from 1 September 2007. [IFRS 1.B1]

It is important to understand that although business combinations that occurred before the date of transition to IFRSs do not have to be 'restated', certain adjustments may be required to the assets and liabilities recognised on such business combinations. The adjustments that may be required are described below.

The exemption for past business combinations also applies to past acquisitions of investments in associates and of interests in joint ventures. The date selected as described above applies equally for all such acquisitions. [IFRS 1.B3]

The following examples illustrate some issues that arise from these requirements.

Example 6.1.1A

Step acquisition completed prior to the date of transition

Company C acquired Company T in stages beginning with a 10 per cent acquisition on 30 June 2005, 30 per cent on 31 December 2005 and 20 per cent on 31 December 2006. It was determined that Company C obtained control of Company T on 31 December 2006. Company C is a first-time adopter with 1 January 2007 as its date of transition to IFRSs and has elected to restate all business combinations after 1 January 2006. It is not choosing to adopt IFRS 3(2008) for its first IFRS financial statements and is instead adopting IFRS 3(2004).How does the election apply to the step acquisition prior to 1 January 2006?

In this example, the date of acquisition is 31 December 2006 and the acquisition should be restated. Company C should also apply IFRS 3(2004) in respect of each step in the acquisition process, back to the first acquisition of 10 per cent on 30 June 2005 (see the guidance on step acquisitions under IFRS 3(2004) set out at **6.8** in **appendix 2**). But this would not affect the date from which all business combinations are restated because the election is based on the date of acquisition of a subsidiary. Therefore, in this example, restatement is not required for any other business combination prior to 1 January 2006.

Example 6.1.1B

The effect of a restatement of a business combination on the acquisition of a joint venture or associate

Company D chooses to restate the acquisition of subsidiaries starting from 1 January 20X0. As a result, all acquisitions of associates and joint ventures from that date must also be restated.

Paragraph B3 of IFRS 1 states that the exemption for past business combinations also applies to past acquisitions of investments in associates and joint ventures. That is, IFRS 1 applies the same guidance to the acquisition of subsidiaries, associates and joint ventures. As a result, entities will have the option to restate acquisitions of associates and joint ventures prior to the date of transition, similar to the acquisition of subsidiaries. As a consequence, if an entity decides to restate an acquisition of a subsidiary at a date prior to the date of transition, all acquisitions of subsidiaries, associates and joint ventures after that date must also be restated. Equally, if an entity chooses to restate an acquisition of an associate at a date prior to the date of transition to IFRSs, all acquisitions of subsidiaries, other associates and joint ventures after that date must also be restated.

Example 6.1.1C

Definition of a business combination for the exemption

In Country E, certain transactions that would be considered business combinations under IFRS 3 would not be considered business combinations under local GAAP. Does a transaction have to be accounted for as a business combination under national accounting standards to qualify for the exemption in IFRS 1?

The determination of whether a transaction qualifies for the business combinations exemption depends on whether that combination meets the definition of a business combination under IFRSs. If the transaction meets that definition, regardless of whether it met the definition under local GAAP, the exemption for business combinations in IFRS 1 would be permitted for that transaction.

UK

This is relatively unlikely to occur for a UK company. Although the definition of a business combination in IFRS 3 is expressed differently from that in FRS 6, the practical effect will be that a transaction that is a business combination under IFRS 3 is likely to have been accounted for as a business combination under UK GAAP. There might, however, be some differences at the margins where a transaction that was accounted for as an asset purchase under UK GAAP might have to be treated as a business combination under IFRSs.

The exemption in IFRS 3 for business combinations involving entities or businesses under common control is broader than the equivalent exemption that permits merger accounting for group reconstructions in FRS 6 (see **chapter 34**). *Transactions that were group reconstructions under FRS 6 are likely to be outside the scope of IFRS 3. Conversely, some transactions that had to be accounted for as acquisitions under FRS 6 will be outside the scope of IFRS 3.*

Example 6.1.1D

Transition to IFRS 3

Company A is adopting IFRSs for the year ended 31 December 20X5. Therefore, Company A's date of transition is 1 January 20X4. Company A purchased Company B on 31 October 20X3, Company C on 15 March 20X4, Company D on 17 July 20X4 and Company E on 15 February 20X5.

Company A does not apply IFRS 3(2008) in its first IFRS financial statements.

The business combinations involving Company C and Company D must be restated because all business combinations after the date of transition (1 January 20X4) must be accounted for in accordance with the accounting requirements in force at the end of the entity's first IFRS reporting period (31 December 20X5). The purchase of Company E will be accounted for in accordance with IFRS 3 when the purchase occurs because it is subsequent to the date of transition to IFRSs.

The purchase of Company B may also be restated provided that Company A applies the requirements of IAS 36 and IAS 38 with the same application date, and the valuation and other information required to apply IFRS 3, IAS 36 and IAS 38 was obtained at the date of acquisition of Company B. If A does not restate the purchase of Company B, the requirements of Appendix B to IFRS 1 must be applied to the transaction in the first financial report prepared in accordance with IFRSs.

If a first-time adopter does not apply IFRS 3 retrospectively to a past business combination, this has the consequences set out in **6.1.2** to **6.1.10** below for that business combination. An exemption relating to the retranslation of goodwill and fair value adjustments arising on past business combinations is considered at **6.1.11** below.

Although IFRS 1 provides an exemption from the need to restate business combinations that occurred before the date of transition to IFRSs, it is very important to appreciate that this does not simply mean that all amounts recorded under local GAAP relating to such business combinations can be carried forward under IFRSs. The detailed rules set out in Appendix B to IFRS 1 and described below are quite complex.

6.1.2 *Classification as an acquisition or merger*

The same classification (e.g. as an acquisition, reverse acquisition or merger) should be used as in the previous GAAP financial statements. [IFRS 1.B2(a)]

UK

> *As a result of this exemption, business combinations prior to the date of transition that have been accounted for as mergers under UK GAAP in accordance with FRS 6 do not have to be restated as acquisitions even though merger accounting is not permitted by IFRS 3.*

6.1.3 Assets and liabilities that should be recognised

All assets and liabilities at the date of transition to IFRSs that were acquired or assumed in a past business combination should be recognised, other than:

- some financial assets and financial liabilities derecognised under previous GAAP (see **chapter 22**); and
- assets, including goodwill, and liabilities that were not recognised in the acquirer's consolidated statement of financial position under previous GAAP and also would not qualify for recognition under IFRSs in the separate statement of financial position of the acquiree (see **6.1.7** and **6.1.8** below).

Any resulting change should be recognised by adjusting retained earnings or, if appropriate, another category of equity, unless the change results from the recognition of an intangible asset that was previously subsumed within goodwill (see **6.1.8** below). [IFRS 1.B2(b)]

The recognition of deferred tax in connection with business combinations that occurred before the date of transition to IFRSs is considered at **6.1.12** below.

6.1.4 Assets and liabilities that should not be recognised

Any item recognised under previous GAAP that does not qualify for recognition as an asset or liability under IFRSs should be excluded from the opening IFRS statement of financial position. The resulting change should be accounted for as follows:

[IFRS 1.B2(c)]

- the first-time adopter may have classified a past business combination as an acquisition and recognised as an intangible asset an item that does not qualify for recognition as an asset under IAS 38. Such an item (and any related deferred tax and non-controlling interest) should be reclassified as part of goodwill unless the entity deducted goodwill directly from equity under previous GAAP (see **6.1.8** below);

- all other resulting changes should be recognised in retained earnings. Such changes include reclassifications from and to intangible assets if goodwill was not recognised under previous GAAP as an asset. This may arise if, under previous GAAP, goodwill was deducted directly from equity or the business combination was not treated as an acquisition.

> *Example 3 in the IFRS 1 Implementation Guidance illustrates this with a provision for restructuring costs which had been recognised under local GAAP but which would not be recognised under IFRSs. This is unlikely to be relevant in the UK because FRS 12 is almost identical to IAS 37.* (UK)

6.1.5 *Assets and liabilities subsequently measured on a basis other than historical cost*

IFRSs require subsequent measurement of some assets and liabilities on a basis that is not based on original cost, for example fair value. These assets and liabilities are measured on that basis in the opening IFRS statement of financial position even if they were acquired or assumed in a past business combination. Any resulting change in carrying amount is recognised by adjusting retained earnings or, if appropriate, another category of equity, rather than goodwill. [IFRS 1.B2(d)]

> *Under UK GAAP, for a business combination that is classified as an acquisition, all assets and liabilities are recorded at fair value at the date of the acquisition. However, in many instances that fair value subsequently becomes deemed cost. If, under IFRSs, the asset or liability would have to be measured at the end of each reporting period at fair value, it should be measured at fair value at the date of transition to IFRSs irrespective of the fact that it was acquired in a business combination. For example, this would apply to certain financial instruments.* (UK)

6.1.6 *Previous GAAP carrying amount to be treated as deemed cost*

Immediately after the business combination, the carrying amounts, under previous GAAP, of assets and liabilities assumed in that business combination are treated as their deemed cost under IFRSs at that date. If IFRSs require a cost-based measurement of those assets and liabilities at a later date, that deemed cost should be the basis for cost-based depreciation or amortisation from the date of the business combination. [IFRS 1.B2(e)]

But if the carrying amount of an intangible asset was zero, the asset should not be recognised in the opening IFRS statement of financial position unless it would qualify under IAS 38 applying the criteria discussed in **5.10** above for recognition in the separate statement of financial position of the acquiree at the date of transition to IFRSs. If those recognition criteria are met, the asset is measured on the basis that IAS 38 would require in the separate statement of financial position of the acquiree. The resulting adjustment affects goodwill. [IFRS 1.IG49]

If there is any indication that the identifiable assets are impaired, they should be tested for impairment based on conditions that existed at the date of transition to IFRSs in accordance with IAS 36. [IFRS 1.IG Example 2]

UK

The effect of this is that accumulated amortisation and depreciation should not normally be restated. Therefore, the carrying amount of such assets in the opening IFRS statement of financial position will equal their carrying amount under UK GAAP at the date of transition to IFRSs. There is an exception to this rule where the depreciation methods and rates under previous GAAP result in amounts that are materially different from those required under IFRSs, for example because they were adopted solely for tax purposes.

This exception will not usually be relevant in the UK given the similarities between UK GAAP and IFRSs for amortisation and depreciation. However, there are some differences which might arise including the possibly more widespread use of component depreciation under IFRSs and the different basis for measuring residual values under IFRSs.

6.1.7 Assets and liabilities not recognised under previous GAAP

If an asset acquired, or liability assumed, in a past business combination was not recognised under previous GAAP, it does not have a deemed cost of zero in the opening IFRS statement of financial position. Instead, it is recognised and measured in the consolidated statement of financial position on the basis that IFRSs would require in the separate statement of financial position of the acquiree. For example, if finance leases acquired in a business combination had not been capitalised under previous GAAP, they should be capitalised in the IFRS consolidated statement of financial position because IAS 17 would require the acquiree to do so in its own separate IFRS statement of financial position. Conversely, if an asset or liability was subsumed in goodwill under previous GAAP but would have been recognised separately under IFRS 3, that asset or liability remains in goodwill unless IFRSs would require its recognition in the separate financial statements of the acquiree. [IFRS 1.B2(f)]

This paragraph of IFRS 1 is amended by IFRS 3(2008) to add an additional example which is as follows. If the acquirer had not, under its previous GAAP, recognised a contingent liability that still exists at the date of transition to IFRSs, the acquirer should recognise that contingent liability at that date unless IAS 37 would prohibit its recognition in the financial statements of the acquiree.

In other words, intangible assets of the acquiree are only recognised in the opening IFRS statement of financial position if they would have satisfied the criteria for recognition under IAS 38 in the statement of financial position of the acquiree. This is in contrast to the requirement in IFRS 3 to recognise all intangible assets acquired at the date of acquisition. The criteria for recognition of such assets are the same as for intangible assets of the acquirer as explained in IFRS 1.IG46 and IFRS 1.IG48 depending on whether the acquiree acquired the intangible asset externally or generated them internally. Accordingly, unless they satisfied the criteria for recognition under IAS 38 at an earlier date (including an assessment and documentation at that date regarding the probability of future economic benefits as well as a reliable system of accumulating the costs- see **5.10** above), intangible assets generated internally by the acquiree such as brands, mastheads, publishing titles and customer lists will not be recognised at the date of transition. Conversely, intangible assets acquired by the acquiree externally will be recognised in most cases because the transaction and invoice are usually sufficient documentation and evidence of future economic benefits at that date.

UK

The example of a finance lease given in IFRS 1 will not usually be relevant to the UK because the requirements of IAS 17 are very similar to those of SSAP 21.

In certain limited circumstances, IFRS 1 requires a reclassification between goodwill and intangibles at the date of transition. However, such circumstances are unlikely to arise for UK companies, because the recognition of intangible assets and goodwill under the requirements of FRS 7 and FRS 10 may be expected to already comply with IFRS 1.

Example 6.1.7

Deferred tax asset acquired in a past business combination

Company K (parent) acquired Company B (subsidiary) on 1 January 20X4. K adopts IFRSs in 20X7 and has a date of transition of 1 January 20X6 and applies the optional exemption in IFRS 1.B2 to this business combination. B had a tax loss that can be carried forward for five years. If B does not use the tax loss before 31 December 20X8, it will expire. At the date of acquisition, K assessed that the tax loss carried forward in B could not be used before it expires at the end of 20X8. Consequently, K did not recognise the related deferred tax asset at the date of acquisition. The nominal value of the unused tax loss remains unchanged at the date of transition.

At the date of transition to IFRSs, 1 January 20X6, K assessed that a portion of the unrecognised tax asset would probably be used before it expires at the end of 20X8.

Therefore, a deferred tax asset should be recognised at the date of transition to IFRSs. IFRS 1 does not include any exceptions to the general principle for deferred tax assets. Therefore, a deferred tax asset is recognised in the opening IFRS statement of financial position for the amount the entity expects will be used at the date of transition to IFRSs. The resulting adjustment is recognised in retained earnings because goodwill is only adjusted at the date of transition for recognition and derecognition of intangible assets, resolution of contingencies related to purchase consideration, and impairment.

6.1.8 *Adjustments to goodwill*

The carrying amount of goodwill in the opening IFRS statement of financial position is its carrying amount under previous GAAP at the date of transition to IFRSs, after the following adjustments:

[IFRS 1.B2(g)]

- goodwill is increased where it is necessary to reclassify an item that was recognised as an intangible under previous GAAP (see **6.1.4** above);
- goodwill is decreased (and, if applicable, deferred tax and non-controlling interests adjusted) where it is necessary to recognise an intangible asset that was subsumed within recognised goodwill under previous GAAP (see **6.1.7** above);
- if IFRS 3(2008) is not being applied, a contingency affecting the amount of the purchase consideration for a past business combination may have been resolved before the date of transition to IFRSs. If a reliable estimate of the contingent adjustment can be made and its

payment is probable, goodwill should be adjusted by this amount. Similarly, the carrying amount of goodwill should be adjusted if a previously recognised contingent adjustment can no longer be measured reliably or its payment is no longer probable; and

- regardless of whether there is any indication that goodwill may be impaired, IAS 36 should be applied in testing goodwill for impairment at the date of transition to IFRSs and in recognising any resulting impairment loss in retained earnings (or, if so required by IAS 36, in revaluation surplus). The impairment test is based on conditions at the date of transition to IFRSs.

UK

All goodwill should be tested for impairment at the date of transition to IFRSs. Although the requirements of IAS 36 are similar to those of FRS 11, the requirement for an impairment test even in the absence of any indicators of impairment will involve considerable extra effort. The impairment testing might reveal the need for impairment write-downs even though there were no indicators of impairment to prompt such testing under UK GAAP. But in most cases, no adjustment should be required.

No other adjustments should be made to the carrying amount of goodwill at the date of transition to IFRSs. For example, the carrying amount should not be restated:

[IFRS 1.B2(h)]

- to exclude in-process research and development acquired in that business combination (unless the related intangible asset would qualify for recognition under IAS 38 in the separate statement of financial position of the acquiree);
- to adjust previous amortisation of goodwill; or
- to reverse adjustments to goodwill that IFRS 3 would not permit, but that were made under previous GAAP because of adjustments to assets and liabilities between the date of the business combination and the date of transition to IFRSs.

UK

The first example would not be relevant in the UK. It is intended to clarify that when in-process research and development is written off to the profit and loss account on acquisition under local GAAP, it should not be reinstated into the carrying value of goodwill on transition to IFRSs. But where development costs meet the recognition criteria in IAS 38, the intangible asset would be recognised and goodwill reduced accordingly (see ***6.1.7*** *above).*

In relation to the second example, goodwill is not amortised under IFRS 3. But goodwill amortisation under UK GAAP prior to the date of transition to IFRSs is not reversed. The carrying amount of goodwill under UK GAAP will become the carrying amount of goodwill under IFRSs, subject to the requirement for impairment testing.

The third example will also not often be relevant in the UK because the restrictions on subsequent adjustments to assets and liabilities in FRS 7 are similar to those in IFRS 3. However, the permitted hindsight period for such adjustments is effectively shorter under IFRS 3 because it is one year from the date of the acquisition whereas FRS 7 permits adjustments in the first full year following the acquisition.

If, under previous GAAP, goodwill was recognised as a deduction from equity:

[IFRS 1.B2(i)]

- that goodwill is not recognised in the opening IFRS statement of financial position;
- that goodwill should not be reclassified to profit or loss if the subsidiary is disposed of or if the investment in the subsidiary becomes impaired; and
- adjustments resulting from the subsequent resolution of a contingency affecting the purchase consideration should be recognised in retained earnings.

UK *Most UK companies wrote off goodwill to reserves prior to the implementation of FRS 10 in 1998. Some companies may wish to reinstate such goodwill on transition to IFRSs given that it will no longer have to be amortised as a result of IFRS 3. However, this is specifically prohibited by IFRS 1. Goodwill can only be reinstated to the extent that it relates to business combinations that are reopened and accounted for under IFRS 3. Goodwill related to business combinations that occurred subsequent to the date from which IFRS 3 applies is recognised and measured in accordance with IFRS 3 regardless of the previous GAAP treatment, even if this was to write it off against equity. It may therefore be possible to achieve reversal from equity of goodwill previously written off related to certain business combinations.*

Also, somewhat surprisingly given that recycling is a feature of IFRSs, there is no requirement along the lines of that in FRS 10 to charge such goodwill to the profit and loss account on a subsequent disposal, closure or impairment. Indeed, this is explicitly prohibited.

6.1.8.1 Reassessment of provisional fair values after the date of transition

Example 6.1.8.1

Reassessment of provisional fair values after the date of transition

Under its local GAAP, Entity A used provisional fair values at the time of a business combination occurring prior to its date of transition to IFRSs. How should it measure goodwill in its first IFRS financial statements?

When IFRS 3 is not applied retrospectively to a business combination prior to the date of transition to IFRSs, the carrying amount of goodwill in the opening IFRS statement of financial position is its amount under local GAAP at the date of transition adjusted only for three items specified in paragraph B2(g) of IFRS 1 (see **6.1.8** above). If the business combination was in the period immediately prior to the date of transition, it is possible that adjustments would have been made in the next period, under local GAAP, to the amount of goodwill because of a reassessment of provisional fair values. It may at first appear that IFRS 1 has the effect of prohibiting the adjustment of goodwill and that the amount would therefore have to remain as originally stated under local GAAP at the date of transition. This is not so.

Under IFRS 3, adjustments to provisional fair values and goodwill may be made in the period subsequent to the business combination although there are two main differences. First, the period during which such an adjustment is permitted is limited to twelve months from the date of acquisition. Second, the adjustment is reflected through a retrospective restatement of the previous period as if the initial accounting had been completed from the date of acquisition.

It is possible to adjust goodwill recognised in the opening IFRS statement of financial position if such an adjustment would be permitted by IFRS 3. The restriction on adjustments to goodwill in IFRS 1 applies only to the amount initially recognised and does not preclude subsequent adjustments as permitted or required by other IFRSs. The amount may be adjusted for the reassessment of fair values on the basis that IFRS 3 requires retrospective restatement for this.

The example above will apply where a UK company has a business combination in the period prior to its date of transition to IFRSs and adjustments are made to provisional fair values during the window permitted by IFRS 3. UK

6.1.9 Subsidiaries not consolidated under previous GAAP

Under previous GAAP, a subsidiary acquired in a past business combination may not have been consolidated. This could arise either because the parent did not prepare consolidated financial statements or because the parent did not regard the entity as a subsidiary under previous GAAP. The carrying amounts of the subsidiary's assets and liabilities are adjusted to the amounts that IFRSs would require in the subsidiary's separate statement of financial position. The deemed cost of goodwill is then the difference, at the date of transition to IFRSs, between the parent's interest in those adjusted carrying amounts and the cost in the parent's separate financial statements of its investment in the subsidiary. [IFRS 1.B2(j)]

An example of the application of this requirement is given in IG Example 6 to IFRS 1.

As noted at **6.1.1** above, the requirements on restatement of business combinations in IFRS 1 apply to associates and joint ventures as well as to subsidiaries. A consequence of this is that if an associate (or joint venture) was not equity accounted under previous GAAP but would have to be equity accounted under IFRSs, it would be within the scope of the requirement in IFRS 1 for subsidiaries not consolidated. This is illustrated in the following example.

Example 6.1.9

Restatement of investment in associates back to original date on which significant influence was originally obtained

Company F acquired 20 per cent of Company A (and obtained significant influence over it) prior to Company F's date of transition to IFRSs. Under local GAAP, Company F accounted for its investment in Company A at cost in its consolidated financial statements.

IAS 28 *Investments in Associates* requires the use of the equity method of accounting for associates in the consolidated financial statements (with certain limited exceptions – see IAS 28.8). IFRS 1 provides guidance on investments in subsidiaries including subsidiaries not previously consolidated and consistently notes that this guidance should also be applied to investments in associates and joint ventures. Therefore, the guidance in IFRS 1.B2 (j) should be applied.

As a result Company F should adjust the carrying amounts of the associate's assets and liabilities to the amounts that IFRSs would require in the associate's statement of financial position, as of the date of transition. Company F's share of the net assets of the associate so adjusted is included in Company F's consolidated opening IFRS statement of financial position as investment in associates, with the difference between this amount and the original cost of the investment in the associate to be considered deemed cost of goodwill. Goodwill relating to an associate is included in the carrying amount of the investment, without subsequent amortisation.

UK

Given the similarities between IAS 27 and FRS 2, and the impact of FRS 5, it is unlikely that this requirement will be relevant to UK companies, except in very rare cases for subsidiaries. However, although the requirements of FRS 9 are broadly similar to those of IAS 28 and IAS 31, there are differences of scope and definitions. There may therefore be instances where an investment that was not accounted for using equity accounting under UK GAAP may have to be equity accounted under IFRSs (see ***5.3*** *in* ***chapter 36****).*

Subsidiaries that were not previously consolidated are considered more generally at **6.5.4** below.

6.1.10 *Effect of restatements on non-controlling interests and deferred tax*

The measurement of non-controlling interests and deferred tax follows from the measurement of other assets and liabilities. Therefore, the adjustments described above to recognise assets and liabilities, affect non-controlling interests and deferred tax. [IFRS 1.B2(k)]

Example 6.1.10

Change in treatment of non-controlling interest on first-time adoption

Under previous GAAP, an entity measured identifiable assets and liabilities acquired in a business combination at:

- The acquirer's interest obtained in the exchange transaction.
- The non-controlling interest's portion of the pre-acquisition carrying amounts.

According to IFRS 3 this treatment is not permitted. The Standard requires that assets and liabilities acquired in a business combination be measured at their fair values at the date of acquisition. As a result, the non-controlling interest will be stated at the non-controlling interest's proportion of the fair values of the identifiable assets and liabilities recognised.

Because the entity has chosen not to restate business combinations that occurred before the date of transition to IFRSs (or another date), IFRS 1.B2(e) requires that 'immediately after the business combination, the carrying amount under previous GAAP of assets acquired and liabilities assumed in that business combination shall be their deemed cost under IFRSs at that date'.

However, the requirements of IFRS 1.B2(e) notwithstanding, IFRS 1.B2(d) and IFRS 1.B2(f) may require some assets acquired, or liabilities assumed, in a business combination to be measured at amounts different from the carrying amounts immediately after the business combination under previous GAAP. IFRS 1.B2(k) states that the measurement of non-controlling interests and deferred tax follows from the measurement of other assets and liabilities. Therefore, adjustments to recognised assets and liabilities required by IFRS 1.B2(d) and IFRS 1.B2(f) affect non-controlling interests and deferred tax. Moreover, an entity that adopts the restatement exemption for business combinations in Appendix B of IFRS 1 and that is required to make adjustments to the carrying amounts of previously acquired assets and liabilities in accordance with the requirements of that Appendix, should also restate non-controlling interests for the effect of those adjustments.

6.1.11 *Retranslation of goodwill and fair value adjustments*

IAS 21 *The Effects of Changes in Foreign Exchange Rates* need not be applied retrospectively to fair value adjustments and goodwill arising in business combinations that occurred before the date of transition to IFRSs. If this election is used, the fair value adjustments and goodwill should be treated as assets and liabilities of the entity rather than assets and liabilities of the acquiree. Such goodwill and fair value adjustments are either already expressed in the entity's functional currency or are non-monetary foreign currency items, which are reported using the exchange rate applied under previous GAAP. [IFRS 1.B1A]

Under IAS 21.47, any goodwill arising on the acquisition of a foreign operation and any fair value adjustments to the carrying amounts of assets and liabilities arising on the acquisition of that foreign operation should be treated as assets and liabilities of the foreign operation. They are therefore expressed in the functional currency of the foreign operation and retranslated at the closing rate at the end of the reporting period. An entity may, under previous GAAP, have treated such goodwill and fair value adjustments as assets and liabilities of the entity rather than as assets and liabilities of the foreign operation. If so, the requirements of IAS 21.47 may be applied prospectively to all acquisitions occurring after the date of transition to IFRSs. [IFRS 1.IG21A]

Alternatively, IAS 21 may be applied retrospectively to goodwill and fair value adjustments arising in either:

[IFRS 1.B1B]

- all business combinations that occurred before the date of transition to IFRSs; or
- all business combinations that the entity elects to restate to comply with IFRS 3 (see **6.1.1** above).

Example 6.1.11

Treating goodwill relating to foreign subsidiaries as an asset of the acquirer

Entity A (A) has goodwill relating to a foreign subsidiary arising on a business combination that occurred before the date of transition. Under previous GAAP, A treated goodwill as its own asset and recorded goodwill in its functional currency based on the exchange rate at the date of acquisition.

On transition, A is not required to restate retrospectively the financial statements to treat goodwill as an asset of the acquiree since the acquisition date and translate goodwill at the closing rate at the end of each reporting period.

Entity A can use the exemption in IFRS 1.B1A to avoid applying IAS 21 *The Effects of Changes in Foreign Exchange Rates* retrospectively to goodwill arising in business combinations that occurred before the date of transition.

When an entity does not apply IAS 21 retrospectively to goodwill, there are no future translation adjustments to the goodwill balance. Instead of treating goodwill as an asset of the acquiree and translating it at the end of each reporting period at the closing rate, the entity treats the goodwill balance as its own asset and records goodwill in its functional currency based on the exchange rate at the date of acquisition (as may have been required by previous GAAP).

The exemption applies to goodwill that is deemed to be an asset of the acquirer at the date of transition. However, the exemption is not available for business combinations that occur after the date of transition. Therefore, for all acquisitions after the date of transition, IAS 21 must be fully complied with and goodwill must be treated as an asset of the acquiree (IFRS 1.IG21A).

UK

IAS 21 requires goodwill and fair value adjustments arising on the acquisition of a foreign operation to be treated as assets and liabilities denominated in the functional currency of that operation. There is no similar requirement in UK GAAP (ignoring for this purpose FRS 23 which is based on IAS 21 but applies to very few entities). In practice, under UK GAAP, fair value adjustments to foreign currency assets and liabilities are usually denominated in foreign currency but goodwill is often treated as an asset of the reporting entity and denominated in the reporting entity's functional currency (i.e. usually Sterling). Full retrospective compliance with IAS 21 would require such goodwill to be treated as an asset denominated in a foreign currency (or currencies) and retranslated at the date of transition to IFRSs and the end of subsequent reporting periods. The exemption provided by IFRS 1 avoids the need for restatement of goodwill arising on acquisitions prior to the date of transition to IFRSs. This is helpful because it may be impracticable, or at least very time consuming, to apply IAS 21 retrospectively to acquisitions that occurred many years ago, particularly if they involved operations with a number of different functional currencies.

It is generally accepted that, although the standard is not completely clear, the exemption in respect of fair value adjustments and goodwill may be applied independently to fair value adjustments and to goodwill. In particular, if fair value adjustments were previously treated as foreign currency assets and liabilities, they can continue to be treated this way even if goodwill was treated as a Sterling asset and the exemption from restatement is applied to this goodwill.

It is possible that UK companies have not previously applied a consistent policy regarding whether to retranslate goodwill each year. For example, goodwill arising in a US sub-consolidation may have been treated as a US dollar asset from the perspective of the group while goodwill arising on the direct acquisition of foreign operations may have been treated as a Sterling asset. It is possible to read IFRS 1.B1A as requiring all existing goodwill to be treated consistently as assets and liabilities of the entity when the exemption is used. This would mean that any amounts that had in fact been treated as foreign currency amounts would have to be restated to the Sterling amounts based on the exchange rate at the date of the acquisition. However, given that the purpose of this exemption was to grandfather the existing treatment under local GAAP, it is regarded as acceptable to apply it only to those assets and liabilities that were not retranslated under UK GAAP. Those that were retranslated under UK GAAP would continue to be retranslated in accordance with IAS 21.

In practice, a decision over whether to apply IAS 21 retrospectively should not be taken in isolation, but in the light of all other factors affecting the transition to IFRSs. The choices made will have consequences in future. For example, if goodwill is left denominated in Sterling, the fact that it will no longer be amortised under IFRS 3 means there is a greater risk that it may become impaired in future, merely as a result of adverse currency movements.

6.1.12 Deferred tax on pre-transition business combinations

On initial adoption of IFRSs, a number of amendments to deferred tax balances may need to be made. Such adjustments will be recognised directly in equity if the entity has not re-stated its past business combinations. Conversely, if the relevant past business combinations are being restated on transition then the goodwill figure will be adjusted to take account of the deferred tax balances that would have been recognised at the date of the business combination if IFRS 3 had been applied.

Example 6.1.12A

Deferred tax on pre-transition business combinations (1)

A parent (P) is preparing its consolidated financial statements in accordance with IFRSs for the first time. Prior to its date of transition it acquired a subsidiary (S) which, at the date of acquisition, owned items of property, plant and equipment that do not attract any tax relief. P has taken advantage of the exemption from restatement of business combinations that took place prior to its transition date to IFRSs. When determining the temporary differences related to assets and liabilities acquired in the business combination, the initial recognition exemption is not relevant, as the assets were acquired in a business combination. Accordingly deferred tax assets and deferred tax liabilities are recognised in respect of the temporary differences. Because P has elected not to restate its past business combination, the effect of the recognition of the deferred tax assets and liabilities is taken to retained earnings or another reserve used by the entity for its IFRS 1 adjustments.

At the date of transition, entities will need to determine whether any tax loss carryforwards or other deferred tax assets not recognised at the date of acquisition meet the recognition criteria. Where a deferred tax asset will be recognised on transition that was not previously recognised in a past business combination the resulting adjustment will be made in retained earnings or another reserve used by the entity for its IFRS 1 adjustments. IFRS 1(Appendix B) specifically limits the adjustments that can be made to goodwill on transition. As adjustments for the recoverability of deferred tax assets are not incorporated in this list, the entity may not adjust the previous carrying amount of goodwill. However, IFRS 1 does not create any ongoing exemptions to the accounting requirements of IFRSs. Therefore, when an entity that has not restated a past business combination, subsequently realises an unrecognised deferred tax asset that did not satisfy the recognition criteria at the date of transition, adjustments to the carrying amount of goodwill will be made in accordance with IFRS 3(2004).65. If IFRS 3(2008) is applied, the equivalent requirement is in IAS 12.68 (as amended) which does not require the adjustment of goodwill beyond the end of the measurement period.

Example 6.1.12B

Deferred tax on pre-transition business combinations (2)

Entity B presents its first IFRS financial statements for the year ended 31 December 20X5. In preparing those financial statements the entity applies IFRS 3(2004) and does not restate prior business combinations.

Entity B had previously acquired Entity C in a business combination in which £300 of goodwill was recognised and £500 of deferred tax assets arising from loss carryforwards was not recognised. The loss carryforwards expire on 31 December 20X6. Under Entity B's previous GAAP goodwill amortisation was prohibited, and the carrying amount of goodwill at the date of transition is £300. At the date of transition, Entity B assesses future profitability and determines that £100 of that deferred tax benefit can be recovered during the year ended 31 December 20X6. As part of the IFRS transition entries the following journal entry is recorded:

	DR	CR
	£	£
Deferred tax asset	100	
Equity – IFRS transition reserve		100

During the year ended 31 December 20X6 Entity B's profitability is even higher than expected, and consequently the full amount of the tax loss carryforwards can be used before they expire. First, Entity B will recognise the recovery of the tax losses in the usual way. Second, Entity B will adjust goodwill arising on the business combination, only to the extent that it does not result in the creation of negative goodwill. The following journal entries would be recorded:

	DR	CR
	£	£
Goodwill reduction (P&L)	300	
Goodwill		300
Current tax liability	500	
Current tax (P&L)		500
Deferred tax (P&L)	100	
Deferred tax asset		100

There is therefore a net credit of £100 in profit or loss in 20X6. This represents the extent to which the value of the tax losses used but not recognised at the date of transition (£400) exceeds the carrying amount of goodwill (£300).

6.2 Fair value or revaluation as deemed cost

IFRS 1 permits an item of property, plant and equipment to be measured at the date of transition to IFRSs at its fair value and for that fair value to be used as the asset's deemed cost at that date. [IFRS 1.16] Where this election is used, the disclosures required by IFRS 1.44 should be made in the entity's first IFRS financial statements (see **8.2.2** below).

This election was originally proposed in ED1 to avoid excessive cost to an entity that had not previously collected the necessary information to apply a cost-based measure. The election would have been available only if determining a cost-based measurement under IFRSs would involve undue cost or effort. However, as explained in IFRS

1.BC42, the IASB decided that IFRS 1 should permit an entity to use fair value as deemed cost in some cases without any need to demonstrate undue cost or effort.

The exemption in IFRS 1.16 is not limited to property, plant and equipment within the scope of IAS 16. Consequently, an entity may elect to measure items of property, plant and equipment that are outside the scope of IAS 16 (e.g. certain mineral rights and reserves) at a deemed cost in accordance with IFRS 1.16. Whether mineral rights and reserves are property, plant and equipment or intangible assets is considered in **section 2** of **chapter 6**. Property, plant and equipment used in exploration activities are within the scope of IAS 16.

UK

A UK company should have the information to apply cost-based measurement because this is required by company law. Even when assets have been revalued under UK GAAP, disclosure is required of the carrying amount that would have been included in the financial statements had the assets been carried at historical cost less depreciation. However, some UK companies may wish to make use of the flexibility provided by this election in IFRS 1 to restate assets to fair value at the date of transition to IFRSs. This might, for example be used to increase the group's asset base without resulting in an obligation to keep the valuations up to date after the transition to IFRSs.

The election may be used selectively for individual items of property, plant and equipment. A first-time adopter need not use fair value as deemed cost for all assets in the same class. However, indications of impairment cannot be ignored for those assets that are not restated. IFRS 1.BC45 explains that some respondents to ED1 suggested that the election should be applied to an entire class of assets. But the IASB rejected this suggestion and IFRS 1 does not restrict the use of fair value as deemed cost to entire classes of assets.

A first-time adopter may also elect to use a previous GAAP revaluation of an item of property, plant and equipment at, or before, the date of transition to IFRSs as deemed cost at the date of revaluation. This is, however, permitted only if the revaluation was, at the date of the revaluation, broadly comparable to:

[IFRS 1.17]

- fair value; or

- cost or depreciated cost under IFRSs, adjusted to reflect, for example, changes in a general or specific price index.

The reference to the revaluation being 'broadly comparable' is explained in IFRS 1.BC47 as allowing a first-time adopter 'to establish a deemed cost using a measurement that is already available and is a reasonable starting point for a cost-based measurement'.

IFRS 1.16 provides the option to measure an item of property, plant and equipment (PPE) at deemed cost without specifying if the assets have been acquired, self-constructed or held under finance leases. Note, however, that the fair value of an item of PPE held under a finance lease will be the fair value of the lessee's interest in the lease, not the fair value of that item.

Example 6.2A

Determining deemed cost under IFRS 1

Under previous GAAP, an airline was required to adjust the carrying amount of its aeroplanes by the amount of the exchange differences incurred on loans obtained to purchase these assets during the four years subsequent to their acquisition. Any accumulated depreciation at the date of this adjustment was restated prospectively. After this four-year period, the cost was considered fixed and no further interest was capitalised. The only limitation on the carrying amount of the asset was, in the case of an upward increase, that the resulting carrying amount could not exceed the lower of market value or depreciated replacement cost of the related asset.

On first-time application of IFRSs, will it be possible to use the carrying amounts of the aeroplanes (as calculated using the accounting treatment detailed above) as their deemed cost?

Yes. IFRS 1.17 states:

A first-time adopter may elect to use a previous GAAP revaluation of an item of property, plant and equipment at, or before, the date of transition to IFRSs as deemed cost **at the date of the revaluation**, if the revaluation was, at the date of the revaluation, broadly comparable to:

- fair value; or
- cost or depreciated cost under IFRSs, adjusted to reflect, for example, changes in a general or specific price index. [Emphasis added]

The revaluation detailed above would be broadly comparable to cost or depreciated cost, adjusted for changes in a price index (i.e. changes in foreign exchange prices). This deemed cost would also be acceptable for assets if the adjustment to the carrying amount has ceased (e.g. assets purchased in 20X5 and adjusted until 20X9). IFRS 1.17 above states that the deemed cost 'at the date of the revaluation' may be used. The entity should note, however, that on adoption of IFRS 1, it will be required to split the aeroplane into its material component parts, in compliance with IAS 16. IFRS 1 would also permit the airline to fair-value its aeroplanes, as a one-off revaluation, on first-time adoption, and then subsequently account for them on a depreciated-cost basis. The airline should ensure that the assets are not overstated on first-time adoption and should review the assets for impairment.

UK

This election in IFRS 1 would permit valuations performed under FRS 15 to be treated as deemed cost on transition to IFRSs. Similarly, any 'frozen valuations' under the transitional provisions of FRS 15 could also be treated as deemed cost under IFRSs.

Where a previous GAAP revaluation is used as deemed cost, it will be necessary to consider how the revaluation surplus recognised in the revaluation reserve under previous GAAP would be recognised under IFRSs. IFRS 1 requires the adjustments arising from first-time adoption to be recognised in retained earnings, or if appropriate, another category of equity. If property, plant and equipment is recognised at its revalued amount as deemed cost, the adjustment is not included in the revaluation reserve. Therefore, a subsequent impairment cannot be recognised against the revaluation reserve, but instead should be charged to profit or loss. The adjustment could be recorded as a separate component of equity but there is nothing in IFRS 1 to require this. Any subsequent impairment would still have to be charged to profit or loss. The determination of how this affects distributable profits is a matter of law and would have to be considered.

UK

*As explained in paragraphs 10.17 to 10.19 of TECH 01/08 (see **chapter 49**), the adjustment is unlikely to be a realised profit available for distribution. It may, therefore, be helpful to exclude it from retained earnings and instead to record it as a separate component of equity even though there is no requirement in IFRS 1 to do this.*

The elections described above for property, plant and equipment are also available for:

- investment property, if an entity elects to use the cost model in IAS 40 *Investment Property*; and
- intangible assets that meet:
  - the recognition criteria in IAS 38 *Intangible Assets* (including reliable measurement of original cost); and

- the criteria in IAS 38 for revaluation (including the existence of an active market).

IFRS 1 states that these elections should not be used for other assets or liabilities. [IFRS 1.18]

The ability to apply this election to intangible assets is likely to be of limited relevance given the restriction that the criteria in IAS 38 for revaluation must be met.

UK *The election might be relevant to a UK company where it holds an investment property and decides to adopt the cost model under IAS 40. The previous valuation under SSAP 19 could be treated as deemed cost for IAS 40.*

A first-time adopter may have established a deemed cost under previous GAAP for some or all of its assets and liabilities by measuring them at their fair value at one particular date because of an event such a privatisation or initial public offering (IPO). IFRS 1 permits the use of such event-driven fair value measurements as deemed cost for IFRSs at the date of that measurement. [IFRS 1.19] This is only possible for an intangible asset if it meets the recognition criteria in IAS 38 (see **5.10** above). [IFRS 1.IG50]

In summary, therefore, one of the following amounts may be used as deemed cost of property, plant and equipment (and in certain cases investment property and intangible assets):

[IFRS 1.IG8]

- fair value at the date of transition to IFRSs;
- a revaluation under previous GAAP that meets the criteria in paragraph 17 of IFRS 1; or
- fair value at the date of an event such as privatisation or IPO.

Subsequent depreciation is based on that deemed cost and starts from the date for which the fair value measurement or revaluation was established. [IFRS 1.IG9]

Under local GAAP, it is possible that the land and buildings components of a property were not recognised separately and were amortised as a whole. In such cases, a first-time adopter should recognise the land and buildings components separately. The recognition of each component should be made using either the asset's original cost restated from the date of acquisition (for depreciation) or its fair value at the date of transition.

This will not usually apply to UK companies because, except in some cases where held under a finance lease, the land and buildings components would typically have been separated under FRS 15. UK

If the revaluation model in IAS 16 is used for some or all classes of property, plant and equipment, the cumulative revaluation surplus is presented as a separate component of equity. The revaluation surplus at the date of transition to IFRSs should be based on a comparison of the carrying amount of the asset at that date with its cost or deemed cost. If the deemed cost is the fair value at the date of transition to IFRSs, the disclosures required by paragraph 44 of IFRS 1 should be given (see **8.2.2** below). [IFRS 1.IG10]

If revaluations under previous GAAP did not satisfy the criteria in paragraphs 17 or 19 of IFRS 1, the revalued assets should be measured in the opening IFRS statement of financial position on one of the following bases:

[IFRS 1.IG11]

- cost (or deemed cost) less any accumulated depreciation and any accumulated impairment losses under the cost model in IAS 16;
- deemed cost, being the fair value at the date of transition to IFRSs; or
- revalued amount, if the entity adopts the revaluation model in IAS 16 as its accounting policy under IFRSs for all assets in the same class.

Example 6.2B

Asset exchanges

IAS 16 *Property, Plant and Equipment* requires that an entity measure an item of property, plant and equipment acquired in exchange for a non-monetary asset or assets, or a combination of monetary and non-monetary assets, at fair value unless the exchange transaction lacks commercial substance. Under the previous GAAP, an entity measured such an acquired asset at fair value unless the exchanged assets were similar. The entity recognised and measured a tangible asset at fair value prior to the date of transition, but the application of IAS 16 would lead to a conclusion that the transaction lacked commercial substance, and IAS 16 would require the new asset to be recognised at the carrying amount of the asset given up. Should the entity adjust accumulated depreciation in its opening IFRS statement of financial position retrospectively to comply with IAS 16?

Under previous GAAP, the acquired asset was recognised at fair value, but IAS 16 would require the acquired asset to be recognised at the carrying amount of the asset given up. For first-time adopters, IFRS 1 has no exemption from applying the IAS 16 requirement retrospectively. Therefore, in theory, restatement is required under IFRS 1. However, provided that the asset was measured at fair value at the date of the transaction, IFRS 1.17 applies. The entity may, therefore, take the fair value at the date of the exchange transaction as the deemed cost of the asset on first-time adoption of IFRSs.

6.3 Employee benefits

6.3.1 The exemption

Under IAS 19 *Employee Benefits*, an entity may elect to use a 'corridor' approach when measuring its obligations under defined benefit pension plans (see **section 7.5** in **chapter 24**) that leaves some actuarial gains and losses unrecognised. Retrospective application of this approach would require the cumulative actuarial gains and losses from the inception of the plan until the date of transition to IFRSs to be split into a recognised portion and an unrecognised portion. A first-time adopter may elect to recognise all cumulative actuarial gains and losses at the date of transition to IFRSs, even if it uses the corridor approach for later actuarial gains and losses. If a first-time adopter uses this election, it must be applied to all its plans. [IFRS 1.20]

As described at **6.5.2** below, if a subsidiary is already reporting under IFRSs and has made an unreserved statement of compliance with IFRSs in previous years, that subsidiary's pensions corridor could not be reset to zero for the purposes of the consolidated financial statements. This is because if a parent adopts IFRSs later than its subsidiary, it must use that subsidiary's date of transition as its own for that subsidiary in accordance with IFRS 1.25.

To the extent the election to reset the pensions corridor is and may be used, the corridor must be reset at the date of transition. It is not possible to select any other date (for example by analogy with the flexibility provided by IFRS 1 for the restatement of past acquisitions).

6.3.2 *The consequences of not using the exemption*

It is likely that most first-time adopters will make use of the election to recognise all cumulative actuarial gains and losses at the date of transition. In practice, this means recognising the full amount of the surplus or deficit at the date of transition to IFRSs (subject to the detailed requirements of IAS 19).

If this election is not made, it would be necessary to go back to the inception of the pension scheme (or, if later, the date on which the scheme was acquired in a business combination) and obtain actuarial valuations at the end of each subsequent reporting period to apply the corridor approach with retrospective effect. For a pension scheme that has been established for more than a few years, this is likely to involve significant cost and may be impracticable.

If a scheme was assumed as part of a business combination, the scheme is only a scheme of the consolidated entity from the date of acquisition. At the date of acquisition, the scheme has a new measurement basis as required by IFRS 3. Also, Example 2 in the IFRS 1 Implementation Guidance clarifies that the pension obligation and corresponding entry to retained earnings are calculated from the date of acquisition. An entity would not be allowed to restate a scheme prior to the date the scheme was assumed in a business combination.

UK

For UK companies, there may be some instances where recognising the full amount of the pension scheme deficit on transition to IFRSs may reduce distributable profits to such an extent as to prevent the payment of dividends. Where this is the case, consideration might be given to applying the corridor approach with retrospective effect but this is likely to involve substantial cost and effort and may be impracticable if the scheme has been established for a long time.

6.3.3 *Exemption from a disclosure requirement in IAS 19*

IAS 19 includes a requirement to disclose the following amounts for the current period and the previous four periods:

- the present value of the defined benefit obligation, the fair value of the plan assets and the surplus or deficit in the plan;
- the experience adjustments arising on the plan liabilities expressed either as an amount or as a percentage of plan liabilities at the end of the reporting period; and

- the experience adjustments arising on the plan assets expressed either as an amount or as a percentage of plan assets at the end of the reporting period.

To be consistent with the transitional rules for this requirement in IAS 19, IFRS 1 states that a first-time adopter may disclose these amounts as they are determined for each accounting period prospectively from the transition date. [IFRS 1.20A]

UK

A similar approach was taken with the equivalent requirements of FRS 17. UK companies may be able to give the complete five year history without significant cost or effort given the similarities between FRS 17 and IAS 19. But they are entitled to use the exemption if they wish.

6.4 Cumulative translation differences

Under IAS 21 some translation differences are initially recognised in other comprehensive income (for entities applying IAS 1(2007)) and accumulated in a separate component of equity. IAS 21 also requires disclosure of the net exchange differences accumulated in a separate component of equity and a reconciliation of the amount of such exchange differences at the beginning and end of the period. On disposal of a foreign operation, IAS 21 requires an entity to reclassify the cumulative translation difference for that foreign operation (including, if applicable, gains and losses on related hedges) to profit or loss as part of the gain or loss on disposal. [IFRS 1.21]

A first-time adopter need not comply with these requirements for cumulative translation differences that existed at the date of transition to IFRSs. If this exemption is used, the cumulative translation differences for all foreign operations are deemed to be zero at the date of transition to IFRSs. The gain or loss on a subsequent disposal of any foreign operation should then exclude translation differences that arose before the date of transition to IFRSs but should include all later translation differences. [IFRS 1.22]

If the election is used to reset all cumulative translation differences for all foreign operations to zero at the date of transition to IFRSs, this treatment applies to translation differences that arise as a result of first-time adoption of IFRSs. The election applies once all adjustments for first-time adoption have been recognised at the date of transition. If the election is used, the balance of cumulative translation differences in the opening IFRS statement of financial position will equal zero.

UK

SSAP 20 is similar to IAS 21 in that it requires certain exchange gains and losses to be taken directly to reserves and not reported in the profit and loss account for the period. However, under UK GAAP there is no requirement to 'reclassify' or 'recycle' these gains and losses on disposal of the related operation. Consequently, few UK companies take such exchange differences to a separate reserve and they are often simply charged and credited to retained profits. Under IAS 21 this is not permitted and they have to be disclosed as a separate component of equity. Detailed records have to be kept of the composition of this balance to enable the amount to be 'reclassified' or 'recycled' on a subsequent disposal to be determined.

However, under IFRS 1, this requirement may be applied prospectively to exchange differences arising after the date of transition to IFRSs. It is not necessary to recreate retrospectively the information about gains and losses prior to that date. Most UK companies will wish to make use of this exemption but, if disposals are planned, it may be worth investigating the potential effect of the exemption on any gains or losses on disposal.

The following example illustrates the application of the exemption in a situation where an entity has to change its functional currency on transition to IFRSs to comply with IAS 21.

Example 6.4

Reassessment of functional currency on transition to IFRSs

Under previous GAAP, an entity had Sterling as its functional currency. At the date of transition, in accordance with IAS 21 *The Effects of Changes in Foreign Exchange Rates*, the entity changes to a functional currency of US dollars. The entity chooses not to use the exemption available in IFRS 1.22 but instead applies IAS 21 retrospectively.

The Foreign currency Translation Reserve (FCTR) must be recalculated from the date the functional currency, in accordance with IAS 21, is considered to be US dollars.

If the functional currency of the entity is determined always to have been US dollars, the FCTR, at the date of transition, will effectively represent the effect of the movements in exchange rates since the acquisition of each asset and liability (including those disposed of). The FCTR must be calculated based on the underlying measurement of assets and liabilities in the functional currency of the entity.

Paragraphs 16 and 17 of IFRS 1 permit deemed cost to be used for certain assets. When this exemption is used, the FCTR will not be calculated from the date of acquisition, but from the date at which the deemed cost amount is determined in relation to the assets to which deemed cost has been applied.

If the functional currency changed from Sterling to US dollars at some point prior to the date of transition (ignoring the use of any deemed cost exemption), the FCTR is only calculated from the date of change, as under IAS 21.35 translation procedures are only applied prospectively.

Irrespective of whether the IAS 21 exemption in IFRS 1.22 is used, and hence the FCTR is reset to zero, balances in the financial statements must be recorded in the entity's functional currency following the IAS 21 requirements.

6.5 Assets and liabilities of subsidiaries, associates and joint ventures

This section deals with the requirements of IFRS 1 where a parent and a subsidiary become first-time adopters at different times. These requirements do not apply when the dates of adoption are the same. When the dates of adoption are the same, the parent and the subsidiary may each apply the exemptions in IFRS 1 independently of each other: they are not required to take the same exemptions.

As explained in **example 6.5.5** below, in the consolidated financial statements of a first-time adopter, the exemptions in IFRS 1 must be applied consistently to all subsidiaries, associates and joint ventures except where the exemption permits otherwise (e.g. the election for deemed cost of property, plant and equipment may be applied on an individual asset basis). This is, however, subject to the requirements described at **6.5.2** below if the subsidiary, associate or joint venture becomes a first-time adopter before the investor.

6.5.1 Subsidiary becomes first-time adopter later than its parent

If a subsidiary becomes a first-time adopter later than its parent, IFRS 1 permits a choice between two measurement bases in the subsidiary's separate financial statements. In this case, a subsidiary should measure its assets and liabilities at either:

- the carrying amount that would be included in the parent's consolidated financial statements, based on the parent's date of transition to IFRSs, if no adjustments were made for consolidation procedures and for the effects of the business combination in which the parent acquired the subsidiary; or
- the carrying amounts required by IFRS 1 based on the subsidiary's date of transition to IFRSs.

The carrying amounts under these alternatives could differ when the exemptions in IFRS 1 result in measurement that depends on the date of transition to IFRSs. They could also differ when the accounting policies used in the subsidiary's financial statements differ from those in the consolidated financial statements. [IFRS 1.24]

> The purpose of this exemption is to avoid the need to keep two parallel sets of records which the IASB accepted would be burdensome and not beneficial to users. [IFRS 1.BC60]

Example 8 in the Implementation Guidance to IFRS 1 provides an illustration of this choice. The example notes that where the assets and liabilities are measured based on the subsidiary's (later) date of transition to IFRSs, this does not change the carrying amount of the assets and liabilities in the consolidated financial statements. [IFRS 1.IG29]

A similar election is available to an associate or joint venture that becomes a first-time adopter later than an entity that has significant influence or joint control over it. [IFRS 1.24]

> *This exemption would be relevant where the subsidiaries in a UK listed group continued to report under UK GAAP from 2005 but change to IFRSs in, say, 2010. It would enable the accounting in the subsidiaries to be consistent with the information used for consolidation purposes.* UK

Paragraphs 24 (discussed in this section) and 25 (discussed at **6.5.2** below) of IFRS 1 do not override the following requirements:

[IFRS 1.IG30]

- to apply Appendix B of IFRS 1 (on business combinations – see **6.1** above) to assets acquired and liabilities assumed in a business combination that occurred before the acquirer's date of transition to IFRSs. But the acquirer should apply paragraph 25 to new assets acquired, and liabilities assumed, by the acquiree after that business combination and still held at the acquiree's date of transition to IFRSs;
- to apply the rest of IFRS 1 in measuring all assets and liabilities for which paragraphs 24 and 25 are not relevant; and
- to give all disclosures required by IFRS 1 as of the first-time adopter's own date of transition to IFRSs (see **section 8** below).

Paragraph 24 of IFRS 1 applies if a subsidiary becomes a first-time adopter later than its parent, for example if the subsidiary previously prepared a reporting package under IFRSs for consolidation purposes but did not present a full set of financial statements under IFRSs. The IFRS 1 Implementation Guidance notes that this may be relevant not only when a subsidiary's reporting package complies fully with the recognition and measurement requirements of IFRSs, but also when it is adjusted centrally for matters such as a review of events after the reporting period and central allocation of pension costs. The Implementation Guidance explains that such adjustments to an unpublished reporting package are not the correction of errors for the purposes of the disclosure requirements of paragraph 41 of the Standard (see **8.2.1** below). However, paragraph 24 does not permit a subsidiary to ignore misstatements that are immaterial to the consolidated financial statements but are material to the subsidiary's own financial statements. [IFRS 1.IG31]

For example, if a subsidiary adopts IFRSs in its December 2008 financial statements, its date of transition to IFRSs will be 1 January 2007. Rather than applying IFRS 1 as at that date, the subsidiary can elect to use the assets and liabilities recorded in the group reporting package as at 31 December 2006 as adjusted for any relevant central adjustments made to bring the reporting package into full compliance with the recognition and measurement requirements of IFRSs. But if there was an error in the reporting package that was material to the subsidiary's financial statements (but ignored as immaterial to the consolidated financial statements) then the amounts would have to be adjusted to comply with IFRSs.

6.5.2 *Parent becomes a first-time adopter later than its subsidiary*

If a parent becomes a first-time adopter later than its subsidiary, the parent should, in its consolidated financial statements, measure the assets and liabilities of the subsidiary at the same carrying amount as in the separate financial statements of the subsidiary, after adjusting for consolidation adjustments and for the effects of the business combination in which the parent acquired the subsidiary. The same approach applies in the case of associates and joint ventures. [IFRS 1.25]

Although this appears in a section of IFRS 1 dealing with exemptions, it is written as a requirement. The reason for this is unclear but the material was presumably included here to contrast with the situation where a subsidiary becomes a first-time adopter later than its parent. The Basis for Conclusions section of IFRS 1 devotes five paragraphs (BC59 to BC63) to explaining the reason for the exemption in the latter case. It then briefly adds 'however, if a parent adopts IFRSs later than a subsidiary, the parent cannot, in its consolidated financial statements, elect to change IFRS measurements that the subsidiary has already used in its financial statements, except to adjust for consolidation procedures and for the effects of the business combination in which the parent acquired the subsidiary'. This is a statement of fact rather than an explanation of the reason for the requirement.

A UK company that adopts IFRSs may have an overseas subsidiary that has previously prepared its local financial statements under IFRSs and included an explicit and unreserved statement of compliance with IFRSs. In this case, the assets and liabilities should be stated at the amounts at which they were included in the IFRS compliant local financial statements. UK

Example 9 in the Implementation Guidance to IFRS 1 provides an illustration of this requirement. [IFRS 1.IG29]

The following example illustrates the effect of this requirement for the recognition of a pension scheme surplus or deficit on transition to IFRSs.

Example 6.5.2

Effect on employee benefit exemption when a parent and subsidiary have different dates of transition to IFRSs

Company S is a publicly listed entity in Europe but is a subsidiary of Company P. Company S adopts IFRSs in 20X5, using 1 January 20X4 as its date of transition. Upon first-time adoption, Company S elected to reset its corridor to zero in accordance with IFRS 1.20 through retained earnings. Company P is adopting IFRSs in 20X8, using 1 January 20X7 as its date of transition.

Company P cannot elect to reset Company S's pension corridor to zero in 20X7 when Company P first adopts IFRSs. If a parent adopts IFRSs later than its subsidiary, it must use the subsidiary's date of transition as its own for that subsidiary in accordance with IFRS 1.25.

But this does not override the need to prepare the consolidated financial statements on the basis of consistent accounting policies. For example, if Company P adopts a policy of immediate recognition of all actuarial gains and losses without the use of the corridor, the amounts reported by Company S (using the corridor) would be adjusted for the purposes of consolidation by Company P.

As explained at **6.5.1** above, IFRS 1.25 does not override certain other requirements of IFRS 1.

6.5.3 *Parent becomes a first-time adopter for its separate financial statements earlier or later than for its consolidated financial statements*

If a parent becomes a first-time adopter for its separate financial statements earlier or later than for its consolidated financial statements, it should measure its assets and liabilities at the same amounts in both financial statements, except for consolidation adjustments. [IFRS 1.25]

UK *This might be relevant to a UK parent company that adopted IFRSs for its consolidated financial statements in 2005 but continues to prepare the separate financial statements of the parent under UK GAAP for a few years. It is interesting to note that, in a similar situation, the UK subsidiaries would have a choice (see* **6.5.1** *above) between using their own date of transition or that of their parent whereas the parent gets no similar choice for its separate financial statements. But, in practice, it would be convenient to use the amounts included in the consolidation, so this should not be a problem.*

It is not immediately obvious how a parent could be a first-time adopter for its separate financial statements earlier than for its consolidated financial statements. Separate financial statements alone would not comply with IAS 27 where that Standard would require consolidated financial statements to be presented. However, the situation might arise if the parent was entitled to the exemption from preparation of consolidated financial statements in IAS 27 (i.e. because a higher parent prepares IFRS consolidated financial statements) but subsequently ceased to be entitled to the exemption or chose not to use it.

6.5.4 *Subsidiaries not previously consolidated*

A first-time adopter consolidates all subsidiaries that it controls, unless IAS 27 requires otherwise. [IFRS 1.IG26]

If a first-time adopter did not consolidate a subsidiary under previous GAAP, then, in its consolidated financial statements, it measures the subsidiary's assets and liabilities at the same carrying amounts as in the separate IFRS financial statements of the subsidiary, after adjusting for consolidation procedures and for the effects of the business combination in which it acquired the subsidiary. If the subsidiary has not adopted IFRSs in its separate financial statements, the carrying amounts required are those that IFRSs would require in those separate financial statements. [IFRS 1.IG27]

If the parent acquired the subsidiary in a business combination before the date of transition to IFRSs, the parent recognises goodwill as explained at **6.1.9** above. If the parent did not acquire the subsidiary in a business combination because it created the subsidiary, the parent does not recognise goodwill. [IFRS 1.IG27]

Given the similarities between the requirements of IAS 27 and FRSs 2 and 5, it will be rare for a company to have to be consolidated under IAS 27 when it was not consolidated under UK GAAP. UK

6.5.5 Application of IFRS 1 exemptions to equity accounting for associates

Example 6.5.5

Application of IFRS 1 exemptions to equity accounting for associates

An associate of an investor may elect to adopt some or all of the voluntary exemptions in IFRS 1 when preparing its own financial statements.

If the investor becomes a first-time adopter later than its associate, the investor is required in its consolidated financial statements to measure the assets and liabilities of the associate based on the same carrying amounts as in the separate financial statements of the associate, after adjusting for the effects of consolidation adjustments (including the alignment of accounting policies) and for the effects of the business combination in which the investor acquired the associate (see **6.5.2** above). The investor's consolidated financial statements will therefore reflect the effects of the elections made by the associate on its own transition to IFRSs. For example, as illustrated in **example 6.5.2** above, if the investor uses the pensions corridor, it cannot elect to reset the associate's pensions corridor to zero at its own date of transition to IFRSs.

However, if the associate first adopts IFRSs at the same time as (or later than) the investor, the IFRS 1 exemptions elected by the investor should be applied consistently to the associate in the former's consolidated financial statements. The exemptions from IFRSs specified in IFRS 1 represent accounting policy choices. IFRS 1.7 states that accounting policies are required to comply with each IFRS effective at the reporting date for its first IFRS financial statements, except as specified in paragraphs 13 to 34. IAS 28.27 requires the accounting policies of an associate to be consistent with those of the investor for the purposes of equity accounting. For most of the exemptions in IFRS 1, the effect of this will be that election choices will need to be consistently applied to an equity-accounted associate in the same way that they are applied to subsidiaries.

An exception to this rule is the use of revaluation or fair value as deemed cost. This is because the deemed cost election can be applied on an individual asset basis. The application of the election can therefore vary for different items of property, plant and equipment in subsidiaries and associates.

Where the deemed cost exemption is not used, the investor should apply consistently the IFRS 1 shortcut in respect of changes in existing decommissioning, restoration and similar liabilities included in the cost of property, plant and equipment. The shortcut only affects the portion of costs to be capitalised into the cost of an asset.

In relation to business combinations undertaken by the associate, the investor's election choices should be consistently applied for any business combinations after it was acquired by the investor.

The above analysis deals only with the consolidated financial statements of the investor. The position regarding the separate financial statements of the investor and the associate are considered at **6.5** below.

6.6 Share-based payments

IFRS 1 includes an exemption for share-based payment transactions that was inserted by IFRS 2. The requirements of IFRS 1, when this exemption is used, are very similar to the transitional provisions in IFRS 2 itself in that the Standard is not required (or in practice permitted) to be applied to certain options previously granted. The relevant requirements of IFRS 1 are described below.

6.6.1 *Equity instruments*

6.6.1.1 *Limitations on retrospective application*

A first-time adopter is encouraged, but not required, to apply IFRS 2 to equity instruments that were:

[IFRS 1.25B]

- granted on or before 7 November 2002; or
- granted after 7 November 2002 and vested before the later of the date of transition to IFRSs and 1 January 2005.

The reference to 1 January 2005 is now of limited relevance because entities adopting IFRSs for the first time will invariably have a date of transition that is later than 1 January 2005. Therefore, the practical effect of this exemption is that equity instruments that vested before the date of transition can be ignored. This is logical because there would be no expense to recognise in the first IFRS reporting period or comparative period for such instruments. Equity instruments granted on or before 7 November 2002 can also be ignored, even if they have not vested at the date of transition, but this is likely to be of limited relevance now.

However, if a first-time adopter elects to apply IFRS 2 to such equity instruments, it may do so only if the entity has disclosed publicly the fair value of those equity instruments, determined at the measurement date, as defined in IFRS 2. [IFRS 1.25B]

The effect of this requirement is to prohibit full retrospective application of IFRS 2 by most entities because they will not have disclosed publicly the fair value of the equity instruments granted in previous years. The Standard does not elaborate on what is meant by 'disclosed publicly' but it appears that the IASB had in mind disclosure in the financial statements in the year when the instruments were granted. Paragraph IG8 in the Implementation Guidance to IFRS 2 gives, as an example, disclosures made in the notes to the financial statements of the information required in the US by SFAS 123. Although the Basis for Conclusions to IFRS 2 does not explain the reasons for the effective prohibition on full retrospective application, it appears that this was due to concerns about the difficulty of obtaining valuations at earlier dates without being influenced by the benefit of hindsight. Therefore, although the letter of the requirement to have publicly disclosed the fair values might be met in other ways (for example a press release prior to the first IFRS financial statements) it is clear that only contemporaneous disclosure in the financial statements would meet the intentions of the Standard.

UK

UK companies were required to adopt FRS 20 for periods commencing on or after 1 January 2005 (listed companies) or 1 January 2006 (unlisted companies). FRS 20 is identical to IFRS 2 in all respects except for the implementation dates. Therefore, companies that are already applying FRS 20 under UK GAAP should not need to make any adjustments on adoption of IFRS 2.

For all grants of equity instruments to which IFRS 2 has not been applied (e.g. equity instruments granted on or before 7 November 2002), a first-time adopter should nevertheless disclose the information required by paragraphs 44 and 45 of IFRS 2 (see **chapter 25**). [IFRS 1.25B]

6.6.1.2 *Modifications to the terms and conditions*

If a first-time adopter modifies the terms or conditions of a grant of equity instruments to which IFRS 2 has not been applied, paragraphs 26 to 29 of IFRS 2 (see **chapter 25**) need not be applied if the modifications occurred before the later of the date of transition to IFRSs and 1 January 2005. [IFRS 1.25B]

6.6.2 *Liabilities arising from share-based payment transactions*

A first-time adopter is encouraged, but not required, to apply IFRS 2 to liabilities arising from share-based payment transactions that were:

- settled before the date of transition to IFRSs; or
- settled before 1 January 2005.

For liabilities to which IFRS 2 is applied, a first-time adopter is not required to restate comparative information to the extent that the information relates to a period or date that is earlier than 7 November 2002. [IFRS 1.25C]

This exemption is now of limited relevance. The date of transition to IFRSs will invariably be later than 1 January 2005 so the practical effect is that liabilities can be ignored if they were settled before the date of transition to IFRSs. Such liabilities would have no effect on the financial statements even if an exemption did not exist.

UK

UK companies that have adopted FRS 20 will not need to make any adjustments to liabilities arising from share-based payment transactions, on transition to IFRSs, because the requirements are the same.

6.7 Insurance contracts

A first-time adopter may apply the transitional provisions of IFRS 4 *Insurance Contracts*. IFRS 4 restricts changes in accounting policies for insurance contracts, including changes made by a first-time adopter. [IFRS 1.25D]

The transitional provisions in paragraphs 41 to 45 of IFRS 4 apply both to an entity that is already applying IFRSs when it first applies IFRS 4 and to a first-time adopter. [IFRS 4.40] The provisions that are still relevant to an entity now adopting IFRSs are set out below.

In applying IFRS 4.39(c)(iii) (see **5.2** in **chapter 44**), it is not necessary to disclose information about claims development that occurred earlier than five years before the end of the first financial year in which an entity applies IFRS 4. Furthermore, if it is impracticable, when an entity first applies IFRS 4, to prepare information about claims development that occurred before the beginning of the earliest period for which the entity presents full comparative information that complies with IFRS 4, that fact is to be disclosed. [IFRS 4.44]

When an insurer changes its accounting policies for insurance liabilities, it is permitted, but not required, to reclassify some or all of its financial assets as 'at fair value through profit or loss' (see **chapter 14**). This reclassification is permitted:

[IFRS 4.45]

- if an insurer changes accounting policies when it first applies IFRS 4 (e.g. on first-time adoption); and
- if it makes a subsequent policy change permitted by IFRS 4.22 (see **4.3** in **chapter 44**) in which case the reclassification is a change in accounting policy and IAS 8 applies.

6.8 Decommissioning liabilities included in the cost of property, plant and equipment

Under IFRIC 1 *Changes in Existing Decommissioning, Restoration and Similar Liabilities* (discussed at **4.4** in **chapter 6**), specified changes in a decommissioning, restoration or similar liability are added to or deducted from the cost of the asset to which it relates, and the adjusted depreciable amount of the asset is then depreciated prospectively over its remaining useful life. A first-time adopter need not comply with these requirements for changes in such liabilities that occurred before the date of transition to IFRSs. Where this exemption is taken, the first-time adopter should:

[IFRS 1.25E]

- measure the liability as at the date of transition to IFRSs in accordance with IAS 37;
- to the extent that the liability is within the scope of IFRIC 1, estimate the amount that would have been included in the cost of the related asset when the liability first arose, by discounting the liability to that date using its best estimate of the historical risk-adjusted discount rate(s) that would have applied for that liability over the intervening period; and

- calculate the accumulated depreciation on that amount, as at the date of transition to IFRSs, on the basis of the current estimate of the useful life of the asset, using the depreciation policy adopted by the entity under IFRSs.

The Implementation Guidance attached to IFRS 1 includes an example illustrating the use of this exemption.

6.9 Leases

A first-time adopter may apply the transitional provisions of IFRIC 4 *Determining whether an Arrangement contains a Lease*. Therefore, a first-time adopter may determine whether an arrangement existing at the date of transition to IFRSs contains a lease on the basis of the facts and circumstances existing at that date. [IFRS 1.25F]

IFRIC 4 specifies criteria for determining, at the inception of an arrangement, whether the arrangement contains a lease. It also specifies when an arrangement should be reassessed subsequently. IFRIC 4 amended IFRS 1 to insert a transitional exemption. Instead of determining retrospectively whether an arrangement contains a lease at the inception of the arrangement and subsequently reassessing that arrangement as required in the periods prior to transition to IFRSs, entities may determine whether arrangements in existence on the date of transition to IFRSs contain leases by applying paragraphs 6 to 9 of IFRIC 4 to those arrangements on the basis of the facts and circumstances existing at that date. [IFRS 1.IG204 – IG205]

6.10 Borrowing costs

6.10.1 Introduction

IAS 23 *Borrowing Costs* prescribes the accounting treatment for borrowing costs. A revised version of the Standard was issued by the IASB in March 2007, and is effective for annual periods beginning on or after 1 January 2009, with earlier application permitted (see **chapter 27**). The revised Standard amends IFRS 1 to insert a new exemption from full retrospective application of IAS 23, which is considered at **6.10.2** below. The position of entities applying the previous version of IAS 23 on transition to IFRSs is explained at **6.10.3** below.

Entities adopting IFRSs in 2008 are not required to adopt the revised version of IAS 23 on transition but should consider doing so to avoid the need for a subsequent change of accounting policy. They may also benefit from being able to apply the transitional provisions described at **6.10.2** below.

UK

The previous version of IAS 23 was similar to FRS 15 in that it permitted a choice of policy between capitalising borrowing costs and not capitalising them. There was nothing to require this choice to be exercised in the same way under IAS 23 as it was under FRS 15 but the factors which led to a particular conclusion under UK GAAP would generally have led to the same conclusion under IFRSs.

When a UK company has previously capitalised borrowing costs under UK GAAP and continues to do so under IAS 23, the amount capitalised will not necessarily be the same because of differences between the two standards.

IAS 23 requires disclosure of interest capitalised in the period. Neither IAS 23 nor IFRS 1 requires disclosure of the cumulative amount capitalised. [IFRS 1.IG24]

6.10.2 *Entities applying the revised version of IAS 23*

Where an entity first adopts IFRSs for a period beginning on or after 1 January 2009, or first adopts IFRSs for an earlier period but chooses to apply the revised version of IAS 23, IFRS 1 permits it either:

[IFRS 1.25I]

- to account for borrowing costs retrospectively, as though the requirements of the revised Standard had always applied; or
- to apply the transitional provisions described in **section 5** of **chapter 27**. Where a first-time adopter chooses this option, references to the effective date are interpreted as 1 January 2009 or the date of transition to IFRSs, whichever is later.

As the transitional provisions allow the revised Standard to be applied prospectively, entities adopting IFRSs before 2009 may find the second option above more attractive than seeking to comply retrospectively with the previous version of IAS 23, as discussed at **6.10.3** below.

On first adopting IFRSs, an entity begins capitalising borrowing costs. In accordance with the above requirement of IFRS 1, the entity:

[IFRS 1.IG23]

- capitalises borrowing costs relating to qualifying assets for which the commencement date for capitalisation is on or after 1 January 2009 or the date of transition to IFRSs (whichever is later); and
- may elect to designate any date before 1 January 2009 or the date of transition to IFRSs (whichever is the later) and to capitalise borrowing costs relating to all qualifying assets for which the commencement date for capitalisation is on or after that date.

However, if the entity establishes a deemed cost for an asset, the entity should not capitalise borrowing costs incurred before the date of the measurement that established the deemed cost.

6.10.3 Entities applying the previous version of IAS 23

Where an entity first adopts IFRSs for a period beginning before 1 January 2009, and does not choose to apply the revised version of IAS 23, no special exemptions in respect of borrowing costs are available. Although the previous version of IAS 23 also contained certain transitional provisions, they are not available to a first-time adopter of IFRSs. Accordingly, such a first-time adopter must account for borrowing costs retrospectively, as though the requirements of the previous version of IAS 23 had always applied. In particular, therefore, where qualifying assets are included on the basis of cost in the statement of financial position at the date of transition, cost must be computed so as to comply with the requirements of the previous version of IAS 23.

UK

The requirement for consistent application of IAS 23 to all qualifying assets may raise a practical issue for some UK companies if they have historically capitalised interest costs for tangible fixed assets but not for other qualifying assets.

6.11 Service concession arrangements

A first-time adopter may apply the transitional provisions in IFRIC 12 (see **10.10** in **chapter 40**).

6.12 Investments in subsidiaries, associates and jointly controlled entities

When an entity prepares separate financial statements, IAS 27 requires it to account for its investments in subsidiaries, associates and jointly controlled entities either:

[IFRS 1.23A]

- at cost; or
- in accordance with IAS 39.

IFRS 1 was amended in May 2008 to permit a first-time adopter to use a deemed cost based on either fair value or previous GAAP carrying amount. The amendment is effective for annual periods beginning on or after 1 January 2009 with earlier application permitted.

The amendment addresses concerns that it may be difficult, or even impossible, and costly to determine cost in accordance with IAS 27. The alternative of accounting for such investments at fair value in accordance with IAS 39 will often be unattractive because of the cost of obtaining annual valuations.

Related amendments were also made to IAS 27 to remove the definition of the cost method and consequently remove the requirement that any dividends received by the parent out of pre-acquisition profits should be deducted from the cost of investment rather than accounted for as income (see **chapter 33**).

UK

This amendment to IFRS 1, and the related amendment to IAS 27, will be very welcome in the UK. Indeed, it was the Institute of Chartered Accountants in England and Wales that first raised the issue with the IASB and has been actively pressing for a solution. The parent companies of many listed groups continue to prepare their separate financial statements under UK GAAP. The reason most often given for this is the need to restate the cost of investment in accordance with IAS 27. In addition to the practical difficulties, such a restatement may have a significant adverse impact on distributable reserves in some cases because of the need to credit against the cost of investment any dividends received out of pre-acquisition profits (as required by IAS 27 before it was amended in May 2008).

However, UK companies will not be able to make use of the new exemption in IFRS 1 or the related amendments to IAS 27 until they have been adopted for use in the EU.

If a first-time adopter measures an investment in a subsidiary, associate or jointly controlled entity at cost, IFRS 1 (as amended in May 2008) requires the investment to be measured in its separate opening IFRS statement of financial position at:

- cost determined in accordance with IAS 27; or

- a deemed cost determined as fair value (determined in accordance with IAS 39) at the entity's date of transition to IFRSs; or
- a deemed cost determined as the previous GAAP carrying amount at that date.

A first-time adopter may choose either method for the determination of deemed cost to measure its investment in each subsidiary, jointly controlled entity or associate that it elects to measure using deemed cost. [IFRS 1.23B]

> That is to say, first-time adopters are permitted to choose which measurement basis to use for each investment on an individual basis. Some could be measured in accordance with IAS 27 and others at deemed cost. For those measured at deemed cost, the choice between fair value and previous GAAP carrying amount may also be made on an individual investment basis.

If an entity uses this exemption, it must make the disclosures described at **8.2.4** below.

7 Exceptions to retrospective application of other IFRSs

IFRS 1 prohibits retrospective application of some aspects of other IFRSs relating to:

[IFRS 1.26]

- derecognition of financial assets and financial liabilities (see **chapter 22**);
- hedge accounting (see **chapter 22**);
- estimates (see **7.1** below); and
- assets classified as held for sale and discontinued operations (see **7.2** below).

> The reason given by the IASB for these requirements is that there is a danger of abuse if retrospective application would require judgements by management about past conditions after the outcome of a particular transaction is already known. [IFRS 1.BC12]

7.1 Estimates

IFRS 1 requires estimates under IFRSs at the date of transition to IFRSs to be consistent with estimates made for the same date under previous GAAP, after adjustments to reflect any difference in accounting policies, unless there is objective evidence that those estimates were in error. [IFRS 1.31]

When restating the opening statement of financial position to IFRSs, an entity may be in possession of information about estimates it made under previous GAAP that was not available at the time when those estimates were made. IFRS 1 requires the receipt of such information to be treated in the same way as non-adjusting events after the end of the reporting period under IAS 10. [IFRS 1.32]

IFRS 1 gives the following example to illustrate this requirement. An entity's date of transition to IFRSs is 1 January 20X4. New information on 15 July 20X4 requires the revision of an estimate made under previous GAAP at 31 December 20X3. The entity does not reflect that new information in its opening IFRS statement of financial position unless the estimate needs adjustment for any differences in accounting policies or there is objective evidence that the estimate was in error as at December 20X3. Instead, the entity reflects the new information in profit or loss (or, if appropriate, other comprehensive income) for the year ended 31 December 20X4. [IFRS 1.32]

It may be necessary to make estimates under IFRSs at the date of transition to IFRSs that were not required at that date under previous GAAP. Those estimates should reflect conditions that existed at the date of transition to IFRSs. In particular, estimates of market prices, interest rates or foreign exchange rates should reflect market conditions at the date of transition to IFRSs. [IFRS 1.33]

If estimates were in error prior to the date of transition, both the impacts of the correction of error due to the change in estimates and the impact of the use of a different accounting policy, if any, should be adjusted for in retained earnings in the opening IFRS statement of financial position. In addition, correction of these errors should be disclosed separately from other changes resulting from the first-time application of IFRSs. This disclosure should be on a gross basis. Presentation of net errors is not allowed.

UK

The IFRS 1 Implementation Guidance provides some examples of the operation of these requirements. For a UK company moving to IFRSs, many

> *of the estimates that will be required will have been required under UK GAAP. In this case the estimates used must be the same and cannot be adjusted with the benefit of hindsight. For example, provisions to write down inventories to net realisable value should be consistent with those used to prepare the original UK GAAP financial statements even though the sale proceeds may now be known to be different from those originally estimated. Another example is provisions for liabilities and charges where FRS 12 and IAS 37 require similar estimates to be made. It would not be possible to revise such provisions with the benefit of hindsight.*
>
> *The exception to this rule is where there is 'objective evidence that those estimates were in error'. Guidance on the circumstances when this might be the case is given in IAS 8 (see* ***chapter 4****). Revision of an estimate for an error on transition to IFRSs would therefore be appropriate only in circumstances where IAS 8 would require a retrospective restatement had the error been made by a company already reporting under IFRSs.*

These requirements also apply to a comparative period presented in an entity's first IFRS financial statements so that references to the date of transition to IFRSs are replaced by references to the end of the comparative period. [IFRS 1.34] That is to say that the estimates made at the end of the comparative period should follow the same rules as the opening IFRS statement of financial position as regards the use of hindsight.

The IFRS 1 Implementation Guidance states that paragraphs 31 to 34 of the Standard do not override the requirements of other IFRSs that base classifications or measurements on circumstances existing at a particular date. Examples given are:

[IFRS 1.IG4]

- the distinction between finance leases and operating leases in IAS 17;
- the restrictions in IAS 38 that prohibit capitalisation of expenditure on an internally generated intangible asset if the asset did not qualify for recognition when the expenditure was incurred; and
- the distinction between financial liabilities and equity instruments in IAS 32.

The use of actuarial assumptions when applying IAS 19 for the first time is considered at **5.6** above.

7.2 Assets classified as held for sale and discontinued operations

An entity with a date of transition to IFRSs before 1 January 2005 was required to apply the transitional provisions of IFRS 5. An entity with a date of transition to IFRSs on or after 1 January 2005 is required to apply IFRS 5 retrospectively. [IFRS 1.34B]

This exemption therefore has no practical effect on entities now adopting IFRSs for the first time.

8 Presentation and disclosure

IFRS 1 does not provide exemptions from the presentation and disclosure requirements of other IFRSs. It imposes additional requirements on first-time adopters. There is an exception to this general rule which concerns non-IFRS comparative information and historical summaries as described at **8.1.1**. [IFRS 1.35]

Also, as explained at **6.3.3** above, IFRS 1 includes an exemption from giving certain five-year trend information required by IAS 19 for dates prior to the date of transition to IFRSs.

IAS 24 requires disclosure of the compensation of key management personnel including separate disclosure of amounts for share-based payments (see **5.2** in **chapter 32**). IAS 24 is a disclosure Standard and does not prescribe the measurement of compensation. Reference should therefore be made to the measurement guidance in other Standards, including IFRS 2 in the case of share-based payments. Accordingly, where no expense is recognised because the arrangements are covered by the exemption in IFRS 1 (see **6.6** above, e.g. for options granted before 7 November 2002), the amount disclosed as share-based payment compensation will not include amounts for these arrangements.

8.1 Comparative information

To comply with IAS 1(2003), an entity's first IFRS financial statements are required to include at least one year of comparative information under IFRSs. [IFRS 1.36]

To comply with IAS 1(2007), an entity's first IFRS financial statements are required to include three statements of financial position, two statements of comprehensive income, two income statements (if presented), two statements of cash flows and two statements of changes in equity and related notes, including comparative information. [IFRS 1.36]

The significance of words 'including comparative information' at the end of IAS 1.36 as revised by IAS 1(2007) is not immediately clear because the paragraph is itself specifying the comparative information that must be presented. They are presumably intended to indicate that comparative information should be given for the disclosures in the notes.

An entity that adopted IFRSs before 1 January 2006 was entitled to certain exemptions concerning comparative information in relation to compliance with IAS 32, IAS 39, IFRS 4, IFRS 6 and IFRS 7. These exemptions have been deleted from IFRS 1 by IAS 1(2007). They are not dealt with in this chapter because they will not be relevant to entities now adopting IFRSs for the first time.

8.1.1 *Historical summaries and previous GAAP comparatives*

Some entities present historical summaries of selected data for periods before the first period for which they present full comparative information under IFRSs. IFRS 1 does not require such summaries to comply with the recognition and measurement requirements of IFRSs. Also, some entities present comparative information under previous GAAP as well as the comparative information required by IAS 1. In any financial statements containing historical summaries or comparative information under previous GAAP, an entity should:

[IFRS 1.37]

- label the previous GAAP information prominently as not being prepared under IFRSs; and
- disclose the nature of the main adjustments that would make it comply with IFRSs. The adjustments need not be quantified.

UK *UK listed companies normally present a five year summary, although this is not a requirement of the Listing Rules (see* ***section 4*** *in* ***chapter 46****). Such summaries do not form part of the financial statements and are not therefore within the scope of this requirement of IFRS 1. But the requirements should nevertheless be regarded as good practice for such summaries.*

Where an entity reporting under IFRSs presents a historical summary, e.g. a five-year summary, the historical information prior to the date of transition may be presented under previous GAAP, e.g. UK GAAP. The previous GAAP information should be clearly labelled as not being prepared under IFRSs and the nature of the main adjustments required to comply with IFRSs should be disclosed, but need not be quantified. An entity may wish to present previous GAAP information adjusted for IFRSs for greater comparability. It may not be feasible in many cases to present adjusted UK GAAP information due to the IFRS 1 exemptions (e.g. business combinations, restating cumulative translation differences to zero, etc). Companies should consider very carefully the implications of presenting adjusted UK GAAP information. Any such adjusted information cannot be described as IFRS information.

8.2 Explanation of transition to IFRSs

An explanation should be given of how the transition from previous GAAP to IFRSs affected the entity's reported financial position, financial performance and cash flows. [IFRS 1.38] IFRS 1 specifies certain disclosures to meet this principle.

8.2.1 Reconciliations

An entity's first IFRS financial statements should include:

[IFRS 1.39]

- reconciliations of its equity reported under previous GAAP to its equity under IFRSs as at:
  - the date of transition to IFRSs; and
  - the end of the latest period presented in the entity's most recent annual financial statements under previous GAAP;
- for entities that are applying IAS 1(2003), a reconciliation of the profit or loss reported under previous GAAP for the latest period in the entity's most recent annual financial statements to its profit or loss under IFRSs for the same period;
- for entities that are applying IAS 1(2007), a reconciliation to total comprehensive income under IFRSs for the latest period in the entity's most recent annual financial statements. The starting point for that reconciliation is total comprehensive income under previous GAAP for the same period or, if the entity did not report such a total, profit or loss under previous GAAP; and

- if the entity recognised or reversed any impairment losses for the first time in preparing its opening IFRS statement of financial position, the disclosures that IAS 36 would have required if the entity had recognised those impairment losses or reversals in the period beginning with the date of transition to IFRSs.

As explained in IFRS 1.BC94, the rationale for the last of these requirements is that there is inevitably subjectivity about impairment losses. The disclosure is intended to provide transparency about impairment losses recognised on transition to IFRSs. These losses might otherwise receive less attention than impairment losses recognised in earlier or later periods.

IFRS 1 requires the above reconciliations to be included in the financial statements. This contrasts with the requirements for an interim report in accordance with IAS 34 (see **8.2.3** below) where a cross reference to another published document will suffice.

UK

Where a parent company adopts IFRSs in its separate financial statements, all reconciliations from previous GAAP to IFRSs as required by IFRS 1 will have to be included in the first full IFRS separate financial statements. A reconciliation of the profit for the comparative period will still be required if the company is making use of the exemption from publication of the profit and loss account in s230 of the 1985 Act or s408 of the 2006 Act. The exemption does not extend to the reconciliation.

The reconciliations described above should give sufficient detail to enable users to understand the material adjustments to the statement of financial position and statement of comprehensive income (or income statement when the entity is applying IAS 1(2003). If a statement of cash flows was presented under previous GAAP, an explanation should be provided of the material adjustments to the statement of cash flows. [IFRS 1.40]

Example 11 in the IFRS 1 Implementation Guidance shows one way of satisfying these requirements. As noted in **section 4** above, there is no requirement to disclose the opening IFRS statement of financial position (i.e. at the date of transition) unless IAS 1(2007) is being applied but the way in which the reconciliations are presented in this example (using a columnar layout) has the effect of doing so.

An entity may become aware of errors made under previous GAAP. The reconciliations required by paragraphs 39(a) and (b) of IFRS 1 (i.e. the reconciliations of equity and profit or loss and/or total comprehensive income) should distinguish the correction of errors from changes in accounting policies. [IFRS 1.41]

The disclosure requirements of IAS 8 about changes in accounting policies do not apply in an entity's first IFRS financial statements. [IFRS 1.42]

If an entity did not present financial statements for previous periods, its first IFRS financial statements should disclose that fact. [IFRS 1.43]

8.2.2 *Use of fair value as deemed cost*

If fair value is used in the opening IFRS statement of financial position as deemed cost for an item of property, plant and equipment, an investment property or an intangible asset (see **6.2** above), the first IFRS financial statements should disclose, for each item in the opening IFRS statement of financial position:

[IFRS 1.44]

- the aggregate of those fair values; and
- the aggregate adjustment to the carrying amounts reported under previous GAAP.

8.2.3 *Interim financial reports*

When an interim financial report is presented under IAS 34 for part of the period covered by the first IFRS financial statements, the following additional requirements apply in addition to those in IAS 34.

Each such interim financial report should, if the entity presented an interim financial report for the comparable period of the immediately preceding financial year, include:

- a reconciliation of its equity under previous GAAP at the end of that comparable interim period to its equity under IFRSs at that date;
- for entities that are applying IAS 1(2003), a reconciliation of its profit or loss under previous GAAP for that comparable interim period (current and year to date) to its profit or loss under IFRSs for that period; and
- for entities that are applying IAS 1(2007), a reconciliation to its total comprehensive income under IFRSs for the comparable interim

period (current and year to date). The starting point for that reconciliation is total comprehensive income under previous GAAP for that period or, if the entity did not report such a total, profit or loss under previous GAAP.

In addition, the first interim financial report under IAS 34 for part of the period covered by the first IFRS financial statements should include the reconciliations and other information described at **8.2.1** above. Alternatively, a cross-reference to another published document that includes these reconciliations may be provided. [IFRS 1.45]

IAS 34 requires minimum disclosures which are based on the assumption that users of the interim financial report also have access to the most recent annual financial statements. But IAS 34 also requires disclosure of 'any events or transactions that are material to an understanding of the current interim period'. Therefore, if a first-time adopter did not, in its most recent annual financial statements under previous GAAP, disclose information material to an understanding of the current interim period, the interim report should disclose that information or include a cross-reference to another published document that includes it. [IFRS 1.46]

IAS 34.6 allows condensed financial statements and footnotes to avoid repetition of information previously reported. IAS 34.6 also states that 'the interim financial report is intended to provide an update on the latest complete set of annual financial statements'. The first interim financial statements under IFRSs, when the most recent annual financial statements have not been prepared under IFRSs, must include additional information to assist users in understanding the financial statements.

For example, the most recent annual financial statements will contain the accounting policies used and the interim report will generally only refer to any changes of policy since that annual report. Therefore, it would be appropriate for the first interim report under IFRSs to include a full description of the accounting policies adopted unless these had already been published in another document to which reference could be made. It would also be appropriate to include expanded footnotes on individual areas where information was not provided in the previous GAAP financial statements.

IAS 34 applies if an entity is required, or elects, to prepare an interim financial report in accordance with IFRSs. Therefore neither IAS 34 nor IFRS 1 requires an entity to present interim financial reports that comply with IAS 34. Neither do they require an entity to prepare a new version of interim financial reports presented under previous GAAP. [IFRS 1.IG37]

However, if an interim financial report is prepared under IAS 34 for part of the period covered by its first IFRS financial statements, the comparative information presented should be restated so that it complies with IFRSs. [IFRS 1.IG37]

IFRS 1 should be applied in each interim financial report that is presented under IAS 34 for part of the period covered by the first IFRS financial statements. In particular, the requirements for reconciliations described above apply. [IFRS 1.IG38]

8.2.4 Use of deemed cost for investments in subsidiaries, associates and jointly controlled entities

If an entity uses a deemed cost in its opening IFRS statement of financial position for an investment in a subsidiary, associate or jointly controlled entity in its separate financial statements (see **6.12** above), it is required to disclose:

[IFRS 1.44A]

- the aggregate deemed cost of those investments for which deemed cost is their previous GAAP carrying amount; and
- the aggregate deemed cost of those investments for which deemed cost is fair value.

9 Effective date

IFRS 1 applies if the first IFRS financial statements are for a period beginning on or after 1 January 2004. The amendments made as a consequence of subsequent new and revised IFRSs have later effective dates but these are of little consequence now particularly as they generally permit early adoption.

The most recent amendments were made in May 2008 and concern the cost of an investment in subsidiaries, jointly controlled entities and associates (see **6.12** above). The amendments are effective for annual periods beginning on or after 1 January 2009 with earlier application permitted.

UK companies are unable to apply these amendments until they are adopted by the EU. UK

10 Future developments

10.1 Restructure of IFRS 1

As part of its annual improvements project, the IASB published proposals to restructure IFRS 1. The main change proposed is to remove some transitional provisions relating to particular IFRSs from the main body of the IFRS to appendices. The restructuring will not alter the technical content of IFRS 1. However, some transitional provisions will be removed as they are no longer relevant.

The revised IFRS 1 was not published as part of *Improvements to IFRSs* in May 2008 following a decision by the IASB to carry it forward as a separate project. It is expected to be published later in 2008.

6 Property, plant and equipment

1 Introduction

IAS 16 *Property Plant and Equipment* specifies the required accounting treatment for property, plant and equipment, and addresses issues such as the recognition of assets, the determination of their carrying amounts, and the depreciation charges and impairment losses to be recognised in relation to them. It was last revised in December 2003 as part of the IASB's Improvements Project, and was most recently amended by *Improvements to IFRSs* issued in May 2008.

This chapter discusses the requirements of IAS 16 in the following sections:

Section 2	Scope
Section 3	Recognition
Section 4	Measurement at recognition
Section 5	Alternatives for measurement after recognition
Section 6	Revaluation model
Section 7	Depreciation
Section 8	Impairment
Section 9	Derecognition
Section 10	Presentation and disclosure

UK

IAS 16 is broadly similar to the UK standard FRS 15 Tangible Fixed Assets, *but there are differences. The most important of these are highlighted below.*

- *IAS 16 requires residual values to be revised using current prices at the end of each reporting period, while FRS 15 requires that prices at the date of acquisition or most recent valuation should be used. Accordingly, where residual value rises over time, the depreciation charge on an asset is likely to decline under IAS 16, and may cease altogether.*

- *When assets are revalued, IAS 16 always requires revaluation to fair value while FRS 15 often requires revaluation based on existing use value. Existing use value may be significantly lower than fair value in circumstances where the latter reflects an alternative use.*

- *FRS 15 requires an annual impairment review for assets with a life longer than 50 years, or where no depreciation is recognised on the grounds of materiality. IAS 16 does not include an equivalent requirement.*

- *FRS 15 provides specific guidance on renewals accounting (although few companies adopt this approach in practice). IAS 16 does not permit renewals accounting and does not allow any departure from the principle that the depreciation expense is determined by reference to the asset's depreciable amount.*

- *FRS 15 requires 5-yearly full valuations, with interim updates. IAS 16 does not specify a maximum period between valuations. Rather, they should be undertaken as often as necessary to ensure that the fair value and carrying amount do not differ materially.*

- *The guidance in IAS 16 covering the approach to valuations is significantly less detailed than that in FRS 15. IAS 16 does not contain a requirement to use an external valuer once every five years, detailed guidance on performing full and interim revaluations, or guidance on the use of indices by directors for valuing plant and machinery. Nor does it include the requirement to consider material notional directly attributable acquisition or selling costs in the valuation, or detailed guidance on valuing 'trading basis' properties and the treatment of specialised 'adaptation works'.*

- *IAS 16 requires that where an item of property, plant or equipment is acquired in exchange for another such item, and the transaction has economic substance, the cost of the item should be measured at fair value. FRS 15 is silent on the measurement of exchanged assets.*

- *FRS 15 gives specific guidance on the treatment of assets donated to charities. IAS 16 is silent on this issue.*

- *Revaluation losses are presented a little differently under IAS 16 and under FRS 15. In particular:*
  - o *under FRS 15, where an impairment loss on a revalued asset is caused by a clear consumption of economic benefits, the loss will be taken to the profit and loss account. Under IAS 16, it will be recognised in other comprehensive income to the extent that there is a revaluation surplus relating to the asset; and*
  - o *under IAS 16, any revaluation loss that exceeds an existing revaluation surplus will be recognised as an expense in profit or*

> *loss. Under FRS 15 such a loss would be recognised in the Statement of Total Recognised Gains and Losses to the extent that the asset's recoverable amount was greater than its revalued amount.*
>
> - *Under UK GAAP, for certain assets held by insurance companies and groups, as part of their insurance business, revaluation gains and losses are taken to the profit and loss account. This treatment is permitted by FRS 15, which includes a specific exemption for such assets. There is no equivalent exemption in IAS 16 (though the IASB is at present working on insurance and performance reporting projects).*

2 Scope

IAS 16 is applicable in accounting for property, plant and equipment, which it defines as tangible items that:

[IAS 16.6]

- are held for use in the production or supply of goods or services, for rental to others, or for administrative purposes; and
- are expected to be used during more than one period.

IAS 16 is applied except when another Standard requires or permits a different accounting treatment. [IAS 16.2] An example of another Standard requiring a different accounting treatment for property, plant and equipment is IAS 17 *Leases* which prescribes a different approach as regards recognition for assets held under leases.

The Standard excludes the following from its scope:

[IAS 16.3]

- property, plant and equipment classified as held for sale in accordance with IFRS 5 *Non-current Assets Held for Sale and Discontinued Operations*;
- biological assets related to agricultural activity (addressed by IAS 41 *Agriculture*); and
- mineral rights and mineral reserves such as oil, natural gas and similar non-regenerative resources.

Although biological assets and mineral rights and reserves are excluded from the scope of IAS 16, the Standard does apply to property, plant and equipment used to develop or maintain those assets. [IAS 16.3] Thus, for example, it applies to agricultural land.

The term 'mineral rights' is not defined in IFRSs. In practice, it is often used to refer to both an 'intangible' right to explore or mine and the 'tangible' underlying mineral reserve. The Illustrative Examples accompanying IFRS 3 *Business Combinations* list 'use rights' such as drilling and mineral rights as an example of a contract-based intangible asset that should be recognised separately from goodwill in a business combination. However, it is not always possible to distinguish the intangible right from the tangible element. In accordance with paragraph 4 of IAS 38 *Intangible Assets* an entity should assess which element is more significant when an asset incorporates both intangible and tangible elements. For that reason, the entity should assess whether the underlying reserve or the right to mine is more significant. If the tangible resource/reserve is the more significant element, the combined mineral rights should be classified as tangible.

Factors to consider in this assessment include:

- whether the rights are granted for extraction of the mineral resource;
- whether the rights include ownership of the land on which the mineral resources are located;
- whether the rights are granted for exploration only.

As discussed at **2.2** in **chapter 7**, for periods beginning on or after 1 January 2009, the requirements of IAS 40 *Investment Property* are amended by *Improvements to IFRSs* issued in May 2008, so that property being constructed or developed for future use as investment property is within the scope of IAS 40. Earlier application of the amendments to IAS 40 is permitted.

Where an entity has not yet adopted this amendment to IAS 40, IAS 16 is applicable to property that is being constructed or developed for future use as an investment property but does not yet satisfy the definition of an investment property in IAS 40 (IAS 40 is applied once the property becomes an investment property). An investment property which is being redeveloped for continuing future use as an investment property, however, continues to be dealt with as an investment property under IAS 40. [IAS 16.5]

When an entity chooses to apply the cost model to investment properties under IAS 40, the cost model is as specified in IAS 16.

2.1 Classification of hotel properties

The question is often asked as to whether hotel properties should be classified as property, plant and equipment within the scope of IAS 16 or as investment properties within the scope of IAS 40. The key determinant is whether the owner acts primarily as the hotel/ restaurant operator or as a landlord. If the property owner's primary source of income from the property depends on day-to-day or week-by-week occupancy of hotel rooms and usage of restaurants and other facilities, and the property owner is providing services directly to hotel guests and diners, the hotel is likely to be property held by the entity for use in the production of services, in which case IAS 16 applies. On the other hand, if the owner's primary source of income from the property comes from longer-term leases (months and years rather than days or weeks), the hotel is likely to be an investment property, in which case IAS 40 applies. That is the case even if the property owner provides a relatively insignificant amount of ancillary services such as cleaning. Management must make the determination based on facts and circumstances. It is not a matter of accounting policy choice.

IAS 40 acknowledges that it may be difficult to determine when ancillary services are so significant that a property does not qualify as an investment property. For example, the owner of the hotel may transfer certain responsibilities to a third party under a management contract. The terms of such management contracts vary widely. At one end of the spectrum, the owner's position may, in substance, be that of a passive investor. At the other end of the spectrum, the owner simply may have outsourced certain day-to-day functions, while retaining significant exposure to variations in the cash flows generated by the operations of the hotel. In the latter case, classification as an investment property is not appropriate.

Classification as an investment property also may be acceptable if the direct involvement of the reporting entity in the operation of the property is short-term. For example, following the acquisition of a hotel, where the reporting entity continues to operate it while seeking a suitable third party manager, the operation of the hotel can be seen to be incidental to the underlying objective of investment return.

2.2 Base stock of assets

It is common for restaurants and similar operations to maintain a base stock inventory of items such as silverware and dishes in an unchanging amount. Additions to the stock are recognised in profit or loss. On average, the turnover of the items is likely to exceed one year. These items are tangible assets held for use in the supply of goods and services and are expected to be used for more than one period. They are therefore appropriately classified as property, plant and equipment and should not be included in current assets.

2.3 Property, plant and equipment used in research activities

Property, plant and equipment used in research activities should be accounted for in the same way as other property, plant and equipment under IAS 16. IAS 38.54, which requires all expenditure on research to be recognised as an expense when it is incurred, does not require that expenditure on property, plant and equipment used in research activities should be recognised in profit or loss when acquired. The depreciation of property, plant and equipment used in research activities constitutes a research expense, however, to which IAS 38 applies.

3 Recognition

3.1 General recognition criteria

The recognition criteria for property, plant and equipment are derived from the general principles for asset recognition established by the *Framework for the Preparation and Presentation of Financial Statements* (see **chapter 2**). An item of property, plant and equipment is to be recognised as an asset if, and only if:

[IAS 16.7]

- it is probable that future economic benefits associated with the asset will flow to the entity; and
- the cost of the asset to the entity can be measured reliably.

3.2 Spare parts and servicing equipment

Spare parts and servicing equipment are usually carried as inventories and recognised as an expense as they are consumed. Major spare parts and stand-by equipment will, however, qualify for recognition as property, plant and equipment when the entity expects to use them during more than one period. Similarly, if the spare parts and servicing equipment can be used only in connection with a particular item of property, plant and equipment, they are accounted for as property, plant and equipment. [IAS 16.8]

Example 3.2

Depreciation of stand-by equipment

An entity has installed two turbines. One will produce energy for the plant, and the other will be used as a backup in case the first turbine fails, or is otherwise rendered out of service. The probability that the spare turbine will ever be used is very low. The spare turbine is necessary, however, to ensure the continuity of the production process if the first turbine fails. The useful life of the stand-by turbine will equal the life of the plant, which is the same as the useful life of the primary turbine.

IAS 16.8 states that items of stand-by equipment qualify as property, plant and equipment when the entity expects to use them during more than one period; it does not state that such use should be regular. Accordingly, the spare turbine is classified as property, plant and equipment and depreciated from the date it becomes available for use, i.e. when it is in the location and condition necessary for it to be capable of operating in the manner intended by management.

3.3 Items acquired for safety or environmental reasons

The acquisition of property, plant and equipment for safety or environmental reasons, while not directly increasing the future economic benefits of any particular existing item of property, plant and equipment, may be necessary in order for the entity to obtain the future economic benefits from its other assets. Such acquisitions qualify for recognition as assets, in that they enable future economic benefits to be derived from related assets in excess of what could otherwise have been derived. The resulting carrying amount of such an asset and the related assets is reviewed for impairment in accordance with IAS 36 *Impairment of Assets*. [IAS 16.11] The Standard cites the following example.

Example 3.3

Items acquired for safety or environmental reasons

[IAS 16.11]

A chemical manufacturer is required to install certain new chemical-handling processes in order to comply with environmental requirements in relation to the production and storage of dangerous chemicals. Related plant enhancements are recognised as an asset because, without them, the entity is unable to manufacture and sell chemicals.

3.4 Aggregation of individually insignificant items

The Standard does not prescribe what constitutes a separate item of property, plant and equipment, and allows a degree of judgement according to the entity's circumstances. It does, however, suggest that, for individually insignificant items (such as moulds, tools and dies), it may be appropriate to aggregate the items and to apply the recognition criteria to the aggregate value. [IAS 16.9]

The determination of whether an item is significant requires a careful assessment of the facts and circumstances. These assessments would include, at a minimum:

- comparison of the cost allocated to the item to the total cost of the aggregated property, plant and equipment; and
- comparison of the effect on depreciation expense between aggregating and not aggregating.

3.5 Subsequent costs

IAS 16 also deals with the recognition of costs incurred subsequently to add to, replace part of, or service a previously recognised item of property, plant and equipment. The general recognition criteria set out in **3.1** above are applied to such expenditure. If the recognition criteria are met, then the expenditure will be added to the carrying amount of the property, plant and equipment. If the recognition criteria are not met, then the expenditure will be expensed when incurred.

3.5.1 Repairs and maintenance

The costs of the day-to-day servicing, repair or maintenance of an item of property, plant and equipment should not be recognised in the carrying amount of the item. These costs are primarily the cost of labour and other items consumed in the service/repair. They may also include the cost of small parts. [IAS 16.12]

3.5.2 *Replacement parts*

Costs incurred on a replacement part for property, plant and equipment are recognised in the carrying amount of the affected item of property, plant and equipment when the costs are incurred if the recognition criteria set out in **3.1** above are met. [IAS 16.13]

If the cost of the replacement part is recognised in the carrying amount of an asset, then the carrying amount of what was replaced is derecognised (regardless of whether it had been identified as a component and depreciated separately), so that the replacement and the replaced item are not both carried as assets. [IAS 16.13] Where it is not practicable to determine the carrying amount of the replaced part, the cost of the replacement may be used as an indication of what the cost of the replaced part was at the time it was acquired or constructed. [IAS 16.70]

Example 3.5.2

Replacement costs

A hotel operator refurbishes its hotels every ten years, on average. The cost of refurbishment is considered a replacement of assets capitalised. That is, if the recognition criteria in IAS 16.7 are met, the expenditure should be capitalised. The replacement indicates, however, that previously-recognised assets may now be required to be derecognised, typically giving rise to a loss to the extent that they have not already been depreciated.

3.5.3 *Major inspections or overhauls*

Major inspections or overhauls may be required at regular intervals over the useful life of an item of property, plant and equipment to allow the continued use of the asset. For example, an entity might acquire a ship that requires a major overhaul, say, once every five years. When each major inspection or overhaul is performed, its cost is recognised in the carrying amount of the item or property, plant and equipment as a replacement if the recognition criteria set out at **3.1** above are met. [IAS 16.14]

Any remaining carrying amount of the cost of the previous inspection is derecognised, regardless of whether the previous inspection was separately identified at the time that the asset was acquired or constructed. Where the previous inspection was not separately identified, the estimated cost of a similar future inspection may, if necessary, be used as an indication of what the cost of the existing inspection component was when the asset was acquired or constructed. [IAS 16.14]

4 Measurement at recognition

4.1 Measurement at cost

Where an item of property, plant and equipment qualifies for recognition as an asset, it should initially be measured at its cost. [IAS 16.15]

Cost is defined as the amount of cash or cash equivalents paid or the fair value of the other consideration given to acquire an asset at the time of its acquisition or construction or, where applicable, the amount attributed to that asset when initially recognised in accordance with the specific requirements of other IFRSs (e.g. IFRS 2 *Share-based Payment*). [IAS 16.6]

At the date of transition to IFRSs, IFRS 1 *First-time Adoption of International Financial Reporting Standards* allows a first-time adopter to use a deemed cost for an item of property, plant and equipment, as discussed at **6.2** in **chapter 5**.

4.2 Elements of cost

4.2.1 Cost of an acquired asset

In the case of an acquired asset, cost comprises:

[IAS 16.16]

- the purchase price, including import duties and non-refundable purchase taxes, after deducting trade discounts and rebates;
- any directly attributable costs of bringing the asset to the location and condition necessary for it to be capable of operating in the manner intended by management; and
- the initial estimate of the costs of dismantling and removing the item and restoring the site on which it is located, the obligation for which the entity incurred either when the item was acquired, or as a consequence of having used the item during a particular period for purposes other than to produce inventories during that period. (See **4.4** for guidance on how to deal with subsequent changes in the estimate of these costs.)

It is perhaps worth emphasising that the final element noted above will be included only when, and to the extent that, the entity has an obligation to dismantle and remove the asset, and has therefore set up a provision in accordance with IAS 37 *Provisions, Contingent Liabilities and Contingent Assets.* For many assets, no such obligation will exist.

Costs cited by IAS 16 as suitable for inclusion in the cost of an item of property, plant and equipment are:

[IAS 16.17]

- costs of employee benefits arising directly from the construction or acquisition of the item of property, plant and equipment;
- costs of site preparation;
- initial delivery and handling costs;
- installation and assembly costs;
- costs of testing whether the asset is functioning properly, after deducting the net proceeds from selling any items produced while bringing the asset to that location and condition (e.g. samples produced when testing equipment); and
- professional fees.

Example 4.2.1A

Land clearing costs

A ski slope operator has developed a piece of land into a ski resort. To do that, the operator has cut the trees, cleared and graded the land and hills, and constructed ski lifts. The tree cutting, land clearing, and grading costs should be capitalised as part of the cost of the land. These costs are expenditures directly attributable to bringing the land to working condition for its intended use and, therefore, are part of the cost of the land, not the ski lifts.

Costs listed in IAS 16 as unsuitable for capitalisation, and therefore to be expensed, are:

[IAS 16.19]

- costs of opening a new facility;
- costs of introducing a new product or service (including costs of advertising and promotional activities);
- costs of conducting business in a new location, or with a new class of customer (including costs of staff training); and
- administration and other general overhead costs.

Example 4.2.1B

Training cost as a component of the cost of an asset

An entity acquires equipment of a type that its employees have never operated before. During the installation period, the employees receive extensive training on the equipment. The cost to the entity includes the incremental cost of hiring experts to conduct the training, and the directly attributable cost of wages of the employees during the training period. The equipment could not be used by the entity unless its employees received the training. Do these training costs qualify as a component of the cost of the equipment?

No. The training costs do not fall within the scope of costs directly attributable to bringing the asset to the location and condition necessary for it to be capable of operating in the manner intended by the management. This piece of equipment would be capable of operating in the manner intended by the management without the entity incurring the training cost – even though the employees would not know how to operate the equipment.

4.2.2 *Cost of a self-constructed asset*

The cost of a self-constructed asset is determined using the same principles as for an acquired asset, as set out at **4.2.1** above. The Standard states that if an entity makes similar assets for sale in the normal course of business, the cost of the asset is usually the same as the cost of constructing the asset for sale, in accordance with the principles of IAS 2 *Inventories*. [IAS 16.22]

Cost is therefore measured at the production cost of the asset, which consists of the purchase price of the raw materials and consumables used, plus other costs incurred (including appropriate overheads) that are directly attributable to the production of the asset.

This concept of 'directly attributable' costs is different from the concepts applied in measurement of costs of conversion in IAS 2 *Inventories*. The latter includes a systematic allocation of fixed and variable production overheads that are incurred in converting materials into finished goods. Such systematic allocation of fixed overheads is not permissible under IAS 16, because IAS 16 looks to capitalise only directly attributable costs.

The Standard gives no further guidance on how to determine which costs may be viewed as 'directly attributable'. Certainly, costs that are directly incremental as a result of the construction of a specific asset appear likely, if they relate to bringing the asset to working condition, to be eligible. Where an entity regularly constructs assets, however, it is possible that some element of apparently 'fixed' costs may also be directly attributable. In such circumstances, it may be helpful to consider which costs would have been avoided if none of those assets had been constructed. For example, a construction company may employ builders who are normally engaged on the construction of properties for sale. If those builders are engaged for part of the year on the construction of a new head office for the company, their direct employment costs should be capitalised.

Administration and other general overhead costs are not a component of the cost of property, plant and equipment because they cannot be directly attributed to the acquisition of the asset or bringing the asset to its working condition.

The costs that may be included in the carrying amount of an asset are limited to those that arise directly from the construction or acquisition of the asset. Where, for example, costs are incurred to demolish existing structures in order to build on a site, the cost of demolition may be incremental to the construction cost or it may be associated with derecognition of a previously-held asset. It depends on whether the existing structures were previously used in the entity's business, or were acquired as part of the site with the specific intention of demolishing them. In the latter case, the demolition costs are clearly incremental and should be included in the cost of the new asset. In the former case, the cost of the old asset should be written off to profit or loss through an accelerated depreciation charge once the decision to demolish is made. Demolition costs incurred relate to derecognition of the old asset.

Example 4.2.2A

Existing building demolished in order to construct new building

In 20X1, Company E purchased land and buildings for £100m (land: £40m and building: £60m). The building is used by E in its business and is classified as property, plant and equipment and is depreciated over its estimated useful life. In 20X3, E demolishes the building and constructs a new building for its own use on the same piece of land. The carrying amount of the building prior to demolition was £55m.

Should the £55m be written off to profit or loss or be capitalised as part of the cost of the new building in accordance with IAS 16?

The carrying amount of £55m should be written off to profit or loss. The cost of the old building is not directly related to the new building as it is more of a 'replacement' in nature as opposed to being directly related to the new building.

The following principles also apply:

[IAS 16.22]

- any internal profits are eliminated in arriving at the cost of an asset;
- the costs of abnormal amounts of wasted material, labour or other resources incurred in the production of the self-constructed asset are excluded from its cost; and
- borrowing costs incurred during the period of production will be included in accordance with IAS 23 *Borrowing Costs* if the self-constructed asset meets the definition of a qualifying asset (see **chapter 27**). The revised version of IAS 23, which is effective for periods beginning on or after 1 January 2009, requires eligible costs to be capitalised. The previous version of IAS 23 permits such costs to be capitalised or expensed as a matter of accounting policy.

Example 4.2.2B

Cost of abnormal amounts of waste in producing a self-constructed asset

A power company (P) signed a contract with a contractor to construct a power plant. P believed that the quality of the construction work was poor and terminated the construction contract. The contractor then sued P for breach of contract, and P lost. P then paid a lump sum to the contractor as compensation for the breach of contract, and the construction work was resumed thereafter. Should the lump sum compensation paid to the contractor be recognised immediately as an expense or added to the construction cost of the power plant?

The amount does not fall within the scope of costs that are directly attributable to bringing the asset to the location and condition necessary for it to be capable of operating in the manner intended by management. This cost is similar in nature to an abnormal cost described in IAS 16.22, and therefore should be expensed.

4.2.3 *Cost of dismantling, removal and site restoration*

Costs incurred by an entity in respect of obligations for dismantling, removing and restoring the site on which an item of property, plant and equipment is located are recognised and measured in accordance with IAS 37 *Provisions, Contingent Liabilities and Contingent Assets*. Where the obligations are incurred when the asset is acquired, or during a period when the item is used other than to produce inventories, they are included in the cost of the item of property, plant and equipment, as specified in **4.2.1** above. Where the obligations are incurred during a period when the entity uses the item of property, plant and equipment to produce inventories, the costs are accounted for under IAS 2 *Inventories*. [IAS 16.18]

(Note that accounting for changes in such obligations is discussed at **4.4** below.)

4.2.4 *Start-up or commissioning period*

It is appropriate to recognise directly attributable costs in the carrying amount of an item of property, plant and equipment during a commissioning period in which it is not possible to operate at normal levels because of the need to run machinery, test equipment, or ensure the proper operation of the equipment. This circumstance generally relates to the physical preparation for use. An example would be a printing press where it is necessary to run it for a period in order to achieve the necessary level of performance.

The following are examples of costs that are *not* included in the carrying amount of an item of property, plant and equipment:

[IAS 16.20]

- costs incurred while an item capable of operating in the manner intended by management has yet to be brought into use or is operated at less than full capacity;
- initial operating losses, such as those incurred while demand for the item's output builds up; and
- costs of relocating or reorganising part or all of an entity's operations.

4.2.5 *Incidental operations*

Some operations occur in connection with the construction or development of an item of property, plant and equipment, but are not necessary to bring the item to the location and condition necessary for it to be capable of operating in the manner intended by management. These incidental operations may occur before or during the construction or development activities. For example, income may be earned through using a building site as a car park until construction starts. Because these incidental operations are not necessary to bring an item of property, plant and equipment to the location and condition necessary for it to be capable of operating in the manner intended by management, the income and related expenses of incidental operations are recognised in profit or loss, and included in their respective classification of income or expense. [IAS 16.21]

The same logic also applies after the construction of an asset is complete, as illustrated in the example at **5.1** below.

4.2.6 *Reimbursement of part of the cost of an asset*

Example 4.2.6

Reimbursement of part of the cost of an asset

Company A enters into a contract with Company B to produce and sell a specific product. Company A needs to transform a major part of its plant to be able to produce that product, and commissions that transformation work from a third party, Company C, unconnected with Company A and Company B. The transformation costs are significant and exclusively for the purpose of this sales contract. Therefore, Company A and Company B enter into an agreement in which Company A will re-invoice to Company B a part of the transformation costs. The question arises as to whether the reimbursement should be deducted from the cost of the transformation.

So far as Company A is concerned, there are two transactions here: the purchase of services (transformation costs) from Company C, and the supply of products to Company B. Accordingly, Company A must determine whether the amount receivable from Company B relates to the former or to the latter.

Company B will only receive the specified products from Company A; it does not gain any rights in respect of the property transformed. Thus, since this is an arm's length transaction, the total amount paid by Company B must relate to those products. If the reimbursement payable to Company A would make the overall price too high, Company B would not be prepared to enter into the transaction.

Similarly, Company C is providing transformation work in exchange for payment from Company A. Since this too is an arm's length transaction, the total amount paid to Company C must relate to that transformation work. If the price charged by Company C for that work was too high, Company A would not be prepared to enter into the transaction with Company C, and would commission the work elsewhere.

Therefore, the amount received as a reimbursement from Company B should be treated as revenue in accordance with IAS 18 *Revenue*, and not as a reduction in the cost of the transformation. As the payment is an integral part of the contract to produce and sell the product, the two transactions should be accounted for together in accordance with IAS 18.13 (see **section 5** in **chapter 23**).

In January 2008, the IFRIC issued a draft Interpretation on this topic, IFRIC D24 *Customer Contributions*, which is discussed at **12.2** in **chapter 23**.

4.2.7 *Broker's commission received by purchaser of property*

Example 4.2.7

Broker's commission received by purchaser of property

During negotiations to purchase a property, the purchaser was unwilling to accept the seller's best offer. To induce the purchaser to agree to the sale, the broker agreed to rebate a portion of the seller-paid commission to the purchaser.

So far as the purchaser is concerned, there is only one transaction here: the purchase of property. Accordingly, the net amount paid by the purchaser is the cost of the property. The seller had already agreed with the broker that part of the selling price would be paid to the broker as commission for services to the seller. In effect, the broker, who is acting as the seller's agent, has been able to agree a lower overall selling price, by accepting that the reduction will reduce its commission without affecting the net amount retained by the seller.

Thus, the rebated commission received is a reduction of the cost of the purchased property. It is not immediate income to the purchaser. The seller's best offer is not the price that the purchaser actually paid. If the purchaser had been required to pay a brokerage commission, that commission would have been part of the cost of the property. In this case, the commission rebate is similarly a component of the cost of the property.

4.2.8 *Utility fees paid to a government*

In some jurisdictions, developers of factories, offices, apartment buildings and shopping malls must pay a 'capacity fee' to the government for the privilege of being able to purchase, on an ongoing basis, defined quantities of electricity and other utilities beyond certain minimum quantities that can be purchased without paying the fee. The fee is paid on a one-off basis and covers supply, either on an indefinite basis or at least for a substantial number of years. The building owner still pays the going rate, however, to purchase the electricity and other utilities. The capacity fee attaches to the entity that owns the building, and it can be transferred to another building if the capacity allowed by the fee is not fully utilised.

As the capacity fees are transferable between buildings, they are not part of the cost of the building but should be capitalised as a purchased intangible asset in their own right. As such, they would be subject to the amortisation and impairment provisions of IAS 38 *Intangible Assets* (see **chapter 8**).

If instead the fees were attached to the building and were not transferable, they would be capitalised as part of the cost of the building and amortised via depreciation.

4.2.9 *Cessation of capitalisation*

Recognition of costs in the carrying amount of an item of property, plant and equipment ceases when the item is in the location and condition necessary for it to be capable of operating in the manner intended by management. Therefore, costs incurred in using or redeploying an item are not included in the carrying amount of that item. [IAS 16.20]

In the case of a self-constructed asset, or the installation of a major asset, a decision should be documented as to what event or activity characterises the moment when an asset's physical construction/installation is complete (i.e. when the item is in the location and condition necessary for it to be capable of operating in the manner intended by management), so that all costs incurred after that point are identified and expensed. Where a commissioning period is involved, it will similarly be essential to determine in principle the point that characterises reaching the capability of operating at normal levels, and then to ensure that costs incurred after reaching that point are captured and expensed.

Where there is delay in achieving final physical completion, costs arising during the period of delay are likely to fall into the category of abnormal costs and so be expensed as incurred. Finance costs incurred during such a period of delay will not qualify for capitalisation under IAS 23 *Borrowing Costs*, which requires that capitalisation should cease when active development is suspended (see **chapter 27**).

Regulatory consents, for example, health and safety clearance, are sometimes required before an asset may be used legally. Cost capitalisation will not necessarily continue until such consents are in place. Management will normally seek to ensure that such consents are in place very close to the time-frame for physical completion and testing, and that they do not slow down the commencement of operations. Avoidable delays in obtaining consents which prevent the start of operations should be seen as abnormal and similar in effect to an industrial dispute, creating a hiatus during which capitalisation should cease.

The words 'capable of operating in the manner intended by management' in IAS 16 cannot be used to justify ongoing capitalisation of costs (and postponement of depreciation) once the asset has actually been brought into use just because the asset does not live up to management's original intentions.

4.3 Measurement of cost

The cost of an item of property, plant and equipment (or of an element of an item) is the cash price equivalent (i.e. the amount that the entity would need to pay if it were to purchase the asset by paying cash immediately upon purchase) at the date on which the asset is recognised. [IAS 16.23]

4.3.1 *Payments deferred beyond normal credit terms*

When payment for an item of property, plant and equipment is deferred beyond normal credit terms, the difference between the cash price equivalent and the total payments is recognised as an interest expense over the period of credit, unless it is capitalised in accordance with the requirements of IAS 23 *Borrowing Costs* (see **chapter 27**). [IAS 16.23]

Example 4.3.1A

Deferred payment terms

On 1 January 20X1, an item of property is offered for sale at £10 million, with payment terms being three equal instalments of £3,333,333 over a two year period (payments are made on 1 January 20X1, 31 December 20X1 and 31 December 20X2). The property developer is offering a discount of 5 per cent (i.e. £500,000) if payment is made in cash at the time of completion of the sale and purchase agreement (which corresponds to an implicit interest rate of 5.36 per cent per annum).

The purchaser will recognise the acquisition of the asset as follows:

	£	£
DR Property, plant and equipment	9,500,000	
CR Cash		3,333,333
CR Accounts payable		6,166,667

The following entry will be required at the end of 20X1:

	£	£
DR Interest expense (5.36% x £6,166,667)	330,459	
DR Accounts payable	3,002,874	
CR Cash		3,333,333

The following entry will be required at the end of 20X2:

	£	£
DR Interest expense	169,541	
DR Accounts payable	3,163,793	
CR Cash		3,333,334

Example 4.3.1B

Payment for an asset deferred beyond 'normal credit terms'

The commercial property market in a particular city is very slow. As an inducement to potential purchasers, a seller of commercial property in that city advertises a property for sale at 'no interest for the first three years after purchase, market rate of interest thereafter'. Other property sellers in the city are making similar offers. A buyer purchases a property on those terms. IAS 16.23 requires imputation of interest if payment for an item of property is 'deferred beyond normal credit terms'. In this circumstance, is the three-year interest-free period 'normal credit terms'?

No. The intent of IAS 16.23 is to ensure that the asset is recognised at its current cash sale price. The 'normal credit terms' provision is intended to recognise that settlement of cash purchases often takes a few days, weeks, or even months (depending on the industry and national laws), and imputation of interest is not required in those circumstances. Particularly for a large item such as a property, however, the cash sale price would be significantly lower if cash payment is made up-front rather than deferred for three years. If the deferral period is greater than what can be considered normal credit terms, the imputed interest element should be recognised.

4.3.2 *Exchanges of assets*

Where an item of property, plant and equipment is acquired in exchange for a non-monetary asset or assets, or a combination of monetary and non-monetary assets, the cost of that item is measured at fair value (even if the entity cannot immediately derecognise the asset given up) unless:

[IAS 16.24]

- the exchange transaction lacks commercial substance; or
- the fair value of neither the asset received nor the asset given up is reliably measurable.

If the acquired item is not measured at fair value, its cost is measured at the carrying amount of the asset given up.

The entity will determine whether an exchange transaction has commercial substance by considering the extent to which its future cash flows are expected to change as a result of the transaction. An exchange transaction has commercial substance if:

[IAS 16.25]

- either:
  - the configuration (risk, timing and amount) of the cash flows of the asset received differs from the configuration of the cash flows of the asset transferred; *or*
  - the entity-specific value of the portion of the entity's operations affected by the transaction changes as a result of the exchange; *and*
- the difference arising in either of the two circumstances outlined above is significant relative to the fair value of the assets exchanged.

Entity-specific value is the present value of the cash flows an entity expects to arise from the continuing use of an asset and from its disposal at the end of its useful life or expects to incur when settling a liability. [IAS 16.6] For the purpose of assessing commercial substance, post-tax cash flows are used. [IAS 16.25]

Example 4.3.2

Exchange of assets

A ship charterer owns land and buildings which are carried in its statement of financial position at an aggregate carrying amount of £10 million, but which have a market value of £15 million. It exchanges the land and buildings for a ship, which has a market value of £18 million, and pays an additional £3 million cash.

Provided that the transaction has commercial substance, the entity will recognise the ship at a cost of £18 million and will recognise a profit on disposal of the land and buildings of £5 million, calculated as follows:

	£'000
Consideration received	18,000
less:	
Carrying amount of land and building disposed of	(10,000)
Cash paid	(3,000)
	5,000

UK

> *The £5,000,000 profit on disposal in this example would not be a realised profit for the purposes of making a distribution because no cash or other qualifying consideration was received.*

The fair value of an asset for which comparable market transactions do not exist is reliably measurable if:

[IAS 16.26]

- the variability in the range of reasonable fair value estimates is not significant for that asset; or
- the probabilities of the various estimates within the range can be reasonably assessed and used in estimating fair value.

Where an entity is able to determine reliably the fair values of either the asset received or the asset given up, then the fair value of the asset given up is used to measure the cost of the asset received, unless the fair value of the asset received is more clearly evident. [IAS 16.26]

4.3.3 Assets held under finance lease

The cost of assets held under finance leases is determined using the principles set out in IAS 17 *Leases* (see **chapter 26** for details). [IAS 16.27]

4.3.4 Government grants

The carrying amount of an item of property, plant and equipment may be reduced by government grants, in accordance with IAS 20 *Accounting for Government Grants and Disclosure of Government Assistance* (see **chapter 41**). [IAS 16.28]

4.3.5 Assets acquired as part of a business combination

IFRS 3 *Business Combinations* requires that property, plant and equipment of a subsidiary acquired as part of a business combination be measured initially at fair value for the purpose of inclusion in the consolidated financial statements (see **chapter 34** for detailed discussion). This fair value exercise does not amount to a revaluation of the assets concerned, but is an allocation of cost to the group, and hence it is not necessary to comply with the revaluation rules prescribed in IAS 16. All other aspects of the accounting treatment for these assets, however, including depreciation, should be determined by reference to the requirements of IAS 16.

4.4 IFRIC 1 *Changes in Existing Decommissioning, Restoration and Similar Liabilities*

IFRIC 1 *Changes in Existing Decommissioning, Restoration and Similar Liabilities* was issued in May 2004. It provides guidance on how to account for the effect of changes in the measurement of existing decommissioning, restoration and similar liabilities. For example, such liabilities may exist for decommissioning a plant, rehabilitating environmental damage in extractive industries, or removing equipment. IFRIC 1 applies to changes in the measurement of any existing decommissioning, restoration or similar liability that is both:

[IFRIC 1.2]

- recognised as part of the cost of an item of property, plant and equipment in accordance with IAS 16; and
- recognised as a liability in accordance with IAS 37.

The guidance below deals with how to account for changes in the measurement of an existing decommissioning, restoration and similar liability that result from changes in the estimated timing or amount of the outflow of resources required to settle the obligation, or a change in the discount rate.

4.4.1 *Cost model*

If the related asset is measured using the cost model:

[IFRIC 1.5]

- changes in the liability are added to, or deducted from, the cost of the related asset in the current period, except that the amount deducted from the cost of the asset must not exceed its carrying amount. If a decrease in the liability exceeds the carrying amount of the asset, the excess is recognised immediately in profit or loss; and
- if the adjustment results in an addition to the cost of an asset, the entity should consider whether this may indicate that the new carrying amount of the asset may not be fully recoverable. If so, the asset should be tested for impairment in accordance with IAS 36 (see **chapter 9**).

4.4.2 *Revaluation model*

If the related asset is measured using the revaluation model:

[IFRIC 1.6]

- changes in the liability alter the revaluation surplus or deficit previously recognised on that asset, so that:

  - a decrease in the liability is generally recognised in other comprehensive income and increases the revaluation surplus within equity, but is recognised immediately in profit or loss:

    - o to the extent that it reverses a revaluation deficit on the asset that was previously recognised in profit or loss; or

    - o to the extent that it exceeds the carrying amount that would have been recognised had the asset been carried under the cost model;

  - an increase in the liability is recognised in other comprehensive income and reduces the revaluation surplus within equity to the extent of any credit balance relating to that asset, with the balance being recognised in profit or loss.

- a change in the liability is an indication that the asset may have to be revalued in order to ensure that the carrying amount does not differ materially from fair value at the end of the reporting period. Any such revaluation is taken into account in determining the amounts to be recognised in profit or loss or in other comprehensive income. If a revaluation is necessary, all assets of that class are revalued; and

- to comply with IAS 1 (see **5.4** and **6.2** in **chapter 3**), the change in the revaluation surplus arising from a change in the liability is separately identified and disclosed as a component of other comprehensive income.

4.4.3 Other requirements

The adjusted depreciable amount of the asset is depreciated over its useful life. Accordingly, once the related asset has reached the end of its useful life, all subsequent changes in the liability are recognised in profit or loss as they occur. This applies under both the cost model and the revaluation model. [IFRIC 1.7]

The periodic unwinding of the discount is recognised in profit or loss as a finance cost as it occurs. Capitalisation under IAS 23 is not permitted. [IFRIC 1.8]

IFRS 1 *First-time Adoption of International Financial Reporting Standards* allows first-time adopters an exemption from full retrospective application of IFRIC 1, as discussed at **6.8** in **chapter 5**.

5 Alternatives for measurement after recognition

IAS 16 permits two different bases for the determination of the carrying amount of property, plant and equipment at the end of subsequent reporting periods – a cost model and a revaluation model. Whichever accounting policy is selected, it is required to be applied to entire classes of property, plant and equipment. [IAS 16.29]

5.1 Cost model

Where the cost model is selected, after recognition as an asset, an item of property, plant and equipment is carried at cost less any accumulated depreciation and any accumulated impairment losses. [IAS 16.30]

When the cost model is used, the cost of the asset will normally remain unchanged until it is derecognised. The treatment of subsequent costs is considered at **3.5** above. The following example confirms that income generated by an asset should not be deducted from its cost.

Example 5.1

Rental income from property acquired through mortgage foreclosure

A bank forecloses on a property under mortgage. As a result of the foreclosure, the property becomes an asset of the bank and the former owner ceases to have any rights over the property or over the income that it generates. The property has rent-paying tenants. By law the bank cannot operate commercial rental property and it is required to put the property up for sale. The bank is permitted to act as landlord while the property is being sold. As a result of the foreclosure, the bank writes off the loan receivable and recognises the property at the lower of the cost (amount of the loan written off) and fair value of the property. Is the rent received rental income or a reduction of the carrying amount of the property (thereby deferring income recognition until the property is sold)?

As noted in paragraph 92 of the Framework, income should be recognised when net assets increase. Therefore, the rent received should be recognised as rent income, not a reduction in the carrying amount of the asset. The property should be evaluated for possible impairment at the time of foreclosure and the bank should also consider whether the property should be classified as 'held for sale' in accordance with IFRS 5 *Non-current Assets Held for Sale and Discontinued Operations* (see **chapter 29**).

Note that the answer would be different if the bank was merely administering the property on behalf of the previous owner, and was only entitled to retain rent in settlement of amounts due from the owner. In that scenario, the bank would not recognise an asset of the property, and would instead continue to recognise the loan receivable, also recognising any necessary impairment loss.

5.2 Revaluation model

Where the revaluation model is selected, after recognition as an asset, an item of property, plant and equipment whose fair value can be measured reliably is carried at a revalued amount, being its fair value at the date of the revaluation less any subsequent accumulated depreciation and any subsequent accumulated impairment losses. Revaluations are required to be carried out with sufficient regularity to ensure that the carrying amount does not differ materially from that which would be determined using fair value at the end of the reporting period. [IAS 16.31]

6 Revaluation model

6.1 Initial adoption of revaluation basis

Where an entity initially adopts a policy to measure property, plant and equipment using the revaluation model, this initial adoption of the valuation basis represents a change in accounting policy. IAS 8.17 specifies, however, that it should be dealt with as a revaluation rather than as a prior period adjustment. Consequently, the valuation uplift or write-down occurring on the initial adoption of the revaluation basis is dealt with in other comprehensive income (as a current year movement in the revaluation surplus) or in profit or loss, as appropriate, in accordance with the requirements of IAS 16 (see **6.8** below). Prior period amounts are not restated.

This is a practical and helpful exemption from the usual rules on changes of accounting policy, which means that it will not be necessary to obtain valuations at the end of earlier reporting periods. One side effect of the approach, however, is that the amounts of depreciation included in current and prior year profit or loss may not be comparable, as they are likely to be based on revaluation and on cost respectively. Where the impact is significant, the entity may wish to provide a brief explanation.

UK *This is a difference from UK GAAP which, at least in principle, requires restatement for such a change of policy (though it seems to be accepted that, at least in some circumstances, restatement may be impracticable).*

6.2 Determination of fair value

Fair value is defined as the amount for which an asset could be exchanged between knowledgeable, willing parties in an arm's length transaction. [IAS 16.6]

The fair value of land and buildings is usually determined from market-based evidence by appraisal that is normally undertaken by professionally qualified valuers. The fair value of items of plant and equipment is usually their market value determined by appraisal. [IAS 16.32]

If there is no market-based evidence of fair value, because of the specialised nature of the item of property, plant and equipment, and the item is rarely sold, except as part of a continuing business, the entity may need to estimate fair value using an income or a depreciated replacement cost approach. [IAS 16.33]

There is an important difference of principle here between IFRSs and UK GAAP. Except where properties are surplus to requirements, the approach of FRS 15 focuses primarily on 'existing use value'. This is a valuation basis that assumes, regardless of whether such a restriction actually exists, that the property can be used for the foreseeable future only for its existing use. IAS 16 focuses on fair value, which will reflect no such assumption. UK

Thus, where a city centre warehouse could profitably be transformed into flats, FRS 15 will value it only as a warehouse, whereas the IAS 16 valuation will reflect the alternative use. It may be expected that valuations under IAS 16 will be higher as a result of this difference, with a correspondingly higher depreciation charge in some cases.

6.3 Frequency of revaluations

IAS 16.31 requires that revaluations should be made with sufficient regularity such that the carrying amount does not differ materially from that which would be determined using fair value at the end of the reporting period.

The Standard therefore does not insist on annual revaluations. The frequency of revaluations will depend upon fluctuations in the fair values of the items of property, plant and equipment under consideration. Some items of property, plant and equipment (e.g. properties situated in countries with high capital asset inflation rates) may experience significant and volatile movements in fair value, thus necessitating annual revaluations. Such frequent revaluations would be unnecessary for items of property, plant and equipment with only insignificant movements in fair value (e.g. machinery situated in countries with relatively low capital asset inflation rates).

Where items of property, plant and equipment have only insignificant changes in fair value, the Standard indicates that it may be necessary to revalue them only every three or five years. [IAS 16.34]

UK

FRS 15 requires 5-yearly full valuations, with interim updates. IAS 16 does not specify a maximum period between valuations. Rather, they should be undertaken as often as necessary to ensure that the fair value and carrying amount do not differ materially.

The guidance in IAS 16 covering the approach to valuations is significantly less detailed than that in FRS 15. IAS 16 does not contain a requirement to use an external valuer once every five years, detailed guidance on performing full and interim revaluations, or guidance on the use of indices by directors for valuing plant and machinery. Nor does it include the requirement to consider material notional directly attributable acquisition or selling costs in the valuation, or detailed guidance on valuing 'trading basis' properties and the treatment of specialised 'adaptation works'.

6.4 Accumulated depreciation at the date of revaluation

IAS 16.35 allows that any depreciation accumulated on an asset at the date of revaluation can be dealt with in one of two ways, i.e. either:

- restated proportionately with the change in the gross carrying amount of the asset so that the carrying amount of the asset after revaluation equals its revalued amount (Method A). The carrying amount is increased to the revalued amount by restating the cost and depreciation proportionately. This method is often used when an asset is revalued to its depreciated replacement cost by means of an index; or
- eliminated against the gross carrying amount of the asset and the resulting net amount restated to the revalued amount of the asset (Method B). The accumulated depreciation is eliminated, and any remaining surplus is used to increase cost. This method is often used for buildings, and for all assets is the most commonly used method in practice.

Example 6.4 illustrates the alternative methods permitted under the Standard.

Example 6.4

Accumulated depreciation at the date of revaluation

A property has a carrying amount of £10m, represented by cost of £12m and accumulated depreciation of £2m. It is revalued to its fair value of £13m.

	Method A	Method B
	£'000	£'000
Cost or valuation		
Before revaluation	12,000	12,000
Revaluation adjustment	3,600*	1,000
After revaluation	15,600	13,000
Depreciation		
Before revaluation	2,000	2,000
Revaluation adjustment	600*	(2,000)
After revaluation	2,600	0
Revalued amount	13,000	13,000

* Allocated in the ratio 12:2

6.5 Revaluation to be made for entire class of assets

When an item of property, plant and equipment is revalued, the entire class of property, plant and equipment to which that asset belongs is required to be revalued. [IAS 16.36] Items within a class of property, plant and equipment are revalued simultaneously to avoid selective revaluation of assets and the reporting of amounts in the financial statements that are a mixture of costs and valuations at different dates. [IAS 16.38] This is intended to prevent the distortions caused by the selective use of revaluation, known colloquially as 'cherry-picking', so as to take credit for gains without acknowledging falls in the value of similar assets.

6.5.1 Definition of a 'class' of assets

A class of property, plant and equipment is defined as a grouping of assets of a similar nature and use in an entity's operations. [IAS 16.37] The following examples are cited of separate classes:

- land;
- land and buildings;
- machinery;
- ships;
- aircraft;
- motor vehicles;

- furniture and fixtures; and
- office equipment.

The examples cited of separate classes are not intended to be prescriptive or comprehensive. In practice, it is not uncommon for some of these classes to be combined. For example, in situations where motor vehicles are not significant to an entity, motor vehicles and machinery may be combined in a plant and machinery class. For similar reasons, office equipment may be included in the furniture and fixtures class.

6.5.2 *Disclosure of classes*

As discussed in **10.2** below, detailed disclosures are specified for each class of property, plant and equipment. This should be borne in mind when distinguishing classes, as multiple classes could lead to voluminous disclosures.

6.5.3 *Revaluation on a rolling basis*

The requirement to revalue entire classes of assets is a potentially onerous requirement since, for some reporting entities, a class of assets could comprise a large number of items. For this reason, IAS 16.38 allows a class of assets to be revalued on a rolling basis, provided that revaluation of the class of assets is completed within a short period of time and that the revaluations are kept up to date.

No further guidance is given on what a 'short period' might be, though given the drafting of the Standard, it is presumably rather less than a financial year. The general approach of IAS 16.38 is, however, to require simultaneous valuations so as to avoid amounts being reported that are a mixture of costs and values as at different dates. Accordingly, it would seem appropriate:

- for all such valuations to take place in the same accounting period (and in the same interim period where an entity produces interim financial statements); and
- for the acceptable length of the period to take into account how stable fair values are, so that greater volatility requires a shorter period over which to perform valuations.

UK

In requiring that valuations be completed within a short period, IAS 16 is apparently more restrictive than FRS 15, which would allow properties to be revalued on a rolling basis over a five year cycle. Unlike FRS 15, however, IAS 16 does not prescribe who can perform valuations. Accordingly, there is no requirement that the valuations to be performed within a short period must be external valuations.

6.6 Assets for which fair value cannot be reliably measured

Even where an entity has selected the revaluation model for its property, plant and equipment, only those assets whose fair value can be measured reliably are carried at revalued amounts. [IAS 16.31]

The Standard provides no guidance as to the circumstances in which it is permissible to conclude that the fair value of an item of property, plant and equipment cannot be measured reliably, nor does it address the appropriate accounting for those assets whose fair value cannot be measured reliably. These 'gaps' in the framework provided by IAS 16 are most likely attributable to the fact that the IASB was, at the time of publication of the revised IAS 16 in 2003, taking part in joint projects with a number of national standard-setters on revaluations of property, plant and equipment. This project no longer appears on the IASB's work programme although other projects, particularly those on fair value measurement and the conceptual framework, may in time lead to amendments to IAS 16.

In the meantime, IAS 40 *Investment Property* contains useful guidance on the circumstances in which it is permissible to conclude that the fair value of an item of property, plant and equipment cannot be measured reliably. Under that Standard, the exception is allowed when, and only when, comparable market transactions are infrequent and alternative reliable estimates of fair value (for example, based on discounted cash flow projections) are not available. IAS 40 is very restrictive, and allows this exception to be invoked only when an entity first acquires an investment property. IAS 16 is not so explicit, and seems to permit a greater degree of flexibility. It seems, however, that the intention of the IASB is that, where the entity has selected the revaluation model as its accounting policy for a particular class of assets, there should be a rebuttable presumption that all of the assets within that class will be carried at revalued amounts. The 'not reliably measurable' exception should be invoked only in exceptional circumstances. Where the entity holds particular types of assets for which it will frequently be difficult to establish fair values (e.g. specialised plant and machinery), then it is preferable to adopt the cost basis for that entire class of assets, so as to avoid the reporting of amounts in the financial statements that are a mixture of costs and valuations at different dates.

Where fair value cannot be reliably measured, the only reasonable approach is to account for those assets using IAS 16's cost model. This is consistent with the treatment required by IAS 40 for those investment properties whose fair value is not reliably measurable. To assist users of the financial statements, additional disclosures should be provided in respect of those assets carried at cost less accumulated depreciation and accumulated impairment losses. Again, useful guidance can be found in IAS 40 which requires that such assets be disclosed separately. In addition, entities are required by IAS 40 to disclose:

- a description of the property;
- an explanation of why fair value cannot be determined reliably;
- if possible, the range of estimates within which fair value is highly likely to lie; and
- on disposal of the property:
  - the fact that the entity has disposed of property not carried at fair value;
  - the carrying amount of the property at the time of sale; and
  - the amount of gain or loss recognised.

Although IAS 16 does not require equivalent disclosures, they should be seen as best practice. In addition, some of these disclosures may on occasions be necessary in order to comply with IAS 1(2007).97 (previously IAS 1(2003).86), which requires that when items of income and expense are material, their nature and amount shall be disclosed separately.

6.7 Voluntary disclosure of revalued amounts

Entities that adopt the cost model of accounting for their property, plant and equipment may wish to disclose the fair value of their property, plant and equipment in a note to the financial statements, when this is materially different from the carrying amount. Such disclosures are encouraged by IAS 16.79(d). In disclosing such fair values, rather than adopting the revaluation model of accounting, such entities are not strictly bound by IAS 16's revaluation rules. Where the amounts disclosed do not represent current fair values, however, they could mislead users of the financial statements. Therefore, the entity should either disclose the current fair values of the assets concerned, or not disclose revalued amounts at all. Similar considerations apply where an entity engages in 'cherry-picking', by disclosing current values only for those assets whose fair values are significantly above carrying amounts and ignoring those assets whose fair values are significantly below their carrying amounts. Accordingly, where fair values are disclosed voluntarily under IAS 16.79(d), they should normally be disclosed for an entire class of assets.

6.8 Treatment of surplus or deficit arising on revaluation

6.8.1 Revaluation surplus

IAS 16 requires that when an asset's carrying amount is increased as a result of a revaluation, the increase (being the difference between the fair value at the date of revaluation and the carrying amount at that date) should generally be recognised in other comprehensive income and accumulated in equity, under the heading of revaluation surplus. [IAS 16.39]

A revaluation increase should be recognised as income, however, to the extent that it reverses a revaluation decrease of the same asset previously recognised as an expense. [IAS 16.39]

When a revaluation surplus is recognised, no amendment is made to profit or loss to reverse depreciation previously recognised.

6.8.2 Revaluation deficit

The Standard requires that when an asset's carrying amount is decreased as a result of a revaluation, the decrease should generally be recognised as an expense. [IAS 16.40]

A revaluation decrease should be recognised in other comprehensive income, however, to the extent of any credit balance existing in the revaluation surplus in respect of that same asset. The decrease reduces the amount of the revaluation surplus accumulated in equity. [IAS 16.40]

UK

There are two differences between how revaluation losses are presented by IAS 16 and by FRS 15:

- *under FRS 15, where an impairment loss on a revalued asset is caused by a clear consumption of economic benefits, the loss will be taken to the profit and loss account. Under IAS 16, it will be recognised in other comprehensive income to the extent that there is a revaluation surplus relating to the asset; and*
- *under IAS 16, any revaluation loss that exceeds an existing revaluation surplus will be recognised as an expense in profit or loss. Under FRS 15 such a loss would be recognised in the Statement of Total Recognised Gains and Losses to the extent that the asset's recoverable amount was greater than its revalued amount.*

6.8.3 *Illustrative examples*

The following examples illustrate the appropriate treatment of valuation movements in a number of circumstances. In each case, the deferred tax implications are ignored and, except for **example 6.8.3D**, the effect of depreciation during each period is ignored.

Example 6.8.3A

Revaluation surplus

An entity purchased a property on 1 July 20X1 for £125 million. At 31 December 20X1, the property was valued at £150 million.

The revaluation surplus of £25 million is recognised in other comprehensive income and credited to a property revaluation reserve within equity.

Example 6.8.3B

Revaluation surplus reversing previous deficit

An entity purchased a property on 1 July 20X1 for £140 million. At 31 December 20X1, the property was valued at £125 million. At 31 December 20X2, the fair value of the property had increased to £150 million.

20X1: Revaluation deficit of £15 million is recognised in profit or loss.

20X2: Revaluation surplus is treated as follows:

- £15 million is credited to profit or loss (i.e. reversal of the previous deficit).
- £10 million is recognised in other comprehensive income and credited to the property revaluation reserve within equity.

Example 6.8.3C

Revaluation deficit reversing previous surplus

An entity purchased a property on 1 July 20X1 for £60 million. At 31 December 20X1, the property was valued at £70 million. At 31 December 20X2, the fair value of the property had decreased to £55 million.

20X1: Revaluation surplus of £10 million is recognised in other comprehensive income and credited to the property revaluation reserve within equity.

20X2: Revaluation deficit is treated as follows:

- £10 million is recognised in other comprehensive income and debited to the property revaluation reserve within equity (i.e. reversal of the previous surplus).
- £5 million is recognised in profit or loss (i.e. excess of deficit over available surplus attributable to the same property).

Example 6.8.3D

Revaluation surplus reversing previous deficit: effect of depreciation

The cost of a property with a useful life of 20 years is £10 million. Depreciation each year is £0.5 million.

At the end of Year 5, the property has a carrying amount of £7.5 million and a fair value of £6 million. At that date, the directors move to the revaluation basis of accounting. The deficit on revaluation of £1.5 million is recognised in profit or loss.

At the end of Years 6 through 9, the directors determine that there is no material difference between the carrying amount of the property and its fair value, and therefore no valuation adjustments are required. Depreciation of £2 million (i.e. 5 x £0.4 million) is recognised in the periods up to the end of Year 10, at which time the property has a carrying amount of £4 million. During Year 10, however, the value of the property increases sharply to a closing fair value of £7 million.

Applying the basic principle as stated in IAS 16.39, the portion of the revaluation surplus that is to be credited to profit or loss at the end of Year 10 might appear to be £1.5 million i.e. the amount of the deficit previously recognised in profit or loss. In effect, however, part of this revaluation decrease has already been reversed through the recognition of a lower depreciation charge for Years 6 to 10.

Accordingly, the amount of the revaluation surplus that is credited to profit or loss should be reduced by the cumulative reduction in depreciation in Years 6 to 10 as a result of recognising the revaluation deficit (i.e. (£0.5m less £0.4m) x 5 years). Therefore the amount of the surplus credited to profit or loss is £1 million. The remaining £2 million of the revaluation surplus is recognised in other comprehensive income and credited to the revaluation reserve within equity. The end result is that the balance on the revaluation reserve (£2m) is the excess of the carrying amount (£7m) over what it would have been had the property never been revalued (£5m).

This treatment is consistent with the treatment prescribed for the reversal of an impairment loss (see **chapter 9**).

6.8.4 Utilisation of revaluation reserve

Under IAS 16.41, the revaluation reserve may be transferred directly to retained earnings when the asset is derecognised. The reserve may be transferred on the retirement or disposal of the asset. Part of the reserve may, however, be transferred over the period for which the asset is used by the entity. In such circumstances, the amount of the reserve transferred is the difference between the depreciation charge based on the revalued carrying amount of the asset and the depreciation charge based on the asset's original cost. The transfer from revaluation reserve to retained earnings, whether on disposal or on a systematic basis over the life of the asset, is not made through profit or loss.

Example 6.8.4

Transfer from revaluation reserve to retained earnings

The cost of a property with a useful life of 20 years is £10 million. Depreciation each year is £0.5 million.

At the end of Year 5, the property has a carrying amount of £7.5 million and a fair value of £12 million. The surplus on revaluation of £4.5 million is credited to the revaluation reserve and the property will be depreciated over its remaining 15-year useful life at the rate of £0.8 million per annum. Assume that, for the remainder of its useful life, the depreciated carrying amount of the property is not materially different from its fair value. Therefore, no further revaluation adjustments are required.

In Years 6 through 20, depreciation has been increased by £0.3 million per annum as a result of the revaluation. Therefore, at the end of each of those years, it is acceptable to make a transfer from the revaluation surplus to retained earnings of an amount of £0.3 million, to reflect the realisation of the revaluation surplus. If such periodic transfers are made, then the revaluation reserve will have been reduced to zero at the point that the property is fully depreciated.

The reserve transfers referred to in IAS 16.41 are implied to be at the option of the reporting entity, rather than being mandated by the Standard. There would therefore appear to be another alternative – to make no reserve transfer. That option will, however, result in the permanent retention of the portion of the revaluation reserve relating to assets that have been fully depreciated or disposed of.

Any transfer between the revaluation reserve and retained earnings, which should be made on a net of tax basis, will reduce the amount that is available for offset against future revaluation deficits in respect of individual assets.

6.9 Deferred tax impact

The revaluation of assets is also likely to have deferred tax implications. For the purposes of the examples in this chapter, the deferred tax impact is ignored. Readers should refer to **chapter 12**, however, for a detailed discussion of the deferred tax impact of revaluations.

7 Depreciation

If an item of property, plant and equipment has a limited useful economic life, then its cost or, if applicable, its fair value, is reduced to its estimated residual value by the systematic allocation of depreciation over the asset's useful economic life. [IAS 16.50]

The depreciation charge for each period should be recognised in profit or loss, unless it qualifies to be capitalised in the carrying amount of another asset. [IAS 16.48] For example, the depreciation of plant and machinery used for construction purposes may be included in the cost of a self-constructed property.

Depreciation, as defined in IAS 16.6, is the systematic allocation of the depreciable amount of an asset (i.e. the cost of the asset, or other amount substituted for cost, less its residual value) over its useful life. In order to comply with the requirements of IAS 16 relating to depreciation, it is necessary to identify:

- the parts (components) of each item of property, plant and equipment that are to be depreciated separately;
- the cost or valuation of each separately depreciable component;
- the estimated residual value of each separately depreciable component;

- the length of time during which the component will be commercially useful to the entity; and
- the most appropriate depreciation method for each separately depreciable component.

Where a first-time adopter uses a deemed cost for an item of property, plant and equipment, subsequent depreciation is based on that deemed cost and starts from the date for which the entity established the fair value measurement or revaluation, as discussed at **6.2** in **chapter 5**.

7.1 Each significant component to be depreciated separately

IAS 16 requires that each part of an item of property, plant and equipment with a cost that is significant in relation to the total cost of the item should be depreciated separately. [IAS 16.43]

UK

When IFRSs were first adopted in the UK, there was discussion about whether IAS 16 takes a more prescriptive approach than FRS 15 in mandating the use of component accounting. Most of that discussion concerned whether component accounting is intended by FRS 15 to be optional or mandatory. Irrespective of the 'right' answer under UK GAAP, it is clear that component accounting is mandatory under IAS 16. It, therefore, seems likely that some UK companies, when adopting IAS 16, may find they have to apply component accounting more extensively than they have done under UK GAAP.

When an item of property, plant and equipment is first recognised, the Standard requires that the entity should allocate the amount initially recognised between the item's significant parts i.e. those separately identifiable components of the item with a cost that is significant to the total cost of the item. Each significant part is required to be depreciated separately. [IAS 16.44]

There may be a number of significant parts which, although separately identifiable, have the same useful life and which are appropriately depreciated using the same depreciation method. Such items will generally be grouped together for the purposes of calculating the depreciation charge. [IAS 16.45]

Once the individually significant parts have been identified, the remaining parts that are not individually significant are grouped together. Although the entity may have varying expectations as to the useful lives and pattern of consumption of the benefits of these remaining components, because they are not individually significant, the Standard allows that they can be depreciated as a group, provided that the depreciation rate and method selected result in a faithful representation of the pattern of consumption of benefits. [IAS 16.46]

A common example of the allocation of the cost of an item of property, plant and equipment is that of an aircraft, as mentioned in IAS 16.44. The airframe, engines and cabin interior of a single plane are likely to have significantly different useful lives. Under IAS 16, these parts are separately identified at the time that the aircraft is acquired, and each is depreciated separately over an appropriate useful life.

This approach of depreciating separate parts of a single item of property, plant and equipment is easily understood in relation to the physical components of a single item, as in the aircraft example discussed above. There will, however, also be 'parts' that are less tangible. An entity may purchase an item of property, plant and equipment that is required to undergo major inspections or overhauls at regular intervals over its useful life. For example, an entity might acquire a ship that requires a major overhaul, say, once every five years. Part of the cost of the ship may be allocable to a separate component representing the service potential required to be restored by the periodic overhauls. That separate component is isolated when the asset is acquired, and depreciated over the period to the next overhaul.

The identification of this inherent component at the time of acquisition may not be simple, as it will generally not have been separately invoiced. Therefore, an estimate of the cost will be required. This will generally be based on the current cost of the expected overhaul or inspection, i.e. the estimated cost of those activities if they were performed at the time of the purchase.

As discussed at **3.5** above, expenditure incurred subsequently on the major inspection or overhaul is capitalised provided that the recognition criteria set out in IAS 16.7 are met. To the extent that the separate component representing the estimated cost of the inspection or overhaul has not been fully depreciated by the time that the inspection/overhaul expenditure is incurred, it is derecognised and will therefore give rise to a loss.

Example 7.1 illustrates the accounting treatment for major inspection or overhaul costs which qualify for separate recognition.

Example 7.1
Separate depreciation of cost of major overhaul

An entity purchases a ship for £40 million. This ship will be required to undergo a dry dock overhaul every five years to restore its service potential. At the time of purchase, the service potential that will be required to be restored by the overhaul can be measured based on the cost of the dry docking if it had been performed at the time of the purchase of the ship, say £4 million.

The following shows the calculation of the depreciation of the ship for Years 1 to 5, using the straight line method.

	Amount	Useful life
	£'000	(years)
Purchase price of ship	40,000	
Comprising:		
The ship, excluding projected overhaul cost	36,000	30
Projected overhaul cost	4,000	5
For years 1 to 5, depreciation charges per annum are:		
	£'000	
Ship (excluding the service potential component)	1,200	
Service potential	800	

By the end of Year 5, the service potential would be fully depreciated. When a dry docking is carried out in Year 6, the expenditure is capitalised to reflect the restoration of service potential, which is then depreciated over the period to the next overhaul in Years 6 to 10.

The process in Years 6 to 10 repeats every five years from Year 11 onwards until Year 30, when both ship and the cost of dry docking are fully depreciated and a new ship is acquired.

Note that the entity is required to use its best efforts to identify separately components such as the service potential component, as described in **example 7.1**, when the asset is first acquired or constructed. That separate identification, and the subsequent separate depreciation of the service potential component, is not, however, a necessary condition for the capitalisation of the subsequent expenditure on the overhaul as part of the cost of the asset. For example, if the entity described in **example 7.1** had, in error, failed to identify the service potential component at the date of acquisition, and had not depreciated it separately during Years 1 to 5, the expenditure on the overhaul in Year 6 would still be capitalised as part of the cost of the asset, provided that the general recognition criteria were met. In this circumstance, the entity would be required to estimate the remaining carrying amount of the service potential component at the date of the first overhaul (which would be approximately £3.33m, i.e. £4m depreciated for 5 years out of 30), and to derecognise that carrying amount at the same time as the expenditure on the overhaul is capitalised.

IAS 16 gives a further example of circumstances in which cost may need to be allocated to significant parts of an asset. If an entity acquires property, plant and equipment subject to an operating lease in which it is the lessor, it may be appropriate to depreciate separately amounts reflected in the cost of the item that are attributable to favourable or unfavourable lease terms relative to market terms. [IAS 16.44]

Land and buildings acquired in such circumstances might qualify as investment property, in which case this guidance would apply where the cost model within IAS 40 *Investment Property* is adopted.

Where lease terms are unfavourable for the lessor (e.g. fixed rentals are below market terms), this will tend to depress the fair value of the asset, so that the component relating to the unfavourable terms will be a credit. Separate depreciation of such a credit component will reduce the total depreciation charge during the period for which unfavourable terms apply.

7.2 Residual value

IAS 16 defines residual value as the estimated amount that an entity would currently obtain from disposal of the asset, after deducting the estimated costs of disposal, if the asset were already of the age and in the condition expected at the end of its useful life. [IAS 16.6]

In practice, the residual value of an asset is often insignificant and, therefore, is immaterial in the calculation of the depreciable amount. However, where the residual value is significant, then it will directly impact on the depreciation charge over the life of the asset.

UK

There is an important difference between FRS 15 and IAS 16 in the way that they approach residual value. Under FRS 15, residual value is measured using prices that existed at the time of initial recognition or most recent revaluation. Although residual value is revised for changes in estimates of expected condition at the end of the asset's useful life, it is not adjusted for changes in prices (i.e. inflation). By contrast, under IAS 16, residual value is reassessed each year at current prices. Therefore over time, all other things being equal, residual value will change with prices under IAS 16 but will not change under FRS 15.

This effect is most pronounced for appreciating assets, such as some buildings. Under FRS 15, depreciation is likely to be recognised throughout the useful life of the buildings. Under IAS 16, it is entirely possible that residual value will rise so that in due course it exceeds carrying amount. When this happens, depreciation will cease.

The residual value of an asset is required to be reviewed at least at each financial year-end. [IAS 16.51] The revised estimate should be based on market conditions current at the end of the reporting period. Where the revised estimate differs significantly from previous estimates of residual value, the effect is accounted for prospectively as a change in estimate, in accordance with the requirements of IAS 8 *Accounting Policies, Changes in Accounting Estimates and Errors*. [IAS 16.51] Effectively, the depreciation charge over the remaining useful life of the asset is adjusted to take account of the revised estimate of residual value.

Where the revised estimate of residual value is equal to or greater than the asset's carrying amount, whether due to inflation or otherwise, then the asset's depreciation charge is zero unless and until its residual value subsequently decreases to an amount below the asset's carrying amount. [IAS 16.54]

The definition of residual value refers to the potential disposal value of the asset if it were already of the age and in the condition expected at the end of its useful life. The amount is therefore quite separate from the current fair value of the asset. Where the fair value of the asset exceeds its carrying amount (generally because the entity has adopted the cost model for accounting for its property, plant and equipment), this does not remove the obligation to recognise depreciation. [IAS 16.52]

Further, the definition focuses on the amount that could currently be obtained on disposal of the asset, rather than the amount that is expected to be obtained at the end of the asset's useful life. Therefore, expectations as to future increases or decreases in that disposal value are not taken into account. Thus, an increase in the expected residual value of an asset because of past events will affect the depreciable amount; expectations of future changes in residual value other than the effects of wear and tear will not. [IAS 16.BC29]

7.3 Estimates of useful lives

The useful life of an asset is defined as:

[IAS 16.6]

- the period over which an asset is expected to be available for use by an entity; or
- the number of production or similar units expected to be obtained from the asset by an entity.

7.3.1 *Commencement of depreciation*

Depreciation of an asset commences when it is available for use, i.e. when it is in the location and condition necessary for it to be capable of operating in the manner intended by management. [IAS 16.55] This is the same point in time at which the entity is required to cease capitalising costs within the carrying amount of the asset. See **4.2.9** above for guidance as to when this point in time occurs.

7.3.2 *Cessation of depreciation*

Depreciation of an asset ceases at the earlier of:

[IAS 16.55]

- the date that the asset is classified as held for sale (or included in a disposal group that is classified as held for sale) in accordance with IFRS 5 *Non-current Assets Held for Sale and Discontinued Operations;* and
- the date that the asset is derecognised.

IFRS 5 requires that a non-current asset (or disposal group) be classified as held for sale if its carrying amount will be recovered principally through a sale transaction rather than through continuing use. [IFRS 5.6] For this to be the case, the asset (or disposal group) must be available for immediate sale in its present condition, and its sale must be 'highly probable'. Readers should refer to **chapter 29** for further guidance.

IAS 16 sets out requirements in respect of the derecognition of items of property, plant and equipment – see **section 9** below.

Therefore, depreciation of an asset does not cease when an asset becomes idle or is retired from active use unless the asset is fully depreciated. Where the depreciation charge is calculated by reference to the usage of the asset, however, the depreciation charge may be zero while there is no production. [IAS 16.55] In any case, when an asset becomes idle, or is retired from active use, this may trigger an impairment loss which will result in the reduction of the carrying amount of the asset to its estimated recoverable amount.

7.3.3 *Factors impacting on the useful life of an asset*

The consumption of the future economic benefits embodied in an asset occurs principally through usage. Other factors should also be taken into account, however, such as technical obsolescence and wear and tear while an asset remains idle, as they may result in a reduction in the economic benefits expected to be derived from the asset. Consequently, all of the following factors need to be considered in determining the useful life of an asset:

[IAS 16.56]

- the expected usage of the asset by the entity. Usage is assessed by reference to the asset's expected capacity or physical output;
- the expected physical wear and tear, which depends on operational factors such as the number of shifts for which the asset is to be used and the repair and maintenance programme of the entity, and the care and maintenance of the asset while idle;
- technical or commercial obsolescence arising from changes or improvements in production, or from a change in the market demand for the product or service output of the asset; and
- legal or similar limits on the use of the asset, such as the expiry dates of related leases.

As the useful life of an asset is defined in terms of its expected utility to the entity, the asset management policy of the reporting entity should be taken into account when estimating the useful life of an asset. For example, an entity may have a policy of disposing of assets after a specified time or after consumption of a specified proportion of the economic benefits embodied in the assets. In such circumstances, the useful life of an asset may be shorter than its economic life. [IAS 16.57] For example, it is often the case that company cars are disposed of well before the end of their economic life.

7.3.4 *Change in estimate of useful life*

IAS 16 requires that the estimate of the useful life of an item of property, plant and equipment should be reviewed at least at each financial year-end. If expectations differ from previous estimates, the change is accounted for as a change in accounting estimate in accordance with IAS 8 *Accounting Policies, Changes in Accounting Estimates and Errors*. [IAS 16.51]

Estimates of useful lives require adjustment from time to time in the light of changes in experience and knowledge. These changes may reflect the extension of estimated useful lives due to exceptional maintenance expenditure, curtailment of estimated useful lives due to excessive use, or obsolescence not allowed for in the original estimates. When the original estimate of the useful life of an asset is revised, the undepreciated cost (or valuation) should be recognised in profit or loss over the revised remaining useful life, except to the extent that the depreciation expense qualifies for capitalisation into the cost of other assets, such as inventories.

Example 7.3.4

Change in estimate of useful life

An entity purchased an item of plant at a cost of £1.2 million with an estimated useful life of 10 years.

At the end of Year 3, the asset has a carrying amount of £840,000. On the basis of experience of similar assets, the item of plant is estimated to have a remaining useful life of 4 years. The asset is not determined to be impaired. Consequently, the carrying amount of £840,000 is depreciated over the remaining 4 years at £210,000 per annum.

Depreciation charges for years 1 to 7 will be as follows:

	£'000		£'000
Year 1	120	Year 5	210
Year 2	120	Year 6	210
Year 3	120	Year 7	210
Year 4	210		

A significant reduction in the estimated useful life of an asset may indicate that the asset has been impaired – because the amount that the entity expects to generate from the use of the asset has been reduced below its carrying amount. In such circumstances, it will be necessary to recognise an impairment loss to reduce the carrying amount of the asset to its recoverable amount (see **chapter 9**). The recoverable amount is then depreciated over the revised estimate of the useful life of the asset.

7.3.5 *Fully-depreciated assets*

If estimates of the useful lives of items of property, plant and equipment are made realistically, and kept under regular review as required by IAS 16.51, there should be few fully depreciated assets still in use. If fully-depreciated assets are no longer in use, they should either be classified as held for sale in accordance with IFRS 5 *Non-current Assets Held for Sale and Discontinued Operations*, or they should be derecognised (see **section 9** below).

7.4 Methods of depreciation

It is necessary to select a method of applying depreciation that results in the carrying amount of the asset being allocated as fairly as possible to the periods expected to benefit from the use of the asset. The method used should be that which reflects most closely the pattern in which the asset's economic benefits are expected to be consumed by the entity. [IAS 16.60]

7.4.1 *Alternative methods of apportioning depreciation*

There are several methods of apportioning depreciation over the anticipated useful life of the asset. Those most commonly employed are the straight-line method and the reducing balance (diminishing balance) method. Straight-line depreciation results in a constant charge over the useful life of the asset, because the annual depreciation charge is a fixed percentage of the original cost (or revalued amount). The reducing-balance method results in a decreasing charge over the life of the asset, because the annual depreciation charge is a fixed percentage of the opening carrying amount. The straight-line method is the most popular, principally because of its simplicity.

Another useful basis is the unit of production method, which apportions the cost of the asset over its productive life measured in terms of the units produced or machine hours utilised in relation to the total of such units or hours estimated to comprise the productive life of the asset. This method is theoretically superior to the straight-line and reducing balance methods in that it more accurately matches costs with revenue, where the life of the asset can be measured with some precision in terms of its ultimate total output. This method is commonly used in the oil, gas and other extractive industries, where the life of an asset may be expressed in terms of a quantity of output and production assets have no further value once mineral reserves have been extracted.

7.4.2 *Increasing charge depreciation*

Entities will often construct items of property, plant and equipment that are expected to generate benefits over many years. customer demand to use the assets may, however, be expected to start slowly and take a number of years to reach an expected 'normal' level. An example of this might be a cable-television distribution network. In such cases, an entity may wish the depreciation charge for the asset to increase gradually to reflect customers' expected phased-in demand.

The appropriateness of such a policy will depend on how the asset's benefits are being consumed. IAS 16.60 requires that depreciation reflect the pattern in which the asset's economic benefits are consumed by the entity. Those benefits should be viewed in terms of physical capacity or physical output (using up physical capability, wear and tear, technical obsolescence) and legal limits on the physical use of the asset (such as by a lease).

While an 'increasing charge' or 'sinking fund' method of calculating depreciation is not appropriate under IAS 16, a unit-of-production method of calculating depreciation will be appropriate if it reflects the pattern of benefit consumption. This method is more likely to be justified for a physical asset, reflecting wear and tear, than for an intangible asset (see **chapter 8**).

Under UK GAAP, the use of annuity depreciation for an asset leased on an operating lease was effectively confirmed as 'not prohibited' through the ASB's issue of an Exposure Draft Amendment to Financial Reporting Standards 15 Tangible Fixed Assets *and 10* Goodwill and Intangible Assets *in June 2000. IAS 17 does not permit the use of annuity depreciation for such assets for the reasons discussed at **8.3** in **chapter 26**.* UK

7.4.3 *Change in depreciation method*

IAS 16 requires that the depreciation method applied to an item of property, plant and equipment should be reviewed at least at each financial year-end. Except where there is a change in the expected pattern of consumption of economic benefits embodied in the asset, the depreciation method adopted should be applied consistently from period to period. If there has been a significant change in the expected pattern of consumption of benefits, the depreciation method is changed to reflect the changed pattern. The change is accounted for as a change in accounting estimate in accordance with IAS 8 *Accounting Policies, Changes in Accounting Estimates and Errors*. [IAS 16.61]

Therefore, a change from one method of providing depreciation to another does not constitute a change in accounting policy. The carrying amount of the asset is written off using the new method over the remaining useful life, commencing with the period in which the change takes place. Separate disclosure of the impact of the change will be required if the change has a material effect in the current period or is expected to have a material effect in subsequent periods.

Example 7.4.3

Change in depreciation method

An entity acquired an asset 3 years ago at a cost of £5 million. The depreciation method adopted for the asset was 10 per cent reducing balance.

At the end of Year 3, the entity estimates that the remaining useful life of the asset is 8 years and determines to adopt straight-line depreciation from that point.

Depreciation charges for years 1 to 11 will be as follows:

	£'000		£'000
Year 1	500	Year 7	455
Year 2	450	Year 8	455
Year 3	405	Year 9	455
Year 4	455	Year 10	455
Year 5	455	Year 11	460
Year 6	455		

7.5 Depreciation of particular classes of asset

7.5.1 Freehold land

Freehold land that is not subject to depletion (e.g. by the extraction of minerals) does not have a limited useful life and, therefore, should not be depreciated. In consequence, it is necessary, where freehold property is purchased, to allocate the purchase consideration between the value of the land and that of the buildings. Similarly, any revaluations of freehold property should distinguish between land and buildings.

Where the cost of site dismantlement, removal and restoration is included in the cost of land, that portion of the land asset is depreciated over the period of benefits obtained by incurring those costs. In some cases, the land itself may have a limited useful life, in which case it is depreciated in a manner that reflects the benefits to be derived from it. [IAS 16.59]

Where the value of freehold land is adversely affected by long-term environmental factors, an impairment loss should be recognised to reflect any decline in its estimated recoverable amount below its carrying amount.

7.5.2 *Freehold buildings*

Buildings have limited useful economic lives and are no different from other depreciable assets. Although their estimated useful lives are usually significantly longer than other items of property, plant and equipment, they should nevertheless be depreciated in a similar manner, generally using the straight-line method. IAS 16 emphasises that an increase in the value of the land on which a building stands does not affect the determination of the useful life of the building. [IAS 16.58] An exception to the general requirement to depreciate buildings is allowed for those properties that qualify as investment properties (see **chapter 7** for details).

IAS 16 does not grant any exemption in respect of historic buildings: the fact that they may have been built centuries earlier, and may be expected to last for centuries more, does not exempt them from depreciation. It is possible that the useful life of such a building may be very long. Also, where an entity intends to sell such a building in due course, rather than use it for the remainder of its physical life, it is possible that the residual value may be relatively high. Both of these factors may lead to the depreciation charge being relatively small. But care should be taken to identify any components (e.g. roofs) that may require replacement at periodic intervals, which will need to be depreciated over a shorter period (see **7.1**).

7.5.3 *Plant and machinery, tools and equipment, ships, vehicles, etc.*

Depreciation charges are, in general, computed using the straight-line method, but the reducing balance and unit of production methods are also suitable in appropriate circumstances. Some small assets with very short useful lives, such as loose tools, jigs and patterns may, however, be dealt with more satisfactorily in aggregate, as discussed at **3.4**.

7.5.4 *Leased assets*

Tangible assets that are held under finance leases are required by IAS 17 *Leases* to be depreciated. That Standard requires that the depreciation policy adopted for depreciable leased assets should be consistent with that for similar assets that are owned, and that the depreciation charge should be calculated in accordance with the principles of IAS 16, as discussed throughout this section. [IAS 17.27]

IAS 17 also stipulates that, if there is reasonable certainty that the lessee will obtain ownership by the end of the lease term, the period of expected use is the useful life of the asset; otherwise, the asset is to be depreciated over the shorter of the lease term and its useful life. [IAS 17.28]

IAS 16.56(d) states that the expiry dates of related leases should be taken into account in determining the useful life of a depreciable asset. Should the renewal option in a lease contract be considered in estimating the useful life of leasehold improvements?

The renewal period(s) should be taken into account if, at the inception of the lease, it is 'reasonably certain' that the lessee will exercise the renewal option. For property acquired by a lessee under a finance lease, IAS 17.27 states that 'if there is no reasonable certainty that the lessee will obtain ownership by the end of the lease term, the asset shall be fully depreciated over the shorter of the lease term and its useful life'. IAS 17.4 defines lease term to include 'any further terms for which the lessee has the option to continue to lease the asset, with or without further payment, when at the inception of the lease it is reasonably certain that the lessee will exercise the option'. This 'reasonable certainty' of renewal test should be applied at the commencement of the lease both in accounting for the lease itself and in assessing the depreciable life of leasehold improvements relating to both finance and operating leases. In particular, therefore, the assumption regarding the lease term should be applied consistently for the lease and for any leasehold improvements.

7.5.5 *Stand-by equipment*

The useful life of stand-by equipment will be determined by the useful life of the equipment for which is serves as a back-up. Take the example cited at **3.2** above, where an entity has installed two turbines. One will produce energy for the plant, and the other will be used as a backup in case the first turbine fails or is otherwise rendered out of service. The stand-by equipment will be depreciated from the date it is made available for use (i.e. when it is in the location and condition necessary for it to be capable of operating in the manner intended by management) over the shorter of the life of the turbine or the life of the plant of which the turbine is part.

7.5.6 *Spare parts*

In contrast to the depreciation of stand-by equipment, the useful life of spare parts classified as property, plant and equipment commences when they are put into use, rather than when they are acquired.

Example 7.5.6

Depreciation of spare parts classified as property, plant and equipment

An entity buys five new machines for use in its production facility. Simultaneously, it purchases a spare motor to be used as a replacement if a motor on one of the five machines breaks. The motor will be used in the production of goods and once brought into service will be operated during more than one period. It is therefore classified as property, plant and equipment.

Since the motor does not qualify as stand-by equipment, in that it will not be ready for use until it is installed, the useful life of the motor commences when it is available for use within the machine rather than when it is acquired. It would, therefore, be depreciated over the period starting when it is brought into service, continuing over the lesser of its useful life and the remaining expected useful life of the asset to which it relates. If the asset to which it relates will be replaced at the end of its useful life and the motor is expected to be used or usable for the replacement asset, a longer depreciation period may be appropriate. During the period before the motor is available for service, any reduction in value should be reflected as an impairment loss under IAS 36 *Impairment of Assets*, at the time impairment is indicated.

8 Impairment

An entity should refer to the requirements of IAS 36 *Impairment of Assets* to determine whether an item of property, plant and equipment is impaired. IAS 36 explains how an entity reviews the carrying amount of its assets, how it determines the recoverable amount of an asset, and when it recognises or reverses an impairment loss (see **chapter 9**). [IAS 16.63]

8.1 Compensation for impairment or loss

Where an asset is impaired, lost or given up, any compensation from third parties is included in profit or loss when the compensation becomes receivable. [IAS 16.65]

Examples of such circumstances include:

- reimbursements by insurance companies after the impairment or loss of items of property, plant and equipment, e.g. due to natural disasters, theft etc.;
- indemnities by governments for items of property, plant and equipment that are expropriated, e.g. compulsory purchase of land to be used for public purposes;
- compensation related to the involuntary conversion of items of property, plant and equipment, e.g. relocation of facilities from a designated urban area to a non-urban area in accordance with government land policy; and
- physical replacement in whole or in part of an impaired or lost asset.

The Standard emphasises that impairments or losses of items of property, plant and equipment, related claims for or payments of compensation from third parties, and any subsequent purchase or construction of replacement assets are separate economic events and should be accounted for as such. The three economic events should be accounted for separately as follows:

[IAS 16.66]

- in respect of impairment or loss:
  - impairments of items of property, plant and equipment should be recognised in accordance with IAS 36;
  - derecognition of items of property, plant and equipment retired or disposed of should be determined in accordance with IAS 16;
- compensation from third parties for items of property, plant and equipment that were impaired, lost or given up should be included in determining profit or loss when it becomes receivable; and
- the cost of items of property, plant and equipment restored, purchased or constructed as replacements should be determined in accordance with IAS 16.

9 Derecognition

IAS 16 requires that the carrying amount of an item of property, plant and equipment should be derecognised:

[IAS 16.67]

- on disposal; or
- when no future economic benefits are expected from its use or disposal.

> **Example 9**
>
> **Disposal of property, plant and equipment**
>
> An entity enters into a transaction whereby it sells an item of property, plant and equipment to a third party. It concurrently enters into a contract with the third party to buy all of the actual output of the asset over its remaining useful life at a fixed per-unit price, but in total not less than a minimum payment equal to the value of 90 per cent of the expected output. The minimum payment must be made even if the actual output is below expectation. Should the entity recognise the sale of the asset by removing it from its statement of financial position?
>
> By entering into the supply contract at a fixed price, the entity has kept the rewards arising from the use of the asset. Similarly, by setting a minimum payment level at a high level, it has retained a significant portion of the risk arising out of operating the asset. It has, therefore, retained significant risks and rewards relating to the asset, and thus the asset should not be derecognised.
>
> In this situation, the entity should also consider the requirements of IFRIC 4 *Determining Whether an Arrangement Contains a Lease* (discussed at **2.1** in **chapter 26**). If it is concluded that the arrangement contains a finance lease, the item of property, plant and equipment will not be derecognised, since the transaction will involve a sale and finance leaseback.

Except where IAS 17 *Leases* requires otherwise in the circumstances of a sale and leaseback, the gain or loss arising on the derecognition of an item of property, plant and equipment must be included in profit or loss when the amount is derecognised. [IAS 16.68]

On the derecognition of an item of property, plant and equipment, the gain or loss arising is determined as the difference between the net disposal proceeds, if any, and the carrying amount of the item. [IAS 16.71] As discussed at **6.8.4** above, where a revalued asset is disposed of, any credit balance on the revaluation reserve attributable to that asset may be transferred directly to retained earnings, though such a transfer is not mandatory, but must not be reflected in profit or loss.

If an item of property, plant or equipment that is measured at revalued amounts under IAS 16.31 is sold or otherwise disposed of, IAS 16 neither precludes nor specifically requires a 'deathbed' revaluation (i.e. a final revaluation of the asset at the time the asset is disposed of). Therefore, a gain or loss will be recognised to the extent of any difference between disposal price and last revaluation.

Entities should adopt a single accounting policy as regards deathbed revaluations, and apply that policy consistently to all revalued assets. If it has, or could have, a material effect, the policy on deathbed revaluations should be disclosed. Where a general policy of revaluation is adopted, significant gains or losses normally would not be expected on disposal since revaluations to fair value should be made with sufficient regularity so that the fair value of a revalued asset does not differ materially from its carrying amount.

The disposal consideration received is measured at its fair value. If payment is deferred beyond normal credit terms, the consideration received is recognised initially at the cash price equivalent. The difference between the nominal amount of the consideration and the cash price equivalent is recognised as interest income on an effective yield basis, in accordance with IAS 18 *Revenue*. [IAS 16.72]

IAS 16 specifically prohibits the classification as revenue of gains arising on the derecognition of property, plant and equipment (but see **9.1** below). [IAS 16.68] The Standard does, however, require that the date of disposal of an item of property, plant and equipment be determined using the criteria for recognising revenue from the sale of goods, as set out in IAS 18 *Revenue* (see **chapter 23**). [IAS 16.69]

9.1 Sales of property, plant and equipment held for rental

For periods beginning on or after 1 January 2009, the requirements of IAS 16 are amended, as described below, by *Improvements to IFRSs* issued in May 2008.

Where an entity, in the course of its ordinary activities, routinely sells items that it has held for rental to others, it transfers those assets to inventories at their carrying amount when they cease to be rented and become held for sale. Sale proceeds from such assets are recognised as revenue in accordance with IAS 18. When such assets are transferred to inventories, IFRS 5 does not apply to them. [IAS 16.68A]

Earlier application of this amendment is permitted, but an entity choosing to apply the amendment early must disclose that fact and must also apply the related amendments to IAS 7 *Statement of Cash Flows* (discussed at **5.1.4** in **chapter 30**).

10 Presentation and disclosure

10.1 Presentation

IAS 1 *Presentation of Financial Statements* requires that, where material, the aggregate carrying amount of the entity's property, plant and equipment should be presented in the statement of financial position. [IAS 1(2007).54(a), previously IAS 1(2003).68(a)]

10.2 Disclosure

10.2.1 General

In respect of each class of property, plant and equipment, an entity is required to disclose:

[IAS 16.73]

- the measurement bases (i.e. cost or valuation) used for determining the gross carrying amount;
- the depreciation methods used;
- the useful lives or the depreciation rates used;
- the gross carrying amount and the accumulated depreciation (aggregated with accumulated impairment losses) at the beginning and end of the period; and
- a reconciliation of the carrying amount at the beginning and end of the period showing:
    - additions;
    - assets classified as held for sale or included as a disposal group classified as held for sale in accordance with IFRS 5 *Non-current Assets held for Sale and Discontinued Operations* and other disposals;
    - acquisitions through business combinations;

- increases or decreases resulting from revaluations and from impairment losses recognised or reversed in other comprehensive income;
- impairment losses recognised in profit or loss during the period;
- impairment losses reversed in profit or loss during the period;
- depreciation;
- the net exchange differences arising on the translation of the financial statements from the functional currency into a different presentation currency, including the translation of a foreign operation into the presentation currency of the reporting entity; and
- other changes.

UK

There are two differences between these IFRS requirements and UK GAAP:

- *the reconciliation above is required both for the current period and for the comparative period, whereas under FRS 15 only a current period reconciliation is required; and*
- *the reconciliation may be presented for the carrying amount, rather than separately for cost (or revalued amount) and depreciation.*

The financial statements are also required to disclose:

[IAS 16.74]

- the existence and amounts of restrictions on title, and property, plant and equipment pledged as security for liabilities;
- the amount of expenditures recognised in the carrying amount of an item of property, plant and equipment in the course of its construction;
- the amount of contractual commitments for the acquisition of property, plant and equipment; and
- if not disclosed separately in the statement of comprehensive income, the amount of compensation from third parties for items of property, plant and equipment that were impaired, lost or given up that is included in profit or loss.

Although the drafting is a little unclear in the Standard, it appears that the second bullet above requires disclosure of the cost of assets that are still in the course of construction at the end of the reporting period (i.e. rather than those that were in the course of construction when the costs were incurred). The drafting is also unclear whether it is the costs incurred in the year or the total cumulative costs incurred on such assets which should be disclosed, although the latter interpretation appears more logical.

Disclosures may also be required by IAS 8 *Accounting Policies, Changes in Accounting Estimates and Errors* in respect of changes in accounting estimates for residual values, useful lives, depreciation methods or provisions for dismantling, removing or restoring assets (see **chapter 4**), or by IAS 36 *Impairment of Assets* (see **chapter 9**). [IAS 16.76 & 78]

10.2.2 *Items stated at revalued amounts*

In respect of items of property, plant and equipment stated at revalued amounts, the entity is required to disclose:

[IAS 16.77]

- the effective date of the revaluation;
- whether an independent valuer was involved;
- the methods and significant assumptions applied in estimating the items' fair values;
- the extent to which the items' fair values were determined directly by reference to observable prices in an active market or recent market transactions on arm's length terms or were estimated using other valuation techniques;
- for each revalued class of property, plant and equipment, the carrying amount that would have been recognised had the assets been carried under the cost model; and
- the revaluation surplus, indicating the movement for the period and any restrictions on the distribution of the balance to shareholders.

The last of these disclosure requirements could be made in the reserves note rather than the property, plant and equipment note.

Under UK law and related guidance, any revaluation surplus relating to property, plant and equipment is very unlikely to be distributable. It may be helpful to disclose this fact but there is no requirement to do so (see ***4.5.2.3*** *in* ***chapter 3****).* UK

10.2.3 Additional recommended disclosures

IAS 16.79 also encourages but does not require the disclosure of the following information:

- the carrying amount of temporarily idle property, plant and equipment;
- the gross carrying amount of any fully depreciated property, plant and equipment that is still in use;
- the carrying amount of property, plant and equipment retired from active use and not classified as held for sale in accordance with IFRS 5 *Non-current Assets Held for Sale and Discontinued Operations*; and
- when the cost model is used, the fair value of property, plant and equipment when this is materially different from the carrying amount.

7 Investment property

1 Introduction

IAS 40 *Investment Property* prescribes the accounting treatment and disclosure requirements for investment property, which is property held to earn rentals, or for capital appreciation, or both. In May 2008, IAS 40 was amended by *Improvements to IFRSs*.

This chapter discusses the requirements of IAS 40 in the following sections:

Section 2	Scope
Section 3	Recognition
Section 4	Measurement at recognition
Section 5	Measurement after recognition
Section 6	Transfers
Section 7	Disposals
Section 8	Presentation and disclosure

There are some important differences between IAS 40 and the equivalent UK standard, SSAP 19 Accounting for investment properties. *The most significant of these are as follows.* UK

- *SSAP 19 requires investment property to be stated at open market value. Under IAS 40, UK entities are permitted to adopt the cost model but this will not avoid the cost and effort of obtaining valuations because the standard requires, except in rare circumstances, disclosure of the fair value when the cost model is used.*
- *When the fair value model is used under IAS 40, the standard requires investment property to be stated at 'fair value' whereas SSAP 19 uses the term 'open market value'. These concepts are similar and it is unlikely that differences in valuations will arise in practice. International Valuation Standards (IVS) define market value as 'the estimated amount for which a property should be exchanged on the date of valuation between a willing buyer and a willing seller in an arm's length transaction after proper marketing wherein the parties*

> *had each acted knowledgeably, prudently, and without compulsion'. Fair value has a broader, more generic meaning than market value. In most circumstances, however, fair value will be best represented by market value. But where no evidenced market exists, the fair value can be represented instead by an income approach or depreciated replacement cost approach.*
>
> - *Although valuations may be similar under the two standards, the reporting of gains and losses is fundamentally different. SSAP 19 requires all gains and losses on investment property to be reported in the Statement of Total Recognised Gains and Losses. IAS 40 requires all gains and losses to be recognised in profit or loss, so that reported profits are more volatile under IAS 40.*
> - *When using the fair value model of IAS 40, the UK GAAP concept of temporary or permanent diminutions in value is no longer relevant as all gains and losses are recognised in profit or loss. However, this distinction may still be relevant in the consideration of distributable profits (as discussed in* ***chapter 49****).*
> - *UK property investment companies are significantly affected by IAS 17 Leases as well as by IAS 40. The requirements of IAS 17 and the related requirements of SIC-15 for operating lease incentives are considered in* ***chapter 26****. Some outward leases (i.e. where the entity is the lessor) that are classified as operating leases under UK GAAP are classified as finance leases under IAS 17 (in respect of the buildings element but not the land element). This has implications for the application of IAS 40 because the buildings elements of such leases are recognised as financial assets and cannot be accounted for as investment property.*

2 Scope

IAS 40 is to be applied in the recognition, measurement and disclosure of 'investment property' (see **2.1** below). [IAS 40.2]

The Standard also deals with the measurement of investment property interests held under lease in the lessee's financial statements, and with the measurement in a lessor's financial statements of investment property leased out under an operating lease. The more general requirements regarding the classification and measurement of leased investment property are not dealt with in IAS 40 but fall within the general requirements of IAS 17 *Leases*. In particular, the following matters are dealt with in IAS 17 rather than in IAS 40:

[IAS 40.3]

- classification of leases as finance leases or operating leases;
- recognition of lease income from investment property;
- measurement in a lessee's financial statements of property interests held under a lease accounted for as an operating lease;
- measurement in a lessor's financial statements of its net investment in a finance lease;
- accounting for sale and leaseback transactions; and
- disclosure about finance leases and operating leases.

Also specifically excluded from the scope of IAS 40 are:

[IAS 40.4]

- biological assets related to agricultural activity (see the discussion of IAS 41 *Agriculture* in **chapter 43**); and
- mineral rights and mineral reserves such as oil, natural gas, and similar non-regenerative resources.

2.1 Investment property – definition

Investment property is defined in IAS 40 as:

[IAS 40.5]

> 'property (land or a building – or part of a building – or both) held (by the owner or by the lessee under a finance lease) to earn rentals or for capital appreciation or both, rather than for:
>
> (a) use in the production or supply of goods or services or for administrative purposes; or
>
> (b) sale in the ordinary course of business'.

Included within this definition are:

[IAS 40.8]

- land held for long-term capital appreciation, and not for short-term sale in the ordinary course of business;
- land held for a currently undetermined future use. If an entity has not decided whether land will be used for owner-occupation or for short-term sale in the ordinary course of business, it should be regarded as held for capital appreciation;

- a building owned or held under finance lease by an entity and leased out under operating lease(s);
- a vacant building that is being held to be leased out under an operating lease (or leases); and
- property that is being constructed or developed for future use as investment property.

The last of these (property under construction or development for future use as an investment property) is brought into the scope of IAS 40 with effect from the implementation of *Improvements to IFRSs* issued in May 2008 – see **2.2**.

Examples of items that are **not** investment property are:

[IAS 40.9]

- property which is being held for sale in the ordinary course of business, or which is under construction or development for such sale (within the scope of IAS 2 *Inventories*, see **chapter 10**). This means that properties acquired specifically for the purpose of subsequent disposal in the near future, or for development and resale, are excluded from the scope of IAS 40;
- property being constructed or developed on behalf of third parties (within the scope of IAS 11 *Construction Contracts*, see **chapter 40**);
- owner-occupied property, which includes property held for future development and subsequent use as owner-occupied property, property held for future use as owner-occupied property, employee-occupied property (whether or not the employees pay rent at market rates) and owner-occupied property awaiting disposal; and
- property leased to another entity under a finance lease.

The Standard acknowledges that judgement is often required to determine whether a property qualifies as an investment property and requires entities to develop criteria to enable them to make that determination in a consistent manner. Disclosure of such criteria is required where classification is difficult (see **8.2**). [IAS 40.14]

2.2 Property under construction or development for future use as an investment property

Improvements to IFRSs issued in May 2008 brought property under construction or development for future use as an investment property within the scope of IAS 40. Previously, such property was accounted for under the requirements of IAS 16 *Property, Plant and Equipment* until the date that construction or development was completed. The IASB has made this change primarily to ensure consistency between the accounting for the construction/ development of a future investment property and the redevelopment of an existing investing property, which has always been included within the scope of IAS 40.

Property under construction had previously been excluded from the scope of IAS 40 due to concerns about the difficulty of estimating reliably the fair value of such property. The Board has addressed these concerns by introducing new guidance into the Standard (see **5.2.2.3**).

The amendments to IAS 40 arising from *Improvements to IFRSs* are effective for annual periods beginning on or after 1 January 2009. The amendments are to be applied prospectively. [IAS 40.85B] Therefore, where an entity has previously accounted for property under construction or development for future use as an investment property under IAS 16, prior period amounts are not restated and the reclassification is presented as a movement in the asset categories in the period of first application.

Entities are permitted to apply the revised requirements from a date earlier than 1 January 2009. Such early adoption is only permitted where the fair values of the investment property under construction were determined at those dates, i.e. entities are not permitted to commission retrospective valuations of those properties. Where the amendments are applied in a period beginning before 1 January 2009, that fact should be disclosed and the amendments to paragraphs 5 and 81E of IAS 16 *Property, Plant and Equipment* (see **section 2** of **chapter 6**) should be applied from the same date. [IAS 40.85B]

The transitional provisions of IAS 40 do not set out explicitly where, at the date on which the amendments are adopted, any difference between the previous carrying amount and fair value of property under construction or development is to be recognised. It appears appropriate for such differences to be recognised in profit or loss. This is because, both before and after the amendment, IAS 40 requires any difference between carrying amount and fair value to be recognised in profit or loss; the amendment has only accelerated the recognition of such gains and losses.

UK

At the time of writing, Improvements to IFRSs *has not yet been endorsed for use in the EU. Since the requirements in respect of property under construction or development for future use as an investment property differ from those of the previous version of IAS 40, EU reporting entities will not be able to apply the revised version in their statutory financial statements until it is endorsed.*

2.3 Property held under an operating lease

A property interest that is held by a lessee under an operating lease may be classified and accounted for as an investment property if, and only if, the property would otherwise meet the definition of an investment property and the lessee uses IAS 40's fair value model (see **5.2**) for the asset recognised. It is important to note that:

[IAS 40.6]

- this is an option (a 'classification alternative'). Entities may elect whether they wish to classify such interests as investment property;
- the classification alternative is available on a property-by-property basis;
- the classification alternative is not available for assets not accounted for using the fair value model;
- once this classification alternative is selected for one property interest held under an operating lease, all property classified as investment property must be accounted for using the fair value model; and
- property interests accounted for under the classification alternative are considered to be part of the entity's investment property for the purposes of IAS 40's disclosure requirements (see **section 8**).

The option above to classify certain property interests under operating leases as investment property is intended to facilitate the classification of assets such as land held under long-term operating leases as investment property, provided that the general criteria for such classification are met. This is particularly relevant in jurisdictions such as Hong Kong and the United Kingdom where interests in property are commonly – or, in the former case, exclusively – held under long-term lease arrangements.

Leased property may also be treated as investment property where the lease meets the definition of a finance lease (see **chapter 26**) and also in the circumstances dealt with in IAS 17.16 where the entire inward lease is classified as a finance lease because the lease payments cannot be allocated reliably between the land and buildings elements (see **5.2.1** in **chapter 26**). The detailed requirements where property or property interests held under leases are classified as investment property are considered further at **4.3** below.

UK

The ability to classify as an investment property an interest held under an operating lease might be attractive for those very long leases, typically of 100 years or more, that are a feature of the UK property market. Although such leases would be classified as finance leases under UK GAAP, this will not necessarily be the case under IFRSs because of the requirements in IAS 17 to separate the land and buildings elements and generally to account for leases of land as operating leases.

Example 2.3

Classification – lease of an investment property

Company A (as lessee) leases a property which meets the definition of an investment property. Company A is unable to obtain a reliable allocation between the land element and the buildings elements of the leased property; accordingly, the entire lease is classified as a finance lease (it is **not** clear that both elements are operating leases, otherwise the entire lease would be classified as an operating lease). Nevertheless, the characteristics of the land element are that it has an indefinite economic life and title is not expected to pass to the lessee by the end of the lease term. For this reason, the unidentifiable land component of the property is in the nature of an operating lease. Does IAS 40 require A to measure the property using the fair value model?

The requirement in IAS 17.19 to adopt the fair value model applies when an entity chooses to account for a property interest held under an operating lease as an investment property. Since the entire property is classified as a finance lease, IAS 40 allows a choice between the cost model and the fair value model. This option is available for finance leases (as determined by IAS 17) irrespective of whether there may be an 'operating lease' component for land which cannot be reliably determined.

2.4 Property held for more than one purpose

In cases where property is held partly for capital appreciation and/or rentals, and partly for the production of goods or services or administrative purposes, the two parts are accounted for separately if they can be sold, or leased out under a finance lease, separately. If they could not be sold (or leased out under a finance lease) separately, the property can be accounted for as an investment property only if an insignificant portion is held for use in the production or supply of goods or services or for administrative purposes. [IAS 40.10]

The Standard does not include any guidance as to what constitutes an 'insignificant' portion for this purpose. This is a deliberate omission – the Basis for Conclusions on IAS 40 explains that quantitative guidance has not been provided because the Board concluded that such guidance could lead to arbitrary distinctions.

2.5 Ancillary services

If an entity provides ancillary services to the occupants of its property, the property is accounted for as investment property provided that the services are an 'insignificant' portion of the arrangement. [IAS 40.11]

Example 2.5A

Services provided by the owner of an office building

The owner of an office building provides cleaning services for the lessees of the building and these services are 'insignificant' in the context of the total arrangement. Therefore, the building is treated as an investment property.

As indicated in the above example, it would be unusual for cleaning services to be so material that they would prevent a property being classified as an investment property. A similar conclusion is likely for security and maintenance services. At the other extreme, some companies rent out fully furnished offices including a whole range of services such as IT systems and secretarial services. Such arrangements are in the nature of the provision of a service rather than property investment and the property would be classified as owner-occupied and accounted for under IAS 16. But there are many instances in between the extremes where the appropriate classification can only be determined based on a detailed assessment of the arrangements and whether or not the services provided are judged to be 'insignificant'.

Example 2.5B

Hotel property as investment property

A hotel operator owns a significant number of buildings. The hotel operator seeks to maximise revenue by selling room occupancy. Can the entity classify these buildings as investment properties?

The property is for use by the entity in the normal course of business and, therefore, is not investment property. IAS 40.12 cites the direct provision of services to hotel guests as services that will generally be considered to be 'significant'. Although the entity may hold the buildings for long-term appreciation, that is not the principal reason for holding them.

The determination of whether ancillary services are significant (thus excluding the property from the scope of IAS 40) will require judgement. The Standard considers the case of hotels and acknowledges the variety of arrangements that may exist. For example, the owner of a hotel property may transfer some responsibilities to third parties under a management contract. The terms of such contracts may vary widely. The owner's role may be restricted to that of a passive investor, in which case the property would be more likely to qualify as investment property. At the other extreme, the contract may simply result in the outsourcing of some day-to-day responsibilities, while the owner retains significant exposure to variations in the cash flows generated by the operation of the hotel. In the latter case, the contract has little effect on the substance of the owner's interest and the property is likely to be classified as owner-managed. [IAS 40.13]

2.6 Property leased to other group members

If an entity owns a property that is leased to, and occupied by, another group member (e.g. a parent or another subsidiary), the property is not recognised as an investment property in the consolidated financial statements because it will be treated as owner-occupied from the perspective of the group. However, from an individual-entity perspective, the property is treated as an investment property if it meets the requirements of IAS 40.5. [IAS 40.15]

This treatment differs from the requirements of UK GAAP. SSAP 19.8 states that property let to, and occupied by, another group entity is not an investment property for the purposes of its own accounts or the group accounts. UK

To meet the definition of an investment property in SSAP 19 it is necessary that the rentals are negotiated at arm's length which would exclude many intragroup leases. There is no such requirement in IAS 40.

3 Recognition

3.1 General requirements

Investment property is recognised as an asset when:

[IAS 40.16]

'(a) it is probable that the future economic benefits that are associated with the investment property will flow to the entity; and

(b) the cost of the investment property can be measured reliably.'

This general principle is used to consider whether capitalisation is appropriate both in respect of the costs incurred initially to acquire or construct an investment property, and costs incurred subsequently to add to, replace part of, or service a property. [IAS 40.17]

3.2 Subsequent costs

Appropriate application of the principle set out at **3.1** results in:

[IAS 40.19]

- the immediate expensing of the costs of the day-to-day servicing of a property (e.g. the costs of labour, consumables and minor parts used for repairs and maintenance); and
- costs incurred to replace parts of the original property being recognised in the investment property where they meet the recognition criteria.

When the costs of replacement parts are capitalised, the carrying amounts of the replaced parts are derecognised. [IAS 40.19]

If the entity has been using the cost model to measure its investment property, but the replaced part was not being depreciated separately, and the carrying amount of the replaced part cannot be determined, the cost of the replacement may be used as an indication of what the cost of the replaced part would have been at acquisition. [IAS 40.68]

When the fair value model is being used, the carrying amount of the investment property may already reflect the deterioration in value of the replaced part. If this is not the case, and the fair value of the replaced part cannot be determined, the cost of the replacement can be added to the carrying amount of the investment property, and the new fair value of the property assessed. [IAS 40.68]

Example 3.2

Recognition of replacement lift as an asset

A lift is replaced in an office building which is being held as an investment property and measured using the fair value model. The fair value of the replaced lift cannot be reliably determined. What is the accounting treatment for this replacement?

The cost of the replacement lift is capitalised and the fair value of the property is assessed. Any movement between the carrying amount and the fair value is recognised in profit or loss.

3.3 Investment property in the course of construction

With effect from the date of implementation of *Improvements to IFRSs* issued in May 2008 (1 January 2009 or date of earlier adoption – see **2.2**), property under construction or development for future use as an investment property falls within the scope of IAS 40. The Standard does not deal specifically with the recognition of the cost of a self-constructed investment property. The appropriate accounting for such property is therefore determined in accordance with general principles.

Over the period of construction, the costs of construction will be capitalised as part of the cost of the investment property in accordance with the general principle outlined at **3.1**. Paragraphs 16 to 22 of IAS 16 (see **section 4.2** of **chapter 6**) provide guidance as to what is appropriately included within such costs.

The capitalisation of borrowing costs is considered in accordance with the general requirements of IAS 23 (see **chapter 27**). IAS 23.4 provides an optional exemption from the requirement to capitalise borrowing costs for qualifying assets that are measured at fair value (which would generally include investment property under construction). Therefore, entities can choose, as a matter of accounting policy, whether to capitalise borrowing costs in respect of such assets. Where relevant to an understanding of the financial statements, that accounting policy should be disclosed.

Where an entity follows the fair value model in accounting for its investment property (see **5.2**), provided that the fair value of the property under construction can be estimated reliably, then the additional costs capitalised during the course of construction will not affect the carrying amount of the investment property under construction, which is remeasured to fair value at the end of each reporting period. Therefore, any costs capitalised during the reporting period will simply reduce the amount recognised in profit or loss for any gain (or increase the amount recognised for any loss) arising on remeasurement to fair value at the end of the reporting period. Although the amount reported in the statement of financial position is not affected, it is important to capitalise construction costs where appropriate, since this may affect the classification of amounts in the statement of comprehensive income.

Prior to the date of implementation of *Improvements to IFRSs* (1 January 2009 or date of earlier adoption – see **2.2**), property under construction or development for future use as an investment property was accounted for under IAS 16 *Property, Plant and Equipment*. Costs were accumulated until the date of completion of construction or development, at which time the property was transferred to investment property and subsequently accounted for under IAS 40. If the entity accounted for its investment property using the fair value model, the difference between the fair value of the property and the carrying amount at the point of completion of construction or development was recognised in profit or loss.

4 Measurement at recognition

4.1 General requirements

An investment property is measured initially at its cost. Transaction costs are included in the initial measurement. [IAS 40.20]

The cost of an investment property includes its purchase price (if purchased) and other directly attributable expenditure, e.g. professional fees for legal services, property transfer taxes and other transaction costs. [IAS 40.21]

Start-up costs are not included unless they are necessary to bring the asset to the condition required for its intended operation. Abnormal costs, and operating losses incurred before the property reaches its required level of occupancy, are excluded from the cost of the investment property. [IAS 40.23]

Example 4.1

Expenditure to be capitalised as part of the cost of an investment property

An entity, R, acquires a building for £95 million in March 20X1 as an investment property. During June, R refurbishes entirely the building at a cost of £5 million to bring it to the condition required by the rental market. R will pay an estate agent two months' rent if the agent locates a lessee. In December, R (the lessor) finally rents the property under an operating lease to entity S (the lessee).

Is it appropriate for R to include the refurbishment costs and the estate agent fees as part of the initial cost of the investment property?

When it buys the building, R should recognise the purchase price as the initial cost of the building under IAS 40. The refurbishment costs are necessary to bring the property to a condition suitable for renting out and therefore these costs should also be included in the initial cost of the building.

The estate agent fees are not part of the initial cost of the building but they are considered to be 'initial direct costs incurred in negotiating and arranging an operating lease' under IAS 17. They are, therefore, capitalised as part of the leased building in accordance with IAS 17.52. Where a cost model is used, the expenses should be depreciated over the lease term. However, where a fair value model is used, these costs will be recognised in profit or loss to the extent that they increase the carrying amount of the building above its fair value.

4.2 Deferred payments

The cost of an investment property for which payment is deferred is the cash price equivalent of these payments. The difference between the cash price equivalent recognised at initial measurement, and the total payments made, is recognised as an interest expense over the period of credit, i.e. the period from the point of receipt of the property until the point of settlement of the related liability. [IAS 40.24]

There is no definition of 'cash price equivalent' in IAS 40. It is presumably intended to equate to the present value of the deferred payment but might also encompass a cash price offered by the vendor as an alternative to the deferred payment terms. Although there is no specific UK GAAP guidance on this issue, in practice a similar approach has generally been taken where the effect is material. UK

4.3 Property held under lease and classified as investment property

The initial cost of a property interest held under a lease and classified as an investment property is prescribed by IAS 17.20. The property is recognised at the lower of its fair value and the present value of the minimum lease payments. An equivalent amount is recognised as a liability in accordance with the same paragraph. [IAS 40.25]

IAS 40.25 applies to all property interests held under leases (whether operating or finance) and classified as investment property. Therefore, in effect, such interests are recognised as if the underlying lease was a finance lease, even if it would be classified as an operating lease under the general requirements of IAS 17.

When a premium is paid on the lease, it is treated as part of the minimum lease payments for this purpose. It is included within the cost of the asset, but excluded from the liability (since it has been paid). If a property interest held under a lease is classified as an investment property, the item accounted for at fair value is that interest and not the underlying property. [IAS 40.26]

This means that it is the fair value of the leasehold interest, rather than the fair value of the property, which is recognised in the financial statements. Normally, in a very long lease with only nominal 'ground rent', the difference between these two values may be very small. However, IAS 40 allows any property held under an operating lease to be classified as an investment property provided that certain criteria are met (see **2.3**). In some cases, therefore, the difference between the fair value of the leasehold interest and the fair value of the property may be significant. For example, in the case of a short lease at market rent, the market value of the leasehold interest will be small compared to the value of the freehold interest in the property.

4.3.1 *Gross value of leasehold interest*

As noted above, a liability will be recognised in the statement of financial position for the present value of the minimum lease payments. If the property is subsequently accounted for under the fair value model, it is important to ensure that the valuation reflected in the statement of financial position is consistent with this. Valuers may value very long leasehold interests on the basis of the freehold interest and then deduct from that value the present value of the ground rent on the head lease and the present value of the estimated residual value at the end of the lease term. But if the liability for the ground rent is recognised separately in the financial statements, it is the gross valuation before any such deduction (but excluding any amount attributable to the residual value) that should be recognised as an asset to avoid double-counting the liability.

4.4 Investment property acquired through exchange of another asset

When an investment property is exchanged for an asset (assets), whether monetary or non-monetary, IAS 40 prescribes the treatment for such an exchange. The cost of the investment property is measured at fair value unless either:

[IAS 40.27]

- the exchange transaction lacks commercial substance; or
- the fair value of neither the asset received nor the asset given up is reliably measurable.

The acquired asset is measured in this way even if an entity cannot derecognise immediately the asset given up. If the acquired asset is not measured at fair value, its cost is measured at the carrying amount of the asset given up. [IAS 40.27]

Whether an exchange transaction has commercial substance is determined by considering the extent to which the future cash flows are expected to change as a result of the transaction. IAS 40 states that a transaction has commercial substance if:

[IAS 40.28]

- the configuration (risk, timing and amount) of the cash flows of the asset received differs from the configuration of the cash flows of the transferred asset; or
- the entity-specific value of the portion of the entity's operations affected by the transaction changes because of the exchange; and
- the difference in either of these is significant relative to the fair value of the assets exchanged.

In determining whether an exchange transaction has commercial substance, the entity-specific value of the portion of the entity's operations affected by the transaction should reflect post-tax cash flows. The Standard notes that the results of these analyses may be clear without having to perform detailed calculations. [IAS 40.28]

> In most instances it will be readily apparent whether or not a transaction lacks commercial substance. The reference in the Standard to the entity-specific value of the portion of the entity's operations affected by the transaction is not explained in detail but clearly is intended to indicate that a transaction will have substance where it has a significant effect on the present value of the entity's future cash flows.

For an asset for which there are no comparable market transactions, the fair value of the asset is reliably measurable if:

[IAS 40.29]

- the variability in the range in estimates of the fair value of the asset is not significant; or
- the probabilities of the various estimates within the range can be reasonably assessed and used in estimating fair value.

If the fair value of either the asset received or the asset given up can be determined reliably, then the fair value of the asset given up is used to measure cost unless the fair value of the asset received is more clearly evident. [IAS 40.29]

5 Measurement after recognition

5.1 Accounting policy

In general, IAS 40 (a) allows an entity to choose whether it adopts a fair value model or a cost model for investment property, and (b) requires that, having decided on its policy, an entity should apply that model to all of its investment property. [IAS 40.30]

There are two exceptions to this general principle. These are: [IAS 40.30]

- where a lessee chooses to classify a property interest held under an operating lease as investment property, the lessee automatically forfeits the choice of model offered by IAS 40 – the fair value model must be used for all investment property (see **2.3**); [IAS 40.6 & 34] and
- where an entity has investment property backing liabilities that pay a return linked directly to the fair value of, or returns from, specified assets including that investment property, the entity is not required to apply the same policy for that property as it does for its other investment property (see **5.1.1**). [IAS 40.32A]

UK

This differs from UK GAAP. SSAP 19 requires investment property to be recognised at open market value. No choice of model is offered.

Once a policy has been adopted, any change will be considered a voluntary change in accounting policy which, under IAS 8 *Accounting Policies, Changes in Accounting Estimates and Errors*, is permitted only if it will result in financial statements providing reliable and more relevant information. IAS 40 notes that it is highly unlikely that a change from the fair value model to the cost model will result in a more relevant presentation. [IAS 40.31]

The drafting of IAS 40.31 was amended by *Improvements to IFRSs* issued in May 2008 to bring the text into line with the relevant requirements in IAS 8. These amendments are not expected to have any impact on accounting.

This guidance would not have the effect of preventing a UK entity from adopting the cost model for its investment property on transition or when an investment property is first acquired because it would never have applied any other policy under IFRSs. UK

If an entity adopts the cost model, it must still determine the fair value of all of its investment property for disclosure purposes, other than in exceptional circumstances when the fair value cannot be reliably determined (see **5.2.2.2** below).

5.1.1 Investment property linked to liabilities

Where an entity has investment property backing liabilities that pay a return linked directly to the fair value of, or returns from, specified assets including that investment property, the entity may choose a model for all such investment property and independently choose a different model for all other investment property. The choice of policy made by an entity for such property does not affect the entity's choice for the rest of its property, e.g. the entity could choose the fair value model for its investment property linked to liabilities, but choose the cost model for the rest of its investment property. [IAS 40.32A]

For an entity that operates an internal property fund that issues notional units whereby some units are held by investors and others are held by the entity, the property held by the fund cannot be held partly at cost and partly at fair value. [IAS 40.32B]

Where different models are chosen, sales of investment property between pools of assets are recognised at fair value and the cumulative change in fair value is recognised in profit or loss. [IAS 40.32C]

5.1.2 Investment property classified as held for sale

Investment property accounted for under IAS 40's cost model falls within the scope of IFRS 5 *Non-current Assets Held for Sale and Discontinued Operations*, both as regards measurement and as regards presentation in the statement of financial position. Therefore, from the point at which a property meets the criteria for classification as held for sale (or is included within a disposal group held for sale), the asset is accounted for under that Standard (see **chapter 29**).

Investment property accounted for under IAS 40's fair value model is excluded from the measurement provisions of IFRS 5, but is otherwise subject to the requirements of that Standard. [IFRS 5.5] Therefore, from the point at which such property meets the criteria for classification as held for sale (or is included in a disposal group held for sale), the asset is presented as held for sale in the statement of financial position, as required by IFRS 5.38 (see **7.2.1** in **chapter 29**), but it continues to be measured at fair value in accordance with the entity's accounting policy for investment property.

5.2 Fair value model

After initial recognition, an entity that chooses the fair value model measures all of its investment property at fair value, except where the requirements of IAS 40.53 apply (inability to determine fair value reliably – see **5.2.2.2**). [IAS 40.33]

5.2.1 Definition of fair value

Fair value is 'the amount for which an asset could be exchanged between knowledgeable, willing parties in an arm's length transaction.' [IAS 40.5]

For this definition, 'knowledgeable' means that both the willing buyer and the willing seller are reasonably informed about the investment property's nature, characteristics, and actual and potential uses, as well as the market conditions at the end of the reporting period. [IAS 40:42]

A 'willing' buyer is motivated, but not compelled, nor over-eager to buy, nor determined to buy at any price. A 'willing' seller is not compelled, nor over-eager to sell, and is not prepared to sell at any price, nor prepared to hold out for a price not considered reasonable in current market conditions. [IAS 40.42 & 43]

An 'arm's length transaction' is one between parties that do not have a particular or special relationship that would make the prices of the transaction uncharacteristic of market conditions. The transaction is presumed to be between unrelated parties, each acting independently. [IAS 40.44]

'Fair value' is different from 'value in use' as defined in IAS 36 *Impairment of Assets*. Fair value is based on the knowledge and estimates of willing and knowledgeable buyers and sellers. Value in use reflects the entity's estimates, including the effects of factors that may be specific to the entity. This means that the following items would be taken into account in determining value in use, but not in assessing fair value to the extent that they would not be generally available to knowledgeable, willing buyers and sellers:

[IAS 40.49]

- additional value derived from the creation of a portfolio of properties in different locations;
- synergies between investment property and other assets;
- legal rights or legal restrictions that are specific only to the current owner; and
- tax benefits or tax burdens that are specific to the current owner.

5.2.2 *Determining fair value*

The Basis for Conclusions on IAS 40 explains, at paragraphs B52 to B54, that when developing the guidance in the Standard on the fair value of investment property, reference was made to the International Valuation Standards (IVS) issued by the International Valuations Standards Committee (IVSC). The guidance in paragraphs 36, 37 and 39 to 44 of IAS 40 is, in substance and largely in wording as well, identical with the guidance in IVS 1. In practice, professional valuers will usually be engaged to perform the required valuations in accordance with IVS (see **5.2.2.1**). Further details about IVS can be found at *www.ivsc.org*.

UK

In the UK, valuations of investment property at open market value have generally been performed in accordance with the Appraisal and Valuation Manual of the Royal Institution of Chartered Surveyors (RICS). This publication is often referred to as the 'red book', and it has been updated to be consistent with IVS. It should be noted that IAS 40 permits other methods of valuation in addition to those mentioned in the red book.

When determining the fair value of an investment property, special terms or circumstances such as atypical financing, sales and leaseback arrangements, special considerations or concessions granted by anyone associated with the sale are ignored. [IAS 40.36]

Fair value is determined without any deduction for transaction costs that may be incurred on sale or other disposal. [IAS 40.37]

The fair value of investment property should reflect market conditions at the end of the reporting period. [IAS 40.38] Fair value is time-specific at a given date because the amount reported as fair value may be incorrect or inappropriate if estimated at another time, due to a change in market conditions. The definition of fair value assumes simultaneous exchange and completion of the contract, without any variation in price that might be made in an arm's length transaction between knowledgeable, willing parties if exchange and completion are not simultaneous. The fair value reflects rental income from current leases, reasonable and supportable assumptions regarding future leases in the light of current conditions, and cash outflows expected on a similar basis for the property. [IAS 40.39 & 40]

The best evidence of fair value is given by current prices in an active market for similar property in the same location and condition and subject to similar lease and other contracts. Where reference is made to transactions in 'similar' properties that are subject to 'similar' contractual arrangements, care is required to ensure that there are no significant variations, whether as regards the characteristics of the property or the contractual obligations applying to the property [IAS 40.45]

In the absence of current prices in an active market as described above, an entity may consider information from a variety of other sources, including:

[IAS 40.46]

- current prices in an active market for properties of different nature, condition or location (or subject to different lease or other contracts), adjusted to reflect those differences;
- recent prices of similar properties on less active markets, with adjustments to reflect any changes in economic conditions since the date of the transactions that occurred at those prices; and
- discounted cash flow projections based on reliable estimates of future cash flows, supported by the terms of any existing lease and other contracts and (when possible) by external evidence such as current market rents for similar properties in the same location and condition, and using discount rates that reflect current market assessments of the uncertainty in the amount and timing of the cash flows.

In some cases, the various sources listed in IAS 40.46 may suggest different estimates for the fair value of an investment property. An entity will need to consider the reasons for those differences, in order to arrive at the most reliable estimate of fair value within a range of reasonable fair value estimates. [IAS 40.47] It will also need to ensure that the variability in the range of reasonable fair value estimates is not so great, and the assessment of the probabilities of the various outcomes so difficult, that the fair value of the property is not reliably measurable (see **5.2.2.2**).

Assets or liabilities recognised elsewhere in the financial statements (e.g. prepaid or accrued operating lease income) should not be double-counted in determining the carrying amount of investment property under the fair value model. For example, if the lifts and air-conditioning system in a property are considered an integral part of the building, they are generally included in the fair value of the investment property and are not recognised as separate assets. Similarly, if an office is leased on a furnished basis, and the rental income relates to the furnished office, the fair value of the office generally includes the fair value of the furniture, and the furniture is, therefore, not recognised as a separate asset. [IAS 40.50]

Example 5.2.2

Acquisition of investment property with existing operating lease in place

Company C acquires an investment property with an operating lease that is not at current market rates. How should the investment property be accounted for?

IAS 40.40 states:

> 'The fair value of investment property reflects, among other things, rental income from current leases and reasonable and supportable assumptions that represent what knowledgeable, willing parties would assume about rental income from future leases in the light of current conditions. It also reflects, on a similar basis, any cash outflows (including rental payments and other outflows) that could be expected in respect of the property. Some of those outflows are reflected in the liability whereas others relate to outflows that are not recognised in the financial statements until a later date (e.g. periodic payments such as contingent rents).'

Additionally, IAS 40.25 states that a premium paid for a lease should be included in the cost of an investment property. This acknowledges the fact that an investment property includes not only land and buildings but other assets (customer relationships, furniture and favourable leases) and liabilities (unfavourable leases) that are interrelated in determining the fair value of the investment property. Hence, the fair value of operating leases at above or below market rates should be incorporated into the fair value of the investment property.

However, in determining the carrying amount of investment property under the fair value model, an entity should not double-count assets or liabilities that are recognised as separate assets or liabilities. Therefore, the carrying amount of the investment property is adjusted to exclude, among other things, prepaid or accrued operating lease income. [IAS 40.50]

These requirements would extend to lease incentives. That is to say that assets/liabilities recognised for lease incentives received/given should not be double-counted in the statement of financial position. There is no guidance within IAS 40 detailing where such assets should be recognised in the statement of financial position; the requirement is merely that they are not double-counted.

Furthermore, the fair value of an investment property held under a lease reflects expected cash flows (including contingent rent that is expected to become payable). Thus, if a valuation obtained for a property is net of all payments expected to be made, any recognised lease liability must be added back to arrive at the carrying amount of the investment property using the fair value model. [IAS 40.50(d)]

The drafting of IAS 40.50(d) was amended by *Improvements to IFRSs* issued in May 2008. The previous wording was considered to be potentially misleading. The amendment is not expected to have any impact on accounting.

Neither future capital expenditure intended to improve or enhance a property, nor related future benefits, should be reflected in the fair value of an investment property. [IAS 40.51]

In many jurisdictions, the tax consequences that would flow from acquiring, holding and selling an investment property will have a significant impact on the value a market participant would be willing to pay to acquire the property. It is common that the difference in the market price will not be directly equal to the tax consequences under existing tax law, as market participants will also factor into the price they are willing to pay the risk that tax law may change. In determining the fair value of an investment property, the valuation should take account of all tax consequences that are available to all market participants, but should not reflect those tax consequences that are unique to the buyer. For example, where the acquisition of the property will enable the entity to recover some unused tax losses, this should not be taken into account in the valuation. But where there is a tax benefit from holding the property that is available to all participants, that should be taken into account in determining the fair value in accordance with IAS 40.49(d).

5.2.2.1 *Use of independent valuers*

Entities are encouraged (but not required) to use, as the basis for determining fair value, a valuation by an independent valuer 'who holds a recognised and relevant professional qualification and has recent experience in the location and category of the investment property being valued'. [IAS 40.32]

UK

This guidance is less specific than that under UK GAAP. As in IAS 40, SSAP 19 does not require valuations to be made by qualified or independent valuers. However, where investment properties represent a substantial proportion of the total assets of a 'major enterprise', the standard says that the valuation of the property would normally be carried out '. . . at least every five years by an external valuer.'

In practice, major listed property investment entities in the UK have external valuations performed at least each year and, in some cases, also at the half-year.

The Board decided that an independent valuation would not be required by the Standard because of the following considerations:

- the cost-benefit ratio of an independent valuation may be inappropriate for some entities; and
- independent valuers with appropriate expertise are not available in some markets.

Thus, paragraphs B55 and B56 of the Basis for Conclusions on IAS 40 explain that it is for the preparers of financial statements to decide, in consultation with auditors, whether an entity has sufficient internal resources to determine reliable fair values. This approach is consistent with the approach to actuarial valuations in IAS 19 *Employee Benefits*.

5.2.2.2 *Inability to determine fair value reliably*

There is a rebuttable presumption that the fair value of an investment property can be determined reliably on a continuing basis. But in exceptional cases, when an investment property is first acquired (or when an existing property first becomes an investment property after a change of use) there may be clear evidence that the fair value of the property is not reliably determinable on a continuing basis. This arises when, and only when, comparable market transactions are infrequent, and alternative reliable estimates of fair value (e.g. based on discounted cash flows) are not available. [IAS 40.53]

Note that this exception is available only when the investment property is first recognised as such. If an investment property has previously been measured at fair value, it should continue to be measured at fair value until disposal (or until it otherwise ceases to be an investment property, for example because it becomes owner-occupied) even if comparable market transactions become less frequent or market prices become less readily available. [IAS 40.55]

Where, in the circumstances described above, it is not possible for an entity which uses the fair value model to determine the fair value of a particular property reliably on initial recognition, that particular investment property is measured using the cost model in IAS 16. In accounting for the property under IAS 16, the entity is required to assume that the residual value of the property is zero. IAS 16 is then applied until the disposal of the property. [IAS 40.53] Special rules apply for investment properties under construction – see **5.2.2.3**.

When an entity is compelled, for the reasons set out above, to measure an investment property using the cost model under IAS 16, it continues to measure all of its other investment property at fair value. [IAS 40.54]

UK

There is no equivalent to this exception to the use of fair values in SSAP 19. Use of this provision of IAS 40 by UK entities should be very rare. The circumstances described above are also relevant to determining the circumstances in which an entity using the cost model would be exempt from disclosing the fair value of investment property (see **8.3** below).

5.2.2.3 *Investment property in the course of construction*

If an entity determines that the fair value of an investment property under construction is not reliably determinable but expects the fair value to be reliably determinable when construction is complete, the entity measures the investment property under construction at cost until the earlier of the fair value becoming reliably measurable or the completion of construction. [IAS 40.53]

Once the entity is able to measure reliably the fair value of the investment property under construction, that property should be measured at fair value. Once construction is complete, it is presumed that fair value can be measured reliably. If this is not the case, following completion, the property is accounted for using the cost model in accordance with IAS 16, under the general requirements of IAS 40.53 (see **5.2.2.2**). [IAS 40.53A]

The presumption that the fair value of investment property under construction can be measured reliably can be rebutted only on initial recognition. An entity that has measured such property at fair value may not conclude that the fair value of the completed investment property cannot be determined reliably. [IAS 40.53B]

The requirements in this section are effective from the date of implementation of *Improvements to IFRSs* issued in May 2008 (1 January 2009 or date of earlier adoption – see **2.2**). Prior to that date, property under construction or development for future use as an investment property was accounted for under IAS 16 *Property, Plant and Equipment*.

5.2.3 *Changes in fair value*

Changes in the fair value of investment property are recognised in profit or loss in the period in which they arise. [IAS 40.35]

UK

This treatment is markedly different from the requirements of UK GAAP. SSAP 19 states that changes in the market value should not be taken to the profit and loss account, but to the STRGL, unless a deficit on a property is expected to be permanent. The judgement regarding whether a diminution in value is permanent or not is therefore not present in IAS 40, although such a distinction may have consequences for distributable profits – see ***chapter 49****.*

5.2.4 *Property held under a lease and classified as investment property*

When a property held under a lease that is negotiated at market rates is classified as an investment property (i.e. accounted for as a finance lease), the fair value of the interest in the leased property at acquisition, net of all expected lease payments including those relating to recognised liabilities, should be zero. This fair value does not change, regardless of whether the leased asset and liability are recognised at fair value or at the present value of minimum lease payments as per IAS 17.20. This means that there should be no initial gain or loss arising from the remeasurement of a leased asset from cost to fair value unless fair value is measured at different times. This could occur when an election to apply the fair value model is made after initial recognition. [IAS 40.41]

5.2.5 *Anticipated liabilities*

When an entity expects that the present value of its payments relating to an investment property (excluding payments relating to recognised liabilities) will exceed the present value of the related cash receipts, IAS 37 *Provisions, Contingent Liabilities and Contingent Assets* should be applied to determine whether a liability should be recognised, and if it should, how it should be measured. [IAS 40.52]

5.3 Cost model

IAS 40.5 defines cost as 'the amount of cash or cash equivalents paid or the fair value of other consideration given to acquire an asset at the time of its acquisition or construction or, where applicable, the amount attributed to that asset when initially recognised in accordance with the specific requirements of other IFRSs ...'.

For example, if the consideration for the purchase of a property was an issue of equity shares in the entity, IFRS 2 *Share-based Payment* would be applied to establish the cost of the property.

After initial recognition, an entity that chooses the cost model measures all its investment property in accordance with IAS 16's requirements for that model, other than those that are classified as held for sale or are included in a disposal group that is classified as held for sale in accordance with IFRS 5 (see **5.1.2**). [IAS 40.56]

6 Transfers

6.1 Point of transfer

Transfers to, or from, investment property are made when, and only when, there is a change in use evidenced by one of the following:

[IAS 40.57]

- commencement of owner-occupation, for a transfer from investment property to owner-occupation;
- commencement of development with a view to sale, for a transfer from investment property to inventories;

- end of owner-occupation, for a transfer from owner-occupied property to investment property; or
- commencement of an operating lease to another party, for a transfer from inventories to investment property.

These circumstances are discussed more fully below.

Paragraphs 60 to 65 of IAS 40 apply to recognition and measurement issues that arise when the fair value model is used for investment property and transfers are made to or from investment property (see **6.1.1** to **6.1.4** below). When the cost model is used, transfers between investment property, owner-occupied property and inventories do not change the carrying amount of the property transferred. They do not, therefore, change the cost of the property for measurement or disclosure purposes. [IAS 40.59]

6.1.1 *Transfer from investment property to owner-occupied property*

The Standard requires an investment property to be transferred to owner-occupied property only when there is a change of use evidenced by commencement of owner-occupation. [IAS 40.57(a)]

When an investment property carried at fair value is transferred to owner-occupied property, the property's deemed cost for subsequent accounting in accordance with IAS 16 is its fair value at the date of change in use. [IAS 40.60]

6.1.2 *Transfer from investment property to inventories*

The Standard requires an investment property to be transferred to inventories only when there is a change of use evidenced by commencement of development with a view to sale. [IAS 40.57(b)]

When an investment property carried at fair value is transferred to inventories, the property's deemed cost for subsequent accounting in accordance with IAS 2 is its fair value at the date of change in use. [IAS 40.60]

6.1.3 *Transfer from owner-occupied property to investment property*

End of owner-occupation signals a potential transfer to investment property. If an owner-occupied property becomes an investment property that will be carried at fair value, IAS 16 is applied up to the date of change of use. Any difference at that date between the carrying amount of the property in accordance with IAS 16 and its fair value is treated in the same way as a revaluation in accordance with IAS 16. [IAS 40.61]

This means that any decrease in the carrying amount of the property is recognised in profit or loss, unless the decrease is the reversal of a previous revaluation surplus, in which case the decrease is recognised in other comprehensive income and reduces that revaluation surplus within equity. [IAS 40.62]

Any increase in the carrying amount is recognised in other comprehensive income and increases the revaluation surplus within equity, unless the increase reverses a previous impairment loss on that property in which case the increase is recognised in profit or loss. The amount recognised in profit or loss should not exceed the amount needed to restore the carrying amount to the amount that would have been determined (net of depreciation) had no impairment loss been recognised. [IAS 40.62]

On subsequent disposal of such a property, the revaluation surplus may be transferred to retained earnings, but not through profit or loss. [IAS 40.62]

6.1.4 *Transfer from inventories to investment property*

This may be evidenced by the commencement of an operating lease to another party. For a transfer to investment property where the property will be carried at fair value, any difference between the fair value and the carrying amount of the property at the date of transfer is recognised in profit or loss. [IAS 40.63] This is consistent with the treatment of sales of inventories. [IAS 40.64]

6.1.5 *Continued classification as investment property*

If an entity decides to dispose of an investment property without development, the property continues to be treated as an investment property until its disposal. It is not treated as inventory. [IAS 40.58]

> Where an entity has decided to dispose of an investment property through sale, the requirements of IFRS 5 need to be considered (see **5.1.2** and **chapter 29**).

Similarly, if redevelopment on an existing investment property commences but the property is intended for future use as an investment property, the property continues to be recognised as an investment property. [IAS 40.58]

Where the fair value model is used, expenditure incurred in the redevelopment of an investment property which remains classified as an investment property (e.g. rebuilding costs) should initially be capitalised. The effect of remeasuring the asset to fair value will result in any gain or loss resulting being taken to profit or loss. Disclosures required by IAS 40.76 distinguish between the cost of additions and fair value movements (see **8.2.2.1**).

Undeveloped land may fall within the definition of investment property in IAS 40 (see **2.3** above) although this will depend on the particular circumstances. Where such land is subsequently developed for future use as an investment property, the property continues to be recognised as an investment property while the development takes place.

7 Disposals

An investment property is derecognised (i.e. removed from the statement of financial position) on disposal or when it is permanently withdrawn from use and no future economic benefits are expected from its disposal. [IAS 40.66]

The disposal of an investment property may occur through sale of the property or through entering into a finance lease. In determining the date of disposal for an investment property, the criteria in IAS 18 *Revenue* for recognising revenue from the sale of goods should be applied and the related guidance in the Appendix to IAS 18 should be considered (see **chapter 23**). IAS 17 applies to a disposal effected by entering into a finance lease and to a sale and leaseback (see **chapter 26**). [IAS 40.67]

7.1 Consideration, gains and losses on disposal

The gain or loss on the retirement or disposal of an investment property is calculated as the difference between the net disposal proceeds and the carrying amount of the property and is recognised in profit or loss in the period of the retirement or disposal. This is subject to the requirements of IAS 17 in the case of a sale and leaseback transaction. [IAS 40.69]

The consideration receivable on the disposal of an investment property is recognised initially at fair value. In particular, if payment is deferred, the consideration is recognised initially at its cash price equivalent. The difference between this amount and the nominal amount is recognised as interest revenue under the effective interest method in accordance with IAS 18. [IAS 40.70]

When any liabilities are retained relating to the property after its disposal, IAS 37 or other relevant standards are applied to those liabilities. [IAS 40.71]

7.2 Compensation for impairment of investment property

Impairments or losses of investment property, related claims for or payment of compensation from third parties and any subsequent purchase or construction of replacement assets are separate economic events and are accounted for separately. Therefore:

[IAS 40.73]

- impairments of investment property are recognised in accordance with IAS 36;
- retirements or disposals of investment property are recognised as set out in this section in accordance with paragraphs 66 to 71 of IAS 40;
- compensation from third parties for investment property that was impaired, lost or given up is recognised in profit or loss when it becomes receivable; and
- the cost of assets restored, purchased or constructed as replacements is determined as set out in **section 4** above in accordance with paragraphs 20 to 29 of IAS 40.

Example 7.2

Insurance claim

A building carried as an investment property burns down before the end of the reporting period. A valuation of the building in its damaged state is performed at the end of the reporting period. Should the value of the property at the end of the reporting period include any amount receivable from insurance?

The amount receivable from insurance should be recognised separately in the statement of financial position as a debtor balance. Any valuation of the property recognised as an investment property should not include the insurance receivable.

8 Presentation and disclosure

8.1 Presentation

IAS 1 *Presentation of Financial Statements* requires that, where material, the aggregate carrying amount of the entity's investment property should be presented in the statement of financial position. [IAS 1(2007).54(b), previously IAS 1(2003).68(b)]

8.2 Disclosure

The disclosures required by IAS 40 are made in addition to the disclosures required by IAS 17 for leases entered into by lessees and lessors.

8.2.1 General disclosures

An entity is required by IAS 40 to disclose:

[IAS 40.75]

- whether it applies the fair value or the cost model;
- whether, and in what circumstances, properties held under operating leases are classified as investment property when the fair value model is used;
- the criteria used to distinguish investment property from owner-occupied property or property held for sale in the normal course of business, when that classification is difficult;
- the methods and significant assumptions applied in determining the fair value of investment property, including a statement of whether the determination of fair value was supported by market evidence or was more heavily based on other factors, which are disclosed, because of the nature of the property and lack of comparable market data;
- the extent to which the fair value of investment property (as measured or disclosed in the financial statements) is based on a valuation by an independent valuer who holds a recognised and relevant professional qualification and has recent experience in the location and category of the investment property being valued. If there has been no such valuation, that fact shall be disclosed; and
- the amounts recognised in profit or loss for:
  - rental income from investment property;

    - direct operating expenses (including repairs and maintenance) arising from investment property that generated rental income during the period;
    - direct operating expenses (including repairs and maintenance) arising from investment property that did not generate rental income during the period; and
    - the cumulative change in fair value recognised in profit or loss on a sale of investment property from a pool of assets, in which the cost model is used, into a pool in which the fair value model is used (see **5.1.2** above);

- the existence and amounts of restrictions on the realisability of investment property or the remittance of income and proceeds of disposal; and
- contractual obligations to purchase, construct or develop investment property or for repairs, maintenance or enhancements.

8.2.1.1 Service charge income and expense

Property investment entities often make service charges to their tenants, for example to cover the cost of repairs and maintenance that are the responsibility of the tenants under the terms of the lease but which are arranged and managed by the lessor. These costs are typically passed on at cost or with a fixed percentage mark-up under the terms of the lease. Where the lessor is in substance merely acting as agent for the payment of these costs, the reimbursement will generally not be recognised as revenue under IAS 18 *Revenue*. Nevertheless, it would be helpful to disclose in the notes the amount of such receipts and related costs.

8.2.2 Fair value model

8.2.2.1 Reconciliation of movements in carrying amounts

In addition to the general disclosure requirements set out at **8.2.1** above, an entity that applies the fair value model is required to disclose a reconciliation between the carrying amounts of investment property at the beginning and end of the period, showing the following:

[IAS 40.76]

- additions, disclosing separately those additions resulting from purchases, those resulting from subsequent expenditure recognised in the carrying amount of an asset and those resulting from acquisitions through business combinations;
- assets classified as held for sale, or included in a disposal group classified as held for sale, in accordance with IFRS 5 and other disposals;
- net gains or losses from fair value adjustments;
- the net exchange differences arising on the translation of the financial statements into a different presentation currency and on translation of a foreign operation into the presentation currency of the entity;
- transfers to and from inventories and owner-occupied property; and
- other changes.

UK

Under UK GAAP, when assets are revalued, there is a requirement to disclose the amounts that would have been reported under the historical cost basis. There is no equivalent requirement in IAS 40. This is a significant relaxation of disclosure requirements for UK property investment entities adopting IFRSs. But records of the historical cost of assets will still have to be maintained, for example for taxation purposes and to determine whether any profits recognised under IAS 40 are unrealised for distribution purposes.

8.2.2.2 Reconciliation of adjustments to valuation of property

When a valuation obtained for investment property is adjusted significantly for the purpose of the financial statements, for example to avoid double-counting of assets or liabilities that are recognised as separate assets and liabilities, the entity is required to disclose a reconciliation between the valuation obtained and the adjusted valuation included in the financial statements, showing separately the aggregate amount of any recognised lease obligations that have been added back, and any other significant adjustments. [IAS 40.77]

8.2.2.3 Details about property exceptionally stated at cost

In the exceptional cases referred to at **5.2.2.2** above, when an entity applying the fair value model measures investment property using the cost model in IAS 16, the reconciliation described at **8.2.2.1** should disclose amounts relating to that investment property separately from amounts relating to other investment property. In addition, the following should be disclosed:

- a description of the investment property;
- an explanation of why fair value cannot be determined reliably; and
- if possible, the range of estimates within which fair value is highly likely to lie.

On disposal of such investment property not carried at fair value, the following should be disclosed:

[IAS 40.78]

- the fact that the entity has disposed of investment property not carried at fair value;
- the carrying amount of that investment property at the time of sale; and
- the amount of gain or loss recognised.

8.2.3 *Cost model*

In addition to the general disclosure requirements set out at **8.2.1** above, an entity that applies the cost model is required to disclose:

[IAS 40.79]

- the depreciation methods used;
- the useful lives or the depreciation rates used;
- the gross carrying amount and the accumulated depreciation (aggregated with accumulated impairment losses) at the beginning and end of the period;
- a reconciliation of the carrying amount of investment property at the beginning and end of the period, showing the following:
  - additions, disclosing separately those additions resulting from acquisitions and those resulting from subsequent expenditure recognised as an asset;
  - additions resulting from acquisitions through business combinations;
  - assets classified as held for sale, or included in a disposal group classified as held for sale, in accordance with IFRS 5 and other disposals;

- depreciation;
- the amount of impairment losses recognised, and the amount of impairment losses reversed, during the period in accordance with IAS 36;
- the net exchange differences arising on the translation of the financial statements into a different presentation currency, and on translation of a foreign operation into the presentation currency of the entity;
- transfers to and from inventories and owner-occupied property;
- other changes; and

- the fair value of investment property. In the exceptional cases described at **5.2.2.2** above, when an entity cannot determine the fair value of the investment property reliably, it should disclose:
  - a description of the investment property;
  - an explanation of why fair value cannot be determined reliably; and
  - if possible, the range of estimates within which fair value is highly likely to lie.

8 Intangible assets

1 Introduction

IAS 38 *Intangible Assets* establishes general principles for the recognition and measurement of intangible assets. The Standard requires an entity to recognise an intangible asset if, and only if, specified criteria are met. The Standard also specifies how to measure the carrying amount of intangible assets, and requires certain disclosures about intangible assets.

IAS 38 was last revised by the IASB in March 2004 as part of its Business Combinations Project, and was most recently amended when *Improvements to IFRSs* was issued in May 2008.

This chapter discusses the requirements of IAS 38 in the following sections:

Section 2	Scope
Section 3	Definition of an intangible asset
Section 4	Recognition and initial measurement
Section 5	Items to be recognised as an expense
Section 6	Alternatives for measurement after initial recognition
Section 7	Revaluation model
Section 8	Determining the useful life of an intangible asset
Section 9	Subsequent accounting for assets with indefinite useful lives
Section 10	Subsequent accounting for assets with finite useful lives
Section 11	Impairment
Section 12	Derecognition
Section 13	Presentation and disclosure
Section 14	Future developments

IAS 38 is the subject of an IASB research agenda project, and is likely to be subject to further revision in the medium term.

UK *The UK material corresponding to IAS 38 is included in FRS 10* Goodwill and Intangible Assets *and SSAP 13* Accounting for research and development. *In overview, the IAS material is broadly similar to those standards, but there are some differences. The most significant of these are highlighted below.*

- *Whereas SSAP 13 permits a choice over whether to capitalise development costs when certain criteria are satisfied, such costs must be capitalised under IAS 38. In addition, IAS 38 expressly prohibits the reinstatement of development costs incurred before the criteria are met, while SSAP 13 is silent on the issue.*
- *Although IAS 38's criteria for recognising internally-generated assets are stringent, there is a single set of rules to cover both development expenditure and other intangible assets. Accordingly, they are designed to allow capitalisation of development expenditure, for which there will be no homogeneous market. This means that they are not as onerous as those of FRS 10 which are designed to deal with intangible assets only and not development expenditure. Under FRS 10, internally-generated intangible assets may not be capitalised unless they have a readily ascertainable market value, i.e. they belong to a homogeneous population of assets for which an active market exists. Accordingly, some assets which could not have been capitalised under UK GAAP may be capitalised under IAS 38.*
- *FRS 10 and IAS 38 take different approaches to recognition based on separability. Under FRS 10, an intangible asset can be recognised only if it 'can be disposed of separately without disposing of a business of the entity.' Under IAS 38, however, non-separable intangible assets are also capable of being recognised if they arise from contractual or other legal rights. This results in more intangible assets being recognised on the acquisition of a business under IFRSs than has historically been the case under UK GAAP.*
- *Under IAS 38, intangible assets with indefinite lives are not permitted to be amortised, but are instead tested for impairment at least annually.*

2 Scope

IAS 38 applies to all intangible assets, except:

[IAS 38.2]

- intangible assets that are within the scope of another Standard, for example:

- intangible assets held by an entity for sale in the ordinary course of business (addressed by IAS 2 Inventories and IAS 11 Construction Contracts);
- deferred tax assets (addressed by IAS 12 Income Taxes);
- leases that fall within the scope of IAS 17 Leases;
- assets arising from employee benefits (addressed by IAS 19 Employee Benefits);
- goodwill acquired in a business combination (addressed by IFRS 3 Business Combinations);
- deferred acquisition costs, and intangible assets arising from an insurer's contractual rights under insurance contracts within the scope of IFRS 4 Insurance Contracts; and
- non-current intangible assets classified as held for sale (or included in a disposal group that is classified as held for sale) in accordance with IFRS 5 Non-current Assets Held for Sale and Discontinued Operations;

- financial assets, as defined in IAS 39 *Financial Instruments: Recognition and Measurement*; and
- mineral rights and expenditure on the exploration for, or development and extraction of, minerals, oil, natural gas and similar non-regenerative resources.

When an intangible asset is contained in or on a physical substance, such as computer software on a compact disc or a motion picture on film, management must assess which element is more significant. For example, software that controls machinery would normally be considered an integral part of the machinery and therefore would be treated as property, plant and equipment rather than as an intangible asset. The same would normally be true for the operating system of a computer. Where the software does not form an integral part of the machinery or computer hardware to which it relates, it is separately accounted for under IAS 38. [IAS 38.4]

Research and development activities may give rise to an asset with physical substance (e.g. a prototype). Because the activities are primarily directed to the development of knowledge, the physical element of the asset is secondary to its intangible component, i.e. the knowledge embodied in it. In such circumstances, the activities are accounted for under IAS 38. [IAS 38.5]

A reporting entity may enter into a lease in respect of an intangible asset. The appropriate classification of the lease is determined in accordance with the requirements of IAS 17 *Leases*. Where the lease is a finance lease, IAS 17 *Leases* directs the lessee to IAS 38 for the requirements as regards the appropriate accounting treatment after initial recognition. However, certain rights are specifically excluded from the scope of IAS 17 (rights under licensing agreements for items such as motion picture films, video recordings, plays, manuscripts, patents and copyrights) and are accounted for under IAS 38. [IAS 38.6]

Although certain specialised activities and transactions associated with the extractive and insurance industries are excluded from the scope of IAS 38, the Standard does apply to other intangible assets used in such industries (such as computer software) and other expenditure incurred (such as start-up costs).

3 Definition of an intangible asset

An intangible asset is defined as an identifiable non-monetary asset without physical substance. [IAS 38.8]

The key components of this definition are:

- identifiability; and
- asset (the definition of which encompasses control).

3.1 Identifiability

Identifiability is the characteristic that conceptually distinguishes other intangible assets from goodwill. In a business combination, it is often difficult to determine whether an intangible item qualifies for recognition as an intangible asset or whether it is merely part of goodwill. The word 'identifiable' in the definition is intended to help in such situations.

An asset is identifiable if either:

[IAS 38.12]

- it is separable, i.e. it is capable of being separated or divided from the entity and sold, transferred, licensed, rented or exchanged, either individually or together with a related contract, identifiable asset or liability, regardless of whether the entity intends to do so; or

- it arises from contractual or other legal rights, regardless of whether those rights are transferable or separable from the entity or from other rights and obligations.

3.1.1 *Identifying intangible assets in a business combination*

The IASB has concluded that all assets that are separable, as defined above, are identifiable. Therefore, any intangible asset that has that characteristic and that is acquired in a business combination should be recognised as an asset separate from goodwill.

However, separability is not the only indication of identifiability. The Standard is clear that, while an asset that is separable meets the identifiability criterion, there are other ways to meet that criterion. For example, a legal right, such as a broadcasting licence, may give rise to future benefits that are 'identifiable' under IAS 38, even if they are not separable from the underlying broadcasting business, since it is unlikely that the broadcasting licence could be sold without disposing of the underlying broadcasting business. Therefore, in a business combination, all intangible assets that arise from contractual or other legal rights, whether or not they are separable, should be identified as assets separate from goodwill.

The Illustrative Examples published with IFRS 3 *Business Combinations* provide a number of examples of items acquired in a business combination that meet the definition of an intangible asset. These examples are not exhaustive, but they do illustrate many of the more common items that arise in the circumstances of a business combination, and they provide a very useful framework for the determination as to whether particular items qualify for recognition as intangible assets. See **7.4.2.3** in **chapter 34** for a summary of the list of examples.

UK

Under FRS 10, an intangible asset can be recognised only if it 'can be disposed of separately without disposing of a business of the entity', i.e. separability is required. As noted above, however, IAS 38 also requires the recognition of non-separable intangible assets arising from contractual or other legal rights.

This results in more intangible assets being recognised on the acquisition of a business under IFRSs than has historically been the case under UK GAAP.

3.2 Asset (control)

IAS 38 takes its definition of an asset from the *Framework for the Preparation and Presentation of Financial Statements,* i.e. it is defined as a resource controlled by an entity as a result of past events and from which future economic benefits are expected to flow to the entity. [IAS 38.8] In the context of intangible assets, it is sometimes difficult to determine whether an entity can exert control over the expected future economic benefits. Control in this context means that the entity has the power to obtain the economic benefits that the asset will generate and to restrict the access of others to those benefits. [IAS 38.13]

Normally, control of an intangible asset is achieved through legal rights (e.g. a brand name is protected by a trademark, a publishing title by copyright, a licence by contract). Less frequently, an intangible asset may be controlled merely through custody (e.g. a product formula or intellectual property may be controlled simply by keeping it a secret from outsiders).

3.2.1 Assembled workforce

Certain intangible items of value to an entity may not be controlled by it. For example, it is unusual for an entity to have control over its employees – usually employee contracts can be terminated with a short period of notice and without penalty. Therefore, when a business combination is accounted for as an acquisition, the benefit of an assembled workforce is more likely to fall to be treated as goodwill than as an intangible asset, since the workforce cannot normally be controlled (at least in the IAS 38 sense). For similar reasons, specific management or technical talent is unlikely to meet the definition of an intangible asset, unless it is protected by legal rights to use it and to obtain the future economic benefits expected from it, and it also meets the other parts of the definition. [IAS 38.15]

3.2.2 Customer relationships and similar items

IAS 38 allows that customer relationships and similar items may meet the definition of intangible assets where either:

[IAS 38.16]

- they are protected or otherwise controlled by legal rights; or
- the ability to control the expected benefits flowing from the relationships, and the separability of the relationships, have been evidenced

by exchange transactions for the same or similar non-contractual customer relationships (other than as part of a business combination).

An established customer base or market share is not usually controlled by the entity. There may be an expectation that customers will continue to buy from the entity but, usually, they are under no obligation to do so. Clearly, where the relationship is protected by a legal right, the entity has control over the future economic benefits. However, such control may also be evidenced where the entity has acquired a non-contractual customer relationship in a separate exchange transaction, or where there have been exchange transactions for similar relationships. Because such exchange transactions also provide evidence that the customer relationships are separable, those customer relationships meet the definition of an intangible asset. [IAS 38.16]

For example, in some industries, such as those providing mobile telephone services, one service provider may purchase subscriber bases of existing customers from another. The price paid for the subscriber bases usually exceeds the value of the existing contracts, the difference representing the expectation that existing subscribers will renew their contracts. The exchange transaction may provide sufficient evidence to enable the entity to recognise this difference as a separable intangible asset in its own right, even if the existing customers are under no obligation to renew their contracts. (However, this should not be confused with the situation where payments are made directly to potential customers as an incentive to enter into a contract.)

The Illustrative Examples published with IFRS 3 *Business Combinations* address various types of customer-related intangible assets acquired in a business combination and whether they meet the definition of an intangible asset (see **7.4.2.3** in **chapter 34**).

3.2.2.1 Commissions paid to acquire contracts

Example 3.2.2.1

Classification of commissions paid to acquire contracts

Company A pays commission to an external party, Company B, which markets its security contracts. When the security contract is signed by the client, Company B earns a commission of CU100. At the time of signing the contract, the client agrees to pay for Company A's security services for a minimum of two years. If, for any reason, the client cancels within those two years, it is required to pay out the remainder of its contract in cash at the time of cancellation. Company A has a history of enforcing these payments in the event of cancellation.

The commission is paid to acquire an asset, the ability to obtain revenues over a minimum two-year period. The asset is controlled by Company A as evidenced by the enforcement of cancellation penalties, and it has arisen as a result of past events (the signing of the contract) from which future economic benefits (security contract revenues) are expected to flow.

More specifically, the asset meets the definition of an intangible asset as it is 'an identifiable non-monetary asset without physical substance.' The amount, which represents a right to receive future revenue from customers, is clearly identifiable; it is non-monetary, as it cannot be readily converted into cash; and it does not have physical substance. [IAS 38.8]

3.2.3 Non-competition agreements

Non-competition agreements (NCAs) are often entered into in conjunction with a business combination and can be structured in a variety of ways. For example, a subsidiary and its parent ('the vendor') may enter into an NCA prior to the subsidiary being sold to an unrelated third party. Alternatively, the acquiring entity ('the acquirer') may enter into an NCA agreement with the vendor. It is presumed for the purposes of the following discussion that a reliable valuation of an NCA can be obtained.

Consolidated financial statements

The Illustrative Examples published with IFRS 3 cite non-competition agreements as items that, when acquired in a business combination, meet the definition of an intangible asset because they arise from contractual or other legal rights. Whilst they may not be separable assets, separability is not a necessary condition to satisfy the IAS 38 recognition criteria for intangible assets acquired in a business combination. Therefore, in the consolidated financial statements, NCAs should be recognised separately as intangible assets.

The value of an NCA will depend on a number of different factors, such as barriers to entry in the market in which the entities operate. For example, the existence of a customer list in the acquired entity alone does not indicate that the NCA is valuable.

Should an NCA be recognised as a separate intangible, it will form part of the same cash-generating unit as the underlying assets of the acquired entity for the purposes of impairment testing in the consolidated financial statements.

Separate financial statements of acquirer

When the NCA is between the subsidiary and vendor, the acquirer does not have the legal rights arising from the contract. Thus, the acquirer would simply recognise an investment in a subsidiary in its separate financial statements (i.e. it would not recognise a separate intangible for the NCA).

Where the NCA is between the acquirer and the vendor, the acquirer does have a separately identifiable legal right with respect to the NCA as well as the investment itself. The right has a value in the entity-only accounts of the acquirer. Therefore, under these circumstances the acquirer should recognise a separate intangible asset for the NCA in addition to the investment in its subsidiary.

Should an NCA be recognised as a separate intangible, the intangible asset (the NCA) and the investment will be tested for impairment jointly.

3.2.4 *Regulatory assets*

In August 2005, the IFRIC considered a request for guidance on operations subject to price regulation, specifically where a regulatory agreement allows an entity to increase its prices in future years to cover outflows of economic resources incurred in current or previous years. An example of such an agreement is set out as **example 3.2.4** below.

The IFRIC observed that it had previously discussed whether a regulatory asset should be recognised in the context of service concession arrangements, either as deferred costs or as an intangible asset to reflect an expectation that the entity will recover these costs as part of the price charged in future periods. The IFRIC concluded that assets should only be recognised if they qualify for recognition in accordance with the IASB's *Framework for the Preparation and Presentation of Financial Statements* and relevant accounting standards such as IAS 11, IAS 18, IAS 16 and IAS 38. Therefore, the determination of whether a regulatory asset should be recognised will be based on the facts of each individual arrangement..

Example 3.2.4

Regulatory assets

Company X, an electricity producer operates in Country B. Electricity producers in Country B are subject to government regulation of electricity charges. Company X has incurred operating losses in the two years ending 20X0 as a consequence of the regulatory pricing mechanism.

The government of Country B subsequently approves a regulatory agreement allowing the electricity producers to increase their prices in future years to offset losses incurred for the previous two years ending 20X0.

Company X should not recognise an asset and associated revenues at the end of 20X0 for the recovery of past operating losses through invoicing future consumption at higher prices. In order to recover operating losses incurred, electricity companies are required to produce electricity for their clients in the future. Even though it is arguable that electricity companies will recover the operating losses, Company X has not, at the end of 20X0, provided the service for which the customers will be paying and therefore the regulatory asset cannot be recognised as it does not qualify for recognition as an asset in accordance with the Framework. Moreover, customers can choose not to purchase electricity from this producer even if electricity is produced. In other words, it is not just a matter of producing electricity for clients in the future but clients purchasing electricity.

Consequently, the authorisation given by the government to increase prices in the future is merely a pricing mechanism that regulates prices for the following periods, and does not give rise to an asset and additional revenue in the current period (i.e. year end 20X0). The recovery of the operating loss is included in the calculation of the price the regulated entity may charge to its customers and should be recognised only when such revenues are received or receivable.

4 Recognition and initial measurement

IAS 38 establishes general principles for the recognition and measurement of intangible assets, as set out in **4.1** below, and discusses the treatment of subsequent expenditure as set out in **4.2**. The Standard then considers in detail the following situations:

- separate acquisition;
- acquisition as part of a business combination;
- acquisition by way of a government grant;
- exchanges of assets; and
- internally-generated intangible assets.

These detailed rules are dealt with in the following sections.

4.1 General principles

Provided that an item meets the definition of an intangible asset, as discussed in **section 3** above, it should be recognised in the financial statements if, and only if:

[IAS 38.18 & 21]

- it is probable that the expected future economic benefits that are attributable to the asset will flow to the entity (the probability criterion); and
- the cost of the asset can be measured reliably.

These recognition criteria apply both to costs incurred to acquire an intangible asset and those incurred to generate an asset internally. The Standard imposes additional criteria, however, for the recognition of internally-generated intangible assets (see **4.7** below).

When assessing the probability of expected future economic benefits, reasonable and supportable assumptions should be used, representing management's best estimate of the set of economic conditions that will exist over the useful life of the asset. [IAS 38.22]

Intangible assets are initially recorded at cost. [IAS 38.24]

At the date of transition to IFRSs, IFRS 1 *First-time Adoption of International Financial Reporting Standards* allows a first-time adopter, in some circumstances, to use a deemed cost for an intangible asset, as discussed at **6.2** in **chapter 5**.

4.2 Subsequent expenditure

The recognition criteria set out above apply equally to those costs incurred to add to, replace part of, or service an intangible asset. [IAS 38.18] Unlike a physical asset, it is not common to add to or replace parts of an intangible asset. Most expenditure incurred on an acquired intangible asset subsequent to its initial recognition, or on an internally-generated intangible asset after completion, will be incurred to maintain the benefits expected from the asset, and therefore will not meet the recognition criteria set out above. Additionally, expenditure incurred on intangible assets will be difficult to differentiate from expenditure related to the business as a whole. Therefore, IAS 38 concludes that only rarely will subsequent expenditure on an intangible asset be recognised in the carrying amount of the asset. [IAS 38.20]

Specifically, the Standard prohibits the capitalisation of any subsequent expenditure incurred on brands, mastheads, publishing titles, customer lists and items similar in substance (whether externally acquired or internally generated). Because such expenditure cannot be distinguished from expenditure to develop the business as a whole, it is always recognised in profit or loss as incurred. [IAS 38.20]

The Standard also addresses specifically subsequent expenditure on an in-process research and development project acquired separately or in a business combination that has been recognised as an intangible asset. Such expenditure is subject to the additional recognition criteria established for internally-generated intangible assets (see **4.7** below). [IAS 38.42] Therefore, the expenditure is:

- recognised as an expense when it is incurred if it is research expenditure;
- recognised as an expense when it is incurred if it is development expenditure that does not satisfy the recognition criteria set out in IAS 38.57 (see **4.7.4** below); and
- added to the carrying amount of the acquired in-process research or development project if it is development expenditure that satisfies the recognition criteria set out in IAS 38.57 (see **4.7.4** below).

If the cost of a replacement for part of an intangible asset is capitalised, in accordance with IAS 38.21, the carrying amount of the replaced part is derecognised. If it is not practicable to determine the carrying amount of the replaced part, the cost of the replacement may be used as an indication. [IAS 38.115] For entities that have adopted IFRS 3(2008), in the case of a reacquired right in a business combination, if the right is subsequently reissued (i.e. sold) to a third party, the related carrying amount, if any, is used in determining the gain or loss on reissue. [IAS 38.115A]

4.3 Separate acquisition

4.3.1 Recognition criteria

Assuming that the asset acquired meets IAS 38's definition of an intangible asset, it will be recognised in the financial statements provided that it is probable that expected future economic benefits will flow to the entity, and that the cost of the asset can be measured reliably.

These conditions are generally met when an asset is acquired separately. The anticipation of future economic benefits, even if there is uncertainty about the timing or the amount, will be built into the price paid for the asset. Therefore, the probability criterion is always considered to be satisfied for separately acquired intangible assets. [IAS 38.25]

Cash or other monetary assets expended will establish a reliable measure of the cost of the asset. The only circumstance where it may not be possible to measure the cost of the asset reliably is where the purchase consideration comprises non-monetary assets (see **4.6** below).

4.3.2 *Measurement of cost*

4.3.2.1 Elements of cost

When an intangible asset is purchased separately, and the consideration given is in the form of cash or other monetary assets, the determination of cost is relatively straight-forward. The cost of the intangible asset comprises:

[IAS 38.27]

- its purchase price, including import duties and non-refundable purchase taxes, after deducting trade discounts and rebates; and
- any directly attributable expenditure on preparing the asset for its intended use.

Examples of directly attributable expenditure are:

[IAS 38.28]

- the salaries, wages and other employment-related costs of personnel directly engaged in bringing the asset to its working condition;
- professional fees arising directly from bringing the asset to its working condition; and
- costs of testing whether the asset is functioning properly.

Examples of expenditure that *does not* form part of the cost of an intangible asset are:

[IAS 38.29]

- costs of introducing a new product or service (including costs of advertising and promotional activities);

- costs of conducting business in a new location or with a new class of customer (including the cost of staff training); and
- administration and general overhead costs.

Example 4.3.2.1

Meaning of 'directly attributable costs'

Scenario 1

Company A (A) is developing a product. The developing process is completed on premises used solely for these activities. The criteria for capitalisation of development costs in IAS 38 have been met. The entity will continue renting the premises after finishing the development activities.

Scenario 2

Company A (as described in Scenario 1) is developing two new products on the same premises instead of one.

Scenario 3

Company A (as described in Scenario 1) is carrying out both research and development activities on the premises.

Can the costs of renting out these premises be capitalised into the cost of the development asset in any of these scenarios?

IAS 38.66 permits only those 'directly attributable costs necessary to create, produce and prepare the asset to be capable of operating in the manner intended by management' to be capitalised. In order to meet the criteria for being 'directly attributable', it would be expected that the costs would have been avoided had the entity not been involved in the development activities.

Accordingly, in Scenario 1 above, it may be possible to demonstrate that the rental costs are directly attributable costs if they would not have been incurred if the development activities were not performed. However, A would need to show that, had the development activities not been carried out, it would never have incurred the rental cost. This could be demonstrated if A had not rented the premises, or would not have rented the premises until some later time (to house the activities that will be housed following completion of the development process), had the development activities not been performed. Alternatively, it could be demonstrated if the building (or area of the building) in which the development activities are performed is separately identifiable and could be separately sub-leased, if not used for these activities.

As IAS 38 requires the expense to be directly attributable (rather than permitting the use of allocation methods as allowed under IAS 2 *Inventories*), it is unlikely that the rental costs would be eligible for capitalisation in Scenario 2 unless the entity can demonstrate that they would otherwise not have been incurred (for example, by demonstrating that the area in which the development activities are performed is separately identifiable and could be separately leased out, if not used for the development activities).

It would be very unlikely in Scenario 3 that any of the rental expense would be directly attributable.

4.3.2.2 *Deferred consideration*

If the payment of consideration is deferred beyond normal credit terms, the asset is recorded at the equivalent cash price and the difference between this amount and the amount actually paid is recognised as interest expense (unless capitalised in accordance with IAS 23 *Borrowing Costs*). [IAS 38.32]

Example 4.3.1A in **chapter 6** illustrates the calculation of an equivalent cash price for an item of property.

4.3.2.3 *Cessation of capitalisation*

Recognition of cost in the carrying amount of an intangible asset ceases when the asset is in the condition necessary for it to be capable of operating in the manner intended by management. The following costs are excluded from the carrying amount of an intangible asset:

[IAS 38.30]

- costs incurred in using or redeploying an asset;
- costs incurred while an asset capable of operating in the manner intended by management has yet to be brought into use; and
- initial operating losses, such as those incurred while demand for the asset's output builds up.

4.4 Acquisition as part of a business combination

4.4.1 *Recognition criteria*

IFRS 3 *Business Combinations* stipulates that, if an intangible asset is acquired in a business combination, the cost of that intangible asset is its fair value at the acquisition date. The fair value of the asset will reflect market expectations as to the economic benefits that will flow from it, even if there is uncertainty about the timing or the amount of those benefits. Therefore, the probability criterion, as set out in **4.1** above, is always considered to be satisfied for intangible assets acquired in a business combination.

The acquirer should recognise an intangible asset acquired in a business combination, separately from goodwill, irrespective of whether the asset was previously recognised by the acquiree. This will include any in-process research and development project of the acquiree if the project meets the definition of an intangible asset, and its fair value can be measured reliably.

IFRS 1 *First-time Adoption of International Financial Reporting Standards* allows a first-time adopter some exemptions in respect of intangible assets acquired in a business combination that were not recognised in the acquirer's consolidated statement of financial position under previous GAAP. These exemptions are discussed at **5.10** in **chapter 5**.

4.4.2 Measuring fair value

Upon adoption of IFRS 3(2008), IAS 38 is amended to state that, where an asset acquired in a business combination is separable or arises from contractual or other legal rights, sufficient information will always exist to measure reliably the asset's fair value. [IAS 38.33]

> The IASB had previously made clear its belief that, in the vast majority of cases, it would be possible to reach a reliable measure of the fair value of an intangible asset acquired in a business combination. Upon adoption of IFRS 3(2008), the Board has removed the possibility of arguing for the non-recognition of such intangible assets on the basis that their value cannot be measured reliably.

Where the entity's estimation process indicates that there is a range of possible outcomes with different probabilities, that uncertainty should be incorporated into the measurement of fair value. [IAS 38.35]

Where an intangible asset acquired in a business combination is separable, but only together with a related tangible or intangible asset, and the individual fair values of the assets in the group are not reliably measurable, the acquirer should recognise the group of assets as a single asset separately from goodwill. [IAS 38.36] Similarly, a group of complementary intangible assets (a trademark and its related trade name, formulas, recipes and technological expertise) may be combined into a single asset (often described as a 'brand') if the individual fair values of the assets are not reliably measurable. If those individual fair values *are* reliably measurable, however, such complementary assets may only be combined if the individual assets have similar useful lives. [IAS 38.37]

An intangible asset acquired in a business combination is recorded at its fair value determined:

- by reference to an active market (see **7.1** below). While quoted market price (usually, current bid price) in an active market provides the most reliable measurement, where current bid prices are unavailable, the price of a similar recent transaction may provide a basis from which to estimate fair value, provided that there has not been a significant change in economic circumstances since the date of the original transaction; [IAS 38.39] or
- if no active market exists for the asset, the fair value reflects the amount that the entity would have paid for the asset, at the date of acquisition, in an arm's length transaction between knowledgeable and willing parties, based on the best information available. In determining this amount, the entity should consider the outcome of recent transactions for similar assets. [IAS 38.40]

In certain industries, where unique intangible assets are regularly traded, techniques have been developed for estimating their fair values indirectly. Such techniques may be used for the initial measurement of an intangible asset acquired in a business combination if their objective is to estimate fair value and if they reflect current transactions and practices in the industry. Such techniques include, when appropriate, applying multiples reflecting current market transactions to certain indicators driving the profitability of the asset, or discounting estimated future net cash flows from the asset. [IAS 38.41]

4.4.2.1 *Inability to measure fair value reliably: entities that have not yet adopted IFRS 3(2008)*

As noted above, IFRS 3(2008) amended IAS 38 to remove the possibility of arguing for the non-recognition of intangible assets on the basis that their value cannot be measured reliably. Previously, IAS 38 indicated that:

- the fair value of an intangible asset acquired in a business combination can normally be measured with sufficient reliability for it to be recognised separately from goodwill; [IAS 38.35]
- where the intangible asset has a finite life, there is a rebuttable presumption that its fair value can be measured reliably; [IAS 38.35] and
- the only circumstances in which it might not be possible to measure reliably the fair value of an intangible asset acquired in a business combination are when the intangible asset arises from legal or other contractual rights, and either:
  [IAS 38.38]

- the asset is not separable; or
- the asset is separable, but there is no history or evidence of exchange transactions for the same or similar assets, and otherwise estimating fair value would be dependant on immeasurable variables.

Given that the exception has now been deleted by IFRS 3(2008), entities which have not yet adopted the new Standard will wish to think carefully before seeking to invoke the limited exception previously granted by IAS 38.38.

4.4.3 Measuring fair value: additional guidance

When it first published IFRS 3 in 2004, the IASB noted in the Basis for Conclusions that, despite the intentions of IAS 22 (the predecessor to IFRS 3), entities did not identify a significant number of assets separately from goodwill when they made acquisitions. The changes made by the IASB were aimed at increasing the frequency and the number of intangible assets identified in acquisitions, in order to ensure that subsequent accounting treatment is appropriate in an accounting model where goodwill is no longer amortised.

Examples of classes of intangible assets are provided in IAS 38.119 (see **7.4** below) and the Illustrative Examples appended to IFRS 3 also include a list of intangibles (see **7.4.2.3** in **chapter 34**).

Three approaches that might be considered for determining fair value are set out below:

- if observable prices for market transactions for identical assets or liabilities at or near the measurement date are available, fair value would be estimated by reference to these prices;
- if observable prices for market transactions for similar assets or liabilities at or near the measurement date are available, fair value could be estimated by reference to these prices, making the necessary adjustments; and
- if the first two approaches do not apply, other valuation methodologies will need to be adopted.

In the majority of cases, there are unlikely to be identical assets with observable prices which can be relied upon to estimate the fair values of the intangible assets of the business being acquired. Some examples of assets where there may be directly comparable prices which could be relied on include taxi licences, allowances for emission rights and fishing rights in some markets.

Other assets can be considered similar by reference to their legal nature (e.g. patents, licences), intended uses, useful economic life, pattern of cash flows, risks and opportunities, etc. Identifying similar assets for which observable prices exist can also be difficult, however, since there are few markets for intangible assets and a majority of asset acquisitions are 'private' transactions, and information is not publicly available. In addition, making adjustments to the observable prices so that they may be used to assess the value of the asset in question can be highly subjective and requires detailed analysis.

Accordingly, in a majority of cases, it should be expected that intangible asset valuations will need to be performed using other valuation methodologies for the purposes of IFRS 3. There is a broad range of valuation techniques that might be appropriate to adopt for the purposes of assessing the fair value of intangible assets, which are discussed below. Where possible, more than one of the valuation techniques may be applied to arrive at fair value. This approach is designed to provide additional support, by way of a cross check, for the fair value assessment made.

4.4.3.1 *Valuation techniques for the purposes of assessing the fair value of intangible assets*

When applying valuation techniques for the purposes of assessing the fair value of intangible assets, the objective of fair value measurement must be considered. Accordingly, the assumptions used should reflect market assumptions.

The most common generally accepted valuation methodologies for the purposes of assessing the fair value of intangible assets include:

- **market methods** – value intangible assets by reference to transactions, or benchmarks, involving similar assets that have occurred recently in similar markets; and

- **income methods** – value intangible assets on the basis of the future economic benefits derived from ownership of the asset. The main income methods include Relief from Royalty and Premium Profits (Excess Earnings).

Note that cost-based methods (which value intangible assets by aggregating the cost of developing the asset to its current condition, or replacing that asset) are sometimes, though not often, used in intangible asset valuations. Paragraph BCZ 29 of IAS 36 (Basis for Conclusions) states, however, that 'IASC believed that replacement cost techniques are not appropriate to measure the recoverable amount of an asset'.

There is a further category of 'hybrid' methods which use elements from more than one method above. These are included below in the category to which they are most closely related (e.g. relief from royalty and avoided cost under income methods, replacement cost plus lost profits under cost-based methods).

IFRS 3 and IAS 38 do not set out detailed criteria for performing a valuation. Listed below, however, are some key criteria, based on common valuation practice, that need to be considered in undertaking a valuation of an intangible asset:

- *credibility* – the valuation methodology should be credible and respectable from both a theoretical and commercial perspective;

- *objectivity* – the choice of methodology may necessitate a trade-off between the intellectual rigour of the methodology and the inherent degree of subjectivity. The valuer must be guided by the quality and quantity of objective information available;

- *versatility* – credibility will be enhanced if standard approaches can be applied across entities, industries and classifications of intangible assets;

- *consistency* – the methodologies should be applicable on a consistent basis year-on-year, and thus facilitate the updating of the valuation;

- *reliability* – the valuation should be verifiable, such that other valuers may replicate the process using similar measurement principles;

- *relevance* – the valuation basis and methodology selected should be relevant to the requirements of the user; and

- *practicability* – the methods and underlying parameters should be clear and relatively easy to apply in practice.

One of the key elements of any valuation exercise is a thorough understanding of the business which is the subject of the transaction. Having obtained this, a valuer will have a better appreciation of the approach that may be adopted for the purposes of the valuation exercise and be able to identify the intangible assets that are important to the business. This will assist in applying the appropriate valuation methodology and assessing the information that will be required, subject to availability. In addition it will help in assessing the lives of the intangible assets that are in existence by understanding their nature and importance to the business.

4.4.3.2 *The process of assessing the fair value of intangible assets*

The approaches set out above include a number of steps that identify and collate the information to enable the valuer to make an assessment of the fair value of the intangible assets. These steps may be summarised as follows:

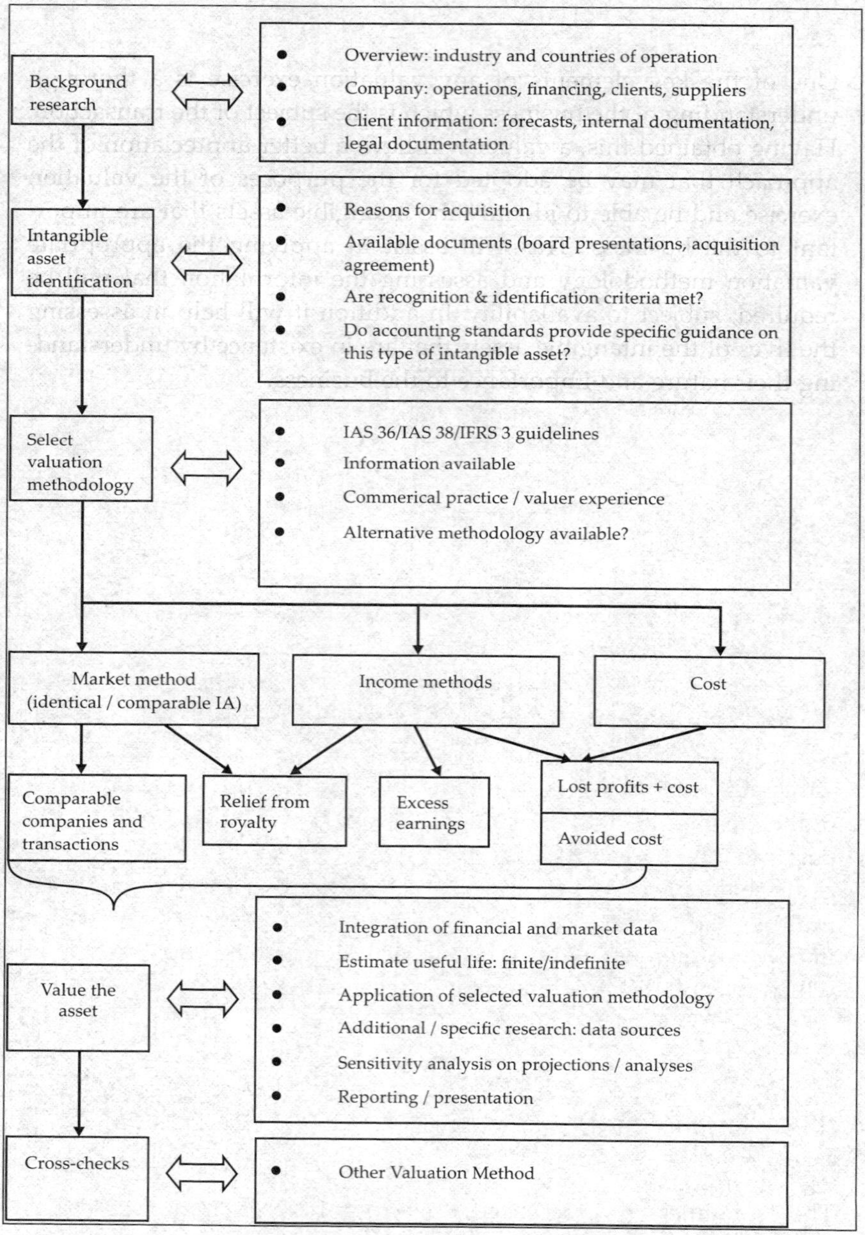

Below are set out brief comments on the application of different valuation methodologies.

4.4.3.3 *Market value method*

Under the comparable market value methodology, the value of an intangible asset is determined by reference to the prices obtained for comparable assets in recent transactions. The methodology is, therefore, theoretically attractive: it is credible, objective and, since the valuation basis is fair value, relevant.

Appropriate adjustments for entities using this method should be made by reference to known, quantifiable differences between the transaction being accounted for and the comparable transaction. (If the differences between the transactions are not capable of quantification, an entity will need to adopt other valuation methodologies).

The main issues with this methodology are that:

- its use in practice is often limited by the scarcity of comparable transactions and publicly disclosed information on any such transactions; and
- it can be difficult to ensure that the asset under consideration and the market transaction are sufficiently comparable.

Transactions in the shares of entities owning similar assets are more frequent. In the majority of these circumstances, separation of the value attributable to the intangible asset from the underlying assets of the business will not be straightforward, particularly for those not party to the transaction. However, the valuer will often find the component parts of the transaction data useful. For example, the multiple of earnings at which the business is sold may be an important reference point when determining an appropriate rate at which to capitalise the intangible asset's earnings.

4.4.3.4 *Income-based methods*

The economic / income-based valuation of any intangible asset has two distinct components:

- identification, separation and quantification of the cash flows (or earnings) attributable to the intangible asset; and

- capitalisation of those cash flows (or earnings).

The main income methods are:

- relief from royalty; and

- premium profits (excess earnings).

Relief from royalty

Principle: the value of an intangible asset to an entity is what it would pay to use it under a licence if it did not own it, or the cost savings of not having to pay a royalty.

Generally applicable to: technologies, patents, brands, know-how.

Steps

- research licensing transactions with comparable assets to establish a range of market levels for royalty rates;

- analyse the strength and importance of the asset and its contribution to the overall economics of the owning entity to determine an applicable royalty rate;

- select a royalty rate or range of royalty rates;

- apply the selected royalty rate to the future revenue stream attributable to the asset;

- use the appropriate marginal tax rate to arrive at an after-tax royalty rate;

- discount the resulting cash flow stream to the present at an appropriate risk-adjusted discount rate; and

- where appropriate, apply a factor to adjust the value of the asset for the effect of tax amortisation.

Issues

- the value of an owned asset may exceed the value of a licensed asset, as ownership may provide additional options, which can be difficult to value separately;

- the process of selecting an appropriate royalty rate range based on market evidence needs to be rigorous, as the value implications of a small change in the royalty rate can be significant;

- factors to consider in establishing the appropriate royalty rate range include the asset's strengths and weaknesses, competing assets, etc;

- what discount rate to use:

  - entity-specific?
  - cash-generating unit-specific? (this may include an additional premium linked to the size of the cash-generating unit)

  - asset-specific? (this may include an additional premium due to the higher risks of an intangible asset compared to a business as a whole)

Excess earnings / premium profits

Principle: the value of an asset is the capitalised amount of incremental profits achievable through use of the intangible asset as compared with the profits of the same business not using it, or the value of an asset is the capitalised amount of earnings relating to that asset less the returns on all other assets that contribute to that earnings stream.

Generally applicable to: customer relationships, technology, know-how, brands.

Two approaches:

- profit and loss based (forecasting profits in excess of 'normal' profits that would be obtained by a business producing a similar good or rendering a similar service, without the use of this intangible asset); and

- balance sheet (i.e. net asset) based (comparing the return on capital of the cash-generating unit using the intangible asset with the return on capital of businesses not using the respective intangibles).

Steps

- forecast a normalised level of income for the cash-generating unit;
- apply an appropriate or 'fair' rate of return to the net asset base to compute the economic income attributable to the tangible and the other intangible assets of the cash-generating unit;
- subtract the fair return on assets from the normalised level of economic income for the cash-generating unit to arrive at the excess earnings;
- capitalise the resulting excess earnings using an appropriate risk-adjusted discount rate to calculate fair value; and
- where appropriate, apply a factor to adjust the value of the asset for the effect of tax amortisation.

Issues

- difficult to find relevant entities which do not own/use a similar intangible asset;
- estimation of discount rate;
- if a business has several intangible assets, how should 'premium profits' value be allocated amongst them?
- what is an appropriate rate of return on other intangible assets?

4.4.3.5 *Some useful information sources used for intangible asset valuations*

For the purposes of valuing intangible assets, various sources can be used for certain elements of the exercise, including:

- third-party licensing agreements;
- *http://www.royaltysource.com/* (a fee is charged for this service);
- *http://www.royaltystat.com/* (a fee is charged for this service);
- Licensing Economics Review;
- in respect of franchise fees:
  - www.minorityfranchising.com;
  - www.franchisingamerica.com;
- SEC EDGAR database for any information filed by comparable entities.

4.5 Acquisition by way of a government grant

An intangible asset may be granted to an entity free of charge or for nominal consideration by a government. This may be the case for assets such as airport landing rights, broadcasting licences, import licences or quotas, or rights to access other restricted resources.

In these circumstances, an entity may either:

[IAS 38.44]

- record both the grant and the intangible asset at fair value; or
- record both the grant and the intangible asset at a nominal amount plus any expenditure that is directly attributable to preparing the asset for its intended use.

The alternatives allowed for under IAS 38, as set out in the previous paragraph, are consistent with those allowed for non-monetary government grants under IAS 20 *Accounting for Government Grants and Disclosure of Government Assistance* (see **section 5** in **chapter 41**).

4.6 Exchanges of assets

When an intangible asset is acquired in exchange for a non-monetary asset or assets, or a combination of monetary and non-monetary assets, the cost of the asset received is measured at fair value (even if the entity cannot immediately derecognise the asset given up), unless either

[IAS 38.45]

- the exchange transaction lacks commercial substance; or
- the fair value of neither the asset received nor the asset given up is reliably measurable.

In either of these circumstances, which result in the acquired asset not being measured at fair value, its cost is measured at the carrying amount of the asset given up. [IAS 38.45]

Whether or not a transaction has commercial substance is determined by considering the extent to which the entity's future cash flows are expected to change as a result of the transaction. An exchange transaction is considered to have commercial substance if:

[IAS 38.46]

- the configuration (i.e. risk, timing and amount) of the cash flows of the asset received differs from the configuration of the cash flows of the asset transferred; *or*
- the entity-specific value (reflecting post-tax cash flows) of the portion of the entity's operations affected by the transaction changes as a result of the exchange; *and*
- the difference arising in either of the two circumstances outlined is significant relative to the fair value of the assets exchanged.

As set out in **4.1** above, no intangible asset can be recognised unless its cost can be measured reliably. In an exchange transaction, if an entity is able to determine reliably the fair value of either the asset received or the asset given up, then the fair value of the asset given up is used to measure cost, unless the fair value of the asset received is more clearly evident. Fair value can be measured reliably if either (a) the variability in the range of reasonable fair value estimates is not significant for that asset or (b) the probabilities of the various estimates within the range can be reasonably assessed and used in estimating fair value. [IAS 38.47]

4.7 Internally-generated intangible assets

Inherently, it is more difficult to assess whether an internally-generated intangible asset qualifies for recognition because of problems in identifying whether and when there is an identifiable asset that will generate future economic benefits, and in determining the cost of the asset reliably. Therefore, IAS 38 includes additional recognition criteria for internally-generated intangible assets which expand on the general recognition criteria. It is assumed that these additional criteria are met implicitly whenever an entity acquires an intangible asset.

Although IAS 38's criteria for recognising internally-generated assets are stringent, they are not as onerous as those of FRS 10. This is because IAS 38 sets a single set of rules both for development costs and other intangibles. Under UK GAAP, these are covered by separate rules in different standards. Under FRS 10, internally-generated intangible assets may not be capitalised unless they have a readily ascertainable market value, i.e. they belong to a homogeneous population of assets for which an active market exists. Accordingly, some assets which could not have been capitalised under UK GAAP may be capitalised under IAS 38. UK

Example 4.7

Development costs paid to an external party

Company A pays Company B, an external party, to develop an asset that would meet the requirements of IAS 38 for recognition as an internally generated intangible asset in A's financial statements (see **4.7.4** below). Company B is performing only development work; all the associated research has already been performed, and the costs expensed, by Company A.

A should recognise an internally generated intangible asset for these development costs under IAS 38. Whether A incurs the costs directly via an internal development function or outsources the development process to an external party does not influence how A should account for the asset in its financial statements.

Therefore, since the expenditure meets the requirements for the recognition of an internally generated intangible asset under IAS 38, A should recognise the asset as an internally generated intangible asset in its financial statements. If the asset being developed did not meet the requirements for recognition of an internally generated intangible asset under IAS 38, the costs would be considered research expenditures and would be expensed as incurred. Similarly, if Company B was paid by Company A to perform both research and development activities, the research element would be expensed as incurred, but the development element would be capitalised provided it met the requirements of IAS 38.

4.7.1 *Items that cannot be recognised as internally-generated intangible assets*

The Standard prohibits the recognition of internally-generated goodwill as an asset. [IAS 38.48]

In addition, certain internally-generated items are specifically identified in IAS 38 as not capable of being distinguished from the cost of developing the business as a whole and therefore are prohibited from being capitalised as internally-generated intangible assets. These are internally-generated:

[IAS 38.63]

- brands;
- mastheads;
- publishing titles;
- customer lists; and
- items similar in substance to any of the above.

Although IAS 38 bans these items from recognition as internally-generated assets, when such assets are purchased either individually or as part of a business combination, they may meet the general recognition criteria for intangible assets and, therefore, potentially may be recognised. This difference means that intangible assets such as brands can be recognised as intangible assets if acquired, but will be expensed if they are generated internally.

4.7.2 *Distinction between research and development*

The Standard distinguishes between two phases in the generation of an intangible asset internally – the research phase and the development phase. Capitalisation is only permitted during the development phase. The additional recognition criteria are discussed at **4.7.4** below.

Research is defined as original and planned investigation undertaken with the prospect of gaining new scientific or technical knowledge and understanding. [IAS 38.8]

Development is the application of research findings or other knowledge to a plan or design for the production of new or substantially improved materials, devices, products, processes, systems or services prior to the commencement of commercial production or use. [IAS 38.8]

If it is not possible to distinguish the research phase from the development phase of an internal project to create an intangible asset, the expenditure on that project is treated as relating only to the research phase. [IAS 38.53]

The following examples of research activities given in the Standard illustrate the fact that the main objective of research activities is the discovery of something new:

[IAS 38.56]

- activities aimed at obtaining new knowledge;
- the search for, evaluation and final selection of, applications of research findings or other knowledge;
- the search for alternatives for materials, devices, products, processes, systems or services; and
- the formulation, design, evaluation and final selection of possible alternatives for new or improved materials, devices, products, processes, systems or services.

The following examples of development activities illustrate the fact that the main objective of development activities is to apply research findings for a business purpose:

[IAS 38.59]

- the design, construction and testing of pre-production or pre-use prototypes and models;
- the design of tools, jigs, moulds and dies involving new technology;
- the design, construction and operation of a pilot plant that is not of a scale economically feasible for commercial production; and
- the design, construction and testing of a chosen alternative for new or improved materials, devices, products, processes, systems or services.

4.7.3 Research phase

Research costs are, by their nature, incurred with the intent of gaining new knowledge rather than creating a practical application from which future economic benefits will flow. Therefore, research costs will not meet the criteria for recognition of an internally-generated asset. Costs incurred during the research phase are required to be expensed. [IAS 38.54]

4.7.4 Development phase (additional recognition criteria)

In limited circumstances, during the development phase of a project, an entity will be able to identify an intangible asset and demonstrate that the asset will generate probable future economic benefits. Criteria in addition to those for externally-acquired intangible assets must be met, however, in order to recognise an internally-generated intangible asset.

Specifically, an intangible asset arising from development (or from the development phase of an internal project) should be recognised if, and only if, an entity can demonstrate all of the following:

[IAS 38.57]

- the technical feasibility of completing the intangible asset so that it will be available for use or sale;
- its intention to complete the intangible asset and use or sell it;
- its ability to use or sell the intangible asset;
- how the intangible asset will generate probable future economic benefits. Amongst other things, the entity can demonstrate the existence of a market for the output of the intangible asset or the intangible asset itself or, if it is to be used internally, the usefulness of the intangible asset;
- the availability of adequate technical, financial and other resources to complete the development and to use or sell the intangible asset; and
- its ability to measure the expenditure attributable to the intangible asset during the development phase.

UK *There is a key difference here from UK GAAP in that, when the necessary criteria for capitalisation are met, SSAP 13 permits a choice over whether to capitalise development costs. Under IAS 38, when the criteria are met, development costs must be capitalised.*

IAS 38 does not provide any guidance in respect of the first criterion as to when technical feasibility is established. While it is difficult to set one guideline, due to the differing types of internally-generated intangible assets, when the asset is the product of 'traditional' research and development activities or software development activities, an appropriate point may be when the entity has completed all the planning, design and testing activities that are necessary to establish that an asset can be produced to meet its design specifications, including functions, features and technical performance requirements.

In respect of the fourth criterion, IAS 38 suggests that an entity can demonstrate that the asset will generate future economic benefits by using the principles in IAS 36 *Impairment of Assets* relating to the estimation of future cash flows. As discussed in more detail in **chapter 9**, cash flow projections should be based on reasonable and supportable assumptions that represent management's best estimate of the set of economic conditions that will exist over the useful life of the asset, with greater weight given to external evidence. Such projections should not normally cover a period of more than five years. The cash flows should be discounted using a pre-tax rate that reflects current market assessments of the time value of money and the risks specific to the asset. If the internally-generated intangible asset will only produce economic benefits together with other assets (e.g. new computer software that will significantly reduce overhead costs), its cash flows cannot be independently assessed. Therefore, it is included in its cash-generating unit and the unit as a whole is evaluated. See **chapter 9** for further discussion of cash-generating units.

The fifth criterion (availability of resources) will normally be met by a business plan that details the planned expenditure on the project and the resources that will be available to fund it. If the project is being financed externally, a lender's indication that it will finance the business plan may be sufficient for the latter. [IAS 38.61]

In order to meet the final criterion (ability to measure attributable expenditure), an entity will need a costing system to track costs incurred related to the specific development project. In many cases, this will be a simple system based on the time sheets of the employees involved in the development of the intangible asset but, on more complex projects, the system will also need to track direct expenses incurred.

4.7.5 Cost of an internally-generated intangible asset

The requirement that an intangible asset should be initially recorded at its cost applies to internally-generated intangible assets as well as purchased intangible assets. Cost includes all costs incurred from the date on which all of the recognition criteria (those for purchased as well as for internally-generated intangible assets) are met. If costs have been expensed prior to the recognition criteria being met, they may not be reinstated upon satisfaction of the criteria. [IAS 38.65 & 71]

Similar to self-constructed items of property, plant and equipment, the cost of an internally-generated intangible asset includes all directly attributable costs necessary to create, produce and prepare an asset to be capable of operating in the manner intended by management. These costs may include:

[IAS 38.66]

- expenditure on materials and services used or consumed in generating the intangible asset;
- the salaries, wages and other employment-related costs of personnel directly engaged in generating the asset;
- borrowing costs, in accordance with the requirements of IAS 23 *Borrowing Costs* – see **chapter 27**; and
- any other expenditure that is directly attributable to generating the asset, such as fees to register a legal right and the amortisation of patents and licences that are used to generate the asset.

IAS 38 specifically prohibits the inclusion of the following items in the cost of an internally-generated intangible asset:

[IAS 38.67]

- selling, administrative and other general overhead expenditure unless this expenditure can be directly attributed to preparing the asset for use;
- clearly identified inefficiencies and initial operating losses incurred before an asset achieves planned performance; and
- expenditure on training staff to operate the asset.

4.7.6 Research and development activities under contract for others

When an entity carries out research and development activities for others, the substance of the arrangement dictates the accounting treatment of the research and development costs for both entities. If the entity carrying out the research and development activities is retaining the risks and rewards of the activities and will control any asset that is developed, it should account for the costs of the research and development activities in accordance with IAS 38. If the entity carrying out the research and development activities is not retaining the risks and rewards of the activities and control of any asset that is developed will lie with the other party, the entity carrying out the activities is providing a service to that other party and should account for its activities in accordance with IAS 18 *Revenue* or IAS 11 *Construction Contracts*, as appropriate. The following factors may indicate that the risks and rewards of the research and development activities are retained by the entity carrying out the activities:

- the entity conducting the research and development activities will retain full rights to any intellectual property that is developed;
- the entity conducting the research and development activities will only receive payment from the other entity if the outcome of the research and development activities is successful (i.e. the outcome meets criteria specified by that other entity);
- the entity conducting the research and development activities is contractually obliged to repay any of the funds provided by the other entity, regardless of the outcome of the research and development activities; or
- even though the contract does not require the entity conducting the research and development activities to repay any of the funds provided by the other entity, repayment could be required at the option of the other entity or the surrounding conditions indicate that repayment is probable.

4.7.7 *Web site costs*

SIC-32 *Intangible Assets – Web Site Costs* addresses the appropriate accounting treatment for internal expenditure to develop, enhance and maintain a web site incurred by an entity (whether for internal or external access). Specifically, the Interpretation addresses the application of IAS 38 to web site development costs.

The Interpretation does not apply to purchasing, developing and operating the hardware associated with a web site (accounted for under IAS 16 *Property, Plant and Equipment*), nor to expenditure on the development or operation of a web site for sale to another entity (accounted for under IAS 2 *Inventories* and IAS 11 *Construction Contracts*).

SIC-32 identifies the following stages of web site development:

[SIC-32.2]

- Planning (including undertaking feasibility studies, defining objectives and specifications, evaluating alternatives and selecting preferences);
- Application and Infrastructure Development (including obtaining a domain name, purchasing and developing hardware and operating software, installing developed applications and stress testing);
- Graphical Design (including designing the appearance of web pages);
- Content Development (including creating, purchasing, preparing and uploading information, either textual or graphical in nature, on the web site before the completion of the web site's development. This information may either be stored in separate databases that are integrated into, or accessed from, the web site or coded directly into the web pages); and
- Operating (including maintaining and enhancing the applications, infrastructure, graphical design and content of the web site).

The Interpretation states that:

[SIC-32.7 & 8]

- a web site developed by an entity for its own use (whether for internal or external access) is an internally-generated intangible asset that is subject to the requirements of IAS 38;
- future economic benefits, as envisaged by IAS 38's criteria for recognition of internally-generated intangible assets, will be generated from a web site only when the web site is capable of generating revenue. For example, the requirement may be satisfied when the web site is capable of generating direct revenues from enabling orders to be placed; and
- where the web site has been developed solely or primarily for promoting or advertising the entity's products and services, the entity will be unable to demonstrate that such a web site will generate future economic benefits, and costs incurred on the development of the web site should be expensed as incurred.

SIC-32 concludes as follows:

[SIC-32.9]

- the nature of each activity for which expenditure is incurred (e.g. training employees and maintaining the web site) and the web site's stage of development or post-development are evaluated to determine the appropriate accounting treatment (additional guidance is provided in the Appendix to SIC-32);

- the Planning stage of a web site development is similar to the research phase described at **4.7.3** above and, therefore, any expenditure incurred in this stage is recognised as an expense when it is incurred;
- the Application and Infrastructure Development stage, the Graphical Design and Content Development stage, are similar in nature to the development phase described at **4.7.4** above. Therefore, expenditure incurred in these stages is recognised as an intangible asset if the expenditure can be directly attributed and is necessary to creating, producing or preparing the web site for it to be capable of operating in the manner intended by management. For example, expenditure on purchasing or creating content (other than content that advertises and promotes an entity's own products and services) specifically for a web site, or to enable use of the content (e.g. a fee for acquiring a licence to reproduce) on the web site, is included in the cost of development when this condition is met;
- expenditure incurred in the Content Development stage, to the extent that content is developed to advertise and promote an entity's own products and services (e.g. digital photographs of products), is recognised as an expense when incurred. For example, when accounting for expenditure on professional services for taking digital photographs of an entity's own products and for enhancing their display, expenditure is recognised as an expense as the professional services are received during the process, not when the digital photographs are displayed on the web site.

In accordance with IAS 38.71 (see **4.7.5**), expenditure on web site development that has previously been recognised as an expense should not be recognised as part of the cost of the web site intangible asset at a later date.

The Operating stage commences once the web site is available for use and, therefore, expenditure to maintain or enhance the web site after development has been completed should be recognised as an expense when it is incurred, unless it meets the criteria discussed at **4.2** above (criteria for recognising subsequent expenditure as an asset). Similarly, when an entity incurs expenditure on an Internet service provider hosting the entity's web site, the expenditure is recognised as an expense when the services are received.

SIC-32 indicates that the best estimate of a web site's useful life, for the purpose of amortisation, is short. [SIC-32.10]

5 Items to be recognised as an expense

As a general rule, expenditure on an intangible item should be recognised as an expense as incurred unless:

[IAS 38.68]

- it forms part of the cost of an intangible asset that meets the appropriate definition and recognition criteria; or
- the item is acquired in a business combination and does not meet the criteria for separate recognition. In such cases, it forms part of the amount recognised as goodwill at the acquisition date.

IAS 38 states that the following types of expenditure should always be recognised as an expense:

[IAS 38.69]

- research (except to the extent that it relates to an intangible acquired in a business combination);
- start-up activities, unless the expenditure qualifies to be included in the cost of an item of property, plant and equipment. Start-up costs include:
  - establishment costs such as legal and secretarial costs incurred in establishing a legal entity;
  - expenditure to open a new facility or business (i.e. pre-opening costs); and
  - expenditure prior to starting new operations or launching new products or processes (i.e. pre-operating costs);
- training activities;
- advertising and promotional activities; and
- relocating or re-organising part or all of an entity.

The Standard does not, however, preclude the recognition of bona fide prepaid costs as an asset when payment for the delivery of goods or services has been made in advance of the delivery of goods or the rendering of services. [IAS 38.70]

For periods beginning on or after 1 January 2009, these requirements of IAS 38 are modified, as described below, by *Improvements to IFRSs* issued in May 2008. Earlier application of the amendment to IAS 38 is permitted, but an entity choosing to apply the amendment early must disclose that fact.

Following the amendment, IAS 38.69 states that expenditure on advertising and promotional activities includes mail order catalogues, which are therefore always recognised as an expense. More generally, the modifications to IAS 38 also make clear that, where expenditure does not give rise to an intangible asset:

[IAS 38.69 & 69A]

- for a supply of goods, an expense is recognised when the entity has a right to access those goods. This is when the entity owns the goods or, if they have been constructed by a supplier in accordance with the terms of a supply contract, when the entity could demand delivery of them in return for payment; and

- for a supply of services, an expense is recognised when the entity receives the services. Services are received when they are performed by a supplier in accordance with a contract to deliver them to the entity and not when the entity uses them to deliver another service, for example to deliver an advertisement to customers.

This does not, however, preclude an entity from recognising a prepayment asset where payment has been made in advance of the entity obtaining a right to access goods, or in advance of receiving services. [IAS 38.70]

These changes to the wording in IAS 38 may result in a change to current practice where a prepayment asset may have been recognised for the costs of production of mail order catalogues or advertising, and only expensed on distribution of the catalogues to the end-customer or once advertisements were broadcast or published. Under the amendment, once the entity has a right to access or has taken delivery of the mail order catalogues or advertisements, any associated expenditure must be recognised as an expense immediately. Where an entity changes its accounting policy as a result of these amendments, the change should be applied retrospectively.

The amendment to IAS 38 also modifies IAS 38.98, as discussed at **10.3** below.

6 Alternatives for measurement after initial recognition

IAS 38 sets out two alternatives for subsequent measurement – the cost model and the revaluation model. The conditions imposed for use of the revaluation model are strict, however, and this alternative is unlikely to be available in practice other than in very rare cases.

6.1 Cost model

If an intangible asset is accounted for using the cost model, after initial recognition, it is carried in the statement of financial position at its cost (measured as described in **section 4** above) less any accumulated amortisation and any accumulated impairment losses. [IAS 38.74]

6.2 Revaluation model

If the revaluation model is adopted, the intangible asset is carried at a revalued amount, which is its fair value at the date of the revaluation less any subsequent accumulated amortisation and any subsequent accumulated impairment losses. [IAS 38.75] The revaluation model is described in **section 7**.

7 Revaluation model

7.1 Which intangibles can be revalued?

In order to use the revaluation model, IAS 38 requires fair value to be determined by reference to an active market. Therefore, only intangibles that are traded on an active market can be revalued under the Standard.

An active market is defined as a market where all of the following conditions are present:

[IAS 38.8]

- the items traded within the market are homogeneous;
- willing buyers and sellers can normally be found at any time; and
- prices are available to the public.

IAS 38 permits no basis for the determination of fair value other than by reference to an active market. It will be quite rare for an active market to exist for intangible assets. Therefore, the revaluation of intangible assets is not expected to be common. Examples of intangible assets where this option might be available are freely transferable taxi licenses, fishing licenses or production quotas.

Other intangible assets may be traded in private transactions, where such intangibles are unique and the price for each transaction is specifically negotiated. In such circumstances, the traded items are not homogeneous and therefore no active market exists.

IAS 38 specifically states that, due to their unique nature, an active market cannot exist for any of the following items:

[IAS 38.78]

- brands;
- newspaper mastheads;
- music and film publishing rights; and
- patents or trademarks.

The revaluation model does not permit:

[IAS 38.76]

- the revaluation of intangible assets that have not previously been recognised as assets; or
- the initial recognition of intangible assets at amounts other than their cost.

Therefore if, in developing an asset internally, the criteria for recognition as set out at **4.7.4** above are not met, and all of the costs are written off as incurred, the asset cannot be subsequently measured at fair value. If, however, only part of the asset was initially recognised as an asset (e.g. because the recognition criteria were met only part way through the project), the whole of that asset can be revalued, if the conditions for revaluation are met. [IAS 38.77]

The Standard also states specifically that the revaluation model may be adopted for intangible assets received by way of government grant and recognised at a nominal amount (see **4.5** above). [IAS 38.77]

Example 7.1
Revaluation of internally generated intangible assets

Over the last two years, a group has developed various items of computer software to be used internally and/or to be sold to prospective buyers. In accordance with IAS 38, the group capitalised the development costs incurred during the development phase and recognised an intangible asset of £1 million. Since the year-end, the group has been in discussions with a third party for the sale of the subsidiary that owns the software, or the sale of that subsidiary's assets. The selling price, under negotiation, is much higher than the carrying amount of the subsidiary's assets (which mainly relate to the intangible asset developed and other computer equipment).

The group may not revalue its internally-generated intangible asset, as no active market exists. [IAS 38.75] An active market is only considered to exist where the items traded in that market are homogenous, willing buyers and willing sellers normally can be found at any time, and prices are available to the public. [IAS 38.8] Although the entity has entered into sale negotiations, this is not sufficient to indicate an active market. If an active market, as defined, genuinely existed, the price for which the asset could be sold would be publicly available and would not be a matter for negotiation. Indeed, IAS 38.78 states that the fact that there is a sale agreement between an entity and a buyer does not provide evidence of an active market.

7.2 Basis for revaluation

When an intangible asset is revalued, it is revalued to its fair value, which is defined as the amount for which the asset could be exchanged between knowledgeable, willing parties in an arm's length transaction. [IAS 38.8] As noted at **7.1** above, for the purpose of revaluing intangible assets, such fair values can only be determined by reference to an active market.

7.3 Frequency of revaluations

IAS 38 does not set a specific requirement for the frequency of revaluations, but states that they should be carried out with sufficient regularity so that, at the end of each reporting period, the carrying amount of a revalued intangible asset does not differ materially from its fair value. [IAS 38.75]

In order to meet this requirement, an entity must estimate the fair value of its revalued intangible assets at the end of each reporting period. This does not mean, however, that revaluation adjustments must be made every year, unless the estimate of fair value differs significantly from the carrying amount of the intangible asset.

Where permitted, the revaluation of intangible assets should, in practice, be a straightforward matter, since it is a pre-requisite that an active market exists and that prices are available to the public.

The frequency of revaluations will be determined by the volatility of the active market on which the intangible asset is traded. Some intangible assets may experience significant and volatile movements in fair value, thus necessitating annual revaluation. Such frequent revaluations are unnecessary for intangible assets with only insignificant movements in fair value. [IAS 38.79]

7.4 Scope of revaluations

When an intangible asset is accounted for using the revaluation model, all of the other assets in its class should also be accounted for using the revaluation model, unless there is no active market for those assets. [IAS 38.72] If there is no active market for a particular intangible asset which is included in a revalued class of intangible assets, that asset is carried at its cost less any accumulated amortisation and any accumulated impairment losses. [IAS 38.81]

A class of intangible assets is defined as a grouping of assets of a similar nature and use in the operations of an entity. Examples of separate classes may include:

[IAS 38.119]

- brand names;
- mastheads and publishing titles;
- computer software;
- licences and franchises;
- copyrights, patents and other industrial property rights, service and operating rights;
- recipes, formulae, model designs and prototypes; and
- intangible assets under development.

If the fair value of a revalued intangible asset can no longer be assessed by reference to an active market, the intangible asset is carried at its fair value at the date of the last revaluation by reference to the active market less any subsequent accumulated amortisation and any subsequent impairment losses. [IAS 38.82] The disappearance of the active market may be an indicator of impairment which triggers an impairment review under IAS

36 *Impairment of Assets* (see **chapter 9**). If the active market re-emerges, the intangible asset should once again be revalued by reference to the active market. [IAS 38.84]

7.5 Accumulated amortisation at the date of revaluation

IAS 38.80 allows the accumulated amortisation relating to an intangible asset that has been revalued to be dealt with in two ways, i.e. either:

- restated proportionately with the change in the gross carrying amount of the asset so that the carrying amount of the asset after revaluation equals its revalued amount. The carrying amount is increased to the revalued amount by restating the cost and amortisation proportionately; or
- eliminated against the gross carrying amount of the asset and the resulting net amount restated to the revalued amount of the asset. The accumulated amortisation is eliminated, and any remaining surplus is used to increase cost.

These treatments are similar to those permitted for accumulated depreciation when an item of property, plant and equipment is revalued. See **example 6.4** in **chapter 6** for a comparison of the two methods described above.

7.6 Treatment of surplus or deficit arising on revaluation

7.6.1 *Revaluation surplus*

When a valuation indicates that the fair value of an intangible asset is greater than its carrying amount, the amount of the surplus is generally recognised in other comprehensive income and accumulated in equity as a revaluation surplus. [IAS 38.85]

If the increase in the fair value of the asset reverses a previously recognised decrease in the fair value of the same asset, however, the increase is recognised in profit or loss to the extent that the previous decrease was recognised in profit or loss. [IAS 38.85]

7.6.2 *Revaluation deficit*

When a revaluation indicates that the fair value of an intangible asset is less than its carrying amount, the amount of the deficit is generally recognised in profit or loss. [IAS 38.86]

If the decrease in the fair value of the intangible asset reverses a previously recognised increase in the fair value of the same asset, however, the decrease is recognised in other comprehensive income to the extent of any credit balance in the revaluation surplus in respect of that asset. The decrease reduces the amount of revaluation surplus. [IAS 38.86]

The treatment of revaluation surpluses and deficits arising on intangible assets is the same as that for items of property, plant and equipment (see the illustrative examples in **6.8.3** of **chapter 6**).

7.6.3 *Realisation of the revaluation surplus*

The revaluation surplus may be transferred to retained earnings as the surplus is realised, though such a transfer is not mandatory. Realisation of the entire surplus may occur on the retirement or disposal of the asset. When the surplus is realised on disposal/retirement, any transfer from the revaluation surplus to retained earnings is not made through profit or loss but by means of a reserve transfer. [IAS 38.87]

Some realisation of the revaluation surplus may occur, however, through the use of the intangible asset. [IAS 38.87] The amount of the surplus that is realised through use of the asset is calculated as the difference between the amortisation calculated on the historical cost of the asset and the amortisation calculated on the revalued amount. This difference may be transferred from the revaluation surplus to retained earnings in each period. If an entity chooses to make such periodic transfers, when a revalued intangible asset is fully amortised in the statement of financial position, the related revaluation surplus will have been reduced to zero.

Whether realised on disposal or on a systematic basis over the life of the asset, any transfer from revaluation reserve to retained earnings is not made through profit or loss.

8 Determining the useful life of an intangible asset

The accounting for an intangible asset is determined on the basis of its useful life. Where the useful life of the asset is determined to be finite, the asset is amortised over that useful life. Where the useful life of the asset is determined to be indefinite, the asset is not amortised. IAS 38 provides a significant amount of guidance to assist in this determination, which is summarised in the following sections.

8.1 Finite or indefinite useful life?

Entities are required to assess whether the useful life of an intangible asset is finite or indefinite and, if finite, the length of, or number of production or similar units constituting, that useful life. [IAS 38.88]

An intangible asset will be regarded as having an indefinite useful life when, based on all of the relevant factors, there is no foreseeable limit to the period over which the asset is expected to generate net cash inflows for the entity. [IAS 38.88] Therefore, where management has the intention and the ability to maintain an intangible asset so that there is no foreseeable limit on the period over which the asset is expected to generate net cash inflows for the entity, the asset is regarded as having an indefinite useful life.

Note that the term 'indefinite' does not mean 'infinite'. [IAS 38.91] There does not need to be an expectation that the cash inflows generated by the asset will go on forever – simply that, at the date of assessment, there is no foreseeable point at which the cash inflows will cease.

Where there is a foreseeable limit to the period over which net cash inflows are expected to flow to the entity, the asset is regarded as having a finite life.

The assessment as to whether an intangible asset has an indefinite useful life is clearly crucial for the purposes of the subsequent accounting treatment for the intangible asset. IAS 38 provides a number of illustrative examples for this determination, which are summarised at **8.4** below.

8.2 Factors for consideration in determining useful life

The useful life of an intangible asset is either:

[IAS 38.8]

- the period over which the asset is expected to be available for use by the entity; or
- the number of production or similar units expected to be obtained from the asset by an entity.

Factors to consider in estimating the useful life of an intangible asset include:

[IAS 38.90]

- the expected usage of the asset by the entity and whether the asset could be efficiently managed by another management team;
- typical product life cycles for the asset and public information on estimates of useful lives of similar types of assets that are used in a similar way;
- technical, technological, commercial or other types of obsolescence;
- the stability of the industry in which the asset operates and changes in the market demand for the products or services output from the asset;
- expected actions by competitors or potential competitors;
- the level of maintenance expenditure required to obtain the expected future economic benefits from the asset and the entity's ability and intent to reach such a level;
- the period of control over the asset, and legal or similar limits on the use of the asset, such as the expiry dates of related leases; and
- whether the useful life of the asset is dependent on the useful life of other assets of the entity.

The useful life of an intangible asset reflects only that level of future maintenance expenditure required to maintain the asset at its standard of performance assessed at the time of estimating the asset's useful life, and the entity's ability and intention to reach such a level. A conclusion that the useful life of an intangible asset is indefinite should not depend on planned future expenditure in excess of that required to maintain the asset at that standard of performance. [IAS 38.91]

The Standard notes that, given the history of rapid changes in technology, computer software and many other intangible assets are susceptible to technological obsolescence. Therefore, it is likely that their useful lives will be short. [IAS 38.92]

8.3 Assets arising from contractual or other legal rights

Control over the future economic benefits from an intangible asset is often achieved through legal rights that have been granted for a finite period. Under most circumstances, the estimated useful life of the intangible asset is the shorter of the period of the legal rights and the period over which economic benefits are expected to be generated. In some cases, however, the legal rights may be renewable. The question then arises as to whether it is appropriate to assume that the legal rights will be extended.

IAS 38 stipulates that the useful life of an intangible asset should include the renewal period(s) only if there is evidence to support renewal by the entity without significant cost. For entities that have adopted IFRS 3(2008), IAS 38 has been amended to clarify that the useful life of a reacquired right recognised as an intangible asset in a business combination is the remaining contractual period of the contract in which the right was granted, and does not include renewal periods. [IAS 38.94]

The following factors are listed which indicate that an entity would be able to renew the contractual or other legal rights without significant cost:

[IAS 38.96]

- there is evidence (possibly based on past experience) that the legal rights will be renewed. If renewal is contingent upon the consent of a third party, this includes evidence that the third party will give its consent;
- there is evidence that the conditions necessary to obtain the renewal of the legal right (if any) will be satisfied; and
- the cost to the entity of renewal is not significant when compared with the future economic benefits expected to flow to the entity from renewal.

If the cost of renewal is significant when compared with the future economic benefits expected to flow to the entity from renewal, the 'renewal' represents, in substance, the acquisition of a new intangible asset at the renewal date. [IAS 38.96]

8.4 Illustrative examples

A number of detailed examples have been published with IAS 38 to provide guidance for the determination of the useful life of an asset in accordance with the Standard. Each details the specific facts and circumstances surrounding the determination of the asset's useful life. The following table summarises the key determinants for each example. Readers should refer to the text of the Standard, however, to obtain a full understanding of each of the circumstances and of the factors assessed in each scenario.

Asset description	Finite or indefinite life?	Amortisation period
Acquired customer list – anticipated to generate benefits for between 1 and 3 years. [IAS 38 Illustrative Examples (Example 1)]	Finite. Although the entity will expect to generate further benefits when new customers are added to the list, the useful life is determined by reference only to customers on the list at the acquisition date.	Management's best estimate of the useful life – say 18 months.
Acquired patent that expires in 15 years. The entity intends to sell the patent to a committed third party in five years for 60 per cent of its fair value at the date of acquisition. [IAS 38 Illustrative Examples (Example 2)]	Finite	The period over which the patent is expected to generate cash inflows for the entity, i.e. five years. The residual value should equal the present value of 60 per cent of the fair value at the date of acquisition.
Copyright with remaining legal life of 50 years, but management estimates that net cash inflows will only be generated for 30 years. [IAS 38 Illustrative Examples (Example 3)]	Finite	30 years

Asset description	Finite or indefinite life?	Amortisation period
Broadcasting licence that expires in five years. Can be renewed indefinitely, at little cost every 10 years, provided that certain conditions are met. Management intends to renew the license indefinitely, and evidence supports its ability to do so. No third party or obsolescence issues that would indicate a problem with indefinite renewal. [IAS 38 Illustrative Examples (Example 4)]	Indefinite. Potential to renew indefinitely is taken into account.	N/a
Same licence as previous example but, when licence has three years remaining, licensing authority decides to auction licenses at future renewal dates. [IAS 38 Illustrative Examples (Example 5)]	Finite. No potential to renew the existing arrangement.	Three years
Acquired airline route authority that expires in three years. Renewable indefinitely, at minimal cost, every five years provided that conditions are complied with. Management expects to renew indefinitely, and no indication that they will not be able to do so. [IAS 38 Illustrative Examples (Example 6)]	Indefinite. Potential to renew indefinitely is taken into account.	N/a

Asset description	Finite or indefinite life?	Amortisation period
Acquired trademark for a market-leading consumer product with a remaining legal life of five years, but renewable every 10 years at little cost. Management intends to renew indefinitely and market indicators support cash inflows for an indefinite period. [IAS 38 Illustrative Examples (Example 7)]	Indefinite. Potential to renew indefinitely is taken into account.	N/a
Acquired trademark for leading consumer product previously regarded as having an indefinite life. Increased competitor activity indicates reduced future cash inflows for an indefinite period. [IAS 38 Illustrative Examples (Example 8)]	Indefinite. Impairment loss recognised for impact of reduced cash inflows.	N/a
Trademark acquired in a business combination some years ago, previously considered to have an indefinite life. Management decides to discontinue related product line over the next four years. [IAS 38 Illustrative Examples (Example 9)]	Finite	Four years

8.5 Subsequent reassessment of useful life

Whether an intangible asset is determined to have a finite useful life, or an indefinite useful life, IAS 38 requires that the initial determination be reviewed at least annually (see **section 9** and **10.2.3** below).

The determination of useful life for each intangible asset requires a comprehensive consideration of all pertinent factors surrounding the assets. Subsequent to the initial determination of useful life, entities must establish sufficient procedures to identify and evaluate appropriately those events or circumstances that, if occurring or changed from the initial determination, may impact the remaining useful life. Some events or circumstances will represent both discrete and readily identifiable events to which the entity should respond (e.g. a change in regulation). Other events or circumstances may develop more gradually over time but, nevertheless, must be monitored and given appropriate consideration by the entity (e.g. obsolescence, competition, and demand). Given the varying nature of the intangible assets, and each entity's unique facts and circumstances, procedures employed by entities to evaluate useful lives of intangible assets are expected to vary.

9 Subsequent accounting for assets with indefinite useful lives

Entities are not permitted to amortise intangible assets that have been assessed as having an indefinite useful life. [IAS 38.107] Rather, in accordance with the requirements of IAS 36 *Impairment of Assets*, such assets are tested for impairment by comparing their recoverable amounts with their carrying amounts once a year, at a minimum. An additional impairment test is required whenever there is an indication that an intangible asset may be impaired. The requirements of IAS 36 are dealt with in detail in **chapter 9**.

Where an asset has been assessed as having an indefinite useful life, resulting in the asset not being amortised in accordance with IAS 38.107, that assessment is revisited each period to determine whether events and circumstances continue to support an indefinite useful life for that asset. If not, the change in the indefinite life assessment is accounted for as a change in accounting estimate in accordance with IAS 8 *Accounting Policies, Changes in Accounting Estimates and Errors.* [IAS 38.109]

Where the useful life of an intangible asset is reassessed as finite rather than indefinite, this is an indicator that the asset may be impaired. Accordingly, the asset is tested for impairment by comparing its recoverable amount, determined in accordance with IAS 36, with its carrying amount, and recognising any excess of the carrying amount over the recoverable amount as an impairment loss. [IAS 38.110]

Following the annual reassessment of the useful life of an asset previously considered to have an indefinite useful life:

- if the intangible asset still has an indefinite useful life, it should be tested for impairment in accordance with the requirements of IAS 38;
- if the intangible asset is determined to have a finite useful life, it should be tested for impairment, and should be amortised over its estimated remaining useful life and accounted for in the same manner as other intangible assets that are subject to amortisation, including further impairment testing where indicators of impairment exist.

10 Subsequent accounting for assets with finite useful lives

The depreciable amount of an intangible asset with a finite useful life is required to be amortised on a systematic basis over its useful life. [IAS 38.97] The depreciable amount of an asset is defined as the cost of the asset, or other amount substituted for cost, less its residual value. [IAS 38.8]

In the majority of cases, the amortisation charges are recognised in profit or loss. If the economic benefits of the intangible asset are used by the entity in the production of other assets, however, the amortisation charge is added to the cost of the other assets and included in their carrying amount. For example, if a patented production process has been capitalised as an intangible asset, as the relevant inventory items are produced using the patented process, the amortisation of the intangible asset is added to the cost of the inventories. [IAS 38.99]

10.1 Residual value

IAS 38 defines residual value as the estimated amount that an entity would currently obtain from disposal of the asset, after deducting the estimated costs of disposal, if the asset were already of the age and in the condition expected at the end of its useful life. [IAS 38.8]

Under most circumstances, the residual value of an intangible asset with a finite life will be zero. A residual value of greater than zero, which implies that the entity expects to dispose of the intangible asset before the end of its useful economic life, may arise if:

[IAS 38.100]

- there is a commitment by a third party to purchase the asset at the end of its useful life; *or*
- there is an active market for the asset, *and*:
  - residual value can be determined by reference to that market; *and*
  - it is probable that such a market will exist at the end of the asset's useful life.

Where residual value is significant, it will directly impact on the depreciation recognised over the life of the asset.

The residual value of an asset is required to be reviewed at least at each financial year-end. [IAS 38.102] The revised estimate should be based on conditions and prices current at the end of the reporting period. Where the revised estimate differs significantly from previous estimates of residual value, the effect is accounted for prospectively as a change in estimate, in accordance with the requirements of IAS 8 *Accounting Policies, Changes in Accounting Estimates and Errors*. Effectively, the amortisation charge over the remaining useful life of the asset is adjusted to take account of the revised estimate of residual value.

Where the revised estimate of residual value is equal to or greater than the asset's carrying amount, whether due to inflation or otherwise, then the asset's amortisation charge is zero unless and until its residual value subsequently decreases to an amount below the asset's carrying amount. [IAS 38.103]

IAS 38 does not allow a reversal of earlier depreciation in these circumstances.

10.2 Amortisation period

The factors to be considered in determining the useful life of an intangible asset are discussed in **section 8** above.

10.2.1 Commencement of amortisation

Amortisation commences from the date the asset is available for use, i.e. when it is in the location and condition necessary for it to be capable of operating in the manner intended by management. [IAS 38.97]

It is important to distinguish the date an asset is available for use from the date on which it is actually brought into use. Amortisation will commence from the former.

Example 10.2.1

Date of commencement of amortisation of an intangible asset

Operators usually are required to purchase a telecom licence prior to the provision of services in a particular location or prior to the provision of certain types of services (e.g. 3G services). Since telecom licences normally are granted for a specified period of time, the cost of the licence has to be amortised over the best estimate of its useful life. The operator generally will have to build and commission its network before it can earn revenues from the use of its licence.

The ability to receive economic benefits from the licence is linked directly to the ability to use the network; therefore, the licence is only available for use when the network is in place. Consequently, amortisation of the licence should commence at the date the network is available for use (i.e. it is in the location and condition necessary for it to be capable of operating in the manner intended by management).

In some countries, the full network may not be operational in the entire targeted areas until a certain date. However, as soon as one area (one connection) is in place and working, the amortisation of the licence should start. In most instances, the amortisation of the licence will begin before the full commercial launch.

10.2.2 Cessation of amortisation

Amortisation ceases at the earlier of:

[IAS 38.97]

- the date that the asset is classified as held for sale (or included in a disposal group that is classified as held for sale) in accordance with IFRS 5 *Non-current Assets Held for Sale and Discontinued Operations*; and
- the date that the asset is derecognised (see **section 12** below).

Amortisation does not cease when an intangible asset is taken out of use, unless one of these conditions is met. [IAS 38.117]

10.2.3 *Review of amortisation period*

At least at each financial year end, the amortisation periods for intangible assets with finite lives should be reviewed. If the expected useful life of the asset is different from previous estimates, the amortisation period should be adjusted accordingly. Any such change is accounted for as a change in estimate in accordance with IAS 8 *Accounting Policies, Changes in Accounting Estimates and Errors,* by adjusting current and future periods. [IAS 38.104]

Where the annual review of the amortisation period of a previously-amortised intangible asset results in a determination that the asset has an indefinite useful life:

- it should be tested for impairment;
- it should no longer be amortised, but should be accounted for in the same manner as other intangible assets that are not subject to amortisation; and
- previous amortisation of that asset is not reversed.

10.3 Amortisation method

There are several methods of apportioning amortisation over the anticipated useful life of the asset. Those most commonly employed are the straight-line method and the reducing balance (diminishing balance) method. These, and other, methods of depreciation and amortisation are discussed in **section 7.4** of **chapter 6**. IAS 38 requires that the entity should select an amortisation method that reflects the pattern in which the asset's future economic benefits are expected to be consumed by the entity. [IAS 38.97]

In some circumstances, it may be difficult to determine reliably the expected pattern of consumption. In such circumstances, use of the straight-line method is mandatory. [IAS 38.97]

At least at each financial year end, the amortisation methods for intangible assets with finite useful lives should be reviewed. If there has been a change in the expected pattern of consumption of the future economic benefits embodied in an asset, the amortisation method should be changed to reflect the changed pattern. Any such change is accounted for as a change in estimate in accordance with IAS 8 *Accounting Policies, Changes in Accounting Estimates and Errors,* by adjusting current and future periods. [IAS 38.104]

For periods beginning on or after 1 January 2009, IAS 38 is amended by *Improvements to IFRSs* issued in May 2008. Prior to this amendment, the Standard noted that there would rarely, if ever, be persuasive evidence to support an amortisation method for intangible assets (e.g. the annuity method) that results in a lower amount of accumulated amortisation than under the straight-line method. [IAS 38.98] The amendment deleted this statement, and also modified IAS 38.69 – 70, as discussed in **section 5** above. Earlier application of the amendment to IAS 38 is permitted, but an entity choosing to apply the amendment early must disclose that fact.

11 Impairment

Entities are required to follow the provisions of IAS 36 *Impairment of Assets* to determine whether an intangible asset is impaired and to measure any such impairment loss (see **chapter 9**). Any impairment loss is then recognised in accordance with the requirements of IAS 36.

For intangible assets with indefinite lives, an impairment review is required at least annually (see **section 9** above).

12 Derecognition

IAS 38 requires that the carrying amount of an intangible asset should be derecognised:

[IAS 38.112]

- on disposal; or
- when no future economic benefits are expected from its use or disposal.

The gain or loss arising from the derecognition of an intangible asset is to be recognised in profit or loss when the asset is derecognised (unless IAS 17 *Leases* requires otherwise in the circumstances of a sale and leaseback). [IAS 38.113]

IAS 38 specifically prohibits the classification as revenue of gains arising on the derecognition of intangible assets. [IAS 38.103] The Standard does require, however, that the date of disposal of an intangible asset be determined using the criteria for recognising revenue from the sale of goods, as set out in IAS 18 *Revenue*. [IAS 38.114]

The gain or loss arising from the derecognition of an intangible asset is determined as the difference between the net disposal proceeds, if any, and the carrying amount of the item. [IAS 38.113] Therefore, as discussed at **7.6.3** above, where a revalued asset is disposed of, any credit balance on the revaluation reserve attributable to that asset is transferred directly to retained earnings, and is not reflected in the statement of comprehensive income.

The disposal consideration received is measured at its fair value. If payment is deferred beyond normal credit terms, the consideration received is recognised initially at the cash price equivalent. The difference between the nominal amount of the consideration and the cash price equivalent is recognised as interest income in accordance with IAS 18 *Revenue*. [IAS 38.116]

13 Presentation and disclosure

13.1 Presentation

IAS 1 *Presentation of Financial Statements* requires that, where material, the aggregate carrying amount of the entity's intangible assets should be presented in the statement of financial position. [IAS 1(2007).54(c), previously IAS 1(2003).68(c)]

13.2 Disclosure

13.2.1 General

The following disclosures should be made for each class of intangible assets, distinguishing between internally-generated intangible assets and other intangible assets:

[IAS 38.118]

- whether the useful lives are indefinite or finite and, if finite, the useful lives or amortisation rates used;
- the amortisation methods used for intangible assets with finite useful lives;
- the gross carrying amount and any accumulated amortisation (aggregated with accumulated impairment losses) at the beginning and end of the period;
- the line item(s) of the statement of comprehensive income in which the amortisation of intangible assets is included; and
- a reconciliation of the carrying amount at the beginning and end of the period showing:

- additions, indicating separately those from internal development, those acquired separately, and those acquired through business combinations;
- assets classified as held for sale or included in a disposal group classified as held for sale in accordance with IFRS 5 *Non-current Assets Held for Disposal and Discontinued Operations*, and other disposals;
- increases or decreases during the period resulting from revaluations and from impairment losses recognised or reversed in other comprehensive income;
- impairment losses recognised in profit or loss during the period;
- impairment losses reversed in profit or loss during the period;
- any amortisation recognised during the period;
- net exchange differences arising on the translation of the financial statements into the presentation currency, and on the translation of a foreign operation into the presentation currency of the entity; and
- other changes in the carrying amount during the period.

UK

There are two differences between these IFRS requirements and UK GAAP:

- *the reconciliation above is required both for the current period and for the comparative period, whereas under FRS 10 only a current period reconciliation is required, and*
- *the reconciliation may be presented either for the carrying amount, or separately for cost* (*or revalued amount*) *and depreciation.*

Examples of classes of intangible assets are listed at **7.4**. Those classes are disaggregated (aggregated) into smaller (larger) classes if this results in more relevant information for the users of the financial statements. [IAS 38.119]

13.2.2 *Intangible assets having an indefinite useful life*

For an intangible asset assessed as having an indefinite useful life, the financial statements should disclose the carrying amount of the asset and the reasons supporting the assessment of an indefinite useful life. In giving these reasons, the entity should describe the factor(s) that played a significant role in determining that the asset has an indefinite useful life. [IAS 38.122(a)]

13.2.3 *Intangible assets that are individually material*

For any individual intangible asset that is material to the entity's financial statements, the financial statements should disclose a description of the asset, its carrying amount and its remaining amortisation period. [IAS 38.122(b)]

13.2.4 *Intangible assets acquired by way of government grant and initially recognised at fair value*

For intangible assets acquired by way of government grant and initially recognised at fair value (see **4.5** above), the financial statements should disclose:

[IAS 38.122(c)]

- the fair value initially recognised for those assets;
- their carrying amount; and
- whether they are measured after recognition under the cost model or the revaluation model.

13.2.5 *Title restrictions and capital commitments*

The financial statements should also disclose:

- the existence and carrying amount of intangible assets whose title is restricted and the carrying amounts of intangible assets pledged as security for liabilities; [IAS 38.122(d)] and
- the amount of contractual commitments for the acquisition of intangible assets. [IAS 38.122(e)]

13.2.6 *Changes in estimates*

In addition to the disclosure requirements included in IAS 38, if there has been a change in estimate during the period, the disclosure requirements set out in IAS 8 *Accounting Policies, Changes in Accounting Estimates and Errors* apply (see **section 4.3** of **chapter 4**). Changes in estimate related to intangible assets include changes in:

- the assessment of an intangible asset's useful life;
- the amortisation method; and
- residual values.

13.2.7 *Impairment losses*

If an intangible asset has suffered an impairment loss, the disclosure requirements set out in IAS 36 *Impairment of Assets* will apply (see **section 11** of **chapter 9**).

13.2.8 *Intangible assets carried at revalued amounts*

In addition to the disclosures listed in the previous sections, if an entity accounts for any intangible assets at revalued amounts, the following disclosures are required:

[IAS 38.124]

- by class of intangible assets:
  - the effective date of the revaluation;
  - the carrying amount of revalued intangible assets; and
  - the carrying amount that would have been included in the financial statements had the revalued intangible assets been accounted for under the cost model;
- the amount of the revaluation surplus that relates to intangible assets at the beginning and end of the period, indicating the changes during the period and any restrictions on the distribution of the balance to shareholders; and
- the methods and significant assumptions applied in estimating the assets' fair values.

Where necessary, it is permissible to aggregate the classes of revalued assets into larger classes for disclosure purposes. Classes are not aggregated, however, if this would result in the combination of a class of intangible assets that includes amounts measured under both the cost and revaluation models. [IAS 38.125]

13.2.9 *Research and development expenditure*

The aggregate amount of research and development expenditure recognised as an expense during the period should be disclosed. [IAS 38.126]

> Note that the requirement is to disclose the amount expensed rather than the amount incurred. Thus, where development expenditure is capitalised, the disclosure will occur in subsequent periods as it is amortised.

13.2.10 *Additional recommended disclosures*

The following disclosures are encouraged but not required:

[IAS 38.128]

- a description of any fully amortised intangible asset that is still in use; and
- a brief description of significant intangible assets controlled by the entity but not recognised as assets because they did not meet the recognition criteria in IAS 38 or because they were acquired or generated before the 1998 version of IAS 38 (which prohibited retrospective recognition) became effective.

14 Future developments

In June 2005, the IASB published an Exposure Draft to amend IAS 37 *Provisions, Contingent Liabilities and Contingent Assets*, which proposes, inter alia, to eliminate the term 'contingent assets'. With the exception of reimbursement rights, which would continue to be accounted for under IAS 37, items previously described as contingent assets but which meet the definition of an asset would fall within the scope of IAS 38. At the time of writing, it is expected that revisions to the Standards will be published in 2009.

9 Impairment of assets

1 Introduction

The objective of IAS 36 *Impairments of Assets* is to prescribe the procedures that an entity applies to ensure that its assets are carried at no more than their recoverable amount. IAS 36 was last revised by the IASB in March 2004 as part of its Business Combinations Project, and was most recently amended when *Improvements to IFRSs* and the Amendments to IFRS 1 and IAS 27 *Cost of an Investment in a Subsidiary, Jointly Controlled Entity or Associate* were issued in May 2008.

This chapter discusses the requirements of IAS 36 in the following sections:

Section 2	Summary of IAS 36 approach
Section 3	Scope
Section 4	Definitions
Section 5	Identifying an asset that may be impaired
Section 6	Measurement of recoverable amount
Section 7	Fair value less costs to sell
Section 8	Value in use
Section 9	Recognition and measurement of an impairment loss
Section 10	Reversals of impairment losses
Section 11	Disclosure

UK

The UK equivalent of IAS 36 is FRS 11 Impairment of Fixed Assets and Goodwill. *In overview, the two standards have much in common, but there are some differences. The most significant of these are highlighted below.*

- *Where an impairment loss on a revalued asset is clearly caused by a consumption of economic benefits, FRS 11 requires the full amount of the impairment to be taken to the profit and loss account. IAS 36 takes to profit or loss only the amount in excess of the relevant part of the revaluation reserve.*

- *FRS 11 allocates impairment losses first to any goodwill, then to any intangibles and then to tangible fixed assets. In recognising reversals, it also applies a more restrictive regime to goodwill and other intangibles than to tangible fixed assets. IAS 36, by contrast, does not distinguish between tangible and intangible fixed assets. Thus, subject to certain constraints, it allocates impairment losses in excess of goodwill pro rata to all other assets, and more readily allows the reversal of impairment losses on intangible fixed assets (though not on goodwill).*
- *IAS 36 does not include any requirement to take into account unrecognised internally generated goodwill when merging acquired and existing businesses.*
- *IAS 36 does not include requirements to monitor cash flows against forecasts in the five years after an impairment review. It does, however, include more extensive disclosure requirements in connection with impairments and their reversals. The additional disclosure requirements may be seen as commercially sensitive, and should not be underestimated.*
- *When allocating goodwill arising on an acquisition to income generating units, it is possible under IAS 36 that some may be allocated to existing businesses (to reflect expected synergies). FRS 11 does not envisage that goodwill arising on an acquisition may be allocated to any income generating units other than those acquired.*

Under IAS 36, impairment testing must be performed every year for any cash generating unit to which goodwill is attached (although the annual test may be conducted at a regular time which is not the end of the reporting period). As a result, UK companies transitioning to IFRSs may need to amend their systems and processes to enable this to become a routine part of annual procedures.

2 Summary of IAS 36 approach

The principles of IAS 36 apply to a wide range of assets (those assets outside its scope are described in **section 3**). The idea is that, for those assets within its scope, the requirements for the recognition of impairment losses should be specified in a single Standard. Thus, other Standards dealing with such asset categories (e.g. IAS 16 *Property, Plant and Equipment*) simply refer to IAS 36 for the requirements regarding impairment testing.

IAS 36 requires that a review for impairment be carried out if events or changes in circumstances indicate that the carrying amount of an asset may not be recoverable. The review will compare the carrying amount of the asset with its recoverable amount, which is the higher of its value if sold (if known) and its value in use.

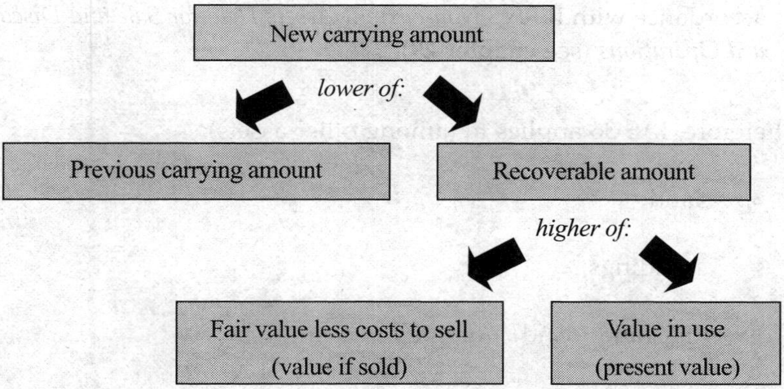

Any shortfall is deemed an impairment loss which, for assets carried at cost, is recognised in profit or loss and, for assets carried at a revalued amount, is treated as a revaluation decrease (which may or may not lead to an expense being recognised in profit or loss).

3 Scope

IAS 36 applies to all assets except:

[IAS 36.2]

- inventories (dealt with in IAS 2 *Inventories* – see **chapter 10**);
- assets arising from construction contracts (dealt with in IAS 11 *Construction Contracts* – see **chapter 40**);
- deferred tax assets (dealt with in IAS 12 *Income Taxes* – see **chapter 12**);
- assets arising from employee benefits (dealt with in IAS 19 *Employee Benefits* – see **chapter 24**);
- financial assets that are within the scope of IAS 39 *Financial Instruments: Recognition and Measurement* (see **chapter 14** and **chapter 18**);
- investment property that is measured at fair value (dealt with in IAS 40 *Investment Property* – see **chapter 7**);
- biological assets related to agricultural activity that are measured at fair value less estimated costs to sell (dealt with in IAS 41 *Agriculture* – see **chapter 43**);

- deferred acquisition costs, and intangible assets, arising from an insurer's contractual rights under insurance contracts within the scope of IFRS 4 *Insurance Contracts* (see **chapter 44**); and
- non-current assets (or disposal groups) classified as held for sale in accordance with IFRS 5 *Non-current Assets Held for Sale and Discontinued Operations* (see **chapter 29**).

Therefore, IAS 36 applies to (among other assets):

- land;
- buildings;
- machinery and equipment;
- investment property carried at cost;
- biological assets carried at cost;
- intangible assets;
- goodwill;
- investments in subsidiaries, associates, and joint ventures; and
- assets carried at revalued amounts under IAS 16 and IAS 38.

Note that, although investments in subsidiaries, associates and joint ventures are financial assets, they are included within the scope of IAS 36.

4 Definitions

The terms used in IAS 36 have specific meanings within the context of the Standard. Therefore, the more important definitions, as set out in IAS 36.6, are set out below for reference.

- Recoverable amount for an asset or a cash-generating unit is the higher of its fair value less costs to sell and its value in use.
- Fair value less costs to sell is the amount obtainable from the sale of an asset or cash-generating unit in an arm's length transaction between knowledgeable, willing parties, less the costs of disposal.

- Costs of disposal are incremental costs directly attributable to the disposal of an asset or cash-generating unit, excluding finance costs and income tax expense.
- Value in use is the present value of the future cash flows expected to be derived from an asset or cash-generating unit.
- An impairment loss is the amount by which the carrying amount of an asset or cash-generating unit exceeds its recoverable amount.
- Carrying amount is the amount at which an asset is recognised in the statement of financial position after deducting any accumulated depreciation (amortisation) and accumulated impairment losses thereon.
- A cash-generating unit (CGU) is the smallest identifiable group of assets that generates cash inflows that are largely independent of the cash inflows from other assets or groups of assets.
- Corporate assets are assets other than goodwill that contribute to the future cash flows of both the cash-generating unit under review and other cash-generating units.
- An active market is a market where all of the following conditions exist:
    - the items traded within the market are homogeneous;
    - willing buyers and sellers can normally be found at any time; and
    - prices are available to the public.

5 Identifying an asset that may be impaired

5.1 Requirements for impairment reviews

An asset is impaired when its carrying amount exceeds its recoverable amount. [IAS 36.8] At the end of each reporting period, entities are required to assess whether there is any indication that an asset may be impaired. If any such indication exists, the entity is required to estimate the recoverable amount of the asset. [IAS 36.9]

Example 5.1

Decline in demand for output

An entity has a machine that was purchased in January 20X1 for £1 million. It is being depreciated over its estimated useful life of 10 years, on a straight-line basis. The carrying amount at 31 December 20X3 is therefore £700,000.

> At 31 December 20X3, the directors become aware that a new technological development means that demand for the output produced by the machine is likely to decline significantly. Under the provisions of IAS 36, they are therefore required to estimate the asset's recoverable amount.

The following items are required to be tested for impairment at least annually, irrespective of whether there is any indication of impairment:

[IAS 36.10]

- intangible assets with an indefinite useful life;
- intangible assets that are not yet available for use; and
- goodwill acquired in a business combination.

Other than in these three specific circumstances (which are discussed at **5.3** below), there is no requirement to make a formal estimate of an asset's recoverable amount if no indication of an impairment loss is present. [IAS 36.8]

5.2 Indications of impairment

The following sections describe a number of indications that an impairment loss may have occurred. In making its assessments as to the possibility of impairment losses having arisen, the entity is required, at a minimum, to consider the indications listed. The lists are not exhaustive, however, and all of the items listed will not apply to every entity. If an impairment indication that is not on these lists exists at the end of the reporting period, a detailed impairment review is required nonetheless. [IAS 36.13]

5.2.1 Internal sources of information

The following internal sources of information may indicate that an asset is impaired:

[IAS 36.12]

- evidence is available of obsolescence or physical damage of the asset;
- significant changes with an adverse effect on the entity have taken place during the period, or are expected to take place in the near future, in the extent to which, or the manner in which, an asset is used or is expected to be used. These changes include the asset becoming idle, plans to discontinue or restructure the operation to

which an asset belongs, plans to dispose of an asset before the previously expected date, and reassessing the useful life of an asset as finite rather than indefinite; or

- evidence is available from internal reporting that indicates that the economic performance of an asset is, or will be, worse than expected.

Such evidence may include:

[IAS 36.14]

- cash flows for acquiring the asset, or subsequent cash needs for operating or maintaining it, that are significantly higher than those originally budgeted; or
- actual net cash flows or operating profit or loss flowing from the asset that are significantly worse than those budgeted; or
- a significant decline in budgeted net cash flows or operating profit, or a significant increase in budgeted loss, flowing from the asset; or
- operating losses or net cash outflows for the asset, when current period figures are aggregated with budgeted figures for the future.

Impairment indicators related to obsolescence or physical damage may be the easiest to identify since they can be observed physically. Items such as unused factory equipment or equipment that has been damaged by fire are two examples that may indicate impairment.

An impairment indication may arise because an asset is to be taken out of use and sold. If the asset qualifies as held for sale, in accordance with IFRS 5 *Non-current Assets Held for Sale and Discontinued Operations*, it will be measured under the rules of that Standard (see **chapter 29**) and will fall outside the scope of IAS 36.

5.2.2 *External sources of information*

The following external sources of information may indicate that an asset is impaired:

[IAS 36.12]

- during the period, the asset's market value has declined significantly more than would be expected as a result of the passage of time or normal use;

Such a decline could be caused by a decrease in the external market value for an asset, such as a head office building, or by a decrease in the sales price of items produced by a group of assets, such as the property, plant and equipment making up a factory.

- significant changes with an adverse effect on the entity have taken place during the period, or will take place in the near future, in the technological, market, economic or legal environment in which the entity operates or in the market to which the asset is dedicated;

For example, if a factory produces a product that is judged harmful to the environment, and the Government introduces a ban on the use of such equipment after a phase-out period, the value of the factory and the associated plant and equipment would need to be assessed. As another example, the value of a luxury hotel would need to be assessed if occupancy rates are declining as a result of a downturn in the economy.

- the carrying amount of the net assets of the reporting entity is more than its market capitalisation;

In some cases, the business prospects of the reporting entity may not have changed, but the sector in which the entity operates may be 'out of favour' with market analysts, resulting in a drop in share price. In such situations, a write-down may not be required, but a formal review should be carried out. In particular, great care should be taken in determining the appropriate discount rate with which to calculate value in use, to ensure that it is consistent with current market assessments.

- market interest rates or other market rates of return on investments have increased during the period, and those increases are likely to affect the discount rate used in calculating the asset's value in use and decrease the asset's recoverable amount materially;

If, in prior years, an asset has been the subject of an impairment test, and, in the current period, there is a change in market interest rates that will affect the discount rate used in the previous calculation, it is appropriate to revisit the calculation. This does not necessarily mean, however, that once an impairment review has been carried out, it must be revisited each year or whenever market rates move. The review is required only when the change in rates is likely to affect materially the recoverable amount of the asset.

- for an investment in a subsidiary, jointly controlled entity or associate, the investor recognises a dividend from the investment and evidence is available that:
    - the carrying amount of the investment in the separate financial statements exceeds the carrying amounts in the consolidated financial statements of the investee's net assets, including associated goodwill; or
    - the dividend exceeds the total comprehensive income of the subsidiary, jointly controlled entity or associate in the period the dividend is declared.

This indicator was added in May 2008 by the Amendments to IFRS 1 and IAS 27 *Cost of an Investment in a Subsidiary, Jointly Controlled Entity or Associate*. As a result of the amendments, dividends paid out of pre-acquisition profits are recognised in profit or loss, rather than as a reduction of the cost of the associated investment (see **6.1.1** in **chapter 33**). Accordingly, where a dividend reduces the recoverable amount of an investment to below its carrying amount, the investment is impaired. The amendment to IAS 36 applies prospectively for annual periods beginning on or after 1 January 2009, but earlier application is permitted. If an entity applies the related amendments to IAS 27 for an earlier period, it must apply the amendment to IAS 36 at the same time

IAS 36.16 specifically states that no formal review is required when the discount rate used in calculating the asset's value in use is:

- unlikely to be affected by the increase in market interest rates or other market rates of return on investments. For example, increases in short-term interest rates may not have a material effect on the discount rate used for an asset that has a long remaining useful life; or
- likely to be affected by the increase in these market rates, but previous sensitivity analysis of recoverable amount shows that:
    - it is unlikely that there will be a material decrease in the recoverable amount because future cash flows are also likely to increase. For example, in some cases, an entity may be able to demonstrate that it adjusts its revenues to compensate for any increase in market rates; or
    - the decrease in recoverable amount is unlikely to result in a material impairment loss.

If there is an indication that the asset may be impaired, the underlying facts should be kept in mind when performing the annual review of the useful life of the asset, the depreciation or amortisation method and the estimated residual value. These items may need to be adjusted even if no impairment loss is recognised. [IAS 36.17]

5.2.3 *Other examples of impairment indicators*

5.2.3.1 Investment property

In addition to the events and circumstances detailed in IAS 36.12, the following conditions may indicate that an investor may be unable to realise the carrying amount of an investment property:

- the investor recently sold a portion of its income-generating investment properties and realised losses on the sale transactions;
- the business plan indicates that the investor may liquidate a portion of its investment property portfolio in the coming year, but has not identified yet which properties will be sold;
- income-generating properties have significant vacancy rates or are expected to be vacant in the near future (e.g. because of non-competitive lease terms);
- depressed market conditions are adversely affecting the rental or sale activities of significant properties.
- the investor does not appear to have the ability to recover the current net carrying amount of investment properties from future cash flows because of a decline in rental rates or occupancy rates; or
- the investor is encountering cash flow difficulties, which may require forced sale of some or all of its investment properties.

The above list is not meant to be all inclusive. Judgement is required to identify circumstances that may indicate impairment in the carrying amount of an investment property or group of properties.

5.2.3.2 *Alternative use of an asset*

Example 5.2.3.2

Alternative use of an asset

A regional railway operator has been in the process of constructing a pier which would accept waterborne freight for transfer onto its railway carriages. The entity is two years into construction, and the project has exceeded its original budget and time schedule. Due to the delays and other advances in waterborne freight transfer, the entity's management is considering alternative uses for the project. Specifically, the entity is considering using the facility as a container yard for offloading bulk products such as salt and construction aggregate. The entity's intent is to begin operating the site as a container yard, as opposed to an off-loading facility for ocean-going vessels, as originally intended.

The entity should perform an impairment test of the asset. In accordance with IAS 36.12(f), the intent to begin operating the site as a container yard clearly represents a significant change in the manner in which an asset is used, and it would appear reasonable that a change such as this may have an adverse effect on the entity. As such, the entity should perform an impairment assessment by comparing recoverable amount, being the higher of value in use and fair value less costs to sell, to the carrying amount of the asset. If the recoverable amount is lower than the carrying amount, an impairment loss must be recognised.

5.2.3.3 *Appraisal or valuation below carrying amount*

The existence of an appraisal or other independent valuation information that indicates the fair value less costs to sell of a held and used asset is below its carrying amount does not, in and of itself, require that an impairment loss be recognised. Where the asset's carrying amount was previously assessed using value in use, the entity should consider whether the appraisal is an indicator of impairment – it is possible that the factors resulting in the lower valuation do not affect the value in use calculations. Where the entity does consider the lower valuation to be an indicator of impairment, the entity should calculate the value in use of the asset. If the recoverable amount of the asset, that is the higher of the asset's fair value less costs to sell and value in use, is less than its carrying amount, then an impairment loss should be recognised.

5.2.3.4 *Capitalised costs of computer software*

In addition to the general indicators of impairment in the Standard, capitalised computer software costs should be tested for impairment if, for example, any of the following events or circumstances occurs:

- the internal-use computer software is not expected to provide service potential as originally planned;
- a significant change occurs in the extent or manner in which the software is used or is expected to be used such that previously capitalised costs are not expected to have further benefit;
- a significant change is made or will be made to the software program such that previously capitalised costs are not expected to have further benefit; or
- the costs of developing or modifying internal-use computer software significantly exceed the amount originally expected to develop or modify the software.

Some software may, during development or after development, no longer be expected to provide any service. When it is no longer probable that computer software being developed will be completed and placed into service, the asset should be impaired.

Indications that the software may no longer be expected to be completed and placed in service include the following:

- a lack of expenditures budgeted or being incurred for the project;
- programming difficulties that cannot be resolved on a timely basis;
- significant cost overruns;
- the costs of internally-developed software will significantly exceed the costs of comparable third-party software, and management intends to acquire the third-party software instead of completing the internally-developed software;
- technologies are introduced in the marketplace, so that management now intends to obtain third-party software instead of completing the internally developed software; or
- the business segment or unit to which the software relates, or relates in part, is unprofitable and has been or will be discontinued.

The above lists are not meant to be all inclusive. Judgement is required to identify circumstances that may indicate impairment in the carrying amount of internal-use computer software.

5.2.3.5 *Impairment indicators after the reporting period*

If information is received after the reporting period that indicates an asset was impaired at the end of the reporting period, then an impairment exercise should be carried out.

However, if management has already assessed impairment indicators as at the end of the reporting period, impairment events (including those arising as a result of management decisions) occurring thereafter usually are not indicative of conditions existing at the end of the reporting period and, therefore, should not be adjusted for. Instead, they should be disclosed when they are of such importance that non-disclosure would affect decisions of the users of the financial statements.

5.2.3.6 *Events and circumstances indicating an impairment of goodwill*

In addition to testing goodwill for impairment annually, goodwill should be tested for impairment whenever there is an indicator that it might be impaired (as for other assets). The following are examples of events and circumstances that might indicate that goodwill is impaired.

- the merger of business information systems does not occur as planned, and the acquirer does not achieve the savings that were expected from operating a merged system;
- industrial agreements do not permit the level of workplace reform that the acquirer had planned, and the employee headcount is higher than that planned at acquisition;
- the acquirer identified at acquisition the feasibility of developing several research projects, and these projects subsequently have been abandoned;

- a regulatory ruling prevents the acquirer from operating in certain markets, and the acquirer will not achieve the level of sales planned at acquisition; or

- a competitor introduces a new product earlier than expected, and the acquirer will not achieve the level of sales planned at acquisition.

The above list is not meant to be all inclusive. Judgement is required to identify circumstances that may indicate impairment of goodwill.

5.2.3.7 *Asset life shortened by physical damage*

Example 5.2.3.7

Asset life shortened by physical damage

An entity has an asset that has been damaged such that the life of the asset has been shortened, but the carrying amount of the asset will still be recovered by the cash flows over the shortened life. The damage to the asset will provide an indicator of impairment in accordance with IAS 36.12(e) and, therefore, the asset must be tested for impairment.

As the carrying amount of the asset will be recovered by the cash flows during the revised useful life, no impairment should be recognised. Nevertheless, the useful life of the asset is changed and the depreciation amount should be recalculated prospectively and accounted for as a change in estimate in accordance with the requirements of IAS 8 *Accounting Policies, Changes in Accounting Estimates and Errors*.

5.3 Requirements for annual reviews

As noted at **5.1** above, irrespective of whether there is any indication of impairment, the following items are required to be tested for impairment at least annually:

[IAS 36.10]

- intangible assets with an indefinite useful life;
- intangible assets that are not yet available for use; and
- goodwill acquired in a business combination.

5.3.1 *Intangible assets*

Intangible assets with an indefinite useful life, and intangible assets not yet available for use, are tested for impairment, by comparing their carrying amounts with their recoverable amounts, both:

[IAS 36.10(a)]

- annually; and
- whenever there is an indication, at the end of a reporting period, that the asset may be impaired.

The Standard allows that the annual impairment test may be performed at any time during the annual period, provided that it is performed at the same time every year. Different intangible assets may be tested for impairment at different times. [IAS 36.10(a)]

In the case of a newly-recognised intangible asset (e.g. an intangible asset with an indefinite useful life purchased in the current period), an impairment test must be carried out before the end of the current annual period. [IAS 36.10(a)]

Although the Standard requires an annual review for the specified intangible assets, it does allow that the most recent detailed calculation of an asset's recoverable amount made in a preceding period may be used in the impairment test for that asset in the current period, provided that the following criteria are met:

[IAS 36.24]

- the most recent recoverable amount calculation resulted in an amount that exceeded the asset's carrying amount by a substantial margin;
- based on an analysis of events that have occurred and circumstances that have changed since the most recent recoverable amount calculation, the likelihood that a current recoverable amount determination would be less than the asset's carrying amount is remote; and
- for intangible assets tested for impairment as part of a cash-generating unit (see **8.1** below), the assets and liabilities making up that unit have not changed significantly since the most recent recoverable amount calculation.

5.3.2 *Goodwill*

Impairment testing for goodwill is always carried out in the context of a cash-generating unit (CGU) or group of CGUs, since goodwill does not generate cash flows independently of other assets. The detailed rules for the allocation of goodwill to cash-generating units are set out in **8.1.2** below.

5.3.2.1 CGUs to which goodwill has been allocated

Where goodwill has been allocated to a CGU, or to a group of CGUs (in the circumstances discussed at **8.1.2**), that unit or group of units is tested for impairment both:

[IAS 36.90]

- annually; and
- whenever there is an indication that the unit, or group of units, may be impaired.

The impairment test is carried out by comparing the carrying amount of the unit (or group of units), including the goodwill, with the recoverable amount of the unit(s). If the recoverable amount of the unit(s) exceeds the carrying amount of the unit(s), the unit(s) and the goodwill allocated to the unit(s) are not regarded as impaired. If the carrying amount of the unit, or group of units, exceeds its (their) recoverable amount, the entity recognises an impairment loss in accordance with the rules set out in **9.2** below. [IAS 36.90]

5.3.2.2 Timing of impairment tests

The annual impairment test for a CGU to which goodwill has been allocated may be performed at any time during the annual period, provided that it is performed at the same time every year. Different CGUs may be tested for impairment at different times. [IAS 36.96]

Where some or all of the goodwill allocated to a CGU was acquired in a business combination during the current annual period, that CGU must be tested for impairment before the end of the current annual period. [IAS 36.96]

Example 5.3.2.2

Timing of impairment tests

An entity routinely tests goodwill for impairment in the second quarter of its annual reporting period. During the current reporting period, the entity makes an acquisition in which goodwill arises. The goodwill is allocated to

CGUs in accordance with the requirements of IAS 36 during the third quarter of the reporting period. There is no indication that the acquired or existing goodwill is impaired.

Although there is no indication that the acquired goodwill is impaired and the annual impairment test for goodwill has already been performed, a further impairment test must be conducted before the end of the current reporting period on each CGU to which the newly acquired goodwill has been allocated.

5.3.2.3 *Individual asset that may be impaired tested before CGU*

Where assets within a CGU (such as intangibles with indefinite lives) are tested for impairment at the same time as the CGU, the assets should be tested first. Similarly, where CGUs are tested for impairment at the same time as the group of CGUs to which they belong and to which goodwill has been allocated in aggregate, the individual CGUs should be tested first. [IAS 36.97]

In addition, at the time of testing a CGU to which goodwill has been allocated, there may be an indication of an impairment of an asset within the CGU. In such circumstances, the individual asset is tested for impairment first (and any identified impairment loss relating to that asset is recognised) before the CGU is tested for impairment. This is so as to ensure that any losses that can be identified with specific assets are not 'lost' in the testing of the CGU. Similarly, where goodwill has been allocated to a group of CGUs, and there is an indication that an individual CGU within the group is impaired, the individual CGU is tested for impairment first (and any identified impairment loss relating to the individual CGU recognised) before testing for impairment the group of units to which goodwill has been allocated. [IAS 36.98]

Example 5.3.2.3A

Assets that provide no future benefit

An entity provides worldwide wireless communications to its customers through a network of ten satellites. The entity has determined appropriately that its satellite business as a whole represents a 'lowest level' for which identifiable cash flows largely are independent of the cash flows of other assets and liabilities. A meteorite destroys one satellite. However, the entity can continue to provide worldwide service with the remaining nine satellites. Although the entity continues to have positive cash flows from its satellite communications business, the entity must recognise the loss of a satellite. IAS 36 does not allow an entity to continue to recognise, as an asset, an item that no longer meets the definition of an asset.

Example 5.3.2.3B

Asset within cash-generating unit that no longer contributes to cash flows

A machine within a cash-generating unit (CGU) has become redundant and is no longer contributing to cash flows. Its carrying amount exceeds its recoverable amount. However, the recoverable amount of the CGU is above its carrying amount.

The entity should recognise an impairment loss for the machine, as its carrying amount is above its recoverable amount. The general principle is that impairment should be identified at the individual asset level, where possible. The recoverable amount should be calculated for the smallest CGU to which the asset belongs only where the recoverable amount for the individual asset cannot be identified. The machine is no longer in use and, therefore, no longer belongs to the CGU. The smallest CGU is now the machine itself. The entity can determine the future cash inflows arising from using this machine; they are nil. Therefore, the entity should determine the fair value less costs to sell of the machine, as it is possible the machine has some scrap or resale value, and recognise the impairment loss identified.

5.3.2.4 *Rolling forward detailed calculations from a preceding period*

Although the Standard requires an annual review for CGUs to which goodwill has been allocated, it does allow that the most recent detailed calculation of the unit's recoverable amount made in a preceding period may be used in the impairment test for that unit in the current period, provided that the following criteria are met:

[IAS 36.99]

- the assets and liabilities making up the unit have not changed significantly since the most recent recoverable amount calculation;
- the most recent recoverable amount calculation resulted in an amount that exceeded the unit's carrying amount by a substantial margin; and
- based on an analysis of events that have occurred and circumstances that have changed since the most recent recoverable amount calculation, the likelihood that a current recoverable amount determination would be less than the unit's carrying amount is remote.

5.3.2.5 *CGUs to which it has not been possible to allocate goodwill*

As discussed in **8.1.2**, it may not be possible to allocate goodwill to an individual CGU to which it relates. Where that is the case the unit concerned is tested for impairment whenever there is an indication that the unit may be impaired, by comparing the unit's carrying amount, excluding any goodwill, with its recoverable amount. Any impairment loss is recognised in accordance with the rules set out in **9.2** below. [IAS 36.88]

Where no goodwill has been allocated to a CGU but the CGU includes an intangible asset that has an indefinite life or that is not yet available for use, it will be necessary to carry out an annual impairment test for that CGU if that asset can be tested for impairment only as part of the CGU. [IAS 36.89] In such circumstances, the rules of **5.3.1** above apply.

6 Measurement of recoverable amount

An asset or CGU is considered to be impaired when its recoverable amount declines below its carrying amount. Following the identification of any indication of impairment, the entity is required to make a formal estimate of the recoverable amount of the asset or CGU. [IAS 36.8] It is only by making such an estimate that the entity can determine whether an impairment loss has occurred.

The recoverable amount of an asset is the higher of its fair value less costs to sell and its value in use. The Standard measures impairment loss based on an assumption that the entity will choose to recover the carrying amount of the asset in the most beneficial way. Therefore, if the entity could earn more by selling the asset than by continuing to use it, it would choose to sell the asset, and vice versa.

Example 6A

Measurement of recoverable amount

An entity buys a machine for £7 million on 1 January 20X1. The asset has a 7 year life, with nil residual value. The carrying amount at 31 December 20X3 is £4 million.

Due to changes in market conditions, the entity considers that the machine may be impaired. It is determined that the asset could be sold for £2 million (with selling costs of £200,000). The directors have estimated that the value in use of the asset is £3.5 million.

First, the fair value less costs to sell of the asset (£1.8 million) is compared with the estimated value in use (£3.5 million). The recoverable amount is the higher of these, i.e. £3.5 million.

The recoverable amount is then compared with the carrying amount and an impairment loss of £500,000 is recognised.

Example 6B

Requirement to determine fair value less costs to sell

An entity is reviewing all of its assets for impairment as a result of a fall in the market price for its products. The entity's plant is 10 years old and has a carrying amount of £80 million and a value in use of £75 million, considering the revised price of the products. A similar plant (belonging to one of the entity's competitors) was sold for £82 million. Costs attributable to the disposal would be around £1 million. There is an active market for the plant assets. Management has no intention to sell the plant.

The fair value less costs to sell (£81 million) is higher than the value in use, and, therefore, is identified as the recoverable amount. The carrying amount is less than the recoverable amount, so no impairment loss should be recognised.

In order to measure an impairment loss, it is sometimes necessary to calculate both fair value less costs to sell and value in use, but often this will not be necessary:

- if either the fair value less costs to sell or the value in use is found to be higher than the carrying amount, the asset is not impaired, and there is no need to calculate the other amount;

- if no reliable estimate of fair value less cost to sell is available, recoverable amount is measured by reference to value in use alone; and

- the detailed calculations involved in measuring value in use may be avoided if a simple estimate is sufficient to show either that value in use is higher than the carrying amount (in which case there is no impairment) or that it is lower than fair value less costs to sell (in which case recoverable amount is the fair value less costs to sell).

Recoverable amount is determined for an individual asset, unless the asset does not generate cash inflows that are largely independent of those from other assets or groups of assets. If this is the case, recoverable amount is determined for the cash-generating unit to which the asset belongs (see **8.1** below), unless either:

[IAS 36.22]

- the asset's fair value less costs to sell is higher than its carrying amount; or

- the asset's value in use can be estimated to be close to its fair value less costs to sell and fair value less costs to sell can be determined.

7 Fair value less costs to sell

This section discusses the measurement of fair value less costs to sell for an asset or CGU. For guidance on the identification of CGUs, see **8.1**.

7.1 Definition

The fair value less costs to sell of an asset or CGU is the amount obtainable from the sale of the asset or CGU in an arm's length transaction between knowledgeable, willing parties, less costs of disposal. [IAS 36.6]

Costs of disposal to be deducted in arriving at fair value less costs to sell include:

[IAS 36.28]

- legal costs;
- stamp duty or similar transaction taxes;
- costs of removing the asset; and
- other direct incremental costs to bring the asset into condition for its sale.

Finance costs and income taxes are excluded from the definition of costs of disposal. [IAS 36.6]

Costs such as termination benefits to employees and reorganisation expenses following a disposal are not considered direct, incremental costs of sale and, as such, are not deducted in arriving at fair value less costs to sell. [IAS 36.28]

> Care should be taken not to include disposal costs twice. For example, where an entity already had an obligation to remove an asset at the end of its life, a provision will have been set up and those costs will already be included in the carrying amount of the asset. Accordingly, in this situation, either:
>
> - the costs should not be included as costs of disposal in arriving at fair value less costs to sell; or

- in some cases, for example where the buyer will have to assume the liability, it may be necessary to deduct the carrying amount of the liability from that of the asset in order to determine a carrying amount that can be compared with fair value less costs to sell, in accordance with IAS 36.29 and IAS 36.78 (see **8.1.1**).

7.2 Revalued assets

As discussed in **section 3**, the scope of IAS 36 includes some assets carried at fair value (e.g. property, plant and equipment accounted for under IAS 16's revaluation model – see **chapter 6**). Intuitively, one might assume that there should be no material difference between the carrying amount of the asset and the amount for which it could be sold. There will be circumstances, however, where IAS 36's determination of the asset's recoverable amount will differ from its recorded fair value. For example:

[IAS 36.5]

- if the asset's fair value is its market value, then the only difference between the carrying amount and the asset's fair value less costs to sell is the direct incremental costs to dispose of the asset:
  - if the disposal costs are negligible, the recoverable amount of a revalued asset is, by definition, close to, or greater than, its revalued amount (i.e. fair value). In this case, after the revaluation requirements have been applied, it is unlikely that the revalued asset is impaired and recoverable amount need not be estimated; but
  - if the disposal costs are not negligible, the fair value less costs to sell of the revalued asset is necessarily less than its fair value. Therefore, the revalued asset will be impaired if its value in use is less than its revalued amount (i.e. fair value). In this case, after the revaluation requirements have been applied, the entity will apply IAS 36 to determine whether the asset may be impaired; and
- if the asset's fair value is determined on a basis other than its market value, its revalued amount (i.e. fair value) may be greater than or lower than its recoverable amount. Hence, after the revaluation requirements have been applied, the entity should apply IAS 36 to determine whether the asset may be impaired.

7.3 Evidence to support estimated fair value less costs to sell

If an estimate of fair value less costs to sell is required, the following sources represent the best evidence (in descending order of preference):

- a price in a binding sale agreement in an arm's length transaction, adjusted for incremental, directly attributable disposal costs; [IAS 36.25]
- the bid price in an active market (as defined in **section 4** above) less costs of disposal. If current bid prices are unavailable, the price of the most recent transaction may provide a basis from which to estimate fair value less costs to sell, if there has not been a significant change in economic circumstances between the transaction date and the estimation date; [IAS 36.26] and
- the best information available to reflect the amount that the entity could obtain, at the end of the reporting period, for the disposal of the asset in an arm's length transaction after deducting the costs of disposal. The outcome of recent transactions for similar assets within the same industry may provide a basis for the estimate. Unless management is compelled to sell immediately, the estimate should not reflect a forced sale. [IAS 36.27]

8 Value in use

The calculation of value in use can be broken down into four stages:

- the identification of cash-generating units;
- the estimation of expected future cash flows;
- the determination of an appropriate discount rate; and
- discounting and aggregating expected cash flows to arrive at value in use.

8.1 Stage 1: The identification of cash-generating units (CGUs)

If the recoverable amount of an asset can be individually determined, this stage is omitted.

It is often not possible to estimate the recoverable amount of an individual asset since assets frequently generate cash when working together rather than singly. When this is the case, an entity should determine the recoverable amount of the CGU to which the asset belongs. [IAS 36.66]

A cash-generating unit is defined as the smallest identifiable group of assets that generates cash inflows that are largely independent of the cash inflows from other assets or groups of assets. [IAS 36.6]

IAS 36.67 specifically states that the recoverable amount of an individual asset cannot be determined when both of the following conditions exist:

- the value in use of the asset cannot be estimated to be close to its fair value less costs to sell (e.g. when the future cash flows from the continuing use of the asset are not negligible); and
- the asset does not generate cash inflows that are largely independent of those from other assets.

Examples 8.1A and **8.1B** below are reproduced from the Standard.

Example 8.1A

Recoverable amount cannot be determined

[IAS 36.67]

A mining entity owns a private railway to support its mining activities. The private railway could be sold only for scrap value and it does not generate cash inflows that are largely independent of the cash inflows from the other assets of the mine.

It is not possible to estimate the recoverable amount of the private railway because its value in use cannot be determined and is probably different from scrap value. Therefore, the entity estimates the recoverable amount of the cash-generating unit to which the private railway belongs, i.e. the mine as a whole.

Example 8.1B

Lowest aggregation of assets that generate largely independent cash flows

[IAS 36.68]

A bus company provides services under contract with a municipality that requires minimum service on each of five separate routes. Assets devoted to each route and the cash flows from each route can be identified separately. One of the routes operates at a significant loss.

Because the entity does not have the option to curtail any one bus route, the lowest level of identifiable cash inflows that are largely independent of the cash inflows from other assets or groups of assets is the cash inflows generated by the five routes together. The cash-generating unit for each route is the bus company as a whole.

When the recoverable amount of an individual asset cannot be determined, its CGU should be identified as the lowest aggregation of assets that generates largely independent cash inflows. [IAS 36.68]

Example 8.1C

Grouping of assets to be held and used

A national wireless communication provider owns each set of antennae, radio transmitters, and receivers (collectively referred to as 'antennae') installed on cell towers which together provide the infrastructure of its telecommunications network. A set of antennae is damaged in an electrical storm to the extent that the antennae will no longer be able to provide services to customers within a particular region. However, a mile away, on another cell tower, a similar set of unused antennae is available to replace the service provided by the damaged set of antennae such that the service to the regional area will be virtually uninterrupted, and all cash flow streams will remain intact. This interchangeability is a feature deliberately built into the integrated logistical design of the network.

The identifiable cash flows of each set of antennae are not largely independent. In this case, there is not a specific cash flow attributable to the individual set of antennae as they are almost instantaneously interchangeable, and as a result, on an individual antennae set basis, their ability or inability to operate does not affect cash inflows. However, the set of antennae is part of a group of assets that make up the entity's national network of towers and antennae, and this national network generates joint cash flows. As the wireless communication provider operates using a national network, the national network infrastructure asset group would be the asset group representing the lowest level of cash generating unit for the purposes of analysing the network infrastructure for impairment. The national wireless communication provider should assess the network infrastructure for impairment based on the joint cash flows provided by the group of assets.

Example 8.1D

Identification of cash generating units in the retail industry

Entity A, a retail company, operates three stores that generate largely independent cash inflows. The three stores share expenditures (cash outflows) such as infrastructure, marketing, pricing policies, and human resources. When A is tested for impairment under IAS 36, can A's cash-generating unit be composed of the three stores, on the basis that the net cash flows associated with the stores are interdependent?

IAS 36.6 defines a cash-generating unit as the smallest identifiable group of assets that generates cash inflows that are largely independent of the cash inflows from other assets or groups of assets.

The definition of a cash-generating unit requires the identification of an asset's cash-generating unit on the basis of independent cash inflows generated by the asset, not independent net cash flows (i.e. cash inflows and outflows). Therefore, outflows such as shared infrastructure and marketing expenditures are not considered when identifying a cash-generating unit. When a store is tested for impairment under IAS 36, the store's cash-generating unit is the store itself.

Example 8.1E

Grouping of assets after disposal of the primary asset

An entity in the retail industry has several retail locations. One of the entity's stores has had negative operating results for the past year. The entity identified the store as a cash-generating unit. Appropriately, the entity performed a test for impairment of its assets as of the year end, 30 June 20X1. The entity is the lessee of the physical store location, and accounts for this lease as a finance lease. Additionally, the entity owned certain assets (computers, forklifts, etc.), which could be sold or transferred to other stores. The entity's impairment calculation determined the assets under finance lease had negative cash flows of 600,000. However, the assets other than the assets under finance lease had positive cash flows of 250,000.

The entity has to determine the value in use of the cash-generating unit, which is the store. The cash inflows of the store and, therefore, the operations of the store depend on the assets under finance lease and the other assets which are inter-related; therefore, the impairment test should be carried out by aggregating all the assets, resulting in a total impairment of 350,000.

However, if the entity subsequently commits to a plan to abandon the finance lease and transfer or sell the other assets, the other assets would be independent of the finance lease, because they would not form part of the generation of cash inflows from the store. Therefore, for purposes of recognition and measurement of an impairment loss, the other assets would no longer be grouped with the assets under the finance lease. The other assets may fall within IFRS 5 (see **chapter 29**) or may be reallocated to other cash generating units if they are to be transferred to other stores.

Cash inflows are inflows of cash and cash equivalents received from parties outside the reporting entity. In general terms, cash inflows are likely to follow the way in which management monitors and makes decisions about continuing or closing the different lines of business of the entity. [IAS 36.69]

Unique intangible assets, such as brands and mastheads, are generally seen to generate cash independently of each other and are usually monitored separately. Hence, they can often be used to identify CGUs. Other CGUs may be identified by reference to major products or services.

If an active market exists for the output produced by an asset or a group of assets, it should be identified as a CGU, even if some or all of the output is used internally. The asset or group of assets forms a separate CGU if the entity could sell this output on an active market. This is because this asset or group of assets *could* generate cash inflows that would be largely independent of the cash flows from other assets or groups of assets. [IAS 36.70 & 71]

In the circumstances described in the previous paragraph, management estimates the expected market price for the output of the unit and uses that estimate not only when determining the value in use of the supplying unit, but also when determining the value in use of the other CGU which is using the output. In other words, market prices rather than internal transfer prices are used when estimating the recoverable amount of a CGU. [IAS 36.70]

Example 8.1F

Active market for product

An entity manufactures 2 products – Product 1 and Product 2. Product 1 is manufactured in the entity's Taiwanese factory, and all of the items produced are transferred to the entity's UK factory where they are used in the assembly of Product 2. The entity does not sell Product 1.

If there is an active market for Product 1, then the Taiwanese factory is treated as a separate CGU. The value in use of the Taiwanese factory is calculated using the market price of the units of Product 1 produced. The estimated value in use of the UK factory will be calculated using the market price of the units of Product 1 purchased as the basis for estimating cash outflows for purchase of subcomponents.

CGUs should be identified consistently from period to period for the same asset or types of assets, unless a change is justified. [IAS 36.72] When a change is made during a period in which an impairment loss is recognised or reversed, disclosure is required of the current and former ways of aggregating assets and the reasons for changing the way the CGU is identified (see **11.3** below).

Example 8.1G illustrates two examples of the identification of CGUs.

Example 8.1G

Interchangeable products

A publisher owns a particular publishing title. The title is sold in both paper and electronic form. In general, customers will purchase either the paper or the electronic version, not both, depending upon their individual circumstances. It has been demonstrated that demand for one affects demand for the other.

The assets used for the production of both the paper and electronic versions of the title comprise one CGU.

Service entities

Some service entities, such as those involved in the telecommunications sector, will have substantial assets to support their services. The arrangement and use of the assets will generally indicate appropriate CGUs.

Other service entities may have very few assets, especially if office buildings are leased. In such entities, the importance of identifying CGUs is not in determining how to allocate assets to the CGUs, but in being able to make accurate estimates of levels of demand for the various services provided.

If an entity provides regional services, it may be appropriate to identify each region as a separate CGU, if economic decisions are taken by region. In contrast, if unprofitable regional offices are supported because overall coverage is necessary to the business as a whole, then 'countrywide' CGUs may be appropriate.

Readers should also refer to the first of the Illustrative Examples published with IAS 36, which includes several examples of the identification of CGUs.

Example 8.1H sets out other examples of the identification of CGUs.

Example 8.1H

Restaurant chains

For restaurant chains with multiple restaurants in one location, demand for one affects demand for the other so it is unlikely to be appropriate to look at the income of one restaurant in isolation from the others in the same location. Also, it is unlikely that any one restaurant would be material. Therefore, where there are many outlets, impairment reviews normally would be carried out on the basis of groupings in the same location/affected by the same economic conditions.

For restaurant chains without multiple restaurants in a single location, each restaurant is likely to be a separate CGU, because its income is independent of the income of other restaurants. The cash inflows of each restaurant can be individually monitored and sensible allocations of costs to each restaurant can be made. However, since any impairment of individual restaurants is unlikely to be material, it is likely that management might monitor goodwill at a higher level than the individual restaurant level for internal reporting purposes. Accordingly, groups of restaurants that are affected by the same economic factors may be reviewed for impairment together if that is the methodology for monitoring the performance of goodwill used by management.

Retailers

Often, it is difficult to determine for retail chains whether a CGU is an individual site, a group of sites in a region, a country, or the whole business. For the majority of modern multi-site retailers, some level of aggregation of sites is normally appropriate. A larger grouping can be treated as a CGU or each site can be taken to be a CGU, though in the latter case a pragmatic view of aggregation may be taken on grounds of materiality, as in the above restaurant example. In some circumstances it may be impractical (or at least costly) to prepare detailed cash flow forecasts for each individual site. Furthermore, forecasts may, to some extent, be based on macro-assumptions about factors that affect larger groupings in a similar way.

Bank branches

Bank branches generally sell a variety of products that are supported by central operations. In many ways, the outlets represent a conduit for the central organisation which determines product pricing on a national basis. Whilst it may be possible to look at the income of each branch as being separate from the others, it is likely that very broad assumptions would need to be made to arrive at a measure of profitability, particularly in respect of recurring products such as life policies and savings schemes. It is unlikely that a branch is a CGU, unless for some reason management addresses profitability or contribution at a branch level. Also, it is unlikely that an individual branch would be material to the organisation.

Hotels

Individual hotels usually would generate income that is largely independent of others, and their performance would be monitored closely by management on an individual basis. It is, therefore, probable that they form individual CGUs, even if there are central sales, marketing, and finance functions. A hotel chain that markets itself centrally to business customers might operate a loss-making hotel in a higher cost location to secure group wide contracts or a nationally advertised price pledge. In such circumstances, it might be argued that the performance of goodwill is managed by reference to a larger group than the individual hotel, and, accordingly, a number of hotels would be combined in testing for impairment of the related goodwill.

> **Petrol stations**
>
> The income of individual petrol stations is likely to be closely monitored by management, and costs are likely to be able to be determined to arrive at a measure of profitability. If management would consider closing one station depending upon its individual performance, each petrol station may be a CGU — similar to the above restaurant example. However, it is unlikely that any one station owned by a major operator would be material, and, therefore, it is likely that the performance of goodwill is measured at a higher level for the purposes of internal reporting. Accordingly, where a large number of outlets is involved, impairment reviews normally would be carried out on the basis of groupings affected by the same economic conditions.

8.1.1 Allocation of assets and liabilities to CGUs

The allocation of assets and liabilities to a CGU, so as to establish the carrying amount of the CGU, should be determined on a basis consistent with the way the recoverable amount of the CGU is determined. [IAS 36.75]

As a general rule, the carrying amount of a CGU:

[IAS 36.76]

- includes the carrying amount of only those assets that can be attributed directly, or allocated on a reasonable and consistent basis, to the CGU and that will generate the future cash inflows used in determining the CGU's value in use; and
- does not include the carrying amount of any recognised liability, unless the recoverable amount of the CGU cannot be determined without consideration of this liability.

This allocation is consistent with the calculation of fair value less costs to sell and value in use of a CGU, which both exclude cash flows that relate to assets outside the CGU and liabilities that have already been recognised in the financial statements (see Stage 2 at **8.2** below). [IAS 36.76]

There will be some assets that contribute to cash flows, such as corporate assets and goodwill, that cannot be allocated to the CGU on a reasonable and consistent basis. These are dealt with in **8.1.2** (goodwill) and **8.1.3** (corporate assets) below.

In some situations, due to the nature of a particular recognised and recorded liability, it may be appropriate to include it in the carrying amount and the recoverable amount of a CGU. This will be the case when a CGU could not be sold without the assumption of the related liability by the buyer. In such circumstances, the fair value less costs to sell of the CGU is the estimated sales price for the assets and the liability together, less disposal costs. In order to be consistent and compare like with like, the carrying amount of the liability should be deducted in determining both the value in use and carrying amount of the CGU. [IAS 36.78]

Example 8.1.1 below is reproduced from the Standard.

Example 8.1.1

Liability included in CGU

[IAS 36.78]

A company operates a mine in a country where legislation requires that the owner must restore the site on completion of its mining operations. The cost of restoration includes the replacement of the overburden, which must be removed before mining operations commence. A provision for the costs to replace the overburden was recognised as soon as the overburden was removed. The amount provided was recognised as part of the cost of the mine and is being depreciated over the mine's useful life. The carrying amount of the provision for restoration costs is CU500, which is equal to the present value of the restoration costs.

The entity is testing the mine for impairment. The cash-generating unit for the mine is the mine as a whole. The entity has received various offers to buy the mine at a price of around CU800. This price reflects the fact that the buyer will assume the obligation to restore the overburden. Disposal costs for the mine are negligible. The value in use of the mine is approximately CU1,200, excluding restoration costs. The carrying amount of the mine is CU1,000.

The cash-generating unit's fair value less costs to sell is CU800. This amount considers restoration costs that have already been provided for. As a consequence, the value in use for the cash-generating unit is determined after consideration of the restoration costs and is estimated to be CU700 (CU1,200 less CU500). The carrying amount of the cash-generating unit is CU500, which is the carrying amount of the mine (CU1,000) less the carrying amount of the provision for restoration costs (CU500). Therefore, the recoverable amount of the cash-generating unit exceeds its carrying amount.

IAS 36.79 states that, for practical purposes, it is sometimes necessary to include assets that are not part of the CGU (e.g. receivables or other financial assets) or liabilities that have already been recognised in the financial statements (e.g. payables, pensions and other provisions) when determining recoverable amount. Where this is the case, these items are also included in the carrying amount of the CGU.

Therefore, although best practice is to exclude these items, if they are included they should be included consistently, i.e. both in the carrying amount of the CGU and in the estimation of recoverable amount. To do otherwise would be to compare unlike items.

8.1.2 *Allocation of goodwill to CGUs*

For the purpose of impairment testing, goodwill acquired in a business combination is, from the acquisition date, required to be allocated to each of the acquirer's CGUs, or groups of CGUs, that are expected to benefit from the synergies of the combination, irrespective of whether other assets or liabilities of the acquiree are assigned to those units or groups of units. [IAS 36.80]

UK

FRS 11 does not envisage that goodwill arising on an acquisition may be allocated to any income generating units other than those acquired.

Goodwill recognised in a business combination is an asset representing the future economic benefits arising from other assets acquired in a business combination that are not individually identified and separately recognised. Goodwill does not generate cash flows independently of other assets or groups of assets and, therefore, it will always be tested for impairment as part of a CGU or a group of CGUs. [IAS 36.81]

In fact, it may not be possible to allocate goodwill to individual CGUs on a reasonable basis. It will often be the case that goodwill can only be allocated to a group of CGUs. IAS 36 permits such aggregation provided that the CGU or group of CGUs to which goodwill is allocated:

[IAS 36.80]

- represents the lowest level within the entity at which goodwill is monitored for internal management purposes; and

- is not larger than an operating segment determined in accordance with IFRS 8 *Operating Segments* (see **chapter 37**). (Where an entity has not yet adopted IFRS 8, each CGU or group of CGUs to which goodwill is allocated should not be larger than a segment based on either the entity's primary or the entity's secondary reporting format determined in accordance with IAS 14 *Segment Reporting* (see **appendix 1**)).

The objective of the IASB in setting these conditions is to require entities to allocate goodwill to the lowest possible level without resorting to arbitrary allocations and without, generally, having to develop new or additional reporting systems to perform impairment testing. The Board's approach is that goodwill should be tested for impairment at a level at which information about the operations of the entity and the assets that support them is provided for internal reporting purposes.

In many cases, the goodwill purchased in a business combination enhances the value of all of the acquirer's pre-existing cash-generating units. Some might argue that, in such circumstances, goodwill should be tested for impairment at the entity level. The Board has rejected this argument and determined that the highest level at which goodwill should be tested for impairment is the segment level. Where the entity monitors goodwill at a level higher than the segment level, which should be unusual, it may be necessary to develop additional reporting systems to perform the impairment testing of goodwill mandated by IAS 36.

For entities that have not yet adopted IFRS 8, IAS 36 permits that the 'segment level' may be determined using either the entity's primary or the entity's secondary format. For most entities, the cut-off will be determined based on the primary format. For some entities, however, such as those that report on a matrix basis (see **appendix 1**), it will be necessary to consider the level of internal reporting that best reflects the way that the operations are managed in order to choose between the primary and secondary formats.

Example 8.1.2

Level at which goodwill is tested for impairment

Company A has three retail divisions, each of which is classified for reporting purposes as an operating segment under IFRS 8 *Operating Segments*. All three divisions consist of a number of individual stores that operate independently of one another. Goodwill was recognised on the acquisition of each division. Management does not monitor goodwill for internal purposes.

However, under the requirements of IAS 36, goodwill is monitored and assessed for impairment annually for financial reporting purposes. Management currently only monitors goodwill for impairment at an operating segment level. However, management also has the ability to allocate goodwill to each store within each operating segment and to monitor goodwill for impairment at that lower level. Given that management is capable of monitoring the impairment of goodwill at a lower level than is currently the case, should management perform its goodwill impairment assessment at that lower level?

Management's current practice is appropriate. IAS 36.80 requires goodwill to be assessed for impairment at a level no larger than an operating segment determined under IFRS 8, and which represents the lowest level at which goodwill is monitored for internal management purposes. Company A complies with both requirements and does not need to alter the level at which goodwill is currently assessed for impairment.

8.1.2.1 Completing the initial allocation of goodwill

Ideally, the initial allocation of goodwill recognised in a business combination should be completed before the end of the annual period in which the business combination is effected. Where this is not possible, the initial allocation should be completed before the end of the first annual period beginning after the acquisition date. [IAS 36.84]

This rule differs from that specified by IFRS 3 *Business Combinations* where the initial accounting for a business combination can be determined only provisionally by the end of the period in which the combination is effected. In such circumstances, IFRS 3 requires the acquirer to:

- account for the combination using the provisional values; and
- recognise any adjustments to those provisional values as a result of completing the initial accounting within the measurement period, which is not to exceed twelve months from the acquisition date.

Therefore, the period allowed to complete the initial allocation of goodwill to CGUs is longer than the period to complete the initial accounting for a business combination. The Board decided to allow this longer period because the allocation of goodwill will often not be possible until after the initial accounting for the combination is complete.

8.1.2.2 Disposal of a portion of a CGU containing goodwill

If goodwill has been allocated to a CGU, or a group of CGUs, and the entity disposes of an operation within that unit or group, the goodwill associated with the operation disposed of should be:

[IAS 36.86]

- included in the carrying amount of the operation when determining the gain or loss on disposal; and
- measured on the basis of the relative values of the operation disposed of and the portion of the CGU retained, unless the entity can demonstrate that some other method better reflects the goodwill associated with the operation disposed of.

In accordance with the requirements set out in the previous sections, the entity will already have allocated goodwill to the CGU, or group of CGUs, at the lowest level to which a portion of the goodwill can be allocated on a reasonable and consistent basis. Therefore, goodwill cannot be identified with smaller operations within that unit or group, except in an arbitrary fashion. Where such smaller operations are being disposed of, however, it is appropriate to assume that some amount of goodwill is associated with the operation being disposed of, and to make an allocation of goodwill for that purpose.

The following example is given by the Standard.

Example 8.1.2.2

Goodwill measured on basis of relative values

[IAS 36.86]

An entity sells for £100 an operation that was part of a CGU to which goodwill has been allocated. The goodwill allocated to that unit cannot be identified or associated with an asset group at a level lower than that unit, except arbitrarily. The recoverable amount of the portion of the CGU retained is £300.

Because the goodwill allocated to the CGU cannot be non-arbitrarily identified or associated with an asset group at a level lower than that unit, the goodwill associated with the operation disposed of is measured on the basis of the relative values of the operation disposed of and the portion of the unit retained. Therefore, 25 per cent of the goodwill allocated to the CGU is included in the carrying amount of the operation that is sold.

Generally, the most appropriate method of allocation will be based on the relative values of the operation disposed of and the portion of the CGU retained. There may be circumstances where some other method better reflects the amount of goodwill associated with the operation disposed of, and the Standard allows the use of another method of allocation, provided that the superiority of the chosen method can be demonstrated. For example, assume that a CGU is acquired and integrated with a pre-existing CGU that did not include any goodwill. Assume that, almost immediately after the business combination, the entity disposes of a pre-existing loss-making operation from within the integrated CGU. In such circumstances, it might reasonably be argued that no part of the goodwill has been disposed of, and therefore no part of its carrying amount should be derecognised by being included in the determination of the gain or loss on disposal.

8.1.2.3 *Reorganisation of reporting structure*

An entity may reorganise its reporting structure in a way that changes the composition of one or more CGUs to which goodwill has been allocated. In these circumstances, the goodwill should be reallocated to the units affected. Unless the entity can demonstrate that some other method better reflects the goodwill associated with the reorganised units, the reallocation should be performed using a relative value approach similar to that discussed in **8.1.2.2** above.

The following example is set out in the Standard.

Example 8.1.2.3

Reorganisation of reporting structure

[IAS 36.87]

Goodwill had previously been allocated to CGU A. The goodwill allocated to A cannot be identified or associated with an asset group at a level lower than A, except arbitrarily. A is to be divided and integrated into three other CGUs, B, C and D.

Because the goodwill allocated to A cannot be non-arbitrarily identified or associated with an asset group at a level lower than A, it is reallocated to units B, C and D on the basis of the relative values of the three portions of A before those portions are integrated with B, C and D.

8.1.2.4 *Goodwill relating to non-wholly owned subsidiaries: entities that have adopted IFRS 3(2008)*

IFRS 3(2008) amended IAS 36 to add a new Appendix C, which sets out requirements for goodwill attributable to non-wholly owned subsidiaries, as discussed below. Entities that have not yet adopted

IFRS 3(2008) will need to continue to apply the rules from the previous version of IAS 36, which are discussed in **8.1.2.5**.

IFRS 3(2008) requires goodwill to be measured as of the acquisition date as the excess of (a) over (b) below:

[IAS 36.C1]

(a) the aggregate of:

(i) the consideration transferred measured in accordance with IFRS 3(2008), which generally requires acquisition-date fair value;

(ii) the amount of any non-controlling interest in the acquiree measured in accordance with IFRS 3(2008); and

(iii) in a business combination achieved in stages, the acquisition-date fair value of the acquirer's previously held equity interest in the acquiree.

(b) the net of the acquisition-date amounts of the identifiable assets acquired and liabilities assumed measured in accordance with IFRS 3(2008).

Goodwill acquired in a business combination is allocated to each of the acquirer's cash-generating units, or groups of cash-generating units, expected to benefit from the synergies of the combination, irrespective of whether other assets or liabilities of the acquiree are assigned to those units, or groups of units. It is possible that some of the synergies resulting from a business combination will be allocated to a cash-generating unit in which the non-controlling interest does not have an interest. [IAS 36.C2]

Example 8.1.2.4A

Allocation of goodwill

Entity A has an existing wholly owned subsidiary, Entity B. Subsequently, Entity A acquires 80% of Entity C in a business combination. Synergies arising from that business combination are expected to benefit Entity B.

Accordingly, some of the goodwill acquired in the business combination may be allocated to cash generating units within Entity B.

Where an entity chooses to measure non-controlling interests as its proportionate interest in the net identifiable assets of a subsidiary at the acquisition date, rather than at fair value, goodwill attributable to non-controlling interests is included in the recoverable amount of the related cash-generating unit but is not recognised in the parent's consolidated financial statements. To deal with this mismatch, for the purposes of impairment testing the carrying amount of goodwill allocated to the unit is grossed up to include the goodwill attributable to the non-controlling interest. This adjusted carrying amount is then compared with the recoverable amount of the unit to determine whether the cash-generating unit is impaired. [IAS 36.C4]

Example 8.1.2.4B

Testing for impairment

Entity A has an existing wholly owned subsidiary, Entity B. Subsequently, Entity A acquires 80% of Entity C in a business combination. Synergies arising from that business combination are expected to benefit Entity B.

Entity A chooses to measure non-controlling interests as its proportionate interest in the net identifiable assets of Entity C at the acquisition date. The resulting goodwill of £20,000 is allocated £14,000 to Entity C and £6,000 to Entity B.

Entity A determines that the amount of goodwill that would have arisen had it instead chosen to measure non-controlling interests at fair value is £25,000 (i.e. £5,000 higher), which would have been allocated £17,500 to Entity C and £7,500 to Entity B. Accordingly, for the purposes of impairment testing, the goodwill allocated to Entity C and Entity B must be grossed up by £3,500 and £1,500 respectively.

	Carrying amount as reported	**Gross up for additional goodwill**	**Adjusted carrying amount**
	£	**£**	**£**
Entity C			
Goodwill	14,000	3,500	17,500
Other net assets	12,000	–	12,000
	26,000	3,500	29,500
Entity B			
Goodwill	6,000	1,500	7,500
Other net assets	25,000	–	25,000
	31,000	1,500	32,500

If a subsidiary, or part of a subsidiary, with a non-controlling interest is itself a cash-generating unit, the impairment loss is allocated between the parent and the non-controlling interest on the same basis as that on which profit or loss is allocated. [IAS 36.C6]

If a subsidiary, or part of a subsidiary, with a non-controlling interest is part of a larger cash-generating unit, goodwill impairment losses are allocated to the parts of the cash-generating unit that have a non-controlling interest and the parts that do not. The impairment losses should be allocated to the parts of the cash-generating unit on the basis of:

[IAS 36.C7]

(a) to the extent that the impairment relates to goodwill in the cash-generating unit, the relative carrying values of the goodwill of the parts before the impairment; and

(b) to the extent that the impairment relates to identifiable assets in the cash-generating unit, the relative carrying values of the net identifiable assets of the parts before the impairment. Any such impairment is allocated to the assets of the parts of each unit pro rata on the basis of the carrying amount of each asset in the part.

In those parts that have a non-controlling interest, the impairment loss is allocated between the parent and the non-controlling interest on the same basis as that on which profit or loss is allocated.

If an impairment loss attributable to a non-controlling interest relates to goodwill that is not recognised in the parent's consolidated financial statements, that impairment is not recognised as a goodwill impairment loss. In such cases, only the impairment loss relating to the goodwill that is allocated to the parent is recognised as a goodwill impairment loss. [IAS 36.C8]

Example 8.1.2.4C

Allocation of impairment loss

Continuing with the facts from **example 8.1.2.4B,** Entity A compares the adjusted carrying amounts of the cash generating units with their recoverable amounts and determines that Entity C is impaired.

	Adjusted carrying amount	Recoverable amount	Impairment
	£	£	£
Entity C	29,500	25,000	(4,500)
Entity B	32,500	40,000	-

The impairment of £4,500 for Entity C relates to goodwill, and is allocated between the parent and the non-controlling interest on the same basis as that on which profit or loss is allocated, i.e. 80% to the parent (£3,600) and 20% to the non-controlling interest (£900). But as the impairment loss attributable to the non-controlling interest relates to goodwill that is not recognised in the parent's consolidated financial statements, that impairment is not recognised as a goodwill impairment loss.

Accordingly, £3,600 is recognised as a goodwill impairment loss, being the impairment loss relating to the goodwill that is allocated to the parent.

Examples 8.1.2.4D to F reproduce Illustrative Examples 7A to 7C published with IAS 36, as amended by IFRS 3(2008), which illustrate the impairment testing of a non-wholly-owned CGU.

Example 8.1.2.4D

Non-controlling interests measured initially as a proportionate share of the net identifiable assets

[IAS 36 Illustrative Examples (Example 7A)]

In this example, tax effects are ignored.

Background

Parent acquires an 80 per cent ownership interest in Subsidiary for CU2,100 on 1 January 20X3. At that date, Subsidiary's net identifiable assets have a fair value of CU1,500. Parent chooses to measure the non-controlling interests as the proportionate interest of Subsidiary's net identifiable assets of CU300 (20% of CU1,500). Goodwill of CU900 is the difference between the aggregate of the consideration transferred and the amount of the non-controlling interests (CU2,100 + CU300) and the net identifiable assets (CU1,500).

The assets of Subsidiary together are the smallest group of assets that generate cash inflows that are largely independent of the cash inflows from other assets or groups of assets. Therefore Subsidiary is a cash-generating unit. Because other cash-generating units of Parent are expected to benefit from the synergies of the combination, the goodwill of CU500 related to those synergies has been allocated to other cash-generating units within Parent. Because the cash-generating unit comprising Subsidiary includes goodwill within its carrying amount, it must be tested for impairment annually, or more frequently if there is an indication that it may be impaired (see paragraph 90 of IAS 36).

At the end of 20X3, Parent determines that the recoverable amount of cash-generating unit Subsidiary is CU1,000. The carrying amount of the net assets of Subsidiary, excluding goodwill, is CU1,350.

Testing Subsidiary (cash-generating unit) for impairment

Goodwill attributable to non-controlling interests is included in Subsidiary's recoverable amount of CU1,000 but has not been recognised in Parent's consolidated financial statements. Therefore, in accordance with paragraph C4 of Appendix C of IAS 36, the carrying amount of Subsidiary is grossed up to include goodwill attributable to the non-controlling interest, before being compared with the recoverable amount of CU1,000. Goodwill attributable to Parent's 80 per cent interest in Subsidiary at the acquisition date is CU400 after allocating CU500 to other cash-generating units within Parent. Therefore, goodwill attributable to the 20 per cent non-controlling interest in Subsidiary at the acquisition date is CU100.

Schedule 1. Testing Subsidiary for impairment at the end of 20X3

End of 20X3	*Goodwill of Subsidiary*	*Net identifiable assets*	*Total*
	CU	CU	CU
Carrying amount	400	1,350	1,750
Unrecognised non-controlling interests	100	–	100
Adjusted carrying amount	500	1,350	1,850
Recoverable amount			1,000
Impairment loss			850

Allocating the impairment loss

In accordance with paragraph 104 of IAS 36, the impairment loss of CU850 is allocated to the assets in the unit by first reducing the carrying amount of goodwill.

Therefore, CU500 of the CU850 impairment loss for the unit is allocated to the goodwill. In accordance with paragraph C6 of Appendix C of IAS 36, if the partially-owned subsidiary is itself a cash-generating unit, the goodwill impairment loss is allocated to the controlling and non-controlling interests on the same basis as that on which profit or loss is allocated. In this example, profit or loss is allocated on the basis of relative ownership interests. Because the goodwill is recognised only to the extent of Parent's 80 per cent ownership interest in Subsidiary, Parent recognises only 80 per cent of that goodwill impairment loss (i.e. CU400).

The remaining impairment loss of CU350 is recognised by reducing the carrying amounts of Subsidiary's identifiable assets (see Schedule 2).

Schedule 2. Allocation of the impairment loss for Subsidiary at the end of 20X3

End of 20X3	*Goodwill*	*Net identifiable assets*	*Total*
	CU	CU	CU
Carrying amount	400	1,350	1,750
Impairment loss	(400)	(350)	(750)
Carrying amount after impairment loss	–	1,000	1,000

Example 8.1.2.4E

Non-controlling interests measured initially at fair value and the related subsidiary is a stand-alone cash generating unit

[IAS 36 Illustrative Examples (Example 7B)]

In this example, tax effects are ignored.

Background

Parent acquires an 80 per cent ownership interest in Subsidiary for CU2,100 on 1 January 20X3. At that date, Subsidiary's net identifiable assets have a fair value of CU1,500. Parent chooses to measure the non-controlling interests at fair value, which is CU350. Goodwill of CU950 is the difference between the aggregate of the consideration transferred and the amount of the non-controlling interests (CU2,100 + CU350) and the net identifiable assets (CU1,500).

The assets of Subsidiary together are the smallest group of assets that generate cash inflows that are largely independent of the cash inflows from other assets or groups of assets. Therefore, Subsidiary is a cash-generating unit. Because other cash-generating units of Parent are expected to benefit from the synergies of the combination, the goodwill of CU500 related to those synergies has been allocated to other cash-generating units within Parent. Because Subsidiary includes goodwill within its carrying amount, it must be tested for impairment annually, or more frequently if there is an indication that it might be impaired (see paragraph 90 of IAS 36).

Testing Subsidiary for impairment

At the end of 20X3, Parent determines that the recoverable amount of cash-generating unit Subsidiary is CU1,650. The carrying amount of the net assets of Subsidiary, excluding goodwill, is CU1,350.

Schedule 1. Testing Subsidiary for impairment at the end of 20X3

End of 20X3	*Goodwill*	*Net identifiable assets*	*Total*
	CU	CU	CU
Carrying amount	450	1,350	1,800
Recoverable amount			1,650
Impairment loss			150

Allocating the impairment loss

In accordance with paragraph 104 of IAS 36, the impairment loss of CU150 is allocated to the assets in the unit by first reducing the carrying amount of goodwill. Therefore, the full amount of impairment loss of CU150 for the unit is allocated to the goodwill. In accordance with paragraph C6 of Appendix C of IAS 36, if the partially-owned subsidiary is itself a cash-generating unit, the goodwill impairment loss is allocated to the controlling and non-controlling interests on the same basis as that on which profit or loss is allocated.

Example 8.1.2.4F

Non-controlling interests measured initially at fair value and the related subsidiary is part of a larger cash-generating unit

[IAS 36 Illustrative Examples (Example 7C)]

In this example, tax effects are ignored.

Background

Suppose that, for the business combination described in paragraph IE68A of Example 7B (**example 8.1.2.4E**), the assets of Subsidiary will generate cash inflows together with other assets or groups of assets of Parent. Therefore, rather than Subsidiary being the cash-generating unit for the purposes of impairment testing, Subsidiary becomes part of a larger cash-generating unit, Z. Other cash-generating units of Parent are also expected to benefit from the synergies of the combination. Therefore, goodwill related to those synergies, in the amount of CU500, has been allocated to those other cash-generating units. Z's goodwill related to previous business combinations is CU800.

Because Z includes goodwill within its carrying amount, both from Subsidiary and from previous business combinations, it must be tested for impairment annually, or more frequently if there is an indication that it might be impaired (see paragraph 90 of IAS 36).

Testing Subsidiary for impairment

At the end of 20X3, Parent determines that the recoverable amount of cash-generating unit Z is CU3,300. The carrying amount of the net assets of Z, excluding goodwill, is CU2,250.

Schedule 3. Testing Z for impairment at the end of 20X3

End of 20X3	*Goodwill*	*Net identifiable assets*	*Total*
	CU	CU	CU
Carrying amount	1,250	2,250	3,500
Recoverable amount			3,300
Impairment loss			200

Allocating the impairment loss

In accordance with paragraph 104 of IAS 36, the impairment loss of CU200 is allocated to the assets in the unit by first reducing the carrying amount of goodwill. Therefore, the full amount of impairment loss of CU200 for cash-generating unit Z is allocated to the goodwill. In accordance with paragraph C7 of Appendix C of IAS 36, if the partially-owned subsidiary forms part of a larger cash-generating unit, the goodwill impairment loss would be allocated first to the parts of the cash-generating unit, Z, and then to the controlling and non-controlling interests of the partially owned Subsidiary.

Parent allocates the impairment loss to the parts of the cash-generating unit on the basis of the relative carrying values of the goodwill of the parts before the impairment. In this example Subsidiary is allocated 36 per cent of the impairment (450/1,250). The impairment loss is then allocated to the controlling and non-controlling interests on the same basis as that on which profit or loss is allocated.

8.1.2.5 Goodwill relating to non-wholly owned subsidiaries: entities that have not yet adopted IFRS 3(2008)

IFRS 3(2008) amended IAS 36 to add a new Appendix C, which sets out requirements for goodwill attributable to non-wholly owned subsidiaries, as discussed in **8.1.2.4**. Entities that have not yet adopted IFRS 3(2008) will need to continue to apply the rules from the previous version of IAS 36, which are discussed below.

For entities that have not yet adopted IFRS 3(2008), the goodwill recognised in a business combination represents the goodwill acquired by the parent (based on the parent's ownership interest) rather than the amount of goodwill controlled by the parent as a result of the business combination. Therefore, in the case of a non-wholly owned subsidiary, goodwill attributable to the minority interest (non-controlling interest) is not reflected in the financial statements.

Where goodwill has been allocated to a CGU that is part of a non-wholly owned subsidiary, the carrying amount of the CGU comprises:

[IAS 36.91]

- both the parent's interest and the minority interest in the identifiable net assets of the CGU; and
- the parent's interest in goodwill.

For the purposes of impairment testing, the carrying amount of such a CGU is notionally adjusted by grossing up the carrying amount of the goodwill allocated to the unit to include the goodwill attributable to the minority interest. This is done so as to arrive at an amount that is appropriately comparable with the recoverable amount of the unit determined in accordance with IAS 36, which is partly attributable to the minority interest in goodwill. [IAS 36.92]

The notionally adjusted carrying amount is compared to the recoverable amount of the unit to determine whether the CGU is impaired. Any resulting impairment loss is first set against the amount of goodwill allocated to the unit, in accordance with the rules set out in **9.2** below. Because the minority's share of goodwill is not recognised in the financial statements, however, the impairment loss relating to goodwill is apportioned between that attributable to the parent, and that attributable to the minority, with only the former being recognised as a goodwill impairment loss. [IAS 36.92 & 93]

Example 8.1.2.5 reproduces Illustrative Example 7 published with IAS 36, before it was amended by IFRS 3(2008), which illustrated the impairment testing of a non-wholly-owned CGU.

Example 8.1.2.5

Impairment testing cash-generating units with goodwill and minority interests

[IAS 36 Illustrative Examples (Example 7)]

In this example, tax effects are ignored.

Background

Entity X acquires an 80 per cent ownership interest in Entity Y for CU1,600 on 1 January 20X3. At that date, Y's identifiable net assets have a fair value of CU1,500. Y has no contingent liabilities. Therefore, X recognises in its consolidated financial statements:

(a) goodwill of CU400, being the difference between the cost of the business combination of CU1,600 and X's 80 per cent interest in Y's identifiable net assets;

(b) Y's identifiable net assets at their fair value of CU1,500; and

(c) a minority interest of CU300, being the 20 per cent interest in Y's identifiable net assets held by parties outside X.

The assets of Y together are the smallest group of assets that generate cash inflows that are largely independent of the cash inflows from other assets or groups of assets. Therefore Y is a cash-generating unit. Because this cash-generating unit includes goodwill within its carrying amount, it must be tested for impairment annually, or more frequently if there is an indication that it may be impaired (see paragraph 90 of IAS 36).

At the end of 20X3, X determines that the recoverable amount of cash-generating unit Y is CU1,000. X uses straight-line depreciation over a 10-year life for Y's identifiable assets and anticipates no residual value.

Testing Y for Impairment

A portion of Y's recoverable amount of CU1,000 is attributable to the unrecognised minority interest in goodwill. Therefore, in accordance with paragraph 92 of IAS 36, the carrying amount of Y must be notionally adjusted to include goodwill attributable to the minority interest, before being compared with the recoverable amount of CU1,000.

Schedule 1. Testing Y for impairment at the end of 20X3

End of 20X3	*Goodwill*	*Identifiable net assets*	*Total*
	CU	CU	CU
Gross carrying amount	400	1,500	1,900
Accumulated depreciation	–	(150)	(150)
Carrying amount	400	1,350	1,750
Unrecognised minority interest	100(a)	–	100
Notionally adjusted carrying amount	500	1,350	1,850
Recoverable amount			1,000
Impairment loss			850

(a) Goodwill attributable to X's 80% interest in Y at the acquisition date is CU400. Therefore, goodwill notionally attributable to the 20% minority interest in Y at the acquisition date is CU100.

In accordance with paragraph 104 of IAS 36, the impairment loss of CU850 is allocated to the assets in the unit by first reducing the carrying amount of goodwill to zero.

Therefore, CU500 of the CU850 impairment loss for the unit is allocated to the goodwill. However, because the goodwill is recognised only to the extent of X's 80 per cent ownership interest in Y, X recognises only 80 per cent of that goodwill impairment loss (i.e. CU400).

The remaining impairment loss of CU350 is recognised by reducing the carrying amounts of Y's identifiable assets (see Schedule 2).

Schedule 2. Allocation of the impairment loss for Y at the end of 20X3

End of 20X3	*Goodwill*	*Identifiable net assets*	*Total*
	CU	CU	CU
Gross carrying amount	400	1,500	1,900
Accumulated depreciation	–	(150)	(150)
Carrying amount	400	1,350	1,750

Impairment loss	(400)	(350)	(750)
Carrying amount after impairment loss	–	1,000	1,000

8.1.3 *Allocation of corporate assets to CGUs*

Corporate assets are assets other than goodwill that contribute to the future cash flows of both the CGU under review and other CGUs. [IAS 36.6] Such assets may include group or divisional assets such as a headquarters building or a research centre. Key characteristics of corporate assets are that:

[IAS 36.100]

- they do not generate cash inflows independently from other assets or groups of assets; and
- their carrying amount cannot be fully attributed to the cash-generating unit under review.

> Other examples of corporate assets may include brands and operating licences.

Because corporate assets do not generate separate cash flows, they are tested for impairment in the context of the CGU or group of CGUs to which the asset belongs. If a portion of the carrying amount of a corporate asset:

[IAS 36.102]

- can be allocated on a reasonable and consistent basis to a CGU, the entity compares the carrying amount of the unit (including the allocated portion of the carrying amount of the corporate asset) with its recoverable amount. Any impairment loss is recognised in accordance with **9.2** below;
- cannot be allocated on a reasonable and consistent basis to that unit, the entity:
  - compares the carrying amount of the unit, excluding the corporate asset, with its recoverable amount, and recognises any impairment loss in accordance with **9.2** below;

- identifies the smallest group of CGUs that includes the CGU under review and to which a portion of the carrying amount of the corporate asset can be allocated on a reasonable and consistent basis; and
- compares the carrying amount of that group of CGUs, including the allocated portion of the carrying amount of the corporate asset, with the recoverable amount of the group of units. Any impairment loss is recognised in accordance with **9.2** below.

Illustrative Example 8 published with IAS 36 illustrates the application of the requirements for corporate assets.

8.2 Stage 2: The estimation of expected future cash flows

8.2.1 General approach to present value

Appendix A to IAS 36 (which is an integral part of the Standard) provides some guidance on the use of present value techniques in measuring value in use. In particular, it considers some of the practical difficulties in estimating future cash flows and arriving at an appropriate discount rate for those cash flows. This section provides a brief summary of the guidance in Appendix A to IAS 36 as regards the general approach to present value. The selection of an appropriate discount rate is dealt with in **8.3**.

IAS 36 identifies the following elements which, taken together, capture the economic differences between assets:

[IAS 36.A1]

- an estimate of the future cash flows the entity expects to derive from the asset;
- the time value of money, represented by the current market risk-free rate of interest;
- expectations about possible variations in the amount or timing of the future cash flows;
- the price for bearing uncertainty inherent in the asset; and
- other factors, such as illiquidity, that market participants would reflect in pricing the future cash flows that the entity expects to derive from the asset.

When estimating the value in use of an asset, the last three elements described in the previous paragraph can be reflected either:

- as adjustments to the discount rate (called the 'traditional' approach); or
- as adjustments to the future cash flows (called the 'expected cash flow' approach).

The traditional approach involves the use of a single set of estimated cash flows, and a single discount rate. It emphasises the selection of an appropriate discount rate, assuming that a single discount rate can incorporate all the expectations about the future cash flows and appropriate risk premium. However, the traditional approach may not be easy to apply, for example, in the case of non-financial assets where no market for the item or a comparable item exists.

IAS 36 supports the expected cash flow approach as being, in some situations, a more effective measurement tool. This approach uses all expectations about possible cash flows instead of the single most likely cash flow. For example, a cash flow might be £100, £200 or £300, with probabilities of 10 per cent, 60 per cent and 30 per cent, respectively. The expected cash flow is £220, i.e. (£100 x 10%) + (£200 x 60%) + (£300 x 30%). The expected cash flow approach therefore differs from the traditional approach by focusing on a direct analysis of the cash flows in question and on more explicit statements of the assumptions used in the measurement. It is highly dependent on assigning probabilities to estimates of future cash flows.

Appendix A to IAS 36 provides a more detailed discussion and comparison of the two approaches. Whichever approach the entity adopts to reflect expectations about possible variations in the amount or timing of future cash flows, the objective is to arrive at an estimate that best reflects the expected present value of future cash flows, i.e. the weighted average of all possible outcomes. [IAS 36.A2]

Whichever approach is selected, key principles to be borne in mind are:

[IAS 36.A3]

- consistent assumptions should be used for the estimation of cash flows and the selection of an appropriate discount rate in order to avoid any double-counting or omissions. For example, a discount rate of 12 per cent might be applied to the contractual cash flows of a loan receivable. That rate reflects expectations about future defaults from loans with particular characteristics. That same 12 per cent should not be used to discount expected cash flows because those cash flows already reflect assumptions about future defaults;

- estimated cash flows and discount rates should be free from both bias and factors unrelated to the asset in question. For example, deliberately understating estimated net cash flows to enhance the apparent future profitability of an asset introduces a bias into the measurement; and

- estimated cash flows or discount rates should reflect a range of possible outcomes, rather than a single, most likely, minimum or maximum possible amount.

8.2.2 *Use of forecasts/budgets/cash flow projections*

When estimating expected future cash flows, the following rules apply:

- projections of cash flows should be based on reasonable and supportable assumptions that represent management's best estimate of the range of economic conditions that will exist over the remaining useful life of the asset. Greater weight should be given to external evidence. [IAS 36.33(a)] The reasonableness of the assumptions on which current cash flow projections are based should be assessed by examining the causes of differences between past cash flow projections and actual cash flows. The assumptions used should be consistent with past actual outcomes, provided the effects of subsequent events or circumstances that did not exist when those actual cash flows were generated make this appropriate; [IAS 36.34]

- cash flow projections should be based on the most recent financial budgets/forecasts that have been approved by management. Projections based on these budgets/forecasts should cover a maximum period of five years, unless a longer period can be justified. [IAS 36.33(b)] Detailed budgets/forecasts for a period of greater than five years are generally not available and, if they are available, are less likely to be accurate. If management has produced budgets/forecasts for a period greater than five years, however, and can demonstrate, based on past experience, that its forecasting methods are reliable for such extended periods, it can use forecasts for periods exceeding five years if it is confident that these projections are reliable. [IAS 36.35] This is expected to be very much the exception, not the rule;

- projections of cash flows beyond the period covered by the most recent budgets/forecasts should be estimated by extrapolating the projections based on the budgets/forecasts using a steady or declining growth rate for subsequent years, unless an increasing rate can be justified based on objective information about patterns over a product or industry lifecycle. This growth rate should not be overly optimistic and should not exceed the long-term average growth rate for the products, industries, or country or countries in which the entity operates, or for the market in which the asset is used, unless a higher rate can be justified. [IAS 36.33(c)] In some cases, it may be appropriate for the growth rate to be zero or negative; [IAS 36.36] and

- projections of cash flows should be consistent with the discount rate assumptions as regards price increases due to general inflation. Thus, if the discount rate includes the effect of price increases due to general inflation, future cash flows are estimated in nominal terms. If the discount rate excludes the effect of price increases due to general inflation, cash flows are estimated in real terms (but including future specific price increases or decreases). [IAS 36.40]

In principle, the guidance in the final bullet above also applies when a currency is hyperinflationary. However, in the case of hyperinflation, frequently there will be difficulties in determining the likely future rate of inflation and the relevant nominal interest rate. Calculating the value in use generally will be easier in real terms.

8.2.3 *Cash flows to be included*

Estimates of future cash flows should include:

- projections of cash inflows from the continuing use of the asset; [IAS 36.39(a)]
- projections of cash outflows that are necessarily incurred to generate the cash inflows from continuing use of the asset. This includes cash outflows to prepare the asset for use (if such preparation has not yet been completed), and future overheads that can be directly attributed, or allocated on a reasonable and consistent basis, to the asset (see **example 8.2.3** below); [IAS 36.39(b)] and
- net cash flows, if any, to be received (or paid) for the disposal of the asset at the end of its useful life. [IAS 36.39(c)] This is the amount that an entity expects to obtain from the disposal of the asset in an arm's length transaction between knowledgeable, willing parties, after deduction of the estimated costs of disposal. [IAS 36.52] In estimating these net cash flows, the same approach is taken as for estimates of fair value less costs to sell, except that:
    - prices used are those prevailing at the date of the estimate for similar assets that have reached the end of their useful life and that have operated under similar conditions; [IAS 36.53(a)] and

- the prices are adjusted for the effect of both future price increases due to general inflation and specific future price increases/decreases. However, if estimates of future cash flows from the asset's continuing use and the discount rate exclude the effect of general inflation, this effect is also excluded from the estimate of net cash flows on disposal. [IAS 36.53(b)]

Example 8.2.3

Estimating future cash flows when testing asset under construction

An entity designs, develops and manufactures components for high speed optical networks. The majority of its customers are buildings communication infrastructures. In December 20X1, the entity purchased a plot of land in an industrial complex with the intent to build a state-of-the-art production facility for the entity's integrated circuit and module products.

Construction of the new facility began in March 20X2 and is expected to be completed by the end of August 20X2. In June 20X2, a number of the entity's customers announced plans to cut the level of capital expenditures related to their infrastructure development, and the entity received several order cancellations. At 30 June 20X2, due to the significant change in business climate, the entity identified indicators of impairment of the new production facility under IAS 36.

The entity shall include the remaining costs associated with completing the production facility in its estimates of future cash flow when assessing the asset group for impairment. IAS 36.42 clearly states that when a carrying amount of an asset does not yet include all the cash outflows to be incurred before it is ready for use, the estimate of future cash outflows includes an estimate of any further cash outflow that is expected to be incurred before the asset is ready for use.

8.2.4 *Cash flows to be excluded*

Estimates of future cash flows should exclude:

- cash inflows from assets that generate cash inflows that are largely independent of the cash inflows from the asset under review (e.g. financial assets such as receivables); [IAS 36.43(a)]
- cash outflows that relate to obligations that have already been recognised as liabilities (e.g. payables, pensions or provisions), except in the limited circumstances described at **8.1.1** above; [IAS 36.43(b)]
- cash outflows or related costs savings (e.g. reductions in staff costs) or benefits that are expected to arise from a future restructuring to which an entity is not yet committed. [IAS 36.45(a)] The guidance in

IAS 37 *Provisions, Contingent Liabilities and Contingent Assets* should be used to determine when an entity is committed to a restructuring (see **chapter 11**). Once an entity is committed to the restructuring, estimates of future cash inflows and cash outflows reflect the cost savings and other benefits from the restructuring based on the most recent financial budgets/forecasts that have been approved by management; [IAS 36.47(a)]

- estimated future cash flows that are expected to arise from improving or enhancing an asset's performance. [IAS 36.44(b)] Estimates of future cash flows do, however, include future cash flows necessary to maintain the level of economic benefits expected to arise from the asset in its current condition. When a CGU consists of assets with different estimated useful lives, the replacement of assets with shorter lives is considered to be part of the day-to-day servicing of the unit when estimating the future cash flows associated with the unit. Similarly, when a single asset consists of components with different estimated useful lives, the replacement of components with shorter lives is considered to be part of the day-to-day servicing of the asset when estimating the future cash flows generated by the asset; [IAS 36.49]

Example 8.2.4

Entity not yet committed to restructuring

The assets of the CGU comprise a factory and plant and machinery. The factory is expected to last 50 years, but will need a new roof in 30 years, and the machinery needs to be replaced every 10 years. The entity expects to be able to reduce costs per unit of production by extending the factory to double production in a few years, but is not yet committed to such a restructuring.

The replacement expenditure for the 50 years, including the new roof and new machinery, should be included in the cash flows. Neither the expenditure to increase the size of the factory nor the additional income and revenue expenditure consequent on that expansion should be included.

- cash inflows or outflows from financing activities. [IAS 36.50(a)] The assumptions underlying the discount rate must be consistent with the estimated future cash flows. Therefore, since the time value of money is considered by discounting the estimated future cash flows, these cash flows exclude cash inflows/outflows from financing activities; [IAS 36.51] and
- income tax receipts or payments. [IAS 36.50(b)] As discussed in Stage 3 (see **8.3** below), a pre-tax discount rate is used and, therefore, future cash flows are also estimated on a pre-tax basis. [IAS 36.51]

Illustrative Examples 5 and 6 published with IAS 36 illustrate, respectively, how future restructurings and improvements or enhancements to asset performance affect a value in use calculation.

8.2.5 *Foreign currency cash flows*

Future cash flows are estimated in the currency in which they will be generated and then discounted using a discount rate appropriate for that currency. The present value obtained is then translated using the spot exchange rate at the date of the value in use calculation. [IAS 36.54]

8.3 Stage 3: The determination of an appropriate discount rate

IAS 36.55 specifies that the discount rate (or rates) used should be:

- a pre-tax rate (or rates);
- that reflect(s) current market assessments of:
  - the time value of money; and
  - the risks specific to the asset for which the future cash flow estimates have not been adjusted (but not those for which the cash flows have been adjusted).

Effectively, the discount rate used is an estimate of the rate that the market would expect on an equally risky investment. This rate is ideally estimated from either:

[IAS 36.56]

- the rate implicit in current market transactions for similar assets; or
- the weighted average cost of capital (WACC) of a listed entity that has a single asset (or portfolio of assets) similar in terms of service potential and risks to the asset under review.

In practice, asset-specific rates, such as those suggested in the previous paragraph, will seldom be available due to the unique nature of different transactions and the fact that there are likely to be few listed entities that offer a readily usable comparison since listed entities generally have a wider product/service base, wider markets and potentially lower risk profile. When an asset-specific rate is unavailable, a discount rate must be estimated. Appendix A to IAS 36, which is an integral part of the Standard, provides additional guidance on estimating the discount rate in such circumstances. This guidance is summarised in the following sections.

8.3.1 *Estimation of a market rate*

The entity may consider one of the following rates as a 'starting point' for its estimation. The rates would then be adjusted as discussed below. The 'starting point' rates include:

[IAS 36.A17]

- the WACC of the entity determined using techniques such as the Capital Asset Pricing Model;
- the entity's incremental borrowing rate; and
- other market borrowing rates.

This 'starting point' rate is then adjusted:

[IAS 36.A18]

- to reflect the way that the market would assess the specific risks associated with the asset's estimated cash flows (such as country risk, currency risk and price risk); and
- to exclude risks that are not relevant to the asset's estimated cash flows or for which the estimated cash flows have been adjusted.

If the 'starting point' rate is post-tax, it must be adjusted to arrive at a pre-tax rate. [IAS 36.A20]

The discount rate is independent of the capital structure of the entity and of the way in which the entity financed the purchase of the asset, because the future cash flows expected to arise from an asset do not depend on the way in which the entity financed the purchase of the asset. [IAS 36.A19]

Generally, a single discount rate is used to estimate the value in use of an asset. Separate discount rates for different future periods should be used, however, where value in use is sensitive to a difference in risks for different periods or to the term structure of interest rates. [IAS 36.A21]

8.4 Stage 4: Discounting and aggregating expected cash flows to arrive at value in use

The formulae for calculating value in use are derived from the following formulae:

Single cash flow

Present value of a single cash flow occurring in n years =

$$\frac{Cashflow}{(1+d)^n}$$

Series of equal cash flows

Present value of n annual cash flows =

$$Cashflow \times \frac{1-(1+d)^{-n}}{d}$$

Perpetuity

Present value of fixed annual cash flow, in perpetuity =

$$\frac{Cashflow}{d}$$

Where d = discount rate

In the first (single cash flow) formula, the cash flow is an actual cash flow. The discount rate will therefore be a nominal rate, matching the cash flow by including a compatible estimate of the effect of inflation.

In the second (series) and third (perpetuity) formulae, it is assumed that all cash flows are the same, with the first cash flow occurring at the end of Year 1. Where these cash flows will increase due to growth and inflation, this effect can be achieved by using a cash flow for Year 1, and reducing the nominal discount rate by both growth and inflation rates. Where the actual cash flow for the previous period is used, it will first be necessary to increase it by the first year's growth and inflation in order to find the cash flow at the end of Year 1. (This adjustment of the discount rate for growth is a substitute for building growth into the cash flows. It should not be confused with a real rate of return that would adjust for inflation only).

At a discount rate of 10 per cent, a perpetuity can be assumed to approximate to 35 years or more, since any amounts beyond that horizon will be immaterial.

Example 8.4A

Assumed steady growth in cash flows to perpetuity

The calculation is based on the perpetuity formula. Cash flow is for Year 1. Thus, where the previous year's actual cash flow is used, it is first necessary to increase it to reflect growth and inflation in Year 1.

Value in use =

$$\frac{CF_o}{d_a}(1 + g)(1 + i)$$

Where:

CF_0= actual cash flow for previous period

i= annual inflation rate

g= annual growth rate in cash flows

d_a= pre-tax discount rate adjusted to reflect inflation and growth in cash flows.

Example 8.4B

Cash flows forecast for five years, and assumed steady growth thereafter

The calculation is the sum of individual present values for the first 5 years, plus a perpetuity from Year 6 onwards re-expressed from Year 5 back to present value at time 0.

Value in use = Present value of each cash flow for Years 1–5

+ Present value of cash flows from Year 6 onwards

=

$$\frac{CF_1}{1 + d_n} + \frac{CF_2}{(1 + d_n)^2} + \frac{CF_3}{(1 + d_n)^3} + \frac{CF_4}{(1 + d_n)^4} + \frac{CF_5}{(1 + d_n)^5} + \frac{CF_5(1 + g)(1 + i)}{d_a x(1 + d_n)^5}$$

Where:

CF_n= Cash flow in nth year

i= annual inflation rate after year five

g= annual growth rate in cash flows after year five

d_n= pre-tax nominal discount rate

d_a= pre-tax discount rate adjusted to reflect growth and inflation in cash flows

Note:

The sixth term in the formula above,

$$\frac{CF_5(1+g)(1+i)}{d_a \times (1+d_n)^5}$$

, is a compound of two functions.

$$\frac{CF_5(1+g)(1+i)}{d_a}$$

is the present value of cash flows from Year 6 onwards expressed as a present value at the beginning of Year 6. Further adjustment to multiply by

$$\frac{1}{(1+d_n)^5}$$

re-expresses this as a present value at the beginning of Year 1.

Example 8.4C

Cash flows are forecast for 2 years

Assume:

Cash flow for year 1: £20m

Cash flow for year 2: £24m

Assumed steady growth thereafter: 2.5%

Inflation: 2.5%

Nominal pre-tax discount rate: 15%

Adjusted pre-tax discount rate: 10%

Value in use=

$$\frac{£20m}{1.15} + \frac{£24m}{1.15^2} + \frac{£24m \times 1.025 \times 1.025}{0.1 \times 1.15^2}$$

= £226m

9 Recognition and measurement of an impairment loss

The following sections discuss the recognition and measurement of an impairment loss for an individual asset (other than goodwill) and for a CGU, respectively.

9.1 Individual asset

If, and only if, the recoverable amount of an asset is less than its carrying amount, the carrying amount of the asset should be reduced to its recoverable amount. That reduction is an impairment loss. [IAS 36.59]

An impairment loss should be recognised in profit or loss immediately unless it relates to an asset carried at a revalued amount. If an asset has been revalued (e.g. an item of property, plant and equipment), the impairment loss is dealt with as a revaluation decrease in accordance with the relevant Standard (in this case IAS 16 – see **chapter 6**). [IAS 36.60] Generally, an impairment loss will first result in a decrease in any revaluation surplus related to the asset. This decrease is recognised in other comprehensive income rather than in profit or loss. Where no related revaluation surplus exists, or to the extent that the impairment loss is greater than the related revaluation surplus, the excess impairment loss is recognised in profit or loss. [IAS 36.61]

Where an impairment loss on a revalued asset is clearly caused by a consumption of economic benefits, FRS 11 requires the full amount of the impairment to be taken to the profit and loss account. IAS 36 includes no such requirement, and takes to profit or loss only the amount in excess of the relevant part of the revaluation surplus. UK

If the impairment loss is greater than the carrying amount of the asset, a liability should be recognised only if it is required by another Standard. [IAS 36.62] A liability will only be recognised in respect of present obligations arising as a result of past events. IAS 37 *Provisions, Contingent Liabilities and Contingent Assets* describes the appropriate recognition criteria (see **chapter 11**).

IAS 16 requires that the estimated useful life, the depreciation method and residual value of an item of property, plant and equipment should be reviewed at the end of each reporting period. After an impairment loss is recognised, these three items are reviewed, and the new carrying amount is depreciated over the asset's remaining useful life. Similar rules for intangible assets are set out in IAS 38 *Intangible Assets*.

Since an impairment loss affects the carrying amount of an asset, it affects the relationship between the asset's carrying amount and its tax base. Therefore, any deferred tax asset or liability is determined by comparing the revised carrying amount of the asset with its tax base (see **chapter 12**). [IAS 36.64]

Example 9.1

Recognition of an impairment loss creates a deferred tax asset

[IAS 36 Illustrative Examples (Example 3)]

An entity has an identifiable asset with a carrying amount of CU1,000. Its recoverable amount is CU650. The tax rate is 30 per cent and the tax base of the asset is CU800. Impairment losses are not deductible for tax purposes. The effect of the impairment loss is as follows:

	Before impairment	*Effect of impairment*	*After impairment*
	CU	CU	CU
Carrying amount	1,000	(350)	650
Tax base	800	-	800
Taxable (deductible) temporary difference	200	(350)	(150)
Deferred tax liability (asset) at 30%	60	(105)	(45)

In accordance with IAS 12, the entity recognises the deferred tax asset to the extent that it is probable that taxable profit will be available against which the deductible temporary difference can be utilised.

The cost of subsequent capital additions to previously impaired assets should be recognised in accordance with IAS 16 and capitalised if they meet the criteria of IAS 16.7.

9.2 Cash-generating unit

An impairment loss should be recognised for a CGU (or the smallest group of CGUs to which goodwill or a corporate asset has been allocated) if, and only if, its recoverable amount is less than its carrying amount. The impairment loss should be allocated to reduce the carrying amount of the assets of the unit or group of units in the following order:

[IAS 36.104]

- first, to goodwill allocated to the CGU (group of CGUs); and
- then, to the other assets of the unit or group on a pro rata basis based on the carrying amount of each asset in the unit or group of units.

Since it is not practicable to estimate the recoverable amount of each individual asset, these rules result in an arbitrary allocation of any impairment loss between the assets of the unit, other than goodwill. These reductions in carrying amounts should be dealt with in the same manner as impairment losses on individual assets as discussed at **9.1**.

This allocation is different to that required under UK GAAP. FRS 11 allocates impairment losses first to any goodwill, then to any intangibles and then to tangible fixed assets. UK

When allocating an impairment loss to individual assets within a CGU, the carrying amount of an individual asset should not be reduced below the highest of:

[IAS 36.105]

- its fair value less costs to sell (if determinable);
- its value in use (if determinable); and
- zero.

If this results in an amount being allocated to an asset which is less than its pro rata share of the impairment loss, the excess is allocated to the remaining assets within the CGU on a pro rata basis. [IAS 36.105]

If the recoverable amount of an individual asset cannot be determined:

[IAS 36.107]

- an impairment loss is recognised for the asset if its carrying amount is greater than the higher of its fair value less costs to sell and the results of the allocation procedures described above; and
- no impairment loss is recognised for the asset if the related CGU is not impaired. This applies even if the asset's fair value less costs to sell is less than its carrying amount.

After the allocation procedures have been applied, a liability is recognised for any remaining impairment loss for a CGU if, and only if, that is required by another Standard. [IAS 36.108]

Example 9.2

Corporate assets

An entity produces different types of packaging based on paper. The three main types of packaging materials produced for its customers are the following:

- tubes;
- corrugated board;
- solid board.

Each of the three main types of packaging associated with the business is identified as an operating segment under IFRS 8 *Operating Segments*, and as a cash-generating unit under IAS 36. Asset M is partly used for the production of tubes (T) and corrugated board (C).

The information regarding the cash-generating unit T is as follows:

- Goodwill = zero
- Carrying amount of machinery used exclusively in manufacturing tubes (excluding M) = 4,500
- Carrying amount of M = 1,000
- Capacity of M used for the tubes production = 60 per cent
- Recoverable amount of T (with M) = 4,000

For cash-generating unit C, the excess of value in use over the carrying amount is equal to 2,000.

In accordance with IAS 36, asset M should be allocated on a reasonable and consistent basis to units T and C. The entity should compare the carrying amount of each CGU, including the portion of the carrying amount of the corporate asset allocated to the CGU, with its recoverable amount. In this case, M is used at 60 per cent for the production of the tubes; therefore, it seems reasonable to allocate 60 per cent of the carrying amount of M to the cash-generating unit T. Therefore, the carrying amount of the cash-generating unit T is equal to 5,100 (1,000 × 60% + 4,500) which is higher than the recoverable amount (4,000) by 1,100. Therefore, an impairment loss should be recognised and should be allocated to all assets of the cash-generating unit T (including M) on a pro-rata basis based on the carrying amount of each asset in the unit:

to M:	1,100 x 600 / 5,100 = 129
to other assets:	1,100 x 4,500 / 5,100 = 971

However, if the entity was able to determine the fair value less costs to sell of M, and that number was 1,000 or more, the impairment loss in respect of cash-generating unit T would be allocated on a pro-rata basis to the other assets of T in accordance with the requirements of IAS 36.104 and 105.

No impairment is recognised in respect of unit C because the amount of M to be allocated (400) is less than the excess of C's value in use over C's carrying amount (2,000).

Even though the difference between the carrying amount and the recoverable amount (2,000) of the cash-generating unit C is higher than the impairment loss of T, an impairment loss should be recognised in T. The entity cannot test for impairment at a higher level to avoid the impairment loss.

10 Reversals of impairment losses

10.1 General rules

An impairment loss on goodwill shall not be reversed. This is discussed in **10.5** below. [IAS 36.124] Note that IAS 39.66 applies a similar requirement to an unquoted equity instrument that is not carried at fair value because its fair value cannot be reliably measured, and to a derivative asset that is linked to and must be settled by delivery of such an unquoted equity instrument (see **chapter 18**).

Where an impairment loss was recognised for an asset other than goodwill (or a CGU) in prior years, an entity is required to assess at the end of each reporting period whether there is any indication that the impairment loss may no longer exist or may have decreased. If such an indication exists, the entity should estimate the recoverable amount of that asset (or CGU). [IAS 36.110]

An impairment loss recognised in a prior period for an asset other than goodwill (or a CGU) may be reversed if, and only if, there has been a change in the estimates used to determine the recoverable amount of the asset (or CGU) since the last impairment loss was recognised. When this is the case, the carrying amount of the asset (or CGU) is increased to its recoverable amount in accordance with the rules set out in **10.3** below (**10.4** below for a CGU). [IAS 36.114]

Example 10.1

Determining whether the reversal of an impairment loss is appropriate

An acquired business produces bottled mineral water. Just before the year end, a consumer group tests the water and publicises the fact that it contains high levels of a harmful chemical. Sales of the mineral water plummet.

Situation 1

Assume that there is great uncertainty about the validity of the consumer group's claim, but it is assumed to be valid and that sales of the product will recover only after the problem has been sorted out, and the product has been re-tested and re-marketed. The future cash flows indicate that the recoverable amount of the CGU (which consists mainly of an intangible asset, being the brand of mineral water) is less than its carrying amount, so the CGU/asset is written down by the entity.

However, in the next period, further tests demonstrate that the consumer group had been wrong in its claims and it retracts them publicly. Sales of the mineral water recover very quickly and soon are back to the previous level.

In this specific case, it is clear that an unforeseen change in the estimates of future cash flows used in determining the recoverable amount has resulted in the recognition of the impairment loss, and later in the reversal of that impairment loss. The CGU/intangible asset can be written back up to the value that would have been recognised had the impairment never occurred (refer to **example 10.3A** below). This write-up is recognised immediately in profit or loss.

Situation 2

Suppose that, by year end, the mineral water company has conducted its own tests and satisfied both itself and independent experts that the consumer group was wrong in its claims. So the entity forecasts that, although there has been a temporary reduction in sales, they will soon recover as the consumer group retracts the claims.

The temporary reduction in sales has caused a small temporary impairment in the value of the CGU/intangible asset as measured at the end of the reporting period. The CGU/intangible asset is written down by this small amount to its recoverable amount.

In the next period, the sales increase back to their previous levels in line with expectations and the value of the CGU/intangible recovers to its original level. But, the (small) impairment loss cannot be reversed in the financial statements. Its reversal was foreseen in the original impairment calculations and has occurred simply because of the passing of time; therefore, the reversal does not arise from a change in the estimates used in completing the original recoverable amount calculation

UK

This approach is slightly different from that required under UK GAAP. In recognising reversals, FRS 11 applies a more restrictive regime to goodwill and other intangibles than to tangible fixed assets.

A reversal of an impairment loss must reflect an increase in the estimated service potential of an asset (or CGU), either from use or sale. Examples of such changes in estimate include:

[IAS 36.115]

- a change in the basis for recoverable amount (i.e. whether recoverable amount is based on fair value less costs to sell or value in use);
- if recoverable amount was based on value in use, a change in the amount or timing of estimated future cash flows or in the discount rate; or
- if recoverable amount was based on fair value less costs to sell, a change in estimate of the components of fair value less costs to sell.

An increase in the recoverable amount of the asset due to the passage of time does not, however, represent an increase in the estimated service potential of an asset and therefore it is not acceptable to recognise a reversal of an impairment loss on this basis. In other words, the value in use of an asset may increase and even become greater than the carrying amount of the asset simply because the present value of future cash inflows increases as they become closer (i.e. 'the discount unwinds'). This does not, however, represent an economic change in the value of the asset. Therefore, a reversal of an impairment loss should not be recognised on this basis. [IAS 36.116]

10.2 Indications of reversals of impairment losses

The indications of the reversal of impairment losses listed in IAS 36.111 are broadly the mirror image of the impairment indications discussed at **5.2** above, and are reproduced in the following paragraphs.

The following external sources of information may indicate that an impairment loss previously recognised for an asset other than goodwill (or a CGU) no longer exists or has decreased:

[IAS 36.111]

- the asset's (or CGU's) market value has increased significantly during the period;
- significant changes with a favourable effect on the entity have taken place during the period, or will take place in the near future, in the technological, market, economic or legal environment in which the entity operates or in the market to which the asset (or CGU) is dedicated; and
- market interest rates or other market rates of return on investments have decreased during the period, and those decreases are likely to affect the discount rate used in calculating the asset's (or CGU's) value in use and increase the asset's (or CGU's) recoverable amount materially.

The following internal sources of information may indicate that an impairment loss previously recognised for an asset other than goodwill (or a CGU) no longer exists or has decreased:

[IAS 36.111]

- significant changes with a favourable effect on the entity have taken place during the period, or are expected to take place in the near future, in the extent to which, or the manner in which, the asset (or

CGU) is used or is expected to be used. These changes include costs incurred during the period to improve or enhance the asset's (or CGU) performance or restructure the operation to which the asset (or CGU) belongs; and

- evidence is available from internal reporting that indicates that the economic performance of the asset (or CGU) is, or will be, better than expected.

If there is an indication that an impairment loss previously recognised for an asset other than goodwill may no longer exist or may have decreased, this may indicate that the remaining useful life, the depreciation/amortisation method or the residual value may need to be reviewed and adjusted in accordance with the Standard applicable to the asset, even if no impairment loss is reversed for the asset. [IAS 36.113]

10.3 Reversal for an individual asset

The increased carrying amount of an asset other than goodwill due to a reversal of an impairment loss should not exceed the carrying amount that would have been determined (net of amortisation or depreciation) had no impairment loss been recognised for the asset in prior years. [IAS 36.117] Any increase in excess of this amount would be a revaluation and would be accounted for under the appropriate Standard (e.g. IAS 16 for an item of property, plant and equipment). [IAS 36.118]

Example 10.3A

Reversal of an impairment loss

An intangible asset costing 10 million is amortised over 20 years. Two years after it is purchased, it becomes impaired and is written down from its carrying amount of 9 million to its estimated recoverable amount of 5 million. Two years after the recognition of that impairment loss, with the carrying amount now 4.4 million, the recoverable amount of the intangible asset is now estimated to be 10 million, following a change in estimates of the future cash flows arising from this asset.

Since the impairment reversal arises from a change in the estimates used to determine the recoverable amount, the impairment loss should be reversed. However, the impairment loss can only be reversed to the extent that it does not increase the carrying amount above what it would have been had the impairment never occurred. Had the impairment never occurred, the carrying amount would be 8 million (9 million – two years depreciation @ 0.5 million per year); therefore, not all of the original 4 million impairment loss can be reversed.

Example 10.3B

Restricted reversal of impairment loss

The cost of a property with a useful life of 20 years is £10 million. Depreciation each year is £0.5 million.

At the end of Year 5, the property has a carrying amount of £7.5 million. Due to changes in the economic environment, the directors perform a detailed impairment review and determine that the property's recoverable amount is its value in use, which is £5 million. Their estimate of the remaining useful life of the asset is 10 years.

Therefore an impairment loss of £2.5 million is recognised in Year 5. In Years 6 and 7, the property is depreciated so that its carrying amount at the end of Year 7 is £4 million.

Due to shortages in the supply of properties, the directors determine that the net selling price of the property at the end of Year 7 is £8 million. The recoverable amount of the asset has therefore increased to £8 million.

The reversal of the impairment loss is restricted, however, to the amount that would restore the carrying amount to what it would have been had no impairment loss been recognised (i.e. £7.5 million – (£7.5 million x 2/10) = 6 million). Therefore, only £2 million of the impairment loss is reversed.

If the reporting entity wishes to recognise the market value of the property in its statement of financial position, the remainder of the uplift would be treated as a revaluation movement. (This will only be possible, however, if the entity decides to adopt the revaluation model for all assets in that class.)

A reversal of an impairment loss for an asset other than goodwill is recognised immediately in profit or loss unless the asset is carried at a revalued amount in accordance with another Standard. When an asset is carried at a revalued amount, the reversal is considered a revaluation increase and treated accordingly. [IAS 36.119] Normally, a revaluation increase is recognised in other comprehensive income and increases the revaluation surplus within equity. But to the extent that an impairment loss on the same revalued asset was previously recognised in profit or loss, a reversal of that impairment loss is recognised in profit or loss. [IAS 36.120]

After the reversal of an impairment loss, the depreciation (amortisation) charge for the asset is adjusted in future periods to allocate the asset's revised carrying amount, less its residual value (if any), on a systematic basis over its remaining useful life. [IAS 36.121]

10.4 Reversal for a CGU

A reversal of an impairment loss for a CGU should be allocated to increase the carrying amount of the assets of the unit, except for goodwill, pro rata based on the carrying amount of each asset in the unit. These increases in carrying amounts should be dealt with as reversals of impairment losses for individual assets in the same manner as discussed at **10.3**. [IAS 36.122]

In allocating a reversal of an impairment loss for a CGU, the carrying amount of an asset should not be increased above the lower of:

[IAS 36.123]

- its recoverable amount (if determinable); and
- the carrying amount that would have been determined (net of amortisation/depreciation) had no impairment loss been recognised for the asset in prior years. (Any further increase would constitute a revaluation.)

It follows, therefore, that the reversal of the impairment loss will be allocated only between those assets (excluding goodwill) against which the original loss was allocated, though not necessarily in the same proportions.

If this results in a reversal being allocated to an asset which is less than its pro rata share of the reversal, the amount of the reversal of the impairment loss that would otherwise have been allocated to the asset should be allocated to the other assets of the unit, other than goodwill, on a pro rata basis. [IAS 36.123]

10.5 Reversal for goodwill

Where an impairment loss has previously been recognised for goodwill, that impairment loss shall not be reversed in a subsequent period. [IAS 36.124]

The IASB has concluded that, since any increase in the recoverable amount of goodwill in the periods following the recognition of an impairment loss is likely to be an increase in internally-generated goodwill, rather than a reversal of an impairment loss, it is inappropriate to recognise any such increase in recoverable amount (since it would result in the recognition of internally generated goodwill, which is prohibited by IAS 38 *Intangible Assets*).

> *Under FRS 11, it is possible in some very limited circumstances to reverse an impairment loss relating to goodwill.*

UK

IFRIC Interpretation 10 *Interim Financial Reporting and Impairment* is effective for annual periods beginning on or after 1 November 2006. The consensus in the Interpretation is that an entity should not reverse an impairment loss recognised in a previous interim period in respect of goodwill or an investment in an equity instrument or a financial asset carried at cost. For further discussion of IFRIC 10, see **5.6.16.1** in **chapter 39**.

11 Disclosure

11.1 General

For each class of assets (defined as a grouping of assets of similar nature and use in the operations of the entity), the financial statements should disclose the amount of:

[IAS 36.126]

- impairment losses recognised in profit or loss during the period and the line item(s) of the statement of comprehensive income in which those impairment losses are included;
- reversals of impairment losses recognised in profit or loss during the period and the line item(s) of the statement of comprehensive income in which those impairment losses are reversed;
- impairment losses on revalued assets recognised in other comprehensive income during the period; and
- reversals of impairment losses on revalued assets recognised in other comprehensive income during the period.

This information may be presented in the reconciliation of the carrying amounts of property, plant and equipment, intangible assets, or elsewhere as appropriate. [IAS 36.128]

> **Example 11.1**
>
> **Impairment loss not included within depreciation expense**
>
> An entity recognises an impairment loss in respect of certain intangible assets with indefinite useful lives in the fourth quarter of 20X1 in accordance

> with IAS 36. The entity has certain debt covenants that state that they must maintain a certain multiple of EBITDA (earnings before interest, taxes, depreciation, and amortisation).
>
> Impairment losses recognised in accordance with IAS 36 cannot be included within depreciation expense. IAS 16 *Property, Plant and Equipment* defines depreciation as the systematic allocation of the depreciable amount of an asset over its useful life. The recognition of an impairment loss is as a result of a valuation exercise, rather than an allocation exercise, and should not be presented in a way which might encourage the belief that it is part of the regular allocation, that is, depreciation expense.

11.2 Entities reporting segment information

Where an entity reports segment information in accordance with IFRS 8 *Operating Segments* (see **chapter 37**), it is required to disclose the following for each reportable segment:

[IAS 36.129]

- the amount of impairment losses recognised in profit or loss and in other comprehensive income during the period; and
- the amount of reversals of impairment losses recognised in profit or loss and in other comprehensive income during the period.

Where an entity has not yet adopted IFRS 8 and applies IAS 14 *Segment Reporting* (see **appendix 1**), it is required to disclose the information above for each reportable segment based on its primary reporting format.

11.3 Impairment losses/reversals individually material to the financial statements

When an impairment loss for an individual asset or a CGU is recognised or reversed which is material to the financial statements taken as a whole, the following disclosures are required:

[IAS 36.130]

- the events and circumstances that led to the recognition (reversal) of the loss;
- the amount of the loss recognised (reversed);
- for an individual asset:
    - the nature of the asset; and

  - if the entity applies IFRS 8, the reportable segment to which the asset belongs (see **chapter 37**);
  - if the entity applies IAS 14, the reportable segment to which the asset belongs based on the primary reporting format of the entity (see **appendix 1**);
- for a CGU:
  - a description of the CGU (such as whether it is a product line, a plant, a business operation, a geographical area, a reportable segment or other);
  - the amount of the loss recognised or reversed by class of assets and, if the entity applies IFRS 8, by reportable segment (if, instead, the entity applies IAS 14, the information should be given by reportable segment based on the primary reporting format of the entity); and
  - if the aggregation of assets for identifying the CGU has changed since the previous estimate of the CGU's recoverable amount (if any), the entity should describe the current and former ways of aggregating assets and the reasons for changing the way the CGU is identified;
- whether the recoverable amount of the asset or CGU is its fair value less costs to sell or its value in use;
- if recoverable amount is fair value less costs to sell, the basis used to determine fair value less costs to sell (such as whether fair value was determined by reference to an active market or in some other way); and
- if recoverable amount is value in use, the discount rate(s) used in the current estimate and previous estimate (if any) of value in use.

11.4 Other impairment losses/reversals material in aggregate to the financial statements

If impairment losses recognised (reversed) during the period, other than those disclosed under **11.3**, are material in aggregate to the financial statements taken as a whole, the entity should disclose a brief description of the following:

[IAS 36.131]

- the main classes of assets affected by those impairment losses (reversals); and

- the main events and circumstances that led to the recognition (or reversal) of those impairment losses.

An entity is encouraged, but not required, to disclose the key assumptions used to determine the recoverable amount of assets (CGUs) during the period. The Standard does, however, require that the entity disclose information about the estimates used to measure the recoverable amount of a CGU when goodwill or an intangible asset with an indefinite useful life is included in the carrying amount of that unit (see **11.6** below). [IAS 36.132]

11.5 Unallocated goodwill

If any portion of the goodwill acquired in a business combination during the period has not been allocated to a CGU (group of CGUs) at the end of the reporting period (see **8.1.2.1** above), the amount of the unallocated goodwill should be disclosed, together with the reasons why that amount remains unallocated. [IAS 36.134]

11.6 CGUs containing goodwill or intangible assets with indefinite useful lives

UK *The disclosures discussed in this section are much more extensive than those required under UK GAAP by FRS 11. In particular, there may be commercial sensitivity around some of the disclosure requirements, such as those relating to key assumptions and the sensitivity of forecasts to variations in those assumptions.*

The following information should be disclosed for each CGU (or group of CGUs) for which the carrying amount of goodwill or intangible assets with indefinite useful lives allocated to that unit (or group of units) is significant in comparison with the entity's total carrying amount of goodwill or intangible assets with indefinite useful lives:

[IAS 36.134]

- the carrying amount of goodwill allocated to the unit (or group of units);
- the carrying amount of intangible assets with indefinite useful lives allocated to the unit (or group of units);
- the basis on which the unit's (or group of units') recoverable amount has been determined (i.e. value in use or fair value less costs to sell);

- if the unit's (or group of units') recoverable amount is based on value in use:
  - a description of each key assumption on which management has based its cash flow projections for the period covered by the most recent budgets/forecasts. Key assumptions are those to which the unit's (or group of units') recoverable amount is most sensitive;
  - a description of management's approach to determining the value(s) assigned to each key assumption, whether those value(s) reflect past experience or, if appropriate, are consistent with external sources of information, and, if not, how and why they differ from past experience or external sources of information;
  - the period over which management has projected cash flows based on financial budgets/forecasts approved by management and, when a period greater than five years is used for a CGU (or group of CGUs), an explanation as to why that longer period is justified;
  - the growth rate used to extrapolate cash flow projections beyond the period covered by the most recent budgets/forecasts, and the justification for using any growth rate that exceeds the long-term average growth rate for the products, industries, or country or countries in which the entity operates, or for the market to which the unit (or group of units) is dedicated; and
  - the discount rate(s) applied to the cash flow projections;
- if the unit's (or group of units') recoverable amount is based on fair value less costs to sell, the methodology used to determine fair value less costs to sell. If fair value less costs to sell is not determined using an observable market price for the unit (or group of units), the following information should also be disclosed:
  - a description of each key assumption on which management has based its determination of fair value less costs to sell. Key assumptions are those to which the unit's (or group of units') recoverable amount is most sensitive; and
  - a description of management's approach to determining the value (or values) assigned to each key assumption, whether those values reflect past experience or, if appropriate, are consistent with external sources of information, and, if not, how and why they differ from past experience or external sources of information.

In addition, if fair value less costs to sell is determined using discounted cash flow projections, the following information shall also be disclosed:

- the period over which management has projected cash flows (*);
- the growth rate used to extrapolate cash flow projections (*); and
- the discount rate(s) applied to the cash flow projections (*); and

- if a reasonably possible change in a key assumption on which management has based its determination of the unit's (or group of units') recoverable amount would cause the unit's (or group of units') carrying amount to exceed its recoverable amount:
  - the amount by which the unit's (or group of units') recoverable amount exceeds its carrying amount;
  - the value assigned to the key assumption; and
  - the amount by which the value assigned to the key assumption must change, after incorporating any consequential effects of that change on the other variables used to measure recoverable amount, in order for the unit's (or group of units') recoverable amount to be equal to its carrying amount.

In May 2008, *Improvements to IFRSs* was issued, which amended IAS 36 to require the disclosures above marked (*) for periods beginning on or after 1 January 2009. Earlier application of this amendment to IAS 36 is permitted, but an entity choosing to apply the amendment early must disclose that fact.

If some or all of the carrying amount of goodwill or intangible assets with indefinite useful lives is allocated across multiple CGUs (or groups of CGUs), and the amount so allocated to each unit (or group of units) is not significant in comparison with the entity's total carrying amount of goodwill or intangible assets with indefinite useful lives, that fact should be disclosed, together with the aggregate carrying amount of goodwill or intangible assets with indefinite useful lives allocated to those units (or groups of units). [IAS 36.135]

In addition to the requirements set out in the previous paragraph, if the recoverable amounts of any such units (or groups of units) are based on the same key assumption(s) and the aggregate carrying amount of goodwill or intangible assets with indefinite useful lives allocated to them is

10 Inventories

1 Introduction

The accounting treatment for inventories is prescribed in IAS 2 *Inventories*, which provides guidance for determining the cost of inventories and for subsequently recognising an expense, including any write-down to net realisable value. It also provides guidance on the cost formulas that are used to assign costs to inventories.

IAS 2 was last revised by the IASB in December 2003 as part of its Improvements Project, and was most recently amended when IFRS 8 *Operating Segments* was issued in November 2006.

This chapter discusses the requirements of IAS 2 in the following sections:

Section 2 Scope

Section 3 Measurement of inventories

Section 4 Presentation and disclosure

UK

The requirements of IAS 2 are for the most part very similar to those for stocks set out in the UK accounting standard SSAP 9 Stocks and long-term contracts. (*Accounting for long-term contracts is addressed by IAS 11* Construction Contracts *and discussed in **chapter 40**.) The main differences relating to inventories are as follows.*

- *Certain biological assets and agricultural produce are outside the scope of IAS 2 and are instead addressed by IAS 41 Agriculture. IAS 41 requires more use of fair values (see **chapter 43**). In the UK, SSAP 9 applies to such assets as UK GAAP has no equivalent of IAS 41.*
- *The requirements in respect of borrowing costs are different under UK GAAP and IFRSs. UK GAAP allows an accounting policy choice over whether borrowing costs are capitalised, and does not require a consistent accounting policy for different kinds of asset. Thus, under UK GAAP, an entity may capitalise borrowing costs in respect of tangible fixed assets but not in respect of inventories. By contrast, to the extent that borrowing costs are eligible for capitalisation, IAS 23 Borrowing Costs requires a consistent accounting policy for all 'qualifying assets' (which may include tangible and intangible fixed*

assets and inventories). The most recent version of IAS 23, which is effective from 2009, requires an accounting policy of capitalising eligible borrowing costs, whereas the previous version of IAS 23 also permitted an accounting policy of expensing such costs. The most recent version of IAS 23 adds a new scope exemption which allows an entity not to apply that Standard to inventories that are manufactured, or otherwise produced, in large quantities on a repetitive basis. The requirements of IAS 23 are discussed in ***chapter 27****.*

- *IAS 2 is more restrictive than SSAP 9 in allowing inventories to be carried at a current value (see* ***section 3*** *below).*
- *As discussed in* ***section 4*** *below, the disclosure requirements of IAS 2 are more extensive than those of SSAP 9.*

2 Scope

IAS 2 defines inventories as assets:

[IAS 2.6]

- held for sale in the ordinary course of business; or
- in the process of production for such sale; or
- in the form of materials or supplies to be consumed in the production process or in the rendering of services.

Inventories held for sale include inventories held by retailers or finished goods of a manufacturer. Inventories in the process of production for such sale may include both work in progress of a manufacturing entity and the labour costs of a service provider related to revenue not yet recognised for a particular project. Inventories in the form of materials or supplies to be consumed in the production process or in the rendering of services are generally referred to as raw materials.

See **example 6.1E** in **chapter 23** for discussion of retention of title clauses.

IAS 2 applies to all inventories, except:

[IAS 2.2]

- work in progress arising under construction contracts, including directly related service contracts (addressed by IAS 11 – see **chapter 40**);

- financial instruments (addressed by IAS 32 and IAS 39 – see **chapters 13 to 22**); and
- biological assets related to agricultural activity and agricultural produce at the point of harvest (addressed instead by IAS 41 – see **chapter 43**).

The Standard does not apply to the measurement of inventories held by:

[IAS 2.3]

- producers of agricultural and forest products, agricultural produce after harvest, and minerals and mineral products, to the extent that they are measured at net realisable value in accordance with well-established practices in those industries; or
- commodity broker-traders who measure their inventories at fair value less costs to sell.

Although inventories held by these entities are excluded from the measurement requirements of IAS 2, the Standard requires that where such inventories are measured at net realisable value / fair value less costs to sell, changes in those values are to be recognised in profit or loss in the period of change. [IAS 2.3] The other requirements of IAS 2, for example on presentation and disclosure, apply in the normal way to such inventories.

For the avoidance of doubt, note that the full requirements of IAS 2 apply to:

- property intended for sale in the ordinary course of business or in the process of construction or development for such sale, e.g. property acquired exclusively with a view to subsequent disposal in the near future or for development and resale; and
- producers of agricultural and forest products, agricultural produce after harvest, and minerals and mineral products, where they are not measured at net realisable value in accordance with well-established practices in those industries.

Example 2A

Accounting for pipeline fill – classification

Entity A operates a pipeline to transport crude oil. Entity A does not produce or distribute crude oil, it merely provides the use of its pipeline to the buyer and seller in a contract for a usage fee. The seller and buyer will independently determine the sales price, and either the buyer or the seller will pay a fee to A for transporting the crude oil via its pipeline.

In order to be operational at all times, the pipeline must be full of crude oil; therefore, A purchases oil to fill the pipeline. When crude oil is pushed into the pipeline at an entry point, it is then pushed out at the other end. When a seller of crude oil pushes product into the line, the end customer receives different oil, albeit, of the same grade and quality.

Entity A charges a fixed rate for its transportation services, and literally swaps crude oil at the entry point for crude oil at the exit point. In the course of transportation, A bears the risk of loss due to theft or line loss, up to the maximums allowed under the contract. Losses, such as these, are rare and normally surround a pipeline spill which is covered by A's insurance.

The pipeline fill meets the definition of an asset and should be recorded at cost when acquired. In accordance with IAS 16 *Property, Plant and Equipment*, the pipeline fill does not meet the definition of property, plant and equipment. [IAS 16.6] Rather, this is an item of inventory, as it is held 'in the form of materials or supplies to be consumed in the production process or in the rendering of services', and, therefore, satisfies the definition of inventory in IAS 2.6.

Because an accounting transaction does not take place at the time of each swap of crude oil, no step-up in the value of inventory is recognised. The pipeline fill is measured at the lower of cost and net realisable value throughout the term of the pipeline's operations in accordance with IAS 2.9.

Example 2B

Classification of assets acquired for sale in the ordinary course of business

Entity X, a lessor, leases assets ordinarily under three-year agreements. At the end of the lease term, the lessee has the option either to return or to acquire the asset. Some of the leases contain an extension option, which allows the lessee an additional three months to return or to acquire the asset. The extension option must be exercised prior to the end of the main lease term.

Entity X enters into 'residual value guarantee' contracts with Entity A, a third party. Under these contracts, Entity A will purchase the assets from Entity X at the end of each lease term at a predetermined price. Entity A receives a fee in return for writing the residual value guarantee.

When an extension option is exercised by the lessee, ownership of the asset is transferred to Entity A at the end of the main lease term for the predetermined price. During the extension period, Entity X passes the rental income to Entity A. At the end of the extension period, Entity A sells the asset either in the market or to the lessee. Rental income received by Entity A during the extension period is considered incidental to Entity A's operating activities, which are providing residual value guarantee contracts and selling the assets acquired.

In order to determine how to recognise the assets in the period from acquisition at the end of the main lease term to the point of sale, Entity A must establish how the assets are used in the business, i.e. whether they represent inventory or property, plant, and equipment.

In this scenario, Entity A acquires the assets at the end of the main lease term to profit from selling them in the market. In accordance with IAS 2, the assets are classified as inventory, since they are assets 'held for sale in the ordinary course of business'.

The assets acquired do not represent property, plant, and equipment, in accordance with IAS 16 *Property, Plant and Equipment*, because they are not held primarily for rental to others and are not expected to be used during more than one period.

2.1 Inventory on consignment

In certain industries it is common to have arrangements where a manufacturer supplies goods to a distributor on consignment. The manufacturer retains title to the product on consignment and the substantial risks and rewards of ownership until some future predetermined event occurs (e.g. sale to a third party customer) and triggers transfer of the title to the distributor.

The distributor should recognise the goods as inventory only when it bears substantial risks and rewards. IAS 18 provides some specific guidance on consignment sales and states that where the recipient of the goods (buyer) undertakes to sell goods on behalf of the shipper (seller), revenue is recognised by the shipper when goods are sold by the recipient to a third party. [IAS 18 Appendix Example 2(c)] Similarly, the risks and rewards of the consignment inventory may not pass to the distributor until it has sold the inventory to a third party customer. The seller would therefore not derecognise its inventory until that point in time.

There is no other guidance on accounting for consignment arrangements in IFRSs and, therefore, in accordance with IAS 8, management should consider the facts and circumstances of its consignment arrangements in order to determine the economic substance of the transactions, not merely their legal form. Until it is established that the transfer to the distributor is substantive and that the risks and rewards of the inventory have passed to the distributor, the goods should be treated as the manufacturer's inventory and excluded from the distributor's statement of financial position.

3 Measurement of inventories

Inventories are measured at the lower of cost and net realisable value. [IAS 2.9] The comparison of cost with net realisable value should, in principle, be carried out on an item-by-item basis but, if this is impracticable, groups of similar items may be considered together. It is unacceptable to compare the total net realisable value of all inventories with their total purchase price or production cost.

UK

The Introduction to IAS 2 makes clear that, with the limited exception of the classes of inventory listed in ***section 2*** *above (i.e. those outside the scope of the standard and those exempt from its measurement rules), it is not acceptable to adopt an accounting policy of carrying inventories at a current value. Although it is not common for UK entities to carry stocks at current value, such an approach is permitted under UK GAAP.*

3.1 Components of cost

IAS 2.10 specifies that the cost of inventories comprises:

- all costs of purchase (see **3.1.1**);
- costs of conversion (see **3.1.2**); and
- other costs incurred in bringing the inventories to their present location and condition (see **3.1.3**).

3.1.1 Costs of purchase

The costs of purchase of inventories include:

- purchase price;
- import duties and other taxes that are not recoverable by the entity (e.g. associated VAT paid to the extent that an entity cannot reclaim it);
- transport and handling costs; and
- other costs directly attributable to the acquisition of finished goods, materials and services.

Any trade discounts or rebates received are deducted in determining the costs of purchase of inventory. [IAS 2.11]

Example 3.1.1

Discounts and rebates

Entity A is granted a 10 per cent settlement discount by its main supplier on all purchases of inventory settled within 30 days of purchase.

In accordance with IAS 2.11, rebates and discounts that have been received as a reduction in the purchase price of inventories should be taken into consideration in the measurement of the cost of those inventories. Rebates that specifically and genuinely refund selling expenses should not be deducted from the cost of inventories.

Entity A should deduct the prompt settlement discount from the cost of the inventory. When measuring the cost of the inventory, the purchaser should estimate the expected settlement discount to be received from the supplier.

This is consistent with the accounting by the supplier required by IAS 18.10, which states that a transaction should be measured 'at the fair value of the consideration received or receivable taking into account the amount of any trade discounts and volume rebates allowed by the entity'.

3.1.1.1 *Direct materials and wastage*

Where raw material is unavoidably subject to wastage and spoilage during production, it will usually be appropriate to include the cost of such normal scrapping and wastage as part of the material cost of the product. Alternatively, if more practicable, the cost of material unavoidably scrapped or wasted may be included in overheads as part of the costs of conversion. It will not be appropriate, however, to include abnormal wastage in the carrying amount of inventories.

3.1.2 *Costs of conversion*

The costs of conversion of inventories include costs directly related to the units of production such as:

[IAS 2.12]

- direct labour, including all related employment taxes, and benefits and any share-based payment charges; and
- a systematic allocation of the fixed and variable production overheads incurred in converting materials into finished goods.

It is sometimes argued that overheads should be excluded from the cost of inventories on the grounds of prudence. Such an approach (sometimes called 'direct costing') is not acceptable under IAS 2, which requires a systematic allocation of production overheads. Similarly, 'marginal costing' approaches, whereby only costs that vary directly with volume of output are included in the measurement of inventory, and costs that accrue on a time basis (such as some overheads) are excluded, will not be acceptable under IAS 2, since they will fail to allocate fixed production overheads.

3.1.2.1 Direct labour

The cost of wages of employees directly engaged in production should be allocated to production on the basis of normal operating conditions. Labour costs that are the result of operating inefficiencies, such as abnormal idle capacity or abnormal rectification work, should not be included in inventory valuation. [IAS 2.13]

3.1.2.2 Overhead costs

Fixed production overheads are those indirect costs of production that remain relatively constant regardless of the volume of production. They may include:

- depreciation;
- rent and rates of the factory building;
- maintenance of the factory building and equipment; and
- factory management and administration.

The allocation of fixed production overheads to inventories should be based on the normal capacity of the production facilities, which is the production expected to be achieved on average over a number of periods under normal circumstances, taking into account the loss of capacity resulting from planned maintenance. The actual level of production may be used if it approximates to normal capacity. [IAS 2.13]

Where production levels are abnormally low, unallocated fixed overheads are recognised in profit or loss in the period in which they are incurred. In periods of abnormally high production, the amount of fixed overhead allocated to each unit of production is decreased so that inventories are not measured at above cost.

Variable production overheads are those indirect costs of production that vary directly, or nearly directly, with the volume of production. [IAS 2.12] Variable overheads may include indirect materials and indirect labour. They are allocated to each unit of production on the basis of the actual use of the production facilities.

Overheads that are properly classified as selling costs should not be included in the cost of inventories.

Other non-production overheads should only be included where this is justified by exceptional circumstances. Where firm sales contracts have been entered into for the provision of goods or services to customer specification, overheads (other than selling costs) relating to design, incurred before manufacture, may be included in arriving at cost.

The problem of determining the amount of overheads to be carried forward in inventories can be considered under two headings – identifying the overheads to be included and allocating those overheads to production in a logical manner. It is necessary first to analyse overheads by function between production, marketing and distribution, and administration. There are practical problems in making this analysis. For example, management salaries may include an element of supervision of production as well as of administration, and pension costs are likely to cover employees in the production function as well as those in sales and general administration departments. Central services departments, such as accounts, may provide identifiable services for production. Costs should be allocated over the functions on a reasonable basis, which should be consistently applied and which should be reviewed regularly.

The method of allocating overheads to production should be one that is appropriate to the nature of the product and the method of production. The most popular methods of allocating overheads are:

- by way of a labour hour or machine hour rate;
- in proportion to direct labour costs;
- in proportion to material costs;
- in proportion to prime costs; and

- equally to each unit of production (this is only appropriate where a single product is being produced in a given cost centre).

Whichever method of allocating overheads is adopted, the overheads should be allocated on the basis of the entity's normal level of activity. Overhead costs that are the result of operating inefficiencies, such as abnormal idle capacity or abnormal rectification work, should not be included in the inventory carrying amount.

Example 3.1.2.2

Capitalisation of lease costs

A company entered into a 50-year lease of land with the intention of constructing a building. The building will be sold together with any remaining lease interest over the land, and was therefore classified as inventory when construction began. Because of various required legal permits, construction began in year 6 of the lease and was completed in year 10.

The operating lease payments for the land should be included in the cost of inventories. IAS 2.10 states that the cost of inventories should include all costs of 'bringing the inventories to their present location and condition'. The operating lease cost of the land is required to construct the building and is therefore a cost of bringing the building to a condition in which it may be sold. However, only the operating lease payments made during the period of construction (i.e. years 6 to 10) may be capitalised. All operating lease payments made outside of this period must be recognised in profit or loss in accordance with IAS 17.33.

3.1.2.3 Allocation of cost to joint products and by-products

Sometimes two products may result from the production process when joint products are produced or when a product and a by-product are produced. In such cases, when it is difficult to allocate costs between the two, a rational and consistent allocation method is chosen. For example, the cost of joint products may be allocated on the basis of relative sales values either at the stage in production when each product becomes identifiable or when production is complete. If an immaterial by-product results from production of the main product, the net realisable value of the by-product is often deducted from the cost of the main product. Since the value of the by-product is immaterial, this deduction does not result in the cost of the main product being understated. [IAS 2.14]

3.1.3 Other costs

Other costs are included in the cost of inventories only to the extent that they are incurred in bringing the inventories to their present location and condition.

IAS 2.16 gives the following as examples of costs that should be excluded from the cost of inventories and recognised as expenses in the period in which they are incurred:

- abnormal amounts of wasted materials, labour, or other production costs;
- storage costs, unless those costs are necessary in the production process before a further production stage;
- administrative overheads that do not contribute to bringing inventories to their present location and condition; and
- selling costs.

> *Under UK GAAP, where a firm sales contract covers the provision of goods to a customer's specification, appendix 1 to SSAP 9 indicates that overheads from marketing and selling costs which were incurred before manufacture may be included in cost.* UK

3.1.4 Borrowing costs

Where an entity has adopted the most recent version of IAS 23 *Borrowing Costs*, or follows the allowed alternative treatment under the previous version of IAS 23, borrowing costs that are directly attributable to the acquisition, construction or production of a qualifying asset are capitalised as part of the cost of the qualifying asset. [IAS 23.8] A qualifying asset is defined as an asset that necessarily takes a substantial period of time to get ready for its intended use or sale. [IAS 23.5] Accordingly, inventories that necessarily take a substantial period of time to get ready for sale are qualifying assets. The basis for determining the appropriate amount of borrowing costs to be capitalised is discussed in **chapter 27**.

Note that the most recent version of IAS 23 adds a new scope exemption which allows an entity not to apply that Standard to inventories that are manufactured, or otherwise produced, in large quantities on a repetitive basis. [IAS 23.4]

Inventories that are manufactured, or otherwise produced, over a short period of time, and assets that are ready for sale when acquired, are not qualifying assets. [IAS 23.7]

UK

UK GAAP allows an accounting policy choice over whether borrowing costs are capitalised, and does not require the same accounting policy for borrowing costs to be applied to all qualifying assets.

An example of circumstances where the capitalisation of borrowing costs will be appropriate is where the reporting entity holds maturing inventories, such as whisky. The maturing period is a necessary part of the period of production and borrowing costs incurred during that period are attributable to bringing the product to its existing condition. Such borrowing costs are therefore appropriately included in the cost of inventories under IAS 2.

3.1.5 Inventories acquired on deferred settlement terms

Where an entity acquires inventories on deferred settlement terms, the transaction may involve a financing element, e.g. where there is a difference between the amount paid and the amount that would have been paid if the inventories had been acquired on normal credit terms. In such circumstances, the financing element is not included in the cost of the inventories, but is recognised as an interest expense over the period of the financing. [IAS 2.18]

3.1.6 Inventories invoiced in a foreign currency

Where inventories are invoiced in a foreign currency, the costs of those inventories should not include exchange differences.

Although this matter is not addressed directly in the body of IAS 2, the introduction to the Standard states that the capitalisation of such exchange differences is not permitted. [IAS 2.IN10] Before the revision of IAS 21 *The Effects of Changes in Foreign Exchange Rates* in 2003, that Standard had permitted the capitalisation of exchange differences in very limited circumstances. However, that exception to the general rule has now been removed from IAS 21 (see **chapter 28**).

However, where the purchase of inventories in a foreign currency has been cash flow hedged and the entity has a policy of basis adjusting (see **chapter 20**) then the effective portion of hedging gains and losses deferred in equity can be included in the initial recognition amount of the inventory.

3.1.7 *Transfer pricing*

Where the manufacturing process involves the transfer of work from one department to another, the transfer may be made at a price different from the cost incurred by the transferring department, either for reasons of convenience in accounting or as part of the system of management control. Where this occurs, it is necessary for the purpose of determining the cost of closing inventories to adjust the carrying amount to actual cost, by eliminating any profits or losses arising at the separate department levels.

3.1.8 *Costs of service providers*

To the extent that service providers have inventories, they measure them at the costs of their production. These costs consist mainly of labour and overhead costs related to any parts of service projects for which revenue has not yet been recognised. The bulk of such costs would relate to the labour costs attributable to the personnel performing the work, with other overheads such as costs associated with photocopying and telephoning allocated to each assignment as appropriate. [IAS 2.19]

Prices charged by service providers will generally reflect a profit margin and an allocation for non-attributable overheads. These items will often be allocated to specific service projects in the internal costing system of the service provider. However, IAS 2 specifically prohibits their inclusion in the cost of inventories of service providers for reporting purposes. [IAS 2.19]

3.1.9 *Cost of agricultural produce harvested from biological assets*

Consistent with IAS 41 *Agriculture*, agricultural produce that an entity has harvested from its biological assets is measured on initial recognition at its fair value less estimated costs to sell at the point of harvest. This is considered the cost of those inventories at that date for application of IAS 2. [IAS 2.20]

3.1.10 *Techniques for the measurement of cost*

Techniques for the measurement of cost, such as the standard cost method or the retail method, may be used providing the results approximate to actual cost. [IAS 2.21]

The standard cost method is a method often used by manufacturing entities to allocate fixed and variable production overheads to each item of inventory produced. The standard cost of a unit of production is based on the budgeted amount of fixed production overheads and the normal capacity of the production facilities. Standard costs are revised to take account of variances that arise when actual performance varies from the budgeted figures on which the standard cost was based.

Standard costs should only be used for year end inventory valuation purposes if they relate to actual costs incurred during the period. This can be achieved by frequent updating of standards or adjusting for the recorded variances.

The retail method may often be used by retailers who sell a large number of relatively homogeneous items with similar gross profit margins. The cost of inventories is determined by deducting the average margin from the selling price of the inventories. Such average margins take into account any reductions from the original selling price of items due to sales or other promotions. When the retail method is used, average margins are often determined on a departmental basis.

Example 3.1.10

Retail method

	Cost £'000	**Retail price £'000**
Opening inventories	300	400
Purchases	1,000	1,600
Total	1,300	2,000
Sales		(1,500)
Closing inventories at retail value		500

To convert closing inventories at retail value to closing inventories at cost, multiply by the ratio of cost: retail price for the year as follows:

£1,300,000 / £2,000,000 = 65%

65% x £500,000 = £325,000 = closing value of inventories

This method results in a valuation of inventories that approximates to average price and is, therefore, acceptable subject to certain constraints. The method only works satisfactorily for an entire department or shop if all of the lines held are expected to generate similar profit margins. For example, the inventories of a newsagent and confectioner normally include lines of widely differing profit margins and, to arrive at an acceptable inventory valuation using the retail method, it is necessary to divide the inventories into categories according to the profit margin achieved. A further problem with the retail method arises if the selling price on slow-moving items has been marked down. If the normal gross profit percentage is then deducted from such items, this will result in their being valued below cost, giving a result that may well be excessively prudent and, hence, unacceptable. It is, therefore, necessary to ensure that the volume of marked-down items is insignificant or, alternatively, they should be segregated and valued separately.

3.2 Cost formulas

Cost may be assigned to individual items of inventory, depending on their nature, either by the specific identification method or by the use of a cost formula. When the use of the specific identification method is inappropriate, IAS 2 allows a choice between two cost formulas: the weighted average formula and the first-in, first out (FIFO) formula.

Although the Standard permits a choice between the weighted average formula and FIFO for those inventories not measured by specific identification, it requires that the same cost formula is used for all inventories having a similar nature and use to the entity. For inventories with a different nature or use, a different cost formula may be justified. [IAS 2.25] Differences of geographical location or of tax rules will not, by themselves, justify the use of different cost formulas. [IAS 2.26]

3.2.1 Specific identification

IAS 2.23 specifies that the cost of inventories of items that are not ordinarily interchangeable, and of goods or services produced and segregated for specific projects, shall be assigned by using specific identification of their individual costs. The specific identification method entails assigning specific costs to identified items of inventory. Thus, this method is appropriate when items of inventory are produced for specific projects or when other items of inventory held could not be substituted for those items, e.g. antique cars or works of art.

The specific identification method is not appropriate for the routine production of inventories that are ordinarily interchangeable, because it would allow an entity to influence its reported profits by choosing whether to sell otherwise identical products having higher or lower specific costs. Some entities may nevertheless have set up computer systems that allocate specific costs to inventories that are ordinarily interchangeable. Whether the valuations produced by such systems will be acceptable will depend on whether they reasonably approximate those that would have resulted from the use of cost formulas.

3.2.2 *Weighted average cost*

The weighted average cost formula assigns a value to each item of inventory based on the weighted average of items in inventory at the beginning of the period and the weighted average of items of inventory purchased or produced during the period. Depending on the inventory system of the reporting entity, the weighted average cost is calculated either on a periodic basis or on a perpetual basis as the inventories are received.

Example 3.2.2

Weighted average cost

An entity had opening inventories of 15,000 units at a weighted average cost of £4 per unit, and made the following purchases during the year:

Date	Number of units	Cost per unit £	Total cost £
1 January	15,000	4.20	63,000
1 April	20,000	4.50	90,000
1 May	25,000	4.10	102,500
1 July	10,000	4.40	44,000
1 October	5,000	4.50	22,500
Total	75,000		322,000

Closing inventory comprised 20,000 units.

Under the weighted average formula, the number of units in closing inventory is multiplied by the weighted average cost per unit for the year:

	Number of units	Cost per unit £	Total cost £
Opening inventories	15,000	4.00	60,000
Purchases:			
1 January	15,000	4.20	63,000
1 April	20,000	4.50	90,000
1 May	25,000	4.10	102,500
1 July	10,000	4.40	44,000
1 October	5,000	4.50	22,500
Total	90,000		382,000

Thus, the weighted average cost per unit for the year is:

£382,000 / 90,000 = £4.24

The value of closing inventories is:

£4.24 x 20,000 = £84,800

3.2.3 *FIFO*

The FIFO cost formula assumes that the items of inventory that were purchased or produced first are sold first. Therefore, at the end of the period, the items in inventory are valued using the prices for the most recent purchases.

Example 3.2.3

FIFO

Same facts as in **example 3.2.2.**

Under the FIFO formula, the first units held are the first units sold. Therefore, closing inventories are valued at the cost per unit of the latest purchases.

Therefore, if 20,000 units are on hand at year end, the value of closing inventories is calculated as follows:

	Number of units	Cost per unit	Total cost
		£	£
October purchases	5,000	4.50	22,500
July purchases	10,000	4.40	44,000
May purchases	5,000	4.10	20,500
Total	20,000		87,000

Thus, closing inventories are valued at £87,000.

3.2.4 *Changing from one cost formula to another*

A reporting entity may decide to change from one cost formula to another (e.g. from the weighted average formula to FIFO) on the basis that the latter is more widely used in its particular industry and will therefore enhance comparability. A common question is whether such a change constitutes a change in accounting policy or a change in estimate. It is sometimes argued that it merely represents a change in estimate, in that it is a revision of the method of estimating cost. On balance, however, it seems appropriate to treat this as a change of accounting policy, for the following reasons.

- For inventories that are ordinarily interchangeable, IAS 2.24 states that a specific identification approach is inappropriate. Accordingly, the use of cost formulas is not merely a method of estimating the aggregate actual cost of individual items, since otherwise a specific identification approach would not be inappropriate, but would instead give the best possible estimate. Rather, cost formulas are used to arrive at a different figure that avoids the unacceptable distortions that would occur if a specific identification approach was adopted.

- IAS 2.36(a) requires disclosure of the accounting policies used for measuring inventories 'including the cost formula used', which reinforces the view that the cost formula selected is a matter of accounting policy.

Similarly, prior to the adoption of IAS 23 (revised March 2007), the decision whether to include borrowing costs as part of the cost of qualifying assets is a matter of accounting policy. Requirements and disclosures relating to changes in accounting policy are discussed in **chapter 4**.

Other changes to the way in which inventories are measured, e.g. any changes to the basis for allocation of overheads or other costs of conversion to inventories are likely to be changes of estimate rather than matters of accounting policy. Under IAS 8.39, the effect of a change in estimate should be separately disclosed, where material.

3.3 Determination of net realisable value

3.3.1 Measurement of net realisable value

IAS 2.6 defines net realisable value as the estimated selling price in the ordinary course of business less the estimated costs of completion and the estimated costs necessary to make the sale. The net realisable value of an item of inventory may fall below its cost for many reasons, including damage, obsolescence, a decline in selling prices, or an increase in the estimate of costs to complete and market the inventories.

The Standard highlights the distinction between net realisable value (as defined in the previous paragraph) and the fair value of inventories, which is defined as the amount for which they could be exchanged between knowledgeable, willing parties in an arm's length transaction. Net realisable value is the net amount that an entity expects to realise from the sale of inventory in the ordinary course of business, and is therefore an entity-specific value. Fair value measures the amount for which the same inventory could be exchanged between knowledgeable and willing buyers and sellers in the marketplace and it is therefore not entity-specific. The net realisable value of inventories may not equal their fair value less estimated costs to sell. [IAS 2.7] This will occur, for example, where the reporting entity has secured favourable binding sales contracts that have not been affected by more recent adverse market conditions.

Generally, estimates of net realisable value are made on an item-by-item basis. In some circumstances, however, it may be appropriate to group items of similar or related inventories. This may be the case when items of inventory:

[IAS 2.29]

- relate to the same product line and have similar purposes or end uses;
- are produced and marketed in the same geographical area; and
- cannot be practicably evaluated separately from other items in that product line.

Service providers generally accumulate costs for each service for which a separate selling price is charged. Thus, when determining net realisable value, it is appropriate to consider separately each service.

When estimating the net realisable value of inventories, management should consider all of the facts relating to the inventories and the operating environment at the time the estimates are made. Estimates are based on the most reliable evidence available at that time as to the amount that the inventories are likely to realise. These estimates take into consideration fluctuations in price or cost directly relating to events occurring after the reporting period to the extent that such events confirm conditions existing at the end of the reporting period. [IAS 2.30]

Example 3.3.1

Sales after the reporting period

An item of inventory which cost £100 is sold after the reporting period for £80. Sale at the lower price will generally provide evidence of the net realisable value of the inventory at the end of the reporting period and the closing inventories will therefore be carried at £80 less any costs to sell.

If, on further investigation, it transpired that the decrease in sales price arose because of damage to the inventory that occurred after the year end, this would indicate that this loss in value did not reflect conditions existing at the end of the reporting period and should not be accounted for until the next period. Instead, it would be necessary to assess whether the item could have been sold undamaged for an amount in excess of its cost (£100) plus any costs to sell.

When estimating the net realisable value of inventories, the purpose for which the inventories are held is taken into consideration. For example, if the inventories are held to satisfy firm sales contracts, the sales prices agreed in those contracts form the basis of the estimation. If the sales contracts are for less than the inventory quantities held, the net realisable value of the excess is based on general selling prices. [IAS 2.31]

3.3.2 *Writing inventories down to net realisable value*

When the net realisable value of an item of inventory is less than its cost, the excess is written off immediately in profit or loss.

Items of inventory are generally written down on an item-by-item basis. IAS 2 indicates that it is generally inappropriate to write down entire classifications of inventories, such as finished goods, or all of the inventories in a particular operating segment. [IAS 2.29]

Materials and other supplies held for use in the production of inventories are not written down below cost if the finished products in which they will be incorporated are expected to be sold at or above cost. However, when a decline in the price of materials indicates that the cost of the finished products will exceed net realisable value, the materials are written down to net realisable value. In such circumstances, the replacement cost of the materials may be the best available measure of their net realisable value. [IAS 2.32]

The costs necessary to make the sale should be determined in a manner consistent with the definition of 'costs of disposal' in IAS 36 *Impairment of Assets*, which states that these are 'incremental costs directly attributable to the disposal of an asset, excluding finance costs and income tax expense'. An incremental cost is one which would not be incurred if the activity was not undertaken. General overheads, therefore, may not be allocated for the purposes of determining costs to sell. Direct transaction costs must be allocated for the purposes of determining costs to sell.

3.3.3 *Reversals of write-downs*

Net realisable value estimates are made at the end of each reporting period. When subsequent evaluations show that the circumstances that previously caused inventories to be written down below cost no longer exist, or when there is clear evidence of an increase in net realisable value because of changed economic circumstances, write-downs of inventories previously recognised are required to be reversed. [IAS 2.33] This occurs, for example, when an item of inventory that is carried at net realisable value because its selling price had declined, is still on hand in a subsequent period and its selling price has increased (though it would still be necessary, where an item had been on hand for a long time, to consider whether there might be obsolescence issues).

The amount of the write-down should be reversed through profit or loss so that the new carrying amount is the lower of the cost and the revised net realisable value. Therefore, the amount of the reversal is limited to the amount of the original write-down.

3.4 Recognition as an expense

The amount of inventories recognised as an expense in the period will generally be:

[IAS 2.34]

- the carrying amount of inventories sold in the period; and
- the amount of any write-down of inventories to net realisable value and all losses of inventories in the period; less
- the amount of any reversal in the period of any write-down of inventories, arising from an increase in net realisable value.

If inventories are used by the entity rather than being sold, their cost may be capitalised as part of the cost of another asset, e.g. property, plant and equipment. Their cost is then recognised as an expense through depreciation of that asset.

4 Presentation and disclosure

4.1 Presentation

IAS 1(2007).54 (previously IAS 1(2003).68) requires that, where material, the total carrying amount of inventories (other than those included in disposal groups – see **chapter 29**) should be presented as a separate item in the statement of financial position. The analysis of items between current and non-current is discussed at **4.1** in **chapter 3**.

4.2 Disclosure

4.2.1 *Accounting policies*

IAS 2.36(a) requires financial statements to disclose the accounting policies adopted in measuring inventories, including the cost formula used.

The description of the accounting policies should be succinct, while making clear to the reader which of the different policies permissible under IAS 2 have been adopted.

4.2.2 *Analysis of carrying amount*

IAS 2.36(b) requires the total carrying amount of inventories to be disclosed, together with an analysis of the carrying amount in a manner appropriate to the entity.

Common classifications of inventories are as follows:

- merchandise;
- production supplies;
- materials;
- work in progress; and
- finished goods.

Entities in specialist industries should use a classification that is meaningful in the context of their operations, e.g. property development entities could analyse their development portfolio as:

- land held for development;
- properties under construction; and
- completed properties held for sale.

The inventories of a service provider may simply be described as work in progress.

4.2.3 *Expected realisation*

IAS 1(2007).61 (previously IAS 1(2003).52) requires that an entity should disclose for each asset that combines amounts expected to be recovered both within twelve months of and after twelve months from the end of the reporting period, the amount expected to be recovered after more than twelve months. It is appropriate for an entity to disclose the amount of inventories that are expected to be recovered after more than one year from the end of the reporting period. [IAS 1(2007).65, previously IAS 1(2003).56]

4.2.4 *Inventories carried at fair value less costs to sell*

IAS 2.36(c) requires separate disclosure of the carrying amount of inventories carried at fair value less costs to sell.

As discussed in **section 2**, this requirement should in practice apply only to certain inventories held by commodity broker-traders. (As explained in **chapter 29**, where inventories are classified as held for sale as part of a disposal group, they continue to be measured in accordance with IAS 2. The disposal group itself may then be written down to fair value less costs to sell, but not the inventories per se.)

4.2.5 *Amounts recognised in profit or loss*

The Standard requires separate disclosure of:

- the amount of inventories recognised as an expense during the period; [IAS 2.36(d)]
- the amount of any write down of inventories to net realisable value recognised as an expense in the period; [IAS 2.36(e)] and
- the amount of any reversal of any write down recognised as a reduction in the inventory expense for the period. [IAS 2.36(f)]

In addition, disclosure is required of the circumstances or events that led to any recognised reversal of a write-down of inventories. [IAS 2.36(g)]

These disclosures are not required under UK GAAP. Accordingly, if a UK entity proposes to adopt IFRSs, it will wish to consider whether its existing accounting systems are capable of tracking the required information, particularly that relating to net realisable value write-downs. UK

IAS 2.38 specifies that the amount of inventories recognised as an expense during the period, which is commonly described as cost of sales, consists of:

- the costs that have previously been included in the measurement of inventory that has now been sold; and
- unallocated production overheads; and
- abnormal amounts of production costs of inventories.

4.2.6 *Inventories pledged as security*

IAS 2.36(h) requires entities to disclose the carrying amount of inventories pledged as security for liabilities.

11 Provisions, contingent liabilities and contingent assets

1 Introduction

IAS 37 *Provisions, Contingent Liabilities and Contingent Assets* deals with the appropriate recognition criteria, measurement bases and the disclosure requirements applied to provisions, contingent liabilities and contingent assets. It has been effective since 1 July 1999, and was most recently amended when the revised version of IFRS 3 *Business Combinations* was issued in January 2008.

This chapter discusses the requirements of IAS 37 in the following sections:

Section 2	Scope
Section 3	Definition and recognition of provisions, contingent liabilities and contingent assets
Section 4	Measurement of provisions
Section 5	Reimbursements
Section 6	Changes in provisions
Section 7	Use of provisions
Section 8	Illustrative examples
Section 9	IFRIC Interpretations
Section 10	Presentation and disclosure
Section 11	Future developments

IAS 37's recognition and disclosure requirements are designed to prohibit three practices:

- the creation of provisions where there is no liability;
- the use of old provisions created for one purpose to meet new expenditure for a different purpose; and

- the undisclosed release of provisions into profit or loss.

UK

The UK equivalent of IAS 37 is FRS 12 Provisions, Contingent Liabilities and Contingent Assets. *The two standards were developed at the same time as part of a joint project between the ASB and the IASB. Accordingly, there are no real differences of substance between them, though FRS 12 does include slightly more guidance than IAS 37 in certain areas.*

2 Scope

The requirements of IAS 37 apply to all provisions, contingent liabilities and contingent assets other than those:

[IAS 37.1]

- resulting from executory contracts, except where the contract is onerous; and
- covered by another Standard.

Note that, unlike IAS 16 *Property, Plant and Equipment* (see **section 2** in **chapter 6**), IAS 37 does not include a scope exclusion for the extractive industries. Therefore, the requirements of IAS 37 should be applied and liabilities recognised for restoration costs (for example) where the recognition and measurement criteria are met. Refer to Examples 2A, 2B and 3 of Appendix C to IAS 37 for examples of the application of IAS 37 to the extractive industries (see **section 8** below).

2.1 Executory contracts

Executory contracts are contracts under which neither party has performed any of its obligations, or both parties have partially performed their obligations to an equal extent. [IAS 37.3] Executory contracts do not fall within the scope of IAS 37, unless they are onerous (see **3.9.2** below).

Examples of executory contracts include:

- employee contracts in respect of continuing employment;
- contracts for future delivery of services such as gas and electricity;

- obligations to pay local authority charges and similar levies; and
- most purchase orders.

2.2 Provisions, contingent liabilities and contingent assets covered by other Standards

There are some instances where another Standard deals with a specific type of provision, contingent liability or contingent asset, in which case the more specific Standard should be applied, as follows:

[IAS 37.5]

- the acquirer's treatment of contingent liabilities assumed in a business combination is addressed by IFRS 3 *Business Combinations* (see **chapter 34**);
- provisions relating to construction contracts are dealt with under IAS 11 *Construction Contracts* (see **chapter 40**);
- provisions relating to income taxes are dealt with under IAS 12 *Income Taxes* (see **chapter 12**);
- provisions relating to leases generally fall within the scope of IAS 17 *Leases* (see **chapter 26**). As IAS 17 contains no specific requirements to deal with operating leases that have become onerous, IAS 37 will apply to such onerous contracts;
- provisions relating to employee benefits are dealt with under IAS 19 *Employee Benefits* (see **chapter 24**); and
- provisions relating to insurance contracts are dealt with under IFRS 4 *Insurance Contracts* (see **chapter 44**). However, IAS 37 applies to provisions, contingent liabilities and contingent assets of an insurer other than those arising from its contractual obligations and rights under insurance contracts within the scope of IFRS 4.

IAS 37 *does* apply to provisions for restructurings (including discontinued operations). When a restructuring meets the definition of a discontinued operation, additional disclosures may be required by IFRS 5 *Non-current Assets Held for Sale and Discontinued Operations* (see **chapter 29**). [IAS 37.9]

2.3 Financial instruments

IAS 37 does not apply to financial instruments (including guarantees) that fall within the scope of IAS 39 *Financial Instruments: Recognition and Measurement* (see **chapter 13**). [IAS 37.2]

Financial guarantee contracts are not within the scope of IAS 37. They are within the scope of IAS 39, except in certain limited circumstances where the issuer may instead elect to apply IFRS 4 *Insurance Contracts* (see the discussion at **2.3.2** in **chapter 13**).

2.4 Use of the term 'provision'

The use of the term 'provision' is restricted to liabilities of uncertain timing or amount. It does not cover adjustments to the carrying amounts of assets (such as depreciation, impairment and allowances for doubtful debts) for which the term 'provision' is used in some jurisdictions. [IAS 37.7]

2.5 Related income and expenditure

Although some amounts treated as provisions may relate to the recognition of revenue (e.g. where an entity gives guarantees in exchange for a fee), IAS 37 does not deal with revenue recognition. IAS 18 *Revenue* identifies the circumstances in which revenue is recognised and provides practical guidance on the application of the recognition criteria (see **chapter 23**). [IAS 37.6]

IAS 37 does not specify whether expenditure should be capitalised as an asset or treated as an expense. These issues are addressed in other Standards. Therefore, IAS 37 itself neither prohibits nor requires capitalisation of the costs recognised when a provision is made. [IAS 37.8]

3 Definition and recognition of provisions, contingent liabilities and contingent assets

3.1 Provisions

IAS 37 defines a provision as a liability of uncertain timing or amount, i.e. a subset of liabilities. [IAS 37.10] The Standard repeats the definition of a liability found in the *Framework for the Preparation and Presentation of Financial Statements*, i.e. a present obligation of the entity arising from past events, the settlement of which is expected to result in an outflow from the entity of resources embodying economic benefits. [IAS 37.10]

A provision should be recognised when and only when:

[IAS 37.14]

- an entity has a present obligation (legal or constructive) as a result of a past event;
- it is probable that an outflow of resources embodying economic benefits will be required to settle the obligation; and
- a reliable estimate can be made of the amount of the obligation.

These recognition criteria cover two elements: the existence of a liability and the measurement of that liability.

Provision = **Liability** + **Ability to measure**

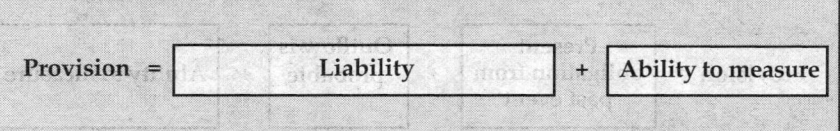

The existence element is further subdivided into two conditions.

Liability

Provision = **Present obligation from past event** + **Outflow is probable** + **Ability to measure**

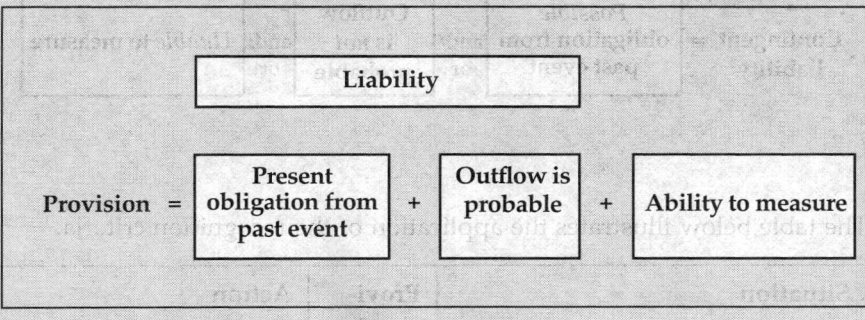

3.2 Contingent liabilities

A contingent liability is defined as:

[IAS 37.10]

- a possible obligation that arises from past events and whose existence will be confirmed only by the occurrence or non-occurrence of one or more uncertain future events not wholly within the control of the entity; or
- a present obligation that arises from past events that is not recognised because:
    - it is not probable that an outflow of resources embodying economic benefits will be required to settle the obligation; or

- the amount of the obligation cannot be measured with sufficient reliability.

Under IAS 37, a reporting entity should not recognise a contingent liability in its statement of financial position. [IAS 37.27]

Therefore, a contingent liability, which is not recognised but is disclosed by way of note, results when one or more of the three recognition criteria for a provision, as outlined at **3.1** above, is not met.

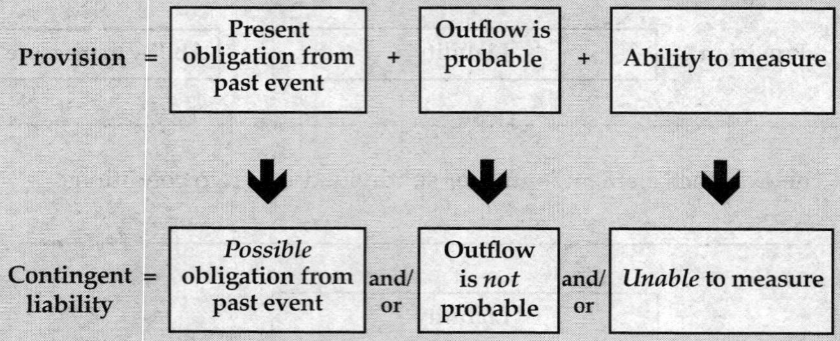

The table below illustrates the application of the recognition criteria.

Situation	**Provision?**	**Action**
Past event has occurred, resulting in a *possible* obligation for which a transfer of benefits is possible but not probable (see **3.6** below).	✘	Unless the possibility of a transfer of benefits is remote, disclose a contingent liability.
Past event has occurred, resulting in a present obligation for which there may *possibly* be a transfer of benefits, but for which there probably will not.	✘	Unless the possibility of a transfer of benefits is remote, disclose a contingent liability.
Past event has occurred, resulting in a present obligation for which it is likely there will be a transfer of benefits, but a *reliable estimate cannot be made* of the amount of the obligation.	✘	Disclose a contingent liability. (N.B. This situation is likely to be very rare – see **3.8** below).

Past event has occurred, resulting in a present obligation for which it is likely there will be a transfer of benefits; a reliable estimate can be made of the amount of the obligation.	✓	Recognise provision and make necessary disclosures.
An obligating *event has not taken place by the end of the reporting period*, but it takes place after the reporting period, resulting in an obligation for which it is likely there will be a transfer of benefits; a reliable estimate can be made of the amount of the obligation.	✗	Consider whether the requirements of IAS 10 *Events after the Reporting Period* require the disclosure of the non-adjusting event that has arisen.

3.3 Contingent assets

A contingent asset is defined as a possible asset that arises from past events and whose existence will be confirmed only by the occurrence or non-occurrence of one or more uncertain future events not wholly within the control of the entity. [IAS 37.10]

Contingent assets are not recognised, but are disclosed by way of note where an inflow of economic benefits is probable. When the realisation of income is virtually certain, however, the related asset is not a contingent asset and its recognition is appropriate. [IAS 37.33]

3.4 Distinguishing provisions from other liabilities

Provisions can be distinguished from other types of liability, including those that involve uncertain amounts, by considering the events that give rise to the obligation and also the degree of uncertainty as to the amount of the liability. In each case, the definition of a liability will be met through the existence of a present obligation arising from a past event.

For example, trade payables are liabilities to pay for goods/services already received/supplied and which have been invoiced or otherwise agreed with the supplier. Accruals, on the other hand, are liabilities to pay for goods/services already received/supplied but which have not been invoiced or otherwise agreed with the supplier. Although it is sometimes necessary to estimate the amount or timing of accruals, the uncertainty is generally much less than for provisions. Accruals are often reported as part of trade and other payables, whereas provisions are reported separately. [IAS 37.11]

Example	Classification	Degree of uncertainty
Goods or services received and invoiced	Trade payable	None
Goods or services received, but not invoiced	Accrual	Some
Legal claim from supplier for breach of exclusive supply agreement	Provision (if conditions met)	Significant

3.5 Present obligations and past events

As will be clear from the table set out at **3.2** above, the existence of a present obligation arising from a past obligating event is a key consideration when determining whether classification as a provision or as a contingent liability is appropriate.

As defined in IAS 37.10, an obligating event is an event that creates a legal or constructive obligation that results in an entity having no realistic alternative to settling that obligation. A legal obligation derives either from the terms of a contract (either explicit or implicit), or legislation or other operation of the law. A constructive obligation is an obligation deriving from an entity's actions where:

- by an established pattern of past practice, published policies or a sufficiently specific current statement, the entity has indicated to other parties that it will accept certain responsibilities; and
- as a result, the entity has created a valid expectation on the part of those other parties that it will discharge those responsibilities.

3.5.1 Events before the end of the reporting period

Financial statements deal with the financial position of an entity at the end of its reporting period and not its possible position in the future. The only liabilities recognised in an entity's statement of financial position are those that exist at the end of the reporting period. Therefore, no provision is recognised for costs that need to be incurred to operate in the future, notwithstanding that such costs may be necessary to continue as a going concern. [IAS 37.18]

3.5.2 *Future actions*

It is only those obligations arising from past events that exist independently of the reporting entity's future actions that are recognised as provisions. [IAS 37.19] One example in which a provision is recognised might be for clean-up costs relating to environmental damage. Even if the entity changes its future business activities (at an extreme, by ceasing to trade), it will still incur the expenses relating to cleaning up, because of its past activities. In contrast, if an airline is legally required to carry out maintenance of its aircraft if it is to continue to operate them, in theory, it could stop flying planes, or stop flying the particular plane, and therefore no present obligation exists.

3.5.3 *Role of third parties*

An obligation always involves a commitment to another party. It is not necessary, however, to know the identity of the party to whom the obligation is owed – the obligation may be to the public at large. [IAS 37.20]

3.5.4 *Management decisions*

It is because of the requirement for a clear commitment to another party, referred to in **3.5.3**, that a decision made by management before the end of the reporting period does not of itself give rise to a present obligation, unless it is communicated to those affected by it in a sufficiently specific manner to raise a valid expectation in them that the entity will discharge its responsibilities. [IAS 37.20]

3.5.5 *New legislation*

It is possible that an event may not give rise to an obligation immediately, but may do so at a later date. This could be as a result of changes in the law or because an act (e.g. a sufficiently specific public statement) by the entity gives rise to a constructive obligation. For example, where an entity causes environmental damage, this may not give rise to an obligation for remedial costs if there is no applicable legislation. The causing of the damage will become an obligating event, however, if a new law requires the existing damage to be rectified or if the entity publicly accepts responsibility for rectification in a way that creates a constructive obligation. [IAS 37.21]

Where details of new legislation have yet to be finalised, an obligation arises only when the legislation is virtually certain to be enacted as drafted. Under IAS 37, such an obligation is treated as a legal obligation. In many cases, however, it will be impossible to be virtually certain of the enactment of a law until it is actually enacted. [IAS 37.22]

3.5.6 *Smoothing of results*

IAS 37 seeks to prevent artificial 'smoothing' of results. By basing the recognition of a provision on the existence of a present obligation, it rules out the recognition of any provision made simply to allocate expenses over more than one period or otherwise to smooth the results reported. For example, entities are not permitted to provide on an annual basis for items such as future repairs, so as to produce a reasonably level charge each year. Unless dealt with through a component approach to depreciation (see **chapter 6**), such costs will instead generally be charged to profit or loss when they are actually incurred, i.e. when the work is done.

3.5.7 *The role of prudence*

As discussed in **chapter 2**, the *Framework for the Preparation and Presentation of Financial Statements* requires the exercise of prudence in the preparation of financial statements, i.e. the observation of a degree of caution in the exercise of the judgements needed in making the estimates required under conditions of uncertainty, such that assets or income are not overstated and liabilities or expenses are not understated. The Framework qualifies this statement, however, by specifying that the exercise of prudence does not allow, for example, the creation of hidden reserves or excessive provisions because this would result in financial statements that were not neutral and, therefore, not providing reliable information to users of financial statements. [FR.37]

A reporting entity may be aware of some future commitment to spend money, and may even feel less well off at the prospect of the expense. But future expenditure, however necessary, does not justify the recognition of a provision unless a liability exists at the period end.

3.6 Situations of uncertainty regarding present obligations

IAS 37.15 states that there will, on rare occasions, be circumstances where it is unclear whether a present obligation exists. In order to determine whether a present obligation exists under such circumstances (for example, where the facts in a law suit are disputed), the Standard advises that account should be taken of all available evidence. Such evidence may include, for example, the opinion of experts. It will also include additional evidence contributed by events occurring after the reporting period. Preparers of financial statements should look at all of the available evidence and come to a reasoned judgement as to whether it is more likely than not that a present obligation exists. If it is more likely than not that a present obligation exists, a provision should be recognised. Otherwise, a contingent liability is disclosed, unless the possibility of any transfer of economic benefits in settlement is remote. [IAS 37.16]

3.7 Transfer of economic benefits

An essential element of the definition of a liability is the existence of an obligation to transfer economic benefits. Recognition of a provision is conditional on the transfer of economic benefits being 'probable'. For the purpose of IAS 37, probable is taken to mean more likely than not to occur. [IAS 37.23]

Thus, 'more likely than not' means that the chance that a transfer of economic benefits will occur is over 50 per cent.

Where a number of similar obligations exist (e.g. product warranties), the overall probability that a transfer of economic benefits will be made is determined by looking at the class of obligations as a whole. A typical situation will be that, despite the likelihood of an outflow of resources for any one item being small, it may well be probable that a transfer of some economic benefits will be needed to settle the class of obligations as a whole. Where this is the case, assuming that the other recognition criteria are met, then a provision is recognised (see **4.2** below). [IAS 37.24]

3.8 Reliable estimate

The use of estimates is an inherent part of preparing financial statements. Provisions are clearly uncertain by nature, but IAS 37 emphasises that it should not be impossible to determine a range of possible outcomes and, from this range, to reach an appropriate conclusion that is sufficiently reliable for the provision to be recognised. IAS 37.26 concludes that the circumstances in which it will not be possible to reach a reliable estimate will be extremely rare. In those extremely rare circumstances, a liability exists that cannot be recognised. That liability will instead be disclosed as a contingent liability.

3.9 Specific applications of recognition criteria

3.9.1 Future operating losses

IAS 37 contains two prohibitions on the recognition of provisions for future operating losses:

- a general prohibition, on the grounds that there is no present obligation and thus no liability (albeit that the expectation of future operating losses may indicate a need to test whether assets have been impaired); [IAS 37.63 – 65] and
- a specific prohibition in respect of future operating losses up to the date of a restructuring – again on grounds that there is no present obligation, unless the losses relate to an onerous contract (see **3.9.2** below). [IAS 37.82]

In both cases, future operating losses relate to an activity that will continue, albeit in a restructured form, and are presumed to be avoidable (e.g. by an immediate closure of the loss-making activities). They are therefore appropriately recognised as the activity occurs.

3.9.2 Onerous contracts

Provision is required for the present obligation arising under an onerous contract. [IAS 37.66] Where assets dedicated to a contract are involved, however, a separate provision is recognised only after any impairment loss has been recognised on those assets. [IAS 37.69]

An onerous contract is defined in IAS 37.10 as a contract in which the unavoidable costs of meeting the obligations under the contract exceed the economic benefits expected to be received under it. In other words, provision should be made for any unavoidable net loss arising from the contract. The unavoidable costs under a contract reflect the least net cost of exiting from the contract, i.e. the lower of:

[IAS 37.68]

- the cost of fulfilling the contract; and
- any compensation or penalties arising from failure to fulfil the contract.

Example 3.9.2A

Long-term contracts

Long-term contracts for the supply of goods or services where costs have risen or current market prices have fallen are onerous, and a provision is recognised, to the extent that future supplies must be made at a loss. No provision is recognised under a contract for the supply of goods which is profitable, but at a reduced margin compared to other contracts, since there is no probable net transfer of economic benefits by the reporting entity.

Example 3.9.2B

Vacant property

A lease for property that has been vacated is onerous, and a provision recognised, to the extent that rentals continue that are not recoverable from subleasing the property. The provision should represent the best estimate of the expenditure required to settle the obligation at the end of the reporting period, which, in this case, might be the amount the landlord would accept to terminate the lease.

Examples of contracts that do not meet the criteria for recognition of a provision are:

- those routine purchase orders, and similar contracts, which realistically could be cancelled by agreement with the vendor without paying compensation; and
- purchase orders where the future benefits from use of the asset exceed its cost, notwithstanding that compensation must be paid if the order is cancelled.

Executory contracts (i.e. contracts under which neither party has performed any of its obligations or both parties have performed their obligations to an equal extent) that are not onerous are excluded from the scope of IAS 37.

With the exception of onerous contracts, therefore, an entity will recognise no liability in respect of the purchase of goods or services until those goods or services are supplied, notwithstanding that the entity may become committed to paying for them at an earlier date.

3.9.3 *Restructuring provisions*

IAS 37 provides specific guidance on how the general recognition criteria for provisions should be applied to restructurings.

3.9.3.1 Definition of a restructuring

A restructuring is defined as a programme that is planned and controlled by management, and materially changes either:

[IAS 37.10]

- the scope of a business undertaken by an entity; or
- the manner in which that business is conducted.

The term 'restructuring' therefore includes events such as:

[IAS 37.70]

- the sale or termination of a line of business;
- the closure of business locations in a country or region or the relocation of business activities from one country or region to another;
- changes in management structure, e.g. the elimination of a layer of management; and
- fundamental reorganisations that have a material effect on the nature and focus of the entity's operations.

3.9.3.2 Specific recognition criteria for restructuring provisions

The two principal requirements for the recognition of a provision for a restructuring are that the entity:

[IAS 37.72]

- has a detailed formal plan; and
- has raised a valid expectation in those affected that the plan will be carried out, by starting to implement that plan or by announcing its main features to those affected by it.

The detailed formal plan must identify:

[IAS 37.72]

- the business or part of a business concerned;
- the principal locations affected;
- the location, function and approximate number of employees who will be compensated for terminating their services;
- the expenditures that will be undertaken; and
- when the plan will be implemented.

Suitable evidence that an entity has started to implement a restructuring plan will, for example, be provided by:

[IAS 37.73]

- dismantling plant; or
- selling assets; or
- by the public announcement of the main features of the plan.

Note, however, that a public announcement of a detailed plan to restructure constitutes a constructive obligation to restructure only if it is made in such a way and in sufficient detail (i.e. setting out the main features of the plan) that it gives rise to valid expectations in other parties such as customers, suppliers and employees (or their representatives) that the entity will carry out the restructuring. [IAS 37.73] Accordingly, for a plan to be sufficient to give rise to a constructive obligation when it is communicated to those affected by it, implementation of the plan should be planned to begin as soon as possible and to be completed within a timeframe that makes significant change to the plan unlikely. Where either there is a long delay before commencement, or execution of the plan will take an unreasonably long time, the timeframe allows opportunities for the plan to be changed. Thus, it is unlikely that the reporting entity has raised a valid expectation that it is sufficiently committed to the restructuring. [IAS 37.74]

The requirement for the existence of a valid expectation in those affected relates to the situation at the end of the reporting period. The fact that implementation has commenced by the date that the financial statements are authorised for issue does not of itself provide evidence that a present obligation existed at the end of the reporting period.

A management or board decision to go ahead with its plan will not, by itself, give rise to a constructive obligation, unless it is accompanied by commencement of the plan, or by a suitable announcement. [IAS 37.75] An obligation may, however, result from earlier events taken together with such a decision. For example, negotiations with employee representatives for termination payments, or with purchasers for the sale of an operation, may have been concluded subject only to board approval. Once that approval has been obtained and communicated to the other parties, the entity has a constructive obligation to restructure, if the general conditions set out above have been met. [IAS 37.76] In addition, a constructive obligation could arise where, as happens in some countries, a board includes non-management representatives such as employees, because a decision by such a board involves communication to those representatives. [IAS 37.77]

A valid expectation is unlikely to exist in either of the following circumstances:

- management has developed a detailed plan, but has not notified those affected by it, even though it can point to previous instances where it has proceeded with a plan; or
- management has developed a plan that involves the closure of one of two possible sites. It has made general indications to employees that one site will close, but has not communicated which of the two sites will close, in order to avoid alienation of employees at that site before implementation commences.

Example 3.9.3.2

Lease termination

An entity has developed a detailed formal plan for restructuring a business, and has announced the key features of the restructuring to all affected by it in a manner that meets the criteria of IAS 37. As part of the restructuring, the entity has entered into an oral agreement (i.e. a commitment has been established) with the landlord to terminate a lease and pay a settlement fee of £1,000,000 to the landlord. The settlement fee represents a direct expenditure resulting from the restructuring. The entity does not expect to be able to sublet the lease; therefore, £1,000,000 represents the minimum expected obligation.

A provision should be recognised for the £1,000,000 settlement fee for the lease because a valid expectation has been created between the lessor and lessee that the lease will be terminated. The entity has a constructive restructuring obligation because it has publicly announced the plan to restructure. Such an announcement gives rise to valid expectations in other parties (e.g. the lessor) that the entity will carry out the restructuring, which includes the termination of the lease.

3.9.3.3 *Sale of an operation as part of a restructuring*

IAS 37.78 specifies that an obligation does not exist for the sale of an operation until the reporting entity is committed to the sale, i.e. there is a binding sale agreement. Until there is such an agreement, the reporting entity will be able to change its mind and, indeed, will be required to take another course of action if a purchaser cannot be found on acceptable terms. [IAS 37.79]

When a sale is only one element of a restructuring plan, a constructive obligation can arise for the other parts of the restructuring before a binding sale agreement exists. In such circumstances, the assets of the operation should be reviewed for impairment. [IAS 37.79]

> Where, at the year end, an entity had signed heads of agreement to dispose of a loss-making part of its business, but a binding sale agreement was not signed until a month later, no provision can be recognised at the end of the reporting period. An impairment review should be carried out, however, and this may cover much of the provision that would otherwise have been made. Also, consideration should be given to whether the business has onerous contracts for which provision should be made.

3.9.3.4 *Amounts to be included in a restructuring provision*

The amounts to be included in a restructuring provision are restricted to the direct expenditures arising from the restructuring, i.e. those that are both:

[IAS 37.80]

- necessarily entailed by the restructuring; and
- not associated with the ongoing activities of the reporting entity.

3.9.3.5 *Amounts to be excluded from a restructuring provision*

Specific items that are excluded from restructuring provisions under IAS 37, on the basis that they relate to the ongoing activities of the business, are:

[IAS 37.81]

- retraining or relocating continuing staff;
- marketing; and
- investment in new systems and distribution networks.

3.9.3.6 *Restructuring provision flowchart*

The flowchart set out below details the steps necessary to determine whether a restructuring provision should be recognised.

Recognition of restructuring provisions

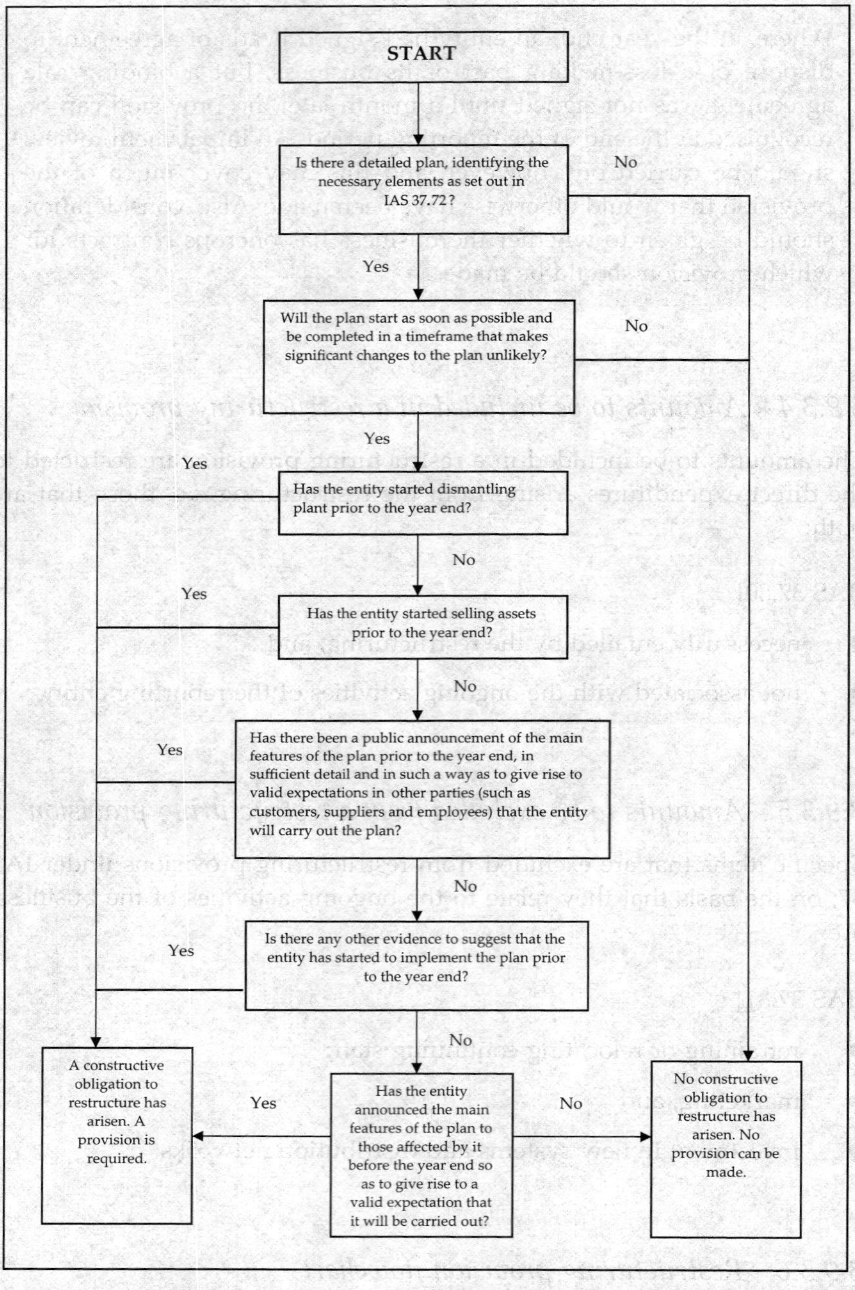

4 Measurement of provisions

4.1 Best estimate

The amount to be recognised as a provision under IAS 37 is the 'best estimate' of the expenditure required to settle the present obligation at the end of the reporting period. [IAS 37.36] The reference to the end of the reporting period does not preclude use of later additional evidence or better information, but indicates that the best estimate will be the amount that a reporting entity would rationally pay at the end of the reporting period to have the obligation taken away – by settlement or by transfer to a third party. [IAS 37.37]

The addition of 'rationally' in IAS 37.37 suggests that, although it may be difficult to arrange settlement or transfer, there is nevertheless a point of balance, and thus a price, at which management, taking all possible outcomes into account, could be willing to settle.

Ultimately, the best estimate will be determined based on the judgement of management and will reflect experience of similar transactions. In reaching their judgement, reports of independent experts may be required. Examples of relevant independent experts are:

- solicitors and barristers;
- surveyors and valuers;
- loss adjusters;
- actuaries; and
- technical experts (e.g. regarding a decommissioning process).

4.2 Use of expected value

4.2.1 *Large populations*

Where the provision relates to a large population of items, the use of an 'expected value' is appropriate to arrive at a best estimate of the obligation. This is the amount that takes account of all possible outcomes, using probabilities to weight the outcomes. [IAS 37.39] Where there is a continuous range of possible outcomes, and each point in that range is as likely as any other, the mid-point of the range is used.

Expected value, as a method of estimation, has a number of desirable features. The method provides an estimate that reflects the entire probability distribution, i.e. all the possible outcomes weighted by their probabilities. For a given assessed distribution, the method has the advantage of objectivity in that different measurers would calculate the same estimate. Furthermore, expected value is additive (i.e. the expected value of a number of items is the sum of the expected values of the individual items).

Example 4.2.1

Best estimate: large populations

An entity faces 100 legal claims, each with a 40 per cent likelihood of success with no cost and a 60 per cent likelihood of failure with the cost of each claim to be £1 million.

Using expected value, the statistical likelihood is that 60 per cent of the claims will result in a cost of £1 million. Thus, the best estimate of the provision should be calculated as 60 per cent x 100 x £1 million = £60 million.

4.2.2 *Single obligations*

Where a single obligation is being measured, IAS 37.40 indicates that the individual most likely outcome may be the best estimate of the liability. Even in such a case, however, it will be necessary to consider other possible outcomes. Where the other possible outcomes are either mostly higher or mostly lower than the most likely outcome, the best estimate will be a higher or lower amount.

Thus, where the provision relates to a single event, or a small number of events, expected value is not a valid technique.

Example 4.2.2A

Best estimate: single obligation

An entity faces a single legal claim, with a 40 per cent likelihood of success with no cost and a 60 per cent likelihood of failure with a cost of £1 million.

Expected value is not valid in this case, since the outcome will never be a cost of £600,000 (60 per cent x £1 million). It will either be nil or £1 million. IAS 37.40 indicates that the provision may be estimated at the individual most likely outcome. In this example, it is more likely that a cost of £1 million will result and, therefore, a provision for £1 million will be made.

Generally, where the most likely outcome is close to the expected value, it will be appropriate to provide for the most likely outcome, since expected value provides evidence of the probable outflow of benefits.

Example 4.2.2B

Best estimate: expected value (1)

An entity is required to replace a major component in an asset under warranty. Each replacement costs £1 million. From experience, there is a 30 per cent chance of a single failure, a 50 per cent chance of 2 failures, and a 20 per cent chance of three failures.

The most likely outcome is two failures, costing £2 million. The expected value is £1.9 million ((30 per cent x £1 million) + (50 per cent x £2 million) + (20 per cent x £3 million)). The expected value supports the provision for the most likely outcome of £2 million.

Where the most likely outcome and the expected value are not close together, it will often be appropriate to provide for whichever possible outcome is nearest to the expected value.

Example 4.2.2C

Best estimate: expected value (2)

An entity is required to replace a major component in an asset under a warranty. Each replacement costs £1 million. From experience, there is a 40 per cent chance of a single failure, a 30 per cent chance of two failures, and a 30 per cent chance of three failures.

The most likely outcome is a single failure, costing £1 million. The expected value is £1.9 million ((40 per cent x £1 million) + (30 per cent x £2 million) + (30 per cent x £3 million)). In this case, the most likely outcome of £1 million has only a 40 per cent probability. There is a 60 per cent probability that the cost will be higher. The outcome closest to expected value is £2 million, i.e. two failures and, therefore, a provision for £2 million will be made.

4.3 Tax

Under IAS 37, provisions are measured before tax. The tax consequences of the provision, and of changes in the provision, are considered separately under IAS 12 *Income Taxes* (see **chapter 12**). [IAS 37.41]

4.4 Risks and uncertainties

IAS 37 indicates that the 'risks and uncertainties that inevitably surround many events and circumstances shall be taken into account in reaching the best estimate of a provision'. [IAS 37.42] A balance needs to be struck between, on the one hand, being imprudent (resulting in overstated assets or profits or understated liabilities or expenses) and, on the other hand, being over-prudent (resulting in excessive provisions or overstated liabilities). Also, adjustments for risk and uncertainty should not be double-counted. The most obvious situation in which this may happen is when risk is reflected both in estimated future cash flows and in the discount rate (see **4.7** below). Disclosures concerning uncertainty required by the Standard should act as a safeguard against obvious error (see **10.2** below).

4.5 Future events

In many cases, future events do not represent present obligations and, therefore, they are not provided for. Future events may, however, affect the measurement of a present obligation. IAS 37 requires that future events that may affect the amount required to settle an obligation should be reflected in the amount of a provision where there is sufficient objective evidence that they will occur. [IAS 37.48]

4.5.1 Changes in technology

A common example is the impact of future technology changes on site clean-up costs at the end of a site's life. The amount recognised as a provision for site clean-up costs should reflect the reasonable expectations of technically qualified, objective observers, taking account of all available evidence, as to the technology that will be available at the time of the clean-up. In this situation, IAS 37.49 requires the current provision to reflect the reduced costs arising from technology expected to be available at the time of the future clean-up. This allows cost reductions to be recognised for:

- increased experience in applying existing technology; and
- applying existing technology to a larger or more complex clean-up operation than has been carried out to date.

The development of a completely new technology should only be taken into account, however, where there is sufficient objective evidence that it will be available and that it will be effective for the required task. [IAS 37.49]

4.5.2 *Changes in legislation*

New legislation should be reflected in the measurement of a provision for an existing obligation when there is sufficient objective evidence that the legislation is virtually certain to be enacted. IAS 37 specifies that this will require evidence:

[IAS 37.50]

- of what the legislation will demand; and
- that the legislation will be enacted and implemented.

In practice, because of varying circumstances, there is no single event in the passage of new legislation prior to enactment that provides a general trigger point. In many cases, sufficient objective evidence will not exist until the new legislation is enacted.

4.6 Expected disposals of assets

Gains from expected disposals of assets should not be taken into account in measuring a provision, even if the expected disposal is closely linked to the event giving rise to the provision. [IAS 37.51 & 52]

Example 4.6

Expected disposals of assets

At the end of 20X1, an entity is demonstrably committed to the closure of some facilities, having drawn up a detailed plan and made announcements. The expected impact of the plan is as follows:

	20X2 £m	20X3 £m
Direct costs	-100	
Gain from sale of property		+20

The provision required at the end of 20X1 is £100 million (ignoring discounting). The expected gain on the sale of the property is dealt with separately under the criteria for asset recognition.

4.7 Present value

IAS 37 requires provisions to be discounted to present value when the effect of the time value of money is material. [IAS 37.45]

It will usually be appropriate to make an initial assessment of whether the impact of discounting might be material before embarking on a potentially complex calculation. Quantifying materiality will depend on a range of factors, e.g. the size of the provision relative to other items in the statement of financial position, the impact of any adjustment on profit for the year etc. The following table summarises the impact of discounting a single future cash flow for a range of future dates and for a range of possible discount rates. Over a 40-year period, discounting typically reduces an amount to less than 10 per cent of its nominal amount (with the effect that most of the charge would be recognised through the unwinding of the discount).

	Discount rate		
Cash flow of 100 after:	**5 per cent**	**7.5 per cent**	**10 per cent**
1 year	95	93	91
2 years	91	87	83
3 years	86	80	75
4 years	82	75	68
5 years	78	70	62
10 years	61	49	39
15 years	48	34	24
20 years	38	24	15
40 years	14	6	2

4.7.1 Choice of discount rate

The discount rate (or rates) selected should:

[IAS 37.47]

- be pre-tax;
- reflect current market assessments of the time value of money; and
- reflect risks specific to the liability.

4.7.2 Adjusting for risk

Under IAS 37, it is acceptable to reflect risk either in the estimation of cash flows or by adjusting the discount rate. The estimation of an adjusted discount rate is not a precise science. It may, therefore, be preferable, on grounds of simplicity, to deal with risk through a detailed estimation of cash flows to include the impact of risk, coupled with the use of a risk-free discount rate. Whichever method is used, care should be taken to avoid double-counting (or omitting) the effect of any risks.

It follows that, where risk is reflected in estimates of cash flows, the appropriate discount rate will be a pre-tax risk-free rate such as a current government bond rate. The following is a general guide:

- a risk-free rate, based on government bond rates, reflects the discount that a creditor will accept to receive a risk-free cash flow now rather than at the due date;
- a risk-adjusted rate based on a general corporate bond rate will reflect general corporate credit risk and will be appropriate for 'blue-chip' entities; and
- a risk-adjusted rate based on an entity-specific corporate bond rate or weighted average cost of capital (adjusted to a gross tax basis) will reflect risk factors specific to an entity and will be appropriate for most entities where risk is not specifically considered in the estimation of cash flows.

Example 4.7.2

Risk-free rate

An entity sells goods subject to a warranty. A provision is calculated for warranty claims based on detailed records of past faults in products. Since the estimation of cash flows takes account of entity specific risks, the appropriate discount rate will be a risk-free rate, for example, a government bond rate.

4.7.3 Pre-tax rates calculated from post-tax rates

Care should be taken in determining a pre-tax discount rate by adjusting a post-tax rate. Because the tax consequences of cash flows may occur in different periods, the pre-tax rate of return is not always the post-tax rate of return grossed up by the standard rate of tax.

4.7.4 Impact of inflation

Where estimated cash flows are expressed in current prices, a real discount rate (i.e. reduced for the impact of future inflation) will be used. Where, alternatively, cash flows are expressed in expected future prices (normally higher than current prices) a nominal discount rate will be used. The effects of inflation on the present value will be the same provided that one of these methods is used:

- current (lower) prices discounted at a real (lower) rate; or
- future (higher) prices discounted at a nominal (higher) rate.

5 Reimbursements

An entity with a present obligation may be able to seek reimbursement of part or all of the expenditure from another party, for example via:

- an insurance contract arranged to cover a risk;
- an indemnity clause in a contract; or
- a warranty provided by a supplier.

The basis underlying the recognition of a reimbursement is that any asset arising is separate from the related obligation. Consequently, such a reimbursement should be recognised only when it is virtually certain that it will be received consequent upon the settlement of the obligation. [IAS 37.53] This treatment is also consistent with guidance on contingent assets.

When a provision has been recognised, the occurrence of the expenditure is taken to be certain for the purposes of assessing the probability of receiving reimbursement and judging whether it is virtually certain.

Note that it is the existence of the reimbursement asset that must be virtually certain, rather than its amount. An entity may be virtually certain that it has insurance to cover a particular provision, but it may not be certain of the precise amount that would be received from the insurer. Provided that the range of possible recoveries is such that the entity can arrive at a reliable prudent estimate, it will be able to recognise this as an asset, even though the amount ultimately received may be different.

The appropriate presentation of a reimbursement is as follows:

- in the statement of financial position, a separate asset is recognised (which must not exceed the amount of the provision); [IAS 37.53] and

- in the statement of comprehensive income, a net amount may be presented, being the anticipated cost of the obligation less the reimbursement. [IAS 37.54]

Example 5

Reimbursements

An entity is a defendant to a lawsuit that has a high probability of loss. If the entity incurs a loss, the entity's insurer may cover the loss. What amount should the entity recognise as an asset and liability, if any?

The loss on the lawsuit and recoverability of the claim from the insurer are due to the same past event. The entity should recognise a provision for the full liability, as it is highly probable to occur. The entity should assess the effectiveness of the insurance policy. Unless there is doubt over the success of the insurance claim, the entity should recognise a reliable estimate of the recovery.

Offset of a provision and the related reimbursement is never appropriate. Where a reporting entity can avoid making payment in respect of an obligation in all circumstances (i.e. there can never be any recourse to the entity), then it has no liability and hence neither a provision nor a reimbursement asset should be recognised. In most cases, however, the entity will remain liable for the whole amount in question and will have to settle the full amount if the third party fails to pay for any reason. In these circumstances, no offset is permitted, irrespective of how unlikely it is that the entity will have to settle the obligation directly. [IAS 37.56 & 57]

Where a reporting entity is jointly and severally liable for an obligation, it should provide for that part of the obligation which it is probable will be settled by the entity. The remainder, expected to be paid by other parties, is a contingent liability. [IAS 37.29 & 58]

If an entity has a provision and a matching reimbursement, and the time value of money is material to both, the question arises as to whether both should be discounted. In principle, both the asset and the liability should be discounted. If there will be a significant interval between the cash outflows and receiving the reimbursement, the reimbursement will be more heavily discounted – so, if the gross inflows and outflows are the same, on initial recognition, there will be a net cost. If (presumably rarely) the reimbursement will be received first, IAS 37.53 will restrict the discounted amount of the reimbursement so that it does not exceed the discounted amount of the provision. In the statement of comprehensive income, the unwinding of the discount on the reimbursement may be offset against that on the provision.

Where a reimbursement will not be received until some significant time after the outflows to which it relates, it is theoretically possible (though perhaps rare) that it may carry interest, or in some other way be increased, so as to reimburse the entity for the lost time value of money. The only restriction in IAS 37 is that the asset recognised (i.e. the discounted amount) must not exceed the provision recognised. It is, in principle, possible for the gross amount of reimbursement used in the discounting calculation to exceed the gross outflows expected, i.e. for the undiscounted asset to be greater than the undiscounted liability.

5.1 Collateralised or guaranteed loan commitments

Example 5.1

Provisions for collateralised or guaranteed loan commitments

Entity A (A) has issued an uncancellable loan commitment at market terms to entity B (B). The loan commitment cannot be settled net, and A has no past practice of selling the assets resulting from its loan commitments shortly after origination. Entity A did not designate this loan commitment at fair value through profit or loss, therefore in accordance with IAS 39.2(h) and IAS 39.4, this loan commitment is scoped out of IAS 39 and should be accounted for according to IAS 37.

Scenario 1:

The loan, subject to the loan commitment, is guaranteed by another (e.g. the parent of the borrowing entity or an insurer). That party will reimburse A for any loss incurred if B fails to make payments when due (i.e. if there is a breach of contract). The loan commitment has not been settled at the end of the reporting period; however, A assesses that B will not be able to repay the loan that it has committed to grant to B.

Scenario 2:

The loan subject to the loan commitment is a collateralised loan; that is, if B fails to make payments when due, A will be transferred the legal ownership of the collateral (e.g. property). The loan commitment has not been settled at the end of the reporting period; however, A assesses that B will not be able to repay the loan that it has committed to grant to B.

How should A account for the loan commitments under Scenarios 1 and 2 at the end of the reporting period?

In general, a provision should be recognised when the conditions set out in IAS 37.14 are met. That is, if A has assessed at the end of the reporting period that B will not be able to repay the loan that it has committed to grant to B, a provision should be recognised.

Under Scenario 1:

- The provision should be measured according to IAS 37.36 at 'the best estimate of the expenditure required to settle the present obligation at the end of the reporting period'. In accordance with IAS 37.53, A shall not take into account the guarantee provided by the parent or insurer when assessing the amount of the provision necessary at the end of the reporting period.
- The guarantee provided by the parent or insurer is a reimbursement right as A 'is able to look to another party to pay part or all of the expenditure required to settle a provision'. [IAS 37.55] The guarantee, therefore, should be recognised as a separate asset. However, this should only be done when the conditions required by IAS 37.53 are met, which requires that a reimbursement from another party is recognised only when it is virtually certain that reimbursement will be received if B fails to make payment when due. The 'virtually certain' criteria may be met once the breach of contract from B has occurred (e.g. at the first interest payment date).
- If the guarantee was part of the same contractual arrangement, then it would be bundled and an alternative treatment would be appropriate (e.g. where the loan commitment issued to B is guaranteed by the parent of B, and the guarantee is part of the same contractual arrangement (see the answer for scenario 2 below)).

Under Scenario 2:

- Collateral held on the loan is not a reimbursement right as A is not 'able to look to another party to pay part or all of the expenditure required to settle a provision'. [IAS 37.55] Accordingly, this collateral is not separate to the loan commitment, and when accounting for the provision, it should be treated as a net arrangement with a single counterparty (i.e. the collateral should be taken into account when measuring the provision amount).
- The provision is measured according to IAS 37.36. Although the loan commitment is within the scope of IAS 37, in practice, a provision will then be recognised at the amount equivalent to the impairment that would have been required under IAS 39.63, which states that 'the amount of the loss is measured as the difference between the asset's carrying amount and the present value of estimated future cash flows'. Additionally, IAS 39.AG84 indicates that 'the calculation of the present value of the estimated future cash flows of a collateralised financial asset reflects the cash flows that may result from foreclosure, less costs for obtaining and selling the collateral, whether or not foreclosure is probable'. Accordingly, the provision is recognised for the present value of the net non-recoverable amount (including the value of the collateral, less the cost for obtaining and selling it).

6 Changes in provisions

Provisions should be reviewed at the end of each reporting period and adjusted to reflect current best estimates. [IAS 37.59]

Adjustments to provisions arise from three sources:

- revisions to estimated cash flows (both amount and likelihood);
- changes to present value due to the passage of time; and
- revisions of discount rates to reflect prevailing current market conditions.

In statements of financial position for years following the initial measurement of a provision at a present value, the present value will be restated to reflect estimated cash flows being closer to the measurement date. This unwinding of the discount relating to the passage of time should be recognised as a finance cost. [IAS 37.60] The effect of revising estimates of cash flows is not part of this unwinding and should be dealt with as part of any adjustment to the previous provision.

Where a provision is no longer required (e.g. if it is no longer probable that a transfer of economic benefits will be required to settle the obligation), the provision should be reversed. [IAS 37.59]

The disclosure requirements in respect of changes in provisions are dealt with in **10.2** below.

7 Use of provisions

One of the objectives of IAS 37 is to increase the transparency of accounting for provisions and, in particular, to prevent the use of an existing provision to meet a different undisclosed obligation. Accordingly, the Standard requires a provision to be used only for expenditures for which the provision was originally recognised. [IAS 37.61]

The disclosure requirements for provisions (see **10.2** below), particularly the requirement to identify movements on each class of provision, are intended to reinforce this requirement.

8 Illustrative examples

The examples set out in Appendix C to IAS 37 are summarised below, but in a tabular format, in order to identify reasons for particular items meeting, or not meeting, the definition of a provision. In all cases, it is assumed that a reliable estimate can be made.

Type of risk or cost	Present obligation as a result of a past event?	Probable transfer of benefits?	Conclusion
Warranty Example 1: Warranty given by a manufacturer under the terms of a contract for sale. Past experience shows that it is probable that claims will be received.	✓	✓	Provide at date of sale for legal obligation.
Contaminated land (1) Example 2A: Contaminated land – entity cleans up only to meet legal requirements, which are virtually certain to be enacted soon after the year end.	✓	✓	Provide for expected legal obligation.
Contaminated land (2) Example 2B: Contaminated land – entity has no legal obligation, but meets widely publicised clean-up policy.	✓	✓	Provide for constructive obligation.
Decommissioning Example 3: Decommissioning – terms of a licence impose a legal obligation to remove an oil rig at the end of its life.	✓	✓	Provide on commissioning of asset and include in cost of oil rig.
Refunds policy Example 4: Refunds – retail store follows a published policy of providing refunds, even though there is no legal obligation.	✓	✓	Provide for constructive obligation.
Closure of a division (1) Example 5A: Closure of a division – board decision taken before the end of the reporting period, but not communicated to those affected and plan not commenced.	✗		No obligating event before the end of the reporting period.
Closure of a division (2) Example 5B: Closure of a division – board decision, detailed plan completed, staff and customers notified before the end of the reporting period.	✓	✓	Provide for expected costs of closure.
Legal requirement to fit smoke filter Example 6: Introduction of legal requirement to fit smoke filters by June 2000.			
(a) At December 1999, the end of the reporting period.	✗		No obligating event at the end of the reporting period.

(b) At December 2000, the end of the reporting period (assuming filters not yet fitted).	✗ ✓	✓	– no obligating event in respect of filters, but – provision may be required for any fines and penalties likely to be suffered.
Staff retraining Example 7: Staff retraining – need to retrain staff to meet new system requirements imposed by change in the law.	✗		No obligating event until training occurs.
Onerous contract Example 8: Onerous contract – operating lease rental payments on vacated property.	✓	✓	Provide for unavoidable lease payments.
Guarantee Example 9: Guarantee – provided for another entity's borrowings.			
(a) At December 1999, the end of the reporting period – other entity is in sound financial condition.	✓	✗	No transfer of benefits is probable.
(b) At December 2000, the end of the reporting period –other entity has filed for protection from creditors.	✓	✓	Provide for estimated call on guarantee.
Court case Example 10: Unsettled court case			
(a) At December 2000, the end of the reporting period – lawyers advise that no liability will be proved.	✗		No obligation exists based on evidence.
(b) At December 2001, the end of the reporting period – lawyers advise that liability will be proved.	✓	✓	Provide for estimated settlement.
Repairs and maintenance Example 11A: Repairs and maintenance – a furnace has a lining that needs to be replaced every five years for technical reasons. At the end of the reporting period, the lining has been in use for three years.	✗		No obligation exists independently of future actions. Expenditure capitalised when incurred and depreciated.
Refurbishment costs Example 11B: Refurbishment costs – legislative requirement – an airline is required by law to overhaul its aircraft once every three years.	✗		No obligation exists independently of future actions (the entity could sell the aircraft). Expenditure capitalised when incurred and depreciated.

8.1 Repairs and maintenance obligations under leases

Under some operating leases, the lessee is required to incur periodic charges for maintenance of the leased asset or to make good dilapidations or other damage occurring during the rental period. Since the lease is a legal contract, it may give rise to legal obligations. Accordingly, the principles of IAS 37, which generally preclude the recognition of provisions for repairs and maintenance, do not preclude the recognition of such liabilities in a lease once the event giving rise to the obligation under the lease has occurred.

Example 8.1

Lease of aircraft

An entity leases an aircraft under an operating lease. The aircraft has to undergo an expensive 'C check' after every 2,400 flying hours.

The requirement to perform a 'C check' does not give rise to a present obligation at the time the lease is signed because, until 2,400 hours have been flown, there is no obligation which exists independently of the entity's future actions. Even the intention to incur the cost of a 'C check' depends on the entity deciding to continue flying the aircraft. Therefore, no provision should be made for a future 'C check'. The cost of each successive 'C check' will instead be capitalised when it is incurred and amortised over the period to the next 'C check'.

This leaves the question of the condition in which the aircraft must be returned to the lessor at the end of the lease and of whether this creates a present obligation, and thus a provision, at the time the lease is signed. The answer depends on what the lease terms state will happen when the aircraft is returned at the end of the lease. If no final 'C check' is required (i.e. in the final period, the client can use the aircraft for up to 2,399 flying hours and then return it without bearing any cost), no provision should be made, since there is no legal obligation.

If a 'C check' is required at the end of the lease, irrespective of how many hours have been flown, full provision for the cost should be made at the start of the lease. The costs should be carried forward and written off over the shorter of the next 2,400 flying hours and the number of flying hours to the end of the lease – and similarly each time a 'C check' is carried out.

If, on returning the aircraft, the client must make a payment towards the 'C check' which is in proportion to the number of hours flown (e.g. 75 per cent of the cost of a 'C check' for 1,800 hours flown), then an obligation is created as the aircraft is used. It will be appropriate to build up a provision based on the number of hours flown.

8.2 Self-insurance – cost of accidents

Where an entity self-insures (for example, a retailer might decide not to insure itself in respect of the risk of minor accidents to its customers), it should provide each year for the costs of accidents that have occurred prior to the end of the reporting period. This provision should cover not only those claims that have been made prior to the end of the reporting period, but also claims potentially incurred but not reported (IBNR) at that date. It will be common that an accident has happened but the entity does not know of its occurrence. This in itself does not preclude the entity from recognising a provision – as long as a reliable estimate can be made of IBNR claims, probably based on past experience. Since the IBNR provision is, by definition, in respect of claims incurred before the end of the reporting period, the obligating event will have occurred by that date. IAS 37 does not, however, permit making provision for the excess of the 'normal annual cost' over the cost of actual accidents in the year. In other words, a self-insuring entity is prevented from 'smoothing' the cost of accidents by making a buffer provision in a year when actual costs are low.

Example 8.2

Claims incurred but not reported

Entity A has an insurance policy with premiums that are adjusted on the basis of actual losses incurred in that year. For example, if losses for a specific period exceed 100, Entity A will have to pay the insurer 80 per cent of the excessive losses in the form of additional premiums in that year. How should Entity A account for this provision in the insurance contract?

Entity A should recognise a provision at the end of each reporting period for the additional premiums due as a result of losses in that year. In estimating that provision, Entity A should consider not only known losses but also losses incurred but not yet reported.

8.3 Vouchers issued for no consideration

A reporting entity may, for no consideration, distribute vouchers that can be used, sometimes within a set period, to obtain discounts on the entity's products and/or third parties' products.(NB Where such vouchers are issued as part of a sales transaction, it will be necessary to consider the unbundling implications of IAS 18 *Revenue* – see **chapter 23**.)

Applying the recognition criteria of IAS 37:

- is there a present obligation? Generally, the answer will be yes, but if the reporting entity reserves the right to terminate the scheme at any time, thus invalidating existing vouchers, then there may or may not be a constructive obligation. In the absence of evidence that schemes have been terminated (and existing vouchers invalidated) in the past, however, it should be presumed that an obligation exists;

- is it probable that economic benefits will be transferred? If, after vouchers are deducted, the entity's products are still being sold at a profit, the answer will be no – therefore no provision will be made. To the extent that products will be sold at a loss, however, or that a third party will be reimbursed for discounts, there will be a transfer of economic benefits;

- can a reliable estimate be made? The answer here should be presumed to be yes, but in making the estimate the entity should consider how many vouchers are likely to be used.

In summary, if the criteria are met, provision should be made for the likely cost to the entity (which may not be the face value of the discounts). The entity will need to form a view as to how many vouchers are likely to be used and should also consider whether discounting is appropriate.

8.4 Costs of decommissioning an oil rig

Commissioning of a new oil rig creates an obligation to incur costs of decommissioning in the future, but also gives access to future economic benefits. A provision for the present value of costs of decommissioning should be recognised at the time of commissioning the oil rig, and the amount recognised should be added to the cost of the rig. The provision should only include the costs that are an obligation resulting from commissioning the rig. The provision should not include any additional costs that will only be triggered by further drilling until that further drilling occurs.

Some related issues are addressed in IFRIC 1 *Changes in Existing Decommissioning, Restoration and Similar Liabilities* (see **4.4** in **chapter 6**) and IFRIC 5 *Rights to Interests arising from Decommissioning, Restoration and Environmental Rehabilitation Funds* (see **9.2** below).

8.5 Late delivery penalties

In some circumstances, a late delivery penalty may be incurred where goods are not supplied by a specified delivery date. At the end of its reporting period, an entity may know that it will not be able to meet the delivery date for goods to be supplied in the next year. At its year end, before the original delivery date, should the entity recognise the penalty provision for the late delivery costs?

If the remaining part of the contract has, as a whole, become onerous as a result of the penalty clause, a provision should be made for any overall loss that is now expected to result. It would not be appropriate, however, merely to provide for the penalty without viewing the remainder of the contract as a whole.

Example 8.5

Late delivery penalties

Entity A (a calendar year-end reporter) signed a firm sales contract with one of its major clients on 1 February 20X1. This contract specifies that 100 units of a product have to be delivered before 1 February 20X2 at a fixed price of £10. The costs of production are £9 per unit. If the products are delivered more than 10 days late, the client will be given a discount of 50 per cent on each delayed product. At the time Entity A signed the contract, it had the ability and the intention to produce the 100 units on time. However, at the end of 20X1, it has only been able to deliver 80 units, and expects to deliver only 10 more before 1 February 20X2 due to manufacturing constraints. Therefore, at year-end Entity A expects to deliver 10 of the remaining 20 units at the discounted price of £5 per unit.

Total revenue from this contract will be £950 [(90 × 10) + (10 × 5)] and total costs will be £900 (100 × 9). Therefore, the overall contract is profitable. However, at year-end Entity A expects to deliver 10 units with delay and at a loss of £40 [(10 × 5) – (10 × 9)], and 10 units on time with a profit of £10 [(10 × 10) – (10 × 9)]. Should a provision be recognised for the expected loss on the 10 units?

A provision of £30 (discounted if material) should be recognised to cover the potential loss arising from the outstanding obligations under the contract. If Entity A is able and expects to mitigate damages by purchasing suitable replacement product and delivering prior to 1 February, the provision should be adjusted to reflect the expected economic loss anticipated to be incurred by Entity A.

If Entity A had entered into this contract knowing that it would not be able to deliver on time, no provision should be recognised, as this is instead a revenue recognition issue under IAS 18 *Revenue*. If, from the outset, Entity A expected to sell 100 units at an average price of £9.50 (£950 ÷ 100) per unit, then revenue of only £9.50 should be recognised for each unit, and not £10.

8.6 Repurchase agreements – trade-in right

Example 8.6

Repurchase agreements – trade-in right

In order to facilitate vehicle sales, a motor dealer offers specified-price trade-in arrangements on vehicles for sale that give customers the right to trade in that vehicle toward the purchase of a new vehicle, at some point in the future. The trade-in may be exercisable by the customer at a specified point in time or during a specified period of time. Should the dealer recognise a provision for the cost of the guaranteed vehicle repurchases?

If the amount of credit that will be received upon exercise of a specified-price trade-in right is equal to or less than the estimated fair value of the vehicle at the trade-in date (determined on the date of the sale of the vehicle subject to the specified-price trade-in right) and if the customer is required to pay a significant incremental amount in addition to the trade-in credit for the new vehicle at the trade-in date, then no revenue from the sale of the vehicle should be allocated to the trade-in right and no provision should be recognised for the trade-in right at the time of the sale. If the motor dealer subsequently determines, however, that it is probable that a loss will be incurred upon the customer's exercise of the specified-price trade-in right (taking into consideration the expected profit on sale of the new vehicle), the motor dealer should recognise a provision based on the best estimate of the loss.

8.7 Employment disputes

Example 8.7

Employment disputes

An entity employs three foreign professional seamen. Maritime law prescribes that registered professionals are paid a premium over unregistered professionals. The entity subsequently discovers that the professionals are not registered and, therefore, have been overpaid. The entity consequently reduces the salaries of these professionals who then take the matter to court. One employee wins the case and is awarded a £70,000 retrenchment package. The other two lose on a technicality, but will appeal the decision. Lawyers are certain that the appeal will be successful.

A provision should be recognised for the best estimate of the costs to settle the appeal. The past event is the underpayment of the employees (after it was thought they were overpaid), and therefore occurred during the year. As a result of the court proceedings, a legal obligation to compensate one employee exists in the current year (for £70,000). With regard to the other two seamen, the past event is the constructive dismissal that occurred during the year. As it is probable (more likely than not) that the entity will be found liable, a present obligation exists. It is probable that economic benefits will flow from the entity.

8.8 Construction contracts

Example 8.8

Recognition of constructive obligations associated with a construction contract

Entity X (X) is in the construction industry. It stores plant and machinery at its site, site A, and transports certain plant and machinery (e.g. cranes) to a construction site (site B), where it is in the process of constructing a hotel. At the end of construction, X will be required to remove the crane from site B and transport it back to site A, or to the site of another contract.

A liability should be recognised for transporting the crane back to site A. IAS 37 applies to provisions which are not dealt with directly in another Standard, such as IAS 11 *Construction Contracts*.

IAS 37.14 requires recognition of a provision when:

- an entity has a present obligation (legal or constructive) as a result of a past event;
- it is probable that an outflow of resources embodying economic benefits will be required to settle the obligation; and
- a reliable estimate can be made of the amount of the obligation.

A constructive obligation should be recognised when, by an established pattern of past practice, published policies, or a sufficiently specific current statement, the entity has created a valid expectation that it will meet certain responsibilities.

IAS 37.19 states that 'it is only those obligations arising from past events existing independently of an entity's future actions (i.e. the future conduct of its business) that are recognised as provisions.' Since the crane cannot be left at site B, Entity X has a constructive obligation to the owners of site B to remove the crane. Therefore, X should recognise a liability for the removal of the crane once it is installed on site B and measure that liability at the best estimate of the cost of transporting the crane back to site A (or the next site at which it is required).

The liability cannot be capitalised to the cost of the crane under the cost model of IAS 16. In accordance with IAS 16.16(c), the cost of an item of property, plant and equipment comprises, inter alia:

'the initial estimate of the costs of dismantling and removing the item and restoring the site on which it is located, the obligation for which an entity incurs either when the item is acquired or as a consequence of having used the item during a particular period for purposes other than to produce inventories during that period.'

The cost of removal of the crane in this instance relates to its redeployment post inventory production, not to restoring the site on which it was located for construction purposes. However, the cost may represent a contract cost under IAS 11 and, if so, would be included in the associated construction asset.

9 IFRIC Interpretations

9.1 Emission Rights (IFRIC 3, since withdrawn)

In December 2004, IFRIC 3 *Emission Rights* was issued to deal with the accounting by participants in a 'cap and trade' scheme. The Interpretation specified that a cap and trade scheme gives rise to an asset for allowances held, a government grant in respect of any allowances granted free of charge, and a liability for the obligation to deliver allowances, equal to the emissions made. However, the accounting required by IFRIC 3 led to a perceived mismatch: assets would either be recognised at historical amounts or revalued with changes recognised in other comprehensive income, whereas liabilities would be remeasured to fair value through profit or loss. Thus, an entity holding precisely the level of assets required to settle its liabilities would nevertheless report gains or losses if there were changes in fair value.

As a result of these perceived problems with IFRIC 3, at its meeting in June 2005, the IASB voted to withdraw IFRIC 3. The IASB intends to conduct a broader assessment of the nature of the various volatilities resulting from the application of IFRIC 3 and to consider whether and how it might be appropriate to amend existing standards to reduce or eliminate some of those volatilities.

In the meantime, entities participating in cap and trade schemes will need to give careful thought to how they account for the assets and liabilities arising. One possible approach would be to follow the guidance set out in IFRIC 3 (see **9.1.1** below). Two other possible approaches are outlined at **9.1.2** and **9.1.3** below. The accounting policy adopted should be applied to all emission allowances and related liabilities on a consistent basis.

9.1.1 *Approach 1: Apply IFRIC 3*

Emission rights are intangible assets that are accounted for in accordance with IAS 38 *Intangible Assets* and would be recognised initially at fair value. When allowances are issued for less than fair value, the difference between the amount paid and fair value is a government grant within the scope of IAS 20 *Accounting for Government Grants and Disclosure of Government Assistance*.

As emissions are made, a liability would be recognised for the obligation to deliver allowances equal to emissions that have been made. This liability is a provision that is within the scope of IAS 37, and would be measured at the best estimate of the expenditure required to settle the present obligation at the end of the reporting period. This would usually be the present market price of the number of allowances required to cover emissions made up to the end of the reporting period.

Offset of the asset (emission credits held) and the liability (to deliver credits to the value of emissions made) would not be permitted.

9.1.2 *Approach 2: Government grant and an intangible asset initially at fair value, emission liability reflects carrying amounts*

9.1.2.1 *Intangible asset*

Allowances allocated would be measured under the alternatives permitted in IAS 20 and IAS 38. It would seem preferable for allowances to be recognised as an asset only when issued. But an acceptable alternative would be for the entire period allocation to be recognised as an asset at the point at which the relevant authority finalises the allocation plan for the allowances.

Allowances represent an intangible asset acquired by an entity free of charge or for nominal consideration. IAS 38.44 provides two possible treatments. The entity may choose to recognise both the intangible asset and the government grant initially at fair value; alternatively, nominal value may be used (see **9.1.3** below). The fair value approach may be preferred as providing better accounting information, in that it results in a better representation of the economic resources and obligations of the entity.

Subsequent to initial recognition, the general requirements for intangible assets in IAS 38 would apply.

(i) IAS 38 permits an intangible asset to be remeasured at fair value where this can be determined by reference to an active market. Remeasurements are recognised directly in other comprehensive income. [IAS 38.85] The revalued amount is subject to amortisation and impairment testing between remeasurements. This accounting treatment precludes any recycling of fair value increments related to the allowances through profit or loss.

(ii) IAS 38 also permits an intangible asset to be measured at cost less amortisation / impairment. [IAS 38.74] If an entity were to use this method, any difference between the carrying amount of the asset and the liability would be recognised in profit or loss upon settlement of the obligation (or sale of the allowances).

For most allowances traded in an active market, no amortisation will be required as the residual value will be the same as cost and therefore the depreciable amount will be zero. If the market value of the allowances falls below cost, or other indicators of impairment exist, then the guidance in IAS 36 *Impairment of Assets* should be followed to determine whether the assets are impaired.

9.1.2.2 *Government grant*

Allowances represent a non-monetary government grant and may be recognised at the fair value of the related asset or at nominal amount. [IAS 20.23] For the reasons noted above, it may be preferable for the government grant to be measured initially at fair value. The grant is recognised as deferred income and recognised in profit or loss on a systematic basis over the compliance period, regardless of whether the allowances received continue to be held by the entity.

9.1.2.3 *Emission liability*

A liability for emissions would be recognised as incurred and measured at the best estimate of the expenditure required to settle the present obligation at the end of the reporting period, in accordance with IAS 37.36. Under cap and trade schemes, entities generally can settle the obligation created by the emission of pollutants only by surrendering allowances to the appropriate authority and cannot settle their obligations by making a cash payment or by transferring other assets.

Where an entity measures allowances at fair value, the liability would be measured at the same amount, since this is the best estimate of the expenditure (economic resources) required to settle the obligation.

Where an entity measures allowances at cost then, provided it has sufficient allowances to satisfy the emission liability, the liability would be measured at the same amount, i.e. as the sum of the cost of the initial allowances received and the cost of any additional allowances purchased. If at the end of the reporting period the liability to deliver allowances exceeds the amount of allowances on hand, then the shortfall would be measured at the current fair (market) value of the short position. Consequently, if an entity chose to sell allowances during the year, and in doing so created a shortfall in the number of allowances held as compared to the total pollutants emitted at that date, it would remeasure the portion of the obligation related to the shortfall at the current market value of the allowances.

9.1.3 *Approach 3: Government grant and an intangible asset measured at nominal amounts* (*net liability approach*)

Under this approach, an intangible asset would be recognised and measured at a nominal amount when allowances are issued or allocated (i.e. the cost / nominal amount alternatives are adopted in IAS 20 and IAS 38). A credit entry for the government grant would be recognised in the statement of financial position at a nominal amount equal to the carrying amount of the allowances. [IAS 20.23]

No liability for emissions would be recognised provided the entity has sufficient allowances to satisfy the emission liability, because the allowances granted (which are recognised only at a nominal amount) will be used to settle the liability. Hence, no entries are required so long as the entity holds sufficient allowances to meet its emission obligations.

If at the end of the reporting period the liability to deliver allowances exceeds the amount of allowances on hand, then the shortfall should be measured at the current fair (market) value of the short position (as in **9.1.2** above).

9.2 IFRIC 5 *Rights to Interests arising from Decommissioning, Restoration and Environmental Rehabilitation Funds*

IFRIC 5 deals with the accounting, in the financial statements of the contributor, for interests in decommissioning, restoration and environmental rehabilitation funds established to fund some or all of the costs of decommissioning assets or to undertake environmental rehabilitation. Contributions to such funds may be voluntary, or required by law. Funds may be established by a single contributor, or they may be established by multiple contributors. Such funds are generally separately administered by trustees. Entities make contributions, which are invested on behalf of the fund by the trustees. The contributors retain the obligation to pay decommissioning costs, but they are able to obtain reimbursement from the fund up to the lower of the decommissioning costs incurred and the contributor's share of the assets of the fund. The contributors may have restricted access or no access to any surplus of assets of the fund over those used to meet eligible decommissioning costs.

The issues under consideration in IFRIC 5 are:

- how should a contributor account for its interest in a fund; and
- when a contributor has an obligation to make additional contributions, e.g. in the event of the bankruptcy of another contributor, how should that obligation be accounted for?

Note that the scope of IFRIC 5 is restricted to funds with separately-administered assets, where the contributor's right to access the assets is restricted. A residual interest in a fund that extends beyond a right to reimbursement, such as a contractual right to distributions once all the decommissioning has been completed or on winding up the fund, may be an equity instrument within the scope of IAS 39 *Financial Instruments: Recognition and Measurement*, and is not within the scope of IFRIC 5.

9.2.1 *Assessing the relationship between the contributor and the fund*

The contributor is required to assess whether it has control, joint control or significant influence over the fund, in accordance with relevant Standards, and to account for its interest by consolidation, proportionate consolidation, or equity accounting, as appropriate under those Standards.

9.2.2 *Accounting for the obligation to pay decommissioning costs*

The contributor's obligation to pay decommissioning costs should be recognised as a liability, separately from its interest in the fund, unless its contributions to the fund have extinguished its obligation to pay decommissioning costs (even in the event that the fund fails to pay). Therefore, when an entity remains liable for expenditure, a provision should be recognised, even where reimbursement is available.

When a contributor has an obligation to make potential additional contributions, e.g. in the event of the bankruptcy of another contributor, or if the value of the investments held by the fund decreases to an extent that they are insufficient to fulfil the fund's reimbursement obligations, this obligation is a contingent liability that is accounted for under IAS 37. The contributor will recognise a liability only if it is probable that additional contributions will be made.

9.2.3 *Accounting for the contributor's interest in the fund*

In the absence of control, joint control, or significant influence, the contributor's right to reimbursement from the fund is accounted for in accordance with the rules set out in IAS 37 in respect of reimbursements. Therefore, if the reimbursement is virtually certain to be received when the obligation is settled, it should be treated as a separate asset.

The reimbursement should be measured at the lower of the amount of the decommissioning obligation recognised, and the contributor's share of the fair value of the net assets of the fund attributable to contributors. Therefore, recognition of an asset in excess of the recognised liability is prohibited. For example, rights to receive reimbursement to meet decommissioning liabilities that have yet to be recognised as a provision are not recognised.

Changes in the carrying amount of the right to receive reimbursement other than contributions to and payments from the fund should be recognised in profit or loss in the period in which those changes occur.

9.2.4 *Disclosure*

Contributors are required to disclose the nature of interests in funds, and any restrictions on access to the assets in the funds. In addition, where the arrangements give rise to contingent liabilities or reimbursement rights that are accounted for under IAS 37, then the relevant disclosure requirements of IAS 37 apply.

9.3 IFRIC 6 *Liabilities arising from Participating in a Specific Market – Waste Electrical and Electronic Equipment*

IFRIC 6 addresses the recognition of liabilities for waste management under the European Union's Directive on Waste Electrical and Electronic Equipment (the WE&EE Directive). Specifically, the Interpretation deals with waste from private households arising from products sold on or before 13 August 2005. It does not apply to waste from sources other than private households, nor to household waste arising from products sold after 13 August 2005.

The Interpretation is therefore quite narrow in scope. The general principles in IAS 37 should be applied to determine the appropriate recognition point for other remediation and recycling obligations. However IFRIC 6.7 states that 'if, in national legislation, new waste from private households is treated in a similar manner to historical waste from private households, the principles of the Interpretation apply by reference to the hierarchy in paragraphs 10–12 of IAS 8'. Therefore, before determining an accounting policy for 'new' household waste, entities will need to determine how the WE&EE Directive has been transposed into local law. The Interpretation will also be a source of authoritative guidance on the appropriate accounting for obligations that are imposed by similar cost attribution models.

Under the WE&EE Directive, the obligation to contribute to waste management costs is allocated proportionately to producers of the relevant type of equipment who participate in the market during a specified period (the measurement period). The IFRIC was asked to determine what constitutes the obligating event for the recognition of a provision for the waste management costs.

The IFRIC decided that the event that triggers liability recognition is participation in the market during a measurement period (and not the production of the equipment, nor the actual incurrence of waste management costs).

9.3.1 *Accounting for Waste Electrical and Electronic Equipment obligations in the UK*

9.3.1.1 *Introduction*

UK

The provisions of the WE&EE Directive were incorporated into UK law by the enactment of the Waste Electrical and Electronic Equipment Regulations 2006 ('the WEEE Regulations').

Note that the WEEE Regulations only cover sales made by producers in the UK. Producers who make sales elsewhere in Europe need to ensure that they comply with the requirements of the regulations enacted in the various countries in which they are trading.

9.3.1.2 *Different types of waste*

UK

In effect, the WEEE Regulations divide WEEE into three categories:

- *WEEE from private households (hereafter referred to as 'domestic waste'), discussed at* **9.3.1.3** *below;*
- *WEEE from users other than private households, arising from products put on the market in the UK on or after 13 August 2005, or from products put on the market before that date where a new product of an equivalent type or fulfilling the same function has been supplied as a replacement (hereafter referred to as 'current non-domestic waste'). Current non-domestic waste is discussed at* **9.3.1.4** *below;*
- *all other WEEE from users other than private households (hereafter referred to as 'historical non-domestic waste'). This consists of WEEE arising from products put on the market in the UK before 13 August 2005, but excluding products put on the market before that date where a new product of an equivalent type or fulfilling the same function has been supplied as a replacement. Historical non-domestic waste is discussed at* **9.3.1.5** *below.*

9.3.1.3 *Domestic waste*

UK

Under the WEEE Regulations, costs incurred during a compliance period in relation to domestic waste are allocated between the producers based on their respective market share during the same period.

As a consequence, the enactment of the WEEE Regulations did not itself give rise to a past obligation for producers in respect of domestic waste. Instead, as explained in IFRIC 6, an obligation only arises as a result of participation in a market during a compliance period, as evidenced by sales in that market. The first compliance period began on 1 July 2007, so no liability was recognised before that date for domestic waste. (Note that the scope of IFRIC 6 is quite narrow, as the Interpretation deals only with domestic waste arising from products sold before 13 August 2005.)

Example 9.3.1.3

Domestic waste

Under the WEEE Regulations, producers are responsible for the cost of domestic waste in proportion to their respective share of the market for that type of equipment in each calendar year. Assume that the government notifies participants in the relevant markets in May each year of their market share for the immediately preceding calendar year.

Entity X

Entity X has been a manufacturer of domestic washing machines since 1980. In May 2008, the government notifies X that its market share for the first compliance period (from 1 July 2007 to 31 December 2007) was 25 per cent. This market share will be used to allocate domestic waste management costs incurred during that period for washing machines estimated at £24 million. Entity X will recognise a liability of £6 million at 31 December 2007, since the recognition of the liability is triggered by participation in the market during 2007, rather than by government notification in May 2008.

Entity Z (new manufacturer)

Entity Z began manufacturing domestic washing machines in July 2007, and is notified by government in May 2008 that its market share for the first compliance period (from 1 July 2007 to 31 December 2007) was 3 per cent. Even though it was not responsible for producing any historical waste, because it participates in the market currently it will contribute to the cost of dealing with domestic waste and will recognise a liability of £0.72 million at 31 December 2007.

Entity T (ceased manufacturing)

Entity T ceased to produce washing machines in 2006. Because T no longer produces domestic washing machines (i.e. its market share in the measurement period was zero), it has no obligation to fund the collection and recycling of historical waste it produced.

9.3.1.4 *Current non-domestic waste*

UK

Under the WEEE Regulations, producers are individually responsible for the costs of current non-domestic waste.

As a consequence, the enactment of the WEEE Regulations triggered a past obligation in respect of such waste. A liability exists for products sold on or after 13 August 2005, and for products sold before that date where a new product of an equivalent type or fulfilling the same function has been supplied as a replacement. Going forward, producers need to provide for the cost of non-domestic waste at the time products are sold.

Example 9.3.1.4

Current non-domestic waste

In December 2008, Entity X, a manufacturer, is paid to replace all the televisions and fridges in a particular hotel. The televisions and fridges replaced were initially installed in 1996. In its December 2008 financial statements, Entity X will provide for the costs associated with the old televisions and fridges as they are being replaced with new equipment fulfilling the same function. In addition, Entity X will provide for estimated costs associated with the new equipment sold.

9.3.1.5 *Historical non-domestic waste*

UK

Under the WEEE Regulations, obligations in respect of historical non-domestic waste fall on the final user.

As a consequence, the enactment of the WEEE Regulations triggered a past obligation in respect of such waste. Final users need to recognise a liability in respect of products purchased before 13 August 2005, except where a new product of an equivalent type or fulfilling the same function has been supplied as a replacement.

10 Presentation and disclosure

10.1 Presentation

IAS 1 *Presentation of Financial Statements* requires that, where material, the aggregate carrying amount of the entity's provisions should be presented in the statement of financial position. [IAS 1(2007).54(l), previously IAS 1(2003).68(k)]

10.2 Disclosure

The objective of IAS 37 with respect to disclosure is to ensure that sufficient information is disclosed in the notes to the financial statements to enable users to understand the nature, timing and amount of provisions, contingent liabilities and contingent assets.

10.2.1 Provisions

For each class of provision, the following should be disclosed (comparative information is not required):

[IAS 37.84]

- the carrying amount at the beginning and end of the period;
- additional provisions made in the period, including increases to existing provisions;
- amounts used (i.e. incurred and charged against the provision) during the period;
- unused amounts reversed during the period; and
- the increase during the period in the discounted amount arising from the passage of time and the effect of any change in the discount rate.

The following should also be disclosed for each class of provision:

[IAS 37.85]

- a brief description of the nature of the obligation and the expected timing of any resulting outflows of economic benefits;
- an indication of the uncertainties about the amount or timing of those outflows. Where necessary to provide adequate information, the entity should disclose the major assumptions made concerning future events (see **4.5**); and
- the amount of any expected reimbursement, stating the amount of any asset that has been recognised for that expected reimbursement.

In determining which provisions may be aggregated to form a class, it is necessary to consider whether the nature of the items is sufficiently similar for a single statement about them to fulfil the requirements outlined above with respect to disclosure of the nature of and uncertainties surrounding such liabilities. [IAS 37.87]

10.2.2 *Contingent liabilities*

For each class of contingent liability (unless the possibility of an outflow in settlement is remote), a brief description of the nature of the contingent liability should be provided. The following information should also be disclosed, where practicable:

[IAS 37.86]

- an estimate of its financial effect (based on the measurement requirements of IAS 37);
- an indication of the uncertainties relating to the amount or timing of any outflow; and
- the possibility of any reimbursement.

In determining which contingent liabilities may be aggregated to form a class, it is necessary to consider whether the nature of the items is sufficiently similar for a single statement about them to fulfil the requirements outlined above with respect to disclosure of the nature of and uncertainties surrounding such items. [IAS 37.87]

Where a provision and a contingent liability arise from the same set of circumstances, the reporting entity should make the required disclosures in a way that clearly shows the link between the provision and the contingent liability. [IAS 37.88]

10.2.3 *Contingent assets*

Where an inflow of economic benefits is probable, the entity should disclose a brief description of the nature of the contingent assets at the end of the reporting period and, where practicable, an estimate of their financial effect (based on the measurement requirements of IAS 37), taking care to avoid giving misleading indications of the likelihood of income arising. [IAS 37.89 & 90]

10.2.4 *Exemptions from disclosure requirements*

10.2.4.1 Exemption applying to disclosure of contingent liabilities and contingent assets

Where any of the information required in respect of contingent liabilities and contingent assets, as set out in **10.2.2** and **10.2.3** above, is not disclosed because it is not practicable to do so, then this fact should be stated. [IAS 37.91]

10.2.4.2 *Exemption applying to all disclosures*

In extremely rare cases, it is conceivable that some or all of the disclosures required by IAS 37 can be expected to prejudice seriously the position of the entity in a dispute with other parties on the subject matter of the provision, contingent liability or contingent asset. In such cases, the reporting entity need not disclose the information, but it should disclose the general nature of the dispute, together with the fact that the information has not been disclosed and the reason why. [IAS 37.92]

11 Future developments

11.1 Amendments to IAS 37

In June 2005, the IASB published an Exposure Draft to amend IAS 37 *Provisions, Contingent Liabilities and Contingent Assets* and IAS 19 *Employee Benefits*. The most significant amendments proposed to IAS 37 are set out below:

- uncertainty over possible outflows will be dealt with in the measurement of a liability, but will not be taken into account for recognition purposes. At present, if an obligation exists, but there is less than a 50 per cent chance that any outflows will be required in settlement, no provision is recognised. Under the new proposals, a 'non-financial liability' (a new term to replace 'provision') will be recognised, measured at an amount that reflects the range of possible outcomes;

- the concept of a 'stand ready obligation' is introduced, being a liability for which the amount that will be required in settlement is contingent on the occurrence or non-occurrence of a future event;

- the term 'contingent liability' is eliminated. Items previously described as contingent liabilities will, as explained above, be recognised as liabilities if there is a present obligation;

- the term 'contingent asset' is also eliminated. Items previously described as contingent assets, but meeting the definition of an asset, will fall within the scope of IAS 38 *Intangible Assets*, except for reimbursement rights, which remain within IAS 37;

- liabilities for the costs associated with a restructuring are recognised on the same basis as other liabilities, i.e. when there is a constructive obligation to another party in respect of that particular cost. This may result in later recognition of restructuring costs in some instances.

At the time of writing, it is expected that revisions to the Standard will be published in 2009.

11.2 Draft Interpretation IFRIC D23 *Distributions of Non-cash Assets to Owners*

Draft Interpretation IFRIC D23 *Distributions of Non-cash Assets to Owners* was issued in January 2008, with a comment deadline of April 2008. It sets out draft guidance on how an entity should measure distributions of assets other than cash when it pays dividends to its owners acting in their capacity as owners. At present, IFRSs do not address the measurement of distributions to owners.

IFRIC D23 would apply to all types of distributions of non-cash assets with one exception: it would not apply to a distribution of an asset to another entity within the same consolidated group. Subject to that exception, IFRIC D23 proposes that all types of distributions of non-cash assets would be measured at the fair value of the assets distributed. Therefore:

- when an entity incurs an obligation to distribute non-cash assets to its owners (a dividend payable), it would measure the obligation at the fair value of the non-cash assets;
- when an entity settles the dividend payable, it would recognise any difference between the carrying amount of the assets distributed and the carrying amount of the dividend payable in profit or loss.

The Interpretation, if finalised, would apply prospectively, i.e. to future distributions.

12 Income taxes

1 Introduction

This chapter sets out the accounting treatment of both current and deferred tax under IAS 12 *Income Taxes*, SIC-21 *Income Taxes – Recovery of Revalued Non-Depreciable Assets* and SIC-25 *Income Taxes – Changes in the Tax Status of an Entity or its Shareholders*.

In January 2008, the requirements of IAS 12 regarding post-acquisition recognition of deferred tax assets acquired in a business combination were amended as a consequential amendment of IFRS 3(2008) (see **5.1.6**).

This chapter sets out the requirements of IAS 12, SIC-21 and SIC-25 in the following sections:

Section 2	Scope
Section 3	Current tax
Section 4	Deferred tax
Section 5	Specific applications
Section 6	Presentation and disclosure
Section 7	Future developments

UK

The requirements of IAS 12 on accounting for current tax do not differ significantly from those in FRS 16 Current Tax, *although some requirements are dealt with in more detail under FRS 16. For instance, whilst IAS 12 requires withholding tax paid by a company to be recognised in equity as part of dividends, it does not deal with how to account for the receipt of dividends that are net of tax. However, IAS 18 requires that revenue should be reported gross and therefore withholding tax paid on behalf of the recipient should not be netted against the dividend income, but disclosed gross with the recipient's unrecovered withholding tax included as tax expense.*

It is in respect of deferred tax that the UK and IFRS treatments differ significantly, despite both standards taking a 'full provision' approach. IAS 12 Income Taxes *is based on a completely different conceptual foundation to FRS 19* Deferred Tax. *This is important to realise because it has a fundamental effect on whether particular accounting entries give rise to deferred tax consequences.*

FRS 19's approach to deferred taxation is based on timing differences, which arise where gains and losses are recognised in the financial statements and tax computations in different periods. Deferred taxation is recognised on timing differences with specific exemptions. The effect is that deferred taxation is recognised where the entity has an obligation to pay more, or a right to pay less, tax at a future date based on amounts that have been recognised in the statement of comprehensive income and/or tax computation.

In contrast, IAS 12 focuses on the tax implication of items recognised in the statement of financial position, requiring deferred tax to be recognised in respect of temporary differences. Temporary differences are differences between the carrying amount of an asset or liability in the statement of financial position and its tax base, which is the amount attributed to that asset or liability for tax purposes. Many temporary differences are also timing differences and may be either taxable or deductible, giving rise to deferred tax liabilities and assets respectively. Temporary differences may also arise from the initial recognition of goodwill, or when the tax base of an asset or liability on initial recognition differs from its initial carrying amount, for example when a non-taxable government grant is received. Such temporary differences, assuming that the 'initial recognition' of the asset or liability is not in a transaction that is a business combination or a transaction affecting accounting profit or taxable profit, are akin to 'permanent differences' and IAS 12 does not permit deferred tax to be recognised on these differences, except deferred tax assets arising on the initial recognition of goodwill.

In contrast to FRS 19, which does not permit deferred tax to be recognised where the entity is not obliged to pay more tax at a future date, IAS 12 requires deferred tax to be recognised for all taxable and deductible temporary differences with some limited exceptions as noted above. Thus, under IAS 12 deferred tax will be recognised in respect of the following items which would not give rise to deferred tax under FRS 19:

- *revaluations of non-monetary assets, irrespective of whether there is a binding sale agreement or not;*
- *unremitted earnings of subsidiaries, associates and joint ventures, except to the extent that the entity is able to control the timing of the reversal of the temporary difference and it is probable that the temporary difference will not reverse in the foreseeable future; and*

- *fair value adjustments arising in business combinations, where carrying amounts are adjusted but the tax base is unaffected.*

Other important differences between FRS 19 and IAS 12 are as follows:

- *IAS 12 does not permit discounting of deferred tax balances;*
- *under IAS 12, deferred tax arising on the elimination of unrealised profits on intragroup transactions is provided at the rate at which it will reverse, namely the purchaser's rate, whereas under FRS 19 it would be at the rate paid by the selling company; and*
- *deferred tax arising on the recognised surplus or deficit in a defined benefit plans should be presented with other deferred tax liabilities or assets and not netted against the recognised defined benefit asset or liability.*

In addition, IAS 1 requires that assets and liabilities for current tax and deferred tax assets and liabilities are shown separately in the statement of financial position.

Income tax is one of a number of areas being considered by the IASB as part of its convergence project with FASB. Tentative agreement has been reached to remove from IAS 12 the general exception to the basic principle of recognising a deferred tax liability or asset for taxable temporary differences that arise from the initial recognition of an asset or liability in a transaction that is (i) not a business combination, and (ii) at the time of the transaction affects neither accounting profit nor taxable profit. However, details as to how the resultant deferred tax assets or liabilities should be accounted for have not yet been finalised. Such an amendment would move IAS 12 and FRS 19 further apart.

For UK companies, the IAS 12 approach is likely to result in more deferred tax balances being recognised in the statement of financial position, because many items will be tax–effected for the first time. For example, revaluations, investments in equity-accounted entities, and business combinations may give rise to deferred tax balances.

2 Scope

IAS 12 deals with accounting for income taxes. The Standard defines these as all domestic and foreign taxes that are based on taxable profits. Income taxes also include taxes, such as withholding taxes, that are payable by a subsidiary, associate or joint venture on distributions to the reporting entity. [IAS 12.2]

The determination of whether or not a tax is an 'income tax' is a matter of careful judgement, based on the specific facts and circumstances. Factors to consider in making this determination include, but are not limited to, the following:

- the 'starting point' for determining the taxable amount (i.e. business income, units of production, etc.); and
- the legal description or characteristics of the tax.

The IFRIC referred to this topic in a rejection notice published in the March 2006 *IFRIC Update*. The IFRIC noted that the definition of taxable profit implies that not all taxes are in the scope of IAS 12, and that the requirement to disclose an explanation of the relationship between tax expense and accounting profit implies that taxable profit need not be the same as accounting profit. However, the term taxable profit does imply a notion of a net rather than a gross amount.

Most sales taxes would not meet the definition of an income tax as they are transactional taxes that are based on sales value rather than on taxable profits. Additionally, a production tax may not meet the definition of income tax (see **example 2.2A** below).

2.1 Interest and penalties

In many jurisdictions, interest and penalties are assessed on underpayment or late payment of income tax. Interest and penalties might arise because the tax amount payable could not be agreed with the taxation authority until significantly after the due date and, therefore, the interest and penalties could not have been avoided by the entity. Alternatively, interest and penalties might arise because the entity made a deliberate choice not to make the appropriate tax payments before the due date. In either case, the interest or penalty does not meet the definition of an income tax in IAS 12 and, accordingly, should be presented based on its nature, i.e. either as a finance cost (interest) or operating expense (penalty).

2.2 Hybrid taxes

Entities are sometimes subject to a tax that has different components. Judgement is required when determining whether each of the components meets the definition of an income tax under IAS 12.

Example 2.2A

Tax comprising both production and profit-based components

Company A is subject to a tax made up of two discrete components – a production-based component and a profit-based component. The production-based component is a fixed minimum amount per ton of product sold. The total tax, however, may exceed the fixed minimum per ton depending on the entity's profitability.

The production-based component of the tax would not be considered an income tax, as it is based on the weight of product sold, rather than taxable profits. It would, therefore, be outside the scope of IAS 12. On the other hand, any amounts due as a result of the profit-based component would be considered an income tax and subject to IAS 12.

The production-based component of tax may be reported within either 'cost of goods sold' or 'operating expenses'. Classification as part of cost of goods sold is preferable, although classification as an operating expense would be acceptable. In either case, the presentation should reflect the substance of the entity's operations, and be consistently applied.

Example 2.2B

Petroleum revenue tax

In many jurisdictions, there are 'petroleum revenue' taxes, which are generally designed to ensure that the taxation authority benefits from the 'super profits' that entities in certain resource sectors are able to generate. The petroleum revenue tax is generally based on revenue from extraction activities reduced by specified items of deductible expenditure. The deductions are mainly items related to the extraction activities, but other deductions relating to administrative costs may be allowable. The amount of petroleum revenue tax paid will often form a deduction in itself when the entity's corporate income tax is calculated.

The key characteristic that defines an income tax is that it be based on a measure of taxable profit. Whether or not the petroleum revenue tax in a particular jurisdiction is considered to be an income tax will depend on the rules in that specific jurisdiction and whether the basis for the tax is judged to be closer to a measure of revenue or a measure of profit.

For the purposes of IAS 12, petroleum revenue tax in the UK is considered to be an income tax because it is judged to be based on a measure of taxable profit. UK

2.3 Investment tax credits

IAS 12 does not deal with methods of accounting for government grants or investment tax credits. [IAS 12.4] 'Investment tax credits' is a term commonly used in many tax jurisdictions to describe a range of tax arrangements. IAS 12 does not provide a definition of 'investment tax credits'. Accordingly, in practice, the first step in accounting for an investment tax credit is determining whether it is an investment tax credit outside the scope of IAS 12, or whether the features of the arrangement are such that it is part of an income tax regime. If the item is determined to be an investment tax credit, an entity must determine how to account for the arrangement. Generally, the most appropriate accounting will be achieved by following the requirements of either IAS 12 or IAS 20 *Accounting for Government Grants and Disclosure of Government Assistance*. However, as investment tax credits are not defined, and are specifically scoped out of both Standards, it is a matter of judgement to determine the most appropriate accounting treatment.

3 Current tax

3.1 Definitions

Current tax is defined as the amount of income taxes payable (recoverable) in respect of the taxable profit (tax loss) for a period. [IAS 12.5] It is the tax that the entity expects to pay (recover) in respect of a financial period.

Taxable profit (tax loss) is defined as the profit (loss) for a period, determined in accordance with the rules established by the taxation authorities, upon which income taxes are payable (recoverable). [IAS 12.5]

3.2 Recognition of current tax assets and liabilities

IAS 12's basic requirement is that, to the extent that current tax for the current and prior reporting periods is unpaid, it should be recognised as a liability. Conversely, if the amount already paid in respect of current and prior periods exceeds the amount due for those periods, the excess should be recognised as an asset. [IAS 12.12]

Similarly, an asset is recognised if a tax loss can be carried back to recover the current tax of an earlier period. [IAS 12.13] Thus, if an entity has a tax loss in one year, say 20X3, and this is carried back and used to recover tax of an earlier period, say 20X2, the benefit of the recovery is recognised in the year in which the loss arises, i.e. 20X3.

Generally, current tax is recognised in profit or loss. There are two exceptions to this:

[IAS 12.58]

- where the current tax arises as a result of a transaction or event which is recognised, in the same or a different period, outside profit or loss, either in other comprehensive income or directly in equity (see **3.2.1**); and
- where the current tax arises from a business combination (see **3.2.2**).

3.2.1 Items recognised outside profit or loss

Current tax is recognised outside profit or loss if the tax relates to items that are recognised, in the same or a different period, outside profit or loss. Where the current tax relates to items that are recognised in other comprehensive income, the tax is also recognised in other comprehensive income. Where the tax relates to items that are recognised directly in equity, the tax is also recognised in equity.[IAS 12.61A]

3.2.1.1 Items recognised in other comprehensive income

Items required or permitted under IFRSs to be recognised in other comprehensive income include:

[IAS 12.62]

- revaluation of property, plant and equipment under IAS 16; and
- exchange differences on the translation of the financial statements of a foreign operation under IAS 21.

3.2.1.2 Items recognised directly in equity

Items required or permitted under IFRSs to be credited or charged directly to equity include:

[IAS 12.62A]

- an adjustment to the opening balance of retained earnings resulting from a change in accounting policy that is accounted for retrospectively under IAS 8; and
- the initial recognition of the equity component of a compound financial instrument under IAS 32.

Another common situation where tax is charged directly to equity is where an entity is required to pay a portion of its dividends over to the tax authorities on behalf of the shareholders (often referred to as a 'withholding tax'). The amount paid or payable to the tax authorities is charged to equity as part of dividends. [IAS 12.65A]

The circumstances in which current tax is recognised directly in equity are quite limited. This treatment will be required where, according to the tax rules in a particular jurisdiction, an item recognised directly in equity for accounting purposes affects the current tax expense or income for the period, for example:

- the transaction costs associated with the issue of an equity instrument are deductible for tax purposes in the period in which they are incurred;
- capital gains tax is charged relating to transactions in the entity's own equity instruments; and
- the current tax deduction for an equity-settled share based payment exceeds the cumulative profit or loss expense recognised in respect of that share-based payment.

Example 3.2.1.2

Tax arising on sale of treasury shares held by a subsidiary

Company S (a subsidiary) holds 10 per cent of the ordinary shares of its parent (Company P). These shares are classified as treasury shares by the group. Company P buys back the shares from Company S. After the buy-back, the shares are cancelled, and the treasury shares are derecognised in the consolidated financial statements. In accordance with the law in the tax jurisdiction in which the group operates, an entity is liable for capital gains tax (CGT) if it sells an asset for more than its base cost. In this case, Company S sells the shares for more than the base cost and therefore incurs CGT on the sale. The group therefore incurs CGT. In the consolidated financial statements, a transfer from one reserve in equity (the treasury share reserve) to another reserve in equity (share capital) is made to reflect the cancellation of shares by the group. The CGT represents a transaction cost of the cancellation (being a transaction with an equity holder) and should therefore be charged directly to equity.

3.2.1.3 *Uncertainty regarding amount to be recognised outside profit or loss*

Where an entity cannot determine the amount of current tax that relates to items recognised outside of profit or loss (either in other comprehensive income or directly in equity), the entity can base the amount on a reasonable pro-rata allocation, or some other method achieving a more appropriate allocation. This is assumed to occur only rarely, but such an uncertainty could arise, for example, when there are graduated rates of income tax, and it is impossible to determine the rate at which a specific component of taxable profit (tax loss) has been taxed. [IAS 12.63]

Example 3.2.1.3

Pro-rata allocation of tax between profit or loss and other comprehensive income

Entity A operates in a jurisdiction in which revaluations of property, plant and equipment are taxed when they are recognised for accounting purposes. In 20X1, Entity A recognises an accounting profit of £1,000 and a revaluation gain in other comprehensive income of £200. Tax is charged at 20 per cent on the first £600 of profit and 30 per cent on any profits above £600.

Total tax for the year: £600*20% + £600*30% =£300

It is not possible to make a determination in this graduated tax regime as to which component of total taxable profit was taxed at each particular rate. Entity A therefore needs to allocate the current tax liability of £300 between profit or loss and other comprehensive income on a reasonable pro-rata basis. Entity A's overall average tax rate is 25 per cent (300/1200), and the entity could use this average rate to make a reasonable allocation. The journal entry to recognise the current tax liability for the year would be:

	Dr	Cr
Current income tax – profit or loss	250	
Current income tax – other comprehensive income (asset revaluation reserve)	50	
Taxes payable		300
(To recognise the current tax liability for the year.)		

3.2.1.4 *Dividends*

In some jurisdictions, income taxes are payable at a higher or lower rate if part or all of the net profit or retained earnings is paid out as a dividend to shareholders of the entity. In some other jurisdictions, income taxes may be refundable or payable if part or all of the net profit or retained earnings is paid out as a dividend to shareholders of the entity. In these circumstances, current and deferred tax assets and liabilities are measured at the tax rate applicable to undistributed profits. [IAS 12.52A]

In the circumstances described above, the income tax consequences of dividends are recognised when a liability to pay the dividend is recognised. The income tax consequences of dividends are more directly linked to past transactions or events than to distributions to owners. Therefore, the income tax consequences of dividends are recognised in profit or loss for the period as required by IAS 12.58 except to the extent that the income tax consequences of dividends arise from the circumstances described in IAS 12.58 (a) & (b) (see **3.2**). [IAS 12.52B]

3.2.1.5 *Withholding tax*

Although IAS 12 does not explicitly address the presentation of withholding taxes, it seems appropriate for dividends to be shown inclusive of any withholding tax. This is based on the view that to show only the net amount of the income received which is subject to withholding tax fails to reflect the full amount taxable in the hands of the recipient. The withholding tax amount would therefore be included within the tax charge for the year of the recipient. The payer is acting as an agent in collecting tax and therefore the total amount of the dividend inclusive of that paid to the tax authorities would be shown as a dividend in the accounts of the payer.

UK *The approach described above is consistent with the requirements of FRS 16* Current Tax.

3.2.2 *Current tax arising from business combinations*

Where current tax arises from a business combination, it will be accounted for as part of the initial accounting for the combination and so affect the goodwill or the bargain purchase gain arising on acquisition. [IAS 12.58(b) & 66]

In the context of a business combination, a change of ownership may have direct tax consequences for the acquiree (e.g. a change in tax rate or loss of tax incentives). Where those consequences result in an adjustment to current tax assets or liabilities, the remeasured tax liability or asset will be included in the identifiable net assets recognised, and the adjustment will therefore affect the amount of the goodwill or the bargain purchase gain recognised. The effects of changes in the tax status of an entity are dealt with in SIC-25, and are considered in **4.6.5** below.

3.3 Measurement of current tax assets and liabilities

Current tax assets and liabilities for both the current and prior periods are measured at the amounts that are expected to be paid to (recovered from) the tax authorities, using the tax rates (and tax laws) that have been enacted or substantively enacted by the end of the reporting period. [IAS 12.46] See **4.5.2** below for a discussion of the general issues that arise in respect of the appropriate tax rate to be used. **Section 4.5.2.2** discusses the meaning of 'substantively enacted'.

Where current tax amounts will be paid in future periods, the current tax should be recognised at a discounted amount if the effect of discounting is material.

Example 3.3

Deferral of current tax

Entity A is a start-up entity. As part of the incentive for creating new business in the tax jurisdiction, the taxation authority has granted a five-year partial deferral of tax payments to new businesses in the jurisdiction, for which Entity A is eligible. Under this arrangement, Entity A must pay 60 per cent of its current year tax bill at the end of the tax year, and 40 per cent is deferred until the end of the tax year five years later. Entity A should recognise a current tax liability of 60 per cent of the total current tax bill, plus 40 per cent of the total current tax bill discounted for five years as a non-current tax liability.

The unwinding of the discount in subsequent periods should be presented as a finance cost, as it does not meet the definition of income tax expense in IAS 12.

3.3.1 *Uncertain tax positions*

In certain circumstances, an entity may not be able to determine the exact amount of its current or future tax liabilities due to ongoing investigations by, or negotiations with, the taxation authority. IAS 12 does not provide clear guidance as to how to measure a tax liability when the exact amount of that tax liability is uncertain. The uncertainty might arise from uncertainty as to interpretation of the tax law, or uncertainty as to the likelihood of detection. In determining the amount to be recognised in respect of an uncertain tax liability, an entity should presume a 100 per cent likelihood of detection by the tax authorities. Accordingly, an entity should presume that the tax authority has all the relevant information and measure deferred tax on the basis of the expected interpretation of that information by the tax authority.

In determining the amount to be recognised in respect of the uncertain tax liability, an entity might have regard to similar considerations as it would use in determining the amount of a provision to be recognised in accordance with IAS 37 *Provisions, Contingent Liabilities and Contingent Assets*. The tax liability so calculated will be disclosed within the entity's current tax liability (current tax asset) rather than with other provisions.

Where the uncertain tax position leads to a contingent liability, i.e. no adjustment is made to the current tax liability because, for example, it is not considered probable that a payment will be made, an entity should follow the requirements of IAS 12.88. That is, the entity will disclose any tax-related contingent liabilities and contingent assets in accordance with IAS 37. Contingent liabilities and contingent assets may arise, for example, from unresolved disputes with the taxation authorities.

3.4 Changes in the tax status of an entity or its shareholders

SIC-25 deals with the appropriate accounting for the consequences of such changes. SIC-25, which applies equally to current and deferred taxes, is discussed in detail in **4.6.5** below.

4 Deferred tax

4.1 General approach

IAS 12 focuses on the statement of financial position by recognising the tax effects of temporary differences, i.e. differences between the carrying amount of an asset or a liability and its tax base.

Deferred tax liabilities are defined as the amounts of income taxes payable in future periods in respect of taxable temporary differences. [IAS 12.5]

Deferred tax assets are defined as the amounts of income taxes recoverable in future periods in respect of:

[IAS 12.5]

- deductible temporary differences;
- the carryforward of unused tax losses; and
- the carryforward of unused tax credits.

Deferred tax assets and liabilities are calculated using the following formulae:

Temporary difference = **Carrying amount** - **Tax base**

Deferred tax asset or liability = **Temporary difference** x **Tax rate**

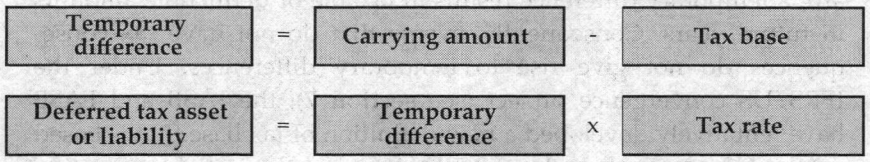

The recognition of deferred tax, therefore, relies on two central concepts:

- tax bases (as defined in **4.2.1** below); and
- temporary differences (as defined in **section 4.3** below).

The principal steps in arriving at deferred tax assets and liabilities under IAS 12 are as follows:

Step 1
Calculate the tax base of each asset and liability in the statement of financial position (see **section 4.2** below). Note that temporary differences can also arise when there is no associated asset or liability recognised for accounting purposes (see **4.2.4** below).

Step 2
Calculate the temporary difference (if any) for each of the above items (see **section 4.3** below).

Step 3
Identify those temporary differences that will give rise to deferred tax assets or liabilities taking into account the recognition criteria and initial exemptions laid down in the Standard (see **section 4.4** below).

Step 4
Calculate the deferred tax attributable to those temporary differences by multiplying each temporary difference by the tax rate that is expected to apply when the temporary difference reverses (see **section 4.5** below).

Step 5
Recognise the movement between the deferred tax balances in the opening and closing statements of financial position in profit or loss, in other comprehensive income, in equity, or as part of the initial accounting for a business combination (thus affecting the goodwill or bargain purchase gain recognised) (see **section 4.6** below).

Although based on temporary differences, the approach of IAS 12 differs from that under US GAAP (SFAS 109). Under the US standard, a temporary difference results in taxable or deductible amounts in future years. Consequently, events that do not have tax consequences do not give rise to temporary differences. Under the IFRS/US convergence project (see **section 7**), the IASB and FASB have tentatively developed a new definition of tax base that is based on the US approach and propose to remove the initial recognition exemptions from IAS 12.

4.2 Calculation of tax bases

4.2.1 Definition of tax base

The tax base of an asset or liability is the amount attributed to that asset or liability for tax purposes. [IAS 12.5] IAS 12 deals separately with the tax base of assets (see **4.2.2** below), and liabilities and revenue received in advance (see **4.2.3** below).

4.2.2 Assets

The tax base of an asset is the amount that will be deductible for tax purposes against any taxable economic benefits that will flow to an entity when it recovers the carrying amount of the asset. [IAS 12.7] Taxable benefits could take the form of proceeds on disposal of an asset, or income earned through the use of an asset (e.g. manufacturing profits).

Future tax consequences are always calculated based on the realisation of the asset at its carrying amount. In reality, an entity will often generate economic benefits in excess of the carrying amount through use or sale. For example, a property may have a market value that is substantially greater than its carrying amount. IAS 12 does not require an estimate of the benefits that will be generated by the asset. Instead, deferred tax is calculated on the assumption that those benefits will be equal to the carrying amount of the asset.

Where the economic benefits that flow from an asset are not taxable, the tax base of the asset is equal to its carrying amount. [IAS 12.7] Deferred taxes only arise when the tax base of an asset or liability differs from its carrying amount. If the economic benefits that flow from an asset are not taxable, and the tax base of the asset is therefore equal to its carrying amount, then the recovery of the asset will not have any deferred tax consequences.

Paragraph 7 of IAS 12 contains several examples of the calculation of the tax base of an asset, including:

- a machine on which tax allowances are received on a different basis to depreciation;
- interest received that is taxed on a receipts basis, but accounted for on a receivable basis;
- trade receivables where revenue has already been recognised and taxed;
- dividends received from a subsidiary which are not taxed;
- a loan receivable on which repayments are not taxed.

Sometimes, the way in which the carrying amount of an asset is recovered can affect the tax base of the asset. Where this is the case, the tax base used should be consistent with the expected manner of recovery. [IAS 12.52(b)]

Example 4.2.2

Expected manner of recovery of asset

[Extracted from IAS 12.52, Example C]

An asset with a cost of 100 and a carrying amount of 80 is revalued to 150. Cumulative depreciation for tax purposes is 30. The carrying amount of the asset is expected to be recovered through sale. If the asset is sold for more than cost, the cumulative tax depreciation of 30 will be included in taxable income and the sale proceeds in excess of an inflation-adjusted cost of 110 will also be taxed. On this basis, the tax base is 80.

If the carrying amount of the asset will be recovered through using the asset, its tax base is 70 (100 less tax depreciation of 30).

4.2.3 *Liabilities*

The tax base of a liability is its carrying amount, less any amount that will be deductible for tax purposes in respect of that liability in future periods. In the case of revenue which is received in advance, the tax base of the resulting liability is its carrying amount, less any amount of the revenue that will not be taxable in future periods. [IAS 12.8]

> Future tax consequences are always calculated based on the settlement of the liability at its carrying amount. There may be occasions where the settlement of a liability is expected to exceed its current carrying amount, for example where a settlement premium is being accrued over the life of a debt instrument. IAS 12 does not require anticipation of the expected settlement amount. Instead, deferred tax is calculated on the assumption that the liability will be settled at its carrying amount.

Where settlement of the liability at its carrying amount would have no tax consequences, the tax base of the liability is equal to its carrying amount. This will be the case where either the transaction has no taxation implications (e.g. accrual of fines and penalties that are not tax deductible), or where the accounting and tax implications occur in the same period (e.g. accrued wages, where the tax deduction is allowed at the same time as the expense is recognised).

Paragraph 8 of IAS 12 contains several examples of the calculation of the tax base of a liability, including:

- accrued expenses that are taxed on a cash basis but accounted for on an accruals basis;
- interest received in advance that is taxed on a cash basis but accounted for on an accruals basis;
- accrued expenses that are taxed and accounted for on an accruals basis;
- accrued expenses that are not deductible for tax purposes; and
- a loan payable on which repayments are not taxed.

In the case of revenue received in advance, the tax base of the liability is the carrying amount of the liability less the portion of the revenue received that has already been taxed (or is never taxable), and hence will not be taxed in the future.

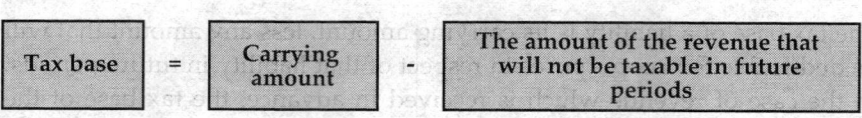

Tax base = **Carrying amount** - **The amount of the revenue that will not be taxable in future periods**

Example 4.2.3A

Revenue received in advance

Company A receives £100 revenue in advance of performing services. It recognises this as deferred revenue in its statement of financial position. For tax purposes, £20 has already been taxed. The carrying amount of the deferred revenue is £100; the amount that will not be taxable in future periods is £20 (as this has already been taxed). Thus, the tax base of the revenue received in advance is £80.

Example 4.2.3B

Receipt of government grant

Company B receives a government grant of CU150 to purchase a certain property. Company B recognises the government grant as deferred income in its statement of financial position, as permitted under IAS 20.

If the government grant is taxable as it is recognised in profit or loss over the life of the related asset, all the grant is taxable in future periods. On initial recognition the tax base will therefore equal the carrying amount of the deferred income.

4.2.4 *Tax bases without an associated carrying amount*

Some items have a tax base but have no carrying amount (i.e. they are not recognised in the statement of financial position for accounting purposes). Where a transaction does not give rise to, or affect the carrying amount of, an asset or liability, but does affect the taxable income of future reporting periods, the tax base is calculated as the amount of the effect on taxable income in future reporting periods. In this case, the carrying amount of the asset or liability associated with the tax base is zero for the purposes of calculating temporary differences. [IAS 12.9]

Example 4.2.4A

Pre-operating costs expensed but not deductible in current period

An entity may incur pre-operating costs. Under IAS 38 *Intangible Assets*, these costs must be expensed when incurred. If local tax laws do not allow an immediate deduction, but do allow a future deduction, the difference between the tax base of the pre-operating costs (i.e. the amount that the taxation authorities will permit as a deduction in future periods) and the carrying amount (of nil) is a temporary difference.

The basic principle of IAS 12 is that entities should (with a few limited exceptions) recognise deferred tax liabilities (assets) whenever settlement or recovery of the carrying amount of an asset or liability would make future tax payments larger (smaller) than they would be if such recovery or settlement were to have no tax consequences. This may be helpful to remember where the tax base of an asset or liability is not immediately apparent. [IAS 12.10]

Example 4.2.4B

Deferred tax assets in respect of goodwill previously written off to reserves

Company D operates in a jurisdiction in which, in accordance with local GAAP requirements, goodwill was written off to reserves prior to the adoption of IFRSs. The local tax authority allows a deduction of one-twentieth of the purchased goodwill in each of the twenty years following an acquisition. Company D acquired a business two years before the adoption of IFRSs, and all related goodwill was written off to reserves at that time. At the date of adoption of IFRSs, Company D will still be able to claim eighteen-twentieths of the amount of purchased goodwill as a deduction over the next eighteen years. Company D should recognise a deferred tax asset, as a deductible temporary difference arises between the carrying amount of the goodwill (nil) and its tax base. At the date of adoption of IFRSs, the deferred tax asset will be recognised as part of the entity's transitional adjustments directly in retained earnings. As the deferred tax asset is subsequently reduced when tax deductions are received, the effect of the reduction in the deferred tax asset will be recognised in profit or loss for the period.

4.2.5 Consolidated financial statements

Where an entity is preparing consolidated financial statements, temporary differences are calculated using:

[IAS 12.11]

- carrying amounts taken from the consolidated statement of financial position; and
- tax bases as determined by reference to the method of tax computation. If the tax authorities calculate tax by reference to each individual entity in the group, the tax bases will be taken from the individual entities' tax computations. Where the tax authorities calculate tax using consolidated figures, the tax bases will be taken from the consolidated tax figures.

Example 4.2.5

Deferred tax asset arising on intragroup transfer

A group undertakes an internal restructuring whereby subsidiary A sells an item of intellectual property with no carrying amount to subsidiary B for 100. Subsidiary B is able to claim a tax deduction for the amortisation of the purchased intangible asset over 5 years.

So far as the group is concerned, the intellectual property has a carrying amount of nil, but a tax base of 100. Accordingly, the group will recognise a deferred tax asset based on the temporary difference of 100. This will be recognised in profit or loss.

The deferred tax impact of eliminations of unrealised profits arising on intragroup transfers is discussed in detail in **section 5.2** below.

4.2.6 *Alternative tax rates and tax bases according to management intent*

Where the amount of tax payable or receivable is dependent upon how the entity recovers the asset or settles the liability, the rate and tax base used to calculate the deferred tax balances should reflect the manner in which the entity expects, at the end of the reporting period, to recover the asset or settle the liability. [IAS 12.51] IAS 12.52 indicates that the manner of recovery may affect either, or both, the tax rate applicable and the tax base of an asset or liability.

Example 4.2.6A

Alternative tax rates for use and disposal of an asset (1)

The carrying amount of an asset is £400,000 (cost of £500,000 less accumulated depreciation of £100,000). The asset's tax written down value (TWDV) is £300,000 (tax depreciation of £200,000 having been claimed to date).

Income generated from the use of the asset is taxed at 25 per cent, and thus the tax depreciation will be recovered at 25 per cent. If the asset were sold, any excess of the disposal proceeds over the asset's tax written down value would be taxed at 30 per cent.

The taxable temporary difference is £100,000. If the entity intends to continue to use the asset in its business, generating taxable income, the deferred tax liability is £25,000 (£100,000 at 25 per cent). If, instead, the entity intends to dispose of the asset, the deferred tax liability is £30,000 (£100,000 at 30 per cent).

Further examples are given in IAS 12.52.

An asset may be recovered through sale, through use, or through use and subsequent sale. Each asset must be assessed to determine the manner in which it is expected to be recovered to determine the appropriate measurement of the related deferred tax. Although the depreciation of an asset to nil is consistent with an expectation of recovery through use, and the depreciation of an asset to a residual amount is consistent with an expectation of recovery through use and subsequent sale, the manner of depreciation is not a conclusive indication of the expected manner of recovery. In particular, non-depreciation does not result in an immediate assumption that an asset is to be recovered through sale. All evidence and economically rational behaviour should be considered in supporting an assumption of recovery of all, or part of , an asset through sale.

Example 4.2.6B

Alternative tax rates for use and disposal of an asset (2)

Assume the same facts as in **example 4.2.6A**, except that the entity intends to use the asset until its carrying amount is £300,000 and its TWDV is £100,000. At that point, the entity will sell the asset, and will be taxed on the difference between the amount recovered through sale and the TWDV. In accordance with the principles of IAS 12, the entity should presume that the value of the asset will be recovered at its carrying amount. The entity will therefore recover another £100,000 from the asset through its use, and receive £200,000 of allowable deductions during that period. The entity will then recover £300,000 from the sale of the asset, and receive £100,000 of allowable deductions. In effect, the entity expects to recover £400,000 from the asset and receive £300,000 of deductions.

The tax rate applicable at the time the temporary difference reverses is 25 per cent in respect of use and 30 per cent in respect of sale. The entity must therefore use both tax rates in determining the deferred tax balance to take account of the fact that the deferred tax will reverse at different rates. Accordingly, the entity's deferred tax liability in respect of the asset is calculated as follows:

[(£100,000 – £200,000)] *25%

+ [(£300,000 – £100,000)]*30%

= £35,000

A more complicated situation arises where in a particular tax jurisdiction the recovery of an asset through use is subject to one type of income tax and recovery through sale is subject to another type of income tax. In some tax jurisdictions the applicable tax rates are the same, and in some jurisdictions there may also be a form of equalisation mechanism such that the total tax deductions obtained for the two types of income tax will together equal the cost for tax purposes, or cannot exceed the tax cost. In other jurisdictions the two tax rates are different and no such equalisation mechanisms exist. Hence, it is often necessary to consider separately the tax bases and temporary differences arising from recovery through use and recovery through sale, particularly where the tax regime is such that there are effectively two distinct tax systems applying to the recovery of the asset. Any deductible temporary difference will need to be assessed for recognition in accordance with the normal requirements, separately from any taxable temporary difference arising.

Example 4.2.6C

Recovery through sale and use under different income taxes

Company D acquires a piece of machinery in a business combination. The machinery is recognised in the consolidated financial statements at a fair value of $150. The entity is not entitled to claim any tax deductions when using or abandoning the asset hence its tax base for recovery through use is nil.

Company D expects to use the asset for a number of years and then sell it for its currently estimated residual value of $50. The income on sale of the asset is subject to a different type of income tax, and at the time of sale a tax deduction of $100 will be available. Therefore its tax base for recovery through sale is $100. The tax rates applicable at the time the temporary differences reverse are 10 per cent in respect of use and 30 per cent in respect of sale.

In the tax jurisdiction in which Company D operates, losses on sale of this type of property, plant and equipment can only be recovered against gains on sale of such property plant and equipment and not against general operating profits.

	Carrying amount	Tax base	Temporary difference	Deferred tax
Recovery through use	100	Nil	100	10
Recovery through sale	50	100	(50)	(15)*

* The possible deferred tax asset that is expected to arise from the sale of the machine must be assessed for recoverability. If it is not probable that suitable future taxable profit will be available against which the deductible temporary difference can be utilised, the deferred tax asset would not be recognised.

4.2.6.1 Non-depreciable assets

A specific issue arises in respect of non-depreciable assets. As noted above, the rate to be used when measuring deferred tax balances should reflect the manner in which the entity intends to recover the carrying amount of the asset. However, where an asset has an unlimited life (i.e. it is non-depreciable), the question arises as to how the term 'recovery' should be interpreted. This issue is addressed in SIC-21 *Income Taxes – Recovery of Revalued Non-depreciable Assets.*

SIC-21 deals with:

- assets that are not depreciated (non-depreciable assets) and are revalued in accordance with IAS 16.31; and
- investment properties that are carried at revalued amounts under IAS 40.33, but would be considered non-depreciable if IAS 16 were to be applied.

When an asset has an unlimited life, the carrying amount of the asset will be recovered through sale, notwithstanding that the asset is being used by the business and that there is no current intention to sell it. SIC-21 concludes that, for revalued non-depreciable assets, deferred tax should be measured based on the tax consequences that would follow from recovery of the carrying amount of the asset through sale.

The basis of conclusion in SIC-21 points to land having an unlimited life and being non-depreciable. Land is the only asset that should be assumed to be non-depreciable. Assets such as some intangible assets that are simply not being depreciated because they have an indefinite life, or because their current residual value is at or above carrying amount, are not non-depreciable for the purposes of SIC-21. The normal rules apply to such assets, namely that temporary differences will be recognised based on the expected manner of recovery.

Example 4.2.6.1A

Non-depreciable asset – freehold land

Company E is carrying freehold land at £900,000, being its current market value. The tax base on sale of the land will be its original cost of £500,000. The land is used for the storage of Company E's raw materials. The tax rate applicable to manufacturing income is 25 per cent but, on disposal of a capital asset, any proceeds in excess of cost are taxed at 30 per cent. There is currently no intention to sell the land.

The taxable temporary difference between the carrying amount and the tax base of the freehold land is £400,000. Although the asset is being used by

Company E to generate manufacturing income, the value of the land is not being recovered in that way. All of the value of the land will be recovered through its eventual sale and, therefore, the applicable tax rate is 30 per cent, and the deferred tax liability arising is £120,000.

If, for tax purposes, there was an indexation allowance on the land, then this indexed amount would be the tax base of the land.

Example 4.2.6.1B

Brand with an indefinite useful life

Company F has a brand, which is carried in its books at £900,000. Under local tax law, only a partial deduction is available in respect of the acquisition cost of intangible assets – the cost attributable to the brand in accordance with those tax rules is £500,000. The brand is considered to have an indefinite useful life, and is therefore not being amortised in accordance with the requirements of IAS 38.107. The tax rate applicable to sales income is 25 per cent but, on disposal of the capital asset, any proceeds in excess of cost are taxed at 30 per cent. There is no intention to sell the brand to realise the tax deduction available through sale.

The taxable temporary difference between the carrying amount and the tax base of the brand is £400,000. The brand is being used by Company F to generate sales income. As there is no intention to sell the asset, it is assessed that the carrying amount of the brand will be recovered through its use. As the value will be recovered through use, the applicable tax rate is 25 per cent, and the deferred tax liability arising is £100,000.

4.2.6.2 *Investment and owner-occupied property*

IFRSs permit or require certain assets to be carried at fair value or to be revalued (for example, IAS 16 *Property, Plant and Equipment*, IAS 39 *Financial Instruments: Recognition and Measurement* and IAS 40 *Investment Property*). In some jurisdictions, the revaluation affects taxable profit (tax loss) for the current period, in which case no temporary difference arises. In other jurisdictions, the revaluation does not affect taxable profit in the period and, consequently, a deferred tax liability or asset arises. This is true even if:

[IAS 12.20]

- the entity does not intend to dispose of the asset. In such cases, the revalued carrying amount of the asset will be recovered through use and this will generate taxable income which exceeds the depreciation that will be allowable for tax purposes in future periods; or

- tax on capital gains is deferred if the proceeds of the disposal of the asset are invested in similar assets. In such cases, the tax will ultimately become payable on sale or use of the similar assets.

UK

The second bullet point above is referring to what, in the UK, is known as rollover relief. IAS 12 requires that when an asset that is expected to be recovered through sale is revalued, deferred tax should be provided on the temporary difference arising even if it is expected that a 'replacement asset' will be acquired and rollover relief obtained. In some jurisdictions, such as the UK, the manner of recovery of the replacement asset will determine whether the rollover relief gives rise to a postponement of tax or to permanent relief. However, until the replacement asset is acquired, deferred tax should be provided on the basis that rollover relief will give rise only to postponement of tax, i.e. the potential permanent relief should not be anticipated. If the original asset is sold and there is a time delay before the replacement asset is acquired the deferred tax would continue to be provided.

SIC-21 includes within its scope investment properties carried at revalued amounts that are accounted for under IAS 40 only if they would be considered non-depreciable if IAS 16 were to be applied. [SIC-21.4]

Therefore, the deferred tax consequences in respect of revalued investment properties will depend on whether they are depreciable or non-depreciable assets.

Although investment properties are not generally depreciated, they are 'depreciable' because they have a limited useful life. SIC-21 is clear that only investment properties 'that would be considered non-depreciable if IAS 16 were to be applied' fall within its scope. This effectively restricts its scope to freehold land.

Thus, if an entity holds investment property that comprises land and buildings, and these are accounted for in accordance with the fair value model in IAS 40 then, except for investment properties that are expected to be sold shortly after the reporting period, the deferred tax consequences of the land and building elements will need to be considered separately for the purposes of IAS 12.

The land element has an unlimited economic life and is therefore a non-depreciable asset within the meaning of IAS 16. Consequently, any deferred tax asset or liability arising on the land element should reflect the tax consequences of selling the asset.

The building element has a finite life, and therefore is a depreciable asset. Any deferred tax asset or liability arising on the building element should reflect the tax consequences that would follow from the manner in which the entity expects, at the end of the reporting period, to recover the asset. This will be use, generally followed by eventual sale for the asset's estimated residual value.

In practice, to the extent that the building's estimated residual value reflects its current fair value, the entire investment property could be viewed as being ultimately recovered through sale, and hence the tax base applicable to a sale is appropriate. However, to the extent that the building's estimated residual value is lower than its current fair value, then a tax base based on the use and consumption of that element of the building should be used. IAS 12 does not specify how the amounts to be recovered through sale and through use should be determined. In practice there are two approaches: one is to determine the amount expected to be recovered through sale, with any residual portion of the carrying amount being considered to be recovered through use. The alternative is to determine the amount expected to be recovered through use, with any residual portion of the carrying amount considered to be recovered through sale. There are differing views in practice as to which of these is most appropriate. As the Standards are silent, each entity must make a judgement as to the most appropriate methodology in their circumstances and apply that methodology consistently across similar transactions.

Example 4.2.6.2A

Investment property building (1)

Entity B has an investment property building that is carried at its fair value of £200,000 in accordance with IAS 40. Entity B intends to hold the investment property for a further two years, after which the entity believes the property will be sold for not less than £200,000. During the two years the entity expects to recover £50,000 from the use of the property but will not receive any tax deductions. The tax base of the property is £100,000. The tax rate for revenue from the use of the property is 25 per cent. The tax rate for profits from the sale of the property is 30 per cent. As the entity expects to recover the entire carrying amount through sale, it is not necessary to allocate portions of the asset between the use rate and the sale rate. The entity would therefore recognise a deferred tax liability of £30,000.

Alternatively, as an accounting policy choice, the entity could choose to allocate portions of the asset between the use rate and the sale rate. The entity would therefore recognise a deferred tax liability of £12,500 in respect of the recovery of £50,000 through use of the asset. In keeping with the principle that the entity should assume recovery at the carrying amount for the purposes of IAS 12, the portion of the carrying amount to be recovered through sale would be £150,000; with a deduction of £100,000. This would give rise to deferred tax liability in respect of the sale of £15,000, resulting in a total deferred tax liability in respect of the asset of £27,500.

Such an accounting policy choice needs to be applied consistently across like transactions in accordance with the requirements of IAS 8.

Example 4.2.6.2B

Investment property building (2)

Presume the same facts as in **example 4.2.6.2A**, except that at the end of the two years Entity B believes the property will be sold for £160,000.

In this case, the entity must make an accounting policy choice as to whether it will consider first the portion that will be recovered through use, or the portion that will be recovered through sale.

If the entity chooses to consider first the portion that will be recovered through sale, then the entity will recognise a deferred tax liability of £18,000 in respect of the sale of the asset [(£160,000 – £100,000)*30%], and a deferred tax liability of £10,000 in respect of the use of the asset (£40,000*25%), resulting in a total deferred tax liability of £28,000.

If the entity chooses to consider first the portion that will be recovered through use, the entity will recognise a deferred tax liability of £12,500 in respect of the use of the asset (50,000*25%), and a deferred tax liability of £15,000 [(£150,000-£100,000)*30%) in respect of the sale of the asset, resulting in a total deferred tax liability of £27,500.

As with investment property, the expected manner of recovery of owner-occupied properties will need to be determined for the purposes of measurement of any deferred tax balances. Generally, this will be use followed by disposal for estimated residual value.

In many jurisdictions it is common for an investment property to be sold within its corporate structure – that is, the corporate structure will hold only one material asset, the investment property itself. When the parent entity disposes of the property, it will dispose of it within that corporate shell, as in many cases this will shield the parent entity from adverse tax consequences.

Generally, deferred tax is recognised in the individual financial statements of the corporate structure entity, calculated on the relevant income tax rate applicable to taxable income of that entity and such deferred tax will be reflected in the parent entity's consolidated financial statements. In addition, the consolidated financial statements may reflect deferred tax in respect of the investment in the corporate structure subsidiary, calculated at the relevant rate applying to taxable income of the parent entity.

However, if it is the case that in a particular jurisdiction, all market participants will purchase and sell property within a corporate shell, such that the purchase of a company containing a property will always be viewed as the purchase of an asset (and not a business combination), in the consolidated financial statements of the parent it may be appropriate to recognise deferred tax in respect of the property on the basis of the rate applicable to the sale of the shares

4.2.6.3 *Changes of intention*

Where there is a change in management's expectation as to the manner in which an asset will be recovered, or a liability settled, the change may impact the measurement of the related deferred tax balances.

The deferred tax impact should be re-measured based on management's revised intentions and the adjustment recognised in profit or loss or, to the extent that it relates to items previously recognised outside profit or loss, in other comprehensive income or directly in equity.

The impact of management intentions on deferred taxes is discussed at **4.2.6** above.

4.2.7 *Rollover relief*

In some jurisdictions, an entity may be entitled to 'rollover relief' when it disposes of a capital asset for a profit and replaces it with an equivalent asset. In such circumstances, the gain on disposal may not be assessed for tax purposes until the replacement asset is disposed of, when it is taken into account via the 'capital' (or sale) tax base of the replacement asset. In many cases this merely postpones, rather than eliminates, the payment of tax, and IAS 12 requires that a deferred tax liability is recognised. [IAS 12.20(b)] If the replacement asset is recovered entirely through use, it may be the case that the tax for which 'rollover relief' was given is not merely postponed, but permanently relieved. Thus, in determining the tax base of a replacement asset, careful consideration should be given to the effect of rollover relief on the tax payments flowing from its recovery, based on the expected manner of recovery.

UK *There is further discussion of rollover relief in the UK at* ***4.2.6.2*** *above.*

4.3 Calculation of temporary differences

Under IAS 12, deferred tax balances are recognised in respect of temporary differences. A temporary difference arises where the carrying amount of an asset or liability differs from its tax base. For many transactions, there is no difference between the accounting and the tax treatment of the transaction. Therefore, no temporary difference and, hence, no deferred tax balance arises.

UK *IAS 12 does not have an equivalent to the 'permanent' differences under FRS 19, i.e. items of income and expense that are never taxable or tax deductible; however, it does have some specific exemptions so that the treatment of some such items is essentially the same as for a 'permanent difference'. As discussed in the previous section, when the recovery of an asset or the settlement of a liability has no tax consequences, then the tax base is equal to the carrying amount, and no deferred tax arises.*

4.3.1 *Definition of temporary difference*

IAS 12 defines a temporary difference as the difference between the carrying amount of an asset or liability in the statement of financial position and its tax base. [IAS 12.5]

Temporary differences can arise in a number of circumstances, for example:

- when income or expenses are included in accounting profit in one period but included in taxable profit in a different period (i.e. timing differences);
- in a business combination, when the carrying amounts of assets and liabilities are adjusted to their fair values at the date of acquisition, but the tax bases of those assets and liabilities are not affected by the business combination or are affected differently;
- where an asset or a liability is revalued, but the tax base of the asset is not adjusted;
- where the taxation authority permits indexation of, or other adjustments to, the cost of an asset for tax purposes, but the asset is not revalued for accounting purposes;

- in respect of non-tax deductible goodwill which arises in a business combination; and
- on the initial recognition of an asset or liability, for example, if part or all of the cost of an asset will not be deductible for tax purposes.

Temporary differences are determined by reference to the carrying amount of an asset or liability. [IAS 12.55]

The carrying amounts used in the calculation of temporary differences are determined from the accounting records. Where applicable, carrying amounts are calculated net of any allowances or deductions, such as allowances for doubtful debts or impairment losses.

There are two types of temporary differences – taxable temporary differences and deductible temporary differences. These are discussed in detail below.

UK

Under IAS 12, where assets and liabilities are remeasured for accounting purposes, but the tax base is not adjusted, a temporary difference will arise. Under UK GAAP, asset revaluations do not give rise to deferred tax assets and liabilities unless there is a binding commitment to sell, and the resulting gain/loss on disposal will be recognised in the financial statements (i.e. no rollover relief is anticipated). Similarly, deferred tax assets and liabilities generally do not arise from adjusting assets to market value as part of a business acquisition. Only where the normal rules require recognition (e.g. binding sales contract) should the liability be recognised.

4.3.2 *Taxable temporary differences*

Taxable temporary differences are temporary differences that will result in taxable amounts in determining the taxable profit (tax loss) of future periods when the carrying amount of the asset or liability is recovered or settled. [IAS 12.5]

Taxable temporary differences are, therefore, differences that will give rise to taxable income in the future: they increase future taxable profit, and so give rise to deferred tax liabilities.

In the context of an asset, a taxable temporary difference arises when the carrying amount of the asset exceeds its tax base (e.g. an asset is depreciated more quickly for tax purposes than for accounting purposes). As the carrying amount of the asset is recovered, the economic benefits subject to tax (i.e. the profits generated by the use of the asset equal to the carrying amount of the asset) will exceed the future tax deductions available (the tax base). The tax effect of this taxable temporary difference gives rise to a deferred tax liability.

In the context of a liability, a taxable temporary difference arises when the tax base of the liability exceeds its carrying amount (e.g. a foreign currency loan payable which has been reduced for accounting purposes by an exchange gain that will be taxable when the loan is settled). If the loan is settled at its carrying amount, a taxable gain will arise. This is a taxable temporary difference.

4.3.3 *Deductible temporary differences*

Deductible temporary differences are temporary differences that will result in amounts that are deductible in determining the taxable profit (tax loss) of future periods when the carrying amount of the asset or liability is recovered or settled. [IAS 12.5]

Deductible temporary differences are, therefore, differences that decrease taxable income in the future, and so they give rise to deferred tax assets.

IAS 12.26 gives some examples of deductible temporary differences that result in deferred tax assets, as follows:

- retirement benefit costs may be deducted in determining accounting profit as service is provided by the employee, but deducted in determining taxable profit either when contributions are paid to a fund by the entity or when retirement benefits are paid by the entity. A temporary difference exists between the carrying amount of the liability and its tax base – the tax base of the liability is usually nil. Such a deductible temporary difference results in a deferred tax asset as economic benefits will flow to the entity in the form of a deduction from taxable profits when contributions or retirement benefits are paid;
- research costs are recognised as an expense in determining accounting profit in the period in which they are incurred but may not be permitted as a deduction in determining taxable profit (tax loss) until a later period. The difference between the tax base of the research costs, being the amount the taxation authorities will permit as a deduction in future periods, and the carrying amount of nil is a deductible temporary difference that results in a deferred tax asset;
- with limited exceptions, an entity recognises the identifiable assets acquired and liabilities assumed in a business combination at their fair values at the acquisition date. When a liability assumed is recognised at the acquisition date but the related costs are not

deducted in determining taxable profits until a later period, a deductible temporary difference arises which results in a deferred tax asset. A deferred tax asset also arises when the fair value of an identifiable asset acquired is less than its tax base. In both cases, the resulting deferred tax asset affects the goodwill or bargain purchase gain recognised; and

- certain assets may be carried at fair value, or may be revalued, without an equivalent adjustment being made for tax purposes. A deductible temporary difference arises if the tax base of the asset exceeds its carrying amount.

In the context of an asset, a deductible temporary difference arises when the tax base of the asset exceeds its carrying amount (e.g. when the carrying amount of a financial asset has been reduced by an allowance for irrecoverable amounts, but the allowance is not deductible for tax purposes until settlement). If the asset is settled at its carrying amount, a net deduction will arise: this is a deductible temporary difference.

In the context of a liability, a deductible temporary difference arises when the carrying amount of the liability exceeds its tax base (e.g. where interest payable has been accrued, but no tax deduction is available until the interest is paid). If the accrual is settled at its carrying amount, a net deduction will arise: this is a deductible temporary difference.

A useful guide for determining whether temporary differences are taxable or deductible is set out below:

	Carrying amount – tax base	**Type of temporary difference**	**Gives rise to . . .**
Asset	Positive	Taxable	Deferred tax liability
Asset	Negative	Deductible	Deferred tax asset
Liability	Positive	Deductible	Deferred tax asset
Liability	Negative	Taxable	Deferred tax liability

4.4 Identification of temporary differences to be recognised

Having identified all of the temporary differences that exist at the end of the reporting period (see **section 4.3** above), the next step is to pinpoint those temporary differences that will give rise to deferred tax assets or liabilities in the statement of financial position, using the recognition criteria laid down in the Standard.

4.4.1 Recognition of taxable temporary differences

A deferred tax liability should be recognised for all taxable temporary differences, unless the deferred tax liability arises from:

[IAS 12.15]

- the initial recognition of goodwill; or
- the initial recognition of an asset or liability in a transaction which:
  - is not a business combination; and
  - at the time of the transaction affects neither accounting profit nor taxable profit (tax loss).

An entity should recognise a deferred tax liability for all taxable temporary differences associated with investments in subsidiaries, branches and associates, and interests in joint ventures, except to the extent that both of the following conditions are satisfied:

[IAS 12.39]

- the parent, investor or venturer is able to control the timing of the reversal of the temporary difference; and
- it is probable that the temporary difference will not reverse in the foreseeable future.

4.4.2 Recognition of deductible temporary differences

A deferred tax asset should be recognised for all deductible temporary differences to the extent that it is probable that taxable profit will be available against which the deductible temporary difference can be utilised, unless the deferred tax asset arises from the initial recognition of an asset or liability in a transaction that:

[IAS 12.24]

- is not a business combination; and
- at the time of the transaction, affects neither accounting profit nor taxable profit (tax loss).

The notion of probability should be applied positively – this approach places the burden of proof on the entity to provide evidence to support recognition.

IAS 12 is silent with regard to the probability threshold. IAS 37 *Provisions, Contingent Liabilities and Contingent Assets* defines the term 'probable' as 'more likely than not'. [IAS 37.23] The footnote to IAS 37.23 acknowledges that this definition is not necessarily applicable to other IFRSs. However, in the absence of any other guidance, the term 'probable' should be applied as 'more likely than not'.

The IASB has tentatively agreed, as part of the IFRS/US convergence project, to clarify that 'probable' means 'more likely than not'.

An entity should recognise a deferred tax asset for all deductible temporary differences arising from investments in subsidiaries, branches and associates, and interests in joint ventures, to the extent that, and only to the extent that, it is probable that:

[IAS 12.44]

- the temporary difference will reverse in the foreseeable future; and
- taxable profit will be available against which the temporary difference can be utilised.

The availability of future profits is discussed in **4.4.8** below.

4.4.3 Recognition exceptions – general

As detailed in **4.4.1** and **4.4.2** above, all deferred tax assets and liabilities should be recognised except for those arising from:

- in relation to deferred tax liabilities only, the initial recognition of goodwill; or
- the initial recognition of an asset or liability in a transaction which (i) is not a business combination and (ii) at the time of the transaction affects neither accounting profit nor taxable profit (tax loss); or
- certain differences associated with investments in subsidiaries, branches and associates, and interests in joint ventures.

In addition to the exceptions noted, a further condition must be met before a deferred tax asset can be recognised in respect of deductible temporary differences – it must be probable that taxable profits will be available against which the deferred tax asset can be utilised. This probability criterion is discussed in detail in **4.4.8** below.

4.4.4 Recognition exceptions – goodwill

The tax deductibility of reductions or impairments in the amount of goodwill recognised varies by jurisdiction according to the tax laws. Where the reduction of goodwill is not deductible against taxable income, the tax base of the goodwill is nil, and a taxable temporary difference arises equal to the carrying amount of the goodwill.

Although a taxable temporary difference exists at initial recognition, IAS 12 prohibits the recognition of the resulting deferred tax liability. The underlying rationale for this exception is that, if a deferred tax liability were set up in respect of the goodwill at the time of the business combination, this would decrease the total for the net assets recognised. Because goodwill is a residual, this would further increase goodwill and the increase would also need to be tax-effected. [IAS 12.21 & 21A]

Subsequent reductions in a deferred tax liability that is unrecognised because it arises from the initial recognition of goodwill are also regarded as arising from the initial recognition of goodwill and, therefore, they are not recognised. [IAS 12.21A]

By contrast, deferred tax liabilities associated with goodwill are recognised to the extent that they do not arise from the initial recognition of that goodwill. [IAS 12.21B]

Example 4.4.4A

Deferred tax liability arising on the initial recognition of goodwill (1)

Company A acquires Company B for consideration of £500. The fair value of the identifiable net assets of Company B at the acquisition date is £400, resulting in goodwill of £100. The goodwill has a tax base of nil, but IAS 12 prohibits recognising the resulting deferred tax liability on the temporary difference of £100.

Subsequently, the goodwill is impaired by £20 and, therefore, the amount of the taxable temporary difference relating to the goodwill is reduced from £100 to £80, with a resulting decrease in the value of the unrecognised deferred tax liability. The decrease in the value of the unrecognised deferred tax liability is also regarded as relating to the initial recognition of the goodwill and is not recognised.

Example 4.4.4B

Deferred tax liability arising on the initial recognition of goodwill (2)

Facts as for **example 4.4.4A**, except that the goodwill is deductible for tax purposes at a rate of 20 per cent per year starting in the year of acquisition. Thus, the tax base of the goodwill is 100 on initial recognition and 80 at the end of the year of acquisition. If the carrying amount of goodwill at the end of the year of acquisition remains unchanged at 100 (i.e. it has not been impaired), a taxable temporary difference of 20 arises at the end of that year. That taxable temporary difference does not relate to the initial recognition of the goodwill and, therefore, the resulting deferred tax liability is recognised. The temporary difference will reverse when the goodwill is sold or impaired.

IAS 12 was previously silent on the recognition of deferred tax assets from the initial recognition of goodwill. IFRS 3(2008) amended IAS 12 to insert IAS 12.32A which states that if the carrying amount of goodwill arising in a business combination is less than its tax base, the difference gives rise to a deferred tax asset that will be recognised as part of the accounting for the business combination to the extent that it is probable that it will be recovered.

This amendment should be applied for annual periods beginning on or after 1 July 2009, or if an entity applies IFRS 3(2008) for an earlier period, from that earlier period.

4.4.5 Recognition exceptions – initial recognition of an asset or liability

IAS 12 requires the recognition of deferred tax in respect of temporary differences arising where an asset or liability results from any one of the following:

- a transaction that affects accounting profit (e.g. anticipation of income receivable (asset), or accrual of costs payable (liability)); or
- a transaction that affects taxable profit (e.g. expenditure on assets such as computer equipment allowed for tax purposes when paid (asset), or deferral of income recognition in respect of funds that are taxable when received (liability)); or
- a business combination.

IAS 12 prohibits the recognition of deferred tax on the initial recognition of an asset or liability in any other circumstances. [IAS 12.22] The flowchart below illustrates these rules.

Temporary difference arising on the initial recognition of an asset or liability

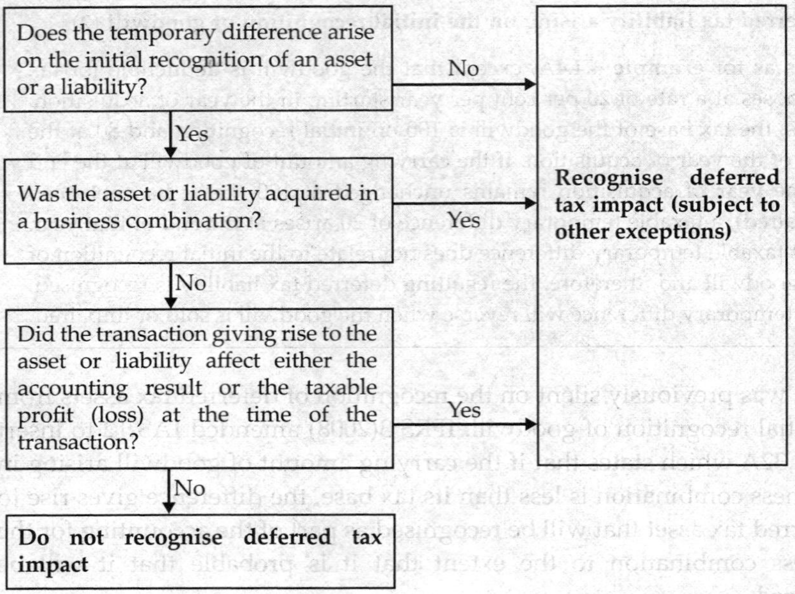

One example given in IAS 12 is that of an asset for which there is no deduction against taxable profits for depreciation. Assuming that the entity intends to recover the value of the asset through use, the tax base of the asset is nil. Therefore, a taxable temporary difference equal to the cost of the asset arises on initial recognition. However, the Standard does not permit a deferred tax liability to be recognised as the initial recognition of the asset is not part of a business combination and doesn't affect either accounting profit or taxable profit. Furthermore, no deferred tax is recognised as a result of depreciating the asset.

The prohibition on recognition is based on the argument that, if a deferred tax liability were recognised, the equivalent amount would have to be added to the asset's carrying amount in the statement of financial position, or be recognised in profit or loss at the date of initial recognition, and this would make the financial statements 'less transparent'.[IAS 12.22(c)] This exception is based on pragmatism and the desire to avoid the particular financial statement effects discussed above, rather than any particular conceptual basis. The exception has a particular effect in jurisdictions where some or all of initial expenditure on assets is disallowed for tax purposes.

Example 4.4.5A

Deferred tax liability arising on the recognition of an asset – asset depreciated at the same rate for tax and accounting purposes

Company A purchases an asset for £100,000. Only £60,000 is qualifying expenditure for tax purposes. The carrying amount of the asset will be recovered through use in taxable manufacturing operations. The asset is depreciated on a straight-line basis at 25 per cent for both tax and accounting purposes.

Year	Carrying amount £	Tax base £	Temporary difference £	Deferred tax £
20X0	100,000	60,000	40,000	-
20X1	75,000	45,000	30,000	-
20X2	50,000	30,000	20,000	-
20X3	25,000	15,000	10,000	-
20X4	-	-	-	-

No deferred tax is ever recognised in respect of the original temporary difference.

Subsequent to initial recognition, additional temporary differences may arise in respect of the same asset or liability. In such circumstances, the deferred tax effect of those additional temporary differences is recognised in accordance with the usual rules.

Effectively what is required, as is illustrated in **example 4.4.5B**, is to deduct from the temporary difference at each period end the proportion of the asset's carrying amount that represents the unrecognised temporary difference at the date of acquisition, as reduced by subsequent depreciation. Deferred tax is provided in respect of remainder of the temporary difference (the recognised temporary difference) in accordance with the usual rules.

Example 4.4.5B

Deferred tax liability arising on the recognition of an asset – different deprecation rates for tax and accounting purposes

Facts as per **example 4.4.5A**, but the asset is depreciated at 25 per cent for accounting purposes and 33⅓ per cent for tax purposes. The tax rate is 30 per cent.

Year	Carrying amount £ A	Tax base £ B	Temporary difference £ A-B = C	Unrecognised temporary difference £ D (as per example 4.4.5A)	Recognised temporary difference £ C-D = E	Deferred tax liability £ E * 30%
20X0	100,000	60,000	40,000	40,000	-	-
20X1	75,000	40,000	35,000	30,000	5,000	1,500
20X2	50,000	20,000	30,000	20,000	10,000	3,000
20X3	25,000	-	25,000	10,000	15,000	4,500
20X4	-	-	-	-	-	-

Additional temporary differences will also arise when the asset is subsequently revalued, as illustrated below.

Example 4.4.5C

Deferred tax liability arising on the recognition of an asset – asset subsequently revalued

Facts as per **example 4.4.5A** (i.e. depreciation at 25 per cent for both tax and accounting purposes), but assume that the asset is revalued for accounting purposes to £120,000 at the end of the first year.

Year	Carrying amount £ A	Tax base £ B	Temporary difference £ A-B = C	Unrecognised temporary difference £ D (as per example 4.4.5A)	Recognised temporary difference £ C-D = E*	Deferred tax liability £ E * 30%
20X0	100,000	60,000	40,000	40,000	-	-
20X1	120,000	45,000	75,000	30,000	45,000	13,500
20X2	80,000	30,000	50,000	20,000	30,000	9,000
20X3	40,000	15,000	25,000	10,000	15,000	4,500
20X4	-	-	-	-	-	-

* The recognised temporary difference is the amount by which the asset has been revalued upwards in comparison with the depreciated original cost (i.e. the difference between £120,000 and £75,000, being the carrying amount of the asset at the time of the revaluation).

4.4.5.1 *Acquisition of investment property*

At the time of acquisition of an investment property, an entity should determine whether the acquisition is considered to be the acquisition of a single asset, or whether it is considered to be a business combination. The acquisition of a single asset is a transaction to which the initial recognition exemption applies and, accordingly, no deferred tax would be recognised as a result of the acquisition. Conversely, the acquisition of assets in a business combination does not attract the initial recognition exemption and, therefore, deferred tax would be recognised on any temporary differences arising from the acquisition.

In determining whether the acquisition is a business combination or not an entity might examine the ancillary activities related to the property. For example, where an entity simply purchases a property with tenancy agreements in place and all other services are carried out by a third party contracting with the tenant, it is likely that the acquisition would be considered to be the acquisition of a single asset. Where a property is acquired that necessarily involves the entity in a number of service arrangements it is more likely that the transaction would be considered to be a business combination. (See **section 4** in **chapter 34** for a discussion of the guidance in FRS 3(2008) on whether a transaction is a business combination.)

4.4.5.2 Government grants

The above examples all deal with deferred tax liabilities arising on the initial recognition of an asset. More rarely, deferred tax assets can arise in such circumstances. The example cited in IAS 12 for a deferred tax asset arising on initial recognition is when a non-taxable government grant related to an asset is deducted in arriving at the carrying amount of the asset but, for tax purposes, is not deducted from the asset's depreciable amount (i.e. its tax base). The carrying amount of the asset is less than its tax base, giving rise to a deductible temporary difference. Under IAS 20, the government grant may also be set up as deferred income, in which case the difference between the deferred income and its tax base of nil is a deductible temporary difference. Whichever method of presentation is adopted, the entity does not recognise the resulting deferred tax asset. [IAS 12.33]

Example 4.4.5.2

Receipt of government grant

Company B receives a government grant of CU150 to purchase a certain property. Company B recognises the government grant as deferred income in its statement of financial position, as permitted under IAS 20.

If the government grant is not taxable, either on receipt, or on recognition as income over the useful life of the related property, applying the formula above will give a tax base of nil. Thus, there will be a deductible temporary difference. However, because this difference arises on the initial recognition of the deferred income it will not be recognised.

If the government grant is taxable on receipt, there will be no revenue taxable in future periods. Therefore the tax base will be nil and a taxable temporary difference will exist. The initial recognition exemption will not apply because tax was payable on initial recognition and a deferred tax asset will be recognised.

4.4.5.3 *Recognition exemptions applied by an acquiree*

An entity acquired in a business combination may, in its financial statements, not have recognised deferred taxes on temporary differences related to some assets or liabilities because on initial recognition of the asset or liability the recognition exemption applied.

Although the acquired entity does not recognise the deferred tax on these items in its financial statements, the recognition exemption does not apply when the assets and liabilities of the acquired entity are initially recognised in the new consolidated group. Deferred tax will be recognised on any temporary differences on these items because the assets and liabilities are acquired in a business combination.

4.4.5.4 *Transfers of assets between group entities*

In some circumstances, an entity within a group will acquire assets and liabilities in a business combination and subsequently transfer one or more of the acquired assets to another entity within the group. In the consolidated financial statements of the group, as the assets were acquired in a business combination, the initial recognition exemption would not apply and deferred tax would be recognised on any temporary differences arising at the date of acquisition and subsequently.

However, from the perspective of an individual entity within the group to which assets have been subsequently transferred, often the transfer will not constitute a business combination, but rather the acquisition of individual assets. Hence, when an asset is transferred to another entity in the group, in the individual financial statements of that other entity, any temporary difference arising on the initial recognition of the asset is subject to the initial recognition exemption and no deferred tax recognised at the point of transfer. In the consolidated financial statements of the group, the unrecognised deferred tax would be reinstated as a consolidation adjustment.

4.4.6 *Recognition exceptions – investments in subsidiaries, branches and associates, and interests in joint ventures*

Temporary differences arise when the carrying amount of an investment differs from its tax base (which is often cost). Examples of situations where temporary differences may arise include:

- the existence of undistributed profits in the subsidiary, branch, associate or joint venture (where profits have been consolidated, equity-accounted or proportionately consolidated);
- movements in the carrying amount of a foreign operation due to changes in foreign exchange rates when a parent and its subsidiary are based in different countries; and
- a reduction in the carrying amount of an investment in an associate to its recoverable amount without a corresponding change in its tax base.

A temporary difference recognised in consolidated financial statements may be different from that in the parent's separate financial statements if the parent carries the investment at cost or revalued amount. [IAS 12.38]

Differences associated with investments in subsidiaries, associates and joint ventures generally arise in consolidated financial statements, because the results of the investee entity have been accounted for (whether by consolidation, proportionate consolidation or equity accounting), and yet the tax base of the investment remains the same. The tax effects of the distribution of those profits (e.g. withholding tax) should be considered. Unlike the 'general' recognition exceptions (see **4.4.3** above), IAS 12 does not prohibit the recognition of deferred tax assets and liabilities in respect of these differences. Instead, it imposes particular conditions for such recognition.

An entity should recognise a deferred tax liability for all taxable temporary differences associated with investments in subsidiaries, branches and associates, and interests in joint ventures, except to the extent that both of the following conditions are satisfied:

[IAS 12.39]

- the parent, investor or venturer is able to control the timing of the reversal of the temporary difference; and
- it is probable that the temporary difference will not reverse in the foreseeable future.

IAS 12 does not define 'foreseeable future'. However, it is referred to in IAS 1 *Presentation of Financial Statements* regarding the going concern assumption. IAS 1(2007).26 (previously IAS 1(2003).24) states that the foreseeable future 'is at least, but not limited to, twelve months from the end of the reporting period'. Therefore, for the purposes of applying IAS 12, it is reasonable to expect that the 'foreseeable future' would be at least twelve months from the end of the reporting period. However, depending on the facts and circumstances (including management intent), it may be a longer period.

UK

Under UK GAAP unremitted earnings of subsidiaries, associates and joint ventures only give rise to deferred tax liabilities to the extent that dividends have been accrued, or if there is a binding agreement to distribute past earnings.

4.4.6.1 Investments in subsidiaries

The temporary difference generally represents the difference between the net investment accounted for in the financial statements (effectively the parent entity's share of the subsidiary's net assets) and the tax base of the investment.

A parent/subsidiary relationship involves the parent controlling its subsidiary, including the subsidiary's dividend policy. Accordingly, the Standard provides that when a parent has stipulated that it is probable that undistributed profits in a subsidiary or branch will not be distributed for the foreseeable future, the parent does not recognise deferred tax on those undistributed profits. [IAS 12.44]

The Standard gives no specific guidance regarding the determination of whether distribution and, therefore, reversal of the temporary difference is probable. The factors that might be considered in making the assessment include:

- any plans for reinvestment to grow the business of the subsidiary;
- the past pattern of dividend payment;
- whether the parent needs a distribution from its subsidiary to enable it to make a dividend payment or satisfy any other cash requirement;

- whether cash and distributable profits are available to pay a dividend;
- whether a binding agreement exists to remit a certain amount of dividend;
- whether there is a policy of paying out a certain percentage of profits each year;
- whether there is intent to sell before any distribution is made; and
- whether any legal or taxation requirements effectively create an economic compulsion to pay distributions.

In the circumstance where an entity requires its subsidiary to remit only a portion of undistributed earnings, the entity should recognise a deferred tax liability only for the portion of the undistributed earnings to be remitted in the future.

If circumstances change and it becomes probable that some or all of the undistributed earnings of a subsidiary will be remitted in the foreseeable future but income taxes have not been recognised, the investor should accrue as an expense of the current period, income taxes attributable to that remittance.

If a subsidiary is loss-making, management may decide to shut down or sell the loss-making division. This may mean that the division meets the definition of a discontinued operation in accordance with IFRS 5 (see **chapter 29**). The fact that a subsidiary is a discontinued operation does not modify the way in which any deductible temporary difference that may exist is recognised. As such, a deferred tax asset should be recognised to the extent that it is probable that the temporary difference will reverse in the foreseeable future, and taxable profit will be available against which the temporary difference can be utilised.

If a parent has recognised deferred income taxes on a temporary difference arising in its investment in a subsidiary, then the amount of deferred income taxes of the parent attributable to the subsidiary should be included in accounting for a disposal through sale or other transaction that reduces the investment, such as a change in investment from a subsidiary to an associate, see **4.4.6.4** below.

Example 4.4.6.1A

Profits in a subsidiary not expected to be distributed in the foreseeable future

Company A has a subsidiary with a carrying amount of £200, and a tax base of £100. Company A controls the distribution of dividends by the subsidiary. Company A does not have any need for the subsidiary to make a distribution, and in fact has active plans for the undistributed profits to be reinvested to grow the business of the subsidiary. Company A should not recognise a deferred tax liability in respect of the temporary difference of £100, because Company A can control the timing of the reversal and the temporary difference is not expected to reverse in the foreseeable future.

Example 4.4.6.1B

Profits in a subsidiary expected to be distributed in the foreseeable future

Presume the same facts as for **example 4.4.6.1A**, except that Company A has encountered a cash flow problem. In order to resolve this problem, Company A needs to extract the increased value in the subsidiary in the form of a cash dividend. In this case, Company A should recognise the deferred tax liability for the portion of the earnings to be remitted because, although it can control the timing of the reversal, it is probable that the temporary difference will reverse in the foreseeable future.

Example 4.4.6.1C

Parent does not control timing of payment of dividends

Presume the same facts as for **example 4.4.6.1A**, except that the subsidiary operates in a foreign jurisdiction. In that jurisdiction, the determination as to whether profits must be returned to foreign investors or can be reinvested in the business is made through regulatory channels. While Company A can express a preference, it is the local regulator who will determine whether profits must be paid out as dividends. In this case, Company A should recognise the deferred tax liability for all unremitted earnings of the subsidiary because it does not control the timing of the reversal of the temporary difference.

Example 4.4.6.1D

Repayment of loan forming part of net investment not expected in foreseeable future

Company B has a functional currency of US dollars. It makes a loan in Euros to its Euro functional currency subsidiary D. The loan is assessed under IAS 21 to be part of Company B's net investment in D. In Company B's separate financial statements the loan is retranslated at the year end with exchange

> differences recognised in profit and loss. The exchange differences arising from the loan will only incur tax when the loan is repaid.
>
> Company B can control the repayment of the loan which forms part of the net investment in the subsidiary. As settlement is neither planned nor likely to occur in the foreseeable future, it is probable that the temporary difference created by the exchange differences will not reverse in the foreseeable future. Company B does not recognise deferred tax on the exchange differences arising on the foreign currency loan to its subsidiary.

Measurement considerations are discussed further in **4.5.3** below.

4.4.6.2 Investments in associates

In consolidated financial statements, investments in associates are generally accounted for using the equity method of accounting. Under the equity method, the investment is originally recognised at cost and the carrying amount is then increased by the investor's share of the profit or loss and other comprehensive income of the investee. The tax arising in respect of the investee's profit or loss and other comprehensive income is recognised in the financial statements of the investee, and is therefore reflected in the amounts accounted for by the investor using the equity method of accounting. Any additional tax arising on any dividends received by the investor will also be reflected in the investor's own financial statements.

There might be additional tax implications if the investor were to realise the investment – whether through distribution of the retained profits of the investee, or through disposal. For example, dividend income might be taxable or partially taxable in the hands of the investor; withholding taxes might be applied in the associate's country of operation; capital gains tax might be payable on disposal of the investment. In any of these circumstances, a temporary difference may exist.

Under IAS 12's recognition rules, (see **4.4.1** above), temporary differences associated with investments in associates should be accounted for except when:

- the investor controls the timing of the reversal of the temporary difference; and

- it is probable that the temporary difference will not reverse in the foreseeable future.

Since an investor/associate relationship does not involve control, the investor should normally recognise deferred tax arising on the undistributed profits of the associate, unless there is a well-evidenced agreement that profits will not be distributed in the foreseeable future.

Example 4.4.6.2

Investment in associate

Company B has an associate, Company A, which operates in Z Land. At 31 December 20X3, Company B had accounted for its £20,000 share of the profits of Company A using the equity method of accounting.

During the period, Company A paid dividends of £5,000 to Company B. No tax arises in Company B's country of operation on receipt of the dividends. However, under the laws of Z Land, additional tax is payable on distributed profits at 25 per cent and is not recoverable.

As Company B is not able to control the timing of the reversal of the temporary difference, it must also recognise the tax consequences of the unremitted earnings of £15,000. A deferred tax liability of £3,750 (£15,000 x 25%) should therefore be recognised in the financial statements to 31 December 20X3, in addition to the recognition of any tax consequences arising from the £5,000 of remitted earnings.

For deductible temporary differences arising in relation to investments, it is not necessary to consider the investor's ability to control distributions from the investee. Recognition of the deferred tax asset is only permitted if it is probable that the temporary difference will reverse in the foreseeable future and taxable profit will be available against which the temporary difference can be utilised.

In determining whether the tax on the temporary differences arising from an investment in an associate should be provided for at the use or sale rate, the entity should have regard to the expected manner of recovery of the investment. Factors to consider in making this judgement include, but are not limited to:

- whether the entity intends to sell its interest;
- the dividend yield on the investment; and
- the reason for acquiring and holding the investment.

The absence of evidence of an intent to sell, even though it may be a possibility at some point in the future, may lead to an assumption of recovery through use.

4.4.6.3 Investments in jointly controlled entities

Under IAS 31 *Interests in Joint Ventures*, jointly controlled entities are accounted for either using proportionate consolidation, or using the equity method of accounting. If the latter method is used, the accounting treatment for investments in jointly controlled entities is the same as that described in the previous paragraphs for investments in associates. Irrespective of the method of accounting for jointly controlled entities, the same considerations as those for associates will apply in respect of deferred tax.

The arrangement between the parties to a joint venture usually deals with the sharing of the profits and identifies whether decisions on such matters require the consent of all the venturers or a specified majority of the venturers. When the venturer can control the sharing of profits and it is probable that the profits will not be distributed in the foreseeable future, a deferred tax liability is not recognised. [IAS 12.43]

The determination as to who controls the timing of the reversal of the temporary difference in the case of jointly controlled entities is not as clear-cut as it is for associates. Investments in jointly controlled entities involve joint control, i.e. there is a contractual agreement to share control and no venturer exercises unilateral control.

The arrangements for distributions or disposals of shareholdings are generally dealt with in the joint venture agreement. In most cases, although each venturer cannot unilaterally declare a dividend, neither can such dividend be declared without each venturer's agreement. Thus, each venturer has the ability to prevent distributions and ,accordingly, prevent the reversal of the temporary difference. If this is the case, no deferred tax liability should be recognised if the venturer does not anticipate that such distributions will be authorised in the foreseeable future.

4.4.6.4 Change in investment from subsidiary to associate

An investment in ordinary shares of a subsidiary may change so that it is no longer a subsidiary because the parent sells a portion of the investment, the subsidiary issues additional shares, or other transactions affect the investment. The change from subsidiary to associate may have deferred tax consequences.

Under IFRS 3(2008) when a transaction results in a change in investment in subsidiary to either an associate or a joint venture and the investment retained is remeasured to fair value, there will be a change to the temporary difference associated with that investment. The temporary difference will include not only the undistributed profits of the entity, and foreign exchange differences etc., but also the fair value uplift of the investment. In many cases because the actions of the associate cannot be controlled, it will be determined that the investor no longer has control of the timing of the reversal of the temporary difference and deferred tax will have to be provided.

Under IFRS 3(2004), when the nature of an investment changes, or part of an investment is sold to result in a retained investment of a different nature, the carrying amount of the investment retained will be the previous carrying amount or portion of the previous carrying amount. If an investment in a subsidiary changes so that the investment becomes an associate, and the associate is accounted for using the equity method under IAS 28, the investor will have to recognise income taxes on its share of undistributed earnings of the associate, even if it did not previously do so. This is because the investor will no longer be able to control the reversal of the temporary difference. The following example illustrates this concept.

Example 4.4.6.4

Subsidiary becomes associate (under IFRS 3(2004))

Company P previously had £1,000 of undistributed earnings from its investment in its subsidiary, Company S. Company P had recognised no deferred income tax liability, because recovery of the undistributed earnings of Company S is within its control and, therefore, Company P can control the timing of the reversal of the temporary difference.

At the beginning of 20X1, Company S issued ordinary shares to an unrelated third party investor such that Company P no longer controlled a majority of Company S's voting shares. As a result of the issue, Company S has become an associate of Company P, and Company P has accounted for its equity interest in Company S as an associate using the equity method.

During 20X1, Company P's share of the earnings of Company S was £2,000 and no dividends were paid or payable. Company S's new dividend policy, beginning in 20X2, is that 100 per cent of retained earnings will be paid to shareholders.

P would recognise an income tax expense for the tax effect of establishing (1) a deferred tax liability for the tax consequences of £2,000 of taxable income attributable to its share of earnings of S during 20X1, and (2) a deferred tax liability for its portion of the 100 per cent undistributed earnings in equity prior to 20X1.

4.4.6.5 *Foreign currency adjustments*

The non-monetary assets and liabilities of an entity are measured in its functional currency (see **chapter 28**). If the entity's taxable profit or tax loss (and, hence, the tax base of its non-monetary assets and liabilities) is determined in a different currency, changes in the exchange rate give rise to temporary differences that result in a recognised deferred tax liability or asset (subject to certain exemptions for deductible temporary differences, see **4.4.2** above). The resulting deferred tax is recognised in profit or loss. [IAS 12.41]

Under FRS 19, such differences would be considered permanent, thus deferred tax would not be provided for. UK

IAS 12 is clear that where the tax base is determined in a different currency to the functional currency of the entity, temporary differences will arise and deferred tax should be calculated. However, there is no guidance on how the deferred tax should be calculated.

In general, the most appropriate methodology will be to convert the tax base into the functional currency using the closing rate. This should be compared with the asset value in the financial statements, which will have been converted at the rate ruling on the date of recognition, and the deferred tax calculated at the effective tax rate expected to apply when the temporary difference reverses. This method provides a systematic best estimate of the exchange rate prevailing when the temporary difference reverses.

Example 4.4.6.5A

Tax base of asset denominated in a foreign currency

Company B, a £ functional currency entity, owns an asset in the United States. At 1 January 20X1, the tax base of the asset is USD120 and the carrying amount is £50. The exchange rate is £0.5 = USD1. At 31 December 20X1 the tax base of the asset is USD120 and the carrying amount is £50. The exchange rate is £0.52 = USD1. At 1 January 20X1, the temporary difference is £10. At 31 December 20X1 the temporary difference is £12. The movement of £2 represents an increase in the temporary difference as a result of the unfavourable movement in the exchange rate.

The movement of £2 will be recognised as part of deferred tax expense for the year, irrespective of the fact that the movement is attributable to the movement in the foreign currency exchange rate.

In practice, because of depreciation, there would be an element of the movement that would arise from the depreciation of the carrying amount, bringing the carrying amount closer to the tax base.

Where an entity owns a subsidiary that is taxed in a currency other than that subsidiary's functional currency, a translation difference will arise on the calculated deferred tax balance in that subsidiary's financial statements. On consolidation, that exchange difference is not transferred to the foreign currency translation reserve because the translation difference does not result from the accounting for the reporting entity's net investment in a foreign operation.

Example 4.4.6.5B

Tax base of subsidiary's assets and liabilities denominated in a foreign currency

Group A prepares consolidated financial statements in Currency Units, and includes a subsidiary with a functional currency of USD. However, that subsidiary pays taxes that are calculated and denominated in Currency Units. Accordingly, the tax bases of the assets and liabilities in the subsidiary's financial statements are denominated in Currency Units. Therefore, changes in exchange rates give rise to temporary differences. The resulting deferred tax is recognised in profit or loss. On consolidation, this expense is not recognised in other comprehensive income as it forms part of the recognised tax expense (income) on consolidation. The amount is a profit or loss item that takes account of the genuine foreign currency exposure between the functional currency of the subsidiary and the tax cash flows of that subsidiary.

4.4.6.6 *Inflation adjustments*

The tax law for a particular foreign jurisdiction may permit or require the taxpayer to adjust the tax basis of an asset or a liability to take into account the effects of inflation. The inflation-adjusted tax base of an asset or a liability would be used to determine the future taxable or deductible amounts. If a foreign subsidiary has such inflation-indexed assets or liabilities, it cannot use the exemptions of IAS 12.39 listed above and not recognise the related deferred tax assets or liabilities.

The temporary differences relate to the foreign operation's own assets and liabilities, rather than to the reporting entity's investment in that foreign operation. Thus, the foreign subsidiary recognises the resulting deferred tax liability or asset as appropriate in its domestic financial statements. The resulting deferred tax is recognised in profit or loss. Such amounts would not be recognised where the usual exemptions for recognising taxable temporary differences (see **4.4.1** above) or deductible temporary differences (see **4.4.2** above) are met.

Example 4.4.6.6

Tax base of assets adjusted for inflation

Assume that Company X (with £ as its functional currency) has an overseas subsidiary (where the inflation rate is not considered hyperinflationary – see **chapter 42**) whose functional currency is the Euro.

At the beginning of 20X2, the foreign jurisdiction enacted tax legislation that increased the tax base of depreciable assets by 10 per cent. That increase will permit the overseas subsidiary to deduct additional depreciation in current and future years. Also, assume that the base of Company X's depreciable assets is €1,000 for tax and financial reporting purposes, the foreign tax rate is 50 per cent, and the current exchange rate between £ and € is £1 equals €2.

Company X would establish a deferred tax asset for the deductible temporary difference resulting from the difference between the £/€ equivalent of the foreign depreciable asset and the indexed tax basis. Thus, at the beginning of 20X2, the overseas subsidiary would recognise a deferred tax asset of €50 ([€1,000 × 10 per cent] × 50 per cent). The deferred tax asset would be remeasured to £25 (€50 × 0.5) based on the current exchange rate.

4.4.7 Recognition of deferred tax assets

Deferred tax assets can arise from deductible temporary differences (e.g. where the carrying amount of an asset is less than its tax base), or from the ability to carry forward unused tax losses and unused tax credits.

Under IAS 12, subject to the exceptions listed in **4.4.2** above, deferred tax assets are recognised for all deductible temporary differences and all unused tax losses and tax credits, but only to the extent that it is probable that future taxable profit will be available against which they can be utilised. [IAS 12.24 & 34]

Where an entity has a deferred tax asset that has not been recognised because it failed this recoverability test, the entity is required to reassess the position at the end of each subsequent reporting period. Where the test is subsequently met, the asset is recognised at that later date. This may occur, for example, if there is an improvement in trading conditions such that it becomes more likely that sufficient taxable profits will be generated in the future. [IAS 12.37]

Conversely, where a deferred tax asset has been recognised in the statement of financial position, its carrying amount should be reviewed at each end of the subsequent reporting period and reduced to the extent that it is no longer probable that sufficient taxable profit will be available to enable its recovery. [IAS 12.56]

4.4.8 Availability of future profits

A deferred tax asset represents a future tax deduction. It is therefore only valuable if the entity will have sufficient future taxable profits against which the deduction can be offset. Thus, an important question to answer is when it can be considered probable that an entity will have sufficient taxable profits available in the future to enable the deferred tax asset to be recovered.

The term 'probable' is not defined in the Standard. As noted in **4.4.2** above, the term is subject to varying interpretations, but is generally agreed to mean at least more likely than not (i.e. a probability of greater than 50 per cent).

The IASB has tentatively agreed, as part of the IFRS/US convergence project (see **section 7**), to make this clarification.

IAS 12 states that it is probable that an entity will have sufficient taxable profit available in the future to enable a deferred tax asset to be recovered when:

- there are sufficient taxable temporary differences relating to the same taxation authority and the same taxable entity which are expected to reverse either in the same period as the expected reversal of the deductible temporary difference or in periods into which a tax loss arising from the deferred tax asset can be carried back or forward; [IAS 12.28] or
- it is probable that the entity will have sufficient taxable profit, relating to the same taxation authority and the same taxable entity, in the same period as the reversal of the deductible temporary difference (or in the periods into which a tax loss arising from the deferred tax asset can be carried back or forward). In making this evaluation, taxable amounts arising from deductible temporary differences that are expected to originate in future periods should be ignored (as these will need further future taxable profits in order to be utilised); [IAS 12.29(a)] or
- tax planning opportunities are available to the entity that will create taxable profit in appropriate periods. [IAS 12.29(b)]

Thus, when looking for future taxable income to justify the recognition of a deferred tax asset, entities can look to:

- future reversals of existing taxable temporary differences (see **4.4.9**);
- future taxable profit (see **4.4.8.1**); and
- tax planning opportunities, i.e. actions that the entity could take to create or increase taxable profits in future periods so as to utilise the available tax deductions before they expire (see **4.4.10** below).

FRS 19 requires consideration of recoverability of an asset against taxation on future profits to take into account the timing of the profit. However, when the entity has deferred tax liabilities, FRS 19 does not require consideration of the timing of the reversal to be taken into account in assessing whether an asset may be recovered against the liability. UK

4.4.8.1 *Indicators on the availability of future taxable profits*

In evaluating whether or not it is probable that taxable profit will be available, the nature and timing of such profit should be considered. The following are some examples of factors that may support the assertion that it is probable that taxable profit will be available.

Contracts or firm sales backlog that will produce sufficient taxable income to realise the deferred tax asset based on existing sales prices and cost structures:

- an entity enters into a long-term contract that will generate sufficient future taxable income to enable it to utilise all existing operating loss carryforwards; or
- during the current year, an entity acquired another entity that operates in a different industry that is characterised by stable profit margins. Assuming that the group is taxed on a consolidated basis or that group relief is available, the acquiree's existing contracts will produce sufficient taxable income to enable utilisation of the loss carryforwards.

An excess of appreciated asset value over the tax basis of an entity's net assets in an amount sufficient to realise the deferred tax asset:

- an entity has invested in land that has appreciated in value. If the land were sold at its current market value, the sale would generate sufficient taxable income to utilise all tax loss carryforwards. The entity will sell the land and realise the gain if the operating loss carryforward would otherwise expire unused. After consideration of the tax planning strategy, the fair value of the entity's remaining net assets exceeds their tax and financial reporting basis.

A strong earnings history exclusive of the loss that created the future deductible amount coupled with evidence indicating that the loss is not a continuing condition:

- an entity incurs operating losses that result in a carryforward for tax purposes. The loss resulted from the disposal of a subsidiary whose operations are not critical to the continuing entity and the entity's historical earnings, exclusive of the subsidiary losses, have been strong.

Conversely, there may be indicators that future taxable profits will not be available. The following are some examples of factors that may rebut the assertion that it is probable that taxable profit will be available.

History of losses in recent years (see also **4.4.11.1** below):

- an entity has incurred operating losses for financial reporting and tax purposes during recent years. The losses for financial reporting purposes exceed operating income for financial reporting purposes as measured on a cumulative basis from the most recent preceding years; or

- a currently profitable entity has a majority ownership interest in a newly-formed subsidiary that has incurred operating and tax losses since its inception. The subsidiary is consolidated for financial reporting purposes. The tax jurisdiction in which the subsidiary operates prohibits it from obtaining group relief (or filing a consolidated tax return) from its parent or other group entities.

A history of operating loss or tax credit carryforwards expiring unused:

- an entity has generated tax credit carryforwards during the current year. During the last several years, tax credits, which originated in prior years, expired unused. There are no available tax planning strategies that would enable the entity to utilise the tax benefit of the carryforwards.

Unsettled circumstances that if unfavourably resolved would adversely affect profit levels on a continuing basis:

- during the last several years, an entity has manufactured and sold devices to the general public. The entity has discovered, through its own product testing, that the devices may malfunction under certain conditions. No malfunctions have been reported. However, management is concerned about the appropriateness of continuing to sell the product; or

- in prior years, the entity manufactured certain products that required the use of industrial chemicals. The entity contracted with a third party to dispose of the by-products. That third party is now out of business, and the entity has learned that the by-products were not disposed of in accordance with environmental regulations. A government agency is investigating and may insist that the entity pay for clean-up costs.

4.4.9 *Future reversals of existing taxable temporary differences*

As noted above, in order to justify the anticipated recovery of a deductible temporary difference against existing taxable differences, the following conditions must be met:

[IAS 12.28]

- the taxable differences must relate to the same taxation authority and the same taxable entity; and

- the taxable differences must be expected to crystallise either in the same period as the deferred tax asset crystallises, or in a period into which any tax loss arising from the reversal of the deferred tax asset can be carried forward or back.

Entities may not take account of future originating temporary differences (e.g. planned future capital expenditure) when assessing future reversals of temporary differences because those differences will only arise as a result of future events or transactions.

To the extent that the conditions set out above are met, the asset should be recognised, irrespective of any trading losses expected to arise in future periods.

Example 4.4.9

Future reversals of existing taxable temporary differences

Company C has made a taxable loss for the year and has identified the following temporary differences at 31 December 20X3:

- taxable temporary differences related to accelerated tax depreciation, expected to reverse in 20X4 and 20X5 – £4,000
- deductible temporary differences in respect of pre-operating costs expensed for accounting purposes in 20X3 but allowed for tax purposes over five years – £2,800

Company C is expected to make losses in 20X4 and 20X5. Tax is payable at 20 per cent. Tax losses may be carried forward, but not back.

Anticipated reversals of temporary differences:

	20X4	20X5	20X6	20X7
	£	£	£	£
Accelerated tax depreciation	(2,000)	(2,000)	-	-
Pre-operating costs	700	700	700	700

At 31 December 20X3, a deferred tax liability is recognised in respect of the accelerated tax depreciation, amounting to £800 (£4,000 x 20 per cent). The deferred tax asset recognised in respect of the pre-operating costs is limited to £280 (£1,400 x 20 per cent). Future tax deductions are available for the remainder of the pre-operating costs. However, because the reversals occur in periods when they cannot be used against existing taxable temporary differences, their recognition cannot be justified on the basis of those temporary differences. Other expected sources of taxable income or tax planning opportunities would need to be identified in order to support the recognition of the remainder of the deferred tax asset. In the above example this seems unlikely, because Company C is, and is forecast to continue to be, a loss-making entity (see **4.4.11** below).

IAS 12 does not specifically address the scheduling of reversal patterns. Because of cost benefit considerations, there may be more than one approach to scheduling reversal patterns. However, it is apparent from the discussion in IAS 12.35 & 36 that two concepts underlie the determination of the reversal patterns for existing temporary differences:

- the year(s) in which temporary differences result in taxable or deductible amounts generally are determined by the timing of the recovery of the related asset or the settlement of the related liability; and
- the tax law determines whether future reversals of temporary differences will result in taxable and deductible amounts that offset each other in future years.

In general, entities should consider all currently available information about the future. However, certain future events should not be anticipated or considered in determining the realisability of deferred tax assets. These items include, but are not limited to, the following:

- changes in tax laws or rates (except those that are substantively enacted);
- changes in tax status;
- expected business combinations;
- anticipating future income from events beyond the entity's control and that are non-recurring or unusual in nature (e.g. forgiveness of indebtedness for purposes of avoiding derecognition of a deferred tax asset); and
- events dependent on future market conditions or otherwise not within the entity's control.

The same method of reversal should be assumed when measuring the deferred tax consequences for a particular category of temporary difference for a particular tax jurisdiction.

If the same category of temporary difference exists in two or more tax jurisdictions, the same method should be used for that temporary difference in those jurisdictions. In addition, the same method should be used consistently from year to year for a particular category within a particular tax jurisdiction and any change in that method of assumed reversal is a change in estimate that should be reported in accordance with IAS 8 *Accounting Policies, Changes in Accounting Estimates and Errors*.

4.4.10 Tax planning opportunities

Tax planning opportunities are actions that the entity can take to create or increase taxable income in a particular period before the expiry of a tax loss or tax credit carryforward. [IAS 12.30] Although such opportunities are future actions, the entity is entitled to consider them in justifying the recognition of a deferred tax asset.

Examples of tax planning opportunities include:

[IAS 12.30]

- being able to elect to have an income source taxed at an earlier point, e.g. electing to have interest income taxed on a receivable, rather than a receipts, basis;
- being able to defer to a future period the claim for certain tax deductible items, e.g. waiving a claim to first year allowances on an item of equipment, and instead taking annual allowances on the full amount in future periods;
- selling and leasing back assets that have appreciated in value, but for which the tax base has not been adjusted to reflect the appreciation; and
- selling an asset that generates non-taxable income in order to purchase another investment that generates taxable income.

In order to take such planning opportunities into account, the entity must have the ability to implement the chosen tax planning strategies. For example, planning to take a pension holiday in order to boost taxable profit in a particular period so as to utilise tax losses that are about to expire can only be taken into account if the strategy can be controlled by the entity, for example, cannot be prevented by pension regulations, and is likely to be accepted by the workforce.

The amount of the asset justified by reference to such proposed strategies must be reduced by the cost of the strategies. The actions must be commercially viable and without significant adverse consequences – otherwise, it is unlikely that management would proceed.

In entering into tax planning strategies, entities will often incur costs payable to the designer of the strategy. In determining whether such costs meet the definition of income tax or should be treated as an operating expense, the entity will need to have regard to whether the payment is to the designer, or whether it is paid to the designer to be paid to the tax authorities on the entity's behalf.

Example 4.4.10

Classification of payments in a tax structuring transaction

Entity A has an effective tax rate of 40 per cent. The entity enters into a transaction with an investment bank which enables a portion of its activities to be taxed in a tax haven country rather than Entity A's domestic taxation regime.

The investment bank receives a 30 per cent fee based on taxable profits before the transaction, of which it pays 10 per cent over to the tax authorities in a tax haven country. Entity A continues to pay tax at an effective rate of 4 per cent. The structuring fee paid to the investment bank is deductible for tax purposes. The following table illustrates the effect of the transaction on taxable profits and tax payments.

	Before structuring	After structuring
	£	£
Profit before tax	1,000	700
Effect of tax restructuring	-	(600)
Taxable profit	1,000	100
Tax (40%)	**(400)**	**(40)**
Profit after tax	**600**	**660**

The effective tax rate and tax charge structure of the deal:

Tax paid/payable by the client	£40	4%
Tax paid/payable by the investment bank	£100	10%
Total tax paid	£140	14%

In determining how the amounts paid should be presented in Entity A's financial statements, only amounts that will ultimately be paid to tax authorities on Entity A's behalf should be considered as tax expenses. An evaluation needs to be performed as to whether in substance Entity A continues to bear the tax risk associated with the tax payment by the investment bank, or whether the bank makes the tax payment of £100 on its own behalf. If Entity A retains substantially all of the tax risk associated with the tax payment by the investment bank, then all direct and indirect payment to the tax authorities should be considered as a tax expense, resulting in the recognition of a tax expense of £140. If the investment bank takes over substantially all the tax risk, then only the direct payment made by Entity A should be considered, resulting in the recognition of a tax expense of £40.

In determining whether Entity A has retained the tax risk, the following factors should be considered:

- whether the taxation authority would have any capacity to demand payment from Entity A if the investment bank did not pay; and
- whether Entity A would be required to make further payments for the tax (or be entitled to refunds) if the onward payment proves to have been miscalculated.

4.4.11 *Tax losses*

Where an entity has incurred losses in recent years, greater caution should be exercised before a deferred tax asset is recognised. The Standard points out that 'the existence of unused tax losses is strong evidence that future taxable profit may not be available'. It goes on to say that, if there are insufficient deferred tax liabilities reversing in appropriate periods and entities, there must be 'convincing other evidence' that there will be sufficient taxable profit. [IAS 12.35]

In assessing the probability that taxable profits will be available, the following should be considered:

[IAS 12.36]

- whether the entity has sufficient taxable temporary differences relating to the same taxation authority and the same taxable entity, which will result in taxable amounts against which the unused tax losses or unused tax credits can be utilised before they expire;
- whether it is probable that the entity will have taxable profits before the unused tax losses or unused tax credits expire;
- whether the unused tax losses result from identifiable causes which are unlikely to recur; and
- whether tax planning opportunities are available to the entity that will create taxable profit in the period in which the unused tax losses or unused tax credits can be utilised.

The entity assesses whether any portion of the total available unused tax losses or tax credits is likely to be utilised before they expire. To the extent that it is not probable that taxable profit will be available against which the unused tax losses or unused tax credits can be utilised, the deferred tax asset is not recognised. [IAS 12.36)]

IAS 12 notes that preparers need to consider whether unused tax losses result from identifiable causes that are unlikely to recur. Where the losses are expected to recur, it is unlikely that a deferred tax asset can be recognised.

The very existence of losses calls future profitability into question. However, the source of the losses may have been addressed, for example, through disposal of loss-making operations, restructurings, or reductions of ongoing costs.

Particular attention needs to be paid to restrictions on:

- the number of years for which the losses can be carried forward; and
- the types of profit against which the losses can be offset.

In some jurisdictions, previous GAAP required that an entity could not look beyond a fixed time period (for example 5 years) in determining whether sufficient future profits would be available. It should be noted that there is no specific time restriction in IAS 12 regarding the length of the 'look-forward' period which is used to determine whether taxable profits will be available. The length of the period used will depend on a number of entity-specific factors, including the entity's historical profitability, accuracy of budgetary controls and expected future activities.

4.4.11.1 *History of recent losses*

The assessment of whether or not an entity will have sufficient taxable profits in the future to realise a deferred tax asset is a matter of careful judgement based on the facts and circumstances available.

A history of recent losses is among the most objectively verifiable evidence and, as a result, carries more weight than other evidence that embodies some degree of subjectivity. For this reason, whenever an entity has suffered cumulative losses in recent years, realisation of a deferred tax asset is difficult to support if those assertions are based on forecasts of future profitable results without a demonstrated turnaround to operating profitability. In other words, an entity that has cumulative losses is generally prohibited from using an estimate of future earnings to support a conclusion that realisation of an existing deferred tax asset is probable, if such forecast is not based on objectively verifiable information that needs to be disclosed in accordance with IAS 12.82 (see **section 6.2** below). Examples of objectively verifiable information include significant new contracts, increase in backlog and disposal of an unprofitable segment.

4.4.11.2 *Non-recurring items*

Non-recurring items generally are not indicative of an entity's ability to generate taxable income in future years.

Examples of non-recurring items that should be excluded in determining future profit or loss include, but are not limited, to the following:

- one-time restructuring costs that permanently remove fixed costs from future cash flows;

- large litigation settlements or awards that are not expected to recur in future years;
- historical interest expense on debt that has been restructured or refinanced as of the date the financial statements are issued;
- historical fixed costs that have been reduced or eliminated as of the date the financial statements are issued;
- large differences that are included in pre-tax accounting income or loss but are not a component of taxable income; and
- severance payments relating to management changes.

Examples of items that should be included in the determination of future profit or loss include, but are not limited to, the following:

- unusual loss allowances (e.g. significant impairment of loans receivable);
- poor operating results caused by an economic downturn, government intervention, or changes in regulation;
- operating losses attributable to a change in the focus of a subsidiary or business unit; and
- the onerous effects on historical operations attributable to prior management decisions when a new management team is engaged (excluding any direct employment cost reductions relating to the replacement of the old management team).

4.5 Measurement of deferred tax assets and liabilities

4.5.1 Computation of deferred tax assets and liabilities

To calculate the amount of a deferred tax asset or liability, the following formula may be useful:

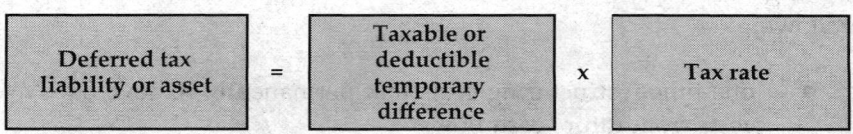

Deferred tax liability or asset = **Taxable or deductible temporary difference** x **Tax rate**

A deferred tax asset can also arise from unused tax losses and tax credits that have been carried forward. These deferred tax assets are calculated as follows:

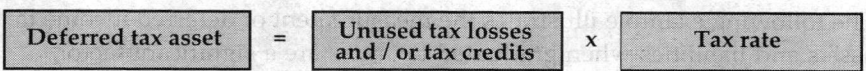

Deferred tax asset	=	Unused tax losses and / or tax credits	x	Tax rate

Thus, an important consideration is what tax rate should be used. This is considered in **4.5.2** below.

4.5.2 Tax rates and laws

Deferred tax balances are calculated using the tax rates that are expected to apply to the reporting period or periods when the temporary differences reverse, based on tax rates and tax laws enacted or substantively enacted at the end of the reporting period. [IAS 12.47]

Where the tax rates that will apply to the entity are expected to vary in coming years (e.g. in start-up situations where tax concessions are granted in the early years), it is necessary to anticipate the year in which the temporary difference will reverse, so that the deferred tax asset or liability can be calculated at the appropriate rate.

4.5.2.1 Progressive or graduated tax rates

In some jurisdictions, the tax rate varies according to the amount of taxable profit earned in a period. This creates a potential issue where it is necessary to predict the tax rate that will apply when a temporary difference reverses. IAS 12 addresses this situation and requires that, in such circumstances, deferred tax assets and liabilities should be measured using the average rates that are expected to apply in the periods in which the temporary differences are expected to reverse. [IAS 12.49]

For entities that expect graduated tax rates to be a significant factor, careful consideration will be needed to determine the average tax rate used to measure deferred tax assets and liabilities.

The determination of the applicable tax rate may require an estimate of future taxable income for the year(s) in which existing temporary differences or carryforwards will enter into the determination of income tax. That estimate of future income includes:

- income or loss exclusive of reversing temporary differences; and

- reversal of existing taxable and deductible temporary differences.

The following example illustrates the measurement of deferred income tax assets and liabilities when graduated tax rates are a significant factor.

Example 4.5.2.1

Graduated tax rates

At the end of 20X1, Company X has £30,000 of deductible temporary differences, which are expected to result in tax deductions of approximately £10,000 for each of the next three years – 20X2 through 20X4.

Company X operates in a jurisdiction that has a graduated tax rate structure. The graduated tax rates are as follows:

Income >	Income <	Tax rate
£	£	
-	50,000	15%
50,000	75,000	25%
75,000	100,000	34%
100,000	335,000	39%
335,000	10,000,000	34%
10,000,000	15,000,000	35%
15,000,000	18,333,333	38%
18,333,333	-	34%

Company X's estimate of pre-tax income for the three years 20X2 through 20X4 is £410,000, £110,000, and £60,000 respectively, exclusive of reversing temporary differences. The estimated taxable income and income taxes payable for those years is computed as follows:

	Future years		
	20X2	20X3	20X4
Estimated pre-tax income, £	410,000	110,000	60,000
Reversing deductible temporary differences, £	(10,000)	(10,000)	(10,000)
Estimated taxable income (A), £	400,000	100,000	50,000
Tax based on graduated tax rates:			
(£50,000 x 15%), £	7,500	7,500	7,500
(£25,000 x 25%), £	6,250	6,250	
(£25,000 x 34%), £	8,500	8,500	
(£235,000 x 39%), £	91,650		
(over £335,000 x 34%), £	22,100		
Estimated tax (B), £	136,000	22,250	7,500
Applicable tax rate (C = B/A)	34%	22.25%	15%
Deferred tax income (£10,000 x C), £	3,400	2,225	1,500

Company X's average applicable tax rate is 23.75 per cent [(£3,400 + £2,230 + £1,500) ÷ £30,000]. Therefore, it recognises a deferred tax asset at the end of 20X1 of £7,125 (£30,000 × 23.75% per cent). Recognition of all or a portion of the deferred tax asset is contingent on meeting the probable realisation criterion established under IAS 12.

If Company X's estimate of taxable income for 20X2 through 20X4 exceeded £335,000 per year, but was less than £10,000,000 per year, the amount of income tax liability would not be affected by the graduated rate structure and, therefore, the requirement to estimate amounts and periods over which existing temporary differences will reverse may be eliminated. In this situation, measurement of the deferred tax asset would be at the average rate (34 per cent in the example), which is the applicable rate expected to apply.

4.5.2.2 Substantively enacted tax rates

The Standard requires that deferred tax assets and liabilities be measured based on rates and laws that have been 'enacted or substantively enacted' by the end of the reporting period. Whether or not a law has actually been enacted by the end of the reporting period is a fact that will be immediately clear. However, where a new rate or law is announced at or before the end of the reporting period, but the formalities of the enactment process have not been finalised, it will be necessary to determine whether such announcement constitutes substantive enactment.

The determination of whether or not new tax rates are considered 'substantively enacted' is a matter of careful judgement, based on the specific facts and circumstances. Factors to consider in assessing that determination include, but are not limited to, the following:

- the legal system and related procedures or processes necessary for enactment of the tax law change;
- the nature and extent of the remaining procedures or processes;
- the extent to which the remaining procedures or processes are perfunctory; and
- the timing of the remaining procedures or processes.

IAS 12 acknowledges that, in some jurisdictions, the announcement of new tax rates and tax laws by the government may have the substantive effect of enactment, even if formal enactment takes place some months later. In these circumstances, tax assets and liabilities are measured using the announced rates. [IAS 12.48] In other countries, it may be necessary for virtually all of the legal stages towards enactment to have been completed before the rates can be considered to be substantively enacted.

This is a grey area that may give rise to differing interpretations, particularly when there may be occasions whereby such proposals can be amended or withdrawn. Therefore, it is not generally appropriate to anticipate changes to tax rates or laws before they have actually been enacted.

The IASB has tentatively decided, as part of the US/IFRS convergence project (see **section 7**), to clarify that 'substantively enacted' means that any expected change in the tax rate is virtually certain. The IASB noted that in some jurisdictions (e.g. the US) enactment may not be virtually certain until the change is signed into law. The Board discussed whether 'substantively enacted' should be based on the probability of enactment or on the process of enactment. The Board decided that reaching a specified stage in the process should be required. It further decided that the specified stage should be that the process of enactment is complete, which is when the remaining steps will not change the outcome.

4.5.2.3 *Changes in tax rates after the reporting period*

Where there is a change in tax rates or laws after the reporting period, no adjustment is made to the carrying amounts of deferred tax assets and liabilities. However, where the effect of the change is such that 'non-disclosure could influence the economic decisions of users taken on the basis of the financial statements', disclosure will be required under IAS 10 *Events after the Reporting Period*. [IAS 10.21]

Example 4.5.2.3

Change in tax rate after the reporting period

Company D has recognised interest receivable of £1,000 in its statement of financial position as at 31 March 20X3. The interest will be taxed when it is received, which will be during the year ending 31 March 20X4. At 31 March 20X3, the tax rate, which has remained unchanged for several years, is 16 per cent. On 5 April 20X3, it is announced that the tax rate for the year ending 31 March 20X4 will be increased to 17.5 per cent, and this change is enacted on 25 April 20X3. The financial statements for the year ended 31 March 20X3 are authorised for issue on 30 June 20X3.

The taxable temporary difference is £1,000. A deferred tax liability of £160 will be included in Company D's financial statements for the year ended 31 March 20X3 in respect of the interest receivable. Although it is known at the time that the financial statements are authorised for issue that the tax rate applying to the interest income when it is received will be 17.5 per cent, IAS 12 precludes using the 17.5 per cent rate to calculate the deferred tax liability, since this rate was neither enacted nor substantively enacted by 31 March 20X3. If the effect of the change is sufficiently important, Company D would include note disclosure.

The tax rate used to measure deferred tax liabilities and deferred tax assets should be the enacted, or substantively enacted, tax rate expected to apply to taxable income in the years that the liability is expected to be settled, or the asset recovered. Consequently, enacted or substantively enacted changes in tax laws or rates that become effective for a particular future year(s) must be considered when determining the tax rate to use in measuring the tax consequences of temporary differences that are expected to reverse in those years. This may require knowledge about the elections that management expect to make in the future, and the amounts of expected income or loss in the future years when those temporary differences are expected to reverse.

4.5.2.4 Phased-in tax rates

A phased-in change in tax rates occurs when an enacted law specifies that in future periods the tax rate applied to taxable income will change (e.g. an enacted tax law provides that the corporate tax rate would be 43 per cent in 20X1, 38 per cent in 20X2, and 35 per cent for 20X3, and thereafter). Phased-in tax rates that are substantively enacted should be considered when measuring deferred tax assets and liabilities that are expected to be realised or settled in future years, particularly through the carryback of a future loss to the current year or a prior year.

4.5.3 Tax rate varies according to whether profits are distributed

Sometimes income taxes are payable at a higher or lower rate if part or all of the net profit or retained earnings are paid out as a dividend to shareholders. Equally, income taxes may be refundable or payable if part or all of the net profit or retained earnings is paid out as a dividend to shareholders of the entity. In such circumstances, IAS 12 stipulates that the rate to be used for the purposes of measurement of both current and deferred tax assets and liabilities is the tax rate applicable to undistributed profits. [IAS 12.52A]

The income tax consequences of a dividend should only be accounted for when the dividend is recognised as a liability in the financial statements. [IAS 12.52B]

Example 4.5.3A

Higher income tax rate on undistributed profits

Company G has undistributed profits of £1,000 in its statement of financial position as at 31 December 20X3. Under local tax regulations, income taxes are payable at a higher rate on undistributed profits (50 per cent), and a lower rate on distributed profits (35 per cent). Company G has traditionally paid dividends to shareholders equivalent to 25 per cent of the taxable profit for the year. It continues that dividend policy by paying an interim dividend in March 20X4, before the 31 December 20X3 financial statements are authorised for issue.

A current tax liability of £500 (£1,000 x 50 per cent) will be included in the financial statements for the year ended 31 December 20X3, even though Company G knows that a portion of the taxable profit will be taxed at a lower rate. In accordance with IAS 10, the liability for the 20X4 interim dividend is not recognised in the financial statements for the year ended 31 December 20X3 and, therefore, the tax consequences of that dividend are not taken into account at 31 December 20X3. However, the lower tax effect will be recognised at the time the dividend is recognised, which will be when the criteria for recognition of a liability are met.

Although tax is always provided at the undistributed rate in the individual financial statements of the entity, on consolidation, the application of IAS 12.39 may require deferred tax to be recognised presuming the distribution of earnings from that subsidiary, associate or joint venture. To the extent that such a distribution is assumed the 'distributed tax rate' is applied.

Although the timing of the recognition of the rate change is related to the recognition of the dividend in the financial statements, IAS 12 clarifies that the liability to pay tax is more directly related to the past events and transactions that gave rise to the tax liability than to the distributions to owners. Thus, the incremental tax effect should not be dealt with in equity (which might be considered appropriate because the dividend is dealt with in equity). Rather, it should generally be dealt with in profit or loss for the period, unless it arose as a result of an underlying transaction or event recognised outside profit or loss, or a business combination, in line with the general rules set out in IAS 12.58 (see **section 4.6**). [IAS 12.52B]

Example 4.5.3B

Recognition of incremental tax effect of dividend payment

Company A has undistributed profits of £1,500 in its statement of financial position at 31 December 20X3, all distributable under local law. £500 of those profits was recognised in other comprehensive income because it arose from the revaluation of and item of property, plant and equipment that was subsequently sold. (the revaluation uplift of £500 was transferred from revaluation surplus to retained earnings when the asset was disposed of). Under local tax regulations, income taxes are payable at a higher rate on undistributed profits (50 per cent), and a lower rate on distributed profits (35 per cent).

Prior to any dividend being declared, current tax was recognised. Of the current tax recognised £250 (£500*50%) was recognised in other comprehensive income and £500 (£1,000*50%) was recognised in profit or loss. Company A decides to distribute all available distributable profits, resulting in a reduction of the tax liability of £225 [£1500*15%]. The journal entry to recognise this reduction is as follows

	Dr	Cr
	£	£
Current tax liability	225	
Income tax (profit or loss)		150
Income tax (other comprehensive income)		75

4.5.4 *Tax holidays*

When a tax jurisdiction grants an exemption from tax on income that otherwise would give rise to an income tax obligation, the event is sometimes referred to as a 'tax holiday'. For example, the jurisdiction may, for economic reasons, forgive income taxes for a specified period if an entity constructs a manufacturing facility located within the jurisdiction.

IAS 12 does not specifically address recognition of tax holidays, but it is unlikely that a tax holiday period would result in the recognition of deferred tax. For each asset and liability, the entity should determine the tax base and calculate any temporary difference in the usual manner. However, for temporary differences that will reverse during the tax holiday period, the appropriate tax rate is 0 per cent. As such, no deferred tax assets or liabilities would be recognised.

4.5.5 *Discounting*

IAS 12 prohibits the use of discounting for the measurement of deferred tax assets and liabilities. [IAS 12.53]

This prohibition is not based on any conceptual argument. Rather, it reflects the practical issues involved in arriving at a reliable determination of deferred tax assets and liabilities on a discounted basis, which would require detailed scheduling of the expected timing of the reversal of every temporary difference. Having concluded that such detailed scheduling would be impracticable or highly complex in many circumstances (and, therefore, that it would be inappropriate to require discounting), the Standard removes the option to discount deferred tax balances, since that would reduce comparability of deferred tax balances between entities.

UK

Under FRS 19, companies are allowed, but not required, to discount deferred tax assets and liabilities. If deferred tax balances are discounted, the discount period(s) should be the number of years between the end of the reporting period and the date(s) on which it is estimated that the underlying timing differences will reverse. Assumptions made when estimating the date(s) of reversal should be consistent with those made elsewhere in the financial statements.

If deferred tax balances are discounted, the discount rates used should be the post-tax yields to maturity that could be obtained at the end of the reporting period on government bonds with maturity dates and in currencies similar to those of the deferred tax assets or liabilities. [FRS 19.52]

4.6 Recognition of movement in deferred tax balances

In determining how the deferred tax effects of a transaction or other event should be recognised, the underlying principle is the accounting for such deferred tax effects should follow the accounting for the transaction or event itself. [IAS 12.57]

Deferred tax should be recognised as income or an expense and included in the profit or loss for the period, except to the extent that the tax arises from:

[IAS 12.58]

- a transaction or event which is recognised, in the same or a different period, outside profit or loss, either in other comprehensive income or directly in equity; or
- a business combination (see **5.1**).

Deferred tax is recognised outside profit or loss if the tax relates to items that are recognised, in the same or a different period, outside profit or loss. Where the deferred tax relates to items that are recognised in other comprehensive income, the tax is also recognised in other comprehensive income (see **4.6.1**). Where the deferred tax relates to items that are recognised directly in equity, the tax is also recognised in equity (see **4.6.2**). [IAS 12.61A]

4.6.1 Items recognised in other comprehensive income

Items required or permitted under IFRSs to be recognised in other comprehensive income include:

- exchange differences on the translation of the financial statements of a foreign operation under IAS 21;
- the recognition of valuation movements on available-for-sale assets (see **5.3.3** below); and
- the revaluation of property, plant and equipment under IAS 16.

4.6.1.1 Asset revaluations

The most common example of deferred tax recognised in other comprehensive income is on the revaluation of an asset.

Where the original deferred tax arising on the revaluation is recognised in other comprehensive income and offset against the revaluation surplus, the subsequent release of that deferred tax liability due to the depreciation of the increased carrying amount is *not* credited in other comprehensive income, but in profit or loss.

This is an important principle to remember. The original recognition of the liability is recognised in other comprehensive income and offset against the revaluation surplus. However, the effects of recovering the asset through use (the recognition of a depreciation charge and the generation of taxable profits), are dealt with in profit or loss. Therefore, the release of the deferred tax liability (against the current tax liability arising) is also dealt with in profit or loss.

It seems logical to offset the deferred tax arising from an asset revaluation against the property revaluation surplus. However, there is no requirement to do so under IFRSs, and an entity may choose to offset the amount against another equity reserve.

Example 4.6.1.1

Deferred tax liability effect of asset revaluation and subsequent recovery of asset

Company I revalues an item of property, plant and equipment from a carrying amount of £95,000 to £150,000. The tax base of the asset is £90,000. The carrying amount of the property is expected to be recovered through use. The applicable tax rate is 30 per cent. A deferred tax liability of £1,500 has been recognised in respect of the taxable temporary difference of £5,000 prior to the revaluation.

An additional taxable temporary difference of £55,000 (£150,000 – £95,000) arises on revaluation, giving rise to a deferred tax liability of £16,500 (£55,000 x 30 per cent). The following entries recognise the revaluation and the deferred tax liability:

	Dr £	Cr £
Property, plant and equipment	55,000	
Property revaluation surplus		55,000
Income tax (other comprehensive income)	16,500	
Deferred tax liability		16,500

In subsequent periods, the property will be depreciated for both accounting and tax purposes, changing the temporary difference. Any movements in the deferred tax liability are recognised in profit or loss. For instance, if the carrying amount of the property at the end of the next reporting period is £130,000 and the tax base is £85,000, there is a taxable temporary difference of £45,000 and a deferred tax liability of £13,500 (£45,000 x 30 per cent). This movement for the year is recognised as follows:

	Dr £	Cr £
Deferred tax liability	3,000	
Income tax (profit or loss)		3,000

IAS 16 does not specify whether an entity should transfer each year from revaluation surplus to retained earnings an amount equal to the difference between the depreciation or amortisation on a revalued asset and the depreciation or amortisation based on the historical cost of that asset. If an entity makes such a transfer, the amount transferred is net of any related deferred tax. Similar considerations apply to transfers made on the disposal of an item of property, plant or equipment. [IAS 12.64]

A more detailed discussion of the appropriate accounting for deferred tax arising in relation to revaluations of investment properties is included in **section 5.4** below.

UK

Under UK GAAP, asset revaluations do not give rise to deferred tax assets and liabilities unless there is a binding commitment to sell, and the resulting gain/loss on disposal will be recognised in the financial statements (where rollover relief is not anticipated). Similarly, deferred tax assets and liabilities generally do not arise from adjusting assets to market value as part of a business acquisition. Only where the general rules require recognition (e.g. binding sales contract) should the liability be recognised.

4.6.1.2 Revaluations for tax purposes

When an asset is revalued for tax purposes and that revaluation is related to an accounting revaluation of an earlier period, or to one that is expected to be carried out in a future period, the tax effects of both the asset revaluation and the adjustment of the tax base are recognised in other comprehensive income in the periods in which they occur. [IAS 12.65]

Where there is a revaluation for tax purposes but there has not been, and is not to be, an accounting revaluation, the tax effects of the adjustment of the tax base are recognised in profit or loss. [IAS 12.65]

There are two common examples of a revaluation for tax, but not accounting, purposes. The first is when tax authorities calculate the taxable gain on disposal of a capital asset by reference to a base cost that represents the original cost of the asset uplifted by an allowance to reflect inflation over the period of ownership.

Example 4.6.1.2

Tax base increased by inflation index in each period

Company J purchases an investment property for £10,000 and does not depreciate it. The carrying amount of £10,000 will be recovered through sale. The allowable cost for tax purposes is increased by an agreed inflation index in each period. Assume the tax rate for capital profits is 30 per cent and the agreed inflation increment in each period under consideration is 5 per cent. The deferred tax consequences for the first three years are calculated as follows:

	Carrying amount	Tax base	Deductible temporary difference	Deferred tax asset
	£	£	£	£
20X0	10,000	10,000	-	-
20X1	10,000	10,500	500	150
20X2	10,000	11,025	1,025	308

The recognition of the resultant deferred tax asset is dependent on the availability of future profits against which the capital loss can be offset.

If the deferred tax asset is recognised, the credit is to profit or loss. Therefore, at the end of 20X1, the required journal entry is:

	Dr	Cr
	£	£
Deferred tax asset	150	
Income tax (profit or loss)		150

The second example is when a group undertakes a transaction between two group entities which is internal to the group (and hence does not change group carrying amounts) but gives rise to a new tax base. An example of such a group restructuring is included as **example 4.2.5**.

4.6.2 *Items recognised directly in equity*

Items required or permitted under IFRSs to be credited or charged directly to equity include:

- an adjustment to the opening balance of retained earnings resulting from a change in accounting policy that is accounted for retrospectively under IAS 8 (see **chapter 4**);
- the initial recognition of the equity component of a compound financial instrument under IAS 32 (see **5.3.4**);
- where the expected tax deduction for an equity-settled share based payment exceeds the cumulative profit or loss expense recognised in respect of that share based payment; and
- where a withholding tax is charged on dividend distributions (see **4.6.2.1**);

4.6.2.1 Withholding tax

A tax jurisdiction may assess an entity with a 'withholding tax', which is paid to the tax authorities on behalf of the shareholders when the entity makes a dividend distribution. Such withholding tax is charged to equity as part of the dividends. [IAS 12.65A]

Where a 'withholding tax' is neither paid on behalf of the shareholders nor gives rise to a future benefit for the entity, it should be dealt with as a higher rate of tax applied to distributed profits – see **4.5.3** above.

If an entity obtains a future benefit from withholding a tax, for example it is deductible against future dividend receipts, the initial payment to the tax authorities is not a 'withholding tax' per IAS 12, and should be recognised as an increase in income tax expense (as opposed to being part of the dividend distribution), with the future tax benefit likewise recognised as a component of tax in the profit or loss. The resulting tax asset will be considered for recoverability – see **4.4.7** above.

IAS 12 requires that when an entity pays withholding tax, it should be charged to equity as part of dividends. IAS 12 does not address how the recipient should deal with withholding tax. However, to the extent that withholding tax is paid entirely on behalf of the recipient, IAS 18 would require that the dividend income be shown as a gross amount and not netted against the tax expense. The tax suffered on the dividend income should be included in the tax line.

Example 4.6.2.1

Withholding tax

Company Z decides to pay a dividend of £100 to its shareholders. The local tax law requires Company Z to withhold 35 per cent of the dividend and pay it to the tax authorities.

Upon payment of the dividend, Company Z would record the following journal entries:

	Dr	Cr
Retained earnings – distribution	100	
Cash		65
Payable		35

(To recognise the dividend payment and related liability to pay tax on shareholders' behalf.)

	Dr	Cr
Payable	35	
Cash		35

(To recognise payment of the taxes withheld.)

4.6.2.2 *Uncertainty regarding the amount to be recognised outside profit or loss*

Where, in exceptional circumstances, an entity is unable to determine the amount of deferred tax that relates to items recognised outside profit or loss, IAS 12 allows the entity to base the amount on a reasonable pro-rata allocation or some other method achieving a more appropriate allocation.

Such uncertainty can arise, for example, when:

[IAS 12.63]

- there are graduated rates of income tax, and it is impossible to determine the rate at which a specific component of taxable profit (tax loss) has been taxed; or
- a change in the tax rate or other tax rules affects a deferred tax asset or liability relating (in whole or in part) to an item that was previously recognised outside profit or loss; or
- an entity determines that a deferred tax asset should be recognised, or should no longer be recognised in full, and the deferred tax asset relates (in whole or in part) to an item that was previously recognised outside profit or loss.

An example of how such an allocation might be made is set out in **3.2.1.3** above.

4.6.3 Recognition of deferred tax arising from a business combination

Where a business combination occurs, deferred tax balances will arise from a number of sources. These are described in detail in **section 5.1** below.

The amount of deferred tax arising from each of these sources is recognised and included as part of the identifiable net assets at the date of acquisition. The combined effect, therefore, impacts on the amount of the goodwill or bargain purchase gain arising on acquisition.

4.6.4 Changes in the carrying amount of a deferred tax asset or liability

The carrying amount of a deferred tax asset or liability may change for reasons other than a change in the temporary difference itself. Such changes might arise as a result of:

- a change in tax rates or laws; or
- re-assessment of the recoverability of a deferred tax asset; or
- a change in the expected manner of recovery of an asset or the expected manner of settlement of a liability.

IAS 12 requires, in such circumstances, that the change in deferred tax balances be recognised in profit or loss, except to the extent that it relates to items previously recognised outside profit or loss. [IAS 12.60]

For example, where a deferred tax amount has previously been recognised in other comprehensive income at the time of the revaluation of an asset, and the deferred tax liability subsequently changes because of a change in tax rates, the adjustment to the deferred tax liability to reflect the revised tax rates is also recognised in other comprehensive income.

The same principle applies to a change of intention. For example, where an entity has previously estimated the deferred tax liability arising on the revaluation of an owner-occupied property on the basis that it would continue to be used to generate taxable manufacturing profits, and a decision is subsequently made to dispose of the property, thus reducing the deferred tax liability, the adjustment to the deferred tax liability is also reflected in other comprehensive income.

4.6.5 Changes in the tax status of an entity or its shareholders

A change in the tax status of an entity or its shareholders may have consequences for the entity by increasing or decreasing its tax assets or liabilities. This may occur, for example, upon the public listing of an entity's equity shares, or upon a controlling shareholder's move to a foreign country. As a result of such an event, the entity may be taxed differently, which may have an immediate effect on its current and deferred tax assets and liabilities. SIC-25 *Income Taxes – Changes in the Tax Status of an Entity or its Shareholders* establishes the accounting treatment for such changes.

SIC-25 requires the current and deferred tax consequences of a change in tax status to be included in profit or loss for the period, unless those consequences relate to transactions or events that result, in the same or a different period, in a direct credit or charge to the recognised amount of equity or in amounts recognised in other comprehensive income. Those tax consequences that relate to changes in the recognised amount of equity, in the same or a different period (not included in profit or loss), should be charged or credited directly to equity. Those tax consequences that relate to amounts recognised in other comprehensive income should be recognised in other comprehensive income. [SIC-25.4]

Effectively, this means that an analysis is required of the original accounting for the transactions or events that gave rise to the current and deferred tax balances. To the extent that those transactions or events were charged or credited directly in equity (e.g. withholding tax on dividend payments), any incremental tax effects should also be charged or credited directly to equity. To the extent that those transactions or events were recognised in other comprehensive income (e.g. certain asset revaluations), any incremental tax effects should also be recognised in other comprehensive income. Thus, the aggregate amount of tax outside profit or loss will be the amount that would have been recognised outside profit or loss if the new tax status had applied previously.

Example 4.6.5

Change in the tax status of an entity

Entity P has a deferred tax liability of £1,000 arising in respect of total temporary differences of £4,000. An £800 temporary difference exists in respect of a previous revaluation of property, plant and equipment. All other temporary differences relate to items recognised in profit or loss. Entity P is sold into foreign ownership, and as a consequence the tax rate rises from 25 per cent to 30 per cent. To recognise the resulting increase in the deferred tax liability the following journal entry is made:

	Dr	Cr
Income tax (profit or loss) [(30%-25%)*(£4,000-£800)]	160	
Income tax (other comprehensive income) [(30%-25%)*£800]	40	
Deferred tax liability		200

Where there is uncertainty as to the amount that was previously dealt with outside profit or loss, it may be necessary to make an allocation on a reasonable basis (see **3.2.1.3** above).

Note that SIC-25 does not permit the effect on deferred tax balances that arose at the time of a previous business combination to be dealt with as an adjustment to goodwill. The change in tax status is a post-acquisition event, and so is accounted for post-acquisition. Since the original deferred tax was not dealt with in equity or in other comprehensive income, the incremental effect must be dealt with in income.

If the change in tax rate is a result of its being acquired by another entity, in the individual financial statements of the acquiree, the adjustments to current and deferred tax assets and liabilities will be accounted for in accordance with SIC-25, as discussed in the previous paragraphs. However, in the consolidated financial statements, the current and deferred tax assets and liabilities will be measured using the revised tax rates – and, consequently, the incremental effect of the acquisition will be reflected as an adjustment to goodwill.

The effect of a voluntary change in the tax status of an entity should be recognised on the date of approval, or on the filing date if no approval is necessary (e.g. if the approval change is perfunctory). A change in tax status that results from a change in tax law will be recognised on the enactment date or the substantively enacted date if applicable. Substantively enacted tax rates are discussed further in **4.5.2.2** above.

5 Specific applications

5.1 Business combinations

Where a business combination occurs, new or adjusted deferred tax balances can arise from the following sources:

- fair value adjustments on consolidation resulting in carrying amounts of assets or liabilities in the consolidated financial statements that differ from the carrying amounts in the acquired entity's financial statements and, consequently, from their tax bases where equivalent adjustments are not recognised for tax purposes (see **5.1.1** below);
- additional assets or liabilities recognised on acquisition that are not recognised in the financial statements of the acquiree (see **5.1.2** below);
- tax balances recognised on acquisition that were not recognised by the acquiree, because of the initial recognition exception (see **5.1.3** below); and
- potential new deferred tax assets where the recoverability criteria can be met at a group level but could not be met at the entity level (e.g. potential for offsetting taxable profits and losses between group entities) (see **5.1.4** below).

Where deferred tax arises at the time of a business combination, and it has not been recognised by the acquiree prior to the acquisition, it must be recognised and taken into account in the initial accounting for the business combination, therefore affecting the measurement of the goodwill or the bargain purchase gain arising on acquisition.

5.1.1 *Fair value adjustments*

With limited exceptions, the identifiable assets, liabilities and contingent liabilities of the acquiree are recognised in the consolidated financial statements at their fair values as at the acquisition date. This will often result in different carrying amounts to those recognised by the entity or operation being acquired. However, the tax bases of the assets and liabilities may remain unchanged.

For example, where the fair value of an asset at the date of acquisition is higher than its carrying amount in the acquiree's financial statements, and the asset is recognised at the higher amount for consolidation purposes, the tax base of the asset is unlikely to be affected. In these circumstances, a taxable temporary difference arises as a result of the acquisition. The deferred tax liability arising from the taxable temporary difference is recognised in the consolidated financial statements to reflect the future tax consequences of recovering the recognised fair value of the asset.

UK *Fair value adjustments in business combinations, where carrying amounts are adjusted but the tax base is unaffected, do not give rise to deferred tax balances under FRS 19.*

5.1.2 *Additional assets or liabilities recognised on acquisition*

On acquisition, additional assets and liabilities may be identified that are not recognised in the financial statements of the acquiree. This will commonly be the case, for example, in respect of intangible assets. Where such additional assets or liabilities are recognised, the deferred tax implications should also be recognised. These additional assets and liabilities will be included as part of the identifiable net assets acquired.

Although the recognition of other assets and liabilities on acquisition may give rise to deferred tax implications, the recognition of goodwill itself does not do so. For the reasons discussed in **4.4.4** above, the recognition of a deferred tax liability in respect of the initial recognition of goodwill is prohibited.

5.1.3 *Additional deferred tax balances recognised on acquisition*

In certain circumstances, the deferred tax impact of temporary differences may not have been recognised in the acquiree's financial statements because those differences fell within one of IAS 12's recognition exceptions. For example, the differences may have arisen on the initial recognition of an asset or liability (see **4.4.5** above) and, consequently, may not have been recognised. In these circumstances, the deferred tax impact of such temporary differences should be recognised in the consolidated financial statements, even though it is not recognised by the acquiree itself.

These additional deferred tax balances are recognised on acquisition because, from the group's perspective, the initial recognition of the asset or liability results from a business combination and, therefore, under the rules set out in **4.4.5**, the deferred tax impact should be recognised.

5.1.4 *Tax assets not previously recognised by the acquiree*

In some circumstances, deferred tax assets (e.g. in respect of tax losses) may not have been recognised by the acquiree due to concerns about the recoverability of the assets in the light of anticipated levels of profitability. However, following the acquisition, in some tax jurisdictions, the losses may become available for use by other group entities, and therefore be considered recoverable. As the asset is now recoverable from a group perspective, the deferred tax asset is recognised at the time of acquisition.

5.1.5 *Tax assets not previously recognised by the acquirer*

Alternatively, as a result of an acquisition, the probability of realising a pre-acquisition deferred tax asset of the acquirer may change so that the acquirer considers it probable that it will recover its own deferred tax asset that was not recognised prior to the business combination. For example, the acquirer may be able to utilise the benefit of its unused tax losses against the future taxable profits of the acquired entity. In such circumstances, the acquirer recognises a deferred tax asset, but does not include it as part of the accounting for the business combination, and therefore does not take it into account in measuring the goodwill or bargain purchase gain arising in the business combination. [IAS 12.67]

Example 5.1.5

Deferred tax arising on a business combination

Company K acquires Company L, which holds two properties and sundry other assets. Property A (carrying amount of £100 in Company L's books) and property B (carrying amount of £150 in Company L's books) are, for tax and accounting purposes, depreciated over 10 years and will be recovered through use in taxable manufacturing activities. The tax rate is 30 per cent.

The following information is relevant at the date of acquisition:

- Company K pays cash consideration of £380 for the acquisition
- the fair values of properties A and B are determined to be £130 and £140 respectively;
- an additional intangible asset in respect of patents held by Company L, with a fair value of £50, is identified for recognition. The tax base of the intangible asset is nil;
- the tax bases of property A and B are £50 and £150 respectively. A temporary difference arose on the acquisition of the property by Company L and, therefore, no deferred tax liability was recognised due to the initial recognition exception; and
- Company L has tax losses available for offset against the future profits of any group entity amounting to £20. It is probable that future taxable profit will be available within the group to absorb these losses. A deferred tax asset had not been recognised in Company L's books in respect of these tax losses.

The goodwill arising on the acquisition of Company L is calculated as follows:

	Carrying amount	Fair value	Tax base	Temporary difference	Tax rate	Deferred tax liability (asset)
Net assets of L	**£**	**£**	**£**	**£**	**£**	**£**
Property A	100	130	50	80	30%	24
Property B	150	140	150	(10)	30%	(3)
Intangible asset	-	50	-	50	30%	15
Other net assets	30	30	30	-	-	-
Tax loss c/f	-	-	-	(20)	30%	(6)
Total	280	350	230	100		30
Deferred tax on acquisition		(30)				
Identifiable net assets acquired		320				
Consideration		380				
Goodwill		60				

UK *The UK GAAP position is the same in that only the position of the acquiree is reassessed. Any changes to the tax position of the acquirer cannot be adjusted against goodwill.*

5.1.6 *Post-acquisition recognition of deferred tax assets*

At the date of acquisition, there may be losses in the acquiree available for carrying forward or deductible temporary differences that do not qualify for recognition as deferred tax assets when the business combination is initially accounted for. These items may subsequently meet the criteria for recognition, and IAS 12 requires that the entity should recognise such acquired deferred tax benefits that it realises after the business combination as follows:

[IAS 12.68]

- acquired deferred tax benefits recognised within the 'measurement period' (i.e. within one year after the acquisition date) that result from new information about facts and circumstances that existed at the acquisition date reduce the amount of any goodwill related to that acquisition. If the carrying amount of that goodwill is zero, any remaining deferred tax benefits are recognised in profit or loss; and

- all other acquired deferred tax benefits realised are recognised in profit or loss (or outside profit or loss if otherwise required by IAS 12).

Example 5.1.6

Realisation of tax loss carryforwards after a business combination

Company Q acquires a new subsidiary, Company R, on 31 March 20X1. Company R has tax losses accumulated in previous periods giving rise to a potential deferred tax asset of £50 million. In the initial accounting for the business combination, Company Q concludes that these losses are not available for offset against the profits of other group entities, and does not recognise a deferred tax asset. The goodwill arising on the acquisition amounts to £20 million.

In February 20X2, within the 'measurement period' the tax authority rules that Company R's losses can be offset against certain of the profits of other group entities – the relevant profits amounting to a deferred tax asset of £30 million at the date of acquisition. Therefore, had the tax ruling been obtained at that time, a deferred tax asset of £30 million could potentially have been recognised in the initial accounting for the business combination. However, the retrospective adjustment of goodwill is limited to the amount of the goodwill. Therefore, only £20 million is adjusted directly against goodwill in the 20X2 financial statements and the balance of £10 million is recognised in profit or loss. Should the other group entities earn profits subsequent to the date of acquisition against which more of Company R losses can be utilised, the effect is recognised in profit or loss.

The requirements of IAS 12.68 have been modified as a consequential amendment of IFRS 3(2008) *Business Combinations*. Prior to this amendment, the subsequent realisation of all deferred tax assets acquired in a business combination was recognised in profit or loss with a consequential reduction in the carrying amount of goodwill to the amount that would have been recognised if the deferred tax asset had been recognised as an identifiable asset from the acquisition date, regardless of the date of realisation. See previous editions of this book for details.

The revised IAS 12.68 is to be applied prospectively from the effective date of IFRS 3(2008) to the recognition of deferred tax assets acquired in business combinations. [IAS 12.93] IFRS 3(2008) is effective for business combinations for which the acquisition date is on or after the beginning of the first annual reporting period beginning on or after 1 July 2009. Earlier application is permitted, but IFRS 3(2008) (and consequently the revised IAS 12.68) cannot be applied in an accounting period beginning before 30 June 2007.

The revised IAS 12.68 therefore applies to changes in recognised deferred tax assets occurring after the date of adoption of IFRS 3(2008), arising from business combinations that occurred before or after the date of adoption of IFRS 3(2008). This means that an acquirer does not adjust the accounting for prior business combinations for previously recognised changes in deferred tax assets outside the relevant 'measurement period'. However, from the date when IFRS 3(2008) is applied, the acquirer recognises, as an adjustment to profit or loss (or if IAS 12 requires, outside profit or loss), changes in recognised deferred tax assets.

5.1.7 *Hedge of net investment in a foreign operation*

Entities sometimes enter into transactions to hedge their net investment in a foreign subsidiary (e.g. through the use of a foreign currency loan, or a forward contract). Under the requirements of IAS 39 *Financial Instruments: Recognition and Measurement*, such a transaction may be designated as a hedge of the foreign currency exposure of a net investment in a foreign operation (see **chapter 20**). Gains and losses on the effective portion of such hedging transactions are recognised in other comprehensive income.

If the tax base of the hedging instrument is different to its carrying amount, this creates a temporary difference and deferred tax should be recognised. This is the case regardless of whether deferred tax has been provided in respect of the parent's investment in a foreign subsidiary. To the extent that the hedge is effective, the tax consequences of establishing a deferred tax asset or liability for the hedging transaction are reported in other comprehensive income in accordance with IAS 12.61. Recognition of amounts outside profit or loss is discussed further in **4.6.1** and **4.6.2** above.

Example 5.1.7

Hedge of a net investment in a foreign subsidiary

Company A (functional currency Currency Units), has a 100 per cent US subsidiary, Company B, which has net assets of US$120,000. Company A hedges its net investment in Company B using a US$100,000 loan. Assuming that the hedge is perfectly effective and that all the other hedging requirements of IAS 39 are met, the exchange gain or loss on retranslating the loan will be recognised in other comprehensive income in Company A's financial statements. Where the retranslation of the loan changes its carrying amount, but not its tax base, deferred tax on the resulting temporary difference is also recognised in other comprehensive income.

5.1.8 *Group relief*

The deferred tax position of each group entity should be determined separately and the results aggregated (with some adjustments) to determine the group position. Adjustments may need to be made to reflect the deferred tax consequences of the availability of group relief altering the view of recoverability of deferred tax assets.

Where losses are expected to be surrendered to another group entity that is expected to pay for the group relief then the 'deferred tax asset' may well be assessed as recoverable and recognised even though the 'asset' is actually a receipt from another group entity that recovers it from the tax authority. Where losses are expected to be surrendered to another group entity but no payment is likely to be received, the entity surrendering the losses would not normally be able to assess the asset as recoverable. However, the deferred tax asset would be recognised on consolidation to the extent that the other entity is expected to utilise the losses.

5.2 Eliminations of unrealised profits

Where a group entity sells goods to another group entity, the seller recognises profits made on those sales in its individual financial statements. If those goods are still held in inventory by the purchaser at the year end, the profit recognised by the seller, when viewed from the standpoint of the group as a whole, has not yet been earned, and will not be earned until the goods are eventually sold outside the group. On consolidation, the unrealised profit on closing inventories is eliminated from the group's profit, and the closing inventories of the group are recognised at cost to the group.

Such consolidation adjustments may have a deferred tax impact in the consolidated financial statements. The intragroup elimination is made as a consolidation adjustment and not in the financial statements of any individual reporting entity. If tax is charged on the results of individual entities, and not on the group, the seller will pay tax on any profits generated from the intragroup sales, even though some of those profits may be unrealised from the group's perspective. Thus, the elimination will result in a temporary difference as far as the group is concerned between the carrying amount of the inventories in the consolidated financial statements and the tax base (assumed to be the carrying amount in the purchaser's individual financial statements). The deferred tax effects arising in respect of this temporary difference should be recognised in accordance with the usual principles.

The tax rate to be used when recognising the deferred tax balance arising from the elimination of unrealised profits on intragroup transactions is determined by reference to the tax jurisdiction where the temporary difference will reverse. This will generally be the tax rate in the purchaser's jurisdiction, as the deduction is available at that rate when the unrealised profit is realised from the sale to an unrelated third party. Under this approach, the deferred tax recognised may not entirely offset the tax currently payable from the sale.

In situations involving the transfer of assets intended for internal use, the deferred taxes should be amortised over the asset's expected useful life consistent with the depreciation method applied under IAS 16 *Property, Plant and Equipment*.

Example 5.2

Elimination of intragroup profits in inventory

Company P sells inventory costing £200 to its overseas subsidiary, Company S, for £300. Company P's tax rate is 40 per cent, Company S's is 50 per cent. At the year end, Company S still holds the inventory.

Company P recognises a current tax liability of £40 (£100 x 40 per cent) relating to the profit on sale of the inventory but does not recognise any deferred tax balances as there are no future tax consequences from Company P's point of view.

Company S is entitled to a future deduction for the £300 paid for the inventory and this is therefore the asset's tax base from Company S's perspective. Thus, in Company S's individual financial statements, the tax base is equal to the carrying amount, and no temporary difference arises.

Company P prepares consolidated financial statements and, for financial reporting purposes, gains and losses on intragroup transactions are eliminated on consolidation. Therefore, on consolidation, the carrying amount of the inventory is reduced from £300 to £200 (to eliminate the unrealised profit). A £100 deductible temporary difference arises, representing the difference between the carrying amount (£200) and the tax base (£300). A deferred tax asset is calculated by multiplying the temporary difference of £100 by 50 per cent, as the deduction is available to Company S at that rate when the unrealised profit is realised outside the group on sale of the inventory by Company S. Available evidence supports a conclusion that realisation of the deferred tax asset representing the tax benefit of Company S's deductible temporary differences is probable. The deferred tax asset arising of £50 is recognised on consolidation. The impact of this intragroup transaction on Company P's consolidated financial statements is shown below in the following journal entries:

	Dr	Cr
Current taxes expense (£100 @ 40%)	40	
Deferred tax asset (£100 @ 50%)	50	
Current taxes payable		40
Deferred income tax benefit		50

Assume in a subsequent period that Company S sells the inventory that it acquired from Company P to an unrelated third party for the exact amount it previously paid Company P – £300. The journal entry to reflect the sales and related tax consequences to be reflected in the consolidated financial statements of Company P are as follows:

	Dr	Cr
Cash	300	
Cost of goods sold	200	
Income tax expense	50	
Sales		300
Inventory		200
Deferred tax asset		50

Under FRS 19 the amount of deferred tax arising from the elimination of the unrealised profit on the intragroup transaction would be provided at the amount paid by the selling company on the basis that it is tax related to a deferred profit. UK

5.3 Financial instruments

5.3.1 General

Investments in securities can often give rise to significant temporary differences. In order to determine the deferred tax implications for various types of investments, it is necessary to understand the tax rules relating to financial instruments. Particularly, an entity should take care to understand the tax implications that arise from the recovery of the investment through dividends ('use'), sale, or a combination of the two. It is then necessary to determine how the carrying amount of the investments will be recovered.

Where an entity has an investment in an equity instrument it may be appropriate to presume the carrying amount will be recovered through sale. This will be the case if the receipt of dividend revenue is not expected to result in an impairment of the carrying amount. For further discussion of circumstances where it may be appropriate to presume recovery through sale refer to **4.2.6.2** above.

Sometimes it will be necessary to consider how a financial asset has been classified under IAS 39 *Financial Instruments: Recognition and Measurement*. For example, financial assets classified as held-to-maturity under IAS 39 are so classified based on the premise that they will not be sold prior to their maturity. When considering any tax implications, the same assumptions should be used.

However, in some cases, the classification of financial instruments under IAS 39 ignores the effect of management expectations. For example, where a convertible instrument exists that is recognised as a liability in accordance with IAS 32, it may be that management expects to settle that liability in equity instruments. Where the tax implications of equity settlement differ from those of liability settlement, it may be possible to account for the deferred tax on the basis of equity settlement. This is because the accounting dictated by IAS 32 does not take account of management expectations, and therefore requires liability treatment. IAS 12 requires that management expectations be taken into account and, accordingly, a different conclusion could be formed. While it is technically possible to account for instruments differently under IAS 12 and IAS 32, in practice it may be difficult to obtain evidence to suggest that the IAS 32 assumptions do not form a valid set of assumptions for the purposes of IAS 12.

5.3.2 *Financial instruments classified as held for trading or at fair value through profit or loss*

Financial instruments that are classified as held for trading or at fair value through profit or loss (see **chapters 14** and **15**) will have fair value gains and losses reported in profit or loss. If these gains and losses are taxable, they may be taxed when they are recognised in the financial statements, or it may be that no tax assessment is raised until the instrument is sold. Where tax is assessed based on fair value movements dealt with in profit or loss, there are no deferred tax implications, because the movements are dealt with in the current tax computation. Conversely, where no taxable gain or loss arises until the asset is disposed of, deferred tax balances may arise.

5.3.3 *Available-for-sale assets*

Similar issues will arise on financial assets classified as available-for-sale (AFS). The main difference is that the change in fair value on these assets is reported in other comprehensive income (excluding impairment losses, exchange gains and losses, and interest and dividend income). Thus, if a deferred tax balance arises on an available-for-sale asset, the deferred tax impact may also be dealt with in other comprehensive income (rather than in profit or loss) in the same manner as the deferred tax effects of revaluations of other assets as described in the following paragraphs.

When a security is eventually sold, the gain or loss that has been recognised in other comprehensive income is reclassified from equity to profit or loss. Consistent with the principle that the tax entries should follow the accounting entries, when the sale of a security occurs, any deferred tax previously recognised in other comprehensive income is reversed in other comprehensive income, and the current tax arising on sale is recognised in the income tax expense line in profit or loss.

In some jurisdictions, tax arises immediately on the movements in the value of available-for-sale financial assets. This tax should be recognised where the movements are recognised, i.e. in other comprehensive income. On eventual disposal, no further tax would arise. It is preferable, however, to reclassify from equity to profit or loss not just the cumulative fair value movement, but also the tax. If such an accounting entry is not processed on sale, then the tax effect may be transferred out of the AFS valuation reserve into another equity component at the date of sale.

Example 5.3.3

Financial assets available-for-sale

Company Y has a portfolio of financial assets classified as available-for-sale in accordance with IAS 39. For financial reporting purposes, unrealised gains and losses on the assets are recognised in other comprehensive income net of any tax consequences. The local tax laws permit an election whereby unrealised gains and losses on investment portfolios are included in the determination of taxable income or loss, and Y has made such an election. Accordingly, the movement in the value of financial assets does not have deferred tax consequences, because each year it affects the current taxes.

At the end of 20X1, the unrealised loss on the assets is £5 million, all of which occurred during the year. The tax rate for 20X1 and 20X2 is 30 per cent. The market value of the assets, determined at the close of 20X1 (i.e. an unrealised loss of £5 million), does not change through the end of 20X2.

On the last day of 20X2, Company Y sells the assets crystallising the previously recognised pre-tax loss of £5 million. Taxable income in 20X2 is zero.

The journal entries for 20X1 would be as follows:

	Dr	Cr
	£	£
Unrealised loss on investments (other comprehensive income)	5,000,000	
Investment portfolio		5,000,000
To recognise the unrealised loss on the available-for-sale assets in equity.		
Current tax liability	1,500,000	
Income tax (other comprehensive income)		1,500,000
To recognise the tax consequences of the unrealised losses on the assets – computed based on mark-to-market accounting as elected under tax law (£5,000,000 x 30 per cent).		

The journal entries for 20X2 would be as follows:

	Dr	Cr
Loss on sale (profit or loss)	5,000,000	
Unrealised loss on investments (other comprehensive income)		5,000,000
To recognise the reclassification from equity to profit or loss of the pre-tax loss on sale of the asset portfolio in 20X2		
Income tax (other comprehensive income)	1,500,000	
Income tax (profit or loss)		1,500,000
To recognise the reclassification from equity to profit or loss of the tax consequences of the realised loss on sale of the assets in 20X2		

For most entities, the assessment concerning the realisation of tax benefits from unrealised losses on an available-for-sale debt securities portfolio will often depend on the inherent assumptions used for financial reporting purposes concerning the ultimate recovery of the carrying amount of the portfolio.

IAS 12.16 concludes that it is inherent in the recognition of an asset that its carrying amount will be recovered in the form of economic benefits that flow to the entity in future periods. Thus, ordinarily, an entity should assume recovery of the carrying amount of its available-for-sale debt securities portfolio will be its fair value at the end of each reporting period. Generally, whenever an unrealised holding loss exists, recovery at fair value would result in a capital loss deduction.

In some jurisdictions, the tax law may allow utilisation of capital losses only through offset of capital gains. In such cases, entities would need to assess whether realisation of the loss is probable based on available evidence. For example, evidence considered might include (1) available capital loss carryback recovery of taxes paid in prior years, and (2) tax planning strategies to sell appreciated capital assets that would generate capital gain income. In these situations, available evidence should be evaluated to determine if it is probable that the entity would have sufficient capital gain income during the carryback and carryforward periods prescribed under tax law.

5.3.4 *Compound financial instruments*

IAS 12 contains guidance on calculating deferred tax in relation to compound financial instruments that are accounted for under IAS 32 *Financial Instruments: Presentation*. Compound financial instruments are instruments that an entity has issued that contain both a liability and an equity component (e.g. issued convertible debt). In the case of convertible debt, the separate components are a liability component, that represents borrowing with an obligation to repay, and an equity component, representing the embedded option to convert the liability into equity of the entity.

Under IAS 32, the equity and liability components of a compound instrument are accounted for separately – the proceeds of issue are allocated between the separate elements. The amount initially recognised as a liability is the present value of the cash flows discounted at a market rate for equivalent debt without the equity feature. As the holders of the compound instrument are effectively purchasing an equity interest, the coupon on the compound instrument is almost always lower than it would be for the equivalent debt without the equity feature. Thus, the value assigned to the debt portion of the compound instrument will be lower than the total proceeds received. For example, £100 proceeds from the issue of a convertible bond could be allocated £90 to debt and £10 to equity – the carrying amount of the liability component (£90) is less than the face value of the instrument (£100). The detailed requirements for accounting for compound instruments are considered in **chapter 15**.

In some jurisdictions, the tax base of the liability component on initial recognition is equal to the initial carrying amount of the sum of the liability and equity components (i.e. £100 in the above example). If the instrument were settled at an amount equal to the carrying amount of its liability component (which is generally less than the face value and, therefore, less than the tax base), a taxable gain arises, and so a deferred tax liability arising from this taxable temporary difference is recognised. In the example cited above, if the bond were settled for £90 (its carrying amount), a gain of £10 would arise which could be taxable.

The rule in IAS 12 of not recognising deferred tax on the initial recognition of an asset or liability does not apply in this situation – a deferred tax liability should be recognised. This is because the temporary difference arises not from the initial recognition of the instrument, but instead from the recognition of the component parts separately. [IAS 12.23]

Because the equity component of the compound financial instrument is recognised directly in equity, the deferred tax liability arising is also recognised directly in equity (i.e. as a reduction in the carrying amount of the equity component). The deferred tax should be charged directly to the carrying amount of the equity component.

However, as the discount associated with the liability component of the compound financial instrument unwinds, the reduction of the associated deferred tax liability is recognised in profit or loss and not directly in equity. The recognition of the deferred tax credit in profit or loss is consistent with the recognition of the associated discount expense in profit or loss. [IAS 12.23]

In jurisdictions where any gain on settlement of the liability would not be taxable, the tax base of the liability is always equal to its carrying amount, and so no temporary difference arises.

Example 5.3.4

Convertible note accounted for as a compound instrument

On 31 December 20X0, Company R issues a convertible note with a face value of £10,000 that matures in three years. There is no interest payable during the period, but the note is convertible into a fixed number of shares at the end of the three-year period. Had Company R issued debt with no conversion rights that matured in three years, the interest rate on the bonds would have been 9 per cent.

Under IAS 32, the note is split into its liability and equity components. Using a discount rate of 9 per cent (i.e. the rate at which Company R could have issued equivalent debt with no conversion rights), the present value of the instrument is £7,722. This is taken to be the value of the liability component, giving rise to an amount recognised directly in equity of £2,278.

The tax base of the instrument is assumed to be £10,000. This is based on there being no tax consequences if the note is repaid at its face value, and a taxable gain arising if the note is settled for less than its face value. The tax rate is 17.5 per cent.

If the liability were settled at its carrying amount (£7,722), a taxable profit would arise. Thus, on the initial separation of the liability and equity components, a taxable temporary difference of £2,278 arises. This gives rise to a deferred tax liability of £399 (£2,278 x 17.5 per cent). This amount is netted against the amount recognised in respect of the equity component of the note.

The following entries are recognised at the date of issue of the convertible note:

	Dr	Cr.
	£	£
Cash	10,000	
Convertible note payable		7,722
Equity (capital reserve)		2,278
Equity (capital reserve)	399	
Deferred tax liability		399

Each year, imputed interest on the liability will be recognised, increasing the carrying amount of the liability component, and reducing the associated deferred tax liability. The reduction in the deferred tax liability is recognised in profit or loss.

The movements over the life of the convertible note can be summarised as follows:

	20X0	20X1	20X2	20X3
	£	£	£	£
Liability & interest				
Opening liability		7,722	8,417	9,174
Imputed interest (9%)		695	757	826
Closing liability	7,722	8,417	9,174	10,000

Deferred tax liability				
Convertible note carrying amount	7,722	8,417	9,174	10,000
Tax base	10,000	10,000	10,000	10,000
Taxable temporary difference	2,278	1,583	826	-
Deferred tax liability (at 17.5%)	399	277	145	-

5.3.5 *Impact of IAS 39 hedging requirements on non-financial items*

The recognition of a 'basis adjustment' for a non-financial asset or liability in accordance with IAS 39.98 may cause the carrying amount of the asset or liability to be different to its tax base. This may occur where the tax value ascribed to the asset or liability under the relevant tax jurisdiction is determined other than by reference to the carrying amount in the financial statements, e.g. the basis adjustment is not recognised for tax purposes until some time after the basis adjustment has been made. Deferred tax should generally be recognised for the temporary difference arising from the different accounting and tax treatments.

Where the different accounting and tax treatments are due to a basis adjustment, the temporary difference effectively arises after the initial recognition of the asset or liability. Accordingly, the initial recognition exceptions in IAS 12.22 and IAS 12.24 do not apply and deferred tax must be recognised. For further information regarding deferral of hedging gains and losses into non-financial assets see **section 2.2.3** of **chapter 20**.

Example 5.3.5

Cash flow hedge of forecast purchases

On 4 January 20X2 Company D has forecast purchases of 100,000 kg of cocoa on or about 31 December 20X2 from a Brazilian supplier, Company B. Company D's functional currency is Currency Units, and Company B has a US$ functional currency. On 4 January 20X2, Company D designates the cash flow of the forecast purchase as a hedged item and enters into a currency forward to buy US$180,000 based on the forecast payment (100,000 kg at US$1.8 per kg). The forward contract locks in the value of the US$ amount to be paid at a rate of US$1.8:£1. At inception of the hedge, the derivative is on-market (i.e. fair value is zero). The terms of the currency forward and the forecast purchase match each other, and the entity designates the forward foreign exchange risk as the hedged risk.

On 31 December 20X2, the transaction occurs as expected. The fair value of the forward is positive £12,500 as the US$ continued to strengthen against

Currency Units. The entity has an accounting policy of reclassifying such gains and losses and including them in the initial cost of the non-financial asset in accordance with IAS 39.88

The inventory is recognised in Company D's financial statements at £100,000, being the cash payment of £112,500 (US$180,000 translated at the spot rate on 31 December 20X2), net of the gain on the forward of £12,500. The applicable tax rate is 30 per cent and the tax authority does not allow a deduction for the value of the hedging instrument. Accordingly, the tax base of the inventory is £112,500. Company D should, subject to the normal recoverability test, recognise a deferred tax asset of £3,750 in respect of the temporary difference arising on the attribution of the hedging gains to the recognised value of the inventory. Because the £3,750 arises on the reclassification, rather than the initial recognition of, the hedging instrument the initial recognition exception does not apply.

5.4 Investments in properties

5.4.1 Revaluation of properties

When a property is revalued, its carrying amount is increased or decreased, but there is generally no effect on the tax base of the property. As a result, deferred tax balances arise. Generally, the recognition of deferred tax arising on a revaluation is consistent with the treatment of the revaluation itself.

Under UK GAAP, asset revaluations do not give rise to deferred tax assets and liabilities unless there is a binding commitment to sell, and the resulting gain/loss on disposal will be recognised in the financial statements (i.e. no rollover relief is anticipated). Similarly deferred tax assets and liabilities generally do not arise from adjusting assets to market value as part of a business acquisition. Only where the general rules require recognition (e.g. binding sales contract) should the liability be recognised. UK

5.4.2 Upward revaluations

The upward revaluation of a property generally gives rise to a deferred tax liability. By increasing the carrying amount of the property, the entity is acknowledging that it expects to generate returns in excess of the original carrying amount, which will lead to future taxable profits, and so tax payable.

When an upward valuation is recognised, the deferred tax liability arising is calculated by reference to the expected manner of recovery of the property. The upward valuation will either be recognised in profit or loss (investment property) or in other comprehensive income (properties other than investment properties). The deferred tax expense will therefore be recognised either in profit or loss or in other comprehensive income, depending on the classification of the property.

If the property is not an investment property, the expense will be recognised in other comprehensive income and be offset in equity against the revaluation surplus. Over the period of use when the temporary difference reverses, the release of the deferred tax liability will be credited to profit or loss (see **4.6.1.1** above). The deferred tax liability recognised at the date of revaluation represents a provision for the tax expected to arise on those benefits. The release of the deferred tax liability to profit or loss over the period in which those future economic benefits (taxable profits) are earned offsets the current tax expense in those years to the extent that it was anticipated at the date of the revaluation.

Example 5.4.2

Deferred tax impact of property revaluation

A property is acquired for £1,000. It is depreciated for tax and accounting purposes over 5 years. At the end of the third year, it is revalued to £1,200. The value of the property is expected to be recovered through use in a taxable manufacturing activity. The tax rate is 30 per cent.

	Carrying amount	Tax base	Temporary difference	Deferred tax liability	Movement for the year
	£	£	£	£	£
20X0	1,000	1,000	-	-	-
20X1	800	800	-	-	-
20X2	600	600	-	-	-
20X3	1,200	400	800	240	240
20X4	600	200	400	120	(120)
20X5	-	-	-	-	(120)

The required journal entries at the end of 20X3 are:

	Dr	Cr
	£	£
Property, plant and equipment	200	
Property, plant and equipment – accumulated depreciation	600	
Gain on revaluation (other comprehensive income)		800
Income tax (other comprehensive income)	240	
Deferred tax liability		240

In both 20X4 and 20X5, the following entry will be recorded, to reflect the reversal of the temporary difference arising on revaluation.

	Dr	Cr
	£	£
Deferred tax liability	120	
Income tax (profit or loss)		120

5.4.3 *Downward revaluations and impairment losses*

Recognition of downward revaluations and impairments of properties is in either profit or loss or in other comprehensive income, depending both on the classification of the property (as an investment property or not) and also on previous gains and losses reported on the property. The accounting for properties is discussed in further detail in **chapters 6** and **7**.

The write-down of a property for accounting purposes can give rise to a deferred tax asset, or a reduction in a deferred tax liability, depending on the tax base of the property. Any deferred tax asset arising can only be recognised to the extent that it is probable that sufficient taxable amounts will be available in the future to allow the benefit of that deferred tax asset to be recovered.

Where a property has previously been revalued, and a downward valuation subsequently occurs which is recognised in other comprehensive income (e.g. because the subsequent downward valuation does not exceed the amount held in the revaluation surplus in respect of that same asset), the deferred tax effects previously recognised in other comprehensive income are reversed through other comprehensive income.

Example 5.4.3

Downward revaluation

A property is acquired for £1,000. It is depreciated for tax and accounting purposes over 10 years. At the end of the third year, it is revalued to £1,050. The value of the property is expected to be recovered through use in a taxable manufacturing activity. At the end of the sixth year, it is revalued downward to £200. The tax rate is 30 per cent.

	Carrying amount						Recognised in	
	Historical cost	Revaluation uplift	Tax base	Temporary difference	Deferred tax liability (asset)	Movement for the year	Other comp. income	Profit or loss
	£	£	£	£	£	£	£	£
20X0	1,000	-	1,000	-	-	-	-	-
20X1	900	-	900	-	-	-	-	-
20X2	800	-	800	-	-	-	-	-
20X3	700	350	700	350	105	105	105	-
20X4	600	300	600	300	90	(15)	-	(15)
20X5	500	250	500	250	75	(15)	-	(15)
20X6	200	-	400	(200)	(60)	(135)	(105)	(30)
20X7	150	-	300	(150)	(45)	15	-	15
20X8	100	-	200	(100)	(30)	15	-	15
20X9	50	-	100	(50)	(15)	15	-	15
20Y0	-	-	-	-	-	15	-	15

If a decision is subsequently taken to dispose of the property, then the deferred tax implications will need to be re-examined. Because the temporary difference is calculated on the basis of management expectations as to the manner of recovery of the property, when those expectations change, the deferred tax position may also change.

5.4.4 *Properties to be recovered through disposal*

Where it is anticipated that a revalued property will be disposed of, the deferred tax implications are determined on the basis of the tax consequences of disposal of the property. It may be that the profit on disposal will be fully taxable, in which case the deferred tax liability arising on any revaluation of the property will be equal to the revaluation uplift multiplied by the tax rate. However, more commonly, the taxation of capital gains is on a different basis (e.g. the taxable gain arising may be limited to the amount of tax allowances previously claimed). This is often referred to as a 'claw-back' of tax allowances.

Example 5.4.4A

Investment property (1)

A building that is assessed as investment property is acquired for £1,000 on 1 January 20X1. No deferred tax arises on initial recognition of the building. It is held at fair value in accordance with IAS 40 *Investment Property*, and therefore not depreciated for accounting purposes. At the end of the first year, the market value of the building is still £1,000. Therefore, no revaluation surplus arises at the end of the first year.

The building is depreciated for tax purposes over five years. If it were disposed of, the taxable gain arising would be limited to the amount of the tax depreciation previously claimed. The tax rate is 30 per cent.

At 31 December 20X1:	Revalued amount = £1,000 Tax base = £800 Temporary difference = £1,000 – £800 = £200 Deferred tax liability = £200 x 30% = £60

Therefore, at the end of 20X1, a deferred tax liability of £60 is recognised in profit or loss.

In the above example, the effect of the recognition of the deferred tax expense in the profit or loss in 20X1 is to offset the tax allowance claimed in the period. Effectively, this recognises that, were the property to be disposed of, the tax allowance would be clawed back.

Example 5.4.4B

Investment property (2)

Facts as per **example 5.4.4A** but, at the end of the second year, the investment property is revalued to £1,500.

At 31/12/X2:	Revalued amount = £1,500 Tax base = £1,100* Temporary difference = £1,500 – £1,100 = £400 Deferred tax liability = £400 x 30% = £120

* The tax base is the carrying amount of £1,500 less future taxable amounts (i.e. the allowances that would be clawed back on disposal) of £400. In these circumstances, the tax base for IAS 12 is not equal to the tax written down value.

5.4.5 *Transfers between categories of assets*

Where properties are transferred between categories (e.g. investment property to property held for own use, or vice versa), the reclassification may have consequences for the deferred tax balances recognised. This may also be the case where the investment property is assessed as recoverable through sale rather than through rental income (as deferred tax consequences arise using the assumption that the asset's value will be realised through disposal), even if it is measured at fair value under both classifications.

5.5 Foreign currency translation

5.5.1 *Assets or liabilities held directly*

Where an entity holds a foreign-currency denominated monetary asset or liability directly, retranslation at each period end will result in a change in the carrying amount for accounting purposes, and a foreign exchange gain or loss that is generally dealt with in profit or loss. Where the tax regulations do not allow for an equivalent change in tax base, and a gain on disposal would be taxable, a temporary difference arises on retranslation which is required to be recognised. In most circumstances, the related deferred tax is recognised in profit or loss. However, where the exchange gain or loss is itself recognised in other comprehensive income, the deferred tax is also recognised in other comprehensive income.

Where the entity holds a non-monetary asset that is located overseas, the asset is recognised at its historical cost, being the original foreign currency purchase price translated at the rate on the date of purchase. Where the realisation of that asset will give rise to tax consequences in the foreign country, the tax base of the asset will change as the exchange rate changes. This will give rise to a temporary difference because the recognised carrying amount of the asset does not change. This effect is consistent with the circumstances arising on the translation of overseas financial statements (see **5.5.2** below).

5.5.2 *Consolidated financial statements*

Where a reporting entity incorporates the financial statements of foreign operations in its consolidated financial statements (whether by equity accounting, or full or proportionate consolidation), the deferred tax consequences will need to be evaluated. A foreign operation is defined as an entity that is a subsidiary, associate, joint venture or branch of a reporting entity, the activities of which are based or conducted in a country or currency other than those of the reporting entity. [IAS 21.8]

Once a foreign operation's own financial statements have been prepared in its functional currency, they must then be translated into the presentation currency of the investing entity or group, before they can be incorporated into the group's consolidated financial statements. This is dealt with in IAS 21 *The Effects of Changes in Foreign Exchange Rates* and discussed further in **chapter 28**.

The basic approach is to translate the statement of financial position using the closing rate of exchange, and income and expenses at the rates ruling on the date of transaction (or an average rate can often be used as an approximation). Exchange differences arising are recognised in other comprehensive income.

From a deferred tax perspective, this approach should not give rise to any additional temporary differences associated with the assets and liabilities of the foreign operation. This is because the carrying amounts and the tax bases of the assets and liabilities of the foreign operation are all translated using the same year-end exchange rate, and any deferred taxes will have already been recognised by the foreign operation.

Although temporary differences do not result directly from the translation of the financial statements of these foreign operations, temporary differences can still arise on their consolidation due to differences between the net investment accounted for in the consolidated financial statements (effectively the parent's share of the net assets of the operation), and the tax base of the investment itself held by the parent (see **4.4.6** above).

Where a parent has a loan to a foreign subsidiary that is considered to be part of the net investment in the foreign operation, the parent will assess the likelihood of reversal of the temporary difference relating to the loan in the same manner as the temporary differences relating to the subsidiary's equity are considered. Therefore, if the parent is able to control the timing of the reversal of those temporary differences and the reversal is not expected to occur in the foreseeable future, the deferred tax would not be recognised. Conversely, if the parent has an interest-earning deposit in the subsidiary, the deferred tax arising from temporary differences would be recognised, as the exemption relates to investments in subsidiaries and not to individual assets within those subsidiaries.

5.6 Share-based payments

In some jurisdictions, entities receive tax deductions for share-based payments, although the deduction may not always equal the accounting expense, nor be in the same period as the accounting expense is recognised. For example, an entity may operate a share option scheme whereby the deduction occurs when the share options are exercised, and the amount is based on the entity's share price on the exercise date. [IAS 12.68A]

The difference between the tax base of the employee services received to date (being the amount accrued to date that the taxation authorities will permit as a deduction in future periods), and the carrying amount for accounting purposes (i.e. nil), is a deductible temporary difference that results in a deferred tax asset. If the amount of the future tax deduction is not known at the end of the period, it should be estimated, based on information available at the end of the period. For example, if the deduction is based on the entity's share price on the exercise date (or some other future date), the measurement of the deductible temporary difference should be based on the entity's share price at the end of the period. [IAS 12.68B]

If the amount of the accrued tax deduction exceeds the amount of the related cumulative remuneration expense, this indicates that the deduction relates not only to the remuneration expense but also to an equity item. Hence, in accordance with IAS 12.58, the excess of the associated current or deferred tax should be recognised directly in equity. [IAS 12.68C]

Although IAS 12.68C does not explicitly state that it relates only to equity-settled share-based payments, the justification given for the accounting treatment is that the excess deduction indicates that the deduction relates to an equity item as well as to the remuneration expense. In the case of a cash-settled share-based payment, there is no equity item recognised to which the deduction could relate and, accordingly, it is appropriate to recognise the entire deduction in profit or loss.

UK *Under UK GAAP, because deferred tax is recognised on timing differences, the maximum amount of the deferred tax will be the tax on the accounting expense to date. When the current tax deduction exceeds the related accounting expense there is no specific guidance on how this excess should be treated, however it appears reasonable to recognise the 'excess' current tax in the profit or loss as it relates to a tax deduction being measured on a different basis but is still in respect of an item in profit or loss.*

IAS 12 Appendix B contains an example of how to calculate the deferred tax asset associated with an employee share remuneration scheme.

Sometimes employee share schemes are modified (e.g. from equity-settled to cash-settled). These modifications can change the accounting for the scheme (e.g. by requiring that a liability be recognised). The accounting implications of employee share schemes are considered in **chapter 25.** However, it is important to note that the modification may affect any deferred tax balances recognised.

6 Presentation and disclosure

6.1 Presentation

6.1.1 Tax expense

The tax expense or income related to the profit or loss from ordinary activities should be presented in the statement of comprehensive income. [IAS 12.77]

If an entity presents the components of profit or loss in a separate income statement (as described in paragraph 81 of IAS 1(2007) – see **section 5** of **chapter 3**), it presents the tax expense or income related to profit or loss from ordinary activities in that separate statement. [IAS 12.77A]

IAS 12 notes that, although IAS 21 requires certain exchange differences to be recognised as income or expense, that Standard does not specify where such differences should be presented in the statement of comprehensive income. Therefore, IAS 12 states that where exchange differences on deferred foreign tax liabilities or assets are recognised in the statement of comprehensive income, such differences may be classified as deferred tax expense (income) if that presentation is considered to be the most useful to financial statement users. [IAS 12.78]

It is possible for an entity to designate a derivative as a cash flow hedge of the cash flow variability of a tax liability arising on the foreign exchange gain or loss on a foreign currency borrowing. Providing that such a hedge has been appropriately designated and documented, the hedge is a qualifying cash flow hedge of a non-financial liability (the tax liability) under IAS 39 *Financial Instruments: Recognition and Measurement*.

IAS 39, the Standard which prescribes the hedge accounting rules in terms of recognition and measurement, is silent on where the gains and losses on derivatives designated as hedging derivatives should be presented within profit or loss. It has become customary, and is useful to the users of the financial statements, for the hedging effects of derivatives to be presented in the statement of comprehensive income in the same line as the item that they hedge. Therefore, although the hedging gain or loss is clearly not an income tax as defined by IAS 12, an argument can be made for including the effects of the derivatives, which an entity has entered into as hedges of its tax liability, in the tax line in the statement of comprehensive income.

Where an entity chooses to present derivative gains/losses relating to designated tax hedging derivatives within the tax line, this accounting policy choice should be applied consistently from period to period. Furthermore, appropriate separate disclosure in the notes of the amount attributable to hedging gains/losses should be made.

6.1.2 *Statement of financial position*

The presentation of both current and deferred tax in the statement of financial position is addressed in IAS 1 *Presentation of Financial Statements* (and not in IAS 12) as follows:

- liabilities and assets for current tax should be presented in the statement of financial position; [IAS 1(2007).54, previously IAS 1(2003).68]
- deferred tax liabilities and deferred tax assets should be presented in the statement of financial position; [IAS 1(2007).54, previously IAS 1(2003).68] and
- when an entity presents current and non-current assets, and current and non-current liabilities, as separate classifications in its statement of financial position, it should not classify deferred tax assets (liabilities) as current assets (liabilities). [IAS 1(2007).56, previously IAS 1(2003).70]

6.1.3 *Offset of tax assets and liabilities*

In a similar approach to that taken in IAS 1, IAS 12 takes a strong line on the extent to which tax assets and liabilities can be offset against one another to present only a net figure in the statement of financial position.

6.1.3.1 *Offset of current tax assets and liabilities*

An entity should offset current tax assets and current tax liabilities if, and only if, the entity:

[IAS 12.71]

- has a legally enforceable right to set off the recognised amounts; and
- intends either to settle on a net basis, or to realise the asset and settle the liability simultaneously.

The Standard explains that an entity normally has a legally enforceable right to set off current tax assets against current tax liabilities when they relate to taxes levied by the same taxation authority, and that authority permits the entity to make or receive a single net payment. [IAS 12.72]

Where an entity is preparing consolidated financial statements, current tax assets and liabilities arising from different group entities should not be offset unless:

[IAS 12.73]

- the entities concerned have a legally enforceable right to make or receive a single net payment; and
- the entities intend to make or receive such a net payment or to recover the asset and settle the liability simultaneously.

6.1.3.2 *Offset of deferred tax assets and liabilities*

An entity should offset deferred tax assets and deferred tax liabilities if, and only if:

[IAS 12.74]

- the entity has a legally enforceable right to set off current tax assets against current tax liabilities; and
- the deferred tax assets and the deferred tax liabilities relate to income taxes levied by the same taxation authority on either:
  - the same taxable entity; or
  - different taxable entities which intend either to settle current tax liabilities and assets on a net basis, or to realise the assets and settle the liabilities simultaneously, in each future period in which significant amounts of deferred tax liabilities or assets are expected to be settled or recovered.

Under the above rules, deferred tax assets and liabilities arising in the same legal entity (which is also a single taxable entity) can generally be offset. However, where, for example, the taxable entity has capital losses carried forward which can only be used to reduce future capital gains, those losses can only be offset against deferred tax liabilities to the extent that recognised deferred tax liabilities arise from unrealised capital gains.

In a consolidation situation, the first condition to overcome is the requirement for the balances to be levied by the same taxation authority. This effectively prohibits the offset of deferred tax assets and liabilities arising in different jurisdictions.

Even for entities operating within the same jurisdiction, except where there are formal group relief or consolidated taxation arrangements, it will be unusual for the taxation authority to permit net settlement between different taxable entities.

Therefore, in preparing consolidated financial statements, the deferred tax balances of the separate entities will generally be aggregated without further setting off the deferred tax balances of one entity against those of another.

The above rules mean that, for disclosure purposes, there is no need for detailed scheduling of the timing of reversals of each temporary difference. In rare circumstances, an entity may have a legally enforceable right of set-off, and an intention to settle net, for some periods but not for others. In such situations, detailed scheduling may be required to establish reliably whether the deferred tax liability of one taxable entity will result in increased tax payments in the same period in which a deferred tax asset of another taxable entity will result in decreased payments by that second taxable entity. [IAS 12.75 & 76]

Where an entity is entitled to offset deferred tax assets and deferred tax liabilities in the statement of financial position, the entity is not necessarily entitled to offset the related deferred tax income and deferred tax expense. The ability to offset the amounts in the statement of financial position does not override the requirement for the income and expense to be appropriately classified.

6.2 Disclosure

6.2.1 Statement of comprehensive income

The major components of tax expense (income) should be disclosed separately, including:

[IAS 12.80 & 81]

- current tax expense (income);
- any adjustments recognised in the period for current tax of prior periods;
- the amount of deferred tax expense (income) relating to the origination and reversal of temporary differences;
- the amount of deferred tax expense (income) relating to changes in tax rates or the imposition of new taxes;

- the amount of the benefit arising from a previously unrecognised tax loss, tax credit or temporary difference of a prior period that is used to reduce current tax expense;
- the amount of the benefit from a previously unrecognised tax loss, tax credit or temporary difference of a prior period that is used to reduce deferred tax expense;
- deferred tax expense arising from the write-down, or reversal of a previous write-down, of a deferred tax asset in accordance with paragraph 56; and
- the amount of tax expense (income) relating to those changes in accounting policies and errors that are included in profit or loss in accordance with IAS 8, because they cannot be accounted for retrospectively.

In respect of discontinued operations, the financial statements should disclose separately the tax expense relating to:

[IAS 12.81(h)]

- the gain or loss on discontinuance; and
- the profit or loss from the ordinary activities of the discontinued operation for the period, together with the corresponding amounts for each prior period presented.

For each type of temporary difference, and each type of unused tax losses and unused tax credits, the financial statements should disclose the amount of the deferred tax income or expense recognised in profit or loss, if this is not apparent from the changes in the amounts recognised in the statement of financial position. [IAS 12.81(g)(ii)]

6.2.1.1 *Reconciliation of tax expense or income*

IAS 12 requires the presentation of an explanation of the relationship between the tax expense (income) and accounting profit in either or both of the following forms:

[IAS 12.81(c) & 86]

- a numerical reconciliation between tax expense (income) and the product of accounting profit multiplied by the applicable tax rate(s), disclosing also the basis on which the applicable tax rate(s) is (are) computed; or

- a numerical reconciliation between the average effective tax rate (being the tax expense (income) divided by the accounting profit) and the applicable tax rate, disclosing also the basis on which the applicable tax rate is computed.

An explanation is required of changes in the applicable tax rate(s) compared to the previous accounting period. [IAS 12.81(d)]

6.2.2 *Statement of financial position*

For each type of temporary difference, and each type of unused tax losses and unused tax credits, the financial statements should disclose the amount of the deferred tax assets and liabilities recognised in the statement of financial position for each period presented. The amount of deferred tax income or expense recognised in profit or loss in respect of each temporary difference must also be disclosed where it is not apparent from the changes in the amounts recognised in the statement of financial position. [IAS 12.81(g)(i)]

The following should also be disclosed:

[IAS 12.81(e) – (f)]

- the amount (and expiry date, if any) of deductible temporary differences, unused tax losses and unused tax credits for which no deferred tax asset is recognised in the statement of financial position; and
- the aggregate amount of temporary differences associated with investments in subsidiaries, branches and associates and interests in joint ventures, for which deferred tax liabilities have not been recognised.

It would often be impracticable to compute the amount of unrecognised deferred tax liabilities arising from investments in subsidiaries, branches and associates and interests in joint ventures, so IAS 12 requires an entity to disclose the aggregate amount of the underlying temporary differences but does not require disclosure of the deferred tax liabilities. Nevertheless, where practicable, entities are encouraged to disclose the amounts of the unrecognised deferred tax liabilities because financial statement users may find such information useful. [IAS 12.87]

An entity should disclose the amount of a deferred tax asset and the nature of the evidence supporting its recognition, when:

[IAS 12.82]

- the utilisation of the deferred tax asset is dependent on future taxable profits in excess of the profits arising from the reversal of existing taxable temporary differences; and
- the entity has suffered a loss in either the current or preceding period in the tax jurisdiction to which the deferred tax asset relates.

Where current and deferred tax assets and liabilities are measured at the tax rate applicable to undistributed profits, but the net income taxes payable will be affected if part of the retained earnings is paid out as a dividend to shareholders, the entity should disclose:

[IAS 12.82A & 87A]

- the nature of the potential income tax consequences that would result from the payment of dividends to its shareholders. This includes the important features of the income tax systems and the factors that will affect the amount of the potential income tax consequences of dividends;
- the amounts of the potential income tax consequences that are practicably determinable; and
- whether there are any potential income tax consequences that are not practicably determinable.

It is not always practicable to compute the total amount of the potential income tax consequences that would result from the payment of dividends to shareholders (e.g. where an entity has a lot of overseas subsidiaries. However, even in such circumstances, usually some consequences may be easily determinable, and these should be disclosed. IAS 12 cites the example of a consolidated group, where the parent and some of its subsidiaries may have paid income taxes at a higher rate on undistributed profits and are aware of the amount that would be refunded on the payment of future dividends to shareholders from consolidated retained earnings. In this case, the refundable amount is disclosed.

Where some or all potential income tax consequences cannot be determined, the entity should disclose that there are additional potential income tax consequences not practicably determinable. In the parent's separate financial statements, the disclosure of the potential income tax consequences relates to the parent's retained earnings. [IAS 12.82B]

Where current and deferred tax assets and liabilities are measured at the tax rate applicable to undistributed profits, but the net income taxes payable will be affected if part of the retained earnings is paid out as a dividend to shareholders, an entity required to provide the disclosures listed above may also be required to provide disclosures related to temporary differences associated with investments in subsidiaries, branches and associates or interests in joint ventures. For example, an entity may be required to disclose the aggregate amount of temporary differences associated with investments in subsidiaries for which no deferred tax liabilities have been recognised. [IAS 12.81(f)] If it is impracticable to compute the amounts of unrecognised deferred tax liabilities there may be amounts of potential income tax consequences of dividends not practicably determinable related to these subsidiaries. [IAS 12.87C]

6.2.3 *Other disclosure requirements*

Other disclosure requirements include:

- the aggregate current and deferred tax relating to items that are charged or credited directly to equity; [IAS 12.81(a)]
- the amount of income tax relating to each component of other comprehensive income (revaluation surplus, foreign exchange reserve, etc.); [IAS 12.81(ab)]
- the amount of income tax consequences of dividends to shareholders of the entity that were proposed or declared before the financial statements were authorised for issue, but are not recognised as a liability in the financial statements; [IAS 12.81(i)]
- if a business combination in which the entity is the acquirer causes a change in the amount recognised for its pre-acquisition deferred tax asset (under IAS 12.67 – see **5.1.5**), the amount of that change; [IAS 12.81(j) – effective for annual periods beginning on or after 1 July 2009 or date of earlier application of IFRS 3(2008)]
- if the deferred tax benefits acquired in a business combination are not recognised at the acquisition date but are recognised after the acquisition date (under IAS 12.68 – see **5.1.6**), a description of the event or change in circumstances that caused the deferred tax benefits to be recognised; [IAS 12.81(k) – effective for annual periods beginning on or after 1 July 2009 or date of earlier application of IFRS 3(2008)]
- any tax-related contingent liabilities and contingent assets in accordance with IAS 37 *Provisions, Contingent Liabilities and Contingent Assets* (e.g. from unresolved disputes with the taxation authorities); [IAS 12.88] and
- where changes in tax rates or tax laws are enacted or announced after the reporting period, any significant impact on the entity's current and deferred tax assets and liabilities. [IAS 10.22(h) & IAS 12.88]

7 Future developments

For some years, the IASB has been working on a project to reduce the differences between IFRSs and US GAAP as regards accounting for income taxes. Both IAS 12 and the equivalent US Standard, SFAS 109 *Accounting for Income Taxes*, are based on the balance sheet liability approach but there are differences because both Standards have numerous exceptions to the basic principle. The Boards' approach to convergence in this project is not to reconsider the underlying approach, but rather to eliminate exceptions to the basic principle. An Exposure Draft is expected in the second half of 2008.

13 Financial instruments: scope

1 Introduction

1.1 Introduction to chapters 13 to 22

Accounting for financial instruments is, for many entities adopting IFRSs, the single biggest challenge. The requirements are complex and many concepts may be unfamiliar; in addition, the sheer volume of the relevant standards and associated material may be daunting. For these reasons, and to make it easier to get to grips with the material, this book deals with financial instruments over the next ten chapters, as follows:

Chapter 13: scope

Chapter 14: financial assets

Chapter 15: financial liabilities and equity

Chapter 16: derivatives

Chapter 17: embedded derivatives

Chapter 18: measurement

Chapter 19: recognition and derecognition

Chapter 20: hedge accounting

Chapter 21: disclosure

Chapter 22: first-time adoption of IFRSs

1.2 IAS 32, IAS 39 and IFRS 7

There are three Standards that deal with the accounting for financial instruments:

- IAS 32 *Financial Instruments: Presentation* deals with the presentation and classification of financial instruments as financial liabilities or equity.
- IAS 39 *Financial Instruments: Recognition and Measurement* contains all the key guidance for recognition and measurement of financial instruments other than equity.

- IFRS 7 *Financial Instruments: Disclosures* prescribes the disclosure of financial instruments.

All three Standards have detailed scoping paragraphs that exclude from their scope certain financial instruments. In addition, the scoping paragraphs of the Standards differ slightly:

- all financial instruments that are scoped out of IAS 32 are also scoped out of IAS 39;
- financial instruments that an entity issues with a discretionary participation feature are accounted for under IFRS 4 *Insurance Contracts* and are scoped out of IAS 39. They are within the scope of IFRS 7, and they are also within the scope of IAS 32 except that, for such contracts, the requirements of IAS 32 regarding the distinction between financial liabilities and equity instruments are not applicable;
- IAS 39 has some additional scope exclusions that go beyond the scope exclusions in IAS 32 (see **section 3** below); and
- IAS 39 excludes all instruments classified as equity from its scope, whereas IFRS 7 appears to only exclude derivatives over own equity classified as equity, making no reference to non-derivative instruments, such as ordinary shares. It appears that this difference does not have any practical effect (see **3.1** below).

The definition of a financial instrument is broad: a financial instrument is defined as any contract that gives rise to a financial asset of one entity and a financial liability or equity instrument of another entity. Trade receivables and payables, bank loans and overdrafts, issued debt, ordinary and preference shares, investments in securities like shares and bonds, and various derivatives are just some of the examples of financial instruments. In addition, certain contracts to buy or sell non-financial items are specifically scoped in on the basis that they behave and are used in a similar way to financial instruments (see **2.5** below). The chapters that follow explain the concepts of financial assets, financial liabilities, equity, derivatives, embedded derivatives and hedge accounting and demonstrate that many items that entities have not previously considered to be financial instruments may well be within the scope of IAS 32 and/or IAS 39 and IFRS 7.

This chapter explains which items that meet the definition of a financial instrument are scoped out of IAS 32 and/or IAS 39 and IFRS 7. In general, items are scoped out of IAS 32, IAS 39 and IFRS 7 if another Standard is more prescriptive. As an example, interests in subsidiaries will be scoped out of all three Standards as they are within the scope of IAS 27 *Consolidated and Separate Financial Statements*. The detailed scope exclusions of IFRS 7 are included in **section 2** of **chapter 21**.

This chapter deals with the scope of all three Standards in the following sections:

Section 2 Financial instruments scoped out of IAS 32, IAS 39 and IFRS 7

Section 3 Additional scope exclusions of IAS 39

2 Financial instruments scoped out of IAS 32, IAS 39 and IFRS 7

A summary of the scope of IAS 32, IAS 39 and IFRS 7 with respect to financial instruments only is included below:

Financial instrument	Within scope of IAS 32?	Within scope of IFRS 7?	Within scope of IAS 39?
Interest in subsidiaries, associates and joint ventures accounted for in accordance with IAS 27, IAS 28 or IAS 31 respectively	No	No	No
Interest in subsidiaries, associates and joint ventures accounted for in accordance with IAS 39 as permitted by IAS 27(2008).38(b) (previously IAS 27(2003).37(b))	Yes	Yes	Yes
Investment in equity securities (available-for-sale investments and fair value through profit or loss)	Yes	Yes	Yes

Financial instrument	**Within scope of IAS 32?**	**Within scope of IFRS 7?**	**Within scope of IAS 39?**
Investment in debt securities (available-for-sale investments, fair value through profit or loss, loans and receivables, held to maturity investments)	Yes	Yes	Yes
Trade receivables and payables	Yes	Yes	Yes
Finance lease receivables of the lessor	Yes	Yes	No
Construction contract receivables accounted for under IAS 11 *Construction Contracts* (see **2.7** below)	No	No	No
Cash and cash equivalents	Yes	Yes	Yes
Borrowings and other financial liabilities such as some preference shares	Yes	Yes	Yes
Derivatives (and non-closely related embedded derivatives)	Yes	Yes	Yes
Derivatives over interests in subsidiaries, associates and joint ventures in the individual financial statements	Yes	Yes	Yes
Derivatives over interests in associates and joint ventures in the consolidated financial statements	Yes	Yes	Yes

Financial instrument	Within scope of IAS 32?	Within scope of IFRS 7?	Within scope of IAS 39?
Contracts over non-financial items that do not meet the purchase, sale or usage exemption in IAS 39.5	Yes	Yes	Yes
Contingent consideration in a business combination (acquirer only)*	No	No	No
Contingent consideration in a business combination (seller)	Yes	Yes	Yes
Deferred consideration in a business combination (acquirer or seller)	Yes	Yes	Yes
Warranty obligations and other provisions under IAS 37 that will be settled by the delivery of cash or other financial assets	Yes	Yes	Yes
Financial guarantee contracts for the writer that are not treated as insurance contracts	Yes	Yes	Yes
Finance lease obligations of the lessee	Yes	Yes	No
Own equity shares	Yes	No **	No
Derivatives over own equity shares that are classified as equity (including derivatives over shares in non-controlling interest in the consolidated financial statements)	Yes	No	No

Financial instrument	Within scope of IAS 32?	Within scope of IFRS 7?	Within scope of IAS 39?
Contracts between an acquirer and a vendor in a business combination to buy or sell an acquiree at a future date	Yes	Yes	No
Loan commitments that cannot be settled net in cash or another financial instrument, and are not designated as at financial liabilities at fair value through profit or loss	Yes	Yes	No
Retirement benefit obligations	No	No	No
Employee share options	No	No	No
Insurance contracts for the writer or holder of insurance (settled in cash or other financial assets)	No	No	No

* if the revised version of IFRS 3 *Business Combinations* issued in 2008 is applied contingent consideration in a business combination for the acquirer is in the scope of all three standards as the scope exemption was removed by IFRS 3(2008)

** scope exclusion refers only to derivatives over own equity but can be applied broadly to all equity instruments of the issuer – see **3.1** below

IAS 32 applies to all financial instruments except for the following items:

- interests in subsidiaries, associates and joint ventures (see **2.1** below);
- employers' rights and obligations under employee benefit plans (see **2.2** below);
- rights and obligations arising under insurance contracts as well as financial instruments that are within the scope of IFRS 4 because they contain a discretionary participation feature (see **2.3** below);

- for acquirers that have not yet adopted IFRS 3(2008), contracts for contingent consideration in a business combination (see **2.4** below); and
- financial instruments, contracts and obligations under share-based payment transactions (see **2.6** below).

IAS 39 also scopes out these instruments, but has some additional scope exemptions (see **section 3** below).

Additionally, IAS 32, IAS 39 and IFRS 7 include within their scopes certain contracts to buy or sell non-financial assets (see **2.5** below) even though they do not meet the definition of a financial instrument.

Each of the above is considered in turn.

2.1 Interests in subsidiaries, associates and joint ventures

Interests in subsidiaries, associates and joint ventures that are accounted for under IAS 27 *Consolidated and Separate Financial Statements*, IAS 28 *Investments in Associates* or IAS 31 *Interests in Joint Ventures* are not within the scope of IAS 32. However, if in certain circumstances specified by IAS 27, IAS 28 or IAS 31 an entity accounts for an interest in a subsidiary, associate or joint venture under IAS 39, then that interest in a subsidiary, associate or joint venture also falls into the scope of IAS 32 and IFRS 7 (see **2.1.1** below). In such a case, the applicable disclosure requirements of IAS 27, IAS 28 and IAS 31 are given in addition to those of IFRS 7. For example, in the parent's separate financial statements, if the parent chooses to record its investment in its subsidiary in accordance with IAS 39 as an available-for-sale financial asset (see **chapter 14**), then that investment having been clearly scoped into IAS 39 also falls into the scope of IFRS 7.

For periods beginning on or after 1 January 2009, *Improvements to IFRSs* issued in May 2008, clarified the interaction of IFRS 7, IAS 28 and IAS 31 in such circumstances (see **section 2** in **chapter 35** and **section 2 in chapter 36**). Earlier application of the amendments made by *Improvements to IFRSs* is permitted, but an entity choosing to apply the amendments early must disclose that fact. The amendments may be applied prospectively.

Derivatives that are linked to interests in subsidiaries, associates and joint ventures are always within the scope of IAS 32. Where a derivative on an interest in a subsidiary meets the definition of equity in the consolidated financial statements in accordance with IAS 32 (see **chapter 15**) that derivative is scoped out of IAS 39 and IFRS 7 and is accounted for as equity under IAS 32. This is the case for a derivative over shares in a subsidiary where the derivative will be settled by delivery of a fixed amount of shares for a fixed amount of cash or other financial asset. The derivative meets the definition of equity in the consolidated financial statements as shares in a subsidiary in the consolidated financial statements are presented as non-controlling interest which is part of consolidated equity. In contrast, shares in an associate or joint venture are never considered part of equity in the consolidated financial statements and therefore in consolidated financial statements a derivative over an interest in an associate or joint venture will never meet the definition of equity and as a result will always be within the scope of IAS 39 and IFRS 7.

Where derivatives over interests in subsidiaries, associates and joint ventures are within the scope of IAS 39 they are covered by the normal measurement requirements for derivatives as detailed in **chapter 16**.

Example 2.1A

Written call over equity of subsidiary (1)

Parent X and Subsidiary Y are part of Group Z.

Subsidiary Y writes a call option to an entity outside the group over a fixed number of its own equity shares that is exclusively physically settled in all cases and the strike price of the option is a fixed amount of cash. For Subsidiary Y, the written call option meets the definition of equity in accordance with IAS 32 and therefore in the financial statements of Subsidiary Y it is treated as an equity item.

In the financial statements of Group Z, the instrument is within the scope of IAS 32 as it is a derivative over an interest in a subsidiary. It is outside the scope of IAS 39 and IFRS 7 because the instrument meets the definition of equity in the financial statements of Subsidiary Y in accordance with IAS 32, and therefore it is non-controlling interest in the consolidated financial statements of Group Z.

Example 2.1B

Written call over equity of subsidiary (2)

As **example 2.1A** above except Parent X writes the call option over a fixed number of shares in Subsidiary Y for a fixed amount of cash.

In the separate financial statements of Parent X the instrument is a derivative that is in the scope of IAS 39 and IFRS 7 as the derivative does not meet the definition of equity in Parent X's financial statements as the derivative is not over Parent X's equity.

In the consolidated financial statements of Group Z, the instrument is within the scope of IAS 32 as it is a derivative over an interest in a subsidiary which is presented as non-controlling interest. The instrument is outside the scope of IAS 39 and IFRS 7 because the instrument meets the definition of equity.

2.1.1 *Investments in subsidiaries, associates and joint ventures*

Where an entity prepares separate financial statements (as defined in IAS 27), an investment in a subsidiary, associate or joint venture should be accounted for:

[IAS 27(2008).38, previously IAS 27(2003).37]

(a) at cost; or

(b) in accordance with IAS 39.

If the investment is accounted for in accordance with IAS 39, then it will be classified as either at fair value through profit or loss or available-for-sale (see **section 3** and **3.5** of **chapter 14**).

Investments that cease to be subsidiaries, but that do not become associates or joint ventures, are accounted for in accordance with IAS 39 from the date they cease to be subsidiaries. Their carrying amount on that date is their initial cost.

Similarly, investments that cease to be associates, but that do not become subsidiaries or joint ventures, are accounted for in accordance with IAS 39 from the date the entity ceases to have significant influence. Investments that cease to be joint ventures, that do not become subsidiaries or associates, are accounted for in accordance with IAS 39 from the date the entity ceases to have joint control. The carrying amount on the date that the investment ceases to be an associate or joint venture is regarded as its initial cost.

Venture capital organisations, mutual funds, unit trusts, investment-linked insurance funds and similar entities that upon initial recognition choose to designate their interests in associates and joint ventures as at fair value through profit or loss or classify them as held for trading in the entity's individual or consolidated financial statements must account for such interests under IAS 39, i.e. measure them at fair value with changes in fair value recognised in profit or loss. [IAS 28.1, IAS 31.1] A venture capital organisation or similar entity is not permitted to apply IAS 39 to their investments in subsidiaries in the consolidated financial statements.

A group may consist of a venture capital entity or similar entity and other operations. This is common in large financial institutions where the organisation consists of a venture capital business as well other banking operations, such as retail and investment banking. It would seem acceptable for the venture capital operation within the larger organisation to choose to apply IAS 39 for its interests in associate and joint ventures. It is not permitted to apply IAS 39 to interests in associates and joint ventures outside of the venture capital operation.

2.2 Employers' rights and obligations under employee benefit plans

Employers' rights and obligations under employee benefit plans are outside the scope of IAS 32, IAS 39 and IFRS 7. They are within the scope of IAS 19 *Employee Benefits*.

2.3 Rights and obligations arising under insurance contracts

Contracts that meet the definition of an insurance contract in IFRS 4 *Insurance Contracts* are outside the scope of IAS 32, IAS 39 and IFRS 7. In addition, financial instruments that are within the scope of IFRS 4 because they contain a discretionary participation feature are outside the scope of IAS 32 and IAS 39. A discretionary participation feature is the right to receive, in addition to guaranteed benefits, significant further benefits that are at the discretion of the issuer and are based on the performance of a specified pool of contracts, investment returns or profit or loss of a company, fund or other entity that issues the contract. [IFRS 4.2 and Appendix A] The issuer of such instruments is exempt from applying the paragraphs in IAS 32 with respect to the distinction between financial liabilities and equity instruments. However, these instruments are subject to all the other requirements of IAS 32. Furthermore, IAS 32 applies to derivatives that are embedded in these instruments that are required to be separately accounted for in accordance with IAS 39 (see **2.3.1** below).

An insurance contract is defined in IFRS 4 as a contract under which one party (the insurer) accepts significant insurance risk from another party (policyholder) by agreeing to compensate the policyholder if a specified uncertain future event (the insured event) adversely affects the policyholder. [IFRS 4, Appendix A] An insurance risk is a pre-existing risk that the policyholder transfers to the insurer and is a risk other than financial risk, i.e. other than a risk of a possible future change in either a financial variable (e.g. interest rate, commodity price, credit rating, etc) or a non-financial variable that is not specific to a party to the contract. The insurance risk has to be significant: it has to have a discernible effect on the economics of the transaction, i.e. significant additional benefits including claims handling and assessment costs could become payable. An adverse effect on a policyholder as a result of an insured event is a precondition for payment, however the payment itself does not have to be limited to the financial loss suffered by the policyholder.

IFRS 4 contains numerous examples of insurance contracts, and also examples of those contracts that do not meet the definition of an insurance contract and may fall within the scope of IAS 32, IAS 39 and IFRS 7.

Example 2.3

Insurance risk

A life insurance contract in which the insurer bears no significant mortality risk will be in the scope of IAS 39 if it creates financial assets or liabilities. [IFRS 4.B19]

2.3.1 *Derivatives embedded in insurance contracts*

Derivatives embedded within insurance contracts are within the scope of IAS 32, IAS 39 and IFRS 7 if they require separation in accordance with IAS 39. The only exception is if a derivative embedded in an insurance contract is itself an insurance contract. [IFRS 4.7]

Example 2.3.1

Embedded derivatives in insurance contracts

[IFRS 4.IG4, Example 2.16]

A contractual feature within an insurance contract provides a return that is contractually linked (with no discretion) to the return on specified assets. The embedded derivative is not an insurance contract and is not closely related to the contract (IAS 39.AG30(h)). Fair value measurement is required [*i.e. the embedded derivative will be separated from the insurance contract and fair valued*].

2.3.2 *Financial guarantee contracts*

If an entity has issued a financial guarantee to a third party, the entity will need to consider whether that instrument meets the definition of a financial guarantee contract as laid out in IAS 39. The Standard defines such contracts as those that require the issuer to make specified payments to reimburse the holder for a loss it incurs because a specified debtor fails to make payment when due in accordance with the original or modified terms of a debt instrument. The issuer of such a contract shall in accordance with the requirements of IAS 39 initially recognise the financial guarantee contract at fair value and subsequently measure it at the higher of:

[IAS 39.47(c)]

- the amount determined in accordance with IAS 37 *Provisions, Contingent Liabilities and Contingent Assets*; and
- the amount initially recognised less when appropriate cumulative amortisation in accordance with IAS 18 *Revenue*.

This treatment in respect of initial recognition and subsequent measurement applies with the following three exceptions:

- if the financial guarantee contract was entered into or retained on a transfer of a financial asset and prevented derecognition of the financial asset or resulted in continuing involvement (see **3.3** and **3.4** in **chapter 19** for further details); [IAS 39.47(b)]
- if the financial guarantee contract was designated at fair value through profit or loss at inception (see **7.1** in **chapter 15** for further details); [IAS 39.47(a)] and
- if the issuer has previously asserted explicitly that it regards such contracts as insurance contracts and has used accounting applicable to insurance contracts; in such cases the issuer may elect to apply either IAS 39 or IFRS 4 *Insurance Contracts*; it should be noted that this election may be made on a contract by contract basis but the election for each contract is irrevocable. [IAS 39.2(e)]

An entity may have written financial guarantee contracts but not as a core business activity. It has historically considered these contracts as insurance and asserted that they were insurance contracts, or alternatively it may have made such an assertion at the time of transition to IFRSs. Evidence is required as to whether the entity's assertion is sufficient for the entity to treat these contracts under IFRS 4.

It should be noted that financial guarantee contracts held, as opposed to those issued, are specifically outside the scope of IAS 39. [IAS 39.IN6]

The following decision tree summarises the treatment of issued financial guarantees:

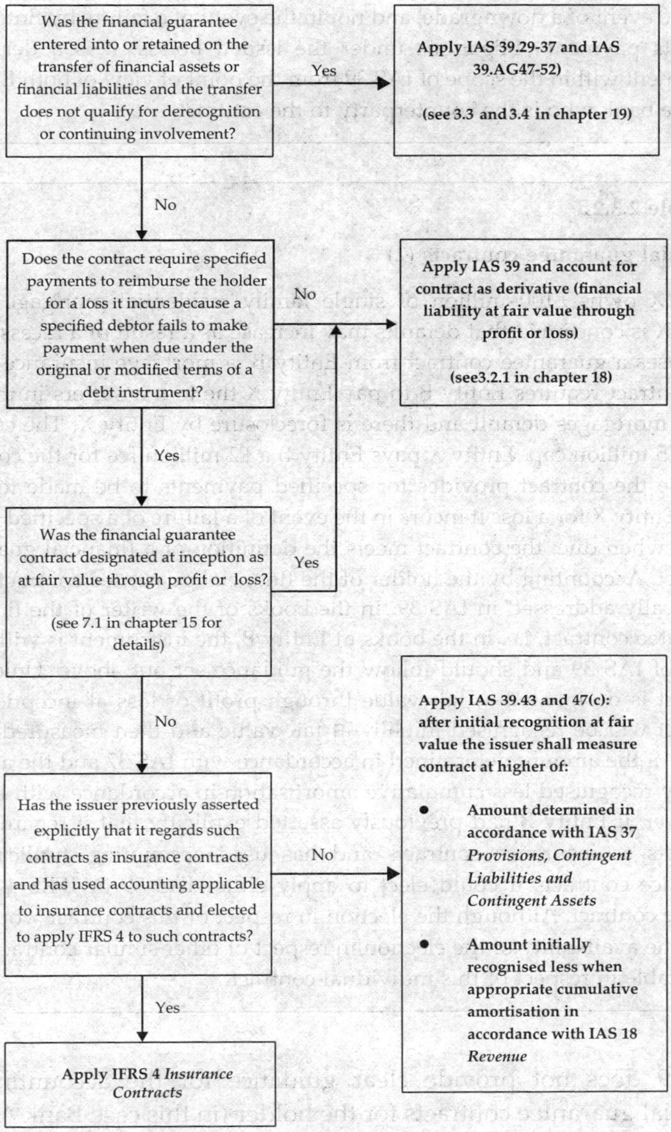
Was the financial guarantee entered into or retained on the transfer of financial assets or financial liabilities and the transfer does not qualify for derecognition or continuing involvement?
Yes
Apply IAS 39.29-37 and IAS 39.AG47-52)
(see 3.3 and 3.4 in chapter 19)
No
Does the contract require specified payments to reimburse the holder for a loss it incurs because a specified debtor fails to make payment when due under the original or modified terms of a debt instrument?
No
Apply IAS 39 and account for contract as derivative (financial liability at fair value through profit or loss)
(see3.2.1 in chapter 18)
Yes
Was the financial guarantee contract designated at inception as at fair value through profit or loss?
(see 7.1 in chapter 15 for details)
Yes
No
Apply IAS 39.43 and 47(c): after initial recognition at fair value the issuer shall measure contract at higher of:
• Amount determined in accordance with IAS 37 Provisions, Contingent Liabilities and Contingent Assets
• Amount initially recognised less when appropriate cumulative amortisation in accordance with IAS 18 Revenue
Has the issuer previously asserted explicitly that it regards such contracts as insurance contracts and has used accounting applicable to insurance contracts and elected to apply IFRS 4 to such contracts?
No
Yes
Apply IFRS 4 Insurance Contracts

Example 2.3.2A

Financial guarantee contracts (1)

Entity A owns £100 million of Entity X bonds that mature in twenty years. Entity X is rated BBB by the rating agencies. Entity A is concerned that Entity X may be downgraded and the value of bonds would decline. To protect against such a decline, Entity A enters into a contract with a bank that will pay Entity A for any decline in the fair value of the Entity X bonds related to a credit downgrade to BB or below. The contract is for a five-year period, and Entity A pays £2 million to enter into the contract. As the contract pays Entity

A in the event of a downgrade, and not in the event of a failure by Entity X to meet its payment obligations under the issued bonds, it is a derivative instrument within the scope of IAS 39 from the point of view of both Entity X and the bank who is the counterparty to the contract.

Example 2.3.2B

Financial guarantee contracts (2)

Entity X owns £100 million of single family residential mortgage loans. Entity X is concerned that defaults may increase as a result of a recession, so purchases a guarantee contract from Entity B, a mortgage insurance entity. The contract requires Entity B to pay Entity X the loss it suffers in the case where mortgages default and there is foreclosure by Entity X. The contract has a £5 million cap. Entity X pays Entity B a £2 million fee for the contract. Because the contract provides for specified payments to be made to reimburse Entity X for a loss it incurs in the event of a failure of a specified debtor to pay when due, the contract meets the definition of a financial guarantee contract. Accounting by the holder of the financial guarantee contract is not specifically addressed in IAS 39. In the books of the writer of the financial guarantee contract, i.e. in the books of Entity B, the instrument is within the scope of IAS 39 and should follow the guidance set out above. Unless the contract is designated at fair value through profit or loss at inception, the contract will be recognised initially at fair value and then measured at the higher of the amount determined in accordance with IAS 37 and the amount initially recognised less cumulative amortisation in accordance with IAS 18. However, if Entity B had previously asserted explicitly that it regards such contracts as insurance contracts and has used accounting applicable to insurance contracts it could elect to apply either IAS 39 or IFRS 4 to the specific contract. Although the election in respect of this contract would not affect the availability of the election in respect of other similar contracts, it is irrevocable in respect of this individual contract.

IAS 39 does not provide clear guidance for the accounting for financial guarantee contracts for the holder (in this case Bank A). IAS 39.IN6 states: "financial guarantee contracts held are not within the scope of the Standard", yet in the body of IAS 39 there is no reference to the scoping out of financial guarantee contracts held. The IASB discussed at its Board meeting in June 2007 an improvement to the introduction to IAS 39 to clarify the reason why financial guarantee contracts held are outside the scope of IAS 39. The clarification was issued in January 2008 as part of editorial changes to standards. The editorial change was made to IAS 39.IN6 only, which now states that the financial guarantee contracts for the holder are not in the scope of IAS 39 because they are insurance contracts. The scope exclusion does not state which standard does apply in accounting for these arrangements.

As financial guarantee contracts held are not in the scope of IAS 39 they will generally be recognised as an asset equal to the premium paid with amortisation of the asset to income over the period in which the benefit of the guarantee is obtained. Only if the entity considers it virtually certain that its claim under the financial guarantee contract will be successful will the asset be remeasured upwards to reflect the claim in accordance with IAS 37. The contract is not accounted for in accordance with IFRS 4 as this standard only applies to the accounting for the issuer of insurance contracts, not the holder.

Example 2.3.2C

Financial guarantee contracts (3)

Entity A has a wholly-owned subsidiary, Entity B. Entity B entered into a third party bank loan. Entity A wrote a financial guarantee contract to the bank over the loan. In the separate financial statements of Entity A, the financial guarantee contract will be accounted for as set out above. In the consolidated financial statements of Group A, the financial guarantee contract is not separately recognised as the group as a single entity has simply borrowed money from a third party.

If Entity A had provided a guarantee directly to Entity B in respect of its bank loan, in the separate financial statements of Entity A, the guarantee is not recognised separately as Entity A has agreed to contribute more money to its subsidiary which will generally be accounted for as a capital contribution as and when it is contributed. The promise by the parent to inject money at a future date is not recognised upfront.

In some jurisdictions, regulatory or statutory requirements state that an ultimate parent company or subsidiary (the guarantor) must, or can elect to, make representations that it will make payments to unspecified parties outside the group should a subsidiary (obligor) fail to make payments under its obligations to those parties. The guarantor will make a payment to the debtor equal to the amount that the obligor has failed to pay. The representation is open-ended (i.e. it relates to all currently recognised obligations as well as to all obligations that the subsidiary may enter into in the future) and does not have a specified counterparty. Care needs to be taken in determining whether such representations by the guarantor are financial guarantee contracts in the guarantor's financial statements.

Before considering whether the representation meets the definition of a financial guarantee contract in accordance with IAS 39.9, the entity must consider whether the instrument meets the definition of a financial instrument. If it does not, the instrument is not within the scope of IAS 39 and cannot be a financial guarantee contract.

Representations to unspecified parties do not meet the definition of a financial instrument because they are not a contractual arrangement between the guarantor and a specified third party or parties. IAS 32.13 states that a contract is "an agreement between two or more parties that has clear economic consequences that the parties have little, if any, discretion to avoid, usually because the agreement is enforceable by law". A representation to meet the subsidiary's obligations should the subsidiary fail to meet its obligations is a representation of unspecified amounts held by unspecified parties. As such, the representation is not a contractual arrangement and is outside the scope of IAS 32 and IAS 39. In addition, IAS 32.AG12 clarifies that "liabilities or assets that are not contractual (such as income taxes that are created as a result of statutory requirements imposed by governments) are not financial liabilities or financial assets". Therefore, the guarantor would apply IAS 37 and provide for the amount it could be required to pay under the arrangement if the criteria in IAS 37.14 are met.

If the representation is a contractual arrangement between the guarantor and a specified third party over a specified amount and, therefore, does meet the definition of a financial instrument and is within the scope of IAS 39, the entity must consider whether the instrument meets the definition of a financial guarantee contract in IAS 39.9. A financial guarantee contract only exists when the guarantor agrees to make specified payments to reimburse the holder for a loss it incurs because a specified debtor fails to make payment when due in accordance with the original or modified terms of a debt instrument. If the guarantor has not explicitly stated that it regards financial guarantee contracts as insurance under IFRS 4 it must measure the contract as described in this section above.

A contractual arrangement that does meet the definition of a financial instrument but does not meet the definition of a financial guarantee contract is measured at fair value through profit or loss because the contractual arrangement meets the definition of a derivative in IAS 39.9. Such a contractual arrangement meets the definition of a derivative because: (1) the initial investment received by the guarantor is small compared with the amount that could be required to be paid if a claim is made under the contractual arrangement, (2) the fair value of the arrangement is driven by the credit risk of the obligor, and (3) the arrangement will be settled either at a future date, should the holder make a claim against the guarantor, or at its maturity since expiration at maturity is a form of settlement. [IAS 39.IG.B.7]

An arrangement whereby a parent agrees to make future contributions or to lend to a subsidiary is not a financial guarantee contract for the parent in its separate financial statements. The arrangement is not a financial guarantee contract as the parent is not making payments in the instance when the subsidiary has suffered loss on a specified debt instrument. Even if the subsidiary only makes a claim from the parent when it is in financial difficulty, the exercise of the claim is more akin to either a claim under a loan commitment (and written and purchased loan commitments are outside the scope of IAS 39 – see **3.5** below) or a commitment for a capital contribution which by analogy to loan commitment accounting would also be considered outside the scope of IAS 39.

A contract that requires an entity to make payments when the counterparty to a derivative contract (for example a foreign currency forward contract or an interest rate swap) fails to make payment is not a financial guarantee contract. A financial guarantee contract is a contract 'that requires the issuer to make specified payments to reimburse the holder for a loss it incurs because a specified debtor fails to make payment when due in accordance with the original or modified terms of a debt instrument'. [IAS 39.9] As a derivative is not a debt instrument, the contract does not meet the definition of a financial guarantee contract.

2.3.3 *Weather derivatives*

Contracts requiring payments based on climatic, geological or other physical variables are inside the scope of IFRS 4 if they meet the definition of an insurance contract. Those based on climatic variables are sometimes referred to as 'weather derivatives'. Examples of climatic, geological and other physical variables include:

- the number of inches of rainfall or snow in a particular area;
- temperature in a particular area or for a specified period of time; and
- the severity of earthquakes.

If these contracts are not within the scope of IFRS 4, and they meet the definition of a derivative in **chapter 16**, they are within the scope of IAS 32, IAS 39 and IFRS 7.

2.4 Contracts for contingent consideration in a business combination

For acquirers that have not yet adopted IFRS 3(2008), contracts for contingent consideration in a business combination are excluded from IAS 32, IAS 39 and IFRS 7. They are subject to the provisions of IFRS 3(2004). This exemption applies only to the acquirer, not to the seller.

The revised version of IFRS 3 *Business Combinations* issued in January 2008 amended IAS 32, IAS 39 and IFRS 7. Under IFRS 3(2008), contracts for contingent consideration are no longer outside the scope of these standards for the acquirer. Thus, if a contract for contingent consideration meets the definition of a financial instrument it will be in the scope of these standards for both the acquirer and the seller. Paragraph BC349 in the Basis for Conclusions accompanying IFRS 3(2008) states that 'the boards noted that most contingent consideration obligations are financial instruments, and many are derivative instruments'. IFRS 3(2008) applies prospectively to business combinations for which the acquisition date is on or after the beginning of the first annual reporting period beginning on or after 1 July 2009.

Irrespective of whether IFRS 3(2008) has been adopted, a seller's contract for contingent consideration is not scoped out of IAS 32, IAS 39 and IFRS 7. The seller will recognise a financial asset for the contract for contingent consideration. The measurement of this financial asset will depend on the facts and circumstances of the contractual arrangement. As the cash flows under the contract for contingent consideration are often derived from an underlying such as the future performance of the entity that has been sold the asset will often meet the definition of a derivative in its entirety (see **chapter 15**) and will therefore be measured as at fair value through profit or loss. Alternatively, the contingent consideration asset may be partly a loan and receivable measured at amortised cost with a non-closely related embedded derivative measured at fair value through profit or loss (see **chapter 16**) if the asset is not designated as at fair value through profit or loss at initial recognition.

2.5 Contracts to buy or sell non-financial items

IAS 32, IAS 39 and IFRS 7 primarily deal with contracts that are financial items, however, they also capture some contracts to buy or sell non-financial items. Contracts to buy or sell non-financial items that can be settled net (either in cash or by exchanging financial instruments) are within the scope of IAS 32, IAS 39 and IFRS 7 unless they were entered into, and continue to be held for the purpose of the receipt of the non-financial item in accordance with the entity's expected purchase, sale or usage requirements. [IAS 39.5]

2.5.1 *Net settlement*

Net settlement can be in cash, another financial instrument, or by exchanging financial instruments. It can be achieved in many ways:

[IAS 39.6]

(a) the contractual terms may permit either party to settle it net in cash or by exchanging financial instruments;

(b) settlement may not be explicit under the terms of the contract, but the entity has a past practice of net settling similar contracts (see **2.5.3** below);

(c) for similar contracts, the entity has a past practice of taking delivery of the underlying and selling it within a short period after delivery for the purpose of generating a profit from short-term price fluctuations or from dealer's margin; or

(d) the non-financial item that is the subject of the contract is readily convertible to cash.

2.5.2 *Non-performance penalties*

The terms of a contract need to be evaluated in detail since net settlement provisions may be implicit rather than explicit.

A non-performance penalty in a purchase order, where the amount of the penalty is calculated by reference to the changes in the price of the item that is the subject of the contract, is an example of an implicit net settlement provision.

Example 2.5.2A

Non-performance penalty equivalent to net settlement

Entity A enters into a forward purchase agreement with Entity B to buy 100 units of a commodity at £1.00 per unit. Entity A defaults on the forward when the prevailing market price of the commodity is £0.75 per unit. Under the non-performance penalty provisions incorporated into the contract, Entity A has to pay Entity B a penalty of £25, i.e. 100 x (£1.00 – £0.75). The non-performance penalty represents an implicit net settlement provision.

Conversely, fixed penalties or normal handling fees do not amount to net settlement.

> **Example 2.5.2B**
>
> **Non-performance penalty not equivalent to net settlement**
>
> Entity A enters into a contract to purchase wheat, which will be used in its manufacturing operations. The delivery contract requires a non-performance penalty of £1 million if A fails to take delivery of the wheat. This is a fixed penalty and does not provide for net settlement because the £1 million payment amount is not based on changes in the price of wheat (the reference asset).

2.5.3 *Past practice*

Contracts where there is a past practice of either net settling or purchasing and selling the underlying within a short period after delivery with a view to making a short-term profit (i.e. (b) or (c) in the above list in **2.5.1**) are always within the scope of the Standards. Such contracts cannot be argued to be entered into and continue to be held for the purpose of the receipt or delivery of the non-financial item in accordance with the entity's expected purchase, sale or usage requirements, since the entity's activities clearly indicate that this is not the case.

> **Example 2.5.3A**
>
> **Rolling contracts until physical delivery**
>
> Entity C is in the business of milling maize and using it as input into its production process. Entity C's procurement strategy for maize includes purchasing futures on a futures exchange. Due to the significant quantity of maize needed, Entity C enters into forward purchases of maize to secure the level required for the running of its business. The intention at the outset is to take physical delivery of the maize under these contracts.
>
> In January 20X6, Entity C procures maize for its 20X6 requirements. The longest available maturity of maize futures contracts is to July 20X6. C's purchasing policy requires it to secure maize at least for 9 months, i.e. as far out as September 20X6. Hence, Entity C enters into a larger number of July 20X6 contracts with a view to rolling some of them to September 20X6.
>
> In April 2006, Entity C will close out some of its July 20X6 forwards at market value at the time, and take out September 20X6 forwards. Entity C will take physical delivery of the maize under the September contracts only.
>
> Entity C's practice of net settling some of its July futures contracts (i.e. its practice of net settling similar contracts) prevents it from arguing that it enters into forward contracts for the receipt of maize in accordance with its

expected purchase, sale or usage requirements. Accordingly, both the July and September contracts are within the scope of IAS 39.

Example 2.5.3B

Choice of cash or physical settlement (1)

[Extract from IAS 39.IG.A.1]

Entity XYZ enters into a fixed price forward contract to purchase one million kilograms of copper in accordance with its expected usage requirements. The contract permits XYZ to take physical delivery of the copper at the end of twelve months or to pay or receive a net settlement in cash, based on the change in fair value of copper.

If XYZ intends to settle the contract by taking delivery and has no history for similar contracts of settling net in cash or of taking delivery of the copper and selling it within a short period after delivery for the purpose of generating a profit from short-term fluctuations in price or dealer's margin, the contract is not accounted for as a derivative under IAS 39. Instead, it is accounted for as an executory contract [*i.e. outside the scope of IAS 39*].

Example 2.5.3C

Choice of cash or physical settlement (2)

Entity A is a copper manufacturer. Entity A enters into forward contracts to sell its copper cathode to its customers. The forward contracts are homogenous and permit the entity to:

- provide physical delivery of copper at the end of the contract; or
- pay or receive a net settlement in cash based on the change in fair value of copper.

Based on its inventory levels and its production capacity, Entity A is able to meet the obligation to deliver copper should it decide to provide physical delivery of copper relating to all of its outstanding forward sales contracts.

Management claims that the intention in entering into the forward sales contracts is for the purpose of delivery of copper in accordance with its sales requirements. Historically, Entity A has a practice of net settling a portion of similar forward contracts, provided the contracts are in the money. For contracts that are out of the money, historically Entity A has opted to physically deliver.

These contracts are all homogenous and the fact that Entity A has a past practice of net settling a portion of similar forward contracts means that it cannot assert that the contracts are held for the purpose of the delivery of copper in accordance with Entity A's expected sale requirements. Hence, the forward contracts are in the scope of IAS 39 and will be accounted for as derivatives.

There are instances where an entity will net settle as part of its normal operating cycle, as opposed to net settling in order to generate profits from short-term movements in prices. This is particularly common for utility entities that need to balance the demand from their customers with the supply contracts. For example, a retail gas supplier purchases gas under long-term take-or-pay contracts. The buyer's intent is to use the contracted volumes to serve its customers. However, the demand in certain periods (usually in the summer months) falls below the minimum required contractual take. The buyer is forced to settle net since the relative scarcity of natural gas storage capacity makes it difficult to store it for later use (storage of electricity is effectively impossible, so a similar situation is likely under a power contract). This 'balancing' activity is common for gas and power entities serving retail customers since customer demand forecasts cannot be precise. The practice of net settling similar contracts makes it difficult to claim that the long-term contracts meet the definition of own use requirements contracts, and therefore they are likely to be scoped into IAS 39.

It is a matter of judgement what is past practice of net settlement. An entity will need to consider its historical behaviour, reasons for past net settlement, and relative frequency. In some cases it may be argued that an occurrence of a net settlement in the past is a result of an isolated non-recurring event that could not have been reasonably anticipated.

2.5.4 *Written options*

In addition to the restriction on contracts where there is a past practice of settling net or a practice of taking delivery of the underlying and selling it within a short period after delivery, a written option to buy or sell a non-financial item that can be settled net contractually or where the non-financial item that is the subject of the option is readily convertible to cash is always within the scope of IAS 39. However, not all written options are necessarily within the scope of IAS 39.

Example 2.5.4A

Written put with no net settlement

Entity XYZ owns an office block. It writes Entity ABC an option, allowing ABC to purchase the office block for a fixed price on a future date. The terms of the contract do not allow for it to be net settled, and the office block is not readily convertible to cash. Therefore, although Entity XYZ has written an option, the option does not fall within the scope of IAS 39.

Example 2.5.4B

Written put with possible net settlement

[Extract from IAS 39.IG.A.2]

Entity XYZ owns an office building. Entity XYZ enters into a put option with an investor that permits XYZ to put the building to the investor for CU150 million. The current value of the building is CU175 million. The option expires in five years. The option, if exercised, may be settled through physical delivery or net cash, at XYZ's option.

XYZ's accounting depends on XYZ's intention and past practice for settlement. Although the contract meets the definition of a derivative, XYZ does not account for it as a derivative [*i.e. the contract would not be in the scope of IAS 39*] if XYZ intends to settle the contract by delivering the building if Entity XYZ exercises its option and there is no past practice of settling net (IAS 39.5 and IAS 39.AG10).

The investor, however, cannot conclude that the option was entered into to meet the investor's expected purchase, sale or usage requirements because the investor does not have the ability to require delivery (IAS 39.7). In addition, the option may be settled net in cash. Therefore, the investor has to account for the contract as a derivative [*i.e. within the scope of IAS 39*]. Regardless of past practices, the investor's intention does not affect whether settlement is by delivery or in cash. The investor has written an option, and a written option in which the holder has a choice of physical settlement or net cash settlement can never satisfy the normal delivery requirement for the exemption from IAS 39 because the option writer does not have the ability to require delivery.

IAS 39 does not define a written option, with only limited discussion of written options provided in the context of hedge accounting. IAS 39.AG94 states that the potential loss on an option an entity writes could be significantly greater than the potential gain in value of a related hedged item.

Different schools of thought exist as to what is considered to be a written option in the context of contracts over non-financial items. Some focus on the existence of a premium received. This treatment is analogous to the approach described in the hedge accounting guidance, as receiving a premium, whether upfront or over the life, indicates that the party to the option is taking on a greater risk of loss and therefore is being compensated by a premium. However, in the context of contracts over a non-financial item this approach has its difficulties, largely because it can be extremely difficult to ascertain whether a premium is received over the life when this 'premium' may be included in the pricing of the non-financial item that will be delivered under the contract.

An alternative approach is to consider whether the holder of the option has the ability to exercise the option in order to make a profit. This approach assesses the pay-off characteristics of the contract. In instances where the behaviour of the holder in exercising the option is independent of price, i.e. the holder exercises the option for reasons other than the value of the underlying being greater than the strike price under the option, it could be argued that the holder exercises the option not in order to profit, but to take delivery of the non-financial item so as to meet the expected purchase, sale or usage requirements. Examples of this are electricity supply contracts to retail customers since generally electricity is considered to be readily convertible to cash in the hands of the writer of the option. As the holder of the option, the retail customer has no ability to take delivery of the electricity, store it, and sell the electricity on at a profit, i.e. the holder is unable to realise a profit from the contract. The holder's behaviour is driven simply from the need for electricity to meet the usage requirements. From the perspective of the writer of the option, i.e. the electricity seller, it can then be argued that it has not written an option.

Often an entity enters into an agreement to buy a fixed quantity of a non-financial item, but has an option to buy further quantities at the contracted price. For example, an entity enters into an agreement to buy 100 units of a non-financial item that is readily convertible into cash, which includes the ability for it to purchase a further 15 units at the same contracted price. These contracts are often referred to as having 'volumetric flexibility'. If the seller concludes that the option on the 15 units is a written option, then the whole contract for 115 units is a written option. This is because IAS 39 looks at the arrangements based on their contractual terms. The contract is a single contract over 115 units and thus it is not possible to split it into (1) a forward over 100 units classified as a normal usage requirements contract outside the scope of IAS 39, and (2) a written option over 15 units in the scope of IAS 39.

In March 2007 the IFRIC finalised a rejection notice titled *Written Options in Retail Energy Contracts*. The IFRIC discussed what is meant by 'written option' within the context of IAS 39.7. The discussion was primarily concerned with the accounting for energy supply contracts to retail customers. The rejection notice states that following an analysis of such contracts the IFRIC believes that in many situations these contracts do not meet the net settlement criteria laid out in IAS 39.5 & 6 and if this is the case, such contracts would not be considered to be within the scope of IAS 39. It is not entirely clear from the IFRIC's rejection notice whether they considered these contracts as written options over an underlying that is not readily convertible into cash and therefore not net settled per IAS 39.6(d), or whether they did not consider them written options at all and therefore viewed an analysis of ready convertibility of the underlying into cash as irrelevant.

IAS 39 does not permit a written option over a non-financial item that is 'readily convertible to cash' to be scoped out of IAS 39. IAS 39 does not provide guidance on what is considered readily convertible to cash and therefore similar guidance in US GAAP is worthy of consideration.

FASB Concepts Statement No. 5 *Recognition and Measurement in Financial Statements of Business Enterprises*, paragraph 83(a), states that assets that are readily convertible to cash 'have (i) interchangeable (fungible) units and (ii) quoted prices available in an active market that can rapidly absorb the quantity held by the entity without significantly affecting the price'. US literature provides further guidance in the Derivative Interpretations Group (DIG) Q&As which considers amongst other issues, the extent to which the cost of converting the item to cash impacts whether the instrument is a derivative or not.

2.5.5 *Expected purchase, sale and usage requirements*

Non-option contracts where either the terms of the contract permit net settlement, or where the non-financial item that is subject to the contract is readily convertible to cash (for example, many commodity contracts) must be assessed to see if they were entered into for the receipt or purchase of the item in accordance with the entity's expected purchase, sale or usage requirements.

Example 2.5.5

Purchase contract with possible net settlement

Entity X enters into a fixed-price forward contract to purchase one million tonnes of copper. Copper is traded on the London Metals Exchange and is readily convertible to cash. The contract permits X to take physical delivery of the copper at the end of 12 months or to pay or receive a net settlement in cash, based on the change in fair value of copper. Entity X does not have a practice of settling similar contracts net or taking physical delivery of copper and selling it within a short period after delivery for the purposes of generating a profit from short-term fluctuations in price.

Entity X needs to demonstrate that the contract was entered into and continues to be held for the purpose of the receipt of copper in accordance with its expected purchase or usage requirements in order for the contract to be scoped out of IAS 39. In addition to past practice, factors like the quantities involved, quality and grades of the commodity, and delivery locations would need to be considered.

Each contract must be evaluated in its entirety. For example, an entity may have a contract for 100 units, yet its expected usage requirement is for 80 units only. The entity intends to net settle the part of the contract it does not need in its normal course of business. Such partial net settlement can be achieved in different ways, for example, by entering into an offsetting contract for 20 units, or by taking delivery of all 100 units and selling 20 straight away. The entire contract falls within the scope of IAS 39 since the entire contract cannot be argued to be in accordance with the entity's expected usage requirements.

The following decision tree illustrates how to evaluate whether contracts to buy or sell non-financial items are within the scope of IAS 32, IAS 39 and IFRS 7:

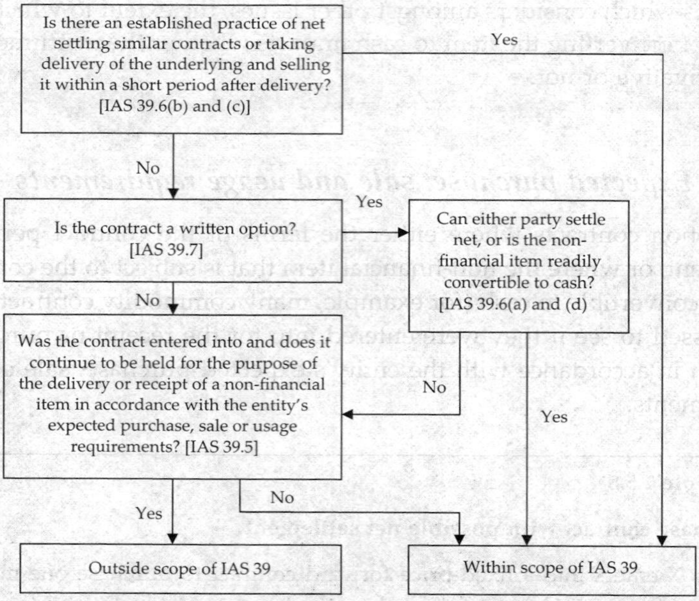

Entities may enter into multiple contracts with the same contractual terms for different reasons. Care needs to be taken in determining whether the contracts themselves should have the same accounting treatment or not. A conglomerate may enter into contracts to buy non-financial items that are used in the conglomerate's production processes for the provision of finished goods. These contracts are always physically delivered. A separate part of the business may enter into contractual arrangements with the same contractual terms but does not always physically receive the non-financial item, rather it cash settles the contract or enters into offsetting contracts as part of a trading strategy. From a group perspective it may be possible to differentiate the two portfolios of contracts in the two separate businesses within the conglomerate and therefore account for them differently only if the contracts are entered into separately and not in contemplation of each other; there are no transfers between the businesses within the group; the businesses are managed independently of each other; and the strategy of each business is sufficiently different that the different settlement behaviour of each business is reasonable. In practice, it is unlikely that such a distinction is possible as different parts of a group often choose to transact with each other as opposed to separately entering into offsetting transactions outside the group and incurring additional transaction costs.

2.5.6 *Change of settlement terms*

The terms of a contract, or the intentions of an entity, may change over time. A contract outside the scope of IAS 39 will continue to be treated as such only if it continues to be held for the purpose of the receipt or delivery of a non-financial item in accordance with the entity's expected purchase, sale or usage requirements.

Example 2.5.6

Change of terms to include net settlement

Two parties enter into a contract for the delivery of a non-financial asset. There is no net settlement provision in the contract, no established market mechanism or side agreement, and no history of net settlement.

Subsequently, the parties agree to settle the contract net. From the time the decision to settle net is made, the contract will be recognised and measured under IAS 39 since from that point the contract no longer continues to be for the purpose of the receipt of the non-financial asset in accordance with the expected purchase, sale or usage requirements.

2.6 Share-based payments

IAS 32, IAS 39 and IFRS 7 exclude from their scope financial instruments, contracts and obligations under share-based payment transactions to which IFRS 2 *Share-based Payment* applies, except for contracts over non-financial items that are within the scope of IAS 39 (see **2.5** above). However, the scope of IAS 32 makes it clear that treasury shares that are purchased, sold, issued or cancelled in connection with employee share option plans, employee share purchase plans, and all other share-based payment arrangements, are in the scope of IAS 32 (see **section 5** of **chapter 15**).

2.7 Construction contract receivables

Construction contract receivables are measured and presented in accordance with IAS 11 *Construction Contracts*. The financial instruments standards do not specifically scope out these contracts and therefore consideration must be given as to whether such receivables are financial instruments. Critical in the definition of a financial asset is a right to cash or another financial asset. In construction contract arrangements the amount of work incurred by the constructor may be in excess of the amount that is billed. IAS 11.42 requires the 'gross amount due from customers for contract work' to be recognised in the statement of financial position. This amount is determined in accordance with IAS 11.43 as the net amount of costs incurred plus recognised profits less the sum of recognised losses and progress billings, for all contracts in progress for which costs incurred plus recognised profits (less recognised losses) exceeds progress billings. An entity must consider whether the amount recognised in accordance with IAS 11 can be contractually billed or recovered.

Example 2.7

Gross amount due from customer for contract work

Entity A has entered into a contract with Entity B for the construction of a single asset, such as a building. The contract is within the scope of IAS 11, but is specifically not within the scope of IFRIC 12 *Service Concession Arrangements*. Because the outcome of the contract can be estimated reliably, contract revenue and contract costs associated with the construction contract are recognised as revenue and expenses, respectively, by reference to the stage of completion of the contract activity at the end of the reporting period in accordance with IAS 11.22. At the end of the reporting period, costs incurred plus recognised profits (less recognised losses) exceed progress billings and Entity A presents an amount in its statement of financial position as 'the gross amount due from customers for contract work'.

Entity A bills Entity B in accordance with the construction contract only when specific work performed by Entity A has been certified as completed. These billings are recognised in the statement of financial position as a separate financial asset because they represent a contractual right to receive cash and thus meet the definition of a financial asset in IAS 32.11.

> The gross amount due from customer for contract work is not a financial asset in accordance with IAS 32.11. Such amounts cannot contractually be billed and recovered from Entity B because Entity A's work has not been certified as completed. The asset is not a financial asset because, in accordance with IAS 32.11, it is not 'a contractual right . . . to receive cash or another financial asset from another entity' at the end of the reporting period. It is only when Entity A's work is certified as completed that (i) Entity A becomes party to a contractual right to receive cash or other financial asset and (ii) the gross amount due from customers for contract work becomes a separate financial asset.

If a construction contract receivable is not a financial instrument then IAS 39 and IFRS 7 do not apply to that balance.

3 Additional scope exclusions of IAS 39

In addition to the above scope exemptions, IAS 39 has some further exemptions as follows:

- financial instruments issued by the entity that meet the definition of equity instruments in accordance with IAS 32 (see **3.1** below);
- contracts to buy or sell an acquiree in a business combination (see **3.2** below);
- certain reimbursement rights (see **3.3** below);
- rights and obligations under leases, although in certain circumstances the derecognition, impairment and embedded derivative provisions of IAS 39 apply (see **3.4** below); and
- certain loan commitments (see **3.5** below).

Each of the above is considered in turn.

3.1 Equity instruments of the entity

Financial instruments issued by an entity that meet the definition of equity instruments in IAS 32 (see **section 2** of **chapter 15**) are outside the scope of IAS 39. This exemption includes standalone equity instruments, such as ordinary shares, as well as derivatives over own equity that exchange a fixed amount of cash or other financial asset for a fixed number of equity instruments. The exemption applies only to the issuer of the equity instrument. The holder of the instrument should apply the recognition and measurement criteria of IAS 39.

Following the amendment to IAS 32, *Puttable financial instruments and obligations arising on liquidation*, issued in February 2008, some instruments previously classified as financial liabilities are classified as equity (see **2.1.2.4** in **chapter 15**). The IAS 32 amendment also amended IFRS 7 to exclude these instruments classified as equity from the scope of IFRS 7. [IFRS 7.3(f)]

IFRS 7 scopes out derivatives over own equity that meet the definition of equity. IFRS 7 does not appear to have a scope exception for non-derivative instruments classified as equity, such as ordinary shares. This appears to be an oversight in the drafting of the Standard as IFRS 7.BC8 states that the scope exception of IFRS 7 is intended to be the same as IAS 32 (prior to IFRS 7 being issued) with one exception, namely 'derivatives based on interests in subsidiaries, associates or joint ventures if the derivatives meet the definition of an equity instrument in IAS 32'. The basis of conclusions justifies this position by stating that these instruments are not remeasured and hence 'do not expose the issuer to balance sheet and income statement risk' and the disclosures about the significance of financial instruments for financial position and performance are not relevant to equity instruments. In addition, it states that these instruments are excluded from the scope of IFRS 7, but they are within the scope of IAS 32 for the purpose of determining whether they meet the definition of equity instruments. It appears reasonable to conclude that the scope exclusions for derivatives over own equity that meet the definition of equity would also apply to non-derivatives that meet the definition of equity as the justification in the basis of conclusions of IFRS 7 would be equally relevant.

3.2 Contracts to buy or sell an acquiree in a business combination

Contracts between an acquirer and a vendor in a business combination to buy or sell an acquiree at a future date are outside the scope of IAS 39. The application of IAS 39.2(g) is assessed at the time the holder enters into the derivative contract. If the contract is a forward contract, whether partly prepaid or not, which will lead to a certain business combination, the exemption applies and the forward contract is outside the scope of IAS 39. The same analysis would be applied to a combination of a put and a call option where the strike prices, exercise dates and notionals are equal, such that the combination of the put and the call is economically equivalent to a forward contract that will result in a business combination that is certain to occur. Equally, an option that is very deeply in-the-money at inception because the strike price is very low compared with the value of the shares to be delivered under it, which is analogous to a forward contract, is also outside the scope of IAS 39. Contracts that have settlement alternatives that may not result in all cases in the delivery of shares to the acquirer will be within the scope of IAS 39 as the exemption within IAS 39.2(g) will not apply.

The above scenarios should be distinguished from contracts between an acquirer and vendor that are options which are not economically equivalent to a forward contract. IAS 27 provides guidance as to whether an option represents a 'potential voting right that is currently exercisable or convertible'. If the option is currently exercisable but is not an in-substance present ownership interest, the appropriate accounting will depend on whether control currently exists. If control does exist, the parent's proportion of the acquiree in the consolidated financial statements is determined taking into account the present ownership interests which do not reflect the possible exercise or conversion of potential voting rights. In such circumstances the ownership interest that excludes the exercise of the currently exercisable option is a subsidiary as there is control and therefore thought will need to be given as to whether the currently exercisable option (to acquire a non-controlling interest) meets the definition of equity in the consolidated financial statements (see **section 6** in **chapter 15**). If the option meets the definition of equity it is outside the scope of IAS 39. Otherwise, it will be within the scope of IAS 39 and the exemption in IAS 39.2(g) does not apply.

If the option (that is not economically equivalent to a forward) is currently exercisable and it gives the holder the ability to control the target entity, and is an in-substance present ownership interest, then control exists and the parent's proportion of the acquiree in the consolidated financial statements is determined reflecting the in substance present ownership interest in accordance with IAS 27. The option is not subject to the requirements of IAS 39 in such a case as it is treated as giving rise to a present ownership interest rather than being a derivative to acquire such an interest in the future.

If the option (that is not economically equivalent to a forward) is not currently exercisable and would give the holder the ability to control the target entity only when it becomes exercisable the scope exemption within IAS 39.2(g) also does not apply. The option will not always result in a business combination to buy or sell an acquiree at a future date and therefore is in the scope of IAS 39.

> The IAS 39.2(g) exemption applies equally to the acquirer as well as the vendor. Therefore, if the acquirer applies the exemption as the contract will result in a future business combination, the vendor equally applies the exemption and scopes out its contract to sell its subsidiary to the acquirer in its consolidated financial statements.

Irrespective of IAS 39.2(g), the contract may also be outside the scope of IAS 39 for the vendor as the contract may meet the definition of equity in the case where the contract is a forward sale of shares in a subsidiary for a fixed amount of functional currency cash.

In 2007 the IFRIC was asked to interpret whether the IAS 39.2(g) scope exemption applies only to binding contracts to acquire shares that constitute a controlling interest in another entity within the period necessary to complete a business combination, or if it applies more widely, and also whether it applies to similar transactions, such as those to acquire an interest in an associate. In January 2008 the IFRIC acknowledged that the wording in IAS 39.2(g) was ambiguous and could lead to diversity in practice. For this reason, the IFRIC referred the issue to the IASB where the Board tentatively decided in April 2008 to amend IAS 39.2(g) as part of the next annual improvements project. The amendment to IAS 39 would clarify that the scope exception applies only to forward contracts entered into before the acquisition date (i.e. before the date the acquirer obtains control of the acquiree) by an acquirer and a vendor in a business combination, to buy or sell an acquiree at a future date. The Board also tentatively decided that the exception in IAS 39.2(g) should not be applied by analogy to investments in associates and other similar transactions.

3.3 Certain reimbursement rights

Rights to payments to reimburse the entity for expenditure it is required to make to settle a liability that it recognises as a provision in accordance with IAS 37 *Provisions, Contingent Liabilities and Contingent Assets*, or for which, in an earlier period, it recognised a provision in accordance with IAS 37, are outside the scope of IAS 39. [IAS 39.2(j)] Such rights are within the scope of IAS 37 and are recognised as a separate asset when, and only when, it is virtually certain that the reimbursement will be received if and when the entity settles the liability. [IAS 37.53]

3.4 Rights and obligations under lease contracts

Rights and obligations under lease contracts may meet the definition of a financial instrument. In a finance lease, a lease receivable recognised by the lessor represents the lessor's right to receive a stream of cash flows. This receivable is substantially the same as blended payments of principal and interest under a loan agreement. Hence, a finance lease is a contract that gives rise to a financial asset in the hands of the lessor and also gives rise to a financial liability in the hands of the lessee. Operating leases, on the other hand, are generally regarded as uncompleted contracts whereby lessors provide the use of assets in exchange for a fee for their service.

Accordingly an operating lease is not regarded as a financial instrument (except as regards individual payments currently due and payable). This continues to be the case even if the operating lease is regarded as an onerous contract and a provision has been recognised in accordance with IAS 37 *Provisions, Contingent Liabilities and Contingent Assets.* IAS 17 *Leases* sets out the accounting framework for leases and hence leases are, for the most part, outside of the scope of all three Standards. However:

- lease receivables recognised by a lessor are subject to the derecognition (see **section 3** of **chapter 19**) and impairment (see **section 6** of **chapter 18**) provisions of IAS 39;
- finance lease payables recognised by a lessee are subject to the derecognition provisions of IAS 39 (see **section 3** of **chapter 19**);
- derivatives embedded in lease contracts are within the scope of IAS 39 (see **section 9** of **chapter 17**); and
- finance leases are within the scope of IFRS 7.

3.5 Loan commitments

Loan commitments that cannot be settled net in cash or another financial instrument are outside the scope of IAS 39, unless the entity designates them as financial liabilities at fair value through profit or loss. If an entity has a past practice of selling the asset resulting from a loan commitment shortly after its origination, it should apply IAS 39 to all loan commitments in the same class.

Loan commitments that can be settled net in cash or another financial instrument are derivatives within the scope of IAS 39. Instalment payments do not constitute net settlement. Thus, for example, a mortgage construction loan that is paid out in instalments in line with the progress of the construction is not within the scope of IAS 39. [IAS 39.2(h)]

A financial institution may write a loan commitment to a large corporate borrower as a lead lender with the expressed intention to sell part of the loan immediately to other financial institutions when lent. The intention to sell part of the loan is part of its predetermined credit risk management. At inception of the loan commitment the financial institution cannot assert that it does not have a past practice of selling the asset resulting from a loan commitment shortly after its origination and therefore cannot consider the loan commitment wholly outside the scope of IAS 39. The financial institution may be able to demonstrate that, consistent with its predetermined credit risk management, only part of the loan that may be originated from the loan commitment is intended to be sold, and if so, only that proportion of the loan commitment is in the scope of IAS 39 and is fair valued through profit or loss. If the loan is originated the part of the loan commitment that is fair valued through profit or loss will be derecognised and will be incorporated into the initial carrying value of the resulting loan.

If an entity commits to providing a loan at a below-market interest rate it should initially recognise the commitment at fair value. Subsequently, the commitment is measured at the higher of:

[IAS 39.47(d)]

(i) the amount determined under IAS 37 *Provisions, Contingent Liabilities and Contingent Assets*; and

(ii) the amount initially recognised less, where appropriate, cumulative amortisation recognised in accordance with IAS 18 *Revenue*.

Loan commitments can either be optional, i.e. provide a borrower with the right to borrow in the future from a specified lender, or be non-optional, i.e. the borrower must borrow from the specified lender. In all cases the lender will lend funds to the borrower either when the borrower exercises its right to borrow or, in the case of non-optional loan commitments, per the specified conditions in the contract. If a contract requires or gives the option for an entity to acquire a debt instrument, this arrangement is not a loan commitment as a lending will not take place. The arrangement is a derivative financial instrument which will be measured as at fair value through profit or loss except if it meets the regular way exemption as described in **section 2** in **chapter 19**.

The scoping out of loan commitments as described above applies equally to the holder (the borrower) as it does to the writer (the lender) of the loan commitment. If a loan commitment is not within the scope of IAS 39, it is accounted for in accordance with IAS 37; however, all loan commitments are subject to the derecognition provisions of IAS 39.

Where the loan to be originated under a loan commitment will include a non-closely related embedded derivative (see **section 3** in **chapter 17**) the question arises as to whether it is still permissible for the loan commitment to be scoped out of IAS 39. Once the loan is originated under the commitment, the non-closely related embedded derivative will be separated from the host loan contract and separately accounted for as at fair value through profit and loss (unless the whole loan is designated at fair value through profit and loss at initial recognition – see **3.1** in **chapter 14** and **7.1.2** in **chapter 15**). It could be argued that applying the scope exemption in such a situation creates a measurement inconsistency between the measurement of the loan commitment (outside the scope of IAS 39 and not measured at fair value) and the subsequent measurement of the loan (within the scope of IAS 39 and either wholly at fair value through profit and loss if so designated or in part measured at fair value in the case of a separately recognised embedded derivative). However, it should be noted that the Standard already allows such a measurement inconsistency where a loan commitment that will result in a loan not containing any embedded derivatives is outside the scope of IAS 39 (and not measured at fair value) and the loan subsequently originated under the commitment is designated at fair value through profit and loss under certain conditions. It seems, therefore, appropriate that the scope exemption for loan commitments that will result in loans with separately accounted embedded derivatives should still apply if the relevant conditions are met, i.e. the loan commitment cannot be settled net in cash, the entity has not designated it as at fair value through profit and loss, and the entity does not have a past practice of selling the assets resulting from loan commitments shortly after origination.

To illustrate, Entity X may enter into a firm commitment to lend to Entity Y. The loan to be originated under the commitment will be a loan which the lender can convert into a fixed number of equity shares of the borrower. Once originated, the lender will have a loan asset with a non-closely related embedded derivative and the analysis in the paragraph above would apply. For Entity X the loan commitment would be outside the scope of IAS 39.

From Entity Y's perspective, the loan commitment is a right to jointly borrow cash and issue a derivative over its own equity. The loan commitment is partly a derivative over debt and partly a derivative over a derivative over Entity Y's equity. The definition of a financial liability (see **section 2** in **chapter 15**) makes it clear that a derivative over a derivative over own equity would itself not meet the definition of equity and therefore it could be argued that the loan commitment cannot be considered as outside the scope of IAS 39. However, IAS 39.BC15 recognises that all loan commitments are in fact derivatives that are excluded from the scope of IAS 39. Consequently, it is reasonable to consider such a loan commitment in the hands of the issuer as also being outside the scope of IAS 39.

14 Financial instruments: financial assets

1 Introduction

IAS 39 prescribes how a financial asset should be classified. The classification of an asset will then drive how the asset is subsequently measured.

All financial assets are required to be classified in one of the four primary classification categories. Two of these categories, 'held-to-maturity' and 'loans and receivables' result in amortised cost measurement and the other two categories 'fair value through profit or loss' and 'available-for-sale' result in fair value measurement.

This chapter discusses financial assets in the following sections:

Section 2	Definition of a financial asset
Section 3	Classification of financial assets
Section 4	Reclassifications
Section 5	Classification of financial assets acquired in a business combination

2 Definition of a financial asset

IAS 32.11 defines a financial asset as any asset that is:

(a) cash;

(b) an equity instrument of another entity;

(c) a contractual right:

 (i) to receive cash or another financial asset from another entity; or

 (ii) to exchange financial assets or financial liabilities with another entity under conditions that are potentially favourable to the entity; or

(d) a contract that will or may be settled in the entity's own equity instruments and is:

(i) a non-derivative for which the entity is or may be obliged to receive a variable number of the entity's own equity instruments; or

(ii) a derivative that will or may be settled other than by the exchange of a fixed amount of cash or another financial asset for a fixed number of the entity's own equity instruments. For this purpose the entity's own equity instruments do not include instruments that are themselves contracts for the future receipt or delivery of the entity's own equity instruments.

A deposit of cash with a bank or similar institution is a financial asset because it represents the contractual right of the depositor to obtain cash from the institution or to draw a cheque or similar instrument against the balance in favour of a creditor in payment of a financial liability.

Common examples of financial assets representing a contractual right to receive cash in the future are trade accounts receivable, notes and loans receivable, and debt securities. Another type of financial asset is one for which the economic benefit to be received is a financial asset other than cash, for example, a note payable in treasury bonds which gives the holder the contractual right to receive treasury bonds, not cash.

Gold bullion is not a financial instrument, it is a commodity. Although bullion is highly liquid, there is no contractual right to receive cash or another financial asset inherent in the bullion. [IAS 39.IG.B.1] Where the future economic benefit is the receipt of goods or services, such as prepaid expenses, the asset is not a financial asset. Also, assets that are a right to receive cash but are not contractual such as tax receivables are not financial assets as they arise from statutory requirements. [IAS 32.AG12]

The definition of a financial asset also includes certain derivative and non-derivative contracts indexed to, or settled in, an issuer's equity instruments.

Example 2

Derivative financial asset

On 1 February 20X0 Entity E enters into a contract with Entity F to receive the fair value of 1,000 of Entity E's own ordinary shares in exchange for a payment of £104,000 in cash (i.e. £104 per share) on 31 January 20X1. Under the terms of the contract, settlement will be net in cash. The market price per share on 1 February 20X0 is £100.

> The initial value of the forward contract on 1 February 20X0 is zero. On 31 December 20X0, the share price has increased and, as a result, the fair value of the forward contract has increased to £6,300. Entity E recognises a derivative asset of £6,300.

For further detail on the classification of contracts indexed to or settled in an entity's own equity instruments as derivative assets or liabilities, gross liabilities or equity, by the issuer, see **section 6** in **chapter 15**.

3 Classification of financial assets

Every financial asset that falls within the scope of IAS 39 must be classified into one of the following four primary categories:

- at fair value through profit or loss (FVTPL);
- available-for-sale (AFS);
- loans and receivables (LR); or
- held-to-maturity (HTM).

This classification is important as it drives the subsequent measurement of the asset (i.e. whether the asset is held at fair value or amortised cost). In the above list, assets in the first two categories are measured at fair value, whilst those in the last two categories are measured at amortised cost. The only exception to this rule is equity instruments that do not have a quoted market price in an active market and whose fair value cannot be reliably measured, and derivatives that are linked to and must be settled by delivery of such an unquoted equity instrument, which are instead held at cost, see **3.1.6** in **chapter 18**.

Different classification categories that are possible for different financial assets are illustrated below:

	Type of instrument		
Classification	**Investment in a debt security**	**Investment in an equity security for which fair value can be reliably measured**	**Derivatives and embedded derivatives**
FVTPL • held for trading	■	■	■

• designated at FVTPL	■	■	
Loans and receivables	■		
Held-to-maturity	■		
Available-for-sale	■	■	

3.1 Financial assets at fair value through profit or loss (FVTPL)

FVTPL has two sub-categories. The first includes any financial asset that is designated on initial recognition as one to be measured at fair value with fair value changes in profit or loss (except for investments in equity instruments and derivatives that are linked to and must be settled by delivery of equity instruments, where the equity instrument does not have a quoted market price in an active market for which fair value is reliably determinable – see **3.1.6** in **chapter 18**). This designation is irrevocable. The second category includes financial assets classified as held for trading. All derivative assets are held for trading financial assets measured at FVTPL, except for derivatives that are designated and effective hedging instruments. If a derivative asset is a hedging instrument in a cash flow hedge or a hedge of a net investment in a foreign operation, part of the fair value gains/losses will be recognised in other comprehensive income. Fair value gains/losses for a derivative asset that is a hedging instrument in a fair value hedge will always be recognised in profit or loss, the same treatment as if the instrument was not in a hedge relationship at all. See **2.2** in **chapter 20** on cash flow hedge accounting and **2.3** in **chapter 20** on hedges of a net investment in a foreign operation.

3.1.1 Designation at FVTPL

There are many reasons why an entity may wish to designate a financial instrument as at FVTPL:

- it eliminates an accounting mismatch;
- it allows an entity to avoid the burden of hedge accounting requirements (see **chapter 20**), for example designating, assessing, and measuring effectiveness where classification of both items at fair value through profit or loss achieves a similar result as if fair value hedge accounting had been applied;
- it de-emphasises interpretative issues of when an item is appropriately considered to be 'held for trading'; or

- when applied to hybrid instruments (see **chapter 17**), it eliminates the burden of separating embedded derivatives that are not considered to be closely related to the host contract as the fair value of the whole contractual arrangement is then recognised in profit or loss.

A financial asset or a financial liability may upon initial recognition be designated as at FVTPL only if it meets one of the following conditions:

(a) it eliminates or significantly reduces a measurement or recognition inconsistency that would otherwise arise from measuring assets or liabilities or recognising the gains and losses on them on different bases (commonly referred to as an 'accounting mismatch');

(b) a group of financial assets, financial liabilities or both is managed and its performance is evaluated on a fair value basis, in accordance with a documented risk management or investment strategy, and information about the group is provided internally on that basis to the entity's key management personnel (as defined in IAS 24 *Related Party Disclosures*), for example the entity's board of directors and chief executive officer; or

(c) in the case of a hybrid contract containing one or more embedded derivatives, an entity may designate the entire hybrid (combined) contract as a financial asset or financial liability as at FVTPL unless:

- the embedded derivative does not significantly modify the cash flows that otherwise would be required by the contract; or
- it is clear with little or no analysis when a similar hybrid instrument is first considered that separation of the embedded derivative is prohibited, for example a prepayment option embedded in a loan that permits the holder to prepay the loan for approximately its amortised cost, (see **7.1** in **chapter 17**).

The election to FVTPL has to be made at initial recognition of the financial instrument. Once an entity has elected to use the fair value option for a financial asset or financial liability it is not allowed to revoke this election. This is the case even if the instrument giving rise to an accounting mismatch is derecognised. This is different from the approach taken when employing hedge accounting (see **chapter 17**) where an entity is free to revoke such a designation at any time.

The fair value option is unavailable for investments in equity instruments that do not have a quoted market price in an active market, and whose fair value cannot be reliably measured (see **section 5** in **chapter 18**).

It should be noted that the requirements for determining a reliable measure of the fair value of a financial asset or financial liability, apply equally to items that are measured at fair value and to those that are only disclosed at fair value (see **3.1.6** in **chapter 18**).

The decision by an entity to designate a financial asset or a financial liability as at FVTPL is similar to an accounting policy choice in that the result of applying the fair value option should provide reliable and more relevant information about the effects of transactions, other events and conditions on the entity's financial position, financial performance or cash flows. [IAS 39.AG4C] However, an important difference between an accounting policy choice and the fair value option is that the latter can be applied on an instrument by instrument basis. The fair value option cannot be applied to a part of a financial instrument, the option must be applied to the financial instrument in its entirety.

3.1.1.1 Eliminates or significantly reduces an accounting mismatch

The following are examples of where applying the fair value option can significantly reduce a measurement or recognition inconsistency.

- In the absence of designation as at FVTPL, a financial asset would often be classified as available-for-sale (with most changes in fair value recognised in other comprehensive income) while a related liability would often be measured at amortised cost (with changes in fair value not recognised). In such circumstances, an entity may conclude that its financial statements would provide more relevant information if both instruments were classified as at FVTPL. [IAS 39.AG4D]

- An entity's liabilities may have cash flows that are contractually linked to the performance of assets that would often be classified as available-for-sale. For example, an insurer may have liabilities that pay benefits based on realised / unrealised investment returns on a specified pool of the insurer's assets. If the measurement of those liabilities reflects current market prices, classifying the assets as at FVTPL means that changes in the fair value of the financial assets are recognised in profit or loss in the same period as related changes in the value of the liabilities. [IAS 39.AG4E(a)]

- An entity may have liabilities under insurance contracts whose measurement incorporates current information (as permitted by IFRS 4 *Insurance Contracts*), and related financial assets would often be classified as available-for-sale or measured at amortised cost. Classifying the assets as at FVTPL means that changes in the fair value of the financial assets are recognised in profit or loss in the same period as related changes in the value of the liabilities. [IAS 39.AG4E(b)]

- An entity may have financial assets, financial liabilities or both that share a risk, such as interest rate risk, that gives rise to opposite changes in fair value that tend to offset each other. Yet, often only some of the instruments are measured at FVTPL (for example, derivatives). Furthermore, the requirements for hedge accounting may not be met, for example because the requirements for effectiveness are not met. Classifying the assets and liabilities at FVTPL will achieve an accounting offset that reflects the existing natural economic offset. [IAS 39.AG4E(c)]
- An entity may have financial assets, financial liabilities or both that share a risk, such as interest rate risk, that gives rise to opposite changes in fair value of those assets and liabilities that tend to offset each other. The assets and liabilities may be measured on a different basis and hedge accounting cannot be applied because none of the instruments is a derivative. Classifying the assets and liabilities at FVTPL will achieve an accounting offset that reflects the existing natural economic offset. [IAS 39.AG4E(d)]

Example 3.1.1.1A

Fair value option: issued fixed rate debt

Entity A issues fixed rate debt. In order to economically hedge the fair value risk associated with interest payments on fixed rate debt, Entity A concurrently enters into an interest rate swap with a bank (receive fixed, pay floating), which has the same terms and payment dates as the debt. The interest rate swap is a derivative that must be fair valued through profit or loss. The entity does not wish to apply fair value hedge accounting as it does not wish to prepare any hedge documentation and does not have the processes in place to monitor hedge effectiveness. By designating the fixed rate debt as at FVTPL on initial recognition, the entity will achieve a natural substantial offset in profit or loss with the held for trading derivative. As the instruments both share a common risk (interest rate risk) the entity will seek to demonstrate that applying the fair value option results in more relevant information because it significantly reduces a measurement inconsistency that would otherwise arise from measuring the derivative at fair value with gains and losses in profit or loss, and carrying the debt at amortised cost. [IAS 39.9]

Example 3.1.1.1B

Fair value option: intragroup derivative

Subsidiary S issues a five-year fixed rate bond. To hedge against the interest rate risk it enters into a pay-variable-receive-fixed interest rate swap with its Parent P. In the subsidiary's financial statements, the bond is designated as at FVTPL. The designation cannot be applied in the consolidated financial statements as the derivative is eliminated on consolidation. If the parent or another group entity had a derivative instrument with a third party that shares a common risk with the bond, a different designation could be made for the bond in the consolidated financial statements provided the designation is made upon initial recognition.

In the examples above, the entity need not have entered into all of the assets and liabilities giving rise to the measurement or recognition inconsistency at exactly the same time. The fair value option is available provided that each transaction is designated as at fair value through profit or loss at its initial recognition, the delay between entering into the separate transactions is reasonably short, and any remaining transactions are expected to occur. [IAS 39.AG4F]

It would not be acceptable to designate only some of the financial assets and financial liabilities giving rise to the inconsistency as at FVTPL if to do so would not eliminate or significantly reduce the inconsistency and would therefore not result in more relevant information. However, it would be acceptable to designate only some of a number of similar financial assets or financial liabilities if doing so achieves a significant reduction (and possibly a greater reduction than other allowable designations) in the inconsistency. [IAS 39.AG4G]

Example 3.1.1.1C

Fair value option: lack of accounting mismatch (1)

Entity A has borrowed (through a single instrument) €1,000,000 with a third party bank and at the same time has used some of the borrowing to acquire 10 similar financial assets each of a value of €50,000 that add up to €500,000 which are all classified as held for trading. Entity A wants to reduce the measurement inconsistency by designating the liability as at FVTPL. However, if the financial liability was fair valued, Entity A would create an accounting mismatch in profit or loss related to the €500,000 of liabilities that are not matched by financial assets that are held for trading. This accounting mismatch is comparable to the mismatch it would have had had it not contemplated applying the fair value option in the first place. Therefore, Entity A cannot apply the fair value option as it does not significantly reduce the accounting mismatch between the assets and the liability.

Example 3.1.1.1D

Fair value option: lack of accounting mismatch (2)

Entity B buys an equity share for £100 which does not meet the definition of held for trading. At the same time the entity buys a put option for £20 over the same share with a strike price of £100. Entity B is contemplating whether it could designate the equity share as a financial asset at fair value through profit and loss at initial recognition by claiming that doing so eliminates or significantly reduces an accounting mismatch that arises as a result of entering into the put option. If the fair value option is not applied the share will be measured at fair value with gains and losses immediately recognised in other comprehensive income unless there is a significant or prolonged decline in fair value in which case the cumulative losses are reclassified from equity to profit or loss prior to derecognition of the share. The put option will be accounted for at fair value through profit or loss in the absence of hedge accounting.

In considering whether an accounting mismatch is eliminated or significantly reduced Entity B considers various share price scenarios.

If the share price increases above £100 the gain in fair value of the share will be recognised in other comprehensive income, while the fall in fair value of the option will be recorded in profit or loss. However, it should be noted that while the share price could rise well beyond £120 (i.e. the fair value gain could be in excess of £20) the corresponding possible fall in the value of the option is limited to £20 as the value of the purchased put option cannot decline below zero). Gains from the shares that arise from increases in the share price above £120 will not have a corresponding loss from the put option. Thus, the degree of offset between the share and the option if the fair value option was applied is limited to certain share price scenarios only. In addition, when the share increases between £100 and £120 the decline in fair value of the option will not be linear compared with the increase in the fair value of the share as the option's fair value includes time value but the share does not.

If the share price falls and the fall is not considered significant or prolonged then the fair value loss will be recognised in other comprehensive income while the increase in the fair value of the option would be recorded in profit or loss. As noted above the increase in fair value of the option will not be fully offset by the decrease in the fair value of the share as the option's fair value will also include changes in time value.

If there is a significant or prolonged decline of fair value below cost the cumulative loss recognised in other comprehensive income will be reclassified from equity to profit or loss as a reclassification adjustment (see **section 6** in **chapter 18**). Once the impairment has occurred, future falls in fair value of the shares and further increases in intrinsic value of the option will be recognised in profit or loss and will achieve the same accounting result had the fair value option not been applied. In the period when the impairment occurs not applying the fair value option would result in a greater one-off loss in profit or loss as a result of reclassification from equity compared to the net loss when applying the fair value option.

Considering all the various scenarios it is not possible for the entity to claim that applying the fair value option does provide an elimination or significant reduction in an accounting mismatch.

3.1.1.2 *Managed and performance evaluated on a fair value basis*

Examples of where an entity can apply the fair value option on the basis that financial assets, financial liabilities or both are managed and their performance evaluated on a fair value basis, in accordance with a documented risk management or investment strategy include the following.

- An entity that is a venture capital organisation, mutual fund, unit trust or similar entity whose business is investing in financial assets with a view to profiting from their total return in the form of interest or dividends and changes in fair value. An entity may designate such investments at FVTPL, provided it does not hold a controlling interest. [IAS 39.AG4I(a)]

- An entity may have financial assets and financial liabilities that share one or more risks and those risks are managed and evaluated on a fair value basis in accordance with a documented policy of asset and liability management. An example could be an entity that has issued 'structured products' containing multiple embedded derivatives and manages the resulting risks on a fair value basis using a mix of derivative and non-derivative financial instruments. [IAS 39.AG4I(b)] This is particularly evident for investment banks that issue structured medium-term note programmes linked to a basket of equities or corporate bonds, where the bank economically hedges its liability by purchasing equity and corporate bonds in the cash market, and/or enters into derivative contracts where the underlying is the referenced equities or corporate bonds. It is common for investment banks to manage the portfolio of assets and liabilities on a fair value basis.

- An insurer holds a portfolio of financial assets, that it manages so as to maximise its total return (i.e. interest / dividends and changes in fair value), and evaluate its performance on that basis. For example, that portfolio may be held to back specific liabilities in which case the investment policy and evaluation on a fair value basis may apply to either the assets and liabilities, or to the assets alone. [IAS 39.AG4I(c)]

An entity that designates financial instruments as at FVTPL on the basis that it manages and evaluates their performance on that basis must designate all eligible financial instruments that are managed and evaluated together, i.e. it cannot cherry-pick. [IAS 39.AG4J]

The risk management or investment strategy must be documented, though documentation need not be extensive. For example, if the performance management system as approved by the entity's key management personnel clearly demonstrates that the performance is evaluated on a total return basis, no additional documentation is required. The documentation need not be on an item-by-item basis, but may be on a portfolio basis, nor need it be at the level of detail required for hedge accounting.

3.1.1.3 *Contracts containing one or more embedded derivative*

IAS 39.11A allows a hybrid contract containing one or more embedded derivatives to be designated in its entirety as at FVTPL unless:

- the embedded derivative does not significantly modify the cash flows that otherwise would be required by the contract; or
- it is clear with little or no analysis when a similar hybrid instrument is first considered that separation of the embedded derivative is prohibited, for example a prepayment option embedded in a loan that permits the holder to prepay the loan for approximately its amortised cost (see **7.1** in **chapter 17**).

Example 3.1.1.3

Fair value option: Commodity-linked debt

Entity Q issues a debt instrument that has interest payments linked to a basket of commodity prices. The linking to commodity prices is considered to be a non-closely related embedded derivative that would require separation and measurement as at FVTPL. Entity Q may choose at initial recognition to designate the whole debt instrument as at FVTPL to avoid separating out the embedded derivative.

IAS 39 applies to financial instruments within its scope. However, certain provisions like embedded derivatives apply to a wider range of contracts. For example, an operating lease that is not a financial instrument may have an embedded derivative that is separately recognised in the statement of financial position. A question arises whether the fair value option provisions can be extended to hybrid contracts where the host contract is a non-financial item or a financial item outside the scope of IAS 39. At its meeting in March 2007, the IFRIC was asked to consider this question. In November 2007 the IFRIC recommended that the Board should clarify IAS 39.11A by specifying whether it applies only to contracts with embedded derivatives that have financial hosts, or whether the fair value option can be applied to all contracts with embedded derivatives. At the date of writing the Board had not considered this question.

It would be surprising to conclude that any host contract that is outside the scope of IAS 39, and in many cases has been specifically excluded from IAS 39 in paragraph 2, could be fair valued through profit or loss as this would override the recognition and measurement guidance of more specific Standards, like IAS 17 *Leases*, IFRS 4 *Insurance Contracts* or IAS 11 *Construction Contracts*. Equally, it would be surprising to conclude that the IASB intended to bring in to the statement of financial position executory host contracts, like sale and purchase contracts, that are normally excluded.

The rules on embedded derivatives contained in non-financial host contracts were introduced as an anti-abuse measure to stop entities from stapling financial instruments on to non-financial contracts. Once the embedded derivative is separated, that part of the hybrid instrument is in the scope of IAS 39, but the host contract always remains outside the scope of IAS 39. The fair value option provisions are contained in IAS 39, the Standard that deals with financial instruments, and contracts that behave like financial instruments, and therefore it seems reasonable to conclude that the fair value option is restricted only to contracts that are in the scope of IAS 39.

IFRIC 9 *Reassessment of Embedded Derivatives* only allows an entity to reconsider whether an embedded derivative is closely related if there is a change in the terms of the contract that significantly modified the cash flows that otherwise would be required under the contract. The fair value option can be applied at initial recognition only. Therefore, only if the cash flows are modified sufficiently for the original instrument to be derecognised would an entity be able to designate the modified instrument as at fair value through profit or loss (see **section 3** in **chapter 17**).

The revised version of IFRS 3 *Business Combinations*, issued in January 2008, clarified that if a contractual arrangement is acquired as part of a business combination the acquirer must determine what is the classification of the contractual arrangement at the date of acquisition as this is the date of initial recognition (see **section 5** below). At the date of acquisition the acquirer will need to consider whether the contractual arrangement has any embedded derivatives that require separation. The acquirer is not *reassessing* an embedded derivative at this point as the acquirer is recognising the contractual arrangement for the first time.

3.1.1.4 Fair valuing through alternative designations

In some cases an entity could achieve fair value accounting through profit or loss by using alternative designation strategies. The choice of that designation strategy must be made at initial recognition of the instruments concerned.

- there is a high turnover rate in the portfolio of financial instrument contracts.

Management and controls:

- compensation and/or performance measures are tied to the short-term results generated from financial instrument transactions (that is, the operation is measured based on trading profits or changes in the market values of its positions);
- the operation communicates internally in terms of 'trading strategy' (that is, management reports identify contractual positions, fair values, hedging activities, risk exposure etc.);
- the operation sets limits on market positions and related strategies, sets policies governing what types of contracts it will transact in, and sets the controls it will follow; in addition, management is involved in reviewing compliance with those limits, strategies, policies, and controls on a daily or frequent basis;
- the word 'trading' appears in the name of or documentation of the operation for internal or external purposes;
- employees of the operation are referred to as 'traders' or 'dealers' or have prior experience in banking, broking, derivatives trading or risk management activities;
- assessment of net market positions of the operation is done on a regular and frequent basis (for example hourly or overnight);
- infrastructure of the operation is similar to that of a trading operation of a bank or investment bank's front office, middle office, and back office (that is, there is a segregation of back office processing and front office trading functions);
- an infrastructure exists that enables the operation to capture price and other risks on a real-time basis;
- the activities are managed on a portfolio or 'book' basis; and
- management searches for opportunities to take advantage of favourable price spreads, arbitrage opportunities, or outright positions in the marketplace.

Transactions/contracts

- the operation has a history of pairing off (entering into offsetting contracts) or otherwise settling the transactions without physically receiving or delivering the underlying item. In other words, past practices of the operation have resulted in net cash settlement, offsetting, as well as netting out, and the type of settlement has changed quickly from one type to another to maximise profits/mitigate losses;

- the contracts do not permit physical delivery and must be settled net in the market or in cash; and

- the financial instrument contracts are not customarily used for general commercial (operational) business purposes or by the industry in general.

3.1.3 Reclassification into the financial assets at FVTPL category

Reclassification into or out of the 'fair value through profit or loss' financial category while an asset is held is prohibited in accordance with IAS 39.50. The following changes in circumstances are not reclassifications:

[IAS 39.50A]

- a derivative that was previously a designated and effective hedging instrument in a cash flow hedge or net investment hedge no longer qualifies as such;
- a derivative becomes a designated and effective hedging instrument in a cash flow hedge or net investment hedge; and
- financial assets are reclassified when an insurance company changes its accounting policies in accordance with IFRS 4.45.

IAS 39.50A was introduced by *Improvements to IFRSs* issued in May 2008. The amendments made to IAS 39 by *Improvements to IFRSs* apply for annual periods beginning on or after 1 January 2009, but earlier application is permitted. An entity choosing to apply the amendments early must disclose that fact. The amendments to IAS 39.50A are to be applied as of the date and in the manner of the 2005 amendments described in IAS 39.105A (i.e. in respect of amendments to the fair value option). [IAS 39.108C]

UK

At the time of writing, Improvements to IFRSs *has not yet been endorsed for adoption in the EU. EU companies may, nevertheless, comply with IAS 39.50A prior to endorsement, since it does not conflict with the existing requirements of IAS 39.*

IAS 39.50 clearly restricts an entity from reclassifying a financial asset into or out of the FVTPL category following initial recognition. Principally, this restriction is designed to prevent an entity from applying the fair value option subsequent to the asset being classified in a different category or, conversely, removing an asset from this category after it applied the fair value option at inception. This restriction also prevents an entity from reclassifying financial instruments into or out of the held for trading category subject to the exceptions described above.

It should be noted that a change in a fair value valuation technique, say from using quoted market prices to using a valuation technique in the instance when there is no longer a quoted market price, is not a reclassification. This applies if the item is classified as at fair value through profit or loss or as an available-for-sale financial asset.

3.2 Held-to-maturity investments (HTM)

HTM investments are financial instruments with fixed or determinable payments and fixed maturity that an entity has the positive intention and ability to hold to maturity, other than those that the entity, upon initial recognition, elects to designate as at FVTPL or available-for-sale or that meet the definition of loans and receivables. [IAS 39.9]

HTM investments are measured at amortised cost using the effective interest rate method.

An asset cannot be classified as HTM if it can be contractually prepaid or otherwise extinguished by the issuer in such a way that the holder would not recover substantially all of its recorded investment, i.e. those contracts where the issuer has a right to settle at an amount significantly below amortised cost. In addition, a debt security with the right of the issuer to redeem early should be evaluated to determine whether it contains an embedded derivative that must be accounted for separately. See **chapter 17** on embedded derivatives.

Some host debt instruments from which an embedded derivative has been separated can be classified as HTM.

3.2.1 Fixed or determinable payments and fixed maturity

HTM investments are financial instruments with fixed or determinable payments and fixed maturity, which means that the contractual arrangement defines the amounts and dates of payments to the holder, such as interest and principal payments.

Equity instruments cannot be HTM investments either because they have an indefinite life (such as ordinary shares) or because the amounts the holder may receive can vary in a manner that is not predetermined (such as for share options, warrants and similar rights). [IAS 39.AG17]

Preference shares with fixed or determinable payments and a fixed maturity, determined to be financial liabilities in accordance with IAS 32 for the issuer, can be classified in the HTM category for the holder, for example, mandatorily redeemable preference shares.

A debt instrument with a variable interest rate can satisfy the criteria for a HTM investment. [IAS 39.AG17] The terms of the contract determine the amounts and dates of payments to the holder. An example is a five-year debt instrument which pays a variable rate of interest specified as LIBOR plus 150 basis points, with interest payments receivable semi-annually in arrears.

Example 3.2.1A

HTM: debt host contract (1)

Entity G has a bond asset with interest payments indexed to the price of gold. The bond has a fixed payment at maturity and a fixed maturity date.

Interest payments contain an embedded derivative (indexation to gold) that is separated and accounted for as a derivative at fair value (unless Entity G elects on initial recognition to designate the bond as a financial asset at FVTPL or it cannot separate and measure the embedded derivative in which case the whole instrument is designated as at FVTPL). Once the embedded derivative is separated, the host debt instrument can be classified as HTM provided Entity G has the positive intention and ability to hold the bond to maturity.

Example 3.2.1B

HTM: debt host contract (2)

Entity A purchases a five-year equity indexed-linked note with an original issue price of £10 at a market price of £12 at the time of purchase. At maturity, the note requires payment of the original issue price of £10 plus a supplemental redemption amount that depends on whether a specified share price index exceeds a predetermined level at the maturity date. The supplemental amount paid at redemption is a formula that incorporates the change in the share index. If the share price index does not exceed or is equal to the predetermined level, no supplemental redemption amount is paid. Entity A has the positive intention and ability to hold the note to its maturity.

Entity A can classify the note as HTM because it has a fixed payment of £10 and fixed maturity and Entity A has the positive intention and ability to hold it to maturity. However, the equity index feature is an embedded derivative that is not closely related to the debt host, and must be separated. The purchase price of £12 is allocated between the host debt instrument and the embedded derivative. For example, if the fair value of the embedded option at acquisition is £4, the host debt instrument is measured at £8 on initial recognition. In this case, the discount of £2 that is implicit in the host bond (principal of £10 minus the original carrying amount of £8) is amortised to profit or loss over the term to maturity of the note using the effective interest method. [IAS 39.IG.B.13]

It is important to note in this example that the instrument has a floor on the redemption equal to £10. Absent that floor, Entity A would not be able to assert an intention to hold to maturity, because an issuer's right to settle a financial asset at an amount significantly below its amortised cost precludes an entity from asserting a positive intention to hold to maturity. [IAS 39.AG16]

If the terms of a 'perpetual' debt instrument (such as 'perpetual' bonds, debentures and capital notes) provide the holder with the contractual right to receive payments of interest at fixed dates into perpetuity, the instrument cannot be classified as HTM because the instrument does not have a fixed maturity date.

It can be argued that a perpetual debt instrument with fixed or determinable payments for which the only cash payments under the terms of the instrument are interest payments during a limited period, for instance, 10 years, can be classified as HTM provided the amount invested is recovered through fixed or determinable payments, and the rights to zero interest after year 10 have no present value at inception. In that case one would need to argue that the final date on which interest is paid is in effect the maturity date of such a financial instrument. Despite the legal form being a perpetual, the substance is that of a finite life instrument.

3.2.2 Positive intention and ability to hold to maturity

An entity cannot classify a financial asset as HTM if the entity intends to hold the financial asset for only an undefined period. A debt security, for example, should not be classified as HTM if the entity anticipates that the security would be available to be sold in response to:

[IAS 39.AG16(b)]

- changes in market interest rates and related changes in the investment's prepayment risk;
- liquidity needs (for example, due to the withdrawal of deposits, increased demand for loans, surrender of insurance policies, or payment of insurance claims);
- changes in the availability of and the yield on alternative investments;
- changes in funding sources and terms; or
- changes in foreign currency risk.

In summary, classification of an investment as HTM means that the entity is indifferent to future opportunities to profit from changes in the asset's fair value.

For this reason IAS 39 prohibits the hedging of a HTM investment for interest rate risk or prepayment risk as the entity, in classifying the investment as HTM, has expressed its commitment to retaining the financial asset and collecting all of its contractual cash flows, irrespective of the impact of changes in market interest rates on the asset's fair value and any option the issuer may have to redeem the asset prior to its contractual maturity.

IAS 39 states that an asset is not classified as HTM if it can contractually be repaid or otherwise extinguished by the issuer in such a way that the holder of the asset would not recover substantially all of its recorded investment. Any premium paid and capitalised transaction costs are considered in determining whether the carrying amount would be substantially recovered. In the circumstances where the holder will recover substantially all of its investment, for example, in the case of a debt instrument where the issuer exercises its call option on the asset and the option's exercise price is approximately equal to the instrument's amortised cost, the debt instrument's maturity date is viewed as being accelerated. The issuer's exercise of a call feature in such circumstances does not invalidate the holder's treatment of the investment as held-to-maturity, provided the holder intends to hold it until it is called.

Convertible debt instruments generally bear a lower interest rate than debt instruments without a conversion feature because the investor pays for the right to benefit from the appreciation in value of the option embedded in the debt instrument. The conversion feature would normally be separated out from the debt host contract and accounted for as an embedded derivative. If the conversion feature can be exercised only at maturity of the instrument, then it may be reasonable for the holder to argue that it has the positive intent and ability to hold the debt host contract to maturity. However, generally, it would be contradictory to assert the positive intention to hold the debt host contract to its maturity if the conversion right that has been purchased by the holder allows the holder to convert the instrument into equity at any point. In the latter case, the holder does not have the positive ability to hold the debt host contract to maturity as exercising the option prior to maturity of the instrument will extinguish the debt host contract early.

For a debt instrument held that is subject to a purchased put option, the existence of the option will prima facie undermine any statement of intention to hold the instrument to maturity. Paying for a put feature is inconsistent with expressing an intention to hold the financial asset until maturity. An entity should not classify a financial asset as HTM if it has the intention to hold the instrument for only an undetermined period or if it stands ready to sell the asset in response to general market conditions. Therefore, unless the terms of the put option are such that it can be exercised only in one of the permitted, isolated, non-recurring circumstances (see **3.3.2** below), it will not be acceptable to classify a puttable security as HTM. [IAS 39.AG19]

Example 3.2.2A

HTM: sale due to credit rating triggers

An investment fund holds high-yield debt securities (bonds, etc) as specified in the portfolio guidelines. The fund only sells assets if the credit rating of the assets deteriorates below a certain specified level (rather than only when significant deterioration has occurred). The fund's assets cannot be classified as HTM because the fund cannot claim at initial recognition that there is a positive intention to hold the assets to maturity – the intention is to hold assets only while their credit rating is within the prescribed parameters.

Example 3.2.2B

HTM: managing debt duration

Entity X has a portfolio of debt securities and wishes to classify the investments as HTM. The investment policy allows management to transfer every HTM security to a more liquid portfolio at a specific predetermined date (e.g. 24 months prior to each security's stated maturity). The policy is designed to permit Entity X the flexibility to sell debt securities and thereby manage the duration of the portfolio.

Entity X's policy would preclude classifying its debt securities as HTM because it does not have the positive intention to hold those securities to maturity – the intention is to hold until the date 24 months prior to stated maturity and that date is not sufficiently close to maturity to meet the exception of tainting certain transfers out of HTM (see **3.3.2** below).

Example 3.2.2C

HTM: regulatory constraint (1)

Entity P would like to designate as HTM its portfolio of high quality assets held for the purpose of complying with regulatory requirements on liquidity.

Entity P cannot designate the portfolio as HTM because Entity P cannot claim that there is a positive intention to hold the assets to maturity – the intention is to hold whilst the assets continue to be of the appropriate quality and Entity P is not required to realise them for regulatory purposes.

A significant risk of default by the issuer does not preclude classification of a financial asset as HTM provided its contractual payments are fixed or determinable and the other criteria for classification as HTM are met. [IAS 39.AG17]

Even if there is a significant risk of default on interest and principal on a bond, for example, due to significant business, financial, or economic uncertainties and, as evidenced, for instance, by a low-grade rating of the bond issue, the contractual payments on the bond may be fixed or determinable. The likelihood of default is not a consideration in qualifying for the HTM category as long as there is an intent and ability, considering the credit condition existing at the acquisition date, to hold the instrument to maturity.

Where an entity classifies a high-risk debt security as HTM knowing that if at some future date there is a further credit deterioration it will sell in response to such a downgrade, it may be difficult, absent a bankruptcy, to substantiate that a significant credit deterioration occurred and that the sale, if significant, does not 'taint' the HTM portfolio.

Securities that have been pledged as collateral for borrowings or are subject to a repurchase agreement or securities lending agreement (i.e. have been transferred to another party under a repo or securities lending transaction but continue to be recognised), can be classified as HTM provided that the entity intends and expects to be able to repay the borrowings without being required to dispose of the asset. [IAS 39.IG.B.18]

For financial assets classified as HTM, management should consider whether the entity has both the financial ability as well as the regulatory ability to obviate the need to dispose of HTM investments prior to maturity. The assessment of an entity's financial ability takes into account such factors as its funding position and its ability to maintain any over-collateralisation requirements. The assessment of an entity's financial ability also takes into account such factors as its regulatory capital requirements, its liquidity position (including specified holdings of liquid assets), its loans-to-one-borrower ratio, growth prospects and related financing requirements and its investment authority (including permitted asset-mix).

Example 3.2.2D

HTM: regulatory constraint (2)

Entity Q, a regulated entity, would like to classify securities as HTM. Its regulators may require Entity Q to dispose of these securities in the normal course of business.

Entity Q cannot classify the securities as HTM. Even though the entity may have the positive intention to hold the securities to maturity, it does not have the ability. Certain financial institution regulators have designated specific financial instruments – such as certain collateralised mortgage obligations (CMOs) or other, similar stripped securities (for example, interest-only and principal-only securities) – as high-risk securities, and may require a regulated entity to sell such securities as a result of changes in interest rates. If a financial instrument is subject to such regulatory provisions, classification as HTM is not appropriate since management would not be able to demonstrate the ability to hold securities to maturity as a result of the regulator being able to require the sale of the security.

3.2.3 *Frequency of assessment of positive intention and ability to hold to maturity*

Both the positive intention and ability to hold are assessed at the end of each reporting period. [IAS 39.AG25]

> **Example 3.2.3**
>
> **HTM: sale after the end of the reporting period**
>
> Entity X, with a 31 December year-end, has a portfolio of financial assets classified as HTM. Early in January 20X2, prior to the issuance of the 20X1 financial statements, Entity X sells a portion of the financial assets held, and the factors motivating the sale do not qualify under the exceptions provided in **3.3.2** below.
>
> The entire HTM securities portfolio is required to be reclassified as available-for-sale in the statement of financial position as at 31 December 20X1, since the actions in January call into question the entity's assertion of intent at year-end.

3.3 Tainting of the HTM portfolio

'Tainting' is the term used to describe the effect of disposing of or reclassifying a HTM investment before its maturity date in situations where such disposal or reclassification disqualifies the entity from using the HTM classification for the remaining portfolio of securities held. Except for certain limited circumstances described in **3.3.2** below, a sale or reclassification of a HTM investment casts doubt on the entity's stated intention or ability to hold the rest of its HTM portfolio to maturity. As a consequence, where an entity has, during the current year, sold or reclassified more than an insignificant amount of HTM investments before maturity, i.e. tainting of the HTM portfolio occurs, then all of the entity's HTM investments generally must be reclassified into the available-for-sale category. Furthermore, the entity is prohibited from classifying any investments as HTM for the next two financial years.

> **Example 3.3**
>
> **HTM: sale of single asset**
>
> Entity X has a portfolio of HTM financial assets comprising both municipal and corporate bonds. A sale or transfer of a single corporate bond which comprises more than an insignificant amount of the portfolio does not meet the specific exceptions in **3.3.2** below and therefore would result in tainting of all remaining bonds, municipal and corporate.

3.3.1 *Sub-categorisation for the purposes of applying the 'tainting' rule*

An entity cannot create two different categories of HTM financial assets, for example, debt securities denominated in US dollars and debt securities denominated in Euros. The 'tainting rule' applies to the portfolio of HTM investments in its entirety. If an entity has sold or reclassified more than an insignificant amount of HTM investments, it cannot classify any financial assets as HTM financial assets. [IAS 39.IG.B.20]

3.3.2 *Sales or reclassification of HTM financial assets which do not taint the HTM portfolio*

Sales or reclassifications in strictly defined and limited circumstances specified in IAS 39 do not taint the remaining HTM portfolio. These are sales or transfers that:

[IAS 39.9]

- are so close to maturity or the financial asset's call date (for example, less than three months before maturity) that changes in the market rate of interest would not have a significant effect on the financial asset's fair value;
- occur after the entity has collected substantially all of the financial asset's original principal through scheduled payments or prepayments; or
- are attributable to an isolated event that is beyond the entity's control, is non-recurring and could not have been reasonably anticipated by the entity; or
- do not involve 'more than insignificant' amount of the entity's HTM portfolio (more than insignificant in relation to the total amount of HTM investments).

Selling an asset close enough to its maturity does not taint the remaining HTM portfolio if the effect of movements in interest rates between the repurchase date and the maturity is expected to have an insignificant impact on the fair value of the asset. For instance, if an entity sells a financial asset less than three months prior to maturity, the present value of the amount received from the sale usually will not be significantly different from the amount received at maturity. This is unlikely to be the case if the instrument's maturity was several months away.

IAS 39 does not provide guidance as to what is considered to be 'substantially all' of the financial asset's original principal. Prior to the 2004 revisions to IAS 39, Implementation Guidance contained an example that illustrated that collecting 90 per cent or more of the original principal was considered to be substantially all. In the amended Implementation Guidance this interpretation has been removed, and therefore judgement must be applied on a case-by-case basis in determining what is considered to be substantially all.

For an event to be isolated, non-recurring, beyond the entity's control and could not have been reasonably anticipated, the event would need to be extremely remote and unlikely to occur in practice. Not many events are likely to meet this criterion.

A sale, or a transfer of a HTM investment due to one of the following isolated, non-recurring events is not considered to be inconsistent with its original classification as HTM and does not raise a question about the entity's intention to hold other investments to maturity:

[IAS 39.AG22]

(a) a significant deterioration in the issuer's credit-worthiness;

(b) a change in tax law that eliminates or significantly reduces the tax-exempt status of interest on the HTM investment (but not a change in tax law that revises the marginal tax rates applicable to interest income);

(c) a major business combination or major disposition (such as sale of a segment) that necessitates the sale or transfer of HTM investments to maintain the entity's existing interest rate risk position or credit risk policy (although the business combination is an event within the entity's control, the changes to its investment portfolio to maintain an interest rate risk position or credit risk policy may be consequential rather than anticipated);

(d) a change in statutory or regulatory requirements significantly modifying either what constitutes a permissible investment or the maximum level of particular types of investments, thereby causing an entity to dispose of a HTM investment;

(e) a significant increase in the industry's regulatory capital requirements that causes the entity to downsize by selling HTM investments; and

(f) a significant increase in the risk weights of HTM investments used for regulatory risk-based capital purposes.

Note that a disaster scenario that is only remotely possible, such as a run on a bank or a similar situation affecting an insurance company, is not something that is assessed by an entity in deciding whether it has the positive intention and ability to hold an investment to maturity. [IAS 39.AG21]

Catastrophic losses or high levels of policy surrenders are 'reasonably probable' of occurring in the insurance industry. They cannot be considered to be non-recurring or isolated and would not meet the exception under IAS 39.9. As a result, the sale of investments classified as HTM in order to meet excessive levels of claim obligations or because of policyholder withdrawals would taint the entity's held-to-maturity category.

The following factors, amongst others, would be relevant in determining whether there has been a significant deterioration in the issuer's creditworthiness. [IAS 39.AG22(a)]

The deterioration in the issuer's creditworthiness should have occurred after the security was acquired. Low credit ratings or creditworthiness concerns existing at acquisition would generally lead to a conclusion that a subsequent not insignificant sale from the HTM category taints the rest of the HTM portfolio.

There should be evidence of actual deterioration of the issuer's creditworthiness. A downgrading by a rating agency may provide objective evidence of a significant credit deterioration. An expectation of deterioration should be supported by objective evidence. Some of the financial measures that may provide objective evidence are:

- cash flows from operations (i.e. decline in cash flows, available cash flows, liquidity);
- broker/analyst reports on the issuer;
- adverse performance compared to projections;
- sustained decline in earnings or other key measures; and
- violation of covenants or other evidence that the issuer is in peril of violating covenants.

An increase in yield relative to a risk-free rate may be indicative of a change in the market's evaluation of the risk associated with holding the issuer's debt. In many situations, an effective measure of a significant deterioration is a significant increase in the yield on the debt of an entity when compared to the change in the yield of a risk-free security of a similar maturity.

Guidance used in determining impairment may also be useful in assessing a significant decline in the issuer's creditworthiness (see **section 6** of **chapter 18**). Information, such as the current and near-term projected financial condition and performance of the issuer, the issuer's dividend payment and earnings performance, the general market conditions and prospects of the region and industry in which the issuer operates, and specific adverse news or events affecting the issuer may provide objective evidence of impairment that may be indicative of a significant decline in the issuer's creditworthiness.

To provide evidence of a significant deterioration in the issuer's creditworthiness, general market or industry factors should have a direct or demonstrable effect on a specific issuer. For example, widespread difficulties experienced by others in the industry (e.g. due to over-leveraging or weak assets) that are not expected to affect the issuer are not relevant.

In contrast, the development of severe competition, adverse tax or regulatory developments, or declining markets may have a direct bearing on the creditworthiness of specific issuers.

A sale of a HTM investment following a downgrade of the issuer's credit rating by a rating agency would not necessarily raise a question about the entity's intention to hold other investments to maturity. A downgrade indicates a decline in the issuer's creditworthiness. IAS 39 specifies that a sale due to a significant deterioration in the issuer's creditworthiness could satisfy the condition in IAS 39 and therefore not raise a question about the entity's intention to hold other investments to maturity. However, the deterioration in creditworthiness must be significant judged by reference to the credit rating at initial recognition. A credit downgrade of a notch within a class or from a rating class to the immediately lower rating class could often be regarded as reasonably anticipated. If the rating downgrade in combination with other information provides evidence of impairment, the deterioration in creditworthiness often would be regarded as significant. [IAS 39.IG.B.15]

However, a not insignificant sale out of HTM would not taint the rest of the HTM portfolio if the significant downgrade in credit was anticipated on initial classification as HTM. A permitted, i.e. non-tainting, sale in accordance with IAS 39.AG22(a) should be in response to an actual deterioration rather than in advance of a deterioration in creditworthiness and should not be based on mere speculation or in response to industry statistics.

The deterioration should be supported by evidence about the issuer's creditworthiness though the entity need not await the formal notification of an actual downgrading in the issuer's published credit rating or inclusion on a 'credit watch' list.

Where an entity uses internal ratings for assessing exposures, changes in those internal ratings may help to identify issuers for which there has been a significant deterioration in creditworthiness, provided the entity's approach to assigning internal ratings and changes in those ratings give a consistent, reliable and objective measure of the credit quality of the issuers.

If an entity does not sell a debt instrument immediately in response to a significant credit deterioration, but continues to classify the instrument in the HTM portfolio, a sale of that instrument at a future date would not satisfy the conditions for permitted sales. As an entity is required to make an ongoing assessment of its ability and intent to hold an instrument to its maturity, by not reclassifying the instrument out of HTM when the credit deterioration occurred, the entity effectively reconfirmed its intent to hold the instrument to its maturity.

An exchange of debt securities classified as HTM pursuant to a bankruptcy generally qualifies as a permitted sale out of HTM since bankruptcy is the ultimate form of credit deterioration. However, if the investor had anticipated the bankruptcy at the acquisition date and was able to control the outcome, then such a sale would not satisfy the conditions for permitted sales due to a significant deterioration in the issuer's creditworthiness.

Example 3.3.2A

HTM: sale due to cash need

Entity P, an insurance entity, sells financial assets that have been classified as HTM due to cash needs arising from the failure of one of its principal reinsurers.

A sale from the HTM portfolio for this reason would be inconsistent with the positive intent and ability to hold the security to maturity. This situation is not analogous to significant deterioration in an issuer's creditworthiness, because the deterioration does not relate specifically to the issuer of the security sold but to the entity's reinsurer. The failure of an insurance entity's principal reinsurer, also, would not be considered an event that is isolated, non-recurring, and unusual, given the environment in which an insurance entity operates.

Example 3.3.2B

HTM: counterparty restructuring

Entity N, a life insurance entity, purchased a debt security in a private placement offering. At acquisition, Entity N classified the debt as HTM. The issuer, a private entity, is currently in bankruptcy proceedings and is restructuring its debt. The issuer is contemplating swapping its debt security to Entity N in exchange for new debt and stock. N has no control over the outcome of the issuer's restructuring arrangements.

Prior to the issuer's determination of the final restructuring arrangements, Entity N can continue to classify the debt security as HTM. The HTM classification is acceptable because the issuer's termination of the original debt is not under Entity N's control. The restructuring is analogous to an issuer's call option. In some circumstances it may not be possible to hold a security to its original stated maturity, such as when the security is called by the issuer prior to maturity. The issuer's exercise of the call option effectively accelerates the security's maturity and is not viewed as being inconsistent with the HTM classification. Under these circumstances, the maturity date is accelerated to the date of early redemption or when the debt security is exchanged. Accordingly, Entity N's classification as HTM is appropriate. Entity N should determine whether impairment has occurred, and if so, write down the financial instrument (see **section 6** of **chapter 18**).

Prior to the issuer's determination of the final restructuring arrangements, Entity N could have transferred the debt security from the HTM to the available-for-sale category if the intention and ability to hold to maturity is no longer appropriate, without tainting its HTM portfolio, since a transfer resulting from evidence of a significant deterioration in the issuer's creditworthiness will not call into question an entity's intent to hold other financial assets.

Sales out of HTM in anticipation of future tax law changes that have not become law will taint the HTM portfolio if sales are significant in comparison to the HTM portfolio. To reduce the risk of tainting the tax change has to already have become law prior to the disposal of the assets.

Example 3.3.2C

HTM: change in tax treaty

Entity X, an entity operating in Canada, has a portfolio of financial assets classified as held-to-maturity, which contains a Malaysian bond issue. At the date that Entity X purchased the security, a tax treaty existed between the Canadian tax jurisdiction and Malaysia which the entity anticipated would continue for the foreseeable future and at least as long as the bonds were outstanding. This treaty allowed the use of Canadian foreign tax credits to reduce the onerous tax consequences that would otherwise result from inclusion of interest on the Malaysian security in taxable income in both tax jurisdictions (assuming Entity X, also, is taxed on the income in Malaysia).

Entity X cannot reclassify the security from its HTM category in anticipation of the treaty's expiration without calling into question the intent to hold other financial assets to maturity. If the treaty does expire, however, reclassification may be permitted which will not taint any remaining HTM securities.

A disposal out of HTM is permitted if it is consequential to a major business combination or disposal of a business and affects existing interest rate risk or credit risk positions which must be maintained in accordance with risk management policies. Hence, an entity may reassess the classification of HTM securities concurrently with or shortly after a major business combination and not necessarily call into question its intent to hold other securities to maturity in the future. As time passes, it becomes increasingly difficult to demonstrate that the business combination, and not other events or circumstances, necessitated the transfer or sale of HTM securities.

Sales in anticipation of a business combination, e.g. for the purpose of financing it, will taint the HTM category.

Sales out of the HTM category as a result of a change in senior management in connection with a restructuring of the entity will result in tainting. A change in management is not identified as an instance of sales or transfers from HTM that does not compromise the classification as HTM as change in management or restructuring cannot be argued to be an isolated, non-recurring event that could not have been reasonably anticipated. [IAS 39.IG.B.16]

In some countries, regulators of banks or other industries may set capital requirements on an *entity-specific* basis based on an assessment of the risk in that particular entity.

Sales of HTM investments in response to an unanticipated significant increase by the regulator in the *industry*'s capital requirements do not taint the entity's intent to hold remaining investments to maturity. However, sales of HTM investments imposed by regulators, due to a significant increase in *entity-specific* capital requirements applicable to a particular entity, but not to the industry, 'taint' the entity's intent to hold other financial assets as HTM. Entity-specific capital requirements could only be disregarded in exceptional cases if it can be demonstrated that the sales result from an increase in capital requirements which is an isolated event that is beyond the entity's control and that is non-recurring and could not have been reasonably anticipated by the entity. [IAS 39.IG.B.17]

In consolidated financial statements, intragroup sales of HTM investments between group entities generally would not taint the HTM portfolio from a group perspective, as long as the business purpose of the transfer and the investment policies of the 'buyer' are consistent with a continued positive intention and ability to hold to maturity.

The impact on each entity's stand-alone financial statements should be assessed separately; in the financial statements of the selling entity, the stated intention of holding securities to maturity will have been undermined, even though the sale was made to another entity within the consolidated group.

Note that an entity cannot apply the conditions separately to HTM financial assets held by different entities in a consolidated group, even if those group entities are in different countries with different legal or economic environments. If the consolidated entity in total across the group has sold or reclassified more than an insignificant amount of investments classified as HTM, it cannot classify any financial assets as HTM investments in its consolidated financial statements unless such sales and transfers do not taint the HTM portfolio.

As a remedy to protect the investor from the issuer's violation of a debt covenant, a contractual right of foreclosure that was negotiated at arm's length at the issuance date would not preclude an investor classifying an investment as HTM. Similarly, the exercise of such a right or foreclosure on the violation of a substantial covenant would not taint an investor's remaining HTM portfolio.

Example 3.3.2D

HTM: sale following acceptance of tender offers

Entity A, an insurance company, initially classified 100 per cent of its property liability fixed income portfolio as available-for-sale, 50 per cent of its life fixed income securities portfolio as HTM, and 50 per cent as available-for-sale. Entity A considered various factors in making these classifications, including its investment policy, security characteristics, liquidity needs, and asset-liability management strategy.

In a subsequent year, Entity A began receiving unsolicited tender offers from issuers with respect to its fixed income portfolio (including its HTM portfolio) which was prompted by a very volatile interest rate environment. Entity A's analysis of these tender offers indicated that generally it would have been economically advantageous to accept them. In addition, Entity A was being approached with increased frequency by issuers who desired to renegotiate the terms of certain previously issued securities which, in some cases, were favourable to Entity A. These renegotiations were for reasons other than deterioration in creditworthiness. Entity A accepted certain tender offers involving the exchange of debt securities classified as HTM as these exchanges were on economically favourable terms.

As a consequence of the tender exchanges, Entity A is required to transfer 100 per cent of previously classified HTM securities to available-for-sale because it can no longer assert it has the positive intent to hold all of these securities to maturity. The sale of a security in response to a tender offer typically is motivated not by a need for cash, but instead by the investor's desire for additional possible profit – a motive inconsistent with the HTM classification. Further, none of the exceptions for sales that do not taint HTM portfolio are met.

In the context of open-ended funds, for example a mutual fund, where investors do not have an investment in equity shares in the fund, but own 'units' in the fund, and can require redemption of their share of the net assets of the fund in cash, it is difficult to argue that the possibility of unit-holders asking for redemption of their units is a non-recurring situation that could not have been reasonably anticipated.

In fact, it could reasonably be argued that the entity, e.g. the mutual fund is *'subject to an existing legal or other constraint that could frustrate its intention to hold the financial asset to maturity'* and therefore that HTM classification of the fund's portfolio of investments would be inappropriate.

Where a large number of unit-holders require redemption of their share in the net assets of the fund, the fund could be obliged to sell assets in order to fulfil its obligation to deliver cash to the unit-holders exiting the fund. Although IAS 39.AG21 states that a *'disaster scenario that is only remotely possible, such as a run on a bank or a similar situation affecting an insurer, is not something that is assessed by an entity in deciding whether it has the positive intention and ability to hold an investment to maturity,'* the possibility of unit-holders asking for their redemption in cash (and in large numbers) and thereby forcing the sale of fund assets does not constitute a disaster scenario but is readily possible in the course of operation of a mutual fund, and consequential liquidity needs have to be considered by the fund manager at any time.

A sale or transfer of a security classified as HTM for reasons other than those that are specifically permitted does not indicate that the previous financial statements were issued in error. As the accounting for financial assets as HTM is based primarily on a representation of intent by management, the sale or transfer of a security classified as HTM does not represent an error of previously issued financial statements, provided there was no evidence that existed at the time the financial statements were issued demonstrating that the entity did not have the positive intent and ability to hold the security to maturity. However, such a sale or transfer may call into question the entity's intent to hold other debt securities to maturity in the future.

If 'tainting' of the HTM portfolio occurs in a period, resulting in reclassification of the portfolio as available-for-sale (see **4.2** below), comparative figures for the period are not restated for the enforced reclassification, since this would disguise the consequences of 'tainting.'

If an entity plans to sell a security from the HTM category in response to one of the permitted conditions that do not taint the HTM portfolio, the instrument can continue to be classified in the HTM category. There is no requirement in IAS 39 for the security to be reclassified as available-for-sale if an entity intends to sell in response to one of the permitted conditions.

3.4 Loans and receivables

Loans and receivables are non-derivative financial assets with fixed or determinable payments that are not quoted in an active market, other than those the entity intends to sell immediately or in the short-term (which must be classified as held for trading), and those that the entity on initial recognition designates as either at FVTPL or available-for-sale. [IAS 39.9]

Note that financial assets that do not meet the definition of loans and receivables may still satisfy the criteria for classification in the HTM category as the HTM definition is different from the loans and receivables definition. See **3.2** above on HTM assets.

Loans and receivables are measured at amortised cost using the effective interest method (see **4.1** of **chapter 18** on measurement).

A financial asset cannot be classified as a loan and receivable if it can be contractually prepaid or otherwise extinguished by the issuer in such a way that the holder would not recover substantially all of its recorded investment, other than because of credit deterioration. [IAS 39.9] Such assets are accounted for as available-for-sale or at FVTPL.

For example, a fixed rate interest-only strip created in a securitisation and subject to prepayment risk cannot be classified as a loan and receivable because there is a risk that the purchaser may not recover substantially all of its investment due to prepayment.

Loans and receivables are created by providing money, goods or services to a debtor. Examples are deposits held in banks, trade receivables, loan assets, including loans originated by the entity, loans acquired in a syndication, and other loans purchased in a secondary market provided that the market is not active and the loans are not quoted. Investments in debt securities that are not quoted in an active market can also be classified as loans and receivables.

When banks make term deposits with a central bank or other banks and the proof of deposit is negotiable, the deposit does meet the definition of a loan and receivable unless the depositor bank intends to sell the deposit immediately or in the near term, in which instance the deposit must be classified as held for trading.

Financial assets purchased after origination do qualify for classification as loans and receivables provided they meet all of the criteria for loans and receivables. However, the purchase of an interest in a pool of assets that are not themselves loans and receivables such as an interest in a mutual fund or a similar fund for example, is not a loan or receivable.

The principal difference between loans and receivables and HTM investments is that loans and receivables are not subject to the tainting provisions that apply to HTM investments. Loans and receivables not held for trading can be classified as such even if an entity does not have the positive intention and ability to hold them until maturity. As a consequence, the ability to measure a financial asset at amortised cost without consideration of the entity's intention and ability to hold the asset until maturity is only appropriate when there is no active market for that asset. [IAS 39.BC27]

Example 3.4

Loan in security form

An entity acquires a debt security issued by a government at original issuance. The debt security will be quoted in an active market.

The debt security does not qualify for classification as a loan and receivable because the debt security is quoted in an active market. The definition of loans and receivables in IAS 39 does not distinguish between loans that take the form of securities and those that do not. However, only debt securities that are not quoted in an active market can be classified in the 'loans and receivables' financial asset category.

As with any financial asset, the characteristics of a loan and receivable should be evaluated to determine whether the contractual arrangement contains an embedded derivative that must be accounted for separately (see **chapter 17**).

Following the separation of an embedded derivative from a debt host contract, the debt host contract may be accounted for as a loan and receivable provided the classification criteria for loans and receivables are met.

3.4.1 Definition of loans and receivables: equity security

Equity instruments cannot be loans and receivables because the amounts the holder may receive can vary in a manner that is not predetermined (such as for ordinary shares, share options, warrants and similar rights). Preference shares with fixed or determinable payments and a fixed maturity that are determined to be financial liabilities for the issuer can be classified in the loans and receivables category provided they are not quoted in an active market [IAS 39.IG.B.22], for example privately issued mandatorily redeemable preference shares.

3.4.2 Securitised loans

The purchase of an interest in a pool of assets that are themselves loans and receivables can be classified as a loan or receivable if it meets the definition of a loan and receivable. If an entity acquires a beneficial interest in a securitised pool of loans and receivables this would not meet the definition of loan and receivable if the beneficial interest is quoted in an active market.

3.5 Available-for-sale financial assets (AFS)

AFS financial assets are those non-derivative financial assets that are designated as AFS, or are not classified as loans and receivables or HTM investments, are not held for trading and are not designated as at FVTPL on initial recognition.

AFS financial assets are measured at fair value with fair value gains or losses recognised in other comprehensive income. On sale or impairment of the asset, the cumulative gain or loss previously recognised in other comprehensive income is reclassified to profit or loss as a reclassification adjustment.

However, interest calculated using the effective interest method on interest-bearing AFS financial assets, impairment losses and foreign exchange gains and losses on monetary AFS financial assets are recognised in profit or loss (see **chapter 18** on measurement).

Dividends on an AFS equity instrument are recognised in profit or loss when the entity's right to receive payment is established.

Examples of AFS financial assets are equity investments that are not designated on initial recognition as at FVTPL, debt securities that are quoted in an active market, which may or may not have put features that would also prohibit them being HTM assets, and other financial assets held for liquidity purposes.

Example 3.5

Held for trading versus available-for-sale

[IAS 39.IG.B.12]

Entity A has an investment portfolio of debt and equity securities. The documented portfolio management guidelines specify that the equity exposure of the portfolio should be limited to between 30 and 50 per cent of total portfolio value. The investment manager of the portfolio is authorised to balance the portfolio within the designated guidelines by buying and selling equity and debt instruments. Is Entity A permitted to classify the instruments as available for sale?

It depends on Entity A's intentions and past practice. If the portfolio manager is authorised to buy and sell instruments to balance the risks in a portfolio, but there is no intention to trade and there is no past practice of trading for short-term profit, the instruments can be classified as available for sale. If the portfolio manager actively buys and sells instruments to generate short-term profits, the financial instruments in the portfolio are classified as held for trading.

4 Reclassifications

4.1 Into and out of FVTPL

Reclassifications into and out of this category are prohibited. However, as explained in **3.1.3** above designation and de-designation of derivatives as hedging instruments is not viewed as reclassification.

4.2 Out of HTM investments

Where, as a result of a change in intention or ability, it is no longer appropriate to classify an investment as HTM, it is reclassified as AFS and remeasured at fair value. [IAS 39.51] Note that the 'tainting' provisions of IAS 39 apply not only to sales but also to reclassifications of HTM investments. Hence, reclassifications of more than an insignificant amount of HTM investments, which do not meet any of the conditions for permitted sales, taint the HTM portfolio and all remaining HTM investments must be reclassified as AFS.

On reclassification out of HTM into the AFS category, as a consequence of tainting, the difference between the assets' carrying amount and their fair value is recognised in other comprehensive income. [IAS 39.51 and IAS 39.55(b)] This difference must be disclosed in addition to the reason for reclassification. [IFRS 7.12]

When an entity taints its HTM portfolio in the current reporting period, and is required to reclassify all of its HTM investments into the AFS category, it does not restate its comparatives for the reporting period to reflect this change of classification, since this would conceal the impact of 'tainting' the portfolio.

4.3 Into HTM investments

When the two-year tainting period subsequent to the period in which tainting occurred has passed, the entity is allowed to transfer the assets back into HTM provided it intends and is able to hold these assets to maturity. On the transfer the assets' carrying amount, i.e. their fair value at the time of the transfer, becomes the assets' new amortised cost. [IAS 39.54]

Any previous fair value gain or loss on the assets that has been recognised in other comprehensive income is amortised to profit or loss over the remaining life of the financial asset using the effective interest method.

4.4 Into and out of loans and receivables

Reclassifications of financial instruments into and out of the loans and receivables category are not permitted. An entity can designate a financial asset that satisfies the loan and receivable definition as AFS or as FVTPL upon initial recognition.

4.5 Investments in equity instruments for which fair value becomes insufficiently reliable

Where fair value becomes insufficiently reliable to warrant an unquoted equity instrument (or derivative linked to it and settled by delivery of an unquoted equity instrument) to be measured at fair value, then the instrument must be measured at cost. The carrying amount of the asset on this date becomes its cost. [IAS 39.55] Any fair value gains and losses recorded in profit or loss to that date will not be reversed; equally any fair value gains and losses that were included in other comprehensive income will remain in equity until the financial asset is sold, at which point these movements will be reclassified to profit or loss. However, even where the asset is carried at cost it is still subject to impairment review (see **section 6** in **chapter 18**).

4.6 Investments in equity instruments for which fair value becomes reliably determinable

When subsequently a reliable measure becomes available for an equity instrument (or derivative that is linked to and must be settled by delivery of an unquoted equity instrument) that was previously held at cost, the asset shall be remeasured at fair value. [IAS 39.53]

The difference between the financial asset's carrying amount and its fair value for an asset remeasured to fair value is recognised in profit or loss for assets classified as at FVTPL or in other comprehensive income for assets classified as AFS.

5 Classification of financial assets acquired in a business combination

When financial assets are acquired in a business combination those assets must be classified in the consolidated financial statements of the acquirer into one of the permitted categories described in **section 3** above. It is entirely possible that the classification of a financial asset for these purposes may differ from its classification in the financial statements of the acquiree. For example, the acquirer in its consolidated financial statements may choose to designate a financial asset as at fair value through profit or loss or as an available-for-sale asset on initial recognition that the acquiree did not when the acquiree initially recognised the asset. Also, the acquirer may choose to classify an asset as held to maturity that the acquiree did not. There are many other variations where the classification in the acquirer could be different to the existing accounting in the acquiree for the same financial asset. These differences arise as the acquirer is recognising the financial assets acquired in a business combination for the first time and therefore makes its classification decisions on that initial recognition.

The revised version of IFRS 3 *Business Combinations* issued in January 2008 provides clear guidance stating that at the acquisition date the acquirer shall make any classifications, designations concerning financial assets acquired or financial liabilities assumed in a business combination in accordance with the contractual terms, economic conditions, the acquirer's operating or accounting policies, and other factors as of that date that are pertinent in subsequently applying other IFRSs. IFRS 3(2008) applies prospectively to business combinations for which the acquisition date is on or after the beginning of the first annual reporting period beginning on or after 1 July 2009.

15 Financial instruments: financial liabilities and equity

1 Introduction

IAS 32 *Financial Instruments: Presentation* requires an issuer of a financial instrument to classify the financial instrument, or its component parts, as a financial liability or as equity in accordance with the substance of the contractual arrangement and the definitions of a financial liability and an equity instrument. The overriding principles are that where the issuer does not have an unconditional right to avoid the obligation to deliver cash, and where the contract does not, in substance, evidence a residual interest in the net assets of the issuer after deducting all of its liabilities, the instrument is not an equity instrument (see **section 2** below).

A more complex area, where the Standard provides additional guidance, is the treatment of derivative and non-derivative contracts indexed to, or settled in, an entity's own equity instruments. The definitions of a financial asset and a financial liability also include certain contracts on own equity and are applied to evaluate whether such contracts are, in substance, equity, financial liabilities or derivatives (derivatives could be either financial assets or financial liabilities). For example, a written put on own shares that will be settled, if the option is exercised by the holder, by delivering cash in exchange for the entity's own shares, is a financial liability as the entity will have an obligation to deliver cash (see **6.3** below).

This chapter addresses the application of the financial liability and equity definitions to various types of financial instruments issued in practice and contracts indexed to and settled in an entity's own equity. It also indicates the implications of classification as either debt, equity or a derivative for the measurement of that contract or its component parts.

This chapter discusses financial liabilities and equity in the following sections:

2 Principles of liability/equity classification

A financial instrument or its component parts should be classified upon initial recognition as a financial liability or equity instrument according to the substance of the contractual arrangement, not its legal form, and the definitions of a financial liability and an equity instrument. [IAS 32.15 & 18] Whilst some instruments may have the legal form of equity, their substance is one of a liability. A preference share, for instance, may display either equity or liability characteristics depending on the substance of the rights that attach to it. The appropriate classification is determined by the entity at the point of initial recognition and is not changed subsequently. When classifying a financial instrument in consolidated financial statements an entity considers all terms and conditions agreed between members of group and the holders of the instrument. A financial instrument issued by a subsidiary could be classified as equity in the individual financial statements and as a liability in the consolidated financial statements if another group entity has provided a guarantee to make payments to the holder of the instrument.

IAS 32 defines a financial liability as any liability that is:

(a) a contractual obligation:

  (i) to deliver cash or another financial asset to another entity (e.g. a payable);

  (ii) to exchange financial assets or financial liabilities with another entity under conditions that are potentially unfavourable to the entity (e.g. a financial option written by the entity); or

(b) a contract that will or may be settled in the entity's own equity instruments and is:

  (i) a non-derivative contract for which the entity is or may be obliged to deliver a variable number of its own equity instruments (e.g. an instrument that is redeemable in own shares to the value of the carrying amount of the instrument); or

  (ii) a derivative contract over own equity that will or may be settled other than by the exchange of a fixed amount of cash (or another financial asset) for a fixed number of the entity's own equity instruments (e.g. a net-share settled written call over own shares). For this purpose the entity's own equity instruments do not include instruments that are themselves contracts for the future receipt or delivery of the entity's own equity instruments.

The Standard defines an equity instrument as any contract that represents a residual interest in the assets of an entity after deducting all of its liabilities. [IAS 32.11]

2.1 Contractual obligation to deliver cash or another financial asset

The key feature in determining whether a financial instrument is a liability is the existence of a contractual obligation of one party (the issuer) to deliver cash or another financial asset to another party (the holder), or to exchange financial assets or liabilities under conditions that are potentially unfavourable. In contrast, in the case of an equity instrument (e.g. ordinary shares) the right to receive cash in the form of dividends or other distributions is at the issuer's discretion and as such no obligation to deliver cash or another financial asset to the holder of the instrument exists.

Items such as deferred revenue or warranty obligations require delivery of goods or services rather than an obligation to deliver cash or another financial asset and therefore are not financial liabilities. [IAS 32.AG11] Obligations to pay tax, company registration fees and other similar charges are obligations to pay cash, however these are statutory rather than contractual requirements and hence are not financial liabilities. Accounting for income taxes is dealt with in IAS 12 *Income Taxes*. Similarly, constructive obligations, as defined in IAS 37 *Provisions, Contingent Liabilities and Contingent Assets*, do not arise from contracts and are not financial liabilities. [IAS 32.AG12]

Liability characteristics are established in practice in a number of ways as demonstrated below.

2.1.1 *Mandatory redemption and/or mandatory interest payments*

Where the instrument requires mandatory redemption by the issuer for a fixed or determinable amount, a contractual obligation to deliver cash at redemption exists and therefore the instrument includes a liability.

Example 2.1.1A

Mandatory redeemable preference shares

Entity A issues preference shares that are mandatorily redeemable at par in 10 years. A contractual obligation to deliver cash exists for the repayment of principal – the issuer cannot avoid the outflow of cash in year 10.

Perpetual instruments provide the holder with no right to require redemption. However, the terms of such instruments often require the issuer to make coupon payments into perpetuity. A perpetual instrument with a mandatory coupon is a liability in its entirety since the whole of its value is derived from the stream of future coupon payments.

Example 2.1.1B

Perpetual coupon bearing preference shares

A perpetual instrument is issued at a par amount of £100 million requiring coupon payments of 6 per cent to be made annually. Provided 6 per cent is the market rate of interest for this type of instrument when issued, the issuer has assumed a contractual obligation to make a future stream of 6 per cent interest payments. The net present value of the interest payments is £100 million and represents the fair value of the liability.

Many traditional debt instruments such as bonds and bank loans involve both mandatory redemption and mandatory interest payments.

Other instruments may require a mandatory payment of a percentage of the profits of an entity (to the extent that such profits are generated) instead of a traditional interest payment. Such an instrument meets the definition of a liability as it is a contractual obligation of the issuer to deliver cash or another financial asset to the holder. The issuer has no discretion over paying out a percentage of its profits.

An entity should take into account not only obligations that exist in the contractual terms of the instrument, but also obligations the entity may have in respect of the issued instrument as a result of statutory conditions. In certain jurisdictions, public companies may under local law be required to distribute to ordinary shareholders a specified proportion of profits based on specified formulae, for example, the higher of (i) x per cent of net profit and (ii) x per cent of ordinary share capital outstanding. An entity will need to consider whether the entity can avoid proposing a dividend under these statutory conditions. If the entity does not have discretion over proposing a dividend then the instrument contains a liability. This liability may be equivalent to all the initial proceeds or may be less than the initial proceeds, indicating that the issued instrument is a compound instrument (see **section 3** below).

If shareholders have the ability to vote against any proposed dividend then this does not negate liability classification. In most jurisdictions the ordinary shareholders of an entity will vote for or against a proposed dividend. The key determinant in whether the instrument is a liability or equity is the issuer's discretion over proposing the payment of a dividend. If the issuer does not have this discretion, the instrument is a liability.

Care is needed in distinguishing those cases where the issuer genuinely contractually has no discretion over the making of interest payments (or payments representing a percentage of profits) and those where, if a payment is not made, there are other consequences (even if significant) to such a decision. For example, in some jurisdictions an entity may issue instruments under which it contractually has the discretion to make payments representing a percentage of profits, though if a payment is not made the entity ceases to benefit from a favourable tax treatment. In such cases, while the entity may in fact always plan to make the payments in light of the significant tax benefits, there is no contractual obligation to deliver cash (or other financial asset) to the holder of the instrument and the instrument is not a financial liability.

2.1.2 *Puttable instruments*

An instrument that gives the holder the right to put the instrument back to the issuer for cash or another financial asset is a financial liability. This is the case where the instrument gives the holder the right (but not the obligation) to require the issuer to redeem the instrument for a fixed amount at or after a particular date. It is also the case where the amount at which the holder can require the instrument to be redeemed is not fixed but is determined by reference to an index or other variable that has the potential to either increase or decrease the redemption value. In this case, there also might be an embedded derivative that may need to be accounted for separately if the whole instrument is not measured at fair value with changes recognised in profit or loss. The put option creates a contractual obligation for the issuer to deliver cash or another financial asset. [IAS 32.18(b)]

The fact that the contractual obligation is conditional upon the holder exercising its right to require redemption does not negate the existence of a financial liability as the issuer does not have the unconditional right to avoid delivering cash or another financial asset. [IAS 32.19(b)] An obligation is not negated where the instrument gives the holder the right to a residual interest in the assets of the issuer, as is the case for example, for a unit in a mutual fund. [IAS 32.18(b)]

Example 2.1.2A

Preference shares puttable at par

An entity issues preference shares that are puttable at par at the option of the holder at a particular date. The issuer recognises a financial liability for the present value of the obligation to redeem the preference shares at par in exchange for cash on that date.

Example 2.1.2B

Instrument puttable at net asset value

Entity A issues Class B shares that allow the holder of the instrument to put the instrument back to Entity A at a price equal to the number of Class B shares owned divided by the total number of Class B shares outstanding, multiplied by the net assets of Entity A (excluding the Class B shares from the net asset calculation). Although Class B shareholders are in a similar position to owners, in that they participate in the performance of the net assets of Entity A, the fact that Entity A has a contractual obligation to pay the holder of the Class B shares cash if the holder chooses to put the instrument back to the Entity, means Entity A must treat the Class B shares as a financial liability. The participation feature is an embedded derivative that is not closely related to the host liability and therefore needs to be separated out from the host contract and accounted for separately. The accounting treatment for embedded derivatives is dealt with in **chapter 17**.

Under IAS 32 the interests in many open-ended mutual funds, unit trusts, partnerships and some co-operative entities, which embody the right of the holder to require the issuer to redeem the interests for a cash amount equivalent to their share of net assets, require classification as financial liabilities. This may lead to a situation where some entities have no equity capital in their financial statements. IAS 32 permits the use of an appropriate description of the line item relating to puttable instruments and provides an illustrative example of such presentation, which is reproduced below:

Example 2.1.2C

Presentation of an entity without equity

[Extracts from IAS 32 Illustrative Examples (Example 7)]

Statement of financial position as at 31 December 20X1

		20X1		20X0
	CU	CU	CU	CU
ASSETS				
Non-current assets (classified in accordance with IAS 1)	91,374		78,484	
Total non-current assets		91,374		78,484
Current assets (classified in accordance with IAS 1)	1,422		1,769	
Total current assets		1,422		1,769
Total assets		92,796		80,253
LIABILITIES				
Current liabilities (classified in accordance with IAS 1)	647		66	
Total current liabilities		(647)		(66)
Non-current liabilities excluding net assets attributable to unitholders (classified in accordance with IAS 1)	280		136	
		(280)		(136)
Net assets attributable to unitholders		91,869		80,051

Statement of comprehensive income for the year ended 31 December 20X1

	20X1	20X0
	CU	CU
Revenue	2,956	1,718
Expenses (classified by nature or function)	(644)	(614)
Profit from operating activities	2,312	1,104
Finance costs:		
– other finance costs	(47)	(47)
– distributions to unitholders	(50)	(50)
Changes in net assets attributable to unitholders	2,215	1,007

Where an entity has no instruments classified as equity the normal requirements for presenting certain gains and losses in other comprehensive income continue to apply. For example, hedging gains and losses on cash flow hedging (see **2.2** in **chapter 20**) and net investment hedging (see **2.3** in **chapter 20**) as well as gains and losses on available-for-sale investments (see **3.5** in **chapter 14**) are recognised in other comprehensive income following the normal recognition and measurement rules.

In the case of some co-operatives, the entity has an unconditional right to refuse a member's request to redeem their shares, as prescribed in the entity's governing charter. In certain jurisdictions, local law, or regulation imposes prohibitions on redemption. Such a prohibition may be absolute in that all redemptions are prohibited; it may also be proportional, in that it prohibits redemption of members' shares if, by redeeming, the number of members' shares or amount of paid-in capital from members' shares would fall below a specified level.

IFRIC Interpretation 2 *Members' Shares in Co-operative Entities and Similar Instruments*, provides guidance on the application of IAS 32's principles to classification of members' shares in a co-operative entity as liabilities or part equity and part liability in accordance with the entity's charter or local legal and regulatory requirements. The Interpretation clarifies the following.

- The contractual right of a member to request redemption of contracts identified as members' shares does not, in itself, give rise to a liability. Rather, the entity must consider all of the terms of the contract in determining classification as a liability or equity (including relevant local laws, regulations and the entity's governing charter in effect at the date of the classification). Expected future amendments to those laws, regulations or charter, however, should not be considered. [IFRIC 2.5]
- Members' shares that give the member a right to request redemption are equity of the entity if the entity has an unconditional right to refuse redemption. [IFRIC 2.7]
- Local law, regulation or the entity's governing charter can impose prohibitions on the redemption of members' shares that are unconditional or dependent on certain conditions being met (or not met), e.g. prohibitions based on liquidity criteria. If redemption is unconditionally prohibited, members' shares are equity. However, provisions in local law, regulation or the entity's governing charter that prohibit redemption only if conditions (e.g. liquidity constraints) are met (or not met) do not result in members' shares being equity. [IFRIC 2.8]
- An unconditional prohibition may be absolute (i.e. all redemptions are prohibited) or partial in prohibiting redemption of members' shares if redemption would cause the number of shares or paid-in capital from members' shares to fall below a specified level. In the latter case, members' shares in excess of the prohibition against

redemption are liabilities, unless the entity has an unconditional right to refuse redemption. [IFRIC 2.9]

In certain cases, the number of shares or amount of paid-in capital subject to a redemption prohibition may change over time. If this is the case, such a change may lead to a transfer between financial liabilities and equity. [IFRIC 2.9] Consistent with the requirements of IAS 39, demand deposits, including current accounts, deposit accounts and similar contracts that arise when members act as customers, are financial liabilities of the entity. [IFRIC 2.6]

2.1.2.1 *Unconditional right to refuse redemption*

Example 2.1.2.1

Discretion to refuse redemption

The entity's governing charter states that redemptions are made at the sole discretion of the entity. There are no other conditions on the level of redemptions or any limitations on the entity's discretion to redeem or make payments to members. In its history, the entity has never refused to redeem members' shares, although the governing board has the right to do so. As the entity does not have an obligation to transfer cash or another financial asset, the members' shares are equity. A history of, or intention to make, discretionary payments does not trigger liability classification. [IAS 32.AG26]

2.1.2.2 *Partial prohibition against redemption*

Example 2.1.2.2

Limited discretion to refuse redemption

Local law governing the operations of co-operatives, or the terms of the entity's governing charter, prohibit an entity from redeeming members' shares if, by redeeming them, it would reduce paid-in capital from members' shares below 90 per cent of the highest amount of paid-in capital from members' shares. The highest amount for a particular co-operative is €1,000,000. At 31 December 20X0 the balance of paid-in capital is €750,000. At this date, the entire balance of paid-in capital €750,000 is classified as equity. At 31 December 20X1 the balance of paid-in capital is €950,000. At this date, €900,000 is classified as equity and €50,000 is classified as a financial liability.

2.1.2.3 *Transfer between equity and financial liabilities*

Example 2.1.2.3

Reclassification due to change in local law

Continuing the example in **2.1.2.2** above, at 31 December 20X2, local law governing the operations of co-operatives, or the terms of the entity's governing charter, change so that redemption of members' share is up to 20 per cent of the highest amount of members' shares, as opposed to 10 per cent. The entity would reclassify €100,000 from equity to financial liabilities, with no gain or loss resulting, at the date the local law or governing charter is amended. The entity must disclose separately the amount, timing and reason for the transfer.

2.1.2.4 *Amendment to IAS 32 for puttable financial instruments and obligations arising on liquidation*

In February 2008 the IASB published an amendment to IAS 32 and IAS 1 *Presentation of Financial Statements*. The amendment is relevant to entities that have issued financial instruments that are (i) puttable financial instruments, or (ii) instruments, or components of instruments, that impose on the entity an obligation to deliver to another party a pro rata share of the net assets of the entity only on liquidation. Subject to specified criteria being met, under the amendments these instruments would be classified as equity, whereas under the requirements in IAS 32 prior to the amendment they may have been classified as a financial liability.

The amendment was developed in response to concerns over the effect of applying the definitions of a financial liability and equity in IAS 32 to financial instruments that are puttable or require payment only at liquidation where either liquidation is certain, as in the case of limited life entities, or liquidation is at the option of the holder of the instrument. Under the existing requirements of IAS 32 the accounting for a puttable instrument could result in the entire market capitalisation of an entity being recognised as a liability and subsequently remeasured if the instrument is puttable at the fair value of the entity. In some instances the entity would have net liabilities as the instrument's carrying amount would be in excess of the entity's recognised assets. Furthermore, counter intuitively, when the entity's performance deteriorates the remeasurement of the liability results in a gain in profit or loss. Similar concerns were raised with the accounting for limited life entities that are obliged to liquidate after a set period of time or at the option of the holder as these entities must recognise a financial liability, instead of equity, as the issuer cannot avoid paying cash.

In response to such concerns the amendment was issued as a 'short term, limited scope amendment' to improve the financial reporting of some puttable financial instruments and instruments with obligations arising on liquidation that have characteristics similar to ordinary shares. It is intended that the amendment should provide an interim solution pending the IASB's long-term project on liabilities and equity. The impact of the amendments is restricted to the specific cases cited – no analogies can be made to these requirements.

The amendment distinguishes between puttable financial instruments and financial instruments that impose on the issuer an obligation to deliver a pro rata share of net assets of the entity only on liquidation. The amendment changes the definition of a financial liability in IAS 32.11 for these two different types of instruments.

Puttable instruments will be presented as equity only if all the following criteria are met:

(i) the holder is entitled to a pro rata share of the entity's net assets at liquidation;

(ii) the instrument is in the class of instruments that is the most subordinate and all instruments in that class are identical;

(iii) the instrument has no other characteristics that would meet the definition of a financial liability; and

(iv) the total expected cash flows attributable to the instrument over its life are based substantially on the profit or loss, the change in the recognised net assets or the change in the fair value of the recognised and unrecognised net assets of the entity. Profit or loss or change in recognised net assets for this purpose is as measured in accordance with relevant IFRSs.

In addition to the above criteria the entity must have no other instrument that has terms equivalent to (iv) above and that has the effect of substantially restricting or fixing the residual return to the holders of the puttable instruments.

Instruments, or components of instruments, that impose on the entity an obligation to deliver to another party a pro rata share of the net assets of the entity only on liquidation have very similar criteria to be presented as equity as described above. The exception is that criteria (iii) and (iv) do not apply. Criterion (iii) does not apply because, if there is a component of the instrument that meets the definition of a liability (other than the right at liquidation itself), this will be recognised separately as a financial liability and the instrument will be presented as a compound instrument, i.e. with both liability and equity components. Criterion (iv) does not apply because should any cash flows be paid to the holder of the instrument during the instrument's life, this will reduce the amount ultimately payable at liquidation.

The amendment permits reclassification from or to equity in the case when the specified criteria for equity are no longer met, or become met. If the instrument presented as equity is reclassified to a financial liability it will be measured at fair value with any difference in the fair value and the carrying value recognised in equity. When the inverse applies, the financial liability will be reclassified to equity at its carrying amount at the date of reclassification.

Where a subsidiary classifies a puttable instrument or instrument imposing an obligation to deliver to another entity a pro-rata share of the net assets of the entity on its liquidation as equity in its individual financial statements, those instruments held by non-controlling parties will not be presented as equity in the group financial statements as it is not the most subordinated class of instrument from the perspective of the group. This is because, if the group were to liquidate, the claims of non-controlling parties to the net assets of the subsidiary have to be satisfied first, before the parent's share of the net assets of the subsidiary could be distributed to the claimants to the assets of the parent.

The amendment also amends the definition of a financial asset and financial liability with respect to a contract that will or may be settled in the entity's own equity instruments (see **section 2** of **chapter 14** and **section 2** of this chapter for current definitions). For the purposes of determining whether a derivative that will or may be settled by the exchange of a fixed amount of cash or another financial asset for a fixed number of the entity's own equity instruments should be classified as equity, own equity instruments do not include puttable financial instruments, or instruments that impose on the entity an obligation to deliver to another entity a pro rata share of the net assets of the entity on its liquidation.

The following illustrate the types of instruments impacted by the new requirements.

Issued financial instrument	**Classification under IAS 32 prior to the amendment**	**Classification under amended IAS 32 after the amendment**
Share puttable throughout its life at fair value, that is also the most subordinate, does not contain any other obligation, with discretionary dividends based on profits of the issuer	Liability	Equity
Share puttable at fair value, that is not the most subordinate	Liability	Liability
Share puttable at fair value only on liquidation, that is also the most subordinate, but contains a fixed non-discretionary dividend	Liability	Compound (part equity, part liability)
Share puttable at fair value only on liquidation, that is also the most subordinate, but contains a fixed discretionary dividend and does not contain any other obligation	Liability	Equity
Any of the instruments described above issued by a subsidiary held by non-controlling parties, in the consolidated financial statements	Liability	Liability

If an entity applies the amendments and as a result would have recognised a financial instrument in the past that would have been a compound instrument, but the financial liability is no longer outstanding at the date of applying the amendments, it does not need to restate retained earnings for the profit or loss impact that would have arisen from that financial liability. This is the same exemption that applies to the accounting for compound instruments in IFRS 1 *First-time adoptions of International Financial Reporting Standards.*

IAS 1 is also amended to require the following additional disclosure if an entity has a puttable instrument that is presented as equity:

- summary quantitative data about the amount classified as equity;

- the entity's objectives, policies and processes for managing its obligation to repurchase or redeem the instruments when required to do so by the instrument holders, including any changes from the previous period;
- the expected cash outflow on redemption or repurchase of that class of financial instruments; and
- information about how the expected cash outflow on redemption or repurchase was determined.

If an instrument is reclassified into and out of each category (financial liabilities or equity) the amount, timing and reason for that reclassification must be disclosed. If an entity is a limited life entity disclosure is required regarding the length of its life.

IFRIC 2 *Members' Shares in Co-operative Entities and Similar Instruments*, see **2.1.2** above, is amended to reflect that the definition of equity is broader following the effective date of the amendment to IAS 32. However, the consensus of IFRIC 2 is not amended.

The amendments are effective retrospectively for annual periods beginning on or after 1 January 2009, with earlier adoption permitted. If entities adopt the amendments for a period beginning before 1 January 2009, consequential amendments to IFRS 7, *Financial Instruments: Disclosures*, IAS 39, and IFRIC 2 should be adopted from the same earlier date. The fact that the amendments have been adopted in advance of their effective date should be disclosed.

UK

At the time of writing, the amendments to IAS 32 have not yet been endorsed for adoption in the EU. EU companies will not be able to adopt the amended version of IAS 32 until it is endorsed.

2.1.3 Restrictions on ability to satisfy contractual obligation

A restriction on the contractual obligation of the entity to deliver cash or another financial instrument, such as the need to obtain regulatory approval for payment, does not in itself negate that obligation. The entity does not in such cases have an unconditional right to avoid delivering cash or another financial asset. [IAS 32.19(a)]

(a) a change in macroeconomic, industry and other indices such as the stock market index, consumer price index, growth in Gross Domestic Product or total sector production;

(b) changes in law, government regulations, and other regulatory requirements (such as changes in taxation, pricing controls or accounting requirements); and

(c) changes in the key performance indicators of the issuer that are beyond the control of both the issuer and the holder such as revenues, net income or debt to equity ratio.

Example 2.1.6A

Contingent settlement provisions: change in accounting or tax law

Entity A issues preference shares bearing 5 per cent non-cumulative dividends that are at the discretion of the issuer. The shares will be redeemed if the applicable taxation or accounting requirements were to change.

Given that the contingent event is outside the control of both the issuer and the holder, is genuine, and can result in the issuer having to deliver cash or another financial asset at a time other than the issuer's liquidation, the instrument is classified as a financial liability. However, the 5 per cent dividend is at the discretion of the issuer and is therefore equity of the issuer. Hence, the preference share contains both debt and equity features, i.e. it is a compound instrument (see **section 3** below).

Example 2.1.6B

Contingent settlement provisions: initial public offering

Entity B issues shares for £1 million. Dividends are discretionary. The issuer must redeem the shares for par in the event of a flotation / Initial Public Offering ('IPO') of the entity. Given that the contingent event, the IPO, is in the control of the issuer, it is not a contingent settlement provision. As the issuer can avoid redeeming the shares, the instrument is classified as equity.

2.2 Equity instruments

In classifying a financial instrument as liability or equity, equity classification is appropriate only if the instrument fails the definition of a financial liability as detailed in **section 2** above.

The key requirement in determining whether an instrument is equity is the issuer's unconditional ability to avoid delivery of cash or another financial asset. That ability is not affected by:

- the history of making distributions;

- an intention to make distributions in the future;
- a possible negative impact on the price of ordinary shares of the issuer if the distributions are not made on the instrument concerned;
- the amount of the issuer's reserves;
- an issuer's expectations of a profit or loss for the period; or
- an ability or inability of the issuer to influence the amount of its profit or loss for the period.

Provided the dividends are at the discretion of the issuer, it is irrelevant whether dividends are cumulative or non-cumulative. [IAS 32.AG26]

Once a dividend is properly declared and the issuer is legally required to pay it, a contractual obligation to deliver cash comes into existence and a financial liability for the amount of the declared dividend needs to be recognised. Similarly, on a winding up a liability arises to distribute to the shareholders the residual assets in the issuer, i.e. any remaining assets after satisfying all of its liabilities.

The existence of an option whereby the issuer can redeem equity shares for cash does not trigger liability classification as the issuer retains the unconditional right to avoid delivering cash or another financial asset. A contractual obligation would only arise at the point where the issuer were to exercise its right to redeem. This principle applies for all instruments that are not derivatives over own equity.

Specific rules apply for derivatives over own equity. For example, a purchased call option over a fixed number of shares will allow the issuer to buy back shares at a fixed price in the future. The issuer always has a choice whether it wishes to pay cash, as it always has a choice as to whether it wishes to exercise its option. However, this instrument is only treated as equity if it is gross physically settled in all cases when the issuer chooses to exercise, i.e. the option cannot ever be net settled.

Often instruments are issued with various links to dividend payments on other types of instruments, most commonly ordinary shares. A 'dividend stopper' is a contractual term that requires no dividend to be paid on the ordinary shares if the payment is not made on the instrument concerned. A 'dividend pusher' is a term that requires a dividend to be paid on the instrument concerned if a payment of dividend is made on ordinary shares.

Provided the link is to the dividends on an instrument like an ordinary share where the issuer has the discretion over the decision whether or not to pay a dividend, a 'dividend pusher' or a 'dividend stopper' does not of itself result in the instrument concerned being classified as a liability. This is because the issuer continues to have the discretion over the decision whether or not to pay on the instrument, though that decision will need to be made in conjunction with the decision on whether to pay on ordinary shares. The fact remains that the issuer has an unconditional right to avoid outflow of cash (or other financial assets).

Example 2.2A

Dividend stopper

Entity Y issues 6 per cent cumulative preference shares with discretionary dividends which are subject to availability of distributable reserves. The directors of Y can decide at each period end whether and the extent to which a dividend on the preference shares will be paid. The terms of the instrument include a dividend stopper, i.e. if no dividend is paid on the preference shares, then no dividend is paid on Entity Y's ordinary shares. Entity Y has an unconditional right to avoid the obligation to deliver cash, as dividends on the preference shares are entirely at Entity Y's discretion.

Example 2.2B

Dividend pusher

Entity M issues preference shares bearing 6 per cent discretionary non-cumulative dividends which are subject to availability of distributable reserves. The directors of M can decide at each period end whether and the extent to which a dividend on the preference shares will be paid. However, the terms of the instrument include a dividend pusher, i.e. if a dividend is paid on Entity M's ordinary shares, then a dividend must be paid on the preference shares. Dividends on its ordinary shares are at the discretion of Entity M and therefore Entity M has an unconditional right to avoid the obligation to pay cash on the preference shares. The preference shares are equity.

Once the amendment to IAS 32 titled *Puttable instruments and obligations arising on liquidation* becomes effective more financial instruments will be classified as equity than prior to the amendment. Provided specified criteria are met certain puttable financial instruments that prior to the amendment would have been classified as a financial liability will be classified as equity. This is not the case for derivatives over puttable financial instruments as the amendment does not permit such instruments to be classified as equity. See **2.1.2.4** above for details of the amendment.

3 Compound instruments

The terms of a financial instrument may be structured such that it contains both equity and liability components (i.e. the instrument is neither entirely a liability, nor entirely an equity instrument). Such instruments are defined in IAS 32 as compound instruments. An example of a compound instrument is a bond that is convertible, either mandatorily or at the option of the holder, into a fixed number of equity shares of the issuer. Compound instruments come in many forms and are not restricted solely to convertible instruments. The liability and equity components of a compound instrument are required to be accounted for separately. [IAS 32.28]

The requirement to separate out the equity and financial liability components of a compound instrument is consistent with the principle that a financial instrument must be classified in accordance with its substance, rather than its legal form. A compound instrument has a legal form of a single instrument, while the substance is that both a liability and equity instrument exist.

For example, a convertible bond that pays fixed coupons and is convertible by the holder into a fixed number of ordinary shares of the issuer has the legal form of a debt contract. Yet, its substance is that of two instruments.

1. A financial liability to deliver cash (by making scheduled payments of coupon and principal) which exists as long as the bond is not converted.
2. A written call option granting the holder the right to convert the bond into a fixed number of ordinary shares of the entity.

The economic effect of the instrument is substantially the same as issuing simultaneously a debt instrument with an early settlement provision, and separately issuing warrants to issue ordinary shares.

3.1 Separating the liability and equity components

Separation of the instrument into its liability and equity components is made upon initial recognition of the instrument and is not subsequently revised. The method used is as follows:

- firstly, the fair value of the liability component is calculated, and this fair value establishes the initial carrying amount of the liability component; and
- secondly the fair value of the liability component is deducted from the fair value of the instrument as a whole, with the resulting residual amount being the equity component.

This method of allocating the liability and equity components is consistent with the definition of equity being a residual interest in the assets of an entity after deducting all of its liabilities. It ensures that no gain or loss arises on initial recognition of the two components.

The fair value of the liability component on initial recognition is the present value of the contractual stream of future cash flows (including both coupon payments and redemption) discounted at the market rate of interest that would have been applied to an instrument of comparable credit quality with substantially the same cash flows, on the same terms, but without the conversion option.

Example 3.1A

Convertible debt

Entity A, a Sterling functional currency entity, issues 2,000 convertible bonds on 1 January 20X5. The bonds have a three-year term, and are issued at par with a face value of £1,000 per bond, giving total proceeds of £2 million. Interest is payable annually in arrears at an annual interest rate of 6 per cent. Each bond is convertible, at the holder's discretion, at any time up to maturity into 250 ordinary shares. When the bonds are issued, the market interest rate for similar debt without the conversion option is 9 per cent.

On initial recognition the liability component is valued first, and the difference between the proceeds of the bond issue (being the fair value of the instrument in its entirety) and the fair value of the liability is assigned to the equity component. The present value (i.e. fair value) of the liability component is calculated using a discount rate of 9 per cent, the market interest rate for similar bonds with the same credit standing having no conversion rights. The calculation, which excludes the income tax entries, is illustrated below:

	£
Present value of principal at the end of 3 years*	1,544,367
Present value of interest –	
– £120,000 payable annually in arrears for 3 years **	303,755
Total liability component (B)	1,848,122
Residual equity component (A-B)	151,878
Proceeds of bond issue (A)	2,000,000
*present value of principal amount at 9%:	
2,000,000/(1.09)^3 =	1,544,367
**present value of interest (£120,000) payable at the end of each of 3 years:	
interest at end of year 1: 120,000/1.09 =	110,092
interest at end of year 2: $120{,}000/(1.09)^2$ =	101,002
interest at end of year 3: $120{,}000/(1.09)^3$ =	92,661
Total net present value of interest payments	303,755

Upon initial recognition of the convertible instrument in the financial statements of the issuer the following entries are appropriate:

Dr	Cash	£2,000,000
Cr	Financial liability	£1,848,122
Cr	Equity	£151,878

Any transaction costs are allocated between the debt component and the equity component, using their relative fair values.

The financial liability component will be subsequently measured in accordance with the measurement requirements in IAS 39 depending on its classification (financial liability at fair value through profit or loss, or other liability, measured at amortised cost using the effective interest rate method).

The equity component will not be re-measured.

Example 3.1B

Perpetual interest bearing preference shares

Entity A, a Euro functional entity, issues non-redeemable preference shares. The preference shares have a cumulative, mandatory dividend fixed at €424 per share per year. If earnings are not sufficient to cover the dividend in any given year, such dividends will be paid in future years. Additional dividends may be declared but must be distributed evenly throughout the different classes of shares.

The preference share is a compound financial instrument that contains both liability and equity components. The liability is the contractual obligation by the issuer to deliver cash (€424 per year), while the equity component is represented by the holder's right to receive an equity return in the form of additional dividends, if declared.

The fair value of the liability will be calculated as the present value of the mandatory dividend of €424 per share per year in perpetuity discounted at the market interest rate for a similar instrument that does not contain a residual benefit to discretionary dividends. The equity component is calculated as the residual amount after deducting from the fair value of the instrument as a whole the amount separately determined for the liability component.

3.2 Separating the liability and equity components where the instrument has embedded derivatives

In addition to the financial liability and equity components, a compound instrument may also have embedded derivatives (see **chapter 17**). For example, the instrument may contain a call option exercisable by the issuer. The value of any such embedded derivative features must be allocated to the liability component. [IAS 32.31] Thus, the carrying amount of the liability component is established by measuring the fair value of a similar liability (with similar terms, credit status and embedded non-equity derivative features) but without an associated equity component. The carrying amount of the equity component is then determined by deducting the fair value of the liability component from the fair value of the compound instrument as a whole.

A further assessment is required to establish whether the embedded derivative is closely related to the liability component (see **chapter 17**). This assessment is made before separating the equity component. No gain or loss arises from initially recognising the components of the instrument separately.

Example 3.2A

Convertible debt with issuer call

A Sterling functional currency entity issues a bond with a principal amount of £60 million carrying a coupon of 5 per cent payable annually in arrears. The instrument is issued for proceeds of £60 million. The instrument is convertible into a fixed number of equity shares of the issuer after a specified date. The instrument has no fixed maturity, however, it contains an issuer call option that allows the issuer to redeem the bond at par at any point in time.

It is established that the value of a similar bond, of similar credit status with similar features except one not containing a call or equity conversion option at current market rates would be £57 million. Based on an option pricing model it is further determined that the value of the issuer purchased call option on a similar bond without a conversion option is £2 million. In this case the value allocated to the liability and equity components should be as follows:

Liability component: £55 million (£57 million less £2 million)

This represents the inclusion of the value of the additional embedded derivative feature in the liability component.

Equity component: £5 million (£60 million – £55 million)

This represents the equity residual arrived at by subtracting from the fair value of the whole instrument the fair value of the liability component (which includes the value of the embedded derivative feature in the form of the purchased call feature).

The issuer call option will not be separately accounted for since its exercise price is set at par (£60 million), which is equal to the amortised cost of the instrument on each exercise date on the basis that the assessment is made prior to separating out the written equity call option, i.e. the embedded derivative is closely related to the host debt instrument.

In the example described above, the initial amortised cost of the financial liability is established as the fair value of issued callable debt. Assuming the call feature over the debt instrument is not separated, the effective interest rate applied at inception and throughout the life of the instrument is the same rate of interest that would apply for plain callable debt. To the extent that interest rates change subsequent to issue, this will impact the likelihood that callable debt will be called by the issuer, and therefore the carrying amount will be updated (see **4.1.1** in **chapter 18**).

Example 3.2B

Convertible debt with issuer call and holder put

Entity X has issued a convertible debt instrument in May 2008 with a contractual maturity of 16 years. One bond allows the holder to obtain, at any time, one share of the issuer (the conversion option). Coupon is 2 per cent payable annually. Issue price is 100 per cent and redemption price is 140 per cent.

The instrument is puttable by the holders on three different dates, during the life of the instrument (May 2012, May 2016 and May 2020).

The instrument is also callable by the issuer, starting 2012, if the price of the issuer's shares increases beyond 125 per cent of the redemption price.

In the case of exercise of the put/call option, the redemption price is equivalent to the amortised cost of the issued instrument (prior to the equity conversion option being separated). The embedded call/put options, therefore, are closely related to the instrument and are not accounted for as derivatives with changes in fair value recognised in profit or loss. On initial recognition, Entity X considers that there is a very high probability that the instrument will be redeemed by the holders on the first exercise date of the put (i.e. 2012), given the low price of its shares.

Entity X will account for the issued bond as a compound instrument. On initial recognition X needs to consider the contractual cash flows in order to measure the value of the debt component of the compound instrument.

The fair value of the straight debt instrument without a call/put or equity conversion option, is equivalent to the present value of the contractually determined stream of future cash flows until maturity (in this case 2024) discounted at the rate of interest that applies to instruments of comparable credit quality and providing substantially the same cash flows on the same terms but without the call, put or conversion option (i.e. debt instruments with a 2024 maturity date).

Entity X then determines the value of the call and put options embedded in the debt instrument using an option pricing model. The call and put options are valued as if they were a call and a put embedded in a debt instrument that did not have any equity conversion feature. Both the purchased call and the written put are deducted and added to the debt in order to obtain the fair value of the total liability component.

Finally, Entity X determines the value of the embedded conversion option (equity component) by subtracting the total liability component from the total net proceeds received on issuance.

If the financial liability is not designated at fair value through profit or loss, the effective interest rate must be applied in determining amortised cost. If an entity designates financial instruments as at fair value through profit or loss it should have a policy as to whether it recognises the effective interest rate in profit or loss separately for such items, see **5.1.1** in **chapter 21**. An issuer must apply the effective interest rate to the financial liability ignoring the likelihood that the financial liability may be forgiven if the equity conversion is exercised. This treatment is consistent with the principle that the likelihood of conversion is recognised as a separate financial instrument in equity.

3.3 Conversion of a compound instrument

Upon conversion of a compound instrument equity is issued and the liability component is derecognised. The original equity component recognised at inception remains in equity (although it may be reclassified from one line item of equity to another). No gain or loss is recognised on conversion. [IAS 32.AG32]

Example 3.3A

Convertible debt: issue of new shares

Assume the facts are as in **example 3.1A** but the date now is 31 December 20X6 (i.e. the end of year 2 of the instrument's life). Assume that due to a rapidly rising share price all holders of the bond exercise their right to convert into a fixed number of equity instruments of the entity at this point in time.

The liability has been accounted for at amortised cost using the effective interest rate method (see **4.1** in **chapter 18**).

At 31 December 20X6 the following applies:

- the amortised cost carrying amount of the liability (determined using the effective interest rate method) just before conversion is £1,944,954;
- the original equity component just before conversion still stands at the original £151,878; and
- upon conversion 500,000 equity shares will be issued (250 equity shares per bond x 2,000 bonds issued) where each equity share has a nominal value of £1.

The accounting entries on conversion are as follows:

Dr	Bond	1,944,954	to remove the liability from the statement of financial position on conversion
Cr	Equity	1,944,954	to record the issue of shares as a result of conversion

The original component of equity, £151,878, may be reclassified to another line item within equity.

Example 3.3B

Convertible debt: issue of treasury shares

Assume the facts as in **example 3.1A** above except that instead of issuing new shares upon conversion the entity satisfies the requirement for equity shares to be delivered to the bondholders through the use of treasury shares. Rather than issuing 500,000 new equity shares the entity will deliver to bondholders upon conversion 500,000 of its own shares that it had previously repurchased and held as treasury shares.

The required journals in this case would be:

Dr	Bond	1,944,954	to remove liability from statement of financial position as a result of conversion
Cr	Equity	1,944,954	to remove the treasury shares from equity

The original component of equity, £151,878, may be reclassified to another line item within equity.

3.4 Early redemption of compound instrument

Where an entity redeems or repurchases a convertible instrument before its maturity (without altering the conversion features) through a tender offer the consideration paid to do so (including any transaction costs) is allocated to the liability and equity components at the date of the early redemption/early repurchase. The method used to make this allocation is the same as that used to make the original allocation of the proceeds of the issue of the instrument between the liability and equity components upon initial recognition. [IAS 32.AG33]

To the extent that the amount of the consideration allocated to the liability component exceeds the carrying amount of the liability component at that point in time, a loss is recorded in profit or loss. Conversely, to the extent that the consideration allocated is smaller than the carrying amount of the liability a gain is recorded in profit or loss.

The amount of consideration allocated to equity is recorded in equity with no gain or loss being recorded (the equity component that is not eliminated may be reclassified to another line item within equity).

Example 3.4

Convertible debt: repurchase

Using the same scenario as in **example 3.1A** assume that one year has elapsed and it is now 31 December 20X5 (i.e. the convertible bonds have been outstanding for one year).

In respect of the first year (y/e 31 December 20X5) the following accounting entries will have been made:

Dr	Interest Expense	166,331
Cr	Bond Liability	166,331

To record the interest expense and amortised cost of the bond using an effective interest rate of 9 per cent.

Dr	Bond Liability	120,000
Cr	Cash	120,000

To record the cash payment of interest.

This gives a carrying amount of the liability at the end of the first year equal to £1,894,453.

	£
Initial carrying amount at inception	1,848,122
Accretion in year 1 using the effective interest method	166,331
Cash coupon payment at end of year 1	(120,000)
Carrying amount at end of year 1	1,894,453

At the end of the first year Entity A repurchases the convertible bonds for a cash amount of £2,100,000. It is established that at the date of repurchase the entity could have issued a non convertible instrument with a term of 2 years bearing a coupon rate of 7 per cent.

The consideration paid is allocated to the liability component and equity component using the same method as used on initial recognition of the convertible bonds. Namely, the fair value of consideration paid is first allocated to the liability component with the residual being assigned to the repurchase of the equity component:

	Fair value of repurchase consideration	Carrying amount prior to repurchase	Difference
	£	£	£
Liability component:			
Present value of 2 remaining interest payments of £120,000 discounted at 7 per cent and 9 per cent respectively	216,963	211,093	
Present value of principal amount due in 2 years time of £2 million discounted at 7 per cent and 9 per cent respectively	1,746,877	1,683,360	
	1,963,840	1,894,453	69,387
Equity component	136,160*	151,878	(15,718)
Total	2,100,000	2,046,331	53,669

* The amount of £136,160 represents the difference between the repurchase price of £2,100,000 and the amount of the consideration paid allocated to the liability component.

Having completed the allocation of the repurchase price, the following entries are made by Entity A in respect of the repurchase of the bonds:

Dr	Bond liability	£1,894,453
Dr	Debt extinguishment loss	£69,387
Cr	Cash	£1,963,840

To record the repurchase of the liability and the loss on doing so

Dr	Equity	£136,160
Cr	Cash	£136,160

To record the portion of the cash paid in respect of the repurchase of the equity component.

The remaining balance of £15,718 can be transferred into a different line item in equity.

Early redemption of convertible bond by the issuer exercising an embedded call option

Repurchase through a tender offer of convertible debt is explicitly addressed in the application guidance to IAS 32 as described above but early redemption via the issuer exercising an embedded call option is not. Consider the following scenario. Entity B (whose functional currency is Euro) issues a convertible bond for €10m on

1 January 20X0. The bond is redeemable at the par amount of €10m at 31 December 20X9. The bond pays interest of 4% on the par amount on 31 December throughout its life. The holder can convert the bond into a fixed number of equity shares at any point from 1 January 20X5 to 31 December 20X9. In addition under the terms of the call option embedded in the convertible bond the issuer may redeem the instrument early by paying the par amount of €10m at any point between 1 January 20X5 and 31 December 20X9.

The convertible bond is classified as a compound instrument with a financial liability and equity component by Entity B. As discussed in **section 7.1** in **chapter 17** the call option is deemed to be closely related and is therefore not separately accounted for on the basis of a comparison of the exercise price of the option (amount repayable if called) to the amortised cost of the instrument before separating the equity component under IAS 32. Assume the issuer does make use of the call option on 1 January 20X5 and redeems the instrument under the terms of the option at this date. The question then arises as to how to account for the redemption of the convertible bond by Entity B.

One way of accounting for the use of the call option would be to account for it as part of the debt instrument to which it is closely related. This would necessitate remeasuring the amortised cost of the financial liability component of the convertible debt under IAS 39.AG8 as discussed in **section 4.1.2** in **chapter 18.** This would involve discounting the revised estimate of cash flows payable under the instrument (to include the €10m that will be payable immediately under the terms of the option) at the original effective interest rate established at initial recognition of the financial liability component of the convertible debt. The difference between the previous amortised cost carrying amount and the newly remeasured amount would be recorded in profit or loss. This would have the effect of recognising a loss equal to par less the carrying amount from the prior reporting period.

Alternatively, it may be argued that the guidance under IAS 32.AG33 discussed earlier in this section should be applied as this refers to redemption. Under this approach the consideration paid to redeem the convertible debt would be allocated to the financial liability and equity components at the date of the early redemption using the same method as that used to make the allocation between the financial liability and equity component on initial recognition of the compound instrument. However, as the fair value of the financial liability component once the option has been exercised is likely to be equal to the redemption price this method would allocate all of the consideration (i.e. the redemption price) to the financial liability component. Therefore the effect would be likely to be substantially the same as the remeasurement under IAS 39.AG8 as discussed above.

3.5 Amendment of the terms of a compound instrument to induce early conversion

An entity may amend the terms of the convertible instrument during its life so as to make conversion more attractive through either offering a more favourable conversion ratio, paying additional consideration in the event of conversion before a specified date, or a combination of both. In such instances the difference between the fair value of the consideration that the holder receives upon conversion under the revised terms and the fair value of the consideration that the holder would have received upon conversion under the original terms, measured at the date when the terms are amended, should be recognised in net profit or loss as a loss. [IAS 32.AG35]

Example 3.5

Convertible debt: inducement to convert

Assume the same scenario as in **example 3.1A**, but at 31 December 20X5 (i.e. the end of year 1 of the instrument's life) to induce holders to convert promptly Entity A amends the terms in one of two ways in respect of conversions that take place prior to 1 March 20X6:

Scenario 1: Entity A alters the terms such that each of the 2,000 bonds converts into 300 equity shares of the entity, instead of 250 equity shares as under the original conversion terms (assume the market value of the equity shares at the date of the amendment is £5).

Scenario 2: Entity A states that it will pay an additional £1 in cash in relation to each share converted.

The liability and equity components have the following carrying amounts in the statement of financial position at 31 December 20X5:

	Carrying amount at 31.12.X5 £
Liability component:	
Present value of 2 remaining interest payments of £120,000 discounted at 9 per cent	211,093
Present value of principal amount of £2m due in 2 years time discounted at 9 per cent	1,683,360
	1,894,453

Equity component	151,878*
Total	2,046,331

* The equity component remains unchanged since the allocation on initial recognition.

The following entries will be necessary to record the amendment of the terms of the convertible:

Scenario 1

Number of equity shares to be issued to bondholders under the *amended* conversion terms:

Number of bonds issued	2,000
Number of shares to be issued per bond on conversion	300
Total number of equity shares to be issued on conversion	600,000

Number of equity shares to be issued to bondholders under *original* conversion terms:

Number of bonds issued	2,000
Number of shares to be issued per bond on conversion	250
Total number of equity shares to be issued on conversion	500,000

Number of incremental equity shares to be issued to bondholders upon conversion: 100,000

Value of incremental equity shares to be issued to bondholders upon conversion:

100,000 * £5 = £500,000

Therefore the entry needed to record the amendment of the terms is:

Dr	Expense on amendment of terms of convertible	£500,000
Cr	Equity	£500,000

Upon conversion the accounting would follow the approach laid out in **example 3.3A**.

Scenario 2

The additional consideration to be paid in the event of conversion would amount to:

500,000 * £1 = £500,000

This would again be recognised through the following double entry:

Dr	Expense on amendment of terms of convertible	£500,000
Cr	Equity	£500,000

Upon conversion the accounting would follow the approach laid out in **example 3.3A** except in so far as an extra entry would be necessary to record the payment of the additional cash inducement as follows:

Dr	Equity	£500,000
Cr	Cash	£500,000

As described in **3.3** above, upon conversion of a compound instrument equity is issued and the liability component is derecognised. The original equity component recognised at inception remains in equity (although it may be reclassified from one line item of equity to another) and no gain or loss is recognised on conversion. This treatment equally applies for conversion of a compound instrument where previously there was an inducement and an expense in profit or loss and increase in equity was recognised. Upon conversion of the compound instrument the financial liability is derecognised and reclassified to equity. Equity will therefore consist of the original equity component recognised on issue of the compound instrument, the amount recognised in equity as a result of inducement, plus the reclassification of the liability upon conversion. Amounts may be transferred within equity from one line item to another upon conversion of the compound instrument.

3.6 Treatment of mandatorily convertible instruments

An entity may issue an instrument that at the end of its life is mandatorily convertible into a fixed number of its equity shares (rather than conversion being at the option of the holder). This instrument is, in substance, a prepaid forward purchase of the entity's equity shares. As the instrument carries an obligation for the issuer to make fixed interest payments during the life of the mandatorily convertible, the instrument includes a financial liability component. The following example illustrates the entries for a mandatorily convertible debt instrument.

Example 3.6

Mandatorily convertible instrument

A Sterling functional currency entity issues a mandatorily convertible instrument for £100,000 on 1 January 20X5. The instrument obligates the entity to make cash coupon payments of £5,000 on both 31 December 20X5 and 31 December 20X6. In addition, at the end of the instrument's life on 31 December 20X6, after the last coupon payment is made, the instrument will mandatorily convert into 5,000 £1 ordinary shares of the entity.

At inception of the instrument the following two elements will be separated.

- A liability component arising from the coupon payments of £5,000 to be made on 31 December 20X5 and 31 December 20X6. This will be determined as the present value of the payments discounted at the rate that would have been applicable if the entity had issued a debt instrument with similar features and of similar credit standing but without the mandatory conversion feature.
- An equity component representing the delivery of equity in the future. This amount will be determined as the residual amount after the

liability component is deducted from the fair value of the whole compound instrument at inception (£100,000).

If on the basis of the above method the liability component is determined to constitute, for example, £9,000 at inception (based on a discount rate of 7.32 per cent) the following entries will be necessary on initial recognition of the instrument:

Dr	Cash	£100,000
Cr	Financial liability	£9,000
Cr	Equity	£91,000

Over the life of the instrument the following entries will be made with respect to the liability such that by the end of the instrument's life the liability component will no longer be present:

Year end 31 December 20X5

Dr	Interest expense	£659
Cr	Financial liability	£659

To account for the liability at amortised cost using the effective interest rate of 7.32 per cent.

Dr	Financial liability	£5,000
Cr	Cash	£5,000

To account for the cash coupon payment of £5,000

Year end 31 December 20X6

Dr	Interest expense	£341
Cr	Financial liability	£341

To account for the liability at amortised cost using the effective interest rate of 7.32 per cent.

Dr	Financial liability	£5,000
Cr	Cash	£5,000

To account for the cash coupon payment of £5,000

When the instrument mandatorily converted into 5,000 ordinary shares of the entity via the issue of new ordinary shares (with nominal value of £1 each) the following entries will be necessary to reclassify the amount originally recognised as equity:

Dr	Equity	£91,000
Cr	Equity – share capital	£5,000
Cr	Equity – share premium	£86,000

3.7 Convertible debt with multiple settlement options

Throughout **section 3** so far, it was assumed that the equity conversion option can only be gross physically settled, i.e. a fixed number of shares is delivered on conversion of the bond. However, this may not always be the case. As explained in **section 6** below, if the settlement of the call option can be achieved in ways other than by delivery of a fixed number of shares for a fixed amount of cash, the call option is treated as a derivative and is carried at fair value with gains and losses recognised in profit or loss.

Some convertible debt instruments include cash settlement options. The contractual terms of such an instrument allow that in the event of the holder of the instrument demanding conversion the issuer has a choice over the manner in which the call option is settled: the issuer may deliver either a fixed number of shares to the holder, or an amount of cash equal to the market value of the fixed number of shares on the date of conversion or an average price in a period before conversion. As the issuer will not always deliver a fixed amount of equity for receipt of a fixed amount of cash upon conversion, the conversion feature does not meet the definition of equity. The written call option is accounted for as a derivative liability. The convertible debt is a hybrid instrument containing a host debt contract and an embedded derivative liability (written call option over own shares). The embedded derivative is measured at fair value with changes in fair value recorded in profit or loss. The treatment of hybrid instruments is explained in **chapter 17**.

Example 3.7

Convertible debt: cash settlement choice at conversion

On 1 January 20X1 Entity X issues a convertible bond with a face value of £10 million at par. The instrument has a maturity of 10 years and pays an annual coupon of 5 per cent on 31 December. The bond is convertible at maturity at the discretion of the holder. However, if the holder does exercise the right to convert Entity X can either:

- deliver a fixed number of Entity X's ordinary shares; or
- pay an amount of cash equal to the fixed number of shares under the conversion option multiplied by the average share price of Entity X's ordinary shares in the 10 days immediately preceding maturity.

As the written call option within the convertible instrument may be settled in cash rather than through the delivery of a fixed number of shares it does not meet the definition of equity and must be accounted for as an embedded derivative. Entity X will need to recognise a derivative liability at fair value on 1 January 20X1. The difference between the fair value of the total hybrid instrument and the fair value of the embedded derivative is assigned to the host contract, with the host accounted for at amortised cost. This accounting treatment applies if the entire financial instrument is not designated at fair value through profit or loss at initial recognition (see **3.1.1** in **chapter 14**).

Assume that at 1 January 20X1 the fair value of the written call option is equal to £1.5 million. The entries on 1 January 20X1 would be as follows:

Dr	Cash	£10,000,000
Cr	Financial liability (host contract)	£8,500,000
Cr	Derivative financial liability	£1,500,000

Entity X will account for the host contract at amortised cost by applying the effective interest rate of 7.15 per cent, and the derivative will be re-measured to its fair value. On 31 December 20X1 the amortised cost of the host debt contract is equal to £9,107,797 and the fair value of the embedded derivative is equal to £2,450,000. Therefore, the entries are as follows:

Dr	Interest expense	£607,797
Cr	Financial liability (host contract)	£607,797
Dr	Financial liability (host contract)	£500,000
Cr	Cash	£500,000

To record the host debt contract at amortised cost and payment of contractual coupon

Dr	Derivative loss	£950,000
Cr	Derivative financial liability	£950,000

To record fair value movement of embedded derivative in profit or loss

3.8 Foreign currency denominated convertible debt

An entity may issue an instrument denominated in a foreign currency (currency other than functional currency of the entity) that is convertible into a fixed number of ordinary shares of the entity. Such an instrument contains a written option to exchange a fixed number of equity instruments for a fixed amount of cash that is denominated in a foreign currency.

As explained in **section 6** of this chapter a derivative contract over an entity's own equity is accounted for as equity only where it will be settled exclusively by the entity delivering (or receiving) a fixed number of its own equity instruments in exchange for a fixed amount of cash or another financial asset.

For foreign currency denominated convertible debt the question arises whether the equity conversion option meets the definition of equity when the consideration the issuer receives for issuing a fixed number of shares is forgiveness of a debt instrument that is variable in functional currency terms. The same question also applies to freestanding instruments, for example, a stand alone physically settled written call over own shares that will be settled at exercise through an exchange of a fixed number of own shares for a fixed amount of foreign currency cash.

A gross physically settled derivative over a fixed number of own equity shares meets the definition of equity only if the amount of cash or financial assets paid or received is fixed in the *functional currency* of the issuer. The following guidance is relevant.

- A derivative over a fixed number of equity shares that is exchanged for a variable amount of cash is a derivative, and not equity. For example, an instrument that requires an exchange of a fixed number of equity shares for a variable amount of cash calculated to equal the value of 100 ounces of gold is a derivative since the fair value of the derivative is driven from movements in the gold price as well as the equity price. [IAS 32.24]

- IAS 39 considers that although foreign denominated monetary items and foreign currency forecast transactions are fixed in foreign currency terms, they are considered variable in functional currency terms and therefore are eligible to be designated in a cash flow hedge. [IAS 39.IG.F.3.3 & F.3.4]

Applying this guidance to foreign currency denominated convertible debt, it is clear that (1) the foreign currency convertible whilst fixed in foreign currency terms, is variable in functional currency terms and therefore a fixed number of shares will be delivered in exchange for a variable amount of cash; and (2) conversion will occur based on the interaction of not only the equity price but the foreign currency value of the bond that is forgiven.

The IFRIC referred the issue to the IASB where, in September 2005, the Board explored whether to amend IAS 32 to permit contracts to be classified as equity if they are to be settled by an entity delivering a fixed number of its own equity instruments for a fixed amount of cash or another financial asset denominated in a foreign currency. The Board noted the amendment would result in equity and foreign exchange features whose values are interdependent being recognised in equity, and that excluding from equity the value attributable to the foreign exchange features would require arbitrary rules. The Board also noted that allowing dual indexed contracts (to share price and foreign exchange rates) to be classified as equity would require additional and detailed guidance to avoid structuring opportunities aimed at obtaining a desired accounting result. The Board therefore decided not to proceed with an amendment to IAS 32.

Example 3.8

Foreign currency denominated convertible debt

Entity A has a Sterling-functional currency. Entity A issues a convertible bond denominated in US dollars that if converted will result in the gross physical delivery of a fixed number of Entity A's Sterling-denominated shares.

The convertible bond will be classified as a financial liability as upon conversion a fixed amount of shares will be delivered in exchange for a variable amount of functional currency cash, being the forgiveness of the bond obligation.

If a parent and subsidiary have the same functional currency and either the parent issues a foreign currency denominated convertible bond that is convertible into a fixed number of subsidiary's shares, or the subsidiary issues a foreign currency convertible bond that is convertible into a fixed number of parent's shares, the instrument in both cases would be classified wholly as a liability in the consolidated financial statements as a fixed number of shares is exchanged for a variable amount of functional currency cash.

The accounting for convertible debt issued by an entity in the group that is convertible into a fixed number of equity instruments of another entity in the group is more complex when the bond is denominated in *one* of the entities' functional currency. The IFRIC discussed this scenario but did not take the issue onto their agenda as they considered the issue was too narrow. In the absence of specific guidance it is not clear whether a group should look to the functional currency of the issuer of the fixed number of shares or the functional currency of the issuer of the convertible bond. A group should establish a policy as to how it determines what is a fixed amount of functional currency cash in the instance when different entities in the group issue the convertible instrument and issue the shares, should the instrument be converted. This policy should be applied consistently to all similar instruments.

3.9 Anti-dilutive provisions in convertible debt

Convertible debt will normally include anti-dilutive provisions within the contractual terms of the instrument to ensure that the holder of the convertible bond's potential interest in the equity of the issuer is not diluted in certain events. For an equity conversion feature to be considered equity it must result in the exchange of a fixed amount of cash or other financial asset for a fixed number of equity instruments (the 'fixed-for-fixed criterion'). As anti-dilutive provisions result in the number of shares that will be delivered to the holder of the convertible bond upon conversion changing subject to specified events, care needs to be taken in determining whether such provisions result in the equity conversion feature failing equity treatment because it fails the fixed-for-fixed criterion.

IAS 32 does not provide any guidance on whether anti-dilutive provisions in convertible debt result in the equity conversion feature failing equity treatment. Most anti-dilutive provisions are structured so as to 'make-whole' the holder of the convertible bond if certain events occur. For example, if the issuer decides to issue more ordinary shares while the convertible debt is outstanding, e.g. through a bonus issue, the conversion feature will be adjusted to reflect the increased number of shares in issue. This adjustment attempts to put the convertible debt holder in the same economic position relative to existing ordinary share holders as they were prior to the issue of the new shares. An adjustment to the number of shares to be delivered under the conversion option that makes whole the holder of the convertible debt relative to existing ordinary shareholders is not deemed to breach the 'fixed-for-fixed' criterion. The same conclusion would be reached in the instance when the number of shares is adjusted due to the issuer entering into a buy back of its own shares in the market while the convertible debt is outstanding. In this instance, the number of shares under the conversion feature will decrease reflecting that there are less ordinary shares outstanding.

Convertible debt may permit the holder to convert into a fixed percentage of the outstanding shares of the entity, say 5% of the entity. In this instance the number of shares does potentially vary, as the number of shares that may be delivered under conversion of the debt is not known until the date of conversion. Even though the number of shares is not fixed in this instance, the conversion feature does not breach the 'fixed-for-fixed' criterion as the feature ensures that the holder of the convertible debt has the same relative potential equity interest in the issuer relative to the existing ordinary shareholders. This feature is economically the same as fixing the conversion ratio at date of issue of the convertible debt but then including anti-dilutive provisions for bonus issues, share buy backs etc as described above to preserve the potential equity interest of the convertible debt holder.

Anti-dilutive provisions linked to dividend payments are also common. Should the issuer pay dividends on its existing ordinary shares an adjustment to the conversion ratio may occur which attempts to compensate the holder of the convertible debt in the instance when dividends paid are in excess of a specified level. This provision attempts to compensate the holder of the convertible bond in the instance when a "special dividend" is paid which is akin to a return of capital to the existing ordinary shareholders. In this instance the conversion ratio that was determined when the convertible bond was issued assumes a certain level of dividend payments between the date when the instrument was issued and the date when conversion can occur. The adjustment to the conversion features makes-whole the difference between the amount of the special dividend and the amount of the dividends expected to be paid. An alternative provision is where the number of shares under the conversion feature is adjusted for the actual dividend paid in a period while the convertible bond is outstanding. In this instance, the conversion ratio that was determined when the convertible bond was issued assumed no dividend payments between the date when the instrument was issued and the date when conversion can occur. The number of shares to be delivered under the conversion feature is adjusted so the conversion price is equal to that which would have been determined had the issuer known at inception exactly what dividends it was going to be paid in the future. Both anti-dilutive provisions in this case are not deemed to breach the 'fixed-for-fixed' criterion as they both compensate the holder of the convertible debt relative to existing ordinary shareholders.

3.10 Other variations in convertible debt

It is not possible to provide an exhaustive list of different variations in conversion features in convertible debt. However, some further examples and discussion of the accounting analysis are included below.

Discounted convertible debt

Convertible debt may be issued such that the investor receives some of the interest on the instrument in the form of fixed cash coupons and some in the form of accretion up to the par amount. For instance an entity may issue convertible debt for £90 that is convertible into a fixed number of equity shares at any time and pays an annual coupon of 1% based on the par amount of £100. If the holder does not choose to convert the instrument into the fixed number of equity shares the bond will be redeemed at maturity for the par amount of £100. When considering whether "fixed cash" is being received as consideration for issuing shares under the conversion option the amount of the liability forgiven needs to be considered. The amount of the liability forgiven could be argued to change with the passage of time, i.e. is variable, because the instrument has been issued at a discount and therefore the investor is giving up a bond piece that is changing over the life as the discount is unwound. However, it would seem inappropriate to consider this a breach of the 'fixed cash' criteria for two reasons. Firstly, the par amount remains constant and therefore the nominal of the bond remains unchanged. Secondly, the unwinding of the discount to par is part of the interest on the bond component. When compared to a conventional fixed rate convertible debt issued at par (i.e. without a discount) the conversion option always results in the holder giving up a variable amount of future interest receipts. As the instrument's life shortens the amount of interest forgiven by the holder reduces. Such variability in the amount forgiven by the holder is not considered variability in cash in determining whether the conversion option meets the definition of equity.

LIBOR-linked convertible debt

Convertible debt usually carries a fixed rate of interest, or as described above may be partly issued at a discount and therefore economically pays a fixed amount of interest at maturity. If the interest on convertible debt is linked to LIBOR and the instrument is not issued at a discount then all interest flows are variable. It could be argued that the conversion feature breaches the 'fixed cash' criteria as the interest forgiveness is always changing. Similar to the analysis above for discounted convertible bond it would be inappropriate to consider variable interest to be a breach of the 'fixed cash' criteria. Firstly, the par amount remains constant and therefore the nominal of the bond remains unchanged Secondly, IAS 32.22 specifically states that *"changes in market interest rates that do not affect the amount of cash or other financial assets to be paid or received"* do not preclude equity classification. If the fixed cash is considered the par amount and the LIBOR interest is considered to be merely servicing the 'fixed cash' criterion is not breached. Such an instrument would therefore be treated as a compound instrument that contains a financial liability and an equity component.

If instead the interest payments were driven not by LIBOR, but say by another variable that was not a market rate of interest, for example changes in inflation, the same conclusion would not be appropriate and therefore the instrument would not be a compound instrument, rather it would be treated as a financial liability in its entirety. The issuer would need to consider whether the inflation linkage was a closely related embedded derivative in the case where the instrument was not classified as at fair value through profit or loss. Guidance on embedded derivatives is detailed in **chapter 17**.

Convertible debt where conversion is into a differing number of shares that depends on the share price at the date of conversion

Convertible debt that permits the holder to convert the instrument into a number of shares that is not always a fixed number as it changes with share price at the date of conversion is not a compound instrument. For example, the conversion feature may be forgiveness of a fixed amount of functional currency debt (i.e. principal and any future interest) for a fixed number of shares, say 10.0 shares, if the share price is above £100 but below £110, but 9.5 shares if the share price is above £110 but below £120, and 9.0 shares if the share price is above £120. The number of shares to be delivered is based on a sliding scale that reduces as the share price increases. In this case, the conversion feature does not meet the definition of equity as the conversion does not result in the delivery of a fixed number of shares.

It is not possible to consider the conversion feature as three separate conversion features that each have a right to convert the same fixed amount of cash (being principal and interest) for a fixed amount of shares as the conversion features are mutually exclusive. There can only ever be one conversion feature that can be exercised (equally there can only ever be one fixed amount of cash that is forgiven as consideration for the issue of shares) as following conversion the instrument is extinguished.

Convertible debt where conversion is into a fixed number of shares or variable number of shares to the value of the debt component

Consider an example where convertible debt permits the holder to convert into a fixed number of shares when the share price is above a specified level, but also allows the holder to forgive the debt component (being principal and interest) by electing for a variable number of shares equal to the par value of the debt component when the share price is below that specified level. On the face of it, and consistent with the example described above, as the instrument does not always result in the delivery of a fixed number of shares it could be argued that the instrument does not have any equity element, i.e. the entire instrument is a financial liability. However, the right for the holder to require repayment of debt in a variable number of shares is not itself a conversion feature, rather it is a settlement alternative inherent in the debt component. The payment of interest and principal, regardless of how it is settled is a financial liability. The inclusion of a feature that permits the holder to early redeem the instrument by requiring the issuer to deliver a variable number of shares equal to the par amount of the debt when the share price is below a specified level is merely an early redemption option. Put another way, when the share price is below a specified level the holder can require the convertible debt to be early redeemed and the issuer is required to use its own shares as currency for this early redemption. The right to convert into a fixed number of shares when the share price is above the specified level is an equity instrument as it permits the holder to require the issuer to deliver a fixed amount of shares in exchange for a fixed amount of cash (being the principal and interest, and the 'shares to the value of' settlement alternative on that principal and interest).

Convertible debt that is convertible only on a contingent event

The issuer of a convertible debt that is convertible only upon the occurrence of a contingent event that is outside the control of the holder and issuer must first determine whether if the event occurs, would the conversion result in the delivery of a fixed number of equity instruments for a fixed amount of functional currency cash. Put another way, ignoring the contingent element, would the instrument be a compound instrument with an equity and debt component? If the answer to this question is yes, then the fact that the holder can only convert if a contingent event has occurred does not prevent the conversion feature being presented as equity. The inclusion of the contingency merely reduces the likelihood of the conversion occurring and therefore for a stated amount of proceeds would result in the value of the equity instrument being lower (because of a corresponding higher contractual interest rate) compared to an equity component on convertible debt without the contingency included in the conversion feature.

4 Treatment of interest, dividends, gains and losses and other items

The classification of a financial instrument or a component of a financial instrument as either a financial liability or an equity instrument determines the treatment of interest, dividends, and other gains and losses relating to that instrument or component of that instrument. Interest, dividends, losses and gains relating to a financial liability, or a component of a compound instrument that is a financial liability, are recognised as income or expense in profit or loss. Distributions to holders of equity instruments are debited directly to equity net of any related income tax benefit; similarly, transaction costs of an equity transaction, other than the costs of issuing an instrument that is directly attributable to the acquisition of a business (which is accounted for under IFRS 3 *Business Combinations*), are accounted for as a deduction from equity. [IAS 32.35]

The following items are treated as income or expense in profit or loss:

[IAS 32.37]

- interest payments on a bond issued by an entity;
- dividend payments on preference shares that are classified as a financial liability;

- gains and losses associated with redemption or refinancing of an instrument classified as a financial liability (notwithstanding the fact that the instrument may take the legal form of a share);
- gains and losses related to the carrying amount of an instrument that is a financial liability notwithstanding the fact that the instrument gives the holder a right to participate in the residual interest of an entity (e.g. certain puttable instruments such as units in a mutual fund that fail equity classification); and
- costs of an equity transaction that is abandoned.

Dividends classified as an expense in profit or loss may be presented either with interest on other liabilities or as a separate item.

The following items are accounted for within equity:

[IAS 32.37]

- dividend payments on shares classified wholly as equity; and
- incremental directly attributable costs incurred in successfully issuing or acquiring an entity's own equity instruments (including transaction costs, regulatory fees, amounts paid to regulatory, legal, accounting and other professional advisers, printing costs, stamp duties).

The amount of transaction costs that are accounted for as a deduction from equity in the period is disclosed in line with the requirements of IAS 1 *Presentation of Financial Statements*. Also, the related amount of income taxes recognised directly in equity is included in the aggregate amount of current and deferred tax credited or charged to equity and is disclosed under IAS 12 *Income Taxes*. [IAS 32.39]

Example 4A

Effective interest rate and dividends for a compound instrument

Entity A issues a non-cumulative preference share that is mandatorily redeemable for cash of £10 million in 10 years' time. During the life of the instrument dividends are payable at the discretion of Entity A. The non-cumulative preference share is issued for £8 million.

The non-cumulative redeemable preference share is a compound instrument. The liability component is determined as the present value of the eventual redemption amount of £10m discounted at the rate at which the entity could issue a similar instrument with a similar credit standing could be issued without the feature of discretionary dividends during its life.

Assuming the liability component is equal to £7.8 million, the residual amount of £0.2 million will be treated as the equity component. The unwinding of the discount (between the redemption of £10 million and its present value of £7.8 million) on the liability component is accounted for using the effective interest rate method as an interest expense and reported in profit or loss. Any dividends actually paid are treated as relating to the equity component and thus are classified as an equity distribution.

Transaction costs that are incremental and directly attributable to the issue of a compound financial instrument (i.e. would have been avoided if not for the issue of the compound instrument) are allocated to the liability and equity components in proportion to the allocation of the proceeds (see **3.1** above). In cases where costs represent the joint cost relating to more than one transaction (for instance a joint and concurrent offering of some equity instruments and an issue of instruments classified as liabilities) these are allocated using a basis that is rational and consistent with similar transactions. [IAS 32.38]

Example 4B

Transaction costs: placing and new issue of shares

Entity B places its privately held ordinary shares that are classified as equity with a stock exchange and simultaneously enters into a new capital raising by issuing new ordinary shares on the stock exchange. Transaction costs are incurred in respect of both transactions. As the issue of new shares is the issue of an equity instrument, but the placing of the existing equity instruments with the exchange is not, the transaction costs will need to be allocated between the two transactions. Transaction costs in respect of the capital raising will be recognised in equity whereas the transaction costs incurred in placing the existing shares with the stock exchange will be recognised in profit or loss.

In July 2008 the IFRIC issued a tentative rejection notice titled *Transaction costs to be deducted from equity*. The IFRIC received a request for guidance on the extent of transaction costs to be accounted for as a deduction from equity in accordance with IAS 32.37 and on how the requirements of IAS 32.38 to allocate transaction costs that relate jointly to more than one transaction should be applied. This issue relates specifically to the meaning of the terms 'incremental' and 'directly attributable'.

The IFRIC noted that only incremental costs directly attributable to issuing new equity instruments or acquiring previously outstanding equity instruments would be related to an equity transaction in accordance with IAS 32. Costs related to other activities undertaken at the same time such as becoming a public company or acquiring an exchange listing are not costs incurred in issuing or acquiring its own equity instruments.

The IFRIC noted that the terms 'incremental' and 'directly attributable' are used with similar but not identical meanings in many IFRSs. The IFRIC recommended that common definitions should be developed for both terms and added to the Glossary as part of the Board's annual improvements project.

At the date of writing the rejection notice had not been finalised.

5 Treasury shares

Where an entity reacquires its own shares, these shares (known as treasury shares) are deducted from equity. No gain or loss is recognised in profit or loss on the purchase, sale, issue or cancellation of an entity's own equity instruments. The acquisition and subsequent resale by an entity of its own equity instruments represents a transfer between owners (specifically between those who have given up their equity interest and those who continue to hold an equity instrument) rather than a gain or loss to the entity. Accordingly, any consideration paid or received is recognised in equity. [IAS 32.33]

Example 5A

Acquisition of equity

Entity A buys back 100,000 of its own equity shares in the market for £5 a share. The shares will be held as treasury shares to enable Entity A to satisfy its obligations under its employee share option scheme. The following entries will be made to record the purchase of the treasury shares as a deduction from equity:

Dr	Equity	£500,000
Cr	Cash	£500,000

Example 5B

Traded treasury shares

Entity F is a large financial institution. The entity's shares are included in the FTSE 100 index. Entity F issues a bond whose principal amount varies with the movement in the FTSE 100 share index (an 'index tracker bond'). In order to hedge economically the equity derivative that is embedded in the bond, F purchases a portfolio of the shares contained in the FTSE 100 index and classifies them as held for trading.

Entity F cannot classify its own purchased shares as held for trading in order to hedge economically the index tracker bond. IAS 39 excludes from its scope instruments issued by an entity that meet the definition of equity in IAS 32. Furthermore, IAS 32 requires that treasury shares are presented in the statement of financial position as a deduction from equity and not as assets, and that no gain or loss should be recognised in profit or loss on such shares.

The amount of treasury shares held is disclosed separately either in the statement of financial position or in the notes in accordance with IAS 1 *Presentation of Financial Statements*. An entity provides disclosure in accordance with the requirements of IAS 24 *Related Party Disclosures* in instances where the entity reacquires its own equity instruments from related parties. [IAS 32.34]

UK

For UK companies, the requirements of the Companies Act relating to treasury shares, and their effects on distributable profits, are discussed at ***3.6 in chapter 49****.*

Where an entity holds its own shares on behalf of others (as is the case when a financial institution holds its own shares on behalf of a client as a custodian), this represents an agency relationship and as a result the shares are not included in the statement of financial position of the entity. [IAS 32.AG36]

6 Derivatives over own equity

A derivative contract over an entity's own equity is accounted for as equity *only* where it will be settled by the entity delivering (or receiving) a fixed number of its own equity instruments and receiving (or delivering) a fixed amount of cash or another financial asset. Any consideration received (such as the premium received in relation to written options over own shares or warrants on the entity's own shares that satisfy the above condition) is added directly to equity. Similarly, any consideration paid for such an instrument (such as premium paid for a purchased option that satisfies the above condition) is deducted from equity. Changes in fair value of the equity instrument are not recognised in the financial statements. [IAS 32.22] At a group level, derivatives over own equity include derivatives over shares of subsidiaries.

Example 6A

Purchased call

On 1 February 20X5 Entity MNO, a Sterling functional currency entity, purchases for £5,000 a call option over 1,000 of its own ordinary shares. The option is a European type option with exercise at a strike price of £102 per share exercisable only on 31 January 20X6. The option is gross physically settled, i.e. Entity MNO takes delivery of 1,000 of its own shares in exchange for an amount of cash paid to the counterparty equal to the option exercise price of £102,000 (£102 per share × 1,000 shares).

The entries are as follows:

1 February 20X5

On inception of the contract the following entry will be needed in order to record the cash paid in exchange for the right to receive a fixed number of own shares in exchange for a fixed amount of cash:

Dr	Equity	£5,000
Cr	Cash	£5,000

The premium is recognised in equity because the instrument meets the definition of an equity instrument.

31 December 20X5

No entry is made on 31 December 20X5 because no cash is paid or received and a contract that gives a right to receive a fixed number of the entity's own shares in exchange for a fixed amount of cash meets the definition of an equity instrument of the entity. Hence, the fair value of the option is irrelevant to the accounting treatment; the equity instrument is not re-measured.

31 January 20X6

The entity exercises the call option and the contract is gross physically settled through the entity taking delivery of 1,000 of its own shares in exchange for a payment of £102,000 to the counterparty. This is recorded as follows:

Dr	Equity	£102,000
Cr	Cash	£102,000

Any contract with a single or multiple settlement option that contains an obligation for the entity to purchase its own equity for cash or another financial asset gives rise to a financial liability for the present value of the repurchase price, even if the obligation to purchase is conditional on the holder exercising its right to sell the shares to the entity. Examples of instruments that give rise to a liability include forward contracts to buy own equity and written put options that allow the holder to put the shares back to the entity at a fixed or variable amount (for example a fixed amount plus inflation). At inception such contracts are recorded at an amount equal to the present value of the obligation inherent in the contract. This is the case notwithstanding the fact that the contract itself may be an equity instrument (as it can be settled only through the entity delivering a fixed amount of cash in exchange for a fixed number of its own shares). [IAS 32.23] The presentation is equivalent to buying back own shares today but with an obligation to still pay the cash under the buy-back to the seller.

The liability is subsequently re-measured through profit or loss, i.e. interest is accrued in accordance with the effective interest method up to the share redemption amount. In the case of a gross liability based on a variable amount of cash, the re-measurement of the amount of the eventual liability (for example, for changes in inflation) would also be recorded through profit or loss.

Example 6B

Forward purchase contract

Assume that, instead of purchasing a call option over own shares that will be gross physically settled, on 1 February 20X5 Entity MNO enters into a forward contract to buy 1,000 of its own ordinary shares on 31 January 20X6 for £104 per share.

This contract will be gross physically settled, i.e. Entity MNO will take delivery of 1,000 of its own shares in exchange for paying to the counterparty an amount of £104,000 (£104 per share × 1,000 shares).

The entries are as follows:

1 February 20X5

The entity has an unconditional obligation to deliver £104,000 in cash in one year's time to the counterparty in exchange for a fixed amount of own equity shares. The following entry is made to record this obligation to deliver £104,000 in one year at its present value of £100,000 discounted using an appropriate interest rate:

Dr	Equity	£100,000
Cr	Liability	£100,000

31 December 20X5

The following entry is necessary to accrue interest in accordance with the effective interest method on the liability for the share redemption amount.

Dr	Interest expense	£3,660
Cr	Liability	£3,660

31 January 20X6

The following entry accrues further interest for the remaining month of January 20X6 in accordance with the effective interest method on the liability for the share redemption amount.

Dr	Interest expense	£340
Cr	Liability	£340

On the same date the following entry will be needed to record the settlement of the liability for the share redemption amount:

Dr	Liability	£104,000
Cr	Cash	£104,000

Example 6C

Written put

On 1 February 20X5 Entity PQR writes a put option over 1,000 of its own ordinary shares and receives a premium of £5,000 for doing so. The option is a European type option with exercise at a strike price of £98 per share exercisable only on 31 January 20X6. The option will be gross physically settled, i.e. if the option is exercised the entity will receive 1,000 of its own shares in exchange for paying to the counterparty an amount equal to the option exercise price of £98,000 (£98 per share × 1,000 shares).

The accounting entries are as follows:

1 February 20X5

On inception of the contract the following entry will be needed in order to record the cash received in exchange for writing the put option giving the counterparty the right to receive a fixed amount of cash in exchange for delivering a fixed number of the entity's own shares:

Dr	Cash	£5,000
Cr	Equity	£5,000

The premium is recognised in equity because the instrument meets the definition of an equity instrument.

The following additional entry is needed in order to record the present value of the £98,000 obligation on 31 January 20X6:

Dr	Equity	£95,000
Cr	Liability	£95,000

31 December 20X5

The following entry is necessary to accrue interest in accordance with the effective interest method on the liability for the share redemption amount.

Dr	Interest expense	£2,745
Cr	Liability	£2,745

31 January 20X6

The following journal accrues further interest for the remaining month of January 20X6 in accordance with the effective interest method on the liability for the share redemption amount.

Dr	Interest expense	£255
Cr	Liability	£255

On the same date the following entry will be needed to record the settlement of the liability for the share redemption amount:

Dr	Liability	£98,000
Cr	Cash	£98,000

If the written put was not exercised by the counterparty, the following entry would be required instead:

Dr	Liability	£98,000
Cr	Equity	£98,000

It is common for a group to acquire an interest in an entity which upon acquisition will be a subsidiary and as part of the acquisition also to enter into a written put option with the seller that permits the seller to put their remaining interest in the acquired entity to the group at a specified price. These puts are written by the acquiring entity to allow the existing owners an exit mechanism for their remaining shares. The acquisition of shares that results in the interest being recognised as a subsidiary will be accounted for in accordance with IFRS 3 *Business Combinations*. If the written put can be physically settled, i.e. subsidiary's shares are physically delivered and paid for by cash or other financial asset, irrespective of whether the strike price of the put is a fixed or variable price, a gross obligation must be recorded equal to the present value of the amount that could be required to be paid to the counterparty in accordance with IAS 32. Changes in the measurement of the gross obligation due to the unwind of the discount or changes in the amount that the group could be required to pay are always recognised in profit or loss. We believe it is not permissible to recognise these gains/losses against the goodwill that arose on acquiring the interest in the subsidiary as changes in the value of the gross obligation relate to the potential *future* acquisition of the remaining shares in the subsidiary.

In November 2006 the IFRIC considered the classification and presentation of written puts and forward purchase arrangements entered into by a parent over shares of a subsidiary, otherwise known as puts and forwards over non-controlling interests (previously known as 'minority interests'). The IFRIC confirmed that in the consolidated financial statements a financial liability must be recognised in accordance with IAS 32.23 for the obligation to pay cash in the future to purchase the shares held by non-controlling interests, even if the payment of that cash is conditional on the option being exercised by the holder. After initial recognition any liability to which IFRS 3 *Business Combinations* is not being applied will be accounted for in accordance with IAS 39. The parent will reclassify the liability to equity if a put expires unexercised.

The IFRIC recognised that there is likely to be divergence in practice in how the related debit to equity is presented. However, the IFRIC did not believe that it could reach a consensus on this matter on a timely basis and therefore it decided not to add this item to its agenda.

The debit that is recognised in equity on initial recognition of a written put or forward purchase over a non-controlling interest may be presented in equity in one of two ways. The debit may be recorded as a deduction from non-controlling interests or may be presented in other reserves, alongside non-controlling interests, illustrating that the transaction represents a future transaction involving the non-controlling interests. The latter seems preferable, i.e. the non-controlling interests balance is unaffected by the transaction, as this preserves the net assets of the subsidiary that are attributed to those non-controlling interest holders.

Example 6D

Written put over equity of subsidiary

On 1 January 20X8 Entity Q, the ultimate parent of Group Q, acquires a 60% interest in Entity P from Entity O. As part of the acquisition agreement Entity Q also writes a put option over 40% of shares in Entity P to Entity O. The written put option allows Entity O to put the 40% interest in Entity P to Entity Q at £275m plus 20% of Entity P's post acquisition cumulative profits. The put can be exercised by Entity O at 1 July 20Y0 and at every anniversary thereafter until 1 July 20Y2. Cumulative profits are determined based on audited financial statements of Entity P up to the year ended immediately prior to exercise of the put option. Group Q's reporting period end is 31 December.

At 1 January 20X8 the fair value of 60% of the shares in Entity P was £1,100m and the fair value of the written put option was £100m. Entity Q's estimation of profits of Entity P for the two year period ending 31 December 20X9 is £50m. Entity Q's cost of debt funding is 10%.

At 31 December 20X8 the fair value of the written put option was £90m. Entity Q revises its estimate of Entity P's profits for the two year period ending 31 December 20X9 to £80m.

Entity Q separate financial statements

The written put is over a third party's equity and therefore does not meet the definition of equity for Entity Q. The put option will be classified as at fair value through profit or loss.

1 January 20X8

Dr	Cost of investment	1,100m	
Cr	Cash		1,000m
Cr	Written put option – FVTPL		100m

To recognise the cost of investment of the subsidiary and the written put option at fair value at initial recognition.

31 December 20X8

Dr	Written put option – FVTPL	10m	
Cr	Profit or loss		10m

To recognise the re-measurement of the put option as at fair value through profit or loss.

Group Q consolidated financial statements

The written put permits a third party, Entity O, to put up to 40% of the shares in a subsidiary of Group Q to Group Q. As Group Q could be required to pay cash or other financial asset as settlement for the acquisition of shares in a subsidiary, in this case non-controlling interest of the group, Group Q must recognise a gross obligation for the potential future acquisition of these equity shares.

1 January 20X8

At the date of acquisition Group Q consolidates Entity P and recognises a 40% non-controlling interest. The fair value of consideration used to acquire 60% of the shares in Entity P for the purposes of determining any goodwill arising on acquisition is £1,100m. The difference between this amount and the total consideration paid to Entity O is the premium that Entity Q received for writing the put option.

The estimated present value of the amount Group Q could be required to pay Entity O should Entity O exercise its put option at the earliest opportunity, being 1 July 20Y0, is £225m. This is determined as follows: [£275m + (£50m x 20%)] x $1/(1.1^{2.5})$.

Dr	Net assets acquired / goodwill, less non-controlling interests arising from acquisition (for simplicity, the non-controlling interests' share of net assets has not been split out)	1,100m
Dr	Equity	125m
Cr	Cash	1,000m
Cr	Gross obligation under put option	225m

To recognise the acquisition of the subsidiary and the recognition of the present value of the gross obligation under the written put over the non-controlling interest.

31 December 20X8

The estimated present value of the amount Group Q could be required to pay Entity O should Entity O exercise its put option at the earliest opportunity, being 1 July 20Y0, is £252m. This is determined as follows: [£275m + (£80m x 20%)] x $1/(1.1^{1.5})$.

Dr	Profit or loss – finance cost	27m
Cr	Gross obligation under put option	27m

To recognise the re-measurement of the present value of the gross obligation under the written put over the non-controlling interest.

All derivatives over own equity other than forward purchases and written puts, where settlement is not by the delivery of a fixed number of equity shares for receipt of a fixed amount of cash (equity) or the receipt of a fixed number of equity shares for the delivery of cash (gross liability), are treated as derivatives (derivative financial assets or liabilities) and are accounted for in accordance with the requirements of IAS 39, namely the fair value of the instrument is recognised in the statement of financial position with changes in fair value recorded in profit or loss.

Hence, the following derivatives over own equity are accounted for as held for trading derivatives:

- those that are net settled in cash (or other financial assets);
- those that are net settled in own equity shares; and
- any derivative over own equity which gives either party a choice over how it is settled unless all the settlement alternatives result in the exchange of a fixed number of own shares for a fixed amount of cash or another financial asset (the only exception being forward purchases and written puts over own shares where one of the settlement alternatives is gross physical settlement).

Example 6E

Forward sale contract: net share settlement

On 1 February 20X5 Entity XYZ, a Sterling functional currency entity, enters into a forward sale contract over 1,000 of its own ordinary shares on 31 January 20X6 at a fixed price of £104 per share. The terms of the contract are that it will be net settled in shares, i.e. settlement will take the form of receipt/delivery by Entity XYZ of a variable number of shares such that the market value of the shares at the date of settlement is equal to the market value of the forward contract.

The accounting entries are as follows:

1 February 20X5

The price per share when the contract is entered into on 1 February 20X5 is £104. The initial fair value of the forward contract on 1 February 20X5 is zero. Thus, no entry is required because the fair value of the derivative is zero and no cash is paid or received.

31 December 20X5

On 31 December 20X5, the market price per share has increased to £110 and, as a result, the fair value of the forward contract has decreased to £6,000.

The following entry is necessary to record the decrease in the fair value of the forward contract:

Dr	Loss	£6,000	
Cr	Forward liability		£6,000

31 January 20X6

On 31 January 20X6, the market price per share has decreased to £106. The fair value of the forward contract is £2,000 ([£106 x 1,000] – £104,000). Thus, the following entry is needed to record the increase in the fair value of the contract:

Dr	Forward liability	£4,000
Cr	Gain	£4,000

On the same day, the contract is settled net in shares (with Entity XYZ delivering an amount of its own shares to the counterparty equivalent to the fair value of the contract). The following entry is therefore necessary to record the settlement of the contract net in own equity shares:

Dr	Forward Liability	£2,000
Cr	Equity	£2,000

For illustrative purposes only the fair value of the forward contract is not discounted.

Example 6F

Total return swap

An entity enters into a total return swap ('TRS') over 1,000 of its own equity shares on 1 February 20X5. The contract matures on 31 January 20X6. Due to the nature of the total return swap (whose fair value is driven by changes in the entity's share price), gross settlement is not possible and it will be settled net (either in cash or in a variable number of shares). Thus, the instrument does not qualify as an equity instrument and therefore will be accounted for as a derivative as follows:

1 February 20X5

The initial fair value of the swap on 1 February 20X5 is zero. No entry is required because the fair value of the derivative is zero and no cash is paid or received.

31 December 20X5

The fair value of the swap at 31 December 20X5 is £4,500, hence the following entry is required to record the increase in fair value:

Dr	Swap asset	£4,500
Cr	Profit or loss	£4,500

31 January 20X6

The fair value of the swap at 31 January 20X6 is £3,750, hence the following entry is required to record the decrease in fair value:

Dr	Profit or loss	£750
Cr	Swap asset	£750

The entries necessary upon settlement will depend on which of the two methods of net settlement is used. If the contract permits only net share settlement, or this method is chosen the following entry will be made:

Dr	Equity	£3,750
Cr	Swap asset	£3,750

In this scenario settlement will take place through the entity taking receipt of 150 of its own shares (£3,750 / £25) (the market value of the entity's share on this date is £25)

If the contract on the other hand only permits net cash settlement, or this method of settlement is chosen the following entry will be recorded at settlement of the contract:

Dr	Cash	£3,750
Cr	Swap asset	£3,750

The following table illustrates application of the above rules to different derivatives over own equity, with different settlement mechanisms:

	Settlement options available			
	A **Net cash settlement***	**B** **Net share settle-ment****	**C** **Gross physical settlement*****	**D** **Settlement options*******
Forward to buy equity shares (the forward may be over a fixed or variable number of equity shares for a fixed or variable amount of functional or foreign currency cash)	Derivative financial asset/ liability	Derivative financial asset/ liability	Gross liability	If C exists as an alternative, treat as a Gross liability If C does not exist as an alternative, treat as a Derivative financial asset/ liability
Forward to sell a fixed number of equity shares for a fixed amount of functional currency cash	Derivative financial asset/ liability	Derivative financial asset/ liability	Equity	Derivative financial asset/ liability
Forward to sell a fixed number of equity shares for a fixed amount of foreign currency cash or variable amount of functional currency cash	Derivative financial asset/ liability	Derivative financial asset/ liability	Derivative financial asset/liability	Derivative financial asset/ liability
Forward to sell a variable number of equity shares for a fixed or variable amount of functional or foreign currency cash	Derivative financial asset/ liability	Derivative financial asset/ liability	Derivative financial asset/liability	Derivative financial asset/ liability

	Settlement options available			
	A	**B**	**C**	**D**
	Net cash settlement*	**Net share settle-ment****	**Gross physical settlement*****	**Settlement options********
Purchased call option on a fixed number of equity shares for a fixed amount of functional currency cash	Derivative financial asset	Derivative financial asset	Equity	Derivative financial asset
Purchased call option on a fixed number of equity shares for a fixed amount of foreign currency cash or variable amount of functional currency cash	Derivative financial asset	Derivative financial asset	Derivative financial asset	Derivative financial asset
Purchased call option on a variable number of equity shares for a fixed or variable amount of functional or foreign currency cash	Derivative financial asset	Derivative financial asset	Derivative financial asset	Derivative financial asset
Written call option on a fixed number of equity shares for a fixed amount of functional currency cash	Derivative financial liability	Derivative financial liability	Equity	Derivative financial liability
Written call option on a fixed number of equity shares for a fixed or variable amount of foreign currency cash or variable amount of functional currency cash	Derivative financial liability	Derivative financial liability	Derivative financial liability	Derivative financial liability
Written call option on a variable number of equity shares for a fixed or variable amount of functional or foreign currency cash	Derivative financial liability	Derivative financial liability	Derivative financial liability	Derivative financial liability
Purchased put option on a fixed number of equity shares for a fixed amount of functional currency cash	Derivative financial asset	Derivative financial asset	Equity	Derivative financial asset

	Settlement options available			
	A	B	C	D
	Net cash settlement*	**Net share settle-ment****	**Gross physical settlement*****	**Settlement options********
Purchased put option on a fixed number of equity shares for a fixed or variable amount of foreign currency cash or variable amount of functional currency cash	Derivative financial asset	Derivative financial asset	Derivative financial asset	Derivative financial asset
Purchased put option on a variable number of equity shares for a fixed or variable amount of functional or foreign currency cash	Derivative financial asset	Derivative financial asset	Derivative financial asset	Derivative financial asset
Written put option on equity shares (the option may be over a fixed or variable number of equity shares for a fixed or variable amount of functional or foreign currency cash)	Derivative financial liability	Derivative financial liability	Gross liability	If C exists as an alternative, treat as a Gross liability If C does not exist as an alternative, treat as a Derivative financial asset/liability

* **Net cash settlement**. Where the one party's net gain/loss is settled in cash and no shares are exchanged.

** **Net share settlement (shares for shares)**. A variable number of shares are delivered/received having an aggregate current fair value equal to the amount of the gain/loss to the relevant party.

*** **Gross physical settlement**. The buyer/seller delivers/receives cash in return for shares from the seller/buyer.

**** **Settlement options**. Where either the issuer or the holder has a right to choose among two or more of the above ways of settlement.

6.1 Other variations of terms of derivatives over own equity

As described immediately above, the guidance on multiple settlement alternatives for standalone derivatives over own equity is consistent with the multiple settlement alternatives guidance for convertible debt described in **3.7** above. The guidance is consistent as in order to determine whether an equity conversion option in convertible debt is considered to be equity for the issuer, the derivatives over own equity guidance is applied. As a result, the guidance on foreign currency convertible debt described in **3.8** above equally applies to standalone derivatives over own equity, i.e. for a derivative over own equity to meet the definition of equity it must be an exchange of a fixed number of shares for a fixed amount of functional currency cash. Also, the guidance on anti-dilutive provisions in **3.9** above also applies to standalone derivatives over own equity.

It is not possible to provide an exhaustive list of different variations in the terms of derivatives over own equity. However, some examples and the accounting analysis are included below.

Contracts where the number of own equity shares or amount of cash is predetermined but still subject to variability

Derivative over own equity may be structured so that they can be exercised at various points in time and the number of shares or the amount of cash is predetermined upfront but varies with time. One must consider whether such derivatives involve exchange of a fixed amount of cash or other financial asset for a fixed amount of equity. Consider the following example:

Entity A, a US$ functional currency, enters into two standalone contracts to deliver own equity to a third party:

- Contract 1: a written call option that gives the counterparty the right to buy equity of Entity A for US$100 over a three year period. The number of shares that will be delivered to the counterparty on exercise will depend on when the counterparty exercises the option. If the counterparty exercises the option at the first anniversary 10 shares are delivered, at the second anniversary 11 shares are delivered, or at the third anniversary 12 shares are delivered. If the option is not exercised by the end of year 3 the call option expires. If the option is exercised at any time in the 3 year period there is no further right to buy shares under the arrangement.

- Contract 2: a written call option that gives the counterparty the right to buy equity of Entity A for US$100 over a three year period. The number of shares that will be delivered to the counterparty on exercise will depend on when the counterparty exercises the option and the rate of LIBOR at that date. If the counterparty exercises the option at the first anniversary the number of shares delivered is 10 x (1+LIBOR), at the second anniversary 10 x $(1+LIBOR)^2$, and at the third anniversary 10 x $(1+LIBOR)^3$. If the option is not exercised by the end of year 3 the call option expires. If the option is exercised at any time in the 3 year period there is no further right to buy shares under the arrangement.

In the case of Contract 1 the contract meets the definition of equity as, if exercised, the issuer will receive a fixed amount of cash for delivering a fixed amount of own equity. Even though the number of shares that the instrument may be converted into does vary, it only varies with the passage of time and not with other variables, i.e. the number of shares is fixed at inception of the contract. The arrangement is considered to be an exchange of a fixed number of shares for a fixed amount of cash. Therefore, the premium received for writing the call option is credited to equity and changes in the fair value of the instrument are not recorded in the financial statements in accordance with IAS 32.

In the case of Contract 2 the contract meets the definition of a financial liability as, if exercised, the issuer will deliver a variable number of shares for a fixed amount of cash. Even though the number of shares is determinable, i.e. it is determined by a specified index, in this case LIBOR, the number of shares is not fixed in advance and does vary due to factors other than the passage of time, in this case, interest rates. The contract is therefore not an exchange of a fixed number of shares for a fixed amount of cash. The written option must be initially recognised at fair value, and subsequently measured as at fair value through profit or loss in accordance with IAS 39.

Contract to exchange a fixed number of shares of a parent for a fixed number of shares in a subsidiary

In the consolidated financial statements such a contract is an exchange of a fixed number of shares of the issuer, being the parent, which are equity instruments, for a fixed number of shares of a subsidiary, being non-controlling interest, which are also equity of the group. IAS 32 does not consider this fact pattern as the standard assumes that for a derivative over equity to be classified as equity the exchange will always involve receipt or delivery of a fixed amount of cash (or other financial asset) for a fixed amount of equity. As the arrangement is an exchange of a fixed number of two equity instruments, at the consolidated level, it is reasonable that the instrument be presented as equity as the holder is exchanging one fixed amount of residual interest in one group entity for another.

Contract to exchange a fixed or variable number of shares of a parent for a fixed number of shares in a subsidiary

Consider an example of such a contract. Entity R (the parent of Group R) writes a call option over 10% of its subsidiary, Entity S, to Entity T. The call option allows Entity T to buy the 10% stake in Entity S by delivering shares in Entity R as consideration at a fixed date in the future. The call option can only be physically settled by the delivery of shares in Entity S to Entity T and the delivery of shares in Entity R from Entity T to Entity R. However, the strike price of the call option, being the consideration that Entity T will pay Entity R if the option is exercised is dependant on the value of Entity S at the exercise date as follows:

(a) if the value of Entity S is equal to £100m or more Entity R will receive from Entity T a fixed number of its own shares, i.e. Entity R shares.

(b) if the value of Entity S is less than £100m Entity T will deliver a variable number of share in Entity R equal to the value of the 10% interest in Entity S.

Assume that both the shares of Entity R and Entity S are equity instruments in accordance with IAS 32.

In the consolidated financial statements the contract is an exchange of a fixed number of shares in a subsidiary (being non-controlling interest that is presented as equity) for a fixed, or under certain scenarios variable, number of equity shares in the parent. IAS 32.21 makes clear that a contract is not an equity instrument solely because it may result in the receipt or delivery of the entity's own equity instruments. IAS 32.21 draws a distinction between two types of arrangements:

(a) obligations to be settled in own equity shares where the fair value of the obligation may be for a fixed amount or an amount that fluctuates in part or in full in response to changes in a variable *other* than the market price of the entity's own equity instruments, and

(b) obligations to be settled in own shares where the fair value fluctuates in response to changes in the market price of an entity's own equity instruments.

The paragraph appears to suggest that contracts to deliver a variable number of own shares may display characteristics of equity, i.e. characteristics of a residual interest in the entity's assets after deducting all of its liabilities. In the above example, Entity R receives its own shares for delivering a fixed number of shares in its subsidiary. The only variable that determines the number of shares to be received is the value of Entity S's shares. Therefore, the principles of IAS 32 would suggest that the contract does evidence a residual interest and therefore Entity R should account for it as equity in its consolidated financial statements.

If the variability in the number of shares was driven by a factor other than the market price of Entity S's shares such as for example the fair value of a certain quantity of gold, as mentioned in IAS 32.21, then it would be inappropriate to classify the contract as an equity instrument. In this case the variable number of equity shares is derived from a variable other than the market price of the shares and the contract does not evidence a residual interest in the entity's assets after deducting all of its liabilities.

In some cases careful judgement is needed in order to determine whether a contractual arrangement is a derivative over own equity. Consider the following example. Entity A enters into an arrangement with a potential investor whereby it receives £100 on day one. Under the terms of the arrangement Entity A has a choice of delivering either a fixed number of equity shares of Entity A to the potential investor or returning £100 back to the potential investor. One way of analysing the transaction would be to regard it as an option purchased by Entity A that would allow it to put a fixed number of its own equity shares to the potential investor under which the strike price of £100 has already been prepaid by the investor and therefore is potentially returnable to the potential investor (should entity A chose not to exercise the put option). However, viewing this transaction as a derivative over own equity does not seem to be the most faithful representation of the contractual arrangement. Under a conventional purchased put option over own equity the purchaser of the option (Entity A in this case) would suffer the cost of the option (in the form of premium) that would not be returnable if the option were not exercised. In this fact pattern Entity A does not suffer any premium. Another possible view might be to liken the arrangement to a prepaid forward to sell own shares with a predetermined requirement for the return of the prepaid cash leg in the case of non-performance by Entity A (i.e. if it chooses not to deliver its own shares). However, this also is not the most faithful representation as a conventional forward to sell own shares would not allow for the potential investor to claim damages for economic losses due to non-performance under the contract. Indeed, the whole nature of the contractual arrangement is that if Entity A chooses not to deliver shares it is entitled to do so and this is not non-performance.

It would therefore seem more appropriate to view the arrangement as an instrument which will be settled by Entity A either delivering cash or issuing a fixed number of own shares and not to apply the rules regarding derivatives over own equity. Viewed in this way the arrangement should, on initial receipt of £100, be accounted for as equity since Entity A has the unconditional right to avoid delivering cash by choosing to deliver own shares. This is the case only if the value of the alternative to deliver shares instead of cash is not determined to exceed substantially the value of the cash alternative. [IAS 32.21] A financial liability would only be recognised at the point where Entity A has chosen not to deliver own shares and has therefore incurred an obligation to deliver cash.

If the value of the share settlement was determined to exceed substantially the value of the cash then the instrument would be considered a financial liability as in substance the holder has been guaranteed receipt of an amount that is at least equal to the cash alternative.

6.2 Share buy-back arrangements

An entity may enter into arrangements with a third party, usually with a financial institution, for that third party to buy back the entity's equity shares in the market for delivery to the entity. It is important to determine in these instances whether the third party is acting as principal or as agent for the entity. If the third party is acting as agent then the contractual arrangement between the entity and third party is not a financial instrument. In such cases, only when shares are acquired by the third party will the entity recognise a financial liability to pay the third party and a debit in equity for the shares to be delivered, and when the shares are delivered to the entity will the entity settle the financial liability with cash or other financial asset and re-present within equity that treasury stock has been acquired or shares cancelled.

In some jurisdictions an entity will enter into an arrangement immediately prior to its period end which allows a financial institution to acquire shares in the entity at the financial institution's discretion with delivery of those shares to the entity. These arrangements are normally subject to a cap and/or floor on the amount of shares the financial institution can acquire and a maximum amount of shares that can be acquired in a trading day. The financial institution acquires the shares in the market and then transfers them to the entity at a market price subject to some adjustments and a fee. These arrangements are entered into to ensure the entity's buy back programme continues during the 'quiet period' (the period between the entity's period end and the release of the financial results) without the entity breaching regulatory rules. The financial institution has the unfettered discretion to buy back shares, is not under instruction from the entity and is therefore considered as a principal.

The entity will need to recognise at the period end that it has a financial obligation to acquire its own equity, i.e. a 'gross obligation'. This financial liability will be initially recognised at the present value of the maximum amount the entity could be required to pay to the financial institution with a corresponding debit in equity. Changes in the present value of this liability, say, due to the unwind of the discount rate, or changes in the market price of the entity's shares, will be recognised in profit or loss. If the arrangement limits the maximum amount the entity can pay to the financial institution, the financial liability will be initially measured at the present value of this amount. In this case, the entity may not have variability in the amount it will pay due to changes in the entity's share price as the entity could always be required to pay the maximum amount to the financial institution.

When the financial institution buys back the entity's shares and delivers them to the entity and the entity settles the obligation with cash or other financial asset, the entity derecognises the part of the financial liability equal to the amount that the entity has paid. If at the end of the buy-back period the financial institution has not acquired the maximum amount of shares or utilised the maximum amount that the entity can spend on buying back shares, a financial liability will remain. This amount should be reversed with a corresponding credit in equity to show that the financial liability has been extinguished.

7 Classification of financial liabilities

IAS 39 *Financial Instruments: Recognition and Measurement* requires that financial liabilities are classified into one of two categories:

- financial liabilities at fair value through profit or loss; and
- other financial liabilities (measured at amortised cost).

7.1 Financial liabilities at fair value through profit or loss

This class of financial liabilities can further be divided into the following two sub-categories:

- financial liabilities classified as held for trading; and
- financial liabilities designated by the entity as at fair value through profit or loss.

7.1.1 *Financial liabilities classified as held for trading*

A financial liability is held for trading if it falls into one of the following categories:

[IAS 39.9]

- financial liabilities incurred with the intention of repurchasing them in the near term;
- financial liabilities that on initial recognition form part of a portfolio of identified financial instruments that are managed together and for which there is evidence of a recent actual pattern of short-term profit-taking; and
- derivative liabilities, unless the derivative forms part of a designated and effective hedging relationship (see **chapter 20**).

In May 2008 the IASB issued *Improvements to IFRSs*. The improvements amended the definition of held for trading to clarify that a non-derivative financial instrument that is traded as part of a portfolio of identified financial instruments that are managed together and for which there is evidence of a recent actual pattern of short-term profit-taking can qualify for the trading classification only if it is included in such a portfolio on initial recognition. The amendments made to IAS 39 by *Improvements to IFRSs* apply for annual periods beginning on or after 1 January 2009, but earlier application is permitted. An entity choosing to apply the amendments early must disclose that fact.

UK

At the time of writing, Improvements to IFRSs *has not yet been endorsed for adoption in the EU. EU companies may, nevertheless, comply with the amended definition of held for trading prior to endorsement, since it does not conflict with the existing requirements of IAS 39.*

The fact that a liability is used to provide funding for trading activities does not of itself mean that liability is to be classified as held for trading. [IAS 39.AG15] Thus, a borrowing that a bank uses to fund its trading portfolio of debt and equity securities would not automatically be classified as held for trading.

Example 7.1.1

Held for trading liabilities

The following are examples of liabilities that would be classified as held for trading and thus included in the fair value through profit or loss category:

(a) an interest rate swap that has negative fair value that is not accounted for as a hedging instrument;

(b) a derivative liability incurred upon writing a foreign exchange option that is not accounted for as a hedging instrument;

(c) an obligation to deliver financial assets borrowed by a short seller (i.e. an entity that sells financial assets it has borrowed and does not yet own); and

(d) a quoted debt instrument that the issuer plans to buy back in the near term depending on movements in the debt instrument's fair value, i.e. a financial liability that is incurred with an intention to repurchase it in the near term.

7.1.2 *Financial liabilities designated as at fair value through profit or loss*

Designation as at fair value through profit or loss is available notwithstanding the fact that in the absence of such a choice the liability would have been classified within the category of 'other financial liabilities' and measured at amortised cost. The ability to fair value through profit or loss a financial liability that is not held for trading is restricted to those instances where specified criteria are met. The criterion for financial liabilities is the same as for financial assets, and is detailed in **3.1.1** in **chapter 14**. The designation is, however, irrevocable so the liability cannot subsequently be reclassified into another category during its life (see **3.1.1** in **chapter 14**).

If an entity has designated a financial liability as at fair value through profit or loss, it must disclose the amount of change in its fair value that is due to credit risk which can be determined as the amount of change that is not attributable to changes in market conditions that give risk to market risk (i.e. benchmark interest rate). [IFRS 7.10] (See **2.8.4** in **chapter 21**.)

7.2 Other financial liabilities

Financial liabilities not classified as at fair value through profit or loss, hence classified in the 'other financial liabilities' category, are measured at amortised cost.

7.3 Reclassification

7.3.1 *Into and out of fair value through profit or loss*

Reclassifications in and out of this category are prohibited. The following changes in circumstances are not reclassifications:

[IAS 39.50A]

- a derivative that was previously a designated and effective hedging instrument in a cash flow hedge or net investment hedge no longer qualifies as such; and
- a derivative becomes a designated and effective hedging instrument in a cash flow hedge or net investment hedge.

IAS 39.50A was introduced by *Improvements to IFRSs* issued in May 2008. The amendments made to IAS 39 by *Improvements to IFRSs* apply for annual periods beginning on or after 1 January 2009, but earlier application is permitted. An entity choosing to apply the amendments early must disclose that fact. The amendments to IAS 39.50A are to be applied as of the date and in the manner of the 2005 amendments described in IAS 39.105A (i.e. in respect of amendments to the fair value option). [IAS 39.108C]

UK

At the time of writing, Improvements to IFRSs *has not yet been endorsed for adoption in the EU. EU companies may, nevertheless, comply with IAS 39.50A prior to endorsement, since it does not conflict with the existing requirements of IAS 39.*

7.4 Classification of financial liabilities acquired in a business combination

When financial liabilities are assumed in a business combination those liabilities must be classified in the consolidated financial statements of the acquirer into one of the permitted categories described in **section 7** above. It is entirely possible that the classification of a financial liability for these purposes may differ from its classification in the financial statements of the acquiree. For example, the acquirer in its consolidated financial statements may choose to designate a financial liability as at fair value through profit or loss at initial recognition that the acquiree did not classify in that category when it initially recognised the liability. The difference in classification arises as the acquirer at the time of acquisition recognises the financial liabilities of the acquiree for the first time and has to make its own classification decision.

The revised version of IFRS 3 *Business Combinations*, issued in January 2008, provides clear guidance stating that at the acquisition date the acquirer shall make any classifications, designations concerning financial assets acquired or financial liabilities assumed in a business combination in accordance with the contractual terms, economic conditions, the acquirer's operating or accounting policies, and other factors as of that date that are pertinent in subsequently applying other IFRSs. IFRS 3(2008) is effective for accounting periods beginning on or after 1 July 2009.

8 Future developments

In February 2008 the IASB issued a discussion paper entitled *Financial Instruments with Characteristics of Equity*. The discussion paper follows the issue in November 2007 of a preliminary views document with the same title issued by the US Financial Accounting Standards Board (FASB). The discussion paper was issued by the IASB as part of its memorandum of understanding with the FASB to issue due process documents relating to a proposed standard on the distinction between liabilities and equity. The discussion paper comprises an invitation to comment on the FASB's preliminary views document. The liabilities and equity project is currently on the IASB's research agenda. Following the publication of this discussion paper, the IASB will consider a proposal to add the project to its active agenda. If the project is added, the IASB intends to undertake it jointly with the FASB. The responses to the discussion paper will be considered in that project as the boards develop a common standard.

The FASB document describes three approaches for distinguishing equity instruments from non-equity instruments: (i) basic ownership, (ii) ownership-settlement and (iii) reassessed expected outcomes. The FASB has reached a preliminary view that the basic ownership approach is the appropriate approach for determining which instruments should be classified as equity. At the date of writing, the IASB had not yet deliberated any of the three approaches, or any other approaches, to distinguishing equity instruments and non-equity instruments.

16 Financial instruments: derivatives

1 Introduction

IAS 39 requires that all derivatives are accounted for in the statement of financial position at fair value, irrespective of whether they are used as part of a hedging relationship. Changes in fair value are recognised in profit or loss unless the contract is part of an effective cash flow or net investment hedging relationship (see **chapter 20** on hedge accounting). If a derivative is part of an effective cash flow or net investment hedge, the change in fair value of the effective portion of the hedge is recognised in other comprehensive income. As the definition of a derivative is so broad, many contracts are likely to be caught, and therefore will have to be accounted for at fair value. For example, certain contracts to buy or sell non-financial items fall within the scope of IAS 39 and meet the definition of a derivative (see **2.5** in **chapter 13**).

A fixed price commitment to buy or sell a financial instrument at a future date meets the definition of a derivative financial instrument. However, as a practical expedient these are not accounted for as derivatives if the commitment has a short duration accepted by market convention. These are referred to as regular way purchases or sales. Regular way contracts are subject to special accounting rules. This is dealt with in **2.2** in **chapter 19**.

This chapter discusses derivatives in the following sections:

Section 2	Definition of a derivative
Section 3	Scoped in contracts
Section 4	Examples of contracts that meet the definition of a derivative
Section 5	Presentation of derivatives

2 Definition of a derivative

IAS 39 defines a derivative as a financial instrument or other contract within the scope of the Standard with all three of the following characteristics:

[IAS 39.9]

- its value changes in response to the change in a specified interest rate, financial instrument price, commodity price, foreign exchange rate, index of prices or rates, credit rating or credit index, or other variable, provided in the case of a non-financial variable that the variable is not specific to a party to the contract (sometimes called the 'underlying');
- it requires no initial net investment or an initial net investment that is smaller than would be required for other types of contracts that would be expected to have a similar response to changes in market factors; and
- it is settled at a future date.

2.1 Underlying

An underlying is a variable that, along with either a notional amount or a payment provision, determines the settlement amount of a derivative.

Examples of underlyings include:

- a security price or security price index;
- a commodity price or commodity price index;
- an interest rate or interest rate index;
- a credit rating or credit index;
- a foreign exchange rate or foreign exchange rate index;
- an insurance index or catastrophe loss index;
- a climatic or geological condition (e.g. temperature, earthquake severity, or rainfall), another physical variable, or a related index; or
- another variable (e.g. volume of sales).

The value or cash flows of all assets, liabilities, and purchase and sale commitments change in response to changes in the market factors in which they are founded. There is nothing unique in this regard about derivatives, except that the market factor is referred to as an index, a variable or an underlying and, in many instances, the referenced underlying is not delivered at settlement but is used as a basis for computing a settlement amount, usually in cash.

Prior to the issue of IFRS 4 *Insurance Contracts*, IAS 39 scoped out derivatives where the variable is based on climatic, geological and other physical variables. However, since IFRS 4 was issued, IAS 39 has been amended to scope these contracts into IAS 39 unless they meet the definition of an insurance contract (see **2.3** of **chapter 13**). If an insurance contract contains an embedded derivative that needs to be separately accounted for, then it is only the embedded derivative part of the insurance contract that will be accounted for as a derivative in accordance with IAS 39. Embedded derivatives are considered in **chapter 17**.

Additionally, a derivative where the underlying is a specific commodity, for example oil, may be scoped out of IAS 39 if the contract is considered a normal purchase, sale or usage requirement contract (see **2.5** of **chapter 13**). Whether the instrument is scoped in or out of IAS 39 is dependent on the entity's normal business requirements as well as the settlement terms of the instrument, the entity's past practice, and whether the instrument is a written option and the underlying is readily convertible to cash.

The definition of a derivative was amended by the IASB when it issued IFRS 4 *Insurance Contracts* to scope out contracts over non-financial variables that are specific to a party to the contract. This amendment was required to ensure that insurance risk was scoped out of IAS 39 and instead accounted for in accordance with IFRS 4. Some argue that the term 'non-financial variable specific to a party to the contract' was intended to scope out contracts beyond just insurance contracts. For example, if the amount of interest payable on issued debt is linked to the sales volume of the issuer, then this could be argued to be 'a non-financial variable specific to a party to the contract.' If this literal interpretation applied then the sales linking feature would never meet the definition of a derivative, and therefore could never be an embedded derivative. However, this would not seem to be a valid interpretation considering that both IAS 39.IG.B.8 and IAS 39.AG33(f)(ii) clearly indicate that derivatives and embedded derivatives can be based on sales volumes and revenue. In addition, IAS 39.IG.A.2 states that an option to put a non-financial asset, such as an office building, is a derivative if it is not scoped out of IAS 39 as a purchase, sale or usage requirements contract (see **2.5** of **chapter 13**). If the literal interpretation described above was appropriate then the implementation guidance Q&A would be incorrect as the put option in that case is over an office building that is a non-financial variable that is specific to a party to the contract. It follows, therefore, from IAS 39.11 that a debt instrument with interest linked to sales volume of the issuer or other non-financial variables contains an embedded derivative that is not closely related to the host debt contract. The embedded derivative is therefore separated from the host contract and accounted for as a derivative under IAS 39. See **chapter 17** on embedded derivatives.

In February 2007 the IFRIC recommended that the Board should make an amendment to IAS 39 to make it clear that the term 'non-financial variable specific to a party to the contract' included in the definition of a derivative is restricted to scoping out insurance contracts from IAS 39. The Board unanimously agreed to this recommendation. In October 2007 the IASB issued an Exposure Draft titled *Improvements to International Financial Reporting Standards* that proposed to amend the definition of a derivative in IAS 39 by deleting the reference to 'non-financial variables specific to a party to the contract' and as a result contracts linked to those variables will be within the scope of IAS 39 and classified as derivatives. The Board recognised that it introduced the exclusion for some non-financial variables when it issued IFRS 4 to exclude from the scope of IAS 39 contracts within the scope of IFRS 4. The Board observed that the proposed amendment would not affect the scope of IAS 39, because contracts within the scope of IFRS 4 are excluded from IAS 39.2(e) anyway. At the date of writing the proposed amendment has not been finalised.

2.2 Notionals and payment provisions

A derivative usually has a notional amount, which is an amount of currency, a number of shares, a number of units of weight or volume or other units specified in the contract. However, instead of having a notional amount, a derivative contract could instead require a fixed payment or payment of an amount that can change (but not proportionally to a change in the underlying) as a result of some future event that is unrelated to a notional. This is referred to as a payment provision.

Example 2.2A

Payment provision based on interest rates

Entity ABC receives £200 to enter into a contract that requires it to pay £500 if six-month LIBOR increases by 75 basis points over the next six months. Even though this contract does not have a notional, it contains a payment provision that does not move proportionally with the underlying.

Example 2.2B

Payment provision based on share price

Entity XYZ enters into a contract that requires it to pay £10 million if Entity ABC share price increases by £5 per share during a six-month period; conversely XYZ will receive £10 million if ABC share price decreases by £5 per share during the same six-month period.

In this example, the underlying is the price of ABC shares. There is no notional amount to determine the settlement amount. Instead, there is a payment provision that does not move proportionally with the underlying. The absence of a notional amount does not preclude the instrument from meeting the definition of a derivative because there is a payment provision.

It is sometimes the case that a contract has neither a notional, nor a fixed payment provision. In addition, a contract may have multiple underlyings.

Example 2.2C

Foreign currency forward contract linked to sales

Entity X, a Euro functional currency entity, sells products in Switzerland. The sales are denominated in Swiss francs. Entity X enters into a contract with an investment bank to convert Swiss francs to Euros at a fixed exchange rate. The contract requires Entity X to remit Swiss francs based on its sales volume in Switzerland in exchange for Euros at a fixed exchange rate of 1.60.

The contract with the bank has two underlyings (sales volume and the Euro/Swiss franc exchange rate). The contract does not have a specified notional amount or a fixed payment provision, but still meets the definition of a derivative.

2.3 Interaction of notional amounts with the underlying

The settlement amount of a derivative instrument with a notional amount is determined by the interaction of that notional amount with the underlying. The interaction may be simple multiplication, or it may involve a formula with leverage factors or other constants.

Example 2.3

Interest rate swap

XYZ enters into an interest rate swap that requires XYZ to pay a fixed rate of interest and receive a variable rate of interest. The fixed interest rate amount is 7.5 per cent, while the variable interest rate amount is three-month LIBOR, reset on a quarterly basis. The notional amount of the swap is £100 million.

The underlying is an interest rate index, three-month LIBOR. Net regular settlements are calculated by applying the difference between 7.5 per cent and three-month LIBOR to the notional of £100 million.

2.4 Initial net investment

The second part of the definition of a derivative is that there is either no initial net investment, or that any initial investment is smaller than would be required for other contracts that are expected to have a similar response to changes in market factors. This is a comparative measure, and excludes any margin accounts (which are instead treated as collateral). Consider the following examples.

2.4.1 Interest rate swaps

Example 2.4.1

Interest rate swap

Entity B enters into a contract with a counterparty that requires it to pay a LIBOR-based variable rate of interest, and receive a fixed rate of 8 per cent. The contract is an interest rate swap with a notional amount of ¥10 billion. Entity B did not pay or receive cash at inception, i.e. the contract is at market at inception, and therefore does not require an initial net investment by either party.

In some instances, the terms of the interest rate swap may be favourable or unfavourable and may require one of the parties to make an up-front initial investment in the contract. If the initial investment represents a premium or discount for market conditions, the initial net investment would normally still be smaller than the notional on the debt instrument from which the interest rate cash flows are derived, so would satisfy the initial net investment criterion of a derivative.

2.4.1.1 Interest rate swap with fixed leg prepaid

Example 2.4.1.1

Prepaid fixed leg

Entity X enters into an eight-year pay-fixed at 7 per cent, receive LIBOR interest rate swap on £100 million. It prepays the fixed leg at inception. The amount it pays is calculated as £7 million (£100 million x 7 per cent) for 8 years, discounted at market rates.

This initial payment is significantly less than the amount Entity X would have to pay to acquire an instrument that would have a similar response to changes in market factors. Entity X would need to acquire £100 million debt with a LIBOR return in order to replicate the return on the floating rate leg of the swap. Therefore, the swap with a prepaid fixed leg will still meet the definition of a derivative.

If the fixed rate payment obligation on the interest rate swap is prepaid after initial recognition the payment would be considered termination of the old swap and an origination of a new instrument that would need to be classified for the first time. [IAS 39.IG.B.4]

2.4.1.2 *Interest rate swap with floating leg prepaid*

Example 2.4.1.2

Prepaid floating leg

Entity A enters into a six-year pay LIBOR, receive-fixed 5 per cent interest rate swap on £100 million. It prepays the variable leg at inception. The cash inflows that the entity continues to receive are akin to those of a financial instrument with a fixed annuity of 5 per cent per year for the next six years.

As the amount prepaid will be about the same as what would have been paid to purchase a fixed annuity instrument paying 5 per cent over the next six years, the initial net investment test is failed. The contract would not be accounted for as a derivative, but instead as a loan made by Entity A. [IAS 39.IG.B.5]

2.4.2 *Options*

For an option the premium paid could be significant. However, it is likely to be smaller than the amount that would be required to buy an instrument with a similar response to changes in market factors, i.e. the underlying instrument to which the option relates.

Example 2.4.2A

Deep in-the-money option (1)

Entity A purchases, for £1.1 million, an option to buy 80,000 shares in Entity B at £75 per share in three months' time. When it purchased the option, Entity B's shares were trading at £70 per share. The cost of the option, £1.1 million, is less than what it would cost to buy 80,000 shares in Entity B, so it meets this part of the definition. This will even be the case for many deep-in-the-money options, as demonstrated below.

Example 2.4.2B

Deep in-the-money option (2)

Entity XYZ purchases a deep-in-the-money call option on Entity ABC shares. ABC's share price is €100 per share. The option is an American option with a 180-day maturity. The option has a strike price of €10 per share and XYZ pays a premium of €91. The initial investment in the option of €91 is less than the notional amount applied to the underlying, i.e. €100 (the notional amount is one share and the underlying is €100 per share).

Although the option has a significant initial net investment, it is smaller than the investment that would be required for other types of contracts that would be expected to have a similar response to changes in market factors. The invested amount of €91 does not approximate the notional amount applied to the underlying (€100) and, therefore, the option meets the initial net investment criterion for a derivative instrument.

2.4.3 *Currency swap*

Currency swaps typically require an initial exchange of currencies. These swaps will still satisfy the initial net investment criterion as the exchange is of amounts with an equal fair value, so that on a net basis the fair value at inception is zero.

Example 2.4.3

Currency swap

Entity X enters into a three-year currency swap with Bank Z. At inception, when the Sterling/Euro exchange rate is 1.5, the swap results in Entity X paying Bank Z £100 million and Bank Z paying Entity X €150 million. Whilst there has been an exchange of cash, the amounts exchanged are of equal fair value.

2.4.4 *Prepaid forward*

Example 2.4.4

Prepaid forward contract

Entity X enters into a forward contract to purchase one million ordinary shares in Entity T in one year. The current market price of Entity T's shares is €50 per share, and the one-year forward price is €55 per share. Entity X prepays the forward contract at inception with a €50 million payment.

The initial net investment approximates the investment that would be required for other types of contracts that would be expected to have a similar response to changes in market factors because one million of Entity T's shares could be purchased at inception for the same price of €50 million. Accordingly, the prepaid forward contract does not meet the initial net investment criterion of a derivative instrument. [IAS 39.IG.B.9]

2.4.5 *Offsetting loans*

Two or more non-derivative contracts should be considered together when the substance of the aggregate position is that of a derivative. IAS 39.IG.B.6 states that indicators of such a situation are when the contracts are:

- entered into at the same time, and in contemplation of each other;
- have the same counterparty;
- relate to the same risk; and
- there is no apparent economic need or substantive business purpose for structuring the transactions separately that could not also have been accomplished in a single transaction.

Example 2.4.5

Offsetting loans

Entity A makes a five-year fixed rate loan to Entity B on market terms. Simultaneously, Entity B makes a five-year variable rate loan to Entity A on market terms over the same notional. The combination of these two loans is akin to an interest rate swap. Even if amounts are exchanged at inception of the two loans, the net fair value of the amounts exchanged is zero. Therefore, the loans must be considered together, and the entire arrangement accounted for as a derivative.

2.5 Future settlement

The third part of the definition of a derivative is that it is settled at a future date. Settlement can occur in different ways, either gross or net [IAS 39.IG.B.3], and does not just mean exchange of cash. For example, it may be expected that an out-of-the-money option will not be exercised. However, expiry of the contract is a form of settlement, even if at maturity of the instrument no cash or underlying changes hands. [IAS 39.IG.B.7]

3 Scoped in contracts

Certain contracts to buy or sell non-financial items are within the scope of IAS 39 (see **2.5** of **chapter 13**). If a contract to buy or sell a non-financial item is within the scope of IAS 39 and meets the definition of a derivative it will be recognised at fair value.

Example 3

Contract over a non-financial item

Entity A enters into a futures contract to purchase 1,000 bushels of corn for £1 per bushel in three months. No cash is paid at inception. Assuming the contract is within the scope of IAS 39 (i.e. because it is not entered into for the purpose of the receipt of the corn bushels), the contract meets the definition of a derivative.

It has an underlying (the price of corn bushels), there is no initial investment, and the contract will be settled in the future. The contract must be recognised in Entity A's statement of financial position at fair value, with changes in fair value recognised in profit or loss unless the contract qualifies as a hedging instrument in an effective hedge relationship.

4 Examples of contracts that meet the definition of a derivative

Some common examples of derivatives are included below:

Contract	Notional/ payment provision	Underlying	Initial invest-ment	Future settlement
A futures contract to buy 1,000 barrels of crude oil at $60 a barrel in 1 month and the contract is not entered into for the physical delivery of oil for the entity's normal business usage requirements	1,000 barrels of crude oil	Price of oil barrels	$0	Yes – 1 month
A forward to buy $500 for £300 in 1 year	$500 (or £300)	£/$ exchange rate	£0	Yes – 1 year
An option to buy 80,000 shares in Entity B at £75 per share in 1 month. The option costs £1.1 million	80,000 shares	Entity B's share price	£1.1 million	Yes – 1 month
A pay LIBOR + 25 basis points, receive fixed 5% interest rate swap over £100 million, settled quarterly	£100 million	LIBOR	£0	Yes – quarterly
A pay-floating £ on £100 million, receive-floating US$ on $170 million currency swap, settled annually	£100 million or $170 million	£/$ exchange rate	£0	Yes – annually
A contract to receive £10 million if Entity A's share price increases by £5 per share at the end of six-months. The contract costs £1.0 million to enter into	Payment provision	Entity A's share price	£1.0 million	Yes – 6 months
A pay-variable Euro amount based on the entity's sales, receive £ at a fixed exchange rate of €1.5:£1 based on the entity's sales, settled monthly	Variable notional	€/£ exchange rate and sales volume	£0	Yes – monthly

Contract	Notional/ payment provision	Underlying	Initial invest- ment	Future settlement
A 5-year interest rate cap over £100 million. The cap will pay if LIBOR increases beyond 8%. The premium paid to enter into the cap is £1.0 million	£100 million	LIBOR	£1.0 million	Yes – if in Year 5 LIBOR exceeds 8%.

The definition of a derivative is very broad and therefore can capture many contractual arrangements that traditionally would not be considered derivatives. One example is bets in the gaming industry. A bookmaker will take a bet from a customer on the outcome of a specified event (for example a horse race, general election, or football match) in cash for stated or variable odds. When the event occurs, depending on the outcome, the bookmaker will pay any winnings to the customer. The contract for the bet is no different to a derivative contract without a notional and with a payment provision. The bookmaker has written an option to the customer, where the bookmaker will receive an up-front premium in return for bearing potential downside risk should the uncertain event occur.

Where the customer does not 'fix' the odds, i.e. has variable odds, the derivative will be far less sensitive to changes in the probability of the uncertain event occurring, and therefore the derivative will be far less sensitive to changes in market prices. However, where the holder of the bet 'fixes' the odds, the fair value of the bet will change with changes in the probability of the uncertain event occurring.

The bookmaker will take bets on many different outcomes for one event and expects to make a profit irrespective of that event's outcome. If a bookmaker has taken too many bets from customers on one outcome, it may 'lay off' bets with another bookmaker, i.e. it enters into an offsetting bet to lay off the risk. This is a form of economic hedging. The entity cannot apply hedge accounting as a derivative is not a qualifying hedged item. As such, in accordance with IAS 39, bookmakers should recognise all bets, whether written or purchased, as derivative assets and liabilities measured at fair value through profit or loss.

In May 2007 the IFRIC issued a rejection notice on gaming transactions stating that an unsettled wager is likely to meet the definition of a derivative and will therefore be accounted for under IAS 39. The IFRIC recognised that, in other situations, a gaming institution does not take a position against a customer but instead provides services to manage the organisation of games between two or more gaming parties. In these instances, the gaming institution earns a commission regardless of the outcome of the wager and therefore it is likely that the commission would meet the definition of revenue and would be recognised when the conditions in *IAS 18 Revenue* were met.

5 Presentation of derivatives

A derivative that has a maturity of less than twelve months from the end of the reporting period or has a maturity greater than twelve months but is expected to be settled within twelve months should be presented as a current asset or liability in the statement of financial position. A derivative that has a maturity of more than twelve months from the end of the reporting period and is not intended to be settled within twelve months will be presented as a non-current asset or liability.

Prior to the issue of *Improvements to IFRSs* in May 2008, there was ambiguity as to whether derivatives with a maturity greater than twelve months that are not intended to be settled within twelve months and were not part of a designated and effective hedge accounting relationship could be presented as non-current as these instrument also met the definition of held for trading in IAS 39.9. An amendment to IAS 1 included as part of *Improvements to IFRSs* clarified that in such instances the derivatives should be presented as non-current as the derivative is not held primarily for trading purposes. The amendments made to IAS 1 by *Improvements to IFRSs* apply for annual periods beginning on or after 1 January 2009, but earlier application is permitted. An entity choosing to apply the amendments early must disclose that fact.

UK *At the time of writing,* Improvements to IFRSs *has not yet been endorsed for adoption in the EU. EU companies may, nevertheless, comply with this amendment to IAS 1 prior to endorsement, since it does not conflict with the existing requirements of IAS 1 and IAS 39.*

For guidance on the presentation of embedded derivatives see **section 13** in **chapter 17**.

5.1 Fair value gains and losses on derivatives that are economic hedges

IAS 39 requires gains and losses on derivatives to be reported in profit or loss when hedge accounting is not applied. However, the Standard does not specify where such gains and losses would be presented within profit or loss.

Example 5.1

Presentation of non-hedge accounting derivative

Entity A enters into a derivative contract (forward contract) to hedge a foreign currency cash flow under a highly probable forecast revenue stream. The entity does not apply hedge accounting.

Presentation of the gains and losses on the derivative within revenue or elsewhere in operating profit is not precluded, provided the chosen presentation is applied consistently from period to period to all similar items and follows the nature of the transaction to which it is linked. The policy adopted should be disclosed in the financial statements.

17 Financial instruments: embedded derivatives

1 Introduction

IAS 39 introduces a new accounting concept, that of an embedded derivative. The definition of an embedded derivative and the principle of separation is relatively simple, but the application is complicated as most of the guidance in the Standard is provided by means of examples. Furthermore, the scope of this application is wide as an entity will need to consider whether embedded derivatives may reside in contracts other than financial instruments. They may be found in any contract, such as a lease, an insurance contract, or a sale or a purchase contract.

The challenge extends beyond searching for all embedded derivatives. Once one has been found, it must then be determined whether the embedded derivative needs to be separately accounted for under IAS 39. Not all embedded derivatives should be separated out from the host contract in which they reside.

Embedded derivatives that have to be separated are accounted for in the same way as stand-alone derivatives, i.e. at fair value with gains and losses recognised in profit or loss at each measurement date, unless the embedded derivative qualifies as an effective hedging instrument in a cash flow or a hedge of a net investment in a foreign operation.

This chapter discusses embedded derivatives in the following sections:

Section 2	Definitions
Section 3	Separation conditions
Section 4	Terms of the embedded derivative and the debt host contract
Section 5	Determination of host contract: debt vs. equity
Section 6	Multiple embedded derivatives
Section 7	Embedded derivatives in debt host contracts
Section 8	Embedded derivatives in equity host contracts
Section 9	Embedded derivatives in lease contracts

2 Definitions

IAS 39 defines an embedded derivative as a component of a hybrid (combined) instrument that also includes a non-derivative host contract – with the effect that some of the cash flows of the combined instrument vary in a way similar to a stand-alone derivative. An embedded derivative causes some or all of the cash flows that otherwise would be required by the contract to be modified according to a specified interest rate, financial instrument price, commodity price, foreign exchange rate, index of prices or rates or other variable (provided in the case of a non-financial variable that the variable is not specific to a party to the contract, see **2.1** of **chapter 16**). [IAS 39.10]

The hybrid contract is the entire contract, within which there may be an embedded derivative. The host contract is the main body of the contract, excluding the embedded derivative. The diagram and examples below demonstrate the application of these terms:

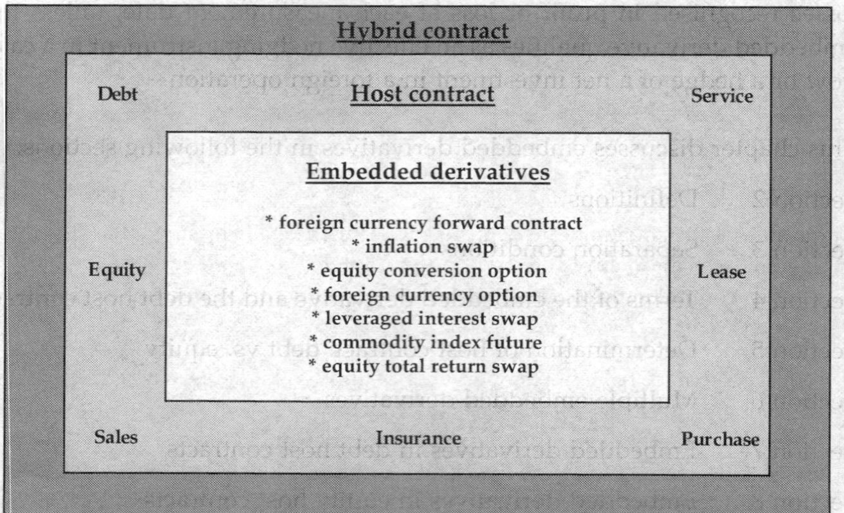

Example 2A

Debt host contract

Entity X holds a bond which is convertible into the ordinary shares of Entity Y. The hybrid contract is the convertible bond; the host contract is the bond asset, and the embedded derivative is the conversion option.

Example 2B

Lease host contract

Entity A enters into a lease with an inflation factor, such that each year rentals are adjusted for changes in a retail price index. The hybrid contract is the entire lease; the host is the lease contract, and the embedded derivative is the adjustment to the retail price index.

Example 2C

Executory host contract

Entity T, a UK entity whose functional currency is Sterling, enters into a contract to sell a non-financial item in US dollars. The hybrid contract is the entire sale contract which will be settled in US dollars; the host contract is the Sterling sale contract; the embedded derivative is the foreign exchange Sterling/US dollar forward.

A derivative that is attached to a financial instrument but is contractually transferable independently of that instrument, or has a different counterparty from that instrument, is not an embedded derivative, but a separate financial instrument. [IAS 39.10]

Example 2D

Contractually separate derivative

Entity A issues floating rate debt. To protect itself against rising interest rates, it purchases an interest rate cap, capping interest payable at 8 per cent. The cap is contractually separate from the debt, so it is not an embedded derivative, but a free-standing derivative.

Entity A could have instead issued floating rate debt, where the debt instrument itself is capped, such that once interest rates go beyond 8 per cent, it only pays out 8 per cent until rates fall below this level. In this case, there is an embedded derivative within the debt, i.e. the interest rate cap, and this cap will need to be assessed to see if it must be separately accounted for.

3 Separation conditions

Not all embedded derivatives should be separated from their host contracts. An embedded derivative is separated from its host contract and accounted for separately as a stand-alone derivative when:

[IAS 39.11]

(a) the economic characteristics and risks of the embedded derivative are not closely related to the economic risks and characteristics of the host contract;

(b) a separate instrument with the same terms as the embedded derivative would meet the definition of a derivative; and

(c) the hybrid instrument is not measured at fair value with changes in fair value recognised in profit or loss.

Condition (b) above means that an embedded feature should only be separated from its host contract if it itself meets the definition of a derivative, i.e. it has an underlying, no initial net investment (or an initial net investment that is smaller than would be required for other types of contracts that would be expected to have a similar response to changes in market factors) and it is settled at a future date (see **chapter 16** for more details on the definition of a derivative).

Example 3A

No underlying

A lease contract contains a provision that rentals increase by £100 each year. The price adjustment feature does not meet the definition of a derivative on a stand-alone basis since its value does not change in response to changes of some 'underlying' – there is no underlying.

Condition (c) means that any financial asset or financial liability that is held at fair value with changes in fair value recognised through profit or loss should not be assessed to see if it contains any embedded derivatives. Any embedded derivative that is not closely related to its host will be accounted for as if it were a stand-alone derivative – i.e. measured at fair value, with changes in fair value recognised in profit or loss. If the entire contract is already being accounted for in this way the embedded derivative is automatically accounted for at fair value and therefore it is not required to be separated.

An entity can elect to classify a hybrid instrument at fair value through profit or loss at initial recognition, even though the instrument would not meet the definition of held for trading (see **3.1** in **chapter 14**).

Such an election cannot be made if:

(a) the embedded derivative does not significantly modify the cash flows that otherwise would be required by the contract; or

(b) it is clear with little or no analysis when a similar hybrid instrument is first considered that separation of the embedded derivative is prohibited, as in the case of a prepayment option embedded in a loan that permits the holder to prepay the loan for approximately its amortised cost (see **7.1** in this chapter).

Designating a hybrid instrument as at fair value through profit or loss may provide benefit to entities with more complex instruments where the search for and analysis of embedded derivatives significantly increases the cost of complying with IAS 39. This will also benefit entities that issue or acquire structured products, for example equity-linked notes or callable range-accrual notes, which may contain more than one embedded derivative that is not closely related to the host contract. For issuers of these instruments, who normally invest in derivatives as an economic hedge of the issued notes, fair valuing the hybrid instrument reduces the accounting mismatch which would have resulted had the host contract been measured at amortised cost. For the acquirer of the notes, assuming the product has been transacted with a financial institution, the fair value of the combined instrument may be more readily available for the hybrid instrument as a whole than for the host contract and the individual embedded derivative separately. [IAS 39.BC77A – 78]

Example 3B

Pricing adjustment to a contract over a non-financial item

An entity enters into a forward contract to purchase wheat. The contract meets the definition of a derivative, but does not meet the 'expected purchase, sale or usage requirements' scope exemption as the entity has a history of net cash settling similar contracts (see **2.5** of **chapter 13**). Embedded in the forward contract is the following price adjustment: if the retail price index were to increase by 3 per cent during the term of the contract, the contracted price is doubled.

As the contract is within the scope of IAS 39 and meets the definition of a derivative, it will be accounted for at fair value with changes in fair value recognised in profit or loss. The embedded derivative will automatically be accounted for at fair value through profit or loss, hence no further considerations are necessary.

Condition (a) is the most difficult of the three to assess, as there is no definition of 'closely related'. In the appendix to IAS 39 there are two lists:

one list gives examples of embedded derivatives that are closely related to their hosts, and the other gives examples of embedded derivatives that are not closely related to their hosts.

When an embedded derivative is not included in one of these lists, a significant degree of judgement will be required and conclusions may need to be drawn by analogy to the specific examples given. Ultimately, the conclusion reached should be consistent with the underlying principle that an embedded derivative should be separated from its host contract when the economic characteristics and risks differ.

In summary, the following decision tree can be used to determine whether an embedded derivative needs to be separated from its host contract:

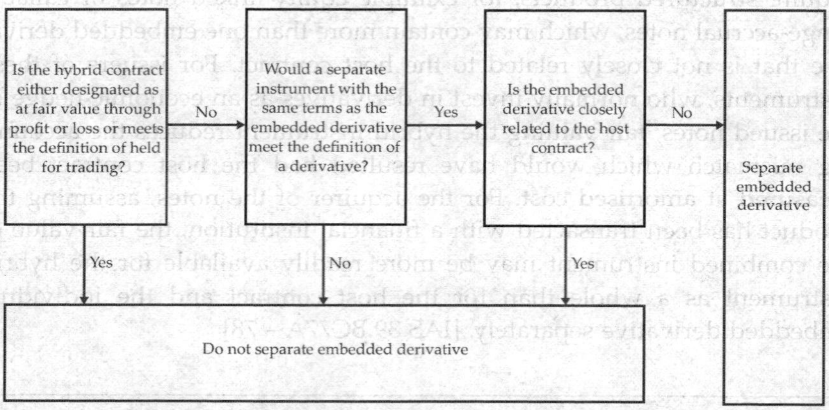

Once it is determined that an embedded derivative is closely related to the host contract, it cannot be separated as the entire hybrid contract is accounted for in accordance with the relevant Standard that deals with the host contract. For example, if an embedded derivative is identified in a lease contract, but it is deemed to be closely related, then the entire contract is accounted for in accordance with IAS 17 *Leases*.

If an identified embedded derivative is not closely related to the host contract, then it must be separately accounted for as if it were a free-standing derivative. This is considered further in **section 12** below.

IFRIC Interpretation 9 *Reassessment of Embedded Derivatives*, published in March 2006, provides guidance on whether an entity shall assess embedded derivatives as closely related at the time the entity first becomes a party to the contract or should be performed on an ongoing basis. The Interpretation clarifies the following.

- An entity is generally prohibited from reassessing its conclusion as to whether an embedded derivative needs to be separated from the hybrid contract after it is initially recognised.
- An entity is required to revisit its assessment if there is a change in the terms of the contract that significantly modifies the cash flows that would otherwise be required under the (original) contract. The significance of the change in cash flows is evaluated by considering the extent of the change in the cash flows of the embedded derivative, the host contract or both and whether these changes are significant relative to the previously expected cash flows of the contract.

A first-time adopter of IFRSs should make its assessment on the basis of conditions existing at the later of the date it first became a party to the contract and the date a reassessment is required. In all cases, the Interpretation shall be applied retrospectively.

Example 3C

Reassessment of embedded derivatives: common currency

Entity G operates in Country Y and had entered into long-dated supply contracts denominated in US$. When Entity G entered into the contracts an assessment was made whether the US$ was considered to be a 'common currency' per IAS 39.AG33(d)(iii) with a view to establishing whether an embedded derivative would need to be separated out. At the time Entity G entered into the contracts the US$ was considered common for Country Y. The functional currency of Entity G and the counterparty to the contracts is not US$.

At the end of the current reporting period the US$ is no longer considered common in Country Y as entities within that country now use the domestic currency instead as this is now traded cross-border and is considered a 'hard' currency by other countries.

Entity G should not reconsider the embedded derivative assessment it made when it originally entered into the contracts as the terms of the arrangement have not changed. The accounting treatment is unchanged even though, had Entity G entered into the same contract today, the US$ would not be considered a common currency and an embedded derivative would need to be recognised.

Example 3D

Reassessment of embedded derivatives: change in correlation of energy prices

Entity T, a coal fired power station, entered into contracts to supply electricity prior to the deregulation of the energy market. The price paid for the supply of electricity was partly linked to the gas price. Entity T always intended to physically deliver electricity to the counterparty so the supply contract was always considered to be an executory contract that was outside the scope of IAS 39. At the date the contract was entered into, the prices for gas and electricity were highly correlated and therefore Entity T considered the linkage to gas prices was a closely related embedded derivative.

Following deregulation of the market the two prices were no longer highly correlated and had Entity T entered into the contract today it would have concluded that the linkage to gas prices was an embedded derivative that was not closely related to the electricity supply contract. Entity T does not reconsider its embedded derivative assessment made when it entered into the electricity supply contract as the terms of the arrangement are unchanged. This is the case even though, had Entity T entered into the same contract today, it would have concluded that the embedded derivative would require separation.

Example 3E

Reassessment of embedded derivatives: equity conversion terms

On 1 January 20X1, Entity Y, a US$ functional currency entity, issued US$ denominated convertible bonds with a par of US$30 million. The convertible bonds will mature on the third anniversary of the date of issue at par unless they are converted into ordinary shares prior to maturity. The conversion price is the lower of US$1.50 and 90 percent of Y's average closing price, determined based on the last 10 trading days immediately before 1 January 20X3.

The equity conversion option does not deliver a fixed amount of cash for a fixed number of equity shares and therefore does not meet the definition of equity (see **example 3.8 in chapter 15**). The instrument is therefore not a compound instrument as it is hybrid financial instrument wholly in the scope of IAS 39. The instrument will be separated into a debt host contract and a non-closely related embedded derivative with respect to the equity conversion option that must be measured as at fair value through profit or loss.

IFRIC 9 does not permit an entity to reconsider its closely related decision made at initial recognition of the hybrid instrument unless there is a significant change to the cash flows under the contract. At 1 January 20X3 Entity Y will know how many shares it will deliver to the holder if the convertible bond is converted but this is not known at the time when the instrument was issued. As the terms of the instrument have not changed, Entity Y must continue to account for the equity conversion option as a non-closely relate embedded derivative.

Example 3F

Reassessment of embedded derivatives: novation within group

Group A has a US$ functional currency subsidiary, Subsidiary B, which enters into contracts to sell non-financial items at a fixed future date with a

Euro functional counterparty, outside of Group A, called Entity D. The contract is denominated in US dollars.

The foreign currency embedded derivative is not separately recognised as Subsidiary B has a US$ functional currency and is a substantial party to the contract. In Group A's consolidated financial statements the same treatment is applied.

Sometime later, Subsidiary B novates the contract to a fellow subsidiary, Subsidiary C, that has a Sterling functional currency. At the date of novation there are no changes to the terms of the contract other than Subsidiary C has stepped into Subsidiary B's place as the seller. Subsidiary C is a principal to the transaction following the novation.

In the individual financial statements of Subsidiary C, at the novation date it becomes a party to the contract for the first time and therefore must consider whether the contract has any embedded derivatives. The contract is not denominated in either Subsidiary C's or Entity D's functional currency and therefore a non-closely related embedded derivative must be recognised by Subsidiary C, being a currency forward contract between Sterling and US$.

In Group A's consolidated financial statements, as the group is presented as a single economic entity, there has been no change in the contractual terms of the contract and therefore the group would not reassess the embedded derivative assessment it made when Subsidiary B entered into the arrangement.

IFRIC 9 does not address remeasurement issues arising from a reassessment of embedded derivatives. [IFRIC 9.4] This will require careful consideration depending on particular facts and circumstances.

Example 3G

Reassessment of embedded derivatives: modification to terms

Entity B, a Euro functional currency entity is party to a contract to purchase a set quantity of electricity at a future date for £10m. The electricity will always be physically delivered under the contract and will be used for Entity B's production processes. The contract is a hybrid contractual arrangement containing a host contract that is an executory contract to purchase electricity in Euros and a non-closely related embedded foreign currency derivative based on the guidance in **10.5** below. The two elements are:

(i) non-closely related embedded Euro/£ forward with an initial fair value of zero to buy Euro12m, sell £10m.

(ii) host purchase contract to buy a set quantity of electricity with a purchase price of Euro12m (that matches the Euro leg of the foreign currency forward in (i) above)

Upon entering into the contract the entity separates out the non-closely related foreign currency embedded derivative and measures it at fair value through profit or loss.

At a later date there is a contractual modification to the terms such that the currency in which the contract is denominated changes to the functional currency of Entity B, i.e. Euro. The embedded derivative had a negative fair value at the date of modification of €1m. Due to the redenomination of the currency of the contract Entity B pays the counterparty €1m which is equal to the value of the change in contractual terms of the arrangement. Entity B derecognises the embedded derivative equal to the cash consideration paid to the counterparty.

The change in denomination of the contract in this case is a significant modification that triggers reassessment under IFRIC 9. As the denomination of the contract after modification is in the functional currency of Entity B the contract no longer has a non-closely related embedded derivative and the entire arrangement will be accounted for prospectively as an executory contract outside the scope of IAS 39.

Care is needed in determining how the carrying value of an embedded derivative is treated when the embedded derivative is no longer closely related. This is particularly relevant when the modification occurs without cash consideration or when the cash consideration differs with the value of the embedded derivative derecognised. The carrying value of the embedded derivative, being its fair value, at the date of modification of the contract, will be recognised in profit or loss, remain in the statement of financial position or be recognised in other comprehensive income in the period or future periods depending on the substance of the modified terms of the contract. Consideration will need to be given as to whether the pricing of the remaining contract is modified to reflect the value of the change in terms of the arrangement; whether any other goods or services are provided or received as part of the modification; or an equity transaction occurs between the entity and the counterparty.

Consideration will also need to be given to the substance of the modification when a non-closely related embedded derivative is recognised for the first time following the modification of a contract where previously the embedded derivative was closely related. As the embedded derivative must be recognised at fair value in accordance with IAS 39.43 consideration will need to given as to whether the counter entry impacts profit or loss, the statement of financial position or other comprehensive income.

A further issue arises when an instrument is acquired in a business combination, since the determination of whether an embedded derivative should be separated, performed at the time of the business combination, may produce a different result compared to the conclusion reached when the assessment was first performed at the time the contract was first entered into by the acquiree. IFRIC 9.5 states specifically that the Interpretation does not address the acquisition of contracts with embedded derivatives in a business combination nor their possible reassessment at the date of acquisition. It is reasonable to argue that whilst the acquiree had become a party to the contract earlier, the group becomes a party to the contract at the time of acquisition. This line of argument would result in reassessment at the time of acquisition and therefore the accounting treatment in the consolidated financial statements may differ to the individual financial statements of the acquiree.

In January 2008, a revised version of IFRS 3 *Business Combinations* was issued. The revised standard is consistent with the above, stating that the assessment as to whether an embedded derivative is closely related to its host contract is to be made on the basis of pertinent factors at the acquisition date. IFRS 3 (2008) applies prospectively to business combinations for which the acquisition date is on or after the beginning of the first annual reporting period beginning on or after 1 July 2009.

4 Terms of the embedded derivative and the debt host contract

The term 'debt host contract' that is applied below includes debt instruments that are issued by an entity, and therefore are financial liabilities, as well as debt instruments that an entity may invest in that are recognised as financial assets.

The terms of the host contract must reflect the stated or implied terms of the hybrid contract; i.e. the embedded feature must be clearly present in the hybrid contract. In the absence of implied or stated terms a judgement may have to be made, but an entity cannot create cash flows that do not contractually exist.

Example 4A

Fixed versus floating debt host contract (1)

Entity A issues floating-rate debt. The contract cannot be seen as fixed-rate debt with an embedded interest rate swap that swaps fixed-rate cash flows into floating-rate cash flows. The terms of the contract do not contain any fixed cash flows, so there can be no embedded feature with fixed rate cash flows.

Example 4B

Fixed versus floating debt host contract (2)

A five-year debt instrument has fixed annual payments, and a principal repayment at the end of the contract which is conditional on changes in the FTSE 100 index. This instrument must be treated as a host fixed-rate debt contract with an embedded equity feature. It cannot be classified as floating-rate debt with an embedded equity swap that has an offsetting floating-rate leg. The host is a fixed-rate contract because there are no variable interest rate payments in it.

Embedded non-optional derivatives must be determined so that they have a fair value of zero at inception of the contract. If this were not stipulated, it would be possible to split one instrument into an infinite number and variety of hosts with embedded derivatives. This could be done by separating embedded derivatives with terms that create leverage, asymmetry or another risk exposure that does not exist in the hybrid contract. [IAS 39.AG21 & IG.C.1]

Embedded optional derivatives will not necessarily have a fair value (or intrinsic value) of zero at inception. The fair value of such an embedded derivative will depend on its strike price or rate. Therefore, the separation of an option from a hybrid contract should be based on the stated terms of the option feature. [IAS 39.AG21 and IG.C.2)]

5 Determination of host contract: debt vs. equity

If a hybrid contract has both debt and equity features, a determination must be made as to whether the host contract is debt or equity. Often, this will be a relatively straightforward task, as the 'majority' of the contract will behave like debt or equity (more usually debt). However, this will not always be the case.

From the perspective of the holder of a contract, if the host contract has no stated or predetermined maturity and represents a residual interest in the net assets of the issuer, then its economic characteristics and risks are those of an equity instrument. Any embedded derivative would need to possess equity characteristics of the issuer to be regarded as closely related. If the host contract is not an equity instrument and meets the definition of a financial asset or liability, then its economic characteristics and risks are those of a debt instrument. [IAS 39.AG27]

Most commonly, the host contract will not represent a residual interest in an entity and, thus, the economic characteristics and risks of a financial host contract will be considered that of a debt instrument. For example, even though an overall hybrid instrument may provide for repayment of principal linked to the market price of the issuer's ordinary shares, the host contract may not involve any existing or potential residual rights in the net assets of the issuer (i.e. rights of ownership) so would not be an equity instrument. The host contract is a debt instrument, and the embedded derivative, the indexation to the market price of the issuer, is not closely related to the host contract.

Example 5A

Debt host contract (1)

[IAS 39.IG.C.5]

Entity A purchases a five-year 'debt' instrument issued by Entity B with a principal amount of CU1 million that is indexed to the share price of Entity C. At maturity, Entity A will receive from Entity B the principal amount plus or minus the change in the fair value of 10,000 shares of Entity C. The current share price is CU110. No separate interest payments are made by Entity B. The purchase price is CU1 million. Entity A classifies the debt instrument as available for sale. Entity A concludes that the instrument is a hybrid instrument with an embedded derivative because of the equity-indexed principal. For the purposes of separating an embedded derivative, is the host contract an equity instrument or a debt instrument?

The host contract is a debt instrument because the hybrid instrument has a stated maturity, i.e. it does not meet the definition of an equity instrument (IAS 32.11 and IAS 32.16). It is accounted for as a zero coupon debt instrument. Thus, in accounting for the host instrument, Entity A imputes interest on CU1 million over five years using the applicable market interest rate at initial recognition. The embedded non-option derivative is separated so as to have an initial fair value of zero (see IAS 39.IG.C.1).

Example 5B

Debt host contract (2)

Entity A invests in instruments that are classified as available-for-sale that are issued by Entity B. The instruments have the legal form of shares, and embedded within them is a put option allowing Entity A to put the 'shares' back to Entity B for the higher of (i) the fair market value of the shares and (ii) an amount based on the initial investment with compounded interest based on LIBOR. The option is exercisable five years after the initial investment is made.

Whilst the instruments have the legal form of shares, they do not evidence a residual interest in Entity B. Entity A will receive a rate of return that is at least equal to the return on a debt instrument. Entity A should account for the instruments as a debt host contract with an embedded derivative.

In January 2007 the IFRIC issued a rejection notice on the classification by the holder of financial instruments that are puttable by the holder at an amount other than fair value. The issuer accounts for the instrument as a financial liability in accordance with IAS 32. The IFRIC was asked whether the holder's accounting should be symmetrical with that of the financial statements of the issuer. The IFRIC noted that IAS 32 and IAS 39 do not directly address whether the accounting for financial instruments in the financial statements of the holder should be symmetrical with that of the issuer. However, the IFRIC noted that the issuer of a financial instrument is required to classify it in accordance with IAS 32, whereas the holder is required to classify and account for it in accordance with IAS 39. The IFRIC also noted that IAS 39 requires the holder to identify embedded derivatives in hybrid financial instruments and requires separate accounting for the embedded derivatives if all the conditions in IAS 39.11 are met. These requirements apply to the holder regardless of whether any embedded derivatives are accounted for separately in the financial statements of the issuer. In light of the existing guidance in IAS 39, the IFRIC decided that the issue should not be taken onto its agenda.

Judgement is required in determining whether the put feature in puttable shares is closely related to the equity host contract where the host is classified as an available-for-sale asset. If the hybrid instrument is classified as at fair value through profit or loss the embedded derivative guidance is not applicable as the whole instrument is fair valued through earnings.

If the shares are puttable at fair value it may be argued that the amount received by the holder upon exercise of the put (being the fair value of the shares) represents the fair value of the equity host, because the amount payable to the holder is the fair value of the residual interest in the assets of the entity after deducting all of its liabilities, and therefore by definition has characteristics of equity. The put would be closely related as its risk characteristics are similar to the equity host. The whole hybrid instrument would be classified as available-for-sale with gains and losses recognised in other comprehensive income and no embedded derivative would be recognised. This treatment could also apply where the issuer is an unquoted entity and the put strike price is derived from a formula which is aimed at being a surrogate for the fair value of the shares of the issuing entity. Greater care would need to be taken in determining whether the put strike is equivalent to the fair value of the underlying shares and therefore the put could be considered closely related.

If the shares are puttable at a fixed amount or an amount determined on the basis of an index that is unrelated to the fair value of the equity host (e.g. the price of gold) then the put would not have equity characteristics and therefore would not be closely related. As the investor can force the issuer to pay an amount not equal to the proportionate share of the net assets of the entity, the holder has downside protection and therefore is not exposed to the residual net assets of the entity. The put would be accounted for separately at fair value through profit or loss and the host contract would be classified as an available-for-sale asset.

6 Multiple embedded derivatives

It is possible for a contract to contain more than one embedded derivative. In such a case, each embedded derivative needs to be individually assessed to see if it is closely related to the host contract.

Example 6

Conversion feature and put option

Entity A holds convertible bonds. In addition to the conversion feature, Entity A can choose to put the bonds back to the issuer. When searching for embedded derivatives, it will be necessary to consider both the conversion option and the put option, and assess each separately.

When contracts contain multiple embedded derivatives they are generally treated as a single compound embedded derivative. Only if the embedded derivatives relate to different risk exposures and are readily separable and independent of each other are they accounted for separately from each other. [IAS 39.AG29]

If an embedded derivative must be separated from its host contract, but it cannot be valued, the entity must first determine both the fair value of the whole contract and the fair value of the host contract, and the balance represents the fair value of the derivative instrument. If an entity is unable to do this, the entity must designate it as fair value through profit or loss.

7 Embedded derivatives in debt host contracts

Financial liabilities are discussed at some length in **chapter 15.** These include traditional debt contracts like bonds and bank borrowings, and also certain other securities that are in substance liabilities, like mandatory redeemable preference shares.

7.1 Puts, calls and prepayment options

Contractual provisions that allow either party to terminate the contract early and accelerate the repayment of the outstanding principal, either in whole or in part, are often embedded derivatives. Examples of such provisions include call options of the issuer, put options of the holder, or prepayment features.

These embedded derivatives are not closely related to the host debt contract unless the exercise price is approximately equal to the debt's amortised cost on each exercise date. [IAS 39.AG30(g)]

From the perspective of the issuer of a convertible debt instrument with an embedded call or put option feature, the assessment of whether the call or put option is closely related to the host debt contract is made before separating the equity element under IAS 32 as discussed in **section 3** of **chapter 15**. [IAS 39.AG30(g)]

Example 7.1A

Issuer call option

Entity A issues a five-year zero-coupon bond for £75 million, with a face value of £100 million. Embedded in the debt is a call option allowing Entity A to repay the debt after three years for £90 million, when its amortised cost will be £89 million. As the repayment amount is approximately equal to its amortised cost on that date, the call option is closely related to the host contract and so is not separated from it. This is the case for both the issuer and holder of the bond.

If the terms were instead such that Entity A could call the debt at any time, but would have to redeem it at a fixed amount, for example at par of £100 million, then the call option would not be closely related, as the repayment amount would not approximately equal the debt's amortised cost on each date that the call can be exercised. For example, the week after issuing the bond (when the bond's amortised cost is approximately £75 million), Entity A could call it back but would have to pay £100 million to do so. This situation arises because the bond was issued at a substantial discount, and hence its amortised cost will not approximate to its par value, except in the years close to its maturity.

Example 7.1B

Investor put option

Entity X issues 10-year bonds with a par value of £1 million for proceeds of £1 million. The bonds have a coupon of 10 per cent. Embedded in the bonds is a provision that allows the investors to put the bonds back to the issuer for

£1 million in the event the FTSE declines by 5 per cent. It is reasonably possible that the FTSE will decline by 5 per cent in the near future. The issue costs are insignificant.

The embedded put option would not be accounted for separately, even though the put is contingent on an event that is not related to the host instrument (i.e. a trigger other than interest rates or credit). The tests in IAS 39 relate to the exercise price (settlement amount), not the trigger. The likelihood of the put being exercised is also irrelevant in determining whether the embedded derivative is closely related, although this will affect valuation. In this case, the bonds will be put back at an amount that approximates amortised cost. It is not relevant that the put only becomes exercisable if an equity index performs in a particular manner.

Example 7.1C

Investor contingent put option

Entity A issues £100 million cumulative preference shares to investors with a dividend of 7 per cent. Dividends are payable quarterly subject to the availability of distributable profits. Issue costs are insignificant. The preference shares are puttable at par to Entity A for cash if interest rates move by 150 basis points. Any dividend that remains accumulated and not paid becomes payable when the shares are put to Entity A.

The embedded put option would not be separated from the host contract under the embedded derivative provisions. The preference shares are classified as a liability under IAS 32 (see **chapter 15**). The put feature is an option that is considered to be closely related to the host since the exercise price of the put is the amortised cost of the preference shares.

Sometimes derivatives may be 'embedded' subsequent to the issuance of the instrument.

Example 7.1D

Remarketable put bonds

Entity X issues 10-year bonds with a 6 per cent coupon to a bank and receives proceeds of €103 million. The debt is puttable by the holder at the end of three years. The three-year debt rate for vanilla debt instruments (i.e. those without put or call features) is 6 per cent. The bank staples a call option and sells the two instruments to an investor. This call option enables the bank to reacquire the bonds in the event that it wishes to exercise its put option inherent in the bond issued by Entity X.

A party other than the issuer (i.e. the bank) has stapled the call option into the debt instrument. Thus, the investor would not be able to consider the call option to be closely related to the host debt instrument. The holder of the call option would have a free-standing derivative that would be recognised at fair value.

Note that Entity X does not have to consider the accounting for the call option because Entity X is not a party to the call option.

A debt instrument that may be called by the issuer or put or prepaid by the holder must be assessed in order to determine whether these features are considered to be closely related. The outcome of this assessment is dependent on comparing the strike price under the option, i.e. the amount the issuer would pay the holder on exercise of the option, with the amortised cost of the instrument. What is less clear is whether calls, puts and prepayment options that are likely to be exercised should be taken into account in determining amortised cost.

Consider the following example. A fixed rate debt instrument is issued at par with a 10 year term. The debt can be put by the holder anytime after year 5 for an amount equal to 110 per cent of par. If the issuer at initial recognition considers it likely that the holder will put at year 5, the host contract could be considered a 10 year host redeeming at 100 per cent or a 5 year host that early redeems at 110 per cent. If the former view is applied the put option is not closely related as 110 per cent is not approximately equal to 100 per cent, whereas if the latter view is applied the put would be closely related as 110 per cent would equal to 110 per cent.

The above example illustrates that where a significant penalty is payable on early redemption the accounting would differ depending on which view is applied. Ironically, if an entity did take into account a put option that is likely to be exercised in determining the host contract it would result in that put option not being recognised. If the put option was less likely to be exercised, it would result in the put option being recognised.

Extending the same example above, assume the holder can put at any time in the ten years for an amount equal to 110 per cent of par. The issuer still believes it is most likely the holder will put at year 5. If the issuer was to consider the 5 year put as part of the amortised cost of the host contract, and thereby not recognise an embedded derivative for that put, it would still need to consider whether the puts from years 2 to 4 were considered closely related. If the host contract is considered a discounted instrument, issued for 100 per cent and redeemable at 110 per cent at year 5, then some of the puts between years 2 to 4 would be non-closely related embedded derivatives as their exercise price of 110 per cent would not be approximately equal to amortised cost.

If early redemption features in debt instruments were reflected in the host contract's amortised cost when determining whether those features are closely related, it is not clear how an entity should account for the instrument should there be changes in the likelihood of the early redemption feature being exercised. Applying the example above, if the issuer subsequently estimated the put was now likely to be exercised after year 5, two views exist. The first view is that the change in timing of cash flows is simply a re-measurement of estimated cash flows and the revised changes in cash flows should be discounted by the original effective interest rate in accordance with IAS 39.AG8. An alternative view is that the host contract is deemed a 5 year instrument; therefore, the right for the holder to put the instrument after year 5 is equivalent to a term extension option, which, if the extension is not at market interest rates, would be considered a non-closely related embedded derivative.

A further consideration is whether the option is a prepayment option over an interest-only or principal-only strip. The embedded derivative will be closely related provided the host contract:

(a) initially resulted from separating the right to receive contractual cash flows of a financial instrument that itself did not contain an embedded derivative; and

(b) does not contain any terms not present in the original host debt.

Example 7.1E

Interest-only strip: no additional terms

A pool of floating rate mortgages is split into an interest-only and principal-only strip, with different entities acquiring each part. The terms of the mortgages allow the borrower to prepay the mortgage at amortised cost prior to the contractual maturity of the mortgage. Because this prepayment option is at amortised cost it does not require separation.

Entity K purchases an interest-only strip from the pool of floating rate mortgages. The floating rate interest only strip has the same terms as the floating rate on the original instrument. Entity K must consider whether the interest only strip has embedded derivatives that require separation.

As the interest-only strip does not contain any terms not present in the original host debt contract and the prepayment option was not separated in the accounting for the original mortgage, the prepayment option is considered closely related to the interest only strip and therefore is not separated. [IAS 39.AG33(e)]

Example 7.1F

Interest-only and principal-only strip: additional terms

Transferor X securitises £100 million of mortgage loans with an 8 per cent coupon in a securitisation structure that meets the requirements for derecognition (derecognition is discussed further in **chapter 19**). The issued beneficial interests consist of a principal-only strip of £100 million and an interest-only strip that pays 8 per cent based on the principal amount.

Transferor X received proceeds of £60 million for the principal-only strip. If market 30-year mortgage rates exceed 10 per cent, the coupon on the interest-only strip increases to 10 per cent. The additional 2 per cent will be paid from the principal-only cash receipts. The conditional 2 per cent payment is an option, sometimes referred to as a caplet.

The embedded caplet is required to be separated because it was not present in the original financial instrument.

Puttable debt and term extending debt are economically the same, however the criteria for assessing the embedded derivative (i.e. the option to extend the term of the debt or to put it back to the holder) are different.

In October 2007 the IASB issued an Exposure Draft titled *Annual Improvements to International Financial Reporting Standards*. Included within the exposure draft was a proposed amendment to IAS 39.AG30(g) for specific prepayment options embedded in a debt host contract that are designed to ensure the lender is compensated for loss of interest when the borrower prepays by reducing the economic loss from reinvestment risk. Such prepayment options are not equal to the amortised cost of the debt host contract because the amount prepaid will include an adjustment to reflect the then market interest rate. At the date of writing the proposed amendment had not been finalised.

7.2 Term extending features

Where the term of the debt is extendable, and there is no concurrent adjustment to the approximate current market rate of interest at the time of the extension, the embedded term extension option is not closely related to the host debt contract. To be closely related the reset to market rates must result in a reset of both current interest rates and current credit spread for the issuer.

If an entity issues a debt instrument and the holder of that debt instrument writes a call option on the debt instrument to a third party, the issuer regards the call option as extending the term to maturity of the debt instrument provided the issuer can be required to participate in or facilitate the remarketing of the debt instrument as a result of the call option being exercised. [IAS 39.AG30(c)]

Example 7.2A

Term extension feature (1)

Entity X issues £10 million fixed rate debt with an 8 per cent coupon and maturity of five years. At the end of five years, Entity X has an option to extend the term for an additional three years. If extended, the coupon will remain at 8 per cent. If the option is exercised it will significantly extend the term of the debt and the coupon will not reset to current market rates. Therefore, this term extending option is an embedded derivative that is not closely related to the host contract.

Example 7.2B

Term extension feature (2)

Entity X issues debt of £10 million with an 8 per cent coupon and a maturity of five years. If LIBOR increases by 200 basis points within any one year, the maturity of the bonds will be extended for another three years at the same 8 per cent coupon rate. The embedded derivative would be accounted for separately from the host contract because the coupon following extension does not reset to the current market rate.

The likelihood of LIBOR increasing by 200 basis points in a year is not a consideration when determining whether the embedded derivative is closely related. It will, however, impact the valuation of the embedded derivative. If the possibility of LIBOR increasing by 200 basis points is considered low, the value of the embedded derivative will be relatively small.

As noted in **section 7** above, five-year fixed rate debt with an option to extend for three years (as detailed in **example 7.2A** above) is economically no different from eight-year fixed rate debt that is puttable at the end of five years. However, the criteria for determining whether there is an embedded derivative in these instruments are different.

The form of the instrument is relevant when determining whether an embedded derivative must be accounted for separately. Thus, two instruments that are economically the same may be treated differently under IAS 39. An entity cannot separate a prepayment option if the debt is prepayable at its amortised cost, but would be required to separate out a term extending option if that option did not result in the interest being reset to market rates.

7.3 Indexed interest and principal payments

Where interest or principal payments in a debt contract are indexed to changes in a specified security price, commodity price, foreign exchange rate, or index of prices or rates, the host debt contract contains an embedded derivative.

Such an embedded derivative will not be closely related to the host debt contract if the amounts of interest or principal are indexed to the price of a commodity or to the change in value of an equity instrument. [IAS 39.AG30(d) & (e)]

Example 7.3A

Commodity price adjustment

Entity X issues 10-year notes with no stated coupon. Embedded in the notes is a provision that adjusts the interest paid by reference to changes in the price of corn.

The embedded derivative would be accounted for separately because the adjustment to interest payments based on changes in corn prices is not closely related to the host debt instrument.

Example 7.3B

Equity price adjustment

Entity X issues 10-year notes to a bank. Embedded in the notes is a provision that requires interest paid to be adjusted based on changes in the share price of Entity Y.

The embedded derivative will be separated because the interest payments are indexed to changes in the share price of Entity Y, and therefore the adjustment is not closely related to the host debt instrument.

Generally, an embedded derivative that adjusts interest and/or principal amounts paid on the debt contract will not be closely related to the host debt where the underlying that drives the value of the derivative is different from the economic factors that drive the value of the host debt contract. The guidance would equally apply to indexation to a basket of commodities, share indices like the FTSE 100, or net asset value changes of a fund.

Example 7.3C

Equity index adjustment

A bank issues 10-year notes with a coupon of 5 per cent to an entity. At maturity, the entity receives cash equal to the higher of the initial proceeds and an amount based on the Standard and Poor's 500 ('S&P 500').

The embedded cash-settled S&P 500 call option is an embedded derivative that is not closely related to the host debt contract.

Even if the interest or principal payments are determined by changes in underlyings that are typically associated with debt (e.g. interest rates, inflation or creditworthiness of the issuer) there may still be an embedded derivative that is not closely related to the host debt contract, for example, when interest or principal repayments are determined based on leveraged, complex or formulaic features.

These features must be such that **either** the holder would not recover substantially all of its recognised investment **or** the issuer would pay more than twice the market rate of the host contract at inception (of issuing the instrument) **and** could result in a rate of return that is at least twice what the market return would be for a similar host contract (sometimes referred to as the 'double double test'). [IAS 39.AG33(a)]

The test is based on the contractual provisions, so the determination is made for both parties to the contract based on the return or loss to the investor. Thus, if the holder separately accounts for an embedded derivative because it could lose substantially all of its initial investment, the issuer would generally do the same.

Example 7.3D

Recovery of recognised investment (1)

Entity X issues £10 million in debt with an 8 per cent coupon. However, if LIBOR increases by 500 basis points within any one year, the bonds mature and the holder receives £8 million in total.

An embedded derivative exists and should be separately accounted for because there is a payment provision that may cause the holder not to recover substantially all of its recognised investment if LIBOR increases by 500 basis points.

The likelihood of LIBOR increasing by 500 basis points in the above example is not relevant when making this determination. The test in IAS

39 is based around the possibility of the holder not recovering its recognised investment or obtaining double its initial rate of return. Even if it is unlikely that LIBOR will increase by 500 basis points, the contingent embedded derivative must be separated from the host contract. However, if the probability of this event occurring is low then the fair value of the embedded derivative at inception will be relatively small compared to the fair value of the host contract.

The condition that the holder will not recover substantially all of its recognised investment is only met if the holder can be forced to accept a settlement amount that is substantially below its recognised investment. If the terms of the contract permit, but do not require the holder to settle the instrument in such a manner, then the feature is closely related to the host contract.

The 'double double test' is performed at the date that the hybrid instrument is initially recognised. The first step is it to determine whether there is a possible future interest rate scenario, no matter how remote, in which the embedded derivative would at least double the investor's initial return on the host contract. In making this assessment, it is important to differentiate the return on the host contract from the return on the hybrid contract. The host contract has terms identical to the hybrid contract being tested, except that it does not contain the embedded derivative. IAS 39.AG33(a) describes this step as requiring that the embedded derivative could at least double the holder's initial rate of return on the host contract. An embedded derivative that does not breach this threshold would be considered closely related to its host. If the embedded derivative does breach the threshold, a second step must be performed to determine whether it is closely related to the host contract. The second step is to review each interest rate scenario identified in the first step for which the investor's initial rate of return on the host contract would be doubled, and determine whether, for any of the scenarios, the embedded derivative would at the same time result in a rate of return that is at least twice what otherwise would be the then-current market return for a contract that has the same terms as the host contract and that involves a debtor with a credit quality similar to the issuer's credit quality at inception. If the embedded derivative does not breach the threshold it would not be considered closely related to its host contract. If the threshold is breached in any one of the scenarios then the embedded derivative whose underlying is an interest rate or interest rate index would be considered not closely related to the host contract and the embedded derivative must be separated.

A vanilla variable rate debt instrument does not contain an embedded derivative even though the investor could pay a rate more than twice the rate at inception. A rate that is always equal to the current market rate is not an embedded derivative.

Example 7.3E

Double-double interest rate test (1)

On 1 January 20X1, an investor purchases a bond where interest payments are linked to LIBOR. The bond also incorporates an interest rate cap provision whereby if LIBOR equals or exceeds 8 percent at any interest rate reset date, the investor will receive a return of 10 percent. On the date the investor purchases the bond, it also could purchase at par a variable-rate bond not containing a cap that pays LIBOR minus 1 percent from a debtor that has the same credit quality as the issuer of the investor's bond. As of 1 January 20X1, LIBOR is 5 percent. The bond cannot be contractually settled such that the investor would not recover substantially all of its initial recorded investment in the bond.

To perform the first test in paragraph IAS 39.AG33(a), the investor must determine whether there is any interest rate scenario, no matter how remote, under which the embedded derivative (the cap) would at least double the investor's initial rate of return on the host contract. This analysis is summarised in the following table:

A **Interest rate change**	B **Return reflecting the effect of the cap**	C **Initial rate of return on the host (LIBOR – 1%)**	D **Initial rate of return on the host doubled**	**Is the first test met, i.e. is A > D?**
0 – 7.99%	0 – 7.99%	4%	8%	No
8% and up	10%	4%	8%	Yes

Since the first test is met, the investor must perform the second test described in paragraph IAS 39.AG33(a) to determine whether the embedded cap is closely related to its bond host. For this test, the investor must determine, for each interest rate scenario identified above for which the investor's initial rate of return on the host contract would be doubled, whether the embedded cap would simultaneously result in a rate of return that is at least twice what otherwise would be the then-current market return for a contract that has the same terms as the host contract and that involves a debtor with a credit quality similar to the issuer's credit quality at inception. The investor's analysis for this test can be summarised as follows:

A	B	C	
Interest rate scenario identified in the first test above for which the cap would at least double the investor's initial rate of return on the host contract	Return reflecting the effect of the cap under the interest rate scenario in A	Current market rate of return for the host contract under the interest rate scenario in A (LIBOR – 1%)	Is the second test met, i.e. is B at least twice C for any scenario?
8% and up	10%	7%	No

As the first test in IAS 39.AG33(a) is met, but the second test is not, the embedded cap is considered closely related to the bond host.

Example 7.3F

Double-double interest rate test (2)

Entity A invests in 30-year variable-rate debt issued by Entity B. The debt is indexed to the three-month LIBOR (3m LIBOR) rate plus 4 percent. As of the date of issuance, the 3m LIBOR rate was 2 percent. The debt's terms also specify that if the 3m LIBOR rate increases to 5 percent, the debt issuer is required to pay 23 percent for the remaining term of the bonds. The bond cannot be contractually settled such that the investor would not recover substantially all of its initial recorded investment in the bond.

If Entity B were to issue 30-year variable-rate debt without any embedded derivatives (i.e. the interest rate reset feature), it would pay a coupon of 3m LIBOR plus 6 percent. Consequently, the initial rate of return on the host contract is 8 percent (3m LIBOR of 2 percent plus 6 percent). It is necessary to determine whether the embedded derivative could at least double the investor's initial rate of return on the host contract, which was 8 percent at the date of issuance, in any of the possible interest rate environments. Therefore, when 3m LIBOR increases to 5 percent, the 23 percent interest rate feature more than doubles the initial rate of return of 8 percent on the host contract.

It is then necessary to perform an analysis to determine whether the embedded derivative results in a rate of return that is at least twice what otherwise would be the then-current market rate of return for a host contract when 3m LIBOR is at 5 percent. When 3m LIBOR increases to 5 percent the rate of return on the host contract would be 11 percent (3m LIBOR of 5 percent plus 6 percent) for a bond of similar credit quality that does not contain any embedded derivatives. Therefore, when 3m LIBOR increases to 5 percent, the 23 percent interest rate feature is more than twice the then-current market rate of return of the host contract of 11 percent (3m LIBOR of 5 percent plus 6 percent.)

Entity A and Entity B each would be required to treat the feature as a non-closely related embedded derivative.

Example 7.3G

Double-double interest rate test (3)

Entity A issues £10 million debt with a coupon of 8 per cent and a term of 10 years. Entity A's market rate for 10-year debt is 8.25 per cent. Embedded in the debt is an interest rate adjustment that resets the interest rate to 16.40 per cent if three-month LIBOR increases to 7 per cent or greater during the first three years of the debt.

The adjustment feature is an embedded derivative, but it would not be accounted for separately. The derivative could not cause the rate of return on the host contract to double.

Example 7.3H

Recovery of recognised investment (2)

Entity X issues £10 million in debt with a coupon of 8.25 per cent and a term of 10 years. Entity X's market rate for 10-year debt is 8 per cent. Embedded in the debt is a provision that states if interest rates increase beyond a specified level, the holder of the debt must give the issuer an additional £1 million in borrowings maturing in 10 years on which the holder will receive no interest.

The adjustment feature is a written option issued by the holder. The issuer pays for this option through a higher interest cost when compared to debt without the option. The embedded derivative would not be accounted for separately because the holder will recover all of its recognised investment, being £10 million advanced at inception and £1 million if it is advanced at a later date. In all cases the investor will recover all its recognised investment. There is no provision that can result in the issuer paying a rate that is more than double the market rate of the host contract at inception.

Note the 'recognised investment' is based on the amount advanced by the holder. The likelihood of the option being exercised or the present value of the loan are not considered when determining whether the holder will recover its recognised investment.

7.4 Inflation features

IAS 39 does not specifically address whether an inflation feature within a debt contract is closely related to the host contract. Where an embedded derivative is not specifically addressed by the Standard, significant judgement will need to be used. In these situations, drawing analogies to specific examples given will often prove helpful.

IAS 39 does address inflation features within lease contracts. Finance lease contracts are similar to debt contracts, and therefore the guidance below is based on the examples given for contracts with lease hosts.

Example 7.4

Inflation-linked bond

Entity X purchases an inflation-linked bond. The bond pays a coupon of 4 per cent annually, with a repayment of principal on maturity of the bond. The principal payment is indexed to the domestic retail price index but cannot decrease below par.

As the bond is denominated in the local currency, the indexation of the principal payment to domestic inflation rates is closely related to the host contract.

An inflation feature in a host debt contract is closely related to the host provided that the inflation index is not leveraged, cannot cause the investor not to recover substantially all of its initial investment and is the inflation rate of the economic environment for the currency in which the debt is denominated.

Inflation features that are leveraged will not be closely related to a host debt contract. This is discussed further in the context of a lease host contract in **9.1** below.

7.5 Credit derivatives and liquidity features

IAS 39 does not explicitly address adjustments to the terms of a debt instrument as a result of issuer default, changes in the issuer's credit rating or creditworthiness. It does, however, provide guidance on embedded credit derivatives that relate to other reference entities. Further, certain credit sensitive contracts embedded in other instruments may meet the definition of a financial guarantee contract (see **2.3.2** of **chapter 13**).

7.5.1 Adjustment for issuer's credit risk

IAS 39 does not provide specific guidance when the cash flows on debt instruments are adjusted for changes in the issuer's creditworthiness.

It is reasonable to conclude that credit features that relate to the credit quality of the issuer (for example the issuer's credit rating, default or ratios indicative of its credit status) should be viewed as closely related to the host debt contract. In economic terms such features directly affect the value of the host debt contract.

Example 7.5.1A

Interest adjustment: debt covenants

Entity X issues bonds with a BBB rating. The bonds have a provision that if Entity X violates a certain debt-to-equity ratio covenant, or Entity X's credit rating is downgraded, the interest rate will reset to the then current market rate for Entity X.

The interest rate reset is considered to be closely related to the host contract and, since it relates to default in a credit risk-related covenant and Entity X's own credit rating, the embedded derivative would not be accounted for separately.

Example 7.5.1B

Interest adjustment: credit risk and share price

Entity Y issues bonds with a BBB rating. The bonds have a provision which states that if both of the below conditions are met the coupon on the bond will be reduced by 50 basis points:

(a) the rating of the bonds by a specific rating agency is upgraded to at least BBB+; and

(b) the average share price of the ordinary shares of Entity Y exceeds a certain level over a certain 20 day period

As the adjustment to the interest payments only occurs if both conditions are met it is appropriate to consider the provision as a single embedded derivative in line with IAS 32.AG29 as discussed in **section 6** above, rather than two embedded derivatives. Although one of the underlyings of the derivative is related to credit quality of the issuer (i.e. Entity Y's credit rating) and the other underlying relates to Entity Y's equity price the whole derivative would be considered not to be closely related to the host debt contract. This is because one of the underlyings (i.e. equity price) is considered not to be closely related to the economic characteristics and risks of debt (see **7.3** above).

By contrast if the feature operated such that there were two independent adjustments to the interest paid on the bond (of 25 basis points each) one of which were triggered by changes to Entity Y's credit rating and the other by movements in Entity Y's equity price it would be appropriate to treat the two features as separate embedded derivatives. The credit rating triggered feature would be closely related but the equity triggered feature would not be closely related to the debt host contract and as a consequence would be accounted for separately as at fair value through profit or loss.

7.5.2 *Adjustment for liquidity of issuer's debt*

IAS 39 does not provide specific guidance when the cash flows of a debt instruments are adjusted for changes in the relative liquidity of that debt instrument. Provided the adjustments are not geared the adjustment is likely to be closely related to the debt host contract as the liquidity of the instrument is inherent in the debt host contract.

> **Example 7.5.2**
>
> **Interest adjustment: liquidity**
>
> Entity X issues a debt instrument that is repayable at par at maturity that pays a fixed rate of interest. On issue of the debt the instrument is not listed. The debt instrument contains a contractual provision specifying that if the debt instrument ever becomes listed then the rate of interest payable on the instrument will decrease by 0.5%. The interest rate will be reset to its initial level should the debt instrument subsequently be delisted.
>
> The listing of the debt instrument is likely to increase the liquidity of the debt instrument. The lower liquidity of an unlisted instrument is a cost borne by the holders as it limits their ability to sell their holding of the debt instrument in the instance when the borrower's ability to meet its obligations as they fall due may be in question. The listing of the debt instrument is likely to improve its liquidity and to provide the holders with an exit mechanism before maturity. The holder's willingness willing to accept a reduction in the interest rate in exchange for increased liquidity would be considered closely related to the host debt contract.

7.5.3 *Adjustment for third party credit*

IAS 39 views a credit derivative that transfers credit risk of a particular reference asset (which the entity, the 'beneficiary', may not own) to another party, the 'guarantor', as not closely related to the host debt contract. [IAS 39.AG30(h)]

> **Example 7.5.3A**
>
> **Credit-linked note**
>
> Entity X issues credit-linked bonds. The bonds are linked to the performance of a portfolio of third party corporate bonds held by a third party bank. The bonds pay a rate of interest in excess of Entity X's normal cost of funds as, in the event that one of the referenced corporate bonds defaults, Entity X will pay a reduced principal to the holders.
>
> The embedded credit-related provision would be accounted for separately because the credit of a third party entity is not considered to be closely related to the debt host contract issued by Entity X.

Example 7.5.3B

Cash versus synthetic credit default obligations

Collateralised debt obligation (CDO) special purpose entities (SPEs) are set up to issue notes to investors which pay based on the performance of specified named corporate debt. The interest and principal on the assets is used to service and repay the CDO liability. If there is default under the named corporate debt, then the investors of the CDO notes will suffer loss. The losses are shared by investors in a pre-agreed manner, often with the most junior notes suffering most of the expected loss.

There are two types of structure:

- the assets in the SPE are actual corporate debt (e.g. GM & Ford corporate bonds), referred to as 'cash CDOs' as the SPE has to own the actual cash instruments; or
- the assets in the SPE are derivatives over the corporate debt (e.g. credit default swaps (CDS) over GM & Ford), referred to as 'synthetic CDOs' as the SPE will or may hold synthetic instruments, as opposed to holding cash instruments.

A CDO is illustrated below:

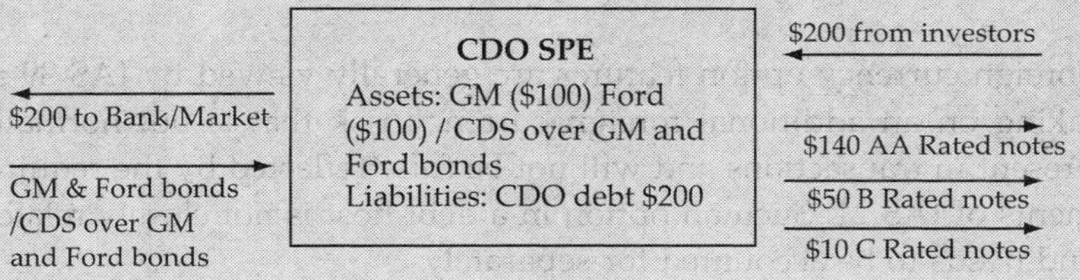

Whether the CDO structure is cash or synthetic will impact the accounting for the notes:

Cash CDO

If an issued CDO liability is not fair valued through profit or loss the SPE will need to assess whether the CDO liability has embedded credit derivatives that require separation. As the entity must own the underlying cash instruments the issued CDO liability does not have a credit derivative that requires separation. The beneficiary (the SPE) is transferring the credit risk of its referenced assets to a guarantor (the investor in the CDO notes).

Synthetic CDO

As the SPE is required to pay returns on the CDO liability that is linked to the performance of corporate bonds, but without actually needing to own these cash instruments (e.g. it can purchase credit derivatives over the reference corporate bonds), the notes issued by the SPE have credit embedded derivatives that require separation. The beneficiary (the SPE) is transferring the credit risk of referenced assets to a guarantor (the investor of the CDO notes) but does not own the underlying referenced assets.

7.6 Foreign currency features

Debt contracts may require the issuer to make payments of interest or principal in a foreign currency. An example of such a contract is a dual currency bond where principal is paid in a foreign currency, whereas interest is paid in the entity's functional currency. The foreign currency feature in a dual currency bond is an embedded derivative (foreign currency swap or foreign currency forward) but it is not separated from the host debt instrument because foreign currency gains and losses on a dual currency bond are already recognised in profit and loss following the requirements of IAS 21 *The Effects of Changes in Foreign Exchange Rates*.

Certain currency features may need to be separated. A debt contract may, for example, contain a provision that would allow the holder to choose to receive interest payments in an alternative currency. This provision is a foreign currency option, written by the issuer.

Foreign currency option features are generally viewed by IAS 39 as taking on an additional foreign currency risk that is not normally present in transactions and will not be fully reflected by the requirements of IAS 21. Such an option in a debt host is not closely related and needs to be accounted for separately.

7.7 Caps, floors and collars on interest rates

Floating rate debt contracts often include features that 'cap', 'floor' or 'collar' the amount of interest payable on the debt.

7.7.1 Definition of 'cap', 'floor', and 'collar'

A 'cap' is an option contract that puts an upper limit on a floating interest rate. The purchaser of the cap is paid the difference between the current floating interest rate and the strike rate of the cap whenever the current floating rate exceeds the strike rate.

Example 7.7.1

Interest rate cap

Entity A purchases an interest rate cap, paying a premium of £1 million. The cap has a notional of £100 million and a strike rate of 6 per cent. Currently, LIBOR is 4.5 per cent.

The cap will pay Entity A the difference between LIBOR and 6 per cent whenever LIBOR exceeds 6 per cent. Thus, if LIBOR moves to 6.5 per cent, the cap will pay Entity A £500,000, i.e. 0.5 per cent (the difference between LIBOR and 6 per cent) applied to the notional of the cap (£100 million).

A 'floor' is an option contract that puts a lower limit on a floating interest rate. The writer of the floor will pay the difference between the current floating interest rate and the strike rate of the floor whenever the current floating rate drops below the strike rate. A floor is effectively the opposite of a cap. The writer of a floor will receive a premium which compensates it for the risk it has taken on (i.e. the risk that rates drop below a certain level).

Entities often want to protect themselves against rises in interest rates, so they purchase caps. However, these can be expensive. To reduce or limit the cost, entities will often simultaneously write a floor. Thus, they have achieved an interest rate collar. A 'collar' is an instrument that combines a cap and a floor. The holder of an interest rate collar will be exposed to interest rate movements only within a specified range. It protects the holder against a significant rise in interest rates, but limits the benefits of a drop in interest rates.

7.7.2 *In-the-money and out-of-the-money caps, floors and collars*

A cap is 'in-the-money' if its strike rate is lower than the market rate of interest. It is 'out-of-the-money' if its strike rate is higher than the market rate of interest. If a cap has a strike rate of 6 per cent, it will be in-the-money whenever interest rates are above 6 per cent and out-of-the-money whenever interest rates are below 6 per cent.

A floor is in-the-money if its strike rate is higher than the market rate of interest. It is out-of-the-money if its strike rate is lower than the market rate of interest. If a floor has a strike rate of 4 per cent, it will be in-the-money whenever interest rates are below 4 per cent and out-of-the-money whenever interest rates are above 4 per cent.

A collar has two strike prices, the upper and lower limits. A collar is out-of-the-money if interest rates are between these two strike rates; it is in-the-money otherwise.

7.7.3 *Embedded caps, floors and collars*

An embedded cap or floor on the interest rate of a debt instrument, where the cap or floor is not leveraged, is closely related to the host debt contract provided the cap is at or above the market interest rate and the floor is at or below the market interest rate when the instrument is issued. The assessment as to whether an embedded cap or floor is closely related to a host debt contract is made at issuance and is not subsequently revised. [IAS 39.AG33(b)]

Example 7.7.3

Embedded interest rate cap

Entity X issues £100 million debt with a five-year maturity. The interest is payable at LIBOR plus a credit spread of 150 basis points. LIBOR at issuance is 4.5 per cent, and therefore the rate at inception of the debt is 6 per cent. There is a provision in the debt contract that if LIBOR were to rise, the rate payable on the debt would not rise above 7 per cent.

The cap is an embedded derivative that is closely related to the host debt contract, since at the time of the issuance of the debt the cap is out-of-the-money.

While the Standard does not specifically address a collar embedded in a debt contract, a simple analogy to caps and floors can be made. If a debt contract has an embedded collar which caps interest rates at 7 per cent and has a floor of 4 per cent, the collar will be closely related to the host debt contract provided both the cap and the floor are out-of-the-money when the debt is issued and are not leveraged.

7.8 Conversion and equity features

A conversion feature that allows the holder of the debt contract to convert the outstanding amount into equity of the issuer is an embedded derivative that is not closely related to the host debt contract.

Accounting for convertible debt is different for the holder and issuer of the instrument if from the issuer's perspective, the conversion feature is an equity instrument which is outside the scope of IAS 39. Issuer accounting is addressed in **chapter 15**.

Example 7.8
Equity conversion feature

Entity X issues debt that is convertible into a fixed number of its ordinary shares in five years. The conversion feature represents an embedded written call option on the shares of Entity X, settled in a fixed number of shares.

For Entity X, the convertible debt is a compound instrument that should be split into its liability and equity components. Entity X will not account for the written call option as an embedded derivative because the option is an equity instrument of Entity X (see **chapter 15**).

The investor will account for the embedded purchased option separately as, under IAS 39, the equity conversion feature is not closely related to the host debt contract.

Another form of equity embedded derivative is an 'equity kicker'. These are debt instruments which provide for the lender to receive shares of the borrower for nothing, or a very low amount if the borrower lists its shares on a stock exchange. The debt remains outstanding following the delivery of the shares. Typically, the lender is a venture capitalist. Similar to convertible debt, debt with an equity kicker carries a coupon that is lower than the rate on a comparable debt without the equity kicker.

The equity kicker meets the definition of a derivative as its value will change in response to changes in the borrower's share price. It has little initial net investment, and is settled at a future date. This is true even though the right to receive the shares is contingent on an unrelated event. [IAS 39.IG.C.4] By analogy to convertible debt, the embedded derivative is not closely related to the host debt contract.

7.9 Non-cash settlement of interest or principal

Debt contracts that allow for the payment of interest or principal in non-cash consideration may contain embedded derivatives that are not closely related to the host debt contract.

For example, Entity A lends Entity B £10 million for 10 years. Each year instead of paying interest, Entity B agrees to give Entity A a predetermined amount of free advertising space in a newspaper. A will not use the advertising space in its own business, so it pre-sells all the advertising space in advance. The feature embedded in the loan meets the definition of a derivative as it has an underlying, which is the price of the advertising space, no initial net investment, and will be settled at future dates. The economic characteristics and risks of the embedded derivative and debt are not closely related. The derivative is net settled and therefore does not get the purchase, sale or usage requirements exemption (see **2.5** of **chapter 13**).

Where Entity A intends to utilise the advertising space in its normal course of business, and therefore does not intend to net settle the advertising space, the provision of advertising space will meet the purchase, sale or usage requirements exemptions and therefore will not be in the scope of IAS 39.

7.10 Unit linking features embedded in host debt instrument

A unit linking feature embedded in a host debt instrument is closely related to the host debt instrument if the unit-denominated payments are measured at current unit values that reflect the fair values of the assets of the fund. A unit linking feature is a contractual term that requires payments denominated in a unit of an internal or external investment fund. [IAS 39.AG33(g)]

IFRS 4.IG Example 2: 2.15 provides the example of a policyholder option to surrender a contract for account value equal to the fair value of a pool of equity investments, possibly after deducting a surrender charge. The example makes reference to IAS 39.AG33(g) and states that if such a feature is embedded in a host investment contract then, if the insurer regards the account value as the amortised cost or the fair value of that portion of its obligation, no further adjustment is needed for the option (unless the surrender value differs significantly from the account value). Otherwise the embedded derivative feature would be required to be classified separately as at fair value through profit or loss. A host investment contract is described in IFRS 4.IG 4 as a financial instrument that does not meet the definition of an insurance contract.

The above guidance suggests that unit linking features would only be considered closely related where the unit denominated payments are measured in such a way that they reflect the fair value of the assets of the fund to which they are linked. In any case, even if the unit linking feature is determined to be closely related to a debt host contract IAS 39.AG8 would be applicable for subsequent measurement of the hybrid instrument if it was measured at amortised cost (see **4.1.2** in **chapter 18**). Applying IAS 39.AG8 would result in the carrying value of the hybrid instrument reflecting the amount expected to be paid or received which would incorporate the unit linking feature.

7.11 Further examples of embedded derivatives in host debt contracts

The table below provides further examples of derivative instruments embedded in debt host contracts.

Type of instrument	Economic characteristics	Embedded derivative	Closely related
Inverse floater	Bond accrues interest at 5.25% for three months to July 20X4; thereafter at 10.75% less six-month LIBOR to January 20X5.	Fixed-to-floating interest rate swap	No. Para AG 33(a)
Leveraged inverse floater	Bond accrues interest at 6% to June 20X5; thereafter, at 14.55% – (2.5 x 3 month LIBOR).	Leveraged interest rate swap	No. Para AG 33(a)
Ratchet floater	Bond accrues interest at three-month LIBOR + 50 basis points. In addition to having a lifetime cap of 7.25%, the coupon will be collared each period between the previous coupon and the previous coupon plus 25 basis points.	Combinations of purchased and written options that create changing caps and floors	Yes. Para AG 33(b)
Fixed-to-floating note	A bond that pays a varying coupon (first-year coupon is fixed; second- and third-year coupons are based on LIBOR).	Forward-starting interest rate swap	Yes. Para AG 33(a)
Indexed amortising note	A bond that repays principal based on a predetermined amortisation schedule or target value. The amortisation is linked to changes in the relevant interest rate index. The maturity of the bond changes as the related index changes.	Conditional exchange option that requires partial or early payment of the note	Yes. Para AG 33(a)
Equity-indexed note	A bond for which the return of interest, principal, or both is tied to a specified equity security or index (for example, the Standard and Poor's 500 (S&P 500) index). This instrument may contain a fixed or varying coupon rate and may place all or a portion of principal at risk.	Forward exchange contracts or option contracts	No. Para AG 30(d)
Variable principal redemption bond	A supplemental principal payment will be paid to the investor, at maturity, if the final S&P 500 closing value (determined at a specified date) is less than its initial value at date of issuance and the 10-year constant maturity treasuries (CMT) is greater than 2% as of a specified date. In all cases, the minimum principal redemption will be 100% of face amount.	Purchased option	No. Para AG 30(d)

Type of instrument	Economic characteristics	Embedded derivative	Closely related
Crude-oil knock-in note	A bond that has a 1% coupon and guarantees repayment of principal with upside potential based on the strength of the oil market.	Option contract	No. Para AG 30(e)
Gold-linked bull note	A bond that has a fixed 3% coupon and guarantees repayment of principal with upside potential if the price of gold increases.	Option contracts	No. Para AG 30(e)
Step-up bond	A bond that provides an introductory above-market yield that is less than twice the market rate at inception and steps up to a new coupon, which will be below then-current market rates or, alternatively, the bond may be called in lieu of the step-up in the coupon rate.	Call option	Yes. Para AG 33(a)
Credit-sensitive bond	A bond that has a coupon rate of interest that resets based on changes in the issuer's credit rating.	Conditional exchange contract or option	Yes. Para AG 33(a)
Inflation bond	A bond with a contractual principal amount that is indexed to the non-leveraged inflation rate of the economic environment of the issuer, but cannot decrease below par; the coupon rate is below that of traditional bonds of a similar maturity.	Conditional exchange contract or option	Yes. Para AG 33(a) and (f)(i)
Specific equity-linked bond	A bond that pays a coupon slightly below that of traditional bonds of similar maturity; however, the principal amount is linked to the stock market performance of an equity investee of the issuer.	Series of forward contracts or option contracts	No. Para AG 30(d)
Dual currency bond	A bond providing for repayment of principal in one currency (e.g. Euro) and periodic interest payments denominated in a different currency (e.g. Yen).	Foreign currency forward	Yes. Para AG 33(c)
Short-term loan with foreign currency option	A US lender issues a loan at an above-market interest rate. The loan is made in US dollars, the borrower's functional currency, and the borrower has the option to repay the loan in US dollars or in a fixed amount of a specified foreign currency.	Foreign currency option	No. Para AG 33(d)
Participating mortgage	A mortgage in which the investor receives a below-market interest rate and is entitled to participate in the appreciation in the market value of the project that is financed by the mortgage upon sale of the project, at a deemed sale date, or at the maturity or refinancing of the loan. The mortgagor must continue to own the project over the term of the mortgage.	Call option	No. Para AG 30(e)

8 Embedded derivatives in equity host contracts

It is not common to find derivatives embedded in equity host contracts. **Chapter 15** provides guidance on when instruments are classified as debt or equity. Sometimes it may be difficult to determine whether the host contract is debt or equity. Further examples are considered in **section 5** above.

8.1 Equity option triggered by an unrelated factor

Example 8.1

Contingent share conversion based on interest rates

Entity A issues €100 million of perpetual, irredeemable preference shares that pay a fixed dividend rate of 10 per cent. The shares meet the definition of equity per IAS 32 as the entity has true discretion as to whether or not, and the extent to which, dividends will be paid.

The shares include a provision stating that if interest rates increase by 200 basis points, the holders will additionally receive 100,000 ordinary shares in Entity A.

The embedded option is not separated by the issuer because it and the host instrument are both equity instruments of the issuer. Although the option is triggered by a change in interest rates, the value of the option is indexed to the change in fair value of, and is settled in, the issuer's shares. Equally, from the holder's perspective, the embedded option is closely related to the host.

8.2 Conditional cash return on perpetual preference shares

Example 8.2

Contingent cash payment based on interest rates

Entity A issues $100 million of perpetual, irredeemable preference shares that pay a discretionary, fixed dividend rate of 8 per cent. The shares meet the definition of equity per IAS 32 as the entity has true discretion as to whether or not, and the extent to which, dividends are paid. Embedded in the shares is a provision that states if LIBOR increases to 12 per cent or more, the holders will become entitled to receive a one-off payment of cash calculated by a predetermined formula.

The issuer cannot avoid an outflow of cash in respect of the amount prescribed by the formula if LIBOR reaches 12 per cent, i.e. the embedded feature is an embedded derivative liability. Both the holder and the issuer account for this derivative separately from the host instrument. Accounting for the host instrument by the issuer is different from that by the holder as for the issuer equity is outside the scope of IAS 39.

8.3 Convertible preference shares

Example 8.3

Convertible preference shares

Entity X issues perpetual preference shares where any dividends are entirely at the discretion of the issuer. The preference shares are convertible into a fixed number of ordinary shares at any time after a specified date. The preference shares meet the definition of equity under IAS 32.

The preference shares are equity of X. The conversion feature represents an embedded call option on Entity X's ordinary shares that also meets the definition of equity. Entity X does not account for the embedded option separately because both the option and the host are equity instruments of Entity X.

The same considerations apply to the investor; however the accounting in the investor's books will be different from that of the issuer since for the issuer equity is outside the scope of IAS 39. For the holder, the perpetual preference share is a financial asset which consists of an equity host contract with a closely related equity embedded derivative.

8.4 Puttable equity instruments

If an instrument has an equity host and is puttable at a fixed amount or an amount determined on the basis of an index that is unrelated to the fair value of the equity host (e.g. the price of gold) then the put would not have equity characteristics and therefore would not be closely related. In the case of fixed strike price the investor has downside protection and therefore does not share in a residual interest in the net assets of the issuer, and in the case of a strike price linked to a variable other than the net assets of the issuer, the investor is not exposed to the residual net assets of the entity. The put would not be considered closely related to the equity host contract and therefore would be separated and classified as at fair value through profit or loss.

9 Embedded derivatives in lease contracts

Embedded derivatives can exist in lease contracts, whether an entity is acting as a lessee or a lessor in either a finance or an operating lease.

9.1 Inflation factors

An embedded derivative in a host lease contract is closely related to the host contract if the embedded derivative is an inflation-related index, for example, where lease payments are indexed to a retail price index, provided that the index is not leveraged, and the index relates to inflation in the entity's own economic environment. [IAS 39.AG33(f)(i)]

9.1.1 Entity's economic environment

IAS 39 does not give any guidance on what constitutes the entity's own economic environment. It is reasonable to assume that where an entity operates in a certain country and enters into a lease agreement on, say, a property located in that country, the inflation of the country concerned will be the relevant inflation index, since that index is related to the value of the lease and is present in the environment in which the entity operates.

Example 9.1.1

Inflation-adjusting lease payments

Entity X, a UK entity, has extensive operations in Europe and the US. Entity Y, Entity X's subsidiary, leases property in Paris with a lease term of 10 years. The functional currency of Entity Y is the Euro. Lease payments are to be made in Euros. Embedded in the lease is a provision that requires the lease payments to be adjusted every two years for the change in the UK consumer price index, which is not the index of the economic environment of Entity Y.

The embedded inflation indexed payment would be accounted for separately because, although the rate of inflation is not leveraged, the inflation index is in a different economic environment from the entity entering into the lease.

9.1.2 Leverage factors

The second consideration when assessing whether an inflation adjustment in a lease contract is an embedded derivative that requires separate accounting is leverage. IAS 39 does not define leverage in the context of inflation. However, the concept of leverage is used in the assessment of the features present in debt contracts. For debt contracts it is assumed that a leverage feature that can double the holder's initial rate of return and could result in a rate of return that is at least twice what the market return would be for a contract with the same terms as the host contract is not closely related to the host debt contract.

By analogy, it can be argued that an inflation adjustment for two times or more of the inflation index will be seen as leveraged. Careful consideration of the terms of the lease is required for a decision on whether any inflation adjustment included in it is indeed leveraged.

Example 9.1.2

Leveraged inflation-adjusting lease payments

Entity X, a UK entity, leases property in London with a lease term of 10 years. Lease payments are to be made in Sterling. Embedded in the lease is a provision that requires the lease payment to be adjusted annually for three times the changes in UK's retail price index.

The embedded inflation adjustment will be accounted for separately because it is leveraged.

In the above example, it is quite clear that there is a leveraged inflation feature that needs to be separated. However, what is less clear is whether the derivative that needs separation is the total inflation adjustment, i.e. three times the retail price index, or just the leveraged portion, i.e. two times the retail price index.

The argument for the latter is that adjustment by the retail price index is seen as closely related. However, there are two counter-arguments to that: firstly, separation of only a portion of the embedded derivative amounts to splitting the derivative into two parts which is not generally permitted under IAS 39; secondly, separation could be argued to create cash flows that are not evident in the contract, which once again is not the general practice under IAS 39. On balance, the total inflation adjustment should be split out.

9.2 Foreign currency features

There are no specific rules addressing currency features in lease contracts. There are two pieces of guidance included in IAS 39 which analyse foreign currency features embedded in contracts: foreign currency derivatives embedded in host debt instruments; and foreign currency derivatives embedded in a host contract that is not a financial instrument.

For the former, the foreign currency feature is not separately accounted for because the instrument is a monetary item and, under IAS 21, foreign currency gains and losses are already recognised in profit or loss. For the latter, the assessment is more complicated. A foreign currency derivative embedded in a host contract that is not a financial instrument is closely related to the host provided it is not leveraged, does not contain an option, and requires payments denominated in:

- the functional currency of any substantial party to the contract;
- the currency in which the price of the related good or service that is acquired or delivered is routinely denominated in commercial transactions around the world; or
- a currency that is commonly used in contracts to purchase or sell non-financial items in the economic environment in which the transaction takes place.

It can be argued that trade receivables and payables recognised under finance leases are akin to a debt host, and therefore are covered by the same requirements in IAS 21 to recognise foreign currency gains and losses in profit or loss on monetary items. Hence, it would be reasonable to analogise from the foreign currency guidance on debt contracts when considering foreign currency features in finance lease payables and receivables.

Operating leases are non-financial instruments. Hence, the considerations that apply to non-financial items detailed in **10.5** below will equally apply to operating leases. These considerations include foreign currency options, leverage factors, the functional currency of substantial parties to the contract, and the currency that is commonly used in contracts in the economic environment in which the transaction takes place.

9.2.1 *Examples of embedded foreign currency features*

The following examples apply the analysis that is described in **9.2** above.

Example 9.2.1A

Operating lease denominated in functional currency of a party

Entity X, a Dutch entity, leases property from Entity Y, a UK entity, under an operating lease. The lease payments are denominated in Sterling. The functional currency of Entity X is the Euro and the functional currency of Entity Y is Sterling.

The provision to pay in Sterling would not require separate accounting, because Sterling is the functional currency of a substantial party to the contract, Entity Y.

Example 9.2.1B

Operating lease not denominated in functional currency of a party

Entity X, a New Zealand entity, leases property under an operating lease from Entity Y, an Australian entity. The lease payments are denominated in US dollars. The primary currency of Entity X is the New Zealand dollar and the primary currency of Entity Y is the Australian dollar.

The provision to pay in US dollars would require separate accounting because it is not the currency of the primary economic environment of either counterparty to the contract, and the price of this asset is not denominated routinely in that currency in international commerce.

If the property was leased under a finance lease (which is a financial instrument), the lease payments would represent monetary items, and therefore be within the scope of IAS 21. The embedded derivative would not be separated.

Example 9.2.1C

Choice of settlement in foreign currencies

A lease contract between a Sterling functional currency entity and a US dollar one, whereby the lessee can choose to make payments in either Sterling or US dollars, contains an embedded option which is not closely related to the host lease contract. This is true even though both of the settlement currencies are functional currencies of one of the counterparties to the lease. This answer would apply regardless of whether the lease was an operating or finance lease.

9.2.2 *Substantial party*

A 'substantial party' to the contract in the examples above is a party acting as a principal to the contract. The criterion for a 'substantial party' would not be satisfied if the party is an agent that is being engaged by the entity solely to comply with the requirement that payments be denominated in the functional currency of any substantial party to the contract.

Example 9.2.2

Substantial party

Entity X would like to lease property from Entity Y under an operating lease and have the payments denominated in US dollars. The functional currency of both entities is Sterling. To accomplish a US dollar-denominated lease, Entity Y leases the property to an investment bank whose functional currency is US dollars. The investment bank then subleases the property to Entity X. The sublease agreement requires Entity X to pay US dollars.

The investment bank is acting solely as an agent for Entity X and, accordingly, is not at risk (i.e. the investment bank would be indemnified by Entity Y for any losses incurred due to a default by Entity X). The bank cannot be viewed as a substantial party to the lease. Hence, the embedded foreign currency derivative requires separate accounting.

9.3 Referenced underlyings

A lease with contingent rentals that are based on related sales or on variable interest rates contain an embedded derivative (linkage to sale or interest) which is deemed to be closely related to the host lease contract.

9.3.1 Contingent rentals based on variable interest rates

Example 9.3.1

Lease linked to interest rates

Entity A, a UK entity, enters into a lease whose payments are indexed to six-month LIBOR. The embedded derivative does not need to be separated as the indexation is to interest rates inherent in its local economy.

IAS 39 does not give any guidance on what constitutes a variable interest rate. It is reasonable to assume that where an entity operates in a certain country and enters into a lease agreement in that country, a variable interest rate would be similar to the benchmark interest rate achieved on a debt instrument where the proceeds are used to invest in an asset where the debt is secured on that asset.

9.3.2 Contingent rentals based on related sales

Example 9.3.2A

Lease linked to sales

Entity X leases a property, which it uses as a retail outlet, selling custom made umbrellas. Embedded in the lease is a provision requiring lease payments to increase for each 1,000 sales after the first 100,000 umbrellas are sold.

Contingent rentals based on related sales are considered to be closely related to the host lease contract, so the sales related option should not be separated from the lease.

Example 9.3.2B

Lease linked to throughput

Entity Y leases shop premises in an airport terminal on an operating lease. The lease payments are contingent on the number of passengers who pass through the terminal.

While the contingent rentals are not based directly on related sales, it is clear that sales are directly affected by the number of passengers passing through the terminal. Thus, the embedded derivative is closely related to the host lease contract and does not need to be separately accounted for.

9.3.3 *Contingent rentals based on other balances*

IAS 39 states that contingent rentals based on related sales are closely related to the host lease contract. However, no guidance is given on contingent rentals based on other balances, such as profit or net assets or based on ratios.

It is not reasonable to extend the guidance given to cover other balances, such as profit. Sales within a retail unit may directly affect how much rent can be charged on the unit, as it will be an indicator of how many customers frequent the premises. However, the sales figure is a gross figure, whereas any profit figure will be a net figure, comprising several balances. To argue that profit is closely related to rentals, it would be necessary to argue that each balance that comprises the profit figure is individually closely related to rentals. It is not clear how figures such as cost of sales can be argued to be closely related to rentals. They are not analogous to sales.

Similarly, a net asset position comprises several asset and liability positions all added together. To argue that net assets are closely related to lease payments, it would be necessary to show that each asset and liability position that makes up the net asset position is individually closely related to the lease payments; i.e. that they have economic characteristics and risks that are similar to those in a lease contract, or that they are analogous to sales. It is not clear how, for example, an overdraft or an investment in securities is closely related to rentals, or analogous to sales.

puts an upper limit on the price A will pay. The cap is out-of-the-money at inception of the contract, i.e. the cap is set above the current price for tin.

The cap is closely related to the host purchase contract, so will not be separated. The cap is closely related to the host contract for the life of the contract, irrespective of whether tin prices rise so that the cap becomes in-the-money.

10.5 Foreign currency features

An embedded foreign currency derivative in a host contract that is not a financial instrument is closely related to the host contract provided it is not leveraged, does not contain an option feature and requires payments denominated in one of the following currencies:

[IAS 39.AG33(d)]

(i) the functional currency of any substantial party to the contract;

(ii) the currency in which the price of the related good or service that is acquired or delivered is routinely denominated in commercial transactions around the world (such as the US dollar for crude oil transactions), or

(iii) a currency that is commonly used in contracts to purchase or sell non-financial items in the economic environment in which the transaction takes place (for example, a relatively stable and liquid currency that is commonly used in local business transactions or external trade).

The three criteria in IAS 39.AG33(d) are not mutually exclusive. For example, an entity in country Y may export oil in US$. One, two or all three of the following may apply: the exporting entity may have US$ as its functional currency; oil is considered a non-financial item that is routinely denominated in US$ throughout the world; or US$ may be a common currency for either internal or external transactions for country Y.

The term 'substantial party' is discussed further in **9.2.2** above.

The assessment of the functional currency of a substantial party to the contract in (i) above requires care. For example, a substantial party to a contract may be a subsidiary of a larger group. The presentation currency of the group (see IAS 21 *The Effects of Changes in Foreign Exchange Rates*) is not relevant to this assessment, as it is the functional currency of the subsidiary that is relevant. In many cases judgement will be required when the subsidiary is in a jurisdiction which does not produce individual entity financial statements under IFRSs and therefore its functional currency is not evident. Too much reliance should not be placed on the country of incorporation or geographical location of a substantial party to the contract as the evaluation of the functional currency in IAS 21 includes many other factors.

The currency in which the price of the related goods or services is routinely denominated in commercial transactions around the world is only a currency that is used for similar transactions all around the world, not just in one local area. For example, if cross-border transactions in natural gas in North America are routinely denominated in US dollars and such transactions are routinely denominated in Euros in Europe, neither the US dollar nor the Euro is the currency in which the goods or services are routinely denominated in commercial transactions around the world. [IAS 39.IG.C.9]

By definition, a currency in which a good or service is routinely denominated around the world has to be one currency. However, the existence of a relatively small proportion of transactions in one or two markets, or a particular jurisdiction, that are denominated in a local currency does not preclude a non-financial item from being considered to be routinely denominated in a particular currency in commercial transactions around the world.

The number of non-financial items that would qualify under IAS 39.AG33(d)(ii) is likely to be limited. In practice, such items will primarily be commodities that are traded in US dollars in commercial transactions throughout the world.

For certain types of commodity transactions, contracts may be based on a dominant currency (such as the US dollar) but may be denominated in local currencies in certain markets for regulatory or other reasons where such local currency transactions are based on the dominant currency price of that commodity translated at the spot rate into local currencies (a "convenience translation" mechanism). For example, although the dominant currency for crude oil transactions as noted in IAS 39.AG33(d)(ii) is the US dollar, some contracts for crude oil may be denominated in Canadian dollars in Canada, where the Canadian dollar price is a convenience translation of the US dollar crude oil price. A simple convenience translation into local currencies of a commodity that is routinely denominated in a dominant currency would not negate the view that the commodity is routinely denominated in a single currency in commercial transactions around the world. On the other hand, if a commodity transaction is regularly denominated in various currencies in commercial transactions around the world where such foreign currency prices are not convenience translations of a dominant currency price, that commodity would not be considered to be routinely denominated in a particular currency.

The existence of an organised commodity exchange where a commodity is traded in a single currency provides a useful starting point in determining the dominant currency in which transactions in that commodity are denominated and, accordingly, whether such a commodity can be considered to be "routinely denominated" in that particular currency. The organised commodity exchanges may establish liquid markets for commodities quoted in a particular currency, and transactions between counterparties that are not conducted through the exchange are also denominated in that particular currency because to do otherwise would present arbitrage opportunities. For example, copper and gold are traded in US dollars on organised commodity exchanges and transactions between various counterparts that are not conducted through the exchange are also denominated in US dollars given the liquid markets established by the exchanges.

Certain commodities are not traded on organised exchanges, but global pricing forums exist that publish "spot prices" denominated in a dominant currency for that particular commodity. Transactions between market participants are based on those published spot prices. For example certain organisations independently may monitor market activities and publish US dollar prices that have become generally accepted as spot prices for the given commodity. Contracts between market participants are denominated in US dollars based on these published spot prices. In Japan and Europe, transactions may be conducted in Japanese Yen or Euros, respectively, but such Yen and Euro price equivalents are convenience translations of the US dollar spot price. Accordingly, the given commodity would in such a scenario be considered to be routinely denominated in US dollars in commercial transactions around the world.

In January 2008 the Emerging Issues Committee of the Canadian Institute of Chartered Accountants issued Abstract EIC 169 "*Determining Whether a Contract is Routinely Denominated in a Single Currency*". The Abstract provides an interpretation regarding paragraph 3855.A34(d) of Canadian GAAP which is equivalent to IAS 39.AG33(d)(ii). The Abstract is therefore **not an interpretation of**

IFRS and it is not issued by the IASB or the IFRIC. Although not issued by the IASB or the IFRIC the Abstract may be a useful starting point when considering what non-financial items are denominated in a common currency and therefore for this reason is reproduced below. The Appendix to the Abstract (which is an integral part of the Abstract) provides examples of commodities and certain other items that are considered to be routinely denominated in US dollars based on consideration of the factors discussed in the Abstract. The list of examples in the Abstract is as follows:

- Aluminium
- Coal (coking and thermal)
- Copper
- Crude oil
- Diamonds [rough/raw and polish (wholesale market)]
- Gold
- Iron ore
- Jet fuel
- Lead
- Nickel
- NBSK pulp
- Palladium
- Platinum
- Silver
- Tin
- Titanium
- Uranium
- Wide-bodied aircraft

- Zinc

The Abstract notes that the list is not intended to be exhaustive. Rather, it is a listing of commodities and certain other items that are routinely denominated in US dollars that have been identified at the date of the Abstract which may be used to support an assertion under paragraph 3855.A34(d) that these goods are routinely denominated in US dollars in commercial transactions around the world. The Abstract notes further that preparers should consider any circumstances arising subsequent to the date of its issue that might impact whether an item should remain on the list.

The concept of a 'currency that is commonly used in contracts to purchase or sell non-financial items in the economic environment in which the transaction takes place' as described in IAS 39.AG33(d)(iii) was introduced to address situations where entities operate in economies in which it is common for business contracts to be denominated in a foreign currency. [IAS 39.BC39]

'Economic environment' should be considered for the country concerned as a whole. It may be the case that more than one currency is commonly used. The Standard provides an example of a common currency as a 'relatively stable and liquid currency that is commonly used in local business transactions **or** external trade' (emphasis added). Therefore, a currency that is common for *either* external or internal transactions will be considered common for that country.

Looking at external trade, it may be possible that a country has multiple currencies that are commonly used to purchase or sell non-financial items. For instance, import and export transactions in and out of a small country (with counterparties in other small countries) may be commonly denominated in a range of internationally liquid, stable currencies (such as the Euro and the US dollar) rather than just one internationally liquid, stable currency. In such a case, if there is a significant level of transactions in each of the currencies, it may be possible that more than one currency is commonly used in the economic environment of external trade for that country.

Similarly, it may be possible that in certain hyperinflationary economies more than one foreign currency is used in local business transactions (because large sections of the general population view amounts in terms of one foreign currency and significant other sections of the population view amounts in another foreign currency). Also, this may be the case where a particular industry dominates the economy and commonly uses a foreign currency in local business transactions whilst the entirety of the remaining part of the economy uses the local currency. The judgement as to whether there is more than one common currency will depend on how significant the use of a particular currency is with respect to the local or external trade transactions of the country as a whole.

In determining whether a currency is common in a particular jurisdiction the analysis should focus on *all* transactions in that jurisdiction. For example, in determining whether external trade is commonly denominated in Euros, transactions with the Euro zone should not be excluded from the analysis. Equally, if an entity is determining whether a country with large oil exports is considered to have US$ as a common currency, the analysis of that country should not exclude exports of oil which would be expected to be denominated in US$ as oil is routinely denominated in US$ throughout the world.

In May 2007 the IFRIC published a tentative rejection notice in response to a submission on the application of IAS 39.AG33(d)(iii), in particular, what is the economic environment when determining whether a currency is commonly used in contracts to buy or sell non-financial items. In the draft rejection notice the IFRIC noted that the paragraph requires an entity to identify where the transaction takes place and to identify currencies that are commonly used in the economic environment in which the transaction takes place. The IFRIC was proposing not to take the issue on to its agenda because any guidance developed would be more in the nature of application guidance than an interpretation.

Following responses by constituents and further debate at IFRIC the IFRIC agreed to refer the matter to the Board for amendment to clarify the standard and eliminate any diversity in practice. At its December 2007 meeting the IASB noted that IAS 39.AG33(d) is intended to prohibit the separation of embedded foreign currency derivatives if the embedded derivatives are integral to the contractual arrangement. The IASB noted that embedded foreign currency derivatives are likely to be integral to the contractual arrangement if the foreign currency has one or more of the characteristics of a functional currency as set out in IAS 21.9. Accordingly, the Board decided to amend IAS 39.AG33(d)(iii) to refer to a currency that has one or more of the characteristics of a functional currency as set out in IAS 21.9. The current intention is to make this amendment through the Annual Improvements process in 2008.

At the time of writing the exposure draft of the 2008 annual improvements had not yet been published.

The following examples demonstrate the application of this guidance.

Example 10.5A

Routinely denominated currency (1)

Two entities, both of whose functional currency is the Japanese yen, enter into a three-year supply contract. If payments were either denominated in or linked to the US dollar, and the US dollar is not the currency in which the service is routinely denominated in commercial transactions around the world, the embedded foreign currency forward would need to be separated from the host supply contract.

Where a transaction is denominated in a currency that is a common currency in the economic environment of one or both of the substantial parties to the contract it is reasonable to consider the currency denomination of the contract is closely related for both parties.

Contracts where a party has the option over which currency the contract may be settled in are foreign currency features that are not closely related to the host purchase or sale contract.

Example 10.5B

Choice of settlement in foreign currencies

Entity A, a car dealership, contracts to purchase cars from Entity B, a car manufacturer. Companies A and B have functional currencies of Sterling and Euro respectively. The purchase agreement allows A to choose whether to settle the contract in a fixed amount of either Sterling or Euros.

The embedded foreign currency option must be separated from the host purchase contract. This treatment applies even though both settlement currencies are functional currencies of counterparties to the sales agreement.

Example 10.5C

Leveraged foreign currency adjustment

Entity X, a UK entity, enters into a sales contract with Entity Z, a US entity. Payments are in US dollars, but embedded in the contract is a clause such that payments are adjusted for twice the change in the US dollar exchange rate for the period that the payment is outstanding.

The sales contract contains an embedded derivative that is not closely related to the host sales contract, as leveraged foreign currency features are not closely related to host sales contracts.

Example 10.5D

Routinely denominated currency (2)

Entity A, a UK entity, contracts to buy oil from Entity B, also a UK entity. The functional currency of both entities is Sterling, however, the contract is to be settled in a fixed number of US dollars.

The embedded foreign currency feature is closely related to the host purchase contract, even though it is not in the functional currency of either counterparty to the contract. This is because oil is routinely denominated in US dollars in commercial transactions around the world. Therefore two Sterling functional currency entities can transact in oil in US dollars and the foreign currency embedded derivative is deemed to be closely related to the host purchase or sale contract.

Example 10.5E

Common currency in local economic environment

Entity A operates in a South American country that is assessed as having a high inflation economy. Like all other local businesses, it chooses to conduct its business in US dollars, a relatively stable currency. Thus, all purchase and sale contracts are denominated in US dollars.

The embedded foreign currency derivative does not need to be separated from a host purchase or sales contract, as these contracts are denominated in a currency that is commonly used in the local economic environment.

If A chose to use the Euro where all other local businesses used the US dollar, this exemption would not be available. To avoid separation of the embedded derivative, A would have to demonstrate that it met one of the other exemptions noted above.

Determination of contractual terms of the separated embedded derivative should be done by reference to the contractual terms of the non-financial host contract. For example, if a foreign currency derivative that needs separation is embedded in a purchase contract of a non-financial item which specifies delivery in two months' time, the maturity of the foreign currency derivative is two months.

The purchase contract stops being an executory (non-financial) contract once the delivery of the non-financial item takes place and a financial instrument, a foreign currency payable, comes into existence. The foreign currency translation of the payable is recognised in profit or loss in

At inception, an entity must determine the fair value of the embedded derivative first. The difference between the consideration paid or received to acquire the entire contract and the fair value of the embedded derivative is assigned to the host contract.

Example 12B

Allocating the proceeds to the embedded derivative

Entity A invests £1 million in a convertible bond. The bond has a coupon of 6 per cent, a maturity of five years, and is convertible into a fixed number of equity shares at maturity of the bond. Using a Black-Scholes model, it is determined that the fair value of the conversion option is £100,000. Assuming that the entire bond is not carried at fair value through profit or loss, separation of the embedded derivative is necessary. The amount assigned to the bond is determined by subtracting the fair value of the option from the consideration paid to purchase the bond. The entry on purchasing the asset is:

Dr	Bond	£900,000
Dr	Equity conversion option	£100,000
Cr	Cash	£1,000,000

It will not always be easy to establish the fair value of embedded derivatives, but there is little room for manoeuvre. If an embedded derivative needs to be separately accounted for, but the entity is unable to determine reliably the fair value of the embedded derivative on the basis of its terms and conditions (e.g. because the embedded derivative results in the delivery of an unquoted equity investment), the entity must determine the fair value of the whole contract and the fair value of the host contract, and the balance represents the derivative instrument. [IAS 39.13] If an entity is unable to do this, the entity must designate the whole contract as at fair value through profit or loss. [IAS 39.12] The entity might conclude, however, in the above example of an equity embedded derivative that results in the delivery of unquoted equity investment, that the equity component of the combined instrument may be sufficiently significant to preclude it from obtaining a reliable estimate of the entire instrument. In that case the combined instrument is measured at cost less impairment. [IAS 39.IG.C.11]

13 Presentation of embedded derivatives

IFRSs do not provide specific guidance on the presentation of embedded derivatives in the statement of financial position or in profit or loss. IAS 39.11 has an explicit statement that it does not address whether an embedded derivative shall be presented separately in the statement of financial position.

It seems appropriate for an entity to choose as an accounting policy whether it presents non-closely related embedded derivatives as separate financial assets or liabilities. This policy should be applied consistently to all hybrid contracts.

In instances where the host contract is a debt instrument held at amortised cost an entity may have a preference for presenting embedded derivatives as separate instruments rather than presenting the hybrid instrument as a single instrument, part measured at fair value and part measured at amortised cost. Conversely, if an entity has available-for-sale investments with separate embedded derivatives, i.e. the hybrid instrument is fair valued in its entirety, an entity may prefer to present the embedded derivative along with the host contract as a single financial instrument. If an entity chooses to present an embedded derivative together with the host contract as a single financial instrument, the entity must be aware of the need to comply with IFRS 7.8 to present either in the statement of financial position or in the notes the carrying amounts of financial instruments classified into appropriate financial instrument categories. Hence, if the contract is presented as a single financial instrument in the statement of financial position, the measurement by category of financial instrument will need to be included in the notes to the financial statements.

IAS 1 *Presentation of Financial Statements* requires an entity to determine whether assets and liabilities are presented as current or non-current. IAS 1 does not provide guidance as to whether in determining current or non-current presentation of embedded derivatives an entity should look to the settlement of the embedded derivative as if it is a standalone derivative (consistent with the way it is measured) or whether the settlement should be considered based on the settlement of the whole hybrid contract (consistent with the fact that the embedded derivative, even if measured separately, is nonetheless part of a hybrid contract).

If an embedded derivative is recognised separately in the statement of financial position from its host contract an entity should choose one of the two following policies in determining whether the embedded derivative is current or non-current:

- consider the timing of the cash flows of the embedded derivative as if it is a standalone contract; or

- consider the timing of the cash flows of the whole hybrid arrangement.

If the first policy is being applied, consideration should be given to *Improvements to IFRSs* issued in May 2008. This amended IAS 1 to clarify that, even though derivatives meet the held for trading definition in IAS 39.9, they are not presented as current unless they are due for settlement or expected to be settled in less than twelve months after the end of the reporting period. The amendments made to IAS 1 by *Improvements to IFRSs* apply for annual periods beginning on or after 1 January 2009, but earlier application is permitted. An entity choosing to apply the amendments early must disclose that fact.

At the time of writing, Improvements to IFRSs *has not yet been endorsed for adoption in the EU. EU companies may, nevertheless, comply with this amendment to IAS 1 prior to endorsement, since it does not conflict with the existing requirements of IAS 1 and IAS 39.* UK

If an embedded derivative is not recognised separately in the statement of financial position from its host contract the entity should determine the presentation as current or non-current based on the timing of the cash flows of the whole hybrid arrangement.

Example 13

Balance sheet presentation of embedded derivative

Entity D issues 5 year callable debt in the period where Entity D has the choice to redeem the instrument prior to maturity at an amount not approximately equal to the amortised cost. Entity D measures the host contract at amortised cost and measures the non-closely embedded derivative, the call option, as at fair value through profit or loss. At the period end Entity D can choose within the next twelve months to call the debt but does not expect to exercise its right to call. As the call option is a right for Entity D to buy the debt back, the embedded derivative will always have a positive fair value for Entity D.

Entity D has an accounting policy choice as to whether it presents the embedded derivative separately, in this case as a derivative financial asset, or together with the host contract as a single financial instrument. If the latter policy is applied, the hybrid financial instrument is presented as a single financial liability (as the embedded derivative will have a fair value less than the amortised cost of the host contract debt liability). If the former policy is applied, Entity D has a further choice as to whether it determines the embedded derivative as current or non-current based on the timing of the cash flows of the embedded derivative as if it is a standalone derivative or based on the timing of cash flows of the whole hybrid arrangement.

Policy based on timing of the cash flows of the embedded derivative as if it is a standalone derivative

Entity D does not have the intention to settle the embedded derivative within twelve months following the end of the reporting period as it does not expect to exercise the call option. The embedded derivative asset that is separately recognised in its statement of financial position will therefore be classified as non-current. The debt host contract liability will be presented as non-current as Entity D cannot be forced to settle the liability within twelve months of the end of the reporting period.

If in a future period Entity D believes it will choose to call the debt within twelve months of the end of the reporting period the embedded derivative will be presented as current at the end of the reporting period. The debt host contract liability will continue to be presented as non-current as Entity D cannot be forced to settle the liability within twelve months of the end of the reporting period.

Should the debt mature within twelve months of the end of the reporting period both the embedded derivative and debt host contract will be presented as current.

Policy based on timing of the cash flows of the whole hybrid instrument

If at the end of a reporting period the contractual maturity of the debt is more than twelve months and Entity D does not intend to call the debt within twelve months the whole instrument will be presented as non-current.

If at the end of a reporting period the contractual maturity of the debt is less than twelve months the whole hybrid contract will be presented as current.

18 Financial instruments: measurement

1 Introduction

IAS 39 requires the use of a mixed measurement model, with certain assets and liabilities measured at fair value and others on a cost basis. The model is based on the classification of financial assets and liabilities discussed in **chapters 14** and **15**. The Standard provides requirements for certain financial assets to be measured at fair value, and an option to measure other financial assets at fair value under specific circumstances. For example, the use of fair value is not required where an asset is to be held to its maturity. Financial liabilities are typically measured at amortised cost, though fair values should be used for derivative liabilities and separate rules apply to liabilities forming part of a hedge.

The rationale for using fair values is that, from a measurement point of view, the most relevant information that can be provided for financial assets is normally the amount that will be realised from their disposal, commonly referred to as 'exit price'. The relevance of fair value information for financial liabilities is less clear. Unless held for speculative or hedging purposes, liabilities generally form part of an entity's financing arrangements. It is often argued that it would be unhelpful for the carrying amount (and associated interest expense) of such liabilities to be remeasured to take account of changes in fair values, particularly those caused by changes in own credit risk. Such concerns are reflected in IAS 39's requirements for financial liabilities and the additional disclosure requirements when the fair value option is applied to financial liabilities. A fair value approach is particularly important for derivative instruments, where cost is typically negligible.

Since IAS 39 was originally issued in 1998 it has continued to have a mixed measurement model. The Joint Working Group of Standard Setters explored the possibility of moving towards a full fair value regime, but progress has been slow and it is expected that the mixed measurement model retained in IAS 39 will be here for some time to come. As part of the memorandum of understanding with the US Financial Accounting Standards Board, the IASB issued a discussion paper, *Reducing Complexity in Reporting Financial Instruments*, in March 2008 that will provide a basis for future discussions of issues related to the measurement of financial instruments (including hedge accounting issues). The ultimate goal of this project is to publish an IFRS that would significantly improve and simplify financial instrument reporting, i.e. would replace IAS 39.

This chapter addresses the approach to measurement that is adopted in the Standard, covering not only the basic rules, but also issues relating to the measurement of fair value and amortised cost, and the Standard's impairment model.

This chapter discusses measurement in the following sections:

2 Initial measurement

2.1 Fair value

IAS 39 requires that financial assets and liabilities are measured initially at 'fair value'. The concept of fair value is central to the approach of the Standard – it is defined as the amount for which an asset could be exchanged, or a liability settled, between knowledgeable, willing parties in an arm's length transaction. [IAS 39.9] (Note that transaction costs will often be added to/deducted from fair value on initial recognition – see **2.2** below.)

Section 5 below contains guidance on the appropriate determination of fair value for financial assets and liabilities.

Assuming transactions are conducted on arm's length terms, the fair value of a financial instrument acquired should normally be equal to the fair value of the consideration given or received (the 'transaction price'). Consequently, IAS 39 states that for initial recognition purposes, the transaction price is normally the best evidence of the fair value of a financial instrument. [IAS 39.AG64]

An exception to this general rule exists where the fair value of an instrument is evidenced by comparison with other observable current market transactions in the same instrument (i.e. without modification or repackaging) or based on a valuation technique whose variables include only data from observable markets. [IAS 39.AG76] This point is of particular significance for some entities, including those operating in the investment banking and insurance industry. An immediate gain may arise on the recognition of a financial instrument only where there is strong, market-based evidence of the fair value of the said instrument. See **5.2.5** below.

In certain situations, it may be difficult to identify and measure the fair value of consideration paid or received for a financial instrument. For example, where part of the amount involved in a transaction represents consideration for something other than the instrument itself. It would then be necessary to value the instrument directly using a valuation technique (see **5.2** below). This issue may arise when a credit card balance is acquired (particularly where there is a discounted rate being offered on the balance transferred and/or on purchases over an introductory period):

Example 2.1A

Separating financial instruments from total consideration (1)

An entity acquires a credit card balance (from the original lender), offering discounted rates on purchases in an introductory 12-month period. The credit card expires in three years.

The purchase consideration consists of four elements.

(i) The financial asset (i.e. the amount outstanding).

(ii) The borrower's option to borrow at preferential rates over the next 12 months.

(iii) The borrower's option to borrow at market rates over the following two years.

(iv) An intangible asset, being the expected future cash flows associated with generating a relationship with the borrower.

Item (i) should be calculated by discounting the expected repayments of the amount outstanding at an interest rate appropriate for the risk profile of the borrower. The commitment to lend at preferential rates should initially be recognised at fair value, and subsequently measured at the higher of (i) the amount recognised under IAS 37 *Provisions, Contingent Liabilities and Contingent Assets*, and (ii) the amount initially recognised less, where appropriate, cumulative amortisation recognised in accordance with IAS 18 *Revenue*. The commitment to lend at future market rates does not have any value for the buyer. However, it might be argued that certain behavioural aspects of credit card relationships (i.e. borrowers will often make purchases even when it would be more rational to obtain finance from another source) would often result in such commitments being viewed as assets (in effect part of the intangible item (iv)). The entity would need to determine whether the relationship met the definition of an intangible asset in IAS 38 *Intangible Assets*.

A similar issue might arise where an entity makes a low-interest, or interest-free, loan to an employee.

Example 2.1B

Separating financial instruments from total consideration (2)

On 1 January 20X0, an entity grants an interest-free loan of £100 to an employee. It is repayable on 31 December 20X0. The market rate of interest for a loan to this individual would be 8 per cent. Consideration paid is made up as follows:

(i) £92.59 is the fair value of the acquired financial asset (i.e. £100/1.08).

(ii) £7.41 is employee remuneration. This amount represents the fair value of the entity providing its employee with interest-free finance and is accounted for under IAS 19 *Employee Benefits*.

Another potential complication may arise if an initial fee is paid or received in compensation for subsequent cash flows that are above or below market rates. A simple example is given below:

Example 2.1C

Fair value of consideration

An entity originates a loan of £100. The entity receives an up-front fee of £10 from the borrower. Interest of £5 is receivable annually over the next five years and the principal amount is repaid at the end of year five.

The entity should recognise its financial asset at its fair value, being the fair value of the net consideration paid, i.e. £90 (principal less fee) and apply the effective interest method (see **4.1** below):

Year	Carrying amount b/f	Interest income at 7.47%	Cash flow	Carrying amount c/f
1	90.00	6.72	(5.00)	91.72
2	91.72	6.85	(5.00)	93.57
3	93.57	6.99	(5.00)	95.56
4	95.56	7.14	(5.00)	97.70
5	97.70	7.30	(105.00)	0.00

The effective interest rate, of 7.47 per cent, will also be the prevailing market rate for this instrument, on the assumption that the arrangement is at arm's length terms.

In some instances the difference between the consideration paid or received and the fair value of the financial instrument may represent a distribution or a capital contribution.

Example 2.1D

Interest free loan

A subsidiary, Entity S, granted an interest free fixed-term loan to its parent, Entity P. As the loan Entity S has provided to Entity P is not on market terms, there will be a difference between the cash advanced to Entity P and the initial recognition amount of the loan at fair value.

This fair value adjustment is, in substance, a distribution from the subsidiary to its parent because it does not meet the definition of an expense under paragraph 70 of the *Framework for the Preparation and Presentation of Financial Statements*. Hence, the adjustment to recognise the loan at its fair value should be taken directly to equity as a deemed distribution.

The deemed distribution would be recognised in equity irrespective of whether the subsidiary had distributable profits. The legal framework in Entity S's jurisdiction will govern whether the transfer of funds from a subsidiary with no legally distributable profits to its parent, by way of a deemed distribution, would render management of the subsidiary in breach of either their fiduciary duties and/or the corporate governance rules in that jurisdiction. Therefore, the level of distributable profits may be a factor affecting Entity S's decision to provide an interest-free loan to its parent but will not impact the accounting if a loan is made.

In May 2008 the IASB issued *Improvements to IFRSs*. The improvements amended IAS 20 *Accounting for Government Grants and Disclosure of Government Assistance* to rectify an apparent inconsistency between IAS 20 and IAS 39. When a loan is received from a government with a below-market rate of interest the pre-amended IAS 20 states that no interest should be imputed for such a loan, whereas IAS 39 requires all loans to be recognised at fair value, thus imputing interest to loans with a below-market rate of interest. The improvements remove this inconsistency by amending IAS 20 so that loans received from a government that have a below-market rate of interest should be recognised and measured in accordance with IAS 39. The benefit of the government loan is quantified by the imputation of interest in accordance with IAS 39. This benefit is accounted for in accordance with IAS 20. The amendment to IAS 20 applies prospectively to government loans received in periods beginning on or after 1 January 2009. If the amendments are applied to an earlier period the entity shall disclose this fact.

At the time of writing, the amended version of IAS 20 has not yet been endorsed for use in the EU. Since the requirements in respect of government UK *loans at below-market rates of interest differ from those of the previous version of IAS 20, EU reporting entities will not be able to apply the revised version in their statutory financial statements until it is endorsed.*

2.2 Transaction costs

For a financial asset or liability that is not classified as 'at fair value through profit or loss' (FVTPL), transaction costs that are directly attributable to the acquisition or issue of the asset or liability should be added to or deducted from the fair value on initial recognition.

The consequences of this are summarised below.

(a) For financial instruments that are carried at amortised cost (see **section 4** below), transaction costs are included in the calculation of the effective interest rate – in effect, they will be amortised through profit or loss over the term of the instrument.

(b) For available-for-sale financial assets where the effective interest method is applied, transaction costs will initially be recognised as part of the carrying amount of the financial asset. The transaction costs will be amortised through profit or loss over the term of the instrument under the effective interest method as with assets and liabilities measured at amortised cost. If the available-for-sale asset does not have fixed or determinable payments or has an indefinite life, and therefore the effective interest rate is not applied (e.g. the asset is an investment in an equity security), transaction costs are recognised in profit or loss only upon impairment or derecognition.

(c) For financial instruments classified as at FVTPL, transaction costs are immediately recognised in profit or loss on initial recognition.

Transaction costs are defined as incremental costs that are directly attributable to the acquisition, issue or disposal of a financial asset or a financial liability. An incremental cost is one that would not have been incurred if the entity had not acquired, issued or disposed of the financial instrument. [IAS 39.9]

Transaction costs are interpreted as including fees and commissions paid to agents, advisers, etc., as well as levies, taxes and duties. However, debt premiums/discounts, financing costs, internal administrative costs and holding costs should not be included. [IAS 39.AG13] In practice, the interpretation of this definition may require significant judgement. A particular issue arises in relation to the treatment of origination fees (see **4.1.3** below).

2.3 Settlement date accounting

The accounting for regular way trades is considered at **2.2** in **chapter 19**. When an entity uses settlement date accounting for an asset that is subsequently measured at cost or amortised cost, the asset is recognised initially at the settlement date, but at the fair value that existed at the trade date (discussed further in **3.5** below). Movements in fair value between trade and settlement date are not recognised (other than impairment losses). For assets carried at fair value, the change in fair value between trade and settlement date is recognised in profit or loss if the asset is measured as at fair value through profit or loss, or in other comprehensive income if the asset is available-for-sale. [IAS 39.57]

3 Subsequent measurement

3.1 Financial assets

As discussed in **section 3** of **chapter 14**, financial assets (including derivatives that are assets) are classified into one of four categories. This classification largely determines their subsequent measurement:

3.1.1 Financial assets as at fair value through profit or loss (FVTPL)

Assets falling within this category, which includes those classified as held for trading and derivative assets that are not designated as effective hedging instruments, are measured at fair value. Gains and losses that arise on changes in fair value are recognised in profit or loss. **Section 5** below contains guidance on the appropriate determination of fair value.

Gains and losses that arise between the end of the last annual reporting period and the date an instrument is derecognised do not constitute a separate 'profit/loss on disposal'. Such gains and losses will have arisen prior to disposal, while the item is still being held as at FVTPL, and should be recognised in profit or loss as they occur.

Transaction costs that might be incurred upon future disposal are **not** deducted from fair value in determining the carrying amount. Some argue that this is inconsistent with the use of exit prices (i.e. fair value) for measurement purposes, but the Standard is clear that such costs are viewed as being related to the act of disposal and, therefore, are recognised only in the period of disposal itself.

3.1.2 *Held-to-maturity investments*

Held-to-maturity investments are measured at amortised cost using the 'effective interest method'. This method is discussed in detail in **section 4** below.

3.1.3 *Loans and receivables*

Loans and receivables are also measured at amortised cost using the effective interest method, as discussed in **section 4** below.

3.1.4 *Available-for-sale financial assets*

Assets classified as available-for-sale are measured at fair value. As with financial assets at FVTPL, no deduction is made for transaction costs that might be incurred upon future disposal. **Section 5** below contains guidance on the appropriate determination of fair value.

Gains and losses that arise on changes in fair value are recognised in other comprehensive income, with three exceptions:

(i) interest, calculated using the effective interest method, is recognised in profit or loss (see **section 4** below);

(ii) impairment losses are recognised in profit or loss (see **section 6** below); and

(iii) foreign exchange gains and losses on monetary financial assets (the approach adopted in relation to foreign currency gains and losses is discussed in **3.3** below).

When an available-for-sale asset is derecognised, the cumulative gain or loss previously recognised in other comprehensive income is reclassified from equity to profit or loss. This reclassification of previous fair value gains and losses is frequently referred to as 'recycling'.

The following example illustrates the concept of 'recycling'.

Example 3.1.4A

Available-for-sale debt instrument

A zero coupon bond is acquired for its fair value of £95 on 1 January 20X0 and classified as available-for-sale. Transaction costs arising on acquisition are £5. The bond redeems for £130 on 31 December 20X4. On 31 December 20X0, the bond's fair value is £103. On 31 December 20X1, the entity sells the bond for its fair value of £108.

In its 20X0 accounts, the entity records the following entries:

(1) Initial recognition (at fair value, including transaction costs)

Dr	Asset	£100
Cr	Cash	£100

(2) Interest income (calculated under the effective interest method – the rate of 5.39 per cent is calculated so as to include transaction costs as explained in **4.1** below)

Dr	Asset	£5.39
Cr	Interest income	£5.39

(3) Fair value adjustment (such that the asset is stated at its fair value of £103)

Dr	Equity	£2.39
Cr	Asset	£2.39

In its 20X1 accounts, the following entries are recorded:

(1) Interest income (calculated under the effective interest method)

Dr	Asset	£5.68
Cr	Interest income	£5.68

(2) Fair value adjustment (such that the asset is stated at its fair value of £108)

Dr	Equity	£0.68
Cr	Asset	£0.68

(3) Sale of asset

Dr	Cash	£108
Cr	Asset	£108

(4) Reclassification to profit or loss of fair value losses previously recognised in other comprehensive income

Dr	Profit or loss	£3.07
Cr	Equity	£3.07

If an available-for-sale asset is derecognised, with the consideration received being another available-for-sale asset, the fair value gain or loss previously recognised in other comprehensive income should nonetheless be reclassified to profit or loss. As the original asset has been derecognised the deferred gain or loss is not attributable to the new asset and does not remain in other comprehensive income. [IAS 39.IG.E.3.1]

Example 3.1.4B

Available-for-sale equity instrument – group restructuring (1)

Entity A has a directly held wholly owned subsidiary, Entity B. Entity A accounts for its investments in subsidiaries in accordance with IAS 39 in its separate financial statements as permitted by IAS 27(2008).38(b) (previously IAS 27(2003).37(b)). Entity A designates its investment in Entity B as an available-for-sale investment in its separate financial statements and therefore measures its investment at fair value with fair value gains/losses recognised in other comprehensive income.

As part of a group reorganisation a new holding entity is created, Entity C, whose shares are issued to Entity A in return for Entity A's investment in Entity B. Entity C has no other assets or liabilities or transactions other than the issue of shares to Entity A and the acquisition of shares in Entity B. At the date of the group reorganisation Entity has a gain in other comprehensive income attributable to the increase in value of Entity B. The group structure is illustrated below:

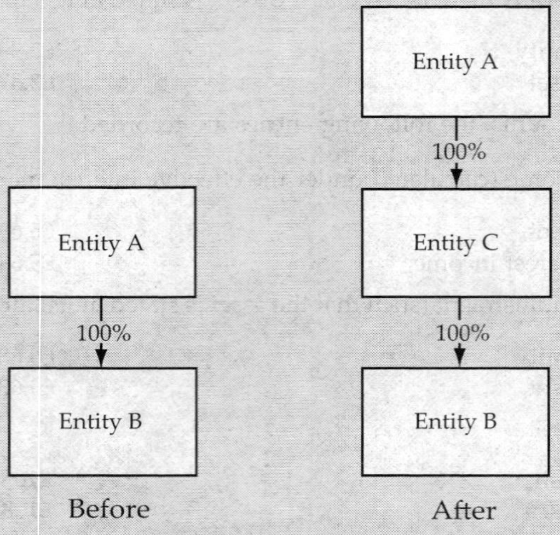

In the separate financial statements of Entity A it will not derecognise its investment in Entity B. Although Entity A has transferred its contractual rights to receive cash flows under the Entity B shares in accordance with IAS 39.18(a), Entity A has not transferred substantially all the risks and rewards of ownership of the Entity B shares in accordance with IAS 39.20(b) as the consideration received for transferring the shares in Entity B are shares in Entity C, the entity whose only asset is the investment in Entity B. Entity A's exposure to the risk and rewards of Entity B are equivalent to its new investment in Entity C. As Entity A has not derecognised the shares in Entity B the fair value gain recognised in other comprehensive income and accumulated in the available-for-sale reserve in equity will not be reclassified to profit or loss at the date of the group reorganisation.

Example 3.1.4C

Available-for-sale equity instrument – group restructuring (2)

Entity X purchases 100 equity shares of Entity Y, a listed entity, for £1,000 (i.e. at a price of £10 per each share). The investment is classified as an available-for-sale investment. At Entity X's period end, 31 December 20X1, the price of the shares has increased to £20 per share. As a result the fair value of Entity

X's holding has increased to £2,000 with Entity X recognising a fair value gain on its available-for-sale financial asset of £1,000 in other comprehensive income.

On 1 January 20X2 Entity Y undergoes a corporate restructuring such that certain assets, liabilities and activities of Entity Y are transferred into a newly created Entity Z whose shares will be distributed to the shareholders of Entity X. The restructuring means Entity Y will continue with certain core activities while Entity Z will undertake certain other activities that were previously undertaken by Entity Y. As part of the demerger shareholders in Entity Y will receive 1 new share in Entity Z (in addition to retaining their existing shares in Entity Y) for each share owned in Entity Y. After the reorganisation Entity X will hold 100 shares in Entity Z in addition to the 100 shares it originally owned in Entity Y. Post the demerger all assets and liabilities within Entity Y and Entity Z were those originally within Entity Y with no new assets or liabilities introduced. The shares in Entity Z are not listed. At the time of the demerger the share price of Entity Y decreases to £5 per share.

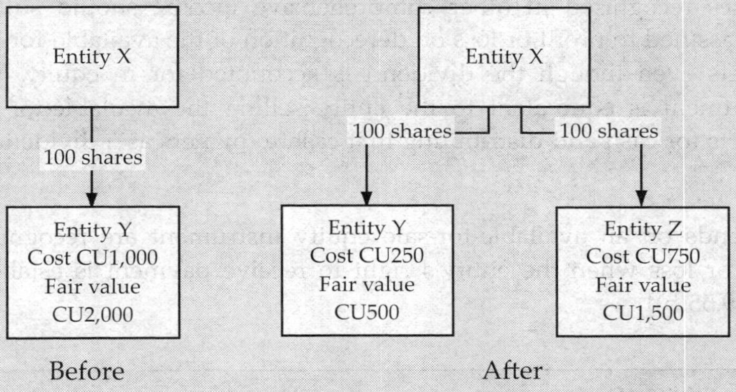

On receipt of the additional shares in Entity Z the available-for-sale reserve should not be reclassified to profit or loss as the original financial asset, Entity Y shares, does not meet the requirements for derecognition. Entity X has not transferred the contractual rights to receive cash flows from the Entity Y shares nor has it retained the contractual rights to receive the cash flows of the financial asset, but assumed a contractual obligation to pay the cash flows to one or more recipients in an arrangement that meets the pass through conditions (IAS 39.18). Furthermore, at the point of the demerger, from the point of view of Entity X, some of the value of the Entity Y shares has been distributed to the newly set up Entity Z. In addition, Entity X's investment in Entity Y is not considered to be impaired as the reduction in fair value of Entity Y shares is only the result of a redistribution of assets to existing shareholders for nil consideration.

Although the gain of £1,000 previously recognised in other comprehensive income should not be reclassified to profit or loss at the point of the demerger, Entity X will need to perform the following:

(i) recognise the shares in Entities Y and Z at their fair values upon the demerger. The fair value of the Entity Y shares upon demerger will be equal to £500 (fair value of £5 multiplied by 100 shares). The fair value of the shares in Entity Z should be estimated using a valuation technique in the absence of a quoted market price. In the event that the fair value of Entity Z shares cannot be estimated reliably the shares will be held at cost less impairment. In such case the cost will be deemed to equal £1,500 (the value of Entity Y shares prior to the demerger, £2,000, less the value of those shares upon demerger, £500).

(ii) allocate the gain of £1,000 in other comprehensive income in relation to the investment in Entity Y shares across the shares in Entity Y and Z. This allocation should be performed in line with the proportions of fair value/estimated cost of the shares upon the demerger as established in (i) above.

If available-for-sale assets are distributed to owners as dividends-in-kind (also known as 'dividends in specie'), the cumulative gains or losses recognised in other comprehensive income should still be reclassified to profit or loss on derecognition of the available-for-sale assets even though the dividend is accounted for in equity. This treatment is equivalent to the entity selling the available-for-sale assets for cash and distributing that cash to owners as a dividend.

Dividends on an available-for-sale equity instrument are recognised in profit or loss when the entity's right to receive payment is established. [IAS 39.55(b)]

Example 3.1.4D

Dividends on available-for-sale equity instruments

On 1 January 20X0, Entity X acquires an equity instrument of Entity Y for its fair value of £100. It is classified as available-for-sale. Y immediately declares a dividend of £10 and, consequently, its fair value decreases to £90. Entity X records the following entries:

(1) Initial recognition

Dr	Asset	£100
Cr	Cash	£100

(2) Dividend income

Dr	Cash	£10
Cr	Dividend income	£10

(3) Fair value adjustment (such that the asset is stated at its fair value of £90)

Dr	Other comprehensive income	£10
Cr	Asset	£10

The accounting treatment in the example above appears unfortunate, since the realisation of part of the value of an asset will lead to the recognition of two offsetting amounts – one in profit or loss and the other in other comprehensive income. (Historically, there was also an apparent conflict here with IAS 18.32, which, until it was amended in May 2008, required dividends out of pre-acquisition profits to be treated as a reduction of the cost of investment, rather than being taken to profit or loss.) Nevertheless, IAS 39 explicitly requires that dividends received are included in profit or loss, and it appears that the IAS 39 requirement should prevail, as it is from the more recent Standard. In addition, an entity would need to consider in all cases whether a reduction in fair value recognised in other comprehensive income needs to be reclassified to profit or loss in the instance when the asset is impaired (see **6.1.2** below).

3.1.5 Hedged items

IAS 39 includes specific requirements to be applied when accounting for a financial asset that is a hedged item. These requirements are discussed in detail in **chapter 20**.

3.1.6 Unquoted equity instruments

Investments in equity instruments that do not have a quoted market price in an active market, and whose fair value cannot be reliably measured, are measured at cost. The term 'active market' is discussed further in **5.1** below. Cost is also applied for derivatives (whether assets or liabilities) that are linked to and must be settled by delivery of such unquoted equity. [IAS 39.46(c)] Examples of such derivatives would include purchased call options over a third party's equity shares requiring physical settlement, or a forward purchase of such shares.

The application guidance to the Standard (IAS 39.AG80 & AG81) makes it clear that it will normally be possible to estimate the fair value of an asset that has been acquired from an outside party. Cost should be used **only** if there is a significant range of possible fair value estimates and the probabilities of the various estimates cannot be reasonably assessed.

3.1.7 Instruments whose fair value is 'unreliable'

If IAS 39 requires a financial instrument to be measured at fair value, there is no exception from measuring on that basis except for equity instruments described above in **3.1.6**. In all other cases, fair value is deemed to be reliable and any measurement assumptions are disclosed. See **chapter 21**.

In November 2006 the IFRIC finalised a rejection notice on the valuation of electricity derivatives where the contract fails to meet the normal purchase, sale or usage exemption in IAS 39.5 and therefore is wholly within the scope of IAS 39. The question that was asked was whether such contracts fell under the exception from fair valuation that applies to derivatives linked to unquoted equity instruments. Valuation issues arise as the derivative in this case has a variable notional amount and the term of the derivative might extend well beyond the period for which there were any observable market data. The IFRIC noted that the only exception in IAS 39 from the requirement to fair value derivatives after initial recognition is given in IAS 39.46(c), amplified by paragraphs AG80 and AG81, which is in respect of unquoted equity investments, and that it was not appropriate to extend this exemption to other derivatives. The IFRIC noted further that IAS 39 contains general principles on how to measure fair value. The IFRIC decided that it should not seek to develop more detailed guidance on this topic, since the subject was too specific.

3.1.8 Negative fair value

If the fair value of a financial instrument, previously recognised as a financial asset, falls below zero, then it is a financial liability and measured as discussed in **3.2** below.

3.2 Financial liabilities

Financial liabilities are measured at amortised cost using the effective interest method (see **section 4** below), with the following exceptions.

3.2.1 Financial liabilities as at fair value through profit or loss (FVTPL)

Such liabilities, which include those classified as held for trading and derivative liabilities that are not designated as effective hedging instruments, and those designated at FVTPL, are measured at their fair value with gains and losses recognised in profit or loss. However, a derivative liability that is linked to, and must be settled by delivery of, an unquoted equity instrument whose fair value cannot be reliably measured is measured at cost (discussed further in **section 5** below).

A consequence of including a financial liability in this category is that the effect of an entity's own credit risk will be reflected in its statement of comprehensive income. For example, if an entity that has elected to fair value its issued debt experiences financial difficulties, it is likely to recognise a gain in profit or loss reflecting the instrument's worsening creditworthiness.

3.2.2 *Financial liabilities arising on the transfer of a financial asset*

A liability may arise when a transfer of a financial asset does not qualify for derecognition or is accounted for using the 'continuing involvement' approach. The approach used when measuring such liabilities is discussed at **3.3** in **chapter 19**.

3.2.3 *Hedged items*

IAS 39 includes specific requirements to be applied when accounting for a financial liability that is a hedged item. These requirements are discussed in detail in **chapter 20**.

3.3 Foreign currency

Where a financial asset or liability is a monetary item under IAS 21 *The Effects of Changes in Foreign Exchange Rates*, foreign exchange gains and losses should be recognised in profit or loss in accordance with that Standard. Monetary items are defined as units of currency held and assets and liabilities to be received or paid in a fixed or determinable number of units of currency. [IAS 21.8]

For financial assets and liabilities that are classified as at FVTPL, this requirement is easy to apply since all gains and losses are recognised in profit or loss in any case. However, the situation is not so straightforward for assets measured at amortised cost and, in particular, for available-for-sale financial assets.

IAS 39 requires that 'for the purpose of recognising foreign exchange gains and losses under IAS 21, a monetary available-for-sale financial asset is treated as if it were carried at amortised cost in the foreign currency.' [IAS 39.AG83] Hence, exchange differences resulting from changes in amortised cost are recognised in profit or loss, with other changes in carrying amount recognised in other comprehensive income under IAS 39.55(b). The result of this is that the cumulative gain or loss recognised in other comprehensive income is the difference between the amortised cost (adjusted for impairment, if any) and the fair value of the instrument in the functional currency of the reporting entity.

IAS 39.IG.E.3.2 illustrates the approach and is reproduced below:

Example 3.3

IAS 39 and IAS 21 – Available-for-sale financial assets: separation of currency component

[IAS 39.IG.E.3.2]

For an available-for-sale monetary financial asset, the entity recognises changes in the carrying amount relating to changes in foreign exchange rates in profit or loss in accordance with IAS 21.23(a) and IAS 21.28 and other changes in the carrying amount in other comprehensive income in accordance with IAS 39. How is the cumulative gain or loss that is recognised in other comprehensive income determined?

It is the difference between the amortised cost (adjusted for impairment, if any) and fair value of the available-for-sale monetary financial asset in the functional currency of the reporting entity. For the purpose of applying IAS 21.28 the asset is treated as an asset measured at amortised cost in the foreign currency.

To illustrate: on 31 December 20X1 Entity A acquires a bond denominated in a foreign currency (FC) for its fair value of FC1,000. The bond has five years remaining to maturity and a principal amount of FC1,250, carries fixed interest of 4.7 per cent that is paid annually (FC1,250 × 4.7 per cent = FC59 per year), and has an effective interest rate of 10 per cent. Entity A classifies the bond as available for sale, and thus recognises gains and losses in other comprehensive income. The entity's functional currency is its local currency (LC). The exchange rate is FC1 to LC1.5 and the carrying amount of the bond is LC1,500 (= FC1,000 × 1.5).

Dr	Bond	LC1,500	
Cr	Cash		LC1,500

On 31 December 20X2, the foreign currency has appreciated and the exchange rate is FC1 to LC2. The fair value of the bond is FC1,060 and thus the carrying amount is LC2,120 (= FC1,060 × 2). The amortised cost is FC1,041 (= LC2,082). In this case, the cumulative gain or loss to be recognised in other comprehensive income and accumulated in equity is the difference between the fair value and the amortised cost on 31 December 20X2, i.e. LC38 (= LC2,120 – LC2,082).

Interest received on the bond on 31 December 20X2 is FC59 (= LC118). Interest income determined in accordance with the effective interest method is FC100 (=1,000 × 10 per cent). The average exchange rate during the year is FC1 to LC1.75. For the purpose of this question, it is assumed that the use of the average exchange rate provides a reliable approximation of the spot rates applicable to the accrual of interest income during the year (IAS 21.22). Thus, reported interest income is LC175 (= FC100 × 1.75) including accretion of the initial discount of LC72 (= [FC100 – FC59] × 1.75). Accordingly, the exchange difference on the bond that is recognised in profit or loss is LC510 (= LC2,082

– LC1,500 – LC72). Also, there is an exchange gain on the interest receivable for the year of LC15 (= FC59 × [2.00 – 1.75]).

Dr	Bond	LC620
Dr	Cash	LC118
Cr	Interest income	LC175
Cr	Exchange gain	LC525
Cr	Fair value change in other comprehensive income	LC38

On 31 December 20X3, the foreign currency has appreciated further and the exchange rate is FC1 to LC2.50. The fair value of the bond is FC1,070 and thus the carrying amount is LC2,675 (= FC1,070 × 2.50). The amortised cost is FC1,086 (= LC2,715). The cumulative gain or loss to be accumulated in equity is the difference between the fair value and the amortised cost on 31 December 20X3, i.e. negative LC40 (= LC2,675 – LC2,715). Thus, the amount recognised in other comprehensive income equals the change in the difference during 20X3 of LC78 (= LC40 + LC38).

Interest received on the bond on 31 December 20X3 is FC59 (= LC148). Interest income determined in accordance with the effective interest method is FC104 (= FC1,041 × 10 per cent). The average exchange rate during the year is FC1 to LC2.25. For the purpose of this question, it is assumed that the use of the average exchange rate provides a reliable approximation of the spot rates applicable to the accrual of interest income during the year (IAS 21.22). Thus, recognised interest income is LC234 (= FC104 × 2.25) including accretion of the initial discount of LC101 (= [FC104 – FC59] × 2.25). Accordingly, the exchange difference on the bond that is recognised in profit or loss is LC532 (= LC2,715 – LC2,082 – LC101). Also, there is an exchange gain on the interest receivable for the year of LC15 (= FC59 × [2.50 – 2.25]).

Dr	Bond	LC555
Dr	Cash	LC148
Dr	Fair value change in other comprehensive income	LC78
Cr	Interest income	LC234
Cr	Exchange gain	LC547

When some portion of the change in carrying amount is recognised in other comprehensive income and some portion is recognised in profit or loss, for example, if the amortised cost of a foreign currency bond classified as available for sale has increased in foreign currency (resulting in a gain in profit or loss) but its fair value has decreased in the functional currency (resulting in a loss in other comprehensive income), an entity cannot offset those two components for the purposes of determining gains or losses that should be recognised in profit or loss or in other comprehensive income. [IAS 39.IG.E.3.4]

IAS 21 specifically scopes out the measurement of foreign currency items that are subject to hedge accounting. These items are discussed in **chapter 20** on hedge accounting.

For available-for-sale financial assets that are not monetary items under IAS 21 (for example, equity investments), the gain or loss that is recognised in other comprehensive income includes any related foreign currency component.

IAS 39.IG.E.3.4 includes a further discussion of the interaction between IAS 39 and IAS 21. It states that the measurement of a financial asset or financial liability at fair value, cost or amortised cost is first determined in the foreign currency in which the item is denominated in accordance with IAS 39. Then, the foreign currency amount is translated into the functional currency using the closing rate or a historical rate in accordance with IAS 21. [IAS 39.AG83]

For example, if a monetary financial asset (such as a debt instrument) is carried at amortised cost under IAS 39, amortised cost is calculated in the currency of denomination of that financial asset. Then, the foreign currency amount is recognised using the closing rate in the entity's financial statements. [IAS 21.23] That applies regardless of whether a monetary item is measured at cost, amortised cost or fair value in the foreign currency. [IAS 21.24] A non-monetary financial asset (such as an investment in an equity instrument) is translated using the closing rate if it is carried at fair value in the foreign currency [IAS 21.23(c)] and at a historical rate if it is not carried at fair value under IAS 39 because its fair value cannot be reliably measured. [IAS 21.23(b) & IAS 39.46(c)]

As an exception, if the financial asset or financial liability is designated as a hedged item in a fair value hedge of the exposure to changes in foreign currency rates under IAS 39, the hedged item is remeasured for changes in foreign currency rates even if it would otherwise have been recognised using a historical rate under IAS 21 [IAS 39.89], i.e. the foreign currency amount is recognised using the closing rate. This exception applies to non-monetary items that are carried in terms of historical cost in the foreign currency and are hedged against exposure to foreign currency rates. [IAS 21.23(b)]

A summary of how foreign currency is treated for the various financial asset and liability classifications is included below:

Classification	Monetary or non-monetary item	Foreign currency gains and losses from re-measurement (prior to its disposal) *
Available-for-sale	Monetary item (e.g. debt security)	Profit or loss
Available-for-sale	Non-monetary item (e.g. equity security)	Equity
Loan and receivable	Always a monetary item	Profit or loss
Held-to-maturity	Always a monetary item	Profit or loss
Fair value through profit or loss	Not applicable	Profit or loss
Liability carried at amortised cost	Always a monetary item	Profit or loss

* assuming the item is not being hedged for foreign currency, or is not a hedging instrument in a foreign currency hedge

3.3.1 *Dual currency bonds*

IAS 39.AG33(c) states that a foreign currency derivative that provides a stream of principal or interest payments that are denominated in a foreign currency and is embedded in a host debt instrument (e.g. a dual currency bond) is closely related to the host debt instrument. Such a derivative is not separated from the host instrument because IAS 21 requires foreign currency gains and losses on monetary items to be recognised in profit or loss.

IAS 39 and IAS 21 do not provide specific guidance on how to measure dual currency bonds. As IAS 39 states that the foreign currency gains and losses are accounted for under IAS 21 it is reasonable to assume that the accounting treatment is equivalent to isolating the foreign currency cash flows and measuring them as if they were a separate instrument. For example, if interest is denominated in a foreign currency, but the principal is not, an entity could measure the interest flows as if it was a foreign currency denominated interest rate strip and treat the principal cash flow as a functional currency denominated zero coupon bond. Conversely, if the principal is denominated in a foreign currency, but the interest is not, an entity could measure the principal as if it was a foreign currency denominated zero coupon bond and treat the interest flows as a functional currency denominated interest rate strip.

Example 3.3.1

Accounting for a dual-currency bond

Entity A, a Sterling functional currency entity, issues a dual currency bond on 1 January 20X4 where the interest is denominated in its functional currency, but the principal is denominated in US dollars. The bond has a notional of US$200m, has a maturity of three years and is issued at par.

Entity A determines the carrying value of a US$-denominated three year zero coupon bond at inception by discounting US$200m by the 3-year US$ zero coupon rate reflecting Entity A's credit quality which is 10% (US$200m / 1.1^3 = US$150.26m). Entity A then converts this amount into its functional currency at the US$:£ spot rate at inception (US$150.26m / US$2:£1 = £75.13m). The difference between this amount and the functional currency equivalent net proceeds received from issuing the dual-currency bond is allocated to the functional currency interest only strip [(US$200m / US$2:£1) – £75.13m = £24.87m]. Each period the US$ effective interest rate of 10% is applied to the US$-denominated zero coupon bond in US$ and this US$ carrying value is converted into £ in accordance with IAS 21.

Entity A determines the £ effective interest rate for the interest only strip which is the 3-year interest rate for an equivalent 3-year amortising loan. For illustration purposes this interest rate is also 10% though in practice the interest rates for the respective currencies will differ.

The foreign exchange rates for the three period were as follows:

	Period end rate (US$:£)	Average rate (US$:£)
20X3	2.00	–
20X4	1.80	1.90
20X5	2.10	1.95
20X6	1.90	2.00

The carrying value of the foreign currency zero coupon bond in US$ is determined by applying the US$ effective interest rate in US$.

	20X4	20X5	20X6
Opening carrying value (US$)	150.26	165.29	181.82
Interest at 10% (US$)	15.03	16.53	18.18
Closing carrying value (US$)	165.29	181.82	200.00

The carrying value of the foreign currency zero coupon bond in £ is determined by converting the opening carrying value in US$ at the opening rate, adding interest at the average rate, adding/subtracting foreign exchange gains or losses so that the closing value in £ is equal to the US$ closing value at the period end rate.

	20X4	20X5	20X6
Opening carrying value (£)	75.13	91.83	86.58
Interest at average rates (£)	7.91	8.48	9.09
Foreign currency (gains) losses (£)	8.79	(13.72)	9.59
Closing carrying value (£)	91.83	86.58	105.26

The carrying value of the interest only strip in £ is determined by adding the effective interest rate and deducting the cash payments for each period.

	20X4	20X5	20X6
Opening carrying value	24.87	17.36	9.10
Interest at 10%	2.49	1.74	0.90
Less cash paid	(10.00)	(10.00)	(10.00)
Closing carrying value	17.36	9.10	-

A summary of the entries are illustrated below:

£	Description	Cash	Debt	Interest expense	Foreign currency gain/(loss)
1/1/X4	Issue debt	100.00	(100.00)		
20X4	Interest on US$ zero coupon bond		(7.91)	7.91	
	Foreign currency movement		(8.79)		(8.79)
	Interest on interest only strip	(10.00)	7.51	2.49	
20X5	Interest on US$ zero coupon bond		(8.48)	8.48	
	Foreign currency movement		13.72		13.72
	Interest on interest only strip	(10.00)	8.26	1.74	
20X6	Interest on US$ zero coupon bond		(9.09)	9.09	
	Foreign currency movement		(9.59)		(9.59)
	Interest on interest only strip	(10.00)	9.10	0.90	
31/12/X6	Repayment of dual currency bond	(105.26)	105.26		

3.4 Reclassifications

The measurement consequences of reclassifying financial assets are discussed in **section 4** of **chapter 14**.

3.5 Settlement date accounting

When an entity uses settlement date accounting for an asset that is subsequently measured at cost or amortised cost, the asset is recognised initially at its fair value on the trade date. Any change in fair value between the trade date and settlement date is not recognised (other than impairment losses). Changes in value between the trade date and settlement date for assets that are subsequently measured at fair value are recognised (i) in profit or loss for financial assets classified as at FVTPL; and (ii) in other comprehensive income for available-for-sale financial assets. This subject is discussed in greater detail at **2.2** in **chapter 19**.

4 Amortised cost

On acquisition, the carrying amount of a financial instrument, being its fair value (normally the transaction price), represents the discounted amount of the expected future cash flows that will arise under that instrument. For financial assets and liabilities that are measured at amortised cost, the unwinding of that discount is included in profit or loss as interest income or interest expense.

Amortised cost is defined as the amount at which the financial asset or financial liability is measured at initial recognition minus principal repayments, plus or minus the cumulative amortisation using the effective interest method of any difference between that initial amount and the maturity amount, and minus any reduction (directly or through the use of an allowance account) for impairment or uncollectibility. [IAS 39.9]

The effective interest method is discussed in **4.1** below.

Amortised cost measurement is required for financial assets that are classified as either 'loans and receivables' or 'held-to-maturity investments', and for financial liabilities that are not at FVTPL. In addition, while interest-bearing available-for-sale financial assets are measured at fair value, with changes in fair value recognised in other comprehensive income, the Standard nonetheless requires interest income or expense (calculated on an amortised cost basis) to be included in profit or loss. This approach is illustrated in **example 3.1.4A** above. For financial assets or liabilities at FVTPL, interest is effectively wrapped up in the fair value adjustment that is included in profit or loss in each accounting period and is not required to be separately disclosed although an entity may choose to do so as an accounting policy choice.

4.1 The effective interest method

IAS 39 requires that the amortised cost of a financial asset or liability is calculated using the 'effective interest method'. This method allocates interest income/expense over the relevant period by applying the 'effective interest rate' to the carrying amount of the asset or liability.

The effective interest rate is defined as the rate that exactly discounts estimated future cash payments or receipts through the expected life of the financial instrument or, when appropriate, a shorter period to the net carrying amount of the financial asset or financial liability. When calculating the effective interest rate, an entity shall estimate cash flows considering all contractual terms of the financial instrument (for example, prepayment, call and similar options) but shall not consider future credit losses. The calculation includes all fees and points paid or received between parties to the contract that are an integral part of the effective interest rate (see IAS 18 *Revenue*), transaction costs, and all other premiums or discounts. There is a presumption that the cash flows and the expected life of a group of similar financial instruments can be estimated reliably. However, in those rare cases when it is not possible to estimate reliably the cash flows or the expected life of a financial instrument (or group of financial instruments), the entity shall use the contractual cash flows over the full contractual term of the financial instrument (or group of financial instruments). [IAS 39.9]

Since transaction costs are taken into account when determining the initial net carrying amount, their recognition in profit or loss is effectively spread over the life of the instrument.

Example 4.1

Effective interest rate

On 1 January 20X0, an entity acquires a bond for consideration of £90, incurring transaction costs of £5. Interest of £4 is receivable annually over the next 5 years (31 December 20X0 to 31 December 20X4). The bond has a mandatory redemption of £110 on 31 December 20X4.

Year	Carrying amount b/f	Interest income at 6.96%	Cash flow	Carrying amount c/f
20X0	95.00	6.61	(4.00)	97.61
20X1	97.61	6.79	(4.00)	100.40
20X2	100.40	6.99	(4.00)	103.39
20X3	103.39	7.19	(4.00)	106.58
20X4	106.58	7.42	(114.00)	0.00

The effective interest rate of 6.96 per cent is the rate that discounts the expected cash flows on the bond to the initial carrying amount, i.e.:

$$4/1.0696 + 4/1.0696^2 + 4/1.0696^3 + 4/1.0696^4 + 114/1.0696^5 = 95$$

The effective interest rate is determined based on the initial carrying amount of the financial asset or liability. Therefore, the effective interest rate applied to any financial instrument, including interest bearing available-for-sale assets is not recalculated to reflect fair value changes in the carrying amount of the asset.

4.1.1 *Cash flows*

When calculating the effective interest rate, the **estimated** cash flows arising from the asset or liability (or, where relevant, the group of assets or liabilities) should be used. The Standard explicitly states that all contractual terms of the instrument (for example prepayment, call and similar options) should be considered, but that future credit losses should **not** be taken into account. This last point is consistent with the fact that the impairment model adopted in the Standard requires impairment losses to be recognised as they are incurred, rather than when they are expected (see **section 6** below).

In contrast, credit losses that have already been incurred on an instrument by the time it is acquired by the reporting entity should be taken into account when calculating the effective interest rate. This might be the case where a financial asset is acquired at a deep discount because credit losses that have occurred are reflected in the transaction price. As mentioned above, IAS 39 requires impairment losses to be recognised as incurred. If previously incurred losses are not factored into the calculation, an overstated interest income amount would be offset by the recognition of impairment losses that have already been incurred.

If a debt instrument has a prepayment, put, or call feature embedded in the terms of the instrument, the entity must firstly determine whether that feature is an embedded derivative that needs to be separately accounted for. See **7.1** in **chapter 17** for further guidance on embedded derivatives. Briefly, such embedded derivatives will be separately accounted for unless the option's exercise price is approximately equal to the instrument's amortised cost on each exercise date. [IAS 39.AG30(g)]

If the embedded derivative is separately accounted, the impact of this feature must not be used in determining the estimated cash flows of the debt host contract when determining the effective interest rate. If the feature was taken into account, it would result in double counting of the prepayment, put or call feature in profit or

loss as it would be included in the effective interest rate on the debt host contract as well as in the fair value movements of the embedded derivative.

4.1.2 *Changes in cash flows*

For floating rate instruments, when cash flows are re-estimated to reflect movements in market rates of interest, the effective interest rate is updated. If the instrument is initially recognised at an amount equal to the amount receivable or payable on maturity, re-estimating future cash flows for this reason will not normally have a significant effect on its carrying amount. [IAS 39.AG7]

The re-estimation of future cash flows for any other reason or in the case of instruments that are not floating rate instruments will normally result in a change in carrying amount, since the revised estimated cash flows are discounted at the instrument's original effective interest rate. The required adjustment is recognised in profit or loss. [IAS 39.AG8] This approach will apply in the case of an instrument for which the timing or amount of interest or principal payments vary but the feature is not accounted for separately as an embedded derivative and the instrument is also not considered a floating rate instrument.

This difference in approach reflects the fact that varying interest receipts/payments are a contractual term of a floating rate instrument. In this situation, it would be inappropriate to determine at inception a single rate to discount estimated future cash flows. Instead, the Standard requires an entity to reflect changes in the interest rate in profit or loss as such changes occur.

Judgement is required in determining what constitutes a floating rate debt instrument. A debt instrument may have variable cash flows linked to market interest rates which differ from standard floating rate debt instruments. If the instrument is considered a floating rate debt instrument then IAS 39.AG7 is applied, if it is not, then IAS 39.AG8 applies.

Consider an example of Sterling functional currency entity that has issued a Sterling denominated bond where principal and interest payments are indexed to unleveraged UK inflation. The inflation-linking feature is considered a closely related embedded derivative (see **7.4 in chapter 17**). Two possible approaches in applying amortised cost could be applied.

The first approach is to treat the instrument as a floating rate instrument and apply IAS 39.AG7. This approach treats the interest payments linked to inflation in the same way as LIBOR linked interest for a LIBOR linked liability. The effective interest rate of the floating rate liability should be updated at each period end in line with the re-estimation of cash flows for changing expectations of inflation. At initial recognition, an effective interest rate should be calculated that discounts the estimated cash flows of principal and interest (which includes the estimation of future inflation) to the initial carrying amount. That initial effective interest rate is used to account for the instrument at amortised cost until the end of the next reporting period. The carrying amount at the end of the first reporting period will be equal to the initial fair value, plus the effective interest on the carrying amount, less any cash payments made in the period. The entity would then determine the new effective interest being the rate that discounts the new estimated cash flows of the instrument (taking into account the revised estimation of future inflation) back to the period end carrying amount. This new effective interest rate is applied for the new reporting period. This approach is repeated at each subsequent reporting period until the instrument is derecognised.

The alternative approach is to treat the inflation-linked debt not as a floating rate instrument, and therefore to apply AG8 instead. The effective interest rate should be calculated at inception, being the rate that exactly discounts the expectations of inflation at initial recognition to the initial carrying amount (being fair value less transaction costs). This effective interest is never updated. At the end of each subsequent reporting period the cash flows are re-estimated, reflecting the then current expectations of future inflation, and are discounted using the *original* effective interest rate. Any difference between the carrying amount of the instrument before and after such re-estimation is recognised in profit or loss.

Applying IAS 39.AG7 will result in a less volatile profit or loss when compared to applying IAS 39.AG8. The application of the latter approach results in changes in expectations of future inflation impacting profit or loss immediately at each re-estimation date.

In July 2008 the IFRIC issued a rejection notice on the application of the effective interest rate method. The rejection notice considered the application of the effective interest rate method to a financial instrument whose cash flows are linked to changes in an inflation index. The IFRIC noted that IAS 39.AG6–AG8 provide the relevant application guidance. The IFRIC recognised that judgement is required to

determine whether an instrument is a floating rate instrument within the scope of IAS 39.AG7 or AG8. As part of its rejection notice the IFRIC agreed to refer the issue to the Board with a recommendation that the Board should consider clarifying or expanding the application guidance.

Changes in any expected cash flows that relate to an embedded prepayment, put or call option will not normally have an effect on carrying amount. This is because one of the following two circumstances will apply.

(i) The embedded derivative is separately accounted for. As discussed in **4.1.1** above, this means that the derivative is ignored when determining the effective interest rate of the host contract.

(ii) The embedded derivative is not separately accounted for because the option's exercise price is approximately equal to the instrument's amortised cost on each exercise date. In this situation, since prepayment/put/call can only occur at an amount (approximately) equal to amortised cost, the discounted amount of future cash flows will be (approximately) unaffected by any change in expectations with respect to the exercise of said options.

This statement is not applicable for embedded prepayment, put or call options embedded in compound instruments because of the unique way in which the embedded prepayment, put or call options are assessed as being closely related and the way the liability component is separated from the instrument as a whole.

Where a prepayment, put or call option is embedded in an issued compound instrument the assessment of whether the prepayment, put or call option is considered closely related to the debt host contract is made *prior* to the instrument being split into liability and equity parts. See **3.2** in **chapter 15**. If the exercise price of the prepayment, put or call option is approximately equal to the amortised cost (prior to splitting the instrument into its liability and equity parts) it is closely related and therefore it is not separately recognised. In the case where the embedded derivative is not separately recognised the embedded prepayment, put or call option is taken into account in determining the timing and amount of the expected cash flows for the liability component when determining its amortised cost in future periods. As the liability is initially recognised at a discount to the proceeds of the instrument as a whole, yet in most cases can be early redeemed at an amount equal to the proceeds of the instrument as a whole, changes in the likelihood that the prepayment, put or call option will be exercised will impact the liability's carrying value.

Example 4.1.2A

Issuer call and holder put in convertible debt

Entity X issued a convertible debt instrument in May 20X2 with a contractual maturity of 16 years. Each bond allows the holder to convert, at any time, into one share of the issuer. The issue price is 100 per cent and redemption price is 140 per cent.

The instrument is puttable by the holders on three different dates, during the life of the instrument (May 20X6, May 20Y0 and May 20Y4). At initial recognition, Entity X considers that there is a very high probability that the instrument will be redeemed by the holders at the first put date (i.e. May 20X6), given the low price of its shares. The instrument is also callable by the issuer, starting May 20X6, if the price of the issuer's shares increases beyond 125 per cent of the redemption price. The issuer does not expect to call the instrument.

All the embedded call and put options over the instrument (excluding the conversion option that is treated as equity) are considered closely related to the debt component as the exercise prices are equal to the amortised cost of the instrument prior to the equity conversion option being separated. The embedded call and put options are therefore not separated and form part of the debt component recognised as a financial liability. The financial liability is not designated as at FVTPL. Rather it is subsequently measured at amortised cost.

The fair value of the debt component at initial recognition is the contractual cash flows of the instrument, being interest and principal at maturity, discounted by the entity's normal borrowing rate, plus the fair value of the written put less the fair value of the purchased call. The effective interest rate is the rate that exactly discounts this carrying amount with the estimated early redemption payment, in this case at May 20X6. This is the instrument's *original* effective interest rate. The difference between the total liability that includes the written put and the net proceeds at issue is assigned to the equity component.

Assuming that the expectation of repayment in May 20X6 does not change, the carrying amount of the debt component will change only for the application of the effective interest rate, i.e. it will increase by the difference between the effective interest rate and interest paid in the period. At May 20X6, the carrying amount of the liability will therefore equal par. If the put is exercised as expected, the early redemption will result in nil gain or loss.

If, however, expectations of repayment were to change (e.g. a change in market conditions were to cause the issuer to consider that the bond will be put back to the issuer on May 20Y0 instead of May 20X6), a recalculation of the carrying amount of the liability component would be required. The new carrying amount of the liability would be the re-estimated cash flows, being interest up to, and principal payable in, May 20Y0, discounted by the *original* effective interest rate. Any difference between the new carrying amount and the old carrying amount will be recognised in profit or loss.

Example 4.1.2B

Example of calculating amortised cost: financial asset

[Extract from IAS 39.IG.B.26]

Entity A purchases a debt instrument with five years remaining to maturity for its fair value of CU1,000 (including transaction costs). The instrument has a principal amount of CU1,250 and carries fixed interest of 4.7 per cent that is paid annually (CU1,250 × 4.7 per cent = CU59 per year). The contract also specifies that the borrower has an option to prepay the instrument and that no penalty will be charged for prepayment. At inception, the entity expects the borrower not to prepay.

It can be shown that in order to allocate interest receipts and the initial discount over the term of the debt instrument at a constant rate on the carrying amount, they must be accrued at the rate of 10 per cent annually. The table below provides information about the amortised cost, interest income and cash flows of the debt instrument in each reporting period.

Year	**(a) Amortised cost at the beginning of the year**	**(b = a x 10%) Interest income**	**(c) Cash flows**	**(d = a + b – c) Amortised cost at the end of the year**
20X0	1,000	100	59	1,041
20X1	1,041	104	59	1,086
20X2	1,086	109	59	1,136
20X3	1,136	113	59	1,190
20X4	1,190	119	1,250 + 59	-

On the first day of 20X2 the entity revises its estimate of cash flows. It now expects that 50 per cent of the principal will be prepaid at the end of 20X2 and the remaining 50 per cent at the end of 20X4. In accordance with IAS 39.AG8, the opening balance of the debt instrument in 20X2 is adjusted. The adjusted amount is calculated by discounting the amount the entity expects to receive in 20X2 and subsequent years using the original effective interest rate (10 per cent). This results in the new opening balance in 20X2 of CU1,138. The adjustment of CU52 (CU1,138 – CU1,086) is recorded in profit or loss in 20X2. The table below provides information about the amortised cost, interest income and cash flows as they would be adjusted taking into account the change in estimate.

Year	(a) Amortised cost at the beginning of the year	(b = a x 10%) Interest income	(c) Cash flows	(d = a + b – c) Amortised cost at the end of the year
20X0	1,000	100	59	1,041
20X1	1,041	104	59	1,086
20X2	1,086 + 52	114	625 + 59	568
20X3	568	57	30	595
20X4	595	60	625 + 30	-

If the debt instrument becomes impaired, say, at the end of 20X3, the impairment loss is calculated as the difference between the carrying amount (CU595) and the present value of estimated future cash flows discounted at the original effective interest rate (10 per cent).

4.1.3 *Fees*

The definition of the effective interest rate goes on to state that 'the calculation includes all fees and points paid or received between parties to the contract that are an integral part of the effective interest rate (see IAS 18).' [IAS 39.9] The appendix to IAS 18 includes material relevant to the determination of whether or not fees should be viewed as an integral part of the effective interest rate (and, therefore, taken into account in the calculation). The interpretation of this material will be far from straightforward in many instances. A number of examples are discussed below.

Origination fees. The appendix to IAS 18 specifically addresses origination fees received by the entity, which may include compensation for activities such as evaluating the borrower's condition, evaluating and recording security arrangements, negotiating terms, preparing and processing documents and closing the transaction. Such fees (relating to the creation or acquisition of a financial asset) are an integral part of generating an ongoing involvement with the resulting financial instrument. As such, they are deferred and recognised as an adjustment to the effective interest rate.

Commitment fees. Where a commitment fee is received by an entity to originate a loan when the loan commitment is outside of the scope of IAS 39, the Standard draws a distinction based on whether it is probable that the entity will enter into the related specific lending arrangement. If it is probable, the fee should be viewed as compensation for an ongoing involvement with the acquisition of a financial instrument (i.e. defer and recognise as an adjustment to the effective interest rate). If it is unlikely that the arrangement will be entered into, the fee is viewed as being compensation for a service provided (i.e. making the borrowing facility available for a period of time) and should be recognised on a time proportion basis over the commitment period. This will be an area in which judgement will be required in many instances.

The choice of the terms 'probable' and 'unlikely' to cover the two possible alternatives is slightly unusual. It is suggested that 'unlikely' should be interpreted as meaning anything less than probable.

Loan servicing fees. Such fees are received for the provision of a service and should be recognised as revenue as those services are provided.

Fees earned on the execution of a significant act. IAS 18 identifies the following examples of such fees: commission on the allotment of shares to a client; placement fees for arranging a loan between two third parties; and loan syndication fees. Such amounts should be recognised as revenue when the significant act has been completed.

Prepayment penalties. A borrower may be required to make a penalty payment to the lender upon early repayment. The definition of the effective interest rate explicitly states that prepayment options, along with all other contractual terms, should be taken into account. This would imply that related penalty payments, along with the effect on cash flows of the early repayment itself, should be included in the calculation. Typically, such penalties represent some form of compensation to the borrower for not receiving interest over the full term of the instrument. However, where such penalties represent only the reimbursement of administrative costs associated with an early repayment, they would not be taken into account in determining the effective interest rate on the instrument. It is also noted that such prepayment options may meet the definition of an embedded derivative that requires separate accounting – the requirements for such instruments are explained in **chapter 17**.

Unless a fee can be clearly demonstrated to relate to a particular service or the execution of a significant act (to use IAS 18 terminology), it will normally be appropriate to view the amount as an adjustment to the effective interest rate. However, it will be necessary to consider such fees carefully, on a case-by-case basis.

The appendix to IAS 18 indicates that, where fees are viewed as an integral part of generating an involvement with a financial instrument (e.g. origination or commitment fees) and are therefore treated as an adjustment to the effective interest rate, 'related transaction costs' should also be deferred. Related transaction costs should include only 'incremental costs that are directly attributable to the acquisition, issue or disposal of a financial asset or financial liability'.

4.1.4 Amortisation period

The definition of the effective interest rate (see **4.1** above) requires the amortisation of premiums/discounts, fees, points paid or received and transaction costs (those that are taken into account in calculating the effective rate) over 'the expected life of the financial instrument or, when appropriate, a shorter period.' A shorter period will be appropriate if it is the period to which the relevant premiums/discounts, fees, points paid or received or transaction costs relate. [IAS 39.AG6] For example, if a fee is received as compensation for a discounted interest rate over an initial period (which ends with a repricing to market interest rates), then that fee should be amortised over that initial period, rather than the expected life of the instrument. In general, where the variable to which the fee, transaction costs, discount or premium relates is repriced to market rates before the expected maturity of the instrument, a shorter period will be used. However, if it is another variable that is repriced, the expected life of the instrument will be used. This would be the case where the premium/discount on an instrument results from changes in the credit spread over the specified floating rate, but it is the interest rate that is repriced.

4.1.5 Measurement

There is a presumption that it will be possible to estimate reliably the cash flows and expected life of an instrument or group of similar instruments, such that the effective interest rate can be determined. However, in those 'rare cases' where that is not so, the rate should be calculated based on the contractual cash flows over the full contractual term of the instrument. [IAS 39.9]

The application of the effective interest method is illustrated in the examples below.

Example 4.1.5A

Example of calculating amortised cost: debt instruments with stepped interest payments

[Extract from IAS 39.IG.B.27]

On 1 January 20X0, Entity A issues a debt instrument for a price of CU1,250. The principal amount is CU1,250 and the debt instrument is repayable on 31 December 20X4. The rate of interest is specified in the debt agreement as a percentage of the principal amount as follows: 6.0 per cent in 20X0 (CU75),

8.0 per cent in 20X1 (CU100), 10.0 per cent in 20X2 (CU125), 12.0 per cent in 20X3 (CU150), and 16.4 per cent in 20X4 (CU205). In this case, the interest rate that exactly discounts the stream of future cash payments through maturity is 10 per cent. Therefore, cash interest payments are reallocated over the term of the debt instrument for the purposes of determining amortised cost in each period. In each period, the amortised cost at the beginning of the period is multiplied by the effective interest rate of 10 per cent and added to the amortised cost. Any cash payments in the period are deducted from the resulting number. Accordingly, the amortised cost in each period is as follows:

Year	**(a) Amortised cost at the beginning of the year**	**(b = a x 10%) Interest income**	**(c) Cash flows**	**(d = a + b – c) Amortised cost at the end of the year**
20X0	1,250	125	75	1,300
20X1	1,300	130	100	1,330
20X2	1,330	133	125	1,338
20X3	1,338	134	150	1,322
20X4	1,322	133	1,250 + 205	-

Example 4.1.5B

Accounting for a loan with a separated embedded derivative

On 1 January 20X0, an entity originates a loan of £100. Interest of £4 is receivable annually over the next 5 years (on 31 December 20X0 to 31 December 20X4). The loan is repayable at an amount of £110 on 31 December 20X4. However, the borrower can prepay (at £111 plus accrued interest for the year) at any time. As the prepayment option will result in the loan potentially being prepaid by the borrower at an amount that is not approximately equal to the amortised cost, the prepayment option is separately accounted for as an embedded derivative. The prepayment option is effectively an option written by the originator allowing the borrower to repay the borrowing at any time. Economically, the borrower will prepay the liability if the fair value of the instrument rises above £111 (plus accrued interest).

On 1 January 20X0, the fair value of the prepayment option for the originator is a £3 liability. Therefore, the remaining balance of £103 is the host contract asset.

(1) Initial recognition at 1 January 20X0

Dr	Asset	£103.00
Cr	Cash	£100.00
Cr	Prepayment option	£3.00

The effective interest rate on the host contract is 5.11 per cent.

At the end of 20X0 interest rates have fallen slightly, and the fair value of the option has risen from £3 to £5. The following entries are recorded in the entity's 20X0 financial statements:

(2) Interest income

Dr	Asset	£5.26
Cr	Interest income	£5.26

(3) Interest receipt

Dr	Cash	£4.00
Cr	Asset	£4.00

The carrying amount of the loan as at 31 December 20X0 is therefore £104.26.

(4) Embedded derivative

Dr	Profit or loss	£2.00
Cr	Embedded derivative liability	£2.00

By the end of 20X1 interest rates have fallen further, so on 31 December 20X1 the borrower repays the borrowing early. At the year end the fair value of the prepayment option is £6

(5) Interest income

Dr	Asset	£5.33
Cr	Interest income	£5.33

(6) Interest receipt

Dr	Cash	£4.00
Cr	Asset	£4.00

The carrying amount of the loan prior to early repayment is therefore £105.59.

(7) Embedded derivative

Dr	Profit or loss	£1.00
Cr	Embedded derivative liability	£1.00

(8) Early repayment of loan

Dr	Cash	£111.00
Dr	Embedded derivative liability	£6.00
Cr	Asset	£105.59
Cr	Profit or loss	£11.41

The credit in profit or loss on early repayment of the loan effectively represents the cumulative catch-up of the fair value of the host contract. As the host contract is not measured at fair value during its life, when the instrument is terminated, this results in a gain in profit or loss due to the impact of movements in interest rates that have not previously been recognised in the financial statements. As interest rates have fallen considerably, the fair value of the host contract has risen.

The above example assumes that at inception the holder of the loan considers that the put option is not likely to be exercised. If the put option was considered likely to be exercised there is an argument that the likely exercise of the put option would form part of the instrument's amortised cost and therefore would result in a different host contract being identified (see **7.1** in **chapter 17**).

Example 4.1.5C

Effective interest rate for fixed-rate perpetual debt

An entity issues a perpetual debt instrument for consideration of £100. Interest of £6 is payable annually in perpetuity. The instrument is not redeemable. The effective rate (i.e. the rate that discounts £6 annually in perpetuity to £100) is 6 per cent. Interest of £6 is recognised in profit or loss and there is no amortisation of the principal amount. This would also be the case for a floating rate instrument since, as discussed in **4.1.2** above, the effective rate is adjusted for changes in market rates for floating rate instruments.

Example 4.1.5D

Effective interest rate for stepped fixed-rate perpetual debt

An entity issues a perpetual debt instrument where the interest rate is fixed at 10% for the first 10 years and 8% for each year thereafter.

The 10% interest payments in the first ten years represent a part payment of redemption. Consequently when these payments are made the difference between 10% and 8% is treated as a reduction in the carrying amount of the liability. In the period from year ten the effective interest will be recognised at 8% as all payments relate to interest and not repayment of principal.

An alternative way of considering the higher payments in the first ten years is the sum of the differential between the 10% and 8% represents repayments on an amortising loan. The value of the amortising loan at inception less the proceeds from the instrument as a whole represents the carrying value of the perpetual debt instrument.

IAS 39.IG.B.26 has a similar fact pattern as **example 4.1.5D** above except that after year ten the interest rate reduces to zero. The implementation guidance states the amortised cost is zero after year ten because the present value of the stream of future cash payments in subsequent periods is zero.

An alternative view to the implementation guidance is that after the final payment is made at year ten the financial liability is derecognised as the entity has fully discharged any obligation to pay cash or other financial asset.

4.1.6 *Interaction of effective interest rate and fair value hedge accounting*

When an entity applies fair value hedge accounting to a hedge of a debt instrument the carrying value of the debt is adjusted for movements in the hedged risk to the extent highly effective. Fair value hedge accounting is explained in detail at **2.1** in **chapter 20**. IAS 39.92 requires the fair value adjustment to be amortised to profit or loss as early as the adjustment is made and no later than when the hedged item ceases to be fair value adjusted. This amortisation is included as part of the revised effective interest rate. Therefore, if an entity chooses to amortise the fair value adjustment as soon as the adjustment is made, then assuming the fair value adjustment changes for each subsequent reporting period as there is a change in the fair value of the hedged risk and the hedge is highly effective, a revised effective interest rate will need to be determined at the start of each reporting period. Alternatively, if an entity chooses to start to amortise the adjustment when hedge accounting ceases the entity will only need to recalculate the effective interest rate at that point.

In May 2008 the IASB issued *Improvements to IFRSs*. The improvements amended IAS 39 to make clear that the effective interest rate that is used when applying IAS 39.AG8 when revisions in estimates of cash flows occur is the original effective interest rate, except when IAS 39.92 as described above applies in which case it is the revised effective interest rate that includes the effects of the fair value hedge adjustment. The amendment to IAS 39.AG8 applies for annual periods beginning on or after 1 January 2009. If the amendment is applied to an earlier period the entity shall disclose this fact.

UK *At the time of writing,* Improvements to IFRSs *has not yet been endorsed for adoption in the EU. EU companies may, nevertheless, comply with the amendment described above prior to endorsement, since it does not conflict with the existing requirements of IAS 39.*

5 Fair value

The concept of fair value is central to the approach of IAS 39. The Standard is based on the premise that the most relevant information to provide to users, in relation to a financial instrument, will normally be its fair value. In this context, fair value is viewed as an 'exit' rather than an 'entry' price, i.e.:

- for an asset, the amount which would be realised from the disposal of the asset, rather than the amount it would cost to acquire it; and

- for a liability, the amount it would cost to discharge the liability, rather than the amount that would be received in return for taking it on.

In determining fair value, the Standard requires the maximum possible use of observable market data and the minimum use of entity-specific factors. [IAS 39.48A] If available, a quoted market price will give the best evidence of fair value, given that fair value is defined as 'the amount for which an asset could be exchanged, or a liability settled, between knowledgeable, willing parties in an arm's length transaction.' [IAS 39.9] The use of such amounts, as opposed to entity-specific information, will also promote consistent measurement across entities.

Nonetheless, the use of fair values gives rise to numerous issues of measurement. IAS 39.AG69 – AG82 provide assistance in the determination of fair value as defined in the Standard. This section outlines and amplifies this material, identifying additional issues that may arise.

It should be noted that IAS 39.AG69 explicitly states that underlying the definition of fair value is a presumption that an entity is 'a going concern without any intention or need to liquidate, to curtail materially the scale of its operations or to undertake a transaction on adverse terms.' In addition, IAS 39.AG71 states that the amount an entity would receive or pay in a forced transaction, involuntary liquidation or distress sale is not fair value.

In November 2006 the IASB issued a discussion paper entitled *Fair Value Measurement*. This discussion paper is equivalent to FAS 157, which was issued by the US FASB some months before. The issue of the discussion paper is part of the IASB and FASB's convergence agenda. The proposals are detailed in the future developments in **section 8** below.

5.1 Quoted in an active market

It will normally be relatively straightforward to determine the fair value of a financial instrument that is quoted in an active market. IAS 39 defines such a market as one in which quoted prices are readily and regularly available from an exchange, dealer, broker, industry group, pricing service or regulatory agency, and those prices represent actual and regularly occurring market transactions on an arm's length basis. [IAS 39.AG71]

'Regularly occurring market transactions' does not mean that there must be a consistent number of market transactions from one period to another. A significantly lower than normal volume of transactions does not automatically mean that either there is not an active market and the observed transactions are forced transactions or distressed sales, or that the transactions that are occurring are motivated other than by normal business considerations. It would not be appropriate to disregard observable prices in an active market even if the market is relatively thinner or illiquid as compared to previous periods.

An imbalance between supply and demand (for example, fewer buyers than sellers, thereby forcing prices down) is not the same as a forced transaction or distressed sale. If transactions are occurring between willing buyers and sellers in a manner that is usual and customary for transactions involving such instruments, then these are not forced transactions or distressed sales. Persuasive evidence is required to establish that an observable transaction is a forced or distressed sale.

Similarly, the absence of transactions for a short period does not automatically mean that a market has ceased to be active. If transactions are occurring frequently enough to obtain reliable pricing information on an ongoing basis, then that market would be considered active. However, if observed transactions are no longer regularly occurring even if prices might be available, or the only observed transactions are forced transaction or distressed sales, then the market would no longer be considered active. What is 'regularly occurring' and a 'forced transaction' or 'distressed sale' is a matter of judgement. The fact that there is no active market in one financial instrument should not be taken to imply that there are no active markets in other similar financial instruments.

Whichever market is referred to, the objective is to determine the price at which a transaction would occur in the relevant instrument, in the instrument as it is without modification or repackaging.

5.1.1 Which market?

Market quotations may vary widely from dealer to dealer and from broker to broker. It may be necessary to obtain more than one quotation from these markets to ensure that the fair value estimate is appropriate. If there is more than one quote, there may be effectively more than one market and the fair value should be based on the most advantageous market to which the entity has immediate access. [IAS 39.AG71]

It is sometimes possible for an entity to have access to more than one exit market for a financial instrument, and prices in those markets may be different – for example, where the same instrument is traded in different geographical markets, or where dealers and brokers give different quotes for the same instrument and effectively create more than one market.

The following considerations are relevant.

- An entity should consider alternative prices only if it has access to the exit markets involved. An entity has access to a market if there is no legal impediment to its participation in that market.

- Where only portfolios of instruments can be traded in a particular market, an entity has access to that market only if it holds a portfolio that could be traded in that market.

- The entity should adjust the price in the more advantageous market to reflect differences in counterparty credit risk.

The term 'most advantageous' should be interpreted in view of the generic objective of maximising profits or net assets. The 'most advantageous' price for an asset is a higher market exit price; for a liability, a lower market exit price is the 'most advantageous'. When estimating the exit value for an instrument, any specific objective of an entity, or management intent, should be disregarded.

It is important that when deciding what is the 'most advantageous' price a comparison is made on a 'like-with-like' basis. Any dissimilarities need to be adjusted for as there could be some differences in transaction costs or value enhancements. Ignoring transaction costs for comparison purposes will not show what is most advantageous to the entity. However, once the comparison is made, the price actually used as an estimate of fair value should not be adjusted to include transaction costs (see **3.1** above and **example 5.1.1A** below).

The following examples are relevant:

Example 5.1.1A

Transactions costs in different markets

An entity can sell a financial asset in two different markets:

Market	Quoted market price	Transaction costs
A	€80	€2
B	€85	€10

Transaction costs should be taken into account when determining the most advantageous market. This will be Market A, since the net cash inflow from disposal of €78 exceeds that available from Market B (€75). Therefore, the estimate of fair value that is appropriate is €80 (i.e. disregarding transaction costs that will be incurred on disposal).

Example 5.1.1B

Most advantageous price

If an entity needs to sell an asset quickly and therefore will not be able to realise the optimum price, it should not adjust the market price and report the asset at a value lower than the 'most advantageous' price. Any subsequent loss is the result of the sub-optimal disposal (and should be recorded only when that disposal occurs).

5.1.2 *Which price?*

Exchange markets provide the most reliable estimate of fair value since closing prices and volumes are readily and regularly available. The fair value is simply the closing price at the end of the last trading day of the reporting period for an instrument identical to the one being measured. Listed stocks, some options, some futures and many fixed income securities are traded on public exchanges like the London Stock Exchange, the New York Stock Exchange and Euronext. IAS 39.AG71 states that where such published price quotations exist, they should be used provided quoted prices represent actual and regularly occurring market transactions.

In dealer markets, such as the US NASDAQ and London's Alternative Investment Market (AIM), dealers stand ready to trade for their own account. Quotations are in the form of bid and ask amounts and are typically more readily available than information about closing prices and volume levels. Dealer markets are the principal exchanges for more narrowly traded securities, corporate bonds, commercial and industrial loans, asset-backed and mortgage-backed securities.

A bid quote normally represents an exit price for an asset, already adjusted for some exit costs (dealer's profit); whilst an ask quote normally represents an exit price for a liability, already adjusted for some exit costs (dealer's profit). The Standard clarifies that when these terms are used, the 'bid-ask spread' (i.e. the difference between the bid and ask for a particular instrument) should be interpreted as including only transaction costs. The quote that will normally be appropriate will differ, depending on whether the relevant instrument is an asset/liability that is held/to be acquired:

	Asset	Liability
Held	Bid	Ask *
To be acquired	Ask *	Bid

* Sometimes referred to as the 'current offer' price

The use of mid-market prices for individual assets and liabilities has been deemed inappropriate, since it would result in the recognition of up-front gains or losses for the difference between the bid/ask price and mid-market. However, if an entity has assets and liabilities with offsetting market risks, it may use mid-market prices when measuring the fair value of the offsetting positions. It will then apply the bid or ask price, as appropriate, to the net open position. [IAS 39.AG72]

Example 5.1.2A

Mid-market prices (1)

Entity X has the following financial instruments:

Asset:
Investment in 100 shares of Entity Y (an unrelated third party). The assets are classified as available-for-sale.

Liability:
Obligation to deliver 80 shares of Entity Y. The liability is held for trading. The liability was created following the entity selling shares in Entity Y that, at the time of the arrangement, Entity X did not own. This is commonly referred to as 'shorting' the shares.

The bid price for shares in Entity Y is £100, the ask price is £102. Therefore, the mid-price is £101 per share.

	Asset	**Liability**
Held	Bid (£100)	Ask (£102)
To be acquired	Ask (£102)	Bid (£100)

Entity X will value its financial instruments as follows:

Asset:

Investment in 80 shares of Entity Y at mid price	£8,080
Investment in 20 shares of Entity Y at bid price	£2,000
Sum	£10,080

Liability:

Obligation to deliver 80 shares of Entity Y at mid price	£8,080

The net of the asset and the liability is equal to £2,000, being the bid price applied to the open net asset position.

Example 5.1.2B

Mid-market prices (2)

An investment fund holds financial assets and puttable financial liabilities linked to the performance of the assets. The entity elects to designate both the assets and liabilities as at fair value through profit or loss. As the assets and liabilities have offsetting market risks, i.e. the market risk of the assets is

> offset by the market risk of the liabilities, it is permitted to apply mid-market prices for both. As the liability is linked to the performance of all invested assets there will be no open net position in this case.

The existence of regulations that require a different measurement for specific purposes is not justification for overriding the general requirements of IAS 39.AG72. For example, a regulator may require investment funds to report net asset values based on mid-market prices. If measuring at mid-prices was not compliant with IAS 39, then the entity could not apply such a technique in measuring its financial instruments. In reporting its net asset values to investors, an investment fund may wish to provide a reconciliation between fair values recognised in its statement of financial position and the prices used for the net asset value calculation. [IAS 39.IG.E.2.1]

In certain types of market, published price quotations will often not be available. Brokered markets, in which brokers attempt to match buyers and sellers but do not trade for their own account, can sometimes provide quotations for comparable completed transactions. Such information, provided it can reasonably be obtained from brokers, may represent 'actual and regularly occurring market transactions', but that will not always be the case. Similarly, prices obtained from industry groups, pricing services, regulatory agencies and other sources will need to be considered on their own merits.

5.1.3 *Other issues*

Components. If a published price quotation does not exist for a financial instrument in its entirety, but active markets exist for its component parts, fair value is determined on the basis of the market prices of those components. [IAS 39.AG72]

Large holdings. The fair value of a large holding of financial instruments is the product of the number of instruments in the holding and the fair value of an individual instrument. [IAS 39.AG72] No adjustment should be made for any premium or discount that might result from selling the portfolio as a whole. For example, an entity with a significant shareholding in another entity would often realise an amount per share in excess of, or perhaps less than, that share's market price if it were to dispose of its entire shareholding in a single transaction. The carrying amount of such a shareholding should not be adjusted to reflect this fact. The IASB's concept of fair value is based on estimating the price that would be achieved in a routine arm's length transaction under the market conditions at the measurement date. The definition is drawn within a going concern context, hence it does not assume that the entity needs to liquidate the whole position or enter into a transaction on adverse terms by accepting a discount to the market price.

Current prices unavailable. Where current prices are not available, the price of the most recent transaction in that instrument will often provide evidence of its current value. This is essentially the use of a valuation technique and is discussed in **5.2** below.

Restrictions. An entity may enter into restrictions which limit its ability to sell an underlying financial instrument. These contractual arrangements must be considered carefully to determine whether the restriction forms part of the underlying financial instrument or is a separate contractual arrangement that has been entered into by the holder of the instrument. Restrictions that form part of the contractual terms of the instrument would be incorporated into the fair value of that instrument. However, restrictions that are not part of the contractual terms of the instrument do not form part of that instrument and should not impact its fair value. For example, if the fair value of an investment in an equity security is traded in an active market but the entity separately agrees not to sell that security within a specified period, the fair value is equal to the price quoted in that active market. The opportunity loss from not being able to sell the security arises because of the separate agreement the holder has entered into (which would not normally be recognised in the statement of financial position) and does not arise from the equity security itself.

5.2 Valuation techniques

If the market for a financial instrument is not active, it will be necessary to use a valuation technique to ascertain fair value. Depending on the type and complexity of the instrument involved, and the availability of reliable input data, the nature of the appropriate technique may differ markedly. The main types are considered in the remainder of this section. Valuation techniques should incorporate all factors that market participants would consider in setting a price. [IAS 39.AG76]

Choosing a valuation technique is a highly judgemental exercise involving the selection of a method, formulae and assumptions. The risk that a technique is incorrectly specified, is based on questionable assumptions, or does not accurately reflect the true behaviour of the market is known as model risk. Model risk will be present whenever a valuation technique is used, since no technique is a perfect substitute for values evidenced by market transactions. Regardless of the level of sophistication, valuation techniques produce only a theoretical representation of market value.

Most valuation techniques are founded on arbitrage arguments, i.e. that there is no such thing as a risk-free profit in the marketplace. If there is no risk-free profit, the theoretical value of a financial instrument will be equal to the value of an equivalent alternative investment. Most techniques therefore involve evaluation of the cash flows of equivalent alternative investments.

In general, if there is a technique that is frequently used and well accepted by market participants, the entity should use that technique. However, care should be taken to ensure that the techniques used have historically provided reliable estimates of the prices obtained in actual transactions. [IAS 39.AG74] In order to assess the validity of the technique used, an entity should periodically calibrate its valuation techniques using prices from a current market transaction or based on any available observable market data. [IAS 39.AG76]

5.2.1 Inputs to valuation techniques

IAS 39.AG75 states explicitly that the valuation techniques used to estimate fair value should make the maximum use of market inputs and rely as little as possible on entity-specific inputs. This approach is consistent with the Standard's overall notion of fair value and promotes comparability between entities. The estimates and assumptions used in a valuation technique should be consistent with those that market participants would use in setting a price for a financial instrument.

The technique used should not just attempt to replicate the market's valuation technique, it should also ensure that the inputs to the technique reflect market conditions on the measurement date and represent the market's assessment of the return required for an instrument of similar risk to that which is being measured (i.e. instrument specific factors).

If a rate, rather than a price, is quoted in an active market, that market-quoted rate should be used as an input into a valuation technique. [IAS 39.AG73]

IAS 39.AG82 identifies a number of factors that may influence the fair value of a financial instrument:

- time value of money (i.e. interest at the risk-free rate);
- credit risk;
- foreign currency exchange rates;
- commodity prices;
- equity prices;

- volatility;
- prepayment or surrender risk; and
- servicing costs.

The list is not intended to be exhaustive.

The extent to which an entity may place reliance on a value or input provided by a third party (for example, a broker quote or pricing service) for an instrument that is not quoted in an active market, will depend on how the third party has derived that valuation and whether it is in accordance with the requirements of IAS 39. Factors to consider include:

- whether it reflects a price at which the entity could be expected to transact (for example, a market to which the entity has access);
- whether and how the valuation incorporates recent market events (for example, does it include 'stale' prices);
- how frequently the valuation is updated to reflect changing market conditions;
- the number of sources from which the valuation is derived (a valuation derived from many quotes or data sources is generally preferable to one based on a small number of observations);
- whether it reflects actual transactions or merely indicative prices; and
- whether it is consistent with available market information, including any current market transactions in the same or similar instruments.

5.2.2 *Recent transaction price*

The most straightforward 'valuation technique' is to base the estimate of fair value on a recent transaction price in an identical instrument. The initial acquisition or origination of a financial asset, or incurrence of a financial liability, is a market transaction for this purpose.

A recent transaction price will provide evidence of current fair value, as long as there has been no significant change in economic conditions since the relevant transaction occurred. If conditions have changed, fair value should be adjusted to reflect that change by reference to current prices or rates for similar instruments. [IAS 39.AG72] For example, a significant announcement made after the date of the most recent transaction might indicate that, if a trade were to take place at the period end, it would not establish the same price as that observed at the time of that transaction.

Example 5.2.2

Valuation including changes in market interest rates

An entity holds an investment in a corporate bond of Entity X. Nominal value is US$100. The most recent transaction price, observed on the day before the measurement date, is US$117. The bond pays interest annually at a rate of 10 per cent. The next interest payment is due on the measurement date itself. On the measurement date, interest rates rose by 0.5 per cent. What is the fair value of the investment at the measurement date?

There is a payment of interest on the measurement date and, all other factors staying equal, the fair value will be reduced to US$107 by the payment of the coupon. The fair value will also need to be adjusted for the change in market conditions: an increase in general interest rates would mean that there will be an upward adjustment to the market rate expected for an instrument of the same terms and credit risk as the bond of Entity X. Hence, the future cash flows of that bond will be discounted at a rate higher than that implied by the most recent transaction price and will produce a valuation lower than US$107.

It will not always be so straightforward to make the appropriate adjustments to a recent transaction price, since the necessary information will not always be readily available. For example, an entity holding a debt instrument that is not actively traded may not be able to determine the level of credit and other risk that market participants would attribute to the relevant counterparty when pricing the instrument. IAS 39.AG78 indicates that, in the absence of evidence to the contrary (e.g. information from other recent transactions that might indicate the appropriate credit spread), it would be reasonable to assume that no adjustment is necessary to the credit spread that existed when the instrument was acquired/originated. However, the entity would be expected to take reasonable steps to determine whether there is evidence that there has been a change in such factors.

Any events post period-end which would affect fair value would not normally be adjusted for since they would be expected to reflect circumstances arising in the following period rather than provide further evidence of the conditions existing at the end of the reporting period. IAS 10 *Events after the Reporting Period* treats a decline in market value of investments between the end of the reporting period and the date when the financial statements are authorised for issue as a non-adjusting event. IAS 10.11 states that 'the decline in market value does not normally relate to the condition of the investments at the end of the reporting period, but reflects circumstances that have arisen subsequently. Therefore, an entity does not adjust the amounts recognised in its financial statements for the investments. Similarly, the entity does not update the amounts disclosed for the investments as at the end of the reporting period, although it may need to give additional disclosure.'

A further complication will arise if it can be demonstrated that the last transaction price was not representative of fair value. This might be the case if, for example:

- the recent transaction occurred between two entities, one or both of which were experiencing severe financial difficulties such as bankruptcy, court orders, orders from regulators, or other extreme legal or financial pressures;
- the price established in a recent transaction would have been different if not for other transactions, contracts, or agreements between the transacting parties;
- the recent transaction is between related parties;
- the recent transaction was the sale of a large holding; and
- some publicly acknowledged errors or irregularities were affecting the observed price at the time of the recent transaction.

An entity will need to consider whether the valuation of a financial instrument should incorporate additional information that adjusts the last transaction price in order for the valuation technique to generate a fair value.

5.2.3 *Comparison to a similar instrument*

Another method of establishing fair value is to draw a comparison with a similar instrument to that being valued. Such an approach will be appropriate, provided the estimation of the effects of differences between the instruments on fair value is practicable.

The process of estimating fair value of an instrument by reference to a market exit price for a similar instrument is a three step process.

(i) Understand the instrument that needs to be measured.

(ii) Identify a similar instrument with a quoted market price (or a recent transaction that can be used to establish its fair value).

(iii) Quantify the effect of any differences and adjust the market price of the similar instrument for this effect.

In order for an instrument to be 'similar' for this purpose, it will be necessary for the two instruments to have contractually specified cash flows which are similar in amounts and timings, and have similar risk attributes. Risk attributes will be similar if both instruments have similar prepayment expectations, credit risk (including collateral) and marketability, and are issued by entities with similar industry and geographical bases.

Similarity can be affected by the absolute size of the investment: £1 million placed on deposit often earns interest at a higher rate than £1,000 placed on deposit. Therefore, the contractual cash flows of a £1 million term deposit will be greater than those one would calculate using 1000 times the return on £1,000, hence an adjustment would be required to achieve similarity.

It is important to note that the effect of any differences must be reasonably determinable. For example, with individual equity investments the differences are so significant that no two equity investments are ever likely to be similar – the value is affected by intangibles and other 'soft' assets like reputation and quality of management which, under the current reporting framework, are not recorded in the statement of financial position or measured in any consistent fashion, but which do affect the market price.

5.2.4 *Other valuation techniques*

It is not always possible to establish the fair value of an instrument by reference to market prices, as outlined above. In such situations it will be necessary to use an alternative technique. Appropriate techniques might range from simple discounted cash flow calculations to complex option pricing models (such as Black-Scholes-Merton and binomial models).

In applying a discounted cash flow analysis, an entity uses discount rates equal to the prevailing rates of return for financial instruments having substantially the same terms and characteristics, including the credit quality of the instrument, the remaining term over which the contractual interest rate is fixed, the remaining term to repayment of the principal and the currency in which payments are to be made. Short-term receivables and payables with no stated interest rate may be measured at the original invoice amount if the effect of discounting is immaterial. [IAS 39.AG79]

As market prices reflect the market's best estimate of the present value of the future cash flows arising from an instrument, in one way or another, an alternative valuation technique will attempt to estimate this present value. The technique/model selected will need to be consistent with the objectives and criteria previously discussed in this section.

5.2.5 *Day 1 P&L*

IAS 39 provides guidance on the initial and subsequent measurement of financial instruments where a valuation technique does not solely use observable market data (this is commonly referred to as 'day 1 p&l'). In such cases no gain or loss should be recognised on initial recognition of a financial instrument. Furthermore, a gain or loss shall be recognised subsequently only to the extent that it arises from a change in a factor (including time) that market participants would consider in setting a price. [IAS 39.AG76A]

Example 5.2.5A

Day 1 P&L (1)

Bank A sells a 30 year cash settled forward sale contract over a commodity to Entity B.

Forward prices for the specific commodity are freely quoted in the market for 10, 15, and 20 year periods. Bank A uses an extrapolation technique and its proprietary pricing system to estimate the 30 year forward rate and incorporates an additional premium on top of this internal price. Some of the premium may be received in cash at inception and some may be included in the contracted price of the forward contract.

The valuation technique uses both the available forward prices and Bank A's estimates of the commodity prices between years 20 and 30. As some of the inputs are entity specific and not observable, a day 1 profit cannot be recognised.

Example 5.2.5B

Day 1 P&L (2)

Investment Bank X issues credit-linked notes to institutional investors.

The credit-linked notes are debt instruments with an interest rate higher than normal bonds issued by the Bank because the performance of the notes is linked to the performance of a basket of underlying corporate bonds. The terms require that if a corporate bond in the basket defaults, then the notional principal will be reset on the next payment date to reflect the outstanding value of the remaining bonds in the basket. This term is commonly referred to as 'first-to-default', as it is the first bond in the basket that defaults which results in the early repayment of the notes at an amount less than was originally invested by the holder.

Bank X does not actually hold the corporate bonds that the credit-linked notes are linked to. Instead Bank X purchases a large number of credit default options over the individual corporate bonds. These purchased options serve as an economic hedge in case any of the referenced credits default. The remaining proceeds from issuing the credit-linked notes are invested in high quality government debt.

If the credit-linked notes are not traded in an active market, then Bank X must use a valuation technique to measure the financial liability. At inception it is assumed that the proceeds received from the issuance of the bonds are equal to the fair value.

It would not be possible to recognise an upfront profit on initial recognition of the credit-linked notes, even if the sum paid to purchase the government bonds and the credit options is less than the proceeds from the notes if:

- there are no other observable current market transactions in the same credit-linked notes with the same terms over the same portfolio of corporate credits; or
- if the valuation of the credit-linked notes includes non-observable market data, e.g. default correlation data between the different corporate credits where this data is not sourced from observable markets.

Using unobservable inputs to calculate a fair value different to the transaction price on day 1 involves a high degree of subjectivity and therefore the day 1 profit should not be recognised immediately. There is little clarity as to when this profit can be recognised. This deferred day 1 p&l could be deferred until all market inputs become observable, or instead released over the life of the transaction using a systematic basis. The simplest technique is straight-line amortisation, though non-linear techniques could, in theory, be adopted particularly in the instance where the item concerned acts in a non-linear fashion, for example option based contracts.

Example 5.2.5C

Day 1 P&L (3)

A bank charges a fee for issuing a short-term loan commitment within the scope of IAS 39 that is higher than the bank's estimate of the fair value of the loan commitment using its proprietary valuation model. The bank does not recognise an upfront gain but measures the derivative loan commitment at the transaction price.

Per IAS 39.AG76A, the bank should recognise in earnings observable changes in the fair value of the derivative that have occurred subsequent to initial recognition that a market participant would consider in setting a price. Unless the bank can demonstrate objectively that the fair value of the derivative loan commitment has changed due to changes in mortgage rates or other factors (that would qualify as observable market data) occurring subsequent to initial recognition, the bank should not recognise a change in the fair value of the loan commitment as profit.

To illustrate, the bank received €500 to issue the loan commitment and the bank's proprietary model valued the commitment at €300. The bank would initially recognise a derivative liability at €500 equivalent to the cash received. Assume that at the next measurement date, adjusting the valuation model for observable market changes, the estimated value was €200 (a decrease of €100 from the previous model estimate). The bank reduces the derivative liability to €400 and recognises €100 as a fair value movement in earnings.

The initial difference of €200 (€500 – €300) can be either amortised or deferred (and recognised in profit or loss at the maturity date if the loan commitment was not exercised, or included in the carrying amount of the loan and recognised in profit or loss through the effective interest rate, if the loan commitment was exercised).

5.2.6 *Applying the fair value hierarchy*

The following table sets out how the fair value hierarchy is applied for instruments commonly used in the energy markets, starting from those quoted in an active market down to those which require other valuation techniques where a greater degree of subjectivity exists and greater use of judgement is required.

Price derivation process	**Example instruments**
Quoted price in an active (liquid) market.	Standard short dated wholesale trades such as NYMEX.
Comparable/proxy instrument with quoted price in an active market if there is a high degree of correlation with the instrument being valued. For example, quoted NBP gas prices may be used to value a contract for gas delivery at delivery point if there is a high level of correlation between NBP and delivery point market prices.	Standard short dated wholesale trades such as NBP '97, IPE, GTMA and oil swaps.
Conventional model based on direct 'market' inputs.	Bilateral deals such as capacity, storage; non-market delivery periods such as overnights and short-dated vanilla options.

Conventional model based on indirect market inputs, such as interpolations of price curves or proxy market inputs. Interpolations can be used for unpriced periods using quoted market prices for points before and after that are not significantly spread apart in price and time, or for implied traded option volatility. Example proxy inputs would be using observable gas prices and heat rates to determine electricity prices if historical evidence and observable market information indicates there is a high degree of correlation with the proxy.	Bilateral deals such as capacity, storage; non-market delivery periods such as overnights and short-dated vanilla options.
Model based on more subjective inputs or proprietary models. Some subjective inputs may include: • estimates of option volatility (e.g. based on historical prices of the underlying); • forward curves constructed using econometric data such as expected supply and demand of commodities; and • extrapolation of price curves for terms beyond the periods in which there are active market quotes.	Complex bilateral contracts which: • are relatively long-term in comparison with similar contracts; • involve underlyings that are not supported by deep and active markets such as with developing contract types; and • involve complex or long-dated optionality.

5.3 Demand features

IAS 39 clarifies the approach that should be adopted in relation to financial liabilities with a demand feature (e.g. demand deposits). It states that the fair value of such liabilities is not less than the amount payable on demand, discounted from the first date that the amount could be required to be paid. [IAS 39.49] Put another way, it is not appropriate to apply a further discount to such liabilities to reflect an expectation that repayment will not be required on the first date possible (even if this expectation is supported by empirical evidence).

6 Impairment

IAS 39 requires all financial assets, with the exception of those measured at FVTPL, to be reviewed for impairment. The approach specified in the Standard is explained in this section.

The two most notable characteristics of the IAS 39 impairment model are:

(i) impairment losses should be recognised when they are incurred, rather than as expected;

(ii) an impairment loss should be regarded as incurred if, and only if, there is objective evidence of impairment as a result of one or more events that occurred after initial recognition (a 'loss event').

6.1 Evidence of impairment

The Standard requires an assessment, at the end of each reporting period, of whether there is any objective evidence that a financial asset or group of financial assets is impaired. An asset is impaired, and an impairment loss recognised, if and only if, such evidence exists. [IAS 39.58]

6.1.1 Loss events

Impairment losses are incurred on a financial asset or a group of financial assets if, and only if, there is objective evidence of an impairment that results from one or more events that occurred after the initial recognition of the asset (a 'loss event'). [IAS 39.59]

The following points are important to note.

- Such loss events must have an impact on the estimated future cash flows of the asset, or group of assets, that can be reliably measured.
- An impairment may occur as the result of the combined effect of several events – it is not always possible to identify a single, discrete event that caused the impairment.
- Losses expected as a result of future events are not recognised (no matter how likely those events might be).

The Standard gives a number of examples of possible loss events:

[IAS 39.59]

(a) significant financial difficulty of the issuer or obligor;

(b) a breach of contract, such as a default or delinquency in interest or principal payments;

(c) the lender, for economic or legal reasons relating to the borrower's financial difficulty, granting to the borrower a concession that the lender would not otherwise consider;

(d) it becoming probable that the borrower will enter bankruptcy or other financial reorganisation;

(e) the disappearance of an active market for that financial asset because of financial difficulties, or

(f) observable data indicating that there is a measurable decrease in the estimated future cash flows from a group of financial assets since the initial recognition of those assets, although the decrease cannot yet be identified with the individual financial assets in the group, including:

  (i) adverse changes in the payment status of borrowers in the group (e.g. an increased number of delayed payments or an increased number of credit card borrowers who have reached their credit limit and are paying the minimum monthly amount); or

  (ii) national or local economic conditions that correlate with defaults on the assets in the group (e.g. an increase in the unemployment rate in the geographical area of the borrowers, a decrease in property prices for mortgages in the relevant area, a decrease in oil prices for loan assets to oil producers, or adverse changes in industry conditions that affect the borrowers in the group).

The following are not, in themselves, evidence of an impairment.

- In contrast to (e) above, the disappearance of an active market because an entity's financial instruments are no longer publicly traded.
- A downgrading of an entity's credit rating, in the absence of other information suggesting the occurrence of a loss event.
- A decline in the fair value of a financial asset below its cost or amortised cost (the Standard gives the example of a decline in the fair value of a debt instrument resulting from an increase in the risk-free interest rate).

A change in the fair value of a fixed rate debt investment due to movements in the *risk-free interest rate* would never by itself be objective evidence of impairment. Also, changes in the fair value of a fixed rate debt investment due to movements in market interest rates will generally not be indicative of impairment as movements in market interest rates are never specific to the credit quality of the investment that is held. [IAS 39.IG.E.4.10]

However, it is possible that a fall in fair value due to an increase in the borrower's specific interest rate (i.e. due to an increase in the credit spread of the borrower) could be indicative of impairment when considered with other evidence supporting that a loss event has been incurred. [IAS 39.AG22(a)]

Losses that are expected to arise as a result of future events are not recognised. This holds true no matter how likely such events might be. The most obvious example of an expected future event in this context is the future default of a counterparty if a default was expected already at origination. Often an entity will have reliable empirical evidence of the rate of default for a particular class of borrower. However, the existence of such evidence does not imply that an impairment loss should be recorded. Otherwise a 'day-one' loss would be recorded upon the origination or acquisition of many financial assets (future cash flows used to calculate the effective interest rate do not reflect future credit losses – see **4.1.1** above). This 'incurred loss', as opposed to 'expected loss', approach is a key characteristic of the impairment model of IAS 39.

There is a subtle difference between not including future credit losses in the effective interest rate, and using the effective interest rate at inception, which may or may not be equivalent to the contractual rate on the instrument that will clearly include a credit spread and reflects the credit quality of the counterparty.

For example, if a financial asset is purchased at a discount to its initial issue price because there has been a worsening of the credit quality of the counterparty (but there is no loss event) between the issue date and the acquisition date, the effective interest rate will reflect the rate that exactly discounts the cash flows until maturity without taking into account expected credit losses. The effective interest rate therefore will be higher than the rate that would have been achieved had the asset been purchased originally at the issue date. Even though the credit spread inherent in the effective interest rate is higher than it is at inception, this is not evidence of impairment itself. When a loss event occurs, only then will an impairment loss be recognised.

In some cases, financial assets are acquired at a deep discount that reflects incurred credit losses. Entities include such incurred credit losses in the estimated cash flows when computing the effective interest rate. [IAS 39.AG5]

It is not necessary to be able to identify a single, discrete event in order to conclude that an impairment loss has occurred. In addition to point (e) of the list above, the following factors should be considered in determining whether there is objective evidence that an impairment loss has been incurred:

[IAS 39.IG.E.4.1]

- information about the counterparty's liquidity, solvency and business and financial risk exposures;
- levels of and trends in delinquencies for similar financial assets;
- national and local economic trends and conditions; and
- the fair value of collateral and guarantees.

In assessing financial assets or groups of financial assets for impairment an entity considers financial guarantees and any existing collateral. IAS 39.AG84 states that when considering impairment an entity should take into account the cash flows from the foreclosure of collateral. IAS 39.IG.E.4.1 states that in determining whether there is objective evidence that an impairment loss has been incurred the entity must consider the existence of guarantees over the financial asset. The accounting for financial guarantee contract is detailed at **2.3.2** in **chapter 13**. As the effect of guarantees are incorporated into the impairment assessment an entity will not recognise both a contingent asset for the claim under a financial guarantee contract in the case of loss under a specified asset and an equal impairment loss on that recognised specified asset. Instead the existence of the guarantee will limit the impairment loss recognised.

6.1.2 *Equity investments*

In addition to the potential loss events discussed above, further factors will apply when considering the impairment of equity investments. Information about significant changes with an adverse effect that have taken place in the technological, market, economic or legal environment in which the issuer operates may constitute objective evidence of an impairment. A significant or prolonged decline in fair value (below cost) is objective evidence of impairment. [IAS 39.61] See **6.4** below.

When considering what is a 'significant or prolonged decline in fair value' of an equity security below cost, the investor must compare the original cost in the investor's functional currency at the date of acquisition compared with the fair value of the equity security, also in the investor's functional currency, on the re-measurement date. If an entity purchased a listed foreign currency denominated equity security whose fair value in local currency terms has remained relatively stable since acquisition, but the currency depreciated significantly or has been depreciating for a prolonged period, this would constitute impairment, as losses that are attributable to foreign currency losses are a portion of the overall net fair value loss of an equity security.

The Standard contains separate rules for the measurement of impairment losses to be applied to financial assets that are (i) carried at amortised cost; (ii) carried at cost; and, (iii) classified as available-for-sale.

6.2 Assets carried at amortised cost

The requirements outlined in this section are relevant for financial assets classified as either loans and receivables or held-to-maturity.

Once an impairment loss has been identified, its amount is measured as the difference between the asset's carrying amount and the present value of estimated future cash flows, discounted at the original effective interest rate. This amount is then recognised in profit or loss. The carrying amount of the asset is reduced, either directly or through use of an allowance account. [IAS 39.63] However, as a practical expedient, the impairment loss can be measured on the basis of an asset's fair value using an observable market price. [IAS 39.AG84]

In circumstances in which there is a range of possible amounts, a loss equal to the best estimate within that range should be recognised. Where there is a continuous range of possible amounts, and each point in that range is as likely as any other, the mid-point of the range is used.

For collateralised assets, the estimated cash flows that should be used to calculate any impairment reflect the cash flows that might result from foreclosure, less the costs of obtaining and selling the collateral. [IAS 39.AG84] Collateral should not be recognised as a separate asset before foreclosure. [IAS 39.IG.E.4.8]

6.2.1 *Discount rate*

In calculating an impairment loss, expected future cash flows are discounted at the original effective interest rate. As a result, **only** the effect of the reduction in cash flows is recognised as a loss – that amount is not affected by other factors (for example, changes in the market interest rate, or the credit rating of the borrower) that might impact on the fair value of the asset.

Where the terms of a loan are renegotiated due to the financial difficulties of the borrower/issuer, any impairment is still measured by reference to the original effective interest rate before the modification of terms. [IAS 39.AG84]

Two particular instances in which a different rate should be used are as follows.

(i) For a variable rate asset, impairment should be measured using the current effective interest rate determined under the contract (see **4.1.2** above).

(ii) The carrying amount of an asset designated as a hedging item in a fair value hedge of interest rate risk will be adjusted for fair value changes attributable to interest rate movements. The original effective interest rate then becomes irrelevant and the rate is recalculated using the adjusted carrying amount of the loan. [IAS 39.IG.E.4.4]

The IAS 39 impairment model is illustrated in the simple example below:

Example 6.2.1

Determining the amount of impairment for a loan

On 1 January 20X0, an entity originates a loan of €100. The loan attracts five annual repayments of €25 on 31 December 20X0 to 31 December 20X4. Ignoring future credit losses, it is expected that all contractual cash flows will be received, hence the effective interest rate is 7.93 per cent and the following entries are recorded in the entity's 20X0 accounts:

(1) Initial recognition		
Dr	Asset	€100.00
Cr	Cash	€100.00
(2) Interest income		
Dr	Asset	€7.93
Cr	Interest income	€7.93
(3) Repayment		
Dr	Cash	€25.00
Cr	Asset	€25.00

The carrying amount of the loan as at 31 December 20X0 is therefore €82.93.

On 1 January 20X1, the entity receives information regarding the future prospects of the sector in which the borrower operates. This information coincides with a downgrading of the borrower's credit rating. Together, these two occurrences are deemed to constitute a loss event and it is now expected that the 20X3 and 20X4 repayments will not be received.

The revised carrying amount of the loan is calculated by discounting the expected future cash flows (i.e. the 20X1 and 20X2 repayments) at the original effective interest rate:

€25/1.0793 + €25/1.0793^2 = €44.62

Therefore an impairment loss of €38.31 (i.e. €82.93 – €44.62) is recorded:

Dr	Profit or loss	€38.31
Cr	Asset	€38.31

6.2.2 *Groups of assets*

IAS 39 contains specific requirements to be employed when considering the impairment of a group of financial assets. It is first necessary to consider whether there is objective evidence of an impairment for financial assets that are 'individually significant'. Assets that are not individually significant may be assessed either individually or collectively. [IAS 39.64] There is no guidance on the appropriate interpretation of the term 'individually significant' and it is, undoubtedly, an area of considerable judgement for management.

Measurement of impairment on a portfolio basis may be applied to groups of small balance items and to financial assets that are individually assessed and found not to be impaired when there is indication of impairment in a group of similar assets and impairment cannot be identified with an individual asset in that group. [IAS 39.IG.E.4.7]

If a collective assessment is to be undertaken, it should include financial assets that have been considered individually, whether or not they are individually significant, for which no impairment has been recorded. Assets that have been considered individually, and for which an impairment is (or continues to be) recognised, are not included in the collective assessment.

Where an asset that is considered individually and no impairment loss is recognised purely due to the existence of a collateral, an issue arises whether that asset should then also be considered in a collective assessment. As the asset itself is not impaired it would seem inappropriate to treat it any differently to an identical uncollateralised asset and, hence, it should not be included in a collective assessment.

The asset groups used for collective assessment of impairment should be defined to include financial assets with similar credit risk characteristics. IAS 39.AG87 gives the example of using 'a credit risk evaluation or grading process that considers asset type, industry, geographical location, collateral type, past-due status and other relevant factors.' If groups sharing similar risk characteristics cannot be identified, the collective assessment cannot be performed.

In determining the impact of external factors on whether an impairment loss should be recognised on an individual or collective basis, each external factor needs to be considered carefully to determine whether that factor relates only to the specific counterparty to the referenced asset, or more widely to the industry in which that counterparty operates in.

For example, if an external factor impacts on a specific loan asset more than other loan assets originated to other entities within the industry, then that factor may be more relevant to an individual assessment of impairment and not on a collective basis. The fact that an external factor exposes the counterparty to a much greater degree than its competitors within the same industry may suggest that this factor is more relevant in an individual impairment analysis. The factor may need to be reapplied along with other factors on a collective impairment assessment if it also impacts on the rest of the industry.

It should be noted that the characteristics of assets that have been assessed individually, and found not to be impaired, will differ from those assets assessed only on a collective basis. This should be taken into account in performing the collective assessment and, as a result, a different amount of impairment may be required.

As soon as information is available that specifically identifies losses on individual assets, those assets are removed from the collective assessment. [IAS 39.AG88]

The application guidance to IAS 39 provides further guidance on how to perform a collective impairment assessment. [IAS 39.AG89-AG92] The main elements of this guidance are as follows.

- Future cash flows for an asset group are estimated on the basis of historical loss experience for assets with similar credit risk characteristics to the group.
- Information about historical loss rates should be applied to groups that are defined in a manner consistent with the groups for which that information was observed.

- Peer-group experience is used if there is no, or insufficient, entity-specific loss experience.
- Historical loss experience is adjusted on the basis of current observable data so that it is consistent with current conditions.
- The methodology and assumptions used to estimate future cash flows are reviewed regularly.

Most importantly, collective assessments of impairment will still reflect the incurred loss model and will not result in the recognition of expected future losses. The aim is to reflect, on a portfolio basis, the effect of loss events that have occurred with respect to individual assets in the group (but have not yet been identified on an individual asset basis). IAS 39 provides an example of an entity that determines on the basis of historical experience that one of the main causes of default on credit card loans is the death of the borrower. The entity may observe that the death rate is unchanged from one year to the next. Nevertheless, some of the borrowers in the entity's group of credit card loans may have died in that year, indicating that an impairment loss has occurred on those loans, even if, at the year-end, the entity is not yet aware which specific borrowers have died. It would be appropriate for an impairment loss to be recognised for these 'incurred but not reported' losses. However, it would not be appropriate to recognise an impairment loss for deaths that are expected to occur in a future period, because the necessary loss event (the death of the borrower) has not yet occurred. [IAS 39.AG90]

Consistent with the principle of only recognising incurred but not reported losses, if a formulae-based approach or statistical method is employed, the method must not give rise to an impairment loss on initial recognition. Such methods may be used only if they are consistent with the guidance above and:

- incorporate the effects of the time value of money;
- consider the cash flows for the whole of the remaining life of an asset; and
- consider the age of loans within the portfolio.

It is not permissible to set aside additional provisions or reserves in excess of the amount of impairment or bad debt losses that are recognised under IAS 39. [IAS 39.IG.E.4.6]

6.2.3 *Reversals*

If the amount of a past impairment loss decreases and the decrease can be related objectively to an event occurring after the impairment was recognised, then the impairment is reversed through profit or loss. However, the carrying amount should not be increased to an amount that exceeds what the amortised cost would have been (at the date of the reversal) had the impairment not been recognised. [IAS 39.65] It should be noted that, to qualify for recognition, a reversal does **not** need to have resulted from the same factor that caused the original impairment.

6.2.4 *Subsequent interest*

Once an impairment loss has been recognised, subsequent interest income is recognised using the rate of interest used to discount the future cash flows in measuring that impairment. [IAS 39.AG93] IAS 39 does not allow for non-accrual of interest following impairment.

In the case of a floating rate financial asset the rate used to discount future cash flows in measuring impairment will be the current effective interest rate since the effective interest rate is updated through the asset's life as the market rates change (see **6.2.1** above). This is consistent with the requirements of IAS 39.AG93 which state that once a financial asset has been written down as a result of an impairment loss, interest income is thereafter recognised using the rate of interest used to discount the future cash flows for the purpose of measuring the impairment loss. In this case, the 'rate' of interest, is a 'floating rate'. Entities may have a preference for 'freezing' the effective interest rate at the date of impairment, as opposed to updating the effective interest rate after the impairment date, but this is contrary to the principle in the Standard that interest income on floating rate loans is recognised at the current floating rate.

6.2.5 *Distressed debt*

An entity must determine the effective interest rate of acquired distressed debt on the date the debt is acquired, ignoring future credit losses that may be expected to occur. The impact of previous impairment will have already been reflected in the purchase of the debt.

Example 6.2.5

Effective interest rate on distressed debt

Entity B acquires distressed debt. The fair value of the consideration paid to acquire the debt is €60. The debt is contracted to redeem at par (€100) at its maturity. The low consideration paid reflects the fact that prior to Entity B's acquisition of the debt, the debt was subject to impairment.

In order to determine the interest to be received on the debt Entity B must determine the effective interest rate at acquisition. The effective interest rate will incorporate the cash flows expected to be received on the debt (i.e. it will incorporate the impact of the impairment event) because incurred credit losses are considered in computing the effective interest rate for financial assets acquired at a deep discount. [IAS 39.AG5] This treatment is consistent with the prohibition on recognising expected future losses in the effective interest rate [IAS 39.59] as upon acquisition of the distressed debt, the impairment event had already occurred. [IAS 39.BC32]

To the extent the recovery of the asset improves as a result of a reversal of factors that led to the original impairment, this shall not be recorded as a reversal of impairment as the original impairment charge was not included in Entity B's financial statements. Instead, Entity B would revise its estimate of expected cash flows and recognise a cumulative catch-up in profit or loss to adjust the carrying amount of the asset by discounting the revised expected cash flows at the original effective interest rate (the effective interest rate computed at initial recognition when Entity B acquired the asset). [IAS 39.AG8]

6.3 Assets carried at cost

Unquoted equity instruments (and derivatives that result in physical delivery of unquoted equity investments) whose fair value cannot be reliably measured are shown at cost (see **3.1.6** above). For such instruments, if there is objective evidence of an impairment (as discussed in **6.1** above), the amount of the impairment loss is measured as the difference between carrying amount and the present value of estimated future cash flows discounted at the current rate of return for a similar financial asset. [IAS 39.66]

Once an impairment loss has been recognised on a financial asset recognised at cost, it is not permitted to recognise a reversal.

6.4 Available-for-sale financial assets

If a decline in the fair value of an available-for-sale financial asset has been recognised in other comprehensive income under the requirements discussed in **3.1.4** above, and there is objective evidence of an impairment (as discussed in **6.1**), the cumulative loss that had been recognised in other comprehensive income is reclassified from equity to profit or loss. The amount of cumulative loss is the difference between the acquisition cost (net of principal repayments and amortisation) and the current fair value, less any impairment loss previously recognised in profit or loss. [IAS 39.67 & 68] Any portion of the cumulative net loss that is attributable to foreign currency movements that had been recognised in other comprehensive income in the case of a non-monetary item is also reclassified from equity to profit or loss. [IAS 39.IG.E.4.9]

An impairment of an available-for-sale equity investment does not establish a new deemed cost for that investment. The test of whether there has been a 'significant or prolonged decline in the fair value of an investment in an equity instrument below its cost' is with reference to the original cost on initial recognition (not the carrying amount after the previous impairment) and 'prolonged' should be evaluated against that period in which the fair value of the investment has been below original cost at initial recognition. [IAS 39.61] IAS 39 does not allow entities to consider only the period since the last impairment loss was recognised in profit or loss nor does it allow entities to segregate different loss events in order to evaluate the significance and duration of each event separately. Therefore, once an impairment loss is recognised in profit or loss any further decline in value must be recognised immediately in profit or loss. [IAS 39.IG.E.4.9] This was confirmed by the IFRIC in April 2005.

It is unlikely that an entity could apply a portfolio approach for assessing impairment of available-for-sale equity securities. As equity securities are issued by different entities they are unlikely to have similar risk characteristics as their exposure to equity price risk will differ.

If an entity holds an investment in a fund that invests in equity securities, and the investment is classified as an available-for-sale investment, the investor should assess impairment based on a comparison of cost and fair value of the investment in the fund, not by looking through the fund to the individual equity securities held by the fund.

6.4.1 *Reversals*

The approach adopted in relation to reversals of past impairments differs for investments in debt and equity instruments:

Equity instruments. Once an impairment loss has been recognised on an available-for-sale equity investment, it is not permitted to recognise a reversal through profit or loss. [IAS 39.69]

Debt instruments. If the fair value of an available-for-sale debt instrument increases and the increase can be related objectively to an event occurring after the impairment was recognised, then the impairment is reversed through profit or loss. [IAS 39.70] It should be noted that, to qualify for recognition, a reversal does **not** need to have resulted from the same factor that caused the original impairment.

IAS 39.BC127 – BC130 explain the rationale for this difference in approach. Primarily, the IASB took the view that reversals of impairments in debt instruments are more objectively determinable than those in equity instruments. In particular, for equity instruments the IASB 'could not find an acceptable way to distinguish reversals of impairment losses from other increases in fair value.' This is consistent with the approach taken for unquoted equity instruments measured at cost (see **6.3** above).

A puttable instrument issued by an entity (e.g. a fund), under which the holder can put it back to the issuer at any time for cash equal to a proportionate share of the net asset value of the entity, should be considered an equity instrument when establishing whether a reversal of impairment is appropriate. As the instrument does not have specified payments and a fixed maturity it is an equity investment and, therefore, any reversal of a previously recognised impairment through profit or loss account is not permitted if it is classified as an available-for-sale financial asset.

6.4.1.1 *Interim financial reporting and impairments*

IFRIC Interpretation 10 *Interim Financial Reporting and Impairment*, published in July 2006, provides guidance on the interaction between the requirements of IAS 34 *Interim Financial Reporting* and the recognition of impairment losses for certain financial assets under IAS 39. In respect of investments in equity instruments or a financial asset carried at cost, the Interpretation clarifies that an entity should not reverse an impairment loss recognised in a previous interim period.

Example 6.4.1.1

Interaction of impairment and interim financial reporting

On 1 January 20X1 Entity A and Entity B each buy small shareholdings of equity instruments of Entity X for €100. Both entities classify their investments in the quoted equity instruments as available-for-sale. Accordingly, IAS 39.55(b) requires gains and losses to be recorded in other comprehensive income except for impairment losses which are recognised in profit or loss.

Entity A is listed on its national stock exchange which requires interim reports in accordance with IFRSs on a semi-annual basis. Entity B is required to prepare IFRS financial statements on an annual basis for statutory purposes. On 30 June 20X1 Entity X shows signs of severe financial difficulties

> with the share price declined to €80. While preparing its interim report Entity A concludes that its investment in Entity X is impaired and recognises an impairment loss of €20 in profit or loss. As Entity B is not required to prepare a semi-annual report it does not review its equity instruments for evidence of impairment at that point in time.
>
> On 31 December 20X1 the financial condition of Entity X has fully recovered due to a successful debt restructuring with the share price having risen to €120. Both Entity A and Entity B conclude that the original cost of the investment is recoverable. However, while Entity B does not recognise an impairment loss in its annual IFRS financial statements, Entity A is prohibited from reversing the impairment loss recognised in its interim report. The result is that Entity A and Entity B have different carrying amounts for exactly the same equity instrument.

6.5 Measurement difficulties

The IASB acknowledges that in some cases, the observable data required to estimate the amount of an impairment loss on a financial asset may not be available or relevant to current circumstances. [IAS 39.62] In such cases, the use of 'experienced judgement' is required. In a collective impairment assessment, **6.2.2** above gives guidance on the approach to be adopted if measurement is less than straightforward.

7 Implications for business combinations

The revised version of IFRS 3 *Business Combinations* issued in January 2008 requires the acquirer to recognise all identifiable assets and liabilities at fair value at the date of the business combination and to reassess classifications and designations of all contractual arrangements, with the exception of classification of leases as finance or operating leases and the classification of insurance contracts. The acquirer in the group financial statements will make all the classification decisions it would have made had the entity acquired the acquiree's financial instruments separately, i.e. not as part of a business combination.

It is worth noting that subsequent measurement of financial instruments by the acquirer in the group financial statements may differ to the acquiree's financial statements. The acquirer may make different classification decisions than those that were originally made by the acquiree. For example, the acquirer may designate a financial instrument carried by the acquiree at amortised cost as at fair value through profit or loss or available-for-sale. Even if classification and the measurement basis are the same, for example, an asset is classified as a loan and receivable held at amortised cost in both the acquiree's financial statements and the acquirer's group financial statements, the amount recognised in the group's statement of financial position and statement of comprehensive income in respect of that asset may be different from the amounts recognised by the acquiree. The acquirer recognises the asset at fair value at the time of acquisition and that amount may be different from the carrying value of the asset in the financial statements of the acquiree both at initial recognition and at the date of acquisition. Thus, going forward, the acquirer will record a different effective interest rate to that recorded by the acquiree. This effective interest rate will impact interest recognition and measurement of any future impairment. Also, the acquiree may reverse an impairment loss in its own financial statements but the acquirer will not if the reversal is an impairment that occurred in the acquiree prior to the acquisition date.

The above illustrations are not exhaustive as there are many other differences that can arise when comparing the subsequent measurement of financial instruments by the acquiree and acquirer.

8 Future developments

8.1 Fair value measurement

In November 2006 the IASB issued a discussion paper titled *Fair Value Measurement*. This discussion paper is equivalent to FAS 157 in US GAAP that is effective for financial statements issued for financial years beginning after 15 November 2007. As the IASB has issued the US standard only as a discussion paper, it will be some time before the IASB issues a standard on fair value measurement and in the meantime GAAP differences will remain between the US standard and the current fair value literature in IFRSs.

Most accounting standards that include fair value focus on what to measure at fair value, whereas the discussion paper instead focuses on how to measure fair value. Dispersed throughout accounting standards are inconsistent definitions of fair value and only limited guidance on application. The discussion paper remedies this by providing a 'one-stop shop' for the definition of fair value and related measurement guidance. In other words, the discussion paper does not propose to introduce any new requirements mandating the use of fair value; instead, it would unify the meaning of fair value and add important disclosures.

Highlights of the discussion paper include the following:

- a new definition of fair value;
- a fair value hierarchy used to classify the source of information used in fair value measurements (i.e. market based or non-market based);

- new disclosures of assets and liabilities measured at fair value based on their level in the hierarchy;

- a modification of the long-standing accounting presumption that the transaction price of an asset or liability equals its initial fair value;

- questions and answers on the application of the discussion paper.

The scope of that the discussion paper is applied to any asset or liability that is measured at fair value, not just financial instruments. The discussion paper defines 'fair value' as 'the price that would be received to sell an asset or paid to transfer a liability in an orderly transaction between market participants at the measurement date.' While the words may have a similar ring to past definitions, there are some key differences. First, the definition is based on an exit price (for an asset, the price at which it would be sold) rather than an entry price (for an asset, the price at which it would be bought), regardless of whether the entity plans to hold or sell the asset. This is the same approach that is currently applied in IAS 39 for subsequent measurement, but is not applied to initial recognition where entry price is applied instead. A second key point of the definition is that it emphasises that fair value is market based rather than entity specific, i.e. fair values must rest on assumptions that market participants would use in pricing the asset or liability, which is equally similar to IAS 39.

A fair value hierarchy underpins the discussion paper. The hierarchy ranks the quality and reliability of information used to determine fair values — quoted prices are the most reliable valuation inputs, whereas model values that include inputs based on unobservable data are the least reliable. The table below provides a description of the levels in the hierarchy and examples:

Level and 'Inputs' (Information Used in Determining Fair Value)	Examples
Level 1 — Quoted market prices for *identical* assets or liabilities in *active* markets	• Entity A common stock traded and quoted on the New York Stock Exchange.

Level and 'Inputs' (Information Used in Determining Fair Value)	Examples
Level 2 — Observable market-based inputs, other than Level 1 quoted prices (or unobservable inputs that are corroborated by market data)	• Entity Z common stock traded and quoted only on an inactive market in an emerging country. • A privately placed bond of Entity Z whose value is derived from a similar Entity Z bond that is publicly traded. • An over-the-counter interest rate swap, valued based on a model whose inputs are observable LIBOR forward interest rate curves.
Level 3 — Unobservable inputs (that are not corroborated by observable market data)	• A long-dated commodity swap whose forward price curve, used in a valuation model, is not directly observable or correlated with observable market data. • Shares of a privately held entity whose value is based on projected cash flows.

The hierarchy requires users to maximise market-based information, and it provides a basis for new disclosures, which, in part, buckets assets and liabilities accounted for at fair value by the level in the hierarchy under which they have been valued. In short, to value an item, start at Level 1, and move down the hierarchy if Level 1 information does not exist.

The proposed disclosures would shed light on the relative reliability of fair value measurements. The discussion paper would require separate disclosures of items that are measured at fair value on a recurring basis (e.g. an investment portfolio) versus items that are measured at fair value on a nonrecurring basis (e.g. an impaired asset). The following briefly summarises the major disclosures proposed for annual and interim statements of financial position.

(a) For items that are measured on a non-recurring basis at fair value:

- a separate table for assets and for liabilities that displays the statement of financial position fair value carrying amount of major categories of assets and of liabilities is required. Within each table, the assets and liabilities measured at fair value in each major category are separated into the level of the hierarchy on which fair value is based. The table also includes total gains and losses recognised for each major category.

(b) For items that are measured on a recurring basis at fair value:

- tables similar to those for non-recurring items (see above); and
- additional information regarding fair values based on Level 3 (unobservable) inputs, including a roll-forward analysis of fair value amounts in the statement of financial position and disclosure of the unrealised gains and losses for Level 3 items held at the end of the reporting period.

A fair value measurement assumes that the transaction to sell the asset or transfer the liability occurs in the principal market for the asset or liability or, in the absence of a principal market, the most advantageous market for the asset or liability. The principal market is the market in which the reporting entity would sell the asset or transfer the liability with the greatest volume and level of activity for the asset or liability. The most advantageous market is the market in which the reporting entity would sell the asset or transfer the liability with the price that maximises the amount that would be received for the asset or minimises the amount that would be paid to transfer the liability, considering transaction costs in the respective market(s). IAS 39 does not distinguish between the principal and the most advantageous market, rather it refers solely to the market that is most advantageous.

The discussion paper proposes to allow an entity to record an upfront profit, 'day 1 p&l', if its valuation technique suggests that fair value is different from the transaction price. This would be a change from IAS 39 which, like US guidance prior to FAS 157 being issued, does not allow an entity to recognise an upfront profit absent observable market data.

Fair value should not be adjusted for transaction costs. Transaction costs that represent the incremental direct costs to sell the asset or transfer are also not an attribute of the asset or liability, instead, they are specific to a transaction and will differ depending on how the reporting entity transacts. However, transaction costs should be taken into account in determining the most advantageous market that the entity has access to. This approach is the same as IAS 39. The discussion paper provides guidance on transportation costs and states that these are an element of fair value in the instance when location is an attribute of the asset or liability (as might be the case for a commodity), but not otherwise. Thus, the price in the principal market used to measure the fair value of the asset or liability should be adjusted for the costs, if any, that would be incurred to transport the asset or liability to (or from) its principal (or most advantageous) market.

When a quoted price in an active market exists, the fair value is the product of the quoted price and the number of units. The fair value of the instrument is not affected by the size of the investment the entity has. The unit of account for Level 1 items is therefore a single instrument. This is the same as IAS 39. On the other hand, the discussion paper does not state what the unit of account would be for items that are not Level 1.

When measuring instruments in active markets the discussion paper is less specific than IAS 39 as to using bid, ask, or mid-market prices. The discussion paper would preserve the ability of securities brokers (and other types of entities) to use a price within the bid-ask spread that is most representative of fair value, as long as this is consistently applied. The discussion paper does not preclude the use of mid-market pricing or other pricing conventions as a practical expedient for fair value measurements within a bid-ask spread.

The discussion paper clarifies that a fair value measurement for a restricted asset should consider the effect of the restriction if market participants would consider the effect of the restriction in pricing the asset. This would usually be the case when the restriction is specific to (an attribute of) the asset and would transfer to market participants.

The IASB has recognised the need for guidance on measuring fair value in IFRSs and for increased convergence with US GAAP. The publication of FAS 157 as a discussion paper is the starting point for its deliberations. Comments from constituents on the paper and feedback from holding round-table meetings will be used in the development of an exposure draft which will ultimately lead to a final IFRS. Although provisions of FAS 157 may be used in the preparation of an exposure draft, they may be reworded or altered to be consistent with other IFRSs and to reflect the decisions of the IASB. At the time of writing the IASB were discussing the comment letters received on the discussion paper with the intention of issuing an exposure draft in 2009. The IASB has yet to determine the expected timing of a final Standard.

8.2 Reducing complexity

In March 2008 the IASB issued a discussion paper *Reducing Complexity in Reporting Financial Instruments*. Although the discussion paper was drafted by the IASB the US Financial Accounting Standards Board also issued the discussion paper as part of the memorandum of understanding between the two standard setters. The aim of the discussion paper is to provide a basis for future discussions of issues related to the measurement of financial instruments (including hedge accounting issues). The ultimate goal of this project is to publish an IFRS that would significantly improve and simplify financial instrument reporting, i.e. it would replace IAS 39.

The discussion paper sets out the IASB's long-term objective of full fair value accounting for all financial instruments, i.e. elimination of the existing mixed measurement approach in IAS 39. The discussion paper acknowledges that instead of immediately moving to its long-term goal the Board may instead consider alternative intermediate approaches which retain a mixed measurement model to some degree. The discussion paper considers three different intermediate approaches on which it requests constituents' views.

19 Financial instruments: recognition and derecognition

1 Introduction

Recognition addresses the question of whether or not a financial instrument is included in the statement of financial position. Derecognition, not surprisingly, is the reverse of recognition and is the removal of a previously recognised financial instrument from the statement of financial position.

A financial instrument is recognised when, and only when, the entity becomes a party to the contractual provisions of the instrument. A previously recognised financial asset is derecognised when, and only when, either the contractual rights to the cash flows from that asset expire, or the entity transfers the asset such that the transfer qualifies for derecognition. A financial liability is derecognised when, and only when, it is extinguished.

The criteria that are applied to transfers of financial assets are a mix of risks and rewards and control tests. IAS 39 establishes a hierarchy of the tests and provides many examples to clarify the meaning of the concepts used and application of the tests to various transfer transactions.

Although the broad principles of derecognition may appear to be simple, a significant degree of judgment will be required when applying these principles in practice. This is particularly so in more mature financial markets where the complexity of transactions is ever increasing.

UK

The approach to derecognition taken by IAS 39 differs significantly from that taken by the UK standard FRS 5 Reporting the Substance of Transactions. *Accordingly, UK companies may find, for example, that assets or liabilities that would have been derecognised under FRS 5 may continue to be recognised under IAS 39.*

This chapter discusses recognition and derecognition in the following sections:

Section 2 Initial recognition

2 Initial recognition

2.1 General principle

An entity should only recognise a financial asset or a financial liability in its statement of financial position when it becomes a party to the contractual provisions of the instrument. [IAS 39.14]

Example 2.1

Recognised and unrecognised financial instruments

Arrangements that are recognised as financial assets and liabilities are as follows.

- Unconditional receivables are recognised as an asset when the entity becomes a party to the contract and, as a consequence, has a legal right to receive cash. [IAS 39.AG35(a)]
- Issued debt is recognised as a liability when the entity that issues it becomes a party to the contractual terms of the debt, and therefore has a legal obligation to pay cash to the debt holder.
- A derivative is recognised as an asset or a liability on the commitment date, rather than on the date on which settlement takes place. At inception the fair values of the right and obligation created by the derivative may be equal, in which case the fair value of the derivative will be zero. [IAS 39.AG35(c)]

Arrangements that are not recognised as financial assets and liabilities are as follows.

- Planned future transactions, no matter how likely, are not assets and liabilities because the entity has not become a party to a contract. [IAS 39.AG35(e)]
- Derivative contracts to buy or sell non-financial items that are scoped out of IAS 39 are not recognised as financial assets and liabilities as they are executory contracts.
- Assets to be acquired and liabilities to be incurred as a result of a firm commitment are generally not recognised until at least one of the parties has performed under the agreement. [IAS 39.AG35(b)]

Firm commitments to acquire a non-financial item are not recognised until the asset is acquired if the commitment itself is deemed to be outside the scope of IAS 39 (see **2.5** of **chapter 13**). A firm commitment to buy a financial asset, or a commitment to buy a non-financial item where the commitment is in the scope of IAS 39, is generally recognised as a derivative on the date the commitment is entered into (see **chapter 16**) unless the 'regular way' exemption is applied (see **2.2** below). If a previously unrecognised firm commitment is subject to a highly effective fair value hedge, changes in the fair value of the hedged risk of the firm commitment are recognised in the statement of financial position. This appears to run counter to non-recognition of certain firm commitments. The argument for permitting such an approach is that all firm commitments are recognised, but generally at a historic cost of nil, and the fair value hedge requirements merely remeasure part of that commitment to fair value. [IAS 39.BC152]

If an entity transfers or receives cash as collateral for an arrangement careful consideration is needed to determine whether the cash should be recognised as a financial asset in the hands of the recipient. If the cash received by the recipient is not legally segregated from the recipients other assets and the recipient can use the cash unfettered then the cash meets the definition of an asset because the ultimate realisation of an financial asset is its conversion into cash and, therefore, no further transformation is required before the economic benefits of the cash transferred by the provider of the collateral are realised by the recipient. In this case, the recipient would recognise the cash as a financial asset and recognise a concurrent financial liability to return the cash to the provider of the collateral. The provider of the collateral would derecognise the cash and recognise a receivable from the collateral holder. [IAS 39.IG.D.1]

Derivatives that prevent a transfer of financial assets from achieving derecognition are not recognised if recognising both the derivative and the asset that failed derecognition would amount to accounting for the same rights and obligations twice. [IAS 39.AG49]

2.1.1 *Linked transactions*

IAS 39 does not contain guidance when two separate financial instruments should be recognised as if the transaction was a single combined instrument. IAS 39 does, however, provide specific implementation guidance in IAS 39.IG.B.6 where a loan receivable and a payable should be considered as a single transaction, in this case an interest rate swap. It seems reasonable that the guidance in this example can be applied to other transactions. Two financial instruments should therefore be recognised and measured as a single combined instrument if:

- they are entered into at the same time and in contemplation of each other;
- they have the same counterparty;
- they relate to the same risk; and
- there is no economic need or substantive business purpose for structuring the transactions separately that could not also have been accomplished in a single transaction.

One of the most common benefits of structuring transactions separately, even if their substance is that of a single arrangement, is tax benefits that accrue. It is difficult to see how it can be argued that structuring for tax benefits is a substantive business purpose, particularly when those tax benefits derive from the accounting treatment adopted (in this example, from treating the transactions separately for accounting purposes).

2.1.2 *Modification that leads to initial recognition of a new instrument*

An entity may become a party to the contractual provisions of a financial instrument as a result of a substantial modification of an instrument that it already recognised in the statement of financial position. The entity will need to consider whether the modification results in derecognition of the existing instrument and recognition of a new instrument. Derecognition of financial assets is detailed in **section 3** below and derecognition of financial liabilities is detailed in **section 4** below.

Example 2.1.2

Initial recognition following modification

An entity had previously issued a perpetual instrument with an issuer option to redeem after 15 years. Under the terms of the instrument the entity had the option to defer interest payments indefinitely, except upon liquidation of the entity. Consequently, the instrument met the definition of an equity instrument and was presented as equity at its net proceeds.

During the year the entity and the holders of the instruments make a modification to the terms of the instrument which creates a contingent settlement provision that is considered to be 'genuine' in accordance with IAS 32.25. If the prescribed contingent event occurred the entity would be required to pay all deferred interest and lose the right to defer future interest. In accordance with IAS 32.25, after this modification the instrument is classified as a financial liability. The modification involves no compensation

> payment to the holders of the instrument or a change in the expected cash flows, and no fees in respect of the modification are paid.
>
> All financial instruments are measured at their fair value at initial recognition. The initial recognition date of the financial liability in this example is the date of the modification of the instrument as at this date the old equity instrument is derecognised and a new financial liability is recognised. Therefore, the entity must recognise this financial liability at its fair value. This fair value will incorporate expectations of cash flows and market interest rates at the date of the modification. Any difference between the previous carrying amount recognised in equity and the fair value of the financial liability is recognised as an adjustment within equity.
>
> If the entity does not designate the financial liability as at fair value through profit or loss, the liability is measured at amortised cost which will include any directly attributable transaction costs.

In November 2006 the IFRIC issued a rejection notice on changes in the contractual terms of an existing equity instrument that results in the instrument being reclassified to a financial liability for the issuer. Two issues were discussed: (i) on what basis the financial liability should be measured at the date when the terms were changed and (ii) how any difference between the carrying amount of the previously recognised equity instrument and the amount of the financial liability recognised at the date when the terms were changed should be accounted for. The IFRIC noted that at the time when the contractual terms were changed, a financial liability was initially recognised, and, furthermore, that a financial liability on initial recognition is measured at its fair value in accordance with IAS 39.43. The IFRIC observed that Example 3 of IFRIC 2 *Members' Shares in Co-operative Entities and Similar Instruments* deals with a similar situation. In that example, at the time when the financial liabilities are recognised, when the terms are changed, they are recognised at their fair value.

The IFRIC observed that the change in the terms of the instrument gave rise to derecognition of the original equity instrument. The IFRIC noted that IAS 32.33 states that no gain or loss shall be recognised in profit or loss on the purchase, sale, issue or cancellation of an entity's own equity instruments. The IFRIC, therefore, believed that, at the time when the terms were changed, the difference between the carrying amount of the equity instrument and the fair value of the newly recognised financial liability should be recognised in equity.

2.2 Trade date and settlement date accounting

'Regular way' purchases and sales of financial assets are recognised by applying either trade or settlement date accounting. A 'regular way' purchase or sale is defined as a transaction whose contractual terms 'require delivery of the asset within a time frame established generally by regulation or convention in the marketplace concerned'. [IAS 39.9] A marketplace is not limited to a formal stock exchange or organised over-the-counter market. Rather, it means the environment in which the financial asset is customarily exchanged. An acceptable time frame would be the period reasonably and customarily required for the parties to complete the transaction and prepare and execute closing documents. [IAS 39.IG.B.28] The trade date is the date of the commitment to buy or sell the financial asset. The settlement date is the date of the delivery of the asset. If a transaction is considered 'regular way' a derivative is not recognised for the time period between trade and settlement date.

Where trade date accounting is applied, the entity recognises the financial asset to be received and the corresponding liability to pay for it at the trade date; on disposal, the financial asset is removed from the statement of financial position on the trade date. [IAS 39.AG55]

Under the settlement date accounting approach, the asset is recognised on the day on which it is received by the entity; on disposal, the asset continues to be recognised until such time as the asset is delivered to the buyer. Between the trade date and settlement date, whilst the asset itself is not yet recognised, the entity is required to account for changes in its fair value applying the same measurement basis that will be used to account for the acquired asset once it is recognised (i.e. changes in fair value are recorded in profit and loss for assets to be classified as at fair value through profit or loss, in other comprehensive income for assets to be classified as available for sale, and not recognised for assets to be carried at amortised cost). [IAS 39.AG56] An entity must choose between trade date and settlement date accounting for each category of financial asset as defined by IAS 39. [IAS 39.AG53]

Example 2.2A

Trade and settlement date accounting for a purchase of an asset

The following example illustrates the amounts to be recorded for a purchase of a financial asset.

The dates that are relevant to the example are:

Trade date: 29 December 20X1

Period end date: 31 December 20X1

Settlement date: 4 January 20X2

TRADE DATE ACCOUNTING

Journal entries	Held to maturity	Available for sale	Fair value through profit or loss
29 December 20X1			
	Dr Asset 1,000 Cr Liability 1,000	Dr Asset 1,000 Cr Liability 1,000	Dr Asset 1,000 Cr Liability 1,000
Description	*To recognise asset and to record payable*	*To recognise asset and to record payable*	*To recognise asset and to record payable*
31 December 20X1			
	– –	Dr Asset 2 Cr Equity 2	Dr Asset 2 Cr Profit or loss 2
Description		*with the increase in fair value to date*	*with the increase in fair value to date*
4 January 20X2			
	– –	Dr Asset 1 Cr Equity 1	Dr Asset 1 Cr Profit or loss 1
Description		*with the increase in fair value to date*	*with the increase in fair value to date*
	Dr Liability 1,000 Cr Cash 1,000	Dr Liability 1,000 Cr Cash 1,000	Dr Liability 1,000 Cr Cash 1,000
Description	*with the amount contracted to pay for the asset*	*with the amount contracted to pay for the asset*	*with the amount contracted to pay for the asset*

SETTLEMENT DATE ACCOUNTING

Journal entries	Held to maturity	Available for sale	Fair value through profit or loss
29 December 20X1			
	– –	– –	– –
31 December 20X1			
	– –	Dr Receivable 2 Cr Equity 2	Dr Receivable 2 Cr Profit or loss 2
Description		*with the increase in fair value to date*	*with the increase in fair value to date*
4 January 20X2			
	– –	Dr Receivable 1 Cr Equity 1	Dr Receivable 1 Cr Profit or loss 1
Description		*with the increase in fair value to date*	*with the increase in fair value to date*
	Dr Asset 1,000 Cr Cash 1,000 –	Dr Asset 1,003 Cr Cash 1,000 Cr Receivable 3	Dr Asset 1,003 Cr Cash 1,000 Cr Receivable 3
Description	*with the amount contracted to pay for the asset*	*with the amount contracted to pay for the asset and its change in fair value since trade date*	*with the amount contracted to pay for the asset and its change in fair value since trade date*

When the settlement provisions of a financial instrument differ between various active markets the entity must apply the provisions that apply in the market in which the purchase or sale under the financial instrument actually takes place.

Example 2.2B

Regular way contracts: which customary settlement provisions apply?

[Extract from IAS 39.IG.B.30]

Entity XYZ purchases one million shares of Entity ABC on a US stock exchange, for example, through a broker. The settlement date of the contract is six business days later. Trades for equity shares on US exchanges customarily settle in three business days. Because the trade settles in six business days, it does not meet the exemption as a regular way trade.

However, if XYZ did the same transaction on a foreign exchange that has a customary settlement period of six business days, the contract would meet the exemption for a regular way trade.

Where the regulation or convention for settlement differs between a derivative over the underlying, say a call option over a share, and the underlying itself, say the share, the regulation or convention that is used to determine whether the financial instrument is regular way would be the regulation or convention specific to that instrument. For example, if the call option over the share is regularly settled within 14 days of exercise of the option in the option markets, but a direct acquisition of a share requires 3 day settlement, the entity will look to the options market in determining whether an option is regular way or not. [IAS 39.IG.B.31]

Example 2.2C

Application of trade and settlement date accounting for different categories of financial asset

Entity P has an accounting policy of settlement date accounting for loans and receivables and trade date accounting for available-for-sale financial assets. Entity P enters into a regular way transactions whereby it will sell a loan in exchange for an available for sale equity instrument. At the date of entering into the arrangement, 30 March 20X8, both assets had the same fair value. The settlement date is 2 April 20X8. Entity P's reporting period is 31 March 20X8.

	Amortised cost US$	Fair value US$
30 March 20X8		
Loan and receivable	10,000	
Available for sale asset		10,400

		Amortised cost	Fair value
		US$	US$
31 March 20X8			
Loan and receivable		10,005	
Available for sale asset			10,350
2 April 20X8			
Loan and receivable		10,015	
Available for sale asset			10,325

30 March 20X8

Dr	Available for sale asset	10,400
Cr	Financial liability	10,400

To record the acquisition of the available-for-sale asset at trade date

31 March 20X8

Dr	Available for sale reserve (equity)	50
Cr	Available for sale asset	50

To record the change in fair value of the available-for-sale equity security

Dr	Loan and receivable	5
Cr	Interest income	5

To record interest earned on an effective interest rate basis

2 April 20X8

Dr	Loan and receivable	10
Cr	Interest income	10

To record interest earned on an effective interest rate basis

Dr	Available for sale reserve (equity)	25
Cr	Available for sale asset	25

To record the change in fair value of the available-for-sale equity security

Dr	Financial liability	10,400
Cr	Loan and receivable	10,015
Cr	Profit or loss	385

To record the gain on disposal of the loan and receivable at the date of derecognition. The gain represents the difference between the proceeds received, being the fair value of the available-for-sale asset at the date the contract is entered into, and amortised cost of the loan and receivable at the settlement date.

If an entity derecognises financial assets using settlement date accounting but receives non-cash consideration for selling the asset which when classified under IAS 39 will be recognised using trade date accounting the entity must apply trade date accounting to the non-cash financial asset to be received.

Example 2.2D

Settlement date accounting: exchange of non-cash financial assets

[Extract from IAS 39.IG.D.2.3]

On 29 December 20X2 (trade date) Entity A enters into a contract to sell Note Receivable A, which is carried at amortised cost, in exchange for Bond B, which will be classified as held for trading and measured at fair value. Both assets have a fair value of CU1,010 on 29 December, while the amortised cost of Note Receivable A is CU1,000. Entity A uses settlement date accounting for loans and receivables and trade date accounting for assets held for trading. On 31 December 20X2 (financial year-end), the fair value of Note Receivable A is CU1,012 and the fair value of Bond B is CU1,009. On 4 January 20X3, the fair value of Note Receivable A is CU1,013 and the fair value of Bond B is CU1,007. The following entries are made:

29 December 20X2

Dr	Bond B	CU1,010
Cr	Payable	CU1,010

31 December 20X2

Dr	Trading loss	CU1
Cr	Bond B	CU1

4 January 20X3

Dr	Payable	CU1,010
Dr	Trading loss	CU2
Cr	Note Receivable A	CU1,000
Cr	Bond B	CU2
Cr	Realisation gain	CU10

In January 2007 the IFRIC issued a rejection notice on accounting for short sales of securities when the terms of the short sales require delivery of the securities within the time frame established generally by regulation or convention in the marketplace concerned. A fixed price commitment between trade date and settlement date of a short sale contract meets the definition of a derivative. As IAS 39.AG55 and AG56 only permit a choice of trade or settlement date accounting for recognition and derecognition of financial assets traded under regular way purchases and regular way sales of long positions, the Standard would require a short sale to be recognised as a derivative until delivery of the security. The IFRIC acknowledged that an interpretation that is applied in practice is that entities choose trade date or settlement date accounting for short sales. Specifically, practice recognises the short sales as financial liabilities at fair value with changes in fair value recognised in profit or loss. Under the industry practice, the same profit or loss amount is recognised as would have been recognised if short sales of securities were accounted for as derivatives but the securities are presented differently in the statement of financial position. The IFRIC acknowledged that requiring entities to account for the short positions as derivatives may create considerable practical problems for their accounting systems and controls with little, if any, improvement to the quality of the financial information presented. For these reasons and because there is little diversity in practice, the IFRIC decided not to take the issue onto the agenda.

IAS 39 does not provide guidance on whether the trade date exemption can be applied if an entity delivers a financial instrument under a regular way contract but the delivery date is delayed, and the asset is delivered outside the normal convention for that type of contract. For example, a contract has a delivery date of t+3 days, but there is a delay in delivery and the instrument is delivered at t+5. A delay should not preclude use of the regular way exemption if the delay is outside the control of the entity.

3 Derecognition of financial assets

A financial asset is derecognised, i.e. removed from the statement of financial position, when, and only when, either the contractual rights to the asset's cash flows expire, or the asset is transferred and the transfer qualifies for derecognition.

The decision whether a transfer qualifies for derecognition is made by applying a combination of risks and rewards and control tests. The risks and rewards tests seek to establish whether, having transferred a financial asset, the entity continues to be exposed to the risks of ownership of that asset and/or continues to enjoy the benefits that it generates. The control tests are designed with a view to understand which entity controls the asset, i.e. which entity can direct how the benefits of that asset are realised.

This approach of using two types of tests is often criticised for being a mix of two accounting models that can create confusion in application. IAS 39 addresses this criticism by providing a clear hierarchy of application of the two sets of tests: risks and rewards tests are applied first, with the control tests used only when the entity has neither transferred substantially all risks and rewards of the asset nor retained them.

Inherent in the IAS 39 derecognition model is the notion of 'stickiness', i.e. it is more difficult to remove an asset from an entity's statement of financial position than it is to recognise that asset in the first place. Derecognition cannot be achieved by merely transferring the legal title to a financial asset to another party. The substance of the arrangement must be assessed in order to determine whether an entity has transferred the economic exposure associated with the rights inherent in the asset, i.e. its risks and rewards, and in some cases control of those rights.

3.1 The IAS 39 derecognition decision tree

IAS 39 provides a decision tree, reproduced below, that clarifies the hierarchy of application of the derecognition tests:

[IAS 39.AG36]

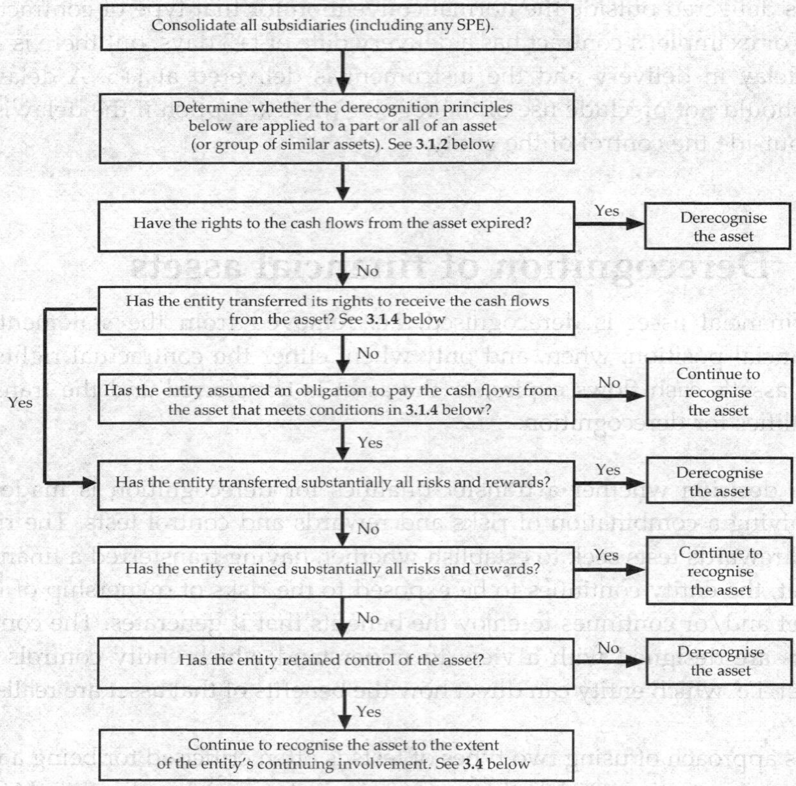

The steps of this decision tree are explained below.

3.1.1 *Consolidate all subsidiaries including any Special Purpose Entity* (*SPE*)

The first step is to define at which level the derecognition decision is to be applied: in the parent's separate financial statements or in the consolidated financial statements. Where derecognition of financial assets is to be applied in the consolidated financial statements, the reporting group must first consolidate all subsidiaries in accordance with IAS 27 *Consolidated and Separate Financial Statements* and SIC-12 *Consolidation – Special Purpose Entities*. [IAS 39.15]

This first step ensures that the derecognition decision is consistent regardless of whether the transfer of assets is direct to investors or through a consolidated SPE that obtains the financial assets, and transfers these financial assets, or their portion, to third party investors.

IAS 27 requires consolidation of all entities that are controlled by the reporting entity. SIC-12 requires consolidation of an SPE when the substance of the relationship between an entity and the SPE indicates that the SPE is controlled by the entity.

Special purpose entities may take the form of a corporation, trust, partnership or unincorporated entity and are often created with legal arrangements that impose strict and sometimes permanent limits on the decision-making powers of their governing board, trustees or management over the operations of the SPE. Frequently, these provisions specify that the policy guiding the ongoing activities of the SPE cannot be modified, other than perhaps by its creator or sponsor (i.e. they operate on so-called 'autopilot').

Structured transactions, such as securitisations and certain other asset-based financing arrangements, typically seek, as their primary economic objective, to isolate legally the assets from the party providing them (and from that party's creditors) to avoid the investor having a credit exposure to the transferor. This isolation is often achieved through a SPE. For many sellers of financial assets, structured arrangements that isolate the assets permit access to capital markets at more favourable prices than might otherwise be available since credit agencies and investors require a lower return from structures that avoid the consequences arising from bankruptcies. This ability is particularly important for those entities whose credit ratings may reflect the adverse effects of financial, operational or environmental risks not directly attributable to the assets being transferred. However, this bankruptcy isolation does not automatically lead to the conclusion that the sponsor is not required to consolidate the SPE. Other factors set out in SIC-12 have to be considered. Consolidation may, through its impact on the sponsor's financial ratios, negate certain of the benefits of isolating the SPE.

A SPE may issue different types of beneficial interests, multiple classes of interests and classes of interests with different maturities.

Several forms of SPE are common, depending on the asset being securitised, the securities issued by the entity and the legal framework governing the entity's operations. These include grantor trusts, owner trusts, revolving trusts, master trusts, special purpose corporations and REMICS (Real Estate Mortgage Investment Conduits).

Typically, the SPE is prevented from selling, assigning or pledging its direct interest in any financial asset it holds; however, the owners of the beneficial interests generally have the right to pledge or exchange their beneficial interests.

In November 2006 the IFRIC issued a rejection notice on the application of SIC-12. The IFRIC was asked the relative weight to be given to the various indicators in SIC-12.10 in determining who should consolidate a SPE. The issue focused on a situation in which all the decisions necessary for the ongoing activities of the SPE had been predetermined by its creator and in which the majority of the 'equity interest tranche' had been transferred to a third party. The question was whether in such a situation the benefits and risks factors specified in SIC-12.10(c) and (d) took precedence over the activities and decision-making factors in SIC-12.10(a) and (b). The IFRIC noted that, under IAS 27 *Consolidated and Separate Financial Statements*, control, which is the basis for consolidation, has two components: power to govern and rights to obtain benefits. The IFRIC noted that the factors set out in SIC-12.10 are indicators only and not necessarily conclusive. The IFRIC believed that this approach was deliberate, in acknowledgement of the fact that circumstances vary case by case. In the IFRIC's view, SIC-12 requires that the party having control over an SPE should be determined through the exercise of judgement and skill in each case, after taking into account all relevant factors.

3.1.2 *Determine whether the derecognition principles are applied to a part or all of an asset (or group of similar assets)*

An entity needs to determine what is being subjected to an evaluation for derecognition: a whole financial asset; a group of financial assets; a part of a financial asset; or a part of a group of similar financial assets.

An entity may apply the derecognition principles to a part of a financial asset (or a group of similar financial assets) if the part comprises one of the following:

- specifically identified cash flows, e.g. an interest or principal strip from a debt instrument;

- a fully proportionate share of the cash flows, e.g. the rights to the cash flows on 90 per cent of all cash flows arising from a debt instrument; or
- a fully proportionate share of specifically identified cash flows, e.g. 90 per cent of the cash flows that arise on the interest strip from a debt instrument.

In all other cases the financial asset (or the group of financial assets) is considered in its entirety. [IAS 39.16]

Example 3.1.2

Determining the part of a financial asset subject to transfer

Entity X, the transferor, transfers the right to the first £90 of cash flows that are derived from a debt instrument, when the fair value of the asset is £100 on the date of transfer.

The transferor cannot apply the derecognition model to part of the asset because the transferor has neither transferred specifically identifiable cash flows, nor a fully proportionate share of all or part of the cash flows. The transferor effectively agrees to absorb the first £10 of losses from the asset that has been subject to the transfer.

It should be noted, however, that if the transferor had transferred a 90 per cent pro rata share of all cash flows from the asset, then the derecognition model could be applied to the part of the asset that has been transferred, i.e. 90 per cent. In this case, the transferor and the transferee have agreed to participate in a fully proportionate share of losses.

The Standard does not provide guidance on what makes assets 'similar'. 'Similar' generally means that the two instruments have contractually specified cash flows which are similar in amounts and timings, and have similar risk attributes. An entity shall consider the similarity of terms, e.g. prepayments features, interest rates, currency denomination. By definition, there will always be some differences between similar instruments, otherwise such instruments would be identical. A portfolio of mortgages transferred by a bank is often deemed to contain similar financial assets. Also, a portfolio of corporate bonds transferred by a bank is often deemed to contain similar financial assets. However, no two portfolios are ever precisely alike. A transfer of a portfolio of mortgages would need to be assessed separately from a transfer of a portfolio of corporate bonds even if the two transfers happen at the same time. With individual equity investments, the differences are so significant that no two equity investments are ever likely to be similar – the value is affected by intangibles and other 'soft' assets, like reputation, which are not recorded on the statement of financial position or measured in any consistent way, but which do affect perceptions and hence market price.

In September 2006 the Board was asked by the IFRIC for input and advice on what is the meaning of 'similar' for group of financial assets (in IAS 39.16). The Board responded with its view which the IFRIC used as a basis for a tentative rejection wording, along with other derecognition issues, in November 2006. The Board believed that derivative assets (which are often transferred together with non-derivative financial assets) are not 'similar' to non-derivative financial assets. Therefore, an entity would apply the derecognition tests in IAS 39 to non-derivative financial assets (or groups of similar non-derivative financial assets) and derivative financial assets (or groups of similar derivative financial assets) separately, even if they are transferred at the same time. The Board also indicated that transferred derivatives that could be either assets or liabilities (such as interest rate swaps) would have to meet both the financial asset and the financial liability derecognition tests.

Following comments from constituents, at the IFRIC meeting in January 2007, the IFRIC decided to withdraw its tentative agenda decision and add a project on derecognition to its agenda. At the date of writing the IFRIC had not completed this project.

3.1.3 Have the rights to the cash flows from the asset expired?

An entity derecognises a financial asset when the rights to the cash flows from that financial asset expire. [IAS 39.17]

The rights to the cash flows expire when, for example, a financial asset reaches its maturity and there are clearly no further cash flows arising from that asset, or a purchased option reaches its maturity unexercised. An entity may have a right to receive certain or all cash flows from a financial asset over a specified period of time which may be shorter than the contractual maturity of that financial asset. In that case, the entity's right to the cash flows expires once the specified period expires.

3.1.4 Has the entity transferred its rights to receive the cash flows from the asset?

An entity may transfer the contractual rights to the cash flows that comprise a financial asset, or it may retain the contractual rights to the cash flows, but assume a contractual obligation to pass on those cash flows to one or more recipients, in what is often referred to as a 'pass-through' arrangement.

In some pass-through arrangements an entity acts as an agent of the eventual recipients of the cash flows that derive from the asset. The entity agrees to receive cash flows and has a concurrent obligation to pay those cash flows to the eventual recipient. For this to be the case, the following conditions on the transfer have to be satisfied:

[IAS 39.19]

- the entity has no obligation to pay amounts to the eventual recipients unless it collects equivalent amounts from the original asset, i.e. the entity does not benefit or suffer from performance or non-performance of the asset;
- the entity is prohibited by the terms of the transfer arrangement from selling or pledging the original asset other than as security to the eventual recipients for the obligation to pay them cash flows, i.e. the entity does not have control of the future economic benefits associated with the transferred asset;
- the entity has an obligation to pass on or remit the cash flows that it has collected on behalf of the eventual recipients *without material delay*, is prohibited from re-investing the cash flows received in the short settlement period between receiving them and remitting them to the eventual recipient in anything other than cash or cash equivalents and any interest earned on such investments must be passed on to the eventual recipients, i.e. the entity has no access to the benefits of the asset.

Even if the entity passes on the interest earned, the delay in passing on the cash flows alters the credit risk characteristics of the original asset such that the eventual recipient of the cash flows is exposed to not only the original asset subject to the arrangement, but to additional credit risk on the investment cash flows from the asset.

Without material delay does not mean instantaneously, nor does it imply an extended length of time. The contractual arrangement will need to be considered in full in order to make an assessment as to whether the timeframe between the collection of cash flows on the underlying assets and the point at which they are passed on to the eventual recipients is material in the context of the contractual arrangements of the transfer.

In some arrangements, the cash collected on the underlying assets occurs sporadically throughout a period of time. For example, if an entity retains the rights to the cash flows arising on a group of credit card receivables, the payments arising on those credit cards are likely to occur on any given day throughout the month. The contractual arrangement of the transfer may require that those cash flows are remitted to the eventual recipients, weekly, monthly, quarterly or even annually. There is a trade-off between passing on the cash flows almost as soon as they arise and the administrative burden that goes along with passing on those cash flows. Half-yearly and certainly annual payments to the eventual recipients would be considered a material delay as the conditions specified above fail and therefore derecognition would be inappropriate in these circumstances. It appears reasonable that the entity can invest the cash flows from the assets for up to three months without breaching the condition that all cash flows must be passed to the eventual recipient without material delay.

An entity may provide credit enhancement in a transfer arrangement so that it suffers the first loss on the asset up to a specified amount. This credit enhancement may be in the form of over-collateralisation or may be in the form of purchasing a subordinated interest in a consolidated SPE (in the latter case the entity is applying the pass-through tests at a consolidated level). Providing credit enhancement will not in itself result in failure of the pass-through tests if all cash received on transferred assets, if received by the transferor, is paid by the transferor to the eventual recipient, though it may result in failure of derecognition due to the entity retaining substantially all the risks and rewards of ownership of the assets. The pass-through tests must be considered prior to considering the entity's exposure to risk and rewards.

An entity may pass all three of the pass-through tests even when it provides credit enhancement. In such cases the entity will pay cash it receives on the asset without material delay to the eventual recipients should the debtor pay. If the debtor fails to pay, the entity will absorb the first loss fully, with the eventual recipient only suffering a loss after the first loss has been fully absorbed.

If a greater amount of cash is realised on the assets than is needed to pay the eventual recipient, i.e. the eventual recipient's initial investment is fully paid, then the entity will retain the remainder of the cash and will not pass it on. In all cases the entity passes 'any cash it collects on behalf of the eventual recipients'.

Example 3.1.4

Pass through arrangements

Entity B enters into an arrangement with Entity C where Entity C pays Entity B £0.9m in return for receiving cash flows on £1.0m of assets when expected losses on the assets are 10 per cent of all cash flows (interest and principal). Entity B retains the contractual rights to receive the cash flows from the assets but assumes an obligation to pay cash flows from the asset to Entity C. The maximum cash flows that Entity C can receive under the arrangement are interest and principal on a notional of £0.9m. If actual credit losses are lower than expected, say only 5 per cent, Entity B will pay Entity C £0.9m and retain £0.05m.

Entity B will pass the pass-through tests, assuming all other conditions are met, as Entity B will pass interest and principal on a notional up to £0.9m of the cash flows to Entity C.

However, if the form of the transaction was different, in that Entity C pays Entity B £1.0m for the assets and purchases a financial guarantee contract from Entity B for £0.1m then the pass-through tests would not be met as Entity B will compensate the eventual recipient, Entity C, even when it does not collect the equivalent amount from the original assets.

In a revolving structure cash received on the assets is reinvested in buying new receivables assets. In other words, cash 'revolves' into new assets instead of being returned immediately to the investors. Upon maturity the reinvested assets are used to repay the beneficial interest holders. Such 'revolving' structures do not meet the pass-through tests as they involve a material delay before the original cash is passed onto the eventual recipients and the reinvestment would typically be not in cash or cash equivalents. The treatment of revolving structures described above was confirmed by the IFRIC in September 2005.

An entity enters into an arrangement with a third party to transfer the contractual rights to receive the cash flows of a financial asset, but may agree to continue to act as an agent to administer collection and distribution of cash flows to the recipient (i.e. it retains servicing rights on the cash flows).

IAS 39.18(a) focuses on whether an entity transfers the contractual rights to receive the cash flows from a financial asset. The determination of whether the contractual rights to cash flows have been transferred is not affected by the transferor retaining the role of an agent to administer collection and distribution of cash flows. Retention of servicing rights by the entity transferring the financial asset does not, in itself, cause the transfer to fail the requirements in IAS

39.18(a). However, careful judgement must be applied to determine whether the entity providing servicing is acting solely as an agent for the owner of the financial asset, i.e. whether it has transferred all risks and rewards.

The IFRIC confirmed in September 2005 that the existence of servicing does not prevent an entity from transferring the contractual rights to the cash flows of the asset.

When the Board considered a number of derecognition issues in September 2006 at the request of the IFRIC it discussed whether the pass-through test is applicable to all transfers in which legal ownership of the financial asset is not transferred. In other words, is transfer of legal ownership of the transferred asset a pre-requisite for the transfer to be considered as a transfer of contractual rights under IAS 39.18(a)? The Board indicated that a transaction in which an entity transfers *all* the contractual rights *to receive the cash flows* [emphasis added in the IASB Update] (without necessarily transferring legal ownership of the financial asset), would not be treated as a pass-through. An example might be a situation in which an entity transfers all the legal rights to specifically identified cash flows of a financial asset (e.g. a transfer of the interest or principal of a debt instrument). Conversely, the pass-through test would be applicable to situations when the entity does not transfer all the contractual rights to cash flows of the financial asset, such as disproportionate transfers (see IAS 39.16(b)).

The Board's view in this case would mean that if an arrangement transferred all the legal rights to cash flows for a full proportionate interest in an asset (say 50 per cent of all cash flows), even though legal title of the asset was not transferred to the transferee, the transferor would apply paragraph 18(a) to the transfer, and therefore would avoid the pass-through tests in paragraph 18(b). The IFRIC agreed to consider this along with other derecognition issues as part of a wider project on derecognition and at the time of writing this had not been completed.

The Board also discussed whether conditional transfers should be treated as pass-through transactions. Conditions attached to a transfer could include provisions ensuring the existence and value of transferred cash flows at the date of transfer or conditions relating to the future performance of the asset. The Board indicated that such conditions would not affect whether the entity has transferred the contractual rights to receive cash flows (under IAS 39.18(a)). However, the existence of conditions relating to the future performance of the asset might affect the conclusion related to the transfer of risks and rewards as well as the extent of any continuing involvement by the transferor in the transferred asset.

The Board's view on conditional transfers would allow the transferor of transferred receivables arising, say, on the delivery of goods to a customer to compensate the transferee should the transferor issue a credit note to the customer should the goods be returned, not to fail the pass-through tests, even though the transferor is obligated to pay cash to the transferee when the transferee did not collect cash from the asset.

The Board's views were included in a draft rejection notice issued by the IFRIC in November 2006. Following comments from constituents, at the IFRIC meeting in January 2007, the IFRIC decided to withdraw the rejection notice and add a project on derecognition to its agenda. At the date of writing the IFRIC had not completed this project.

3.1.5 Has the entity transferred substantially all of the risks and rewards of ownership of the asset?

Determining the extent to which the risks and rewards of the transferred asset have been transferred and retained is critical in determining the accounting outcome for a transfer. The greater the risks and rewards retained the greater is the likelihood of continued recognition. The degree to which risks and rewards have been transferred and its effect on the accounting outcome can be illustrated as follows:

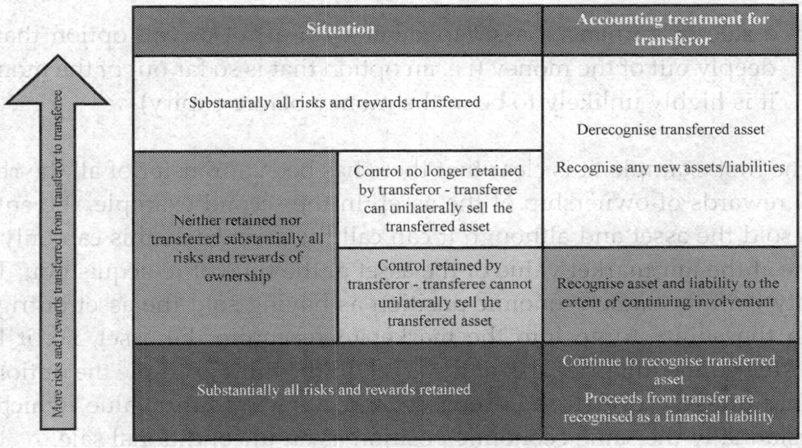

Situation
Accounting treatment for transferor
More risks and rewards transferred from transferor to transferee
Substantially all risks and rewards transferred
Derecognise transferred asset
Recognise any new assets/liabilities
Neither retained nor transferred substantially all risks and rewards of ownership
Control no longer retained by transferor - transferee can unilaterally sell the transferred asset
Control retained by transferor - transferee cannot unilaterally sell the transferred asset
Recognise asset and liability to the extent of continuing involvement
Substantially all risks and rewards retained
Continue to recognise transferred asset
Proceeds from transfer are recognised as a financial liability

Where the entity transfers substantially all of the risks and rewards of ownership of the financial asset, the asset should be derecognised. The entity may have to recognise separately any rights and obligations created or retained in the transfer. [IAS 39.20(a)]

> There is no 'bright line' provided in IAS 39 as to what is meant by 'substantially all' and a significant degree of judgement is required when applying the risks and rewards test.

There are other references in the Standard to various yardsticks that need to be met when applying certain paragraphs. For example, when comparing the old and new terms of a financial liability, the terms are considered to be 'substantially different' if the present value of the cash flows under the new terms is at least 10 per cent different from the discounted present value of the remaining cash flows of the original financial liability (see **4.1** below).

While IAS 39 does not apply the 90 per cent test to derecognition of financial assets, it would seem imprudent to conclude that substantially all risks and rewards of ownership have been transferred where the computations show that the entity still retains more than 10 per cent of the exposure to the variability in present value of the expected future cash flows post transfer.

IAS 39 provides three examples of when an entity has transferred substantially all of the risks and rewards of ownership:

[IAS 39.AG39]

- an unconditional sale of a financial asset;
- a sale of a financial asset together with an option to repurchase the financial asset at its fair value at the time of repurchase, and
- a sale of a financial asset together with a put or call option that is deeply out of the money (i.e. an option that is so far out of the money, it is highly unlikely to be in the money before expiry).

In the first example, it is clear that there has been a transfer of all the risks and rewards of ownership of the asset. In the second example, the entity has sold the asset and although it can call the asset back, this can only be done at the fair market value of the asset at the time of re-acquisition. The entity is in the same economic position as having sold the asset outright, with the ability to go into the market to reacquire the asset, i.e. it has transferred the full price risk of the asset. In the third example the option is highly unlikely ever to be exercised and has very little value, which is substantially the same economic position as an unconditional sale.

Pass-through arrangements that meet the criteria in **3.1.4** above may not satisfy the transfer of substantially all risks and rewards test.

Example 3.1.5A

Interaction of pass-through tests and risk and reward tests

Entity A originates a portfolio of five-year interest-bearing loans of £10,000. Entity A enters into an agreement with Entity C whereby in exchange for a

> cash payment of £9,000, Entity A agrees to pay to Entity C the first £9,000 (plus interest) of cash collected from the loan portfolio. Entity A retains rights to the last £1,000 (plus interest), i.e. it retains a subordinated residual interest. If Entity A collects, say, only £8,000 of its loans of £10,000 because some debtors default, Entity A would pass on to Entity C all of the £8,000 collected and Entity A keeps nothing of the £8,000 collected. If Entity A collects £9,500, it passes £9,000 to Entity C and retains £500. Expected losses are £500.
>
> Even though all cash flows that derive from the portfolio of assets are passed onto Entity C up to a maximum of £9,000, Entity A has not transferred substantially all the risks and rewards of ownership because of the subordinated retained interest. The residual interest absorbs the likely variability in net cash flows, i.e. the expected losses.

IAS 39 acknowledges that in many cases it will be clear whether or not the entity has transferred substantially all of the risks and rewards of ownership following a transfer of an asset. Where it is unclear whether or not there has been a transfer of substantially all of the risks and rewards of ownership of the financial asset, then the entity will have to evaluate its exposure before and after the transfer by comparing the variability in the amounts and timing of the net cash flows of the transferred asset. [IAS 39.21] If the exposure to the present value of the future net cash flows from the financial asset does not change significantly as a result of the transfer, then the entity has not transferred substantially all of the risks and rewards of ownership.

The computational comparison is made using an appropriate current market interest rate as the discount rate. All reasonably possible outcomes should be considered and a greater weight given to those outcomes that are more likely to occur. This is an expected cash flow model and should include all risks inherent in the cash flows.

There is no example in the Standard that describes the methodology that should be used in performing the risks and rewards assessment. A methodology that is used should be consistently applied to all transfers that are similar in nature. It would be inappropriate to use multiple methodologies for similar transactions and to 'cherry pick' the methodology that produced the desired degree of transfer of risks and rewards.

A common approach is to use a standard deviation statistic as the basis for determining how much variability has been transferred and retained by the transferor. To apply this approach the transferor will need to consider various future scenarios that will impact the amount and timing of cash flows of the transferred assets and calculate the present value of these amounts both before and after the transfer. In the case of a transfer of loans and receivables, scenarios will incorporate among other factors, changes in the amount of cash flows due to changes in the rate of default by the borrower and recovery of any collateral in the case of default; changes in the timing of when cash flows are received due to changes in prepayments rates. The expected cash flows on the transferred assets will be allocated to the transferor and the transferee based on the rights and obligations following the transfer. For example, if the transferor guarantees part of the transferred assets or invests in a subordinated loan, a subordinated interest only strip or excess spread issued by the transferee, this will result in some of the exposure to the assets coming back to the transferor.

The transferor will need to assess the probability of the various scenarios occurring so it can take the various present values described above and multiply them by those probabilities in order to determine probability weighted present values. These values are used for calculating the standard deviation, which can be thought of as the exposure, or volatility, that the transferor has to the transferred asset both before and after the transfer. This will form the basis for judging whether the transferor has retained or transferred substantially all the risks and rewards of ownership of the transferred assets.

The example below is aligned with the fact pattern included in the illustration in IAS 39.AG52, reproduced in **example 3.4.2** below, where prepayable loans are transferred to a transferee in return for cash proceeds and an investment in a subordinated interest only strip, subordinated principal only strip, and an excess spread. The illustration in the Standard concludes that the transferor has neither retained nor transferred substantially all the risks and rewards of ownership.

Example 3.1.5B

Determining the extent of risk and reward transferred

Entity A has a portfolio of similar prepayable fixed rate loans with a remaining maturity of two years, a coupon and effective interest rate of 10% and whose principal and amortised cost is £10,000. On 1/1/X0 Entity A transfers the loans for cash consideration of £9,115 to Entity B, an entity not consolidated in Entity A's consolidated financial statements. In order to acquire the loans Entity B issues a senior note, linked to the performance of the transferred assets, to third parties where the holders of the notes obtain the right to £9,000 of any collections of principal plus interest thereon at 9.5 per cent. Entity A agrees to retain rights to £1,000 of any collections of principal plus interest thereon at 10 per cent, plus the excess spread of 0.5 per cent on the remaining £9,000 of principal. Collections from prepayments are allocated between the transferor and the transferee proportionately in the ratio of 1:9, but any defaults are deducted from the entity's interest of £1,000 until that interest is exhausted. Entity A's retained interest is therefore more subordinate to the senior notes as it suffers the loss of any defaults on the transferred assets prior to the holders of the senior notes.

Interest is due on the transferred assets annually on the anniversary of the date of transfer.

In order to determine the extent to which Entity A has retained the risks and rewards of the transferred assets Entity A considers a number of scenarios where amounts and timings of cash flows on the transferred assets vary and assigns a probability for each scenario occurring in the future. For illustration purposes only four scenarios are included below, though in practice a greater number of scenarios is likely to be required. A risk-free rate of 8.5% is used to determine net present values and all amounts are denominated in Sterling.

Scenario		**Total**	**Senior note holders**	**Retained by Entity A**
1. All loans prepay immediately with no defaults. Probability is 20%	1/1/X0 – undiscounted	10,000	9,000	1,000
	Total net present value	*10,000*	*9,000*	*1,000*
2. All loans prepay in one year with no defaults. Probability is 30%	1/1/X0 – undiscounted	–	–	–
	1/1/X1 – undiscounted	11,000	9,855 (9.5% x 9,000) + 9,000	1,145 (0.5% x 9,000) + (10% x 1,000) + 1,000
	Total net present value	*10,138*	*9,083*	*1,055*
3. All loans run to their contractual maturity of 1/1/X2 with no defaults. Probability is 30%	1/1/X0 – undiscounted	–	–	–
	1/1/X1 – undiscounted	1,000	855 (9.5% x 9,000)	145 (0.5% x 9,000) + (10% x 1,000)
	1/1/X2 – undiscounted	11,000	9,855	1,145
	Total net present value	*10,265*	*9,159*	*1,106*
4. All loans default at 1/1/X1 and due to immediate foreclosure and sale of the collateral, a total of £10,741 is recovered. Probability is 20%	1/1/X0 – undiscounted	–	–	–
	1/1/X1 – undiscounted	10,741	9,855	886 Proceeds from sale of collateral less amount paid to senior note holders
	Total net present value	*9,900*	*9,083*	*817*

The net present values for each scenario are multiplied by the probability of each scenario to determine a probability weighted present value. The variance before and after the transfer is determined using the profitability weighted present values as illustrated below:

Entity A's variability before the transfer

Scenario	PV of cash flows	Probability	Probability weighted PV	Variability in PV	Probability weighted variability
	a	b	c = a x b	e = a – d	f = e² x b
1	10,000	20%	2,000	(101)	2040
2	10,138	30%	3,041	37	411
3	10,265	30%	3,080	164	8,069
4	9,900	20%	1,980	(201)	8,080
Total			10,101 [d]		18,600
Square root of f					**136**

Entity A's variability after the transfer

Scenario	PV of cash flows	Probability	Probability weighted PV	Variability in PV	Probability weighted variability
	a	b	c = a x b	e = a – d	f = e² x b
1	1,000	20%	200	(12)	29
2	1,055	30%	317	43	555
3	1,106	30%	332	94	2,651
4	817	20%	163	(195)	7,605
Total			1,012 [d]		10,840
Square root of f					**104**

Senior note holders' variability after the transfer

Scenario	PV of cash flows	Probability	Probability weighted PV	Variability in PV	Probability weighted variability
	a	b	c = a x b	e = a – d	f = e² x b
1	9,000	20%	1,800	(90)	1,620
2	9,083	30%	2,725	(7)	15
3	9,159	30%	2,748	69	1,428
4	9,083	20%	1,817	(7)	10
Total			9,090 [d]		3,073
Square root of f					**55**

Entity A determines whether substantially all of the risks and rewards of ownership of the transferred assets are retained by dividing the variability retained after the transfer by the variability of the portfolio as a whole [$^{104}/_{136}$ = 76%]. Consequently, Entity A concludes that substantially all the risks and rewards of ownership are neither transferred nor retained. Entity A would then need to address whether it has control of the transferred asset as described in detail in **3.1.7** below to determine whether Entity A can derecognise the asset in full or continue to recognise its continuing involvement in the transferred assets.

It is worth noting that the sum of variability of Entity A after the transfer (£104) plus variability of the senior note holders (55) is greater than the variability of the portfolio as a whole (£136). This arises because the portfolio of loans as a whole has less risk due to the diversification of the loans within the portfolio. Some of this diversification is reversed when the portfolio is split into pieces. More complex mathematical techniques can be applied to show Entity B's variability to the loans after transfer that include the diversification effect that exists in the portfolio prior to the transfer. Such techniques are not covered in this publication.

3.1.6 *Has the entity retained substantially all of the risks and rewards of ownership of the asset?*

If the entity has retained substantially all of the risks and rewards of ownership of a financial asset, the entity shall continue to recognise that financial asset. [IAS 39.20(b)]

Once again, where it is unclear whether the entity has retained substantially all of the risks and rewards of ownership of the asset it should look at its exposure before and after the transfer by comparing the variability in the amounts and timing of the net cash flows of the transferred asset. [IAS 39.21]

IAS 39 provides examples of transfers where substantially all of the risks and rewards of ownership have been retained and therefore derecognition is not permitted:

[IAS 39.AG40]

- a sale and repurchase transaction where the repurchase price is a fixed price or the sale price plus a lender's return;
- a securities lending transaction;
- a sale of a financial asset together with a total return swap that transfers the market risk back to the entity;
- a sale of a financial asset together with a deep in-the-money written put or purchased call option (i.e. an option that is so far in the money that it is highly unlikely to go out of the money before expiry); and
- a sale of short-term receivables in which the entity guarantees to compensate the transferee for credit losses that are likely to occur.

In a typical repurchase agreement, the entity might, for example, own government securities that it sells to a third party with an agreement to repurchase the securities at a specified price, generally within a short period of time. At inception, the lender transfers the securities to the borrower and receives cash or other consideration as collateral; if the consideration is cash, it is then invested in other assets that earn a return. At a defined date, the transferor repurchases the securities. Dollar repurchase agreements (dollar rolls) are similar transactions in which the transferor repurchases similar but not identical assets to those originally sold. Economically, the lender is motivated in these transactions by the liquidity afforded by the agreement and/or the excess returns it expects to earn on the collateral.

Repurchase agreements are commonly referred to as repos. In many countries, these are actively traded on listed exchanges or in the over-the-counter market and often are used as a source of funding or yield enhancement mechanism. The terminology, however, varies from country to country and the form taken, also, can be different. In some countries, a distinction is made between a repurchase agreement where legal title passes (also known as 'sell/ buy-backs') and a carry (typically, a short term repo that is sometimes known as a classic repo) where title does not pass. Terminology also differs depending on which party is 'buying' or 'selling' the security (hence the use of terms such as reverse repos, inward and outward carries).

In a securities lending transaction the transferor (lender of the security) transfers a security to the transferee (borrower of the security) for a period of time. The transferee generally is required to provide collateral, which may be cash, other securities, or a standby letter of credit with a value that can be slightly higher than the value of the security borrowed (sometimes referred to as a 'haircut'). These transactions are typical when an entity needs a specific security to cover a short sale or a customer's failure to deliver securities sold. The transferor is compensated for lending the security by earning a fee or a return on the collateral invested if the collateral is cash.

A sale and repurchase transaction with a fixed price establishes a lending arrangement whereby the transferor is always going to reacquire the asset in the future. The fixed price is usually set to reflect the cost of borrowing over the period of the transaction. As the transferor is required to reacquire the asset for a fixed price, the transferor is exposed to the market risk of the asset. The same analysis applies to a securities lending transaction. [IAS 39.AG51(a)]

A sale of a financial asset together with a total return swap that transfers the market risk back to the entity also establishes the economic equivalent of a lending arrangement. Under the terms of the total return swap, the transferor will usually pay an amount equivalent to a borrowing rate to the transferee over time and the transferee will reimburse the transferor for the performance of the asset. For example, the transferred asset may be an equity security: if the equity price goes up, the transferor receives the benefits of the rise in value of the transferred equity security from the transferee and pays an amount equivalent to a borrowing rate to the transferee; if the equity security price falls, the transferor pays an amount equivalent to a borrowing rate and, in addition, pays an amount equivalent to the fall in value of the equity security. The transferor continues to be exposed to the rise and fall in the equity security price after the transfer and hence, has retained substantially all of the risks and rewards of ownership of the asset. [IAS 39.AG51(o)]

Where an entity sells an asset, but retains the right to buy the asset back at a price that is sufficiently low (option is deep in the money) that the option is highly likely to be exercised, the entity retains substantially all the risks and rewards of ownership. Similarly, where an entity sells an asset and gives the transferee the right to put the asset back at a sufficiently advantageous price (option is deep in the money) so that the option is likely to be exercised, the entity retains substantially all the risks and rewards of ownership. [IAS 39.AG51(f)]

Example 3.1.6A

Transfer of receivables with a deep in-the-money written put option (1)

Transferor X transfers receivables that are carried at amortised cost with a carrying amount of $90 and a put option which expires in 10 days to Transferee Y. Transferee Y pays $150 for the receivables, which have a fair value of $100. Under the terms of the put option, Transferee Y may put the receivables to Transferor X for $151. The possibility of the fair value of the receivables increasing to $151 in 10 days is considered remote and, therefore, exercise of the option appears virtually assured at inception.

Since at inception it is virtually certain that the put option will be exercised, Transferor X has retained substantially all of the risks and rewards of ownership over the receivables, and this transaction should be accounted for as a secured borrowing of $150 with the difference between the consideration received and the put strike price, being $1, amortised to profit or loss using the effective interest rate method.

However, the same analysis is not appropriate where the option is not deep in the money and therefore further derecognition tests should be applied.

In a sale of short-term receivables where the main risk of ownership is credit risk (i.e. the risk that the debtor will fail to pay) and the entity guarantees to compensate the transferee for credit losses that are likely to occur, the transferor has retained substantially all of the risks of ownership. [IAS 39.AG40(e)]

All the terms of a transfer need to be carefully evaluated. For example, penalty provisions attached to the agreement may affect the analysis of whether the risks and rewards have been transferred.

Example 3.1.6B

Transfer of receivables with a deep in-the-money written put option (2)

Transferor X transfers receivables with a carrying amount of $90 and a put option that expires in 10 days' time to Transferee Y. In the exchange, Transferee Y pays Transferor X $100, the fair value of the receivables. Under the terms of the put option, Transferee Y may put the receivables back to Transferor X for $101. However, if Transferee Y does not put the receivables back to Transferor X, Transferee Y must pay Transferor X an additional $50. The possibility of the fair value of the receivables increasing to $151 in 10 days is remote and, therefore, exercise of the option appears virtually assured at inception.

Since at inception it is virtually certain that the put option will be exercised, Transferor X has effectively retained substantially all the risks and rewards of ownership, and therefore the transaction should be accounted for as a secured borrowing of $100 with the difference between the consideration received of $100 and the put strike price, of $101, amortised to profit or loss using the effective interest rate method.

Typical risks included in a risk and reward analysis are interest rate risk, credit risk (i.e. risk of default), late payment risk, and currency risk. In many securitisation transactions an entity, typically a special purpose entity ('SPE'), acquires assets and issues notes that are backed by those assets. The overall securitisation has liquidity risk associated with the fact that there is a mismatch in the timing of cash inflows and outflows. It is important to recognise that liquidity risk differs between late payment risk and default risk. If an asset pays late, the transferee may have liquidity risk as it cannot immediately meet its obligations under the notes. This risk is not part of the transferred asset as it only results when the assets are placed inside the securitisation structure. The liquidity risk associated with late payment risk is therefore not included in the transferor's risk and rewards assessment in determining derecognition for the transferor. However, the impact of liquidity risk will be included as part of the risks and rewards analysis of the SPE in determining whether an entity should consolidate that SPE.

Derivatives are often included in the contractual arrangements that transfer financial assets and may affect the analysis of whether the risks and rewards of those assets have been transferred. Their presence and contractual terms may not be obvious and careful review of all the terms of the transfer agreement is required.

In some instances, derivatives are included in a transfer or a securitisation structure and are not explicitly defined as derivatives. For example, the terms of a securitisation may call for the allocation of all principal cash flows to outside investors, with any remainder going to the retained interest of the seller. This provision may be in the form of a call option, put option, or forward contract. Identifying the implicit derivative in this example requires a thorough understanding of the transfer structure, terms, and conditions. A further assessment is required in these circumstances to determine the applicability of the embedded derivative provisions (see **chapter 17**).

Derivatives commonly found in transfers of financial assets include put options, call options, forward or repurchase contracts, forward sales contracts and swap agreements. Put options provide the transferee with the right to require the transferor to repurchase some or all of the financial assets that were sold, for example, to repurchase delinquent receivables. Call options provide the transferor with the right to repurchase some or all of the financial assets sold to the transferee. Forward or repurchase agreements require the transferee to sell and the transferor to buy some or all of the financial assets that were sold before their scheduled maturity. Forward sales contracts require the transferor to sell and the transferee to buy additional financial assets in the future. Swap agreements effectively change one or more cash flows of the underlying transferred assets (or debt issued by a special purpose entity). For example, an interest rate swap may convert a variable rate asset to a fixed rate.

Derivatives can operate automatically or require exercise by one of the parties; they can be exercised freely or only after the occurrence of a future event. Such a future event may be certain of occurring, such as the passage of time, or may be conditional upon another event, such as a loan becoming delinquent. The certainty of occurrence varies with conditional events. Some conditional events may be probable of occurring, possible of occurring, or their occurrence may be considered remote. The exercise price of a derivative can be fixed above, below or equal to the market value of the financial assets at inception or it can be variable, equal to the market value at exercise date, or the result of a formula that is a function of market conditions or other future events. Derivatives can be combined to form different types of derivatives. Each of these factors impacts the extent to which risks and rewards have been retained by the transferor.

Where a transferor transfers a fixed rate debt instrument for cash or other consideration and at the same time enters into an interest rate swap with the transferee so that the transferor receives a fixed rate and pays floating rate based on a notional equal to the par amount of the transferred debt instrument the interest rate swap does not preclude derecognition of the debt instrument as long as payments under the swap are not conditional on payments being made on the transferred debt. [IAS 39.AG51(p)] Even though the interest rate swap results in the transferor receiving cash flows similar to the underlying cash flows it would have received under the debt instrument, this does not prevent derecognition as the transferor's exposure before and after the transfer is different. Prior to the transfer the transferor is exposed to fixed interest only and the credit risk of the issuer of the debt instrument. After the transfer the transferor is exposed to the net of fixed and floating interest rates and the credit risk of the transferee to the extent that the transferee owes the transferor any amounts under the interest rate swap. If the cash flows under the swap were contingent on the cash flows received under the debt instrument then credit risk of the interest flows under the debt instrument would be retained by the transferor and a different derecognition conclusion is likely to result.

Where a transferor transfers a prepayable fixed rate debt instrument for cash or other consideration and at the same time enters into an amortising interest rate swap with the transferee so that the transferor receives fixed rate and pays floating rate the transferor will have retained prepayment risk if the repayment profile on the debt instrument matches the amortising profile of the interest rate risk. In this case, the transferor will either continue to fully recognise the fixed rate debt instrument or will recognise the transferred asset to the extent of its continuing involvement. If the amortisation of the notional of the swap is not linked to the principal amount outstanding of the transferred asset, the swap will not result in the transferor retaining prepayment risk on the asset. [IAS 39.AG51(q)] For the same reasons as described above for non-amortising swaps, as long as the interest flows on the swap are not conditional on the cash flows under the debt instrument and the swap does not result in the transferor retaining any other significant risks and rewards of the ownership then derecognition of the asset would apply.

3.1.7 *Has the entity retained control of the asset?*

Where an entity determines that it has neither transferred nor retained substantially all of the risks and rewards of ownership of the transferred assets it has to make an assessment as to whether or not it has retained control of the asset.

- If the entity has not retained control of the financial asset, the entity shall derecognise the financial asset and recognise separately as assets or liabilities any rights and obligations created or retained in the transfer.
- If the entity has retained control of the financial asset, the entity shall continue to recognise the financial asset to the extent of its continuing involvement in the financial asset. [IAS 39.20(c)]

An entity controls a financial asset when it is able to sell that asset. Where the transferee has the *practical ability* to sell the asset in its entirety to an *unrelated* third party and is able to exercise that ability *unilaterally* and *without* the imposition of additional *restrictions* on the transfer, the transferee controls the asset, and hence the transferor must have relinquished control. [IAS 39.23]

Where the transferred asset is traded in an active market the transferee generally has the practical ability to sell the asset. This is because there is a ready market and the transferee can repurchase the asset if and when it is required to return the asset back to the transferor. [IAS 39.AG42]

However, the fact that the transferred asset is traded in an active market is not in itself sufficient to conclude that the transferee has the 'practical ability' to sell the asset. For example, the settlement terms of repurchase, which are driven by the market conventions, may differ significantly from the settlement terms in the transfer agreement such that the transferee will not be able to get hold of the asset quickly enough to deliver the asset to the transferor so as to comply with the contractual provisions of the transfer agreement. In this case the transferee is forced to hold the asset in order to ensure that it can deliver the asset back to the transferor when required.

Other factors may affect the entity's practical ability to sell the asset:

- a financial asset that would satisfy the call option or forward contract may have to be purchased from a third party at a price significantly above its estimated fair value, thus indicating that the assets are not liquid;

- financial assets available to satisfy the call option or forward contract may be held by one or a small number of investors, thus indicating that the assets are not liquid; or
- the quantity of financial assets necessary to satisfy the call option or forward contract may be too large compared to that traded in the market and the terms of the transfer do not allow delivery of the assets over a period of time.

Intuitively, the wider the range of assets that may be used to satisfy the call option, the more likely it is that the entity has practical ability to sell the asset. For instance, assets identical to those originally transferred may not be readily obtainable, but, if the call option permits delivery of assets that are similar to the transferred assets, they may be readily obtainable. Where a call option permits settlement in cash as an alternative to delivering the financial asset, and the cash settlement alternative does not contain an economic penalty rendering it unfeasible, the transferee has the practical ability to sell the asset as cash is a readily obtainable asset.

Unilateral and unrestricted ability to sell means that there can be no 'strings' attached to the sale. If the transferee has to attach a call option over the asset when it sells it, or introduce conditions over how the asset is serviced, in order to satisfy the terms of the original transfer, then 'strings' exist and the test of 'practical ability' is failed.

The 'strings' can be created by other instruments that form a contractual part of the transfer arrangement and are sufficiently valuable to the transferee, so that if the transferee were to sell the asset it would rationally include similar features within that sale. For example, a guarantee may be included in the initial transfer and may have such potential value to the transferee that the transferee would be reluctant to sell the asset and forgo any payments that may fall due under the guarantee.

The transfer agreement may have an explicit restriction that prohibits the transferee from selling the asset. When that restriction is removed or lapses, and as a result the transferee has the practical ability to sell the asset, derecognition would then be appropriate.

The fact that the transferee may or may not choose to sell the asset should not form part of the decision making process, it is the transferee's practical ability to do so that is important.

Example 3.1.7A

Transfer of readily obtainable bonds with written put option

Transferor X sells South African government bonds that are readily obtainable in the market with a book value of 100 Rand to Transferee Y for 103 Rand. The transfer includes an option for Transferee Y to put the assets back to Transferor X up to one year after the transfer date at 103.50 Rand. Transferee Y exercises its option 30 days after the initial sale. The option had a fair value of 2 Rand at the exchange date consisting of time value of 1.50 Rand and intrinsic value of 0.50 Rand.

In this example, the transferor has neither transferred nor retained substantially all the risks and rewards of ownership because the option is neither deeply in, or deeply out of the money. The transferor has not retained control because the assets are readily obtainable. This put option does not therefore preclude derecognition.

Example 3.1.7B

Transfer of mortgage loans with right to call

Transferor X transfers a portfolio of mortgage loans to a third party, Transferee Y. The transferred loans can be repurchased by Transferor X at any time prior to their maturity. The agreement contains no explicit conditions restraining Transferee Y from selling, exchanging or pledging the assets to a third party.

Transferee Y does not have the practical ability to sell the portfolio of mortgage loans since it must have access to the original mortgage loans that were transferred in the event Transferor X exercises its right under the call option, and the mortgage loans cannot be readily obtained from another source.

IAS 39 envisages instances where the transferee does not have the unilateral and unrestricted ability to sell the asset due to arrangements such as a call option held by the transferor. The Standard is less clear on the treatment when a call option is held by a party other than the transferor. Consider the following example.

Bank A transfers loans to a non-consolidated SPE. The funds that the SPE used to purchase the loans were generated through a securitisation involving notes being issued by the SPE to third parties. Bank A invests in a note that comprises an interest-only strip on the transferred loans and also provides a subordinated loan to the SPE. The SPE is consolidated by Bank B (independent third party relative to Bank A) due to it providing a larger subordinated loan and investing in the most junior notes of the SPE such that it is exposed to the majority of the risks and rewards of the vehicle. Bank B has a call on the assets of the SPE that is exercisable at a fixed price.

As Bank A has invested in the interest-only strip and provided the subordinated loan it is considered to neither have transferred nor retained substantially all of the risks and rewards of the transferred loans. Bank A must assess whether it has retained control of the asset. Much of the guidance in this area focuses on whether the *transferee* has the practical ability to sell the asset in its entirety to an unrelated third party and is able to exercise that ability unilaterally and without imposition of additional restrictions.

In this example, if the SPE is considered to be the transferee, it does not have such practical ability to sell the loans without restrictions. If it were to sell the loans it would need to attach restrictions such that it could honour its obligations under the call option which allows Bank B to call the remaining loans. However, this conclusion is contrary to the principle that the transferor should retain an interest in the asset for it to have a continuing involvement. If the transferee in this case is viewed as the consolidated group of Bank B (which therefore includes the SPE) then the transferee does have the unrestricted ability to sell the assets as the call option is eliminated on consolidation. Also, it can be argued that Bank A has not retained control of the asset, given that it has no mechanism within the arrangements for buying back the loans or being forced to acquire the loans. It is acceptable in this case for Bank A to derecognise the loans, and therefore not to apply continuing involvement accounting (see **3.4** below), and instead recognise the interest only strip and subordinated loan at fair value.

3.2 Transfers that qualify for derecognition

Where an entity concludes that derecognition of a financial asset is appropriate (the rights to the cash flows from the asset expired, or the entity has transferred substantially all of its risks and rewards, or the entity no longer retains control of the asset), the asset is removed from the statement of financial position and any new financial assets obtained, financial liabilities assumed and any servicing obligation are recognised at fair value. [IAS 39.25]

Often the transferor continues to service the transferred assets for a fee, which may take the form of part of the interest receipts on the transferred assets that an entity retains as compensation for servicing those assets.

Servicing refers to activities associated with the collection of cash flows from receivables or other financial assets after origination and the distribution of that cash to investors if the receivables are owned by other entities. Servicing may include the temporary investment and distribution to the financial asset owners of all or a portion of the cash collected. Servicing activities, also, may include monitoring delinquencies, advancing delinquent payments, restructuring receivables, and foreclosing on the collateral underlying the receivables when necessary. If the receivables are mortgage loans, servicing activities often include collecting and disbursing escrow payments for taxes and insurance. Servicing activities are inherent in all receivables; however, they do not need to be performed by the owner of the receivables. If the receivables are being serviced for another entity, the servicer generally receives a fee for performing these activities. This fee is usually a contractual amount received based on a fixed percentage of the outstanding receivables for the period. Servicers may also receive additional compensation by retaining late charges, other ancillary fees, and the float, which is the net interest earned on funds held by the servicer before disbursement. The compensation received by the servicer is referred to as the benefits of servicing.

Where the benefits of servicing are not expected to cover the costs of servicing the assets, then the entity should recognise a liability for the fair value of the service obligation that it has entered into as a result of the transfer. [IAS 39.24] The servicing in this instance represents an obligation, because the servicer would have to pay another entity to assume the servicing contract or use its assets in the future to perform under the servicing contract.

When the benefits of servicing exactly compensate the servicer for performing the servicing but provide no additional benefits, the servicer has neither an asset nor a liability and the fair value of this servicing contract is zero. A servicing contract with a positive fair value is considered to be one that would be favourable for a substitute servicer should one be required, and includes the profit that would be demanded in the marketplace. The amount allocated to a servicing right is treated as a retained interest and the amount allocated to it is determined by allocating the carrying amount of the larger financial asset. [IAS 39.24]

Example 3.2

Allocating consideration received between sold and retained interests

Entity A owns £1,000,000 face amount of loans that contractually yield 10 per cent interest over their life. The carrying amount of these loans after recognising impairment of £20,000 is £980,000. Entity A sells 90 per cent of the principal, plus the right to receive interest income of 8 per cent without recourse to an investor for £900,000 in cash. The part of the asset that has been transferred meets all the criteria for derecognition.

Entity A retains the right to service these loans, and the servicing contract stipulates a 1 per cent fee as compensation for performing the servicing. Entity A also retains an interest-only strip for the portion of the interest coupon not sold (1 per cent). At the date of transfer, the fair value of the retained 10 per cent of the loan is £100,000; the fair value of the servicing asset is £15,000; and the fair value of the interest-only strip is £35,000.

The following table demonstrates the allocation of this loan between the sold and retained interests assuming the entity has already determined that it has transferred substantially all risks and rewards of ownership of the transferred asset (for example substantially all the credit losses and the majority of interest rate risk on the loans transferred):

Interest	**Fair value**	**Percentage of total fair value**	**Allocated carrying amount (1)**	**Sold interests**	**Retained interests**
Loans sold	£900,000	85.71	£840,000	£840,000	–
Loans retained	£100,000	9.53	£93,333	–	£93,333
IO strip	£35,000	3.33	£32,667	–	£32,667
Servicing asset	£15,000	1.43	£14,000	–	£14,000
Total	£1,050,000	100.00	£980,000	£840,000	£140,000

(1)The allocated carrying amount is calculated as the percentage of total fair value multiplied by the aggregate carrying amount prior to the transfer (£980,000).

The difference between:

- the carrying amount allocated to the part derecognised; and
- the sum of (i) the consideration received for the part derecognised (including any new asset obtained less any new liability assumed) and, for available-for-sale assets, (ii) any cumulative gain or loss allocated to it that had been recognised in other comprehensive income;

is recognised in profit or loss. A cumulative gain or loss, for available-for-sale assets, that had been recognised in other comprehensive income is allocated between the part that is derecognised and the part that continues to be recognised on the basis of their relative fair values. [IAS 39.27]

In the above example the assets were carried at amortised cost and the amount recognised in the profit or loss is calculated as the difference between the consideration of £900,000 and the allocated carrying amount of the derecognised asset of £840,000.

There are likely to be instances in which applying basis allocation based on the 'relative fair value method' is difficult to apply because it is difficult to obtain the fair value of the parts of the asset that are subject to derecognition and continued recognition. The Standard acknowledges that where an entity has a historical practice of selling parts similar to the part that is continued to be recognised, or other market transactions for such parts exist, recent prices for actual transactions would best reflect the fair value of the parts. Where there are no price quotes available, the best estimate of the fair value is the difference between the fair value of the larger financial asset as a whole and the consideration received from the transferee for the part of the asset that is derecognised. [IAS 39.28]

3.3 Transfers that do not qualify for derecognition

Where a financial asset is precluded from being derecognised in its entirety, i.e. the transferor retains substantially all of the risks and rewards of ownership, the entity continues to recognise the asset in its entirety and recognises a financial liability for the consideration received. [IAS 39.29] The asset and liability cannot be offset and, similarly, any income arising from the asset cannot be offset against any expense incurred on the liability. [IAS 39.36] The asset's classification, measurement basis and income recognition does not change as a result of the transfer. This accounting treatment is often referred to as 'gross presentation' or 'secured borrowing' presentation.

Example 3.3

Transfer of receivables with credit guarantee

Entity X transfers short term receivables to Entity Y and provides a credit guarantee to Entity Y over the expected losses of those receivables.

Entity X continues to recognise the receivables in its statement of financial position because it has retained substantially all the risks and rewards of ownership of the receivables. Entity X will recognise a financial liability for the proceeds received. The substance of the arrangement is that of a secured borrowing, i.e. short term receivables provide security for the cash advanced by Entity Y.

Where a derivative financial instrument forms part of the transfer arrangement and precludes the asset from being derecognised, the derivative is not accounted for separately as this would result in the derivative being effectively counted twice. [IAS 39.AG49]

IAS 39 does not provide specific guidance on the accounting for the transferee in the case where the transferor continues to recognise the asset in its entirety. It is reasonable to assume that the accounting for the transferee is the inverse of the accounting for the transferor in this case. For example, if the transferor continues to recognise the asset and therefore recognises a collateralised borrowing for the consideration received then the transferee will not recognise the asset but will instead recognise a collateral lending to the transferor. If a derivative is entered into between the transferor and transferee as part of the arrangement but is not recognised by the transferor because it is an impediment to derecognition, then similarly the derivative will not be recognised by the transferee. The terms of the collateralised lending will include the cash consideration paid at the date of transfer, the contractual cash flows of the derivative, as well as the imputed repayment of principal.

3.4 Continuing involvement in the transferred assets

Where an entity neither transfers, nor retains substantially all of the risks and rewards of ownership of a financial asset, and retains control of that asset, the entity continues to recognise the asset to the extent of its continuing involvement. Continuing involvement represents the extent to which the transferor continues to be exposed to the changes in the value of the transferred asset. A corresponding liability is also recognised and measured in such a way that the *net* carrying amount of the asset and the liability is:

- the amortised cost of the rights and obligations retained, if the asset is measured at amortised cost; or
- the fair value of the rights and obligations retained, if the asset is measured at fair value. [IAS 39.31]

The liability that is recognised at the date of transfer will not necessarily equate to the proceeds received in transferring the asset which would ordinarily be the case if the asset continued to be fully recognised and the proceeds received were recognised as a collateralised borrowing. In some cases, the liability appears to be the 'balancing figure' that is the result of applying the specific guidance for continuing involvement accounting. IAS 39 acknowledges that measuring the liability by reference to the interest in the transferred asset is not in compliance with the other measurement requirements of the standard. [IAS 39.31]

This requirement for consistent measurement of the asset and associated liability means that designation of the liability as at fair value through profit or loss is not available if the transferred asset is measured at amortised cost (see **7.1.2** in **chapter 15**).

The entity cannot offset the asset and the associated liability. Any subsequent changes in the fair value of that asset and that liability are measured consistently and are not offset. [IAS 39.33] Any income on the asset to the extent of the entity's continuing involvement and any expense incurred on the associated liability are not offset. [IAS 39.32]

Where an entity transfers assets, but retains a guarantee over the transferred assets that absorb future credit losses and that guarantee (as well as other continuing involvement) results in the transferor neither transferring nor retaining substantially all the risks and rewards of ownership, the transferor must recognise the guarantee as part of its continuing involvement. Assuming for illustration only, that the guarantee represents the transferor's only continuing involvement in the transferred asset, then:

- the transferred asset at the date of transfer will be measured at the lower of (i) the carrying value of the asset; and (ii) the maximum amount of the consideration received in the transfer that the entity could be required to repay; and
- the associated liability is measured initially at the amount in (ii) above plus the fair value of the guarantee.

The initial fair value of the guarantee is recognised in profit or loss on a time proportion basis in accordance with IAS 18 *Revenue* and the carrying value of the asset is reduced by any impairment losses. [IAS 39.AG48(a)]

Example 3.4A

Continuing involvement: guarantee over first default losses

Transferor X transfers an asset that is carried at, and is worth, £100 on the date of transfer to Transferee Y. Transferee Y pays £105. Transferor X provides a guarantee to Transferee Y to pay for the first default losses up to a value of £8. The fair value of the guarantee at the date of transfer is £5. Expected future losses on the portfolio are £12. Transferor X considers that substantially all the risks and rewards of ownership have neither been transferred, nor retained. Transferee Y does not have the practical ability to sell the assets, i.e. Transferor X controls the asset.

Transferor X determines its continuing involvement as the extent to which it continues to be exposed to the changes in the value of the transferred asset, i.e. the lower of:

(i) the carrying amount of the asset (£100); and

(ii) the maximum amount of the consideration received in the transfer that Transferor X could be required to repay ('the guarantee amount') (£8).

Transferor X records its continuing involvement in the asset at £8, and derecognises the part of the asset transferred, i.e. £92. The associated liability is initially measured at £13, being the guarantee amount (£8) plus the fair value of the guarantee (£5). Subsequently, the initial fair value of the guarantee is recognised in profit or loss on a time proportion basis.

The following entries would be made at the date of transfer:

Dr	Cash	£105
Cr	Financial asset	£92
Cr	Financial liability	£13

If at the end of the guarantee period, no amounts have been paid under the guarantee then the following entries will be required:

Dr	Financial liability	£8	(the fair value of the guarantee of £5 will have been fully amortised by the end of the guarantee period)
Cr	Financial asset	£8	

If at the end of the guarantee period, the full amount of the guarantee is claimed by Transferee Y then the following entries will be required:

Dr	Financial liability	£8	
Cr	Cash	£8	
Dr	Profit or loss	£8	(the fair value of the guarantee of £5 will have been fully amortised by the end of the guarantee period)
Cr	Financial asset	£8	

Example 3.4B

Continuing involvement: guarantee over slow payment risk

Entity A transfers short term receivables to Bank B under a factoring arrangement. Entity A transfers the credit risk of the receivables but retains the slow payment risk up to a maximum of 120 days. If the receivable is outstanding after 120 days the risk is absorbed by Bank B as the receivables is deemed to be in default. Entity A is charged a market interest rate of 10% for the slow payment risk on the outstanding balance for the period it is deemed to be a slow paying receivable. At the date of transfer receivables with a face value and amortised cost of £300m are transferred and the fair value of the late payment guarantee is £1m. The total consideration received by Entity A receives is 96% of the face value of the receivables at the date of transfer.

Entity A considers it has neither retained nor transferred substantially of all the risks and rewards of ownership and is deemed to control the receivables as Bank B does not have the practical ability to sell the transferred assets.

Entity A determines its continuing involvement as the extent to which it continues to be exposed to the late payment risk of the transferred asset, i.e. the lower of:

(i) the carrying amount of the asset (£300m); and

(ii) the maximum amount of the consideration received in the transfer that Entity A could be required to repay ('the guarantee amount') (£3m, being £300m x 120/360 x 10%).

Entity A records its continuing involvement in the asset at £3m, and derecognises the part of the asset transferred, i.e. £297m. The associated liability is initially measured at £4m, being the guarantee amount (£3m) plus the fair value of the guarantee (£1m). Subsequently, the initial fair value of the guarantee is recognised in profit or loss on a time proportion basis.

Dr	Cash	288
Dr	Continuing involvement in the transferred asset	3
Dr	Loss on disposal	13
Cr	Receivables	300
Cr	Continuing involvement liability	4

To record the derecognition of the receivables and the recognition of the continuing involvement.

The interest in the continuing involvement asset of £3m less the continuing involvement liability £4m is equal to the fair value of the guarantee at the date of transfer, being £1m.

3.4.1 Continuing involvement through options

Transfer arrangements often contain written or purchased options, or combinations thereof, so that the transferor neither retains, nor transfers substantially all the risks and rewards of ownership, and controls the transferred asset. This is the case when the option is neither deeply-in, nor deeply-out of the money at the date of transfer. In such transfer arrangements, with the exception of arrangements that contain a put option written by the transferor and the transferor measures the asset at its fair value, the entity's continuing involvement in the asset is the amount of the transferred asset that the entity may repurchase. In the case of the arrangement that contains a put option written by the transferor where the transferor measures the asset at its fair value, the continuing involvement is the lower of the asset's fair value and the option exercise price. [IAS 39.30(b)] This is because in such a transfer arrangement the entity has no right to increases in fair value of the transferred asset above the exercise price of the option.

The table below sets out the measurement bases for the asset and associated liability for transfers that contain written or purchased options, or combinations thereof, where the transferor continues to recognise its continuing involvement in the asset. The manner of settlement of the options, gross or net cash settled, does not affect the accounting analysis below. However, a cash settled option in of itself is less likely to restrict the transferee's practical ability to sell the transferred asset, so may not result in the transferor retaining control of the transferred asset, and therefore continuing involvement accounting would not apply.

Derivative involved	**Measurement basis of transferred asset prior to the transfer**	**Measurement basis of transferred asset after the transfer**	**Measurement basis of the associated financial liability**
Purchased call option	Amortised cost	Amortised cost	Amortised cost: cost on initial recognition (being consideration received) is adjusted for amortisation of the difference between that cost and amortised cost of the asset on the expiration date of the option.
Written put option	Amortised cost	Amortised cost	Amortised cost: cost on initial recognition (being consideration received) is adjusted for amortisation of the difference between that cost and amortised cost of the asset on the expiration date of the option.
Purchased call option	Fair value	Fair value	Where the *option is in or at the money* - the call option exercise price less the time value of the option. Where the *option is out of the money* - the fair value of the transferred asset less the time value of the option. This ensures that the net carrying amount of the asset and associated liability is the fair value of the call option right.
Written put option	Fair value	Fair value (limited to the lower of the fair value of the asset and the option exercise price)	Option exercise price plus the time value of the option. This ensures that the net carrying amount of the asset and associated liability is the fair value of the put option obligation.
Collar (combination of purchased call and a written put)	Amortised cost	Amortised cost	Amortised cost: cost on initial recognition (being consideration received) is adjusted for amortisation of the difference between that cost and amortised cost of the asset on the expiration date of the options.

Derivative involved	Measurement basis of transferred asset prior to the transfer	Measurement basis of transferred asset after the transfer	Measurement basis of the associated financial liability
Collar (combination of purchased call and a written put)	Fair value	Fair value	Where the *call option is in or at the money* - the sum of the call exercise price and fair value of the put option less the time value of the call option. Where the *call option is out of the money* - the sum of the fair value of the asset and the fair value of the put option less the time value of the call option. This ensures that the net carrying amount of the asset and associated liability is the fair value of the options held and written.

The examples below apply the requirements set out in the table above:

Example 3.4.1

Continuing involvement: options

(a) Out of the money purchased call

Entity A transfers an asset to Bank X and receives $92. The amortised cost of the asset on the date of transfer is $98. The amortised cost of the asset on the expiration of the option will be $100. The fair value of the asset on the date of transfer is $95. The exercise price of the purchased call option is $99 (being out of the money at the date of transfer) and therefore the premium paid to purchase the option consists entirely of the time value, being $3, at the date of transfer.

The asset is held at amortised cost. On the date of transfer the asset will continue to be recognised at $98. The associated liability will be recognised at the fair value of the consideration received, $92, with the difference between $92 and $100 being recognised in profit or loss using the effective interest rate method.

The asset is held at fair value. On the date of transfer the asset will continue to be recognised at $95. The associated liability will be recognised at $92, being the fair value of the transferred asset, $95, less the time value of the option, $3.

(b) In or at the money purchased call

Entity A transfers an asset to Bank X and receives $87. The amortised cost of the asset on the date of transfer is $98. The amortised cost of the asset on the expiration of the option will be $100. The fair value of the asset on the date of transfer is $95. The exercise price of the purchased call option is $90 (being in the money at the date of transfer) and therefore the premium paid to purchase the option consists of intrinsic value, being $5, and time value, being $3, at the date of transfer.

The asset is held at amortised cost. On the date of transfer the asset will continue to be recognised at $98. The associated liability will be recognised at the fair value of the consideration received, $87, with the difference between $87 and $100 being recognised in profit or loss using the effective interest rate method.

The asset is held at fair value. On the date of transfer the asset will continue to be recognised at $95. The associated liability will be recognised at $87, being the option exercise price, $90, less the time value of the option, $3.

(c) Written put

Entity A transfers an asset to Bank X and receives $95. The amortised cost of the asset on the date of transfer is $98. The amortised cost of the asset on the expiration of the option will be $100. The fair value of the asset on the date of transfer is $92. The exercise price of the written put is $90 (out of the money at the date of transfer) and therefore the premium received for writing the option consists entirely of time value, being $3.

The asset is held at amortised cost. On the date of transfer the asset will continue to be recognised at $98. The associated liability will be recognised at the fair value of the consideration received, $95, with the difference between $95 and $100 being recognised in profit or loss using the effective interest rate method.

The asset is held at fair value. The asset will be recorded at the lower of its fair value and the option exercise price, i.e. at $90. The associated liability will be recognised at $93, being the option exercise price, $90, plus the time value of the option, $3.

(d) Collar

Entity A transfers an asset to Bank X and receives $98. The amortised cost of the asset on the date of transfer is $98. The amortised cost of the asset on the expiration of the option will be $100. The fair value of the asset on the date of transfer is $92. The cost of the collar at the date of transfer is zero. The exercise price of the written put is $80 (out of the money at the date of transfer) and the exercise price of the purchased call is $120 (out of the money at the date of transfer).

The asset is held at amortised cost. On the date of transfer the asset will continue to be recognised at $98. The associated liability will be recognised at the fair value of the consideration received, $98, with the difference between $98 and $100 being recognised in profit or loss using the effective interest rate method.

The asset is held at fair value. On the date of transfer the asset will continue to be recognised at $92. The associated liability will be recognised at $92, which is calculated as the sum of the fair value of the asset, $92, and the fair value of the put, less the time value of the call. The fair value of the put will be equal to the time value of the call, as the put's fair value represents only time value, and the sum of the two premiums on the options (both representing time value only) is zero.

Where an option expires unexercised, the transferor derecognises financial assets that were subject to the option and also derecognises the associated liability. The transferee recognises the financial assets and eliminates the receivable due from the transferor.

3.4.2 *Continuing involvement in a part of a financial asset*

In a situation where an entity has a continuing involvement in only a part of a financial asset, the entity allocates the previous carrying amount of the financial asset between the part it continues to recognise under continuing involvement, and the part it no longer recognises based on the relative fair values of those parts at the date of transfer. [IAS 39.34]

The allocation exercise and the calculation of the gain or loss on the disposal of the part of the asset are done in the same way as in **3.2** above. In addition to the part retained, the transferor also recognises its continuing involvement in the asset and the associated liability. IAS 39.AG52 contains a numerical illustrative example of continuing involvement in a part of an asset which is reproduced below.

Example 3.4.2

Continuing involvement: part of a financial asset

[Extract from IAS 39.AG52]

Assume an entity has a portfolio of prepayable loans whose coupon and effective interest rate is 10 per cent and whose principal amount and amortised cost is CU10,000. It enters into a transaction in which, in return for a payment of CU9,115, the transferee obtains the right to CU9,000 of any collections of principal plus interest thereon at 9.5 per cent. The entity retains rights to CU1,000 of any collections of principal plus interest thereon at 10 per cent, plus the excess spread of 0.5 per cent on the remaining CU9,000 of principal. Collections from prepayments are allocated between the entity and the transferee proportionately in the ratio of 1:9, but any defaults are deducted from the entity's interest of CU1,000 until that interest is exhausted. The fair value of the loans at the date of the transaction is CU10,100 and the estimated fair value of the excess spread of 0.5 per cent is CU40.

The entity determines that it has transferred some significant risks and rewards of ownership (for example, significant prepayment risk) but has also retained some significant risks and rewards of ownership (because of its subordinated retained interest) and has retained control. It therefore applies the continuing involvement approach.

To apply this Standard, the entity analyses the transaction as (a) a retention of a fully proportionate retained interest of CU1,000, plus (b) the subordination of that retained interest to provide credit enhancement to the transferee for credit losses.

The entity calculates that CU9,090 (90 per cent × CU10,100) of the consideration received of CU9,115 represents the consideration for a fully proportionate 90 per cent share. The remainder of the consideration received (CU25) represents consideration received for subordinating its retained interest to provide credit enhancement to the transferee for credit losses. In addition, the excess spread of 0.5 per cent represents consideration received for the credit enhancement. Accordingly, the total consideration received for the credit enhancement is CU65 (CU25 + CU40).

The entity calculates the gain or loss on the sale of the 90 per cent share of cash flows. Assuming that separate fair values of the 90 per cent part transferred and the 10 per cent part retained are not available at the date of the transfer, the entity allocates the carrying amount of the asset in accordance with paragraph 28 as follows:

	Estimated fair value	Percentage	Allocated carrying amount
Portion transferred	9,090	90%	9,000
Portion retained	1,010	10%	1,000
Total	**10,100**		**10,000**

The entity computes its gain or loss on the sale of the 90 per cent share of the cash flows by deducting the allocated carrying amount of the portion transferred from the consideration received, i.e. CU90 (CU9,090 – CU9,000). The carrying amount of the portion retained by the entity is CU1,000.

In addition, the entity recognises the continuing involvement that results from the subordination of its retained interest for credit losses. Accordingly, it recognises an asset of CU1,000 (the maximum amount of the cash flows it would not receive under the subordination), and an associated liability of CU1,065 (which is the maximum amount of the cash flows it would not receive under the subordination, i.e. CU1,000 plus the fair value of the subordination of CU65).

The entity uses all of the above information to account for the transaction as follows:

	Debit	Credit
Original asset	–	9,000
Asset recognised for subordination or the residual interest	1,000	–
Asset for the consideration received in the form of excess spread	40	–

	Debit	Credit
Profit or loss (gain on transfer)	–	90
Liability	–	1,065
Cash received	9,115	–
Total	**10,155**	**10,155**

Immediately following the transaction, the carrying amount of the asset is CU2,040 comprising CU1,000, representing the allocated cost of the portion retained, and CU1,040, representing the entity's additional continuing involvement from the subordination of its retained interest for credit losses (which includes the excess spread of CU40).

In subsequent periods, the entity recognises the consideration received for the credit enhancement (CU65) on a time proportion basis, accrues interest on the recognised asset using the effective interest method and recognises any credit impairment on the recognised assets. As an example of the latter, assume that in the following year there is a credit impairment loss on the underlying loans of CU300. The entity reduces its recognised asset by CU600 (CU300 relating to its retained interest and CU300 relating to the additional continuing involvement that arises from the subordination of its retained interest for credit losses), and reduces its recognised liability by CU300. The net result is a charge to profit or loss for credit impairment of CU300.

A number of observations can be drawn from the example in IAS 39.AG52 reproduced above. A concern that is often cited is that the example advocates 'double-counting', i.e. the continuing involvement in the asset is accounted for twice. Using the numbers in the example above, the transferor continues to recognise a fully proportionate interest in 10% of all cash flows which equals an amortised cost of CU1,000 (being 10% x CU10,000 carrying amount), yet also recognises an additional CU1,000 being the 'asset recognised for subordination or the residual interest'. The reason for presenting the transferor's interest in the transferred asset this way is to reflect that the transferor's interest in 10% of the asset is in fact subordinated (and therefore is not a fully proportionate interest) as any losses borne by the transferred assets continue to be borne by the transferor until their remaining interest is exhausted. In order to recognise the transferor's continuing involvement liability the entity needs to 'gross-up' its statement of financial position by recognising a further asset.

As the transferor's interest in the transferred asset is considered to be a fully proportionate share of the asset (plus that interest being subordinated) the calculation of the gain/loss on partial disposal of the asset is also based on a fully proportionate basis. On the face of it this calculation may appear odd as the entity has not economically sold a fully proportionate share in the asset to the transferee.

The example also recognises another new asset that it refers to as the 'asset for the consideration received in the form of excess spread'. It is worth noting that the amount recognised for the excess spread is equal to the fair value of the excess spread at the date of transfer, being CU40, even though it appears the loans themselves were not originally measured at fair value, i.e. they were originally measured at amortised cost. As the objective of accounting for continuing involvement is to ensure that the measurement of the net involvement (being the net of the continuing involvement asset and continuing involvement liability) is consistent with the measurement of the transferred assets, it is surprising that the excess spread in the example is initially recognised at fair value, as opposed to amortised cost. We suspect this was an oversight when the example was developed.

3.4.3 *Accounting by the transferee in the case of continuing involvement*

Bank S owns a 16 per cent equity stake in a thinly traded entity. The investment is classified by Bank S as an available-for-sale financial asset. Bank S enters into an agreement with Entity K whereby Entity K pays £102 to Bank S in return for:

- the 16 per cent equity interest in the thinly traded entity; and
- a put option that allows Entity K to put the shares back to Bank S for a price of £96 at a pre-specified date.

On the date of the transfer, the fair value of the shares is £97 and the time value of the put option is £5 (£102 minus £97), i.e. the option is out of the money at inception.

Transferor accounting

Bank S, the transferor, will apply continuing involvement accounting as it is considered to control the shares as it has neither transferred nor retained substantially all the risks and rewards of the shares and Entity K does not have the practical ability to sell the shares since it is a significant holding in an entity that is thinly traded.

As the arrangement involves the transferor writing a put option on an asset that is measured at fair value, the extent of the continuing involvement for Bank S is limited to the lower of the fair value of the shares and the option exercise price. [IAS 39.30(b) & AG48]

At the transaction date, the following entries will be required:

Dr	Cash	102
Cr	Available-for-sale financial asset	1
Cr	Financial liability	101

This entry recognises a liability of £101, consisting of a strike price of £96 and time value of the put option of £5.

The shares continue to be recognised by Bank S and measured as an available-for-sale financial asset, though changes in their value above the strike price of £96 are not recognised.

Transferee accounting

Entity K has paid cash of £102 in return for a right to receive cash of £96 (through exercise of its purchased put option) and rights to all the upside on the shares above £96 (i.e. by not exercising its put and physically retaining the transferred shares). Entity K economically has an investment in shares with no downside risk below £96.

Entity K should recognise its interest in the arrangement as an available-for-sale financial asset, but not recognise any changes in fair value below the strike price of £96, as Entity K has no exposure to fair value movements below this amount. This is the inverse of the accounting by the transferor, Bank S. Both parties recognise an available-for-sale investment with Entity K recognising fair value gains above £96, and Bank S recognising fair value gains below £96.

At the date of transfer the following entry will be required:

Dr	Available-for-sale financial asset	102
Cr	Cash	102

This entry will recognise the financial asset consisting of the fair value of the shares of £97 plus the value of the put option of £5. Increases in the fair value of the available-for-sale investment above £96 will be recognised in other comprehensive income. The available-for-sale asset and the purchased put will be re-measured in other comprehensive income. As the purchased put provides a 'floor' of £96, changes in fair value of the security below this amount will not be recognised. At maturity of the option the time value of the option will have been fully eroded resulting in the security either being put at £96 and thereby being derecognised, or continuing to be fair valued in other comprehensive income as the transferee has not exercised the put. The put option is not fair valued through profit or loss since for the transferor it is not recognised as it is an impediment to derecognition, and for the transferee it forms part of its involvement in the asset.

If the put is exercised by Entity K because the share price is below £96 the following entry will be required:

Dr	Cash	96
Cr	Available-for-sale financial asset	96

An amount of £1 would have already been recognised in other comprehensive income when the fair value of asset had decreased to £96. Fair value movements below £96 are not recognised. The £1 in other comprehensive income is reclassified from equity to profit or loss when the put is exercised by Entity K and the available-for-sale asset is derecognised.

If the put is not exercised by Entity K because the share price is above £96 no further entry will be required to recognise the shares as they are already recognised in Entity K's statement of financial position. After the expiration of the option all gains or losses on the available-for-sale investment will be recognised in other comprehensive income (except impairment losses recognised in profit or loss) as Entity K will be exposed to movements in the share price in both directions.

3.5 Collateral

A transfer arrangement may require a transferor to provide non-cash collateral (e.g. a debt or an equity instrument) to the transferee. The transferee's entitlement to the collateral is conditional upon the transferor's default and while the transferor continues to perform under the contract, the transferor continues to benefit from substantially all of the collateral's risks and rewards. Normal recognition and derecognition principles apply to the collateral: the transferee is not entitled to recognise the collateral until it becomes contractually entitled to it, which will not be the case until the transferor defaults under the terms of the contract; the transferor retains all of the risks and rewards of ownership of the asset pledged as collateral and therefore cannot derecognise it.

Where the transferee has the right by contract or custom to sell or repledge the collateral then the asset that has been pledged by the transferor should be reclassified in its statement of financial position separately from its other assets and described as a loaned asset, pledged equity instrument or repurchase receivable. Where the transferee uses that right and sells the collateral, it shall recognise the proceeds from the sale and a liability measured at fair value for its obligation to return the collateral. [IAS 39.37]

In the event of a default by the transferor the risks and rewards of the collateral, within the confines of the collateral agreement, are transferred to the transferee. Hence, the transferor derecognises the collateral and the transferee, who after the default becomes contractually entitled to it, recognises the collateral at its fair value, unless the transferee has already sold the collateral, in which case, it derecognises its obligation to return the collateral to the transferor.

3.6 Sale and repurchase agreements and stock lending

A sale and repurchase agreement usually takes the form of an agreement to sell a security (i.e. transfer all the rights attaching to a security) with a simultaneous agreement to repurchase it at a specified price at a fixed future date. The consideration involved is either in the form of cash or security. The repurchase price is normally structured higher than the sale price; alternatively, the two prices can be the same, but with an explicit rate charged instead. The transferee will require that it is assured of a lender's return on its investment and the transferor will require that the transferee earns no more than this return. In the event that the transferee is entitled to retain any coupons or dividends that are paid on the asset during the term of the repurchase agreement, the transaction price is adjusted to reflect the fact (see **3.1.6** above).

The table below considers some common terms of sale and repurchase transactions and applies IAS 39 derecognition principles to those transactions.

Features	**Applying derecognition in IAS 39**
The repurchase price is an agreed price higher than the market value at the date of sale.	If the repurchase price results in a lender's return for the transferee then the transferor has not transferred, but has retained substantially all of the risks and rewards of ownership of the asset. The lender's return earned by the transferee is consistent with the arrangement being a collateralised borrowing for the transferor, and a collateralised lending for the transferee.
The repurchase provision is an option for the transferor to repurchase the asset at a fixed price (where the call option is neither deeply in nor out of the money), and the asset is readily obtainable in the market.	The asset is derecognised since the transferor neither transferred nor retained substantially all of the risks and rewards of ownership, and has lost control over the asset. The transferor will recognise a standalone call option in the statement of financial position at fair value with gains or losses recognised in profit or loss.

Features	Applying derecognition in IAS 39
The repurchase provision is an option for the transferor to repurchase the asset at a fixed price (where the call option is neither deeply in nor out of the money), and the asset is *not* readily obtainable in the market.	The transferor has neither transferred nor retained substantially all of the risks and rewards of ownership but has retained control of the asset. Hence, the transferor continues to recognise the asset to the extent of its continuing involvement: where the asset is measured at fair value and the option is out of the money the transferor records a liability for the fair value of the transferred asset less the time value of the option; where the asset is measured at fair value and the option is at or in the money the transferor records a liability for the option exercise price less the time value of the option; where the asset is measured at amortised cost the transferor records a liability for the consideration received and adjusts it for the amortisation between the consideration received and amortised cost of the asset on the expiration date of the option.
The repurchase provision is a put option at a fixed price (where the put option is neither deeply in nor out of the money) and the asset is readily obtainable in the market.	The asset is derecognised since the transferor has neither retained nor transferred substantially all of the risks and rewards of ownership, and has lost control over the asset. The transferor recognises a standalone put option in the statement of financial position at fair value with gains or losses recognised in profit or loss.
The repurchase provision is a put option at a fixed price (where the put option is neither deeply in nor out of the money) and the asset is *not* readily obtainable in the market.	The transferor has neither transferred nor retained substantially all of the risks and rewards of the asset and has retained control of the asset; hence, it continues to recognise the asset to the extent of its continuing involvement. Hence, the transferor continues to recognise the asset to the extent of its continuing involvement: where the asset is measured at fair value the transferor records a liability equal to the option exercise price plus the time value of the option; where the asset is measured at amortised cost the transferor records a liability for the consideration received and adjusts it for the amortisation between the consideration received and amortised cost of the asset on the expiration date of the option.
The asset sold is subject to the transferor receiving a deferred consideration receipt/payment based on the increases/decreases in the fair value of the asset respectively for a specified period of time.	The deferred consideration passes the changes in the fair value of the asset back to the transferor, thus the transferor has retained substantially all of the risks and rewards of ownership of the asset; hence, the transferor continues to recognise the asset and recognises a liability for the initial cash consideration received.

Features	Applying derecognition in IAS 39
The asset is subject to a varying repurchase price such that original purchase price is adjusted retrospectively to pass variations in the value of the asset to the transferor.	The variation in the repurchase price so as to pass the changes in the value of the asset back to the transferor means that the transferor retains substantially all the risks and rewards of ownership; hence, the transferor continues to recognise the asset and recognises a liability for the cash consideration received.
The transferor provides a residual value guarantee to the transferee or subordinated debt to protect the transferee from falls in the value of the asset.	Provided the asset has upside potential, the transferor neither retained nor transferred substantially all the risks and rewards of ownership (transferred the upside, but retained the downside). The transferor continues to control the asset where the guarantee is sufficiently valuable to the transferee and limits its ability to transfer the asset, and therefore the transferor continues to recognise the asset to the extent of its continuing involvement, i.e. at the date of the transfer the asset is measured at the lower of its carrying amount and the guarantee amount. The transferor records an associated liability equal to the guarantee amount plus the fair value of the guarantee. Where the guarantee does not restrict the transferee's ability to sell the asset, the transferor derecognises the asset.
The repurchase price, whether put/call or forward, is the market price at the time of repurchase.	The transferor has transferred substantially all of the risks and rewards of ownership of the asset since the transferor can only repurchase it at its fair value. Hence, the asset is derecognised.
Asset repurchased is substantially the same as the asset that is transferred or the transferee can substitute the asset with one that is similar or is of equal fair value.	The transferor retains substantially all the risks and rewards of ownership of the asset and therefore derecognition is precluded.

3.7 Debt factoring

Debt factoring is used extensively as a method for obtaining one or more of the following benefits: obtaining financing, bad debt protection or sales ledger administration. A factoring transaction normally takes the form of an entity receiving cash consideration in exchange for the rights to cash collected from its receivables. In many situations the rights to the cash flows on the receivables are subject to certain restrictions or guarantees. Sometimes the transferee may have recourse to the transferor over the performance of the receivables either up to a certain limit or to the extent to which there is a shortfall of the cash collected on the receivables. In a non-recourse transaction, there is no obligation of the transferor to make good the transferee for any shortfall on the assets. In order to receive a market return from the receivables (the receivables are collected over time) the transferee charges interest.

The table below sets out some of the common features of debt factoring transactions and application of derecognition principles to a 'vanilla' debt factoring transaction (an entity receives cash consideration in exchange for the rights to cash collected from its receivables) with each of those features. It is assumed that the transferee cannot sell receivables, i.e. the transferor continues to control them.

Features	Applying derecognition in IAS 39
For all receivables not recovered after a certain period, e.g. 120 days, whether due to late payment or default, the transferor provides a guarantee.	The guarantee may represent substantially all the risks of ownership of receivables (e.g. where most receivables are long term due to the credit terms offered). If so, derecognition is precluded. Where the transferor has neither transferred nor retained substantially all the risks and rewards of ownership, the transferor continues to recognise receivables to the extent of its continuing involvement, i.e. to the extent that amounts may be repaid under the guarantee.
In the event of a receivable going bad beyond but not prior to a certain period (e.g. the period commencing after 120 days), the transferor provides credit protection on that receivable.	The credit protection may represent substantially all the risks of ownership (e.g. where credit terms are 120 days or more and thus the risk of a receivable going bad stays with the transferor). If it does, derecognition is precluded. Depending on the likelihood of default prior to 120 days and other risks transferred to the transferee, the transferor may determine that substantially all the risks and rewards of ownership are neither transferred nor retained and thus the transferor continues to recognise receivables to the extent of its continuing involvement, i.e. to the extent that amounts may be repaid under the credit protection.
The transferor receives an element of non-returnable consideration for the receivables, but either the transferor or the transferee has rights to some further sums from the other party to the transaction. This further sum depends on whether or when cash is collected from the receivables, e.g. through deferred consideration, a retrospective adjustment to the sale price or rebates of certain charges.	Where the further sums from the other party are not considered to be substantially all of the risks and rewards of ownership, the transferor has neither transferred nor retained substantially all the risks and rewards of ownership and continues to recognise the receivables to the extent of its continuing involvement. The transferor derecognises receivables to the extent of the non-returnable consideration.

Features	Applying derecognition in IAS 39
The transferor provides a warranty over the quality/condition of the receivables at the moment of transfer, e.g. at the point of delivery of the goods, the customer had not breached their credit limit.	The warranty provision may result in the transferor retaining some risks and rewards, for example, if the transferor has to reimburse the transferee should the transferor's representations as to the quality/condition of the asset prove to be wrong. If the warranty results in the transferor neither transferring nor retaining substantially all the risks and rewards of ownership it continues to recognise the receivables to the extent of its continuing involvement, i.e. to the extent that amounts may be repaid under the warranty. If the warranty as to quality/condition of the assets at the date of transfer results in the entity transferring substantially all the risks and rewards of ownership then the transferor will derecognise the assets. (The IFRIC considered conditional transfers in November 2006 – see **3.1.4** above.)
The transferor continues to service the receivables by administering the sales ledger for a fee that is based upon the total amount of receivables factored at each month end. The charge is at market price. The transferor is not subject to any recourse and the transferor has not retained any residual interest in the receivables.	A servicing arrangement at a market price with no further continuing involvement in the receivables is considered to be a transfer of substantially all of the risks and rewards of ownership of the assets, and therefore derecognition by the transferor is appropriate. If the charge for the servicing arrangement is not at market price such that the benefits of servicing the assets are not commensurate with the administration charges, but did not otherwise involve further transfer of exposure to risk back to the transferor, a servicing asset or servicing liability will arise and be recorded separately.
The transferor has a call option to purchase outstanding receivables from the transferee at a predetermined price when the amount of outstanding assets falls to a specified level at which the cost of servicing those assets is too high as compared to the benefits of servicing. This is sometimes known as a clean-up call.	Provided that the clean-up call results in the entity neither retaining nor transferring substantially all the risks and rewards of ownership, it precludes derecognition only to the extent of the amount of the assets subject to the call option.

3.8 Securitisations

Securitisation is a means of making use of a portfolio of assets, usually receivables held by an entity (such as loans, mortgages, credit cards, etc.), to obtain cost effective funding. These assets are usually purchased by a transferee who then re-packages the receivables as asset-backed securities and sells them on in the market to investors for cash consideration. The normal process is to re-package these securities in a vehicle specifically set up for that purpose, a Special Purpose Entity ('SPE', see **3.1.1** above). The notes issued to the investors are secured on the underlying assets that have been transferred to the SPE. It is usual for investors to require a form of credit enhancement which can take many forms:

- subordination: typically the transferor acquires a junior (often the most junior) note issued by the SPE that absorbs the first losses incurred by the transferred assets;
- over-collateralisation: the face amount of the transferred assets is larger than the funding used to buy the assets;
- excess spread: after all interest has been received and paid and expenses of the SPE settled, an amount is retained in the arrangement which will absorb first losses should they occur;
- reserve fund: similar to excess spread except a separate fund is created;
- guarantees: the SPE may obtain guarantees either from the transferor or from third parties, for example from well rated insurance companies;
- letters of credit: the SPE may obtain letters of credit from well rated banks where the bank will stand ready to reimburse the SPE for losses incurred up to a specified amount;
- cash collateral account: similar to a letter of credit except the bank lends cash upfront which is invested in highly rated short-term commercial paper. The SPE has some credit risk on its investments but this is less than would be the case for a letter of credit where the borrower runs the risk that the lender will fail to meet its lending commitment when demanded by the borrower. Alternatively, the transferor may deposit a percentage of its proceeds from the securitisation in a cash collateral or maintenance account.

Some forms of credit enhancement, like subordination and over-collateralisation, some cash collateral accounts deposited by the transferor, transfer risks and rewards of the transferred asset back to the transferor. Others, like letters of credit and some cash collateral accounts, transfer risks and rewards to third parties. The types of risk transfer determine whether the transferor is able to achieve derecognition for the transferred assets.

As explained in **3.1.1** above, it is important to determine whether or not the entity needs to consolidate the SPE. If the SPE is consolidated, the extent of derecognition achieved is the same irrespective of whether the transfer is direct to investors or through a consolidated SPE that obtains the financial assets and, in turn, transfers them to third party investors.

In many securitisations the SPE is consolidated and the assets are not transferred to a third party, i.e. the right to receive the cash flows from the assets remains with the group. The group may assume a contractual obligation to pass on those cash flows to ultimate investors in a 'pass-through' arrangement that meets all three conditions detailed in **3.1.4** above. Nevertheless, the group may still have retained all the risks and rewards of ownership of the assets (e.g. where credit risk is the main risk and credit enhancement provided by the group covers all expected losses) and may still need to continue to recognise the assets. The IASB recognises that many securitisations will not qualify for derecognition either because one of the three conditions in the pass-through test will not be met or because the credit enhancement required by the ultimate investors will mean that the group retains substantially all the risks and rewards of ownership of the assets. [IAS 39.BC63] Where credit enhancement provided by the group is such that the group neither retains nor transfers all the risks and rewards of ownership, the group will continue to recognise the assets only to the extent of its continuing involvement, i.e. the credit enhancement provided.

The table below sets out some of the common features of securitisations where the SPE that purchases the assets is *not consolidated* by the transferor and application of derecognition principles to securitisations with each of those features. It is assumed that the SPE cannot sell receivables, i.e. the transferor continues to control them and the transferor has no exposure to the assets other than stated.

Features	**Applying derecognition in IAS 39**
Credit enhancement is provided for the transferred receivables by an independent third party, e.g. third party credit insurance or guarantee.	The transferor has transferred the rights to receive cash flows on the assets to the SPE and also transferred substantially all the risks and rewards of ownership of those assets, hence full derecognition is appropriate.
As above, but the transferor acts as the servicing agent on the portfolio of the assets.	The retention of a servicing right at market price does not preclude derecognition, since substantially all of the risks and rewards of the assets have been transferred and accordingly derecognition is appropriate. If the charge for the servicing asset is not at market price such that the benefits of servicing the assets are not commensurate with the administration charges, but do not otherwise involve further retention of exposure to risk, a servicing asset or liability arises and is recorded separately.

Features	Applying derecognition in IAS 39
A call option is held by the transferor that allows it to call back some of the assets from the portfolio. The transferor has the choice of which balances can be recalled but the total amount of balances that can be recalled is restricted.	Assuming the transferor is economically rational, the transferor will repurchase those assets that will yield the highest return, thereby avoiding assets that are expected to default. This interest in the assets indicates that the transferor has neither transferred nor retained substantially all the risks and rewards of ownership, and hence is required to continue to recognise the assets to the extent of its continuing involvement, i.e. the extent to which the transferred assets are subject to the call option.
The transferor has a call option enabling it to insist on the return of some specific assets from the portfolio; the amount of balances that can be recalled is restricted and the transferor cannot choose the balances to be recalled.	Assuming the call option is not deeply in nor out of the money, the transferor has neither retained nor transferred all the risks and rewards of ownership and will continue to recognise the assets to the extent of its continuing involvement, i.e. the extent to which the transferred assets are subject to the call option. If the call option is deeply out of the money, e.g. the assets that can be recalled are in default, derecognition is appropriate.
The transferor services the assets and has a clean-up call to purchase outstanding receivables from the SPE when the amount of outstanding assets falls to a specified level at which the cost of servicing those assets is too high as compared to benefits of servicing.	Provided the clean-up call results in the transferor neither retaining nor transferring substantially all the risks and rewards of ownership, the clean-up call precludes derecognition only to the extent of the amount of the assets subject to the call option.

The table below sets out some of the common features of securitisations where the SPE that purchases the assets *is consolidated* by the transferor and application of derecognition principles to securitisations with each of those features. It is assumed that the SPE has not transferred the assets to a third party, but instead assumed a contractual obligation to pass the cash flows to external investors. Other than indicated, the pass-through tests (see **3.1.4** above) are met and the group has not retained substantially all the risks and rewards of ownership.

Features	Applying derecognition in IAS 39
The SPE has provisions for a revolving investment facility (i.e. securitisation of revolving assets such as credit card receivables) in which for a given time period the SPE reinvests cash receipts in similar assets. This is common where the receivables have a much shorter life than the securitisation programme.	The pass-through conditions are not met as the reinvestment is in assets other than cash and cash equivalents and the cash flows are not passed on without material delay. Derecognition by the group is precluded.

Features	Applying derecognition in IAS 39
A rebalancing swap is taken on by the SPE to ensure that the cash flows due on the notes are met at their predetermined payment dates as the timing of cash flows on the underlying assets is often unpredictable.	Short term advances to the investors from the group do not violate the pass through tests as long as the investors still bear the risk of recovery of the assets. Hence, provided the amounts paid to investors are recovered by the group if the group suffers loss on the assets and any advances are only short term, derecognition is appropriate.
The group is granted rights to cash collected from the portfolio of assets and any remaining cash after the payments due on the securities issued to the investor, e.g. deferred sale consideration, dividend payments or other fees.	This right to collect the excess cash flows is often designed to create a similar payoff profile for the group as if the group had retained a subordinated interest in a non-consolidated SPE. The extent of subordination as compared to expected credit losses on the assets determines whether the group has retained substantially all the risks and rewards of ownership and thus continues to recognise the assets or whether the group has neither retained nor transferred substantially all of the risks and rewards of ownership and thus continues to recognise the assets only to the extent of its continuing involvement, i.e. to the extent of its subordinated interest.

Example 3.8

Securitisation

A Bank creates a special purpose entity (SPE) in order to facilitate the acquisition of specified assets (long-term loans) from third parties. The consideration received by the third party transferors from the SPE is less than the fair value of the assets transferred, i.e. the SPE is overcollateralised, and as such the transferors suffer expected losses. The SPE raises external debt through the issue of a rolling short-term commercial paper programme (i.e. the commercial paper is repaid and new paper is issued over the life of the arrangement). All the proceeds of the initial issue are used to finance the acquisition of the assets from the third parties which are co-mingled in the SPE. When all the underlying assets have been repaid the proceeds from the assets will be used to repay the final round of commercial paper. In order to support the whole programme the sponsoring bank will provide the SPE with a short-term liquidity facility should it require any short-term funds. In addition, the sponsoring bank will agree to be the lender to the SPE should the SPE fail to issue short-term commercial paper to investors (this facility is generally known as programme wide credit enhancement).

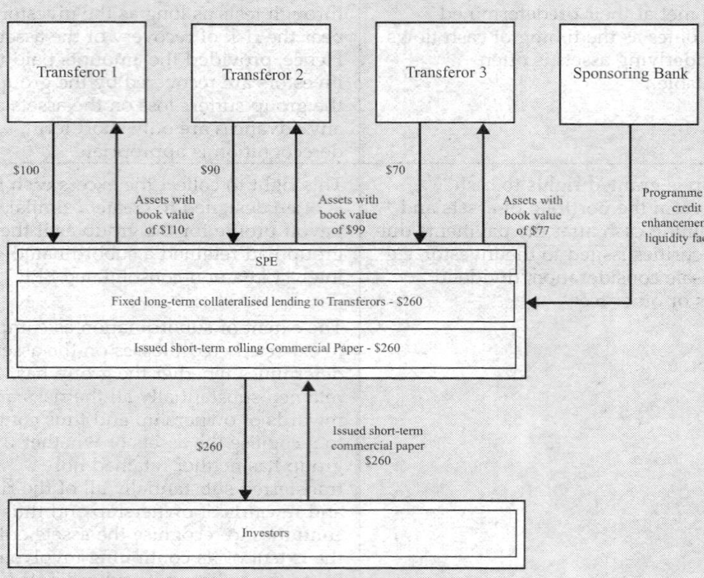

Transferor accounting

The transferors must firstly consider whether they consolidate the SPE. Applying the tests in SIC-12 to each transferor, the SPE is not controlled by any of the transferors as the SPE's activities are not being conducted on behalf of any one particular transferor; the transferors do not have the decision making powers to obtain the majority of benefits of the SPE; they do not have the right to the majority of the benefits and majority of residual risks of the SPE.

Each transferor must therefore apply the derecognition model to the transfer of the assets to the SPE. As each transferor retains substantially all the risks and rewards of ownership of the transferred asset due to the over-collateralisation, each transferor fails derecognition, and recognises a collateralised borrowing equal to the proceeds received from the SPE.

Sponsoring bank accounting

The Sponsoring Bank needs to consider whether it consolidates the SPE. The assets of the SPE are collateralised loans to the third party transferors (not the underlying transferred long-term loans as these continue to be recognised by the transferors) and liabilities under the short-term commercial paper. The Sponsoring Bank consolidates the SPE for the following reasons.

The Bank has agreed to provide support to the SPE through the programme wide credit enhancement and liquidity facility. If the assets of the SPE under-perform, which are driven by the performance of the assets transferred by the transferors, the Bank has to step in and finance the programme.

As the assets will already under-performing in excess of the expected loss the bank's lending is not likely to be fully repaid, i.e. it bears the residual risk of the SPE.

If the assets perform better than expected the cash retained in the SPE after repaying all will pass to the Bank. The Bank therefore has the majority of the residual benefits.

The Bank has the decision making powers through the setting of the autopilot mechanism (the Bank chose the underlying assets, predetermined the nature of the funding and sourced investors).

The activities of the SPE are being conducted on behalf of the Bank as it receives remuneration through providing banking facilities.

3.9 Loan transfers

A loan transfer is an agreement under which payments of principal and interest collected under the original loan are passed to a transferee or transferees for an immediate cash payment. There are several ways in which a loan transfer can be enacted. The three most common ways are as follows.

(a) Novation – this is normally where the rights and obligations of the loan are cancelled or amended and renegotiated such that the identity of the lender has been changed. In this case, the borrower is released from its obligation to the transferor and instead has an obligation to the transferee.

(b) Assignment – this is a similar process to novation but the original borrower may or may not be made aware of the change in assignment depending on whether or not the assignment is statutory or equitable respectively. Any cash flows paid to the transferor are passed on to the transferee.

(c) Sub-participation – the borrower still has an obligation to the transferor but at the same time the transferor enters into a non-recourse back-to-back agreement with the transferee to pass on the cash flows collected on the original loan.

Under novation the transferor's rights to the cash flows expire and hence derecognition is appropriate. In an assignment or sub-participation where the cash flows paid to the transferee reflect in full the collections from the original loan and there is no recourse to the transferor it is likely that the pass-through tests in **3.1.4** above are met and the transferor does not retain the risks and rewards of ownership of the assets i.e. derecognition is appropriate.

The table below sets out common features of loan sub-participations and application of derecognition principles to sub-participations with each of those features. Other than indicated, the pass-through tests are met and there is no recourse to the transferor (i.e. risks and rewards are transferred).

Features	Applying derecognition in IAS 39
The terms of the transfer provide that additional funds that are not part of the terms of the original loan will be made available to the borrower in the event of restructuring of the debt; this facility is not provided to the transferee under the terms of the sub-participation.	In the event of restructuring, the entity will not pass all the restructured cash flows to the transferee, i.e. pass-through tests are not met and derecognition is precluded.
A proportionate share of all future cash flows on the original loan is transferred, e.g. 40 per cent.	A fully proportionate share of the cash flows from the original loan (40 per cent) constitutes part of the loan. It is assumed that the pass-through tests applied to that part of the loan are met and the transferor has transferred all the risks and rewards of ownership of that part of the loan. Hence, derecognition of the part of the loan is appropriate.
The transferor continues to administer the original loan for a fee.	The servicing right at market price does not preclude derecognition since substantially all of the risks and rewards of the asset have been transferred. If the charge for the servicing asset is not at market price such that the benefits of servicing the asset are not commensurate with the administration charges, but does not otherwise involve further transfer of exposure to risk, a servicing asset or liability arises and is recorded separately.
The assigned loan or sub-participation is floating rate, whilst the original loan carries a fixed rate coupon.	The pass-through tests are not met since the transferor may be required to pay amounts that are not collected on the original loan to the transferee and equally not all cash flows collected on the original loan are passed to the transferee. Hence, derecognition is precluded.
Both the original loan and the assigned loan or sub-participation are floating rates instruments but they are priced off different floating rate indices, e.g. 6 month LIBOR and 6 month EURIBOR.	The pass-through tests are not met since the transferor may be required to pay amounts that are not collected on the original loan to the transferee and equally not all cash flows collected on the original loan are passed to the transferee. Hence, derecognition is precluded.
The original loan and the assigned loan or sub-participation are in different currencies.	The pass-through tests are not met since the transferor may be required to pay amounts that are not collected on the original loan to the transferee and equally not all cash flows collected on the original loan are passed to the transferee. Hence, derecognition is precluded.

Features	Applying derecognition in IAS 39
The sub-participation is in the same currency, but concurrently the transferor and transferee enter into a cross currency swap over the same notional as the original loan which converts the payments made to the transferee into a different currency. If the original loan defaults the swap can be terminated at its fair value at the time; the amounts and timing of the payments on the swap are not adjusted to reflect any changes that may occur in the amounts and timing of the cash flows of the original loan.	The sub-participation qualifies for derecognition since all of the risks and rewards of ownership of the original loan are transferred to the transferee. The cross currency swap is recognised separately as a derivative at fair value through profit or loss and may qualify for hedge accounting in the books of the transferee.

3.9.1 Loan syndication

Loan syndication is an agreement between several lenders to jointly fund a large loan. Each lender will advance a loan of a specific amount to the borrower and has the right to repayment from the borrower. Such a syndication agreement does not involve a loan transfer and should be accounted for as recognition of a financial asset by each of the lenders involved.

In some loan syndications, a lead lender may advance cash to the borrower and transfer the loan to a number of other lenders so that repayments by the borrower are made to the lead lender who then distributes the collections to the other lenders in the syndicate. Such loan syndications are just another form of a loan sub-participation and the lead lender would need to consider whether the pass-through tests are met. In other syndications, the pass-through tests are not relevant as the lead lender transfers the contractual rights to a proportion of the loan to third parties.

3.10 Transfers with total return swaps

A total return swap is a derivative that transfers the exposure of a referenced asset between two parties. Typically, one entity would pay amounts equal to increases in the fair value of the referenced asset to the counterparty, and at the same time receive amounts equal to decreases in the fair value of the asset plus a floating rate interest return calculated on a fixed notional amount. This floating funding interest compensates the entity for the theoretical cost of borrowing cash in order to buy the referenced asset, or put another way, is equal to a cost that would have been borne by the entity if the entity had instead chosen to expose itself to the referenced asset by acquiring the referenced asset as opposed to entering into the total return swap. These types of instruments are common in transfers of financial assets as they allow the transferor some or all of the participation in the underlying asset. As discussed in **3.1.6** above a transfer of an asset for cash consideration and a total return swap would not result in the transferor derecognising the transferred asset as the transferor continues to be exposed to substantially all the risks of rewards of ownership as a result of the total return swap. However, total return swaps can be used in transfer arrangements in other ways. Below are some illustrations which explain the consideration that would need to be given in assessing whether derecognition is appropriate.

Example 3.10

Transfers of financial assets with total return swaps

(*i*) *Transfer of financial asset with deferred consideration and a TRS*

Transferor A transfers a debt instrument where the transfer agreement requires Transferee B to pay the transferor a fixed sum in 6 months time. The transferor and transferee also enter into a total return swap whereby the transferor receives cash equal to increases in fair value of the asset from the transferee and pays cash equal to decreases in the fair value of the asset plus LIBOR plus a fixed spread every quarter based on a notional equal to the fair value of the debt instrument at the date of transfer. The transferee also pays the transferor any interest that it receives on the transferred asset.

Transferor A must first determine whether the contractual rights to cash flows have been transferred to Transferor B in accordance with IAS 39.18(a). As Transferee B has all rights to cash flows under the asset the answer is yes. Transferor A must then consider whether it has transferred substantially all the risks and rewards of ownership to Transferor B. The existence of the total return swap results in the transferor continuing to be exposed to the risks and rewards of ownership of the transferred asset, being both fair value risk and the interest earned. The risks and rewards are retained by the transferor and therefore derecognition is not appropriate even though the transferor has taken on an additional risk that it did not have prior to the transfer, being the credit risk of the transferee who has yet to pay the transferor cash consideration for the transferred asset.

As the total return swap is an impediment to derecognition it will not be recognised by the transferor in accordance with IAS 39.AG49. Transferor A will continue to recognise the assets until maturity of the total return swap. At that date, the total return swap will not be an impediment to derecognition as it will have matured and therefore the transferor will not have retained substantially all the risks and rewards of ownership, cash consideration for the asset will be received from the transferee and a gain/loss will be recognised by the transferor on disposal.

(*ii*) *Transfer of financial asset with deferred delivery of the asset at maturity of a TRS*

Entity C enters into a 6 month TRS with Entity D over Entity C's debt instrument whereby Entity C will pay Entity D cash equal to increases in fair value of the asset and receive from Entity D cash equal to decreases in the fair value of the asset plus LIBOR plus a fixed spread every quarter based on a notional equal to the fair value of the debt instrument at the date of entering into the arrangement. Entity C will also pay Entity D any interest that it receives on the transferred asset immediately after Entity C receives the interest from the issuer of the debt instrument. If Entity C does not receive interest on the debt instrument it has no obligation to pay Entity D. Equally, Entity C does not provide Entity D with any guarantee to pay further amounts. At maturity of the TRS Entity C will physically deliver the referenced asset to Entity D for a fixed amount of cash determined upon entering into the arrangement.

Entity C must firstly determine whether the contractual rights to cash flows have been transferred to Entity D in accordance with IAS 39.18(a). As the transferor retains all the rights to cash flows under the asset then the answer is no. Entity C must then consider whether the pass-through requirements in IAS 39.18(b) are met. It is clear that *all* the contractual cash flows under the asset are not passed to Entity D as the only cash flows that are passed to Entity D are interest flows on the asset for 6 months. As these interest flows are specifically identified cash flows from a financial asset, i.e. they constitute a portion of the asset, under IAS 39.16(a)(i) and the cash flows are immediately paid by Entity C to Entity D when Entity C receives the cash, then Entity C could apply the pass-through requirements to the portion of the asset that represents the interest flows for 6 months only. Assuming that both the pass through and risks and rewards tests lead to the conclusion that the portion of the asset representing the interest flows for 6 months should be derecognised, Entity C would need to recognise a debtor from Entity D as no upfront consideration is received by Entity C. The debtor recognised would be equal to the fair value of the interest flows for the next 6 months and may differ in amount to the portion of the asset derecognised in the case where the asset is not measured at fair value, i.e. it is measured at amortised cost, with the difference recognised in profit or loss as a gain/loss on disposal.

The remaining portion of the financial asset is not subject to a transfer and therefore will continue to be recognised and measured consistently with the period prior to the transaction occurring. The TRS will be recognised as at fair value through profit or loss. When the referenced asset is physically delivered to Entity D at maturity of the TRS Entity C transfers the contractual right to cash flows under the asset and derecognition it. This scenario is illustrated below.

- Entity C's fixed-rate debt instrument has an amortised cost of €100, and fair value of €110 at 1/1/X8. The amortised cost of the remaining interest flows, being the present value discounted at the original effective interest rate, is €3, and the fair value, being the present value discounted at current market rates, is €4.

- Entity C enters into a TRS with Entity D for 6 months over the fixed-rate debt instrument. Entity C will pay Entity D increases in fair value of the debt instrument and Entity D will pay Entity C decreases in fair value as well as a funding rate of 6m LIBOR + 50 basis points set in advance. At the maturity of the TRS Entity C will transfer the debt instrument to Entity D for €110. LIBOR at 1/1/X8 was 5.5%.

- At 30/6/X8 the fair value of the debt instrument is €106.

1/1/X8

Dr	Loan and receivable	€4
Cr	Debt instrument	€3
Cr	Profit or loss	€1

To recognise the profit on derecognition of the portion of the debt instrument representing the 6m interest flows that were subject to the pass-through tests.

No further entries are required at 1/1/X8 as the contractual rights to the cash flows of the remaining portion of the asset have not been transferred and the pass-through requirements for the remaining portion of the asset do not apply.

30/6/X8

Dr	Total return swap asset	€7
Cr	Profit or loss	€7

To recognise the TRS as at FVTPL. For illustration purposes, the fair value of the TRS is equal to the decrease in fair value of the debt instrument (€4) plus 6m LIBOR accrued for 6 months (6% x 6/12).

Dr	Cash	€117
Cr	Total return swap asset	€7
Cr	Debt instrument	€97
Cr	Loan and receivable	€4
Cr	Profit or loss	€9

To recognise the consideration received on transfer of the debt instrument with the corresponding derecognition of the TRS, the debt instrument, and the receivable that was recognised on entering into the pass-through arrangement.

The gain on disposal represents the unrealised gain of the debt instrument immediately prior to entering into the arrangement, being €10, less the gain of €1 recognised on 1/1/X8 upon entering into the pass-through arrangement.

4 Derecognition of a financial liability

A financial liability is derecognised when, and only when, it is extinguished, i.e. when the obligation in the contract is *discharged*, *cancelled* or *expired*. [IAS 39.39]

An entity discharges its obligation by paying amounts of cash, other financial assets, or by delivering other goods or services to the counterparty. An obligation may expire due to the passage of time (e.g. an unexercised written option). An obligation is cancelled when through the process of law, or via negotiation with a creditor, an entity is released from its primary obligation to pay the creditor.

Example 4

Extinguishment of financial liabilities

Situations may arise where a liability is considered unlikely to result in an outflow of economic resources. The following examples illustrate three scenarios in which a liability might never be extinguished absent a statute of limitation in the applicable jurisdiction:

Unredeemed travellers cheques

Entity A is in the business of issuing travellers cheques to customers. Historical statistical analysis indicates that five per cent of travellers cheques will never be redeemed. Travellers cheques do not have an expiry date.

As travellers cheques do not have an expiry date, the entity is obliged to honour the redemption of travellers cheques on demand. The financial liability will measured at the amount the Entity A can be required to pay on demand. This obligation may carry on indefinitely into the future unless the jurisdiction allows for legal release from that obligation when a specified period of time has passed.

Goods received but not invoiced

Entity B is a media buying entity that purchases advertising space in newspapers, television and radio on behalf of its customers, thereby incurring a liability to pay for that advertising space. Historical analysis shows that invoices have never been received by Entity B in respect of five per cent of the advertising space purchased. The jurisdiction of Entity B contains a 'statute of limitations' under which the counterparty is no longer able legally to enforce payment if it does not claim payment from Entity B within a period of six years from the date the goods or services are provided.

Until six years have expired since the transaction, Entity B is legally obligated to pay the counterparty should they make a claim. The financial liability will be measured at the amount the Entity B can be required to pay on demand. At six years, Entity B should derecognise the financial liability.

Dormant bank accounts

Bank C cannot locate all its customers that deposit cash with the bank. The depositor may have moved from their home without notifying the bank and there have been no transactions on the account for a considerable period of time (the account is dormant). However, the depositor or its legal representatives, including the depositor's executor of the estate, have the right to claim the deposited amounts indefinitely. Historically, five per cent of dormant accounts held with the bank are never reclaimed.

In the absence of a statute of limitation in Bank C's jurisdiction Bank C will continue to recognise the financial liability to return the cash to the depositor at the amount repayable on demand. In other jurisdictions the law may allow the bank, or the bank may be forced, to transfer the deposit to a third party, for example, a government body, after a specified period of time. The legal release on transfer to the government body is a legal release for the bank if the depositor has no recourse to the bank.

Where an entity pays another party to assume its obligation under a contract, sometimes referred to as 'in substance defeasance', the liability is not extinguished until a legal release from the obligation is obtained. [IAS 39.AG59]

Legal release from an obligation extinguishes the liability, but if concurrently an entity assumes another obligation to a third party or indeed to the original creditor, the new obligation is recognised. For example, an entity may be released from its primary obligation to the creditor, but assumes a guarantee if the party assuming the primary obligation defaults, in which case it derecognises the original liability and recognises the new liability for the guarantee. [IAS 39.AG60]

When a liability is extinguished, the difference between its carrying amount and consideration paid including any non-cash assets transferred and any new liabilities assumed is recognised in profit or loss. [IAS 39.41] In the above example, the difference between the carrying amount of the liability and consideration paid to the creditor including the fair value of the guarantee provided to the creditor is recognised in profit or loss. Where only part of a liability is extinguished (e.g. repurchased by an entity), the allocation of the previous carrying amount between the amount that continues to be recognised and the part that is derecognised is performed by reference to the relative fair values of those parts on the date of repurchase (see **3.2** above).

4.1 Renegotiation of a financial liability

Often entities will seek to renegotiate debt instruments for a variety of reasons. Sometimes the entity will be seeking more favourable terms from the lender. Sometimes the borrower may be in financial difficulty and need to alter the contractual terms of the liability such as the maturity of the instrument or the coupon on the instrument.

Where the existing borrower and lender exchange instruments with terms that are substantially different, the exchange is accounted for as an extinguishment of the original liability and recognition of a new liability. Similarly, modification of the terms of a liability is accounted for as an extinguishment of the original liability and recognition of a new liability where the modification is substantial. [IAS 39.40]

The terms are deemed to be substantially different if the net present value of the cash flows under the new liability, including any fees paid and received, is at least 10 per cent different from the net present value of the remaining cash flows of the existing liability, both discounted at the original effective interest rate of the original liability. Similarly, modification is deemed to be substantial if the net present value of the cash flows under the modified terms, including any fees paid or received, is at least 10 per cent different from the net present value of the remaining cash flows of the liability prior to the modification, once again in both cases discounted at the original effective interest rate of the liability prior to the modification. [IAS 39.AG62]

When performing the 10 per cent test described above the entity must exclude from the original effective interest rate the effects of hedge accounting (whether fair value hedging or cash flow hedging). For example, if the issuer is fair value hedge accounting the interest rate risk portion of its issued fixed rate debt, the effective interest rate on this debt will reflect current floating rates at the date of exchange. As the terms of the original debt are fixed, not floating, the original effective interest determined at initial recognition of the debt prior to any hedge accounting, should be the rate that is used in applying the 10 per cent test.

The above treatment for fair value hedge accounting is consistent with applying the original effective rate at initial recognition had the issuer designated the debt as at fair value through profit or loss. Designating the debt as at fair value through profit or loss for subsequent measurement does not negate the issuer determining the original effective interest rate at the date the instrument was initially recognised for the purposes of applying the 10 per cent test.

Example 4.1A

Debt modification: change in interest and term

Entity A borrowed £1 million on 1 January 20X0, at a fixed rate of 9 per cent per annum for 10 years. Entity A incurred issue cost of £50,000. Interest on the loan is payable annually in arrears. The original effective interest rate ('EIR') is 9.807 per cent. During 20X5, Entity A approached the lender for a modification of the terms of the debt (this modification could have been as a result of a deteriorating financial condition of the borrower or because of a fall in interest rates). The following modified terms were agreed with effect from 1 January 20X6:

- Interest rate will be reduced to 7.5 per cent payable yearly in arrears.
- The original amount, payable on maturity, remains unchanged but the maturity of the loan is extended by two years to 31 December 20Y1.

No fees for renegotiating the finance are payable.

	Opening	Interest	Payments	Closing
		EIR of 9.807%	-950,000	
31 Dec 20X0	950,000	93,166	90,000	953,166
31 Dec 20X1	953,166	93,477	90,000	956,643
31 Dec 20X2	956,643	93,818	90,000	960,461
31 Dec 20X3	960,461	94,192	90,000	964,654
31 Dec 20X4	964,654	94,604	90,000	969,257
31 Dec 20X5	969,257	95,055	90,000	974,312
31 Dec 20X6	974,312	95,551	90,000	979,863
31 Dec 20X7	979,863	96,095	90,000	985,958
31 Dec 20X8	985,958	96,693	90,000	992,651
31 Dec 20X9	992,651	97,349	1,090,000	0

The present value of the modified debt at the original effective interest rate is calculated is as follows:

	Payments
31 Dec 20X6	75,000
31 Dec 20X7	75,000
31 Dec 20X8	75,000
31 Dec 20X9	75,000
31 Dec 20Y0	75,000
31 Dec 20Y1	1,075,000
Present value at 1 January 20X6 discounting at original EIR of 9.807%	**898,954**

The entity must determine whether the modification is considered to be an extinguishment of the original debt. [IAS 39.AG62] As the difference between the amortised cost of the debt instrument at the date of modification and the present value of the new debt instrument, discounted by the original effective interest rate, is less than 10 per cent, the modification is not considered an extinguishment of the original debt. The difference, £75,359, will be recognised in profit or loss in future periods through the revised effective interest rate.

For the avoidance of doubt, at the date of modification only, the issuer should not apply IAS 39.AG8, as this will result in an immediate gain/loss in profit or loss on modification which is contrary to the issuer not achieving derecognition. The issuer will apply IAS 39.AG8 following the date of modification if the estimates of future cash flows change. The revised cash flows must be discounted at the revised effective interest rate that was determined at the date of modification.

A modification of debt terms may include changes to any one or a combination of the following:

- stated interest rate for the remaining original life of the debt;
- maturity date or dates;
- face amount of the debt;

- accrued interest;
- recourse or non-recourse features;
- priority of the obligation;
- collateral (requirement for or changes in the type of the collateral);
- covenants and/or waivers;
- currency denomination;
- the guarantor (or elimination of the guarantor); or
- option features.

Example 4.1B

Debt modification: change in notional, interest, term

Entity P borrowed £100 million on 1 January 20X0 at a fixed interest rate of 10 per cent per annum for 10 years. Entity A incurred no issue costs. Interest on the loan is payable annually in arrears. The original effective interest rate is 10 per cent. At the end 20X4, Entity P is offered a number of alternatives to refinance its issued debt with effect from 1 January 20X0. The current market interest rate including a credit premium for Entity P's credit risk (which has remained unchanged) is 5 per cent for the remaining time to maturity of its existing debt, i.e. half the contractual cash flows on the original debt issued at the start of 20X0.

All proposed new borrowings are with the same counterparty and are used to buy back existing debt with the issue and buy back being in contemplation of one another. Assume for illustrative purposes only the yield curve is flat at 1 January 20X5. All amounts are in £million.

The fair value of the outstanding debt at 31 December 20X4 is determined as follows:

Period	Cash flows 10% x £100	Discount factor at 5%	Present value
20X5	10	0.952	9.52
20X6	10	0.907	9.07
20X7	10	0.864	8.64
20X8	10	0.823	8.23
20X9	110	0.784	86.19
		Fair value	121.65

Scenario 1 – new borrowing at current market interest rate of 5% with notional equal to the amount needed to buy back the outstanding debt at market price

Entity P determines the present value of remaining cash flows on its existing debt at the original effective interest rate and compares this with the cash flows on the new debt also discounted at the same original effective interest rate.

The new debt has a notional of £121.65m and an interest rate of 5% and matures in 20X9.

Period	Cash flows Existing debt	Cash flows New debt 5% x £121.65	Discount factor at 10%	Present value Existing debt	Present value New debt
20X5	10	6.08	0.909	9.09	5.53
20X6	10	6.08	0.826	8.26	5.03
20X7	10	6.08	0.751	7.51	4.57
20X8	10	6.08	0.683	6.83	4.15
20X9	110	127.73	0.621	68.31	79.31
				100.00	98.59

The difference between the present value of the existing and new debt discounted at the original effective interest rate is £1.41 (1.41%). As the difference is within the '10% test' the existing debt will not be derecognised.

Scenario 2 – same as Scenario 1 but term of new debt is extended by one year (assuming yield curve is flat)

The new debt has a notional of £121.65m and an interest rate of 5% and matures in 20Y0.

Period	Cash flows New debt 5% x £121.65	Discount factor at 10%	Present value New debt
20X5	6.08	0.909	5.53
20X6	6.08	0.826	5.03
20X7	6.08	0.751	4.57
20X8	6.08	0.683	4.15
20X9	6.08	0.621	3.78
20Y0	127.73	0.564	72.10
			95.16

The difference between the present value of the existing and new debt discounted at the original effective interest rate is £4.84 (4.84%). As the difference is within the '10% test' the existing debt will not be derecognised.

The difference in the present value calculations of the new debt in scenario 1 and new debt in scenario 2 arises because scenario 2 has an additional interest flow at current market rates and deferral of the principal by a year.

Scenario 3 – same as Scenario 2 but the yield curve is not flat in 20Y0

The yield curve remains flat until 20X9 as in scenario 2 but then falls in 20Y0 and beyond. The 6-year yield curve at 1/1/X5 (i.e. until 20Y0) is 4.85% compared to 5% in scenario 2.

Period	Cash flows New debt 4.85% x £121.65m	Discount factor at 10%	Present value New debt
20X5	5.90	0.909	5.37
20X6	5.90	0.826	4.88
20X7	5.90	0.751	4.43
20X8	5.90	0.683	4.03
20X9	5.90	0.621	3.67
20Y0	127.55	0.564	71.99
			94.37

The difference between the present value of the existing and new debt discounted at the original effective interest rate is £5.63 (5.63%). As the difference is within the '10% test' the existing debt will not be derecognised.

The difference in the present value calculations of the new debt in scenario 2 and the new debt in scenario 3 has increased because even though both scenarios 2 and 3 have the same maturity and notional the effective interest rate on the new debt differs. As the additional contractual interest flows on the new debt extending beyond the term of the existing debt are locking in a lower interest rate environment this exaggerates the difference in present value calculations between the existing and new debt. If the term was to extend further, and/or interest rates were even lower, then the present value of the new debt may be greater than 10% of the existing debt which would result in derecognition of the existing date and recognition of the new debt at fair value in accordance with IAS 39.43.

It is possible in a scenario of higher interest rates that when the term of the debt is extended beyond the term of the existing date that the '10% test' is breached and derecognition of the existing debt is required.

Example 4.1C

Debt modification: change in basis of interest

Entity C issued 5 year debt at a fixed rate of interest of 7 per cent on 1/1/X3 at par for €100m. The debt is measured at amortised cost. On 1/1/X5 the debt is exchanged with a new debt instrument that has floating rate, LIBOR, for the remaining 3 year term that is set annually in advance. The current LIBOR rate is 4 per cent and the yield curve is flat for the next 3 years. As interest rates have fallen from 7 per cent to 4 per cent, and credit spreads have remained unchanged, the fair value of the debt has risen above par. In order to put the current debt holders in the same economic position following the debt exchange the issuer agrees to increase the notional of the new debt to €108.70m.

Entity C applies the 10 per cent per cent test to the debt exchange. Entity C sums the cash flows on the new debt discounted by the original effective interest rate of 7 per cent:

- €4.3m for 3 years (4 per cent x €108.70m, as the LIBOR curve is flat at the date of exchange); and
- the principal of €108.70m payable at the end of year 3.

The net present value of the new debt discounted using the original effective interest rate is €100m.

Entity C then sums the remaining cash flows on the old debt of €7m for 3 years and a principal of €100m discounted by the original effective interest rate of 7 per cent, which is also €100m.

The 10 per cent test is failed as the net present value of the old debt and modified debt discounted by the original effective interest rate are the same, i.e. €100m. Entity C therefore does not derecognise the old debt.

For the remaining three years Entity C applies a modified effective interest rate that consists of current LIBOR for the period plus the amortisation from €100m to €108.70m based on a constant yield. The internal rate of return for the amortisation is 2.82 per cent per year and represents the current discount to par on the modified debt. This is the same accounting as for a discounted floating rate bond. The amortisation for the remaining three years is:

Period ending 31/12/05: 2.82% x €100m = €2.82m
Period ending 31/12/06: 2.82% x €102.82m = €2.90m
Period ending 31/12/07: 2.82% x €105.72m = €2.98m

At 31/12/05 Entity C accrues both LIBOR for the period plus the amortisation less the LIBOR interest paid in the period. As LIBOR is set in advance the interest paid during the year was €4.3m, being 4 per cent on the modified notional of the debt of €108.70m. The period end carrying value is therefore €102.82m (being €100m + €4.3m + €2.82m – €4.3m).

For illustrative purposes, assuming LIBOR remained the same for the remaining term of the instrument the period end carrying values for 31/12/06 and 31/12/07 would be as follows:

1/1/06	€102.82m
LIBOR	€4.3m
Amortisation of discount	€2.90m
Less cash paid	(€4.3m)
31/12/06	€105.72m
LIBOR	€4.3m
Amortisation of discount	€2.98m
Less cash paid	(€4.3m)
31/12/07	€108.70m

At 31/12/07 Entity C settles the modified debt instrument for €108.70m, being its par amount.

Even though the new and old debt instruments have a different basis of interest, the former fixed and the latter floating, the 10 per cent test is still applicable. Had the 10 per cent test not been applied Entity C would have recognised a loss on redemption of the old debt of €8.70m, being the fair value movement in the old debt since issue to the date of exchange. It would not be appropriate to recognise this loss upfront at the date of exchange, and after the exchange recognise lower interest rate costs than under the old debt simply because interest rates have fallen since the old debt was issued.

In most instances 'substantially different' will be determined by using the 10 per cent test, however, in limited cases a simple qualitative assessment will be sufficient to establish that the terms of the modified liability are substantially different from those of the original one. One example of modification where a qualitative assessment is relevant is where the denomination of the original liability is changed to a different currency such that the entity is left in a different economic position due to the new currency exposure taken on.

In some instances entities renegotiate debt in such a way that under the new terms the lender is granted equity instruments in full settlement of the obligation under the former terms and conditions of the contract (i.e. a debt for equity swap). Such a restructuring is treated as an extinguishment of debt and a simultaneous issuance of new shares. The shares are recognised at the fair value of the consideration received with any difference to the carrying amount of the debt being recognised in profit or loss.

The approach above is consistent with the rationale that the restructuring could be seen as a 'shortcut' for issuing shares to the lender and using the consideration received to repay the debt. The alternative school of thought is that the consideration for the shares is the carrying value of the debt then the debt will be reclassified at its carrying value with no gain or loss recognised. As the transaction is with a third party it seems appropriate to assume that shares are issued at fair value and therefore if this amount differs to the carrying value of the debt a gain or loss will be recognised in profit or loss.

The guidance on renegotiations and exchanges of debt instruments in IFRS is broadly based on the equivalent guidance in US GAAP. However, US GAAP has a greater amount of guidance in certain areas. An entity may find the guidance in EITF 96–19 *Debtor's Accounting for a Modification or Exchange of Debt Instruments* useful in applying IFRS.

The following guidance included in the EITF 96–19 may be relevant in applying the '10 per cent' test under IFRS:

- the cash flows have to include all cash flows specified by the terms of the new debt instrument (plus any amounts paid by the debtor to the creditor and less any amounts received by the debtor from the creditor as part of the exchange or modification);
- if either the old or the new debt instrument or both have a variable interest rate, an entity has to use the rate effective as at the date of exchange or modification to calculate the cash flows;

- if either the old or the new debt instrument has a call or a put option then separate cash flow analyses for exercise and non-exercise has to be performed and the scenario that generates the smaller change would be used to decide whether the 10 per cent hurdle is breached;
- judgement is to be used when determining the cash flows if the instrument contains contingent payment terms or unusual interest rate terms; and
- if the exchanged or modified debt instrument is exchanged or modified again within one year, the terms of the original debt should be used as starting point to perform the '10 per cent' test.
- in the case of an intermediary acting as an agent for the debtor, the assessment of the transaction should "look through" that intermediary;
- if the intermediary is identified as acting as a principal it is treated like any other creditor.

Where an investment bank is used to facilitate a debt exchange it is important to establish all the terms of the arrangement in order to establish whether the investment bank is acting as agent or principal to the transaction. An investment bank can undertake a number of roles in debt exchanges. For example, if an entity wishes to exchange its issued debt it may request an investment bank to seek out the holders of the debt in order for those holders to be offered the new debt instrument. If the investment bank is remunerated by way of a predetermined fee for this service, it is likely the bank is acting as an agent to enable the issuer to exchange its existing debt instruments.

If the existing debt holders acquire the new debt in exchange for returning the old debt to the issuer, and the investment bank simply facilitates this exchange as an agent of the issuer, then this is considered a debt exchange between the issuer and existing debt holders and therefore the 10 per cent test would need to be applied by the issuer. On the other hand, if debt is transferred from one debt holder to another, the issuer's accounting is not impacted as long as funds do not pass through the issuer or its agent.

In some instances the investment bank buys the existing debt from the debt holders by using its own funds and bears market risk of the debt, and therefore is considered principal to the original debt. If the investment bank subsequently exchanges or modifies the debt with the issuer, the investment bank is considered the original debt holder and the issuer must determine whether the debt exchange between the investment bank and the issuer breaches the 10 per cent test. The investment bank would not be acting as principal, i.e. would be acting as agent, if it merely was placing the new notes in the market and only buys the new debt that it has contractually agreed to sell to others.

Where the terms of the new/modified instrument are not substantially different, then any fees or costs paid in the exchange/modification are treated as an adjustment to the carrying amount of the original liability and are amortised over the remaining life of the new/modified liability. [IAS 39.AG62]

Fees paid on an exchange of liabilities or for a modification of a liability may include fees paid to third parties, such as legal fees, provided they are directly attributable to the exchange/modification. Any fees paid need to be considered carefully since they are often used as a mechanism for amending the terms of the loan.

20 Financial instruments: hedge accounting

1 Introduction

Entities enter into many transactions that aim to reduce risk, and ultimately reduce the variability in cash flows that arise from these risks. Entities enter into hedging transactions to hedge risks that are evident in items that are already recognised in the statement of financial position, as well as hedge risks for future transactions that have yet to occur.

Hedge accounting is a method of presentation that may be voluntarily applied to hedging transactions. The objective of hedge accounting is to ensure that the gain or loss on the hedging instrument is recognised in profit or loss in the same period when the item that is being hedged affects profit or loss. In other words, applying hedge accounting results in the 'matched' timing of recognition of gains and losses in profit or loss. Where an entity is perfectly hedged, the gains and losses on the hedging instrument and the hedged item perfectly offset in profit or loss in the same period.

IAS 39 allows an entity to apply hedge accounting if an entity specifically designates the hedging instrument and the hedged item at inception of the hedge accounting relationship. Generally, there are two ways in which hedge accounting achieves the matching of gains and losses on the hedging instrument and the hedged item:

- changes in the fair value of the hedging instrument are recognised in profit or loss at the same time that a recognised asset and liability that is being hedged is adjusted for movements in the hedged risk and that adjustment is also recognised in profit or loss in the same period. This is referred to as a fair value hedge because it is the exposure to changes in the fair value of the hedged item due to the designated risk that is being hedged; or
- changes in the fair value of the hedging instrument are recognised initially in other comprehensive income and reclassified from equity to profit or loss when the hedged item affects profit or loss. This is known as a cash flow hedge because it is the exposure to the variability in future cash flow that is being hedged.

A third and final category of hedge accounting is hedging a net investment in a foreign operation. This is accounted for similarly to cash flow hedges.

There are specific rules in the Standard that limit which financial instrument can be considered a hedging instrument, and which item can be considered a hedged item. In summary, a hedging instrument can be a derivative financial instrument or a non-derivative financial instrument (for hedges of foreign exchange risk only). The hedged item must be an identified hedged item or group of items that could affect profit or loss.

When an entity wishes to apply hedge accounting, it must formally document in writing its intention to apply hedge accounting prospectively. Hedge accounting cannot be applied retrospectively. Additionally, hedge accounting must be consistent with the entity's established risk management strategy for that hedge relationship. The hedge documentation must identify the hedging instrument, the hedged item or transaction, the nature of the risk being hedged and specify how the 'effectiveness' of the hedge relationship will be assessed and ineffectiveness measured.

Hedge accounting is only permitted if the hedge relationship is expected to be highly effective and it is actually effective within a quantitative range. To the extent that the hedging instrument and hedged item are not perfectly effective at offsetting each other, this ineffectiveness is immediately recognised in profit or loss.

IAS 39 does not mandate the use of hedge accounting. Hedge accounting is voluntary. If an entity does not wish to use hedge accounting it does not need to designate and document its hedging relationships. Where an entity applies the normal recognition and measurement requirements of IAS 39 it may find in some cases that the effect on profit or loss of applying hedge accounting could be substantially the same as where hedge accounting is not applied. In such cases, an entity may well choose not to apply hedge accounting because there is very little benefit in doing so.

In some instances the fair value option (see **3.1.1** in **chapter 14**) can be used as an alternative to hedge accounting. If an accounting mismatch exists, which will result in profit or loss volatility, an entity may apply the fair value option to reduce this volatility instead of complying with the onerous conditions of hedge accounting. For example, where a derivative provides an economic hedge of a financial instrument that is not measured at fair value through profit or loss, an accounting measurement mismatch exists. In that situation, the fair value option applied to the hedged item would reduce the measurement mismatch. The simplicity of applying the fair value option does, however, come at a cost:

- hedge accounting can be discontinued at any time but fair value through profit or loss designation is irrevocable; and
- if fair value option is used, the entire change in fair value of the designated item must be recognised in profit or loss. This amount will not be an exact offset to the change in fair value of the hedging instrument where the hedging instrument is not hedging all the risks of the item that is designated under the fair value option. Hedge accounting allows the specific hedged risk to be designated, and therefore can achieve a greater reduction in profit or loss volatility.

The approach taken by IAS 39 to hedge accounting is fundamentally different from that typically applied in the UK by companies outside the scope of FRS 26. For some companies, the degree of planning and monitoring associated with hedge accounting under IAS 39 may be very significant. UK

This chapter discusses hedge accounting in the following sections:

Section 2	Definitions and mechanics of hedge accounting
Section 3	Hedged items
Section 4	Hedging instruments
Section 5	Hedge effectiveness
Section 6	Cash flow hedge accounting for a portfolio hedge of interest rate risk
Section 7	Fair value hedge accounting for a portfolio hedge of interest rate risk
Section 8	Documentation

2 Definitions and mechanics of hedge accounting

IAS 39 recognises three types of hedge accounting depending on the nature of the risk exposure:

- a fair value hedge;
- a cash flow hedge; and
- a hedge of a net investment in a foreign operation ('net investment hedge').

2.1 Definition of a fair value hedge

A fair value hedge is a hedge of the exposure to changes in fair value of a recognised asset or a liability or an unrecognised firm commitment or an identified portion of such an asset, a liability or a firm commitment that is attributable to a particular risk and could affect profit or loss. [IAS 39.86(a)]

2.1.1 Examples of fair value exposure

Fair value exposures arise from existing assets or liabilities, including firm commitments. Fixed-rate financial assets and liabilities, for example, have a fair value exposure to changes in market rates of interest and changes in credit quality. Non-financial assets have a fair value exposure to changes in their market price, e.g. a commodity price. Some assets and liabilities have fair value exposures arising from more than one type of risk, e.g. interest rate, credit, foreign currency risk.

The following assets and liabilities are commonly fair value hedged:

- fixed rate liabilities like loans;
- fixed rate assets like investments in bonds;
- investments in equity securities; and
- firm commitments to buy/sell non-financial items at a fixed price.

Examples of fair value hedges include:

- a hedge of exposure to changes in the fair value of fixed rate debt as a result of changes in market interest rates (such a hedge could be entered into either by the issuer or by the holder);
- a hedge of the foreign currency risk of an unrecognised contractual commitment by an airline to purchase an aircraft for a fixed amount of a foreign currency at a future date; and
- a hedge of the change in fuel price relating to an unrecognised contractual commitment by an electricity utility to purchase fuel at a fixed price at a specified date, with payment in its functional currency.

2.1.2 Firm commitment

A firm commitment is a binding agreement for the exchange of a specified quantity of resources at a specified price on a specified future date or dates. [IAS 39.9]

A commitment is binding if it is enforceable either legally or otherwise. If the commitment is with a related party, consideration should be given as to whether in practice the right can be enforced. To be enforceable, the agreement should provide for remedies that are available to the parties to the contract in the event of non-performance. For example, a penalty could be specified at a fixed amount or equal to the change in market price of the item under the contract. Alternatively, the penalty may not be specifically stipulated in the agreement but may otherwise be applicable (for example remedies under law). When an entity is preparing its individual entity only financial statements the entity needs to consider carefully whether transactions between group entities meet the definition of a firm commitment as they may not be subject to remedies for non-performance. In many instances, particularly, in the absence of non-controlling interests that may require protection from the controlling interest, the agreement between group entities would not be binding.

Hedges of firm commitments are generally treated as fair value hedges under IAS 39. However, there is one exception: if an entity is hedging the foreign currency risk in a firm commitment this may be accounted for either as a fair value hedge or a cash flow hedge. [IAS 39.87]

Example 2.1.2A

Hedging foreign currency risk of a firm commitment

Entity B sells machinery at fixed prices in many jurisdictions. Entity B's functional currency is Sterling. Entity B enters into a contract with Entity D, whose functional currency is Euro, to sell machinery for delivery in six months' time at a fixed price in Euro that is determined today. In other words, Entity B has entered into a firm commitment with Entity D.

Entity B simultaneously enters into a foreign currency forward contract to hedge its future exposure to Euro arising from its firm commitment. This foreign currency forward contract can either be designated as a hedging instrument in a fair value hedge or a cash flow hedge as it is hedging the foreign currency risk of a firm commitment.

Example 2.1.2B

Fair value hedging a firm commitment

Entity E is a discount grocery chain with over 400 stores in the US, which enters into forward contracts to purchase various inventory items for its stores. On 1 June 20X0, Entity E enters into a forward contract to purchase

300,000 bushels of wheat from a wheat producer for a fixed price of US$1.40 per bushel on 1 August 20X0. Entity E will use the wheat in its bakery operations. Entity E intends taking physical delivery of the wheat in accordance with its expected purchase requirements. If Entity E failed to take delivery of the wheat, it would be required to pay for any decrease in the value of the wheat and legal remedies will be available to the wheat producer.

The transaction is a firm commitment because it is a binding agreement for the exchange of a specified quantity of wheat at a specified price on a specified future date. The forward contract is not accounted for as a derivative because Entity E intends to take physical delivery of wheat and has no past practice of settling similar contracts net. Entity E could enter into a fair value hedge to hedge the fair value exposure of the firm commitment due to the change in the price of wheat between 1 June 20X0 and 1 August 20X0 by entering into a net cash settled forward contract to sell wheat for a fixed price on 1 August that qualifies as a hedging instrument.

2.1.3 *Fair value hedge accounting*

A fair value hedge that meets all the hedge accounting criteria is accounted for as follows:

[IAS 39.89]

(a) the gain or loss from re-measuring the hedging instrument at fair value (for a derivative hedging instrument) or the foreign currency component of its carrying amount (for a non-derivative hedging instrument) is recognised immediately in profit or loss; and

(b) the carrying amount of the hedged item is adjusted through profit or loss for the gain or loss on the hedged item attributable to the hedged risk. This applies even if the hedged item is an available-for-sale asset measured at fair value with changes in fair value recognised in other comprehensive income. This also applies if the hedged item is otherwise measured at cost.

Example 2.1.3A

Fair value hedging fixed rate debt

On 1 January 20X0, Entity C issued £100 million of five-year 8 per cent fixed rate debt. Entity C has a BBB credit rating at the issuance date. The fixed interest rate on the debt is 150 basis points higher than the five-year swap rate. Interest on the debt is payable annually. Entity C's interest rate risk policy requires that all debt is at variable rates which is achieved either through issuing variable rate debt or by issuing fixed rate debt and swapping it into variable.

In order to maintain compliance with this policy Entity C entered into an interest rate swap on 1 January 20X0 to 'convert' the debt from fixed rate to variable and designated the swap (identifying and documenting all critical terms) as a fair value hedge of interest rate risk on the fixed rate debt (credit spreads are purposely not hedged). The swap is a five-year pay LIBOR, receive 6.50 per cent fixed interest rate swap.

Entity C satisfies the hedge accounting criteria.

- The fair value of Entity C's issued fixed rate debt will vary with changes in market interest rates. Such changes could have an impact in profit or loss if the debt is extinguished early. Hence, the debt qualifies for fair value hedge accounting (it is not a non-qualifying exposure).
- Entity C has formally documented the hedging relationship from inception, identifying all critical terms.
- The hedge is consistent with Entity C's risk management policy for that hedging relationship.
- Entity C expects its hedge to be highly effective and has documented this assessment –the primary potential source of ineffectiveness in a fair value hedge of fixed rate debt is credit risk. Entity C is using an interest rate swap to hedge interest rate risk only. Hence, changes in credit spreads between Entity C's BBB rate and swap rates will not generate hedge ineffectiveness.

Note that the principal terms of the hedged item and the hedging instrument match. IAS 39 recognises that if the principal terms of the hedging instrument and the hedged item are the same, then the changes in fair value attributable to the risk being hedged may be likely to offset each other fully, both at inception and afterwards. [IAS 39.AG108] Entity C is required, however to assess effectiveness on an ongoing basis. [IAS 39.IG.F.4.7]

The fair value of the swap and the carrying amount of the debt following the adjustment for changes in fair value attributable to the hedged risk are as follows:

	1/1/20X0	**30/6/20X0**	**31/12/20X0**
Issued debt	£(100m)	£(105m)	£(102m)
Swap	£nil	£5m	£2m

The required entries are as follows (£):

1 January 20X0

Dr	Cash	100,000,000
Cr	Debt	100,000,000

To record the issuance of debt.

No entries are required in respect of the swap as it was entered into at the money when the fair value was zero.

30 June 20X0

Dr	Profit or loss	5,000,000
Cr	Debt	5,000,000

Dr	Swap	5,000,000
Cr	Profit or loss	5,000,000

The net impact in profit or loss of £nil reflects that the changes in fair value of the swap offset fully the changes in the fair value of the debt for the designated risk.

31 December 20X0

Dr	Debt	3,000,000
Cr	Profit or loss	3,000,000
Dr	Profit or loss	3,000,000
Cr	Swap	3,000,000

The net impact in profit or loss of £nil reflects that the changes in fair value of the swap offset fully the changes in the fair value of the debt for the designated risk.

Note that the carrying amount of the debt in the statement of financial position will not represent its full fair value but will be a hybrid of amortised cost and an element of its fair value which is due to movements in interest rates since the inception of the hedging relationship. As the entity's credit spread was purposely not hedged, the hedged item is not adjusted for movements in that risk.

Where an entity issues debt at a negative spread to LIBOR (i.e. the coupon is set at a rate below the LIBOR rate at inception), it cannot designate a 'LIBOR' portion as the hedged risk. This would entail splitting the fixed rate of the debt into a LIBOR portion and a discount to LIBOR (or negative credit spread component). IAS 39 specifies that if a portion of the cash flows of a financial asset or a financial liability is designated as the hedged item that designated portion must be less than the total cash flows of the asset or liability. [IAS 39.AG99C]

Example 2.1.3B

Fair value hedging sub-LIBOR fixed rate debt

Entity XYZ issues fixed rate debt at 3.75 per cent when LIBOR is 4 per cent. Entity XYZ would like to hedge its debt for interest rate risk arising from changes in the benchmark interest rate, i.e. LIBOR.

Entity XYZ cannot designate a LIBOR component (4 per cent) as the hedged risk as this amount is greater than the contractual cash flow on the hedged item. However, XYZ can designate all of the cash flows of the debt instrument as the hedged item and specify that these cash flows are hedged for changes that are attributable to LIBOR. In order for XYZ to have a high expectation of hedge effectiveness, XYZ may need to choose a hedge ratio other than one to one in order to improve the effectiveness of the hedge as described in **5.1.2** below.

If an entity enters into a fair value hedge of a fixed rate asset or a liability some time after its initial recognition, IAS 39 permits the entity to designate as the hedged item a portion of the cash flows equal to the benchmark rate (e.g. LIBOR) that is higher than the contractual fixed rate received or paid on the asset or liability, provided the benchmark rate is less than the recalculated effective interest rate on the asset or liability calculated as if the entity had purchased or issued the instrument on the date it first designates the hedged item. [IAS 39.AG99D]

Example 2.1.3C

Fair value hedging fixed rate debt when interest rates have moved since issue

Entity FGH originated a four-year 5 per cent fixed-rate loan of £10,000 on 1 January 20X2, with a maturity date of 31 December 20X5. Of the 5 per cent coupon, 0.4 per cent represents credit spread, i.e. the market rate of interest was 4.6 per cent. Interest is receivable annually. The effective interest rate of FGH's loan at inception is 5 per cent.

Scenario 1: Interest rates fall between 1/1/20X2 and 31/12/20X2

One year later interest rates have fallen. At 31 December 20X2, the loan has a fair value of £10,251. FGH wishes to protect its loan asset against an increase in interest rates by entering into a fair value hedge of interest rate risk. The current market rate of interest is now 3.5 per cent, rather than 4.6 per cent.

Entity FGH enters into a receive-variable rate, pay-fixed rate of 3.5 per cent interest rate swap on 31 December 20X2 with a maturity of 31 December 20X5 to hedge its fair value interest rate exposure. The swap is on-market, i.e. it has a fair value of zero at inception.

If FGH had originated the loan when the hedging swap was entered into, it would not have originated the loan at 5 per cent, but rather at 3.9 per cent, i.e. at the benchmark interest market rate plus the appropriate margin given the counterparty's credit rating (3.5 per cent + 0.4 per cent). In this case, the effective interest rate of the loan would have been 3.9 per cent and not 5 per cent. The benchmark interest rate of 3.5 per cent is lower than the effective interest rate of this 'hypothetical loan' and hence FGH is permitted to designate as the hedged item a portion equal to the benchmark rate (e.g. LIBOR).

Scenario 2: Interest rates increase between 1/1/20X2 and 31/12/20X2

One year later interest rates have increased. At 31 December 20X2, the loan has a fair value of £9,081. FGH wishes to protect its loan asset against a further increase in interest rates by entering into a fair value hedge of the interest rate risk. The current market rate of interest is now 6 per cent, rather than 4.6 per cent.

Entity FGH enters into a receive-variable rate, pay-fixed rate of 6 per cent interest rate swap on 31 December 20X2 with a maturity of 31 December

20X5 to hedge its fair value interest rate exposure. The swap is on-market, i.e. it has a fair value of zero at inception.

If FGH had originated the loan when the hedging swap was entered into, it would not have originated the loan at 5 per cent, but at 6.4 per cent, i.e. at the benchmark interest market rate plus the appropriate margin given the counterparty's credit rating, i.e. the (6 per cent + 0.4 per cent), in which case the effective interest rate of the loan would have been 6.4 per cent and not 5 per cent. The benchmark interest rate of 6 per cent is lower than the effective interest rate of this 'hypothetical loan' and hence FGH is permitted to designate as the hedged item a portion equal to the benchmark rate (e.g. LIBOR) that is higher than the contractual fixed rate received on the asset.

2.1.4 Fair value hedges of unrecognised firm commitments

When an unrecognised firm commitment is designated as a hedged item, the subsequent cumulative change in the fair value of the firm commitment attributable to the hedged risk is recognised as an asset or a liability with a corresponding gain or loss recognised in profit or loss. [IAS 39.93]

The changes in the fair value of the hedging instrument will also be recognised in profit or loss.

The initial carrying amount of the asset or the liability that results from the entity fulfilling the firm commitment is adjusted to include the cumulative change in the fair value of the firm commitment attributable to the hedged risk that was recognised in the statement of financial position. **Example 4.1A** demonstrates the entries required when an entity hedges foreign currency risk of a firm commitment.

2.1.5 Discontinuance of fair value hedge accounting

An entity must discontinue prospectively fair value hedge accounting if:

- the hedging instrument expires or is sold, terminated or exercised (the replacement or rollover of a hedging instrument into another hedging instrument is not an expiration or termination if it formed part of the entity's documented hedging strategy from inception, for rollover hedging strategies see **4.12** below);
- the hedge no longer meets the hedge accounting criteria (for example, it is no longer highly effective or its effectiveness is no longer measurable); or
- the entity de-designates the hedge relationship. [IAS 39.91]

Any adjustment to the carrying amount of the hedged item for the designated risk for interest-bearing financial instruments is amortised to profit or loss, with amortisation commencing no later than when the hedged item ceases to be adjusted. [IAS 39.92] The amortisation is based on a recalculated effective interest rate at the date amortisation commences such that the adjustment is fully amortised by maturity.

Where amortisation begins as soon as a fair value adjustment exists, the adjustment to the carrying amount affects the effective interest rate calculation for the hedged item. In practice, to ease the administrative burden of amortising the adjustment while the hedged item continues to be adjusted for changes in fair value attributable to the hedged risk, it may be easier to defer amortising the adjustment until the hedged item ceases to be adjusted for the designated hedged risk. This is particularly true when the life of the hedge is the same as that of the hedged item. For example, if a fixed rate loan is issued at par and redeems at par, its fair value will move away from par over its life in response to changes in interest rates but will be pulled back to par on maturity. Therefore, any fair value adjustments to the carrying amount of the bond under a fair value hedge for interest rate risk will be reversed by the end of the hedge and will not require amortisation.

However, if an interest-bearing instrument is hedged for only a portion of its term to maturity (see **3.8.2** for partial term hedging), deferring amortisation until cessation of the hedge relationship will result in a skewed effective interest rate in the remaining years to the maturity of the hedged item.

An entity must apply the same amortisation policy for all of its debt instruments, i.e. it cannot defer amortising fair value adjustments on some items and not on others.

Example 2.1.5

Amortising fair value hedge adjustments

Bank J has a ¥10 million fixed-rate loan asset that is classified as an available-for-sale asset. Bank J hedged the fair value exposure of the asset using a forward contract. As a result of the hedge, the loan asset has been adjusted for changes in the fair value of the risk being hedged and that adjustment is recognised in profit or loss. If Bank J does not elect to start amortising the hedging gain or loss while the hedge is outstanding, the adjustment will remain as part of the available-for-sale asset, until the loan is sold or until the loan is no longer hedged. If hedge accounting ceases prior to the loan being sold, the fair value adjustment of the loan will be amortised through the revised effective interest over the expected remaining life of the loan.

If an entity discontinues hedge accounting by de-designating the hedging relationship, an entity may elect to designate prospectively a new hedging relationship with the same derivative hedging instrument provided the new hedging relationship meets the requirements for hedge accounting.

2.2 Definition of a cash flow hedge

A cash flow hedge is a hedge of the exposure to variability in cash flows that:

- is attributable to a particular risk associated with a recognised asset or liability (such as all or some future interest payments on variable rate debt) or a highly probable forecast transaction; and
- could affect profit or loss. [IAS 39.86(b)]

Common assets and liabilities and forecast transactions that are cash flow hedged include:

- variable rate liabilities like loans;
- variable rate assets like investments in bonds;
- highly probable future issuance of fixed rate debt;
- forecast reinvestment of interest and principal received on fixed rate assets; and
- highly probable forecast sales and purchases.

An example of a cash flow hedge is a hedge of variable rate debt with a floating to fixed interest rate swap. The variability in cash flow arises due to the reset of interest rates. The cash flow hedge reduces future variability of interest cash flows on the debt. Another cash flow hedge is a hedge of anticipated reinvestment of cash inflows and the anticipated refinancing or rollover of a financial liability. A hedging instrument that swaps one variable rate for another, e.g. LIBOR for EURIBOR, would not qualify in a cash flow hedge relationship as it does not reduce cash flow variability, it merely swaps the existing cash flow variability of the debt for cash flow variability determined on a different basis.

2.2.1 Forecast transactions

A forecast transaction is an uncommitted but anticipated future transaction. [IAS 39.9]

It is important to distinguish between forecast transactions and firm commitments as forecast transactions are always cash flow hedged, whereas firm commitments are generally fair value hedged. The following table illustrates some examples of forecast transactions and, also illustrates the difference between a forecast transaction and a firm commitment:

Example 2.2.1

Examples of forecast transactions and firm commitments

Forecast transaction	Firm commitment
In May 20X1 an entity forecasts the purchase of 100,000 bushels of corn to be used in its manufacturing process in October 20X1.	An entity has signed a legally binding purchase agreement to take delivery of 100,000 bushels of corn on 30 September 20X1 for US$2 per bushel.
Corporate Treasury forecasts the sale of an available-for-sale debt instrument at the end of the fourth quarter.	Corporate Treasury signs a legally binding agreement with a third party to sell a specific available-for-sale debt instrument for par on 30 December 20X1.
Corporate Treasury forecasts the purchase of a £25 million bond on 23 March 20X1 from an investment bank.	Corporate Treasury enters into a legally binding purchase agreement with a bank to take delivery of a £25 million bond for par on 23 March 20X1.

Cash flow hedge accounting can be applied to a forecast transaction only if the transaction is highly probable. [IAS 39.88(c)]

Highly probable is not defined in IAS 39. The probability of occurrence must be significantly in excess of a 50 per cent likelihood, but not necessarily as high as 100 per cent as the entity can never claim a transaction that is not yet committed can be guaranteed to occur. IFRS 5.BC81 also refers to 'highly probable' although in a different context. It states that in IFRS 'probable' is defined as "more likely than not" and that the 'highly probable' is regarded as implying a significantly higher probability than 'more likely than not' and as being equivalent to the phrase "likely to occur".

Probability is assessed based on observable facts and the relevant circumstances. In assessing the likelihood that a transaction will occur, consideration should be given to the following:

- the frequency of similar past transactions;

- the financial and operational ability of the entity to carry out the transaction;
- substantial commitments of resources to a particular activity (for example, a manufacturing facility that can be used in the short run only to process a particular type of commodity);
- the extent of loss or disruption of operations that could result if the transaction does not occur;
- the likelihood that transactions with substantially different characteristics might be used to achieve the same business purpose (for example, an entity that intends to raise cash may have several ways of doing so, ranging from a short-term bank loan to a common stock offering); and
- the entity's business plan.

In addition, both the length of time until a forecast transaction is projected to occur and the quantity of the forecast transaction should be considered in determining probability. Other factors being equal, the more distant a forecast transaction is, the less likely it is that the transaction would be considered probable and the stronger the evidence that would be needed to support an assertion that it is probable. For example, a transaction forecast to occur in five years may be less likely than a transaction forecast to occur in one year.

Other factors being equal, the greater the physical quantity or future value of a forecast transaction, the less likely it is that the transaction would be considered probable and the stronger the evidence that would be required to support an assertion that it is highly probable. For example, it is easier to support forecast sales of 100,000 units in a particular month than support forecast sales of 300,000 units in that month by an entity, where recent sales have averaged 300,000 units per month for the past three months. [IAS 39.IG.F.3.7]

IAS 39.IG.F.2.4 provides an example of an airline entity that could use sophisticated models based on experience and economic data to project its revenues in various currencies. If it can demonstrate that forecast revenues for a period of time into the future in a particular currency are 'highly probable' it may designate a currency borrowing as a cash flow hedge of the future revenue stream.

To meet the 'highly probable' requirement an entity is not required to predict and document the exact date a forecast transaction is expected to occur. However, it is required to identify and document the time period during which the forecast transaction is expected to occur within a reasonably specific and generally narrow range of time from a most probable date, as a basis for assessing hedge effectiveness. To determine that the hedge will be highly effective it is necessary to ensure that changes in the fair value of the expected cash flows are offset by changes in the fair value of the hedging instrument and this test may be met only if the cash flows occur within close proximity to each other. [IAS 39.IG.F.3.11]

A pattern of discovering that hedged forecast transactions are no longer expected to occur would call into question both an entity's ability to predict accurately forecast transactions and the propriety of using hedge accounting in the future for similar transactions. [IAS 39.IG.F.3.7]

A hedged forecast transaction must be identified and documented with sufficient specificity so that when the transaction occurs, it is clear whether the transaction is the designated hedged transaction. Hence, a forecast transaction may be identified as the sale of the first 15,000 units of a specific product during a specified three-month period, but it could not be identified as the last 15,000 units of that product sold during a three-month period because the last 15,000 units cannot be identified with sufficient specificity: it could be units 20,001 to 35,000 or units 120,001 to 135,000. [IAS 39.IG.F.3.10]

For the same reason, a forecast transaction cannot be specified solely as a percentage of sales or purchases during a period.

While sufficient specificity is required when identifying forecast transactions, a description of the transaction that is *too* specific increases the risk of failure of hedge accounting in its entirety. For example, an entity may have a forecast fixed rate debt issuance of £100m in six months' time. The movement in interest rates between the date of designation and the date the debt is to be issued is hedged using a forward starting interest rate swap which will be closed out on the date the debt is issued. The changes interest rates prior to the date of issuing the debt influences the determination of the fixed rate on that future debt.

If the entity designated the forecast debt issuance as being a fixed rate debt issuance then, should the forecast debt issuance not occur, the hedge will be entirely ineffective and hedge accounting will not be permitted. This will be the case even where the entity decides at debt issuance to issue floating rate debt instead of fixed rate debt. All gains/losses recognised in other comprehensive income on the forward starting interest rate swap would need to be reclassified from equity to profit or loss. The reclassification of amounts from equity to profit or loss is required because the specific forecast fixed rate debt issuance did not occur, even though economically at the date of issuance the entity would be indifferent as to whether it chooses to issue fixed or floating rate debt.

As an alternative, the entity could make its designation a bit less specific as to the ultimate basis of interest that will be issued. Instead, it could designate the hedged risk more broadly, for example, as changes in interest rates between the date of designation and the date when £100m of debt is issued. As long as the debt when issued is referenced to the same interest rate as is evident in the forward starting interest rate swap the hedge will, all other things being equal, be highly effective and therefore the entity will continue to recognise the effective gains and losses in the cash flow hedge reserve in equity irrespective of whether ultimately the entity chooses to issue fixed or floating rate debt. The amounts recognised in other comprehensive income will be reclassified from equity to profit or loss when the interest impacts profit or loss.

2.2.2 *Cash flow hedge accounting*

A cash flow hedge (assuming it meets all other hedge accounting requirements) is accounted for as follows:

(a) the portion of the gain or loss on the hedging instrument that is determined to be an effective hedge is recognised in other comprehensive income; and

(b) the ineffective portion of the gain or loss on the hedging instrument is recognised immediately in profit or loss. [IAS 39.95]

In particular:

(a) the separate component of equity associated with the hedged item is adjusted to the lesser of the following (in absolute amounts):

- the cumulative gain or loss on the hedging instrument from inception of the hedge; and
- the cumulative change in fair value (present value) of the expected future cash flows on the hedged item from inception of the hedge; and

(b) any remaining gain or loss on the hedging instrument (which is not an effective hedge) is included in profit or loss.

31 Dec		Cash	CCS	Debt	CFH reserve	Interest expense	Translation loss (gain)
	Net interest on CCS	(1,259)				1,259	
	Fair value of cross currency CCS		1,743		(62)		(1,681)
20X3	Pay interest on debt	(2,788)				2,788	
	Revalue debt to spot			(3,676)			3,676
	Net interest on CCS	(1,476)				1,476	
	Fair value of cross currency CCS		3,777		(101)		(3,676)
20X4	Pay interest on debt	(2,469)				2,469	
	Revalue debt to spot			(4,167)			4,167
	Net interest on CCS	(1,952)				1,952	
	Fair value of cross currency CCS		4,150		17		(4,167)
20X5	Pay interest on debt	(2,879)				2,879	
	Revalue debt to spot			11,111			(11,111)
	Net interest on CCS	(1,042)				1,042	
	Fair value of cross currency CCS		(11,294)		183		11,111
20X6	Pay interest on debt	(3,171)				3,171	
	Revalue debt to spot			(3,268)			3,268
	Net interest on CCS	(1,321)				1,321	

31 Dec	Cash	CCS	Debt	CFH reserve	Interest expense	Translation loss (gain)
Fair value of cross currency CCS		3,305		(37)		(3,268)
Settlement of swap	1,681	(1,681)				
Repayment of debt	(58,824)		58,824			
	(20,676)	0	0	0	20,676	0
Key				A	B	

* Numbers rounded.

Key

A Nets to zero reflecting that all amounts in the cash flow hedge reserve in equity have been reclassified to profit or loss to offset retranslation of the debt to spot each period and the recognition of interest.

B Reflects the total interest expense from US$ Debt and CCS. This amount equals the total interest expense that would have been incurred had Entity A actually issued £ debt at inception (£57,143 * (LIBOR + 106bp)) * 5 years = £20,675.

Entries in the consolidated financial statements for 20X2 for illustrative purposes

1 January 20X2

No entry required for CCS as fair value is nil at inception.

Dr	Cash	57,143
Cr	Debt	57,143

To record issue of 4% US$ bond in £ (retranslated at spot).

31 December 20X2

Dr	Interest expense	2,319
Cr	Cash	2,319

To record payment of the interest on US$ debt converted at average rates.

Dr	Retranslation loss (profit or loss)	1,681
Cr	Debt	1,681

To record loss on retranslation of the US$ debt at year end spot rates.

Dr	Interest expense	1,259
Cr	Cash	1,259

To record net interest paid on CCS.

Dr	CCS asset	1,743
Cr	Other comprehensive income (cash flow hedging reserve)	1,743

To record fair value movement in CCS in other comprehensive income (as 100 per cent effective).

Dr Other comprehensive income (cash flow hedging reserve)		1,681
Cr Retranslation gain (profit or loss)		1,681

To record reclassifying the effective portion of CCS from equity to profit or loss to offset the retranslation of the debt.

Similar entries would be recorded for the remaining term of the hedging relationship (20X3 -20X6).

Interest expense totalling £20,675 is recognised over the term of the hedging instrument and net profit or loss impact is as if Entity A had issued Sterling LIBOR + 106bp debt at inception. The CCS is fair valued at the end of each reporting period (after interest payments have been made as all interest payments are deemed to have taken place on last day of year which is also reset date for swap) with amounts recognised in other comprehensive income (and taken to the cash flow hedge reserve in equity). The amount of the CCS is reclassified from equity to profit or loss at the end of each reporting period to offset the amount recorded for retranslation of the US$ debt to Sterling spot rates and finally to offset the translation loss on repayment of principal at maturity of the debt.

It is worth noting that if there was no margin on the legs of the CCS, the CCS would reset at par each reset date (i.e. 31 December). In this case, the net figure in the statement of financial position (Debt and CCS) would be the same as if Entity A had issued Sterling debt at inception and therefore no amount would be taken to other comprehensive income at the end of each reporting period as the value of the CCS would be fully offset by the retranslation of the debt for spot rates. If there are margins on the legs of the swap, the changing yield curves result in fair value movements with respect to those margins, and therefore the CCS will not offset the retranslation of the debt notional for spot rates. Hence, where there is a margin, the fair value in respect of those amounts is initially recognised in other comprehensive income (and taken to the cash flow hedge reserve), to the extent it is effective, and reclassified from equity to profit or loss when interest on the debt is paid such that by the maturity of the debt and hedge relationship the amounts in the cash flow hedge reserve will be fully reclassified from equity to profit or loss.

Example 2.2.2D

Cash flow hedging the foreign currency risk of issued fixed rate debt with a cross currency swap that receives fixed foreign currency and pays fixed functional currency

On 1 January 20X2, Entity A, a Sterling functional currency entity, issues a 4 per cent annual fixed coupon debt instrument denominated in US dollars (US$) with a notional amount of US$100,000, that will mature on 31 December 20X6 at par, and therefore the effective interest rate is 4 per cent. At 1 January 20X2, the spot rate on the US$ / £ is 1.75/1 so the notional of US$100,000 is equivalent to £57,143. On 1 January 20X2, Entity A also enters into a cross currency swap ('CCS') to exchange interest payments and principal at redemption on the same terms as the above debt and designates the CCS as a cash flow hedge of the variability of the £ functional currency equivalent cash flows on the debt. The terms are such that on each interest payment date (assume interest is paid annually on 31 December each year for both the debt and the cross currency swap), Entity A will receive 4 per cent on a notional of US$100,000 and pay 6 per cent based on a notional of £57,143. Because the currency, notional, coupons and interest payment dates match on both the cross currency swap and the debt, Entity A expects that the hedge relationship will be highly effective.

Date	Spot rate US$ / £	Carrying amount of debt in US$	Carrying amount of debt in £	Cross currency swap fair value £	Net interest payment on the swap £ (£ 6% – US$ 4%)
1/1/X2	1.75	100,000	57,143	0	0
31/12/X2	1.7	100,000	58,824	2,560	1,110
31/12/X3	1.6	100,000	62,500	7,723	1,004
31/12/X4	1.5	100,000	66,667	9,513	848
31/12/X5	1.8	100,000	55,556	(1,452)	1,004
31/12/X6	1.7	100,000	58,824	1,681	1,143

Entity A's documentation of the hedge is as follows:

Risk management objective and nature of risk being hedged	Cash flow hedge of the variability in functional currency equivalent cash flows associated with the foreign currency debt due to changes in forward rates.
Date of designation	1 January 20X2
Hedging instrument	Cross currency swap to receive US$ 4 per cent, pay £6 per cent interest annually based on notional of US$100,000 over the term of the instrument and exchange US$100,000 for £57,143 at maturity.
Hedged item	Changes in the £ functional currency equivalent cash flows relating to the changes in foreign currency spot rates related to the debt and to the annual interest payments.

Assessment of hedge effectiveness	The critical terms of the derivative match (exchange of principal at maturity and annual interest payments), accordingly there is an expectation of high effectiveness. The entity will assess counterparty credit risk and probability of cash flows under the swap occurring every period.
Measurement of hedge effectiveness	Hypothetical derivative method. The actual hedging instrument is the same as a hypothetical cross currency swap with exactly matching terms and therefore, no ineffectiveness is anticipated.

The following table illustrates the accounting entries for the transaction during its life in Sterling. Dr or (Cr) as indicated.

31 Dec		Cash	CCS statement of financial position	Debt	CFH reserve	Interest expense	Translation loss (gain)
20X2	Issue debt	57,143		(57,143)			
	Pay interest on debt	(2,319)				2,319	
	Revalue debt to spot			(1,681)			1,681
	Net interest on CCS	(1,110)				1,110	
	Fair value of cross currency CCS		2,560		(879)		(1,681)
20X3	Pay interest on debt	(2,424)				2,424	
	Revalue debt to spot			(3,676)			3,676
	Net interest on CCS	(1,004)				1,004	
	Fair value of cross currency CCS		5,163		(1,487)		(3,676)
20X4	Pay interest on debt	(2,581)				2,581	

31 Dec		Cash	CCS statement of financial position	Debt	CFH reserve	Interest expense	Translation loss (gain)
	Revalue debt to spot			(4,167)			4,167
	Net interest on CCS	(848)				848	
	Fair value of cross currency CCS		1,790		2,377		(4,167)
20X5	Pay interest on debt	(2,424)				2,424	
	Revalue debt to spot			11,111			(11,111)
	Net interest on CCS	(1,004)				1,004	
	Fair value of cross currency CCS		(10,965)		(146)		11,111
20X6	Pay interest on debt	(2,286)				2,286	
	Revalue debt to spot			(3,268)			3,268
	Net interest on CCS	(1,143)				1,143	
	Fair value of cross currency CCS		3,133		135		(3,268)
	Settlement of swap	1,681	(1,681)				
	Settlement of debt	(58,824)		58,824			
		(17,143)	0	0	0	17,143	0
	Key				A	B	

*Numbers rounded.

Key

A: Nets to zero reflecting that all amounts in cash flow hedge reserve in equity have been reclassified to profit or loss.

B: Reflects the total interest expense from US$ debt and CCS. Equals the

total interest expense that would have been incurred had Entity A actually issued £ debt at inception (£57,143*6%) * 5 years = £17,143.

Entries in the consolidated financial statements for 20X2 for illustrative purposes

1 January 20X2

No entry required for CCS as fair value is nil at inception.

Dr	Cash	57,143
Cr	Debt	57,143

To record issue of 4 per cent US$ debt in £ (retranslated at spot).

31 December 20X2

Dr	Interest expense	2,319
Cr	Cash	2,319

To record payment of the interest on US$ debt converted at average rates.

Dr	Retranslation loss (profit or loss)	1,681
Cr	Debt	1,681

To record loss on retranslation of the US$ debt at year end spot rates.

Dr	Interest expense	1,110
Cr	Cash	1,110

To record net interest paid on CCS (£ 6% – US$ 4%).

Dr	CCS asset	2,560
Cr	Other comprehensive income (cash flow hedging reserve)	2,560

To record fair value movement in CCS in other comprehensive income (as 100% effective).

Dr	Other comprehensive income (cash flow hedging reserve)	1,681
Cr	Retranslation gain (profit or loss)	1,681

To record reclassifying the effective portion of CCS from equity to profit or loss to offset the retranslation of the debt.

Similar entries would be recorded for the remaining term of the hedging relationship (20X3 -20X6)

Interest expense totalling £17,143 is recognised over the term of the hedging instrument which is equivalent to Entity A having issued Sterling 6 per cent debt at inception. The CCS is fair valued at the end of each reporting period (after interest payments have been made as all interest payments for purposes of this illustration are deemed to have taken place on last day of year which is the reset date for the swap) with amounts recognised in other comprehensive income (and taken to the cash flow hedge reserve in equity). The amount of the CCS is reclassified from equity to profit or loss at the end of each reporting period to offset the amount recorded for retranslation of the US$ debt to Sterling spot rates.

Example 2.2.2E

Cash flow hedging the foreign currency risk of zero coupon debt with a forward exchange contract

On 1 January 20X2, Entity A, a £ functional currency entity, issues 5-year US$ denominated zero coupon debt with a notional amount of US$1,812,052 for US$1,419,791. The interest rate implicit in the debt is 5 per cent. The zero coupon debt will mature on 31 December 20X6. On the same date Entity A entered into a forward contract to buy US$1,812,052 for £1,000,000 at the forward rate of US$1.812:£ at 31 December 20X6. The £ interest rate implicit in the forward contract is 6 per cent. The carrying value of the zero coupon debt at initial recognition in Entity A's functional currency, is £747,258 as spot rates at the date of issue are US$1.90:£.

The entity designates the forward exchange contract as a hedge of the variability of the £ functional currency equivalent cash flows on the zero coupon debt. As the currency, notional amount and maturity of the forward contract match that of the zero coupon debt Entity A expects the hedge relationship to be highly effective.

Date	Spot rate US$ / £	Forward rate US$/£	US$ amortised cost (effective interest rate of 5%)	Synthetic £ zero coupon debt (effective interest rate of 6%)	Fair value of forward contract (£)
1/1/X2	1.900	1.812	1,419,791	747,258	0
31/12/X2	1.800	1.733	1,490,780	792,094	36,117
31/12/X3	1.900	1.847	1,565,319	839,619	(15,767)
31/12/X4	1.900	1.900	1,643,585	889,996	(41,196)
31/12/X5	1.900	1.900	1,725,764	943,396	(43,668)
31/12/X6	1.900	1.900	1,812,052	1,000,000	(46,288)

The change in forward rates over the period reflects a combination of factors: (i) the pull of spot rates to forward rates over the period ending 31/12/X6; and (ii) an increase in US$ interest rates from 31/12/X4 to 31/12/X6 from 5% to 6%. Forward rates and spot rates coincide from 20X4 as there is no interest rate differential between US$ and £ as both are 6 per cent.

Entity A's documentation of the hedge is as follows:

Risk Management objective and nature of risk being hedged	Cash flow hedge of the variability in functional currency equivalent cash flows associated with the foreign currency zero coupon debt due to changes in US$:£ forward rates.
Date of designation	1 January 20X2
Hedging instrument	Forward contract entered into on 1 January 20X2 maturing on 31 December 20X6 to buy US$1,812,052 and sell £1,000,000.

Hedged item	Zero coupon debt issued on 1 January 20X2 maturing on 31 December 20X6 with a notional amount of US$1,812,052 and issued for proceeds of US$1,419,791.
Assessment of hedge effectiveness	The critical terms of the derivative match those of the hedged item (in terms of maturity and notional), accordingly there is an expectation of high effectiveness. The entity will assess counterparty credit risk every period.
Measurement of hedge effectiveness	Hypothetical derivative method. The actual hedging instrument is the same as the hypothetical forward with exactly matching terms and therefore, no ineffectiveness is anticipated.

The following table illustrates the accounting entries for the transaction during its life in Sterling. Dr or (Cr) as indicated.

Date		Cash	Forward	Debt	CFH reserve	Interest expense	Foreign currency loss (gain)
1/1X2	Issue zero coupon debt	747,258		(747,258)			
31/12/X2	Accrue interest on debt			(39,439)		39,439	
	Revalue debt to spot			(41,514)			41,514
	Fair value forward contract		36,117			5,397	(41,514)
31/12/X3	Accrue interest on debt			(39,231)		39,231	
	Revalue debt to spot			43,590			(43,590)
	Fair value of forward contract		(51,885)			8,295	43,590
31/12/X4	Accrue interest on debt			(41,193)		41,193	
	Fair value of forward contract		(25,428)		16,245	9,183	
31/12/X5	Accrue interest on debt			(43,252)		43,252	
	Fair value of forward contract		(2,472)		(7,676)	10,148	
31/12/X6	Accrue interest on debt			(45,415)		45,415	
	Fair value of forward contract		(2,620)		(8,569)	11,189	

Date		Cash	Forward	Debt	CFH reserve	Interest expense	Foreign currency loss (gain)
	Settlement of forward	(46,288)	46,288				
	Settlement of debt	(953,712)		953,712			
		(252,742)	0	0	0	252,742	0
	Key				A	B	

Key

A nets to zero reflecting that all amounts in the cash flow hedge reserve in equity have been reclassified to profit or loss to offset retranslation of the debt to spot each period and the recognition of total interest in £ at the £ rate implicit in the forward contract of 6 per cent.

B reflects the total interest expense from the US$ denominated zero coupon debt and the foreign currency forward contract. This is equal to a rate of 6 per cent as applied to the £747,258 (the £ equivalent of the proceeds at the spot rate when the zero coupon debt was issued). The interest amounts comprise two elements:

(i) the underlying 5 per cent interest on the US$ zero coupon debt retranslated into the functional currency; and

(ii) the systematic reclassification of the fair value movements of the forward contract from equity to profit or loss so as to increase the effective interest rate to 6 per cent.

Entries in the financial statements for 20X2 for illustrative purposes:

1 January 20X2

No entry required for forward contract as fair value is nil at inception.

Dr	Cash	747,258
Cr	Debt	747,258

To record the issue of the US$ denominated zero coupon debt in the £ functional currency (retranslated at spot).

31 December 20X2

Dr	Interest expense (profit or loss)	39,439
Cr	Debt	39,439

To record accrual of interest on zero coupon debt (5 per cent on US$1,419,791 translated at year end spot rate of US$1.8:£. Translation at year end spot rates is used for illustrative purposes only.

Dr	Retranslation loss (profit or loss)	41,514
Cr	Debt	41,514

To record loss on retranslation of US$ zero coupon debt at year end spot rate.

Dr	Forward contract	36,117
Dr	Interest expense (profit or loss)	5,397
Cr	Retranslation gain (profit or loss)	41,514

To record the fair value movement of the forward contract with the effective gain recognised in other comprehensive income (and taken to the cash flow hedge reserve) together with the appropriate reclassification from equity to profit or loss so as to offset the retranslation of the zero coupon debt to spot and to increase interest expense in profit or loss to total the rate that would have been accrued had the entity issued the zero coupon debt in Sterling.

In this period the effective gain recognised in other comprehensive income is reclassified from equity to profit or loss in the same period and therefore for illustrative purposes only the gross entries of recognising in other comprehensive income and reclassifying to profit or loss are not presented.

Similar entries would be recorded for the remaining term of the hedging relationship (20X3 -20X6).

Interest expense totalling £252,742 is recognised over the term of the hedging instrument and the net profit or loss is the same as if Entity A had issued £ denominated zero coupon debt for £747,258 on 1 January 20X2 which accrued interest at an effective rate of 6 per cent and matured with a payment of the notional of £1,000,000 at 31 December 20X6.

Example 2.2.2F

Cash flow hedging the foreign currency risk of a forecast sale of a non-financial item

On 4 January 20X2 Entity D has a forecast sale of €4,000,000 of confectionery on or about 31 December 20X2 to a German retail outlet (Entity AG). Entity D has a Sterling functional currency, and Entity AG has a Euro functional currency. On 4 January 20X2, Entity D designates the cash flow of the forecast sale as a hedged item and enters into a currency forward to sell €4 million based on the forecast receipt. The forward contract locks in the value of the Euros to be received at a rate of €1.5:£. At inception of the hedge, the derivative is on-market (i.e. fair value is zero). The terms of the currency forward and the forecast sale match each other. The entity designates the forward foreign exchange risk as the hedged risk.

Potential sources of ineffectiveness include non-occurrence of the forecast transaction and changes in the date of sale. Any ineffectiveness will be recognised in profit or loss.

On 30 June 20X2, the fair value of the currency forward is negative £100,000 because the forward rate has changed, reflecting the fact that the Euro has strengthened against Sterling.

On 31 December 20X2 the transaction occurred as expected. The fair value of the forward is negative £111,111 as the Euro continued to strengthen against Sterling.

The required entries are as follows:

4 January 20X2
No entries are required since the forward was entered into 'on-market', and

therefore had a fair value of zero at inception. Normally, there will be margin to be posted, associated with trading on a currency exchange, but this has been ignored for illustration purposes only. There may also be fees if the foreign exchange contract is an over-the-counter (OTC) transaction.

30 June 20X2

Dr	Other comprehensive income	£100,000
Cr	Forward	£100,000

To recognise the forward at fair value, reflecting that the forward contract is fully effective in hedging the forward rate of the forecast transaction.

31 December 20X2

Dr	Other comprehensive income	£11,111
Cr	Forward	£11,111

To record the change in fair value of the forward. The forward contract remains fully effective in hedging the forward rate of the forecast transaction.

Dr	Forward	£111,111
Cr	Cash	£111,111

To record the cash paid in settling the forward contract.

Dr	Cash	£2,777,778
Cr	Sales	£2,777,778

To record the receipt of €4m from the sale of confectionery translated at the spot rate of €1.44:£.

Dr	Sales	£111,111
Cr	Other comprehensive income	£111,111

To record the cumulative effective portion of the hedging instrument included in other comprehensive income that is reclassified from equity to profit or loss when the sale occurs.

The net effect of reclassifying the amount from equity to profit or loss when the sale occurred is equivalent to recognising in profit or loss the sale translated at the contracted rate inherent in the forward (i.e. €4,000,000 / €1.5:£).

Translation of sale at spot rate at 31 December 20X2	£2,777,778
Reclassified from equity to profit or loss at 31 December 20X2	(£111,111)
Sum	£2,666,667

Note: for the purposes of illustration only, the forward contract has not been discounted.

Example 2.2.2G

Cash flow hedging the foreign currency risk of a forecast sale and the subsequent receivable with a forward exchange contract

On 1 January 20X2, Entity A, a £ functional currency entity, has a highly probable forecast sale of US$100,000 in June 20X2. The receivable that is due with respect to the sale will be on 6 months credit terms. Entity A wishes to hedge the forecast sale and the receivable for foreign currency risk. Entity A will designate the forward US$:£ exchange rate, as opposed to the spot exchange rate. Entity A enters into a forward contract to sell US$100,000 and buy £50,481. As the currency, notional amount and maturity of the forward contract coincide with that of the highly probable forecast sale, Entity A expects the hedge relationship to be highly effective.

Date	Spot rate US$ / £	US$ interest rates	£ interest rates	Forward rate US$ / £	Fair value of forward contract (£)	Fair value movement of forward contract (£)
1/1/X2	2.000	4%	5%	1.981	0	0
31/3/X2	1.900	5%	6%	1.887	(2,418)	(2,418)
30/6/X2	1.850	4%	6%	1.832	(3,973)	(1,555)
30/9/X2	1.900	7%	8%	1.896	(2,230)	1,743
31/12/X2	2.100	8%	9%	2.100	2,862	5,092

The exchange of US$ at the spot rate at inception, being US$2.0:£, is equal to £50,000. The difference between this amount and the £50,481 contracted in the forward contract is £481 and represents the forward point differential in functional currency terms. This amount can be converted into a daily interest rate for use in allocating the systematic release of forward points to the periods pre and post the sale. The daily forward point differential is 0.0026%, calculated as $(1+(481/50{,}000))^{\wedge 1/365}$.

Period	£-equivalent US$	Forward point differential
1/1/X2	50,000	–
1/1/X2 to 30/6/X2	50,238	238
1/7/X2 to 30/9/X2	50,359	121
1/10/X2 to 31/12/X2	50,481	122

Entity A's documentation of the hedge is as follows:

Risk Management objective and nature of risk being hedged	Cash flow hedge of the variability in functional currency equivalent cash flows associated with a forecast sale in 6 months and the cash to be paid on resulting receivable due in 12 months with respect to change in forward rates.
Date of designation	1 January 20X2
Hedging instrument	Forward contract entered into on 1 January 20X2 maturing on 31 December 20X2 to buy £50,481 and sell US$100,000.
Hedged item	Forecast US$100,000 denominated sale in June 20X2 with resulting receivable due December 20X2.

Assessment of hedge effectiveness	The critical terms of the derivative match that of the hedged item (in terms of maturity and notional), accordingly there is an expectation of high effectiveness. The entity will assess counterparty credit risk every period.
Measurement of hedge effectiveness	Hypothetical derivative method. The actual hedging instrument is the same as the hypothetical forward with exactly matching terms and therefore, no ineffectiveness is anticipated.

The following table illustrates the accounting entries for the transaction during its life in Sterling. Dr or (Cr) as indicated.

Date		Profit or loss	Receivable	Derivative	CFH reserve	Cash
31/3/X2	Fair value forward contract			(2,418)	2,418	
30/6/X2	Fair value of forward contract			(1,555)	1,555	
	Sale	(54,054)	54,054			
	Reclassification – spot	4,054			(4,054)	
	Reclassification – forward points	(238)			238	
30/9/X2	Fair value of forward contract			1,743	(1,743)	
	Translation of receivable	1,422	(1,422)			
	Reclassification – spot	(1,422)			1,422	
	Reclassification – forward points	(121)			121	
31/12/X2	Fair value of forward contract			5,092	(5,092)	
	Translation of receivable	5,013	(5,013)			
	Reclassification – spot	(5,013)			5,013	
	Reclassification – forward points	(122)			122	
	Settle receivable		(47,619)			47,619
	Settle forward contract			(2,862)		2,862
		(50,481)	0	0	0	50,481
	Key	A			B	C

Key

A the amounts in profit or loss account can be considered as a sale at £50,000 (being a US$100,000 sale at the contracted forward rate of US$2.0:£), the retranslation loss on the receivable of £6,435 in accordance with IAS 21 with a corresponding fair value gain due to spot movements with respect to the forward contract of £6,435, plus the fair value gain of £481 arising from the forward point differential.

B nets to zero reflecting that all amounts in the cash flow hedge reserve in equity have been reclassified to profit or loss to offset the sale and the retranslation of the receivable to spot each period.

C reflects the £-equivalent cash from the receivable plus the receipt under the forward contract.

Entries in the financial statements for 20X2 are as follows:

1 January 20X2

No entry required as the forward contract has a fair value of nil at inception.

31 March 20X2

Dr	Other comprehensive income (cash flow hedge reserve)	2,418	
Cr	Derivative		2,418

To recognise the fair value movements of the forward contract and the effective amount recognised in other comprehensive income (and taken to the cash flow hedge reserve in equity).

30 June 20X2

Dr	Other comprehensive income (cash flow hedge reserve)	1,555	
Cr	Derivative		1,555

To recognise the fair value movements of the forward contract and the effective amount recognised in other comprehensive income (and taken to the cash flow hedge reserve in equity).

Dr	Receivable	54,054	
Cr	Revenue		54,054

To recognise the sale at the spot rate.

Dr	Profit or loss	3,816	
Cr	Other comprehensive income (cash flow hedge reserve)		3,816

To recognise the reclassification from equity (the cash flow hedge reserve) to profit or loss.

31 September 20X2

Dr	Derivative	1,743	
Cr	Other comprehensive income (cash flow hedge reserve)		1,743

To recognise the fair value movements of the forward contract and the effective amount recognised in other comprehensive income (and taken to the cash flow hedge reserve in equity).

Dr	Profit or loss	1,422
Cr	Receivable	1,422

To recognise the retranslation of the receivable to spot rates in accordance with IAS 21.

Dr Other comprehensive income (cash flow hedge reserve)		1,543
Cr	Profit or loss	1,543

To recognise the reclassification from equity (the cash flow hedge reserve) to profit or loss.

31 December 20X2

Dr	Derivative	5,092
Cr	Other comprehensive income (cash flow hedge reserve)	5,092

To recognise the fair value movements of the forward contract and the effective amount recognised in other comprehensive income (and taken to the cash flow hedge reserve in equity).

Dr	Profit or loss	5,013
Cr	Receivable	5,013

To recognise the retranslation of the receivable to spot rates in accordance with IAS 21.

Dr Other comprehensive income (cash flow hedge reserve)		5,135
Cr	Profit or loss	5,135

To recognise the reclassification from equity (the cash flow hedge reserve) to profit or loss.

Dr	Cash	47,619
Cr	Receivable	47,619

To recognise the settlement of the receivable with the receipt of US$100,000 at the spot rate.

Dr	Cash	2,862
Cr	Derivative	2,862

To recognise the settlement of the derivative with receipt of £2,862 from the derivative counterparty.

In a cash flow hedge of a forecast transaction where the spot foreign exchange rate is being hedged, the effective amount recognised in other comprehensive income is calculated on a discounted basis, i.e. it is based on the present value of the spot element of the derivative. [IAS 39.IG.F.5.6]

Where an entity hedges the spot foreign exchange rate in a forecast transaction using a non-derivative hedging instrument, such as foreign currency denominated debt, the amount recognised in other comprehensive income should be the undiscounted spot rate as this is the rate that the foreign currency denominated debt is translated at in accordance with IAS 21.

For hedges of forecast transactions, it is permitted, but not required, to adjust the carrying amount of an acquired non-financial asset or non-financial liability by the effective gain or loss on the hedging instrument as explained below.

2.2.3 *Basis adjustments*

An entity has a choice of accounting policy regarding the presentation of gains and losses recognised in other comprehensive income if a cash flow hedge of a forecast transaction subsequently results in the recognition of a *non-financial* asset (or a *non-financial* liability), or if a forecast transaction for a non-financial asset or a non-financial liability becomes a firm commitment for which fair value hedge accounting is applied. The accounting policy chosen must be applied consistently to all such hedges. [IAS 39.99]

The accounting policy choices are as follows. The entity can either:

(a) reclassify the associated gains and losses from equity to profit or loss in the same period or periods during which the asset acquired or liability assumed affects profit or loss (such as in the periods that depreciation expense or cost of sales is recognised); or

(b) remove the associated gains and losses that were recognised in other comprehensive income and include them in the initial cost or other carrying amount of the asset or liability (in which case they will automatically impact profit or loss when the item is depreciated or sold). [IAS 39.98]

However, if an entity expects that all or a portion of a loss recognised in other comprehensive income will not be recovered in one or more future periods, it must reclassify the amount that is not expected to be recovered into profit or loss immediately.

IAS 39 only allows a basis adjustment for non-financial items. This exception simplifies the accounting and tracking of gains and losses that would have otherwise been retained in equity. This exception does not apply for financial items as allowing basis adjustments would be contrary to recognising all financial instruments at fair value on initial recognition.

Example 2.2.3

Basis adjusting forecast acquisition of a non-financial item

On 4 January 20X2 Entity D has a forecast purchase of 100,000 kg of cocoa on or about 31 December 20X2 from a Brazilian supplier, Entity B. Entity D has a Sterling functional currency, and Entity B has a US$ functional currency. On 4 January 20X2, Entity D designates the cash flow of the forecast purchase as a hedged item and enters into a currency forward to buy US$180,000 based on the forecast payment (100,000 kg at US$1.8 per kg). The forward contract locks in the value of the US$ amount to be paid at a rate of US$1.8:£1. At inception of the hedge, the derivative is on-market (i.e. fair value is zero). The terms of the currency forward and the forecast purchase match each other, and the entity designates the forward foreign exchange risk as the hedged risk.

Potential sources of ineffectiveness include non-occurrence of the forecast transaction and changes in the date of purchase. Any ineffectiveness will be recognised in profit or loss.

On 30 June 20X2, the fair value of the currency forward is positive £10,000 because the forward rate has changed, reflecting the fact that the US$ has strengthened against Sterling.

On 31 December 20X2 the transaction occurred as expected. The fair value of the forward is positive £12,500 as the US$ continued to strengthen against Sterling.

The required entries are as follows:

4 January 20X2

No entries are required since the forward was entered into 'on-market', and therefore had a fair value of zero at inception. Normally, there will be margin to be posted associated with trading on a currency exchange, but this has been ignored for illustration purposes only. There may also be fees if the foreign exchange contract is an over-the-counter (OTC) transaction.

30 June 20X2

Dr	Forward	£10,000
Cr	Other comprehensive income	£10,000

To recognise the forward at fair value, reflecting that the forward contract is fully effective in hedging the forward rate of the forecast transaction.

31 December 20X2

Dr	Forward	£2,500
Cr	Other comprehensive income	£2,500

To record the change in fair value of the forward. The forward contract remains fully effective in hedging the forward rate of the forecast transaction.

Dr	Cash	£12,500
Cr	Forward	£12,500

To record the cash received in settling the forward contract.

Dr	Stock	£112,500
Cr	Cash	£112,500

To record the payment of US$180,000 to purchase cocoa translated at the spot rate of $1.6:£1.

Dr	Other comprehensive income	£12,500
Cr	Stock	£12,500

To record the cumulative effective portion of the hedging instrument included in other comprehensive income that is removed from equity and included as a basis adjustment in the initial carrying value of the inventory.

The net effect of removing the amount from equity and including it in the carrying amount of the stock is equivalent to recognising the inventory at the contracted rate inherent in the forward (i.e. US$180,000 / US$1.8:£1)

Translation of purchase at spot rate at 31 December 20X2	£112,500
Release from equity at 31 December 20X2	(£12,500)
Sum	£100,000

Note: for the purposes of illustration only, the forward contract has not been discounted.

2.2.4 *Discontinuance of cash flow hedge accounting*

An entity must discontinue prospectively hedge accounting if:

- the hedging instrument expires or is sold, terminated or exercised (the replacement or rollover of a hedging instrument into another hedging instrument is not an expiration or termination if it formed part of the entity's documented hedging strategy from inception);
- the hedge no longer meets the hedge accounting criteria (for example, it is no longer highly effective or its effectiveness is no longer measurable);
- the forecast transaction is no longer expected to occur; or
- the entity de-designates the hedge relationship. [IAS 39.101]

The cumulative gain or loss on the hedging instrument recognised in other comprehensive income continues to be separately classified in equity until the forecast transaction occurs, at which point it is reclassified from equity to profit or loss.

When a forecast transaction is no longer highly probable but is still expected to occur, it no longer qualifies for cash flow hedge accounting as it does not satisfy the 'highly probable' criterion. Further recognition of fair value gains and losses on the hedging instrument in other comprehensive income is prohibited, i.e. subsequent changes in the fair value of the hedging instrument are recognised in profit or loss.

The cumulative gain or loss on the hedging instrument recognised in other comprehensive income prior to the transaction ceasing to be highly probable remains in equity until the transaction occurs, or until it is determined that the forecast transaction is no longer expected to occur. In the former case, the gain or loss is reclassified from equity to profit or loss when the hedged item impacts profit or loss or is used to adjust the initial cost of the carrying amount of a non-financial item. In the latter case, the gain or loss is reclassified from equity to profit or loss as soon as it is discovered that the transaction is no longer expected to occur.

Example 2.2.4A

Change in term of forecast debt issuance

Entity D, a Euro functional entity intends to issue Euro denominated debt in six months' time with a maturity of five years that will pay fixed interest on a six monthly basis. The transaction is highly probable and therefore there is a stream of ten highly probable six monthly interest payments. In order to hedge its future profit or loss exposure as a result of the fixed interest payments on the debt due to changes in the six-month LIBOR rate between now and the issuance of the debt (in six months' time), Entity D enters into a forward starting receive six-month LIBOR pay fixed interest rate swap with terms matching the critical terms of the forecast debt issuance such as start date, maturity, notional and payment dates. The entity designates the swap as a cash flow hedge of the profit or loss exposure arising from the series of six monthly interest payments on the forecast issuance of debt. Assuming all conditions necessary for hedge accounting under IAS 39 are satisfied, the effective portion of the gain and loss on the swap will be recognised in other comprehensive income.

On the forecast issue date Entity D issues seven-year Euro denominated fixed rate debt, rather than debt with a five-year term as previously anticipated. The entity closes out the swap at the date of issuance. Ten forecast highly probable interest payments are still likely to occur, even though they will now be interest payments on debt with a seven-year maturity. The gain or loss recognised in other comprehensive income will be reclassified from equity to profit or loss when the individual interest payments for the first five years of the debt impact profit or loss. An allocation of the amount deferred in equity when the debt is issued will be required to determine the amount of the swap that relates to the individual interest payments that were forecast and are still expected to occur. As the fair value of the swap recognised in other comprehensive income consists of the present value of 10 future fixed cash flows, this present value amount is allocated specifically to those 10 future interest periods, and accordingly is released to profit or loss in those future periods.

Where the timing of a transaction moves forward, i.e. the transaction is expected to occur sooner, the forecast transaction continues to be highly probable and hence continues to qualify as a hedged item. [IAS 39.IG.F.5.4]

Example 2.2.4B

Change in timing of forecast sale of a non-financial item

Entity S designates a derivative as a hedging instrument in a cash flow hedge of a forecast sale of silver. The hedging relationship meets all the hedge accounting conditions, including the requirement to identify and document the period in which the transaction is expected to occur within a reasonably specific and generally narrow range of time.

In a subsequent period, the forecast transaction is expected to occur in an earlier period than originally anticipated.

The change in timing of the forecast transaction does not affect the validity of the designation. Entity S can conclude that the transaction is the same as the one that was designated as being hedged. However, the change in timing of the hedged transaction may affect the assessment of hedge effectiveness going forward since the hedging instrument must continue to be designated for the whole of its remaining period to maturity. Also, the amount recognised in other comprehensive income up to this point will need to be adjusted to be the lower of the cumulative gain or loss on the derivative from inception of the hedge and the cumulative change in fair value of the future cash flows of the forecast transaction.

If the hedged transaction is no longer expected to occur then the cumulative amounts in other comprehensive income are reclassified from equity to profit or loss. [IAS 39.101(c)]

Example 2.2.4C

Change in timing of forecast debt issuance

Entity D is hedging the forecast issuance of £100 million of 10-year, fixed-rate debt using a rate lock agreement (a derivative). The entity designates the rate lock agreement as a hedge of the variability in the total cash flows arising on the forecast debt issuance. Entity D expects to issue the debt in the second quarter of 20X0. Entity D's credit rating is BB. In the first quarter of 20X0, the spreads between government and corporate bond rates widen significantly. As a result, Entity D does not expect to issue its bonds in the second quarter. Entity D's advisors believe that the markets may stabilise in the first quarter of 20X1. Entity D will now make a decision on the type of funding in the first quarter of 20X1 and therefore closes out its rate lock agreement. At the time of closure the fair value of the lock agreement was negative.

Entity D should recognise the entire loss in income because the forecast debt issuance is not expected to occur.

An entity can de-designate a hedge relationship at any point in time. Any gains or losses recognised in other comprehensive income up to the point of de-designation will remain in equity until the forecast transaction occurs. [IAS 39.101(d)] Gains or losses on the hedging instrument after de-designation will be recognised in profit or loss if the hedging instrument continues to be held.

2.2.5 *Reclassification from equity to profit or loss after a business combination*

Following a business combination, where the acquiree has applied cash flow hedging and recognised gains or losses in other comprehensive income prior to the acquisition, the acquirer will not be able to reclassify those gains and losses to consolidated profit or loss. Because the pre-acquisition reserves of the subsidiary do not exist in the consolidated financial statements of its new parent, any amounts recognised in other comprehensive income by the subsidiary prior to the business combination cannot be reclassified. Thus, the group can only hedge account for the specific relationship that the acquiree has prospectively from the date of acquisition with only post acquisition amounts in other comprehensive income being reclassified from equity to consolidated profit or loss in accordance with IAS 39.95.

2.3 Net investment hedge

A hedge of a net investment in a foreign operation is a hedge of the foreign currency exposure to changes in the reporting entity's share in the net assets of that foreign operation. IAS 21 *The Effects of Changes in Foreign Exchange Rates* requires that the reporting entity's share in the net assets of a foreign operation is translated into the functional currency of the ultimate parent with the retranslation gain or loss recognised in other comprehensive income. It does not matter what denomination the monetary assets and liabilities are in the foreign operation, as all those monetary items are firstly retranslated into the foreign operation's functional currency. It is the translation of those net assets of the foreign operation into the parent's functional currency that is the designated hedged risk.

IFRIC 16 *Hedges of a Net Investment in a Foreign Operation* was issued in July 2008 and is effective for annual periods beginning on or after 1 October 2008. One of the questions it addressed was whether the hedged risk in a net investment hedge was the difference between the functional currency of the foreign operation and the presentation currency of the group, or the functional currency of the foreign operation and the functional currency of the parent. The IFRIC consensus was the latter. The IFRIC acknowledged that this question will only be relevant to the extent that the presentation currency of the group differs from the functional currency of the parent. The IFRIC recognised that there were arguments for either view but on balance considered the arguments in favour of looking to the functional currency of the parent were more compelling. The IFRIC concluded that the presentation currency does not create an exposure to which an entity may apply hedge accounting. The functional currency is determined on the basis of the primary economic environment in which the entity operates. Accordingly, functional currencies create an economic exposure to changes in cash flows or fair values; a presentation currency never will. [IFRIC 16.BC14]

At the time of writing, IFRIC 16 has not yet been endorsed for adoption in the EU. EU companies may, nevertheless, comply with its requirements prior to endorsement, since it does not conflict with the existing requirements of IAS 39. UK

A hedge of a net investment in a foreign operation, including a hedge of a monetary item that is accounted for as part of the net investment as defined in IAS 21, assuming it meets all other requirements for hedge accounting, is accounted for similarly to a cash flow hedge:

(a) the portion of the gain or loss on the hedging instrument that is determined to be an effective hedge is recognised in other comprehensive income; and

(b) the ineffective portion of the gain or loss on the hedging instrument is recognised immediately in profit or loss. [IAS 39.102]

The descriptions of fair value and cash flow hedges in **2.1** and **2.2** above respectively make specific reference to the presence of an exposure attributable to a particular risk that could affect profit or loss. The equivalent statement is not made with respect to a hedge of a net investment in a foreign operation. However, this can be seen as simply an omission rather than a substantive difference. The hedged risk in a net investment hedge, being the foreign currency exposure on the retranslation of the reporting entity's share of the net assets of the foreign operation under IAS 21, does affect profit or loss because IAS 21.48 & 48C require the cumulative exchange differences of the foreign operation to be reclassified from equity to profit or loss on the disposal (or, in some cases, the partial disposal) of that foreign operation.

Goodwill and any fair value adjustments arising on acquisition of a foreign operation are treated as assets and liabilities of the foreign operation, expressed in the foreign currency and translated at the closing rate, and thus are considered net assets of the foreign operation. [IAS 21.47] Equally, a monetary item that is receivable from or payable to a foreign operation for which settlement is neither planned nor likely to occur in the foreseeable future is, in substance, part of the entity's net investment in that foreign operation, and therefore forms part of the net assets of that foreign operation. [IAS 21.15]

Example 2.3

Identifying net assets available to be hedged

Parent A, £ functional currency, has an investment in a foreign operation, its wholly-owned Subsidiary B that has a US$ functional currency. Parent A heads Group A. The investment in Subsidiary B was made at 1 January 20X0 when Parent A acquired 100 per cent of the share capital for US$100m. At the date of acquisition the fair value of the identifiable net assets of Subsidiary B was US$70m with no contingent liabilities. Therefore, in applying purchase accounting under IFRS 3 *Business Combinations* US$30m of goodwill was recognised in the consolidated financial statements of Parent A. At the acquisition date, Parent A extended a loan of £10m to Subsidiary B when the US$/£spot exchange rate was US$2:£1. Settlement of this loan is neither planned nor likely to occur in the foreseeable future.

At the acquisition date, Group A wishes to designate as a hedged item its net investment in its foreign operation, Subsidiary B, in the consolidated financial statements. The maximum amount of the net investment in the foreign operation that can be designated as a hedged item is US$120m. This comprises three elements:

- US$70m of the identifiable net assets of the foreign operation acquired upon acquisition;
- US$30m of goodwill that forms part of the net assets of the foreign operation; and
- US$20m of additional net assets as a result of the loan extended by Parent A to Subsidiary B, being a monetary item for which settlement is neither planned nor likely to occur in the foreseeable future and the item, thus, in substance, forms part of the net investment in Subsidiary B.

It should be noted that if the loan extended to Subsidiary B was expected to be settled in the foreseeable future the maximum amount of the net investment in the foreign operation that could be designated would be US$100m as the loan would not form part of the net investment in Subsidiary B.

The gain or loss on the hedging instrument relating to the effective portion of the hedge that has been recognised in other comprehensive income is reclassified from equity to profit or loss when the net investment affects profit or loss, i.e. on the disposal (or, in some cases, partial disposal) of the net investment in the foreign operation. [IAS 39.102] This makes it necessary to track the amount of gains and losses on hedging instruments recognised in other comprehensive income in relation to the hedge of each individual foreign operation separately, so as to be able to identify how much of the total amount recognised in other comprehensive income should be reclassified from equity to profit or loss on the sale of a particular foreign operation. This may be complex in large groups with many foreign operations and with many hedging instruments used over different periods of time.

IAS 21 *The Effects of Changes in Foreign Exchange Rates* defines what a net investment in a foreign operation is. IAS 21 defines a net investment in a foreign operation as the amount of the reporting entity's interest in the net assets of that operation. [IAS 21.8]

Net investment hedging is only permitted in consolidated financial statements, as it is only in consolidated financial statements that the net assets of the foreign operation are recognised. The only exception to this is where a foreign operation is not a separate legal entity but is a branch of the reporting entity and the branch has a functional currency different to the functional currency of the reporting entity. In this instance the reporting entity may apply net investment hedging in the individual financial statements of the investor in the branch by designating the translation risk of the net assets of the foreign operation branch. This view is acknowledged in IFRIC 16.2.

In the individual financial statements of the investor, an investment in a subsidiary is recognised either at cost or in accordance with IAS 39, i.e. as an available-for-sale asset or at fair value through profit or loss. [IAS 27(2008).38, previously IAS 27(2003).37] Similarly, an investment in an associate or a jointly controlled entity is recognised either at cost or in accordance with IAS 39. [IAS 28.35 & IAS 31.46] The carrying amount under either of these methods will not be equivalent to the net assets of that operation.

However, as an alternative, the investor may wish to apply fair value hedge accounting for the foreign exchange risk of its investment in its foreign operation. For example, if an investor makes an investment in a foreign operation that meets the definition of a subsidiary, the investor will hold its investment either at cost or in accordance with IAS 39. [IAS 27(2008).38, previously IAS 27(2003).37] The investing entity will be exposed to a risk that will impact profit or loss, i.e. the foreign currency risk that arises upon disposal of the foreign subsidiary. If the investing entity has a foreign exchange derivative, or a foreign denominated liability that was used to fund the investment in the foreign operation, it could designate it as a hedging instrument in respect of a portion of the foreign currency risk of the investment in the subsidiary equivalent to the notional on the hedging instrument. Applying fair value hedge accounting would result in the gain or loss on the hedging instrument being recognised in profit or loss along with the associated foreign currency risk on the designated portion of the investment in the subsidiary.

It is worth noting that this approach is very different to applying net investment in a foreign operation hedge accounting at a consolidated level where both the hedging instrument and the foreign exchange translation on the net assets of the foreign operation are recognised in other comprehensive income. Additionally, it should be noted that fair value hedge accounting cannot be applied in the consolidated financial statements to an equity method investment or an investment in a consolidated subsidiary. [IAS 39.AG99] Fair value hedge accounting for such items can only be applied in the separate financial statements of the investor.

2.3.1 *Hedging net investments with loans*

In the absence of hedge accounting the foreign exchange gains and losses on re-translating the net assets of the foreign operation would be recognised in other comprehensive income and taken to a separate component of equity (in accordance with IAS 21), whilst those on the loan would be recognised in profit or loss. This creates a mismatch in foreign currency translation. When net investment hedge accounting is applied, this mismatch is eliminated as the gains and losses on the loan, to the extent effective, are recognised in other comprehensive income.

When the hedging instrument in a net investment hedge is a foreign denominated non-derivative financial liability, for example, a foreign denominated loan, it is always the spot re-translation risk that is the hedged risk (as opposed to the forward rate) as it is only the spot rate that is recognised from retranslating the foreign currency non-derivative liability.

2.3.1.1 *Loan is less than or equals net assets of subsidiary*

Example 2.3.1.1

Loan is less than or equals net assets of subsidiary

Entity A, a UK entity with a Sterling functional currency, has a US subsidiary with a US dollar functional currency, Entity B. To finance this subsidiary,

Entity A has a US$50 million US dollar loan with a third party bank. Entities A and B have the same 31 December year end and the net assets of Entity B at 31 December 20X1 and 31 December 20X2 were US$70 million.

The loan is designated as a hedging instrument of the first US$50 million of net assets of Entity B. The designation is spot retranslation risk only. The hedge is determined to be highly effective. The US$/£ spot rate on 31/12/X1 is 1.6 and on 31/12/X2 it is 1.7.

On 31/12/X2 the entries are as follows:

Dr	Loan	£1.84m
Cr	Other comprehensive income	£1.84m

To recognise the foreign exchange gain on the loan. This is the difference between US$50m translated at 1.6 and 1.7.

Dr	Other comprehensive income	£2.57m
Cr	Net assets	£2.57m

To retranslate the net assets. This is the difference between US$70m translated at 1.6 and 1.7.

The entire exchange difference on retranslating the net assets of the foreign operation is taken to other comprehensive income in accordance with IAS 21. The application of hedge accounting results in the remeasurement of the loan being recognised in other comprehensive income as opposed to profit or loss. No hedge ineffectiveness has been recognised. Hedge ineffectiveness would have arisen if the net assets of the foreign operation fell below US$50m at the period end.

2.3.1.2 *Loan exceeds net assets of subsidiary*

Hedge accounting is still possible when the amount of the loan exceeds the net assets of the foreign operation.

Example 2.3.1.2

Loan exceeds net assets of subsidiary

The same scenario applies as in **example 2.3.1.1** except the loan is US$100m.

The entity designates US$70 million of the loan as a hedging instrument of the first US$70 million net assets of Entity B. The designation is spot retranslation risk only. The hedge is determined to be highly effective. The US$/£ spot rate on 31/12/X1 is 1.6 and on 31/12/X2 it is 1.7.

On 31/12/X2 the entries are as follows:

Dr	Loan	£3.68m
Cr	Other comprehensive income	£2.57m
Cr	Profit or loss	£1.11m

To recognise the foreign exchange gain on the loan.

The entire loan must be reported at the closing rate, giving rise to an exchange gain. The exchange gain that relates to the designated and effective hedging instrument (i.e. US$70 million of the loan) is reported in other comprehensive income. The remainder is reported in profit or loss.

Dr	Other comprehensive income	£2.57m
Cr	Net assets	£2.57m

To retranslate the net assets.

2.3.1.3 *Net assets of the foreign operation change*

Both of the above examples were simplified as the net assets of the subsidiary remained the same at the start and at the end of the reporting period. In practice this will rarely be the case. As documentation and designation must be in place at inception of the hedge, the hedged item will be based on the opening net asset position. Hedge ineffectiveness arises to the extent to which the net asset position falls below the designated amount of net assets at the date that hedge effectiveness is assessed, which is, at a minimum, at the end of each reporting period.

Example 2.3.1.3

Net assets of foreign operation change

Entity A, a UK entity with a Sterling functional currency, has a US subsidiary with a US dollar functional currency, Entity B. To finance this subsidiary, Entity A has a US$80 million US dollar loan with a third party bank. The year end of both entities is 31 December. On 31 December 20X1 the net assets of Entity B were US$90m, and are expected to remain at approximately this level, so the entire loan was designated as hedging the spot retranslation risk associated with the first US$80 million net assets of Entity B.

On 31 December 20X2, the net assets of B were US$75m. The US$/£ spot rate on 31/12/X1 is 1.6 and on 31/12/X2 is 1.7.

Hedge ineffectiveness arises as there are no longer US$80 million of net assets that are being hedged. The effectiveness can be measured as 75/80, i.e. 93.75 per cent, or as 80/75, i.e. 106.67 per cent. In either case the effectiveness is within 80–125 per cent range, so hedge accounting is permitted for the period. Hedge ineffectiveness must be reported immediately in profit or loss.

Dr	Loan	£2.94m
Cr	Other comprehensive income	£2.76m
Cr	Profit or loss	£0.18m

To recognise the foreign exchange gain on the loan.

The foreign exchange gain that relates to the designated and effective hedging instrument is recognised in other comprehensive income (i.e. the exchange gain on US$75 million), whilst the ineffective portion is recognised in profit or loss.

On 31 December 20X2 the group may choose to redesignate prospectively the hedging instrument to be only US$75 million of the loan.

In the above example, ineffectiveness was caused by the net assets of the foreign operation falling below the level of the loan hedging it. This ineffectiveness can be minimised by monitoring the net assets of the foreign operation and redesignating as appropriate.

2.3.2 *Hedging net investments with forward contracts*

If no hedge accounting was applied, then the foreign exchange gains and losses on re-translating the net assets of the foreign operation would be taken to other comprehensive income (in accordance with IAS 21.39) and the change in fair value of the forward contract would be recognised in profit or loss.

When hedging net investments with forward contracts, it is important to specify what risk is being hedged: i.e. the forward or the spot foreign currency exchange rate. If the forward rate is hedged, the full change in fair value of the forward is recognised in other comprehensive income if it is fully effective whereas if the spot rate is hedged, the spot element of the forward is recognised in other comprehensive income and the remainder (being the forward points) is recognised in profit or loss. Any element recognised in other comprehensive income as an effective gain or loss is reclassified from equity to profit or loss when the underlying net investment is sold.

2.3.2.1 *Hedging the spot rate*

Example 2.3.2.1

Net investment hedging the spot foreign currency rate

On 1 November 20X1, Entity XYZ enters into a forward contract to sell US$1,000,000 and buy Sterling at a fixed rate of US$1.57:£1 on 30 January 20X2. Group XYZ has a 31 December year end and is headed by Entity XYZ, which has a Sterling functional currency. The forward contract is entered into to hedge the foreign exchange translation risk associated with movements in the spot rate relating to its investment in its US subsidiary with a US dollar functional currency, Entity ABC, which has net assets of US$1,000,000 in Group XYZ's consolidated group accounts.

The forward and spot US$/£ translation rates are as follows:

	1/11/X1	31/12/X1	30/1/X2
Spot	1.55	1.59	1.61

Forward (to 30/1/X2)	1.57	1.60	n/a

On 30 January 20X2, Entity XYZ closes out the forward contract, and also sells Entity ABC for US$1,200,000 which is equal to £745,342 translated at US$1.61:£1.

Translating US$1,000,000 at the above rates gives the following Sterling amounts:

	1/11/X1	**31/12/X1**	**30/1/X2**
Spot	1.55	1.59	1.61
Sterling amount	£645,161	£628,931	£621,118
Forward (to 30/1/X2)	1.57	1.60	n/a
Sterling amount	£636,943	£625,000	

Therefore, the value of the derivative is (for purposes of illustration, ignoring the time value of money):

Date	**Derivative value**	**How calculated**
31/12/X1	£11,943	£636,943 – £625,000
30/1/X2	£15,825	£636,943 – £621,118

Movements in the fair value of the premium (or discount) implicitly inherent in the fair value of the forward contract will not give rise to hedge ineffectiveness, as the designated hedged risk is movements in spot rate only and, therefore, those movements are excluded from the designated hedging relationship. However, movements in the fair value of these forward points will give rise to volatility in profit or loss.

The entries are as follows:

31 December 20X1

Dr	Other comprehensive income	£16,230	
Cr	Net assets	£16,230	

To recognise the foreign exchange difference on translation of the net assets at the spot rate (i.e. translating the investment at 1.59 rather than 1.55).

Dr	Derivative	£11,943	
Dr	Profit or loss	£4,287	(relates to forward points)
Cr	Other comprehensive income	£16,230	

To recognise the change in the fair value of the derivative, the effective portion in other comprehensive income and the undesignated portion in profit or loss.

30 January 20X2

Dr	Other comprehensive income	£7,813	
Cr	Net assets	£7,813	

To recognise the foreign exchange difference on translation of the net assets at the spot rate (i.e. translating the investment at 1.61 rather than 1.59).

Dr	Derivative	£3,882	

Dr	Profit or loss	£3,931	(relates to forward points)
Cr	Other comprehensive income	£7,813	

To recognise the change in the fair value of the derivative, the effective portion in other comprehensive income and the undesignated portion in profit or loss.

Dr	Cash	£15,825
Cr	Derivative	£15,825

To reflect cash settlement of the derivative at its maturity.

Dr	Cash	£745,342
Cr	Profit or loss	£100,181
Cr	Net assets	£621,118
Cr	Other comprehensive income	£24,043

To recognise the sale proceeds and profit on disposal.

Dr	Other comprehensive income	£24,043
Cr	Profit or loss	£24,043

To recognise the reclassification of the hedging gains and losses from equity to profit or loss.

The total, post hedge, profit on disposal is £124,224 (£100,181 + £24,043).

It is assumed for illustrative purposes only that the total net assets of the foreign operation are unaffected by the application IFRS 5 *Non-current assets held for sale and discontinued operations* to the disposal group, i.e. the net assets are lower than the fair value less costs to sell.

For the purpose of both assessing effectiveness and measuring ineffectiveness in net investment hedging it is possible to identify the spot element of a forward contract as the undiscounted spot. This is because the risk being hedged is the risk of the retranslation of the net assets of the net investment in accordance with IAS 21 *The Effects of Changes in Foreign Exchange Rates*, which is calculated on an undiscounted basis. This is equally true when an entity designates foreign currency denominated debt as a hedge of a net investment in a foreign operation. In this case, both the hedged item and hedging instrument are retranslated to undiscounted spot in accordance with IAS 21 and therefore the hedged risk is the undiscounted spot.

2.3.2.2 *Hedging the forward rate*

In **example 2.3.2.1**, the spot rate was hedged. Consider the same example where the forward rate is hedged.

Example 2.3.2.2

Net investment hedging the forward foreign currency rate

Movements in the fair value of the premium (or discount) implicit in the forward contract, the forward points, will now be recognised in other comprehensive income (rather than in profit or loss) and will therefore give rise to equity volatility. These amounts will be reclassified from equity to profit or loss when the subsidiary is sold.

The required entries are as follows:

31 December 20X1

Dr	Other comprehensive income	£16,230
Cr	Net assets	£16,230

To recognise the foreign exchange difference on translation of the net assets at the spot rate (i.e. translating the investment at 1.59):

Dr	Derivative	£11,943
Cr	Other comprehensive income	£11,943

To recognise the change in the fair value of the derivative that is fully effective.

30 January 20X2

Dr	Other comprehensive income	£7,813
Cr	Net assets	£7,813

To recognise the movements in the investment relating to the spot rate movement (i.e. translating the investment at 1.61):

Dr	Derivative	£3,882
Cr	Other comprehensive income	£3,882

To recognise the change in the fair value of the derivative that is fully effective.

Dr	Cash	£15,825
Cr	Derivative	£15,825

To reflect cash settlement of the derivative at its maturity.

Dr	Cash	£745,342
Cr	Profit or loss	£100,181
Cr	Net assets	£621,118
Cr	Other comprehensive income	£24,043

To recognise the sale proceeds and the profit on disposal.

Dr	Other comprehensive income	£15,825
Cr	Profit or loss	£15,825

To recognise the reclassification of the hedging gains and losses from equity to profit or loss

The total, post hedge, profit on disposal is £116,006 (£100,181 + £15,825).

Compared to **example 2.3.2.1**, the profit on disposal is £8,218 lower as in the previous example the fair value of the forward points was recognised in profit or loss throughout the life of the hedge relationship.

It is assumed for illustrative purposes only that the total net assets of the foreign operation are unaffected by the application IFRS 5 *Non-current assets held for sale and discontinued operations* to the disposal group, i.e. the net assets are lower than the fair value less costs to sell.

Whether the spot rate or the forward rate is the designated hedged risk, the overall effect on profit or loss is the same, but the timing of the recognition of the fair value of the forward points is different.

It is not permitted in any hedge relationship to amortise any premium or discount on a forward contract. Derivatives must always be measured at fair value in the statement of financial position. Changes in fair value are either recognised in profit or loss, or in other comprehensive income, if the derivative is designated as an effective hedge in a cash flow or net investment hedge. [IAS 39.IG.F.6.4]

2.3.3 *Hedging net investments with currency swaps*

Hedging net investments with foreign currency swaps is very similar to hedging with forwards. This is to be expected, as swaps with fixed cash flows are simply a series of forwards. As with forwards, it is important to be clear which risk is being hedged (i.e. the spot or forward rate).

Whilst foreign currency swaps that swap from one currency to another can be used as hedging instruments of net investment hedges, it is difficult to be highly effective with cross currency fixed-for-floating interest rate swaps as the interest element of the swap does not reduce foreign exchange risk of the net investment in the foreign operation. This is the case when an entity is swapping currency as well as the basis of interest from floating to fixed rates and vice versa. Furthermore, since a derivative instrument must be designated in its entirety (except for the limited circumstances noted in **4.2**), the element that does not reduce foreign exchange risk cannot be excluded from the hedge designation.

Where the currency swap is fixed for fixed, or floating to floating, the derivative may qualify as a hedge of a net investment in a foreign operation. Hedging instruments such as floating to floating currency swaps respond closely to movements in spot rates. Thus, provided the notional of such an instrument does not exceed the net investment, it is likely to be an effective hedging instrument for a hedge of the spot risk associated with the net investment.

Fixed for fixed currency swaps may be used as hedging instruments in a hedge of either the forward or spot risk associated with the net investment. In either case there are potentially two ways of designating such an instrument. One would be to hedge an amount of net assets that is equal to the present value of the foreign currency interest and principal. This is in line with viewing the cross currency swap as comprising a combination of a loan payable in foreign currency and a loan receivable in the other currency. In this case an amount of net assets equal to the foreign currency principal of the swap should be designated as the hedged item. Alternatively, an amount of net assets equal to the sum of the undiscounted foreign currency principal and undiscounted foreign currency interest payments can be designated as the hedged item. This is in line with viewing the fixed for fixed swap as a combination of forwards with respect to interest payments and final principal exchange at maturity. Note that a greater amount of net assets would have to be available for the second method to be an effective hedge relationship. Whichever approach is applied it should applied consistently where fixed for fixed currency swaps are designated as hedges of net investments in a foreign operation.

Example 2.3.3A

Hedging a net investment in a foreign operation with a cross currency swap that receives floating functional currency pays floating foreign currency

On 1 January 20X2, Entity A, a Sterling functional currency entity, acquires a US subsidiary with a US dollar functional currency which has net assets of US$150,000. Entity A will be subject to foreign currency risk (between the US$ and £) on retranslation of the net investment in the consolidated financial statements and therefore wants to achieve hedge accounting for a specific level (US$100,000) of the net assets in the foreign operation. Entity A wishes to designate the first US$100,000 of net assets as the hedged item in a net investment in a foreign operation. At 1 January 20X2, the spot rate on the US$ / £ is 1.75/1 so the notional of US$100,000 is equivalent to £57,143. On the same date, Entity A enters into a cross currency swap ('CCS') to exchange interest payments and principal at redemption with a notional equal to the designated amount of net assets, and designates the cross currency swap as a hedge of the variability of the £ equivalent cash flows on the US$100,000 of the net assets of the foreign operation. The terms are such that on each interest payment date (assume interest is paid annually on 31 December each year for the cross currency swap), Entity A will pay US$ LIBOR + 100 basis points on a notional of US$100,000 and receive Sterling LIBOR + 106 basis points based on a notional of £57,143. Because the currency and notional on the swap match the net investment, and the swap is on-market at inception, Entity A expects that the hedging relationship will be highly effective.

Date	Spot rate US$ / £	Net assets of foreign operation in US$	Carrying amount of US$100,000 of net assets in £	Cross currency swap fair value £	Net interest receipt on the swap (£ LIBOR +106bp – US$ LIBOR +100bp)
31/12/X1	1.75	150,000	57,143	0	0
31/12/X2	1.7	160,000	58,824	(1,743)	1,259
31/12/X3	1.6	141,000	62,500	(5,520)	1,476
31/12/X4	1.5	121,000	66,667	(9,670)	1,952
31/12/X5	1.8	106,000	55,556	1,624	1,042
31/12/X6	1.7	115,000	58,824	(1,681)	1,321

Entity A's documentation of the hedge is as follows:

Risk management objective and nature of risk being hedged	Net investment hedge of the foreign currency exposure (due to US$/£ spot rate) to changes in the reporting entity's interest in the first US$100,000 of net assets in the foreign operation.
Date of designation	1 January 20X2
Hedging instrument	Cross currency swap to exchange US$100,000 at maturity and pay US$ LIBOR +100bp, receive £ LIBOR +106bp interest annually over the term of the instrument.
Hedged item	The first US$100,000 of net assets in the foreign operation.
Assessment of hedge effectiveness	The critical terms of the derivative (currency, notional) match that of the net investment. Although there are no interest payments from the net investment, the cross currency float to float swap responds closely to movements in undiscounted spot rates as the interest payments are made at the end of the reporting period. Accordingly there is an expectation of high effectiveness. The entity will assess counterparty credit risk and probability of cash flows under the swap occurring every period.
Measurement of hedge effectiveness	Comparison of the period-to-period retranslation on the first US$100,000 of net assets of the foreign operation using undiscounted spot rates compared to the fair value movement on the CCS.

Period-to-period assessment of hedge effectiveness using the dollar offset test:

Period	Fair value movement in spot rates in period for first US$100,000 of net assets £	Fair value movement in CCS in period £	% effective using period to period gains / losses	Hedge accounting permitted in period (80–125%)
20X2	1,681	1,743	96%	YES
20X3	3,676	3,777	97%	YES
20X4	4,167	4,150	100%	YES
20X5	(11,111)	(11,294)	98%	YES
20X6	3,268	3,305	99%	YES

The hedging relationship is deemed to be highly effective (80%-125%) throughout each period and therefore hedge accounting is permitted. Any ineffectiveness, being the difference between fair value movement of the CCS and the retranslation of the first US$100,000 of net assets using undiscounted spot rates, will be recognised in profit or loss in the period.

The following table illustrates the accounting entries for the transaction during its life in Sterling: Dr or (Cr) as indicated. For illustrative purposes only, the entries have recognised the translation on only US$100,000 of net assets and not actual net assets. IAS 21 would require translation of all net assets of the foreign operation to the cumulative translation reserve. As the total net assets never fall below US$100,000 at a period end, the illustrative journal for 'Consolidated net assets' is always the retranslation of US$100,000.

31 Dec		Cash	CCS	Consolidated net assets	Profit or loss (ineffective)	Interest income	Other comprehensive income (cumulative translation reserve)
20X2	Revalue US$100,000 net assets to spot			1,681			(1,681)
	Net interest on CCS	1,259				(1,259)	
	Fair value of CCS		(1,743)		62		1,681
20X3	Revalue US$100,000 net assets to spot			3,676			(3,676)
	Net interest on CCS	1,476				(1,476)	
	Fair value of CCS		(3,777)		101		3,676
20X4	Revalue US$100,000 net assets to spot			4,167			(4,167)

31 Dec		Cash	CCS	Consolidated net assets	Profit or loss (ineffective)	Interest income	Other comprehensive income (cumulative translation reserve)
	Net interest on CCS	1,952				(1,952)	
	Fair value of CCS		(4,150)		(17)		4,167
20X5	Revalue US$100,000 net assets to spot			(11,111)			11,111
	Net interest on CCS	1,042				(1,042)	
	Fair value of CCS		11,294		(183)		(11,111)
20X6	Revalue US$100,000 net assets to spot			3,268			(3,268)
	Net interest on CCS	1,321				(1,321)	
	Fair value of CCS		(3,305)		37		3,268
20X6		(7,050)	(1,681)	1,681	0	(7,050)	0
	Key		A	A	B		C

Key

A: the remaining value on the CCS is the difference between the net assets retranslated at US$1.75/£ (original rate) and the US$1.70/£ (spot rate at date termination of swap). Hence total statement of financial position before final settlement of CCS is (net assets £58,824 – CCS £1,681) = £57,123 at 31/12/X6 which is equivalent to the original US$100,000 net assets at the original spot rate of US$1.75/£.

B: Nets to zero as all amounts have been taken to profit or loss as ineffectiveness.

C: As at least US$100,000 of net assets existed at each reporting period throughout the relationship, the hedge relationship was fully effective in hedging the first US$100,000 of net assets.

Entries in the consolidated financial statements for 20X2 for illustrative purposes.

1 January 20X2

No entry required by CCS as fair value is nil at inception.

31 December 20X2

Dr	Net assets	1,681

Cr	Other comprehensive income (cumulative translation reserve)		1,681

To record gain on retranslation of the US$100,000 of net assets at year-end spot rates.

Dr	Cash	1,259	
Cr	Interest income		1,259

To record net interest income on the CCS

Dr	Other comprehensive income (cumulative translation reserve)	1,681	
Dr	Profit or loss	62	
Cr	Cross currency swap liability		1,743

To record fair value movement in CCS with corresponding entries to other comprehensive income (cumulative translation adjustment in equity to offset retranslation of net assets) and remainder recognised as ineffectiveness in profit or loss.

Similar entries would be recorded for the remaining term of the hedging relationship (20X3 -20X6). The amount in cumulative translation reserve will be reclassified from equity to profit or loss on disposal of the foreign operation.

Interest income totalling £7,050 is recognised over the term of the hedging instrument in profit or loss as the interest receipts represent the net financing on the swap. The reason the swap is not 100 per cent effective in hedging undiscounted spot is because the fair value of the swap is the present value of all future cash flows on the swap, which include some fixed cash flows. As both legs on the swap have fixed margins, the present value of these fixed margins will result in some hedge ineffectiveness. In the above example, the amount of ineffectiveness is not sufficient for the hedge relationship to fail hedge accounting.

Example 2.3.3B

Hedging a net investment in a foreign operation with a cross currency swap that receives fixed functional currency pays fixed foreign currency

On 1 January 20X2, Entity A, a Sterling functional currency entity, acquires a US subsidiary with a US dollar functional currency which has net assets of US$150,000. Entity A will be subject to foreign currency risk (between the US$ and £) on retranslation of the net investment in the consolidated financial statements and therefore wants to achieve hedge accounting for a specific level (US$100,000) of the net assets in the foreign operation. Entity A wishes to designate the first US$100,000 of net assets as the hedged item in a net investment hedge. At 1 January 20X2, the spot rate on the US$ / £ is 1.75/1 so the notional of US$100,000 is equivalent to £57,143. On the same date, Entity A enters into a cross currency swap ('CCS') to exchange interest payments and principal at redemption with a notional equal to the designated amount of net assets, and designates the cross currency swap as a hedge of the variability of the £ equivalent cash flows on the US$100,000 of the net assets of the foreign operation. The terms are such that on each interest payment date (assume interest is paid annually on 31 December each year for the cross currency swap), Entity A will pay US$ 4 per cent on a notional of US$100,000 and receive Sterling 6 per cent on a notional of £57,143. Because the currency and notional on the swap match the net investment, and the swap is on-market at inception, Entity A expects that the hedging relationship will be highly effective.

Date	Spot rate US$ / £	Net assets of foreign operation in US$	Carrying amount of US$100,000 of net assets in £	Cross currency swap fair value £ (liability)	Net interest receipts on the swap (US$ 4% – £ 6%)
31/12/X1	1.75	150,000	57,143	0	0
31/12/X2	1.7	160,000	58,824	(2,560)	1,110
31/12/X3	1.6	141,000	62,500	(7,723)	1,004
31/12/X4	1.5	121,000	66,667	(9,513)	848
31/12/X5	1.8	106,000	55,556	1,452	1,004
31/12/X6	1.7	115,000	58,824	(1,681)	1,143

Entity A's documentation of the hedge is as follows:

Risk management objective and nature of risk being hedged	Net investment hedge of the foreign currency exposure (due to US$/£ forward rates) to changes in the reporting entity's interest in the first US$100,000 of net assets in the foreign operation.
Date of designation	1 January 20X2
Hedging instrument	Cross currency swap to exchange US$100,000 at maturity and pay US$ 4%, receive £ 6% interest annually over the term of the instrument.
Hedged item	The first US$100,000 of net assets in the foreign operation.
Assessment of hedge effectiveness	The critical terms of the derivative (currency, notional) match those of the net investment. There is an expectation of high effectiveness. The entity will assess counterparty credit risk and probability of cash flows under the swap occurring every period.
Measurement of hedge effectiveness	Comparison of the fair value movement of the CCS and a hypothetical CCS with a notional amount equal to the hedged amount and terms that mirror those of the actual CCS.

The following table illustrates the accounting entries for the transaction during its life in Sterling: Dr or (Cr) as indicated. For illustrative purposes only, the entries have recognised the translation on only US$100,000 of net assets and not actual net assets. IAS 21 would require translation of all net assets of the foreign operation to the cumulative translation reserve. As the total net assets never fall below US$100,000 at a period end, the illustrative journal for 'Consolidated net assets' is always the retranslation of US$100,000.

For illustrative purposes the hedge relationship is deemed to be fully effective throughout its life.

31 Dec		Cash	CCS	Consolidated net assets	Profit or loss (ineffective)	Interest expense	Other comprehensive income (cumulative translation reserve)
20X2	Revalue US$100,000 net assets to spot			1,681			(1,681)
	Net interest on CCS	1,110				(1,110)	
	Fair value of CCS		(2,560)				2,560
20X3	Revalue US$100,000 net assets to spot			3,676			(3,676)
	Net interest on CCS	1,004				(1,004)	
	Fair value of CCS		(5,163)				5,163
20X4	Revalue US$100,000 net assets to spot			4,167			(4,167)
	Net interest on CCS	848				(848)	
	Fair value of CCS		(1,790)				1,790
20X5	Revalue US$100,000 net assets to spot			(11,111)			11,111
	Net interest on CCS	1,004				(1,004)	
	Fair value of CCS		10,965				(10,965)
20X6	Revalue US$100,000 net assets to spot			3,268			(3,268)
	Net interest on CCS	1,143				(1,143)	
	Fair value of CCS		(3,133)				3,133
20X6		5,109	(1,681)	1,681	0	(5,109)	0
	Key		A	A	B		C

Key

A: the remaining value on the CCS is the difference between the net assets retranslated at US$1.75/£ (original rate) and the US$1.70/£ (spot rate at date termination of swap). Hence, total statement of financial position before final settlement of CCS is (net assets £58,824 – CCS £1,681) = £57,143 at 31/12/X6 which is equivalent to the original US$100,000 net assets at the original spot rate of US$1.75/£.

B: Totals to zero as the hedge relationship was fully effective.

C: As at least US$100,000 of net assets existed at each reporting period throughout the relationship, the hedge relationship was fully effective in hedging the first US$100,000 of net assets.

Entries in the consolidated financial statements for 20X2 for illustrative purposes

1 January 20X2

No entry required as fair value of CCS is nil at inception.

31 December 20X2

Dr	Net assets	1,681
Cr	Other comprehensive income (cumulative translation reserve)	1,681

To record gain on retranslation of the US$100,000 of net assets at year-end spot rates.

Dr	Cash	1,110
Cr	Interest expense	1,110

To record net interest receipt on the CCS

Dr	Other comprehensive income (cumulative translation reserve)	2,560
Cr	CCS liability	2,560

To record fair value movement in CCS with corresponding entries to other comprehensive income (cumulative translation adjustment in equity).

Similar entries would be recorded for the remaining term of the hedging relationship (20X3 -20X6). The amount in cumulative translation reserve will be reclassified from equity to profit or loss on disposal of the foreign operation.

Interest income totalling £5,109 is recognised over the term of the hedging instrument in profit or loss as the interest receipts represent the net financing on the swap.

2.3.4 *Hedging by multiple parent entities*

IFRIC 16 clarified that within consolidated financial statements a parent that hedges a foreign operation can be an immediate parent, intermediate parent, or ultimate parent. The fact that the net investment is held through an intermediate parent does not affect the nature of the economic risk arising from the foreign currency exposure to the ultimate parent entity.

[IFRIC 16.12] However, an exposure to foreign currency risk arising from a net investment in a foreign operation may qualify for hedge accounting only once in the consolidated financial statements. Therefore, if the same net assets of a foreign operation are hedged by more than one parent entity within the group (for example, both a direct and an indirect parent entity) for the same risk, only one hedging relationship will qualify for hedge accounting in the consolidated financial statements of the ultimate parent. [IFRIC 16.13]

If a hedging relationship is designated by one parent entity in its consolidated financial statements it does need not be to maintained by another higher level parent entity. However, if it is not maintained by the higher level parent entity, the hedge accounting applied by the lower level parent must be reversed before the higher level parent's hedge accounting is recognised. [IFRIC 16.13] This is not unique to net investment hedging as hedge accounting by a subsidiary or by a sub-consolidated group need not be maintained in the consolidated financial statements that include the subsidiary or a sub-consolidated group. Conversely, hedge accounting could be designated in the consolidated financial statements but is not designated in the subsidiary only financial statements or the financial statements of a sub-consolidated group that forms part of the larger group. This flexibility is possible because hedge accounting is entirely voluntary.

Example 2.3.4

Hedge designations

The group structure of Group P is as follows:

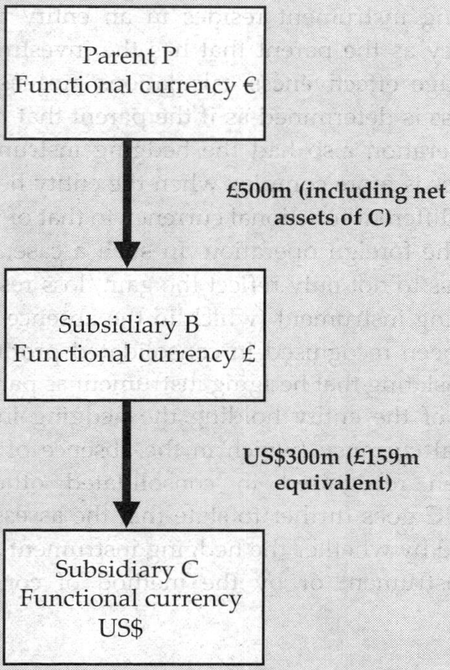

In the consolidated financial statements headed by Group P the maximum amount of net assets available to be hedged for the respective hedged risk in a qualifying hedge relationship is:

- $300m net assets for €/US$ risk between P and C; or
- £500m net assets for €/£ risk between P and B; or
- $300m net assets for £/US$ risk between B and C; or
- $300m net assets for £/US$ risk between B and C; and £500m net assets for €/£ risk between P and B; or
- $300m net assets for €/US$ risk between P and C; and £341m net assets for €/£ risk between P and B.

2.3.5 *Location of hedging instrument within the group*

IFRIC 16.14 states that the hedging instrument(s) may be held by any entity or entities within the group (except the foreign operation that itself is being hedged), as long as the designation, documentation and effectiveness requirements of IAS 39.88 for the net investment hedge are satisfied. IFRIC 16 notes that the hedge strategy must be clearly documented because of the possibility of different designations at different levels of the group.

Where the hedging instrument resides in an entity that has the same functional currency as the parent that has the investment in the foreign operation the hedge effectiveness calculations are easier to perform as hedge effectiveness is determined as if the parent that has the investment in the foreign operation also had the hedging instrument. Determining hedge effectiveness is more complex when the entity holding the hedging instrument has a different functional currency to that of the parent that has the exposure to the foreign operation. In such a case, IFRIC 16 requires hedge effectiveness to not only reflect the gain/loss residing in the entity holding the hedging instrument (which in the absence of hedge accounting would have been recognised in consolidated profit or loss), but also the effect of retranslating that hedging instrument as part of the translation of the net assets of the entity holding the hedging instrument into the parent's functional currency (which in the absence of hedge accounting would have been recognised in consolidated other comprehensive income). The IFRIC goes further to state that the assessment of effectiveness is not affected by whether the hedging instrument is a derivative or a non-derivative instrument or by the method of consolidation. [IFRIC 16.15]

Example 2.3.5

Assessing hedge effectiveness based on parent's functional currency

Parent P has a Euro functional currency and has two foreign operations, Subsidiary A which has a US dollar functional currency and Subsidiary B which has a New Zealand dollar functional currency. Subsidiary B holds a foreign currency forward contract to sell a fixed amount of US$ for a fixed amount of € at a specific date in the future. Parent P wishes to designate the foreign currency forward as a net investment hedge of its investment in Subsidiary A. The hedged risk is the €/US$ foreign currency exposure with respect to the translation of Subsidiary A's US$ net assets into €.

Parent P wishes to designate the spot foreign currency risk only (not the forward foreign currency risk). The opening net assets of Subsidiary A are $1,000 and the entire opening net assets are intended to be designated as being hedged by Parent P in its consolidated financial statements. For illustrative purposes the foreign currency forward's fair value is calculated using undiscounted spot rates and the foreign currency spot and forward rate are presumed to be the same (i.e. there is no gain/loss in respect of fair valuing the forward point differential).

	Opening spot rate	Closing spot rate	Average spot rate
€/US$	1.400	1.520	1.460
€/NZ$	2.200	1.850	2.025
US$/NZ$	1.571	1.217	1.394

Parent P's translation of Subsidiary A's designated net assets in the consolidated financial statements:

Opening designated net assets	US$1,000 @ 1.400 =	€714
Closing designated net assets	US$1,000 @ 1.520 =	€658
Loss on translation of Subsidiary A's net assets		€56

Gain/loss on the foreign currency forward with respect to spot rates in Subsidiary B's financial statements:

Receive €	(Buy €714 @ 1.850) =	NZ$1,321
Pay US$	(Sell US$1,000 @ 1.217) =	NZ$1,217
Gain/loss in the period		NZ$104

Impact of the derivative in consolidated profit or loss in the absence of hedge accounting with respect to the hedged risk:

Gain/loss NZ$104 @ 2.025 (average spot rate) = €51

If the translation of the hedging instrument from Subsidiary B's functional currency, NZ$, to the Parent P's functional currency, €, was ignored, the hedge relationship is partly ineffective. The hedge relationship would be 91% effective (€51/€56). As this remains within the 80% to 125% parameter it would have been deemed highly effective in the period.

IFRIC 16 requires the effectiveness to be determined by reference to the parent's functional currency. The effect of applying this approach is to include the difference between the average spot rate and the closing spot rate that is recognised in consolidated other comprehensive income with respect to the translation of the derivative in Subsidiary B, as part of the assessment of hedge effectiveness.

Gain/loss	NZ$104 @ 2.025 (average rates) =	€51
Gain/loss	NZ$104 @ 1.850 (closing rates) =	€56
Difference	=	€5

When the additional amount described above is included in the assessment of hedge effectiveness the hedge is 100% effective ((€51 + €5) / €56).

Had Parent P held the foreign currency forward, the gain/loss derived from the foreign currency forward would be driven solely by US$ as the € receive leg of the foreign currency forward does not generate foreign currency risk because Parent P has a € functional currency. The gain/loss on the hedging instrument would be an offset to the translation of Subsidiary A's US$ net assets to €. Considered differently, in the group accounts of Parent P the group has a long US$ position being the net assets of Subsidiary A, and a short US$ position being the US$ pay leg of the foreign currency forward contract and therefore the derivative would have been fully effective.

2.3.6 *Hedging a portfolio of net investments with a single derivative*

If a group has multiple foreign operations that have the same functional currency, the group can hedge the foreign operations either as a group, or individually. For example, Parent heads a group that includes two US$ subsidiaries, A and B, each with $500k of net assets, and $1m of third party borrowings. The Parent's interest in subsidiary A and B is held directly, i.e. Subsidiary B is not a subsidiary of Subsidiary A. The group may either designate the borrowings of $1m as a hedge of a group of foreign operations of $1m, or designate 50 per cent of the borrowings as hedging $500k of subsidiary A, and 50 per cent of the borrowings as hedging $500k of subsidiary B. When the designation is on a group basis the hedge documentation can be done on a group basis; however, hedge effectiveness must be assessed for each subsidiary individually.

Example 2.3.6

Hedging a portfolio of net investments with a single derivative

Entity P is a Sterling functional currency entity that has US$400m foreign currency denominated issued debt which it wishes to designate as a hedging instrument of the net investment in its US dollar foreign operations. The group structure is as follows:

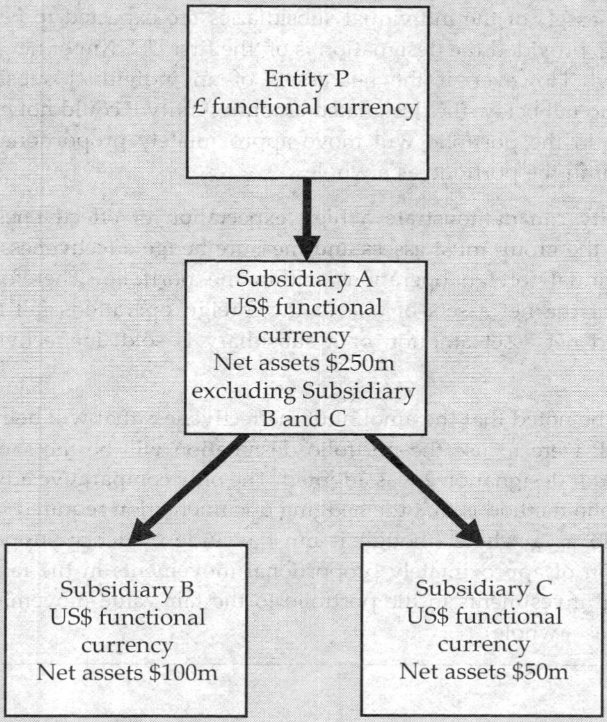

The following designations are permitted by IAS 39:

1. Entity P may designate US$400m debt as a hedging instrument of a net investment in the consolidated net assets of the sub-group headed by Subsidiary A;

2. Entity P may designate relevant proportions of the US$ debt as hedges of net investments in Subsidiary A, Subsidiary B, and Subsidiary C individually, i.e. 62.5 per cent of the US$ debt as a hedge of the net investment in subsidiary A, 25 per cent of the US$ debt as a hedge of the net investment in Subsidiary B, and 12.5 per cent of the US$ debt as the hedge of the net investment in Subsidiary C; or

3. Entity P may designate US$400m debt as a hedge of a portfolio of net investments in US$ subsidiaries.

IAS 21 *The Effects of Changes in Foreign Exchange Rates* views a net investment in a foreign operation as 'the amount of the reporting entity's interest in the net assets of that operation'. [IAS 21.8] The 'operation' is not defined and can be considered to be either the consolidated net assets of the sub-group headed by Entity A, or as a collection of net assets held by each of the three subsidiaries.

If Entity P chooses to designate a portfolio (designation 3 in the list above) it must have an expectation that each individual item in the portfolio will change in fair value approximately proportionally to the change in the fair value of the portfolio as a whole. Such an expectation would be appropriate if the net assets of the individual subsidiaries are expected to be stable or increasing, provided the designation is of 'the first US$ Xm of net assets of a subsidiary'. However, if the net assets of an individual subsidiary are expected to fall below the designated amount, Entity P could not expect that the items in the portfolio will move approximately proportionally to the movement in the portfolio as a whole.

If an entity can demonstrate a high expectation of effectiveness for the portfolio, the group must assess and measure hedge effectiveness based on the individual foreign operations within the portfolio. Therefore, to the extent that the net assets of one of the foreign operations fall below the designated net asset amount, or a subsidiary is sold, ineffectiveness will arise.

It should be noted that the amount of ineffectiveness that will be recognised if Entity P were to use the portfolio designation will be the same as that recognised if designation 2 was adopted. The only comparative advantage of the portfolio method is that the hedging documentation required is done for a portfolio as a whole (though it must include evidence supporting the expectation of approximately proportional movements in the fair value of individual investments in the portfolio to the fair value movements of the portfolio as a whole).

2.4 Exposures and types of hedges: summary

The following table provides examples of assets, liabilities, forecast transactions, firm commitments that may be hedged, and the type of hedge accounting that could apply.

Exposures and types of hedges

Fixed-rate assets and liabilities		*Variable-rate assets and liabilities*	
Examples:		Examples:	
Fixed-rate loans and receivables		Variable-rate loans and receivables	
Fixed-rate debt securities		Variable-rate debt securities	
Fixed-rate issued debt of the entity		Variable-rate debt of the entity	
Fixed-rate deposit liabilities		Variable-rate deposit liabilities	
Exposure	*Hedge accounting*	*Exposure*	*Hedge accounting*
Overall fair value	FV (Fair Value)	Overall fair value	FV
Interest rates	FV	Interest rates	FV* or CF (Cash flow)
Credit of the issuer	FV or CF**	Credit of the issuer	FV or CF**
Foreign currency	FV or CF	Foreign currency	FV or CF
Termination options	FV	Termination options	FV

Firm commitments to purchase or sell financial instruments		*Forecast purchases and sales of financial instruments*	
Examples:		Examples:	
Commitment to purchase fixed-rate debt		Forecast purchase of fixed-rate debt	
Fixed-rate loan commitments		Forecast loan originations	
Exposure	*Hedge accounting*	*Exposure*	*Hedge accounting*
Overall fair value	FV	Overall fair value	CF
Interest rates	FV	Interest rates	CF
Credit	FV	Credit	CF
Foreign currency	FV or CF***		

Firm commitment to purchase or sell non-financial assets		*Forecast purchases and sales of non-financial instruments*	
Examples:		Examples:	
Committed sale of inventory		Forecast sale of inventory	
Committed purchase of inventory		Forecast purchase of inventory	
Exposure	*Hedge accounting*	*Exposure*	*Hedge accounting*
Overall fair value	FV	Overall fair value	CF
Foreign currency	FV or CF	Foreign currency	CF

Other Assets	
Examples:	
Equity investments	
Exposure	*Hedge accounting*
Overall fair value	FV
Foreign currency	FV or CF

* FV hedging is generally permitted for hedging the fair value risk associated with the fixing of interest between floating reset dates.

** CF hedging would only be appropriate if the credit spread on the instrument was variable.

*** IAS 39 recognises that firm commitments create fair value exposure. However, it does allow hedges of the foreign currency risk of a firm commitment to be accounted for as either a fair value hedge or a cash flow hedge. [IAS 39.87]

3 Hedged items

IAS 39 defines a hedged item as follows:

A hedged item is a recognised asset, liability, unrecognised firm commitment, highly probable forecast transaction or net investment in a foreign operation that:

(a) exposes the entity to risk of changes in fair value or future cash flows; and

(b) is designated as being hedged. [IAS 39.9]

A hedged item can be:

(a) a single asset, liability, firm commitment, highly probable forecast transaction or net investment in a foreign operation;

(b) group of assets, liabilities, firm commitments, highly probable forecast transactions or net investments in foreign operations with similar risk characteristics; or

(c) in a portfolio hedge of interest rate risk only a portion of the portfolio of financial assets/liabilities that share the risk being hedged.

3.1 Unrecognised assets

Unrecognised assets (other than unrecognised firm commitments) cannot be designated as hedged items. For example, it is not possible to hedge account for an unrecognised intangible asset such as a core deposit intangible that is not recognised in the statement of financial position. [IAS 39.IG.F.2.3]

3.2 Intragroup items

As a general rule only assets, liabilities, firm commitments or highly probable forecast transactions that are with a party or parties external to the reporting entity can be a designated hedged item. Transactions between entities within the same group can only be designated as hedged items in the entity only financial statements and not in the consolidated financial statements of the group. This is because intragroup transactions do not generally expose the group to a risk that affects consolidated profit or loss. [IAS 39.80]

There are two exceptions to this general rule. The first is where the foreign currency exposure of an intragroup monetary item does not fully eliminate on consolidation under IAS 21 *The Effects of Changes in Foreign Exchange Rates* (discussed further in **3.2.1** below). The second is for the foreign currency risk of forecast intragroup transactions (discussed further in **3.2.2** below).

Within a group, an entity exposed to a hedged risk is not required to be party to the hedging instrument if hedge accounting is applied at the group level. An entity may decide not to apply hedge accounting in its individual financial statements, but hedge accounting can be applied in the consolidated financial statements which include that entity. For example, it is common in many groups that trading subsidiaries do not enter into derivative transactions; instead corporate treasury does so on their behalf. Unless there are internal derivatives transactions between the trading subsidiary and corporate treasury, the subsidiary would not be able to apply hedge accounting in its entity only financial statements because it has not entered into any hedging instruments. Hedge accounting may, though, be applied at the consolidated group level if the external hedging instrument entered into by corporate treasury is an effective instrument at the consolidated group level.

3.2.1 *Intragroup monetary items*

In accordance with IAS 21, foreign currency gains and losses on intragroup monetary assets and liabilities do not fully eliminate on consolidation when the intragroup monetary item is transacted between two group entities that have different functional currencies. As these gains and losses impact consolidated profit or loss, foreign currency risk on such intragroup monetary assets and liabilities is eligible to be hedged. [IAS 39.80]

Example 3.2.1

Foreign currency risk on intra-group loans

A UK parent entity makes a US$ denominated loan to its US subsidiary. The loan does not form part of the parent's investment in the US subsidiary. In the parent's separate financial statements, this loan will need to be remeasured at the end of each reporting period in accordance with IAS 21, and will give rise to an exchange gain or loss. However, there will be no corresponding foreign currency gain or loss in the subsidiary's financial statements as its functional currency is the US dollar and the loan is in US dollars.

In the consolidated financial statements, the exchange gain or loss on the intragroup balance will not be eliminated, but will be reported in the profit or loss as an exchange gain or loss on a monetary item. The loan may be designated as a hedged item in both the parent only accounts and in the consolidated accounts.

3.2.2 *Foreign currency risk of a highly probable forecast intragroup transaction*

Foreign currency risk of a highly probable intragroup transaction qualifies as a hedged item in the consolidated financial statements provided the following two conditions are met:

[IAS 39.80]

- the transaction is denominated in a currency other than the functional currency of the entity entering into that transaction; and
- the foreign currency risk will affect consolidated profit or loss.

The entity can be a parent, subsidiary, associate, joint venture or branch. [IAS 39.AG99A]

In many cases the forecast intragroup transaction does not affect consolidated profit or loss, as is the case for royalty payments, interest payments or management charges, unless there is a related external transaction. Transactions for which there are no related external transactions do not qualify as hedged items. By contrast, in the case of forecast sales or purchases of inventories between members of the same group where there is an onward sale of the inventory to a party external to the group and such a forecast sale or purchase of inventory does qualify as a hedged item there will be an effect on consolidated profit or loss (see **example 3.2.2B** below). Similarly, a forecast intragroup sale of plant and equipment from the group entity that manufactured it to a group entity that will use the plant and equipment in its operation will affect consolidated profit or loss. This is because the amount initially recognised by the purchasing entity for the plant and equipment, and thus depreciated through its profit or loss, will vary with movements in foreign currency prior to the plant and equipment being recognised when the forecast intragroup transaction is denominated in a currency other than the functional currency of the purchasing entity (see **example 3.2.2A** below). [IAS 39.AG99A]

If a hedge of a forecast intragroup transaction qualifies for hedge accounting, any gain or loss recognised in other comprehensive income is reclassified from equity to profit or loss in the same period or periods during which the foreign currency risk of the external hedged transaction affects consolidated profit or loss. [IAS 39.AG99B]

Example 3.2.2A

Hedging foreign currency risk of intragroup transactions (1)

Entity A (a Sterling functional currency entity) is expecting, with a high degree of probability, to purchase a machine from Entity B (a Euro functional currency entity) for €10m in 1 year's time. Entity A and Entity B are part of the same group and Entity A will use the machine in its production process to make goods for external sale. The cost of the machine will be capitalised and depreciated over its useful economic life in both the individual financial statements of Entity A and the consolidated financial statements (including both Entity A and Entity B). Entity A enters into a buy Euro sell Sterling forward contract with a third party to hedge the expected foreign currency risk on the forecast purchase.

The forecast intragroup purchase will qualify as a hedged item in the consolidated financial statements in a cash flow hedge of the currency risk since:

- the purchase is highly probable;

- the purchase is denominated in a currency (Euro) other than Entity A's functional currency (Sterling); and
- the depreciation of the machine will result in the foreign currency risk of the forecast transaction affecting consolidated profit or loss. The Euro/Sterling exchange rate at the date of purchase will affect the amount initially recognised in respect of the machinery, and thus will impact the associated depreciation charge.

Example 3.2.2B

Hedging foreign currency risk of intragroup transactions (2)

In all scenarios below, the group has two subsidiaries (Entity C – Euro (€) functional currency and Entity D – US dollar (US$) functional currency).

Scenario 1

Entity C incurs external production costs in € towards goods it manufactures and sells on in € to a fellow subsidiary Entity D. This creates a foreign currency risk in Entity D to the €/US$ exchange rate with regard to its forecast purchase from Entity C (purchase of goods in €). Entity D also intends to sell the goods externally outside of the group in US$. In order to hedge the exposure associated with the forecast purchase from Entity C, Entity D enters into a forward contract with a third party (buy €/ sell US$). The group wishes to designate the forward contract as hedging the foreign currency risk of the forecast intragroup purchase by Entity D from Entity C in a cash flow hedging relationship in the consolidated financial statements.

Scenario 2

Same as Scenario 1 above except that the sale of goods from Entity C to Entity D is denominated in US$ and therefore there is foreign currency risk for Entity C on the sale of goods to Entity D. Entity C enters into a forward contract with a third party to mitigate its foreign currency risk of the forecast sale to Entity D in US$ (buy €/ sell US$). The group wishes to designate the forward contract as hedging the foreign currency risk of the forecast intragroup sale by Entity C to Entity D in a cash flow hedging relationship in the consolidated financial statements.

Scenario 3

Same as Scenario 1 above except that the sale of goods from Entity C to Entity D is denominated in Sterling and therefore there is foreign currency risk for Entity C on the sale of goods to Entity D and there is also foreign currency risk for Entity D on the purchase of goods from Entity C. Entity C enters into a buy €/ sell £ forward contract with a third party to mitigate its foreign currency risk of the forecast sale to Entity D, and Entity D enters into a buy £/sell US$ forward contract with a third party to mitigate its foreign currency risk of the forecast purchase from Entity C.

In both scenarios 1 and 2 the internal transaction being designated is denominated in a currency other than the functional currency of the entity entering into it: in Scenario 1 the forecast intragroup purchase by Entity D (functional currency of US$) is denominated in €; in Scenario 2 the forecast intragroup sale by Entity C (functional currency €) is denominated in US$. Also, in both cases the onward sale of the goods by Entity D will affect consolidated profit or loss. Thus, in both cases the forecast intragroup transaction could be designated as the hedged item in a cash flow hedge of foreign currency risk in the consolidated financial statements, assuming all other conditions of hedge accounting are met.

In Scenario 3, in the individual financial statements of both entities, cash flow hedge accounting can be applied. The provision to hedge intragroup forecast transactions was included in IAS 39 for situations where one of the parties to the internal transaction passes their foreign currency risk to the other, as in Scenarios 1 and 2 above. This is the currency risk that exists and cannot be avoided because the two parties have different functional currencies. In Scenario 3 the parties to the internal transaction are taking on a new foreign currency risk and therefore the amendment cannot be applied. Furthermore, although the sum of the two derivatives result in a net buy €/sell US$ position, these two derivatives cannot be designated in combination in the consolidated financial statements as a hedge of the external € purchases or a hedge of the external US$ sales, as Entity C does not have a US$ exposure, and Entity D does not have a € exposure.

Example 3.2.2C

Hedging foreign currency risk of intragroup transactions (3)

Entity E (Sterling functional currency entity) has a wholly-owned subsidiary, Entity F (Yen functional currency entity). Entity F generates substantial profits and regularly pays Yen dividends on its ordinary shares to its sole shareholder and parent, Entity E. In order to hedge the Yen exposure associated with the dividend income Entity E enters into a series of sell Yen buy Sterling forward contracts. Entity E also expects to pay dividends on its own ordinary shares (classified as equity in accordance with IAS 32 *Financial Instruments: Presentation*) using the proceeds from dividends received from its shareholding in Entity F.

The forecast intragroup transaction (the dividend income in the hands of Entity E) will not qualify as a hedged item in the consolidated financial statements of the group in a cash flow hedge of the currency risk as the foreign currency risk will not affect consolidated profit or loss. Even though Entity E may expect to make an onward declaration and payment of dividends on its own shares, IAS 32 requires that distributions to holders of an equity instrument shall be debited by the entity directly to equity and thus, this will not give rise to a gain or loss in consolidated profit or loss.

Example 3.2.2D

Hedging foreign currency risk of intragroup transactions (4)

Entity A is a Euro functional currency entity that has a fellow subsidiary Entity B, a US$ functional currency entity. Entity A borrows a specified amount of Euro from a party external to the group at fixed interest rates. Entity A lends the proceeds of the borrowing to Entity B on the same terms as the external borrowing. As Entity B has borrowed in Euro at fixed rates and has a US$ functional currency, it enters into a Receive Euro fixed Pay US$ fixed cross currency swap with a party external to the group to hedge the foreign currency risk of the interest and principal payments on its borrowing from Entity A.

In the separate financial statements of Entity B it can designate the foreign currency risk arising from the Euro denominated interest payments and principal of its borrowing from Entity A in a hedging relationship with the hedging instrument being the external cross currency swap.

In the consolidated financial statements the cross currency swap cannot be designated as a hedge of the foreign currency risk of the forecast intragroup interest payments by Entity B as the interest payments in Entity B are eliminated against the interest receipts in Entity A. Entity B's interest payments do not impact consolidated profit or loss and therefore cannot be designated as a hedged item in the consolidated financial statements.

The foreign currency exposure generated on the intragroup loan will not be fully eliminated on consolidation in accordance with IAS 21 as the loan is measured in Entity B in US$ but measured in Entity A in Euro. It is unlikely that this foreign currency risk could be designated as a hedged item in an effective hedge relationship with the external cross currency swap as a hedging instrument in the consolidated financial statements as the swap's fair value is derived from both interest and principal payments and receipts where as the foreign currency risk that survives consolidation is limited to Entity B's translation of the opening and closing carrying amounts of the intragroup loan.

3.3 Foreign currency risk of a forecast foreign currency debt issuance

An entity that has a highly probable forecast debt issuance may wish to cash flow hedge the interest rates and/or the foreign currency risk associated with the issuance. Hedging the interest rate risk is permitted and is described in **example 2.2.4A** above and also in IAS 39.IG.F.5.5.

IAS 39 does not provide guidance on whether a hedge of the variability in functional currency equivalent proceeds attributable to foreign exchange risk that is to be received from a highly probable forecast issue of debt denominated in a currency other than the entity's functional currency can qualify for hedge accounting. It would not appear to be possible to designate the variability in the functional currency equivalent cash flows of a forecast debt issuance in a foreign currency as the foreign currency risk does not impact profit or loss. Foreign currency risk only arises from the date the debt is recognised in the statement of financial position as it is translated thereafter into the entity's functional currency under IAS 21. The quantum of this foreign currency risk that will impact profit or loss following the issue of the debt bears no relation to the quantum of foreign currency risk that arises prior to the date the debt is issued.

Example 3.3

Hedging foreign currency risk of forecast foreign currency debt issuance

On 1 January, Entity C, a US$ functional currency entity, has a highly probable forecast 10% fixed rate debt issuance of €100m in one month's time and wishes to hedge the variability in the US$ equivalent proceeds that it will receive from the point in time when the hedging instrument is entered into and the point in time when the debt is issued. Entity C will enter into a foreign currency forward contract to sell €100m and to buy an equivalent amount of US$ based on the forward rate for delivery when the debt is expected to be issued. At the date Entity C enters into the foreign currency forward contract, it is expected that the combination of the net cash flows from the forward contract and the Euros to be received from issuing the debt should equal $100m, all other things being equal.

Entity C cannot designate the changes in foreign currency risk between the date of entering into the derivative and the date the forecast debt is expected to be issued as a qualifying hedge exposure. This is due to the foreign currency risk on the debt will only arise and impact profit or loss from the date it is a recognised liability and retranslated from Euro to Entity C's US$ functional currency during the period it remains outstanding. The gains/losses on the forward contract prior to the debt being issued bear no relationship to the foreign currency gains/losses that will be recognised after the debt is issued. In addition, the functional currency amount of interest in future periods is unaffected by movements in foreign currency prior to the debt being issued, as is illustrated below.

Assume the foreign currency exchange rate at 1 January is $1:€1 and at 1 February is $1:€1.5. Using the 1 January exchange rate, the annual interest in US$ would be $10m. At the rate of exchange rate prevailing on 1 February, the amount of Euro proceeds necessary to raise $100m would be €67m. The related annual interest, assuming constant interest rates, would be €6.7m. However, translating € into US$, the annual interest is still $10m (since €6.7m / 1.5 = $10m). As demonstrated, the annual interest expense in functional currency terms is unaffected by a change in exchange rates between the date the foreign currency forward contract is entered into and the date the debt is issued.

Once the debt is issued it will be a recognised monetary item and will be retranslated from Euro to US$ on an ongoing basis in accordance with IAS 21 with any resulting foreign exchange gains or losses recognised in profit or loss. Once recognised, the debt could be designated in either a cash flow or fair value hedge of foreign currency risk.

3.4 Overall business risks

Overall business risk cannot be hedged because it cannot be specifically identified and measured. [IAS 39.AG98] For example, an entity could not apply hedge accounting to a hedge of a risk of a transaction not occurring which will result in less revenue. This is an overall business risk. [IAS 39.IG.F.2.8]

A firm commitment to acquire a business in a business combination cannot be a hedged item, except for foreign exchange risk, because the other risks being hedged cannot be specifically identified and measured. These other risks are general business risks. [IAS 39.AG98]

Example 3.4

Hedging foreign currency risk of a firm commitment to acquire a business

Entity D, a € functional currency entity, is the parent company of Group D. Entity D enters into an agreement to acquire Entity E in two months' time for US$50m. Entity D will produce consolidated financial statements. To hedge the US$ foreign currency risk of the purchase consideration, Entity D enters into a foreign currency forward contract to buy US$50m and sell € at a specified foreign currency rate that matures in two months.

As Entity D is hedging the foreign currency risk of a firm commitment, it may designate the foreign currency forward contract as a fair value or as a cash flow hedge.

If Entity D designates the derivative in a fair value hedge, the gains or losses will be recognised in profit or loss, and the movements in the fair value of the firm commitment due to foreign currency risk will also be recognised in profit or loss with the other side of the entry recognised in the statement of financial position. At acquisition, this balance will be derecognised and will adjust the amount of goodwill.

If Entity D designates the derivative in a cash flow hedge, the gain or loss will be recognised in other comprehensive income. As discussed in **2.2.3** above, the entity has a choice as to whether to apply a basis adjustment when cash flow hedging the acquisition of a non-financial item (the acquisition of a business). If Group D applies a basis adjustment, it will remove the gain or loss on the derivative from equity and basis adjust the goodwill that is recognised on acquisition. The amount of the basis adjustment will impact profit or loss, for example, if any resulting goodwill is impaired. If Group D does not apply a basis adjustment, it will continue to recognise the gain or loss on the derivative in other comprehensive income until it would have affected profit or loss had goodwill been basis adjusted.

3.5 Held-to-maturity assets

A held-to-maturity (HTM) investment cannot be a hedged item with respect to interest rate risk or prepayment risk. This is irrespective of whether the interest is fixed or variable. To be able to designate an asset as HTM, an entity must be indifferent to future profit opportunities for that asset, i.e. it must have the positive intent to hold the asset to maturity irrespective of changes in its market value (see **3.2** in **chapter 14**). However, an HTM asset can be a hedged item with respect to foreign currency risk and credit risk. [IAS 39.79]

A forecast purchase of a financial asset that an entity intends to classify as HTM can be a hedged item. The prohibition for hedges of interest rate risk and prepayment risk is only for HTM assets already held, hence until the asset is acquired, it may be a hedged item. [IAS 39.IG.F.2.10]

Example 3.5A

Hedging interest risk for forecast acquisition of a held-to-maturity asset

Entity A forecasts the purchase of a fixed rate financial asset that it intends to classify as HTM. To protect itself against movements in interest rates between now and when the asset is purchased, Entity A enters into a derivative contract that will mature when the forecast transaction occurs with the intent of locking in the current forward rate for the day when the asset is expected to be purchased. The derivative is designated as a hedge of the forecast purchase of the financial asset, and qualifies for hedge accounting.

IAS 39 does not prohibit an entity from hedging its forecast interest receipts on debt instruments resulting from the reinvestment of interest receipts from an HTM asset. [IAS 39.IG.F.2.11]

Example 3.5B

Hedging interest risk of forecast reinvestment of cash flows from a held-to-maturity asset

Entity XYZ owns a variable rate asset that it has classified as HTM. The variable interest rate receipts are reinvested in debt instruments. Entity XYZ enters into a derivative to lock in the current interest rate on the reinvestment of the variable cash flows, and designates the derivative as a cash flow hedge of the forecast future interest receipts on debt instruments.

Entity XYZ qualifies for hedge accounting, even though the interest payments that are being reinvested derive from an HTM asset. Whilst an HTM asset itself cannot be hedged with respect to interest rate risk, it is possible to designate the derivative as hedging cash flow risk from debt instruments that were purchased using the interest receipts from the HTM asset. The source of the funds used to purchase the debt instruments in the future is not relevant.

The same would be true if Entity XYZ's HTM assets had been fixed rather than variable rate assets.

3.6 Loans and receivables

Assets classified as loans and receivables are measured at amortised cost. Even though a loan or receivable is not measured at fair value, it can still be a hedged item in a fair value hedge or cash flow hedge. For example, if a loan earns fixed rate interest, it could be hedged for changes in fair value due to movements in interest rates. Further, as there is no presumption of holding loans and receivables until their maturity it is possible to hedge the cash flows that arise from their future disposal where their disposal is considered to be highly probable.

3.7 Derivatives

Derivatives cannot be designated as hedged items. [IAS 39.IG.F.2.1] As an exception, IAS 39 permits a written option to qualify as a hedging instrument if it is designated as an offset to a purchased option, including one that is embedded in another financial instrument (for example, a written call option used to hedge a callable liability). [IAS 39.AG94]

3.8 Designation of financial items

Provided that effectiveness can be measured, it is possible to designate only a portion of either the cash flows or fair value of a financial instrument as the hedged item.

It is possible to designate:
[IAS 39.81]

- one or more contractual cash flows of an instrument;
- one or more portions of one or more contractual cash flows of an instrument; or
- a proportion (i.e. percentage) of the cash flows or fair value of the instrument.

Example 3.8A

Permitted hedge designations of financial items

Entity B has a 5-year fixed rate bond asset. Entity B wishes to hedge part, or all, of the bond. The instrument is not classified as held-to-maturity. There are many options available to Entity B in applying hedge accounting:

- hedge the full fair value of the cash flows on the debt (all contractual cash flows);
- hedge the fair value on a proportion of debt, e.g. fair value of 50 per cent of the debt (proportion of all the contractual cash flows);
- hedge the fair value on all cash flows due to the impact of a specific risk only such as the impact of changes in risk-free interest rates (rather than all risks);
- hedge part of the cash flows due to a specific risk, e.g. designate the impact of movements in interest rates on 50 per cent of the cash flows (hedging a specific risk on a proportion of all cash flows);
- hedge an isolated set of cash flows due to all risks, e.g. hedging the fair value movement on the principal only (hedging a portion of cash flows);
- hedge an isolated set of cash flows due to a specific risk, e.g. hedging the fair value movement due to interest rate risk on the principal only (hedging a specific risk only on a portion of cash flows); or
- hedging the full fair value above or below a specified amount, e.g. hedging fair value decreases below a specified amount (hedging a part of the fair value).

IAS 39 does not require risk reduction on an entity-wide basis as a condition for hedge accounting. Exposure is assessed on a transaction basis. [IAS 39.IG.F.2.6]

Example 3.8B

Risk reduction

An entity has a fixed rate asset and a fixed rate liability, each having the same principal amount. The entity receives interest on the asset of 10 per cent, and pays interest of 8 per cent on the liability, with payments and receipts occurring in the same period, so the entity always has a net cash inflow of 2 per cent.

The entity enters into a receive-floating, pay-fixed interest rate swap on a notional amount equal to the principal of the asset and designates the interest rate swap as a fair value hedge of the fixed rate asset. The entity qualifies for hedge accounting, even though the effect of the swap on an entity-wide basis is to create an exposure to interest rate changes that did not previously exist. The specific asset being hedged has a fair value exposure to interest rate movements that is offset by the interest rate swap.

3.8.1 Hedges of portions

As illustrated in **example 3.8A** above, an entity has many options available to it on how to dissect the cash flows of a hedged financial item. An entity may hedge part or all of the cash flows due to all risks inherent in the hedged item, or it may choose to hedge part or all of the cash flows due to specific risks only. This approach is known as hedging portions and is only allowed if the risk can be identified and hedge effectiveness can be assessed and measured reliably.

Hedging portions of cash flows and risks can be helpful in ensuring that the designated terms of the hedged item are similar to the terms of the hedging instrument, which reduces hedge ineffectiveness.

Example 3.8.1A

Hedging interest rate risk portion (1)

Entity A wishes to issue 5-year fixed rate debt. Based on market rates of interest and A's credit rating, it is able to issue debt at 6.5 per cent. This comprises a 5-year interest rate risk of 4.5 per cent, and a credit spread of 2 per cent. Entity A may designate the hedged risk as changes in fair value of the debt associated with changes in interest rate risk only, i.e. it may exclude from the designation its own credit spread.

Excluding the credit spread from the designation will increase the effectiveness of the hedge relationship as the equivalent credit risk inherent in the debt is not reflected in the terms of the interest rate swap.

An individual leg on an interest rate swap (or other derivative) that is not exactly the same as the cash flows on the hedged item does not necessarily preclude hedge accounting. The fair value of a hedging instrument is determined by the valuation of its net cash flows, and therefore when determining whether a hedging relationship is effective, an entity would not consider the terms of a single leg of the swap, without also considering the impact of the other leg of the swap.

Instead of entering into swaps that receive or pay a LIBOR flat equivalent amount (i.e. LIBOR without a credit spread), entities often enter into swaps where one of the legs exactly matches the cash flows on their debt.

Example 3.8.1B

Hedging interest rate risk portion (2)

Entity Z has a credit rating of B. It issues fixed-rate debt at 6 per cent, which includes a credit spread of 100 basis points, i.e. the rate comprises a LIBOR rate of 5 per cent and a credit spread of 1 per cent. To hedge its exposure to changes in interest rate movements, it enters into a receive-fixed, pay-floating interest rate swap.

Instead of entering into a swap where the pay leg exactly matches the equivalent of LIBOR (i.e. receive 5 per cent, pay LIBOR), Entity Z enters into a swap where the fixed leg exactly matches its debt. As the receive leg is 6 per cent, the pay leg is increased correspondingly, to LIBOR + 100 basis points. As the fair value of the swap is derived from its net settlements, the receive 5 per cent, pay LIBOR swap and the receive 6 per cent, pay LIBOR + 100 basis points will have the same fair value for a given movement in interest rates. Therefore, Entity Z may still designate the LIBOR portion of its debt as the hedged item.

As it is a requirement for all hedge relationships that effectiveness can be assessed and measured [IAS 39.88(d)], it is essential that the hedged portion is identifiable and separately measurable. For instance, the risk free rate or benchmark interest rate risk component of either a fixed or floating interest-bearing asset or liability is an identifiable and separately measurable portion (as illustrated in **example 3.8.1A** above). However, in other cases it may not be possible to establish that a given variable is an identifiable and separately measurable portion if that portion is not identifiable when the instrument was originally issued and priced. This is illustrated in the following example:

Example 3.8.1C

Ineligible portion of interest rate risk

Entity C has issued Euro denominated debt with a floating interest rate based on the European Central Bank (ECB) rate. It has also entered into a receive EURIBOR pay fixed Euro interest rate swap with a notional equal to the principal of the debt.

The receive EURIBOR pay fixed interest rate swap cannot be designated as a hedge of the portion of the ECB cash flows that are due to changes in EURIBOR. There is no EURIBOR component in the ECB variable cash flows. The interest rate risk that can be designated as the hedged risk is variability in the ECB rate.

Alternatively, Entity C could hedge the variability of the ECB floating interest rate with a EURIBOR swap, however this is unlikely to be a perfectly effective hedging instrument even if the notional amounts of the two swaps are the same, because of the basis difference between ECB rate and EURIBOR. Changes in the cash flows of the floating interest rate on the debt will not necessarily be offset by variability in EURIBOR on the swap.

It may be possible to adjust continually the number of EURIBOR swaps to be equivalent to the variability in cash flows generated by variability in the ECB rate in order to achieve a highly effective hedge relationship. This is a dynamic hedging strategy. If a sufficiently high correlation can be demonstrated between EURIBOR and ECB rates then a statistical relationship could be used to adjust the hedge ratio in order to demonstrate prospectively a highly effective hedge in line with the principles described in **5.1.2** below.

It is possible to hedge the benchmark interest rate risk portion of a fixed rate loan some time after its issue. Assume an entity issues a fixed rate bond at par that will redeem at par. Some time later it enters into an interest rate swap to hedge its exposure to changes in the fair value of the liability attributable to the benchmark interest rate. If the swap has a fair value of zero at inception and interest rates have fallen since the bond was issued, the coupons on the bond will be higher than the contracted fixed receipts on the interest rate swap. As the fixed receipts on the swap are lower than the contractual fixed rate coupons on the bond, the entity can designate as the hedged item a portion of each coupon cash flow equal to the fixed receipts of the swap. The fixed receipts of the swap and the cash flows on the designated portion of the bond will match and the hedge is likely to be highly effective.

If interest rates have risen since the bond was issued, the coupons on the bond may be lower than the contractual fixed receipts on the interest rate swap. The entity can designate the bond as hedged for the benchmark interest rate portion of its fair value interest rate risk provided the benchmark rate is less than the effective interest rate of the hedged item calculated based on the assumption that the entity had issued the bond on the date the hedge is designated. [IAS 39.AG99D] This is achieved by designating as the hedged risk both the contractual coupon payments and an amount of discount which is included in the difference between the current fair value of the bond and the amount repayable at maturity. A hedge designated in this way is likely to exhibit ineffectiveness because the fixed cash flows on the swap will have a different profile to the fixed cash flows of the hedged item: the fixed interest cash flows of the swap are composed of equal payments, while the hedged interest cash flows on the bond comprise lower contractual payments and a discount to par. The different cash flow profiles will result in different changes in fair value in response to changes in interest rates.

To minimise ineffectiveness an entity may need to enter into a swap with a fixed leg rate equal to or lower than the contractual coupons on the bond. Such a swap does not have a zero fair value at inception as it is not entered into at market interest rates. Where the upfront payment on the swap is structured to be equivalent to the discount on the bond, the swap will be more effective at hedging the bond.

In July 2008 the IASB issued an amendment to IAS 39 titled *Eligible hedged items*. The aim of the amendment was to clarify two issues in relation to hedge accounting: (i) identifying inflation as a hedged risk or portion; and (ii) hedging with options. The amendments are to be applied retrospectively for annual periods beginning on or after 1 July 2009.

The amendments make clear that inflation may only be hedged in the instance where changes in inflation are a contractually-specified portion of cash flows of a recognised financial instrument. This may be the case where an entity acquires or issues inflation-linked debt. In such circumstances, the entity has a cash flow exposure to changes in future inflation that may be cash flow hedged. The amendments, therefore, do not permit an entity to designate an inflation component of issued or acquired fixed-rate debt in a fair value hedge as the Board considers that such a component is not separately identifiable and reliably measurable. The amendments also clarify that a risk-free or benchmark interest rate portion of the fair value of a fixed-rate financial instrument will normally be separately identifiable and reliably measurable and therefore may be hedged.

The clarification on hedging with options is detailed in **4.7** below.

3.8.2 Partial term hedging

Hedging only a part of a financial instrument's term is an extension of hedging portions of cash flows of the instrument. An entity is not allowed to designate a hedging relationship for only a portion of the time period during which a hedging instrument remains outstanding. [IAS 39.75] However, as an entity is able to hedge portions of cash flows, it is possible to hedge for a shorter period than the term of the whole hedged item, by hedging only selected cash flows in that item. As with all hedge relationships, this is only permitted if hedge effectiveness can be demonstrated and measured (and the other hedge criteria are met). [IAS 39.IG.F.2.17]

Example 3.8.2A

Partial term hedging fixed rate debt (1)

XYZ plc issues 10-year fixed-rate debt. To hedge against changes in interest rates, it enters into a 6-year receive-fixed pay-floating interest rate swap. XYZ may designate the swap as hedging the fair value exposure of the interest rate payments relating to the first 6 years of the debt with respect to movements in interest rates only.

The concept of being able to hedge on a partial term basis is driven by the relationship between spot rates and forward rates for any given yield curve. The spot rate today, and the anticipated spot rates in the future periods are used to construct the yield curve today. The yield curve is a reflection of the anticipated rates in the future based on an assessment today.

By dissecting a longer dated current yield curve into 'mini-curves' it is possible to isolate the fair value movements of a longer dated instrument due to movements in the shorter part of the yield curve.

Example 3.8.2B

Partial term hedging fixed rate debt (2)

Facts as in **example 3.8.2A**.

At issuance of the bond the entity can obtain the yield curve for the stated maturity of the whole instrument, in this case, a ten year yield curve.

The ten year yield curve can be dissected into mini-yield curves.

- Spot interest rate today (t0) for interest due in a year (t1).
- Expected spot interest rate starting in a year's time (t1) due at the end of that year (t2) [one-year forward rate starting in a year].
- Expected spot interest rate starting at year 2 (t2) due at the end of that year (t3) [one-year forward rate starting in year 2].

If the entity wishes to fair value hedge for movements in the interest rate curve that matures in six years' time, it only has to consider movements in the first six years of the ten year yield curve in computing the change in the fair value of the hedged item. Because a six-year interest swap is priced of the six-year yield curve, in order to demonstrate hedge effectiveness, the entity discounts the six years of cash flows using the spot rates at the date hedge effectiveness is measured.

In one year's time, the entity will compare the change in the fair value of the derivative (with five years remaining) with the change in fair value of the hedged selected cash flows on the bond as well as the principal payment due at maturity to the extent affected by changes in the spot yield curve for the next five years, and so on.

An entity is permitted to partial term cash flow hedge a financial instrument as IAS 39 provides greater flexibility in designating portions when hedging financial instruments compared to hedging non-financial items. For hedges of non-financial items an entity is limited to hedging all foreign currency risk or all risks in their entirety (see **3.9** below). An entity that has a derivative that has a maturity that is shorter than the timing of the cash flow exposure of the non-financial hedged item must designate all of the derivative (with the exception of the forward points in a forward contract or time value in an option) as hedging all foreign currency risk or all risks in their entirety up to the timing of the cash flow of the hedged item. As the hedged item is non-financial the entity cannot designate a derivative for part of the time period until the forecast transaction occurs.

For example, a derivative that matures in 9 months' time could be perfectly effective as a hedge of a forecast sale or purchase of a non-financial item that is highly probable of occurring in 9 months' time. If the transaction is highly probable of occurring in 10 months' time, the same derivative could not be designated as a hedge of the 9 month portion of time until the transaction is expected to occur as a non-financial item cannot be partial-term hedged.

3.9 Designation of non-financial items

If the hedged item is a non-financial asset or liability, it may only be designated as a hedged item:

(a) for foreign currency risk; or

(b) in its entirety for all risks. [IAS 39.82]

It is often difficult to isolate and directly measure the change in cash flows or fair value associated with a specific risk for a non-financial item, other than foreign currency risk, when compared to measuring separately specific risks of financial items, for example, interest rate risk. For this reason, the Standard only permits hedging of a non-financial item for foreign currency risk or in its entirety for all risks, even though it may be argued that in some cases it is possible to, at least indirectly, isolate the changes in cash flows or fair value attributable to a particular risk. This position was confirmed by the IFRIC in October 2004 where the IFRIC also noted that to allow separation of a non-financial asset into price risk components with the separate components being designated as the hedged item would require an amendment to IAS 39 rather than an Interpretation.

Example 3.9A

Hedging a forecast acquisition of a non-financial item: foreign currency risk

Entity D, a € functional currency entity, has a highly probable forecast transaction to purchase tyres from an external US$ functional currency entity. Because the tyres are a non-financial item, Entity D can either hedge the purchase of tyres for all risks or for just the foreign currency risk.

Entity D is able to hedge the foreign currency risk that will arise from buying the tyres as the foreign currency risk between the Euro and the US$ is identifiable and measurable. However, it is not possible to hedge just the cost of rubber in the purchase of tyres as this is not the entirety of all risks in the forecast transaction.

Example 3.9B

Hedging a forecast acquisition of a non-financial item: all risk

Entity B purchases bronze for its inventory of raw materials used in manufacturing its products. Entity B enters into a forward contract indexed to copper and wishes to designate it as a hedge of the copper component in forecasted purchases of bronze.

The price of copper is only a portion of the exposure to changes in the price of bronze. Entity B cannot designate as the hedged item changes in the value of the future purchase of bronze due to changes in the price of copper. However, if Entity B is able to demonstrate that the hedging instrument will be highly effective in hedging the price of bronze, it may be able to designate the forward contract as a hedging instrument in hedging the price of bronze. Any hedge ineffectiveness that arises from the hedge relationship must be reported in profit or loss.

The term 'entirety of all risks' in IAS 39.82 does include variability in cash flows that will be incurred in getting the non-financial item to its deliverable condition and location where these costs are included by the seller as a single unit price. For example, if an entity has forecast purchases of non-financial items where the buyer is billed for the cost of the non-financial item (which includes some conversion of a commodity into a finished good) plus the delivery of that finished good to the buyer, the entirety of all risks is the entire variability in cash flows, which includes the cost of conversion and delivery.

Where transportation is undertaken by a third party provider, not the counterparty, the variability in the cost of transportation does not form part of the non-financial item, as it a separate service undertaken by an unrelated party.

The restriction to hedge the item in its entirety for all risks or just foreign currency risk can give rise to practical problems for entities that hedge the purchase or sale of commodities where the grade of the hedging instrument is not equivalent to the grade of the commodity in the purchase. This is often referred to as a basis risk.

Example 3.9C

Hedging a forecast acquisition of a non-financial item: basis risk

Entity E hedges the forecast purchase of cocoa using cocoa futures. The cocoa futures contracts specify a grade of quality of cocoa that differs from the grade of quality of the forecast purchase of the non-financial item. The difference in the grade of the quality of cocoa between the hedged item and the hedging instrument is referred to as basis risk. The basis risk will cause hedge ineffectiveness.

Example 3.9D

Hedging a forecast acquisition of a non-financial item: transportation

Entity C acquires commodities for use in its business. Entity C acquires the commodities at spot prices on the date Entity C requires the commodity for use in its business. The amount Entity C pays for the commodity from the supplier is an amount referenced to the London Metal Exchange (LME), plus an amount for transportation of the commodity from the supplier to the entity.

If an entity designates a non-financial item as a hedged item it must be designated as a hedged item for (a) foreign currency risk only, or (b) in its entirety.

If Entity C is hedging the cash flow price variability of its future commodity purchases in its entirety, the entity must include the costs, whether fixed or variable, it will pay the supplier in bringing the non-financial item to its current location. Should the transportation paid to the supplier be variable this would result in greater cash flow variability that will potentially result in greater hedge ineffectiveness.

If Entity C enters into the hedging instrument to hedge the variability in the LME price only, yet the transportation costs also are paid to the supplier and are variable, Entity C may choose to adjust the hedge ratio (i.e. so it is not 1-to-1) to reduce the amount of hedge ineffectiveness that may result from changes in the cash flow variability of transportation costs.

Example 3.9E

Hedging a non-financial item: operating leases

Entity A is a leasing entity which rents out machinery on both operating and finance lease arrangements. Entity A may wish to hedge future lease receipts. The ability to hedge these future receipts depends on whether the lease arrangement is a finance lease or an operating lease. An operating lease is an executory contract committing the lessor to provide the use of an asset in future periods in exchange for cash receipts. As the lease is a non-financial item, Entity A would need to either hedge account all the risks of the future lease receipts or foreign currency risk only. This is different from a finance lease, since a finance lease is a financial instrument which gives Entity A greater flexibility in designating the hedged item in a qualifying hedge relationship.

Example 3.9F

Hedging a non-financial item: inventory

[Extract from IAS 39.IG.F.3.6]

Can an entity designate inventories, such as copper inventory, as the hedged item in a fair value hedge of the exposure to changes in the price of the inventories, such as the copper price, although inventories are measured at the lower of cost and net realisable value under IAS 2 *Inventories*?

Yes. The inventories may be hedged for changes in fair value due to changes in the copper price because the change in fair value of inventories will affect profit or loss when the inventories are sold or their carrying amount is written down. The adjusted carrying amount becomes the cost basis for the purpose of applying the lower of cost and net realisable value test under IAS 2.

As described in **2.2.3** above IAS 39 permits an accounting policy choice as to whether to basis adjust non-financial items that are subject to a cash flow hedge. As described above, IAS 39.IG.F.3.6 states that a basis adjustment impacts the determination of cost that will impact the measurement of inventory at the lower of cost or net realisable value for the purposes of IAS 2. IFRS is not clear if an entity has an accounting policy of not basis adjusting non-financial items subject to a cash flow hedge whether the lack of a basis adjustment results in amounts being reclassified from the cash flow hedge reserve in equity to profit or loss differently than had the entity adopted a policy of basis adjusting.

It is reasonable to assume that the absence of specific guidance in this area does not change the overall objective that should any choose to basis adjust or not the impact in profit or loss is the same. Therefore, if an entity does not basis adjust the reclassification from equity to profit or loss should result in the same net profit or loss amount that would have been achieved had the entity basis adjusted the non-financial item.

3.9.1 *Hedging foreign currency risk of non-financial asset held at cost*

If an entity is hedging foreign currency risk, this risk must be separately measurable. A non-financial asset that was purchased in a foreign currency cannot be hedged for foreign currency risk because foreign currency risk is not evident in that non-financial item. However, the foreign currency risk associated with a forecasted sale of that non-financial item could qualify as a hedged item.

It is important to distinguish between hedging foreign currency risk of a non-financial item and hedging foreign currency risk in relation to the forecast sale and purchase of that non-financial item.

Example 3.9.1 below illustrates that it is not possible to hedge the foreign currency risk of a non-financial item as the foreign currency risk is not evident and not separately measurable. However, if an entity is purchasing or selling a non-financial item in a foreign currency, it is a fixed amount of foreign currency that will be needed to buy or will be received from selling that non-financial item, and a qualifying foreign currency exposure therefore exists.

Example 3.9.1

Hedging a non-financial item: held at cost

Entity A, a Sterling functional currency entity acquires some plant and machinery in US$ from Entity B, an unrelated third party US$ functional currency entity. In the financial statements of Entity A the plant and machinery will be translated at the US$:£ exchange rate at the date of the purchase (i.e. at historic rate).

If Entity A used US$ borrowing to finance the purchase of the plant and machinery, these US$ borrowings cannot be used as a hedging instrument in a fair value hedge of the foreign currency risk of the plant and machinery because the hedged item does not contain any separately measurable foreign currency risk.

If Entity A was to demonstrate that the disposal of the plant and machinery in US$ was highly probable, then the US$ denominated debt could be used as a hedging instrument against the forecast sale in US$ provided that the timing of the future cash flows on the debt coincided with the timing of the future cash flow on the disposal.

Non-derivatives can be used as hedging instruments only when hedging foreign currency risk. This is discussed further in **4.1** below.

3.9.2 Hedging all risks except foreign currency

IAS 39 is clear that hedges of a non-financial instrument are possible for all risks or just foreign currency risk. Therefore, by deduction, it is possible to hedge all risks except foreign currency risk, assuming all other hedge accounting criteria are met. IAS 39.IG.E.3.4 on the interaction between IAS 39 and IAS 21 supports the assertion above. For financial instruments fair value is firstly determined in the currency in which the contract is denominated, and translation of the contract into the functional currency of the entity is secondary. If it can be clearly demonstrated that the exposure to fair value of the non-financial instrument excluding foreign currency risk can be identified and measured, and hedged for all risks except foreign currency risk, such exposure is a permissible hedging designation.

Example 3.9.2

Hedging a non-financial item: all risks except foreign currency

Entity O has an anticipated purchase of 1,000 barrels of oil in 6 months that is highly probable of occurring. The purchase price will be the market price at the date of purchase and will be priced in US$. Entity O's functional currency is the Australian dollar.

Entity O purchases oil futures on 500 barrels of oil to fix the price at US$60 for those 500 barrels. The duration (and other terms) of the forecast transaction and the futures contracts match so that Entity O believes the hedge will be highly effective over its term.

Entity O has two risk exposures: foreign currency risk and fair value risk.

The oil futures hedge price risk only. Entity O does not co-terminously hedge its exposure to the US$ on the purchase contract.

The oil futures can be designated as a hedge of the forecast purchase of oil (provided the other hedge accounting criteria are satisfied). A forward purchase of oil (a non-financial asset) does not have inherent foreign exchange risk. The foreign exchange risk arises from the fact that the reporting entity's functional currency is not the US$, not from the market price risk inherent in a forward purchase of oil.

3.9.3 *Hedging own equity*

Transactions in own equity cannot be designated as hedged items. An entity's own equity transactions cannot be hedged because they do not expose the entity to a risk that can affect reported profit or loss. For example, a forecast dividend payment could not be designated as a hedged item, as IAS 32 requires that distributions to owners are debited directly to equity and therefore do not impact on profit or loss. However, a properly declared dividend that has not yet been paid and is recognised as a financial liability by the payer or financial asset by the recipient may qualify as a hedged item for foreign currency risk if it is denominated in a foreign currency as changes in the foreign currency will impact on profit or loss. [IAS 39.IG.F.2.7]

An entity may be able to designate share based payment transactions that are exclusively cash settled in an effective hedge accounting relationship. Even though the amount of cash payable varies by reference to the entity's share price there is a cash flow variability that will impact profit or loss.

Example 3.9.3

Hedging share appreciation rights

On 1 January 20X1, Entity A awarded its employees exclusively cash-settled share appreciation rights (SARs) that vest and can be exercised at 31 December 20X3 if the employees are still working for the entity on that date. Each of the 100 employees is granted one SAR with a strike price of £10. Therefore, each right provides for a cash payment equal to the amount by which the share price of Entity A exceeds the strike price on the exercise date. No payment will be made if Entity A's share price is at or below £10; Entity A's share price on 1 January 20X1 is £10. Entity A estimates that 85 per cent of employees granted a SAR will be employed at 31 December 20X3 (it is estimated five employees leave the entity each year).

Entity A purchases a net cash-settled call option for £70 with a strike price of £10 that can only be settled at maturity on 31 December 20X3. The notional of the call option is over 70 shares, i.e. less than the 85 employees that are expected to be employed at the end of the scheme. Entity A hedges only 70 out of the 85 SARs that are expected to vest in order to reduce the risk over over-hedging should more employees leave than expected. Entity A excludes the time value of the option from the hedge designation to demonstrate prospectively that the relationship is expected to be highly effective. Entity A designates the intrinsic value of the derivative as hedging the cash flow variability of 70 employees' SARs and their profit or loss impact recognised in accordance with IFRS 2 *Share-based Payment*. At any given period, the IFRS 2 liability and corresponding cumulative profit or loss charge will be equal to the degree to which the hedging instrument is "in-the-money" apportioned for the period from the grant date to the vesting date.

The time value and intrinsic value of the hedging instrument are summarised below:

	1/1/X1	31/12/X1	31/12/X2	31/12/X3
Time value	70	40	20	-
Intrinsic value	-	210	280	140
Fair value	70	250	300	140

All amounts are expressed in Sterling.

1 January 20X1

Dr	Derivative asset	70
Cr	Cash	70

To recognise the fair value of the hedging instrument at initial recognition.

31 December 20X1

Entity A's share price is £13, and three employees have left the entity in the period. Entity A changes its estimate of the number of employees expected to be employed at 31 December 20X3 to 91.

The share-based payment charge and liability is £91 [((£13 – £10) × 91) × $^1/_3$ = £91].

Dr	Employee expense	91
Cr	Share based payment liability	91

To recognise the share-based payment expense in the period.

The hedge was highly effective for the period since 70 employees are still expected to be employed at 31 December 20X3, and the hedging instrument provides a perfect offset to the cash flow variability of the liability for the payments to these employees.

Dr	Derivative asset	180 [250 – 70]
Dr	Profit or loss	30
Cr	Other comprehensive income (cash flow hedge reserve)	210

To recognise the fair value movement of the derivative with the time value recognised in income and the effective portion recognised in other comprehensive income.

The period-end cash flow hedge reserve must be equal to the intrinsic value of 70 employee SARs that are still considered to be highly probable and that have not yet affected profit or loss through the IFRS 2 charge. Because the scheme is one-third through its life, the cash flow hedge reserve at the end of the period is £140 [((£13 – £10) × 70) × $^2/_3$ = £140].

Dr	Other comprehensive income (cash flow hedge reserve)	70
Cr	Profit or loss	70

To recognise the reclassification from the cash flow hedge reserve in equity to profit or loss for the portion of intrinsic value of the derivative as a result of the SAR impacting profit or loss. The amount reclassified is determined as ((13–10) x 70) x $^1/_3$ = 70.

31 December 20X2

Entity A's share price is £14, and four employees have left the entity in the period. The entity revises its estimates of the number of employees expected to be employed at 31 December 20X3 to 89.

The share-based payment liability is £237 [((£14 – £10) × 89) × $^2/_3$ = £237].

Dr	Employee expense	146
Cr	Share-based payment liability	146 [237 – 91]

To recognise the share-based payment expense in the period.

The hedge was highly effective for the period since 70 employees are still expected to be employed at 31 December 20X3, and the hedging instrument provides a perfect offset to the cash flow variability of the liability for the payments to these employees.

Dr	Derivative asset	50 [300 – 250]
Dr	Profit or loss	20
Cr	Other comprehensive income	70

To recognise the fair value movement of the derivative with the time value recognised in income and the effective portion recognised in other comprehensive income.

The period-end cash flow hedge reserve must be equal to the intrinsic value of 70 employee SARs that are still considered to be highly probable and that have not yet affected profit or loss through the IFRS 2 charge. Because the scheme is two-thirds through its life, the cash flow hedge reserve at the end of the period is £93 [((£14 – £10) × 70) × $^1/_3$ = £93].

Dr	Other comprehensive income (cash flow hedge reserve)	117
Cr	Profit or loss	117

To recognise the reclassification from the cash flow hedge reserve in equity to profit or loss for the portion of intrinsic value of the derivative as a result of the SAR impacting profit or loss. The amount reclassified is determined as [((14–10) x 70) x $^2/_3$*] – 70 recognised in previous period = 117.*

31 December 20X3

Entity A's share price is £12, and five employees have left the entity in the period. In all, 12 employees have left over the three-year period [three in 20X1, four in 20X2, and five in 20X3].

The share-based payment liability is £176 [((£12 – £10) × 88) × $^3/_3$ = £176].

Dr	Share-based payment liability	61 [176 – 237]
Cr	Employee expense	61

To recognise the share-based payment expense in the period.

The hedge was highly effective for the period since 70 employees were employed at 31 December 20X3, and the hedging instrument provided a perfect offset to the cash flow variability of the liability for the payments to these employees.

Dr	Profit or loss	20
Dr	Other comprehensive income	140
Cr	Derivative asset	160 [140 – 300]

To recognise the fair value movement of the derivative with the time value recognised in income and the effective portion recognised in other comprehensive income.

Since the 70 SARs vested at the period end, no amount should be left in the cash flow hedge reserve. Because the scheme is at the end of its life, the cash flow hedge reserve at the end of the period is £0.

Dr	Other comprehensive income (cash flow hedge reserve)	117

Cr	Profit or loss	117

To recognise the reclassification from the cash flow hedge reserve in equity to profit or loss for the portion of intrinsic value of the derivative as a result of the SAR impacting profit or loss. The amount reclassified is determined as [((12–10) x 70) x 3/3] – (70 + 117) recognised in period periods = 47.

Dr	Share-based payment liability	176 [(12–10) x 88]
Cr	Cash	176

To recognise payment to employees on exercise of the SARs.

Dr	Cash	140
Cr	Derivative asset	140

To recognise cash received on settlement of the hedging instrument.

Summary of entries

Dr/(Cr)

Description	Derivative asset	Cash-settled share-based payment liability	Cash	Profit or loss	Other comprehensive income (cash flow hedge reserve)
1/1/X1					
Hedging instrument	70		(70)		
31/12/X1					
Share-based payment		(91)		91	
Hedging instrument	180			(40)	(140)
31/12/X2					
Share-based payment		(146)		146	
Hedging instrument	50			(97)	47
31/12/X3					
Share-based payment		61		(61)	
Hedging instrument	(160)			67	93
Share-based payment		176	(176)		
Hedging instrument	(140)		140		
Total	–	–	(106)	106	–

The net cash impact of hedging the cash-settled share-based payments is the total share-based payments of £176, plus the up-front premium spent to acquire the hedging instrument of £70, less the cash received on settlement of the hedging instrument of £140. The profit or loss impact equates to the IFRS 2 charge of £176 plus the net gain from the hedging instrument of £70.

The net income in each period is not fully offset for the following reasons:

- Entity A did not hedge all its expected cash-settled share-based payment transactions. The entity hedged the first 70 share-based payment transactions, even though it expected at 1 January 20X1 that 85 of 100 employees would still be employed at 31 December 20X3.
- The time value of the SAR is not designated as part of the hedge relationship, which results in net income volatility in all periods.

In the above example the entity is negatively exposed to favourable movements in its own share price. The more the share increases in value, the greater the share-based payment liability that must be carried in the statement of financial position in accordance with IFRS 2, and the greater the ultimate cash payout will be at the maturity of the scheme. The cash-settled share-based payment presents an exposure to cash flows that affect profit or loss because the entity's liability under the scheme is remeasured with the movement in the share price. The transaction is deemed highly probable as a number of employees are expected to remain in employment for the period to enable them to exercise their SARs. It is possible to designate the cash flow variability arising from the SARs as the population of forecast transactions is homogenous, i.e. the SARs have the same maturity and the same strike price, and therefore result in the same cash payment at maturity.

To improve hedge effectiveness the time value of the hedging option will generally be excluded from the hedge designation. The effectiveness of the hedge will also be influenced by the number of SARs hedged compared to the number that is expected to, and ultimately does, vest. The effective portion of the gain and loss on the hedging instrument is recognised in other comprehensive income and is subsequently reclassified from equity to profit or loss in the same period during which the hedged item affects profit or loss. The ineffective portion of the gain or loss on the derivative must be recognised in profit or loss immediately.

3.10 Hedging foreign currency exposure in equity securities

Available-for-sale ('AFS') assets are held at fair value with changes in fair value recognised in other comprehensive income. A non-monetary AFS asset, such as a listed equity security in an unrelated party can be hedged provided there is a clear and identifiable exposure to changes in foreign exchange rates. This would normally be the case where:

- the equity instrument is not traded on an exchange (or in another established marketplace) where trades are denominated in the same currency as the functional currency of the entity; and
- dividends received by the investor are not in the same currency as the functional currency of the investor.

If a share is traded in multiple currencies and one of those currencies is the functional currency of the reporting entity, hedge accounting for the foreign currency component of the share price is not permitted.

[IAS 39.IG.F.2.19]

Example 3.10A

Hedging foreign currency of a equity security: qualifying

Entity ABC is a UK-based manufacturing entity. Entity ABC owns shares in Entity X, which is listed on the New York Stock Exchange. The security is classified as available-for-sale. Dividends are paid in US dollars and the share price is quoted in US dollars.

As the shares in Entity X are not traded on a Sterling-denominated exchange and the dividends are not in the functional currency of Entity ABC, there is a clear and identifiable exposure to changes in foreign exchange rates, and the investment in shares can qualify as a hedged item.

Entity ABC could hedge its exposure to foreign currency risk by, for example, entering into a forward foreign currency contract to sell US dollars. Additionally, it could choose to designate only a portion of the shares, provided effectiveness can be measured. For example, if the fair value of the shares was US$1,000, it could designate the foreign currency risk associated with, say, US$800 of the fair value of the shares.

Entity ABC could designate the forward contract as a fair value hedge of the investment in Entity X, or as a cash flow hedge of the forecast sale of the shares if the timing of the sale is highly probable.

Example 3.10B

Hedging foreign currency of a equity security: non-qualifying

Group A is a group headed by a Japanese resident parent whose shares are publicly traded on the Tokyo Stock Exchange (TSE). Group A has a secondary listing on the New York Stock Exchange (NYSE) where the parent's shares are listed as American Deposit Receipts (ADRs). Trading on the NYSE is comparatively low compared to trading on the TSE as Group A has a small number of US investors. The prices on the NYSE closely approximate the prices of the shares on the TSE multiplied by the current foreign exchange rate between Japanese Yen and US dollars.

An investor is prohibited from hedging the foreign currency risk of an investment in a share denominated in multiple currencies where one of the currencies is the functional currency of the investor. Even where the trading volume is low compared to its primary listing as in the above scenario the Parent's shares remain dual listed. As the investor is a US dollar functional currency investor, and the shares are denominated in US dollars on a stock exchange, the investor cannot hedge their foreign currency risk in respect of the shares acquired from the TSE that are denominated in Japanese Yen. [IAS 39.IG.F.2.19]

3.11 Designation of groups of items

It is possible to group together similar assets or similar liabilities and hedge them as a group, but only if the individual items within the group share the same risk exposure that is designated as being hedged. The change in fair value attributable to the hedged risk of each item in the group must be approximately proportional to the change in fair value attributable to the hedged risk of the entire group. [IAS 39.83]

IAS 39 does not provide specific guidance as to what is approximately proportional, however it does not expect that the items within a portfolio have exactly the same sensitivity to the hedged risk, but the items must show a high degree of similarity for a given movement in the hedged risk.

Investments in debt instruments that have different credit ratings and different maturities can be combined and hedged as a portfolio. In order to comply with the requirement that all items in the portfolio share the same risk exposure for which they are designated and that changes in their fair values are expected to be approximately proportional to the overall change in the fair value attributable to the hedged risk of the group, only portions of risks related to these instruments can be designated as being hedged and only for a portion of their terms that is common to all instruments in the portfolio. For example, the risk-free interest rate component that is shared by these instruments can qualify as being hedged. Alternatively, if an entity wanted to designate the entire risk of each instrument in the portfolio as being hedged, it would have to segregate the loans into portfolios in which each item in the portfolio is similar. This can be done by classifying loans according to their predominant risk characteristics, including:

- date of origination;
- loan type;
- loan size;

- geographical location;
- nature and location of collateral;
- interest rate type (fixed or variable) and the coupon interest rate (if fixed) or the timing of reset dates (if variable);
- scheduled maturity, prepayment history of the loans; and
- expected prepayment performance in varying interest rate scenarios.

Example 3.11

Hedging a group of similar items

On 1 April 20X4, Bank S has a £100 million portfolio of corporate bonds that have a range of coupons from 7.5 per cent to 9.0 per cent and a maturity range of 10–11 years. Bank S would like to hedge the interest rate exposure on the £100 million bond portfolio. It performs a sensitivity analysis and determines that the fair value exposure with respect to movement in interest rate risk only of all of the items individually respond within a range of 95 to 105 per cent of the overall change in price of the portfolio as a whole.

Bank S can designate an interest rate swap as a hedge of interest rate risk of the portfolio as a whole since all items within the portfolio share the same risk exposure and the change in value of the items within the portfolio is expected to be approximately proportional to the change in value of the portfolio as a whole.

It is unlikely that a pool of shares could be grouped together and hedged as a portfolio. For example, it would not be possible to hedge a portfolio of shares that equate to the FTSE-100 index with a FTSE-100 total return swap. Although on an aggregated basis the hedge may be highly effective, it is clear that the individual equity securities that make up the portfolio do not share the exposure to risk, in that the fair value of each individual equity share does not move proportionally to the changes in value of the overall FTSE-100 index. [IAS 39.IG.F.2.20]

3.12 Hedging net positions

A hedge of an overall net position, does not qualify for hedge accounting since hedge effectiveness is required to be measured by comparing the change in fair value or cash flows of a hedging instrument and a specific hedged item (or group of similar items). However, almost the same effect on profit or loss can be achieved by designating part of the underlying items, assets or liabilities, equal to the net position as the hedged item. [IAS 39.AG101]

Example 3.12A

Hedging a net payable

Entity A, a Sterling functional currency entity, has payables of US$100, and receivables of US$80. Instead of entering into two separate derivatives, it wishes to hedge the net US$20 position for foreign currency risk. Whilst the Standard does not allow it to designate the net position as the hedged item, Entity A can instead designate US$20 of payables as the hedged item.

Similarly, if an entity had £500 fixed rate assets and £350 fixed rate liabilities and entered into a hedge of the net position, it could designate £150 of assets as being a hedged item in a fair value hedge of interest rate risk.

The net exposure from a forecast purchase and a forecast sale cannot be designated as a hedged item. Once again, almost the same effect on profit or loss can be achieved by designating part of the forecast purchases or forecast sales equal to the net position as the hedged item.

Example 3.12B

Hedging a net sale

Entity A, a UK entity, has highly probable forecast sales of US$100, and highly probable forecast purchases of US$80. Entity A enters into a single foreign currency forward contract to hedge the net exposure of US$20. Entity A can designate that derivative as hedging the first US$20 of sales.

An entity cannot hedge net profit as this is also a net number of many items. If an entity has sufficiently stable net profit margins it may be able to hedge the net number by designating as the hedged item a portion of sales equal to that amount.

Example 3.12C

Hedging a net profit

Entity A's functional currency is Sterling. A fifth of Entity A's profits is generated in US$ and thereby this exposes the entity's net profit to foreign currency risk. The US$ sales are expected to be $100m per month and have a relatively stable net profit margin of 15 per cent (i.e. US$ purchases are expected to be $85m per month).

Entity A wishes to hedge the exposure of net profit to changes in US$ / Sterling currency rate. As Entity A cannot hedge a net amount, and therefore cannot hedge the net profit, Entity A chooses instead to designate the hedging instrument as a cash flow hedge of the first $15m of US$ sales per month.

As long as Entity A makes at least $15m of US$ sales per month, the hedge relationship will be effective.

3.13 Equity method investments and investments in consolidated subsidiaries

An equity method investment cannot be a hedged item in a fair value hedge in consolidated financial statements because the equity method recognises the investor's share of the associate's profit or loss, rather than changes in the investment's fair value.

For a similar reason, an investment in a consolidated subsidiary cannot be a hedged item in consolidated financial statements in a fair value hedge because consolidation recognises the subsidiary's profit or loss, rather than changes in the investment's fair value. [IAS 39.AG99]

Although in the consolidated financial statements it is not possible to apply fair value hedge accounting for an equity method investment or investment in a consolidated subsidiary, it may be possible to apply fair value hedge accounting to such a hedge in the investor's separate financial statements.

Whether fair value hedge accounting is permitted is dependent on whether the investment in the equity security can actually be fair valued. It is inconsistent to claim fair value hedge accounting when the fair value of the investment cannot be reliably measured, e.g. where the investment is in an unquoted equity and the variability in the range of reasonable fair value estimates is too high.

A hedge of a net investment in a foreign operation is different because it is a hedge of the foreign currency exposure, not a fair value hedge of the change in the value of the investment. Hedges of net investments in foreign operations are dealt with in **2.3** above.

3.14 Instruments subject to prepayment

An instrument that contains an embedded prepayment option may still be designated as a hedged item. However, the effect of the prepayment option should be considered when designating the hedged item and assessing whether the hedge relationship will be highly effective.

If the entire asset or liability is designated as being hedged, for the hedging instrument to be highly effective it may have to include an equivalent option that coincides with the prepayment option in the hedged item. Inclusion of such an option in the hedging instrument ensures that fair value of the hedging instrument is as sensitive as the hedged item with respect to the designated hedged risk.

Alternatively, the hedging relationship could be designated for just a portion of the term of the instrument prior to the prepayment option ever being capable of being exercised provided the hedging instrument is designated for the entirety of its term (see **4.2** below). For example, if a debt instrument can be prepaid by the issuer after year five, the investor may wish to hedge the debt instrument for a period before the prepayment option can be exercised, i.e. for the first five years only.

An investor in a prepayable asset may decide to hedge cash flows in the period in which the prepayment option is exercisable (or in the period after the date on which the option can be exercised). In order to demonstrate that the hedging instrument is expected to be highly effective in the period, the cash flows must be highly probable. For example, cash flows in the period when the prepayment option is exercisable may qualify as highly probable if they result from a group or pool of similar assets (for example, mortgage loans) for which prepayments can be estimated with a high degree of accuracy or if the prepayment option is significantly out of the money. [IAS 39.IG.F.2.12]

Example 3.14A

Hedging prepayable loans for interest rate risk (1)

Entity A purchases a perpetual debt instrument which pays a market rate of interest of 5 per cent on par. The issuer of the debt instrument has an option to prepay the perpetual debt at an amount that is equal to the instrument's par amount after 5 years.

As the debt instrument is not quoted in an active market, Entity A classifies the instrument as a loan and receivable and determines that the embedded prepayment option is closely related to the host contract since the option's exercise price is approximately equal to the debt instrument's amortised cost on the exercise date of the option (i.e. par). Entity A enters into a non-prepayable swap with Bank B to pay fixed 5 per cent and to receive LIBOR for 20 years. The interest rate swap is designated as a partial term fair value hedge of the LIBOR portion of the perpetual debt instrument for 20 years. Apart from the issuer call prepayment option, all terms and conditions of the swap match those of the hedged item.

Entity A must compare the changes in fair value of the interest rate swap to the changes in the fair value of the perpetual debt instrument, where the latter includes both the change in fair value of the contractual cash flows and the change in fair value of the prepayment option. Hedge ineffectiveness will arise since the hedged item is prepayable, whilst the hedging instrument is not. Hedge ineffectiveness is likely to be so significant in that it will be difficult to demonstrate prospective hedge effectiveness. If 5 years after the issue, the perpetual debt has not been called by the issuer, Entity A may be able to designate the interest rate swap as a partial term hedge of the LIBOR portion of the perpetual debt for the next 15 years. It is not appropriate to exclude the prepayment risk out of the designation of the hedging relationship since prepayment risk and interest rate risk are closely interrelated.

Example 3.14B

Hedging prepayable loans for interest rate risk (2)

Facts as in **example 3.14A**, except that Entity A enters into a swap with Bank B whereby the swap can be terminated after 5 years at Entity A's option. The swap will be terminated at the swap's then fair value.

Entity A must compare the changes in fair value of the interest rate swap to the changes in the fair value of the perpetual debt instrument. In both cases the change in fair value includes both the change in fair value of the contractual cash flows as well as the change in fair value of the prepayment option which for the swap has negligible value as the swap terminates at fair value. Hedge ineffectiveness will still arise since the hedged item is prepayable at par whilst the hedging instrument can only be terminated at its then fair value which will include the fair value of the expected future cash flows on the remaining 15 years of the swap. Thus, changes in the fair value of the hedged item will not be offset by changes in the fair value of the hedging instrument. The lack of offset may be significant enough to prevent hedge accounting.

Example 3.14C

Hedging prepayable loans for interest rate risk (3)

Facts as in **example 3.14A**, except that Entity A enters into a swap with Bank B whereby the swap can be terminated after 5 years at Entity A's option. The swap will be terminated at zero value.

Entity A must compare the changes in fair value of the interest rate swap to the changes in the fair value of the perpetual debt instrument. In both cases the change in fair value includes the change in fair value of the contractual cash flows as well as the change in fair value of the prepayment option. The hedging relationship is expected to be highly effective at hedging the interest rate risk of the debt for part of its term since both the hedging instrument and the hedged item are pre-payable at par.

3.15 Hedging convertible debt

As explained at **3.1** in **chapter 15**, convertible debt is separated at issue into a financial liability and equity conversion option which is included in equity. The financial liability is recognised at the present value of the contractual interest flows and principal, discounted at an interest rate for a debt without the equity conversion option. As the financial liability is measured as if the entity had issued a partly discounted bond, the hedging of the interest rate risk on this financial liability must also take into account this discount. In addition, because the financial liability will be extinguished when the convertible bond is converted, the hedging instrument should mirror this termination feature in order to increase hedge effectiveness.

3.16 Hedging capitalised borrowing costs

IAS 39 and IAS 23 *Borrowing Costs* do not provide guidance on whether an entity can cash flow or fair value hedge interest rate risk when the interest is partly or fully capitalised under IAS 23 as part of a qualifying asset. IAS 23 (Revised 2007) makes references in its basis of conclusions that US GAAP does provide specific guidance in this area for fair value hedges. IAS 23.BC21 states that "EITF Issue No. 99–9 concludes that derivative gains and losses (arising from the effective portion of a derivative instrument that qualifies as a fair value hedge) are part of the capitalised interest cost. IAS 23 does not address such derivative gains and losses".

The capitalisation of borrowing costs in and of itself should not prohibit any entity from applying hedge accounting for interest rate risk for debt that is used to fund a qualifying asset under IAS 23. IAS 39 requires that a hedge must result in the hedged risk impacting profit or loss which will be the case when interest on debt is capitalised as the qualifying asset will impact profit or loss either through amortisation, impairment or sale. The example below sets out two scenarios where cash flow and fair value hedge accounting of interest rate risk is applied when the interest on the borrowing is capitalised under IAS 23.

Example 3.16

Hedging capitalised borrowing costs

Entity A borrows £10m to finance the construction of a 'qualifying asset' in accordance with IAS 23. The related borrowing costs are eligible for capitalisation.

Scenario 1: Entity A borrows at fixed rates

Entity A enters into an interest rate swap (with the same notional and term as the debt) to receive fixed pay 3m LIBOR and designates this as a hedge of the fair value exposure to changes in interest rates (say 3m LIBOR) of its debt. Entity A will capitalise under IAS 23 the synthetic floating rate borrowing costs that have been achieved as a result of entering into the effective hedge accounting relationship.

Entity A will:

(i) Determine the effectiveness of the fair value hedge and recognise any ineffectiveness in profit or loss. If the hedge is highly effective the debt will be fair value adjusted for changes in interest rates with the corresponding entry in profit or loss. The fair value adjustment will be amortised to profit or loss either immediately when the adjustment is made or no later than the debt ceases to fair value hedge adjusted.

(ii) The synthetic floating interest rate that is achieved as a result of the highly effective hedge that would have been recognised in profit or loss in the absence of applying IAS 23 is capitalised. This amount will include the actual fixed rate on the debt plus the effect of swapping this fixed rate into floating rates.

Scenario 2: Entity A borrows at floating rates

Entity A enters into an interest rate swap to receive 3m LIBOR pay fixed rates (same notional and term as debt) and designates the swap as hedging the variability in its debt due to changes in 3m LIBOR. Entity A intends to cash flow hedge the variability in interest rates on its borrowings even though the interest on the borrowings is capitalised under IAS 23.

Entity A can apply cash flow hedge accounting of the interest rate risk on its variable rate borrowings but the gain/loss on the derivative that is recognised in other comprehensive income is reclassified from equity to profit or loss when the interest component of the qualifying asset impacts profit or loss.

Entity A will applies the following steps in order:

(i) Capitalise the variable rate interest on the borrowing in accordance with IAS 23.

(ii) Determine the effectiveness of the cash flow hedge and recognise any ineffectiveness in profit or loss. Recognise the effective gain/loss on the derivative in other comprehensive income.

(iii) The amount recognised in other comprehensive income will be reclassified from equity to profit or loss when the hedged risk impacts profit or loss. The hedged interest that is capitalised as part of the qualifying asset will impact profit or loss when the qualifying asset is amortised, impaired, or is sold. The net effect in profit or loss from this reclassification is that the impact in profit or loss will be equivalent to the entity borrowing at fixed rates and capitalising fixed borrowing costs.

If an entity does not apply hedge accounting and therefore the derivatives are classified as at fair value through profit or loss it is not appropriate for the entity to capitalise part of the derivative as part of the borrowing costs under IAS 23. All gains/losses on non-hedging derivatives must be immediately recognised in profit or loss.

4 Hedging instruments

A hedging instrument is a designated derivative, or for a hedge of the risk of changes in foreign currency exchange rates a designated non-derivative financial asset or non-derivative financial liability, whose fair value or cash flows are expected to offset changes in the fair value or cash flows of a designated hedged item. [IAS 39.9]

Unless it is a written option (see **4.6** below), a derivative carried at fair value may always be designated as a hedging instrument, provided it:

(a) meets the effectiveness requirements (see **section 5** below); and

(b) the necessary documentation is in place that supports the hedging relationship (see **section 8** below).

A derivative that is linked to and must be settled by delivery of an unquoted equity instrument whose value cannot be reliably measured is measured at cost, and cannot be considered an effective hedging instrument as it is not possible to determine hedge effectiveness when the fair value of the hedging instrument cannot be determined. [IAS 39.AG96]

A derivative may only be designated as an effective hedging instrument if it is a derivative in the scope of IAS 39. The term 'derivative' does not extend to other types of derivatives that are scoped out of IAS 39. For example, a derivative over own equity that meets the definition of equity in accordance with IAS 32 also meets the definition of a derivative in IAS 39 as it has an underlying, requires a small initial net investment, and is settled at a future date. However, such a derivative is an equity instrument recognised and measured in accordance with IAS 32 and cannot therefore be designated as a hedging instrument.

4.1 Hedging with non-derivatives

A non-derivative financial instrument may only be designated as a hedging instrument when hedging foreign currency risk. [IAS 39.72] An entity can use foreign currency denominated loans, deposits and other non-derivative financial instruments as hedging instruments. A common example of a non-derivative financial instrument used as a hedging instrument is a foreign denominated debt liability used in a hedge of a net investment in a foreign operation (see **2.3.1** above).

Example 4.1A

Hedging a firm commitment with a non-derivative (1)

On 1 January 20X4, Entity B has a firm commitment to purchase equipment (a non-financial asset) from Entity M, a French entity. Entity B's functional currency is Sterling and Entity M's is Euro. The firm commitment requires B to pay €30 million for the equipment for delivery on 1 January 20X5. Entity B has a 31 March year-end.

Entity B currently has €30 million on deposit with a European bank maturing on 1 January 20X5 on which it currently recognises in profit or loss foreign exchange gains and losses at the end of each reporting period. Entity B would like to use its Euro deposit balance as a hedge of its commitment to purchase the equipment.

Entity B can designate the cash deposit as a hedging instrument in either a cash flow or a fair value hedge of the spot foreign currency risk of the firm commitment (see **2.1.2** above).

The spot foreign exchange rates are as follows:

Date	Exchange rate	Sterling equivalent of €30m	Movement
1 January 20X4	1.4321	20,948,257	
31 March 20X4	1.4282	21,005,461	57,204
1 January 20X5	1.4511	20,673,971	(331,490)

The entries below do not consider the accounting for the deposit before 1 January 20X4. Up to this date, the monetary asset will have been reported at the spot rate at the end of each reporting period, with exchange gains and losses reported in profit or loss.

Entity B designates the hedge as a *fair value hedge* of the spot foreign currency risk of the firm commitment.

1 January 20X4

There are no entries. The firm commitment has a fair value of zero.

31 March 20X4

Dr	Deposit	57,204
Cr	Profit or loss	57,204

To recognise the foreign exchange gain on remeasurement of the deposit.

Dr	Profit or loss	57,204
Cr	Firm commitment	57,204

To recognise the change in fair value of the firm commitment relating to the hedged risk (foreign currency spot movements).

1 January 20X5

Dr	Profit or loss	331,490
Cr	Deposit	331,490

To recognise the exchange loss on remeasurement of the deposit.

Dr	Firm commitment	331,490
Cr	Profit or loss	331,490

To recognise the change in fair value of the firm commitment relating to the hedged risk (foreign currency spot movements).

Dr	Property, plant, equipment	20,948,257
Cr	Firm commitment	274,286
Cr	Cash	20,673,971

To recognise the acquisition of the asset and derecognise the firm commitment that has now been extinguished. The carrying value of the non-financial asset is the Sterling equivalent of €30 million, translated at the spot rate when the hedge was entered into.

Dr	Cash	20,673,971
Cr	Deposit	20,673,971

To account for the repayment of the deposit upon its maturity on 1 January 20X5.

Entity B designates the hedge as a *cash flow hedge* of the spot foreign currency risk of the firm commitment.

1 January 20X4

There are no entries.

31 March 20X4

Dr	Deposit	57,204
Cr	Other comprehensive income	57,204

To recognise the foreign exchange gain on remeasurement of the deposit being fully effective in hedging the foreign currency risk of the forecast purchase.

1 January 20X5

Dr	Other comprehensive income	331,490
Cr	Deposit	331,490

To recognise the exchange loss on remeasurement of the deposit being fully effective in hedging the foreign currency risk of the forecast purchase.

Dr	Property, plant, equipment	20,948,257
Cr	Other comprehensive income	274,286
Cr	Cash	20,673,971

To recognise the cash paid on acquisition of the asset and perform a basis adjustment to remove the effective amount from equity and include it in the carrying amount of the asset. The carrying value of the non-financial asset is the Sterling equivalent of €30 million, translated at the spot rate when the hedge was entered into.

Dr	Cash	20,673,971
Cr	Deposit	20,673,971

To account for the repayment of the deposit upon its maturity on 1 January 20X5.

If Entity B has an accounting policy not to apply basis adjustments to non-financial items in cash flow hedges, the amount recognised in other comprehensive income will be retained in equity at the acquisition date of the equipment and will be reclassified from equity to profit or loss in future periods when the depreciation of the equipment will impact profit or loss (see **2.2.3** above). In this case, the carrying amount of the equipment would be €20,673,971.

Example 4.1B

Hedging a financial asset with a non-derivative

Entity J, whose functional currency is Sterling, has issued 5 million five-year US$ fixed rate debt. It also acquired a 5 million five-year fixed rate US$ bond which it has classified as available-for-sale.

Entity J cannot designate its US$ liability as a hedging instrument in a fair value hedge of the entire fair value exposure of its US$ bond, as a non-derivative may only be used as a hedging instrument of foreign currency risk.

Entity J could consider the use of the fair value option (see **3.1.1** in **chapter 14**) at initial recognition of the loan and liability. By designating both items as at fair value through profit or loss this designation would result in substantial offset of gains and losses in profit or loss, and unlike treating the asset as available-for-sale and the liability at amortised cost, it will result in no or little volatility in equity.

If Entity J did not apply the fair value option it could designate the US$ liability as a hedge of the foreign currency component of the bond (as either a fair value or cash flow hedge), but hedge accounting will not provide any advantage over not applying hedge accounting at all: the foreign currency gains and losses on both the monetary asset and monetary liability are already recognised in profit or loss in the period, in accordance with IAS 21, i.e. there is already a natural offset of foreign currency risk in profit or loss.

It should be noted that this natural offset would not apply if the hedged item was a non-monetary financial instrument, such as an equity security held as available-for-sale. Because the foreign exchange gains and losses on an equity security that is recognised at fair value will be recognised in other comprehensive income, there will not be a natural offset as the foreign exchange gains and losses from reporting the monetary financial liability would continue to be recognised in profit or loss under IAS 21. An entity could therefore attempt to apply either fair value or cash flow hedge accounting to achieve offset in profit or loss or other comprehensive income respectively but variations in the US$ fair value of the equity security could result in ineffectiveness as the foreign currency component of the shares are derived from the fair value of the shares in local currency, being US$.

Example 4.1C

Hedging a firm commitment with a non-derivative (2)

Entity XYZ's functional currency is Euro. It has issued a US$5m fixed rate debt instrument with semi-annual interest payments that matures in two years. Entity XYZ has also entered into a US$5m fixed price sale commitment of a non-financial item that matures in two years and is not accounted for as a derivative because it meets the exemption as a contract that is entered into and continues to be held for the purpose of the delivery of a non-financial item in accordance with the entity's expected sale requirements.

Entity XYZ cannot designate its US$ liability as a fair value hedge of the entire fair value exposure of its fixed price sale commitment as a non-derivative liability can only be used as a hedging instrument for a hedge of a foreign currency risk.

However, Entity XYZ can designate its US$ liability as a fair value or cash flow hedge of the foreign currency risk of its fixed price sale commitment.

Note that Entity XYZ cannot designate the fixed price sale commitment as the hedging instrument instead of the hedged item, as only a derivative or non-derivative financial instrument can be designated as a hedging instrument in a hedge of a foreign currency risk. The fixed price sale commitment in this case is neither, as it is scoped out of IAS 39.

If the foreign currency component of the sale commitment was separated as an embedded derivative that was not considered to be closely related to the sale contract, the embedded derivative could be designated as a hedging instrument of the foreign currency risk of the fixed rate debt instrument. However, applying hedge accounting would not provide the entity with any presentation benefit as both the foreign currency risk on the debt and the embedded derivative hedging instrument would be recognised in profit or loss.

A financial asset that is classified as held-to-maturity may be designated as a hedging instrument in a hedge of foreign currency risk.

4.2 Splitting a derivative

A hedging relationship must be designated for a hedging instrument in its entirety. This is because there is usually only one fair value for a hedging instrument, and each of the factors contributing to that fair value are co-dependent. Two exceptions to designating a hedging instrument in its entirety are:

(i) the intrinsic and time value of an option may be separated, with only the intrinsic element designated as the hedging instrument; and

(ii) the interest and spot elements of a forward may be separated, with only the spot element designated as the hedging instrument. [IAS 39.74]

In both of these situations, the element of the derivative that is not designated as a hedging instrument (i.e. the time value on an option, or the interest element on a forward) will be fair valued through profit or loss.

The above exceptions are permitted because the intrinsic value of an option and the spot element of a forward can usually be measured separately. However, the principle of reliable separate measurement cannot be extended. Even if it can be demonstrated that a reliable measure of an element of a derivative can be determined it cannot be excluded from the hedge designation except if it is one of the two exceptions described above.

As part of a hedge relationship an entity can choose to designate only a proportion of the derivative as the hedging instrument (e.g. 50 per cent of the notional), and then apply one of the exceptions as described above should it wish to. Designation of proportions of hedging instruments is discussed in **4.3** below.

Example 4.2

Fair value hedging with a purchased put

Entity A has an investment in shares of Entity XYZ, which it has classified as available-for-sale ('AFS'). To protect itself against a decrease in the share price, it purchases a put option over those shares. A designates the intrinsic value of the put as a hedging instrument in a fair value hedge of the XYZ shares.

The put has a strike price of £50 per share – i.e. it allows A to sell the shares at £50. When Entity A purchased the put, Entity XYZ shares were trading at £55 per share. The put option will be fully effective in offsetting any price decrease below £50, as A is designating only the intrinsic value. Any change in price above £50 is not hedged.

Changes in the fair value of Entity XYZ shares are recognised in other comprehensive income. To the extent that the shares are hedged, changes in the fair value attributable to the hedged risk are recognised in profit or loss and offset with the gains and losses on the hedging instrument (i.e. the gains or losses on the hedged item below £50 will be recognised in profit or loss and offset with the gains or losses on hedging instrument). Changes in the fair value of the option that relate to time value will be recognised in profit or loss.

It is not possible to split the embedded financing from a non-optional derivative that has a fair value other than zero at the time of designation and account for it as a separate amortising loan whilst designating the zero fair value derivative as the hedging instrument.

If a non-optional derivative, such as a forward contract or swap, has a fair value other than zero at inception of the hedge, future changes in its fair value are impacted by that starting value. The derivative includes an embedded financing element which contributes to its fair value movements and causes them to differ from the changes in fair value of the hedged item when the hedged item does not have an equal and opposite financing element.

IAS 39 does not prohibit non-zero fair value non-optional derivatives being designated as hedging instruments as long as the hedging instrument is expected to be highly effective. In fact, IAS 39 allows hedging instruments to be designated part way through their lives, and therefore it is quite common for a derivative to have a starting value on designation other than zero. If the derivative can pass the prospective assessment of hedge effectiveness, the non-zero element of the derivative at initial designation will cause ineffectiveness that will be recognised in profit or loss over the term of the hedge. This is particularly the case for cash flow hedges as the 'hypothetical derivative' is deemed to be on-market at the date of designation, which for a non-optional derivative would have a fair value of zero (see **5.7.2.3** below).

The ineffectiveness arises because the embedded financing element is economically similar to a fixed rate amortising loan embedded in the derivative and this 'loan' will change in fair value as interest rates move. By the time the derivative matures, the loan will have been fully eliminated along with the derivative.

4.3 Designation of portions and proportions of hedging instruments

A proportion of the entire hedging instrument may be designated as the hedging instrument in a hedge relationship. [IAS 39.75]

Example 4.3A

Designating part of a derivative: qualifying

Entity A has a pay-fixed, receive-variable interest rate swap that it wishes to designate as hedging its issued variable rate debt. The notional on the swap is £100 million and the notional on the debt is £60 million. Entity A may designate £60 million of the swap (i.e. 60 per cent) as the hedging instrument of the variable rate debt. The remaining £40 million (i.e. 40 per cent) of the notional of the swap will be treated as a held for trading item, unless it is designated as a hedging instrument in another hedge relationship.

A hedging relationship may not be designated for only a portion of the time period that the hedging instrument is outstanding. [IAS 39.75]

Example 4.3B

Designating part of a derivative: non-qualifying

Entity A has a pay-fixed, receive-variable interest rate swap that it wishes to designate as hedging its issued variable rate debt. The swap has a 10-year term and the debt has a 7-year term. Entity A may not designate seven of the ten years of the swap as the hedging instrument.

Note that the converse can be applied as IAS 39 permits partial term hedging. If in the above example the terms of the debt and swap were reversed, it would be possible to hedge the debt for the first seven years that it remains outstanding. Partial term hedges are discussed further in **3.8.2** above.

The inability to designate a hedging instrument for only a portion of the time period that the hedging instrument remains outstanding is an extension of the rule that does not allow derivatives to be split up. It is not permitted to designate part of a derivative that is not a proportion of the derivative as a whole, unless the part of the derivative excluded from the hedge relationship is the time value of an option or forward points in a forward as discussed in **4.2** above.

This should not be confused with designating a hedging instrument for only part of its life, if for that part of its life it is expected to be a highly effective hedge. For example, it is possible to hedge a 10 year debt instrument using a 10-year interest rate swap, but apply hedge accounting for only one year. Hedge accounting is permitted, assuming the relationship is highly effective, for as long as the designation is applied. An entity may choose to de-designate any hedge relationship if it chooses at any time because hedge accounting is in all cases a voluntary exercise.

4.4 Hedging more than one risk

A hedging instrument is often designated as hedging one risk only.

However, a hedging instrument can be designated as hedging more than one risk provided that:

[IAS 39.76]

(i) the risks being hedged can be clearly identified;

(ii) the effectiveness of the hedge can be demonstrated; and

(iii) it is possible to ensure that there is specific designation of the hedging instrument and different risk positions.

If a single hedging instrument is hedging more than one risk, and each risk is being hedged using a different form of hedge accounting (for example one as a fair value hedge and one as a cash flow hedge), separate disclosures will be needed for each.

4.4.1 Hedging more than one risk in a single hedged item

IAS 39 allows the use of one instrument to hedge more than one risk. Cross currency interest rate swaps are commonly used to swap foreign currency variable rate debt back into functional currency fixed rate debt, or to swap foreign currency fixed into functional currency variable.

Example 4.4.1

Hedging both interest rate and foreign currency risk

Entity A, a Sterling functional currency entity, issues variable US dollar debt. To hedge its exposure to foreign currency exchange rates and to interest rate risk it enters into a cross currency interest rate swap. The terms of the swap match those of the debt. Under the swap, Entity A receives floating US dollars and pays fixed Sterling. IAS 39 allows the swap to be designated as a cash flow hedge of interest rate risk, and either a cash flow hedge or fair value hedge of the foreign currency risk.

Similarly, Entity A could have issued fixed US dollar debt, and used a cross currency interest rate swap to convert the position into variable Sterling debt. IAS 39 would permit the entity to designate the swap as a fair value hedge of both the interest rate and foreign currency risk or a fair value hedge of US$ interest rate risk and a cash flow hedge of the foreign currency risk.

Assuming all other hedge accounting criteria are met it is possible to use a single derivative to hedge both foreign currency and interest rate risks if both risks are evident in the hedged item.

4.4.2 Hedging multiple hedged items

IAS 39 provides limited guidance on how to assess hedge effectiveness when an entity uses a single hedging instrument to hedge multiple hedged items. There are many instances where an entity could use a single derivative financial instrument to hedge one risk (say foreign currency risk) or multiple risks (say foreign currency risk and interest rate risk) where those risks reside in more than one hedged item.

IAS 39.IG.F.1.13 provides an example of an entity hedging two hedged items for the same risk. The example describes a Japanese Yen functional currency entity that has a 5-year floating rate US$ liability and a 10-year fixed rate £-denominated note receivable and chooses to hedge both items with a single foreign currency forward contract where it will receive US$ and pay £ in 5 years. As the principal amounts of the asset and liability when converted into Japanese Yen are the same, the entity designates the dual foreign currency forward contract as hedging foreign currency risk for both items. Even though foreign currency risk is defined by reference to the entity's functional currency, and the foreign currency forward contract does not have a cash flow in the functional currency, i.e. Japanese Yen, the foreign currency forward contract may still be designated as hedging *both* foreign currencies as the exposure to both currencies has been eliminated by the forward. Put another way, if the entity entered into a receive US$ pay Japanese Yen forward, and a receive Japanese Yen pay £ forward, each forward could have been designated separately as hedging the foreign currency risk of the liability and asset respectively, even the fair value of the two Japanese Yen legs would offset each other perfectly. In a single forward to receive US$ pay £, the receive Japanese Yen leg and the pay Japanese Yen leg do not exist but this does not create hedge ineffectiveness as the fair value of both legs offsets to zero. However, in assessing and measuring hedge effectiveness with a single forward contract the entity will need to impute the two notional Japanese Yen legs into the hedge designation in order to determine the hedge effectiveness of the two hedges of foreign currency risk. Imputing the two notional cash flows for assessing hedge effectiveness is permitted as doing so does not create any additional cash flows as both notional cash flows offset each other perfectly.

In July 2007 the IFRIC issued a rejection notice on hedging multiple risks with a single derivative financial instrument. The IFRIC recognised that IAS 39's interpretative guidance does result in an entity needing to impute a notional leg as a means of splitting the fair value of the derivative into multiple components in order to assess hedge effectiveness. IFRIC considered that this was acceptable in assessing hedge effectiveness as this conclusion did not conflict with IAS 39.IG.C.1 which prohibits an entity from recognising embedded derivatives that result in the *recognition* [emphasis added in the July 2007 IFRIC Update] of cash flows that do not contractually exist. The IFRIC's rejection notice highlights that should any entity need to notionally split a derivative for assessing hedge effectiveness when that derivative is hedging multiple risks then the process of splitting should not result in any new cash flows and any new risks arising which were not evident in the contractual terms of the derivative.

Example 4.4.2A

Hedging a net investment in a foreign operation and interest rate risk of issued debt

Parent P, a € functional currency entity, has issued a €100m denominated fixed rate debt. Parent P consolidates Subsidiary S, a US$ functional currency foreign operation with opening net assets of US$300m. Parent P's objective is to hedge (i) the foreign currency risk of part of its foreign operation (being the € equivalent of US$150m net assets) and (ii) the fair value due to changes in interest rates on its issued debt (being interest rate risk on €100m). In order to minimise transaction costs the entity enters into a single derivative to Receive € fixed on €100m, Pay US$ 3m-US$ LIBOR on US$150m with the fair value of the cross-currency interest rate swap equal to zero at the transaction date, i.e. the derivative is on-market.

Parent P designates in the consolidated financial statements the cross-currency interest rate swap as a hedge of the foreign currency risk of Subsidiary S's net assets equal to US$150m and the fair value interest rate risk on €100m of its €-denominated debt. In order to assess hedge effectiveness for net investment hedge and fair value hedge Parent P notionally splits the derivative into the following: (i) Receive fixed €100m, Pay 3m-EURIBOR on €100m (notional derivative 1), and (ii) Receive 3m-EURIBOR on €100m, Pay 3m-US$ LIBOR US$150m (notional derivative 2). Parent P fair values the two notional derivatives at inception and both have a fair value of zero so the sum of the fair values equals the fair value of the actual contractual derivative. Each period the notional derivatives are fair valued in order to assess and measure hedge effectiveness and to ensure that the sum of these fair values equals the fair value of the actual contractual derivative entered into.

Example 4.4.2B

Hedging cash flow variability of both an asset and liability

Entity B, a Sterling functional currency entity, has issued 3m-LIBOR £200m denominated debt and has an investment in an inflation-linked bond that receives 3% + UK CPI on a notional of £200m (the inflation linkage is considered a closely related embedded derivative). The asset and liability have the same 5 year maturity.

Entity B's objective is to hedge the cash flow variability on both its asset and its liability. In order to minimise transaction costs the entity enters into 5-year Receive 3m-LIBOR £200m Pay 3% + UK CPI £200m and designates this basis swap as a hedge of the cash flow variability of both its assets and its liability. In order to assess hedge effectiveness Entity B notionally splits the derivative into the following: (i) 5-year Receive 3m LIBOR £200m, Pay 6% £200m (notional derivative 1), and (ii) Receive 6% £200m, Pay 3% + UK CPI £200m (notional derivative 2). Entity B fair values the two notional derivatives at inception and both have a fair value of zero so the sum of the fair values equals the fair value of the actual contractual derivative. Each period the notional derivatives are fair valued in order to assess and measure hedge effectiveness and to ensure that the sum of these fair values equals the fair value of the actual contractual derivative entered into.

Judgement is required in determining what is an appropriate split when allocating the fair value of derivative to multiple hedged items for assessing hedge effectiveness. It would not be appropriate to create multiple notional derivatives which introduce notional legs over risks which did not exist in the contractual derivative or are not specific to the entity entering into the transaction, for example the entity's functional currency. Taking **example 4.4.2A** above, the notional legs introduced are in the functional currency of the entity, being Euro, which is a reference point that is specific to the entity; the frequency of reset of EURIBOR on the notional leg is equal to the frequency of reset on the US$-LIBOR leg of the actual derivative. Taking **example 4.4.2B** above, the notional legs introduced are the Sterling fixed rate for a 5-year interest rate swap priced off the Sterling 5-year LIBOR curve. In both examples it would be unacceptable to impute notional legs which although could offset each other would introduce an unrelated risk, say equity prices or an unrelated currency.

If a single hedging instrument is designated as a hedge of more than one risk the hedge accounting criteria must be satisfied in respect of all the designated hedged risks. If the criteria are not met in respect of one of the risks being hedged no hedge accounting treatment is allowed for the period. If one designation fails to meet the effectiveness test or no longer exists, continuing hedge accounting would result in split accounting for the hedging instrument, treating one part as a hedge and the other as a trading instrument which is not allowed. (see **4.2** above)

4.5 Hedging with more than one derivative

Two or more offsetting derivatives, or proportions thereof, can be jointly designated as a hedging instrument if none of them are a written or net written option. [IAS 39.77] Further, when hedging foreign currency risk, two or more non-derivatives (or proportions) or a combination of non-derivatives and derivatives can be viewed in combination. Common situations where two or more offsetting derivatives are designated in combination as a hedging instrument are:

- where an entity issues fixed-rate debt, swaps the entirety of the debt instrument to floating, and then re-fixes some of the instrument's cash flows;
- where an entity uses a combination of long and short foreign currency forwards to hedge its net investments in a foreign operation (e.g. when it manages foreign currency risk on the net assets of the foreign operation where the value of those net assets changes on a frequent basis); and
- where an entity uses a combination of a basis swap and a floating to fixed interest rate swap in the instance where there is not enough liquidity directly to enter into a floating to fixed interest rate swap that has a floating leg that matches the specific risk of the hedged item

Example 4.5A

Hedging with multiple derivatives (1)

Entity A has a forecast purchase of copper. To hedge the price risk associated with the forecast purchase it enters into a futures contract to buy copper. However, the grade of copper in the futures contract is lower than that required by the entity. It therefore also enters into a basis swap which swaps between the different grades of copper between the futures contracts and the forecast purchase. Subject to the other hedge accounting criteria being satisfied, Entity A may jointly designate the futures and the basis swap as hedging its forecast purchase of copper.

Where a combination of derivatives, (or non-derivative instruments with respect to hedges of foreign currency risk only) is used as a hedging instrument, the hedge effectiveness of this relationship is based on the combination as a whole.

Example 4.5B

Hedging with multiple derivatives (2)

Entity X issues fixed-rate 10-year debt. At the same time, it enters into a receive-fixed, pay-floating interest rate swap whose terms exactly match those of the debt.

The swap was entered into as Entity X did not want to be exposed to changes in interest rates over the 10-year period of the debt. However, it would like to fix its cash flows for the next 12 months, so enters into a 1-year receive-floating, pay-fixed interest rate swap. Entity X has now re-fixed its cash flows for the first year of the debt.

Subject to the other hedge accounting criteria being satisfied, Entity X may designate both swaps as a partial term fair value hedge of interest rate risk for years 2 to 10 (even though the second swap partially offsets the effects of the first swap). Partial term hedging is discussed further in **3.8.2** above.

Example 4.5C

Hedging with derivatives and non-derivatives

Entity A, a UK entity, has a US subsidiary, Entity Z. Entity A hedges its net investment in Entity Z in its consolidated financial statements using forward foreign currency contracts and loans. It manages the net asset position quarterly, and as the net asset position changes, it enters into further forwards to sell US$ and buy £ that cover the increased exposure (if the US$ net asset position increases), or if the exposure decreases (if the US$ net asset position falls) the entity enters into forward contracts to sell £ and buy US$. In the latter case any sold US$ forwards will partially offset the purchased US$ forwards.

The loans and forwards may be viewed in combination and jointly designated as a hedge of the spot foreign currency risk of the net investment in Entity Z, even though some of the forward positions may offset each other. This is discussed further in net investment hedging in **2.3** above.

Example 4.5D

Hedging with multiple derivatives (3)

Entity C is a Euro functional currency entity. Entity C issues Mexican Peso floating rate debt. Entity C has a policy of swapping all floating rate debt into fixed and into its functional currency. Because of limited liquidity for Peso/Euro swaps, Entity C does not enter into a Receive Mexico Peso floating, Pay Euro fixed cross currency interest rate swap. Instead, Entity C enters into a Receive Mexico Peso floating, Pay US Dollar floating cross currency swap, and a Receive US Dollar floating, Pay Euro fixed cross currency interest rate swap, and designates these two swaps in combination as a cash flow hedge of both interest rates and foreign currency of its Mexican Peso floating debt.

Where an entity enters into two derivative transactions at the same time and in contemplation of each other with the same counterparty, so that the terms of the second derivative fully offset the terms of the first one, the two derivatives are viewed as one unit and cannot be used in separate hedge designations. [IAS 39.IG.B.6] This is commonly referred to as 'round-tripping'. However, where there is a substantive business purpose for structuring transactions separately, then the two derivatives are not viewed as one unit. Judgement is applied to determine whether there is a substantive business purpose. Achieving hedge accounting treatment with respect to one of the two derivative transactions is not by itself considered a substantive business purpose. [IAS 39.IG.F.1.14]

Example 4.5E

Roundtripping

[Extract from IAS 39.IG.F.1.14]

Some entities have a policy that requires a centralised dealer or treasury subsidiary to enter into third-party derivative contracts on behalf of other subsidiaries within the organisation to hedge the subsidiaries' interest rate risk exposures. The dealer or treasury subsidiary also enters into internal derivative transactions with those subsidiaries in order to track those hedges operationally within the organisation. Because the dealer or treasury subsidiary also enters into derivative contracts as part of its trading operations, or because it may wish to rebalance the risk of its overall portfolio, it may enter into a derivative contract with the same third party during the same business day that has substantially the same terms as a contract entered into as a hedging instrument on behalf of another subsidiary. In this case, there is a valid business purpose for entering into each contract.

4.5.1 *Hedging with a combination of a derivative and a non-derivative*

If an entity is hedging foreign currency risk it may designate a non-derivative as a hedging instrument. An entity can also designate a combination of derivatives or a combination of a derivative and a non-derivative in a hedge of foreign currency risk. If a combination of a derivative and a non-derivative is jointly designated as a hedge of foreign currency risk the derivative cannot be a written or a net written option. [IAS 39.77]

Example 4.5.1

Hedging with derivatives and non-derivatives

Parent A, a Sterling functional currency entity, has an investment in a Yen functional currency foreign operation. Parent A has US$100 million floating issued debt. Parent A also has a cross-currency swap to receive US$ floating over a notional of US$100 million, pay Yen floating over a fixed notional of Yen (equivalent to US$100 million on the trade date of the swap). Both the US$ debt and the cross-currency swap have the same maturity. The Yen notional on the swap is less than the net assets of the Yen foreign operation.

Group A can designate the US$ denominated debt and US$/Yen cross-currency swap jointly as a hedging instrument in hedging the £/Yen foreign currency risk of its net investment in its Yen foreign operation.

Even though the US$ debt and the US$/Yen swap have a shared risk, being US$, that offsets when the two instruments are used in combination, the non-derivative and the derivative may be designated in combination as a hedging instrument of foreign currency risk, being £/Yen foreign currency risk, as the swap is not a written or net written option. It is assumed all other hedge accounting criteria are met.

4.6 Written options and combinations of written options

4.6.1 Written options

The Standard does not allow a written option to be designated as a hedging instrument unless it is designated as an offset to a purchased option (including one that is embedded in another financial instrument). The written option is not effective in reducing the profit or loss exposure of a hedged item since the potential loss on an option that an entity writes could be significantly greater than the potential gain in value of a related hedged item. [IAS 39.AG94]

Example 4.6.1A

Hedging an available-for-sale asset with a written put

Entity A owns shares in Entity XYZ, an unrelated entity. It classifies these shares as available-for-sale. Entity A purchased the shares when the share price was £10. The share price is currently £15. Entity A writes an option over its shares in XYZ, allowing the purchaser of the option to acquire the shares for £17, and for this Entity A receives a premium of £0.50.

A may not designate the option as a hedge of its shares in XYZ because it is a written option.

All hedging instruments must be assessed to consider whether they contain a written option as this will often disqualify their designation as hedging instruments.

Example 4.6.1B

Embedded written options in interest rate swaps

Entity A issues twenty-year fixed rate debt. To hedge its fair value exposure to interest rate risk, it enters into a receive fixed, pay floating interest rate swap, such that all the terms of the swap match the debt. Owing to the long-term nature of the swap, the counterparty to the swap, the Bank, inserts a break clause into the swap giving the Bank the option to terminate the swap after ten years, so that on termination no cash will be exchanged. No cash is exchanged at the start of the transaction.

Entity A has effectively written an option to the bank allowing it to terminate the swap after ten years. While no cash was exchanged up-front, Entity A will have been recompensed for writing this option by receiving a favourable rate on one of the legs of the swap.

The swap cannot be designated as a hedge of the issued debt, as it contains a written option. The written option cannot be split out of the swap contract (leaving a vanilla twenty year interest swap) since a derivative must be designated as a hedging instrument in its entirety (with only two exceptions as described in **4.2** above).

If the terms of the break-clause resulted in termination of the swap at fair value at the time of termination, and fair value excluded any additional compensation paid/receivable to either party in excess of the interest rate swap, the swap would still contain a written option, but the value of the option would be zero. The legs of the swap would be no different from a swap without a break clause. In this case the swap could be used as a hedging instrument.

IAS 39.AG94 states that a written option can only be used as a hedging instrument where it is designated as an offset to a purchased option. The purchased option can be either a stand-alone derivative, or one embedded in another contract. Thus, a written option could be designated as hedging a callable liability where the issuer has the right to call the debt back early.

4.6.2 Net written options

If two options, one written and one purchased, are structured as a single instrument (for example as a collar), this instrument must be assessed to see whether overall it is a net written option.

Even where the critical terms and conditions of the written option component and the purchased option component are largely the same (e.g. underlying variable(s), currency denomination and maturity date are the same) a combination of written and purchased options is deemed to be net written (and therefore not allowed to be designated as a hedging instrument) if:

(i) a net premium is received, either at inception or over the life of the combination of options; or

(ii) the notional on the written option exceeds that on the purchased option. [IAS 39.IG.F.1.3]

Example 4.6.2

Hedging with a collar

Entity A issues £100 million variable rate debt. To hedge against interest rate increases, it purchases an interest rate collar at the date of issuance of the debt that hedges interest rates above 8 per cent and below 4 per cent. Current fixed interest rates for the same term as the debt are 6 per cent. The collar costs £0.5 million as forward rates indicate that interest rates are expected to rise over the term of the debt and therefore there is a greater likelihood that the purchased cap will be in the money, when compared to the written floor. The purchased cap at 8 per cent and written floor at 4 per cent included in the collar have the same notional of £100 million.

Entity A may designate the collar as a cash flow hedge of the variable rate debt, as there is no net premium received (there is a net premium payable of £0.5 million) and the notional on the floor does not exceed that on the cap.

If there was a premium received on the collar, it could not have been designated as a hedging instrument. Equally, if the notional on the floor was greater than £100 million, the collar could not have been designated as a hedging instrument.

It is not permissible to split a single instrument that consists of a number of options, for example an interest rate collar, and designate just the purchased option component as a hedging instrument. IAS 39.74 specifies that a derivative is designated as a hedging instrument in its entirety except when splitting the time value and intrinsic value of an option and splitting the interest element and spot price on a forward. [IAS 39.IG.F.1.8]

As is the case for all hedging instruments, in order for a combination of interest rate options structured as a single instrument to qualify as a hedging instrument, the combination of options must be expected to be highly effective in achieving offsetting changes in fair value or cash flows attributable to the hedged risk.

4.6.3 *Combination of derivatives that includes a written option*

Only a combination of separate contractual derivatives that does not include a written or a net written option can be designated as a single qualifying hedging instrument. [IAS 39.77]

When an entity enters into purchased and sold options at the same time it is necessary to consider by analogy to the following indicators contained in IAS 39.IG.B.6, whether the two options are separate instruments or the combination of the two options is in substance a single arrangement. Factors that indicate that the instrument is a single arrangement are:

- they are entered into at the same time and in contemplation of one another;
- they have the same counterparty;

- they relate to the same risk; and
- there is no apparent economic need or substantive business purpose for structuring the transactions separately that could not also have been accomplished in a single transaction.

If the combination of options is not considered to be one arrangement, and one of the instruments is a written option or net written option, the combination of options cannot be designated as a hedging instrument.

However, a combination of options structured as a single instrument (that may economically be equivalent to options in a combination of contractually separate instruments) qualifies for designation as a hedging instrument as long as the single instrument is not a net written option as described in **4.6** above. This is the case for a zero cost collar that combines a purchased option and a written option and passes the test of not being a net written option overall.

4.7 Purchased options

Unlike written options, a purchased option may be designated as a hedging instrument, provided all the other criteria for hedge accounting are met. This is because a purchased option has a potential gain equal to or greater than the loss on a hedged item and therefore has the potential to reduce profit or loss exposure from changes in fair values or cash flows. [IAS 39.AG94]

Example 4.7A

Hedging an available-for-sale asset with a purchased put

Entity XYZ owns 1,000 shares of Entity ABC which are publicly traded, and has classified the shares as available-for-sale. At 1 January 20X0, these shares are trading at £50 per share and Entity XYZ has an unrealised gain of £25,000 recognised in other comprehensive income. XYZ would like to lock in the unrealised gain and purchases a put option on Entity ABC's shares from Entity A for £9,000. The purchased put option allows Entity XYZ to put the 1,000 shares to Entity A at £50 per share on 31 December 20X2. Subject to the other hedge accounting criteria being met, the purchased put option may be designated as a hedge of the exposure to the decline in the fair value of the investment in ABC shares below £50 per share.

In order to demonstrate the hedge will be highly effective Entity XYZ designates just the intrinsic value of the purchased put as a hedging instrument so when the fair value of the shares falls below £50 the option will be fully effective. When the share price rises above £50 per share the put option is out of the money and has no intrinsic value. Accordingly, gains and losses on the 1,000 shares in Entity ABC above £50 are not attributable to the hedged risk for the purposes of assessing hedge effectiveness and recognising gains and losses on the hedged item.

Entity XYZ reports a change in the fair value of the shares in other comprehensive income if it is associated with the price increases above £50. [IAS 39.55 & 90] Changes in the fair value of the shares associated with price decreases below £50 form part of the designated fair value hedge and are recognised in profit or loss under IAS 39.89(b). Assuming the hedge is effective, those changes are offset by changes in the intrinsic value of the put, which are also recognised in profit or loss. [IAS 39.89(a)] Changes in the time value of the put are excluded from the designated hedge relationship and recognised in profit or loss under IAS 39.55(a). Changes in the intrinsic value of the put provide protection against the changes in the fair value of the investment in ABC shares below £50 per share. [IAS 39.IG.F.1.10]

Example 4.7B

Hedging variable-rate debt with a purchased interest rate cap (1)

On 4 January 20X0, Entity X issued a 5-year US$100 million variable-rate bond. The bond pays interest based on LIBOR plus a spread of 200 basis points on an annual basis, reset on December 31 (i.e. is reset in arrears). Entity X wants to hedge against increases in interest rates by capping the maximum interest rate at 9 per cent (LIBOR of 7.00 per cent + 2.00 per cent spread). Entity X purchased an interest rate cap that is indexed to LIBOR with a US$100 million notional amount. The cap pays Entity X the difference between 7 per cent and LIBOR if LIBOR rises above 7 per cent. The interest rate cap (intrinsic value only) is designated as a cash flow hedge of the variable-rate debt. The terms of the cap are as follows:

Notional amount	US$100 million
Trade date	04/01/X0
Start date	04/01/X0
Expiration date	31/12/X4
Strike price	7.00 per cent
Index	12 month LIBOR
Initial LIBOR	5.56 per cent
Premium	US$1.44 million
Caplet expirations	31 December 20X0, 20X1, 20X2 and 20X3

The payments on each caplet are made at expiration. For example, the caplet that expires on 31 December 20X0 will be paid, if applicable, on that date. The fair value of the cap throughout the term of the cap is summarised below:

Date	LIBOR	Cap rate	Fair value of cap	Intrinsic value of cap (1)	Time value of cap	Cap cash payments
4 January 20X0	5.56 per cent	7.00 per cent	1,440,000	$ —	$1,440,000	$ —

Date	LIBOR	Cap rate	Fair value of cap	Intrinsic value of cap (1)	Time value of cap	Cap cash payments
31 December 20X0	5.00	7.00	1,000,000	—	1,000,000	—
31 December 20X1	5.50	7.00	850,000	—	850,000	—
31December 20X2	7.50	7.00	1,500,000	895,000	605,000	500,000
31 December 20X3	8.00	7.00	1,000,000	1,000,000	—	1,000,000

(1) Intrinsic fair value is computed on a discounted basis.

The following entries are required:

4 January 20X0

Dr	Cash	US$100,000,000
Cr	Debt	US$100,000,000

To record the issuance of debt.

Dr	Option asset	US$1,440,000
Cr	Cash	US$1,440,000

To record the purchase of the interest rate cap.

31 December 20X0

Dr	Interest expense	US$7,000,000
Cr	Cash	US$7,000,000

To record the interest expense (LIBOR at reset plus 200 basis points (5.00 per cent + 2.00 per cent)) on the US$100m principal amount.

Dr	Derivative loss	US$440,000
Cr	Option asset	US$440,000

To record the cap option asset at fair value with changes in time value recognised in income (there was no intrinsic value to record).

31 December 20X1

Dr	Interest expense	US$7,500,000
Cr	Cash	US$7,500,000

To record the interest expense (LIBOR at reset plus 200 basis points (5.50 per cent + 2.00 per cent)) on the US$100m principal amount.

Dr	Derivative loss	US$150,000
Cr	Option asset	US$150,000

To record the cap option asset at fair value with changes in time value recognised in income (there was no intrinsic value to record).

31 December 20X2

Dr	Interest expense	US$9,500,000
Cr	Cash	US$9,500,000

To record the interest expense (LIBOR at reset plus 200 basis points (7.50 per cent + 2.00 per cent)) on the US$100 m principal amount.

Dr	Option asset	US$650,000
Dr	Derivative loss	US$245,000
Cr	Other comprehensive income	US$1,395,000

Dr	Other comprehensive income	US$500,000
Dr	Cash	US$500,000
Cr	Interest expense	US$500,000

To record the cap option asset at fair value with changes in time value recognised in income, changes in intrinsic value recognised in other comprehensive income and reclassification of amounts in other comprehensive income to profit or loss. The receipt under the interest-rate cap ((7.50 per cent LIBOR – 7.00 per cent cap rate) × 100 million) results in an interest expense of 9.00 per cent.

31 December 20X3

Dr	Interest expense	US$10,000,000
Cr	Cash	US$10,000,000

To record the interest expense (LIBOR at reset plus 200 basis points (8.00 per cent + 2.00 per cent)) on the US$100m principal amount.

Dr	Derivative loss	US$605,000
Cr	Other comprehensive income	US$105,000
Cr	Option asset	US$1,500,000
Dr	Other comprehensive income	US$1,000,000
Dr	Cash	US$1,000,000
Cr	Interest expense	US$1,000,000

To record the cap option asset at fair value with changes in time value recognised in income, changes in intrinsic value recognised in other comprehensive income and reclassification of amounts in other comprehensive income to profit or loss. The receipt under the interest-rate cap ((8.00 per cent LIBOR – 7.00 per cent cap rate) × 100 million) results in an interest expense of 9.00 per cent.

When designating an option in a cash flow hedge accounting relationship it is common to designate just the intrinsic value of the option as permitted by IAS 39.74(a) and not designate the time value of the option. This approach ensures that when the option is 'in-the-money' the option is fully effective at hedging the variability in cash flows of the hedged item. As the time value of the option is not designated as part of the hedge relationship the gains/losses relating to time value are immediately recognised in profit or loss. These gains/losses are not considered hedge ineffectiveness as time value did not form part of the hedge accounting relationship. Had an entity chosen instead to designate the entirety of the option, the fair value gains/losses that result from changes in time value would cause hedge ineffectiveness, perhaps to such a great degree that the entity could not claim that the hedge is expected to be highly effective.

In July 2008 the IASB issued an amendment to IAS 39 titled *Eligible hedged items*. The amendment clarified that a purchased (or net purchased) option can be designated as a hedging instrument in a hedge of a financial or non-financial item. An entity may designate an option as a hedge of changes in the cash flows or fair value of a hedged item above or below a specified price or other variable (a one-sided risk). The amendments make clear that the intrinsic value, not the time value, of an option reflects a one-sided risk and therefore an option designated in its entirety cannot be perfectly effective. The time value of a purchased option is not a component of the forecast transaction that impacts profit or loss. Therefore, if an entity designates an option in its entirety as a hedge of a one-sided risk arising from a forecast transaction hedge ineffectiveness will arise. Alternatively, an entity may choose to exclude time value as permitted by the Standard in order to improve hedge effectiveness. As a result of this designation, changes in the time value of the option will be recognised immediately in profit or loss.

If a purchased option or net purchased option is in-the-money at the date of designation and the entity excludes time value from the hedge relationship a question arises as to whether the intrinsic value that exists at the date of designation is itself effective at hedging future cash flows in a cash flow hedge. As the objective of a cash flow hedge is to hedge against future changes in cash flow variability and any intrinsic value that exists at the date of designation does not itself hedge this future variability then in determining hedge effectiveness in this case an entity should compare the actual in-the-money option with an at-the-money option in determining the future change in intrinsic value that should be recognised in other comprehensive income. Only future changes in intrinsic value that result in the at-the-money option being in the money in future periods are deemed effective and therefore can be recognised in other comprehensive income. This can be illustrated in the example below.

Example 4.7C

Hedging variable-rate debt with a purchased interest rate cap (2)

Entity B has a purchased European-style cap at 6% that matures in 6 months that has a notional of £100m that corresponds with issued variable rate debt with the same notional that has a variable interest reset date also in 6 months time. Entity B wishes to designate the intrinsic value of the option as a hedge of future cash flow variability on its variable rate debt for the next 6 months with respect to changes in interest rates.

At the date of designation current interest rates are 8% and therefore the option is in-the-money. It is assumed for illustrative purposes the interest rate curve is flat and therefore both current and forward rates are 8%. The intrinsic value would be equal to (8%-6%) x £100m discounted for 6 months. The fair value of the purchased cap with respect to intrinsic value will be included in the overall fair value of the derivative asset at the date of designation. At the date of designation the fair value of the intrinsic value is

£2m (for illustration purposes only discounting has been ignored throughout this example and fair value movements in time value are excluded as these gains/losses will always immediately be recognised in profit or loss as they are excluded from the hedge designation).

The date of designation is 1 October 20X9 and the reporting period end is 31 December 20X9. At the reporting period end four scenarios could arise.

Scenario 1 – interest rates rise (to 9%)

The option is further in-the-money.

Dr	Derivative asset	£1m
Cr	Other comprehensive income – cash flow hedge reserve	£1m

The option is fully effective at hedging increases in interest rates. In this case increases in interest rates of 1% would result in the at-the-money option being in-the-money by £1m.

Scenario 2 – interest remain the same (at 8%)

The option remains in-the-money by the same degree as at the date of designation.

No entries are required as intrinsic value has remained the same as there has been no increase or decrease in interest rates. In this case as there is no change in interest rates an at-the-money option would continue to be at-the-money.

Scenario 3 – interest rates fall but remain above the cap (to 7%)

The option remains in-the-money but by a lesser amount.

Dr	Profit or loss	£1m
Cr	Derivative asset	£1m

The purchased cap is not effective at hedging changes in interest rates in the instance when interest rates fall below the level that existed when the option was designated. £1m cannot be recognised in other comprehensive income as the option is not effective in the period in hedging future variability in interest rates. In this case a fall in interest rates for an at-the-money option would result in the option being out-of-the-money and therefore no intrinsic value could be recognised in other comprehensive income.

Scenario 4 – interest rates fall below the cap (to 5%)

The option is out of the money.

Dr	Profit or loss	£2m
Cr	Derivative asset	£2m

The purchased cap is not effective at hedging changes in interest rates in the instance when interest rates fall below the level that existed when the option was designated. £2m cannot be recognised in other comprehensive income as the option is not effective in the period in hedging future variability in interest rates. In this case a fall in interest rates for an at-the-money option would result in the option being out-of-the-money and therefore no intrinsic value could be recognised in other comprehensive income. In this instance the actual option is out-of-the-money so all intrinsic value that was recognised as an asset in the statement of financial position at the date of designation is recognised in profit or loss in the period.

If Scenario 1 occurred in the first quarter, but in the second quarter interest rates fell below the level of the cap then the amount recognised in the cash flow hedge reserve in the first quarter will be reversed through the cash flow hedge reserve until the cash flow hedge reserve is nil, and any excess is recognised in profit or loss.

If Scenario 4 occurred in the first quarter, but in the second quarter interest rates rose above the level of the cap then the amount recognised in profit or loss in the first quarter will be reversed in the second quarter in profit or loss. Any increase in intrinsic value above £2m (being the intrinsic value at the date of designation) will be recognised in other comprehensive income.

4.8 Investments in unquoted equity

Investments in unquoted equity that are carried at cost (because their fair value cannot be reliably measured) and derivatives that are linked to and must be settled by delivery of such an unquoted equity instrument, cannot be designated as hedging instruments. [IAS 39.AG96]

This is because a hedging instrument is defined as a designated financial instrument whose fair value or cash flows are expected to offset changes in the fair value or cash flows of a designated hedged item. However, if the instrument is carried at cost because it is not possible to reliably measure it, then there can be no expectation that its change in fair value or cash flows will offset those of the hedged item.

Any derivative, other than one that is linked to and will result in the delivery of an unquoted equity investment, is considered to be measurable with sufficient reliability. Therefore, an entity may designate any derivative as a hedging instrument, assuming all other qualifying criteria are met, even though the derivative's valuation may use a significant amount of unobservable data. However, significant judgement will need to be exercised in these circumstances when assessing hedge effectiveness, determining the gain/loss attributed to the hedged risk for the hedged item in a fair value hedge (pursuant to IAS 39.89(b)), and for cash flow hedges determining the cumulative change in fair value of the expected future cash flows on the hedged item from inception of the hedge.

4.9 Dynamic hedging strategies

IAS 39.74 states that 'a dynamic hedging strategy that assesses both the intrinsic value and time value of an option contract can qualify for hedge accounting', i.e. the standard permits an entity to apply hedge accounting for a 'delta-neutral' or other dynamic hedging strategy under which the quantity of the hedging instrument is constantly adjusted in order to maintain a desired hedge ratio. For example, an entity may wish to achieve a delta-neutral position insensitive to changes in the fair value of the hedged item.

Example 4.9

Delta-neutral hedging

An entity hedges the fair value of an equity security by using a combination of purchased options that aims to achieve a delta-neutral position. As the delta of the options changes, the number of options required will change to ensure the hedge is considered to be highly effective for movements in the fair value of the equity securities. This strategy can qualify for hedge accounting.

To qualify for hedge accounting, all the usual conditions must be met. These will include documenting how effectiveness will be assessed and measured, and demonstrating an ability to track properly all terminations and re-designations of the hedging instrument. Also, the entity must be able to demonstrate an expectation that the hedge will be highly effective for any specified short period of time during which the hedge is not expected to be adjusted. [IAS 39.IG.F.1.9]

4.10 'All-in-one' hedges

A derivative instrument within the scope of IAS 39 that will be settled by physical delivery of an underlying asset at a fixed price can be designated as the hedging instrument in a cash flow hedge of that gross settlement. Without the derivative there would be an exposure to variability in the purchase or sale price. The derivative eliminates this exposure, i.e. it acts as a hedging instrument. [IAS 39.IG.F.2.5] This hedge strategy is suitable when the underlying hedged item, when it is recognised, will not subsequently be measured at fair value.

The rationale for allowing hedge accounting for 'all-in-one' hedges is that an entity should not be disadvantaged from not achieving hedge accounting if a transaction is structured as a single instrument or as a combination of two transactions. Consider the following example:

Entity A normally sells products at variable prices. Entity A could concurrently enter into derivative transactions to fix the price of its forecast sales. Derivative instruments would be recognised at fair value with gains or losses recorded in profit or loss, unless hedge accounting is applied. Assuming the sales are highly probable and cash flow hedge accounting is applied, Entity A would recognise the gains and losses on its hedging instruments in other comprehensive income and reclassify them from equity to profit or loss when the sales occur.

Entity A now decides that it is no longer going to sell its products at variable prices and swap them back into fixed prices via derivatives, but instead is going to fix the sales price today directly with the customer. If the fixed price contract with the customer fell within the scope of IAS 39 it will be recognised at fair value with gains and losses recognised in profit or loss. By applying an all-in-one hedge accounting strategy, Entity A can obtain the same accounting treatment (i.e. recognise gains and losses on the derivative in other comprehensive income until the sale occurs under cash flow hedging), as had been the case in the former scenario where hedge accounting was applied to the derivative and the forecast sale separately.

Example 4.10A

All-in-one hedge of a non-financial item

An entity enters into a fixed price contract to sell a commodity and that contract is accounted for as a derivative under IAS 39. (This may be because the entity has a practice of settling similar contracts net in cash or taking delivery of the underlying and selling it within a short period after delivery for the purpose of generating a profit from short-term fluctuations in price or dealer's margin.) The entity may designate the fixed price contract as a cash flow hedge of the variability of the consideration to be received on the sale of the asset (a future transaction) even though the fixed price contract is the contract under which the asset will be sold.

Example 4.10B

All-in-one hedge of a debt instrument

An entity enters into a forward contract to purchase a debt instrument that will be settled by physical delivery of the debt instrument. The forward contract is a derivative in the scope of IAS 39 because its term exceeds the regular way delivery period in the marketplace. The entity may designate the forward as a cash flow hedge of the variability of the consideration to be paid to acquire the debt instrument (a forecast transaction), even though the derivative is the contract under which the debt instrument will be acquired.

Example 4.10C

All-in-one hedge of an equity instrument

Entity P, a US$ functional currency entity, enters into a forward contract to buy an equity share of Entity XYZ in 6 months' time at $10. The current share price of Entity XYZ is $10. At maturity of the forward contract the share price is $15 and therefore the forward contract has a positive fair value at maturity of $5.

Entity P cannot designate the forward as an all-in-one hedge of the future acquisition of a share in Entity XYZ in 6 months' time if Entity P intends to classify the share as at fair value through profit or loss, either because it is designated as such, or Entity P intends to sell the share in the short-term after initial recognition and therefore would meet the definition of held for trading. If the share is measured as at fair value through profit or loss there is no systematic basis in which the hedged risk impacts profit or loss and therefore Entity P cannot determine how the amount recognised in other comprehensive income can be reclassified from equity to profit or loss.

To illustrate why the forward cannot be designated in an all-in-one hedge consider the accounting entries that would result if cash flow hedging was applied: (i) at initial recognition of the equity security there would be a gain of $5 in other comprehensive income that would require reclassification from equity to profit or loss when the hedged risk of the hedged item impacts profit or loss, and (ii) the shares will be recognised at fair value, being $15 (Dr Shares $15, Cr Cash $10, Cr Derivative asset $5). If the share price rose or fell and thus affected profit or loss, there would be no basis for determining how much of the gain recognised in other comprehensive income should be reclassified. If the equity security was classified as an available-for-sale asset on initial recognition the amount recognised in other comprehensive income as a cash flow hedge would be reclassified from equity to profit or loss when the equity security was disposed of, or earlier if the security is impaired.

4.11 Internal hedges

In a group that has a central treasury function a group entity or division that wishes to enter into hedging transactions uses their central treasury function rather than using an external group counterparty. The central treasury function then aggregates all its internal positions and enters into external transactions to offset the internal ones on a net basis thereby taking advantage of any natural offsets and hedging the exposures of the group in a cost efficient way.

At a group level, if the central treasury function enters into external derivatives these can be used as hedging instruments, but only as a hedge of a gross position. As discussed in **3.12** above, a net position cannot be a hedged item. Therefore, even though the external derivative was entered into to offset a net position, it can be used as a hedging instrument but only if it is designated as hedging (a portion of) a gross position.

Example 4.11A

Hedging an external gross position (1)

Entity A has a central treasury division. The central treasury division aggregates the internal derivative contracts with other group entities, and enters into external derivatives that offset the internal derivatives on a net basis.

Central treasury has three internal receive-fixed, pay-variable interest rate swaps and one internal receive-variable, pay-fixed interest rate swap. It enters into an interest rate swap with an external counterparty that exactly offsets the four internal swaps as follows:

Swap	Counterparty	Description	Notional
1	Internal	Receive-fixed, pay-variable	£100 million
2	Internal	Receive-fixed, pay-variable	£60 million
3	Internal	Receive-fixed, pay-variable	£30 million
4	Internal	Receive-variable, pay-fixed	£150 million
5	External	Receive-variable, pay-fixed	£40 million

Swap 5 cannot hedge an overall net position, i.e. it cannot be used to hedge all of the items that the internal derivatives 1–4 are hedging. IAS 39 states that an overall net position cannot qualify as a hedged item.

However, Swap 5 can qualify as a hedging instrument in a hedge of the underlying hedged items residing in the group companies on a gross basis, i.e. it could hedge US$40 million of fixed rate assets or US$40 million of variable rate liabilities.

IAS 39.IG.F.1.4 gives further guidance on the use of internal derivatives. The guidance derives from the principles of preparing consolidated financial statements in IAS 27 *Consolidated and Separate Financial Statements*, which require that 'intragroup balances, transactions, income and expenses shall be eliminated in full'. [IAS 27(2008).20, previously IAS 27(2003).24]

Only a derivative that is external to the reporting entity, i.e. external to the group or individual entity that is being reported, can be designated as a hedging instrument. In the consolidated financial statements intragroup derivatives cannot be hedging instruments as these are not external to the reporting entity and eliminate on consolidation. However, they may be used in the entity only financial statements since from that entity's perspective such derivatives are with a third party. [IAS 39.73]

Example 4.11B

Hedge accounting in the group versus entity only financial statements

Entity A has a 100 per cent subsidiary, Entity B. The group treasury policy requires that only Entity A enters into derivatives with external parties. If Entity B wishes to enter into a foreign currency forward it notifies Entity A. Entity A enters into a forward with a bank (forward 1), and then enters into an equal and opposite forward contract with Entity B (forward 2).

From a consolidated perspective, only the forward contract with the bank, forward 1, can be a designated hedging instrument. In Entity B's entity only financial statements, forward 2 may be designated as a hedging instrument. This would be true even if Entity A had not entered into forward 1 with the bank.

In Entity A's entity only financial statements there will be two equal and opposite derivatives. These must be presented separately in its statement of financial position. They cannot be offset as they do not meet the offset requirements of IAS 32 (see **section 4** in **chapter 21**).

Entities sometimes enter into netting agreements with a bank such that derivatives held with that bank are settled on a net basis. This does not in itself preclude those instruments being designated as hedging instruments. [IAS 39.IG.F.2.16]

Example 4.11C

Hedging an external gross position (2)

Entity A has several subsidiaries. Entity A acts as a central treasury function, so that if any subsidiary wants to lay off risk it must do so with Entity A. For each internal derivative Entity A enters into an equal and opposite external contract with a bank. Thus, if it has a 3-year pay 6 per cent receive LIBOR interest rate swap with a subsidiary, it will enter into a 3-year receive 6 per cent pay LIBOR interest rate swap with a bank, such that all of the terms of the two contracts match. Each internal derivative is hedging a gross exposure.

The external derivatives can be designated as hedging instruments of the underlying gross exposures in the group's consolidated financial statements. This is true even if the external derivatives are settled on a net basis. Provided the contracts are legally separate and serve a valid business purpose (such as laying off risk exposures on underlying gross positions) they qualify as hedging instruments.

Entities sometimes have external positions that offset each other. This can arise (as in the above example) because there is a policy of hedging every exposure separately (i.e. gross), or because an entity wishes to manage its external portfolio in a certain way.

Example 4.11D

Hedging an external gross position (3)

Continuing with **example 4.11C**, assume Entity A manages the portfolio of offsetting external derivatives separately from other exposures of the entity and enters into an additional, single derivative to offset the risk of the portfolio.

The individual external derivative contracts in the portfolio can still be designated as hedging instruments of the underlying gross exposures even though a single external derivative is used to offset fully the market exposure created by entering into these external contracts.

The purpose of structuring the external derivative contracts in this manner is consistent with the entity's risk management objectives and strategies. As noted in **4.5** above, external derivative contracts that are structured separately and serve a valid business purpose qualify as hedging instruments. [IAS 39.IG.F.2.16]

Detailed guidance on achieving hedge accounting in the group consolidated financial statements where a central treasury function exists, is provided in the Implementation Guidance of IAS 39. Specifically, IAS 39.IG.F.1.5 provides guidance on offsetting internal derivative contracts used to manage interest rate risk, and IAS 39.IG.F.1.6 and IAS 39.IG.F.1.7 provide guidance on offsetting internal derivative contracts used to manage foreign exchange risk.

4.12 Rollover hedging strategies

A combination of more than one derivative or a derivative and a non-derivative may be used in 'rollover' hedging strategies when applying cash flow hedge accounting. IAS 39 envisages hedging strategies may include the replacement or rollover of one hedging instrument into another as they are referred to in IAS 39.101(a): an entity shall discontinue prospectively hedge accounting when "the hedging instrument expires or is sold, terminated or exercised (for this purpose, the replacement or rollover of a hedging instrument into another hedging instrument is not an expiration or termination if such replacement or rollover is part of the entity's documented hedging strategy)" (see **2.2.4** above).

The benefit of a rollover strategy is that derivatives that have a maturity shorter than the timing of the underlying exposure of the hedged item can be designated as part of a rollover strategy as a hedge of that long-dated exposure. Where the hedged item is a financial instrument this technique offers no advantage as an entity could instead apply partial term hedging, i.e. hedge a risk of the hedged item for part of its life (see **3.8.2** above), but for hedges of non-financial items it is beneficial as for non-financial items an entity can only hedge foreign currency risk or all risk in its entirety, i.e. it is not possible to apply partial term hedging.

The following example illustrates how a rollover hedging strategy can be applied in a cash flow hedge relationship.

Example 4.12

Rollover strategies

On 1 January 20X1, Entity A, a £ functional currency, determines with high probability that it will have US$10m worth of sales on 30 September 20X1. Entity A enters into short dated forward contracts as part of a rollover strategy in order to hedge the US$:£ risk on its highly probable US$ sales.

On 1 January 20X1 Entity A enters into a 6-month forward contract (F1) to sell US$10m and buy £ which is intended to rollover into a new 3-month US$:£ forward contract (F2), also with a notional of US$10m, to coincide with the timing of the highly probable sales.

Entity A could designate the hedge relationship in one of two ways:

Designation 1

Designate the US$:£ foreign currency *spot* rate risk relating to the first US$10m of highly probable sales due to occur on 30 September 20X1 with the hedging instrument being the original forward contract (F1) recognised in the statement of financial position at the date of designation and rolled over into a new forward contract (F2) as part of the entity's hedging strategy.

In determining hedge effectiveness (see **5** below for detail), the hypothetical derivative will be the spot element of an on-market forward contract for US$:£ that is entered into on 1 January 20X1 and matures on 30 September 20X1. The forward points will be excluded from the fair value of the hypothetical derivative as it does not form part of the hedge relationship. The hypothetical derivative has a maturity date of 30 September 20X1 to coincide with the timing of the forecast transaction.

This designation will not be perfectly effective for a hedge of spot rates as there will be some ineffectiveness in the first six months as the fair value of the spot element of F1 will be discounted from 30 June 20X1, whereas the fair value of the hypothetical derivative will be discounted from 30 September 20X1. In the second period there will be no additional ineffectiveness due to discounting as both F2 and the hypothetical derivative terminate on the same date. Changes in the fair value of the forward points of the derivatives, F1 in the first period and F2 in the second period, will be immediately recorded in profit or loss as forward points do not form part of the hedge relationship.

Designation 2

Designate the US$:£ foreign currency *forward* rate risk relating to the first US$10m of highly probable sales due to occur on 30 September 20X1 with the hedging instrument being the original forward contract (F1) recognised in the statement of financial position at the date of designation and rolled over into a new forward contract (F2) as part of the entity's hedging strategy.

In determining hedge effectiveness, the hypothetical derivative will be a forward contract for US$:£ that is entered into on 1 January 20X1 and matures on 30 September 20X1 when the forecast transaction is expected to occur.

As the forward points form part of the hedge relationship the fair value of this hypothetical derivative will be compared with the fair value of the hedging instrument. Forward points in this case are not excluded from the hedge designation as Entity A is hedging the forward foreign currency exchange rate.

The effectiveness of the hedging relationship will be evaluated by comparing the cumulative change in the present value of the hedged item's cash flows due to the hedged risk (being the *forward* foreign currency exposure), which will equal the hypothetical derivative, with the fair value of the hedging instrument. This hedge will not be perfectly effective. Like in Designation 1, the differing maturities of F1 and the hypothetical derivative in the first period will be a source of ineffectiveness. In addition, the forward rate that is locked into in F1 will differ from the forward rate implicit in the hypothetical derivative which will be a further source of ineffectiveness.

If F1 is rolled over into a non-derivative financial instrument, a liability to deliver US$10m on 30 September 20X1, Entity A could apply the following designation:

Rollover of a derivative to a non-derivative

Assume the first derivative, F1, is gross cash settled (gross exchange of US$ and £) and Entity A borrows US$ at 30 June 20X1 in order to deliver under the gross cash settled derivative, F1, and the borrowing matures on 30 September 20X1. Entity A could intend to designate the anticipated rollover of derivative, F1, into a non-derivative, the US$ borrowing, as a hedging instrument of the US$:£ foreign currency *spot* rate relating to the first US10$m of highly probably sales due to occur on 30 September 20X1. Entity A can only designate the *spot* US$:£ rate, not the *forward* US$:£ rate, as the liability is only subject to spot retranslation under IAS 21. The same level of ineffectiveness would result as per Designation 1.

4.13 Forwards versus futures

Forward contracts and futures contracts share similar characteristics in that both contracts result in the exchange of a specified amount of cash or other financial asset for an underlying at a specific future date. The terms of a forward contract are negotiable as the two parties will agree the notional, forward price, maturity date, etc, subject to their specific needs. Futures are traded via a third party futures exchange which acts as an intermediary between two parties in a contract. The futures contract is normally standardised in size and over one of the pre-established underlyings (in the case of non-financial items, one of the pre-established grades and locations). A party to the futures contract will generally cash settle the market value of the futures contract on a regular basis, usually daily, with the futures exchange. Assuming the futures exchange has a buyer and a seller of equivalent futures contracts, the daily cash settlements will be paid to the futures exchange by one party and paid by the future exchange to the other party. These daily settlements are referred to as variation margin. In addition, the future exchange will also require the posting of collateral with the future exchange at inception, referred to as initial margin, to reduce the counterparty credit risk in the case where a party owes the futures exchange but fails to pay.

For the purposes of hedge accounting, the most significant difference between forwards and futures is the regular settlement of the fair value of futures contracts with the futures exchange which results in futures having a different fair value to a comparable forward contract with the same underlying, maturity and specified price for the underlying. To determine the fair value of the forward contract the cash flows will be discounted because the cash flows will occur at a future date, whereas the futures contract will not be discounted as the cash flows (being the settlements of the daily fair value movements) are occurring every day. The difference in fair value between a forward and a future will result in these instruments having different degrees of hedge effectiveness. Whether forwards or futures are more effective for hedge accounting depends on the individual circumstances and the hedge designation.

Example 4.13

Forwards versus futures

Entity P has an investment in Entity W which is classified as available-for-sale equity security. Entity P is considering entering into one of two contracts described below to hedge the available-for-sale equity security. Entity P believes it is highly probable that it will sell the investment in Entity W in six months' time, being the end of June 20X9. Assume that the forward price of the available-for-sale security is equal to the spot price at the start of January 20X9 when the hedging instrument will be entered into.

Entity P is considering the following two contracts:

- A forward contract to sell the available-for-sale equity security in six months' time for a fixed amount, equal to the spot price when the forward is entered into. The instrument is net cash settled with all cash flows settled at maturity of the contract.
- A futures contract to sell the available-for-sale equity security in six months' time for a fixed amount, equal to the spot price when the future is entered into. Entity P provides an initial margin to the futures

> exchange and pays/receives a daily variation margin equal to the fair value movements in the futures contract. The initial margin is deemed to be a collateral for the futures contract in accordance with IAS 39.IG.B.10 and therefore does not impact the fair value of the futures contracts as it is a separate financial asset. The daily settlement of daily variation margin is not a collateral and is deemed to be daily settlement of the futures contract.

Entity P considers designating one of these hedging instruments in a fair value hedge of the available-for-sale equity security.

If Entity P enters into the forward contract the hedge will not be perfectly effective as the change in fair value of the forward contract will not equal the change in fair value of the available-for-sale equity security. The difference is due to the discounting of the fair value of the forward as settlement is not due until six months' time, whereas the fair value movements of the available-for-sale equity security are not discounted as they are recognised as they arise.

If Entity P enters into the futures contract the hedge will be perfectly effective (all other things being equal) as the change in fair value of the futures contract will equal the change in fair value of the available-for-sale equity security. The futures contract is not discounted as there is daily settlement equal to the change in its fair value which is equal to the recognised gains/losses on the available-for-sale equity security.

For this designation the future is more effective than the forward for a given period.

If a forward contract is used Entity P could improve hedge effectiveness by designating a proportion, i.e. a percentage, of the equity security. The proportion of the equity security hedged would be equal to the fair value of the security at inception of the hedge discounted for 6 months. As the effect of discounting reduces over the life of the forward contract the hedge designation would need to be adjusted continuously by increasing the proportion the equity hedged.

Entity P considers designating one of these hedging instruments in a cash flow hedge of the forecast sale of the available-for-sale equity security in six months' time.

If Entity P enters into the forward contract the hedge will be perfectly effective (all other things being equal) as the cumulative change in fair value of the forward contract is expected to equal the cumulative change in fair value of the expected future cash flow on the hedged item. This is because the forward contract and the forecast transaction occur on the same date in the future and therefore are discounted by the same factor.

If Entity P enters into the futures contract the hedge will not be perfectly effective as the cumulative change in fair value of the futures contract is not expected to equal the cumulative change in fair value of the expected future cash flow on the hedged item. The futures contract is not discounted whereas the cash flow on the forecast transaction is when calculating the expected hedge effectiveness. The futures contract will 'over-hedge' the forecast transaction as it is expected to generate more gains/losses than the hedged item.

For this designation the forward is more effective than the future for a given period.

The technique described in the above example is often applied in practice when hedging forecast transactions with futures. It involves entering into futures contracts with a lower notional (or less futures contracts) compared with that of the hedged item. For a given notional the futures contract will have a larger fair value movement than the forecast transaction, so this technique attempts to ensure that the fair value movements of the futures contracts (which are undiscounted) match the fair value movements in the fair value of the forecast cash flows (which are discounted). The effect of discounting which is greater at the start of the hedge and all other things being equal reduces over time as the timing of the forecast transaction gets nearer. Adjusting the size of the notional of the futures to compensate for these differences is known as "tailing" the futures hedge. This technique improves hedge effectiveness, and may also be applied for economic reasons as the benefit of a lower notional offsets the downside of financing the variation margin receipts and payments.

5 Hedge effectiveness

IAS 39 requires a hedge to be 'highly effective', prospectively and retrospectively, for it to qualify for hedge accounting. [IAS 39.88] Any ineffectiveness is required to be measured and recorded immediately in profit or loss.

The Standard does not prescribe a specific method for assessing effectiveness. [IAS 39.AG107] However, it requires an entity to specify at inception of the hedge relationship the method it will apply to assess effectiveness, and to apply that method consistently for the duration of the hedging relationship. The method specified must be consistent with management's risk management strategy and objective. A method of assessing effectiveness must be applied consistently to all similar hedges unless different methods are explicitly justified. [IAS 39.IG.F.4.4]

Several mathematical techniques can be used to assess hedge effectiveness, including ratio analysis and various statistical methods like regression analysis. The appropriateness of a given method will depend on the nature of the risk being hedged and the type of hedging instrument used.

5.1 The 'highly effective' criterion

IAS 39.AG105 specifies that a hedge is regarded as highly effective only if both of the following conditions are met:

(a) at the inception of the hedge and in subsequent periods, the hedge is expected to be *highly effective* in achieving offsetting changes in fair value or cash flows attributable to the hedged risk during the period for which the hedge is designated. Such an expectation can be demonstrated in various ways, including a comparison of past changes in the fair value or cash flows of the hedged item that are attributable to the hedged risk with past changes in the fair value or cash flows of the hedging instrument ('ratio analysis' or the 'dollar offset method' – see **5.6.1** below), or by demonstrating a high statistical correlation between the fair value or cash flows of the hedged item and those of the hedging instrument (for example 'regression analysis' – see **5.6.2** below). The entity may choose a hedge ratio of other than one to one in order to improve the effectiveness of the hedge (see **5.1.2** below).

(b) The actual results of the hedge are within a range of 80–125 per cent.

When actual results are within a range of 80–125 per cent, but not 100 per cent exactly, any deviation from 100 per cent means that the hedge relationship is partly ineffective and ineffectiveness must be recognised in profit or loss.

Hedge ineffectiveness arises in a fair value hedge when the change in the fair value of the hedging instrument differs from that of the hedged risk of the hedged item. Since changes in fair value of the hedging instrument are recognised in profit or loss so as to offset changes in the fair value due to the hedged risk on the hedged item, all hedge ineffectiveness is automatically recognised in profit or loss in the period. Hedge ineffectiveness is recognised in profit or loss for both under and over hedges, i.e. ineffectiveness is recognised when the fair value of the hedging instrument changes, either to a lesser or greater extent respectively when compared to the changes in the fair value of the hedged item.

In a cash flow hedge, the portion of the hedging instrument that is considered to be effective, and therefore is recognised in other comprehensive income, is the lesser of (i) and (ii):

(i) the cumulative gain or loss on the hedging instrument from inception of the hedge; and

(ii) the cumulative change in fair value (present value) of the expected future cash flows on the hedged item from inception of the hedge. [IAS 39.96]

In an over-hedge, where the change in fair value of the hedging instrument is greater than the change in fair value of the expected future cash flows on the hedged item, the difference is recognised in profit or loss as hedge ineffectiveness. However, where the change in fair value of the hedging instrument is less than the change in the fair value of expected future cash flows on the hedged item, the entire change in fair value of the hedging instrument is recognised in other comprehensive income, i.e. no ineffectiveness arises in an under-hedge, unless the hedge is determined no longer to be highly effective.

Example 5.1.A

Cash flow hedge ineffectiveness

[Extract from IAS 39.IG.F.5.2]

Entity A has a floating rate liability of CU1,000 with five years remaining to maturity. It enters into a five-year pay-fixed, receive-floating interest rate swap in the same currency and with the same principal terms as the liability to hedge the exposure to variable cash flow payments on the floating rate liability attributable to interest rate risk. At inception, the fair value of the swap is zero. Subsequently, there is an increase of CU49 in the fair value of the swap. This increase consists of a change of CU50 resulting from an increase in market interest rates and a change of minus CU1 resulting from an increase in the credit risk of the swap counterparty. There is no change in the fair value of the floating rate liability, but the fair value (present value) of the future cash flows needed to offset the exposure to variable interest cash flows on the liability increases by CU50. Assuming that Entity A determines that the hedge is still highly effective, is there ineffectiveness that should be recognised in profit or loss?

No. A hedge of interest rate risk is not fully effective if part of the change in the fair value of the derivative is attributable to the counterparty's credit risk (IAS 39.AG109). However, because Entity A determines that the hedge relationship is still highly effective, it recognises the effective portion of the change in fair value of the swap, i.e. the net change in fair value of CU49, in other comprehensive income. There is no debit to profit or loss for the change in fair value of the swap attributable to the deterioration in the credit quality of the swap counterparty, because the cumulative change in the present value of the future cash flows needed to offset the exposure to variable interest cash flows on the hedged item, i.e. CU50, exceeds the cumulative change in value of the hedging instrument, i.e. CU49.

Dr	Swap	CU49
Cr	Other comprehensive income	CU49

If Entity A concludes that the hedge is no longer highly effective, it discontinues hedge accounting prospectively as from the date the hedge ceased to be highly effective in accordance with IAS 39.101.

Would the answer change if the fair value of the swap instead increases to CU51 of which CU50 results from the increase in market interest rates and CU1 from a decrease in the credit risk of the swap counterparty?

Yes. In this case, there is a credit to profit or loss of CU1 for the change in fair value of the swap attributable to the improvement in the credit quality of the swap counterparty. This is because the cumulative change in the value of the hedging instrument, i.e. CU51, exceeds the cumulative change in the present value of the future cash flows needed to offset the exposure to variable interest cash flows on the hedged item, i.e. CU50. The difference of CU1 represents the excess ineffectiveness attributable to the derivative hedging instrument, the swap, and is recognised in profit or loss.

Dr	Swap	CU51
Cr	Other comprehensive income	CU50
Cr	Profit or loss	CU1

Hedge effectiveness testing is based on comparing changes in the fair value of the hedging instrument and changes in the fair value of the hedged item. In determining the change in fair value of the hedging instrument an entity considers gains and losses, not the carrying amount in the statement of financial position. It is the gains/losses that are recognised in profit or loss, whereas changes in the carrying amount of the hedging instrument may result from receipts or payments of cash which do not impact profit or loss. Similarly for the hedged item, it is the impact of the hedged risk of the hedged item that impacts profit or loss and is therefore considered in assessing hedge effectiveness and not the carrying amount of the hedged item itself.

Example 5.1B

Chas flow hedge ineffectiveness: off-market swaps

Entity B designates an off-market receive LIBOR, pay 7% interest rate swap in a cash flow hedge of variability in interest rates on its issued variable rate debt. The interest rate swap is off-market because at initial designation the swap has a negative fair value as expectations of interest rates have fallen since the swap was originally priced. The current yield curve for the remaining time to maturity is 5%.

Entity B assesses hedge effectiveness using the hypothetical derivative method and at the date of designation determines that a hypothetical derivative that would have a fair value of zero is the same as the actual derivative except that it would receive LIBOR, pay 5% (not receive LIBOR, pay 7%). In assessing hedge effectiveness Entity B models the actual and hypothetical derivative under various interest rate scenarios and compares the two in reaching its conclusion that the actual derivative, even though off-market, will still be effective at cash flow hedging its variable debt and therefore can qualify as a hedging instrument in a qualifying hedge relationship. The 2% extra that Entity B will pay 2% on the actual derivative compared to the hypothetical derivative is not the amount of hedge ineffectiveness that will arise in the future periods. The 2% is part of the cash flows of the actual derivative. The amount of hedge ineffectiveness will depend on how future interest rates affect the cumulative fair value gains/losses on the actual derivative from inception of the hedge as compared to the effect they will have on the hypothetical derivative. Another way of viewing the 2% difference between the pay leg of the actual derivative and hypothetical derivative can is viewing Entity B as paying loan instalments equal to 2% of the notional of the swap every period to the swap counterparty on an amortising loan. The cash payments on the 'loan' do not impact profit or loss, but changes in fair value of these future cash flows do.

5.1.1 *Designating a cash flow hedge in layers*

In order to improve effectiveness an entity may choose to hedge forecast transactions in layers. For example, instead of hedging a single layer of the first US$1m of forecast sales, an entity could designate the hedge relationship in layers: the first US$0.6m of forecast sales and a second layer of US$0.4m forecast sales. Designation in layers will only result in better hedge effectiveness where in future periods the amount of previously designated highly probable forecast transactions falls. In such a situation an entity may be able to recognise a greater amount in other comprehensive income if it designates in layers as hedge effectiveness will be assessed on each individual layer.

Example 5.1.1

Designating a cash flow hedge in layers

Entity A, € functional currency, has a substantial export business to the United States where Entity A receives US$ receipts from the sales of goods. Entity A is exposed to variability of its future revenue from export sales due to fluctuations in currency rates between US$ and €.

Entity A reports under IFRS on a semi-annual basis and its period end is 31 December. On 1 January 20X0 Entity A establishes that it will have highly probable US$ sales amounting to US$10m on 30 June 20X1. In order to hedge its exposure to changes in the US$:€ forward exchange rate it enters into a forward contract to sell US$10m and buy € on 30 June 20X1. Entity A designates and documents the forward contract as a hedging instrument in a cash flow hedge of the US$:€ forward risk on a designated amount of highly probable US$ revenue.

The changes in the fair value of the derivative are shown in the table below:

Date	Fair value of forward (€ m)	Fair value change in period (€ m)
01.01.20X0	0	0
30.06.20X0	0.5	0.5

Date	Fair value of forward (€ m)	Fair value change in period (€ m)
31.12.20X0	2.5	2.0
31.06.20X1	4.0	1.5

On 31 December 20X0 the entity revises its estimates of the US$ sales that will take place on 30 June 20X1 and determines that now only $7.5m of sales are highly probable. The entity is unable to identify a single event or change in circumstances responsible for this revision in accordance with IAS 39.AG113. In addition to this, a further $0.5m of sales is expected to occur (but is not highly probable).

Whether Entity A designates and documents the forecast sales in multiple layers or a single layer does have an impact on the amount of the effective portion of the gain or loss on the derivative that is recognised in other comprehensive income in a cash flow hedge. The impact on profit or loss and other comprehensive income of the two designations is illustrated below.

The entries below are for the 6 months to 30 June 20X0 and 31 December 20X0 only.

Entity A specifies as part of its hedge documentation put in place on 1 January 20X0 that it has two designated hedge relationships, identified by two different layers:

- L1: a 75% proportion of the US$10m forward is designated as hedging the first $7.5m of US$ sales that are highly probable of occurring on 30 June 20X1;
- L2: a 25% proportion of the US$10m forward is designated as hedging the next US$2.5m of highly probable US$ sales occurring on 30 June 20X1, i.e. sales US$ US$7.5m – US$10m.

6 months to 30 June 20X0

The full $10m forecast sales remain highly probable and therefore the total fair value movement of €0.5m will be recognised in other comprehensive income under L1 and L2 (both designations being perfectly effective hedging relationships).

Dr	Derivative asset	€0.5m
Cr	Other comprehensive income	€0.5m

To recognise the effective amount of the derivative gain in other comprehensive income

6 months to 31 December 20X0

(i) Entity A must assess whether any of the amounts recognised in other comprehensive income in equity at 30 June 20X0 should be reclassified from equity to profit or loss in the instance when some of the previously considered highly probable forecast transactions are no longer expected to occur. [IAS 39.101(c)] As US$8m of sales are still expected to occur (being US$7.5m that are highly probable and US$0.5m that are still expected to occur), compared to US$10m of sales at 30 June 20X0, 80 per cent of the €0.5m fair value movement previously recognised in other comprehensive income should remain in other comprehensive income with 20 per cent reclassified from equity to profit or loss. This in line with the principles outlined in **2.2.4** above.

Dr	Other comprehensive income	€0.1m
Cr	Profit or loss	€0.1m

To reclassify a fifth of the cash flow hedge gain from equity to profit or loss as a fifth of previously designated forecast transactions are no longer expected to occur

(ii) Entity A must assess whether the two hedging relationships (L1 and L2) have been highly effective for the 6 months to 31 December 20X0. Based on the revised estimates at 31 December 20X0 only US$7.5m of sales are highly probable. The L1 designation is considered to be highly effective as the total fair value movement in the designated proportion of the derivative is €1.5m (being 75 per cent of the total movement of €2.0m) and the change in fair value of the hedged cash flows, being US$7.5m, is €1.5m. L1 is therefore 100 per cent effective [€1.5m / €1.5m = 100 per cent].

All of the fair value movement of designation L2 (€0.5m, being 25 per cent of total movement of €2.0m) will be recognised in profit or loss as the hedge relationship is not highly effective due to the fall in the level of highly probable sales. As the amount of highly probable forecast sales between US$7.5m and US$10m is now nil, the hedge relationship is 0 per cent effective.

Dr	Derivative asset	€2.0m
Cr	Cash flow hedge reserve	€1.5m
Cr	Profit or loss	€0.5m

To recognise the effective amount of the derivative gain in other comprehensive income and remainder in profit or loss.

The amount of ineffectiveness recognised in profit or loss in the 6 months to 31 December 20X0 would be different were Entity A to designate the hedge of the forecast sales in a single layer.

As on 31 December 20X0, only US$7.5m of sales are considered to be highly probable, the hedging relationship is not highly effective: it is only 75 per cent effective as the total fair value movement in the derivative is €2.0m and the change in fair value of the hedged cash flows, being $7.5m, is €1.5m [€2.0m / €1.5m = 75 per cent]. Since hedge effectiveness is outside the range of 80 per cent – 125 per cent the entire fair value movement in the period of €2.0m will be recognised in profit or loss.

5.1.2 *A hedge ratio of other than one to one*

For the purposes of designating a hedge relationship that satisfies the highly effective criterion, the amount of the hedging instrument designated may be greater or less than that of the hedged item if this improves the effectiveness of the hedging relationship.

For example, if an entity hedges an item with a hedging instrument with a different basis (IAS 39.100 uses the example of a transaction based on Brazilian coffee prices hedged with a transaction based on Columbian coffee prices), a regression analysis (see **5.6.2** below) could be performed to establish a statistical relationship between the two items. If a valid statistical relationship between the two variables (i.e. between the unit prices of Brazilian coffee and Columbian coffee) can be demonstrated, the slope of the regression line could be used to establish the hedge ratio that would maximise expected effectiveness.

If the slope of the regression line is, say, 1.02, a hedge ratio based on 0.98 quantities of hedged items to 1.00 quantities of the hedging instrument will maximise expected effectiveness.

Example 5.1.2

Hedge ratio other than one

Entity R periodically issues new bonds to refinance maturing bonds, provide working capital, and for various other purposes. Entity R hedges the risk of changes in the long-term interest rates from the date it decides to issue the bonds to the date the bonds are issued.

Entity R performed historical correlation studies and determined that a treasury bond of the same maturity adequately correlates to the bonds Entity R expects to issue, assuming a hedge ratio of 0.93 futures on treasury bonds to one debt unit. In order to achieve an effective hedge of the future issuance of the bond, Entity R enters into the futures on treasury bonds using this ratio.

Hedge ineffectiveness is measured on the basis of the actual amounts designated. It is not possible to designate an exposure based on a specified notional, but measure ineffectiveness on a different notional.

5.1.3 *Hedging on an after-tax basis*

IAS 39 permits assessment of hedge effectiveness on an after-tax basis, provided this approach is documented formally at inception. [IAS 39.IG.F.4.1]

It may be advantageous to assess hedge effectiveness on a post tax basis where the hedged item and hedging instrument are taxed differently. However, it must be borne in mind that any subsequent changes in the basis or rate of tax of either the hedged item or hedging instrument, will result in hedge ineffectiveness.

Example 5.1.3

Hedging a net investment in a foreign operation on an after-tax basis

Entity T, a Sterling functional currency, has an investment in a wholly owned subsidiary Entity U, a Euro functional currency. The consolidated financial statements headed by Entity T are presented in Sterling. Entity T's consolidated interest in its foreign operation, Entity U is equal to €840,000 of net assets as of 1/1/X1. Assume that the amount of net assets remains unchanged and that the foreign currency retranslation of the investment in the net assets of Entity U will not attract any taxation. On 1/1/X1 Entity T enters into a forward contract to sell €1,200,000 and buy Sterling at a rate of €1.5: £1 on 31/12/X2. The gain or loss arising on remeasurement of the forward contract at spot rates is subject to current tax at 30 per cent.

The forward and the spot EUR/£ translation rates are as follows:

	1/1/X1	**31/12/X1**	**31/12/X2**
Spot	1.4	1.6	1.7
Forward (to 31/12/X2)	1.5	1.66	-

Reporting €1,200,000 at the above rates gives the following Sterling amounts:

	1/1/X1	**31/12/X1**	**31/12/X2**
Spot	1.4	1.6	1.7
Sterling amount	£857,143	£750,000	£705,882
Forward (to 31/12/X2)	1.5	1.66	-
Sterling amount	£800,000	£722,892	

Therefore the fair value of the forward is:

Date	**Derivative value**	**Calculated as:**
31/12/X1	£77,108	£800,000 – £722,892
31/12/X2	£94,118	£800,000 – £705,882

(For illustration purposes only, the fair value of the forward ignores the time value of money.)

Reporting €840,000 at the above spot rates gives the following Sterling amounts:

	1/1/X1	**31/12/X1**	**31/12/X2**
Spot	1.4	1.6	1.7
Sterling amount	£600,000	£525,000	£494,118

The forward contract is designated as the hedging instrument in an after tax hedge of the spot retranslation risk on the first €840,000 net assets of the investment in the foreign operation in the consolidated financial statements. The notional of the forward contract is purposefully greater than the amount of net assets being designated as a hedged item to compensate for the fact that foreign currency movements on the hedged item (net assets) are not taxable while those on the hedging instrument (forward contract) are. The notional of the derivative of €1,200,000 equals the net assets grossed up for the tax rate (€840,000 / 1 – 0.30 tax rate).

Movements in the fair value due to the forward points will not give rise to hedge ineffectiveness, as the designated hedged risk is movements in spot rate only (on an after tax basis), i.e. these movements do not form part of the hedging relationship and will be recognised directly in profit or loss.

In accordance with the requirements of IAS 12 *Income Taxes* the current tax relating to the gain or loss remeasurement of the forward contract at spot rates will be recognised in other comprehensive income since the gain or loss itself is recognised in other comprehensive income.

The required entries are as follows:

31 December 20X1

Dr	Other comprehensive income	£75,000
Cr	Net assets	£75,000

To recognise the foreign exchange difference on translation of the net assets at the spot rate (i.e. translating the investment at 1.6 rather than 1.4).

Dr	Derivative	£77,108
Dr	Profit or loss	£30,035 (relates to forward points)
Cr	Other comprehensive income	£107,143

To recognise the change in the fair value of the derivative, the effective portion in other comprehensive income based on undiscounted spot rates, and the undesignated portion in profit or loss. It is presumed that the hedge relationship is fully effective, so the amount recognised in profit or loss is only the change in the fair value of forward points.

Dr	Other comprehensive income	£32,143 (30% of £107,143)
Cr	Tax liability	£32,143

To recognise the tax in respect of the gain on the derivative recognised in other comprehensive income.

On a post-tax hedge effectiveness assessment the hedge relationship has been fully effective. The post-tax foreign exchange loss on the net assets, £75,000, is equal to the post-tax foreign exchange gain on the derivative, £75,000 (£107,143 – £32,143).

31 December 20X2

Dr	Other comprehensive income	£30,882
Cr	Net assets	£30,882

To recognise the foreign exchange difference on translation of the net assets at the spot rate (i.e. translating the investment at 1.7 rather than 1.6).

Dr	Derivative	£17,010
Dr	Profit or loss	£27,108 (relates to forward points)
Cr	Other comprehensive income	£44,118

To recognise the change in the fair value of the derivative, the effective portion in other comprehensive income based on undiscounted spot rates, and the undesignated portion in profit or loss. It is presumed that the hedge relationship is fully effective, so the amount recognised in profit or loss is only the fair value of forward points.

Dr	Other comprehensive income	£13,236 (30% of £44,118)
Cr	Tax liability	£13,236

To recognise the tax in respect of the gain on the derivative recognised in other comprehensive income.

On a post-tax hedge effectiveness assessment the hedge relationship has been fully effective. The post-tax foreign exchange loss on the net assets, £30,882, is equal to the post-tax foreign exchange gain on the derivative, £30,882 (£44,118 – 13,236).

Dr	Cash	£94,118
Cr	Derivative	£94,118

To reflect cash settlement of the derivative at its maturity.

5.1.4 *Assessment on cumulative basis*

IAS 39 permits the assessment of hedge effectiveness either on a period-by-period basis or cumulatively over the life of the hedging relationship, provided the approach to be taken is documented formally at inception of the hedge relationship. [IAS 39.IG.F.4.2]

If hedge effectiveness is assessed on a cumulative basis and the hedge is not expected to be highly effective in a particular period, hedge accounting is not precluded if effectiveness is expected to remain sufficiently high over the life of the hedging relationship. The entity is still required to recognise any ineffectiveness in profit or loss as it occurs.

Example 5.1.4

Assessment on cumulative basis

Entity S designates a LIBOR-based interest rate swap that resets every 3 months as a hedge of its LIBOR based borrowing which carries interest at LIBOR plus a credit spread, where LIBOR resets every 6 months. Entity S documents that it will assess hedge effectiveness on a cumulative basis. Over the life of the hedge relationship, the hedge is expected to be almost perfect. However, there will be periods when the variability in cash flows on the borrowing is not perfectly offset by the variability in the interest rate swap.

Entity S is required to recognise any ineffectiveness in profit or loss as it arises. Because it assesses hedge effectiveness on a cumulative basis, Entity S will be able to hedge account for this relationship provided hedge effectiveness is expected to remain sufficiently high over the remainder of the life of the hedge.

5.1.5 *Effectiveness outside the 80 to 125 per cent range*

Effectiveness outside the range of 80 to 125 per cent at any measurement period may preclude hedge accounting not only in the period but also for future periods if it is an indication of further expected ineffectiveness.

A hedge relationship must be discontinued for the period in which the hedge fails to meet the effectiveness criteria. [IAS 39.88] IAS 39.IG.F.6.2 issue (i) states that "if there is a hedge effectiveness failure, the ineffective portion of the gain or loss on the derivative instrument is recognised immediately in profit or loss and hedge accounting based on the previous designation of the hedge relationship cannot be continued. In this case, the derivative instrument may be redesignated prospectively as a hedging instrument in a new hedging relationship provided this hedging relationship satisfies the necessary conditions". Generally, hedge accounting will be discontinued from the previous effectiveness testing date, though where it is possible to identify the event that caused the hedging relationship to fail the effectiveness test and to demonstrate that the hedge was effective before the event occurred, hedge accounting will be discontinued from the date the event occurred. [IAS 39.AG 113]

Where hedge effectiveness is outside the 80–125 per cent range, hedge accounting in subsequent periods would only be appropriate if a strong historical relationship exists and there is an expectation that the hedge will be highly effective in future periods. The same hedge relationship can be re-designated for hedge accounting prospectively provided the entity can demonstrate that the new hedge relationship is expected to be highly effective in the future. An entity may wish to change the hedge ratio of the existing hedged item and hedging instrument, designate a new hedging instrument, or utilise the hedging instrument in hedging a different hedged item in order to improve effectiveness.

Where a hedge is re-designated after an effectiveness failure, the previous hedge relationship is considered to be extinguished and a new hedge relationship created. Accordingly, subsequent retrospective effectiveness testing will only assess hedge effectiveness since the date of the new hedge designation and will not be tainted by the poor historical performance. Prospective tests will, nevertheless, be affected where the entity's chosen method of prospective effectiveness testing incorporates historical performance data.

5.2 Principal terms of the hedged item and hedging instrument match

If the principal terms of the hedged item and the hedging instrument match, then there is likely to be a high degree of offset between the hedged item and the hedging instrument. The principal terms of a hedged item and a hedging instrument will include: the notional and principal, the maturity, and the underlying. Different hedge relationships will have different principal terms.

For fair value hedges of investments in equity securities, if the underlying of the derivative equals that of the equity security and the derivative has a fair value of zero, then there will be an expectation of a high degree of offset in theirs fair values.

For hedges of interest rate risk there is a greater number of principal terms to consider, in particular depending on whether:

- the notional amount of the derivative matches the principal amount of the interest-bearing asset or liability;
- for cash flow hedges, repricing dates and interest rate indices match;
- the derivative is on-market at inception and therefore has a fair value of zero;
- the formula for computing net settlements under the interest rate swap is the same for each net settlement (i.e. the fixed rate is the same throughout the term, and the variable rate is based on the same index and includes either the same constant adjustment or no adjustment, say, for credit spread); and
- if the hedged item has prepayment features, these features are also reflected in the derivative.

For hedges of firm commitments, the principal terms will depend on which risk is being hedged. If the foreign currency risk of a firm commitment is being hedged then the principal terms will include the maturities of the commitment and the derivative, the underlying (i.e. the foreign currency), and the notional of each. Where an entity is hedging all the fair value of a firm commitment, the underlying will reflect the exact quality, grade, type, if the underlying is a non-financial item, or exact index, timing of cash flows, if the underlying is a financial item.

Similarly, for cash flow hedges of forecast transactions, the maturity of the hedging instrument is compared to the period when the designated forecast transactions are expected to impact profit or loss. Other principal terms that need to be considered are similar to those described above for hedges of firm commitments. In addition, where a forward contract is designated as a hedging instrument, for the terms to match, either the change in the discount or premium on the forward contract needs to be excluded from the assessment of effectiveness and recognised in profit or loss, or the change in expected cash flows on the highly probable forecast transaction needs to be based on the forward price for the non-financial item.

Even where the principal terms of the hedging instrument and of the entire hedged asset or liability or hedged forecast transaction are the same, an entity cannot assume hedge effectiveness without subsequent effectiveness testing as significant hedge ineffectiveness may arise from other sources, for example, as a result of changes in the liquidity of the hedging instruments or their credit risk. [IAS 39.IG.F.4.7]

Example 5.2A

Hedge effectiveness not assumed

Entity X enters into a firm commitment to buy 10,000 ounces of gold at the current six-month forward rate of US$310. This contract is not recognised as a financial instrument as it is a purchase or usage requirements contract in accordance with IAS 39.5. On the same day, Entity X enters into a cash settled forward contract to sell 10,000 ounces of gold at the current six-month forward rate of US$310 which is designated as a fair value hedge of all risks with respect to the firm commitment to purchase gold. Hedge effectiveness will be measured based on changes in the six-month forward price of gold.

Because the principal terms of the firm commitment and the forward contract match (quantity of gold, contract maturity, forward rate) Entity X may conclude that the changes in the fair value of the firm commitment are expected to offset the change in the fair value of the derivative. However, ineffectiveness must still be assessed, at a minimum, at the end of each reporting period.

Example 5.2B

Fair value derived from net settlements

If the form of an interest rate swap is such that the variable leg is adjusted for a fixed spread, for example LIBOR + 150 basis points, the adjustment can be considered as an adjustment of the fixed leg of the swap.

For example, for a fair value hedge of a 7 per cent fixed rate issued debt where the credit spread at issue was 1 per cent, the hedged risk, being the LIBOR portion, would be equivalent to 6 per cent. If the terms of the derivative were receive 7.5 per cent, pay LIBOR + 150 basis points, the terms of the swap would not invalidate a conclusion of minimal ineffectiveness as the swap's fair value is derived from its net settlements, and the net receive leg is equivalent to 6 per cent, being the hedged risk.

If the principal terms of the hedging instrument and the hedged item do not match, an entity will be subject to a larger degree of hedge ineffectiveness. For example, if, at inception of a cash flow hedge, the fair value of the swap is not zero, i.e. it is off-market, there will be ineffectiveness due to the interest rate risk on an up-front payment or receipt. For example, where an entity enters into an interest rate swap that has been structured to be significantly in-the-money at inception, the price paid to purchase the interest rate swap will be reimbursed to the buyer via a higher receive leg, or a lower pay leg. The upfront payment of cash by the buyer of the swap is like financing, and therefore any costs or income with respect to the financing will result in hedge ineffectiveness.

5.3 Assessing effectiveness: basis risk

It is not always possible for an entity to find a hedging instrument with exactly the same terms as the item it wishes to hedge. Basis differences result from using a hedging instrument that is based on a specific risk that is similar, but not identical to the risk being hedged in the hedged item. For example, there may not always be an active market for the grade or location of a commodity that an entity is seeking to hedge.

For interest sensitive items, basis differences result from differences in interest indices, e.g. LIBOR versus Treasury rates, in terms, e.g. three-month LIBOR versus six-month LIBOR, and in credit risk differences.

Example 5.3A

Basis risk: commodities

Entity Z has 20,000 therms of natural gas stored at its location in the United Kingdom. Entity Z ultimately intends on selling this gas to customers in continental Europe, and is concerned that prices may fall in the future. To hedge the exposure of its sales of natural gas, Entity Z sells the equivalent of 20,000 therms of natural gas under a forward contract (which the entity intends on net settling in cash by entering into an offsetting position in the spot market at delivery). The forward contract's price is based on delivery of natural gas at the Zeebrugge gas collection point in Belgium. Because prices in the UK (as based on the price quoted in the UK National Balancing Point, or NBP, market) and at Zeebrugge will differ as a result of regional factors (e.g. location, pipeline transmission costs, and supply and demand), Entity Z cannot assume that the hedge will be highly effective in achieving offsetting changes in fair value. Entity Z appropriately documents the hedging strategy and states that effectiveness will be measured based on the spot prices of natural gas in the UK NBP market and the spot prices at the Zeebrugge hub.

Entity Z is required to demonstrate effectiveness at inception and on an ongoing basis. This is achieved typically, through a correlation method such as regression analysis, or ratio analysis. If such analysis does not result in an expectation that correlation would be between 80 to 125 per cent, Entity Z is not permitted to apply hedge accounting. However, even if the effectiveness test is met, Entity Z may have ineffectiveness due to the difference in the basis of the hedged item and the hedging instrument and such ineffectiveness is recognised in profit or loss.

Example 5.3B

Basis risk: interest rate resets

Entity D designates an interest rate swap as hedging a debt instrument. The interest rate swap's rate settles every three months but is indexed to the six-month LIBOR rate and the debt settles every three months but is indexed to the three-month LIBOR rate, i.e. the three-month LIBOR index on the debt does not match the six-month LIBOR index on the swap. To the extent that there is high empirical correlation between these rate indices, Entity D may designate the swap as the hedge of the interest rate risk on the debt instrument, but the different rate indexation may result in ineffectiveness that needs to be measured and recognised.

Example 5.3C

Basis risk: foreign currency risk

Entity X's functional currency is the Euro. Entity X's forecast purchase of equipment from Brazil is expected to cost R$100,000. Entity X wishes to hedge its foreign currency risk. As the US$/ Euro currency market is more liquid than the R$/ Euro dollar currency market, Entity X enters into a forward contract to receive US$33,300 and pay €27,000. The US$ will then be converted into Brazilian Real in the liquid spot market for payment to the supplier.

Because the bases of foreign currency for the purchase of the equipment and the foreign exchange forward contract are different (R$ vs. US$), Entity X will have to demonstrate that US$/€ is highly effective in hedging R$/€ both at inception and on an ongoing basis. The entity could use a correlation method to demonstrate the effectiveness of this relationship.

To the extent that there is a basis difference between R$ and US$, hedge ineffectiveness will result and will be recognised in profit or loss.

In **example 5.3D** below, basis risk exists between the risk exposure of the derivative, which is solely interest rates, and the risk exposure of the hedged item, which includes both interest rate risk and credit risk of the debt that has been issued. Even though there is basis risk, in this example, applying cash flow hedge accounting does not result in hedge ineffectiveness in profit or loss (as the hedge underperforms in the first period and is perfectly effective on a cumulative assessment basis for the second period).

Example 5.3D

Basis risk: interest rate basis

Entity X is expecting to issue €100 million of five-year fixed-rate bonds on 30 June 20X0. Entity X has a single A credit rating, it believes that interest rates may increase during the next six months and wants to hedge against such an increase by locking-in existing five-year fixed rates. Entity X enters into a forward starting five-year swap on 1 January 20X0 (the swap starts in six months) with a notional amount equal to the expected principal amount of the anticipated debt issuance. At the date of the hedge, swap rates were 5.50 per cent and five-year single A rates were 5.60 per cent.

Entity X assesses effectiveness based on the cumulative change in fair value of the derivative and the cumulative change in the discounted present value or fair value of expected future interest and principal payments on fixed-rate single A bonds. Changes in spreads during the hedge period will result in hedge ineffectiveness. At the inception of the hedge the spread between the swap rates and five-year single A corporate bonds was 10 basis points. Historically there is a high degree of correlation between swaps and single A corporate bonds.

The required entries are as follows:

1 January 20X0

No entry required as the derivative has a fair value of zero.

31 March 20X0

On 31 March 20X0 five-year swap rates are 5.10 per cent and five-year single A rates are 5.15 per cent. The derivative has a negative fair value of €1.744 million as a result of a decrease in five-year swap rates of 40 basis points subsequent to 1 January 20X0. The spread between five-year swap rates and five-year single A corporate bond rates decreased to 5 basis points. Because the hedge underperformed the changes in single A rates, the loss on the hedge is smaller than the present value decrease in expected future interest expense on the anticipated issuance of debt and, therefore, the hedge is fully effective. If the decrease in the expected future interest expense on the anticipated issuance of debt was lower than the loss on the hedge, a portion of the loss on the derivative would be recognised in profit or loss.

Dr	Other comprehensive income	€1,744,000
Cr	Derivative liability	€1,744,000

To record the derivative at fair value with changes in fair value recorded in other comprehensive income.

30 June 20X0

On 30 June 20X0 five-year swap rates are 5.30 per cent and five-year single A rates are 5.40 per cent. The derivative has a negative fair value of €867,000 as a result of an increase in five-year swap rates of 20 basis points from

31 March 20X0; spreads at 31 March 20X0 returned to 10 basis points. The hedge is completely effective on a cumulative basis as the spreads returned to 10 basis points.

Dr	Derivative Liability	€877,000
Cr	Other comprehensive income	€877,000

To record the derivative at fair value with changes in fair value recorded in other comprehensive income.

On 30 June 20X0 Entity X issues €100 million of five-year bonds at a rate of 5.40 per cent. Entity X also closes out the derivative.

Dr	Cash	€100,000,000
Cr	Debt Obligation	€100,000,000
Dr	Derivative Liability	€867,000
Cr	Cash	€867,000

To record the debt issuance and close out of the derivative.

The €867,000 debit will be reclassified from equity to profit or loss when the interest on the debt is recognised in profit or loss. It will effectively result in a yield adjustment over the life of the bond (since the bond is issued at a greater discount) and an effective yield on the bond of approximately 5.60 per cent, which is the rate in effect at 1/1/X0, the date the hedge is initiated.

5.4 Minimising ineffectiveness

To improve hedge effectiveness, an entity can elect to designate only certain risks inherent in a hedged item as being hedged. The ability to hedge portions of cash flows or fair value generally applies to hedges of financial items only. The ability to designate only certain risks in non-financial items is limited and is discussed in **3.9** above. 'Hedging portions', i.e. designating an identifiable and separable portion of the risk on the financial asset or liability as the hedged item [IAS 39.81], can result in a higher degree of effectiveness as the designated risk is a specifically identifiable risk inherent in the hedged item. Designating portions is discussed in greater detail in **3.8.1** above.

Example 5.4

Hedging the LIBOR swap rate

Entity A enters into a receive-fixed, pay-variable LIBOR interest rate swap and designates the swap as a fair value hedge of its issued fixed rate debt. As the interest rate index in the hedging instrument is LIBOR, and the LIBOR rate reflects the credit quality of AA financial institutions, even though Entity A is not a AA rated entity, it may designate the portion of risk inherent in its issued debt equivalent to this rate, i.e. hedge the LIBOR swap rate only. Entity A designates the risk of fair value movements in respect of the LIBOR swap rate on its issued fixed rate debt. By hedging just this portion of risk,

Entity A has purposely excluded from the designation fair value movements of the debt due to movements in its own credit quality.

It should be noted that if Entity A is charged an additional spread on the interest rate swap by the counterparty because Entity A's credit quality relative to the counterparty is worse, this may impact hedge effectiveness. The spread on the derivative will be relatively small when compared to the credit spread charged on the cash instrument, i.e. the debt. The entity will need to monitor the impact of the credit spread of the interest rate swap as part of its assessment of hedge effectiveness.

5.4.1 *Minimising ineffectiveness: forward points*

Where a forward contract is designated as a hedging instrument in a cash flow hedge of a forecast transaction the entity can choose to exclude the fair value movements of the forward points from the hedge relationship. In other words, an entity may include in its designation the whole fair value movements of the forward contract, or just the fair value movements of the forward contract that relate solely to movements in spot rates.

Example 5.4.1

Hedging the forward foreign currency rate

Entity X is a Euro functional entity. Entity X makes sales to US customers in US$. Entity X wishes to hedge its exposure to US$ by entering into a forward contract to sell US$ and buy € at a fixed rate at a specified delivery date that coincides with the timing of the sales.

Entity X can choose to designate the hedged risk as movements in either the spot US$/€ rate, or the forward US$/€ rate that terminates when the sales occur and the hedging instrument matures.

If the entity chooses to hedge the spot rate, then movements in the fair value of the forward contract due to movements in spot rate from period to period are recognised in other comprehensive income (to the extent this is effective). The fair value movements in the forward contract due to the fair value of the forward points will be recognised immediately in profit or loss throughout the hedge relationship.

If the entity chooses to hedge the forward rate, then the full movement in the fair value of the forward contract is recognised in other comprehensive income (to the extent this is effective). Compared to designating the spot rate only, the fair value changes of the forward points are recognised in other comprehensive income (instead of profit or loss) throughout the hedge relationship. If the hedge was perfectly effective over the life, then the fair value of the forward points would never be recognised in profit or loss (at maturity of the hedging relationship and hedging instrument the fair value of the forward points will be zero as there will be no more forward points left). The fair value of the forward contract at maturity will be equivalent to the difference between the spot rate at maturity and the contracted rate.

5.4.2 *Minimising ineffectiveness: option time value*

By splitting the time and intrinsic value of an option that is a qualifying hedging instrument, and designating only the intrinsic value in the hedging relationship, a higher level of effectiveness may be achieved. Depending on the length of time to the maturity of the option, the relative volatility of the option, and other factors that affect the time value, this designation may make the difference as to whether the relationship qualifies for hedge accounting.

Generally, if options are being used to hedge financial instruments that have a linear response to changes in the hedged risk, such as cash instruments, it is beneficial to exclude the time value of the option from the hedge relationship as the time value evident in the option is not evident in the hedged item. Designating the gains and losses on the hedging instrument with respect to intrinsic value only as an offset of the gains and losses on the hedged item creates a greater likelihood that the hedge will be highly effective in achieving offsetting changes in fair value or cash flows attributable to the hedged risk.

The disadvantage of not including time value in the hedge designation is that changes in the value of the component that is not designated in the hedging relationship, i.e. change in time value, must be recognised immediately in profit or loss.

Example 5.4.2

Hedging intrinsic value only

Entity X owns 1,000 shares of Entity A worth £50 each. Entity X classifies these securities as available-for-sale and recognises changes in the fair value of these securities in other comprehensive income. Entity X would like to hedge its downside equity price risk. Entity X purchases an at-the-money put option (i.e. the put option has a strike price of £50) on 1,000 Entity A shares expiring in three years' time. The premium paid for the option is £9,000.

Entity X designates the intrinsic value of the put option as a fair value hedge of its investment in Entity A. The hedge strategy is consistent with Entity X's established risk management strategies. Entity X measures effectiveness by comparing decreases in fair value of the investment below the £50 strike price with changes in the intrinsic value of the option on a quarterly basis. The time value of the option is not included in the assessment of effectiveness.

Because the hedging instrument and the hedged item have the same basis and are based on the same number of shares, increases in the intrinsic value of the option are expected to be fully effective in offsetting decreases in the fair value of the investment.

In this example, the entire £9,000 premium is time value because the option purchased was at-the-money. This time value and subsequent changes in time value are recognised directly in profit or loss. Effectiveness of the hedge is assessed based on the intrinsic value rather than the fair value of the option. To the extent that the fair value of the option changes due to other variables such as volatility and the risk free rate, Entity X calculates the fair value of the option and then deducts the intrinsic value to arrive at the 'time' value component. In other words, the time value component reflects the effect of all variables on the option's price other than the intrinsic value. Based on Entity X's designation of effectiveness, the time value component is not part of the hedge relationship and is therefore recognised directly in profit or loss.

When the fair value of the shares falls below the strike price of the option, i.e. £50, the entity will recognise fair value movements on the hedged item below this amount in profit or loss (instead of other comprehensive income) which will offset the intrinsic value on the hedging instrument that will be recognised in profit or loss in the same period.

The Standard does not provide a definition of time value or intrinsic value for the purposes of identifying these two elements. This raises the question of what should be taken as intrinsic value, especially in the case of European options where the value of the option is driven from the expected price of the underlying in the future, and not its current price. For example, in the case of a cap on an interest rate index that is exercisable at the maturity of the option, there is a question whether intrinsic value at any point in time should be measured based on the current level of the given index (i.e. intrinsic value based on the spot rate) or by reference to the forward rate of the index that coincides with the actual exercise date (i.e. intrinsic value based on the forward rate)?

The latter view would seem to be more in line with the economic reality for a European option as the intrinsic value of the option is entirely a function of where the rate of interest is predicted to be at the exercise date as opposed to where it currently is, given that the option cannot be presently exercised. This view of intrinsic value is supported by the fact that there is a readily observable prediction of future interest rates, i.e. the forward rates derived from the yield curve. In this respect European options over interest rate indices are different from those over other underlyings such as equity shares. IFRS 2 *Share-based Payment* Appendix A defines the intrinsic value of a share option as the difference between the fair value of the shares and the exercise price of the option, pointing towards a spot based view of intrinsic value, which is consistent with the fact that for equity shares there is no readily observable prediction of future prices as there is for interest rates.

Consider the case of a purchased European interest rate cap in an environment of an inverted interest rate curve (i.e. a yield curve that predicts that future interest rates will be below current levels). An entity may purchase a European interest rate cap at 5 per cent with a maturity of 2 years when the current spot rate is 6 per cent and the current market prediction as illustrated by the yield curve is that the interest rate is expected to be 4.5 per cent at the exercise date of the option. If intrinsic value is based on the spot rate, the intrinsic value will effectively 'build in' an assumption of the interest rate remaining at 6 per cent, i.e. in excess of the cap even though the yield curve predicts that this will not be the case. This will lead to a value being attributed to intrinsic value that is in excess of the total fair value of the option. As a result 'negative' value will be attributed to the time value in order for the sum of the time and intrinsic values to equal the total fair value of the option. It would seem strange that IAS 39 would require an entity to attribute 'negative' time value to a purchased option and therefore it is reasonable for an entity to assess intrinsic value based on forward rather than spot interest rates, assuming it documents this as part of its risk management strategy and applies this consistently for similar hedging relationships.

5.4.3 *Assessing effectiveness: embedded call, prepayment or termination features*

Any derivative feature embedded in the hedged item or features embedded in the hedging instrument will have some impact on the changes in the fair value of these instruments. Differences in terms between the hedged item and hedging instrument will lead to differences in changes in fair value of the respective instruments. A termination, cancellation, call or prepayment feature embedded in the hedged item which is not replicated in the hedging instrument may result in a hedge relationship failing to qualify for hedge accounting.

Example 5.4.3A

Hedging callable issued debt

Entity X issues 10-year fixed-rate debt that is callable at the end of the sixth year. It decides to convert the interest payments on the bond from fixed-rate to floating-rate by entering into a 10-year receive-fixed, pay-floating interest rate swap. The interest rate swap is not cancellable at the end of year six. Entity X would like to designate the swap as the hedging instrument in a fair value hedge of the interest rate risk only on the fixed-rate debt.

The call feature may impede designation of the hedging relationship, particularly if it is probable that during the first six years of the debt it will be in-the-money. The assessment of whether it will be in the money can be based on a probability-weighted analysis of possible future changes in interest rates. Even if the option is unlikely to be exercised, the fact that there is a possibility of exercise, i.e. time value, will impact the debt's sensitivity to changes in interest rates.

If, during the first six years, interest rates decrease, the gain on the swap will be greater than the loss on the debt because the fair value of the debt will take into consideration the call feature, which will be in-the-money when interest rates fall below the rate on the debt. Economically, the debt will behave more like 6-year term debt, rather than 10-year term debt. Consequently, the changes in fair value of the debt due to movements in interest rates and the interest rate swap are unlikely to fully offset, potentially resulting in the prospective or retrospective hedge effectiveness tests being failed.

Example 5.4.3B

Hedging puttable issued debt

Bank C has a fixed-rate commercial loan maturing in five years. The borrower can prepay the loan without penalty after year two.

If Bank C wants to hedge the fair value of the loan due to changes in interest rate risk, it must consider the effect on fair value of the embedded option (a prepayment option forms a sub-component of the overall interest rate risk). A five-year receive-variable, pay-fixed swap might or might not be sufficiently effective to qualify as a hedging instrument. A swap, cancellable at Bank C's option after year two with the same terms as the prepayment feature in the loan, would be a more effective hedging instrument because it hedges all of the interest rate risk, including the embedded prepayment option.

5.4.4 *Assessing effectiveness: counterparty credit risk*

The effect of counterparty credit risk on hedge effectiveness cannot be disregarded. An entity must consider the counterparty's creditworthiness (and changes therein) in assessing hedge effectiveness. [IAS 39.IG.F.4.3]

For a cash flow hedge, if it becomes probable that a counterparty will default, an entity will be unable to conclude that the hedge is expected to be highly effective in achieving offsetting cash flows. As a consequence, hedge accounting would be discontinued.

A change in the creditworthiness of the counterparty of the derivative in a fair value hedge would have an immediate impact on the assessment of whether the hedge relationship is effective and qualifies for hedge accounting because the fair value of the hedging derivative will change and will result in immediate recognition of ineffectiveness in profit or loss.

5.4.5 *Assessing effectiveness: clean versus dirty prices*

Clean prices are prices that exclude any interest accruals. Dirty prices include interest accruals.

Clean prices can be used when assessing whether a hedge is expected to be highly effective.

Where a retrospective test of hedge effectiveness is performed using dirty prices for a hedge of a debt instrument with an interest rate swap, ineffectiveness will be observed if the test is performed between interest payment dates. The swap's value will include a net interest accrual being the net of the interest receivable on the receive leg and the interest payable on the pay leg. The loan's value will include a gross interest accrual. The accrued interest component of the swap's value will therefore be far smaller than that of the debt causing hedge ineffectiveness.

It is important to note that excluding accrued interest in an effectiveness test does not eliminate the ineffectiveness that can be caused by the first fixing of the swap. When an interest rate swap fixes in advance, the interest rate on the floating leg of the swap is fixed until the next reset date. Therefore, between reset dates, as market interest rates change, this fixed portion of the floating leg builds up value. The build up of value between reset dates is not mirrored in the fair value movements of the hedged debt. This ineffectiveness is not eliminated by excluding accrued interest from the hedge effectiveness testing.

When measuring the actual results of the hedge (see **5.7 below**) the dirty value of the instruments must be used.

5.4.6 *Assessing effectiveness: deal contingent forwards*

An entity that expects to enter into transactions whose occurrence depends on a future event sometimes enter into derivatives that mirror the possibility of non-occurrence of the future event, i.e. the derivative has a knock-out option that is exercised if the future event does not occur. These are often referred to as deal contingent derivatives. If the future event occurs the derivative remains outstanding, if the event does not occur, the derivative ceases to exist and no settlements between the parties are made. It is unlikely that these instruments can be considered qualifying hedging instruments as illustrated in the example below.

Example 5.4.6

Hedging with deal contingent forwards

An entity believes it will enter into a highly likely business combination at a future date where the consideration for the acquiree is specified in a foreign currency. The prospective acquirer is awaiting approval by the acquiree's current shareholders, regulatory agencies, governments, or other parties etc. The prospective acquirer chooses to economically hedge their exposure by entering into a deal contingent foreign currency forward contract, such that if the business combination does not proceed the forward contract knocks-out and is terminated with no cash settlement between the parties. The value of this derivative contract is driven not only by the foreign currency component but also by the probability of the business combination occurring.

The business combination is unlikely to be seen as being highly probable, and therefore it would be inappropriate to designate the deal contingent forward contract as a hedge of the currency risk of the forecast business combination. The existence of a knock-out option adds strength to the argument that the business combination is not highly probable as the knock-out feature would not be needed if it was. IAS 39 presupposes that if an entity is hedging a transaction that it claims to be highly probable it expects the transaction to occur, while here the entity is economically entering into an additional hedge: the hedge of the non-occurrence of the transaction. The fair value of the deal contingent forward includes the probability that the business combination will not occur, which when compared to the fair value of a hypothetical derivative, a vanilla forward that assumes the transaction will occur, will be different. This difference may be so significant that the entity cannot claim on a prospective assessment of hedge effectiveness that the hedge is expected to be highly effective.

The ineffectiveness cannot be minimised by designating additionally the risk of non-occurrence of the transaction for two reasons: (i) the risk of non-occurrence is considered to be a general business risk and hence is not eligible to be a hedged item [IAS 39.IG.F.2.8] and, (ii) with the exceptions set out in IAS 39.74 an entity must designate a derivative instrument in its entirety.

Bank C has a fixed-rate commercial loan maturing in five years. The borrower can prepay the loan without penalty after year two.

If Bank C wants to hedge the fair value of the loan due to changes in interest rate risk, it must consider the effect on fair value of the embedded option (a prepayment option forms a sub-component of the overall interest rate risk).

A five-year receive-variable, pay-fixed swap might or might not be sufficiently effective to qualify as a hedging instrument. A swap, cancellable at Bank C's option after year two with the same terms as the prepayment feature in the loan, would be a more effective hedging instrument because it hedges all of the interest rate risk, including the embedded prepayment option.

5.5 Frequency of hedge effectiveness assessment

Effectiveness must be assessed, at a minimum, at inception and at the end of each reporting period, including interim financial statements. [IAS 39.AG106]

5.6 Ratio analysis and regression analysis

Hedge effectiveness is the degree to which changes in the fair value or cash flows of the hedged item that are attributable to a hedged risk are offset by changes in the fair value or cash flows of the hedging instrument.

A perfect hedge relationship might be illustrated as follows:

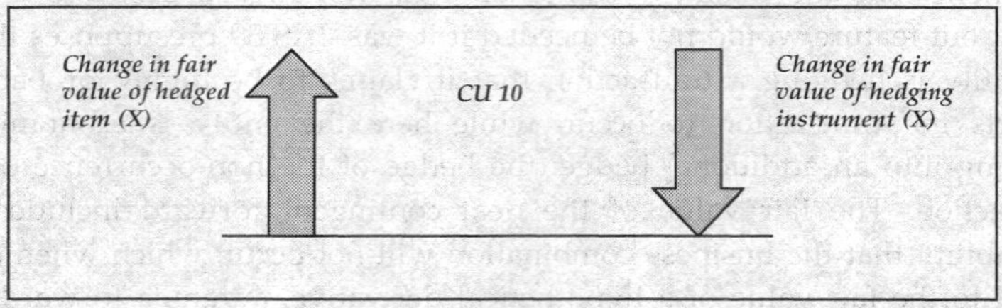

For each £10 change in value of the hedged item, there is an equal and opposite (£10) change in value of the hedging instrument, i.e. the hedging instrument is perfectly negatively correlated in this example with the risk it hedges. The negative sign results from the offsetting effect between the derivative and the hedged item.

Correlation is a term that originates from probability theory and relies on statistical analysis, but it is often estimated from historical data. It is a measure of the extent to which two variables move in relation to one another. The correlation can range from perfectly negative through totally uncorrelated to perfectly positive. Quantitatively, it is expressed as a value ranging from -1 (perfectly negatively correlated) to 1 (perfectly positively correlated).

5.6.1 *Ratio analysis*

Ratio analysis establishes, as a percentage, the extent of effectiveness of the hedging instrument in offsetting the hedged item for the designated risk over a defined period of time, i.e. the degree to which the changes in fair value of the hedging instrument and the hedged item are negatively correlated. It is relatively simple to compute and is well suited for measuring the effectiveness of short-term hedges (where there may be insufficient data to perform a statistical test, such as regression) and is also used to measure the level of actual offset.

5.6.2 *Regression analysis*

Regression analysis is a statistical measurement technique for determining the validity and extent of a relationship between an independent and dependent variable. It is more complex than ratio analysis and requires appropriate interpretation and understanding of the statistical inferences. Where regression analysis is used, the entity's documented policies for assessing effectiveness must specify how the results of the regression will be assessed. A regression analysis can be used for either a cash flow or a fair value hedge.

Example 5.6.2A

Regression analysis (1)

Where the changes in value of a hedged item in Euros is X(t) and the change in value of the hedging instrument in Euros is Y(t), then if Y is a 'good hedge' for X then the observed points (X,Y) should be clustered close to a straight line with a slope equal to -1 and intercept equal to the value of the hedged position, C.

$Y(t) - X(t) = C$ or $Y = X + C$

C is the (constant) value of the hedged position.

For the purposes of illustration, assuming a constant of zero, the slope of the regression equation is equivalent to the ratio of effectiveness and, therefore, should lie within the range of -0.8 to -1.25 (corresponding to a ratio of 80 to 125 per cent) for a 1 to 1 hedge relationship. In the absence of further statistical evidence derived from the same data, a correlation coefficient, R^2, between the values of 0.8 to 1 typically is representative of a highly effective offsetting relationship between the hedged item and the hedging instrument. In other words, an R^2 of 0.8 indicate that 80 per cent of the movement in the dependent variable is 'explained' by variation in the independent variable. As the objective of hedge effectiveness is to assess the degree of offset between two variables, a simple linear regression is an acceptable technique for demonstrating the effectiveness of a hedge relationship.

The slope coefficient is the slope of the straight line of best fit of the regression. For a fully effective hedge relationship the slope coefficient will approximate to -1. A slope coefficient of -1 means that for a specified movement in the hedged item the hedging instrument will move by an equal but opposite extent. A slope coefficient of -0.85 means that for every €1 change in the hedged item it will generally result in an opposite change of €0.85 in the hedging instrument.

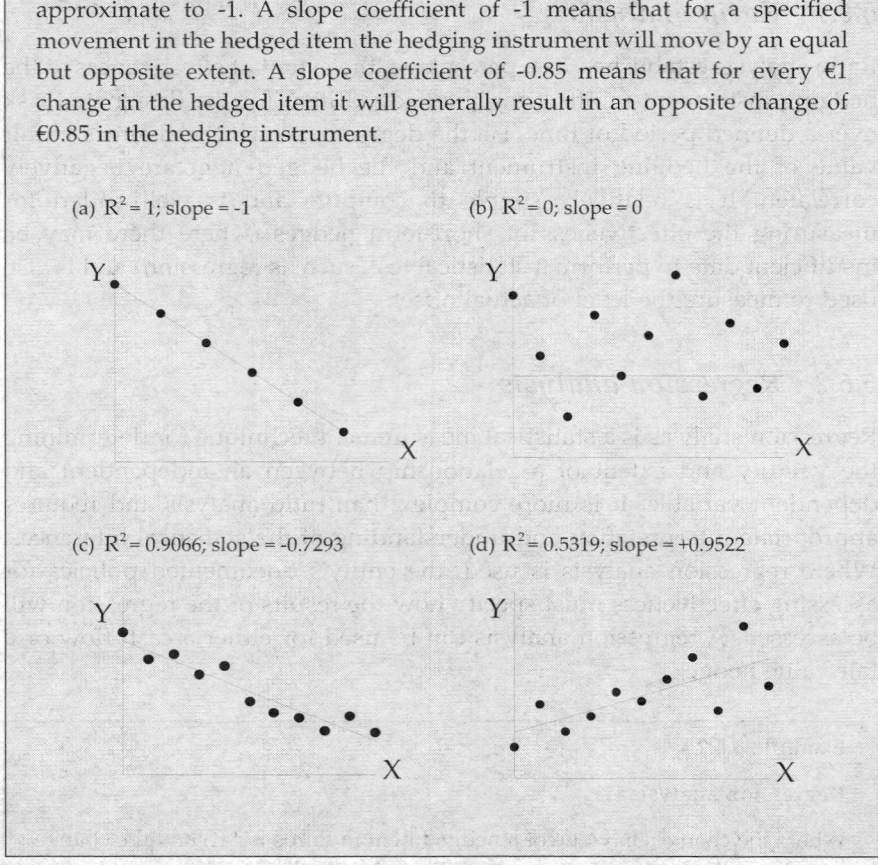

(a) $R^2 = 1$; slope = -1

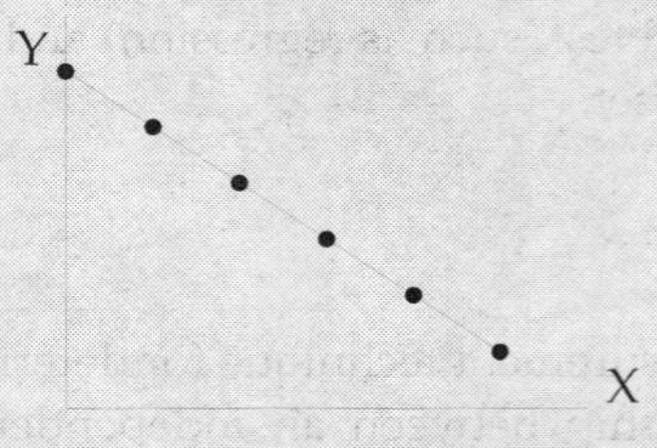

(b) $R^2 = 0$; slope = 0

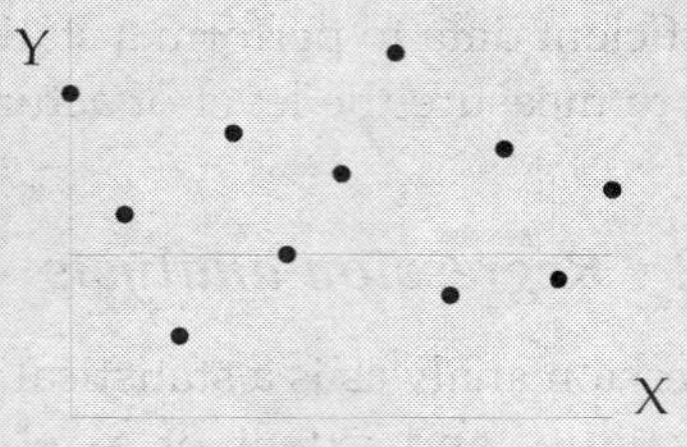

(c) $R^2 = 0.9066$; slope = -0.7293

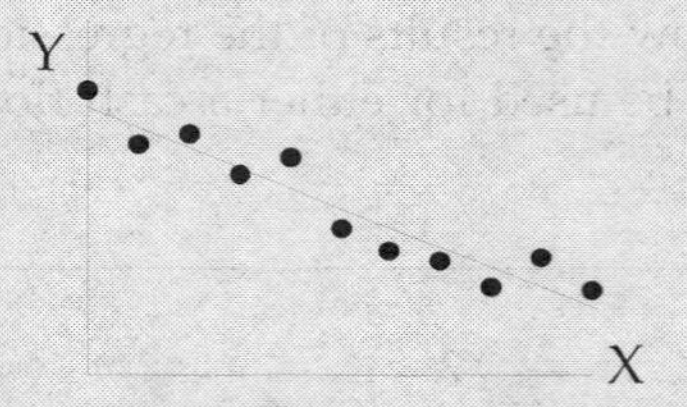

(d) $R^2 = 0.5319$; slope = +0.9522

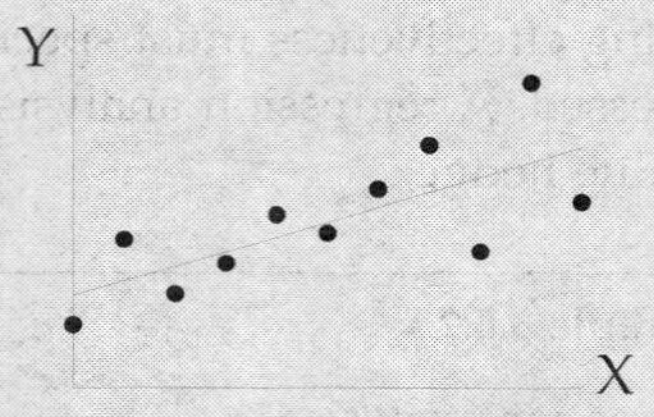

Regression analysis is best suited for measuring the strength of empirical relationships. This relationship can then be used to assess probability of offset, and establish hedge ratios. Such analysis is essential for indirect hedges, i.e. hedges with basis risk where the hedging instrument (e.g. a futures or options contract) has a different underlying to that of the hedged item or transaction. An example is a hedge of petrol prices using oil futures. A simple linear regression may establish a statistical relationship between the two variables, i.e. the price of oil and the price of petrol. The most common method to determine the regression line is called the least squares method. The method finds the best-fitting equation that minimises the sum of the (squared) distances between the data points and the regression line. Where there is a valid statistical relationship, the slope of the regression line can be used to establish the hedge ratio that will maximise expected effectiveness. [IAS 39.AG100]

More complex hedging strategies establish a relationship between one dependent and two or more independent variables by using multiple linear regression. However, as the objective of hedge effectiveness is to compare two variables, namely (i) the changes in fair value of the hedged risk of a hedged item with the change in fair value of a hedging instrument in a fair value hedge, or (ii) the cumulative change in fair value of the expected future cash flows on the hedged item from inception of the hedge with the cumulative gain or loss on the hedging instrument, a simple linear regression will normally be applied.

In order to conclude that the hedging relationship is highly effective using a regression analysis, R^2 should be equal to, or greater than 0.8, and the slope should be between a negative 0.8 and 1.25; and the F and *t* statistics should be evaluated at a 95 per cent confidence level. Only when all of these statistical objectives have been met can an entity claim a highly effective hedge relationship for the period.

The formula for a linear regression is as follows:

$y = mx + b + x1.$

where y — represents the dependent variable
m — represents the slope of the line
x — represents the independent variable
b — represents the y intercept
x1 — represents the error term

The table below provides information on how to evaluate the validity of a linear regression.

Factors that prove a regression analysis Is valid	Confidence level or numerical requirement	How to evaluate the confidence level or numerical requirement
R^2	> = 0.8	The R^2 output should be greater than or equal to 0.8. R^2 is the coefficient of determination which is the square of the coefficient of correlation or r. r indicates when two variables are linearly related. The value of r can range from –1 to +1. R^2 measures the proportion of variability in y that derives from x (i.e. how much of the change of y is explained by a change in x). The higher the value the higher the indication that y is related to x. R^2 is always positive as it is a squared number and cannot exceed 1 as x cannot explain more than 100 per cent in the change of y.

Factors that prove a regression analysis Is valid	Confidence level or numerical requirement	How to evaluate the confidence level or numerical requirement
m — slope factor	Between –0.8 & –1.25	In the regression equation, the slope should be in the range provided. The slope of a line is the change in y over the change in x. An increasing or decreasing value indicates the positive or negative change in y for every change in x. For example, a slope of +1 would indicate that y is increasing at a positive rate with each change in x. In a hedging relationship, a hedge is used to achieve offsetting changes in the value of the hedged item, therefore, a regression equation for a hedging relationship should have a negative slope within the range previously specified as an entity will be long the exposure with the hedged item and short the exposure with the hedging instrument or vice versa. Additionally, 'm' represents the optimal hedge ratio for the hedge, indicating you need 'more' or 'less' of the hedging instrument to compensate for changes in the hedged item.
t — Statistic	95 Per cent Confidence Level	The t statistic for the x coefficient evaluates the probability that the slope is zero. A slope of zero indicates that there is no relationship between the x and y variables. A high t statistic for the x coefficient, positive or negative, generally is a good indicator of correlation and thus a linear relationship. This statistic may be further evaluated by examining the p-value; a statistical output of the t statistic calculation. A low p-value associated with the t-statistic for the x variable, e.g. less than five per cent, indicates a low probability of the slope being zero and thus a high probability that the independent variable is useful in predicting the dependent variable.

Factors that prove a regression analysis Is valid	Confidence level or numerical require-ment	How to evaluate the confidence level or numerical requirement
F — Statistic	95 Per cent Confidence Level	The F statistic evaluates the probability that there is no linear relationship between the x and y variables. To achieve a 95 per cent confidence level, the significance of F should be less than five per cent. If the significance of F is less than five per cent then there is a less than five per cent probability that no linear relationship is present.

It has to be noted that all the factors have to be considered in determining whether a hedge relationship is highly effective. For example, if R^2 has a value near 1 then an m near the ranges of 80%-125% can be acceptable and vice versa.

If a hedge ratio other than one-for-one is applied (see **5.5.1** above), and historical regression analysis is used to determine this hedge ratio, when an entity actually assesses hedge effectiveness using regression values based on this hedge ratio, the entity would expect the 'perfect hedge' to have a gradient of 1 (not that of the hedge ratio). For example, if an entity has a hedge ratio of 0.7, i.e. 0.7 hedged items to 1 hedging instrument, for the purpose of assessing hedge effectiveness, the entity would still be expecting a gradient of the regression line of 0.8 to 1.25 in order to establish that the hedge was highly effective.

Users of regression must be aware of the concept of autocorrelation (i.e. serial correlation). This concept applies when the data points are correlated to each other over time, i.e. the data points are not random. One of the assumptions of a least squares regression is that the data points are uncorrelated to each other. If the data points are correlated to each other this will impact the output of the regression and will result in the R^2, m slope etc being misstated. When data points are taken over a period of time autocorrelation can occur if the different data points are sourced from the same period. For example, if one data point is the change in fair value of a derivative from 1 June to 30 August, and the second data point is the change in fair value from 1 August to 31 October, there is autocorrelation with respect to the month of August as it overlaps in both data points. Users of regression should ensure data is taken from discrete periods to avoid the data points being correlated with each other. Statistical techniques like the Durbin-Watson test can be applied to determine whether there is autocorrelation. Other statistical techniques, like the Prais-Winsten test can be used to restate the output from the model by removing the effects of autocorrelation. As IAS 39 provides no guidance on the use of statistical techniques, entities should use established statistical techniques that are known to provide a meaningful output that is consistent with the Standard's objective of assessing hedge effectiveness.

Example 5.6.2B

Regression analysis (2)

Bank A owns a €100 million portfolio of 10-year BBB corporate bonds. The bonds are eligible to be hedged as a portfolio because each item in the portfolio shares the same hedged risk (interest rate risk) and the change in fair value attributable for each individual item in the portfolio is expected to be approximately proportional to the overall change in the fair value attributable to the hedged risk of the group of items.

On 1 July 20X0, Bank A executes a fair value hedge of the interest rate risk on the bond portfolio using a Euro-bond indexed derivative. To establish a basis for hedge accounting at inception, Bank A computed a historical regression analysis on the monthly results for the previous six months and has assessed offset on a monthly and cumulative basis as summarised below. (For illustrative purposes only six data points have been regressed. As stated in **5.6.3** below more data points will generally be required.)

Month	Current period gain/(loss) on hedging instrument (€)	Current period gain/(loss) on hedged item (€)	(1) Current period R^2	(1) Current period slope	Current period ratio (per cent)
January	-700,000	300,000			-233.33
February	1,600,000	-1,500,000	0.970	1.11	-106.67
March	-2,050,000	2,200,000	0.980	0.99	-93.18
April	1,100,000	-1,020,000	0.988	1.00	-107.84
May	3,900,000	-3,980,000	0.995	0.99	-97.99
June	-12,350,000	11,900,000	1.000	1.03	-103.78

(1) Constant set to zero

	Cumulative gain/(loss) on hedging instrument (€)	Cumulative gain/(loss) on hedged item (€)	Cumulative ratio (per cent)
January	-700,000	300,000	-233.33
February	900,000	-1,200,000	-75.00
March	-1,150,000	1,000,000	-115.00
April	-50,000	-20,000	250.00
May	3,850,000	-4,000,000	-96.25
June	-8,500,000	7,900,000	-107.59

Based on the historical regression analysis, Bank A has a basis for concluding that the hedge is expected to be effective in offsetting changes in fair value. The ratio on a cumulative basis from January to June was within the acceptable 80 to 125 per cent range. Although there were two observations where the cumulative ratio was outside the acceptable 80 to 125 per cent range, based on the per-period ratio results and the strong statistical (regression) results, Bank A could conclude that the hedge was expected to be effective at providing offset. On a per-period basis, the ratio was within the acceptable 80 to 125 per cent range in all periods after the initial period. The regression statistics, with the constant set to zero, were well within the acceptable range of 0.80 to 1.25 for slope, while the range of 0.8 to 1.0 for R^2 indicates that a large element of changes in the fair value of the dependent variable are explained by fair value changes in the independent variable.

The **actual** cumulative and current period changes in fair value of the interest rate risk on the bond portfolio and the Euro-bond indexed derivative, from the date the hedge was initiated on 1 July, are summarised below. The R^2 and slope values were computed using the monthly observations from July to December.

Month	Current period gain/(loss) on hedging instrument (€)	Current period gain/(loss) on hedged item (€)	(1) current period R^2	(1) Current period slope	Current period ratio (per cent)	Current period ineffective portion of hedge
July	€8,575,000	€-7,885,000	1.000	1.05	-108.75	€690,000
August	425,000	-765,000	0.998	1.04	-55.56	-340,000
September	750,000	-350,000	0.998	1.05	-214.29	400,000
October	-1,000,000	800,000	0.998	1.05	-125.00	-200,000
November	2,500,000	-2,300,000	0.998	1.05	-108.70	200,000
December (2)	-2,775,000	2,775,000	0.998	1.05	-100.00	0

(1) Constant set to zero

(2) Note that only six observations were used for illustrative purposes to compute the regression statistics. Sufficient data points are required to render the results meaningful. However, there are also instances whereby data sourced over inappropriate lengths of time can obscure a change in the relationship between the hedged risk and the hedging instrument. Therefore, the context of how and why the data points have been sourced should be considered when judging which data should be applied to the assessment of effectiveness.

Month	Cumulative gain/(loss) on hedging instrument (€)	Cumulative gain/(loss) on hedged item (€)	Cumulative ratio (per cent)
July	75,000	15,000	500.00
August	500,000	-750,000	-66.67
September	1,250,000	-1,100,000	-113.64
October	250,000	-300,000	-83.33
November	2,750,000	-2,600,000	-105.77
December	-25,000	175,000	-14.29

Using a regression test measured on a period basis with the constant set to zero, the hedge was highly effective because the R^2 showed a strong level of explained changes in fair value, i.e. that was due to movements in interest rates, and the slope was within the range of negative 0.8–1.25. If the hedge was evaluated using period to period changes, the hedging relationship had periods of ineffectiveness in August and September using a ratio test and was always effective using a regression test. An entity's risk management policy should address when a failure to establish a hedging relationship, using either ratio or regression, would preclude hedge accounting.

Even though on a ratio basis the hedge failed the 80 to 125 per cent test in two months, the entity may conclude that hedge accounting was appropriate based on the strength of historical period to period offset provided that the entity had documented that it would assess hedge effectiveness on a cumulative basis. This assessment would only be appropriate if the entity's risk management policy specifically addresses hedge failures and indicates when such failures preclude hedge accounting.

It should be noted, however, that the measurement and recognition of the ineffective portion, which is computed on a monthly basis in the above example, is based on the degree of offset. Hence, for example, in July, €90,000 is recognised in profit or loss (€75,000 on the hedging instrument plus €15,000 on the hedged item). Although hedge accounting is permitted for the full period, the full extent of ineffectiveness is recognised in profit or loss for each month. For the months in which the effectiveness ratio fell outside the acceptable range, a relatively higher amount of hedge ineffectiveness is recognised in profit or loss.

Further, in this example it has been demonstrated that different methods of assessing hedge effectiveness can be applied, e.g. cumulative or period-to-period. An entity would need to document at the outset of the hedge relationship which method of assessment is going to be applied, and then use this method consistently. This method will also be documented in the entity's risk management strategy. It is not acceptable to switch methods part-way through a hedge relationship in order to 'cherry-pick' the method that produces the more acceptable results.

5.6.3 *Inputs in a regression analysis*

Past data can be used to demonstrate that a hedge relationship is expected to be highly effective in a prospective hedge effectiveness test, and was highly effective in a retrospective hedge effectiveness test.

The data used in a regression is a series of matched-pair observations from a specified period of time. For example, an entity may wish to regress the change in fair value of an interest rate swap with the change in fair value of the interest rate portion of fixed rate debt on the first day of each month for a three year period. This will generate 36 matched-pair observations which will input into the regression model. An entity should apply a consistent number of data points as the regression is updated at a minimum at the end of each reporting period. If an entity is using a regression model for both prospective and retrospective hedge effectiveness tests it should also use the same number of data points in both tests, and should apply this consistently to other similar hedges.

It is typical to regress observations over the same period as the length of the hedge relationship. For example, if an entity is fair value hedging 5 year fixed rate debt from the date of issue for its full term, an entity would use observations from the last 5 years to demonstrate prospectively that a 5 year receive fixed pay floating interest rate swap is highly effective in fair value hedging the interest rate portion of the debt.

The more data points that are included in the data set will generally result in a more robust regression analysis. However, care must be taken not to include so many data points from such a long period that the data set is not representative of the hedge relationship. It is typical to use at least 30 observations, though in theory it is possible to have a highly effective hedge relationship with less than 30 observations when this is supported with an F-statistic and t-statistic that pass the required confidence levels if the underlying distribution can be assumed to be normal or approximately normal. However, as the number of observations must remain fixed throughout the hedge relationship, and therefore must be stated at inception in the hedge documentation, it is beneficial to use at least 30 observations in order to maximise the number of chances of passing the hedge effectiveness test in future reporting periods.

In both prospective and retrospective hedge effectiveness tests an entity will update the regression by adding new observations and excluding the same number of the oldest observations from the data set. This methodology ensures that the regression is consistently updated and interpreted throughout the hedge relationship.

If an entity wishes to designate a hedging relationship at initial recognition of the hedging instrument (in the case of a cash flow hedge) or at initial recognition of the hedging instrument and the hedged item (in the case of a fair value hedge) it will not necessarily have the data history for those particular instrument(s). This would be the case if the contract did not exist prior to the initial recognition date, or historical fair value data is not available for an instrument that did exist but was held by a different party. In this case the entity should consider using data from similar instruments or instead generate data points by calculating the hypothetical fair value of the instrument using historic market data assuming that instrument had existed prior to the initial recognition date.

5.6.4 *Differences in the results of regression and ratio analysis*

Ratio and regression analysis are clearly very different statistical techniques for assessing hedge effectiveness. Whichever technique is applied, whether for a prospective or/and retrospective assessment of hedge effectiveness, they are unlikely to achieve the same results for each period. The only exception to this perhaps is if the terms of the hedging instrument and hedged item are exactly the same and therefore for all periods the hedge effectiveness assessment would be highly effective. In such instances, entities may have a preference in applying ratio analysis instead of regression because it is simpler.

If an entity chooses to use regression analysis, and therefore must apply this technique consistently throughout the hedge relationship, the entity should be aware of other statistical techniques whose results could call into question the validity of the regression. An example would be a comparison of regression to ratio analysis. If an entity had chosen regression analysis and failed to be highly effective for a period using ratio analysis, it does not mean that the results of the regression are considered not highly effective for that period. Instead, the entity should be aware that if the entity would have failed using ratio analysis on multiple consecutive periods then this does call into question the validity and robustness of the regression analysis. In these instances, the entity should investigate the reasons for the divergence between ratio analysis and regression and if the reasons are not expected to recur in future periods the entity will pass the highly effective test in the current period, and can continue to apply regression analysis in future periods. For example, assume an entity was regressing Brent crude oil prices with aviation fuel prices over a 3 year period as it is hedging its forecast aviation fuel purchases in 3 years' time. After 4 quarters since the start of the hedge relationship, the retrospective hedge effectiveness assessment using regression passed every quarter, but ratio analysis failed every quarter. Upon further investigation of the difference, the entity noted there was a structural event in the market that will result in ratio analysis continuing to fail based on the current hedge designation. It is worth noting that the impact of this structural event will ultimately impact the regression analysis in future periods as new data is added each quarter and the oldest data is removed from the data set. Because the reasons for the divergence in regression and ratio analysis are expected to continue in future periods the entity would not achieve hedge accounting for the period, but the entity could re-designate the hedge relationship using a different hedge ratio and attempt to claim prospective hedge effectiveness based on the new designation.

In November 2006 the IFRIC issued a rejection notice that addressed testing of hedge effectiveness on a cumulative basis. One of the points made in the rejection notice was if the dollar-to-dollar comparison (i.e. ratio analysis) of the changes in the fair value or cash flows of the hedged items and the changes in the fair value or cash flows of the hedging instrument falls outside a range of 80–125 per cent this does not necessarily result in the entity failing to qualify for hedge accounting, provided that the dollar-to-dollar comparison is not the method documented at inception of the hedge for assessing hedge effectiveness. While this conclusion is certainly logical it is worth noting that the existence of a failing ratio analysis may provide evidence that the data being added to a regression analysis will result in a future failure of regression, which ultimately will impact an entity's ability to pass the prospective hedge effectiveness assessment. In short, entities should not be blinded by the output from statistical techniques nor should they look at the output in isolation as this will hinder their ability to assess the quality of the output and the soundness of statistical relationships.

5.7 Measuring hedge ineffectiveness

Section 5.4 above looked at the various ways in which hedge effectiveness can be assessed. These techniques are used to support the entity's claim that a hedge relationship has been highly effective in the period, and will continue to be so for future periods. Consistent application of these techniques in assessing hedge effectiveness is used to support the continued application of hedge accounting.

Measurement of hedge effectiveness relates to the actual amount of ineffectiveness that needs to be reported in the period's profit or loss.

In many instances, the techniques used for assessing hedge effectiveness, i.e. whether the hedge relationship is effective for this period and future periods, will be different to the technique used in measuring ineffectiveness for the period. The difference arises because recognition of ineffectiveness is based on actual offset. The degree of offset is more consistent with ratio analysis techniques (otherwise known as 'the dollar offset test') as opposed to statistical techniques such as regression. Equally, where clean prices are used for assessing hedge effectiveness the measurement of the actual results of the hedge must be based on the actual performance of the derivative, i.e. it is not possible to exclude from its measurement a portion of fair value that is due to the interest accrual. This means that measurement of hedge effectiveness is always based on dirty prices.

The extent to which hedge ineffectiveness will be recognised will depend on whether the hedge is a fair value hedge, or a cash flow hedge.

5.7.1 *Fair value hedge effectiveness measurement*

Once a fair value hedge has been assessed as being highly effective for the period, and there is an expectation of high effectiveness for future periods, the entity has earned the right to measure the hedged item in a manner consistent with fair value hedging, i.e. adjusting the hedged item for fair value movements in the hedged risk.

Actual measurement of hedge ineffectiveness will be recognised in profit or loss of the period because both the adjustment to the hedged item with respect to fair value movements in the hedged risk, and the fair value movements on the hedging instrument are both recognised in profit or loss. To the extent that these two amounts do not fully offset, this difference, being hedge ineffectiveness, will be recognised in profit or loss.

If an entity was applying a retrospective assessment of hedge effectiveness using ratio analysis (i.e. dollar offset test) using period-to-period data, then the percentage of hedge ineffectiveness derived from using this technique would be consistent with the measurement of ineffectiveness in the period.

5.7.2 *Cash flow hedge effectiveness measurement*

As described in **5.1** above, effectiveness measurement in a cash flow hedge effectiveness is different from effectiveness measurement in a fair value hedge. With cash flow hedges, no hedge ineffectiveness is recognised in profit or loss if the cumulative gain or loss on the hedging instrument from inception of the hedge is less than the cumulative change in fair value of the expected future cash flows on the hedged item from inception of the hedge. As described in **5.1** this results in hedge ineffectiveness being recognised in profit or loss only when the change in the hedging instrument's fair value exceeds the change in the present value of future cash flows on the hedged item.

If an entity was applying a retrospective assessment of hedge effectiveness using ratio analysis (i.e. dollar offset test) using cumulative data, then in the case of over-hedging, the percentage of hedge ineffectiveness derived from using this technique would be consistent with the measurement of the cumulative ineffectiveness over the life.

5.7.2.1 *Cash flow hedges: forecast transaction occurs prior to the specified period*

Where the forecast transaction that an entity has designated as a hedged item in a cash flow hedge, for example a forecast sale of a commodity, is expected to occur in an earlier period than originally anticipated, the entity can conclude that this transaction is the same as the one that was designated as being hedged. The change in timing of the forecast transaction does not affect the validity of the designation. [IAS 39.IG.F.5.4]

However, it may affect the assessment of the effectiveness of the hedging relationship as the hedging instrument would need to be designated as a hedging instrument for the whole remaining period of its existence in order for it to continue to qualify as a hedging instrument. If the forecast transaction was expected to occur prior to the date documented in the hedge documentation, the relationship is likely to be ineffective because the hedging instrument matures after the transaction has occurred. The hedging instrument cannot be split into a part that is fully effective up to the date of the transaction, and a part that is excluded from the designation. However, if the forecast transaction was delayed, and was expected to occur after the date documented in the hedge documentation, the hedge could be re-designated as a hedge for the period up to the maturity of the hedging instrument. The effective part of this hedge will be recognised in other comprehensive income, and reclassified from equity to profit or loss when the transaction impacts profit or loss. In the latter case, the hedging instrument is being designated for its full life.

5.7.2.2 Methods for measuring effectiveness for cash flow hedges

IAS 39 does not provide specific guidance as to how an entity should measure hedge effectiveness. However, IAS 39.IG.F.5.5 provides an illustrative example of measuring hedge effectiveness in a cash flow hedge of forecast issuance of fixed rate debt. The implementation guidance recognises that there are at least two methods of accomplishing this measurement. The two methods: the hypothetical derivative method and changes in fair value method, are explained in the following section.

5.7.2.3 The 'hypothetical derivative' method

The hypothetical derivative method measures hedge ineffectiveness by comparing the change in fair value of the actual derivative designated as the hedging instrument and the change in fair value of a 'hypothetical derivative' that would result in perfect hedge effectiveness for the designated hedged item, i.e. the hypothetical derivative would have terms that identically match the critical terms of the hedged item. For example, for a hedge of a variable rate financial asset or liability, the hypothetical derivative would be a swap with the same notional amount and same repricing dates as the hedged asset or liability. In addition, the index on which the hypothetical swap's variable rate is based would match the index on which the asset or liability's variable rate is based, including, where present, any caps and floors and any other embedded features in the hedged item. Further, it would be an on-market swap, i.e. have a zero fair value at inception.

Under the 'hypothetical derivative method' the change in the fair value of the 'perfect' hypothetical swap is regarded as a proxy for the change in the present value of the expected future cash flows on the hedged transaction.

The determination of the fair value of both the 'perfect' hypothetical swap and the actual swap will use discount rates based on the relevant swap curves.

The amount of ineffectiveness recognised in profit or loss for a cash flow hedge equals the excess of the cumulative change in the fair value of the actual swap over the cumulative change in the fair value of the 'perfect' hypothetical swap.

Example 5.7.2.3A

Identifying the hypothetical derivative

Entity PQR has a 4-year variable rate loan asset with a notional of €100 and a maturity of 31/12/X5. The benchmark rate on the loan (i.e. the coupon excluding credit spread) is 3-month EURIBOR. Interest is received quarterly. Entity PQR does not hedge its loan asset on origination, 1/01/X2.

However, at the end of 20X2, Entity PQR forecasts a fall in interest rates and designates a pay variable overnight indexed swap rate (OIS), receive 5 per cent fixed interest rate swap with a notional of €100 and annual interest payments as a cash flow hedge of the interest rate risk on the loan.

Entity PQR formally designates the hedging relationship and meets all of the hedge accounting criteria including the prospective effectiveness test.

To measure effectiveness of the hedging relationship Entity PQR compares the change in fair value of the hedging pay variable OIS, receive 5 per cent fixed interest rate swap to the changes in value of the 'hypothetical derivative,' i.e. the derivative that would result in perfect hedge effectiveness for a hedge of the loan. In this instance the hypothetical derivative is a pay 3-month EURIBOR, receive 4.9 per cent interest rate swap with quarterly payment dates. The 4.9 per cent fixed rate for the remaining 3 years is the market EURIBOR swap rate.

Note that the fixed rates on the actual hedging swap and the hypothetical swap differ as they are priced off different yield curves (i.e. OIS versus EURIBOR).

The hypothetical derivative method can be used universally for all cash flow hedge relationships where a derivative is used as a hedging instrument. This method would not be appropriate in the case of hedging foreign currency risk with a non-derivative instrument as clearly the hedging instrument is not a derivative.

The other method discussed below, the change in fair value method, will have greater applicability when determining hedge effectiveness on variable rate financial assets and liabilities and the forecast issuance of fixed rate debt.

The hypothetical derivative method is referred to as Method B in IAS 39.IG.F.5.5.

Hedge ineffectiveness will arise if the timing or amount of a forecast transaction changes as the fair value (present value) of the expected future cash flows on the hedged item from inception of the hedge will not equal the cumulative fair value on the hedging instrument from inception of the hedge.

Determining the degree of hedge ineffectiveness when the timing or amount of forecast transactions change can be a complex exercise. If an entity applies the hypothetical derivative method in assessing hedge effectiveness then this method will also be reapplied when the timing or amount of the hedged item changes. For example, if the timing of the cash flows on the derivative hedging instrument and the hedged item coincide at inception of the hedge and the derivative is deemed to be the hypothetical derivative, then only to the extent that the cash flows continue to coincide will the hedge be fully effective. If the timing of the forecast cash flows changes during the life of the hedge relationship then a new hypothetical derivative needs to be determined which will be equal to the hypothetical derivative that the entity would have determined when they entered into the hedge accounting relationship that reflects the revised timing of the forecast cash flows. Put another way, the revised hypothetical derivative is the one the entity would have determined had it been able to foresee the revised timing of the forecast cash flows. A comparison of the cumulative gain/loss on the actual hedging instrument and the revised hypothetical derivative will determine the degree of hedge effectiveness and the amount of hedge ineffectiveness to be measured under IAS 39.96(a). The technique is best illustrated with an example.

Example 5.7.2.3B

Identifying the hypothetical derivative

On 1 July 20X1, Entity A considers with high probability that it will issue 5 year fixed rate debt with a notional of £100m in six months' time. Interest will be payable semi-annually when the debt is issued. Entity A is concerned that interest rates will change during the next six months and therefore decides to hedge this exposure by entering into a forward starting interest rate swap to receive 6m-LIBOR pay fixed on a notional of £100m for 5 years where the cash flows on the swap will be receivable and payable every six months starting in six months time. In six months time' when the fixed rate debt is issued Entity A will close out the forward starting interest rate swap and settle with the swap counterparty as Entity A will no longer be exposed to changes in interest rates because the fixed rate on the debt will have been determined. The forward starting interest rate swap has a fair value of zero at 1 July 20X1. The hypothetical derivative would have the same terms as the interest rate swap and is deemed to be perfectly effective at hedging changes in the six month forward 5-year LIBOR swap rate which will be an offset to the variability in the ten to-be-fixed interest payments on the debt that is forecast to be issued on 1 January 20X2.

The hedging instrument will be receive 6m-LIBOR (set in advance) pay 5% every six months starting 1 January 20X2 ending 31 December 20X6. Entity A has a calendar year reporting period and chooses to assess hedge effectiveness every quarter.

1 July 20X1

No entries are required as the fair value of the hedging instrument is zero at inception.

30 September 20X1

The derivative is remeasured to fair value and the effective portion of the gains/losses is recognised in other comprehensive income and taken to the cash flow hedge reserve in equity. As the timing of the forecast transaction and the credit quality of the counterparty remains unchanged the fair value of the derivative is deemed to be fully effective, i.e. the hypothetical derivative still equals the actual derivative. In the three month period since the derivative was entered into interest rates have fallen and therefore the derivative's fair value is negative, i.e. it is a financial liability. The valuation of the derivative is for illustrative purposes only.

Dr	Other comprehensive income (cash flow hedge reserve)	450,000	
Cr	Derivative financial liability		450,000

To record the fair value movement of the derivative and the effective amount in other comprehensive income.

Reporting period	Fair value gain (loss) of derivative in the period	Cumulative fair value gain (loss) of derivative	Fair value gain (loss) of forecast transactions in the period	Cumulative fair value gain (loss) of forecast transactions	(Debit) credit in other comprehensive income (taken to cash flow hedge reserve in equity)	(Debit) credit to profit or loss	(Debit) credit to profit or loss
1 July to 30 September 20X1	(450,000)	(450,000)	450,000	450,000	(450,000)	-	100%

At 1 October 20X1 Entity A revises its estimates of forecast debt issuance due to changes in its funding needs and considers that the fixed rate debt is no longer expected to be issued at 1 January 20X2 and forecasts a 30 day delay. In addition Entity A no longer believes it will issue £100m of debt, rather it

will issue £95m. All other terms of the debt, e.g. frequency of interest payments, denomination, maturity remain the same as originally forecast. Two sources of hedge ineffectiveness have arisen: (i) change in timing of forecast transactions and (ii) reduction in amount of the forecast transaction. Entity A redefines the hypothetical derivative to reflect these changes in expectations. Entity A defines the hypothetical derivative that would have had a fair value of zero at 1 July 20X1 as the forward starting swap that will receive 6m-LIBOR (set in advance) pay fixed every six months starting 1 February 20X2 ending 31 January 20X7 with a notional of £95m. The fixed rate that Entity A would have locked into for this revised hypothetical derivative would have been 5.2% (not the 5% fixed that the actual derivative and original hypothetical derivative achieved). The fair value of the revised hypothetical derivative at 1 October 20X1 is £475,000.

Entity A decides to retain the actual derivative and continue to apply hedge accounting with the actual derivative to the extent that Entity A can be highly effective. The ten forecast interest payments are still expected to occur, though all ten forecast interest payments have shifted back 30 days and will be priced 30 days later because the issue date of the debt is delayed.

31 December 20X1

Interest rates continue to fall during the reporting period ended 31 December 20X2 and the fair value of the actual derivative liability is £800,000. Entity A fair values the revised hypothetical derivative at 31 December 20X1 and the fair value is equal to (£780,000). The difference in value between the revised hypothetical derivative and the actual derivative arises because the revised hypothetical derivative has a smaller notional but a higher fixed rate.

Period	Fair value gain (loss) of derivative in the period	Cumulative fair value gain (loss) of derivative	Fair value gain (loss) of forecast transactions in the period (revised cash flows)	Cumulative fair value gain (loss) of forecast transactions	(Debit) credit in other comprehensive income (taken to the cash flow hedge reserve in equity)	(Debit) credit to profit or loss	Hedge effectiveness
1 October to 31 December 20X1	(350,000)	(800,000)	305,000	780,000	(330,000)	(20,000)	97.5% (780,000 / 800,000)

Dr	Other comprehensive income (cash flow hedge reserve)	330,000
Dr	Profit or loss	20,000
Cr	Derivative financial liability	350,000

To record the fair value movement of the derivative in the period and the effective amount in other comprehensive income and ineffective amount in profit or loss.

The effect of the revision to the change in timing and amount of the forecast transaction is that for the quarter ending 31 December 20X1 not all the gains/losses of the actual derivative are recognised in other comprehensive income (and taken to the cash flow hedge reserve in equity) as the hedge is

> not fully effective. The hedge is only 97.5% effective and £20,000 is recognised as ineffectiveness in the period as the cumulative gain/loss on the actual derivative from inception of the hedge is greater than the cumulative gain/loss on the revised hypothetical derivative from inception of the hedge.
>
> At the start of each period for which hedge effectiveness is assessed Entity A would need to demonstrate that prospectively the hedge relationship will be highly effective. Even though the hedge was highly effective for the period ending 31 December 20X1 this of itself is not assurance that the hedge is expected to be highly effective for future periods. On 1 January 20X2 Entity A will perform the prospective hedge effectiveness test that will take into account the revised timing and amount of the forecast transactions.
>
> Had the change in timing and amount of the forecast transaction been so significant that the entity failed hedge accounting in the period then Entity A would need to redesignate the hedge relationship in its entirety. A new hypothetical derivative would be determined for the new hedge relationship which as interest rate swap is a non-optional derivative, would have a fair value of zero at the new designation date.

Phase 1 of the Business Combinations project that led to the publication of the original version of IFRS 3 *Business Combinations* in 2003 had no specific guidance about whether hedge relationships that exist in the acquiree need to be re-designated by the acquirer should the acquirer wish to continue hedge accounting in the group financial statements. IAS 39 also has no specific requirements with respect to business combinations. Phase 2 of the Business Combinations project that led to the issue of the revised version of IFRS 3 *Business Combinations* in January 2008 has specific guidance on reassessment of contractual arrangements, including financial instruments. IFRS 3(2008) applies prospectively to business combinations for which the acquisition date is on or after the beginning of the first annual reporting period beginning on or after 1 July 2009.

The revised standard requires reassessment of classification and designation of all contractual arrangements based on the pertinent conditions as they exist at the acquisition, with the exception of two cases which are classification of leases as finance or operating leases, and the classification of insurance contracts. IFRS 3(2008).16(b) and BC185 specifically refer to designation of a derivative instrument as a hedging instrument in accordance with IAS 39 and requires reassessment of classification and designation.

The implication of the requirement to reassess hedge relationships at the date of business combinations is that, without re-designation at the group level, the hedge accounting that may continue to be applied at the level of the acquiree will not be applied by the group. If the group wishes to apply hedge accounting at the group level immediately post-acquisition a new hedge relationship will need to be designated at the date of the business combination. When designating cash flow hedges the hypothetical derivative will reflect the conditions that exist at the date of re-designation and therefore may be substantially different to the hypothetical derivative that was originally designated in the acquiree's financial statements. Assuming the group attempts to designate the existing derivative of the acquiree in the same hedge relationship as the acquiree, any difference in the hypothetical derivative will result in a different amount of hedge effectiveness recognised at the group level. The hypothetical derivative may be so different to the actual derivative that the group is unable to pass the assessment of prospective hedge effectiveness and therefore is unable to apply hedge accounting post-acquisition. It is worth noting that any re-designation by the group does not affect the acquiree's financial statements assuming the acquiree retains its original hedge designation.

5.7.2.4 The 'change in fair value' method

The change in fair value method requires a computation of the change in fair value of the cash flows that would have been achieved had the variable cash flow exposure been a fixed cash exposure. For example, if an entity is hedging variable rate debt, the change in fair value method will compare the cumulative changes in the present value of the fixed cash flows that would have been achieved at inception, discounted at the new interest rate, with the fair value of the derivative that is designated as the hedging instrument.

In the instance that an entity is hedging the variable interest rate risk of a variable rate financial asset or liability, the fair value of the hedged item is generally equal to its par amount, as it is not sensitive to fair value movement when interest rates change. This method overcomes this problem by discounting the cash flows that would have been achieved had the instrument been fixed from inception.

Example 5.7.2.4

Change in fair value method

Facts as in **example 5.7.2.3A**.

Applying the change in fair value method, Entity PQR will determine the fixed rate that would have been achieved on 4-year fixed rate loan that is priced off EURIBOR.

The entity will discount the fixed cash flows that would have been achieved on a 4 year fixed rate loan at the new EURIBOR interest rate curve. The cumulative present value of these cash flows will be compared with the fair value of the interest rate swap that is priced off OIS. The change in fair value method will recognise ineffectiveness due to the different basis of interest rates between the hedging instrument and the hedged item.

The change in fair value method is referred to as Method A in IAS 39.IG.F.5.5.

5.7.2.5 *The 'change in variable cash flows' method*

The change in variable cash flows method compares the floating rate cash flows of the hedged item with the floating rates cash flows on the derivative. For example, if an entity was assessing hedge effectiveness for a variable rate financial asset or liability, the entity would compare the present value of the cumulative changes in the expected future cash flows on the variable leg of an interest rate swap with the present value of the cumulative change in expected future interest cash flows on the hedged item. The fixed rate leg of the interest rate swap is excluded from the analysis as it is assumed that the derivative's fair value that is attributable to the fixed rate leg is not relevant to the variability of the variable cash flows on the hedged item. Such an assumption is only valid when the derivative has a fair value of zero at inception, i.e. it is an on-market instrument. If the derivative did not have a fair value of zero at inception, the derivative would have a higher or lower fixed rate leg to compensate the entity for the upfront payment or receipt at inception. Because the fixed rate leg is adjusted to reflect this upfront payment or receipt, the fixed rate leg includes a financing element that cannot be ignored. It is for the above reason that IAS 39.IG.F.5.5 purposely prohibits use of the variable cash flows method. In practice, in the circumstances where the derivative does not include a financing element, the variable cash flows method should amount to using the hypothetical derivative and change in fair value method.

In March 2007, the IFRIC finalised a rejection notice titled *Assessing hedge effectiveness of an interest rate swap in a cash flow hedge*. The IFRIC stated that it was not permissible to consider only the undiscounted changes in cash flows of the hedging instrument and the hedged item in assessing hedge effectiveness in a cash flow hedge of interest rate risk when using an interest rate swap. The IFRIC noted that such a method for assessing hedge effectiveness would not be in accordance with IAS 39.74 that does not allow the designation of a portion of a derivative as the hedging instrument, and would ignore the fact that one of the reasons for ineffectiveness is the mismatch of the timing of interest payments or receipts of the swap and the hedged item.

6 Cash flow hedge accounting for a portfolio hedge of interest rate risk

An entity may wish to designate a derivative, or portfolio of derivatives, as a hedge of multiple variable interest rate payments or receipts. Instead of allocating each individual derivative to an individual cash inflow or outflow, the derivatives and the hedged cash flows are 'pooled' and hedged as a portfolio. IAS 39.IG.F.6.2 provides a series of questions and answers for an entity wishing to undertake such a hedge accounting strategy. IAS 39.IG.F.6.3 provides an illustrative example of the hedge strategy. The implementation guidance is very detailed and is complex. The objective of this section is to simplify the concepts and highlight some relevant conclusions that can be reached from this implementation guidance.

6.1 Hedged item

As stated in **2.2** above a recognised floating rate debt instrument can either be hedged as a recognised financial instrument, or instead the floating interest inflows or outflows can be hedged as forecast transactions. If an entity regularly borrows or invests in floating rate debt instruments the entity has an exposure not only from the recognised debt instruments but also the debt instruments that it will invest or borrow in the future. An entity may, for example, borrow through short-term commercial paper, say up to a maturity of 90 days, that has an interest rate that resets monthly, but will rollover the recognised commercial paper into further commercial paper when the recognised commercial paper reaches its maturity. The entity has variability in cash flows with respect to its recognised commercial paper, but also the commercial paper it believes, with high probability, it borrow in the future.

IAS 39 provides flexibility in hedging forecast cash flows when an entity expects, with high probability, to reinvesting cash flows from one instrument into another. When cash flow hedging interest rate risk, say LIBOR, an entity can have cash flow variability with respect to the following:

- the variability in LIBOR inflows or outflows on a recognised acquired or issued debt instrument when the basis of interest is determined by future LIBOR rates; or
- the variability in LIBOR inflows or outflows from a highly probable reinvestment or future borrowing of a new floating rate LIBOR debt instrument. As future interest inflows or outflows will be derived from future rates of LIBOR, the entity has an exposure to variability in LIBOR; or

- the effective interest rate that will be earned or paid if an entity has a highly probable forecast investment or issuance of fixed rate debt where the debt is priced off the LIBOR curve at the date the debt is issued; or
- the effective interest rate that will be earned or paid if an entity has a highly probable forecast investment or issuance of a fixed rate debt and the fixed interest rate is determined of the LIBOR curve prior to the debt being issued, and therefore the amount of proceeds received by the issuer, or paid by the acquirer has not yet been determined, i.e. it is variable. The resulting premium or discount to par at issue will impact profit or loss through the effective interest rate determined when the debt is issued.

The entity can aggregate its floating rate LIBOR exposures from the four examples above and plot them in time buckets so that the entity can determine when the LIBOR cash flows are set (i.e. when they fix), and therefore determine up to what period it has an exposure to LIBOR. For example, if an entity has issued 5-year floating rate 3-month LIBOR debt where the floating rate is set in advance, at the date of issue, the floating rate for the next 3 months will be determined based on the rate of LIBOR at the date the debt is issued. An entity cannot cash flow hedge the first payment of interest as that first payment is not actually variable as it has been fixed in advance. This payment will be excluded from the hedge designation. (If LIBOR was priced in arrears, or was priced in advance but some of the interest receipts or payments have not yet been set then this is the variability in LIBOR that could be designated.) However, all future interest payments that will be determined in 3 months' time and beyond, are today all variable, and until those floating rates are set, at the start of each respective quarter, the entity has exposure to LIBOR which it can hedge. As future LIBOR interest payments are set at the start of each quarter, the number of forecast transactions with respect to that debt instrument, falls, but is likely to be replaced by more forecast interest exposures in future periods if the entity expects to borrow more floating rate debt.

An entity does not need to state the maturity of the forecast floating or fixed debt it is expecting with high probability to invest in or borrow at. As long as the entity has a high probability of being exposed to LIBOR, as the entity is expected to invest in LIBOR debt instruments or borrow at LIBOR rates, the exact maturity of the instrument is not relevant. If an entity believes it will have an exposure to LIBOR for 3 years, it does not matter whether the entity expects to invest in a floating rate asset with a maturity of 6 months, that then rolls into another five 6-month term floating rate assets, or whether it expects to invest in a 12-month floating rate asset, and a subsequent investment in a further three 12-month floating rate assets. In both cases, and any other combination, the entity's *future* exposure to LIBOR is the same.

An entity also does not need to state whether it will invest or borrow in floating rate debt instruments, or fixed rate debt instruments, as long as any debt instrument it invests in or borrows is derived from the LIBOR curve. For example, if an entity expects to borrow in 6 months' time, up to the date it draws down the borrowing, it has an exposure to LIBOR. From today until 6-months' time, changes in LIBOR will impact the future interest payments on future floating rate debt, or will impact the fixed rate or amount of proceeds that will only be determined at the date the entity draws down the fixed rate borrowing. In both cases, the entity may designate its exposure to LIBOR for the next 6 months.

The portfolio approach to cash flow hedging interest rate risk is a dynamic approach in that an entity may choose to re-designate, almost on a continuous basis, though more likely every quarter if LIBOR resets quarterly. As the cash flows that are due to fix in the next period fall away from the designation, new forecast cash flows may be added to the designation. As long as the entity can claim these new forecast transactions are highly probable and the entity has qualifying hedging instruments that are expected to be highly effective, the entity can pursue hedge accounting.

6.2 Hedging instrument

In the instance where the hedged risk is LIBOR the hedging instrument could be a LIBOR for fixed rate interest rate swap. Alternatively, it could be a LIBOR based purchased option. If the entity has an exposure to LIBOR inflows, and it chooses to hedge with a swap, it will have a pay LIBOR receive fixed rate interest rate swap; if the entity has an exposure to LIBOR outflows, and it chooses to hedge with a swap, it will have a receive LIBOR pay fixed rate interest swap. The entity must designate all, or a proportion, of the interest rate swap as a hedging instrument relating to the designated hedged item (forecast LIBOR interest inflows or outflows).

6.3 Hedge designation

In a hedge of forecast interest payments or receipts an entity will schedule the forecast transactions and will hedge these floating inflows or outflows up to the date they fix, i.e. when LIBOR is set. In more simple hedge designations, the timing of the fixing of the cash flows on the hedged items coincides with the timing of the refixing of the variable rate on the swap. This is considered a full term hedge, compared to a partial term hedge, as the full period up to the date when the forecast transaction is no longer subject to cash flow variability is hedged.

An entity will have exposure to LIBOR as long as the entity has a high probability of investing or borrowing in LIBOR-based debt instruments (whether floating or fixed of the future LIBOR curve). In order to designate all these exposures an entity can choose to partial term hedge these exposures until the next time LIBOR is set. As described in **6.1** above, if a LIBOR interest inflow or outflow is set, it no longer is variable and therefore cannot be hedged. An entity can use partial term hedging to hedge all variable LIBOR exposure for its forecast LIBOR-based transactions from today until the next time LIBOR resets. If LIBOR resets every quarter, the entity can partial term hedge all the future LIBOR exposures for just 3 months only. After 3 months, the entity will re-designate, for the next 3 months, and so on.

Example 6.3

Cash flow hedging the variability in reinvestment: designation

Entity A has a short-term recognised variable rate asset with 3 months remaining to maturity. At maturity of that asset Entity A will reinvest the proceeds from the asset into either fixed rate asset(s) or floating rate asset(s) of maturities that are not determined until those instruments are acquired. Entity A forecasts with high probability that it will reinvest for up to 4 years. As Entity A is exposed to interest rates from its reinvestment into new assets (irrespective of whether the asset is fixed or floating), it enters into a receive fixed pay floating 3m-LIBOR interest rate swap (IRS) that has a 2 year maturity (Entity A has a policy of hedging out only 2 years) to hedge the risk of variability in LIBOR. It is assumed that the floating rate on the recognised floating rate liability has already been set in advance and therefore there is no cash flow variability that can be hedged.

Entity A does not need to be specific as to the maturity of the future reinvested debt instruments. The instruments could have maturities of 3 months, 6 months, 9 months etc, and could also be fixed or floating. Up to the date the reinvestment occurs, Entity A has an exposure to LIBOR that it can cash flow hedge.

Entity A plots the notionals for the various time periods over the next 2 years which will determine the extent to which Entity A is exposed to LIBOR:

	t0	3m	6m	9m	12m	15m	18m	21m	24m
Specific 3m floating LIBOR asset (notional £m)	100								
Hedged item:									

	t0	3m	6m	9m	12m	15m	18m	21m	24m
Non specific assets that have LIBOR exposure (notional £m)		100	100	100	100	100	100	100	100
Hedging instrument: Receive fixed pay 3m-LIBOR (notional £m)	100	100	100	100	100	100	100	100	100

t0 = 1/1/X0

As the interest rate swap and the recognised floating rate asset have LIBOR set in advance, in this case on 1/1/X0, there is no cash flow variability on the LIBOR based asset with 3 months to maturity. All cash flows of that debt instrument are fixed, not variable, being the principal and one interest payment that have been determined at the date of designation. Therefore, the recognised floating rate LIBOR asset cannot be a hedged item in a cash flow hedge.

Entity A, therefore, can only designate the cash flow variability due to changes in LIBOR with respect to forecast transactions that occur after the first reset date of the swap (the first cash flows under the swap are already fixed at t0 as LIBOR is set in advance). The forecast transactions that Entity A chooses to hedge are the non-specific forecast exposure to LIBOR from reinvesting in LIBOR based assets from 1/4/X0 until 31/12/X1 (equal to the maturity of the IRS). At t0, Entity A designates the exposure of variability in LIBOR that occurs between 1/1/X0 and 31/3/X0 with respect to its forecast transaction (being the LIBOR variability on its forecast transactions occurring from 1/4/X0 to 31/12/X1). The exposure for the subsequent periods is specifically not hedged in this designation. Entity A has entered into a hedge of its exposure to LIBOR with respect to its reinvestment and rollover of LIBOR-based asset that are expected to occur in the 21 month period beginning 1/4/X0, due to changes in LIBOR that occur between 1/1/X0 and 31/3/X0.

Entity A is not specific as to the maturity of its reinvested assets that are acquired after 1/4/X0 as all assets will be subject to exposure to LIBOR until the date they are priced. As all non-specific forecast transaction are exposed to LIBOR and are deemed as highly probable Entity A is highly effective on a prospective basis.

6.4 Partial term cash flow hedging

Where there is a difference between the timing of the fixing of the LIBOR-based inflows or outflows of the hedged item and the timing of the fixing of LIBOR on the swap hedge ineffectiveness will generally arise as an entity hedges the full term of the forecast transaction, being the time period up to the date the interest receipt or payment is set to LIBOR.

Partial term cash flow hedging is an alternative technique which can be applied to hedged items that are financial instruments. Partial term cash flow hedging does not apply to non-financial items as explained in **3.8.2** above. In this instance where a forecast variable interest receipt or payment fixes at a date later than the respective fixing on the variable leg of the interest rate swap, an entity can purposely designate a partial term hedge of the period up to the date the variable leg on the interest rate swap refixes. For example, if the variable leg on the interest rate swap fixes for LIBOR on 1 October, yet the hedged item fixes for LIBOR on 1 November, the difference in timing of resetting cash flows is not part of the hedge designation. In this instance, variations in LIBOR between the designation date and 1 October are considered a partial term hedge of the variability in LIBOR that exists on the hedged item that will reset on 1 November. Partial term hedging 'carves' up the period to the next resetting on the hedged item and hedges only part of that period.

IAS 39.IG.F.6.3 endorses this type of designation as it states that 'when the interest rate swap is repriced in three months at the then current variable rate, the fixed rate and the variable rate on the interest rate swap become known and no longer provide hedge protection for the next three months. If the next forecast transaction does not occur until three months and ten days, the ten-day period that remains after the repricing of the interest rate swap is not hedged'. The term of the hedge designation is only for the next 3 months. The implementation guidance explains that the 'period of the exposure to interest rate changes on the portion of the cash flow exposures being hedged is:

- the period from the designation date to the repricing date of the interest rate swap that occurs within the quarterly period in which, but not before, the forecast transactions occur, and
- its effects for the period after the forecast transactions occur equal to the repricing interval of the interest rate swap.'

As the designation is the variability due to LIBOR prior to the debt instrument being acquired or issued, the fact that following the acquisition or recognition of the borrowing, LIBOR continues to change is irrelevant with respect to this specific partial term hedge designation, as the period following recognition of the asset or liability does not form part of this specific hedge.

6.5 Hedge effectiveness

Hedge ineffectiveness can be greatly reduced by using the above hedge accounting strategy for a number of reasons:

- The entity designates the LIBOR risk only, and excludes credit risk on the hedged items. Changes in the credit risk of the hedged item will not impact the effectiveness of the hedge as credit risk is not a designated hedged risk. The credit risk of the interest rate swap, however, must be monitored as this may be a source of ineffectiveness.

- Duration differences between the interest rate swap and the hedged forecast cash flow are not a source of ineffectiveness as the interest rate risk that is hedged is the risk relating to changes in the portion of the yield curve that corresponds with the period in which the variable rate leg of the interest rate swap is repriced.

- Timing differences between the date the swap resets to LIBOR and the date the hedged item resets to LIBOR are not a source of ineffectiveness when partial term hedging is applied.

Example 6.5

Cash flow hedging the variability in reinvestment: hedge effectiveness

Continuing with **example 6.3**, assuming Entity A is subject to quarterly reporting where the period end coincides with the repricing on the swap, i.e. 31/3/X0, Entity A must perform a retrospective assessment of hedge effectiveness for the period gone, plus a prospective assessment if it wishes to continue to apply hedge accounting.

As part of the retrospective assessment of hedge effectiveness for the period it looks back at the transactions that occurred in the period to determine whether it has been highly effective. As at 1/1/X0 Entity A never claimed it was hedging cash flow variability for the first 3 months of 20X0 for its recognised asset as LIBOR had already been determined on that floating rate recognised asset and therefore it never formed part of the designation. However, Entity A must assess whether the forecast transactions that it had designated at 1/1/X0, being the full-term hedge of forecast reinvestments after 1/4/X0, is highly effective. Entity A did not need to apply partial term hedging as the date of the LIBOR reset on the interest rate swaps coincides with the date of the LIBOR reset of the forecast reinvestments. Where the forecast reinvestments remain highly probable the hedge will have been fully effective on a retrospective basis, assuming all other criteria are met. Entity A may therefore recognise the full amount of the fair value of the derivative in other comprehensive income at 31/3/X0 in accordance with IAS 39.96.

As part of the prospective assessment of hedge effectiveness at 1/4/X0 Entity A must reassess whether the future exposure to LIBOR is still highly probable. As the next reset date on the interest rate swap is 1/7/X0, Entity A is hedging those forecast transactions that are subject to LIBOR in the future that reset after 1/7/X0. Any LIBOR-based interest inflows that are fixed at 1/4/X0 are not designated as they are no longer variable, and any interest inflows that fix within the next 3 months are not part of the designation as they are not subject to variability in LIBOR for the next 3 months. Entity A can pass the prospective assessment of hedge effectiveness as long as all the forecast transactions are deemed to be highly probable.

7 Fair value hedge accounting for a portfolio hedge of interest rate risk

The IASB published an amendment to IAS 39 in March 2004 that details how an entity can apply fair value hedge accounting to a portfolio of financial assets and/or financial liabilities for interest rate risk only. The main reasons for amending IAS 39 and a summary of the amendments are as described below.

7.1 Prepayable financial items

Fixed rate prepayable debt instruments may be prepaid prior to their contracted maturity. When interest rates move the change in the fair value of a prepayable item is caused by changes in the fair value of the contractual cash flows and changes in the fair value of the prepayment option. If the hedging instrument, e.g. an interest rate swap, is not prepayable, changes in the fair value of the hedged item are not expected to be offset by changes in fair value of the hedging instrument. This results in hedge ineffectiveness.

IAS 39 permits prepayable financial assets and liabilities to be hedged for changes in fair value attributable to changes in the hedged interest rate on the basis of expected rather than contractual repricing dates. [IAS 39.81A] This is achieved by analysing the portfolio of hedged items into time periods based on the expected repricing dates. The expected repricing date of an item is the earlier of the dates when the item is expected to mature or to reprice to market rates. [IAS 39.AG117] As a result, the computation of the effect of a change in interest rates on the fair value of the prepayment option embedded in a prepayable item is not required. Though, if the estimates of the time periods in which items are expected to repay change, ineffectiveness will arise.

7.2 Hedging a portfolio of items

IAS 39 allows similar assets or similar liabilities to be aggregated and hedged as a group only if the individual assets or individual liabilities in the group share the risk exposure that is designated as being hedged. Furthermore, the change in fair value attributable to the hedged risk for each individual item in the group must be expected to be approximately proportional to the overall change in fair value attributable to the hedged risk of the group of items. [IAS 39.83] As the individual hedged items are expected to behave differently in so far as they may prepay at different times, the change in the fair value of each hedged item cannot be expected to be proportional to the change in the fair value of the portfolio.

The general requirement is modified for a hedge of a portfolio for interest rate risk only. The items in the hedged portfolio must be items whose fair value changes in response to the hedged interest rate and must be items that could have qualified for fair value hedge accounting had they been designated individually. However, an entity is not required to demonstrate that the change in fair value of the individual hedged items is approximately proportional to the overall change in fair value of the portfolio due to interest rate risk. [IAS 39.AG118] For this type of hedge the designated hedged item is expressed as an 'amount of currency' (e.g. an amount of Sterling, US dollars, Euros etc) rather than as individual assets or liabilities. [IAS 39.81A]

7.3 Fair value hedge adjustments

IAS 39 requires that in an effective fair value hedge relationship the hedged item is adjusted by the change in its fair value due to the hedged risk. The adjustment to the hedged item may be amortised to profit or loss as soon as the adjustment exists, but shall begin no later than when the item ceases to be adjusted for the hedged risk. For a portfolio hedge this would require an adjustment to many items, as well as tracking the amortisation of the resultant adjustment to profit or loss. In most cases complex systems solutions would be required.

IAS 39 is modified to permit the adjustment to the hedged items for a portfolio hedge of interest rate risk to be recognised in two separate line items within assets or liabilities for those repricing time periods for which the hedged item is an asset or liability respectively. This adjustment shall be presented next to financial assets or financial liabilities. [IAS 39.89A] Furthermore, that adjustment may be amortised to profit or loss using a straight line method where amortising using a recalculated effective interest rate is not practicable. The adjustment should also be amortised to profit or loss by the expiry of the relevant repricing time period. [IAS 39.92]

7.4 Hedging a net position

Whilst IAS 39 prohibits the designation of an overall net position (e.g. the net of fixed rate assets and fixed rate liabilities), entities that hedge the net position in economic terms may designate a proportion of either the assets or liabilities as the hedged item. The net exposure will change each period due to the re-pricing of items, or through derecognition, impairment and origination of new instruments. It follows that the designated proportion of assets or liabilities will also need to be changed following such changes in the net exposure.

In the case of a portfolio hedge for interest rate risk only, the hedged item may be expressed as a *gross currency amount* of either assets or liabilities rather than as an individual asset (or liability). [IAS 39.81A] The benefit of this approach is that the effect of changes in interest rates on the amount of designated currency is determined in aggregate and not individually for each hedged item. [IAS 39.81A]

7.5 Demand deposits

IAS 39 states that the fair value of a financial liability with a demand feature is not less than the amount payable on demand, discounted from the first date that the amount could be required to be paid. [IAS 39.49] Many entities economically hedge their demand deposits on the basis that a certain core level of the demand deposits is not repaid on demand. For the core deposits the expected life extends well beyond the demand date and the balance of the portfolio is relatively stable because withdrawals on some accounts are offset by new deposits into others. The hedge relationships are entered into on the basis of the expected repayment dates of the total balance of the portfolio of deposits.

In a fair value hedge, accounting for demand deposits on the basis of their expected repayment dates is inconsistent with the measurement principle for a financial liability with a demand feature. Thus, for fair value hedges, demand deposits cannot be hedged beyond their demand date. Nevertheless, the deposits may be included in determining the entity's net exposure and the designated hedged item with one restriction: if the net exposure is a net liability and that liability is made up entirely or partly of demand deposits, the designated liability can only be up to an amount equal to the amount of non-demand deposit liabilities. The reason for this is that the fair value determined in accordance with IAS 39 of a demand deposit is not affected by changes in interest rates, i.e. there is no fair value exposure to hedge for accounting purposes.

7.6 Ineffectiveness

In a fair value hedge of a portfolio hedge of interest rate risk, in addition to hedge ineffectiveness that arises on other fair value hedging relationships, additional hedge ineffectiveness may arise for the following reasons in a portfolio hedging relationship:

- actual repricing dates differ from those expected, or expected repricing dates are revised; and
- items in the hedged portfolio become impaired or are derecognised.

7.7 Application

IAS 39 sets out a number of steps that should be followed in achieving hedge accounting for a portfolio hedge of interest rate risk. These steps are summarised in the example below.

Example 7.7

Fair value hedging a portfolio of interest rate risk

Step 1: As part of its risk management process, Bank A identifies a portfolio of items whose interest rate risk it wishes to hedge. The portfolio may comprise only of financial assets, financial liabilities, or both. Since Bank A hedges its fixed rate originated mortgages, fixed rate liabilities and core deposits on a net basis, it identifies a portfolio containing these items as the portfolio it wishes to hedge. [IAS 39.AG114(a)]

Step 2: Bank A analyses the portfolio into repricing time periods based on expected, rather than contractual, repricing dates. The expected repricing dates are based on historical experience and other available information, including information and expectations regarding prepayment rates, interest rates and their interaction. Whilst the analysis into repricing time periods may be performed by scheduling cash flows into the periods in which they are expected to occur, the Bank schedules the notional principal amounts into all periods until repricing is expected to occur as follows: [IAS 39.AG114(b)]

	T1	**T2**	**T3**
Fixed rate assets	30	40	25
Fixed rate liabilities	(20)	(30)	(15)
Demand deposits	-	-	(35)
Net exposure	10	10	(25)

In addition to complying with all other hedge designation and documentation criteria, Bank A documents:

- which assets and liabilities are included in the portfolio hedge and the basis used for removing them from the portfolio; [IAS 39.AG119(a)]
- how Bank A estimates its repricing dates, including what interest rate assumptions underlie estimates of prepayments rates and the basis for changing those estimates; the same method is used for both the initial estimates made at the time an asset or liability is included in the hedged portfolio and for any later revisions to those estimates; [IAS 39.AG119(b)] and
- The number and duration of repricing time periods. [IAS 39.AG119(c)]

(for further documentation requirements see steps 3 and 5)

Step 3: Bank A determines the amount it wishes to hedge and designates as the hedged item in each repricing time period a gross currency amount of assets and/or liabilities from the identified portfolio equal to that amount.

	T1	T2	T3
Amount of assets (liabilities) designated as hedged item	10	10	(15)

This amount is converted into a percentage of assets or liabilities from the identified portfolio in each time period, which is used in testing hedge effectiveness. [IAS 39.AG114(c)]

	T1	T2	T3
Net Exposure	10	10	(25)
Amount of assets (liabilities) designated as hedged item	10	10	(15) *
Hedge ratio (hedged item as a percentage of amount of qualifying assets (liabilities)	33.33% (10/30)	25% (10/40)	100% (15/15)

(* Note that the amount hedged may only be drawn from the fixed rate liabilities and not from the demand deposits as demand deposits cannot be a hedged item beyond their demand date.)

Bank A is therefore hedging 33.33 per cent of its assets in repricing time period T1, 25 per cent of its assets in repricing time period T2 and 100 per cent of its fixed rate liabilities in repricing time period T3.

In addition to complying with all other hedge accounting criteria, Bank A documents the methodology used to determine the amount of assets or liabilities that are designated as the hedged item, the hedge ratio and the percentage measure used when testing effectiveness. [IAS 39.AG119(e)]

Step 4: Bank A designates the interest rate risk hedged as a particular benchmark rate, e.g. LIBOR. [IAS 39.AG114(d)]

Step 5: Bank A designates one or more hedging instruments for each repricing time period. [IAS 39.AG114(e)] The derivatives designated for a repricing time period may comprise a number of derivatives with offsetting risk positions all of which contain exposure to LIBOR. None of the derivatives however may be a written option, or net written option as the Standard does not permit such options to be designated as hedging instruments except in certain limited circumstances (see **4.6** above for details). [IAS 39.AG120]

Bank A has the following interest rate swaps (by maturity):

<table>
<tr><th></th><th>T1</th><th>T2</th><th>T3</th></tr>
<tr><td>Swap 1</td><td colspan="2">35</td><td></td></tr>
<tr><td>Swap 2</td><td colspan="3">10</td></tr>
<tr><td>Swap 3</td><td colspan="3">(35)</td></tr>
</table>

Bank A designates the following swaps or combination of swaps to hedge each of the time periods:

	T1	T2	T3
Swap 1	–	–	–
Swap 2	10	10	10
Swap 3	–	–	(25)
Total designated hedging instruments	10	10	(15)

In the above example swap 2 hedges more than one repricing time period and is thus allocated to all the time periods it hedges. [IAS 39.AG120]

Step 6: Using the designations made in steps 3–5 above, Bank A assesses at inception and in subsequent periods, whether the hedge is expected to be highly effective during the period for which the hedge is designated. [IAS 39.AG114(f)] It is not appropriate to assume that changes in the fair value of the hedged item equal changes in the value of the hedging instrument. [IAS 39.AG122] IAS 39 does allow the use of two techniques to measure the effectiveness of the hedging relationship: Bank A can calculate the effectiveness of the hedging relationship as the difference between the change in the fair value of the hedging instrument and the change in the fair value of the entire hedged item attributable to the hedged risk; [IAS 39.AG126(a)] or it can elect to use an approximation approach. [IAS 39.AG126(b)] Bank A applies this approximation method as is illustrated in steps A to E and step 7 below.

In addition to complying with all other hedge accounting criteria, Bank A documents:

- how often Bank A will test effectiveness (monthly in this case); [IAS 39.AG119(d)]
- which of the two effectiveness testing techniques Bank A is using; [IAS 39.AG119(d)] and
- when effectiveness is tested using the approximation approach, whether effectiveness will be assessed for each repricing time period individually, for all time periods in aggregate, or by using some combination of the two (in this case Bank A elects to assess effectiveness for all time periods in aggregate). [IAS 39.AG119(f)]

After one month, Bank A assesses the effectiveness of the hedging relationship using the approximation approach as follows:

Step A: Fair value changes of the hedged item (before determining the impact of changes in fair value due to revised repayment expectations and ignoring changes in fair value not attributable to interest rate movements) and of the hedging instruments are determined to be as follows:

	T1	T2	T3
Changes in fair value: hedged item	2	3	(1)

	T1	T2	T3
% change in fair value (as a percentage of the hedged assets (liabilities))	20% (2/10)	30% (3/10)	6.67% (1/15)
Changes in fair value: hedging instrument	(2)	(3)	1

Step B: A revised estimate of the amount of assets and liabilities in each repricing time period is determined in order to calculate the amount of the hedged item based on the revised estimates. Following a decrease in LIBOR, the assets and liabilities have repaid faster than initially expected. Bank A determines that its portfolio of assets and liabilities is now expected to reprice as follows:

	T1	T2	T3
Fixed rate assets	27	32	20
Fixed rate liabilities	(15)	(20)	(10)
Demand deposits	–	–	(20)
Net Exposure *	12	12	(10)

(*Note that the above new net position is irrelevant for the purposes of determining the effectiveness of the hedging relationship for this period. It may however be relevant in the next period in determining the amount of hedged assets and liabilities.)

Step C: The percentage of the assets and liabilities hedged (as determined in step 3 above) is applied to the revised amount of assets and liabilities in each repricing period.
[IAS 39.AG126(b)(ii)]

	T1	T2	T3
Hedge ratio (from Step 3)	33.33%	25%	100%
Revised assets	27	32	–
Revised liabilities	–	–	(10)
Revised hedged assets	9 (33.33%*27)	8 (25%*32)	–
Revised hedged liabilities	–	–	(10) (100%*10)

Step D: The change in the fair value of the revised estimate of the hedged item that is attributable to the hedged risk is calculated by multiplying the change in fair value (as determined in Step A) by the new amount of assets (liabilities) in that repricing period (as determined in Step C) [IAS 39.AG126(b)(iii)]:

	T1	T2	T3
% change in fair value (Step A)	20%	30%	6.67%
Revised assets and liabilities (Step C)	9	8	(10)
Changes in fair value of the hedged item	1.8	2.4	(0.667)

Step E: The effectiveness of the hedging relationship is determined by comparing the change in the fair value of the hedging instrument to the change in the fair value of the hedged item:

	T1	T2	T3
Changes in fair value of the hedged item	1.8	2.4	(0.667)
Change in fair value of the hedging instrument(s)	(2)	(3)	1
Effectiveness (each time period)	90% (1.8/2)	80% (2.4/3)	66.7% (0.667/1)
Effectiveness (all time periods)		88.33% (1.8+2.4–0.667)/(-2–3+1)	

As the portfolio hedge is effective for all repricing time periods, in accordance with the documented method of testing hedge effectiveness (see step 6 above), Bank A concludes that the hedge is effective for the designated period.

In this example, for illustrative purposes only, all hedge ineffectiveness is due to changes in the amount of assets and liabilities at the start and the end of the reporting period due to changes in prepayment rates. In practice, ineffectiveness will also result due to impairment of assets, derecognition of assets and liabilities, and other valuation differences between the hedging instrument and hedged item like in any conventional fair value hedge.

Step 7: Bank A measures the change in the fair value of the hedged item attributable to the hedged risk on the basis of the expected repricing dates. Bank A recognises the change in fair value of the hedged item as a gain or loss in profit or loss and in one of two line items in the statement of financial position. Bank A recognises the following entry based on Step D above: [IAS 39.AG114(g)]

Dr	Separate statement of financial position line item (assets) [1.8+2.4]	4.2
Cr	Separate statement of financial position line item (liabilities)	0.667
Cr	Profit or Loss	3.533

Step 8: Bank A measures the change in fair value of the hedging instrument(s) and recognises it as a gain or loss in profit or loss. The fair value of the hedging instrument(s) is recognised as an asset or liability in the statement of financial position. Bank A recognises the following journal entry based on Step A above:
[IAS 39.AG114(h)]

Dr	Profit or Loss (fair value gains and losses on derivatives)	4
Dr	Derivative asset	1
Cr	Derivative liability	5

Step 9: Any ineffectiveness will be recognised in profit or loss as the difference arising from steps 7 and 8. The above hedging relationship resulted in an amount of 0.467 [4–3.533] being recognised in profit or loss as hedge ineffectiveness for the period. [IAS 39.AG114(i)]

Step 10: Bank A then establishes a new estimate of the total assets (liabilities) in each repricing time period, including new assets (liabilities) that have been originated since it last tested effectiveness, and designates a new amount as the hedged item and a new percentage as the hedged percentage. [IAS 39.AG127] The procedures set out above are then repeated at the next date the Bank tests effectiveness.

Step 11: The adjustment determined in Step 7 above should be amortised to profit or loss. Amortisation may begin as soon as an adjustment exists and shall begin no later than when the hedged item ceases to be adjusted for changes in its fair value attributable to the risk being hedged. Bank A concludes that amortising the adjustment using a recalculated effective interest rate is not practicable and instead will amortise the adjustment to profit or loss using a straight line approach. The adjustment will be amortised fully to profit or loss by the expiry of the relevant repricing time period. [IAS 39.92] Any amount relating to a particular time period that remains when the repricing time period expires should be recognised in profit or loss at that time. [IAS 39.AG129]

The example above does not account for the instances where, following the calculation of the hedge gain or loss, the hedged items are derecognised (e.g. through earlier than expected prepayment, impairment or sale). Should this occur, then the amount of change in fair value included in the statement of financial position (within a separate line item) that relates to the derecognised item shall be removed from the statement of financial position and be included in the gain or loss that arises on derecognition of the item. The knowledge of which repricing time period(s) the derecognised item was included in determines the repricing time periods from which to remove it, and therefore the amount to be removed from the separate line item. If it can be determined in which time period the derecognised item was included, it is removed from that time period. If not, it is removed from the earliest time period if the derecognition resulted from higher than expected prepayments or allocated to all time periods containing the derecognised item on a systematic and rational basis if the item was sold or became impaired. [IAS 39.AG128]

8 Documentation

There are several conditions to achieving hedge accounting under IAS 39. In the previous sections of this chapter the conditions have focused on what is considered to be an eligible hedged item and hedging instrument. Even if the hedge relationship is considered to be eligible for hedge accounting, documentation of the hedge relationship must be in place at inception of the hedge relationship. Until the necessary documentation is in place, an entity cannot apply hedge accounting. There can be no retrospective designation of a hedge relationship. [IAS 39.IG.F.3.8]

Example 8

Timing of hedge documentation

Entity A issues fixed rate debt on 1 January. On the same date it enters into a receive-fixed, pay-floating interest rate swap, with all the terms of the debt and swap matching. Entity A does not complete the required documentation until 1 February.

A may adopt hedge accounting from 1 February. From 1 January to 1 February, it will account for the debt and the derivative on the normal measurement basis, i.e. amortised cost for the debt, and fair value for the derivative, with changes in fair value recognised in profit or loss.

IAS 39 states that at the inception of the hedge there must be formal designation and documentation of:

- the hedging relationship; and
- the entity's risk management objective and strategy for undertaking the hedge.

That documentation shall include identification of:

- the hedging instrument;
- the hedged item or transaction;
- the nature of the risk being hedged; and
- how the entity will assess the hedging instrument's effectiveness in offsetting the exposure to changes in the hedged item's fair value or cash flows attributable to the hedged risk. [IAS 39.88]

Broadly, the documentation requirements fall into two categories:

- specific documentation for every hedge entered into. This will give details of the hedged item, hedged risk, hedging instrument, how effectiveness will be assessed prospectively and retrospectively, and how effectiveness will be measured retrospectively; and
- overall risk management objectives and strategies.

8.1 Risk management objectives and strategies

There are no rules governing this area, except that to achieve hedge accounting, an entity must have documented its objectives and strategies. The hedge relationships that the entity wishes to apply hedge accounting to, must be consistent with these stated policies. Therefore the policies and objectives should as a minimum include a list of the risks that the entity is exposed to, and how the entity intends to manage those risks.

8.2 Specific hedge documentation

Below is one example of how the specific documentation requirements for each hedge relationship could be met. It is based on the minimum that could reasonably be provided.

Example 8.2

Entity XYZ

Accounting hedge designation and assessment summary

Policy declaration

This relationship is in accordance with our Risk Management and Accounting Policies for IAS 39 [insert specific reference to policy within the policy manual]. The risk management objective and strategy for undertaking the hedge is as follows [to be inserted].

Risk identification

Nature of risk hedged

e.g. overall fair value, interest, credit, foreign currency, equity risk.

Specific hedged risk

e.g. for overall fair value, commodity price risk, for foreign currency, forward or spot rate; for interest rate risk, specific portion such as the benchmark interest rate.

Hedge type

	Yes	No
Cash Flow Hedge		
Fair Value Hedge		
Net Investment Hedge		

Date of designation of hedging relationship

Indicate date of designation of the hedging relationship.

Process required for the de-designation of the hedging relationship, including date on which the hedging relationship was de-designated

Indicate process required to formally de-designate the hedging relationship and date of de-designation.

Details of Hedging Instrument

Nature of hedging instrument	
Deal reference number	
Contractual parties of the hedging instrument	
Start date	
Maturity date	
Currency	
Principal/Notional	
Cash flows to be received and paid – amount, basis (e.g. LIBOR) and timing	
Amount of Principal/Notional designated as a hedging instrument	
If non-optional derivative is used, will movements in forward points be excluded?	
If optional derivative is used, will the movement in time value be excluded?	
Attachments (include any other information to explain the nature and profile of the instrument, e.g. the swap has an amortising notional)	

Details of hedged item

Nature of hedged item	
Deal reference number (if applicable)	
Contractual parties of the hedged item	
Start date	
Maturity date	
Currency, amount (and basis e.g. LIBOR) and timing	
Principal/Notional	
Amount designated as hedged item	
Attachments (e.g. if cash flow hedging forecasts sales then sales forecasts will be attached which show the level of designated sales compared with the total forecast	

Effectiveness testing

Prospective effectiveness testing

Can hedge effectiveness be reliably measured?	
Expectation of hedge effectiveness	
Type of test	
Period by period or cumulative assessment	
Frequency of hedge effectiveness test	

Results of prospective effectiveness testing

Date of test					
Results of Test					
Attachments (include any details of the results of the assessment)					

Retrospective effectiveness testing

Can hedge effectiveness be reliably measured?	
Expectation of hedge effectiveness	
Type of test	
Period by period or cumulative assessment	
Frequency of hedge effectiveness test	

Result of retrospective effectiveness testing

Date of test					
Results of Test					
Attachments (include any details of the results of the assessment)					

Result of retrospective effectiveness testing

Date of test					
Results of Test					
Attachments (include any details of the results of the assessment)					

Accounting

Basis Adjustment

If the hedge is a cash flow hedge and results in the recognition of a non-financial asset or non-financial liability, whether the gains and losses are reclassified directly out of equity into profit or loss or whether the gains and losses are removed from equity on initial recognition of the non-financial asset or liability and included in the initial carrying value of the asset or liability.

Reconciliation of gain or loss deferred in equity for cash flow and net investment hedges

	Cash flow hedging	Net investment hedging
Balance brought forward in equity as effective gains/losses		
Effective gains and losses recognised in equity in period		
Gains and losses reclassified out of equity in period		
Balance carried forward in equity as effective		

Hedge documentation prepared by: ________________

Hedge documentation reviewed by: ________________

Date: ________________

21 Financial instruments: disclosure

1 Introduction

In August 2005, the IASB issued IFRS 7 *Financial Instruments: Disclosures*. IFRS 7 is effective for annual periods beginning on or after 1 January 2007, and supersedes both IAS 30 *Disclosures in the Financial Statements of Banks and Similar Financial Institutions* and the disclosure requirements of IAS 32 *Financial Instruments: Disclosure and Presentation*. Following the introduction of IFRS 7, IAS 32 was renamed IAS 32 *Financial Instruments: Presentation* and continues to address the presentation requirements of financial instruments including classification of instruments as liabilities or equity, compound financial instruments, treasury shares, and the criteria for offsetting financial assets and financial liabilities.

Consequential amendments were made to a number of other Standards when IFRS 7 was issued. In particular, the disclosure requirements of IFRS 4 *Insurance Contracts* were realigned with those of IFRS 7. Also IAS 1 *Presentation of Financial Statements* was amended to include disclosures regarding an entity's capital.

The objective of IFRS 7 is to require entities to provide disclosures in their financial statements that enable users to evaluate:

[IFRS 7.1]

(i) the significance of financial instruments for the entity's financial position and performance; and

(ii) the nature and extent of risks arising from financial instruments to which the entity is exposed during the period and at the end of the reporting period, and how the entity manages those risks.

These disclosures are designed to provide users of financial statements with additional information that would influence their assessment of the financial position, financial performance and of the amount, timing and uncertainty of future cash flows for that entity. Further disclosures are required to enable users to determine what accounting elections and judgements have been made when applying the requirements of IAS 32 and IAS 39, and their impact on the financial statements.

This chapter discusses the requirements of IFRS 7 and IAS 32 in the following sections:

Section 2	Scope
Section 3	Classes of financial instruments
Section 4	Significance of financial instruments
Section 5	Nature and extent of risks arising from financial instruments
Section 6	Disclosure checklist
Section 7	Offsetting a financial asset and a financial liability

Whilst each disclosure requirement of IFRS 7 has been discussed separately, disclosures would, in practice, normally be presented as an integrated package with individual disclosures, in some instances, satisfying more than one requirement.

IFRS 7 contains mandatory application and non-mandatory Implementation Guidance, with the latter providing examples and guidance on how the requirements of IFRS 7 may be fulfilled. This chapter includes both. It also includes further examples of the application of IFRS 7.

2 Scope

IFRS 7 is applicable to *all* entities and to *all* risks arising from *all* financial instruments, whether recognised or unrecognised, except where specifically mentioned below. Recognised financial instruments include financial assets and financial liabilities that are within the scope of IAS 39. Unrecognised financial instruments include some financial instruments that, although outside the scope of IAS 39, are within the scope of IFRS 7, such as certain loan commitments that are not designated or required to be carried at fair value through profit or loss. [IFRS 7.4]

> Whilst a loan commitment may eventually give rise to a recognised financial asset for the lender, to the extent that funds have not been drawn down by the counterparty, the commitment to lend meets the definition of a financial liability as the lender is *contractually obligated to deliver cash or another financial asset to another entity*. [IAS 32.11] Even though this commitment is not recognised and measured in accordance with IAS 39 it is considered to be an unrecognised financial liability to which IFRS 7 disclosure requirements apply. Similarly, the party with the right to draw down funds (the borrower) with respect to a loan commitment has an unrecognised

financial asset to the extent that the funds have not yet been drawn down to which IFRS 7 disclosure requirements apply.

The table included in **section 2** of **chapter 13** summarises whether certain arrangements are in the scope of IFRS 7 or not.

Regular way sales and purchases of financial assets accounted for using a settlement date accounting policy also give rise to unrecognised financial asset or liabilities that are within the scope of IFRS 7. See **2.2** in **chapter 19** for settlement date accounting.

IFRS 7 includes within its scope leases which meet the definition of a financial instrument. Finance leases are financial instruments whereas operating leases are not (except as regards individual payments currently due and payable). For further discussion see **3.4** in **chapter 13**.

IFRS 7 applies to the financial statements of subsidiaries. There is no exemption even if full disclosures are provided in the consolidated financial statements in which the subsidiary is included. The IASB has stated that where an entity prepares any financial statements in accordance with IFRSs, users of those financial statements should receive information of the same quality as users of general purpose financial statements prepared in accordance with IFRSs. [IFRS 7.BC11]

IFRS 7 applies to all contracts linked to interests in subsidiaries, associates or joint ventures that meet the definition of a derivative unless they meet the definition of an equity instrument. [IFRS 7.3(a)]

IFRS 7 scopes out derivatives over own equity that meet the definition of equity. This will include derivatives over shares in a subsidiary that meet the definition of equity in the consolidated financial statements. IFRS 7 does not appear to have a scope exception for non-derivative instruments classified as equity, such as ordinary shares and certain preference shares. This appears to be an oversight in the drafting of the Standard as IFRS 7.BC8 states that the scope exception of IFRS 7 is intended to be the same as IAS 32 (prior to IFRS 7 being issued) with one exception, namely 'derivatives based on interests in subsidiaries, associates or joint ventures if the derivatives meet the definition of an equity instrument in IAS 32'. The basis of conclusions justifies this position by stating that these instruments are not remeasured and hence "do not expose the issuer to balance sheet and income statement risk", and the disclosures about the significance of financial instruments for financial position and performance are not relevant to equity instruments. In addition, it states that these instruments are excluded from the scope of IFRS 7, but they are within the scope of IAS 32 for the purpose of determining whether they meet the definition of equity instruments. It seems reasonable that the scope exclusions for derivatives over own equity that meet the definition of equity would also apply to non-derivatives that meet the definition of equity as the justification in the basis of conclusions would be equally relevant.

IFRS 7 excludes from its scope those interests in subsidiaries, associates and joint ventures that are accounted for in accordance with IAS 27 *Consolidated and Separate Financial Statements*, IAS 28 *Investments in Associates* or IAS 31 *Interests in Joint Ventures*. [IFRS 7.3(a)] The only exception is where the entity applies IAS 39 for measuring its interests in a subsidiary, joint venture or associate as specifically permitted by IAS 27(2008).38 (previously IAS 27(2003).37), IAS 31.1 and IAS 28.1. IAS 27(2008).38 (previously IAS 27(2003).37) applies to the separate financial statements, IAS 31.1 and IAS 28.1 apply to investment in joint ventures and associates held by venture capital organisations, mutual funds, unit trusts and similar entities including investment-linked insurance funds.

Consolidated financial statements include all financial instruments of the subsidiary except those intragroup financial instruments that are fully eliminated on consolidation. Only if the financial instrument is fully eliminated on consolidation is it excluded from the scope of IFRS 7 in the consolidated financial statements.

IFRS 7 does not apply to an investment in an associate or joint venture accounted for under the equity method as the carrying amount represents the investor's initial cost adjusted for the post-acquisition changes in the investor's share of net assets of the investee.

It is less clear as to whether IFRS 7 applies to financial instruments of a proportionately consolidated joint venture. The application of proportionate consolidation means that the statement of financial position of the venturer includes its share of the assets that it controls jointly and its share of the liabilities for which it is jointly responsible. [IAS 31.33] As the assets and liabilities will include the venturer's share of financial instruments that are recognised and measured in accordance with IAS 39, it would seem reasonable that these financial instruments are subject to the disclosure requirements of IFRS 7.

IFRS 5 *Non-current Assets held for sale and Discontinued Operations* specifically states in paragraph 2 that the classification and presentation requirements of IFRS 5 apply to all non-current assets (or disposal groups) classified as held for sale and discontinued operations. A question arises as to whether IFRS 7 disclosures are also required for financial assets and financial liabilities classified as held for sale or part of disposal groups as there is no scope exemption in IFRS 7 in this respect. At the IFRIC's September 2007 meeting the IFRIC considered whether the disclosure requirements of other standards, in the absence of specific exclusion, would apply to non-current assets (or disposal groups) classified as held for sale or discontinued operations in accordance with IFRS 5. The IFRIC decided to refer the matter to the IASB for their consideration as part of the 2008 annual improvements process. At the time of writing the exposure draft of *Improvements to International Financial Reporting Standards* had not been issued.

Without clear guidance from the IASB it is questionable whether such financial instruments are outside the scope of IFRS 7. Irrespective of the lack of clarity the financial risk disclosures detailed in IFRS 7.31–42 and discussed in **section 5** below are likely to be relevant for financial assets and liabilities classified as held for sale or part of a disposal group under IFRS 5 as those financial instruments do expose the entity to significant financial risks. If IFRS 7 is not applied in full to assets and liabilities held for sale or part of a disposal group care should be taken in providing sufficient information that is consistent with the objectives of IFRS 7, namely providing information about the significance of financial instruments for the entity's financial position and performance, the nature and extent of risks arising from financial instruments and how those risks are managed.

It is important to remember that contracts to buy or sell non-financial items that may not be typically considered financial instruments, are within the scope of IFRS 7 if they are in the scope of IAS 39. Guidance on the recognition and measurement of contracts over non-financial items is detailed in **2.5** in **chapter 13**.

The extent to which an entity will provide financial instrument disclosures will depend on the entity's use of financial instruments and the associated risks. As many of the requirements of IFRS 7 are based on information provided internally to key management personnel, the depth of disclosure will reflect partly the information provided for use within the business. Entities with few financial instruments and associated risks will provide less disclosure than those entities that have significant financial instruments and related exposures to financial risk.

3 Classes of financial instruments

IFRS 7 specifies a number of disclosure requirements to be provided by 'class of financial instrument'. These include derecognition of financial assets (see **4.1.5** below); allowance account for credit losses if an entity chooses under IAS 39 to have a separate allowance account (see **4.1.7** below); impairment losses in the period (see **4.2.4** below); fair value of all financial instruments (see **4.3.3** below); 'day 1 profit or losses' (see **4.3.3** below); and, credit risk (see **5.2.1** below).

IFRS 7 requires the entity to group financial instruments into classes that are appropriate to the nature of the information disclosed and that take into account the characteristics of those financial instruments. The classes are to be reconciled to the line items presented in the statement of financial position. [IFRS 7.6] The classes are determined by the entity and are distinct from the categories of financial instruments specified by IAS 39. [IFRS 7.B1] At a minimum, the classes are required to distinguish between those financial instruments that are measured at amortised cost and those that are measured at fair value. The entity should treat as a separate class or classes those financial instruments that are outside the scope of IFRS 7 (where the entity wishes to provide additional disclosure over and above the requirements of IFRS 7). [IFRS 7.B2] In many instances, classes of financial instruments will be more granular than the categories of financial instruments. For example, loans and receivables is a financial instrument category that could comprise various classes like home loans, credit card loans, unsecured medium term loans etc.

The preparer of the financial statements must strike a balance between providing excessive detail and obscuring information as a result of too much aggregation. [IFRS 7.B3]

IFRS 7 is not clear whether the same classes of financial instruments are applied universally to all the disclosures that IFRS 7 requires by class. An advantage of applying the same classes of financial instruments across all the required disclosures is that it will enhance comparability and understanding between disclosures. However, such an approach may be in conflict with IFRS 7 in the following instances:

(i) disclosure by class is required for certain quantitative disclosures, yet, IFRS 7.34 requires this information to be consistent with that provided internally to key management personnel. If the information provided to key management for the quantitative disclosures required by the Standard is aggregated differently, depending on the applicable risk disclosure, this information must be disclosed. It would be inappropriate to aggregate classes differently to the aggregation provided to key management.

(ii) IFRS 7.IG21 indicates that in determining classes for credit risk disclosures an entity should group financial instruments that share economic characteristics with respect to the risk being disclosed, for example, residential mortgages, unsecured consumer loans and commercial loans. This implies that classes vary depending on the type of information being disclosed. The classes applied to credit risk disclosure, therefore, may not be appropriate for the classes of financial instruments applied to fair value disclosure, for example the specific disclosures required for 'day 1 profit or loss' (see **4.3.3** below). If only a small number of items are included in the day 1 profit or loss disclosure but the characteristics of the instruments or valuation techniques differ an entity may consider it more appropriate to choose classes for this specific disclosure that differ to other required disclosures.

Care should be taken to ensure that the determination of classes is relevant to the disclosure requirement and provides the most meaningful information. If different classes of financial instrument are used for different disclosures then the entity should place greater emphasis on making clear how the classes are reconciled to the statement of financial position and between notes.

As IFRS does not prescribe captions for the statement of financial position, other than the minimum required by IAS 1 and other specific standards, an entity could choose to use its classes of financial instruments as a basis for its captions in the statement of financial position. Such an approach is likely to result in many more captions in the statement of financial position compared to the presentation where an entity uses the categories of financial assets in IAS 39 as the basis for captions in the statement of financial position.

4 Significance of financial instruments

One of the two key objectives of IFRS 7 is to require entities to provide disclosures in its financial statements that enable users to evaluate the significance of financial instruments for the entity's financial position and performance. To achieve this, disclosures must be provided for the statement of financial position, statement of comprehensive income and equity.

4.1 Statement of financial position disclosures

IFRS 7 requires specific statement of financial position disclosures. Some are very broad, for example, disclosing financial asset and financial liabilities by classification category, whereas some are very specific, for example, disclosures on collateral and derecognition.

4.1.1 Categories of financial assets and financial liabilities

An entity is required to disclose the carrying amount for each financial instrument category as defined by IAS 39 either in the statement of financial position or in the notes to the financial statements. Disclosure of carrying amount is required specifically of the following:

[IFRS 7.8]

(a) financial assets at fair value through profit or loss, showing separately (i) those designated as such upon initial recognition and (ii) those classified as held for trading;

(b) held-to-maturity investments;

(c) loans and receivables;

(d) available-for-sale financial assets;

(e) financial liabilities at fair value through profit or loss, showing separately (i) those designated as such upon initial recognition and (ii) those classified as held for trading; and

(f) financial liabilities measured at amortised cost.

These disclosures are intended to assist users in understanding the extent to which accounting policies affect the amounts at which financial assets and financial liabilities are recognised. [IFRS 7.BC14] Together with the disclosures of the gains and losses by category of financial instrument, the disclosure of the carrying amounts for each category of financial instrument allows users to appraise management on its decisions to buy, sell or hold financial assets and to incur, maintain or discharge financial liabilities.

Recognised derivative financial instruments other than those that are designated and effective hedging instruments are included within the fair value through profit or loss category. Derivatives that are designated as effective hedging instruments, however, are excluded from that category and IAS 39 does not include them in any other category or create a new category for them. It is reasonable, however, to include derivatives that are effective hedging instruments as a separate category in order to aid reconciliation between disclosures by category and the statement of financial position. Some entities choose to show derivatives in effective hedging relationship in a separate caption both in the statement of financial position and in the notes.

4.1.2 *Financial assets at fair value through profit or loss*

IFRS 7.9 requires extensive disclosure where an entity has designated loans and receivables as at fair value through profit or loss (FVTPL), since applying the fair value option to these instruments may result in a significant impact on the financial statements caused by fair value movements, and in particular those movements caused by changes in credit risk.

IFRS 7 requires disclosure of:

[IFRS 7.9]

(a) the maximum exposure to *credit risk* of the loan or receivable designated as at fair value through profit or loss (or group of loans or receivables) at the end of the reporting period;

(b) the amount by which any related credit derivatives or similar instruments mitigate that maximum exposure to credit risk;

(c) the amount of change, during the period and cumulatively, in the fair value of the loan or receivable (or group of loans or receivables) that is attributable to changes in the credit risk of the financial asset determined either:

   (i) as the amount of change in its fair value that is not attributable to changes in market conditions that give rise to *market risk*; or

   (ii) using an alternative method the entity believes more faithfully represents the amount of change in its fair value that is attributable to changes in the credit risk of the asset.

   Changes in market conditions that give rise to market risk include changes in an observed (benchmark) interest rate, commodity price, foreign exchange rate or index of prices or rates; and

(d) the amount of the change in the fair value of any related credit derivatives or similar instruments that has occurred during the period and cumulatively since the loan or receivable was designated.

In addition, an entity shall disclose:

[IFRS 7.11]

(a) the methods used to comply with the requirements in (c) above;

(b) if the entity believes that the disclosure it has given to comply with the requirements in (c) above does not faithfully represent the change in the fair value of the financial asset attributable to changes in its credit risk, the reasons for reaching this conclusion and the factors it believes are relevant.

The maximum exposure to credit risk for a derivative is its carrying amount. [IFRS 7.BC50] The Standard is not clear whether the maximum exposure to credit risk for loans and receivables can also equal the carrying amount, which is fair value, when an entity designates those loans and receivables as at FVTPL.

The information to be disclosed regarding the maximum exposure to credit risk depends on whether exposure to credit loss is viewed as 'cash loss' or as loss to the statement of comprehensive income. Credit risk is defined as *the risk that one party to a financial instrument will cause a financial loss for the other party by failing to discharge an obligation*. [IFRS 7(Appendix A)] Where the maximum exposur to credit risk is viewed as a cash loss, then the amount to be disclosed would be the amount owed, e.g. if the fair value of the debt is £70 and the amount owed is £100, then the maximum 'cash loss' is £100. If, however, the maximum exposure to credit risk is viewed as loss to the statement of comprehensive income, then the carrying amount, which is fair value of the loans and receivables in this instance, will be the amount that is required to be disclosed.

While either approach is supportable an entity must apply a consistent policy in disclosing the maximum exposure to credit risk for the loans and receivables that are designated as at FVTPL.

Example 4.1.2

Loans and receivables designated as at fair value through profit or loss

Entity A acquired at the start of the prior period a group of 9 per cent non-amortising unsecured long term loans with five years remaining to maturity and designated them as at FVTPL. The loans were acquired for £905m when the effective interest rate was 10 per cent, consisting of 8 per cent interest rate and 2 per cent credit spread. The par amount of the loans is £1bn. At the date of acquisition Entity A entered into a credit default swap with a financial institution to provide credit protection on the loans with a notional of £500m. The credit default swap had an initial fair value of zero and remains outstanding at the year end.

The fair value of loans is £896m at the year end (prior year: £852m). At the year end interest rates for the remaining maturity are 8 per cent and credit spreads are 2.5 per cent (prior year: 9 per cent and 3 per cent respectively). The credit default swap has a fair value at the year end of £35m (prior year: £46m)

The items to be disclosed in accordance with IFRS 7.9 are as follows:

(*a*) *Maximum exposure to credit risk at the end of the reporting period*

If maximum exposure to credit risk is viewed as being loss to the statement of comprehensive income, then the amount to be disclosed would be £896m (prior year: £852m), being the fair value of the loans at the year end.

If the maximum exposure to credit risk is viewed as being equal to a cash loss, then the amount to be disclosed would be £1bn (prior year: £1bn), being the amount owed by the borrower at the year end.

Note: the entity cannot offset the loans and the credit default swaps as there is no right of set off and the financial instruments are with a different counterparty.

(*b*) *Amount by which any related credit derivatives or similar instruments mitigate that maximum exposure to credit risk*

The credit default swap provides credit protection on half of the loans. On a fair value basis, the maximum protection is equivalent to 56 per cent (prior year: 59 per cent) and on a cash loss basis is equivalent to 50 per cent (prior year: 50 per cent).

(*c*) *Amount of change, during the period and cumulative, in the fair value of loans that is attributable to changes in credit risk*

The cumulative change in fair value due to credit risk of the loans is a £16m loss (prior year: £27m loss). The change in fair value due to credit risk for the period was a £11m gain.

(*d*) *Change in the fair value of any related credit derivatives*

The cumulative change in fair value of the credit default swap is a £35m gain (prior year: £46m gain). The change in fair value of the credit default swap for the period was a £11m loss.

4.1.3 Financial liabilities at fair value through profit or loss

Where an entity has designated financial liabilities as at FVTPL, IFRS 7.10 requires extensive disclosure and in particular disclosure about creditworthiness. These disclosures have been included to help alleviate concerns that users may misinterpret the profit or loss effects of changes in issuer's credit risk. The perceived 'anomaly' of recording gains in profit or loss when the entity's credit rating deteriorates should be helped by disclosure of the changes in fair value attributable to credit risk.

IFRS 7 requires disclosure of:

[IFRS 7.10]

(a) the amount of change, during the period and cumulatively, in the fair value of the financial liability that is attributable to changes in the credit risk of that liability determined either:

  (i) as the amount of change in its fair value that is not attributable to changes in market conditions that give rise to market risk; or

  (ii) using an alternative method the entity believes more faithfully represents the amount of change in its fair value that is attributable to changes in the credit risk of the liability.

  Changes in market conditions that give rise to market risk include changes in a benchmark interest rate, the price of another entity's financial instrument, a commodity price, a foreign exchange rate or an index of prices or rates. For contracts that include a unit-linking feature, changes in market conditions include changes in the performance of the related internal or external investment fund.

(b) the difference between the financial liability's carrying amount and the amount the entity would be contractually required to pay at maturity to the holder of the obligation.

IFRS 7.BC22 states that the fair value may differ significantly from the settlement amount, i.e. amount contractually required to be paid at maturity in particular for financial liabilities with a long duration when an entity has experienced a significant deterioration in creditworthiness since their issue. When complying with IFRS 7.10(b) as stated above the amount contractually required to be paid at maturity should be an undiscounted amount not affected by the entity's own credit risk. To the extent the amount payable at maturity is subject to variability, for example because the principal is indexed linked, an estimation of this amount should also be included, whether the index-linked feature is a separately accounted for embedded derivative or not. This is consistent with the principle applied for liquidity risk disclosures in IFRS 7.B16 as discussed in **5.2.2** below where the effects of any embedded derivatives are included on an undiscounted basis based on conditions existing at the end of the reporting period (incorporating forward rates as applicable).

The Standard also requires disclosure of:

[IFRS 7.11]

(a) the methods used to comply with the requirements in IFRS 7.10(a) above; and

(b) if the entity believes that the disclosure it has given to comply with the requirements in IFRS 7.10(a) above does not faithfully represent the change in the fair value of the financial liability attributable to changes in its credit risk, the reasons for reaching this conclusion and the factors it believes are relevant.

Example 4.1.3

Financial liabilities designated as at fair value through profit or loss

On the first day of its current financial period Entity B issued a 5-year bond in order to finance the expansion of its operations. The bond trades on a recognised bond exchange. Entity B's year-end is 31 December 20X1.

Maturity date:	31 December 20X5
Nominal value:	£500million
Coupon:	9%, payable annually on 31 December in arrears
Issue price (1 January 20X1):	£450million
Fair value (31 December 20X1):	£400million
5-year LIBOR (1 January 20X1):	10.5%
4-year LIBOR (31 December 20X1):	12.75%

IFRS 7 requires disclosure of the amount of change in the fair value of the financial liability that is attributable to changes in the liability's credit risk. IFRS 7 permits an entity to determine this amount as the amount of change in the liability's fair value that is not attributable to changes in market conditions that give rise to market risk. If the only relevant changes in market conditions for a liability are changes in an observed (benchmark) interest rate, then this amount may be estimated as follows: [IFRS 7.B4]

(a) Determine the liability's internal rate of return at the start of the period using the observed market price of the liability and the liability's contractual cash flows at the start of the period.

Year 0	**Year 1**	**Year 2**	**Year 3**	**Year 4**	**Year 5**
-450,000,000[1]	45,000,000[2]	45,000,000[2]	45,000,000[2]	45,000,000[2]	545,000,000[3]

1 The bonds are recognised initially at fair value, being an amount of £450million.

2 Yearly cash flows are determined as being 9% x £500million.

3 The terminal cash flow is determined as the nominal value of the bonds plus the interest coupon.

The internal rate of return, equal to the effective interest rate, at issue is 11.76%.

(b) Deduct the observed (benchmark) interest rate at the start of the period from the internal rate of return to arrive at an instrument-specific component of the internal rate of return (i.e. the portion of the effective interest that relates to credit risk).

11.76% – 10.5% = 1.26% instrument specific component of the IRR

(c) Compute the present value of the cash flows of the liability using the liability's contractual cash flows at the end of the period and a discount rate equal to the sum of the observed benchmark interest rate at the end of the period and the instrument specific component of the internal rate of return determined above in (b).

Remaining cash flows to be discounted using an internal rate of return of 14.01% (12.75% + 1.26%)

Year 2	**Year 3**	**Year 4**	**Year 5**
45,000,000	45,000,000	45,000,000	545,000,000

Present value is equal to £427,059,828 as at the end of the reporting period.

(d) Compute the change in the fair value of the liability that is not attributable to changes in the observed (benchmark) interest rate as being the difference between the observed market price of the liability and the amount determined above.

Change in fair value due to changes in credit risk is determined as £27,059,828 (£427,059,828 – £400,000,000).

The disclosures may be provided as follows:

Financial liabilities

During the year, the group issued a commercial bond with a nominal value of £500,000,000 with a maturity of five years that is designated as at fair value through profit or loss at initial recognition. The fair value and the change in that fair value that can be ascribed to changes in underlying credit risk are set out below:

	31 December 20X6	**31 December 20X5**
Fair value of commercial bond	£400,000,000	–
Change in fair value of bonds not attributable to changes in market conditions	£(27,059,828)	–
Difference between carrying amount and amount contractually required to be paid at maturity	£100,000,000	–

The group estimates changes in fair value due to credit risk, by estimating the amount of change in the fair value that is not due to changes in market conditions that give rise to market risk.

The example above assumes that changes in the fair value arising from factors other than changes in the bond's credit risk or changes in interest rates are not significant. Had the bond above contained an embedded prepayment option, then the change in the fair value of the embedded derivative would need to be excluded in determining the amount to be disclosed. [IFRS 7.B4] Whether the embedded is closely related or not, the effects of the embedded derivative need to be excluded.

The methodology illustrated above in **example 4.1.3** is a reasonable approach in determining the fair value movements due to credit risk for plain vanilla debt instruments. Where there are other factors that affect the change in the instrument's fair value, such as embedded derivatives, then alternative methods may be used to calculate the amount of change in the fair value attributable to changes in credit risk of the liability. Such methods are required to be disclosed, as well as why those methods provide a more faithful representation than the method described in IFRS 7. [IFRS 7.BC21(a)] Liabilities, such as unit-linked insurance contracts, for which the amount of the liability reflects the performance of a defined pool of assets, present particular challenges.

4.1.4 Reclassification

Where an entity reclassifies financial assets in accordance with the requirements of IAS 39, from cost or amortised cost to fair value or vice versa, disclosure of the amount that has been reclassified into and out of each category is required, together with the reason for that reclassification. [IFRS 7.12]

Some classification decisions depend on management's intent, for example, classification as held-to-maturity investments. Reclassifications from cost/amortised cost to fair value and vice versa may occur in limited circumstances and it is important to understand the reasons for such reclassifications since the understanding of the reasons may assist the users in judging how management follows through with its stated intentions. Such information is also useful to the user in understanding the performance of the entity since reclassifications of such instruments can have a significant effect on their measurement. [IFRS 7.BC23]

IFRS 7 requires disclosure of financial assets that are reclassified from cost or amortised cost to fair value and vice versa. Whilst reclassification of financial liabilities is equally possible, the disclosure requirements in IFRS 7 do not refer to financial liabilities.

Although IFRS 7 appears not to require the same disclosure for financial liabilities, it is preferable to provide similar disclosures. For example, if an entity had written a call option over a non-listed third party equity security, where a fixed amount of the equity security would be delivered to the option holder upon exercise, the derivative instrument will be a financial liability. If the entity had previously held the derivative at cost as it could not measure the instrument reliably, and a reliable measure became available at a later date, the entity would be required to remeasure the derivative liability at fair value with changes in fair value recognised in profit or loss. [IAS 39.53] The amount and the reason for the reclassification would be equally relevant for a reclassification of the liability as it would be for a reclassification of an asset.

4.1.5 Derecognition

Some transfers of financial assets do not qualify for derecognition. It is important for the users to be able to evaluate the significance of such transactions and the risks retained, the nature of the risks and rewards to which the entity continues to be exposed to and the extent of its continuing involvement with the asset. Disclosure is required of:

[IFRS 7.13]

(a) the nature of the assets involved;

(b) the nature of the risks and rewards of ownership to which the entity remains exposed;

(c) when the entity continues to recognise all of the assets, the carrying amounts of the assets and of the associated liabilities; and

(d) when the entity continues to recognise the assets to the extent of its continuing involvement, the total carrying amount of the original assets, the amount of the assets that the entity continues to recognise, and the carrying amount of the associated liabilities.

For example, a sale of a portfolio of receivables with a limited guarantee may result in the entity continuing to recognise the receivables and retaining some exposure to the receivables, but to a lesser extent than prior to the transfer.

IAS 1(2007).122 (previously IAS 1(2003).113 requires an entity to disclose in its accounting policies the judgements management make in the process of applying its accounting policies. IAS 1(2007).123(b) (previously IAS 1(2003).114(b)) makes specific reference to disclosure of the judgement management makes in determining when substantially all the significant risks and rewards of ownership of financial assets and lease assets are transferred to other entities.

The disclosures for derecognition required by IFRS 7 are by class of financial asset and can be provided either by type of financial assets (i.e.

differentiating by characteristics of the assets) or by type of risks or rewards of ownership to which the entity remains exposed.

4.1.6 *Collateral*

The entity is required to disclose the carrying amount of financial assets it has pledged as collateral (non-cash financial assets) for liabilities or contingent liabilities, including amounts the transferor has reclassified in accordance with IAS 39.37(a) where the transferee has the right to sell or pledge the collateral. The entity is also required to disclose the terms and conditions relating to its pledge. [IFRS 7.14] The terms and conditions may include:

- how much collateral needs to be maintained as security for the loans; and
- the type of collateral that needs to be provided as security for the loans.

Where an entity holds collateral (both financial and non-financial assets) as security for financial assets loaned to another entity and that it is permitted to sell or repledge in the absence of default by the owner of the collateral, the entity is required to disclose:

- the fair value of the collateral held;
- the fair value of any such collateral that has been sold or repledged, and whether the entity has an obligation to return it; and
- the terms and conditions associated with its use of the collateral. [IFRS 7.15]

The disclosure of the existence of such collateral is important since it provides information to the user of the financial statements of the amount of collateral used and available for use that may not be recognised in the statement of financial position of the entity.

Disclosure of collateral that the entity does not have the right to sell or pledge in the absence of default by the borrower is required in the credit risk disclosures note – see **6.2.1.2** below.

4.1.7 *Allowance account for credit losses*

Where financial assets are impaired by credit losses, and the entity records the impairment in a separate allowance account rather than by directly reducing the carrying amount of an asset, the entity is required to disclose a reconciliation of changes in that account during the period. [IFRS 7.16]

This disclosure is required by class of financial asset. The reconciliation is useful in assessing the adequacy of the allowance for impairment losses and enables comparison between entities.

IFRS 7 does not, however, specify components of the reconciliation. As the impairment for financial assets is determined differently from one entity to another, preparers are given flexibility in determining the most appropriate format for their needs. [IFRS 7.BC26]

For example, the reconciliation of the allowance account for credit losses may be presented with the following line items:

Opening balance	XX
Plus: impairment losses recognised	XX
Less: reversals of impairment losses	XX
Less: amounts written off during the year	XX
Plus/less: exchange gains and losses on foreign denominated items	XX
Less: unwind of discount	XX
Closing balance	XX

Entities may wish to expand on each of the above items. For instance:

- impairment losses recognised could be analysed between losses due to breach of contract, bankruptcy of the underlying debtor, adverse changes in payment status of borrowers and national or local economic conditions that correlate with defaults on the assets in the group and increases due to increases in effective interest rates (floating rate debt);
- reversals of impairment may similarly be analysed according to the underlying cause of the reversal; and
- amounts written off during the year may be analysed, for example, by type of exposure, type of client, geographical or industry segment.

The allowance account may be expanded to include any other items that the preparer of the financial statements considers to be material to the user's understanding of the financial statements.

4.1.8 Compound financial instruments with multiple embedded derivatives

IAS 32 prescribes how a compound financial instrument should be separated into its liability and equity components. For a compound financial instrument, the value of the debt or equity component may be affected by the other component. For instance, for convertible debt, the value of the debt component may depend in part on the relative attractiveness of early conversion. Hence, the aggregate fair value of the convertible bond could differ from the sum of the estimated fair values of the debt and equity components if these were valued independently of each other. IAS 32 assigns the full value of these interdependencies to the liability component and treats equity as the residual. This is arbitrary and can be argued to misstate the amount of the liability and thereby misstate the 'true' interest cost.

The interdependencies become even more significant when a compound instrument contains multiple embedded features whose values are also interdependent, e.g. the value of an embedded purchased call option and a written equity conversion option feature in a callable convertible debt instrument depend in part on each other as the equity conversion option is extinguished if the issuer exercises its purchased call option to redeem early, and vice versa the value of the issuer purchased call option depends on the likelihood that the holder will exercise its right to convert early into shares. Because of the importance of these features, IFRS 7.17 requires an issuer of a compound instrument that has multiple embedded derivatives whose values are interdependent to disclose the existence of those features.

4.1.9 Defaults and breaches

For loans payable recognised at the end of the reporting period, disclosure is required of any defaults during the period of principal, interest, sinking fund, or redemption terms. In addition, the entity is required to disclose the carrying amount of any such loans that are in default at the end of the reporting period and whether the default was remedied, or the terms of the loans payable were renegotiated, before the financial statements were authorised for issue. [IFRS 7.18] Loans payable are defined as *'financial liabilities, other than short-term trade payables on normal credit terms'*. [IFRS 7(Appendix A)] It is important to note that disclosure of defaults is required of loans even where those defaults were rectified by the end of the reporting period.

If, during the period, there were breaches of loan agreement terms other than those described in the previous paragraph, the entity is required to disclose the same information as required above if those breaches permitted the lender to demand accelerated repayment (unless the breaches were remedied, or the terms of the loan were renegotiated, on or before the end of the reporting period). [IFRS 7.19] Examples of such defaults include breaches of collateral requirements or loan covenant features, or a failure to administer the loan in terms of the loan agreement.

Such disclosures are designed to provide the users with the relevant information about the entity's creditworthiness and its prospects of obtaining future loans. [IFRS 7.BC32]

The presentation of such loans as either current or non-current in accordance with the requirements of IAS 1 *Presentation of Financial Statements* may also be affected by such defaults.

4.2 Statement of comprehensive income disclosures

IFRS 7 requires disclosure of certain income, expense, gains or losses either in the statement of comprehensive income or in the notes to the financial statements.

4.2.1 Net gains or net losses

Disclosure of net gains or net losses is required for:

[IFRS 7.20(a)]

(i) financial assets or financial liabilities at fair value through profit or loss, showing separately those on financial assets or financial liabilities designated as such upon initial recognition, and those on financial assets or financial liabilities that are classified as held for trading in accordance with IAS 39;

(ii) available-for-sale financial assets, showing separately the amount of gain or loss recognised in other comprehensive income during the period and the amount reclassified from equity to profit or loss for the period;

(iii) held-to-maturity investments;

(iv) loans and receivables; and

(v) financial liabilities measured at amortised cost;

These disclosures are intended to assist users in understanding the extent to which accounting policies affect the performance of the entity and understanding the nature of such gains and losses. [IFRS 7.BC33] The disclosures also provide useful financial information, together with the disclosures of the carrying amounts by category of financial instruments, which is designed to allow users to appraise management on the manner in which it has classified financial instruments and ultimately its decisions to buy, sell or hold financial assets and to incur, maintain or discharge financial liabilities.

IFRS 7.BC33 states that that the above disclosure of statement of comprehensive income "gains and losses by the measurement categories in IAS 39" complement the statement of financial position disclosures described in **5.1** above. Despite this claim it would appear that there is a difference between the requirements of the statement of financial position and statement of comprehensive income disclosures. As explained in **5.1** above IFRS 7.8 requires disclosure of the carrying amounts of: financial assets *and* financial liabilities designated at fair value through profit or loss upon initial recognition, as well as financial assets *and* financial liabilities classified as held for trading in accordance with IAS 39. The equivalent statement of comprehensive income disclosures refer to financial assets *or* financial liabilities. It is reasonable to presume this difference in wording was an oversight in the drafting and therefore an entity should disclose information on net gain or net losses in relation to *both* financial assets *and* financial liabilities.

Derivative financial instruments (or non-derivative financial instruments when hedging foreign currency risk) that have been designated as effective hedging instruments are not included in any of the financial instrument categories. Instead, the changes in fair values of those instruments will be reported in accordance with the hedge accounting disclosure requirements.

4.2.2 *Interest income and interest expense*

IFRS 7 requires disclosure of total interest income and total interest expense, determined using the effective interest method, for financial assets or financial liabilities that are not classified as at fair value through profit or loss. [IFRS 7.20(b)] Total interest expense is a component of the finance costs that are required to be disclosed as a line item in the statement of comprehensive income in accordance with IAS 1(2007).82(b) (previously IAS 1(2003).81(b)). Finance costs that are required to be disclosed in accordance with IAS 1 may also include amounts that arise on non-financial liabilities such as pension liabilities and income taxes. Separate disclosure of total interest expense allows the user to understand the extent to which financial instruments contribute to finance costs.

4.2.3 *Fee income and expense*

IFRS 7 requires disclosure of fee income and expense, other than those amounts that are included in determining the effective interest rate, that arise from financial assets or financial liabilities that are not at fair value through profit or loss. Such items may include fee income earned as services are provided and fees that are earned on execution of a significant act. [IAS 18(Appendix Example 14(b) & (c)] In addition, disclosure is required of trust and other fiduciary activities that result in the holding or investing of assets on behalf of individuals, trusts, retirement benefit plans, and other institutions. [IFRS 7.20(c)] This information indicates the level of such activities and helps users to estimate possible future income of the entity. [IFRS 7.BC35]

The extent of fees to which this disclosure requirement relates will depend on the type of business. Lenders are likely to be subject to a significant level of disclosure. Examples of fees will include annual membership fee income for credit cards (payable irrespective of whether the card holder borrows using the card); interchange fees received each time a credit card is used; merchant service commission fees for processing debit and credit transactions; fees for withdrawing cash on a credit card; overdraft fee income received irrespective of whether the borrower utilises the overdraft facility, etc. Many fees with respect to specific borrowing and lending will meet the definition of a transaction cost and therefore will form part of the effective interest rate and thereby will not be subject to separate disclosure.

4.2.4 *Interest on impaired financial assets*

Interest income on impaired financial assets is determined using the rate of interest used to discount the future cash flows for the purposes of measuring the impairment loss. [IFRS 7.20(d)]

The above requirement needs careful consideration in the case of financial assets impaired on a portfolio basis (see **6.2.2** in **chapter 18**).

If a loan within a portfolio is not individually assessed as being impaired, but is impaired on a collective basis prior to the loan being individually identified, and all cash flows with respect to the impaired loan are not recoverable, then no interest income will be disclosed in accordance with IFRS 7.20(d). In this case, following the impairment loss, there is no interest income on the loan that remains unidentified in the portfolio that is fully impaired (since no cash flows are expected).

In contrast, the entity may determine that an impairment loss is required in the instance where some, but not all, cash flows on unidentified loans are not recoverable. For disclosure of interest recognition post impairment the entity should use the effective interest rate that was applied in discounting the cash flows in determining the impairment loss. Even though the loans that are impaired are not identified yet, the entity is still required to disclose the amount of interest on the portfolio of loans that is impaired.

If an impairment loss is recognised in the period but is reversed prior to the period end an entity should still disclose the interest that arose during the part of the reporting period that the loan was impaired. As interest will be recognised throughout the instrument's life the entity will need to isolate the period immediately following the impairment event and prior to the impairment loss being reversed and determine the interest that was recognised during that period.

4.2.5 Impairment losses

IFRS requires disclosure of the amount of any impairment loss for each class of financial asset. [IFRS 7.20(e)] These amounts may be combined with the disclosures that are required for the allowance account mentioned above.

4.3 Other disclosures

4.3.1 Accounting policies

IAS 1 requires disclosure of the measurement bases used in preparing the financial statements and the other accounting policies used that are relevant to an understanding of the financial statements. For financial instruments these would normally include:

[IFRS 7.B5]

(a) for financial assets or financial liabilities designated as at fair value through profit or loss:

  (i) the nature of the financial assets or financial liabilities that have been designated as at fair value through profit or loss;

  (ii) the criteria for so designating financial assets or financial liabilities on initial recognition; and

  (iii) how the entity has satisfied the criteria in IAS 39 for such designation. That disclosure includes a narrative description of the circumstances underlying the measurement or recognition inconsistency that would otherwise arise and a narrative description of how designation at fair value through profit or loss is consistent with the entity's documented risk management or investment strategy where applicable.

(b) the criteria for designating financial assets as available for sale;

(c) whether regular way purchases and sales of financial assets are accounted for at trade date or at settlement date;

(d) when an allowance account is used to reduce the carrying amount of financial assets impaired by credit losses:

 (i) the criteria for determining when the carrying amount of impaired financial assets is reduced directly (or, in the case of a reversal of a write-down, increased directly) and when the allowance account is used; and

 (ii) the criteria for writing off amounts charged to the allowance account against the carrying amount of impaired financial assets;

(e) how net gains or net losses on each category of financial instrument are determined, for example, whether the net gains or net losses on items at fair value through profit or loss include interest or dividend income;

It appears that the objective of the Standard in requiring an entity to disclose whether interest or dividends are shown separately from other fair value gains/losses was to make clear how interest and dividends were presented in income for non-derivative instruments that are carried at FVTPL. It is reasonable that if a derivative is not in a qualifying hedge relationship and is therefore is classified as a held for trading instrument, its fair value is a single number recognised in income and should not be split further across other profit or loss captions.

For non-derivative financial instruments carried at FVTPL, some entities include interest income and expense and dividend income in gains and losses on financial assets and financial liabilities respectively and others include them in separate line items for interest and dividends. The disclosure of whether net gains and losses on financial assets or financial liabilities that are carried as at FVTPL include interest income and expense or dividend income is designed to aid comparability between entities.

It seems reasonable to have a separate policy for interest-bearing instruments, such as debt, and non-interest bearing instruments that earn a dividend, such as equity securities, but it is not acceptable to have a separate policy for interest bearing assets and a separate policy for interesting bearing liabilities as this would have the appearance of overstating or understating interest income and expense.

(f) the criteria the entity uses to determine that there is objective evidence that an impairment loss has occurred; and

(g) when the terms of financial assets that would otherwise be past due or impaired have been renegotiated, the accounting policy for financial assets that are the subject of renegotiated terms.

The disclosure required is the entity's policy as to how it accounts for renegotiated debt assets, specifically how it determines whether the renegotiated debt is considered new debt and therefore old debt is derecognised, or whether it is considered the original debt with the original effective interest rate and the carrying amount adjusted according to IAS 39.AG8 at the date of renegotiation. This disclosure would be relevant since the only guidance in IFRSs on the accounting for debt modifications is with respect to financial liabilities in IAS 39.40 & AG62, whilst no guidance is provided for financial assets other than in the case of impairment. [IAS 39.IG.E.4.3]

Information that includes a description of the manner in which debt is renegotiated and the terms and conditions of the renegotiated debt may also provide valuable information.

4.3.2 *Hedge accounting*

Disclosures are required for entities that apply hedge accounting in accordance with IAS 39. [IFRS 7.22–24]

Hedging activities are integral to an entity's financial risk management and are often significant. Hedge accounting for such activities is a matter of choice under IAS 39 and this accounting choice can have a significant impact on the financial statements. In the absence of hedge accounting, changes in the fair value of all derivatives are reflected in profit or loss as they arise, often creating a mismatch with the timing of recognition of the gains and losses on the exposure that is being hedged. Hedge accounting corrects this measurement or recognition mismatch.

Hedge accounting disclosures are provided to allow the user to understand the nature of the entities' hedge relationships and the effect that those hedge relationships had on the performance of the entity both during the current period and what is expected in future periods.

For each type of hedge accounting that is applied (fair value hedge, cash flow hedge, or a hedge of net investment in a foreign operation), the entity must disclose the following:

[IFRS 7.22]

(a) a description of each type of hedge;

(b) a description of the financial instruments designated as hedging instruments and their fair values at the end of the reporting period; and

(c) the nature of the risks being hedged.

Additional disclosures are required for cash flow hedges as the entity has to make significant judgements about the expectation of future cash flows that are being hedged. Also, as cash flow hedging requires recognition of gains/losses in other comprehensive income and frequent reclassification from equity to profit or loss, the Standard requires these amounts to be transparent. An entity shall disclose:

[IFRS 7.23]

(a) the periods when the cash flows are expected to occur and when they are expected to affect profit or loss;

(b) a description of any forecast transaction for which hedge accounting had previously been used, but which is no longer expected to occur;

(c) the amount that was recognised in other comprehensive income during the period;

(d) the amount that was reclassified from equity to profit or loss for the period, showing the amount included in each line item in the statement of comprehensive income; and

(e) the amount that was removed from equity during the period and included in the initial cost or other carrying amount of a non-financial asset or a non-financial liability whose acquisition or incurrence was a hedged highly probable forecast transaction.

IFRS 7 requires an entity to disclose the extent to which hedge accounting has been effective in the period. For cash flow hedges and hedges of a net investment in a foreign operation, the amount of ineffectiveness may be disclosed either in the statement of comprehensive income (as all hedge effectiveness is recognised in profit or loss), or alternately in a note to the financial statements.

The disclosure requirements for fair value hedges are somewhat different, although the objective of disclosing hedge ineffectiveness is the same. In a fair value hedge, the gain or loss on the hedging instrument and the gain or loss on the hedged item are immediately recognised in profit or loss in all periods. The net of these amounts is equivalent to the hedge ineffectiveness that is recognised in profit or loss in the period. IFRS 7, therefore, requires an entity to disclose separately the gains or losses on the hedging instrument and on the hedged item that are attributable to the hedged risk. [IFRS 7.24] This may be disclosed either in the statement of comprehensive income or alternatively in a note to the financial statements.

If a fair value hedge is not highly effective, i.e. hedge effectiveness is outside the 80–125 per cent range, then hedge accounting cannot be applied for the period. The entity has not achieved hedge accounting and therefore is not required to disclose hedge ineffectiveness for that period with respect to that designated hedge.

For cash flow hedges and hedges of a net investment in a foreign operation if the hedge is not highly effective in the period, i.e. it is outside the 80–125 per cent range, hedge accounting is not applied in the period. The gains or losses on the hedging instrument will be recognised directly in profit or loss. The entity is not required to disclose hedge ineffectiveness. If previously designated forecast transactions are no longer expected to occur, this will generally result in reclassification from equity to profit or loss for some or all of the cumulative gains/losses brought forward from the prior period recognised in other comprehensive income (and accumulated in the cash flow hedging reserve in equity). This amount must be disclosed along with the other disclosures listed above.

4.3.3 *Fair value*

Fair value disclosures should be provided for each class of financial asset and financial liability, in a way that allows a comparison to be made to the corresponding carrying amounts in the statement of financial position. [IFRS 7.25] Financial assets and financial liabilities should be grouped into appropriate classes, but shall only be offset to the extent that their carrying amounts are offset in the statement of financial position. [IFRS 7.26]

Fair values reflect the financial markets' judgement about the present value of expected future cash flows from a financial instrument, and therefore provide a neutral basis of assessing management's decision to enter into financial instruments. Some financial instruments are already carried at fair value in the statement of financial position and their fair values need not be disclosed in the notes. However, for the instruments accounted for on a different basis, e.g. cost or amortised cost, fair value disclosures are required. An exception to this is for those financial instruments whose carrying amount reasonably approximates fair value, as is the case for most short-term trade receivables and payables. Additional exceptions exist for investments in unquoted equity instruments and derivatives linked to unquoted equity instruments when their fair value cannot be measured reliably, and contracts that contain a discretionary participation feature if their fair value cannot be measured reliably. [IFRS 7.29] However, where fair value cannot be measured reliably, additional disclosures are required to assist users of the financial statements in making their own judgements about the extent of possible differences between the carrying amount of those financial assets or financial liabilities and their fair value. These disclosures include a statement that fair value disclosure has not been provided as fair value cannot be measured reliably, a description of the instrument, its carrying amount, an explanation of why fair value cannot be measured reliably, information about the market for the instruments, and information about whether and how the entity intends to dispose of the financial instruments. Furthermore, if such instruments are subsequently derecognised, disclosures should be provided of the carrying amount at the date of disposal, the fact that fair value could not be reliably measured, and the gain or loss that results. [IFRS 7.30]

As noted above, IFRS 7 permits an entity to omit the fair value disclosure for derivatives that are *linked to equity instruments* that do not have a quoted market price in an active market and are measured at cost in accordance with IAS 39. It is worth noting that IAS 39.46 states that derivatives that are *linked to <u>and must be settled by delivery</u> of such unquoted equity instruments*, [emphasis added] shall be measured at cost. Thus, there is a difference in wording between the disclosure requirements of IFRS 7 and the measurements requirements of IAS 39. IAS 39 requires delivery of the unquoted equity instrument whereas IFRS 7 does not. However, while there is a difference in wording, the exception in IFRS 7 is not wider than in IAS 39 as a derivative that is linked to, but is not settled by the delivery of an unquoted equity is measured at fair value in accordance with IAS 39, and therefore supplementary disclosure of fair value would not be necessary.

In the case of compound financial instruments (i.e. an instrument including a financial liability and equity component as described in **section 3** in **chapter 15**) the fair value disclosure will relate only to the financial liability component of the compound instrument as the equity component is scoped out of IFRS 7 (see **section 2** above). The

	LIBOR at inception and at each reset date	Fair value of the interest rate swap
31 December 20X2	6.79 per cent	US$2,303,000
31 December 20X3	5.76 per cent	US$241,000

Entity X accrues its interest expense at LIBOR plus 200 basis points on the debt and accrues the swap payments or receipts at the end of each reporting period as an adjustment to interest expense. The effect of the debt and swap accruals is a 7.50 per cent fixed rate. The fair value of the swap is recognised as an asset or liability with an offsetting amount in other comprehensive income to the extent the hedge relationship is effective. Any ineffectiveness is immediately recognised in net profit or loss.

1 January 20X0

Dr	Cash	US$100,000,000
Cr	Debt	US$100,000,000

To record the issuance of debt.

No entries are required in respect of the interest rate swap since it has a fair value of zero at inception.

Interest rates increased during the period ended 31 December 20X0 resulting in a fair value of the interest rate swap of US$4,068,000. Hedge ineffectiveness is assessed and measured at the end of the reporting period (determined to be zero), so the total change in fair value of the swap is recorded in other comprehensive income. Entity X paid US$500,000 in net cash settlements on the swap at 31 December 20X0. The LIBOR rate for the next period is 6.57 per cent.

31 December 20X0

Dr	Swap asset	US$4,068,000
Cr	Other comprehensive income	US$4,068,000

To record the fair value of derivative as a cash flow hedge.

Dr	Interest expense	US$7,000,000
Cr	Cash	US$7,000,000
Dr	Interest expense	US$500,000
Cr	Cash	US$500,000

To record payment of LIBOR plus 200 basis points (5.00 per cent + 2.00 per cent) on debt obligation and the net cash settlement payment on the swap as an adjustment to the yield on the debt. Effective yield is 7.50 per cent.

31 December 20X1

Interest rates increased further during the period ended 31 December 20X1 resulting in a fair value of the interest rate swap of $5,793,000. Hedge ineffectiveness is assessed and measured at the end of the reporting period (determined to be zero), so the total change in fair value of the swap is recorded in other comprehensive income. Entity X received US$1,070,000 in net cash settlements on the swap at 31 December 20X1. The LIBOR rate for the next period is 7.70 per cent.

Dr	Swap asset	US$1,725,000
Cr	Other comprehensive income	US$1,725,000

To record the change in fair value of derivative as a cash flow hedge.

Dr	Interest expense	US$8,570,000
Cr	Cash	US$8,570,000
Dr	Cash	US$1,070,000
Cr	Interest expense	US$1,070,000

To record payment of LIBOR plus 200 basis points (6.57 per cent + 2.00 per cent) on debt obligation and the net cash settlement receipt on the swap as an adjustment to the yield on the debt. Effective yield is 7.50 per cent.

Interest rates decreased during the period ended 31 December 20X2 resulting in a fair value of the interest rate swap of US$2,303,000. Hedge ineffectiveness is assessed and measured at the end of the reporting period (determined to be zero), so the total change in fair value of the swap is recorded in other comprehensive income. Entity X received US$2,200,000 in net cash settlements on the swap at 31 December 20X2. The LIBOR rate for the next period is 6.79 per cent.

31 December 20X2

Dr	Other comprehensive income	US$3,490,000
Cr	Swap asset	US$3,490,000

To record the fair value of derivative in other comprehensive income as a cash flow hedge.

Dr	Interest expense	US$9,700,000
Cr	Cash	US$9,700,000
Dr	Cash	US$2,200,000
Cr	Interest expense	US$2,200,000

To record payment of LIBOR plus 200 basis points (7.70 per cent + 2.00 per cent) on debt obligation and the net cash settlement receipt on the swap as an adjustment to the yield on the debt. Effective yield is 7.50 per cent.

Interest rates decreased during the period ended 31 December 20X3 resulting in a fair value of the interest rate swap of US$241,000. Hedge ineffectiveness is assessed and measured at the end of the reporting period (determined to be zero), so the total change in fair value of the swap is recorded in other comprehensive income. Entity X received US$1,290,000 in net cash settlements on the swap at 31 December 20X3. The LIBOR rate for the next period is 5.76 per cent.

31 December 20X3

Dr	Other comprehensive income	US$2,062,000
Cr	Swap asset	US$2,062,000

To record the change in fair value of derivative as a cash flow hedge.

Dr	Interest expense	US$8,790,000
Cr	Cash	US$8,790,000
Dr	Cash	US$1,290,000
Cr	Interest expense	US$1,290,000

Dr	Cash	US$1,075,000	
Dr	Cost of goods sold	US$1,000,000	
Cr	Revenue		US$1,075,000
Cr	Inventory		US$1,000,000

To record the inventory sale

Dr	Other comprehensive income	US$25,000	
Cr	Revenue		US$25,000

Revenue of US$1,100,000 is recognised. This represents US$1,075,000 from the sale of wheat at spot prices, plus the gain on the derivative. The sum of the two equals the sale of wheat at the hedged rate.

Example 2.2.2B

Cash flow hedging: variable rate debt

Entity X issued US$100 million of five-year variable-rate debt on 1 January 20X0. The variable-rate on the debt is LIBOR plus a spread of 200 basis points. Initial LIBOR is 5 per cent. The debt pays interest on an annual basis and the swap resets on an annual basis on 31 December.

On 1 January 20X0, Entity X entered into a five-year pay fixed, receive LIBOR interest rate swap with a notional amount of US$100 million. The swap is designated as a cash flow hedge of the forecast interest payments on the LIBOR portion of the debt. Entity X does not intend to repurchase the debt prior to its maturity. The interest rate swap is on-market at inception and has a fair value of zero.

The terms of the interest rate swap are as follows:

Notional amount	US$100 million
Trade date	01/01/X0
Start date	01/01/X0
Maturity date	31/12/X4
Entity X pays	5.50 per cent
Entity X receives	LIBOR
Pay and receive dates	Annually on the debt-payment dates
Variable reset	Annually (on 31 December)
Initial LIBOR	5.00 per cent
First pay/receive date	31/12/X0
Last pay/receive date	31/12/X4

The interest rate swap is expected to be highly effective because the principal terms of the debt and the swap match. Hedge effectiveness will be assessed and measured, at a minimum, at the end of each reporting period. For illustration purposes only, this hedge relationship is deemed to be perfectly effective.

	LIBOR at inception and at each reset date	Fair value of the interest rate swap
1 January 20X0	5.00 per cent	US$0
31 December 20X0	6.57 per cent	US$4,068,000
31 December 20X1	7.70 per cent	US$5,793,000

An entity may exclude the time value of an option or interest element of a forward from the hedge designation, in which case the component of the fair value gain or loss related to that component is recognised in profit or loss. Alternatively, an entity may exclude a proportion of a derivative (or a non-derivative instrument for hedges of foreign currency risk), for example 50 per cent of a derivative, or a proportion of hedged item, for example, 50 per cent of a debt instrument, from the hedge relationship, in which case the gain or loss on the proportion excluded from the designation is recognised by applying the instrument's normal classification guidance (see **chapter 14** for financial assets and **chapter 15** for financial liabilities). [IAS 39.96]

The effective portion of the gain or loss on the hedging instrument recognised in other comprehensive income is subsequently reclassified from equity to profit or loss in the same period or periods during which the hedged item affects profit or loss, so as to offset the changes in the cash flows of the hedged item for the designated risk (e.g. if sales are hedged, the reclassification from equity to profit or loss will occur when the sales occur).

Example 2.2.2A

Cash flow hedging: forecast sale of non-financial item

On 4 January 20X0 Entity B has a forecast sale of 500 tonnes of wheat expected to occur on or about 31 December 20X0.

On 4 January 20X0 Entity B designates the cash flows of the forecasted sale as a hedged item and enters into a wheat futures contract to sell 500 tonnes at US$1.1 million on 31 December 20X0.

At inception of the hedge, the derivative is at-the-money (fair value is zero). The terms of the forecast sale and the derivative match. On 31 December 20X0, the wheat futures contract has a fair value of US$25,000 and is closed out. Entity B sells the inventory for US$1,075,000.

The required entries are as follows:

31 December 20X0

Dr	Wheat futures contract	US$25,000
Cr	Other comprehensive income	US$25,000

To record the wheat futures contract at fair value (note that the changes in fair value of the derivative are recorded in other comprehensive income until the hedged forecast sale occurs).

31 December 20X0

Dr	Cash	US$25,000
Cr	Wheat futures contract	US$25,000

To record the settlement of the wheat futures contract.

Date	Spot rate US$ / £	Carrying amount of debt in US$	Carrying amount of debt in £	Cross currency swap fair value £	Net interest payment on the swap (£ LIBOR + 106 bp) – (US $ LIBOR + 100 bp)
31/12/X4	1.5	100,000	66,667	9,670	1,952
31/12/X5	1.8	100,000	55,556	(1,624)	1,042
31/12/X6	1.7	100,000	58,824	1,681	1,321

Entity A's documentation of the hedge is as follows:

Risk management objective and nature of risk being hedged	Cash flow hedge of the variability in functional currency equivalent cash flows associated with the foreign currency debt due to changes in spot rates.
Date of designation	1 January 20X2
Hedging instrument	Cross currency swap to exchange US$100,000 for £57,143 at maturity and receive US$ LIBOR + 100bp, pay £ LIBOR + 106bp interest annually over the term of the instrument.
Hedged item	The cross currency swap is designated as a hedge of the changes in the cash flows relating to the changes in foreign currency spot rates related to the debt and to the annual interest payments.
Assessment of hedge effectiveness	The critical terms of the derivative match (exchange of principal at maturity and annual interest payment), accordingly there is an expectation of high effectiveness. The entity will assess counterparty credit risk and probability of cash flows under the swap occurring every period.
Measurement of hedge effectiveness	Hypothetical derivative method. The actual hedging instrument is the same as the hypothetical cross currency swap with exactly matching terms and therefore, no ineffectiveness is anticipated.

The following table illustrates the accounting entries for the transaction during its life in Sterling. Dr or (Cr) as indicated.

31 Dec		Cash	CCS	Debt	CFH reserve	Interest expense	Translation loss (gain)
20X2	Issue debt	57,143		(57,143)			
	Pay interest on debt	(2,319)				2,319	
	Revalue debt to spot			(1,681)			1,681

To record payment of LIBOR plus 200 basis points (6.79 per cent + 2.00 per cent) on debt obligation and the net cash settlement receipt on the swap as an adjustment to the yield on the debt. Effective yield is 7.50 per cent.

The swap matured at 31 December 20X4. Entity X received US$260,000 in net cash settlements on the swap at 31 December 20X4.

31 December 20X4

Dr	Other comprehensive income	US$241,000
Cr	Swap asset	US$241,000

To record the change in fair value of derivative as a cash flow hedge.

Dr	Interest expense	US$7,760,000
Cr	Cash	US$7,760,000
Dr	Cash	US$260,000
Cr	Interest expense	US$260,000

To record payment of LIBOR plus 200 basis points (5.76 per cent +2.00 per cent) on debt obligation and the net cash settlement receipt on the swap as an adjustment to the yield on the debt. Effective yield is 7.50 per cent.

Example 2.2.2C

Cash flow hedging the foreign currency risk of issued floating rate foreign currency debt with a cross currency swap that pays floating foreign currency and receives floating functional currency

On 1 January 20X2, Entity A, a Sterling functional currency entity, issues a US$ LIBOR +100 basis points (bp) floating rate debt instrument denominated in US dollars with a principal amount of US$100,000, that will mature on 31 December 20X6 at par. At 1 January 20X2, the spot rate on the US$ / £ is 1.75/1 so the principal of US$100,000 is equivalent to £57,143. On 1 January 20X2, Entity A also enters into a cross currency swap ('CCS') to exchange interest payments and principal at redemption on the same terms as the above debt and designates the CCS as a hedge of the variability of the £ functional currency equivalent cash flows on the debt. The terms are such that on each interest payment date (assume interest is paid annually on 31 December each year for both the debt and the cross currency swap), Entity A will receive US$ LIBOR + 100 basis points on a notional of US$100,000 and pay Sterling LIBOR + 106 bp based on a notional of £57,143. Because the currency, notional, coupons and interest payment dates match on both the CCS and the debt, Entity A expects the hedge relationship to be highly effective.

Date	Spot rate US$ / £	Carrying amount of debt in US$	Carrying amount of debt in £	Cross currency swap fair value £	Net interest payment on the swap (£ LIBOR + 106 bp) – (US $ LIBOR + 100 bp)
1/1/X2	1.75	100,000	57,143	0	0
31/12/X2	1.7	100,000	58,824	1,743	1,259
31/12/X3	1.6	100,000	62,500	5,520	1,476

fair value of the financial liability component will incorporate interest rate risk and the entity's own credit risk but will exclude any consideration of equity price risk.

Disclosure is required of the methods and significant assumptions used in arriving at fair values. This includes disclosure of whether a market price or a valuation model has been used. Where a valuation technique has been used, disclosures are required as to whether any inputs into the valuation model are based on assumptions that are not supported by observable prices from observable current market transactions in the same instrument and not based on available observable market data. Where such fair values are recognised in the financial statements, if changing one or more assumptions would change fair value significantly, disclosure of this fact and the effect of those changes should be provided. [IFRS 7.27] Only those changes in assumptions that could result in a significantly different estimate of fair value are required, and such disclosures are not required to reflect interdependencies between those assumptions. [IFRS 7.BC38] Further disclosure shall also be provided of the total amount of change in fair value that has been estimated using such a valuation technique that was recognised in profit or loss for the period. [IFRS 7.27]

Disclosure of the method and significant assumptions used is very important as the use of valuation models inevitably involves a significant degree of judgement. Users of the financial statements should be in a position to understand the subjective and judgemental nature of the fair value numbers and to judge for themselves whether the assumptions made by management are reasonable.

Example 4.3.3

Fair value disclosures

Entity B (31 March 20X1)

	31 March 20X1		**31 March 20X0**	
	Carrying amount	Fair value	Carrying amount	Fair value
Investments	£m	£m	£m	£m
Loans and receivables	3,428	3,543	5,200	5,602
Held-to-maturity investments	6,870	7,243	9,304	9,730

The assumptions used to estimate current fair values of investments are summarised below.

(i) For short-term loans and receivables (e.g. trade receivables) the carrying amount approximates to fair value because of their short maturities.

(ii) For long-term loans and receivables where the market rate of interest for that specific issuer is not readily determinable (e.g. non-quoted corporate debt issued by non-quoted companies), fair value has been calculated by discounting the future cash flows at the market rate of interest for a similar issuer with the same credit quality.

(iii) The fair values of held-to-maturity quoted corporate debt are derived from their external quoted prices.

	At 31 March 20X1		At 31 March 20X0	
Fair value of financial liabilities	Carrying amount £m	Fair value £m	Carrying amount £m	Fair value £m
Short-term creditors and borrowings	631	631	907	907
Current portion of long-term debt				
Bank Loans	50	52	32	31
Eurobonds	70	74	45	44
Sterling bond 20X1	82	84	52	50
Total current portion of long-term debt	202	210	129	125
Non-current portion of long-term debt				
Eurobonds	590	640	361	385
Sterling bond 20X1	674	732	413	441
European Investment Bank Loans	421	457	258	275
Total long-term debt	1,685	1,829	1,032	1,101

The assumptions used to estimate current fair values of debt and other financial instruments are summarised below:

(i) For short-term creditors and short-term borrowings (e.g. commercial paper and short-term borrowings under committed facilities) the carrying amount approximates to fair value because of their short maturities.

(ii) The fair values of the Sterling bond 20X1 and Bank loans have been calculated by discounting their future cash flows at the market rate that reflects current interest rates and current spreads for the entity.

(iii) The fair values of the Eurobonds have been derived from their external quoted prices.

IAS 39 requires that no gain or loss should be recognised on initial recognition of a financial instrument where the valuation technique for that instrument does not solely use observable market data. A gain or loss shall be recognised subsequently only to the extent that it arises from a change in factor (including time) that market participants would consider in setting a price. As noted at **5.2.5** in **chapter 18** there is little clarity as to when day 1 profit or loss should be recognised since the standard does not specify how entities should account for those initial differences in subsequent periods. Disclosure is required, by class of financial instrument, of the accounting policy used to recognise that difference in profit or loss. In addition, the aggregate difference yet to be recognised in profit or loss at the beginning and end of the period should be disclosed together with a reconciliation of the changes in the balance during the period. [IFRS 7.28]

5 Nature and extent of risks arising from financial instruments

IFRS 7 has two key objectives: firstly to show the significance of financial instruments as discussed in **section 4** above; and, secondly, to require entities to disclose information that enables users of its financial statements to evaluate the nature and extent of risks arising from financial instruments to which the entity is exposed at the end of the reporting period as discussed below.

Both qualitative and quantitative disclosures are required about the risks that arise from financial instruments and how these risks have been managed. These risks typically include, but are not limited to, credit risk, liquidity risk and market risk. [IFRS 7.32] The disclosures provided should depend on the extent of an entity's use of financial instruments and the extent to which it assumes associated risks, though certain minimum disclosures are required for all entities. The guidance on how the disclosures should be provided has been developed so as to be consistent with the Basel Committee disclosure requirements for banks to allow banks (so called 'Pillar 3' of Basel II) to prepare a single set of co-ordinated disclosures about financial risk. [IFRS 7.BC41] It is of note that Pillar 3 disclosures are broader than those of IFRS 7 as they include operational risks

The disclosures shall either be provided in the financial statements or incorporated by clear cross-reference from the financial statements to some other statement, such as a management commentary or risk report. Such a report must be available to users on the same terms as the financial statements and be available at the same time. Without such information the financial statements are incomplete. [IFRS 7.B6]

Where the disclosures are provided in a separate statement, the information should be clearly referenced as being part of the IFRS financial statements.

5.1 Qualitative disclosures

For each type of risk that an entity is exposed to, disclosure is required of the exposures to that risk, explanation of how the exposures arose, the entity's objective, policies and processes for managing the risk and the method used to measure it. Any changes from the previous period are also required to be disclosed. [IFRS 7.33]

Disclosure may be provided on a gross basis or net of any risk transfer and other risk mitigating transactions. [IFRS 7.IG15(a)] Such information is useful since it highlights the relationship between financial instruments and provides the user of the financial statements with information to understand the effect that those relationships have on the nature, timing and uncertainty of future cash flows.

Disclosure of the entity's policies and processes for accepting, measuring, monitoring and controlling risk may include disclosure of the following:

[IFRS 7.IG15(b) & (c)]

- the structure and organisation of the entity's risk management function;
- the scope and nature of risk reporting or measurement systems;
- policies for hedging or mitigating risk, including policies and procedures for taking collateral;
- the entity's processes for monitoring the continuing effectiveness of such hedges or mitigating devices; and
- disclosure of the policies and procedures that are undertaken to avoid excessive concentrations of risk.

An entity is required to disclose any changes in the qualitative information from the previous period. Such changes may result from changes in the risk exposure or from changes in the way in which the exposures are managed. [IFRS 7.IG17] This information is important since the user of the financial statements needs to understand the effect that such changes have on the nature, timing and uncertainty of future cash flows.

One of the objectives of the disclosure requirements is to enable users to evaluate an entity's ability to generate returns, and to appreciate the risks and uncertainties of those expected returns. This evaluation can only be meaningful if it is carried out in the context of the entity's risk management policies.

5.2 Quantitative disclosures

For each type of risk that an entity is exposed to IFRS 7 requires an entity to provide quantitative information about exposure to that risk at the end of the reporting period, based on information reported internally to key management personnel. [IFRS 7.34(a)] Where more than one method is used to manage and report information about risk exposures, then disclosure of the method that provides the most relevant and reliable information shall be disclosed. [IFRS 7.B7] Disclosure based on management information provides a useful insight into how risk is viewed and managed by the entity, is based on information that has a more predictive value than information based on assumptions and methods that management does not use, provides disclosures which adapt to changes in the manner in which risk is measured and managed and allows users to use the same data that management uses to measure and manage risk. [IFRS 7.BC47]

Key management personnel are defined as *'those persons having authority and responsibility for planning, directing and controlling the activities of the entity, directly or indirectly, including any director (whether executive or otherwise) of that entity.'* [IAS 24.9]

Following the definition, any director, whether executive or non-executive, will be considered to be key management personnel. The definition of key management personnel is, however, wider than just directors of an entity. Key management personnel might in some instances include directors of subsidiaries who are not directors of the parent entity and senior managers who are not directors. Other managers may be included as key management personnel in some cases, and not in others. Consideration needs to be given to the relative autonomy of management and whether their decisions are subject to the approval of the Board of Directors. Take for instance a Treasury Manager in an organisation. Where that manager unilaterally reviews exposures and acts independently following only Board guidelines and objectives established by the Board , then that person may be considered to be included as part of the key management personnel of that entity. Where, however, that manager acts purely in accordance with the detailed treasury risk policy and framework as set out and approved by the board, then that person may in most instances be excluded from the definition of key management personnel. In all instances, a thorough understanding of that person's role within the organisation and the realms within which they operate and report needs to be clearly understood in concluding whether that person is indeed included in the definition of key management personnel.

In addition to the above disclosures which are based on information provided to key management personnel, IFRS 7 requires, to the extent that these are not covered, disclosures of credit, liquidity and market risk, unless the risk is not material. [IFRS 7.34(b)] Furthermore, disclosure of concentrations of risk shall be provided if not apparent from those disclosures. [IFRS 7.34(c)] Concentrations of risk arise from financial instruments that have similar characteristics and are affected similarly by changes in economic or other conditions. The identification of concentrations of risk requires judgement and must take into account the specific circumstances of the entity. Disclosures may include:

[IFRS 7.B8]

- description of how concentrations are determined;
- description of the shared characteristic that identifies each concentration, e.g.: counterparty credit rating, geographical distribution, industry sector and other risks such as liquidity and market risks; and
- the amount of the risk exposure associated with all financial instruments that share that risk characteristic.

The quantitative information shall, in all instances, be provided for the risk exposures that exist at the end of the reporting period. Where such information is unrepresentative of the exposure to financial risk during the period, an entity should provide additional information, which may include, but not be limited to, disclosure of the highest, lowest and average amount of risk the entity was exposed to during the period. [IFRS 7.IG20]

5.2.1 Credit risk

Credit risk is defined as 'the risk that one party to a financial instrument will cause a financial loss for the other party by failing to discharge an obligation'. [IFRS 7(Appendix A)] IFRS 7 disclosures about credit risk are substantial and are discussed in detail below. These disclosures are intended to provide the user with a sufficient understanding of the net risk position of financial assets at all stages and the extent of financial assets that are more likely to become impaired in the future. The disclosure requirements can be summarised in the following diagram.

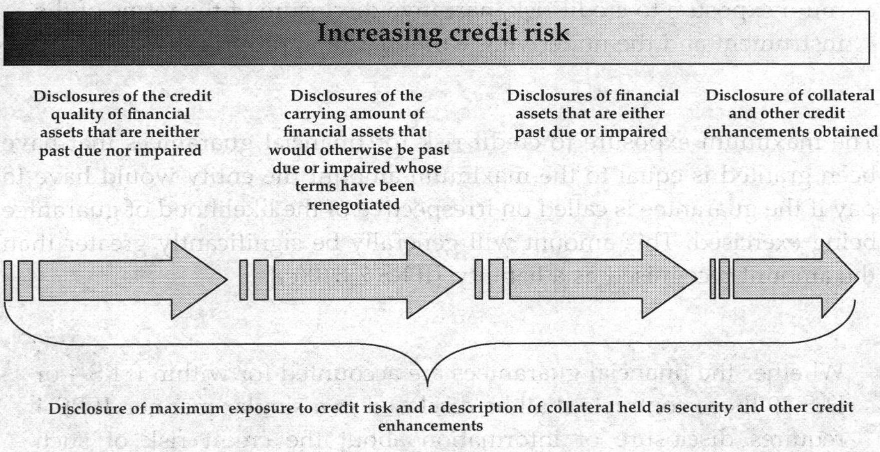

5.2.1.1 *Disclosure of the maximum exposure to credit risk*

For each class of financial asset disclosure is required of the amount that best represents its maximum credit risk exposure at the end of the reporting period, *excluding* any collateral and other amounts that do not qualify for offset in accordance with IAS 32. [IFRS 7.36(a)]

These disclosures are designed to provide users of the financial statements with a consistent measure of the amounts exposed to credit risk and to allow for the possibility that the maximum exposure to loss may differ from the carrying amount of financial assets recognised at the end of the reporting period. [IFRS 7.BC49]

For financial assets exposed to credit risk, the maximum exposure to credit risk is typically the gross carrying amount, net of any amounts offset in accordance with IAS 32 and any impairment losses that are recognised in accordance with IAS 39. [IFRS 7.B9] In the case of derivatives that are measured at fair value, the maximum exposure to credit risk at the end of the reporting period will equal its carrying amount. [IFRS 7.B10(b)]

A derivative that will result in the delivery or receipt of an unquoted equity security where the underlying security cannot be fair valued with sufficient reliability will be recognised at cost in accordance with IAS 39.46(c) & 47(a). IFRS 7 does not state how to determine the maximum exposure to credit risk when the derivative is held at cost. For example, a gross physically settled purchased call over an unquoted equity security has a maximum exposure to credit risk equal to the value of the equity security that will be physically delivered to the entity less the exercise price to be paid. However, as the fair value of the instrument cannot be determined with sufficient reliability and cost will generally be unrepresentative of the maximum exposure to credit risk, narrative disclosure of the terms of the instrument and the underlying would seem appropriate.

The maximum exposure to credit risk for financial guarantees that have been granted is equal to the maximum amount the entity would have to pay if the guarantee is called on irrespective of the likelihood of guarantee being exercised. This amount will generally be significantly greater than the amount recognised as a liability. [IFRS 7.B10(c)]

Whether the financial guarantees are accounted for within IFRS 4 or IAS 39 those contracts shall be disclosed in a similar manner. IFRS 4 requires disclosure of information about the credit risk of such contracts in the same manner as IFRS 7 requires credit risk disclosure for instruments that are measured in accordance with IAS 39. [IFRS 4.39(d)]

The maximum exposure to credit risk for a loan commitment that is irrevocable over the life of the facility, or is revocable only in response to a material adverse change, is the full amount of the commitment if the loan commitment cannot be settled net in cash or another financial asset. This is because it is uncertain whether the amount of any undrawn portion may be drawn upon in the future. Thus, the amount of the maximum exposure to credit risk for a loan commitment may be significantly greater than the amount recognised as a liability. [IFRS 7.B10(d)] Loan commitments that will be settled net in cash or other financial instruments are treated as derivative financial instruments and thus the maximum exposure to credit risk will, in that instance, be equal to their carrying value.

Whilst loan commitments that will not be settled net in cash or other financial instruments are outside the scope of IAS 39, they are within the scope of IFRS 7 as they are unrecognised financial assets or financial liabilities. [IFRS 7.4] If a loan commitment cannot be settled net but is designated as at FVTPL and therefore is within the scope of IAS 39, the Standard is not clear whether it is possible to consider the maximum exposure to credit risk as being its fair value, as is the case for other derivative financial assets. As a loan commitment that cannot be settled net will always result in the origination of a loan if the commitment is exercised by the borrower, the most appropriate amount representing the maximum exposure to credit risk would seem to be the maximum that can be borrowed under the commitment. Disclosing this amount is consistent with the majority of gross settled loan commitments that are outside the scope of IAS 39.

The exposure under the loan to be originated under a loan commitment is the same as the exposure under a financial guarantee that can be claimed if the loan is in default. From the lender's perspective, both have credit risk.

IFRS 7.B10(c) states that the maximum exposure to credit risk for a written guarantee is the amount the entity could have to pay if the guarantee is called upon. It is reasonable to conclude that this amount should be based on the amount that could be required to be paid if the guarantee was called upon in its entirety, as opposed to the amount that could be claimed under the guarantee at the end of the reporting period based on the then level of lending that the lender has made to the borrower. This approach equally applies to loan commitments.

Example 5.2.1.1A

Maximum exposure to credit risk: loan commitment

Entity A issues a loan commitment to Entity B for US$100m. The maximum exposure to credit risk that will be disclosed in the bank's financial statements with respect to the loan commitment will be equal to the full amount of the loan that has been offered, US$100m. Assume Entity C issues a financial guarantee to Entity A with respect to their loan commitment to Entity B over US$100m. The guarantee will provide protection against Entity B defaulting on its loan to Bank A should Entity B draw down on the loan commitment. The maximum exposure to credit risk for Entity A will be US$100m, being the maximum potential loan under the loan irrespective of the guarantee it has acquired to reduce this potential loss. This amount will be disclosed at the end of the reporting period even if no draw down on the loan commitment is made by Entity B.

Entity C has credit risk on the financial guarantee written to Entity A. The maximum exposure to credit risk is also US$100m as this is the maximum amount Entity C could have to pay to Entity A if the guarantee is called on.

Example 5.2.1.1B

Maximum exposure to credit risk: receivables

Group F is a listed retail group with a large customer base. Customers purchase goods under the group's standard credit terms. Group F also purchases goods from some of its major customers.

	30 June 20X2	30 June 20X1
	US$	US$
Gross trade receivables	365,500	323,700
Impairment loss	(14,620)	(12,948)
Net carrying amount	350,880	310,752
Amounts owed to customers	(75,500)	(62,250)

The group has an agreement with its customers to set off amounts owed by customers and amounts owed to customers, but only if the customer defaults. Group F does not meet the requirements to offset the asset and liability and there is not the intention and legal ability to set off the recognised amounts.

The maximum credit exposure to credit risk at the end of each reporting period is the gross amount less the allowance for impairment losses. The payables are excluded from the analysis as they are not offset in the statement of financial position.

Example 5.2.1.1C

Maximum exposure to credit risk: financial guarantee contracts

Entity B is a wholly owned operating subsidiary of Entity A, the ultimate parent of Group A. To finance its working capital requirements, Entity B has short-term banking facilities of €300million with various banks. Entity A has issued a variety of guarantees on behalf of its subsidiary and in favour of the banks which meet the definition of a financial guarantee contract. The schedule below details the drawn down banking facilities of Entity B and the amount guaranteed by Entity A at the period-end.

	30 June 20X2	30 June 20X1
	€m	€m
Short-term banking facilities drawn down at year end	100	100
Guarantees issued by Entity A to lenders	250	250

The following amount will be disclosed as the maximum exposure to credit risk in Entity B, Entity A, and in the Group A financial statements.

- Entity B: € nil (20X1: €0) since Entity B is the borrower, it does not have an exposure to credit risk.
- Entity A: €250,000 (20X1: €250,000) – being the full amount of the guarantee that would be required to be paid if the guarantee is called upon. [IFRS 7.B10(c)]
- Group A: € nil (20X1: nil) since from a group perspective the group is the borrower and it does not have exposure to credit risk. The amount repayable is the same irrespective of whether Entity B repays the debt or Entity A repays the debt on Entity B's behalf.

5.2.1.2 Disclosure of collateral held as security and other credit enhancements

IFRS 7 requires disclosure of the collateral held and other credit enhancements. [IFRS 7.36(b)] This requirement may be met by disclosing:

[IFRS 7.IG23]

- the policies and processes for valuing and managing collateral and other credit enhancements obtained;
- a description of the main types of collateral and other credit enhancements (examples of the latter being guarantees, credit derivatives, and netting agreements that do not qualify for offset in accordance with IAS 32);
- the main types of counterparties to collateral and other credit enhancements and their creditworthiness; and
- information about risk concentrations within the collateral or other credit enhancements.

5.2.1.3 Disclosure of information of the credit quality of financial assets that are neither past due nor impaired

Disclosures shall be provided of the credit quality of financial assets that are neither past due nor impaired. [IFRS 7.36(c)] A financial asset is not past due where the debtor has not missed a contractual payment (interest or capital) when contractually due [IFRS 7(Appendix A)], and a financial asset is not impaired where there is no objective evidence of impairment. [IAS 39.59] In providing these disclosures, the following information may be provided:

[IFRS 7.IG22]

(a) an analysis of credit exposures using an external or internal credit grading system;

(b) the nature of the counterparty;

(c) historical information about counterparty default rates; and

(d) any other information used to assess credit quality.

Such disclosures provide useful information and greater insight into the credit risk of assets and allow users to assess whether assets are more or less likely to become impaired in the future. Since all entities are different, each entity may determine its own way of providing the required information. [IFRS 7.BC54]

When an entity considers external ratings for managing and monitoring credit quality, the entity might disclose information about:

[IFRS 7.IG24]

(a) the amounts of credit exposures for each external credit grade;

(b) the rating agencies used;

(c) the amount of an entity's rated and unrated credit exposures; and

(d) the relationship between internal and external ratings.

When an entity considers internal credit ratings for managing and monitoring credit quality, the entity might disclose information about:

[IFRS 7.IG25]

(a) the internal credit ratings process;

(b) the amounts of credit exposures for each internal credit grade; and

(c) the relationship between internal and external ratings.

Disclosing information of exposures by credit grade reflects the strength of the debtors, especially where that debt is rated externally. The disclosure of one's internal credit rating process together with exposures by credit rating provides a useful insight into how the credit risk of financial assets is monitored internally and reflects how management measures and manages credit risk. Since comparative financial information will also be provided, the user will be able to understand how the credit risk of those financial assets that are neither past due nor impaired has changed over the financial period.

5.2.1.4 *Disclosure of information of financial assets that would otherwise be past due or impaired whose terms have been renegotiated*

Disclosure shall be provided of the carrying amount of financial assets that would otherwise be past due or impaired whose terms have been renegotiated. [IFRS 7.36(d)]

> An example where financial assets that would otherwise be past due whose terms have been renegotiated would be where the dates for repayment of a loan have been changed, e.g. previously a debtor was required to service a loan monthly but the loan has been renegotiated

to require payments on a yearly basis. Were it not for the renegotiation of the terms, the loan would be past due as soon as a monthly repayment was missed.

If the terms of a financial asset are renegotiated or otherwise modified because of financial difficulties of the borrower or issuer, impairment may or may not have been recognised prior to the renegotiation as it will have depended if an impairment trigger event had occurred. Where the lender, for economic or legal reasons relating to the borrower's financial difficulty, grants to the borrower a concession to the lender, this is evidence of impairment. [IAS 39.59(c) & IG.E.4.3] The renegotiation of the contractual cash flows of the debt may have avoided an impairment, and similarly, if there was an impairment prior to the renegotiation, the loan may no longer be impaired following the renegotiation because the contractual cash flows have changed.

An example where financial assets would otherwise be impaired whose terms have been renegotiated is where additional collateral or security has been provided on the loan as part of the terms of the debt renegotiation, e.g. previously the loan was unsecured and because of the debtor's worsening credit status, the debtor is required to provide collateral. If by taking the collateral into account on the financial asset the loan is no longer assessed to be impaired then such a loan would be classified as a loan that would otherwise be impaired whose terms have been renegotiated.

5.2.1.5 *Disclosure of financial assets that are either past due or impaired*

Disclosure of financial information shall be provided by class of financial asset for financial assets that are either past due or impaired. [IFRS 7.37]

A financial asset is past due when the counterparty has failed to make a payment when contractually due. [IFRS 7(Appendix A)] Past due status can trigger various actions such as renegotiation, enforcement of covenants, or even legal proceedings. [IFRS 7.IG26] The new terms and conditions of debt that has been renegotiated apply in determining whether the financial asset is past due for the purposes of this disclosure item. [IFRS 7.IG27]

There is a subtle distinction between past due and impaired. Past due occurs when a payment that was contractually due is not made. This may not necessarily be equivalent to an impairment as the late

> payment may be added to the outstanding balance, with interest applied to the outstanding payment missed that is still deemed recoverable, so that from the lender's perspective the recoverable amount of the asset is the same, i.e. there is no impairment.

This disclosure shall include analysis of the age of financial assets that are past due but not impaired at the end of the reporting period. [IFRS 7.37(a)] An entity shall use its judgement to determine an appropriate number of time bands. [IFRS 7.IG28]

> Since the quantitative disclosures of IFRS 7 should be based on the information that is provided internally to key management personnel of the entity, the disclosures for the ageing analysis based on internally reported time bands should be provided where available.

Providing an analysis of the age of financial assets that are past due, but not impaired, as at the end of the reporting period allows the user of the financial statements to understand the extent of financial assets that are more likely to become impaired because they are past due. This, in turn, assists users in estimating the level of future impairment losses. [IFRS 7.BC55(a)]

> The disclosure of past due items may be particularly onerous for entities with accounts receivable. For example, if an entity has debtor repayment terms of 30 days from invoice date, yet it is customary for payment to be received after 60 days, then those receivables that remain outstanding at the end of the reporting period that are older than 30 days shall be disclosed as past due. This disclosure requirement is more onerous than that for breaches of loans payable, where short-term trade payables on normal credit terms are specifically excluded.

The disclosure shall include an analysis of financial assets that are individually determined to be impaired at the end of the reporting period and the factors that were considered in determining that those assets were impaired. [IFRS 7.37(b)] Such an analysis may include the carrying amount, before deducting any impairment losses, the amount of any related impairment losses, and the nature and fair value of collateral available and other credit enhancements obtained. [IFRS 7.IG29]

An analysis of impaired financial assets other than by age is useful because it helps users to understand why the impairment occurred. [IFRS 7.BC55(b)]

The disclosure shall also include disclosure of a description of collateral held by the entity as security and other credit enhancements and, unless impracticable, an estimate of their fair value. [IFRS 7.37(c)] Disclosure of the fair value of collateral for such debts provides useful information on the net risk position of those receivables.

5.2.1.6 Disclosure of collateral and other credit enhancements obtained

Where an entity obtains financial or non-financial assets by taking possession of collateral or calling on other credit enhancements (e.g. financial guarantee contracts) at foreclosure, and such assets are required to be recognised in accordance with IAS 39 or another Standard, disclosure shall be provided of the nature and carrying amount of assets obtained. When those assets are not readily convertible into cash, then the entity's policies for disposing of those assets or using them in its operations shall also be disclosed. [IFRS 7.38] Disclosure of collateral in this instance is useful since it provides information about the frequency of such activities and the entity's ability to obtain and realise the value of the collateral.

IFRSs do not define what readily convertible to cash means. As explained at **2.5.4** in **chapter 13**, the guidance in US literature may prove helpful in determining what is readily convertible into cash.

Consideration shall be given to the type of assets that are obtained as collateral and the ability to sell those assets. The mere fact that the collateral consists of listed securities does not indicate that it is readily convertible to cash as the liquidity of those assets and the size of holding should be considered.

Example 5.2.1.6

Collateral and other credit enhancements obtained

Scenario 1

Bank A lends £100,000 to a homeowner with property specified as collateral for the loan. During the period the homeowner defaults under loan and the property meets the criteria for recognition in the statement of financial position of Bank A before being disposed of. Bank A must comply with the disclosure requirements of IFRS 7.38 as noted above.

Scenario 2

Bank B lends £1,000 to a retail customer. Concurrently it enters into a financial guarantee contract with Entity C under which if the retail customer fails to make payments under the loan agreement when due Entity C will reimburse Bank B the £1,000 in cash. During the period the retail customer defaults under the loan and Bank B claims under the financial guarantee contract. The amount of £1,000 is required to be disclosed following the requirements of IFRS 7.38.

5.2.2 *Liquidity risk*

Liquidity risk is defined as the risk that an entity will encounter difficulty in meeting obligations associated with financial liabilities. [IFRS 7(Appendix A)] Liquidity risk also arises because of the possibility (which may often be remote) that the entity could be required to pay its financial liabilities earlier than expected. Disclosure of a maturity analysis for all financial liabilities at the end of the reporting period that shows the remaining contractual maturities for all financial liabilities at the end of the reporting period together with a description of how it manages that liquidity risk is required. [IFRS 7.39] The analysis is by reference to the earliest contractual maturity date since this disclosure represents the worst case scenario. [IFRS 7.BC57] An entity shall exercise its judgement in determining the appropriate number of the time bands in that analysis.

Since quantitative information is required to be reported based on information reported to key management personnel, the time bands should, where applicable, be equivalent to those reported internally. Some entities may have many more time bands than others, such as banks that disclose liquidity for 1 day, 1–3 days, 3–7 days, 7–30 days etc. In any event, the entity should evaluate whether the liquidity analysis provides sufficient disclosure of the liquidity requirements by considering the relative timing of its liquidity needs. For example, an entity may have significant obligations due in a month's time, in which case aggregating all obligations of the first year into one band will not be appropriate.

5.2.2.1 *Determining which time band*

When a counterparty has a choice of when an amount is required to be paid, the liability is included on the basis of the earliest date on which the entity can be required to pay it, e.g. demand deposits shall be included in the earliest time band as the deposit holder can require repayment on demand. [IFRS 7.B12] Therefore, American-style written options that can be exercised by the holder at any time should be disclosed in the earliest time band in which the holder can exercise, whilst a European style option, which is only exercisable by the holder at maturity, should be included in the time period equivalent to its maturity date.

Where the counterparty has the choice of when an amount is to be paid liquidity analysis is based on the 'worst case' scenario, i.e. the earliest period that the holder could be required to pay. [IFRS 7.BC 57] This also has implications for the treatment of financial liabilities that are callable by the issuer. Both IFRS 7.BC 57 & IG30 seem to imply that an issuer call is not taken account for the purposes of the liquidity analysis. Therefore, for liquidity risk purposes, perpetual fixed rate debt that can be called by the issuer will be presented as if the call feature were absent and therefore the issuer has an obligation to pay cash flows into perpetuity. Similarly, if a financial liability has a maturity of 10 years but is callable by the issuer after 5 years the cash flows included in the liquidity analysis would assume the instrument will remain outstanding until its contractual maturity. This approach applies even if it is highly likely that the call will be exercised by the issuer and also if the effect of the call has been included in the determining the effective interest rate of the liability for the purpose of its measurement at amortised cost (see **section 4.1** in **chapter 18** for details).

When an entity is committed to make amounts available in instalments each instalment is allocated to the earliest period in which the entity can be required to pay it, e.g. an undrawn loan commitment shall be included in the time band containing the earliest date that it can be drawn down. [IFRS 7.B13] If loan commitments can be drawn by the holder at any time they should be included in the earliest time period.

While the loan commitment is undrawn it is generally an unrecognised financial liability. However, the requirement for a lender to include in the maturity analysis of liquidity risk its obligation to pay cash under undrawn loan commitments is reasonable as it demonstrates the amount of cash that the entity may be committed to pay to a borrower.

If an entity has issued perpetual debt the entity must consider how the cash flows which are due to perpetuity will be included in the liquidity analysis. As the cash flows are perpetual it would be reasonable to determine the number of time bands based on all other financial liabilities that are not perpetual (i.e. that are term liabilities) and include undiscounted interest cash flows in relation to perpetual liabilities as appropriate in these time bands. In addition, it will be necessary to make clear through additional disclosure (in narrative form or a combination of an additional column with narrative disclosure) that the entity is subject to a stream of interest cash flows in relation to the perpetual instrument into infinity with disclosure of the key terms of the perpetual (such as rate of interest and notional).

5.2.2.2 *What amount to include in the time band*

The amounts to be provided in the liquidity analysis are contractual, undiscounted cash flows. These amounts will differ from the amounts disclosed in the statement of financial position for financial liabilities since these are typically discounted amounts.

Although not specifically mentioned in IFRS 7, the financial liabilities to be disclosed as part of the liquidity risk analysis should be after any amounts offset in accordance with IAS 32.

Examples of amounts included on an undiscounted basis include:

[IFRS 7.B14]

- gross finance lease obligations, before deduction of finance charges;
- forward prices specified in forward agreements to purchase financial assets for cash;
- net amounts for pay (receive) floating/ receive (pay) fixed interest rate swaps for which net cash flows are exchanged (where the variable cash flow leg of the derivative is determined by reference to the interest rate yield curve at the end of the reporting period);
- contractual amounts to be exchanged in a derivative financial instrument, such as a cross currency swap, for which gross cash flows are exchanged (where the variable cash flow leg of the derivative is determined by reference to the interest rate yield curve at the end of the reporting period); and
- gross cash flows in respect of loan commitments.

For foreign denominated fixed or floating rate debt instruments the disclosure of principal and interest in the appropriate time bands is determined based on the interest rates curves in the foreign currency interest rate environment. These amounts may be disclosed in the foreign currency. Alternatively, they may be disclosed in the functional currency when preparing company only financial statements, or alternatively disclosed in the group presentation currency when preparing consolidated financial statements.

Where the amount payable is not fixed, as is the case for issued debt that has a variable interest rate, the amount to be disclosed shall be determined by reference to the conditions existing at the end of the reporting period. If amount payable varies with changes in an index, the amount disclosed may be based on the level of the index at the end of the reporting period. [IFRS 7.B16]

What is not clear with IFRS 7.B16 is whether 'conditions existing at the end of the reporting period' is referring solely to the absolute level of the index at the end of the reporting period, say the LIBOR rate at the end of the reporting period, or whether it is referring to conditions relating to future LIBOR that exist at the end of the reporting period. The former would result in say a five-year LIBOR based issued debt having five interest payments of the same amount whereas the latter would have five interest payments based on the prevailing forward curve at the end of the reporting period, i.e. on what LIBOR is expected to be in the future. The most appropriate disclosure would seem to be the latter as it recognises the conditions at the period end relating to the entity's expected payments of cash.

Where appropriate, an entity shall disclose the analysis of derivative financial instruments separately from that of non-derivative financial instruments in the contractual maturity analysis for financial liabilities. For example, it would be appropriate to distinguish cash flows between derivative financial instruments and non-derivative financial instruments if the cash flows arising from the derivative financial instruments are settled gross. This is because the gross cash outflow may be accompanied by a related inflow. [IFRS 7.B15]

A derivative may be an asset in one period and a liability in another period depending on its fair value at the end of the reporting period. In order to provide some comparability an entity may choose to project the undiscounted cash flows on the derivative (whether it is settled net or gross) and disclose these undiscounted cash flows in the appropriate time bands, irrespective of whether in a particular time band the entity is expecting a net cash inflow or a net cash outflow.

In the case of gross settled derivatives that are liabilities at the end of the reporting period the Standard only requires disclosure of the gross outflow leg. However given that IFRS 7.B15 specifically mentions that the entity may want to disclose these separately because the gross outflow will be accompanied by a gross inflow, an entity may also choose to provide the information in relation to the accompanying gross inflow. If it does so it should take care to disclose the information in such a way that it is clear that this is not information required by the Standard and is provided in addition to its requirements.

Disclosure of the gross outflow leg of gross settled derivative liabilities is required even if the outflow leg is not a cash leg. For instance an entity may have entered into a forward contract to sell a particular corporate bond in exchange for £100m cash in 9 months' time with the contract being exclusively gross settled through delivery of the bond and receipt of the cash. Alternatively an entity may have entered into a contract, within the scope of IAS 39 and IFRS 7, to sell a fixed quantity of a physical commodity such as copper in exchange for cash in the future. The forward contract may again be in a liability position at the end of the reporting period. A similar issue arises in the case of a gross settled derivative liability over own equity where the entity has an obligation to deliver a fixed number of its own equity shares in exchange for a variable amount of cash that does not meet the definition of equity and is thus accounted for as a derivative. Liquidity risk is defined in Appendix A to IFRS 7 as "the risk that an entity will encounter difficulties in meeting obligations associated with financial liabilities". This does not seem to limit the concept of liquidity risk to difficulties in meeting obligations to pay cash only. Given this fact, it would seem appropriate to include the outflow legs in the liquidity analysis in the case of the examples such as those mentioned above.

Consideration needs to be given how to present optional derivative liabilities (whether standalone or embedded) and written financial guarantee contracts as part of the liquidity risk analysis. Written financial guarantee contracts should be included in the liquidity analysis in the earliest time band in which the holder of the financial guarantee contract could claim an amount from the writer should the debtor fail to make payment when due in accordance with the terms of the debt instrument. This is in line with the 'worst case' approach as regards timing discussed earlier in this section. However, with respect to the amount that shall be disclosed, IFRS 7.B16 requires this to be based on conditions existing at the end of the reporting period. For many written financial guarantee contracts where there is no indication that the debtor is likely to default this will result in a nil amount being disclosed. In contrast where, based on conditions at the end of the reporting period, the underlying debtor is likely to default or has done so already the undiscounted amount expected to be paid out under the financial guarantee contract will be disclosed.

In the case of written options (standalone or embedded) the same analysis applies. For instance, if a written credit default option does not meet the definition of a financial guarantee contract because payout under the contract is driven not only by non-payment of a debtor but also by the credit rating of the borrower, it will be measured as at fair value through profit or loss. The fair value of the written option will at each period end comprise intrinsic value and time value. In determining the amount to be included in the liquidity analysis it would seem reasonable to draw on the principle in IFRS 7.B16 and disclose an undiscounted amount that represents the expected payout under the option based on conditions at the end of the reporting period. Under this approach an amount of nil would be disclosed for options that are out of the money (based on forward rates if applicable) at the end of the reporting period. For options that are in the money (based on forward rates if applicable) the amount of the expected payout would be included in the liquidity risk analysis. It should be noted that this amount will not take account of any of the option's time value as the time value is not payable by the writer to the counterparty, and will also differ from the intrinsic value of the option as this will include the effect of discounting.

IFRS 7 does not provide guidance on how to disclose in the liquidity analysis non-closely related embedded derivatives that are liabilities at the end of the reporting period that are embedded in non-financial host contracts. Consider the example of a Sterling functional currency entity which enters into an electricity sales contract to sell set quantities of electricity in the future in exchange for fixed amounts of Euro. The host contract to sell electricity in exchange for Sterling is considered to be an executory contract to sell a non-financial item that is outside the scope of IAS 39 and IFRS 7 (see **2.5** in **chapter 13**). However, on the basis of IAS 39.33(d), see **10.5** in **chapter 17**, the entity determines there is a non-closely related embedded derivative with respect to the foreign currency element. This embedded derivative is defined as a forward contract to sell Sterling and buy Euro that is within the scope of IAS 39 and IFRS 7. If the embedded derivative is a financial liability at the period end it must be included within the liquidity risk analysis. The standard does not state whether for this purpose the derivative liability should be considered as a gross or a net settled derivative. Given that the embedded derivative has been separated only for accounting purposes and there is no exchange of gross amounts of Sterling for gross amounts of Euro, it would seem most appropriate to treat the embedded derivative as net settled for the purposes of the liquidity analysis and provide appropriate disclosure of such treatment.

Example 5.2.2.2

Liquidity risk disclosure: maturity analysis of financial liabilities

Bank M is a financial institution with a reporting period ending 31 December 20X1. Bank M accepts deposits from a wide range of investors with a variety of rates and maturities. The bank manages its exposure to liquidity risk through a separate and independent liquidity risk management board which reports monthly to the Board with a maturity analysis on the term structure of its deposit book. The schedule below sets out the financial liabilities at the 31 December 20X2 (ignores comparative figures and assumes that all figures quoted in the table are the notional amounts only (where applicable).

Instrument type	**£'000**
5.35% 15-day notice deposits	4,550
4.5% demand deposits	6,750
Fixed rate deposits	6,200
10% preference shares[4]	5,000
LIBOR-based financial liabilities[5]	10,000
Interest rate swaps[6]	1,200
Total	33,700

1 The notice deposits have a clause that allows for a depositor to elect to liquidate his/her deposit within 15 days. At the end of the reporting period, 40 per cent of the outstanding balance is in respect of depositors who have made this election.

2 The demand deposits are repayable within 30 days of notice being given. No persons had given notice at the end of the reporting period.

3 The fixed rate deposits vary between 60 days, 90 days and 120 days at varying rates. The year-end balance is made up as follows:

Maturity	**Rate**	**Notional (£'000)**
60 days	4.90%	1,240
90 days	6.50%	1,860
120 days	7.36%	3,100

Interest is payable on maturity.

4 The preference shares are redeemable after 5 years. The interest on the preference shares is paid yearly on 31 December.

5 The LIBOR-based financial liabilities pay interest monthly with the interest rate re-setting to LIBOR in advance, with a bullet repayment of principal in 1 year's time. The forward curve at the end of the reporting period was as follows:

Month	**Interest rate**
January 20X2	5.53%
February 20X2	5.61%
March 20X2	6.12%
April 20X2	6.57%

Month	Interest rate
May 20X2	6.59%
June 20X2	6.69%
July 20X2	6.71%
August 20X2	6.95%
September 20X2	7.06%
October 20X2	7.06%
November 20X2	7.30%
December 20X2	7.18%

6 The interest rate swaps net settle on a quarterly basis. The undiscounted future cash flows for all interest rate swap liabilities based on the forward curve at the end of the reporting period were as follows (negatives represent cash inflows):

Month	Net cash flow
March 20X3	600
June 20X3	500
September 20X3	400
December 20X3	350
March 20X4	300
June 20X4	200
September 20X4	100
December 20X4	50
March 20X5	-100
June 20X5	-150
September 20X5	-250
December 20X5	-300

Liquidity risk– maturity analysis
£'000

	≤1 month	1-≤3 months	3-≤12 months	1-≤3 years	3-≤5 years
Notice deposits	4,560[1]				
Demand deposits	6,775[2]				
Fixed deposits		3,140[3]	3,175[3]		
Preference shares			500[4]	1,000[4]	6,000[4]
LIBOR-based financial liabilities		142[5]	10,520[5]		
Interest rate swaps	—	600[6]	1,250[6]	(150)[6]	—
Total	11,335	3,882	15,445	850	6,000

Amounts determined as follows:

1 (4,550 x 5.35% x 40% x 15/365) + (4,550 x 5.35% x 60% x 16/365) + 4,550 = £4,560

Whilst 40% of the depositors have indicated they will liquidate their deposit, on a worst case scenario basis, the remaining 60% will also all liquidate their deposits, by giving notice the very next day for their funds to be repaid within the next 15 days. Hence, the total liability will be settled within the next month, and the disclosure will need to include the principle plus interest due.

2 (6,750 x 4.5% x 30/365) + 6,750 = £6,775

On a worst case basis, all of the demand deposits will be called within the following month. The amount to be disclosed will be the principal plus the interest for 30 days.

3 60 days: (1,240 x 4.90% x 60/365) + 1,240 = £1,250
90 days: (1,860 x 6.50% x 90/365) + 1,860 = £1,890

The fixed deposit is payable in tranches. The first two tranches fall due within the first 3 months. Total for 1–3 month time period = £3,140

120 days: (3,100 x 7.36% x 120/365) + 3,100 = £3,175

The fixed deposit is payable in tranches. The last tranche falls due in 120 days' time, i.e.: 3–12 month period.

4 1 year: (5,000 x 10%) = £500
2, 3 years: (5,000 x 10% x 2) = £1,000
4, 5 years: (5,000 x 10% x 2) +5,000 = £6,000

The interest payment for the preference share falls due at the end of each year, with the capital being repaid at the end of 5 years.

5 Interest due is determined using the yield curve at the end of the reporting period, and is calculated as the product of the notional of the loan, the interest rate and the number of days.

Total for 1–3 months:

Month	Days	Time band	Rate	Cash flow
January 20X2	31	1–3 months	5.53%	47.00
February 20X2	28	1–3 months	5.61%	43.00
March 20X2	31	1–3 months	6.12%	52.00
Total				142.00

Total for 3–12 months:

Month	Days	Time band	Rate	Cash flow
April 20X2	30	3–12 months	5.53%	54.00
May 20X2	31	3–12 months	6.57%	56.00
June 20X2	30	3–12 months	6.59%	55.00
July 20X2	31	3–12 months	6.69%	57.00
August 20X2	31	3–12 months	6.71%	59.00
September 20X2	30	3–12 months	6.95%	58.00
October 20X2	31	3–12 months	7.06%	60.00

Month	Days	Time band	Rate	Cash flow
November 20X2	30	3–12 months	7.06%	60.00
December 20X2	31	3–12 months	7.30%	61.00
December 20X2	–	3–12 months	-	10,000
Total				10,520

[6] The undiscounted forecasted cash flow for:

March 20X3 =	£600
June, September and December 20X3 =	£1,250
March 20X4 to December 20X7	(£150)

An entity may choose to disclose an expected maturity analysis of both its financial assets and financial liabilities where it manages its liquidity risk on that basis. When using expected maturities, it is recommended that disclosure be provided of how expected maturities are determined, how the estimates have been determined and why this differs from its contractual maturity analysis. [IFRS 7.IG30]

Other factors that an entity may wish to disclose in describing how it manages its liquidity risk include, but are not limited to, whether the entity:

[IFRS 7.IG31]

(a) expects some of its liabilities to be paid later than the earliest date on which the entity can be required to pay (as may be the case for customer deposits placed with a bank);

(b) expects some of its undrawn loan commitments not to be drawn;

(c) holds financial assets for which there is a liquid market and that are readily saleable to meet liquidity needs;

(d) has committed borrowing facilities (e.g. commercial paper facilities) or other lines of credit (e.g. stand-by credit facilities) that it can access to meet liquidity needs;

(e) holds financial assets for which there is not a liquid market, but which are expected to generate cash inflows (principal or interest) that will be available to meet cash outflows on liabilities;

(f) holds deposits at central banks to meet liquidity needs;

(g) has very diverse funding sources; or

(h) has significant concentrations of liquidity risk in either its assets or its funding sources.

There is an apparent conflict between IFRS 7 which requires the disclosure of a liquidity analysis for all *financial liabilities* and IAS 1(2007).65 (previously IAS 1(2003).56) which states that 'IFRS 7 requires disclosure of the maturity dates of *financial assets and financial liabilities*' [emphasis added]. It seems reasonable to conclude that IFRS 7 continues to only require disclosure of a maturity analysis for financial liabilities. Disclosure of a maturity analysis for financial assets is permitted, while a liquidity analysis for financial liabilities is required.

5.2.3 Market risk

Market risk is defined as 'the risk that the fair value or future cash flows of a financial instrument will fluctuate because of changes in market prices. Market risk comprises three types of risk: currency risk, interest rate risk and other price risk'. [IFRS 7(Appendix A)] Each of these risks is defined as follows:

[IFRS 7(Appendix A)]

(a) **Currency risk:** the risk that the fair value or future cash flows of a financial instrument will fluctuate because of changes in foreign exchange rates. Currency risk arises on financial instruments that are denominated in a different currency to the entity's functional currency.

(b) **Interest rate risk:** the risk that the fair value or future cash flows of a financial instrument will fluctuate because of changes in market interest rates. Interest rate risk arises on interest-bearing financial instruments that are recognised in the statement of financial position, e.g. loans and receivables and on some financial instruments that are not recognised in the statement of financial position, like some loan commitments.

(c) **Other price risk:** the risk that the fair value or future cash flows of a financial instrument will fluctuate because of changes in market prices (other than those arising from **interest rate risk** or **currency risk**), whether those changes are caused by factors specific to the individual financial instrument or its issuer, or factors affecting all similar financial instruments traded in the market'

Examples of other price risks include equity price risk, commodity price risk, prepayment risk and residual value risk.

For a financial asset or a liability that is classified as at fair value through profit or loss, whether a non-derivative or a derivative, credit risk will be a factor affecting its fair value and will impact profit or loss. For a debt security designated as available-for-sale, credit risk associated with the security will affect equity. However, it is questionable whether credit risk is a 'market price risk' in the same way that an equity price, foreign exchange rate or interest rate are. Also, as credit risk is specifically covered by a different set of detailed disclosures in IFRS 7, see **5.2.1** above, it is reasonable to assume credit risk was not intended to be included. While changes in the likelihood of the obligor defaulting under a financial instrument would not be treated as a type of *other price risk*, changes in fair value of an instrument due to, or cash flow payments contractually linked to, a variable such as a credit index which is not based on the ability of the obligor to meet its obligations under the financial instrument, which be viewed as a type of *other price risk*.

Market risk sensitivity analysis is required for each type of market risk to which the entity is exposed at the end of the reporting period showing how profit or loss and equity would have been affected by changes in the relevant risk variable that were reasonably possible at the end of the reporting period. In addition, disclosure should be provided of the methods and assumptions that were used in preparing the sensitivity analysis, any changes from the previous period in the methods and assumptions used, and the reasons for those changes. [IFRS 7.40]

An entity shall decide how it aggregates information to display the overall picture without combining information with different characteristics about exposures to risks from significantly different economic environments. For example:

(a) an entity that trades financial instruments might disclose this information separately for financial instruments held for trading and those not held for trading;

(b) an entity that has exposure to market risks from areas of hyperinflation and areas of very low inflation would disclose the information sensitivity for the two areas.

If an entity has exposure to only one type of market risk in only one economic environment, it would not show disaggregated information. [IFRS 7.B17]

The sensitivity analysis provides useful information since it is relatively easy to calculate and understand, is suitable for all entities and highlights the nature and extent of risks that arise from financial instruments. [IFRS 7.BC59]

It is not necessary to prepare an analysis that reflects inter-dependencies between risk variables, e.g. in preparing an interest rate sensitivity analysis an entity does not need to determine the impact of changes in interest rates would have on the relative strengthening and weakening of the currency with other currencies. Rather a simple sensitivity analysis that shows the change in only one variable is sufficient. [IFRS 7.BC60]

The preparation of a market risk sensitivity analysis requires the following steps:

(i) **Identify risk exposures**

All market risks to which the entity is exposed need to be identified.

(ii) **Identify the exposures at the end of the reporting period and how those exposures affect the sensitivity analysis**

All financial instruments at the end of the reporting period whose fair value and/ or cash flows are affected by changes in risk factors need to be identified.

Examples of financial instruments and their impact in *profit or loss* are included below.

- Floating rate debt instruments, whether an asset or liability, have a sensitivity to interest rates. The entity will flex interest rates for floating rate instruments that are outstanding at the period end showing how profit or loss would have varied in the period assuming the instruments at the period end were outstanding for the entire period.

- Foreign currency denominated debt instruments are sensitive to foreign currency rates as monetary items are retranslated into the functional currency of the entity at the period end. The sensitivity to foreign currency rates applies irrespective of whether the instrument is an asset or a liability, whether it is measured at fair value or amortised cost. This includes intercompany foreign currency denominated loans that are expected to be repaid in the foreseeable future where the foreign currency risk does not eliminate on consolidation.

- Any financial instrument at the period end that is designated as at fair value through profit or loss or is held for trading. The sensitivity will depend on the underlying risks of the instrument. A debt instrument may be sensitive to changes in interest rate, foreign currency risk, whereas an equity instrument may be sensitive to changes in equity prices and foreign currency risk.

- All derivatives in designated and qualifying fair value hedge accounting relationships.
- Fixed rate debt instruments that are hedged items in qualifying fair value hedges of interest rate risk are sensitive to changes in interest rates.

Examples of financial instruments and their impact in *equity* (*other comprehensive income*) are included below:

- foreign currency denominated debt instruments that are designated as a qualifying hedging instrument in a foreign currency cash flow or net investment hedge are sensitive to foreign currency rates;
- intragroup foreign currency denominated debt instruments to or from a foreign operation that are not expected to be repaid in the foreseeable future in accordance with IAS 21.15 are sensitive to foreign currency rates where the foreign currency risk does not eliminate on consolidation. Even though the debt instrument may form part of the foreign operation in accordance with IAS 39.102 it remains within the scope of IAS 39 and IFRS 7 and therefore should be included within sensitivity analysis;
- derivatives and embedded derivatives designated as effective hedging instruments in a cash flow hedge or a hedge of a net investment in a foreign operation;
- foreign currency denominated equity securities classified as available for sale are sensitive to foreign currency rates and equity prices;
- debt securities classified as available for sale are sensitive to interest rate risk and credit risk, and may also be sensitive to foreign currency risk.

Any recognised financial instrument at the end of the reporting period whose cash flows are contractually linked to a variable or whose fair value is dependent on a variable should be included in a sensitivity analysis to the extent changes in the variable will impact profit or loss or equity. For example, if an entity has issued debt that is contractually linked to inflation where the inflation linkage is considered a closely related embedded derivative, the carrying value of the debt and its impact in profit or loss will depend on the level of inflation throughout the reporting period and at the period end.

Alternatively, if the inflation linkage was not closely related it would impact profit or loss through its re-measurement as a derivative at fair value through profit or loss.

An example of a financial instrument that has no impact on profit or loss or equity is a fixed rate debt instrument without any non-closely related embedded derivatives that is denominated in the entity's functional currency, whether an asset or liability, provided that it is measured at amortised cost. Changes in interest rates or currency rates do not impact profit or loss or equity.

IFRS 7(Appendix A) defines currency risk as the *risk that the fair value or future cash flows of a financial instrument will fluctuate because of changes in foreign exchange rates.* IFRS 7.B23 states that *currency risk* (*or foreign exchange risk*) *arises on financial instruments that are denominated in a foreign currency, i.e. in a currency other than the functional currency in which they are measured.* The Standard is clear that any foreign currency monetary item at the period end will be included in the foreign currency risk sensitivity analysis. What is less clear is whether IFRS 7 requires an entity to also include in the foreign currency risk sensitivity analysis the extent to which the effective interest rate that is recognised in profit or loss in the period in respect of the period end monetary item would have differed had foreign currency rates differed. The foreign currency interest recognised in profit or loss is usually translated using the average monthly foreign currency rate and therefore profit or loss is sensitive to changes in foreign currency rates irrespective of whether the loan has fixed or floating foreign currency interest. As the monetary item impacts profit or loss through the recognition of interest, as well as the translation of the period end carrying amount, it would be meaningful to include both interest and principal of a monetary item within the foreign currency sensitivity analysis. This approach is consistent with the view that foreign currency interest is variable in the functional currency of the entity.

Financial instruments that are classified as equity in accordance with IAS 32 are not remeasured and therefore do not impact profit or loss or equity when sensitivity analysis is performed. [IFRS 7.B28]

It should be noted that if the entity is party to derivatives over own equity that are not classified as equity (e.g. if the entity has issued warrants with an exercise price in a currency other than the functional currency of the entity) then its own equity price risk will be a relevant example of an *other price risk*. As the instruments will be accounted for as derivatives at fair value through profit or loss with the underlying being the entity's own equity price they will need to be considered for the purposes of the sensitivity analysis.

(iii) Determine what is a reasonably possible change in the relevant risk variable that were reasonably possible at that date

An entity needs to determine what it considers to be a reasonably possible change in the relevant risk variable and should consider both the economic environment in which it operates and the time frame over which it is making the assessment. A reasonably possible change in a relevant risk variable in one environment may not be the same in another environment, e.g. a reasonable possible change in interest rates may be 100bp for Sterling denominated debt, but the same could not be said for Yen denominated debt where a reasonably possible change may be substantially smaller. Entities are required to judge what those reasonably possible changes are and should not include remote or 'worse case scenarios' or 'stress tests'. A reasonably possible change in the relevant risk variable should be assessed over a time frame until the entity next presents these disclosures, which is usually the end of its next annual reporting period. [IFRS 7.B19]

While the range of reasonably possible changes may be wide, disclosure is not required for each change within that range. It is sufficient to disclose the effects of the changes at the limits of the reasonably possible range. [IFRS 7.B18(b)]

IFRS 7 requires comparative information to be presented. If the volatility of a given risk variable changes and therefore an entity alters its view of what is a reasonably possible change in that risk variable in relation to the prior year this would not prompt restatement of the comparative risk disclosures. The entity should, however, carefully disclose the fact that there has been a change in what is considered a reasonably possible change in the risk variable.

(iv) Determine the appropriate level of aggregation that should be provided in the disclosures

An entity should aggregate the output from sensitivity analysis in order to provide a broad view of the entity's overall sensitivity to market risk but without combining information with different characteristics about exposures to risks from significantly different economic environments. Disclosure may, for instance, be provided separately for financial instruments that are held for trading from those that are not. Alternatively, disclosures may be disclosed for each risk. As a minimum, disclosure of sensitivity

analyses for each currency to which an entity has a significant exposure shall be provided.
[IFRS 7.B24]

An entity shall provide sensitivity analyses for the whole of its business but may provide different types of sensitivity analyses for different classes of financial instruments. [IFRS 7.B21]

> An entity could provide different types of sensitivity analysis for different parts of its business if this is consistent with how it manages risk internally. For example, a financial institution may comprise a retail banking division and an investment banking division. The entity could choose to provide a conventional sensitivity analysis as described in the steps above in relation to the retail banking division and a value-at-risk analysis in relation to the investment banking division if the latter analysis is used for internal risk management purposes within the investment banking division. However, the entity in this case would need to consider carefully how to treat any transactions and exposures between the two divisions so that the disclosure is not misleading. See (vi) below for discussion of VaR as an alternative disclosure of market risk.

(v) Calculate and present the sensitivity analyses

Entities shall disclose the effect on profit or loss and equity for exposures at the end of the reporting period assuming that a reasonably possible change in the relevant risk variable had been applied to those exposures at the end of the reporting period. [IFRS 7.B18]

The sensitivity may be reported separately for different lines in profit or loss or for consolidated profit or loss and equity. An entity might disclose a sensitivity analysis for interest rate risk for each currency in which the entity has material exposures to interest rate risk. [IFRS 7.IG34]

The sensitivity of profit or loss and the sensitivity of equity shall be disclosed separately. [IFRS 7.B27]

> The sensitivity analysis is prepared based on financial instruments that are recognised at the end of the reporting period. This is the case even where those exposures did not exist for the entire period or where the exposure changed materially during the period.
>
> For example, an entity is building a road. To finance the construction of the road, it negotiates a floating rate debt facility. The entity starts to draw down on the facility half way through the year and at year

end it has fully drawn down on the facility. A sensitivity analysis will be prepared for the loan showing profit or loss sensitivity assuming that the loan was in place for the entire period. A similar situation would arise in the case of an amortising loan where the exposure has reduced over the period due to part repayments of principal. In that instance, the sensitivity analysis would be prepared on the basis of the exposure at the end of the reporting period although it had significantly higher exposures during the period.

IFRS 7.35 does state that if the quantitative data disclosed as at the end of the reporting period is unrepresentative of an entity's exposure to risk during the period, an entity shall provide further information that is representative. For sensitivity analysis, an entity may provide supplementary disclosure illustrating the impact on profit or loss and equity based on the timing of recognition and derecognition of financial instruments in the period in addition to the analysis based on financial instruments recognised at the period end.

Whilst IFRS 7 provides some guidance on the determination of reasonably possible changes in the relevant risk variable, no guidance is available on whether the degree of change at the end of the reporting period in the relevant risk variable should be extrapolated to the risk variables during the period, or whether the change should be determined as a fixed amount of change.

For example, an entity has a floating rate liability at year end. The current LIBOR rate is 5 per cent, and the entity estimates that a reasonably possible change in LIBOR is 100bp. During the year LIBOR was 2 per cent in the first half of the year, 3 per cent at half year and 4 per cent during the last 6 months. The volatility in cash flows during the year may either be expressed as:

(a) An *absolute change* of 100bp's to all rates. Thus, the sensitivity would be of 100bp increase and decrease to the loan's cash flows during the year; or

(b) A *percentage change*, where the change at the end of the reporting period is 20 per cent ($^{1}/_{5th}$) and hence all rates should change by 20 per cent during the period. Thus, the volatility in cash flows will be determined as the change of the above interest rate of 1.6 and 2.4 per cent, 2.4 and 3.6 per cent and 3.2 and 4.8 per cent (all increased and decreased by 20 per cent).

While either approach would be acceptable under IFRS 7, approach (a) provides information that seems more relevant and reliable than approach (b) since the sensitivity analysis will be more comparable with past periods. Whichever approach is used, disclosure of the method and assumptions should be provided.

IFRS 7 requires disclosure of a sensitivity analysis showing how profit or loss and equity would have been affected by changes in the relevant risk variable. The Standard is not clear whether sensitivity analysis should be provided on a pre or post tax basis. As equity is defined in IAS 32 as *the residual interest in the assets of the entity after deducting all of its liabilities* and tax on gains or losses recognised in other comprehensive income (and taken to equity) will also be recognised in other comprehensive income (and taken to equity), it is reasonable to assume that for the purposes of the sensitivity analysis the analysis should be net of tax. Additionally, IFRS 7.IG36 provides an example of a sensitivity analysis which is determined on an after-tax basis.

Example 5.2.3A

Market risk disclosures: sensitivity analysis

Company D (ZAR functional currency) is a diversified oil and gas group. The earnings of the group are exposed to movements due to changes in market interest rates, equity prices, exchange rates and commodity prices. The entity expects the following to be reasonably possible changes in the relevant risk variable at the end of the reporting period:

ZAR market interest rates =	100 basis points
ZAR equity prices =	8%
ZAR/USD exchange rate =	15%
USD Brent crude price =	25%

Assume a tax rate of 30%. Profit after tax for the year ended 31 December 20X0 was:

ZAR 2,750million and equity was ZAR 1,000million. Company D has the following financial instruments that have an exposure to the relevant risk variable at the end of the reporting period.

1. USD denominated short term accounts receivable with a carrying value of ZAR 235million are held at amortised cost.

2. ZAR denominated listed equity investments that are classified as held for trading with a carrying value of ZAR 500million.

3. ZAR denominated listed equity investments that are classified as available-for-sale with a carrying value of ZAR 200million.

4. ZAR denominated fixed rate cash deposits with a carrying value ZAR

1,245million. The cash deposits are classified as loans and receivables and return a rate of 10 per cent per annum. The deposits were initially recognised at the beginning of the year.

5. ZAR denominated treasury bonds that have a fixed rate of interest of 12 per cent per annum with a carrying value of ZAR 765million. The bonds are designated as at fair value through profit or loss. A 100 basis point change in market interest rates is equivalent to a 4 per cent change in the fair value of the bond.

6. Purchased brent crude futures denominated in USD that are classified as held for trading and have a carrying value of ZAR 490million. A 100 basis point change in the ZAR market interest rate is equivalent to a 1 per cent change in the fair value of the futures and a 25 per cent change in the Brent crude oil price is equivalent to a 20 per cent change in the fair value of the futures.

7. USD denominated fixed rate borrowings initially recognised at the beginning of the year. The interest rate is 10 pr cent. The borrowings have been classified as a liability to be carried at amortised cost. The weighted average exchange rate during the reporting period was ZAR7:$1.These borrowings were designated as a hedge of a net investment of its foreign operation and had a carrying value at year end of ZAR 730million (USD100 million at a closing exchange rate of ZAR7.3:$1)

8. ZAR denominated floating rate borrowings of ZAR 350million that are classified as a financial liability held at amortised cost and were entered into at the beginning of the year for an amount of ZAR 350million. The floating interest resets on a quarterly basis in advance, with the quarterly rates during the past reporting period being as follows:

Month	Rate
1 January 20X0	14%
1 April 20X0	13%
1 July 20X0	12%
1 October 20X0	13%
1 January 20X1	14%

Company D wishes to present its sensitivity analysis by risk variable. Comparative financial data has been ignored for the purposes of this example.

The following represents the calculation of the market risk sensitivity analysis as required by IFRS 7.40.

Market interest rates

Items (1), (2), (3) and (4) do not affect profit or loss or equity if market interest rates change. In the case of item (4), the ZAR denominated fixed rate cash deposits that are classified as loans and receivables do not affect profit or loss or equity given a reasonably possible change in market interest rates since they are neither measured at fair value nor do they contain variable cash flows.

Item (5), the ZAR denominated fixed rate bonds that are designated at fair value through profit or loss will result in sensitivity in profit or loss of ZAR 765 million x 4% = **+/-ZAR 30.60million**.

Item (6), the Brent crude futures will result in sensitivity in profit or loss of +/-ZAR490 million x 1% = **+/-ZAR 4.90million**.

Item (7), the USD denominated fixed rate liability is designated as a hedging instrument for foreign currency risk only, with the carrying amount in foreign currency measured at amortised cost. This liability does not affect profit or loss or equity if market interest rates change since it is neither measured at fair value nor does it contain variable cash flows.

Item (8), the ZAR denominated floating rate borrowings are subject to floating interest rates. If market rates changed by 100 basis points during the period the sensitivity in interest cash flows would be 1.0% x ZAR 350million = **+/-ZAR 3.50million**

The treasury bond assets and the issued floating rate borrowings have the same directional sensitivity to interest rates with respect to their impact on profit or loss. As interest rates rise, the treasury bond assets fall in value, resulting in a loss in profit or loss, and the floating rate borrowing results in a higher interest expense in profit or loss. The vice versa is equally true when interest rates fall. Total profit or loss sensitivity as a result of changes in ZAR market interest rates is **+/-ZAR 39.00 million** after tax (30.60+4.90+3.50) * (1–30%).

ZAR Equity prices

Items (1), (4) – (8) do not affect profit or loss or equity is ZAR equity prices change.

Item (2), the ZAR listed investments that have been classified as held for trading will result in profit or loss sensitivity of ZAR 500million * 8% = +/-ZAR 40.00million.

Item (3), the ZAR listed investments that have been classified as available for sale will result in equity sensitivity of ZAR 200 million * 8% = +/-ZAR 16.00million.

Total profit or loss sensitivity as a result of changes in ZAR equity prices is **+/-ZAR 28.00million** after tax 40.00 * (1–30%).

Total equity sensitivity as a result of changes in ZAR equity prices is **+/-ZAR 11.20million** after tax 16.00 * (1–30%).

ZAR/USD exchange rate

Items (2), (3) (5) and (8) do not affect profit or loss or equity if ZAR/USD exchange rates change.

Item (1), the USD denominated accounts receivable will result in profit or loss sensitivity of ZAR 235million * 15% = +/-ZAR 35.25million.

Item (6), the USD denominated Brent crude derivatives will result in profit or loss sensitivity of ZAR 490million * 15% = +/-ZAR ZAR73.50million.

Item (7), the USD denominated borrowings will result in equity sensitivity of ZAR 730million * 15% = +/-ZAR 109.50million, being the re-translation of the borrowings at the end of the reporting period. Sensitivity of profit or loss due to recording interest cash flows during the year at a different exchange rate is determined as USD 100million * 10% interest rate * weighted average exchange rate during the year of ZAR7:$1 * sensitivity of 15% = ZAR 10.50 million

Total profit or loss sensitivity as a result of changes in the ZAR/USD exchange rate is
+/-ZAR 83.48million after tax (35.25+73.5+10.5) * (1–30%).

Total equity sensitivity as a result of changes in the ZAR/USD exchange rate is
+/-ZAR 76.65million after tax (109.5) * (1–30%).

USD Brent crude price

Items (1) – (5), (7) and (8) do not affect profit or loss or equity if USD Brent crude prices change.

Item (6), the USD denominated Brent crude futures will result in profit or loss sensitivity of ZAR 490million x 20% = +/- ZAR 98.00million.

Total profit or loss sensitivity as a result of changes in the Brent crude price is +/-ZAR 68.60million after tax 98.00 * (1–30%).

Disclosure

For financial instruments held, the company has used a sensitivity analysis technique that measures the change in the fair value and cash flows of the company's financial instruments for hypothetical changes in all relevant market risk variables.

The amounts generated from the sensitivity analysis are forward-looking estimates of market risk assuming certain market conditions. Actual results in the future may differ materially from those projected results due to the inherent uncertainty of global financial markets. The methods and assumptions used are the same as those applied in the previous reporting period.

The sensitivity of profit or loss and equity due to changes in the relevant risk variables as at 31 December 20X0 are set out in the table below. The methods and assumptions used in calculating are set out in note X1 to the financial statements.

The estimated change in fair values and cash flows for changes in market interest rates are based on an instantaneous increase or decrease of 100 basis points at the end of the reporting period, with all other variables remaining constant.

The estimated change in fair values for changes in ZAR equity prices are based on an instantaneous increase or decrease of 8 per cent for instruments at the end of the reporting period, with all other variables remaining constant.

The estimated change in fair values for changes in the ZAR/USD exchange rate are based on an instantaneous increase or decrease of 15 per cent for instruments at the end of the reporting period, with all other variables remaining constant.

The estimated change in fair values for changes in Brent crude prices are based on an instantaneous increase or decrease of 25 per cent for instruments at the end of the reporting period, with all other variables remaining constant.

The above-mentioned changes in the risk variables may result in non-proportional changes in fair values or cash flows due to the specific terms and nature of the relevant risk exposures.

The sensitivity analysis is for illustrative purposes only – in practice market rates rarely change in isolation and are likely to be interdependent.

The sensitivity of the relevant risk variables, on an after tax basis is as follows:

Market risk exposure	Profit or loss sensitivity ZAR million	Equity sensitivity ZAR million
Market interest rates	+/-39.00	-
ZAR equity prices	+/-28.00	+/-11.20
ZAR/USD exchange rates	+/-83.48	+/-76.65
USD Brent crude	+/-68.60	-

Example 5.2.3A above includes only non-optional derivatives, in this case Brent crude oil futures. Other non-optional derivatives include swaps and forward contracts. If these non-optional derivatives do not contain options embedded within their contractual terms, like knock-out or knock-in options, early termination clauses that terminate at an amount other than at fair value, then the sensitivity to the underlying is likely to be the same irrespective of whether the price of the underlying moves up or down. This would not be the case for optional derivatives like options, or derivatives that are constructed using combinations of options, for example collars. As an option provides one-directional exposure, for example, protection against rising interest rates, then the fair value sensitivity of the option to increasing interest rates will be different from sensitivity to falling interest rates. The fair value sensitivity of optional derivatives will vary depending on the directional movement in the underlying market risk. The fair value sensitivity of an option to the underlying market risk will also depend on the price of the underlying at the end of the reporting

period compared to the strike price of the option. If an option is nearly at-the-money it will have a greater sensitivity to changes in market risk when compared to an option that is deeply out-of-the-money.

Impairment of financial assets can also be affected by changes in an underlying market risk. However, it seems appropriate that for debt instruments only changes in existing impairment losses should be considered in the determination of the market risk sensitivity analysis. An entity should not project additional impairment losses that might have occurred given a movement in an underlying market risk. For example, if a loan is not impaired at the period end it will not be treated as impaired for the purposes of the sensitivity analysis.

If an available-for-sale debt instrument is impaired at the end of the reporting period and all the accumulated loss has been recognised in profit or loss in accordance with IAS 39.67–68 then the sensitivity of the fair value of the debt instrument for changes in interest rates will impact the extent of impairment recognised in profit or loss. Had interest rates been higher or lower the amount of impairment recognised in profit or loss in the period would have differed as a different market interest rate would have resulted in a different fair value.

If an available-for-sale debt instrument is not impaired at the end of the reporting period changes in the relevant risk variable should not result in an impairment charge. For example, the increased likelihood of a borrower defaulting in a higher interest rate environment should not result in the lender recognising an impairment charge in its interest rate sensitivity analysis. This view is consistent with the view that credit risk is not a market risk, as discussed at the start of this section.

If a floating rate financial asset is impaired at the end of the reporting period the amount of interest income in the period will be sensitive to changes in the floating rates for the period. If the floating rate cash flows are themselves impaired, as opposed to the principal cash flow, then changes in the floating rate will impact the amount of impairment at the period end. This is not the case for a fixed rate asset as all cash flows are fixed and the effective interest rate is not sensitive to changes in interest rates.

In the case of sensitivity analysis of equity price risk of non-monetary available-for-sale financial assets it is necessary to give careful consideration to whether a reasonably possible change in the relevant equity price would affect equity or profit or loss. Consider the case of an investment in an equity security that has already suffered impairment by the end of the reporting period. As reversals of impairment on equity securities classified as available-for-sale may not be recorded through profit or loss in such a case a reasonably possible downward fall in the equity price will be shown as affecting profit or loss, but an equivalent upward shift would be shown as affecting equity. The fair value of an available-for-sale equity security that has not previously been impaired could become impaired depending on what is considered a reasonably possible downward shift in equity prices (based on a significant or prolonged decline in fair value of an investment in an equity security below cost in accordance with IAS 39.61). In such a case consideration must be given to whether a reasonably possible downward movement in the equity price would affect equity or profit or loss, taking into account an entity's impairment policy.

(vi) Provide additional disclosures

When the sensitivity analysis is unrepresentative of a risk inherent in a financial instrument, disclosure of that fact and the reason why the entity believes the sensitivity analysis is unrepresentative shall be provided. [IFRS 7.42] Examples where this may be the case include:

[IFRS 7.IG37]

(a) financial instruments contain terms and conditions whose effects are not apparent from the sensitivity analysis, e.g. options that are deep out of (or in) the money for the chosen change in risk variable;

(b) financial assets that are illiquid, such that the calculated changes in profit or loss are difficult to realise where there are low volumes of transactions or lack of counterparties to trade at those prices or rates;

(c) large holdings in financial assets that would be sold at a discount or premium to the quoted prices.

In these cases, additional disclosure may be provided of the terms and conditions of the financial instruments, the effect on profit or loss if the term or condition were met, description of how the risk is hedged and the reasons for illiquidity of the instruments concerned. [IFRS 7.IG38 and IG39]

IFRS 7.IG38(b) states that when financial instruments contain terms and conditions whose effects are not apparent from the sensitivity analysis, an entity may wish to state the effect on profit or loss if the term or condition were met. An entity may also wish to state the impact on equity, as this is consistent with the objective of sensitivity analysis of providing the user with the impact on profit or loss and equity. For example, an entity may have designated a purchased interest cap as a cash flow hedge of highly probable forecast floating interest payments where the option is so deeply out-of-the-money at the period end that no intrinsic value is recognised in other comprehensive income (and taken to equity). As the option is so deeply out-of-the-money, a moderate change in interest rates has little fair value sensitivity. If interest rates were to increase significantly, the option's fair value would be subject to fair value movements in profit or loss, and potentially would result in part of the fair value being recognised in other comprehensive income (and taken to equity) if interest rates are higher than the strike price of the cap. As the derivative is an effective hedging instrument in a cash flow hedge, illustrating the impact on equity is equally appropriate to illustrating the impact in profit or loss.

The sensitivity analysis may not give a true presentation of exposure to risk in the cases where the hedging instrument is in the scope of IFRS 7 but the hedged item is not. An example is a hedge of a net investment in a foreign operation. Changes in the sensitivity of the fair value of derivatives or foreign currency risk for non-derivative financial instruments will be reported in other comprehensive income if it is a qualifying hedging instrument in a net investment hedge. The changes in the hedged item, being the re-translation of the net assets in accordance with IAS 21 is not required to be reported in the sensitivity analysis since it is not a financial instrument within the scope of IFRS 7. An entity may choose to provide additional disclosure to explain that the retranslation of the net assets of the foreign operation would reduce the sensitivity of the hedging instrument in equity. For example, if the entity designates spot foreign currency risk as being hedged and the hedge is fully effective, the gains and losses on the hedging instrument recognised in other comprehensive income (and taken to equity) will be offset by the losses and gains on foreign currency translation on the net assets of the foreign operation which are also recognised in other comprehensive income (and taken to equity). Similarly, additional disclosure may be appropriate for cash flow hedges or fair value hedges of non-financial items (including unrecognised 'off balance sheet' items). An entity may designate a foreign exchange forward contract in a highly effective hedge of a firm commitment to acquire plant and equipment with the hedged risk being spot foreign currency risk. The forward contract will be included in the sensitivity analysis while the fair value adjustment to the firm commitment to acquire a non-financial item will be outside the scope of IFRS 7. Additional disclosures may be useful to explain that the retranslation of the firm commitment at spot rates reduces the sensitivity of the hedging instrument in profit or loss.

Example 5.2.3B

Interest rate risk

[IFRS 7.IG36]

At 31 December 20X2, if interest rates at that date had been 10 basis points lower with all other variables held constant, post-tax profit for the year would have been CU1.7 million (20X1 – CU2.4 million) higher, arising mainly as a result of lower interest expense on variable borrowings, and other comprehensive income would have been CU2.8 million (20X1 – CU3.2 million) higher, arising mainly as a result of an increase in the fair value of fixed rate financial assets classified as available for sale. If interest rates had been 10 basis points higher, with all other variables held constant, post-tax profit would have been CU1.5 million (20X1 – CU2.1 million) lower, arising mainly as a result of higher interest expense on variable borrowings, and other comprehensive income would have been CU3.0 million (20X1 – CU3.4 million) lower, arising mainly as a result of a decrease in the fair value of fixed rate financial assets classified as available for sale. Profit is more sensitive to interest rate decreases than increases because of borrowings with capped interest rates. The sensitivity is lower in 20X2 than in 20X1 because of a reduction in outstanding borrowings that has occurred as the entity's debt has matured (see note X).

Foreign currency exchange rate risk

At 31 December 20X2, if the CU had weakened 10 per cent against the US dollar with all other variables held constant, post-tax profit for the year would have been CU2.8 million (20X1 – CU6.4 million) lower, and other comprehensive income would have been CU1.2 million (20X1 – CU1.1 million) higher. Conversely, if the CU had strengthened 10 per cent against the US dollar with all other variables held constant, post-tax profit would have been CU2.8 million (20X1 – CU6.4 million) higher, and other comprehensive income would have been CU1.2 million (20X1 – CU1.1 million) lower. The lower foreign currency exchange rate sensitivity in profit in 20X2 compared with 20X1 is attributable to a reduction in foreign currency denominated debt. Equity is more sensitive in 20X2 than in 20X1 because of the increased use of hedges of foreign currency purchases, offset by the reduction in foreign currency debt.

As an alternative to sensitivity analysis, disclosure may be provided of a ***value-at-risk analysis*** that reflects interdependencies between risk variables. An entity may only disclose value-at-risk analysis where the entity uses such a model to manage risk internally. Disclosure shall include an explanation of the method used in preparing such an analysis, how the model works (such as whether the model is based on a delta-normal variance-covariance approach, historical simulation or Monte Carlo simulation), the main parameters and assumptions underlying the data provided such as the holding period, confidence interval, historical observation period and weightings assigned to the observations, how options are dealt with and which volatilities and correlations are used. Disclosure of the objective of the method used and of the limitations that may result in the information not fully reflecting the fair value of the assets and liabilities involved shall also be provided [IFRS 7.41 & B20]

The value-at-risk analysis used internally may measure the potential for loss or gain including the effects of items that are outside the scope of IFRS 7 (e.g. contracts to buys or sell non-financial items outside the scope of IAS 39, hedged items that are outside the scope of IFRS 7 or risks such as credit risk which are not market risks). In contrast to conventional sensitivity analysis as discussed above, a value-at-risk analysis including such items would, if used as a model to manage risk internally, satisfy the requirements of the Standard. If such items are included this fact should be clearly disclosed as part of the method used in preparing the analysis.

Example 5.2.3C

Market risk disclosures: value at risk

The Group manages the market risk in its trading and treasury portfolios through the use of value-at-risk (VaR) limits as well as stress testing, position and sensitivity limits. VaR is a technique that produces estimates of the potential negative change in the market value of a portfolio over a specified time horizon at a given confidence level. The table below sets out the trading and treasury VaR for the Group, which assumes a 95 per cent confidence level and a one-day time horizon. The VAR model uses largely historical data from the preceding three years to simulate scenarios of the future.

Year	**Period end**	**Minimum**	**Maximum**	**Average**
	£m	**£m**	**£m**	**£m**
Trading VaR				
20X1	17.2	13.4	24.3	19.1
20X0	16.2	14.0	22.3	18.1
Treasury VaR				
20X1	8.1	6.6	12.1	9.5
20X0	8.0	6.9	13.1	8.5

The Group's VaR should be interpreted in light of the limitations of the methodologies used. These limitations include the following.

- Historical data may not provide the best estimate of the joint distribution of risk factor changes in the future and may fail to capture the risk of possible extreme adverse market movements which have not occurred in the historical window used in the calculations.

- VaR using a one-day time horizon does not fully capture the market risk of positions that cannot be liquidated or hedged within one day.
- The Group largely computes the VaR of the trading portfolios at the close of business and positions may change substantially during the course of the trading day. Controls are in place to limit the Group's intra-day exposure such as the calculation of VaR for selected portfolios.
- VaR using a 95 per cent confidence level does not reflect the extent of potential losses beyond that percentile.

These limitations and the nature of the VaR measure mean that the Group can neither guarantee that losses will not exceed the VaR amounts indicated nor that losses in excess of the VaR amounts will not occur more frequently than once in 20 business days.

6 Disclosure checklist

This checklist was up-to-date at the time of going to press. The IASB continues to refine its standards via editorial corrections and annual improvements. Accordingly, reference should be made to the most recent versions of these standards when financial statements are being prepared.

IFRS 7 Reference	IFRS 7 Disclosure Checklist
7	An entity shall disclose information that enables users of its financial statements to evaluate the significance of financial instruments for its financial position and performance. **Statement of financial position** *Categories of financial assets and financial liabilities* The carrying amounts of each of the following categories, as defined in IAS 39, shall be disclosed either in the statement of financial position or in the notes:
8(a)	(a) financial assets at fair value through profit or loss, showing separately: i. those designated as such upon initial recognition; and ii. those classified as held for trading in accordance with IAS 39;
8(b)	(b) held-to-maturity investments;

IFRS 7 Reference	IFRS 7 Disclosure Checklist
8(c)	(c) loans and receivables;
8(d)	(d) available-for-sale financial assets;
8(e)	(e) financial liabilities at fair value through profit or loss, showing separately: i. those designated as such upon initial recognition; and ii. those classified as held for trading in accordance with IAS 39; and
8(f)	(f) financial liabilities measured at amortised cost.
	Financial assets or financial liabilities at fair value through profit or loss
	If the entity has designated a loan or receivable (or group of loans or receivables) as at fair value through profit or loss, it shall disclose:
9(a)	(a) the maximum exposure to credit risk of the loan or receivable (or group of loans or receivables) at the end of the reporting period;
36(a)	Note: The maximum exposure to credit risk reported should not take account of any collateral held or other credit enhancements (e.g. netting agreements that do not qualify for offset in accordance with IAS 32 (see also IFRS 7.B9 & B10).
9(b)	(b) the amount by which any related credit derivatives or similar instruments mitigate that maximum exposure to credit risk;
9(c)	(c) the amount of change, during the period and cumulatively, in the fair value of the loan or receivable (or group of loans or receivables) that is attributable to changes in the credit risk of the financial asset determined either: i. as the amount of change in its fair value that is not attributable to changes in market conditions that give rise to market risk; or ii. using an alternative method the entity believes more faithfully represents the amount of change in its fair value that is attributable to changes in the credit risk of the asset;
9(c)	Note: Changes in market conditions that give rise to market risk include changes in an observed (benchmark) interest rate, commodity price, foreign exchange rate or index of prices or rates.

IFRS 7 Reference	IFRS 7 Disclosure Checklist
9(d)	(d) the amount of the change in the fair value of any related credit derivatives or similar instruments that has occurred during the period and cumulatively since the loan or receivable was designated.
	If the entity has designated a financial liability as at fair value through profit or loss in accordance with paragraph 9 of IAS 39, it shall disclose:
10(a)	(a) the amount of change, during the period and cumulatively, in the fair value of the financial liability that is attributable to changes in the credit risk of that liability determined either: i. as the amount of change in its fair value that is not attributable to changes in market conditions that give rise to market risk (see also IFRS 7.B4); or ii. using an alternative method the entity believes more faithfully represents the amount of change in its fair value that is attributable to changes in the credit risk of the liability;
10(a)	Note: Changes in market conditions that give rise to market risk include changes in a benchmark interest rate, the price of another entity's financial instrument, a commodity price, a foreign exchange rate or an index of prices or rates. For contracts that include a unit-linking feature, changes in market conditions include changes in the performance of the related internal or external investment fund.
10(b)	(b) the difference between the financial liability's carrying amount and the amount the entity would be contractually required to pay at maturity to the holder of the obligation.
	The entity shall disclose:
11(a)	(a) the methods used to determine the amount of change that is attributable to changes in the credit risk in compliance with the requirements in paragraphs 9(c) and 10(a) of IFRS 7 (see above).
11(b)	(b) if the entity believes that the disclosure it has given to comply with the requirements in paragraph 9(c) or 10(a) of IFRS 7 does not faithfully represent the change in the fair value of the financial asset or financial liability attributable to changes in its credit risk, the reasons for reaching this conclusion and the factors it believes are relevant.

IFRS 7 Reference	IFRS 7 Disclosure Checklist
	Reclassification
12(a)	If the entity has reclassified a financial asset as one measured: (a) at cost or amortised cost, rather than at fair value; or (b) at fair value, rather than at cost or amortised cost, it shall disclose the amount reclassified into and out of each category and the reason for that reclassification.
	Derecognition
	An entity may have transferred financial assets in such a way that part or all of the financial assets do not qualify for derecognition. The entity shall disclose for each class of such financial assets:
13(a)	(a) the nature of the assets;
13(b)	(b) the nature of the risks and rewards of ownership to which the entity remains exposed;
13(c)	(c) when the entity continues to recognise all of the assets, the carrying amounts of the assets and of the associated liabilities; and
13(d)	(d) when the entity continues to recognise the assets to the extent of its continuing involvement, the total carrying amount of the original assets, the amount of the assets that the entity continues to recognise, and the carrying amount of the associated liabilities.
	Collateral
	An entity shall disclose:
14(a)	(a) the carrying amount of financial assets it has pledged as collateral for liabilities or contingent liabilities, including amounts that have been reclassified in the statement of financial position separately from other assets as the transferee has the right to sell or repledge the collateral.
14(b)	(b) the terms and conditions relating to its pledge.
	When an entity holds collateral (of financial or non-financial assets) and is permitted to sell or repledge the collateral in the absence of default by the owner of the collateral, it shall disclose:
15(a)	(a) the fair value of the collateral held;
15(b)	(b) the fair value of any such collateral sold or repledged, and whether the entity has an obligation to return it; and
15(c)	(c) the terms and conditions associated with its use of the collateral.

IFRS 7 Reference	IFRS 7 Disclosure Checklist
	Allowance account for credit losses
16	When financial assets are impaired by credit losses and the entity records the impairment in a separate account (e.g. an allowance account used to record individual impairments or a similar account used to record a collective impairment of assets) rather than directly reducing the carrying amount of the asset, it shall disclose a reconciliation of changes in that account during the period for each class of financial assets.
	Compound financial instruments with multiple embedded derivatives
17	If an entity has issued an instrument that contains both a liability and an equity component and the instrument has multiple embedded derivatives whose values are interdependent (such as a callable convertible debt instrument), it shall disclose the existence of those features.
	Defaults and breaches
	For loans payable recognised at the end of the reporting period, an entity shall disclose:
18(a)	(a) details of any defaults during the period of principal, interest, sinking fund, or redemption terms of those loans payable;
18(b)	(b) the carrying amount of the loans payable in default at the end of the reporting period; and
18(c)	(c) whether the default was remedied, or the terms of the loans payable were renegotiated, before the financial statements were authorised for issue.
19	If, during the period, there were breaches of loan agreement terms other than those described in paragraph 18 of IFRS 7 (see above), an entity shall disclose the same information as required by paragraph 18 if those breaches permitted the lender to demand accelerated repayment (unless the breaches were remedied, or the terms of the loan were renegotiated, on or before the end of the reporting period).
	Statement of comprehensive income
	Items of income, expense, gains or losses
	An entity shall disclose the following items of income, expense, gains or losses either in the statement of comprehensive income or in the notes:

IFRS 7 Reference	IFRS 7 Disclosure Checklist
20(a)	(a) net gains or net losses on: i. financial assets or financial liabilities at fair value through profit or loss, showing separately those on financial assets or financial liabilities designated as such upon initial recognition, and those on financial assets or financial liabilities that are classified as held for trading; ii. available-for-sale financial assets, showing separately the amount of gain or loss recognised in other comprehensive income during the period and the amount reclassified from equity to profit or loss for the period; iii. held-to-maturity investments; iv. loans and receivables; and v. financial liabilities measured at amortised cost;
20(b)	(b) total interest income and total interest expense (calculated using the effective interest method) for financial assets or financial liabilities that are not at fair value through profit or loss;
20(c)	(c) fee income and expense (other than amounts included in determining the effective interest rate) arising from: i. financial assets or financial liabilities that are not at fair value through profit or loss; and ii. trust and other fiduciary activities that result in the holding or investing of assets on behalf of individuals, trusts, retirement benefit plans, and other institutions;
20(d)	(d) accrued interest income on impaired financial assets; and
20(e)	(e) the amount of any impairment loss for each class of financial asset.
	Other disclosures *Accounting policies*
21	In accordance with paragraph 117 of IAS 1 *Presentation of Financial Statements* (as revised in 2007), an entity discloses, in the summary of significant accounting policies, the measurement basis (or bases) used in preparing the financial statements and the other accounting policies used that are relevant to an understanding of the financial statements, including:

IFRS 7 Reference	IFRS 7 Disclosure Checklist
B5(a)	for financial assets or financial liabilities designated as at fair value through profit or loss: (i) the nature of the financial assets or financial liabilities the entity has designated as at fair value through profit or loss; (ii) the criteria for so designating such financial assets or financial liabilities on initial recognition; and (iii) how the entity has satisfied the conditions for such designation including where appropriate a narrative description of the circumstances underlying the measurement or recognition inconsistency that would otherwise arise, or how designation at fair value through profit or loss is consistent with the entity's documented risk management or investment strategy.
B5(b)	the criteria for designating financial assets as available for sale.
B5(c)	whether regular way purchases and sales of financial assets are accounted for at trade date or at settlement date.
B5(d)	when an allowance account is used to reduce the carrying amount of financial assets impaired by credit losses: (i) the criteria for determining when the carrying amount of impaired financial assets is reduced directly (or, in the case of a reversal of a write-down, increased directly) and when the allowance account is used; and (ii) the criteria for writing off amounts charged to the allowance account against the carrying amount of impaired financial assets.
B5(e)	how net gains or net losses on each category of financial instrument are determined, for example, whether the net gains or net losses on items at fair value through profit or loss include interest or dividend income.
B5(f)	the criteria the entity uses to determine that there is objective evidence that an impairment loss has occurred.

IFRS 7 Reference	IFRS 7 Disclosure Checklist
27(d)	(d) if paragraph 27(c) of IFRS 7 applies (see above), the total amount of the change in fair value estimated using such a valuation technique that was recognised in profit or loss during the period.
27(c)	In the circumstances described in paragraph 27(c) of IFRS 7 (see above), for fair values that are recognised in the financial statements, if changing one or more of those assumptions to reasonably possible alternative assumptions would change fair value significantly, the entity shall state this fact and disclose the effect of those changes.
27(c)	Note: For this purpose, significance shall be judged with respect to profit or loss, and total assets or total liabilities, or, when changes in fair value are recognised in other comprehensive income, total equity.
	If a difference exists between the fair value at initial recognition and the amount that would be determined at that date using a valuation technique (see note below), an entity shall disclose, by class of financial instrument:
28(a)	(a) its accounting policy for recognising that difference in profit or loss to reflect a change in factors (including time) that market participants would consider in setting a price; and
28(b)	(b) the aggregate difference yet to be recognised in profit or loss at the beginning and end of the period and a reconciliation of changes in the balance of this difference.
28	Note: If the market for a financial instrument is not active, an entity establishes its fair value using a valuation technique. Nevertheless, the best evidence of fair value at initial recognition is the transaction price, unless the fair value of the instrument concerned is evidenced by comparison with other observable current market transactions in the same instrument or based on a valuation technique whose variables include only data from observable markets. It follows that there could be a difference between the fair value at initial recognition and the amount that would be determined at that date using the valuation technique.

IFRS 7 Reference	IFRS 7 Disclosure Checklist
	Disclosures of fair value are not required:
29(a)	(a) when the carrying amount is a reasonable approximation of fair value, for example, for financial instruments such as short-term trade receivables and payables;
29(b)	(b) for an investment in equity instruments that do not have a quoted market price in an active market, or derivatives linked to such equity instruments, that is measured at cost because its fair value cannot be measured reliably; or
29(c)	(c) for a contract containing a discretionary participation feature (as described in IFRS 4 *Insurance Contracts*) if the fair value of that feature cannot be measured reliably.
	In the cases described in paragraphs 29(b) and (c) of IFRS 7 (see above), an entity shall disclose information to help users of the financial statements make their own judgements about the extent of possible differences between the carrying amount of those financial assets or financial liabilities and their fair value, including:
30(a)	(a) the fact that fair value information has not been disclosed for these instruments because their fair value cannot be measured reliably;
30(b)	(b) a description of the financial instruments, their carrying amount, and an explanation of why fair value cannot be measured reliably;
30(c)	(c) information about the market for the instruments;
30(d)	(d) information about whether and how the entity intends to dispose of the financial instruments; and
30(e)	(e) if financial instruments whose fair value previously could not be reliably measured are derecognised, that fact, their carrying amount at the time of derecognition, and the amount of gain or loss recognised.
	Nature and extent of risks arising from financial instruments
31	An entity shall disclose information that enables users of its financial statements to evaluate the nature and extent of risks arising from financial instruments to which the entity is exposed at the end of the reporting period.

IFRS 7 Reference	IFRS 7 Disclosure Checklist
	Notes:
32	1. The disclosures required by paragraphs 33 to 42 of IFRS 7 (see below) focus on the risks that arise from financial instruments and how they have been managed. These risks typically include, but are not limited to, credit risk, liquidity risk and market risk.
B6	2. The disclosures required by paragraphs 31–42 shall be either given in the financial statements or incorporated by cross-reference from the financial statements to some other statement, such as a management commentary or risk report, that is available to users of the financial statements on the same terms as the financial statements and at the same time. Without the information incorporated by cross-reference, the financial statements are incomplete.
	Qualitative disclosures
	For each type of risk arising from financial instruments, an entity shall disclose:
33(a)	(a) the exposures to risk and how they arise;
33(b)	(b) its objectives, policies and processes for managing the risk and the methods used to measure the risk; and
33(c)	(c) any changes in 33(a) or (b) (see above) from the previous period.
	Quantitative disclosures
	For each type of risk arising from financial instruments, an entity shall disclose:
34(a)	(a) summary quantitative data about its exposure to that risk at the end of the reporting period. This disclosure shall be based on the information provided internally to key management personnel of the entity (as defined in IAS 24 *Related Party Disclosures*), for example the entity's board of directors or chief executive officer.
B7	Note: When an entity uses several methods to manage a risk exposure, the entity shall disclose information using the method or methods that provide the most relevant and reliable information.
34(b)	(b) the disclosures required by paragraphs 36 to 42 of IFRS 7 (see below), to the extent not provided in paragraph 34(a) (see above), unless the risk is not material.

IFRS 7 Reference	IFRS 7 Disclosure Checklist
34(b)	Note: See paragraphs 29 to 31 of IAS 1 *Presentation of Financial Statements* for a discussion of materiality.
34(c) B8	(c) concentrations of risk if not apparent from 34(a) and (b) (see above), including: 1. a description of how management determines concentrations; 2. a description of the shared characteristic that identifies each concentration (e.g. counterparty, geographical area, currency or market); and 3. the amount of the risk exposure associated with all financial instruments sharing that characteristic.
B8	Note: Concentrations of risk arise from financial instruments that have similar characteristics and are affected similarly by changes in economic or other conditions. The identification of concentrations of risk requires judgement taking into account the circumstances of the entity.
35	If the quantitative data disclosed as at the end of the reporting period are unrepresentative of an entity's exposure to risk during the period, an entity shall provide further information that is representative.
	Credit risk An entity shall disclose by class of financial instrument:
36(a)	(a) the amount that best represents its maximum exposure to credit risk at the end of the reporting period without taking account of any collateral held or other credit enhancements (e.g. netting agreements that do not qualify for offset in accordance with IAS 32 *Financial Instruments: Presentation*) (see also IFRS 7.B9 & B10);
B9, B10	Notes: 1. For a financial asset the entity's maximum exposure to credit risk is typically the gross carrying amount net of any amounts offset in accordance with IAS 32 and any impairment losses. 2. Activities that give rise to credit risk include granting loans, receivables, financial guarantees, making irrevocable loan commitments and entering into derivative contracts. Further guidance is included in IFRS 7.B10.

IFRS 7 Reference	IFRS 7 Disclosure Checklist
36(b)	(b) in respect of the amount disclosed in 36(a) (see above), a description of collateral held as security and other credit enhancements;
36(c)	(c) information about the credit quality of financial assets that are neither past due nor impaired; and
36(d)	(d) the carrying amount of financial assets that would otherwise be past due or impaired whose terms have been renegotiated.
	Financial assets that are either past due or impaired
	An entity shall disclose by class of financial asset:
37(a)	(a) an analysis of the age of financial assets that are past due as at the end of the reporting period but not impaired;
37(b)	(b) an analysis of financial assets that are individually determined to be impaired as at the end of the reporting period, including the factors the entity considered in determining that they are impaired; and
37(c)	(c) for the amounts disclosed in 37(a) and (b) (see above), a description of collateral held by the entity as security and other credit enhancements and, unless impracticable, an estimate of their fair value.
	Collateral and other credit enhancements obtained
	When an entity obtains financial or non-financial assets during the period by taking possession of collateral it holds as security or calling on other credit enhancements (e.g. guarantees), and such assets meet the recognition criteria in other Standards, an entity shall disclose:
38(a)	(a) the nature and carrying amount of the assets obtained; and
38(b)	(b) when the assets are not readily convertible into cash, its policies for disposing of such assets or for using them in its operations.
	Liquidity risk
39(a)	An entity shall disclose a maturity analysis for financial liabilities that shows the remaining contractual maturities.
B11 to B16	Notes:
	1. An entity must use its judgement to determine an appropriate number of time bands;

IFRS 7 Reference	IFRS 7 Disclosure Checklist
	2. when a counterparty has a choice of when an amount is paid, the liability is included on the basis of the earliest date on which the entity can be required to pay;
	3. when an entity is committed to make amounts available in instalments, each instalment is allocated to the earliest period in which the entity can be required to pay;
	4. the amounts disclosed in the maturity analysis are the contractual undiscounted cash flows. Such undiscounted cash flows differ from the amount included in the statement of financial position because the amount in the statement of financial position is based on discounted cash flows;
	5. if appropriate, an entity shall disclose the analysis of derivative financial instruments separately from that of non-derivative financial instruments in the contractual maturity analysis for financial liabilities; and
	6. when the amount payable is not fixed, the amount disclosed is determined by reference to the conditions existing at the end of the reporting period.
	Further guidance is included in IFRS 7.B11 – B16.
39(b)	An entity shall disclose a description of how it manages the liquidity risk inherent in 39(a) (see above).
	Market risk
B17 to B28	*Sensitivity analysis*
	Unless an entity complies with paragraph 41 of IFRS 7 (see below), it shall disclose:
40(a)	(a) a sensitivity analysis for each type of market risk to which the entity is exposed at the end of the reporting period, showing how profit or loss and equity would have been affected by changes in the relevant risk variable that were reasonably possible at that date;

IFRS 7 Reference	IFRS 7 Disclosure Checklist
B17 to B28	Notes: 1. An entity decides how it aggregates information to display the overall picture without combining information with different characteristics about exposures to risks from significantly different economic environments. If an entity has exposure to only one type of market risk in only one economic environment, it would not show disaggregated information; 2. an entity discloses the effect on profit or loss and equity at the end of the reporting period assuming that a reasonably possible change in the relevant risk variable had occurred at the end of the reporting period and had been applied to the risk exposures in existence at that date; 3. an entity is not required to disclose the effect on profit or loss and equity for each change within a range of reasonably possible changes of the relevant risk variable. Disclosure of the effects of the changes at the limits of the reasonably possible range would be sufficient; and 4. an entity shall provide sensitivity analyses for the whole of its business, but may provide different types of sensitivity analysis for different classes of financial instruments. Further guidance is included in IFRS 7.B17 – B28.
40(b)	(b) the methods and assumptions used in preparing the sensitivity analysis; and
40(c)	(c) changes from the previous period in the methods and assumptions used, and the reasons for such changes.
41	If an entity prepares a sensitivity analysis, such as value-at-risk, that reflects interdependencies between risk variables (e.g. interest rates and exchange rates) and uses it to manage financial risks, it may use that sensitivity analysis in place of the analysis specified in paragraph 40 of IFRS 7 (see above).
B20	Notes: 1. This applies even if such a methodology measures only the potential for loss and does not measure the potential for gain.

IFRS 7 Reference	IFRS 7 Disclosure Checklist
	2. An entity may also disclose the historical observation period and weightings applied to observations within that period, an explanation of how options are dealt with in the calculations, and which volatilities and correlations (or, alternatively, Monte Carlo probability distribution simulations) are used. The entity shall also disclose:
41(a)	(a) an explanation of the method used in preparing such a sensitivity analysis, and of the main parameters and assumptions underlying the data provided; and
41(b)	(b) an explanation of the objective of the method used and of limitations that may result in the information not fully reflecting the fair value of the assets and liabilities involved. Other market risk disclosures
42	When the sensitivity analyses disclosed in accordance with paragraph 40 or 41 of IFRS 7 (see above) are unrepresentative of a risk inherent in a financial instrument (for example because the year-end exposure does not reflect the exposure during the year), the entity shall disclose that fact and the reason it believes the sensitivity analyses are unrepresentative. **Adoption of Standard before effective date**
43	If an entity applies IFRS 7 for a period beginning before 1 January 2007, it shall disclose that fact. **Exemption in the first period of adoption before 1 January 2006 from presenting certain comparative information**
44	If an entity applies IFRS 7 for annual periods beginning before 1 January 2006, it need not present comparative information for the disclosures required by paragraphs 31 to 42 of the Standard about the nature and extent of risks arising from financial instruments (see above).

UK *In addition, UK companies are required under the Companies Acts 2006 and 1985 to disclose information about investments in certain undertakings. These disclosure requirements are discussed at* **7.3** *in* ***chapter*** **33**.

7 Offsetting a financial asset and a financial liability

7.1 General principle

IAS 32 requires that a financial asset and a financial liability shall be offset as a net amount in the statement of financial position when, and only when, both of the following conditions are satisfied:

- the entity currently has a legally enforceable right to set off the recognised amounts of the asset and liability; and
- the entity intends to settle on a net basis, or to realise the asset and settle the liability simultaneously.

In the case of a transfer of a financial asset that does not qualify for derecognition under IAS 39, the entity shall not offset the transferred asset and the associated liability (for further details on derecognition refer to **3.3** in **chapter 19**). [IAS 32.42]

When offset is applied, the entity will have the right to pay or receive a single net amount in relation to the two instruments, and intends to do so, and therefore in effect, the entity only has a single financial asset or financial liability. If the conditions of offset are not met then the two financial instruments are presented separately. Whether or not a financial asset and a financial liability is offset, they shall be measured in accordance with the normal measurement guidance with respect to financial assets and financial liabilities.

It should be noted that offsetting a financial asset and a financial liability (and the consequent net presentation in the statement of financial position) is different to the derecognition of those financial instruments. In contrast to offsetting, derecognition of a financial asset or a financial liability not only removes the financial instrument in question from the statement of financial position but also may give rise to a gain or loss on derecognition. [IAS 32.44] Offset does not result in the asset or liability being removed from the statement of financial position, but in net presentation of the asset and liability as either a net asset or a net liability. A gain or loss does not arise because of the offsetting requirements, although it may arise because of the measurement requirements applicable to the asset or liability, respectively.

7.2 Legal right of offset

IAS 32 defines the right of offset as a debtor's legal right, by contract or otherwise, to settle or otherwise eliminate all or a portion of an amount due to a creditor by applying against that amount an amount due from the creditor. As the right is specifically a legal right, the circumstances that give rise to such a right will vary from one legal jurisdiction to another. Thus, for each relationship between the two parties (of debtor and creditor) it will be necessary to consider the particular laws applicable to it. [IAS 32.45]

In certain circumstances the debtor may have a legal right to apply an amount due from a third party against the amount due to a creditor provided that there is an agreement between the three parties that clearly establishes the debtor's right to offset. [IAS 32.45]

> Legal rights do not need to be established in a single document between the three parties. For example, a debtor might obtain set-off rights separately from the third party and from the creditor. In establishing the validity of the legal right to set-off, it is necessary to understand the terms of the particular contracts as well as the context within which set-off is to be applied. The legal right to set-off could, inter alia, be evidenced with reference to a legal opinion, or be established by statutory or regulatory provisions which have been clearly demonstrated as applicable to and governing the particular transaction.

For a discussion of considerations surrounding master netting agreements refer to **7.6** below.

7.3 Intention to settle on a net basis, or to realise the asset and settle the liability simultaneously

The existence of the legal right of offset (while it affects the entity's rights and obligations and may affect its credit exposure) is not sufficient in itself for offsetting. Where there is a legal right, and an entity intends to exercise the right of offset, or to settle simultaneously, the entity is, in effect, exposed to a net amount, which reflects the timing of the expected cash flows and the risks to which those cash flows are exposed, and therefore presentation of the financial instruments on a net basis is appropriate. [IAS 32.46]

The intention by one or both parties to settle on a net basis without the legal right to do so is not sufficient to justify offsetting a financial asset and financial liability. This is due to the fact that the legal rights and obligations pertaining to the individual financial assets and financial liabilities are not altered. [IAS 32.45]

Intention may be demonstrated through management representations that are not contradicted by past experience or other relevant circumstances (e.g. normal business practices, requirements of financial markets, circumstances that limit the ability to settle net) and, also, may take into account reference to the entity's risk management policies, if appropriate. There is no requirement for an assessment of the counterparty's intent.

The operation of a clearing house in an organised financial market, or a face to face exchange may facilitate the simultaneous settlement of two financial instruments. In such circumstances the cash flows are, in effect, equivalent to a single net amount and the exposure to credit or liquidity risk does not pertain to the gross amounts. This is different from a situation where the entity will settle two instruments separately by receiving and paying the gross amounts, even if the period between settlement of the two instruments is short. In the latter case the entity is exposed to credit risk on the asset and liquidity risk on the liability, both of which may be significant. In such circumstances net presentation is not appropriate. Realisation of a financial asset and settlement of a financial liability are treated as simultaneous only when the transactions occur at the same moment. [IAS 32.48]

Example 7.3

Offset: unmatched payments and receipts

Assume that the legal right of offset exists in the following scenario. Company X owes Company Y four payments of £10 million each at the end of each calendar quarter (31 March, 30 June, 30 September, 31 December), totalling £40 million. As part of another contract, Company Y owes Company X two payments of £15 million at 30 June and 31 December, totalling £30 million.

The intention to settle simultaneously can only be demonstrated in respect of the 30 June and 31 December cash flows. At the beginning of the year, Company X will, therefore, reflect a financial liability of £20 million (being the 31 March and 30 September payments) and a separate financial asset of £10 million (representing the difference between the £10 million payable and £15 million receivable from Company Y on 30 June and 31 December). Although Company X's net position over the whole year is a financial liability of £10 million, since it cannot demonstrate the intention to settle net or simultaneously for all payments, the criteria for offset are not satisfied in respect of those unmatched payments and separate presentation is required. Company Y correspondingly has an asset of £20 million and a liability of £10 million.

7.4 Circumstances in which offsetting is usually not appropriate

Due to the principles outlined in **7.1** above not being met, offsetting is specifically identified in IAS 32 as not being appropriate where:

(a) several different financial instruments are used to emulate the features of a single financial instrument (known as a 'synthetic instrument').

Example 7.4

Offset: synthetic instrument accounting

Assume an entity issues long term floating rate debt in the market and concurrently enters into an interest rate swap with the bank that involves receiving floating rate payments and making fixed rate payments with a maturity equal to that of the debt. The combination of the issued debt and the interest rate swap could be seen as synthetically amounting to fixed rate long term debt.

Each of the two instruments (floating rate liability and receive floating rate pay fixed rate interest rate swap) represent contractually separate arrangements with their own terms and conditions and each may be transferred or settled separately. Moreover, each of the two instruments will be exposed to risks that differ from those to which the other instrument is exposed. The offset conditions are not met since there is no legal right of set-off and while the cash flows under the two instruments may occur within a short space of time from each other, they are not simultaneous. Hence, the debt and swap are not presented on a net basis in the entity's statement of financial position.

(b) financial assets and financial liabilities arise from financial instruments with the same primary risk exposure (for example, assets and liabilities within a portfolio of forward contracts or other derivative instruments) but with different counterparties;

(c) financial or other assets are pledged as collateral for non-recourse financial liabilities;

(d) financial assets are set aside in trust by a debtor for the purpose of discharging an obligation without those assets having been accepted by the creditor in settlement of the obligation (for example, a sinking fund arrangement); or

(e) obligations incurred as a result of events giving rise to losses are expected to be recovered from a third party by virtue of a claim made under an insurance policy. [IAS 32.49]

7.5 Circumstances in which offset conditions are met only in relation to some cash flows

There may be circumstances where the offset requirements are met only in relation to some of the cash flows of a contractually single financial asset and a contractually single financial liability. In such circumstances the offset requirements are applied to the extent that the conditions are met. This is illustrated in the following example:

Example 7.5

Offset: partial offset of cash flows

Company A and Company B are independent entities. On 1 January 20X1 Company A borrows £100 from Company B ('instrument 1'). The terms of instrument 1 require repayment after 6 years (at 31 December 20X6) of £100 and annual interest of 6 per cent on the notional of £100. One year later, on 1 January 20X2 Company A lends £50 to Company B ('instrument 2') on terms that require repayment of £50 after 5 years (at 31 December 20X6) and annual interest of 6 per cent on the notional of £50.

The terms of the instruments give both parties the legally enforceable right to settle the principal amounts repayable on a net basis on maturity of the instruments (i.e. through Company A paying a net amount of £50 to Company B on 31 December 20X6). Both parties intend to settle the principal amounts on this basis. In respect of the 6 per cent interest payments/receipts over the life of the two instruments there is no ability to settle on a net basis.

Company A measures both the financial liability (instrument 1) and the financial asset (instrument 2) at amortised cost using the effective interest rate method.

Company A should offset the financial asset and liability to the extent that the financial asset and financial liability meet the condition for offset. The offset conditions are met in respect of a proportion of the principal payments on the two instruments at 1 January 20X2 onwards. Therefore, offsetting is appropriate in respect of these amounts. However, offsetting is not appropriate in respect of the interest amounts.

Assume that at initial recognition of the lending, 1 January 20X1, the amortised cost carrying value of £100 of instrument 1 (before considering offset) comprises an amount of £75 being the present value of the principal payment and an amount of £25 being the present value of the interest payments. Similarly the amortised cost carrying value of instrument 2 (before considering offset) comprises an amount of £37.5 representing the present value of the principal payment and an amount of £12.5 representing the present value of the interest payments.

Applying offset to the proportion of principal payments but not to the interest components of the financial asset and financial liability will result in a liability of £62.5 and asset of £12.5 being shown in the statement of financial position of Company A. This balance is summarised below:

	£	£
Asset		
Present value of interest flows on instrument 2		12.5
Liability		
Present value of interest flows on instrument 1		25
Present value of principal flow on instrument 1	75	
Less offset of principal flow on instrument 2	(37.5)	
Net principal flow		37.5
		62.5

The offset that is achieved by Company A can equally apply to Company B, Company B will present a liability of £12.5 to Company A, and a loan and receivable of £62.5 from Company A.

7.6 Master netting agreements

An entity that undertakes a number of financial instrument transactions with a single counterparty may enter into a 'master netting agreement' covering all of its transactions with that counterparty. Such an agreement creates a legally enforceable right of offset that comes into effect and affects the realisation of individual financial assets and settlement of individual financial liabilities only on the occurrence of a specified event of default or other events not expected to happen in the normal course of business. Such agreements are typically used by financial institutions to provide a degree of protection in the event of bankruptcy or other circumstances that render a counterparty unable to meet its obligations. Once the triggering event takes place the contract will typically provide for a single net settlement of all financial instruments covered by the agreement.

The existence of a master netting agreement does not in itself provide a basis for offsetting assets and liabilities covered by the agreement: firstly, the master netting agreement creates only a conditional right to set off recognised amounts, which falls short of the IAS 32 requirement that the entity must have the *currently enforceable* legal right to set off recognised amounts; and secondly, the entity may not have the intention or ability to either settle on a net basis or realise the asset and settle the liability simultaneously. [IAS 32.50]

Example 7.6A

Offset: master netting agreement

Bank X, an investment bank, enters into several swap transactions with different reset dates to manage the interest rate risk arising from its corporate loans portfolio. Although these transactions are with a range of other banks as counterparties, Bank X's systems aggregate all exposures on a daily basis to enable them to recognise the net profit or loss due to the change in fair value of all open (i.e. unexpired) contracts. Certain contracts have a positive fair value while others are in a loss position. ISDA (International Swaps and Derivatives Association) Master Netting Agreements are in place with some, but not all of these counterparties. Bank X does not net the settlements across swap positions with counterparties on reset dates.

Bank X does not meet the criteria for offsetting financial assets and liabilities related to its swap positions. It does not settle on a net basis and, due to the mismatch in reset dates across its swaps book, cannot demonstrate the simultaneous settlement of swap cash flows. Additionally, the ISDA Master Netting Agreements are not, in themselves sufficient to provide the Bank with the legal right to set off its settlement cash flows across contracts except in the conditional event of default or termination by one of the parties.

Example 7.6B

Offset: options

Company X, a gold producer in South Africa, manages its exposure to changes in the gold price and locks in the cost of funding future capital expenditure by entering into option strategies with several investment banks. These strategies require Company X to both purchase call options and to write put options at various strike prices and with various maturity dates. The transactions are expected to be settled in cash and hence meet the definition of a derivative in IAS 39.

The investment banks require Company X to enter into ISDA Master Netting agreements which give either party the legal right of offset on termination of the contract, or on default of the other party. These agreements do not provide for the offset of settlements in the ordinary course of business.

Company X may not offset the financial assets and financial liabilities arising from the premiums paid and received and subsequent measurement of these options to fair value. The master netting agreement establishes a legally enforceable right of offset only in the event of a contingent event (i.e. default or on termination by one of the parties) and not in respect of ongoing settlements. Additionally, by virtue of the different maturity dates, the company does not demonstrate the intention to settle on a net basis or to realise the asset and liability simultaneously. Therefore, the requirements in IAS 32 are not satisfied. Even in the case where the premiums are settled on the same date, the continuing exposure to credit risk on the party writing the option precludes set-off.

22 Financial instruments: first-time adoption of IFRSs

1 Introduction

1.1 First-time adoption

A first-time adopter of IFRSs is an entity that prepares its first IFRS annual financial statements containing an explicit and unreserved statement of compliance with IFRSs. [IFRS 1.3] The date of transition to IFRSs for a first-time adopter is the beginning of the earliest period for which an entity presents full comparative information under IFRSs in its first IFRS financial statements. [IFRS 1(Appendix A)]

In general, IFRS 1 *First-time Adoption of International Financial Reporting Standards*, which applies to first-time adopters, requires an entity to comply retrospectively with each IFRS effective at the end of the reporting period for its first IFRS financial statements. [IFRS 1.7] IFRS 1 grants limited exemptions from these requirements in specified areas, including financial instruments (e.g. see **3.7** below) and prohibits retrospective application in others, also including financial instruments (see **section 4** below).

In addition, IFRS 1.36A grants an exemption for first-time adopters before 1 January 2006 (i.e. those entities adopting IFRSs in their 2005 financial statements) from presenting comparative information that complies with IAS 32 and IAS 39.

Additionally, such a first-time adopter is not required to present the comparative disclosures required by IFRS 7 if it rly adopts IFRS 7 in advance of the Standard's effective date in its first IFRS financial statements. [IFRS 1.36C] As this book is aimed at those entities either currently applying IFRSs or first-time adopting IFRSs in 2008, the exemption from preparing comparative information under the three Standards for those first-time adopting IFRS before 1 January 2006 is not dealt with in detail in this edition.

This chapter explores some of the aspects of first-time adoption of IFRSs on an entity's accounting for financial instruments that are within the scope of IAS 32 and IAS 39:

- the requirement to identify, classify and measure as appropriate all financial instruments in the scope of IAS 32 and IAS 39 (see **sections 3** to **3.6** below);
- IFRS 1's elective exemption from retrospective application of IAS 32 to compound instruments where the liability component is no longer outstanding (see **3.7** below); and
- IFRS 1's mandatory prohibitions from retrospective application of IAS 39 in respect of derecognition, hedge accounting, and estimates (see **4.1**, **4.3** and **3.5** below).

This chapter is set out differently from preceding financial instruments chapters, as a series of questions and answers, and constitutes an amalgamation of questions frequently asked by first-time adopters. It includes the following sections:

Section 2 Reconciliations for first-time adopters

Section 3 Transition to IFRSs with respect to financial instruments

Section 4 Prohibition on retrospective application of IAS 32 and IAS 39

2 Reconciliations for first-time adopters

Example 2

Reconciliations for first-time adopters

Question

Which reconciliations must a first-time adopter, Entity Y, with a 31 December 2008 year-end, provide in the 2008 financial statements?

Answer

On transition, a first-time adopter is required to explain how the transition from previous GAAP to IFRSs affected its reported financial position, financial performance, and cash flows. [IFRS 1.38] In order to explain how the transition from previous GAAP to IFRSs has affected its financial position and financial performance, IFRS 1.39 requires the following reconciliations to be included in the entity's first IFRS financial statements:

(a) reconciliations of equity reported under previous GAAP to equity under IFRSs (with sufficient detail to enable users to understand the material adjustments to the statement of financial position) for the following dates:

(i) the date of transition to IFRSs; and

(ii) the end of latest period presented in the entity's most recent annual financial statements under previous GAAP; and

(b) a reconciliation of profit or loss reported under previous GAAP for the latest period in the entity's most recent annual financial statements to its profit or loss under IFRSs (with sufficient detail to enable users to understand the material adjustments to the statement of comprehensive income).

Entity Y is required therefore to provide the following reconciliations in accordance with IFRS 1.39 in its first IFRS financial statements:

- a reconciliation of equity under previous GAAP to equity under IFRSs (including IAS 32 and IAS 39) as at 1 January 2007 (this being Entity Y's date of transition to IFRS);
- a reconciliation of equity under previous GAAP to equity under IFRS (including IAS 32 and IAS 39) as at 31 December 2007 (this being the end of latest period presented in the Entity Y's most recent annual financial statements under previous GAAP); and
- a reconciliation of profit or loss under previous GAAP to profit or loss under IFRSs (including IAS 32 and IAS 39) for the year ended 31 December 2007 (this being the latest period in the Entity Y's most recent annual financial statements).

3 Transition to IFRSs with respect to financial instruments

IFRS 1 contains specific transitional provisions in respect of financial instruments. These are discussed in this section and **section 4** below. A first-time adopter is required to identify, recognise, classify and measure as appropriate all financial assets and financial liabilities at the date of transition that qualify for recognition in accordance with IAS 32 and IAS 39, and treat any adjustment to the carrying amount of a financial asset or financial liability as a result of the adoption of the two Standards as a transition adjustment to be recognised in the opening balance of retained earnings at the date of transition to IFRSs. [IFRS 1.IG58A]

IAS 8 applies to adjustments resulting from changes in estimates. Where it not possible to determine whether a particular portion of the adjustment is a transition adjustment or a change in estimate, it should be treated as a change in accounting estimate under IAS 8, with appropriate disclosures. [IFRS 1.IG58B]

At the date of transition a first-time adopter is required to derecognise assets and liabilities that do not qualify for recognition in accordance with IAS 32 and IAS 39, for example, gains and losses deferred as assets and/or liabilities in the statement of financial position in respect of hedge relationships under previous GAAP that do not qualify for recognition as assets and liabilities under IFRSs (see **4.3** below).

3.1 The key steps to conversion to IFRSs for financial instruments

Example 3.1

Key steps for first-time adoption

Question

What are the key steps an entity should consider for conversion to IFRSs in respect of financial instruments?

Answer

The key steps to ensure that an entity complies with IAS 32 and IAS 39 can be summarised as follows:

(a) identify all financial instruments and other contracts that fall within the scope of IAS 32 and IAS 39 including embedded derivatives and other contracts scoped into those two standards, not accounted for as financial instruments under previous GAAP (see **chapter 13**);

(b) recognise and classify all financial instruments in accordance with the financial asset and financial liability classifications of IAS 39 and the rules on equity or liability classification in IAS 32 (see **chapters 14** and **15**);

(c) derecognise items if IAS 32 and IAS 39 do not permit their recognition, for example, gains and losses deferred as assets and/or liabilities in the statement of financial position in respect of hedge relationships under previous GAAP that do not qualify for recognition as assets and liabilities under IFRSs (see **4.3** below);

(d) designate and document qualifying hedge relationships before the date of transition to IAS 39 to ensure these comply with IAS 39's hedge accounting criteria should an entity wish to apply hedge accounting prospectively from the date of transition to IAS 39 (see **4.1** below and **chapter 20**);

(e) apply IAS 32 and IAS 39 in measuring all financial assets and financial liabilities in accordance with their classification (see **3.4** below and **chapters 14, 15** and **18**); and

(f) design and implement controls and procedures for continued compliance with (a) to (e) above.

3.2 Identification of all financial assets and financial liabilities on first-time adoption

Example 3.2

Unrecognised financial instruments under previous GAAP

Question

For a first-time adopter of IFRSs in 2008, which previously unrecognised items under previous GAAP will require first-time recognition as financial assets and financial liabilities?

Answer

It depends. Typically a number of items would **not** have been recognised under previous GAAP compared to IFRSs. These include:

(a) all derivatives, including:

(i) contracts to buy or sell a non-financial item, scoped into IAS 39 if they can be settled net in cash or another financial instrument, or by exchanging financial instruments, and are not entered into or held in accordance with the entity's expected purchase, sale or usage requirements (see **2.5** in **chapter 13**);

(ii) issued guarantees falling within the scope of IAS 39 that do not meet the definition of a financial guarantee contract (see **2.3.2** in **chapter 13**);

(iii) derivatives on an interest in a subsidiary, associate or joint venture unless they meet the definition of an equity instrument of the entity in accordance with IAS 32 or because they will result in a business combination at a future date (see **2.1** and **3.2** in **chapter 13**);

(iv) derivatives based on climatic, geological or other physical variables unless they meet the definition of an insurance contract and are within the scope of IFRS 4 (see **2.3.3** in **chapter 13**); and

(v) loan commitments that can be settled net in cash or another financial instrument, loan commitments that the issuer designates as financial assets or liabilities at fair value through profit or loss or loan commitments to provide a loan at a below-market interest rate (see **3.3** in **chapter 13**);

(b) all embedded derivatives that are required to be separately accounted for, i.e. the entire contract is not one measured at fair value through profit or loss and the embedded derivative is not closely related to the non-derivative financial host contract (see **chapter 17**);

(c) other interests, such as servicing rights or servicing liabilities, retained after a derecognition transaction and still existing at the date of transition to IFRSs (see **chapter 19**);

(d) financial instruments that are held in special purpose entities (SPEs) that were not consolidated under the previous GAAP, but are consolidated under IFRS because the entity controls the SPE at the date of transition to IFRSs (see **3.1.1** in **chapter 19**).

3.2.1 *Embedded derivatives*

Example 3.2.1

Embedded derivative

Question

IAS 39 requires separate accounting treatment for embedded derivatives not closely related to the host contract, where the entire contract is not one measured at fair value through profit or loss. On transition to IFRSs, does an entity assess whether an embedded derivative is closely related to the host contract or not, at the date of transition, or at the date when that contract would have been initially recognised if IAS 39 had always been applied?

Answer

Full retrospective application of IAS 39 is required in this area. IFRIC 9 *Reassessment of Embedded Derivatives* clarifies that a first-time adopter should make its assessment of whether an embedded derivative is to be separated on the later of when becoming party to the contract or when the contract is substantially modified (for a discussion of the 'substantially modified' criterion see **section 3** in **chapter 17**). Assuming in the above scenario there was no substantial modification of the arrangement the assessment of whether the embedded derivative is closely related is made at the date when the entity first became party to the contract and not on the date of transition to IFRSs. The initial carrying amounts of the embedded derivative and the host contract reflect circumstances at the date the whole instrument satisfied the recognition criteria of IAS 39. [IFRS 1.IG55] Once the carrying amount at initial recognition of an embedded derivative that is not closely related to the host contract is separately determined (see **chapter 17**), it is then possible to determine the appropriate carrying values at the date of transition. These adjustments are recognised in the opening balance of retained earnings at the date of transition to IFRSs.

If the entity cannot determine the initial carrying amounts of the embedded derivative and host contract reliably, it treats the entire combined contract as a financial instrument held for trading (see **section 12** in **chapter 17**) measured at fair value through profit or loss. [IFRS 1.IG55]

3.3 Recognition of all financial instruments on first-time adoption

Subject to the exception discussed in **4.1** below on the retrospective application of IAS 39's derecognition rules, at the date of transition to

IFRSs an entity recognises all financial assets and financial liabilities that qualify for recognition under IAS 39, for example, all derivative instruments that have not qualified for derecognition under IAS 39. [IFRS 1.IG53]

3.4 Classification and measurement of financial assets and financial liabilities on transition

A first-time adopter applies IAS 39's classification and measurement criteria to its financial assets and financial liabilities at the date of transition to IFRSs.

For those financial assets and financial liabilities classified at the date of transition in an amortised cost category, an entity determines their amortised cost on the basis of circumstances existing when the assets and liabilities first satisfied the recognition criteria in IAS 39. However, if the entity acquired those financial assets and financial liabilities in a past business combination, their carrying amount under previous GAAP immediately following the business combination is their deemed cost under IFRSs at that date. [IFRS 1.IG57]

Example 3.4A

Determining classification and measurement at date of transition to IFRSs

Question

Entity ABC is a Norwegian listed entity with a 31 December year-end and a first-time adopter in 2008. Its date of transition to IFRSs is 1 January 2007. How does Entity ABC apply the requirements of IAS 39 in respect of the classification and measurement of its financial assets and financial liabilities?

Answer

At 1 January 2007, Entity ABC applies IAS 39's classification and measurement criteria to its financial assets and financial liabilities as if it had initially recognised those financial assets and financial liabilities in accordance with the Standard as illustrated:

- Entity ABC can classify those financial assets meeting the criteria for classification as held-to-maturity (HTM) investments (see **3.2** in **chapter 14**) in that category; its intent and ability to hold such assets to their maturity is made at the date of transition. [IFRS 1.IG56(a)] Entity ABC recognises any adjustment to financial assets classified in the HTM category to measure them at the appropriate amortised cost balance, as if that measurement basis had been applied since the date they first qualified for recognition in accordance with IAS 39, directly in retained earnings. [It follows that sales or transfers of held-to-maturity investments before the date of transition to IFRSs do not trigger the 'tainting' rules (see **3.3** in **chapter 14**).]

- It can classify those financial assets that satisfied the loans and receivables definition (see **3.4** in **chapter 14**) when the financial assets first satisfied the recognition criteria in IAS 39 for that category. [IFRS 1.IG56(b)] Entity ABC recognises any adjustment to financial assets classified in the loans and receivables category to measure them at the appropriate amortised cost amount, as if that measurement basis had been applied since the date they first qualified for recognition as loans and receivables in accordance with IAS 39, directly in retained earnings.

- Entity ABC can designate any non-derivative financial asset that is not held for trading (see **3.5** in **chapter 14**) and required to be measured at fair value through profit or loss, as available-for-sale. [IFRS 1.25A] Like the designation of available-for-sale assets at initial recognition, the designation in this category on transition to IFRSs is irrevocable. The fair value gain or loss on transition for assets designated as available-for-sale financial assets on the date of transition and hence measured at fair value is taken to a separate component of equity as if those assets had been accounted for since initial recognition as available-for-sale financial assets, except for impairment losses, foreign exchange gains or losses on monetary assets and interest income calculated using the effective interest method on those assets. [IFRS 1.IG59]

- Entity ABC recognises any derivative financial assets and derivative financial liabilities that are in the scope of IAS 39 at fair value (see **3.1.2** in **chapter 14** and **7.1.1** in **chapter 15**) with fair value gains or losses on transition accounted for as an adjustment to retained earnings, except for derivatives that were part of a net investment hedge or cash flow hedge under previous GAAP.

- Entity ABC classifies non-derivative financial assets or non-derivative financial liabilities in its opening IFRS statement of financial position as held for trading (hence measured at fair value through profit or loss) if, the assets or liabilities were: (i) acquired or incurred principally for the purpose of selling or repurchasing in the near term; or (ii) at the date of transition to IFRSs, part of a portfolio of identified financial instruments that were managed together and for which there was evidence of a recent actual pattern of short-term profit-taking. [IFRS 1.IG56(d)] The fair value gain or loss on transition is accounted for as an adjustment to retained earnings.

- At the date of transition to IAS 39, Entity ABC is also permitted to designate any financial asset or financial liability as one to be measured at fair value through profit or loss if specified criteria are met, i.e. the 'fair value option' (see **3.1.1** in **chapter 14** and **7.1.2** in **chapter 15**) is available as a one-off choice on transition. [IFRS 1.25A] The fair value gain or loss on transition for financial assets or financial liabilities designated as at fair value through profit or loss at the date of transition, is accounted for as an adjustment through retained earnings, i.e. the assets or liabilities are accounted for as if designated at fair value through profit or loss from the date of initial recognition.

Entity ABC must disclose the fair value of any financial assets or financial liabilities designated into the 'financial assets at fair value through profit or loss' and 'financial liabilities at fair value through profit or loss' categories and their classification and carrying amount in its previous financial statements. [IFRS 1.43A]

- Entity ABC classifies financial liabilities that are not measured at fair value through profit or loss, either because the 'fair value option' has not been applied or because the items are not held for trading, as other financial liabilities measured at amortised cost (see **7.2** in **chapter 15**). It recognises any adjustment to measure them at the appropriate amortised cost amount as if that measurement basis had been applied since the date they first qualified for recognition in accordance with IAS 39, in retained earnings.

Example 3.4B

Derivative not fair valued under previous GAAP

Question

Entity P is a first-time adopter of IFRSs and has a financial year-end of 31 March. Entity P prepares its first annual IFRS financial statements for the year ended 31 March 2008.

Entity P has some derivative financial instruments. Under previous GAAP these instruments were not recognised at fair value in the statement of financial position as they were considered to be hedging instruments. The derivatives were instead held on an accruals basis and were included in the carrying amount of the item being hedged. At the date of transition the instruments have a fair value of £(2) million and do not qualify as hedging instruments in accordance with IAS 39 as they are net written options. How does Entity P account for these derivative instruments on first-time adoption of IFRSs?

Answer

On Entity P's date of transition to IFRSs, i.e. 1 April 2007, it shall recognise the derivative liability in its statement of financial position with the corresponding entry recognised in retained earnings. The entity cannot include the loss in a cash flow hedge accounting reserve as the derivative is not a qualifying hedge accounting instrument under IAS 39.

Under previous GAAP the derivatives had been netted against the item being hedged. Not only is the measurement basis not compliant with IFRSs, but also the financial instruments could not be offset unless the criteria for offset in IAS 32 were met (see **section 4** in **chapter 21**).

An adjustment will be required to the hedged items to recognise them at the appropriate carrying amounts (see **4.3** below).

Example 3.4C

Determining amortised cost

Question

Entity MNO's year-end is 31 December 2008. Entity MNO's date of transition to IFRSs is 1 January 2007. Entity MNO has the following two zero coupon bond assets, which are not quoted in an active market.

- Bond 1 was purchased at original issuance on 1 January 2004 for €1,000. It is redeemable in 5 years' time at €1,250. The effective interest rate on this instrument is 4.56 per cent.
- Bond 2 has the same terms as Bond 1, but the bond was acquired in a business combination on 1 January 2005. The fair value of the bond on the date of the business combination was €1,100. The bond has risen in value since it was issued because of the accretion of the zero coupon and because interest rates have fallen since the bond had been issued. The effective interest rate calculated at the time of the business combination is 3.25 per cent.

How does Entity MNO recognise its investments in Bonds 1 and 2 on the date of transition to IFRSs?

Answer

The bonds are not quoted in an active market and the entity chooses not to designate the bonds as available-for-sale financial assets. Hence, at the date of its transition to IFRS, 1 January 2007, Entity MNO classifies both bonds as loans and receivables (see **3.4** in **chapter 14**) measured at amortised cost. Entity MNO determines the carrying amount of Bond 1 as if it had been accounted for at amortised cost since acquisition using the bond's effective interest rate of 4.56 per cent. The amortised cost on 1 January 2007 is €1,092, representing two years of amortisation at 4.56 per cent.

Entity MNO determines the carrying amount of Bond 2 as if it had been accounted for at amortised cost since acquired in the business combination using the bond's effective interest rate of 3.25 per cent. The amortised cost on 1 January 2007 is €1,136, representing 1 year of amortisation at 3.25 per cent.

Alternatively, the fair value option could have been applied to the bonds on transition to IFRSs if the specified criteria were met.

3.5 Impairment and other estimates

IFRS 1 prohibits retrospective application of IFRSs in respect of estimates, unless there is objective evidence that previous estimates were in error. [IFRS 1.31]

The principal area where estimates are involved in the measurement of financial instruments is in assessments of impairment. IFRS 1.IG58 confirms that an entity's estimates of loan impairments at the date of transition to IFRS are consistent with estimates made for the same date under previous GAAP (after adjustments to reflect any difference in accounting policies), unless there is objective evidence that those assumptions were in error. [IFRS 1.31] It is important to distinguish between a change in estimate and a change in accounting policy for the purpose of recognition of impairment on transition. For example, a change in accounting policy would be moving from an undiscounted basis of measuring impairment under previous GAAP to a discounted basis under IFRSs. The effect of such a change in accounting policy would be reflected in the adjustment to the opening balance of retained earnings on transition. Generally, reconsidering the extent of cash flows that are then subject to discounting under IFRSs is reassessment of an estimate. Such a change in estimate would not be reflected in the adjustment to the opening balance of retained earnings on transition. An exception may arise in the case of purchased guarantees. In this case, the accounting treatment of the guarantee may differ between previous GAAP and IFRSs, thus resulting in an adjustment to the carrying value of loans and potentially retained earnings on transition. This is because IFRSs include the potential recovery under the guarantee as part of the impairment analysis whereas previous GAAP may not (e.g. the guarantee may be recognised separately if cash is due). Impairment is described in greater detail in **chapter 18**.

3.5.1 Change in impairment policy

Example 3.5.1

Change in impairment policy

Question

Under previous GAAP, Entity A measured impairment of financial assets carried at cost on an undiscounted basis. Entity A is a first-time adopter of IFRSs.

IAS 39 requires impairment losses to be measured using discounted cash flows. [IAS 39.63] Therefore, at the date of transition to IFRS, Entity A makes an adjustment to the carrying amount of those financial assets that are measured at amortised cost under IAS 39 to reflect the effect of discounting expected future cash flows.

Is this adjustment recognised as an adjustment to the opening balance of retained earnings at the date of transition in accordance with IFRS 1?

Answer

Yes. In accordance with IFRS 1.11, 31 & IG58, Entity A should recognise this measurement adjustment as a consequence of change in accounting policy in respect of the impairment of financial assets (e.g. loans and receivables) in the opening balance of retained earnings at the date of transition to IFRSs.

3.6 Classification as a financial liability or equity

In its opening IFRS statement of financial position, an entity applies the criteria in IAS 32 to classify financial instruments issued (or components of compound instruments issued) as either financial liabilities or equity instruments in accordance with the substance of the contractual arrangement when the instrument first satisfied the recognition criteria in IAS 32.15, without considering events after that date, other than changes to the terms of the instruments. [IFRS 1.IG35]

Example 3.6

Assessing terms at date of transition to IFRSs

Question

Entity P issued a capital instrument two years before its date of transition to IFRSs, 1 January 2004. Entity P's date of transition to IFRS is 1 January 2007. If IAS 32 was applied at the date of issue of the instrument, the instrument would have been classified as a liability as the instrument's contingent settlement provision (requiring redemption in cash) would have been judged to be genuine, i.e. the circumstances in which redemption is triggered would not have been considered to be extremely rare. At transition date these circumstances (not the terms of the instrument) have changed such that redemption is now extremely rare.

Answer

In its opening IFRS statement of financial position an entity classifies financial instruments issued or their component parts as either financial liabilities or equity instruments based on the substance of the contractual arrangements and the definitions of a financial liability and equity at the time when the instrument first satisfied the recognition requirements of IAS 32 (see **section 2** in **chapter 15**). Subsequent events or changes in market conditions are not taken into account, except for changes in the terms of the instrument. [IFRS 1.IG35]

Entity P therefore classifies its instrument as a financial liability on transition notwithstanding the fact that if it issued an instrument with the same terms at 1 January 2007 it would recognise an equity instrument.

3.7 Compound instruments

To the extent that the liability component is no longer outstanding at the date of transition to IFRSs, full retrospective application of IAS 32 with regard to such compound financial instruments is not required. Full retrospective application would involve separating two components of equity: one portion representing the cumulative interest accrued on the liability component during its life using the effective interest rate method, which would normally reside in retained earnings; and the second portion representing the original equity component that would have been separated on initial recognition of the instrument. [IFRS 1.23]

Example 3.7A

Convertible debt: outstanding at date of transition to IFRSs

Question

Entity H is a first-time adopter in 2008. Entity H issued 2,000 convertible bonds on 1 January 2005. The bonds have a four-year term, and were issued at par with a face value of £1,000 per bond, giving total proceeds of £2 million. Interest is payable annually in arrears at an annual interest rate of 6 per cent. Each bond is convertible, at the holder's discretion, at any time up to maturity into 250 ordinary shares. When the bonds were issued, the market interest rate for similar debt without the conversion option was 9 per cent.

How does Entity H account for its convertible debt on first-time adoption of IFRSs?

Answer

An entity that has an issued compound instrument outstanding at the date of transition to IFRSs determines the initial carrying amounts of the liability and equity components based on circumstances existing when the instrument was issued. [IFRS 1.IG36]

IAS 32 requires that the liability component is valued first. The liability component is calculated as the present value of the contractual cash flows using the discount rate of 9 per cent, which was the market interest rate for similar bonds with the same credit standing having no conversion rights when the bonds were issued. The difference between the proceeds of the bond issue and the fair value of the liability at the time of original issuance is assigned to the equity component. The equity component is not re-measured. An adjustment in the opening balance of retained earnings is required to measure the liability component at its appropriate amortised cost at the date of transition.

Example 3.7B

Convertible debt: not outstanding at date of transition to IFRSs

Question

Entity Q, on the other hand, also a first-time adopter in 2008 (with a December year-end), issued convertible bonds on 1 January 2002. The bonds had a three-year term, were convertible at any time up to maturity into 250 ordinary shares of the entity, and were redeemed at maturity.

How does Entity Q account for its convertible debt on first-time adoption of IFRSs?

Answer

The liability component of Entity Q's convertible instruments is no longer outstanding at its date of transition to IFRSs, 1 January 2007. Entity Q is not required to do a full retrospective application of IAS 32 with regard to its convertible. IFRS 1 permits a first-time adopter not to separate the two components of equity which would have resulted if full retrospective application had been applied: one component representing the cumulative interest accrued on the liability component during its life using the effective interest rate method, which would normally reside in retained earnings; and the second portion representing the original equity component that would have been separated on initial recognition of the instrument.

Example 3.7C

Convertible debt: redeemed after date of transition to IFRSs

Question

Using the facts as in **example 3.7B** above, if Entity Q's convertible had a maturity of 1 January 2008, i.e. it had a six-year term, and was expected to be redeemed on its maturity on 1 January 2008, would Entity Q be exempted from full retrospective application of IAS 32 for its convertible?

Answer

No. Entity Q's date of transition to IFRS is the beginning of its first IFRS reporting period, 1 January 2007. The liability component of its convertible instrument, in this instance, is still outstanding at the date of transition. Hence, Entity Q would be required to apply IAS 32 retrospectively to its convertible debt and separate out the equity component that would have been separated on initial recognition of the instrument in accordance with IAS 32.

3.8 Designation of previously recognised financial instruments

Any entity is permitted to designate any financial asset, other than an asset that meets the definition of held-for-trading, as an available-for-sale financial asset at the date of transition to IFRSs. [IFRS 1.25A(a)]

A first-time adopter of IFRSs must de-designate financial assets and financial liabilities that under previous GAAP were designated as at fair value through profit or loss (FVTPL), but they do not qualify for such designation under IAS 39. An entity that presents its first IFRS financial statements for an annual period beginning on or after 1 September 2006 is permitted to designate, *as at the date of transition to IFRSs*, any financial asset or financial liability as at fair value through profit or loss provided the asset or liability meets the criteria for such classification at that date. [IFRS 1.25A(b)] The criterion is detailed in IAS 39.9(b)(i), (9)(b)(ii) and (11A) and is described in more detail at **3.1.1** in **chapter 14**.

Example 3.8

Date of designation

Entity B prepares its first set of IFRS financial statements for the year ended 31 December 2008. In February 2007, Entity B issued fixed rate debentures which are measured at amortised cost on initial recognition. At the same time, Entity B uses the proceeds of the debt to acquire a portfolio of fixed rate assets which it designates as available-for-sale with changes in fair value recognised in other comprehensive income. The fair value changes on the assets tend to offset the fair value movements on the debenture liabilities. During 2008, Entity B realises the measurement and recognition inconsistency in measuring the fixed rate debt liability at amortised cost whilst measuring the fixed rate assets at fair value with gains and losses recognised in other comprehensive income.

Entity B cannot re-designate the fixed rate debt instruments after initial recognition. At initial recognition, in February 2007, Entity B chose to designate the fixed rate debentures at amortised cost and not at fair value through profit or loss. A designation as at fair value through profit or loss must be made at the later of initial recognition or date of transition to IFRSs.

If the fixed rate debentures were acquired prior to the date of transition to IFRSs, i.e. prior to 1 January 2007, Entity B could have designated those fixed rate debentures as at fair value through profit or loss as at the date of transition to IFRSs if the specified criteria were met.

The entity shall disclose the fair value of the financial assets or financial liabilities designated into each category (available-for-sale or at fair value through profit or loss) at the date of designation and their classification and carrying amount in the previous financial statements. [IFRS 1.43A]

Special guidance exists for entities that present their first IFRS financial statements for an annual period beginning before 1 September 2006. [IFRS 1.25A(c), (d) & (e)] This detailed guidance is not included in this edition as this publication is aimed at those entities either already applying IFRS or that are first-time adopters of IFRS in 2008.

3.9 Fair value measurement of financial assets or financial liabilities

As all financial assets and liabilities must be initially recognised at fair value an entity must consider the specific guidance in IAS 39 on fair value when determining the carrying value of financial assets and liabilities at the date of transition to IFRSs. This applies even if the financial asset or financial liability is not subsequently measured at fair value, as fair value at initial recognition will the opening carrying values at the date of transition to IFRSs.

IAS 39 has very specific guidance on determining fair value at initial recognition for financial assets and liabilities that are not traded in an active market. The Standard limits upfront gain/loss recognition unless the fair value of the instrument is evidenced by comparison with other observable current market transactions in the same instrument (i.e. without modification or repackaging) or based on a valuation technique whose variables include only data from observable markets. This is often referred to as "day 1 P&L" and is discussed in more depth at **5.2.5** in **chapter 18**. IFRS 1.25G has specific transition requirements when applying the day 1 P&L guidance. IFRS 1 permits an entity to apply the day 1 P&L guidance, referred specifically in IFRS 1 as the last sentence of IAS 39AG76 & 76A in any one of the following ways:

- retrospectively;
- prospectively to transactions entered into after 25 October 2002; or
- prospectively to transactions entered into after 1 January 2004.

The unique transition requirements listed above were introduced when the day 1 P&L guidance was originally included in IAS 39. Full retrospective application was not required as constituents raised concerns that retrospective application would diverge from the requirements of US GAAP, would be difficult and expensive to implement, and might require subjective assumptions about what was observable and what was not.

4 Prohibition on retrospective application of IAS 32 and IAS 39

IFRS 1.26 prohibits retrospective application of IFRSs relating to:

(a) derecognition of financial assets and financial liabilities except as specified in **4.2** below;

(b) hedge accounting; and

(c) estimates (see **3.5** above).

4.1 The transition provisions on derecognition for first-time adopters

A first-time adopter is required by IFRS 1.27 to apply the derecognition rules in IAS 39 prospectively from the effective date of IAS 39, 1 January 2004 (i.e. the effective date of the revised version of the Standard published in December 2003) unless it chooses to apply the derecognition rules of IAS 39 retrospectively from a date of its choosing in accordance with IFRS 1.27A (see **4.2** below). Hence, if a first-time adopter derecognised financial assets under its previous GAAP in a securitisation, transfer or other derecognition transaction that occurred before 1 January 2004, it does not recognise those assets and liabilities at the date of transition (even if these would not have qualified for derecognition under IAS 39), unless they qualify for recognition as a result of a later transaction or event.

Example 4.1A

Transfers after 1 January 2004

Question

If a securitisation, transfer, or other derecognition transaction was entered into before 1 January 2004, and derecognition treatment was permitted under previous GAAP, are further transfers of financial assets as part of the same scheme after this date (for example, to maintain a specified balance of mortgage or credit card receivables) subject to the derecognition criteria of IAS 39?

Answer

Yes. Any further transfers of financial assets as part of the same scheme after 1 January 2004 (effective date of application of the recognition requirements in IAS 39) would have to satisfy the derecognition criteria of IAS 39 in order to qualify for derecognition treatment. [IFRS 1.27 – 27A]

A first-time adopter must recognise, however, any financial interest retained as a result of a derecognition transaction prior to 1 January 2004 which still exists at the date of transition to IFRSs, for example, any derivatives and other interests, such as servicing rights or servicing liabilities.

Furthermore, the exemption from applying the derecognition requirements prior to 1 January 2004 is not extended to consolidation. A first-time adopter must consolidate all special purpose entities (SPEs) that it controls at the date of transition to IFRSs, even if the SPEs existed before the date of transition to IFRS or hold financial assets or financial liabilities that were derecognised under previous GAAP. [IFRS 1.IG26] Hence, although a group may have derecognised financial assets under its previous GAAP as a result of a transfer of assets to a SPE occurring before 1 January 2004, those assets may be consolidated back into the group's statement of financial position if the SPE to which the financial assets were transferred is deemed to be controlled by the group in accordance with SIC-12 *Consolidation – Special Purpose Entities*, and the SPE did not derecognise the assets under the previous GAAP. If this is the case, the IAS 39 derecognition decision tree will be applied to the new group as defined by IFRSs.

Example 4.1B

Transfers to a consolidated entity

Entity X is part of Group Y. The date of transition to IFRSs is 1 January 2007 for Entity X and for the group. The entity and group do not apply the election available under IFRS 1.27A (see **4.2** below) to apply the derecognition rules to transactions derecognised prior to 1 January 2004.

Entity X derecognised financial assets under its previous GAAP on 30 September 2003. These assets were transferred to Entity Z. Entity Z is not a member of Group Y under previous GAAP. Entity Z is a special purpose entity that issues beneficial interests in the underlying financial assets transferred to it by Entity X to unrelated third party investors, and provides servicing of those financial assets.

On the date of transition to IFRSs, in accordance with SIC-12, Entity Z is now considered to be part of Group Y and must be consolidated by Group Y.

Individual financial statements of Entity X under IFRS

As Entity X derecognised the financial assets under its previous GAAP in a transaction occurring prior to 1 January 2004, the transferred assets continue to be derecognised under IFRSs.

Group Y's financial statements under IFRS

As Group Y now includes Entity Z, the derecognition requirements must be applied to the enlarged group. If Entity Z could not derecognise the financial assets under its previous GAAP, and the assets continue to be recognised under IFRSs, then the Group continues to recognise those assets. If Entity Z did derecognise the financial assets under its previous GAAP, the assets will remain derecognised ('off balance sheet') under IFRSs because they were derecognised under previous GAAP in a transaction occurring prior to 1 January 2004.

Where the entity and group had made the election available under IFRS 1.27A to apply the derecognition requirements of IAS 39 to derecognition transactions occurring before 1 January 2004 (see **4.2** below), the derecognition requirements of IAS 39 would be applied to the transaction on 30 September 2003. If the transfer of financial assets qualified for derecognition by both Entity X and Group Y (including Entity Z) under IAS 39, the assets would remain derecognised ('off-balance sheet') on the adoption of IFRSs by Group Y on 1 January 2007.

4.2 Option to apply derecognition rules retrospectively from a chosen date

Notwithstanding the requirement to apply IAS 39's rules on derecognition prospectively from 1 January 2004, an entity may choose to apply them retrospectively from a date of the entity's choosing, provided that the information needed to apply IAS 39 to financial assets and financial liabilities derecognised as a result of past transactions was obtained at the time of initially accounting for those transactions. [IFRS 1.27A] (See **example 4.1B** above.)

4.3 Hedge accounting

IFRS 1 prohibits retrospective application of IAS 39 in respect of hedge accounting. [IFRS 1.28 – 30] This is consistent with the general hedging provisions of IAS 39 where hedge accounting is only ever available prospectively if the hedge relationship is appropriately designated, documented, is expected to be highly effective and satisfies all other hedge accounting criteria (see **chapter 20**).

At the date of transition to IFRS, an entity must measure all derivatives at fair value and eliminate all deferred gains and losses arising on derivatives that were reported under previous GAAP as assets or liabilities in the statement of financial position in respect of hedge relationships under previous GAAP since these do not qualify for recognition as assets and liabilities under IFRSs. [IFRS 1.28]

If, before the date of transition to IFRSs, a transaction had been designated as a hedge but the hedge does not meet the conditions for hedge accounting in IAS 39, the requirements of IAS 39.(91) and (101) should be applied to discontinue hedge accounting. [IFRS 1.30]

The designation and documentation of a hedge relationship must be completed on or before the date of transition to IFRSs if the hedge relationship is to qualify for hedge accounting from that date. Hedge accounting can be applied prospectively only from the date that the hedge relationship is fully designated and documented. [IFRS 1.IG60]

4.3.1 *Re-designation or discontinuation of hedge relationships that do not comply with IAS 39*

Where a first-time adopter has a hedge relationship of a type that does not qualify for hedge accounting under IAS 39, for example, where the hedging instrument is a cash instrument or written option or where the hedged item is a net position, or the designated risk is interest rate risk in a held-to-maturity investment (see **sections 3** and **4** in **chapter 20** on qualifying hedged items and qualifying hedging instruments respectively), the entity shall not reflect that hedge relationship in its opening IFRS statement of financial position. However, if an entity designated a net position as a hedged item under previous GAAP, it may designate an individual item within that net position as a hedged item under IFRSs, provided that it does so no later than the date of transition to IFRSs and provided all other hedge accounting criteria are met. [IFRS 1.29]

4.3.1.1 *Fair value hedge under previous GAAP that does not qualify as a fair value hedge under IFRS*

Example 4.3.1.1A

Non-qualifying hedge accounting (1)

Question

Entity H is fair value hedging a fixed rate debt instrument for interest rate risk under previous GAAP. Entity H intends to classify the instrument as held-to-maturity under IFRSs. Held-to-maturity investments cannot be hedged items with respect to interest rate risk under IFRSs because designation of an investment as held-to-maturity requires an intention to hold the investment till maturity without regard to the changes in fair value attributable to changes in interest rates. Hence, the hedge relationship does not qualify for hedge accounting under IAS 39, and the entity is not permitted to reflect the hedge relationship in its opening IFRS statement of financial position. [IFRS 1.29] Under IFRSs, the held-to-maturity debt security will be accounted for at amortised cost. How should the previous fair value adjustments to the carrying amount of the hedged item be accounted for on the first-time adoption of IFRSs, and thereby, the initial application of IAS 39?

Answer

As the held-to-maturity investments are not qualifying hedged items under IFRSs in respect of interest rate risk, the carrying amount on the date of transition to IFRSs should reflect the balance that would have existed had the entity always applied IFRSs, i.e. the balance that would have existed had the entity never applied hedge accounting. The held-to-maturity investment will be measured at amortised cost and thus any previous adjustments recognised under previous GAAP should be reversed to the extent that they have resulted in a carrying amount that differs from the amortised cost balance that would have been reported had the entity applied IFRSs and measured the item at amortised cost throughout its life.

The derivative will be recognised in the statement of financial position at its fair value with an adjustment to retained earnings on the date of transition.

Example 4.3.1.1B

Non-qualifying hedge accounting (2)

Question

Entity J is fair value hedging a fixed rate, non pre-payable debt instrument for interest rate risk under previous GAAP with an interest rate swap whereby Entity J receives a fixed rate of interest and pays LIBOR. The interest rate swap contains an option for the Bank to cancel the swap at any time at a settlement amount of zero (the bank will cancel the swap where it is out of the money to them). Under IFRSs, the debt instrument will be carried at amortised cost. How should this relationship be accounted for on the first time adoption of IFRSs, and thereby, the initial application of IAS 39?

Answer

Entity J has written an option embedded in the swap. A written option or net written option does not qualify as a hedging instrument unless it is designated as an offset to a purchased option, including one that is embedded in another financial instrument. [IAS 39.77 and (AG94)] As the debt is non pre-payable, and therefore does not have an equal and opposite embedded purchased option, the hedging instrument is not a qualifying instrument. [IAS 39.AG94] The difference between the fair value of the interest rate swap and its previously reported carrying value, together with the difference between the debt's amortised cost value and its previously reported carrying amount should be recognised directly in opening retained earnings. No fair value hedging adjustment to the hedged debt is allowed.

4.3.1.2 *Cash flow hedge under previous GAAP that does not qualify as a cash flow hedge under IFRS*

Example 4.3.1.2

Non-qualifying hedge accounting (3)

Question

If a forecasted transaction is not expected to occur at the date of transition to IFRSs how should any net cumulative gains or losses arising on measurement at fair value of the hedging instrument be accounted for at the date of transition?

Answer

If, at the date of transition to IFRSs, the forecasted transaction is not expected to occur the hedge does not qualify as a cash flow hedge. A first-time adopter reclassifies any net cumulative gain or loss reported in other comprehensive income under previous GAAP to retained earnings at the date of transition in accordance with IFRS 1.11.

If the derivative instrument was carried at cost, and no changes in value of the derivative were recognised in other comprehensive income, the full amount of the adjustment to the derivative asset or liability necessary to recognise the derivative at fair value should be recorded in retained earnings where hedge accounting is not permitted. If the derivative instrument was carried at an amount other than fair value with a deferred debit or credit in the statement of financial position recorded as an offset, that deferred debit or credit should be reversed through retained earnings if it does not meet the appropriate recognition criteria under IFRSs, and the value of the derivative brought up to its fair value at the date of transition.

4.3.2 Hedge relationships that continue to qualify under IAS 39

For a hedge relationship to continue to qualify as a hedge relationship at the date of transition to IFRSs, it must meet all the hedge accounting criteria (see **chapter 20**). In particular, the designation and documentation of a hedge relationship must be completed on or before the date of transition to IFRSs if the hedge relationship is to qualify for hedge accounting from that date. Hedge accounting can be applied prospectively only from the date that the hedge relationship is fully designated and documented.

For a first-time adopter of IFRSs this may be a significant change to previous GAAP which may not have required such rigorous hedge designation and documentation. Hedge accounting under IAS 39, and hence on first-time adoption of IFRSs, can only be applied prospectively from the date that the hedge relationship is fully designated and documented subject to all other hedge accounting requirements of IAS 39 being met.

4.3.2.1 Qualifying fair value hedges

Under its previous GAAP, an entity may have deferred or not recognised gains and losses on a fair value hedge of a hedged item that is not measured at fair value. In these circumstances IFRS 1 requires an adjustment (in the opening balance of retained earnings) to the carrying amount of the hedged item at the date of transition provided the hedge is a qualifying hedge relationship under IAS 39. This adjustment is the lower of:

(a) that portion of the cumulative change in the fair value of the hedged item that reflects the designated hedged risk and was not recognised under previous GAAP; and

(b) that portion of the cumulative change in the fair value of the hedging instrument that reflects the designated hedged risk and, under previous GAAP, was either (i) not recognised or (ii) deferred in the statement of financial position as an asset or liability. [IFRS 1.IG60A]

These provisions result in the hedged item being adjusted by the cumulative change in the fair value of the hedged item due to the designated risk where the fair value of the hedging instrument is more than the exposure on the hedged item. This entry is equivalent to the entry that would have been recognised had the entity always applied IFRSs.

If the derivative is less than exposure of the hedged item, the hedged item is adjusted to the value of the derivative which would have been different had the entity always applied IFRSs.

Example 4.3.2.1

Qualifying fair value hedges

Assume for both the following scenarios that the hedge relationship is one that is a qualifying hedge relationship under IAS 39 and hence, qualifies for hedge accounting at the date of transition to IFRSs.

Scenario A

Entity D has an issued fixed rate bond (£100 million) and a receive fixed rate £ pay floating 3 month £ LIBOR interest rate swap that it has designated in a fair value hedge of the fixed rate bond (with the designated risk being fair value interest rate exposure due to changes in 3 month £ LIBOR. Under Entity D's previous GAAP changes in the fair value of the swap were not recognised in the financial statements and the carrying value of the debt was not adjusted for changes in fair value attributable to the designated risk (3 month £ LIBOR).

At the date of transition to IFRSs the fair value of the bond is £70 million. Of the £30 million cumulative changes in the value of the bond since its issue (when its fair value was equal to £100 million) £20 million is determined to be due to changes in the 3 month £ LIBOR interest rate while £10 million relates to changes in Entity D's credit risk. At the date of transition the cumulative changes in fair value of the swap (not reflected in the financial statements under previous GAAP) amount to £21 million of which £19.5 million is attributable to the hedged risk (changes in the 3 month £ LIBOR rate).

In accordance with IFRS 1.IG60A, on transition to IFRSs, the hedged item (the fixed rate bond) is adjusted by £19.5 million such that its carrying value in the opening statement of financial position is £80.5 million (£100 million less the adjustment of £19.5 million). The £19.5 million adjustment is the lower of the portion of the cumulative change in the fair value of the hedged item due to the designated hedged risk and the portion of the cumulative change in the fair value of the hedging instrument due to the designated hedged risk (£20 million and £19.5 million respectively).

At the date of transition Entity D makes the following entries:

Dr Fixed rate bond	£19.5 million
Cr Retained earnings	£19.5 million

To adjust the hedged item for the designated risk.

Dr Retained Earnings	£21.0 million
Cr Derivative liability	£21.0 million

To recognise the swap at fair value

Scenario B

Entity F has a fixed rate investment that is not classified as held-to-maturity that it originally acquired for £100 million some years ago. On acquisition of the investment Entity F also entered into a receive floating 1 month £ LIBOR pay fixed £ interest rate swap that it designated under previous GAAP as a hedging instrument in a fair value hedge of the fixed rate investment (with the hedged risk being fair value interest rate risk due to changes in the one-month £ LIBOR rate).

At the date of transition to IFRSs, the fair value of the fixed rate investment is £115 million. Changes in fair value of the investment have not been recognised under previous GAAP. Of the £15 million cumulative change in the value of the fixed rate investment since it was acquired (when its fair value was equal to £100 million), £13 million is determined to be due to fair value changes due to changes in the one-month £ LIBOR rate while £2 million relates to changes in the issuer's credit risk. At the date of transition the cumulative change in the fair value of the swap (not reflected in the financial statements under previous GAAP) amounts to £12 million, all of which is determined to relate to the hedged risk (changes in the one-month £ LIBOR rate).

At the date of transition, the fixed rate investment is adjusted by £12 million such that its carrying value in the opening statement of financial position is £112 million (£100 million plus the adjustment of £12 million). This adjustment is the lower of the portion of the cumulative change in the fair value of the hedged item due to the designated hedged risk and the portion of the cumulative change in the fair value of the hedging instrument due to the designated hedged risk (£13 million and £12 million respectively).

On transition Entity D makes the following entries:

Dr Fixed rate investment	£12 million
Cr Retained earnings	£12 million

To adjust the hedged item.

Dr Retained earnings	£12 million
Cr Derivative liability	£12 million
To recognise the swap at fair value	

4.3.2.2 *Qualifying cash flow hedges*

An entity may have deferred gains and losses on a cash flow hedge of a forecast transaction. If, at the date of transition to IFRSs, the hedge relationship is a qualifying hedge relationship under IAS 39, i.e. the forecast transaction is highly probable, or if it is not highly probable, it is still expected to occur, the entire deferred gain or loss on the hedging instrument is recognised in equity. [IFRS 1.IG60B] Note that this initial entry in or reclassification into equity (depending on whether the gains and losses were either previously not recognised or deferred in the statement of financial position outside of equity) comprises the entire cumulative gain or loss on the hedging instrument as at the date of transition regardless of its effectiveness up to that date.

Any net cumulative gain or loss that is reclassified to equity on initial application of IAS 39 remains in equity until:

(a) the forecast transaction subsequently results in the recognition of a non-financial asset or non-financial liability and the amount deferred in equity, depending on the accounting policy choice of the entity, is either included in the initial carrying value of the non-financial asset or non-financial liability, i.e. it is accounted for as a basis adjustment to the item, or remains in equity and is reclassified from equity to profit or loss when the item affects profit or loss (see **2.2.3** in **chapter 20**);

(b) the forecast transaction affects profit or loss and the amount deferred in equity is reclassified from equity to profit or loss, for example, when a hedged highly probable forecast sale actually occurs; or

(c) the forecast transaction is no longer expected to occur, in which case any related net cumulative gain or loss is reclassified from equity to profit or loss.

Example 4.3.2.2

Qualifying cash flow hedges

Prior to the date of transition, a Sterling functional currency entity expects, with a high degree of probability, to sell goods to one of its customers for €1 million on a date after the date of transition to IFRSs. The entity enters into a forward contract to sell €1 million and buy £ at a forward rate of £0.7:€1 on the expected date of sale of the goods. Under previous GAAP the entity did not recognise the fair value of the forward contract in its statement of financial position.

Assume that on date of transition:

- the fair value of the forward contract is £(200,000), i.e. it is a liability; and
- the sale of goods for €1 million at the date originally forecast is still a highly probable forecast transaction.

At the date of transition, the entire cumulative loss on the forward contract to date is recorded in equity as follows:

Dr Equity	£200,000
Cr Forward contract	£200,000

After the date of transition the accounting treatment depends on the likelihood of the forecast transaction occurring.

(a) If the forecast transaction is no longer expected to occur, the entire cumulative gain/loss on the forward contract deferred in equity until that date (including that portion deferred on transition) is immediately reclassified from equity to profit or loss.

(b) If after the date of transition the forecast transaction becomes no longer highly probable but is still expected to occur, the hedged transaction no longer qualifies for hedge accounting (since it is no longer highly probable). Hence, subsequent gains and losses on the forward contract are recognised in profit or loss. However, the cumulative gain/loss on the forward contract deferred in equity (including that portion deferred on transition) up until the forecast transaction is no longer highly probable, remains in equity until either the transaction takes place (see (c) below) or it is no longer expected to occur (see (a) above).

(c) The highly probable forecast transaction takes place as expected. The cumulative gains/losses on the hedging instrument (including that portion deferred on transition) will be released to profit or loss at the same time as the highly probable forecast transaction (in the form of € denominated revenues) affects profit or loss, i.e. when the Euro denominated sale occurs.

4.3.2.3 *Qualifying net investment hedges*

IAS 39 and IFRS 1 do not contain any explicit guidance as to the transitional provisions in respect of hedges of a net investment in a foreign operation.

In accordance with IAS 39.102 hedges of a net investment in a foreign operation are accounted for similarly to cash flow hedges. It may therefore be argued that similar transitional provisions to those for cash flow hedging should be applied in the case of hedges of a net investment in a foreign operation. This would imply that, providing the hedge relationship qualifies for hedge accounting under IAS 39 the cumulative gain/loss on the hedging instrument at the date of transition (that under previous GAAP may or may not have been recorded in the statement of financial position) is recognised in equity. Hence, for a derivative hedging instrument (e.g. cross currency swap or foreign currency forward contract) not previously reflected in the statement of financial position under previous GAAP, the following journal entry is required:

Dr/Cr Fair value of derivative (statement of financial position)	X
Cr/Dr Equity	X

This amount classified in equity is released to profit or loss upon disposal of the foreign operation in accordance with the requirements of IAS 39.102 (see **2.3** in **chapter 20** for more details on hedging a net investment in a foreign operation). The reclassification of the deferred fair value gains/losses on the hedging instrument from equity to profit or loss will offset either fully or partially the foreign exchange gains/losses recognised in other comprehensive income arising on the retranslation of the net assets of the foreign operation in accordance with IAS 21 *The Effects of Changes in Foreign Exchange Rates*.

Pre-transition gains and losses recognised in equity will not be reclassified from equity to profit or loss in accordance with IAS 39.102 when an entity has elected to reset the cumulative translation reserve in equity to zero in accordance with IFRS 1.22. Applying the exemption in IFRS 1.22, the cumulative translation differences for all foreign operations are deemed to be zero at the date of transition and therefore only subsequent translation differences that arise after the date of the transition will be reclassified from equity to profit or loss on disposal of the foreign operation. If an entity has applied net investment hedge accounting in the consolidated financial statements under previous GAAP and the related hedging reserve is set to zero at the date of transition to IFRSs, the gains and losses on the hedging instrument prior to the date of transition, shall be recognised in the opening balance of retained earnings.

23 Revenue

1 Introduction

IAS 18 *Revenue* sets out recognition criteria for revenue, identifies the circumstances in which those criteria will be met and provides practical guidance on the application of the criteria. It was most recently amended in May 2008 when the IASB issued Amendments to IFRS 1 *First-time Adoption of International Financial Reporting Standards* and IAS 27 *Consolidated and Separate Financial Statements* in respect of the cost of an investment in a subsidiary, jointly controlled entity or associate.

This chapter discusses the requirements of IAS 18 in the following sections.

Section 2	Scope
Section 3	Definition of revenue
Section 4	Measurement of revenue
Section 5	Identification of the transaction
Section 6	Recognition criteria – sale of goods
Section 7	Recognition criteria – rendering of services
Section 8	Recognition criteria – interest revenue
Section 9	Recognition criteria – royalty revenue
Section 10	Recognition criteria – dividend revenue
Section 11	Disclosure
Section 12	Future developments

IAS 18 is the subject of an active IASB project, leading to revision in the medium term (see **12.1**).

UK

Under UK GAAP, Application Note G to FRS 5 Reporting the Substance of Transactions *and UITF Abstract 40* Revenue recognition and service contracts *are concerned with revenue recognition but do not purport to deal comprehensively with the subject. Accordingly, in the absence of a full UK standard, it is not possible to identify all differences that may exist between revenue practices adopted under UK GAAP and the detailed guidance in the IAS.*

2 Scope

IAS 18 is applied in accounting for revenue arising from:

[IAS 18.1]

- the sale of goods (including goods produced for sale and goods purchased for sale, such as merchandise purchased by a retailer or land and other property held for resale);
- the rendering of services; and
- the use by others of entity assets yielding interest, royalties and dividends.

IAS 18 does not deal with revenue arising from:

[IAS 18.6]

- leases (dealt with in IAS 17 *Leases* – see **chapter 26**);
- dividends arising from investments accounted for under the equity method (dealt with in IAS 28 *Investments in Associates* – see **chapter 35**);
- insurance contracts within the scope of IFRS 4 *Insurance Contracts* – see **chapter 44**;
- changes in the fair value of financial assets and financial liabilities or their disposal (dealt with in IAS 39 *Financial Instruments: Recognition and Measurement* – see **chapter 18** and **chapter 19**);
- changes in the value of other current assets;
- the initial recognition, and changes in the fair value, of biological assets related to agricultural activity (dealt with in IAS 41 *Agriculture* – see **chapter 43**);
- the initial recognition of agricultural produce (also dealt with in IAS 41); and
- the extraction of mineral ores (dealt with in IFRS 6 *Exploration for and Evaluation of Mineral Resources*).

Also excluded from the scope of IAS 18 are contracts for the rendering of services that are directly related to construction contracts, e.g. those for the services of project managers and architects. These service contracts fall within the scope of IAS 11 *Construction Contracts* (see **chapter 40**). That chapter also discusses IFRIC 12 *Service Concession Arrangements*, which gives guidance on the accounting by operators for public-to-private service concession arrangements. [IAS 18.4]

2.1 IFRIC 15 *Agreements for the Construction of Real Estate*

IFRIC 15 *Agreements for the Construction of Real Estate* was issued in July 2008. It addresses whether an agreement is within the scope of IAS 11 or IAS 18, and when revenue from the construction of real estate should be recognised. [IFRIC 15.6]

The Interpretation applies to agreements for the construction of real estate, and to entities that undertake that construction directly or through subcontractors. [IFRIC 15.4] In addition to the construction of real estate, such agreements may include the delivery of other goods or services. [IFRIC 15.5]

> Agreements for the construction of real estate take diverse forms, in part because the underlying substance of such agreements varies. While some agreements are for the provision of construction services, others are in substance for the delivery of goods (e.g. housing units) that are not complete at the time of entering into the agreement. Thus, the percentage of completion method is appropriate for some agreements for the construction of real estate, but for others revenue should be recognised only at the point that the constructed real estate is delivered to the customer. The Interpretation provides guidance on how to determine which approach is appropriate in which circumstances.

IFRIC 15 is accompanied by an information note which, although not part of the Interpretation, summarises its requirements in the form of two flowcharts, reproduced as **Table 2.1.1** and **Table 2.1.2** below.

The detailed guidance in IFRIC 15 is written on the assumption that the entity has previously analysed the agreement for the construction of real estate and any related agreements and concluded that any other criteria for revenue recognition (discussed later in this chapter) are met. In particular, the entity must not retain continuing managerial involvement to the degree usually associated with ownership; and it must not retain effective control over the constructed real estate to an extent that would preclude recognition of some or all of the consideration as revenue. If recognition of some of the consideration as revenue is precluded, the detailed guidance in IFRIC 15 applies only to the part of the agreement for which revenue will be recognised. [IFRIC 15.7]

2.1.1 Splitting an agreement into separately identifiable components

It is possible that a single agreement may cover the delivery of certain goods or services in addition to the construction of real estate. For example, an agreement to construct real estate may also specify that property management services are to be provided.

As discussed in **section 5**, IAS 18.13 indicates that, in some circumstances, agreements may need to be split into separately identifiable components, with each such component being accounted for separately. Where this is necessary, the fair value of the total consideration received or receivable for the agreement is allocated to each component. The seller then applies the requirements of IFRIC 15 to any components for the construction of real estate in order to determine whether each component is within the scope of IAS 11 or IAS 18. [IFRIC 15.8]

The segmenting criteria of IAS 11 then apply to any component of the agreement that is determined to be a construction contract. [IFRIC 15.8]

Table 2.1.1

[Information note accompanying IFRIC 15]

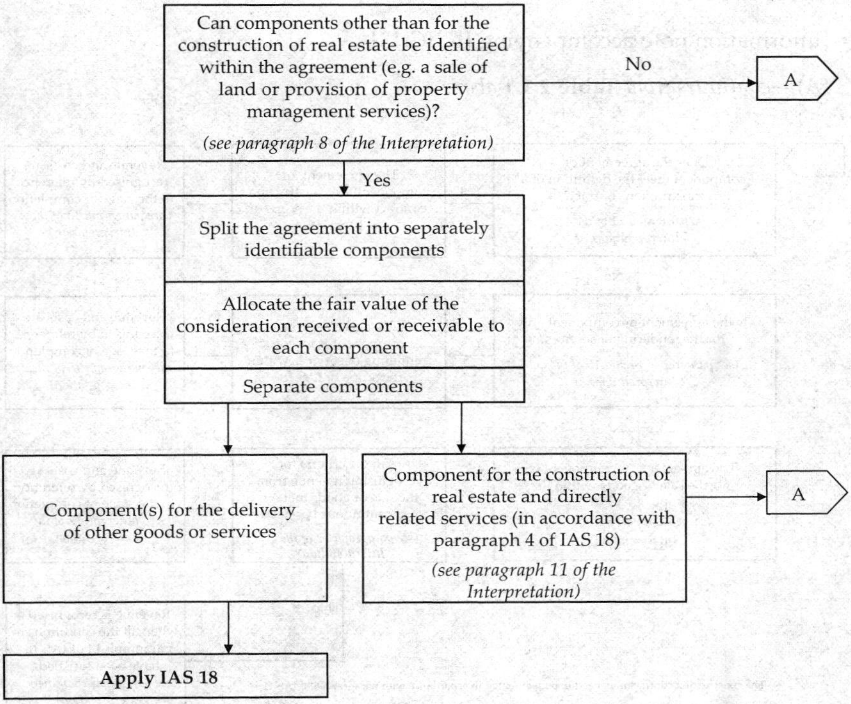

(A) – continues in **Table 2.1.2** *below.*

2.1.2 *Accounting for the construction of real estate*

The appropriate accounting for an agreement to construct real estate (or, where an agreement is split into separately identifiable components, for a component for the construction of real estate) depends on whether the agreement (or component):

- meets the definition of a construction contract; or
- is only for the rendering of services; or
- is for the sale of goods, in which case it is necessary to consider whether the criteria for recognising revenue from the sale of goods are met on a continuous basis.

Whether an agreement (or component) is within the scope of IAS 11 or IAS 18 depends on the terms of the agreement and all the surrounding facts and circumstances, and judgement will be required with respect to each agreement. [IFRIC 15.10]

Table 2.1.2

[Information note accompanying IFRIC 15]

(A) – continues from **Table 2.1.1** *above.*

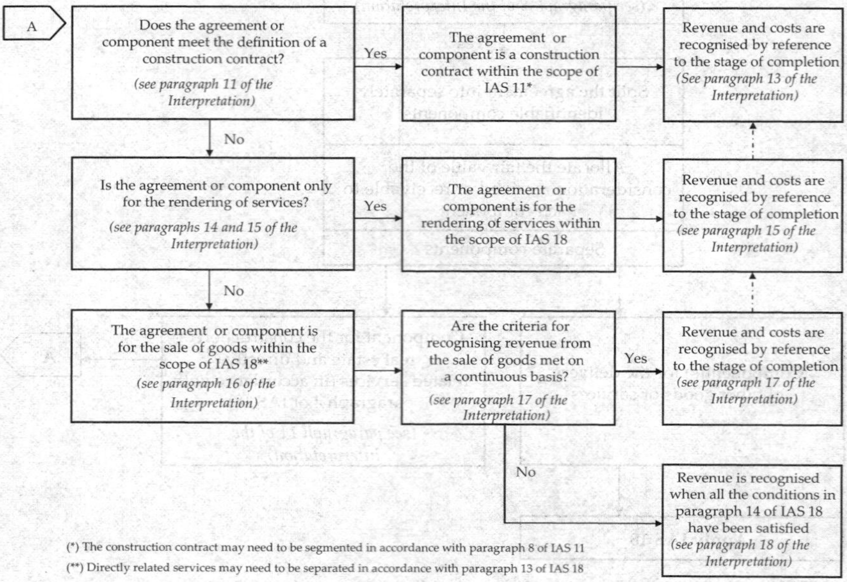

(*) The construction contract may need to be segmented in accordance with paragraph 8 of IAS 11

(**) Directly related services may need to be separated in accordance with paragraph 13 of IAS 18

2.1.2.1 *Construction contracts*

IAS 11 applies when the agreement (or component) meets the definition of a construction contract set out in IAS 11.3, namely 'a contract specifically negotiated for the construction of an asset or a combination of assets …'

IFRIC 15.11 states that an agreement for the construction of real estate will meet the definition of a construction contract when the buyer is able to:

- specify the major structural elements of the design of the real estate before construction begins; and/or

> Where construction will take place on land that was already the buyer's asset before the agreement to construct real estate was envisaged, it is likely that IAS 11 will apply. This is because an

owner of land will, subject to planning constraints, usually be able to decide whether to construct real estate on that land, and to specify the major structural elements of the design of any such real estate before construction.

- specify major structural changes once construction is in progress, whether it exercises that ability or not.

Generally, it is likely that a buyer will be able to specify major structural changes once construction is in progress only if such a right is explicit in the agreement. But it is possible that such a right may be established by the law of a jurisdiction in which a transaction occurs.

In contrast, if buyers have only limited ability to influence the design (for example, to select from a range of entity-specified options, or to specify only minor variations to the basic design), IFRIC 15.12 states that the agreement will be for the sale of goods, and within the scope of IAS 18.

Although IFRIC 15.12 states that such an agreement will be for the sale of goods, it would seem possible in some circumstances (e.g. where construction materials will be sourced directly by the buyer) for the agreement to be for the rendering of services, as discussed at **2.1.2.2**. But it is clear that the agreement will not be a construction contract.

When IAS 11 applies, the construction contract also includes any contracts or components for the rendering of services that are directly related to the construction of the real estate in accordance with IAS 11.5(a) and IAS 18.4. [IFRIC 15.11] If the outcome of the agreement (or component) can be estimated reliably, revenue is recognised by reference to the stage of completion of the contract activity in accordance with IAS 11. [IFRIC 15.13] The recognition of revenue for construction contracts is discussed in **chapter 40**.

2.1.2.2 Agreements for the rendering of services

If an agreement (or component) does not meet the definition of a construction contract, it will be within the scope of IAS 18. The Interpretation provides further guidance on how to determine whether the agreement is for the rendering of services (see below) or for the sale of goods (see **2.1.2.3**). [IFRIC 15.14]

In some cases, the entity is not required to acquire and supply construction materials because they will be sourced directly by the buyer. Where this is the case, the agreement may be only an agreement for the rendering of services in accordance with IAS 18, in which case, providing the criteria in IAS 18.20 are met, revenue will be recognised using the percentage of completion method. IAS 18.21 indicates that the requirements of IAS 11 are generally applicable to the recognition of revenue and the associated expenses for such a transaction. [IFRIC 15.15] The recognition of revenue from the provision of services is discussed in **section 7** below.

2.1.2.3 Agreements for the sale of goods

Conversely, if the entity is required to provide services together with construction materials in order to perform its contractual obligation to deliver real estate to the buyer, then, assuming it does not qualify as a construction contract (see **2.1.2.1**), the agreement is for the sale of goods and the criteria set out in IAS 18.14 apply. [IFRIC 15.16]

If an agreement is determined to be for the sale of goods, the timing of revenue recognition will depend on when control and the significant risks and rewards of ownership are transferred to the buyer. IFRIC 15 envisages two possibilities:

- The entity may transfer to the buyer control and the significant risks and rewards of ownership of the real estate in its entirety at a single time (e.g. at completion, upon or after delivery). In this case, revenue will be recognised only when all the criteria in IAS 18.14 are satisfied. [IFRIC 15.18] Those criteria are discussed in **section 6** below.
- Alternatively, the entity may transfer to the buyer control and the significant risks and rewards of ownership of the work in progress in its current state as construction progresses. In this case, if all the criteria in IAS 18.14 are met continuously as construction progresses, revenue will be recognised using the percentage of completion method. The requirements of IAS 11 are generally applicable to the recognition of revenue and the associated expenses for such a transaction. [IFRIC 15.17]

The idea that the criteria in IAS 18.14 can be met continuously as construction progresses is relatively new. In the Basis for Conclusions accompanying IFRIC 15, the IFRIC noted that agreements with 'continuous transfer' might not be encountered frequently. [IFRIC 15.BC26] Where an entity adopts such accounting, specific disclosures are required, including how it determines which agreements meet all the criteria in IAS 18.14 continuously as construction progresses (see **2.1.3**).

The Interpretation itself does not give further guidance on how to assess whether 'continuous transfer' is present, but some further commentary is included at IE3, IE8 and IE11 in the illustrative examples accompanying IFRIC 15 (see **2.1.5**). One of the important indicators of 'continuous transfer' appears to be that, if the agreement is terminated before construction is complete, the buyer retains the work in progress and the entity has the right to be paid for the work performed to date.

When the entity is required to perform further work on real estate already delivered to the buyer, it recognises an expense in accordance with IAS 18.19 (see **6.5**), measuring the liability in accordance with IAS 37 (see **chapter 11**). When the entity is required to deliver further goods or services that are separately identifiable from the real estate already delivered to the buyer, it will already have identified the remaining goods or services as a separate component of the sale, in accordance with IFRIC 15.8 (see **2.1.1**). [IFRIC 15.19]

2.1.3 *Disclosures*

When an entity recognises revenue using the percentage of completion method for agreements that meet all the criteria in IAS 18.14 continuously as construction progresses (see **2.1.2.3**), the following disclosures are required:

[IFRIC 15.20]

(a) how the entity determines which agreements meet all the criteria in IAS 18.14 continuously as construction progresses;

(b) the amount of revenue arising from such agreements in the period; and

(c) the methods used to determine the stage of completion of agreements in progress.

For any such agreements that are in progress at the reporting date, the following disclosures are also required:

[IFRIC 15.21]

(a) the aggregate amount of costs incurred and recognised profits (less recognised losses) to date; and

(b) the amount of advances received.

IFRIC 15.BC32 notes that these disclosures are similar to those required for construction contracts by IAS 11.39 & 40.

2.1.4 Effective date and transition

IFRIC 15 applies for annual periods beginning on or after 1 January 2009. Entities are permitted to apply the Interpretation for a period beginning before 1 January 2009, but those so choosing must disclose that they have applied the Interpretation early. [IFRIC 15.24] The Interpretation supersedes the guidance in Example 9 in the Appendix to IAS 18 (see **example 6.6I**).

Where an entity changes its accounting policy in order to comply with IFRIC 15, that change is accounted for retrospectively in accordance with IAS 8. [IFRIC 15.25]

2.1.5 Illustrative Examples

The following examples accompany, but are not part of, IFRIC 15.

Example 2.1.5A

Separately identifiable component for sale of land

[IFRIC 15 Illustrative Example 1]

IE1 An entity buys a plot of land for the construction of commercial real estate. It designs an office block to build on the land and submits the designs to planning authorities in order to obtain building permission. The entity markets the office block to potential tenants and signs conditional lease agreements. The entity markets the office block to potential buyers and signs with one of them a conditional agreement for the sale of land and the construction of the office block. The buyer cannot put the land or the incomplete office block back to the entity. The entity receives the building permission and all agreements become unconditional. The entity is given access to the land in order to undertake the construction and then constructs the office block.

IE2 In this illustrative example, the agreement should be separated into two components: a component for the sale of land and a component for the construction of the office block. The component for the sale of land is a sale of goods within the scope of IAS 18.

IE3 Because all the major structural decisions were made by the entity and were included in the designs submitted to the planning authorities before the buyer signed the conditional agreement, it is assumed that there will be no major change in the designs after the construction has begun. Consequently, the component for the construction of the office block is not a construction contract and is within the scope of IAS 18. The facts, including that the construction takes place on land the buyer owns before construction begins and that the buyer cannot put the incomplete office block back to the entity, indicate that the entity transfers to the buyer control and the significant risks and rewards of ownership of the work in progress in its current state as construction progresses. Therefore, if all the criteria in paragraph 14 of IAS 18 are met continuously as construction progresses, the entity recognises revenue from the construction of the office block by reference to the stage of completion using the percentage of completion method.

IE4 Alternatively, assume that the construction of the office block started before the entity signed the agreement with the buyer. In that event, the agreement should be separated into three components: a component for the sale of land, a component for the partially constructed office block and a component for the construction of the office block. The entity should apply the recognition criteria separately to each component. Assuming that the other facts remain unchanged, the entity recognises revenue from the component for the construction of the office block by reference to the stage of completion using the percentage of completion method as explained in paragraph IE3.

IE5 In this example, the sale of land is determined to be a separately identifiable component from the component for the construction of real estate. However, depending on facts and circumstances, the entity may conclude that such a component is not separately identifiable. For example, in some jurisdictions, a condominium is legally defined as the absolute ownership of a unit based on a legal description of the airspace the unit actually occupies, plus an undivided interest in the ownership of the common elements (that includes the land and actual building itself, all the driveways, parking, lifts, outside hallways, recreation and landscaped areas) that are owned jointly with the other condominium unit owners. In this case, the undivided interest in the ownership of the common elements does not give the buyer control and the significant risks and rewards of the land itself. Indeed, the right to the unit itself and the interest in the common elements are not separable.

Example 2.1.5B

Agreement for sale of goods

[IFRIC 15 Illustrative Example 2]

IE6 An entity is developing residential real estate and starts marketing individual units (apartments) while construction is still in progress. Buyers enter into a binding sale agreement that gives them the right to acquire a specified unit when it is ready for occupation. They pay a deposit that is refundable only if the entity fails to deliver the completed unit in accordance with the contracted terms. Buyers are also required to make progress payments between the time of the initial agreement and contractual completion. The balance of the purchase price is paid only on contractual completion, when buyers obtain possession of their unit. Buyers are able to specify only minor variations to the basic design but they cannot specify or alter major structural elements of the design of their unit. In the jurisdiction, no rights to the underlying real estate asset transfer to the buyer other than through the agreement. Consequently, the construction takes place regardless of whether sale agreements exist..

IE7 In this illustrative example, the terms of the agreement and all the surrounding facts and circumstances indicate that the agreement is not a construction contract. The agreement is a forward contract that gives the buyer an asset in the form of a right to acquire, use and sell the completed real estate at a later date and an obligation to pay the purchase price in accordance with its terms. Although the buyer might be able to transfer its interest in the forward contract to another party, the entity retains control and the significant risks and rewards of ownership of the work in progress in its current state until the completed real estate is transferred. Therefore, revenue should be recognised only when all the criteria in paragraph 14 of IAS 18 are met (at completion in this example).

IE8 Alternatively, assume that, in the jurisdiction, the law requires the entity to transfer immediately to the buyer ownership of the real estate in its current state of completion and that any additional construction becomes the property of the buyer as construction progresses. The entity would need to consider all the terms of the agreement to determine whether this change in the timing of the transfer of ownership means that the entity transfers to the buyer control and the significant risks and rewards of ownership of the work in progress in its current state as construction progresses. For example, the fact that if the agreement is terminated before construction is complete, the buyer retains the work in progress and the entity has the right to be paid for the work performed, might indicate that control is transferred along with ownership. If it does, and if all the criteria in paragraph 14 of IAS 18 are met continuously as construction progresses, the entity recognises revenue by reference to the stage of completion using the percentage of completion method taking into account the stage of completion of the whole building and the agreements signed with individual buyers.

Example 2.1.5C

Continuing managerial involvement

[IFRIC 15 Illustrative Example 3]

IE9 Determining whether the entity will retain neither continuing managerial involvement to the degree usually associated with ownership nor effective control over the constructed real estate to an extent that would preclude recognition of some or all of the consideration as revenue depends on the terms of the agreement and all the surrounding facts and circumstances. Such a determination requires judgement. The Interpretation assumes the entity has reached the conclusion that it is appropriate to recognise revenue from the agreement and discusses how to determine the appropriate pattern of revenue recognition.

IE10 Agreements for the construction of real estate may include such a degree of continuing managerial involvement by the entity undertaking the construction that control and the significant risks and rewards of ownership are not transferred even when construction is complete and the buyer obtains possession. Examples are agreements in which the entity guarantees occupancy of the property for a specified period, or guarantees a return on the buyer's investment for a specified period. In such circumstances, recognition of revenue may be delayed or precluded altogether.

IE11 Agreements for the construction of real estate may give the buyer a right to take over the work in progress (albeit with a penalty) during construction, e.g. to engage a different entity to complete the construction. This fact, along with others, may indicate that the entity transfers to the buyer control of the work in progress in its current state as construction progresses. The entity that undertakes the construction of real estate will have access to the land and the work in progress in order to perform its contractual obligation to deliver to the buyer completed real estate. If control of the work in process is transferred continuously, that access does not necessarily imply that the entity undertaking the construction retains continuing managerial involvement with the real estate to the degree usually associated with ownership to an extent that would preclude recognition of some or all of the consideration as revenue. The entity may have control over the activities related to the performance of its contractual obligation but not over the real estate itself.

3 Definition of revenue

IAS 18 defines revenue as the gross inflow of economic benefits during the period arising in the course of the ordinary activities of an entity when those inflows result in increases in equity, other than increases relating to contributions from equity participants. [IAS 18.7] Revenue includes such items as sales, fees, interest, dividends, royalties and rent.

The definition of revenue excludes contributions from equity participants. For example, where an entity issues warrants (options issued on the entity's own shares) for cash, the cash is credited to equity as the proceeds are received from an equity instrument. Where the warrants lapse unexercised, no revenue is recognised. The fact that an equity participant no longer has an equity claim on the assets of the entity does not convert the equity contribution to income.

The disposal of non-current assets is a transaction that does not generate revenue. Instead, gains and losses on the disposal of non-current assets, including investments and operating assets, are reported by deducting from the proceeds on disposal the carrying amount of the asset and related selling expenses. [IAS 1(2007).34, previously IAS 1(2003).34]

3.1 Gross or net presentation

Revenue includes only gross inflows of economic benefits that are received or receivable by the entity on its own account. The use of the word 'gross' in the definition of revenue is not intended to include amounts collected on behalf of others. For example, sales taxes collected by the entity and remitted to a customs authority will not be included as revenue. Likewise, collection agency revenue does not include the amounts actually collected on behalf of customers, but is restricted to the fee or commission relating to the collection. [IAS 18.8]

In an agency relationship, gross amounts collected by the agent on behalf of the principal are not benefits that flow to the agent and, therefore, they are not revenue. The agent's revenue is the amount of the commission. [IAS 18.8]

IAS 18 does not provide guidance or indicators of when a seller is an agent or a principal. Determining whether a seller is an agent or principal requires judgement and will depend on the particular facts and circumstances of each arrangement.

Factors indicating, individually or in combination, that the seller may be acting as a principal, and that therefore gross revenue reporting is appropriate, include situations in which the seller:

- is the primary obligor in the arrangement (this is often a strong indicator);
- has general inventory risk (before the customer order is placed or on customer return);
- has latitude in establishing price;
- changes the product or performs part of the service;
- has discretion in supplier selection;
- is involved in determining product or service specifications;
- has physical loss inventory risk (after the customer order or during shipping);

- has credit risk; or
- is responsible for warranty or quality risk on the product(s) sold or service(s) rendered.

Examples indicating individually or in combination that the seller may be acting as an agent, and that therefore net revenue reporting is appropriate, include situations in which:

- the supplier (and not the seller) is the primary obligor in the arrangement (this is often a strong indicator);
- the seller earns a fixed or determinable amount; or
- the supplier (and not the seller) has credit risk.

These lists are not exhaustive. Circumstances may require that some factors be weighted more heavily than others, and conclusions should not be based solely on the number of factors present. In addition, although IFRSs do not contain any guidance on this issue, other guidance is available and may be useful in reaching a judgement if the factors taken into account are applied consistently and do not conflict with IFRSs.

Example 3.1A

Sales incentives – gross or net?

A vendor which sells its products and services through a retailer gives the retailer a cash incentive payment when a related service is sold to end customers in combination with the main product. For example, a retailer sells a warranty along with the vendor's product. The vendor's tariff schedules an additional £10 to be received on this package. The retailer may or may not be required to follow the vendor's pricing policy. This warranty is serviced by the vendor, and therefore the retailer's cost is zero. The retailer then remits £8 (regardless of the actual price received from the end customer) to the vendor (or £10 with a subsequent payment from the vendor to the retailer of £2).

Whether the vendor should account for the incentive payment of £2 as a reduction of revenue or as a promotion expense will depend on whether the retailer (intermediary) is acting as a principal or as an agent.

If the retailer is acting as an agent, the incentive payment to the retailer of £2 is similar in substance to a commission and, therefore, should be treated as an expense by the vendor under IAS 18.8.

If, however, the retailer is acting as a principal, the incentive payment should be treated as a volume rebate and, accordingly, as a reduction in revenue under IAS 18.10.

Example 3.1B

Income tax withheld in a different country

Company X performs consulting services for Company C, which is in a different country from Company X. Company C withholds 20 per cent of Company X's fee as local income tax and transmits this amount to its local government on behalf of Company X. Company C pays the remaining 80 per cent balance to Company X. The countries do not have a tax treaty and Company X is not required to file a tax return in Company C's country. However, Company X may, at its option, file a tax return in Company C's country to recover taxes withheld in excess of its share of income. Company X was fully aware that the 20 per cent income tax would be withheld in Company C's country when it agreed to perform the consulting services for Company C. If Company X's fee is £100 and Company C remits £80 to Company X and £20 to the local government, does Company X have revenue of £100 and tax expense of £20, or net revenue of £80?

Company X has revenue of £100 and income tax expense of £20. Under Company C's local law, Company X is the primary obligor in the arrangement. However, the amount is paid by Company C on behalf of Company X.

Example 3.1C

Value Added Tax (VAT) rebate

In Country C, software developers must pay 17 per cent VAT (this rate is consistent with VAT on other similar items) to the government when software is sold to distributors or end users, but 14 per cent is rebated by the government to the developer almost immediately, resulting in an effective three per cent VAT rate. This is well known by both the developer and the buyer, who factor it into the selling price. Even though the seller effectively pays three per cent, the buyer gets credit for 17 per cent if the software is resold. Assume software is sold for £103 inclusive of VAT. This was negotiated based on selling price of £100 plus effective VAT of £3. How much revenue should the seller recognise?

IAS 20 *Accounting for Government Grants and Disclosure of Government Assistance* defines a government grant as 'assistance by government in the form of transfers of resources to an entity in return for past or future compliance with certain conditions relating to the operating activities of the entity'. The 14 per cent VAT rebate is regarded as a government grant to encourage the software development industry. Therefore, the seller will record revenue of £88 (£103 ÷ 1.17) and government grant income of £12 [(£103 – £88) × (14 ÷

17)]. In accordance with IAS 20.29, government grants related to income may be presented separately or as 'other income'. The £3 VAT is excluded from revenue under IAS 18.8.

Example 3.1D

Severance taxes

A government requires a mining or oil and gas producer to pay a 'severance tax' or other similar tax based on the value of minerals produced. The tax is payable even if the minerals are not sold.

In this case, the severance tax is an expense related to the production of the asset to be sold, because the burden of the tax falls on the producer and is not dependent on sales. The producer is not considered an agent of the government for the purposes of collection of the severance tax. Therefore, the full amount of the sale should be included in revenue. This answer is appropriate even if, when the minerals are ultimately sold, the invoice shows the severance tax as a separate item.

If, on the other hand, the government levies tax only on products sold and such amounts are re-invoiced to the purchaser, the amount should be regarded as a sales tax that is excluded from revenue under IAS 18.8. In effect, the entity is acting as a collection agent for the government.

(Although revenue from the extraction of mineral ores is excluded from the scope of IAS 18, the severance tax issue is not excluded.)

Example 3.1E

Royalty payments

An entity is required by contract to pay a royalty to the government in respect of certain intangible assets. The royalty is specified as a percentage of gross proceeds from sales less costs applicable to the royalty owner's share of production. The entity can pay the royalty in cash or in kind. Should the royalty be netted against the operating company's revenue or recognised as an operating expense?

The entity should record its revenue on a gross basis as it is the primary obligor in the arrangement. The royalty is recognised as an operating expense.

If the government was also a shareholder in the entity, these royalty payments should be differentiated from a distribution to shareholders in the form of a royalty.

4 Measurement of revenue

Revenue is measured at the fair value of the consideration received or receivable. [IAS 18.9] Fair value is defined as the amount for which an asset could be exchanged, or a liability settled, between knowledgeable, willing parties in an arm's length transaction. [IAS 18.7]

4.1 Trade discounts allowed and similar items

In practice, revenue is usually determined by agreement between the entity and the buyer or user of the goods or services. Thus, the amount of revenue recognised for a transaction is net of any trade discounts or volume rebates given, since these discounts and rebates are not received as consideration by the seller. [IAS 18.10]

At the IFRIC meeting in July 2004, IFRIC members agreed that prompt settlement discounts should be estimated at the time of sale, and presented as a reduction in revenues.

Example 4.1

Cash discounts

A seller offers a cash discount for immediate or prompt payment (i.e. payment earlier than required by the normal credit terms). A sale is made for £100 with the balance due within 90 days. If the customer pays within 10 days, the customer will receive a two per cent discount on the total invoice. How should the seller account for this early payment incentive?

IAS 18.10 states that the amount of revenue arising on a transaction is the amount agreed by the buyer and seller. If the agreement between buyer and seller calls for payment within a relatively short period such as 90 days, and the environment is not hyperinflationary, a cash discount for prompt payment is not intended as a financing transaction. It is simply a way of identifying the amount agreed by the buyer and seller. It also can be viewed as a mechanism to enhance collectibility of the agreed amount. Therefore, the seller should recognise revenue net of the amount of cash discount taken. In the example above, revenue is £100 if the discount is not taken and £98 if the discount is taken. Where necessary, the seller should recognise revenue based on an estimate of the number of customers that will take the discount, and true up in the next reporting period for the actual number.

This answer is consistent with the guidance in IAS 2.11, which states that trade discounts, rebates, and other similar items are deducted in determining the costs of purchase.

4.2 Deferred consideration

In the majority of cases, the nominal amount of the consideration received or receivable will not vary materially from its fair value because most trade receivables are due within a relatively short time-frame. In the unusual circumstances when consideration is to be received outside such a short time-frame, the fair value of the consideration to be received will not, due to the time value of money, be the same as the nominal amount of the consideration. Such an arrangement effectively includes a financing transaction. Therefore, to calculate the fair value of the consideration receivable, future receipts are discounted using an imputed interest rate which is the more clearly determinable of:

[IAS 18.11]

- the prevailing rate for a similar instrument of an issuer with a similar credit rating; or
- a rate of interest that discounts the nominal amount of the instrument to the current cash sales price of the goods or services.

Where the second approach is taken, the resulting interest rate should be assessed for reasonableness. If the rate appears unrealistically low, this may indicate that the current cash sales price that would be appropriate for this particular customer has not been correctly identified.

IFRIC members considered the accounting for extended payment terms, such as six-months interest-free credit, at the meeting in July 2004. They agreed that IAS 39 *Financial Instruments: Recognition and Measurement* applies to the receivable in such circumstances, and that the effect of the time value of money should be reflected when this is material, in accordance with IAS 39 (AG69-AG82).

If material, the difference between the nominal amount of the consideration to be received and the discounted amount is recognised as interest revenue over the credit period, in accordance with the requirements of IAS 18 (see **section 8** below) and IAS 39 (see **section 4.1** of **chapter 18**).

Example 4.2A

Deferred consideration: discounting based on interest rate

An entity sells an item of equipment for £100,000 under a financing agreement which has no stated interest rate. Annual instalments of £20,000 are due each year for five years from the date of purchase. Thus, it is a 'zero percent' financing arrangement. The policy of not charging interest is consistent with normal industry practice.

Because industry practice is to allow deferred payment with no interest, there are no recent cash transactions from which the entity could make a reliable estimate of the cash sales price. The seller believes, however, that the buyer would be able to obtain financing from other sources at an interest rate of 10 per cent.

Step 1 Calculate the fair value of the stream of payments

Assuming no down payment, five annual instalments of £20,000, and an interest rate of 10 per cent, the fair value of the stream of payments forming the consideration is £75,816. Therefore, on the date of the sale, £75,816 is recorded as revenue from the sale of goods and a related receivable is recognised.

Step 2 Calculate the amount of interest earned each period

The difference between £100,000 and £75,816 of £24,184 will be recognised as interest revenue as it becomes due each year, as calculated below.

	Principal amount outstanding {A} £	Interest element of payment {Ax10% = B} £	Principal element of payment {C-B} £	Total payment {C} £
End of year 1	75,816	7,581	12,419	20,000
End of year 2	63,397	6,340	13,660	20,000
End of year 3	49,737	4,974	15,026	20,000
End of year 4	34,711	3,471	16,529	20,000
End of year 5	18,182	1,818	18,182	20,000
Total		24,184	75,816	100,000

Example 4.2B

Deferred consideration: discounting to current cash sales price

Annual instalments of £20,000 are due each year for five years from the date of purchase. If the buyer had paid cash for the equipment, the sales price would have been £80,000.

The selling entity should record the consideration at its fair value. Since there is a £20,000 difference between the cash price of £80,000 and the amount due if the equipment is paid for in instalments, the arrangement is effectively a financing transaction as well as the sale of goods. The amount of the consideration attributable to the sale of goods is the cash price of £80,000. The remaining £20,000 is interest revenue and is recognised as it becomes due each year using the effective interest method as illustrated below.

Step 1 Calculate the effective rate of interest

Since the cash price offered is £80,000, it is necessary to determine the interest rate which discounts £100,000 to £80,000 over a five-year period, assuming no down payment and five annual instalments of £20,000. This interest rate is 7.93 per cent.

Step 2 Calculate the amount of interest earned each period

The difference of £20,000 between £100,000 and £80,000 will be recognised as interest revenue as it becomes due each year, as calculated below.

	Principal amount outstanding {A}	Interest element of payment {Ax7.93% = B}	Principal element of payment {C-B}	Total payment {C}
	£	£	£	£
End of year 1	80,000	6,345	13,655	20,000
End of year 2	66,345	5,262	14,738	20,000
End of year 3	51,607	4,093	15,907	20,000
End of year 4	35,700	2,831	17,169	20,000
End of year 5	18,531	1,469	18,531	20,000
Total		20,000	80,000	100,000

4.3 Exchanges of goods or services

When goods or services are exchanged or swapped for goods or services of a similar nature and value, no revenue is recognised. [IAS 18.12] Such transactions occur in a limited number of commodity industries such as the oil or milk industries. These exchanges are generally made to help suppliers in the distribution of their products when they need a specific quantity of a commodity at a specific time in a particular location. In practice, this type of exchange of similar goods is relatively uncommon outside those industries. Another scenario in which this might apply, however, is where a wholesaler agrees that a retailer may return certain goods in exchange for others.

When goods or services are exchanged for dissimilar goods or services, a transaction that generates revenue has taken place and revenue is recognised. The revenue is measured at the fair value of the goods or services received, adjusted for any cash payments made by either the buyer or the seller. If the fair value of the goods or services received cannot be measured reliably, revenue is recognised at the fair value of the goods or services given up, adjusted for any cash payments made or received. [IAS 18.12]

IAS 18 does not include any guidance on how to determine whether goods or services are of 'a similar nature or value', but in the case of goods it will often be helpful to contrast the different markets on which the entity normally buys and sells.

For example, when a dealer in used goods transacts with a customer and accepts other used goods in exchange, the allowance granted to the customer will typically be less than the price at which the dealer expects to resell. In effect, the customer is being charged a 'retail' price for the goods purchased but being granted only a 'wholesale' price for the goods traded in. Thus, even if the goods exchanged are similar (e.g. vehicles or compact discs), their value is dissimilar because of the difference between wholesale and retail prices, and so the transaction will give rise to revenue. By contrast, when a dealer exchanges goods with a fellow dealer, both sides of the transaction are likely to be priced by reference to the 'wholesale' price. Thus, the goods will be similar in nature and value, and no revenue will be recognised.

Example 4.3A

Transport sales of oil

Company A owns and operates a pipeline to transport crude oil. Company A does not produce or distribute crude oil, but merely provides for use of its pipeline to the buyer and the seller in a contract for a use fee. The seller and buyer will independently determine the sales price and either the buyer or seller will pay a fee to Company A to transport the oil purchased/sold in its pipeline.

The pipeline needs to be full of product at all times to be operational. Therefore, during initial construction of the pipeline, Company A purchases oil to fill the pipeline. Company A charges a fixed fee for its transportation services and, literally, swaps crude oil at one entry point for crude oil at another exit point. Company A bears the risk of loss due to theft or line loss in excess of maximums allowed under the contract. This loss is rare and normally arises in a pipeline spill that is covered by insurance. How should Company A record revenue, gross of the oil sold or net equal to the fee received?

While the entity initially purchases product for the pipeline, it effectively exchanges that product with equivalent product from customers when the crude oil is pushed in, and then pushed out, of the pipeline. Therefore, this transaction is regarded as an exchange of similar assets and only the fee charged for use of the pipeline should be recorded as revenue.

Example 4.3B

Transfer of inventories for an entity's own shares

Company A has produced inventory at a cost of £80 that is normally sold to unrelated third parties at a price of £100. Company A enters into a transaction to buy £100 of its ordinary shares from a shareholder in return for £100 of its inventory (priced at the retail rate). How should Company A account for this transaction?

> Company A should record revenue for the sale of its inventory for £100 and treasury shares for £100. The form of consideration should not have an impact on whether revenue is recorded. Company A would then record cost of sales and reduce inventory by £80.

4.4 Barter transactions involving advertising services

SIC-31 *Revenue – Barter Transactions Involving Advertising Services* deals with the circumstances where an entity (the Seller) enters into a barter transaction to provide advertising services in exchange for receiving advertising services from its customer (the Customer). Such advertisements may be displayed on the Internet, poster sites, broadcast on television or radio, published in magazines or journals, or presented in another medium.

Where the services exchanged are similar, the principles outlined in **4.3** above mean that no revenue can be recognised. Where the services exchanged are dissimilar, revenue can be recognised provided that the amount of the revenue can be measured reliably. SIC-31 discusses the circumstances under which a Seller can reliably measure revenue at the fair value of advertising services received or provided in a barter transaction.

The Interpretation concludes that revenue from a barter transaction involving advertising services can never be measured reliably at the fair value of the advertising services received. [SIC-31.5]

The fair value of such barter transactions can only be determined by reference to other transactions with knowledgeable and willing parties in an arm's length transaction. For such transactions to provide a relevant and reliable basis for support, the services involved must be similar, there must be many transactions, valuable consideration that can be reliably measured must be exchanged, and independent third parties must be involved. [SIC-31.8] The conditions set out below are designed to ensure that these characteristics are present.

Under SIC-31, a Seller can reliably measure revenue at the fair value of the advertising services it provides in a barter transaction, by reference only to non-barter transactions that:

[SIC-31.5]

- involve advertising similar to the advertising in the barter transaction;
- occur frequently;

- represent a predominant number of transactions and amount when compared to all transactions to provide advertising that is similar to the advertising in the barter transaction;
- involve cash and/or another form of consideration (such as marketable securities, non-monetary assets, and other services) that has a reliably measurable fair value; and
- do not involve the same counterparty as in the barter transaction.

UK

The overall approach taken by SIC-31 is broadly consistent with that taken under UK GAAP by UITF 26 Barter transactions for advertising, *but there are some differences in the detail. In particular, UITF 26 requires that substantially all of the turnover from advertising within the accounting period is represented by cash sales. It also specifies factors (such as circulation, timing, prominence, demographic and duration) to be considered in deciding whether the advertising on which prices are based is the same in all material respects as that exchanged in a barter transaction. Overall, the criteria specified by UITF 26 are more onerous than those of SIC-31. Accordingly, it is possible that some barter transactions not giving rise to revenue under UK GAAP may nevertheless give rise to revenue under SIC-31.*

4.5 Price regulation

Example 4.5

Revenue recognition in the pharmaceutical industry

The Pharmaceutical Price Regulation Scheme (PPRS) in Country A is a joint initiative between the pharmaceutical industry and the Department of Health (DH). The PPRS applies to all entities supplying branded, licensed medicines to the Public Health Service (PHS). The objectives of the PPRS are to ensure that the PHS buys medicines at reasonable prices while allowing pharmaceutical entities to earn a reasonable profit so that they are able to continue to invest in research and development activities. The PPRS operates by limiting the profits an entity can make from the supply of medicines to the PHS. The entity's return on capital employed is calculated based on the annual financial return. All excess profits earned over the prescribed limits for the current period should be refunded to the DH.

In this scenario, the pharmaceutical entities are effectively operating in a regulated market in which the prices they can charge are governed by an agreement with the DH. When the pharmaceutical entities are required to pay a refund to the DH because their profits have exceeded the allowed profits for the period, this is a reduction of the revenue already recognised and should be accounted for as such.

However, note that the accounting for government schemes to regulate the prices of pharmaceutical products should be based on the particular facts and circumstances of the government scheme under which the entity operates. Different types of regulations may exist in different jurisdictions, some being in the nature of rebates or limits on profits, whereas others may be in the nature of an expense.

5 Identification of the transaction

The recognition criteria specified by IAS 18 (as discussed in **sections 6** to **10** below) are usually applied separately to each transaction. To present the substance of a transaction appropriately, however, it may sometimes be necessary to apply the recognition criteria to the separately identifiable components of a single transaction. [IAS 18.13]

For example, a contract to sell software may include an element related to after-sales servicing over a period of time. In such circumstances, it is appropriate to split the transaction into two components, a sale element and a servicing element, and to apply the revenue recognition criteria to each component individually.

In other circumstances, several related transactions may, in substance, be part of one larger transaction when the transactions are linked in such a way that the commercial effect cannot be understood without reference to the series of transactions as a whole. For example, a seller may enter into a contract to sell goods but agree in a separate contract to repurchase the goods at a later date. In such circumstances, the revenue recognition criteria are applied to both transactions together to determine if revenue is recognised. [IAS 18.13]

5.1 Sales arrangements in which the seller has partially performed its obligations

Failure to deliver one item or to perform one service specified by a sales arrangement does not necessarily preclude the immediate recognition of any revenue for that sales arrangement. IAS 18.13 notes that the revenue recognition criteria should be applied to the separately identifiable components of a single transaction. If all other recognition criteria are met, revenue can be recognised for a sales arrangement, notwithstanding the seller's remaining obligation for additional performance or delivery, as set out below.

Revenue from the sales arrangement can be recognised in full if the seller's remaining obligation is inconsequential or perfunctory. In this case, costs expected to be incurred to fulfil the remaining obligation must be reliably estimable and accrued when the revenue is recognised. A remaining performance obligation is not inconsequential or perfunctory if:

- it is essential to the functionality of the delivered products or services (for example, installation and/or training); or

- failure to complete the activities would result in the customer's receiving a full or a not insignificant partial refund or the right to reject the products delivered or services performed to date.

Additionally, a remaining performance obligation may not be inconsequential or perfunctory if:

- the seller does not have a demonstrated history of completing the remaining tasks in a timely manner and reliably estimating their costs;

- the cost or time to perform the remaining obligations for similar contracts historically has varied significantly from one instance to another;

- the skills or equipment required to complete the remaining activity are specialised or are not readily available in the marketplace;

- the cost of completing the obligation, or the fair value of the obligation, is more than insignificant in relation to such items as the total contract fee, gross profit and operating income;

- the period before the remaining obligation will be extinguished is lengthy; or

- the timing of payment of a portion of the sales price is coincident with completing performance of the remaining activity.

A portion of the revenue under the sales arrangement is also recognised when the seller has substantially fulfilled the terms of a separately identifiable component of the arrangement. The examples set out in the Appendix to IAS 18 illustrate a number of such circumstances (see later sections of this chapter).

5.2 Up-front fees

In general, unless up-front fees are paid in exchange for products delivered or services performed and, therefore, substantial risks and rewards have been transferred to the buyer in a separate transaction as described in IAS 18.13, such fees are not recognised as revenue up front but rather as unearned revenue (even if they are non-refundable). An up-front fee might not be regarded as relating to a separate transaction if, for example:

- the up-front fee is negotiated in conjunction with the pricing of other elements;
- the customer would ascribe a lower value, or no value, to the up-front activity in the absence of the performance of the other elements of the arrangement; or
- the vendor does not often sell the initial right or activities separately.

The up-front, non-refundable fees should be recognised as revenue over the life of the agreement(s) to which they relate, by reference to the goods and services supplied under the agreement(s).

Example 5.2A

Upfront payment by customer – lifetime membership fees in a private club

Company A owns and operates a private club. New members have an option of paying a single up-front, non-refundable lifetime membership fee rather than monthly or annual payments. That fee entitles members to most, but not all, of the club's services for the member's life. Lifetime members must pay separately for those services not covered by the lifetime membership fee. How should revenue from the lifetime membership fee be recognised?

Revenue should be recognised rateably over the time the individual may be expected to require the services of the club. IAS 18.20 requires that income from a service transaction be recognised by reference to the stage of completion of the transaction. The club member would not pay an up-front membership fee in the absence of on-going usage of the club's services. Moreover, the pricing of the lifetime membership fee and the monthly usage fee are interrelated.

Example 5.2B

Upfront payment by supplier – outsourcing contracts

In signing an outsourcing contract with a client, a service provider may make an up-front payment to the client. How should up-front payments made to clients by service providers in the context of outsourcing contracts be treated?

The amount of the up-front payment and the price charged for the service provided are generally part of a global pricing agreement for that service. To the extent that the up-front payment does not correspond to an identifiable service received by the service provider from the client, or to the reimbursement by the service provider of costs necessary for the contract incurred by the client, the amount of the up-front payment should be accounted for by the service provider as a reduction of revenue.

As a result, the up-front payment would be accounted for by the service provider as an asset (rebate paid in advance) and amortised against revenue over the contract period.

5.3 IFRIC 13 *Customer Loyalty Programmes*

Entities use customer loyalty programmes to incentivise customers to buy their goods or services. Customers buying goods or services are granted customer award credits (often described as 'points') by the entity, which can be redeemed for awards such as free or discounted goods or services.

IFRIC 13 *Customer Loyalty Programmes* addresses the accounting by the entity that grants award credits. It applies to customer loyalty award credits that:

[IFRIC 13.3]

- entities grant to their customers as part of an IAS 18 sales transaction (a sale of goods, rendering of services or use by the customer of entity assets); and
- the customers can redeem in future for free or discounted goods or services, subject to meeting any further qualifying conditions.

Customer loyalty programmes operate in a number of ways. Customers may not be permitted to redeem award credits until they have accumulated a specified minimum number or value. Award credits may be linked to individual purchases or groups of purchases, or to continued custom over a specified period. Entities may operate their own customer loyalty programmes or may participate in programmes operated by third parties. And the awards offered may include goods or services supplied by the entity itself and/or rights to claim goods or services from a third party. [IFRIC 13.2]

IFRIC 13 will also apply where the sales transaction giving rise to award credits involves the entity receiving consideration from an intermediate party rather than directly from the customer to whom it grants the award credits. For example, credit card providers may provide services and grant award credits to credit card holders but receive consideration for doing so from vendors accepting payment by credit card. [IFRIC 13.BC4]

The Interpretation is not applicable to 'money off' vouchers that are distributed free of charge, or any other sort of promotion that is not connected to sales of an entity's goods or services. It also does not cover the accounting for the goods acquired initially or the accounting for the award credits in the books of the customer.

IFRIC 13 requires entities to account for award credits supplied in the context of a customer loyalty programme as a separately identifiable component of the sales transaction(s) in which they are granted (applying the requirements of IAS 18.13). The fair value of the consideration received or receivable is allocated between the award credits and the other components of the sale. [IFRIC 13.5] The consideration allocated to the award credits is measured by reference to their fair value, being the amount for which the award credits could be sold separately. [IFRIC 13.6]

Accordingly, when accounting treatment for customer loyalty programmes, an entity is required to:

- allocate some of the consideration received or receivable from the sales transaction to the award credits and defer the recognition of that revenue; and

- recognise its share of revenue allocated to the award credits when it has fulfilled its obligations in respect of the award credits. Note that the amount and timing of revenue will typically be different depending on whether the awards are supplied by the entity itself (as principal) or by a third party (with the entity acting as an agent in respect of the award credits).

5.3.1 *Measuring the fair value of award credits*

The consideration allocated to award credits is measured by reference to their fair value – the amount for which the award credits could be sold separately. If the fair value is not directly observable, it must be estimated, e.g. by reference to the fair value of the awards for which they could be redeemed. That fair value is adjusted to take into account the fair value of awards that would be offered to customers who have not earned award credits from an initial sales transaction and the proportion of the award credits not expected to be redeemed. [IFRIC 13.AG1 – AG2]

Example 5.3.1A

Impact of awards granted without an initial sales transaction

All visitors to Supermarket B can pick up a voucher entitling them to a reduction of £1 off the price of Product X, irrespective of whether they make any purchases. Customers who make a purchase receive a voucher entitling them to a reduction of £5 off the price of Product X. Only one voucher can be used for any purchase of Product X.

The £1 vouchers are outside the scope of IFRIC 13 because they are distributed free of charge.

In assessing the fair value of the £5 vouchers for the purposes of IFRIC 13, Supermarket B will take into account both the number of vouchers not expected to be redeemed, and the fact that customers not making a purchase could still have claimed a £1 voucher. Although the £5 vouchers are not sold separately, it is clear that no customer would rationally pay more than £4 for such a voucher, because it would instead be cheaper to buy Product X using one of the free £1 vouchers. Thus, the fair value of the £5 vouchers will not exceed £4, and may be considerably lower depending on the proportion of vouchers expected to be redeemed.

If there is a range of awards that customers may choose from, the fair value of the award credits will reflect the fair values of the range of available awards, weighted in proportion to the frequency with which each award is expected to be selected. [IFRIC 13.AG2]

A range of estimation techniques may be available for the purposes of estimating the fair value of awards. The Application Guidance to IFRIC 13 gives as an example the scenario in which a third party will supply the awards and the entity pays the third party for each award credit it grants: in these circumstances, the entity could estimate the fair value of the award credits by reference to the amount it pays the third party, adding a reasonable profit margin. Importantly, judgement is required to select and apply the estimation technique that satisfies the requirements of IFRIC 13.6 and is most appropriate in the circumstances. [IFRIC 13.AG3]

As noted above IFRIC 13 states that award credits shall be measured '**by reference to** their fair value'. But it does not mandate any particular method for allocating amounts to the award credits. In particular, it does not specify whether the amount allocated to the award credits should be:

[IFRIC 13.BC14]

(a) equal to their fair value (irrespective of the fair values of the other components); or

(b) a proportion of the total consideration based on the fair value of the award credits relative to the fair values of the other components of the sale.

This is because the IFRIC decided that the Interpretation should not be more prescriptive than IAS 18, which does not specify which of these methods should be applied, or in what circumstances. Management must apply judgement in deciding to select one or other method.

The former approach involves estimating the fair value of award credits (e.g. by reference to the goods and services that may be selected, as discussed above), and then allocates any residual revenue to the original sale. This is illustrated in **example 5.3.1B** below.

Example 5.3.1B

Valuing award credits by reference to goods and services that may be selected

Customers buying Product A from Company X for £100 receive an award credit. The award credit can be used to obtain Product B free of charge, or to purchase Product C at a discounted price of £10.

The normal selling prices of Products B and C are:

Product B £5

Product C £17

Company X estimates that 60% of customers will select Product B, and 40% will select Product C.

The fair value of the award credit may be estimated as:

(60% x £5) + (40% x [£17 – £10]) = £5.80

Accordingly, the revenue recognised in respect of Product A is £100.00 – £5.80, i.e. £94.20.

An alternative approach is to make an allocation based on relative fair value as illustrated in **example 5.3.1C** below.

Example 5.3.1C

Valuing award credits by reference to relative fair values

The facts are the same as in **example 5.3.1B.**, but Company X decides to use a relative fair value approach to allocate revenue to the award credits.

The normal selling price of Product A, after taking into account discounts that are usually offered but which are not available during this promotion, is £95.

The total revenue of £100 is allocated between Product A and the award credit by reference to their relative fair values of £95 and £5.80 respectively. Accordingly:

Revenue for Product A = £100 x (£95 ÷[£95 + £5.80]) = £94.25

Revenue for award credit = £100 x (£5.80 ÷[£95 + £5.80]) = £5.75

5.3.2 *Awards supplied by the reporting entity*

Where the entity will supply the awards itself, it recognises the consideration allocated to award credits as revenue when award credits are redeemed and it fulfils its obligations to supply awards. The amount of revenue recognised is based on the number of award credits that have been redeemed in exchange for awards, relative to the total number expected to be redeemed. [IFRIC 13.7]

5.3.2.1 *Changes in expectations*

After granting award credits, the entity may revise its expectations about the proportion that will be redeemed. The change in expectations does not affect the consideration that the entity has received for supplying awards (this is fixed at the outset), but it affects the amount of revenue recognised in respect of award credits that are redeemed in the period. The change in expectations is thus accounted for as a change in estimate in the period of change and future periods, in accordance with IAS 8.36 (see **4.2** in **chapter 4**). [IFRIC 13.BC16]

Example 5.3.2.1

Awards supplied by the entity

[IFRIC 13 Illustrative Example 1]

A grocery retailer operates a customer loyalty programme. It grants programme members loyalty points when they spend a specified amount on groceries. Programme members can redeem the points for further groceries. The points have no expiry date. In one period, the entity grants 100 points. Management expects 80 of these points to be redeemed. Management estimates the fair value of each loyalty point to be one currency unit (CU1), and defers revenue of CU100.

Year 1

At the end of the first year, 40 of the points have been redeemed in exchange for groceries, i.e. half of those expected to be redeemed. The entity recognises revenue of (40 points / 80[1] points) × CU100 = CU50.

Year 2

In the second year, management revises its expectations. It now expects 90 points to be redeemed altogether.

During the second year, 41 points are redeemed, bringing the total number redeemed to 40[2]+ 41 = 81 points. The cumulative revenue that the entity recognises is (81 points / 90[3] points) × CU100 = CU90. The entity has recognised revenue of CU50 in the first year, so it recognises CU40 in the second year.

Year 3

In the third year, a further nine points are redeemed, taking the total number of points redeemed to 81 + 9 = 90. Management continues to expect that only 90 points will ever be redeemed, i.e. that no more points will be redeemed after the third year. So the cumulative revenue to date is (90 points / 90[4] points) × CU100 = CU100. The entity has already recognised CU90 of revenue (CU50 in the first year and CU40 in the second year). So it recognises the remaining CU10 in the third year. All of the revenue initially deferred has now been recognised.

[1] total number of points expected to be redeemed

[2] number of points redeemed in year 1

[3] revised estimate of total number of points expected to be redeemed

[4] total number of points still expected to be redeemed

It is possible, particularly if there are changes in expectations regarding redemption rates or revised cost expectations, for the unavoidable costs of meeting award obligations to exceed the consideration received and receivable for them (i.e. including any further consideration receivable when the customer redeems the award credits). Where this occurs, the entity has onerous contracts and a liability will be needed for the excess in accordance with IAS 37. [IFRIC 13.9]

The interpretation does not imply that award credits need to be accounted for on an individual transaction-by-transaction basis. Varying degrees of aggregation by the accounting period in which such awards are generated may be appropriate depending on the circumstances, as confirmed in *IFRIC Update* in May 2007.

5.3.3 *Awards supplied by a third party*

If a third party supplies the awards, the entity is required to assess whether it is collecting the consideration allocated to the award credits on its own account or on behalf of the third party. In other words, it much assess whether it is acting as principal in the transaction or as an agent for the third party. [IFRIC 13.8]

There is no detailed guidance in IFRSs on identifying agency relationships. Determining whether a seller is an agent or principal requires judgement and will depend on the particular facts and circumstances of each arrangement, and some relevant factors are discussed at **3.1** above.

Where an entity is collecting consideration on behalf of a third party it:

[IFRIC 13.8]

- measures its revenue as the net amount retained on its own account, i.e. the difference between the consideration allocated to the award credits and the amount payable to the third party for supplying the awards; and
- recognises this net amount as revenue when the third party is obliged to supply the awards and entitled to receive consideration for doing so. (These events may occur as soon as the award credits are granted. Alternatively, if the customer can choose to claim awards from either the entity or a third party, these events may occur only when the customer chooses to claim awards from the third party.)

Where an entity is collecting consideration on its own account, it measures its revenue as the gross consideration allocated to the award credits and recognises the revenue when it fulfils its obligations in respect of the awards. [IFRIC 13.9]

Example 5.3.3

Awards supplied by a third party

[IFRIC 13 Illustrative Example 2]

A retailer of electrical goods participates in a customer loyalty programme operated by an airline. It grants programme members one air travel point with each CU1 they spend on electrical goods. Programme members can redeem the points for air travel with the airline, subject to availability. The retailer pays the airline CU0.009 for each point.

In one period, the retailer sells electrical goods for consideration totalling CU1 million. It grants 1 million points.

Allocation of consideration to travel points

The retailer estimates that the fair value of a point is CU0.01. It allocates to the points 1 million × CU0.01 = CU10,000 of the consideration it has received from the sales of its electrical goods.

Revenue recognition

Having granted the points, the retailer has fulfilled its obligations to the customer. The airline is obliged to supply the awards and entitled to receive consideration for doing so. Therefore the retailer recognises revenue from the points when it sells the electrical goods.

Revenue measurement

If the retailer has collected the consideration allocated to the points on its own account, it measures its revenue as the gross CU10,000 allocated to them. It separately recognises the CU9,000 paid or payable to the airline as an expense. If the retailer has collected the consideration on behalf of the airline, i.e. as an agent for the airline, it measures its revenue as the net amount it retains on its own account. This amount of revenue is the difference between the CU10,000 consideration allocated to the points and the CU9,000 passed on to the airline.

Where, at the time of the original transaction, it is made clear to the customer that a third party will be obliged to supply the awards, it is likely that the entity is collecting consideration on behalf of that third party. Conversely, where the customer believes that the entity itself is obliged to supply the awards, it is likely that the entity is collecting consideration on its own account.

5.3.4 *Effective date and transition*

The Interpretation applies for annual periods beginning on or after 1 July 2008, but earlier application is permitted. Where an entity chooses to apply the Interpretation for a period beginning before 1 July 2008, that fact is to be disclosed. [IFRIC 13.10] Where adoption of the Interpretation requires a change of accounting policy, this is accounted for in accordance with IAS 8. [IFRIC 13.11]

> Where an entity (acting as a principal) has previously recognised revenue for award credits at the time of the original transaction, and provided for the expected future costs of meeting awards, adoption of IFRIC 13 is likely to involve a change of accounting policy.

6 Recognition criteria – sale of goods

Revenue from the sale of goods should be recognised when all of the following criteria have been satisfied:

[IAS 18.14]

- the entity has transferred to the buyer the significant risks and rewards of ownership of the goods;
- the entity retains neither continuing managerial involvement to the degree usually associated with ownership nor effective control over the goods sold;
- the amount of revenue can be measured reliably;
- it is probable that the economic benefits associated with the transaction will flow to the entity; and
- the costs incurred or to be incurred in respect of the transaction can be measured reliably.

UK

> *Under UK GAAP, FRS 5* Reporting the Substance of Transactions *allows a partial sale treatment where a non-financial asset is sold with an agreement to repurchase that asset in a substantially depreciated form (e.g. the sale of a car by a car dealer whereby the dealer agrees to repurchase the car at a fixed price after three years). Under FRS 5, a sale is recorded, but an asset (stock) and a liability equal to the present value of the obligation to repurchase may be retained in the balance sheet (i.e. statement of financial position).*

There is no equivalent treatment in IFRSs. Instead, a detailed analysis of the substance of the arrangement is needed to determine whether the appropriate accounting treatment is sale of the total asset (under IAS 18) or operating or finance lease treatment (under IAS 17 Leases). Where a sale is recorded, the entity would consider whether the repurchase option amounts to an onerous contract under IAS 37.

IAS 18 offers no guidance on how to determine whether a contract is for the supply of goods or services, and in some circumstances careful judgement may be required. In particular, merely because a contract requires items to be supplied that have not yet been manufactured, it does not necessarily follow that the contract is for manufacturing services.

6.1. Risks and rewards of ownership

The circumstances of the transaction must be examined to assess when a seller has transferred the significant risks and rewards of ownership to the buyer. Generally, the transfer of the risks and rewards of ownership coincides with the transfer of the legal title or the passing of possession to the buyer, as for example with most retail sales. Sometimes, however, the transfer of risks and rewards of ownership occurs at a different time from the transfer of legal title or the passing of possession. [IAS 18.15]

If significant risks of ownership are retained by the seller, the transaction is not a sale and revenue is not recognised. Such significant risks of ownership may be retained in a number of ways. Examples given by IAS 18 are:

[IAS 18.16]

(a) when the seller retains an obligation for unsatisfactory performance not covered by normal warranty provisions;

(b) when the receipt of the revenue from a particular sale is contingent on the derivation of revenue by the buyer from its sale of the goods;

(c) when the goods are shipped subject to installation and the installation is a significant part of the contract which has not yet been completed by the entity; and

(d) when the buyer has the right to rescind the purchase for a reason specified in the sales contract and the seller is uncertain about the probability of return.

If only an insignificant risk of ownership is retained by the seller, the transaction is a sale and revenue is recognised. For example, solely to protect the collectibility of the amount due, a seller may retain the legal title to goods. Providing the seller has transferred the significant risks and rewards of ownership, the transaction is a sale and revenue is recognised. Similarly, an insignificant risk of ownership may be retained by the seller in a retail sale when a refund is offered if the customer is not satisfied. Revenue in such cases is recognised at the time of sale provided the seller can reliably estimate future returns and recognises a liability and corresponding reduction in revenue for returns based on previous experience and other relevant factors. [IAS 18.17]

The examples below illustrate some common situations in which the risks have or have not been transferred.

Example 6.1A

Warranty

An entity manufactures an item of customised machinery and gives a three-month warranty covering the cost of any adjustments or repairs subsequent to delivery. The product is likely to have some serious problems that will need to be remedied after delivery, due to the need to suit the particular customer's environment. It is not possible to estimate with reliability the cost to the seller of carrying out any such adjustments or repairs. Under the terms of the sales contract, title passes on delivery.

The risks and rewards of ownership do not pass until the three-month period has expired, since it is not possible to estimate, and therefore accrue, any costs of repairs or adjustments, which could be material.

Example 6.1B

Magazines distributed on the basis of sale or return

A magazine distributor sells and delivers magazines to a local shop. If the local shop does not sell the magazines, they are returned to the distributor for a refund or credit. It is not possible to estimate reliably at the time the magazines are delivered how many magazines will be unsold.

The risks and rewards of ownership do not pass from the distributor until the shop has sold the magazines, since the receipt of revenue by the distributor is contingent on the sale of the magazines by the shop.

Example 6.1C

Equipment sold subject to right of return

A heavy equipment manufacturer sells an item of machinery to a customer who is anticipating being awarded a particular road-building contract from the Government. In the sales contract, the seller gives the customer the right to return the machinery if the customer does not win the contract. There is no way to estimate reliably whether the customer will return the machinery.

The risks and rewards of ownership do not pass until the customer has been granted the road-building contract from the Government.

Example 6.1D

Retail guarantee

A retail shop offers a lifetime guarantee on its products. A customer may return any item for any reason at any time and have its money refunded. Based on reliable, historical data, 0.95 per cent of sales are returned under this policy.

Based on historical data, the shop retains only insignificant risks and rewards of ownership by offering this guarantee. Provided that the other revenue recognition criteria are met, revenue should be recognised at the time of sale and a corresponding provision of 0.95 per cent of the amount of the sale should be recognised to cover the cost of expected sales returns.

Example 6.1E

Retention of title

As a matter of policy, a manufacturer writes its sales contracts in such a way that legal title does not pass on delivery but when consideration for the goods is received. A sale is made and the related goods are delivered to a customer who is not a particular credit risk.

The risks and rewards of ownership have passed even though title has not. Transfer of title may be an indicator that the risks and rewards of ownership have passed to the buyer, but it is not a required condition. Therefore, provided that the other revenue recognition criteria are met, revenue can be recognised if the only rights that a seller retains with the title are those enabling recovery of the goods in the event of customer default on payment.

Example 6.1F

'Trade loading' and 'channel stuffing'

Sometimes manufacturers or dealers try to enhance the apparent volume of their sales, profits, and/or market share by inducing their wholesale customers to buy more product than they can promptly resell. The result is accelerated, but not increased, volume, because the wholesalers' inventories become bloated and their future orders from the manufacturers are reduced. This practice is known as 'trade loading' or 'channel stuffing'.

Entities may induce wholesale customers to buy more product than they can promptly resell for reasons other than enhancing the appearance of their financial figures (e.g. to improve cash flows or to spread production more evenly throughout the year when sales are seasonal). If the revenue recognition criteria in IAS 18.14 for sales of goods are met, the revenue should be recognised. In many situations, however, products sold during 'channel stuffing' programmes are merely held by the wholesaler to be returned in a future accounting period when it is determined the products cannot be sold to the end user. Assuming the criteria in IAS 18.14 are met, which will require that the level of returns can be estimated reliably, revenue is recorded net of the expected returns. Therefore, management must estimate the amount of product to be returned. Historical return rates may not capture appropriately the high level of returns usually related to 'channel stuffing' programmes. If the level of returns cannot be estimated reliably, revenue should not be recognised.

Example 6.1G

Unlimited right of return

Company A distributes CDs and DVDs. Its key customers are department stores. It also sells to small shops. The sales agreement with key customers allows these customers to return any slow-moving goods, but there is no definition of slow-moving in the agreement. The returns could result in replacement of the returned goods with other CDs and DVDs or return of cash. For customers other than the key customers, the sales agreement limits their returns of slow-moving goods to not more than 10 per cent of purchases. In both cases, based on experience, Company A is able to make a reliable estimate of the amount of returns. How should Company A account for its revenues from (a) key customers (whose right to return goods is unlimited) and (b) other customers (whose right of return is limited)?

A condition for recognising revenue from the sale of goods in IAS 18.14(a) is that the entity has transferred to the buyer the significant risks and rewards of ownership of the goods. In this case, both classes of customers have assumed all of the significant rewards of ownership of the goods, because they have an unrestricted right to resell the goods. Furthermore, because a reliable estimate of the amount of returns can be made for both classes of customers, the extent to which the buyer has assumed the significant risks also can be measured for both classes of customers. Therefore, revenue should be recognised on initial delivery of the goods in an amount that reflects a reduction for the estimated amount to be returned.

The answer would be different for the key customers if the effect of their right to return all slow-moving goods could not be measured. In those circumstances, Company A would have retained an immeasurable risk of marketability and obsolescence. The condition in IAS 18.14(a) would not be met, and Company A would recognise revenue on a consignment basis (i.e. recognise revenue when the key customers resell the goods to third-party customers).

Example 6.1H

Customer acceptance provision

A sales contract may give the customer the unilateral right, for a certain period of time after delivery, to accept or reject the goods. The appropriate point for revenue recognition will depend on the probability of customer acceptance. If the seller is uncertain about the probability of acceptance, revenue recognition should not occur until the earlier of customer acceptance and expiry of the acceptance period. If the probability of customer acceptance is uncertain, the risks of ownership must be regarded as remaining with the seller.

Example 6.1I

Sale of gift certificates

Gift certificates sold by a retailer can be used by the holder to buy merchandise up to the amount indicated on the gift certificate.

Sales revenue should not be recognised for gift certificates at the time that the gift certificate is purchased. Gift certificates represent prepayments of cash that can be redeemed for merchandise at a later date. Revenue is not recognised until the gift certificate is redeemed for merchandise. Instead, the retailer recognises the proceeds from gift certificates as a liability, representing the obligation to deliver merchandise at a future time.

Example 6.1J

Sale of products with a time restriction on resale or use

Company A, a manufacturer of designer clothing, ships clothing for the spring season to customers (clothing retailers) in December 20X1. While the customers take title to the goods when they receive them, the terms of the sales prohibit the customers from displaying or selling the clothing until 15 February 20X2. The terms of the arrangement are such that payment generally is not due until the restriction is lifted. When is revenue recognised — when the goods are delivered (20X1) or when the restriction on resale expires (20X2)?

The limitation on when the product can be sold would not, of itself, preclude revenue recognition in 20X1. IAS 18.14(a) prohibits revenue recognition when goods are sold, until the seller has transferred to the buyer the significant risks and rewards of ownership of the goods. In the above situation, the timing is short compared to the life cycle of the inventory and the timing of the restriction does not affect the value of the inventory to be sold. If the timing was longer, however, for example until the summer season, a review of whether the significant rewards of ownership had been transferred should be performed.

6.1.1 *Impact of national law*

The transfer of the risks and rewards of ownership is determined on an individual basis. National law may affect the timing of such transfer and, therefore, the timing of revenue recognition can differ between countries. This does not mean that different revenue recognition criteria are applied in different countries but, rather, the recognition criteria are met at different times in different countries. The principle is that the significant risks and rewards of ownership must have passed from the seller to the buyer. [IAS 18(Appendix)]

Examples of legal provisions that can affect the transfer of risks and rewards and, therefore, the timing of revenue recognition, include:

- in some jurisdictions, title does not legally transfer until the buyer obtains physical possession of the goods; and
- a 'cooling off' period is required in property transactions (often residential property transactions) in certain jurisdictions, during which the buyer has an absolute legal right to rescind the transaction.

6.1.2 *When are risks and rewards transferred?*

Products may be delivered based on oral arrangements (e.g. either a telephone call from a customer or walk-in business) or on the basis of a detailed contract with specified shipping terms, with many variations in between. The judgement as to when all risks and rewards of ownership have been transferred is a determination that should consider the laws of the jurisdiction in which the sale is made, particularly if the contract does not specify shipping terms. In complex circumstances, it may be useful to obtain the advice of legal counsel regarding the rights and obligations of the parties.

The revenue recognition criteria in IAS 18 should be evaluated based on the mutually understood terms of the transaction. IAS 18 does not require a written sales agreement as a condition for revenue recognition. What is required is that the seller has transferred the significant risks and rewards of ownership of the goods to the buyer. This means that both the buyer and the seller should have a clear understanding of all terms of the transaction, including pricing, payment terms, return rights, shipping, installation and warranty rights. Where there is a written sales agreement, these terms should be clearly set out. Where an entity routinely provides goods or services based on an oral agreement, there is an expectation that, where necessary, the entity will have clearly articulated its policies and terms of sale to its customers through brochures, store signage, notices on invoices, advertising and similar written means.

Although IAS 18 does not require a written contract as evidence of an agreement, if such a contract is being prepared and has not yet been signed, this may be evidence that agreement has not yet been reached. Great care should be taken before recognising revenue in such circumstances, as the apparent absence of a contractual understanding between the parties may make it unlikely that the conditions in IAS 18.14 have been met.

Example 6.1.2A

Goods shipped FOB shipping point, but seller arranges shipping

When goods are shipped 'free on board' (FOB) shipping point, title passes to the buyer when the goods are shipped and the buyer is responsible for any loss in transit. On the other hand, when goods are shipped FOB destination, title does not pass to the buyer until delivery and the seller is responsible for any loss in transit.

Company A sells goods FOB shipping point and it is clear that title transfers to the buyer at the time of shipment. Company A's business practice is to arrange for shipping the goods to the buyer and to deal directly with the shipping company. Company A bills the buyer for the shipping costs separately from the product. Company A's business practice is also that if there is any damage or physical loss during transit, Company A provides the buyer with replacement products at no additional cost. If the loss or damage in transit is substantial, Company A's insurance would cover all or most of the loss.

In these circumstances, Company A may not recognise revenue at the time its products have been shipped. While title has passed, Company A has retained a significant risk of ownership (i.e. responsibility for damage or loss in transit). The fact that Company A's insurance would cover a substantial loss is evidence that it has managed its risk, but Company A has still retained the risk. The criterion for recognising revenue set out in IAS 18.14(a) has not been met.

Example 6.1.2B

Goods shipped FOB destination, but shipping company assumes risk of loss

Company A sells goods 'free on board' (FOB) destination, which means that title does not pass to the buyer until delivery and Company A is responsible for any loss in transit. To protect itself from loss, Company A contracts with the shipping company for the shipping company to assume total risk of loss while the goods are in transit.

In these circumstances, Company A may not recognise revenue when the goods are shipped. While Company A has managed its risk, it has not transferred risk to the buyer. Therefore, the criterion in IAS 18.14(a) has not been met until the goods have been delivered.

Example 6.1.2C

Seller arranges for manufacturer to ship directly to buyer ('drop shipment')

A seller who arranges for direct shipping of products from a manufacturer to a buyer must first consider whether it should report revenue on a gross or net basis. This determination will depend on whether the seller is acting as a principal or an agent (see **3.1** above).

If the seller arranges to have the manufacturer ship the products directly to the buyer, and the seller is a principal rather than an agent, the seller should recognise revenue as if it had shipped the product(s) itself. Therefore, if those terms specify FOB shipping point, the seller recognises revenue when the manufacturer ships the goods. If those terms specify FOB destination, the seller recognises revenue when the buyer receives the goods.

Example 6.1.2D

Written sales agreement has expired but shipments continue

An entity's normal practice is to obtain written sales agreements signed by the buyer. The agreement has a fixed termination date and no provision for automatic extension. The seller has continued to ship product to a customer after the written agreement expires. Should revenue be recognised?

This is essentially a legal question as to what the seller's and buyer's rights are in the circumstances. The expiry of the agreement may indicate that the seller has retained significant risks of ownership, that the amount of revenue cannot be measured reliably, or that collectibility (flow of benefits to the seller) is not probable. If any of those is the case, IAS 18.14 would preclude revenue recognition.

Even if it is determined that revenue should be recognised in this case, a question arises as to the measurement of the revenue. If the vendor has a history of providing price or other concessions as an inducement for renewal of a sales agreement, that practice must be taken into account in measuring the revenue from the product shipped after the sales agreement has expired.

Example 6.1.2E

Vendor installation – customer acceptance

Company A sells a machine and is required to install it on the customer's premises. The sales contract requires the customer to inspect and accept or reject the installation. Based on A's experience, the probability of customer acceptance of the equipment after installation is completed is very high. Should revenue be recognised (1) when the machine is delivered (if necessary, with a provision for estimated additional installation costs) or (2) after customer acceptance?

This depends on whether the transaction can be unbundled into two separately identifiable components of revenue: delivery of the machine and its installation. If the installation cannot be unbundled, i.e. the installation cannot be accounted for separately from the sale of the machine, then revenue should be recognised on delivery of the machine only if, among other criteria:

- it is probable that the customer will accept the machine (if relevant — see **example 6.1H**); and
- the installation process is simple in nature, for example the installation of a factory tested television receiver which only requires unpacking and connection of power and antennae (see **example 6.6B**).

The Appendix to IAS 18 provides additional examples which illustrate the appropriate time to recognise revenue from the sale of goods. For convenience, these examples are reproduced in **6.6** below.

6.2 Continuing managerial involvement and effective control

This criterion generally goes hand-in-hand with the risks and rewards of ownership (see **6.1**). It would be unusual for an entity to retain managerial involvement to the degree usually associated with ownership or to retain effective control over goods without retaining the risks and rewards of ownership. Each situation should, however, be considered individually. It may be the case that continuing managerial involvement is not to the degree usually associated with ownership. For example, a software consultancy firm may install a software system for a client and then oversee and manage the computer department that uses the software. This outsourcing of managerial control over the computer department, which includes the newly-installed software, does not necessarily prohibit revenue recognition for the provision of the software. It will be necessary to consider the terms of the agreement to determine whether the risks and rewards stemming from the software have been transferred to the client.

6.3 Reliable measurement of revenue

Until the amount of revenue to be received can be measured reliably, revenue cannot be recognised. This does not imply, however, that the consideration must have been received in all cases for revenue to be recognised. Generally, consideration will be agreed in advance and the revenue from a sale will be recognised when all of the other recognition criteria are met.

Example 6.3

Vendor installation – settlement terms

A sales contract requires payment of 90 per cent on completion of the delivery and installation of a machine, and the remaining 10 per cent at the earlier of customer acceptance or 90 days. In this particular case, the seller has determined that it is not appropriate to account for installation as a separate component.

In this case, the arrangements for customer acceptance do not affect the amount of revenue to be received, only the timing of payment. Therefore, those arrangements do not affect the timing of recognition of revenue.

Since installation is not a component of revenue to be accounted for separately, 100 per cent of the revenue should be recognised when the significant risks and rewards of ownership of the machine have been transferred to the buyer. Depending on the particular facts and circumstances, this will either be on delivery (with an appropriate accrual for any estimated additional installation costs to be incurred) or on completion of installation (see **example 6.1.2E** for further guidance).

The recognition of revenue is not affected by the settlement terms unless there is uncertainty regarding the flow of the economic benefits related to the transaction to the entity.

6.4 Probability of receipt of economic benefits

Revenue cannot be recognised unless it is probable that the economic benefits or consideration associated with the transaction will flow to the entity. For example, it may not be probable that consideration will be received from a particular customer due to exchange controls in the country in which the customer operates, which limit the amount of currency that can be remitted from that country. In such cases, when it is not probable that the consideration will be received, revenue is not recognised until the consideration is received.

If revenue has been recognised and it later emerges that the related consideration will not be collectible, an expense for bad debts is recognised rather than reversing the related revenue. [IAS 18.18]

6.5 Measurement of costs incurred related to the transaction

When the costs incurred or to be incurred in a transaction cannot be measured reliably, revenue is not recognised. This criterion flows from the matching principle. Under this principle, when revenue is recognised, the related expenses are also recognised. A common example of the type of expense that should be estimated and accrued is warranty costs. If such costs cannot be estimated reliably, revenue is deferred until the amount of such expenses can be more reliably estimated or have been incurred. In these circumstances, any consideration already received from the sale of goods is recognised as a liability. [IAS 18.19]

6.6 Additional examples

The following examples of the application of the revenue recognition criteria for the sale of goods are taken from the Appendix to IAS 18. Although the Appendix is not part of the Standard, it provides useful application guidance. Unless stated otherwise, the examples generally assume that the amount of revenue can be measured reliably, it is probable that the economic benefits will flow to the entity and the costs incurred or to be incurred can be measured reliably.

Example 6.6A

'Bill-and-hold' sales, in which delivery is delayed at the buyer's request, but the buyer takes title and accepts billing

[IAS 18 Appendix Example 1]

Revenue is recognised when the buyer takes title, provided that:

- it is probable that delivery will be made;
- the item is on hand, identified and ready for delivery to the buyer at the time the sale is recognised;
- the buyer specifically acknowledges the deferred delivery instructions; and
- the usual payment terms apply.

Revenue is not recognised when there is simply an intention to acquire or manufacture the goods in time for delivery.

Example 6.6A, as extracted from the Appendix to IAS 18, describes a bill-and-hold sale in which revenue would be recognised on completion of manufacture if shipping is delayed at the buyer's request. But the facts in that example are that the buyer has taken title and accepts billing. If this were not the case, so that the seller retains title and the buyer is not obligated to pay until the goods are delivered, then revenue should not be recognised until the goods are delivered. This is the case even if the order is non-cancellable.

Consistent with the revenue recognition criteria set out in **example 6.6A**:

- revenue recognition at completion of manufacture may be inappropriate if there is no fixed delivery schedule or if the delivery schedule is significantly longer than those customary in the industry; and

- revenue recognition at completion of manufacture would not be appropriate if the seller, rather than the buyer, has requested that the transaction be on a bill-and-hold basis. Also, the buyer must have a substantial business purpose for ordering the goods on a bill-and-hold basis.

Example 6.6B

Goods shipped subject to conditions

[IAS 18 Appendix Example 2]

(*a*) *Installation and inspection*

Revenue is normally recognised when the buyer accepts delivery, and installation and inspection are complete. However, revenue is recognised immediately upon the buyer's acceptance of delivery when:

- the installation process is simple in nature, e.g. the installation of a factory-tested television receiver which only requires unpacking and connection of power and antennae; or

- the inspection is performed only for the purposes of final determination of contract prices, e.g. shipments of iron ore, sugar or soya beans.

(*b*) *On approval when the buyer has negotiated a limited right of return*

If there is uncertainty about the possibility of return, revenue is recognised when the shipment has been formally accepted by the buyer or the goods have been delivered and the time period for rejection has elapsed.

(*c*) *Consignment sales under which the recipient (buyer) undertakes to sell the goods on behalf of the shipper (seller)*

Revenue is recognised by the shipper when the goods are sold by the recipient to a third party.

(*d*) *Cash on delivery sales*

Revenue is recognised when delivery is made and cash is received by the seller or its agent.

Example 6.6C

Lay away sales under which the goods are delivered only when the buyer makes the final payment in a series of instalments

[IAS 18 Appendix Example 3]

Revenue from such sales is recognised when the goods are delivered. However, when experience indicates that most such sales are consummated, revenue may be recognised when a significant deposit is received, provided that the goods are on hand, identified and ready for delivery to the buyer.

The determination of whether a deposit is considered significant is a matter of careful judgement, based on all of the relevant facts and circumstances. Factors to consider in making this determination include, but are not limited to, the following:

- the entity's policy on lay away sales, including the amount of deposit generally required;
- the nature and amount of the goods sold; and
- the history of lay away sales, including the extent to which sales are consummated.

In any case, the final conclusion should be supported by sufficient objective evidence.

If a customer forfeits its deposit under a lay away programme, so that the seller is entitled to keep the deposit without having any further obligations, the retained deposit will satisfy the definition of revenue in IAS 18.7 and should be presented as such. The fact that the seller has retained the deposit without having delivered any goods is an event that is part of the ordinary course of business of a lay away seller. If forfeitures are significant, it may be appropriate to disclose the amount separately.

If such forfeited deposits do not remain the property of the seller, but rather must be remitted to the Government under 'escheat laws', then no revenue is recognised. As noted above, the deposit for lay away sales is normally recorded as a liability, not revenue. Sometimes the seller may recognise revenue, however, when a 'significant deposit is received'. If that is the case, and the seller will be required to remit any forfeited deposits to the government, the seller should establish an allowance for estimated forfeitures at the time the revenue is recognised. If no such reliable estimate can be made, no revenue should be recognised.

Example 6.6D

Orders when payment (or partial payment) is received in advance of delivery for goods not currently held in inventory (e.g. the goods are still to be manufactured or will be delivered directly to the customer from a third party)

[IAS 18 Appendix Example 4]

Revenue is recognised when the goods are delivered to the buyer.

Example 6.6E

Sale and repurchase agreements (other than swap transactions), under which the seller concurrently agrees to repurchase the same goods at a later date, or when the seller has a call option to repurchase, or the buyer has a put option to require the repurchase, by the seller, of the goods

[IAS 18 Appendix Example 5]

For a sale and repurchase agreement on an asset other than a financial asset, the terms of the agreement should be analysed to ascertain whether, in substance, the seller has transferred the risks and rewards of ownership to the buyer and hence revenue is recognised. When the seller has retained the risks and rewards of ownership, even though legal title has been transferred, the transaction is a financing arrangement and does not give rise to revenue. (IAS 39 *Financial Instruments: Recognition and Measurement* applies for a sale and repurchase agreement on a financial asset – see **chapter 19**.)

In the circumstances described in **example 6.6E**, if the seller has an option (meaning a right but not an obligation) to buy the goods back at a fixed price for a fixed period of time, the seller has retained an important benefit of ownership, namely the ability to profit from the difference between the strike price of the option and the fair value of the goods at the time the option is exercised. The significance of this benefit is to be considered at the date the transaction is being reviewed for the determination of whether to recognise revenue. If the benefits retained are significant, revenue should not be recognised until expiry of the repurchase period. On the other hand, if the seller has the right to buy the goods back at market price at the time of repurchase, and the goods are readily available in the market, then revenue is recognised at the time of delivery. The determination of whether to recognise revenue is a matter of judgement.

Example 6.6F

Sales to intermediate parties, such as distributors, dealers or others for resale

[IAS 18 Appendix Example 6]

Revenue from such sales is generally recognised when the risks and rewards of ownership have passed. However, when the buyer is acting, in substance, as an agent, the sale is treated as a consignment sale.

Example 6.6G

Subscriptions to publications and similar items

[IAS 18 Appendix Example 7]

When the items involved are of similar value in each time period, revenue is recognised on a straight-line basis over the period in which the items are despatched. When the items vary in value from period to period, revenue is recognised on the basis of the sales value of the item despatched as a proportion of the total estimated sales value of all items covered by the subscription.

Example 6.6H

Instalment sales, under which consideration is receivable in instalments

[IAS 18 Appendix Example 8]

Revenue attributable to the sales price, exclusive of interest, is recognised at the date of sale. The sale price is the present value of the consideration, determined by discounting the instalments receivable at the imputed rate of interest. The interest element is recognised as revenue as it is earned, using the effective interest rate method.

In some cases, because of the nature of the industry in which an entity operates, goods are sold and delivered even though collection of the sales price is not reasonably assured. Often in those cases, payment is required in periodic instalments over an extended period of time. The seller generally will retain a lien on the product sold until payment is completed. For such instalment sales, where collection of the sales price is not reasonably assured, revenue recognition is deferred. A fundamental condition for revenue recognition in IAS 18.14(d) is that it is probable that the economic benefits associated with the transaction will flow to the entity. Example 8 of the Appendix presumes that collectibility is not an issue.

Example 6.6I

Real estate sales

[IAS 18 Appendix Example 9]

Revenue is normally recognised when legal title passes to the buyer. However, in some jurisdictions, the equitable interest in a property may vest in the buyer before legal title passes and, therefore, the risks and rewards of ownership have been transferred at that stage. In such cases, provided that the seller has no further substantial acts to complete under the contract, it may be appropriate to recognise revenue. In either case, if the seller is obliged to perform any significant acts after the transfer of the equitable and/or legal title, revenue is recognised as the acts are performed. An example is a building or other facility on which construction has not been completed.

In some cases, real estate may be sold with a degree of continuing involvement by the seller such that the risks and rewards of ownership have not been transferred. Examples are sale and repurchase agreements that include put and call options, and agreements whereby the seller guarantees occupancy of the property for a specified period, or guarantees a return on the buyer's investment for a specified period. In such cases, the nature and extent of the seller's continuing involvement determines how the transaction is accounted for. It may be accounted for as a sale, or as a financing, leasing or some other profit-sharing arrangement. If it is accounted for as a sale, the continuing involvement of the seller may delay the recognition of revenue.

The seller must also consider the means of payment and evidence of the buyer's commitment to complete payment. For example, when the aggregate of the payments received, including the buyer's initial down payment, or continuing payments by the buyer, provides insufficient evidence of the buyer's commitment to complete payment, revenue is recognised only to the extent that cash is received.

For annual periods beginning on or after 1 January 2009, the guidance in IAS 18 Appendix Example 9 above is superseded by IFRIC 15 (see **2.1**). Earlier application of IFRIC 15 is permitted.

7 Recognition criteria – rendering of services

IAS 18 requires the use of the percentage of completion method when accounting for the rendering of services. Under the percentage of completion method, revenue is recognised as work progresses based on the percentage of work completed at the end of the reporting period. IAS 18 requires the use of this method for revenue recognition, but the recognition of related contract expenses is beyond its scope (though there is some guidance on the treatment of associated expenses in the Appendix to IAS 18). The Standard refers users to IAS 11 *Construction Contracts* for further guidance on the percentage of completion method as it applies to both revenue and expenses. The requirements and guidance included in IAS 18 are set out below and a more detailed discussion of the percentage of completion method is included in **chapter 40**.

As with the supply of goods, when an uncertainty arises about the collectibility of an amount already included in revenue in relation to services, the uncollectible amount, or the amount for which recovery has ceased to be probable, is recognised as a bad debt expense, rather than as an adjustment of the amount of revenue originally recognised. [IAS 18.22]

7.1 Outcome of transaction can be estimated reliably

When the outcome of a transaction involving the rendering of services can be estimated reliably, revenue associated with the transaction is recognised by reference to the stage of completion of the transaction at the end of the reporting period (i.e. using the percentage of completion method). IAS 18 lists the following conditions for the outcome of a transaction to be estimated reliably:

[IAS 18.20]

- the amount of revenue can be measured reliably;
- it is probable that the economic benefits associated with the transaction will flow to the entity;

- the stage of completion of the transaction at the end of the reporting period can be measured reliably; and
- the costs incurred for the transaction and the costs to complete the transaction can be measured reliably.

An entity is usually able to make reliable estimates after it has agreed the following with the other parties to the transaction:

[IAS 18.23]

- each party's enforceable rights regarding the service to be provided and received by the parties;
- the consideration to be exchanged; and
- the manner and terms of settlement.

In addition, it will be necessary for an entity to have an effective internal budgeting and reporting system for it to make reliable estimates and, in subsequent periods, to compare those estimates to the actual costs incurred to date.

The Standard emphasises that the need to revise the estimates of revenue as the service is performed does not necessarily indicate that the outcome of the transaction cannot be estimated reliably. [IAS 18.23]

The stage of completion of a transaction at the end of the reporting period can be determined in a variety of ways. Progress payments and advances received from customers are, however, generally not reliable indicators of the stage of completion, as these payments are often made for reasons other than compensating for work performed. Depending on the nature of the transaction, methods for determining the stage of completion may include:

[IAS 18.24]

- surveys of work performed;
- services performed to date as a percentage of total services to be performed; or
- the proportion that costs incurred to date bear to the estimated total costs of the transaction. Only costs that reflect services performed to date are included in costs incurred to date and only costs that reflect services performed or to be performed are included in the estimated total costs of the transaction.

When services are performed by an indeterminate number of acts over a specified period of time, revenue is recognised on a straight-line basis, unless there is evidence that some other method better represents the stage of completion. For example, if a service contract relates to daily cleaning services, for practical reasons, the revenue relating to those services will be recognised on a straight-line basis as the work is performed. If one specific act is much more significant than any other acts, the recognition of revenue is postponed until the significant act is executed. [IAS 18.25]

Example 7.1A

Claims processing and billing services

Company A performs claims processing and medical billing services for health care providers. It prepares and submits claims to government agencies and insurance companies, tracks the outstanding billings, collects the amounts billed, and remits payments to the health care provider. Company A's fee is 5 per cent of the amount collected. Company A has reliable, historical evidence indicating that the government agencies and insurance companies pay 85 per cent of the claims submitted with no further effort on A's part.

Under IAS 18.20, revenue from rendering services should be recognised by reference to the stage of completion of the transaction. How is that principle applied in this case? Specifically, may A recognise as revenue its 5 per cent fee on 85 per cent of the gross billings at the time it prepares and submits the billings, or must it wait until collections occur?

The recognition of revenue in such a case will depend on whether the amount that will be received by A is sufficiently predictable to be a reliable measurement. If A can make a reliable estimate of collections, revenue related to at least 85 per cent of the claims can be recognised. The entity shall determine the pattern of revenue recognition that best reflects the stage of completion.

Similar arrangements should be analysed to ascertain whether a transaction contains multiple elements to be accounted for separately. If so, revenue will be recognised separately for the different activities performed by A.

Example 7.1B

Membership or services when the customer is entitled to a full refund

Company A sells one-year memberships in a facility it operates. The terms state that if the customer is unhappy with the facility for any reason within 30 days of joining the facility, the customer can request a full refund of the membership fee paid upon sign up. After 30 days, the membership is non-refundable. Company A's experience is that approximately 20 per cent of its customers do request a refund during the 30-day period. When should A begin to recognise revenue?

If it is possible to make a reliable estimate of the level of expected refunds, A should begin recognising the membership fee from the date the membership contract is signed, with appropriate provision for estimated refunds. If it is not possible to make a reliable estimate of the level of expected refunds, revenue recognition should be deferred until the 30-day money-back period elapses.

Example 7.1C

Performance-based fee part way through the performance period

Company A, an investment manager, will earn a bonus of £1 million if a managed fund's performance exceeds the performance of the S&P 500 by 20 per cent for the calendar year 20X1. Company A's financial year ends 30 June 20X1. At that time, the fund is outperforming the S&P 500 by 25 per cent. Should the investment manager recognise revenue (bonus) at 30 June 20X1 and, if so, £500,000 (one-half year's worth) or £1 million (the expected total bonus)?

IAS 18.20 states that revenue can be recognised when the amount of revenue can be measured reliably and it is probable that the economic benefits will flow to the entity. The investment manager has not earned the bonus until the annual return exceeds the performance of the S&P 500 by 20 per cent. As the markets are very volatile, the annual performance of the S&P 500 cannot be estimated reliably before the end of the year. Consequently, no amount of the bonus can be determined reliably before the bonus measurement date. Therefore, the fund manager should not recognise any of the bonus at 30 June 20X1.

7.2 Outcome of transaction cannot be estimated reliably

When the outcome of a transaction involving the rendering of services cannot be estimated reliably, either:

[IAS 18.26 – 28]

- revenue is recognised to the extent of expenses incurred that are likely to be recovered. Thus, no profit is recognised on the transaction; or
- if it is not probable that the costs incurred will be recovered, no revenue is recognised and the costs incurred are recognised as an expense.

When the uncertainties that led to no profit being recognised on the transaction no longer exist, revenue is recognised on the percentage of completion basis.

- **Origination fees received on issuing financial liabilities measured at amortised cost.** These fees are an integral part of generating an involvement with a financial liability. When a financial liability is not classified as 'at fair value through profit or loss', the origination fees received are included, with the related transaction costs (as defined in IAS 39) incurred, in the initial carrying amount of the financial liability and recognised as an adjustment to the effective yield. An entity distinguishes fees and costs that are an integral part of the effective interest rate for the financial liability from origination fees and transaction costs relating to the right to provide services, such as investment management services.

* In *Improvements to IFRSs* issued in May 2008, the IASB replaced the term 'direct costs' with 'transaction costs' as defined in IAS 39.9. This amendment removed an inconsistency for costs incurred in originating financial assets and liabilities that should be deferred and recognised as an adjustment to the underlying effective interest rate. 'Direct costs', as previously defined, did not require such costs to be incremental.

(*b*) *Fees earned as services are provided*

- **Fees charged for servicing a loan.** Fees charged by an entity for servicing a loan are recognised as revenue as the services are provided.

- **Commitment fees to originate a loan when the loan commitment is outside the scope of IAS 39.** If it is unlikely that a specific lending arrangement will be entered into and the loan commitment is outside the scope of IAS 39, the commitment fee is recognised as revenue on a time proportion basis over the commitment period. Loan commitments that are within the scope of IAS 39 are accounted for as derivatives and measured at fair value.

- **Investment management fees.** Fees charged for managing investments are recognised as revenue as the services are provided.
  Incremental costs that are directly attributable to securing an investment management contract are recognised as an asset if they can be identified separately and measured reliably and if it is probable that they will be recovered. As in IAS 39, an incremental cost is one that would not have been incurred if the entity had not secured the investment management contract. The asset represents the entity's contractual right to benefit from providing investment management services, and is amortised as the entity recognises the related revenue. If the entity has a portfolio of investment management contracts, it may assess their recoverability on a portfolio basis.
  Some financial services contracts involve both the origination of one or more financial instruments and the provision of investment management services. An example is a long-term monthly saving contract linked to the management of a pool of equity securities. The provider of the contract distinguishes the contract cost relating to the origination of the financial instrument from the costs of securing the right to provide investment management services.

(c) Fees that are earned on the execution of a significant act

The fees are recognised as revenue when the significant act has been completed, as in the examples below.

- **Commission on the allotment of shares to a client.** The commission is recognised as revenue when the shares have been allotted.
- **Placement fees for arranging a loan between a borrower and an investor.** The fee is recognised as revenue when the loan has been arranged.
- **Loan syndication fees.** A syndication fee received by an entity that arranges a loan and retains no part of the loan package for itself (or retains a part at the same effective interest rate for comparable risk as other participants) is compensation for the service of syndication. Such a fee is recognised as revenue when the syndication has been completed.

Example 7.3F

Admission fees

[IAS 18 Appendix Example 15]

Revenue from artistic performances, banquets and other special events is recognised when the event takes place. When a subscription to a number of events is sold, the fee is allocated to each event on a basis that reflects the extent to which services are performed at each event.

Example 7.3G

Tuition fees

[IAS 18 Appendix Example 16]

Revenue is recognised over the period of instruction.

Example 7.3H

Initiation, entrance and membership fees

[IAS 18 Appendix Example 17]

Revenue recognition depends on the nature of the services provided. If the fee permits only membership, and all other services or products are paid for separately, or if there is a separate annual subscription, the fee is recognised as revenue when no significant uncertainty as to its collectibility exists. If the fee entitles the member to services or publications to be provided during the membership period, or to purchase goods or services at prices lower than those charged to non-members, it is recognised on a basis that reflects the timing, nature and value of the benefits provided.

Some care should be taken before concluding that a fee permits only membership, particularly where goods or services are not made available to non-members at any price. In such circumstances, it will often be the case that the membership fee also provides the member with a valuable option to buy those goods and services, in which case the fee will permit more than just membership.

Example 7.3I

Franchise fees

[IAS 18 Appendix Example 18]

Franchise fees may cover the supply of initial and subsequent services, equipment and other tangible assets, and know-how. Accordingly, franchise fees are recognised as revenue on a basis that reflects the purpose for which the fees were charged. The following methods of franchise fee recognition are appropriate:

- **Supplies of equipment and other tangible assets.** The amount, based on the fair value of the assets sold, is recognised as revenue when the items are delivered or title passes.

- **Supplies of initial and subsequent services.** Fees for the provision of continuing services, whether part of the initial fee or a separate fee, are recognised as revenue as the services are rendered. When the separate fee does not cover the cost of continuing services together with a reasonable profit, part of the initial fee, sufficient to cover the costs of continuing services and to provide a reasonable profit on those services, is deferred and recognised as revenue as the services are rendered.

  The franchise agreement may provide for the franchisor to supply equipment, inventories, or other tangible assets, at a price lower than that charged to others or a price that does not provide a reasonable profit on those sales. In these circumstances, part of the initial fee, sufficient to cover estimated costs in excess of that price and to provide a reasonable profit on those sales, is deferred and recognised over the period the goods are likely to be sold to the franchisee. The balance of an initial fee is recognised as revenue when performance of all of the initial services and other obligations required of the franchisor (such as assistance with site selection, staff training, financing and advertising) has been substantially accomplished.

  The initial services and other obligations under an area franchise agreement may depend on the number of individual outlets established in the area. In this case, the fees attributable to the initial services are recognised as revenue in proportion to the number of outlets for which the initial services have been substantially completed.

If the initial fee is collectible over an extended period, and there is a significant uncertainty that it will be collected in full, the fee is recognised as cash instalments are received.

- **Continuing franchise fees.** Fees charged for the use of continuing rights granted by the agreement, or for other services provided during the period of the agreement, are recognised as revenue as the services are provided or the rights used.

- **Agency transactions.** Transactions may take place between the franchisor and the franchisee which, in substance, involve the franchisor acting as agent for the franchisee. For example, the franchisor may order supplies and arrange for their delivery to the franchisee at no profit. Such transactions do not give rise to revenue.

Example 7.3J

Fees from the development of customised software

[IAS 18 Appendix Example 19]

Fees from the development of customised software are recognised as revenue by reference to the stage of completion of the development, including completion of services provided for post-delivery service support.

8 Recognition criteria – interest revenue

Interest revenue should be recognised using the effective interest method when:

[IAS 18.29 & 30(a)]

- it is probable that the economic benefits associated with the transaction will flow to the entity; and

- the amount of the revenue can be measured reliably.

IAS 18 refers to IAS 39.9 and IAS 39.AG5 – AG8 for a description of the effective interest method, as discussed at **section 4.1** of **chapter 18**.

When unpaid interest has accrued before the acquisition of an interest-bearing investment, the subsequent receipt of interest is allocated between the pre-acquisition and post-acquisition periods. [IAS 18.32] Only the post-acquisition portion is recognised as revenue. The pre-acquisition portion will offset the amount recognised at acquisition for interest receivable.

Example 8

Unpaid interest accrued before acquisition of investment

An entity purchases £1 million face value bonds for £1,030,000 on 1 April 20X1. The bonds pay interest at 12 per cent per annum on 31 December and 30 June each year.

The investor will receive £60,000 as interest for the period from 1 January 20X1 to 30 June 20X1, but only £30,000 of this is to be treated as interest revenue.

Therefore, the entries to record the acquisition of the bond and the receipt of interest on 30 June 20X1 will be as follows:

	£'000 Dr	£'000 Cr
Investments	1,000	
Debtor – interest receivable	30	
Cash		1,030
Cash	60	
Debtor – interest receivable		30
Statement of comprehensive income – interest income		30

Interest revenue is recognised only when it is probable that the economic benefits associated with the transaction will flow to the entity. However, when an uncertainty arises about the collectibility of an amount already included in revenue, the uncollectible amount, or the amount in respect of which recovery has ceased to be probable, is recognised as a bad debt expense, rather than as an adjustment of the amount of revenue originally recognised. [IAS 18.34]

9 Recognition criteria – royalty revenue

Royalty revenue should be recognised on an accrual basis in accordance with the substance of the relevant agreement when:

[IAS 18.29 & 30(b)]

- it is probable that the economic benefits associated with the transaction will flow to the entity; and
- the amount of the revenue can be measured reliably.

Royalties accrue in accordance with the terms of the relevant agreement and are usually recognised on that basis unless, having regard to the substance of the agreement, it is more appropriate to recognise revenue on some other systematic and rational basis. [IAS 18.33]

The Appendix to IAS 18 contains the following illustration of the principle of revenue recognition for royalty income.

Example 9

Licence fees and royalties

[IAS 18 Appendix Example 20]

Fees and royalties paid for the use of an entity's assets (such as trademarks, patents, software, music copyright, record masters and motion picture films) are normally recognised in accordance with the substance of the agreement. As a practical matter, this may be on a straight-line basis over the life of the agreement, e.g. when a licensee has the right to use certain technology for a specified period of time.

An assignment of rights for a fixed fee or non-refundable guarantee under a non-cancellable contract which permits the licensee to exploit those rights freely and the licensor has no remaining obligations to perform is, in substance, a sale. An example is a licensing agreement for the use of software when the licensor has no obligations subsequent to delivery. Another example is the granting of rights to exhibit a motion picture film in markets where the licensor has no control over the distributor and expects to receive no further revenues from the box office receipts. In such cases, revenue is recognised at the time of sale.

In some cases, whether or not a licence fee or royalty will be received is contingent on the occurrence of a future event. In such cases, revenue is recognised only when it is probable that the fee or royalty will be received, which is normally when the event has occurred.

Royalty revenue is recognised only when it is probable that the economic benefits associated with the transaction will flow to the entity. When an uncertainty arises about the collectibility of an amount already included in revenue, however, the uncollectible amount, or the amount in respect of which recovery has ceased to be probable, is recognised as a bad debt expense, rather than as an adjustment of the amount of revenue originally recognised. [IAS 18.34]

Royalty agreements vary, but essentially their purpose is to sell a right to use an entity's assets, such as trademarks, patents, and software, for a certain period of time. Under royalty agreements, should revenue recognition be up front upon signing the agreement or should it be deferred and spread over the duration of the agreement?

Example 20 in the Appendix to IAS 18 states that recognition of revenue under royalty agreements should be recognised in accordance with the substance of the arrangements. It further clarifies that the overriding factor in determining the accounting treatment for such arrangements should be whether the licensor has any remaining obligation to perform. The outcome of each arrangement depends on the circumstances. Below are two typical examples.

License to use a trademark

The sale of the right to use a trademark often requires that the licensor (seller) continue to ensure the 'quality' of the trademark. When the requirement imposes a genuine performance obligation (i.e. the licensee could realistically seek redress for non-performance), revenue recognition shall be deferred and spread over the period of performance (i.e. the license term) by the seller. If, however, the requirement is a mere formality and the seller has no remaining obligation to perform, then revenue shall be recognised immediately.

Software licensing arrangement

Software licensing arrangements allow the licensee (customer) to use intellectual property. Upon delivery of the software license, in the absence of any requirement that the licensor (seller) provide technical support, software upgrades, or enhancements, a sale has occurred and revenue from the sale can be fully recognised.

If the licensor sells technical support or software upgrades together with the license, the arrangement should be analysed as to whether it is a multiple-element arrangement, in which case revenue shall be recognised separately for each of the identified components.

10 Recognition criteria – dividend revenue

Dividend revenue should be recognised when:

[IAS 18.29 & 30(c)]

- it is probable that the economic benefits associated with the transaction will flow to the entity;
- the amount of the revenue can be measured reliably; and
- the shareholder's right to receive payment is established.

The timing of the establishment of the shareholders' right to receive payment may vary based on the laws of particular countries. In some countries, it may occur when the board of directors of an entity formally declares its intention to pay a dividend. In other countries, it may occur only after such a declaration has been approved by shareholders. In any case if, subsequent to revenue recognition but before receipt of the dividend, it becomes apparent that the investee will not be able to pay the dividend, the amount of dividend revenue previously recognised is dealt with as a bad debt expense rather than as a reversal of dividend revenue. [IAS 18.34]

10.1 Dividends on equity investments declared from pre-acquisition profits

Until it was amended in May 2008, IAS 18 required that, when dividends on equity investments are declared from pre-acquisition profits, those dividends are deducted from the cost of the investment. If it is difficult to make such an allocation except on an arbitrary basis, dividends are recognised as revenue unless they clearly represent a recovery of part of the cost of the equity investment. [IAS 18.32]

In May 2008, the IASB issued Amendments to IFRS 1 *First-time Adoption of International Financial Reporting Standards* and IAS 27 *Consolidated and Separate Financial Statements* in respect of the cost of an investment in a subsidiary, jointly controlled entity or associate. For annual periods beginning on or after 1 January 2009, the requirement above is deleted. Instead, as discussed at **6.1.1** in **chapter 33**, dividend revenue is recognised in profit or loss irrespective of whether it is declared from pre- or post-acquisition profits and, separately, in some cases it is necessary to consider whether the equity investment may be impaired.

Earlier application of the Amendments is permitted. If an entity applies the amendments to IAS 27.4 & 38A (see **6.1.1** in **chapter 33**) for an earlier period, this amendment to IAS 18 should be applied at the same time.

UK

At the time of writing, the Amendments to IFRS 1 and IAS 27 have not yet been endorsed for use in the EU. Since the amended requirements of IAS 18 are not compatible with those of the previous version, EU reporting entities will not be able to apply the amendment to IAS 18 in their statutory financial statements until endorsement has occurred.

11 Disclosure

Entities are required to disclose the accounting policies adopted for revenue recognition, including the methods adopted to determine the stage of completion of transactions involving the rendering of services. [IAS 18.35(a)]

The following should be considered, depending on circumstances, for disclosure in the revenue recognition accounting policy:

- if an entity has different policies for different types of revenue transactions, the policy for each material type of transaction should be disclosed;
- if sales transactions have multiple elements, such as product and service, the disclosure should include the accounting policy for each element as well as how multiple elements are determined and valued;
- changes in estimates that underlie revenue recognition, such as changes in estimated returns, should be disclosed; and
- any specific revenue transactions that are unusual because of their nature, size, or frequency of occurrence may require separate disclosure.

The amount of each significant category of revenue recognised during the period is also required to be disclosed, including revenue arising from:

[IAS 18.35(b)]

- the sale of goods;
- the rendering of services;
- interest;
- royalties; and
- dividends.

The entity is also required to disclose the amount of revenue arising from exchanges of goods or services included in each significant category of revenue. [IAS 18.35(c)]

UK

Under UK GAAP, there are no requirements to analyse revenue between goods and services or to disclose revenue arising from exchanges of goods or services. Accordingly, some UK companies transitioning to IFRSs may need to amend their financial reporting systems to make this disclosure possible.

12 Future developments

12.1 Revenue recognition project

IAS 18 (as well as IAS 11 *Construction Contracts*, discussed in **chapter 40**) is currently under review in a project entitled *Revenue Recognition.* The IASB is working with the US Financial Accounting Standards Board on a joint project to develop concepts for revenue recognition and a general standard based on those concepts.

At the time of writing, a discussion paper outlining the approaches discussed by the boards is expected to be published towards the end of 2008.

12.2 Draft Interpretation IFRIC D24 *Customer Contributions*

Draft Interpretation IFRIC D24 *Customer Contributions* was issued in January 2008, with a comment deadline of April 2008. Customer contributions are transactions in which an entity – the access provider – receives an asset it uses to provide access to an ongoing supply of goods or services to a customer or customers. In some cases, the access provider receives cash which it must use to acquire or construct the asset that will provide access. IFRIC D24 addresses a number of areas where practice is diverse. It seeks to clarify:

- whether a customer contribution should be recognised as an asset and, if so, whether it should be initially recognised at cost or fair value;
- whether an agreement to provide ongoing services using a contributed asset contains a lease;
- how to account for the credit that arises from the recognition of a customer contribution at fair value; and
- how to account for a cash contribution.

IFRIC D24 proposes that all access providers will be required to recognise contributed assets and revenue from providing access to a supply of goods or services over the period access is provided.

If finalised, the Interpretation would be applied prospectively, that is, for all future transactions.

24 Employee benefits

1 Introduction

Accounting and disclosure requirements for employee benefits are principally set out in IAS 19 *Employee Benefits*. The Standard was most recently amended when *Improvements to IFRSs* was issued in May 2008.

This chapter discusses the requirements of IAS 19 in the following sections:

Section 2	Scope
Section 3	Short-term employee benefits
Section 4	Post-employment benefits
Section 5	Multi-employer plans, group plans and state plans
Section 6	Defined contribution plans
Section 7	Defined benefit plans
Section 8	Defined benefit plans and business combinations
Section 9	Presentation and disclosure for defined benefit plans
Section 10	Other post-employment benefits
Section 11	Other long-term employee benefits
Section 12	Termination benefits
Section 13	Future developments

Related disclosure requirements are also set out in:

- IAS 1 *Presentation of Financial Statements*, which requires that staff costs are disclosed (see **section 8.1.2** of **chapter 3**); and
- IAS 24 *Related Party Disclosures*, which requires disclosure of employee benefits including share-based payments for key management personnel (see **section 5.2** of **chapter 32**);

In addition, for UK companies, there are related disclosure requirements set out in: UK

- *the Companies Act, which specifies certain disclosures in respect of directors' emoluments (see* **chapter 48***), and*
- *the Listing Rules, which require additional disclosures in respect of the remuneration of directors, share option schemes, and also disclosures in respect of the retirement benefit schemes of listed entities (see* **section 7** *of* **chapter 48***).*

IAS 26 *Accounting and Reporting by Retirement Benefit Plans* deals with the financial statements of pension schemes. Its requirements are outside the scope of this publication, as explained in **section 4.1** of the **Introduction**.

UK *The largest part of IAS 19 is concerned with accounting for defined benefit pension plans. IAS 19 and its UK equivalent, FRS 17* Retirement Benefits, *have much in common in how they deal with such plans, but the most significant difference relates to how actuarial gains and losses are recognised. Whereas under FRS 17 such gains and losses are recognised immediately in the Statement of Total Recognised Gains and Losses, IAS 19 allows the use of a 'corridor' approach to defer recognition of some actuarial gains and losses (see* **section 7.5***).*

Other potentially significant differences from a UK perspective are that:

- *group defined benefit plans are not eligible to be treated as multi-employer plans (see* **5.1***). Under IAS 19, a liability relating to a group plan will always be allocated to one or more of the individual group entities (see* **14.1.2***). This contrasts with the position under FRS 17, where it is possible for none of the plan participants to recognise a liability;*
- *plan assets will be valued at bid price under IAS 19; originally they were valued at mid-market price under FRS 17, but for periods beginning on or after 6 April 2007 the UK standard is amended to require bid price (see* **7.7.7***);*
- *the various components of defined benefit plan expense may be presented separately in the income statement (as under FRS 17), or as a single net figure (see* **9.1***); and*
- *IAS 19 includes specific guidance on dealing with short-term employee benefits (such as holiday pay), for which there is no UK equivalent (see* **section 3***).*

2 Scope

IAS 19 defines employee benefits as all forms of consideration given by an entity in exchange for service rendered by employees. [IAS 19.7] The Standard divides the employee benefits within its scope into four categories, which are discussed in the following sections of this chapter:

- **section 3** – short-term employee benefits, such as wages, salaries and social security contributions, paid annual leave, paid sick leave, profit-sharing, bonuses payable within 12 months of the end of the reporting period, and non-monetary benefits for current employees;
- **sections 4 to 10** – post-employment benefits (e.g. pensions, other retirement benefits, post-employment life insurance and post-employment medical care);
- **section 11** – other long-term employee benefits (e.g. long-service leave and bonuses not wholly payable within 12 months of the end of the reporting period); and
- **section 12** – termination benefits.

Share-based compensation is outside the scope of IAS 19 and is dealt with in IFRS 2 *Share-based Payment*.

3 Short-term employee benefits

3.1 Definition

Short-term employee benefits are defined as employee benefits (other than termination benefits) that are due to be settled within twelve months after the end of the period in which the employees render the related service. [IAS 19.7] They include items such as:

[IAS 19.8]

- wages, salaries and social security contributions;
- short-term compensated absences (e.g. vacation or annual leave, sickness and short-term disability, maternity or paternity leave, jury service and military service) where the compensation for the absences is due to be settled within twelve months after the end of the period in which the employees render the related service;
- profit-sharing and bonus payments (where payable within twelve months after the end of the period in which the employees render the related service); and

- non-monetary benefits (e.g. access to medical care, housing, cars, subsidised goods).

Paragraphs 7 and 8 of IAS 19 were amended by *Improvements to IFRSs* issued in May 2008. These amendments were made because of a perceived inconsistency in the wording of the paragraphs. Previously, the definition of short-term employee benefits referred to benefits 'which fall due wholly within twelve months after the end of the period ...' and the description of short-term compensated absences referred to absences 'expected to occur within twelve months after the end of the period ...'. The definition of short-term employee benefits and the description of short-term compensated absences have been amended to refer to when the benefits are 'due to be settled' because the timing of expected settlement is considered to be the critical factor in distinguishing between short-term and long-term benefits.

The amendments are effective for annual accounting periods beginning on or after 1 January 2009, and should be applied retrospectively. Earlier application of these amendments is permitted, but an entity choosing to apply the amendments early must disclose that fact.

UK *At the time of writing, the amendments made by* Improvements to IFRSs *have not yet been endorsed for use in the EU.*

3.2 Recognition of short-term employee benefits

An entity should recognise the undiscounted amount of short-term employee benefits earned by an employee in exchange for services rendered during the accounting period:

[IAS 19.10]

- in the statement of financial position, as a liability (accrued expense), after deducting any amounts already paid, or as an asset (prepaid expense), if the amount already paid exceeds the undiscounted amount of the benefits, to the extent that the prepayment will be recoverable (e.g. by means of a reduction in future payments or a cash refund); and

- in profit or loss, as an expense, unless another Standard requires or permits inclusion of the benefits in the cost of an asset (e.g. as part of staff costs capitalised in a self-constructed property – see **chapter 6**).

The cost of all short-term employee benefits is recognised as noted above. No actuarial assumptions are required (hence there are no actuarial gains or losses to address) and, due to their short-term nature, obligations are dealt with on an undiscounted basis.

3.2.1 *Short-term compensated absences*

Short-term compensated absences may be classified as accumulating or non-accumulating. Accumulating compensated absences are those that can be carried forward and used in future accounting periods if the current accounting period's entitlement is not used in full. Accumulating compensated absences may be further sub-divided as vesting (where employees are entitled to a cash payment for unused entitlement on leaving the entity) or non-vesting (where no such entitlement arises).

Non-accumulating compensated absences cannot be carried forward, i.e. any unused entitlement is lost at the end of the current period and the employee is not entitled to a cash payment for unused entitlement on leaving the entity.

In applying the general requirements set out at **3.2** above to the expected cost of short-term compensated absences:

[IAS 19.11 & 14]

- for accumulating compensated absences, the expense should be recognised when the employees render service that increases their entitlement to future compensated absences, based on the additional amount that the entity expects to pay as a result of the unused entitlement accumulated at the end of the reporting period; and
- for non-accumulating compensated absences, the expense should be recognised as the absences occur.

For accumulating absences, the difference between vesting and non-vesting does not affect whether an obligation exists and should be recognised, but does affect the measurement of that obligation, as there is a possibility that employees may leave before they use an accumulating non-vesting entitlement. Thus, the expense is measured as the additional amount that the entity expects to pay, rather than the maximum amount that it could be obliged to pay.

Example 3.2.1

Short-term compensated absences

Company A has 200 employees, who are each entitled to 20 working days of paid leave each year. Paid leave is first taken out of the current year's

> entitlement and then out of the balance brought forward from the previous year (a LIFO basis). Unused leave cannot be carried forward more than one year.
>
> At 31 December 20X1, the average unused entitlement was 3 days per employee (i.e. 600 days in total). The entity expects, based on past experience, that 175 employees will take no more than their annual entitlement in 20X2 and that the remaining 25 employees will, in total, use 70 days of the entitlement brought forward from 20X1.
>
> The entity recognises a liability and an expense at 31 December 20X1 based on 70 days.
>
> Had the employees been permitted to carry forward holiday indefinitely, and been entitled to a cash payment for unused holiday entitlement on leaving the entity (i.e. a vested entitlement), then the full 600 days would be accrued at 31 December 20X1.

3.3 Profit-sharing and bonus plans

In applying the general requirements set out at **3.2** above to the expected cost of profit-sharing and bonus plans, an entity should recognise the expected cost when, and only when:

[IAS 19.17]

- it has a present legal or constructive obligation to make such payments as a result of past events; and
- a reliable estimate of the obligation can be made.

In this context, a present obligation exists when, and only when, the entity has no realistic alternative but to make the payments. The requirements therefore follow closely the general recognition criteria for provisions under IAS 37 *Provisions, Contingent Liabilities and Contingent Assets* (see **chapter 11**). Even where an entity has no legal obligation to pay a bonus, past practice of paying bonuses may give rise to a constructive obligation, if this has led to a valid expectation on the part of the employees.

An employee's entitlement to a profit-share may depend on the employee remaining with the entity for a specified period. In such circumstances, the plan creates a constructive obligation as employees render service that increases the amount to be paid if they remain in service until the end of that specified period. The fact that some employees may leave without receiving payments is reflected in the measurement of the obligation. It is not appropriate to defer recognition of the obligation until the employee completes the entitlement period. [IAS 19.18]

Example 3.3

Profit-sharing plan

A profit-sharing plan requires Company B to pay a specified proportion of its profit before tax for the financial year to 30 June 20X1 to employees who serve throughout the calendar year 20X1. If no employees leave during the year, the total profit-sharing payments for the year will be 3 per cent of profit before tax. The entity estimates that staff turnover will reduce the payments to 2.5 per cent of profit before tax.

Although the payment is measured as a proportion of the profits for the financial year to 30 June 20X1, performance is based on an employee's service during the calendar year 20X1. Accordingly, the entity recognises a liability and an expense of 2.5 per cent of 50 per cent of the profit before tax at 30 June 20X1. A further expense of 2.5 per cent of 50 per cent will be recognised in the next period, together with a true-up for any difference between the estimated amounts and the actual amounts paid.

If the plan had been in existence in the calendar year 20X0, an expense would also be recognised in the financial year to 30 June 20X1 in respect of the last six months of the entitlement period for 20X0. That amount would be fixed as it would have been paid before 30 June 20X1 or the actual staff turnover for 20X0 would have been known.

The costs of profit-sharing and bonus plans are recognised as an expense (and not as a distribution of profit) because they result from employee service and not from a transaction with the entity's owners. [IAS 19.21]

If profit-sharing and bonus payments are not due wholly within twelve months after the end of the period in which the employees render the related service, those payments are classified as 'other long-term employee benefits' (see **section 11**).

3.3.1 *When is a reliable estimate possible?*

An entity can make a reliable estimate of its legal or constructive obligation under a profit-sharing or bonus plan when, and only when:

[IAS 19.20]

- the formal terms of the plan contain a formula for determining the amount of the benefit; or
- the amounts to be paid are determined before the financial statements are authorised for issue; or

- past practice gives clear evidence of the amount of the constructive obligation.

3.4 Disclosure

IAS 19 does not specify any particular disclosure requirements for short-term employee benefits, but other Standards may require disclosures. For example:

- IAS 24 *Related Party Disclosures* requires disclosures about employee benefits for key management personnel; and
- IAS 1 *Presentation of Financial Statements* requires disclosure of the employee benefits expense.

4 Post-employment benefits

Post-employment benefits are defined as employee benefits (other than termination benefits) which are payable after the completion of employment. [IAS 19.7]

This definition captures pensions, other retirement benefits and other post-employment benefits such as post-employment life insurance or access to medical care. If an entity provides such benefits, the requirements of IAS 19 apply irrespective of whether a separate entity is established to receive contributions and to pay benefits.

4.1 Post-employment benefit plans

Post-employment benefit plans are formal or informal arrangements under which an entity provides post-employment benefits for one or more employees. [IAS 19.7]

4.2 Types of post-employment benefit plans

The accounting treatment and required disclosures for a post-employment benefit plan depend upon whether it is classified as a defined contribution or a defined benefit plan. In addition to addressing defined contribution and defined benefit plans generally, the Standard also gives guidance as to how its requirements should be applied to insured benefits, multi-employer plans, group plans and state plans.

There are two main types of post-employment benefit plans:

[IAS 19.7]

- **defined contribution plans** are post-employment benefit plans under which an entity pays fixed contributions into a separate entity (a fund) and will have no legal or constructive obligation to pay further contributions if the fund does not hold sufficient assets to pay all employee benefits relating to employee service in the current and prior periods; and
- **defined benefit plans** are post-employment benefit plans other than defined contribution plans.

The classification as either a defined contribution plan or a defined benefit plan depends on the economic substance of the plan as derived from its principal terms and conditions.

IAS 19 explains that, under a defined contribution plan, the amount of benefits received by an employee is determined by the amount of contributions paid to a post-employment benefit plan or to an insurance company, together with any investment returns arising from the contributions, so that actuarial risk (that benefits will be less than expected) and investment risk (that assets invested will be insufficient to meet expected benefits) fall on the employee. Thus, for example, a plan that includes either:

[IAS 19.26]

- a benefit formula that is not linked solely to the amount of contributions, or
- a guarantee, either indirectly through the plan or directly from the entity, of a specified return on contributions,

is a defined benefit plan.

Example 4.2

Defined contribution plan with target benefits

An employer has a target benefit plan, the contributions to which are determined based on each employee's age on joining the plan, projected average salary at retirement, projected mortality, and retirement age. On joining the plan, a contribution percentage is computed for each employee based on the relevant demographic information. Thereafter, the employer contributes that specific percentage of the employee's salary to the plan. If the employee's salary or other factors change, the employer's contribution rate will not change.

The plan is structured so that the employer's contributions accumulate to each individual employee's account. Investment gains or losses on assets in the plan accrue to the employees on a pro-rata basis and are not considered in computing the employer's future contributions. If an employee's account balance at retirement or termination either exceeds or falls short of the target amount, then the account balance will not be adjusted by the employer. Employees receive only the funds credited to their accounts.

This plan meets the definition of a defined contribution plan. The target benefit plan has a complex formula to compute the employer's pension contributions. However, the benefit computation is not adjusted for investment gains/losses/forfeitures on the assets contributed to the employee's individual account. As a result, the actuarial and investment risks associated with the plan effectively fall to the employee and, therefore, the plan is a defined contribution plan.

4.3 Funded and unfunded retirement plans

Retirement benefit plans can be either funded or unfunded. Funded plans are those where contributions are paid into a separate entity, usually under the supervision of an administrator. The administrator will typically manage the investment of contributions and the payment of benefit entitlements to employees in accordance with the plan rules. Defined contribution plans are, by definition, funded plans.

Although IAS 19 does not define funded and unfunded plans, it does define assets held by a long-term employee benefit fund. These are assets (other than non-transferable financial instruments issued by the reporting entity) that:

[IAS 19.7]

(a) are held by an entity (a fund) that is legally separate from the reporting entity and exists solely to pay or fund employee benefits; and

(b) are available to be used only to pay or fund employee benefits, are not available to the reporting entity's own creditors (even in bankruptcy), and cannot be returned to the reporting entity, unless either:

(i) the remaining assets of the fund are sufficient to meet all the related employee benefit obligations of the plan or the reporting entity; or

(ii) the assets are returned to the reporting entity to reimburse it for employee benefits already paid.

Where, or to the extent that, these criteria are not met, it appears that the plan should be regarded as unfunded for the purposes of IAS 19. The entity should consider whether the assets underlying employee benefit plans which do not qualify as plan assets should instead appear in its own statement of financial position, either because they are held directly by the entity or, for example, by a Special Purpose Entity (SPE) controlled by it, which would be consolidated in accordance with SIC-12 *Consolidation – Special Purpose Entities* (see **chapter 33**).

4.4 Insured benefits

A post-employment benefit plan that is funded by insurance premiums is treated as a defined benefit plan if the reporting entity (either directly or indirectly through the plan) has a legal or constructive obligation to either:

[IAS 19.39]

- pay the employee benefits directly when they fall due; or
- pay further amounts if the insurer does not pay all future employee benefits relating to service in the current or prior periods.

In the absence of such a legal or constructive obligation, the plan is treated as a defined contribution plan. [IAS 19.39]

Thus, insured plans are subject to the same distinction as other plans. If there is no legal or constructive obligation, payment of the insurance premium is, in substance, settlement of the obligation for a specified plan participant or group of participants. If a legal or constructive obligation remains, payment of the insurance premium is, in substance, an investment to meet the obligation. Where the entity retains a legal or constructive obligation, it will need to account for its 'qualifying' insurance policies as plan assets (see **section 7.7.2**) and recognise other insurance policies as reimbursement rights (if the policies satisfy certain criteria – see **section 7.7.4**). [IAS 19.41]

It should not be assumed, merely because an entity insures the benefits arising under a defined benefit plan, that the plan assets will necessarily be equal to the plan liabilities. IAS 19.40 notes that the benefits insured by an insurance contract need not have a direct or automatic relationship with the entity's obligation for employee benefits.

5 Multi-employer plans, group plans and state plans

5.1 Multi-employer plans

Multi-employer plans are defined contribution plans (other than state plans) or defined benefit plans (other than state plans) that:

[IAS 19.7]

- pool the assets contributed by various entities that are not under common control; and
- use those assets to provide benefits to employees of more than one entity, on the basis that contribution and benefit levels are determined without regard to the identity of the entity that employs the employees concerned.

Multi-employer plans should be classified as defined contribution or defined benefit plans based on the criteria discussed in **section 4**, and accounted for accordingly. If a multi-employer plan is classified as a defined benefit plan, an entity should account for its proportionate share of the plan assets, obligations and costs, and provide disclosures, in the same way as for any other defined benefit plan, unless the exemption discussed at **5.1.1** below is available. [IAS 19.29]

UK

> *The definition of multi-employer plans under IAS 19 differs from FRS 17, in that it excludes assets pooled by entities under common control (i.e. group schemes). Under FRS 17, it is possible for all of the participants in a group plan to adopt defined contribution accounting, so that none of them recognises a scheme asset or liability. This treatment is not available under IAS 19; an asset or liability relating to a group plan will always be allocated to one or more of the individual group entities.*

5.1.1 Exemption for insufficient information

The Standard acknowledges that an entity may not be able to identify its share of the underlying financial position and performance of the plan with sufficient reliability for accounting purposes. This may occur if:

[IAS 19.32]

- the entity does not have access to information about the plan that satisfies the requirements of IAS 19; or
- the plan exposes the participating entities to actuarial risks associated with the current and former employees of other entities, with the result that there is no consistent and reliable basis for allocating the obligations, plan assets and costs to individual entities participating in the plan.

In such circumstances (i.e. the entity participates in a multi-employer plan that is a defined benefit plan, but there is not sufficient information available to use defined-benefit accounting), the entity:

[IAS 19.30]

- accounts for the plan as if it were a defined contribution plan; and
- makes appropriate disclosures (see **5.1.4**).

The Standard emphasises that, if a participant in a defined benefit multi-employer plan:

- accounts on a defined contribution basis because it has insufficient information to apply defined benefit accounting, but
- is party to a contractual agreement that determines how a surplus would be distributed or a deficit funded,

it should recognise the asset or liability arising from that contractual agreement, and the resulting income or expense in profit or loss. [IAS 19.32A] This requirement is illustrated in **example 5.1.1**, which is included in the Standard.

> **Example 5.1.1**
>
> **Multi-employer plans**
>
> [Example illustrating IAS 19.32A]
>
> An entity participates in a multi-employer defined benefit plan that does not prepare plan valuations on an IAS 19 basis. It therefore accounts for the plan as if it were a defined contribution plan. A non-IAS 19 funding valuation shows a deficit of 100 million in the plan. The plan has agreed under contract a schedule of contributions with the participating employers in the plan that will eliminate the deficit over the next five years. The entity's total contributions under the contract are 8 million.
>
> *The entity recognises a liability for the contributions adjusted for the time value of money, and an equal expense in profit or loss.*

5.1.2 *Group administration plans*

Multi-employer plans may be differentiated from group administration plans (also known as common investment funds). Group administration plans allow participating employers to pool their assets for investment purposes, thus reducing administration and investment management costs. The claims of the different participating employers on the assets are segregated for the sole benefit of their employees and other beneficiaries of their plans, so that there is no particular accounting problem in obtaining the information relating to a particular employer. Participating employers are not exposed to the actuarial risks attaching to the obligations of the other participating employers.

Plans of this nature should be classified as either defined contribution or defined benefit in the usual manner. [IAS 19.33]

5.1.3 *Change from defined contribution to defined benefit accounting for a multi-employer plan*

Example 5.1.3

Change from defined contribution to defined benefit accounting for a multi-employer plan

Company A contributes to a multi-employer defined benefit plan. However, because the plan has never been able to provide its participants with sufficient information for them to apply the accounting requirements in IAS 19.29, Company A has always accounted for the plan as if it were a defined contribution plan in accordance with the exemption in IAS 19.30 (see **5.1.1** above).

As at 31 December 20X1, the plan is, for the first time, able to provide the participants with sufficient information for them to apply the accounting requirements in IAS 19.29.

The effect of the change from defined contribution accounting to defined benefit accounting should be treated as a change in estimate in accordance with IAS 8 *Accounting Policies, Changes in Accounting Estimates and Errors*, and not as a change in accounting policy. For the reasons set out below, Company A is not changing its accounting policy.

Although Company A's accounting policy has always been to recognise its defined benefit liability (or asset), prior to being provided with the necessary information at 31 December 20X1, Company A was not in a position to do so. Company A was required to account for the plan as a defined contribution plan, with the cost of the plan measured at an amount equal to the contributions made. From 31 December 20X1, Company A has sufficient information to enable it to measure reliably the defined benefit liability (or asset) at that date, and the cost going forward. The best estimate of the liability, and not the basis of accounting for the plan, has changed and the adjustment to the carrying amount is therefore a change in estimate. The effect of the change in estimate should be recognised in profit or loss in the year in which the new information is obtained.

5.1.4 *Disclosure*

Where the entity participates in a multi-employer plan that is a defined benefit plan, but there is not sufficient information available to use defined-benefit accounting, the entity:

[IAS 19.30]

- discloses the fact that the plan is a defined benefit plan, and the reason why sufficient information is not available to account for the plan as a defined benefit plan; and
- to the extent that a surplus or deficit in the plan may affect the amount of future contributions, discloses any available information about that surplus or deficit, the basis used to determine that surplus or deficit, and any implications for the entity.

In addition, in accordance with IAS 37 *Provisions, Contingent Liabilities and Contingent Assets* (see **chapter 11**), the entity is required to disclose information about contingent liabilities arising from, for example:

[IAS 19.32B]

- actuarial losses relating to other participating entities because each entity that participates in a multi-employer plan shares in the actuarial risks of every other participating entity; or
- any responsibility under the terms of a plan to finance a shortfall in the plan if other entities cease to participate.

Paragraph 32B of IAS 19 was amended by *Improvements to IFRSs* issued in May 2008. The previous wording stated that contingent liabilities might be recognised – which would be inconsistent with the general principles of IAS 37. The amendment is unlikely to have a significant effect in practice.

The amendment is effective for annual accounting periods beginning on or after 1 January 2009, and should be applied retrospectively. Earlier application is permitted, but an entity choosing to apply the amendments made by *Improvements to IFRSs* to IAS 19 early must disclose that fact.

At the time of writing, the amendments made by Improvements to IFRSs *have not yet been endorsed for use in the EU.* UK

5.2 Group plans

A defined benefit plan that shares risks between various entities under common control (e.g. various subsidiaries within a group) is not a multi-employer plan for the purposes of IAS 19. [IAS 19.34] IAS 19.34A & 34B specify the accounting and disclosure requirements for such plans (referred to below as 'group plans').

Information is obtained about the group plan as a whole measured in accordance with IAS 19 on the basis of assumptions that apply to the group plan. The amounts recognised in individual entities will vary, however, depending on the arrangements that exist for charging the net IAS 19 cost to individual group entities:

[IAS 19.34A]

- if there is a contractual agreement or stated policy for charging the net defined benefit cost for the group plan as a whole measured in accordance with IAS 19 to individual group entities, each group entity recognises in its separate or individual financial statements the net defined benefit cost so charged; or
- if there is no such agreement or policy, the net defined benefit cost is recognised in the separate or individual financial statements of the group entity that is legally the sponsoring employer for the plan. Each of the other group entities recognises, in its separate or individual financial statements, a cost equal to its contribution payable for the period.

UK *Thus, a liability relating to a group plan will always be allocated to one or more of the individual group entities under IAS 19. This contrasts with the position under FRS 17, where it is possible for none of the individual plan participants to recognise a liability. (Note that, under FRS 17, the accounting treatment for individual plan participants is unaffected by whether group financial statements are prepared under IFRSs, or under UK GAAP, or are not prepared at all.) This GAAP difference can have a significant impact on distributable reserves, and it is a factor that UK companies will wish to consider when deciding whether to adopt IFRSs for their individual financial statements.*

IAS 19 emphasises that participation in a group plan is a related party transaction. Accordingly, each group entity participating in such a plan is required to disclose in its separate or individual financial statements:

[IAS 19.34B]

- the contractual agreement or stated policy for charging the net defined benefit cost or the fact that there is no such policy;
- the policy for determining the contribution to be paid by the entity;
- if the entity accounts for an allocation of the net defined benefit cost in accordance with IAS 19.34A (see above), all the information about the plan as a whole required by IAS 19.120, 120A and 121(see **9.2**); and

- if the entity accounts for the contribution payable for the period rather than an allocation of the net defined benefit cost, as is permitted in some circumstances under IAS 19.34A (see above), the information about the plan as a whole required by IAS 19.120A(b) – (e), (j), (n), (o), (q) and 121 (see **9.2**). In these circumstances, the other disclosures required by IAS 19.120A do not apply.

5.3 State plans

IAS 19.37 explains that state plans:

> 'are established by legislation to cover all entities (or all entities in a particular category, for example, a specific industry) and are operated by national or local government or by another body (for example, an autonomous agency created specifically for this purpose) which is not subject to control or influence by the reporting entity.'

Normally, state plans will be defined contribution plans. For these plans, a participating employer's liability will be restricted to contributions payable in a period, with the plan being funded on a pay-as-you-go basis. If the entity ceases to employ members of the state plan, it will no longer be liable for further payments even if the benefits of employees for prior periods under the state plan require additional funding. In rare cases, a state plan may be considered a defined benefit plan. IAS 19 requires that such state plans should be treated in the same way as multi-employer plans (see **5.1** above). [IAS 19.36]

Where a plan is established by an entity to provide both compulsory benefits which substitute for benefits that would otherwise be covered under a state plan and additional voluntary benefits, it is not considered to be a state plan. [IAS 19.37]

6 Defined contribution plans

6.1 Basic principles

An entity should recognise the contribution payable to a defined contribution plan in exchange for services rendered by an employee in an accounting period:

[IAS 19.44]

- in the statement of financial position, as:

    - a liability (accrued expense), after deducting any contribution already paid (to the extent that not all of the contributions due for service before the end of the reporting period have been paid at that date); or
    - an asset (prepaid expense), if the amount already paid exceeds the contributions due for service before the end of the reporting period, to the extent that the prepayment will be recoverable (e.g. by means of a reduction in future payments or a cash refund); and
- as an expense, unless another Standard requires or permits inclusion of the contribution in the cost of an asset.

If outstanding contributions to a defined contribution plan do not fall due wholly within twelve months after the end of the period in which the employees render the related service, they should be discounted using the discount rate specified by the Standard for post-employment benefit obligations (see **7.4.3**). [IAS 19.45] All other defined contribution liabilities and expenses are measured on an undiscounted basis. [IAS 19.43]

Example 6.1

Defined contribution plan where forfeitures revert to employer

An employer sponsors a defined contribution plan. Under the terms of the plan, the employer's contributions are discretionary, and amounts forfeited by participants who leave the entity before vesting revert to the employer. In the current year, the employer has made a contribution to the plan. The employer estimates that a portion of its contribution will eventually revert due to forfeitures.

IAS 19.44 provides guidance for contributions that may lead to a reduction in future payments or a cash refund: 'When an employee has rendered service to an entity during a period, the entity shall recognise the contribution payable to a defined contribution plan in exchange for that service . . . If the contribution already paid *exceeds the contribution due for service before the end of the reporting period*, an entity shall recognise that excess as an asset (prepaid expense) to the extent that the prepayment will lead to, for example, a reduction in future payments or a cash refund . . .'. [Emphasis added]

In the circumstances under consideration, all of the contributions paid related to services rendered before the end of the reporting period. As the employer has contributed the amount required for the period, the entire contribution should be recognised as an expense. No reduction is recognised for the amount expected eventually to revert to the employer. Any forfeitures reverting to the employer will be recognised as a reduction of employer contributions in the year that they are forfeited.

6.2 Disclosure

The amount recognised as an expense for defined contribution plans should be disclosed. [IAS 19.46]

Additional disclosures regarding contributions to defined contribution plans for key management personnel may be required in accordance with IAS 24 *Related Party Disclosures* (see **section 5.2** of **chapter 32**). [IAS 19.47]

7 Defined benefit plans

7.1 Basic principles

Accounting for defined benefit plans is much more complex than the accounting for defined contribution plans. It requires the use of actuarial techniques and assumptions to measure the obligation and expense, with the obligation being measured on a discounted basis. The possibility of actuarial gains and losses also arises, as assumptions used will very often differ from actual outcomes.

When accounting for a defined benefit plan, an entity should consider both its legal and constructive obligations. A constructive obligation arises when an entity has no realistic alternative but to pay employee benefits (e.g. where a change in the entity's informal practices would cause unacceptable damage to its relationship with employees). [IAS 19.52] An example cited by IAS 19 is where the formal terms of a plan permit the employer to terminate its obligations under the plan. In practice, it would generally be very difficult for an employer to take such a course of action so that, unless there is evidence to the contrary, it will be assumed that the employer will continue to provide benefits over the remaining working lives of employees. [IAS 19.53]

Example 7.1

Employer with history of improving pension benefits retrospectively

Company O is a manufacturer with a work force whose compensation and other employee benefits are governed by a union contract established through a collective bargaining process. Company O has a history of granting improvements in pension benefits, to both retirees and active employees, during the collective bargaining process. The improvements sometimes have taken the form of fixed monetary increases in monthly benefits, or lump-sum payments made outside the pension plans, or formula-based cost-of-living adjustment (COLA) increases in the monthly benefit. There is no evidence of a present commitment to increase plan benefits other than Company O's history of retrospective plan amendments.

Careful judgement should be applied in assessing whether a constructive obligation has arisen.

In the circumstances described, the employer's practice is to provide improvements only during the collective bargaining process, not during any informal process. The increases in benefits historically have been awarded in several different forms. Therefore, it does not appear that the employer has set a pattern of increases in pension benefits that can be projected reliably to give rise to a constructive obligation. However, if the practice established by an employer were that of a consistent pension-benefit enhancement as part of union negotiations that clearly established a pattern (always a COLA increase, or always fixed monetary increases), it could be concluded that a constructive obligation exists and that those additional benefits should be included in the measurement of the projected benefit obligation.

7.2 Recognition and measurement

7.2.1 *Statement of financial position*

7.2.1.1 Amount to be recognised

The amount recognised as a defined benefit liability is calculated as the net total of:

[IAS 19.54]

- the present value of the defined benefit obligation at the end of the reporting period (i.e. the gross obligation before deducting the fair value of plan assets –see **section 7.3**);
- plus any actuarial gains, or less any actuarial losses, not yet recognised (i.e. as a result of adopting the 'corridor approach'–see **section 7.5**);
- minus any past service cost not yet recognised (see **section 7.6**);
- minus the fair value at the end of the reporting period of plan assets (if any) out of which the obligations are to be settled directly (see **section 7.7**).

Although IAS 19 describes the amount to be included in the statement of financial position as a liability, it is possible that the net balance could be an asset. This would occur where the fair value of plan assets and deferred costs exceeds the gross obligation plus any deferred gains.

7.2.1.2 *The 'asset ceiling'*

If the amount calculated in accordance with IAS 19.54 (see above) is negative, the resulting asset should be measured at the lower of:

[IAS 19.58]

(a) the net total calculated in accordance with IAS 19.54; and

(b) the total of:

  (i) any cumulative unrecognised net actuarial losses and past service cost; and

  (ii) the present value (using the discount rate specified in the Standard – see **7.4.3**) of any economic benefits available in the form of refunds from the plan or reductions in future contributions to the plan.

The restriction described above seeks to ensure that any asset recognised does not exceed the future economic benefit that it represents for the entity. This restriction does not override the delayed recognition of certain actuarial losses (see **7.5.1**) and certain past service cost (see **7.6**), other than as specified in **7.2.1.4** below. Where any amount is not recognised as an asset because of the limit imposed by IAS 19.58, the impact is disclosed (see **section 9.2**).

The following example from IAS 19 illustrates the effect of the 'asset ceiling' requirements.

Example 7.2.1.2

Limit on asset recognised

[Example illustrating IAS 19.60]

A defined benefit plan has the following characteristics:

Present value of the obligation	1,100
Fair value of plan assets	(1,190)
	(90)
Unrecognised actuarial losses	(110)
Unrecognised past service cost	(70)
Unrecognised increase in the liability on initial adoption of the Standard under paragraph 155(b)	(50)
Negative amount determined under paragraph 54	(320)
Present value of available future refunds and reductions in future contributions [see following sections for further consideration]	90

The limit under IAS 19.58(b) is computed as follows:

Unrecognised actuarial losses	*110*
Unrecognised past service cost	*70*
Present value of available future refunds and reductions in future contributions	*90*
Limit	*270*

270 is less than 320. Therefore, the entity recognises an asset of 270 and discloses that the limit reduced the carrying amount of the asset by 50 (see IAS 19.120A(f)(iii)).

In practice, there had been diversity in the interpretation of IAS 19.58(b)(ii), particularly as regards when economic benefits in the form of refunds from the plan or reductions in future contributions to the plan should be regarded as 'available'. As a consequence, in July 2007 the IFRIC issued IFRIC 14 *IAS 19 – The Limit on a Defined Benefit Asset, Minimum Funding Requirements and their Interaction*, which addresses three issues:

- when refunds or reductions in future contributions should be regarded as available in accordance with IAS 19.58 and how the available economic benefit should be measured;
- how a minimum funding requirement might affect the availability of reductions in future contributions; and
- when a minimum funding requirement might give rise to a liability.

These points are discussed in **7.2.1.3** to **7.2.1.6** below.

The Interpretation applies to all post-employment defined benefits and other long-term employee defined benefits. See **7.2.1.7** for a discussion of its effective date.

7.2.1.3 When are refunds 'available'?

IFRIC 14 requires that the availability of a refund or reduction in future contributions should be determined on the basis of the terms and conditions of the plan, and any relevant statutory requirements. [IFRIC 14.7] As a general principle, an economic benefit in the form of a refund or reduction in future contributions is available if the entity can realise that benefit at some point during the life of the plan or when the plan liabilities are settled, even if the benefit is not realisable immediately at the end of the reporting period. [IFRIC 14.8]

The economic benefit available does not depend on how the entity intends to use the surplus – it is the maximum economic benefit that is available from refunds, reductions in future contributions, or a combination of both. In making such estimates, the assumptions made regarding refunds and reductions in future contributions should not be mutually exclusive. [IFRIC 14.9]

In the absence of statutory or contractual minimum funding requirements (see **section 7.2.1.5**) **a refund** is generally available to an entity only when the entity has an unconditional right to the refund:

[IFRIC 14.11]

(a) during the life of the plan, without assuming that the plan liabilities must be settled in order to obtain the refund (e.g. in some jurisdictions, the entity may have a right to a refund during the life of the plan, irrespective of whether the plan liabilities are settled); or

(b) assuming the gradual settlement of the plan liabilities over time until all members have left the plan; or

(c) assuming the full settlement of the plan liabilities in a single event (i.e. as a plan wind-up).

If the entity's right to a refund of a surplus depends on the occurrence or non-occurrence of one or more uncertain future events not wholly within its control, the entity does not have an unconditional right and should not recognise an asset. [IFRIC 14.12]

Whether or not a pension surplus is 'available' will depend on a careful assessment of the legal requirements and the rules of the particular plan, often codified in a trust deed. In some jurisdictions, trustees have the ability or right to protect the interests of members, and to prevent entities from acting 'unreasonably'. Trustees or other third parties may have rights such as the ability to prevent or restrict the payment of a refund, the freedom to determine investment policy and/or the ability to increase benefits in certain circumstances.

Where the trustees have the ability to prevent any or all of a surplus being refunded to an entity, this circumstance would clearly fall within the guidance of IFRIC 14.12, and be a contingent event beyond the entity's control that would prevent it from having an unconditional right to the refund and hence from recognising an asset. However, in some jurisdictions, the ability to prevent a refund may apply to only part of a surplus.

IFRIC 14.11(b) requires consideration of whether a refund would be available assuming the gradual settlement of pension liabilities. When considering gradual settlement, it is necessary to consider what happens at final settlement and, perhaps more importantly, when the plan is closed and members are reducing. For example, once only a limited number of employees are left in the plan, trustees may be required to wind up the plan and secure employees' benefits by purchasing matching insurance policies. IFRIC 14.14 requires an entity to 'include the costs to the plan of settling the plan liabilities' and to deduct 'costs of any insurance premiums that may be required to secure the liability'.

The Basis for Conclusions for IAS 19 (IAS 19.BC10) makes it clear that the entity's ability to improve benefits should not be taken into consideration until such a decision is made. However, a unilateral unlimited right of the trustees to enhance benefits would prevent an entity from having an unconditional right to the surplus.

7.2.1.4 Measurement of the economic benefit

The entity should measure the economic benefit available **as a refund** as the amount of the surplus at the end of the reporting period (i.e. the fair value of the plan assets less the present value of the defined benefit obligation) that the entity has a right to receive as a refund, less any associated costs (e.g. taxes other than income tax). [IFRIC 14.13]

IFRIC 14.13 refers specifically to the fair value of plan assets at the end of the reporting period. Hence, a change of investment strategy (e.g. a move into bonds), whether determined by the entity or by the trustees, represents a potential future change in the fair value of plan assets that should not be taken into account until the investment decision is actually made and the fair value of plan assets changes.

In measuring the amount of a refund available when the plan is wound up (under IFRIC 14.11(c) – see above), the entity should include the costs of settling the liabilities and making the refund (e.g. professional fees and insurance costs should be deducted to the extent that they would be paid by the plan). [IFRIC 14.14]

If the refund is determined as the full amount or a proportion of the surplus, rather than a fixed amount, the amount is calculated without further adjustment for the time value of money, even if the refund is realisable only at a future date, as both the defined benefit obligation and the fair value of plan assets are already measured on a present value basis. [IFRIC 14.15]

If there is no minimum funding requirement, the economic benefit available as **a reduction in future contributions** should be measured as the lower of:

[IFRIC 14.16]

- the surplus in the plan; and
- the present value of the future service cost to the entity (i.e. excluding any part of the future cost that will be borne by employees) for each year over the shorter of the expected life of the plan and the expected life of the entity.

The benefit should be determined using assumptions consistent with those used to determine the defined benefit obligation (including the discount rate) and based on conditions that exist at the end of the reporting period. This means, an entity should assume:

[IFRIC 14.17]

- no change to the benefits provided by a plan in the future until the plan is amended; and
- a stable workforce unless it is demonstrably committed at the end of the reporting period to make a reduction in the number of employees covered by the plan.

7.2.1.5 *The impact of minimum funding requirements*

In many jurisdictions, entities are required, either by law or by agreement with plan managers/trustees, to provide a minimum amount or level of contributions to post-employment benefit plans over a given period, so as to improve the security of the post-employment benefit promise made to the members of such plans. Such commitments are generally referred to as minimum funding requirements.

For the purposes of IFRIC 14, minimum funding requirements are defined as any requirements to fund a post-employment or other long-term defined benefit plan. [IFRIC 14.5] Therefore, both statutory and contractual requirements are covered by the Interpretation.

If a minimum funding requirement is in place for a particular plan, IFRIC 14 distinguishes between contributions that are required to cover:

(a) any existing shortfall for past service on the minimum funding basis; and

(b) the future accrual of benefits.

Under (a), the minimum funding requirement relates to services already received by an entity and does not affect future contributions for future service. To the extent that the contributions payable to cover an existing shortfall on a funding basis will not be available after they have been paid into the plan for a refund or reduction in future contributions, the entity recognises a liability when the obligation to make such contributions arises. [IFRIC 14.24] In other words, if paying the contribution would give rise to an IAS 19 surplus or an increased surplus that would be irrecoverable, this is akin to an onerous contract and a liability should be recognised.

The liability recognised will reduce an existing defined benefit asset or increase a defined benefit liability so that no gain or loss is expected to result from applying IAS 19.58 when the contributions are paid. [IFRIC 14.24]

The liability in respect of the minimum funding requirement, and any subsequent measurement of that liability, should be recognised immediately either through profit or loss or through other comprehensive income, according to the entity's general policy for recognising actuarial gains and losses (see **section 7.5**). [IFRIC 14.26]

For those contributions covered under (b) above (i.e. those that are required to cover the future accrual of benefits), an entity should determine the economic benefit available as a reduction in future contributions as the present value of:

[IFRIC 14.20]

- the estimated future service cost in each year; less
- the estimated minimum funding contributions required in respect of the future accrual of benefits in that year.

This calculation should:

[IFRIC 14.21]

- take into account the effect of any existing surplus on the minimum funding requirement basis;
- be based on assumptions required by the minimum funding requirement and, for any factors not specified by the minimum funding

requirement, on assumptions consistent with those used to determine the defined benefit obligation and with the situation that exists at the end of the reporting period as determined by IAS 19; and

- include any changes expected as a result of the entity paying the minimum contributions due; but
- exclude the effect of expected changes in the terms and conditions of the minimum funding requirement that are not substantively enacted or contractually agreed at the end of the reporting period.

To the extent that the minimum funding contribution required in respect of the future accrual of benefits exceeds the future IAS 19 service cost in any given year, the present value of that excess reduces the amount of the asset available as a reduction in future contributions at the end of the reporting period. However, the amount of that asset can never be less than zero. [IFRIC 14.22]

In some jurisdictions, contribution rates will be determined by law, while in others individual entities and the plan managers/trustees will negotiate the appropriate level of funding. Where the latter is the case, the assumptions to be used for determining the minimum funding requirement may not be clearly defined. It may be necessary to consider the overall funding objective and the basis on which the current contribution schedule was agreed to assess how contributions may be determined in the future. Contribution schedules tend to be more flexible for immature plans (i.e. plans with a high proportion of active employees) than for mature or closed plans. If future contribution levels will be revised to reflect changes in the economic circumstances of the plan (i.e. if contributions may be adjusted downwards or if entities may even take 'contribution holidays' in the event that the scheme is in surplus, an 'economic benefit in the form of reductions in future contributions' will generally be available. On the other hand, if contributions will always be higher than the IAS 19 cost, an analysis of the rules on refunds (see **7.2.1.3** above) would be required.

Example 7.2.1.5

Minimum funding requirements

The following examples are based on those accompanying IFRIC 14 and illustrate the impact of a minimum funding requirement (MFR) on the availability of an economic benefit in the form of a refund or reductions in future contributions and the required accounting treatment under three different scenarios:

A IAS 19 surplus and MFR contributions payable are fully refundable to the entity.

B IAS 19 deficit and MFR contributions payable are not fully available.

C IAS 19 deficit and MFR contributions payable are not fully available, effect on future contribution reduction.

Scenario	A	B	C
Fair value of plan assets	1,200	1,000	1,150
Present value of defined benefit obligation under IAS 19	(1,100)	(1,100)	(1,100)
Defined benefit asset/(liability) (before consideration of MFR)	100	(100)	50
Funding level specified by the MFR (measured on a different basis from IAS 19)	82%	77%	95%
Additional contributions required under the MFR rules	200	300	300
Percentage refundable under the rules of the plan	100%	60%	< 100%*
Adjustment in respect of MFR	0	(80)	(294)
Net asset/(liability) before payment of MFR contributions	100	(180)	(244)

*Contributions to be made over 3 years
For simplicity, it is assumed under all scenarios that there are no unrecognised amounts.

Under Scenario A, payment of the contributions of 200 will increase the IAS 19 surplus (the excess of plan assets over the defined benefit obligation) from 100 to 300. Under the rules of the plan, this amount will be fully refundable to the entity with no associated costs. Therefore, no liability is recognised for the obligation to pay the contributions.

Under Scenario B, the payment of 300 would turn the IAS 19 deficit into a surplus of 200, of which 60 per cent (120) would be refundable to the entity. The remaining 80 (40 per cent of 200) of the contributions paid is not available to the entity. Therefore, the entity increases the defined benefit liability by 80. When the contributions of 300 are paid, the net asset will be 120.

Under Scenario C, the MFR requires the entity to increase the funding level to 100 per cent over the next three years. The contributions are required to make good the deficit on the MFR basis and cover the accrual of benefits in each year on the MFR basis. The nominal amounts are shown in the table below

Year	Total MFR contribution	MFR contribution required to cover the shortfall	MFR contributions required to cover future accrual
1	135	120	15
2	125	112	13
3	115	104	11

Assuming a discount rate of 6 per cent, the present value of the entity's obligation to cover the shortfall is approximately 300 [$120/(1.06) + 112/(1.06)^2 + 104/(1.06)^3$]. Once paid to the plan, the present value of the IAS 19 surplus would increase to 350 (300 + 50). Applying the principles of IFRIC 14, the amounts available as a future contribution reduction are set out below:

Year	IAS 19 service cost	MFR contribution required to cover future accrual	Amount available as contribution reduction
1	13	15	(2)
2	13	13	0
3	13	11	2
4+	13	9	4

Again assuming a discount rate of 6 per cent, the economic benefit available as a future contribution reduction is approximately 56 [$(2)/(1.06) + 0/(1.06)^2 + 2/(1.06)^3 + 4/(1.06)^4 \ldots 4/(1.06)^{50} \ldots$]. As a consequence, the entity would reduce the defined benefit asset by 294 (50 + 300 – 56). The resulting net liability of 244 is recognised immediately in the statement of financial position in accordance with the entity's adopted policy for recognising the effect of the limit in IAS 19.58.

7.2.1.6 Disclosure

IFRIC 14 does not specify any additional disclosure requirements, but notes that, under IAS 1(2007).125 (previously IAS 1(2003).116 – see **7.3** in **chapter 3**), entities are required to disclose information about the key sources of estimation uncertainty that have a significant risk of causing an adjustment to the carrying amount of assets and liabilities within the next financial year. Therefore, the entity should disclose information about the key sources of estimation uncertainty at the end of the reporting period that have a significant risk of causing a material adjustment to the carrying amount of the net asset or liability in the statement of financial position. This might include disclosure of any restrictions on the realisability of the surplus or disclosure of the basis used to determine the amount of the economic benefit available. [IFRIC 14.10]

7.2.1.7 IFRIC 14 – effective date and transition

IFRIC 14 is applicable for annual periods beginning on or after 1 January 2008. Earlier application is permitted. [IFRIC 14.27]

IFRIC 14 is to be applied prospectively from the beginning of the first period presented in the first financial statements to which the Interpretation applies. Any initial adjustment arising should be recognised in retained earnings at the beginning of that period.

Therefore, where the requirements of IFRIC 14 result in a change in accounting policy, entities are not permitted to apply that change retrospectively.

UK

At the time of writing, IFRIC 14 has not yet been endorsed for use in the EU.

7.2.1.8 Restrictions relating to the 'asset ceiling'

The application of the 'asset ceiling' should not result in a gain being recognised solely as a result of an actuarial loss or past service cost in the current period, nor in a loss being recognised solely as a result of an actuarial gain in the current period. [IAS 19.58A] Accordingly, while the defined benefit asset is being measured in accordance with IAS 19.58(b) (i.e. restricted to any cumulative unrecognised net actuarial losses and past service cost plus the present value of any future refunds and contribution reductions –see **7.2.1.2**), any of the following that arise should be recognised immediately:

- net actuarial losses of the current period and past service cost of the current period to the extent that they exceed any reduction in the present value of the economic benefits relating to refunds and reductions in future contributions (i.e. the amounts specified in IAS 19.58(b)(ii) – see **7.2.1.2**). If there is no change or an increase in the present value of those economic benefits, the entire net actuarial losses of the current period and past service cost of the current period should be recognised immediately; [IAS 19.58A(a)] and
- net actuarial gains of the current period after the deduction of past service cost of the current period to the extent that they exceed any increase in the present value of the economic benefits relating to refunds and reductions (i.e. the amounts specified in IAS 19.58(b)(ii) – see **7.2.1.2**). If there is no change or a decrease in the present value of those economic benefits, the entire net actuarial gains of the current period after the deduction of past service cost of the current period should be recognised immediately. [IAS 19.58A(b)]

These restrictions apply only where an entity has, at the beginning or end of the accounting period, a surplus in a defined benefit plan and cannot, based on the current terms of the plan, recover that surplus fully through refunds or reductions in future contributions. [IAS 19.58B] The objective of the restrictions is to prevent the inappropriate recognition of gains and losses. Appendix C to IAS 19 illustrates how these restrictions are applied.

The requirement of IAS 19.58A not to recognise a gain (increase in asset)/loss (decrease in asset) as a result of an actuarial loss or past service cost/actuarial gain in the current period may be illustrated by adapting the circumstances cited in **example 7.2.1.2** above, if it is assumed that an additional unrecognised actuarial loss of 10 arose in the current period, all other factors being kept equal. The surplus recognised under the requirements of IAS 19.58(b) would increase the asset to 280, resulting in the recognition of a gain. If an entity cannot, based on the current terms of the plan, recover that surplus fully through refunds or reductions in future contributions, this increase will have to be offset by a corresponding decrease in the present value of economic benefits that qualify for recognition. In such cases, actuarial losses or past service cost/actuarial gains will effectively have to be recognised immediately.

7.2.2 *Profit or loss*

The net total of the following amounts is recognised in profit or loss (or in the cost of an asset, to the extent that capitalisation is required or permitted):

[IAS 19.61]

- current service cost (see **section 7.3**);
- interest cost (see **section 7.4.1**);
- expected return on plan assets (see **section 7.7.6**) and on any reimbursement rights (see **section 7.7.4**);
- actuarial gains and losses as required in accordance with the entity's accounting policy (see **section 7.5**);
- past service cost to the extent recognised (see **section 7.6**);
- the effect of curtailments or settlements (see **section 7.8**); and
- the effect of the limit in IAS 19.58(b) (see **sections 7.2.1.1** to **7.2.1.8** above) unless it is recognised outside profit or loss in accordance with IAS 19.93C (see **section 7.5.3**).

Neither IAS 19 nor IAS 1 prescribes how the amount(s) recognised in profit or loss should be presented. **Section 9.1** considers the options available for classification in the statement of comprehensive income.

Where employee costs are capitalised as part of the cost of an asset (e.g. inventories under IAS 2 *Inventories* or self-constructed property in accordance with IAS 16 *Property, Plant and Equipment*), the appropriate proportion of the net total above is included in the employee costs capitalised. [IAS 19.62]

7.3 Defined benefit obligation and current service cost

7.3.1 Definitions

The present value of a defined benefit obligation is the present value, without deducting any plan assets, of expected future payments required to settle the obligation resulting from employee service in the current and prior periods. [IAS 19.7]

Current service cost is the increase in the present value of the defined benefit obligation resulting from employee service in the current period. [IAS 19.7]

In 2007, the IFRIC considered two issues in relation to the treatment of employee contributions to the cost of retirement benefits (see *IFRIC Update*, November 2007). The first issue was how employee contributions should be accounted for in general. The second issue was how to account for a pension plan in which the cost of providing the benefits is shared between the employees and the employer.

On the first issue, the IFRIC noted the IAS 19.7 definition of current service cost and that IAS 19.120A (see **section 9.2**) implies that contributions by employees to the ongoing cost of the plan reduce the current service cost to the entity. The IFRIC also noted that, in accordance with IAS 19.91, employee contributions payable when benefits are paid, such as contributions to a post-employment healthcare plan, are to be taken into account in determining the defined benefit obligation.

On the second issue, the IFRIC noted that IAS 19.85 states that 'If the formal terms of a plan (or a constructive obligation that goes beyond those terms) require an entity to change benefits in future periods, the measurement of the obligation reflects those changes'. Therefore, the IFRIC noted that:

- if the terms of a defined benefit plan include surplus-sharing provisions, the employer's obligation to use any surplus in the plan for the benefit of plan participants (e.g. adjusting participants' benefits) should be considered when measuring its obligation) and
- if the terms of a defined benefit plan include cost-sharing provisions, the requirement for employees to make contributions to reduce or eliminate an existing deficit should be considered when measuring the employer's obligation.

The final cost of a defined benefit plan is influenced by many uncertain variables (e.g. final salaries, employee turnover and mortality, medical cost trends and investment earnings). [IAS 19.63] The use of actuarial techniques to value an obligation and allocate it to accounting periods allows an entity to measure an obligation with sufficient reliability to justify recognition of a liability. The whole of the obligation is discounted, even if part of it falls due within twelve months after the reporting period. [IAS 19.66]

7.3.2 *Measurement of the present value of a defined benefit obligation*

A number of steps are required in order to measure the present value of a defined benefit obligation and the associated current service cost. These steps, which are considered in the following paragraphs, are:

- to apply an actuarial valuation method (see **7.3.3**);
- to attribute benefit to the employees' periods of service (see **7.3.4**);
- to make actuarial assumptions (see **7.3.5**);
- to perform actuarial valuations (see **7.3.6**); and
- to consider the impact of tax and social security payments (see **7.3.7**).

7.3.3 *Actuarial valuation method*

The Projected Unit Credit Method should be used to determine the present value of an entity's defined benefit obligation, the related current service cost and, where applicable, past service cost. [IAS 19.64] IAS 19.65 explains that the Projected Unit Credit Method treats each period of service as giving rise to an additional unit of benefit entitlement and measures each unit separately to build up the final obligation.

No other valuation method is permitted under IAS 19.

The Projected Unit Credit Method referred to by IAS 19 is sometimes also called the 'accrued benefit method pro-rated on service', the 'benefit/years of service' method or the 'projected unit' method. [IAS 19.65]

UK

Although they are given slightly different names, the Projected Unit Credit Method referred to by IAS 19 is the same as the projected unit method mandated by FRS 17.

Example 7.3.3, which is included in the Standard, provides a simple illustration of the application of the Projected Unit Credit Method.

Example 7.3.3

Projected Unit Credit Method

[Example illustrating IAS 19.65]

A lump sum benefit is payable on termination of service and equal to 1% of final salary for each year of service. The salary in year 1 is 10,000 and is assumed to increase at 7% (compound) each year. The discount rate used is 10% per year. The following table shows how the obligation builds up for an employee who is expected to leave at the end of year 5, assuming that there are no changes in actuarial assumptions. For simplicity, this example ignores the additional adjustment needed to reflect the probability that the employee may leave the entity at an earlier or later date.

Year	**1**	**2**	**3**	**4**	**5**
Benefit attributed to					
- prior years	*0*	*131*	*262*	*393*	*524*
- current year (1% of final salary)	*131*	*131*	*131*	*131*	*131*
- current and prior years	*131*	*262*	*393*	*524*	*655*
Opening obligation	*0*	*89*	*196*	*324*	*476*
Interest at 10%	*0*	*9*	*20*	*33*	*48*
Current service cost	*89*	*98*	*108*	*119*	*131*
Closing obligation	*89*	*196*	*324*	*476*	*655*

Note:

1. *The opening obligation is the present value of benefit attributed to prior years.*
2. *The current service cost is the present value of benefit attributed to the current year.*
3. *The closing obligation is the present value of benefit attributed to current and prior years.*

7.3.4 *Attributing benefit to periods of service*

When determining the present value of the defined benefit obligation, current service cost and (where applicable) past service cost, an entity should attribute benefit to periods of service using the plan's benefit formula. [IAS 19.67]

An exception to the foregoing is made where the benefit levels are skewed to the later years of an employee's service (see below).

The measurement of the liability for vested benefits must reflect the expected date of employees leaving service and must be discounted to a present value (as illustrated in the examples below). It is not acceptable to measure the liability at an undiscounted amount (i.e. at the amount that would be payable if all employees left the entity at the end of the reporting period). This issue has been discussed by the IFRIC and the treatment confirmed (see *IFRIC Update*, June 2002).

The following examples are included in IAS 19 to illustrate the attribution of benefit to periods of service.

Example 7.3.4A

Attributing benefit to periods of service (1)

[Examples illustrating IAS 19.68]

1. A defined benefit plan provides a lump-sum benefit of 100 payable on retirement for each year of service.

   A benefit of 100 is attributed to each year. The current service cost is the present value of 100. The present value of the defined benefit obligation is the present value of 100, multiplied by the number of years of service up to the end of the reporting period.

   If the benefit is payable immediately when the employee leaves the entity, the current service cost and the present value of the defined benefit obligation reflect the date at which the employee is expected to leave. Thus, because of the effect of discounting, they are less than the amounts that would be determined if the employee left at the end of the reporting period.

2. A plan provides a monthly pension of 0.2% of final salary for each year of service. The pension is payable from the age of 65.

   Benefit equal to the present value, at the expected retirement date, of a monthly pension of 0.2% of the estimated final salary payable from the expected retirement date until the expected date of death is attributed to each year of service. The current service cost is the present value of that benefit. The present value of the defined benefit obligation is the present value of monthly pension payments of 0.2% of final salary, multiplied by the number

> *of years of service up to the end of the reporting period. The current service cost and the present value of the defined benefit obligation are discounted because pension payments begin at the age of 65.*

Employee service gives rise to an obligation under a defined benefit plan even if the benefits are not vested (e.g. if they are conditional on future employment). The probability that some employees may not ultimately satisfy any vesting conditions is reflected in the measurement of the defined benefit obligation. [IAS 19.69]

Similarly, although certain post-employment benefits (e.g. post-employment medical benefits) become payable only if a specified event occurs when an employee is no longer employed, an obligation is created when the employee renders service that will provide entitlement to the benefit if the specified event occurs. The probability that the specified event will occur affects the measurement of the obligation, but does not determine whether the obligation exists. [IAS 19.69]

The following examples, which are included in the Standard, illustrate the application of IAS 19.69.

Example 7.3.4B

Attributing benefit to periods of service (2)

[Examples illustrating IAS 19.69]

1. A plan pays a benefit of 100 for each year of service. The benefits vest after ten years of service.

   A benefit of 100 is attributed to each year. In each of the first ten years, the current service cost and the present value of the obligation reflect the probability that the employee may not complete ten years of service.

2. A plan pays a benefit of 100 for each year of service, excluding service before the age of 25. The benefits vest immediately.

   No benefit is attributed to service before the age of 25 because service before that date does not lead to benefits (conditional or unconditional). A benefit of 100 is attributed to each subsequent year.

The obligation increases until the date when further service by the employee will lead to no material amount of further benefits. Therefore, all benefit is attributed to periods ending on or before that date. Benefit is attributed to individual accounting periods under the plan's benefit formula. However, if an employee's service in later years will lead to a materially higher level of benefit than in earlier years, an entity attributes benefit on a straight-line basis until the date when further service by the employee will lead to no material amount of further benefits. That is because the employee's service throughout the entire period will ultimately lead to benefit at that higher level. [IAS 19.67 & 70]

Example 7.3.4C

Attributing benefit to periods of service (3)

[Examples illustrating IAS 19.70]

1. A plan pays a lump-sum benefit of 1,000 that vests after ten years of service. The plan provides no further benefit for subsequent service.

   A benefit of 100 (1,000 divided by ten) is attributed to each of the first ten years. The current service cost in each of the first ten years reflects the probability that the employee may not complete ten years of service. No benefit is attributed to subsequent years.

2. A plan pays a lump-sum retirement benefit of 2,000 to all employees who are still employed at the age of 55 after twenty years of service, or who are still employed at the age of 65, regardless of their length of service.

   For employees who join before the age of 35, service first leads to benefits under the plan at the age of 35 (an employee could leave at the age of 30 and return at the age of 33, with no effect on the amount or timing of benefits). Those benefits are conditional on further service Also, service beyond the age of 55 will lead to no material amount of further benefits. For these employees, the entity attributes benefit of 100 (2,000 divided by 20) to each year from the age of 35 to the age of 55.

   For employees who join between the ages of 35 and 45, service beyond twenty years will lead to no material amount of further benefits. For these employees, the entity attributes benefit of 100 (2,000 divided by 20) to each of the first twenty years.

   For an employee who joins at the age of 55, service beyond ten years will lead to no material amount of further benefits. For this employee, the entity attributes benefit of 200 (2,000 divided by 10) to each of the first ten years.

   For all employees, the current service cost and the present value of the obligation reflect the probability that the employee may not complete the necessary period of service.

3. A post-employment medical plan reimburses 40% of an employee's post-employment medical costs if the employee leaves after more than ten and less than twenty years of service and 50% of those costs if the employee leaves after twenty or more years of service.

   Under the plan's benefit formula, the entity attributes 4% of the present value of the expected medical costs (40% divided by ten) to each of the first ten years and 1% (10% divided by ten) to each of the second ten years. The current service cost in each year reflects the probability that the employee may not complete the necessary period of service to earn part or all of the benefits. For employees expected to leave within ten years, no benefit is attributed.

4. A post-employment medical plan reimburses 10% of an employee's post-employment medical costs if the employee leaves after more than ten and less than twenty years of service and 50% of those costs if the employee leaves after twenty or more years of service.

Service in later years will lead to a materially higher level of benefit than in earlier years. Therefore, for employees expected to leave after twenty or more years, the entity attributes benefit on a straight-line basis under IAS 19.68. Service beyond twenty years will lead to no material amount of further benefits. Therefore, the benefit attributed to each of the first twenty years is 2.5% of the present value of the expected medical costs (50% divided by twenty).

For employees expected to leave between ten and twenty years, the benefit attributed to each of the first ten years is 1% of the present value of the expected medical costs. For these employees, no benefit is attributed to service between the end of the tenth year and the estimated date of leaving.

For employees expected to leave within ten years, no benefit is attributed.

Note that, in the third illustration in **example 7.3.4C**, the level of benefit after twenty years is considered to be materially higher than after ten years, whereas in the fourth illustration it is not.

Where the amount of a benefit is a constant proportion of final salary for each year of service, future salary increases will affect the amount required to settle the obligation that exists for service before the end of the reporting period, but do not create an additional obligation. Therefore:

[IAS 19.71]

- for the purpose of IAS 19.67(b) (see above), salary increases do not lead to further benefits, even though the amount of the benefits is dependent on final salary; and
- the amount of benefit attributed to each period is a constant proportion of the salary to which the benefit is linked.

Example 7.3.4D

Attributing benefit to periods of service (4)

[Example illustrating IAS 19.71]

Employees are entitled to a benefit of 3% of final salary for each year of service before the age of 55.

Benefit of 3% of estimated final salary is attributed to each year up to the age of 55. This is the date when further service by the employee will lead to no material amount of further benefits under the plan. No benefit is attributed to service after that age.

By completing the allocation of current service cost at the time that no further benefit accrues, this cost is allocated over a period that is shorter than the period when an employee is expected to provide service to the employer. The reason for this, as explained in IAS 19.67, is that the subsequent period of employment yields no material amount of further benefits.

7.3.4.1 *Death-in-service benefits*

IAS 19 does not specifically address the question of accounting for death-in-service benefits. See **11.3** for a discussion of the considerations regarding the appropriate accounting treatment of such benefits.

7.3.4.2 *Career Average Re-valued Earnings plans*

In some jurisdictions, entities may offer 'Career Average Re-valued Earnings' (CARE) pension plans, also referred to as 'Pension Builder Plans', to their employees. Such plans generally provide a defined benefit pension based on the employee's number of years of service and the average salary earned over the period of service. The plan formula is stated as:

> a member shall accrue for each year of service: accrual rate x current (or average) salary *

* The salary in each year is typically re-valued (either to give an adjusted current salary or to determine the adjusted average salary) in line with a specified index (e.g. price inflation) between the date of accrual and the date of retirement to maintain purchasing power. The index used to re-value salaries earned in past years is typically lower than the wage increase over the service period.

Such plans should be measured using the Projected Unit Credit Method, taking into account estimated future salary increases as required by IAS 19.83(a) and IAS 19.84. IAS 19.67 states that in determining the defined benefit obligations

> "an entity shall attribute benefit to periods of service under the plan's benefit formula. However, if an employee's service in later years will lead to a materially higher level of benefit than in earlier years, an entity shall attribute benefit on a straight-line basis."

The CARE plan formula described above does attribute a higher level of benefit to later years and therefore an entity will need to assess whether this is likely to be materially higher, in which case the benefits will need to be attributed on a straight-line basis.

7.3.5 *Actuarial assumptions*

The actuarial assumptions used for the purposes of measuring a defined obligation should be unbiased and mutually compatible. [IAS 19.72] They are an entity's best estimates of the variables that will determine the ultimate cost of providing post-employment benefits. They should be neither imprudent nor excessively conservative, and should reflect the economic relationships between factors such as inflation, rates of salary increase, return on plan assets and discount rates. [IAS 19.74 & 75]

IAS 19.73 explains that actuarial assumptions comprise:

(a) demographic assumptions about the future characteristics of current and former employees (and their dependants) who are eligible for benefits. Demographic assumptions deal with matters such as:

- (i) mortality, both during and after employment;
- (ii) rates of employee turnover, disability and early retirement;
- (iii) the proportion of plan members with dependants who will be eligible for benefits; and
- (iv) claim rates under medical plans; and

(b) financial assumptions, dealing with items such as:

- (i) the discount rate (see **section 7.4.3** below);
- (ii) future salary and benefit levels (see **sections 7.3.5.2** and **7.3.5.3** below);
- (iii) in the case of medical benefits, future medical costs, including, where material, the cost of administering claims and benefit payments (see **section 7.3.5.4** below); and

(iv) the expected rate of return on plan assets (see **section 7.7.6**).

7.3.5.1 *Financial assumptions*

Financial assumptions should be based on market expectations at the end of the reporting period, for the period over which the post-employment benefit obligations will be settled. [IAS 19.77] Discount rates and other financial assumptions should not be inflation-adjusted unless such measures are more reliable (e.g. in a hyperinflationary economy, or where benefits are index-linked). [IAS 19.76]

7.3.5.2 *Future salary increases*

When considering future salary increases, account should be taken of inflation, seniority, promotion and any other relevant factors (both internal and external), such as the scarcity or surplus of potential employees with the required skills. [IAS 19.84]

7.3.5.3 *Benefit levels*

The post-employment benefit obligation should reflect plan terms relating to benefit levels, and any constructive obligation that extends those terms, at the end of the reporting period. This would include any obligation to increase benefits to mitigate the effects of inflation (either as required by the terms of the plan or in line with the entity's past history of increasing benefits, i.e. a constructive obligation) or a benefit improvement (required by the plan terms, legislation or established practice of the entity) arising from an actuarial gain that has already been recognised in the financial statements. [IAS 19.83 & 85]

Some post-employment benefits are linked to levels of state-provided benefits, such as state-provided retirement benefits and medical care. In such cases, the post-employment benefit obligation should reflect estimated future changes in those state benefits, based on past history and other reliable evidence. [IAS 19.87]

Such changes will be reflected if they were enacted before the end of the reporting period, or if past history and other reliable evidence indicate that the state benefits will change in a predictable manner (e.g. in line with general salary or price levels).

Future benefit changes that are not included in the actuarial assumptions because they do not arise from the formal terms of the plan or from a constructive obligation (such as the entity's established practice) will, when they are introduced, result in past service cost (to the extent that they have a retrospective impact) and current service cost (to the extent that they change benefits for service after the change). [IAS 19.86]

7.3.5.4 Post-employment medical benefits

When measuring the obligation arising in respect of post-employment medical benefits, additional assumptions are required. They include general inflation and specific changes in future medical costs, level and frequency of claims, technological advances, changes in the health status of participants in the plan, and changes in the utilisation and delivery of health care. In making these assumptions, reference may be made to historical data from the entity's own records and external data from other entities, insurers, medical providers and other sources. It is important that such assumptions are adjusted where the population providing the historical data differs from that for which the obligation arises. For example, the level and frequency of claims may be sensitive to age, sex and current health status of those benefiting under the plan. The estimate of future medical costs should take account of contributions due from beneficiaries towards medical cost, based upon the terms of the plan, or additional constructive obligations, at the end of the reporting period, and also any cost that may be met by the state or other medical providers. [IAS 19.88 – 91]

7.3.5.5 Pension promises based on performance targets

Defined benefit plans may include pension promises that are based on achieving specific performance targets, such as additional pensionable earnings in the form of bonuses for achieving specified performance targets, arrangements relating to additional sponsor contributions, or additional years of deemed service.

The impact of such promises on the measurement of the defined benefit obligation has been considered by the IFRIC (see *IFRIC Update*, January 2008). The IFRIC noted that IAS 19.73 defines actuarial assumptions as an entity's best estimates of the variables that will determine the ultimate cost of providing post-employment benefits. Performance targets are variables that will affect the ultimate cost of providing post-employment benefits and should, therefore, be included in the determination of the defined benefit obligation.

The IFRIC also noted that IAS 19.67 also requires benefits to be attributed to 'periods of service under the plan's defined benefit formula' unless 'an employee's service in later years will lead to a materially higher level of benefit than in earlier years ...'. Consequently, when benefits are affected by performance targets, the effect on the attribution of benefits must also be considered.

7.3.5.6 *Subsequent introduction of new state cost*

Where a state introduces in an unpredictable manner a new significant state cost (e.g. tax) for an existing employer's defined benefit obligation, with no impact on the ultimate benefit to be received by employees, the change should be treated as a change in actuarial assumptions (and not as a plan amendment).

IAS 19.73 states that actuarial assumptions are an entity's best estimates of the variables that will determine the ultimate cost of providing post-employment benefits. Where an entity does not explicitly state an assumption about such a variable, it is effectively making an assumption of zero value for that element. Any resulting differences from actual numbers are experience adjustments.

Where there is a change in a post-employment benefit cost without a change in the benefits to be paid to employees, this change should be accounted for as a change in actuarial assumptions.

7.3.5.7 *Changes in legislation*

In 2007, the IFRIC was asked to provide guidance on accounting for the effects of a change to a defined benefit arrangement resulting from action by government (see *IFRIC Update*, November 2007).

The IFRIC noted that IAS 19 already provides guidance on whether the identity of the originator of the change affects the accounting. Paragraph 55 of the Basis for Conclusions to IAS 19 explains the IASC Board's decision to reject the proposal that 'past service costs should not be recognised immediately if the past service cost results from legislative changes (such as a new requirement to equalise retirement ages for men and women) or from decisions by trustees who are not controlled, or influenced by, the entity's management'. In other words, the IASC did not believe that the source of the change should affect the accounting. Therefore, the accounting for changes caused by government should be the same as the accounting for changes made by an employer.

The IFRIC acknowledged that, in some circumstances, it might be difficult to determine whether the change affects actuarial assumptions or benefits payable and noted that judgement is required.

Example 7.3.5.7

Accounting for the effect of a change in legislation

Entity X operates a defined benefit pension plan. Under the plan rules, members can choose, on retirement, to receive an annual pension or to exchange part of the pension for a tax-free lump sum payment. The plan rules specify a commutation rate of 9:1, which means that a member can exchange one unit of annual pension for a tax-free lump sum payment of nine units. The lump sum amount is subject to a maximum set by the tax authority.

Changes in tax legislation increase the maximum lump sum amount that a member can receive tax-free.

In the past, members generally preferred to take the immediate lump sum payment rather than the ongoing pension, either from a liquidity perspective or because they underestimated the effective value of the pension.

The increased lump sum maximum might allow X to mitigate the adverse effects of increasing longevity and falling interest rates. For example, when the applicable commutation rate no longer reflects a cost-neutral exchange rate of pension versus lump sum, an increase in the maximum lump sum amount (with the same commutation rate), will lead to a reduction in the defined benefit obligation on the basis of the assumption that members will choose the maximum lump sum payment on retirement.

Because of the change in tax legislation, X amends the scheme rules to permit members to opt for the 'increased' lump sum amount on retirement. No other amendments are made to the scheme rules, and the commutation rate remains the same.

The legislative change alters how members can choose to receive the benefits, not the overall benefits that members are entitled to. The amount available to members on retirement, which can be taken as an annual pension or a lump sum, does not change. Because members are no better or worse off, amending the pension scheme solely to reflect this legislative change does not substantively alter the defined benefit plan and, therefore, should not be treated as a plan amendment.

The pension fund retains the long-term risk for any amounts taken as a pension (i.e. amounts the employee chooses not to receive as a lump sum). As part of the actuarial valuation, the employer assesses how many employees are expected to take part of their overall benefits as a lump sum and (2) how much each employee is expected to take. If the legislation changes to allow more to be taken as a lump sum, it is likely that the actuarial assumptions regarding the amounts taken as a lump sum would change, resulting in an actuarial gain or loss that should be accounted for in accordance with the entity's accounting policy for actuarial gains and losses.

7.3.6 *Actuarial valuations*

IAS 19 does not specify the frequency of valuations, either for the measurement of plan assets or the determination of the present value of the defined benefit obligation. It requires that the valuations be performed with sufficient regularity that the amounts recognised in the financial statements do not differ materially from the amounts that would be determined at the end of the reporting period. [IAS 19.56]

7.3.6.1 *Involvement of an actuary*

IAS 19 does not require the involvement of a qualified actuary but, in practice, it will usually be difficult to value material defined benefit obligations without actuarial involvement.

7.3.6.2 *Date of valuation*

An entity is not precluded from using a detailed valuation of the obligation at a date prior to the end of the reporting period provided that it is updated for any material transactions or other changes up to the end of the reporting period. Although many entities carry out actuarial valuations annually, at the end of the reporting period, some carry out full actuarial valuations less frequently (e.g. every three years) and update approximately to the end of each reporting period.

Although local legislation may not require a full plan valuation every year, in order to meet the requirement of IAS 19.56 (see **7.3.6**), it may be necessary for some aspects of the valuation to be reviewed at the end of each reporting period (e.g. the fair value of plan assets and financial assumptions such as the discount rate and the rate of salary increase). Demographic assumptions, such as mortality rates and rate of employee turnover, may not need to be reviewed annually.

7.3.6.3 *Interim reporting*

IAS 19 does not give any guidance as to what is expected in terms of an actuarial valuation for an interim reporting period under IAS 34 *Interim Financial Reporting*. In appendix B9, IAS 34 states as follows.

'Pension cost for an interim period is calculated on a year-to-date basis by using the actuarially determined pension cost rate at the end of the prior financial year, adjusted for significant market fluctuations since that time and for significant curtailments, settlements, or other significant one-time events.'

Although there is no requirement to conduct a full actuarial valuation at the end of each interim reporting period, clearly there is a requirement to consider any significant changes in the performance of the plan assets, or in interest rates or other factors affecting the computation, and their impact on the net defined benefit asset or obligation. In practice, it may be that valuations will not be updated for interim periods unless there are significant valuation movements. Instead, the probable effects of any valuation changes from expectations would be disclosed in the notes.

7.3.7 *Tax and social security payments*

7.3.7.1 *Tax gross-up of pension benefit*

Some entities settle their defined benefit obligation for employees through the purchase of non-participating annuity contracts that are distributed to the employees. These contracts do not require any contribution ('participation') from employees. The receipt of the non-participating annuity contracts by the employee may trigger a taxable event for the employee upon distribution. Some entities compensate the employees so that the after-tax benefit to the employee is the same as if the contracts were not distributed, although this is commonly not a formal feature of the plan.

A tax gross-up payment made by an employer to an employee is an amendment of the defined benefit plan only if the employer actually amends its post-employment benefit plan to provide for this benefit. If the employer does not amend its plan to provide the additional benefit, the cash payment is regarded as additional compensation expense and recognised in the current period.

However, if the employer establishes a pattern of providing such benefits, a constructive obligation may arise, in which case the benefits are considered part of the substantive written plan and included in the basis for accounting for the plan pursuant to IAS 19.52.

7.3.7.2 Social security contributions by employer

Example 7.3.7.2

Social security contributions by employer

An entity operates a defined benefit plan.

- The benefit to be paid out at the age of 60 amounts to £1,000.
- The entity, at the time the benefit is paid, will pay employer social security tax of £200.
- The entity is also required to withhold the employee's social security tax of £150.
- The net benefit received by the employee is £850 (£1,000 – £150).
- Cash paid out by the entity is £1,200 (£1,000 + £200).
- The amount of social security tax contributed by the employer is calculated as a percentage of the employee benefits granted.

Employer social security tax levied on the benefits paid out to the employee is a directly related inherent cost of receiving services from employees and, consequently, is part of the consideration paid for those services.

In the above scenario, the social security contributed by the employer can be seen as part of a defined benefit of £1,200 under which the employee will have to pay 100 per cent of the employer and employee social security contributions that would reduce the net pay-out to £850. Therefore, the entity by assuming a percentage of that contribution, either voluntarily or by legislation, should recognise the cost of the social security payment in the same manner as the underlying benefit, by including its cost in the calculation of the present value of the defined benefit obligation.

7.4 Interest cost and discount rate

7.4.1 Interest cost

Interest cost is the increase during a period in the present value of a defined benefit obligation which arises because the benefits are one period closer to settlement. [IAS 19.7]

7.4.2 Calculation of interest cost

Interest cost is calculated as follows:

[IAS 19.82]

Discount rate determined at start of period	x	Present value of the defined benefit obligation throughout that period

Note that interest cost is calculated on the defined benefit obligation (i.e. the gross obligation before deducting the fair value of plan assets) not the (net) liability presented in the statement of financial position. Since the reference is to the obligation throughout the period, the calculation should reflect changes in the obligation.

7.4.3 *Discount rate*

The discount rate is one of the most important assumptions utilised in measuring defined benefit obligations. The rate used should reflect the time value of money, but not credit risk specific to an entity, nor the risk that actual experience may differ from assumptions, nor the actuarial or investment risk. [IAS 19.79]

The Standard specifies that:

[IAS 19.78]

- the rate used to discount post-employment benefit obligations (both funded and unfunded) should be determined by reference to market yields at the end of the reporting period on high quality corporate bonds;
- in countries where there is no deep market in such bonds, the market yields (at the end of the reporting period) on government bonds should be used; and
- the currency and term of the corporate bonds or government bonds should be consistent with the currency and estimated term of the post-employment benefit obligations.

IAS 19 does not provide any further guidance on the meaning of the term 'high quality corporate bonds'. In practice, the term is generally taken to refer to corporate bonds with one of the two highest ratings from a recognised rating agency in jurisdictions in which such an agency exists.

The determination as to whether a deep market for high quality corporate bonds exists is based on the economy in which the retirement benefit plan is located and whether the bonds are considered high quality in that economy. It is essential to look at comparisons with the government bond market and the rates for those bonds, Where the market for AA- and AAA-rated bonds is narrow, judgement is required to determine whether high quality corporate bonds should be considered to exist at all in the particular economy. For example, because of an economic downturn, the market for AA- or AAA- rated bonds may be temporarily very narrow, but there may be a deep market in A-rated bonds.

In 2005, the IFRIC was asked to consider whether, in circumstances where there is no deep market in high quality corporate bonds in a country, it is appropriate to use a discount rate based on a synthetic equivalent constructed by reference to the market in another country instead of using the yield on government bonds (see *IFRIC Update*, June 2005). The IFRIC took the view that IAS 19.78 is clear that the use of such a synthetically-constructed equivalent is not appropriate, and that the yield on government bonds should be used.

However, the IFRIC observed that the reference to 'in a country' could reasonably be read as including high quality corporate bonds that are available in a regional market to which the entity has access provided that the currency of the regional market and the country are the same (e.g. the Euro).

The amount of the yield on such bonds over time has a material effect on the measurement of pension obligations. For example, if the pension liability discussed previously in **example 7.3.3** was discounted using a rate of 5% (instead of 10%), the present value of the obligation would change substantially, as demonstrated below.

Year	**1**	**2**	**3**	**4**	**5**
Opening obligation	0	108	226	356	499
Interest at 5%	0	5	11	18	25
Current service cost	108	113	119	125	131
Closing obligation@ 5%	108	226	356	499	655
Closing obligation@ 10% (per **example 7.3.3**)	89	196	324	476	655

Comparing the results above, it becomes apparent that the longer the period remaining until retirement (i.e. the higher the number of younger active employees in a pension plan), the more dramatic the impact of changes in interest rates will be. For example, at the end of year 1, the obligation discounted at 5% is 20% higher than that measured at 10%, while that gap would narrow to about 5% in year 4. In practice, actuaries estimate that, depending on the circumstances, a decrease in the discount rate of 0.5% could cause the liability to rise by up to 20%, while a 2% decline could increase the liability by more than 150%. Fluctuations in the discount rate over time are one of the major sources of actuarial gains and losses, discussed in detail in **section 7.5** below.

7.4.3.1 Term of bonds and obligations

The requirement for the term of the bonds to be consistent with the term of the obligations means that they should reflect the estimated timing of the benefit payments. The Standard notes that, in practice, this may be achieved by applying a single weighted average discount rate that reflects the estimated timing and amount of benefit payments and the currency in which the benefits are to be paid.

If there is no deep market for bonds of a sufficiently long maturity date to match that of all of the obligation payments, the entity may extrapolate current market rates for a shorter period along the yield curve. [IAS 19.81]

7.5 Actuarial gains and losses

Actuarial gains and losses comprise:

[IAS 19.7]

- experience adjustments (the effects of differences between the previous actuarial assumptions and what has actually occurred); and
- the effects of changes in actuarial assumptions.

Actuarial gains and losses can arise from changes in the present value of the defined benefit obligation or the fair value of the related plan assets. They arise because actual outcomes or current forecasts differ from the forecasts of earlier periods. For example, the actual return on plan assets may differ from the expected return, the actual rate of employee turnover may differ from the expected rate, or changes may occur in forecast salary increases.

IAS 19 permits a number of policies for the recognition of actuarial gains and losses.

- **10% corridor** The minimum requirement is that actuarial gains and losses that breach a pre-determined 'corridor' should be recognised over a specified period (see **section 7.5.1** below). Under this corridor approach, the 'excess' gains and losses are recognised in profit or loss.

- **Faster recognition** The Standard permits any systematic method for recognition that results in faster recognition of actuarial gains and losses (see **section 7.5.2**), provided that the same basis is applied to both gains and losses, and the basis is applied consistently from period to period. Where any such method is adopted, other than immediate recognition (see below), then the gains and losses are recognised in profit or loss.
- **Immediate recognition** Where actuarial gains and losses are recognised in full as they occur, entities are permitted to recognise those gains and losses either in profit or loss or in other comprehensive income (see **section 7.5.3**).

In purely numerical terms, the choice of approaches above represents the most significant difference between IAS 19 and FRS 17, in that the latter requires actuarial gains and losses to be recognised immediately in the Statement of Total Recognised Gains and Losses. UK

7.5.1 *Minimum recognition requirement – 'corridor' approach*

The corridor approach is based on the view that, in the long term, actuarial gains and losses may offset each other and the adoption of a range (referred to as a 'corridor') around the best estimate of the post-employment benefit obligation. The minimum requirement of IAS 19 is that, to the extent that the unrecognised gains and losses exceed a corridor of 10 per cent (discussed below), the excess is recognised in profit or loss over a specified time span, generally the average remaining working lives of the current and former employees participating in the plan. The unrecognised cumulative actuarial gains and losses are one component in the calculation of the net defined benefit liability or asset (see **section 7.2**). The unrecognised cumulative actuarial gains and losses comprise both those within the 10 per cent corridor that are being deferred indefinitely and that portion outside the corridor that has not yet been recognised in profit or loss at the end of the reporting period. [IAS 19.95]

The steps involved in applying the corridor approach are as follows.

Step 1 Consider each defined benefit plan separately

Step 2 Calculate the excess amount falling outside the 'corridor' as:

[IAS 19.92]

- the net cumulative unrecognised actuarial gain or loss at the end of the previous accounting period; less
- 10% of the greater of:
  - the present value of the defined benefit obligation at that date (before deducting plan assets); and
  - the fair value of the plan assets at that date.

Step 3 Recognise in profit or loss an amount equal to the excess (as calculated at Step 2) divided by the expected average remaining working lives of the employees participating in the scheme. [IAS 19.93]

Step 4 Include the cumulative unrecognised actuarial gains and losses (which comprise both those within the 10% corridor that are being deferred indefinitely and that portion outside the corridor that has not yet been recognised in profit or loss at the end of the reporting period) within the net defined benefit liability or asset presented in the statement of financial position.

The effect of this basis of calculation is that amortisation of actuarial gains and losses falling outside the corridor does not commence in the period in which the gains and losses arise, but in the following accounting period.

Example 7.5.1

Corridor approach to recognising actuarial gains and losses

At 31 December 20X1, a defined benefit plan had a net cumulative unrecognised actuarial loss of £1,200. At the same date, the present value of the defined benefit obligation was £10,200 and the fair value of the associated plan assets was £9,500. The expected average remaining working life of the employees participating in the scheme was 9 years.

Actuarial losses of £20 will be recognised in profit or loss for the 12 months to 31 December 20X2. This is calculated as follows:

	£
Net cumulative unrecognised actuarial loss	1,200
Less the greater of:	
10% of £10,200 and 10% of £9,500	(1,020)
Excess	180
Average remaining working life	9 years
Actuarial loss to be recognised	£20

The higher the number of retired employees covered by a pension plan, the shorter the average remaining working life and amortisation period for actuarial gains and losses is likely to be. For plans which only cover retired and former employees, all actuarial gains and losses exceeding the corridor will be recognised immediately.

7.5.2 *Faster recognition of actuarial gains and losses in profit or loss*

As an alternative to the minimum recognition requirement discussed at **7.5.1**, an entity may adopt any systematic method that results in faster recognition of actuarial gains and losses in profit or loss (including immediate recognition of the full amount), provided that:

[IAS 19.93]

- the same basis is applied to both gains and losses; and
- the basis is applied consistently from period to period.

An entity may apply such systematic methods to actuarial gains and losses even if they fall within the 10% corridor described at **7.5.1**.

Thus, entities have considerable choice if they wish to recognise actuarial gains and losses in profit or loss more quickly than in accordance with the minimum recognition requirement. For example, an entity's options could include recognising in profit or loss:

- gains and losses outside the corridor over average remaining working lives, but deferring indefinitely gains and losses inside the corridor;
- gains and losses outside the corridor over a shorter period, but deferring indefinitely gains and losses inside the corridor;
- gains and losses outside the corridor immediately, but deferring indefinitely gains and losses inside the corridor;
- all gains and losses (i.e. both outside and inside the corridor) over average remaining working lives;
- all gains and losses (i.e. both outside and inside the corridor) over a shorter period; or

- all gains and losses immediately ('immediate recognition').

If a policy of immediate recognition is selected, entities may also consider recognition in other comprehensive income (see **7.5.3** below).

Example 7.5.2

Consistent recognition policy where the entity has more than one plan

An entity has several employee defined benefit plans. The entity has chosen to apply the corridor approach for the recognition of actuarial gains and losses. However, it would like to recognise actuarial gains and losses in profit or loss immediately for some plans that include a large proportion of retirees.

It is not acceptable to use different accounting policies for the recognition of actuarial gains and losses for different defined benefit plans. The treatment for the recognition of actuarial gains and losses should be consistent for all defined benefit plans in accordance with IAS 8.13 (see **3.1** in **chapter 4**), which requires that an entity select and apply its accounting policies consistently for similar transactions, events and conditions.

However, even though the corridor approach must be applied in the same way to all plans, the period over which gains and losses will be recognised is likely to be shorter for employee benefit plans that include a large portion of retirees, as this factor must be considered in determining the expected average remaining working lives of the employees participating in each plan.

7.5.3 Immediate recognition of actuarial gains and losses in other comprehensive income

IAS 19 includes an additional option to recognise actuarial gains and losses in full as they occur for all defined benefit plans, but in other comprehensive income rather than in profit or loss. If this option is chosen, it must be applied to all defined benefit plans and all actuarial gains and losses. [IAS 19.93A]

UK

The option is equivalent to the requirement in FRS 17 to take such gains and losses to the Statement of Total Recognised Gains and Losses. It was added in 2004, reflecting the IASB's concerns over the appropriateness of the 'corridor' approach, and its perceived inconsistency with the IASB Framework for the Preparation and Presentation of Financial Statements.

Where an entity chooses this option, it should also recognise any adjustments arising from the 'asset ceiling' limit in IAS 19.58(b) (see **7.2.1.2**) in other comprehensive income. [IAS 19.93C] Neither those adjustments nor the actuarial gains and losses should be reclassified to profit or loss in a subsequent period. [IAS 19.93D]

7.5.4 Selecting an accounting policy for the recognition of actuarial gains and losses

The choice of accounting policy for actuarial gains and losses can have a very significant impact on an entity's statement of financial position, equity and reported earnings. Although avoiding any impact on profit or loss, recognising such gains and losses in other comprehensive income in the period in which they arise can result in considerable volatility in the statement of financial position and reported equity. On the other hand, the corridor approach is likely to impact future reported earnings.

Once an entity has selected and applied one of the methods available, any subsequent change in method will be a voluntary change in accounting policy in accordance with IAS 8 *Accounting Policies, Changes in Accounting Estimates and Errors* and will only be justified if it results in 'financial statements providing reliable and more relevant information about the effects of transactions, other events or conditions on the entity's financial position, financial performance or cash flows' (see **3.2** in **chapter 4**). [IAS 8.14(b)]

7.6 Past service cost

The detailed definition and description of past service cost as summarised in the following paragraphs have been amended by *Improvements to IFRSs* issued in May 2008. The objective of these amendments (and those relating to curtailments – see **7.8.2**) is to clarify the distinction between curtailments and negative past service cost. The amendments relating to past service costs and curtailments are effective for annual periods beginning on or after 1 January 2009, and are to be applied prospectively to changes in benefits that occur on or after 1 January 2009.

At the time of writing, the amendments made by Improvements to IFRSs *have not yet been endorsed for use in the EU.* UK

Past service cost is defined as 'the change in the present value of the defined benefit obligation for employee service in prior periods, resulting in the current period from the introduction of, or changes to, post-employment benefits or other long-term employee benefits. Past service cost may be either positive (when benefits are introduced or changed so that the present value of the defined benefit obligation increases) or negative (when existing benefits are changed so that the present value of the defined benefit obligation decreases)'. [IAS 19.7]

Past service cost may arise when a defined benefit plan is introduced that attributes benefits to past service, or when benefits payable for past service under an existing plan are amended. Although the cost is determined by reference to employee service rendered in past periods, the changes to benefits are in return for employee service over the period until the benefits concerned are vested. Therefore, IAS 19 requires that the cost be recognised as an expense on a straight-line basis over the average period until the benefits vest (subject to the restrictions discussed at **7.2.1.1** and **7.2.1.2**). To the extent that the benefits vest immediately following the introduction of, or changes to, the benefit plan, the entity should recognise the past service cost immediately. [IAS 19.96 & 97] Therefore, an increase in benefits for former employees who have retired is recognised in full immediately.

Example 7.6A, which is included in the Standard, illustrates the application of IAS 19.97.

Example 7.6A

Past service cost

[Example illustrating IAS 19.97]

An entity operates a pension plan that provides a pension of 2% of final salary for each year of service. The benefits become vested after five years of service. On 1 January 20X5, the entity improves the pension to 2.5% of final salary for each year of service starting from 1 January 20X1. At the date of the improvement, the present value of the additional benefits for service from 1 January 20X1 to 1 January 20X5 is as follows:

Employees with more than five years' service at 1/1/X5	150
Employees with less than five years' service at 1/1/X5 (average period until vesting: three years)	120
	270

The entity recognises 150 immediately because those benefits are already vested. The entity recognises 120 on a straight-line basis over three years from 1 January 20X5.

Example 7.6B

New plan member with benefits already vested

In connection with an acquisition, Company C has given an executive of the acquired entity a three-year employment contract that includes 100 per cent vested participation in C's supplemental executive retirement scheme (SERS). Under the scheme, the executive will receive credit for prior service at the acquired entity. As a result, the SERS's projected benefit obligation will increase. Company C does not intend to fund any of the increase in the accumulated benefit obligation.

Company C should immediately recognise the additional SERS obligation created by the admission of the executive into the plan. The admission of the executive results in past service cost. In general, IAS 19.96 requires that the cost of providing retrospective benefits of plan amendments be amortised over the period until the benefits become vested. However, in this case, the benefits become vested when the executive becomes a member of the plan. Therefore, Company C should recognise the past service cost immediately.

The amount of the past service cost is measured as the change in the present value of the defined benefit obligation resulting from the change in benefits. Any unrecognised past service cost is one component in the calculation of the net defined benefit liability or asset (see **section 7.2**). Having established the amortisation schedule for past service cost when the benefits are introduced or established, that schedule is only amended if there is a curtailment or settlement (see **section 7.8**).

Because past service cost includes both positive (debits) and negative (credit) amounts, and IAS 19.96 requires the past service cost to be recognised as an expense, any negative past service cost is also recognised as an expense in profit or loss. It is recognised over the average period until the reduced portion of the benefits vests (i.e. immediately to the extent that the reduction in benefits vests immediately).

Past service cost is dealt with on a net basis where, under the same plan and for the same employees, some benefits are reduced and, at the same time, other benefits are increased. [IAS 19.101]

Past service cost arises due to changes in post-employment benefits or other long-term employee benefits. It does not include differences between actuarial assumptions and actual performance, or curtailments. Thus, it excludes:

[IAS 19.98]

- the effect of differences between actual and previously-assumed salary increases, and underestimates and overestimates of discretionary pension increases (where there is a constructive obligation to grant such increases), as these effects will have been allowed for in the actuarial assumptions;
- an increase in vested benefits due to employees completing vesting requirements (rather than new or improved benefits being introduced) as the cost of the benefits now vesting will have been recognised as current service cost when the employee service was rendered;
- estimates of benefit improvement (required by the plan terms, legislation or established practice of the entity) arising from an actuarial gain that has already been recognised in the financial statements; and
- the effect of a curtailment that reduces benefits for future service (see 7.8.2).

7.6.1 Amortisation schedule not subsequently amended

IAS 19.99 specifies that, once the amortisation schedule for part service cost has been established when the benefits are introduced or changed, that schedule is subsequently changed only if there is a curtailment or settlement. In particular, the amortisation schedule is not amended for subsequent changes in the average remaining working life of the employees, unless there is a curtailment or settlement. [IAS 19.BC56]

Example 7.6.1

Change in average remaining working life of plan members

Company N established a supplemental executive retirement scheme (SERS) for three key executives. When the plan was established, it granted benefits based on services rendered in prior periods (past service cost). Under the provisions of IAS 19.96, past service cost is being amortised on a straight-line basis over the average period until the benefits become vested, which is approximately 15 years.

Subsequent to the initial determination of the amortisation method, one executive resigned. Additionally, because a second executive is nearing retirement, it is apparent that the current amortisation schedule will result in amortisation of unrecognised past service cost during a period when only one participant will be providing service.

IAS 19.99 prohibits Company N from changing the amortisation schedule to an amortisation method that recognises the cost of each individual's added benefits over that individual's remaining service period. IAS 19.BC56 confirms that the amortisation schedule is not amended for subsequent changes in the average remaining working life, unless there is a curtailment or settlement. Consequently, as the events described above do not represent a curtailment or settlement, the amortisation period should not be modified.

Note though that, as one of the executives resigned, the estimate of the past service cost will have changed and the revised estimate will be amortised over the remainder of the original schedule.

7.7 Plan assets

Plan assets comprise:

[IAS 19.7]

- assets held by a long-term employee benefit fund; and
- qualifying insurance policies.

Plan assets exclude:

[IAS 19.103]

- unpaid contributions due from the reporting entity to the fund; and
- any non-transferable financial instruments issued by the entity and held by the fund.

Plan assets are reduced by any liabilities of the fund that do not relate to employee benefits (e.g. trade and other payables, and liabilities resulting from derivative financial instruments). [IAS 19.103]

7.7.1 Assets held by a long-term employee benefit fund

These are assets (other than non-transferable financial instruments issued by the reporting entity) that:

[IAS 19.7]

- are held by an entity (a fund) that is legally separate from the reporting entity and exists solely to pay or fund employee benefits; and
- are available to be used only to pay or fund employee benefits, are not available to the reporting entity's own creditors (even in bankruptcy) and cannot be returned to the reporting entity, unless either:
  - the remaining assets of the fund are sufficient to meet all of the related employee benefit obligations of the plan or the reporting entity; or

- the assets are returned to the reporting entity to reimburse it for employee benefits already paid.

Entities should consider whether any funding arrangements that they have in place meet these criteria, paying particular attention to any supplementary schemes such as separate arrangements for directors. If not, any assets that have been put aside for funding purposes will not be regarded as plan assets, and the plan should be treated as unfunded for the purposes of IAS 19. The entity should consider whether the assets intended to fund its pension obligation should instead appear on its own statement of financial position, either because they are held directly by the entity or in accordance with SIC-12 *Consolidation – Special Purpose Entities*.

7.7.2 *Qualifying insurance policy*

A qualifying insurance policy is an insurance policy issued by an insurer that is not a related party of the reporting entity (as defined by IAS 24 *Related Party Disclosures*), if the proceeds of the policy:

[IAS 19.7]

- can be used only to pay or fund employee benefits under a defined benefit plan; and
- are not available to the reporting entity's own creditors (even in bankruptcy) and cannot be paid to the reporting entity, unless either:
    - the proceeds represent surplus assets that are not needed for the policy to meet all of the related employee benefit obligations; or
    - the proceeds are returned to the reporting entity to reimburse it for employee benefits already paid.

Example 7.7.2

Insurance policy issued by a related party

Company A offers its employees defined pension benefits through a pension fund. The pension fund acquires an insurance policy from Company A's subsidiary, Company B.

The insurance policy can be included as part of plan assets in Company A's financial statements (consolidated or separate) only if it meets the definition of either:

- an asset held by a long-term employee benefit fund; or

- a qualifying insurance policy.

The policy does not meet the definition of a qualifying insurance policy (see above) because it is issued by a related party. Therefore, to qualify as a plan asset, the insurance policy must meet the definition of an asset held by a long-term employee benefit fund. That definition sets out certain criteria that must be met (see **7.7.1**), but it automatically excludes non-transferable financial instruments issued by the reporting entity.

Thus, in Company A's consolidated financial statements, the insurance policy cannot qualify as a plan asset unless it is a 'transferable financial instrument' (because the policy is issued by an entity within the consolidated group). An insurance policy issued by a group entity that covers the employees in a fund will often be non-transferable and, thus, will not meet the definition of a plan asset.

However, for A's separate financial statements, the insurance policy is not considered to be issued by the 'reporting entity'. Accordingly, in those financial statements, the insurance policy will qualify as a plan asset if the criteria in **7.7.1** are met, even if the policy is a non-transferable financial instrument.

See **chapter 32** for guidance on whether an entity is a related party. In particular, **example 4.1** in that chapter discusses whether an insurer is a related party of the reporting entity if it is a subsidiary of an associate of the reporting entity's parent.

7.7.3 Measurement of plan assets

The fair value of plan assets is deducted in arriving at the net defined benefit liability (asset) in the statement of financial position (see **section 7.2**). An estimate will need to be made of the fair value of an asset if no market price is available. One method would be to discount expected future cash flows from the asset at a rate reflecting the risk associated with the asset and its expected maturity or disposal date. If the asset does not have a maturity date, reference should be made to the settlement date of the related obligation.

Where plan assets include qualifying insurance policies that exactly match the amount and timing of part or all of the benefits payable under the plan, the fair value of those insurance policies is deemed to be the present value of the related obligations (subject to any reduction required if the amounts receivable under the insurance policies are not recoverable in full). [IAS 19.104]

Example 7.7.3

Measurement of qualifying insurance policies

Company A sponsors a defined benefit pension plan. Its defined benefit obligation under IAS 19 is measured at £100. Company A buys an insurance policy from an insurance company, Company B, that will cover the entire obligation and exactly match the payments due to the employees in accordance with the benefit formula in the plan, both in amount and timing. Company B is not a related party as defined in IAS 24 *Related Party Disclosures*. It is determined that the policy represents a qualifying insurance policy in accordance with IAS 19. The insurer charges £120 for the insurance policy. What value should be attributed to the insurance policy for the purposes of measuring plan assets and, if that value is not cost, how should Company A account for the difference?

In accordance with IAS 19.104 (see above), where the policy acquired meets the definition of a qualifying insurance policy, the insurance policy would be reflected in plan assets at the value of the related defined benefit obligation, i.e. £100. In respect of the difference between this amount and the cost of the policy (£120), either of the following treatments would generally be acceptable:

(a) the excess amount of £20 is considered a transaction cost of having the obligation effectively taken over by Company B and is immediately recognised as an expense in profit or loss; or

(b) Company A initially recognises the insurance policy at £120. The policy is then immediately remeasured in line with IAS 19.104, and its fair value on remeasurement is deemed to be the present value of the related obligation i.e. £100. The difference of £20 is treated as an actuarial loss and is accounted for in line with the entity's policy for recognising actuarial gains and losses.

In certain instances, it may be possible to determine that the difference (or a part of it) relates clearly to transaction costs. In those instances, the amount determined to represent transactions costs is immediately recognised as an expense in profit or loss. Any remaining difference is recognised using either treatment A or B above, based on the entity's accounting policy.

7.7.4 Reimbursements

When, and only when, it is virtually certain that another party (e.g. an insurer) will reimburse some or all of the expenditure required to settle a defined benefit obligation, an entity should recognise its right to reimbursement as a separate asset. The entity should measure the asset at fair value. In all other respects, the entity should treat that asset in the same way as plan assets. In the statement of comprehensive income, the expense relating to a defined benefit plan may be presented net of the amount recognised for reimbursement. [IAS 19.104A]

The previous paragraph deals with the circumstances where the reimbursement right does not meet the definition of a qualifying insurance policy (see **7.7.2**). In such cases, the reimbursement right is not a plan asset and, therefore, should not be presented as a deduction in determining the defined benefit liability. However, the defined benefit liability is increased (reduced) to the extent that net cumulative actuarial gains (losses) on the defined benefit obligation and on the related reimbursement right remain unrecognised (see **section 7.5**). [IAS 19.104C]

Example 7.7.4, which is included in the Standard, illustrates the requirements of IAS 19.104A – 104C.

Example 7.7.4

Reimbursements

[Example illustrating IAS 19.104A – 104C]

Present value of obligation	1,241
Unrecognised actuarial gains	17
Liability recognised in statement of financial position	1,258
Rights under insurance policies that exactly match the amount and timing of some of the benefits payable under the plan. Those benefits have a present value of 1,092.	1,092

The unrecognised actuarial gains of 17 are the net cumulative actuarial gains on the obligation and on the reimbursement rights.

If the right to reimbursement arises under an insurance policy that exactly matches the amount and timing of part or all of the benefits payable under the plan, the fair value of the reimbursement is deemed to be the present value of the related obligations (subject to any reduction required if reimbursement is not recoverable in full). [IAS 19.104D]

7.7.5 *Frequency of valuation*

As regards the required frequency of valuations, similar considerations apply as for the determination of the present value of the defined benefit obligation (see **7.3.6**).

7.7.6 *Return on plan assets*

The movement in plan assets may be expressed as follows:

Ending fair value	=	Beginning fair value	+	Contributions received	–	Benefits paid	+	Actual return on plan assets

The return on plan assets comprises interest, dividends and other revenue derived from the plan assets, together with realised and unrealised gains or losses on the plan assets, less any costs of administering the plan (other than those included in the actuarial assumptions used to measure the defined benefit obligation) and less any tax payable by the plan itself. [IAS 19.7] There are two measures of return on plan assets – expected and actual. The difference between the expected and actual return on plan assets is included in net actuarial gains and losses (see **section 7.5**).

The definition of the 'return on plan assets' was amended by *Improvements to IFRSs* issued in May 2008 to specify that plan administration costs should be deducted only to the extent that such costs have not been reflected in the actuarial assumptions used to measure the defined benefit obligation. The amendment (which has been made to avoid double-counting such costs) is effective for annual periods beginning on or after 1 January 2009, and should be applied retrospectively. Earlier application is permitted, but an entity choosing to apply the amendments made by *Improvements to IFRSs* to IAS 19 early must disclose that fact.

UK *At the time of writing, the amendments made by* Improvements to IFRSs *have not yet been endorsed for use in the EU.*

The expected return on plan assets reflects market expectations, at the start of the accounting period, of the returns over the life of the related obligation and reflects changes in the fair value of plan assets held during the period. The expected return on plan assets is one part of the net income or expense recognised in profit or loss (see **section 7.2**). [IAS 19.106]

The development of future rate of return assumptions should be based on a coherent methodology that is prudent and reasonable. The following factors may be considered when a plan sponsor is developing its long-term rate of return assumption (the list is not exhaustive):

- the assumed asset allocation of pension plan assets (common stock, bonds, etc.);
- the assumed volatility of the portfolio;

- the location of the assets;
- the methods of constructing a best estimate range of investment returns, such as the Building Block method or the Cash Flow Matching method;
- historical return data by asset category;
- rolling averages by asset category over a long-term period (e.g. five, ten years);
- current trends with respect to economic conditions, inflation, and market sentiment;
- views and forecasts by market analysts;
- views of the plan sponsor;
- views of external investment managers;
- investment manager performance; and
- investment policy.

The actual and expected return on plan assets are measured net of any administrative expenses that have not otherwise been included within the actuarial assumptions used to measure the obligation. [IAS 19.107]

The expected return on plan assets affects profit or loss in the current period, but the difference between expected return and actual return may be deferred as part of actuarial gains and losses, or recognised outside of profit or loss. This distinction is included within IAS 19 in order to reduce volatility in profit or loss. Care should be taken to ensure that the expected return is not consistently misstated. To provide transparency, disclosure is required of the expected return and the actual return – see **9.2**).

Example 7.7.6, which is included in the Standard, illustrates the calculation of the expected and the actual return on plan assets.

Example 7.7.6

Return on plan assets

[Example illustrating IAS 19.106]

At 1 January 20X1, the fair value of plan assets was 10,000 and net cumulative unrecognised actuarial gains were 760. On 30 June 20X1, the plan paid benefits of 1900 and received contributions of 4900. At 31 December 20X1, the fair value of plan assets was 15,000 and the present value of the defined benefit obligation was 14,792. Actuarial losses on the obligation for 20X1 were 60.

At 1 January 20X1, the reporting entity made the following estimates, based on market prices at that date:

	%
Interest and dividend income, after tax payable by the fund	9.25
Realised and unrealised gains on plan assets (after tax)	2.00
Administration costs	(1.00)
Expected rate of return	10.25

For 20X1, the expected and actual return on plan assets are as follows:

Return on 10,000 held for 12 months at 10.25%	*1025*
Return on 3,000 held for six months at 5% (equivalent to 10.25% annually, compounded every six months)	*150*
Expected return on plan assets for 20X1	*1,175*
Fair value of plan assets at 31 December 20X1	*15,000*
Less fair value of plan assets at 1 January 20X1	*(10,000)*
Less contributions received	*(4,900)*
Add benefits paid	*1,900*
Actual return on plan assets	*2,000*

The difference between the expected return on plan assets (1,175) and the actual return on plan assets (2,000) is an actuarial gain of 825. Therefore, the cumulative net unrecognised actuarial gains are 1,525 (760 plus 825 less 60). Under IAS 19.92, the limits of the corridor are set at 1,500 (greater of: (i) 10% of 15,000 and (ii) 10% of 14,792). In the following year (20X2), the entity recognises in profit or loss an actuarial gain of 25 (1,525 less 1,500) divided by the expected average remaining working life of the employees concerned.

The expected return on plan assets for 20X2 will be based on market expectations at 1/1/X2 for returns over the entire life of the obligation.

7.7.7 *Price used to value plan assets*

Plan assets are measured at fair value, defined as the amount for which an asset could be exchanged or a liability settled between knowledgeable, willing parties in an arm's length transaction. [IAS 19.7]

IAS 19 gives no further guidance on the fair value of plan assets, but the Application Guidance to IAS 39 *Financial Instruments: Recognition and Measurement* states that the appropriate quoted market price for an asset held is usually the current bid price, i.e. the price for which the asset could be sold. [IAS 39.AG72] It follows that bid price should generally be used when establishing the fair value of quoted plan assets.

UK

This is different from the position under FRS 17 as originally issued, which specified the use of mid-market value. Thus, the value of plan assets was typically a little lower under IAS 19 than under FRS 17. For periods beginning on or after 6 April 2007, an amendment to FRS 17 requires, inter alia, plan assets to be valued at bid price.

7.8 Curtailments and settlements

In calculating the present value of a defined benefit obligation, demographic assumptions (e.g. mortality rates during employment, rate of employee turnover etc.) and financial assumptions (e.g. future salary and benefit levels) will project the continuance of the plan in its current form and of the entity and its operations as a going concern. Such assumptions do not allow for curtailments or settlements which crystallise in full or in part the obligations of the plan.

7.8.1 Settlements

A settlement occurs when an entity eliminates all of its legal or constructive obligations for part or all of the defined benefits under a plan (e.g. by purchasing an annuity for, or making a lump sum payment to, plan participants in exchange for their rights to receive specified post-employment benefits). [IAS 19.112] It should be noted that the definition of a settlement does not require the discontinuance of a plan nor does it require that the plan participants receiving the settlement should earn no further benefits under the plan.

An entity may acquire an insurance policy to fund some or all of the employee benefits relating to employee service in current and prior periods. The acquisition of such a policy is not a settlement if the entity retains a legal or constructive obligation to pay further amounts if the insurer does not pay the employee benefits specified in the insurance policy. [IAS 19.113]

7.8.2 Curtailments

The detailed definition and description of curtailments as summarised in the following paragraphs have been amended by *Improvements to IFRSs* issued in May 2008. The objective of these amendments (and those relating to past service cost – see **7.6**) is to clarify the distinction between curtailments and negative past service costs. In particular, the amendments have clarified how a reduction in the extent to which future salary increases are linked to the benefits payable for past service should be treated.

The amendments relating to past service costs and curtailments are effective for annual periods beginning on or after 1 January 2009 and are to be applied prospectively to changes in benefits that occur on or after 1 January 2009.

UK *At the time of writing, the amendments made by* Improvements to IFRSs *have not yet been endorsed for use in the EU.*

A curtailment occurs when an entity either:

[IAS 19.111]

- is demonstrably committed to making a significant reduction in the number of employees covered by a plan; or
- amends the terms of a defined benefit plan so that a significant element of future service by current employees will no longer qualify for benefits or will qualify only for reduced benefits.

A curtailment may arise from an isolated event (e.g. the closure of a plant, discontinuance of an operation, termination or suspension of a plan) or a reduction in the extent to which future salary increases are linked to the benefits payable for past service. Curtailments are often linked with a restructuring. When this is the case, the curtailment is accounted for at the same time as the related restructuring. [IAS 19.111]

A curtailment gain or loss may result from an amendment to a post-retirement benefit plan that is approved by an entity's board of directors and announced to the participants during the current period, but is effective in the subsequent period. IAS 19.111 indicates that the gain should be recognised when the plan is amended, not when it is effective. As curtailments frequently are linked with a restructuring, in determining when the plan is amended it is relevant to determine when the conditions to recognise a restructuring provision under IAS 37.72 would have been met (see **section 3.9.3** of **chapter 11**).

Example 7.8.2A

Termination over an extended period

Entity R has a defined benefit pension plan that covers substantially all of its employees. Entity R is in the process of restructuring its operations, which includes an involuntary termination of its workforce and a spin-off of one of its subsidiaries. The involuntary redundancies of employees are expected to occur over a 36-month period, commencing on the announcement date of the restructuring.

Timing and measurement of impact of curtailment of defined benefit plan

IAS 19.111 requires a curtailment to be accounted for at the same time as the related restructuring. Accordingly, any gain or loss arising on curtailment should be recognised in the period in which the conditions for recognising a provision for termination benefits are met pursuant to IAS 19.133 (see **12.2**). If the number of employees expected to be made redundant, or the value of the related curtailment gain or loss, is not reliably measurable at that date, the gain or loss should be recognised when it becomes reliably measurable.

Changes in the number of employees

Any difference between the number of employees originally considered in the restructuring and the number of employees actually made redundant should be accounted for as a gain or loss as terminations occur and should not be included in the accumulated unrecognised gains and losses. Ordinarily, there should not be significant differences between the number of employees considered in the restructuring and the number of employees actually made redundant. A significant increase in the number of employees included in the restructuring provision would require consideration of whether these employees were part of the original plan. If that were not the case, a new curtailment should be accounted for.

A gain or loss arising on the curtailment or settlement of a defined benefit plan should be recognised immediately when the curtailment or settlement occurs. Such a gain or loss will comprise the aggregate of:

[IAS 19.109]

- resulting changes in the present value of the defined benefit obligation (i.e. the gross obligation before deducting the fair value of plan assets);
- resulting changes in the fair value of plan assets; and
- related actuarial gains and losses and past service costs that have not previously been recognised.

The defined benefit obligation, and related plan assets, should be remeasured using current actuarial assumptions (e.g. current interest rates), before determining the changes resulting from the curtailment or settlement.

Where a curtailment relates to only some of the members covered by a plan (e.g. where there is a material reduction in the workforce following a reorganisation) or where the obligation is only partly settled, then the gain or loss arising on the curtailment or settlement will incorporate a proportion of any previously unrecognised past service costs and actuarial gains and losses. The proportion will be based on the present value of the obligation before and after the curtailment or settlement, unless a more rational basis is appropriate. [IAS 19.115]

A curtailment will be combined with a settlement when a plan is terminated and the outstanding obligation is settled such that the plan ceases to exist. However, where the plan is to be replaced by a new plan offering benefits that are in substance identical, it should not be considered as a settlement or curtailment and, consequently, no gain or loss on curtailment or settlement should be recognised. [IAS 19.114]

8 Defined benefit plans and business combinations

IFRS 3 *Business Combinations* specifies that, in accounting for a business combination, the acquirer should recognise and measure a liability (or asset, if any) related to the acquiree's employment benefit arrangements in accordance with IAS 19. [IFRS 3(2008).26] Therefore, the accounting is determined in accordance with the specific requirements of IAS 19 dealing with business combinations (see below).

Whereas the 2008 version of IFRS 3 (quoted above) simply refers the reader to IAS 19 for the detailed rules for assets and liabilities arising from employee benefit arrangements in the context of business combinations, the previous version of IFRS 3 included explicit requirements regarding net employee benefit assets or liabilities for defined benefit plans. However, the text of IAS 19 (which is more detailed) remains unchanged and, therefore, the requirements effectively remain unchanged.

IAS 19 states that, in a business combination, an entity should recognise assets and liabilities arising from post-employment benefits as the present value of the defined benefit obligation less the fair value of any plan assets. The present value of the defined benefit obligation would include all of the following, even if the acquiree had not recognised them at the date of acquisition:

[IAS 19.108]

- actuarial gains and losses that arose before the acquisition date (whether or not they fall inside the 10% corridor);
- past service cost that arose from benefit changes, or the introduction of a plan, before the acquisition date; and
- amounts that, under the transitional provisions of IAS 19.155(b), the acquiree had not recognised.

If the subsidiary uses the corridor method, at the acquisition date it is likely to have unrecognised actuarial gains or losses in its individual financial statements. In the measurement of the subsidiary's assets and liabilities for the purposes of the business combination (under IAS 19.108 – see above), such actuarial gains and losses are included (i.e. the corridor is effectively set to zero on initial recognition by the group). Subsequently, any recognition of those actuarial gains and losses in the subsidiary's individual financial statements will be eliminated on consolidation and recognition of actuarial gains and losses in the consolidated financial statements will be based on the actuarial gains and losses arising after the acquisition.

9 Presentation and disclosure for defined benefit plans

9.1 Presentation

An asset relating to one plan should be offset against a liability relating to another plan when, and only when, an entity:

[IAS 19.116]

- has a legally enforceable right to use a surplus in one plan to settle obligations under the other plan; and
- intends either to settle the obligations on a net basis, or to realise the surplus in one plan and settle its obligation under the other plan simultaneously.

IAS 19.117 notes that these offsetting criteria are similar to those established for financial instruments in IAS 32 *Financial Instruments: Presentation*.

In practice, such offset will be available only rarely.

IAS 19 does not specify whether an entity should distinguish current and non-current portions of assets and liabilities arising from post-employment benefits. [IAS 19.118] Nor does it specify whether an entity should present current service cost, interest cost and the expected return on plan assets as components of a single item of income or expense in the statement of comprehensive income. [IAS 19.119]

Accordingly, it appears that entities have a choice as to whether to present the different components of income and expense separately or as a single net figure. Such a decision would be an accounting policy choice, and should therefore be disclosed appropriately and applied consistently for all plans.

UK *In this respect, IAS 19 differs from FRS 17, which mandates where the various components are to be presented in profit or loss (e.g. the net of interest cost and expected return on plan assets must be classified as finance costs or income).*

It is important that the accounting policy choice results in a fair presentation in profit or loss. For example, where an entity chooses to disclose results from operating activities or 'operating profit' as a separate line item in profit or loss, it may be appropriate either to present interest cost and the expected return on plan assets both within or both outside operating profit. But it appears unlikely that a fair presentation could be achieved if one of these items is presented within 'operating profit' but the other is presented outside 'operating profit'.

9.2 Disclosure

IAS 19 requires extensive disclosures in respect of defined benefit plans, ranging from the accounting policy for recognised gains and losses, through to a reconciliation of the various categories discussed at **7.2** to the net totals in the statement of financial position and the statement of comprehensive income, any investment by the plan in the entity, and principal actuarial assumptions.

Appendix B, which accompanies but is not part of IAS 19, illustrates how the disclosure requirements set out in the following sections can be met.

9.2.1 *Required disclosures*

An entity should disclose information that enables users to evaluate the nature of its defined benefit plans and the financial effects of changes in those plans during the period. [IAS 19.120]

The detailed disclosure requirements for defined benefit plans are as follows (note that only the items marked * need be disclosed for a plan sharing risks between entities under common control, as discussed at **5.2**, by an entity accounting for the contribution payable for the period rather than an allocation of the net defined benefit cost):

[IAS 19.120A]

(a) the entity's accounting policy for recognising actuarial gains and losses;

(b) * a general description of the type of plan (see below);

(c) * a reconciliation of opening and closing balances of the present value of the defined benefit obligation showing separately, if applicable, the effects during the period attributable to each of the following:

(i) current service cost;

(ii) interest cost;

(iii) contributions by plan participants;

(iv) actuarial gains and losses;

(v) foreign currency exchange rate changes on plans measured in a currency different from the entity's presentation currency;

(vi) benefits paid;

(vii) past service cost;

(viii) business combinations;

(ix) curtailments; and

(x) settlements;

(d) * an analysis of the defined benefit obligation into amounts arising from plans that are wholly unfunded and amounts arising from plans that are wholly or partly funded;

(e) * a reconciliation of the opening and closing balances of the fair value of plan assets and of the opening and closing balances of any reimbursement right recognised as an asset in accordance with IAS 19.104A (see **7.7.4**) showing separately, if applicable, the effects during the period attributable to each of the following:

(i) expected return on plan assets;

(ii) actuarial gains and losses;

(iii) foreign currency exchange rate changes on plans measured in a currency different from the entity's presentation currency;

(iv) contributions by the employer;

(v) contributions by plan participants;

(vi) benefits paid;

(vii) business combinations; and

(viii) settlements;

(f) a reconciliation of the present value of the defined benefit obligation in (c) and the fair value of the plan assets in (e) to the assets and liabilities recognised in the statement of financial position, showing at least:

(i) the net actuarial gains or losses not recognised in the statement of financial position;

(ii) the past service cost not recognised in the statement of financial position;

(iii) any amount not recognised as an asset, because of the limit in IAS 19.58(b) (see **7.2.1.2**);

(iv) the fair value at the end of the reporting period of any reimbursement right recognised as an asset in accordance with IAS 19.104A (see **7.7.4**), with a brief description of the link between the reimbursement right and the related obligation; and

(v) the other amounts recognised in the statement of financial position;

(g) the total expense recognised in profit or loss for each of the following, and the line item(s) in which they are included:

(i) current service cost;

(ii) interest cost;

(iii) expected return on plan assets;

(iv) expected return on any reimbursement right recognised as an asset in accordance with IAS 19.104A (see **7.7.4**);

(v) actuarial gains and losses;

(vi) past service cost;

(vii) the effect of any curtailment or settlement; and

(viii) the effect of the limit in IAS 19.58(b);

(h) the total amount recognised in other comprehensive income for each of the following:

(i) actuarial gains and losses; and

(ii) the effect of the limit in IAS 19.58(b);

(i) for entities that recognise actuarial gains and losses in other comprehensive income in accordance with IAS 19.93A, the cumulative amount of actuarial gains and losses recognised in other comprehensive income;

(j) * for each major category of plan assets, which includes, but is not limited to, equity instruments, debt instruments, property, and all other assets, the percentage or amount that each major category constitutes of the fair value of the total plan assets;

(k) the amounts included in the fair value of plan assets for:

(i) each category of the entity's own financial instruments; and

(ii) any property occupied by, or other assets used by, the entity;

(l) a narrative description of the basis used to determine the overall expected rate of return on assets, including the effect of the major categories of plan assets;

(m) the actual return on plan assets, as well as the actual return on any reimbursement right recognised as an asset in accordance with IAS 19.104A (see **7.7.4**);

(n) * the principal actuarial assumptions used as at the end of the reporting period, including, when applicable:

(i) the discount rates;

(ii) the expected rates of return on any plan assets for the periods presented in the financial statements;

(iii) the expected rates of return for the periods presented in the financial statements on any reimbursement right recognised as an asset in accordance with IAS 19.104A (see **7.7.4**);

(iv) the expected rates of salary increases (and of changes in an index or other variable specified in the formal or constructive terms of a plan as the basis for future benefit increases);

(v) medical cost trend rates; and

(vi) any other material actuarial assumptions used.

For example, it will often be appropriate to provide information about assumed mortality rates, where these have had a material impact on the present value of the defined benefit obligation.

An entity should disclose each actuarial assumption in absolute terms (e.g. as an absolute percentage) and not just as a margin between different percentages or other variables;

(o) * the effect of an increase of one percentage point and the effect of a decrease of one percentage point in the assumed medical cost trend rates on:

(i) the aggregate of the current service cost and interest cost components of net periodic post-employment medical costs; and

(ii) the accumulated post-employment benefit obligation for medical costs.

For the purposes of this disclosure, all other assumptions should be held constant. For plans operating in a high inflation environment, the disclosure should be the effect of a percentage increase or decrease in the assumed medical cost trend rate of a significance similar to one percentage point in a low inflation environment;

(p) the amounts of the current annual period and previous four annual periods of:

(i) the present value of the defined benefit obligation, the fair value of the plan assets and the surplus or deficit in the plan; and

(ii) the experience adjustments arising on:

(A) the plan liabilities expressed either as (1) an amount or (2) a percentage of the plan liabilities at the end of the reporting period; and

(B) the plan assets expressed either as (1) an amount or (2) a percentage of the plan assets at the end of the reporting period.

An entity may disclose the amounts required by IAS 19.120A(p) as they are determined for each annual period prospectively from the first annual period presented in the financial statements in which the entity first gives the disclosures required by IAS 19.120A. [IAS 19.160]

(q) * the employer's best estimate, as soon as it can reasonably be determined, of contributions expected to be paid to the plan during the annual period beginning after the reporting period.

For the purposes of IAS 19.120A(b), the general description of the type of plan will distinguish, for example, flat salary pension plans from final salary pension plans and from post-employment medical plans, and will include informal practices that give rise to constructive obligations included in the measurement of the defined benefit obligation. Further detail is not required. [IAS 19.121]

9.2.2 *Entities with more than one defined benefit plan*

Where an entity has more than one defined benefit plan, disclosures may be made

[IAS 19.122]

- in total; or
- separately for each plan; or
- in useful groupings, based on criteria such as:
  - geographical location (e.g. by distinguishing domestic plans from foreign plans); or
  - whether plans are subject to materially different risks (e.g. by distinguishing flat salary pension plans from final salary pension plans and from post-employment medical plans).

When disclosures are provided in total for a grouping of plans, they should be in the form of weighted averages or of relatively narrow ranges.

9.3 Additional disclosures for UK reporters: ASB Reporting Statement *Retirement Benefits – Disclosures*

UK *In January 2007, the ASB issued a Reporting Statement* Retirement Benefits – Disclosures. *Its objective is to set out best practice for entities operating or sponsoring defined benefit schemes, and it is not mandatory. The publication of this Reporting Statement followed an amendment to FRS 17 which brought its disclosure requirements into line with those of IAS 19 for periods beginning on or after 6 April 2007. The Reporting Statement is equally applicable to companies reporting under IFRSs and those reporting under UK GAAP, although it is not mandatory for either. In fact, it was primarily concern about the disclosures made by listed companies for their retirement benefit obligations which resulted in the amendment to FRS 17 and the publication of the Reporting Statement, although most listed companies now report under IFRSs. UK listed companies may therefore come under market pressure from investors and other stakeholders to make disclosures in accordance with the Reporting Statement.*

The recommended disclosures complement the requirements set out in IAS 19 (FRS 17) in six areas:

- *the relationship between the entity and trustees (managers) of the defined benefit scheme;*
- *the principal assumptions used to measure scheme liabilities;*
- *the sensitivity of the principal assumptions used to measure scheme liabilities;*
- *how the liabilities arising from the scheme are measured;*
- *the future obligations in relation to the defined benefit scheme; and*
- *the nature and extent of the risks arising from financial instruments held by the defined benefit scheme.*

Where retirement benefits are established as trusts, the Reporting Statement recommends explaining significant and unusual powers that have been granted to the trustees (managers) of the scheme that could have a material financial effect on the entity. It recommends disclosing information about assumptions used to measure the scheme's liabilities, where this is not otherwise required by IAS 19 (or FRS 17). Additionally, the ASB proposes that the financial statements should include a sensitivity analysis showing how the measurement of scheme liabilities would have been affected by changes in the relevant assumptions that were reasonably possible at the balance sheet date.

An entity may also disclose information that enables users to understand the funding obligations that the entity has in relation to defined benefit schemes, the duration of scheme liabilities (the projected cash outflow profile), as well as, for each type of risk arising from financial instruments held by defined benefit schemes, outlining the exposures to risk and how they arise, the objectives, policies and processes for managing the risk and the methods used to measure it, and any changes from the previous period. Disclosure is also suggested of the expected rate of return for each major category of scheme assets.

The Reporting Statement contains illustrative examples of the recommended disclosures.

10 Other post-employment benefits

Employers may provide other post-employment benefits such as health care or welfare plans to their employees.

For example, entities may provide employees with medical insurance which continues, at the entity's expense, when the employees retire. The provision of such benefits is comparable to that of an unfunded retirement scheme and, therefore, the cost of such benefits should be accrued over the working lives of the employees. The accounting treatment required for other post-employment benefits, whether funded or unfunded, is as discussed in **sections** 4 to 9 above for retirement benefit plans.

11 Other long-term employee benefits

Other long-term employee benefits are employee benefits (other than post-employment benefits and termination benefits) which do not fall due wholly within twelve months after the end of the period in which the employees render the related service. [IAS 19.7]

Other long-term employee benefits will therefore include such items as:

[IAS 19.126]

- compensated long-service or sabbatical leave;
- jubilee or other long-service benefits;
- profit-sharing and bonus payments payable 12 months or more after the end of the period in which the employee renders the related service; and

- deferred compensation paid 12 months or more after the end of the period in which it is earned.

11.1 Recognition and measurement

IAS 19's requirements relating to other long-term employment benefits are a simplified version of those applied to post-employment benefits. All past service cost and actuarial gains and losses are recognised immediately and there is no application of a corridor.

11.1.1 Statement of financial position

The liability recognised in the statement of financial position for other long-term employee benefits is the net total of:

[IAS 19.128]

- the present value of the defined benefit obligation at the end of the reporting period (i.e. the gross obligation before deducting the fair value of plan assets) (see IAS 19.64);
- less the fair value at the end of the reporting period of any plan assets out of which the obligations are to be settled directly (see IAS 19.102 – 104).

In measuring the liability, the entity applies paragraphs 49 – 91 of IAS 19 (which set out the recognition and measurement requirements for defined benefit plan liabilities other than those dealing with actuarial gains and losses and past service cost), but excluding:

- IAS 19.54 (which lists the components of the defined benefit liability; in the case of other long-term benefits, this is replaced by IAS 19.128 above); and
- IAS 19.61 (which lists the components to be recognised in profit or loss for defined benefit plans; in the case of other long-term benefits, this is replaced by IAS 19.129 below).

IAS 19.104A is applied in recognising and measuring any reimbursement right (see **7.7.4**).

If the net total arrived at above is an asset, the amount recognised may be restricted (see **7.2.1.2**).

Note that the definition of plan assets here is the same as discussed in **section 7.7** above. Accordingly, assets that have been set aside to fund an obligation may not always qualify as plan assets.

11.1.2 Amount recognised as income or expense

The expense recognised in profit or loss (or in the cost of an asset, where capitalisation is permitted) for other long-term employee benefits is the net total of:

[IAS 19.129]

- current service cost;
- interest cost;
- expected return on any plan assets and on any reimbursement right recognised as an asset;
- actuarial gains and losses (which should all be recognised immediately);
- past service cost (which should all be recognised immediately); and
- the effect of curtailments and settlements.

If the net total calculated above is a credit, it may be limited by the restriction on the size of any associated asset (see **7.2.1.2**).

An example of a long-term employee benefit discussed in IAS 19 is a long-term disability benefit. If the amount of such a benefit is independent of years of service (i.e. the level of benefit is the same for any disabled employee regardless of years of service), then a cost is not recognised until an event occurs that causes a long-term disability. If the level of benefit is dependent on years of service, then an obligation should be recognised as the service is rendered, based upon the probability and timing of payments expected to be made. [IAS 19.130]

11.2 Disclosure

IAS 19 has no specific disclosure requirements for other long-term employment benefits, but notes that disclosures may be required under IAS 1 (where the expense is material) or under IAS 24 (if in relation to key management personnel).

11.3 Death-in-service benefits

Accounting for death-in-service benefits (payments to employees if they die while employed) raises several issues that are not addressed in IAS 19. There was some consideration of these issues in E54, the Exposure Draft upon which IAS 19 was based, but this material was omitted from IAS 19. No reason for this was given in the Basis for Conclusions on IAS 19.

The issue has also recently been discussed by the IFRIC (see *IFRIC Update*, January 2008). The IFRIC discussions concerning death-in-service benefits focused on the appropriate manner for attributing those benefits to periods of service. The IFRIC noted the requirement in IAS 19.67(b) to attribute the cost of benefits until the date when future service by the employee will lead to no material amount of future benefits under the plan, other than from salary increases.

In the case of death-in-service benefits, the IFRIC noted that:

- the anticipated date of death would be the date at which no material amount of further benefit would arise from the plan;
- using different mortality assumptions for a defined benefit pension plan and an associated death-in-service benefit would not comply with the requirement in IAS 19.72 to use actuarial assumptions that are mutually compatible; and
- if the conditions in IAS 19.39 were met, then accounting for death-in-service benefits on a defined contribution basis would be appropriate.

The appropriate accounting for death-in-service benefits will depend on the nature of the arrangements, including:

- whether the benefits depend on the length of service or are the same irrespective of the length of service; and
- whether the benefits are provided through a post-employment benefit plan or through a stand-alone arrangement.

Benefits related to length of service

IAS 19 does not specifically mention death-in-service benefits but it refers to long-term disability benefits as an example of other long-term benefits (see above). IAS 19.130 states that if the level of benefit depends on the length of service, an obligation arises when the service is rendered. Measurement of that obligation reflects the probability that payment will be required and the length of time for which payment is expected to be made. The related cost should be attributed over the service period until the date of the expected death of the employee.

If death-in-service benefits are provided as part of a defined benefit plan, an entity would recognise actuarial gains and losses arising on the death-in-service benefits in line with its general policy for recognising such gains and losses under defined benefit plans.

If death-in-service benefits related to the period of service are provided through a stand-alone plan, they would represent an 'other long-term employee benefit'. Applying IAS 19.130 by analogy, such benefits would be attributed over the service period until the date of the expected death of the employee. However, actuarial gains and losses arising on such plans would be recognised in profit or loss immediately, in accordance with IAS 19.127.

Benefits unrelated to length of service – stand-alone plans

IAS 19.130 states that if the level of benefits is the same regardless of years of service (e.g. a lump-sum fixed amount), the expected cost of those benefits is recognised when an event occurs that causes long-term disability. Applying IAS 19.130 by analogy for death-in-service benefits that are fixed irrespective of any period of service, it would be appropriate to record an expense only when an employee dies.

Benefits unrelated to length of service – benefits provided under a defined benefit plan

The calculation of the liabilities of a defined benefit retirement benefit plan will include an assumption about employees dying before reaching normal retirement age. This will generally reduce the liability recognised. It might therefore be thought imprudent to reduce the liabilities under the plan in this way without recognising the additional liabilities that will arise under the death-in-service benefit arrangements in the event that an employee dies before normal retirement age.

The basic approach of IAS 19 for defined benefit plans is to calculate the expected obligation and attribute that benefit to periods of service. Where the death-in-service benefit is a lump sum amount, there is no plan benefit formula that can be used to attribute the benefit to periods of service. In the absence of such a formula, it would seem appropriate to attribute the benefit on a straight-line basis until the date of the employee's expected death, although it appears that the alternative (i.e. recognition of an expense only when an employee dies) may be justified by reference to IAS 19.130.

Example 11.3

Measurement of incapacity benefit or death-in-service benefit based on service life

An entity operates a defined benefit post-employment plan. Under the terms of the plan, the employee is entitled to a pension of 1/60th of final earnings for each year of service until retirement. If an employee dies or becomes incapacitated prior to the normal retirement date, the benefit paid (to the employee or the employee's dependant) is based on the years of employment until the date of incapacity/death, and credit is given for 50 per cent of the years from that date until the normal retirement date.

For example, an employee works for 20 years and then becomes incapacitated 10 years prior to the normal retirement date. The benefit paid is 25/60ths based on 25 years service (the 20 actually worked plus 50 per cent of the remaining years to normal retirement date).

In these circumstances, the assumptions used for attributing benefits to service periods should reflect that, for employees expected to die or become incapacitated prior to their normal retirement date, the service period would only encompass the period until the expected death or incapacity. A consistent benefit formula should be used over the years of service to reflect the value of the benefit. The expense should be attributed to the periods of service under the benefit formula because the employee's service does not result in a materially higher level of benefit in later years than in early years.

In determining costs, actuaries will make assumptions about the number of employees who are expected to die or become incapacitated prior to normal retirement date. Therefore, for the employees not expected to reach retirement age, the total expected benefit payable, including that related to credited years not actually worked (in this example, 50 per cent of the years between the date of expected death or incapacity and the normal retirement date) will be attributed to the years of expected service up to the date of expected death or incapacity.

12 Termination benefits

Termination benefits are defined as employee benefits payable as a result of either:

[IAS 19.7]

- an entity's decision to terminate an employee's employment before the normal retirement date; or
- an employee's decision to accept voluntary redundancy in exchange for those benefits.

Termination benefits include:

[IAS 19.135]

- lump sum payments;
- enhanced retirement benefits or other post-employment benefits (provided directly or through an employee benefit plan); and
- salary paid until the end of a specified period even though the employee renders no service that provides economic benefits to the entity in that period.

Termination benefits differ from post-employment benefits in that an entity can avoid paying them if it does not terminate an employee's contract of employment. Thus, termination benefits (or redundancy payments) arise not from the rendering of service by an employee, but from the termination of that service. Consequently, they do not relate to future benefits and should be recognised as an expense immediately. Situations that give rise to termination benefits may also impact other employee benefits or give rise to a curtailment of retirement benefits (see **section 7.8**).

Example 12

Payments for early retirement accounted for as termination benefits

Company A is an entity that encourages employees to retire at the age of 58 instead of the national retirement age of 65. The post-retirement programme in Company A's country is a state pension plan. The state sets out the conditions for an employee to receive retirement benefits before the age of 65. This benefit does not form part of an employee's contractual terms and conditions of employment and, each year, Company A can decide whether or not to offer early retirement to its employees. Company A is not, therefore, obligated to make such an offer. Although the retirement benefit for persons between the ages of 58 and 65 is paid for by the government, Company A is required to fund a portion of those payments.

An employee who is offered an early retirement plan can either accept or reject the offer. The offer is normally made prior to the employee's early retirement date (this period may vary from a few months to a couple of years). If the employee does not accept the offer, he or she will continue service until normal retirement age. Early retirement plans are normally implemented to reduce the work force by a means other than compulsory redundancy. An entity may propose early retirement plans to a selected category of employees.

Under IAS 19.7, termination benefits include those payable as a result of an employee's decision to accept voluntary redundancy in exchange for those benefits. Accordingly, these arrangements are accounted for as termination benefits. The full expense will be recognised when the employer is demonstrably committed to the payment, since the payment is not related to future employee service.

12.1 Employee benefits payable irrespective of reason for employee departure

Employee benefits that are payable irrespective of the reason for an employee's departure (subject to any vesting or minimum service requirements) are post-employment benefits rather than termination payments, and should be accounted for as such under IAS 19. In some cases, a higher benefit may be payable in the event of an involuntary termination, at the request of the entity, than is paid for a voluntary termination, at the request of the employee. Such an additional benefit payable on involuntary termination would be a termination benefit. [IAS 19.136]

12.2 Timing of recognition

A termination benefit liability and the corresponding expense are recognised if, and only if, the entity is demonstrably committed to either:

[IAS 19.133]

- terminating the employment of an employee or group of employees before their normal retirement date; or
- providing termination benefits as a result of an offer made to encourage voluntary redundancy.

The approach outlined above is broadly similar to that taken by IAS 37 *Provisions, Contingent Liabilities and Contingent Assets* related to reorganisation provisions in that, by being demonstrably committed, the entity is creating a legal (by legislation or contractual) or constructive (based on business practice, custom or a requirement to act equitably) obligation.

For a termination benefit to be recognised, the entity should be demonstrably committed to the termination at the end of the reporting period.

In order to be demonstrably committed, an entity must have a detailed formal plan from which it cannot realistically withdraw. Although worded slightly differently, this is similar to the requirements for restructuring provisions in IAS 37 (see **chapter 11**). At a minimum, IAS 19 requires that the detailed plan for the termination should include:

[IAS 19.134]

- the location, function, and approximate number of employees whose services are to be terminated;
- the termination benefits for each job classification or function; and
- the time at which the plan will be implemented. Implementation should begin as soon as possible and the period of time to complete implementation should be such that material changes to the plan are not likely.

Example 12.2

Termination benefits requiring regulatory approval

An entity has offered voluntary special termination benefits to specific union employees. The identified employees have accepted the termination benefits. The entity has obtained approval of the benefit packages from the employees' union.

The entity has not received required approval from a National Employment Agency in the relevant jurisdiction. However, the entity has for many years routinely obtained similar approval without challenge.

The special termination benefits should be recognised in accordance with IAS 19 prior to receiving regulatory approval if the required approval from the National Employment Agency is virtually automatic (i.e. there are no situations envisaged in which the approval would be denied). The entity's history of obtaining approval of similar special termination benefits without challenge appears to support the position that the required approval is perfunctory.

Although IAS 19 gives no guidance on how to assess whether withdrawal from a detailed formal termination plan is realistically possible, it does give further guidance in IAS 19.134 on when an entity is 'demonstrably committed'. That further guidance appears to be essentially consistent with the approach taken by IAS 37 to restructuring provisions. Accordingly, in assessing whether an entity is demonstrably committed to a termination under IAS 19, it will usually be helpful to consider whether the requirement of IAS 37.72(b) has been satisfied – namely that the entity 'has raised a valid expectation in those affected that it will carry out the restructuring by starting to implement that plan or by announcing its main features to those affected by it' (see **section 3.9.3.2** of **chapter 11**).

12.3 Measurement

If termination benefits fall due more than 12 months after the end of the reporting period, they should be discounted to their present value, using the same discount rate as for defined benefit obligations (see **7.4.3** above). [IAS 19.139]

If the termination benefits relate to a voluntary redundancy, the provision should reflect the number of employees expected to accept the offer. [IAS 19.140]

12.4 Disclosures

There are no specific disclosure requirements for termination benefits in IAS 19, but disclosures may be required by other Standards, for example:

- IAS 24 *Related Party Disclosures*, where termination benefits relate to key management personnel;
- IAS 37 *Provisions, Contingent Liabilities and Contingent Assets*, where there is uncertainty as to the number of employees who will accept an offer of termination benefits; and
- IAS 1 *Presentation of Financial Statements*, where the expense for termination benefits is material.

13 Future developments

13.1 Short-term convergence with US-GAAP

In June 2005, the IASB published a number of proposed changes to IAS 19 *Employee Benefits*. The proposed changes originally related to phase II of the Board's project on business combinations, and are part of a convergence project with FASB to reduce differences between IFRSs and US GAAP.

The most significant amendments proposed to IAS 19 are as follows:

- voluntary redundancy would be classified as a termination benefit only if offered for a short period. Ongoing programmes to encourage employees to leave before retirement date would be classified as post-retirement benefits;
- obligations in respect of voluntary termination benefits would be recognised only when employees accept the offer of such benefits.

Although the IASB issued revised versions of IFRS 3 and IAS 27 in January 2008, the proposals to amend IAS 19 have been split off from the business combinations project (together with related proposals to amend IAS 37) and will be progressed separately. At the time of writing, the Board expects this project to result in a final Standard in the first half of 2009.

13.2 IASB-FASB project on post-employment benefits

In July 2006, the IASB added a project on post-employment benefits to its agenda, to be conducted in two phases and to involve a fundamental review of all aspects of post-employment benefit accounting. As a first step in Phase I of this project, the IASB published a Discussion Paper entitled *Preliminary Views on Amendments to IAS 19 Employee Benefits* in March 2008. The Discussion Paper is limited in scope and addresses the following issues:

- deferred recognition of some gains and losses arising from defined benefit plans;
- presentation of defined benefit liabilities;
- accounting for benefits that are based on contributions (actual and notional) and a promised return; and
- accounting for benefits with a 'higher-of' option.

The Discussion Paper considers how post-employment defined benefit costs might be allocated between profit or loss and other comprehensive income, and outlines three possible approaches. It also proposes to clarify the definitions underlying the classification of post-employment benefit plans, and suggests creating a new category of 'contribution-based' plans, which would include traditional defined contribution plans, together with more complex benefit formulas of a return based on actual or notional contributions, career average and current salary plans.

Comments on these draft proposals were invited by 26 September 2008.

25 Share-based payment

1 Introduction

Entities often grant shares or share options to directors and employees or other parties in return for services or goods. Until IFRS 2 was issued in February 2004, there was no IFRS covering the recognition and measurement of these transactions. The Standard was effective for periods beginning on or after 1 January 2005.

It is important to appreciate that the Standard may be applicable even when the counterparty receives cash from the entity. This is because the scope of the Standard includes cash-settled share-based payment transactions as explained in **section 2** below.

In January 2008, the IASB published *Amendments to IFRS 2 Share-based Payment: Vesting Conditions and Cancellations*. The amendments are effective for periods beginning on or after 1 January 2009, with earlier application permitted. If an entity applies the amendments for an earlier period, that fact should be disclosed. This chapter explains the relevant requirements of IFRS 2 both before and after the amendments (see **3.2.1** and **5.2** below).

UK

The amendments have not yet been adopted by the European Commission. However, it is arguable that the accounting treatment required by the amended standard was not previously prohibited. Therefore, UK companies may adopt the amendments early, if they wish.

The amendments will have a significant effect on UK companies with SAYE schemes and matching share schemes. Although the total expense recognised over time should not be significantly affected, it may become more volatile.

This chapter discusses the requirements of IFRS 2 in the following sections:

Section 2 Scope

Section 3 Recognition

Section 4 Measurement: equity-settled transactions

Section 5	Modifications including cancellations and settlements
Section 6	Measurement: cash-settled transactions
Section 7	Transactions with settlement alternatives
Section 8	Disclosure and presentation
Section 9	Employee share ownership plans (ESOPs)
Section 10	Employment taxes on share-based payments
Section 11	Accounting by entities within groups
Section 12	Future developments

Appendix A to IFRS 2 includes a list of defined terms which are an integral part of the IFRS. These defined terms are dealt with in the relevant sections of this chapter rather than in a separate definitions section.

UK

In April 2004, the UK Accounting Standards Board issued FRS 20 Share-based Payment. *This standard is identical to IFRS 2 with two exceptions. Unlisted entities (defined, in effect, as those companies not within the scope of the IAS Regulation) had an extra year to prepare for adoption of the standard. For such companies the standard applied for accounting periods beginning on or after 1 January 2006. The second exception is that those entities that prepare their financial statements in accordance with the Financial Reporting Standard for Smaller Entities (FRSSE) are exempt from the standard (as they are exempt from all other standards). However, note that the FRSSE, effective for periods beginning on or after 1 January 2007, requires certain disclosures.*

Therefore, for most UK companies, there will be no change in this area if they move to reporting under IFRSs.

2 Scope

2.1 General

2.1.1 Definitions

IFRS 2 should be applied to each 'share-based payment transaction', defined as follows:

[IFRS 2(Appendix A)]

> 'A transaction in which the entity receives goods or services as consideration for equity instruments of the entity (including shares or share options), or

> acquires goods or services by incurring liabilities to the supplier of those goods or services for amounts that are based on the price of the entity's shares or other equity instruments of the entity.'

IFRS 2 also uses the term 'share-based payment arrangement' which is defined as follows:

[IFRS 2(Appendix A)]

> 'An agreement between the entity and another party (including an employee) to enter into a share-based payment transaction, which thereby entitles the other party to receive cash or other assets of the entity for amounts that are based on the price of the entity's shares or other equity instruments of the entity, or to receive equity instruments of the entity, provided that the specified vesting conditions, if any, are met.'

'Equity instrument' is defined as follows:

[IFRS 2(Appendix A)]

> 'A contract that evidences a residual interest in the assets of an entity after deducting all of its liabilities.'

This definition is consistent with paragraph 11 of IAS 32.

'Equity instrument granted' is defined as follows:

[IFRS 2(Appendix A)]

> 'The right (conditional or unconditional) to an equity instrument of the entity conferred by the entity on another party, under a share-based payment arrangement.'

The Standard does not include a formal definition of either goods or services, although IFRS 2.5 specifies that goods would include inventories, consumables, property, plant and equipment, intangible assets and other non-financial assets. In January 2006, the IASB issued IFRIC Interpretation 8 *Scope of IFRS 2* which confirms that the goods or services do not have to be identifiable to be within the scope of IFRS 2. IFRIC 8 is considered at **2.6** below.

2.1.2 *Types of share-based payment*

Three types of transactions are identified:

[IFRS 2.2]

- equity-settled share-based payment transactions, in which the entity receives goods or services as consideration for equity instruments of the entity (including shares or share options);
- cash-settled share-based payment transactions, in which the entity acquires goods or services by incurring liabilities to the supplier of those goods or services for amounts that are based on the price (or value) of the entity's shares or other equity instruments of the entity. Transactions involving share appreciation rights fall into this category; and
- transactions in which the entity receives or acquires goods or services and the terms of the arrangement provide either the entity or the supplier of those goods or services with a choice of whether the entity settles the transaction in cash (or other assets) or by issuing equity instruments.

IFRS 2 includes separate measurement requirements for each of these, which are discussed in the remainder of this chapter. Business combinations and certain arrangements within the scope of IAS 32 are excluded from the scope of IFRS 2 as discussed at **2.4** and **2.5** below respectively.

2.1.3 Conflict between IFRS 2 and IAS 32

The liability/equity distinction in IFRS 2 is drawn along different lines to the general requirements of IAS 32 (see **chapter 15**). This is explained in the following example.

Example 2.1.3

Equity settlement or cash settlement

Company A issues 1,000 share options to an employee with an exercise price of £15 per share. After completion of the vesting period, the employee will receive shares with the total value equal to the intrinsic value of the options (referred to below as an equity-settled SAR).

The share options should be accounted for as equity-settled because settlement will be by delivery of equity instruments.

The amount of shares that could be issued under the equity-settled share appreciation rights (SAR) and the value of each share issued is variable. IFRS 2.BC106 notes that if the debt/equity requirements of IAS 32 *Financial Instruments: Presentation* were applied to share-based payment transactions, instruments where the number of shares issued is variable would be considered a liability. They would therefore be treated similar to a cash-settled share-based payment. As a result, IFRS 2.BC110 explains that the debt/equity requirements in IAS 32, whereby some obligations to issue equity instruments are classified as liabilities, should not be applied in the IFRS on share-based payment. IFRS 2.BC107 gives an SAR settled in shares as an example of an instrument that would be accounted for differently between IAS 32 and IFRS 2.

2.1.4 *Identifying share-based payment transactions*

It may not always be immediately straightforward to identify transactions falling within the scope of IFRS 2 as shown by the following example.

Example 2.1.4

Scope of IFRS 2

Company L provides an interest-free loan in the amount of £100 to one of its executives to purchase shares with a fair value of £100 in the open market. The shares are used as collateral for the loan balance and, therefore, cannot be sold by the executive during the four-year vesting period. If the executive remains employed with L at the end of four years, the entire amount of the loan is forgiven and the shares are released from all restrictions. If the executive leaves the employ of L during the vesting period, the shares are returned to L and, regardless of value, are considered full payment of the loan.

Since the executive has no risk of owing more than the shares are worth, the substance of the transaction is the issue of restricted shares that vest at the end of four years and, therefore, the transaction is within the scope of IFRS 2. As a result, the fair value of the restricted shares at the grant date should be expensed over the vesting period.

2.1.5 *Awards made by shareholders*

Transfers of an entity's equity instruments by its shareholders to parties (including employees) that have supplied goods or services to the entity are share-based payment transactions within the scope of IFRS 2, unless the transfer is clearly for a purpose other than the payment for goods and services. [IFRS 2.3]

Where a shareholder provides shares for the purposes of an employee share scheme, it will generally be clear that these benefits form part of the remuneration of the employees for their services to the entity. A charge to profit or loss will therefore be required in accordance with IFRS 2 for the services received.

On the other hand, a shareholder may make a gift of shares to a close relative who is coincidentally an employee of the entity. Such a gift might not form part of the remuneration of the employee but it will be necessary to look carefully at the facts of each case. For example, it would be necessary to consider whether similar benefits were given to other employees and whether the gift of shares was in any way conditional on continuing employment with the entity.

The most common instance when equity instruments are provided by a shareholder rather than the entity that has received the goods or services is within groups. This is considered at **2.2** below.

2.2 Groups

2.2.1 Parent and subsidiaries

It is often the case that employees of a subsidiary will receive part of their remuneration in the form of shares in the parent, or less commonly in some other group entity. Where this is the case, IFRS 2 requires the entity that has received the benefit of the services to recognise an expense. This is so even if the equity instruments issued are those of another entity.

Transfers of equity instruments of the entity's parent, or of equity instruments of another entity in the same group, to parties that have supplied goods or services to the entity are within the scope of IFRS 2 unless the transfer is clearly for a purpose other than payment for goods and services. [IFRS 2.3]

Example 2.2.1

Services received in equity-settled share-based transaction

Company P is a publicly listed entity that applies US GAAP. Company P has a majority-owned subsidiary, Company S, which applies IFRSs. Company P issues share options in P's ordinary shares to certain employees of S.

Company S receives the benefit of the services provided by its employees. As a result, S should record the expense related to the share-based payment, regardless of whether S, or another group entity, issues the share options. Where P issues the share options, there may be also a capital contribution to be recognised by P and S (see **section 11** below).

2.2.2 Associates and joint ventures

IFRS 2.3 does not address the situation where employees of an associate or joint venture are granted equity instruments in the investor in connection with their employment. However, a similar approach should generally be adopted because the associate or joint venture will have received the benefit of services provided by the employees and a capital contribution from the investor.

2.2.3 *Meaning of 'entity'*

Various definitions included in Appendix A to IFRS 2 make reference to 'the entity.' In the context of groups, certain such references will sometimes need to be interpreted to mean another group entity.

IFRS 2 is clear that an expense must be recognised in the entity that has received the benefit of the goods or services. It is also clear that, where the parent provides the shares, the other side of this accounting entry is a credit to equity which is in the nature of a capital contribution. However, IFRS 2 does not address the accounting in the other group entity that issued equity instruments or the effect of charges made between group entities in connection with share-based payment arrangements. Neither does it provide guidance on the circumstances where an arrangement is equity-settled from the perspective of the group but may appear to be cash-settled from the perspective of the subsidiary (and vice versa). For example, the subsidiary that receives the benefit of the employee's services might buy shares in its parent in the market for cash to satisfy the arrangement. Some of these issues have been addressed in IFRIC 11 *IFRS 2 – Group and Treasury Share Transactions*. The requirements of IFRIC 11 and some related issues not addressed by the Interpretation are considered in detail in **section 11** below.

2.3 Transactions with owners as owners

The requirements of IFRS 2 should not be applied to transactions with parties (employees, for example) in their capacity as holders of equity instruments of the entity (referred to as 'owners' in IAS 1(2007)). For example, a rights issue may be offered to all holders of a particular class of equity. If an employee is offered the chance to participate purely because he/she is a holder of that class of equity, IFRS 2 is not applied. The requirements of the Standard are only relevant for transactions in which goods or services are acquired. [IFRS 2.4]

Example 2.3

Transaction outside the scope of IFRS 2

Company D purchases its own shares from employees for an amount that equals the fair value of those shares. This transaction would be considered a purchase of treasury shares and would not be within the scope of IFRS 2.

> However, if Company D pays an amount in excess of fair value only to its employees, that excess would be considered remuneration expense.

2.4 Business combinations

IFRS 2 applies to share-based payment transactions in which an entity acquires or receives goods or services. Goods include inventories, consumables, property, plant and equipment, intangible assets and other non-financial assets. However, the IFRS is not applied to transactions in which an entity acquires goods as part of the net assets acquired in a business combination to which IFRS 3 applies. Therefore, equity instruments issued in a business combination in exchange for control of the acquiree are not within the scope of the IFRS. But equity instruments granted to employees of the acquiree in their capacity as employees (e.g. in return for continued services) are within the scope of IFRS 2. Similarly, the cancellation, replacement or other modification of share-based payment arrangements because of a business combination or other equity restructuring are accounted for in accordance with IFRS 2. [IFRS 2.5]

Where shares are issued in a business combination, it is necessary to determine to what extent they are purchase consideration and to what extent they are share-based payments. IFRS 3(2008) provides guidance on determining whether equity instruments issued in a business combination are part of the consideration transferred in exchange for control of the acquiree (and therefore within the scope of IFRS 3) or are in return for continued service to be recognised in the post-combination period (and therefore within the scope of IFRS 2). [IFRS 2.5 as amended] This guidance is considered at **section 8.3** of **chapter 34.**

Section 5.7 of **appendix 2** discusses factors to be considered in deciding whether IFRS 2 should be applied to share-based payment transactions associated with a business combination when IFRS 3(2004) is applied.

IFRS 3(2008).B56-B62 provides guidance on acquirer share-based payment awards exchanged for awards held by the acquiree's employees (see **section 8.3.4** of **chapter 34**).

2.5 Financial instruments

IFRS 2 does not apply to share-based payment transactions in which the entity receives or acquires goods or services under a contract within the scope of paragraphs 8–10 of IAS 32 or paragraphs 5–7 of IAS 39. [IFRS 2.6]

IAS 32 and IAS 39 both state that they should be applied to contracts to buy or sell a non-financial item that can be settled net in cash or by another financial instrument, or by exchanging financial instruments, as if the contracts were financial instruments (subject to one exception). Such contracts are considered in **chapter 13**. Paragraph BC28 of IFRS 2 explains that the IASB concluded that such contracts should remain within the scope of IAS 32 and IAS 39 and, therefore, excluded them from the scope of IFRS 2.

Example 2.5

Interaction with IAS 32 and IAS 39

Company C enters into a forward contract to buy 1,000 units of a commodity at a price equal to 2,000 of Company C's ordinary shares. Company C can settle the contract net, but does not intend to do so (nor has it a practice of doing so). This transaction would be within the scope of IFRS 2. However, if Company C had a practice of settling these contracts net, or did not intend to take physical delivery, then the forward contract would be within the scope of IAS 32 and IAS 39.

2.6 Goods or services cannot be specifically identified (IFRIC 8)

IFRIC 8 *Scope of IFRS 2* addresses whether IFRS 2 applies to transactions in which the entity cannot identify specifically some or all of the goods or services received. It was issued in January 2006 and applied for annual periods beginning on or after 1 May 2006.

The IFRIC first considered this issue in response to uncertainties about the application of IFRS 2 when an entity is required by local legal or regulatory requirements to issue shares at below their fair value to certain (e.g. disadvantaged) sections of the community. This is unlikely to be relevant in the UK. However, IFRIC 8 deals with the issue more broadly and could be relevant in the UK. For example, a UK company might issue shares to a charity at below their market price as a form of charitable giving. IFRIC 8 confirms that an expense should be recognised for the charitable donation in this case. UK

IFRS 2 applies to transactions in which an entity, or an entity's shareholders, have granted equity instruments or incurred a liability to transfer cash or other assets for amounts based on the price (or value) of the entity's shares or other equity instruments. IFRIC 8 applies to such transactions when the identifiable consideration received (or to be received) by the entity, including cash and the fair value of identifiable non-cash consideration, appears to be less than the fair value of the equity instruments granted or the liability incurred. However, the Interpretation does not apply to transactions that are excluded from the scope of IFRS 2 in accordance with paragraphs 3 to 6 of the Standard (e.g. a rights issue at a discount to the market price). [IFRIC 8.6]

IFRS 2 applies to particular transactions in which goods or services are received, such as transactions in which an entity receives goods or services as consideration for equity instruments of the entity. IFRIC 8 confirms that this includes transactions in which the entity cannot identify specifically some or all of the goods or services received. [IFRIC 8.8]

In the absence of specifically identifiable goods or services, other circumstances may indicate that goods or services have been, or will be, received. In this case IFRS 2 applies. If the identifiable consideration received appears to be less than the fair value of the equity instruments granted, or the liability incurred, typically this circumstance indicates that other consideration (i.e. unidentifiable goods or services) has been, or will be, received. [IFRIC 8.9]

The entity measures any identifiable goods and services in accordance with IFRS 2. Any unidentifiable goods or services received are then measured as the difference between the fair value of the share-based payment and the fair value of any identifiable goods or services received. The unidentifiable goods or services are measured at grant date although, for cash-settled arrangements, the liability is remeasured at the end of each reporting period until it is settled. [IFRIC 8.10–12]

IFRIC 8 gives the example of a grant of shares to a charitable organisation for nil consideration as an instance where it might be difficult to demonstrate that goods or services have been, or will be, received. It notes that a similar situation might arise in transactions with other parties. [IFRIC 8.2]

An illustrative example that accompanies IFRIC 8 deals with a situation where an entity grants shares for no consideration to parties who form a particular section of community, as a means of enhancing its corporate image. The example notes that the economic benefits might take a variety of forms such as increasing the entity's customer base, attracting and retaining employees, and improving its chances of being awarded contracts.

There may be no obvious benefits of this kind in cases where shares are required by law to be issued at below their market value.

However, IFRIC 8 should still be applied and an expense recognised. This might be viewed as 'the price of staying in business' or a form of taxation.

For transactions with parties other than employees, IFRS 2 specifies a rebuttable presumption that the fair value of the goods or services received can be estimated reliably. The IFRIC concluded that goods or services that are unidentifiable cannot be reliably measured and so the rebuttable presumption is relevant only for identifiable goods or services. Therefore, in this case, it is necessary to derive the value of the unidentifiable goods or services received from the value of the equity instruments. [IFRIC 8.BC8]

This approach might be seen to imply that it is always necessary to consider the fair value of the equity instruments granted to see if this is greater than the fair value of the goods or services received. This is not so. IFRIC 8.BC7 states that 'the IFRIC noted that it is neither necessary nor appropriate to measure the fair value of goods or services as well as the fair value of the share-based payment for every transaction in which the entity receives goods or non-employee services'. In practice, it will be necessary to consider this issue only in those cases where the value of the goods and services received 'appears to be' less than the fair value of the equity instruments granted. For example, it would not be necessary to obtain a valuation of unquoted shares that had been issued as consideration for non-employee services unless there were indications that some other non-identifiable goods or services had also been obtained.

The phrase 'the fair value of the share-based payment' refers to the value of the particular share-based payment concerned. For example, an entity might be required by legislation to issue some portion of its shares to nationals of a particular country, which may be transferred only to other nationals of that country. Such transfer restrictions may affect the fair value of the shares concerned. They may have a fair value that is less than the fair value of otherwise identical shares that do not carry the transfer restrictions. In this case, if it is the restricted shares that are granted, the phrase 'the fair value of the share-based payment' in IFRIC 8 refers to the fair value of the restricted shares and not to the fair value of the unrestricted shares. [IFRIC 8.5]

3 Recognition

3.1 General

The goods or services received or acquired in a share-based payment transaction are recognised as the goods are obtained or the services are received. A corresponding increase in equity is recognised if the goods or services were received in an equity-settled transaction. A liability is recognised if the goods or services were acquired in a cash-settled transaction. [IFRS 2.7]

The goods or services received in a share-based payment transaction may qualify for recognition as an asset. If not, they are recognised as an expense. [IFRS 2.8]

Services are typically consumed immediately, in which case an expense is recognised as the counterparty renders service. Goods might be consumed over a period of time or, in the case of inventories, sold at a later date, in which case an expense is recognised when the goods are consumed or sold. However, sometimes it is necessary to recognise an expense before the goods or services are consumed or sold, because they do not qualify for recognition as assets. For example, an entity might acquire goods as part of the research phase of a project to develop a new product. Although those goods have not been consumed, they might not qualify for recognition as assets under the applicable IFRS. [IFRS 2.9]

3.2 Timing

As explained at **3.1** above, the goods or services involved in a share-based payment transaction should be recognised when they are acquired/received. It will normally be relatively straightforward to ascertain when goods are received, but this is not necessarily so when services are involved.

3.2.1 Equity-settled share-based payment transactions

The approach to be adopted in relation to the timing of recognition depends largely on the concept of vesting. IFRS 2, as amended in January 2008, defines 'vest' as follows:

[IFRS 2(Appendix A)]

> 'To become an entitlement. Under a share-based payment arrangement, a counterparty's right to receive cash, other assets, or equity instruments of the entity vests when the counterparty's entitlement is no longer conditional on the satisfaction of vesting conditions.'

For those entities that have not applied the amended standard, the definition is as follows:

[IFRS 2(Appendix A)]

> 'To become an entitlement. Under a share-based payment arrangement, a counterparty's right to receive cash, other assets, or equity instruments of the entity vests upon satisfaction of any specified vesting conditions.'

As explained at IFRS 2.BC171B, this change was made to address the question of whether particular restrictive conditions, such as 'non-compete provisions', are vesting conditions. The Board noted that a share-based payment vests when the counterparty's entitlement to it is no longer conditional on future service or performance conditions. Therefore, conditions such as non-compete provisions and transfer restrictions, which apply after the counterparty has become entitled to the share-based payment, are not vesting conditions. The Board amended the definition of 'vest' accordingly.

If equity instruments vest immediately then, in the absence of evidence to the contrary, it is presumed that the consideration for the instruments (employee services, for example) has been received. The consideration (i.e. an expense or asset, as appropriate) should, therefore, be recognised in full, with a corresponding increase in equity. [IFRS 2.14]

If equity instruments do not vest immediately, the terms 'vesting conditions' and 'vesting period', as defined by IFRS 2, are important. In IFRS 2, as amended in January 2008, 'Vesting conditions' are:

[IFRS 2(Appendix A)]

> 'The conditions that determine whether the entity receives the services that entitle the counterparty to receive cash, other assets or equity instruments of the entity, under a share-based payment arrangement. Vesting conditions are either service conditions or performance conditions. Service conditions require the counterparty to complete a specified period of service. Performance conditions require the counterparty to complete a specified period of service and specified performance targets to be met (such as a specified increase in the entity's profit over a specified period of time). A performance condition might include a market condition.'

For those entities that have not applied the amended standard, the definition is as follows:

[IFRS 2(Appendix A)]

> 'The conditions that must be satisfied for the counterparty to become entitled to receive cash, other assets or equity instruments of the entity, under a share-based payment arrangement. Vesting conditions include service conditions, which require the other party to complete a specified period of service, and performance conditions, which require specified performance targets to be met (such as a specified increase in the entity's profit over a specified period of time).'

The original definition of vesting conditions indicates that they include service conditions and performance conditions, without limiting them to these two types of conditions. The revised definition restricts vesting conditions to only service conditions and performance conditions. It also clarifies that a performance condition must not only require a specified performance target to be met but also require the counterparty to complete a specified period of service. This appears to make performance conditions a sub-set of service conditions. IFRS 2.BC171A notes that 'the feature that distinguishes a performance condition from a non-vesting condition is that the former has an explicit or implicit service requirement and the latter does not'.

The amendment was originally intended to address uncertainty about the treatment of SAYE share options schemes in which employees save a regular amount, usually through deduction from salary, which is applied to cover the exercise price of the options when they are exercised. Employees are free to stop contributing to the scheme and obtain a refund of contributions at any time, but forfeit their entitlement to exercise the options if they do so. The question that arose was whether the continued payment of contributions into the scheme should be regarded as a vesting condition. Prior to the amendment to IFRS 2, some have taken the view that the payment of contributions is a performance condition or some other form of vesting condition. Accordingly, any expense recognised for the options is reversed if an employee stops making contributions and withdraws from the scheme.

The IASB did not agree with this point of view and amended the Standard to make it clear that the payment of contributions into an SAYE scheme is not a vesting condition. It does not meet the revised definition of a performance condition because it has no link to service. The amended standard introduces the concept of a 'non-vesting condition'. Examples of non-vesting conditions are the payment of contributions to an SAYE scheme and a requirement to subscribe for shares to become entitled to be granted free 'matching shares' in certain types of share schemes.

IFRS 2 has been amended to clarify that non-vesting conditions are taken into account when estimating the fair value of the equity instruments at grant date (see **4.3.1** below). This is the same as the treatment of a market-based vesting condition. The Standard has also been amended to clarify that failure to meet a non-vesting condition, for example by ceasing to contribute to an SAYE scheme, should be accounted for as a cancellation of the options so that the expense will be accelerated (see **5.2** below).

For example, on a grant of SAYE options, an estimate should be made of the number of employees who will cease to contribute to the scheme, otherwise than through termination of their employment, before the options vest. The grant date fair value should be reduced accordingly. It can therefore be seen that there should be no overall increase in the expense recognised for such schemes if the initial estimate of the number of members withdrawing from the scheme is accurate. However, the expense may be more volatile due to the acceleration of the expense when employees withdraw from the scheme.

IFRS 2.IG4A provides the following flowchart to illustrate the application of the amended definition of vesting conditions.

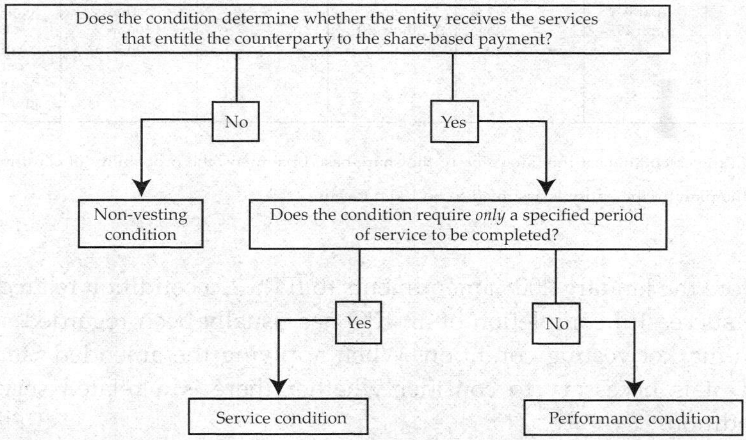

IFRS 2.IG15A provides a numerical example, under the amended Standard, of a share-based payment with vesting and non-vesting conditions when the counterparty can choose whether the non-vesting condition is met. The example is not reproduced here.

IFRS 2.IG24 provides the following table which categorises, with examples, the various conditions that determine whether a counterparty receives an equity instrument granted and the accounting treatment of share-based payments with those conditions under the amended IFRS 2.

Summary of conditions that determine whether a counterparty receives an equity instrument granted

	VESTING CONDITIONS			NON-VESTING CONDITIONS		
	Service conditions	Performance conditions				
		Performance conditions that are market conditions	Other performance conditions	Neither the entity nor the counterparty can choose whether the condition is met	Counterparty can choose whether to meet the condition	Entity can choose whether to meet the condition
Example conditions	Requirement to remain in service for three years	Target based on the market price of the entity's equity instruments	Target based on a successful initial public offering with a specified service requirement	Target based on a commodity index	Paying contributions towards the exercise price of a share-based payment	Continuation of the plan by the entity
Include in grant date fair value?	No	Yes	No	Yes	Yes	Yes[(a)]
Accounting treatment if the condition is not met after the grant date and during the vesting period	Forfeiture. The entity revises the expense to reflect the best available estimate of the number of equity instruments expected to vest. (paragraph 19)	No change to accounting. The entity continues to recognise the expense over the remainder of the vesting period. (paragraph 21)	Forfeiture. The entity revises the expense to reflect the best available estimate of the number of equity instruments expected to vest. (paragraph 19)	No change to accounting. The entity continues to recognise the expense over the remainder of the vesting period. (paragraph 21A)	Cancellation. The entity recognises immediately the amount of the expense that would otherwise have been recognised over the remainder of the vesting period. (paragraph 28A)	Cancellation. The entity recognises immediately the amount of the expense that would otherwise have been recognised over the remainder of the vesting period. (paragraph 28A)

(a) In the calculation of the fair value of the share-based payment, the probability of continuation of the plan by the entity is assumed to be 100 per cent.

Before the January 2008 amendments to IFRS 2, a condition related to the successful completion of an IPO has usually been regarded as a non-market vesting condition. When applying the amended Standard, it is necessary to consider whether there is a related service condition.

One of the examples of a vesting condition in the above table [IFRS 2.IG24] is the successful completion of an IPO **together with** a specified service requirement (i.e. an employee is required to be employed at the time an IPO is successfully completed). It is also clear that, under the amended Standard, the successful completion of an IPO **without** any related service condition is a non-vesting condition.

If the service period is shorter than the period to the IPO, the IPO should be treated as a non-vesting condition under the amended Standard. This would be the case if there is a service condition for a limited period (e.g. two years) and the employees are then free to leave while retaining their right to exercise the options at a later date if the IPO is achieved. In this case, any expense recognised for the options granted to employees who leave before meeting the two-year service condition will be reversed. There will be no reversal, if the IPO does not occur, in relation to the employees who remain at the end of the two-year service period. However, as noted above, the grant date fair value will have been adjusted to take account of the probability that the IPO will not occur.

The 'vesting period' is:

[IFRS 2(Appendix A)]

> 'The period during which all the specified vesting conditions of a share-based payment arrangement are to be satisfied.'

If the equity instruments granted do not vest until the counterparty completes a specified period of service, it is presumed that the service period equals the vesting period. The services are accounted for as they are rendered by the counterparty during the vesting period, with a corresponding increase in equity. [IFRS 2.15]

A simple scenario would see employees granted share options which vest only once they have completed a specified period of employment – say three years. In this scenario, the entity will record an expense over the three-year vesting period. [IFRS 2.15(a)] However, if the employees are granted share options which are conditional upon the employees working for the entity for the three financial years beyond the current one, generally, the IFRS 2 expense will be recognised over a vesting period of four years beginning on the date of grant because, in substance, the vesting is conditional on the employee continuing to render service for another four years (i.e. remain employed for the current year, plus three subsequent years).

The question arises of whether failure to complete the specified period of service because of redundancy should be treated in the same way as a voluntary termination of employment by the employee. The Standard does not specify whether redundancy should be treated as forfeiture or cancellation. This is key because forfeiture would enable the employer to 'true up' and therefore reverse the IFRS 2 expense previously recognised, whereas cancellation would trigger accelerated recognition of the remaining charges. IFRS 2 specifies that failure to meet a service condition by an employee, for example due to voluntary departure, should be treated as forfeiture. The January 2008 amendments to IFRS 2 introduced a relevant principle. This principle is that a cancellation, whether by an employee or the employer, should be accounted for in the same way. Building on this principle, the employer's decision to make an employee redundant should be treated in the same manner as a voluntary departure and consequently this should be accounted for as a forfeiture.

However, attention should be paid to cases where the severance of an employee's contract is accompanied by a compensation package at the time of termination of employment. In such instances, facts and circumstances should be considered to assess whether the severance package (or part thereof) should be treated as a modification and settlement of the original awards.

If an employee is granted share options conditional upon the achievement of a performance condition and remaining in the entity's employ until that performance condition is satisfied, and the length of the vesting period varies depending on when that performance condition is satisfied, the entity presumes that the services to be rendered by the employee as consideration for the share options will be received in the future, over the expected vesting period. The entity estimates the length of the expected vesting period at grant date, based on the most likely outcome of the performance condition. If the performance condition is a market condition (see **section 4** below), the estimate of the length of the expected vesting period should be consistent with the assumptions used in estimating the fair value of the options granted, and should not be subsequently revised. If the performance condition is not a market condition, the entity revises its estimate of the length of the vesting period, if necessary, if subsequent information indicates that the length of the vesting period differs from previous estimates. [IFRS 2.15(b)]

3.2.2 *Cash-settled share-based payment transactions*

IFRS 2.32 makes it clear that the principles discussed in **3.2.1** above also apply to cash-settled share-based payments. The consideration for such payments is recognised when it is received (i.e. immediately or over any vesting period), with a corresponding liability.

There are specific requirements that relate to arrangements with a choice of settlement method (see **section 7** below).

4 Measurement: equity-settled transactions

4.1 General

4.1.1 Fair value

In an equity-settled transaction, the goods or services received, and the corresponding increase in equity, should be measured at the fair value of those goods/services.

'Fair value' is defined as follows:

[IFRS 2(Appendix A)]

> 'The amount for which an asset could be exchanged, a liability settled, or an equity instrument granted could be exchanged, between knowledgeable, willing parties in an arm's length transaction.'

Market vesting conditions are taken into account when estimating the fair value of the equity instruments granted. All non-vesting conditions are similarly taken into account. However, non-market vesting conditions are not taken into account for this purpose. This is explained further at **4.3.1** below.

4.1.2 Transactions with employees and non-employees

For equity-settled share-based payment transactions, the goods or services received and the corresponding increase in equity are measured directly at the fair value of the goods or services received, unless that fair value cannot be estimated reliably. If it is not possible to estimate reliably the fair value of the goods or services received, the fair value of the equity instruments granted is used as a proxy. [IFRS 2.10] There is a limited exception to this requirement in rare cases where the entity is unable to estimate reliably the fair value of the equity instruments granted at the measurement date. This exception is considered at **4.6** below.

The IASB has taken the view that the fair value of the equity instruments granted should be used for transactions with employees and others providing similar services. This is because, in such transactions, 'typically it is not possible to estimate reliably the fair value of the services received.' The fair value of those equity instruments is measured at grant date. [IFRS 2.11–12]

IFRS 2 defines 'employees and others providing similar services' as:

[IFRS 2(Appendix A)]

> 'Individuals who render personal services to the entity and either (a) the individuals are regarded as employees for legal or tax purposes, (b) the individuals work for the entity under its direction in the same way as individuals who are regarded as employees for legal or tax purposes, or (c) the services rendered are similar to those rendered by employees. For example, the term encompasses all management personnel, i.e. those persons having authority and responsibility for planning, directing and controlling the activities of the entity, including non-executive directors.'

Further references to employees in this chapter will include others providing similar services.

The determination as to whether an individual is similar to an employee or a non-employee is a matter of careful judgement.

The following factors may be considered as indicators of employees and others providing similar services.

- The purchasing entity is paying for the right to use certain individuals and not the actual output from the individuals (i.e. the purchasing entity has the risk of downtime).
- The individuals are under the direct supervision of the purchasing entity.
- The contract depends on the services from a specified individual.
- The purchasing entity receives substantially all of the output from the individual for a specified period of time.
- The individuals perform services that are similar to services currently provided by employees.

Factors that would indicate an individual is not an employee or providing services similar to an employee include the following.

- The individual performs services that cannot legally be provided by employees.
- The individual uses technology that is not legally available to the purchasing entity to perform the services.

For transactions with parties other than employees, there is a rebuttable presumption that the fair value of the goods or services received can be estimated reliably. This fair value should be measured at the date the entity receives the relevant goods or services. This presumption should be rebutted only in those 'rare cases' in which the fair value of the goods or services received cannot be estimated reliably. In such circumstances, the fair value is measured indirectly by reference to the fair value of the equity instrument granted, measured at the date the entity receives the relevant goods or services. [IFRS 2.13]

4.1.3 *More than one measurement date*

If the goods or services are received on more than one date, the entity should measure the fair value of the equity instruments granted on each date when goods or services are received. The entity should apply that fair value when measuring the goods or services received on that date. [IFRS 2.IG6]

It is possible to use an approximation in some cases. If an entity received services continuously during a six-month period, and its share price did not change significantly during that period, the entity could use the average share price during the six-month period when estimating the fair value of the equity instruments granted. [IFRS 2.IG7]

These principles are illustrated in the following examples.

Example 4.1.3A

Issue of shares for goods or services from non-employees

Company P (a private entity) issues shares to its external lawyers for services related to the successful completion of a lawsuit that Company P is currently defending. The lawyers spent 100 hours working on the case. From recent invoices from the lawyers, Company P determined the fair value of the services received to be £300 per hour. Company P would record an expense for £30,000 [100 x £300] and would not be required to determine the fair value of the shares granted to the lawyers since the fair value of the services could be reliably measured.

Example 4.1.3B

Measurement date for fair valuation purposes

Company G is a start-up entity that wants to build a website. Company G contacts Supplier W on 15 March and offers 100 shares in G if W builds a website to G's specifications. The offer is valid for six months. Supplier W neither rejects nor accepts G's offer. On 30 June, W agrees to build G's website for the 100 shares. On 30 October, the website is delivered to G. On the same date, G delivers the 100 shares to W.

Company G has determined that it cannot measure reliably the fair value of the services received and, therefore, measures the share-based payment by reference to the fair value of the shares issued.

The measurement date under IFRS 2 will be 30 October. For transactions with parties other than employees (and those providing similar services), the measurement date is defined as '. . . the date the entity obtains the goods or the counterparty renders service'. The 100 shares, therefore, would be valued at 30 October, based on current market prices. Since no further action is required by W and the shares issued are fully vested, the full fair value should be expensed or capitalised as an intangible asset in accordance with IAS 38 *Intangible Assets*.

In certain jurisdictions G may be required to present interim financial statements at 30 June. Under IFRS 2, there is no requirement to recognise an interim expense for this transaction. Therefore, G would need only to provide the disclosures required for such commitments (if material).

4.1.4 *Cash received from employees entering a share purchase plan*

Example 4.1.4

Cash received from employees entering a share purchase plan

An entity offers all its employees the opportunity to participate in an employee share purchase plan. The employees have a limited time to decide whether to accept the offer. The plan entitles the employees to purchase a maximum of 100 shares each at a purchase price of 10 pence per share (the nominal value of a share). The purchase price is lower than the fair value of the shares as of the grant date.

The employees are required to pay the purchase price on accepting the offer and receive the shares immediately. However, they must remain employed with the entity for five years before being permitted to sell the shares. If an employee ceases employment before the vesting period ends, the entity will automatically redeem the shares at 10 pence per share. The employees are not entitled to dividends on the shares during the vesting period.

How should this employee share purchase plan and the 10 pence received by the entity as of the grant date be accounted for?

This scheme is an equity-settled share-based payment arrangement because the employees are ultimately only entitled to receive shares. However, the distinctive feature of this share purchase plan is that the shares are delivered immediately on receipt of the cash payment for the nominal value of the shares even though they do not vest for five years. In substance, the employees do not receive the shares until they vest unconditionally.

To reflect the prepaid purchase price and the employer share redemption mechanism, the entity should recognise the cash received as a financial liability until the end of the vesting period, at which time it will be reclassified to equity as long as the employee remains employed. If the employee leaves the entity before the vesting period ends, the entity repays the employee the initial investment and derecognises the financial liability.

Because the financial liability could be repaid at any time within the vesting period, it will be measured at 10 pence per share. The 'pre-payment' of the exercise price will be factored into the grant date fair value of the share option.

Entitlement to dividends during the vesting period would be factored into the fair value determination, but would otherwise not alter this answer.

4.2 Determining the fair value of equity instruments granted

4.2.1 The measurement date

Where transactions are measured by reference to the fair value of the equity instruments granted, that fair value should be determined at the 'measurement date' which is defined in IFRS 2 as:

[IFRS 2(Appendix A)]

> 'The date at which the fair value of the equity instruments granted is measured for the purposes of this IFRS. For transactions with employees and others providing similar services, the measurement date is grant date. For transactions with parties other than employees (and those providing similar services), the measurement date is the date the entity obtains the goods or the counterparty renders service.'

This definition uses the term 'grant date' which is in turn defined as:

[IFRS 2(Appendix A)]

> 'The date at which the entity and another party (including an employee) agree to a share-based payment arrangement, being when the entity and the counterparty have a shared understanding of the terms and conditions of the arrangement. At grant date the entity confers on the counterparty the right to cash, other assets, or equity instruments of the entity, provided the specified vesting conditions, if any, are met. If that agreement is subject to an approval process (for example, by shareholders), grant date is the date when that approval is obtained.'

Example 4.2.1A

Grant date

At the beginning of year one, 1 January 20X1, Company A and each of its executives enter into an agreement where A will issue shares to each

> executive. The number of shares depends on a formula that considers growth in revenue and profits for the year to 31 December 20X1. Depending on audited revenue and profit growth, which will be known at 31 March 20X2, A could issue between nil and 100 restricted shares. The restricted shares will vest in the employees if they remain in A's employment at the end of a further three years. Therefore, the earliest each executive could sell his/her restricted shares is at the end of year four. The Board has already approved the formula and no further approvals are needed. The question that arises is whether the grant date is 1 January 20X1 or 31 March 20X2.
>
> Grant date is defined as 'the date at which the entity and another party ... agree to a share-based payment arrangement, being when the entity and the counterparty have a shared understanding of the terms and conditions of the arrangement ...'. At 1 January 20X1, all parties understand the terms and, therefore, this should be viewed as the grant date.
>
> An estimate of the number of shares that will vest is made at 1 January 20X1. A fair value is assigned to each share. As the formula is considered a non-market vesting condition that should be accounted for using the true up method in IFRS 2, the number of shares is adjusted at 31 March 20X2 based on the amount of restricted shares actually issued to the executives. The fair value of each share is based on the value at 1 January 20X1.

Two key factors that need to be considered when deciding on the grant date are:

- both parties need to 'agree' to a share-based payment; and
- both parties must have a shared understanding of the terms and conditions.

The word 'agree' is used in its usual sense and means that there must be both an offer and acceptance of that offer. The date of grant is when the other party accepts an offer and not when the offer is made. In some instances the agreement might be implicit (i.e. not by signing a formal contract) and this is the case for many share-based payment arrangements with employees. In these cases, the employees' agreement is evidenced by their commencing to render services. [IFRS 2.IG2]

For both parties to have agreed to the share-based payment arrangement, they must have a shared understanding of the terms and conditions of the arrangement. If some of the terms and conditions of the arrangement are agreed on one date, with the remainder of the terms and conditions agreed on a later date, then grant date is on that later date, when all of the terms and conditions have been agreed. For example, consider the situation where an entity agrees to issue share options to an employee, but the exercise price of the options will be set by a remuneration committee that meets in three months' time. The grant date is when the exercise price is set by the remuneration committee. [IFRS 2.IG3]

The scenario described in the previous paragraph differs from that described in **example 4.2.1A**. In **example 4.2.1A** the number of restricted shares to be issued, although not known, is the subject of an agreed formula which considers revenue and profit growth. In the scenario of the previous paragraph the exercise price is not agreed until it is set by the remuneration committee because until then it remains subject to the committee's discretion.

In some cases, a grant date might occur after the employees to whom the equity instruments were granted have begun rendering services. For example, if a grant of equity instruments is subject to shareholder approval, grant date might occur some months after the employees have begun rendering services in respect of that grant. The IFRS requires the entity to recognise the services when received. In this situation, the entity should estimate the grant date fair value of the equity instruments (e.g. by estimating the fair value of the equity instruments at the end of the reporting period), for the purposes of recognising the services received during the period between service commencement date and grant date. Once the date of grant has been established, the entity should revise the earlier estimate so that the amounts recognised for services received in respect of the grant are ultimately based on the grant date fair value of the equity instruments. [IFRS 2.IG4]

The following example considers the effect of employee-acceptance provisions on the determination of grant date.

Example 4.2.1B

Effect of employee-acceptance provisions on grant date

In Country B, an individual is taxed in the period that share-based payments are received. As a result, prior to issuing share-based payments to its employees, Company X first issues an offer letter to each employee detailing the amount of shares or share options and the exercise price. Each employee has 30 days in which to return the offer letter to accept the options.

Is the grant date the date of the offer or the date of the acceptance?

In many cases, the determination of whether the requirement for rejection or acceptance is explicit or implicit requires careful analysis of the facts and circumstances. On the facts presented, the requirement to accept is explicit and has substance, given that the employee will be taxed immediately on the options received. While the employee understands all of the terms and conditions, the employer does not, until acceptance, have a full understanding of how many share options will be issued. Therefore, due to the explicit acceptance requirement, grant date would be the date of acceptance.

The date of grant determines the date the options should be measured, but does not affect the recognition period of the expense. That is, the option should be recognised as an expense over the service period. If the service period begins prior to the date of grant (e.g. the offer date), Company X should begin expensing the share-based payment at the date of offer at an amount that will approximate to the fair value to be determined at grant date. Once an employee accepts, that date would be the grant date and the fair value would be determined at that date.

4.2.2 *Fair value by reference to the fair value of goods or services*

When determining fair value by reference to the value of the goods or services, care should be taken to ensure that volume rebates or other discounts are considered. Where the value of the goods or services received is not commensurate with the value of the equity instruments issued, the difference may be due to volume rebates. If this is the case, the amount recorded should be the fair value net of any volume rebates.

Example 4.2.2

Volume rebates

For example, assume Company A purchases 1,000 computers in return for 5,000 of Company A's ordinary shares, trading at £100 each. The seller generally sells the same computers for £700 each. Company A currently trades several thousand shares a day, such that 5,000 shares would be readily convertible to cash by the seller. The difference between £500,000 [5,000 x £100] and £700,000 [1,000 x £700] may relate to a volume rebate that should be considered in the valuation. Therefore, £500,000 may be the more appropriate measure for the computers.

4.2.3 *Fair value by reference to the fair value of equity instruments*

When share-based payment transactions are measured by reference to the fair value of the equity instruments granted, ideally that fair value should be determined by reference to market prices. For example, in the case of an issuance of shares that must be forfeited if the employee leaves service over a three-year period, the share-based payment will be measured at the fair value of the shares at the date of grant. A share price or valuation of the entity at the date of grant would be sufficient to determine the fair value of those shares and it would not be necessary to recalculate this value unless the grant was modified.

When market prices do not exist for share options, the fair value should be determined by applying a valuation technique, usually in the form of an option pricing model. [IFRS 2.B4]

The three most common models are the Black-Scholes model, the binomial model and Monte Carlo model. These models are further considered in **4.2.4** below.

The entity should consider factors that knowledgeable, willing market participants would consider in selecting the option pricing model to apply. For example, employee options are often exercised early, have quite long lives and are usually exercisable during the period between vesting date and the end of the options' life. These factors should be considered when determining the grant date fair value of the options. IFRS 2 states that for many entities 'this might preclude the use of the Black-Scholes-Merton formula, which does not allow for the possibility of exercise before the end of the option's life and may not adequately reflect the effects of expected early exercise. It also does not allow for the possibility that expected volatility and other model inputs might vary over the option's life'. [IFRS 2.B5]

It may be acceptable, and even necessary, to use different models for different schemes to reflect their particular features. It may also sometimes be appropriate to use different models for different grants under the same scheme, for example to change to a more complex model as amounts become more material. However, other than in the case of material error, the grant date fair value should not be adjusted, once it has been determined using a particular model, even if that model is no longer used for new grants.

Appendix B to IFRS 2 discusses measurement of the fair value of shares and share options granted, focusing on specific terms and conditions that are common features of a grant of shares or share options to employees. Examples of the types of decisions related to measurement that entities are required to make include:

Items to determine	Accounting decisions
Pricing model	Black-Scholes, binomial, Monte Carlo, etc.
Expected life assumption/ employee behaviour	For variable exercise dates, assumptions are needed as to when employees are likely to exercise their options (e.g. in a financially optimal manner; when the option is in the money at a certain time, e.g. vesting date; when the share price hits a specified share price ('barrier'); or based on historical behaviour).
Current share price	Share price can be determined on the basis of closing price on grant date or the average price on grant date.
Expected volatility	There are various methods to calculate this amount (e.g. based on historical experience, implied volatility of traded options, volatility of comparator entities, or industry index).
Expected dividends	This should be the expected future dividends over the expected life of the award. This should be in line with the entity's policy, although this may be derived from historical experience or experience of competitors.
Risk-free interest rate	This should generally be the implied yield available at the date of grant on zero-coupon government issues of the country in whose currency the exercise is expressed and of duration that is similar to the expected life of the award.

These items are addressed in more detail in the sections below.

The fair value of cash-settled share-based payments, such as share appreciation rights (SARs), should be measured by using a model similar to one used for share options. That is, future share price increases and other variables have a similar effect on the fair value of many forms of cash-settled share-based payment transactions.

4.2.4 *Valuation models*

As referred to in **4.2.3**, the three most common option pricing models are the Black-Scholes model, the binomial model and Monte Carlo model.

The Black-Scholes model for valuing share options was first published in 1973 and has been used as the basis to value share options and other share-based payments the fair value of which reacts similar to that of share options. The binomial model was introduced to provide a simplified explanation to the Black-Scholes model and to extend its usefulness beyond some Black-Scholes narrow confines. When awards have market-based vesting conditions, a Monte Carlo model (or equivalent numerical approach) that allows for these conditions should be used.

This section compares and contrasts the three models.

4.2.4.1 *Black-Scholes*

Application of the Black-Scholes model tends to be a straightforward calculation, which requires only six inputs. These are:

- share price at grant date;
- exercise price;
- dividend yield;
- expected life;
- risk-free interest rate; and
- volatility

The Black-Scholes approach assumes that exercise of the option can only take place at one point in time. It requires an expected life assumption as to when the option is likely to be exercised and does not allow for variable exercise dates.

The strengths of the Black-Scholes model are:

- generally accepted method for valuing share options, with wide acceptance in the market;
- many entities with share option plans use the Black-Scholes model to compute the fair value of their share awards. The consistent use of this model also enhances the comparability between the entities; and

- formula required to calculate the fair value is straightforward and can be easily included in spreadsheets.

The weaknesses of the Black-Scholes model are:

- the Black-Scholes model assumes that the exercise of the option can only take place at one point in time. It does not allow for variable exercise dates. This model may undervalue the plan option as options that are out-of-the money at the end of the expected life are assumed to expire worthless. However, there is additional value arising from the possibility that the options may subsequently come back into the money before the end of the full contractual term. This can be a major issue for options that have a long exercise window, where one point in the exercise window has to be chosen when exercise takes place;

- the Black-Scholes model is described as a 'closed form solution' because inputs and assumptions are made to cover the entire period during which the option is outstanding. For example, volatility of the underlying shares may be expected to change over the period. The Black-Scholes model cannot take this into account; and

- the Black-Scholes model cannot typically take account of most market-based performance conditions (although certain variations are possible to cope with some such conditions).

4.2.4.2 Binomial model

The binomial model breaks down the time to expiration into potentially a large number of time-intervals or steps. A tree of share prices is initially produced working forward from the present time to expiration of the option. At each step it is assumed that the share price will move up or down by an amount calculated using the volatility assumption and the length of each time-interval. The probabilities of upward and downward movements are calculated using risk-neutral probabilities derived from the size of the upward and downward steps and the risk-free rate of return. This produces a binomial distribution, or tree, of underlying share prices. The tree represents all possible paths that the share price could take during the life of the option. Factors that affect the share price, such as dividends, are adjusted for in the binomial tree as they are paid during the contractual life. At the end of the tree – that is, the expiration of the option – all the terminal option payoffs for each of the final possible share prices are known as they simply equal their intrinsic values.

Next, the option values at each step of the tree are calculated working back from expiration to the present. The option values at each step are used to derive the option values at the preceding step of the tree using a risk-neutral valuation. This risk-neutral valuation uses the risk-free rate of interest as a discount factor and risk-neutral probabilities of the share price moving up or down. Certain adjustments to option prices (e.g. market-based vesting features) can be worked into the calculations at the required point in time (although not all market-based conditions can be incorporated, meaning that another approach, e.g. Monte Carlo, may be required – see below). At the start of the tree, the option's fair value is obtained.

If the inputs and assumptions used in the Black-Scholes and the binomial models were the same, the results would be similar.

The strengths of the binomial model are:

- the binomial model is described as an 'open form solution' as it can incorporate different values for variables (such as volatility) over the term of the option. Therefore, many believe the inputs into the model are better reflective of an option with a longer term. In particular, it can take account of exercise on variable dates, whereas the Black-Scholes model assumes any exercise takes place at one particular time;

- the model can be adjusted to take account of market conditions and other factors; and

- the binomial model has also been generally accepted as a more flexible alternative to the Black-Scholes model.

The weaknesses of the binomial model are:

- the Black-Scholes model allows the value of an option to be calculated using a relatively simple spreadsheet. However, the binomial model requires a considerably more complex spreadsheet or program to calculate the option value; and

- in addition, it is necessary to make a number of judgemental decisions as to how various factors (e.g. employee exercise behaviour) are taken into account.

4.2.4.3 *Monte Carlo model*

A Monte Carlo model works by simulating a large number of projected random outcomes for how the share price may move in future. The relevant share price may be that of the entity and, if applicable, those of comparator entities (for example, where there are market-based performance conditions based on relative Total Shareholder Return rankings).

Based on each simulated share price (or set of comparator entity share prices), the proportion of awards that would vest and the resultant pay-off is determined. This is then discounted back to the valuation date at the risk-free interest rate. The procedure is then repeated a large number of times to determine the expected (average) value of the award at the valuation date.

The strengths of the Monte Carlo model are:

- it is the most flexible of the models described. It can take account of complex market-based vesting conditions, exercise behaviours and factors;
- it may be easier to explain/understand the results; and
- it can be used to look at the distribution of payoffs.

The weaknesses of the Monte Carlo model are:

- it requires a program or complex spreadsheet with an embedded program to calculate the option value; and
- it may require in excess of 10,000 simulations or more to obtain a sufficiently accurate answer. Depending on the features of the model, this can require a large amount of computer processing time and as such it would generally be used only where it is not possible or appropriate to use other methods.

4.2.5 *Basic factors affecting the valuation of share-based payments*

Most employee share-based payments granted will not have an equivalent instrument traded in an active market and, therefore, when the determination of their fair values is required by IFRS 2, valuation models will need to be applied. IFRS 2 requires, at a minimum, that all valuation models consider the following six basic inputs:

[IFRS 2.B6]

- the exercise price of the option (see **4.2.5.1** below);
- the current price of the underlying shares (see **4.2.5.2** below);
- the life of the option (see **4.2.5.3** below);
- the expected volatility of the share price (see **4.2.5.4** below);
- the dividends expected on the shares (see **4.2.5.5** below); and
- the risk-free interest rate for the life of the option (see **4.2.5.6** below).

These variables have been widely accepted as required inputs into valuations. Therefore, it is useful first to review these basic inputs. Other factors affecting the valuation of share-based payments are addressed in **4.2.6** below.

For some of the inputs listed above it is likely that there will be a range of reasonable expectations, e.g. for exercise behaviour of employees. If this is the case, the fair value should be calculated by weighting each amount within the range of probabilities of occurrence. [IFRS 2.B12]

4.2.5.1 *Exercise price*

IFRS 2 does not provide guidance on the determination of the exercise price. The exercise price should be determined from the agreement.

4.2.5.2 *Current share price*

IFRS 2 does not provide guidance on the determination of the current share price.

The current share price should be determined in accordance with an entity's accounting policy. That policy may dictate the closing price or average price at the grant date. Whichever method is chosen, it should be used consistently between periods and among plans.

4.2.5.3 *Expected life*

There are several factors that affect the expected life of a typical non-traded share option given to employees, such as vesting features and various behavioural considerations. These factors and others will be discussed in greater detail in the next section.

Some ways that the expected life of a share option may be determined are:

- by creating a binomial lattice that includes all the appropriate factors – the lattice outcomes will determine when the exercise date is most likely to occur; or

- by taking factors, such as listed below, employee risk aversion and behaviour into consideration and estimating an expected life that is then used in, for example, a Black-Scholes model.

Factors to consider in estimating the expected exercise date of a share option include:

[IFRS 2.B18]

- the length of the vesting period, as share options typically cannot be exercised before they vest;
- historical experience related to actual lives of share options;
- the price of underlying shares. Employees may tend to exercise options when the share price reaches a specified level above the exercise price;
- the expected volatility of the underlying shares. Employees tend to exercise options earlier on highly volatile shares; and
- the employee's level within the organisation.

IFRS 2 suggests that different groups of employees may have homogeneous exercise behaviours and therefore determining the expected life for each homogeneous group may be more accurate than an expected life for all recipients of an option grant. [IFRS 2.B20] That is, one share option granted to the Chief Executive Officer may have a different value from one share option granted to a factory worker at the same time with the same term. For example, the Chief Executive Officer might have a greater understanding of when it is optimal to exercise the award and might have less restrictive cash flow constraints compared to the average worker. If the Black-Scholes model is used, IFRS 2 requires the use of the expected life of the option. Alternatively, exercise behaviours can be modelled into a binomial or similar option pricing model that uses contractual life.

4.2.5.4 Expected volatility

Volatility is a measure of the amount by which a share price is expected to fluctuate during a period. [IFRS 2.B22] Many of the concerns about determining the fair value of non-traded employee share options relate to determining the estimate of expected volatility over the term of the option.

> Volatility may be measured by reference to the implied volatility in traded options. However, the trading of such options is quite thin and the terms tend to be much shorter than the terms of most employee share options. There is also empirical evidence that options with the same term but different strike prices have different implied volatility. This is a factor that cannot be included in the Black-Scholes model, which assumes a constant volatility.
>
> Historical volatility is often used as a rebuttable presumption for long-term options because there is evidence that volatilities are mean-reverting and, therefore, using the long-term average historical volatility for long-term options would be sufficient if there were no reasons to assume that historical volatility would not generally be representative of future volatility. Some have suggested a blended approach utilising both implied volatility and historical volatility.

The historical volatility may be problematic for newly listed and unlisted entities. If a newly listed entity does not have sufficient historical information, it should nevertheless compute historical volatility for the longest period for which trading activity is available. It can also consider the historical volatility of similar entities following a comparable period in their lives. [IFRS 2.B26]

The unlisted entity will not have historical information to consider when estimating expected volatility. Instead, it should consider other factors, including historical or implied volatility of similar listed entities. [IFRS 2.B27–28]

Many factors should be considered when estimating expected volatility. For example, the estimate of volatility might first focus on implied volatilities for the terms that were available in the market and compare the implied volatility to the long-term average historical volatility for reasonableness.

In addition to implied and historical volatility, IFRS 2 suggests the following factors to be considered in estimating expected volatility:

[IFRS 2.B25]

- the length of time an entity's shares have been publicly traded;
- appropriate and regular intervals for price observations; and
- other factors indicating that expected future volatility might differ from past volatility (e.g. extraordinary volatility in historical share prices).

4.2.5.5 *Expected dividends*

Whether expected dividends should be included in the measurement of share-based payments depends on whether the holder is entitled to dividends or dividend equivalents. For example, if employees are granted options and are entitled to dividends on the underlying shares or dividend equivalents (which might be paid in cash or applied to reduce the exercise price) between grant date and exercise date, the options granted should be valued as if no dividends will be paid on the underlying shares. That is to say, the input to the option pricing model for expected dividends should be zero. [IFRS 2.B31-B32] If the holder of the option or share is entitled to dividends between the grant date and the exercise date, expected dividends should not be included in the fair value measurement. [IFRS 2.B33]

If the employees are not entitled to dividends or dividend equivalents during the vesting period (or, in the case of options, before exercise), the grant date valuation of the rights to shares or options should take expected dividends into account. That is to say, when the fair value of an option is estimated, expected dividends should be included in the application of the option pricing model. When the fair value of a share grant is estimated, that valuation should be reduced by the present value of dividends expected to be paid during the vesting period. [IFRS 2.B34]

IFRS 2 notes that assumptions about expected dividends should generally be based on publicly available information. An entity that does not pay dividends and has no plans to do so should assume an expected dividend yield of zero. However, a newly formed entity with no history of paying dividends might expect to begin paying dividends during the expected lives of its employee share options. Those entities could use an average of their past dividend yield (zero) and the mean dividend yield of an appropriately comparable peer group. [IFRS 2.B36]

Option pricing models usually require expected dividend yield, as input into the models. However, the models can be modified to use an expected dividend amount rather than a yield. If an entity uses the amount, it should consider its historical patterns of increases in dividends. For example, if an entity's policy has generally been to increase dividends by 3 per cent per year, its estimated option value should not assume a fixed dividend amount throughout the option's life unless there is evidence to support this. [IFRS 2.B35]

Example 4.2.5.5

Accounting for dividends paid on share options

Company B (B) provides money to a trust to purchase shares in B in the market. These shares are then granted to certain employees of B on B's instruction. When the shares are granted, the trust provides an interest-free limited recourse loan (recourse is limited to the shares being financed) to the employee to finance the purchase of the shares. In substance, B has granted share options to certain employees (see **example 2.1B** above). The exercise price equals the loan amount. The shares held by the trust are treated as treasury shares in B's consolidated financial statements until the shares fully vest in B's employees.

If an employee leaves B during the first three years, the employee forfeits the shares and any difference between the value of the shares and the outstanding loan balance is forgiven. After three years of service, the shares will only fully vest in an employee once the remaining loan balance has been repaid (i.e. the exercise price has been paid).

Consider the following three scenarios:

Scenario A: Employees are not entitled to dividends on the shares held in trust.

Scenario B: Employees are entitled to dividends in cash on the shares held in trust, which are paid to the employees. These dividends do not need to be used to reduce the value of the loan. If the shares are forfeited, the employees retain the dividends declared and paid up to that date.

Scenario C: Employees are entitled to dividends, but they are automatically applied to reduce the value of the loan. If the shares are forfeited, the employee loses the right to dividends accrued and offset.

How should:

- a dividend declared and paid for the share held in trust be treated in measuring the share options; and
- a dividend be accounted for in the consolidated financial statements of B, which include the trust, when paid?

IFRS 2.B32 and IFRS 2.B34 clarify that when dividends are paid to the option holders before the exercise of the options, the value of these options is greater than the value of options for which there is no dividend entitlement prior to exercise.

Scenario A

When no dividends accrue to employees, the fair value of the share options at the grant date should be reduced by the present value of dividends expected to be paid during the vesting period.

When the share-based payment related to these options is recognised, provided that they are considered an equity-settled share-based payment, the appropriate journal entry is:

Dr	Share-based payment expense	XXX	
Cr	Equity		XXX

Dividends accrued on the shares held in trust are attributable to Company B. On consolidation, the dividends are eliminated because they relate to treasury shares and have not been paid outside the group.

Scenario B

When dividends are paid to the option holders before the exercise date of the options, the share options should be valued as if no dividends will be paid on the underlying shares during the vesting period. As a result, the grant date valuation is not reduced by the present value of the dividends expected to be paid during the vesting period. The exercise price is the value of the loan.

When the share-based payment related to these options is recognised, provided that they are considered to be an equity-settled share-based payment, the appropriate journal entry is:

Dr	Share-based payment expense	XXX	
Cr	Equity		XXX

When the dividend is paid, the entry is:

Dr	Equity/retained earnings	XXX	
Cr	Cash		XXX

Provided that the share-based payment is equity-settled, IFRS 2 treats the employees as holders of share options. Therefore, any dividend paid on these share options is recorded in equity. This is consistent with the principles of IAS 32.35 *Financial Instruments: Presentation* which states that '... distributions to holders of an equity instrument shall be debited by the entity directly to equity, net of any related income tax benefit'. In addition, expensing the dividend through profit or loss as additional compensation when paid would result in double counting of an expense (on the basis that there are effectively two transactions, (1) the compensation paid to employees when the right to dividends has been included in the grant date fair value and (2) the dividends paid to the option equity class).

Scenario C

When dividends are automatically applied to reduce the value of the loan, the input for dividends into the valuation of the option is the same as in Scenario B, as indicated in IFRS 2.B32.

When the share-based payment related to these options is recognised, provided that they are considered to be an equity-settled share-based payment, the appropriate journal entry is:

Dr	Share-based payment expense	XXX	
Cr	Equity		XXX

When the dividend is declared, the entity may make a transfer from retained earnings to another component of equity for the amount of the dividend since this represents a part of the exercise price 'paid' by the employee. This is relevant only if the credit to equity under IFRS 2 is made to a separate reserve (see **8.5.1** below).

4.2.5.6 Risk-free interest rate

The risk-free interest rate affects the price of an option in a less intuitive way than expected volatility or expected dividends. As interest rates increase, the value of a call option also increases. This is because the present value of the exercise price will decrease.

IFRS 2 states that the risk-free interest rate should be the implied yield available at the date of grant on zero-coupon government issues in whose currency the exercise price is expressed, with a remaining term equal to expected life of the option being valued. It may be necessary to use an appropriate substitute in some circumstances. [IFRS 2.B37]

4.2.6 Other factors affecting the valuation of share-based payments

There are certain variables that impact the value of many employee share options that are not factored into the standardised Black-Scholes model. The inability to incorporate these factors directly into the Black-Scholes model limits its usefulness in estimating the fair value of the options. While the approach in IFRS 2 attempts to 'fix' this fault through adjustments to the inputs to the Black-Scholes calculation (e.g. expected life versus contractual life), many believe these adjustments are just not enough. This section will discuss in more detail some of these additional assumptions. However, depending upon materiality levels, the costs of preparing a model that involves these assumptions may not be worth the additional benefits derived from that model.

4.2.6.1 *Performance conditions*

Examples of performance conditions include the vesting of options based upon:

- the Total Shareholder Return of the entity, either in absolute terms or relative to a comparator group or index (market-based);
- meeting a specific target share price (market-based); or
- levels of revenues (non-market-based).

As a result of those conditions, the holder of the right to an option or share may receive some or all of the vested option / shares.

As further explained in **4.3** below, IFRS 2 requires that market-based performance related vesting features be included in the determination of the fair value at the date of grant. Additionally, IFRS 2 requires the entity to estimate the vesting period at the date of grant and recognise the related expense over that period. There is no subsequent adjustment to the vesting period when the performance condition is market-based.

Under IFRS 2, a non-market-based performance condition should not be included in the determination of the fair value at the grant date. For grants with such vesting conditions, at the end of each reporting period, the cumulative expense should equal that proportion of the charge that would have been expensed based on the multiple of the latest estimate of the number of awards that will meet that condition and the fair value of each award, i.e. it should be trued up at the end of each reporting period.

4.2.6.2 *Non-transferability*

Many believe non-transferability after the vesting period does not have a material impact on the valuation of an option from the perspective of the issuer. However, since the share holding is typically a disproportionate part of an employee's wealth, it may have a significant impact on their behaviour and, therefore, the expected life of the option. Several valuation experts have stated that the inability to transfer an employee share option does not violate option pricing model assumptions because there is no assumption about the transferability of the option in the calculation.

When estimating the fair value of an employee share option at the grant date, IFRS 2 requires the use of expected life to exercise instead of the option's contractual life to expiration to take into account the option's non-transferability. However, valuation experts agree that the use of an average expected life to exercise is not a theoretically accurate way to capture the option's non-transferability. They argue that looking only at the average expected life of the share option distribution could not capture information about that distribution. Therefore, some believe employee behaviours that result in early exercise should be explicitly modelled using a more dynamic option pricing model – such as the binomial model.

Furthermore, many valuation experts now believe that no discount is warranted for non-transferability during the vesting period. If the premise of fair value, as discussed above, is to estimate the amount that a hypothetical market participant would pay for such an option, then the estimate should incorporate employee characteristics only to the extent that they would affect the amount and timing of cash flows of the option. The only alternatives facing the employee during the vesting period are to vest or not to vest – and those two alternatives are addressed under the modified grant date approach in IFRS 2.

Example 4.2.6.2

Effect of post-vesting transfer restrictions when measuring fair value of equity instruments

Company A operates a share purchase plan for its employees. A's shares are listed and are actively traded. There are no vesting conditions; therefore, the shares vest immediately on grant date.

The plan stipulates post-vesting transfer restrictions as employees cannot sell their shares until the end of a five-year period beginning on the grant date. The sale of those shares is legally prohibited before the end of the five-year period. Consequently, employees are required to pay the subscription price on the grant date, but they are unable to take advantage of market fluctuations during the ensuing five years. The shares are held in a trust until the transfer restrictions expire. Dividends distributed during the restriction period are held by the trust.

IFRS 2.B3 indicates that post-vesting transfer restrictions should be taken into account when estimating the fair value of the shares granted, but only to the extent that the post-vesting transfer restrictions affect the price that a knowledgeable willing market participant would pay for those shares. If the shares are actively traded in a deep and liquid market, post-vesting transfer restrictions may have little, if any, effect on the price that a knowledgeable, willing market participant would pay for those shares.

In order to measure the effect of the post-vesting transfer restrictions, A considers a methodology that combines bank borrowings as if to acquire unrestricted shares on the market (the same number as granted in the plan) at the beginning of the five-year period and a forward to sell shares kept in the trust at the end of the five-year period. The fair value determined by such a methodology depends mainly on the interest rate applied to the borrowings.

IFRS 2(Appendix A) defines fair value as the 'amount for which an asset could be exchanged, a liability settled, or an equity instrument granted could be exchanged, between knowledgeable, willing parties in an arm's length transaction'. Based on this definition, under A's valuation methodology, the interest rate applied to the borrowings should be the rate applicable to the instrument. Therefore, an employee's ability to source such borrowings is not considered.

4.2.6.3 *Stated exercise restrictions*

Stated exercise restrictions (e.g. restrictions on exercise or sale of shares by employees) will affect the value both directly and through their impact on the behaviour of holders. The easiest way to see this is to note that employees may find themselves holding a large proportion of their wealth in the form of shares whereas, in the absence of such restrictions, they would hold a more diversified portfolio. This, in turn, will affect their behaviour and, generally (but not invariably) will cause them to exercise as early as possible so as to be out of the restricted period as fast as possible. A history of exercising options as early as possible demonstrates that the value given by the employer is less than the amount attributable to the full term of the option.

The effects of exercise restrictions will be similar to the effects of non-transferability features as discussed above. Therefore, stated exercise restrictions should be evaluated when estimating the fair value of employee share options based on their effect on the expected future cash flows from the options.

4.2.6.4 *Behavioural considerations*

As can be seen from the above discussion, there are many factors that affect the value of share options through their impact on employee behaviour. Behavioural considerations are critical and should be included in the valuation of share options. This is a familiar consideration in the financial markets. The entire mortgage market, for example, revolves around estimation of the behavioural influences on prepayments.

IFRS 2 requires behavioural considerations to be included in the model through an adjustment to the expected life of the option. Many believe, however, that this will generally be inadequate since the life of the option will depend on the returns for both the entity and for the market and the mechanism for this dependency will be determined by the group characteristics noted, such as risk aversion, diversification, and tax considerations. For example, as individuals grow wealthier in a rising market, the costs of poor diversification may decline and that will reduce occurrences of early exercise of the share options.

4.2.6.5 Long-term nature

The long-term nature of employee share option grants is significant and will clearly impact valuation. The Black-Scholes model uses one set of assumptions at grant date that do not change during the expected life of the options, while a binomial model can use varying assumptions at grant date depending on expected changes to the inputs during the expected life. A typical employee share option can have a contractual life of 10 years. Therefore, the use of static model inputs is not grounded in reality. Because changes in those factors over time can have a significant impact on option value, failure to model such changes over the term of the option can result in overstating or understating the fair value of an option.

Based on the results of research and discussions with valuation experts, fair value for an employee share option should incorporate at the measurement date volatility factors for discrete time periods over the term of the option, interest and dividend rates and exercise patterns over the term of the option, to correspond with historical evidence and/or current expectations, to the extent material. It is to be expected that applying a more dynamic option pricing model with changing inputs will be more difficult and therefore a cost benefit analysis (taking into consideration materiality) should be completed.

4.2.6.6 Effects on the capital structure of an entity

Typically, the shares underlying traded options are acquired from existing shareholders and, therefore, have no dilutive effect. [IFRS 2.B38]

Capital structure effects of non-traded options, such as dilution, can be significant and are generally anticipated by the market at the date of grant. Nevertheless, except in most unusual cases, they should have no impact on the individual employee's decision. The market's anticipation will depend, among other matters, on whether the process of share returns is the same or is altered by the dilution and the cash infusion. In many situations the number of employee share options issued relative to the number of shares outstanding is not significant and, therefore, the effect of dilution on share price can be ignored.

IFRS 2 suggests that the issuer should consider whether the possible dilutive effect of the future exercise of options granted has an effect on the fair value of those options at grant date by an adjustment to option pricing models and factor it into the valuation. [IFRS 2.B41]

4.2.7 Example of employee share purchase plan

The following example is taken from the IFRS 2 Implementation Guidance (IG Example 11) and illustrates some issues about the valuation of equity instruments.

Example 4.2.7

[IFRS 2 Implementation Guidance (IG Example 11)]

Employee share purchase plan

BACKGROUND

An entity offers all its 1,000 employees the opportunity to participate in an employee share purchase plan. The employees have two weeks to decide whether to accept the offer. Under the terms of the plan, the employees are entitled to purchase a maximum of 100 shares each. The purchase price will be 20 per cent less than the market price of the entity's shares at the date the offer is accepted and the purchase price must be paid immediately upon acceptance of the offer. All shares purchased must be held in trust for the employees, and cannot be sold for five years. The employee is not permitted to withdraw from the plan during that period. For example, if the employee ceases employment during the five-year period, the shares must nevertheless remain in the plan until the end of the five-year period. Any dividends paid during the five-year period will be held in trust for the employees until the end of the five-year period.

In total, 800 employees accept the offer and each employee purchases, on average, 80 shares, i.e. the employees purchase a total of 64,000 shares. The weighted-average market price of the shares at the purchase date is CU30 per share, and the weighted-average purchase price is CU24 per share.

APPLICATION OF REQUIREMENTS

For transactions with employees, IFRS 2 requires the transaction amount to be measured by reference to the fair value of the equity instruments granted (IFRS 2.11). To apply this requirement, it is necessary first to determine the type of equity instrument granted to the employees. Although the plan is described as an employee share purchase plan (ESPP), some ESPPs include option features and are therefore, in effect, share option plans. For example, an ESPP might include a 'lookback feature', whereby the employee is able to purchase shares at a discount, and choose whether the discount is applied to the entity's share price at the date of grant or its share price at the date of purchase. Or an ESPP might specify the purchase price, and then allow the employees a significant period of time to decide whether to participate in the plan. Another example of an option feature is an ESPP that permits the participating employees to cancel their participation before or at the end of a specified period and obtain a refund of amounts previously paid into the plan.

However, in this example, the plan includes no option features. The discount is applied to the share price at the purchase date, and the employees are not permitted to withdraw from the plan.

Another factor to consider is the effect of post-vesting transfer restrictions, if any. Paragraph B3 of IFRS 2 states that, if shares are subject to restrictions on transfer after vesting date, that factor should be taken into account when estimating the fair value of those shares, but only to the extent that the post-vesting restrictions affect the price that a knowledgeable, willing market participant would pay for that share. For example, if the shares are actively traded in a deep and liquid market, post-vesting transfer restrictions may have little, if any, effect on the price that a knowledgeable, willing market participant would pay for those shares.

In this example, the shares are vested when purchased, but cannot be sold for five years after the date of purchase. Therefore, the entity should consider the valuation effect of the five-year post-vesting transfer restriction. This entails using a valuation technique to estimate what the price of the restricted share would have been on the purchase date in an arm's length transaction between knowledgeable, willing parties. Suppose that, in this example, the entity estimates that the fair value of each restricted share is CU28. In this case, the fair value of the equity instruments granted is CU4 per share (being the fair value of the restricted share of CU28 less the purchase price of CU24). Because 64,000 shares were purchased, the total fair value of the equity instruments granted is CU256,000.

In this example, there is no vesting period. Therefore, in accordance with paragraph 14 of IFRS 2, the entity should recognise an expense of CU256,000 immediately.

However, in some cases, the expense relating to an ESPP might not be material. IAS 8 *Accounting Policies, Changes in Accounting Estimates and Errors* states that the accounting policies in IFRSs need not be applied when the effect of applying them is immaterial (IAS 8, paragraph 8). IAS 8 also states that an omission or misstatement of an item is material if it could, individually or collectively, influence the economic decisions that users make on the basis of the financial statements. Materiality depends on the size and nature of the omission or misstatement judged in the surrounding circumstances. The size or nature of the item, or a combination of both, could be the determining factor (IAS 8.5). Therefore, in this example, the entity should consider whether the expense of CU256,000 is material.

UK *The above example is taken from the Implementation Guidance to IFRS 2. The type of plan described in the example is not common in the UK although there are similarities with UK Save As You Earn (SAYE) schemes which provide a right to acquire shares at a discount to market value. However, UK SAYE schemes generally provide for the possibility for employees to withdraw from the scheme and obtain a refund. As stated in the example, this means that the arrangements have 'option features'. The question arises of whether an employee withdrawing from the scheme should be regarded as a failure to meet a vesting condition, as a cancellation of the options, or be dealt with in some other way. This issue has been addressed by the IASB in the amendments to IFRS 2 published in January 2008 which are effective for periods beginning on or after 1 January 2009. As explained at* **3.2.1** *above and* **5.2** *below, the effect of the amendments is to require withdrawal from an SAYE scheme by an employee to be treated as a cancellation, resulting in an acceleration of expense recognition.*

It is unusual that the example in the IFRS 2 Implementation Guidance explicitly refers to the possibility that the charge might not be material. This might equally be true of most other requirements of this or other accounting standards. Caution should be exercised in deciding that a charge otherwise required by IFRS 2 is not material. IAS 8 provides guidance on the meaning of 'material' in the context of errors.

4.6 below looks at the approach to be adopted if it is not possible to estimate reliably the fair value of the equity instrument granted.

4.3 Treatment of vesting conditions

4.3.1 Basic approach

A grant of equity instruments might be conditional upon satisfying specified vesting conditions (see **3.2.1** above for the definition of vesting conditions). For example, a grant of shares or share options to an employee is often conditional on the employee remaining in the employment of the entity for a specified period of time. Alternatively, or in addition, there may be performance conditions that must be satisfied, such as the entity achieving a specified growth in earnings per share or a specified increase in the entity's share price. [IFRS 2.19]

The following diagram summarises the treatment of vesting conditions in IFRS 2 as more fully described below:

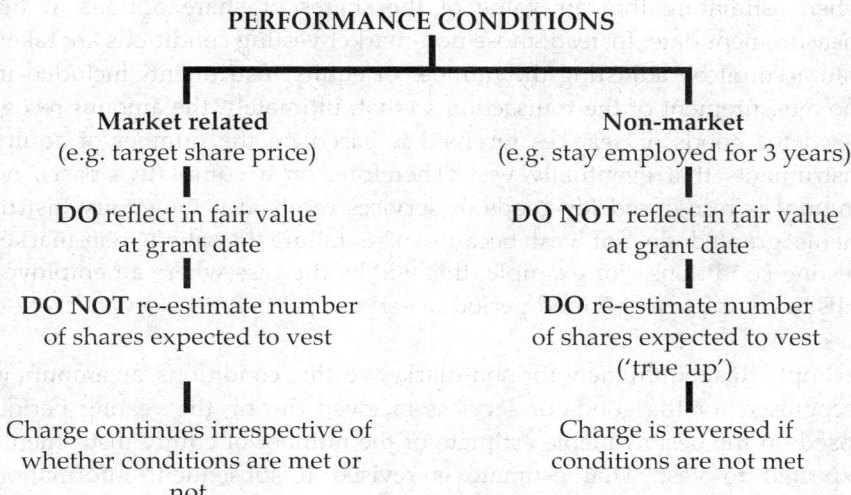

PERFORMANCE CONDITIONS

Market related (e.g. target share price)	**Non-market** (e.g. stay employed for 3 years)
DO reflect in fair value at grant date	**DO NOT** reflect in fair value at grant date
DO NOT re-estimate number of shares expected to vest	**DO** re-estimate number of shares expected to vest ('true up')
Charge continues irrespective of whether conditions are met or not	Charge is reversed if conditions are not met

IFRS 2 distinguishes between 'market conditions' and conditions other than market conditions (referred to generally as 'non-market conditions'). A market condition is defined by IFRS 2 as:

[IFRS 2(Appendix A)]

> 'A condition upon which the exercise price, vesting or exercisability of an equity instrument depends that is related to the market price of the entity's equity instruments, such as attaining a specified share price or a specified amount of intrinsic value of a share option, or achieving a specified target that is based on the market price of the entity's equity instruments relative to an index of market prices of equity instruments of other entities.'

Market conditions, such as a target share price upon which vesting is conditional, are taken into account when estimating the fair value of the equity instruments granted. Therefore, for grants of equity instruments with market conditions, the entity recognises the goods or services received from a counterparty who satisfies all other vesting conditions (e.g. service conditions) irrespective of whether that market condition is satisfied. [IFRS 2.21]

Similarly, under IFRS 2 as amended in January 2008 (see **3.2.1** above), all non-vesting conditions are taken into account when estimating the fair value of the equity instruments granted. Therefore, for grants of equity instruments with non-vesting conditions, the goods or services received from a counterparty that satisfies all vesting conditions that are not market conditions (e.g. services received from an employee who remains in service for the specified period of service) are recognised, irrespective of whether those non-vesting conditions are satisfied. [IFRS 2.21A]

Vesting conditions other than market conditions are not taken into account when estimating the fair value of the shares or share options at the measurement date. Instead, those non-market vesting conditions are taken into account by adjusting the number of equity instruments included in the measurement of the transaction so that, ultimately, the amount recognised for goods or services received is based on the number of equity instruments that eventually vest. Therefore, on a cumulative basis, no amount is recognised for goods or services received if the equity instruments granted do not vest because of a failure to satisfy non-market vesting conditions. For example, this will be the case where an employee fails to complete a specified period of service. [IFRS 2.19]

To apply this requirement for non-market vesting conditions, an amount is recognised for the goods or services received during the vesting period based on the best available estimate of the number of equity instruments expected to vest. That estimate is revised if subsequent information indicates that the number of equity instruments expected to vest differs from previous estimates. On vesting date, the estimate is revised to equal the number of equity instruments that ultimately vest. [IFRS 2.20]

This approach, which is generally referred to as the 'modified grant date method', was adopted by the IASB for two primary reasons: measurement practicalities and US GAAP convergence.

Valuation models used to determine the fair value of share-based payments could be modified to incorporate non-market conditions. However, the inclusion of these conditions would increase the difficulty and reduce the reliability of the fair value measurement. Therefore, non-market conditions are not included in the grant date fair value calculation due to the practical difficulties of measuring these conditions as noted in paragraph BC184 of IFRS 2.

Although IFRS 2 does not achieve complete convergence with US GAAP on the treatment of vesting conditions, the requirement to 'true up' for non-market vesting conditions is similar to US GAAP. In particular, the requirements of IFRS 2 are much closer to US GAAP than those proposed in the Exposure Draft that preceded the Standard, which involved including all performance and service conditions in the measurement of fair value coupled with the 'unit of service' method (see the Basis for Conclusions section of IFRS 2 for further explanations).

The operation of these requirements in practice is illustrated by the examples set out in the following sections.

4.3.2 Non-market vesting condition

The following example, which is taken from the IFRS 2 Implementation Guidance (IG Example 1), illustrates the basic approach to be adopted in relation to a non-market vesting condition.

Example 4.3.2A

Non-market vesting condition

[IFRS 2 Implementation Guidance (IG Example 1)]

BACKGROUND

An entity grants 100 share options to each of its 500 employees. Each grant is conditional upon the employee working for the entity over the next three years. The entity estimates that the fair value of each share option is CU15.

On the basis of a weighted average probability, the entity estimates that 20 per cent of employees will leave during the three-year period and therefore forfeit their rights to the share options.

APPLICATION OF REQUIREMENTS

Scenario 1

If everything turns out exactly as expected, the entity recognises the following amounts during the vesting period, for services received as consideration for the share options.

Year	Calculation	Remuneration expense for period CU	Cumulative remuneration expense CU
1	50,000 options × 80% × CU15 × 1/3 years	200,000	200,000
2	(50,000 options × 80% × CU15 × 2/3 years) – CU200,000	200,000	400,000
3	(50,000 options × 80% × CU15 × 3/3 years) – CU400,000	200,000	600,000

Scenario 2

During year 1, 20 employees leave. The entity revises its estimate of total employee departures over the three-year period from 20 per cent (100 employees) to 15 per cent (75 employees). During year 2, a further 22 employees leave. The entity revises its estimate of total employee departures over the three-year period from 15 per cent to 12 per cent (60 employees). During year 3, a further 15 employees leave. Hence, a total of 57 employees forfeited their rights to the share options during the three-year period, and a total of 44,300 share options (443 employees × 100 options per employee) vested at the end of year 3.

Year	Calculation	Remuneration expense for period CU	Cumulative remuneration expense CU
1	50,000 options × 85% × CU15 × 1/3 years	212,500	212,500
2	(50,000 options × 88% × CU15 × 2/3 years) – CU212,500	227,500	440,000
3	(44,300 options × CU15) – CU440,000	224,500	664,500

The following example illustrates the use of probabilities when assessing non-market vesting conditions.

Example 4.3.2B

Use of probabilities to assess vesting conditions

BACKGROUND

Company A (A) has issued 10 options to 10 employees (i.e. 100 options in total). The options will vest at the end of year 2 of an employee's continued employment (i.e. the 'service period condition') and after A has met a specified level of earnings-per-share (EPS) growth compared with the EPS for year 0. However, the number of options that vest will depend on the extent of the EPS growth. If all employees remain in employment, the options will vest according to the following EPS percentages at the end of year 2:

- Less than 4 per cent: none of the options will vest.
- Between 4 per cent and 10 per cent: 50 per cent of the options will vest.
- More than 10 per cent: all options will vest.

The number of options expected to eventually vest can only be 0, 50, or 100.

APPLICATION OF REQUIREMENTS

Scenario 1

All employees are expected to remain in employment until the end of year 2.

The target EPS growth vesting condition is a non-market-based vesting condition. During the vesting period, an entity is required to recognise an expense (or asset, if applicable) by determining the total number of equity instruments that are expected to vest eventually as a result of the fulfilment of non-market-based conditions (IFRS 2.19). An entity should only use probabilities when determining whether a non-market-based condition will be met. For example, if an entity believes that there is a 90 per cent chance that a performance target will be met, the accounting for this transaction during the vesting period should reflect the target being met. The entity would recognise 100 per cent of the total expense for the reporting period (as long as all other vesting conditions are met), not 90 per cent of the total expense for the reporting period.

At the end of year 1, A should estimate the most probable EPS growth figure for the end of year 2 (using, for example, budget information or historical EPS growth) and should use this estimate to determine the number of options that will vest.

At each future reporting date, A should reassess expected EPS growth and 'true up' the expense accordingly. This requirement may result in greater volatility in the amount of expense recognised from year to year.

Scenario 2

Only eight employees are expected to remain until the end of year 2.

If only 80 per cent of the employees are expected to remain employed by the company at the end of two years, the number of options expected to vest would need to be adjusted to incorporate the impact of the service period condition (e.g. staff turnover rate should be analysed). Therefore, the actual number of options expected to vest, after the impact of the service period condition and the number of employees expected to remain with the company are taken into account, can only be one of the following:

- Zero (i.e. no options are expected to vest).
- Forty (50 per cent of 80 per cent of 100 – i.e. 50 per cent of the options are expected to vest).

- Eighty (100 per cent of 80 per cent of 100 – i.e. all options are expected to vest).

Many of the examples in the IFRS 2 implementation guidance employ percentages for determining the number of employees expected to meet a service period condition. These percentages are used to estimate the number of equity instruments that will actually vest, not the probability that the employee will meet the service condition. That is, an entity expects that 80 per cent of its employees will meet the service condition, not that there is an 80 per cent chance of the service condition being met.

4.3.3 *Vesting period varies with a non-market condition*

The length of the vesting period might vary depending on when a performance condition is met. If an employee is granted share options that are conditional on the achievement of a performance condition and on remaining in employment until that performance condition is satisfied, it is presumed that the services to be rendered by the employee will be received in the future, over the expected vesting period. Where this is the case, the length of the estimated vesting period at grant date is estimated based on the most likely outcome of the performance condition. [IFRS 2.15] If the performance condition is a market condition, the estimated length of the vesting period should be consistent with the assumptions used in estimating the fair value of the options granted and should not be subsequently revised. If the performance condition is a non-market condition, the initial estimate of the length of the vesting period should be revised if subsequent information indicates that the length of the vesting period differs from the previous estimate.

The following example, taken from the IFRS 2 Implementation Guidance (IG Example 2), illustrates the case where the vesting period varies according to the achievement of a non-market condition (a specified increase in earnings).

Example 4.3.3

Grant with a performance condition, in which the length of the vesting period varies

[IFRS 2 Implementation Guidance (IG Example 2)]

BACKGROUND

At the beginning of year 1, the entity grants 100 shares each to 500 employees, conditional upon the employees' remaining in the entity's employ during the vesting period. The shares will vest at the end of year 1 if the entity's earnings increase by more than 18 per cent; at the end of year 2 if the entity's earnings increase by more than an average of 13 per cent per year over the two-year period; and at the end of year 3 if the entity's earnings increase by more than an average of 10 per cent per year over the three-year period. The shares have a fair value of CU30 per share at the start of year 1, which equals the share price at grant date. No dividends are expected to be paid over the three-year period.

By the end of year 1, the entity's earnings have increased by 14 per cent, and 30 employees have left. The entity expects that earnings will continue to increase at a similar rate in year 2, and therefore expects that the shares will vest at the end of year 2. The entity expects, on the basis of a weighted average probability, that a further 30 employees will leave during year 2, and therefore expects that 440 employees will vest in 100 shares each at the end of year 2.

By the end of year 2, the entity's earnings have increased by only 10 per cent and therefore the shares do not vest at the end of year 2. 28 employees have left during the year. The entity expects that a further 25 employees will leave during year 3, and that the entity's earnings will increase by at least 6 per cent, thereby achieving the average of 10 per cent per year.

By the end of year 3, 23 employees have left and the entity's earnings had increased by 8 per cent, resulting in an average increase of 10.67 per cent per year. Therefore, 419 employees received 100 shares at the end of year 3.

APPLICATION OF REQUIREMENTS

Year	Calculation	Remuneration expense for period CU	Cumulative remuneration expense CU
1	440 employees × 100 shares × CU30 × ½	660,000	660,000
2	(417 employees × 100 shares × CU30 × 2/3) – CU660,000	174,000	834,000
3	(419 employees × 100 shares × CU30 × 3/3) – CU834,000	423,000	1,257,000

Granting share options contingent on an Initial Public Offering (IPO) of an entity is another example of an award with a variable non-market vesting period. However, no expense will be recognised unless and until the IPO is probable. This may not be the case on grant date. Therefore, in practice, the expense may sometimes be recognised over a relatively short period between the IPO becoming probable and taking place. As explained at **3.2.1** above an IPO may be a non-vesting condition, under IFRS 2 as amended in January 2008, where the exercise of the options is not linked to service continuing until the IPO.

4.3.4 *Number of options vesting is dependent on a non-market performance condition*

A similar approach will be adopted where the number of equity instruments that might vest with each employee varies. This is illustrated in the following example which is taken from the IFRS 2 Implementation Guidance (IG Example 3).

Example 4.3.4

Grant with a performance condition, in which the number of equity instruments varies

[IFRS 2 Implementation Guidance (IG Example 3)]

BACKGROUND

At the beginning of year 1, Entity A grants share options to each of its 100 employees working in the sales department. The share options will vest at the end of year 3, provided that the employees remain in the entity's employ, and provided that the volume of sales of a particular product increases by at least an average of 5 per cent per year. If the volume of sales of the product increases by an average of between 5 per cent and 10 per cent per year, each employee will receive 100 share options. If the volume of sales increases by an average of between 10 per cent and 15 per cent each year, each employee will receive 200 share options. If the volume of sales increases by an average of 15 per cent or more, each employee will receive 300 share options.

On grant date, Entity A estimates that the share options have a fair value of CU20 per option. Entity A also estimates that the volume of sales of the product will increase by an average of between 10 per cent and 15 per cent per year, and therefore expects that, for each employee who remains in service until the end of year 3, 200 share options will vest. The entity also estimates, on the basis of a weighted average probability, that 20 per cent of employees will leave before the end of year 3.

By the end of year 1, seven employees have left and the entity still expects that a total of 20 employees will leave by the end of year 3. Hence, the entity expects that 80 employees will remain in service for the three-year period. Product sales have increased by 12 per cent and the entity expects this rate of increase to continue over the next 2 years.

By the end of year 2, a further five employees have left, bringing the total to 12 to date. The entity now expects only three more employees will leave during year 3, and therefore expects a total of 15 employees will have left during the three-year period, and hence 85 employees are expected to remain. Product sales have increased by 18 per cent, resulting in an average of 15 per cent over the two years to date. The entity now expects that sales will average 15 per cent or more over the three-year period, and hence expects each sales employee to receive 300 share options at the end of year 3.

By the end of year 3, a further two employees have left. Hence, 14 employees have left during the three-year period, and 86 employees remain. The entity's sales have increased by an average of 16 per cent over the three years. Therefore, each of the 86 employees receives 300 share options.

APPLICATION OF REQUIREMENTS

Year	Calculation	Remuneration expense for period CU	Cumulative remuneration expense CU
1	80 employees × 200 options × CU20 × 1/3	106,667	106,667
2	(85 employees × 300 options × CU20 × 2/3) – CU106,667	233,333	340,000
3	(86 employees × 300 options × CU20 × 3/3) – CU340,000	176,000	516,000

4.3.5 *Exercise price dependent on a non-market condition*

The exercise price might vary depending on whether non-market vesting conditions are satisfied. This is illustrated in the following example taken from the IFRS 2 Implementation Guidance (IG Example 4).

Example 4.3.5

Grant with a performance condition, in which the exercise price varies

[IFRS 2 Implementation Guidance (IG Example 4)]

BACKGROUND

At the beginning of year 1, an entity grants to a senior executive 10,000 share options, conditional upon the executive's remaining in the entity's employ until the end of year 3. The exercise price is CU40. However, the exercise price drops to CU30 if the entity's earnings increase by at least an average of 10 per cent per year over the three-year period.

On grant date, the entity estimates that the fair value of the share options, with an exercise price of CU30, is CU16 per option. If the exercise price is CU40, the entity estimates that the share options have a fair value of CU12 per option.

During year 1, the entity's earnings increased by 12 per cent, and the entity expects that earnings will continue to increase at this rate over the next two years. The entity therefore expects that the earnings target will be achieved, and hence the share options will have an exercise price of CU30.

During year 2, the entity's earnings increased by 13 per cent, and the entity continues to expect that the earnings target will be achieved.

During year 3, the entity's earnings increased by only 3 per cent, and therefore the earnings target was not achieved. The executive completes three years' service, and therefore satisfies the service condition. Because the earnings target was not achieved, the 10,000 vested share options have an exercise price of CU40.

APPLICATION OF REQUIREMENTS

Because the exercise price varies depending on the outcome of a performance condition that is not a market condition, the effect of that performance condition (i.e. the possibility that the exercise price might be CU40 and the possibility that the exercise price might be CU30) is not taken into account when estimating the fair value of the share options at grant date. Instead, the entity estimates the fair value of the share options at grant date under each scenario (i.e. exercise price of CU40 and exercise price of CU30) and ultimately revises the transaction amount to reflect the outcome of that performance condition, as illustrated below.

Year	Calculation	Remuneration expense for period CU	Cumulative remuneration expense CU
1	10,000 options × CU16 × 1/3	53,333	53,333
2	(10,000 options × CU16 × 2/3) – CU53,333	53,334	106,667
3	(10,000 options × CU12 × 3/3) – CU106,667	13,333	120,000

4.3.6 *A market condition and a non-market condition*

The following example, taken from the IFRS 2 Implementation Guidance (IG Example 5), illustrates the operation of the requirements of IFRS 2 for a grant of options with a market condition (a specified increase in share price) and a non-market service condition (continuing employment).

Example 4.3.6A

Grant with a market condition

[IFRS 2 Implementation Guidance (IG Example 5)]

BACKGROUND

At the beginning of year 1, an entity grants to a senior executive 10,000 share options, conditional upon the executive remaining in the entity's employ until the end of year 3. However, the share options cannot be exercised unless the share price has increased from CU50 at the beginning of year 1 to above CU65 at the end of year 3. If the share price is above CU65 at the end of year 3, the share options can be exercised at any time during the next seven years, i.e. by the end of year 10.

The entity applies a binomial option pricing model, which takes into account the possibility that the share price will exceed CU65 at the end of year 3 (and hence the share options become exercisable) and the possibility that the share price will not exceed CU65 at the end of year 3 (and hence the options will be forfeited). It estimates the fair value of the share options with this market condition to be CU24 per option.

APPLICATION OF REQUIREMENTS

Because paragraph 21 of IFRS 2 requires the entity to recognise the services received from a counterparty who satisfies all other vesting conditions (e.g. services received from an employee who remains in service for the specified service period), irrespective of whether that market condition is satisfied, it makes no difference whether the share price target is achieved. The possibility that the share price target might not be achieved has already been taken into account when estimating the fair value of the share options at grant date. Therefore, if the entity expects the executive to complete the three-year service period, and the executive does so, the entity recognises the following amounts in years 1, 2 and 3:

Year	Calculation	Remuneration expense for period	Cumulative remuneration expense
		CU	CU
1	10,000 options × CU24 × 1/3	80,000	80,000
2	(10,000 options × CU24 × 2/3) – CU80,000	80,000	160,000
3	(10,000 options × CU24) – CU160,000	80,000	240,000

As noted above, these amounts are recognised irrespective of the outcome of the market condition. However, if the executive left during year 2 (or year 3), the amount recognised during year 1 (and year 2) would be reversed in year 2 (or year 3). This is because the service condition, in contrast to the market condition, was not taken into account when estimating the fair value of the share options at grant date. Instead, the service condition is taken into account by adjusting the transaction amount to be based on the number of equity instruments that ultimately vest, in accordance with paragraphs 19 and 20 of the IFRS.

Another example of the case where share options are granted with both market conditions and non-market conditions is set out below.

Example 4.3.6B

Share option grant with both market and non-market performance conditions

Company H issued 100 share options to certain of its employees that will vest once revenues reach £1 billion and its share price exceeds £50. The employees will have to be employed with Company H at the time the share options vest to receive the options. The share options will expire in 10 years.

Paragraph 21 of IFRS 2 states that the grant date fair value of the share-based payment with market-based performance conditions that has met all its other vesting conditions should be recognised, irrespective of whether that market condition is achieved. Company H determines the grant date fair value of the share-based payment excluding the non-market-based performance factor, but including the market-based performance factor.

Assuming Company H determines the fair value of the share-based payment at the date of grant is £20 per option, the expense recorded over the expected vesting period in the following fact patterns would be:

- If all options vest, £2,000 [100 options x £20].
- If all vesting conditions are met, except the market-based performance condition of share price exceeding £50, £2,000 [100 options x £20].
- If all vesting conditions are met, except the non-market-based performance condition of revenues reaching £1billion is not achieved, nil expense.
- If all vesting conditions are met, except half of the employees who received options left the entity prior to the vesting date, £1,000 [50 options x £20].

Therefore, where there are both market and non-market conditions, an entity will still need to estimate whether non-market conditions will be satisfied even if ultimately no share options vest due to market conditions.

4.3.7 A market condition where the vesting period varies

The effect of a vesting condition may be to change the length of the vesting period. In this case, paragraph 15 of the IFRS requires the entity to presume that the services to be rendered by the employees as consideration for the equity instruments granted will be received in the future, over the expected vesting period. Hence, the entity will have to estimate the length of the expected vesting period at grant date, based on the most likely outcome of the performance condition. If the performance condition is a market condition, the estimate of the length of the expected vesting period must be consistent with the assumptions used in estimating the fair value of the share options granted and is not subsequently revised.

The following example, taken from the IFRS 2 Implementation Guidance (IG Example 6), illustrates the application of IFRS 2 where the vesting period varies with a market condition (a specified increase in the share price).

Example 4.3.7

Grant with a market condition, in which the length of the vesting period varies

[IFRS 2 Implementation Guidance (IG Example 6)]

BACKGROUND

At the beginning of year 1, an entity grants 10,000 share options with a ten-year life to each of ten senior executives. The share options will vest and become exercisable immediately if and when the entity's share price increases from CU50 to CU70, provided that the executive remains in service until the share price target is achieved.

The entity applies a binomial option pricing model, which takes into account the possibility that the share price target will be achieved during the ten-year life of the options, and the possibility that the target will not be achieved. The entity estimates that the fair value of the share options at grant date is CU25 per option. From the option pricing model, the entity determines that the mode of the distribution of possible vesting dates is five years. In other words, of all the possible outcomes, the most likely outcome of the market condition is that the share price target will be achieved at the end of year 5. Therefore, the entity estimates that the expected vesting period is five years. The entity also estimates that two executives will have left by the end of year 5, and therefore expects that 80,000 share options (10,000 share options x 8 executives) will vest at the end of year 5.

Throughout years 1–4, the entity continues to estimate that a total of two executives will leave by the end of year 5. However, in total three executives leave, one in each of years 3, 4 and 5. The share price target is achieved at the end of year 6. Another executive leaves during year 6, before the share price target is achieved.

APPLICATION OF REQUIREMENTS

Paragraph 15 of the IFRS requires the entity to recognise the services received over the expected vesting period, as estimated at grant date, and also requires the entity not to revise that estimate. Therefore, the entity recognises the services received from the executives over years 1–5. Hence, the transaction amount is ultimately based on 70,000 share options (10,000 share options × 7 executives who remain in service at the end of year 5). Although another executive left during year 6, no adjustment is made, because the executive had already completed the expected vesting period of 5 years. Therefore, the entity recognises the following amounts in years 1–5:

Year	Calculation	Remuneration expense for period CU	Cumulative remuneration expense CU
	‘		
1	80,000 options × CU25 × 1/5	400,000	400,000
2	(80,000 options × CU25 × 2/5) – CU400,000	400,000	800,000
3	(80,000 options × CU25 × 3/5) – CU800,000	400,000	1,200,000
4	(80,000 options × CU25 × 4/5) – CU1,200,000	400,000	1,600,000
5	(70,000 options × CU25) – CU1,600,000	150,000	1,750,000

4.3.8 Contingent issue of shares for goods or services from non-employees

Example 4.3.8

Contingent issue of shares for goods or services from non-employees

Company G enters into an agreement with its lawyers currently assisting G in defending a lawsuit. If G is successful in winning the case, it will issue 100 of its own shares to the lawyers. If G is not successful in winning the case, it will issue 20 of its own shares to its lawyers. G expenses the amount it expects to pay to the lawyers over the service period. At the end of each reporting period, G should make its best estimate of whether the lawyers will win the case as well as the most likely outcome of the period over which the case will be settled. This estimate should be revised at the end of each reporting period as long as the case is not settled. In the end, the expense should equal the multiple of the shares issued and their fair value (determined by either reference to the value of the services received, or, if not reliable, the fair value of the equity instruments granted, in accordance with the measurement guidance for share-based payment transactions with non-employees).

4.3.9 Equity instruments vesting in instalments

Example 4.3.9

Equity instruments vesting in instalments

Company A grants its employees 1,000 share options each, which will vest in instalments of 200 share options at the end of each year over the next five years.

To apply the requirements of the IFRS, the entity should treat each instalment as a separate share option grant, because each instalment has a different vesting period and hence the fair value of each instalment is likely to be different. This is because the length of the vesting period will affect, for example, the likely timing of cash flows arising from the exercise of the options.

4.3.10 *Distinguishing market and non-market vesting conditions*

For the majority of vesting conditions, it is straightforward to determine whether they should be viewed as market or non-market conditions. However, it is not always so straightforward to make this distinction as illustrated in the following examples.

Example 4.3.10A

Market and non-market vesting conditions (index)

Company A issues share options to certain of its employees that vest if, and when, A's share price growth (as a percentage) exceeds the average share price growth of A's 10 most significant competitors. Share price growth is calculated based on share prices only and does not factor in dividends or other factors.

IFRS 2 defines one form of a market condition as a condition upon which the exercise price, vesting, or exercisability of an equity instrument depends on '. . . achieving a specified target that is based on the market price of the entity's equity instruments relative to an index of market prices of equity instruments of other entities'. IFRS 2 does not provide guidance on what constitutes an index.

While the term 'index' would appear to require a comparison of more than one entity, there clearly is no requirement that the index be a published, standard index such as the S&P 500 or FTSE 100. The following criteria should be considered in determining whether an index exists:

- the fair value at the date of grant can be reliably determined by reference to the index;
- the share prices of the entities in the index are readily available in an active market such that accurate and reliable measurements of fair value can be determined at a specific point in time; and
- a consistent and reasonable formula is used to determine the effects of the entities' performance on the performance of the index.

If these criteria are met, A would have a strong case for demonstrating that the vesting condition was a market condition.

Example 4.3.10B

Ranking of shares within a population

Company A issues share options to certain employees that vest if A's share price growth (as a percentage) ranks in the top quartile of the largest 100 companies in its market. Share price growth is calculated based on share price only and does not take account of dividends or other factors.

Should this vesting condition be considered a market condition?

The ranking within an index or group of companies may be representative of an index if it meets the criteria for an index described in **example 4.3.10A** above. Notably, the vesting condition is measurable based on quoted market prices and a consistent formula is used. Therefore, a vesting condition based on a ranking should be considered a market condition.

Example 4.3.10C

TSR as a market condition

Total Shareholders' Return (TSR) is the internal rate of return on the entity's shares calculated by assuming that (a) someone bought the share at the start of the performance period, (b) any dividends received on the share had been used to buy more shares when received, and (c) the shares (plus dividend shares) were sold at the end of the performance period. For example, if no dividends were paid and the share price increased from £100 to £107 after one year, the TSR would be 7 per cent. The way that TSR performance conditions typically work is by comparing the entity's TSR with those of an index of other entities. For example, if the entity's TSR were to be placed in the top 30th percentile, then 90 per cent of an award may vest.

A TSR calculation includes not only changes in the entity's share price, but the effects of dividends. Nevertheless, a TSR condition should be considered a market condition because movements in the share price are the predominant factor in its calculation. This conclusion is consistent with the generally accepted interpretation of SFAS 123 under US GAAP which, according to IFRS 2.BC184, applies the same approach to distinguishing between market and non-market conditions.

4.4 Reload features

Some share options have a 'reload feature'. This entitles the employee to automatic grants of additional share options whenever he/she exercises previously granted share options and pays the exercise price in the entity's shares rather than in cash. Typically, the employee is granted a new share option, called a reload option, for each share surrendered when exercising the previous share option. The exercise price of the reload option is usually set at the market price of the shares on the date the reload option is granted. [IFRS 2.BC188]

Reload features are not a common feature of UK employee share schemes but may be significant in other countries such as the USA. UK

A 'reload feature' is defined in IFRS 2 as:

[IFRS 2(Appendix A)]

> 'A feature that provides for an automatic grant of additional share options whenever the option holder exercises previously granted options using the entity's shares, rather than cash, to satisfy the exercise price.'

A 'reload option' is defined as:

[IFRS 2(Appendix A)]

> 'A new share option granted when a share is used to satisfy the exercise price of a previous share option.'

IFRS 2 requires that for options with a reload feature, the feature should not be taken into account when estimating the fair value of options granted at the measurement date. Instead, a reload option should be accounted for as a new option grant, if and when a reload option is subsequently granted. [IFRS 2.22]

As discussed in paragraphs BC189 to BC192 of IFRS 2, it may theoretically be preferable to take account of reload features when measuring the fair value of options granted. ED 2 proposed this treatment 'where practicable'. However, in the light of comments received, the IASB decided to require the treatment set out above in all cases.

4.5 Adjustments after vesting date

Having recognised the goods or services received in accordance with the requirements of IFRS 2 (and a corresponding increase in equity) no subsequent adjustment should be made to equity after vesting date. For example, the amount recognised for services received from an employee is not subsequently reversed if the vested equity instruments are later forfeited or, in the case of share options, are not exercised. This requirement does not, however, preclude a transfer from one component of equity to another. [IFRS 2.23]

For example, the expense recognised in accordance with IFRS 2 is not reversed if options vest but are not exercised because they are 'out of the money' or simply because the employee elects not to do so.

4.6 If fair value is not measurable

IFRS 2 provides an exemption from fair value when the fair value of the equity instruments issued cannot be reliably measured. In these rare cases, the grant is initially measured at its intrinsic value and adjusted at the end of each reporting period for any change in intrinsic value until the options are either exercised, forfeited or lapse.

IFRS 2 defines 'intrinsic value' as:

[IFRS 2(Appendix A)]

> 'The difference between the fair value of the shares to which the counterparty has the (conditional or unconditional) right to subscribe or which it has the right to receive, and the price (if any) the counterparty is (or will be) required to pay for those shares.'

For example, a share option with an exercise price of £15 on a share with a fair value of £20 has an intrinsic value of £5.

When the IASB developed the Exposure Draft preceding IFRS 2, it concluded that there should be no exceptions to the requirement to apply a fair value measurement basis. It therefore was not necessary to include in the proposed IFRS specific requirements for share options that were difficult to value. The IASB noted that share options form part of the employee's remuneration package and that it seemed reasonable to presume that an entity's management would consider the value of the share options to satisfy itself that the package was fair and reasonable. However, after considering respondents' comments, particularly with regard to unlisted entities, the IASB reconsidered this issue.

The IASB concluded that 'in rare cases only' in which it is not possible to estimate the grant date fair value of the equity instrument granted, the alternative treatment of using intrinsic values should be permitted. [IFRS 2.BC199]

No further guidance is provided in IFRS 2 regarding the nature of the rare circumstances which would justify the use of this approach. Although unlisted entities may find it particularly difficult to apply

IFRS 2, it should be remembered that even when the intrinsic value approach is used, it will still be necessary to have an estimate of the fair value of the shares at the end of each reporting period. Also, entities may be discouraged from following this route because the expense recognised using the intrinsic value approach will, in most circumstances, be higher (and more volatile) than that which would be recognised on the basis of fair value at grant date.

In the rare cases described above, the equity instruments granted are measured at their intrinsic value, initially at the date when the entity obtains the goods or the counterparty renders the services. The instrument is subsequently remeasured at intrinsic value at the end of each reporting period and at the date of final settlement, with any change in intrinsic value recognised in profit or loss. For a grant of share options, the share-based payment arrangement is finally settled when the options are exercised, are forfeited (e.g. upon cessation of employment) or lapse (e.g. at the end of the option's life). [IFRS 2.24(a)]

When this approach is used, the goods or services received should be recognised based on the number of equity instruments that ultimately vest or, where applicable, are ultimately exercised. This means that in the case of share options, the goods or services received are recognised during the vesting period in accordance with paragraphs 14 and 15 of the Standard (see **3.2.1** above) except that the requirements of paragraph 15(b) concerning market conditions do not apply. The amount recognised for goods or services received during the vesting period is based on the number of share options expected to vest. That estimate is revised if subsequent information indicates that the number of options expected to vest differs from previous estimates. On vesting date, the estimate is revised to equal the number of equity instruments that ultimately vested. After vesting date, the amount recognised for goods or services received is reversed if the options are later forfeited, or lapse at the end of the option's life. [IFRS 2.24(b)]

If the intrinsic value approach is used, it is not necessary to apply paragraphs 26 to 29 of the Standard which deal with modifications to the terms and conditions on which equity instruments were granted, including cancellation and settlement (see **section 5** below). This is because any modifications to the terms and conditions on which the equity instruments were granted will be taken into account when applying the intrinsic value method described above. [IFRS 2.25]

However, if an equity instrument to which the intrinsic value method has been applied is settled and the settlement occurs during the vesting period, the settlement is accounted for as an acceleration of vesting. The amount that would otherwise have been recognised for services received over the remainder of the vesting period is therefore recognised immediately. In this case, any payment made on settlement is accounted for as the repurchase of equity instruments (i.e. as a deduction from equity) except to the extent that the payment exceeds the intrinsic value of the equity instruments measured at the repurchase date. Any such excess is recognised as an expense. [IFRS 2.25]

The application of the intrinsic value method is illustrated in the following example which is taken from the IFRS 2 Implementation Guidance (IG Example 10).

Example 4.6

Grant of share options that is accounted for by applying the intrinsic value method

[IFRS 2 Implementation Guidance (IG Example 10)]

BACKGROUND

At the beginning of year 1, an entity grants 1,000 share options to 50 employees. The share options will vest at the end of year 3, provided the employees remain in service until then. The share options have a life of 10 years. The exercise price is CU60 and the entity's share price is also CU60 at the date of grant.

At the date of grant, the entity concludes that it cannot estimate reliably the fair value of the share options granted.

At the end of year 1, three employees have ceased employment and the entity estimates that a further seven employees will leave during years 2 and 3. Hence, the entity estimates that 80 per cent of the share options will vest.

Two employees leave during year 2, and the entity revises its estimate of the number of share options that it expects will vest to 86 per cent.

Two employees leave during year 3. Hence, 43,000 share options vested at the end of year 3.

The entity's share price during years 1–10, and the number of share options exercised during years 4–10, are set out below. Share options that were exercised during a particular year were all exercised at the end of that year.

Year	Share price at year-end	Number of share options exercised at year-end
1	63	0
2	65	0
3	75	0
4	88	6,000
5	100	8,000
6	90	5,000
7	96	9,000
8	105	8,000
9	108	5,000
10	115	2,000

APPLICATION OF REQUIREMENTS

In accordance with paragraph 24 of the IFRS, the entity recognises the following amounts in years 1–10.

Year	Calculation	Expense for period CU	Cumulative expense CU
1	50,000 options × 80% × (CU63 – CU60) × 1/3 years	40,000	40,000
2	50,000 options × 86% × (CU65 – CU60) × 2/3 years – CU40,000	103,333	143,333
3	43,000 options × (CU75 – CU60) – CU143,333	501,667	645,000
4	37,000 outstanding options × (CU88 – CU75) + 6,000 exercised options × (CU88 – CU75)	559,000	1,204,000
5	29,000 outstanding options × (CU100 – CU88) + 8,000 exercised options × (CU100 – CU88)	444,000	1,648,000
6	24,000 outstanding options × (CU90 – CU100) + 5,000 exercised options × (CU90 – CU100)	(290,000)	1,358,000
7	15,000 outstanding options × (CU96 – CU90) + 9,000 exercised options × (CU96 – CU90)	144,000	1,502,000
8	7,000 outstanding options × (CU105 – CU96) + 8,000 exercised options × (CU105 – CU96)	135,000	1,637,000
9	2,000 outstanding options × (CU108 – CU105) + 5,000 exercised options × (CU108 – CU105)	21,000	1,658,000
10	2,000 exercised options × (CU115 – CU108)	14,000	1,672,000

4.7 Share price denominated in a foreign currency

Example 4.7

Share price denominated in a foreign currency

Company E is a UK entity with Sterling as its functional currency. E is registered on the New York Stock Exchange with a current market price of

US$15 per share. E issues 100 options to its employees with an exercise price of US$15 per share and a vesting period of three years. The share options can only be equity-settled. How should these arrangements be accounted for given that the share price is quoted in a currency other than the functional currency of the entity?

E does not have an embedded derivative in this share-based payment to employees that needs to be accounted for under IAS 39. Equity-settled share-based payments do not give rise to assets or liabilities that would be denominated in a currency other than the entity's own functional currency. That is, the transaction is an equity transaction that should be denominated in Sterling for E. For example, if the total fair value of the options was determined to be US$1,500 at the date of grant and the exchange rate was US$1.5/£1, the total amount that would be expensed under IFRS 2 would be £1,000 [1,500 / 1.5] or £10 per share. This amount would not change over the life of the options even if the exchange rate fluctuates.

For cash-settled share options, the liability recorded would be considered a US$ denominated liability and would need to be remeasured at the end of each reporting period. Since the remeasurement is at fair value with changes recognised in profit or loss, no embedded derivative would need to be identified and separated.

5 Modifications including cancellations and settlements

5.1 Modifications

An entity may decide to modify the terms of an existing equity instrument granted in a share-based payment transaction. For example, if there is decline in the entity's share price an employer may decide to reduce the exercise price of options previously issued to employees, thus increasing their fair value. The requirements of the Standard in this area are expressed in the context of transactions with employees. However, the requirements also apply to share-based payment transactions with parties other than employees that are measured by reference to the fair value of the equity instruments granted. In this case, any references to grant date are instead used to refer to the date the entity obtains the goods or the counterparty renders service. [IFRS 2.26]

As a minimum, the services received are measured at the grant date fair value, unless the instruments do not vest because of a failure to satisfy a non-market vesting condition that was specified at grant date. This applies irrespective of any modifications to the terms and conditions on which the instruments were granted (including cancellation or settlement). In addition, the effects of modifications that increase the total fair value of the share-based payment arrangement, or are otherwise beneficial to the employee, are recognised. [IFRS 2.27]

Therefore, a modification that results in a decrease in the fair value of equity instruments does not result in a reduction in the expense recognised in future periods. However, the effects of modifications that increase fair value are recognised. Appendix B of IFRS 2 provides guidance on how this requirement should be implemented. This guidance, which forms an integral part of the Standard, is summarised below.

5.1.1 *The modification increases the fair value of the equity instruments granted*

The fair value of the equity instruments granted may be increased, for example by reducing the exercise price of share options. Where this happens, the incremental fair value is measured by comparing the fair value of the instrument immediately before and immediately after the modification. This incremental fair value is then included in the measurement of the amount recognised for services received.

If the modification occurs during the vesting period, the incremental fair value granted is included in the measurement of the amount recognised for services received over the period from the modification date until the date when the modified equity instruments vest. The amount based on the grant date fair value of the original equity instruments continues to be recognised over the remainder of the original vesting period.

If the modification occurs after vesting date, the incremental fair value granted is recognised immediately. If the employee is required to complete an additional period of service before becoming unconditionally entitled to the modified equity instruments, the incremental fair value granted will be recognised over the vesting period. [IFRS 2.B43(a)]

The following example, which is taken from the IFRS 2 Implementation Guidance (IG Example 7) illustrates the approach that should be adopted for a simple option repricing.

Example 5.1.1

Grant of share options that are subsequently repriced

[IFRS 2 Implementation Guidance (IG Example 7)]

BACKGROUND

At the beginning of year 1, an entity grants 100 share options to each of its 500 employees. Each grant is conditional upon the employee remaining in service over the next three years. The entity estimates that the fair value of each option is CU15. On the basis of a weighted average probability, the entity estimates that 100 employees will leave during the three-year period and therefore forfeit their rights to the share options.

Suppose that 40 employees leave during year 1. Also suppose that by the end of year 1, the entity's share price has dropped, and the entity reprices its share options, and that the repriced share options vest at the end of year 3. The entity estimates that a further 70 employees will leave during years 2 and 3, and hence the total expected employee departures over the three-year vesting period is 110 employees. During year 2, a further 35 employees leave, and the entity estimates that a further 30 employees will leave during year 3, to bring the total expected employee departures over the three-year vesting period to 105 employees. During year 3, a total of 28 employees leave, and hence a total of 103 employees ceased employment during the vesting period. For the remaining 397 employees, the share options vested at the end of year 3.

The entity estimates that, at the date of repricing, the fair value of each of the original share options granted (i.e. before taking into account the repricing) is CU5 and that the fair value of each repriced share option is CU8.

APPLICATION OF REQUIREMENTS

Paragraph 27 of the IFRS requires the entity to recognise the effects of modifications that increase the total fair value of the share-based payment arrangement or are otherwise beneficial to the employee. If the modification increases the fair value of the equity instruments granted (e.g. by reducing the exercise price), measured immediately before and after the modification, paragraph B43(a) of Appendix B requires the entity to include the incremental fair value granted (i.e. the difference between the fair value of the modified equity instrument and that of the original equity instrument, both estimated as at the date of the modification) in the measurement of the amount recognised for services received as consideration for the equity instruments granted. If the modification occurs during the vesting period, the incremental fair value granted is included in the measurement of the amount recognised for services received over the period from the modification date until the date when the modified equity instruments vest, in addition to the amount based on the grant date fair value of the original equity instruments, which is recognised over the remainder of the original vesting period.

The incremental value is CU3 per share option (CU8 – CU5). This amount is recognised over the remaining two years of the vesting period, along with remuneration expense based on the original option value of CU15.

The amounts recognised in years 1–3 are as follows:

Year	Calculation	Remuneration expense for period CU	Cumulative remuneration expense CU
1	(500 – 110) employees ×100 options × CU15 × 1/3	195,000	195,000
2	(500 – 105) employees × 100 options × (CU15 × 2/3 + CU3 × 1/2) – CU195,000	259,250	454,250
3	(500 – 103) employees × 100 options × (CU15 + CU3) – CU454,250	260,350	714,600

5.1.2 *The modification increases the number of equity instruments granted*

If the modification increases the number of equity instruments granted, the fair value of the additional equity instruments granted, measured at the date of the modification, is included in the measurement of the amount recognised for services received, consistent with the requirements in **5.1.1** above.

For example, if the modification occurs during the vesting period, the fair value of the additional equity instruments granted is included in the amount recognised for services received over the period from the modification date until the date when the additional equity instruments vest. This is in addition to the amount based on the grant date fair value of the equity instruments originally granted which is recognised over the remainder of the original vesting period. [IFRS 2.B43(b)]

The additional equity instruments granted as a result of the modification are therefore accounted for in the same way as a new grant of equity instruments on the date of the modification. The related expense is recognised over the remainder of the vesting period, in addition to the expense on the original grant.

Example 5.1.2

Additional equity instruments granted

On 1 January 20X1, Company A puts in place a share-based payment arrangement under which employees will receive 10,000 shares in Company A if they stay in employment for three years. At 1 January 20X1, the grant date, Company A's share price is £6.

During the first half of 20X1, Company A's share price falls significantly. On 1 July 20X1, Company A modifies the scheme so that participating employees who are still employed at 31 December 20X3 will receive twice as many shares, i.e. 20,000 shares rather than 10,000 shares. On 1 July 20X1, Company A's share price is £2.50.

At 31 December 20X1, Company A expects that shares will vest for 90 per cent of the employees (i.e. 18,000 shares are expected to vest).

The modification is accounted for in the same way as a new grant of equity instruments. At the end of 20X1, Company A is 1/3 (12 of 36 months) of the way through the vesting period for the original grant, and 1/5 (6 of 30 months) of the way through the vesting period for the additional grant. Therefore, the charge for 20X1 is calculated as:

(9,000 x £6 x 1/3) + (9,000 x £2.50 x 1/5) = £225.

5.1.3 *The vesting conditions are modified in a manner that is beneficial to the employee*

The vesting conditions may be modified in a way that is beneficial to the employee. For example, the vesting period may be reduced or a performance condition might be eliminated or made less demanding. Where the modification affects a market condition it is accounted for as described at **5.1.1** above. In all other cases, the modified vesting conditions are taken into account when applying the requirements of paragraphs 19 to 21 of the Standard (see **4.3** above). [IFRS 2.B43(c)]

The following example illustrates a modification which is beneficial to the employee as a result of the removal of a market condition.

Example 5.1.3A

Removal of a market condition

Company A issues 100 options each to 100 employees. The options vest if:

a) the employees remain in employment for 3 years; and

b) the share price increases to £9 by the end of the 3-year vesting period.

The share price at grant date is £5 and the fair value of the options is £3. It is expected that 90 of the employees will remain for the 3 years.

In year 1, the charge is:

Dr	Profit or loss	£9,000	
Cr	Equity		£9,000

{100 options x £3 x 90 employees x 1/3}

At the beginning of year 2, the market-based vesting condition (share-price target) is removed. At this date, the fair value of the option with the share-price target is £2 and the fair value of the option without the share-price target is £3.50. Thus, there is an incremental fair value of £1.50 per option being given to the employees. It is expected that 92 employees will remain for the 3 years.

In year 2, the charge is:

In respect of the original scheme

Dr	Profit or loss	£9,400	
Cr	Equity		£9,400

{100 options x £3 x 92 employees x 2/3} – £9,000

In respect of the modification

Dr	Profit or loss	£6,900	
Cr	Equity		£6,900

{100 options x £1.50 x 92 employees x ½}

At the end of year 3, 88 employees are still in employment. The charge is:

In respect of the original scheme

Dr	Profit or loss	£8,000	
Cr	Equity		£8,000

{100 options x £3 x 88} – £9,000 – £9,400

In respect of the modification

Dr	Profit or loss	£6,300	
Cr	Equity		£6,300

{100 options x £1.50 x 88} – £6,900

The following example illustrates a modification which is beneficial to the employee as a result of the removal of a non-market condition. The removal of a non-market vesting condition will increase the likelihood of the instruments vesting. This will be reflected by an increased charge in profit or loss if, and to the extent that, more instruments are likely to vest as a result of the modification.

Example 5.1.3B

Removal of a non-market condition

Company A issues 100 options each to 100 employees. The options vest if:

a) the employees remain in employment for 3 years; and

b) EPS reaches 25p by the end of the 3-year vesting period.

The fair value of the options is £3. It is expected that 90 of the employees will remain for the 3 years. At the start of year 1, it is expected that the EPS condition will be met.

In year 1, the charge is:

Dr	Profit or loss	£9,000	
Cr	Equity		£9,000

{100 options x £3 x 90 employees x 1/3}

At the end of year 2, it is expected that the EPS condition won't be met, so in year 2, the charge is reversed:

Dr	Equity	£9,000	
Cr	Profit or loss		£9,000

During year 3, it is still expected that the EPS condition will not be met but the EPS condition is removed. At the end of year 3, 88 employees are still in employment, so the charge is:

Dr	Profit or loss	£26,400	
Cr	Equity		£26,400

{100 options x £3 x 88 employees} – nil

The effect of modifications which replace a market condition with a non-market condition is considered at **5.1.7** below. The effect of a modification which replaces a non-market condition with a market condition is considered at **5.1.8** below.

5.1.4 *The terms or conditions are modified in a way that is not beneficial to the employee*

The terms and conditions of the equity instruments granted may be varied in a manner that reduces the total fair value of the share-based payment arrangement, or is otherwise not beneficial to the employee. In this case, the entity continues to account for the services received as if the modification had not occurred (other than for a cancellation of some or all of the equity instruments granted which is considered at **5.2** below). [IFRS 2.B44]

This situation is unlikely to be common in practice because it is difficult to see why employees would consent to their agreed benefits being made less attractive. However, if this requirement of the Standard did not exist it would be possible for management to reduce or eliminate the expense for 'out-of-the money' options because the employees might accept that they would receive no benefit anyway.

If the modification reduces the fair value of the equity instruments granted, measured immediately before and after the modification, the decrease in fair value is not taken into account. The amount recognised for services received continues to be measured based on the grant date fair value of the instrument originally granted. [IFRS 2.B44(a)]

If the modification reduces the number of equity instruments granted to an employee, the reduction is accounted for as a cancellation of that portion of the grant (see **5.2** below). [IFRS 2.B44(b)]

If the vesting conditions are modified in a manner that is not beneficial to the employee, for example by increasing the vesting period, the modified vesting conditions are not taken into account when applying the requirements of paragraphs 19 to 21 of the Standard (see **4.3** above). [IFRS 2.B44(c)]

The following example, taken from the IFRS 2 Implementation Guidance (IG Example 8), illustrates the application of this requirement.

Example 5.1.4

Grant of share options with a vesting condition that is subsequently modified

[IFRS 2 Implementation Guidance (IG Example 8)]

BACKGROUND

At the beginning of year 1, the entity grants 1,000 share options to each member of its sales team, conditional upon the employee's remaining in the entity's employ for three years, and the team selling more than 50,000 units of a particular product over the three-year period. The fair value of the share options is CU15 per option at the date of grant.

During year 2, the entity increases the sales target to 100,000 units. By the end of year 3, the entity has sold 55,000 units, and the share options are forfeited. Twelve members of the sales team have remained in service for the three-year period.

APPLICATION OF REQUIREMENTS

Paragraph 20 of the IFRS requires, for a performance condition that is not a market condition, the entity to recognise the services received during the vesting period based on the best available estimate of the number of equity instruments expected to vest and to revise that estimate, if necessary, if subsequent information indicates that the number of equity instruments expected to vest differs from previous estimates. On vesting date, the entity revises the estimate to equal the number of equity instruments that ultimately vested. However, paragraph 27 of the IFRS requires, irrespective of any modifications to the terms and conditions on which the equity instruments were granted, or a cancellation or settlement of that grant of equity instruments, the entity to recognise, as a minimum, the services received, measured at the grant date fair value of the equity instruments granted, unless those equity instruments do not vest because of failure to satisfy a vesting condition (other than a market condition) that was specified at grant date. Furthermore, paragraph B44(c) of Appendix B specifies that, if the entity modifies the vesting conditions in a manner that is not beneficial to the employee, the entity does not take the modified vesting conditions into account when applying the requirements of paragraphs 19–21 of the IFRS.

Therefore, because the modification to the performance condition made it less likely that the share options will vest, which was not beneficial to the employee, the entity takes no account of the modified performance condition when recognising the services received. Instead, it continues to recognise the services received over the three-year period based on the original vesting conditions. Hence, the entity ultimately recognises cumulative remuneration expense of CU180,000 over the three-year period (12 employees × 1,000 options × CU15).

The same result would have occurred if, instead of modifying the performance target, the entity had increased the number of years of service required for the share options to vest from three years to ten years. Because such a modification would make it less likely that the options will vest, which would not be beneficial to the employees, the entity would take no account of the modified service condition when recognising the services received. Instead, it would recognise the services received from the twelve employees who remained in service over the original three-year vesting period.

5.1.5 *Modifications involving changes to whether instruments will be equity-settled or cash-settled*

Paragraph 27 of IFRS 2 which is considered in this section deals only with the modification to the terms and conditions on which equity instruments were granted. This would include the addition of a cash alternative to share options originally issued on terms that they would be equity-settled. Guidance on changes regarding terms of settlement are dealt with in **section 7** below.

5.1.6 *Modifications that are intended to preserve the rights of the holders*

The terms of share options or other share-based payment arrangements may be modified with the intention of preserving the rights of the holders in the case of capital changes such as bonus issues, rights issues and demergers. For example, in the event of a one-for-one bonus issue, the number of shares in issue will double and the share price will fall by half. Therefore, to avoid the option holders being disadvantaged, it would be usual to adjust the terms of the options by halving the exercise price and doubling the number of options.

UK *It is normal practice in the UK for share option agreements to provide for such adjustments to be made. These clauses normally permit, rather than require, the directors to make such adjustments. However, they would generally be expected to exercise this right and might be compelled to do so to maintain the tax approved status of the scheme. The clauses may provide details of the circumstances in which adjustments are permitted or required. They typically require any adjustments to be 'fair and reasonable' rather than prescribing the method of calculation.*

Such an adjustment will be a modification for the purposes of IFRS 2. However:

- an additional expense should not arise where the clear intention of the modification is just to preserve the existing rights of the option holders;
- it will not be necessary to value the options using an option pricing model immediately before and after the modification where it is clear that the formula used achieves that intention (e.g. in the case of a one-for-one bonus issue, the number of options is doubled and the exercise price is halved); and
- this is so even if there is not strictly a contractual obligation to make the adjustment. It is not necessary to take the view that by making an adjustment that is not contractually required, the entity has conferred an extra benefit on the employees. It has instead merely reinstated what would have been taken away without the modification.

In cases where it is not clear whether the formula used confers any additional benefit on the employees, it will be necessary to compare the fair value of the rights immediately before and immediately after the modification in accordance with IFRS 2.

5.1.7 Replacement of a market condition with a non-market condition

The following example is similar to **example 5.1.3A** above in that a market condition has been removed but in this case it has been replaced with a non-market condition. There will usually be an incremental fair value because an equity instrument with no market conditions attached will be more valuable than the same equity instrument with a market condition attached. However, whether that incremental fair value is charged as an expense will depend on whether the replacement non-market condition is met.

Example 5.1.7

Replacement of a market condition with a non-market condition

Company A issues 100 options each to 100 employees. The options vest if:

a) the employees remain in employment for 3 years; and

b) the share price increases to £9 by the end of the 3-year vesting period.

The share price at grant date is £5 and the fair value of the options is £3. It is expected that 90 of the employees will remain for the 3 years.

In year 1, the charge is:

Dr	Profit or loss	£9,000	
Cr	Equity		£9,000

{100 options x £3 x 90 employees x 1/3}

At the beginning of year 2, the market-based vesting condition (share-price target) is removed and replaced with an EPS condition such that, to vest, EPS must reach 25p at the end of the 3-year period.

At this date, the fair value of the option with the share-price target is £2 and the fair value of the option without the share-price target is £3.50. Thus, there is an incremental fair value of £1.50 per option being given to the employees. It is expected that 92 employees will remain for the 3 years, and that the EPS target will be met.

In year 2, the charge is:

In respect of the original scheme

Dr	Profit or loss	£9,400	
Cr	Equity		£9,400

{100 options x £3 x 92 employees x 2/3} – £9,000

In respect of the modification

Dr	Profit or loss	£6,900	
Cr	Equity		£6,900

{100 options x £1.50 x 92 employees x ½}

At the end of year 3, 88 employees are still in employment and the EPS target is met. The charge is:

In respect of the original scheme

Dr	Profit or loss	£8,000	
Cr	Equity		£8,000

{100 options x £3 x 88} – £9,000 – £9,400

In respect of the modification

Dr	Profit or loss	£6,300	
Cr	Equity		£6,300

{100 options x £1.50 x 88} – £6,900

Alternatively, at the end of year 3, the EPS target may not be met. As a result, the incremental charge should be reversed because the non-market condition (i.e. the EPS target) has not been met. However, the original charge is still recognised because, although the options have failed to vest, this was not because of not meeting an *original* non-market condition.

Therefore, the charge in year 3 is:

In respect of the original scheme

Dr	Profit or loss	£8,000	
Cr	Equity		£8,000

{100 options x £3 x 88} – £9,000 – £9,400

In respect of the modification (reversal of prior charge)

Dr	Equity	£6,900	
Cr	Profit or loss		£6,900

It is possible that the modification may be structured with the intention that the fair value to the employee is the same before and after the modification. For example, this might be the case if the probability of the replacement non-market condition being met is the same as probability of the original market condition being met. However, as illustrated in the example above, such a modification may result in an additional expense in accordance with the requirements of IFRS 2. This is a consequence of the different manner in which IFRS 2 treats market and non-market conditions.

5.1.8 *Replacement of a non-market condition with a market condition*

The following example is similar to **example 5.1.3B** above in that a non-market condition has been removed but in this case it has been replaced with a market condition.

Example 5.1.8

Replacement of a non-market condition with a market condition

Company A issues 100 options each to 100 employees. The options vest if:

a) the employees remain in employment for 3 years; and

b) EPS reaches 25p by the end of the 3-year vesting period.

The fair value of the options is £3. It is expected that 90 of the employees will remain for the 3 years. At the start of year 1, it is expected that the EPS condition will be met.

In year 1, the charge is:

Dr	Profit or loss	£9,000	
Cr	Equity		£9,000

{100 options x £3 x 90 employees x 1/3}

At the end of year 1, the EPS condition is removed and replaced with a market-based condition such that the share price must reach £9 per share by the end of the vesting period. It is expected that 92 employees will remain for the 3 years.

The removal of a non-market condition means that paragraph B43(c) must be applied. At the date of the modification, the fair value of the option with the share-price target is £2 and the fair value of the option without the share-price target is £3.50. Value to the employees is decreased but under B44 this decrease is not accounted for.

The original grant date fair value must continue to be charged, except to the extent that the shares do not vest because a non-market condition that was present at grant date is not met. The only non-market condition that continues to exist once the EPS condition is removed is the employment condition.

In year 2, the charge is:

Dr	Profit or loss	£9,400	
Cr	Equity		£9,400

{100 options x £3 x 92 employees x 2/3 – £9,000}

At the end of year 3, 88 employees are still in employment, so the charge is:

Dr	Profit or loss	£8,000	
Cr	Equity		£8,000

{100 options x £3 x 88 employees – £9,000 – £9,400}

Replacement of a non-market condition will therefore result in the need to recognise an expense equal to the whole of grant date fair value irrespective of whether the replacement market condition is more or less likely to be met than the original non-market condition. In particular, replacement of a non-market condition which is unlikely to be met with a market condition which is equally unlikely to be met will result in the need to recognise an expense which would not otherwise have been recognised. This is a consequence of the different manner in which IFRS 2 treats market and non-market conditions.

5.2 Cancellations and settlements

An entity may cancel or settle a grant of equity instruments during the vesting period. IFRS 2 includes requirements that deal with such situations. This does not cover those cases when a grant is cancelled by forfeiture when the vesting conditions are not satisfied which are dealt with in accordance with the requirements of the Standard for vesting conditions (see **4.3** above).

Before the amendments published in January 2008, IFRS 2.28 referred to circumstances where 'the entity cancels or settles a grant of equity instruments during the vesting period'. The standard did not address the circumstances where the counterparty (e.g. the employee) cancels the arrangement. Following the amendments, which must be applied for periods beginning on or after 1 January 2009, IFRS 2.28 refers to circumstances where 'a grant of equity instruments is cancelled or settled during the vesting period'. Therefore, when the amended standard is applied, all cancellations must be dealt with in accordance with IFRS 2.28 irrespective of whether it is the entity or the counterparty which cancels the arrangements.

The January 2008 amendments also added an additional paragraph to the Standard which addresses a failure to meet a non-vesting condition (see **3.2.1** above). This states that if an entity or counterparty can choose whether to meet a non-vesting condition, the entity treats the counterparty's failure to meet that non-vesting condition during the vesting period as a cancellation. [IFRS 2.28A]

> A practical example of this is where an employee stops making payments into an SAYE option scheme and therefore forfeits his entitlement under the scheme. Under the amended Standard, the failure to make contributions would be a failure to meet a non-vesting condition and should therefore be accounted for as a cancellation.

The cancellation or settlement of an equity instrument is accounted for as an acceleration of vesting. The amount that would otherwise have been recognised for services received over the remainder of the vesting period is therefore recognised immediately. [IFRS 2.28(a)]

Any payment made to the employee on cancellation or settlement is accounted for as a repurchase of an equity interest (i.e. as a deduction from equity) except to the extent that the payment exceeds the fair value of the equity instrument granted, measured at the repurchase date. Any such excess is recognised as an expense. [IFRS 2.28(b)]

The January 2008 amendments to IFRS 2 added two additional sentences at the end of IFRS 2.28(b). They require that, if the share-based payment arrangement included liability components, the fair value of the liability at the date of cancellation or settlement should be remeasured. Any payment made to settle the liability component is accounted for as an extinguishment of the liability.

IFRS 2 also deals with the situation where new equity instruments may be granted to an employee in connection with the cancellation of existing equity instruments. If new equity instruments are granted and they are identified, on the date when they are granted, as replacement equity instruments for the cancelled equity instruments, this is accounted for as a modification of the original equity instruments (see **5.1** above). The incremental fair value granted is the difference between the fair value of the replacement equity instruments and the net fair value of the cancelled equity instruments at the date the replacement equity instruments are granted. The net fair value of the cancelled equity instruments is their fair value, immediately before the cancellation, less the amount of any payment made to the employee that is accounted for as deduction from equity in accordance with IFRS 2.28(b). [IFRS 2.28(c)]

If the entity does not identify new equity instruments granted as replacement equity instruments for those cancelled, the new equity instruments are accounted for as a new grant.

The Standard appears to imply a free choice as to whether an entity decides to identify replacement instruments. As indicated by **example 5.2A** below, it will often be attractive to identify the new options as replacements because this will avoid accelerating the expense recognised for the original options. However, it would not give a fair presentation to characterise equity instruments as replacements when they were clearly unrelated to the cancelled instruments.

The determination of whether the issue of new options is a replacement of cancelled options requires careful assessment of the facts and circumstances surrounding such transactions. IFRS 2 does not provide specific guidance in this area. Factors that may indicate that a new issue of options identified as a replacement of the cancelled options is a replacement include:

- the new share options are with the same participants as the cancelled options;
- the new share options are issued at a fair value that is broadly consistent with the fair value of the cancelled options determined either at their original grant date (indicating a repricing) or the cancellation date (indicating a replacement);

- the transactions to issue and cancel the options are part of the same arrangement;
- the cancellation of the options would not have occurred unless the new options were issued; and
- the cancellation of the options does not make commercial sense without the issue of the new options (and vice-versa).

If vested equity instruments are repurchased from employees, the payment made is accounted for as a deduction from equity, except to the extent that the payment exceeds the fair value of the repurchased instruments, measured at the repurchase date. Any such excess is recognised as an expense. [IFRS 2.29]

These requirements are illustrated by the following example.

Example 5.2A

Replacement of share options

Company O issued options with a 4-year vesting period to employees in 20X3. The options had an exercise price of £10 per share and the fair value determined at the grant date was £100,000. In 20X5, O cancelled those options and issued new options with an exercise price of £3 per share. The fair value of the new share options at the grant date is £75,000. If the new issue of share options is not considered a replacement of the existing share options, the remaining portion of the original fair value of £100,000 should be expensed immediately and the fair value of the new issue should be recognised over its vesting period. Therefore, a total of £175,000 would be expensed related to these options, much of the expense in earlier periods.

However, if O identifies the new issue of options as a replacement of the cancelled options, O accounts for the transaction similar to a modification. Therefore, O will continue to expense the portion of the £100,000 not yet recognised over the original vesting period. Additionally, O will expense the incremental fair value of the new instruments over the old instruments determined at the date of modification over the remaining vesting period. If the old share options had a fair value of £20,000 at the date they were cancelled, an incremental expense of £55,000 [75,000–20,000] should be recognised. Therefore, a total of £155,000 would be expensed related to these options.

The following example considers the situation where the replacement options are issued by a different entity in a group.

Example 5.2B

Issue of new options as a replacement of cancelled options

Company S is a publicly listed subsidiary of Company P (P) which is also publicly listed. P decides to de-list S by purchasing all of its outstanding shares from existing shareholders at an amount determined to be fair value. As part of the transaction, all outstanding share options in S were cancelled. In return, P issued share options in P to the same employees of S whose share options in S were cancelled. The fair value of the new share options determined at the grant date approximates the fair value of the replaced options determined at the cancellation date. In addition, the vesting terms and option lives of the new share options were adjusted to ensure consistency with the cancelled options.

Even though the share options are in a different entity that has different risks than S, the intention is to replace value held by the employees. Therefore, the transaction should be considered a replacement of equity instruments and accounted for in accordance with IFRS 2.28(c).

6 Measurement: cash-settled transactions

6.1 Basic requirements

As indicated in **2.1** above, IFRS 2 applies to transactions in which the entity acquires goods or services by incurring a liability to transfer cash or other assets for amounts based on the price (or value) of the entity's shares or other equity instruments of the entity.

The most common example of such arrangements are cash-settled Share Appreciation Rights (SARs) which are also sometimes referred to as 'phantom option schemes'. Typically, these schemes put the employees in the same position as if they had been granted options. But they involve a cash payment to the employees equal to the gain that would have been made by exercising the notional options and immediately selling the shares in the market.

It may not be immediately apparent why such arrangements are within the scope of the Standard. Paragraph BC242 of IFRS 2 notes that because cash-settled SARs involve an outflow of cash, rather than the issue of equity instruments, they should be accounted for 'in accordance with usual accounting for similar liabilities'. The paragraph goes on to note that while this sounds straightforward, there are some questions to consider. The Standard therefore provides guidance, for example, on how the liability should be measured (see IFRS 2 paragraphs BC243 to BC255 for further details).

For cash-settled share-based payment transactions, the goods or services acquired and the liability incurred are measured at the fair value of the liability. Until the liability is settled, the liability is remeasured at fair value at the end of each reporting period (and the settlement date). Any changes in fair value are recognised in profit or loss for the period. [IFRS 2.30]

It is an explicit requirement of IFRS 2.30 that any changes in fair value are recognised in profit or loss. IFRS 2.IG19 confirms that if the amount recognised for the goods or services received was included in the carrying amount of an asset recognised in the entity's balance sheet (e.g. inventory), the carrying amount of that asset is not adjusted for the effects of liability remeasurement.

Changes in fair value will include the effect of truing up for any vesting conditions (see **6.2** below).

The services received and the liability to pay for those services are recognised as the employees render service. For example, some SARs vest immediately and the employees are not therefore required to complete a specified period of service to become entitled to the cash payment. In the absence of evidence to the contrary, it should be presumed that the services rendered by the employees in exchange for the SARs have been received. In this case the expense for the services received and the liability to pay for them should be recognised immediately. But if the rights do not vest until the employees have completed a specified period of service, the services received and the liability to pay for them should be recognised as the employees render service during the period. [IFRS 2.32]

The liability is measured, initially and at the end of each reporting period until settled, at the fair value of the SARs by applying an option pricing model, taking into account the terms and conditions upon which the rights were granted and the extent to which the employees have rendered service to date.

A simpler approach would have been to base the liability on the intrinsic value of the SARs at the end of the reporting period. It can be argued that the additional cost and effort of using an option pricing model is not justified given that the cumulative expense is always trued up to the actual cash payment. However, the IASB rejected this approach and concluded that measuring SARs at intrinsic value would be inconsistent with the fair value measurement basis applied in the rest of the IFRS.

The following example, which is taken from the IFRS 2 Implementation Guidance (IG Example 12), illustrates the application of these requirements.

Example 6.1

Cash-settled share appreciation rights

[IFRS 2 Implementation Guidance (IG Example 12)]

BACKGROUND

An entity grants 100 cash share appreciation rights (SARs) to each of its 500 employees, on condition that the employees remain in its employ for the next three years.

During year 1, 35 employees leave. The entity estimates that a further 60 will leave during years 2 and 3. During year 2, 40 employees leave and the entity estimates that a further 25 will leave during year 3. During year 3, 22 employees leave. At the end of year 3, 150 employees exercise their SARs, another 140 employees exercise their SARs at the end of year 4 and the remaining 113 employees exercise their SARs at the end of year 5.

The entity estimates the fair value of the SARs at the end of each year in which a liability exists as shown below. At the end of year 3, all SARs held by the remaining employees vest. The intrinsic values of the SARs at the date of exercise (which equal the cash paid out) at the end of years 3, 4 and 5 are also shown below.

Year	Fair value	Intrinsic value
1	CU14.40	
2	CU15.50	
3	CU18.20	CU15.00
4	CU21.40	CU20.00
5		CU25.00

APPLICATION OF REQUIREMENTS

Year	Calculation		Expense CU	Liability CU
1	(500 – 95) employees × 100 SARs × CU14.40 × 1/3		194,400	194,400
2	(500 – 100) employees × 100 SARs × CU15.50 × 2/3 – CU194,400		218,933	413,333
3	(500 – 97 – 150) employees × 100 SARs × CU18.20 – CU413,333	47,127		460,460
	+ 150 employees × 100 SARs × CU15.00	225,000		
	Total		272,127	
4	(253 – 140) employees × 100 SARs × CU21.40 – CU460,460	(218,640)		241,820
	+ 140 employees × 100 SARs × CU20.00	280,000		
	Total		61,360	
5	CU0 – CU241,820	(241,820)		0
	+ 113 employees × 100 SARs × CU25.00	282,500		
	Total		40,680	
	Total		787,500	

Note that re-measurement of the liability is not recognised as one amount immediately. Instead this amount is spread over the remaining vesting period of the liability.

6.2 Treatment of vesting conditions

An issue which arises is whether vesting conditions should be considered in determining the fair value of cash-settled share-based payments. IFRS 2 provides no specific requirements about this.

IFRS 2.30 requires that the liability incurred from a cash-settled share-based payment transaction should be measured at the fair value of the liability. IFRS 2.BC248 states that the fair value of one form of cash-settled share-based payment (share appreciation rights or SARs) includes both the intrinsic value and the time value. Time value in this context is explained as '. . . the value of the right to participate in future increases in the share price, if any, that may occur between the valuation date and the settlement date'. Furthermore, IFRS 2.BC250 states that the exclusion of time value would lead to an inadequate measure of the liability. There is no mention in IFRS 2 of whether the fair value of the liability for a cash-settled share-based payment should include the effects of vesting conditions.

Example 6.1 above (which is taken from the Implementation Guidance to IFRS 2) provides an illustration of the accounting for SARs. In this illustration, employees must remain in the entity's employment for the next 3 years for their SARs to vest. The illustration does not include the effects of this vesting condition in determining the fair value of the SARs at the end of each reporting period, but bases the total liability on the best estimate of SARs that will vest. Non-market vesting conditions are excluded from the grant date fair value of equity-settled share-based payment because the 'true up' model is applied to those transactions. As noted in IFRS 2.19, the exclusion of vesting conditions from the measurement of equity-settled share-based payments has the effect of creating a measurement that is not a true fair value measurement. Similar statements are not made for the measurement of cash-settled share-based payment.

While **example 6.1** excludes one type of non-market vesting condition (remaining in the employment of an entity for a specified period of time), it is not clear whether the implication of this exclusion should extend to vesting conditions based on achieving a target revenue or share price. The definition of fair value is 'the amount for which an asset could be exchanged, a liability settled, or an equity instrument granted could be exchanged, between knowledgeable, willing parties in an arm's length transaction'. From this perspective, the fair value measurement should include all terms and conditions, including all vesting conditions.

From a pragmatic perspective, the effect of including vesting conditions in the measurement of fair value may not be materially different from applying the approach described in IFRS 2 (IG Example 12) using a best estimate approach. While this approach may provide a materially similar measurement when the only vesting condition is to remain in employment, this may not be the case if the vesting conditions are based on achieving a target share price or level of revenues.

6.3 Disclosure of liability

The following example considers the presentation and disclosure of the liability for cash-settled SARs.

Example 6.3

Presentation and disclosure of SARs

Company C issues twelve cash-settled share appreciation rights (SARs) to certain of its employees. The SARs vest over a three-year period. At the end of the vesting period, C expects that three of the SARs will be exercised within one year and the remaining nine SARs will be exercised after one year. The question is how C should present the liability for share-based payments?

IFRS 2 does not require a separate presentation of the carrying amount of liabilities relating to share-based payments in the statement of financial position but requires this information to be disclosed in the financial statements. Liabilities arising from share-based payments are financial liabilities, although they are excluded from the scope of IAS 32 and IAS 39.

Therefore, an entity should consider whether share-based payment liabilities are grouped with other financial liabilities in the statement of financial position. IAS 1(2007).29 and IAS 1(2003).29 require each material class of similar items to be presented separately in the financial statements. Items of a dissimilar nature or function are presented separately unless they are immaterial. IAS 1(2007).30 and IAS 1(2003).30 explain that if a line item is not individually material, it is aggregated with other items either on the face of the financial statements or in the notes. Share-based payment liabilities are likely to be different from other financial liabilities in nature and function.

IAS 1(2007).60 and IAS 1(2003).51 require separate presentation in the statement of financial position for current and non-current liabilities. Based on the above facts, since all SARs can be exercised within the next year, the liabilities should be presented as current liabilities. If C determines that presentation on a liquidity basis is more relevant, the current portion of the liability should be disclosed in accordance with IAS 1(2007).61 or IAS 1(2003).52.

6.4 Share price denominated in a foreign currency

This issue is considered at **4.7** above in relation to equity-settled share-based payments.

Consider the situation where an entity has Sterling as its functional currency but its share price is quoted in US$. For cash-settled share options, the liability recorded would be considered a US$ denominated liability and would need to be remeasured at the end of each reporting period. Since the remeasurement is at fair value with changes recognised in profit or loss, no embedded derivative would need to be identified and separated.

7 Transactions with settlement alternatives

7.1 Basic principles

In certain circumstances, share-based payment transactions may provide either the entity or the counterparty with a choice as to whether settlement occurs in equity instruments or cash. The basic principle to be applied is as follows.

For share-based payment transactions in which the terms of the arrangement provide either the entity or the counterparty with the choice of whether the entity settles the transaction in cash (or other assets) or by issuing equity instruments, the transaction, or the components of that transaction, are accounted for:

[IFRS 2.34]

- as a cash-settled share-based payment transaction if, and to the extent that, the entity has incurred a liability to settle in cash or other assets; or
- as an equity-settled share-based payment transaction if, and to the extent that, no such liability has been incurred.

IFRS 2 contains more detailed requirements concerning how to apply this principle to share-based payment transactions in which the terms of the arrangement:

- provide the counterparty with a choice of settlement (see **7.2** below); and
- provide the entity with a choice of settlement (see **7.3** below).

Circumstances where there is a modification to the terms of settlement are considered at **7.4** below.

References to cash, in the remainder of this section, also include other assets.

7.2 Counterparty's choice

If the counterparty has the choice as to whether an entity settles a share-based payment transaction in cash or with equity instruments, the entity has granted a compound financial instrument, similar to convertible debt. The instrument has:

- a debt component – the counterparty's right to demand cash; and
- an equity component – the counterparty's option to receive equity instruments rather than cash.

Each component is accounted for separately, similar to the equivalent requirements of IAS 32 as described below.

The following example illustrates the need to consider the substance of the arrangement where the cash alternative is provided through a separate agreement.

Example 7.2

Counterparty choice in settlement of a share-based payment

Company A grants share options to its employees that vest over a three-year period. These share options can only be settled by the issue of A's shares at the end of the vesting period. In a separate legal agreement consummated at the same time as the grant of the share options, A issues a put option to its employees that can (at the option of the employee) require A to settle the share options in cash based on the higher of a predetermined price (equal to the grant date fair value) or the fair value of the shares underlying the options. The put is only exercisable between the vesting date and the expiration of the options.

The two contracts (share options and written put) should be linked and the transaction accounted for as a share-based payment with a cash alternative.

The substance of this arrangement is the issue of an equity instrument to employees with a cash alternative. Therefore, the accounting should be the same whether the transaction is consummated through one or more contracts. As a result, A should fair value the liability component and any residual should be assigned to the equity component. Since the remaining amount to be assigned to equity in this example would be nil (see **7.2.1** below), the transaction is accounted for similar to a cash-settled share-based payment up to the date of exercise.

7.2.1 *Measurement*

For transactions with parties other than employees, the fair value of goods or services is measured directly (if that is possible with sufficient reliability – see **4.1** above). For such transactions, the equity component is measured as the difference between the fair value of the goods or services received and the fair value of the debt component, at the date when goods or services are received. [IFRS 2.35] This is the basic approach that is adopted for compound instruments that are accounted for under IAS 32 (see **section 3** in **chapter 15**).

For other transactions, including those with employees, the fair value of the compound financial instrument is measured at the measurement date, taking into account the terms and conditions on which the rights to cash or equity instruments were granted. [IFRS 2.36] To do this, the debt component is measured first and then the equity component is measured. The fact that the counterparty must forfeit the right to receive cash to receive the equity instrument should be taken into account. The fair value of the compound financial instrument is the sum of the fair values of the two components. [IFRS 2.37]

Under IAS 32.32 the carrying amount of the equity instruments is determined by deducting the fair value of the financial liability from the fair value of the compound financial instrument as a whole. This is straightforward when the fair value of the combined instrument is reliably known, for example where it is the proceeds of an issue for cash. However, IFRS 2.BC260 explains that, where this is not the case, it will be necessary to estimate the fair value of the compound instrument itself. The IASB therefore concluded, as stated above, that the compound instrument should be measured first by valuing the liability component (i.e. the cash alternative) and then valuing the equity component and adding the two components together.

Entities will often structure share-based payment transactions in which the counterparty has the choice of settlement in such a way that the fair value of one settlement alternative is the same as the other. For example, the counterparty might have the choice of receiving share options or cash-settled share appreciation rights. In such cases, the fair value of the equity component is zero, and hence the fair value of the compound financial instrument is the same as the fair value of the debt component. [IFRS 2.37]

IFRS 2 notes that, conversely, if the fair value of the settlement alternatives differ, the fair value of the equity component will usually be greater than zero. In this case the fair value of the compound financial instrument will be greater than the fair value of the debt component.

IFRS 2.BC259 explains that the fair value of the compound financial instrument will usually exceed both:

- the individual fair value of the cash alternative – because of the possibility that the shares or share options may be more valuable than the cash alternative; and
- that of the shares or options – because of the possibility that the cash alternative may be more valuable than the shares or options.

But, as explained above, in many practical situations the fair value of the settlement alternatives will be the same and there will be no equity component.

7.2.2 *Subsequent accounting*

Once the debt and equity components have been separately identified and measured, the goods or services received in respect of each component are accounted for separately. For the debt component, the goods or services received, and a corresponding liability, are recognised in accordance with the requirements applying to cash-settled transactions (see **section 6** above). For the equity component, if any, the goods or services received are recognised as the counterparty supplies goods or renders services in accordance with the requirements for equity-settled transactions (see **section 4** above). [IFRS 2.38]

At the date of settlement, the liability is remeasured at its fair value. If equity instruments are issued in settlement rather than cash, the liability is transferred direct to equity as the consideration for the equity instruments issued. [IFRS 2.39]

If settlement is in cash rather than equity instruments, the payment made is applied to settle the liability in full. Any equity component previously recognised remains in equity. By electing to receive cash settlement, the counterparty forfeited the right to receive equity instruments. But this does not preclude a transfer from one component of equity to another. [IFRS 2.40]

The application of these requirements is illustrated by the following example which is taken from the IFRS 2 Implementation Guidance (IG Example 13). It illustrates the circumstances where the cash alternative is less favourable than the equity-settled alternative and so the equity component is not zero.

Example 7.2.2

Subsequent accounting where counter-party has choice of settlement

[IFRS 2 Implementation Guidance (IG Example 13)]

BACKGROUND

An entity grants to an employee the right to choose either 1,000 phantom shares (i.e. a right to a cash payment equal to the value of 1,000 shares) or 1,200 shares. The grant is conditional upon the completion of three years' service. If the employee chooses the share alternative, the shares must be held for three years after vesting date.

At grant date, the entity's share price is CU50 per share. At the end of years 1, 2 and 3, the share price is CU52, CU55 and CU60 respectively. The entity does not expect to pay dividends in the next three years. After taking into account the effects of the post-vesting transfer restrictions, the entity estimates that the grant date fair value of the share alternative is CU48 per share.

At the end of year 3, the employee chooses:

Scenario 1: The cash alternative

Scenario 2: The equity alternative

APPLICATION OF REQUIREMENTS

The fair value of the equity alternative is CU57,600 (1,200 shares × CU48). The fair value of the cash alternative is CU50,000 (1,000 phantom shares × CU50). Therefore, the fair value of the equity component of the compound instrument is CU7,600 (CU57,600 – CU50,000).

The entity recognises the following amounts:

Year		Expense CU	Equity CU	Liability CU
1	Liability component: (1,000 × CU52 × 1/3)	17,333		17,333
	Equity component: (CU7,600 × 1/3)	2,533	2,533	
2	Liability component: (1,000 × CU55 × 2/3) – CU17,333	19,333		19,333
	Equity component: (CU7,600 × 1/3)	2,533	2,533	
3	Liability component: (1,000 × CU60) – CU36,666	23,334		23,334
	Equity component: (CU7,600 × 1/3)	2,534	2,534	
End Year 3	Scenario 1: cash of CU60,000 paid			(60,000)
	Scenario 1 totals	67,600	7,600	0
	Scenario 2: 1,200 shares issued		60,000	(60,000)
	Scenario 2 totals	67,600	67,600	0

7.3 Entity's choice

The terms of a share-based payment transaction may provide an entity with the choice as to whether to settle in cash or by issuing equity instruments. In this case, it is necessary to determine whether the entity has a present obligation to settle in cash and to account for the transaction accordingly. IFRS 2 states that the entity has a present obligation to settle in cash if:

[IFRS 2.41]

- the choice of settlement in equity instruments has no commercial substance, for example because the entity is legally prohibited from issuing shares; or
- the entity has a past practice or stated policy of settling in cash; or
- the entity generally settles in cash whenever the counterparty asks for cash settlement.

When the entity has a present obligation to settle in cash, the transaction is accounted for as a cash-settled transaction (see **section 6** above). [IFRS 2.42]

If no such obligation exists, the transaction is accounted for in accordance with the requirements of the Standard applying to equity-settled transactions (see **section 4** above).

The application of these classification requirements is illustrated by the following example:

Example 7.3

Classification of an employee share option plan in which the entity has the choice of settlement

Company A, a listed entity, grants its employees options to acquire ordinary shares in A. A's shares trade in an active market. The exercise of the options is conditional upon the achievement of certain performance conditions during the vesting period. In addition, the holders of the options have to be employed within the group headed by A or can be retired, if they retire at the normal retirement age.

Employees can exercise the options over a period of 5 years. Following the exercise of an option, the employee is required to sell the shares obtained immediately. Company A has first right to purchase these shares at a price equal to the market price at the moment employees exercise the underlying options. Should the entity not purchase the shares, there are no constraints on how the employees dispose of the shares, or to whom. There is no enforcement mechanism by the entity.

Company A has the legal ability to buy its own shares in the market, and has sufficient authorised capital to issue new shares to deliver the required number of shares to the employees upon exercise.

The share option scheme is a new arrangement, and there have been no other arrangements in the past where the entity has had a choice of cash or equity settlement; hence, there is no historical fact pattern of A exercising its rights. The share option scheme has been approved by the shareholders without objection, and no indication was provided as to what course of action the entity would take when the exercise date is reached — whether the entity would seek to acquire the shares based on its pre-emptive right or choose not to do so.

Company A represents that it will act in its own interest every time it has the right to buy back shares, and that it does not believe any situation exists which would force it to buy back the shares given to the employees under the scheme.

According to the listing rules, employees cannot exercise their rights during a 'closed period'. Therefore, employees will not be able to sell shares in a closed period.

When employees exercise the options granted by A, they are obliged to sell the shares on the date of exercise. Company A has first right to purchase these shares. In substance, this right to repurchase shares immediately gives A an option to settle the share-based payment transaction in cash. Therefore, paragraphs 41–43 of IFRS 2 apply.

Paragraph 41 of IFRS 2 requires an entity that has a choice of settlement to determine whether it has a present obligation to settle the share-based payment transaction in cash.

The entity has a present obligation to settle in cash if the choice of settlement in equity instruments has no commercial substance (e.g. because the entity is legally prohibited from issuing shares), or the entity has a past practice or a stated policy of settling in cash, or generally settles in cash whenever the counterparty asks for cash settlement.

If an entity with a choice of settlement has no present obligation to settle the transaction in cash, paragraph 43 of IFRS 2 states 'the entity shall account for the transaction in accordance with the requirements applying to equity-settled share-based payment transactions, in paragraphs 10–29'.

The management of Company A considers all facts and circumstances to determine whether there are any factors that could create an obligation to deliver cash and concludes that there are no situations in which the entity would have a legal obligation, or has created a constructive obligation, to repurchase the shares and thereby deliver cash.

In particular:

- there is an active market in which the shares could be sold;
- from a legal perspective, A has sufficient authorised share capital in order to be able to issue new shares;
- current shareholders raised no objection to the scheme in the general shareholders' meeting and the entity did not raise an expectation of a particular action;
- no restrictions on trading in a closed period apply as exercise is prohibited in this period; and
- there is no stated policy or constructive obligation created by past practice.

Hence, this scheme should be accounted for as an equity-settled share-based payment arrangement.

On settlement:

[IFRS 2.43]

- if the entity elects to settle in cash, the cash payment is accounted for as the repurchase of an equity interest. It is therefore treated as a deduction from equity except as described below; and

- if the entity elects to settle by issuing equity instruments, no further accounting is required except as noted below and except for a transfer from one component of equity to another component of equity, if necessary.

These requirements are not consistent with the requirements of IAS 32 for other circumstances where the entity has a choice of settlement. IAS 32 requires such arrangements to be classified wholly as a liability (if the contract is a derivative contract) or as a compound instrument (if the contract is a non-derivative contract). The IASB decided to retain this difference pending the outcome of its longer-term project on the distinction between liabilities and equity. [IFRS 2.BC266]

If the entity elects for the settlement alternative with the higher fair value, as at the date of settlement, the entity should recognise an additional expense for the excess value given. That is:

[IFRS 2.43]

- the difference between the cash paid and the fair value of the equity instruments that would have been issued; or
- the difference between the fair value of the equity instruments issued and the amount of cash that would otherwise have been paid.

Thus, there is an additional expense recognised when an entity elects to use the settlement alternative with the higher fair value. But this does not mean that the expense recognised will be the same as it would have been if the method of settlement assumed at the outset was the same as the actual method of settlement. For example, consider the case of share appreciation rights where the cash-settled and equity-settled alternatives have the same fair value because the cash payment is equal to the gain that would arise on exercise of the options. If these were assumed to be cash-settled from the outset, the cumulative expense recognised would be based on the actual cash payment made (i.e. intrinsic value on exercise). If these were assumed to be equity-settled from the outset, the cumulative expense recognised would be based on fair value at grant date (which would usually be lower).

Now suppose that the entity concluded, at the outset, that there was no obligation to settle in cash but subsequently did so. The expense recognised would be based on fair value at grant date and would not be adjusted to the amount of the cash payment made. The IASB considered and rejected the argument that an additional expense should be recognised in these circumstances as described in IFRS 2.BC267.

Where the entity has the choice of settlement, it may therefore appear advantageous to conclude that there is no obligation to settle in cash and to account for the arrangements as equity-settled. Where the entity has no past practice or stated policy of settling in cash, there is nothing in the Standard to prevent this. But an entity that tried to exploit this could do so only for a limited time because it might, in due course, establish a practice of settling in cash.

7.4 Changes to method of settlement

IFRS 2 contains specific requirements for modifications to the terms and conditions on which equity instruments are granted (see **section 5** above). It also deals with circumstances where there is choice between cash settlement and equity settlement (see **7.1** to **7.3** above). But it contains no specific requirements relating to the variation of terms to alter the method of settlement.

7.4.1 Addition of a cash alternative

An entity may decide, during the vesting period for an equity-settled transaction, to add an employee option to choose a cash alternative. From the date of such a modification, the transaction should be accounted for as a compound instrument as outlined at **7.2** above. This approach is illustrated in the following example which is taken from the IFRS 2 Implementation Guidance (IG Example 9).

Example 7.4.1A

Grant of shares, with a cash alternative subsequently added

[IFRS 2 Implementation Guidance (IG Example 9)]

BACKGROUND

At the beginning of year 1, the entity grants 10,000 shares with a fair value of CU33 per share to a senior executive, conditional upon the completion of three years' service. By the end of year 2, the share price has dropped to CU25 per share. At that date, the entity adds a cash alternative to the grant, whereby the executive can choose whether to receive 10,000 shares or cash equal to the value of 10,000 shares on vesting date. The share price is CU22 on vesting date.

APPLICATION OF REQUIREMENTS

Paragraph 27 of the IFRS requires, irrespective of any modifications to the terms and conditions on which the equity instruments were granted, or a cancellation or settlement of that grant of equity instruments, the entity to recognise, as a minimum, the services received measured at the grant date fair value of the equity instruments granted, unless those equity instruments do not vest because of failure to satisfy a vesting condition (other than a market condition) that was specified at grant date. Therefore, the entity recognises the services received over the three-year period, based on the grant date fair value of the shares.

Furthermore, the addition of the cash alternative at the end of year 2 creates an obligation to settle in cash. In accordance with the requirements for cash-settled share-based payment transactions (paragraphs 30–33 of the IFRS), the entity recognises the liability to settle in cash at the modification date, based on the fair value of the shares at the modification date and the extent to which the specified services have been received. Furthermore, the entity remeasures the fair value of the liability at the end of each reporting period and at the date of settlement, with any changes in fair value recognised in profit or loss for the period. Therefore, the entity recognises the following amounts:

Year	Calculation	Expense CU	Equity CU	Liability CU
1	Remuneration expense for year: 10,000 shares × CU33 × 1/3	110,000	110,000	
2	Remuneration expense for year: (10,000 shares × CU33 × 2/3) – CU110,000	110,000	110,000	
	Reclassify equity to liabilities: 10,000 shares × CU25 × 2/3		(166,667)	166,667
3	Remuneration expense for year: (10,000 shares × CU33 × 3/3) – CU220,000	110,000	26,667*	83,333*
	Adjust liability to closing fair value: (CU166,667 + CU83,333) – (CU22 × 10,000 shares)	(30,000)		(30,000)
	Total	300,000	80,000	220,000

* Allocated between liabilities and equity, to bring in the final third of the liability based on the fair value of the shares as at the date of the modification.

The following example is based on similar facts to the one above but assumes that the share price has increased rather than decreased by the end of year 2.

Example 7.4.1B

Accounting for an equity-settled share-based payment when a cash alternative is subsequently offered

At the beginning of year 1, an entity grants 10,000 shares with a fair value of CU33 per share to a senior executive, conditional on the completion of three years of service. By the end of year 2, the share price has increased to CU50 per share. At that date, the entity adds a cash alternative to the grant, whereby the executive can choose whether to receive 10,000 shares, or take the cash equivalent to the value of the 10,000 shares on the vesting date. This cash alternative has the same value as the shares. The share price decreased to CU45 at the end of year 3. How should these transactions be treated under IFRS 2?

IFRS 2.27 requires an entity to 'recognise, as a minimum, services received measured at the grant date fair value of the equity instruments granted, unless those equity instruments do not vest because of failure to satisfy a vesting condition (other than a market condition)'. In addition, the entity must recognise in profit or loss the effects of modifications that increase the total fair value of the share-based payment arrangement.

Since the modification to the share-based payment to add a cash alternative does not increase the total fair value of the share-based payment arrangement at the date of the modification, the entity continues to recognise an IFRS 2 charge for the services received during the three-year period, based on the grant date fair value of the shares.

However, the addition of the cash alternative at the end of year 2 creates an obligation to settle in cash. In accordance with the requirements for cash-settled share-based payment transactions (IFRS 2.30–33), the entity recognises the liability to settle in cash at the modification date. In a manner consistent with **example 7.4.1A** above, the liability is measured at the value of the shares on the date of modification, pro-rated for the effect of the service vesting condition. This effect of the modification is recognised in equity and not in profit or loss. Thereafter, the cost of the original equity grant is recognised in profit or loss. The increase in the liability for the remaining service period, which is based on the modification date value, is recognised in equity. Subsequent remeasurement of the liability to fair value at each reporting date and at the date of settlement is recognised in profit or loss.

Year	Calculation	Expense CU	Equity CU	Liability CU
1	Remuneration expense for year: 10,000 shares × CU33 × 1/3	110,000	110,000	
2	Remuneration expense for year: (10,000 shares × CU33 × 2/3) – CU110,000	110,000	110,000	
	Reclassify equity to liabilities: 10,000 shares × CU50 × 2/3		(333,333)	333,333
3	Remuneration expense for year: (10,000 shares × CU33 × 3/3) – CU220,000	110,000	110,000	
	Final third of liability at modification value: (10,000 shares × CU50 × 3/3) – CU333,333		(166,667)	166,667
	Remeasurement of liability: (10,000 shares × CU45 ×3/3) – CU500,000	(50,000)		(50,000)
	Total	280,000	(170,000)	450,000

In the entry in year 2, therefore, the value of the cash modification is recognised in equity and not in profit or loss. In year 3, the cost of the original equity grant is recognised in profit or loss, along with the remeasurement in the liability value to CU450,000 at the end of the year. The remaining unvested portion of the fair value of the liability at the modification date, which is CU166,667 ([10,000 shares × CU50 × 3/3] – 333,333), is recognised in equity.

7.4.2 *Change from cash-settled to equity-settled*

IFRS 2 does not specify how to account for a modification of a share-based payment arrangement from being cash-settled to equity-settled. The principles of IFRS 2 are generally consistent with those of US GAAP, namely FAS123(r) *Share-based Payment*. For example, modifications to the terms and conditions of equity-settled share-based payments are generally treated consistently under IFRS 2 and FAS123(r). While the guidance in IFRS 2 is limited to modifications to the terms and conditions of equity-settled arrangements, FAS123(r) also specifies how to account for a modification to a share-based payment arrangement which results in a change in its classification from being cash-settled to equity-settled. Specifically, the cash-settled share-based payment expense recognised up to the date of modification is not adjusted and the expense recognised from the date of modification over the remainder of the vesting period is determined based on the fair value of the re-classified equity award at the date of the modification. In other words, the modification is accounted for as if the cash-settled liability existing at the date of modification is effectively settled in exchange for an equity award with the same fair value. Given the similarity in underlying principles between FAS123(r) and IFRS 2 in this area, it is considered appropriate that a modification of an award from being cash-settled to equity-settled should be accounted for in the same way under IFRS 2. An example of this accounting treatment is given below.

Example 7.4.2

Change from cash-settled to equity-settled

On 1 January 20X3, Company A issues 100 share options to some of its employees with a strike price of £15 per option. The share options vest if the employee remains in A's employment after four years. The share options can only be cash-settled. Company A determines the fair value of the instruments to be £5 per option at the date of grant.

At 31 December 20X4, the fair value of the cash-settled share-based payment is £6 per option hence Company A has recognised a cumulative share-based payment expense of £300 [(£6 × 100) × 2/4 years] as A expects all of the options to vest. On 1 January 20X5, A modifies the options such that they can only be settled by delivery of A's equity instruments (one share option entitles the employee to one ordinary share of A). No other terms or vesting conditions of the share-based payment arrangement are amended.

At the date of modification, 1 January 20X5, A is required to derecognise the existing cash-settled liability as the cash-settled liability award has effectively been settled by the issue of an equity instrument. The existing cash-settled liability is therefore reclassified to equity. The cash-settled compensation cost recognised to date is not adjusted. The compensation cost to be recognised over the remaining vesting period is determined based on the fair value of the equity instrument at the time of the modification, which is £6 per option, such that the cumulative compensation cost recognised for the share-based payment arrangement reflects fair value for the equity award at 1 January 20X5. The cost to be recognised in each of years 3 and 4 of the award, provided all awards vest, will be £150.

7.4.3 *Change from equity-settled to cash-settled*

The following example considers a change in the terms whereby options that were originally to be equity-settled will be cash-settled.

Example 7.4.3

Modification from an equity-settled to a cash-settled share-based payment arrangement

On 1 January 20X3, Company A (A) issued 100 share options to certain employees, with a strike price of £15 per option. The options vest if the employees remain in A's employ after four years. The share options can only be settled by delivery of A's equity instruments and therefore are classified as equity-settled share-based payments. Company A determined the fair value of the instruments to be £5 per option.

As of 31 December 20X4, A had recorded a cumulative expense of £250 [(£5 × 100) × 2/4 years], since A expected all options to vest. On 1 January 20X5, A modified the options so that they could only be settled in cash. Therefore, upon settlement, A will pay the employees in cash the amount equal to the intrinsic value on the settlement date. On the date of modification, the fair value of the share options is £400. How should this modification be accounted for?

IFRS 2.B43, which contains guidance on the application of paragraph 27, states, in part, that 'if the modification increases the fair value of the equity instruments granted ..., measured immediately before and after the modification, the entity shall include the incremental fair value granted in the measurement of the amount recognised for services received as consideration for the equity instruments granted'. IFRS 2.B43 further clarifies that the 'incremental fair value granted is the difference between the fair value of the modified equity instrument and that of the original equity instrument, both estimated as at the date of the modification'.

Therefore, the fair value of the share options, which was £400, is reclassified from equity to liability. That is, £150 (the difference between the cumulative grant date fair value of the original instrument and the fair value on the date of modification of the original instrument) is debited to equity (IFRS 2.BC267-BC268).

7.5 Equity awards settled net of tax

Sometimes employees with equity-settled awards agree to 'net settlement' whereby they receive a reduced number of shares in return for the entity settling the related tax liability on their behalf. The value of the shares received is reduced by the amount of tax paid on their behalf. The question arises of whether this makes the award partly cash-settled.

Such arrangements should generally be treated as entirely equity-settled on the basis that the cash payment made by the entity is, in effect, as agent for the employee. However, before reaching a conclusion on any specific arrangements, it will be helpful to ask the following questions.

- Is the employee entitled to ask for all the shares and take responsibility for settling the tax liability either through deduction from salary or making a payment to the entity or to the tax authorities?
- Is the employee unable to receive cash from the arrangements (i.e. any cash paid is paid only to the tax authorities)?

If the answer to both of these questions is yes, the arrangements can be assumed to be equity-settled. If the answer to either question is no, the particular facts and circumstances should be considered and may indicate that the arrangements should be treated as partly cash-settled.

8 Disclosure and presentation

Paragraphs 44 to 52 of IFRS 2 give detailed disclosure requirements for share-based payments. The main requirements are summarised below. Additional information should be disclosed if the detailed information required to be disclosed by the IFRS does not satisfy the principles in paragraphs 44, 46 and 50 of the Standard (see **8.1**, **8.2** and **8.3** below). [IFRS 2.52]

Where separate financial statements of the parent are presented using IFRSs, these disclosures will be required for both the parent entity's separate financial statements and for the consolidated financial statements of the group. Some of the disclosures (e.g. regarding the nature of the schemes and the option pricing models used) will be common to both and need not be repeated. However, some details (e.g. regarding the numerical details of the number of options outstanding, etc.) will have to be given separately for the parent entity as well as for the group.

8.1 Nature and extent of share-based payments

An entity should disclose information that enables users of the financial statements to understand the nature and extent of share-based payment arrangements that existed during the period. [IFRS 2.44] To give effect to this principle, IFRS 2 specifies that at least the following should be disclosed:

[IFRS 2.45]

- a description of each type of share-based payment arrangement that existed at any time during the period, including the general terms and conditions of each arrangement such as:
  - the vesting requirements;
  - the maximum term of options granted; and
  - the method of settlement (e.g. whether in cash or equity).

  An entity with substantially similar types of share-based payment arrangements may aggregate this information, unless separate disclosure of each arrangement is necessary to satisfy the principle in paragraph 44 of the Standard;
- the number and weighted average exercise prices of share options for each of the following groups of options:
  - outstanding at the beginning of the period;
  - granted during the period;
  - forfeited during the period;
  - exercised during the period;

  - expired during the period;
  - outstanding at the end of the period; and
  - exercisable at the end of the period;
- for share options exercised during the period, the weighted average share price at the date of exercise. If options were exercised on a regular basis throughout the period, the weighted average share price during the period may instead be disclosed; and
- for share options outstanding at the end of the period, the range of exercise prices and weighted average contractual life. If the range of exercise prices is wide, the outstanding options should be divided into ranges that are meaningful for assessing the number and timing of additional shares that may be issued and the cash that may be received upon exercise of those options.

As explained at **11.2.1** below, a parent may grant rights to its equity instruments to the employees of its subsidiaries which are conditional upon the completion of continuing service with the group, rather than a specified subsidiary, for a specified period. In accordance with IFRIC 11.9–10, each subsidiary will recognise an expense for the period of service of the employee with that subsidiary and may also need to 'true up' for the outcome of any non-market vesting conditions. The question arises of whether the disclosure requirements described above apply only in relation to the current employees of a subsidiary or extend to former employees who are now employed elsewhere in the group.

When deciding on the appropriate disclosures, regard should be had to the principle in IFRS 2.44 that the information should enable users of the financial statements to understand the nature and extent of share-based payment arrangements that existed during the period. Therefore, disclosures should, at a minimum, deal with options held by employees of the entity during the financial year. The table of options should include a line or column to adjust for the numbers for employees transferring in or out of the entity. On this basis, the number of options outstanding at the end of the period will include only current employees. Employees who have transferred to another subsidiary will be included in that subsidiary's disclosures.

A subsidiary may remain exposed to adjustments to the expense recognised for former employees when there are non-market vesting conditions. This may require disclosure, in some cases, if the effect is expected to be material.

8.2 How fair value is determined

An entity should disclose information that enables users of the financial statements to understand how the fair value of the goods or services received, or the fair value of the equity instruments granted, during the period was determined. [IFRS 2.46]

To give effect to this principle, IFRS 2 specifies that at least the following should be disclosed if the entity has measured the fair value of goods and services received indirectly, by reference to the fair value of the equity instruments granted:

[IFRS 2.47]

- for share options granted during the period, the weighted average fair value of those options at the measurement date and information on how the fair value was measured, including:
  - the option pricing model used and the inputs to that model, including the weighted average share price, exercise price, expected volatility, option life, expected dividends, the risk-free interest rate and any other inputs to the model, including the method used and the assumptions made to incorporate the effects of expected early exercise;
  - how expected volatility was determined, including an explanation of the extent to which it was based on historical volatility; and
  - whether and how any other features of the option grant were incorporated into the measurement of fair value, such as a market condition;
- for other equity instruments granted during the period (i.e. other than share options) the number and weighted average fair value of those equity instruments at the measurement date, and information on how that fair value was determined, including:
  - if the fair value was not measured on the basis of observable market price, how it was determined;
  - whether and how expected dividends were incorporated into the measurement of fair value; and
  - whether and how any other features of the equity instruments granted were incorporated into the measurement of fair value; and
- for share-based payment arrangements that were modified during the period:

- an explanation of those modifications;
- the incremental fair value granted as a result of those modifications; and
- information on how the incremental fair value was measured.

If the entity has measured directly the fair value of goods or services received during the period, disclosure is required of how that fair value was determined (e.g. whether fair value was measured at a market price for those goods or services). [IFRS 2.48]

If the presumption in paragraph 13 of the Standard has been rebutted, that fact should be disclosed together with an explanation of why the presumption was rebutted. The presumption in paragraph 13 is that in the case of transactions with parties other than employees, the fair value of the goods or services received can be estimated reliably (see **4.1** above). [IFRS 2.49]

8.3 Effect of share-based payment transactions on the profit or loss and financial position

An entity should disclose information that enables users of the financial statements to understand the effect of share-based payment transactions on its profit or loss for the period and on its financial position. [IFRS 2.50] To give effect to this principle, IFRS 2 specifies that at least the following should be disclosed:

[IFRS 2.51]

- the total expense recognised for the period arising from share-based payment transactions in which the goods or services received did not qualify for recognition as assets and hence were recognised immediately as an expense, including separate disclosure of that portion of the total expense that arises from transactions accounted for as equity-settled share-based payment transactions; and
- for liabilities arising from share-based payment transactions:
  - the total carrying amount at the end of the period; and
  - the total intrinsic value at the end of the period of liabilities for which the counterparty's right to cash or other assets had vested by the end of the period (e.g. vested share appreciation rights).

8.4 Illustrative disclosures

Illustrative disclosures for share-based payment transactions are included in the IFRS 2 Implementation Guidance at paragraph IG32 and also *iGAAP 2009 Financial statements for UK listed groups*.

8.5 Movements in reserves

8.5.1 Entries arising from IFRS 2

For the IFRS 2 expense, the Standard requires a 'corresponding increase in equity'. There is nothing in IFRSs to require or prohibit the credit entry going to a separate component of equity.

There is also nothing in IFRSs to prevent the credit entry being taken to retained earnings. Paragraph 48W of the Basis for Conclusions to IAS 19 explains that the phrase 'retained earnings' is not a defined term and, in particular, it is not defined as the cumulative total of profit or loss less amounts distributed to owners.

Local legal and regulatory requirements may have to be taken into account when determining the most appropriate treatment. Local legal and regulatory requirements in some jurisdictions may require the credit entry to be regarded as capital and therefore prohibit its inclusion in retained earnings.

UK

In the UK, the preference, in general, for share options that will be settled by a new issue of shares, is to credit the amount back to retained earnings. If the credit is taken to a separate reserve, the balance will accumulate indefinitely as there is no future event that would cause it to be eliminated. The balance does not have any significance other than being the historical accumulation of the IFRS 2 expenses. Another argument to support the credit being taken to retained earnings is that the expense does not reduce distributable profits (see ***5.7.2*** *in* ***chapter 49****).*

A note of legal consideration attached to UITF Abstract 17 confirmed that where new shares are issued in connection with an employee share scheme, the share premium account will normally have to reflect only the cash subscribed for the shares. In such cases, any difference between the cash subscribed for the shares (which must be at least as much as the nominal value because shares cannot be issued at a discount) and the amount recognised as an expense should be credited to reserves other than share

premium account. This is on the basis that the services of the employees do not, as a matter of law, form part of the consideration received for the shares issued.

In other cases it will generally be necessary to take the credit entry arising from IFRS 2 to share capital and share premium. This will, for example, be the case where shares are issued to a supplier for the supply of services. The law requires a share premium to be recognised based on the fair value of the consideration received and this will generally correspond with the expense recognised under IFRS 2.

The position becomes more complicated where an ESOP trust is involved which is often the case with employee share schemes. For example, it may appear to be attractive to take the IFRS 2 credit entry to the 'ESOP reserve' which represents the deduction within equity for own shares held. However, the IFRS 2 credit entry based on grant date fair value is unlikely to equal the purchase price of the shares in the trust less any exercise price, so a difference will build up. These issues are addressed at **8.5.2** below.

8.5.2 *Entries relating to ESOP trusts*

The use of ESOP trusts is considered in **section 10** below. This section considers the accounting entries that may be required within consolidated reserves when an entity's own shares are held by the trust. From the perspective of the consolidated financial statements, such shares are 'treasury shares' and are deducted from equity in accordance with IAS 32.33. In accordance with IAS 32.34, the amount of treasury shares held may be disclosed either in the statement of financial position (e.g. as a separate component of equity) or in the notes (e.g. as a component of retained earnings).

In the UK, most companies show the deduction as a separate reserve, often described as 'ESOP reserve' or simply 'own shares'. The use of the caption 'treasury shares' will not generally be appropriate because it may give the misleading impression that the shares are treasury shares as defined in s724 of the 2006 Act and s162A of the 1985 Act. UK

If the deduction is not shown as a separate reserve (e.g. because it is deducted from the balance of retained earnings), the amount

included should be shown by way of note. It will generally be clearer to use a separate reserve where the amount is material.

For the purposes of the following illustration, it is assumed that a separate ESOP reserve is maintained.

Where shares are purchased in the market by an ESOP trust, they will initially be recorded as a debit to the ESOP reserve for the price paid. For example, assuming that the price paid is £1,000:

Dr	ESOP reserve	£1,000	
Cr	Cash		£1,000

Now if options are granted over these shares with an exercise price of £800, the following entry will be necessary on exercise:

Dr	Cash	£800	
Dr	Retained earnings	£200	
Cr	ESOP reserve		£1,000

This is because it is illogical to leave a balance on the ESOP reserve which relates to shares that are no longer held. The difference must go somewhere and retained earnings will generally be the most appropriate caption.

UK *In the UK, the difference is a realised loss that reduces the company's profits available for distribution. Based on TECH 01/08 (see* ***5.7.1*** *in* ***chapter 49****), this reduction in distributable profits should be regarded as accruing over the vesting period. To avoid the possibility of making an unlawful dividend payment, it may therefore be advisable to make an annual transfer between the ESOP reserve and the profit and loss account reserve. In aggregate, over the vesting period, this entry would be:*

Dr	Retained earnings	£200	
Cr	ESOP reserve		£200

If this entry was made, the balance on the ESOP reserve would be reduced over the vesting period so that it would equal the cash received on exercise:

Dr	Cash	£800	
Cr	ESOP reserve		£800

However, this does not deal with the accounting entries in reserves that may be required by IFRS 2. These are discussed at **8.5.1** above. They will generally involve a credit to equity equal to the expense

recognised. This credit will usually be taken to retained earnings but there is nothing to prohibit it from being credited to a separate reserve.

It may be tempting to take this credit entry to the ESOP reserve where one exists and the options are to be satisfied by using the shares held by the trust. But, in practice, this does not generally make sense. The credit entry is based on fair value at grant date and is unlikely to coincide with the difference between the purchase price of the shares by the trust and the option exercise price (if any). Therefore, taking the credit entry to the ESOP reserve would be likely to result in that reserve increasing each year and never being eliminated. It is therefore generally preferable for the credit entry arising from IFRS 2 to be taken to retained earnings and for the effects of any purchase of own shares through the ESOP trust to be considered separately.

9 Employee share ownership plans (ESOPs)

ESOP trusts, created by a sponsoring entity for employees, are designed to facilitate employee shareholding and are often used as vehicles for distributing shares to employees under remuneration schemes. The detailed structures of individual trusts are many and varied, as are the reasons for establishing them.

Reasons for establishing ESOPs include the following although it should be noted that some of these are not permitted in some jurisdictions:

- to fund a matching programme for a sponsor's defined contribution plan or other employee benefits:
- to raise new capital or to create a marketplace for existing shares;
- to replace lost benefits from the termination of other employee benefit plans or to provide benefits under post-retirement plans (particularly medical benefits);
- to be part of the financing package in leveraged buy-outs;

- to provide tax-advantaged means for owners to terminate ownership;
- to be part of a long-term programme to restructure the equity section of a sponsor's statement of financial position; and
- to defend the entity against a hostile takeover.

ESOPs can be leveraged or non-leveraged. In a leveraged ESOP, the plan borrows money to purchase shares, usually guaranteed by the sponsor.

UK

In the UK, ESOP trusts have been widely used in connection with employee share schemes. To a large extent the need for such trusts was driven by the legal prohibition on companies owning their own shares or their parent company's shares. This prohibition was partially relaxed in December 2003 and some companies can hold 'treasury shares' without cancelling them, subject to various restrictions (see ***chapter 49****). Nevertheless, the use of ESOP trusts remains widespread in the UK.*

The provision of finance to an ESOP trust to facilitate the purchase of the company's own shares, or those of a parent company, is covered by the statutory prohibition on the provision of financial assistance for the acquisition of own shares. However, there is an exemption where the assistance is provided in good faith in the interests of the company for the purposes of an employee share scheme. Therefore, it can be seen that some of the reasons listed above for establishing ESOP trusts would be unlawful in the UK. The statutory prohibition on the provision of financial assistance is repealed for private companies under the 2006 Act with effect from 1 October 2008. However, the rules continue to apply to public companies and subsidiaries of public companies.

The IFRIC was asked by the IASB to consider whether the scope exclusion in SIC-12 *Consolidation – Special Purpose Entities* (see **chapter 33**) for equity compensation plans should be removed when IFRS 2 became effective. Prior to IFRS 2 becoming effective, these plans were within the scope of IAS 19, although the Standard did not specify any recognition and measurement requirements for such benefits. Once IFRS 2 became effective, IAS 19 no longer applied to equity compensation plans. Also, IFRS 2 amended IAS 32 so that its requirement to deduct treasury shares from equity also applies to shares purchased, sold, issued or cancelled in connection with employee share option plans, employee share purchase plans and all other share-based payment arrangements.

The IFRIC concluded that, to ensure consistency with IFRS 2 and IAS 32, the scope of SIC-12 should be amended to remove the scope exclusion for equity compensation plans. This proposal was approved and issued in final form in November 2004. The amendment was effective for annual periods beginning on or after 1 January 2005 (i.e. the same as IFRS 2). The Press Release issued by the IASB on publication of the amendment commented that, as a consequence of the amendment 'an entity that controls an employee benefit trust (or similar entity) set up for the purposes of a share-based payment arrangement will be required to consolidate that trust'.

When considering the amendment to SIC-12 to remove the exemption for equity compensation plans, the IFRIC noted that there were further issues about such arrangements that might be considered. These included the question of whether the arrangements should be accounted for by consolidation or by inclusion in the separate financial statements of the sponsoring entity. However, this matter is not on the IFRIC's current agenda and, in the absence of further clarification from the IFRIC, it is reasonable to assume that, at least in some circumstances, accounting for trust assets and liabilities may be required only in the consolidated financial statements (see also the discussion below and at **3.3.2** in **chapter 33**).

UK

Under UK GAAP, there has been a requirement to account for the assets and liabilities of an ESOP trust in the financial statements of the sponsoring company since 1995. This requirement was originally in UITF Abstract 13 which was superseded by UITF Abstract 38 for periods ending on or after 22 June 2004. Abstract 38 changed the treatment of investments in own shares so that they are presented as a deduction in arriving at shareholders' funds, rather than as assets, which is consistent with the requirements of IAS 32. However, both Abstracts are based on the principle that the sponsoring company of an ESOP trust should recognise certain assets and liabilities of the trust as its own whenever it has de facto control of the shares held by the trust and bears their benefits and risks.

Therefore, under UK GAAP, the assets and liabilities (and deduction for own shares) are recorded in the separate financial statements of the sponsoring company. This is a different approach from that under IFRSs which may require ESOP trusts to be included in consolidated financial statements only. This will have no effect on the consolidated financial statements of UK groups but will have a beneficial effect on profits available for distribution where the investment in own shares is not reflected in the separate financial statements of the sponsoring company.

Trusts created by a sponsoring entity for employees are designated to facilitate employee shareholdings and often used as vehicles for distributing shares to employees under remuneration schemes. The sponsoring entity must consolidate these trusts if the sponsoring entity has control over them. As noted above, IAS 27 *Consolidated and Separate Financial Statements* and SIC-12 contain the primary criteria for determining whether the entity has control over an ESOP trust. In addition to those factors, the following indicators may also provide evidence of control over the trust. However, no one factor, or the absence of one factor, is a determinant of control, or absence of control, without a complete analysis of all the relevant facts and circumstances.

Indicators of control:

- the trust is designed to serve the purposes of the sponsoring entity – that is to compensate the sponsoring entity's employees;
- the sponsoring entity appoints trustees to the trust;
- trustees usually act on advice from the sponsoring entity, e.g. letter of wishes indicating how funds of the trust might be allocated;
- the assets of the trust can be recaptured by the sponsoring entity or its creditors (e.g. in a bankruptcy situation);
- the liabilities of the trust are guaranteed by the sponsoring entity;
- the assets of the trust revert to the sponsoring entity if shares do not vest;
- the sponsoring entity determines the level of future funding to the trust;
- the sponsoring entity has a practice of buying shares from the trust (instead of requiring the trust to sell the shares on the market to be able to pay the employee who wants to exercise his/her right);
- the sponsoring entity determines the allocation of shares to employees;

- the sponsoring entity provides guarantees (or other contracts) to protect the trust from liquidity risks;
- at the end of the life of the trust, any surplus in the trust is to be paid to the entity, and any shortfall owing to the entity will constitute a loss by it (or the subsidiaries);
- if the trust makes any profit during a year (with its portfolio), this profit is ceded to the sponsoring entity; and
- the sponsoring entity guarantees a minimum value of the shares.

When a sponsoring entity has control, the assets, liabilities and treasury shares should be recognised in the consolidated financial statements, and:

- consideration paid or received for the purchase or sale of the entity's own shares in a trust should be shown as separate amounts in the reconciliation of movements in equity;
- no gain or loss should be recognised in profit or loss on purchase, sale, issue or cancellation of the entity's own shares;
- finance costs and any administration expenses should be charged as they accrue and not as funding payments are made to the trust; and
- any dividend income on the entity's own shares should be excluded in determining profit before tax and deducted from the aggregate of dividends paid and proposed.

Sufficient information should be disclosed in the financial statements of the sponsoring entity to enable readers to understand the significance of the trust in the context of the sponsoring entity.

Some of the factors listed above would not be applicable in the UK because they would be contrary to trust law. In practice, it is likely that those entities that are regarded as ESOP trusts for the purposes of UITF Abstract 38 (or employee benefit trusts within the scope of UITF Abstract 32) will be regarded as Special Purpose Entities under SIC-12 in virtually all cases. UK

10 Employment taxes on share-based payments

In some jurisdictions, employment taxes may be payable which are determined by reference to the gain made by the employee on the exercise of shares options. Such payments of tax are outside the scope of IFRS 2 because they are not payments to the suppliers of goods or services.

When the amount of tax is based on the gain made by the employee (i.e. intrinsic value at exercise date) the following issues may arise:

- does the entity have a liability before the employee exercises the options; and
- if so, how should that liability be measured at the end of each reporting period.

These are similar to the questions addressed in IFRS 2 for cash-settled share-based payments. A liability should therefore be recognised at the end of each reporting period for such tax. This is consistent with the requirements of IAS 37 as well as IFRS 2 because the 'obligating event' is the granting of the options by the entity rather than the exercise of them by the employees. The liability could be measured on the same basis as required by IFRS 2 although it is acceptable to use intrinsic value at the end of the reporting period rather than fair value determined using an option pricing model, given that the liability is outside the scope of IFRS 2. Measuring the liability at fair value in accordance with IFRS 2 is nevertheless to be preferred. Under IFRSs, staff costs generally are within the scope of IAS 19 and that Standard recognises staff costs over the period that services are provided. Therefore, in the absence of any conflicting interpretation by the IFRIC, the liability could be built up over the vesting period.

UK *In the UK, this issue is addressed in UITF Abstract 25* National insurance contributions on share option gains. *The UITF reached a consensus that provision should be made for National Insurance contributions (NIC) on outstanding share options that are expected to be exercised. It should be calculated at the latest enacted NIC rate applied to the difference between the market value of the underlying shares at the balance sheet date and the option exercise price and allocated over the period from the date of grant to the end of the performance/service period. From that date to the actual date of exercise, the provision is adjusted by using the current market value of the shares. Where there is no performance period, full provision is made immediately.*

Under IFRSs, staff costs generally are within the scope of IAS 19 and that Standard recognises staff costs over the period that services are provided. Therefore, in the absence of any conflicting interpretation by IFRIC, Abstract 25 might be seen as relevant guidance to follow. Abstract 25 was not withdrawn when the requirements of IFRS 2 were implemented in the UK through FRS 20. Therefore, unless the ASB or UITF reconsiders this issue, companies reporting under UK GAAP will be required to continue to comply with Abstract 25 even if they are reporting share-based payment transactions under FRS 20.

The charge to NIC arises only on certain share options, in particular those granted after 5 April 1999 under 'unapproved' share option schemes. The question of whether a liability arises in connection with a particular scheme is a matter of tax law rather than financial reporting. However, the NIC charge arises only where the shares are deemed to be 'readily convertible assets'. That is, they can be sold on a stock exchange or alternative arrangements exist enabling employees to obtain cash for shares. This condition is applied when the options are exercised rather than when they are granted. Therefore NIC may become payable in respect of outstanding share options as a result of an IPO. The issue arises of whether it is necessary to make a provision for NIC in financial statements that are approved prior to the IPO. This issue was not addressed in Abstract 25. Under UK GAAP, the approach has generally been to consider whether the IPO is probable at the date of approval of the financial statements.

11 Accounting by entities within groups

As explained at **2.2** above, it is often the case that employees of a subsidiary will receive part of their remuneration in the form of the shares in the parent, or less commonly in some other group entity. Where this is the case, IFRS 2 requires the entity that has received the benefit of the services to recognise the expense. This is so even if the equity instruments issued are those of another entity within the group. However, IFRS 2 provides no further guidance on the issues that arise from applying IFRS 2 to the individual entities within the group.

Further guidance is provided in IFRIC 11 *IFRS 2 – Group and Treasury Share Transactions* and is addressed in **11.1** and **11.2** below. Although IFRIC 11 focuses on transactions with employees, it also applies to similar share-based payment transactions with other suppliers of goods or services. [IFRIC 11.6]

IFRIC 11 applies to periods beginning on or after 1 March 2007, with earlier application permitted. IFRIC 11 must be applied retrospectively in accordance with IAS 8, subject to the transitional provisions of IFRS 2. [IFRIC 11.13]

11.1 Share-based payment arrangements involving an entity's own equity instruments

The first issue addressed by IFRIC 11 is whether the following transactions should be accounted for as equity-settled or cash-settled under the requirements of IFRS 2:

[IFRIC 11.1]

- an entity grants to its employees rights to equity instruments of the entity (e.g. share options) and either chooses or is required (either by contract or necessity) to buy equity instruments (i.e. treasury shares) from another party, to satisfy its obligation to its employees; and
- an entity's employees are granted rights to equity instruments of the entity (e.g. share options), either by the entity itself or by its shareholders, and the shareholders of the entity provide the equity instruments needed.

Share-based payment transactions in which an entity receives services as consideration for its own equity instruments are accounted for as equity-settled. IFRIC 11 confirms that this applies regardless of whether the entity chooses or is required to buy those equity instruments from another party to satisfy its obligations to its employees. This also applies regardless of whether:

[IFRIC 11.7]

- the employee's rights to the entity's equity instruments were granted by the entity itself or by its shareholders; or
- the share-based payment arrangement was settled by the entity or by its shareholders.

These requirements of IFRIC 11 are straightforward and simply remove any residual doubt that such transactions should be accounted for as equity-settled even though the entity may not itself issue or transfer any equity instruments as part of the transaction.

IFRIC 11.BC6 notes that an entity should recognise a separate financial liability when it enters into a contractual arrangement to acquire its own equity instruments. This is not dealt with in IFRIC 11 because the requirements of IAS 32 were thought to be clear in this respect.

11.2 Share-based payment arrangements involving equity instruments of the parent

The second issue addressed by IFRIC 11 concerns share-based payment arrangements that involve two or more entities within the same group. For example, the employees of a subsidiary may be granted rights to equity instruments of its parent as consideration for the services they provide to the subsidiary. It is clear from IFRS 2.3 that such arrangements are within the scope of IFRS 2. However, the Standard does not give guidance on how to account for such transactions in the individual or separate financial statements of each group entity. [IFRC 11(2)]

IFRIC 11 addresses the following share-based payment arrangements:

[IFRIC 11.3]

- a parent grants rights to its equity instruments direct to the employees of its subsidiary so that the parent (and not the subsidiary) has the obligation to provide the employees of the subsidiary with the equity instruments needed (addressed in **11.2.1** below); and
- a subsidiary grants rights to equity instruments of its parent to its employees so that the subsidiary (and not the parent) has the obligation to provide its employees with the equity instruments needed (addressed in **11.2.2** below).

IFRIC 11 assumes that it is clear whether the parent or the subsidiary granted the rights to equity instruments and prescribes a different accounting treatment in each case. It may not, in practice, be clear which entity in a group granted the rights to the employees. Often this is done by mutual agreement between the subsidiary and the parent. How to apply IFRIC 11 in these circumstances is considered at **11.2.3** below.

IFRIC 11 does not address the accounting in the parent (which is considered at **11.3** below); nor does it address accounting for any intragroup payments that may be made in the scenarios described (addressed in **11.4** below). However, it does state that classification of the share-based arrangement is not affected by the existence (or otherwise) of payment arrangements between a subsidiary and parent.

11.2.1 *A parent grants rights to its equity to employees of its subsidiary*

Where a parent grants rights to its equity instruments to employees of its subsidiary and the arrangement is accounted for as equity-settled in the consolidated financial statements, the subsidiary should in its own separate financial statements measure the services received from its employees in accordance with the requirements of IFRS 2 applicable to equity-settled share-based payment transactions. There will be a corresponding increase recognised in equity as a capital contribution from the parent. [IFRIC 11.8]

IFRIC 11.BC8 explains that from the perspective of the subsidiary, such a transaction does not meet the definition of either an equity-settled transaction or a cash-settled transaction in IFRS 2. The IFRIC concluded that it is not appropriate to account for such an arrangement as cash-settled in the subsidiary's financial statements because the subsidiary does not have an obligation to deliver cash or other assets to its employees. The IFRIC concluded that the equity-settled basis was more consistent with the principles of IFRS 2.

This requirement of IFRIC 11 is straightforward to apply. The expense recognised in the consolidated financial statements is 'pushed down' into the accounts of the relevant subsidiaries that receive the services of the employees.

Example 11.2.1

Parent grants rights to its equity to employees of its subsidiary

P grants 100 of S's employees 30 shares in P each, provided that they remain in employment for 3 years and provided that S meets a particular profit target. The fair value on grant date is £5 per share. Assume that at the outset, and at the end of years 1 and 2, it is expected that the profit target will be met and that no employees leave.

At the end of year 3, the profit target is met.

Accounting by S

In years 1–3, S will record an IFRS 2 charge in profit or loss, and a corresponding entry in equity which reflects the capital contribution it is receiving from P:

Dr	Profit or loss	5,000	(£5 x 30 x 100 / 3 years)	
Cr	Equity (capital contribution)			5,000

S makes no further entries when the shares are provided to the employees by its parent.

There is no requirement in IFRSs to credit the capital contribution to a separate component of equity. Therefore, it may be credited to retained earnings if this is permitted in the legal jurisdiction in which S operates (see general discussion of this issue at **8.5** above).

In the UK, the credit entry will be a realised profit and so there is no net impact on distributable reserves of accounting for the equity-settled share-based payment in accordance with IFRS 2. UK

A parent may grant rights to its equity instruments to the employees of its subsidiaries which are conditional upon the completion of continuing service with the group (rather than a specified subsidiary) for a specified period. An employee may therefore transfer employment from one subsidiary to another during the specified vesting period without the employee's rights under the arrangements being affected. Where this is the case, each subsidiary measures the services received from its employee by reference to the fair value of the equity instruments at the date when the rights were originally granted by the parent and the proportion of the vesting period served by the employee with that subsidiary. [IFRIC 11.9]

Such an employee, after transferring between group entities, may fail to satisfy a vesting condition (e.g. the employee may leave the group before completing the required period of service) other than a market condition. In this case, each subsidiary adjusts the amount previously recognised in respect of the services received from the employee in accordance with IFRS 2.19. Consequently, if the rights to equity instruments do not vest because of a failure to meet a vesting condition (other than a market condition), no amount is recognised on a cumulative basis for the services received from that employee in the financial statements of both subsidiaries. [IFRIC 11.10]

This requirement for all affected entities to 'true up' at vesting date means that a subsidiary may need to make adjustments to its share-based payment expense several years after an employee has transferred elsewhere within the group.

IFRIC 11 does not address the effect of employees transferring between group entities for cash-settled arrangements. Guidance on this issue is provided at **11.5** below.

11.2.2 *A subsidiary grants rights to equity instruments of its parent to its employees*

Where the subsidiary grants rights to equity instruments of its parent to employees, the subsidiary accounts for the transaction with its employees as cash-settled. This requirement applies irrespective of how the subsidiary obtains the equity instruments to satisfy the obligations to its employees. [IFRIC 11.11]

IFRIC 11.BC13 explains that from the perspective of the subsidiary, such a transaction does not meet the definition of either an equity-settled transaction or a cash-settled transaction in IFRS 2. The IFRIC concluded that accounting for this transaction as cash-settled is more consistent with the principles of IFRS 2 because the subsidiary has an obligation to provide its employees with equity instruments of the parent, which are treated as assets of the subsidiary when acquired by the subsidiary. The practical implications of accounting for arrangements as cash-settled in the subsidiary while they are equity-settled from the perspective of the group are considered further at **11.7** below.

IFRIC 11 does not address the accounting required in the subsidiary when it has recognised a liability for an arrangement as cash-settled but subsequently makes no cash payment because the parent provides the shares without any reimbursement. IFRS 2 addresses transactions with settlement alternatives (see **section 7** above) but these do not apply to this situation because they envisage only the grantor of the rights or the counterparty having the choice, whereas in this case the choice lies with a third party – the parent. If the parent satisfies the subsidiary's obligation, the liability will be removed from the statement of financial position of the subsidiary with the credit recognised in equity as a capital contribution from the parent. The expense recognised in respect of the services received is not reversed.

11.2.3 *Determining which entity has granted the rights*

To apply the requirements of IFRIC 11 set out at **11.2.1** and **11.2.2** above, it will be necessary to determine which entity in the group granted the rights to the employees. This will require a careful assessment of the particular facts and circumstances. The factors to be considered include but are not limited to:

- the contractual terms of the share scheme;

- any formal documentation provided to the employees that are granted the rights;
- any other communications provided to employees;
- whether the scheme is specific to one subsidiary or covers a number of subsidiaries within a group; and
- any other aspects of the arrangements, whether formally documented or not.

As explained above, IFRIC 11 states that the arrangements should be accounted for as cash-settled by the subsidiary where it is the subsidiary that has granted the rights, irrespective of how the subsidiary obtains the equity instruments to satisfy the obligation to the employees.

UK

In the UK, it will be common that arrangements accounted for as equity-settled in the consolidated financial statements will also be accounted for as equity-settled in a subsidiary. Share schemes are often set up by a group of companies and rights are then granted to employees of subsidiaries as part of that group scheme. Share schemes set up by listed companies are generally subject to approval by shareholders of the listed parent company. The management of any subsidiary would be unlikely to have the power to grant rights under the scheme autonomously without approval by the parent company.

However, there may be cases where the subsidiary has set up a share scheme independently of its parent company and is clearly obliged to purchase shares in the market to satisfy the obligations into which it has entered. This might, for example, be the case where a UK subsidiary sets up a UK share scheme with little or no involvement by a foreign parent.

Each case should be judged carefully on its merits.

11.3 Accounting in the parent's separate financial statements

IFRIC 11 addresses whether arrangements that are accounted for as equity-settled in the consolidated financial statements should be accounted for as equity-settled or cash-settled in the financial statements of the subsidiary. It does not address the accounting in the parent entity.

The illustrative example accompanying IFRIC D17 (the exposure draft upon which IFRIC 11 was based) included entries in separate financial statements of the parent. These entries are omitted from the illustrative example accompanying IFRIC 11 because IFRIC decided that accounting by the parent entity was outside of the scope of the Interpretation. The illustrative example accompanying D17 dealt with the case where the parent has granted the rights so that the arrangement is equity-settled for both the group and the subsidiary but it is possible to apply the same principles in other cases (see **11.3.1** to **11.3.3** below).

11.3.1 *Equity-settled for the group and the subsidiary*

The illustrative example accompanying D17 suggested that the parent should record an entry each year to debit the cost of investment in subsidiary and credit equity with an amount equal to the expense recognised in the subsidiary in accordance with IFRS 2. This was not explained in the Basis for Conclusions which accompanied D17 but the rationale was that the parent had made a capital contribution to the subsidiary (assuming the subsidiary has not paid fair value as the reimbursement to the parent) by taking on the cost of remunerating the subsidiary's employees that the subsidiary would otherwise have had to bear, and had also granted an equity instrument in accepting the obligation to those employees. This is consistent with the credit to equity recognised in the subsidiary which IFRIC 11 refers to as 'contribution from parent'. It is understood that the entry illustrated in D17 was not explained or justified because the members of the IFRIC regarded it as uncontentious generally accepted practice. Such an entry should be recorded as a necessary consequence of the requirement to follow GAAP.

Increasing the cost of investment in a subsidiary may in rare cases give rise to impairment issues and this should be considered where appropriate.

UK *In the UK the credit to equity in the parent will not be a realised profit and will not therefore be available for distribution. This is because the credit to equity is represented by an increase in the cost of the investment in the subsidiary which will not meet the definition of 'qualifying consideration' in TECH 01/08. Therefore, it may be desirable to take the credit to a separate non-distributable reserve rather than to retained earnings to avoid the possibility that it will inadvertently be distributed as a dividend.*

Example 11.3.1A

Equity-settled for the group and the subsidiary (1)

The facts are the same as in **example 11.2.1** above.

Accounting by P

In years 1–3, P will record the enhancement to its investment in S, and a corresponding entry in equity which reflects the capital contribution being made to S and the equity instrument being granted to S's employees:

Dr	Cost of investment	5,000	
Cr	Equity		5,000

P will have to make further entries when it transfers the shares to the employees. These entries will depend on whether P issues new shares or utilises shares purchased in the market and held as treasury shares. The entries may also be affected by the involvement of an ESOP trust.

In the same way that the subsidiary will true up the IFRS 2 expense to reflect changes in non-market vesting conditions, so will the parent 'true up' its contributions to the subsidiary. This will usually result in symmetrical accounting for the capital contribution between the parent and subsidiary.

Example 11.3.1B

Equity-settled for the group and the subsidiary (2)

The facts are the same as in **example 11.2.1** above except that at the end of year 3, the profit target is not met.

Accounting by P

In years 1 and 2, P will record an enhancement to its investment in S, and a corresponding entry in equity which reflects the capital contribution being made to S and the equity instrument being granted to S's employees:

Dr	Cost of investment	5,000	
Cr	Equity		5,000

At the end of year 3, the profit target is not met, so P must true up the amounts recorded to reflect the non-market vesting condition not being met:

Dr	Equity	10,000	
Cr	Cost of investment		10,000

This true up in P therefore mirrors the accounting entries posted by S.

11.3.2 *Cash-settled for the group and the subsidiary*

There are two different scenarios in which a scheme might be accounted for as cash-settled both by the group and by the subsidiary. The first is where the subsidiary itself has the obligation to transfer cash or other assets (other than equity instruments of the group) to its employees. The second is where the parent has the obligation to transfer cash or other assets (other than equity instruments of the group) to its subsidiary's employees.

No accounting is required by the parent when the subsidiary has the obligation to its employees and makes a cash payment to satisfy the obligation. Where the parent makes a cash payment to satisfy the obligation of its subsidiary, the parent records the amount of the cash payment as a capital contribution, increasing the cost of investment in its subsidiary. Such arrangements are considered further at **11.5** below.

Where the parent has the obligation to its subsidiary's employees, it will need to record a liability in accordance with IFRS 2, and should record the other side of the entry as an increase in the cost of investment in its subsidiary, as it is effectively making a capital contribution by taking on the liability on behalf of its subsidiary.

11.3.3 *Equity-settled for the group but cash-settled for the subsidiary*

No accounting is required by the parent when the subsidiary has the obligation to its employees and satisfies that obligation, for example by purchasing its parent's shares in the market.

Assuming that no formal intragroup settlement arrangements were in place, where the parent subsequently provides shares to the subsidiary's employees for no consideration, the subsidiary records the credit arising from derecognition of the liability as a capital contribution in equity (see **11.3.2** above). There are two possible views on the amount that should be recognised as a capital contribution by the parent:

- the equity-settled amount recognised in the consolidated financial statements; or

- the cash-settled amount recognised in the subsidiary's financial statements.

Where the parent has not made a cash payment but has issued equity securities to satisfy the obligation, some might argue that the credit to equity in the parent's separate financial statements should be the same as the equivalent credit in the consolidated financial statements because they relate to the same equity instrument.

The second view is, however, more logical and consistent with IFRIC 11. The reasoning implicit in IFRIC 11 means that, although the group has created an equity instrument at grant date, the parent has not; instead, the parent first creates an equity instrument when it actually issues the shares. Moreover, the parent has relieved the subsidiary of its obligation, which means the contribution received by the subsidiary equals the amount of the obligation recorded in its financial statements. Thus, it is this amount that should be recognised by the parent.

Practical application of these principles is considered further at **11.7** below.

11.4 Accounting for intragroup recharges

The IFRIC discussed whether IFRIC 11 should address how to account for an intragroup payment arrangement under which the subsidiary pays the parent for the provision of equity instruments to the employees. As explained in IFRIC 11.BC12, IFRIC decided not to address the issue because it did not wish to widen the scope of the Interpretation to an issue that relates to the accounting for intragroup payment arrangements generally.

The illustrative example accompanying IFRIC D17 (the exposure draft upon which IFRIC 11 is based) included guidance on this issue. This guidance is omitted from the illustrative example accompanying IFRIC 11.

The illustrative example accompanying D17 indicated that if the parent levies an intragroup recharge on the subsidiary, the amount of that recharge is offset against the capital contribution arising from the share-based payment in the individual and separate financial statements of the subsidiary and in any separate financial statements of the parent. It also indicated that if the amount of the recharge exceeds the capital contribution, that excess is accounted for as a distribution from the subsidiary to the parent. Thus, in effect, IFRIC D17 proposed to account for any difference between share-based payment expense and reimbursement as a transaction with shareholders (i.e. a capital contribution or distribution).

The same logic applies irrespective of whether an arrangement is an equity-settled share-based payment arrangement or a cash-settled one.]

There is no specific requirement in IFRS literature to present intragroup recharges of share-based payments in this way, but the net approach illustrated in IFRIC D17 appears reasonable and has been used as the basis for the guidance set out below. Nevertheless, other approaches may also be acceptable, provided that they do not misstate the amount of share-based payment expense recognised. For example, an entity may elect to account separately for services received (as a capital contribution) and for payments made (as a distribution), without offsetting the two. Moreover, when the amount payable to the parent is conditional on share awards vesting, a reimbursement obligation might be accounted for as a derivative financial instrument. Whatever the approach adopted, careful judgement should be applied to ensure that the accounting properly reflects the substance of the arrangement.

Some complexities may arise if the timing of the intragroup charges is different from the recognition of the expense under IFRS 2. For example, it is possible that the charge might be levied only when the options are exercised by the employees. Some of these issues are considered in the illustrative examples below.

When the recharge made exceeds the expense recognised in accordance with IFRS 2, as will typically be the case when the charge is based on the intrinsic value on exercise of options, the excess will be accounted for as a distribution. Consequently, it will not be recognised as an expense in the subsidiary's financial statements, but will be recognised as income in the parent entity.

The fact that the excess recharge will be accounted for as a distribution does not necessarily mean that it will be a distribution as a matter of law. The position may vary according to the legal jurisdiction. Legal advice should be sought when necessary.

UK *In the UK, TECH 01/08 (7.54) confirms that the accounting treatment of any such charge does not affect whether or not it is a distribution as a matter*

of law. Any excess charge will not be a distribution as a matter of law if there is a commercial basis for the charge. An example of a commercial basis would be where the charge is the amount of the expense that the subsidiary would have incurred if it had purchased the shares in the market to satisfy the obligation. Consequently, it will not be unlawful for the subsidiary to make the reimbursement payment, even in the absence of distributable profits, provided that the payment is not a distribution as a matter of law.

The following examples distinguish between circumstances when there is a right to reimbursement and circumstances when there is no such right. A right to reimbursement may exist in the absence of a written contract. For example, it may exist when the clear intention of the parties, when the share-based payment arrangement is established, is that reimbursement will occur and the basis for calculating the amount of that reimbursement is also agreed at that time.

Example 11.4A

Reimbursement over the term of the arrangement

A parent P (P) grants 30 of its shares to each of 100 employees of its subsidiary (S), provided that the employees remain employed by S for 3 years. Assume that at the outset, and at the end of years 1 and 2, it is expected that all of the employees will remain employed for the full 3 years. At the end of year 3, none of the employees have left. The fair value of the shares on grant date is £5 per share.

S agrees to reimburse P, over the term of the arrangement, 75 per cent of the final charge reflected in S's profit or loss. Over that period, S expects to recognise a charge totalling £15,000, and therefore expects to reimburse P £11,250 (£15,000 x 75 per cent). S therefore reimburses P £3,750 (£11,250 / 3) each year.

Illustrated below is one of several acceptable approaches for accounting for recharges of share-based payment costs in the individual financial statements of the parent and subsidiary.

Accounting by S

In years 1 – 3, S will recognise an IFRS 2 expense in profit or loss, the cash paid to P, and the balance of the capital contribution it has received from P:

Dr	Profit or loss	5,000	
Cr	Cash		3,750
Cr	Equity (capital contribution)		1,250

Accounting by P

In years 1 – 3, P will recognise an entry to equity for the instruments being granted, the cash reimbursed by S, and the balance of the capital contribution it has made to S:

Dr	Cost of investment	1,250	
Cr	Cash		3,750
Cr	Equity		5,000

Example 11.4B

Reimbursement (if any) at the end of the arrangement – no right to reimbursement

The facts are as in **example 11.4A**, except that, before vesting, there was no right to reimbursement. At the end of the arrangement (i.e. when the shares vest), S agreed to pay P 75 per cent of the final charge reflected in S's statement of comprehensive income.

Illustrated below is one of several acceptable approaches for accounting for recharges of share-based payment costs in the individual financial statements of the parent and subsidiary.

Accounting by S

In years 1 – 3, S will recognise the IFRS 2 expense in profit or loss and a capital contribution from P:

Dr	Profit or loss	5,000	
Cr	Equity (capital contribution)		5,000

At the end of year 3, all the shares will vest and S will pay P £11,250. The payment is treated as a distribution to P:

Dr	Equity (distribution)	11,250	
Cr	Cash		11,250

Accounting by P

In years 1 – 3, P will recognise an entry to equity for the instruments being granted and the capital contribution made to S:

Dr	Cost of investment	5,000	
Cr	Equity		5,000

At the end of year 3, all the shares will vest and S will pay P £11,250. The payment is treated as dividend income by P and will be accounted for in accordance with IAS 27:

Dr	Cash	11,250	
Cr	Dividend income		11,250

When necessary, P should also recognise an impairment loss for the cost of its investment in S.

Example 11.4C

Reimbursement at the end of the arrangement – right to reimbursement

The facts are as in **example 11.4A**, except that, on grant date, S and P enter into a binding agreement under which S will reimburse P 75 per cent of the

final charge reflected in S's profit or loss. The payment will be made at the end of the arrangement (i.e. when the shares vest).

Illustrated below is one of several acceptable approaches for accounting for recharges of share-based payment costs in the individual financial statements of the parent and subsidiary.

Accounting by S

In years 1 – 3, S will recognise the IFRS 2 expense in profit or loss, a payable for 75 per cent of this amount, and a capital contribution from P for the balance:

Dr	Profit or loss	5,000	
Cr	Intragroup payables		3,750
Cr	Equity (capital contribution)		1,250

At the end of year 3, all the shares will vest and S will pay P £11,250, settling the liability recognised.

Dr	Intragroup payables	11,250	
Cr	Cash		11,250

Accounting by P

In years 1 – 3, P will recognise an entry to equity for the instruments being granted and a receivable from S:

Dr	Intragroup receivables	3,750	
Dr	Cost of investment	1,250	
Cr	Equity		5,000

At the end of year 3, all the shares will vest and S will pay P £11,250:

Dr	Cash	11,250	
Cr	Intragroup receivables		11,250

For simplicity, this example assumes that any effect of discounting would not be material. When reimbursement balances are very large, consideration should be given to whether any discounting might be necessary.

A common situation is where the reimbursement is made based on the intrinsic value on vesting (or on actual exercise in the case of options). This will often result in a reimbursement that exceeds the grant date fair value recognised under IFRS 2. The excess of the amount of the reimbursement over the IFRS 2 expense will be accounted for as a distribution by the subsidiary. This is illustrated in the following example. For the sake of simplicity, it has been assumed that there is no entitlement to the reimbursement and that it is therefore accounted for only when made. Otherwise it would be necessary for S to estimate the amount of the accrued reimbursement to be recognised at the end of each reporting period.

Example 11.4D

Reimbursement at the end of the arrangement equal to the intrinsic value at that date – no right to reimbursement

The facts are as in **example 12.4A**, except that S pays P at the end of the arrangement an amount equal to the intrinsic value at that date. This amount is assumed to be £25,000.

Accounting by S

In years 1 – 3, S will recognise the IFRS 2 expense in profit or loss and a capital contribution from P:

Dr	Profit or loss	5,000	
Cr	Equity (capital contribution)		5,000

At the end of year 3, all the shares will vest and S will pay P £25,000. The payment is treated as a distribution by P.

Dr	Equity (distribution)	25,000	
Cr	Cash		25,000

Accounting by P

In years 1 – 3, P will recognise an entry to equity for the instruments being granted and the capital contribution made to S:

Dr	Cost of investment	5,000	
Cr	Equity		5,000

At the end of year 3, all the shares will vest and S will pay P £25,000. The payment is treated as dividend income by P, and will be accounted for in accordance with IAS 27.

Dr	Cash	25,000	
Cr	Profit or loss (distribution from subsidiary)		25,000

When necessary, P should also recognise an impairment loss for the cost of its investment in S.

11.5 Cash-settled arrangements in the consolidated financial statements

IFRIC 11 deals with the case when share-based payment arrangements are accounted for as equity-settled in the consolidated financial statements but may be cash-settled from the perspective of a subsidiary. It does not include any requirements in the case where the arrangement is accounted for as cash-settled in the consolidated financial statements. The IASB is now proposing to address this issue (see **12.1** below).

The position is straightforward in the simple case when the subsidiary has the obligation to its employee and makes a cash payment to

satisfy the obligation. The expense recognised in the consolidated financial statements and in the financial statements of the subsidiary will be the same amount. No entries will be recorded by the parent.

In a cash-settled arrangement like share appreciation rights where cash is payable by the parent to the employees of a subsidiary, the subsidiary has no obligation to make any cash payments or to issue any of its own equity instruments.

Applying the principles of IFRIC 11, the subsidiary would recognise an expense of the same amount as that recognised in the consolidated financial statements with the credit going to equity as a capital contribution from the parent. The parent will debit the cash payment to the cost of investment in the subsidiary as a capital contribution.

11.5.1 *Transfers of employees between group entities*

IFRIC 11 addresses the effect of employees transferring between group entities for equity-settled arrangements (addressed in **11.2.1** above) but not for cash-settled arrangements. In each case it will be necessary to consider which entity or entities in the group have the obligation to settle with the employee and recognise their liabilities accordingly. This will depend on the particular terms of the scheme.

It may be that the subsidiary which has the obligation to settle the liability to the employee is the one where he or she is employed at vesting. The question that arises is how, on movement of employment between subsidiaries, the transfer of the accrued liability should be treated. The first subsidiary has received a capital contribution while the second has made a distribution by relieving the sister subsidiary of its obligation for no charge (i.e. it has effectively made a distribution on direction of the parent). The first subsidiary should credit the release of the liability to equity while the second charges the recognition of the liability to equity.

Although the first subsidiary derecognises the liability; it also neither reverses nor adjusts the expense it had previously recognised for the cash-settled amount. This is consistent with the guidance in IFRS 2.IG19 which says that the amount recognised for the services received and included in the carrying amount of an asset recognised for the entity's statement of financial position should not be adjusted for subsequent re-measurements of the liability.

In situations when the parent has the obligation to settle the liability, subsidiaries treat their liabilities in the same way as in the previous scenario. The expense amount, however, should continue to be adjusted until vesting so that the subsidiary bears the proportion of the total cash-settled amount related to the period of the employee's employment with that subsidiary (see **example 11.5.1** below). This is consistent with the IFRIC 11's logic in respect of the transfers of employees in equity-settled arrangements. [IFRIC 11.9] This adjustment is taken to equity as an adjustment to the amount credited to equity when the liability was derecognised.

Example 11.5.1

Parent has obligation to settle the liability

A group employee is awarded a cash-settled share-based payment by the group's parent, P, such that an amount will be payable if he works for the group for three years. The amount payable will be cash to the value of 1,000 shares of P. The share price of P is £10 at the grant date, £14 at the end of year 1, £13 at the end of year 2 and £16 at vesting date. The award will be settled by P, and there are no intragroup payment arrangements.

The employee works for subsidiary A throughout the first year, but transfers to subsidiary B for years 2 and 3.

The expense to be recognised by the group is as follows:

	Cumulative £	Recognised in the year £
Year 1: 1,000 x £14 x 1/3	4,667	4,667
Year 2: 1,000 x £13 x 2/3	8,667	4,000
Year 3: 1,000 x £16 x 3/3	16,000	7,333

This is allocated between subsidiaries A and B as follows:

	Subsidiary A		**Subsidiary B**	
	Cumulative £	*Recognised in the year* £	*Cumulative* £	*Recognised in the year* £
Year 1:				
A = 1,000 x £14 x 1/3	4,667	4,667	-	-
Year 2:				
A = 1,000 x £13 x 1/3	4,333	(334)		
B = 1,000 x £13 x 1/3			4,333	4,333
Year 3:				
A = 1,000 x £16 x 1/3	5,333	1,000		
B = 1,000 x £16 x 2/3			10,667	6,334

11.6 Effect of the use of ESOP trusts

ESOP trusts may potentially be accounted for in two different ways depending on the circumstances (see **section 9** above). Where the assets and liabilities of the trust are recognised as those of the sponsoring entity, any obligations of the trust will be regarded as obligations of the sponsoring entity.

The analysis will be different where the trust is regarded as a subsidiary. In this case the rights and obligations of the trust will be reflected in its own individual financial statements, rather than those of the sponsoring entity.

It will be necessary to apply the requirements of IFRIC 11 and the other guidance in this section to the particular facts of each case. In particular, the guidance at **11.2.3** above will be relevant to determining which entity has granted the rights and therefore has the obligation to employees.

The analysis might be further complicated when in practice three entities are involved in the arrangement. The third entity might be a fellow subsidiary or intermediate parent which grants the options and delivers the shares to the employees (either directly or via an ESOP trust).

11.7 Subsidiary purchases parent's shares

To settle its obligation to employees, the subsidiary will often need to acquire parent's shares either in the market or directly from the parent.

When the subsidiary purchases shares in the market to satisfy its obligation at the vesting date, the price paid will normally be the same as the liability recognised so that no gain or loss will arise on settlement. The subsidiary will not have any entries in equity arising from the arrangements because it has not issued any equity instruments and has not received any capital contribution from its parent. The parent will have no entries to record because it is not a party to the arrangement.

Alternatively, the subsidiary may purchase shares in the market prior to vesting date, and hold them as an asset to provide an economic hedge against the uncertain liability for the cash-settled amount. Such arrangements cannot qualify for hedge accounting under IAS 39 for the reasons explained at **11.7.1** below. They are, however, sometimes referred to in practice as hedging arrangements because they may eliminate or reduce uncertainty about the cash cost of meeting the cash-settled obligation.

When the parent issues its shares to the subsidiary at the market price, from the subsidiary's perspective this is no different from purchasing shares in the market and the guidance above is relevant. The parent would record an issue of shares for full consideration in the normal way.

If a subsidiary purchases shares in its parent they will be financial assets in the individual financial statements of the subsidiary even though they will be treasury shares in the consolidated financial statements of the parent. They will therefore either be classified as 'available-for-sale' (which is the default category) or designated as 'at fair value through profit or loss' if the relevant requirements of IAS 39 can be met.

One of the circumstances in which an asset may be designated as 'at fair value through profit or loss' is where doing so results in more relevant information because it eliminates or significantly reduces a measurement or recognition inconsistency (sometimes referred to as 'an accounting mismatch') that would otherwise arise from measuring assets or liabilities or recognising the gains and losses on them on different bases. Judgement on whether designation as at fair value through profit or loss would significantly reduce a measurement or recognition inconsistency will need to be based on a careful analysis of the specific facts and circumstances in each case.

Where shares are classified as available-for-sale, the cumulative gains or losses accumulated in equity will be reclassified to profit or loss on disposal (i.e. when the shares are delivered to employees).

11.7.1 Hedge accounting under IAS 39

Although 'economic hedges' can be achieved for some share-based arrangements, as described in **12.7** above, IAS 39 *Financial Instruments: Recognition and Measurement* sets out detailed rules on hedge accounting, including which items can be hedged and which instruments can qualify as hedging instruments.

Under IAS 39, it is not possible to apply hedge accounting to an equity-settled share-based payment arrangement as the Standard prohibits own equity as a hedged item.

A liability recognised under a cash-settled share-based payment arrangement can qualify as a hedged item. But it is important to note that the subsidiary cannot designate shares in its parent (whether held directly or via an ESOP trust) as a hedging instrument. A subsidiary might consider purchasing options over parent shares and designating them as a hedging instrument in hedging the forecast employee expense. However, it will still need to meet the detailed requirements of IAS 39 in order to achieve hedge accounting, including those relating to effectiveness. In practice, many groups may conclude that the benefits of obtaining hedge accounting in a subsidiary are insufficient to outweigh the associated practical difficulties.

12 Future developments

12.1 Proposed amendments to IFRS 2 and IFRIC 11 for group cash-settled share-based payment transactions

In December 2007, the IASB published an Exposure Draft of amendments to IFRS 2 and IFRIC 11 to deal with group cash-settled share-based payment transactions.

IFRS 2.3 requires an entity to recognise as share-based payment transactions, transfers of equity instruments of the entity's parent (or another entity in the same group) to parties that have supplied goods or services to the entity. IFRIC 11 provides guidance on how the entity that receives the goods or services from its suppliers should account for such transactions in its financial statements. The purpose of the proposed amendments is to specify the accounting, in the financial statements of an entity that receives goods or services from its suppliers (including employees), for similar arrangements that are share-based and cash-settled. For example:

- Arrangement 1 – the suppliers of the entity will receive cash payments that are linked to the price of the equity instruments of the entity; and
- Arrangement 2 – the suppliers of the entity will receive cash payments that are linked to the price of the equity instruments of the parent of the entity.

Under either arrangement, the parent of the entity has an obligation to make the required cash payments to the suppliers of the entity. The entity itself does not have any obligation to make such payments to its suppliers or provide them with equity instruments. The proposed amendment to IFRS 2 clarifies that an entity that receives goods or services from its suppliers must apply IFRS 2 even though the entity has no obligation to make the required share-based cash payments. The proposed amendment to IFRIC 11 specifies that an entity that receives goods or services from its suppliers under the arrangements described above (i.e. Arrangement 1 and Arrangement 2) should measure the goods or services in accordance with the requirements applicable to cash-settled share-based payment transactions. The proposed amendment to IFRIC 11 does not change its existing requirements.

Comments on the Exposure Draft were requested by 17 March 2008.

26 Leases

1 Introduction

IAS 17 *Leases* prescribes, for lessees and lessors, the appropriate accounting policies and disclosures for both finance leases and operating leases. IAS 17 was last revised by the IASB in December 2003 as part of its Improvements Project, and was most recently amended when IAS 1 *Presentation of Financial Statements* was revised in September 2007.

This chapter discusses the requirements of IAS 17 in the following sections:

Section 2 Scope

Section 3 Definition of a lease

Section 4 Classification of leases

Section 5 Characteristics of a finance lease

Section 6 Calculating the minimum lease payments

Section 7 Accounting and disclosure by lessees

Section 8 Accounting and disclosure by lessors

Section 9 Future developments

UK

IAS 17 has much in common with its UK counterpart, SSAP 21 Leases and hire purchase contracts, *but there are certain important differences that may have a pronounced impact for some UK companies. The most significant differences between the two standards are highlighted below.*

- *When SSAP 21 is applied in practice to distinguish between finance and operating leases, considerable emphasis is placed on the present value of minimum lease payments (the so-called '90 per cent test'). IAS 17 does not include a 90 per cent test, so that greater weight is placed on other factors in assessing lease treatment. Some leases that have historically been classified as operating under UK GAAP are classified as finance leases under IAS 17.*

- *Under IAS 17, unlike SSAP 21, it is necessary to split a single lease of land and building between the two elements. Accordingly, when adopting IAS 17, UK companies may find that they have to reclassify some leases. For example:*

  - o *where a lease of land and buildings has been treated as an operating lease under UK GAAP, it may be that the buildings element, when considered separately, will be classified as a finance lease under IAS 17; and*

  - o *where a lease of land and buildings has been treated as a finance lease under UK GAAP (which might include the 'outright purchase' of a long leasehold interest), it may be that the land element, when considered separately, will be classified as an operating lease under IAS 17.*

- *IAS 17, unlike SSAP 21, suggests that leases of land will be operating leases unless title passes. Thus, a lease of land classified as a finance lease under UK GAAP (which could include the purchase of a long leasehold interest for full payment at the outset) may need to be reclassified as an operating lease under IAS 17.*

- *In some cases, SSAP 21 allows lessors to use either the net investment method or the net cash investment method for finance leases, though it prefers (and sometimes requires) the latter. IAS 17 permits only the former.*

- *The period over which lease incentives are spread may be different under SIC-15 (the relevant IAS interpretation) from that under the UK equivalent, UITF 28.*

As explained above, some leases may be reclassified (for example, from operating to finance) on transition to IFRSs. The absence of any transitional reliefs may lead to practical difficulties, particularly where a lease (for example, of land and buildings) that has been classified as operating under UK GAAP may be treated as a finance lease under IFRSs. It will be necessary to perform lease calculations as at the time of entering into the lease, which may have been many years earlier, and there may be difficulties in obtaining all the relevant information for these calculations.

2 Scope

IAS 17 applies in accounting for all leases other than:

[IAS 17.2]

- lease agreements to explore for or use minerals, oil, natural gas and similar non-generative resources; and
- licensing agreements for such items as motion picture films, video recordings, plays, manuscripts, patents and copyrights.

Rights under licensing agreements for items such as motion picture films, video recordings, plays, manuscripts, patents and copyrights are excluded from the scope of IAS 17. Intangible assets are within the scope of IAS 17, however, if they establish rights for the exclusive use of the intangible asset. Brands and trademarks often are licensed exclusively and, therefore, are examples of leases of intangible assets that are included in the scope of IAS 17.

In addition, the Standard should not be applied as the measurement basis for:

[IAS 17.2]

- property held by lessees that is accounted for as investment property (dealt with under IAS 40 *Investment Property* – see **chapter 7**);
- investment property provided by lessors under operating leases (dealt with under IAS 40 *Investment Property* – see **chapter 7**);
- biological assets held by lessees under finance leases (dealt with under IAS 41 *Agriculture* – see **chapter 43**); or
- biological assets provided by lessors under operating leases (dealt with under IAS 41 *Agriculture* – see **chapter 43**).

IAS 17 applies to contracts that transfer the right to use assets even though substantial services by the lessor are required in connection with the operation or maintenance of such assets. [IAS 17.3] Examples include the supply of property, motor vehicles and photocopiers.

A contract that includes both assets and services should be separated where two or more identifiable streams operate independently of each other, e.g. where payments increase in response to different factors, parts of the contract run for different periods, or they can be terminated or renegotiated separately. In such cases, IAS 17 should be applied to the part relating to asset provision or use. (See also the discussion of IFRIC Interpretation 4 at **2.1** below.)

Conversely, IAS 17 does not apply to agreements that are contracts for services that do not transfer the right to use assets from one contracting party to the other, e.g. employment contracts. [IAS 17.3] It follows that it does not apply to the separable service component of contracts that include both assets and services. Examples would include the maintenance element of property and motor vehicle contracts.

It is also possible for an agreement to lease part of an asset to fall within the scope of IAS 17. This will be the case as long as the agreement has fully conveyed the right to use that portion of the asset. In some instances, this 'right to use' may only pertain to a portion of a larger asset (e.g. a transponder on a satellite, part of a building). IAS 40 *Investment Property* specifically allows that a portion of a property can be sold separately or leased out separately under a finance lease.

2.1 IFRIC 4 *Determining whether an Arrangement contains a Lease*

In recent years, arrangements have developed that do not take the legal form of a lease but which convey rights to use assets in return for a payment or series of payments. Examples of such arrangements include:

- outsourcing arrangements;
- telecommunication contracts that provide rights to capacity; and
- take-or-pay and similar contracts, in which purchasers must make specified payments regardless of whether they take delivery of the contracted products or services.

These arrangements share many features of a lease, because a lease is defined in IAS 17.4 as 'an agreement whereby the lessor conveys to the lessee in return for a payment or series of payments *the right to use an asset* for an agreed period of time'. The IFRIC concluded that all arrangements meeting this definition should be accounted for in accordance with IAS 17 (subject to the scope of that Standard), regardless of whether they take the legal form of a lease. The objective of IFRIC 4 *Determining whether an Arrangement contains a Lease* is to provide guidance to assist in determining whether an arrangement is, or contains, a lease.

The Interpretation does not address arrangements that are, or contain, leases that are excluded from the scope of IAS 17 nor, for leases falling within the scope of IAS 17, how such leases should be classified under that Standard.

In November 2006, the IASB published IFRIC 12 *Service Concession Arrangements*. IFRIC 12 applies for annual periods beginning on or after

1 January 2008, with earlier application permitted. When assessing the contractual terms of some arrangements it is possible that they could fall within the scope of both IFRIC 4 and IFRIC 12. To eliminate any inconsistencies between the accounting treatment for contracts which have similar economic effects, Appendix B to IFRIC 12 includes an amendment to IFRIC 4 to specify that if a contract appears to fall within the scope of both Interpretations then the requirements of IFRIC 12 prevail.

> *At the time of writing, IFRIC 12 has not yet been endorsed by the European Commission for adoption in Europe, and so the amendments made by Appendix B to IFRIC 12 are not yet effective. Where an entity within the scope of the IAS Regulation (see* **1.2** *in* **chapter 1***) has an arrangement to which IFRIC 12 would apply, but which is currently within the scope of IFRIC 4, it will not be possible to adopt the requirements of IFRIC 12 for reporting in the EU until the Interpretation has been endorsed. Until then, the entity should continue to apply IFRIC 4 to such an arrangement.* UK

2.1.1 *Determining whether an arrangement is, or contains, a lease*

IFRIC 4 specifies that an arrangement that meets *both* of the following criteria is, or contains, a lease that should be accounted for in accordance with IAS 17:

[IFRIC 4.6 – 8]

- fulfilment of the arrangement is dependent on the use of a specific asset or assets ('the asset'). The asset need not be explicitly identified by the contractual provisions of the arrangement. Rather it may be implicitly specified because it is not economically feasible or practical for the supplier to fulfil the arrangement by providing use of alternative assets; and
- the arrangement conveys a right to use the asset.

An arrangement conveys the right to use an asset if the arrangement conveys to the purchaser (lessee) the right to control the use of the underlying asset. This will be the case if *any* of the following conditions is met:

[IFRIC 4.9]

- the purchaser in the arrangement has the ability or right to operate the asset or direct others to operate the asset (while obtaining or controlling more than an insignificant amount of the output of the asset); or

- the purchaser has the ability or right to control physical access to the asset (while obtaining more than an insignificant amount of the output of the asset); or
- there is only a remote possibility that parties other than the purchaser will take more than an insignificant amount of the output of the asset and the price that the purchaser will pay is neither fixed per unit of output nor equal to the current market price at the time of delivery.

Example 2.1.1

Identification of a specific asset under IFRIC 4

Company A enters into a three-year agreement to provide internet access to Company B. The agreement requires B to make monthly payments and specifies the amount of bandwidth B needs. In order to provide B with the necessary bandwidth, A installs a router on B's premises. The router is not explicitly specified in the agreement, but is necessary to provide the required service and bandwidth to B. Company A has 24-hour access to the router to undertake any necessary maintenance or service. The useful life of the router is estimated to be three years.

Company A can replace the router at any time during the contract period provided that the replacement can provide the same service. Generally, A would only replace the router if it is damaged or needs to be upgraded. Company A has an excess inventory of these routers and does not have a history of replacing or exchanging the routers before the end of the contracts.

Is the router an asset that is implicitly identified in the agreement?

Company A's 24-hour access to the router, immediate access to replacement routers, and contractual permission to change the router at any time indicate that the router installed on B's premises is not an implicit asset under IFRIC 4.8. In effect, A can choose (1) which router to use in providing B with internet access for the three-year contract period and (2) whether to replace that router.

When fulfilment of the agreement to provide internet access does not depend on the use of a specific asset (i.e. the criteria in IFRIC 4.6(a) are not met), the agreement does not contain a lease. In such cases, the agreement is a contract for the provision of services and should be accounted for in accordance with the relevant standards.

2.1.2 *Assessing or reassessing whether an arrangement is, or contains, a lease*

The assessment of whether an arrangement contains a lease is made at the inception of the arrangement (being the earlier of the date of the arrangement and the date of commitment by the parties to the principal terms of the arrangement). A reassessment of the arrangement is permitted (and indeed required) only in the event of certain changes in circumstances, namely:

[IFRIC 4.10]

- a change in the contractual terms (unless the change only renews or extends the arrangement); or
- a renewal option being exercised or an extension being agreed to by the parties to the arrangement (unless the term of the renewal or extension was initially included in the lease term – see **6.1**). Note that a renewal or extension of the arrangement that does not include modification of any of the terms in the original arrangement before the end of the term of the original arrangement is evaluated only with respect to the renewal or extension period; or
- a change in the determination of whether fulfilment is dependent on a specified asset; or
- a substantial change to the asset, for example a substantial physical change to property, plant or equipment.

Changes in estimate (e.g. the estimated amount of output to be delivered to the purchaser or other potential purchasers) would not trigger a reassessment. If an arrangement is reassessed and is determined to contain a lease (or not contain a lease), lease accounting should be applied (or should cease to apply) from the date of change in circumstances. [IFRIC 4.11]

2.1.3 Separating payments for the lease from other payments

For the purpose of applying IAS 17, payments and other consideration required by the arrangement are separated into those for the lease and those for other elements in the arrangement on the basis of their fair values. The minimum lease payments for the purposes of IAS 17 include only payments for the lease (i.e. for the right to use the asset) and exclude payments for other elements in the arrangement (e.g. for services and the cost of inputs). [IFRIC 4.13] Specific rules are set out in IFRIC 4.15 where a purchaser determines that it is impracticable to separate the payments reliably.

3 Definition of a lease

A lease is defined as an agreement whereby the lessor conveys to the lessee, in return for a payment or series of payments, the right to use an asset for an agreed period of time. [IAS 17.4] The definition includes hire purchase contracts, i.e. contracts for the hire of an asset which contain a clause giving the hirer an option to acquire title to the asset upon fulfilment of agreed conditions. [IAS 17.6]

3.1 Arrangements involving the legal form of a lease

Not all transactions that involve the legal form of a lease will fall within the definition of a lease for the purposes of IAS 17. In some cases, such transactions may be designed to achieve a particular tax effect, which is shared between the parties, rather than conveying the right to use an asset. SIC-27 *Evaluating the Substance of Transactions Involving the Legal Form of a Lease* addresses issues that may arise when an entity (the Entity) enters into a transaction or a series of structured transactions with an unrelated party or parties (the Investor) that involves the legal form of a lease. For example, the Entity may lease assets to the Investor and lease the same assets back or, alternatively, sell assets and lease the same assets back. The form of each arrangement and its terms and conditions can vary significantly. In the lease and leaseback example, it may be that the arrangement is designed to achieve a tax advantage for the Investor that is shared with the Entity in the form of a fee, and not to convey the right to use an asset.

3.1.1 Evaluating the substance of an arrangement

Consistent with the general principles of IAS 17, SIC-27 states that the accounting for arrangements between the Entity and the Investor should reflect the substance of the arrangement. A series of transactions should be considered as linked and accounted for as one transaction when the overall economic effect cannot be understood without reference to the series of transactions as a whole. [SIC-27.3] All aspects of the arrangement should be evaluated to determine its substance, with weight given to those aspects and implications that have an economic effect. [SIC-27.4]

3.1.2 Indicators that an arrangement does not involve a lease

The key characteristic of a lease is that it includes the conveyance of the right to use an asset for an agreed period of time. [SIC-27.5] Indicators that may suggest that an arrangement does not, in substance, involve a lease under IAS 17 include:

[SIC-27.5]

- the Entity retains all the risks and rewards incidental to ownership of the underlying asset and enjoys substantially the same rights to its use as before the arrangement;
- the primary reason for the arrangement is to achieve a particular tax result, and not to convey the right to use an asset; and
- an option is included on terms that make its exercise almost certain (e.g. a put option that is exercisable at a price sufficiently higher than the expected fair value when it becomes exercisable).

3.1.3 *Assets and liabilities in an arrangement that does not involve a lease*

If an arrangement does not meet the definition of a lease, the principles of the *Framework for the Preparation and Presentation of Financial Statements* (see **chapter 2**) are used to determine whether, in substance, a separate investment account and lease payment obligations represent assets and liabilities of the Entity. Indicators that collectively demonstrate that, in substance, a separate investment account and lease payment obligations do *not* meet the definitions of an asset and a liability and should not be recognised by the Entity include:

[SIC-27.6]

- the Entity is not able to control the investment account in pursuit of its own objectives and is not obligated to pay the lease payments. This occurs when, for example, a prepaid amount is placed in a separate investment account to protect the Investor and may only be used to pay the Investor, the Investor agrees that the lease payment obligations are to be paid from funds in the investment account, and the Entity has no ability to withhold payments to the Investor from the investment account;
- the Entity has only a remote risk of reimbursing the entire amount of any fee received from an Investor and possibly paying some additional amount, or, when a fee has not been received, only a remote risk of paying an amount under other obligations (e.g. a guarantee). Only a remote risk of payment exists when, for example, the terms of the arrangement require that a prepaid amount is invested in risk-free assets that are expected to generate sufficient cash flows to satisfy the lease payment obligations; and
- other than the initial cash flows at inception of the arrangement, the only cash flows expected under the arrangement are the lease payments that are satisfied solely from funds withdrawn from the separate investment account established with the initial cash flows.

Other obligations of an arrangement, including any guarantees provided and obligations incurred upon early termination, should be accounted for under IAS 37 *Provisions, Contingent Liabilities and Contingent Assets* (see **chapter 11**), IAS 39 *Financial Instruments: Recognition and Measurement* (see **chapters 13 – 22**) or IFRS 4 *Insurance Contracts* (see **chapter 44**), as appropriate. [SIC-27.7]

3.1.4 Accounting for fees received by the Entity

The criteria in IAS 18.20 (see **section 7.1** of **chapter 23**) should be applied to the facts and circumstances of each arrangement in determining when to recognise any fee that the Entity receives as income. Factors such as whether there is continuing involvement in the form of significant future performance obligations necessary to earn the fee, whether there are retained risks, the terms of any guarantee arrangements, and the risk of repayment of the fee, should be considered. Indicators that individually demonstrate that recognition of the entire fee as income when received, if received at the beginning of the arrangement, is *inappropriate* include:

[SIC-27.8]

- obligations either to perform or to refrain from certain significant activities are conditions of earning the fee received and, therefore, execution of a legally binding arrangement is not the most significant act required by the arrangement;
- limitations are put on the use of the underlying asset that have the practical effect of restricting and significantly changing the Entity's ability to use (e.g. deplete, sell or pledge as collateral) the asset;
- the possibility of reimbursing any amount of the fee and possibly paying some additional amount is not remote. This occurs when, for example:
  - the underlying asset is not a specialised asset that is required by the Entity to conduct its business and, therefore, there is a possibility that the Entity may pay an amount to terminate the arrangement early; or
  - the Entity is required by the terms of the arrangement, or has some or total discretion, to invest a prepaid amount in assets carrying more than an insignificant amount of risk (e.g. currency, interest rate or credit risk). In this circumstance, the risk of the investment's value being insufficient to satisfy the lease payment obligations is not remote and, therefore, there is a possibility that the Entity may be required to pay some amount.

The presentation of the fee in the statement of comprehensive income should be based on its economic substance and nature. [SIC-27.9]

3.1.5 *Disclosure*

All aspects of an arrangement that does not, in substance, involve a lease under IAS 17 should be considered in determining the appropriate disclosures that are necessary to understand the arrangement and the accounting treatment adopted. An Entity should disclose the following in each period that such an arrangement exists:

[SIC-27.10]

- a description of the arrangement including:
  - the underlying asset and any restrictions on its use;
  - the life and other significant terms of the arrangement; and
  - the transactions that are linked together, including any options; and
- the accounting treatment applied to any fee received, the amount recognised as income in the period, and the line item of the statement of comprehensive income in which it is included.

These disclosures should be provided individually for each arrangement or in aggregate for each class of arrangement. A class is a grouping of arrangements with underlying assets of a similar nature (e.g. power plants). [SIC-27.11]

3.1.6 *Illustrative examples*

The Appendices to SIC-27 provide and discuss illustrations of the application of the Interpretation, including:

- an arrangement designed predominantly to generate shared tax benefits; [SIC-27.A2(a)]
- arrangements that offset so that, in substance, no transaction has occurred; [SIC-27.A2(b)] and
- two arrangements that are, in substance, secured borrowings. [SIC-27.A2(c) & (d)]

4 Classification of leases

The key distinction to be made in accounting for leases is whether the lease in question is a simple short-term hire arrangement (an operating lease), whereby rentals are dealt with in profit or loss with the only impact on the statement of financial position relating to the timing of payments, or whether the lease is akin to an arrangement for financing the acquisition of an asset (a finance lease), where the financial statements presentation will depart from the legal form of the transaction and be based on the economic substance, i.e. as if the asset had been purchased by the user.

Since the classification of a lease as an operating lease will often present a better picture of financial gearing, lessees will often prefer to see a lease classified as an operating lease rather than as a finance lease. As a consequence of this preference, many leasing entities will structure the specific conditions of their contracts in an attempt to ensure that a lease will not fall to be classified as a finance lease. The classification of a lease is based on an analysis of those terms of the lease agreement that are likely to have commercial effect, and ignores those terms that are not likely to have commercial effect. This analysis plays an important part in determining the appropriate accounting treatment for the lease.

UK *Unlike SSAP 21, IAS 17 does not include a '90 per cent test' so that, in practice, greater weight is placed on other factors in assessing lease treatment. Some leases that have historically been classified as operating under UK GAAP are classified as finance leases under IAS 17.*

4.1 Definitions

A finance lease is a lease that transfers substantially all the risks and rewards incidental to ownership of an asset to the lessee. Title may or may not eventually be transferred. [IAS 17.4]

An operating lease is any lease other than a finance lease. [IAS 17.4]

The classification of leases under the Standard is therefore based on the extent to which the risks and rewards incidental to ownership of a leased asset lie with the lessor or the lessee. The risks incidental to ownership include the possibility of losses from idle capacity or technological obsolescence, and of variations in the future economic benefits expected to flow to the entity due to changing economic conditions. The rewards incidental to ownership may be represented by the expectation of profitable operation over the asset's economic life and of gain from appreciation in value or realisation of a residual value. [IAS 17.7]

The Standard notes that, although a consistent definition of finance lease is used for both lessee and lessor accounting, and the transaction will be based on the same agreement between the parties, it is possible that the two parties will arrive at a different classification of the same lease because of their different circumstances (see **section 8.1** below). [IAS 17.9]

4.2 Lease classification determined at the inception of a lease

Lease classification is determined at the inception of the lease. Changes to the particulars of a lease after inception, other than by renewing the lease, which would have resulted in a different classification of the lease had the revised terms been in effect at the inception of the lease, should be considered as the inception of a revised agreement over the remaining term. However, changes in estimates (e.g. changes in estimates of the economic life or of the residual value of the leased asset), or changes in circumstances (e.g. default by the lessee), do not give rise to a new lease classification. [IAS 17.13]

Note that when a group acquires a new subsidiary, the leases to which that subsidiary is a party will be classified in the consolidated financial statements based on their terms at original inception, and not by looking at the remaining lease term from the acquisition date. Thus, in particular, where a subsidiary has appropriately treated a lease as a finance lease, that lease will also be treated as a finance lease in the consolidated financial statements, even if nearly all the lease term has expired by the acquisition date. This follows from the requirement in IFRS 3 *Business Combinations* that the acquirer should recognise the acquiree's identifiable assets and liabilities, because the asset and the associated finance lease creditor will qualify as identifiable assets and liabilities.

4.2.1 Inception of the lease vs commencement of the lease term

IAS 17 makes an important distinction between the inception of a lease and the commencement of the lease term.

> The inception of the lease is defined as the earlier of the date of the lease agreement and the date of commitment by the parties to the principal provisions of the lease. [IAS 17.4]

> The commencement of the lease term is the date from which the lessee is entitled to exercise its right to use the leased asset. [IAS 17.4]

There may be a time lag between these two dates, and the amounts involved in the lease arrangement may change between the two – most commonly where the asset is being constructed and the final cost is not known at inception. It is therefore important to clarify the significance of each of these dates.

The classification of a lease and, in the case of finance leases, the amounts to be recognised in the statement of financial position are determined at the inception of the lease. The assets, liabilities, income and expenses resulting from the lease, however, are not recognised in the financial statements until the commencement of the lease term. [IAS 17.4]

If lease payments are adjusted for changes in the lessor's costs (e.g. of construction, acquisition or financing), or for changes in some other measure of cost or value, such as general price levels, between the inception of the lease and the commencement of the lease term, the effect of any such changes is deemed to have taken place at inception. [IAS 17.5]

4.3 Changes in lease classification

As noted at **4.2** above, if the provisions in the lease are changed to such an extent that the lease would have been classified differently at inception had the changed provisions been in effect at that time, the revised agreement is considered as a new agreement over its remaining term.

For lessees, if a lease previously classified as an operating lease now becomes a finance lease, the lease should be capitalised by the lessee at the present value of the remaining minimum lease payments, and accounted for as a finance lease from that point forward. No prior year adjustments should be made. If a finance lease is reclassified as an operating lease, the lessee should follow the guidance for sale and leaseback transactions (see **7.3**).

For lessors, if a lease previously classified as an operating lease now becomes a finance lease, the lease receivable should be recognised at the present value of the remaining minimum lease payments, and the leased asset should be derecognised. No prior year adjustments should be made. A profit or loss may arise on derecognition of the asset and recognition of the finance lease receivable. If a finance lease is reclassified as an operating lease, the lessor should remove the lease receivable from the statement of financial position, and recognise a leased asset for the same amount.

Example 4.3

Upgrade of leased assets

A lessee is entitled to upgrade leased computers prior to the end of the initial lease term. A new lease agreement is concluded for each upgrade. What impact will the upgrade have on the lease?

The upgraded computers are distinct from the original leased computers. The lease provisions are renegotiated for each upgrade. Therefore, the provisions of the lease change on upgrade of the computers and the lease of the upgrades should be assessed as a new lease over the renegotiated term.

4.4 Leases of several assets

Where a lease agreement involves more than one asset, the lease should be assessed separately for each significant asset which operates independently (e.g. where payments increase in response to different factors, the lease runs for different periods, or the lease can be terminated and renegotiated separately).

For example, an equipment lease may include virtually all items necessary to operate a store such as refrigeration cases, air conditioning, alarm and phone systems, and office furniture. In such instances, where the items of leased equipment clearly have differing economic useful lives, it is appropriate to view the agreement as a lease of several distinct groups of assets based on similar attributes and economic lives. The lease classification should be assessed for each distinct group of assets. The allocation of assets to the finance and operating lease components should be based on their fair values at the inception of the lease.

5 Characteristics of a finance lease

5.1 Situations that will generally lead to finance lease classification

Having established a definition for a finance lease, as set out in **section 4** above, IAS 17 then proceeds to list examples of situations that, individually or in combination, would normally lead to a lease being classified as a finance lease. The indicators in IAS 17.10 relate to transfer of title and other factors in the primary period of the lease and should be regarded as the primary indicators. IAS 17.11 sets out additional indicators, which will sometimes be relevant. IAS 17.12 – 19 provide additional guidance.

Primary indicators of a finance lease are:

[IAS 17.10]

- the lease transfers ownership of the asset to the lessee by the end of the lease term;

This condition would hold where transfer of legal title, and thus continued ownership of risks and rewards, is automatic either within the agreement or within a side agreement which forms part of the overall transaction. This condition will be met, in substance, where the lessor has a put option requiring the lessee to acquire legal title, and the option is structured such that it is very likely to be exercised by the lessor.

- the lessee has the option to purchase the asset at a price that is expected to be sufficiently lower than the fair value at the date the option becomes exercisable such that, at the inception of the lease, it is reasonably certain that the option will be exercised;

This condition extends that referred to in the previous bullet point to a lessee call option at a price that makes its exercise commercially likely to occur. An option to purchase at a nominal amount is a typical example of this type of arrangement.

In some lease arrangements, rather than the lessee having a bargain purchase option, its parent (perhaps with no operations other than to act as an investment holding company) has the option to acquire the leased asset at less than market value at the end of the lease term. In these circumstances, it is reasonably certain that the parent will exercise the option to acquire the asset as the exercise price is less than the expected market value. The option to acquire the asset is not held by the lessee, but the substance is that only the lessee will have use of the asset. As a result, such arrangements will normally lead the lessee to classify the lease as a finance lease.

Where a lease involves identical put and call options (at the end of the lease term, the lessee has a call option to acquire the leased asset at a fixed price and the lessor has a corresponding put option for the same value), the substance is that of a forward contract. At the end of the lease term, the lessee will exercise the call option if the market value of the leased asset exceeds the exercise price of the option. The lessor will exercise the put option if the market price is less than the exercise price of the option. Therefore, either the put or the call option will be exercised at the end of the lease term, and the lessee will acquire the asset at the end of the lease term. Consequently, the lease should normally be classified as a finance lease from the perspective of both the lessee and the lessor.

- the lease term is for the major part of the economic life of the asset, even if title is not transferred;

This condition covers the situation where substantially all the risks and rewards occur during the lease term for which the lessee controls the asset. There is no definitive threshold in IAS 17 for what is 'the major part' of an asset's economic life and thresholds established by other GAAPs should not be considered definitive. Instead, it is necessary to consider the substance of a lease and classify it depending on whether the agreement transfers substantially all of the risks and rewards of ownership. These include, but are not limited to, the possibilities of losses from idle capacity or technological obsolescence, variations in return due to changing economic conditions, the expectation of profitable operation over the asset's economic life, and of gain or loss from movements in value or realisation of a residual value.

- at the inception of the lease, the present value of the minimum lease payments amounts to at least substantially all of the fair value of the leased asset;

This condition tests whether the lessor receives a full return of its initial investment. As with economic life, there is no definitive threshold in IAS 17 for what constitutes 'substantially all' of the fair value of a leased asset and thresholds established by other GAAPs should not be considered definitive. Instead, as discussed above, it is necessary to consider the substance of a lease and classify it depending on whether the agreement transfers substantially all of the risks and rewards of ownership.

SSAP 21 indicates (as a rebuttable presumption) a threshold of 90 per cent as the point at which the present value of minimum lease payments amounts to substantially all of the fair value of a leased asset. IAS 17 does not indicate a threshold at which this test is met. A lease that has been classified as operating under UK GAAP, because it falls below the 90 per cent threshold, may nevertheless be a finance lease under IAS 17. UK

- the leased assets are of such a specialised nature that only the lessee can use them without major modifications.

Where this condition is met, it is likely that the asset will have been constructed to the lessee's specifications such that its market value is limited. It follows that the lessor will seek to recover its investment from the primary lease term.

Other indicators that, individually or in combination, could also lead to a lease being classified as a finance lease are:

[IAS 17.11]

- if the lessee can cancel the lease, the lessor's losses associated with the cancellation are borne by the lessee.

Where the possibility of cancellation is relied on to reduce minimum lease payments, the likelihood of cancellation occurring in practice must be considered, and the consequences of a lessee's decision to terminate must be evaluated. Evidence that the lessee suffers a financial penalty for cancelling the lease suggests that the original intention of the parties is that cancellation is not expected to occur. Conversely, arrangements for termination that are unlikely to be applicable in practice (e.g. following insolvency of the lessee or failure to pay rentals when due) will be less relevant;

- gains or losses from fluctuations in the fair value of the residual fall to the lessee (e.g. in the form of a rent rebate equalling most of the sales proceeds at the end of the lease);

Where the lessee does not acquire legal title, it may nevertheless bear the risk of variation in residual values of the asset through payment of a substantial fixed final rental (a 'balloon rental') followed by a repayment equal to all or substantially all of the sales proceeds.

- the lessee has the ability to continue the lease for a secondary period at a rent that is substantially lower than market rent.

Rental for a secondary period either at a nominal amount or substantially below market rates suggests both that the lessor has received the required return from its initial investment, and that the lessee is likely to choose to enter into such a secondary period.

A bargain renewal option occurs when a lessee has the ability to continue the lease for a secondary period at a rent that is substantially lower than market rent. The rent for a secondary period would be considered substantially lower than market rent if it would be economically rational for the lessee to continue the lease at that lower rent. Factors to consider in determining whether a renewal represents a bargain are:

- the nature of the leased asset;
- the possibility of technological obsolescence;
- the possibility of higher operating and maintenance costs over the secondary rent period; and
- costs to be incurred by the lessor to find a new lessee and to prepare the asset for a new lessee.

For example, a lessee has a renewal option for a secondary rent period. The lease payments are indexed to the Consumer Price Index (CPI) during any renewal periods, at 75 per cent of the CPI existing at the time of the renewal. A 25 per cent discount may, depending on the circumstances, be regarded as a significant saving that would lead to the renewal option being classified as a bargain.

If the rental payments in the renewal period are equal to a specified percentage of the original monthly payments, one approach to assess whether this represents a bargain would be to compare the implicit interest rate determined by assuming that the lease is terminated at the end of the original lease term, with the implicit interest rate determined by assuming that the lease is renewed at the reduced rental rates. Appropriate estimates of the residual value of the asset at the end of the original term and at the end of the renewal period should be included in the computations. If the implicit interest rate increases or remains substantially the same when the renewal option is assumed to be exercised, it is appropriate to conclude that the renewal option is not a bargain. The assessment of whether the interest rate differential is a bargain will be made at the inception of the lease and will depend on economic conditions prevailing in that jurisdiction taken together with the circumstances of the parties to the lease agreement.

Although the factors set out above are intended to identify the key characteristics of a finance lease, they are not always conclusive. IAS 17 underlines the requirement to consider the whole of the arrangement, and the extent to which the risks and rewards incidental to ownership are transferred. Although a lease may appear to fall within the definition of a finance lease, having regard to the characteristics referred to above, there may be other features that demonstrate that the lease does not transfer substantially all risks and rewards incidental to ownership. By way of example, the Standard cites the circumstances where ownership of the asset transfers at the end of the lease, but for a variable payment equal to its then fair value. Similarly, if there are contingent rents, as a result of which the lessee does not have substantially all such risks and rewards, the lease will not be classified as a finance lease. [IAS 17.12]

The evaluation of a lease will require an examination of the lease agreement, including any supporting schedules and side letters (particularly where these include the monetary amounts of rental payments), and arrangements for the return and disposal of the asset. It follows that a lease agreement without a schedule of rental payments cannot be adequately assessed. The most relevant evidence will be found from clauses dealing with:

- rental payments and rebates (normally contained in a schedule to the lease agreement) to be used to consider whether the minimum lease payments amount to at least substantially all of the fair value of the leased asset; and

- arrangements that apply once the lease has run its normal full term, e.g. the existence of options, balloon payments, guarantees, process for disposal of the asset, etc.

Clauses dealing with the following issues will be of less relevance:

- maintenance and insurance (not normally a significant element of overall cost); and

- arrangements for termination that are unlikely to be applicable in practice, e.g. following insolvency of the lessee or failure to pay rentals when due.

5.2 Leases of land and buildings

Leases of land and buildings are classified as operating or finance leases in the same way as leases of other assets. A characteristic of land is that it normally has an indefinite economic life and, if title is not expected to pass to the lessee by the end of the lease term, the lessee does not receive substantially all of the risks and rewards incidental to ownership, in which case the lease of land will be an operating lease. Any premium paid for such a leasehold interest represents prepaid lease payments that are amortised over the lease term in accordance with the pattern of benefits provided. [IAS 17.14]

It is common for a new lessee to pay the incumbent tenant a lump sum when transferring the lease contract. If the lease is an operating lease, the lump sum payment should be accounted for as pre-paid lease payments, which are amortised over the lease term in accordance with the pattern of benefits provided. If the lease is a finance lease, the lump sum payment should be capitalised as part of the value of the asset to the extent that the carrying amount of the asset does not exceed its fair value. Alternatively, such a lump sum payment might be attributable to the purchase of other rights separate from the leased asset.

The land and buildings elements of a lease of land and buildings are considered separately for the purposes of lease classification. If title to both elements is expected to pass to the lessee at the end of the lease term, both elements are classified as a finance lease, unless it is clear from other features that the lease does not transfer substantially all the risks and rewards incidental to ownership of one or both elements. As the land normally has an indefinite life, the land element is normally classified as an operating lease unless title is expected to pass to the lessee by the end of the lease term. The buildings element will be classified as a finance or operating lease according to the extent to which the risks and rewards incidental to ownership have been transferred. [IAS 17.15]

UK

Under SSAP 21, it is not necessary to split a single lease of land and building between the two elements. Accordingly, when adopting IAS 17, UK companies may find that they have to reclassify some leases. For example:

- *where a lease of land and buildings has been treated as an operating lease under UK GAAP, it may be that the buildings element, when considered separately, will be classified as a finance lease under IAS 17; and*
- *where a lease of land and buildings has been treated as a finance lease under UK GAAP (which might include the 'outright purchase' of a long leasehold interest), it may be that the land element, when considered separately, will be classified as an operating lease under IAS 17.*

The basis on which leases of land and buildings are split is discussed further at ***5.2.1*** *below.*

IAS 17.14 & 15 appear to indicate that a lease of land will be an operating lease, unless substantially all of the economic life is transferred (e.g. through title passing). This is in some ways surprising, in that economic life is only one of five primary tests set out in IAS 17.10 (see **5.1** above), any one of which could normally cause a lease to be classified as a finance lease. For example, where a lease of land is granted for a period of 500 years for a fixed sum payable in full at the outset, and with no further amounts being payable, it might be expected that the fixed sum would represent substantially all of the fair value of the land. Thus, the fourth test in IAS 17.10 would be passed and the lease might be expected to be classified as a finance lease. (In effect, although the risks and rewards after 500 years remain with the lessor, their present value is only a tiny proportion of the value of the land.)

The IFRIC referred to this topic in a rejection published in the March 2006 IFRIC Update. IAS 17.BC8 explains that, because land normally has an indefinite economic life, and therefore there are significant risks and rewards associated with the land at the end of lease terms that do not pass to the lessee, land will 'normally' be classified as an operating lease. Although in the case of a long lease the time value of money would reduce the residual value of the land to a negligible amount, this does not alter the conclusion that significant risks and rewards associated with the land are not passed to the lessee.

The IFRIC did note one example of a lease classification affected by the introduction of the word 'normally', being a lease of land in which the lessor had agreed to pay the lessee the fair value of the property at the end of the lease period. In such circumstances, significant risks and rewards associated with the land at the end of the lease term would have been transferred to the lessee despite there being no transfer of title.

Thus, given that the comments about leases of land in IAS 17.14 & 15 are very specific, it appears that they should generally take precedence over the indicators in IAS 17.10, particularly in light of the IFRIC's comments. Moreover, leases of land (and buildings) for long periods will often be subject to rent reviews, which may mean that the lessor has not transferred substantially all the risks and rewards.

UK

Unlike IAS 17, SSAP 21 does not suggest that leases of land will be operating leases unless title passes. Thus, a lease of land classified as a finance lease under UK GAAP (which could include the purchase of a long leasehold interest for full payment at the outset) may need to be reclassified as an operating lease under IAS 17.

5.2.1 *Splitting leases of land and buildings*

In order to determine the appropriate accounting for the land and buildings elements of a lease, the minimum lease payments should generally be allocated in proportion to the relative fair values of the leasehold interests in the land element and the buildings element of the lease at the inception of the lease. [IAS 17.16]

Note that this split is *not* on the basis of the relative fair values of the land and buildings. The IASB concluded that the allocation of the minimum lease payments should reflect the extent to which they are intended to compensate the lessor for the use of the separate elements. The future economic benefits of a building are likely to be consumed to some extent over the term of a lease. Therefore, the lease payments allocated to the building should reflect not only the lessor's return on its investment in the building, but also the recovery of the value of the building consumed over the lease term. In contrast, land with an indefinite useful life should maintain its value beyond the lease term and, therefore, the lessor does not normally need compensation for any consumption of the economic benefits inherent in the land. [IAS 17.BC10 & BC11]

If the lease payments cannot be allocated reliably between the land and buildings elements, the entire lease is classified as a finance lease, unless it is clear that both elements are operating leases, in which case the entire lease is classified as an operating lease. [IAS 17.16]

One of the most common applications of the previous paragraphs is likely to be in legal jurisdictions where the ownership of property is held only via leasehold interests. Typically, the government retains ownership of all land, and leasehold interests in land and buildings are the only means of purchasing such assets. In these circumstances, because similar land and buildings are not sold or leased separately, it may not be possible to arrive at a meaningful allocation of the minimum lease payments.

For a lease of land and buildings where the present value of the minimum lease payments allocated to the land at the inception of the lease is immaterial, IAS 17 allows that the land and buildings may be treated as a single unit for the purposes of lease classification. The IASB considers that, in such cases, the benefits of separating the two elements and accounting for each separately may not outweigh the costs. The lease is classified in accordance with the general criteria set out above. In such cases, the economic life of the buildings is regarded as the economic life of the entire leased asset. [IAS 17.17]

5.3 Investment property

In the case of investment property held under a lease, generally there is no requirement for separate measurement of the land and buildings elements of a lease when the fair value model is adopted. It is possible for a lessee to classify a property interest held under an operating lease as investment property. In such circumstances, the property interest is accounted for as if it were a finance lease and, in addition, the fair value model is used for the asset recognised. These rules are discussed in detail in **chapter 7**.

If a lessee's property interest held under an operating lease is classified as an investment property, the lessee must continue to account for the lease as if it were a finance lease, even if a subsequent event changes the nature of the lessee's property interest so that it is no longer classified as investment property. The Standard indicates that this will be the case if, for example, the lessee:

[IAS 17.19]

(a) occupies the property, which is then transferred to owner-occupied property at a deemed cost equal to its fair value at the date of change in use; or

(b) grants a sublease that transfers substantially all of the risks and rewards incidental to ownership of the interest to an unrelated third party. Such a sublease is accounted for by the lessee as a finance lease to the third party, although it may be accounted for as an operating lease by the third party.

6 Calculating the minimum lease payments

The calculation of the minimum lease payments involved in a lease can be critical for the purposes of lease classification, and also for the subsequent accounting for finance leases. This section examines in detail the provisions of IAS 17 regarding the calculation of minimum lease payments.

The minimum lease payments are the payments over the lease term that the lessee is, or can be, required to make, excluding contingent rents, costs for services and taxes to be paid by and reimbursed to the lessor, together with:

[IAS 17.4]

- in the case of a lessee, any amount guaranteed by the lessee or by a party related to the lessee; or
- in the case of a lessor, any residual value guaranteed to the lessor by the lessee, or a party related to the lessee, or a third party unrelated to the lessor that is financially capable of meeting this guarantee.

If the lessee has an option to purchase the asset at a price that is expected to be sufficiently lower than the fair value at the date the option becomes exercisable that, at the inception of the lease, is reasonably certain to be exercised, the minimum lease payments comprise the minimum payments payable over the lease term to the expected date of exercise of this purchase option and the payment required to exercise it.

In focusing on minimum lease payments, it is important to consider the extent to which a lease is cancellable. IAS 17.4 defines a non-cancellable lease as a lease that is cancellable only:

(a) upon the occurrence of some remote contingency;

(b) with the permission of the lessor;

(c) if the lessee enters into a new lease for the same or an equivalent asset with the same lessor; or

(d) upon payment by the lessee of such an additional amount that, at inception of the lease, continuation of the lease is reasonably certain.

In addition, as noted above, minimum lease payments exclude contingent rents. IAS 17.4 defines contingent rent as that portion of the lease payments that is not fixed in amount but is based on the future amount of a factor that changes other than with the passage of time (e.g. percentage of future sales, amount of future use, future price indices, future market rates of interest). (See **6.2.2** for further discussion of variable rentals.)

6.1 Lease term

The lease term is the non-cancellable period for which the lessee has contracted to lease the asset, together with any further terms for which the lessee has the option to continue to lease the asset, with or without further payment. An option is only taken into account in the lease term if, at the inception of the lease, it is judged to be reasonably certain that the lessee will exercise the option. [IAS 17.4]

As noted at **4.2.1**, the commencement of the lease term is the date from which the lessee is entitled to exercise its right to use the leased asset. [IAS 17.4]

Careful judgement will be required in considering whether it is reasonably certain that a renewal option will be exercised. Situations that normally would result in a renewal option being reasonably certain of exercise include, but are not limited to, the following:

- the lessee has the right to prescribe the lease terms on renewal of the lease;
- the lease rentals on renewal are expected to be lower than market rates; and
- the lessee is economically compelled to renew based on the nature of the assets being leased or the existence of penalties.

Break clauses, i.e. clauses offering the lessee an opportunity to return equipment and cancel remaining rentals, may be included in a lease. Where, in order to classify a lease as an operating lease, a lessee places reliance on its ability to invoke a break clause and thus limit the lease term to the period then ended, it will be important to ensure that:

- there is a genuine likelihood of the break clause being used; and
- all financial consequences of a decision to break the contract are taken into consideration.

The classification of the lease should be based on the most likely course of events. There are instances where an artificial break clause is inserted purely in an attempt to ensure that the lease will be classified as an operating lease, but where there is no commercial possibility of the break clause being invoked. For example, a clause may allow the lessee to terminate a three-year lease after one month of operation but, in return, requires the lessee to pay a penalty of 75 per cent of the asset's cost. Although the penalty payment might not qualify as 'substantially all' of the fair value of the asset, there may be little commercial possibility of a lessee paying 75 per cent of the cost of an asset in return for one month's use. Accordingly, such a break clause should be disregarded.

Similar considerations apply when evaluating upgrade options, whereby a lessee can return existing equipment provided that it enters into a new lease. In particular, the impact on new lease rentals should be considered. For example, a lessor may seek to recover the remaining rentals on the old lease by increasing the rentals on new equipment. To the extent that classification of the old lease assumes exercise of an upgrade option, any increase in rentals on the new lease should be regarded as part of the guaranteed minimum payments under the old lease.

6.1.1 *Exercising option to extend a lease*

Where, at inception of a lease, an option to extend the lease is not reasonably certain to be exercised, this potential future lease extension should not be taken into account when calculating the lease term under IAS 17.4. In such a case, it is possible that the lessee may subsequently decide to exercise the option. The extended period would then be treated as a separate lease agreement to be classified and accounted for under IAS 17.

For example, an entity enters into a 10-year lease with a 5-year lease extension option. The exercise of the option to extend is not considered reasonably certain at the inception of the lease. Hence, the lease in this example is determined to be an operating lease with a 10-year term. Subsequently the option to extend the lease is exercised. The extension of the lease is accounted for as a new lease agreement, i.e. a separate lease agreement for 5 years which is classified as either an operating lease or a finance lease at the date of exercise of the option in accordance with IAS 17.

Example 6.1.1A

Exercise of a renewal option in an operating lease arrangement

Company A leases a property from Company B for ten years. The lease includes a renewal option under which A may extend the lease contract with

B at the end of the lease. At inception of the lease, exercise of the renewal option is not considered probable, and the lease is classified as an operating lease.

Company A must give notice if it intends to exercise the renewal option no later than two years before the end of the lease term. The commercial rationale for this is to allow B to market the leased asset for sale or lease to another party if Company A chooses not to exercise the renewal option. Towards the end of the eighth year of the lease, A serves notice that it will renew the lease contract, thereby extending the lease.

The notification that a renewal option will be exercised does not require reassessment of the classification of the lease. IAS 17.13 states:

> 'Lease classification is made at the inception of the lease. If at any time the lessee and the lessor agree to change the provisions of the lease, **other than by renewing the lease**, in a manner that would have resulted in a different classification of the lease under the criteria in paragraphs 7–12 if the changed terms had been in effect at the inception of the lease, the revised agreement is regarded as a new agreement over its term. However, changes in estimates . . ., or changes in circumstances . . ., do not give rise to a new classification of a lease for accounting purposes.' [Emphasis added.]

In the above scenario, the lease contains a renewal option, but exercise is not considered reasonably certain at inception of the lease. Subsequent notification by A represents a change in circumstance indicating the intention to renew, but does not alter the existing lease agreement. Therefore, the lease is not reassessed. On actual renewal of the lease at the end of the lease term, A effectively enters into a new lease which is classified according to IAS 17.8.

However, if the original lease did not include a renewal option and the lease is renegotiated to include one, or the terms of an existing renewal option in a lease are changed, this is a modification in accordance with IAS 17.13. Hence, classification of the lease should be reassessed at the date of modification and exercise, i.e. in year eight.

Example 6.1.1B

Renewal option in a finance lease

An asset is leased under a finance lease where the lease term is shorter than the useful life of the leased asset. Subsequent to initial recognition, an option to renew the lease is now exercised. At inception of the lease, it was not reasonably certain that the option would be exercised; therefore, the renewal option was not taken into account in assessing the lease term.

In substance, the renewal of the lease is a separate lease agreement; hence, the existing lease should continue to be accounted for as a finance lease to the end of its original term. Subsequently, the renewal of the lease needs to be classified as a finance or an operating lease according to the facts and circumstances. Where the renewal of the lease is classified as a finance lease,

IAS 17.20 applies for initial measurement at commencement of the renewal lease term, and IAS 17.25 applies for subsequent measurement. If the renewal of the lease is classified as an operating lease, it should be accounted for as any other operating lease in accordance with IAS 17.33.

Example 6.1.1C

Depreciation of an asset held under a finance lease with a renewal option

An asset is leased under a finance lease where the lease term is shorter than the useful life of the asset. Subsequent to initial recognition, it becomes certain that an option to renew the lease will be exercised. At inception this option was not reasonably certain. There is no provision in the lease contract for the lessee to acquire the asset at the end of the lease term.

The depreciation period should not be revised to include the expected renewal of the lease since IAS 17.27 requires that the asset should be depreciated over the **shorter** of the lease term and its useful life. The term of the original lease is not revised when it becomes certain that the renewal option will be exercised. Thus, depreciation continues to be calculated by reference to the term of the original lease. When the renewal option is exercised, in effect a new lease agreement is created and is classified and accounted for as a new lease. If the new lease is classified as a finance lease, the asset will be depreciated over the shorter of its remaining useful life at the time of renewal and the new lease term.

6.1.2 *Exercise of a purchase option in a lease arrangement*

Example 6.1.2

Exercise of a purchase option in a lease arrangement

Company A leases a property from Company B for ten years. The lease includes an option under which A may purchase the asset from B at the market price of the asset at the end of the lease. Company A may exercise the option no later than two years before the lease expires. The commercial rationale for this is to allow B to market the leased asset for sale or lease to a third party if A chooses not to exercise the purchase option. At inception of the lease, A assesses that there is a reasonable commercial possibility that it will not exercise the purchase option and hence classifies the lease as an operating lease.

Towards the end of the eighth year of the lease, A serves notice that it will purchase the property, thereby creating a binding purchase commitment. Company A will not acquire legal title to the property until exercise of the option at the end of year ten.

Notification that the purchase option will be exercised does not lead to reassessment of the classification of the lease. IAS 17.13 clarifies that lease classification is made at the inception of the lease unless the lease terms are subsequently modified (other than by renewing) and that modification would have resulted in a different classification if the modified terms had been in effect at inception.

In this case, the purchase price for the asset will be determined at the end of the original ten-year lease term, and paid for on exercise at the end of year ten. The original operating lease terms have not been modified. Company A continues to account for the operating lease until the purchase option is exercised at the end of year ten when A will account for an acquisition of the property.

However if, at the date of notification, the option price is renegotiated to be the market price for the asset at the date of notification and the original lease term is shortened to eight years, this would be a termination of the original lease and acquisition of the asset, and, therefore, would be accounted for as such.

6.2 Components of minimum lease payments

6.2.1 *Security deposits*

If the lessee is required to make a security deposit at the commencement of the lease that is refundable at the end of the lease term, the payment and subsequent refund of the deposit should both be considered in the calculation of the present value of the minimum lease payments. The effect of the deposit and subsequent refund is to accelerate the cash outflows of the lessee in the early years of the lease, so that there is an incremental effect on the present value of the minimum lease payments. However, where the refundable deposit is of such magnitude that it would distort the economics of the lease, the substance of the deposit may be that it relates to a separate transaction and should be accounted for accordingly.

6.2.2 *Variable rentals*

Lease payments may be linked to a change in a variable such as an inflation index or a prime interest rate.

The definition of contingent rent refers to payment 'that is not fixed but is based on the future amount of a factor that changes other than with the passage of time (e.g. percentage of future sales, amount of future use, future price indices, future market rates of interest)'. Therefore, where an agreement specifies that at the beginning of the lease, the annual payment will be a fixed amount, but in future years will be increased by a variable, that future increase in rental payments will not form part of the minimum lease payments but will be contingent rent.

Example 6.2.2A

Impact of variable rentals on minimum lease payments – inflation

A lease agreement specifies that the amount of the annual lease payments will be equal to £100 multiplied by the change in an inflation index. At the beginning of the lease, the index is 1.21, while at the end of Year 1 it is 1.24.

The minimum lease payments would be assumed to be £100 for every year of the lease because £100 is considered to be the base rent for the whole contract. In Year 2, an increase in the rent of £ 3 (£100*(1.24–1.21)) is contingent rent.

In addition, careful consideration of the terms of the lease may be required where any inflation adjustment in it is leveraged. This might represent an embedded derivative (see **chapter 17**).

Example 6.2.2B

Impact of variable rentals on minimum lease payments – prime interest rate

A lease agreement specifies that lease payments will increase each year by the prime interest rate, LIBOR.

It is considered that the link of lease payments to an interest rate such as LIBOR is an adjustment to the lease payments for the time value of money. At the inception of the lease, the future minimum lease payments should be determined on the basis of LIBOR at that date, i.e. using the assumption that LIBOR remains at that rate for the remainder of the lease.

Contingent rentals are those linked to the future amount of a factor that changes 'other than with the passage of time'. Contingent rents, therefore, are considered to be those arising from future changes in the prime interest rate. Thus, any future changes in the level of lease payments caused by future changes to the existing LIBOR rate represent contingent rentals, which will be recognised as incurred.

Careful consideration of the terms of the lease is required to determine whether any prime interest rate adjustment included in it is leveraged, in which case it might represent an embedded derivative (see **chapter 17**).

6.2.3 *Maintenance*

Lease instalments may include payments related to maintenance incurred by the lessor on behalf of the lessee. To the extent that the substance of the lease payments is for maintenance, they should be excluded from the calculation of minimum lease payments as they represent a cost for services to be paid by and reimbursed to the lessor.

Sometimes operating lease contracts may stipulate that the leased equipment must be returned to the lessor in the same condition as when originally leased. The accounting treatment depends on the particular lease clause. For example, the equipment may suffer general wear and tear that is merely a result of being used. In such circumstances, it may be necessary gradually to build up a provision to repair or maintain the equipment over the lease term, so that it can be returned to the lessor in its original condition. Generally, in these circumstances, it would be inappropriate to set up the full provision at the outset of the lease. Conversely, other contracts may require specific work to be performed. For example, the contract may stipulate that the equipment must be painted at the end of the lease, before being returned to the lessor. In such circumstances, it may be appropriate to recognise a provision at the outset of the lease, as by signing the contract the entity has committed itself to painting the asset, irrespective of any wear and tear suffered.

Repairs and maintenance obligations under leases are discussed further at **8.1** in **chapter 11**.

6.2.4 *Administration costs*

Lease instalments may also include payments related to administration costs incurred by the lessor on behalf of the lessee. These administration costs represent executory costs and should be excluded from the calculation of minimum lease payments.

6.2.5 *Termination penalties*

In some leases the terms include a termination penalty if the lessee terminates the contract prior to the end of the agreed lease term, which may, or may not, be explicitly expressed as a termination penalty. The inclusion or exclusion of termination penalties in the minimum-lease-payments calculation should be consistent with the determination of the lease term under the arrangement. The Standard defines the lease term as the 'non-cancellable period', together with further periods for which the lessee has the option to extend the lease and for which, at inception, it is reasonably certain the lessee will exercise that option.

The same lease could instead be expressed as a 'longer' period with an option (either explicit or implied by the inclusion of termination penalty clauses) to cancel the lease at an earlier date. The amount of termination payment will be one of the factors considered in determining whether it is reasonably certain that the lease will continue to full term. If it is not reasonably certain to continue to full term, the lease term is the shorter non-cancellable period. In such cases, any associated termination penalties would form part of the minimum lease payments. Where it is assessed that the lease term is the full length of the arrangement, termination penalties should be excluded from the minimum lease payments.

6.2.6 *Lease incentives given by a lessor*

SIC-15 *Operating Leases — Incentives*, which is discussed at **7.2.1** below, provides guidance for incentives in operating leases. All incentives for the agreement of a new or renewed operating lease should be recognised as an integral part of the net consideration agreed for the use of the leased asset, irrespective of the incentive's nature or form, or the timing of payments.

Likewise, if incentive payments are given in respect of finance leases, the incentives should be included as a reduction of the minimum lease payments to be received by the lessor.

Where there are tenant incentives paid at the start of a lease, even when they are not part of the actual lease documentation, they should be included in the minimum lease payments calculation.

6.2.7 *Rent reviews*

The definition of minimum lease payments specifically excludes contingent rents. Rent reviews, whether to market rates or upward-only, give rise to contingent rent. Therefore, at the inception of the lease the minimum lease payments throughout the lease term will be equal to the initial payments before any rent reviews have occurred.

Whether a lease specifies a rent of CU 100 annually plus market increases, or CU 100 annually resetting up or down to market every five years, the minimum lease payments are CU 100 annually. Any increase or decrease as a result of the review will be contingent rent.

The basis of any rent review under the lease should be evaluated carefully to determine whether the rent review resets the lease payments to market at the date of the review or whether, in substance, the amount of change in the lease payments at the date of the review was fixed at inception.

7 Accounting and disclosure by lessees

7.1 Accounting for finance leases

7.1.1 Initial recognition

At the commencement of the lease term, both the leased asset and the related lease obligation should be recorded in the statement of financial position at an amount equal to the fair value of the leased asset or, if lower, the present value of the minimum lease payments, each determined at the inception of the lease. [IAS 17.20] If liabilities are split between current and non-current in the statement of financial position, the same split is made for lease liabilities; they should not be shown as a deduction from the leased assets. [IAS 17.23]

IAS 17.4) defines initial direct costs as incremental costs that are directly attributable to negotiating and arranging a lease, except for such costs incurred by manufacturer or dealer lessors. Where the lessee incurs initial direct costs in connection with specific leasing activities (e.g. in negotiating and securing lease arrangements), those costs are included as part of the amount recognised as an asset under a finance lease to the extent that they can be directly attributed to that lease. [IAS 17.20]

7.1.1.1 The present value of the minimum lease payments

The present value of the minimum lease payments should be calculated using the interest rate implicit in the lease. [IAS 17.20] The interest rate implicit in the lease is the discount rate that, at the inception of the lease, causes the aggregate present value of (a) the minimum lease payments and (b) the unguaranteed residual value to be equal to the sum of (i) the fair value of the leased asset and (ii) any initial direct costs of the lessor. [IAS 17.4]

The residual value should be determined by using information relevant to the specific market at the time of inception of the lease; a guaranteed residual value may, however, be agreed at a higher amount. IAS 17 does not define 'residual value'. The unguaranteed residual value in the lease should be determined in accordance with the definition in IAS 16 as 'the estimated amount that an entity would currently obtain from disposal of the asset, after deducting the estimated costs of disposal, if the asset were already of the age and in condition expected at the end of its useful life' (i.e. at current value).

IAS 17.4) defines the interest rate implicit in the lease to be the rate that discounts the present value of (a) minimum lease payments and (b) unguaranteed residual value to be equal to the sum of (i) the fair value of the leased asset and (ii) any initial direct costs of the lessor. However, the estimate of the unguaranteed residual value is already a current value in accordance with IAS 16, rather than an estimated cash flow at the end of the lease. Hence, the implicit interest rate will be obtained by considering the rate that is necessary to discount the minimum lease payments such that (a) the present value of minimum lease payments and (b) the current value of the unguaranteed residual value together equate to the amount of the fair value of the leased asset, including initial direct costs.

For example, the residual value of a motor vehicle at the end of a three-year lease should be determined as the value of a three-year-old vehicle of the same or similar model at inception of the lease. The possible effects of future inflation in estimating residual values should not be considered, because anticipated increases in residual values, as a result of inflation, represent gain contingencies that should be recognised only when realised.

The fair value of the leased asset should be determined as follows.

- When the lessor is a manufacturer or dealer, the fair value of the equipment should be its **normal selling price**, reflecting any volume or trade discounts that may be applicable, using the market conditions prevailing at the time.

- When the lessor is not a manufacturer or dealer, the fair value of the property generally should be its **market price**, reflecting any volume or trade discounts that may be applicable.

- When the lessor is not a manufacturer or dealer and there has been a significant lapse of time between the acquisition of the property by the lessor and the inception of the lease, the determination of fair value should consider market conditions prevailing at the inception of the lease, which may indicate that the fair value of the property is greater or less than its cost or carrying amount, if different.

- When the leased asset is a second hand or specialised asset, and a fair market value is not determinable, the fair value should, as a last resort, be based on a depreciated replacement cost of a comparable new asset.

If the interest rate implicit in the lease is not determinable, then the lessee's incremental borrowing rate should be used. [IAS 17.20] The lessee's incremental borrowing rate of interest is the rate of interest the lessee would have to pay on a similar lease or, if that is not determinable, the rate that, at the inception of the lease, the lessee would incur to borrow over a similar term, and with a similar security, the funds necessary to purchase the asset. [IAS 17.4]

The determination of the lessee's incremental borrowing rate should be based on the facts and circumstances of the leasing practices in the specific jurisdiction. Generally, most lease arrangements are secured, and therefore a secured loan rate would be appropriate. There may be situations, however, in which lease arrangements are unsecured and, consequently, an unsecured loan rate would be appropriate (as the lessor would have appropriately considered the unsecured leasing arrangement in its pricing).

Where the lease is denominated in a foreign currency, the lessee's incremental borrowing rate should be the rate at which the lessee could obtain funding for the asset in the foreign currency.

7.1.2 *Subsequent measurement*

7.1.2.1 *Allocation of finance charges*

The difference between the total minimum lease payments (including any guaranteed residual amounts) and the amount at which the lessee records the outstanding liability at the inception of the lease represents a finance charge. This is allocated to accounting periods over the term of the lease so as to produce a constant periodic rate of interest (or, in practice, a reasonable approximation thereto) on the remaining balance of the lease obligation for each period. [IAS 17.25]

Note that the definition of minimum lease payments excludes contingent rents (see **section 6** above). IAS 17 requires that contingent rents are charged as expenses in the periods in which they are incurred. [IAS 17.25]

The allocation of the finance charge to accounting periods is achieved by apportioning each rental payment between a finance charge and a reduction of the lease obligation. IAS 17 does not specify any particular method for allocating the finance charge to each period – but it does allow that some form of approximation can be used to simplify the calculation.

The most common methods used are:

- the actuarial method;
- the sum-of-digits method; and
- the straight-line method (though this will generally be a poor approximation to a constant periodic rate of interest, and is likely to be acceptable only where the amounts involved are small).

Where a lease contains variation clauses which adjust the rentals to take account of movements in base rates of interest or changes in taxation, no adjustment need normally be made to the calculations carried out at the start of the lease. Any increase or reduction in rentals should be accounted for as an increase or reduction in finance charges in the period in which it arises, i.e. the adjustments should be treated as contingent rentals.

Actuarial method This method achieves an accurate apportionment of interest cost at a constant periodic rate over the term of the lease. Often the lessor will provide to the lessee the information necessary to adopt this basis. Alternatively, computer spreadsheets generally have suitable functions for such calculations to be performed.

Sum-of-digits method This is also referred to as the 'Rule of 78'. In most cases, this method produces an acceptable approximation of the results obtained by the actuarial method, but is simpler to apply. It is probably the method most frequently used in situations where the lessor does not provide to the lessee the information necessary to adopt the actuarial method.

Example 7.1.2.1

Sum-of-digits method

An asset is leased under a finance lease as follows:

- 3 year period;
- 12 quarterly rental payments;
- total finance charges of £10m.

If rentals are paid quarterly in arrears:

The digit assigned for the first period will be 12 and for the last period, 1.

Period	Quarter	Digit	Finance charge allocation	£'000
Year 1	1	12	10 x 12/78	1,539
	2	11	10 x 11/78	1,410
	3	10	10 x 10/78	1,282
	4	9	10 x 9/78	1,154
Year 2	1	8	10 x 8/78	1,026
	2	7	10 x 7/78	897
	3	6	10 x 6/78	769
	4	5	10 x 5/78	641
Year 3	1	4	10 x 4/78	513
	2	3	10 x 3/78	385
	3	2	10 x 2/78	256
	4	1	10 x 1/78	128
		78		10,000

If rentals are paid in advance:

Since there is no capital outstanding during the final quarter of the last year, there is no finance charge allocation to that quarter. Consequently, the digit for the last period will be zero, and for the first period, 11. The sum of the digits becomes 66, and this (rather than 78) is the denominator to be used in the fractions that are applied to allocate the total interest charge.

Straight-line method The finance charge is spread equally over the period of the lease. Thus, if it were applied in the circumstances of **example 7.1.2.1**, the finance charge would be £833,000 (i.e. £10m ÷ 12) in each quarter. This method does not attempt to produce a constant periodic rate of charge and does not, therefore, comply with IAS 17. It is only appropriate, on grounds of simplicity, if the difference between the figures thus produced and those that would be produced by the actuarial method would not be material to the financial statements. This is unlikely to be the case where the aggregate amount of finance leases is other than small relative to the size of the entity.

7.1.2.2 Depreciation

If there is no reasonable certainty that the lessee will obtain ownership of the asset by the end of the lease term, the leased asset should be depreciated over the shorter of the lease term and its useful life. [IAS 17.27] Where there is reasonable certainty that the lessee will obtain ownership by the end of the lease term, the asset should be depreciated over its useful life. The lease term should, for this purpose, be determined as discussed at **6.1** above.

The depreciation policy used for leased assets should be consistent with that for depreciable assets that are owned, and the principles of IAS 16 *Property, Plant and Equipment* or IAS 38 *Intangible Assets* should be applied, as appropriate. [IAS 17.27]

A lessee will also be required to recognise any impairment of a leased asset. To determine whether a leased asset is impaired, i.e. whether the recoverable amount of the leased asset is lower than its carrying amount, IAS 36 *Impairment of Assets* should be applied (see **chapter 9**).

7.1.3 Lease terminations

When a finance lease is terminated early, the appropriate accounting will depend on whether:

- the asset is purchased by the lessee;
- a further finance lease is entered into over the same asset;
- an operating lease is entered into over the same asset; or
- the entity ceases to have use of the asset.

In the last of these situations, the lessee should remove both the leased asset (in accordance with IAS 16 *Property, Plant and Equipment* or IAS 38 *Intangible Assets*, as appropriate) and the lease liability from its statement of financial position and should recognise any resulting difference in profit or loss.

Where a finance lease is terminated and replaced with an operating lease over the same asset, however, the transaction will be a sale and leaseback and should be accounted for in the manner discussed at **7.3** below.

7.1.4 *Lease incentives (rent-free periods)*

Where a lease contains an incentive, such as a rent-free period, the lessee will, at the commencement of the lease, recognise a leased asset and a finance lease payable either at the amount of the fair value of the leased asset or, if lower, at the amount of the present value of the minimum lease payments.

The lessee will also treat the finance lease payable as prescribed by IAS 17.25 (i.e. with a constant periodic rate of interest on the remaining balance of the liability during the lease term, including the rent-free period). Although there will be no payments made during the rent-free period (i.e. no reduction in the liability), finance charges will be recognised (at the rate implicit in the lease) in profit or loss with corresponding increases in the liability.

For example, the lessee has recorded a lease liability of £100 at the commencement of the lease. The rent-free period is one year and the implicit interest rate is 10 per cent. At the end of Year 1, the liability is increased by an interest charge of £10, because no payment is made. The liability balance will be reduced by payments in subsequent years.

7.2 Accounting for operating leases

Rentals payable under an operating lease should be charged on a straight-line basis over the lease term, even if the payments are not made on that basis, unless another systematic basis is more representative of the time pattern of the user's benefit. [IAS 17.33] For example, where the rental payments for an asset are based on the actual usage of that asset, or are revised periodically to reflect the efficiency of the asset or current market rates, the rentals actually payable may be an appropriate measure.

Example 7.2

Lease payments on unused property

Company XYZ currently is performing a major expansion of its oil production capacity; production will start in 20X2. In order to ensure shipping capacity, the entity will enter into operating lease transactions in 20X1 for rail cars that will be stored on XYZ's premises. Expected use in 20X1 will be minimal. Company XYZ is optimistic that it will be able to rent out the cars to other producers in 20X1 but this activity will be minimal. The sole reason for the leases is to ensure that the rail cars will be available to XYZ in 20X2. When should XYZ commence recognising the lease payments in its financial statements?

In accordance with IAS 17.4, assets, liabilities, income and expenses resulting from a lease are recognised in the financial statements at the commencement of the lease term. The commencement of the lease term is the date from which the lessee is entitled to exercise its right to use the leased asset. In 20X1, XYZ has the right to use the leased rail cars. Irrespective of whether XYZ chooses to exercise its right, and in accordance with IAS 17.33, it should commence recognising the lease expense in 20X1 on a straight-line basis over the lease term.

7.2.1 *Lessee incentives*

The question of operating lease incentives is dealt with in SIC-15 *Operating Leases – Incentives*. Examples of such incentives are an up-front cash payment to the lessee or the reimbursement or assumption by the lessor of costs of the lessee, such as relocation costs, leasehold improvements and costs associated with a pre-existing lease commitment of the lessee. Another form of incentive is the agreement for a rent-free or reduced rent period at the beginning of the lease.

7.2.1.1 *Rental holidays, reverse premiums and other lease incentives*

SIC-15 requires that all incentives for the agreement of a new or renewed operating lease should be recognised as an integral part of the net consideration agreed for the use of the leased asset, irrespective of the incentive's nature or form or the timing of payments. [SIC-15.3]

The lessee should recognise the aggregate benefit of incentives as a reduction of rental expense over the lease term, on a straight-line basis unless another systematic basis is representative of the time pattern of the lessee's benefit from the use of the leased asset. [SIC-15.5]

Example 7.2.1.1A

Lease incentive

The total payments under an operating lease are as follows:

Years 1 to 5: £200 per year

Years 6 to 20: £100 per year

In addition, the lessor provides a lease incentive with a value of £500. The lessee's benefit under the lease arises on a straight-line basis over the full lease term.

Applying IAS17 to the lease payments:

Total payments: (£200 x 5) + (£100 x 15) = £2,500

Length of lease: 20 years

Charge per year: £125

Applying SIC-15 to the incentive:

£500 / 20 years = reduction of £25 per year

Net charge per year = £125 – £25 = £100

UK *The approach taken by SIC-15 is different from that of its UK equivalent, UITF 28* Operating lease incentives. *UITF 28 indicates that benefit should be spread over the shorter of the lease term and a period ending on a date from which it is expected that a prevailing market rental will be payable. Thus, where there is a rent review date at which rentals will genuinely reset to market, UITF 28 spreads lease incentives over the period to that date. (Where a lease specifies upwards only rent reviews, however, there can be no genuine reset to market, and so the incentive is spread over the entire lease term.)*

Example 7.2.1.1B

Recognition of operating lease incentives under SIC-15

What is the appropriate method and period over which to recognise an incentive for an operating lease when an incentive is provided to the lessee and the lease contains a clause that requires lease payments to be repriced to market rates?

IAS 17.33 requires lease payments under an operating lease to be recognised as an expense on a straight-line basis over the lease term unless another systematic basis is more representative of the time pattern of the user's benefit. Moreover, SIC-15.5 states:

> 'The lessee shall recognise the aggregate benefit of incentives as a reduction of rental expense over the lease term, on a straight-line basis unless another systematic basis is representative of the time pattern of the lessee's benefit from the use of the leased asset.'

Even if an operating lease is repriced to market rates during the lease term, it does not mean that the lease expenses of a lessee should be comparable to the lease expense of an entity entering into an operating lease at the same time at market rates. Moreover, the repricing itself should not be considered representative of a change in the time pattern of the lessee's benefit referred to in SIC-15.5. Consequently, an incentive for an operating lease should be recognised on a straight-line basis over the full term of the operating lease, unless thorough assessment shows that another systematic basis is more representative of the time pattern of the lessee's benefit from use of the leased asset.

Costs incurred by the lessee, including costs in connection with a pre-existing lease (e.g. costs for termination, relocation or leasehold improvements), should be accounted for by the lessee in accordance with the Standard applicable to those costs, including costs which are effectively reimbursed through an incentive arrangement. [SIC-15.6]

The question often arises as to whether the lessee in an operating lease can defer initial direct costs it has incurred entering into the lease.

By way of example, Company A enters into an operating lease of a property and incurs a statutory levy (e.g. stamp duty) at a fixed percentage of the fair value of the leased property. The statutory levy is a tax payable to the tax authorities on entering into the lease and is payable at inception of the lease. IAS 8.11 requires that, in the absence of a specific standard applying to the transaction, the requirements and guidance in IFRSs dealing with similar and related issues should be considered. IAS 17 is silent on the subject of initial direct costs incurred by a lessee in an operating lease. SIC-15.6 states that costs incurred by the lessee should be accounted for in accordance with the Standards applicable to those costs. One way to account for the stamp duty cost, in the absence of any applicable specific guidance allowing its deferral, would be to expense it as incurred. Alternatively, guidance on similar issues found elsewhere in IFRSs (as set out below) recognises that costs incurred to obtain benefit over time should be expensed over time, hence, by analogy would support recognition of the statutory levy and amortisation over the lease term on a straight line basis. In particular:

- initial direct costs incurred by a lessor in negotiating and arranging an operating lease are added to the carrying amount of the leased asset and recognised as an expense over the lease term; [IAS 17.52]

- initial direct costs of a lessee on entering into a finance lease are added to the amount recognised as an asset; [IAS 17.20, 24]

- IAS 16.16(b) requires directly attributable costs in relation to an asset to be added to the carrying amount of the asset and depreciated over the asset's useful life; and
- transaction costs incurred on entering into financial instruments not held at fair value through profit or loss are included in the initial measurement of the financial instrument. [IAS 39.43]

7.2.1.2 *Vacant property following removal to new property*

When a leased property is vacated, it is necessary to consider whether an onerous contract provision may be required under IAS 37 *Provisions, Contingent Liabilities and Contingent Assets*. This will be the case if the costs associated with the property are likely to exceed the benefits to be obtained from it (for example, through sub-letting). This issue is discussed at **3.9.2** in **chapter 11**.

7.2.2 *Lease payments increase by fixed annual percentage*

Some contracts provide for annual payments in an operating lease to increase by a fixed annual percentage over the life of the lease. It is sometimes suggested that, where such increases are intended to compensate for expected annual inflation over the lease period, it may be acceptable to recognise them in each accounting period as they arise.

Such a treatment is not appropriate, as it would not be consistent with the time pattern of the user's benefit. IAS 17 does not incorporate adjustments to reflect the time value of money (e.g. by deferring a portion of a level payment to a later period). Rather, under an operating lease, IAS 17.33 requires lease payments to be recognised on a straight-line basis over the lease term unless another systematic basis is more representative of the time pattern of the user's benefit.

7.2.3 *Discounting of operating lease payments*

In determining the operating lease expense to be charged in each year, the future payments are not discounted to their present value. IAS 17 requires the operating lease expense to be recognised on a straight-line basis, unless another systematic basis is more representative of the time pattern of the user's benefits. In most standard operating leases, the user's benefits do not vary from year to year; consequently, discounting is not appropriate. Alternatives to a straight-line basis are only appropriate where the benefit from the leased asset is received on some other basis — for example, by reference to units of production. But even where another systematic basis is used, it is not appropriate to discount lease payments.

When payments increase with time, whereas the rentals are recognised on a straight-line basis, an accrual will be built up over the first half of the lease and run back down again in its second half. This accrual should not be discounted to its present value. Consistent with the way the lease expense is calculated (by analysing undiscounted payments), the liability should be recognised without taking into account the effect of discounting.

7.3 Accounting for sale and leaseback and similar transactions

A sale and leaseback transaction is a linked arrangement whereby the owner of an asset sells that asset and immediately leases it back from the purchaser. The subject of the sale and leaseback is commonly a building, but may be another item of property, plant and equipment. The lease payment and sale price are usually interdependent, as they are negotiated as a package. [IAS 17.58]

Often, an entity entering into a sale and leaseback transaction will, prior to the transaction, have had title to the asset being sold. This is not, however, essential: sale and leaseback accounting, as discussed below, would also apply where the asset 'sold' was previously held by the entity under a finance lease. Thus, where the terms of a lease are modified, so that it ceases to be a finance lease and becomes instead an operating lease, this should be accounted for as a sale and leaseback transaction.

Note that the disclosure requirements for leases (discussed at **7.4** and **8.5** below) apply to sale and leaseback arrangements just as to any other leases. In addition, such transactions may include unique or unusual provisions requiring disclosure as material leasing arrangements, and they may trigger the separate disclosure criteria in IAS 1 *Presentation of Financial Statements* (see **chapter 3**). [IAS 17.65 & 66]

7.3.1 *Finance leasebacks*

The leaseback may be a finance lease if it meets the condition that substantially all the risks and rewards of ownership remain with the lessee, or it may be an operating lease (in which case, some significant risks and rewards of ownership will have been transferred to, and remain with, the purchaser). The accounting treatment of a sale and leaseback transaction depends on the type of lease involved.

If the transaction gives rise to a finance lease, the substance of the transaction is that no disposal of the asset has taken place and therefore no gain or loss on disposal should be recognised. The transaction is merely a means by which the lessor provides finance to the lessee, with the asset as security. In such circumstances, any excess of the sales proceeds over the carrying amount should not be immediately recognised as income in the financial statements of the seller/lessee. Instead, it should be deferred and amortised over the lease term. [IAS 17.59]

In practice, the most straightforward treatment is to continue to recognise the asset at its previous carrying amount and to account for the asset as if the sale and leaseback transaction had not occurred. This reflects the reality that the sale and leaseback transaction has not resulted in any change to the seller's interest in the risks and rewards incidental to ownership. Consequently, there is unlikely to be any change to the asset's useful life or residual value so far as the seller is concerned.

Nevertheless, the seller/lessee should consider whether the transaction has resulted in an impairment in value, in which case the carrying amount is reduced to recoverable amount in accordance with IAS 36 *Impairment of Assets*.

The proceeds from the 'sale' transaction are credited to a liability account representing the initial net obligation under the finance lease. Subsequent accounting for the lease liability is as described in **section 7.1** above.

7.3.2 *Operating leasebacks*

If the related leaseback is an operating lease, it is necessary to determine the fair value of the asset and compare this with the contract sale price. Because the sale and lease transactions are connected, the sale may be arranged at other than fair value, with the impact of any difference being recognised in the rentals payable.

The appropriate accounting treatment is as follows:

[IAS 17.61]

- if the sale price is equal to the fair value, there has, in effect, been a normal sales transaction and any profit or loss on sale should be recognised immediately;
- if the sale price is above the fair value:
  - the difference between fair value and carrying amount may be recognised immediately; but
  - the excess of proceeds over fair value should be deferred and amortised over the period for which the asset is expected to be used. The excess of the sale price over the fair value will be reflected in higher rental charges; and
- if the sale price is below the fair value, the difference between sale price and carrying amount should be recognised immediately except that, if a loss arising is compensated by future rent at below market price, it should be deferred and amortised in proportion to the rent payments over the period for which the asset is expected to be used.

Thus, for operating leases, if the fair value at the time of the transaction is less than the carrying amount of the asset, a loss equal to the amount of the difference between the carrying amount and the fair value should be recognised immediately. [IAS 17.63]

Example 7.3.1 illustrates these rules for sale and leaseback transactions that are classified as operating leases.

Example 7.3.1

Sale and operating leaseback

(i) Sale price above fair value:

	£000
Carrying amount (book value)	100
Fair value	110
Sale price	125
Profit to be recognised	10
Profit to be deferred	15

(ii) Sale price below fair value:

	Asset A	Asset B
	£'000	£'000
Carrying amount (book value)	100	100
Fair value	125	110

Sale price	110	95
Profit to be recognised	10	–
Apparent loss to be deferred if compensated by below market rentals	–	(5)

There can be other arrangements involving the use of leases where legal title and risks and rewards of ownership may be separated, e.g. lease and leaseback arrangements, and leases where there is a future commitment to purchase the entity that is the other party to the lease. In such circumstances, the series of transactions should be considered as a whole, and the accounting should reflect the substance of the arrangements. The rules set out above for sale and leaseback transactions may provide a useful framework for the consideration of such transactions. Note also the requirements of SIC-27, as discussed in **section 3.1** above – it is possible that a transaction involving the legal form of a lease may not fall to be accounted for under IAS 17.

7.4 Disclosure requirements for lessees

7.4.1 Finance leases

Finance leases fall within the definition of financial instruments as set out in IAS 32 *Financial Instruments: Presentation*. Therefore, in addition to the specific disclosure requirements set out below, an entity must also meet the requirements of IFRS 7 *Financial Instruments: Disclosures* in respect of its finance lease arrangements (see **chapter 21**).

Lessees are required to make the following disclosures for finance leases:

[IAS 17.31]

- for each class of asset, the net carrying amount at the end of the reporting period;
- a reconciliation between the total of future minimum lease payments at the end of the reporting period, and their present value;
- the total of future minimum lease payments at the end of the reporting period, and their present value, for each of the following periods:
  - not later than one year;
  - later than one year and not later than five years; and
  - later than five years;

- contingent rents recognised as an expense in the period;
- the total of future minimum sublease payments expected to be received under non-cancellable subleases at the end of the reporting period; and
- a general description of the lessee's material leasing arrangements including, but not limited to, the following:
  - the basis on which contingent rent payable is determined;
  - the existence and terms of renewal or purchase options and escalation clauses; and
  - restrictions imposed by lease arrangements, such as those concerning dividends, additional debt, and further leasing.

In addition, the disclosure requirements of IAS 16 *Property, Plant and Equipment*, IAS 40 *Investment Property*, IAS 38 *Intangible Assets*, IAS 36 *Impairment of Assets* and IAS 41 *Agriculture* (see **chapters 6**, **7**, **8**, **9** and **43** respectively) apply equally to assets held under finance leases. [IAS 17.32]

7.4.2 *Operating leases*

Lessees are required to make the following disclosures for operating leases:

[IAS 17.35]

- the total of future minimum lease payments under non-cancellable operating leases for each of the following periods:
  - not later than one year;
  - later than one year and not later than five years; and
  - later than five years;

> *UK companies should note that, whereas SSAP 21 requires disclosure of the minimum lease payments falling due within the next year (analysed by when the lease terminates), the disclosure required by IAS 17 is of the total minimum lease payments (i.e. the aggregate payments for all future periods).* UK

- the total of future minimum sublease payments expected to be received under non-cancellable subleases at the end of the reporting period;

- lease and sublease payments recognised as an expense in the period, with separate amounts for minimum lease payments, contingent rents, and sublease payments; and
- a general description of the lessee's significant leasing arrangements including, but not limited to, the following:
  - the basis on which contingent rent payable is determined;
  - the existence and terms of renewal or purchase options and escalation clauses; and
  - restrictions imposed by lease arrangements, such as those concerning dividends, additional debt, and further leasing.

In disclosing the future minimum operating lease payments, disclosure should be made of the cash payments expected in terms of the lease agreement, rather than of the straight-line expense recognised as a result of IAS 17.33, if different.

7.4.3 Arrangements involving the legal form of a lease

As discussed at **3.1** above, SIC-27 requires that where an arrangement involves the legal form of a lease but does not, in substance, involve a lease under IAS 17, all aspects of the arrangement should be considered in determining the appropriate disclosures that are necessary to understand the arrangement and the accounting treatment adopted.

As noted at **3.1.5**, an entity should disclose the following in each period in which an arrangement of the type described in **section 3.1** exists:

[SIC-27.10]

- a description of the arrangement, including:
  - the underlying asset and any restrictions on its use;
  - the life and other significant terms of the arrangement; and
  - the transactions that are linked together, including any options;
- the accounting treatment applied to any fee received;
- the amount recognised as income in the period; and
- the line item of the statement of comprehensive income in which it is included.

These disclosures should be provided individually for each arrangement, or in aggregate for each class of arrangements (i.e. each grouping of arrangements with underlying assets of a similar nature). [SIC-27.11]

8 Accounting and disclosure by lessors

The approach required by IAS 17 for finance leases is to recognise the substance of the transaction, namely that the lessor is providing finance to the lessee to enable the lessee to obtain the use of a specific asset. Consequently, the asset recognised by the lessor under a finance lease is the amount receivable from the lessee rather than the asset that is the subject of the lease. Under an operating lease, the lessor treats the leased asset as a non-current asset and the rentals received as income.

8.1 Classification of leases

The circumstances under which a lease is presumed to be a finance lease are the same for a lessor as for a lessee. There may be differences in circumstances, however, including differences in the cash flows arising, which result in the lessor classifying a lease in a different manner from the lessee. In particular, some leases that are regarded as finance leases by lessors may be operating leases as far as lessees are concerned. [IAS 17.9]

In determining the minimum lease payments, a lessee takes account only of payments to be made by it, and any amounts guaranteed by it or by a party related to the lessee. On the other hand, the lessor may be able to arrange at or before the commencement of the lease that, at its conclusion, the asset will be sold to a third party at a guaranteed minimum price. The lessor will take account of any such guaranteed residual value in determining the minimum lease payments. The classification of leases is based on the extent to which risks and rewards incidental to ownership of a leased asset have been transferred by the lessor or received by the lessee. When an independent third party is involved in the lease, it may result in the lessor transferring substantially all the risks and rewards of ownership. The lessee may not receive substantially all the risks and rewards of ownership, however, if some of the risks and rewards are transferred to a third party through a residual value guarantee.

8.2 Accounting for finance leases

8.2.1 Initial measurement

Lessors are required to present finance lease assets as receivables in their statements of financial position, at an amount equal to the net investment in the lease. [IAS 17.36]

The net investment in the lease is the gross investment in the lease discounted at the interest rate implicit in the lease. [IAS 17.4] The gross investment in the lease is the aggregate of the minimum lease payments receivable by the lessor under a finance lease and any unguaranteed residual value accruing to the lessor. [IAS 17.4]

The interest rate implicit in the lease is the discount rate that, at the inception of the lease, causes the aggregate present value of (a) the minimum lease payments and (b) the unguaranteed residual to be equal to the sum of (i) the fair value of the leased asset and (ii) any initial direct costs of the lessor. [IAS 17.4]

The difference between the gross investment in the lease and the net investment in the lease is unearned finance income. [IAS 17.4]

Where a lessor (other than a manufacturer or dealer lessor) incurs initial direct costs in connection with specific leasing activities, the definition of the interest rate implicit in the lease set out above results in such costs being included in the finance lease receivable. These costs should include only costs that are incremental, and that are directly attributable to negotiating and arranging a lease (e.g. commissions, legal fees and incremental internal costs). General overheads, such as costs of sales and marketing, are excluded. [IAS 17.38]

UK

In some cases, SSAP 21 allows lessors to use either the net investment method or the net cash investment method when accounting for finance leases, though it prefers (and sometimes requires) the latter. As described above, only the net investment method is permitted under IAS 17.

If the lessor grants any incentives to the lessee, such as an initial rent-free period, then, at the inception of the lease, the calculation of the minimum lease payments and determination of the interest rate implicit in the lease will factor in nil payments by the lessee during such a rent-free period.

The lessor will recognise a finance lease receivable, initially, under IAS 17.36, at the amount equal to the net investment in the lease.

Subsequently, finance income will be recognised at a constant rate on the net investment under IAS 17.39. During the 'rent-free' period this will result in the accrued finance income increasing the finance lease receivable.

8.2.2 *Subsequent measurement*

The lessor recognises finance income so as to reflect a constant periodic rate of return on its net investment in the finance lease. [IAS 17.39] This is achieved by allocating the rentals (net of any charges for services etc.) received by the lessor between finance income to the lessor and repayment of the debtor balance.

Example 8.2.2

Finance lease: initial and subsequent accounting by a lessor

Company A which is not a manufacturer-dealer, leases a machine to Company B for 25 years. The rents are £10 million per year.

- At inception, the fair value of the machine is £120 million.
- The carrying amount of the machine is £95 million.
- Company A incurred £5 million of initial direct costs relating to negotiating and arranging the lease.
- The machine also has an unguaranteed residual value for A. The present value of the unguaranteed residual value is £10 million.
- The present value of minimum lease payments is £115 million.

At the commencement of the lease, the lessor (A) will reclassify the machine from equipment to finance lease receivables in its statement of financial position. The net investment in the lease will be the lease receivable, calculated as the total of the present value of the minimum lease payments, including annual rents, and the unguaranteed residual value. The present value of the minimum lease payments is calculated using the interest rate implicit in the lease. IAS 17.4 defines this rate as the discount rate that, at the inception of the lease, causes the aggregate present value of (a) the minimum lease payments and (b) unguaranteed residual value to be equal to the sum of (i) the fair value of the leased asset [£120 million] and (ii) any initial direct costs of the lessor [£5 million]. This sum is £125 million.

Therefore, the lease receivable at the inception of the lease is £125 million.

As A is not a manufacturer-dealer, the difference between the original carrying amount of the machine and the net investment in the lease is recognised in profit or loss as a gain on disposal of the machine: this is a gain of £25 million (£125 – £95 – £5 million).

The accounting entries required at commencement of the lease are as follows:

	£'000	£'000
Dr Finance lease receivable	125	
Cr Income statement		25
Cr Property, plant and equipment		95
Cr Cash (initial direct costs paid)		5

IAS 17.39 requires that finance income should be recognised on a pattern that reflects a constant periodic rate-of-return on the lessor's net investment in the finance lease, using the rate implicit in the lease. Company A will recognise annual rental payments received (£10 million) as partly being the repayment of the finance lease receivable and partly as interest income.

The accounting entry for Year 1 will be as follows (the constant periodic rate of return is 7.15 per cent):

	£million	£million
Dr Cash	10.00	
Cr Finance income (125 million x 7.15%)		8.94
Cr Finance lease receivable (10 million – 8.94 million)		1.06

The accounting entry for Year 2 will be as follows (the constant periodic rate of return continues to be 7.15 per cent):

	£million	£million
Cash	10.00	
Finance income ((125 million – 1.06 million) x 7.15%)		8.86
Finance lease receivable (10 million – 8.86 million)		1.14

The Standard emphasises that estimated unguaranteed residual values used in computing the lessor's gross investment in a lease should be reviewed regularly. Where there has been a reduction in the estimated unguaranteed residual value, the income allocation over the lease term is revised and any reduction in respect of amounts already accrued is recognised immediately. [IAS 17.41]

Changes in the unguaranteed residual value of the leased asset will only impact the finance lease receivable if the changes indicate impairment of the receivable and, subsequently, reversal of impairment.

IAS 17.36 requires the lessor's net investment in the finance lease to be shown as a finance lease receivable. The net investment in the finance lease is equal to the unguaranteed residual value accruing to the lessor plus the minimum lease payments, discounted at the interest rate implicit in the lease. The subsequent measurement of the lease receivable is specified by IAS 17 and by the derecognition and impairment requirements of IAS 39 *Financial Instruments: Recognition & Measurement*. The recognition of finance income is based on a constant rate of return on the net investment. Finance income is recognised at the rate implicit in the lease on the total net investment including the unguaranteed residual value.

Over the term of the lease, IAS 17.41 requires the estimated unguaranteed residual value to be reviewed regularly for any potential reductions in the estimated amount. Hence, the portion of lease receivable representing the unguaranteed residual value should be regularly compared with the current assessment of residual value. If the current assessment of the residual value is below the carrying amount of this portion of the finance lease receivable, an immediate loss should be recognised. IAS 39.63 specifies that any impairment loss will be measured as the difference between the carrying amount and the present value of the estimated future cash flows, i.e. the minimum lease payments discounted at the originally assessed interest rate implicit in the lease and current assessment of unguaranteed residual value. Subsequent to an impairment loss, interest will be accrued using the rate implicit in the lease on the basis of the revised carrying amount. The interest rate implicit in the lease is as determined at the inception of the lease and remains unchanged.

The guidance on reversal of an impairment loss for financial assets in IAS 39.65 applies. Any reversal of an impairment loss of the residual value, where permitted in accordance with IAS 39, is limited to the amount of the residual value estimated at the inception of the lease with accreted interest.

Where an asset under a finance lease is classified as held for sale (or included in a disposal group that is classified as held for sale) in accordance with IFRS 5 *Non-current Assets Held for Sale and Discontinued Operations*, it is accounted for in accordance with that Standard (see **chapter 29**). [IAS 17.41A]

8.2.3 Lease terminations

The derecognition of a lease receivable by a lessor is included in the scope of IAS 39 *Financial Instruments: Recognition and Measurement*. Accordingly, the derecognition criteria of IAS 39 should be applied (see **chapter 19**).

8.3 Accounting for operating leases

Lessors should present assets subject to operating leases in their statements of financial position according to the nature of the asset. [IAS 17.49]

Rental income, excluding charges for services such as insurance and maintenance, should be recognised on a straight-line basis over the lease term even if the payments are not made on that basis, unless another systematic basis is more representative of the time pattern in which use benefit derived from the leased asset is diminished (e.g. where rentals are based on usage). [IAS 17.50]

Costs, including depreciation, incurred in earning the lease income are recognised as an expense. [IAS 17.51]

Where initial direct costs are incurred by lessors in negotiating and arranging an operating lease, these are added to the carrying amount of the leased asset and recognised as an expense over the lease term on the same basis as the lease income. [IAS 17.52]

The depreciation of leased assets should be on a basis consistent with the lessor's normal depreciation policy for similar assets, and the depreciation charge should be calculated on the basis set out in IAS 16 *Property, Plant and Equipment* or IAS 38 *Intangible Assets*, as appropriate (see **chapters 6** and **8** respectively). [IAS 17.53]

A problem of income and cost matching may arise where a lessor arranges specific finance for the purchase of an asset that is leased under an operating lease. Where the finance is repaid from cash generated by rental receipts, the application of the previous paragraphs will result in:

- rental income recognised on a straight-line basis;
- depreciation expense recognised, say, on a straight-line basis; and
- finance costs front-end loaded since they will be charged as a constant percentage of capital outstanding.

The effect may be that the three items taken together show a loss in earlier years, and a profit in later years. It is sometimes argued that one way to address this issue is to view the leased asset as having some of the attributes of a financial asset. A method of depreciation that would be consistent with viewing the asset as having attributes of a financial asset is one which reflects the time value of money, for example the annuity method. This would result in a lower depreciation charge in earlier years and a more constant net profit after interest.

Use of the annuity method of depreciation, however, is not permitted. IAS 17.53 states that the lessor should apply its normal depreciation policy for similar assets and the depreciation charge should be calculated on the basis set out in IAS 16 *Property, Plant and Equipment*. IAS 16.60 states that the depreciation method used should reflect the pattern in which the asset's economic future benefits are expected to be consumed. The method should be based on the economic depreciation of the asset, not on the return from the asset. Therefore, the consideration of the time value of money in the depreciation calculation is not permitted.

Moreover, IAS 38.98 states explicitly that there is rarely, if ever, persuasive evidence to support an amortisation method for intangible assets with finite useful lives that results in a lower amount of accumulated amortisation than under the straight-line method.

To determine whether a leased asset has become impaired, i.e. when the recoverable amount of the asset is lower than its carrying amount, an entity applies the principles of IAS 36 *Impairment of Assets* (see **chapter 9**).

Note that *Improvements to IFRSs* issued in May 2008 amended IAS 16 for entities that, in the course of their ordinary activities, routinely sell items that they have held for rental to others. For periods beginning on or after 1 January 2009, such entities are required to transfer those assets to inventories at their carrying amount when they cease to be rented and become held for sale. This amendment is discussed further at **9.1** in **chapter 6**.

8.3.1 *Lessee incentives*

The treatment of operating lease incentives from the perspective of the lessor is also dealt with in SIC-15 *Operating Leases – Incentives* (see **7.2.1** above).

SIC-15 requires that all incentives for the agreement of a new or renewed operating lease should be recognised as an integral part of the net consideration agreed for the use of the leased asset, irrespective of the incentive's nature or form or the timing of payments. [SIC-15.3]

The lessor recognises the aggregate cost of incentives as a reduction of rental income over the lease term, on a straight-line basis unless another systematic basis is representative of the time pattern over which the benefit of the leased asset is diminished. [SIC-15.4]

8.4 Accounting by manufacturer and dealer lessors

Where a manufacturer or dealer offers leasing terms as an option in addition to normal selling terms (termed in the United States, a 'sales-type lease'), the question arises as to whether an immediate selling profit should be recognised when the asset is first leased. The answer will depend on whether there has, in effect, been a disposal of that asset. This in turn will depend on whether the lease is an operating or a finance lease.

In the case of an operating lease, the manufacturer or dealer has retained the asset with a view to using it to generate rental income. Consequently, no selling profit should be recognised and the asset should be included in the statement of financial position as a non-current asset, initially at its purchase price or production cost. [IAS 17.55]

In the case of a finance lease, there are two types of income associated with the contract: the selling profit or loss (i.e. an amount equivalent to the profit or loss arising on the outright sale of the asset at normal selling prices) and the finance income over the period of the lease. As a general principle, the selling profit or loss should be recognised at the commencement of the lease, in accordance with the entity's usual accounting policies. The sales revenue recognised is the fair value of the asset, or, if lower, the present value of the minimum lease payments accruing to the lessor, computed at a market rate of interest. Thus, if artificially low rates of interest are charged, the amount of the selling profit will be restricted to the profit that would have been earned if a commercial rate of interest had been charged over the lease term. [IAS 17.42 – 44]

Manufacturer or dealer lessors are required to recognise the costs of negotiating and arranging a finance lease as an expense when the selling profit is recognised. [IAS 17.42] Such costs are not included in the initial measurement of the finance lease receivable (as in the case of other lessors – see **8.2.1** above) because they are regarded as mainly relating to earning the manufacturer's or dealer's selling profit. [IAS 17.46] For manufacturer or dealer lessors, costs incurred in connection with negotiating and arranging a lease are excluded from the definition of initial direct costs (see **7.1.1**). As a result, they are excluded from the net investment in the lease and are recognised as an expense when the selling profit is recognised, which for a finance lease is normally at the commencement of the lease term. [IAS 17.38]

8.5 Disclosure requirements for lessors

8.5.1 Finance leases

Finance leases fall within the definition of financial instruments as set out in IAS 32 *Financial Instruments: Presentation*. Therefore, in addition to the specific disclosure requirements set out below, an entity must also meet the requirements of IFRS 7 *Financial Instruments: Disclosures* in respect of its leasing arrangements (see **chapter 21**).

Lessors are required to make the following disclosures for finance leases:

[IAS 17.47]

- a reconciliation between the gross investment in the lease at the end of the reporting period, and the present value of minimum lease payments receivable at the end of the reporting period;
- the gross investment in the lease and the present value of minimum lease payments receivable at the end of the reporting period, for each of the following periods:
  - not later than one year;
  - later than one year and not later than five years; and
  - later than five years;
- unearned finance income;
- the unguaranteed residual values accruing to the benefit of the lessor;
- the accumulated allowance for uncollectible minimum lease payments receivable;
- contingent rents included in income in the period; and
- a general description of the lessor's material leasing arrangements.

IAS 17.48 suggests that, as an indicator of growth it is often useful also to disclose the gross investment less unearned income in new business added during the period, after deducting the relevant amounts for cancelled leases.

8.5.2 Operating leases

Lessors are required to make the following disclosures for operating leases:

[IAS 17.56]

- the future minimum lease payments under non-cancellable operating leases, in aggregate and for each of the following periods:
    - not later than one year;
    - later than one year and not later than five years; and
    - later than five years;
- total contingent rents recognised in income in the period; and
- a general description of the lessor's leasing arrangements.

For the disclosure of minimum lease payments, the Standard requires disclosure of the anticipated cash flows from future minimum lease payments, and not the amounts expected to be recognised as income (if the cash flows are structured differently to the economic use of the asset).

In addition, the disclosure requirements of IAS 16 *Property, Plant and Equipment*, IAS 40 *Investment Property*, IAS 38 *Intangible Assets*, IAS 36 *Impairment of Assets* and IAS 41 *Agriculture* (see **chapters 6**, **7**, **8**, **9** and **43** respectively) apply equally to assets leased out under operating leases. [IAS 17.57]

8.5.3 *Arrangements involving the legal form of a lease*

As discussed at **3.1** above, SIC-27 requires that where an arrangement involves the legal form of a lease but does not, in substance, involve a lease under IAS 17, all aspects of the arrangement should be considered in determining the appropriate disclosures that are necessary to understand the arrangement and the accounting treatment adopted.

As noted at **3.1.5**, an entity should disclose the following in each period in which an arrangement of the type described in **section 3.1** exists:

[SIC-27.10]

- a description of the arrangement, including:
    - the underlying asset and any restrictions on its use;
    - the life and other significant terms of the arrangement; and
    - the transactions that are linked together, including any options;
- the accounting treatment applied to any fee received;
- the amount recognised as income in the period; and

- the line item of the statement of comprehensive income in which it is included.

These disclosures should be provided individually for each arrangement, or in aggregate for each class of arrangements (i.e. each grouping of arrangements with underlying assets of a similar nature). [SIC-27.11]

9 Future developments

The IASB has an active research project dealing with leases, which will seek to improve the accounting for leases by developing an approach that is more consistent with the conceptual framework definitions of assets and liabilities. The project would result in an amendment or replacement of IAS 17. An earlier G4+1 Study recommended capitalising property rights inherent in all leases – in effect 'abolishing' the concept of operating leases. At the time of writing, a discussion paper is expected at the end of 2008.

27 Borrowing costs

1 Introduction

IAS 23 *Borrowing Costs* prescribes the accounting treatment for borrowing costs.

The Standard was significantly revised in March 2007, when the option to expense all borrowing costs (including those directly attributable to the acquisition, construction or production of qualifying assets) was removed. This chapter discusses the requirements of the Standard as revised. However, the option to expense all borrowing costs as incurred continues to be available for accounting periods beginning before 1 January 2009. For entities that have previously followed that option, and that are required to change their accounting policies as a result of the revised Standard, specific transitional provisions apply (see **section 5**).

In May 2008, IAS 23 was further amended by *Improvements to IFRSs*. The amendments deleted from IAS 23 certain of the specific descriptions of the components of borrowing costs and replaced them with a reference to the guidance in IAS 39 *Financial Instruments: Recognition and Measurement* on calculating the interest expense using the effective interest rate method (see **section 2** below). These amendments were made to address a potential inconsistency between the Standards.

UK

At the time of writing, the revised version of IAS 23 has not yet been endorsed for use in the EU, with endorsement expected by the end of 2008. Until it is endorsed, entities reporting under IFRSs in the EU will only be able to adopt the revised version if it does not conflict with the previous (endorsed) version of IAS 23. In most respects, the revised version is consistent with the allowed alternative treatment in the previous version of the Standard, so that early adoption would be possible. However, the new scope exemptions (see ***section 2*** *below) and transitional provisions (see* ***section 5*** *below) will not be available to entities reporting under IFRSs in the EU until the revised version is endorsed.*

This chapter discusses the requirements of IAS 23 in the following sections:

Section 2 Core principle and scope

UK

UK GAAP requirements in respect of capitalising interest costs are included in FRS 15 Tangible Fixed Assets. *FRS 15 allows a choice of accounting policy over whether to capitalise borrowing costs. In overview, the two standards take broadly similar approaches when calculating the amount to be capitalised, but the most significant differences are highlighted below.*

- *Whereas FRS 15 allows a choice of accounting policy over whether to capitalise borrowing costs, and requires a consistent policy only for tangible fixed assets, IAS 23 requires a policy of capitalisation for all 'qualifying assets', being assets that necessarily take a substantial period of time to get ready for intended use or sale. Thus, the policy must be applied not only to property, plant and equipment but also, for example, to any qualifying assets within inventories and intangible assets.*
- *Under IAS 23, the amount to be capitalised is the actual borrowing costs on the related funds less any investment income on the temporary investment of those borrowings. This differs from FRS 15 which permits capitalisation only on the amount expended to date.*

2 Core principle and scope

The core principle of IAS 23 is that borrowing costs directly attributable to the acquisition, construction or production of a qualifying asset form part of the cost of that asset. Other borrowing costs are recognised as an expense. [IAS 23.1]

This core principle was added when the Standard was revised in March 2007. The previous version also allowed all borrowing costs to be expensed as a matter of accounting policy.

Borrowing costs are defined as interest and other costs that an entity incurs in connection with the borrowing of funds. [IAS 23.5]

Borrowing costs may include:

[IAS 23.6]

- interest expense calculated using the effective interest rate method as described in IAS 39 *Financial Instruments: Recognition and Measurement;*

- finance charges in respect of finance leases recognised in accordance with IAS 17 *Leases;* and

- exchange differences arising from foreign currency borrowings to the extent that they are regarded as an adjustment to interest costs.

The effective interest method is a method of calculating the amortised cost of a financial asset or a financial liability and of allocating the interest income or interest expense over the relevant period. The effective interest rate is the rate that exactly discounts estimated future cash payments or receipts through the expected life of the financial instrument or, when appropriate, a shorter period to the net carrying amount of the financial asset or financial liability. The calculation includes all fees and points paid or received between parties to the contract that are an integral part of the effective interest rate, transaction costs, and all other premiums or discounts. [IAS 39.9] See **section 4.1** of **chapter 18** for further discussion.

Paragraph 6 of IAS 23 is amended with effect from the date of adoption of *Improvements to IFRSs* issued in May 2008 (annual periods beginning on or after 1 January 2009 or date of earlier adoption). Previously, the text corresponding to the first bullet above referred to (a) interest on bank overdrafts and short-term borrowings, (b) amortisation of discounts or premiums relating to borrowings, and (c) amortisation of ancillary costs incurred in connection with the arrangement of borrowings. These descriptions were deleted and replaced with the reference to the interest expense as calculated under the requirements of IAS 39 so as to remove any potential for inconsistency between the two Standards. Although these amendments were included in Part I of *Improvements to IFRSs* (and, therefore, in the opinion of the Board could result in accounting changes), it appears unlikely that they will often have a significant impact in practice. The effect of the change, if any, should be accounted for retrospectively.

An entity is not required to apply IAS 23 to borrowing costs directly attributable to the acquisition, construction or production of:

[IAS 23.4]

(a) a qualifying asset (see **3.1** below) measured at fair value (e.g. a biological asset); or

(b) inventories that are manufactured, or otherwise produced, in large quantities on a repetitive basis.

The two scope exemptions set out above were added when IAS 23 was revised in 2007. No such exemptions were included in the previous version of the Standard.

The exemption for assets measured at fair value recognises that the measurement of such assets will not be affected by the amount of borrowing costs incurred during their construction or production period. The exemption for inventories manufactured in large quantities on a repetitive basis acknowledges the difficulty both in allocating borrowing costs to such inventories and monitoring those borrowing costs until the inventory is sold. The Board concluded that it should not require entities to capitalise borrowing costs on such inventories because the costs of capitalisation were likely to exceed the potential benefits.

These exemptions are optional rather than mandatory. Accordingly, an entity can choose, as a matter of accounting policy, whether or not to apply the requirements of IAS 23 to borrowing costs that relate to assets measured at fair value and / or inventories produced in large quantities on a repetitive basis.

Improvements to IFRSs issued in May 2008 amended IAS 16 *Property, Plant and Equipment* and IAS 40 *Investment Property* to bring investment property in the course of construction within the scope of the latter (see **section 2** of **chapter 6** and **2.2** in **chapter 7**). Accordingly, the first scope exemption above will also be available where an entity adopts the fair value model for investment properties.

UK

At the time of writing, the revised version of IAS 23 has not yet been endorsed for use in the EU, with endorsement expected by the end of 2008. Until it is endorsed, entities reporting under IFRSs in the EU will only be able to adopt the revised version if it does not conflict with the previous (endorsed) version of IAS 23. In most respects, the revised version is consistent with the allowed alternative treatment in the previous version of the Standard, so that early adoption would be possible. However, as these scope exemptions are new, they will not be available to entities reporting under IFRSs in the EU until the revised version is endorsed.

2.1 Exchange differences to be included in borrowing costs

IAS 23 includes no further clarification as to what is meant by the inclusion of exchange differences 'to the extent that they are regarded as an adjustment to interest costs'. The question has been addressed by the IFRIC but not added to its agenda (see *IFRIC Update*, January 2008). The IFRIC reaffirmed that how an entity applies IAS 23 to foreign currency borrowings is a matter of accounting policy requiring the exercise of judgement. Where the accounting policy adopted is relevant to an understanding of the financial statements, it should be disclosed as required by IAS 1 *Presentation of Financial Statements*.

It is clear that not all exchange differences arising from foreign currency borrowings can be regarded as an adjustment to interest costs — otherwise there would be no requirement for the qualifying terminology used in IAS 23.6(e). The extent to which exchange differences can be so considered depends on the terms and conditions of the foreign currency borrowing.

At a minimum, qualifying interest costs denominated in the foreign currency, translated at the actual exchange rate on the date on which the expense is incurred, should be classified as borrowing costs. Although exchange rate fluctuations may mean that this amount is substantially higher than the interest costs contemplated when the original financing decision was made, the full amount is appropriately treated as borrowing costs.

It is arguable that some exchange differences relating to the principal may also be included within borrowing costs. Assuming that the entity borrowed funds in the foreign currency in an attempt to reduce its cost of borrowing below that which would have been incurred if the funds were borrowed in the local currency, it follows that the entity would not have been willing to incur a cost of borrowing greater than the commercial interest rate prevailing in its local currency at the time the borrowing was originally taken out. Therefore, to the extent that the entity has incurred exchange losses on borrowings taken out in a foreign currency at lower interest rates, it seems reasonable to consider those exchange losses as one element of total borrowing costs, subject to the limit that the total borrowing costs capitalised (interest costs translated at actual rates plus exchange differences on the principal) do not exceed a notional borrowing cost based on commercial interest rates prevailing in the local currency as at the drawdown date of the borrowing.

The extent to which foreign exchange losses can be regarded as borrowing costs is illustrated in **example 2.1**.

Example 2.1

Exchange differences to be included in borrowing costs

An entity which prepares its financial statements in Thai Baht (the entity's functional currency) enters into a borrowing arrangement, with the following terms and conditions:

Drawdown amount (in the foreign currency)	US$100 million
Drawdown date	1 January 20X1
Exchange rate at drawdown	Baht 25:US$1
Interest rate on foreign borrowings	6% per annum (fixed)
Interest rate on similar borrowing in Thailand as at the drawdown date	12% per annum (fixed)
Average exchange rate for 20X2	Baht 36:US$1
Closing exchange rate for 20X2	Baht 47:US$1

The following interest payments were made in 20X2:

Interest payments (6% x US$100 million)	US$ 6,000,000
Translated at average rate	Baht 216 million

The borrowing costs that would have been incurred in the 20X2 reporting period if the funds had been borrowed in Thailand are calculated as follows:

Baht equivalent of US$100 million at 1 January 20X1	Baht 2,500 million
Annual interest expense based on Thai interest rates (12%)	Baht 300 million

This is the limit on the amount to be classified as borrowing costs. The difference between this amount and the actual US$ interest payments translated at the average rate is Baht 84 million.

The foreign exchange loss incurred on the retranslation of the principal amount of the US$100 million borrowings during 20X2 is calculated as follows:

Baht equivalent at opening rate of Baht 25:US$1	Baht 2,500 million
Baht equivalent at closing rate of Baht 47:US$1	Baht 4,700 million
Foreign exchange loss	Baht 2,200 million

The amount of borrowing costs included in the cost of assets under construction for the 20X2 accounting period is Baht 300 million, being the Baht equivalent of the US$ interest paid *plus* Baht 84 million of the exchange loss arising on the principal amount. This is equal to the interest expense that would have been incurred if the funds had been borrowed in Thailand based on commercial interest rates at that time.

The remaining exchange loss on the principal (Baht 2,116 million) is recognised in profit or loss in the year.

2.2 Costs associated with shares and similar instruments classified as financial liabilities

IAS 23 does not deal with the actual or imputed cost of equity, including preferred capital not classified as a liability. [IAS 23.3]

By implication, the requirements of the Standard *do* apply to costs associated with shares and similar financial instruments that are classified as liabilities, in accordance with the requirements of IAS 32 *Financial Instruments: Presentation*. Under IAS 32.35, the dividends arising on such instruments are recognised in profit or loss as an expense. IAS 32.36 states that '... dividend payments on shares wholly recognised as liabilities are recognised as expenses in the same way as interest on a bond.' Although IAS 23 does not define what is meant by 'the borrowing of funds', the classification of shares and similar instruments as liabilities means that they should be considered to represent such borrowings. Hence, the cost of servicing those shares, the dividends, will fall within the definition of borrowing costs.

2.3 Imputed interest on convertible debt instruments

Where an entity has issued a convertible debt instrument, IAS 32 requires that the liability component of the instrument be presented on an amortised cost basis using the coupon rate for an equivalent non-convertible debt. The imputed interest is recognised in profit or loss under IAS 39's effective interest rate method. Therefore, it is appropriate for the imputed interest expense in relation to the liability component of the convertible debt instrument to be included in borrowing costs eligible for capitalisation.

3 Recognition of borrowing costs

Borrowing costs that are directly attributable to the acquisition, construction or production of a qualifying asset are capitalised as part of the cost of the qualifying asset. Other borrowing costs are recognised as an expense in the period in which they are incurred. [IAS 23.8 & 9]

Before amendment in 2007, IAS 23 allowed a choice of accounting policy for borrowing costs directly attributable to the acquisition, construction or production of a qualifying asset. The benchmark treatment was for such costs to be expensed, with capitalisation being an allowed alternative treatment. The Standard has been amended to delete the previous benchmark treatment, so that the previous allowed alternative treatment is now mandatory. These changes are effective for annual periods beginning on or after 1 January 2009. Therefore, the option to expense all borrowing costs when incurred is available for accounting periods beginning before that date. **Section 5** deals with the transitional provisions where the change has resulted in a change in accounting policy.

When an entity applies IAS 29 *Financial Reporting in Hyperinflationary Economies*, it recognises as an expense the part of borrowing costs that compensates for inflation during the same period in accordance with IAS 29.21 (see **5.1.4** in **chapter 42**). [IAS 23.9]

3.1 Qualifying assets

A qualifying asset is defined as an asset that necessarily takes a substantial period of time to get ready for its intended use or sale. [IAS 23.5] Depending on the circumstances, any of the following may be qualifying assets:

[IAS 23.7]

- inventories;
- intangible assets;
- investments properties;
- manufacturing plants; and
- power generation facilities.

The following are *not* qualifying assets:

[IAS 23.7]

- assets that are ready for their intended use or sale when acquired;
- financial assets; and
- inventories that are manufactured, or otherwise produced, over a short period of time.

3.1.1 Assets with an extended delivery period

IAS 16 *Property, Plant and Equipment* identifies delivery and handling costs as part of the cost of an item of property, plant and equipment.

It includes such activities as part of the process of preparing the asset for its intended use. The shipping of an asset is therefore part of its acquisition and, consequently, borrowing costs attributable to the shipping period can be considered to be borrowing costs directly attributable to the acquisition of the asset as required by IAS 23.

For example, an entity orders and pays for a large piece of equipment from overseas that will take six months to arrive. A loan is raised to finance the acquisition. The equipment is already manufactured and available for shipment. Therefore, the period between payment for the equipment and its installation is only caused by shipping time. The asset is recognised by the entity on the date of shipping by the supplier, since that is the date on which (in this particular example) the risks pass to the entity. Borrowing costs incurred on the loan raised to finance the acquisition will be capitalised as part of the cost of the equipment up to the date that the asset arrives at its destination, is installed, and is ready for its intended use.

3.1.2 *Equity-accounted investments*

Example 3.1.2

Determining whether an equity-accounted investment can be a qualifying asset

Company X invests in construction contracts via participating interests in single-purpose entities. The entities are generally either associates (as defined in IAS 28 *Investments in Associates*) or jointly controlled entities (as defined in IAS 31 *Interests in Joint Ventures*) of Company X, which accounts for all such investments using the equity method of accounting. Where Company X borrows funds for the purpose of funding its investments, should it capitalise borrowing costs as part of the carrying amount of the equity-accounted investments?

Borrowing costs should not be capitalised in these circumstances. IAS 23.7 states that financial assets are not qualifying assets. It is sometimes argued, where a financial asset is an equity-accounted investment in a vehicle established for the purpose of constructing a qualifying asset, that the substance of the arrangement is that the investment is a qualifying asset for the investor. The logic is most appealing in the case of projects organised by a limited number of investors to pool resources in developing production facilities or properties. It is argued that, from the investor's perspective, the amount of borrowing costs capitalised should not be different simply because construction of the qualifying asset is through a separate investee vehicle, rather than by the investing entity itself. However, this approach is not permitted by IAS 23.

In contrast, where a jointly controlled entity is accounted for using proportionate consolidation under IAS 31's benchmark treatment, capitalisation of borrowing costs is required in similar circumstances (see **3.1.3**).

3.1.3 *Jointly controlled entities accounted for using proportionate consolidation*

In contrast to the prohibition on capitalisation of borrowing costs in respect of equity-accounted investments as described in **example 3.1.2**, it appears that where a jointly controlled entity is accounted for using proportionate consolidation under IAS 31's benchmark treatment, capitalisation of borrowing costs is required.

The investor's share of the qualifying assets of a jointly controlled entity accounted for using proportionate consolidation can be considered to be qualifying assets for the purposes of the consolidated financial statements and, therefore, capitalisation of borrowing costs incurred by any group entity to fund the construction of those qualifying assets is required, provided that all of the conditions of IAS 23 are met.

3.1.4 *Investment property subject to lessee fit-out*

Where a lessor completes a property subject to fit-out, and transfers it to the lessee, who then carries out further work to bring the property to the condition necessary for its intended use, the lessor in effect completes its work on the property at the time that the lessee takes possession. This will be the 'commencement of the lease term' [IAS 17.4] and the date at which the lessor ceases capitalisation of borrowing costs (unless there is a delay between the lessor completing work and the lessee taking possession, in which case capitalisation will cease at the earlier date).

3.2 Borrowing costs eligible for capitalisation

The borrowing costs that are eligible for capitalisation are those borrowing costs that would have been avoided if the expenditure on the qualifying asset had not been made. [IAS 23.10]

3.2.1 *Specific borrowing costs*

When funds are borrowed specifically for the purpose of acquiring or constructing a qualifying asset, the amount of borrowing costs eligible for capitalisation is the actual borrowing costs incurred on those funds during the period. [IAS 23.12]

The financing arrangements may result in the specific borrowings being drawn down prior to some or all of the funds being utilised to finance the qualifying asset. In such circumstances, any investment income earned on the temporary investment of the funds, pending their expenditure on the qualifying asset, should be deducted from the actual borrowing costs incurred to arrive at the borrowing costs eligible for capitalisation. [IAS 23.13]

This is different from the approach taken by FRS 15, which permits capitalisation only on the amount expended to date. UK

Example 3.2.1

Specific borrowings to finance factory construction

An entity borrows £20 million to finance the construction of a factory. The funds are to be drawn down on a monthly basis in four equal amounts. Payment of construction costs occurs throughout each month, rather than coinciding with the draw-downs. During each month, the entity invests any excess funds, drawn down in accordance with the financing arrangements, in short-term bank deposits.

In its financial statements for the year, the entity should capitalise, as part of the cost of construction of the factory, the actual borrowing costs incurred on the £20 million borrowing (incurred during the period of construction), less the interest income derived from the temporary investments in bank deposits.

3.2.2 *General borrowing costs*

When a qualifying asset is funded from a pool of general borrowings, the amount of the borrowing costs eligible for capitalisation is not so obvious. While the basic principles still apply, there may be practical difficulties in identifying a direct relationship between the particular borrowings utilised and the qualifying assets.

3.2.2.1 Calculation of capitalisation rate

In these circumstances, IAS 23.14 requires that the amount of the borrowing costs to be capitalised should be determined by applying an appropriate capitalisation rate to the expenditure on the qualifying asset.

The capitalisation rate is calculated as follows:

[IAS 23.14]

$$\frac{\text{Total general borrowing costs for the period (i.e. other than specific borrowings relating to qualifying assets)}}{\text{Weighted average total general borrowings (i.e. other than those specific borrowings)}}$$

Example 3.2.2.1

Qualifying asset funded from a general borrowing pool

An entity centrally co-ordinates its financing activities through a treasury function, with borrowings being raised to finance general requirements, including the acquisition and development of qualifying assets.

During the year ended 31 December 20X1, the entity commenced a property development project and incurred the following expenditure:

	£'000
1 June	5,000
1 October	10,000
1 November	10,000

The entity had total borrowings outstanding during the period, and incurred interest on those borrowings, as follows:

		Balance outstanding	Interest
		£'000	£'000
Long-term loans			
	10 years at 10%	35,000	3,500
	5 years at 8%	10,000	800
Short-term loans*		12,000	1,600
Bank overdraft*		5,000	500
		62,000	6,400

* The amounts disclosed for short-term loans and the bank overdraft represent the average amounts outstanding during the period and the interest incurred at variable rates.

The appropriate capitalisation rate to be applied to the expenditure is calculated as follows:

$$\frac{\text{Total borrowing costs for the period}}{\text{Weighted average total borrowings}} = \frac{6{,}400}{62{,}000} = 10.32\%$$

Interest capitalised is therefore calculated as follows:

	£'000
£5 million x 7/12 x 10.32%	301
£10 million x 3/12 x 10.32%	258
£10 million x 2/12 x 10.32%	172
Interest capitalised for the period	731

3.2.2.2 *Expenditure to which the capitalisation rate is applied*

The amount of expenditure on a qualifying asset used in the calculation should consist only of payments of cash, transfers of other assets or the assumption of interest-bearing liabilities, and should be reduced by any pre-sale deposits, progress payments or grants received in connection with the qualifying asset. The average carrying amount of the asset during a period, including borrowing costs previously capitalised, is normally a reasonable approximation of the expenditures to which the capitalisation rate is applied in that period. [IAS 23.18]

3.2.2.3 *Borrowing costs capitalised limited to the borrowing costs incurred*

The capitalisation of general borrowing costs calculated using the capitalisation rate is subject to the condition that the amount of borrowing costs capitalised should not exceed the actual borrowing costs incurred during that same period. [IAS 23.14]

Since the amount of borrowing costs capitalised may not exceed the amount of borrowing costs actually incurred, 'notional' interest expenses may not be capitalised. This point has particular relevance for groups. Some groups have centralised banking arrangements whereby the 'banking' entity charges or credits interest to the other group entities on the basis of its balances with those entities. Interest charged by one member of a group to another cannot be capitalised in the consolidated financial statements except to the extent that it represents an interest expense actually borne by the group on capital borrowed externally to finance the construction or production of the relevant asset. Intragroup interest is eliminated on consolidation.

Example 3.2.2.3

Borrowing costs limited to the borrowing costs incurred

A group consists of the parent P and two subsidiaries, S1 and S2. S1 is engaged in the construction of a power plant that is wholly financed by fellow subsidiary S2, which obtains the necessary funds through bank borrowings. No intragroup interest is charged by S2 to S1.

Under these circumstances, no interest should be capitalised in either of the individual financial statements of S1 Limited or S2 Limited. S1 has incurred no borrowing costs, and S2 has no qualifying asset.

However, it will be appropriate to capitalise interest in the consolidated financial statements of P, provided that the amount capitalised fairly reflects the interest cost to the group of borrowings from third parties which could have been avoided if the expenditure on the qualifying asset had not been made.

3.2.2.4 *Investment income on excess funds*

Where funds are borrowed generally, interest income earned on excess funds should not be offset against the interest cost in determining the appropriate capitalisation rate, nor in determining the limit on capitalisation by reference to the amount of borrowing costs incurred during the period.

3.2.2.5 *Assets funded from specified cash balances*

Where an entity has a general borrowing pool, it may nevertheless consider that expenditure on certain assets is met out of specified cash balances. In such circumstances, the question arises as to whether the entity is required to capitalise 'deemed' borrowing costs in respect of the expenditure on such assets.

This question is not specifically dealt with in IAS 23. IAS 23.14 refers to '. . . the extent that an entity borrows funds generally and uses them for the purpose of obtaining a qualifying asset ...'. Therefore, it appears that to the extent that the asset is demonstrably not paid for out of borrowings (e.g. it is paid for out of the cash proceeds of an equity issue), there is no requirement to capitalise a deemed interest cost.

To understand this position, contrast the IAS 23 requirements with those of US GAAP, which state that the interest cost to be capitalised is that which would theoretically have been avoided by using the funds expended to repay existing borrowings. Therefore, whenever an entity has a general borrowing pool, it is required to capitalise the borrowing costs that would have been avoided if the cash balances had been used to repay those borrowings.

Under IAS 23.14, there is no requirement to capitalise a 'deemed' interest cost, although it appears that adopting the approach required by US GAAP will be acceptable.

3.2.2.6 *Use of insurance proceeds to fund the reconstruction of an asset*

Example 3.2.2.6

Use of insurance proceeds to fund the reconstruction of an asset

Company A had a factory that was destroyed by fire. Insurance proceeds have been received and are being used to reconstruct the factory. Company A has a general borrowing pool. Because costs are incurred on the general borrowing pool, must Company A capitalise a deemed interest cost in respect of the reconstruction, even though the construction is funded from the insurance proceeds which are lodged in a separate bank account?

The capitalisation of borrowing costs is not necessarily required in these circumstances. The construction of the replacement asset is a distinct event and should be assessed separately for the purpose of determining the appropriateness of capitalisation of borrowing costs. The general question as to whether an entity is required to capitalise borrowing costs, even when it has identified the source of the funding for the qualifying asset as cash balances, is dealt with in **3.2.2.5**.

The only distinction in the case of insurance proceeds is that the entity may be legally required to use the insurance proceeds for the purposes of the reconstruction. Where this is the case, the option of repayment of the borrowings is not available, and the borrowing costs are not avoidable. Therefore, the option of capitalising a 'deemed' interest cost is not available in such circumstances.

3.3 Interaction of capitalisation of borrowing costs and hedge accounting

The interaction between the capitalisation of borrowing costs and hedge accounting is discussed at **3.16** in **chapter 20**.

3.4 Period of capitalisation

3.4.1 *Commencement of capitalisation*

IAS 23.17 states that borrowing costs should be capitalised from the commencement date. The commencement date for capitalisation is the date when the following three conditions are first met:

- expenditures for the asset are being incurred;
- borrowing costs are being incurred; and
- activities that are necessary to prepare the asset for its intended use or sale are being undertaken.

The term 'activities' in this context is interpreted as having a broad meaning and should include all steps necessary to prepare the asset for its intended use. Such activities include initial technical and administrative work, such as activities associated with obtaining permits, prior to the commencement of the physical construction of the asset. [IAS 23.19]

The mere holding of an asset, however, without any associated development activities, does not entitle an entity to capitalise related borrowing costs. [IAS 23.19] A typical example is the holding of land banks that are not undergoing activities necessary to prepare them for their intended use. Capitalisation of borrowing costs should only commence when such activities are being undertaken as part of a specific development plan to change an asset's condition.

3.4.2 Suspension of capitalisation

Capitalisation of borrowing costs should generally continue as long as the three conditions listed at **3.4.1** are met. If, however, the entity suspends activities related to development for an extended period, capitalisation of borrowing costs should also cease until such time as activities are resumed. [IAS 23.20] Such interruptions in development may occur, for example, due to cash flow difficulties or a desire to hold back development while the market is in depression, in which case the borrowing costs incurred during the period of suspension are not considered to be a necessary cost of development and therefore cannot be capitalised. On the other hand, temporary delays that are necessary or expected in the process of getting an asset ready for its intended use, or which result from a natural delay such as adverse weather conditions that are common to the location, do not require the suspension of capitalisation. [IAS 23.21]

3.4.3 Cessation of capitalisation

Borrowing costs should only be capitalised to the extent that they accrue during the period of production. In accordance with IAS 23.22, capitalisation should cease when substantially all of the activities necessary to prepare the qualifying asset for its intended use or sale are complete.

> Capitalisation will therefore generally cease when the physical construction of an asset is complete, because at that stage the asset will

be substantially ready for its intended use, notwithstanding that further time might be necessary to complete routine administrative work, market the asset or, in the case of an investment property, find a tenant.

For maturing inventories, it is sometimes difficult to determine when the 'period of production' ends, i.e. when inventories are being held for sale as opposed to being held to mature. For example, whisky is 'mature' after three years, but goes on improving with age for many more years. Providing it is management's intention to hold such items so that they mature further, it would seem acceptable to continue to add borrowing costs to the value of such maturing inventories for as long as it can be demonstrated that the particular item of inventory continues to increase in value solely on account of increasing age, rather than because of market fluctuations or inflation. If this cannot be demonstrated, then the inventories should be regarded as held for sale and no further borrowing costs should be capitalised.

IAS 23.22 does not permit continued capitalisation where the completion of an asset is intentionally delayed. In the case of property development, it is customary for the developer to defer installation of certain fixtures and fittings and the decoration work until units are sold, so that purchasers may choose their own specifications. Such delays relate more to the marketing of units than to the asset construction process.

When a qualifying asset is constructed in stages, and each stage or part can be used or sold individually while construction of the remaining development continues, capitalisation of the borrowing costs related to that part should cease when substantially all of the activities necessary to prepare that part for its intended use or sale are completed. [IAS 23.24] A development comprising several buildings or units, each of which can be used or sold individually, is an example of this type of qualifying asset. For an asset that must be completed in its entirety before any part of the asset can be used as intended, however, the borrowing costs should be capitalised until all of the activities necessary to prepare the entire asset for its intended use or sale are substantially complete. An example of this might be a manufacturing facility involving a sequence of processes, where production cannot begin until all the processes are in place.

Example 3.4.3

Cessation of capitalisation where construction completed in stages

A cable service supplier is building a cable network covering many franchise areas. The construction is carried out sequentially for each franchise area.

Once the construction in each franchise area is completed, the network is available for use in that area. The expenditure is being funded from a general borrowing pool. Should capitalisation of borrowing costs cease at the end of the entire project, or at the completion of each individual franchise area?

Capitalisation related to each stage ceases on the completion of the individual stage of the project, rather than when the project as a whole is completed. Under IAS 23.24, when the construction of a qualifying asset is completed in parts, and each part is capable of being used while construction continues on other parts, capitalisation of borrowing costs should cease when substantially all the activities necessary to prepare that part for its intended use or sale are completed. In this example, therefore, capitalisation of borrowing costs for each franchise area ceases as and when substantially all of the activities necessary to prepare the cable network in the particular franchise area for use are completed. Note that capitalisation of borrowing costs in other franchise areas still under construction may continue.

3.5 Recognition of an impairment loss or write-down

When the carrying amount or the expected ultimate cost of the qualifying asset exceeds its recoverable amount or net realisable value, the carrying amount is written down or written off in accordance with the requirements of other IFRSs. In certain circumstances, the amount of the write-down or write-off is written back in accordance with those other IFRSs. [IAS 23.16]

Accordingly, once borrowing costs have been identified as appropriate for capitalisation, they should be capitalised as part of the cost of the qualifying asset. This is so, even in those circumstances where the expected ultimate cost of the qualifying asset exceeds its recoverable amount (or net realisable value for inventories). In such cases, the appropriate treatment is to capitalise the interest cost as part of the gross carrying amount of the asset, and then recognise an impairment loss for any excess over the estimated recoverable amount or net realisable value in accordance with the requirements of IAS 36 *Impairment of Assets* or IAS 2 *Inventories*, as appropriate.

4 Disclosure

Entities are required to disclose:

[IAS 23.26]

- the amount of borrowing costs capitalised during the period; and

- the capitalisation rate used to determine the amount of borrowing costs eligible for capitalisation.

UK

UK listed companies are required to state the amount of interest capitalised by the group during the year, together with an indication of the amount and treatment of any related tax relief. [LR 9.8.4R(1)] The first part of this requirement effectively duplicates the requirement in IAS 23.26 discussed above. There is no choice over the treatment of related tax relief because IAS 23 requires capitalisation on a pre-tax basis; nevertheless, this fact should be stated in order to comply with the Listing Rule.

5 Effective date and transitional provisions

5.1 Elimination of option to expense all borrowing costs – effective 1 January 2009

The 2007 revisions to IAS 23 are effective for annual periods beginning on or after 1 January 2009, but earlier application is permitted. If an entity applies the revised Standard from a date before 1 January 2009, that fact should be disclosed. [IAS 23.29]

When application of the revised version of IAS 23 constitutes a change in accounting policy, the revised Standard is applied to borrowing costs relating to qualifying assets for which the commencement date for capitalisation is on or after the effective date. [IAS 23.27] However, an entity may designate any date before the effective date and apply the revised Standard to borrowing costs relating to all qualifying assets for which the commencement date for capitalisation is on or after that date. [IAS 23.28)]

Where an IFRS reporter had previously adopted the benchmark treatment of expensing all borrowing costs, the new accounting policy of capitalisation will be applied prospectively for qualifying assets with a commencement date on or after the effective date, or any earlier date designated in accordance with IAS 23.28. Thus, the new policy (of capitalisation) will not be applied to qualifying assets with an earlier commencement date, and all borrowing costs relating to such assets, including any incurred after the effective (or designated) date, will continue to be expensed.

Where an IFRS reporter had previously adopted the allowed alternative treatment of capitalising borrowing costs relating to qualifying assets, there will generally be no change of accounting policy on application of the revised Standard. An exception may be where the entity takes one of the new scope exemptions discussed in **section 2**, having previously capitalised borrowing costs for such assets. In accordance with IAS 23.27 & 28, such a change of accounting policy would be accounted for prospectively from the effective date, or from any earlier date designated in accordance with IAS 23.28. Thus, the new policy (of expensing borrowing costs for such exempt assets) will not be applied to assets with an earlier commencement date, and borrowing costs relating to such assets, including any incurred after the effective (or designated) date, will continue to be capitalised in accordance with the previous version of the Standard.

In all cases, the effect of the transitional provisions of the revised Standard is that assets with a commencement date before the effective (or designated) date will not be restated.

UK

At the time of writing, the revised version of IAS 23 has not yet been endorsed for use in the EU, with endorsement expected by the end of 2008. Until it is endorsed, entities reporting under IFRSs in the EU will only be able to adopt the revised version if it does not conflict with the previous (endorsed) version of IAS 23. In most respects, the revised version is consistent with the allowed alternative treatment in the previous version of the Standard, so that early adoption would be possible. However, the new scope exemptions (see ***section*** *2) and transitional provisions (see above) will not be available to entities reporting under IFRSs in the EU until the revised version is endorsed.*

5.2 Amendments to description of components of borrowing costs – effective 1 January 2009

The revisions to IAS 23 arising from *Improvements to IFRSs* issued in May 2008 are effective for annual periods beginning on or after 1 January 2009, but earlier application is permitted. If an entity applies the revised Standard from a date before 1 January 2009, that fact should be disclosed. [IAS 23.29A]

The effect of any change in accounting policy resulting from the implementation of the amendments should be accounted for retrospectively i.e. prior period amounts are required to be restated.

28 Foreign exchange

1 Introduction

IAS 21 *The Effects of Changes in Foreign Exchange Rates* prescribes how to account for transactions in a foreign currency and how to include foreign operations in the financial statements of an entity.

The requirements of IAS 21 regarding disposals and partial disposals of foreign operations have been amended as consequential amendments of IAS 27(2008) *Consolidated and Separate Financial Statements*. Details of the new requirements, and of the effective date and transitional provisions, are set out in **section 5**. IAS 21 was most recently amended in May 2008 when the IASB issued Amendments to IFRS 1 *First-time Adoption of International Financial Reporting Standards* and IAS 27 *Consolidated and Separate Financial Statements* in respect of the cost of an investment in a subsidiary, jointly controlled entity or associate.

This chapter discusses the requirements of IAS 21 in the following sections:

Section 2	Foreign currency transactions and the scope of IAS 21
Section 3	Definitions
Section 4	Reporting foreign currency transactions in the functional currency
Section 5	Presentation currency
Section 6	Tax effects of all exchange differences
Section 7	SIC-7 *Introduction of the Euro*
Section 8	Presentation and disclosure

Under UK GAAP, FRS 23 The Effects of Changes in Foreign Exchange Rates *embodies IAS 21, but makes amendments for UK entities, primarily to exempt FRSSE companies and to adjust references to other accounting standards. FRS 23 is mandatory for some entities and optional for others, but may only be adopted as part of a package of standards that also includes FRSs 24 to 26 and 29.* UK

UK companies not adopting FRS 23 continue to follow its predecessor, SSAP 20 Foreign currency translation. *The most significant differences between SSAP 20 and IAS 21 are set out below.*

- *SSAP 20 allows transactions to be reported at a future contracted rate. Under IAS, the transaction date (or average) rate must be used, and any matching foreign exchange contracts may be dealt with as hedges in accordance with IAS 39 Financial Instruments: Recognition and Measurement.*

- *IAS 21 has two concepts: functional currency (the currency in which the entity measures the items in the financial statements) and presentation currency (the currency in which the entity presents its financial statements). IAS 21 is prescriptive as to which currency should be used as its functional currency by each business, but allows wide discretion over the choice of presentation currency. The functional currency is the currency of the primary economic environment in which the entity operates. Functional currency broadly equates to SSAP 20's 'local currency' and, like IAS 21, SSAP 20 requires each entity to determine its functional/local currency and measure its results in that currency. However, whereas IAS 21 permits the entity to report those results in any currency it chooses (the presentation currency), SSAP 20 implicitly assumes that the local currency in which the company operates will be the same as the currency in which the company will present its financial statements.*

- *SSAP 20 requires the use of different methods of preparing consolidated financial statements (closing rate/net investment method and temporal method) depending on the relationship between the investing company and the foreign entity. Under IAS 21, where the affairs of a foreign entity are such that its results are more dependent on the economic environment of the investing company's currency than that of its own currency, the functional currency of the foreign entity should be the same as that of the investing company. Consequently, although IAS 21 has no separate concept of a temporal method, the effect should be the same.*

- *IAS 21 permits an average rate (or rates) to be used for the translation of the profit and loss account of a foreign entity into a presentation currency for the purpose of inclusion in the reporting entity's consolidated financial statements, but does not permit the use of closing rate. SSAP 20 allows the translation of the profit and loss account of a foreign entity using either average rate or closing rate.*

- *Under IAS 21, any goodwill arising on the acquisition of a foreign operation, and any fair value adjustments to the carrying amounts of assets and liabilities arising on the acquisition of that foreign operation, are treated as assets and liabilities of the foreign operation.*

> *Hence, they are expressed in the functional currency of the foreign operation and translated at the closing rate. In the past, some UK companies have not retranslated such items since SSAP 20 does not include similar guidance.*
>
> - *Although SSAP 20 and IAS 21 both use the net investment method, and both take net exchange differences to reserves (i.e. other comprehensive income), SSAP 20 prohibits the recycling of differences to the income statement on disposal of a subsidiary, whereas IAS 21 requires recycling (i.e. reclassification from other comprehensive income to profit or loss). Thus, under IAS 21, the gain or loss on disposal of a subsidiary is adjusted by the amount of exchange differences historically reported in other comprehensive income.*
> - *Under SSAP 20, loans to (and deferred balances with) foreign entities that are 'as permanent as equity' are sometimes not retranslated in the individual financial statements of the investor, in which case no exchange differences are recognised on such items in those individual financial statements. Under IAS 21, such balances are retranslated and any exchange gains and losses arising are recognised in profit or loss in the individual financial statements of the investor.*
> - *SSAP 20 includes limited ability to hedge account net borrowings which finance a net investment. IAS 21 does not include any material on hedging, which is dealt with in IAS 39. Under IAS 39, the conditions for using hedge accounting for a hedge of a net investment in a foreign entity are the same as for other kinds of hedges under IAS 39 (see* ***chapter 20****). This requires any ineffectiveness that arises on a hedge of a net investment in a foreign entity to be reported in profit or loss.*

2 Foreign currency transactions and the scope of IAS 21

An entity may enter into foreign currency transactions in two main ways:

- it may enter directly into transactions denominated in a foreign currency; and
- it may have foreign operations.

In addition, an entity may present its financial statements in a foreign currency.

> *Whilst it is customary for most UK entities to produce their statutory financial statements in Sterling, there are no restrictions in UK company* UK

law which prevent companies from using a foreign currency for this purpose, if there are good reasons for doing so. The choice of a 'presentation currency' is discussed in **section 5** *below.*

IAS 21 prescribes how to account for transactions in a foreign currency and how to translate foreign operations for inclusion in the financial statements of an entity (whether by consolidation, proportionate consolidation or the equity method). It also addresses how to translate financial statements into a presentation currency. [IAS 21.3]

IAS 21 excludes from its scope those foreign currency derivatives to which IAS 39 applies (see **chapters 16** and **17**). Foreign currency derivatives that are not within the scope of IAS 39 (e.g. some foreign currency derivatives that are embedded in other contracts) are within the scope of IAS 21. In addition, IAS 21 applies when an entity translates amounts relating to derivatives from its functional currency to its presentation currency. [IAS 21.4]

Although IAS 21 defines a net investment in a foreign operation (see **section 3** below), IAS 39 actually addresses the accounting treatment for a hedge of a net investment of a foreign operation. Similarly, IAS 39 applies to hedge accounting for a designated hedged item for foreign exchange risk. IAS 21 specifically scopes out the measurement of foreign currency items that are subject to hedge accounting. [IAS 21.5] These items are discussed in **section 2.3** of **chapter 20** on hedge accounting.

IAS 21 does not apply to the presentation in a statement of cash flows of cash flows arising from transactions in a foreign currency, nor to the translation of cash flows of a foreign operation, which are addressed in IAS 7 *Statement of Cash Flows* (see **chapter 30**). [IAS 21.7]

Example 2

Hedging a net investment in a foreign operation

S, a Swedish entity, has a foreign subsidiary with a different functional currency. S's investment in the subsidiary is US$2,000,000. S has a third party long-term debt agreement in the amount of US$4,000,000. S designates US$ 2,000,000 of the debt at the beginning of the year as a hedge of its net investment in the foreign subsidiary.

That part of the debt qualifying as a hedging instrument is outside the scope of IAS 21 and is instead dealt with by IAS 39. The portion of the debt instrument that is not designated in the hedging relationship is, however, still within the scope of IAS 21.

See **chapter 20** for guidance on hedges of net investments in a foreign operation and on hedge effectiveness.

3 Definitions

The following definitions are from IAS 21:

[IAS 21.8]

Foreign operation is an entity that is a subsidiary, associate, joint venture or branch of a reporting entity, the activities of which are based or conducted in a country or currency other than those of the reporting entity.

Functional currency is the currency of the primary economic environment in which the entity operates.

Monetary items are units of currency held and assets and liabilities to be received or paid in a fixed or determinable number of units of currency.

Net investment in a foreign operation is the amount of the reporting entity's interest in the net assets of that operation.

Presentation currency is the currency in which the financial statements are presented.

3.1 Monetary items

Under IAS 21, foreign currency monetary items are treated differently from foreign currency non-monetary items. The essential feature of a monetary item (see definition above) is the right to receive (or the obligation to deliver) a fixed or determinable number of units of currency. [IAS 21.16] Conversely, a non-monetary item does not carry this right or obligation.

Examples of *monetary items* include trade payables and receivables, debt securities, deferred taxes, employee benefits to be paid in cash, cash dividends recognised as a liability, cash and bank balances.

Examples of *non-monetary items* include amounts prepaid for goods and services (e.g. prepaid rent), goodwill and other intangible assets (e.g. patents, trademarks, licences and formulas), deferred income, equity instruments (e.g. equity securities), inventories and property, plant and equipment, and provisions to be settled by the delivery of a non-monetary asset.

A contract to receive (or deliver) a variable number of the entity's own equity instruments or a variable amount of assets in which the fair value to be received (or delivered) equals a fixed or determinable number of currency units is also a monetary item. [IAS 21.16] For example, an issued US$100,000 loan note repayable in ordinary shares to the value of US$100,000 meets the definition of a monetary item.

Where preference shares are classified as debt by the issuer, they will typically be a monetary liability for the issuer and a monetary asset for the holder. Where preference shares are classified as equity by the issuer, they will be recorded in equity by the issuer, typically using the rate on the date that they were issued. They will be a non-monetary asset for the holder and will, on initial recognition, typically be recorded using the rate on the date that they were acquired. Such assets may often subsequently be measured at fair value and the fair value will reflect the rate at the date of the valuation.

Example 3.1

Foreign currency defined benefit pension scheme

UK Entity A has a defined benefit pension scheme that invests in UK equities under which the benefits to employees will be denominated in Sterling. The functional currency of Entity A, determined in accordance with IAS 21, is the US dollar.

Pensions and other employee benefits to be paid in cash are classified as monetary items in accordance with IAS 21.16. Therefore, at the end of each reporting period, the pension balance should be translated using the closing rate. The foreign exchange exposure arises as a result of the functional currency of Entity A (i.e. the pension scheme itself is not affected by the US dollar). Consequently, any exchange difference arising from the translation of the pension balance at the end of the reporting period represents a foreign currency exposure for Entity A, and should be recognised in profit or loss in accordance with IAS 21.28. Amounts recognised in profit or loss in accordance with IAS 19.61 are generally translated using the average rate as an approximation of the exchange rates ruling at the dates of the transactions.

3.2 Monetary item that forms part of a net investment in a foreign operation

An entity may have a monetary item that is receivable from or payable to a foreign operation. An item for which settlement is neither planned nor likely to occur in the foreseeable future is, in substance, part of the entity's net investment in that foreign operation. An example is a long-term financing loan to the foreign operation where there are no fixed repayment terms, where management confirms that repayment is neither planned nor likely in the future. Such monetary items may include long-term receivables or loans. They do not include trade receivables or trade payables. [IAS 21.15]

Exchange gains or losses on such monetary items are recognised in accordance with IAS 21.32 – 33 (see **4.2.3.4** below).

IAS 21 does not specify a time period that might qualify as the 'foreseeable future'. Therefore, the term 'foreseeable future' is not meant to imply a specific time period, but is an intent-based indicator, i.e. an intragroup receivable or payable may qualify as part of the net investment in the foreign operation where:

- the parent does not intend to require repayment of the intragroup account (which cannot be represented if the debt has a maturity date that is not waived); and
- the parent's management views the intragroup account as part of its investment in the foreign operation.

A history of repayments is likely to be indicative that an advance or loan does not form part of the investment in a foreign operation.

Example 3.2A

Rolling balance intragroup accounts

Company A, with the Singapore dollar as its functional currency, advances Euros to its foreign subsidiary, Company B. Company B has identified the Euro as its functional currency. Company B may repay some of the advances but, generally, they are replaced with new advances in a very short time frame (e.g. three to five days). In total, Company B generally has 50 million Euro advances outstanding at all times. Can the Euro advances be treated by Company A as part of its net investment in Company B?

Rolling balance and minimum balance intragroup accounts generally do not form part of the net investment in a foreign operation under IAS 21. IAS 21.15 specifically excludes trade receivables and trade payables as qualifying assets and liabilities. Intragroup transactions must be evaluated on an individual basis, not on an aggregate or net basis.

Example 3.2B

Parent guarantee of foreign subsidiary's debt

A Swiss entity, AA, has a Mexican subsidiary, BB, with the Mexican peso as its functional currency. BB borrows Swiss francs from a Swiss bank and AA guarantees repayment of the loan. AA has the ability to provide an intragroup loan to BB, but decided not to do so for tax reasons. Interest payments are made by BB, rather than AA. It is not anticipated that the subsidiary itself will repay the loan in the foreseeable future.

Although AA has guaranteed its subsidiary's foreign-currency denominated debt to a third party, that guarantee will not bring the third party loan within the scope of its net investment in the subsidiary as set out in IAS 21.15. Consequently, the translation gains or losses on the Swiss franc-denominated bank debt are recognised in profit or loss, both in BB's individual financial statements and in AA's consolidated financial statements.

Example 3.2C

Foreign-currency denominated intragroup payables arising in the normal course of business

Company J, a Japanese parent, has a wholly-owned Mexican subsidiary, Company M. Company M's management has previously identified the Mexican peso as the entity's functional currency because Company M's sales to third parties are denominated in Mexican pesos, as are its labour costs. Raw material purchases from Company J are denominated in Japanese yen and have resulted in intragroup payables to Company J that are also denominated in Japanese yen. In previous reporting periods, Company M has made cash repayments to Company J relating to these payables. However, no fixed repayment terms have been agreed for the intragroup payables. Although no specific amount has been formally designated as such, the management of Company M believes that a portion of the amounts due to Company J are of a long-term nature. Can that portion of the amounts due be considered part of Company J's net investment in Company M?

IAS 21.15 specifically excludes trade receivables and payables from forming part of an entity's net investment in a foreign operation. Therefore, such balances do not qualify for the exception in IAS 21.15. Moreover, the fact that Company M has made previous cash repayments to Company J leads to a presumption that Company M had the intent to repay the intragroup payables.

However, if Company M negotiates a separate financing long-term advance with its parent, Company J, such that repayment of the advance is not planned or anticipated in the foreseeable future, gains or losses resulting from future foreign currency fluctuations may be accounted for as part of Company J's net investment prospectively from the date of the advance or note payable.

Example 3.2D

Short-term intragroup debt

Company C is a wholly-owned US subsidiary of Company D, a Dutch-based parent. Company C has notes due to Company D that are denominated in

Euros. The notes have stated maturities ranging from six months to one year. Although the notes are short-term by contract, the parent provides a representation each year that it will not demand repayment in that year. Historically, the notes have been renewed each year.

The short-term notes do not qualify for the exception in IAS 21.15.

In order to qualify as long-term investment, settlement must neither be planned nor likely to occur in the foreseeable future. Rolling intragroup balances generally do not form part of the net investment in a foreign operation under IAS 21.15. In the circumstances described, the parent has only represented that it will not require repayment in that year on the rolled-over short-term notes. It has not represented that it will not demand repayment of the notes in the foreseeable future.

Example 3.2E

Replacement of foreign-currency denominated debt with a long-term advance

Company L is a Lesotho subsidiary of Company S, a South African parent. Company L has the loti as its functional currency and Company S has the South African rand as its functional currency. Company L has taken out third-party rand-denominated debt which gives rise to exchange losses. In a restructuring of finances, Company S will repay Company L's foreign currency (rand) denominated debt and Company S will advance replacement funds to Company L denominated in the loti.

It would not be appropriate in this transaction for Company S to consider the exchange differences arising on settlement of the rand-denominated debt as relating to its net investment in Company L. The intragroup borrowing and settlement of third-party debt should be accounted for separately.

Although IAS 21.15 discusses the accounting for an intragroup foreign currency advance that is of a long-term nature, the transactions should be accounted for as they occur. Therefore, any foreign currency adjustments related to settlement of the third-party debt should be recorded in profit or loss in the period in which the exchange rate changes. However, if the advance from Company S to Company L is of a long-term nature for which settlement is not planned or anticipated in the foreseeable future, it may be treated as part of Company S's net investment in Company L pursuant to IAS 21.15.

3.2.1 Loans or advances from other group entities

The entity that has a monetary item receivable from or payable to the foreign operation may be the parent entity or any subsidiary in the group, including another foreign operation. [IAS 21.15A]

For example, an entity has two subsidiaries, A and B. Subsidiary B is a foreign operation. Subsidiary A grants a loan to Subsidiary B. Subsidiary A's loan receivable from Subsidiary B would be part of the entity's net investment in Subsidiary B if settlement of the loan is neither planned nor likely to occur in the foreseeable future. [IAS 21.15A]

3.2.2 *Loans or advances denominated in another currency*

Most frequently, a monetary item that meets the requirements in paragraphs 15 and 15A will be denominated in the functional currency of the foreign operation or alternatively in the functional currency of the reporting entity. However, it may be denominated in a currency other than the functional currency of either entity. For example, the monetary item may be denominated in a currency that is more readily convertible than the local domestic currency of the foreign operation.

IAS 21.33 is clear that foreign exchange differences on a monetary item denominated in a currency other than the functional currency of either the reporting entity or the foreign operation also qualify for initial recognition in other comprehensive income in the consolidated financial statements, provided the requirements in paragraphs 15 and 15A are met (see **4.2.3.4** below).

3.3 Functional currency

As stated above, an entity's functional currency is the currency of the primary economic environment in which the entity operates. In preparing financial statements, each entity is required to determine its functional currency in accordance with IAS 21.9 – 14. This applies whether the entity is a stand-alone entity, an entity with foreign operations (such as a parent) or a foreign operation (such as a subsidiary or branch). There is no concept of a 'group functional currency' in IFRSs.

3.3.1 *Primary indicators of a functional currency*

IAS 21.9 explains that the primary economic environment in which an entity operates is normally the one in which it primarily generates and expends cash. When determining its functional currency, an entity considers:

[IAS 21.9]

(a) the currency that mainly influences sales prices for goods and services (which is often the currency in which those sales prices are denominated and settled) and the currency of the country whose competitive forces and regulations mainly determine the sales prices of its goods and services; and

(b) the currency that mainly influences labour, material and other costs of providing goods or services (which will often be the currency in which such costs are denominated and settled).

3.3.2 *Further indicators of a functional currency*

When determining its functional currency, an entity may also need to consider:

[IAS 21.10]

(a) the currency in which funds from financing activities (i.e. issuing debt and equity instruments) are generated; and
(b) the currency in which receipts from operating activities are usually retained.

3.3.3 *Assessing whether the functional currency of a foreign operation is the same as that of a reporting entity to which it is related*

Where the entity is a foreign operation, additional factors are set out in IAS 21.11 to consider in determining whether its functional currency is the same as that of the reporting entity of which it is a subsidiary, branch, associate or joint venture:

[IAS 21.11]

(a) whether the activities of the foreign operation are carried out as an extension of that reporting entity, rather than being carried out with a significant degree of autonomy. If the foreign operation only sells goods imported from that reporting entity and remits the proceeds to it, this will be an example of the former. An example of the latter is when the foreign operation accumulates cash and other monetary items, incurs expenses, generates income and arranges borrowings, all substantially in its local currency;

(b) whether transactions with that reporting entity are a high or a low proportion of the foreign operation's activities;

(c) whether cash flows from the activities of the foreign operation directly affect the cash flows of that reporting entity and are readily available for remittance to it; and

(d) whether cash flows from the activities of the foreign operation are sufficient to service existing and normally expected debt obligations without funds being made available by that reporting entity.

The functional currency of a foreign operation that is integral to the group will be the same as that of the parent; it would be contradictory for an integral foreign operation that carries on business as if it were an extension of the parent entity's operations to operate in a primary economic environment different from its parent. [IAS 21.BC6]

3.3.4 *Applying the guidance*

When the indicators above are mixed and the functional currency is not obvious, management should use judgement to determine the functional currency that most faithfully represents the economic effects of transactions, events and conditions. As part of this approach, management should give priority to the primary indicators in **3.3.1** above before considering the indicators in **3.3.2** and **3.3.3**. [IAS 21.12]

Consideration of the following additional factors, based on the nature of the foreign operation, may assist in the determination of functional currency.

- Where an intermediate parent carries out duties related to the sub-group in which it holds investments (e.g. when the entity has different directors/employees from the ultimate parent entity, has its own reporting responsibilities and produces consolidated financial statements including the sub-group, and actively manages a series of operations in a geographical area, and, therefore, incurs costs in a local currency), this would indicate that the functional currency of the entity is not the same as that of the ultimate parent. Where the intermediate parent exists solely in order for the ultimate parent to obtain a tax, regulatory, jurisdictional or legal type of benefit it would not otherwise receive, this indicates that it is an extension of its parent entity.

- Where the foreign operation is clearly set up as a special purpose entity (SPE), its activities are being conducted on behalf of the parent entity (e.g. employee benefit trusts, leasing vehicles, etc.) and the SPE is an extension of the reporting entity, it should have the same functional currency as that of the reporting entity.

- For treasury entities, it is necessary to assess whether they exist to serve the funding and cash management needs of the group as a whole (i.e. constitute an extension of the parent entity), or whether they exist solely to service a specific sub-group. In the latter case, the functional currency of the treasury entity may be different to that of the parent entity.

- A 'money-box' entity is an entity that holds cash only. In accordance with the factors in IAS 21.9 – 12, it is not the currency of the cash that the entity holds that is the deciding factor in determining functional currency. Consistent with the bullet points above, it is necessary to consider for whose benefit the 'money-box' entity exists, which will determine its functional currency.

Example 3.3.4

Functional currency of an operating entity versus a shell corporation

Company M has identified the Euro as its functional currency. Company M establishes two entities, Company P and Company Q. Company P is incorporated in the US and Company Q is incorporated in the UK. The following transactions occurred:

- Company M loaned £2 million each to Company P and Company Q, and both recorded the transaction as an intragroup payable;
- Company Q borrowed an additional £3 million from an unrelated third party. Company P guaranteed this third party loan;
- Company Q invested its entire £5 million in building a manufacturing facility to serve the domestic UK market. Company Q intends to repay the loan to the third party from the profit generated through its manufacturing operations; and
- Company P used its £2 million loan from Company M to invest in marketable securities in international markets.

What are the functional currencies of Company P and Company Q?

In line with the guidance in the previous sections, in general, the functional currency identified for an entity should provide information about the entity that is useful and reflects the economic substance of the underlying events and circumstances relevant to that entity. If a particular currency is used to a significant extent in, or has a significant impact on, the entity, that currency may be an appropriate currency to be used as the functional currency.

Consequently, Sterling would be identified as Company Q's functional currency because that is the currency of the country that influences the sale prices and costs of its goods, as well as the regulations and competitive forces under which it operates.

On the other hand, even though Company P is domiciled in the US, its activities (investing in marketable securities) are carried out as an extension of Company M, such that those activities could have been carried directly in the parent's books. Therefore, in accordance with IAS 21.11(a), Company P should identify the Euro as its functional currency.

3.3.4.1 Functional currency of investment funds

Some features common to investment funds include the following (not an exhaustive list).

- Investors in the fund subscribe and redeem their investments in a specific currency. It may not be permitted, depending on the fund's policies or regulatory requirements, to subscribe or redeem such investments in any other currency.
- The fund may conduct its investment activities through subsidiaries set up in various jurisdictions to take advantage of tax treaties, double taxation agreements, and concessions.
- The investment fund's policies may allow it to invest in various securities regardless of jurisdiction, industry or currency. Consequently, investment transactions and the related income and expenses may be denominated in several currencies.
- Investment management fees may be invoiced and received in a specific currency.
- Other costs of operating the fund may be denominated in the local currency of the jurisdiction in which the fund physically operates.

Given these complexities, how should the functional currency of an investment fund be determined?

As noted above, IAS 21.12 clarifies that, in determining the functional currency of a foreign operation, management should consider the guidance in IAS 21.9 – 11 (see **sections 3.3.1 – 3.3.3**) – giving IAS 21.9 priority before considering IAS 21.10 and 11.

In the context of an investment fund, IAS 21.9 does not seem immediately relevant and is difficult to apply because its factors are directed towards manufacturing entities that provide goods and services. However, the same underlying principle can be applied to a fund with a mandate to buy and sell securities to generate a return for investors. Hence, the currency of the country whose competitive forces and regulations mainly determine the fund's revenue should be considered when determining the functional currency.

The currency in which management fees are charged may provide an indication of the functional currency. In addition, the currencies in which the fund's labour costs, and operating expenses are sourced and incurred should also be considered.

However, when a fund's functional currency is not obvious from the analysis above, consideration of the secondary indicators in paragraph 10 (see **3.3.2**) may provide additional evidence. The currency in which the fund raises finance from investors (i.e. the investor's participation in a fund) and makes distributions to investors (e.g. on redemption) should be considered. The currency in which dividends on investments or interest inflows are received will provide additional evidence of the functional currency.

The indicators in IAS 21.11 (see **3.3.3**) should also be considered if they are relevant to an investment fund (in a foreign operation).

IAS 21.12 states that, when the indicators in IAS 21.9 – 11 are mixed and the functional currency is not obvious, 'management uses its judgement to determine the functional currency that most faithfully represents the economic effects of the underlying transactions, events and conditions'.

3.4 Functional currency is the currency of a hyperinflationary economy

Where the functional currency is the currency of a hyperinflationary economy, the entity's financial statements are restated in accordance with IAS 29 *Financial Reporting in Hyperinflationary Economies* (see **chapter 42**). An entity cannot avoid restatement in accordance with IAS 29 by, for example, adopting as its functional currency a currency other than the functional currency determined in accordance with IAS 21 (such as the functional currency of its parent). [IAS 21.14]

4 Reporting foreign currency transactions in the functional currency

A foreign currency transaction is a transaction that is denominated or requires settlement in a foreign currency. [IAS 21.20] A foreign currency is a currency other than the functional currency of the parent. [IAS 21.8] For example, an entity may:

- buy or sell goods or services at a price denominated in a foreign currency;
- borrow or lend funds where the amounts payable or receivable are denominated in a foreign currency, and/or;
- acquire or dispose of assets, or incur or settle liabilities, denominated in a foreign currency.

When an entity directly enters into such transactions, it is exposed to the cash flow effects of changes in value of the foreign currency. An entity must convert foreign currency items into its functional currency for recognising those items in its accounting records. Once recognised, exchange differences will arise where changes in exchange rates affect the carrying amounts.

4.1 Initial recognition

The functional currency amount at which transactions denominated in foreign currencies should initially be recognised will be determined by using the exchange rate appropriate to the transaction. This is the spot rate between the functional currency and the foreign currency at the date of the transaction. [IAS 21.21] The date of the transaction is the date on which the transaction first qualifies for recognition in accordance with IFRSs. [IAS 21.22]

Example 4.1

Initial recognition of purchase of inventory

An entity with a functional currency of Sterling buys inventory for US$15,000. The spot rate is £1 = US$1.50. The inventory is measured at initial recognition at £10,000 (= 15,000/1.50).

For practical reasons, a rate that approximates the actual rate at the date of the transaction is often used. For example, an average rate for a week or a month might be used for all transactions in each foreign currency occurring during that period. If exchange rates fluctuate significantly, however, the use of the average rate for a period is inappropriate. [IAS 21.22]

It is common practice for entities that engage in a large number of foreign currency transactions to fix, for a period, the rate of exchange used to measure those transactions in their accounting records and to disregard day-to-day fluctuations in exchange rates. Where this approach is used, care must be taken to ensure that the carrying amount of non-monetary assets, particularly inventory, is not materially different from what it would have been if actual rates had been used for translation. The actual rates should be used if a material difference would arise compared to average rates, for example to measure large one-off transactions such as the acquisition of property, plant and equipment, or in the event of severe currency devaluation.

4.2 Reporting at the end of subsequent reporting periods

The treatment of foreign currency items at the end of each reporting period depends on whether the item is:

- monetary or non-monetary; and
- carried at historical cost or fair value.

4.2.1 *Monetary items*

At the end of each reporting period, foreign currency monetary items are translated using the closing rate, i.e. the spot exchange rate at the end of the reporting period. [IAS 21.23(a)]

4.2.2 *Non-monetary items*

The carrying amount of an item is determined in conjunction with other relevant IFRSs.

Non-monetary items that are measured in terms of historical cost in a foreign currency are translated using the spot exchange rate at the date of the transaction, i.e. they remain at the initial recognised amount and are not retranslated. [IAS 21.23(b)] These balances reflect the historical cost in the functional currency of acquiring the items.

Example 4.2.2A

Non-monetary item measured at historical cost

Company T holds an investment in a Japanese entity. The investment is accounted for appropriately under IAS 39.46(c) at cost because the securities

> do not have a quoted market price in an active market and their fair value cannot be reliably measured. Company T's initial investment was made in Japanese yen and represented 4.3 million Euros at the date of acquisition of the investment. At the end of the reporting period, the historical cost in Japanese yen, if translated at the closing rate, would correspond to 6 million Euros.
>
> It would not be appropriate to recognise the 1.7 million Euro increase as a translation gain. IAS 21.23 states that non-monetary items denominated in a foreign currency measured in terms of historical cost should be reported using the exchange rate at the date of the transaction. Accordingly, the investment will continue to be measured at 4.3 million Euros.

Non-monetary items that are measured at fair value in a foreign currency are translated using the spot exchange rates at the date when the value was determined. [IAS 21.23(c)]

Sometimes the carrying amount of assets is determined by comparing two or more amounts, for example:

- the lower of cost and net realisable value for inventory (IAS 2 *Inventories*); or
- the lower of an asset's previous carrying amount and its recoverable amount to determine the amount of an impairment loss (IAS 36 *Impairment of Assets*).

Where the asset is non-monetary and is measured in a foreign currency, the carrying amount is determined as the lower of:

[IAS 21.25]

- the cost or carrying amount translated at the exchange rate at the date that amount was determined (the rate at the transaction date for items carried at historical cost); and
- the net realisable value or recoverable amount translated at the exchange rate at the date that value or amount was determined. This will be the closing rate if the value was determined at the end of the reporting period.

The effect of this may be that an impairment loss is recognised in the functional currency but would not be recognised in the foreign currency, or vice versa.

> **Example 4.2.2B**
>
> **Write-down of non-monetary asset**
>
> Company A is a UK entity, and has Sterling as its functional currency.

Company A purchases inventory, which it plans to sell in Euros, for €150 when the exchange rate is £1: €1.50. At the end of the reporting period, the inventory is slightly damaged and Company A determines the net realisable value (NRV) to be €120. At the end of the reporting period, the exchange rate is £1: €1.2.

At the end of the reporting period, the inventory is impaired in Euros (by €30) but not in Sterling, as the exchange rate has moved.

The inventory is initially recognised at £100 (= €150/€1.5).

When determining the net realisable value (NRV), the currency in which the inventory will be sold is used. For Company A, this is Euros.

At the end of the reporting period, the carrying amount is determined by comparing:

- cost of €150 translated at the transaction date rate of £1: €1.50, and
- NRV of €120 translated at the closing rate of £1: €1.20.

These are both £100, so there is no write-down of inventory in the financial statements of Company A.

4.2.3 *Recognition of exchange differences*

4.2.3.1 *Exchange differences on monetary items*

Exchange differences arise on:

- the settlement of monetary items at a date subsequent to initial recognition; and
- remeasuring an entity's monetary items at rates different from those at which they were either initially recognised (if in the period) or previously measured (at the end of the previous reporting period).

Such exchange differences must be recognised as income or expenses in profit or loss in the period in which they arise, except as described in **4.2.3.4** below. [IAS 21.28]

As noted in **section 2**, however, where an item is within the scope of IAS 39 (for example, it is a foreign currency derivative within the scope of IAS 39 or a debt instrument that qualifies as a hedging instrument), IAS 21 does not apply and IAS 39 should be applied instead.

An exchange difference on a foreign currency monetary item occurs when there is a change in the exchange rate between the transaction date and the date of settlement. When the transaction is settled within the same accounting period as that in which it occurred, the entire exchange difference is recognised in that period. When the transaction is settled in a different accounting period to that in which it occurred, the exchange difference to be recognised in each period is determined by the change in exchange rates during that period. [IAS 21.11]

Example 4.2.3.1

Exchange differences arising on borrowings denominated in a foreign currency

Transaction gains or losses are the result of movements in the exchange rate between the functional currency of an entity and the foreign currency in which receivables or payables are denominated. For example, an entity has the US dollar as its functional currency and it has borrowed Japanese yen resulting in a yen-denominated payable. Transaction gains or losses will be recognised in profit or loss on the outstanding yen-denominated debt for changes in the spot rate of exchange between the Japanese yen and the US dollar at the end of the reporting period.

4.2.3.2 Exchange differences on non-monetary items

When a gain or loss on a non-monetary item is recognised in profit or loss (e.g. the sale of investments carried at historical cost), any exchange component of that gain or loss is also recognised in profit or loss. When a gain or loss on a non-monetary item is recognised in other comprehensive income, any exchange component of that gain or loss is also recognised in other comprehensive income. [IAS 21.30]

For example, IAS 16 requires some gains and losses arising on a revaluation of property, plant and equipment to be recognised in other comprehensive income. When such an asset is measured in a foreign currency, IAS 21.23(c) requires the revalued amount to be translated using the rate at the date the value is determined, resulting in an exchange difference that is also recognised in other comprehensive income.

Example 4.2.3.2

Non-monetary asset measured at fair value in a foreign currency

On 1 November 20X1, Company A (Sterling functional currency) buys a building for US$50,000,000, with full payment being made on that date. The exchange rate is US$1.68:£1. At the end of Company A's reporting period, 31 December 20X1, the building is not depreciated as it is not yet available for use. The exchange rate is US$1.71:£1 and the fair value of the building is US$60,000,000 at that date.

The journal entries are as follows:

1 November 20X1

Dr	Property, plant and equipment	£29,761,905	
Cr	Cash		£29,761,905

To recognise the US$ transaction in the functional currency at the exchange rate at the time of the transaction US$1.68:£1.

Depending on whether Company A accounts for its buildings at cost less accumulated depreciation and any impairment loss, or at a revalued amount, subsequent accounting entries are as follows:

At cost less accumulated depreciation and any impairment loss

31 December 20X1

The building is a non-monetary item and held at historical cost. It continues to be measured at £29,761,905, i.e. at the transaction rate.

At revalued amount

31 December 20X1

The building is a non-monetary item and held at fair value. It is retranslated at the rate of exchange at the date of valuation.

Dr	Property, plant and equipment	£5,325,814	
Cr	Revaluation gain (other comprehensive income)		£5,325,814

To recognise a gain in fair value of £5,325,814 (35,087,719 – 29,761,905), which includes the exchange component.

Note: where an asset's revalued amount is less than its carrying amount, and no credit balance exists in the revaluation surplus in respect of the asset, an expense is recognised in profit or loss.

4.2.3.3 *Foreign-currency denominated available-for-sale financial assets*

In accordance with IAS 39, available-for-sale financial assets are measured at fair value with fair value gains or losses recognised in other comprehensive income and reclassified from equity to profit or loss when the asset is derecognised or impaired (see **3.5** in **chapter 14**).

For the purpose of recognising foreign exchange gains and losses in respect of available-for-sale financial assets that are monetary items, IAS 39.AG83 requires that such items be treated as if they are carried at amortised cost in the foreign currency. Therefore, exchange differences resulting from changes in amortised cost are recognised in profit or loss, with other changes in the carrying amount recognised in other comprehensive income in accordance with IAS 39.55(b).

This treatment results in the cumulative gain or loss recognised in other comprehensive income being the difference between the amortised cost (adjusted for impairment, if any) and the fair value of the instrument in the functional currency of the reporting entity. The approach is illustrated in a numerical example (IAS 39.IG.E.3.2) – which is reproduced as **example 3.3** in **chapter 18**.

For non-monetary available-for-sale financial assets (e.g. equity investments), the gain or loss that is recognised in other comprehensive income includes any related foreign currency component.

4.2.3.4 *Exchange differences on monetary items to be recognised outside profit or loss*

Certain monetary items are outside the scope of IAS 21 because they are instead dealt with by IAS 39 (for example, an item designated as a hedging instrument). For monetary items within the scope of IAS 21, however, there is only one exception to the requirement that exchange differences are recognised in profit or loss. Where a monetary item forms part of a reporting entity's net investment in a foreign operation (see **3.2**):

[IAS 21.32]

- exchange differences are recognised in profit or loss in the separate financial statements of the reporting entity and of the foreign operation, as appropriate; but
- in any financial statements that include both the reporting entity and the foreign operation (e.g. consolidated financial statements if the foreign operation is a subsidiary), such exchange differences are recognised initially in other comprehensive income and reclassified from equity to profit or loss on disposal of the net investment in accordance with IAS 21.48) (see **5.5**).

The effect of this in the 'consolidated' financial statements (i.e. those that combine the reporting entity and the foreign operation) will be as follows:

[IAS 21.33]

- a monetary item denominated in the functional currency of the reporting entity will give rise to an exchange difference in the foreign operation, and this is recognised in other comprehensive income as above;
- a monetary item denominated in the functional currency of the foreign operation will give rise to an exchange difference in the reporting entity, and this is recognised in other comprehensive income as above; and

- a monetary item denominated in a currency other than the functional currency of either the reporting entity or the foreign operation will give rise to an exchange difference in the separate financial statements of both the foreign operation and the reporting entity, and these are recognised in other comprehensive income as above.

UK

SSAP 20(20) includes a similar concept of loans to (and deferred balances with) foreign entities that are 'as permanent as equity', and the treatment of such balances in consolidated financial statements is similar to that under IAS 21. However, under SSAP 20, such balances are sometimes not retranslated in the individual financial statements of the investor, in which case no exchange differences are recognised on such items in the individual financial statements. Under IAS 21, such balances are retranslated and any exchange gains and losses arising are recognised in profit or loss in the individual financial statements of the investor.

Example 4.2.3.4A

Transaction gains or losses on dividends

If a foreign subsidiary, with a functional currency different to that of the parent, declares a dividend to its parent (the legal effect being such that the parent's right to the dividend is established), and there is a significant time lag between the date of recognition of the dividend revenue and the date when the dividend is received, what is the appropriate accounting for the translation gain or loss arising on the parent's dividend receivable account?

IAS 21 does not address this issue specifically. However, the receivable is a monetary item and will not meet the criteria to be treated as part of the net investment in the subsidiary (on the basis that payment is expected in the foreseeable future). Accordingly, gains and losses on retranslating the monetary item will be taken to profit or loss by the parent, and will not be reclassified on consolidation of the subsidiary.

This may be contrasted with the exchange gains and losses arising when an interest in a subsidiary is retranslated on consolidation, which are recognised in other comprehensive income (see **5.2**). IAS 21.41 states that the reason for not recognising those translation adjustments in profit or loss for the period is that the changes in the exchange rates have little or no direct effect on the present and future cash flows from operations of either the foreign entity or the reporting entity. Where a dividend has already given rise to an asset in the parent, however, changes in exchange rates will have a direct effect on the parent's future cash inflows (see also the discussion in **5.4.1**.)

Example 4.2.3.4B

Changing the form of a long-term investment which forms part of the net investment in a foreign operation

A UK entity, Company A, has a Canadian subsidiary to which it has made advances that are denominated in Canadian dollars. Company A has previously represented its intention that the advances are a long-term investment. Consequently, exchange gains and losses on the advances have been recognised in other comprehensive income in the consolidated financial statements in accordance with IAS 21.32. There have been no previous repayments of these advances. Company A now proposes to contribute cash to the Canadian subsidiary in the form of a capital contribution and the Canadian subsidiary will immediately use the cash received to repay the advances.

In the proposed transaction, Company A is replacing one form of long-term investment (long-term advances) with another form of long-term investment (capital contribution). The translation adjustment attributable to the long-term intragroup advances should remain as a component of equity until the disposal or partial disposal of the Canadian subsidiary, at which time they will be reclassified from equity to profit or loss as a reclassification adjustment.

4.2.4 Exchange rates – other considerations

4.2.4.1 Several exchange rates available

In some circumstances there may be several exchange rates available, for example where a country is experiencing turmoil and its government has imposed an exchange rate that is different from the spot exchange rate, in order to discourage the outflow of capital from that country.

Where several exchange rates are available, the rate to be used is that at which the future cash flows represented by the transaction or balance could have been settled if those cash flows had occurred at the measurement date. [IAS 21.26]

4.2.4.2 Unofficial exchange rate for translation and remeasurement

When there is both an official exchange rate, *and* an unofficial exchange rate, and the unofficial exchange rate is used both widely and legally for the purposes of currency conversions, a parallel or dual exchange rate situation exists.

In such circumstances, if it can be demonstrated reasonably that transactions have been or will be settled at the unofficial rate (including currency exchanges for dividend or profit repatriations), it is appropriate to use the unofficial rate for translation and remeasurement purposes.

Example 4.2.4.2

Dividend remittance rate specified by government

A country is experiencing turmoil, and the government has imposed an exchange rate different from the spot market exchange rate in order to discourage capital from leaving the country. The new rate is the dividend remittance rate. This specific exchange rate applies to all remittances of earnings or dividends distributed outside the country.

IAS 21.8 defines the closing rate as 'the spot exchange rate at the end of the reporting period.' The closing rate should be the rate the entity currently would pay/receive in the market. Therefore, under the above scenario, the dividend remittance rate would be appropriate for translation purposes because cash flows to the reporting entity can only occur at this rate, and the realisation of a net investment is dependent upon cash flows from that foreign entity.

Unusual circumstances that may permit an entity to use the market exchange rate in translating a foreign subsidiary in the circumstances described above would include (1) a history of obtaining the market exchange rate for such transactions, and (2) the ability to source funds at the market exchange rate. Otherwise, the dividend remittance rate should be used.

Careful judgement should be applied to determine whether those circumstances result in the loss of control in accordance with IAS 27(2008).32 (see **4.3.4** in **chapter 33**).

4.2.4.3 Lack of exchangeability between two currencies

Where exchangeability between two currencies is temporarily lacking, the rate used is the first subsequent rate at which exchanges could be made. [IAS 21.26]

4.2.4.4 Exchange rate movements after the end of the reporting period

Example 4.2.4.4

Exchange rate movements after the end of the reporting period

Company G is a German entity with a Russian subsidiary. The subsidiary's functional currency is the Russian ruble. The subsidiary has Euro-denominated debt. The Russian ruble exchange rate against the Euro has fluctuated significantly in the two months before and after the end of the reporting period.

IAS 21.23(a) states that foreign currency monetary items should be reported at the end of each reporting period using the closing rate, with no exceptions provided. It would not be appropriate to use an exchange rate subsequent to the end of the reporting period, even though exchange rates are volatile.

Due to the significant volatility in exchange rates, however, the effect on foreign currency monetary items of a change in exchange rates occurring after the end of the reporting period should be disclosed if the change is of such significance that non-disclosure would affect the ability of users of the financial statements to make proper evaluations and decisions (see **section 6.1** in **chapter 31**.)

4.2.5 *Accounting records in a currency other than the functional currency*

When an entity keeps its accounting records in a currency other than its functional currency, at the time the entity prepares its financial statements all amounts are translated into the functional currency in accordance with IAS 21.20 – 26, so as to produce the same amounts in the functional currency as would have occurred had the items been recognised initially in the functional currency. [IAS 21.34]

4.3 Change in functional currency

As noted in **3.3**, the functional currency of an entity reflects the underlying transactions, events and conditions that are relevant to the entity. Accordingly, once determined, the functional currency can be changed only if there is a change to those underlying transactions, events and conditions. [IAS 21.13] For example, a change in the currency that mainly influences the sales prices of goods and services may lead to a change in an entity's functional currency. [IAS 21.36]

Example 4.3A

Impact of foreign currency borrowings on functional currency

Company K's functional currency is the Euro. Company K accounts for its 43 per cent investment in Company M, a Mexican entity, using the equity method of accounting. Company M's functional currency is the Mexican peso. During the current year, Company M entered into a 200 million Euro third-party borrowing denominated in Euros. Most of Company M's operations, labour costs and purchases are denominated in the peso and incurred in the domestic market. Is it appropriate for Company M to change its functional currency from the peso to the Euro?

Since the majority of Company M's operations, sales, purchases, labour costs, etc. are denominated in the Mexican peso, and Mexico is the country that drives the competitive forces and regulations of that entity, Company M should continue using the Mexican peso as its functional currency. Although, in accordance with IAS 21.10, a large third-party financing in the significant shareholder's functional currency may in some circumstances provide evidence to support a change in functional currency, greater weight must be given to the factors discussed in IAS 21.9 (sales, purchases, labour costs etc.). Accordingly, in this situation, the new financing is not sufficient to demonstrate a change in the functional currency from the peso to the Euro.

Example 4.3B

Change in functional currency

KI, located in Ireland, is a wholly-owned subsidiary of Company K. The US dollar is Company K's functional currency and KI has previously identified the Euro as its functional currency. The functional currency was identified because KI's sales and purchases were denominated primarily in Euros, as were all of KI's labour costs. During the fourth quarter, KI's operations began to change. KI's sales decreased due to a loss of some sizable contracts while Company K's sales increased due to new significant contracts. Company K began using KI's manufacturing facilities in order to meet its sales orders. KI closed down its sales department because KI will no longer need to generate its own sales because more than 80 per cent will originate from Company K's operations. Company K has built a new facility to produce the materials needed in its manufacturing processes. As of the end of the fiscal year, KI began receiving all materials from Company K instead of from outside suppliers.

Based on the changes in KI's business, KI expects cash inflows and outflows, except for wages, primarily to be denominated in US dollars.

IAS 21.36 states that a change in the currency that influences mainly the sales prices of goods and services may lead to a change in functional currency. In addition, the changes in KI's activities may be such that they are now primarily an extension of the reporting entity, Company K, as discussed in IAS 21.11(a).

There is evidence to suggest that KI's functional currency may have changed. For example, the currency of revenues has changed from the Euro to primarily the US dollar. This change does not appear to be temporary since the sales department has been closed down. Secondly, the currency of cash outflows for materials has also changed to the US dollar. Company K has built a new facility that will make these materials, so this change does not appear to be temporary either. Lastly, the position of KI's operations within Company K's overall operating strategy has changed, from a self-supporting, stand-alone operating entity to what is primarily a manufacturing facility of Company K.

The change in functional currency should be reported as of the date it is determined that there has been a change in the underlying events and circumstances relevant to that entity that justifies a change in the functional currency. This could occur on any date during the year. For convenience, and as a practical matter, there is a practice of using a date at the beginning of the most recent period (annual or interim, as the case might be).

In accordance with IAS 21.35, when there is a change in an entity's functional currency, the entity applies the translation procedures applicable to the new functional currency prospectively from the date of the change.

In other words, all items are translated into the new functional currency using the exchange rate at the date of the change. The resulting translated amounts for non-monetary items are treated as their historical cost. Exchange differences arising from the translation of a foreign operation previously recognised in other comprehensive income are not reclassified from equity to profit or loss until the disposal of the operation (see **5.5**). [IAS 21.37]

An entity must disclose when there has been a change in functional currency, and the reasons for the change (see **8.2**).

5 Presentation currency

The presentation currency is defined as the currency in which the financial statements are presented. [IAS 21.8] Unlike the functional currency, the presentation currency can be any currency of choice.

Presenting the financial statements in a currency other than the functional currency does not change the way in which the underlying items are measured. It merely expresses the underlying amounts, which are measured in the functional currency, in a different currency.

5.1 Choice of presentation currency

The most common use of a presentation currency is in the context of a consolidated group. When a group contains entities with different functional currencies, the results and financial position of each entity must be expressed in a common currency in order to produce the consolidated financial statements. The presentation currency of the consolidated financial statements of the group is often, but not always, the functional currency of the parent.

A corporate group may have extensive operations in many countries and conduct its business largely in international markets. It may be difficult to identify the most appropriate presentation currency. An international currency such as Sterling, the US dollar or the Euro might be used. For example, for entities that raise capital in international markets, the use of an international currency may be of benefit to the users of the financial statements.

Individual entities, or groups where all of the entities have the same functional currency, may also choose to present their financial statements in a currency other than their functional currency. This option may be selected, for example:

- to provide information to overseas shareholders; or
- for the purpose of preparing statutory financial statements in some jurisdictions where entities are required to present their financial statements in the local currency even if this is not their functional currency; or
- by a subsidiary who wishes to present its financial statements in the functional currency of its parent where that is different from its own functional currency.

Whilst it is customary for a UK entity to produce its statutory financial instruments in Sterling, there are no restrictions in UK company law which prevent a company from using a foreign currency for this purpose, if there are good reasons for doing so. UK

5.2 Translation to the presentation currency

Except where the functional currency is the currency of a hyperinflationary economy (see **5.3**), an entity's results and financial position are translated from its functional currency into a different presentation currency using the following procedures:

[IAS 21.39]

(a) assets and liabilities for each statement of financial position presented (i.e. including comparatives), are translated at the closing rate at the date of that statement of financial position;

(b) for each period presented (i.e. including comparative periods) income and expenses recognised in the period are translated at the exchange rates at the dates of the transactions; and

(c) all resulting exchange differences are recognised in other comprehensive income.

Cash flows are translated on a basis similar to that required for income and expenses, i.e. using the exchange rates at the transaction dates. [IAS 7.25 – 6]

Equity transactions (e.g. contributions to equity share capital, distributions to owners of equity) are also translated at the exchange rates at the transaction dates.

For practical reasons, a rate that approximates the exchange rates at the dates of the transactions (e.g. an average rate for the period) is often used to translate income and expense items in step (b) above. If exchange rates fluctuate significantly, however, the use of the average rate for a period is inappropriate. [IAS 21.40]

IAS 21.41 explains that exchange differences resulting from translation into a presentation currency are not recognised in profit or loss because those changes in exchange rates have little or no direct effect on the present and future cash flows from operations.

The exchange differences arising on translation to the presentation currency result from:

[IAS 21.41]

- translating income and expenses at the exchange rates at the dates of the transactions and assets and liabilities at the closing rate; and
- translating the opening net assets at an exchange rate (closing rate) different from that at which they were previously reported.

IAS 21.39 provides rules for the translation of income, expenses, assets and liabilities. It does not refer to the translation, or retranslation, of share capital or other equity reserves. But, as explained above, it mandates the amounts to be recognised in other comprehensive income, and later reclassified to profit and loss on disposal or partial disposal. Those amounts do not reflect any retranslation of share capital or other equity reserves.

Although IAS 21 does not specifically prohibit the retranslation of share capital and other equity reserves, such a retranslation would have no meaning for financial reporting purposes, and might confuse or even mislead users of financial statements. Moreover, where an entity accumulates the exchange differences recognised in other comprehensive income as a separate component of equity (a 'foreign currency translation reserve'), it would not be appropriate for that reserve to include any amounts for the retranslation of share capital or other equity reserves – such 'differences' will never be reclassified to profit or loss.

Accordingly, it is appropriate to translate share capital and other components of equity using the historical rate, i.e. the exchange rate at the date of issue of share capital, or at the date of the associated transaction for other equity reserves. In particular:

- when translating share capital into the presentation currency, the rate at the date of issue should be used. Thus, more than one historical rate will apply when share capital is issued at different times; and

- when translating a revaluation reserve (for example, when an item of property, plant, or equipment is revalued in accordance with IAS 16 *Property, Plant and Equipment*) into the presentation currency, the rate at the date of the latest revaluation should be used. Thus, more than one historical rate will apply when a revaluation reserve relates to different assets that have been revalued at different times.

5.3 Translation to presentation currency from the currency of a hyperinflationary economy

Where an entity's functional currency is the currency of a hyperinflationary economy, the entity must first restate its financial statements in accordance with IAS 29 *Financial Reporting in Hyperinflationary Economies* before translating its results into its chosen presentation currency (see **chapter 42**). Note, however, that the treatment of comparative amounts translated into the currency of a non-hyperinflationary economy is different, as discussed below. [IAS 21.43]

Once the entity's financial statements have been restated in accordance with IAS 29, if the entity chooses to present them in a different presentation currency, the results and financial position of that entity are translated into a different presentation currency as follows:

[IAS 21.42]

- all amounts (i.e. assets, liabilities, equity items, income and expenses, including comparatives) are translated at the closing rate at the date of the statement of financial position, except that

- where comparative amounts are translated into the currency of a non-hyperinflationary economy, all amounts are those presented in the prior financial statements (i.e. they are not adjusted for subsequent changes in the price level or subsequent changes in exchange rates).

Note that the different treatment of comparatives described above does not apply when the presentation currency is that of a (different) hyperinflationary economy. In those circumstances, all amounts are translated at the closing rate of the most recent statement of financial position presented (i.e. last year's comparatives, as adjusted for subsequent changes in the price level, are translated at this year's closing rate).

When the economy ceases to be hyperinflationary and the entity no longer restates its financial statements in accordance with IAS 29, it uses as the historical costs for translation into the presentation currency the amounts restated to the price level at the date the entity ceased restating its financial statements. [IAS 21.43]

5.4 Translation of a foreign operation

In addition to the procedures discussed in **5.2** and **5.3**, there are other rules in IAS 21 that apply when the results and financial position of a foreign operation are translated into a presentation currency for inclusion in the financial statements of a reporting entity (whether by consolidation, proportionate consolidation or the equity method). These rules deal with:

- exchange differences on intragroup transactions;

- financial statements of foreign operations prepared to a different date; and

- goodwill and fair value adjustments.

The incorporation of the results and financial position of a foreign operation in the financial statements of a reporting entity follows normal consolidation procedures as set out in IAS 27 *Consolidated and Separate Financial Statements*, IAS 28 *Investments in Associates* and IAS 31 *Interests in Joint Ventures*. These Standards are discussed in **chapter 33, chapter 35** and **chapter 36** respectively.

Where a foreign operation is consolidated but is not wholly-owned, accumulated exchange differences arising from translation and attributable to non-controlling interests are allocated to, and recognised as part of, non-controlling interests in the consolidated statement of financial position. [IAS 21.41]

5.4.1 *Exchange differences on intragroup transactions*

An intragroup monetary asset (or liability), whether short-term or long-term, cannot be eliminated against the corresponding intragroup liability (or asset) without showing exchange differences in the consolidated financial statements.

The monetary item represents a commitment to convert one currency into another and, hence, the entity is exposed to an exchange gain or loss.

Accordingly, in the consolidated financial statements of the reporting entity, such an exchange difference is recognised in profit or loss unless it is a monetary item that forms part of the reporting entity's net investment in the foreign operation in accordance with **3.2** above. [IAS 21.45]

5.4.2 *Financial statements of a foreign operation as of a different date*

A foreign operation may prepare financial statements as of a date different from that of the reporting entity, e.g. for tax reasons or if legislation in its country requires financial statements to be prepared to a specific date. Often the foreign operation will prepare additional statements as of the same date as those of the reporting entity (investor) for inclusion in the consolidated financial statements.

Where it is impracticable to prepare additional statements, IAS 27 allows the use of a different date, provided that the difference is no greater than three months and adjustments are made for the effects of any significant transactions or other events that occur between the different dates.

If the foreign operation's financial statements are prepared as of a different date, the assets and liabilities of the foreign operation are translated at the exchange rate at that date (i.e. at the end of the reporting period of the foreign operation). In accordance with IAS 27, adjustments are made for significant changes in exchange rates up to the end of the reporting period of the reporting entity. For example, significant movements may arise between the two dates if the functional currency of the foreign operation devalues significantly against that of the reporting entity.

Example 5.4.2

Financial statements of a foreign operation as of a different date

A parent includes a foreign subsidiary's financial statements for the year ended 30 November in the parent's consolidated financial statements for the year ended 31 December. Between 30 November and 31 December, the functional currency of the subsidiary devalues significantly against the parent's functional currency (which is also the presentation currency of the group).

Where the financial statements of a subsidiary used in the consolidated financial statements are prepared as of a date different from that of the parent, IAS 27(2008).23 requires adjustments to be made for the effects of significant events or transactions that occur between that date and the date of the parent's financial statements. The rate used for the translation of the foreign subsidiary's financial statements should be the spot rate at 30 November, as required by IAS 21.46, but, separately, it will be necessary to consider which assets and liabilities might be affected significantly by the devaluation. Different items may be affected in different ways. For example:

- a further adjustment may be required for significant non-monetary assets of the subsidiary, to retranslate them using the rate at 31 December, with a corresponding adjustment to the exchange differences recognised in other comprehensive income;
- conversely, there may be little impact on the statement of financial position for any significant monetary assets of the subsidiary that are denominated in the functional currency of the parent. But a further adjustment may be required to recognise in profit or loss the exchange gains that arose on those items in the subsidiary during December, with a corresponding adjustment to the exchange differences recognised in other comprehensive income.

The same approach is used in applying the equity method to associates and jointly controlled entities and in applying proportionate consolidation to jointly controlled entities in accordance with IAS 28 and IAS 31. [IAS 21.46]

5.4.3 *Goodwill and fair value adjustments*

Any goodwill arising on the acquisition of a foreign operation and any fair value adjustments to the carrying amounts of assets and liabilities arising on the acquisition of that foreign operation are:

[IAS 21.47]

- treated as assets and liabilities of the foreign operation, and therefore expressed in the functional currency of the foreign operation; and

- translated at the closing rate in accordance with IAS 21.39 and IAS 21.42.

5.4.4 *Multi-level consolidations*

Example 5.4.4

Multi-level consolidation

A Swiss parent wholly owns a second-tier German subsidiary. The German subsidiary wholly owns a third-tier British subsidiary. The local currency is the functional currency for all entities, and the presentation currency of the consolidated entity is the Swiss franc. Each entity has third-party foreign-currency-denominated debt. Under IAS 21, what is the appropriate accounting for the foreign-currency transactions and the foreign-currency financial statements in the consolidation of the subsidiaries with the Swiss parent?

The British and German subsidiaries recognise translation gains and losses on their respective third-party foreign-currency-denominated debt in their individual financial statements using the closing rate at the end of the reporting period in accordance with IAS 21.23. The translation gains and losses are recognised in profit or loss and are not reversed out of profit or loss on consolidation.

In its separate financial statements, the Swiss parent recognises translation gains and losses on its third-party foreign-currency-denominated debt in profit or loss, just as its subsidiaries do for their foreign-currency-denominated debt.

If an intermediate consolidation exercise is performed, the German subsidiary translates the British subsidiary's Sterling-denominated financial statements into Euro-denominated financial statements. The Sterling-to-Euro exchange differences are recognised in other comprehensive income in the intermediate consolidated financial statements. The Swiss parent then translates the Euro-denominated, consolidated financial statements of the German subsidiary into Swiss francs and recognises the resulting exchange differences in other comprehensive income in the ultimate consolidated financial statements.

If an intermediate consolidation exercise is not performed, the Swiss parent translates the Sterling-denominated financial statements of the British subsidiary and the Euro-denominated financial statements of the German subsidiary into Swiss francs. The exchange differences arising are recognised in other comprehensive income.

IFRIC 16 *Hedges of a Net Investment in a Foreign Operation*, which was issued in July 2008, notes that the aggregate net amount recognised in the foreign currency translation reserve in respect of all foreign operations is not affected by whether the ultimate parent uses the direct or the step-by-step method of consolidation. IFRIC 16 is discussed at **2.3** in **chapter 20**.

5.5 Disposal or partial disposal of a foreign operation

An entity may dispose or partially dispose of its interest in a foreign operation through sale, liquidation, repayment of share capital or abandonment of all, or part, of that entity. [IAS 21.49]

In May 2008, IAS 21 was amended when the IASB issued Amendments to IFRS 1 *First-time Adoption of International Financial Reporting Standards* and IAS 27 *Consolidated and Separate Financial Statements* in respect of the cost of an investment in a subsidiary, jointly controlled entity or associate. As a result of these amendments, in separate financial statements dividend revenue is recognised in profit or loss irrespective of whether it is declared from pre- or post-acquisition profits. Prior to its amendment, IAS 21 noted that the payment of a dividend is part of a disposal only when it constitutes a return of the investment, for example when the dividend is paid out of pre-acquisition profits. For annual periods beginning on or after 1 January 2009, this statement is deleted. [IAS 21.49]

5.5.1 Disposals

On disposal of a foreign operation, the cumulative amount of the exchange differences relating to that operation, recognised in other comprehensive income and accumulated in the separate component of equity, is reclassified from equity to profit or loss (as a reclassification adjustment) when the gain or loss on disposal is recognised. [IAS 21.48]

In addition to the disposal of an entity's entire interest in a foreign operation, the following events, transactions or changes in circumstance are accounted for as disposals, even if the entity retains an interest in the former subsidiary, associate or jointly controlled entity:

[IAS 21.48A]

- the loss of control of a subsidiary that includes a foreign operation;
- the loss of significant influence over an associate that includes a foreign operation; and
- the loss of joint control over a jointly controlled entity that includes a foreign operation.

IAS 21.48A was added to IAS 21 as a consequential amendment of IAS 27(2008) *Consolidated and Separate Financial Statements*. It requires that the loss of control, significant influence or joint control of an entity be accounted for as a disposal (not as a partial disposal) under IAS 21. Therefore, all of the exchange differences previously accumulated in equity are reclassified to profit or loss – none are attributed to the interest retained by the entity.

This amendment is effective from the date of application of IAS 27(2008), i.e. for annual periods beginning on or after 1 July 2009. Earlier adoption is only permitted where IAS 27(2008) is also applied from that earlier date (see **section 8** of **chapter 33** for discussion of the transitional provisions of IAS 27(2008)).

Prior to the addition of paragraph 48A, IAS 21 was not clear on the appropriate treatment of exchange differences in the circumstances outlined, and practice varied. The application of paragraph 48A may therefore result in a change in accounting treatment for some entities, which will be accounted for retrospectively, but subject to the transitional requirements of IAS 27, as discussed at **section 8** in **chapter 33**. In particular, IAS 27(2008).45(c) notes that an entity shall not restate the carrying amount of an investment in a former subsidiary if control was lost before it applies the amendments to IAS 27 (and the related amendments to IAS 21). In addition, an entity shall not recalculate any gain or loss on the loss of control of a subsidiary that occurred before those amendments are applied.

Example 5.5.1

Loss of control of a foreign operation

A parent, P, has held a 100% interest in a subsidiary, S, for a number of years. S has been classified as a foreign operation and, in accordance with IAS 21.39, exchange differences of £2.5 million relating to S have been recognised in other comprehensive income and accumulated in a separate component of equity.

P disposes of 51% of its interest in S, resulting in a loss of control. Its retained interest of 49% ensures that it retains significant influence over S. Notwithstanding this continuing influence, all of the exchange differences of £2.5 million are reclassified from equity to profit or loss and are included in the calculation of the profit or loss on disposal of S.

UK

Under IAS 21, the gain or loss on disposal of a subsidiary is adjusted by the amount of exchange differences historically recognised in other comprehensive income. This is different from the position under SSAP 20, which prohibits the recycling of such exchange differences to the income statement on disposal of a subsidiary.

5.5.2 *Differences attributable to non-controlling interests*

When an entity disposes of a partially-owned subsidiary, the cumulative amount of the exchange differences relating to that foreign operation that have previously been attributed to the non-controlling interests are derecognised, but are not reclassified to profit or loss. [IAS 21.48B]

The cumulative amount of the exchange differences attributable to the non-controlling interests will have been allocated to, and recognised as part of, non-controlling interests in the consolidated statement of financial position, in accordance with IAS 21.41 and IAS 21.48C. The gain or loss recognised in profit or loss on the disposal of a partially-owned subsidiary includes the amount of non-controlling interests that is derecognised – thus it will already reflect those cumulative exchange differences.

Paragraph 48B has also been added to IAS 21 as a consequential amendment of IAS 27(2008). It may result in a change in accounting treatment for some entities. The effective date and transitional arrangements are discussed in **5.5.1**.

Example 5.5.2

Loss of control of a partially-owned foreign operation

A parent, P, has held an 80% interest in a subsidiary, S, for a number of years. S has been classified as a foreign operation and, in accordance with IAS 21.39, exchange differences of £2.5 million relating to S have been recognised in other comprehensive income. 80% of the exchange differences (£2 million) have been accumulated in P's foreign currency translation reserve in equity, and the remainder have been attributed to non-controlling interests.

P disposes of a 31% interest in S, resulting in a loss of control. Its retained interest of 49% ensures that it retains significant influence over S. Notwithstanding this continuing influence, all of the exchange differences of £2.5 million are derecognised:

- The exchange differences attributable to the parent (£2 million) are reclassified to profit or loss from the foreign currency translation reserve in equity and included in the calculation of the profit or loss on disposal of S.
- The exchange differences attributable to the non-controlling interest (£0.5 million) were already reflected as part of non-controlling interests in the consolidated statement of financial position. Those non-controlling interests are derecognised upon loss of control and included in the calculation of the profit or loss on disposal of S (see **5.7** in **chapter 33**).

5.5.3 *Partial disposals (no loss of control, joint control or significant influence)*

The requirements referred to below have been added to IAS 21 as a consequential amendment of IAS 27(2008). They may result in a change in accounting treatment for some entities. The effective date and transitional arrangements are discussed in **5.5.1**.

IAS 21.48D defines a partial disposal of an entity's interest in a foreign operation as any reduction in an entity's ownership interest in a foreign operation, except those reductions in paragraph 48A that are accounted for as disposals (see **5.5.1**).

IAS 21 does not give any further guidance on what it means by a 'reduction in an entity's ownership interest in a foreign operation'. Accordingly, does a partial disposal occur only when an entity's relative ownership interest is reduced (i.e. there is an increase in the relative ownership interest attributable to other parties), or can it occur for example when invested capital is returned to the parent without any changes in ownership? The references to non-controlling interest in IAS 21.48C and the fact that an impairment loss does not represent a partial disposal (as per IAS 21.49) appear to indicate that the former is the case, i.e. a partial disposal occurs only when an entity's relative ownership interest is reduced.

A reduction in relative ownership interest could arise directly or indirectly. For example, the entity's relative ownership interest could be reduced by the entity selling shares to a third party, through the entity choosing not to participate in a rights issue by the investee, or by the investee repurchasing equity shares from the entity but not from other investors. But a repurchase of equity shares by an investee that affected all equity holders equally (e.g. a repurchase of

10% of the shares held by each investor) would not be a partial disposal, because there would be no change in relative ownership interest. Thus, a share repurchase by the investee would only give rise to a partial disposal to the extent that the proportion of shares repurchased from the entity exceeded that for other investors.

The table below classifies various transactions as either disposals or partial disposals under IAS 21.48A and 48D

Effect of transaction	Disposal (IAS 21.48A)	Partial disposal (IAS 21.48D)	Reason
Subsidiary to subsidiary		X	Control remains
Subsidiary to jointly controlled entity (JCE)	X		Control lost
Subsidiary to associate	X		Control lost
Subsidiary to investment	X		Control lost
JCE to JCE		X	Joint control remains
JCE to associate	X		Joint control lost
JCE to investment	X		Joint control lost
Associate to associate		X	Significant influence remains
Associate to investment	X		Significant influence lost

For partial disposals as defined, the Standard distinguishes between:

[IAS 21.48C]

- the partial disposal of a subsidiary that includes a foreign operation; and
- all other partial disposals (i.e. of associates and jointly controlled entities).

Where there is a partial disposal of a subsidiary that includes a foreign operation, entities are required to re-attribute the proportionate share of the cumulative amount of the exchange differences recognised in other comprehensive income to the non-controlling interests in that foreign operation. [IAS 21.48C]

The transfer will be recognised in equity. Therefore, the exchange differences relating to the portion of the investment disposed of are not recognised in profit or loss as a reclassification adjustment at the date of the transaction. Nor are they recognised in profit or loss at the date of ultimate disposal of the partially owned subsidiary (see **5.5.2**). This treatment, illustrated in the following example, reflects the general approach adopted under IAS 27(2008) that changes in a parent's ownership interest in a subsidiary that do not result in a loss of control are accounted for as equity transactions.

Example 5.5.3A

Partial disposal of a foreign operation

A parent, P, has held a 100% interest in a subsidiary, S, for a number of years. S has been classified as a foreign operation and, in accordance with IAS 21.39, exchange differences of £2.5 million relating to S have been recognised in other comprehensive income and accumulated in a separate component of equity (the foreign currency translation reserve).

P disposes of 20% of its interest in S, but retains control over the subsidiary. At the date of the transaction, 20% (£0.5 million) of the cumulative exchange differences are transferred within equity from the foreign currency translation reserve to non-controlling interests. No amounts are reclassified to profit or loss.

For any other partial disposal of a foreign operation, entities are required to reclassify to profit or loss only the proportionate share of the cumulative amount of the exchange differences recognised in other comprehensive income. [IAS 21.48C]

Given that this category excludes (a) transactions that are accounted for as disposals (i.e. those involving the loss of control, joint control or significant influence), and (b) partial disposals of subsidiaries that do not involve the loss of control, it will include only partial disposal of jointly controlled entities and associates that do not result in a loss of joint control or significant influence.

Example 5.5.3B

Partial disposal of an associate

An investor, I, has held a 40% interest in an associate, A, for a number of years. A has been classified as a foreign operation and, in accordance with IAS 21.39, exchange differences of £8 million relating to A have been recognised in other comprehensive income and accumulated in a separate component of equity.

I disposes of a 15% interest in A, but retains significant influence. The proportionate share of accumulated exchange differences (15/40 x £8 million, i.e. £3 million) is derecognised and is recognised in profit or loss as a reclassification adjustment.

5.5.4 *Write-downs*

A write-down of the carrying amount of a foreign operation, either because of its own losses or because of an impairment loss recognised by the investor, does not constitute a partial disposal. Accordingly, no part of the foreign exchange gain or loss recognised in other comprehensive income is reclassified to profit or loss at the time of a write-down. [IAS 21.49]

5.5.5 *Repayment of a long-term financing loan*

As discussed at **3.2** above, an entity may have a monetary item (such as a long-term financing loan to an overseas subsidiary) that forms part of its net investment in a foreign operation. IAS 21.32 requires that the exchange differences arising on such items are recognised in other comprehensive income and accumulated in a separate component of equity (see **4.2.3.4**). Such differences are reclassified from equity to profit or loss on disposal of the net investment in accordance with IAS 21.48.

The question arises whether repayment of a loan of this nature would constitute a 'disposal' for the purposes of IAS 21.32 & 48, such that it would result in a reclassification of the relevant exchange differences to profit or loss.

Prior to the 2008 amendments to IAS 21, this point was not clear. It was considered that repayment of the loan could constitute a partial disposal of a foreign operation and, because the Standard was not explicit as to treatment of partial disposals, that it could trigger the reclassification. Following the 2008 amendments, the situation has been clarified. The Standard now includes clear rules regarding partial disposals and they are dealt with in paragraphs 48C and 48D of IAS 21 (not in paragraph 48). A partial disposal occurs only on a reduction in an entity's ownership interest; where the repayment of a loan does not alter an entity's relative ownership interest, that repayment will not be a partial disposal.

Thus, for a foreign operation that is a subsidiary:

- the reference in IAS 21.32 to reclassification of exchange differences on the monetary items under consideration from equity to profit or loss on '. . . disposal of the net investment in accordance with IAS 21.48' makes it clear that such differences are not reclassified in the event of a partial disposal; and

- therefore, the exchange differences relating to such monetary items will only be recognised in profit or loss when the entity disposes of its entire interest in the subsidiary, or, in the circumstances described in IAS 21.48A, when it disposes of an interest that results in a loss of control (see **5.5.1**).

For a foreign operation that is an associate or jointly controlled entity:

- in accordance with IAS 21.48A & 48C, exchange differences are only reclassified to profit or loss on a disposal or partial disposal;

- thus, unless the loan repayment arises on the loss of significant influence or joint control (a disposal), or it has the effect of reducing the entity's relative ownership interest (a partial disposal), no exchange differences will be reclassified on repayment of the loan;

- in accordance with IAS 21.48C, if there is a partial disposal (i.e. there is no loss of significant influence or joint control, but there is a reduction in the entity's relative ownership interest – see **5.5.3**), only the proportionate share of the cumulative amount of exchange differences is reclassified to profit or loss; and

- cumulative exchange differences relating to such monetary items will be recognised in profit or loss in full when the entity disposes of its entire interest in the associate or jointly controlled entity, or, in the circumstances described in IAS 21.48A, when it disposes of an interest that results in a loss of joint control or significant influence (see **5.5.1**).

The requirements referred to above have been added to IAS 21 as consequential amendment of IAS 27(2008). They may result in a change in accounting treatment for some entities. The effective date and transitional arrangements are discussed in **5.5.1**.

6 Tax effects of all exchange differences

Gains and losses on foreign currency transactions and exchange differences arising on translating the results and financial position of an entity (including a foreign operation) into a different currency may have tax effects. IAS 12 *Income Taxes* applies to these tax effects (see **chapter 12**). [IAS 21.50] IAS 12.61A requires current and deferred tax to be recognised outside profit or loss if the tax relates to items that are recognised, in the same or a different period, outside profit or loss.

7 SIC-7 *Introduction of the Euro*

SIC-7 *Introduction of the Euro* explains that the requirements of IAS 21 regarding the translation of foreign currency transactions and financial statements of foreign operations should be applied to the fixing of exchange rates when countries join the Economic and Monetary Union (EMU) and change over to the Euro, as follows:

(a) foreign currency monetary assets and liabilities resulting from transactions continue to be translated into the functional currency at the closing rate. Any resulting exchange differences are recognised as income or expense immediately, except that an entity continues to apply its existing accounting policy for exchange gains and losses relating to hedges of the currency risk of a forecast transaction;

(b) cumulative exchange differences relating to the translation of financial statements of foreign operations, recognised in other comprehensive income, are accumulated in equity and are reclassified from equity to profit or loss only on the disposal or partial disposal of the net investment in the foreign operation; and

(c) exchange differences resulting from the translation of liabilities denominated in participating currencies should not be included in the carrying amount of related assets.

8 Presentation and disclosure

8.1 General requirements

The following should be disclosed:

[IAS 21.52]

(a) the amount of exchange differences recognised in profit or loss except for those arising on financial instruments measured at fair value through profit or loss in accordance with IAS 39; and

(b) net exchange differences recognised in other comprehensive income and accumulated in a separate component of equity, and a reconciliation of the amount of such exchange differences at the beginning and end of the period.

The presentation of foreign currency exchange gains and losses should follow the nature of the transactions to which they are linked. As such, recognising foreign currency gains and losses relating to operational activities (e.g. on trade receivables/trade payables, etc.) within income from operations, and recognising foreign currency exchange gains and losses related to debt in finance costs, would be appropriate.

8.2 Change in functional currency

If there has been a change in the functional currency of either

- the reporting entity; or
- a significant foreign operation,

that fact should be stated, and the reason for the change in functional currency disclosed. [IAS 21.54]

8.3 Presentation currency different from functional currency

If the presentation currency is not the same as the functional currency (or, for a group, the functional currency of the parent), that fact should be stated. The functional currency should be disclosed, together with the reason for using a different presentation currency. [IAS 21.53]

When an entity presents its financial statements in a currency other than its functional currency (or, for a group, in a currency other than the functional currency of the parent), the financial statements may be described as complying with International Financial Reporting Standards only if they comply with all the requirements of each applicable Standard and each applicable Interpretation of those Standards including the translation method set out in IAS 21.39 and IAS 21.42 (see **5.2** and **5.3**). [IAS 21.55]

8.4 Supplementary information in other currencies

When an entity displays its financial statements or other financial information in a currency that is different from either its functional currency or its presentation currency and the requirements of IAS 21.55 are not met (see **8.3**), it is required to:

[IAS 21.57]

(a) clearly identify the information as supplementary information, to distinguish it from the information that complies with International Financial Reporting Standards;

(b) disclose the currency in which the supplementary information is displayed; and

(c) disclose the entity's functional currency and the method of translation used to determine the supplementary information.

Entities sometimes present their financial statements or other financial information in a currency that is not the functional currency without meeting the requirements of IAS 21.55. For example, an entity may convert into another currency only selected items from its financial statements; alternatively, an entity whose functional currency is not that of a hyperinflationary economy may convert the financial statements into another currency by translating all items at the most recent closing rate. Such conversions are not in accordance with International Financial Reporting Standards and the disclosures set out above are required. [IAS 21.56]

29 Non-current assets held for sale and discontinued operations

1 Introduction

IFRS 5 *Non-current Assets Held for Sale and Discontinued Operations* deals with the presentation of discontinued operations in the statement of comprehensive income. It also covers the measurement and presentation of non-current assets (and disposal groups) held for sale in the statement of financial position.

IFRS 5 was most recently amended by the IASB as part of the *Improvements to IFRSs* issued in May 2008. The amendments clarify the requirements of IFRS 5 in circumstances where an entity is planning to sell a controlling interest in a subsidiary (see **3.4**).

This chapter discusses the requirements of IFRS 5 in the following sections:

Section 2	Scope
Section 3	Classification of non-current assets (or disposal groups) as held for sale
Section 4	Measuring assets (and disposal groups) held for sale
Section 5	Assets acquired exclusively with a view to subsequent disposal
Section 6	Discontinued operations
Section 7	Other presentation and disclosure requirements
Section 8	Future developments

UK

Under UK GAAP, there is no special treatment for non-current assets (and disposal groups) held for sale. They are measured in the same way as, and presented with, all other assets and liabilities. IFRS 5 requires different treatment for such assets and liabilities in that they:

- *are segregated on the balance sheet (see* ***section 7.2****);*
- *cease to be depreciated; and*

- *are written down to fair value less costs to sell where this is less than the previous carrying amount* (see **section 4**). *For disposal groups, aggregate fair value less costs to sell is compared with aggregate previous carrying amount.*

IFRS 5 also differs from UK GAAP in its treatment of discontinued operations.

- *Under IFRS 5, operations will often be classified as discontinued earlier than under the UK standard, FRS 3 Reporting Financial Performance* (see **section 6**).
- *IFRS 5 allows a single figure to be shown on the face of the income statement, combining the results of discontinued operations with any write downs for disposal groups and non-current assets held for sale within those discontinued operations* (see **section 6.2**).

In effect, this can be seen as a different focus for the income statement. Under UK GAAP, the primary figures on the face of the profit and loss account are for total operations, with some further analysis between continuing and discontinued. Under IFRS 5, the primary figures on the face of the income statement are for continuing operations: income and expenses for discontinued operations may be collapsed into a single figure.

2 Scope

Although IFRS 5 deals with the measurement and presentation of non-current assets (and disposal groups) held for sale, it does *not* cover liability recognition for costs associated with the disposal of non-current assets (or disposal groups) such as one-time termination benefits, lease termination costs, facility-closing costs, and employee-relocation costs. Liability recognition for such costs is covered by other Standards, such as IAS 19 *Employee Benefits* (see **chapter 24**) and IAS 37 *Provisions, Contingent Liabilities and Contingent Assets* (see **chapter 11**).

2.1 Classification and presentation requirements

The classification and presentation requirements of IFRS 5 apply to all recognised non-current assets and disposal groups of an entity, but certain assets are not subject to its measurement requirements and instead continue to be measured in accordance with other Standards (see **2.2.1** below). [IFRS 5.2]

2.1.1 *Non-current assets*

Non-current assets are assets that do not meet the definition of a current asset. An entity classifies an asset as current when:

[IFRS 5(Appendix A)]

(a) it expects to realise the asset, or intends to sell or consume it, in its normal operating cycle;

(b) it holds the asset primarily for the purpose of trading;

(c) it expects to realise the asset within twelve months after the reporting period; or

(d) the asset is cash or a cash equivalent (as defined in IAS 7 *Statement of Cash Flows*), unless the asset is restricted from being exchanged or used to settle a liability for at least twelve months after the reporting period.

2.1.2 *Disposal groups*

A disposal group is a group of assets to be disposed of, by sale or otherwise, together as a group in a single transaction and liabilities directly associated with those assets that will be transferred in the transaction. [IFRS 5(Appendix A)] A disposal group may be a group of cash-generating units, a single cash-generating unit or part of a cash-generating unit.

If the group includes a cash-generating unit to which goodwill has been allocated under IAS 36 *Impairment of Assets* (see **section 8.1.2 of chapter 9**), or includes an operation within such a cash-generating unit, the associated goodwill is included within the disposal group.

Where an asset is being sold individually, IFRS 5 will apply only if it is a non-current asset. Where a group of assets is being disposed of in a single transaction, the classification and presentation requirements of IFRS 5 will apply to the disposal group as a whole.

Thus, where a business is being sold, IFRS 5 will apply to all recognised assets and liabilities of that business, including goodwill. The definition of a disposal group is, however, much wider than this. It requires neither that the disposal involve a 'business', nor that the group include any non-current assets. At an extreme, therefore, it is apparently possible for a group of inventories intended to be sold in a single transaction to constitute a disposal group. In practice, it is doubtful whether it would be helpful to users for such items to be removed from inventories and classified separately as assets held for sale. Accordingly, some care and judgement may be necessary when interpreting and applying the definition of a disposal group.

2.2 Measurement requirements

2.2.1 *'Scoped-out' non-current assets*

The measurement requirements of IFRS 5 do not apply to the following assets (which are covered by the Standards listed):

[IFRS 5.5]

(a) deferred tax assets (IAS 12 *Income Taxes* – see **chapter 12**);

(b) assets arising from employee benefits (IAS 19 *Employee Benefits* – see **chapter 24**);

(c) financial assets within the scope of IAS 39 *Financial Instruments: Recognition and Measurement* (see **chapter 14**);

(d) non-current assets that are accounted for in accordance with the fair value model in IAS 40 *Investment Property* (see **chapter 7**);

Note that where investment property is accounted for in accordance with the cost model in IAS 40, it will be within the scope of the measurement requirements of IFRS 5.

(e) non-current assets that are measured at fair value less costs to sell in accordance with IAS 41 *Agriculture* (see **chapter 43**); and

(f) contractual rights under insurance contracts as defined in IFRS 4 *Insurance Contracts* (see **chapter 44**).

The non-current assets listed above are excluded from the measurement requirements of IFRS 5 when they are held for sale either as individual assets or when they form part of a disposal group.

The exclusions relate only to the measurement requirements of IFRS 5 – the classification and presentation requirements of IFRS 5 apply to all non-current assets (see **2.1** above).

For convenience, the term 'scoped-out non-current assets' is used elsewhere in this chapter to refer to the assets listed at (a) to (f) above. Non-current assets other than those listed are referred to as 'scoped-in non-current assets'.

Disposal groups may include both scoped-in and scoped-out non-current assets. Where a disposal group includes any scoped-in non-current asset, the measurement requirements of IFRS 5 apply to the group as a whole, so that the group is measured at the lower of its carrying amount and fair value less costs to sell. [IFRS 5.4]

Where 'scoped-out non-current assets' form part of a disposal group, the measurement requirements of IFRS 5 can be more complex than they may at first appear. Those requirements are discussed at **4.2** below.

2.2.2 *Current assets*

It follows from the discussion so far that current assets can be affected by the requirements of IFRS 5, but only when they are part of a disposal group. Thus, in particular:

- where a current asset is part of a disposal group that also contains scoped-in non-current assets, the disposal group as a whole will be subject both to the measurement and to the classification and presentation requirements of IFRS 5;
- where a current asset is part of a disposal group that does not contain any scoped-in non-current assets, the disposal group as a whole will be subject to the classification and presentation requirements of IFRS 5, but not to the Standard's measurement requirements; and
- a current asset being sold as an individual asset (i.e. not as part of a disposal group) will never be classified as held for sale under IFRS 5.

3 Classification of non-current assets (or disposal groups) as held for sale

3.1 Assets that are to be sold

The overall principle of IFRS 5 is that a non-current asset (or disposal group) should be classified as held for sale if its carrying amount will be recovered principally through a sale transaction rather than through continuing use. [IFRS 5.6] The Standard specifies certain requirements and conditions that must be met for this to be the case, as discussed in the following sections.

It is worth emphasising that the separate presentation of certain non-current assets and disposal groups in the statement of financial position under IFRS 5 is not retrospective. Assets held for sale will be presented as such if they meet IFRS 5's conditions at the end of the reporting period. Accordingly, comparative amounts are not restated. If an asset qualifies as held for sale during 20X5, it will be classified as such in the statement of financial position at the end of 20X5, but not in the 20X4 comparative amounts.

This contrasts with IFRS 5's requirements regarding the presentation of discontinued operations in the statement of comprehensive income (see **section 6** below), which do require re-presenting the results of those operations for comparative periods. Thus, if an operation qualifies as discontinued during 20X5, it will be classified as discontinued in the statement of comprehensive income for the whole of 20X5 and also in the 20X4 comparative amounts.

It is also worth noting that there need be no link between assets (and disposal groups) held for sale and operations classified as discontinued. In particular, it may be the case that:

- a disposal group that is classified as held for sale does not qualify as a discontinued operation (e.g. because it does not represent a separate major line of business or geographical area of operations); or
- an operation is classified as discontinued even though none of its assets has ever qualified as held for sale.

3.1.1 *General requirements*

The two general requirements for a non-current asset (or disposal group) to be classified as held for sale are that:

[IFRS 5.7]

- the asset (or disposal group) must be available for immediate sale in its present condition subject only to terms that are usual and customary for sales of such assets (or disposal groups); and
- its sale must be highly probable.

These requirements are discussed further in **3.1.2** to **3.1.5** below.

Where the held-for-sale criteria are not met until after the reporting period, non-current assets (or disposal groups) should not be classified as held for sale. Instead, the disclosures required by IFRS 5.41(a), (b) & (d) (discussed at **7.3** below) should be provided. [IFRS 5.12] Furthermore, unless and until they meet the held-for-sale criteria:

- assets of a class that an entity would normally regard as non-current that are acquired exclusively with a view to resale, and
- assets classified as non-current in accordance with IAS 1 *Presentation of Financial Statements*

should not be classified as current assets. [IFRS 5.3] The treatment of assets acquired exclusively with a view to resale is discussed in **section 5** below.

3.1.2 *Available for immediate sale*

IFRS 5.7 requires that 'the asset (or disposal group) must be available for immediate sale in its present condition subject only to terms that are usual and customary for sales of such assets (or disposal groups)'. No further guidance on what this might mean is included within the Standard itself, but the Implementation Guidance accompanying IFRS 5 states that a non-current asset (or disposal group) is available for immediate sale if an entity currently has the intention and ability to transfer the asset (or disposal group) to a buyer in its present condition. The Implementation Guidance also sets out various examples illustrating this point, which are reproduced below.

Example 3.1.2A

Availability for immediate sale (1)

[Guidance on Implementing IFRS 5 (Example 1)]

An entity is committed to a plan to sell its headquarters building and has initiated actions to locate a buyer.

(a) The entity intends to transfer the building to a buyer after it vacates the building. The time necessary to vacate the building is usual and customary for sales of such assets. The criterion in IFRS 5.7 would be met at the plan commitment date.

(b) The entity will continue to use the building until construction of a new headquarters building is completed. The entity does not intend to transfer the existing building to a buyer until after construction of the new building is completed (and it vacates the existing building). The delay in the timing of the transfer of the existing building imposed by the entity (seller) demonstrates that the building is not available for immediate sale. The criterion in IFRS 5.7 would not be met until construction of the new building is completed, even if a firm purchase commitment for the future transfer of the existing building is obtained earlier.

Example 3.1.2B

Availability for immediate sale (2)

[Guidance on Implementing IFRS 5 (Example 2)]

An entity is committed to a plan to sell a manufacturing facility and has initiated actions to locate a buyer. At the plan commitment date, there is a backlog of uncompleted customer orders.

(a) The entity intends to sell the manufacturing facility with its operations. Any uncompleted customer orders at the sale date will be transferred to the buyer. The transfer of uncompleted customer orders at the sale date will not affect the timing of the transfer of the facility. The criterion in IFRS 5.7 would be met at the plan commitment date.

(b) The entity intends to sell the manufacturing facility, but without its operations. The entity does not intend to transfer the facility to a buyer until after it ceases all operations of the facility and eliminates the backlog of uncompleted customer orders. The delay in the timing of the transfer of the facility imposed by the entity (seller) demonstrates that the facility is not available for immediate sale. The criterion in IFRS 5.7 would not be met until the operations of the facility cease, even if a firm purchase commitment for the future transfer of the facility were obtained earlier.

Example 3.1.2C

Availability for immediate sale (3)

[Guidance on Implementing IFRS 5 (Example 3)]

An entity acquires through foreclosure a property comprising land and buildings that it intends to sell.

(a) The entity does not intend to transfer the property to a buyer until after it completes renovations to increase the property's sales value. The delay in the timing of the transfer of the property imposed by the entity (seller) demonstrates that the property is not available for immediate sale. The criterion in IFRS 5.7 would not be met until the renovations are completed.

(b) After the renovations are completed and the property is classified as held for sale but before a firm purchase commitment is obtained, the entity becomes aware of environmental damage requiring remediation. The entity still intends to sell the property. However, the entity does not have the ability to transfer the property to a buyer until after the remediation is completed. The delay in the timing of the transfer of the property imposed by others before a firm purchase commitment is obtained demonstrates that the property is not available for immediate sale. The criterion in IFRS 5.7 would not continue to be met. The property would be reclassified as held and used in accordance with IFRS 5.26.

More generally, where there are certain, relatively minor, pre-selling activities outstanding, and those activities are usually performed immediately before an asset is transferred, the asset could nevertheless be appropriately treated as available for immediate sale.

Conversely, where an asset is still in the course of construction, and significant activities will need to be performed before it can be transferred, it is unlikely that it could be regarded as available for immediate sale.

In the Basis of Conclusions for IFRS 5, the Board has confirmed that assets that are being used are not precluded from classification as held for sale if they meet the criteria set out in IFRS 5.7. This will be the case, for example, where an entity continues to operate an asset while actively marketing it. This is because, if a non-current asset is available for immediate sale, the remaining use of the asset is incidental to its recovery through sale and the carrying amount of the asset will be recovered principally through sale. [IFRS 5.BC23]

The following additional examples illustrate further circumstances in which assets (or disposal groups) may or may not be regarded as available for immediate sale.

Example 3.1.2D

Operational requirement to operate a non-current asset group to be disposed of by sale

Company D is a joint venture between two multi-national diversified manufacturers. On 28 December 20X2, management having the appropriate level of authority approved and committed Company D to a restructuring plan that included both employee terminations and plant disposals. The plan specifically identified all significant actions to be taken to complete the plan, activities that will not be continued, including the location of those activities and the method of disposal, and the expected date of completion (within one year). As part of the restructuring plan, Company D will continue to operate Plant B until June 20X3, at which time an alternative plant (Plant L) will be able to absorb Plant B's capacity.

Company D may not classify Plant B as held for sale at 31 December 20X2. Company D has an operational requirement to continue to operate Plant B until June 20X3 and, as such, Plant B has not met the requirement of IFRS 5.7

because it is not available for immediate sale. Additionally, Company D should reconsider the period over which Plant B is being depreciated and perform a detailed impairment review of Plant B in accordance with IAS 36 *Impairment of Assets*.

Example 3.1.2E

Completion of planned overhauls prior to disposal by sale

On 1 March 20X2, an entity announced plans to close and sell one of its manufacturing facilities. The entity will be required to perform major building and equipment overhauls to be able to market the facility effectively. The facility was closed on 30 April 20X2, and the overhauls were completed on 31 May 20X2. Immediately after the overhauls were completed, the entity began marketing the facility and the facility was sold on 15 July 20X2.

The entity may not classify the manufacturing facility as held for sale in its statement of financial position at 31 March 20X2. At that date, the entity had not met the conditions of IFRS 5.7 which require that the asset 'must be available for immediate sale in its present condition . . .'. Assuming all the other criteria of IFRS 5.7 were met, the entity would classify the asset as held for sale on 31 May 20X2, the date that the overhauls were completed and the entity began to market the facility.

Example 3.1.2F

Capital expenditures in the normal course of business of a held-for-sale component

Company G owns and operates cable television franchises throughout Europe. In June 20X2, Company G committed to a plan and entered into an agreement to sell its franchises in France and Germany to Company J, subject to approval by regulators. During the time that Company G waits for regulatory approval, it is required by the sales agreement to continue to expand the cable networks of the franchises to be sold, as subscribers demand service. Such capital expenditures are common to all cable franchises and Company G would have to make the expenditures even if it did not sell the franchises. Company G expects to invest €125 million in the French and German franchises before their sale to Company J is consummated.

Assuming that regulatory approval is usual and customary for these sales, and all the other criteria of IFRS 5.7 & 8 have been met, Company G should classify the French and German franchises as held for sale in its statement of financial position at 30 June 20X2, because the capital expenditures that it is required to make are usual and customary for the operation of such assets (i.e. the assets are available for immediate sale in their present condition regardless of the capital expenditures to be incurred). Company G is operating and selling a live cable franchise and there is an expectation that

Company G will have to make certain capital expenditures in the normal course of business to accommodate new subscribers.

3.1.3 *Highly probable: specific conditions*

The Standard defines 'highly probable' as meaning 'significantly more likely than probable', where 'probable' means 'more likely than not'. [IFRS 5(Appendix A)]

A number of specific conditions must be satisfied for the sale of a non-current asset (or disposal group) to qualify as highly probable:

[IFRS 5.8]

- the appropriate level of management must be committed to a plan to sell the asset (or disposal group);
- an active programme to locate a buyer and complete the plan must have been initiated;
- the asset (or disposal group) must be actively marketed for sale at a price that is reasonable in relation to its current fair value; and
- except as discussed at **3.1.5** below, the sale should be expected to qualify for recognition as a completed sale within one year from the date of classification, and actions required to complete the plan should indicate that it is unlikely that significant changes to the plan will be made or that the plan will be withdrawn.

The Implementation Guidance accompanying the Standard includes the following illustration of the application of the criteria in IFRS 5.7 & 8.

Example 3.1.3A

Completion of sale expected within one year

[Guidance on Implementing IFRS 5 (Example 4)]

To qualify for classification as held for sale, the sale of a non-current asset (or disposal group) must be highly probable (IFRS 5.7), and transfer of the asset (or disposal group) must be expected to qualify for recognition as a completed sale within one year (IFRS 5.8). That criterion would not be met if, for example:

(a) an entity that is a commercial leasing and finance company is holding for sale or lease equipment that has recently ceased to be leased and the ultimate form of a future transaction (sale or lease) has not yet been determined; or

(b) an entity is committed to a plan to 'sell' a property that is in use, and the transfer of the property will be accounted for as a sale and finance leaseback.

The following additional examples focus on approval by the appropriate level of management.

Example 3.1.3B

Board approval of a plan to split off an operating segment

Company D is contemplating a non pro-rata split-off (i.e. issuance of shares) of one of its operating segments, Company E. Company D anticipates that the split-off will occur prior to the end of its calendar year ending 31 December 20X2, and that it will receive a ruling from the taxing authority that the transaction may be accounted for as tax-free. Subsequent to issuing the second quarter interim report, the following events occur:

- Company D receives a ruling from the taxing authority indicating that the proposed split-off will be considered a non-taxable transaction; and
- Company D's board of directors appoints a committee to explore the split-off. The committee is charged to explore the following: (a) the precise ratio at which Company E shares will be offered for exchange to the Company D shareholders, (b) the minimum number of shares required for Company D to complete the distribution to make the split-off economically feasible, and (c) other criteria that must be met for Company D to complete the distribution. The committee is required to report to the board for approval of the conditions related to the proposed split-off.

Company D has indicated that if the structure, timing and terms of the split-off transaction are not approved by the board, Company D will continue to control and operate Company E. There are currently no alternative disposal plans being contemplated.

At the point in time that the ruling is received from the taxing authority and the committee of the board is appointed, D does not meet the criteria to classify the operating segment as held for sale. IFRS 5.8 clarifies that for a sale to be highly probable, the 'appropriate level of management must be committed to a plan to sell the asset'. Approval by the board of directors would generally constitute this level of commitment.

3.1.3.1 Plan of sale requiring shareholder approval

It is not unusual for local laws or regulations (or the entity's own constitution) to require that asset disposals be approved by a majority of the entity's shareholders (generally for transactions above a certain size threshold or transactions with connected parties). In such cases, approval by the board of directors (or equivalent level of management) will generally precede shareholder approval. Where, at the end of the reporting period, the board has approved a plan to dispose of a non-current asset by sale, but the required shareholder vote has not yet taken place, the question arises as to whether an 'appropriate level of management' is committed to the sale (as required by IFRS 5.8) at the reporting date.

To satisfy the criterion in IFRS 5.8, the board of directors (or the appropriate level of management) must have the power to commit the entity to the plan to sell the asset (or disposal group). Approval of the plan by the board of directors, if it does not represent a commitment by the entity, would not be sufficient to meet the criterion. The determination as to whether the board of directors has the power to commit the entity to a plan to sell the asset requires a careful assessment of the facts and circumstances surrounding the transaction, taking into account relevant jurisdictional and legal requirements. In particular, an assessment must be made as to whether the shareholders' approval is substantive in nature.

The following examples illustrate two possible scenarios.

Example 3.1.3.1A

Plan of sale requiring shareholder approval (1)

At the end of the reporting period, an entity's board of directors has approved a plan to sell a non-current asset. The eventual disposal requires approval by a majority of the entity's shareholders through a formal vote which will take place after the reporting period. At the end of the reporting period, a majority of the entity's shareholders have provided the entity with signed irrevocable agreements stating that they will vote their shares in favour of the disposal.

The criterion that an 'appropriate level of management' be committed to the plan is met because the shareholders have irrevocably committed to approving the transaction and, therefore, the formal vote by the shareholders is merely a formality.

Example 3.1.3.1B

Plan of sale requiring shareholder approval (2)

Company A holds an 80% interest in a subsidiary, Company B. At the year end, the board of directors of Company B has approved a plan to sell a non-current asset to Company A. The eventual disposal requires approval by a majority of B's shareholders through a formal vote which will take place after the reporting period. For a transaction with a major shareholder (in this case, the parent), the minority shareholders are given protection in law if the value of the transaction exceeds a certain threshold. The law prevents Company A from participating in the formal vote on such a transaction. Company B has not received any undertakings to vote in a particular manner from any of the shareholders.

From Company B's perspective, the criterion that an 'appropriate level of management' must be committed to the plan to sell the asset is not met at the end of the reporting period because the formal vote by the remaining shareholders is substantive in nature.

3.1.4 *Impairment reviews for assets not qualifying as held for sale*

The criteria for classifying an asset (or disposal group) as held for sale set out in IFRS 5.7 & 8 are very rigorous. Failure to meet these criteria should not, however, result in potentially impaired assets not being written down to their recoverable amounts.

When an entity has indicated an intent to sell an asset with a carrying amount that may exceed its fair value less costs to sell, but the asset does not qualify as held for sale, the entity should consider this to be an impairment loss indicator under IAS 36 *Impairment of Assets*, which would require the entity to perform an impairment review. The holding period used in estimating the future cash flows for the purpose of determining the asset's value in use should reflect the entity's intent to sell the asset.

IAS 36.21 notes that the fair value less costs to sell of an asset to be disposed of will often approximate its value in use, as the value in use calculation will consist mainly of the net disposal proceeds. This is because the future cash flows from continuing use of the asset until its disposal are likely to be negligible.

3.1.5 *Extension of the period required to complete a sale*

IFRS 5.9 notes that, on occasion, events or circumstances may extend the period to complete the sale beyond one year. Provided that the delay is caused by events or circumstances beyond the entity's control and there is sufficient evidence that the entity remains committed to its plan to sell the asset (or disposal group), such an extension does not preclude an asset (or disposal group) from being classified as held for sale.

Appendix B to IFRS 5 specifies that held-for-sale classification will continue to be available in the following situations:

[IFRS 5.B1]

> '(a) at the date an entity commits itself to a plan to sell a non-current asset (or disposal group) it reasonably expects that others (not a buyer) will impose conditions on the transfer of the asset (or disposal group) that will extend the period required to complete the sale, and:
>
> (i) actions necessary to respond to those conditions cannot be initiated until after a firm purchase commitment is obtained, and
>
> (ii) a firm purchase commitment is highly probable within one year.
>
> (b) an entity obtains a firm purchase commitment and, as a result, a buyer or others unexpectedly impose conditions on the transfer of a non-current asset (or disposal group) previously classified as held for sale that will extend the period required to complete the sale, and:
>
> (i) timely actions necessary to respond to the conditions have been taken, and
>
> (ii) a favourable resolution of the delaying factors is expected.
>
> (c) during the initial one-year period, circumstances arise that were previously considered unlikely and, as a result, a non-current asset (or disposal group) previously classified as held for sale is not sold by the end of that period, and:
>
> (i) during the initial one-year period the entity took action necessary to respond to the change in circumstances,
>
> (ii) the non-current asset (or disposal group) is being actively marketed at a price that is reasonable, given the change in circumstances, and
>
> (iii) the criteria in paragraphs 7 and 8 [of the Standard] are met.'

A firm purchase commitment is an agreement with an unrelated party, binding on both parties and usually legally enforceable, that (a) specifies all significant terms, including the price and timing of the transactions, and (b) includes a disincentive for non-performance that is sufficiently large to make performance highly probable. [IFRS 5(Appendix A)]

The criteria in paragraphs 7 and 8 of IFRS 5, referred to above, are respectively the general requirements discussed at **3.1.1** and the specific conditions discussed at **3.1.2** and **3.1.3**.

The Implementation Guidance accompanying the Standard includes the following examples of the limited situations in which the period required to complete a sale may extend beyond one year but not breach the held-for-sale criteria.

Example 3.1.5A

Completion of sale expected within one year – exceptions (1)

[Guidance on Implementing IFRS 5 (Example 5)]

An entity in the power generating industry is committed to a plan to sell a disposal group that represents a significant portion of its regulated operations. The sale requires regulatory approval, which could extend the period required to complete the sale beyond one year. Actions necessary to obtain that approval cannot be initiated until after a buyer is known and a firm purchase commitment is obtained. However, a firm purchase commitment is highly probable within one year. In that situation, the conditions in IFRS 5.B1(a) for an exception to the one-year requirement in IFRS 5.8 would be met.

Example 3.1.5B

Completion of sale expected within one year – exceptions (2)

[Guidance on Implementing IFRS 5 (Example 6)]

An entity is committed to a plan to sell a manufacturing facility in its present condition and classifies the facility as held for sale at that date. After a firm purchase commitment is obtained, the buyer's inspection of the property identifies environmental damage not previously known to exist. The entity is required by the buyer to make good the damage, which will extend the period required to complete the sale beyond one year. However, the entity has initiated actions to make good the damage, and satisfactory rectification of the damage is highly probable. In that situation, the conditions in IFRS 5.B1(b) for an exception to the one-year requirement in IFRS 5.8 would be met.

Example 3.1.5C

Completion of sale expected within one year – exceptions (3)

[Guidance on Implementing IFRS 5 (Example 7)]

An entity is committed to a plan to sell a non-current asset and classifies the asset as held for sale at that date.

(a) During the initial one-year period, the market conditions that existed at the date the asset was classified initially as held for sale deteriorate and, as a result, the asset is not sold by the end of that period. During that period, the entity actively solicited but did not receive any reasonable offers to purchase the asset and, in response, reduced the price. The asset continues to be actively marketed at a price that is reasonable given the change in market conditions, and the criteria in IFRS 5.7 & 8 are therefore met. In that situation, the conditions in IFRS 5.B1(c) for an exception to the one-year requirement in IFRS 5.8 would be met. At the end of the initial one-year period, the asset would continue to be classified as held for sale.

(b) During the following one-year period, market conditions deteriorate further, and the asset is not sold by the end of that period. The entity believes that the market conditions will improve and has not further reduced the price of the asset. The asset continues to be held for sale, but at a price in excess of its current fair value. In that situation, the absence of a price reduction demonstrates that the asset is not available for immediate sale as required by IFRS 5.7. In addition, IFRS 5.8 also requires an asset to be marketed at a price that is reasonable in relation to its current fair value. Therefore, the conditions in IFRS 5.B1(c) for an exception to the one-year requirement in IFRS 5.8 would not be met. The asset would be reclassified as held and used in accordance with IFRS 5.26.

The following additional example illustrates further circumstances in which assets may qualify as held for sale despite an extension beyond one year.

Example 3.1.5D

Non-current assets to be disposed of by sale requiring bankruptcy court approval

Company S has filed for reorganisation under a local bankruptcy code, and has entered into an agreement to sell certain assets and liabilities of one of its wholly-owned subsidiaries to a third party. The sale has been authorised by the directors and approved by the creditors. However, the sale requires approval from the bankruptcy court. The role of the bankruptcy court in this jurisdiction primarily is to ensure compliance with legal procedures regarding bankruptcy filings. Management considers that it is highly probable that the bankruptcy court will approve the sale, but Company S has not received approval from the bankruptcy court as of the period end.

Company S is not precluded from classifying the disposal group as held for sale. In accordance with IFRS 5.8, the appropriate level of management has committed to the plan to dispose of the group of assets and liabilities. The criteria in IFRS 5.7 require that the disposal group be available for immediate sale. As the sale agreement must be approved by the bankruptcy court prior to finalisation of the sale, circumstances may arise that extend the period to complete the sale beyond one year. Such an extension does not preclude a disposal group from being classified as held for sale if the delay is caused by events or circumstances beyond the entity's control and there is sufficient evidence that the entity remains committed to its plan to sell the disposal group.

Note, however, that bankruptcy courts may have different roles in different jurisdictions and this could affect the above conclusion. Further, in certain situations, the appropriate level of management may not yet have committed to the plan to dispose, while they await the ruling of the bankruptcy court. Where the appropriate level of management is not yet committed to disposal, classification of the assets and liabilities as held for sale would be inappropriate.

3.2 Assets that are to be abandoned

As noted at **3.1**, assets held for sale are those whose carrying amounts will be recovered principally through a sale transaction rather than through continuing use. Where assets or disposal groups are to be abandoned, rather than sold, there will be no sale transaction, so that their carrying amounts can only be recovered through continuing use. Accordingly, assets to be abandoned will not qualify as held for sale and should not be classified as such in the statement of financial position. [IFRS 5.13]

For non-current assets retired from active use, the IASB decided that where such assets do not meet the criteria for classification as held for sale, they should not be presented separately in the statement of financial position because their carrying amounts may not be recovered principally through sale. [IFRS 5.BC23]

Example 3.2A

Non-current assets to be abandoned as part of a corporate restructuring

An entity has committed to a plan of restructuring and expects that certain assets will be disposed of through abandonment. The assets will continue to be used until their abandonment. As the sale proceeds will be nil, should all of the assets to be abandoned as a result of the restructuring be written down to zero carrying amount as of the commitment date?

No. Non-current assets to be disposed of by abandonment, whether or not as the result of a restructuring, will not qualify as held for sale because their carrying amounts will not be recovered principally through sale. Thus, the measurement requirements of IFRS 5 do not apply.

Instead, the assets should be evaluated for impairment in accordance with IAS 36 *Impairment of Assets*. Additionally, the entity should revise the estimated useful lives of the assets in accordance with IAS 16 *Property, Plant and Equipment*, to reflect the use of the assets over their shortened useful lives, and recognise the depreciation expense in continuing operations until the date of disposal. Only in unusual situations would the recoverable amount of a non-current asset to be abandoned be zero while it is being used, as the continued use of the non-current asset demonstrates the presence of service potential.

If an impairment loss is recognised relating to assets that are part of a component that has qualified for discontinued-operation presentation in accordance with IFRS 5.30, the impairment loss should be presented in discontinued operations.

Nevertheless, for the purpose of presentation in the statements of comprehensive income and cash flows, a disposal group to be abandoned could meet the definition of a discontinued operation at the date on which it ceases to be used (see **6.1** below). The Implementation Guidance accompanying the Standard illustrates this point as follows.

Example 3.2B

Presenting a discontinued operation that has been abandoned

[Guidance on Implementing IFRS 5 (Example 9)]

In October 2005 an entity decides to abandon all of its cotton mills, which constitute a major line of business. All work stops at the cotton mills during the year ended 31 December 2006. In the financial statements for the year ended 31 December 2005, results and cash flows of the cotton mills are treated as continuing operations. In the financial statements for the year ended 31 December 2006, the results and cash flows of the cotton mills are treated as discontinued operations and the entity makes the disclosures required by IFRS 5.33 & 34 (see **6.2.1**).

Example 3.2C

Classification of non-current assets (or disposal groups) that are to be abandoned

Company A, operating in the construction industry, made a decision to abandon its property rental interests (Company B) with effect from 30 June 20X2. The business of Company B operates via a number of property leases, including both finance leases and operating leases. Selected properties are also occupied by the Company A and Company B group as well as subleased to tenants. Company A has determined that Company B represents a component of its entity. Company B plans to allow the leases to run to the end of the lease terms as this is the lowest cost option for exiting the business. No alterations will be made to any of the leases and effectively the business runs on 'autopilot'. This process will take a number of years.

Company A cannot classify the operations of Company B as discontinued operations in its 31 December 20X2 financial statements. For an operation to be classified as discontinued, it must either have been disposed of or meet the held-for-sale criteria (IFRS 5.32). In addition, IFRS 5.13 states that an operation to be abandoned may only be treated as a discontinued operation if it has actually been abandoned. Although Company A and Company B are not seeking new tenants, they continue to provide landlord services and maintain the buildings in a good state of repair, etc. Therefore, the operations have not yet been abandoned, have not been disposed of and do not meet the criteria for classification as held for sale. Consequently, they cannot be classified as 'discontinued operations'.

Where a non-current asset has been temporarily taken out of use, it should not be accounted for as if it had been abandoned. [IFRS 5.14] The Implementation Guidance accompanying the Standard includes the following illustration.

Example 3.2D

Determining whether an asset has been abandoned

[Guidance on Implementing IFRS 5 (Example 8)]

An entity ceases to use a manufacturing plant because demand for its product has declined. However, the plant is maintained in workable condition and it is expected that it will be brought back into use if demand picks up. The plant is not regarded as abandoned.

In practice, when an entity is closing an operation, it may intend to sell some assets and to scrap others. Care will be needed, as the former may qualify as held for sale while the latter will not.

3.3 Assets that are to be exchanged

For an asset to qualify as held for sale, it is necessary that the carrying amount will be recovered principally through sale, i.e. that sale proceeds will be received. It is not necessary that the intended sale of a non-current asset should be in exchange for cash. It is, however, necessary that the expected exchange would qualify for recognition as a completed sale (see **3.1.3** above). Thus, if an entity intends to exchange a non-current asset for another non-current asset, the IFRS 5 conditions for classification as held for sale cannot be met unless the exchange will have commercial substance in accordance with IAS 16 *Property, Plant and Equipment*. [IFRS 5.10]

IAS 16 states that an entity should determine whether an exchange transaction has commercial substance by considering the extent to which its future cash flows are expected to change as a result of the transaction (see **4.3.2** in **chapter 6**). An exchange transaction has commercial substance if:

[IAS 16.25]

- either:
  - the configuration (risk, timing and amount) of the cash flows of the asset received differs from the configuration of the cash flows of the asset transferred; *or*
  - the entity-specific value of the portion of the entity's operations affected by the transaction changes as a result of the exchange; *and*
- the difference arising in either of the two circumstances outlined above is significant relative to the fair value of the assets exchanged.

3.4 Disposals and partial disposals

Where an entity is committed to a sale plan involving loss of control of a subsidiary, all of the assets and liabilities of that subsidiary are classified as held for sale, regardless of whether the entity will retain a non-controlling interest in its former subsidiary after the sale. [IFRS 5.8A]

Paragraph 8A was added to IFRS 5 as part of the *Improvements to IFRSs* issued in May 2008. The effective date and transitional provisions are discussed at **3.4.1** below.

The IASB has concluded that loss of control is a significant economic event that changes the nature of an investment. The parent-subsidiary relationship ceases to exist and an investor-investee relationship begins that differs significantly from the former parent-subsidiary relationship. The new investor-investee relationship is recognised and measured initially at the date when control is lost. Extrapolating from the principle introduced in IFRS 5.8A, a disposal will occur either when the entire holding in an investment is sold or when the nature of the holding changes substantively as a result of a sale. A change between controlling interest, joint control, significant influence and trade investment represents such a substantive change in the nature of the holding in the investment.

The table below illustrates how this guidance should be applied.

Type of transaction	IFRS 5 held-for-sale classification?	Reason
Subsidiary to subsidiary	No	Control remains
Subsidiary to jointly controlled entity (JCE)	Yes	Control lost
Subsidiary to associate	Yes	Control lost
Subsidiary to investment	Yes	Control lost
JCE to JCE	No	Joint control remains
JCE to associate	Yes	Joint control lost
JCE to investment	Yes	Joint control lost
Associate to associate	No	Significant influence remains
Associate to investment	Yes	Significant influence lost

Example 3.4A

Disposal of subsidiary undertaking with retention of associate interest

An entity has a 70 per cent interest in a subsidiary that it consolidates in accordance with IAS 27 *Consolidated and Separate Financial Statements*. On 1 July 20X6, the entity enters into an unconditional, binding agreement to dispose of 30 per cent of its interest. The 30 per cent interest is disposed of in February 20X7, at which point the entity ceases to have control and instead has significant influence.

The planned disposal of shares results in the subsidiary being classified as a disposal group held for sale that should be accounted for in accordance with IFRS 5 from the date the criteria for classification as held for sale are met.

For the purposes of the 20X6 financial statements, the subsidiary continues to be consolidated (i.e. 100 per cent of the assets and liabilities of the subsidiary are consolidated), but presentation is collapsed into two lines in the statement of financial position (i.e. non-current assets held for sale and associated liabilities). If the disposal group qualifies as a discontinued operation, the presentation in the statement of comprehensive income is collapsed into one single line in accordance with IFRS 5.33 (see **section 6**).

In 20X7, the entity consolidates the subsidiary in accordance with IAS 27 for the first 2 months of the financial year (classifying amounts as arising from discontinued operations, where appropriate). Following the disposal of shares, the entity accounts for the disposal of the subsidiary, recognising any gain or loss in profit or loss. Thereafter, the ongoing 40 per cent interest will be accounted for as an associate, i.e. using the equity method. (Note that the calculation of the gain or loss on disposal, and the measurement of the associate, will be different depending on whether the entity has adopted IFRS 3(2008) – see the discussion at **5.7.1** and **5.7.2** in **chapter 33**.)

Example 3.4B

Dilution of interest in a subsidiary through a rights offer

Company H has a wholly-owned subsidiary, Company B. Company B makes a rights offer to Company H's shareholders, proposing to issue 10 of its own shares for each share held in Company H. To receive the rights, the shareholders must pay fair value for the shares issued and accept the offer by a specified deadline.

After the issuance of shares under the rights offer, Company H will hold 35 per cent of B. As a result, Company H will relinquish control over Company B but will retain significant influence. Should the rights offer be regarded as a sale transaction under IFRS 5?

The rights offer is effectively Company H's disposal of a portion of its interest in Company B to a preferred group of bidders if the rights are taken up. Since the shares will be issued at fair value, Company H will receive proceeds for the sale of 65 per cent of its investment in Company B to its shareholders.

This disposal will change the nature of the investment in Company B from a subsidiary to that of an associate. Accordingly, the entire investment in Company B will be recognised as a disposal group held for sale if the investment is available for sale in its present condition and the sale is regarded as highly probable (i.e. it is highly probable that the rights will be taken up).

3.4.1 *Amendments to IFRS 5 (May 2008) – effective date and transition*

Prior to the amendment of IFRS 5, many entities will have developed their own accounting policies for the application of IFRS 5 to disposals and partial disposals. The adoption of the new paragraph 8A will have no impact for those entities that have previously applied an accounting policy that is consistent with the requirements of that paragraph, as discussed in the previous section. Entities that will be affected by the transitional provisions for the 2008 amendments are those that have previously applied an accounting policy that is inconsistent with the requirements of IFRS 5.8A and they, therefore, will need to consider the extent to which restatement of prior financial statements is appropriate.

The requirements of IFRS 5.8A (see above) are effective for annual periods beginning on or after 1 July 2009 (which is later than the effective date for most of the other components of the improvements project, so as to align the effective date with that of the January 2008 amendments to IAS 27 *Consolidated and Separate Financial Statements*). The early adoption and transitional provisions are a little complicated to work through – although, for the majority of entities, they should not present a problem.

The requirements of IFRS 5.8A may be applied before 1 July 2009 – but only if the entity applies IAS 27(2008) from the same date. Early adoption of IAS 27(2008) is itself linked to the adoption of IFRS 3(2008), which may not be applied for an accounting period that begins before 30 June 2007. The effect of these various interactions is that the earliest financial statements for which the requirements of IFRS 5.8A may be adopted are those for a period beginning 30 June 2007.

The amendments are to be applied *prospectively* from the date at which the entity first applied IFRS 5 (generally for periods beginning on or after 1 January 2005, unless the entity opted for early application). However, this is subject to the transitional provisions in paragraph 45 of IAS 27(2008).

Paragraph 45 of IAS 27(2008) states that an entity should not restate the carrying amount of an investment in a former subsidiary if control was lost before the requirements of IAS 27(2008) are applied. Therefore, although the transitional provisions for the 2008 amendments to IFRS 5 would, at first glance, require retrospective restatements of transactions from the date of adoption of IFRS 5 (generally from 2005), the override of the IAS 27(2008) transitional provisions means that no restatements are made in respect of transactions or events resulting in a loss of control that occurred before the beginning of the first period in which IAS 27(2008) is applied.

Example 3.4.1A

Adoption of IFRS 5.8A

The end of Company X's reporting period is 31 December, and it is currently producing its financial statements for 2008.

Company X is permitted to adopt the 2008 improvements to IFRS 5 for its 2008 reporting period (i.e. commencing 1 January 2008) – but only if it also adopts IAS 27(2008) and IFRS 3(2008). If it does, it will not restate the carrying amount of an investment in a former subsidiary if control was lost before 1 January 2008. Accordingly, if Company X lost control of a subsidiary during 2007, that transaction will not be restated; but the requirements of IFRS 5.8A would be applied if it lost control of a subsidiary during 2008.

Company X could instead choose to adopt IAS 27(2008) and IFRS 3(2008) for its 2008 reporting period (i.e. commencing 1 January 2008), but without adopting the improvements to IFRS 5. If it chose subsequently to adopt the improvements to IFRS 5 for its 2010 reporting period, it would at that point apply IFRS 5.8A retrospectively – but only in respect of transactions or events resulting in a loss of control that occurred after 1 January 2008, i.e. the beginning of the first period in which it applied IAS 27(2008).

3.5 Demergers

Sometimes an entity may dispose of a non-current asset or disposal group without the receipt of proceeds, such as where the entity distributes that non-current asset or disposal group to its shareholders. For example, in a demerger, an entity may distribute a segment of its business to its shareholders.

IFRS 5.6 states that an entity 'shall classify a non-current asset (or disposal group) as held for sale if its carrying amount will be recovered *principally through a sale transaction* rather than through continuing use'. [Emphasis added]

The detailed requirements of IFRS 5 regarding classification as held for sale are based, therefore, on an assumption that there will be a sale transaction (i.e. there will be sales proceeds). In the case of a distribution to shareholders, the entity will not 'recover' the carrying amount of the non-current asset or disposal group or, as in the example above, the segment to be divested. Therefore, the asset or disposal group/segment to be divested will not qualify as held for sale.

However, at the date of the distribution, where a segment is sufficiently significant to qualify as a discontinued operation, it should be presented as such (see **section 6**).

3.6 Assets ceasing to qualify as held for sale

Where an asset (or disposal group) has been classified as held for sale, but the requirements and conditions discussed in this section are no longer met, the asset (or disposal group) should be removed from the held-for-sale category. [IFRS 5.26] The measurement requirements that apply in such circumstances are discussed in **4.6** below.

4 Measuring assets (and disposal groups) held for sale

Where non-current assets and disposal groups are classified as held for sale, they are required to be measured at the lower of their carrying amount and fair value less costs to sell. [IFRS 5.15]

> The comparison of carrying amount and fair value less costs to sell is carried out on the date the non-current asset (or disposal group) is first classified as held for sale, and then again at each subsequent reporting date while it continues to meet the held-for-sale criteria.

4.1 Individual assets held for sale

Certain assets (listed at **2.2.1**) are outside the scope of IFRS 5's measurement requirements. When classified as held for sale, those scoped-out non-current assets will continue to be measured in accordance with the Standards that applied before they were classified as held for sale, although the presentation and disclosure requirements of IFRS 5 apply.

All other individual non-current assets held for sale (i.e. 'scoped-in non-current assets') are measured at the lower of their carrying amount and fair value less costs to sell. [IFRS 5.15] Fair value is the amount for which an asset could be exchanged, or a liability settled, between knowledgeable, willing parties in an arm's length transaction. [IFRS 5(Appendix A)] Costs to sell are discussed at **4.3** below.

> If assets are carried at fair value prior to initial classification, the requirement to deduct costs to sell from fair value will result in the immediate recognition of a loss in profit or loss.

The detailed requirements are as follows.

- The carrying amount of the non-current asset is measured in accordance with applicable IFRSs immediately before initial classification as held for sale. [IFRS 5.18]

> For example, a property accounted for using the revaluation model in accordance with IAS 16 *Property, Plant and Equipment* would be revalued in accordance with IAS 16 immediately before classification as held for sale. Any revaluation gain or loss would be accounted for as usual under IAS 16.

For assets within the scope of IAS 36, if there is any indication of an impairment loss, the recoverable amount of the asset is calculated and, where required, the impairment loss recognised in accordance with IAS 36. Although IAS 36 specifically excludes from its scope assets classified as held for sale, that Standard still applies immediately before initial classification as held for sale.

- If the carrying amount determined in accordance with IFRS 5.18 exceeds the asset's fair value less costs to sell, an impairment loss is recognised to reduce the carrying amount to fair value less costs to sell. [IFRS 5.20]

For example, immediately on classification as held for sale and at each subsequent reporting date, the property, which was previously measured under IAS 16, is remeasured in accordance with IFRS 5. In accordance with IFRS 5.20 and IFRS 5.37, any impairment loss arising subsequent to the classification as held for sale is recognised in profit or loss.

- Once classified as held for sale, a non-current asset is no longer depreciated or amortised. [IFRS 5.25]

A non-current asset is no longer depreciated or amortised, even if the entity continues to use it within the business.

- A gain should be recognised for any subsequent increase in fair value less costs to sell of an asset, but not in excess of the cumulative impairment loss recognised in accordance with IFRS 5 or previously in accordance with IAS 36. [IFRS 5.21]

Where assets had been impaired prior to classification as held for sale, it is possible that a net remeasurement gain may be recognised while they are held for sale. It should, however, be noted that, although earlier impairment losses may in effect be reversed, the same is not true for accumulated depreciation.

Assets acquired exclusively with a view to their subsequent disposal, for example as part of a business combination, are discussed in **section 5** below.

Example 4.1A

Measuring non-current assets held for sale (1)

A freehold property was originally acquired for £400,000. Some years later, after cumulative depreciation of £110,000 has been recognised, the property is classified as held for sale.

At the time of classification as held for sale:

- carrying amount is £290,000; and
- fair value less costs to sell is assessed at £300,000.

Accordingly, there is no write-down on classification as held for sale and the property is carried at £290,000.

At the next reporting date, the property market has declined and fair value less costs to sell is reassessed at £285,000. Accordingly, a loss of £5,000 is recognised in profit or loss and the property is carried at £285,000.

Subsequently, the property is sold for £288,000, at which time a gain of £3,000 is recognised.

Example 4.1B

Measuring non-current assets held for sale (2)

A freehold property was originally acquired for £400,000. Some years later, after cumulative depreciation of £110,000 has been recognised, an impairment loss of £35,000 is recognised, taking the carrying amount to £255,000, which represents the estimated value in use of the property. Shortly thereafter, as a consequence of a proposed move to new premises, the freehold property is classified as held for sale.

At the time of classification as held for sale:

- carrying amount is £255,000; and
- fair value less costs to sell is assessed at £250,000.

Accordingly, the initial write-down on classification as held for sale is £5,000 and the property is carried at £250,000.

At the next reporting date, the property market has improved and fair value less costs to sell is reassessed at £265,000. The gain of £15,000 is less than the cumulative impairment losses recognised to date (£35,000 + £5,000 = £40,000). Accordingly, it is credited in profit or loss and the property is carried at £265,000.

Six months after that, the property market has continued to improve, and fair value less costs to sell is now assessed at £300,000. This further gain of

£35,000 is, however, in excess of the cumulative impairment losses recognised to date (£35,000 + £5,000 – £15,000 = £25,000). Accordingly, a restricted gain of £25,000 is credited in profit or loss and the property is carried at £290,000.

Subsequently, the property is sold for £300,000, at which time a gain of £10,000 is recognised.

Example 4.1C

Non-current asset previously accounted for under revaluation model

An entity has adopted a policy of carrying a particular class of property, plant and equipment (PPE) at revalued amounts. An item of PPE in that class now satisfies the criteria for classification as held for sale. On the date of reclassification, the fair value less costs to sell is lower than the current carrying amount of the particular item. The write-down to fair value less costs to sell should be accounted for as follows.

Step 1: update valuation (fair value)

Immediately before the asset is initially classified as held for sale, the carrying amount of the asset should be measured in accordance with applicable IFRSs. [IFRS 5.18]

Given that the asset is carried at a revalued amount under IAS 16, any decrease in value would be accounted for in other comprehensive income to the extent that any credit balance exists in the revaluation reserve for that asset, with any excess being recognised in profit or loss.

Step 2: consider recoverable amount (higher of fair value less costs to sell and value in use)

Before the asset's classification as held for sale, the entity must assess whether there is any indication that the asset is impaired. If there is an indication of an impairment loss, the recoverable amount of the asset should be determined under IAS 36.

If recognition of an impairment loss is required, the impairment loss should be accounted for as a revaluation decrease in accordance with IAS 16, to the extent that a revaluation reserve for the asset remains. Any impairment loss in excess of the available reserve should be recognised in profit or loss.

Step 3: write-down to fair value less costs to sell (if lower than step 2)

Upon reclassification of the asset as held for sale, if fair value less costs to sell equates to value in use, there should be no further impairment loss to recognise. However, if value in use is higher, a further impairment loss should be recognised in profit or loss in accordance with IFRS 5.20 & 37. This impairment loss is recognised in profit or loss in the same way as any asset that before classification as held for sale had not been revalued. [IFRS 5.BC47 – 48]

Example 4.1D

Reversal of impairment losses on an asset with a prior revaluation decrease but no prior impairment loss

An entity holds land (original cost £100,000), previously carried at a revalued amount of £250,000 in accordance with IAS 16, which is classified as held for sale in accordance with IFRS 5.

- Before its reclassification as held for sale, a revaluation decrease was recognised on the land in accordance with IAS 16. The revaluation decrease of £50,000 was recognised in other comprehensive income.

- Immediately before its reclassification as held for sale, the land was carried at a revalued amount of £200,000 in accordance with IAS 16, which was also the appropriate measure on initial classification as held for sale under IFRS 5.

- Since the land's reclassification as held for sale, the entity has recognised an impairment loss of £20,000 in profit or loss (in accordance with IFRS 5) because its fair value less costs to sell fell to £180,000.

- On the reporting date, the land has not been sold and it still satisfies the criteria for classification as held for sale. Its fair value less costs to sell has increased to £215,000.

Summary of the land's history:	£
Revalued carrying amount prior to revaluation decrease	250,000
Revaluation decrease recognised in other comprehensive income in accordance with IAS 16	(50,000)
Revalued carrying amount immediately before classification as held for sale	200,000
Impairment loss recognised in profit or loss in accordance with IFRS 5	(20,000)
Fair value less costs to sell under IFRS 5	180,000
Fair value less costs to sell on the reporting date	215,000
Fair value movement	35,000

IFRS 5 only allows the reversal of impairment losses and not revaluation decreases. Consequently, the impairment-loss reversal is limited to £20,000 (i.e. the amount of the impairment loss recognised under IFRS 5). The additional fair value gain of £15,000 (£35,000 – £20,000) cannot be recognised because it was initially recognised in other comprehensive income as a revaluation decrease and not as an impairment loss.

Example 4.1E

Reversal of impairment losses on an asset previously classified as property, plant and equipment with prior impairment loss

Summary of asset's history:	£
Property purchased on 1 July 20X4 at cost (nil residual value and a useful life of 10 years)	500,000
Depreciation for 2 years (500,000/10 x 2)	(100,000)
Impairment loss recognised in accordance with IAS 36 at 30 June 20X6	(100,000)
Carrying amount at 30 June 20X6	300,000
Depreciation for the year (300,000/8)	(37,500)
Carrying amount at 30 June 20X7 immediately before classification as held for sale under IFRS 5	262,500
Write-down to fair value less costs to sell in accordance with IFRS 5 on classification as held for sale at 30 June 20X7	(100,000)
Carrying amount at 30 June 2007 after classification as held for sale	162,500

On 30 June 20X8, the asset is still held for sale and fair value less costs to sell has increased by £200,000 to £362,500.

The reversal of prior impairment losses is limited to the carrying amount that would have been determined at the date the property was classified as held for sale under IFRS 5, as if no prior impairment loss had been recognised under IAS 36. The carrying amount cannot be increased beyond £350,000 because that is the amount that would have been determined at the date the property was classified as held for sale if no previous impairment loss had been recognised under IAS 36 (i.e. the original cost of £500,000 less accumulated depreciation of £150,000 over three years). Accordingly, even though the fair value less costs to sell has increased by £200,000 (i.e. by an amount equivalent to all prior impairment losses and write-downs under IAS 36 and IFRS 5), the reversal is limited to £187,500 (i.e. £350,000 – £162,500).

Example 4.1F

Interest in associate reclassified as held for sale

Company X has a 25 per cent associate, Company A, which it accounts for using the equity method in accordance with IAS 28 *Investments in Associates*. Prior to the end of the reporting period, Company X has decided to sell its interest in Company A and all the criteria in IFRS 5 for classification as held for sale have been met. At the date of classification as held for sale, Company X ceases to equity account for the associate and accounts for its interest in Company A at the lower of carrying amount and fair value less costs to sell. [IFRS 5.15] For IFRS 5 measurement purposes, the carrying amount at the date of classification as held for sale is the 'frozen' equity-accounted carrying amount, i.e. the amount at which the associate was recognised under equity accounting immediately prior to reclassification.

4.2 Disposal groups

The measurement requirements for disposal groups are for the most part similar to those relating to individual non-current assets. But they are complicated by the treatment of those assets (listed at **2.2.1**) that are outside the scope of IFRS 5's measurement requirements (the scoped-out non-current assets).

The general principle is that a disposal group held for sale is measured at the lower of its carrying amount and fair value less costs to sell. [IFRS 5.15] The detailed requirements on initial classification are as follows.

- Immediately before initial classification as held for sale, the carrying amounts of all the individual assets and liabilities in the disposal group are measured in accordance with applicable IFRSs. [IFRS 5.18]

  For example, investment property held at fair value will be measured in accordance with IAS 40 *Investment Property,* factory equipment in accordance with IAS 16 *Property, Plant and Equipment*, inventories in accordance with IAS 2 *Inventories* and derivative financial liabilities in accordance with IAS 39 *Financial Instruments: Recognition and Measurement*. Any changes in the carrying amounts of the assets and liabilities are recognised as usual in accordance with their applicable IFRSs.

  If there is any indication of an impairment loss for assets falling within the scope of IAS 36, an impairment review is carried out and an impairment loss is recognised in accordance with IAS 36, if necessary.

- If fair value less costs to sell for the disposal group is below the aggregate carrying amount of all of the assets and liabilities included in the disposal group, the disposal group is written down. The impairment loss is recognised in profit or loss for the period. [IFRS 5.20 & 37]

On subsequent remeasurement of a disposal group, the detailed requirements are as follows.

- Assets and liabilities that are not within the scope of the measurement requirements of IFRS 5 – namely the scoped-out non-current assets (listed at **2.2.1**), current assets and all liabilities – are first remeasured in accordance with applicable IFRSs, and the carrying amount of the disposal group is adjusted to reflect these remeasurements. [IFRS 5.19]

For example, the carrying amounts for inventories will be adjusted to the lower of cost and net realisable value.

- Interest and other expenses attributable to liabilities within the disposal group continue to be recognised. [IFRS 5.25]
- Other non-current assets (i.e. those within the scope of IFRS 5's measurement requirements – the scoped-in non-current assets) are no longer depreciated or amortised. [IFRS 5.25]
- The fair value less costs to sell of the disposal group is calculated.
- If the updated carrying amount of the disposal group exceeds its fair value less costs to sell, the excess is written off as a further impairment loss. [IFRS 5.20]
- A gain is recognised for any subsequent increase in fair value less costs to sell of a disposal group:

[IFRS 5.22]

  - to the extent that it has not been recognised in the remeasurement of scoped-out non-current assets, current assets and liabilities; but
  - not in excess of the cumulative impairment loss recognised, either in accordance with IFRS 5 or previously in accordance with IAS 36, on the scoped-in non-current assets (note that the requirements of IFRS 5.22 are discussed in more detail at **4.2.1** below).

Where an impairment loss is recognised (or reversed) for a disposal group, it is allocated between the scoped-in non-current assets using the order of allocation set out in IAS 36.104(a) & (b) and IAS 36.122. [IFRS 5.23] The order of allocation of impairment losses under IFRS 5 is therefore:

- first, to reduce the carrying amount of any goodwill allocated to the disposal group;
- then, to the other scoped-in non-current assets of the group, pro-rata on the basis of the carrying amount of each of those assets.

The allocation of disposal-group impairment losses under IFRS 5 is different from that specified by IAS 36. Disposal-group impairment losses can only be allocated between the scoped-in non-current assets, whereas impairment losses recognised under IAS 36 may, in principle, be allocated between all assets of a cash-generating unit. Further, the purpose of the restricted references to IAS 36 is to make clear that, unlike IAS 36.105, IFRS 5 does not establish a limit below which the carrying amount cannot be reduced. Accordingly, it is possible for a scoped-in non-current asset within a disposal group to be written down to a lower amount than would result if IAS 36 alone were applied. The reference to IAS 36.104 is not to the entire paragraph, but is limited to the specific criteria in (a) and (b). Therefore, the reference is intentionally only to the order of allocation and not to the entire paragraph.

Where a disposal group is written down to fair value less costs to sell, the methodology described by the Standard allocates the adjustment against the scoped-in non-current assets in the disposal group – no element of the adjustment is allocated to the other assets and liabilities of the disposal group. This is true even where the adjustment has arisen because the fair value of liabilities (e.g. fixed-rate borrowings) is higher than their carrying amount. Accordingly, although the net amount included for the disposal group will be the fair value less costs to sell of the disposal group as a whole, the gross amounts presented separately for assets and liabilities may differ significantly from the fair value less costs to sell of those individual assets and liabilities.

IFRS 5 does not discuss the possibility that the carrying amount of scoped-in non-current assets may be less than the amount by which a disposal group's carrying amount exceeds its fair value less costs to sell. Such a scenario could arise if, for example, the carrying amount of scoped-in non-current assets is small, but there are fixed-rate borrowings (carried at amortised cost) with a fair value significantly in excess of carrying amount. In such circumstances, a number of different approaches might be possible. For example, to the extent that the write-down exceeds the carrying amount of scoped-in non-current assets, that excess:

- might also be allocated against the scoped-in non-current assets, so that their carrying amount becomes negative;
- might be allocated against other assets (i.e. those outside the scope of IFRS 5's measurement requirements);
- might be recognised as an additional liability; or
- might not be recognised at all.

In the absence of relevant guidance from the IASB or the IFRIC, in these circumstances it would seem appropriate for an entity to adopt one of the above approaches as an accounting policy choice.

Example 4.2A

Initial and subsequent measurement of a disposal group (1)

A disposal group includes an investment property (previously accounted for under the fair value model in IAS 40) and other assets. None of the assets has been previously impaired and they are all within the scope of IFRS 5's measurement requirements. Immediately prior to classification as held for sale, the investment property is remeasured under IAS 40 to fair value of £300,000. The aggregate carrying amount of the other assets under applicable IFRSs is £250,000, giving a total of £550,000.

The fair value less costs to sell of the disposal group as a whole is initially estimated at £560,000. Accordingly, there is no initial write-down on classification as held for sale, and the disposal group is carried at £550,000.

At the next reporting date, the fair value of the investment property has fallen to £280,000, and the fair value less costs to sell of the disposal group as a whole is reassessed at £515,000. Accordingly:

- the loss of £20,000 on the investment property is recognised under IAS 40;
- this brings the carrying amount of the disposal group down to £530,000, but the fair value less costs to sell of the disposal group is only £515,000; and
- accordingly, a further loss of £15,000 is recognised, bringing the carrying amount of the disposal group down to £515,000.

In accordance with IFRS 5.23, this further impairment loss is allocated first to reduce any goodwill in the disposal group, and then pro-rata between the other scoped-in non-current assets (without allocation to the investment property as it is scoped out).

Example 4.2B

Initial and subsequent measurement of a disposal group (2)

A disposal group includes an investment property (previously accounted for under the fair value model in IAS 40) and other assets. None of the assets has been previously impaired and they are all within the scope of IFRS 5's measurement requirements. Immediately prior to classification as held for sale, the investment property is remeasured under IAS 40 to fair value of £300,000. The aggregate carrying amount of the other assets under applicable IFRSs is £250,000, giving a total of £550,000.

The fair value less costs to sell of the disposal group as a whole is initially estimated at £520,000. Accordingly, the initial write-down on classification as held for sale is £30,000 and the disposal group is carried at £520,000. The £30,000 impairment loss is allocated first to reduce any goodwill in the disposal group, and then pro-rata between the other scoped-in non-current assets (without allocation to the investment property as it is scoped out).

At the next reporting date, the fair value of the investment property has increased to £310,000 and the fair value less costs to sell of the disposal group as a whole is reassessed at £570,000. Accordingly:

- the gain of £10,000 on the investment property is recognised under IAS 40;
- this brings the carrying amount of the disposal group up to £530,000, which is less than the fair value less costs to sell;
- the fair value less costs to sell of the disposal group has increased by £50,000 (£570,000 – £520,000), but under IFRS 5.22 this must be reduced by the amount already recognised in respect of scoped-out non-current assets – the £10,000 gain on the investment property in this case;
- the remaining £40,000 is then capped at the amount of cumulative impairment losses, namely £30,000 (assuming there were no previous impairment losses under IAS 36);
- accordingly, a further gain of £30,000 is recognised, bringing the carrying amount of the disposal group up to £560,000. The reversal is allocated to the scoped-in non-current assets, except for goodwill.

The Implementation Guidance accompanying the Standard includes the following illustration of the allocation of an impairment loss to the assets of a disposal group.

Example 4.2C

Allocation of an impairment loss to a disposal group

[Guidance on Implementing IFRS 5 (Example 10)]

An entity plans to dispose of a group of its assets (as an asset sale). The assets form a disposal group, and are measured as follows:

	Carrying amount at the reporting date before classification as held for sale	Carrying amount as remeasured immediately before classification as held for sale
	CU	CU
Goodwill	1,500	1,500
Property, plant and equipment (carried at revalued amounts)	4,600	4,000
Property, plant and equipment (carried at cost)	5,700	5,700
Inventory	2,400	2,200
AFS [available for sale] financial assets	1,800	1,500
Total	**16,000**	**14,900**

The entity recognises the loss of CU1,100 (CU16,000-CU14,900) immediately before classifying the disposal group as held for sale.

The entity estimates that fair value less costs to sell of the disposal group amounts to CU13,000. Because an entity measures a disposal group classified as held for sale at the lower of its carrying amount and fair value less costs to sell, the entity recognises an impairment loss of CU1,900 (CU14,900 – CU13,000) when the group is initially classified as held for sale.

The impairment loss is allocated to non-current assets to which the measurement requirements of the IFRS are applicable. Therefore, no impairment loss is allocated to inventory and AFS financial assets. The loss is allocated to the other assets in the order of allocation set out in paragraphs 104 and 122 of IAS 36 (as revised in 2004).

The allocation can be illustrated as follows:

	Carrying amount as remeasured immediately before classification as held for sale	Allocated impairment loss	Carrying amount after allocation of impairment loss
	CU	CU	CU
Goodwill	1,500	(1,500)	–
Property, plant and equipment (carried at revalued amounts)	4,000	(165)	3,835
Property, plant and equipment (carried at cost)	5,700	(235)	5,465
Inventory	2,200	–	2,200
AFS financial assets	1,500	–	1,500
Total	**14,900**	**(1,900)**	**13,000**

First, the impairment loss reduces any amount of goodwill. Then, the residual loss is allocated to other assets pro-rata based on the carrying amounts of those assets.

A further example is set out below.

Example 4.2D

Allocation of an impairment loss to a disposal group

Company Z intends to sell a division, Division D, which is not a separate legal entity. Division D (the disposal group) meets all the criteria in IFRS 5 to be classified as held for sale. Division D is a service organisation with few non-current assets. The carrying amounts of assets and liabilities held in D are as follows:

	Carrying amount
	£
Property, plant and equipment: Asset A	75
Property, plant and equipment: Asset B	25
Receivables	300
Cash	50
Total assets	450
Post-employment benefits	130
Trade payables	180
Other current liabilities	100
Total liabilities	410
Net assets	40

The fair value of the disposal group is £30. All financial liabilities are accounted for at amortised cost, and costs to sell are estimated at £2. The disposal group, therefore, should be written down to £28 [£30 – £2].

IFRS 5.20 requires that the full write-down of £12 [£40 – £28] be recognised against the disposal group. In accordance with IFRS 5.23, the whole £12 should reduce the non-current assets within the scope of IFRS 5 (in this case property, plant, and equipment) to £88 in total. The write-down is allocated pro-rata on the basis of the carrying amount of each asset in the group. This would require the entity to recognise £9 [(75 ÷ 100) × 12] against Asset A and £3 [(25 ÷ 100) × 12] against Asset B.

4.2.1 *Recognising gains in relation to a disposal group*

As discussed above, although under IFRS 5.19 gains and losses relating to scoped-out non-current assets will continue to be recognised in accordance with the applicable IFRSs, IFRS 5.22 restricts the extent to which gains can separately be recognised in respect of a disposal group:

> 'An entity shall recognise a gain for any subsequent increase in fair value less costs to sell of a disposal group:
>
> (a) to the extent that it has not been recognised in accordance with paragraph 19; but
>
> (b) not in excess of the cumulative impairment loss that has been recognised, either in accordance with this IFRS or previously in accordance with IAS 36, on the non-current assets that are within the scope of the measurement requirements of this IFRS.'

At first glance, it might appear that the purpose of IFRS 5.22 is to isolate gains and losses relating to scoped-out non-current assets and then to recognise gains relating to the rest of the disposal group only to the extent that they reverse previous impairment losses. In fact, the drafting of IFRS 5.22 is not as equitable as this. Care is needed when applying it, as illustrated in the following example.

Example 4.2.1

Recognising subsequent measurement gains on disposal groups classified as held for sale

A disposal group held for sale includes a freehold property carried under IAS 16's cost model on which an impairment loss of £100,000 was recognised prior to the asset being classified as held for sale. No adjustments are necessary when the disposal group is classified as held for sale. Some time after the disposal group has been classified as held for sale, the property increases in value by £50,000, causing a corresponding increase of £50,000 in the fair value less costs to sell of the disposal group. How will this gain be recognised?

Scenario 1

Assume that scoped-out non-current assets have increased in value by £10,000 and the increase in value has been recognised in accordance with the requirements of other Standards, so that the disposal group as a whole has increased in value by £60,000. Applying the requirements of IFRS 5.22, this total gain of £60,000 is restricted by £10,000 (being the amount in respect of scoped-out non-current assets), leaving a balance of £50,000. This is less than the cumulative impairment loss, so a gain of £50,000 will be recognised (in addition to the scoped-out non-current asset gains of £10,000 recognised).

Scenario 2

Assume instead that scoped-out non-current assets have decreased in value by £40,000, and the value of the property has increased by £50,000 so that the disposal group as a whole has increased in value by a net £10,000. Applying the requirements of IFRS 5.22, only this net increase in the fair value less costs to sell can be considered for recognition. This is not restricted by any amounts recognised in respect of scoped-out non-current assets (which are negative), and is less than the cumulative impairment loss on the property, so a gain of only £10,000 will be recognised. Since losses of £40,000 will have been recognised on the scoped-out non-current assets, the net effect will be to recognise losses of £30,000.

Scenario 3

Finally, assume instead that scoped-out non-current assets have decreased in value by £60,000, and the value of the property has increased by £50,000, so that the disposal group as a whole has decreased in value by a net £10,000. Applying the requirements of IFRS 5.22, there is no increase in the fair value less costs to sell of the disposal group, so no gain can be recognised. Thus, only the losses of £60,000 will be recognised (on the scoped-out non-current assets), even though the disposal group has decreased in value by only £10,000.

Thus, the recognition of subsequent changes in measurement can be affected by how the scoped-out non-current assets in the disposal group have changed in value.

4.2.2 *Accumulated translation adjustments relating to a foreign subsidiary held for sale*

Where a disposal group classified as held for sale consists of the assets and liabilities of a foreign subsidiary, in respect of which accumulated translation adjustments have been recognised in other comprehensive income, the question arises as to whether the accumulated foreign currency translation adjustments should be taken into account in determining the recoverability of the subsidiary.

Such differences should not be included when measuring the carrying amount of the disposal group. IAS 21 *The Effects of Changes in Foreign Exchange Rates* requires exchange differences to be reclassified from equity to profit or loss at the time of disposal of the operation. IFRS 5.BC37 & BC38 clarify that exchange differences should not be so reclassified at the time when the asset or disposal group is classified as held for sale. Including these translation adjustments in the carrying amount of the asset or disposal group to calculate the impairment loss (if any) would be tantamount to reclassifying them from equity to profit or loss. The accumulated foreign currency translation adjustments, therefore, should be excluded from the carrying amount. They will not be taken into account until the asset or disposal group is sold.

4.3 Measuring costs to sell

Costs to sell are the incremental costs directly attributable to the disposal of an asset (or disposal group), excluding finance costs and income tax expense. [IFRS 5(Appendix A)]

4.3.1 Facility-holding costs

Facility-holding costs (e.g. insurance, security services, utility expenses etc.) to be incurred between the date of classifying the asset as held for sale and the date of ultimate disposal should not be recognised as costs to sell. Such costs are not incremental costs directly attributable to the disposal of an asset (or disposal group) because they would be incurred whether or not the facility was being sold.

4.3.2 Costs to sell measured at present value

If the sale of an asset (or disposal group) is expected to occur beyond one year, costs to sell are measured at their present value, i.e. discounted for the time value of money. The subsequent unwinding of the discount is presented in profit or loss as a financing cost. [IFRS 5.17] accumulated translation adjustments have been recognised in other comprehensive income, the question arises as to whether the accumulated foreign currency translation adjustments should be taken into account in determining the recoverability of the subsidiary.

Such differences should not be included when measuring the carrying amount of the disposal group. IAS 21 *The Effects of Changes in Foreign Exchange Rates* requires exchange differences to be reclassified from equity to profit or loss at the time of disposal of the operation. IFRS 5.BC37 & BC38 clarify that exchange differences should not be so reclassified at the time when the asset or disposal group is classified as held for sale. Including these translation adjustments in the carrying amount of the asset or disposal group to calculate the impairment loss (if any) would be tantamount to reclassifying them from equity to profit or loss. The accumulated foreign currency translation adjustments, therefore, should be excluded from the carrying amount. They will not be taken into account until the asset or disposal group is sold.

4.3 Measuring costs to sell

Costs to sell are the incremental costs directly attributable to the disposal of an asset (or disposal group), excluding finance costs and income tax expense. [IFRS 5(Appendix A)]

4.3.1 *Facility-holding costs*

Facility-holding costs (e.g. insurance, security services, utility expenses etc.) to be incurred between the date of classifying the asset as held for sale and the date of ultimate disposal should not be recognised as costs to sell. Such costs are not incremental costs directly attributable to the disposal of an asset (or disposal group) because they would be incurred whether or not the facility was being sold.

4.3.2 *Costs to sell measured at present value*

If the sale of an asset (or disposal group) is expected to occur beyond one year, costs to sell are measured at their present value, i.e. discounted for the time value of money. The subsequent unwinding of the discount is presented in profit or loss as a financing cost. [IFRS 5.17] asset as held for sale in its annual financial statements and wrote down the carrying amount of the asset to its estimated fair value less costs to sell. Subsequent to the end of the reporting period, but prior to the issuance of the financial statements, Company T enters into a final agreement to sell the asset at a value which is less than the estimated fair value less costs to sell. Should Company T consider the final agreement and adjust the fair value less costs to sell of the asset at the end of the reporting period?

Company T should evaluate the factors that led to the decrease in value of the asset between its classification as held for sale and the determination of the actual sales price. If the value of the asset changed after the end of Company T's reporting period, Company T should not adjust the carrying amount of the asset as of the end of the reporting period. However, if facts and circumstances indicate that the value of the asset remained unchanged between the time Company T classified it as held for sale and the determination of the final sales price, and the sales price determined after the end of the reporting period provided additional evidence of conditions that existed at the end of the reporting period, which were indicative of the true estimate of the fair value, then Company T should use the price established in the sales agreement as the basis of its estimate of fair value less costs to sell.

4.6 Changes to a plan of sale

Where an asset or disposal group has been classified as held for sale, but the held-for-sale criteria (see **3.1** above) are no longer met, the asset/disposal group should be removed from the held-for-sale category. [IFRS 5.26]

4.6.1 *Remeasuring a non-current asset that is no longer held for sale*

When a non-current asset ceases to be classified as held for sale (or ceases to be included in a disposal group classified as held for sale), it is measured at the lower of:

[IFRS 5.27]

(a) its carrying amount before the asset (or disposal group) was classified as held for sale, adjusted for any depreciation, amortisation or revaluations that would have been recognised had the asset (or disposal group) not been classified as held for sale; and

(b) its recoverable amount at the date of the subsequent decision not to sell.

This effectively restates the asset at the value at which it would have been recognised had it never been classified as held for sale in the first place, taking into account any impairment losses. Part (b) includes an impairment assessment, which seems appropriate since an impairment loss indicator (e.g. a fall in market value) could be driving the decision not to sell the asset.

Recoverable amount is the higher of fair value less costs to sell and value in use, where value in use is the present value of estimated future cash flows expected to arise from the continuing use of an asset and from its disposal at the end of its useful life. [IFRS 5(Appendix A)] If a non-current asset is part of a cash-generating unit, its recoverable amount is the carrying amount that would have been recognised after the allocation of any impairment loss arising on that cash-generating unit in accordance with IAS 36.

Where the above requirement triggers an adjustment to the asset's carrying amount, the adjustment is generally included in profit or loss from continuing operations in the period in which the held-for-sale criteria are no longer met. If the asset is property, plant and equipment or an intangible asset that had been revalued in accordance with IAS 16 or IAS 38 before classification as held for sale, the adjustment is treated as a revaluation increase or decrease. The adjustment should be included in the same caption in the statement of comprehensive income used to present other gains or losses on held-for-sale items not meeting the definition of discontinued operations (see **7.1** below). [IFRS 5.28]

4.6.2 Removing an asset or liability from a disposal group

If an individual asset or liability is removed from a disposal group classified as held for sale, the remaining assets and liabilities of the disposal group will continue to be measured as a group only if the group continues to meet the held-for-sale criteria (see **3.1**). Otherwise:

[IFRS 5.29]

- any non-current assets of the group that individually meet the criteria to be classified as held for sale are measured individually at the lower of their carrying amounts and fair values less costs to sell at that date; and
- any non-current assets that do not meet the criteria are removed from the held-for-sale category and measured in accordance with **4.6.1** above.

Example 4.6.2

Sale of a subsidiary with the exception of certain assets

Company C has a wholly-owned subsidiary, Company D, which manufactures and sells athletic equipment. In January, Company C adopted a plan to sell all of the assets and liabilities of Company D. Having met the requirements of IFRS 5.7 & 8 at the end of the first quarter, Company C appropriately classified Company D as held for sale and reported the results of Company D's operations in discontinued operations.

In June, Company C elected not to sell certain existing trademarks and license arrangements owned by Company D. Subsequent to the sale of Company D, Company C will continue to generate revenue (and incur the associated costs) from its trademark and license arrangements. Such revenue represented approximately five per cent of Company D's total revenue for the year.

If Company C removes the trademark and license arrangements from the asset group to be disposed of, should Company C continue to account for the remaining assets and liabilities as held for sale?

If the remaining assets and liabilities of Company D continue to meet the criteria of IFRS 5.7 & 8, Company C should continue to classify those remaining assets and liabilities as held for sale. Company C must reclassify the trademarks and license arrangements to assets held and used. Additionally, Company C should measure the trademarks and license arrangements at the lower of (a) their carrying amounts before being classified as held for sale less any amortisation expense that would have been recognised if they had not been classified as held for sale, and (b) their recoverable amount at the date of the subsequent decision not to sell.

5 Assets acquired exclusively with a view to subsequent disposal

An entity may acquire a non-current asset (or disposal group) exclusively with a view to its subsequent disposal, for example as part of a business combination. In such circumstances, the non-current asset (or disposal group) is classified as held for sale at the acquisition date only if:

[IFRS 5.11]

- the requirement that a sale is expected within one year (see **3.1.3**) is met (unless the exceptions discussed in **3.1.5** apply); and

- it is highly probable (i.e. significantly more likely than probable) that any of the other general requirements (see **3.1.1**) and specific conditions (see **3.1.2** and **3.1.3**) that are not met at that date will be met within a short period following the acquisition (usually within three months).

UK *Under UK GAAP, where a subsidiary is acquired exclusively with a view to subsequent resale, it is excluded from consolidation in accordance with FRS 7.16. There is no similar exemption under IFRS 5, and accordingly such a subsidiary will be consolidated. However, providing the criteria above are met, the subsidiary's assets and liabilities will be presented as held for sale in the balance sheet, and its results will be presented as part of discontinued operations in the income statement (see* **6.1**).

If a newly-acquired asset (or disposal group) meets the criteria to be classified as held for sale, it will be measured on initial recognition at the lower of its carrying amount had it not been so classified (for example, cost) and fair value less costs to sell. Accordingly, if an asset or a disposal group is acquired as part of a business combination, it will be measured at fair value less costs to sell. [IFRS 5.16]

6 Discontinued operations

The overall objective of IFRS 5's presentation and disclosure requirements is to enable users to evaluate the financial effects of discontinued operations and disposals of non-current assets or disposal groups. [IFRS 5.30] To this end, the Standard distinguishes discontinued operations from other operations and presents them separately.

Certain operations that are to be disposed of will be classified as discontinued operations, resulting in gains and losses relating to them (including those for any corresponding disposal group) being presented separately in the statement of comprehensive income. Other operations, disposal groups and assets held for sale will not be classified as discontinued operations and gains and losses relating to them will be presented as part of continuing operations.

6.1 Definition of a discontinued operation

A discontinued operation is a component of an entity that either has been disposed of or is classified as held for sale and:

[IFRS 5.32 and IFRS 5(Appendix A)]

(a) represents a separate major line of business or geographical area of operations; or

(b) is part of a single co-ordinated plan to dispose of a separate major line of business or geographical area of operations; or

(c) is a subsidiary acquired exclusively with a view to resale.

IFRS 5.31 explains that a component of an entity 'comprises operations and cash flows that can be clearly distinguished, operationally and for financial reporting purposes, from the rest of the entity. In other words, a component of an entity will have been a cash-generating unit or a group of cash-generating units while being held for use.' As in IAS 36, a cash-generating unit is defined as the smallest identifiable group of assets that generates cash inflows that are largely independent of the cash inflows from other assets or groups of assets. [IFRS 5(Appendix A)]

UK

This approach, which links the treatment of an operation as discontinued to the held for sale criteria, is quite different to that taken in UK GAAP under FRS 3.

- *Where an operation is to be sold, it is likely that it will be classified as discontinued earlier under IFRS 5. This is because an operation cannot be presented as discontinued under FRS 3 unless it has actually been sold within three months of the balance sheet date or by the time the financial statements are approved if earlier. Under IFRS 5, such a sale need only be expected within the next year.*
- *Conversely, where an operation is to be closed or abandoned, rather than sold, it will only be presented as a discontinued operation under IFRS 5 if it has actually been disposed of by the balance sheet date (see* **3.2**). *This is a tougher requirement than that of FRS 3, which only requires that the operation has been terminated within three months of the balance sheet date or by the time the financial statements are approved if earlier.*

Example 6.1

Classification of a component that is to be abandoned

Company M, which has a 31 December year end, announced a plan to abandon the operations of its subsidiary, Company E, on 15 December 20X2. Company M has determined that Company E represents a component of the entity as defined in IFRS 5. Under the plan for abandonment, Company E will cease to accept any new business as of 31 December 20X2. Company M anticipates that Company E will be able to wrap up production of all remaining orders, ancillary operations and close both the plant and office facilities by 15 March 20X3. Should Company M classify the operations of Company E as discontinued operations in its 31 December 20X2 financial statements?

IFRS 5.13 states that while assets or disposal groups to be abandoned may not be classified as held for sale, a disposal group may be classified as a discontinued operation if the group represents a component of an entity and meets the criteria in IFRS 5.32. IFRS 5.32 requires a component to be disposed of, or classified as held for sale, prior to being presented as a discontinued operation. Since an item to be abandoned cannot be classified as held for sale (per IFRS 5.13), it will not meet the IFRS 5.32 criteria until it is actually abandoned. Therefore, in the circumstances described, Company M should not classify the operations of Company E as discontinued operations in its 31 December 20X2 financial statements.

However, at 15 December 20X2, Company M may have an impairment loss indicator under IAS 36 *Impairment of Assets*, and may need to test the assets of Company E for recoverability. In addition, Company M may need to revise its depreciation estimates in accordance with IAS 16 *Property, Plant and Equipment* to reflect the use of Company E's assets over their shortened useful life.

6.1.1 *Equity-method investees*

In some circumstances, the disposal of a stand-alone investment in equity securities accounted for by the equity method may be classified as a discontinued operation in the investor's consolidated financial statements. If the entity's business model includes conducting operations through strategic investments in associates and jointly controlled entities accounted for using the equity method, it may be possible to demonstrate that the investment is a component of the entity as described in IFRS 5.31. In many cases, however, the operations relating to an equity-method investment (an investor's share of the earnings and losses of an equity-method investee) are not sufficient to establish a component of the investor-entity as described in IFRS 5.31. If a component of an entity has operations that include, but are not limited to, operations related to an equity-method investment, and the conditions for reporting discontinued operations are met (as set out in IFRS 5.32), all of the operations of the component should be reported as discontinued operations.

An investor should not present its share of an equity-method investee's discontinued operations as a discontinued operation in its consolidated financial statements. IAS 1(2007).54 (previously IAS 1(2003).68) requires a separate line item in the statement of comprehensive income for investments accounted for using the equity method. It would not be appropriate to break out of that line item an amount that relates to the discontinued operations of the associate. In addition, it is unlikely that a component of an equity-method investment could be determined to be a component of the investor-entity.

6.1.2 *Disposal achieved in stages*

Example 6.1.2

Disposal achieved in stages

On 15 December 20X1, Company Z decided to sell 65 per cent of its wholly-owned subsidiary, Company X. At that time, it was determined that the subsidiary met the requirements to be classified as a disposal group held for sale and a discontinued operation (as Company X represented a major line of business). On 1 April 20X2, Z sold 65 per cent of its wholly-owned subsidiary Company X to Company Y. Subsequent to the disposal, Company Z's investment in Company X was classified as an associate. On 30 June 20X3, Company Z decided to sell its remaining 35 per cent interest in Company X to Company Y. The sale was completed on 31 August 20X3. When should Company Z classify the results of Company X's operations as a discontinued operation, if at all?

A subsidiary that represents a major line of business should be classified as a discontinued operation at the earlier of its disposal date, or when that subsidiary meets the held-for-sale criteria in IFRS 5.7. A subsidiary meets the highly probable sale criteria in IFRS 5.7 when the controlling entity, as a result of the disposal, will lose control over the former subsidiary (see **3.4**). Therefore, provided that the other criteria are met, Company X should be presented as a discontinued operation in Company Z's first financial statements on or after 15 December 20X1.

6.1.3 *Sale of a component to more than one buyer*

Example 6.1.3

Sale of a component to more than one buyer

Company C manufactures and markets men's shoes and coats. Company C discloses two operating segments under IFRS 8 *Operating Segments*, the Shoe Group and the Coat Group. Company C also discloses certain trademark and license agreements within each segment.

The operations and cash flows of the Shoe Group can be clearly distinguished operationally and for financial reporting purposes from the rest of Company C. Therefore, the Shoe Group is a component of Company C. In the fourth quarter of 20X2, Company C completed a transaction to sell the majority of the Shoe Group's manufacturing and distribution operations to

Company E. In addition, management, having the appropriate level of authority, has committed to a formal plan of sale for the remaining assets of the Shoe Group. Should Company C account for the sale of the majority of the Shoe Group together with the formalised plan by management to dispose of the remaining Shoe Group assets as a discontinued operation at 31 December 20X2?

Yes. While the definition of a disposal group requires a sale in a single transaction, a discontinued operation may comprise several disposal groups. At 31 December 20X2, one disposal group (the majority of the Shoe Group's operations) has already been sold and a second (the remaining assets of the Group) is classified as held for sale (assuming all of the requirements of IFRS 5.7 are met). Therefore, the operating segment qualifies for classification as discontinued.

6.1.4 Allocation of part of an asset's cost to discontinued operations

Example 6.1.4

Allocation of part of an asset's cost to discontinued operations

Company T, a public entity, currently reports three operating segments. In the current year, Company T implemented a new centralised computer system to be used by each of the three operating segments. Subsequent to the implementation of the computer system, Company T entered into an agreement to sell one of the operating segments. The disposal of the segment will be accounted for as a discontinued operation. Is it appropriate for Company T to allocate a portion of the costs incurred on the new computer system to the operating segment being sold in determining the gain or loss on the disposal of the segment?

No. In order for an asset to be classified as held for sale, it must be available for immediate sale in its present condition. There are no plans to sell the central computer system, and, thus, it should not be included in the assets to be disposed of. Therefore, Company T may not allocate the overall costs incurred on the new computer system to the operating segment being disposed of. Additionally, any impairment loss recognised by Company T in respect of the central computer system should not be included in discontinued operations.

6.1.5 Normally occurring discontinued operations

Certain entities (e.g. real estate investment trusts, retailers and restaurants) routinely dispose of asset groups that meet the definition of a component of an entity in IFRS 5.31. Such routine disposals of components will not generally represent a separate major line of business or geographical area of operations, as required by IFRS 5.32(a). Therefore, many routine disposals of components will not be classified as discontinued operations.

6.2 Presenting discontinued operations

6.2.1 Presentation in the statement of comprehensive income

IFRS 5.33(a) requires the presentation of a single amount in the statement of comprehensive income comprising the total of:

(i) the post-tax profit or loss of discontinued operations; and

(ii) the post-tax gain or loss recognised on the measurement to fair value less costs to sell or on the disposal of the assets or disposal group(s) constituting the discontinued operation.

In addition, this single amount must be analysed, either in the notes or in the statement of comprehensive income, into:

[IFRS 5.33(b)]

(i) the revenue, expenses and pre-tax profit or loss of discontinued operations;

(ii) the related income tax expense as required by IAS 12.81(h);

(iii) the gain or loss recognised on the measurement to fair value less costs to sell or on the disposal of the assets or disposal group(s) constituting the discontinued operation; and

(iv) the related income tax expense as required by IAS 12.81(h).

Where this analysis is included in the statement of comprehensive income, it is shown separately from continuing operations, in a section identified as relating to discontinued operations. The analysis is not required for disposal groups that are newly-acquired subsidiaries that meet the criteria to be classified as held for sale on acquisition (see **section 5**).

With effect from the implementation of IAS 27(2008) (see **chapter 33**), entities are also required to disclose the amount of income from continuing operations and from discontinued operations attributable to owners of the parent. These disclosures (which are illustrated in the Implementation Guidance accompanying IFRS 5, reproduced at **example 6.2.1** below) may be presented either in the notes or in the statement of comprehensive income. [IFRS 5.33(d)]

Where an entity presents the components of profit or loss in a separate income statement as described in IAS 1(2007).81, that statement is also required to present a separate section identified as relating to discontinued operations. [IFRS 5.33A]

Where amounts relating to discontinued operations are separately presented, the comparative figures for prior periods are also re-presented, so that the disclosures relate to all operations that have been discontinued by the end of the reporting period for the latest period presented. [IFRS 5.34]

When IFRS 5 was issued, the IASB made no change to the requirement in IAS 1 *Presentation of Financial Statements* that revenue should be shown in the statement of comprehensive income. However, the option set out in IFRS 5.33 to present revenue from discontinued operations only in a note apparently conflicts with this requirement of IAS 1. It appears that the failure to amend IAS 1 was an oversight on the part of the IASB, since it would make little sense for IFRS 5 to include an option that can never be adopted. Accordingly, notwithstanding that this disclosure requirement has been carried forward to IAS 1(2007).82(a), it seems acceptable to present only revenue from continuing operations in the statement of comprehensive income, and to show revenue for discontinued operations in a note.

The Implementation Guidance accompanying the Standard includes the following illustration of presentation in the statement of comprehensive income.

Example 6.2.1

Presenting discontinued operations in the statement of comprehensive income

[Guidance on Implementing IFRS 5 (Example 11)]

XYZ GROUP – STATEMENT OF COMPREHENSIVE INCOME FOR THE YEAR ENDED 31 DECEMBER 20X2 (illustrating the classification of expenses by function)

(in thousands of currency units)	20X2	20X1
Continuing operations		
Revenue	X	X
Cost of sales	(X)	(X)
Gross profit	X	X
Other income	X	X
Distribution costs	(X)	(X)
Administrative expenses	(X)	(X)
Other expenses	(X)	(X)
Finance costs	(X)	(X)
Share of profit of associates	X	X
Profit before tax	X	X
Income tax expense	(X)	(X)
Profit for the period from continuing operations	X	X
Discontinued operations	–	–
Profit for the period from discontinued operations [a]	X	X
Profit for the period	X	X
Attributable to:		
Owners of the parent		
Profit for the period from continuing operations	X	X
Profit for the period from discontinued operations	X	X
Profit for the period attributable to owners of the parent	X	X
Non-controlling interests		
Profit for the period from continuing operations	X	X
Profit for the period from discontinued operations	X	X
Profit for the period attributable to non-controlling interests	X	X
	X	X

(a) The required analysis would be given in the notes.

6.2.1.1 *Disclosure of components of income and expense*

When IFRS 5 was issued, the Board appears not to have considered the disclosure requirements of other Standards relating to the statement of comprehensive income and the extent to which they should apply to the components of income and expense included in discontinued operations. Items affected include:

- disclosure of analysis of expenses under IAS 1;

- disclosure of finance costs and finance income under IAS 1 and IFRS 7; and

- disclosure of the components of income tax under IAS 12.

In recent months, the IASB has discussed this issue and has proposed amendments to IFRS 5 (see **8.1**). If implemented, these proposed changes would clarify that the disclosure requirements of other Standards do not generally apply to discontinued operations and, therefore, that the amounts disclosed under the requirements listed above need relate only to continuing operations.

6.2.1.2 *Allocated corporate overhead costs included in discontinued operations*

An entity may include in amounts reported for discontinued operations only those costs that are clearly identifiable as costs of the component that is being disposed of and that will not be recognised on an ongoing basis by the entity.

Example 6.2.1.2A

Allocated corporate overhead costs included in discontinued operations (1)

An entity has a general workers' compensation insurance policy for all of its operations, the cost of which is allocated to each operation based on the number of employees in the operation. The entity's insurance costs will be reduced by £1 million as a result of the disposal of an operation which meets the criteria for classification as discontinued. The allocation of £1 million insurance costs to the discontinued operation is appropriate.

Example 6.2.1.2B

Allocated corporate overhead costs included in discontinued operations (2)

An entity allocates the salary costs of its executive committee to all of its operations based on total revenues. No executive has direct responsibility for the operation being disposed of, which meets the criteria for classification as discontinued. However, two of the executives will transfer with the operation. The entity may not allocate the salaries of the transferred executives to discontinued operations because the costs are not clearly identifiable as costs of the component.

6.2.1.3 *Earnings per share presentation of discontinued operations*

Earnings per share amounts should be shown separately when an entity reports discontinued operations. IAS 33.68 requires an entity that reports discontinued operations to present basic and diluted per-share amounts for discontinued operations either in the statement of comprehensive income or in the notes to the financial statements. This disclosure is required in addition to the presentation of basic and diluted per-share amounts for profit or loss from continuing operations and profit or loss for the year, both of which should be shown in the statement of comprehensive income with equal prominence.

6.2.1.4 *Classification of non-controlling interest in discontinued operations*

Example 6.2.1.4

Classification of non-controlling interest in discontinued operations

Company T owns 85 per cent of Company V. Company T consolidates Company V and accounts for the remaining 15 per cent ownership in Company V as a non-controlling interest. On 31 August 20X2, Company T committed to a plan to sell its 85 per cent interest in Company V. All the criteria of IFRS 5.7, IFRS 5.31 and IFRS 5.32 were met as of 31 August, and Company T classified Company V as a discontinued operation as of that date. How should Company T present the 15 per cent non-controlling interest in Company V in Company T's 30 September 20X2 financial statements?

IAS 1 (and the accompanying Implementation Guidance) make clear that in the statement of comprehensive income, the amount reported as non-controlling interests is an allocation of profit or loss for the period. Therefore, the amount reported in respect of non-controlling interests is unaffected by whether an operation is continuing or discontinued.

Note that, with effect from the date of implementation of IAS 27(2008), IFRS 5.33(d) requires entities to disclose the amount of income from continuing operations and from discontinued operations attributable to owners of the parent – thereby effectively requiring an analysis of non-controlling interests between continuing and discontinued operations. These disclosures (which are illustrated in **example 6.2.1** above) may be presented either in the notes or in the statement of comprehensive income.

6.2.1.5 Intragroup sales

Example 6.2.1.5A

Intragroup sales to a discontinued operation with external sales

Company N is a paper manufacturer with factories around the country. Company N also owns a distribution business, Company X, which buys paper from Company N and then sells the paper to external customers. Company N is planning to discontinue the operations of Company X and sell Company X to another paper manufacturer. In its consolidated financial statements, Company N has appropriately eliminated the intragroup sales between itself and Company X and, therefore, only recognises the sales from Company X to the external customers. Company X will be classified as a discontinued operation in the second quarter financial statements.

Following its disposal, Company X will continue to purchase paper from Company N to sell to external customers. Therefore, Company N will continue to have sales to Company X that will not be eliminated once it is no longer a consolidated subsidiary. How should sales, cost of sales, and profit be reported in Company N's consolidated financial statements following classification of Company X as a discontinued operation?

The sales from Company N to Company X should continue to be eliminated in the consolidation. Any profit made from sales to external parties by the discontinued operation (Company X) would be presented outside continuing operations. Therefore, the profit on the corresponding sales made by Company N should be shown in the continuing operations of Company N.

For example: Company N sells paper to Company X for £6 with a cost of £4. Company N's profit is £2. Company X sells paper to external customers for £7 with a cost (Company X's purchase price from Company N) of £6. Company X's profit is £1. In the consolidated financial statements of Company N, the intragroup sales of £6 will be eliminated along with the £6 cost of sales, leaving a profit of £3. The £3 margin will come through as £2 in continuing operations (representing the sales from Company N to Company X) and £1 in discontinued operations (representing the sales from Company X to the external customers).

Therefore, Company N's consolidated financial statements would present sales from continuing operations of £6, cost of sales from continuing operations of £4, a profit of £2 from continuing operations, and a profit of £1 in discontinued operations since the sale was to an external entity. In the following year (assuming the same facts), when Company N sells paper to Company X, it will have sales of £6, £4 cost of sales and £2 profit in its continuing operations (and will not have the additional £1 profit from sales to external customers).

In accordance with IFRS 5.33(b), the single amount for discontinued operations (£1 in the above example) should be analysed between its components either in the statement of comprehensive income or in the notes: revenue of £1, cost of sale of nil, and profit of £1.

Example 6.2.1.5B

Intragroup sales to a discontinued operation without external sales

Company N is a paper manufacturer with factories around the country. Company N owns a distribution business, Company X, which buys paper from Company N and then sells the paper to external customers. Company N is planning to discontinue the operations of Company X and sell Company X to another paper manufacturer. In its consolidated financial statements, Company N has appropriately eliminated the intragroup sales between itself and Company X and, therefore, only recognises the sales from Company X to the external customers. Company X will be classified as a discontinued operation in the second quarter financial statements.

Following its disposal, Company X will continue to purchase paper from Company N to sell to external customers. Therefore, Company N will continue to have sales to Company X that will not be eliminated once it is no longer a consolidated subsidiary. Should the intragroup sales between Company N and Company X that have not been passed on to external customers remain in continuing operations?

No. While IFRS 5 requires the separate presentation of discontinued operations, the requirement to eliminate intragroup sales is not changed from that in IAS 27 *Consolidated and Separate Financial Statements*. Therefore, the sales should be fully eliminated and not reported by N until an external sale occurs.

6.2.2 *Disclosures in the statement of cash flows*

The net cash flows attributable to the operating, investing and financing activities of discontinued operations must be shown, either in the notes or in the statement of cash flows. These disclosures are not required for disposal groups that are newly-acquired subsidiaries that meet the criteria to be classified as held for sale on acquisition (see **section 5**). [IFRS 5.33]

Once again, the comparative figures for prior periods are also re-presented, so that the disclosures relate to all operations that have been discontinued by the end of the reporting period for the latest period presented. [IFRS 5.34]

Example 6.2.2

Presentation of taxes on sale of discontinued operations in statement of cash flows

Company P sold its international business to Company J for £12 billion. As a result of the sale, Company P paid taxes related to the gain on the sale of approximately £3 billion. Company P has appropriately determined to report the sale of the international business as a discontinued operation in its statement of comprehensive income. In its statement of cash flows, P has proposed including the taxes on the gain as a component of cash flows from investing activities, below the net proceeds from the sale of the international business.

Is it appropriate to present taxes associated with the proceeds from the sale of a component of an entity as part of investing activities in the statement of cash flows?

Yes. IAS 7.35 states that taxes shall be classified as operating activities '... unless they can be specifically identified with financing and investing activities'. The disposal of non-current assets would be considered investing activities and, therefore, allocation of the tax effect of the sale to investing activities would be appropriate.

6.2.3 Adjustments to prior period disposals

It may be necessary occasionally to estimate a gain or loss on disposal of a discontinued operation, so that further adjustments arise in a subsequent period. Where adjustments are made to amounts previously presented in discontinued operations that are directly related to the disposal of a discontinued operation in a prior period, they are classified separately in discontinued operations, and the nature and amount of such adjustments are disclosed. [IFRS 5.35]

IFRS 5.35 gives the following examples of circumstances that may trigger such adjustments:

(a) the resolution of uncertainties arising from the terms of the disposal transaction, such as the resolution of purchase price adjustments and indemnification issues with the purchaser;

(b) the resolution of uncertainties arising from and directly related to the operations of the component before its disposal, such as environmental and product warranty obligations retained by the seller; and

(c) the settlement of employee benefit plan obligations if the settlement is directly related to the disposal transaction.

6.2.3.1 Reporting retained equity interest sold in a subsequent period

Example 6.2.3.1

Reporting retained equity interest sold in a subsequent period

Company D is proposing to sell a subsidiary, Company T, which qualifies as a discontinued operation under IFRS 5. Because this transaction arose from an unexpected offer from Company X, a third party, Company D does not have immediate plans for use of the proceeds from this sale. Accordingly, Company D would like to retain an equity interest (common stock) of up to 10 per cent in Company T for the next four to five years. Company D's retained equity interest in Company T would not be sufficient to enable Company D to exercise significant influence over Company T.

Additionally, Company D will have a put option on the retained equity interest in Company T to sell this interest over a four to five year period to Company X. Company X also will receive a call option to purchase the equity interest retained by D at the end of the four to five-year period. How should Company D report gains on the sale of the retained interest in Company T in subsequent periods?

Changes in the carrying amount of assets received as consideration on the disposal, or of residual interests in the business, should be classified within continuing operations. IFRS 5.35 requires adjustments to amounts previously reported in discontinued operations that are directly related to the disposal of a component of an entity in a prior period to be classified separately in the current period in discontinued operations. Developments subsequent to the disposal date that are not directly related to the disposal of the component or the operations of the component prior to disposal will not meet the criteria in IFRS 5.35. Subsequent changes in the carrying amount of assets received upon disposal of a component do not affect the determination of gain or loss at the disposal date, but represent the consequences of management's subsequent decisions to hold or sell those assets. Gains and losses, dividend and interest income, and portfolio management expenses associated with assets received as consideration for discontinued operations should be reported within continuing operations.

The gains resulting from Company D exercising its put option to sell a portion of its retained interest in Company T, or gains resulting from Company X exercising its call option to purchase the remaining interest in Company T, should be reported within continuing operations since they are not related directly to Company D's initial sale of Company T to Company X, and are the result of management's decision to hold and then sell an investment. Furthermore, any increases or decreases that may need to be reflected under IAS 39 *Financial Instruments: Recognition and Measurement* would be reported as part of continuing operations.

6.2.3.2 *Interest income on note receivable from discontinued operations*

Example 6.2.3.2

Interest income on note receivable from discontinued operations

In October 20X2, Company P properly accounted for a component of its entity as a discontinued operation in accordance with IFRS 5. As part of the discontinuation, Company P retained a note receivable from the component. Subsequent to October 20X2, Company P received interest income from the note receivable. Interest income recognised totalled £43,000 in 20X2, and £250,000 in 20X3.

During the fourth quarter of 20X3, the disposed component defaulted on the note receivable and stopped paying interest. Based upon the current default as well as other factors, Company P believes that the note receivable has been impaired and that the amount will be written off during the fourth quarter of 20X3.

Company P believes the 20X2 financial statements did not contain an error since there was no oversight or misuse of available facts that would have indicated the existence of the impairment loss.

What is the proper accounting for the interest income on the note receivable subsequent to the discontinuation?

Income from a financial asset received as part of the proceeds of disposal of discontinued operations should be reported as part of continuing operations. The carrying amount of assets received as consideration in the disposal or of residual interests in the business should be classified within continuing operations. Subsequent changes in the carrying amount of assets received upon disposal of a component do not affect the determination of the gain or loss at the disposal date, but represent the consequences of management's subsequent decisions to hold those assets.

Thus, the interest income associated with assets received as consideration for discontinued operations or with residual interests in the business should be reported within continuing operations. Company P should also recognise any impairment loss on the note receivable within continuing operations in the current year.

6.2.3.3 *Ongoing pension obligations*

Example 6.2.3.3

Ongoing pension obligations

Company B, a publicly-held entity, previously closed two of its four chemical plants and retained the obligation for the defined benefit pension plans at the facilities. In the current year, Company B has spun-off its remaining chemical division through a share distribution to its current shareholders. Prior to approving the spin-off, the Pension Governmental Agency (PGA) required Company B to retain the pension obligations for the two chemical plants that were previously closed. This agreement was required because the PGA believed Company B was an entity more financially viable than the spun-off division and, accordingly, was more likely to remain in existence in order to settle the pension obligations as they continue to come due.

At the end of Company B's current reporting period, the pension obligations for the closed plants are underfunded by approximately £22 million. Since the participants are no longer earning additional pension benefits under the plans, the only components of net periodic pension cost each year are interest cost, return on plan assets and amortisation of gains and losses. Historically, Company B has recognised the net periodic pension cost for the plans at the closed plants within continuing operations each year.

Management contends that since the entire division was spun-off in the current year, all future interest costs associated with these plans should be accrued as part of discontinued operations in the current year. Accordingly, management has proposed calculating the total future interest cost on the plans (over their remaining payout period) and accruing this amount as part of discontinued operations in the current year.

Would it be acceptable for Company B to recognise as an immediate cost to discontinued operations an accrual for the future interest cost on the pension obligations that were retained?

No. Company B made a decision not to settle the pension obligations at the time the plants were closed and a second decision not to fund fully the obligations. As a result of these decisions, Company B continues to incur interest cost on the unfunded pension obligations. Therefore, the interest cost is a component of net periodic pension cost and should be recognised as a period cost. Net periodic pension cost is comprised of a number of different components that should be included in the determination of profit from continuing operations.

6.2.4 *Changes to a plan of sale*

As discussed in **4.6** above, sometimes an entity's plans will change so that a component ceases to qualify as held for sale. When this occurs, the results of that operation should be reclassified from discontinued operations to continuing operations, both for the current and prior periods. The amounts for prior periods should be described as having been re-presented. [IFRS 5.36]

7 Other presentation and disclosure requirements

7.1 Gains or losses relating to continuing operations

Gains or losses on the remeasurement of a non-current asset (or disposal group) classified as held for sale that does not meet the definition of a discontinued operation are included in profit or loss from continuing operations. [IFRS 5.37]

Where a non-current asset ceases to qualify as held for sale, IFRS 5.28 requires any resulting measurement adjustment (see **4.6.1**) to be presented 'in the same caption in the statement of comprehensive income used to present a gain or loss, if any, recognised in accordance with paragraph 37'. The intention appears to be that all gains and losses relating to any particular asset (or disposal group) should be presented within the same caption in the statement of comprehensive income – not that gains and losses on all items held for sale should be aggregated within a single caption. Thus, for example, gains and losses relating to properties held for sale might be presented in a different caption in the statement of comprehensive income from those relating to subsidiaries acquired exclusively with a view to resale.

7.2 Non-current assets and disposal groups classified as held for sale

7.2.1 Presentation of non-current assets and disposal groups held for sale

Non-current assets held for sale and the assets of a disposal group held for sale are presented separately from other assets in the statement of financial position. Similarly, the liabilities of a disposal group held for sale are presented separately from other liabilities in the statement of financial position. Those assets and liabilities should not be offset and presented as a single amount. [IFRS 5.38]

There should be separate disclosure, either in the statement of financial position or in the notes, of the major classes of assets and liabilities classified as held for sale (except where the disposal group is a newly-acquired subsidiary that meets the criteria to be classified as held for sale on acquisition). Any cumulative income or expense recognised in other comprehensive income relating to a non-current asset (or disposal group) classified as held for sale (e.g. fair value changes on a financial asset classified as available for sale under IAS 39) should also be presented separately. [IFRS 5.38]

Although IFRS 5 states that non-current assets held for sale, and assets of disposal groups held for sale, should be presented separately in the statement of financial position, it does not specifically address the issue as to whether those assets should be presented as current or non-current. The illustrative example issued with IFRS 5 (reproduced at **example 7.2** below) presents them as current assets –

and this will generally be the case since the general condition for classification as held for sale is that disposal be anticipated within one year of the reporting period (see **3.1.3** above). However, as discussed at **3.1.5** above, there are exceptions to this general principle, and the entity may be aware that the disposal will not occur until after one year. In such circumstances, if none of the other criteria for classification as a current asset (see **2.1.1** above) are met, it appears that the assets would be presented as non-current assets.

Where the disposal group is a newly-acquired subsidiary that meets the criteria to be classified as held for sale on acquisition (see **section 5**), disclosure of the major classes of assets and liabilities is not required. [IFRS 5.39]

Comparative figures for non-current assets or for the assets and liabilities of disposal groups held for sale in the statements of financial position for prior periods are not reclassified or re-presented to reflect the classification in the statement of financial position for the latest period presented. [IFRS 5.40]

The Implementation Guidance accompanying the Standard includes the following illustration of presentation in the statement of financial position.

Example 7.2

Presenting non-current assets or disposal groups classified as held for sale

[Guidance on Implementing IFRS 5 (Example 12)]

At the end of 20X5, an entity decides to dispose of part of its assets (and directly associated liabilities). The disposal, which meets the criteria in IFRS 5.7 & 8 to be classified as held for sale, takes the form of two disposal groups, as follows:

	Carrying amount after classification as held for sale	
	Disposal group I: CU	Disposal group II: CU
Property, plant and equipment	4,900	1,700
AFS financial asset	1,400[(a)]	-
Liabilities	(2,400)	(900)
Net carrying amount of disposal group	**3,900**	**800**
(a)An amount of CU400 relating to these assets has been recognised in other comprehensive income and accumulated in equity.		

The presentation in the entity's statement of financial position of the disposal groups classified as held for sale can be shown as follows:

	20X5	20X4
ASSETS		
Non-current assets		
AAA	X	X
BBB	X	X
CCC	X	X
	X	X
Current assets		
DDD	X	X
EEE	X	X
	X	X
Non-current assets classified as held for sale	8,000	–
	X	X
Total assets	X	X
	20X5	**20X4**
EQUITY AND LIABILITIES		
Equity attributable to equity holders of the parent		
FFF	X	X
GGG	X	X
Amounts recognised in other comprehensive income and accumulated in equity relating to non-current assets held for sale	400	–
	X	X
Non-controlling interest	X	X
Total equity	X	X
Non-current liabilities		
HHH	X	X
III	X	X
JJJ	X	X
	X	X

Current liabilities		
KKK	X	X
LLL	X	X
MMM	X	X
	X	X
Liabilities directly associated with non-current assets classified as held for sale	3,300	–
	X	X
Total liabilities	X	X
Total equity and liabilities	X	X

The presentation requirements for assets (or disposal groups) classified as held for sale at the end of the reporting period do not apply retrospectively. The comparative statements of financial position for any previous periods are therefore not re-presented.

7.2.2 *Disclosures required for non-current assets and disposal groups held for sale*

The question as to the level of disclosures required for non-current assets and disposal groups held for sale has been the subject of debate since the implementation of IFRS 5. The debate centres around whether the disclosure requirements of Standards other than IFRS 5, in the absence of specific exclusion, should apply to non-current assets (or disposal groups) classified as held for sale. The IASB is currently considering this matter as part of its 2008 Annual Improvements Process – see **8.1**. If implemented, these proposed changes would clarify that the disclosure requirements of other Standards do not generally apply to items classified as held for sale.

7.3 Additional disclosures

In any period in which a non-current asset (or disposal group) has been either classified as held for sale or sold, the following information should be provided in the notes to the financial statements:

[IFRS 5.41]

(a) a description of the non-current asset (or disposal group);

(b) a description of the facts and circumstances of the sale, or leading to the expected disposal, and the expected manner and timing of that disposal;

(c) the gain or loss recognised in accordance with IFRS 5.20 – 22 (see **section 4**) and, if not separately presented in the statement of comprehensive income, the caption in the statement of comprehensive income that includes that gain or loss; and

(d) if applicable, the reportable segment in which the non-current asset (or disposal group) is presented in accordance with IFRS 8 *Operating Segments*. (For entities that have not yet adopted IFRS 8, the requirement is to disclose, if applicable, the segment in which the non-current asset or disposal group is presented in accordance with IAS 14 *Segment Reporting*).

IFRS 5.42 requires certain disclosures where there has been a change to a plan of sale, such that either an asset (or disposal group) previously classified as held for sale no longer meets the criteria, or an individual asset or liability has been removed from a disposal group classified as held for sale. In the period of the decision to change the plan to sell the non-current asset (or disposal group), the financial statements should disclose:

- a description of the facts and circumstances leading to the decision; and
- the effect of the decision on the results of operations for the period and any prior periods presented.

8 Future developments

8.1 Annual Improvements

The IASB is currently considering the disclosure requirements for non-current assets and disposal groups held for sale as part of its Annual Improvements project. At its January 2008 meeting, the Board tentatively decided to add a paragraph in the scope section of IFRS 5 to clarify that:

- IFRS 5 specifies disclosures required in respect of non-current assets (or disposal groups) classified as held for sale or discontinued operations;
- disclosures in other IFRSs do not apply to such assets (or disposal groups) unless those other IFRSs specifically require a disclosure in respect of non-current assets (or disposal groups) classified as held for sale or discontinued operations; and
- additional disclosures about such assets (or disposal groups) may be necessary to comply with the general requirements of IAS 1 *Presentation of Financial Statements*.

The Exposure Draft for the Annual Improvements, planned for issue in the fourth quarter of 2008, is expected to include proposed changes to IFRS 5 to clarify these points.

8.2 IFRS/US convergence

In their joint project on financial statement presentation, the IASB and the FASB are working to develop a common definition of discontinued operations based on operating segments as defined in their standards on segment reporting and to require common disclosures related to components of an entity that have been disposed of. The amounts presented in the statement of comprehensive income and related note disclosures would continue to be based on applicable IFRSs rather than the amounts provided to the chief operating decision maker. An Exposure Draft to amend IFRS 5 on this basis is expected later in 2008.

30 Statement of cash flows

1 Introduction

IAS 7 *Statement of Cash Flows* requires the presentation of information about the historical changes in the cash and cash equivalents of an entity by means of a statement of cash flows, which classifies cash flows during the period according to operating, investing and financing activities.

In September 2007, the IASB amended the title of IAS 7 from *Cash Flow Statements* to *Statement of Cash Flows* to reflect the new title for the statement introduced by IAS 1(2007) *Presentation of Financial Statements*. Note, however, that entities are not required to use the new title for the statement. [IAS 1(2007).10]

IAS 7 was further amended with effect from the date of implementation of IAS 27(2008) – as regards the classification of cash flows arising on changes in interests in subsidiaries and other businesses where there is no loss of control (see **7.1.2**).

In May 2008, the Standard was further amended by *Improvements to IFRSs* (effective 1 January 2009) to clarify that, for entities that routinely sell items of property, plant and equipment that they have previously held for rental to others, the resulting cash flows are cash flows from operating activities (see **5.1.4**).

At the time of writing, Improvements to IFRSs *has not yet been endorsed for adoption by EU companies.*

UK

This chapter discusses the requirements of IAS 7 in the following sections:

Section 2 Scope

Section 3 Form of statement of cash flows

Section 4 Cash and cash equivalents

Section 5 Classification of cash flows

Section 6 Investments in subsidiaries, associates and joint ventures

UK

There are various differences between IAS 7 and its UK GAAP equivalent, FRS 1 Cash Flow Statements. *The most significant of these are highlighted below.*

- *Whereas FRS 1 exempts certain entities (including small companies and certain subsidiary undertakings) from preparing a cash flow statement, IAS 7 offers no such exemptions. All financial statements prepared in accordance with IFRSs are required to include a statement of cash flows. Moreover, where entity financial statements are presented together with consolidated financial statements, a statement of cash flows is required for each.*
- *FRS 1 lists nine headings under which cash flows are to be classified, and the order in which they are to be set out. IAS 7 specifies only three headings (operating, investing and financing) and does not mandate the order in which they are presented.*
- *FRS 1 focuses on movements in cash, whereas IAS 7 is concerned with movements in cash and cash equivalents, being certain highly liquid short-term investments. This approach is similar to the version of FRS 1 which was effective from 1992 to 1996. Under the current version of FRS 1, cash equivalents would be classified within management of liquid resources.*

2 Scope

IAS 7 requires all reporting entities to present a statement of cash flows prepared in accordance with that Standard. The statement of cash flows should be presented as an integral part of the financial statements. [IAS 7.1]

UK

In terms of the practical impact on UK groups, this is perhaps the most significant difference from FRS 1, in that there are no exemptions for small companies or subsidiary undertakings under IAS 7. In particular, UK subsidiaries choosing to adopt IFRSs must ensure that their financial statements include a statement of cash flows.

3 Form of statement of cash flows

The basic requirement of IAS 7 is that an entity should prepare and present a statement of cash flows that reports the cash flows of the entity during the period classified into operating, investing and financing activities. [IAS 7.10]

Under the general requirements of IAS 1 *Presentation of Financial Statements*, comparative information in respect of the previous period should be presented for all amounts reported in the current period's statement of cash flows and the supporting notes. [IAS 1(2007).38, previously IAS 1(2003).36]

Where an entity prepares only individual financial statements, the statement of cash flows will be for the individual entity. Where consolidated financial statements are prepared, a consolidated statement of cash flows will be prepared. Where an entity produces both separate (as defined in IAS 27) and consolidated financial statements, a statement of cash flows will be required for each.

> *This is a significant difference between IAS 7 and FRS 1, since the latter does not require a cash flow statement for the parent in addition to a consolidated cash flow statement.* UK

3.1 Reporting cash flows on a net basis

Cash inflows should generally be reported separately from outflows. However, the Standard does permit the following cash flows to be reported on a net basis:

[IAS 7.22]

- receipts and payments on behalf of customers when the cash flows reflect the activities of the customer rather than those of the entity (such as the collection of rent on behalf of the owner of a property, funds held for customers by an investment entity, or the acceptance and repayment of demand deposits by a bank); and
- receipts and payments for items in which the turnover is quick, the amounts are large and the maturities are short (such as advances and repayments of principal amounts relating to credit card customers, purchases and sales of investments, and commercial paper or other short-term borrowings with a maturity period of three months or less).

For financial institutions, the following additional cash flows may be reported on a net basis:

[IAS 7.24]

- cash receipts and payments for the acceptance and repayment of deposits with a fixed maturity date;
- the placement of deposits with and withdrawal of deposits from other financial institutions; and
- cash advances and loans made to customers and the repayment of those advances and loans.

3.2 Exclusion of non-cash transactions

As a general principle, only transactions that require the use of cash or cash equivalents should be included in a statement of cash flows. Note, however, that where the indirect method of presenting cash flows from operating activities is used (as discussed at **5.1.2** below), this will result in certain non-cash items appearing in the statement of cash flows as adjustments to profit or loss for the period. Investing and financing activities that do not require the use of cash or cash equivalents are, however, always excluded from a statement of cash flows. [IAS 7.43]

Examples of investing and financing transactions that do not result in cash flows, and consequently are excluded from the statement of cash flows, include:

- the acquisition of an asset by way of a finance lease (but the payments of lease rentals are cash flows);
- the acquisition or disposal of assets (other than cash) in return for equity securities;
- exchanges of non-monetary assets such as property, plant and equipment, and inventories;
- the issue of bonus shares to holders of the entity's equity;
- the receipt of bonus shares from another entity in which the reporting entity holds an investment; and
- the conversion of debt securities into equity securities.

The inception of a finance lease contract is one of the most commonly encountered non-cash transactions. Such a transaction, although reflected in the statement of financial position by recognising an asset and a matching liability, should not be reflected in the statement of cash flows because the reporting entity neither pays nor receives cash. It is not appropriate to show a cash outflow in respect of an asset purchase and the drawdown of a loan. A sale and leaseback arrangement, however, *will* generate cash flows and therefore should be included in the statement of cash flows (see **5.3.1** below).

Where transactions of a non-cash nature occur, the Standard requires that they be disclosed elsewhere in the financial statements in a way that provides all of the relevant information about those investing and financing activities. [IAS 7.43]

3.3 Exclusion of movements between items that constitute cash or cash equivalents

Movements between items that constitute cash or cash equivalents are excluded from cash flows, because these components are part of the cash management of an entity rather than part of its operating, investing or financing activities. Cash management includes the investment of excess cash in cash equivalents. [IAS 7.9] For example, where an entity uses cash to purchase a short-term investment meeting the definition of a cash equivalent, the purchase is not shown in the statement of cash flows.

4 Cash and cash equivalents

Cash flows are defined as inflows and outflows of cash and cash equivalents. [IAS 7.6]

4.1 Cash

Cash comprises cash on hand and demand deposits. [IAS 7.6]

The term 'demand deposits' is not defined in IAS 7, but the term may be taken to refer to deposits where the reporting entity can withdraw cash without giving any notice and without suffering any penalty. A seven-day call deposit would therefore not qualify as cash, because notice of withdrawal is required. The deposit could, however, be reported as a cash equivalent.

4.2 Cash equivalents

Cash equivalents are defined as short-term, highly liquid investments that are readily convertible to known amounts of cash and which are subject to an insignificant risk of changes in value. [IAS 7.6]

4.2.1 *Held to meet short-term cash commitments*

The Standard explains that cash equivalents are held for the purpose of meeting short-term cash commitments rather than for investment or other purposes. [IAS 7.7] Therefore, in order to determine whether a particular investment qualifies for classification as a cash equivalent, it is necessary to look at the purpose for which it is held. Even though the investment may meet the definition set out in the previous paragraph, unless it is held for the purpose of meeting short-term cash commitments, it will not be classified as a cash equivalent.

4.2.2 *Presumption of maturity of three months or less*

The definition of cash equivalents includes the requirement that they be held for the 'short-term'. In order to qualify as such, the Standard states that the investment will *normally* have a maturity of three months or less from the date of acquisition. [IAS 7.7] Thus, the requirement for a three-month maturity is not part of the definition, but will nevertheless be a presumption except in very exceptional circumstances.

The Standard implicitly suggests that only in unusual cases will investments with more than three months to maturity nevertheless be free from significant risk of changes in value (arising, for example, from changes in interest rates). An entity purchasing a two-year bond in the market when the bond only has three months remaining before its redemption date could therefore classify the bond as a cash equivalent (assuming that there are no other factors causing it to be subject to a significant risk of change in value, and that the underlying purpose of holding the bond is to meet short-term cash commitments). However, the reference to three months or less 'from the date of acquisition' means that, if the entity instead purchased the same two-year bond when it had four months remaining before maturity, the entity could not classify the bond as a cash equivalent either at the date of purchase or once it has less than three months remaining to maturity (unless it could justify a departure from the three-month guideline, in which case the instrument would be classified as a cash equivalent throughout the entire four months).

The three-month limit may appear somewhat arbitrary, but the intention is to promote consistency between entities.

Example 4.2.2

Repurchase agreements as cash equivalents

An entity invests excess funds in short-term repurchase agreements with a term of two months. The underlying debt securities involved in the transaction have maturities in excess of three months. These repurchase agreements will be classified as cash equivalents provided that (a) there are no other factors that would subject the instruments to a significant risk of change in value, and (b) the underlying purpose for holding the repurchase agreements is to meet short-term cash commitments. The critical factor is the maturity of the repurchase agreements themselves, not the underlying debt securities.

4.2.3 *Foreign currency investments*

Provided that the definition of cash equivalent is met, there is no reason why an investment acquired in a foreign currency could not be classified as a cash equivalent. Indeed, the Standard refers specifically to cash and cash equivalents held or due in a foreign currency. [IAS 7.28]

4.2.4 *Equity investments*

Equity investments will not normally meet the definition of a cash equivalent since, even where they are readily convertible to cash, the amount of that cash is generally not known and the risk of changes in value is generally not insignificant, although there are exceptions. The example given in the Standard is that of preferred shares with a specific redemption date which, when acquired, are close to maturity. The majority of equity instruments will not meet the definition, however, and therefore cannot be classified as cash equivalents. [IAS 7.7]

4.2.5 *Gold bullion*

Gold (and similar traded commodities) will not qualify as cash equivalents for the same reason as equity investments (see above). In addition, IAS 39 confirms that gold bullion 'is a commodity. While highly liquid, there is no contractual right to receive cash or another financial asset inherent in bullion.' [IAS 39.IG.B.1]

4.2.6 *Bank borrowings*

The definition of cash equivalents makes no reference to the inclusion of bank borrowings. The Standard acknowledges, however, that bank overdrafts repayable on demand may form an integral part of an entity's cash management, in which case they should be included as a component of cash and cash equivalents. A characteristic of such banking arrangements is that the bank balance often fluctuates from being positive to being overdrawn. [IAS 7.8]

IAS 7 does not therefore mandate the inclusion of bank overdrafts in cash equivalents in all circumstances. But it does require their inclusion where the bank overdraft forms an integral part of the entity's cash management. IAS 7.8 also emphasises that bank borrowings are generally considered to be financing activities. Therefore, the Standard does not allow for other short-term loans (e.g. short-term bank loans, advances from factors or similar credit arrangements, credit import loans, trust receipt loans) to be classified as cash equivalents, because they are financing in nature.

4.3 Change in policy for components of cash equivalents

IAS 7.47 states that the effect of any change in the policy for determining components of cash and cash equivalents (e.g. a change in the classification of financial instruments previously considered to be part of an entity's investment portfolio) is reported in accordance with IAS 8 *Accounting Policies, Changes in Accounting Estimates and Errors*. IAS 8 requires that comparative amounts are restated and additional disclosures (e.g. the reasons for the change) are made.

These disclosures are not triggered, however, simply because an entity presents an instrument as a cash equivalent in a particular year that was not there the previous year. For example, in Year 2 an entity has, for the first time, classified an investment in a 90-day notice account as a cash equivalent. If the 90-day account is included in cash equivalents for the first time because the account was only opened during Year 2, then this does not represent a change in accounting policy. If the entity held equivalent balances in Year 1, but classified them as investing, and during Year 2 decided that they were more appropriately classified as cash equivalents, even though its reasons for holding them have not changed, then this is a change in accounting policy (provided that there has been no change of substance in the accounts and the level of funds kept in them) and the requirements of IAS 8 are triggered.

Because IAS 7 focuses on the reason for holding a particular balance, the same types of investments may be classified differently from year to year, without this constituting a change in accounting policy. For example, in Year 1, an entity may hold short-term bonds for the purpose of generating investment returns, and they are therefore not classified as cash equivalents. In Year 2, perhaps because of a change in the cash flow profile of the entity, the same type of investments may be held, but they may be held for the purpose of meeting short-term cash commitments, and therefore be classified as cash equivalents. In such circumstances, the bonds will be classified in a different manner in Years 1 and 2, but this will not constitute a change in accounting policy.

5 Classification of cash flows

Cash flows should be classified by operating, investing or financing activities. [IAS 7.10]

Unlike IFRS requirements for other financial statements (e.g. statement of financial position and statement of comprehensive income), the headings for the statement of cash flows are standard, and should not be altered to suit individual circumstances (unless, very exceptionally, the use of the standard wording is likely to mislead readers of the financial statements). There are no requirements, however, that would prevent further sub-classifications or analyses being shown within these three headings in the statement of cash flows.

Cash flows should be classified under the standard headings in the most appropriate manner for the entity's business. [IAS 7.11] Thus, for example, the purchase of an investment might be an investing activity for a manufacturing entity but might be part of the operating activities of a financial institution.

Where a single payment or receipt of cash represents a number of smaller payments or receipts, each should be classified according to its nature. [IAS 7.12] For example, where the settlement of a financial liability involves the repayment of principal and interest, the cash flows will be dealt with separately (see **5.4.3**). Similarly, finance lease payments will be segregated between their capital and interest components.

Example 5

Classification of finance lease payments

An entity makes a payment of £100,000 under a finance lease. In its financial statements, it allocates £20,000 to interest and £80,000 as a repayment of loan capital.

In its statement of cash flows, £80,000 will be classified as a financing cash flow and £20,000 will be classified according to the entity's general classification for interest (see **5.4.1** below).

5.1 Operating activities

Operating activities are defined as the principal revenue-producing activities of the entity and other activities that are not investing or financing activities. [IAS 7.6]

Therefore, 'operating' is the residual category for the purpose of presenting cash flows. If a cash flow does not fall within the scope of investing or financing activities (see **5.2** and **5.3**) then it will be classified as operating.

Examples of cash flows from operating activities are:

- cash received in the year from customers (in respect of sales of goods or services rendered either in the year, or in an earlier year, or received in advance in respect of the sale of goods or services to be rendered in a later year);
- cash payments in the year to suppliers (for raw materials or goods for resale whether supplied in the current year, or an earlier year, or to be supplied in a later year);
- the payment of wages and salaries to employees;
- tax and other payments on behalf of employees;
- the payment of rent on property used in the business operations;
- royalties received in the year;
- cash receipts and cash payments of an insurance entity for premiums and claims, annuities and other policy benefits;
- the payment of insurance premiums;
- cash payments or refunds of income taxes that cannot be specifically identified with financing or investing activities (see **5.5** below);

- cash flows arising from futures contracts, forward contracts, option contracts or swap contracts hedging a transaction that is itself classified as operating; and

- cash flows arising from the purchase and sale of securities and loans held for dealing or trading purposes.

Cash flows from operating activities should be reported using either the direct method or the indirect method. [IAS 7.18] The Standard encourages the use of the direct method.

5.1.1 Direct method

Under the direct method, each major class of gross cash receipts and gross cash payments is disclosed separately. [IAS 7.18(a)] **Example 5.1.1** illustrates the operating cash flows section of a statement of cash flows using the direct method.

Example 5.1.1

Direct method of presenting operating cash flows

	20X1	**20X1**
	£'000	**£'000**
Cash flows from operating activities		
Cash receipts from customers	252,376	
Cash paid to suppliers	(127,045)	
Cash paid to and on behalf of employees	(78,014)	
Other cash payments	(12,038)	
Cash generated from operations	35,279	
Interest paid	(5,933)	
Income taxes paid	(13,447)	
Net cash from operating activities		15,899

5.1.2 Indirect method

The indirect method starts with the profit or loss and adjusts it for:

[IAS 7.18(b)]

- any non-cash items included in its calculation (such as depreciation or movements in provisions);

- any cash flows in the year that were reported in the profit or loss of an earlier year or will be reported in profit or loss of a future year (e.g. operating accruals and prepayments, settlement of a liability for restructuring costs accrued in the prior year); and

- any items of income and expense that are related to investing or financing cash flows.

IAS 7 describes two ways of presenting operating cash flows using the indirect method. The first (and the most commonly used) starts with profit or loss and then adjusts it for:

[IAS 7.20]

- changes during the period in inventories and operating receivables and payables;
- non-cash items such as depreciation, provisions, deferred taxes, unrealised foreign currency gains and losses, undistributed profits of associates, and non-controlling interests; and
- all other items for which the cash effects are investing or financing cash flows.

The presentation for operating cash flows using the indirect method is illustrated in **example 5.1.2A**.

IAS 7 is not explicit as to whether these adjustments should be presented in the statement of cash flows or in a supporting note. The illustrative example in Appendix A to IAS 7 shows them in the statement of cash flows, and this is accordingly the preferred presentation. It is the most common presentation used by entities applying IAS 7, and is also the presentation used in the IFRS illustrative financial statements published by the IASB. However, presentation of the adjustments in the notes is generally acceptable.

UK *This is a change for UK companies adopting IFRSs. Under FRS 1, the reconciliation between operating profit and net cash flow from operating activities may not be shown as part of the primary cash flow statement.*

Example 5.1.2A

Indirect method of presenting operating cash flows (1)

	20X1 £'000	20X1 £'000
Cash flows from operating activities		
Profit before taxation	19,696	
Adjustments for:		
Depreciation	6,174	
Foreign exchange loss	829	
Interest expense*	7,305	
Profit before working capital changes	34,004	
Increase in trade and other receivables	(7,601)	
Increase in trade payables	5,224	
Decrease in inventories	3,652	
Cash generated from operations	35,279	
Interest paid*	(5,933)	
Income taxes paid	(13,447)	
Net cash from operating activities		15,899

* 'Interest expense' is included above as an 'adjustment' to profit before tax. If interest is considered an operating activity, the adjustment from profit to cash flow is the difference between the interest expense in the statement of comprehensive income and the interest actually paid during the period, i.e. £1,372,000. In order that the amount of interest paid can be disclosed separately as required by IAS 7.31, however, the above example adds back the interest expense in full and then deducts the full amount of interest paid.

The alternative indirect method of presentation shows the revenues and expenses that are disclosed in the statement of comprehensive income and adjusts these for the changes during the period in operating receivables and payables and in inventories. [IAS 7.20] This alternative is rarely used in practice. The alternative presentation is illustrated in **example 5.1.2B**.

Example 5.1.2B

Indirect method of presenting operating cash flows (2)

	20X1 £'000	20X1 £'000
Cash flows from operating activities		
Revenue	259,376	
Operating expenses excluding depreciation	(225,372)	
Profit before working capital changes	34,004	
Increase in trade and other receivables	(7,601)	
Increase in trade payables	5,224	
Decrease in inventories	3,652	
Cash generated from operations	35,279	
Interest paid	(5,933)	
Income taxes paid	(13,447)	
Net cash from operating activities		15,899

5.1.2.1 Indirect method: which profit or loss?

When using the indirect method of presentation for operating cash flows, IAS 7.18(b) requires that 'profit or loss' be adjusted for (1) the effects of transactions of a non-cash nature, (2) any deferrals or accruals of past or future operating cash receipts or payments, and (3) items of income or expense associated with investing or financing cash flows. But which 'profit or loss' is the appropriate starting point for the presentation of these adjustments?

The illustrative example in Appendix A to IAS 7 starts with 'profit before taxation', and, accordingly, this is the preferred presentation.

Entities that choose to present an operating result in the statement of comprehensive income (or in a separate income statement, where applicable) (see **5.2.5** in **chapter 3**) may, however, wish to use that operating result as the starting point for the presentation of adjustments. Unless the entity has a discontinued operation (see below), the items presented between operating result and profit/loss before taxation are generally non-operating cash flows (share of results of associates, interest paid etc.). Where this is the case, rather than using profit/loss before taxation as the starting point, and subsequently adjusting for all of the items between that amount and operating result, it appears generally acceptable to use the operating result as the starting point.

Where an entity has a discontinued operation, the results of which are presented under IFRS 5 *Non-current Assets Held for Sale and Discontinued Operations*, the 'profit before tax' presented in the statement of comprehensive income (or separate income statement) relates only to continuing operations. In these circumstances, there is more than one way in which the requirements of IAS 7.18(b) can be met.

The first approach, which is the preferred approach, is to start with the 'profit for the year' as presented in the statement of comprehensive income (or separate income statement) under IAS 1(2007).82(f) (previously IAS 1(2003).81(f)). This includes both continuing and discontinued operations. The amount can then be adjusted for the items required under IAS 7.18(b). The advantage of this approach is that it results in a very clear link between the amounts presented in the statement of comprehensive income (or separate income statement), and the amounts presented in the statement of cash flows. The disadvantage is that it can result in a long list of adjustments being presented in the statement of cash flows. This approach is illustrated in **example 5.1.2.1A**.

Another solution, for entities presenting an operating result, would be to start with the operating figure presented in the statement of comprehensive income (or separate income statement) (i.e. the operating profit from continuing operations) and to add to this the operating profit from discontinued operations, to arrive at an operating profit for the reporting entity as a whole. As discussed above, this would reduce the number of adjustments presented in the statement of cash flows, and may provide a clearer presentation for the user of the statement of cash flows. The disadvantage is that it is not so easily linked to the amounts presented in the statement of comprehensive income (or separate income statement). This approach is illustrated in **example 5.1.2.1B**.

Example 5.1.2.1A

Presentation of adjustments from profit to operating cash flows (1)

	Notes	Year ended 31 Dec 20X1 £'000	Year ended 31 Dec 20X0 £'000
Operating activities			
Profit for the year		100,366	19,626
Adjustments for:			
Share of profit of associates		(12,763)	(983)
Investment revenues		(3,501)	(717)
Other gains and losses		563	44
Finance costs	8	36,680	32,995
Income tax expense	9	17,983	4,199
Gain on disposal of discontinued operation	10	(8,493)	-
Depreciation of property, plant and equipment		29,517	19,042
Impairment loss on fixtures and equipment		4,130	247
......			

Example 5.1.2.1B

Presentation of adjustments from profit to operating cash flows (2)

	Notes	Year ended 31 Dec 20X1 £'000	Year ended 31 Dec 20X0 £'000
Operating activities			
Operating profit from continuing operations		126,342	49,774
Operating profit from discontinued operations		4,493	5,390
Total operating profit		130,835	55,164
Adjustments for:			
Depreciation of property, plant and equipment		29,517	19,042
Impairment loss on fixtures and equipment		4,130	247
......			

5.1.3 Sales taxes

IAS 7 does not explicitly address whether cash flows reported in accordance with IAS 7 should be measured as inclusive or exclusive of sales taxes.

The IFRIC was asked to consider this issue in 2005, specifically in connection with Value Added Tax (VAT) (see *IFRIC Update*, August 2005). Different practices were expected to emerge, the differences being most marked for entities that adopt the direct method of reporting operating cash flows (see **5.1.1**). The IFRIC did not add the project to its agenda, but recommended that the treatment of VAT should be considered by the IASB as part of the project on performance reporting (now titled *Financial Statement Presentation* – see **section 10**).

In advance of the publication of any explicit guidance, the issue should be considered in the context of IAS 7.50 which encourages disclosure of additional information when it may be relevant to users in understanding the financial information and liquidity of an entity. Hence, an entity should disclose whether gross cash flows are presented inclusive or exclusive of sales taxes. In addition, such disclosure would be considered necessary to comply with IAS 1. In particular, IAS 1(2007).112(c) (previously IAS 1(2003).103(c)) requires that the notes provide additional information that is not presented in the statement of financial position, statement of comprehensive income, statement of changes in equity or statement of cash flows, but is relevant to an understanding of any of them.

5.1.4 *Cash flows associated with assets held for rental to others*

For entities that are in the business of renting out assets to others, the cash inflows arising from renting out the assets and the associated operating costs are classified as operating cash flows. However, where such entities, in the course of their ordinary activities, routinely sell items of property, plant and equipment that they have previously held for rental to others, the appropriate classification for the cash flows arising on the acquisition and disposal of such assets has been the subject of varying interpretations. *Improvements to IFRSs* issued in May 2008 addressed and concluded on this question.

The IASB decided that the proceeds of sale of such assets should be recognised as revenue in accordance with IAS 18 *Revenue* (rather than a net gain or loss being presented as is generally the case for disposals of property plant and equipment). As a consequential amendment, the following text has been added to IAS 7.14:

> 'However, cash payments to manufacture or acquire assets held for rental to others and subsequently held for sale as described in paragraph 68A of IAS 16 *Property, Plant and Equipment* are cash flows

> from operating activities. The cash receipts from rents and subsequent sales of such assets are also cash flows from operating activities.'

This amendment is effective for annual periods beginning on or after 1 January 2009. Earlier application is permitted, provided that the related amendments to IAS 16 are applied at the same time (see **9.1** in **chapter 6**).

In the absence of specific transitional provisions, the amendments should be applied retrospectively. Therefore, when the amendments are first implemented, an entity that has previously classified the cash flows associated with the acquisition and disposal of such assets as investing activities should re-present cash flows for the comparative period.

UK *At the time of writing,* Improvements to IFRSs *has not yet been endorsed for adoption by EU companies.*

5.2 Investing activities

Investing activities are defined as the acquisition and disposal of long-term assets and other investments not included in cash equivalents. [IAS 7.6] Major classes of gross cash receipts and gross cash payments arising from investing activities should be reported separately, except to the extent that cash flows described in IAS 7.22 and IAS 7.24 are reported on a net basis (see **3.1** above). [IAS 7.21]

Examples of cash flows arising from investing activities include:

[IAS 7.16]

- payments to acquire property, plant and equipment (including self-constructed property, plant and equipment – but see **5.4.2** in respect of interest capitalised), intangible assets and other long-term assets;
- payments in respect of development costs that have been capitalised (but see **5.4.2** in respect of interest capitalised);
- cash received from the sale of property, plant and equipment, intangible assets and other long-term assets;
- payments to acquire equity or debt instruments of other entities or interests in joint ventures (although, in some circumstances, these may need to be classified either as cash equivalents or, if they are held for dealing purposes, as operating cash flows);

- cash receipts from the sale of equity or debt instruments of other entities or interests in joint ventures (although, again, these may instead need to be classified either as cash equivalents or, if the assets were held for dealing purposes, as operating cash flows);
- cash advances and loans made to other parties (other than loans made by a financial institution);
- cash received following the repayment of advances and loans made to other parties (other than loans made by a financial institution); and
- payments for and receipts from futures contracts, forward contracts, option contracts and swap contracts provided that the contracts:
  - are not held for dealing or trading purposes,
  - are not financing in nature; and
  - are not hedging a transaction that itself is classified as operating or financing.

As noted above, cash flows associated with the acquisition and disposal of property, plant and equipment, intangibles and other long-term assets will generally be classified as investing activities. However, IAS 7 was amended by *Improvements to IFRSs* issued in May 2008 so that, for entities that routinely sell items of property, plant and equipment that they have previously held for rental to others, the resulting cash flows are cash flows from operating activities (see **5.1.4**).

5.2.1 *Classification of expenditure as operating or investing*

Some types of expenditure can be recognised (based on the entity's accounting policy and/or the criteria established by the relevant Standards) either as an asset or as an expense. For example, expenditure during the development phase of an internal project will be recognised as an expense up to the point at which the criteria established in IAS 38.57 are met, but will be capitalised as part of the cost of an intangible asset thereafter (see **4.7.4** of **chapter 8**). This issue also arises in respect of exploration and evaluation activities. In practice, some entities classify expenditure of this nature that does not result in the recognition of an asset as cash flows from operating activities, while others classify such expenditure as part of investing activities. IAS 7 does not provide any guidance as to which classification is appropriate – although the definition of investing activities (as set out at **5.2**) would seem to suggest that a cash flow should only be classified as investing if it relates to the acquisition of a long-term asset or an investment that is not a cash equivalent.

The IFRIC received a request for guidance on the appropriate classification of cash flows in these circumstances. The IFRIC decided not to add the issue to its agenda and concluded (see *IFRIC Update*, March 2008) that the issue could be best resolved by referring it to the Board with a recommendation that IAS 7 should be amended to make explicit that only an expenditure that results in a recognised asset can be classified as a cash flow from investing activity.

The IFRIC noted that advertising and promotional activities, staff training and research and development could also raise the same issue.

5.3 Financing activities

Financing activities are defined as activities that result in changes in the size and composition of the contributed equity and borrowings of the entity. [IAS 7.6] Major classes of gross cash receipts and gross cash payments arising from financing activities should be reported separately, except to the extent that cash flows described in IAS 7.22 and IAS 7.24 are reported on a net basis (see **3.1** above). [IAS 7.21]

Examples of cash flows arising from financing activities are:

[IAS 7.17]

- cash receipts from issuing shares or other equity instruments;
- payments to owners to purchase or redeem shares in the entity;
- cash flows arising from futures contracts, forward contracts, option contracts or swap contracts hedging a transaction that is itself classified as financing;
- cash receipts from issuing debentures, loans, notes, bonds, mortgages and other borrowings, whether short or long-term;
- repayments of borrowings; and
- where the reporting entity is a lessee, that part of the payments under a finance lease that will be treated in the statement of financial position as a repayment of the loan from the lessor (i.e. the capital element).

5.3.1 *Sale and leaseback transactions*

Under certain sale and leaseback arrangements, the substance of the arrangements is that the asset is not 'sold', but that the lessor makes a loan to the lessee (i.e. a sale and finance leaseback) with the asset as security. From an accounting perspective, the entity has not disposed of the asset. In this case, the receipt from the 'sale' of the asset should be included as a financing cash flow rather than an investing cash flow, this treatment being consistent with that in the statement of comprehensive income and the statement of financial position. In contrast, where the substance of the transaction is that the asset is sold and then an operating lease is put in place, the receipt from the disposal of the asset will be included as an investing cash flow.

5.3.2 *Factoring*

IAS 7 does not provide any guidance on the treatment of factored debts in a statement of cash flows. Where debts are factored without recourse in circumstances qualifying for derecognition of the debts, no special problems arise. The receipt of the proceeds from the factor will simply be treated as an operating cash flow, just as if it had come from the debtor. Where debts are factored with recourse, however, and the advances from factors are treated as financing creditors in the balance sheet, the position is less clear.

IAS 7 requires cash flows to be analysed under the standard headings according to the substance of the transactions that give rise to them. Where factoring is viewed as being, in substance, a financing transaction, it might be argued that all of the cash flows received from the factor should be viewed as financing cash inflows. This would be consistent with the treatment of finance leases prescribed by IAS 7, where entering into the lease is viewed as a non-cash transaction and so does not appear in the statement of cash flows. The capital elements of the lease payments then appear as a financing outflow. This could be argued as leading to an overstatement of the financing outflows, and an understatement of the investing outflows. But the treatment for finance leases is specifically required by IAS 7 and is well established.

It could be argued that a similar principle should be applied to factored debts. The distortion would be more significant, however, and potentially the entity would have no operating cash inflows at all if all of its debts were factored. It appears questionable whether showing all of an entity's sales revenue as cash flows from financing could be said to give a true and fair view of its cash flows. Also, importantly, the treatment of factored debts is not addressed in IAS 7, whereas the treatment of leases is addressed.

If it is concluded that the receipts from the factor should be viewed as operating cash flows rather than financing cash flows (because they are, in substance, the receipts from trade debtors), there is a second question to be addressed. This is whether all of the cash flows should be shown as operating or whether the movement on the financing creditor should be treated as a financing cash flow. The preferable treatment is to show this movement as a financing cash flow because this results in operating cash flows including the cash flows from the debtors as if the factoring had not been entered into. It also results in financing cash flows as if the debtors had been financed by a loan. Finally, it also reflects the definition of financing activities as those 'that result in changes in the size and composition of . . . borrowings'.

Due to lack of clarity in IAS 7 as to the appropriate treatment of such transactions, it is important that the policy adopted is clearly stated and explained.

5.4 Interest and dividends

IAS 7.31 states that cash flows from interest and dividends paid and received:

- should each be disclosed separately; and
- should be classified in a consistent manner from period to period as either operating, investing or financing activities.

5.4.1 *Classification of interest and dividends paid and received*

The Standard permits each entity to choose how it wishes to classify its interest and dividends, provided that the classification is consistently applied from period to period.

The Standard suggests that dividends paid should be reported in either financing or operating activities. The argument for the classification of dividends paid as financing outflows is that the dividends represent a cost of obtaining financial resources. The argument in favour of classification within operating activities is that such classification will assist users to determine the ability of an entity to pay dividends out of operating cash flows. [IAS 7.34]

Interest paid, and interest and dividends received, should generally be classified as operating cash flows by a financial institution. For other entities, the Standard suggests that these items might similarly be classified as operating activities because they are included in arriving at profit or loss for the period. Interest paid could be classified as a financing cash flow, however, and interest and dividends received could be classified as investing cash flows, because the first is a cost of obtaining financial resources, and the last two are returns on investments. [IAS 7.33]

5.4.2 *Presentation of interest capitalised*

The total amount of interest paid during a period is disclosed in the statement of cash flows whether it has been recognised as an expense in profit or loss or capitalised in accordance with IAS 23 *Borrowing Costs*(see **chapter 27**). [IAS 7.32]

5.4.3 *Debt securities issued at a discount or premium*

For more complex financial instruments, it is important not to confuse principal amounts of finance with the nominal amounts of the instruments concerned. The principal amount of a financing arrangement is the amount borrowed at the beginning of the arrangement. It is not necessarily the same as any amount shown as the nominal amount of the financial instrument. This distinction is necessary to ensure that cash flows relating to finance costs are appropriately classified.

If an entity issues debt securities at a discount or a premium (e.g. zero coupon debt securities), the proceeds received from issuing the debt securities should be classified as a financing cash inflow. The excess of the amounts repaid (during the life of the instrument and at maturity) over the amount received when the debt securities were issued should be reported as a cash outflow, classified in the same way as interest paid.

Example 5.4.3

Zero coupon bond issued at a discount

An entity receives £100,000 on 1 January 20X1, when it issues a zero coupon bond. On 31 December 20X5, it redeems the bond by paying cash of £140,255 to the bondholder. In its statement of comprehensive incomes for the five years ended 31 December 20X5, the entity classifies the £40,255 as interest expense.

In its statement of cash flows for the year ended 31 December 20X5, £100,000 is classified as a financing cash flow and £40,255 is classified according to the entity's general classification for interest (see **5.4.1**).

5.4.4 *Investments acquired at a discount or a premium*

If an entity invests in debt securities at a discount or a premium (e.g. zero coupon bonds), the cash paid at acquisition is classified as an investing cash flow. The excess of the amounts received (during the life of the instrument and on maturity) over the amount of the original investment should be reported as a cash inflow, classified in the same way as interest received.

5.5 Taxes

Unless they can be specifically identified with financing or investing activities, cash flows arising from taxes on income should be classified as operating cash flows. Cash flows arising from taxes are required to be separately disclosed. [IAS 7.35]

Clearly, transactions of all types may have tax consequences. Identifying whether each amount of income or expense included in the tax computation derives from operating, investing or financing activities is a relatively simple task. Identifying the *cash flows*, however, is not always so easy. IAS 7 points out that, because it is often impracticable to identify tax cash flows in respect of investing and financing activities, and because such cash flows often arise in a different period from the cash flows of the underlying transaction, taxes paid should generally be classified as cash flows from operating activities. [IAS 7.36]

When it is practicable to identify a tax cash flow with an individual transaction that is classified as investing or financing, the tax cash flow will be classified as investing or financing in accordance with the underlying transaction. In these circumstances, the total amount of taxes paid is also disclosed.

6 Investments in subsidiaries, associates and joint ventures

Where an entity prepares a consolidated statement of cash flows, that statement of cash flows includes the cash flows of consolidated subsidiaries, but excludes any that are intragroup.

Where a consolidated subsidiary is only partly owned by the group, the dividends paid to the non-controlling interests (but not the dividends paid to group entities) are classified as either financing or operating cash outflows, consistently with the classification of dividends paid by the parent (see **5.4.1**).

Where an interest in an associate or joint venture is accounted for using the equity or the cost method, the investor's statement of cash flows reports only the cash flows between itself and the investee, such as dividends and advances. [IAS 7.37 & 38]

Where an entity has an interest in a joint venture that is accounted for using proportionate consolidation, the consolidated statement of cash flows includes the investor's proportionate share of the cash flows of the joint venture. [IAS 7.38]

7 Changes in ownership interests in subsidiaries and other businesses

7.1 Separate presentation of cash flows relating to changes in ownership interests

7.1.1 Changes in ownership interests involving a change in control

Where an entity has obtained or lost control of subsidiaries or other businesses during the reporting period, the aggregate cash flows arising should be presented separately and classified as investing activities. [IAS 7.39] The single-line entry in the statement of cash flows comprises the amount of cash paid or received as consideration for obtaining or losing control, net of the cash and cash equivalents in the subsidiaries or businesses at the date of the transaction, event or change in circumstance. [IAS 7.42] The cash flow effects of losing control are not to be deducted from those of obtaining control. Rather, each is to be shown separately. [IAS 7.41]

The requirements of IAS 7.39 – 42 apply to all transactions, events or other circumstances that result in a parent obtaining or losing control of a subsidiary. This can occur without the parent receiving or paying out cash (e.g. in the circumstances of a rights issues by the subsidiary – see **7.2**) and also where there is a change in circumstance but no change in absolute or relative ownership interests. The focus of the requirements is on whether or not control has been obtained or lost; if so, associated cash flows will always be classified as investing.

Where the parent obtains or loses control without receiving or paying out cash, investing cash flows will still be presented if there were cash balances in the subsidiary at the time of acquisition or disposal, as illustrated in **example 7.2**. This is because the entry in the statement of cash flows for consideration is reported net of cash and cash equivalents in the subsidiary.

Example 7.1.1

Cash flows arising on sale of a subsidiary

On 30 June 20X1, an entity sells its 100 per cent holding in a subsidiary for £900,000. At that date, the net assets of the subsidiary included in the consolidated statement of financial position were:

	£'000
Property, plant and equipment	500
Inventories	150
Accounts receivable	230
Cash	80
Cash equivalents	100
Trade payables	(110)
Long-term debt	(300)
	650

The consideration was received during the year ended 31 December 20X1 and comprised cash of £300,000 and equity shares of £600,000.

In the investing activities section of the statement of cash flows for the year ended 31 December 20X1, the entry in respect of the sale of the subsidiary will be an inflow of £120,000 (being £300,000 cash received less cash and cash equivalents of £180,000 in the subsidiary at the date of sale). The cash and cash equivalents of £180,000 in the subsidiary at the date of sale are deducted from the cash received because the cash and cash equivalents of the group are reduced by this amount as a result of the sale of the subsidiary.

Had the cash consideration of £300,000 been received over two years with £150,000 being received in 20X1 and £150,000 being received in 20X2, the investing section of the statement of cash flows would present an outflow in

> 20X1 of £30,000 (being £150,000 less the cash and cash equivalents of £180,000) and an inflow in 20X2 of £150,000.
>
> The group's property, plant and equipment is reduced by £500,000 as a result of the sale. However, this is not presented in the statement of cash flows as a sale of property, plant and equipment for cash.
>
> Where the indirect method is used to present the operating activities section of the statement of cash flows, the increase or decrease in inventories and accounts receivable and payable will need to be adjusted for the sale of the subsidiary. Taking inventories as an example, on 31 December 20X1 the inventories in the consolidated statement of financial position totalled £950,000 and at 31 December 20X0 totalled £1,000,000. In the adjustments from profit before taxation to the operating cash flow, the movement in inventories will be an increase of £100,000 (being the decrease in the year of £50,000 offset by the subsidiary's inventories in the consolidated statement of financial position at the date of sale of £150,000).

Each of the following should be disclosed, in aggregate, in respect of obtaining control of subsidiaries or other businesses during the period:

[IAS 7.40]

- the total consideration paid;
- the portion of the consideration consisting of cash and cash equivalents;
- the amount of cash and cash equivalents in the subsidiaries or other businesses over which control is obtained; and
- the amount of the assets and liabilities other than cash or cash equivalents in the subsidiaries or other businesses over which control is obtained, summarised by each major category.

Similarly, each of the following should be disclosed, in aggregate, in respect of losing control of subsidiaries or other businesses during the period:

[IAS 7.40]

- the total consideration received;
- the portion of the consideration consisting of cash and cash equivalents;
- the amount of cash and cash equivalents in the subsidiaries or other businesses over which control is lost; and

- the amount of the assets and liabilities other than cash or cash equivalents in the subsidiaries or other businesses over which control is lost, summarised by each major category.

7.1.2 *Changes in ownership interests in a subsidiary not resulting in a loss of control*

Upon adoption of IAS 27(2008), IAS 7 is amended to require that, where there has been a change in ownership interests in a subsidiary, but the transaction, event or circumstance has not resulted in a loss of control, the associated cash flows are classified as financing activities (in contrast to cash flows associated with a loss of control, as discussed at **7.1.1**, which are classified as investing activities). [IAS 7.42A]

Such changes will arise from transactions such as the purchase or sale by a parent of a subsidiary's equity instruments. From the date of implementation of IAS 27(2008) (see **chapter 33**), such transactions are accounted for as equity transactions – i.e. as transactions with owners in their capacity as owners. The requirements of IAS 7.42A (which was inserted in IAS 7 as a consequence of IAS 27(2008)) ensures that the cash flows are classified in the same way as other transactions with owners described in IAS 7.17 (see **5.3**).

Prior to the amendments discussed in the previous paragraphs, IAS 7 did not deal specifically with changes in ownership interests in subsidiaries other than those involving a change in control. Often, however, cash flows relating to purchases or sales of shares in subsidiaries will have been classified as investing activities, consistent with the treatment of other transactions in shares. For many entities, the requirements of IAS 7.42A will therefore result in a re-presentation of such cash flows.

These amendments should be made from the date that the entity applies IAS 27(2008), and prior period amounts should be restated accordingly. [IAS 7.54]

7.2 Cash flows arising from shares issued by a subsidiary

IAS 7.17(a) states that cash proceeds from issuing shares should be classified as financing activities. IAS 7.39 states that cash flows arising as a result of a transaction, event or change in circumstance where control of a subsidiary is lost should be classified as investing activities. The question arises as to how the cash flows from a rights issue by a partly-owned subsidiary should be reflected in the statement of cash flows.

Take, for example, a rights issue where the shares of the subsidiary are issued on a pro-rata basis to its parent and minority shareholders. In the subsidiary's own statement of cash flows, the entire proceeds from the rights issue should be shown under financing activities because they clearly represent a cash inflow from issuing shares. In the consolidated statement of cash flows, where shares are issued to the parent and minority shareholders on a pro-rata basis such that the percentage interest held by the group is not changed, the cash received from issuing shares to the parent will be eliminated on consolidation, leaving the receipt from the minority shareholders as a cash inflow to the group. Since there is no change in the group's interest in the subsidiary, this cash flow is also financing in nature, and should be classified as such in the consolidated statement of cash flows.

Where shares are issued only to minority shareholders, the treatment in the subsidiary's own statement of cash flows is the same as that described above. From the group perspective, although the minority shareholders have injected new funds into the subsidiary, the issue of shares outside the group gives rise to a reduction in the group's interest in the subsidiary The presentation in the consolidated statement of cash flows will depend on whether control has been lost as a result of that reduction. Following the principles outlined in **7.1** above, where the transaction has resulted in a loss of control, the cash flows will be classified as investing activities in accordance with IAS 7.39. Where control remains with the parent, following the adoption of IAS 27(2008) the transaction is considered an equity transaction and the cash flows are classified as financing in accordance with IAS 7.42A (see **7.1.2**). Previously, in the absence of guidance within IAS 7, entities may have classified such cash flows as investing, in which case that treatment will need to be amended upon adoption of IAS 27(2008).

Example 7.2

Loss of control as a result of shares issued by a subsidiary

Company P enters into a joint venture agreement with Company Q under which Company Q acquires a 50 per cent interest in Company R, formerly a wholly-owned subsidiary of Company P. Company R, which issues new shares to Company Q for cash, has a bank overdraft of £250,000 at the date that it ceases to be a subsidiary of Company P. How should the change in status from a subsidiary to a jointly controlled entity be reflected in the consolidated statement of cash flows, assuming that Company R will be accounted for subsequent to the transaction using the equity method of accounting?

Although Company P retains a 50 per cent interest, Company R is no longer part of the group, and its cash flows will no longer be consolidated. Under IAS 7.39 (see **7.1.2**), where a transaction results in the loss of control of a subsidiary, the amount to be shown under investing activities comprises cash and cash equivalents received as consideration plus or minus any cash or cash equivalents transferred. In this case, because the shares were issued directly to Company Q by Company R, Company P receives no disposal proceeds. Therefore, the only amount to be presented in the consolidated statement of cash flows is an investing cash inflow of £250,000, representing the balance on the subsidiary's overdraft at the date it ceases to be a subsidiary.

7.3 Cash flows arising subsequent to an acquisition

Cash flows relating to an acquisition may arise subsequent to the acquisition. Examples of cash outflows include the payment of deferred and contingent consideration. Examples of cash inflows include the receipt of proceeds of a warranty claim or in respect of an indemnification asset. IAS 7 provides no explicit guidance on the treatment of such items.

Where consideration is payable shortly after the acquisition date, so that no adjustment is necessary for the effects of discounting, the cash outflow will be classified as investing. This is because there is no significant financing element and the payment clearly represents the cost of making the acquisition.

In the case of deferred consideration, both the principal and any interest element could be presented as financing cash flows on the basis that the payments represent the servicing and settlement of a financing liability recognised on the acquisition. This approach is consistent with IFRS 3 *Business Combinations* (2008) which requires the discounting of deferred consideration. It is also consistent with the treatment of finance leases under IAS 17 *Leases*, where the inception of the lease is treated as a non-cash transaction so that the cash cost of acquiring the asset is recognised in financing cash flows over the lease term.

In the case of contingent consideration, under IFRS 3(2008) it is only the acquisition-date fair value of contingent consideration which is recognised as part of the consideration transferred in exchange for the acquiree (and, hence, adjusts goodwill). Changes in fair value of contingent consideration which do not relate to facts and circumstances that existed at the acquisition date, but result from events after that date, do not adjust goodwill. Where contingent consideration is not equity, changes in its fair value will be recognised in profit or loss, consistent with changes in measurement for any financial liability or IAS 37 liability. Since these changes are not treated as a cost of the acquisition, and do not adjust goodwill, the payment of contingent consideration could be presented as a financing cash flow.

Warranties may be received from the seller regarding the value and condition of the assets of the target company and its business, and are often short term in nature. For example, the seller may warrant that, at the acquisition date, there will be at least a specified level of working capital within the business, with a warranty payment becoming due to the extent that the actual level of working capital turns out to be lower. Where a warranty payment is determined based on the facts and circumstances that existed at the acquisition date, any receipt by the acquirer is, in substance, an adjustment to the consideration paid for the acquisition (and, consequently, gives rise to a reduction in goodwill). Generally, such a payment will be made shortly after the acquisition date and will not include any significant financing element, in which case it should be shown as an investing cash flow in the statement of cash flows. Where such a payment is deferred and includes a significant financing element, it should be classified as a financing cash flow, following the logic for deferred consideration.

Where a seller provides an indemnity, giving rise to an indemnification asset, it is agreeing to reimburse the buyer for specific outflows it may incur. As receipts under indemnities are a direct reimbursement of an outflow incurred, the receipt should be classified in accordance with the nature of the cash outflow. This matching of inflows and outflows is consistent with the treatment of reimbursement assets under IAS 37 *Provisions, Contingent Liabilities and Contingent Assets*.

8 Foreign currency cash flows

Foreign currency cash flows arise in two instances – where the reporting entity enters into an external transaction involving inflows or outflows in a foreign currency, and where the reporting group includes an overseas subsidiary and there are cash movements between that subsidiary and other entities in the group.

Where the reporting entity enters into an external transaction involving inflows or outflows in a foreign currency, the cash flows should be presented in the statement of cash flows in the entity's functional currency by translating the foreign currency cash flow at the rate of exchange applying on the date of the cash flow. [IAS 7.25]

Example 8

Foreign currency cash flows

An entity, whose functional currency is Sterling, buys an item of equipment for US$100,000. It recognises the purchase in its accounting records on the date of delivery of the equipment. The rate of exchange on that date ($2 to £1) results in the equipment being recognised at £50,000. The invoice for the equipment is settled by bank transfer 30 days later, at which date £55,000 is needed to settle the liability. The exchange difference of £5,000 is recognised in the statement of comprehensive income.

The purchase of the equipment will be presented in the statement of cash flows as an investing cash outflow of £55,000. Thus, if the operating cash flows are shown using the indirect method, one of the adjustments to net profit will be to adjust for the exchange difference of £5,000.

Had the item purchased been goods for resale, then the cash flow for the purchase should be reported in operating (not investing) cash flows. Under the rules in IAS 7, a cash outflow of £55,000 should be included in the operating cash flows section of the statement of cash flows in respect of the purchase. In the statement of comprehensive income, the cost of the goods, recognised at £50,000, will have been included in purchases and the exchange difference of £5,000 will have been recognised in arriving at profit for the year. Thus, the full £55,000 will have already been recognised in the statement of comprehensive income in arriving at the net profit for the year. Consequently, if the operating cash flows are shown using the indirect method, there will be no need to adjust for the exchange difference of £5,000.

The cash flows of a foreign subsidiary should be included in the group statement of cash flows translated at the exchange rate between the functional currency and the foreign currency ruling on the dates of the cash flows. [IAS 7.26]

IAS 7.27 states that cash flows denominated in a foreign currency are to be reported in a manner consistent with IAS 21 *The Effects of Changes in Foreign Exchange Rates*. IAS 21 permits the use of an average exchange rate that approximates to the actual rate. For example, a weighted average exchange rate for the period may be used for the translation of foreign currency transactions or the translation of the cash flows of a foreign subsidiary. IAS 21 does not permit the cash flows of a foreign subsidiary to be translated using the rate of exchange ruling at the end of the reporting period.

For individually significant transactions, however, it may be necessary to use the actual exchange rate. This would particularly be the case where a significant level of additional cash funding is passed from a parent to an overseas subsidiary, since otherwise it will not be possible to eliminate the intragroup cash flows.

Unrealised gains and losses arising from movements in exchange rates do not represent cash flows. However, the effect of exchange rate changes on cash and cash equivalents held or due in a foreign currency is reported in the statement of cash flows in order to reconcile the balance of cash and cash equivalents at the start and end of the period. This amount is to be presented separately from cash flows from operating, investing and financing activities. The amount includes the differences, if any, had those cash flows been reported using the rate of exchange ruling at the end of period. [IAS 7.28]

9 Additional disclosure requirements

9.1 Non-cash transactions

Where an entity enters into an investing or financing transaction that does not involve the use of cash or cash equivalents, the transaction is excluded from the statement of cash flows (see **3.2** above). The entity should, however, disclose sufficient information in the financial statements to give a user all the relevant information about the transaction. [IAS 7.43]

9.2 Components of cash and cash equivalents

The components of cash and cash equivalents should be disclosed, and a reconciliation is required between the amounts in the statement of cash flows and the equivalent items reported in the statement of financial position. [IAS 7.45] As required by IAS 1, the policy adopted in determining the composition of cash and cash equivalents should also be disclosed. [IAS 7.46]

9.3 Balances not available for use by the group

The amount of significant cash and cash equivalent balances that are not available for use by the group should be disclosed, together with a commentary by management. [IAS 7.48] This disclosure requirement might be triggered by a subsidiary operating in a country where exchange controls or other legal restrictions apply and, thus, the cash and cash equivalents in that subsidiary are not available for general use by other members of the group. Another example might be where substantial amounts of cash are held in escrow accounts and are only available for use on a particular project.

Restrictions on the use of cash or cash equivalents do not alter the classification of the restricted amounts in the statement of financial position or statement of cash flows. For example, where there are restrictions on the transfer of amounts from a foreign subsidiary, the amounts are treated as part of group cash and cash equivalents in the statement of cash flows if they meet the definition of cash and cash equivalents in the foreign subsidiary, and disclosure is made in accordance with IAS 7.48.

9.4 Additional recommended disclosures

IAS 7.50 suggests that additional information may be relevant to users in understanding the financial position and liquidity of an entity. Disclosure of this information, together with a commentary by management, is encouraged and may include:

- the amount of undrawn borrowing facilities that may be available for future operating activities and to settle capital commitments, indicating any restrictions on the use of these facilities;
- the aggregate amounts of cash flows under each classification related to interests in joint ventures that are accounted for using proportionate consolidation;
- the aggregate amount of cash flows that represent increases in operating capacity separately from those cash flows that are required to maintain operating capacity; and
- the amount of the cash flows arising from the operating, investing and financing activities of each reportable segment under IFRS 8 *Operating Segments*. (For entities that have not yet adopted IFRS 8, disclosure is encouraged in respect of each reported business and geographical segment under IAS 14 *Segment Reporting*.)

10 Future developments

The format and content of statements of cash flows in future accounting periods will be dictated by the outcome of the IASB's current project entitled *Financial Statement Presentation*, which is a joint project with the FASB. Phase A of that project has already been finalised and resulted in a number of amendments to IAS 1 *Presentation of Financial Statements* (see

chapter 3). Phase B will address the more fundamental issues for presentation of information in the financial statements (including the statement of cash flows). Phase B topics include:

- developing principles for aggregating and disaggregating information in each financial statement;
- defining the totals and subtotals to be reported in each financial statement (this might include categories such as business and financing); and
- reconsidering IAS 7 (and FASB Statement No. 95 *Statement of Cash Flows*) including whether to require the use of the direct or indirect method.

At the time of writing, it is expected that a discussion document on these topics will be published in the third quarter of 2008.

31 Events after the reporting period

1 Introduction

IAS 10 *Events after the Reporting Period* prescribes when an entity should adjust its financial statements for events after the reporting period, and the disclosures that an entity should make about the date when the financial statements were authorised for issue and about events after the reporting period.

In September 2007, the IASB amended the title of IAS 10 from *Events after the Balance Sheet Date* as a consequential amendment of IAS 1(2007) *Presentation of Financial Statements*.

In May 2008, paragraph 13 of the Standard was amended by *Improvements to IFRSs* (see **4.1**). The amendment, which has clarified the explanation as to why a dividend declared after the reporting period does not result in the recognition of a liability, is not expected to have a significant impact in practice.

This chapter discusses the requirements of IAS 10 in the following sections:

Section 2 Definitions

Section 3 Adjusting events

Section 4 Non-adjusting events

Section 5 Going concern

Section 6 Disclosure

UK

> *Under UK GAAP, FRS 21* Events After the Balance Sheet Date *embodies IAS 10, but makes amendments for UK entities, primarily to exempt FRSSE companies and to adjust references to other accounting standards.*

2 Definitions

IAS 10 defines events after the reporting period as those events, both favourable and unfavourable, that occur between the end of the reporting period and the date on which the financial statements are authorised for issue. [IAS 10.3]

Events after the reporting period include all events up to the date when the financial statements are authorised for issue. The Standard states explicitly that events occurring after the publication of a profit announcement or of other selected financial information but before the financial statements are authorised for issue fall within the scope of the Standard. [IAS 10.7]

A distinction is drawn between two types of events after the reporting period:

- adjusting events – being those that provide evidence of conditions that existed at the end of the reporting period; and
- non-adjusting events – being those that are indicative of conditions that arose after the reporting period.

2.1 Date when financial statements are authorised for issue

Although the date when financial statements are authorised for issue is not defined, IAS 10 gives some guidance on how the phrase should be interpreted.

- Where an entity is required to submit its financial statements to its shareholders for approval after the financial statements have been issued, the financial statements are nevertheless authorised for issue on the date of issue, not the date when shareholders approve the financial statements. [IAS 10.5]
- Where the management of an entity is required to issue its financial statements to a supervisory board (made up solely of non-executives) for approval, the financial statements are authorised for issue when the management authorises them for issue to the supervisory board. [IAS 10.6]

3 Adjusting events

Adjusting events are defined as those events after the reporting period that provide evidence of conditions that existed at the end of the reporting period. [IAS 10.3]

The general principle established by IAS 10 is that financial statements should be prepared so as to reflect events occurring up to the end of the reporting period and conditions existing at the end of the reporting period. As adjusting events provide additional evidence of conditions existing at the end of the reporting period, the amounts recognised in the financial statements are adjusted for their effect. [IAS 10.8]

The following are examples of adjusting events:

[IAS 10.9]

- a court case may be resolved after the reporting period which, because it confirms that the entity already had a present obligation at the end of the reporting period, requires the entity to adjust a provision already recognised, or to recognise a provision instead of merely disclosing a contingent liability;
- information may be received after the reporting period indicating that an asset was impaired at the end of the reporting period, or that the amount of a previously recognised impairment loss for that asset needs to be adjusted. For example:
  - if a customer's bankruptcy occurs after the reporting period, this usually confirms that a loss already existed at the end of the reporting period on a trade receivable account and that the entity needs to adjust the carrying amount of the trade receivable (but see **example 4B** regarding bankruptcy as a result of events occurring after the reporting period); and
  - the sale price achieved for inventories sold after the reporting period may provide evidence about their net realisable value at the end of the reporting period;
- the cost of assets purchased, or the proceeds from assets sold, before the end of the reporting period may be determined after the reporting period;
- the amount of profit-sharing or bonus-payment provisions may be determined after the reporting period, if the entity had a present legal or constructive obligation at the end of the reporting period to make such payments as a result of events before that date; and
- fraud or errors may be discovered that show that the financial statements were incorrect.

4 Non-adjusting events

Non-adjusting events are defined as events after the reporting period that are indicative of conditions that arose after the reporting period. [IAS 10.3]

Non-adjusting events do not give rise to a need for changes in the amounts recognised in the financial statements, but should be disclosed if they are material, such that non-disclosure could affect the economic decisions that users make on the basis of the financial statements. [IAS 10.10 & 21]

The following are examples of non-adjusting events generally requiring disclosure:

[IAS 10.22]

- a major business combination after the reporting period (IFRS 3 *Business Combinations* requires specific disclosures in such cases – see **section 13.1** of **chapter 34**) or disposing of a major subsidiary;
- announcing a plan to discontinue an operation;
- major purchases of assets, classification of assets as held for sale in accordance with IFRS 5 *Non-current Assets Held for Sale and Discontinued Operations*, other disposals of assets, or expropriation of major assets by government;
- the destruction of a major production plant by a fire after the reporting period;
- announcing, or commencing the implementation of, a major restructuring (dealt with in IAS 37 *Provisions, Contingent Liabilities and Contingent Assets* – see **chapter 11**);
- major ordinary share transactions and potential ordinary share transactions after the reporting period. (IAS 33 *Earnings per Share* requires an entity to disclose a description of such transactions, other than when such transactions involve capitalisation or bonus issues, share splits or reverse share splits, all of which are required to be adjusted under IAS 33);
- abnormally large changes after the reporting period in asset prices or foreign exchange rates;
- changes in tax rates or tax laws enacted or announced after the reporting period that have a significant effect on current and deferred tax assets and liabilities (see **4.2** below);
- entering into significant commitments or contingent liabilities (e.g. by issuing significant guarantees); and
- commencing major litigation arising solely out of events that occurred after the reporting period.

Example 4A

Decline in value of share portfolio after the reporting period

An entity has a portfolio of shares. After the end of the reporting period, there has been a substantial fall in the value of the stock market. The entity's accounting policy is to measure the shares at fair value. The entity is not permitted to adjust the fair value of the shares for the decline in value subsequent to the end of the reporting period (i.e. the event is a non-adjusting event after the reporting period). If the impact is significant, however, the entity may be required to disclose the decline in fair value between the end of the reporting period and the date when the financial statements are authorised for issue (see **6.1**).

Example 4B

Default by debtor after the reporting period

An entity sells inventory on credit to a third party. At the end of the reporting period, there was no doubt about the debtor's ability to pay. In the process of the finalisation of the financial statements, the entity is informed that the debtor is going into liquidation as a result of events that occurred after the reporting period. No impairment of the trade receivable should be recognised in the financial statements, because the statement of financial position appropriately reflects the circumstances as at the end of the reporting period. If the impact is significant, however, the entity may be required to disclose the impact of the debtor's default after the reporting period (see **6.1**).

Example 4C

Significant movements in exchange rates after the reporting period

An entity translates foreign currency items at spot-rate at the end of each reporting period. In 20X1, due to significant economic upheaval in Country A, that country's currency was devalued after the end of the reporting period. Nevertheless, for the purposes of the year-end financial statements, items should be translated using the closing rate at the end of the reporting period. If the effect of the exchange rate movements after the reporting period is significant, disclosure may be required (see **6.1**).

Most often, a customer's bankruptcy after the end of the reporting period will be the culmination of a sequence of events that started before the reporting date, so that the impairment of the trade receivables will need to be recognised in the financial statements. It is, nevertheless, not impossible for such bankruptcy to be triggered entirely after the reporting period (e.g. through mismanagement of large derivative contracts).

UK *For UK companies, the Companies Act also requires disclosure in the directors' report of particulars of important events affecting the company or its subsidiaries which have occurred after the end of the year (see* **3.6** *in* **chapter 46**). *To avoid duplication of information, the directors' report may cross refer to details given in the notes to the financial statements or vice versa.*

4.1 Dividends proposed after the reporting period

Dividends to holders of equity instruments (as defined in IAS 32 *Financial Instruments: Presentation*) that are declared after the reporting period should not be recognised as a liability at the end of the reporting period. [IAS 10.12] This is because no obligation exists to pay the dividends until they are appropriately authorised and no longer at the discretion of the entity. [IAS 10.13]

Disclosure is required where such dividends are declared after the reporting period, but before the financial statements are authorised for issue (see **6.4**).

The Standard is clear regarding the treatment of dividends declared after the reporting period. Other situations may arise that are more complex – and the appropriate treatments will be affected by the legal requirements in the jurisdiction concerned. The following examples illustrate three such circumstances.

Example 4.1A

Rescinding of illegal dividends paid before the end of the reporting period

Company A distributes dividends to its shareholders at the end of each quarterly interim reporting period. Therefore, at the end of the annual reporting period, Company A has paid out all of the dividends allocated for the period. After the end of the annual reporting period, but before the financial statements are authorised for issue, Company A discovers an error in its final interim financial report relating to conditions that existed at the end of the reporting period. The financial statements are adjusted accordingly, in accordance with IAS 10. The adjustment reduces profits available for dividend distribution below the level at which dividends were paid (i.e. a portion of the dividends distributed during the period should not have been paid out). In the jurisdiction in which Company A operates, there is a legally binding requirement that dividends distributed in excess of available profits be repaid. Therefore, Company A issues demands to its shareholders for return of the appropriate portion of the dividend.

The rescinding of the dividend is an adjusting event. The need to rescind the dividend arises as a result of the discovery of an error that has been accounted for as an adjusting event. Moreover, the rescinding of the dividends itself meets the definition of an adjusting event as it provides evidence of conditions that existed at the end of the reporting period (at the end of the reporting period, the dividends were illegal).

Example 4.1B

Rescinding of dividends paid before the end of the reporting period due to cash flow shortage

At the end of the annual reporting period, Company A has paid out all of the dividends allocated for the period. After the end of the reporting period, A has a cash-flow shortage and requests shareholders to return a portion of the dividends paid during the reporting period.

This is not an adjusting event. This request for the dividends to be returned arises as a result of circumstances that arose after the end of the reporting period. If the dividends are returned, they should be accounted for as a capital contribution in the subsequent period, not a reduction of the dividends paid.

Example 4.1C

Legal right to rescind interim dividend declared but not paid

An entity declares an interim dividend during the reporting period — it remains unpaid at the end of the reporting period. Under local law, the directors have the right subsequently to vary or rescind this dividend.

The dividend should not be recognised as an obligation in the financial statements. IAS 10.13 confirms that dividends should not be recognised unless an obligation to pay exists at the end of the reporting period. Such an obligation does not arise until the dividends are no longer at the discretion of the entity.

4.2 Changes in tax rates after the reporting period

For current and deferred tax balances, the amounts recognised in the financial statements are based on tax rates and laws enacted or substantively enacted at the end of the reporting period. In certain circumstances, they may reflect the impact of changes to tax rates and laws that have been announced at the end of the reporting period, where such announcement has the substantive effect of actual enactment. To the extent that changes have not been substantively enacted at the end of the reporting period, however, they should not be reflected in the amounts recognised in the financial statements (see **chapter 12**).

4.3 Dividends receivable

Dividends receivable, including those receivable from subsidiaries and associates, should be accounted for in accordance with the general principles established by IAS 18 *Revenue*. Therefore, dividend income should be recognised when the shareholder's right to receive payment is established. [IAS 18.30(c)]

Where dividends are declared by the investee after the reporting period such that, at the end of the reporting period, the investor had no right to receive payment, then neither the investor nor the investee should adjust their financial statements.

5 Going concern

An entity's financial statements should not be prepared on a going concern basis if management determines after the reporting period either that it intends to liquidate the entity or to cease trading, or that it has no realistic alternative but to do so. [IAS 10.14]

If operating results and financial position deteriorate after the reporting period, this may indicate a need to consider whether the going concern assumption is still appropriate. If the going concern assumption is no longer appropriate, the effect is so pervasive that IAS 10 requires a fundamental change in the basis of accounting, rather than an adjustment to the amounts recognised within the original basis of accounting. [IAS 10.15]

Example 5

Voluntary liquidation after the reporting period

An owner-managed entity's reporting date is 31 December 20X1. At the reporting date, the entity is trading profitably, and the owner-managers expect that it will continue to do so; they have no intention to liquidate the entity or to cease trading. But in March 20X2, before the financial statements are authorised for issue, the owner-managers experience an unexpected change in personal circumstances, and decide to put the entity into voluntary liquidation.

> The entity's financial statements should be prepared on a basis other than that of a going concern.

6 Disclosure

6.1 Non-adjusting events

Where non-adjusting events after the reporting period are so material that non-disclosure could influence the economic decisions of users taken on the basis of the financial statements, the entity should disclose the following information for each material category of non-adjusting event after the reporting period:

[IAS 10.21]

- the nature of the event; and
- an estimate of its financial effect, or a statement that such an estimate cannot be made.

6.2 Date of authorisation for issue

The entity is required to disclose the date when the financial statements were authorised for issue and who gave that authorisation. If the entity's owners or others have the power to amend the financial statements after issue, that fact should be disclosed. [IAS 10.17]

6.3 Updating disclosures about conditions at the end of the reporting period

IAS 10 also requires that, if an entity receives information after the reporting period about conditions that existed at the end of the reporting period, it should update disclosures that relate to those conditions in the light of the new information. [IAS 10.19] For example, where new evidence becomes available after the reporting period about a contingent liability that existed at the end of the reporting period, the disclosures about the contingent liability in the financial statements, made in accordance with IAS 37, will be updated based on the new information.

6.4 Dividends proposed or declared after the reporting period

Where dividends are proposed or declared after the reporting period, but before the financial statements are authorised for issue, the entity is required to disclose in the notes to the financial statements the amount of such dividends and the related amount per share. [IAS 1(2007).137(a), previously IAS 1(2003).125(a)]

6.5 Going concern

Disclosures are required by IAS 1 where:

(a) the financial statements are not prepared on a going concern basis; or

(b) management is aware of material uncertainties related to events or conditions that may cast significant doubt upon the entity's ability to continue as a going concern. The events or conditions requiring disclosure may arise after the reporting period.

These disclosures are discussed at **2.4** in **chapter 3**.

32 Related party disclosures

1 Introduction

The disclosure of related party relationships and transactions with related parties is dealt with in IAS 24 *Related Party Disclosures*. The Standard was revised by the IASB in December 2003, and was most recently amended when the revised version of IAS 3 *Presentation of Financial Statements* was issued in September 2007.

This chapter discusses the requirements of IAS 24 in the following sections:

Section 2	Purpose of related party disclosures
Section 3	Scope
Section 4	Definitions
Section 5	Disclosure requirements
Section 6	Additional disclosure requirements for UK companies
Section 7	Future developments

In overview, IAS 24 is broadly similar to its UK equivalent, FRS 8 Related Party Disclosures, *but there are some differences, the most significant of which are highlighted below.* UK

- *FRS 8 exempts subsidiary undertakings 90 per cent or more of whose voting rights are controlled within a group from disclosure of transactions and outstanding balances with the group and its investees, provided group financial statements including the subsidiary are publicly available. IAS 24 does not include an equivalent exemption.*
- *FRS 8 requires the names of transacting related parties to be disclosed. IAS 24 does not include this requirement (though it does require the names of controlling parties to be disclosed). Instead, it requires the nature of the relationship to be disclosed, and separate disclosures to be given for transactions with entities in each of certain specified categories. (Note that, in practice, UK companies will still need to disclose the names of transacting parties where transactions are also caught by the UK disclosure requirements discussed in* **section 6** *below.)*

- *Where an individual is a related party under FRS 8, the related party relationship also encompasses any entities in which that individual (or members of the close family) has a controlling interest. IAS 24 extends this so that it also applies to entities over which the individual (or members of the close family) has joint control or significant influence.*
- *IAS 24 does not repeat the guidance from FRS 8 on materiality, including materiality for transactions with directors and key managers.*
- *FRS 8 states that the required related party disclosures do not over-ride an entity's duties of confidentiality arising by operation of law. IAS 24 does not include a similar exemption but, as explained above, nor does it require disclosure of the names of transacting related parties.*
- *IAS 24 requires disclosure of the compensation of key management personnel. Such disclosure is outside the scope of FRS 8, although the Companies Act and Listing Rules require detailed disclosures in relation to directors' remuneration (see* ***chapter 48****).*

2 Purpose of related party disclosures

The objective of IAS 24 is to ensure that financial statements contain the disclosures necessary to draw attention to the possibility that the reported financial position and results may have been affected by the existence of related parties and by transactions and outstanding balances with related parties. [IAS 24.1]

The Standard notes that related party relationships are a normal feature of business and commerce. It is common, for example, for entities to operate separate parts of their activities through subsidiaries, associates or joint ventures. Such relationships can have an effect on the operating results and financial position of the reporting entity. They may lead to transactions being entered into between the related parties that would not be entered into between unrelated parties, or to transactions being effected at different amounts from those that would prevail between unrelated parties.

The Standard also considers the implications of the existence of related party relationships – even where there are no transactions between the parties concerned. It acknowledges that the mere existence of the relationship may be sufficient to affect the transactions of the reporting entity with other parties. For example, a subsidiary might terminate relations with a trading partner following the acquisition by its parent of a fellow subsidiary engaged in the same trade as the former partner. Alternatively, one party might refrain from acting because of the significant influence of another – for example, a subsidiary might be instructed by its parent not to engage in research and development.

For these reasons, the Standard concludes that knowledge of related party transactions, outstanding balances and relationships may affect assessments of an entity's operations by users of financial statements, including assessments of the risks and opportunities facing the entity.

3 Scope

IAS 24 should be applied in:

[IAS 24.2]

- identifying related party relationships and transactions;
- identifying outstanding balances between an entity and its related parties;
- identifying the circumstances in which disclosure of such relationships, transactions and balances is required; and
- determining the disclosures to be made about those items.

IAS 24 does not apply to the measurement of related party transactions.

3.1 Consolidated financial statements

IAS 24 contains no specific exemptions for intragroup transactions in consolidated financial statements. Such intragroup transactions and outstanding balances are, however, eliminated on consolidation. Therefore, because they do not form part of the consolidated financial statements, related party transactions and outstanding balances between group members are not disclosed under IAS 24. [IAS 24.4]

3.2 Separate financial statements

Where a parent, venturer or investor presents separate financial statements in accordance with IAS 27 *Consolidated and Separate Financial Statements*, IAS 24 applies equally to those separate financial statements. [IAS 24.3] In addition, there are no exemptions available to subsidiaries in respect of transactions and balances with other group entities. Related party transactions and outstanding balances with other entities in a group are disclosed in an entity's separate or individual financial statements. [IAS 24.4]

At one time, IAS 24 exempted disclosures about related party transactions in parent financial statements published with consolidated statements, and in the financial statements of a wholly-owned subsidiary in limited circumstances. However, this exemption was withdrawn when IAS 24 was revised in 2003. Under the current Standard, individual financial statements of group entities are dealt with on a stand-alone basis, and are required to comply with all of the requirements of IAS 24.

UK *This is a key difference between IAS 24 and FRS 8, as the latter offers exemptions both to certain subsidiaries and in respect of separate financial statements of a parent. From a practical viewpoint, UK companies adopting IFRSs need to ensure that they have adequate systems to track intragroup transactions if those transactions may, in aggregate, be material to their individual financial statements.*

3.3 Relationships that change during the period

IAS 24 does not specify whether, in order for two parties to be considered related, a relationship should exist at the end of the reporting period, throughout the reporting period or simply at any time during the reporting period. Consequently, it is unclear whether transactions between parties should be disclosed if the entities were related parties for part of the reporting period, but have ceased to be related by the end of the reporting period.

Equally, it is unclear how to treat the situation where parties were not related at the time when a transaction took place between them, but they become related parties before the end of the reporting period. For example, where an entity is acquired by A Group Limited during the period, and it has transacted with members of A Group Limited throughout the period (i.e. both before and after acquisition), to what extent are pre-acquisition transactions disclosable?

The most appropriate interpretation seems to be that, where there is no related party relationship at the time of a particular transaction, it is not a related party transaction. If the objective of IAS 24 is to highlight transactions that may have been affected by the relationship between two parties, then disclosure of transactions entered into prior to the existence of that relationship does not appear to contribute to that objective.

For transactions with parties that were related at the time of a transaction, but that are no longer related by the end of the reporting period, a similar logic applies. Such transactions will be disclosable, because there was a related party relationship at the time the transactions were entered into.

In the absence of more detailed guidance within IAS 24, it seems appropriate that related party relationships between parents and subsidiaries, and the amount of outstanding balances and related provisions for doubtful debts, should be disclosed if they are related parties either at the end of the reporting period, at the time when the financial statements are authorised for issue, or at any time during the reporting period when a related party relationship exists.

3.4 Parties related to a group

IAS 24 does not specifically address the use of the term 'related party' in the context of consolidated financial statements. The most appropriate approach, however, appears to be to disclose only those transactions with parties who are related parties of the group as a whole. This approach, by implication, means considering the group in its role as reporting entity and considering which parties are related to it under IAS 24. Thus, for example, the Chief Financial Officer of a subsidiary may be a member of the key management personnel of the subsidiary, but may not be viewed as a member of the key management personnel for the group unless he or she has authority and responsibility for planning, directing and controlling activities at a group level. This degree of influence at a group level may arise as a consequence of the individual having a management role at the parent entity level or, if the subsidiary is significant, directly as a result of his or her authority over and responsibility for a significant component of the group.

3.5 State-controlled entities

IAS 24.IN6 emphasises that state-controlled entities are within the scope of IFRSs (i.e. those that are profit-oriented are not exempted from disclosing transactions with other state-controlled entities).

See **section 7** below regarding proposals to provide limited relief from IAS 24's requirements for state-controlled entities.

4 Definitions

This section addresses the extended definitions provided in IAS 24 for the identification of related parties. The Standard requires the substance of each potential related party relationship to be considered, and not merely the legal form. [IAS 24.10]

4.1 Related party

IAS 24 provides the following definition of a related party.

[IAS 24.9]

> 'A party is related to an entity if:
>
> (a) directly, or indirectly through one or more intermediaries, the party:
>
> (i) controls, is controlled by, or is under common control with, the entity (this includes parents, subsidiaries and fellow subsidiaries);
>
> (ii) has an interest in the entity that gives it significant influence over the entity; or
>
> (iii) has joint control over the entity;
>
> (b) the party is an associate (as defined in IAS 28 *Investments in Associates*) of the entity;
>
> (c) the party is a joint venture in which the entity is a venturer (see IAS 31 *Interests in Joint Ventures*);
>
> (d) the party is a member of the key management personnel of the entity or its parent;
>
> (e) the party is a close member of the family of any individual referred to in (a) or (d);
>
> (f) the party is an entity that is controlled, jointly controlled or significantly influenced by, or for which significant voting power in such entity resides with, directly or indirectly, any individual referred to in (d) or (e); or
>
> (g) the party is a post-employment benefit plan for the benefit of employees of the entity, or of any entity that is a related party of the entity.'

The list of related party relationships falling within the scope of the Standard, as set out above, is exhaustive. Types of relationships not included in the list are outside the scope of the Standard. However, the determination as to whether a relationship falls within one of the categories listed can involve considerable judgement – focusing on the substance of a relationship and not merely its legal form.

It follows from the definition in IAS 24.9 that all of the following are related parties of Company A:

- Company A's parents, subsidiaries, fellow subsidiaries, associates and jointly controlled entities;
- those entities having significant influence or joint control over Company A;
- individuals having control, joint control or significant influence over Company A, and also:
  - close members of their family;
  - any other entities over which such individuals or family members have control, joint control or significant influence; and
  - any other entities for which significant voting power resides, directly or indirectly, with those individuals or family members;
- members of the key management personnel of Company A or its parent, and also:
  - close family members of such key management personnel;
  - any other entities over which such key management personnel or their close family members have control, joint control or significant influence; and
  - any other entities for which significant voting power resides, directly or indirectly, with such key management personnel or their close family members;
- post-employment benefit plans for the benefit of employees of Company A, or of any entity that is a related party of Company A.

A number of differences between IAS 24 and FRS 8 may be observed. UK

- *FRS 8 lists certain parties that will always be regarded as related and others for which that presumption may be rebutted. There is no rebuttable presumption in IAS 24; the parties listed are always related.*

- *Where an individual is a related party under FRS 8, the related party relationship also encompasses any entities in which that individual (or members of the close family) has a controlling interest. IAS 24 extends this so that it also applies to entities over which the individual (or members of the close family) has joint control or significant influence.*
- *FRS 8 states that two parties are related if, in entering a transaction, they are subject to influence from the same source to such an extent that one has subordinated its own separate interests. IAS 24 does not deal with such circumstances.*
- *FRS 8 and IAS 24 differ in how they define the degree of influence that will establish a related party relationship. FRS 8 refers to one party having influence over the financial and operating policies of the other to the extent that the latter might be inhibited from pursuing at all times its own separate interests. IAS 24 refers to significant influence, being the power to participate in financial and operating policy decisions.*

IAS 24 states that the following are not *necessarily* related parties:

[IAS 24.11]

- two entities simply because they have a director or other member of key management personnel in common;
- two venturers simply because they share joint control over a joint venture;
- providers of finance, trade unions, public utilities, and government departments and agencies simply by virtue of their normal dealings with an entity (even though they may affect the freedom of action of an entity or participate in its decision-making process); and
- a customer, supplier, franchisor, distributor or general agent with whom an entity transacts a significant volume of business, merely by virtue of the resulting economic dependence.

It is important to understand that IAS 24.11 does not provide a blanket exemption from the requirements of the Standard for the relationships listed. If the reporting entity has a related party relationship, as defined in IAS 24, with one of these entities, the general requirements apply. Essentially, IAS 24.11 is saying that disclosure of economic dependence is not required in the absence of a related party relationship for some other reason.

It may be the case that a supplier operates a system of inducements (e.g. loans or bank guarantees) in exchange for a customer agreeing to source supplies solely from that supplier. This, of itself, will not normally create a related party relationship. However, consideration will need to be given as to whether the agreement allows the supplier to direct the financial or operating policies of the customer. For example, provided that it is not economically prohibitive for the customer to terminate the relationship with the supplier if more favourable terms are available elsewhere, then such an agreement will not create a related party relationship.

A bank may provide loan finance to an entity and charge it a fee for doing so. IAS 24.11 does not require disclosure of the relationship and transactions between the entity and its providers of finance simply as a result of those dealings; disclosures will not be required unless the bank and the entity are otherwise related. This may be contrasted with the situation in which a venture capitalist, with an equity stake giving it significant influence over an entity, procures external loan finance for that entity and charges a fee for doing so. In the latter case, the investee and the venture capitalist are already related (because the venture capitalist has significant influence over the entity). Therefore, the exemption does not apply and all transactions (including the fees) should be disclosed.

Example 4.1

Determining whether an associate is a related party of the investor's subsidiary

C purchased an insurance policy from D to cover its post-retirement medical liability. As discussed at **7.7.2** in **chapter 24**, this can only be classified as a plan asset (i.e. a 'qualifying insurance policy)', if D is not a related party of C.

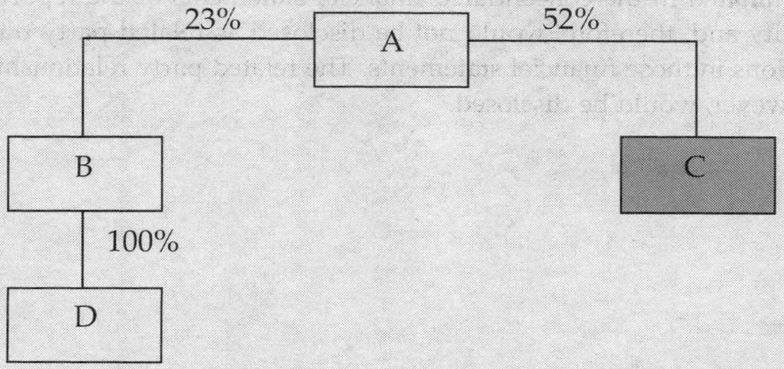

The question in this case is whether or not Company B (and, consequently, D) and C are related parties in C's separate financial statements.

B and C are not related parties provided that the two entities do not have common management personnel who control, jointly control, significantly influence , or have significant voting power in B.

IAS 24.9(f) states that a party is related to an entity if 'the party is an entity that is controlled, jointly controlled or significantly influenced by, or for which significant voting power in such entity resides with, directly or indirectly, any individual referred to in (d) or (e)'. IAS 24.9(d) refers to members of the key management personnel of the entity or its parent, and IAS 24.9(e) to close family members of the individuals described in (d).

Where it is evidenced that the entities do not have common management personnel who meet the criteria in IAS 24.9(f), B and C are not related parties in accordance with the Standard.

Note that if A were the reporting entity, B (and, consequently, D) and C would be considered related parties.

4.1.1 *Related parties in a group*

The following example provides guidance for identifying related parties in a group scenario. Entities in the boxes marked (1) and (2) are considered to be related parties of the reporting entity (shaded box). Transactions between entities in the boxes marked (2) would be eliminated in the consolidated financial statements of the reporting entity and, therefore, would not be disclosed as related party transactions in those financial statements. The related party relationships, however, would be disclosed.

The associates in the boxes marked (3) are not considered to be related parties of the reporting entity in accordance with IAS 24.9(a)(ii).

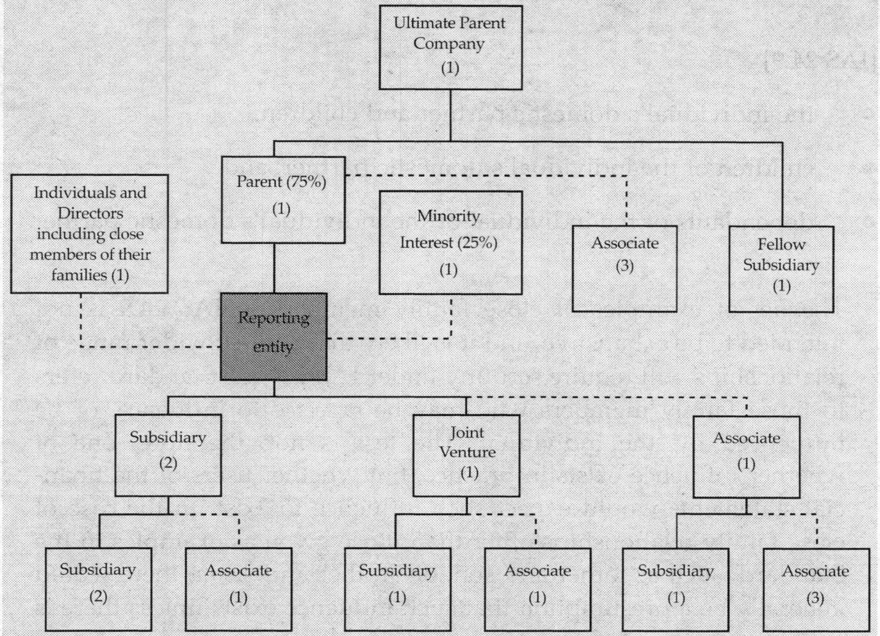

4.2 Control

Control is defined as the power to govern the financial and operating policies of an entity so as to obtain benefits from its activities. [IAS 24.9]

4.3 Joint control

Joint control is the contractually agreed sharing of control over an economic activity. [IAS 24.9]

4.4 Significant Influence

Significant influence is the power to participate in the financial and operating policy decisions of an entity, but not control over those policies. Significant influence may be gained by share ownership, statute or agreement. [IAS 24.9]

4.5 Close members of the family of an individual

Close members of the family of an individual are those family members who may be expected to influence, or be influenced by, that individual in their dealings with the entity. They may include:

[IAS 24.9]

- the individual's domestic partner and children;
- children of the individual's domestic partner; and
- dependants of the individual or the individual's domestic partner.

The list of examples of close family members in IAS 24.9 is not intended to be exhaustive, and it is likely that a much wider range of relationships will require scrutiny under IAS 24. The Standard refers to those family members who may be *expected* to influence, or be influenced by, the individual. The test is not, therefore, one of whether influence exists in practice, but whether users of the financial statements would expect such influence to exist. In the case of close family relationships other than those given as examples in the Standard, such as father and son, or brother and sister, there would generally be a presumption that such influence exists unless there is evidence to the contrary. Conversely, in the case of more distant family relationships, there would generally be a presumption that no influence exists unless there is evidence to the contrary.

The Standard does not clarify what is meant by the 'dependants' of an individual or the individual's domestic partner. The word is defined in the Oxford Concise English Dictionary as 'a person who relies on another, especially for financial support, or a servant or a subordinate'.

4.6 Key management personnel

Key management personnel are those persons having authority and responsibility for planning, directing and controlling the activities of an entity, directly or indirectly, including any director (whether executive or otherwise) of that entity. [IAS 24.9]

Individuals other than directors may fall to be classified as key management personnel, according to the degree of their authority and responsibility. This is significant for many reporting entities, as the explicit requirement to disclose the remuneration of key management personnel (see **5.2**) may result in the disclosure of remuneration of individuals other than statutory directors.

Key management personnel might in some instances include directors of subsidiaries who are not directors of the parent and senior managers who are not directors. It will usually be the case, however, that those with authority and responsibility for planning, directing and controlling the activities of the group will be the board of directors of the parent. There may be exceptions to this general rule: for example, if an entity's board was entirely comprised of non-executive directors, it would be possible that the most senior executives would be the key management personnel. Similarly, in the case of an overseas subsidiary with no directors based in the overseas location, a 'general manager' might be regarded as key management personnel of the subsidiary. Where an entity has a major trading subsidiary which represents a substantial proportion of the group, the management of that subsidiary might be regarded as key management personnel of the group. But it would be necessary to have regard to the amount of autonomy that they had and whether all major decisions were subject to the approval of the parent's board.

4.7 Related party transaction

A related party transaction is defined as a transfer of resources, services or obligations between related parties, regardless of whether a price is charged. [IAS 24.9]

The last point means that it is not possible to rely only on an entity's normal accounting records (general ledger, cash book, sales ledger etc.) to identify related party transactions. In addition, there will need to be a process for tracking any goods or services received or provided free of charge (see **5.3.4**).

It is not uncommon for directors to give guarantees in respect of the borrowings of an entity, often without making a charge to the entity. The provision of such a guarantee will be a related party transaction.

5 Disclosure requirements

5.1 Relationships

Regardless of whether there have been transactions with related parties, an entity is required to disclose:

[IAS 24.12]

- the name of its parent and, if different, the ultimate controlling party; and
- if neither the entity's parent nor the ultimate controlling party produces financial statements available for public use, the name of the next most senior parent that does so. The next most senior parent is the first parent in the group, above the immediate parent, that produces consolidated financial statements available for public use.

IAS 24 indicates that relationships where control exists should be disclosed, even where there have been no transactions between the parties, in order to enable users of financial statements to form a view about the effects of related party relationships on the entity.

The requirements of IAS 24.12 are in addition to the disclosure requirements of IAS 27 *Consolidated Financial Statements and Separate Financial Statements*, IAS 28 *Investments in Associates* and IAS 31 *Interests in Joint Ventures*, which require an appropriate listing and description of the entity's significant investments in subsidiaries, associates and jointly controlled entities.

The ultimate controlling party may or may not be a corporate entity. The requirement to disclose the entity's ultimate controlling *party* means that, where such control is exercised by an individual, or by a group of individuals acting in concert, their identity must be disclosed.

UK *Schedule 4 of the Accounting Regulations (previously Schedule 5 to the Companies Act 1985) continues to apply to UK companies preparing their financial statements under IFRSs. Accordingly, in addition to the disclosures required by IAS 24.12, a UK subsidiary company will need to disclose details concerning:*

[Acc Regs Sch. 4: 8 and 9, previously CA 1985 Sch. 5: 11, 12, 30 and 31]

(a) the company (if any) regarded by the directors as the company's ultimate parent company (which may be different from the ultimate controlling party); and

(b) the parent undertaking of the largest group of undertakings for which group financial statements are drawn up and of which the reporting company is a member, and also the parent undertaking of the smallest such group.

In (a) above references to a company include any body corporate, e.g. a foreign company.

The details to be disclosed for each parent company or undertaking identified above are:

- *its name; and*
- *its country of incorporation, if outside the United Kingdom (under the Companies Act 1985, this disclosure is required if the country of incorporation is outside Great Britain).*

In addition, in respect of the parent undertakings of the largest and smallest group for which group financial statements are drawn up and of which the reporting company is a member, the following should be disclosed:

(a) *the address from which copies of the group financial statements can be obtained (if they are available to the public); and*

(b) *the principal place of business (if the parent undertaking is unincorporated).*

5.2 Compensation of key management personnel

The total compensation paid to key management personnel must be disclosed, and analysed between:

[IAS 24.16]

- short-term employee benefits;
- post-employment benefits;
- other long-term benefits;
- termination benefits; and
- share-based payment.

Compensation includes all employee benefits, as defined in IAS 19 *Employee Benefits* (see **chapter 24**). It therefore includes all forms of consideration provided in exchange for services rendered to the entity, including those benefits to which IFRS 2 *Share-based Payment* applies. Compensation includes:

[IAS 24.9]

- short-term employee benefits, such as wages, salaries, and social security contributions, paid annual leave and paid sick leave, profit-sharing and bonuses (if payable within twelve months of the end of the period) and non-monetary benefits (such as medical care, housing, cars, and free or subsidised goods or services) for current employees;

- post-employment benefits such as pensions, other retirement benefits, post-employment life insurance and post-employment medical care;
- other long-term employee benefits, including long-service leave or sabbatical leave, jubilee or other long-service benefits, long-term disability benefits and, if they are not payable wholly within twelve months after the end of the period, profit-sharing, bonuses and deferred compensation;
- termination benefits; and
- share-based payment.

The amount disclosed should include consideration paid on behalf of a parent of the entity in respect of the entity. [IAS 24.9]

UK

As discussed in ***chapter 48****, UK listed companies must produce a directors' remuneration report under Schedule 8 of the Accounting Regulations (previously Schedule 7A to the Companies Act 1985), containing extensive details of the remuneration policies and the remuneration of individual directors. Also, certain disclosures about the aggregate remuneration of the directors are required by Schedule 5 of the Accounting Regulations (previously Schedule 6 to the Companies Act 1985) to be given in the notes to the financial statements. These disclosures are often made in the directors' remuneration report and linked to the financial statements through a cross reference. Note, however, that IAS 24 requires a different analysis, which will need to be provided in addition to the Act disclosures.*

Example 5.2

Negative compensation amount for key management personnel

Members of key management personnel have been granted options under an entity's executive share option plan. The options vest over a three-year period and include a non-market vesting condition. In 20X1 and 20X2, it is estimated that the non-market vesting condition will be satisfied and, accordingly, under IFRS 2 *Share-based Payment*, the entity recognises an expense for these options on this basis. In 20X3 (the current reporting period), the non-market vesting condition is not satisfied and, therefore, the entity reverses the cumulative expense recognised in 20X1 and 20X2 in accordance with the requirements of IFRS 2.20. Should this 'negative expense' be included in the amounts disclosed for the compensation of key management personnel when the non-market vesting condition is not satisfied and the entity 'trues-up' its recognised IFRS 2 expense in 20X3?

Yes. IAS 24 requires disclosure of key management personnel compensation, which is defined to include all employee benefits (as defined in IAS 19 *Employee Benefits* and including those employee benefits to which IFRS 2 applies). IAS 24 does not prescribe any requirements for the measurement of the amounts to be disclosed for such compensation. Reference should therefore be made to the measurement guidance contained in other Standards (such as IAS 19 and IFRS 2) in order to determine amounts to be disclosed. Accordingly, it is appropriate to 'true-up' the amount disclosed as share-based payment compensation when options do not vest as a consequence of non-market vesting conditions not being satisfied in a manner that is consistent with the treatment adopted in the measurement of the expense recognised under IFRS 2.

In such circumstances, entities should consider whether they ought to provide additional disclosure to explain this negative amount included in the measurement of the amounts disclosed for the compensation of key management personnel, particularly in the light of any comparative amount provided.

5.2.1 *Compensation of key management personnel who are members of an entity's defined benefit retirement benefit plan*

IAS 24 does not provide guidance as to the amounts to be disclosed with respect to members of key management personnel who are also members of an entity's defined benefit retirement benefit plan. Reference should therefore be made to the measurement guidance contained in other Standards, such as IAS 19 *Employee Benefits*, in order to determine the measurement of the compensation to be disclosed. The entity should include in the amounts disclosed the cost of an employee benefit, attributable to the services rendered by the employee to the entity, with respect to the employee's participation in the defined benefit plan. The entity may establish its own accounting policy regarding how the amount is determined. The entity should disclose the method adopted and as much information as possible given the information available. The policy adopted should be applied on a consistent basis.

IAS 19 does not prescribe whether an entity should present current service cost, interest cost, and expected return on plan assets as components of a single item of income or expense in profit or loss. The following accounting policies might be considered acceptable, depending on an entity's circumstances:

- disclosure of the amount of the total IAS 19 expense recognised in profit or loss that is attributable to the key management personnel; or

- disclosure of the amount of the IAS 19 service cost that is attributable to the key management personnel.

The following accounting policies would be considered unacceptable:

- no disclosure of key management personnel employee benefits because of the complexity of calculation;

- disclosure of the IAS 19 service cost together with the expected return on plan assets (but excluding all other aspects of the IAS 19 expense) that is attributable to the key management personnel; or

- disclosure of the contribution by the entity to the employee defined benefit plan with respect to the key management personnel only.

In determining the amount to be disclosed as compensation, entities should consider all of the relevant facts, circumstances and complexities associated with IAS 19, including, amongst others:

- how the amount to be recognised under IAS 19.61 has been disclosed, i.e. the amounts reflected as compensation expense versus those amounts reflected as financing (if any);

- whether the employee defined benefit plan is for key management personnel only, or whether it includes other employees as well; and

- the practicalities of allocating actuarial gains and losses to particular employees in a manner that is not arbitrary.

5.2.2 *Disclosure of non-monetary benefits to key management*

Example 5.2.2

Disclosure of non-monetary benefits to key management

A member of key management personnel is given, as part of his employment package, the benefit of staying in a residential property owned by the reporting entity. The property was bought by the entity fifty years ago. The value of the property has increased significantly compared to its cost. The market rental of a similar property is £100,000 per annum. The depreciation recognised on the property is £5,000 per annum. How should the non-monetary benefit to the member of key management personnel be disclosed?

IAS 24.17 states that if 'there have been transactions between related parties, an entity shall disclose the nature of the related party relationship as well as information about the transactions and outstanding balances necessary for an understanding of the potential effect of the relationship on the financial statements. These disclosure requirements are in addition to the requirements in paragraph 16'.

For the purposes of IAS 24.17, it would be appropriate to disclose the depreciation recognised in the period, because that is the amount the entity has recognised in profit or loss in respect of the benefits.

The Standard does not require disclosure of fair value of the benefit provided. The entity should consider whether the amount recognised reflects the nature of the benefit provided. If the fair value of the benefit could be determined reliably, disclosure of additional information that is relevant to users, including a description of the terms and conditions of the compensation, would be encouraged.

5.3 Other related party transactions

In addition to the compensation of key management personnel, an entity is required to disclose details of any other transactions with its related parties. Where such transactions have occurred, the Standard requires disclosure of:

[IAS 24.17]

- the nature of the related party relationship; and
- information about the transactions and outstanding balances necessary for an understanding of the potential effect of the relationship on the financial statements.

Unlike FRS 8, IAS 24 includes no explicit guidance on how to assess the materiality of transactions for disclosure purposes. Nevertheless, the two standards have essentially the same objective – to draw attention to the possibility that financial position and profit or loss may have been affected by the existence of related parties and by transactions with them. In that light, the following guidance from FRS 8 may be helpful when assessing materiality in the context of IAS 24: UK

[FRS 8.20]

> *'Transactions are material when their disclosure might reasonably be expected to influence decisions made by the users of general purpose financial statements. The materiality of related party transactions is to be judged, not only in terms of their significance to the reporting entity, but also in relation to the other related party when that party is:*
>
> *(a) a director, key manager or other individual in a position to influence, or accountable for stewardship of, the reporting entity; or*
>
> *(b) a member of the close family of any individual mentioned in (a) above; or*
>
> *(c) an entity controlled by any individual mentioned in (a) or (b) above.'*
>
> *There is some further discussion of materiality at* **6.3.1.3**.

The following examples are cited in the Standard of related party transactions that require disclosure:

[IAS 24.20]

- purchases or sales of goods (finished or unfinished);
- purchases or sales of properties or other assets;
- rendering or receiving of services;
- leases;
- transfers of research and development;
- transfers under licence agreements;
- transfers under finance arrangements (including loans and equity contributions in cash or in kind);
- provision of guarantees or collateral; and
- settlement of liabilities on behalf of the entity or by the entity on behalf of another party.

The list of examples in IAS 24.20 is not intended to be exhaustive, and any event meeting the definition of a related party transaction (see **4.7**) should be disclosed if it is material.

The payment of a dividend to a related party will constitute a related party transaction. However, in some cases, the information may already be disclosed and additional disclosure may be unnecessary to meet the requirements of IAS 24. For example, if disclosure is made of the fact that the reporting entity is wholly-owned, that the ownership has not changed in the reporting period, and of details of dividends paid and proposed, then it is not necessary to state explicitly that the dividend has been paid to the owner.

5.3.1 *Details to be disclosed*

The following *minimum* disclosures are required:

[IAS 24.17]

- the amount of the transactions;
- the amount of outstanding balances and:
  - their terms and conditions, including whether they are secured, and the nature of the consideration to be provided in settlement; and
  - details of any guarantees given or received;
- provisions for doubtful debts related to the amount of the outstanding balances; and
- the expense recognised during the period in respect of bad or doubtful debts due from related parties.

The details listed in IAS 24.17 are not exhaustive, and other significant aspects of the transactions will be required to be disclosed, if such disclosure is necessary for an understanding of the financial statements.

UK

FRS 8 requires the names of transacting related parties to be disclosed. IAS 24 does not include this requirement (though it does require the names of controlling parties to be disclosed, as discussed in **5.1***). Instead, IAS 24 requires the nature of the relationship to be disclosed, and separate disclosures to be given for transactions with entities in each of certain specified categories, which are listed in* **5.3.3***. In practice, UK companies will still need to disclose the names of transacting parties where transactions are also caught by the UK disclosure requirements discussed in* ***section 6*** *below.*

5.3.2 *Aggregation*

IAS 24 provides that items of a similar nature may be disclosed in aggregate, except where separate disclosure is necessary for an understanding of the effects of related party transactions on the financial statements. [IAS 24.22]

Related parties may include a number of parties who have the same or similar relationships with the entity, such as a group of owners, members of key management personnel, etc. IAS 24 is not specific as to whether transactions with such related parties with similar relationships to the entity can be disclosed in aggregate, nor as to the circumstances which might lead to separate disclosure of items.

The principal objective of IAS 24 is to provide useful information to the users while avoiding excessive disclosure where the related party transactions comprise many items of a routine nature, such as in a normal trading relationship between group entities. Therefore, transactions with related parties with similar relationships with the entity may be disclosed in aggregate unless a transaction is individually significant. A significant transaction with a specific related party should not be concealed within an aggregated disclosure.

5.3.3 *Analysis of transactions and balances*

The disclosures set out in previous paragraphs are required to be made separately for each of the following categories:

[IAS 24.18]

- the parent;
- entities with joint control or significant influence over the entity;
- subsidiaries;
- associates;
- joint ventures in which the entity is a venturer;
- key management personnel of the entity or its parent; and
- other related parties.

The classification of amounts payable to, and receivable from related parties in the different categories set out above is an extension of the disclosure requirements in IAS 1 *Presentation of Financial Statements* for information to be presented either in the statement of financial position or in the notes. The categories are intended to provide a more comprehensive analysis of related party balances and apply to related party transactions. [IAS 24.19]

5.3.4 *Reference to transactions carried out at arm's length*

The Standard specifically states that it is inappropriate to indicate that transactions were carried out at arm's length unless such an assertion can be substantiated. [IAS 24.21]

By their nature, it would be unusual for the pricing of related party transactions not to reflect the relationship between the parties. One would therefore expect references to transactions being 'on normal commercial terms' or 'on an arm's length basis' to be rare – particularly in relation to trading transactions.

If no price is charged for a transaction that would have given rise to a cost if the transaction had been entered into with an unrelated party, then this fact should be disclosed. In a group context, it is particularly important to consider services that are provided by the parent free of charge. For example, administrative services provided free of charge or group banking arrangements that result in lower finance costs may be disclosable if their effect is material (i.e. if the financial effect of such arrangements has a material impact on the results disclosed in the financial statements).

In addition to the related party disclosures discussed above, where goods and services are provided by a parent or owner free of charge, it will be appropriate to consider whether a capital contribution should be recognised.

5.3.5 *Comparative amounts*

The general requirement to present comparative amounts included within IAS 1 *Presentation of Financial Statements* means it is necessary to present comparatives for related party transactions. There are various areas of uncertainty, however, as to which are the comparatives for related party disclosures. For example:

- a party is a related party in the current year, but was not in the prior year. Should transactions with that party in the prior year be disclosed as comparatives, even though it was not a related party in that prior year?

- a party was a related party in the prior year, but is not in the current year. Should transactions with that party in the prior year (which were disclosed in that year's financial statements) be disclosed again?

IAS 24 does not address these issues specifically, and again it is necessary to look at the underlying objective of the Standard. The purpose of the disclosures required by IAS 24 is to draw attention to the possibility that the financial statements have been affected by related party transactions. The transactions that may have affected the current period's results are those with parties that were related in the current period. The appropriate comparative information, i.e. transactions that may have affected the comparative period's results, would therefore be transactions with parties that were related in the comparative period. Under this approach, the financial statements should disclose:

- the impact on amounts reported in the current year of transactions with parties who are related during the current year; and
- as a comparative, the impact on amounts reported in the prior year of transactions with parties who were related during the prior year.

Where this is deemed to give insufficient explanation, then additional disclosure may be given.

Example 5.3.5A

Transactions with party related in the current year, but not in the prior year

Sales were made to A Limited in both the current and prior years. If A Limited is a related party in the current year, but was not a related party in the prior year, should comparatives be disclosed?

Comparatives should not be disclosed, as there was no related party relationship that may have affected the comparative period's results. Where the absence of comparatives may create confusion, then an additional explanation might be provided, stating that, while similar transactions were entered into in the prior period, they were not related party transactions, as the related party relationship did not exist in that period.

Example 5.3.5B

Transactions with party related in the prior year, but not in the current year

Sales were made to B Limited in both the current and prior years. If B Limited was a related party in the prior year, but is not a related party in the current year, should the prior year's sales be disclosed as related party transactions again in the current year's financial statements? If so, should the current year's sales also be disclosed even though B Limited is no longer related?

The prior year's sales should be disclosed again, since the related party transactions may have impacted the comparative figures in the financial statements. The current year's sales should not be disclosed, since B Limited is no longer related. Where the inclusion of comparatives but not current period figures may create confusion, then an additional explanation might be provided, stating that, while similar transactions occurred in the current period, they are not related party transactions, as the related party relationship did not exist in that period.

6 Additional disclosure requirements for UK companies

6.1 Introduction

6.1.1 Sources of disclosure requirements

In addition to the requirements of IAS 24, discussed above, UK companies adopting IFRSs will nevertheless find that disclosure of transactions with related parties continues to be required by: UK

(*a*) *statute (**sections 6.2** and **6.3** below);*

(*b*) *the Listing Rules (**section 6.4** below); and*

(*c*) *the AIM Rules (**section 6.5** below).*

In many cases, transactions caught by the above requirements will also be caught by IAS 24. Note, however, that additional disclosures (such as the names of transacting parties) may be needed to comply with these UK requirements.

*The requirements under the Companies Act 2006 are summarised at **6.2** and the requirements under the Companies Act 1985 are summarised at **6.3**. The disclosure requirements under the Companies Act 2006 supersede those of the Companies Act 1985 for periods beginning on or after 6 April 2008. The requirements of the Companies Act 2006 in respect of loans to directors (and similar transactions with or on behalf of directors) supersede those of the Companies Act 1985 from 1 October 2007.*

The requirements of the Listing Rules and of the AIM Rules that are addressed here are only those relating to the disclosures required in the annual financial statements of listed or AIM companies. It should be noted that there are additional requirements in certain cases, e.g. to notify the Financial Services Authority or, for AIM companies, the London Stock

Exchange in writing of the proposed transaction. Reference should be made to the Listing Rules (for listed companies) or the AIM Rules (for AIM companies) for additional detail.

6.2 Companies Act 2006

6.2.1 *Statutory disclosures of transactions with directors*

6.2.1.1 Introduction

UK

The disclosure requirements for directors' loans and transactions in Part II of Schedule 6 to the 1985 Act have been replaced with new provisions in section 413 of the 2006 Act. These provisions are more limited than the requirements of the 1985 Act (see ***6.3*** *below) in terms of the transactions covered and the disclosures required. However, as directors and certain parties closely related to them are related parties under IAS 24, in practice there will be little difference in the disclosures required in most cases.*

The disclosure requirements of the 2006 Act are effective for financial years beginning on or after 6 April 2008.

6.2.1.2 *Persons affected*

UK

Disclosure is required of relevant transactions with persons who were directors of the company at any time during the financial year to which the accounts relate. In contrast to the 1985 Act, 'shadow directors' are not included for the purpose of the disclosure requirement, although they remain included for the purpose of approval of loans and similar arrangements (see ***6.2.2*** *below).*

Furthermore, in contrast to the 1985 Act, these disclosures are not required for persons 'connected with' directors.

6.2.1.3 *Transactions which require disclosure*

UK

Section 413 of the 2006 Act requires the disclosures set out below.

In the case of a parent company that prepares group accounts, the notes to the group accounts must disclose details of:

(*a*) *advances and credits granted to the directors of the parent company, by that company or by any of its subsidiary undertakings; and*

(*b*) *guarantees of any kind entered into on behalf of the directors of the parent company, by that company or by any of its subsidiary undertakings.*

In the case of a company that does not prepare group accounts, the notes to the individual accounts must disclose details of:

(*a*) *advances and credits granted by the company to its directors; and*

(*b*) *guarantees of any kind entered into by the company on behalf of its directors.*

These requirements apply in relation to every advance, credit or guarantee subsisting at any time in the financial year to which the accounts relate:

(*a*) *whenever it was entered into;*

(*b*) *whether or not the person concerned was a director of the company in question at the time it was entered into; and*

(*c*) *in the case of an advance, credit or guarantee involving a subsidiary undertaking of that company, whether or not that undertaking was such a subsidiary undertaking at the time it was entered into.*

6.2.1.4 *Particulars to be disclosed*

UK

The details required of an advance or credit are:

(*a*) *its amount;*

(*b*) *an indication of the interest rate;*

(*c*) *its main conditions; and*

(*d*) *any amounts repaid.*

Banking companies need only to state details of the amount of the advance or credit.

The details required of a guarantee are:

(*a*) *its main terms;*

(*b*) *the amount of the maximum liability that may be incurred by the company (or its subsidiary); and*

(c) *any amount paid and any liability incurred by the company (or its subsidiary) for the purpose of fulfilling the guarantee (including any loss incurred by reason of enforcements of the guarantee).*

Banking companies need only to state details of the amount of the maximum liability that may be incurred by the company (or its subsidiary).

In contrast with the requirements under the 1985 Act, there is no specific requirement to name the director or directors concerned.

The notes to the accounts must also disclose the totals (i.e. for all such arrangements for all directors) of:

(a) *the amounts of any advances or credits;*

(b) *the amounts repaid of any advances or credits;*

(c) *the maximum amount of any liability that may be incurred by the company, or its subsidiary, in the case of a guarantee; and*

(d) *any amounts paid, and any liabilities incurred, by the company, or its subsidiary, for the purpose of fulfilling a guarantee (including any loss incurred by reason of enforcement of the guarantee).*

6.2.2 *Loans to directors*

6.2.2.1 Restrictions on loans to directors

UK *The legislation concerning restrictions on loans to, and similar transactions with or on behalf of, directors is contained in sections 197 to 214 of the Companies Act 2006 and is effective from 1 October 2007. Any loan entered into before 1 October 2007 must comply with the approval requirements of the 1985 Act. If such a loan remains outstanding at 1 October 2007 no further approval is required under the 2006 Act.*

A company is able to carry out the required approval procedures of the 2006 Act for a transaction entered into after 1 October 2007 before that date, provided that the procedures are carried out fully in accordance with the 2006 Act.

Certain transactions can only be entered into with directors (or persons connected with directors) if the transaction has been approved by a resolution of the members of the company, and, in the case of a transaction with a director (or persons connected with directors) of the company's holding company, approved by a resolution of the members of the holding company.

In order for the resolution to be passed, a memorandum must be made available to the members setting out:

(*a*) *the nature of the transaction;*

(*b*) *the amount of the loan and the purpose for which it is required; and*

(*c*) *the extent of the company's liability under any transaction connected with the loan.*

The transactions which require this approval are:

- *for all companies, a loan to the director of the company or holding company or a guarantee given to provide security in connection with a loan made by any person to such a director.*
- *for public companies or companies associated with public companies, a loan to a person connected with directors of the company or holding company or a guarantee given to provide security in connection with a loan made by any person to a person connected with such a director.*
- *for public companies or companies associated with public companies, a quasi-loan to the director or a person connected with directors of the company or holding company or a guarantee given to provide security in connection with a quasi-loan made by any person to such a director or person connected with such a director.*
- *for public companies or companies associated with public companies, entering into a credit transaction as creditor for the benefit of a director or person connected with such a director of the company or holding company or giving a guarantee to provide security in connection with a credit transaction entered into by any person for the benefit of such a director or person connected with such a director.*

A quasi-loan is defined in section 199 of the 2006 Act and is an arrangement whereby the company pays or agrees to pay sums on behalf of the person affected to be reimbursed at later date (e.g. a credit card transaction). A credit transaction is defined in section 202 of the 2006 Act and includes, for example, leasing transactions, hire purchase transactions conditional sales and other sales on deferred payment terms.

Section 203 of the 2006 Act contains provisions to ensure that companies cannot avoid obtaining the required approval from members of the company by structuring the transactions listed above using more indirect methods.

Sections 252 to 254 of the 2006 Act define persons connected with a director more broadly than did the 1985 Act. These include but are not limited to:

(*a*) *his/her spouse, civil partner, child or step-child;*

(b) *any person with whom the director lives as a partner in an enduring relationship, and the children or step-children of that person under 18 who also live with the director;*

(c) *the director's parents; and*

(d) *a company in respect of which the director and other persons connected with him/her are interested in at least 20 per cent of the equity share capital or are entitled to exercise more than 20 per cent of the voting power at a general meeting.*

Section 256 of the 2006 Act states that companies are associated if one is a subsidiary of the other or both are subsidiaries of the same body corporate. Thus, companies will be associated if there is a group of which they are both part.

6.2.2.2 *Exemptions*

UK

Sections 204 to 209 of the 2006 Act state the following circumstances in which approval of the members is not required for companies to enter into loans, quasi-loans and credit transactions for the benefit of one or more of the directors:

(a) *when a director incurs expenditure on company business and has received funds to meet this expenditure (providing the total value is less than £50,000);*

(b) *when a director is being funded for expenditure incurred either defending criminal or civil proceedings in connection with any alleged negligence, default, breach of duty or breach of trust by him/her in relation to the company or an associated company, or in connection with any application for relief, providing certain terms are met (see below);*

(c) *when a director is being funded to defend himself/herself in an investigation by a regulatory authority or against action proposed by a regulatory authority in connection with any alleged negligence, default, breach of duty or breach of trust by him/her in relation to the company or an associated company;*

(d) *when the total value of the loan or quasi-loan and any other relevant transaction or arrangement is less than £10,000, or the total value of the credit transaction and any other relevant transaction or arrangement is less than £15,000;*

(e) *when the credit transaction is entered into by the company in the usual course of business and is on the same terms as would be offered to a comparable but unconnected person;*

(f) *when the transaction is between two companies in the same group; and*

(g) *when the company is a money lending company and the transaction is in the ordinary course of the company's business.*

Additionally, wholly-owned subsidiaries are exempt from the requirement to obtain members' approval.

In the case of (b) above, if a company agreed to provide funds to a director for legal proceedings prior to 1 October 2007 and the case continues running past that date, the company is permitted to fulfil that agreement without requiring further approval under the 2006 Act.

6.2.3 *Transactions with officers other than directors*

In contrast to the 1985 Act, there are no requirements for disclosures in respect of arrangements made by the company or any of its subsidiaries for persons who were officers of the company, but not directors, at any time during the financial year. However, an officer of the company who is not a director may fall within the scope of the disclosure requirements of IAS 24 for 'key management personnel' (see **4.6** *above).* UK

6.2.4 *Shareholder approval*

A transaction in which a director is interested may need shareholder approval, even if the company's articles permit such interests. Similarly, sections 190 to 195 of the 2006 Act state that a company may not enter into an arrangement with a director for the sale or purchase of a substantial non-cash asset unless the arrangement has been approved or is to be approved by a resolution of the company's members. This is effective from 1 October 2007, replacing a similar requirement under the 1985 Act (see **6.3.4** *below).* UK

An asset is substantial in relation to a company if its value exceeds 10% of the company's asset value and is more than £5,000, or exceeds £100,000.

Exemptions from the requirement for approval include when:

(*a*) *the transaction is between a holding company and its wholly-owned subsidiary or two wholly-owned subsidiaries of the same holding company;*

(*b*) *a company is being wound up or is in administration;*

(*c*) *a transaction is on a recognised investment exchange and is effected through the agency of a person who acts as an independent broker on that transaction; and*

(*d*) *a transaction is between a company and a person in his character as a member of the company.*

Arrangements entered into without the requisite approval may be voided at the instance of the company, unless certain terms are met. [CA 2006 s195]

Where a transaction or arrangement is entered into without the requisite approval, but within a reasonable period is affirmed by a resolution of the members of the relevant company, the transaction or arrangement may no longer be avoided under section 195.

6.3 Companies Act 1985

6.3.1 *Statutory disclosures of transactions with directors*

6.3.1.1 *Persons affected*

UK *Disclosure is required of relevant transactions with:*

(*a*) *persons who were directors, including 'shadow directors', of the company or its holding company, at any time during the financial year; and*

(*b*) *persons connected with them.*

A shadow director is a person in accordance with whose directions or instructions other directors are accustomed to act. However, a person is not deemed to be a shadow director by reason only that the directors act on advice given by him in a professional capacity.

Persons connected with a director were defined in section 346 of the 1985 Act, but this section was repealed with effect from 1 October 2007. Schedule 6 to the 1985 Act was amended with effect from the same date to say that references to connected persons in that Schedule should be interpreted according to the definition given in sections 252 to 255 of the 2006 Act. As noted at **6.2.2.1** *above, that definition is broader in some respects than the one in section 346 of the 1985 Act.*

However, in relation to years ending on or after 6 April 2008, further amendments were made to Schedule 6 to remove the references to connected persons such that transactions with them were no longer within the scope of the disclosure requirements. This change was made after the Government recognised that it had inadvertently made the requirements more onerous by applying the broader definition of connected persons in the 2006 Act to these disclosures.

6.3.1.2 *Transactions which require disclosure*

The following transactions should be disclosed if they were made for any person affected (as described in **6.3.1.1** *above) by the company or any of its subsidiaries:* UK

[CA 1985 Sch. 6: 15 and 16]

(a) loans;

(b) quasi-loans (i.e. arrangements whereby the company pays or agrees to pay sums on behalf of the person affected to be reimbursed at a later date, e.g. credit card transactions);

(c) credit transactions (i.e. leasing transactions, hire purchase transactions, conditional sales and other sales on deferred payment terms);

(d) guarantees or provisions of security for any loans, quasi-loans or credit transactions made by a third party;

(e) any agreement to enter into any of the above transactions; and

(f) any other transaction or arrangement in which the person affected had directly or indirectly a material interest (see **6.3.1.3** *below for the definition of material interest).*

The Companies Act 1985 does not define a loan, but a definition which has received judicial approval is 'a sum of money lent for a time to be returned in money or money's worth'. Thus, an essential ingredient of a loan is that there should be an intention of the parties that it should be repaid at some future time. On this basis, an amount drawn by a director on account of remuneration (e.g. of a bonus which only becomes payable when approved at the annual meeting or a prepayment of a salary) would not necessarily be classified as a loan. Similarly, advances of sums which are intended to meet expenses to be incurred on the company's business are not necessarily loans.

Every case should be considered on its merits, however, and on the substance of the transaction. If a sum advanced to a director purports to be on account of remuneration, then PAYE ought to be applied at the time of payment and, if this is not done, then the payment may assume the characteristics of a loan. Similarly, advances made on account of expenses, which are clearly in excess of any amount a director could reasonably be expected to incur within a reasonable time, are probably entered into in order to give the director the benefit of the use of the money and should therefore be classified as loans. In any case, amounts advanced may require the approval of shareholders (see **6.3.2.2** *and* **6.3.4** *below).*

It is specifically enacted that disclosure is required even if:

[CA 1985 Sch. 6: 19]

(*a*) *the transaction or arrangement is prohibited under the applicable company law (the 2006 Act requirements replaced those of the 1985 Act with effect from 1 October 2007);*

(*b*) *the person for whom it was made was not a director or connected person at the time it was made; or*

(*c*) *the company making the transaction is a subsidiary company which was not a subsidiary at the time it was made.*

Any transaction with a director or with a person connected with him is treated as a transaction in which that director is interested, but disclosure is not required if:

(*a*) *a director is interested in a transaction or arrangement with another company only by virtue of being a director of that other company (this would not apply if he was also a shareholder of that company);*

(*b*) *it is in respect of a director's contract of service; or*

(*c*) *the transaction or arrangement was not entered into during the financial year and did not subsist at any time during it. [CA 1985 Sch. 6: 18]*

A loan from a director to his company or to a subsidiary company is a 'transaction or arrangement' which must be disclosed, unless it can be excluded as not material, as discussed in **6.3.1.3** *below.*

6.3.1.3 Materiality

UK *Transactions and arrangements which should be disclosed under* **6.3.1.2**(*f*) *above are restricted to those in which the director's interest is 'material', but there are some differences of view as to how materiality should be judged in this context.*

It is suggested that the best way to approach the matter is to consider whether disclosure of the transactions might reasonably be expected to influence decisions made by the users of the financial statements. The required disclosure is of significant information concerning the existing relationship between the company and its directors and of matters which might affect this relationship in the future. On this basis, it is not necessary to disclose a director's interest in a transaction on the grounds that the interest is material to the transaction as a whole if the transaction itself is insignificant; on the other hand, an item should not be excluded from disclosure merely because the amount involved is small in relation to the amounts included in the accounts, such as turnover or profit.

The Companies Act 1985 specifically provides that if a majority of the directors (excluding the director whose interest is under consideration) resolve that an interest in a particular transaction or arrangement is not material, then that is conclusive and the interest need not be disclosed under the requirement in ***6.3.1.2****(f) above. [CA 1985 Sch. 6: 17] However, this would not, of itself, preclude the transaction from disclosure under IAS 24.*

6.3.1.4 *Permitted exemptions from the statutory disclosures*

There are no exemptions from the disclosure requirements of (a) to (e) in the first paragraph of ***6.3.1.2*** *above.* UK

In addition to the exemptions in ***6.3.1.2*** *above, other exemptions from the requirement in (f) in the first paragraph of* ***6.3.1.2*** *above (to disclose transactions or arrangements in which a director has a material interest) are:*

(*a*) *transactions or arrangements entered into by a company in the ordinary course of business and on an arm's-length basis (i.e. on terms not less favourable to either party to the arrangement, than would have been obtained if there had been no director's interest); [CA 1985 Sch. 6: 20]*

(*b*) *transactions or arrangements entered into by a company when the following conditions are met:*

[CA 1985 Sch. 6: 21]

(*i*) *the company is a member of a group;*

(*ii*) *either the company is wholly owned or no other group member (other than the company or a subsidiary of the company) is involved in the transaction or arrangement;*

(*iii*) *the director in question was at some time during the relevant period associated (see (c) in* **6.3.1.1** *above) with the company; and*

(*iv*) *the material interest of the director would not have arisen if he had not been associated with the company at any time during the relevant period; and*

(*c*) *transactions or arrangements in which any director was interested if the aggregate value of the transactions or arrangements for that director made after the commencement of the financial year, together with any liability outstanding in respect of transactions or arrangements entered into before the beginning of that year, did not exceed £1,000 or, if they did exceed £1,000, did not exceed the lower of £5,000 or one per cent of the net assets of the company at the year end, whichever is the less. [CA 1985 Sch. 6: 25]*

The Companies Act 1985 refers to exemption (a) above in terms of each party to the transaction being a member of the same group of companies. Therefore, it has been suggested that the exemption cannot apply where the transacting parties are not group companies. However, it appears that the drafting of the Act is deficient as the Explanatory Note to the 1984 Statutory Instrument that first inserted the exemption stated that 'these Regulations amend …. so as to exempt from disclosure …. any transactions in which a director has a material interest if that transaction is entered into at arm's length and in the ordinary course of business'. Accordingly, in the past the view has been taken that in interpreting this opaque wording in the Act, it is reasonable to look at the intention of the provision and not restrict the exemption to transactions between group companies. But this point is now of less relevance because material transactions would have to be disclosed to comply with IAS 24 even if exempted by the Companies Act 1985.

The example below illustrates the exemptions noted above.

Example 6.3.1.4

Permitted exemptions from statutory disclosures

Mr X has a 60 per cent shareholding in company A, which has two direct subsidiaries, B and C. (Hence, as discussed in (c) in **6.3.1.1** above, Mr X is associated with A, B and C.) Mr X is a director of all three companies.

Suppose that B transacts with C, and that the transaction is not at arm's-length (so the exemption in (a) above is not available). So far as B is concerned, Mr X has an interest in the transaction because he is associated with C (and vice versa so far as C is concerned). If Mr X's interest is material, in which companies' accounts, if any, does the Companies Act 1985 require it to be disclosed?

Applying the exemption in (b) above, no disclosure will be required in A's accounts because the only group members involved in the transaction are subsidiaries of A. So far as the accounts of B and C are concerned, the answer will depend on whether they are wholly-owned subsidiaries:

(a) if B and C are both wholly-owned subsidiaries, no disclosure is required;

(b) if one is wholly-owned but not the other, the exemption will be available only to the wholly-owned subsidiary;

(c) if neither B nor C is wholly-owned, disclosure will be required in both subsidiaries' accounts.

Accordingly, disclosure is made in the accounts of any subsidiary that is not wholly-owned. In effect, the exemption in (b) above is not available where there is a non-controlling interest that might be affected by a transaction not at arm's-length.

There is also an exemption from disclosure of credit transactions, guarantees of credit transactions and agreements to enter into credit transactions in respect of any individual director if the aggregate outstanding balance of such transactions entered into for that director and persons connected with him did not exceed £5,000 at any one time during the financial year. [CA 1985 Sch. 6: 24] Only reduced disclosures are required for loans or quasi-loans between two companies where one is a wholly owned subsidiary of the other or both are wholly owned subsidiaries of another company. In such cases, only the disclosures in (a), (b) and (c) in ***6.3.1.5*** *below are required. [CA 1985 Sch. 6: 23]* UK

6.3.1.5 *Particulars to be disclosed*

The particulars to be disclosed are: UK

[CA 1985 Sch. 6: 22]

(a) *the principal terms of the transaction;*

(b) *a statement that the loan, guarantee, transaction, etc. was made or subsisted during the financial year;*

(c) *the name of the person for whom it was made (if the person is a connected person, the name of the director with whom he is connected must also be given);*

(*d*) *in the case of a loan made or to be made, the amount of the liability in respect of principal and interest at the beginning and end of the financial year, the maximum amount of the liability during the financial year, any interest due which has not been paid and the amount of any provision made against the loan or accrued interest;*

(*e*) *where a company has guaranteed or provided security for a loan, the amount for which the company (or its subsidiary) was liable at the beginning and end of the financial year, the maximum potential liability and the amount of any actual liability incurred;*

(*f*) *in the case of quasi-loans and credit transactions, the value of the transaction; and*

(*g*) *in the case of any other transaction or arrangement in which a director had a material interest, the name of the director concerned, the nature of the interest and the value of the transaction or arrangement.*

The value of a transaction or arrangement is the value which would be attached on an arm's-length basis in the ordinary course of business to the goods or services which are the subject of the transaction. If the transaction is a loan or guarantee, it is the principal of the loan or the amount guaranteed or secured. In the case of a quasi-loan it is the amount, or maximum amount, which the person to whom the quasi-loan is made, is liable to reimburse the creditor. [CA 1985 s340]

The above rules are summarised in the table below. Corresponding amounts are not required.

Table 6.3.1.5

Particulars to be discussed	Loans	Quasi-loans	Credit transactions	Guarantee (for security)	Other material transactions exc. service contracts
1. The principal terms of the transaction etc., including: 2. A statement that the transaction etc., was made or subsisted during the year; 3. The name of the director (and, where applicable, the connected person);	Yes	Yes	Yes – except where the aggregate outstanding sum for a director (including connected persons) did not exceed £5,000 during the financial year	Yes	Yes – except where the aggregate interest in each transaction with a director (including connected persons) did not exceed the higher of either: i) the lower of £5,000 and 1% of net assets; or ii) £1,000 during the financial year.

Table 6.3.1.5

Particulars to be discussed	Loans	Quasi-loans	Credit transactions	Guarantee (for security)	Other material transactions exc. service contracts
4. The nature of the director's interest in the transaction (including a deemed interest in relation to a connected person);	N/A	N/A	N/A	N/A	Yes – except as above.
5. The amount due (including interest) at the beginning and end of the financial year; 6. The maximum amount due during the financial year; 7. The amount of unpaid interest; 8. The amount of any provision;	Yes	No – but see 9. below	No	No – but see 10 to 12 below	No
9. The value of the transaction etc.;	No – but see 5 to 8 above	Yes	Yes – except as above	No – but see 10 to 12 below	Yes – except as above
10. The amounts guaranteed (secured) at the beginning and end of the financial year; 11. The maximum liability guaranteed (secured); and 12. Any amounts paid or incurred since the inception of the guarantee (security).	No	No	No	Yes	No

If the financial statements do not give the information detailed above, the auditor must give it in his report. [CA 1985 s237(4)]

There are specific exemptions relating to banking companies [CA 1985 Sch. 9: Pt IV: 2], which are not covered by the table above. Where advantage is taken of the exemption for banking companies, s343 of the Companies

Act 1985 sets out specific requirements in respect of keeping a register of transactions with directors and the resulting auditor's responsibilities.

6.3.2 *Loans to directors*

6.3.2.1 *Restrictions on loans to directors*

UK

The legislation concerning restrictions on loans to and similar transactions with or on behalf of directors and persons connected with them is contained in sections 330 to 347 of the Companies Act 1985. These sections were repealed with effect from 1 October 2007 and replaced with different (and less onerous) requirements under the 2006 Act which are summarised at ***6.2.2.1*** *above.*

The Act provides that:

[CA 1985 s330]

(*a*) *a company shall not make a loan to a director or to a director of its holding company or guarantee or provide security in connection with a loan made by any person to such a director;*

(*b*) *a 'relevant' company shall not make a loan or a quasi-loan to, enter into a credit transaction as creditor for, or guarantee or provide security in connection with a loan, quasi-loan or credit transaction to its director or a director of its holding company or to a person 'connected' with such a director. A 'relevant' company is defined by the Companies Act 1985 as a company which is either a public limited company or a member of a group which includes a public limited company; [CA 1985 s331(6)]*

(*c*) *a company shall not arrange for the assignment to it, or the assumption by it, of any rights, obligations or liabilities under a transaction which, if the company had entered into it, would have been prohibited by (a) and (b) above;*

(*d*) *a company shall not take part in any arrangement whereby another person enters into a transaction described in (a), (b) and (c) above and in return that person obtains some benefit from the company or another company in the group.*

Thus, provided that the company is not a relevant company, e.g. a private company which is a member of a group consisting entirely of private companies, it may lawfully:

(*a*) *make a loan to a person connected with a director (see* **6.3.1.1** *above for details of a connected person); or*

(*b*) *make a quasi-loan to a director or to a person connected with a director; or*

(*c*) *enter into a credit transaction with a director or a person connected with a director.*

6.3.2.2 *Exemptions*

The following are excepted from the rules in **6.3.2.1** *above concerning the restriction of loans to and similar transactions with directors. However, it should be noted that these exemptions relate to the legality of the transaction, and not to the disclosure requirements of the Companies Act 1985. All transactions and arrangements in section 330 of the Act should be disclosed in the financial statements including the following permitted transactions:* UK

(*a*) *loans to directors if the aggregate amount to any director does not exceed £5,000; [CA 1985 s334]*

(*b*) *loans and quasi-loans to, and credit transactions in respect of, a holding company and entering into guarantees or providing security to a third party in connection with loans, quasi-loans and credit transactions in respect of a holding company; [CA 1985 s336]*

(*c*) *relevant companies making loans and quasi-loans to, or guarantees for, a fellow group company where the connection is only that the director of one company is associated (see* **6.3.1.1** *above) with the other; [CA 1985 s333]*

(*d*) *credit transactions, and guarantees and security in connection with credit transactions, up to £10,000 or where entered into in the normal course of business and on normal commercial arm's-length terms; [CA 1985 s335]*

(*e*) *provision to a director of a company (but not to a director of its holding company) of funds to meet expenditure for the purposes of the company or to enable him to perform his duties as an officer of the company. The provision must either be approved in advance at a general meeting or made on conditions that, unless it is approved at or before the next annual general meeting, it will be repaid within the six months thereafter. In a relevant company, the provision must not exceed £20,000; [CA 1985 s337] and*

(*f*) *quasi-loans aggregating not more than £5,000 which are required to be repaid within two months. [CA 1985 s332]*

A loan made to an employee before he is appointed to the board is not of itself illegal, since it is the making of a loan to a director, rather than the existence of the loan, which is addressed by the Companies Act 1985. However, once the employee becomes a director, any increase in the loan due to further advances or the accruing of interest would be subject to the restrictions.

Money carried by a director on behalf of a company is often not a provision of funds to that director. For example, cash (or traveller's cheques) given to a director to settle company expenses incurred on an overseas visit, but which is not available for the director's own use, will, in many cases, not need to be disclosed, because the director obtains no benefit from carrying such cash. Generally speaking, expense advances therefore would not constitute a loan. The reason for this is that ordinary expense advances are not intended to be repaid by the recipient; the intention is that the recipient should use the amount advanced in his/her capacity as agent for, and for the benefit of, the company. The position will not usually change if the amount advanced exceeds the subsequent expenditure, provided that the recipient accounts promptly to the company for the difference. However, it should be borne in mind that in circumstances where the amount advanced is clearly excessive, remains unspent for an unduly long time or if the money had been paid into the director's bank account, then the recipient is likely to have derived some personal benefit. The transaction then takes on the nature of a loan and is disclosable if the recipient is a director or an officer. If the sum advanced is large, it may be illegal. It is important, therefore, that companies have procedures for keeping expense advances within bounds.

There are additional exemptions for money lending companies which are summarised along with the above rules in the table below.

Table 6.3.2.2

Permitted for:	Loans	Quasi-loans	Credit transactions
Any company	A company may make a loan to a director if the aggregate amount does not exceed £5,000. [CA 1985 s334] A company may provide a director with funds (up to £20,000 in the case of a public company or member of a group which includes a public company) to meet expenditure for the purposes of the company or to enable him to perform his duties. Approval of the company in a general meeting is required, failing which the loan etc., is repayable within six months. [CA 1985 s337]		

Permitted for:	Loans	Quasi-loans	Credit transactions
Public company or member of a group which includes a public company	Not permitted (except as above).	Only if reimbursable within two months, and the total for the director does not exceed £5,000. [CA 1985 s332] Not permitted to a connected person	Either: where the transaction is under normal commercial terms; or where the total for the director does not exceed £10,000 [CA 1985 s335]
Private company not a member of a group which includes a public company	Not permitted to a director (except as above). May be made to a connected person.	Permitted.	Permitted.
Money lending company	Either: where loan etc., is under normal commercial terms, with an upper limit of £100,000 per director (no upper limit for a recognised bank or for a private company not being a member of a group which includes a public company); or where the loan etc., is in the ordinary course of business, on terms available to other employees and is in connection with the purchase or improvement of the director's main residence, with an upper limit of £100,000 per director. [CA 1985 s338]		No special rules

In each case noted above, the monetary amounts must take into account not just the value of any proposed transaction, but also:

(*a*) *the amount outstanding in respect of any existing transaction of the same type made under the same exception by the company (or its subsidiary); and*

(*b*) *the value of any existing arrangements under section 330(6) or 330(7) of the Companies Act 1985 made under the same exception by the company (or its subsidiary).*

6.3.3 *Transactions with officers other than directors*

6.3.3.1 *Statutory disclosure requirements*

The notes to the accounts should disclose information in respect of arrangements made by the company or any of its subsidiaries for persons who were officers of the company at any time during the financial year, but who were not directors. [CA 1985 s232] UK

Under the Companies Act 1985, an officer includes a director, manager or secretary of a corporate entity. [CA 1985 s744]

Courts have laid different interpretations on what constitutes a manager, but in the case Re a Company (1980) 1 All ER 284, the judge stated: 'The expression "manager" should not be too narrowly construed. It is not to be equated with a managing or other director or a general manager. As I see it, any person who in the affairs of a company exercises a supervisory control which reflects the general policy of the company for the time being or which is related to the general administration of the company is in the sphere of management.' Although it is not clearly stated in the Companies Act 1985, it seems that an auditor of the company will be considered by the courts to be an officer.

The information to be disclosed is the aggregate amount, for all officers other than directors, outstanding at the end of the financial year under each of the following headings:

[CA 1985 Sch. 6: 28 and 29]

- *loans;*
- *quasi-loans; and*
- *credit transactions.*

In each case, guarantees and securities for these items and agreements to enter into such arrangements are to be included under the appropriate heading.

The number of officers for whom they were made in each case should also be stated.

If the aggregate of such arrangements outstanding at the end of the financial year in respect of any individual officer does not exceed £2,500, then the arrangements in respect of that officer may be excluded from the amounts disclosed.

6.3.3.2 Other requirements

UK

An officer of the company, who is not a director, may fall within the scope of the disclosure requirements of IAS 24 for 'key management personnel' (see **4.6** *above).*

6.3.4 *Shareholder approval*

UK

A transaction in which a director is interested may need shareholder approval, even if the company's articles permit such interests. For example, amounts advanced to directors may require shareholder approval (see (e) in **6.3.2.2** *above). Similarly, unless approval is first given in the general meeting, a company may not enter into a substantial property transaction whereby a director of the company or its holding company (or a person connected with such a director) acquires non-cash assets of the requisite value from the company or the company acquires non-cash assets of the requisite value from such a person. A non-cash asset is of the requisite value if it exceeds the lower of:*

(i) *£100,000; and*

(ii) *10 per cent of the company's 'net assets', subject to a de minimis limit of £2,000.*

If the company has failed to obtain prior approval, the directors should take legal advice, although it may be possible to reduce the likelihood of an action being brought to enforce the civil remedies available under the Companies Act 1985 [CA 1985 s322] by ratifying the transaction.

6.4 Listing Rules requirements

6.4.1 *Contracts of significance and transactions with controlling shareholders*

UK

The Listing Rules require listed companies to disclose the following:

[LR 9.8.4R(10) and (11)]

(a) *details of any contract of significance (see below for the definition) subsisting during the period under review, to which the company, or one of its subsidiary undertakings, is a party and in which a director of the company is or was materially interested;*

(b) *details of any contract of significance subsisting during the period between the company, or one of its subsidiary undertakings, and a controlling shareholder; and*

(c) *details of any contract for the provision of services to the company or any of its subsidiary undertakings by a controlling shareholder, subsisting during the period under review; an exception is allowed if*

the services provided are those which it is the principal business of the shareholder to provide and the contract is not a 'contract of significance'.

A 'contract of significance' is defined as one which represents in amount or value (or, as the case may be, in annual amount or value) a sum equal to one per cent or more, calculated on a group basis where relevant, of:

[Glossary to FSA Handbook]

(*a*) *in the case of a capital transaction or a transaction of which the principal purpose or effect is the granting of credit, the aggregate of the group's share capital and reserves; or*

(*b*) *in other cases, the total annual purchases, sales, payments or receipts, as the case may be, of the group.*

The UK Listing Authority does not specify where this information is to be given in the annual report and accounts, but it is usual to comply with the UK Listing Authority requirements in the directors' report. However, if a 'contract of significance' requires disclosure as a material contract under the statutory rules or under IAS 24, it should also be disclosed in the financial statements or cross-referenced to the directors' report in the notes to the financial statements.

6.4.2 *Related party transactions*

UK

Chapter 11 of the Listing Rules sets out requirements that apply to transactions between a listed company (or any of its subsidiary undertakings) and a related party. The main requirements of that chapter, which will apply to large transactions or arrangements, involve the company making a notification, sending a circular containing specified information to shareholders, and obtaining shareholder approval for the transaction before it is entered into or, if conditional on such approval, before it is completed. [LR 11.1.7R]

However, certain related party transactions are exempt, as listed in LR 11 Annex 1R, and, in addition, there are less onerous requirements for certain 'smaller related party transactions' meeting the criteria set out in LR 11.1.10R (see below for details). The Listing Rules require listed companies to make disclosure of those smaller related party transactions. [LR 9.8.4R(3)] Companies must undertake in writing to the UK Listing Authority to include details of the transaction or arrangement in the company's next published annual accounts including, if relevant:

[LR 11.1.10R(2)(c)]

(*a*) *the identity of the related party;*

(*b*) *the value of the consideration for the transaction or arrangement; and*

(*c*) *all other relevant circumstances.*

These rules apply to a related party transaction where each of the percentage ratios (as calculated in the class tests set out in LR 10 Annex 1, i.e. gross assets, profits, consideration and gross capital) is less than five per cent, but one or more exceeds 0.25 per cent. [LR 11.1.10R(1)] In computing the above ratios, it is necessary to aggregate all transactions which are entered into by the company (or any of its subsidiary undertakings) with the same related party (and any of its associates) in any 12-month period and which have not been approved by shareholders. [LR 11.1.11R(1)]

6.4.2.1 *Definition of 'related party transaction'*

A 'related party transaction' means: UK

[LR 11.1.5R]

(*a*) *a transaction (other than a transaction of a revenue nature in the ordinary course of business) between a listed company, or any of its subsidiary undertakings, and a related party; or*

(*b*) *any arrangements pursuant to which a listed company, or any of its subsidiary undertakings, and a related party each invests in, or provides finance to, another undertaking or asset; or*

(*c*) *any other similar transaction or arrangement (other than a transaction of a revenue nature in the ordinary course of business) between a listed company, or any of its subsidiary undertakings, and any other person the purpose and effect of which is to benefit a related party.*

In assessing whether a transaction is in the ordinary course of business, the UK Listing Authority will have regard to the size and incidence of the transaction and also whether the terms and conditions of the transaction are unusual. [LR 11.1.5A]

6.4.2.2 *Definition of 'related party'*

A 'related party' means: UK

[LR 11.1.4R]

(*a*) *a person who is (or was within the 12 months before the date of the transaction or arrangement) a substantial shareholder;*

(*b*) *a person who is (or was within the 12 months before the date of the transaction or arrangement) a director or shadow director of the listed company or of any other company which is (and, if he has ceased to be such, was while he was a director or shadow director of such other company) its subsidiary undertaking or parent undertaking or a fellow subsidiary undertaking of its parent undertaking; or*

(*c*) *a person exercising significant influence; or.*

(*d*) *an associate of a related party within (a) to (c) above.*

A 'substantial shareholder' means any person who is entitled to exercise or to control the exercise of 10 per cent or more of the votes able to be cast on all or substantially all matters at general meetings of the company (or of any company which is its subsidiary undertaking or parent undertaking or of a fellow subsidiary undertaking of its parent undertaking). Disregard for this purpose any voting rights which such a person exercises (or controls the exercise of) independently in its capacity as bare trustee, investment manager, collective investment undertaking or a long term insurer in respect of its linked long term business if no associate of that person interferes by giving direct or indirect instructions, or in any other way, in the exercise of such voting rights (except to the extent any such person confers or collaborates with such an associate which also acts in its capacity as investment manager, collective investment undertaking or long term insurer). [Glossary to FSA Handbook]

6.4.2.3 *Definition of 'associate'*

UK *The definition of an associate is set out in the Glossary to the FSA Handbook.*

(1) *In relation to a director, substantial shareholder or person exercising significant influence who is an individual, an 'associate' means:*

(*a*) *that individual's spouse, civil partner or child (together 'the individual's family');*

(*b*) *the trustees (acting as such) of any trust of which the individual or any of the individual's family is a beneficiary or discretionary object (other than a trust which is either an occupational pension scheme or an employees' share scheme which does not, in either case, have the effect of conferring benefits on persons all or most of whom are related parties);*

(c) *any company in whose equity securities the individual or any member or members (taken together) of the individual's family or the individual and any such member or members (taken together) are directly or indirectly interested (or have a conditional or contingent entitlement to become interested) so that they are (or would on the fulfilment of the condition or the occurrence of the contingency be) able:*

(i) *to exercise or control the exercise of 30 per cent or more of the votes able to be cast at general meetings on all, or substantially all, matters; or*

(ii) *to appoint or remove directors holding a majority of voting rights at board meetings on all, or substantially all, matters.*

For the purpose of (c) above, if more than one director of the listed company, its parent undertaking or any of its subsidiary undertakings is interested in the equity securities of another company, then the interests of those directors and their associates will be aggregated when determining whether that company is an associate of the director.

(2) *In relation to a substantial shareholder or person exercising significant influence which is a company, an 'associate' means:*

(a) *any other company which is its subsidiary undertaking or parent undertaking or fellow subsidiary undertaking of the parent undertaking;*

(b) *any company whose directors are accustomed to act in accordance with the substantial shareholder's or person exercising significant influence's directions or instructions;*

(c) *any company in the capital of which the substantial shareholder or person exercising significant influence and any other company under paragraph (1) or (2) taken together, is (or would on the fulfilment of a condition or the occurrence of a contingency be) able to exercise power of the type described in paragraph (1)(c)(i) or (ii) of this definition.*

6.5 Alternative Investment Market companies

AIM companies are required to disclose, in their annual audited accounts, any transaction with a related party (whether or not previously disclosed under AIM rules) where any of the class tests which are set out in schedule 3 to the AIM Rules exceed 0.25 per cent. [AIM Rule 19] The tests are: a UK *gross assets test; a profits test; a turnover test; a consideration test; and a gross capital test. As well as disclosing the transaction, the accounts must specify the identity of the related party and the consideration for the transaction. [AIM Rule 19] Where any transaction with a related party exceeds 5% in any of the class tests, an AIM company must issue notification without delay as soon as the terms of the transaction with the related party are agreed. [AIM Rule 13]*

The glossary to the AIM Rules defines a 'related party' as follows:

(*a*) *any person who is a director of an AIM company or of any company which is its subsidiary or parent undertaking, other subsidiary undertaking of its parent company;*

(*b*) *a substantial shareholder;*

(*c*) *an associate of (a) or (b) being;*

(*i*) *the family of such a person;*

(*ii*) *the trustees (acting as such) of any trust of which the individual or any of the individual's family is a beneficiary or discretionary object (other than a trust which is either an occupational pension scheme as defined in regulation 3 of the Financial Services and Markets Act 2000 (Regulated Activities) Order 2001, or an employees' share scheme which does not, in either case, have the effect of conferring benefits on persons all or most of whom are related parties).*

(*iii*) *any company in whose equity shares such a person individually or taken together with his or her family (or if a director, individually or taken together with his family and any other director of that company) are directly or indirectly interested (or have a conditional or contingent entitlement to become interested) to the extent that they are or could be able:*

- *to exercise or control the exercise of 30% or more of the votes (excluding treasury shares) able to be cast at general meetings on all, or substantially all, matters or*
- *to appoint or remove directors holding a majority of voting rights at board meetings on all, or substantially all, matters;*

(*iv*) *any other company which is its subsidiary undertaking, parent undertaking or subsidiary undertaking of its parent undertaking;*

(*v*) *any company whose directors are accustomed to act in accordance with (a)'s directions or instructions;*

> (*vi*) *any company in the capital of which* (*a*), *either alone or together with any other company within* (*iv*) *or* (*v*) *or both taken together, is* (*or would on the fulfilment of a condition or the occurrence of a contingency be*) *interested in the manner described in* (*iii*);
>
> (*d*) *for the purposes of rule 13, any person who was a director of an AIM company or any of its subsidiaries, sister or parent undertakings or a substantial shareholder within the twelve months preceding the date of the transaction.*

7 Future developments

As part of a limited project to update and clarify the requirements of IAS 24, the IASB published an exposure draft in February 2007, which proposed to amend:

- the requirements of IAS 24 for state-controlled entities when they transact with similar entities; and
- certain aspects of the definition of a related party.

Under the proposals, state-controlled entities (including associates of the state), i.e. entities controlled by national, regional or local governments, would be granted relief from the requirements of IAS 24 to disclose the relationship and transactions between themselves and fellow state-controlled entities.

The ED also proposed that the definition of related party be completely rewritten, with a view to improving its clarity. In addition, a limited number of substantive changes were proposed regarding the status of:

- an associate of a subsidiary's controlling investor;
- two associates of a person; and
- investments of members of key management personnel.

At the time of writing, it is expected that the IASB will issue a final Standard before the end of 2008.

33 Consolidated and separate financial statements

1 Introduction

IAS 27 *Consolidated and Separate Financial Statements* deals with:

- the preparation and presentation of consolidated financial statements for a group of entities under the control of a parent; and
- the accounting for investments in subsidiaries, jointly controlled entities, and associates when an entity elects, or is required by local regulations, to present separate (non-consolidated) financial statements.

The Standard was significantly revised by the IASB in January 2008 as part of its Business Combinations Project. It was most recently amended when *Improvements to IFRSs* and the Amendments to IFRS 1 and IAS 27 *Cost of an Investment in a Subsidiary, Jointly Controlled Entity or Associate* were issued in May 2008.

The most significant changes made when the Standard was revised in January 2008 were as follows:

- The revised Standard specifies that changes in a parent's ownership interest in a subsidiary that do not result in the loss of control must be accounted for as equity transactions (see **5.6.1**). The previous version did not include any guidance for such transactions.

- The revised Standard modifies how an entity measures any gain or loss arising on the loss of control of a subsidiary. Any such gain or loss is recognised in profit or loss. Any investment retained in the former subsidiary is measured at its fair value at the date when control is lost (see **5.7.1**). The previous version required the carrying amount of an investment retained in the former subsidiary to be regarded as its cost on initial measurement of the financial asset in accordance with IAS 39 *Financial Instruments: Recognition and Measurement*.

- The revised Standard requires total comprehensive income to be attributed to the owners of the parent and to the non-controlling interests even if this results in the non-controlling interests having a deficit balance (see **5.3.1.2**). The previous version required excess losses to be allocated to the owners of the parent, except to the extent that the non-controlling interests had a binding obligation and were able to make an additional investment to cover the losses.

- The term minority interest was replaced by the term non-controlling interest, with a new definition (see **5.3**). For ease of reading, the new term is used throughout this chapter, except where the context demands otherwise.

The amendments also changed the structure of IAS 27, moving and renumbering some paragraphs. Where paragraphs of the revised Standard have been amended or renumbered, this chapter makes clear to which version reference is being made (e.g. IAS 27(2008).24, previously IAS 27(2003).28). Where a paragraph is unchanged, for ease of reading, the references draw no such distinction (e.g. IAS 27.9).

UK *At the time of writing, the amended version of IAS 27 has not yet been endorsed for use in the EU. Since the requirements of the amended Standard differ in important respects from those of its predecessor, EU reporting entities will not be able to apply the revised version in their statutory financial statements until it is endorsed.*

This chapter discusses the requirements of IAS 27 in the following sections:

Section 2	Scope
Section 3	Identifying a subsidiary
Section 4	Presentation of consolidated financial statements
Section 5	Consolidation procedures
Section 6	Separate financial statements
Section 7	Disclosures
Section 8	Effective date and transition: IAS 27 (2008)
Section 9	Future developments

Note that business combinations are discussed in **chapter 34**.

IAS 27 is broadly similar to the UK standard FRS 2 Accounting for Subsidiary Undertakings*, but there are various differences. The most important of these are highlighted below.* UK

- *The definition of a subsidiary in IAS 27 differs in a number of respects from that used under UK GAAP, but in practice it is unlikely that different conclusions will be reached over whether control exists.*

- *Under IAS 27, consolidated financial statements are required (subject to exemptions) if the parent disposed of all its subsidiaries during the financial year. This differs from the position under UK GAAP, where consolidated financial statements are not prepared if the parent has no subsidiaries at the year end.*

- *The exemptions from preparing group accounts under IAS 27 are different from those set out in UK GAAP. A UK company producing IFRS accounts will only be exempt from preparing group accounts if it satisfies both IFRS and UK legal exemption criteria.*

- *Under UK GAAP, all distributions (whether out of pre- or post-acquisition profits) are taken to profit or loss and, separately, the investment is written down if impaired. In May 2008, IAS 27 was amended to require a similar approach, but at the time of writing that amendment has not yet been endorsed for use in the EU. For entities not yet applying the amended version of the Standard, distributions received out of pre-acquisition profits are deducted from the cost of an investment. Accordingly, the cost of a subsidiary undertaking for the purposes of IFRS financial statements may not be the same as the figure currently recorded in UK financial statements.*

- *Where a UK parent company producing IFRS solus accounts records an investment in a subsidiary at cost, it will not be able to take advantage of section 615 of the Companies Act 2006 (previously s133 of the Companies Act 1985), relating to merger relief and group reconstruction relief, so as to record such an investment in its solus statement of financial position at an amount less than the fair value of the consideration paid to acquire that subsidiary. This follows from the IASB Glossary definition of 'cost' which includes 'the fair value of the other consideration given'. In May 2008, IFRS 1 was amended to allow the use of deemed cost for investments in subsidiaries, jointly controlled entities and associates when entities first adopt IFRSs, but at the time of writing that amendment has not yet been endorsed for use in the EU. Until the amendment is endorsed, where a UK parent company has, prior to transition, taken advantage of CA 2006 s615*

> *(or previously CA 1985 s133) and recorded an investment in subsidiary at a lower amount, it will be necessary on first-time adoption of IFRSs to restate the investment to the full cost calculated in accordance with IAS 27.*

2 Scope

2.1 Consolidated financial statements

IAS 27 applies in the preparation and presentation of consolidated financial statements for a group of entities under the control of a parent. [IAS 27.1] Consolidated financial statements are the financial statements of a group presented as those of a single economic entity. [IAS 27.4]

A group is defined as a parent taken together with its subsidiaries. A parent is defined as an entity that has one or more subsidiaries. A subsidiary is an entity, including an unincorporated entity such as a partnership, that is controlled by another entity (the parent). [IAS 27.4]

IAS 27 sets out detailed rules as regards:

- which entities are required to prepare consolidated financial statements;
- the identification of subsidiaries;
- the procedures for the preparation of consolidated financial statements; and
- disclosures in consolidated financial statements.

2.2 Separate financial statements

IAS 27 also applies in accounting for investments in subsidiaries, jointly controlled entities and associates when an entity elects, or is required by local regulations, to present separate financial statements. [IAS 27.3]

Separate financial statements are defined as those presented by a parent, an investor in an associate, or a venturer in a jointly controlled entity, in which the investments are accounted for on the basis of the direct equity interest rather than on the basis of the reported results and the net assets of the investees. [IAS 27.4]

The Standard does not mandate which entities prepare separate financial statements – but specifies the rules to be followed in accounting for investments where such financial statements are prepared voluntarily (e.g.

for the purposes of supporting a tax return) or are required by local regulations (e.g. certain jurisdictions require the preparation and publication of stand-alone financial statements for parent entities).

> UK
>
> *Where a UK company prepares group accounts in accordance with international accounting standards, it may nevertheless choose to prepare its separate financial statements in accordance with UK GAAP, in which case these requirements of IAS 27 would not be relevant (see* ***section 3*** *of* ***chapter 1****).*

3 Identifying a subsidiary

A subsidiary is an entity, including an unincorporated entity such as a partnership, that is controlled by another entity (the parent). [IAS 27.4]

> UK
>
> *This definition of a subsidiary differs in a number of respects from that used under UK GAAP (see* ***2.3.1*** *in* ***chapter 1****), but in practice it is unlikely that different conclusions will be reached over whether control exists.*

3.1 Control

Control is the power to govern the financial and operating policies of an entity so as to obtain benefits from its activities. [IAS 27.4]

> Financial and operating policies are not defined in IAS 27. Operating policies generally would include those policies that guide activities such as sales, marketing, manufacturing, human resources, and acquisitions and disposals of investments. Financial policies generally would be those policies that guide capital expenditures, budget approvals, credit terms, dividend policies, issue of debt, cash management and accounting policies.
>
> The definition of control encompasses both the notion of governance and the economic consequence of that governance (i.e. benefits and risks). Governance relates to the power to make decisions. In the definition of control, the phrase 'power to govern' implies having the capacity or ability to accomplish something – in this case, to govern the decision-making process through the selection of financial and operating policies. This does not require active participation or ownership of shares.

Benefits may relate to current or future cash inflows either remitted to the controlling entity or remaining in control of the controlling entity. Benefits also may encompass non-monetary increases in value to the controlling entity. Risks may relate to current or future cash or non-monetary outflows paid either by the controlling entity or through assets controlled by the entity.

Ultimately, the assessment of whether or not an entity controls another is a matter of careful judgement based on all relevant facts and circumstances.

As a general rule, control is presumed to exist when an investor owns, either directly or indirectly through subsidiaries, more than 50 per cent of the voting power of an entity. In exceptional cases, however, it may be possible to demonstrate that such ownership does not constitute control. The substance of the arrangements in each case will need to be considered. [IAS 27.13]

Control can also exist, even if the parent owns 50 per cent or less of the voting power of an entity, when there is:

[IAS 27.13]

- power over more than one half of the voting rights by virtue of an agreement with other investors;
- power to govern the financial and operating policies of the entity under a statute or an agreement;
- power to appoint or remove the majority of the members of the board of directors or equivalent governing body and control of the entity is by that board or body; or
- power to cast the majority of votes at meetings of the board of directors or equivalent governing body and control of the entity is by that board or body.

The Implementation Guidance attached to IAS 27 states explicitly that the definition of control permits only one entity to have control (as distinct from joint control – see **chapter 36**) over another entity. Therefore, when two or more entities each hold significant voting rights, the factors set out in IAS 27.13 are reassessed to determine which party has control. [IAS 27.IG4]

In addition to the control indicators in IAS 27.13, the following factors should be considered in evaluating whether or not control exists. No one factor is a determinant of control, however, without a complete analysis of all the relevant facts and circumstances:

- potential voting rights (see **3.2**);
- the level of total equity or 'at risk' capital, thereby resulting in potential influence beyond voting share percentage (e.g. financial obligations due to the owner);
- the ability to sell, lease, or otherwise dispose of the entity's assets;
- the ability to enter into contracts or commitments on behalf of the entity;
- the ability to establish or take any action that could change the operating or capital policies of the entity, including selecting, terminating, or setting the compensation of the entity's management responsible for implementing the entity's policies;
- responsibility for all supervision, operation and maintenance of the entity's business and property;
- whether or not the entity is a mechanism to finance a project, and the investor will eventually acquire the project;
- whether or not the entity is an integral part of the investor's business;
- guarantee of the entity's debt; and
- possession of the right or obligation to offer to buy out the other ownership interests in the entity.

In some instances, the powers of a shareholder with a majority voting interest to control the operations or assets of an entity are restricted in certain respects by approval or veto rights granted to the minority shareholder. Those minority rights may have little or no impact on the ability of a shareholder with a majority voting interest to control an entity's financial and operating policies. In certain cases, however, those rights may be so restrictive as to call into question whether control rests with the majority owner.

The following are illustrative minority rights (whether granted by contract or by law) that may require careful consideration in the determination of control:

- selecting, terminating and setting the compensation of management responsible for implementing the investee's policies and procedures;
- establishing operating and capital decisions of the investee, including budgets, in the ordinary course of business;
- the ability to participate in determining the priority directions of an investee's activities;
- the ability of a minority investor to veto certain decisions to maintain the operation of an investee, such as the addition or deletion of certain essential services of an investee; and
- the right to veto the termination of management responsible for implementing the investee's policies and procedures.

While the existence of minority rights should be considered, the primary focus of such assessment should be on whether or not one entity controls another. This assessment should take into consideration the rights of all parties involved.

3.1.1 *De facto control*

Following a discussion at its October 2005 meeting, the IASB issued a statement that acknowledged that the concept of *de facto* control exists under IAS 27. 'De facto control' is a commonly used term for a situation where an entity owns less than 50 per cent of the voting shares in another entity, but has control for reasons other than potential voting rights, contract or other statutory means.

The circumstances in which *de facto* control can arise are likely to be very rare, and careful judgement taking account of all facts and circumstances is essential before concluding whether *de facto* control is present. In particular, the fact that the remaining share ownership in an investee is widely dispersed does not, in itself, provide sufficient evidence that an investor with a significant minority stake has control rather than significant influence. For *de facto* control to exist, other factors will need to be present having the overall effect that it is not possible, in practice, for others to prevent the investor from governing the financial and operating policies of the investee.

One scenario in which it is sometimes asserted that a company has *de facto* control over another is as follows:

- an entity has a significant ownership interest in another but that interest does not give it more than 50 per cent of the voting shares, for example 45 per cent of the voting shares;
- the investee is a publicly listed company and has an otherwise widely dispersed group of shareholders with individually insignificant shareholdings; and
- attendance at shareholder meetings aside from the significant shareholder is poor, i.e. the other shareholders are passive in practice as demonstrated by no history of collective decision-making against the significant shareholder.

Absent other factors, the 45 per cent shareholder in the example above would not have control under IAS 27. Although the other shareholders have not historically done so, they could vote together and veto certain financial and operating policy decisions requiring shareholder approval. As such, although the investee's financial and operating policies may currently be determined in accordance with the wishes of the 45 per cent shareholder, absent other factors that shareholder does not have the power to control in accordance with IAS 27's definition of control: 'control is the power to govern the financial and operating policies of an entity so as to obtain benefits from its activities'. [IAS 27.9]

Where ownership or other legal rights do not confer a majority of voting rights, 'power to govern' should be presumed not to exist unless there is very strong evidence to the contrary. It is most unlikely that a minority shareholder will be able to demonstrate that it has *de facto* control unless it has evidence that, over a period of time, it has been able to exercise control in practice, that there is a lack of institutional shareholder activism in the country and that the economic environment is one in which hostile takeovers are rare.

In summary, judgement is required in determining whether a company controls another. A conclusion that consolidation is appropriate, where an entity has less than 50 per cent of the voting power, on the basis of other factors, will be appropriate only in rare situations.

A company that consolidates on the basis of *de facto* control is required to provide clear disclosure of the basis for consolidating a subsidiary.

3.2 Potential voting rights

Potential voting rights can arise through share warrants, share call options, debt or equity instruments that are convertible into ordinary shares, or similar instruments that have the potential, if exercised or converted, to give the holder additional voting power or reduce another party's voting power over the financial and operating policies of another entity. Where an investor owns such instruments, the existence and effect of potential voting rights that are currently exercisable or currently convertible are considered when assessing whether the investor has control. Such voting rights, when they are currently exercisable or convertible, may provide the holder with a current ability to exercise control. [IAS 27.14]

Potential voting rights are not currently exercisable or convertible when, for example, they cannot be exercised or converted until a future date or until the occurrence of a future event.

The investor needs to consider the potential voting rights held by other parties in addition to those it holds itself. Although the investor may believe, after considering the impact of its own potential voting rights, that it has the power to exercise control, that impact may be negated by other potential voting rights held by other parties that are also currently exercisable or currently convertible.

In assessing whether potential voting rights contribute to the power to control, the investor examines the facts and circumstances that affect the potential rights, such as the terms of exercise of the instruments and any other contractual arrangements. IAS 27 requires that all of these factors be taken into account – but excludes consideration of the intention of management and the financial ability to exercise or convert such rights. [IAS 27.15]

The ability to exercise power does not exist when potential voting rights lack economic substance (e.g. the exercise price is set in a manner that precludes exercise or conversion in any feasible scenario). Consequently, potential voting rights are considered when, in substance, they provide the ability to exercise power. [IAS 27.IG2]

The Implementation Guidance attached to IAS 27 sets out five examples, each of which considers one aspect of a potential voting right. These examples are reproduced below for convenience.

Example 3.2A

Options are out of the money

[IAS 27.IG Example 1]

Entities A and B own 80 per cent and 20 per cent respectively of the ordinary shares that carry voting rights at a general meeting of shareholders of Entity C. Entity A sells one half of its interest to Entity D and buys call options from Entity D that are exercisable at any time at a premium to the market price when issued, and if exercised would give Entity A its original 80 per cent ownership interest and voting rights.

Though the options are out of the money, they are currently exercisable and give Entity A the power to continue to set the operating and financial policies of Entity C, because Entity A could exercise its options now. The existence of the potential voting rights, as well as the other factors described in IAS 27.13, are considered and it is determined that Entity A controls Entity C.

Example 3.2B

Possibility of exercise or conversion

[IAS 27.IG Example 2]

Entities A, B and C own 40 per cent, 30 per cent and 30 per cent respectively of the ordinary shares that carry voting rights at a general meeting of shareholders of Entity D. Entity A also owns call options that are exercisable at any time at the fair value of the underlying shares which, if exercised, would give it an additional 20 per cent of the voting rights in Entity D and reduce Entity B's and Entity C's interests to 20 per cent each. If the options are exercised, Entity A will have control over more than one half of the voting power. The existence of the potential voting rights, as well as the other factors described in IAS 27.13 and IAS 28.6 & 7, are considered and it is determined that Entity A controls Entity D.

Example 3.2C

Other rights that have the potential to increase an entity's voting power or reduce another entity's voting power

[IAS 27.IG Example 3]

Entities A, B and C own 25 per cent, 35 per cent and 40 per cent respectively of the ordinary shares that carry voting rights at a general meeting of shareholders of Entity D. Entities B and C also have share warrants that are exercisable at any time at a fixed price and provide potential voting rights. Entity A has a call option to purchase these share warrants at any time for a nominal amount. If the call option is exercised, Entity A would have the potential to increase its ownership interest, and thereby its voting rights, in Entity D to 51 per cent (and dilute Entity B's interest to 23 per cent and Entity C's interest to 26 per cent).

Although the share warrants are not owned by Entity A, they are considered in assessing control because they are currently exercisable by Entities B and C. Normally, if an action (e.g. purchase or exercise of another right) is required before an entity has ownership of a potential voting right, the potential voting right is not regarded as held by the entity. However, the share warrants are, in substance, held by Entity A, because the terms of the call option are designed to ensure Entity A's position. The combination of the call option and share warrants gives Entity A the power to set the operating and financial policies of Entity D, because Entity A could currently exercise the option and share warrants. The other factors described in IAS 27.13 and IAS 28.6 & 7 are also considered, and it is determined that Entity A, not Entity B or C, controls Entity D.

Example 3.2D

Management intention

[IAS 27.IG Example 4]

Entities A, B and C each own $33^{1/3}$ per cent of the ordinary shares that carry voting rights at a general meeting of shareholders of Entity D. Entities A, B and C each have the right to appoint two directors to the board of Entity D. Entity A also owns call options that are exercisable at a fixed price at any time that, if exercised, would give it all the voting rights in Entity D. The management of Entity A does not intend to exercise the call options, even if Entities B and C do not vote in the same manner as Entity A. The existence of the potential voting rights, as well as the other factors described in IAS 27.13 and IAS 28.6 & 7 are considered and it is determined that Entity A controls Entity D. The intention of Entity A's management does not influence the assessment.

Example 3.2E

Financial ability

[IAS 27.IG Example 5]

Entities A and B own 55 per cent and 45 per cent respectively of the ordinary shares that carry voting rights at a general meeting of shareholders of Entity C. Entity B also holds debt instruments that are convertible into ordinary shares of Entity C. The debt can be converted at a substantial price, in comparison with Entity B's net assets, at any time and if converted would require Entity B to borrow additional funds to make the payment. If the debt were to be converted, Entity B would hold 70 per cent of the voting rights and Entity A's interest would reduce to 30 per cent.

Although the debt instruments are convertible at a substantial price, they are currently convertible and the conversion feature gives Entity B the power to set the operating and financial policies of Entity C. The existence of the potential voting rights, as well as the other factors described in IAS 27.13 are considered and it is determined that Entity B, not Entity A, controls Entity C. The financial ability of Entity B to pay the conversion price does not influence the assessment.

It is important to emphasise that each illustrative example focuses only on one factor, but in practice it will always be necessary to consider all factors.

Although in **example 3.2E** above, the debt can be converted at a substantial price in comparison with Entity B's net assets, the implication is that the conversion option nevertheless has real economic substance, i.e. it is conceivable that it might be exercised. If the option price was so high as to preclude exercise in any feasible scenario, the potential voting rights would be ignored. As noted previously, potential voting rights are only considered when, in substance, they provide the ability to exercise power.

The proportion allocated to the parent and non-controlling interests in preparing consolidated financial statements in accordance with IAS 27 is determined solely on the basis of present ownership interests, because potential voting rights do not currently entitle an investor to a different share of net assets. [IAS 27.IG5]

In some circumstances, however, an entity has, in substance, a present ownership as a result of a transaction that gives it access to the economic benefits associated with an ownership interest. In such circumstances, the proportion allocated is determined taking into account the eventual exercise of those potential voting rights and other derivatives that give the entity access to the economic benefits at present. [IAS 27.IG6]

Example 3.2F

Allocation of ownership interests

Entity A has a 75 per cent ownership interest in Entity C, with Entity B holding the remaining 25 per cent interest. Entity A sells 10 per cent of its ownership interest at its fair value of £100 to Entity B and simultaneously enters into a forward agreement with Entity B to repurchase the 10 per cent ownership interest at £115. Entity B receives a 7 per cent return when the forward settles.

The sale and forward repurchase agreements are linked and the terms of the forward agreement are such that Entity A retains access to the economic benefits associated with the 10 per cent ownership interest. Therefore, the proportions allocated to Entities A and B are 75 per cent and 25 percent respectively when preparing consolidated financial statements.

Instead of entering into a forward purchase agreement, Entity A could have simultaneously written put options to and purchased call options from Entity B in relation to the 10 per cent ownership interest, with the options having substantially the same fixed strike price and exercisable at the same future date. In this circumstance, the proportions allocated to Entities A and B are still 75 per cent and 25 per cent respectively when preparing the consolidated financial statements.

When instruments containing potential voting rights in substance currently give access to the economic benefits associated with ownership interest (such as those described in **example 3.2F**), and the investment is consolidated, accounted for using the equity method, or proportionately consolidated in accordance with IAS 27, IAS 28 and IAS 31 respectively, the instruments are not subject to the requirements of IAS 39 *Financial Instruments: Recognition and Measurement*. In all other cases, instruments containing potential voting rights are accounted for in accordance with IAS 39. [IAS 27.IG7]

See also the discussion of potential voting rights at **3.2** in **chapter 13**.

3.3 Special purpose entities

SIC-12 *Consolidation – Special Purpose Entities* provides explicit guidance on the extent to which special purpose entities should be considered under the control of an investor. The Interpretation requires that such entities should be consolidated when the substance of the relationship between the parties indicates control. [SIC-12.8]

SIC-12 does not apply to post-employment benefit plans or other long-term employee benefit plans to which IAS 19 applies (see **chapter 24**). The amendment in November 2004 removed a previous scope exclusion in SIC-12 for equity compensation plans, with the effect that an entity that controls an employee benefit trust (or similar entity) set up for the purposes of a share-based payment arrangement will be required to consolidate that trust. [SIC-12.6] See **3.3.2** below and **section 9** in **chapter 25** for more guidance on employee share ownership trusts.

UK *Under UK GAAP, the assets and liabilities of an employee benefit trust are accounted for as assets and liabilities of the sponsoring entity, in accordance with UITF 38* Accounting for ESOP trusts. *This contrasts with the position under SIC-12, where, in some circumstances, such trusts might only be consolidated in group financial statements – in other words, under SIC-12 the trust assets and liabilities might, in some circumstances, only be recognised in the consolidated statement of financial position, and not in any separate statement of financial position of the sponsoring entity. This is discussed further at* ***3.3.2*** *below.*

A special purpose entity (SPE) is a corporation, trust or unincorporated entity that has been created to accomplish a narrow and well-defined objective (e.g. to effect a lease, research and development activities, or a securitisation of financial assets). [SIC-12.1]

SPEs are often created with legal arrangements that impose strict legal limits on the decision-making powers of their governing body over the operations of the SPE. Frequently, these provisions specify that the policy guiding the ongoing activities of the SPE cannot be modified, other than perhaps by its creator or sponsor (i.e. they operate on so-called 'autopilot'). The sponsor (or entity on whose behalf the SPE was created) may transfer assets to the SPE, obtain the right to use assets held by the SPE or perform services for the SPE, while other parties (the 'capital providers') may provide the funding for the SPE. A beneficial interest in an SPE may, for example, take the form of a debt instrument, an equity instrument, a participation right, a residual interest or a lease. Some beneficial interests may simply provide the holder with a fixed or stated rate of return, while others give the holder rights or access to other future economic benefits of the SPE's activities. In most cases, the creator or sponsor retains a significant beneficial interest in the SPE's activities, even though it may own little or none of the SPE's equity. [SIC-12.1 – 3]

Central to the determination of whether an entity is, in substance, an SPE is the extent to which there are limitations or restrictions on the entity's operations or activities and decision-making ability. The following factors, at a minimum, should be considered in determining whether an entity is, in substance, an SPE:

- the nature and scope of the entity's activities (e.g. are the activities limited to a single transaction type; are they limited to certain industries; are there limits on the number or amount of activities or transactions that can be entered into?);

- the ability of another entity (e.g. a sponsor or entity on whose behalf the entity was created) to limit or restrict the activities of the entity;

- the extent to which the entity can modify or change the nature and scope of its operations and activities;
- the nature and scope of the entity's customer base (e.g. is the entity restricted to serving a limited number of customers?);
- the nature and scope of the entity's decision-making ability (e.g. what is the relationship between the entity's permitted activities and its ability to effect or carry out those activities?); and
- the extent to which the entity's ability to make decisions is contingent on approval by another entity (e.g. a sponsor or entity on whose behalf the entity was created).

SIC-12 requires that an SPE should be consolidated when the substance of the relationship between the reporting entity and the SPE indicates that the SPE is controlled by that entity. [SIC-12.8] In this context, control may arise through the predetermination of the activities of the SPE (operating on 'autopilot') or otherwise. This is possible even in cases where an entity owns little or none of the SPE's equity. [SIC-12.9]

In addition to the circumstances described in IAS 27.13 (see **3.1**), where control may exist despite the absence of a majority shareholding, SIC-12 describes circumstances that may indicate that a relationship exists in which the reporting entity controls an SPE and consequently should consolidate the SPE:

[SIC-12.10]

- in substance, the activities of the SPE are being conducted on behalf of the reporting entity according to its specific business needs so that the entity obtains benefits from the SPE's operation;
- in substance, the reporting entity has the decision-making powers to obtain the majority of the benefits of the activities of the SPE or, by setting up an 'autopilot' mechanism, the entity has delegated those decision-making powers;
- in substance, the reporting entity has rights to obtain the majority of the benefits of the SPE and therefore may be exposed to risks incident to the activities of the SPE; or
- in substance, the reporting entity retains the majority of the residual or ownership risks related to the SPE or its assets in order to obtain benefits from its activities.

The application of the indicators listed above should be consistent with the notion of control, as defined in IAS 27 (see **3.1**) – that is, control encompasses both governance and benefits aspects. The first two indicators listed relate to the governance aspect of control (i.e. the activities of the SPE and its decision-making powers), while the second two indicators relate to the benefits aspect of control (i.e. benefits and risks). In its November 2006 meeting to discuss possible agenda items, the IFRIC emphasised that the factors are indicators only and not necessarily conclusive, because circumstances vary case by case. SIC-12 requires that the party having control over an SPE should be determined through the exercise of careful judgement and skill in each case, after taking into account all relevant factors.

Example 3.3

Special purpose entity

Bank A sets up a SPE which is used to issue credit-linked notes to third party investors. Bank A sets up the SPE in order to raise funding from investors whose return on that funding is driven from the performance of the underlying assets in the SPE, usually investments in corporate debt. Bank A markets the credit-linked notes to third party investors. The notes will be issued in different tranches to reflect the relative credit risk on the underlying cash that may be paid to the investors. All notes bear risk of the underlying assets, though the most junior notes will bear the first loss. The expected loss on the assets may be greater than the maximum absolute loss on the most junior notes. In this case, the note holders other than the most junior note holders also bear some of the expected losses. Bank A will acquire the most junior of the notes, i.e. the 'equity' tranche, with the intention of either retaining them, or selling them to third party investors in the future.

Bank A will also act as fund manager in the instance where the fund is actively managed, where the manager can trade and substitute assets within a specified mandate. Profits and losses from trading the assets accrue to the holders of the notes. Bank A will be remunerated at market rates for the fund management service.

Entity B, independent from the Bank, acquires 51 per cent of the equity tranche from Bank A some time after the SPE has been set up (i.e. in the secondary market). Entity B had no involvement in the SPE at inception and it cannot exercise any decision-making powers as those are retained by the fund manager acting in accordance with the investment mandate on behalf of all note holders.

The consolidation decision is based on a balanced assessment of all indicators.

Bank A will consolidate the SPE at inception because it set up the SPE, acquired a significant beneficial interest in the SPE by acquiring the equity tranche, and it is counterparty to the fund management contract with the SPE.

At the date Bank A sells 51 per cent of its equity tranche, Bank A would need to reconsider its consolidation decision. As Bank A retains a significant beneficial interest (49 per cent of equity tranche), and remains the party that set up the SPE at inception, it is likely Bank A will continue to consolidate.

Entity B is unlikely to consolidate as its interest in part of the equity tranche is simply an interest in a high yielding security. This security does not give the investor any decision making powers nor was Entity B involved in the setting up of the activities of the SPE when it was created. But it is necessary to consider all facts and circumstances in each specific case, so it is not possible to apply a generalised answer to all potential scenarios.

3.3.1 Indicators of control over an SPE

The Appendix to SIC-12 contains additional guidance to illustrate the application of the requirements of IAS 27 to SPEs, which is set out in the following sections. The objective of including these examples is to illustrate the types of circumstances that should be considered in evaluating the substance of the relationship between an investor and an investee. The factors listed are indicators only, however, and do not necessarily provide conclusive evidence of a control relationship. Further, the Appendix does not provide an exhaustive list of the circumstances in which consolidation of an SPE might be appropriate. The appropriate treatment in each case will be based on the substance of the arrangements, taking into account all of the significant aspects of the structures.

3.3.1.1 Activities

The activities of the SPE, in substance, are being conducted on behalf of the reporting entity which, directly or indirectly, created the SPE according to its specific business needs.

Examples are:

- the SPE is principally engaged in providing a source of long-term capital to an entity or funding to support an entity's ongoing major or central operations; or
- the SPE provides a supply of goods or services that is consistent with an entity's ongoing major or central operations which, without the existence of the SPE, would have to be provided by the entity itself.

Economic dependence of an entity on the reporting entity (such as the relationship between a supplier and a significant customer) does not, by itself, lead to control.

3.3.1.2 *Decision-making*

The reporting entity, in substance, has the decision-making powers to control or to obtain control over the SPE or its assets, including certain decision-making powers coming into existence after the formation of the SPE. Such decision-making powers may have been delegated by establishing an 'autopilot' mechanism.

Examples are:

- power to unilaterally dissolve an SPE; or
- power to change the SPE's charter or bylaws; or
- power to veto proposed changes to the SPE's charter or bylaws.

3.3.1.3 *Benefits*

The reporting entity, in substance, has rights to obtain a majority of the benefits of the SPE's activities through a statute, contract, agreement, or trust deed, or any other scheme, arrangement or device. Such rights to benefits in the SPE may be indicators of control when they are specified in favour of an entity that is engaged in transactions with an SPE and that entity stands to gain those benefits from the financial performance of the SPE.

Examples are:

- rights to a majority of any economic benefits distributed by an entity in the form of future net cash flows, earnings, net assets, or other economic benefits; or
- rights to majority residual interests in scheduled residual distributions or in a liquidation of the SPE.

3.3.1.4 *Risks*

An indication of control may be obtained by evaluating the risks of each party engaging in transactions with an SPE. Frequently, the reporting entity guarantees a return or credit protection, directly or indirectly through the SPE, to outside investors who provide substantially all of the capital to the SPE. As a result of the guarantee, the entity retains residual or ownership risks and the investors are, in substance, only lenders because their exposure to gains and losses is limited.

Examples are:

- the capital providers do not have a significant interest in the underlying net assets of the SPE; or
- the capital providers do not have rights to the future economic benefits of the SPE; or
- the capital providers are not substantively exposed to the inherent risks of the underlying net assets or operations of the SPE; or
- in substance, the capital providers receive mainly consideration equivalent to a lender's return through a debt or equity instrument.

3.3.2 *Accounting for employee share trusts in separate financial statements*

Depending on the nature of an employee share trust, it may be appropriate in separate financial statements either to adopt a 'look-through' approach (accounting for the trust as, in substance, an extension of the sponsoring entity), or to account for the employee share trust as a subsidiary.

For example, a 'look-through' approach may be appropriate where, as a result of its investment in the trust, the sponsoring entity's only exposure is to its own equity. One such situation would be where the trust has been financed by the sponsoring entity with an interest-free loan, the trust acts solely as a warehouse for the sponsoring entity's shares, any shares that are distributed are distributed directly to the sponsoring entity's employees and shares held by the trust are under option to employees but have not vested yet. Where a trust has external funding, the substance may also be that the trust is acting solely as a warehouse for the sponsoring entity's shares – for example, where the funding is entirely guaranteed by the sponsoring entity or the sponsoring entity provides the trust with the necessary contributions for the trust to be able to pay interest on the third party funding.

Conversely, where the trust creates additional risk exposures (for example it has other risk exposures such as unguaranteed loans or any other obligations, and hence creates exposures other than to the equity of the sponsoring entity), it may be that, in substance, the sponsoring entity has an investment in another entity, which it should account for as an investment in a subsidiary, at cost or in accordance with IAS 39 (per IAS 27(2008).38, previously IAS 27(2003).37) or, if applicable, in accordance with IFRS 5.

3.4 Problem areas in the identification of subsidiaries

3.4.1 Horizontal groups

The term 'horizontal group' is sometimes used to describe the situation where two or more reporting entities are controlled by a common shareholding, such as that held by a private individual. Since this individual is not subject to a requirement to prepare financial statements, there is no mechanism, either legal or professional, by which consolidated financial statements can be required. Under the disclosure requirements of IAS 24 *Related Party Disclosures*, the existence of the controlling individual, and transactions between entities that are under common control, will be disclosed (see **chapter 32**).

3.4.2 Limited partnerships

The structure of a limited partnership and the functions of a sole general partner of a limited partnership vary widely from partnership to partnership and from jurisdiction to jurisdiction. A limited partnership generally must meet certain legal and tax criteria to qualify as a limited partnership. Therefore, the structure is often form-driven. The rights and obligations of general partners in limited partnerships are usually different from those of limited partners. Some general partners perform a function designed solely to satisfy the criteria to qualify the entity as a limited partnership. Those general partners may have little, if any, real economic or beneficial interest in the partnership, but will exercise control.

Applying the definition of a subsidiary, which requires both control of operating and financial policies, and the ability to benefit:

- a partnership in which the general partner has no beneficial interest in the partnership net assets or net income is unlikely to meet the definition of a subsidiary of the general partner;

- similarly, a partnership in which a limited partner has an economic interest, but no ability to control the operating and financial policies, is unlikely to meet the definition of subsidiary of the limited partner (though care should be taken also to consider the requirements of SIC-12, as discussed at **3.3**, when assessing whether control is present);
- however, a limited partner who is also the general partner, or who holds the power to remove the general partner, may have both the elements of control and benefit such that the partnership meets the definition of a subsidiary.

The determination of whether or not a general partner controls the partnership is a matter of careful judgement based on the relevant facts and circumstances.

3.4.3 *Investment managers*

Where an investment manager has discretion over the investment decisions of a fund, it might be considered that the manager has control over the fund and should therefore consolidate the fund with its own activities. However, this argument fails to take into consideration the fact that the nature of the manager's business is the provision of expertise for a fee, with the benefit of investment returns accruing to investors in the fund. The manager's business is thus different from that of the fund.

Where the other investors have the power to remove and replace the investment manager at relatively short notice, and could exercise that power in practice, the fund is unlikely to be a subsidiary. The manager would not seem to have the power to govern the fund's financial and operating policies, in that it can be removed from its role. Where this is not the case, however, it will be necessary to consider the nature of the manager's interest in the fund. Provided that the manager takes only an insignificant equity stake in the fund, so that its return from the fund (if any) is equivalent to a normal performance-related fee, the fund is unlikely to meet the definition of a subsidiary since, although the investment manager has some powers associated with control of policies, it does not derive benefit from the exercise of those powers. Where, alternatively, the manager does hold a significant equity interest in the capital and income of the fund, and cannot be removed by the other investors, it may have more difficulty arguing that it is not the parent of the fund.

Example 3.4.3

Consolidation of funds

An unlisted fund with sub-funds has both voting shares and preference shares. Its voting shares are owned by a management company who also make up the board of directors of the fund. The preference shareholders, however, have the power to remove and replace the fund's board of directors (i.e. the management company) with directors of their choice.

The management company receives a management fee which is based on the fund's net asset value, including realised and unrealised gains. The preference shareholders, whose return is based on the performance of the sub-funds less the management fee, receive their return at the time they redeem their shares.

The management company does not control the fund. Control is the power to govern the financial and operating policies of an entity so as to obtain benefits from its activities. [IAS 27.4] Control relates to the ability to govern the decision-making through the selection of financial and operating policies, regardless of whether this power is actually exercised. The ability to govern the decision-making alone, however, is not sufficient to establish control, and, therefore, must be accompanied by the objective of obtaining benefits from the entity's activities.

Where a party has the power to appoint or remove the majority of the board of directors or equivalent governing body, a careful analysis of the policies regarding the replacement of these members is essential. In addition, it is essential to consider the party's ability to remove the majority of these members without delay and expense. If the evidence shows that the board of directors only 'temporarily' exercise decision-making powers, because another party has the right to remove and replace the majority of the board of directors at their choice with immaterial delay and expense, those with the ultimate power to remove and replace the majority of the board members have the power to govern the decision-making of the entity.

However, control only exists if the party which has the power to govern the financial and operating policies also obtains benefits from its activities. The criterion to obtain these benefits has to be viewed as benefits derived from having the power to govern the financial and operating policies. Therefore, in addition to analysing the control rights in IAS 27.13, an analysis of the benefits obtained is required. In circumstances, in which the fee received by a management party represents only a 'normal' level for the management service provided and no more, the party receives no further benefits from its activities.

Due to the right, held by the preference shareholders, to replace the management company with directors of their choice with no delay or at no expense, and the fact that the fee is at a 'normal' rate for the level of service provided, the current holding of the management company in the fund does not constitute control. Overall, its relationship with the fund can be viewed as a fiduciary relationship rather than one of control.

4 Presentation of consolidated financial statements

4.1 Requirement to prepare consolidated financial statements

Subject to one exception when all of the conditions set out in **4.2** are met, IAS 27 requires that parents should prepare consolidated financial statements in which they consolidate their investments in subsidiaries in accordance with the Standard. [IAS 27.9]

IAS 27(2008).26 (previously IAS 27(2003).30) makes it clear that a subsidiary is consolidated until the date when the parent ceases to control it. Accordingly, where a parent had subsidiaries at any time during the year, IAS 27 will require consolidated financial statements to be produced (unless the exemption in **4.2** is available). Subsidiaries classified as held for sale are discussed at **4.3.1**.

UK *This differs from the position under UK GAAP, where the legal requirement for consolidated financial statements only exists where the parent has subsidiaries at the year end. Thus, under UK GAAP, a group that disposes of all subsidiaries during the year will not produce consolidated financial statements.*

4.2 Exemption from the requirement to prepare consolidated financial statements

A parent need not prepare consolidated financial statements if, and only if, all of the following conditions are met:

[IAS 27.10]

- the parent is itself a wholly-owned subsidiary, or is a partially-owned subsidiary of another entity and its other owners, including those not otherwise entitled to vote, have been informed about, and do not object to, the parent not presenting consolidated financial statements;
- the parent's debt or equity instruments are not traded in a public market (i.e. a domestic or foreign stock exchange or an over-the-counter market, including local and regional markets);

- the parent did not file, nor is it in the process of filing, its financial statements with a securities commission or other regulatory organisation for the purpose of issuing any class of instruments in a public market; and
- the ultimate or any immediate parent of the parent produces consolidated financial statements available for public use that comply with International Financial Reporting Standards.

A parent taking this exemption may prepare separate financial statements as its only IFRS financial statements – see **section 6**. [IAS 27.8]

UK

The criteria described above will not be met by a UK parent company that is required to prepare IFRS accounts under the EU regulation, but they may be met by a UK parent company that voluntarily chooses to prepare IFRS accounts. Such a company must, however, also comply with the requirements of the Companies Act 2006 or the Companies Act 1985 (whichever is applicable) in respect of group accounts. In most respects those requirements are essentially the same in both Acts. Accordingly, for ease of reading, in the guidance below 'the Act' refers to both the Companies Act 2006 and the Companies Act 1985.

Under the Act, exemption from producing group accounts may be available if:

- *the parent is included in group accounts of a larger European Economic Area (EEA) group (see* **4.2.1***); or*
- *the parent is included in group accounts of a larger non-EEA group (see* **4.2.2***); or*
- *all subsidiary undertakings are permitted to be excluded from consolidation (see* **4.2.4***); or*
- *the group qualifies as small (or, under the Companies Act 1985, medium-sized) (see* **4.2.5***). Note that the Companies Act 2006 removed the previous exemption for medium-sized groups, but retained the exemption for a parent company that is subject to the small companies regime.*

Subject to the point discussed below concerning IFRSs as adopted by the EU, a UK parent company producing IFRS accounts will only be exempt from producing group accounts if it meets the criteria of IAS 27.10, discussed above, and can also claim one of the UK exemptions discussed below. This is because a company preparing its individual financial statements under IFRSs must comply with IAS 27, which includes a requirement to prepare IFRS consolidated financial statements unless the exemption in IAS 27 applies. It must also comply with the requirement in CA 2006 s399 (previously CA 1985 s227) to prepare consolidated financial statements if, at the end of the financial year, it is a parent, subject to the Act's exemptions listed above.

For example, a small company entitled not to prepare group accounts under CA 2006 s398 (previously CA 1985 s248), or a subsidiary of a US parent entitled to the exemption in CA 2006 s401 (previously CA 1985 s228A), would have to prepare consolidated financial statements to be able to claim compliance with IFRSs as issued by the IASB.

However, it appears that a company which makes use of one of the exemptions in the law but would be required by IAS 27 to prepare consolidated financial statements will nevertheless be able to claim compliance with IFRSs as adopted by the EU. This matter has been discussed on various occasions by the Accounting Regulatory Committee of the European Commission. No formal guidance has yet been issued by the Commission on this matter but substantive agreement has been reached that the requirements of IAS 27 for consolidated financial statements do not apply, for IFRSs as adopted by the EU, if the company is not required by the Seventh Directive to prepare group accounts. This is a surprising conclusion given that IAS 27 was adopted by the EU without any amendments. Nevertheless, it is the view of the Commission that those parts of IAS 27 that deal with consolidated financial statements are relevant only in those cases where such financial statements are required by EU law. Companies which make use of this interpretation of EU law should recognise that they will not be able to claim compliance with 'full' IFRSs as issued by the IASB and consider any commercial or regulatory implications of this.

4.2.1 *Additional UK exemption criteria: larger EEA group*

UK *The Act exempts a parent undertaking, which is itself a subsidiary undertaking and whose immediate parent undertaking is established under the law of an EEA State, from the requirement to prepare group accounts providing certain conditions are met. [CA 2006 s400, previously CA 1985 s228] This exemption applies only where the UK parent is either wholly owned, or majority owned ('more than 50 per cent of the allotted shares') by the immediate parent (which is established under the law of an EEA State). In determining whether a subsidiary undertaking is majority owned, shares held by a wholly-owned subsidiary of the parent undertaking, or held on behalf of the parent undertaking or a wholly-owned subsidiary, shall be attributed to the parent undertaking. [CA 2006 s400(3), previously CA 1985 s228(5)] In determining whether a subsidiary undertaking is wholly owned, shares held by directors of a company for the purpose of complying with any share qualification requirement shall be disregarded. [CA 2006 s400(5), previously CA 1985 s228(4)]*

The other conditions for this exemption to apply are set out below.

The UK parent must be included in consolidated financial statements (not necessarily those of its immediate parent) which are:

(*a*) *prepared by a parent undertaking established under the law of an EEA State;*

(*b*) *in English (or if not in English, accompanied by a certified translation into English);*

(*c*) *drawn up to the same date, or an earlier date in the same financial year, as the UK parent;*

(*d*) *prepared in accordance with law based on the EU Seventh Directive on company law or in accordance with international accounting standards;*

(*e*) *audited; and*

(*f*) *filed with the UK Registrar of Companies, together with the UK parent's individual accounts (which must contain various additional disclosures – see below for those upon which exemption from preparing group accounts is conditional).*

The company must disclose in its individual accounts that it is exempt from the obligation to prepare and deliver group accounts.

The company must state in its individual accounts the name of the parent undertaking which draws up the group accounts referred to above and:

(*a*) *if it is incorporated outside Great Britain, the country in which it is incorporated; or*

(*b*) *if it is unincorporated, the address of its principal place of business.*

For a parent that is a UK company, a further condition imposed by the Act is that, to claim exemption from producing group accounts, it must not have any securities listed on an EEA regulated market. [CA 2006 s400(4), previously CA 1985 s228(3)]

Finally, if the parent is itself not wholly-owned, the exemption is not available if minority shareholders holding in aggregate either more than half the remaining allotted shares or five per cent of the total allotted shares have requested group accounts. Such notice must be served (the onus being on the minority shareholders) not later than six months after the end of the previous financial year, i.e. normally within six months of the beginning of the financial year to which it relates.

Section 400 of the Companies Act 2006 (previously CA 1985 s228) makes a number of references to the European Economic Area (EEA). The EEA came into effect on 1 January 1994 and extended the European Community single market to participating Member States. The term therefore covers Norway, Iceland and Liechtenstein as well as the European Union (EU) countries.

4.2.2 Additional UK exemption criteria: larger non-EEA group

UK *The Act exempts a parent undertaking, which is itself a subsidiary undertaking and whose parent undertaking is not established under the law of an EEA State, from the requirement to prepare group accounts providing certain conditions are met. [CA 2006 s401, previously CA 1985 s228A] This exemption applies only where the UK parent is either wholly owned, or majority owned ('more than 50 per cent of the allotted shares') by the parent undertaking. In determining whether a subsidiary undertaking is majority owned, shares held by a wholly-owned subsidiary of the parent undertaking, or held on behalf of the parent undertaking or a wholly-owned subsidiary, shall be attributed to the parent undertaking. [CA 2006 s401(3), previously CA 1985 s228A(5)] In determining whether a subsidiary undertaking is wholly owned, shares held by directors of a company for the purpose of complying with any share qualification requirement shall be disregarded. [CA 2006 s401(5), previously CA 1985 s228A(4)]*

The other conditions for this exemption to apply are set out below.

The UK parent and all of its subsidiary undertakings must be included in consolidated financial statements which are:

(*a*) *prepared by a parent undertaking;*

(*b*) *in English (or if not in English, accompanied by a certified translation into English);*

(*c*) *drawn up to the same date, or an earlier date in the same financial year, as the UK parent;*

(*d*) *prepared in accordance with law based on the EU Seventh Directive on company law or in a manner equivalent (see* **4.2.3** *below) to consolidated accounts and consolidated annual reports so drawn up (this requirement also applies, where appropriate, to the group's annual report);*

(*e*) *audited by one or more persons authorised to audit accounts under the law under which the parent undertaking which draws them up is established; and*

(*f*) *filed with the UK Registrar of Companies, together with the UK parent's individual accounts (which must contain various additional disclosures – see below for those upon which exemption from preparing group accounts is conditional) and, where appropriate, the consolidated annual report.*

The company must disclose in its individual accounts that it is exempt from the obligation to prepare and deliver group accounts.

The company must state in its individual accounts the name of the parent undertaking which draws up the group accounts referred to above and:

(*a*) *if it is incorporated outside Great Britain, the country in which it is incorporated; or*

(*b*) *if it is unincorporated, the address of its principal place of business.*

For a parent that is a UK company, a further condition imposed by the Act is that, to claim exemption from producing group accounts, it must not have any securities admitted to trading on a regulated market of any EEA State. [CA 2006 s401(4), previously CA 1985 s228A(3)]

Finally, if the parent is itself not wholly-owned, the exemption is not available if minority shareholders holding in aggregate either more than half the remaining allotted shares or five per cent of the total allotted shares have requested group accounts. Such notice must be served (the onus being on the minority shareholders) not later than six months after the end of the previous financial year, i.e. normally within six months of the beginning of the financial year to which it relates.

4.2.3 *Equivalence and UITF Abstract 43*

4.2.3.1 *The UITF consensus*

In October 2006, the UITF issued Abstract 43 The interpretation of equivalence for the purposes of section 228A of the Companies Act 1985. *Although that section has been superseded by section 401 of the Companies Act 2006, there is no change of substance to the requirements and, accordingly, the UITF Abstract continues to be relevant to companies now within the scope of the Companies Act 2006.* UK

The UITF noted that the analysis of whether or not a particular set of accounts is drawn up in a manner equivalent to accounts drawn up in accordance with the Seventh Directive has to be made on a case by case basis. However, the UITF decided that it should be possible to identify some GAAPs that usually result in consolidated accounts being drawn up in such a manner. [UITF 43.6 – 7]

The approach taken in Abstract 43 is that the reference to equivalence in s228A (subsequently CA 2006 s401) does not mean compliance with every detail of the Seventh Directive. Rather, a qualitative approach which focuses on compliance with the basic requirements of the Directive and, in particular, the requirement to give a true and fair view, should be taken. This is more in keeping with the deregulatory nature of the exemption than consideration of the detailed requirements on a checklist basis. [UITF 43.8]

The consensus reached by the UITF is that:

(*a*) *when assessing whether consolidated accounts of a higher non-EEA parent are drawn up in a manner equivalent to consolidated accounts drawn up in accordance with the Seventh Directive, it is necessary to consider whether they meet the basic requirements of the Fourth and Seventh Directives, in particular the requirement to give a true and fair view, without implying strict conformity with each and every provision; and*

(*b*) *the consequences of adopting the principle in (a) above are:*

(*i*) *consolidated accounts of the higher parent that give a true and fair view and comply with accounting standards applicable in the UK and Republic of Ireland will meet the test of equivalence with the Seventh Directive;*

(*ii*) *consolidated accounts of the higher parent prepared in accordance with IFRSs as adopted by the EU will meet the test of equivalence with the Seventh Directive;*

(*iii*) *consolidated accounts of the higher parent prepared in accordance with IFRSs as issued by the IASB will meet the test of equivalence with the Seventh Directive subject to the consideration of the reasons for any failure by the European Commission to adopt a Standard or Interpretation;*

(*iv*) *consolidated accounts of the higher parent prepared using GAAPs which are closely related to IFRSs will meet the test of equivalence with the Seventh Directive subject to consideration of the effect of any differences from IFRSs as adopted by the EU;*

(*v*) *consolidated accounts of the higher parent prepared in accordance with US GAAP, Canadian GAAP and Japanese GAAP will normally meet the test of equivalence with the Seventh Directive subject to consideration of developments in those GAAPs following the date of issue of the Abstract and:*

- *ensuring the scope of entities included in those consolidated accounts is consistent with the Seventh Directive;*
- *ensuring that consistent accounting policies have been used for all entities included in those consolidated accounts; and*
- *evaluating the effect of any exemptions or modifications to the GAAPs allowed by specialised industry standards which have been applied in those consolidated accounts; and*

(*vi*) *consolidated accounts of the higher parent prepared using other GAAPs should be assessed for equivalence with the Seventh Directive based on the particular facts, including the similarities to, and differences from, the GAAPs considered specifically in the Abstract.*

4.2.3.2 US GAAP, Canadian GAAP and Japanese GAAP

The UITF Abstract contains some additional material explaining the reasons for these conclusions. The position in relation to UK GAAP, IFRSs and those GAAPs closely related to IFRSs is straightforward. The position in relation to US GAAP, Canadian GAAP and Japanese GAAP is more complicated because the UITF imposed three specific additional tests, as well as a general caveat about changes after the date of publication of the Abstract. The UITF felt unable to give a blanket assurance that these three GAAPs would always meet the test of equivalence although in practice they will do so in many cases. UK

The first area of concern was that some entities might be excluded from consolidation even though they would be required to be consolidated under the Seventh Directive. The UITF considered the scope of the consolidation as being something that is fundamental to the true and fair view. The concern was primarily in respect of 'qualifying SPEs' under US GAAP although the drafting of the consensus applies this test to Canadian and Japanese GAAP as well.

However, the Seventh Directive is significantly less onerous than UK GAAP as regards the scope of the consolidation. The relevant requirements are set out in appendix 1 to Abstract 43. In particular, the requirement that an undertaking should be consolidated on the grounds of actual exercise of, or power to exercise, a dominant influence is a Member State option which was taken up in the UK but which need not be considered for the purposes of assessing equivalence. Consequently, some entities that would have to be consolidated under UK GAAP would not have to be consolidated under the requirements of the Seventh Directive. [UITF 43.17 – 18]

The position in relation to those companies comprising the UK sub-group which is seeking the exemption is, however, tougher due to the drafting of s228A. There is a specific requirement that the UK parent company and all of its subsidiary undertakings (as defined in the Act) are included in the consolidated accounts of the larger group. [UITF 43.16]

Enquiries should therefore be made, where relevant, concerning the extent of any 'off balance sheet arrangements' which are excluded from the consolidated accounts of the larger group. Judgement should then be applied to decide whether such arrangements are so significant as to prevent equivalence being achieved.

The second area of concern identified by the UITF was the need for consistent accounting policies to have been used for all entities included within the consolidation. This concern is primarily aimed at parent companies reporting under Japanese GAAP which permits different policies to be used in some cases. This should not be an issue for companies reporting under US GAAP or Canadian GAAP. Where the consolidated accounts of the larger group are prepared under Japanese GAAP, enquiries should be made to ascertain whether this might be a material issue that could result in a lack of equivalence. [UITF 43.19]

The third area of concern identified by the UITF was the use of specialised industry standards. The specific example given in the Abstract is that US GAAP grants an exemption from the requirement to consolidate certain subsidiaries of some types of investment vehicles. More generally, the UITF was unable to assess all of the possible specialised industry requirements and exemptions that might arise and therefore took the cautious approach of saying that these should be considered where relevant. Enquiries should therefore be made, when the parent company operates in a specialised industry, to establish whether there are any unusual policies that might lead to a lack of equivalence. [UITF 43.21]

4.2.3.3 *Annual report*

UK

Section 228A(2)(b) (subsequently CA 2006 s401(2)(b)) imposes a condition that 'where appropriate' the 'annual report' of the larger group must be drawn up in accordance with the provisions of the Seventh Directive or in a manner equivalent to reports so drawn up. The term 'annual report' is used in the section in the sense that it is used in the Directive and should be read as 'directors' report' in the UK context. [UITF 43.22]

Neither the Act nor the Directive provide any further elaboration of the expression 'where appropriate'. Abstract 43 notes that this might mean 'where the larger group prepares an annual report' or 'where the larger group would be required to prepare an annual report under the Directive'. It does not indicate which is the correct interpretation. The former interpretation does not appear logical because the requirements would be tougher for a company that prepared an annual report than for one that did not do so. Therefore the second interpretation appears more likely and is more cautious. The Directive permits Member states to waive the requirement for small companies to prepare an annual report. However, the small company exemption would almost inevitably not be available to the non-EEA parent so an 'annual report' will be required to enable the UK parent to qualify for the exemption.

Abstract 43 notes that, in keeping with the approach to equivalence of financial statements taken in the Abstract, any consideration of equivalence of the annual report would be at a high level rather than considering the detailed requirements on a checklist basis. The relevant requirements of the Fourth Directive concerning the contents of the annual report are set out in Appendix 2 to Abstract 43. [UITF 43.24]

For example, the MD&A prepared by a US quoted company would meet the requirement for an annual report.

4.2.4 Additional UK exemption criteria: all subsidiary undertakings excluded

These criteria are discussed at **2.3.2** *in* ***chapter 1****.* (UK)

4.2.5 Additional UK exemption criteria: small or medium-sized group

The Companies Act 1985 exempts a group which is small or medium-sized and which is not an ineligible group from preparing consolidated financial statements. [CA 1985 s248] The Companies Act 2006 restricts this exemption so that it is only available to a parent company that is subject to the (UK) *small companies regime, i.e. the exemption is no longer available for medium-sized groups. [CA 2006 s398] The relevant criteria are discussed further below.*

4.2.5.1 *Companies Act 2006: exemption criteria for small groups*

UK

If at the end of a financial year a company subject to the small companies regime is a parent company the directors, as well as preparing individual accounts for the year, may prepare (but are not required to prepare) group accounts for the year. [CA 2006 s398] The small companies regime for accounts and reports applies to a company for a financial year in relation to which the company:

[CA 2006 s381]

(*a*) *qualifies as small (the size criteria are set out in CA 2006 sections 382 and 383); and*

(*b*) *is not excluded from the regime.*

The small companies regime does not apply to a company that is, or was at any time within the financial year to which the accounts relate:

[CA 2006 s384(1)]

(*a*) *a public company;*

(*b*) *a company that:*

  (*i*) *is an authorised insurance company, a banking company, an e-money issuer, an ISD investment firm or a UCITS management company; or*

  (*ii*) *carries on insurance market activity; or*

(*c*) *a member of an ineligible group.*

Note that (c) in the list above is more restrictive than the equivalent requirement of the Companies Act 1985. Under the 1985 Act, it was necessary to assess whether the group headed by the parent was an ineligible group (see **4.2.5.2***); under the 2006 Act it is necessary to consider whether the parent itself is a member of an ineligible group. In other words, the test now applies to the largest group of which the parent is a member, and not just the sub-group of which it is the parent.*

A group is ineligible if any of its members is:

[CA 2006 s384(2)]

(a) *a public company;*

(b) *a body corporate (other than a company) whose shares are admitted to trading on a regulated market in an EEA State;*

(c) *a person (other than a small company) who has permission under Part 4 of the Financial Services and Markets Act 2000 to carry on a regulated activity;*

(d) *a small company that is an authorised insurance company, a banking company, an e-money issuer, an ISD investment firm or a UCITS management company; or*

(e) *a person who carries on insurance market activity.*

For the purposes of assessing whether a group is ineligible, a company is a small company if it qualified as small in relation to its last financial year ending on or before the end of the financial year to which the accounts relate. Note that (b) in the list above represents a slight relaxation compared to the position under the Companies Act 1985, as discussed at **4.2.5.2**.

4.2.5.2 *Companies Act 1985: exemption criteria for small and medium-sized groups*

UK

A group is ineligible if any of its members is a public company, a person who has permission under Part 4 of the Financial Services and Markets Act 2000 to carry on a regulated activity, or a person who carries on an insurance market activity. In addition, if a parent undertaking is a company reporting under the Companies Act 1985, a group will also be ineligible if any of its members is a body corporate which has power under its constitution to offer its shares or debentures to the public and may lawfully exercise that power. The qualifying size criteria for classification as small or medium-sized are set out in CA 1985 s249.

Under the Companies Act 1985 consolidated accounts are not required in respect of a year 'in relation to which the group ***headed*** *by that company qualifies as a small or medium-sized group and is not an ineligible group' (our emphasis). Consequently, where a parent company is itself a subsidiary undertaking in a larger group, and is not otherwise exempt from the requirement to prepare consolidated accounts by CA 1985 s228 (see* **4.2.1***) or CA 1985 s228A (see* **4.2.2***), it will nevertheless be exempt via CA 1985 s248 providing the group that it heads is not ineligible and is small or medium-sized.*

4.3 Scope of consolidated financial statements

The consolidated financial statements are required to include all subsidiaries of the parent. [IAS 27.12]

4.3.1 *Subsidiaries classified as held for sale*

Under IAS 27, there is no basis on which a subsidiary may be excluded from consolidation. If, on acquisition, a subsidiary meets the criteria to be classified as held for sale in accordance with IFRS 5 *Non-current Assets Held for Sale and Discontinued Operations*, it is included in the consolidation but is accounted for under that Standard (see **chapter 29**). [IAS 27.12]

Under IFRS 5, the assets of such a subsidiary will be combined as a single figure separately from other assets and liabilities, as will the liabilities, and the results of the subsidiary will be excluded from continuing operations, and instead classified as discontinued operations.

UK

Under UK GAAP, where a subsidiary is acquired exclusively with a view to subsequent resale, it is excluded from consolidation in accordance with FRS 7.16.

4.3.2 *Investments held by venture capital organisations and similar entities*

A subsidiary is not excluded from consolidation simply because the investor is a venture capital organisation, mutual fund, unit trust or similar entity. [IAS 27(2008).16, previously IAS 27(2003).19]

Note that, although the IASB has excluded investments in associates and interests in joint ventures held by venture capital organisations and similar entities from the scope of IAS 28 and IAS 31 respectively, the exemption has not been extended to subsidiaries of such organisations. The Board concluded that if an investor controls an investee, the investee is part of the structure through which the group operates its business, and thus consolidation of the investee is appropriate.

4.3.3 *Subsidiaries with dissimilar activities*

IAS 27 explicitly states that it is inappropriate to exclude subsidiaries from consolidation on the grounds that their activities are substantially different from those of the parent and/or the rest of the group. As long as the parent retains control over such subsidiaries, they are required to be consolidated. Information regarding the different nature of the activities of a subsidiary can be appropriately disclosed by listed entities in accordance with IFRS 8 *Operating Segments* (or, for entities that have not yet adopted IFRS 8, in accordance with IAS 14 *Segment Reporting*). [IAS 27(2008).17, previously IAS 27(2003).20]

4.3.4 Loss of control

When a parent loses control, the investee no longer meets the definition of subsidiary, and so it is no longer consolidated. A parent loses control when it loses the power to govern the financial and operating policies of an investee so as to obtain benefit from its activities.

The loss of control can occur with or without a change in absolute or relative ownership levels. It could occur, for example, when a subsidiary becomes subject to the control of a government, court, administrator or regulator. It could also occur as a result of a contractual agreement. [IAS 27(2008).32, previously IAS 27(2003).21]

A common example of loss of control is when a subsidiary becomes subject to insolvency proceedings involving the appointment of a receiver or liquidator, if the effect is that the shareholders cease to have the power to govern the financial and operating policies. Although this will often be the case in a liquidation, a receivership or administration order may not involve loss of control by the shareholders.

Another example of loss of control would be the seizure of the assets or operations of an overseas subsidiary by the local government.

Short-term restrictions on cash flows from a subsidiary, perhaps because of exchange controls or restrictions on distributions of profits in a foreign jurisdiction, do not generally result in a loss of control. The fact that a parent may not be able to remit dividends from the subsidiary, or use the funds for other parts of the group outside the country of operation, does not by itself indicate that the ability to transfer funds in the longer term has been significantly impaired. Indeed, subsidiaries are often set up in the face of such restrictions and are, presumably, expected to produce economic benefits for the parent.

It is possible for a parent to lose control of a subsidiary as a result of two or more arrangements (transactions). Where this is the case, it is necessary to consider all of the terms and conditions of the arrangements and their economic effects in order to determine whether the multiple arrangements should be accounted for as a single transaction. IAS 27(2008) states that one or more of the following may indicate that the parent should account for the multiple arrangements as a single transaction:

[IAS 27(2008).33]

(a) They are entered into at the same time or in contemplation of each other.

(b) They form a single transaction designed to achieve an overall commercial effect.

(c) The occurrence of one arrangement is dependent on the occurrence of at least one other arrangement.

(d) One arrangement considered on its own is not economically justified, but it is economically justified when considered together with other arrangements. An example is when one disposal of shares is priced below market and is compensated for by a subsequent disposal priced above market.

> Although IAS 27(2003) did not include equivalent guidance, these principles would seem equally relevant for entities that have not yet adopted IAS 27(2003).

5 Consolidation procedures

When preparing consolidated financial statements, the individual balances of the parent and its subsidiaries are aggregated on a line-by-line basis, and then certain consolidation adjustments are made. [IAS 27(2008).18, previously IAS 27(2003).22] For example, the cash, trade receivables and prepayments of the parent and each subsidiary are added together to arrive at the cash, trade receivables and prepayments of the group, before consolidation adjustments are made. The objective is that the consolidated financial statements should present the information contained in the consolidated financial statements of a parent and its subsidiaries as if they were the financial statements of a single entity.

The consolidation adjustments required will vary depending on the circumstances. The adjustments include (but are not restricted to):

- the elimination of the carrying amount of the parent's investment in each subsidiary and the parent's portion of equity of each subsidiary. Any resultant goodwill is recognised in accordance with IFRS 3 *Business Combinations* (IFRS 3(2008) is dealt with in **chapter 34**; IFRS 3(2004) is dealt with in **appendix 2**); [IAS 27(2008).18(a), previously IAS 27(2003).22(a)]
- the identification of the non-controlling interest in the profit or loss of consolidated subsidiaries for the reporting period; [IAS 27(2008).18(b), previously IAS 27(2003).22(b)]
- the elimination of all intragroup balances and intragroup transactions, and the resulting unrealised profits and losses; [IAS 27(2008).20, previously IAS 27(2003).24] and
- adjustment of the consolidated results for dividends related to outstanding cumulative preference shares of a subsidiary that are classified as equity and are held by non-controlling interests, regardless of whether dividends have been declared. [IAS 27(2008).29, previously IAS 27(2003).36]

For consolidation purposes, the income and expenses of a subsidiary are based on the values of the assets and liabilities recognised in the parent's consolidated financial statements at the subsidiary's acquisition date. For example, depreciation expense recognised in the consolidated statement of comprehensive income after the acquisition date is based on the fair values of the related depreciable assets recognised in the consolidated financial statements at the acquisition date. [IAS 27(2008).26]

5.1 Reciprocal interests

Reciprocal interests represent situations in which a parent and a subsidiary have equity interest in each other. An analogy to IAS 32.33 is appropriate, i.e. reciprocal interests should be treated in a similar manner to own shares. In its consolidated financial statements, reciprocal interests should be presented by a parent as a reduction of both its investment in the subsidiary and its equity in the earnings of the subsidiary.

Example 5.1

Reciprocal interests

Company A owns a 90 per cent interest in Company B, and B owns a 10 per cent interest in A. Company A and B respectively have 10,000 and 5,000 ordinary shares in issue.

Both paid £100 per share for their respective ownership interests in each other. Company A's shares are publicly traded, and B has classified its investment in A as held for trading under IAS 39 *Financial Instruments: Recognition and Measurement*.

Company A's investment in B, B's investment in A, and A's reciprocal interest in B are calculated as follows:

A's investment in B = £100/share × (90% × 5,000 shares) = £450,000

B's investment in A = £100/share × (10% × 10,000 shares) = £100,000

A's reciprocal interest in B = 90% × £100,000 = £90,000.

Company A's investment in B is reduced for its ownership interests in itself through the reciprocal holdings by B of A's shares.

5.2 Elimination of intragroup transactions

5.2.1 *General rules*

In order to present financial statements for the group in a consolidated format, the effects of transactions between group entities should be eliminated. IAS 27 requires that intragroup transactions (including sales, expenses and dividends) and the resulting unrealised profits and losses be eliminated in full. [IAS 27(2008).21, previously IAS 27(2003).25]

Liabilities due to one group entity by another will be set off against the corresponding asset in the other group entity's financial statements; sales made by one group entity to another should be excluded both from revenue and from cost of sales or the appropriate expense heading in consolidated profit or loss.

Adjustments such as those referred to in the previous paragraph are not required to be made for transactions between group entities and investments that are dealt with by equity accounting in the consolidated financial statements (e.g. associates and jointly controlled entities) – see **section 4.3** of **chapter 35**.

To the extent that the buying entity has on-sold the goods in question to a third party, the eliminations to sales and cost of sales are all that is required, and no adjustments to consolidated profit or loss for the period, or to net assets, are needed. However, to the extent that the goods in question are still on hand at year end, where they are carried at an amount that is in excess of cost to the group, the amount of the intragroup profit must be eliminated, and assets reduced to cost to the group.

For transactions between group entities, unrealised profits resulting from intragroup transactions that are included in the carrying amount of assets, such as inventories and property, plant and equipment, are eliminated in full. The requirement to eliminate such profits in full applies to the transactions of all subsidiaries that are consolidated – even those in which the group's interest is less than 100 per cent.

For entities that are dealt with by equity accounting in the consolidated financial statements (e.g. associates and jointly controlled entities), unrealised profits on intragroup transactions are generally eliminated to the extent of the investor's interest in the associate (see **section 4.3.6** of **chapter 35**).

5.2.2 *Unrealised profit in inventories*

Where a group entity sells goods to another, the selling entity, as a separate legal entity, recognises profits made on those sales. If these goods are still held in inventory by the buying entity at the year end, however, the profit recognised by the selling entity, when viewed from the standpoint of the group as a whole, has not yet been earned, and will not be earned until the goods are eventually sold outside the group. On consolidation, the unrealised profit on closing inventories will be eliminated from the group's profit, and the closing inventories of the group will be recorded at cost to the group.

When the goods are sold by a parent to a subsidiary, all of the profit on the transaction is eliminated, irrespective of the percentage of the shares held by the parent. In other words, the group is not permitted to take credit for the share of profit that is attributable to any non-controlling interest.

Example 5.2.2A

Unrealised profit in inventories (1)

A Limited has an 80 per cent subsidiary, B Limited. During 20X1, A Limited sells goods, which originally cost £20,000, to B Limited for £30,000. At 31 December 20X1, B Limited continues to hold half of those goods as inventories.

The inventories held by B Limited include an unrealised profit of £5,000. This profit must be eliminated in full – irrespective of any non-controlling interest.

Therefore, the required journal on consolidation, to eliminate all of the effects of the transaction, is as follows:

	DR £	CR £
Consolidated revenue	30,000	
Consolidated cost of sales		30,000
Consolidated cost of sales (closing inventories)	5,000	
Closing inventories		5,000

Where the goods are sold by a subsidiary in which there is a non-controlling interest to another group entity, whether the parent or a fellow subsidiary, the whole of the unrealised profit should also be eliminated.

In these circumstances, however, a question arises as to how the amount of profit to be shown as attributable to non-controlling interests should be calculated.

- One approach would be to allocate to non-controlling interests their proportionate share of the unrealised profit. This approach eliminates the profit in the selling entity.
- Another approach would be to allocate no part of the unrealised profit to the non-controlling interests, acknowledging that they are still entitled to their full share of profit arising on intragroup sales. Under this approach, the figure for non-controlling interests reflects their entitlement to the share capital and reserves of the subsidiary.

IAS 27 does not specify which treatment is more appropriate and, in practice, both alternatives are commonly adopted.

Example 5.2.2B

Unrealised profit in inventories (2)

C Limited has two subsidiaries: D Limited, in which it has an 80 per cent interest; and E Limited, in which it has a 75 per cent interest. During the accounting period, D Limited sold goods to E Limited for £100,000. The goods had been manufactured by D Limited at a cost of £70,000. Of these goods, E Limited had sold one half by the end of the reporting period.

In the preparation of C Limited's consolidated financial statements, the unrealised profit remaining in inventories still held by E Limited will be eliminated. These inventories were transferred from D Limited to E Limited at a value of £50,000, and their cost to the group was £35,000. The intragroup profit to be eliminated from inventories, therefore, is £15,000.

The proportion attributed to non-controlling interests, assuming the first method described above is adopted, is determined by reference to the group's proportionate interest in the selling company, D Limited, of which C

Limited owns 80 per cent and the non-controlling interests own 20 per cent. The amount is therefore £15,000 x 20 per cent = £3,000.

5.2.3 *Unrealised profit on transfers of non-current assets*

Similar to the treatment described above for unrealised profits in inventories, unrealised profits arising from intragroup transfers of non-current assets are also eliminated from the consolidated financial statements.

Example 5.2.3

Unrealised profit on transfer of non-current asset

Assume that F Limited holds 80 per cent of the issued share capital of G Limited. G Limited purchased a machine on 1 January 20X1 at a cost of £4 million. The machine has a life of 10 years.

On 1 January 20X3, G Limited sells the machine to F Limited at a price of £3.6 million.

In preparing the consolidated financial statements of F Limited at 31 December 20X3, the effects of the sale from G Limited to F Limited have to be eliminated.

At 31 December 20X3, the carrying amount of the machine in the books of F Limited will be £3.15 million, with a depreciation charge of £450,000 (i.e. assuming that the cost to F Limited of £3.6 million will be written off over the asset's remaining life of 8 years).

G Limited will have recognised a profit on transfer of the asset of £400,000.

If there had been no transfer, the asset would have been included in the statement of financial position at 31 December 20X3 at £2.8 million and a depreciation charge of £400,000 would have been recognised.

Therefore, the consolidation entry that is required is:

	Dr £'000	Cr £'000
Consolidated profit or loss (profit on sale)	400	
Consolidated profit or loss (excess depreciation)		50
Machine (restore to original cost)	400	
Accumulated depreciation (based on original date of acquisition)		750

The proportion of the profit or loss adjustment attributable to the non-controlling interests, assuming the first method described in **5.2.2** above is adopted, is determined as:

	£'000
Non-controlling interests' share of profit on sale (20 per cent x 400)	80

Non-controlling interests' share of excess depreciation (20 per cent x 50)	(10)
	70

5.2.4 *Construction contracts*

Special considerations apply if a construction or contracting entity is a member of a group and carries out work for other group entities:

- if the building or other asset being constructed will, on completion, be acquired as an item of property, plant and equipment by another group entity (e.g. a new factory or an investment property) then, as indicated above, any profit made by the constructing entity should be eliminated on consolidation. However, if the asset being constructed is the subject of a contract for sale by the buying entity to a third party, then any profit made by the constructing entity need not be eliminated, provided that it is measured in accordance with the rules set out in IAS 11 *Construction Contracts* (see **chapter 40**); and

- if the constructing entity includes borrowing costs in the cost of construction, and the group's policy is also to capitalise borrowing costs relating to qualifying assets, the amount capitalised will need to be recomputed from the group's perspective and adjusted if necessary. If finance for the project is being provided by another group entity which is charging interest, the interest charged may not correspond to the amount that is to be capitalised by the group in accordance with IAS 23 *Borrowing Costs* (see **chapter 27**). The most recent version of IAS 23, which is effective for periods beginning on or after 1 January 2009, requires eligible costs to be capitalised. Under the previous version of IAS 23, such costs could be capitalised or expensed as a matter of accounting policy.

5.2.5 *Unrealised losses*

Intragroup losses may indicate an impairment that requires recognition in the consolidated financial statements. [IAS 27(2008).21, previously IAS 27(2003).25]

Example 5.2.5

Unrealised losses

Consider the facts as per **example 5.2.3**, except that the machine was transferred from G Limited to F Limited at £2.4 million.

At 31 December 20X3, the carrying amount of the machine in the books of F Limited will be £2.1 million, after a depreciation charge of £300,000 (i.e. assuming that the cost of £2.4 million will be written off over the asset's remaining life of 8 years).

G Limited will have recognised a loss on transfer of the asset of £800,000.

If there had been no transfer, the asset would have been included in the statement of financial position at 31 December 20X3 at £2.8 million and a depreciation charge of £400,000 would have been recognised.

Provided that the entity is satisfied that the original carrying amount of the asset can be recovered, the following consolidation entry is required:

	DR £'000	CR £'000
Consolidated profit or loss (additional depreciation)	100	
Consolidated profit or loss (loss on sale)		800
Machine (restore to original cost)	1,600	
Accumulated depreciation (based on original date of acquisition)		900

However, where transfer at the lower amount indicates that the previous carrying amount of the asset cannot be recovered, the impairment loss will be recognised in accordance with IAS 36 *Impairment of Assets*.

5.2.6 *Deferred tax*

IAS 12 *Income Taxes* applies to temporary differences that arise from the elimination of profits and losses resulting from intragroup transactions. [IAS 27(2008).21, previously IAS 27(2003).25] See **chapter 12** for a detailed discussion of the issues arising.

5.3 Non-controlling interest (previously minority interest)

As indicated above, the basic consolidation process involves the aggregation of the assets, liabilities, income and expenditure of the individual group entities. Therefore, where the group does not hold the whole of the share capital of a subsidiary, an adjustment is necessary to take account of the interests of the outside shareholders. Their interests in the net assets of the subsidiary need to be recognised within equity of the group and their share of the subsidiary's profit or loss for the year needs to be disclosed as an allocation of total profit or loss.

IAS 27(2008) defines non-controlling interest as the equity in a subsidiary not attributable, directly or indirectly, to a parent. [IAS 27(2008).4]

For entities that have not yet adopted IAS 27(2008), IAS 27(2003) defines minority interest as that part of the profit or loss and of the net assets of a subsidiary attributable to equity interests that are not owned, directly or indirectly through subsidiaries, by the parent. [IAS 27.4]

> IAS 27(2008).BC28 explains that this change in terminology reflects the fact that the owner of a minority interest in an entity might control that entity and, conversely, that the owners of a majority interest might not control the entity. 'Non-controlling interest' is a more accurate description than 'minority interest' of the interests of those owners who do not have a controlling interest in an entity.

5.3.1 *Measurement of non-controlling interests*

The amount of non-controlling interests in the net assets of consolidated subsidiaries is calculated as:

[IAS 27(2008).18(c), previously IAS 27(2003).22(c)]

- the amount of non-controlling interests arising at the date of the original combination, as calculated in accordance with IFRS 3 *Business Combinations* (IFRS 3(2008) is dealt with in **chapter 34**; IFRS 3(2004) is dealt with in **appendix 2**); plus
- the non-controlling interests' share of changes in equity since the date of the combination.

When potential voting rights exist, the proportions of profit or loss and changes in equity allocated to the parent and non-controlling interests are determined on the basis of present ownership interests and do not reflect the possible exercise or conversion of potential voting rights. [IAS 27(2008).19, previously IAS 27(2003).23]

5.3.1.1 *Two classes of shares*

IAS 27 explicitly provides that if a subsidiary has outstanding cumulative preference shares that are classified as equity and held by non-controlling interests, the parent computes its share of profits or losses after adjusting for the subsidiary's dividends, whether or not the dividends have been declared. [IAS 27(2008).29, previously IAS 27(2003).36] By comparison, dividends in respect of non-cumulative shares classified as equity only affect the allocation of profits or losses when declared.

5.3.1.2 *Profits and losses attributable to non-controlling interests: entities that have adopted IAS 27(2008)*

Profit or loss and each component of other comprehensive income are attributed to the owners of the parent and to the non-controlling interests. Total comprehensive income is attributed to the owners of the parent and to the non-controlling interests even if this results in the non-controlling interests having a deficit balance. [IAS 27(2008).28]

The previous version of IAS 27 did not generally allow a deficit balance, as explained below. The change is to be applied prospectively, as discussed in **section 8**.

This approach differs from UK GAAP. Under FRS 2, where the losses in a subsidiary undertaking attributable to the minority interest (i.e. non-controlling interest) result in its interest being one in net liabilities rather than net assets, the group makes provision to the extent that it has any commercial or legal obligation (whether formal or implied) to provide finance that may not be recoverable in respect of the accumulated losses attributable to the minority interest. UK

5.3.1.3 *Profits and losses attributable to minority interests: entities that have not yet adopted IAS 27(2008)*

The profit or loss is attributed to the parent shareholders and minority interests. Because both are equity, the amount attributed to minority interests is not income or expense. [IAS 27(2003).34] Where a subsidiary included in the consolidation reports losses, the minority interest should reflect an appropriate share of those losses.

The losses attributable to the minority may exceed the minority's interest in the subsidiary's equity. In such circumstances, the excess, and any further losses applicable to the minority are allocated against the majority interest except to the extent that there is a binding obligation on minority shareholders to make good losses incurred which they are able to meet. [IAS 27(2003).35]

Therefore, the excess of the losses attributable to the minority over the minority's interest in the equity of the subsidiary is charged against the group. When the subsidiary subsequently reports profits, the minority does not participate until the group has recovered all of the losses of the minority it previously absorbed. [IAS 27(2003).35]

UK

> *This approach differs from UK GAAP. Under FRS 2, where the losses in a subsidiary undertaking attributable to the minority interest result in its interest being one in net liabilities rather than net assets, the group makes provision to the extent that it has any commercial or legal obligation (whether formal or implied) to provide finance that may not be recoverable in respect of the accumulated losses attributable to the minority interest.*

5.3.2 *Presentation of non-controlling interests*

For the presentation of non-controlling interests, the requirements are:

- non-controlling interests should be presented in the consolidated statement of financial position within equity, separately from the equity of the owners of the parent; [IAS 27(2008).27, previously IAS 27(2003).33] and
- total comprehensive income for the period attributable to (i) non-controlling interests and (ii) owners of the parent should be separately disclosed in the statement of comprehensive income as allocations of profit or loss for the period. [IAS 1(2007).83, previously IAS 1(2003).82(a)]

5.4 Reporting periods of subsidiaries

For the purposes of preparing consolidated financial statements, the financial statements of all subsidiaries should, wherever practicable, be prepared:

[IAS 27(2008).22 & 23, previously IAS 27(2003).26 & 27]

- as of the same date; and
- for the same reporting period as the parent.

When a subsidiary and its parent have differing reporting periods, the subsidiary prepares additional financial statements corresponding to the group's reporting period for consolidation purposes, unless it is impracticable to do so. [IAS 27(2008).22, previously IAS 27(2003).26]

If the subsidiary does not prepare financial statements corresponding to the group's reporting period, adjustments should be made for the effects of significant transactions or events that occur between the end of the subsidiary's reporting period and the end of the parent's reporting period. [IAS 27(2008).23, previously IAS 27(2003).27]

IAS 27 does not define 'significant transactions or events', but they may include business combinations, asset impairments, and the crystallisation of contingent liabilities. A potentially significant transaction or event requires a careful analysis of the relevant facts and circumstances to determine if an adjustment is required.

Where a subsidiary prepares financial statements for a different reporting period, it is also necessary to review the subsidiary's statement of financial position to ensure that items are still correctly classified as current or non-current at the end of the parent's reporting period.

Example 5.4

Classification as current or non-current when parent and subsidiary have different reporting periods

A subsidiary that has an accounting year end of 31 December 20X1 has a loan outstanding which is due for repayment on 1 January 20X3. The debt is appropriately classified as non-current in the subsidiary's statement of financial position.

The subsidiary is consolidated in the financial statements of its parent, which are prepared to 31 March 20X2. Due to the time lag, the subsidiary's debt falls due in less than twelve months from the end of the parent's reporting period. The classification of the debt as current or non-current should be determined by reference to the year-end of the parent which, in this case, results in a current classification since the debt maturity is nine months from the parent's year end.

IAS 27 includes an additional restriction that, in any case, the difference between the ends of the reporting periods should be no more than three months either earlier or later. [IAS 27(2008).23, previously IAS 27(2003).27] The time lag should be consistent from year to year.

Under UK GAAP, it is possible to use financial statements of a subsidiary prepared for a reporting period ending up to three months earlier than that of the parent, but not financial statements prepared for a reporting period ending later than that of the parent. UK

There are circumstances that make it necessary or appropriate for a subsidiary to have a different reporting period. For example:

- legislation in certain countries requires financial statements to be prepared to a specified date;
- the normal trading cycle in certain activities (e.g. agriculture) may make it desirable for subsidiaries to have financial years which end at a particular time of the year (e.g. when crops have been harvested). In addition, subsidiaries with cyclical trades such as retail businesses may wish to avoid a year end routine during busy pre-Christmas trading when inventory levels are high; and
- a change in accounting date may have seriously adverse tax consequences, or significant tax advantages may arise from having a different accounting date.

Nevertheless, in such circumstances, the subsidiary should prepare additional financial statements corresponding to the group's reporting period for consolidation purposes, unless it is impracticable to do so. Such impracticability may arise where entities in remote territories are unable to comply with the parent's timetable for preparing annual financial statements (which will usually be framed with a view to avoiding undue delay in publication). This may result in some foreign subsidiaries closing their accounts one or two months earlier than the parent in order to allow time to complete and transmit information for consolidation. Even then, a time lag between the ends of the reporting periods of longer than three months is not permitted.

5.5 Uniform accounting policies

Consolidated financial statements should be prepared using uniform accounting policies for like transactions and other events in similar circumstances. [IAS 27(2008).24, previously IAS 27(2003).28]

Where such group accounting policies are not adopted in the financial statements of a subsidiary, appropriate adjustments should be made in preparing the consolidated financial statements. [IAS 27(2008).25, previously IAS 27(2003).29]

5.6 Changes in a parent's ownership interest in a subsidiary without loss of control

5.6.1 Changes in a parent's ownership interest in a subsidiary without loss of control: entities that have adopted IAS 27(2008)

Where there is a change in a parent's ownership interest in a subsidiary, but the parent does not cease to have control, this is accounted for as an equity transaction, i.e. a transaction with owners in their capacity as owners. [IAS 27(2008).30]

In particular, therefore, when a parent increases or decreases its stake in an existing subsidiary without losing control, no adjustment is made to goodwill or any other assets or liabilities, and no gain or loss is reported.

When such a change occurs, the carrying amounts of the controlling and non-controlling interests are adjusted to reflect the changes in their relative interests in the subsidiary. Any difference between (i) the amount by which the non-controlling interests are adjusted and (ii) the fair value of the consideration paid or received is recognised directly in equity and attributed to the owners of the parent. [IAS 27(2008).31]

For a transaction between the parent and non-controlling interests, IAS 27(2008) does not give detailed guidance on how to measure the amount to be allocated to the parent and non-controlling interests to reflect a change in their relative interests in the subsidiary. More than one approach may be possible, as discussed in **example 5.6.1.1B** and **example 5.6.1.1C** below.

IAS 32.35 requires that the costs of any equity transaction be recognised in equity. Therefore, the costs associated with a transaction between a parent and non-controlling interests are recognised in equity.

The requirements of IAS 27(2008).30 & 31 are to be applied prospectively, as discussed in **section 8**.

5.6.1.1 Implications of the measurement basis of non-controlling interests

The adjustment to the carrying amount of non-controlling interests and the consequential adjustment to equity following a transaction with the parent will be affected by the choice of measurement basis for the non-controlling interest at acquisition date (see **7.3.1** in **chapter 34**). The IASB explained the difference as follows:

[IFRS 3(2008).BC218]

> 'The third difference [due to the choice of measurement basis for non-controlling interests] arises if the acquirer subsequently purchases some (or all) of the shares held by the non-controlling shareholders. If the non-controlling interests are acquired, presumably at fair value, the equity of the group is reduced by the non-controlling interests' share of any unrecognised changes in the fair value of the net assets of the business, including goodwill. If the non-controlling interest is measured initially as a proportionate share of the acquiree's identifiable net assets, rather than at fair value, that reduction in the reported equity attributable to the acquirer is likely to be larger. This matter was considered further in the IASB's deliberations on the proposed amendments to IAS 27.'

The difference is highlighted in the following examples.

Example 5.6.1.1A

Parent acquires non-controlling interest

In 20X1, A acquired a 75% equity interest in B for cash consideration of £90,000. B's identifiable net assets at fair value were £100,000. The fair value of the 25% non-controlling equity interest (NCI) was £28,000. Goodwill, on the two alternative bases for measuring non-controlling interests at acquisition, is calculated as follows:

	NCI @ % of net assets	**NCI @ fair value**
	£	£
Fair value of consideration	90,000	90,000
Non-controlling interests	25,000	28,000
	115,000	118,000
Fair value of net assets	100,000	100,000
Goodwill	15,000	18,000

In the subsequent years, B increased net assets by £20,000 to £120,000. This is reflected in the carrying amount within equity attributed to non-controlling interests as follows:

	NCI @ % of net assets	**NCI @ fair value**
	£	£
Non-controlling interests at acquisition	25,000	28,000

	NCI @ % of net assets	NCI @ fair value
Increase (25% x £20,000)	5,000	5,000
Carrying amount	30,000	33,000

In 20X6, A then acquired the 25% equity interest held by non-controlling interests for cash consideration of £35,000. The adjustment to equity will be:

	NCI @ % of net assets	NCI @ fair value
	£	£
Fair value of consideration	35,000	35,000
Carrying amount of non-controlling interests	30,000	33,000
Negative movement in parent equity	5,000	2,000

As indicated in IFRS 3(2008).BC218, the reduction in equity is greater where the option was taken to measure non-controlling interests at acquisition date as a proportionate share of the acquiree's identifiable net assets. The treatment has the effect of including the non-controlling interest's share of goodwill directly in equity. This outcome will always occur where the fair value basis is greater than the net asset basis at acquisition date.

Example 5.6.1.1B

Parent acquires part of a non-controlling interest

The facts are as in **example 5.6.1.1A** above except that, rather than acquire the entire non-controlling interest, A acquires an additional 15% equity interest held by non-controlling interests for cash consideration of £21,000. The adjustment to the carrying amount of non-controlling interests will be:

	NCI @ % of net assets	NCI @ fair value
	£	£
Balance as in **example 5.6.1.1A**	30,000	33,000
Transfer to parent (15/25ths) *	18,000	19,800
10% interest carried forward	12,000	13,200

The adjustment to equity will be:

	NCI @ % of net assets	NCI @ fair value
	£	£
Fair value of consideration	21,000	21,000

Change to non-controlling interests (as above)	18,000	19,800
Negative movement in parent equity	3,000	1,200

* In this example, it is assumed that non-controlling interests are reduced proportionately. Under the fair value option, the closing balance represents 10/25th of the acquisition date fair value (11,200) plus 10% of the change in net assets since acquisition (2,000). As discussed at **5.6.1**, other approaches may also be acceptable to determine the amount by which non-controlling interests are adjusted.

Example 5.6.1.1C

Parent disposes of part of its interest to non-controlling interests

In 20X1, A acquired a 100% equity interest in B for cash consideration of £125,000. B's identifiable net assets at fair value were £100,000. Goodwill of £25,000 was identified and recognised.

In the subsequent years, B increased net assets by £20,000 to £120,000. This is reflected in equity attributable to the parent.

A then disposed of 30% of its equity interest to non-controlling interests for £40,000. The adjustment to equity will be:

	£
Fair value of consideration received	40,000
Amount recognised as non-controlling interests (30% x 120,000) *	36,000
Positive movement in parent equity	4,000

* In this example, it is assumed that non-controlling interests are measured based on their share of identifiable assets. As discussed at **5.6.1**, other approaches may also be acceptable to determine the amount by which non-controlling interests are adjusted (e.g. non-controlling interests might instead be measured at fair value, £40,000).

Note that there is no adjustment to the carrying amount of goodwill of £25,000 because control has been retained.

5.6.2 *Changes in a parent's ownership interest in a subsidiary without loss of control: entities that have not yet adopted IAS 27(2008)*

Before IAS 27(2008) was issued, IFRSs contained no guidance on how to account when a parent's ownership interest in a subsidiary changed without there being any change in control. Prior to adoption of IAS 27(2008), various methods may be adopted to account for changes in a parent's ownership interest, and these are discussed at **6.8.2** in **appendix 2**.

5.7 Disposal of a subsidiary

The income and expenses of a subsidiary are included in the consolidated financial statements from the acquisition date (as defined in IFRS 3 *Business Combinations*) until the date when the parent ceases to control the subsidiary. [IAS 27(2008).26, previously IAS 27(2003).30]

There may be circumstances when the disposal of a subsidiary should not be recognised as a sale. These circumstances typically relate to when the parent sells the subsidiary but retains a degree of continuing involvement such that risks and rewards of ownership and control have not been transferred. Examples of circumstances that should be considered include, but are not limited to, the following:

- the seller has effective veto power over major contracts or customers;
- the buyer or any successor has the ability to put (sell) the subsidiary back to the seller at other than fair value;
- the seller can require the buyer or any successor owner to sell the subsidiary back to it at other than fair value;
- the seller has significant voting power on the subsidiary's board;
- the seller has continuing involvement in the subsidiary's affairs with risks and management authority similar to ownership;
- the buyer does not make a significant financial investment in the subsidiary (e.g. a minimal down payment);
- the buyer's repayment of debt that constitutes the principal consideration in the acquisition is dependent on future profitable operations of the acquired subsidiary;
- the seller continues to guarantee debt or contract performance of the acquired subsidiary.

When any of the above circumstances exist, careful judgement should be exercised in determining if such circumstances would preclude the seller from accounting for the transaction as a disposal.

5.7.1 *Accounting for loss of control: entities that have adopted IAS 27(2008)*

When a parent loses control of a subsidiary, the steps set out below are followed. [IAS 27(2008).34]

- The assets (including any goodwill) and liabilities of the subsidiary are derecognised at their carrying amounts at the date when control is lost.
- The carrying amount of any non-controlling interests in the former subsidiary at the date when control is lost (including any components of other comprehensive income attributable to them) is derecognised
- The parent recognises the fair value of the consideration received, if any, from the transaction, event or circumstances that resulted in the loss of control.
- If the transaction that resulted in the loss of control involves a distribution of shares of the subsidiary to owners in their capacity as owners, that distribution is recognised.
- Any investment retained in the former subsidiary is recognised at its fair value at the date when control is lost.
- The amounts recognised in other comprehensive income in relation to the former subsidiary are reclassified to profit or loss, or transferred directly to retained earnings if required in accordance with other IFRSs (see further discussion below).
- Any resulting difference is recognised as a gain or loss in profit or loss attributable to the parent.

When a parent loses control of a subsidiary, all amounts recognised in other comprehensive income in relation to that subsidiary are accounted for on the same basis as would be required if the parent had directly disposed of the related assets or liabilities. Accordingly:

[IAS 27(2008).35]

- if a gain or loss previously recognised in other comprehensive income would be reclassified to profit or loss on the disposal of the related assets or liabilities, the parent reclassifies the gain or loss from equity to profit or loss (as a reclassification adjustment) when it loses control of the subsidiary. For example, if a subsidiary has available-for-sale financial assets and the parent loses control of the subsidiary, the gain or loss previously recognised in other comprehensive income in relation to those assets is reclassified to profit or loss; and

- if a revaluation surplus previously recognised in other comprehensive income would be transferred directly to retained earnings on the disposal of the asset, the revaluation surplus is transferred directly to retained earnings when the parent loses control of the subsidiary.

Note that this applies to the entire amount recognised in other comprehensive income, irrespective of whether the parent will continue to hold a residual interest in the former subsidiary.

Any investment retained in the former subsidiary and any amounts owed by or to the former subsidiary are accounted for in accordance with other IFRSs from the date when control is lost. [IAS 27(2008).36]

The fair value of any investment retained in the former subsidiary at the date when control is lost is regarded as the fair value on initial recognition of a financial asset in accordance with IAS 39 *Financial Instruments: Recognition and Measurement* or, when appropriate, the cost on initial recognition of an investment in an associate or jointly controlled entity. [IAS 27(2008).37]

The requirements of IAS 27(2008).34 – 37 are to be applied prospectively, as discussed in **section 8**.

Example 5.7.1

Parent disposes of its controlling interest but retains an associate interest

In 20X1, A acquired a 100% equity interest in B for cash consideration of £125,000. B's identifiable net assets at fair value were £100,000. Goodwill of £25,000 was identified and recognised.

In the subsequent years, B increased net assets by £20,000 to £120,000. Of this, £15,000 was reported in profit or loss and £5,000, relating to fair value movements on an available-for-sale financial asset, was reported within other comprehensive income.

A then disposed of 75% of its equity interest for cash consideration of £115,000. The resulting 25% equity interest is classified as an associate under IAS 28 and has a fair value of £38,000.

The gain recognised in profit or loss on disposal of the 75% equity interest is:

	£
Fair value of consideration received	115,000

Fair value of residual interest	38,000
Gain previously reported in other comprehensive income	5,000
	158,000
Less: net assets and goodwill derecognised	145,000
Gain	13,000

Subsequent accounting under IAS 28 on an equity-accounting basis will require an exercise to assess the fair value of B's identifiable net assets on the date that control is lost. Goodwill will be identified by comparing the initial fair value of the interest of £38,000 with the residual share (25%) of identifiable net assets at fair value.

IAS 27(2008).41(f) requires disclosure of 'the portion of that gain or loss attributable to recognising any investment retained in the former subsidiary at its fair value at the date when control is lost'. The amount would be determined as follows:

	£
Fair value of residual interest	38,000
25% of net assets and goodwill derecognised (25% x £145,000)	36,250
Portion of gain	1,750

5.7.2 *Accounting for loss of control: entities that have not yet adopted IAS 27(2008)*

Where a parent loses control over a subsidiary, the investment will be accounted for under IAS 39 *Financial Instruments: Recognition and Measurement* from the date of loss of control, unless the investor retains significant influence (in which case the investment will be accounted for under IAS 28 – see **chapter 35**) or joint control (in which case the investment will be accounted for as a jointly controlled entity under IAS 31 – see **chapter 36**). [IAS 27(2003).31]

The carrying amount of the investment at the date the entity ceases to be a subsidiary will be regarded as the cost on initial measurement of a financial asset for the purposes of IAS 39. [IAS 27(2003).32]

On disposal of a subsidiary, the gain or loss on disposal is recognised in consolidated profit or loss, and is calculated as the aggregate of:

[IAS 27(2003).30]

- the difference between the proceeds of disposal of the subsidiary and its carrying amount as of the date of disposal; and

- the cumulative amount of any exchange differences that relate to the subsidiary recognised in equity, in accordance with IAS 21 *The Effects of Changes in Foreign Exchange Rates*.

*Under UK GAAP, exchange differences taken to equity are not recycled on the disposal of a subsidiary. The IFRS requirements relating to such exchange differences are discussed further in **chapter 28**.* UK

For the purposes of the gain or loss on disposal calculation, the carrying amount of the subsidiary would include any amount of goodwill carried in the statement of financial position in respect of the subsidiary. However, where goodwill has previously been eliminated against reserves prior to transition to IFRSs, IFRS 1 prohibits it from being recycled to profit or loss on subsequent disposal.

By contrast, whereas 'old' eliminated goodwill is prohibited from recycling to profit or loss by IFRS 1, UK GAAP requires such goodwill to be included in the profit or loss on disposal. UK

5.7.3 *Partial disposals*

When part of an investment in a subsidiary is sold during the reporting period, the status of the investment immediately after the disposal should determine the accounting. For example:

- if a parent sells a portion of its investment in a subsidiary, but still retains a controlling interest, the consolidated financial statements at the end of the period should include the assets, liabilities, and operations of the subsidiary, and reflect the new non-controlling interest from the date of the transaction. Under IAS 27(2008), no gain or loss will be reported, as this is an equity transaction (see **5.6.1**); under IAS 27(2003), it is possible that a gain or loss may be reported (see **5.6.2**);

- if the parent sells a controlling interest in the subsidiary, but still retains significant influence over the entity, that remaining investment should be reflected in the statement of financial position at the end of the period as a single line item, using the equity method in accordance with IAS 28 *Investments in Associates*. The subsequent results of operations should also be reported using the equity method. If the disposal qualifies as a discontinued operation, presentation of the discontinued operation should follow IFRS 5 *Non-current Assets Held for Sale and Discontinued Operations* from the date that the operations qualify as held for sale (see **3.4** in **chapter 29**); and

- when almost all of a subsidiary is sold (except for an interest which does not allow the parent to exert significant influence over the subsidiary), and if the sale of the subsidiary qualifies as a discontinued operation, presentation of the discontinued operation should follow IFRS 5 *Non-current Assets Held for Sale and Discontinued Operations* from the date that the operations qualify as held for sale (see **3.4** in **chapter 29**). The remaining interest in the entity should be accounted for in accordance with IAS 39 *Financial Instruments: Recognition and Measurement* from the date of the disposal.

5.7.4 *Deemed disposals*

A deemed disposal of an interest in a subsidiary, joint venture or associate may arise through the parent not taking up its full entitlement in a rights issue, a payment of scrip dividends not taken up by the parent, the issue of shares to other shareholders, or the exercise of options or warrants granted to another party. As a result, the parent's shareholding is reduced or diluted.

Any gain or loss arising as a result of a deemed disposal should be recognised in profit or loss. (Note that, under IAS 27(2008), a gain or loss can arise only where control is lost as a result of the deemed disposal. By contrast, under IAS 27(2003), it is possible for gains or losses to be reported when a parent reduces its stake in a subsidiary without losing control.)

UK *Under Schedule 1 of the Accounting Regulations (previously Schedule 4 of the Companies Act 1985), only profits realised at the balance sheet date (i.e. the end of the reporting period) are included in the profit and loss account. Therefore, under UK GAAP it is necessary to determine whether a deemed disposal gives rise to a realised or unrealised profit. Any unrealised profit arising as a result of a deemed disposal should be recognised in the STRGL. (See* ***section 5.3*** *of* ***chapter 49*** *for further guidance on realised and unrealised profits.)*

IFRSs do not contain a similar realisation test. Therefore, all gains and losses arising from deemed disposals should be recognised in profit or loss.

6 Separate financial statements

IAS 27 also deals with the appropriate treatment for investments in subsidiaries, jointly controlled entities and associates when an entity elects, or is required by local regulations, to present separate financial statements. [IAS 27.3]

IAS 27 defines separate financial statements as those presented by a parent, an investor in an associate or a venturer in a jointly controlled entity, in which the investments are accounted for on the basis of the direct equity interest rather than on the basis of the reported results and net assets of the investees. [IAS 27.4]

The financial statements of an entity that does not have a subsidiary, associate or venturer's interest in a jointly controlled entity are not separate financial statements. [IAS 27.7]

Where an entity with investments in associates and/or joint ventures produces consolidated financial statements, those consolidated financial statements must also comply with IAS 28 *Investments in Associates* and IAS 31 *Interests in Joint Ventures* respectively. [IAS 27.5] Separate financial statements are those prepared and presented in addition to such consolidated financial statements. IAS 27 does not require them to be appended to, or to accompany, the consolidated financial statements. [IAS 27.6]

UK

But a UK company that prepares statutory group accounts for a financial year must not publish its statutory individual accounts for that year without also publishing with them its statutory group accounts. [CA 2006 s434(2), previously CA 1985 s240(2)]

Particularly when dealing with associates and joint ventures, it is important to understand that the term 'separate financial statements' does not simply mean 'financial statements other than consolidated financial statements'. For example, where an entity has no subsidiaries, and therefore does not produce consolidated financial statements, it may nevertheless be required to use equity accounting for associates in its 'main' financial statements.

'Separate financial statements' are best understood as financial statements presented in addition to the 'main' financial statements. They will most often occur when an entity that is required to produce consolidated financial statements also produces non-consolidated financial statements for the parent as a separate entity; the latter would be separate financial statements. But the definition is not as narrow as this, and would in principle also apply where an entity other than a parent prepares, in addition to its 'main' financial statements (which would use equity accounting for associates), separate 'parent' financial statements (which would not use equity accounting).

The Standard does not mandate which entities prepare separate financial statements – but specifies the rules to be followed in accounting for investments where separate financial statements are prepared voluntarily (e.g. for the purposes of supporting a tax return) or are required by local regulations (e.g. certain jurisdictions require the preparation and publication of stand-alone financial statements for parent entities).

UK *As explained in* ***chapter 1****, UK parent companies are required by law to prepare separate financial statements but can choose to present these under IFRSs or UK GAAP when the consolidated financial statements are prepared under IFRSs.*

Where an entity does produce separate financial statements, the general requirements of IFRSs will apply to those financial statements if they are described as complying with IFRSs. The supplementary rules set out below for accounting for investments are required because, in separate financial statements, investments are accounted for on the basis of the direct equity interest rather than on the basis of the reported results and net assets of the investees. [IAS 27.4]

When separate financial statements are prepared, investments in subsidiaries, jointly controlled entities and associates that are not classified as held for sale (or included in a disposal group that is classified as held for sale) in accordance with IFRS 5 *Non-current Assets Held for Disposal and Discontinued Operations*, should be accounted for either:

[IAS 27(2008).38, previously IAS 27(2003).37]

- at cost (less any impairment loss); or
- in accordance with IAS 39 *Financial Instruments: Recognition and Measurement*.

See **6.1** below for a discussion of the treatment of dividends when investments in subsidiaries, jointly controlled entities or associates are accounted for at cost in IFRS financial statements.

For each category of investments (subsidiaries, jointly controlled entities, associates) the selected accounting policy should be applied consistently. [IAS 27(2008).38, previously IAS 27(2003).37]

Where an investment in a jointly controlled entity or an associate is accounted for in accordance with IAS 39 in the consolidated financial statements (e.g. an investment held by a venture capital organisation), it should be accounted for in the same way in the investor's separate financial statements. [IAS 27(2008).40, previously IAS 27(2003).39] Therefore, cost is not an allowed alternative for such investments in the investor's separate financial statements.

The appropriate accounting for investments in subsidiaries, jointly controlled entities and associates that are classified as held for sale is discussed at **6.2** below.

6.1 Accounting for investments in subsidiaries, jointly controlled entities or associates at cost

In May 2008, the IASB amended IAS 27 and IFRS 1 to change, inter alia, the treatment of dividends out of pre-acquisition profits (discussed below) and to allow the use of deemed cost for investments in subsidiaries, jointly controlled entities and associates when entities first adopt IFRSs (see **6.12** in **chapter 5**).

The amendments remove an important difference between IFRSs and UK GAAP, and should make it easier for UK companies to adopt IFRSs in future. At the time of writing, these amendments to IAS 27 and IFRS 1 have not yet been endorsed for use in the EU. Since the requirements of the amended Standards differ in important respects from those of the previous versions, EU reporting entities will not be able to apply the revised versions in their statutory financial statements until the revised Standards are endorsed. UK

6.1.1 *Accounting for investments in subsidiaries, jointly controlled entities or associates at cost: entities that have adopted the May 2008 amendments to IFRS 1 and IAS 27*

Prior to its amendment in May 2008, IAS 27 included a definition of the 'cost method' which explained that distributions received in excess of post-acquisition profits should be recognised as a reduction of the cost of the investment (see **6.1.2**). The May 2008 amendment deleted this definition, and inserted a new paragraph (38A), which explains that an entity recognises a dividend from a subsidiary, jointly controlled entity or associate in profit or loss in its separate financial statements when its right to receive the dividend is established. [IAS 27(2008).38A]

The amendments above apply prospectively for annual periods beginning on or after 1 January 2009, but earlier application is permitted. If an entity applies the changes for an earlier period, that fact is to be disclosed, and the entity must apply the related amendments to IAS 18, IAS 21 and IAS 36 at the same time (see **10.1** in **chapter 23**, **5.5** in **chapter 28** and **5.2.2** in **chapter 9**, respectively). [IAS 27(2008).45B]

Thus, all distributions received from subsidiaries, jointly controlled entities and associates after the date from which an entity adopts the amendments will be recognised in profit or loss – irrespective of whether they arose from pre- or post-acquisition profits. But the cost of investment in such entities is not restated for earlier distributions.

UK

This revised treatment of dividends out of pre-acquisition profits is the same as that adopted under UK GAAP. As noted at **6.1**, *EU reporting entities will not be able to apply these amendments in their statutory financial statements until they have been endorsed.*

The May 2008 amendment also added two new paragraphs (38B and 38C) relating to group reorganisations. When a parent reorganises the structure of its group by establishing a new entity as its parent such that the following criteria are met:

[IAS 27(2008).38B]

(a) the new parent obtains control of the original parent by issuing equity instruments in exchange for existing equity instruments of the original parent;

(b) the assets and liabilities of the new group and the original group are the same immediately before and after the reorganisation; and

(c) the owners of the original parent before the reorganisation have the same absolute and relative interests in the net assets of the original group and the new group immediately before and after the reorganisation

and the new parent accounts for its investment in the original parent at cost in its separate financial statements, the new parent measures cost at the carrying amount of its share of the equity items shown in the separate financial statements of the original parent at the date of the reorganisation.

Thus, in the straightforward scenario where the original parent becomes a wholly-owned subsidiary of the new parent, the cost shown in the new parent's separate financial statements will simply be the total equity (assets less liabilities) of the original parent shown in the separate financial statements of the parent at the date of the reorganisation.

The amendment does not explain what happens if the original parent has net liabilities. Consistent with the general accounting for investments in subsidiaries in separate financial statements, the investment will presumably be recorded at nil. But this treatment would only be appropriate to the extent that the transferee does not assume a liability beyond the cost of the shares at the time of the transfer.

Where the new parent does not acquire all of the equity instruments of the original parent, care will be needed in assessing whether condition (c) is met. But providing all three conditions are met, the cost shown in the new parent's separate financial statements will be its share of the total equity (assets less liabilities) of the original parent at the date of the reorganisation.

Note that the treatment described above is not a choice: it is required if the conditions are met.

Similarly, an entity that is not a parent might establish a new entity as its parent in a manner that satisfies the criteria in paragraph 38B. The requirements in paragraph 38B apply equally to such reorganisations. In such cases, references to 'original parent' and 'original group' are to the 'original entity'. [IAS 27(2008).38C]

Example 6.1.1

Cost for new parent in group reorganisation

Company S has one class of equity instruments, 70% of which are held by Company P. A new company, Company X, is created and it issues equity instruments to P in exchange for P's 70% interest in S. Company X therefore becomes P's wholly-owned subsidiary. X has no other assets or liabilities. At the time of this reorganisation, the total equity (assets less liabilities) of S as reported in its separate financial statements is £10,000.

The requirements of IAS 27(2008).38B & 38C are met in that:

- X has obtained control of S by issuing equity instruments to P in exchange for existing equity instruments of S;
- the assets and liabilities of the X group and S are the same immediately before and after the reorganisation; and
- the owners of S before the reorganisation have the same absolute and relative interests in the net assets of S and the X group immediately before and after the reorganisation.

If X accounts for its investment in S at cost in its separate financial statements, cost is measured at the carrying amount of X's share of the equity items shown in the separate financial statements of S at the date of the reorganisation, i.e.:

cost = 70% x £10,000 = £7,000

Note that, providing the requirements of IAS 27(2008).38B & 38C are met, the calculation of cost is the same irrespective of whether S is itself a parent.

New paragraphs 38B and 38C apply prospectively to reorganisations occurring in annual periods beginning on or after 1 January 2009, but earlier application is permitted. Paragraphs 38B and 38C may also be applied retrospectively to past reorganisations within their scope, but if an entity chooses to restate any reorganisation to comply with paragraph 38B or 38C, it must also restate all later reorganisations within the scope of those paragraphs. If an entity applies paragraph 38B or 38C for a period beginning on or after 1 January 2009, that fact is to be disclosed. [IAS 27(2008).45C]

UK *Again, as noted at **6.1**, EU reporting entities will not be able to apply these amendments in their statutory financial statements until they have been endorsed.*

6.1.2 *Accounting for investments in subsidiaries, jointly controlled entities or associates at cost: entities that have not yet adopted the May 2008 amendments to IFRS 1 and IAS 27*

Prior to the May 2008 amendment discussed above, IAS 27 defined the cost method as follows:

[IAS 27(2003).4]

> 'The cost method is a method of accounting for an investment whereby the investment is recognised at cost. The investor recognises income from the investment only to the extent that the investor receives distributions from retained earnings of the investee arising

> after the date of acquisition. Distributions received in excess of such profits are regarded as a recovery of investment and are recognised as a reduction of the cost of the investment.'

Prior to the May 2008 amendment discussed above, IAS 18.32 noted that when it is difficult to allocate dividends between pre- and post-acquisition net income except on an arbitrary basis, dividends are recognised as revenue unless they clearly represent a recovery of part of the cost of the equity securities.

UK

Under UK GAAP, when accounting for distributions received from a subsidiary, no distinction is drawn between pre- and post-acquisition profits; all amounts are taken to profit or loss and, separately, the investment is written down if impaired. The definition of the cost method means that, in some cases, cost for the purposes of IFRS financial statements will not be the same as the figure currently recorded in UK financial statements. Moreover, until the amendments discussed at ***6.1.1*** *are endorsed, there are no exemptions on first-time adoption in respect of this figure. Accordingly, UK companies adopting IFRSs before the amendments are endorsed will need to consider whether, at any stage, subsidiaries have paid dividends out of pre-acquisition profits and, hence, whether the cost of investment needs to be adjusted for IFRS purposes.*

It is likely that any adjustment, on first-time adoption, to reduce the cost of an investment in respect of dividends out of pre-acquisition profits, will also reduce the balance of profits available for distribution by the parent.

6.1.3 *Merger relief and group reconstruction relief*

UK

In certain circumstances, s133 of the Companies Act (relating to merger relief and group reconstruction relief) allows a parent to record an investment in a subsidiary in its individual statement of financial position at an amount less than the fair value of the consideration paid to acquire that investment. This relief will not be available to a UK parent company producing IFRS solus accounts. This follows from the IASB Glossary definition of 'cost' which includes '... the fair value of the other consideration given'; the only exceptions to recording such an investment at the fair value of the consideration paid will arise once the amendments discussed at ***6.1.1*** *are endorsed.*

Where a UK parent company adopting IFRSs before the amendments discussed at ***6.1.1*** *are endorsed has, under UK GAAP, taken advantage of these reliefs and recorded an investment in subsidiary at a lower amount, it* *will be necessary on first-time adoption of IFRSs to restate the investment to the full cost calculated in accordance with IAS 27.*

6.1.4 *New intermediate parent*

Where a new intermediate parent is introduced into an existing group through an exchange of shares, the ultimate parent will have exchanged an investment in one or more subsidiaries for an investment in the new intermediate parent. The question arises as to what carrying amount should be attributed to the new intermediate parent in the separate financial statements of the ultimate parent. (Note that the discussion at **6.1.1** relates only to the accounting required in the financial statements of the new intermediate parent itself.)

Where the new intermediate parent has no net assets, and the exchange is for shares, the exchange will not have commercial substance (by analogy with the principle described in IAS 16.24 – 25, and discussed at **section 4.3.2** in **chapter 6**). Moreover, the disposal of the shares previously owned directly by the parent would not meet the derecognition criteria of IAS 39 in the parent's accounting records. Accordingly, the parent's investment in the new intermediate parent should be initially recorded at the previous carrying amount of the assets given in exchange. In addition, for the purpose of determining whether dividends are paid out of pre-acquisition profits (see **6.1.2**), the relevant date will continue to be that on which the former subsidiaries were acquired, and not the date on which the new intermediate parent was introduced.

Example 6.1.4

Cost of new intermediate shell company in parent's financial statements

Company A originally acquired 100 per cent of Company B for cash consideration of £1,000. Some time later, when the fair value of B had increased to £9,000 and the total equity reported in B's separate financial statements was £4,000, a new intermediate parent, Company C, was inserted into this structure. C issued 500 £1 shares (being the whole of its share capital) to A in exchange for the latter's entire shareholding in B. C has no other assets or liabilities. B has never paid any dividends to A.

From the perspective of A, the exchange of shares in B for shares in C does not have commercial substance; the underlying interests of A have not changed. Accordingly, the cost of C in the books of A should be £1,000 (the original cost of B), and not £9,000.

From the perspective of C, however, the acquisition of B does have commercial substance. Thus:

- if C has adopted IAS 27(2008).38B & 38C (as discussed at **6.1.1**) then, provided the specified criteria are met, the cost of B in the books of C will be £4,000 (being the carrying amount of C's share of the equity items shown in the separate financial statements of B);
- otherwise, the cost of B in the books of C will be £9,000.

6.2 Investments in subsidiaries, jointly controlled entities and associates that are classified as held for sale

For periods beginning on or after 1 January 2009, the requirements of IAS 27.38 are modified, as described below, by *Improvements to IFRSs* issued in May 2008. Earlier application of the amendment to IAS 27 is permitted, but an entity choosing to apply the amendment early must disclose that fact.

Following the amendment, the option within IAS 27(2008).38 to account for investments in subsidiaries, jointly controlled entities and associates either (i) at cost or (ii) in accordance with IAS 39 also applies to such investments that are classified as held for sale. Thus, when investments in subsidiaries, jointly controlled entities and associates that have been accounted for in accordance with IAS 39 are classified as held for sale, they continue to be measured in accordance with IAS 39. [IAS 27(2008).38]

Before the amendment was made, IAS 27 stated that investments in subsidiaries, jointly controlled entities and associates that are classified as held for sale (or included in a disposal group that is classified as held for sale) in accordance with IFRS 5 should be accounted for under that Standard (see **chapter 29**). [IAS 27(2008).38, previously IAS 27(2003).37]

The purpose of the amendment was to eliminate any apparent inconsistency in this requirement as previously drafted. The measurement requirements of IFRS 5 do not apply to financial assets within the scope of IAS 39. But it was not clear, prior to the amendment, whether a subsidiary that had been accounted for under IAS 39 should be regarded as still within the scope of IAS 39 once it was classified as held for sale. Two different interpretations were possible:

- that IAS 39 continued to apply, and therefore such subsidiaries were outside the scope of IFRS 5's measurement requirements; or

- that IAS 39 no longer applied, and therefore such subsidiaries were now within the scope of IFRS 5's measurement requirements.

In modifying the Standard, the IASB has favoured the former interpretation. Nevertheless, it was clearly possible to read the words of the standards so as to reach the other view. In light of this, where an entity has not yet adopted the amendment to IAS 27, either interpretation appears acceptable.

UK *At the time of writing, the amendments made to IAS 27 by* Improvements to IFRSs *issued in May 2008 have not yet been endorsed for use in the EU. However, as explained above, it may be argued that the accounting required as a result of the amendment does not conflict with the previous requirements of IAS 27 and IFRS 5. Accordingly, EU reporting entities may choose to follow the revised guidance in their statutory financial statements immediately.*

7 Disclosure

7.1 Consolidated financial statements

The following disclosures are required in consolidated financial statements:

[IAS 27(2008).41, previously IAS 27(2003).40]

- the nature of the relationship between the parent and a subsidiary when the parent does not own, directly or indirectly through subsidiaries, more than one half of the voting power;
- the reasons why the ownership, directly or indirectly through subsidiaries, of more than half of the voting power or potential voting power of an investee does not constitute control;
- the end of the reporting period of the financial statements of a subsidiary when such financial statements are used to prepare consolidated financial statements and are as of a date or for a period that is different from that of the parent's financial statements, and the reason for using a different date or period; and
- the nature and extent of any significant restrictions (e.g. resulting from borrowing arrangements or regulatory requirements) on the ability of subsidiaries to transfer funds to the parent in the form of cash dividends or to repay loans or advances.

7.1.1 *Additional disclosures required for entities that have adopted IAS 27(2008)*

For an entity that has adopted IAS 27(2008), the following additional disclosures are required in consolidated financial statements:

[IAS 27(2008).41]

- a schedule that shows the effects of any changes in a parent's ownership interest in a subsidiary that do not result in a loss of control on the equity attributable to owners of the parent; and
- if control of a subsidiary is lost, the gain or loss, if any, recognised in accordance with IAS 27(2008).34 (see **5.7.1**), and:
  - the portion of that gain or loss attributable to recognising any investment retained in the former subsidiary at its fair value at the date when control is lost; and
  - the line item(s) in the statement of comprehensive income in which the gain or loss is recognised (if not presented separately in the statement of comprehensive income).

7.2 Separate financial statements

7.2.1 *Parent exempt from preparing consolidated financial statements*

The following disclosure requirements apply when separate financial statements are prepared for a parent that, in accordance with IAS 27.10 (see **4.2** above) is not required to prepare consolidated financial statements and elects not to do so. In these circumstances, the separate financial statements should disclose:

[IAS 27(2008).42, previously IAS 27(2003).41]

- the fact that the financial statements are separate financial statements;
- that the exemption from consolidation has been used;
- the name and country of incorporation or residence of the entity whose consolidated financial statements that comply with IFRSs have been produced for public use; and
- the address where those consolidated financial statements can be obtained.

UK

> *Similarly, under the Companies Act 2006, the reason why the company is not required to prepare group accounts must be stated. If the reason is that all the subsidiary undertakings of the company fall within the exclusions provided for in CA 2006 s405 (see* **2.3.2** *in* ***chapter 1****), for each subsidiary undertaking it must be stated which of those exclusions applies. [Acc Regs Sch. 4: 10]*

In addition, the separate financial statements should disclose:

[IAS 27(2008).42, previously IAS 27(2003).41]

- a list of significant investments in subsidiaries, jointly controlled entities and associates, including:
  - the name;
  - country of incorporation or residence;
  - the proportion of ownership interest held; and
  - if different, the proportion of voting power held; and
- a description of the method used to account for such investments.

7.2.2 *Parent not exempt from preparing consolidated financial statements*

When a parent (other than a parent covered by **7.2.1**), venturer with an interest in a jointly controlled entity or an investor in an associate elects or is required to prepare separate financial statements in addition to its 'main' financial statements, those separate financial statements should disclose:

[IAS 27(2008).43, previously IAS 27(2003).42]

- the fact that the statements are separate financial statements and the reasons why those statements are prepared if not required by law;
- a list of significant investments in subsidiaries, jointly controlled entities and associates, including:
  - the name;
  - country of incorporation or residence;
  - the proportion of ownership interest held; and
  - if different, the proportion of voting power held; and
- a description of the method used to account for such investments.

The separate financial statements are also required to identify the 'main' financial statements to which they relate. [IAS 27(2008).43, previously IAS 27(2003).42]

7.3 Additional disclosures required for UK companies

For UK companies, certain additional disclosures are required by the Companies Act. The disclosures needed under the Companies Act 2006 are set out at **7.4**, *and supersede those of the Companies Act 1985 for periods beginning on or after 6 April 2008. The disclosures needed under the Companies Act 1985 are set out at* **7.5**. *In both cases, the disclosure requirements should be read in conjunction with the additional guidance in* **sections 7.3.1** *to* **7.3.3** *below.* UK

The disclosure requirements under the Companies Act 2006 are structured and drafted differently from those of the 1985 Act. For the most part, the impact of changes is likely to be small, but UK companies should note, in particular, that some references to Great Britain in the 1985 requirements have been widened to refer to the United Kingdom (i.e. including Northern Ireland) in the 2006 requirements.

7.3.1 *Definitions*

Note that the following terms used in **sections 7.3** *to* **7.5** *should be interpreted according to their UK GAAP definitions:* UK

- *subsidiary undertaking – see the definition at* **2.3.1** *in* **chapter 1**;
- *associated undertaking –an undertaking in which an undertaking included in the consolidation has a participating interest and over whose operating and financial policy it exercises a significant influence, and which is not:*
  [Acc Regs Sch. 6: 19, previously CA 1985 Sch. 4A: 20]
  - o *a subsidiary undertaking of the parent company; or*
  - o *an unincorporated joint venture that is proportionally consolidated.*

7.3.2 *Exemptions from disclosure requirements*

If the undertakings referred to in **7.4** *or* **7.5** *are too numerous, the directors need only give the information for undertakings which principally affect the* UK *figures shown in the accounts and for subsidiary undertakings which have been excluded from consolidation. They should include a statement to this effect and annex the full information to the company's next annual return. [CA 2006 s410, previously CA 1985 s231(5) and (6)]*

Where an undertaking is established, or carries on business, outside the United Kingdom, most of the disclosures listed in **7.4** *or* **7.5** *may be omitted if, in the opinion of the directors, disclosure would be seriously prejudicial to the business or to the group and the Secretary of State agrees to the exclusion. Where advantage is taken of this exemption, this fact should be stated in the notes to the accounts. [CA 2006 s409, previously CA 1985 s231(3) and (4)]*

Application to the Secretary of State to gain his agreement, although a formal procedure, is not one for which guidance is available from BERR. A letter would seem necessary, explaining why the directors believe disclosure would be seriously prejudicial, and experience suggests that the reasons given should be seen to have real substance. The criteria applied by the Secretary of State tend to vary according to the overseas country concerned and from time to time.

7.3.3 Comparative information

UK

Companies reporting under UK GAAP do not need to provide corresponding information for certain of the disclosures listed in **sections 7.4** *and* **7.5***, but it is not clear to what extent the same exemption should be available to companies reporting under IFRSs.*

The exemption in question was previously set out in CA 1985 Sch. 4: 58(3), but is now reflected in FRS 28 Corresponding Amounts. *The uncertainty for IFRS reporters arises because they are not within the scope of FRSs, and IAS 1* Presentation of Financial Statements *requires comparative information for all amounts reported in the financial statements, except when an IFRS permits or requires otherwise. The disclosures to which the FRS 28 exemption applies are listed in* **sections 7.4** *and* **7.5** *and marked (*).*

To the extent that these disclosures are also required by IAS 27 (e.g. the proportion of ownership interest held – see **7.1** *and* **7.2***), it seems clear that comparative information is required. To the extent that the disclosures marked (*) go beyond those required by IFRSs, it seems unlikely that the disclosure regime is intended to be more onerous for IFRS reporters than for UK GAAP reporters, and it may therefore be judged acceptable to omit* *comparative information. But in many cases it may be simplest to provide comparative information for all disclosures.*

7.4 Additional disclosures required for UK companies under the Companies Act 2006

UK

The disclosures described in this section apply to all UK companies other than those which are subject to the small companies regime. The disclosures described in **7.4.1** *apply irrespective of whether group accounts are required. In addition, UK companies not required to prepare group accounts should provide the disclosures described in* **7.4.2***; and UK companies required to prepare group accounts should provide the disclosures described in* **7.4.3***. The disclosures apply for periods beginning on or after 6 April 2008.*

For the purposes of the disclosures described in ***sections 7.4.1*** *to* ***7.4.3****, shares held by way of security must be treated as held by the person providing the security:*

[Acc Regs Sch. 4: 14, 22]

(*a*) *where apart from the right to exercise them for the purpose of preserving the value of the security, or of realising it, the rights attached to the shares are exercisable only in accordance with that person's instructions; and*

(*b*) *where the shares are held in connection with the granting of loans as part of normal business activities and apart from the right to exercise them for the purpose of preserving the value of the security, or of realising it, the rights attached to the shares are exercisable only in that person's interests.*

7.4.1 Disclosures needed irrespective of whether group accounts are required

7.4.1.1 Disclosures relating to subsidiary undertakings

UK

The following information must be given where at the end of the financial year the company has subsidiary undertakings:

[Acc Regs Sch. 4: 1]

- *the name of each subsidiary undertaking;*

- *if it is incorporated outside the United Kingdom, the country in which it is incorporated; and*
- *if it is unincorporated, the address of its principal place of business.*

For each subsidiary undertaking not included in consolidated accounts by the company, the company must disclose (a) the aggregate amount of its capital and reserves as at the end of its relevant financial year (see below), and (b) its profit or loss for that year. This information need not be given if:

[Acc Regs Sch. 4: 2, 14]

- *the company is exempt under CA 2006 s400 or s401 from preparing group accounts (see* **4.2.1** *and* **4.2.2***); or*
- *the company's investment in the subsidiary undertaking is included in the company's accounts under the equity method; or*
- *the subsidiary undertaking is not required by any provision of the 2006 Act to deliver a copy of its balance sheet for its relevant financial year and does not otherwise publish that balance sheet in the United Kingdom or elsewhere, and the company's holding (including any shares held by a subsidiary undertaking, or by a person acting on behalf of the company or a subsidiary undertaking, but excluding any shares held on behalf of a person other than the company or a subsidiary undertaking) is less than 50% of the nominal value of the shares in the undertaking; or*
- *the information is not material.*

The relevant financial year of a subsidiary undertaking is:

[Acc Regs Sch. 4: 2(6)]

- *if its financial year ends with that of the company, that year, and*
- *if not, its financial year ending last before the end of the company's financial year.*

The number, description and amount of the shares in the company held by or on behalf of its subsidiary undertakings must be disclosed, except where the subsidiary undertaking is concerned as:

[Acc Regs Sch. 4: 3]

- *personal representative or,*
- *as trustee, provided that neither the company, nor any of its subsidiary undertakings, is beneficially interested under the trust, otherwise*

than by way of security only for the purposes of a transaction entered into by it in the ordinary course of a business which includes the lending of money.

7.4.1.2 Disclosures relating to other significant holdings

UK

Where at the end of the financial year the company has a significant holding (see below) in an undertaking which is neither a subsidiary undertaking of the company, nor an associated undertaking nor an unincorporated joint venture that is proportionally consolidated, it must disclose:

[Acc Regs Sch. 4: 5]

- *the name of the undertaking;*
- *if the undertaking is incorporated outside the United Kingdom, the country in which it is incorporated;*
- *if it is unincorporated, the address of its principal place of business;*
- *the identity of each class of shares in the undertaking held by the company; (*) and*
- *the proportion of the nominal value of the shares of that class represented by those shares. (*)*

A holding is significant if:

[Acc Regs Sch. 4: 4]

- *it amounts to 20% or more of the nominal value of any class of shares in the undertaking; or*
- *the amount of the holding (as stated or included in the company's individual accounts) exceeds one-fifth of the amount (as so stated) of the company's assets.*

The company must also disclose (a) the aggregate amount of the capital and reserves of the undertaking as at the end of its relevant financial year, and (b) its profit or loss for that year. This information need not be given if:

[Acc Regs Sch. 4: 6, 13]

- *the undertaking is not required by any provision of the 2006 Act to deliver a copy of its balance sheet for its relevant financial year and does not otherwise publish that balance sheet in the United Kingdom or elsewhere, and the company's holding is less than 50% of the nominal value of the shares in the undertaking; or*

- *the company is exempt by virtue of CA 2006 s400 or s401 from the requirement to prepare group accounts (see* **4.2.1** *and* **4.2.2***), and the investment of the company in all undertakings in which it has such a holding is shown, in aggregate, in the notes to the accounts under the equity method; or*
- *the information is not material.*

The relevant financial year of an undertaking is:

[Acc Regs Sch. 4: 6(4)]

- *if its financial year ends with that of the company, that year, and*
- *if not, its financial year ending last before the end of the company's financial year.*

For the purposes of the disclosures in this section, shares held on the company's behalf by any person are included, but shares held on behalf of a person other than the company are excluded. [Acc Regs Sch. 4: 14, 22]

7.4.1.3 Disclosures relating to membership of qualifying undertakings

UK

A qualifying undertaking is:

[Acc Regs Sch. 4: 7]

- *a qualifying partnership; or*
- *an unlimited company each of whose members is:*
  - o *a limited company; or*
  - o *another unlimited company each of whose members is a limited company; or*
  - o *a Scottish partnership each of whose members is a limited company.*

  References to a limited company, another unlimited company or a Scottish partnership include a comparable undertaking incorporated in or formed under the law of a country or territory outside the United Kingdom.

Where at the end of the financial year the company is a member of a qualifying undertaking, unless the information is not material, the company must disclose:

[Acc Regs Sch. 4: 7]

- *the name and legal form of the undertaking, and*
- *the address of the undertaking's registered office (whether in or outside the United Kingdom) or, if it does not have such an office, its head office (whether in or outside the United Kingdom).*

If the undertaking is a qualifying partnership, the company must also state either:

- *that a copy of the latest accounts of the undertaking has been or is to be appended to the copy of the company's accounts sent to the registrar under CA 2006 s444; or*
- *the name of at least one body corporate (which may be the company) in whose group accounts the undertaking has been or is to be 'dealt with on a consolidated basis' (note that this encompasses equity accounting and proportional consolidation as well as full consolidation). But this information need not be given if the notes to the company's accounts disclose that advantage has been taken of the exemption conferred by regulation 7 of the Partnerships (Accounts) Regulations 2008.*

7.4.2 UK companies not required to prepare group accounts

UK

For each class of share held by the company in a subsidiary undertaking, the company must disclose:

[Acc Regs Sch. 4: 11]

- *the identity of the class; (*) and*
- *the proportion of the nominal value of the shares of that class represented by those shares; (*)*

distinguishing shares held by or on behalf of the company itself from those attributed to the company which are held by or on behalf of a subsidiary undertaking.

Where information is disclosed in respect of a subsidiary undertaking not included in consolidated accounts by the company (see **7.4.1.1***) and that undertaking's financial year does not end with that of the company, the date on which that undertaking's last financial year ended must be disclosed (i.e. the last before the end of the company's financial year). [Acc Regs Sch. 4: 12]*

For the purposes of the disclosures in this section, any shares held by a subsidiary undertaking, or by a person acting on behalf of the company or a subsidiary undertaking, are attributed to the company; but any shares held on behalf of a person other than the company or a subsidiary undertaking are excluded. [Acc Regs Sch. 4: 14]

7.4.3 UK companies required to prepare group accounts

UK

*For the purposes of **sections 7.4.3.1** to **7.4.3.5**, references to shares held by the group are to any shares held by or on behalf of the parent company or any of its subsidiary undertakings; but any shares held on behalf of a person other than the parent company or any of its subsidiary undertakings are not to be treated as held by the group. [Acc Regs Sch. 4: 22]*

7.4.3.1 Disclosures relating to subsidiary undertakings

UK

*As well as the information described in **7.4.1.1**, the following information must be given for those undertakings which are subsidiary undertakings of the parent company at the end of the financial year:*

[Acc Regs Sch. 4: 16, 17]

- *whether the subsidiary undertaking is included in the consolidation and, if it is not, the reasons for excluding it;*
- *for each subsidiary undertaking, by virtue of which of the conditions specified in CA 2006 s1162(2) or (4) it is a subsidiary undertaking of its immediate parent undertaking (see **2.3.1** in **chapter 1**). This disclosure is not required if the relevant condition is that specified in s1162(2)(a) (i.e. holding a majority of the voting rights) and the immediate parent undertaking holds the same proportion of the shares in the undertaking as it holds voting rights;*
- *the identity of each class of shares held; (*) and*
- *the proportion of the nominal value of the shares of that class represented by those shares, disclosing those held by the parent company and, if different, those held by the group (i.e. the parent company and its subsidiary undertakings). (*)*

For the purposes of these disclosures, shares held on the company's behalf by any person are included, but shares held on behalf of a person other than the company are excluded. [Acc Regs Sch. 4: 22]

7.4.3.2 Disclosures relating to joint ventures

Where an unincorporated joint venture is included in the consolidated accounts using proportional consolidation, the company must disclose: (UK)

[Acc Regs Sch. 4: 18]

- *the name of the joint venture;*
- *the address of its principal place of business;*
- *the factors on which joint management of the joint venture is based; and*
- *the proportion of the capital of the joint venture held by undertakings included in the consolidation. (*)*

If the joint venture's year end was different from that of the company, the date of the joint venture's last year end before that of the company must be disclosed.

7.4.3.3 Disclosures relating to associated undertakings

Where any undertaking included in the consolidation has an interest in an associated undertaking, the company must disclose: (UK)

[Acc Regs Sch. 4: 19]

- *the name of the associated undertaking;*
- *if the undertaking is incorporated outside the United Kingdom, the country in which it is incorporated;*
- *if it is unincorporated, the address of its principal place of business.*
- *the identity of each class of shares held; (*) and*
- *the proportion of the nominal value of the shares of that class represented by those shares, showing separately the shares held by the company and the shares held by the group (i.e. the parent company and its subsidiary undertakings). (*)*

This information must be given even if equity accounting has not been applied because the amounts in question are not material for the purpose of giving a true and fair view

For the purposes of these disclosures, shares held on the company's behalf by any person are included, but shares held on behalf of a person other than the company are excluded. [Acc Regs Sch. 4: 22]

7.4.3.4 Disclosures relating to other significant holdings

UK

The disclosures described at **7.4.1.2** *must also be given where at the end of the financial year the group has a significant holding in an undertaking which is neither a subsidiary undertaking of the parent company, nor an associated undertaking nor an unincorporated joint venture that is proportionally consolidated. For this purpose, references to the company in* **7.4.1.2** *are treated as a reference to the group (i.e. the parent company and its subsidiary undertakings). [Acc Regs Sch. 4: 20]*

A holding is significant if:

- *it amounts to 20% or more of the nominal value of any class of shares in the undertaking; or*
- *the amount of the holding (as stated or included in the group accounts) exceeds one-fifth of the amount of the group's assets (as so stated).*

The relevant financial year of an outside undertaking is:

- *if its financial year ends with that of the parent company, that year, and*
- *if not, its financial year ending last before the end of the parent company's financial year.*

7.4.3.5 Disclosures relating to membership of qualifying undertakings

UK

The disclosures described at **7.4.1.3** *must also be given where at the end of the financial year the group is a member of a qualifying undertaking. [Acc Regs Sch. 4: 21]*

7.5 Additional disclosures required for UK companies under the Companies Act 1985

UK

UK companies required to prepare group accounts should provide the disclosures described in **7.5.1**. *UK companies not required to prepare group* *accounts should provide the disclosures described in* ***7.5.2****. The disclosures apply for periods beginning before 6 April 2008.*

7.5.1 UK companies required to prepare group accounts

7.5.1.1 Disclosures relating to subsidiary undertakings

The disclosures listed below are required for each undertaking that is a subsidiary undertaking at the end of the financial year: UK

[CA 1985 Sch. 5: 15, 16]

- *the name of each undertaking;*
- *if it is incorporated outside Great Britain, its country of incorporation;*
- *if it is unincorporated, the address of its principal place of business;*
- *whether it is included in the consolidation and, if not, the reasons for excluding it;*
- *which of the conditions listed at* ***2.3.1*** *in* ***chapter 1*** *are satisfied, i.e. explaining why it meets the definition of a subsidiary (this disclosure is not required where a majority of the voting rights is held and the immediate parent holds the same proportion of shares as it holds voting rights); and*
- *for each class of shares held, the identity and proportion of the nominal value held of that class. (*)*

The information required by the final bullet should be given separately for shares held by the parent company and shares held by the group (if different).

In addition, the number, description and amount of shares in the company held by or on behalf of its subsidiary undertakings should be disclosed. This requirement does not apply to shares in the case of which the subsidiary undertaking is concerned as:

[CA 1985 Sch. 5: 20]

- *personal representative; or*
- *trustee, providing neither the company nor any of its subsidiary undertakings is beneficially interested under the trust (other than by*

way of security only for the purposes of a transaction entered into by it in the ordinary course of a business which includes the lending of money).

Where a subsidiary undertaking is excluded from consolidation, the notes to the accounts should disclose the aggregate amount of the capital and reserves of the excluded subsidiary undertaking at the end of its relevant financial year and its profit or loss for that year. The relevant financial year is that ending at the same date as that of the parent or, if year ends are not coterminous, the most recent year ending before that date. This information need not be given if:

[CA 1985 Sch. 5: 17]

(i) the investment in that undertaking is accounted for by way of the equity method; or

(ii) the subsidiary undertaking is not required by the Act to deliver a copy of its balance sheet (i.e. statement of financial position) and does not otherwise publish that balance sheet in Great Britain or elsewhere and the holding of the group is less than 50 per cent of the nominal value of the shares in the undertaking; or

(iii) the information is not material.

7.5.1.2 Disclosures relating to certain joint ventures

UK

The disclosures listed below are required for each unincorporated joint venture that is proportionally consolidated:

[CA 1985 Sch. 5: 21]

- *the name of each undertaking;*
- *the address of its principal place of business;*
- *the factors on which joint management of the undertaking is based;*
- *the proportion of the undertaking's capital that is held by undertakings included in the consolidation; (*) and*
- *where the undertaking's year end is different from that of the group's parent, the date of the most recent year ending before that of the parent.*

7.5.1.3 Disclosures relating to associated undertakings

UK

The disclosures listed below are required for each associated undertaking (see the definition at **7.3.1***) of the parent and its consolidated subsidiary undertakings:*

[CA 1985 Sch. 5: 22]

- *the name of each undertaking;*
- *if it is incorporated outside Great Britain, its country of incorporation;*
- *if it is unincorporated, the address of its principal place of business; and*
- *for each class of shares held, the identity and proportion of the nominal value held of that class. (*)*

The information required by the final bullet should be given separately for shares held by the parent company and shares held by the group.

7.5.1.4 Disclosures relating to other significant holdings of the parent company

UK

The disclosures listed below are required for undertakings that represent significant holdings of the parent company at the end of its financial year, excluding undertakings already covered under **7.5.1.1** *to* **7.5.1.3** *(for this purpose, a holding is significant if it is 20 per cent or more of the nominal value of any class of shares, or the amount at which the holding is included in the parent company's individual balance sheet (i.e. statement of financial position) exceeds 20 per cent of the parent company's assets):*

[CA 1985 Sch. 5: 24]

- *the name of each such undertaking;*
- *if it is incorporated outside Great Britain, its country of incorporation;*
- *if it is unincorporated, the address of its principal place of business; and*
- *for each class of shares held by the parent company, the identity and proportion of the nominal value held of that class. (*)*

In addition, the notes to the accounts should disclose the aggregate amount of the capital and reserves of each such undertaking at the end of its relevant financial year and its profit or loss for that year. The relevant financial year is that ending at the same date as that of the parent or, if year ends are not coterminous, the most recent year ending before that date. This information need not be given if:

[CA 1985 Sch. 5: 25]

(*i*) *the undertaking is not required by the Act to deliver a copy of its balance sheet and does not otherwise publish that balance sheet in Great Britain or elsewhere and the holding of the parent is less than 50 per cent of the nominal value of the shares in the undertaking; or*

(*ii*) *the information is not material.*

7.5.1.5 Disclosures relating to other significant holdings of the group

UK

The disclosures listed below are required for undertakings that represent significant holdings of the group at the end of the financial year, excluding undertakings already covered under **7.5.1.1** *to* **7.5.1.3** *(for this purpose, a holding is significant if it is 20 per cent or more of the nominal value of any class of shares, or the amount at which the holding is included in the group's balance sheet (i.e. statement of financial position) exceeds 20 per cent of the group's assets):*

[CA 1985 Sch. 5: 27]

- *the name of each such undertaking;*
- *if it is incorporated outside Great Britain, its country of incorporation;*
- *if it is unincorporated, the address of its principal place of business; and*
- *for each class of shares held by the group, the identity and proportion of the nominal value held of that class.* (*)

In addition, the notes to the accounts should disclose the aggregate amount of the capital and reserves of each such undertaking at the end of its relevant financial year and its profit or loss for that year. The relevant financial year is that ending at the same date as that of the parent or, if year ends are not coterminous, the most recent year ending before that date. This information need not be given if:

[CA 1985 Sch. 5: 28]

(i) *the undertaking is not required by the Act to deliver a copy of its balance sheet and does not otherwise publish that balance sheet in Great Britain or elsewhere and the holding of the group is less than 50 per cent of the nominal value of the shares in the undertaking; or*

(ii) *the information is not material.*

7.5.1.6 Disclosures relating to membership of qualifying undertakings

UK

The disclosures listed below are required where, at the end of the financial year, the parent company or group was a member of a qualifying partnership or of a qualifying company (as defined in the Partnerships and Unlimited Companies (Accounts) Regulations 1993):

[CA 1985 Sch. 5: 28A]

- *the name and legal form of each undertaking; and*
- *the address of its registered office (whether in or outside Great Britain) or, if it has no registered office, the address of its head office (whether in or outside Great Britain).*

The information above is not required if it is not material. [CA 1985 Sch. 5: 28A(4)]

Where, at the end of the financial year, the parent company or group was a member of a qualifying partnership, the notes to the accounts should disclose (as appropriate) either:

[CA 1985 Sch. 5: 28A]

- *that a copy of the latest accounts of the partnership has been or is to be appended to the copy of the company's accounts sent to the registrar under CA 1985 s242; or*
- *the name of at least one body corporate (which may be the company) in whose group accounts the partnership has been or is to be 'dealt with on a consolidated basis' (note that this encompasses equity accounting and proportional consolidation as well as full consolidation); or*
- *that advantage has been taken of the exemption conferred by regulation 7 of the Partnerships and Unlimited Companies (Accounts) Regulations 1993.*

7.5.2 UK companies not required to prepare group accounts

7.5.2.1 Disclosures relating to subsidiary undertakings

UK

The reason why the company is not required to prepare group accounts should be given. If the reason is that all the subsidiary undertakings are excluded under CA 1985 s229 (see ***2.3.2*** *in* ***chapter 1****), the exclusions applicable to each subsidiary undertaking should be stated. [CA 1985 Sch. 5: 1]*

The disclosures listed below are required for each undertaking that is a subsidiary undertaking at the end of the financial year:

[CA 1985 Sch. 5: 1, 2]

- *the name of each undertaking;*
- *if it is incorporated outside Great Britain, its country of incorporation;*
- *if it is unincorporated, the address of its principal place of business; and*
- *for each class of shares held, the identity and proportion of the nominal value held of that class. (*)*

The information given for the final bullet should distinguish between shares held by the company itself and shares attributed to it which are held by or on behalf of a subsidiary undertaking.

In addition, the number, description and amount of shares in the company held by or on behalf of its subsidiary undertakings should be disclosed. This requirement does not apply to shares in the case of which the subsidiary undertaking is concerned as:

[CA 1985 Sch. 5: 6]

- *personal representative; or*
- *trustee, providing neither the company nor any of its subsidiary undertakings is beneficially interested under the trust (other than by way of security only for the purposes of a transaction entered into by it in the ordinary course of a business which includes the lending of money).*

For each subsidiary undertaking, the notes to the accounts should disclose the aggregate amount of its capital and reserves at the end of its relevant financial year and its profit or loss for that year (giving the date of the year end if different from that of the parent). [CA 1985 Sch. 5: 3, 4] The relevant financial year is that ending at the same date as that of the parent or, if year ends are not coterminous, the most recent year ending before that date. This information need not be given if:

[CA 1985 Sch. 5: 3]

(i) *the company is exempt from producing group accounts under CA 1985 s228 (but the relief does not apparently extend to a company that is exempt under CA 1985 s228A); or*

(ii) *the company's investment in that undertaking is accounted for in the company's accounts by way of the equity method; or*

(iii) *the subsidiary undertaking is not required by the Act to deliver a copy of its balance sheet (i.e. statement of financial position) and does not otherwise publish that balance sheet in Great Britain or elsewhere and the holding of the group is less than 50 per cent of the nominal value of the shares in the undertaking; or*

(iv) *the information is not material.*

7.5.2.2 Disclosures relating to other significant holdings

UK

The disclosures listed below are required for undertakings that represent significant holdings of the parent company at the end of its financial year, excluding subsidiary undertakings (for this purpose, a holding is significant if it is 20 per cent or more of the nominal value of any class of shares, or the amount at which the holding is included in the parent company's individual balance sheet (i.e. statement of financial position) exceeds 20 per cent of the parent company's assets):

[CA 1985 Sch. 5: 7, 8]

- *the name of each such undertaking;*
- *if it is incorporated outside Great Britain, its country of incorporation;*
- *if it is unincorporated, the address of its principal place of business; and*
- *for each class of shares held by the company, the identity and proportion of the nominal value held of that class. (*)*

In addition, the notes to the accounts should disclose the aggregate amount of the capital and reserves of each such undertaking at the end of its relevant financial year and its profit or loss for that year. The relevant financial year is that ending at the same date as that of the parent or, if year ends are not coterminous, the most recent year ending before that date. This information need not be given if:

[CA 1985 Sch. 5: 9]

(*i*) *the company is exempt from producing group accounts under CA 1985 s228 and the investment of the company in all such undertakings is shown, in aggregate, in the notes to the accounts by way of the equity method of valuation (but the relief does not apparently extend to a company that is exempt under CA 1985 s228A); or*

(*ii*) *the undertaking is not required by the Act to deliver a copy of its balance sheet and does not otherwise publish that balance sheet in Great Britain or elsewhere and the holding of the parent is less than 50 per cent of the nominal value of the shares in the undertaking; or*

(*iii*) *the information is not material.*

7.5.2.3 *Disclosures relating to membership of qualifying undertakings*

UK *The disclosures listed below are required where, at the end of the financial year, the company was a member of a qualifying partnership or of a qualifying company (as defined in the Partnerships and Unlimited Companies (Accounts) Regulations 1993):*

[CA 1985 Sch. 5: 9A]

- *the name and legal form of each undertaking; and*
- *the address of its registered office (whether in or outside Great Britain) or, if it has no registered office, the address of its head office (whether in or outside Great Britain).*

The information above is not required if it is not material. [CA 1985 Sch. 5: 9A(4)]

Where, at the end of the financial year, the company was a member of a qualifying partnership, the notes to the accounts should disclose (as appropriate) either:

[CA 1985 Sch. 5: 9A]

- *that a copy of the latest accounts of the partnership has been or is to be appended to the copy of the company's accounts sent to the registrar under CA 1985 s242; or*

- *the name of at least one body corporate (which may be the company) in whose group accounts the partnership has been or is to be 'dealt with on a consolidated basis' (note that this encompasses equity accounting and proportional consolidation as well as full consolidation); or*
- *that advantage has been taken of the exemption conferred by regulation 7 of the Partnerships and Unlimited Companies (Accounts) Regulations 1993.*

8 Effective date and transition: IAS 27 (2008)

The 2008 amendments to IAS 27 are effective for annual accounting periods beginning on or after 1 July 2009. [IAS 27(2008).45] This is the same effective date as for IFRS 3(2008), as discussed in **chapter 34**. The amendments can be applied early, but only if IFRS 3(2008) is adopted early and disclosure is made of early adoption. Because the adoption of IAS 27(2008) is linked to the adoption of IFRS 3(2008), this has the effect of limiting early adoption of IAS 27(2008) to annual reporting periods that begin on or after 30 June 2007 (see **14.1.2** in **chapter 34**).

The requirements of IAS 27(2008) are applied retrospectively with the following exceptions (which are applied prospectively):

[IAS 27(2008).45]

- attribution of total comprehensive income to the parent and non-controlling interests even if this results in the non-controlling interests having a deficit balance (see **5.3.1.2**). Therefore, entities are not permitted to restate the allocation of profit or loss between the parent and the non-controlling interests for reporting periods before the amendment is applied;
- accounting for changes in ownership interests in a subsidiary after control is obtained (see **5.6.1**). Therefore, these requirements should not be applied to changes in ownership interests that occurred before the amendments are applied; and
- accounting for loss of control (see **5.7.1**). Entities are not permitted to restate the carrying amount of an investment in a former subsidiary, nor to recalculate any gain or loss on the loss of control of a subsidiary, if control was lost before the amendments are applied.

At the time of writing, the amended version of IAS 27 has not yet been endorsed for use in the EU. Since the requirements of the amended Standard UK *differ in important respects from those of its predecessor, EU reporting entities will not be able to apply the revised version in their statutory financial statements until it is endorsed.*

9 Future developments

9.1 Consolidation (including Special Purpose Entities)

The IASB is currently working on an agenda project, *Consolidation (including Special Purpose Entities)*, which addresses both the basis (policy) on which a parent entity should consolidate its investments in subsidiaries, and the procedures for consolidation. It will result in the introduction of more rigorous guidance around the concept of control, which is the basis for consolidation under IAS 27. Most standard setters (including the IASB) have identified control as the appropriate basis for consolidation, but there appear to be differences in the way control is interpreted in deciding whether consolidation is required. As a result, there may be differences in how a reporting entity is defined.

The work on the consolidations project is likely to result in an amendment to, or replacement of, IAS 27 and SIC-12. At the time of writing, an exposure draft is expected in the fourth quarter of 2008, with a final IFRS in the second half of 2009.

34 Business combinations

1 Introduction

1.1 IFRS 3(2008) and IFRS 3(2004)

In January 2008, the IASB issued a revised version of IFRS 3 *Business Combinations,* which is effective for business combinations for which the acquisition date is on or after the beginning of the first annual reporting period after 1 July 2009. For business combinations with earlier acquisition dates, entities may continue to apply the previous version of IFRS 3 (as issued in 2004), which is discussed in **appendix 2**. Alternatively, subject to certain rules on transition, entities may choose to apply the revised version of IFRS 3 in advance of the 2009 effective date, provided that they disclose that fact.

At the same time as IFRS 3(2008), the IASB also issued a revised version of IAS 27 *Consolidated and Separate Financial Statements*. The changes to IAS 27 are discussed in **chapter 33**, but the most significant impacts are listed below.

UK

At the time of writing, the revised versions of IFRS 3 and IAS 27 have not yet been endorsed for use in the EU. Since the requirements of the revised Standards differ in important respects from those of the previous versions, EU reporting entities will not be able to apply the revised versions of IFRS 3 and IAS 27 in their statutory financial statements until the revised Standards are endorsed.

Some key drivers behind the changes to IFRS 3 and IAS 27 are:

- a greater emphasis on the use of fair value, potentially increasing the judgement and subjectivity around business combination accounting and requiring greater input by valuation experts;

- a focus on change in control as a significant economic event – introducing requirements to re-measure interests to fair value at the time control is achieved or lost, and recognising the impact of all transactions between controlling and non-controlling shareholders, not involving a loss of control, directly in equity; and

- a focus on what is given to the vendor as consideration, rather than what is spent to achieve the acquisition. Transaction costs, changes in the value of contingent consideration, settlement of pre-existing contracts, share-based payments and similar items will generally be accounted for separately from the business combination and affect profit or loss.

An overview of the most significant impacts for IFRS reporters of adopting IFRS 3(2008) and IAS 27(2008) is set out below.

- Costs incurred to effect a business combination (e.g. finder's fees, advisory, legal, accounting, valuation, and other professional or consulting fees) are expensed in the period incurred. (Costs incurred to issue debt or equity securities continue to be recognised in accordance with IAS 39 *Financial Instruments: Recognition and Measurement*.)

- Where the acquirer has a pre-existing equity interest in the entity acquired, it remeasures that previously-held interest to fair value as at the date of obtaining control, and recognises any resulting gain or loss in profit or loss.

- The term 'non-controlling interest' (NCI) replaces minority interest. At an acquisition date, the acquirer may choose, on a transaction by transaction basis, whether to measure NCI at:

  - fair value; or

  - the NCI's proportionate share of the net identifiable assets of the entity acquired.

  In order to measure NCI at fair value it may be possible to use market prices for the equity shares not held by the acquirer. When a market price is not available, because the shares are not publicly traded, an alternative valuation technique will need to be used to measure the NCI's fair value.

- Goodwill is measured at the acquisition date as the difference between:

- the aggregate of:
  - o the acquisition-date fair value of the consideration transferred;
  - o the amount of any non-controlling interests (NCI) in the entity acquired; and
  - o the acquisition-date fair value of any previously-held equity interest in the entity acquired (in a business combination achieved in stages); and
- the net of the acquisition-date fair value of the identifiable assets acquired and the liabilities assumed.

Accordingly, where an acquirer chooses to measure NCI at fair value at the acquisition date, the goodwill reported will typically be higher, reflecting goodwill attributable to the NCI.

- Once control is obtained, all subsequent increases and decreases in ownership interests that do not involve the loss of that control are treated as transactions among owners. Goodwill is not remeasured or adjusted. Instead, any difference between the change in the NCI and the fair value of the consideration paid or received is recognised directly in equity and attributed to the owners of the parent.

- Consideration for an acquisition, including contingent consideration, is measured at fair value at the acquisition date. Changes resulting from events after the acquisition date, such as the acquiree meeting an earnings target or reaching a specified share price, are recognised in profit or loss.

- The revised IAS 27 requires an entity to attribute their share of profit or loss to the NCI even if this results in the NCI having a deficit balance.

- When a parent ceases to have control of a subsidiary, the parent derecognises all assets, liabilities and NCI at their carrying amount. Any interest retained in the former subsidiary is recognised at its fair value at the date control is lost. Any gain or loss arising on loss of control is recognised in profit or loss. Note that a parent can lose control of a subsidiary through a sale or distribution, or through some other transaction or event in which it takes no part (e.g.

expropriation or the subsidiary being placed in administration or bankruptcy). If the loss of control of a former subsidiary involves the distribution of equity interests to owners of the parent acting in their capacity as owners, that distribution is recognised at the date control is lost.

- Other important changes include the following:
  - The scope of the revised IFRS 3 has been widened to include business combinations between mutual entities and business combinations achieved by contract alone.
  - The revised IFRS 3 includes specific guidance on whether replacement share based payment awards are part of the consideration transferred, and measurement of reacquired rights on initial recognition.
  - The revised Standard clarifies that an entity needs to reassess the classification of contractual arrangements on acquisition with the exception of insurance contracts and leases (for which the original classification as finance or operating stands). This is particularly relevant when looking at financial instruments, embedded derivatives and hedging relationships.

1.2 IFRS 3 *Business Combinations* (2008)

This chapter discusses the requirements of IFRS 3(2008) in the following sections:

Section 2	Scope
Section 3	The acquisition method of accounting
Section 4	Identifying a business combination
Section 5	Identifying the acquirer
Section 6	Determining the acquisition date
Section 7	Recognising and measuring the identifiable assets acquired, the liabilities assumed and any non-controlling interest in the acquiree
Section 8	Identifying and measuring consideration
Section 9	Recognising and measuring goodwill or a gain from a bargain purchase

Section 10	Post-combination accounting
Section 11	Step acquisitions
Section 12	Reverse acquisitions
Section 13	Disclosure
Section 14	Effective date and transition

Throughout this chapter, certain examples reproduced from the Illustrative Examples accompanying IFRS 3(2008) use the abbreviations AC and TC for Acquirer Company and Target Company respectively.

This chapter includes consideration of issues in IAS 38 *Intangible Assets* (see **section 6**) which are specific to IFRS 3. More detailed guidance on this Standard is included in **chapter 8**.

UK

Following the adoption of IFRS 3(2008), the most significant differences between IFRSs and UK GAAP in respect of business combinations are that, under IFRSs:

- *merger accounting is not permitted for business combinations which are not group reorganisations;*
- *there may be identification and recognition of more acquired intangible assets, and consequent reduction in the residual balance of goodwill;*
- *there is no amortisation of goodwill;*
- *costs incurred to effect a business combination are expensed in the period incurred;*
- *where the acquirer has a pre-existing equity interest in the entity acquired, it remeasures that previously-held interest to fair value as at the date of obtaining control, and recognises any resulting gain or loss in profit or loss;*
- *at an acquisition date, the acquirer may choose, on a transaction by transaction basis, to measure NCI at fair value;*
- *consideration for an acquisition, including contingent consideration, is measured at fair value at the acquisition date. Changes resulting from events after the acquisition date, such as the acquiree meeting an earnings target or reaching a specified share price, are recognised in profit or loss; and*
- *when a parent ceases to have control of a subsidiary, the parent derecognises all assets, liabilities and NCI at their carrying amount. Any interest retained in the former subsidiary is recognised at its fair*

value at the date control is lost, and any gain or loss arising on loss of control is recognised in profit or loss.

1.3 Principles underlying the revised standards

Underlying the 2008 versions of IAS 27 and IFRS 3 is the development of two important principles.

1.3.1 Entity concept

Although the Standards do not use the term 'entity concept', and the Board has noted that it 'did not consider comprehensively the entity and proprietary approaches as part of the amendments to IAS 27 in 2008', nevertheless, throughout the various phases of the business combinations project, the Standards have changed conceptually both in respect of classification and measurement.

In respect of classification, the Standards have changed from the position where non-controlling interests were recognised separately from both shareholders' equity and liabilities in a consolidated statement of financial position, and as a deduction in arriving at the 'bottom line' of a statement of comprehensive income, (which is usually described as a 'parent concept' or 'proprietary concept') to a position where non-controlling interests are part of equity (which is a feature of the 'entity concept'). This change has occurred in two stages.

- Firstly, as part of the 2003 revision of IAS 27, the Board required minority interests (as they were then called) to be presented in the consolidated statement of financial position within equity, but separately from the equity of the shareholders of the parent. In the statement of comprehensive income, the minority's share of net income was presented as an allocation rather than as a deduction within the statement. This reflected the Board's view that a minority interest is not a liability of a group.

- Secondly, the 2008 amendments to IAS 27 implemented further changes as a consequence of their view that non-controlling interests (as they are now called) are part of equity. The effect is that transactions between non-controlling interests and parent shareholders which do not affect control are now reported as movements within equity, such that goodwill is not recognised when parent interests are increased, and no profit or loss is recognised when parent interests are decreased (see **chapter 33**).

In respect of measurement, the Board did not fully implement the proposal in the 2005 Exposure Draft to focus on the fair value of the business combination and thereby require goodwill to be based on both parent and non-controlling interests measured at fair value (sometimes referred to as the 'gross-up' of goodwill, or the 'full goodwill' method). Rather, the Board has provided an option on an acquisition-by-acquisition basis which allows non-controlling interests to be measured initially at fair value or at a proportionate share of identifiable net assets (see **7.3**). The policy adopted to measure non-controlling interests impacts the initial measurement of goodwill, which is a residual number.

The position in the 2008 versions of IFRS 3 and IAS 27 could therefore be described as a 'partial entity concept'. As part of its Conceptual Framework project, the IASB has decided to issue an invitation to comment requesting comment on the 'entity view' of financial reporting. The IASB believes the 'entity view' is the only appropriate view and that the 'proprietary/parent entity' view is not appropriate.

Transactions that are reported wholly within equity

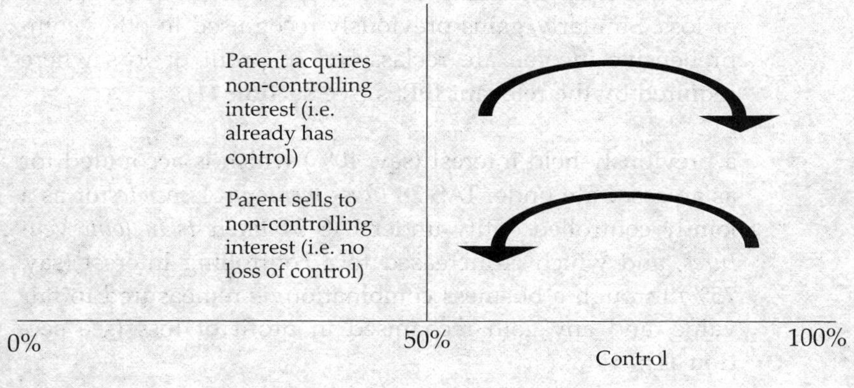

1.3.2 *Crossing an accounting boundary involves a disposal*

'Crossing an accounting boundary' describes a change in the method of accounting (e.g. measurement at fair value, equity accounting, proportionate consolidation or full consolidation) as a result of increasing or decreasing an equity interest in another entity. Prior to the 2008 revisions, a controlling interest achieved in stages was dealt with as a series of separate acquisition transactions with goodwill recognised as the sum of the goodwill arising on the separate transactions. On disposal, various approaches were used to measure residual interests, but commonly these were measured by reference to the residual proportion of previous carrying amounts (e.g. the residual share of net assets and goodwill).

Under the 2008 revisions, a business combination accounted for under IFRS 3 occurs only at the time that one entity obtains control over another, and does not apply to previous or subsequent transactions not involving a change in control. Any change in equity interests which crosses an accounting boundary causing a change in the method of accounting is regarded as a significant economic event. Such a transaction is therefore accounted for as if the original asset (in the case of an increase in equity interest), or the residual asset (in the case of a reduction in equity interest) were disposed of for fair value, and immediately reacquired for the same fair value. The implications of this change of principle are:

- a previously-held interest (say, 10%) which is accounted for under IAS 39 *Financial Instruments: Recognition and Measurement*, and which is increased to a controlling interest (say, 75%) through a business combination, is remeasured to fair value at acquisition date, and any gain recognised in profit or loss. Similarly, gains previously recognised in other comprehensive income are reclassified to profit or loss where required by the relevant IFRSs (see **section 11**);

- a previously-held interest (say, 40%) which is accounted for as an associate under IAS 28 *Investments in Associates* or as a jointly controlled entity under IAS 31 *Interests in Joint Ventures*, and which is increased to a controlling interest (say, 75%) through a business combination, is remeasured to fair value, and any gain recognised in profit or loss (see **section 11**);

- on disposal of a controlling interest, any retained interest in the former subsidiary is measured at fair value on the date that control is lost. This fair value is reflected in the calculation of the gain or loss on disposal attributable to the parent, and becomes the initial carrying amount for subsequent accounting for the retained interest under IAS 28, IAS 31 or IAS 39 as appropriate (see **chapter 33**); and

- similar considerations apply to the partial disposal of an interest in an associate or jointly controlled entity where the residual interest is accounted for as a financial asset under IAS 39 (see **4.3.9.1** in **chapter 35** and **8.3.3.1** in **chapter 36** respectively).

Although the revised Standards expressly deal with the above situations, they do not deal with a '15% to 25%' transaction- i.e. a transaction that takes an investment accounted for under IAS 39 to an associate interest accounted for under IAS 28 or a jointly controlled entity accounted for under IAS 31 (see **4.3.3.4** in **chapter 35**).

Transactions that involve remeasurement of an existing interest

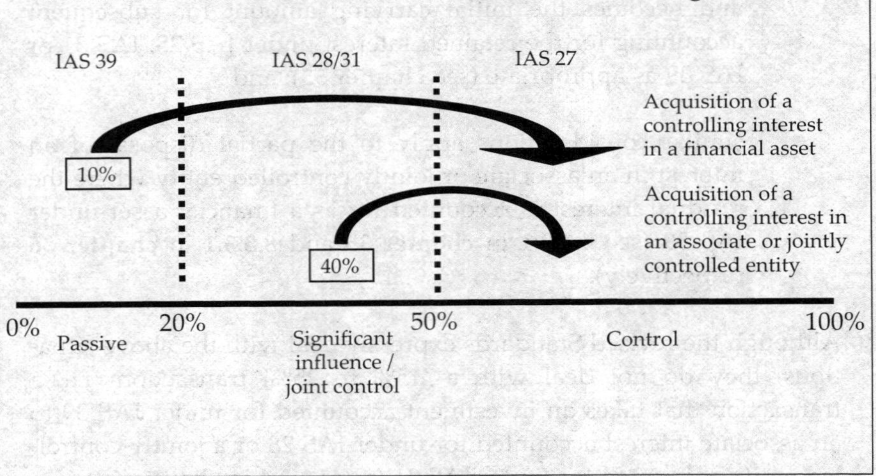

Transactions that involve remeasurement of a retained interest

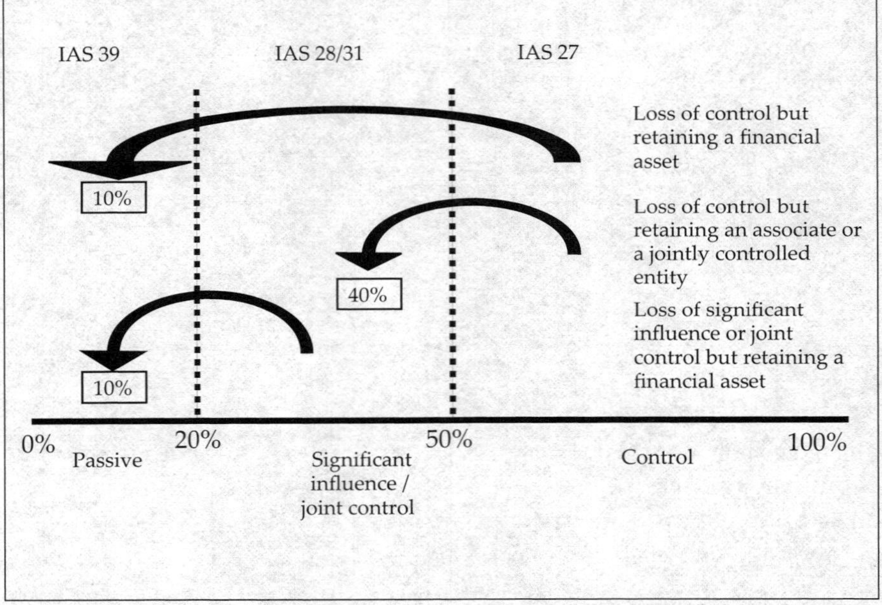

Business combinations achieved in stages are considered in more detail in **section 11**.

2 Scope

IFRS 3(2008) applies to a transaction or other event that meets the definition of a business combination. [IFRS 3(2008).2]

2.1 Definition of a business combination

A business combination is defined as:

[IFRS 3(2008)(Appendix A)]

> 'A transaction or other event in which an acquirer obtains control of one or more businesses. Transactions sometimes referred to as 'true mergers' or 'mergers of equals' are also business combinations as that term is used in this IFRS.'

2.2 Transactions outside the scope of IFRS 3(2008)

IFRS 3(2008) does not apply to the following transactions:

[IFRS 3(2008).2]

- the formation of a joint venture;
- the acquisition of an asset or a group of assets that does not constitute a business (discussed in **section 4**); and
- a combination between entities or businesses under common control (see **2.2.2**).

Business combinations involving mutual entities are within the scope of IFRS 3(2008), but were not in the scope of IFRS 3(2004). Similarly, combinations achieved by contract alone rather than through an exchange transaction are within the scope of IFRS 3(2008) but were excluded from IFRS 3(2004).

2.2.1 *Formation of a joint venture*

The Basis for Conclusions to IFRS 3(2008) suggests that further work would be necessary before the Board could proceed to provide guidance on accounting for the formation of a joint venture, and that the Board did not wish to delay the issue of IFRS 3(2008).

However, where a parent contributes a subsidiary to a joint venture arrangement, and receives in exchange an equity interest in the joint venture which qualifies as a jointly controlled entity under IAS 31, the transaction falls within the scope of IAS 27 so far as the parent is concerned with the effect that the residual interest in the former subsidiary would be remeasured to fair value – see **chapter 33**. The IFRS 3(2008) scope exemption would apply to the financial statements of the jointly controlled entity (i.e. entity B below).

Example 2.2.1

Formation of a joint venture that is outside the scope of IFRS 3 but within the scope of IAS 27

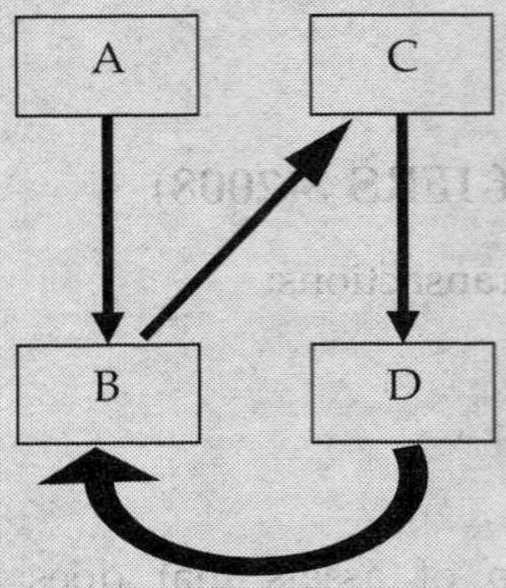

B and D are respectively wholly-owned subsidiaries of A and C. A and C form a new joint venture whereby B issues equity interests representing 50% of B's equity to C in return for the transfer of C's equity interest in D. In A's consolidated financial statements, A has disposed of its controlling interest in B. Accordingly, A's residual interest in B should be fair valued – see **chapter 33**.

2.2.2 *Common control transactions*

A combination of entities or businesses under common control (commonly referred to as a 'common control transaction') is '... a business combination in which all of the combining entities or businesses are ultimately controlled by the same party or parties both before and after the combination, and that control is not transitory'. [IFRS 3(2008).B1]

Examples of ultimate controlling parties include:

- an individual, or a group of individuals who, as a result of contractual arrangements, collectively control an entity (even where those individuals are not subject to financial reporting requirements); [IFRS 3(2008).B2 – B3] and
- a parent entity (even where the controlled entity is excluded from its consolidated financial statements). [IFRS 3(2008).B4]

There is currently no specific guidance on accounting for common control transactions under IFRSs. However, in December 2007, the IASB added a project on this topic to its agenda. The project will examine the definition of common control and the methods of accounting for business combinations under common control in the acquirer's consolidated and separate financial statements.

In the absence of specific guidance, entities involved in common control transactions should select an appropriate accounting policy using the 'hierarchy' described in paragraphs 10 – 12 of IAS 8 *Accounting Policies, Changes in Accounting Estimates and Errors* (see **3.1** in **chapter 4**). As the hierarchy permits the consideration of pronouncements of other standard-setting bodies, the guidance on group reorganisations in both UK and US GAAP may be useful in some circumstances – this guidance produces a result that is similar to pooling.

Example 2.2.2

Example of a common control transaction

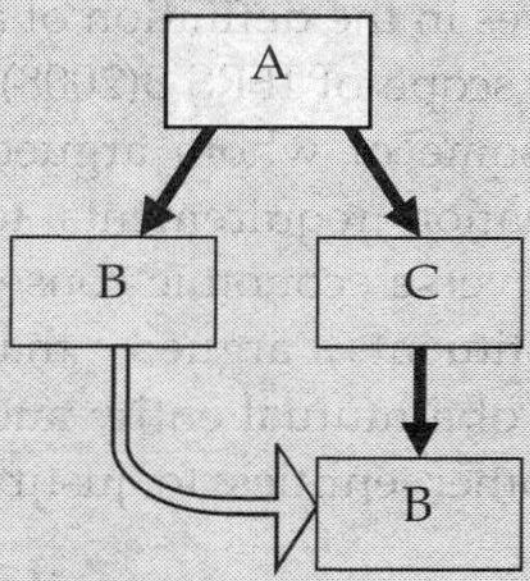

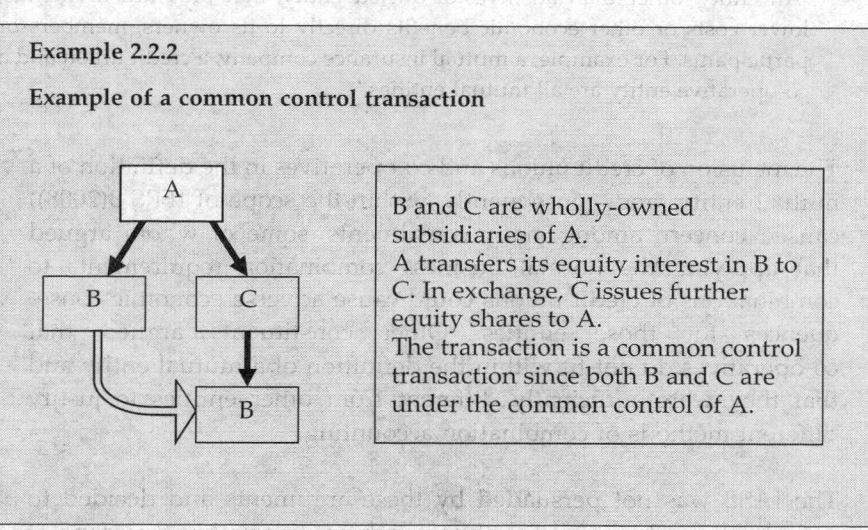

B and C are wholly-owned subsidiaries of A.
A transfers its equity interest in B to C. In exchange, C issues further equity shares to A.
The transaction is a common control transaction since both B and C are under the common control of A.

A new entity may be formed by a parent to issue equity instruments to acquire one or more subsidiaries that are part of the parent's existing group. A reorganisation involving the formation of such a new entity to facilitate the sale of part of an organisation is not a business combination within the scope of IFRS 3. This is because the combining entities that existed before the combination were entities under common control that was not transitory.

Under IFRS 3(2008).B18, when an entity is formed to issue equity instruments to effect a business combination, one of the combining entities that existed before the combination is identified as the acquirer on the basis of the evidence available. To be consistent with the principle in IFRS 3(2008).B18, the test of whether the entities or businesses are under common control should be applied to the combining entities that existed before the combination, excluding the newly formed entity. Therefore, where an existing parent forms a new entity to undertake a pre-sale restructuring, the transaction is excluded from the scope of IFRS 3 as a 'business combination involving entities or businesses under common control'.

This was confirmed by an IFRIC agenda rejection published in the March 2006 *IFRIC Update*.

2.2.3 *Combinations involving mutual entities*

A mutual entity is defined as follows:

[IFRS 3(2008)(Appendix A)]

> 'An entity, other than an investor-owned entity, that provides dividends, lower costs or other economic benefits directly to its owners, members or participants. For example, a mutual insurance company, a credit union and a co-operative entity are all mutual entities.'

The inclusion of credit unions and co-operatives in the definition of a mutual entity (and, consequently, within the scope of IFRS 3(2008)) caused concern among many constituents, some of whom argued that applying the normal business combination requirements to combinations of credit unions could cause adverse economic consequences for those entities. Other constituents argued that co-operatives do not fit within the definition of a mutual entity and that they were sufficiently different from other entities to justify different methods of combination accounting.

The IASB was not persuaded by these arguments and decided to include all combinations involving such entities within the scope of the revised IFRS 3(2008) without amendment, but with limited additional guidance as to how the relevant requirements should be applied.

Combinations involving mutual entities are considered in two sections:

- identification of the acquirer is considered in **5.3.2**; and
- measurement issues, including goodwill, are considered in **9.2.3**.

3 The acquisition method of accounting

IFRS 3(2008) requires that all business combinations be accounted for by applying the acquisition method. [IFRS 3(2008).4] In addition to determining whether a transaction or other event is a business combination (IFRS 3(2008).3), four stages in the application of the acquisition method are listed:

[IFRS 3(2008).5]

(a) identifying the acquirer;

(b) determining the acquisition date;

(c) recognising and measuring the identifiable assets acquired, the liabilities assumed and any non-controlling interest in the acquiree; and

(d) recognising and measuring goodwill or a gain from a bargain purchase.

However, taking all the requirements of the Standard into account, there are seven distinct steps to be considered and these are described in the following chart:

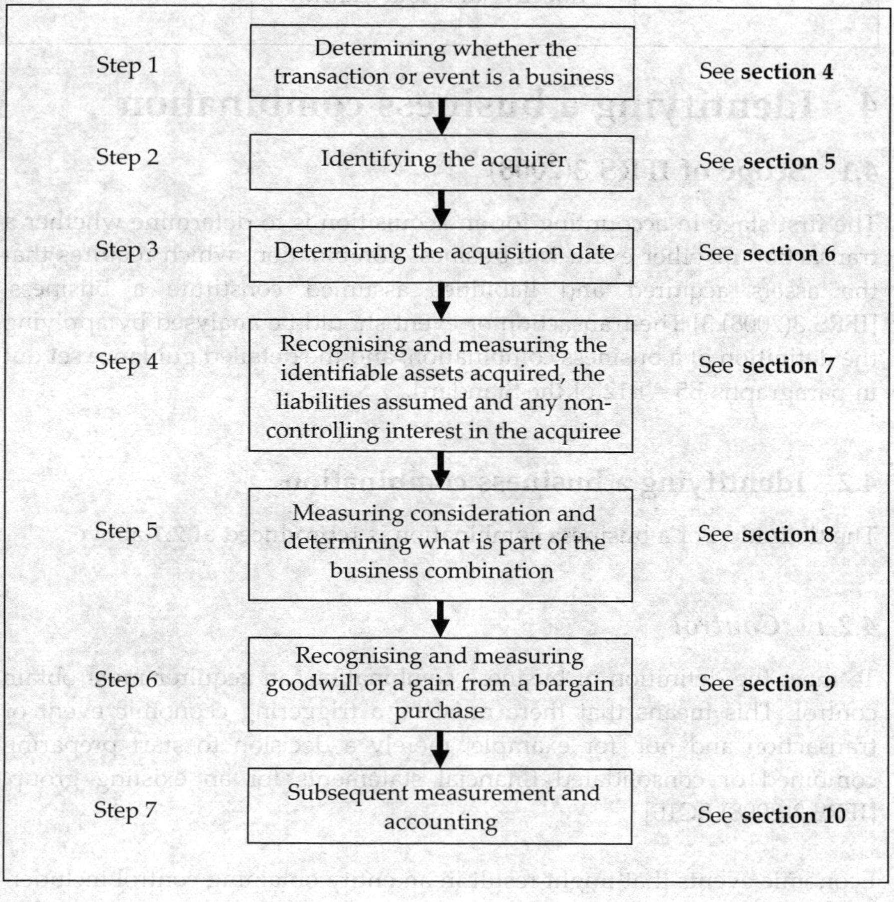
Step 1
Determining whether the transaction or event is a business
See section 4
Step 2
Identifying the acquirer
See section 5
Step 3
Determining the acquisition date
See section 6
Step 4
Recognising and measuring the identifiable assets acquired, the liabilities assumed and any non-controlling interest in the acquiree
See section 7
Step 5
Measuring consideration and determining what is part of the business combination
See section 8
Step 6
Recognising and measuring goodwill or a gain from a bargain purchase
See section 9
Step 7
Subsequent measurement and accounting
See section 10

Subsequent sections deal with special situations:

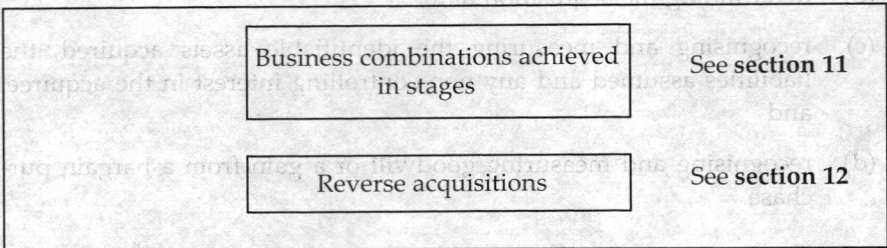

Business combinations achieved in stages	See **section 11**
Reverse acquisitions	See **section 12**

Finally, two sections deal with disclosure and transition:

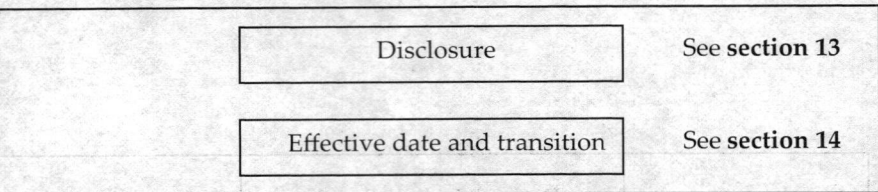

Disclosure	See **section 13**
Effective date and transition	See **section 14**

4 Identifying a business combination

4.1 Scope of IFRS 3(2008)

The first stage in accounting for an acquisition is to determine whether a transaction or other event is a business combination, which requires that the assets acquired and liabilities assumed constitute a business. [IFRS 3(2008).3] The transaction or event should be analysed by applying the definition of a business combination, and the detailed guidance set out in paragraphs B5 – B12 of the Standard.

4.2 Identifying a business combination

The definition of a business combination is reproduced at **2.1** above.

4.2.1 Control

To meet the definition of business combination, an acquirer must obtain control. This means that there must be a triggering economic event or transaction and not, for example, merely a decision to start preparing combined or consolidated financial statements for an existing group. [IFRS 3(2008).BC10]

Economic events that might result in an entity obtaining control include:

[IFRS 3(2008).B5]

(a) transferring cash or other assets (including net assets that constitute a business);

(b) incurring liabilities;

(c) issuing equity instruments;

(d) a combination of the above;

(e) a transaction not involving consideration, such as a combination by contract alone (e.g. a dual listed structure – see **section 8**).

Other examples of events that might result in an entity obtaining control:

- potential voting rights (options, convertible instruments, etc) held by the entity in an investee becoming exercisable;
- an investee undertaking a selective buy-back transaction which results in the entity achieving a majority ownership in the investee without changing the number of equity instruments held in the investee;.
- the expiry of an agreement with other shareholders where that agreement prevented the entity from controlling the investee (e.g. another shareholder had participative rights (right of veto) over major financing and operating policy decisions); and.
- a 'creep acquisition' of equity instruments in an investee through a dividend reinvestment plan or bonus issue that increases the entity's holding to a controlling level.

4.2.2 *Possible structures*

The structure of a business combination may be determined by a variety of factors, including legal and tax strategies. Other factors might include market considerations and regulatory considerations. Examples of structures include:

[IFRS 3(2008).B6]

(a) one business becomes a subsidiary of another;

(b) two entities are legally merged into one entity;

(c) one entity transfers its net assets to another entity;

(d) an entity's owners transfer their equity interests to the owners of another entity;

(e) two or more entities transfer their net assets, or the owners transfer their equity interests, to a newly-formed entity (sometimes termed a 'roll-up' or 'put-together' transaction); and

(f) a group of former owners of one entity obtains control of a combined entity.

Examples of other legal structures that might be used to effect business combinations include:

- transactions that involve the dual listing and equalisation arrangements between two entities (see **8.5.2.2**);
- a contractual arrangement between two entities that has the effect of creating one entity in substance (i.e. a 'stapling' arrangement);
- a contractual arrangement that provides a third party with all economic returns, and responsibility for risks, in relation to an investee, even though the legal ownership of ordinary capital is with another entity (e.g. a 'pass-through' arrangement); and
- arrangements whereby an entity is the beneficial owner of an interest held in trust but the trustee is the legal owner of that interest.

4.3 Identifying a business

A business is defined as follows.

[IFRS 3(2008)(Appendix A)]

> 'An integrated set of activities and assets that is capable of being conducted and managed for the purpose of providing a return in the form of dividends, lower costs or other economic benefits directly to investors or other owners, members or participants.'

The application guidance in IFRS 3.B7 – B12, which is consistent with the previous version of IFRS 3, is a theoretical description of a business. While there are some useful clues, it does not provide a practical checklist for what constitutes a business.

4.3.1 *Presence of goodwill*

Paragraph B12 provides an over-arching test based on the presence of goodwill.

[IFRS 3(2008).B12]

> 'In the absence of evidence to the contrary, a particular set of assets and activities in which goodwill is present shall be presumed to be a business. However, a business need not have goodwill.'

No further guidance on identifying the presence of goodwill is provided in the Standard. Goodwill may be likely to occur where the particular set of assets or activities includes a trade or operating activity that generates revenue. In addition, the requirements in relation to accounting for transactions that are not business combinations (see **4.4**) require an entity to determine the fair values of the acquired assets and liabilities so as to proportionately allocate the cost of the group of assets and liabilities. This analysis may quickly identify that the total consideration paid exceeds the aggregate fair value of the assets acquired and liabilities assumed, potentially indicating the existence of goodwill.

4.3.2 *Inputs, processes and outputs*

The guidance describes a business as consisting of inputs and processes applied to those inputs that have the ability to create outputs. Although outputs are usually present, they are not required for an integrated set of activities and assets to qualify as a business. [IFRS 3(2008).B7]

The following points are summarised from IFRS 3(2008).B7 – B11:

(a) inputs are economic resources including employees, materials and non-current assets including rights of use;

(b) processes are systems, standards, protocols, conventions or rules that, when applied to inputs, create outputs. Examples would include strategic management, operations and resource management. Accounting, billing, payroll and similar administrative systems typically are not used to create outputs;

(c) outputs provide a return in the form of dividends, lower costs or other economic benefits to stakeholders;

(d) as a result of an acquisition, an acquirer may combine the acquiree's inputs and processes with its own with the result that it is not necessary that all pre-acquisition inputs and processes remain unchanged;

(e) a business may not have outputs (e.g. where it is in a development stage);

(f) a business may or may not have liabilities; and

(g) the assessment as to whether a particular set of assets and activities is a business is made by reference to whether the integrated set is capable of being conducted and managed as a business by a market participant – it is not relevant whether the seller operated the set as a business or whether the acquirer intends to operate the set as a business.

Example 4.3.2A

Outsourcing arrangements

The application of the revised guidance around the identification of a business can, in some circumstances, lead to different conclusions under IFRS 3(2008) and IFRS 3(2004) as to whether a business exists. One of these areas, depending on the nature of the arrangement, can be the treatment of an outsourcing arrangement.

For example, an entity may decide to outsource its information technology or call centre operations to a third party. Before the outsourcing, these functions generally will have been operated as a cost centre for the business as a whole, rather than as a business per se. Generally, the staff, plant and equipment and other working capital of the outsourced department are transferred to the third party, and a contractual arrangement entered into with the third party for the provision of the service to the outsourcing entity on an ongoing basis.

While they were part of the outsourcing entity, the operations generally would not have been considered a business and would not have been operated as such. However, the third party that acquires the assets and liabilities and takes on the staff could be seen to have acquired a business, as the transferred set of assets and activities is *capable* of being operated as a business. The conclusion is even clearer where the transferred assets and employees are used as the 'seed capital' to offer similar services to other parties.

Example 4.3.2B

Industries where the required inputs are minimal

When assessing whether a particular set of assets and activities is a business, it is important to consider the normal nature of the assets and activities in the relevant business sector or industry. In some industries, there may be a relatively low number of assets required as inputs, working capital requirements may be low, or the number of employees used in the process of creating outputs may be low. The acquisition of assets and activities in these types of industries must be assessed by reference to these normal levels.

For example, an entity may acquire a set of assets and activities that represents the ownership and management of a group of pipelines used for the transport of oil, gas and other hydrocarbons on behalf of a number of customers. The operation has a limited number of employees (mainly used in maintenance of the pipelines and billing of customers), a system used for tracking transported hydrocarbons and a minor amount of working capital. The transaction involves the transfer of employees and systems, but not the working capital.

Notwithstanding that the inputs into the process are minimal, the group of pipelines will meet the definition of a business and so the transaction will be accounted for as a business combination.

4.4 Accounting for a transaction that is not a business combination

Where a transaction or other event does not meet the definition of a business combination due to the acquiree not meeting the definition of a business, it is termed an 'asset acquisition'. In such circumstances, the acquirer:

[IFRS 3(2008).2(b)]

- identifies and recognises the individual identifiable assets acquired (including those assets that meet the definition of, and recognition criteria for, intangible assets in IAS 38 *Intangible Assets* – see **section 4** of **chapter 8**) and liabilities assumed; and
- allocates the cost of the group of assets and liabilities to the individual identifiable assets and liabilities on the basis of their relative fair values at the date of purchase.

Such a transaction or event does not give rise to goodwill.

Example 4.4A

Incorporation of a new subsidiary

In corporate groups it is common for subsidiaries to be incorporated for specific purposes (e.g. to house particular operations, to act as service companies, or for other structuring purposes). In such circumstances, the acquisition of a 'shell' or 'shelf' company is not a business combination as defined in IFRS 3(2008) because no business is being acquired.

Accordingly, the acquisition or incorporation of such an entity should be accounted for in the separate financial statements of the legal parent in accordance with IAS 27, which would require initial measurement at cost (i.e. the cost of incorporating or acquiring the 'shelf' entity). In the consolidated financial statements, the costs would be recognised as start-up, restructuring or similar costs in accordance with IAS 38 *Intangible Assets*.

Example 4.4B

Exploration and evaluation assets held in corporate shells

In some jurisdictions, it is common for rights to tenure over exploration and evaluation interests to be held in separate companies for each tenement, area of interest, field, etc. Management of the entity's exploration and evaluation activities is centralised, including any plant and equipment used, employees, service and other contracts, and similar items.

In many cases, transactions involving the transfer of a particular exploration and evaluation interest involves the legal transfer of the company, rather than the underlying right or title over the interest.

Where an entity acquires a company in these circumstances, it is likely that the acquisition will not meet the definition of a business combination, because the acquisition is in substance the acquisition of the exploration and evaluation interest, rather than the acquisition of a business. Accordingly, in the consolidated financial statements, such a transaction would be accounted for in accordance with the entity's accounting policy for exploration and evaluation under IFRS 6 *Exploration for and Evaluation of Mineral Resources*, rather than as a business combination.

5 Identifying the acquirer

IFRS 3(2008) continues the requirement of IFRS 3(2004) that, for each business combination, one of the combining entities should be identified as the acquirer (i.e. the entity that obtains control of the acquiree). [IFRS 3(2008).6 & (Appendix A)]

The acquirer and the acquiree are identified by applying the guidance in IAS 27(2008) regarding the concept of control. Where identification is not achieved by this analysis, application guidance in IFRS 3(2008).B14 – B18 provides additional guidance (see **5.2**). [IFRS 3(2008).7]

5.1 Meaning of control

The definition of control, and added guidance, in IFRS 3(2008) is consistent with IAS 27 *Consolidated and Separate Financial Statements*. Thus, control is defined as:

[IFRS 3(2008)(Appendix A)]

> 'The power to govern the financial and operating policies of an entity or business so as to obtain benefits from its activities'

See **chapter 33** for discussion of the guidance on control in IAS 27 and in SIC-12 *Consolidation – Special Purpose Entities.*

5.2 Additional guidance in marginal cases

Where application of IAS 27(2008) does not clearly indicate which of the combining entities is the acquirer, a number of additional factors for consideration are set out in IFRS 3(2008).B14 – B18 as follows.

Factor	Acquirer is:
Consideration primarily cash, other assets or incurring liabilities.	Usually the entity that transfers the cash or other assets, or incurs the liabilities. [IFRS 3(2008).B14]
Consideration primarily in equity interests.	Usually the entity that issues its equity interests. However, in a reverse acquisition, the acquiree may issue equity interests (see **section 12**). [IFRS 3(2008).B15]
Relative size.	Usually the entity whose relative size (measured in, for example, assets, revenues or profit) is significantly greater than that of the other combining entities. [IFRS 3(2008).B16]
More than two combining entities.	Consider which entity initiated the combination (as well as relative sizes). [IFRS 3(2008).B17]
New entity formed which issues equity interests.	One of the combining entities that existed before the combination, identified by applying the guidance in other paragraphs (see **5.3.1**). [IFRS 3(2008).B18]
New entity formed which transfers cash, other assets or incurs liabilities.	New entity may be the acquirer (see **5.3.1**). [IFRS 3(2008).B18]

In addition, in the case of a share exchange, other pertinent facts and circumstances may be as follows. [IFRS 3(2008).B15]

Factor	Acquirer is:
Relative voting rights in the combined entity after the combination.	Usually the entity whose owners as a group retain or receive the largest portion of the combined voting rights, after considering the existence of any unusual or special voting arrangements and options, warrants or convertible notes.
No majority interest in the combined entity, but single large minority interest.	Usually the entity whose single owner or group of organised voters holds the largest minority voting interest in the combined entity.
	Care should be taken in applying this test to ensure that the IAS 27 test of 'power to control' is met.
Composition of the governing body of the combined entity.	Usually the entity whose owners have the ability to elect or appoint a majority of the members of the governing body.
Senior management of the combined entity.	Usually the entity whose (former) management dominates the combined management.
Terms of the exchange of equity interests.	Usually the entity that pays a premium over pre-combination fair value of the other entity or entities

5.3 Application to specific cases

5.3.1 *Combinations effected by creating a new entity*

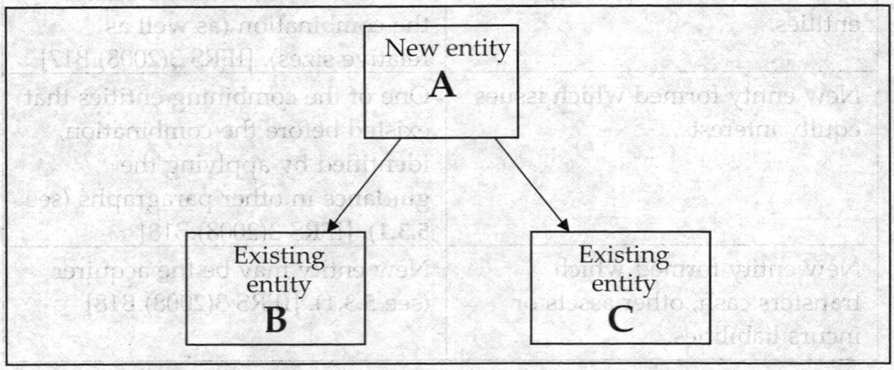

Where a new entity A is formed to effect a combination between two or more entities, say B and C, IFRS 3(2008) identifies two distinct scenarios:

[IFRS 3(2008).B18]

- where A issues equity instruments in itself in exchange for equity instruments in B and C, then either B or C should be identified as the acquirer by applying the guidance in IAS 27 and IFRS 3; and
- where A transfers cash (or other assets) in exchange for equity instruments in B and C (e.g. from the proceeds of a debt issue to new investors or to existing investors holding a minority interest in B or C), then A may be identified as the acquirer.

Example 5.3.1A

New entity issues equity instruments

B and C are existing entities, and combine through a new entity A which issues new equity shares in itself in the proportion four-fifths to the equity shareholders of B and one-fifth to the equity shareholders of C.

On the basis of the relative voting rights, and in the absence of other factors suggesting otherwise, B is identified as the acquirer.

Accounting for the combination is developed on the principle that the consolidated financial statements of the A group are presented on the same basis as if B had legally acquired C, noting that A lacks commercial substance because it is effectively a legal mechanism to achieve this outcome. Accordingly, the combination of A and B will be accounted for as a capital restructuring whereby:

- the net assets of B remain at their previous carrying amounts;
- the consolidated statement of comprehensive income of the A group, including comparatives, will be based on the reporting period of B and will include the pre-combination results of B;
- the equity of the group will be that of B plus the fair value of A; and
- the share capital of the group, if any, will be that of A the legal parent.

The combination of the A group and C will be a 'normal' acquisition whereby:

- the identifiable net assets of C are fair valued on acquisition; and
- the consolidated statement of comprehensive income of the A group will only include C's post-acquisition results.

Example 5.3.1B

New entity transfers cash

B and C are existing entities, and combine through a new entity A. The equity investors in A are a private equity business that own 60% of A and the former equity investors in C who own 40%. A pays cash to acquire the equity interests of B, and issues equity interests in A to acquire C.

C is not identified as the acquirer since the equity investors in C do not hold a majority of the equity shares in A. In this case, A is identified as the acquirer.

The combination of A and B, and A and C, are 'normal' acquisitions whereby:

- the identifiable net assets of both B and C are fair valued on acquisition; and
- the consolidated statement of comprehensive income of the A group will include only the post-combination results of B and C.

5.3.2 *Mutual entities*

The definition of a mutual entity is set out at **2.2.3**.

Since a combination of mutual entities involves an exchange (albeit typically of membership interests), IFRS 3(2008) allows no exemption from its general requirements in respect of applying the acquisition method. Consequently, an acquirer must be identified in any combination of mutual entities. [IFRS 3(2008).BC104]

The Board further concluded that the guidance on identifying the acquirer in IFRS 3(2008) is applicable to mutual entities and no additional guidance is needed. [IFRS 3(2008).BC105]

However, additional guidance is provided to assist in measuring the fair value of equity or membership interests exchanged in paragraphs B47 – B49 of IFRS 3(2008). This guidance is considered in **9.2.3**.

6 Determining the acquisition date

6.1 Definition of acquisition date

The acquisition date is defined as the date on which the acquirer obtains control of the acquiree. [IFRS 3(2008)(Appendix A)] This is consistent with the definition in IFRS 3(2004). However, the additional guidance given in IFRS 3(2004) on successive share purchases and dates of exchange, which was necessary in the context of that Standard's approach to step acquisitions, is rendered redundant. This is due to the 2008 Standard's stipulation that a business combination occurs, and goodwill is identified, only on the date that control is achieved.

6.2 Relationship to the timing of the payment of consideration

IFRS 3(2008) explains that the date on which the acquirer obtains control of the acquiree is generally the date on which the acquirer legally transfers the consideration, acquires the assets and assumes the liabilities of the acquiree – the closing date. However, the acquirer should consider all pertinent facts and circumstances in identifying the acquisition date, and it might be that control is achieved on a date that is either earlier or later than the closing date. For example, the acquisition date precedes the closing date if a written agreement provides that the acquirer obtains control of the acquiree on a date before the closing date. [IFRS 3(2008).9]

The reference to a written agreement is taken to mean the purchase agreement or a separate agreement signed before the closing date that grants rights to the acquirer. Since the date of acquisition will be a matter of fact, it cannot be retrospectively altered (e.g. by indicating in the purchase agreement that control is deemed to exist from an earlier date, or that profits accrue to the purchaser from some earlier or later date). This latter feature may represent a mechanism to adjust the amount of purchase consideration.

In some cases, the entire purchase price may be in the form of deferred or contingent consideration. In such circumstances, the timing of the payment of the consideration will have little or no bearing on the determination of the acquisition date.

6.3 Equity securities transferred as consideration

Consistent with the requirements in the previous version of the Standard, IFRS 3(2008) requires that the measurement date for equity securities transferred as consideration is the acquisition date (see **8.1**). [IFRS 3(2008).37]

The Basis for Conclusions to IFRS 3(2008) summarises the Board's discussion of the measurement date for equity securities transferred. This is mainly to explain the Board's decision to reject the approach reflected in certain US accounting literature. There is consequently no change to the previous position that the fair value of equity securities transferred is measured on a single date, being the date control passes. No consideration is given to movements in share prices before or after this date. [IFRS 3(2008).BC342]

6.4 Practical guidance

IFRS 3(2008) does not contain any further detailed guidance on the determination of the acquisition date. The following examples may be a useful guide in some circumstances.

Public offer of shares

Where a public offer of shares is made, the date that control passes is the date when the offer becomes unconditional and a controlling interest in the acquiree has therefore been achieved. This is usually the date that the number of acceptances passes a predetermined threshold and that threshold is sufficient to provide control (i.e. usually more than 50%). In the absence of such a threshold, the acquisition date may be the date the offer is declared unconditional. In making this assessment, other factors will also need to be considered, including where offers are declared unconditional before a controlling shareholding is achieved. In these cases, the acquisition date may occur when the level of shareholding has exceeded a particular level and the acquirer is able to effect change in the board of directors of the acquiree.

Private transfer

For a private transfer, the date that control passes will be the date that an unconditional offer is accepted. Where agreements are subject to substantive preconditions, the acquisition date will usually be the date that the last of those preconditions is satisfied.

Other scenarios

A number of indicators may be relevant, including:

(a) the date that the acquirer commences direction of operating and financial policies;

(b) the date from which the flow of economic benefits changes;

(c) the date that consideration passes (although this is not conclusive, since it is capable of being adjusted either forwards or backwards or settled in instalments);

(d) the appointment of the majority of the board of directors of the acquiree (although this may serve as a measure of the *latest* possible date that control passes in many cases); and

(e) the date that competition authorities provide clearance of a referred bid.

In practice, the date identified as the acquisition date should reflect all the various circumstances surrounding the transfer of control.

7 Recognising and measuring the identifiable assets acquired, the liabilities assumed and any non-controlling interest in the acquiree

IFRS 3(2008) sets out basic principles for the recognition and measurement of identifiable assets acquired, liabilities assumed and non-controlling interests (see **7.1, 7.2** and **7.3**).

7.1 Recognition principle

IFRS 3(2008) requires that, as of the acquisition date, the acquirer should recognise, separately from goodwill, the identifiable assets acquired, the liabilities assumed and any non-controlling interest in the acquiree. [IFRS 3(2008).10]

7.1.1 Conditions for recognition

To qualify for recognition as part of applying the acquisition method, an item acquired should:

- meet the definition of an asset or liability in the *Framework for the Preparation and Presentation of Financial Statements* (see **chapter 2**) at the acquisition date; [IFRS 3(2008).11] and
- be part of the business acquired (the acquiree) rather than the result of a separate transaction (see **8.3**). [IFRS 3(2008).12]

The following are outcomes as a result of applying the first recognition condition above.

- **Post-acquisition reorganisation** Costs that the acquirer expects but is not obliged to incur in the future to effect its plan to exit an activity of an acquiree or to terminate the employment of or relocate an acquiree's employees are not liabilities at the acquisition date. [IFRS 3(2008).11] This exclusion of an acquirer's post-acquisition initiated costs is consistent with IFRS 3(2004).

- **Unrecognised assets and liabilities** The acquirer may recognise some assets and liabilities that the acquiree had not previously recognised in its financial statements. For example, the acquirer recognises the acquired identifiable intangible assets (e.g. brand names, patents or customer relationships) that the acquiree did not recognise as assets in its financial statements because it developed them internally and charged the related costs to expense. [IFRS 3(2008).13] The recognition of assets and liabilities that were not recognised by the acquiree is consistent with IFRS 3(2004).

The following recognition criteria, which were included in IFRS 3(2004), have been eliminated from IFRS 3(2008).

- Reliability of measurement as a criterion for recognising an asset or liability separately from goodwill – the Board considered this an unnecessary duplication of the overall recognition criteria in the *Framework*. [IFRS 3(2008).BC125] The requirement to recognise a contingent liability only where its fair value can be measured reliably remains (see **7.5.1** below).

- Probability of an inflow or outflow of economic benefits – as a result, there is a greater focus on the presence of an unconditional right or obligation. [IFRS 3(2008).BC130]

7.1.2 *Classifying or designating identifiable assets acquired and liabilities assumed in a business combination*

7.1.2.1 Conditions at the acquisition date

IFRS 3(2008) requires that, *at the acquisition date*, the identifiable assets acquired and liabilities assumed should be classified or designated as necessary to apply other IFRSs subsequently. The acquirer makes those classifications or designations on the basis of contractual terms, economic conditions, its operating or accounting policies, and other pertinent conditions as they exist at the acquisition date. [IFRS 3(2008).15]

Examples of classifications or designations made at the acquisition date include:

[IFRS 3(2008).16]

(a) classification of financial assets as at fair value through profit or loss, available-for-sale or held-to-maturity;

(b) classification of financial liabilities as at fair value through profit or loss;

(c) designation of a derivative as a hedging instrument; and

(d) assessment of whether an embedded derivative should be separated from a host contract (which is a classification matter).

7.1.2.2 *Conditions not at the acquisition date*

The Standard provides two exceptions to the principle (set out above) that classifications or designations are based on the terms of the instruments and conditions at the acquisition date. The two exceptions relate to:

[IFRS 3(2008).17]

(a) the classification of a lease contract as either an operating lease or finance lease in accordance with IAS 17 *Leases* (see **chapter 26**); and

(b) the classification of a contract as an insurance contract in accordance with IFRS 4 *Insurance Contracts* (see **chapter 44**).

The acquirer classifies such leases and insurance contracts on the basis of the contractual terms and other factors **at the inception of the contract** (or, if the terms of the contract have been modified in a manner that would change its classification, at the date of that modification, which might be the acquisition date).

7.2 Measurement principle for assets and liabilities

Identifiable assets acquired and liabilities assumed are measured at their acquisition-date fair values. [IFRS 3(2008).18]

7.2.1 *Assets with uncertain cash flows (valuation allowances)*

An acquirer is not permitted to recognise a separate valuation allowance as of the acquisition date for assets acquired in a business combination that are measured at their acquisition-date fair values because the effects of uncertainty about future cash flows are included in the fair value measure. For example, because IFRS 3(2008) requires the acquirer to measure acquired receivables, including loans, at their acquisition-date fair values, the acquirer does not recognise a separate valuation allowance for the contractual cash flows that are deemed to be uncollectible at that date. [IFRS 3(2008).B41]

This is a change from IFRS 3(2004), which required receivables, beneficial contracts and other identifiable assets to be measured at the present values of the amounts to be received, determined at appropriate current interest rates, less allowances for uncollectibility and collection costs.

The principle of 'no valuation allowance' also extends to property, plant and equipment such that, following a business combination, such assets are stated at a single fair value amount, and not at a gross 'deemed cost' and accumulated depreciation.

7.2.2 *Assets that the acquirer intends not to use or to use in a way that is different from the way other market participants would use them*

For competitive or other reasons, the acquirer may intend not to use an acquired asset (e.g. a research and development intangible asset or a brand name of an acquired competitor that is going to be taken out of service), or it may intend to use the asset in a way that is different from the way in which other market participants would use it. In these circumstances, the general principle applies and the fair value of the asset is determined in accordance with its use by other market participants. [IFRS 3(2008).B43]

This requirement is an application of the principle that the fair value of an asset should reflect its highest and best use. The requirement has been stated explicitly in IFRS 3(2008) to avoid inconsistencies in practice. [IFRS 3(2008).BC262]

Example 7.2.2

Acquisition of an intangible that will not be used

A acquires B. The identifiable net assets of B include a trademark, being the logo previously used by B as a direct competitor to A. A has no intention of using this logo in the future.

The logo is considered to be separable because it could, for example, be licensed to a third party. It also arises from legal rights. Therefore, the intangible asset should be recognised as part of the accounting for the acquisition (**7.4.2** below deals more fully with intangible assets).

In practice, if A has no intention of using the logo after the acquisition, it will not be possible to allocate the logo to existing cash-generating units. Consequently, it should be identified as a cash-generating unit by itself as management intends to exclude the logo from the operating process. The cash inflows related to the logo are nil. However, immediately after acquisition, it would appear reasonable that the fair value less costs to sell are not significantly different from the amount recognised and, accordingly, an impairment loss is not recognised. However, the asset must be amortised over its useful life. The useful life to the entity is the length of time for which holding the logo will be effective in discouraging competition, which is likely to be a fairly short period, as an unexploited logo loses value very quickly. As A acquired the asset with the express intention of denying others the opportunity to use the asset, it appears unlikely that the asset will be sold in the future and, accordingly, the residual value is zero. As a result, an amortisation charge for the full carrying amount of the asset is recognised over the useful life (which may be as short as a single accounting period).

7.3 Non-controlling interest (NCI) in an acquiree

7.3.1 Choice of method

For each business combination, any non-controlling interest in the acquiree is measured either:

[IFRS 3(2008).19]

- at fair value; or
- at the non-controlling interest's proportionate share of the acquiree's identifiable net assets.

This choice is available for each business combination, so an entity may use fair value for one business combination and the proportionate share of the acquiree's identifiable net assets for another.

IFRS 3(2008).19 states that the choice of measurement is available for each business combination. The Basis for Conclusions reiterates that this choice is available on a transaction-by-transaction basis. [IFRS 3(2008).BC216] IAS 8 *Accounting Policies, Changes in Accounting Estimates and Errors* indicates that where specific guidance is available in another Standard, that guidance overrides the requirements of IAS 8.13 to select and apply accounting policies consistently for similar transactions, other events or conditions. There is no requirement within IFRS 3(2008) to measure non-controlling interests on a consistent basis for similar types of business combinations and, therefore, an entity has a free choice between the two options for each transaction undertaken.

An example illustrating the choice, and its impact on goodwill, is set out in **9.1**.

When measuring non-controlling interest at the proportionate share of the acquiree's identifiable net assets, an entity should not take into account any goodwill recognised in the acquiree's own financial statements. The non-controlling interest is calculated as the proportionate share of the acquiree's identifiable assets and liabilities that satisfy the recognition criteria at the acquisition date. [IFRS 3(2008).19] Any pre-existing goodwill recognised in the acquiree's separate financial statements is ignored, as goodwill is not an identifiable asset.

7.3.2 *Implications of choice between alternatives for measuring non-controlling interests*

Where the option is taken to measure non-controlling interests at fair value (which is generally higher than the proportionate share of identified net assets), there is a corresponding impact on the residual amount of goodwill.

Further considerations include:

- the choice only affects initial measurement of a non-controlling interest – the fair value option is not available for subsequent changes in non-controlling interests;
- an increased amount attributed to goodwill as a result of the non-controlling interest measurement choice is a permanent difference in the carrying amount of goodwill;
- this would suggest that the amount of goodwill that is subject to impairment testing under IAS 36 *Impairment of Assets* will differ. However, IFRS 3(2008) amends IAS 36 such that this effect is equalised (see **8.1.2.4** in **chapter 9**). Where an entity measures a non-controlling interest at its proportionate interest in the net identifiable assets of a subsidiary at the acquisition date, rather than at fair value, for the purposes of impairment testing, the carrying amount of goodwill allocated to the unit is grossed up to include the goodwill attributable to the non-controlling interest. This adjusted carrying amount is then compared with the recoverable amount of the unit to determine whether the cash-generating unit is impaired; [IAS 36.C4] and

- where the option to measure non-controlling interests at fair value is not taken, any goodwill relating to non-controlling interests acquired subsequently will never be recognised since additional transactions after control has been obtained are accounted for as equity transactions. This feature is discussed further at **11.3.1**.

7.3.3 *Measuring the fair value of NCI*

For the purpose of measuring non-controlling interests at fair value, it may be possible to determine the acquisition-date fair value on the basis of active market prices for the equity shares not held by the acquirer. When a market price for the equity shares is not available because the shares are not publicly traded, the acquirer should measure the fair value of the non-controlling interests using other valuation techniques. [IFRS 3(2008).B44]

The fair values of the acquirer's interest in the acquiree and the non-controlling interest on a per-share basis may differ. The main difference is likely to be the inclusion of a control premium in the per-share fair value of the acquirer's interest in the acquiree or, conversely, the inclusion of a discount for lack of control in the per-share fair value of the non-controlling interest. [IFRS 3(2008).B45]

Example 7.3.3

Potential for fair values reflecting different circumstances

A acquired B in two separate transactions:

- a one-third equity interest for which A paid £10 per share, which resulted in A having significant influence over B; and
- a further one-third equity interest for which A paid £15 per share, which resulted in A having a controlling interest.

Based on the market prices of the remaining shares, A assesses the fair value of the non-controlling interest at £9 per share.

In this case, it appears that three different fair values have been attributed to similar sized equity interests. However, each fair value reflects a different fact pattern and, therefore, a different market:

- £10 represents the fair value of an equity interest carrying significant influence in an entity where other holdings are dispersed and the holder has the potential to launch a bid for a controlling interest;
- £15 represents the fair value of a controlling interest, including a control premium; and

- £9 represents the fair value of a minority non-controlling interest in an entity which is controlled by another party.

7.3.4 *Statutory obligation to launch a takeover bid*

Example 7.3.4

Statutory obligation to launch a takeover bid

Entity A has an agreement with the shareholders of Entity B to acquire a 60 per cent interest in B, a listed company. Under local law, an investor purchasing at least 30 per cent of a listed company is obliged to launch a takeover bid on the remaining shares. All conditions for the acquisition of the 60 per cent interest have been satisfied. Should the obligation to launch a takeover bid for the remaining interest in the listed company result in the recognition of a liability?

Entity A is obliged under local law to offer to acquire the remaining shares of B. A financial instrument is any contract that gives rise to a financial asset of one entity and a financial liability or equity instrument of another entity. In addition, IAS 32.AG12 clarifies that liabilities or assets that are not contractual (such as income taxes that are created as a result of statutory requirements imposed by governments) are not financial liabilities or financial assets.

For the holders of the remaining 40 percent of the shares in B, this statutory offer is not a contractual right to receive cash evidenced by a financial instrument and is not a financial asset. For A, the statutory offer is not a contractual obligation evidenced by a financial instrument and no financial liability should be recognised.

The acquisition of the non-controlling interest is accounted for when it occurs. Therefore, when A acquires all or some of the non-controlling interest after the 60 per cent interest acquisition, the non-controlling interest acquisition will be accounted for separately as an equity transaction in accordance with IAS 27(2008).30 (see **5.6.1** in **chapter 33**).

Entity A should consider whether a provision for an onerous contract should be recognised in accordance with IAS 37 as a result of the statutory obligation to launch a takeover bid.

7.4 Guidance on specific assets and liabilities

7.4.1 *Operating leases*

IFRS 3(2008) includes specific guidance on how operating leases should be recognised and measured when accounting for a business combination.

- **Classification as operating or finance** Classification of a lease contract as either an operating or a finance lease at the acquisition date is based on factors at the inception of the lease, which is generally before the acquisition date. If the terms of the contract have been changed subsequent to the inception of the lease such that the classification of the lease would change, then the classification at the acquisition date is based on the contractual terms and other factors at the date of that change. This means that an acquiree's lease classifications are not changed when accounting for the business combination, unless a lease contract is modified at the date of acquisition. [IFRS 3(2008).17]
- **Measurement where acquiree is the lessee** In general, the acquirer should not recognise any asset or liability related to an operating lease in which the acquiree is the lessee. [IFRS 3(2008).B28] It follows that any lease incentive that is being amortised by the acquiree will not be recognised by the acquirer. However, the acquiree may be party to operating lease arrangements that involve future lease payments at below or above market rates. The acquirer determines whether the terms of each operating lease in which the acquiree is the lessee are favourable or unfavourable. The acquirer recognises an intangible asset if the terms of an operating lease are favourable relative to market terms, and a liability if the terms are unfavourable relative to market terms. [IFRS 3(2008).B29]
- **Separate identifiable intangible** An identifiable intangible asset may be associated with an operating lease, which may be evidenced by market participants' willingness to pay a price for the lease even if it is at market terms. For example, a lease of gates at an airport or of retail space in a prime shopping area might provide entry into a market or other future economic benefits that qualify as identifiable intangible assets (e.g. as a customer relationship). In such circumstances, a separate identifiable intangible is recognised – see **7.4.2** below. [IFRS 3(2008.B30]
- **Measurement where acquiree is the lessor** Where an asset such as a building or a patent is leased out by the acquiree under an operating lease, the acquirer takes the terms of the lease into account in measuring the acquisition-date fair value of the leased asset. In other words, the acquirer does not recognise a separate asset or liability if the terms of the operating lease are either favourable or unfavourable when compared with market terms (as is required for leases in which the acquiree is the lessee), but instead reflects the terms of the lease in the determination of the fair value of the leased asset (see **example 7.4.3**). [IFRS 3(2008).B42]

7.4.2 *Intangible assets*

The acquirer should recognise, separately from goodwill, the identifiable intangible assets acquired in a business combination. An asset is identifiable if it meets either the separability or contractual-legal criteria in IAS 38.12 (see below). [IFRS 3(2008).B31]

7.4.2.1 Separability criterion

An intangible is separable if it is capable of being separated or divided from the entity and sold, transferred, licensed, rented or exchanged, either individually or together with a related contract, identifiable asset or liability, regardless of whether the entity intends to do so. [IAS 38.12(a)] An acquired intangible meets the separability criterion if there is evidence of exchange transactions for that type of asset or an asset of a similar type, even if those transactions are infrequent and regardless of whether the acquirer is involved in them. [IFRS 3(2008).B33]

Example 7.4.2.1A

Customer lists

[IFRS 3(2008).B33]

Customer and subscriber lists are frequently licensed and thus meet the separability criterion. Even if an acquiree believes its customer lists have characteristics different from other customer lists, the fact that customer lists are frequently licensed generally means that the acquired customer list meets the separability criterion. However, a customer list acquired in a business combination would not meet the separability criterion if the terms of confidentiality or other agreements prohibit an entity from selling, leasing or otherwise exchanging information about its customers.

An intangible asset that is not individually separable from the acquiree or combined entity meets the separability criterion if it is separable in combination with a related contract, identifiable asset or liability. [IFRS 3(2008).B34]

Example 7.4.2.1B

Depositor relationships

[IFRS 3(2008).B34(a)]

Market participants exchange deposit liabilities and related depositor relationship intangible assets in observable exchange transactions. Therefore, the acquirer should recognise the depositor relationship intangible asset separately from goodwill.

Example 7.4.2.1C

Trademarks

[IFRS 3(2008).B34(b)]

An acquiree owns a registered trademark and documented but unpatented technical expertise used to manufacture the trademarked product. To transfer ownership of a trademark, the owner is also required to transfer everything else necessary for the new owner to produce a product or service indistinguishable from that produced by the former owner. Because the unpatented technical expertise must be separated from the acquiree or combined entity and sold if the related trademark is sold, it meets the separability criterion.

7.4.2.2 Contractual-legal criterion

An intangible that arises from contractual or other legal rights is identifiable regardless of whether those rights are transferable or separable from the acquiree or from other rights and obligations. [IAS 38.12(b)]

IFRS 3(2004) included reliability of measurement as a recognition condition for intangible assets. IFRS 3(2008) presumes that where an intangible asset satisfies either of the criteria above, sufficient information should exist to measure its fair value reliably.

Example 7.4.2.2A

Manufacturing facility under an operating lease

[IFRS 3(2008).B32)(a)]

An acquiree leases a manufacturing facility under an operating lease that has terms that are favourable relative to market terms. The lease terms explicitly prohibit transfer of the lease (through either sale or sublease). The amount by which the lease terms are favourable compared with the terms of current market transactions for the same or similar items is an intangible asset that meets the contractual-legal criterion for recognition separately from goodwill, even though the acquirer cannot sell or otherwise transfer the lease contract.

Example 7.4.2.2B

Nuclear power plant subject to a licence

[IFRS 3(2008).B32)(b)]

An acquiree owns and operates a nuclear power plant. The licence to operate that power plant is an intangible asset that meets the contractual-legal criterion for recognition separately from goodwill, even if the acquirer cannot sell or transfer it separately from the acquired power plant. An acquirer may recognise the fair value of the operating licence and the fair value of the power plant as a single asset for financial reporting purposes if the useful lives of those assets are similar.

Example 7.4.2.2C

Technology patent

[IFRS 3(2008).B32)(c)]

An acquiree owns a technology patent. It has licensed that patent to others for their exclusive use outside the domestic market, receiving a specified percentage of future foreign revenue in exchange. Both the technology patent and the related licence agreement meet the contractual-legal criterion for recognition separately from goodwill even if selling or exchanging the patent and the related licence agreement separately from one another would not be practical.

The recognition and measurement of intangible assets has always been one of the difficult areas of IFRS 3 to apply in practice. Valuation practices have developed over time and their interpretation and implementation remains varied.

7.4.2.3 Examples of identifiable intangible assets

The following examples of identifiable intangible assets are taken from the Illustrative Examples accompanying IFRS 3(2008), and are not intended to be all-inclusive. They include examples under 5 headings: marketing-related, customer-related, artistic-related, contract-based, and technology-based intangible assets. The text indicates whether examples are contractual or non-contractual. Intangible assets identified as having a contractual basis are those that arise from contractual or other legal rights. Those designated as having a non-contractual basis do not arise from contractual or other legal rights but are separable. Intangible assets identified as having a contractual basis might also be separable but separability is not a necessary condition for an asset to meet the contractual-legal criterion. [IFRS 3(2008).IE17]

Example 7.4.2.3A

Marketing-related intangible assets

[IFRS 3(2008).IE18-IE22]

Marketing-related intangible assets are used primarily in the marketing or promotion of products or services. Examples of marketing-related intangible assets are:

Class	Basis
Trademarks, trade names, service marks, collective marks and certification marks	Contractual
Trade dress (unique colour, shape or package design)	Contractual
Newspaper mastheads	Contractual
Internet domain names	Contractual
Non-competition agreements	Contractual

Trademarks, trade names, service marks, collective marks and certification marks

Trademarks are words, names, symbols or other devices used in trade to indicate the source of a product and to distinguish it from the products of others. A service mark identifies and distinguishes the source of a service rather than a product. Collective marks identify the goods or services of members of a group. Certification marks certify the geographical origin or other characteristics of a good or service.

Trademarks, trade names, service marks, collective marks and certification marks may be protected legally through registration with governmental agencies, continuous use in commerce or by other means. If it is protected legally through registration or other means, a trademark or other mark acquired in a business combination is an intangible asset that meets the contractual-legal criterion. Otherwise, a trademark or other mark acquired in a business combination can be recognised separately from goodwill if the separability criterion is met, which normally it would be.

The terms *brand* and *brand name*, often used as synonyms for trademarks and other marks, are general marketing terms that typically refer to a group of complementary assets such as a trademark (or service mark) and its related trade name, formulas, recipes and technological expertise. IFRS 3 does not preclude an entity from recognising, as a single asset separately from goodwill, a group of complementary intangible assets commonly referred to as a brand if the assets that make up that group have similar useful lives.

Internet domain names

An Internet domain name is a unique alphanumeric name that is used to identify a particular numeric Internet address. Registration of a domain name creates an association between that name and a designated computer on the Internet for the period of the registration. Those registrations are renewable. A registered domain name acquired in a business combination meets the contractual-legal criterion.

Example 7.4.2.3B

Customer-related intangible assets

[IFRS 3(2008).IE23-IE31]

Examples of customer-related intangible assets are:

Class	Basis
Customer lists	Non-contractual
Order or production backlog	Contractual
Customer contracts and related customer relationships	Contractual
Non-contractual customer relationships	Non-contractual

Customer lists

A customer list consists of information about customers, such as their names and contact information. A customer list also may be in the form of a database that includes other information about the customers, such as their order histories and demographic information. A customer list does not usually arise from contractual or other legal rights. However, customer lists are often leased or exchanged. Therefore, a customer list acquired in a business combination normally meets the separability criterion.

Order or production backlog

An order or production backlog arises from contracts such as purchase or sales orders. An order or production backlog acquired in a business combination meets the contractual-legal criterion even if the purchase or sales orders can be cancelled.

Customer contracts and the related customer relationships

If an entity establishes relationships with its customers through contracts, those customer relationships arise from contractual rights. Therefore, customer contracts and the related customer relationships acquired in a business combination meet the contractual-legal criterion, even if confidentiality or other contractual terms prohibit the sale or transfer of a contract separately from the acquiree.

A customer contract and the related customer relationship may represent two distinct intangible assets. Both the useful lives and the pattern in which the economic benefits of the two assets are consumed may differ.

A customer relationship exists between an entity and its customer if (a) the entity has information about the customer and has regular contact with the customer and (b) the customer has the ability to make direct contact with the entity. Customer relationships meet the contractual-legal criterion if an entity has a practice of establishing contracts with its customers, regardless of whether a contract exists at the acquisition date. Customer relationships may also arise through means other than contracts, such as through regular contact by sales or service representatives.

As noted in IFRS 3(2008).IE25, an order or a production backlog arises from contracts such as purchase or sales orders and is therefore considered a contractual right. Consequently, if an entity has relationships with its customers through these types of contracts, the customer relationships also arise from contractual rights and therefore meet the contractual-legal criterion.

Examples

The following examples illustrate the recognition of customer contract and customer relationship intangible assets acquired in a business combination.

(a) Acquirer Company (AC) acquires Target Company (TC) in a business combination on 31 December 20X5. TC has a five-year agreement to supply goods to Customer. Both TC and AC believe that Customer will renew the agreement at the end of the current contract. The agreement is not separable.

The agreement, whether cancellable or not, meets the contractual-legal criterion. Additionally, because TC establishes its relationship with Customer through a contract, not only the agreement itself but also TC's customer relationship with Customer meet the contractual-legal criterion.

(b) AC acquires TC in a business combination on 31 December 20X5. TC manufactures goods in two distinct lines of business: sporting goods and electronics. Customer purchases both sporting goods and electronics from TC. TC has a contract with Customer to be its exclusive provider of sporting goods but has no contract for the supply of electronics to Customer. Both TC and AC believe that only one overall customer relationship exists between TC and Customer.

The contract to be Customer's exclusive supplier of sporting goods, whether cancellable or not, meets the contractual-legal criterion. Additionally, because TC establishes its relationship with Customer through a contract, the customer relationship with Customer meets the contractual-legal criterion. Because TC has only one customer relationship with Customer, the fair value of that relationship incorporates assumptions about TC's relationship with Customer related to both sporting goods and electronics. However, if AC determines that the customer relationships with Customer for sporting goods and for electronics are separate from each other, AC would assess whether the customer relationship for electronics meets the separability criterion for identification as an intangible asset.

(c) AC acquires TC in a business combination on 31 December 20X5. TC does business with its customers solely through purchase and sales orders. At 31 December 20X5, TC has a backlog of customer purchase orders from 60 per cent of its customers, all of whom are recurring customers. The other 40 per cent of TC's customers are also recurring customers. However, as of 31 December 20X5, TC has no open purchase orders or other contracts with those customers.

Regardless of whether they are cancellable or not, the purchase orders from 60 per cent of TC's customers meet the contractual-legal criterion.

Additionally, because TC has established its relationship with 60 per cent of its customers through contracts, not only the purchase orders but also TC's customer relationships meet the contractual-legal criterion. Because TC has a practice of establishing contracts with the remaining 40 per cent of its customers, its relationship with those customers also arises through contractual rights and therefore meets the contractual-legal criterion even though TC does not have contracts with those customers at 31 December 20X5.

(d) AC acquires TC, an insurer, in a business combination on 31 December 20X5. TC has a portfolio of one-year motor insurance contracts that are cancellable by policyholders.

Because TC establishes its relationships with policyholders through insurance contracts, the customer relationship with policyholders meets the contractual-legal criterion. IAS 36 *Impairment of Assets* and IAS 38 *Intangible Assets* apply to the customer relationship intangible asset.

Non-contractual customer relationships

A customer relationship acquired in a business combination that does not arise from a contract may nevertheless be identifiable because the relationship is separable. Exchange transactions for the same asset or a similar asset that indicate that other entities have sold or otherwise transferred a particular type of non-contractual customer relationship would provide evidence that the relationship is separable.

Example 7.4.2.3C

Artistic-related intangible assets

[IFRS 3(2008).IE32-IE33]

Examples of artistic-related intangible assets are:

Class	**Basis**
Plays, operas and ballets	Contractual
Books, magazines, newspapers and other literary works	Contractual
Musical works such as compositions, song lyrics and advertising jingles	Contractual
Pictures and photographs	Contractual
Video and audiovisual material, including motion pictures or films, music videos and television programmes	Contractual

Artistic-related assets acquired in a business combination are identifiable if they arise from contractual or legal rights such as those provided by copyright. The holder can transfer a copyright, either in whole through an assignment or in part through a licensing agreement. An acquirer is not precluded from recognising a copyright intangible asset and any related assignments or licence agreements as a single asset, provided they have similar useful lives.

Example 7.4.2.3D

Contract-based intangible assets

[IFRS 3(2008).IE34-IE38]

Contract-based intangible assets represent the value of rights that arise from contractual arrangements. Customer contracts are one type of contract-based intangible asset. If the terms of a contract give rise to a liability (for example, if the terms of an operating lease or customer contract are unfavourable relative to market terms), the acquirer recognises it as a liability assumed in the business combination.

Examples of contract-based intangible assets are:

Class	Basis
Licensing, royalty and standstill agreements	Contractual
Advertising, construction, management, service or supply contracts	Contractual
Lease agreements (whether the acquiree is the lessee or the lessor)	Contractual
Construction permits	Contractual
Franchise agreements	Contractual
Operating and broadcast rights	Contractual
Servicing contracts, such as mortgage servicing contracts	Contractual
Employment contracts	Contractual
Use rights, such as drilling, water, air, timber cutting and route authorities	Contractual

Servicing contracts, such as mortgage servicing contracts

Contracts to service financial assets are one type of contract-based intangible asset. Although servicing is inherent in all financial assets, it becomes a distinct asset (or liability) by one of the following:

(a) when contractually separated from the underlying financial asset by sale or securitisation of the assets with servicing retained;

(b) through the separate purchase and assumption of the servicing.

If mortgage loans, credit card receivables or other financial assets are acquired in a business combination with servicing retained, the inherent servicing rights are not a separate intangible asset because the fair value of those servicing rights is included in the measurement of the fair value of the acquired financial asset.

Employment contracts

Employment contracts that are beneficial contracts from the perspective of the employer because the pricing of those contracts is favourable relative to market terms are one type of contract-based intangible asset.

Use rights

Use rights include rights for drilling, water, air, timber cutting and route authorities. Some use rights are contract-based intangible assets to be accounted for separately from goodwill. Other use rights may have characteristics of tangible assets rather than of intangible assets. An acquirer should account for use rights on the basis of their nature.

Example 7.4.2.3E

Technology-based intangible assets

[IFRS 3(2008).IE39-IE44]

Examples of technology-based intangible assets are:

Class	Basis
Patented technology	Contractual
Computer software and mask works	Contractual
Unpatented technology	Non-contractual
Databases, including title plants	Non-contractual
Trade secrets, such as secret formulas, processes and recipes	Contractual

Computer software and mask works

Computer software and program formats acquired in a business combination that are protected legally, such as by patent or copyright, meet the contractual-legal criterion for identification as intangible assets.

Mask works are software permanently stored on a read-only memory chip as a series of stencils or integrated circuitry. Mask works may have legal protection. Mask works with legal protection that are acquired in a business combination meet the contractual-legal criterion for identification as intangible assets.

Databases, including title plants

Databases are collections of information, often stored in electronic form (such as on computer disks or files). A database that includes original works of authorship may be entitled to copyright protection. A database acquired in a business combination and protected by copyright meets the contractual-legal criterion. However, a database typically includes information created as a consequence of an entity's normal operations, such as customer lists, or specialised information, such as scientific data or credit information. Databases that are not protected by copyright can be, and often are, exchanged, licensed or leased to others in their entirety or in part. Therefore, even if the future economic benefits from a database do not arise from legal rights, a database acquired in a business combination meets the separability criterion.

Title plants constitute a historical record of all matters affecting title to parcels of land in a particular geographical area. Title plant assets are bought and sold, either in whole or in part, in exchange transactions or are licensed. Therefore, title plant assets acquired in a business combination meet the separability criterion.

Trade secrets, such as secret formulas, processes and recipes

A trade secret is 'information, including a formula, pattern, recipe, compilation, program, device, method, technique, or process that (a) derives independent economic value, actual or potential, from not being generally known and (b) is the subject of efforts that are reasonable under the circumstances to maintain its secrecy.' If the future economic benefits from a trade secret acquired in a business combination are legally protected, that asset meets the contractual-legal criterion. Otherwise, trade secrets acquired in a business combination are identifiable only if the separability criterion is met, which is likely to be the case.

7.4.2.4 *Assembled workforce and other items that are not identifiable*

The acquirer subsumes into goodwill the value of an acquired intangible asset that is not identifiable as of the acquisition date. [IFRS 3(2008).B37]

Example 7.4.2.4A

Assembled workforce

[IFRS 3(2008).B37]

An acquirer may attribute value to the existence of an assembled workforce, which is an existing collection of employees that permits the acquirer to continue to operate an acquired business from the acquisition date. An assembled workforce does not represent the intellectual capital of the skilled workforce – the (often specialised) knowledge and experience that employees of an acquiree bring to their jobs, which would be included in the fair value of an entity's other intangible assets, such as proprietary technologies and processes and customer contracts and relationships. Because the assembled workforce is not an identifiable asset to be recognised separately from goodwill, any value attributed to it is subsumed into goodwill.

Example 7.4.2.4B

Agreements with independent contractors

Although an entity's arrangements with its independent contractors are similar in many ways to its arrangements with its at-will employees making up an assembled workforce, the existence of contractual arrangements with independent contractors can represent an intangible asset in some cases. Although individual employees might have employment contracts that are similar to arrangements with independent contractors, it is the collection of employees that permits the acquirer to continue to operate an acquired business from the acquisition date and this collection is not an identifiable asset.

Independent contractors are often engaged to perform specific tasks and are not employees of the organisation. There are often negotiated rights for the contractor to retain intellectual property generated during a contract phase. They usually provide services to a number of different entities. Accordingly, the nature of the relationship with independent contractors is often quite different to that with employees and, where that relationship leads to the existence of an intangible asset, it should be recognised and measured in accordance with IFRS 3(2008).

The acquirer also subsumes into goodwill any value attributed to items that do not qualify as assets at the acquisition date. [IFRS 3(2008).B38]

Example 7.4.2.4C

Potential contracts

[IFRS 3(2008).B38]

The acquirer might attribute value to potential contracts the acquiree is negotiating with prospective new customers at the acquisition date. The acquirer does not recognise those potential contracts separately from goodwill, because they are not themselves assets at the acquisition date. The acquirer should not subsequently reclassify the value of those contracts from goodwill for events that occur after the acquisition date. However, the acquirer should assess the facts and circumstances surrounding events occurring shortly after the acquisition to determine whether a separately recognisable intangible asset existed at the acquisition date.

Example 7.4.2.4D

Expansion of business

In negotiating the purchase consideration, an acquirer may place significant value on the 'critical mass' or 'base' that an entity's existing customers, sales channels and other systems may provide to allow a significant expansion of the business after the combination. Sometimes, the acquiree's resources and systems are planned to be used in conjunction with the acquirer's own.

In such an acquisition, the customer base of the acquiree at the acquisition date will usually be a separately identifiable intangible asset. However, where the acquirer attributes value to the future customers that the acquiree might obtain, this will not represent a separately identifiable asset and this amount should be subsumed within goodwill.

Example 7.4.2.4E

Future growth in monopoly businesses

An acquiree may operate its business under a monopoly created by legislation. This might occur in telecommunications, utilities and similar industry sectors where individual entities are given rights to be the exclusive supplier of a utility or telecommunication service in a particular geographical region. Because of these monopoly rights, any future customers in that region will be *required* to use the acquiree to provide its service.

In these cases, the acquirer will usually ascribe significant value to the monopoly licence asset rather than customer-related intangible assets. In addition, future growth expected in the geographical region would be factored into the value of the monopoly licence rather than being subsumed within goodwill.

The identifiability criteria determine whether an intangible asset is recognised separately from goodwill. However, the criteria neither provide guidance for measuring the fair value of an intangible asset nor restrict the assumptions used in estimating the fair value of an intangible asset. [IFRS 3(2008).B40]

Example 7.4.2.4F

Contract renewal

[IFRS 3(2008).B40]

The acquirer would take into account assumptions that market participants would consider, such as expectations of future contract renewals, in measuring fair value. It is not necessary for the renewals themselves to meet the identifiability criteria. (However, see IFRS 3(2008).29, which establishes an exception to the fair value measurement principle for reacquired rights recognised in a business combination.) Paragraphs 36 and 37 of IAS 38 provide guidance for determining whether intangible assets should be combined into a single unit of account with other intangible or tangible assets.

Reacquired rights are discussed at **7.5.2** below.

7.4.2.5 In-process research and development

IAS 38 generally requires research expenditure and development expenditure not meeting certain criteria to be expensed. However, it is likely that in-process research and development (IPR&D) projects will have a fair value, and this is recognised if the requirements of IFRS 3(2008).B31 are met.

Neither IFRS 3 nor IAS 38 includes any guidance on the subsequent accounting for the fair value recognised at the date of acquisition. Therefore, the general requirements of IAS 38 regarding measurement after recognition, and amortisation, will apply. This is confirmed in the IAS 38 Basis for Conclusions. [IAS 38.BC84] The subsequent basis of accounting is thus:

(a) cost less any accumulated amortisation and any accumulated impairment losses; or

(b) revalued amount, being the asset's fair value, determined by reference to an active market, at the date of revaluation less any subsequent accumulated amortisation and any subsequent accumulated impairment losses.

Amortisation would be based on the useful life of the IPR&D. [IAS 38.88]

It is unlikely that the conditions for revaluation will exist, since it is unlikely that an active market will exist for IPR&D and, consequently, the cost method will be used. In the event that a research project does not lead to future economic benefits, the amount carried would be subject to impairment testing. Where future economic benefits are forecast, amortisation would be based on the useful life assessed by number of production, or similar, units representing that useful life.

Subsequent to the business combination, capitalisation of further expenditure is subject to the usual requirements of IAS 38. [IAS 38.42]

Example 7.4.2.5

In-process research and development

Entity N acquires a research laboratory. The lab is involved in the development of medical research techniques. At the date of acquisition, the entity has two projects in progress. One is the development of a proven cure for a common disease into a commercially viable drug, and the second is research into the curative characteristics of a particular chemical compound.

On initial acquisition the intangible assets arising from these projects are measured at their fair value and recognised as assets acquired in the business combination.

In subsequent years, providing the IAS 38 recognition criteria are met, development expenditure directly attributable to the first project is capitalised, and the asset tested for impairment if any indicators of impairment are considered to exist. All subsequent expenditure attributable to the second project is expensed when incurred, until such time as the project meets all the criteria in the standard for recognition as a development asset. Once the criteria are satisfied, expenditure that has been previously expensed cannot be reinstated into the development asset.

7.4.3 *Investment property*

Example 7.4.3

Acquisition of investment property with existing operating lease in place

Company A acquires Company B which is acting as a lessor over an investment property with an operating lease that is not at current market rates.

The fair value of an operating lease over an investment property should not be recognised separately from the fair value of the investment property. Where an acquiree is acting as a lessor over an investment property with operating leases at above or below current market rates, the fair value of the operating lease should be incorporated as part of the value of the investment property.

Example 5.2.2 in **chapter 7** deals with the acquisition, outside a business combination, of an investment property where an operating lease is not at current market rates.

7.4.4 *Performance obligations*

Example 7.4.4

Treatment of performance obligations

Company A acquires Company B in a business combination. As of the acquisition-date, B has recognised deferred income related to a customer contract. The deferred income represents a prepayment received by B for future services.

IFRS 3(2008).18 requires the acquirer to 'measure the identifiable assets acquired and the liabilities assumed at their acquisition-date fair values'. As of the acquisition-date, A should recognise a liability in its consolidated financial statements to the extent that the deferred income represents an obligation to provide future services that will be the combined entity's responsibility after the acquisition-date. That is, a liability should be recognised because A has a performance obligation to provide future services for which payment has already been received. This liability should be measured at fair value as of the acquisition-date and consideration should be given to whether any intangible assets should be recognised as part of the business combination with respect to B's customer contracts (see **example 7.4.2.3B**).

7.4.5 *Contractual provisions*

Example 7.4.5

Recognition of contractual provisions

Entity F acquires Entity G. Prior to the date of acquisition, Entity G has entered into a retrenchment package for directors, such that if the entity is acquired by another party the directors will become entitled to a one-off aggregate payment of £50,000. In addition, a restructuring plan with a total cost of £115,000 would be implemented.

At the acquisition-date, Entity F recognises the liability of £50,000 to the directors, because this represents a contractual obligation of Entity G that has become payable by virtue of the consummation of the business combination, but does not recognise the liability for the restructuring of £115,000 – this amount would be recognised as an expense when the recognition criteria in IAS 37 are met.

7.4.6 *Non-competition agreements*

Non-competition agreements are discussed at **3.2.3** in **chapter 8**.

7.4.7 *Inventories*

Fair value at the point of acquisition (i.e. the date of combination) typically includes profit attributed to past production effort, i.e. in bringing the goods to their current condition. Except on grounds of materiality, it is not generally appropriate to assign the acquiree's carrying amount to the cost of acquired inventories, because the acquiree's cost does not reflect the manufacturing profit that is recognised by the acquiree through the normal selling process. This manufacturing profit should be considered as part of the fair value assigned to the inventory.

The fair value of finished goods and merchandise is likely to be lower than selling price, to reflect the costs of disposal and a reasonable profit allowance for the selling effort of the acquirer based on profit for similar finished goods and merchandise. In determining a reasonable profit allowance, the following factors should be considered:

- the historical turnover rate for inventories of the acquiree and for the acquiree's industry;
- industry statistics for normal profit allowances and turnover rates; and
- the nature of the selling network and marketing techniques employed by the acquiree or that will be employed by the acquirer, if significantly different.

In the case of retail operations, costs to dispose may include inventory stocking costs and warehousing and distribution costs for the acquired inventory. However, it is inappropriate to allocate general and administrative overhead costs to finished goods inventory in the acquisition.

7.4.8 Emission rights acquired in a business combination

Example 7.4.8

Emission rights

Entity A acquires Entity B. Entity B's accounting policy is to adopt the net liability approach for recognition of emission rights (see **9.1.3** in **chapter 11**). It has been granted emission rights by the government for no charge and, at acquisition date, it holds emission rights in excess of actual emissions made. Accordingly, no asset or provision is recognised in the financial statements of B in respect of emissions.

On acquisition, A's consolidated financial statements will include the emission rights held by B as an asset and will include a separate provision for the actual emissions made as at that date. Both the asset and the provision will need to be recognised at fair value, in accordance with IFRS 3. Accordingly, the net liability approach may not be applied in the consolidated financial statements; instead, the consolidated financial statements will thereafter reflect an expense for actual emissions made.

Fair value at acquisition date will be determined by reference to an active market for emission rights or, if no active market exists, on a basis that reflects the amount the acquirer would have paid for the rights in an arm's length transaction between knowledgeable willing parties, based on the best information available.

7.5 Exceptions to the recognition and measurement principles

IFRS 3(2008) sets out limited exceptions to its general recognition and measurement principles. This results in particular items being:

[IFRS 3(2008).21]

(a) recognised either by applying recognition conditions in addition to those set out at **8.1** above or by applying the requirements of other IFRSs, with results that differ from applying the recognition principle and conditions; or

(b) measured at an amount other than their acquisition-date fair values.

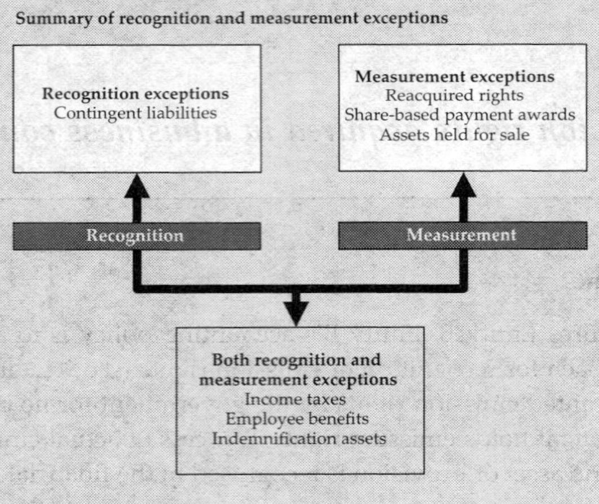

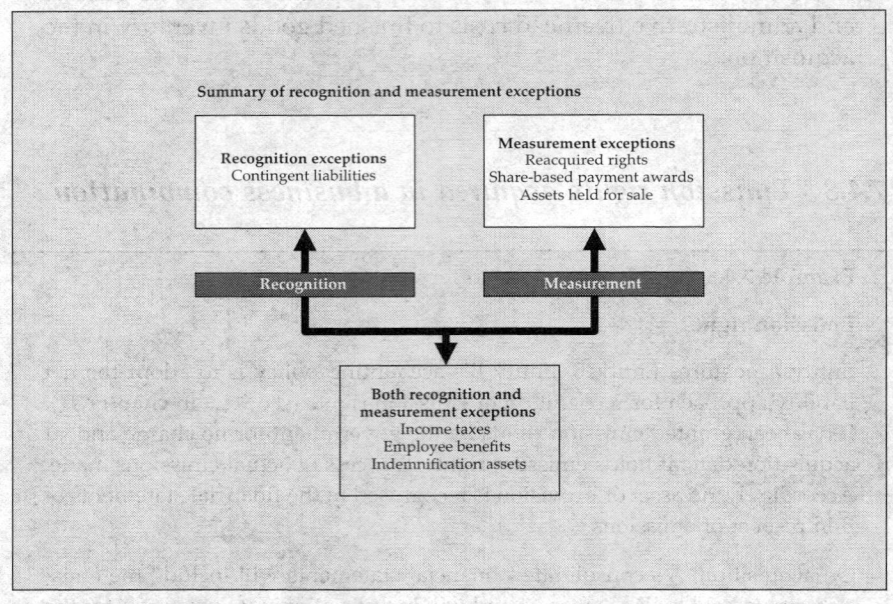

7.5.1 Contingent liabilities

7.5.1.1 Background

IFRS 3(2004) required the contingent liabilities of the acquiree to be recognised and measured in a business combination at acquisition-date fair value. IFRS 3(2008) effectively reapplies the requirement of IFRS 3(2004) to measure at acquisition-date fair value regardless of probability, and retains a filter based on whether fair value can be measured reliably.

This may result in the recognition of contingent liabilities that would not qualify for recognition under IAS 37 *Provisions, Contingent Liabilities and Contingent Assets* (see **chapter 11**). Consequently, IFRS 3(2008) also includes guidance on the subsequent measurement of contingent liabilities recognised in a business combination.

7.5.1.2 Requirements

IAS 37 defines a contingent liability as:

[IAS 37.10]

(a) a possible obligation that arises from past events and whose existence will be confirmed only by the occurrence or non-occurrence of one or more uncertain future events not wholly within the control or the entity; or

(b) a present obligation that arises from past events but is not recognised because:

(i) it is not probable that an outflow of resources embodying economic benefits will be required to settle the obligation; or

(ii) the amount of the obligation cannot be measured with sufficient reliability.

In a business combination, the requirements of IAS 37 are not applied in determining which contingent liabilities should be recognised as of the acquisition date. Instead, IFRS 3(2008) requires that the acquirer should recognise a contingent liability assumed in a business combination as of the acquisition date if:

[IFRS 3(2008).23]

- it is a present obligation that arises from past events; and
- its fair value can be measured reliably.

Therefore, contrary to IAS 37, the acquirer recognises a contingent liability assumed in a business combination at the acquisition date even if it is not probable that an outflow of resources embodying economic benefits will be required to settle the obligation. [IFRS 3(2008).23]

7.5.1.3 *Implications*

In practice, the application of IAS 37 to past events focuses on the future outcome of those events. Where the occurrence or non-occurrence of an uncertain future event will determine whether an obligation will arise, it is classified as 'possible' under IAS 37, included within contingent liabilities, and therefore not recognised as a liability in the statement of financial position, but disclosed by way of note.

Under the fair value principle of IFRS 3(2008), the fact that there is a past event giving rise to ongoing uncertainty and, therefore, a present obligation, means that the risk has a fair value since the entity would rationally pay to have the risk removed. This is true regardless of the probability of outcomes. In practice, it will be necessary to determine whether a present obligation exists (recognised if reliably measurable), or whether there is just a possible obligation (not recognised).

The Board's original intention was to revise IAS 37 as part of phase II of the business combinations project. At the time of writing, the Board is continuing its deliberations on this related topic.

7.5.1.4 *Subsequent remeasurement*

As noted above, contingent liabilities recognised in a business combination are initially measured at their acquisition-date fair values. After initial recognition and until the liability is settled, cancelled or expires, the acquirer should measure a contingent liability recognised in a business combination at the higher of:

[IFRS 3(2008).56]

(a) the amount that would be recognised in accordance with IAS 37 (see **chapter 11**); and

(b) the amount initially recognised less, if appropriate, cumulative amortisation recognised in accordance with IAS 18 *Revenue* (see **chapter 23**).

This requirement does not apply to contracts accounted for in accordance with IAS 39.

7.5.2 *Pre-existing relationships and reacquired rights*

7.5.2.1 Overview

IFRS 3(2008) deals with reacquired rights and the wider issue of pre-existing relationships in three inter-related sections:

- first, the section on identifying and measuring assets acquired includes a requirement to identify and recognise reacquired rights;
- second, the section on determining what is part of the business combination requires an adjustment to be made to the purchase consideration for transactions that in effect settle pre-existing relationships between the acquirer and the acquiree; and
- third, the section on subsequent measurement and accounting includes a requirement in respect of reacquired rights.

7.5.2.2 Recognition of reacquired rights as an intangible

As part of a business combination, an acquirer may reacquire a right that it had previously granted to the acquiree to use one or more of the acquirer's recognised or unrecognised assets. Examples of reacquired rights include a right to use the acquirer's trade name under a franchise agreement or a right to use the acquirer's technology under a technology licensing agreement. A reacquired right is an intangible asset that the acquirer recognises separately from goodwill. [IFRS 3(2008).B35]

There are two specific requirements regarding the measurement of a reacquired right.

- **Ignoring the potential for contract renewal** The acquirer is required to measure the value of a reacquired right recognised as an intangible asset on the basis of the remaining contractual term of the related contract, regardless of whether market participants would consider potential contractual renewals in determining its fair value. [IFRS 3(2008).29]
- **Recognition of a settlement gain or loss** If the terms of the contract giving rise to a reacquired right are favourable or unfavourable to the acquirer relative to the terms of current market transactions for the same or similar items, the acquirer should recognise a settlement gain or loss. [IFRS 3(2008).B36] The consequence of this requirement is that the consideration for the business combination is adjusted down (and that amount recognised as an expense) where part of the consideration effectively settles an unfavourable exposure from the

acquirer's perspective, and adjusted up (a gain) where the consideration is lower due to the effective settlement of a favourable arrangement from the acquirer's perspective. The measurement of any such gain or loss is described in **7.5.2.3** below.

The effect of these requirements is that the amount recognised for the reacquired right asset is based on the 'at market' valuation of the contract, but only by reference to the contracted term of the right.

7.5.2.3 *Measurement of gain or loss on settlement of a pre-existing relationship*

The acquirer and acquiree may have a relationship that existed before they contemplated the business combination, referred to as a 'pre-existing relationship'. A pre-existing relationship between the acquirer and the acquiree may be contractual (e.g. vendor and customer, or licensor and licensee) or non-contractual (e.g. plaintiff and defendant). [IFRS 3(2008).B51]

If the business combination in effect settles a pre-existing relationship, the acquirer recognises a gain or loss, measured as follows:

[IFRS 3(2008).B52]

(a) for a pre-existing non-contractual relationship (such as a lawsuit), fair value.

(b) for a pre-existing contractual relationship, the lesser of (i) and (ii):

(i) the amount by which the contract is favourable or unfavourable from the perspective of the acquirer when compared with terms for current market transactions for the same or similar items. (An unfavourable contract is a contract that is unfavourable in terms of current market terms. It is not necessarily an onerous contract in which the unavoidable costs of meeting the obligations under the contract exceed the economic benefits expected to be received under it); and

(ii) the amount of any stated settlement provisions in the contract available to the counterparty to whom the contract is unfavourable.

If (ii) is less than (i), the difference is included as part of the business combination accounting.

The amount of gain or loss recognised may depend in part on whether the acquirer had previously recognised a related asset or liability, and the reported gain or loss therefore may differ from the amount calculated by applying the above requirements. [IFRS 3(2008).B52]

A pre-existing relationship may be a contract that the acquirer recognises as a reacquired right. If the contract includes terms that are favourable or unfavourable when compared with pricing for current market transactions for the same or similar items, the acquirer recognises, separately from the business combination, a gain or loss for the effective settlement of the contract, measured in accordance IFRS 3(2008).B52. [IFRS 3(2008).B53]

Summary of accounting for a pre-existing relationship

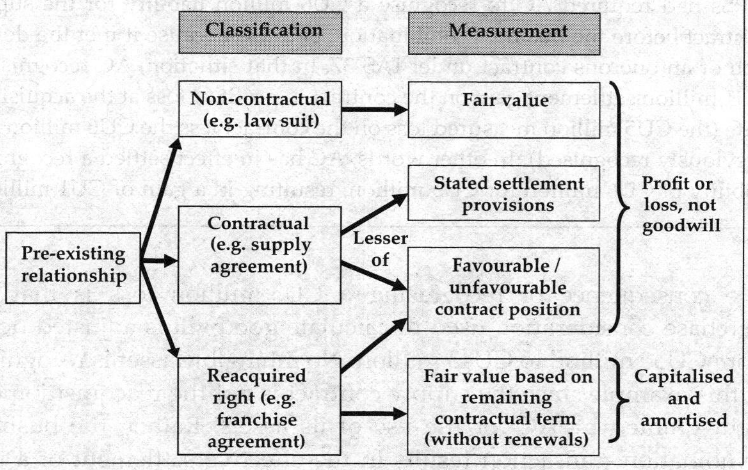

Example 7.5.2.3A

Settlement of a pre-existing relationship – contractual supply agreement

[IFRS 3(2008).IE54-IE57]

AC purchases electronic components from TC under a five-year supply contract at fixed rates. Currently, the fixed rates are higher than the rates at which AC could purchase similar electronic components from another supplier. The supply contract allows AC to terminate the contract before the end of the initial five-year term but only by paying a CU6 million penalty. With three years remaining under the supply contract, AC pays CU50 million to acquire TC, which is the fair value of TC based on what other market participants would be willing to pay.

Included in the total fair value of TC is CU8 million related to the fair value of the supply contract with AC. The CU8 million represents a CU3 million component that is 'at market' because the pricing is comparable to pricing for current market transactions for the same or similar items (selling effort, customer relationships and so on) and a CU5 million component for pricing that is unfavourable to AC because it exceeds the price of current market transactions for similar items. TC has no other identifiable assets or liabilities related to the supply contract, and AC has not recognised any assets or liabilities related to the supply contract before the business combination.

In this example, AC calculates a loss of CU5 million (the lesser of the CU6 million stated settlement amount and the amount by which the contract is unfavourable to the acquirer) separately from the business combination. The CU3 million 'at-market' component of the contract is part of goodwill.

Whether AC had recognised previously an amount in its financial statements related to a pre-existing relationship will affect the amount recognised as a gain or loss for the effective settlement of the relationship. Suppose that IFRSs had required AC to recognise a CU6 million liability for the supply contract before the business combination, perhaps because it met the definition of an onerous contract under IAS 37. In that situation, AC recognises a CU1 million settlement gain on the contract in profit or loss at the acquisition date (the CU5 million measured loss on the contract less the CU6 million loss previously recognised). In other words, AC has in effect settled a recognised liability of CU6 million for CU5 million, resulting in a gain of CU1 million.

The consequence of recognising a CU5 million loss is that the purchase consideration used to calculate goodwill is adjusted down from CU50 million to CU45 million. No intangible asset is recognised in this example since the supply contract is not the reacquisition of a right granted by AC for the use of its assets. Rather, the business combination transaction results in the effective settlement of a pre-existing contractual supply arrangement between AC and TC.

Example 7.5.2.3B

Reacquired right at market terms

X grants a franchise right to Y to operate under X's name in the northeast region of the country in which it operates. Two years later, X decides to expand its business and enters into an agreement to acquire 100% of Y for £50,000. Y's business consists of the franchise right (fair value £20,000), a customer list (fair value £10,000), some operating assets and liabilities (net fair value £15,000), an assembled workforce (recognised as part of goodwill) and processes. At the time of the acquisition, the franchise right is at market terms and, therefore, X does not recognise an off-market settlement gain or loss. Assume that the franchise right has a fixed term and is not renewable.

Under IFRS 3(2008), X recognises an identified intangible asset for the reacquired right at its fair value of £20,000. This right will be amortised over the remaining term of the franchise agreement.

Goodwill will therefore be £5,000 (£50,000 less (20,000 + 10,000 + 15,000)).

Example 7.5.2.3C

Reacquired right at off-market terms

The facts are as in **example 7.5.2.3B**, except that the franchise right contract terms are favourable to X compared to market terms at the acquisition date by £3,000.

As before, X recognises an identified intangible asset for the reacquired right at its fair value of £20,000. This right will be amortised over the remaining term of the franchise agreement.

In addition, X recognises a gain of £3,000 for the effective settlement of the contract and consequently increases the consideration used in the acquisition accounting to £53,000.

Goodwill will therefore be £8,000 (£53,000 less (20,000 + 10,000 + 15,000)).

7.5.2.4 Subsequent measurement

A reacquired right recognised as an intangible asset shall be amortised over the remaining contractual period of the contract in which the right was granted. An acquirer that subsequently sells a reacquired right to a third party should include the carrying amount of the intangible asset in determining the gain or loss on the sale. [IFRS 3(2008).55] In such cases, care should be taken to ensure that the intangible asset being sold is the same asset that was previously reacquired. Thus, the reacquisition through a business combination of a 'master franchise agreement', and the subsequent granting of sub-franchises for specific geographical areas to third parties, would be dealt with separately and the master franchise agreement retained in the acquirer's statement of financial position.

7.5.3 Share-based payment awards

Where an acquirer issues share-based payment awards to replace those of an acquiree, it is necessary to allocate the replacement awards between:

- the element which represents purchase consideration for accrued share rights earned before the acquisition; and
- the element which represents compensation for post-acquisition services.

As an exception to the fair value measurement principle, any liability or equity instrument recognised by the acquirer is based on a 'market-based measure' determined in accordance with IFRS 2 *Share-based Payment*. Share-based payments are dealt with in **8.3.4** below.

7.5.4 *Assets held for sale*

The acquirer should measure an acquired non-current asset (or disposal group) that is classified as held for sale at the acquisition date in accordance with IFRS 5 *Non-current Assets Held for Sale and Discontinued Operations* at fair value less costs to sell in accordance with paragraphs 15 -18 of that Standard (see **chapter 29**). [IFRS 3(2008).31]

7.5.5 *Income taxes*

IFRS 3(2008) requires the acquirer to recognise and measure a deferred tax asset or liability arising from the assets acquired and liabilities assumed in a business combination in accordance with IAS 12 *Income Taxes* (see **chapter 12**). [IFRS 3(2008).24]

The acquirer should account for potential tax effects of temporary differences and carry forwards of an acquiree that exist at the acquisition date or that arise as a result of the acquisition in accordance with IAS 12. [IFRS 3(2008).25]

Amendments to IAS 12 relating to the post-acquisition recognition of deferred tax assets are discussed in **10.3.6**. Transitional arrangements are discussed in **14.2.3**.

7.5.6 *Employee benefits*

The acquirer should recognise and measure a liability (or asset, if any) related to the acquiree's employee benefit arrangements in accordance with IAS 19 *Employee Benefits* (see **chapter 24**). [IFRS 3(2008).26]

7.5.7 *Indemnification assets*

7.5.7.1 *Initial measurement*

The seller in a business combination may contractually indemnify the acquirer for the outcome of a contingency or uncertainty related to all or part of a specific asset or liability. For example, the seller may indemnify the acquirer against losses above a certain amount on a liability arising from a particular contingency, such as legal action or income tax uncertainty. As a result, the acquirer obtains an indemnification asset. [IFRS 3(2008).27]

IFRS 3(2008) requires the acquirer to recognise an indemnification asset at the same time that it recognises the indemnified item and that the indemnification asset be measured on the same basis as the indemnified item, assuming that there is no uncertainty over the recovery of the indemnification asset. Therefore, if the indemnification relates to an asset or liability that is recognised at the acquisition date and that is measured at fair value, the acquirer should recognise the indemnification asset at the acquisition date measured at its fair value. [IFRS 3(2008).27]

For an indemnification asset measured at fair value, the effects of uncertainty about future cash flows because of collectibility considerations are included in the fair value measure and a separate valuation allowance is not necessary. [IFRS 3(2008).27]

In some circumstances, the indemnification may relate to an asset or liability that is an exception to the recognition or measurement principles. For example, an indemnification may relate to a contingent liability that is not recognised at the acquisition date because its fair value is not reliably measurable at that date. Alternatively, an indemnification may relate to an asset or liability (e.g. one that results from an employee benefit) that is measured on a basis other than acquisition-date fair value. In those circumstances, the indemnification asset is recognised and measured using assumptions consistent with those used to measure the indemnified item, subject to management's assessment of the collectibility of the indemnification asset and any contractual limitations on the indemnified amount. [IFRS 3(2008).28]

The requirement that an indemnification asset be measured using assumptions consistent with the measurement of the indemnified item does not necessarily mean that the indemnification asset and indemnified item are measured at the same amount. For instance, an indemnity may be capped at a certain amount, be determined as a portion of any final settlement amount, represent an amount over a particular amount, or be recovered in a later time period than when the indemnified item is settled. In these cases, it is likely that the indemnified item will be recognised at a different amount to the indemnification asset because the cash outflows and inflows will be different.

However, the recognition and measurement of the asset and liability will be determined on a consistent basis, by reference to any relevant Standards. Therefore, an indemnification asset in relation to:

- an employee benefit will be measured using the principles of IAS 19 (see **chapter 24**);
- a liability recognised as a provision will be measured in accordance with IAS 37 (see **chapter 11**); and

- an income tax exposure, will be measured by reference to IAS 12 (see **chapter 12**).

7.5.7.2 *Subsequent measurement*

At the end of each subsequent reporting period, the acquirer should measure an indemnification asset that was recognised at the acquisition date on the same basis as the indemnified liability or asset, subject to any contractual limitations on its amount and, for an indemnification asset that is not subsequently measured at its fair value, management's assessment of the collectibility of the indemnification asset. The acquirer should derecognise the indemnification asset only when it collects the asset, sells it or otherwise loses the right to it. [IFRS 3(2008).57]

The effect of the requirements for indemnification assets is to achieve matching of the asset recognised with the item that is the subject of the indemnity. In most cases, it is expected that remeasurement of both asset and liability would be in profit or loss, although IFRS 3(2008) does not provide for this.

8 Identifying and measuring consideration

8.1 Consideration transferred

IFRS 3(2008) requires the consideration transferred in a business combination to be measured at fair value. This is calculated as the sum of the acquisition-date fair values of:

[IFRS 3(2008).37]

- the assets transferred by the acquirer;
- the liabilities incurred by the acquirer to former owners of the acquiree; and
- the equity interests issued by the acquirer.

However, any portion of the acquirer's share-based payment awards exchanged for awards held by the acquiree's employees that is included in the consideration transferred in the business combination should be measured in accordance with IFRS 2 *Share-based Payment* (see **8.3.3**). [IFRS 3(2008).37]

Potential forms of consideration include cash, other assets, a business or a subsidiary of the acquirer, contingent consideration (see **8.2**), ordinary or preference equity instruments, options, warrants and member interests of mutual entities. [IFRS 3(2008).37]

The consideration transferred may include assets or liabilities of the acquirer with carrying amounts that differ from their fair values at the acquisition date (e.g. non-monetary assets or a business of the acquirer). If so, the acquirer should remeasure the transferred assets or liabilities to their fair values as of the acquisition date and recognise any resulting gains or losses in profit or loss. [IFRS 3(2008).38]

The recognition of a gain or loss on assets or liabilities transferred is a further application of the principle that crossing an accounting boundary involves a disposal (see **1.3.2**). It is also consistent with the definition of cost in the IASB *Glossary* which defines cost as 'the amount of cash or cash equivalents paid or *the fair value of the other consideration* given to acquire an asset at the time of its acquisition ...'. In the case of a subsidiary, this would imply the date of acquisition of the subsidiary.

However, sometimes the transferred assets or liabilities remain within the combined entity after the business combination (e.g. because the assets and liabilities were transferred to the acquiree rather than to its former owners), and the acquirer therefore retains control of them. In that situation, the acquirer should measure those assets and liabilities at their carrying amount immediately before the acquisition date. No gain or loss should be recognised in profit or loss in respect of assets or liabilities controlled by the acquirer both before and after the business combination. [IFRS 3(2008).38]

The implication of not remeasuring assets and liabilities that remain within the group to fair value is that goodwill will be correspondingly lower than the situation where assets and liabilities are transferred outside the group and remeasured to fair value.

8.2 Contingent consideration

8.2.1 Recognition at acquisition date

The consideration the acquirer transfers in exchange for the acquiree includes any asset or liability resulting from a contingent consideration agreement. [IFRS 3(2008).39] Contingent consideration is defined as follows.

[IFRS 3(2008)(Appendix A)]

> 'Usually, an obligation of the acquirer to transfer additional assets or equity interests to the former owners of an acquiree as part of the exchange for control of the acquiree if specified future events occur or conditions are met. However, contingent consideration may also give the acquirer the right to the return of previously transferred consideration if specified conditions are met'.

Contingent consideration is recognised as part of the consideration transferred in exchange for the acquiree, measured at its acquisition-date fair value. [IFRS 3(2008).39]

An obligation to pay contingent consideration is classified as a liability or as equity on the basis of the definitions of an equity instrument and a financial liability in paragraph 11 of IAS 32 *Financial Instruments: Presentation* (see **section 2** of **chapter 15**). [IFRS 3(2008).40]

Where the purchase agreement includes a right to the return of previously-transferred consideration if specified conditions for a repayment are met, that right to return is classified as an asset by the acquirer. [IFRS 3(2008).40]

Example 8.2.1

Contingent consideration

A acquires B. The consideration is payable in 3 tranches:

- an immediate payment of £1m;
- a further payment of £0.5m after one year if profit before interest and tax for the first year following acquisition exceeds £200,000; and
- a further payment of £0.5m after two years if profit before interest and tax for the second year following acquisition exceeds £220,000.

The two payments that are conditional upon reaching earnings targets are contingent consideration. At the date of acquisition, the fair value of these two payments is assessed as £250,000.

Consequently, on the date of acquisition, consideration of £1,250,000 is recognised.

8.2.2 *Subsequent accounting*

As noted above, contingent consideration is measured at its acquisition-date fair value. IFRS 3(2008) has introduced a new approach to the accounting for changes in the value of contingent consideration subsequent to the acquisition date.

8.2.2.1 *Changes based on additional information about facts and circumstances at the acquisition date*

Changes that are the result of the acquirer obtaining additional information about facts and circumstances that existed at the acquisition date, and that occur within the measurement period (which may be a maximum of one year from the acquisition date), are recognised as adjustments against the original accounting for the acquisition (and so may impact goodwill) – see **10.1**. [IFRS 3(2008).58]

8.2.2.2 *Post-combination changes*

Changes resulting from events after the acquisition date (e.g. meeting an earnings target, reaching a specified share price or reaching a milestone on a research and development project) are not measurement period adjustments. Such changes are therefore accounted for separately from the business combination. The acquirer accounts for changes in the fair value of contingent consideration that are not measurement period adjustments as follows:

[IFRS 3(2008).58]

(a) contingent consideration classified as equity is not remeasured and its subsequent settlement is accounted for within equity; and

(b) contingent consideration classified as an asset or a liability that:

(i) is a financial instrument and is within the scope of IAS 39 is measured at fair value, with any resulting gain or loss recognised either in profit or loss or in other comprehensive income in accordance with IAS 39; and

(ii) is not within the scope of IAS 39 is accounted for in accordance with IAS 37 or other IFRSs as appropriate.

In practice, most changes in contingent consideration will be recognised in profit or loss. However, the above requirements mean that shares, some options and other equity instruments issued by the acquirer are not remeasured once initially recognised when accounting for the business combination.

8.2.3 *Implications*

The requirements in respect of contingent consideration represent a fundamental change to IFRS 3(2004) in two respects:

- under IFRS 3(2004), contingent consideration was only recognised at the date of acquisition where it met both a 'probable' test and a 'reliably measurable' test. If either test was only met after the date of acquisition, the additional consideration was recognised at that later date and treated as an adjustment to goodwill. IFRS 3(2008) requires contingent consideration to be measured at fair value at the date of acquisition irrespective of the level of probability or measurement reliability, in order to provide a complete picture of liabilities; and

- once the fair value of the contingent consideration at the acquisition date has been determined, any subsequent adjustments which do not reflect fair value at the acquisition date, or which occur outside the measurement period, are treated in accordance with other Standards – typically this means remeasurement of financial liabilities through profit or loss.

Importantly, contingent consideration arising in relation to business combinations that occur prior to the initial application of the IFRS 3(2008) will continue to be accounted for under IFRS 3(2004), meaning that retrospective adjustments to the initial accounting for these business combinations will still be possible. The treatment of contingent consideration relating to business combinations that occurred prior to the implementation of IFRS 3(2008) is considered in **14.2.1**.

8.3 Determining what is part of the business combination transaction

8.3.1 Principles to determine what is part of the business combination

The acquirer and the acquiree may have a pre-existing relationship or other arrangement before negotiations for the business combination begin, or they may enter into an arrangement during the negotiations that is separate from the business combination. [IFRS 3(2008).51]

In either situation, the acquirer is required to identify any amounts that are not part of what the acquirer and the acquiree (or its former owners) exchanged in the business combination, i.e. amounts that are not part of the exchange for the acquiree. [IFRS 3(2008).51]

The acquirer is required to recognise as part of applying the acquisition method only the consideration transferred for the acquiree, and the assets acquired and liabilities assumed in exchange for the acquiree. Separate transactions are accounted for in accordance with the relevant Standards. [IFRS 3(2008).51]

A transaction entered into by or on behalf of the acquirer or primarily for the benefit of the acquirer or the combined entity, rather than primarily for the benefit of the acquiree (or its former owners) before the combination, is likely to be a separate transaction. [IFRS 3(2008).52]

An acquirer should consider the following factors, which are neither mutually exclusive nor individually conclusive, to determine whether a transaction is part of the exchange for the acquiree or whether the transaction is separate from the business combination.

[IFRS 3(2008).B50]

(a) **The reasons for the transaction** Understanding the reasons why the parties to a combination entered into a particular transaction or arrangement may provide insight into whether it is part of the consideration transferred and the assets acquired or liabilities assumed. For example, if a transaction is arranged primarily for the benefit of the acquirer or the combined entity rather than primarily for the benefit of the acquiree or its former owners before the combination, that portion of the transaction price paid (and any related assets or liabilities) is less likely to be part of the exchange for the acquiree. Accordingly, the acquirer would account for that portion separately from the business combination.

Example 8.3.1A

Acquirer pays vendor's costs

In some cases, the vendor and the acquirer may agree, for tax or other reasons, that the acquirer will pay selling expenses incurred by the vendor in the sale and purchase transaction. Although these amounts are not paid directly to the vendor, they will still form part of the purchase consideration for the business combination as the acquirer is acting on behalf of the vendor in making the payments, which are primarily for the benefit of the former owners. However, this principle would not apply to any costs incurred by the acquirer on its own behalf in making the acquisition, as these must be accounted for outside the business combination (see **8.3.5**)

(b) **Who initiated the transaction** Understanding who initiated the transaction may also provide insight into whether it is part of the exchange for the acquiree. For example, a transaction or other event that is initiated by the acquirer may be entered into for the purpose of providing future economic benefits to the acquirer or combined entity with little or no benefit received by the acquiree or its former owners before the combination. On the other hand, a transaction or arrangement initiated by the acquiree or its former owners is less likely to be for the benefit of the acquirer or the combined entity and more likely to be part of the business combination transaction.

Example 8.3.1B

Acquisition from government with employee obligations

An acquirer may acquire a business from government in a privatisation transaction. These legal arrangements sometimes have obligations that are effectively imposed upon the acquirer by the government (e.g. a requirement to retain a certain level of staff, to maintain a presence in a certain geographical location, or to meet other government policy objectives). In some cases, these arrangements may impact the purchase consideration that the acquirer is prepared to pay, which might generally be higher if the obligations did not exist.

These transactions are generally initiated by the relevant government as the vendor for its own benefit (i.e. meeting the policy objectives). Therefore, no adjustment would be made to the purchase consideration as a result of the obligations. However, in some cases, a liability may be recognised as part of the business combination accounting where the relevant criteria are met.

(c) **The timing of the transaction** The timing of the transaction may also provide insight into whether it is part of the exchange for the acquiree. For example, a transaction between the acquirer and the acquiree that takes place during the negotiations of the terms of a business combination may have been entered into in contemplation of the business combination to provide future economic benefit to the acquirer or the combined entity. If so, the acquiree or its former owners are likely to receive little or no benefit from the transaction except for the benefits they receive as part of the combined entity.

The following are examples of separate transactions that are not to be included in applying the acquisition method:

[IFRS 3(2008).52]

(a) a transaction that settles pre-existing relationships between the acquirer and the acquiree (see **7.5.2** above)

(b) a transaction that remunerates employees or former owners of the acquiree for future services (see **8.3.3** for contingent payments to employees or selling shareholders, and **8.3.4** for share-based payment awards); and

(c) a transaction that reimburses the acquiree or its former owners for paying the acquirer's acquisition-related costs (see **8.3.5**).

8.3.2 Settlement of a pre-existing relationship between the acquirer and acquiree in a business combination

This is discussed in **7.5.2** above, which deals with both reacquired rights and the wider issue of pre-existing relationships.

8.3.3 Arrangements for contingent payments to employees or selling shareholders

The acquirer or vendor may make payments to the employees of the acquiree (who may or may not also be selling shareholders), which are contingent on a post-acquisition event such as a period of continuing service as an employee. In such cases, it is necessary to determine what element of the payment qualifies as consideration, and what element is for post-acquisition services. IFRS 3(2008) provides guidance as to how to make the allocation.

As discussed in **8.3.1** above, understanding the reasons why the acquisition agreement includes a provision for contingent payments, who initiated the arrangement, and when the parties entered into the arrangement may be helpful in assessing the nature of the arrangement. [IFRS 3(2008).B54]

The acquirer should consider the following indicators to determine whether an arrangement for payments to employees or selling shareholders is part of the exchange for the acquiree or a separate transaction:

[IFRS 3(2008).B55]

(a) **Continuing employment** A contingent consideration arrangement in which the payments are automatically forfeited if employment terminates is remuneration for post-combination services. Arrangements in which the contingent payments are not affected by employment termination may indicate that the contingent payments are additional consideration rather than remuneration.

(b) **Duration of continuing employment** If the period of required employment coincides with or is longer than the contingent payment period, that fact may indicate that the contingent payments are, in substance, remuneration.

(c) **Level of remuneration** Situations in which employee remuneration other than the contingent payments is at a reasonable level in comparison with that of other key employees in the combined entity may indicate that the contingent payments are additional consideration rather than remuneration.

(d) **Incremental payments to employees** If selling shareholders who do not become employees receive lower contingent payments on a per-share basis than the selling shareholders who become employees of the combined entity, that fact may indicate that the incremental amount of contingent payments to the selling shareholders who become employees is remuneration.

(e) **Number of shares owned** The relative number of shares owned by the selling shareholders who remain as key employees may be an indicator of the substance of the contingent consideration arrangement. If the selling shareholders who owned substantially all of the shares in the acquiree continue as key employees, that fact may indicate that the arrangement is, in substance, a profit-sharing arrangement intended to provide remuneration for post-combination services. If selling shareholders who continue as key employees owned only a small number of shares of the acquiree and all selling shareholders receive the same amount of contingent consideration on a per-share basis, that fact may indicate that the contingent payments are additional consideration.

(f) **Linkage to the valuation** If the initial consideration transferred at the acquisition date is based on the low end of a range established in the valuation of the acquiree and the contingent formula relates to that valuation approach, that fact may suggest that the contingent payments are additional consideration. Alternatively, if the contingent payment formula is consistent with prior profit-sharing arrangements, that fact may suggest that the substance of the arrangement is to provide remuneration.

(g) **Formula for determining consideration** The formula used to determine the contingent payment may be helpful in assessing the substance of the arrangement. For example, if a contingent payment is determined on the basis of a multiple of earnings (i.e. more than one year's earnings), that might suggest that the obligation is contingent consideration in the business combination and that the formula is intended to establish or verify the fair value of the acquiree. In contrast, a contingent payment that is a specified percentage of earnings (i.e. a proportion of one year's earnings) might suggest that the obligation to employees is a profit-sharing arrangement to remunerate employees for services rendered.

(h) **Other agreements and issues** The terms of other arrangements with selling shareholders (such as agreements not to compete, executory contracts, consulting contracts and property lease agreements) may indicate that contingent payments are attributable to something other than consideration for the acquiree. For example, in connection with the acquisition, the acquirer might enter into a property lease arrangement with a significant selling shareholder. If the lease payments specified in the lease contract are significantly below market, some or all of the contingent payments to the lessor (the selling shareholder) required by a separate arrangement might be, in substance, payments for the use of the leased property that the acquirer should recognise separately in its post-combination financial statements. In contrast, if the lease contract specifies lease payments that are consistent with market terms for the leased property, the arrangement for contingent payments to the selling shareholder may be contingent consideration in the business combination.

Example 8.3.3A

Contingent payments to employees recognised as a liability

[IFRS 3(2008).IE58-IE59]

TC appointed a candidate as its new CEO under a ten-year contract. The contract required TC to pay the candidate CU5 million if TC is acquired before the contract expires. AC acquires TC eight years later. The CEO was still employed at the acquisition date and will receive the additional payment under the existing contract.

In this example, TC entered into the employment agreement before the negotiations of the combination began, and the purpose of the agreement was to obtain the services of the CEO. Thus, there is no evidence that the agreement was arranged primarily to provide benefits to AC or the combined entity. Therefore, the liability to pay CU5 million is included in the application of the acquisition method.

Example 8.3.3B

Contingent payments to employees recognised as post-acquisition remuneration

Facts as in **example 8.3.3A**, except that TC entered into the agreement with the CEO at the suggestion of AC during the negotiations for the business combination, and the payment is contingent on the CEO remaining in employment for 3 years following a successful acquisition.

The primary purpose of the agreement appears to be to retain the services of the CEO. Since the CEO is not a shareholder, and the payment is contingent on continuing employment, the payment is accounted for as post-acquisition remuneration separately from the application of the acquisition method.

8.3.4 Acquirer share-based payment awards exchanged for awards held by the acquiree's employees

8.3.4.1 Overview

An acquirer may exchange its share-based payment awards (replacement awards) for awards held by employees of the acquiree. IFRS 3(2008) introduces a number of guidelines and examples for when to treat particular replacement share-based payment awards as part of the cost of the combination and when to treat the amounts as employee compensation.

Exchanges of share options or other share-based payment awards in conjunction with a business combination are accounted for as modifications of share-based payment awards in accordance with IFRS 2 *Share-based Payment* (see **chapter 25**). [IFRS 3(2008).B56] IFRS 3(2008) uses the term 'market-based measure' to describe the basis of measurement in IFRS 2.

8.3.4.2 Acquirer obliged to replace awards

Where the acquirer is obliged to replace the acquiree awards, either all or a portion of the market-based measure of the acquirer's replacement awards is included in measuring the consideration transferred in the business combination. [IFRS 3(2008).B56] The basis of allocating awards between consideration and post-combination service is described in **8.3.4.4** below.

The acquirer is considered to be obliged to replace the acquiree awards if the acquiree or its employees have the ability to enforce replacement. For example, for the purposes of applying this requirement, the acquirer is considered to be obliged to replace the acquiree's awards if the replacement is required by:

[IFRS 3(2008).B56]

(a) the terms of the acquisition agreement;

(b) the terms of the acquiree awards; or

(c) applicable laws and regulations.

8.3.4.3 Acquirer makes voluntary awards

If the acquiree's awards expire as a consequence of a business combination and the acquirer replaces those awards even though it is not obliged to do so, all of the market-based measure of the replacement awards is recognised as remuneration cost in the post-combination financial statements.

This means that none of the market-based measure of those awards is included in measuring the consideration transferred in the business combination. [IFRS 3(2008).B56]

8.3.4.4 Allocating awards to consideration and post-combination service

The requirements of IFRS 3(2008) are best explained by working through an example.

A has awarded share options to its employees, which vest if employees remain in employment for 3 years. A has accounted for the award in accordance with IFRS 2. After 2 years, A is acquired by B. B is obliged to exchange the share options for new share options which vest after two further years of employment.

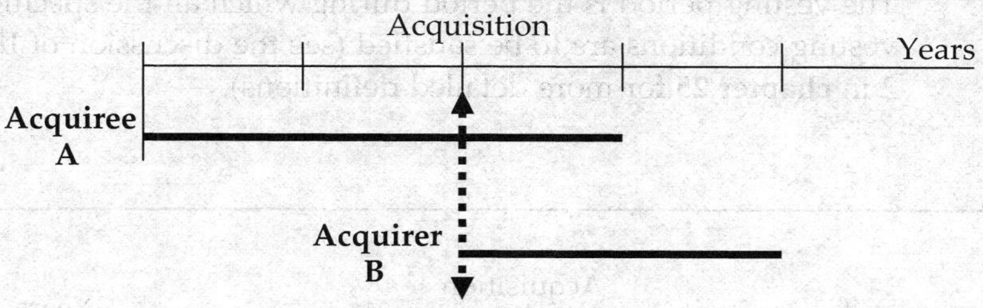

Step 1 To determine the portion of a replacement award that is part of the consideration transferred for the acquiree and the portion that is remuneration for post-combination service, the acquirer measures both the replacement awards granted by the acquirer and the acquiree awards as of the acquisition date in accordance with IFRS 2. [IFRS 3(2008).B57]

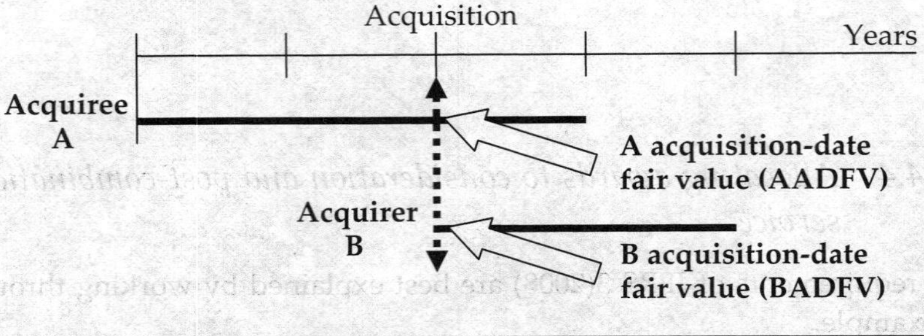

Step 1: B measures the fair value of both A's original share options and the replacement share options at the acquisition date in accordance with IFRS 2.

Step 2 Identify three periods of time:

- the vesting period completed at the date of acquisition;
- the total vesting period; and
- the original vesting period.

The vesting period is the period during which all the specified vesting conditions are to be satisfied (see the discussion of IFRS 2 in **chapter 25** for more detailed definitions).

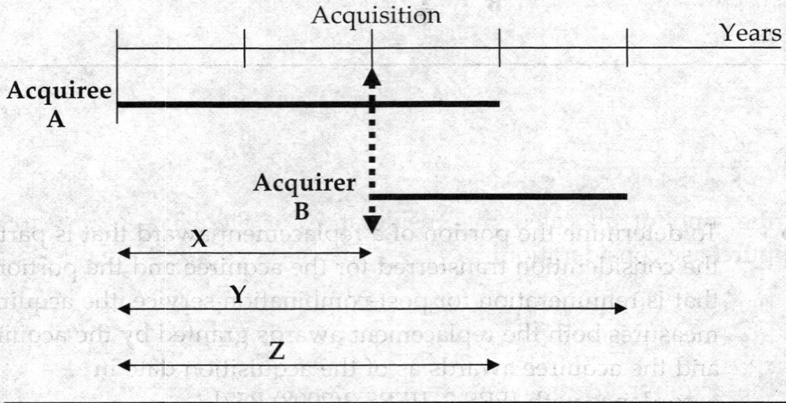

Step 2: B identifies the vesting period completed (X), the total vesting period (Y), and the original vesting period (Z).

Step 3 The portion of the replacement award attributable to pre-combination service (which is the portion that is accounted for as part of the consideration in the business combination) is the 'market-based measure' of the acquiree award multiplied by the ratio of the portion of the vesting period completed to the greater of the total vesting period or the original vesting period of the acquiree award. [IFRS 3(2008).B58]

> **Step 3:** Amount allocated to consideration is:
>
> $$AADFV \times \frac{X}{Higher\ of\ Y\ and\ Z}$$

Step 4 The amount attributable to post-combination service, and so recognised as remuneration cost in the post-combination financial statements, is determined as the difference between the market-based measure of the acquirer's replacement award and the amount allocated to purchase consideration in Step 3. Therefore, the acquirer attributes any excess of the market-based measure of the replacement award over the market-based measure of the acquiree award to post-combination service and recognises that excess as remuneration cost in the post-combination financial statements. This expense is recognised immediately if there is no further service period. [IFRS 3(2008).B59]

> **Step 4:** Amount allocated to post-combination service is:
>
> *BADFV less Amount calculated at Step 3*

Further requirements:

- the amount allocated to consideration at Step 3 is added to the purchase consideration;
- the amount allocated to post-combination service at step 4 is recognised as a post-combination expense in accordance with IFRS 2;
- the acquirer attributes a portion of a replacement award to post-combination service if it requires post-combination service, regardless of whether employees had rendered all of the service required for their acquiree awards to vest before the acquisition date; [IFRS 3(2008).B59]

- the allocation between purchase consideration and post-combination service should reflect the best estimate of the number of replacement awards that are expected to vest. For example, if the market-based measure of the portion of a replacement award attributed to pre-combination service is £100 and the acquirer expects that only 95 per cent of the award will vest, the amount included in consideration transferred in the business combination is £95; [IFRS 3(2008).B60]

- subsequent changes in the estimated number of replacement awards expected to vest are reflected in remuneration cost for the period in which the changes or forfeitures occur and are not adjusted against the initial accounting for the acquisition; [IFRS 3(2008).B60]

- the effects of other events, such as modifications or the ultimate outcome of awards with performance conditions, that occur after the acquisition date are accounted for in accordance with IFRS 2 in determining remuneration cost for the period in which an event occurs (see **chapter 25**); [IFRS 3(2008).B60]

- the same requirements for determining the portions of a replacement award attributable to pre- and post-combination service apply regardless of whether a replacement award is classified as a liability or as an equity instrument in accordance with IFRS 2. All changes in the market-based measure of awards classified as liabilities after the acquisition date and the related income tax effects are recognised in the acquirer's post-combination financial statements in the period(s) in which the changes occur; [IFRS 3(2008).B61] and

- the income tax effects of replacement awards of share-based payments are recognised in accordance with the requirements of IAS 12 *Income Taxes* (see **chapter 12**). [IFRS 3(2008).B62]

The following examples (which assume that all awards are classified as equity) illustrate replacement awards that the acquirer (AC) was obliged to issue in the following circumstances:

[IFRS 3(2008).IE61]

		Acquiree awards Has the vesting period been completed before the business combination?	
		Completed	**Not completed**
Replacement awards Are employees required to provide additional service after the acquisition date?	**Not required**	**Example 8.3.4.4A**	**Example 8.3.4.4D**
	Required	**Example 8.3.4.4B**	**Example 8.3.4.4C**

Example 8.3.4.4A

Vesting period completed, no additional services required

[IFRS 3(2008).IE62-IE64]

Acquiree awards	*Vesting period **completed** before the business combination*
Replacement awards	*Additional employee services **are not** required after the acquisition date*

AC issues replacement awards of CU110 (market-based measure) at the acquisition date for TC awards of CU100 (market-based measure) at the acquisition date. No post-combination services are required for the replacement awards and TC's employees had rendered all of the required service for the acquiree awards as of the acquisition date.

The amount attributable to pre-combination service is the market-based measure of TC's awards (CU100) at the acquisition date; that amount is included in the consideration transferred in the business combination. The amount attributable to post-combination service is CU10, which is the difference between the total value of the replacement awards (CU110) and the portion attributable to pre-combination service (CU100). Because no post-combination service is required for the replacement awards, AC immediately recognises CU10 as remuneration cost in its post-combination financial statements.

Applying the steps outlined earlier:

Step 1 Acquiree acquisition date fair value = CU100

Acquirer acquisition date fair value = CU110

Step 2 Vesting period completed = (say) 3 years

Original vesting period = (say) 3 years

Total vesting period = (say) 3 years

Step 3 Amount allocated to consideration =

$$100 \times \frac{3}{\textit{Higher of } 3 \textit{ and } 3} = 100$$

Step 4 Amount allocated to post-combination service = 110–100 = 10

Example 8.3.4.4B

Vesting period completed, but additional services required

[IFRS 3(2008).IE65-IE67]

Acquiree awards	*Vesting period* ***completed*** *before the business combination*
Replacement awards	*Additional employee services* ***are*** *required after the acquisition date*

AC exchanges replacement awards that require one year of post-combination service for share-based payment awards of TC, for which employees had completed the vesting period before the business combination. The market-based measure of both awards is CU100 at the acquisition date. When originally granted, TC's awards had a vesting period of four years. As of the acquisition date, the TC employees holding unexercised awards had rendered a total of seven years of service since the grant date.

Even though TC employees had already rendered all of the service, AC attributes a portion of the replacement award to post-combination remuneration cost in accordance with paragraph B59 of IFRS 3, because the replacement awards require one year of post-combination service. The total vesting period is five years—the vesting period for the original acquiree award completed before the acquisition date (four years) plus the vesting period for the replacement award (one year).

The portion attributable to pre-combination services equals the market-based measure of the acquiree award (CU100) multiplied by the ratio of the pre-combination vesting period (four years) to the total vesting period (five years). Thus, CU80 (CU100 × 4/5 years) is attributed to the pre-combination vesting period and therefore included in the consideration transferred in the business combination. The remaining CU20 is attributed to the post-combination vesting period and is therefore recognised as remuneration cost in AC's post-combination financial statements in accordance with IFRS 2.

Applying the steps outlined earlier:

Step 1 Acquiree acquisition date fair value = CU100

Acquirer acquisition date fair value = CU100

Step 2 Vesting period completed = 4 years

Original vesting period = 4 years

Total vesting period = 5 years

Step 3 Amount allocated to consideration =

$$100 \times \frac{4}{\textit{Higher of } 4 \textit{ and } 5} = 80$$

Step 4 Amount allocated to post-combination service = 100–80 = 20

Example 8.3.4.4C

Vesting period not completed, additional services required
[IFRS 3(2008).IE68-IE69]

Acquiree awards	*Vesting period* ***not completed*** *before the business combination*
Replacement awards	*Additional employee services* ***are*** *required after the acquisition date*

AC exchanges replacement awards that require one year of post-combination service for share-based payment awards of TC, for which employees had not yet rendered all of the service as of the acquisition date. The market-based measure of both awards is CU100 at the acquisition date. When originally granted, the awards of TC had a vesting period of four years. As of the acquisition date, the TC employees had rendered two years' service, and they would have been required to render two additional years of service after the acquisition date for their awards to vest. Accordingly, only a portion of the TC awards is attributable to pre-combination service.

The replacement awards require only one year of post-combination service. Because employees have already rendered two years of service, the total vesting period is three years. The portion attributable to pre-combination services equals the market-based measure of the acquiree award (CU100) multiplied by the ratio of the pre-combination vesting period (two years) to the greater of the total vesting period (three years) or the original vesting period of TC's award (four years). Thus, CU50 (CU100 × 2/4 years) is attributable to pre-combination service and therefore included in the consideration transferred for the acquiree. The remaining CU50 is attributable to post-combination service and therefore recognised as remuneration cost in AC's post-combination financial statements.

Applying the steps outlined earlier:

Step 1 Acquiree acquisition date fair value = CU100

Acquirer acquisition date fair value = CU100

Step 2 Vesting period completed = 2 years

Original vesting period = 4 years

Total vesting period = 3 years

Step 3 Amount allocated to consideration =

$$100 \times \frac{2}{\textit{Higher of } 4 \textit{ and } 3} = 50$$

Step 4 Amount allocated to post-combination service = 100–50 = 50

Example 8.3.4.4D

Vesting period not completed, but no additional services required

[IFRS 3(2008).IE70-IE71]

Acquiree awards	*Vesting period **not completed** before the business combination*
Replacement awards	*Additional employee services **are not** required after the acquisition date*

Assume the same facts as in **example 8.3.4.4C** above, except that AC exchanges replacement awards that require no post-combination service for share-based payment awards of TC for which employees had not yet rendered all of the service as of the acquisition date. The terms of the replaced TC awards did not eliminate any remaining vesting period upon a change in control. (If the TC awards had included a provision that eliminated any remaining vesting period upon a change in control, the guidance in **example 8.3.4.4A** would apply.) The market-based measure of both awards is CU100. Because employees have already rendered two years of service and the replacement awards do not require any post-combination service, the total vesting period is two years.

The portion of the market-based measure of the replacement awards attributable to pre-combination services equals the market-based measure of the acquiree award (CU100) multiplied by the ratio of the pre-combination vesting period (two years) to the greater of the total vesting period (two years) or the original vesting period of TC's award (four years). Thus, CU50 (CU100 × 2/4 years) is attributable to pre-combination service and therefore included in the consideration transferred for the acquiree. The remaining CU50 is attributable to post-combination service. Because no post-combination service is required to vest in the replacement award, AC recognises the entire CU50 immediately as remuneration cost in the post-combination financial statements.

Applying the steps outlined earlier:

Step 1 Acquiree acquisition date fair value = CU100

Acquirer acquisition date fair value = CU100

Step 2 Vesting period completed = 2 years

Original vesting period = 4 years

Total vesting period = 2 years

Step 3 Amount allocated to consideration =

$$100 \times \frac{2}{\textit{Higher of } 4 \textit{ and } 2} = 50$$

Step 4 Amount allocated to post-combination service = 100–50 = 50

8.3.5 *A transaction that reimburses the acquiree or its former owners for paying the acquirer's acquisition related costs.*

Section 8.4 below deals with the treatment of acquisition-related costs as expenses, which represents a significant change from the previous version of IFRS 3. The Basis for Conclusions for IFRS 3(2008) recognises that this change creates the potential for abuse.

'Some constituents, including some respondents to the 2005 Exposure Draft, said that if acquirers could no longer capitalise acquisition-related costs as part of the cost of the business acquired, they might modify transactions to avoid recognising those costs as expenses. For example, some said that a buyer might ask a seller to make payments to the buyer's vendors on its behalf. To facilitate the negotiations and sale of the business, the seller might agree to make those payments if the total amount to be paid to it upon closing of the business combination is sufficient to reimburse the seller for payments it made on the buyer's behalf. If the disguised reimbursements were treated as part of the consideration transferred for the business, the acquirer might not recognise those expenses. Rather, the measure of the fair value of the business and the amount of goodwill recognised for that business might be overstated.' [IFRS 3(2008).BC370]

To mitigate such concerns, IFRS 3(2008) includes in its list of examples of transactions that should be separated from the business combination '. . . a transaction that reimburses the acquiree or its former owners for paying the acquirer's acquisition-related costs'. [IFRS 3(2008).52(c)] It follows that where such a transaction is identified, that element is deducted from the consideration used to calculate goodwill, and is expensed by the acquirer.

8.4 Acquisition related costs

Acquisition-related costs are costs the acquirer incurs to effect a business combination. Those costs include finder's fees; advisory, legal, accounting, valuation and other professional or consulting fees; general administrative costs, including the costs of maintaining an internal acquisitions department; and costs of registering and issuing debt and equity securities. Under IFRS 3(2008), the acquirer is required to account for acquisition-related costs as expenses in the periods in which the costs are incurred and the services are received, with one exception. The costs to issue debt or equity securities are recognised in accordance with IAS 32 (for equity – see **section 4** of **chapter 15**) and IAS 39 (for debt – see **2.2** in **chapter 18**). [IFRS 3(2008).53]

This requirement is a change from IFRS 3(2004) where direct costs were included in the acquisition cost, but indirect costs were excluded. In explaining this change, the Basis for Conclusions notes: 'The boards concluded that acquisition-related costs are not part of the fair value exchange between the buyer and seller for the business. Rather, they are separate transactions in which the buyer pays for the fair value of services received. The boards also observed that those costs, whether for services performed by external parties or internal staff of the acquirer, do not generally represent assets of the acquirer at the acquisition date because the benefits obtained are consumed as the services are received.' [IFRS 3(2008).BC366]

The Board rejected arguments that certain costs are unavoidable, or are taken into account by the buyer in deciding what it is willing to pay for the acquiree. The Board noted that the amount that a seller is willing to accept as consideration for its business does not vary with the costs incurred by different potential buyers. Also, the recoverability of costs is considered to be a matter that is separate from 'the fair value measurement objective in the revised standards'. [IFRS 3(2008).BC368]

It has been pointed out that this change results in the treatment of acquisition-related costs in a business combination transaction being inconsistent with the treatment of direct incremental costs incurred in acquiring, for example, property, plant and equipment (capitalised in accordance with IAS 16 *Property, Plant and Equipment*), or inventory (capitalised in accordance with IAS 2 *Inventories*). The Board notes, in the 'Feedback Statement' issued with the new Standards, that it does not see this as a reason to delay change in the treatment of business combination costs.

It is suggested that, since the Board has introduced the requirement to expense acquisition costs within IFRS 3(2008), it only applies to financial statements in which a business combination is accounted for under IFRS 3(2008). It follows that this requirement does not extend to the individual financial statements of the investing or parent entity.

The Board has also identified a potential for abuse, whereby the acquirer might arrange for the seller to pay certain acquisition-related costs on its behalf in return for increased purchase consideration for the business combination. This is considered in **8.3.5** above.

8.5 Business combinations with no transfer of consideration

8.5.1 Accounting requirement and examples

An acquirer may obtain control of an acquiree without transferring consideration. In such cases, IFRS 3(2008) requires an acquirer to be identified, and the acquisition method to be applied. Examples of such circumstances include:

[IFRS 3(2008).43]

(a) acquiree repurchases a sufficient number of its own shares for an existing investor (the acquirer) to obtain control;

(b) minority veto rights lapse that previously kept the acquirer from controlling an acquiree in which the acquirer held the majority voting rights; and

(c) a combination by contract alone (see **8.5.2.2**).

8.5.2 *Combinations by contract alone*

In a business combination achieved by contract alone, two entities enter into a contractual arrangement which covers, for example, operation under a single management and equalisation of voting power and earnings attributable to both entities' equity investors. Such structures may involve a 'stapling' or formation of a dual listed corporation.

8.5.2.1 *Example of a dual listed structure*

BHP Billiton Annual Report 2007

Merger terms

On 29 June 2001, BHP Billiton Plc (previously known as Billiton Plc), a UK listed company, and BHP Billiton Limited (previously known as BHP Limited), an Australian listed company, entered into a Dual Listed Companies' (DLC) merger. This was effected by contractual arrangements between the Companies and amendments to their constitutional documents.

The effect of the DLC merger is that BHP Billiton Plc and its subsidiaries (the BHP Billiton Plc Group) and BHP Billiton Limited and its subsidiaries (the BHP Billiton Limited Group) operate together as a single economic entity (the BHP Billiton Group). Under the arrangements:

- the shareholders of BHP Billiton Plc and BHP Billiton Limited have a common economic interest in both Groups
- the shareholders of BHP Billiton Plc and BHP Billiton Limited take key decisions, including the election of Directors, through a joint electoral procedure under which the shareholders of the two Companies effectively vote on a joint basis
- BHP Billiton Plc and BHP Billiton Limited have a common Board of Directors, a unified management structure and joint objectives
- dividends and capital distributions made by the two Companies are equalised

- BHP Billiton Plc and BHP Billiton Limited each executed a deed poll guarantee, guaranteeing (subject to certain exceptions) the contractual obligations (whether actual or contingent, primary or secondary) of the other incurred after 29 June 2001 together with specified obligations existing at that date

If either BHP Billiton Plc or BHP Billiton Limited proposes to pay a dividend to its shareholders, then the other Company must pay a matching cash dividend of an equivalent amount per share to its shareholders. If either Company is prohibited by law or is otherwise unable to declare, pay or otherwise make all or any portion of such a matching dividend, then BHP Billiton Plc or BHP Billiton Limited will, so far as it is practicable to do so, enter into such transactions with each other as the Boards agree to be necessary or desirable so as to enable both Companies to pay dividends as nearly as practicable at the same time.

The DLC merger did not involve the change of legal ownership of any assets of BHP Billiton Plc or BHP Billiton Limited, any change of ownership of any existing shares or securities of BHP Billiton Plc or BHP Billiton Limited, the issue of any shares or securities or any payment by way of consideration, save for the issue by each Company of one special voting share to a trustee company which is the means by which the joint electoral procedure is operated. In addition, to achieve a position where the economic and voting interests of one share in BHP Billiton Plc and one share in BHP Billiton Limited were identical, BHP Billiton Limited made a bonus issue of ordinary shares to the holders of its ordinary shares.

8.5.2.2 *Accounting for a combination by contract*

IFRS 3(2008) requires one of the combining entities to be identified as the acquirer, and one to be identified as the acquiree – see **section 5** for guidance. In reaching the conclusion that combinations achieved by contract alone should not be excluded from the scope of IFRS 3, the Board noted that:

[IFRS 3(2008).BC79]

- such business combinations do not involve the payment of readily measurable consideration and, in rare circumstances, it might be difficult to identify the acquirer;
- difficulties in identifying the acquirer are not a sufficient reason to justify a different accounting treatment, and no further guidance is necessary for identifying the acquirer; and
- the acquisition method is already being applied for such combinations in the United States and insurmountable issues have not been encountered.

Under IFRS 3(2004), combinations achieved by contract alone were outside the scope of the Standard. Accordingly, they were often accounted for as poolings of interests.

8.5.3 *Application of the acquisition method to a combination in which no consideration is transferred*

8.5.3.1 *Deemed consideration*

In a business combination achieved without the transfer of consideration, the acquirer substitutes the acquisition-date fair value of its interest in the acquiree for the acquisition-date fair value of the consideration transferred to measure goodwill or a gain on a bargain purchase. [IFRS 3(2008).33 & B46]

The acquirer measures the fair value of its interest in the acquiree using one or more valuation techniques that are appropriate in the circumstances and for which sufficient data is available. If more than one valuation technique is used, the acquirer should evaluate the results of the techniques considering the relevance and reliability of the inputs used and the extent of the available data. [IFRS 3(2008).B46]

The acquirer's interest in the acquiree may be limited to its right to equalisation payments. In practice, the fair value may be negligible.

8.5.3.2 *Amount attributed to non-controlling interests*

The amount attributed to non-controlling interests in a business combination achieved by contract alone is dealt with in IFRS 3(2008).44, which states as follows: 'In a business combination achieved by contract alone, the acquirer shall attribute to the owners of the acquiree the amount of the acquiree's net assets recognised in accordance with this IFRS. In other words, the equity interests in the acquiree held by parties other than the acquirer are a non-controlling interest in the acquirer's post-combination financial statements even if the result is that all of the equity interests in the acquiree are attributed to the non-controlling interest.'

9 Recognising and measuring goodwill or a gain from a bargain purchase

9.1 Measuring goodwill or a gain from a bargain purchase

Goodwill arising from a business combination is determined as:

[IFRS 3(2008).32]

Consideration transferred	→	Generally acquisition-date fair value – see **section 8**
plus		
The amount of any non-controlling interest	→	See **7.3**
plus		
The fair value of any previously-held equity interest in the acquiree	→	See **section 11**
less		
The fair value of the identifiable net assets of the acquiree	→	See **section 7**

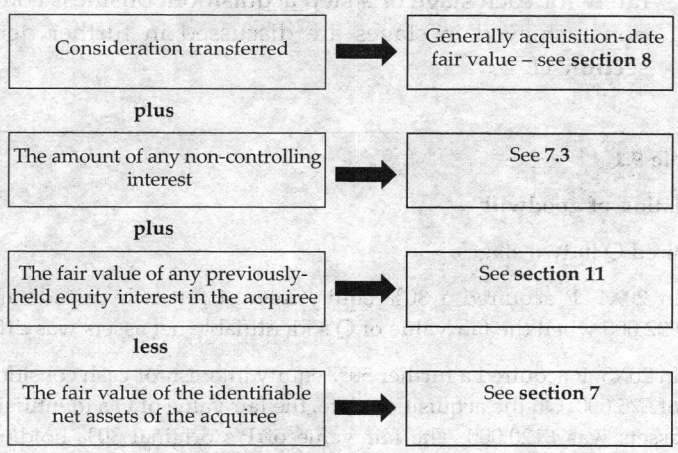

Under IFRS 3(2004) the calculation of goodwill compared just two numbers, being the excess of the cost of the business combination over the acquirer's interest in the net fair value of the identifiable assets, liabilities and contingent liabilities. In a business combination achieved in stages, goodwill was determined as the sum of goodwill arising at each stage (or 'step') of the acquisition.

The revised treatment has expanded the calculation to involve potentially four numbers.

- As noted in **7.3**, under IFRS 3(2008), non-controlling interests can be measured on two bases – by reference to their share of the identifiable net assets of the acquiree or the fair value of the non-controlling interests. The latter measure results in the recognition of the non-controlling interest's share of goodwill. Because non-controlling interests can be measured by alternative methods, it is necessary to include the non-controlling interests within the calculation, and also to deduct the entire identifiable acquiree net assets (rather than only the acquirer's share of those net assets). **Example 9.1** below provides an illustration.

- Under IFRS 3(2008) a business combination occurs only at the date when an acquirer obtains control of an acquiree.

Accounting for a business combination therefore reflects the fair value of any previously-held equity interests in the acquiree. Under IFRS 3(2004), goodwill was calculated separately for each stage of a step acquisition. Business combinations achieved in stages are discussed in further detail in **section 11**.

Example 9.1

Calculation of goodwill

P acquired Q in two stages.

- In 20X1, P acquired a 30% equity interest for cash consideration of £32,000 when the fair value of Q's identifiable net assets was £100,000.
- In 20X5, P acquired a further 50% equity interest for cash consideration of £75,000. On the acquisition date, the fair value of Q's identifiable net assets was £120,000. The fair value of P's original 30% holding was £40,000 and the fair value of the 20% non-controlling interest is assessed as £28,000.

Goodwill is calculated, on the alternative bases that P records non-controlling interests (NCI) at their share of net assets, or at fair value, as follows:

	NCI @ % of net assets	NCI @ fair value
Fair value of consideration	75,000	75,000
Non-controlling interests	24,000	28,000
Previously-held interest	40,000	40,000
	139,000	143,000
Fair value of identifiable net assets	120,000	120,000
Goodwill	19,000	23,000

The implications of the choice between the alternatives for measuring non-controlling interests are discussed in **7.3.2**.

9.2 Special situations

9.2.1 Share for share exchange

In a business combination in which the acquirer and the acquiree (or its former owners) exchange only equity interests, the fair value of the acquiree's equity interests may be more reliably measurable than the fair value of the acquirer's equity interests. If so, the acquirer should determine the amount of goodwill by using the fair value of the acquiree's equity interests rather than the fair value of the equity interests transferred. [IFRS 3(2008).33]

Use of the fair value of the acquiree's equity interests in this situation, as an alternative to measuring the fair value of consideration transferred by the acquirer, is on grounds of reliable measurement only.

Example 9.2.1

Consideration measured using acquiree's equity

An unlisted private equity entity acquires a listed entity through an exchange of equity instruments. The published price of the quoted equity instruments of the acquiree at the date of exchange is likely to provide a more reliable indicator of fair value than the valuation methods used to measure the fair value of the private acquirer's equity instruments.

9.2.1.1 *Merger relief and group reconstruction relief*

Merger relief and group reconstruction relief are reliefs offered by the Companies Act, in certain restricted circumstances discussed below, from recognising the full share premium that would otherwise have resulted on certain share issues. Despite their names, the reliefs are not restricted to situations in which merger accounting or group reconstruction accounting are adopted. UK

For companies reporting under UK GAAP, the Act offers a related option to record shares acquired at an amount less than the fair value of shares issued. As explained at ***9.2.1.5****, this option is not available to UK companies choosing to report under IFRSs.*

9.2.1.2 *Merger relief – CA 2006 section 612 (previously CA 1985 section 131)*

Merger relief, or relief from recording a share premium, was originally written into company law as a foundation for merger accounting. However, the conditions of section 612 and 613 of the Companies Act 2006 (previously section 131 of the Companies Act 1985) mean that it applies in a wider set of circumstances. UK

The conditions for merger relief are:

[CA 2006 s612 & 613, previously CA 1985 s131]

- *equity shares are issued as part of an acquisition 'arrangement';*
- *in consideration, the issuer takes its interest in another body corporate from below 90 per cent equity holding to a 90 per cent or above equity holding (excluding any treasury shares held by that body corporate);*
- *for this purpose, holdings of the issuing company, its holding company, subsidiaries and fellow subsidiaries, and nominees of any of those entities, are aggregated;*
- *where the acquired body corporate has more than one class of equity shares, the 90 per cent condition must be met in respect of each separate class of equity share (i.e. must exceed 90 per cent on all classes to achieve merger relief on any); and*
- *the conditions for group reconstruction relief are not met (see* **9.2.1.3** *below).*

The implications of the relief are:

- *it applies to the entity that issues shares;*
- *it applies only to equity shares issued to acquire equity shares, including a part payment in equity shares; if company A acquires 100 per cent of the equity share capital of company B, paying £80,000 in cash and £20,000 in shares, being 1,000 shares of £1 nominal value each, the merger relief will apply to the issue of 1,000 shares provided all the conditions in section 612 and 613 of the Companies Act 2006 (previously section 131 of the Companies Act 1985) are met;*
- *where the arrangement includes the acquisition of non-equity shares in another body corporate, then merger relief extends to any shares issued, both equity and non-equity; [CA 2006 s612(3), previously CA 1985 s131(3)]*
- *where the conditions are met, the wording of section 612(2) of the Companies Act 2006 (previously section 131(2) of the Companies Act 1985) '. . . section 610 [130] does not apply to the premiums …' means that the relief is mandatory; consequently any premium which is voluntarily recorded should not be classified as a share premium but as an 'other reserve' such as 'merger reserve';*
- *the term 'arrangement' is widely defined in section 616(1) of the Companies Act 2006 (previously section 131(7) of the Companies Act 1985) and would include an acquisition which is consummated through a series of stages (provided it can be demonstrated that there was an ultimate plan to acquire in excess of 90 per cent), a scheme of arrangement under Part 26 of the Companies Act 2006 (previously an arrangement under section 425 of the Companies Act 1985), and an arrangement with a liquidator;*

- *in a partial acquisition which is not part of an 'arrangement', the relief is available on the transaction which results in the holding passing the 90 per cent threshold. Thus, if company A acquired 15 per cent of company B 10 years ago and now acquires a further 80 per cent, the relief will be available on the acquisition of the 80 per cent.*

9.2.1.3 *Group reconstruction relief – CA 2006 section 611 (previously CA 1985 section 132)*

Group reconstruction relief is founded on the presumption that assets will sometimes be transferred within a wholly-owned group at book value, that is avoiding the recognition of any unrealised gain or loss. Consequently, it does not totally exempt intragroup transactions from recording a share premium, but restricts the amount of share premium by reference to previous carrying value. UK

The conditions for group reconstruction relief are:

[CA 2006 s611, previously CA 1985 s132]

- *the issuing company is a wholly-owned subsidiary;*
- *the issuing company allots shares, equity or non-equity, to another member of the wholly-owned group (i.e. any holding company of which the issuer is a wholly-owned subsidiary, and any other wholly-owned subsidiaries of that holding company);*
- *consideration for the issue is the transfer of non-cash assets from another member of the wholly-owned group.*

The issuing company is required to record share premium on the issue of shares equal to the 'minimum premium value'. This is calculated as:

	£
Lower of cost and carrying value of assets transferred	x
Less: Carrying value of liabilities transferred	(x)
Base value of consideration	x
Less: Nominal value of shares issued	(x)
Minimum premium value	x

The implications of the relief are:

- *share premium is not avoided, but is restricted to avoid unrealised gains or losses arising;*

- *where base value of consideration is less than the nominal value of shares issued, shares are recorded at nominal value to avoid an issue at a discount (N.B fair value must exceed nominal value to avoid an illegal issue at a discount);*

- *where the conditions are met, the wording of section 611(2) of the Companies Act 2006 (previously section 132(2) of the Companies Act 1985) '. . . is not required by section 610 [130]...' means that the relief is voluntary; consequently any premium in excess of the required minimum which is voluntarily recorded may either be classified as a share premium or alternatively as an 'other reserve'.*

9.2.1.4 *Deciding which relief applies*

UK

Merger relief is not available for any issue of shares that qualifies for group reconstruction relief. Therefore, in particular, merger relief is not available where the issuing company is a wholly-owned subsidiary and it acquires shares in a body corporate from another member of the wholly-owned group (i.e. any holding company of which the issuer is a wholly-owned subsidiary, and any other wholly-owned subsidiaries of that holding company).

Where a new intermediate holding company is being inserted within an existing group, it can be structured to achieve either merger relief or group reconstruction relief as follows:

- *merger relief is applicable where the issuing company is first formed, or an off-the-shelf company acquired, independently (for example, any arrangement that avoids a group company being the founder shareholder for a newly formed company or the shareholder in the off-the-shelf purchase) and, as a result of the share exchange, it becomes a subsidiary;*

- *group reconstruction relief is applicable where the issuing company is first formed, or an off-the-shelf company acquired, as a wholly-owned subsidiary, and then issues further shares in exchange for another body corporate.*

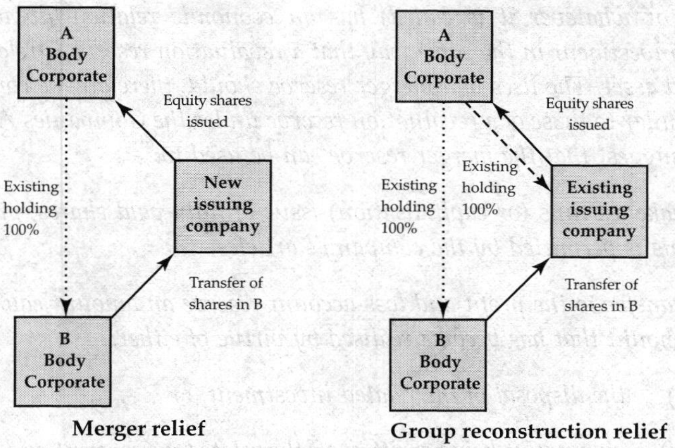

If the merger relief route is taken, the initial shares, say, two £1 shares, in the new issuing company could be owned by, say, the directors or lawyers of A. Once the new shares have been issued to A in exchange for the shares in B, the initial shares could be sold to A for their original cost or they could be purchased by Newco for cost and cancelled.

9.2.1.5 *Carrying value of investments – CA 2006 section 615 (previously CA 1985 section 133)*

Where an interest in another body corporate is acquired by issuing shares, to the extent that relief from recording share premium is available (whether merger relief or group reconstruction relief), section 615 of the Companies Act 2006 (previously section 133(1) of the Companies Act 1985) allows an option to reduce the carrying value of the related investment by a similar amount. For example, if shares with a fair value of £1,000 are acquired through the issue of shares with an aggregate nominal value of £200, and merger relief applies, then this section allows the option of recording the cost of investment as £200 rather than £1,000. UK

However, this option is not available to UK companies that report under IFRSs, because it conflicts with the requirement in IAS 27 to record an investment in a subsidiary either at cost or at fair value. The IASB Glossary definition of 'cost' includes '... the fair value of the other consideration given'.

9.2.1.6 *Uses of a merger reserve*

UK

Once established, a merger reserve (group reconstruction reserve, capital reserve or whatever it is called) has an economic relationship with the related investment in the same way that a revaluation reserve is related to a revalued asset. The uses of a merger reserve should, therefore, be considered to be similar to those of a revaluation reserve under the Companies Act. This would suggest that the merger reserve can be used to:

(*a*) *make a bonus (or capitalisation) issue of fully paid shares, providing this is permitted by the company's articles;*

(*b*) *transfer to the profit and loss account reserve an amount equal to the amount that has become realised by virtue of either:*

(*i*) *the disposal of the related investment; or*

(*ii*) *an amount being written off the related investment and charged against the profit and loss account, for example, as the result of an impairment.*

9.2.2 *Business combinations with no consideration*

Paragraph 33 of IFRS 3(2008) also deals with the situation of a business combination in which no consideration is transferred. This could occur where the acquiree repurchases equity interests from other investors such that the acquirer's unchanged equity interest becomes a controlling interest, or a business combination achieved by contract alone.

In a business combination achieved without the transfer of consideration, goodwill is determined by using the acquisition-date fair value of the acquirer's interest in the acquiree (measured using a valuation technique) rather than the acquisition-date fair value of the consideration transferred. [IFRS 3(2008).33]

The acquirer measures the fair value of its interest in the acquiree using one or more valuation techniques that are appropriate in the circumstances and for which sufficient data is available. If more than one valuation technique is used, the acquirer should evaluate the results of the techniques, considering the relevance and reliability of the inputs used and the extent of the available data. [IFRS 3(2008).B46]

Business combinations with no transfer of consideration are considered in more detail in **8.5**.

9.2.3 *Mutual entities*

Earlier sections of this chapter dealt with the change to include combinations involving mutual entities within the scope of IFRS 3(2008) (see **2.2.3**), and identification of the acquirer in such circumstances (see **5.3.2**). This section deals with measurement issues.

When two mutual entities combine, the entity identified as the acquirer gives member interests in itself in exchange for the member interests in the acquiree. Thus, consideration is paid, but its fair value is not readily determinable by reference to a market. IFRS 3(2008) recognises that it may be easier to fair value the entire member interest of the acquiree, rather than the incremental member interests given by the acquirer.

9.2.3.1 *Consideration given*

Accordingly, IFRS 3(2008) provides that where the fair value of the equity or member interests in the acquiree (or the fair value of the acquiree) is more reliably measurable than the fair value of the member interests transferred by the acquirer, the acquirer should determine the amount of goodwill by using the acquisition-date fair value of the acquiree's equity interests instead of the acquisition-date fair value of the acquirer's equity interests transferred as consideration. [IFRS 3(2008).B47]

This is an example of IFRS 3(2008) using the fair value of the acquiree to measure consideration as it is more reliably measurable than consideration given by the acquirer.

9.2.3.2 *Basis of valuation*

Although they are similar in many ways to other businesses, mutual entities have distinct characteristics that arise primarily because their members are both customers and owners. Members of mutual entities generally expect to receive benefits for their membership, often in the form of reduced fees charged for goods and services or patronage dividends. The portion of patronage dividends allocated to each member is often based on the amount of business the member did with the mutual entity during the year. [IFRS 3(2008).B48]

A fair value measurement of a mutual entity should include the assumptions that market participants would make about future member benefits as well as any other relevant assumptions market participants would make about the mutual entity. For example, an estimated cash flow model may be used to determine the fair value of a mutual entity. The cash flows used as inputs to the model should be based on the expected cash flows of the mutual entity, which are likely to reflect reductions for member benefits, such as reduced fees charged for goods and services. [IFRS 3(2008).B49]

9.2.3.3 *Identifiable net assets acquired*

The acquirer in a combination of mutual entities recognises the acquiree's net assets as a direct addition to capital or equity in its statement of financial position, not as an addition to retained earnings, which is consistent with the way in which other types of entities apply the acquisition method. [IFRS 3(2008).B47]

Member interests given by the acquirer will be recognised directly in equity. IFRSs do not usually prescribe where within equity such items are classified. In this case, however, IFRS 3(2008) is specific that the amount recognised (equal to the acquiree's identifiable net assets) should not be added to retained earnings.

Example 9.2.3.3

Combination of mutual entities

X and Y are co-operative institutions owned by their customers who receive dividends in proportion to the amount of goods purchased. They combine, with X identified as the acquirer. Members of Y become members of X.

A valuation of Y as an entity indicates a fair value of £500,000. The fair value of Y's identifiable net assets is £400,000.

X records its acquisition of Y in its consolidated financial statements as follows:

	£	£
Dr Identifiable net assets acquired	400,000	
Dr Goodwill	100,000	
Cr Member interests issued		500,000

The classification of member interests as either equity or a financial liability is determined by applying IAS 32.

9.3 Bargain purchases

A bargain purchase is a business combination in which the net fair value of the identifiable assets acquired and liabilities assumed exceeds the aggregate of the consideration transferred, the non-controlling interests and the fair value of any previously-held equity interest in the acquiree.

A bargain purchase might happen, for example, in a business combination that is a forced sale in which the seller is acting under compulsion. However, the recognition and measurement exceptions for particular items, as discussed in **section 7**, might also lead to the recognition of a gain (or a change in the amount of a recognised gain) on a bargain purchase. [IFRS 3(2008).35]

9.3.1 Accounting for a bargain purchase gain

If, after applying the requirements in **9.3.2** below, it is determined that the acquisition is a bargain purchase, the acquirer recognises the resulting gain in profit or loss on the acquisition date. The gain is attributed to the acquirer. [IFRS 3(2008).34]

9.3.2 Consequences of identifying a bargain purchase

An acquirer's initial calculations under IFRS 3(2008).32 (see **9.1** above) may indicate that the acquisition has resulted in a bargain purchase. Before recognising any gain, the Standard requires that the acquirer should reassess whether it has correctly identified all of the assets acquired and all of the liabilities assumed. The acquirer should recognise any additional assets or liabilities that are identified in that review. [IFRS 3(2008).36]

The acquirer is then required to review the procedures used to measure the amounts that IFRS 3(2008) requires to be recognised at the acquisition date for all of the following:

[IFRS 3(2008).36]

(a) the identifiable assets acquired and liabilities assumed;

(b) the non-controlling interest in the acquiree, if any;

(c) for a business combination achieved in stages, the acquirer's previously-held equity interest in the acquiree; and

(d) the consideration transferred.

The objective of the review is to ensure that the measurements appropriately reflect consideration of all available information as of the acquisition date. [IFRS 3(2008).36]

Example 9.3.2

Gain on a bargain purchase

[IFRS 3(2008).IE46-IE49]

On 1 January 20X5 AC acquires 80 per cent of the equity interests of TC, a private entity, in exchange for cash of CU150. Because the former owners of TC needed to dispose of their investments in TC by a specified date, they did not have sufficient time to market TC to multiple potential buyers. The management of AC initially measures the separately recognisable identifiable assets acquired and the liabilities assumed as of the acquisition date in accordance with the requirements of IFRS 3. The identifiable assets are measured at CU250 and the liabilities assumed are measured at CU50. AC engages an independent consultant, who determines that the fair value of the 20 per cent non-controlling interest in TC is CU42.

The amount of TC's identifiable net assets (CU200, calculated as CU250 – CU50) exceeds the fair value of the consideration transferred plus the fair value of the non-controlling interest in TC. Therefore, AC reviews the procedures it used to identify and measure the assets acquired and liabilities assumed and to measure the fair value of both the non-controlling interest in TC and the consideration transferred. After that review, AC decides that the procedures and resulting measures were appropriate. AC measures the gain on its purchase of the 80 per cent interest as follows:

			CU
Amount of the identifiable net assets acquired (CU250 – CU50)			200
Less:	Fair value of the consideration transferred for AC's 80 per cent interest in TC; plus	150	
	Fair value of non-controlling interest in TC	42	
			192
Gain on bargain purchase of 80 per cent interest			8

AC would record its acquisition of TC in its consolidated financial statements as follows:

	CU	CU
Dr Identifiable assets acquired	250	
Cr Cash		150
Cr Liabilities assumed		50
Cr Gain on the bargain purchase		8
Cr Equity—non-controlling interest in TC		42

If the acquirer chose to measure the non-controlling interest in TC on the basis of its proportionate interest in the identifiable net assets of the acquiree, the recognised amount of the non-controlling interest would be CU40 (CU200 × 0.20). The gain on the bargain purchase then would be CU10 (CU200 – (CU150 + CU40)).

10 Post-combination accounting

This section covers two aspects of post-combination accounting:

- adjustments to provisional fair values in the 'measurement period'. This is dealt with in **10.1**; and
- specific and general guidance for measurement and accounting for assets, liabilities and equity following a business combination. This is dealt with in **10.2.**

10.1 Adjustments to provisional values

IFRS 3(2008) permits adjustments to items recognised in the original accounting for a business combination, for a maximum of one year after the acquisition date, where new information about facts and circumstances existing at the acquisition date is obtained. Any such adjustments are made retrospectively as if those adjustments had been made at the acquisition date.

10.1.1 Use of provisional values

If the initial accounting for a business combination is incomplete by the end of the reporting period in which the combination occurs, the financial statements should be prepared using provisional amounts for the items for which the accounting is incomplete. [IFRS 3(2008).45]

10.1.2 The measurement period

The measurement period is the period after the acquisition date during which the acquirer may adjust the provisional values recognised for a business combination. [IFRS 3(2008).46] The measurement period begins on the acquisition date and ends as soon as the acquirer receives the information it was seeking about facts and circumstances that existed as of the acquisition date or learns that more information is not obtainable. However, the measurement period cannot exceed one year from the acquisition date. [IFRS 3(2008).45]

10.1.3 What can be adjusted?

Adjustments may be made in the measurement period to the following components:

[IFRS 3(2008).46]

(a) the identifiable assets acquired, liabilities assumed and any non-controlling interest in the acquiree;

(b) the consideration transferred for the acquiree (or the other amount used in measuring goodwill);

(c) in a business combination achieved in stages, the equity interest in the acquiree previously held by the acquirer; and

(d) the resulting goodwill or gain on a bargain purchase.

10.1.4 Retrospective adjustments

The adjustments to provisional amounts should be recognised as if the accounting for the business combination had been completed at the acquisition date. Therefore, comparative information for prior periods presented in the financial statements is revised as required, including making any change in depreciation, amortisation or other income effects recognised in completing the initial accounting. [IFRS 3(2008).49]

Adjustments to recognised items During the measurement period, the acquirer retrospectively adjusts the provisional amounts recognised at the acquisition date to reflect new information obtained about facts and circumstances that existed as of the acquisition date and that, if known, would have affected the measurement of the amounts recognised as of that date. [IFRS 3(2008).45]

Adjustments to unrecognised items During the measurement period, the acquirer also recognises additional assets or liabilities if new information is obtained about facts and circumstances that existed as of the acquisition date and that, if known, would have resulted in the recognition of those assets and liabilities as of that date. [IFRS 3(2008).45]

Information to be considered The acquirer is required to consider all pertinent factors in determining whether information obtained after the acquisition date should result in an adjustment to the provisional amounts recognised or whether that information results from events that occurred after the acquisition date. Pertinent factors include the date when additional information is obtained and whether the acquirer can identify a reason for a change to provisional amounts. Information that is obtained shortly after the acquisition date is more likely to reflect circumstances that existed at the acquisition date than is information obtained several months later. For example, unless an intervening event that changed its fair value can be identified, the sale of an asset to a third party shortly after the acquisition date for an amount that differs significantly from its provisional fair value determined at that date is likely to indicate an error in the provisional amount. [IFRS 3(2008).47]

Revising goodwill The acquirer recognises an increase (decrease) in the provisional amount recognised for an identifiable asset (liability) by means of a decrease (increase) in goodwill. However, new information obtained during the measurement period may sometimes result in an adjustment to the provisional amount of more than one asset or liability. For example, the acquirer might have assumed a liability to pay damages related to an accident in one of the acquiree's facilities, part or all of which are covered by the acquiree's liability insurance policy. If the acquirer obtains new information during the measurement period about the acquisition-date fair value of that liability, the adjustment to goodwill resulting from a change to the provisional amount recognised for the liability would be offset (in whole or in part) by a corresponding adjustment to goodwill resulting from a change to the provisional amount recognised for the claim receivable from the insurer. [IFRS 3(2008).48]

Example 10.1.4

Measurement period

[IFRS 3(2008).IE51–53]

Suppose that AC acquires TC on 30 September 20X7. AC seeks an independent valuation for an item of property, plant and equipment acquired in the combination, and the valuation was not complete by the time AC authorised for issue its financial statements for the year ended 31 December 20X7. In its 20X7 annual financial statements, AC recognised a provisional fair value for the asset of CU30,000. At the acquisition date, the item of property, plant and equipment had a remaining useful life of five years. Five months after the acquisition date, AC received the independent valuation, which estimated the asset's acquisition-date fair value as CU40,000.

In its financial statements for the year ended 31 December 20X8, AC retrospectively adjusts the 20X7 prior year information as follows:

(a) the carrying amount of property, plant and equipment as of 31 December 20X7 is increased by CU9,500. That adjustment is measured as the fair value adjustment at the acquisition date of CU10,000 less the additional depreciation that would have been recognised if the asset's fair value at the acquisition date had been recognised from that date (CU500 for three months' depreciation);

(b) the carrying amount of goodwill as of 31 December 20X7 is decreased by CU10,000; and

(c) depreciation expense for 20X7 is increased by CU500.

In accordance with paragraph B67 of IFRS 3, AC discloses:

(a) in its 20X7 financial statements, that the initial accounting for the business combination has not been completed because the valuation of property, plant and equipment has not yet been received; and

(b) in its 20X8 financial statements, the amounts and explanations of the adjustments to the provisional values recognised during the current reporting period. Therefore, AC discloses that the 20X7 comparative information is adjusted retrospectively to increase the fair value of the

> item of property, plant and equipment at the acquisition date by CU9,500, offset by a decrease to goodwill of CU10,000 and an increase in depreciation expense of CU500.

10.1.5 *Adjustments after the measurement period*

After the measurement period ends, the accounting for a business combination can be amended only to correct an error in accordance with IAS 8 *Accounting Policies, Changes in Accounting Estimates and Errors* (see **section 5** of **chapter 4**). [IFRS 3(2008).50]

10.1.6 Deferred tax arising from a business combination

The requirements of IFRS 3(2008) have resulted in amendments to IAS 12 *Income Taxes* (see **chapter 12**). In addition to consequential changes in terminology, a more significant change is made in respect of the post-combination recognition of deferred tax assets acquired in a business combination as follows:

[IAS 12.68 (as amended by IFRS 3(2008).C4)]

- acquired deferred tax benefits recognised within the measurement period that result from new information about facts and circumstances that existed at the acquisition date reduce the carrying amount of any goodwill related to that acquisition. If the carrying amount of that goodwill is zero, any remaining deferred tax benefits are recognised in profit or loss; and

- all other acquired deferred tax benefits realised are recognised in profit or loss (or outside profit or loss if otherwise required by IAS 12).

Prior to this amendment, under IAS 12, the subsequent realisation of all deferred tax assets acquired in a business combination reduced the carrying amount of goodwill to the amount that would have been recognised if the deferred tax asset had been recognised as an identifiable asset from the acquisition date, regardless of the date of realisation.

See **14.2.3** for specific transitional provisions regarding this change.

10.2 Guidance on subsequent measurement and accounting

10.2.1 *Guidance in other IFRSs*

In general, assets acquired, liabilities assumed or incurred, and equity instruments issued in a business combination are subsequently measured and accounted for in accordance with other applicable IFRSs, according to their nature. [IFRS 3(2008).54]

Examples of other IFRSs that provide guidance on subsequently measuring and accounting for assets acquired and liabilities assumed or incurred in a business combination include:

[IFRS 3(2008).B63]

- IAS 38 *Intangible Assets* prescribes the accounting for identifiable intangible assets acquired in a business combination (see **chapter 8**). The acquirer measures goodwill at the amount recognised at the acquisition date less any accumulated impairment losses;
- IAS 36 *Impairment of Assets* prescribes the accounting for impairment losses (see **chapter 9**);
- IFRS 4 *Insurance Contracts* provides guidance on the subsequent accounting for an insurance contract acquired in a business combination (see **chapter 44**);
- IAS 12 *Income Taxes* prescribes the subsequent accounting for deferred tax assets (including unrecognised deferred tax assets) and liabilities acquired in a business combination (see **chapter 12**);
- IFRS 2 *Share-based Payment* provides guidance on subsequent measurement and accounting for the portion of replacement share-based payment awards issued by an acquirer that is attributable to employees' future services (see **chapter 25**); and
- IAS 27 *Consolidated and Separate Financial Statements* (as amended in 2008) provides guidance on accounting for changes in a parent's ownership interest in a subsidiary after control is obtained (see **chapter 33**).

10.2.2 *Specific guidance*

IFRS 3(2008) provides specific guidance in relation to the following assets acquired, liabilities assumed or incurred, and equity instruments issued in a business combination:

- reacquired rights (see **7.5.2**);

- contingent liabilities (see **7.5.1**);
- indemnification assets (see **7.5.7**); and
- contingent consideration (see **8.2**).

11 Step acquisitions

This section applies where an equity investment in one of the following categories is increased to become a controlling interest: a financial asset under IAS 39, an associate under IAS 28 or a jointly controlled entity under IAS 31.

Transactions where control is achieved through two transactions

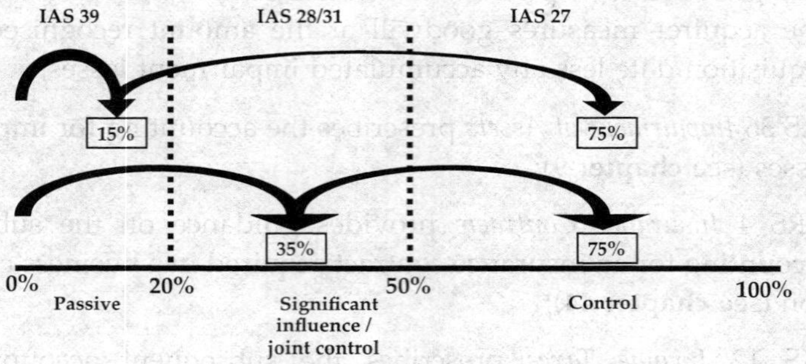

The principles to be applied are:

- a business combination occurs only in respect of the transaction that gives one entity control of another; [IFRS 3(2008)(Appendix A)]
- identifiable net assets of the acquiree are remeasured to their fair value on the date of acquisition (i.e. the date that control passes); [IFRS 3(2008).18]
- non-controlling interests are measured on the date of acquisition under one of the two options permitted by IFRS 3(2008); [IFRS 3(2008).19]
- an equity interest previously held in the acquiree which qualified as a financial asset under IAS 39 is treated as if it were disposed of and reacquired at fair value on the acquisition date. Accordingly, it is remeasured to its acquisition-date fair value and any resulting gain or loss is recognised in profit or loss. Consistent with the treatment as

if it were a direct disposal, any changes in value of the equity interest that were previously recognised in other comprehensive income (e.g. because the investment was classified as available-for-sale) are reclassified from equity to profit or loss; [IFRS 3(2008).42]

- an equity interest previously held in the acquiree which qualified as an associate under IAS 28 or a jointly controlled entity under IAS 31 is similarly treated as if it were disposed of and reacquired at fair value on the acquisition date. Accordingly, it is remeasured to its acquisition-date fair value, and any resulting gain or loss compared to its carrying amount under IAS 28 or IAS 31 is recognised in profit or loss. Any amount that has previously been recognised in other comprehensive income, and that would be reclassified to profit or loss following a disposal, is similarly reclassified from equity to profit or loss; [IFRS 3(2008).42] and
- goodwill (or a gain from a bargain purchase) is measured as: [IFRS 3(2008).32]

Consideration transferred to obtain control
plus
Amount of non-controlling interest (using either option)
plus
Fair value of previously-held equity interest
less
Fair value of the identifiable net assets of the acquiree (100%)

Example 11A

Financial asset under IAS 39 becomes a subsidiary

A acquired a 75% controlling interest in B in two stages.

- In 20X1, A acquired a 15% equity interest for cash consideration of £10,000. A classified the interest as available-for-sale under IAS 39. From 20X1 to the end of 20X5, A reported fair value increases of £2,000 in other comprehensive income (OCI).
- In 20X6, A acquired a further 60% equity interest for cash consideration of £60,000. A identified net assets of B with a fair value of £80,000. A elected to measure non-controlling interests at their share of net assets. On the date of acquisition, the previously-held 15% interest had a fair value of £12,500.

In 20X6, A will include £2,500 in profit or loss, being:

£

Gain on 'disposal' of 15% investment (£12,500 – £12,000)	500
Gain previously reported in OCI (£12,000 – £10,000)	2,000
Total	2,500

In 20X6, A will measure goodwill as follows:

	£
Fair value of consideration given for controlling interest	60,000
Non-controlling interest (25% x £80,000)	20,000
Fair value of previously-held interest	12,500
Sub-total	92,500
Less: fair value of net assets of acquiree	(80,000)
Goodwill	12,500

Example 11B

Associate becomes a subsidiary

C acquired a 75% controlling interest in D in two stages.

- In 20X1, C acquired a 40% equity interest for cash consideration of £40,000. C classified the interest as an associate under IAS 28. At the date that C acquired its interest, the fair value of D's identifiable net assets was £80,000. From 20X1 to 20X6, C equity accounted for its share of undistributed profits totalling £5,000, and included its share of an IAS 16 revaluation gain of £3,000 in other comprehensive income (OCI). Therefore, in 20X6, the carrying amount of C's interest in D was £48,000.
- In 20X6, C acquired a further 35% equity interest for cash consideration of £55,000. C identified net assets of D with a fair value of £110,000. C elected to measure non-controlling interests at fair value of £30,000. On the date of acquisition, the previously-held 40% interest had a fair value of £50,000.

In 20X6, (ignoring any profits earned prior to the acquisition) C will include £2,000 in profit or loss, being:

	£
Fair value of previously-held interest	50,000
Less: carrying amount under IAS 28	48,000
Total	2,000

The revaluation gain of £3,000 previously recognised in OCI is not reclassified to profit or loss because it would not be reclassified if the interest in D were disposed of.

In 20X6, C will measure goodwill as follows:

	£
Fair value of consideration given for controlling interest	55,000
Non-controlling interest (fair value)	30,000
Fair value of previously-held interest	50,000
Sub-total	135,000

Less: fair value of net assets of acquiree	(110,000)
Goodwill	25,000

12 Reverse acquisitions

12.1 Identifying a reverse acquisition

12.1.1 Meaning of reverse acquisition

A reverse acquisition occurs when the entity that issues securities (the legal acquirer) is identified as the acquiree for accounting purposes on the basis of the guidance in **section 5**. The entity whose equity interests are acquired (the legal acquiree) must be the acquirer for accounting purposes for the transaction to be considered a reverse acquisition. [IFRS 3(2008).B19]

Example 12.1.1

Private entity reversing into a public entity

[IFRS 3(2008).B19]

Reverse acquisitions sometimes occur when a private operating entity wants to become a public entity but does not want to register its equity shares. To accomplish that, the private entity will arrange for a public entity to acquire its equity interests in exchange for the equity interests of the public entity. In this example, the public entity is the **legal acquirer** because it issued its equity interests, and the private entity is the **legal acquiree** because its equity interests were acquired. However, application of the guidance in paragraphs B13 – B18 (see **section 5**) results in identifying:

(a) the public entity as the **acquiree** for accounting purposes (the accounting acquiree); and

(b) the private entity as the **acquirer** for accounting purposes (the accounting acquirer).

12.1.2 Acquiree must meet the definition of a business

IFRS 3(2008) limits business combinations to circumstances where the acquiree is a business. [IFRS 3(2008).3] It follows, for reverse acquisitions, that the accounting acquiree must meet the definition of a business for the transaction to be accounted for as a reverse acquisition. [IFRS 3(2008).B19]

This restriction appears to exclude from the scope of IFRS 3(2008) two circumstances that, in the past, were identified as reverse acquisitions:

- a private entity reversing into a publicly-listed 'cash shell' (i.e. an entity with a public listing but with no ongoing activities); and

- a new entity becoming the new parent of an existing group through an exchange of equity instruments.

Under IFRS 3(2008), such transactions should not be described as reverse acquisitions. An appropriate accounting policy may describe them as 'capital restructurings' or 'reverse asset acquisitions'. Such an accounting policy may result in consolidated financial statements that are similar to those produced under reverse acquisition accounting.

12.1.3 *More complex cases*

The guidance on identifying the acquirer in **section 5** is relevant in a reverse acquisition transaction. Beyond this, IFRS 3(2008) does not provide detailed guidance for more complex arrangements (e.g. where the accounting acquirer had a previously-held interest in the accounting acquiree). It is suggested that the two primary factors might lead to the conclusion that the transaction involves a reverse acquisition are:

- the former shareholders of the entity whose shares are acquired own the majority of shares, and control the majority of votes, in the combined entity; and

- the management of the combined entity is drawn predominantly from the entity whose shares are acquired.

12.2 Accounting for a reverse acquisition

There are no substantive differences between the accounting treatment prescribed for reverse acquisitions under IFRS 3(2004) and under IFRS 3(2008). Both versions of IFRS 3 aim to achieve an accounting outcome that reflects the consolidated financial statements as if the accounting acquirer had legally acquired the accounting acquiree. In other words, the legal form of the business combination should not impact the accounting for the substance of the business combination.

12.2.1 *Accounting periods*

Consolidated financial statements prepared following a reverse acquisition are issued under the name of the legal parent (accounting acquiree) but described in the notes as a continuation of the financial statements of the legal subsidiary (accounting acquirer), with one adjustment, which is to adjust retroactively the accounting acquirer's legal capital to reflect the legal capital of the accounting acquiree. That adjustment is required to reflect the capital of the legal parent (the accounting acquiree). Comparative information presented in those consolidated financial statements also is retroactively adjusted to reflect the legal capital of the legal parent (accounting acquiree). [IFRS 3(2008).B21]

Separate entity financial statements for the legal parent, if required, would be prepared on a stand-alone basis. Where the entity was formed shortly before the combination, its entity financial statements would cover only its actual accounting period.

12.2.2 *Detailed accounting entries*

IFRS 3(2008).B19 – B27 contains detailed guidance on the preparation of consolidated financial statements for a reverse acquisition. For understanding, this guidance is set out below as a comparison with a 'conventional' acquisition, (i.e. a business combination where the accounting acquirer and the legal acquirer are the same entity). The terminology used for a reverse acquisition is that the accounting acquirer is the legal subsidiary, and the accounting acquiree is the legal parent.

	Conventional acquisition	**Reverse acquisition** [IFRS 3(2008).B19 – B27]
Consolidated financial statements issued	In the name of the legal parent.	In the name of the legal parent (with disclosure in the notes that they are a continuation of the financial statements of the legal subsidiary).

	Conventional acquisition	**Reverse acquisition** [IFRS 3(2008).B19 – B27]
Consideration transferred	Fair value of consideration given by legal parent.	Fair value of the notional number of equity instruments that the legal subsidiary would have had to issue to the legal parent to give the owners of the legal parent the same percentage ownership in the combined entity.
Net assets of legal subsidiary (accounting acquirer)	Recognised and measured in accordance with IFRS 3(2008) – generally restated to fair value.	Not restated from pre-combination carrying amounts.
Net assets of legal parent (accounting acquiree)	Not restated from pre-combination carrying amounts.	Recognised and measured in accordance with the requirements for acquirees under IFRS 3(2008) – generally restated to fair value.
Goodwill / gain on bargain purchase	Consideration transferred less identified net assets of legal subsidiary.	Consideration transferred less identified net assets of legal parent.
Consolidated retained earnings and other equity balances at date of combination.	Legal parent only.	Legal subsidiary only.
Consolidated equity instruments.	Equity instruments of legal parent.	Issued equity instruments of legal subsidiary outstanding before the business combination plus the fair value of the legal parent.

	Conventional acquisition	Reverse acquisition [IFRS 3(2008).B19 – B27]
Non-controlling interests in legal subsidiary	Non-controlling interest's proportionate share of legal subsidiary net assets, or at fair value.	Non-controlling interest's proportionate share of legal subsidiary net assets at pre-combination carrying amounts. No fair value option.
Comparative information	Legal parent only.	Legal subsidiary only, but retroactively adjusted to reflect the legal capital of the legal parent.
Earnings per share of current period	Earnings based on consolidated earnings. Weighted average number of shares reflects actual shares issued for legal subsidiary from date of acquisition.	Earnings based on consolidated earnings. Weighted average number of shares reflects legal subsidiary's weighted average pre-combination ordinary shares multiplied by the exchange ratio established in the acquisition, and the weighted average total actual shares of the legal parent in issue after the date of acquisition.
Earnings per share of comparative period	Acquirer only.	Earnings of legal subsidiary. Legal subsidiary's weighted average ordinary shares multiplied by exchange ratio established at acquisition.
Separate financial statements of legal parent.	Legal parent.	Legal parent.

12.2.3 *Presentation of equity and comparative information*

Pre-combination net income and net assets are those of the legal subsidiary (accounting acquirer), and present no particular problems.

Pre-combination equity is, in theory, the pre-combination equity of the legal subsidiary but adjusted retroactively to reflect the legal capital of the legal parent. IFRS 3(2008) describes the position at the date of combination as follows:

[IFRS 3(2008).B22(c) & (d)]

- the consolidated financial statements reflect the retained earnings and other equity balances of the legal subsidiary (accounting acquirer) before the business combination; and
- the amount recognised as issued equity interests in the consolidated financial statements is determined by adding the issued equity interest of the legal subsidiary (the accounting acquirer) outstanding immediately before the business combination to the fair value of the legal parent (accounting acquiree) determined in accordance with the requirements of IFRS (2008). However, the equity structure (i.e. the number and type of equity interests issued) reflects the equity structure of the legal parent (the accounting acquiree), including the equity interests the legal parent issued to effect the combination. Accordingly, the equity structure of the legal subsidiary (the accounting acquirer) is restated using the exchange ratio established in the acquisition agreement to reflect the number of shares of the legal parent (the accounting acquiree) issued in the reverse acquisition.'

Applying this guidance to periods before the combination:

- the total amount shown as equity is the total shown as equity in the legal subsidiary; and
- the amount shown as equity instruments (e.g. share capital) is the amount shown in the legal subsidiary adjusted by the exchange ratio. In the case of share capital with a fixed nominal value, the result may be higher or lower than the legal subsidiary's actual share capital pre-combination. The resulting adjustment is reflected as a reduction in, or addition to, equity reserves.

Example 12.2.3

Presentation of equity for an entity with share capital

The statements of financial position of Company A and Company B include the following amounts.

	Company A	Company B
	£	£
Share capital – £1 nominal shares	100	300
Retained earnings	200	500
Net assets at carrying amount	300	800

	Company A	Company B
	£	£
Net assets at fair value	500	2,000
Fair value of whole business	5,000	25,000

On the date that the statements of financial position were drawn up, Company A issued 500 new shares in exchange for the entire share capital of Company B.

Since the owners of Company B obtain a 5/6ths share of the equity of Company A, Company B is identified as the acquirer. Since Company A issued 500 shares in itself in exchange for 300 shares in Company B, the exchange ratio is 5/3rds.

The consideration transferred would be £5,000. This equals the fair value of 60 new shares in Company B, being the notional number that Company B would issue to give the shareholders of Company A 1/6th of the combined entity. It also represents the fair value of Company A as an entity.

	Date of combination	Pre-combination comparative
	£	£
Share capital – £1 nominal	600	500
Other reserves	4,700	(200)
Issued equity instruments	5,300	300
Retained earnings	500	500
Total equity	5,800	800

Share capital at the date of combination is 600, being the actual Company A shares in issue. Share capital pre-combination is £500, being the issued shares of Company B (£300) adjusted for the exchange ratio.

Issued equity instruments at the date of combination are the issued equity instruments of Company B (£300) plus the consideration transferred (£5,000). Issued equity instruments pre-combination are those of Company B (£300).

Retained earnings at the date of combination, and pre-combination, are those of B (£500).

The balance of other reserves pre-combination (£200 debit) represents the capitalisation of reserves into share capital (500 shares in Company A issued in exchange for 300 shares in Company B).

Earnings per share would be based on the consolidated earnings (pre-combination earnings of Company B, and post-combination earnings of Company A + B. The weighted average number of shares would be based on 500 shares pre-combination (being the number of shares in Company A issued to shareholders of Company B) and 600 shares post-combination.

12.2.4 *Worked example of a reverse acquisition*

Example 12.2.4

Reverse acquisition

[IFRS 3(2008).IE1-IE15]

This example illustrates the accounting for a reverse acquisition in which Entity B, the legal subsidiary, acquires Entity A, the entity issuing equity instruments and therefore the legal parent, in a reverse acquisition on 30 September 20X6. This example ignores the accounting for any income tax effects.

The statements of financial position of Entity A and Entity B immediately before the business combination are:

	Entity A (legal parent, accounting acquiree)	**Entity B** (legal subsidiary, accounting acquirer)
	CU	**CU**
Current assets	500	700
Non-current assets	1,300	3,000
Total assets	1,800	3,700
Current liabilities	300	600
Non-current liabilities	400	1,100
Total liabilities	700	1,700
Shareholders' equity		
Retained earnings	800	1,400
Issued equity		
100 ordinary shares	300	
60 ordinary shares		600
Total shareholders' equity	1,100	2,000
Total liabilities and shareholders' equity	1,800	3,700

This example also uses the following information:

(a) On 30 September 20X6 Entity A issues 2.5 shares in exchange for each ordinary share of Entity B. All of Entity B's shareholders exchange their shares in Entity B. Therefore, Entity A issues 150 ordinary shares in exchange for all 60 ordinary shares of Entity B.

(b) The fair value of each ordinary share of Entity B at 30 September 20X6 is CU40. The quoted market price of Entity A's ordinary shares at that date is CU16.

(c) The fair values of Entity A's identifiable assets and liabilities at 30 September 20X6 are the same as their carrying amounts, except that the fair value of Entity A's non-current assets at 30 September 20X6 is CU1,500.

Calculating the fair value of the consideration transferred

As a result of Entity A (legal parent, accounting acquiree) issuing 150 ordinary shares, Entity B's shareholders own 60 per cent of the issued shares of the combined entity (i.e. 150 of 250 issued shares). The remaining 40 per cent are owned by Entity A's shareholders. If the business combination had taken the form of Entity B issuing additional ordinary shares to Entity A's shareholders in exchange for their ordinary shares in Entity A, Entity B would have had to issue 40 shares for the ratio of ownership interest in the combined entity to be the same. Entity B's shareholders would then own 60 of the 100 issued shares of Entity B— 60 per cent of the combined entity. As a result, the fair value of the consideration effectively transferred by Entity B and the group's interest in Entity A is CU1,600 (40 shares with a fair value per share of CU40).

The fair value of the consideration effectively transferred should be based on the most reliable measure. In this example, the quoted market price of Entity A's shares provides a more reliable basis for measuring the consideration effectively transferred than the estimated fair value of the shares in Entity B, and the consideration is measured using the market price of Entity A's shares—100 shares with a fair value per share of CU16.

Measuring goodwill

Goodwill is measured as the excess of the fair value of the consideration effectively transferred (the group's interest in Entity A) over the net amount of Entity A's recognised identifiable assets and liabilities, as follows:

	CU	CU
Consideration effectively transferred		1,600
Net recognised values of Entity A's identifiable assets and liabilities		
Current assets	500	
Non-current assets	1,500	
Current liabilities	(300)	
Non-current liabilities	(400)	(1,300)
Goodwill		300

Consolidated statement of financial position at 30 September 20X6

The consolidated statement of financial position immediately after the business combination is:

	CU
Current assets [CU700 + CU500]	1,200
Non-current assets [CU3,000 + CU1,500]	4,500
Goodwill	300
Total assets	6,000
Current liabilities [CU600 + CU300]	900
Non-current liabilities [CU1,100 + CU400]	1,500
Total liabilities	2,400

Shareholders' equity	
Retained earnings	1,400
Issued equity	
250 ordinary shares [CU600 + CU1,600]	2,200
Total shareholders' equity	3,600
Total liabilities and shareholders' equity	6,000

The amount recognised as issued equity interests in the consolidated financial statements (CU2,200) is determined by adding the issued equity of the legal subsidiary immediately before the business combination (CU600) and the fair value of the consideration effectively transferred (CU1,600). However, the equity structure appearing in the consolidated financial statements (i.e. the number and type of equity interests issued) must reflect the equity structure of the legal parent, including the equity interests issued by the legal parent to effect the combination.

Earnings per share

Assume that Entity B's earnings for the annual period ended 31 December 20X5 were CU600 and that the consolidated earnings for the annual period ended 31 December 20X6 were CU800. Assume also that there was no change in the number of ordinary shares issued by Entity B during the annual period ended 31 December 20X5 and during the period from 1 January 20X6 to the date of the reverse acquisition on 30 September 20X6. Earnings per share for the annual period ended 31 December 20X6 is calculated as follows:

Number of shares deemed to be outstanding for the period from 1 January 20X6 to the acquisition date (i.e. the number of ordinary shares issued by Entity A (legal parent, accounting acquiree) in the reverse acquisition)	150
Number of shares outstanding from the acquisition date to 31 December 20X6	250
Weighted average number of ordinary shares outstanding [(150 x 9/12) + (250 x 3/12)]	175
Earnings per share [800/175]	CU4.57

Restated earnings per share for the annual period ended 31 December 20X5 is CU4.00 (calculated as the earnings of Entity B of 600 divided by the number of ordinary shares Entity A issued in the reverse acquisition (150)).

13 Disclosure

13.1 Business combinations in the current period or after the reporting period

IFRS 3(2008) requires that the acquirer should disclose information that enables users of its financial statements to evaluate the nature and financial effect of a business combination that occurs either:

[IFRS 3(2008).59]

- during the current reporting period; or
- after the end of the reporting period but before the financial statements are authorised for issue.

Detailed guidance as to disclosures required to meet the objectives of IFRS 3(2008).59 is set out in Appendix B to the Standard. These requirements are set out below, accompanied by extracts from the Illustrative Examples issued with IFRS 3(2008) which illustrate some of the requirements (not all of the requirements are illustrated).

If the specific disclosures set out below and those required by other IFRSs do not meet the objectives set out in IFRS 3(2008).59, the acquirer should disclose whatever additional information is necessary to meet those objectives. [IFRS 3(2008).63]

The disclosures are generally required for each business combination that occurs during the reporting period and after the end of the reporting period (see **13.1.12** below). However, for individually immaterial business combinations occurring during the reporting period that are material collectively, the disclosures may be made in aggregate. [IFRS 3(2008).B65]

For the purposes of the illustrative examples, AC (the acquirer) is assumed to be a listed entity and TC (the acquiree) is an unlisted entity.

13.1.1 Details of the business combination

The acquirer is required to disclose:

[IFRS 3.64(a) – (d)]

- the name and a description of the acquiree;
- the acquisition date;
- the percentage of voting equity interests acquired; and
- the primary reasons for the business combination and a description of how the acquirer obtained control of the acquiree.

Example 13.1.1

Details of the business combination

[Extract from IFRS 3(2008).IE72]

On 30 June 20X0 AC acquired 15 per cent of the outstanding ordinary shares of TC. On 30 June 20X2 AC acquired 60 per cent of the outstanding ordinary shares of TC and obtained control of TC. TC is a provider of data networking products and services in Canada and Mexico. As a result of the acquisition, AC is expected to be the leading provider of data networking products and services in those markets. It also expects to reduce costs through economies of scale.

13.1.2 Goodwill

The acquirer is required to provide a qualitative description of the factors that make up the goodwill recognised, such as expected synergies from combining operations of the acquiree and the acquirer, intangible assets that do not qualify for separate recognition or other factors. [IFRS 3(2008).B64(e)]

The acquirer is also required to disclose the total amount of goodwill that is expected to be deductible for tax purposes. [IFRS 3(2008).B64(k)]

Example 13.1.2

Goodwill

[Extract from IFRS 3(2008).IE72]

The goodwill of CU2,500 arising from the acquisition consists largely of the synergies and economies of scale expected from combining the operations of AC and TC.

None of the goodwill recognised is expected to be deductible for income tax purposes.

13.1.3 Fair value of consideration and details of contingent consideration

The acquirer is required to disclose the acquisition-date fair value of the total consideration transferred and the acquisition-date fair value of each major class of consideration, such as:

[IFRS 3(2008).B64(f)]

- cash;
- other tangible or intangible assets, including a business or subsidiary of the acquirer;
- liabilities incurred (e.g. a liability for contingent consideration); and

- equity interests of the acquirer, including the number of instruments or interests issued or issuable and the method of determining the fair value of those instruments or interests.

For contingent consideration arrangements and indemnification assets, the acquirer is required to disclose:

[IFRS 3(2008).B64(g)]

- the amount recognised as of the acquisition date;
- a description of the arrangement and the basis for determining the amount of the payment; and
- an estimate of the range of outcomes (undiscounted) or, if a range cannot be estimated, that fact and the reasons why a range cannot be estimated. If the maximum amount of the payment is unlimited, the acquirer should disclose that fact.

Example 13.1.3

Fair value of consideration and details of contingent consideration

[Extract from IFRS 3(2008).IE72]

At 30 June 20X2

Consideration	**CU**
Cash	5,000
Equity instruments (100,000 ordinary shares of AC)	4,000
Contingent consideration arrangement	1,000
Total consideration transferred	10,000

The fair value of the 100,000 ordinary shares issued as part of the consideration paid for TC (CU4,000) was determined on the basis of the closing market price of AC's ordinary shares on the acquisition date.

The contingent consideration arrangement requires AC to pay the former owners of TC 5 per cent of the revenues of XC, an unconsolidated equity investment owned by TC, in excess of CU7,500 for 20X3, up to a maximum amount of CU2,500 (undiscounted). The potential undiscounted amount of all future payments that AC could be required to make under the contingent consideration arrangement is between CU0 and CU2,500.

The fair value of the contingent consideration arrangement of CU1,000 was estimated by applying the income approach. The fair value estimates are based on an assumed discount rate range of 20–25 per cent and assumed probability-adjusted revenues in XC of CU10,000–20,000.

13.1.4 Details of acquired receivables

For acquired receivables, the acquirer is required to disclose:

[IFRS 3(2008).B64(h)]

- the fair value of the receivables;
- the gross contractual amounts receivable; and
- the best estimate at the acquisition date of the contractual cash flows not expected to be collected.

These disclosures are required by major class of receivable, such as loans, direct finance leases and any other class of receivables.

Example 13.1.4

Details of acquired receivables

[Extract from IFRS 3(2008).IE72]

The fair value of the financial assets acquired includes receivables under finance leases of data networking equipment with a fair value of CU2,375. The gross amount due under the contracts is CU3,100, of which CU450 is expected to be uncollectible.

13.1.5 Details of assets acquired and liabilities assumed

The acquirer is required to disclose the amounts recognised as of the acquisition date for each major class of assets acquired and liabilities assumed. [IFRS 3(2008).B64(i)]

Example 13.1.5

Details of assets acquired and liabilities assumed

[Extract from IFRS 3(2008).IE72]

Recognised amounts of identifiable assets acquired and liabilities assumed	**CU**
Financial assets	3,500
Inventory	1,000
Property, plant and equipment	10,000
Identifiable intangible assets	3,300
Financial liabilities	(4,000)
Contingent liability	(1,000)
Total identifiable net assets	12,800

13.1.6 Details of contingent liabilities recognised

For each contingent liability recognised in accordance with IFRS 3(2008).23 (see **7.5.1**), the acquirer is required to disclose the information required in paragraph 85 of IAS 37 *Provisions, Contingent Liabilities and Contingent Assets*. [IFRS 3(2008).B64(j)]

IAS 37 sets out the general disclosure requirements for provisions recognised under that Standard. The effect of IFRS 3(2008).B64(j) is to require the same disclosures for contingent liabilities recognised in a business combination, as follows:

[IAS 37.85]

- a brief description of the nature of the obligation and the expected timing of any resulting outflow of economic benefits;
- an indication of the uncertainties about the amount or timing of those outflows. Where necessary to provide adequate information, the acquirer should disclose the major assumptions made concerning future events; and
- the amount of any expected reimbursement, stating the amount of any asset that has been recognised for that expected reimbursement.

Example 13.1.6

Details of contingent liabilities recognised

[Extract from IFRS 3(2008).IE72]

A contingent liability of CU1,000 has been recognised for expected warranty claims on products sold by TC during the last three years. We expect that the majority of this expenditure will be incurred in 20X3 and that all will be incurred by the end of 20X4. The potential undiscounted amount of all future payments that AC could be required to make under the warranty arrangements is estimated to be between CU500 and CU1,500.

If a contingent liability is not recognised because its fair value cannot be measured reliably, the acquirer is required to disclose:

[IFRS 3(2008).B64(j)]

- the information required by paragraph 86 of IAS 37 (see below); and
- the reasons why the liability cannot be measured reliably.

IAS 37 sets out the general disclosure requirements for contingent liabilities, as follows:

[IAS 37.86]

- a brief description of the nature of the contingent liability; and
- where practicable:
  - an estimate of the financial effect;
  - an indication of the uncertainties relating to the amount or timing of any outflow; and
  - the possibility of any reimbursement.

13.1.7 Details of transactions recognised separately

For transactions that are recognised separately from the acquisition of assets and assumption of liabilities in the business combination in accordance with IFRS 3(2008).51 (see **8.3**), the acquirer is required to disclose:

[IFRS 3(2008).B64(l)]

- a description of each transaction;
- how the acquirer accounted for each transaction;
- the amounts recognised for each transaction and the line item in the financial statements in which each amount is recognised; and
- if the transaction is the effective settlement of a pre-existing relationship, the method used to determine the settlement amount.

The disclosure of separately-recognised transactions required by IFRS 3(2008).B64(l) should include the amount of acquisition-related costs and, separately, the amount of those costs recognised as an expense and the line item or items in the statement of comprehensive income in which those expenses are recognised. The amount of any issue costs not recognised as an expense and how they were recognised should also be disclosed. [IFRS 3(2008).B64(m)]

Example 13.1.7

Details of transactions recognised separately

[Extract from IFRS 3(2008).IE72]

Acquisition-related costs (included in selling, general and administrative expenses in AC's statement of comprehensive income for the year ended 31 December 20X2) amounted to CU1,250.

13.1.8 *Details of bargain purchases*

In a bargain purchase (see **9.3**), the acquirer is required to disclose:

[IFRS 3(2008).B64(n)]

- the amount of any gain recognised in accordance with IFRS 3(2008).34 and the line item in the statement of comprehensive income in which the gain is recognised; and
- a description of the reasons why the transaction resulted in a gain.

IFRS 3(2008) does not specify that the amount of the gain recognised must be shown as a separate line item. It could be shown as part of 'other gains and losses'. However, the requirements of IFRS 3(2008).B64(n) ensure that the amount is separately disclosed in the notes.

13.1.9 *Details of non-controlling interests*

For each business combination in which the acquirer holds less than 100 per cent of the equity interests in the acquiree at the acquisition date, the acquirer is required to disclose:

[IFRS 3(2008).B64(o)]

- the amount of the non-controlling interest in the acquiree recognised at the acquisition date and the measurement basis for that amount; and
- for each non-controlling interest in an acquiree measured at fair value, the valuation techniques and key model inputs used for determining that value.

Example 13.1.9

Details of non-controlling interests

[Extract from IFRS 3(2008).IE72]

The fair value of the non-controlling interest in TC, an unlisted company, was estimated by applying a market approach and an income approach. The fair value estimates are based on:

(a) an assumed discount rate range of 20–25 per cent;

(b) an assumed terminal value based on a range of terminal EBITDA multiples between 3 and 5 times (or, if appropriate, based on long term sustainable growth rates ranging from 3 to 6 per cent);

(c) assumed financial multiples of companies deemed to be similar to TC; and

(d) assumed adjustments because of the lack of control or lack of marketability that market participants would consider when estimating the fair value of the non-controlling interest in TC.

13.1.10 *Business combinations achieved in stages*

In a business combination achieved in stages, the acquirer is required to disclose:

[IFRS 3(2008).B64(p)]

- the acquisition-date fair value of the equity interest in the acquiree held by the acquirer immediately before the acquisition date; and
- the amount of any gain or loss recognised as a result of remeasuring to fair value the equity interest in the acquiree held by the acquirer before the business combination and the line item in the statement of comprehensive income in which that gain or loss is recognised.

Example 13.1.10

Business combination achieved in stages

[Extract from IFRS 3(2008).IE72]

The fair value of AC's equity interest in TC held before the business combination amounted to CU2,000. AC recognised a gain of CU500 as a result of measuring at fair value its 15 per cent equity interest in TC held before the business combination. The gain is included in other income in AC's statement of comprehensive income for the year ending 31 December 20X2.

13.1.11 *Impact of acquiree on amounts reported in the statement of comprehensive income*

The acquirer is required to disclose the following information:

[IFRS 3(2008).B64(q)]

- the amounts of revenue and profit or loss of the acquiree since the acquisition date included in the consolidated statement of comprehensive income for the reporting period; and
- the revenue and profit or loss of the combined entity for the current reporting period as though the acquisition date for all business

combinations that occurred during the year had been as of the beginning of the annual reporting period.

If disclosure of any of the information required by IFRS 3(2008).B64(q) is impracticable, the acquirer should disclose that fact and explain why the disclosure is impracticable. IFRS 3(2008) uses the term 'impracticable' with the same meaning as in IAS 8 *Accounting Policies, Changes in Accounting Estimates and Errors* (see **2.8** in **chapter 4**). [IFRS 3(2008).B64(q)]

Example 13.1.11

Impact of acquiree on amounts reported in the statement of comprehensive income

[Extract from IFRS 3(2008).IE72]

The revenue included in the consolidated statement of comprehensive income since 30 June 20X2 contributed by TC was CU4,090. TC also contributed profit of CU1,710 over the same period. Had TC been consolidated from 1 January 20X2, the consolidated statement of comprehensive income would have included revenue of CU27,670 and profit of CU12,870.

13.1.12 Business combinations after the reporting period

If the acquisition date of a business combination is after the end of the reporting period but before the financial statements are authorised for issue, the disclosures set out in sections **13.1.1** to **13.1.11** are required unless the initial accounting for the business combination is incomplete at the time the financial statements are authorised for issue. [IFRS 3(2008).B66]

In that situation, the acquirer should describe which disclosures could not be made and the reasons why they cannot be made. [IFRS 3(2008).B66]

13.2 Adjustments recognised for business combinations that occurred in the current or previous reporting periods

The acquirer is required to disclose information that enables users of its financial statements to evaluate the financial effects of adjustments recognised in the current reporting period that relate to business combinations that occurred in the current or previous reporting periods. [IFRS 3(2008).61]

If the specific disclosures set out below and other those required by IFRSs do not meet the objectives set out in IFRS 3(2008).61, the acquirer should disclose whatever additional information is necessary to meet those objectives. [IFRS 3(2008).63]

The information should be disclosed separately for each material business combination or in the aggregate for individually immaterial business combinations that are material collectively. [IFRS 3(2008).67]

13.2.1 *Business combinations for which the initial accounting is incomplete*

If the initial accounting for a business combination is incomplete (see **10.1.1**), and the amounts recognised in the financial statements for the business combination thus have been determined only provisionally, the following information should be disclosed for particular assets, liabilities, non-controlling interests or items of consideration:

[IFRS 3(2008).B67(a)]

- the reasons why the initial accounting for the business combination is incomplete;
- the assets, liabilities, equity interests or items of consideration for which the initial accounting is incomplete; and
- the nature and amount of any measurement period adjustments recognised during the reporting period in accordance with IFRS 3(2008).49 (see **10.1.4**).

Example 13.2.1

Business combinations for which the initial accounting is incomplete

[Extract from IFRS 3(2008).IE72]

The fair value of the acquired identifiable intangible assets of CU3,300 is provisional pending receipt of the final valuations for those assets.

13.2.2 *Contingent assets and contingent liabilities*

For each reporting period after the acquisition date until the entity collects, sells or otherwise loses the right to a contingent consideration asset, or until the entity settles a contingent consideration liability or the liability is cancelled or expires, the acquirer should disclose:

[IFRS 3(2008).B67(b)]

- any changes in the recognised amounts, including any differences arising upon settlement;
- any changes in the range of outcomes (undiscounted) and the reasons for those changes; and
- the valuation techniques and key model inputs used to measure contingent consideration.

For contingent liabilities recognised in a business combination, the acquirer should disclose the information required by IAS 37.84 – 85 for each class of provision. [IFRS 3(2008).B67(c)]

The requirements of IAS 37.85 are set out at **13.1.6** above. IAS 37.84 requires the following to be disclosed for each class of provision (and, in these circumstances, each class of recognised contingent liability):

- the carrying amount at the beginning and end of the period;
- additional contingent liabilities recognised in the period, included increases to existing contingent liabilities;
- amounts used (i.e. incurred and charged against the contingent liability) during the period;
- unused amounts reversed in the period; and
- the increase during the period in the discounted amount arising from the passage or time and the effect of any change in the discount rate.

13.2.3 Goodwill

The acquirer is required to disclose a reconciliation of the carrying amount of goodwill at the beginning and end of the reporting period, showing separately:

[IFRS 3(2008).B67(d)]

- the gross amount and accumulated impairment losses at the beginning of the reporting period;
- additional goodwill recognised during the reporting period, except goodwill included in a disposal group that, on acquisition, meets the criteria to be classified as held for sale in accordance with IFRS 5 *Non-current Assets Held for Sale and Discontinued Operations* (see **chapter 29**);

- adjustments resulting from the subsequent recognition of deferred tax assets during the reporting period in accordance with IFRS 3(2008).67 (see **14.1.1**);
- goodwill included in a disposal group classified as held for sale in accordance with IFRS 5 and goodwill derecognised during the reporting period without having previously been included in a disposal group classified as held for sale;
- impairment losses recognised during the reporting period in accordance with IAS 36. (IAS 36 requires disclosure of information about the recoverable amount and impairment of goodwill in addition to this requirement – see **11.6** in **chapter 9**);
- net exchange rate differences arising during the reporting period in accordance with IAS 21 *The Effects of Changes in Foreign Exchange Rates*;
- any other changes in the carrying amount during the reporting period; and
- the gross amount and accumulated impairment losses at the end of the reporting period.

13.2.4 Material gains and losses recognised in the period

The acquirer is required to disclose the amount and an explanation of any gain or loss recognised in the current reporting period that both:

[IFRS 3(2008).B67(e)]

- relates to the identifiable assets acquired or liabilities assumed in a business combination that was effected in the current or previous reporting period; and
- is of such a size, nature or incidence that disclosure is relevant to understanding the combined entity's financial statements.

14 Effective date and transition

14.1 IFRS 3(2008) – effective date

14.1.1 Mandatory application

IFRS 3(2008) is applicable to business combinations for which the acquisition date is in annual reporting periods beginning on or after 1 July 2009. [IFRS 3(2008).64] With certain exceptions, the requirements of IFRS 3(2008) apply prospectively, meaning that there is no amendment to the accounting for earlier business combinations.

Specific transitional provisions override the requirements of IFRS 3(2008) in relation to deferred taxes, meaning that no goodwill adjustments can be recognised where deferred taxes arising in a pre-transition business combination are recognised for the first time after the beginning of the annual reporting period in which the IFRS 3(2008) is applied. [IFRS 3(2008).67]

There are also specific transitional provisions in relation to entities (such as mutual entities) that have not yet applied IFRS 3(2004) and had one or more business combinations that were accounted for using the purchase method (see **14.2.2**). [IFRS 3(2008).67]

14.1.2 *Early adoption*

The Standard may be adopted early but only for annual reporting periods beginning on or after 30 June 2007. If an entity chooses to adopt IFRS 3(2008) before 1 July 2009:

- it should disclose that fact; and
- it should apply the 2008 amendments to IAS 27 at the same time (see **chapter 33**).

14.1.3 *Effect on a calendar year period*

For an entity with a calendar-year accounting period:

- application of IFRS 3(2008) is mandatory for the year ended 31 December 2010; and
- early adoption is allowed from the year ended 31 December 2008.

At the time of writing, the revised versions of IFRS 3 and IAS 27 have not yet been endorsed for use in the EU. Since the requirements of the revised Standards differ in important respects from those of the previous versions, UK

> *EU reporting entities will not be able to apply the revised versions of IFRS 3 and IAS 27 in their statutory financial statements until the revised Standards are endorsed.*

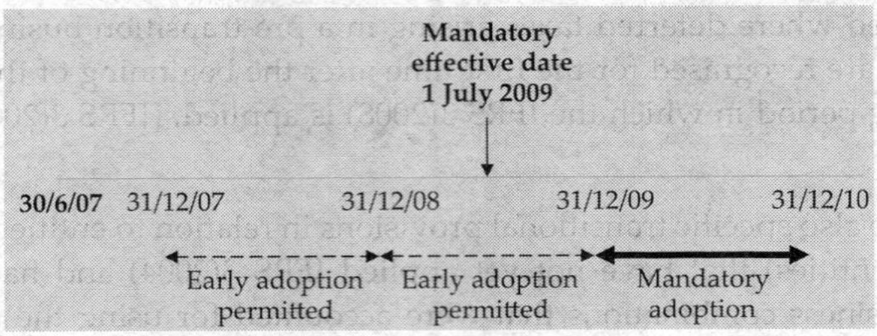

14.1.4 *Summary table for various reporting periods*

The table below shows the mandatory application date of IFRS 3(2008) and the earliest business combination that could be accounted for under IFRS 3(2008) if the Standard is adopted early.

End of annual reporting period	First mandatory application date in annual reporting periods ending	Date of earliest acquisition date for a business combination to which IFRS 3(2008) could be applied if early adopted
January	31 January 2011	1 February 2008
February	28 February 2011	1 March 2008
March	31 March 2011	1 April 2008
April	30 April 2011	1 May 2008
May	31 May 2011	1 June 2008
June	30 June 2010	1 July 2007
July	31 July 2010	1 August 2007
August	31 August 2010	1 September 2007
September	30 September 2010	1 October 2007
October	31 October 2010	1 November 2007
November	30 November 2010	1 December 2007
December	31 December 2010	1 January 2008

Note: *Different dates will apply where an entity changes its reporting period during the transitional period.*

14.2 Transition

14.2.1 *General principles*

Assets and liabilities that arose from business combinations whose acquisition dates preceded the application of the Standard are not adjusted upon application of IFRS 3(2008). [IFRS 3(2008).65] Similarly, many of the changes introduced in IAS 27(2008) only apply on a prospective basis, and the accounting adopted for transactions that occurred prior to the beginning of the first annual reporting period in which IAS 27(2008) is applied is not adjusted. [IAS 27(2008).45]

The acquisition date in a business combination, combined with the relevant annual reporting period to which IFRS 3(2008) is first applied, determines which version of IFRS 3 to apply when accounting for a particular business combination.

Acquisition date after IFRS 3(2008) is applied Where the acquisition date is on or after the beginning of the annual reporting period during which the IFRS 3(2008) is first applied, then IFRS 3(2008) must be applied in full to the transaction.

Acquisition date before IFRS 3(2008) is applied Where the acquisition date is before the beginning of the annual reporting period during which the IFRS 3(2008) is first applied, IFRS 3(2004) is applied when accounting for the business combination. Therefore:

- the initial accounting for the business combinations is in accordance with IFRS 3(2004);
- the initial accounting for the business combination (e.g. capitalised acquisition costs, initial measurement of non-controlling interests, adjustments to goodwill for the different method of accounting for step acquisitions, and so on) is not restated to reflect the new or revised requirements in IFRS 3(2008) when the revised Standard is first adopted;
- contingent consideration adjustments that arise in respect of the business combination are adjusted against the initial accounting for the business combination in accordance with IFRS 3(2004), resulting in an adjustment to goodwill; and
- comparative information is not adjusted.

However, the new requirements in IFRS 3(2008) and IAS 27(2008) are applied to:

- changes in ownership interests in a subsidiary occurring after the beginning of the annual reporting period in which IFRS 3(2008) and IAS 27(2008) are first applied, regardless of whether or not the subsidiary was acquired in a business combination that occurred prior to initial application of IFRS 3(2008) and IAS 27(2008); and
- deferred taxes adjustments occurring after the beginning of the annual reporting period in which IFRS 3(2008) and IAS 27(2008) are first applied – see **14.2.3** below.

Contingent consideration The intent of the Board appears to be that contingent consideration arising on business combinations occurring before IFRS 3(2008) is applied continues to be accounted for under IFRS 3(2004). Consequently, any adjustments continue to be made against goodwill. However, the interaction of this requirement in IFRS 3(2008) and the consequential amendment to IAS 39 is currently the subject of debate. As a consequence of IFRS 3(2008), paragraph 2(f) of IAS 39 is deleted with the effect that contracts for contingent consideration in a business combination are no longer excluded from the scope of IAS 39. The amendment to IAS 39 does not provide any transitional relief for contingent consideration relating to business combinations occurring before the implementation of IFRS 3(2008) with the effect that IAS 39 would apply to such 'brought forward' contingent consideration. On the basis that the US version of this requirement provides such transitional relief, it is suggested that the Board's drafting does not reflect their intent.

14.2.2 Entities previously outside the scope of IFRS 3

Mutual entities and combinations by contract alone were previously outside the scope of IFRS 3. IFRS 3(2008) will apply to those entities prospectively, as described above. For business combinations occurring in earlier periods:

[IFRS 3(2008).B68 – B69]

- classification – earlier business combinations continue to be classified in accordance with the entity's previous accounting policy;
- previously-recognised goodwill – elimination of any amortisation accumulated under the entity's previous accounting policy, but no change to net carrying amount;
- goodwill previously recognised as a deduction from equity – not recognised as an asset. Nor is the goodwill recognised in profit or loss when the business to which it relates is disposed of or when the relevant cash-generating unit is determined to be impaired;
- subsequent accounting for goodwill – discontinue amortisation (if any) and test for impairment; and
- previously-recognised negative goodwill – derecognise any amount carried as a deferred credit and adjust retained earnings.

14.2.3 *Income taxes*

Paragraph 68 of IAS 12 *Income Taxes*, which deals with changes in the measurement of deferred tax assets arising in business combinations, has been amended by IFRS 3(2008) (see **10.1.6**). These amendments are to be applied prospectively to the recognition of deferred tax assets acquired in business combinations from the effective date of IFRS 3(2008). [IAS 12.93]

Therefore, following the adoption of IFRS 3(2008), the rules of the revised Standard as regards subsequent recognition or remeasurement of deferred tax assets arising in business combinations apply both to business combinations occurring after the adoption of IFRS 3(2008), and prospectively to the recognition or remeasurement of deferred tax assets acquired in business combinations occurring before the adoption of IFRS 3(2008). Therefore, following the adoption of IFRS 3(2008), irrespective of the date of the original acquisition, the impact of the recognition or remeasurement of such deferred tax assets is recognised in profit or loss unless the benefits are recognised within the measurement period and those adjustments result from new information about facts and circumstances that existed at the acquisition date. [IAS 12.94]

Example 14.2.3A

Deferred tax assets determined provisionally

Company M has an annual reporting period that ends in December. On 15 November 2009, Company M acquires a 100% controlling interest in Company N and the business combination is accounted for in accordance with IFRS 3(2004). At the acquisition date, Company N has certain carry-forward tax benefits. It is not clear that Company N will be able to carry forward those tax benefits following its acquisition – the position requires detailed assessment under the relevant tax law of the jurisdiction in which Company N operates.

Company M engages tax advisors to assess whether the tax benefits will be available to Company N after the acquisition. At 31 December 2009, this assessment has not been completed and, based on preliminary assessment of the application of the relevant laws, a deferred tax asset is not recognised in the initial accounting for the business combination in accordance with IFRS 3(2004). Accounting for the acquired deferred tax benefits is identified as an item determined only provisionally in the 31 December 2009 financial statements.

Company M first applies IFRS 3(2008) in the accounting period ending 31 December 2010. On 30 April 2010, Company M's tax advisers conclude that 50 per cent of Company N's tax benefits can be carried forward. Accordingly, the deferred tax asset arising from 50 per cent of the tax benefits is recognised and an adjustment is made to the goodwill arising in the initial accounting for the business combination (which is sufficient to absorb the adjustment).

In February 2011, when the case comes for final ruling by the taxation authorities, it is determined that all of the tax benefits are available for carry-forward. Under the requirements of IFRS 3(2008), because this adjustment arises after the end of the measurement period, the benefit is not adjusted against goodwill but is recognised in profit or loss. The requirements of IFRS 3(2008 are applied even though the acquisition of Company N was originally accounted for under IFRS 3(2004).

Example 14.2.3B

Favourable change in tax law during the measurement period

Assume the same facts as in **example 14.2.3A** except that, in making their assessment in April 2010, the tax advisers make reference to a favourable change in the tax law that is substantively enacted in February 2010. Without this change in tax law, the tax benefits could not have been carried forward by Company N.

In this case, the recognition of the deferred tax asset is a direct result of the change in tax law that occurs in February 2010 and, therefore, it does not result from new information about facts and circumstances that existed at the acquisition date. Accordingly, the recognition of the deferred tax asset in April 2010 is recognised in profit or loss, even though it is recognised during the measurement period.

35 Investments in associates

1 Introduction

The appropriate accounting treatment for associates is dealt with in IAS 28 *Investments in Associates*. IAS 28 was last revised by the IASB in December 2003, and was most recently amended when *Improvements to IFRSs* was issued in May 2008.

This chapter discusses the requirements of IAS 28 in the following sections:

Section 2 Scope

Section 3 Significant influence

Section 4 Equity accounting for investments in associates

Section 5 Separate financial statements

Section 6 Presentation and disclosure

UK

The accounting for associates under IAS 28 is, in most respects, reasonably similar to that required under the UK standard, FRS 9 Associates and Joint Ventures, *but there are some important differences. The most significant of these are as follows.*

- *Under IAS 28, equity accounting can, in some circumstances, be required in financial statements other than consolidated financial statements. Under FRS 9, equity accounting is only possible in consolidated financial statements.*
- *When applying equity accounting under IAS 28, losses of an associate are recognised only until the point at which the investor's interest is reduced to nil. A liability in respect of an investment in an associate is recognised only to the extent that the investor has incurred legal or constructive obligations or made payments on behalf of the associate. This contrasts with FRS 9, under which losses continue to be recognised for as long as significant influence exists.*
- *Under FRS 9, the investor's shares of the associate's operating profit and of each line item after operating profit are presented separately in the profit and loss account. Under IAS 1* Presentation of Financial

> *Statements, a single figure is shown in the statement of comprehensive income, being the investor's share of profit or loss after tax.*
>
> *In addition, there are some other differences of presentation and disclosure.*

2 Scope

IAS 28 generally applies to investments in associates. An associate is an entity, including an unincorporated entity such as a partnership, over which the investor has significant influence, and which is neither a subsidiary nor an interest in a joint venture. [IAS 28.2] The concept of significant influence is discussed in **section 3** below.

IAS 28 excludes from its scope certain investments in associates held by venture capital organisations, and by mutual funds, unit trusts and similar entities (including investment-linked insurance funds). Where investments held by such entities are, at the time of their initial recognition, designated as at fair value through profit or loss or classified as held for trading and accounted for in accordance with IAS 39 *Financial Instruments: Recognition and Measurement*, these investments are excluded from the scope of IAS 28 and are measured at fair value in accordance with IAS 39, with changes in fair value recognised in profit or loss in the period of change. [IAS 28.1]

For periods beginning on or after 1 January 2009, where an entity holds such an investment, it must provide the disclosures required by IAS 28.37(f) (see **6.2.1** below). This amendment to IAS 28 was made by *Improvements to IFRSs* issued in May 2008, which also amended IAS 28.33 (see **4.3.3.5** below). Earlier application of these amendments to IAS 28 is permitted, but an entity choosing to apply the amendments early must disclose that fact and must also apply the related amendments to IFRS 7.3, IAS 31.1 (see **section 2** in **chapter 36**) and IAS 32.4 (see **2.1** in **chapter 13**). The amendments may be applied prospectively.

> Note that, in order to qualify for exclusion, the investments held by venture capital organisations and similar entities must be identified and appropriately designated at the time of their initial recognition. Investments held by such entities that are not designated at the time of their initial recognition as at fair value through profit or loss or classified as held for trading will fall within the scope of IAS 28.

Example 2

Accounting for an associate at the group level

Company P, which is not a venture capital organisation, is a parent entity in a group that has an 80 per cent ownership in a subsidiary, Company S. Company S has a 40 per cent ownership in an associate, Company A. Company S is a venture capital organisation, and has made the designation under IAS 28.1(a) to account for its interest in the associate at fair value through profit or loss.

The designation made by S under IAS 28.1(a) can be carried forward to P's consolidated financial statements. Hence, P has an accounting policy choice either to carry the associate at fair value under IAS 39, or to apply the equity method in its consolidated financial statements. This accounting policy choice can be made on an associate-by-associate basis (provided that the associate is held by a subsidiary that qualifies for the scope exemption), i.e. some associates may be accounted for at fair value and some may be accounted for under the equity method.

The accounting policy choice should be made upon recognition of an associate and should be applied consistently from one period to the next.

3 Significant influence

The key question in determining whether an investment should be accounted for as an associate is whether the investor has significant influence over it. Significant influence is the power to participate in the financial and operating policy decisions of the investee, but is not control or joint control over those policies. [IAS 28.2]

Financial and operating policies are not defined in IAS 28. Operating policies generally would include those policies that guide activities such as sales, marketing, manufacturing, human resources, and acquisitions and disposals of investments. Financial policies generally would be those policies that guide accounting policies, budget approvals, credit terms, dividend policies, issuance of debt, cash management and capital expenditures.

3.1 Indicators of significant influence

When an investor exercises significant influence over the investee, one or more of the following indicators is usually present:

[IAS 28.7]

- representation on the board of directors or equivalent governing body of the investee;
- participation in policy-making processes, including participation in decisions about dividends or other distributions;
- material transactions between the investor and the investee;
- interchange of managerial personnel; or
- provision of essential technical information.

3.2 Holding 20 per cent or more of voting power

As a general rule, significant influence is presumed to exist when an investor holds, directly or indirectly through subsidiaries, 20 per cent or more of the voting power of the investee. [IAS 28.6]

This presumption relates to voting rights, which can arise not just in relation to an ordinary shareholding. For example, where 50 per cent of the voting rights in an entity are held by the ordinary shareholders, and the other 50 per cent of the voting rights are attached to voting preferred shares, an investment in four per cent of the ordinary shares and 36 per cent of the voting preferred shares will result in a presumption that the four per cent ordinary share ownership will be accounted for under the equity method, provided the voting preferred share investment is, with respect to voting rights, substantively the same as an investment in ordinary shares.

As with the classification of any investment, the substance of the arrangements in each case will need to be considered. If it can be clearly demonstrated that an investor holding 20 per cent or more of the voting power of the investee does not exercise significant influence, the investment will not be accounted for as an associate. [IAS 28.6]

A substantial or majority ownership by another investor does not necessarily preclude an investor from having significant influence. [IAS 28.6]

Circumstances that may indicate that an investor lacks the ability to exercise significant influence include:

- the chairman of the investee owns a large, but not necessarily controlling, block of the investee's outstanding stock. The combination of his substantial shareholding and his position with the investee may preclude the investor from having an ability to influence the investee;

- adverse political and economic conditions exist in the foreign country where the investee is located;

- opposition by the investee, such as litigation or complaints to governmental regulatory authorities, challenges the investor's ability to exercise significant influence;

- the investor and the investee sign an agreement under which the investor surrenders significant rights as shareholder;

- majority ownership of the investee is concentrated among a small group of shareholders who operate the investee without regard to the views of the investor; and

- litigation against an investee, particularly where the investee is in bankruptcy, is to be settled by the investee issuing shares to the settling parties, and it is probable that the new shares, when issued, will reduce the investor's ownership percentage.

3.3 Holding less than 20 per cent of voting power

If the investor holds, directly or indirectly through subsidiaries, less than 20 per cent of the voting power of the investee, it is presumed that the investor does not have significant influence, unless such influence can be clearly demonstrated. [IAS 28.6] The presence of one or more of the indicators set out in **3.1** may indicate that an investor exercises significant influence over a less than 20 per cent-owned corporate investee.

In addition, the following indicators could provide evidence of significant influence:

- the investor has veto power over significant operating and financial decisions but affirmative voting is not required for their approval;

- the investor's extent of ownership is significant relative to other shareholdings (i.e. a lack of concentration of other shareholders);

- the investor's significant shareholders, its parent, fellow subsidiaries, or officers of the investor, hold additional investment in the investee (indirect ownership); and

- the investor is a member of significant investee committees, such as the executive committee or the finance committee.

Example 3.3

Significant influence in a group scenario

Company A has two subsidiaries, Company B and Company C. Company B has a 15 per cent ownership interest in C. The group structure is as follows:

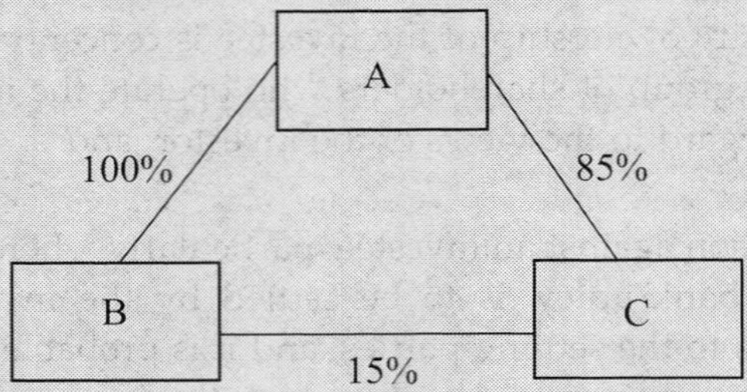

Company A has appointed an executive of B as a director to the board of C. Because of the number of directors on the board, this director is able to influence significantly C's board. Company A has the right to remove the executive from the board at any time. Company B has also been directed by A to manage C in a way that maximises the return from both B and C, which are located in the same jurisdiction. Company A can amend this directive at any time.

IAS 28.6 indicates that a substantial or majority ownership by another investor does not necessarily preclude an investor from having significant influence. In this scenario, however, B does not have significant influence over C. Although B can participate in policy-making decisions, A can remove B's executive from C's board at any time. Therefore, B's apparent position of significant influence over C can be removed by A and B does not have the power to exercise significant influence over C.

3.4 Potential voting rights

Potential voting rights can arise through share warrants, share call options, debt or equity instruments that are convertible into ordinary shares, or similar instruments that have the potential, if exercised or converted, to give the holder additional voting power or reduce another party's voting power over the financial and operating policies of another entity. Where an investor owns such instruments, the existence and effect of potential voting rights that are currently exercisable or currently convertible are considered when assessing whether the investor has significant influence over that other entity. Potential voting rights are not currently exercisable or convertible when, for example, they cannot be exercised or converted until a future date or until the occurrence of a future event. [IAS 28.8]

The investor needs to consider the potential voting rights held by other parties in addition to those it holds itself. Although the investor may believe, after considering the impact of its own potential voting rights, that it exercises significant influence, that impact may be negated by other potential voting rights held by other parties that are also currently exercisable or currently convertible.

In assessing whether potential voting rights contribute to significant influence, the investor examines all facts and circumstances that affect the potential rights, such as the terms of exercise of the instruments and any other contractual arrangements. IAS 28 requires that all of these factors be taken into account – but excludes consideration of the intention of management and the financial ability to exercise or convert. [IAS 28.9]

Example 3.4

Options to purchase investments in an entity

Company A holds a 15 per cent voting ordinary share interest in Company B, as well as a European call option (i.e. one that can only be exercised at the end of the option period) to acquire an additional 10 per cent voting ordinary share interest in Company B which matures in three years. Company A's ownership of the call option, which, if converted, would give Company A a 25 per cent voting interest in Company B, does not create the presumption that Company A currently exercises significant influence over Company B, as the call option is not currently exercisable. If, however, rather than a European call option Company A held an American call option (i.e. one that can be exercised at any time during the option period), Company A may effectively exert significant influence over Company B as the call option would be currently exercisable.

Further implementation guidance in relation to the consideration of potential voting rights accompanies IAS 27 *Consolidated and Separate Financial Statements*. The guidance, which is equally applicable to the determination of significant influence under IAS 28, is discussed at **3.2** in **chapter 33**.

3.5 Investments in preferred shares

When an investment in preferred shares is determined to be substantively the same as an investment in ordinary shares, the investment may give the investor significant influence in which case the investment should be accounted for using the equity method. Factors that either individually or collectively may indicate that a preferred share investment is substantively the same as an ordinary share investment include:

- the investee has little or no significant ordinary shares or other equity, on a fair value basis that is subordinate to the preferred shares;

- the investor, regardless of ownership percentage, has demonstrated the power to exercise significant influence over the investee's operating and financial decisions. The power to participate actively is an important factor in determining whether an equity interest exists by virtue of preferred shareholdings;

- the investee's preferred shares have essentially the same rights and characteristics as the investee's ordinary shares as regards voting rights, board representation, and participation in, or rate of return approximating, the ordinary share dividend; and

- the preferred shares have a conversion feature (with significant value in relation to the total value of the shares) to convert the preferred shares to ordinary shares.

An investor may have a variety of interests in an associate, both long-term and short-term, including ordinary or preferred shares, loans, advances, debt securities, options to acquire ordinary shares, and trade receivables. For the purposes of IAS 28.29, which considers the extent to which losses of an associate should be recognised (see **4.3.8** below), the investor's interest in the associate is the carrying amount of the investment in the associate under the equity method together with any long-term interests that, in substance, form part of the investor's net investment in the associate. [IAS 28.29]

For example, an item for which settlement is neither planned nor likely to occur in the foreseeable future is, in substance, an extension of the entity's investment in that associate. Such items may include preference shares and long-terms receivables or loans. Items such as trade receivables, trade payables and any long-term receivables for which adequate collateral exists, such as secured loans, will not fall to be treated as part of the investor's interest in an associate for this purpose. [IAS 28.29]

The implication of IAS 28.29 is apparently that only ordinary shares (and other shares that are substantively the same as ordinary shares) will be presented as part of the carrying amount of the investment in the associate under the equity method. Other long-term interests that, in substance, form part of the investor's net investment in the associate, will be taken into account in recognising losses, but will nevertheless be presented separately from the carrying amount of the investment in the associate under the equity method.

Example 3.5

Accounting for a long-term loan to an equity-accounted investment

An entity (investor) grants a long-term interest-free loan to one of its equity-accounted associates (investee). The loan has no fixed repayment terms and settlement of the loan is neither planned nor likely to occur in the foreseeable future.

From the standpoint of the investee, the investee has a contractual obligation to deliver cash or another financial asset to the investor. Accordingly, the loan payable will be classified as a financial liability within the scope of IAS 39 *Financial Instruments: Recognition and Measurement* as it does not meet the definition of equity.

While the investor has the contractual right to receive cash or another financial asset from the investee, the investor views the loan as part of the net investment in the investee as, in accordance with IAS 28.29, the settlement of the loan is neither planned nor likely to occur in the foreseeable future.

In the investor's financial statements (both consolidated and, if applicable, separate), the interest-free loan is classified and measured in accordance with IAS 39. In general, the loan asset will be classified as a loan and receivable or may be designated as an available-for-sale financial asset.

IAS 28 determines whether the long-term interest-free loan can be viewed as part of the interest in the investee when accounting for losses of the investee in accordance with IAS 28.29, which states, in part:

> 'The interest in an associate is the carrying amount of the investment in the associate under the equity method together with any long-term interests that, in substance, form part of the investor's net investment in the associate.'

For the purpose of accounting for losses of an investee, the loan would form part of the investor's net investment in the investee as its settlement is neither planned nor likely to occur in the foreseeable future.

3.6 Ceasing to have significant influence

Significant influence over an investee is lost when the investor loses the power to participate in the financial and operating policy decisions of that investee. The loss of significant influence can occur with or without a change in absolute or relative ownership levels. It could occur, for example, when an associate becomes subject to the control of a government, court, administrator or regulator. It could also occur as a result of a contractual agreement. [IAS 28.10]

4 Equity accounting for investments in associates

4.1 Associates generally accounted for using the equity method

IAS 28 defines the equity method as a method of accounting whereby the investment is initially recognised at cost and adjusted thereafter for the post-acquisition change in the investor's share of net assets of the investee. The profit or loss of the investor includes the investor's share of the profit or loss of the investee. [IAS 28.2]

The general rule is that investments in associates are accounted for using the equity method of accounting. [IAS 28.13] Since the investor exerts significant influence over the associate, the equity method of accounting is appropriate as it communicates the stewardship of management in carrying out its responsibilities related to the associate more clearly than if the investment were accounted for on the basis of the direct equity interest.

Equity accounting is used whether or not the investor, because it also has subsidiaries, prepares consolidated financial statements. However, the investor does not apply the equity method when presenting separate financial statements prepared in accordance with IAS 27 *Consolidated and Separate Financial Statements* (see **section 5** below).

UK

The requirement, in certain circumstances, to apply equity accounting other than in group accounts is different from UK GAAP, which permits equity accounting only in consolidated financial statements. UK companies with interests in associates but no subsidiaries should be mindful of this difference when transitioning to IFRSs.

4.2 Exemptions from applying the equity method

An investment in an associate is not accounted for using the equity method when:

[IAS 28.13]

- the investment is classified as held for sale in accordance with IFRS 5 *Non-current Assets Held for Sale and Discontinued Operations*, in which case it should be accounted for under that Standard (see **chapter 29**);
- the investor is a parent that is exempt from preparing consolidated financial statements under IAS 27 (see **4.2** in **chapter 33**) and prepares separate financial statements as its primary financial statements. In those separate statements, the investment in the associate may be accounted for at cost or under IAS 39 *Financial Instruments: Recognition and Measurement*; or
- all of the following apply:
  - the investor is a wholly-owned subsidiary, or is a partially-owned subsidiary of another entity and its other owners, including those not otherwise entitled to vote, have been informed about, and do not object to, the investor not applying the equity method;
  - the investor's debt or equity instruments are not traded in a public market;
  - the investor did not file, nor is it in the process of filing, its financial statements with a securities commission or other regulatory organisation for the purpose of issuing any class of instruments in a public market; and
  - the ultimate or any intermediate parent of the investor produces consolidated financial statements available for public use that comply with IFRSs.

A public market here means a domestic or foreign stock exchange or an over-the-counter market, including local and regional markets.

4.3 Application of the equity method

Under the equity method, an investment is initially recorded at cost, and the carrying amount is adjusted thereafter for:

[IAS 28.11]

- the investor's share of the post-acquisition profits or losses of the investee, which are recognised in the investor's profit or loss;
- distributions received from the investee, which reduce the carrying amount of the investment; and
- changes in the investor's proportionate interest in the investee arising from changes in the investee's other comprehensive income (such as the impact of property revaluations and some exchange differences). These are recognised in other comprehensive income of the investor.

The investor's share of the associate's profits or losses after acquisition is also adjusted to take account of items such as additional depreciation of depreciable assets based on their fair values at the acquisition date.

4.3.1 *Share of profits or losses*

4.3.1.1 Proportionate ownership interest

The investor's share of the associate's profits or losses, or other changes in the associate's equity, is determined on the basis of its proportionate ownership interest.

> The investor generally records its share of the investee's earnings and losses based on the percentage of the equity interest owned by the investor. When, however, agreements designate allocations among the investors of profits and losses, certain costs and expenses, distributions from operations, or distributions upon liquidation that are different from ownership percentages, recording equity method income based on the percentage of the equity interest owned may not be appropriate. The substance of these agreements should be reflected in determining how an increase or decrease in net assets of the investee will affect cash payments to the investor over the life of the investee and upon its liquidation.

4.3.1.2 Potential voting rights

When potential voting rights exist (see **3.4** above), only the investor's present ownership interests are taken into account in determining the investor's share of the associate's profits or losses. That share does not reflect the possible exercise or conversion of potential voting rights. [IAS 28.12]

4.3.1.3 *Aggregation of group interests*

Where the investor is a parent, the group's share of the associate is the aggregate of the holdings in that associate by the parent and its subsidiaries. The holdings of the parent's other associates and joint ventures are ignored for this purpose. [IAS 28.21]

When an associate has subsidiaries, associates or joint ventures, the profits or losses and net assets taken into account in applying the equity method are those recognised in the associate's financial statements (including the associate's share of the profits or losses and net assets of its associates and joint ventures), after any adjustments necessary to give effect to uniform accounting policies (see **4.3.5** below). [IAS 28.21]

4.3.1.4 *Cumulative preference shares*

If the associate has outstanding cumulative preference shares held by outside interests and classified as equity, the investor computes its share of profits or losses after adjusting for the preference dividends, whether declared or not. [IAS 28.28]

4.3.1.5 *Reciprocal interests*

Example 4.3.1.5A

Accounting for treasury shares held by an associate

Company A, an investor, owns an interest in an associate entity, Company B, and B concurrently owns an interest in A. Company A applies the equity method of accounting to its investment in B. Company B's investment is determined to be a reciprocal interest. (Note that judgement is required when determining whether the interest held by B is a reciprocal interest rather than an investment held as part of a trading portfolio. This example does not address the factors affecting such a judgement.)

How should A account for the reciprocal equity interest held by B when the reciprocal equity interest is accounted for in Company B's financial statements:

- using the equity method under IAS 28?
- as an investment (either at cost or in accordance with IAS 39 *Financial Instruments: Recognition and Measurement*)?

The reciprocal interest should be eliminated. The requirements of IAS 28.20 apply to accounting for reciprocal equity interests regardless of how the investee has accounted for the reciprocal interest. Consequently, the accounting treatment of the investment in B's financial statements does not affect how A should account for the reciprocal interest.

IAS 28.20 states that many of the procedures appropriate for the application of the equity method are similar to the consolidation procedures described in IAS 27, and that the concepts underlying the procedures used in accounting for the acquisition of a subsidiary are also adopted in accounting for the acquisition of an investment in an associate.

Reciprocal interests should be treated in a similar manner to an investor's own shares, resulting in consolidation elimination entries to eliminate the investor's share of the reciprocal interests. Therefore, Company A, the investor, will show a reduction in its investment in the equity method investee and its own share capital as though it held treasury shares. It will also eliminate any dividends received on these shares by the associate from its share of the associate profits.

To illustrate, Company A owns a 30 per cent interest in Company B, and B owns a 20 per cent interest in A. Company A and Company B have 10,000 shares and 5,000 shares, respectively, of common stock issued and outstanding, and each paid £100 per share for their respective ownership interests in each other.

Company A's basis in its investment in B, and B's corresponding reciprocal interest in A, are calculated as follows:

B's basis in A = £100/share × (20 per cent × 10,000 shares) = £200,000

A's reciprocal interest in B = 30 per cent × £200,000 = £60,000

The reduction in A's investment should be offset by a decrease in retained earnings, and the offset to the reduction may be presented as a separate line item in the equity section in a manner similar to treasury stock.

Company B's investment in A, and A's reciprocal interest in B, would be calculated and accounted for in a similar fashion:

A's basis in B = £100/share × (30 per cent × 5,000 shares) = £150,000

B's reciprocal interest in A = 20 per cent × £150,000 = £30,000

If earnings of Company A exclusive of any equity in Company B total £100,000 ('direct earnings of A'), and earnings of B exclusive of any equity in A total £50,000 ('direct earnings of B'), net income and earnings per share for A and B, respectively, are calculated as follows:

Income of A before equity in B = £100,000

Equity in direct earnings of B = 30 per cent × £50,000 = £15,000

Net income of A = £100,000 + £15,000 = £115,000

10,000 shares of A – [30 per cent × (20 per cent × 10,000 shares held by B)] = 10,000 – 600 = 9,400

Earnings per share of A = £115,000 ÷ 9,400 shares = £12.23 per share

Although A owns 30 per cent of B, A's investment in B is reduced for its ownership interests in itself through the reciprocal holdings by B of A's stock. Company B's ownership of A is reduced in a similar fashion as shown below:

Income of B before equity in A = £50,000

Equity in direct earnings of A = 20 per cent × £100,000 = £20,000

Net income of B = £50,000 + £20,000 = £70,000

5,000 shares of B – [20 per cent × (30 per cent × 5,000 shares held by A)] = 5,000 – 300 = 4,700

Earnings per share of B = £70,000 ÷ 4,700 shares = £14.89 per share

Example 4.3.1.5B

Accounting for treasury shares of venture capital organisations

Company A owns an interest in an associate entity, Company B, and B concurrently owns an interest in A. The investments are determined to be reciprocal interests. A is a venture capital organisation that measures its investment in B at fair vale in accordance with IAS 39 *Financial Instruments: Recognition and Measurement*. How should A account for the reciprocal equity interest held by B?

The reciprocal interest should not be eliminated. Although IAS 28.20 states, in part, that "the concepts underlying the procedures used in accounting for the acquisition of a subsidiary are also adopted in accounting for the acquisition of an investment in an associate", venture capitalists that measure their investment at fair value in accordance with IAS 39 are not required to apply IAS 28. Therefore, IAS 28.20 does not apply. Consequently, the reciprocal equity interests are not eliminated at the investor level.

4.3.2 *Distributions received from an associate*

Distributions received from an associate reduce the carrying amount of the investor's interest in the associate. [IAS 28.11]

IAS 28 does not address the accounting for distributions by equity method investees to an investor in excess of the investor's carrying amount. If distributions by an equity method investee to an investor are in excess of the investor's carrying amount, and (a) the distributions are not refundable by agreement or law, and (b) the investor is not liable for the obligations of the investee or otherwise committed to provide financial support to the investee, then cash distributions received in excess of the investment in the investee should be recorded as income. If the investee subsequently reports net income, the investor should resume applying the equity method in accordance with IAS 28 once the investee has made sufficient profits to cover the aggregate of any investee losses not recognised by the investor (due to the investor's zero balance in the investment) and any income previously recognised for excess cash distributions.

Example 4.3.2A

Accounting for distributions by an equity method investee in excess of the investor's carrying amount (1)

Company A has invested £1 million for a 50 per cent ownership interest in Company C. Company A uses the equity method to account for its investment in Company C. Company C subsequently incurs a loss of £2.4 million, which exceeds Company A's investment balance by £200,000. As the losses are due to non-cash depreciation expense and Company C has available cash, it distributes £100,000 to Company A.

The £100,000 distribution made to Company A is not refundable by agreement or law, and Company A is not liable for the obligations of Company C or otherwise committed to provide financial support to Company C. Therefore, Company A should reduce its investment in Company C to zero and record the £100,000 received as income. When Company C becomes profitable such that Company A's share of Company C's earnings exceeds the distributions and share of unrecognised losses attributable to Company A (i.e. £300,000), Company A will resume applying the equity method in accordance with IAS 28.

Even where the investor is not legally obliged to refund the distribution, the need for judgement and consideration of specific facts and circumstances, including the relationship among the investors, is still required. If distributions by an investee to an investor are in excess of the investor's carrying amount, and (a) the distribution may be refundable by convention, or (b) the investor may become liable for the obligations of the investee or is otherwise expected to provide financial support to the investee, then cash distributions received in excess of the investment in the investee should be recorded as a liability. If the investee subsequently reports net income, the investor should first reverse the liability and then record its investment in the investee as an asset.

In circumstances where the investor has undertaken to provide financial support to the investee, it will be necessary to consider whether any additional provision or disclosure is required in accordance with IAS 37 *Provisions, Contingent Liabilities and Contingent Assets* (see **chapter 11**).

Example 4.3.2B

Accounting for distributions by an equity method investee in excess of the investor's carrying amount (2)

Company B has invested £1 million for a 50 per cent ownership interest in Company C. Company B uses the equity method to account for its investment in Company C. Company C subsequently incurs a loss of £2.4 million, which exceeds Company B's investment balance by £200,000. As the losses are due to non-cash depreciation expense and Company C has available cash, it distributes £100,000 to Company B.

The £100,000 distribution made to Company B is not refundable by agreement or law, and Company B is not liable for Company C's obligations. However, Company B has committed to providing financial support to Company C. Therefore, Company B should reduce its investment in Company C to zero, but also record a liability of £300,000 for equity in losses of £200,000 and the £100,000 cash received. When Company C becomes profitable such that Company B's share of Company C's earnings exceeds the distributions and share of unrecognised losses attributable to Company B, Company B will reverse the liability before increasing the carrying amount of its investment in Company C.

Separately, Company B should consider whether any additional provision or disclosure is required in accordance with IAS 37 *Provisions, Contingent Liabilities and Contingent Assets* (see **chapter 11**).

4.3.3 *Commencing use of the equity method*

4.3.3.1 *Date of commencing use of the equity method*

An investment in an associate is accounted for under the equity method as from the date on which it falls within the definition of an associate. [IAS 28.23]

Commencement of equity-method accounting will generally occur at the date that the investor acquires or increases its interest in the associate such that significant influence is achieved. Other events that might qualify an investment to be accounted for under the equity method include:

- an investee in which the investor holds more than 20 per cent emerges from bankruptcy. During the bankruptcy, the investee's board of directors had no power to direct the investee's operating and financial policies, with all decisions instead being made by an independent administrator appointed following a vote by the investee's creditors. The investor had stopped applying the equity method of accounting for its investment during the bankruptcy because it was unable to exercise significant influence over the investee, and

- an investor's representation on the board of directors of an investee increases without a corresponding increase in the investor's investment (e.g. a board member resigns and is not replaced, thereby increasing the investor's representation, or alternatively, the investor is given or gains another seat on the board for no consideration).

4.3.3.2 *Investments previously classified as held for sale*

When an investment in an associate previously classified as held for sale in accordance with IFRS 5 no longer meets the criteria to be so classified, it should be accounted for using the equity method as from the date of its classification as held for sale. Financial statements for periods since classification as held of sale are amended accordingly. [IAS 28.15]

4.3.3.3 *Recording the initial investment*

On the acquisition of an investment in an associate, any difference between the cost of the investment and the investor's share of the net fair value of the associate's identifiable assets and liabilities is accounted for as follows:

[IAS 28.23]

- goodwill relating to an associate is included in the carrying amount of the investment. IAS 38 *Intangible Assets* does not permit the amortisation of goodwill (see **4.3.3.5**); and
- any excess of the investor's share of the net fair value of the associate's identifiable assets and liabilities over the cost of the investment is included as income in the determination of the investor's share of the associate's profit or loss in the period in which the investment is acquired.

The investor's proportionate share of the assets acquired and liabilities assumed would be adjusted for write-ups or write-downs to fair value in the same manner as a business combination accounted for using the purchase method under IFRS 3. The investor would then amortise its proportionate share of any purchase accounting adjustments over the period necessary to match them against the related assets and liabilities. Any further acquisitions of ownership interests of the investee would also be accounted for as purchase acquisitions.

Example 4.3.3.3A

Recording of initial investment (1)

Company A purchased 35 per cent of Company B's outstanding shares for an amount in excess of the recorded value of 35 per cent of Company B's net assets. Company B's assets are composed solely of investments in debt securities that Company B has classified as held-to-maturity in accordance with IAS 39, and there are no liabilities. The fair value of the debt securities is in excess of the carrying amount, and the proportionate difference between the amount Company A paid for its investment and its proportionate interest in Company B's net assets is equal to the difference between the carrying amount and fair value of the debt securities after consideration of income taxes.

In this case, the difference can be attributed to the specific assets and the amounts should be recorded accordingly. Any future gain or loss on disposal of the assets reported by Company B would be adjusted by Company A to reflect the fair value recognised on acquisition.

Example 4.3.3.3B

Recording of initial investment (2)

Company A purchased 35 per cent of Company B's outstanding shares for an amount in excess of the recorded value of 35 per cent of Company B's net assets. Company A's purchase price cannot be attributed to specific assets of Company B. Therefore, the difference would remain a component of the recorded investment as goodwill accounted for under IFRS 3. Such goodwill is not amortised, but is tested for impairment as part of the carrying amount of the investment (see **4.3.3.5**).

4.3.3.4 Associate acquired in stages

Prior to the adoption of IFRS 3(2008), when an associate is acquired in stages, goodwill may be calculated on a mixed measurement basis as the aggregate of the amounts of goodwill determined for each tranche of shares purchased. Under this approach, for each tranche, the associated goodwill is determined by deducting the share of the net fair value of the identifiable assets and liabilities acquired from the price paid for that tranche. This is by analogy to the guidance in IFRS 3(2004) on business combinations achieved in stages or 'piece-meal' acquisitions as they are commonly known.

With the introduction of IFRS 3(2008) and consequential amendments to IAS 28, as reflected in IAS 28.23, goodwill is calculated on the acquisition of significant influence only, as the difference between the cost of the investment and the investor's share of the net fair value of the associate's identifiable assets and liabilities. Therefore, it is no longer appropriate to calculate goodwill on a mixed measurement basis.

In accordance with IAS 28.11, the investment in the associate undertaking is initially recognised at cost. The fair value of the original investment at the date of re-categorisation and the cost paid for the additional stake will be the deemed cost of the investment in the associate. But it is not clear from IAS 28 whether any gains or losses arising on the original investment since its acquisition should be reflected in profit or loss at this point.

As IAS 28 provides no clear guidance on this matter, by way of accounting policy choice, an entity may either:

- treat the transaction as a disposal of the original investment for fair value and an acquisition of an associate, by analogy to IFRS 3(2008), with the result that a gain or loss on the disposal will typically be reflected in profit or loss; or

- recognise a revaluation gain on the original tranche in an appropriate component of equity in order to get to the appropriate starting point for equity accounting. Under this approach, where the original investment has been classified previously as an available-for-sale financial asset under IAS 39 *Financial Instruments: Recognition and Measurement*, the revaluation gain or loss recognised in other comprehensive income should not be reclassified from equity to profit or loss as this investment continues to be held. Where the original investment was measured at cost in accordance with IAS 39.46(c), a revaluation gain is required to recognise the investment at fair value and to calculate goodwill. No gain or loss should be recognised in profit or loss under this approach, as there has been no realisation event, e.g. a disposal.

This accounting policy should be applied consistently for all situations where the acquisition of an associate undertaking is achieved in stages.

Therefore, where an entity has classified its equity interest in the original investment as available-for-sale and measured it at fair value with changes taken to other comprehensive income, it will have an accounting policy choice either:

- to reclassify the changes in value on this tranche from equity to profit or loss on acquisition of the additional stake, by analogy to IFRS 3(2008); or
- to leave the gains or losses in equity.

If the entity has measured the original investment at cost (for example, because the instruments did not have a quoted market price in an active market and their fair value could not be measured reliably), it will have an accounting policy choice either:

- to treat the increase in stake as a disposal of the original investment and an acquisition of an associate with a resulting gain or loss reflected in profit or loss; or
- to recognise a revaluation gain in other comprehensive income in order to measure the original tranche at fair value.

4.3.3.5 *Subsequent accounting for goodwill*

The portion of the difference between the cost of an investment and the amount of the underlying equity in net assets of an associate that is recognised as goodwill in accordance with IAS 28 should not be amortised. Since goodwill that forms part of the carrying amount of an equity accounted investment is not separately recognised, neither is it tested for impairment separately by applying the requirements for impairment testing goodwill in IAS 36 *Impairment of Assets*. Instead, the entire carrying amount of the investment is tested for impairment in accordance with IAS 36 as a single asset, by comparing its recoverable amount with its carrying amount whenever, based on the requirements in IAS 39 *Financial Instruments: Recognition and Measurement*, there is an indication of impairment (see **4.3.10**). [IAS 28.33] (Note that this is different from the position for goodwill recognised separately, for which impairment testing is required annually irrespective of whether there are indicators of impairment.)

For periods beginning on or after 1 January 2009, IAS 28 is amended to make it clear that an impairment loss recognised in the circumstances above is not allocated to any asset, including goodwill, that forms part of the carrying amount of the investment in the associate. Accordingly, any reversal of that impairment loss is recognised in accordance with IAS 36 to the extent that the recoverable amount of the investment subsequently increases.

This amendment to IAS 28 was made by *Improvements to IFRSs* issued in May 2008, which also amended IAS 28.1 (see **section 2** above). Earlier application of these amendments to IAS 28 is permitted, but an entity choosing to apply the amendments early must disclose that fact and must also apply the related amendments to IFRS 7.3, IAS 31.1 (see **section 2** in **chapter 36**) and IAS 32.4 (see **2.1** in **chapter 13**). The amendments may be applied prospectively.

4.3.4 Reporting periods of associates

When applying the equity method, the investor uses the most recent financial statements of the associate. When the associate's reporting period is different from that of the investor, the associate will prepare additional financial statements, for the investor's use, corresponding to the investor's reporting period, unless it is impracticable to do so, in which case financial statements prepared for a different reporting period may be used. [IAS 28.24] The difference between the end of the reporting period of the associate and that of the investor, however, can never be more than three months. [IAS 28.25]

The length of the reporting periods used and any difference between the ends of the reporting periods should be consistent from period to period. [IAS 28.25]

When financial statements of an associate with a different reporting period are used, adjustments are made for the effects of any significant events or transactions that occur between the end of the associate's reporting period and the end of the investor's reporting period. [IAS 28.25]

4.3.5 Uniform accounting policies

The investor's financial statements should be prepared using uniform accounting policies for like transactions and events in similar circumstances. [IAS 28.26] Where an associate uses different accounting policies for like transactions and events, the associate's financial statements used for the purposes of equity accounting are adjusted to conform the associate's accounting policies to those of the investor. [IAS 28.27]

4.3.6 *Transactions with associates*

Where an associate is accounted for using the equity method, unrealised profits and losses resulting from upstream (associate -> group) or downstream (group -> associate) transactions should be eliminated to the extent of the investor's interest in the associate. [IAS 28.22]

Upstream: If an investor purchases goods from an associate and the goods have not been sold by the investor to a third party at period end, the entry to eliminate the investor's share of the unrealised profit on the inventories would be taken against income from associates.

Downstream: If an investor sells goods to an associate and the goods have not been sold by the associate to a third party at period end, the journal entry to eliminate the investor's share of the unrealised profit on the inventories would be taken against consolidated profit or loss (usually cost of sales).

Example 4.3.6A

Elimination of profits and losses on transactions with associates

Assume the following:

- An investor owns 30 per cent of an investee.
- The investment is accounted for under the equity method.
- The income tax rate for both investor and investee is 40 per cent.
- Both are able, under IAS 12 *Income Taxes*, to recognise deferred tax assets for net deductible temporary differences.

Downstream

The investor sells inventory items to the investee. On the investee's balance sheet date, the investee holds inventory for which the investor has recorded a gross profit of £300,000. The investor's net income would be reduced by £54,000 to reflect a £90,000 (300,000 × 30 per cent) reduction in gross profit and a £36,000 (90,000 × 40 per cent) reduction in income tax expense. The investor reduces its investment in the investee by £90,000 and recognises a £36,000 deferred tax asset (subject to the IAS 12 recognition criteria).

Upstream

The investee sells inventory items to the investor. On the investor's balance sheet date, the investor holds inventory for which the investee has recorded a gross profit of £200,000. In the computation of the investor's equity in the investee's earnings, £120,000 (£200,000 less 40 per cent of income tax) would be deducted from the investee's net income and £36,000 (the investor's 30 per cent share of the intercompany gross profit after income tax) would be eliminated from the investor's equity income. The investor also would reduce the carrying amount of its inventory by £60,000 (the investor's share of the investee's gross profit) and recognise a deferred tax asset of £24,000 (£60,000 × 40 per cent).

No adjustment is required to be made to the investor's sales figure in its financial statements (because the purchases of the associate are not included in the cost of sales figure). However, sales to associates are disclosable as related party transactions (see **chapter 32**).

The investor's income tax provision usually will equal the sum of current and deferred tax expense, including any tax consequences of its interest in earnings and temporary differences attributable to its investment in an equity method investee. The tax consequences of the investor's interest in earnings and temporary differences attributable to its investment in the investee should not be offset against the investor's interest in earnings, because it is the investor's tax provision, not the investee's

Example 4.3.6B

Elimination of intragroup transactions when applying the equity method

An entity lends £10,000 to an associate in which it has a 20 per cent interest. The entity earned finance income of £1,000 during the year on this loan. In applying the equity method, should the entity eliminate its interest in the finance income earned on its loan to the associate against the related finance cost included in the earnings of the associate?

IAS 28.22 requires the elimination of profits and losses resulting from downstream transactions. However, it does not address the treatment of revenue derived by group companies from transactions with associates (e.g. revenue from the sale of goods, or interest revenue) and whether that revenue should be eliminated from the consolidated financial statements.

IAS 28.20 indicates that many of the procedures appropriate for the application of the equity method are similar to consolidation procedures, so the entity may choose to apply IAS 27(2008).20 (previously IAS 27(2003).24) and eliminate its interest in the finance income. However, such elimination is not required.

The entity should select an accounting policy for such transactions that it discloses and applies consistently.

Example 4.3.6C

Profit elimination on sale to an associate

Entity A (A) has a 30 per cent stake in an associate, Entity B (B). A equity accounts for B, and the carrying amount of B in A's consolidated financial statements is £15m.

A sells plant and equipment to B in exchange for cash of £100m, which B finances through bank borrowings. Immediately before the sale, the plant and equipment was carried in A's books at a depreciated amount of £20m. A will have no further involvement with the plant and equipment, and the derecognition criteria in IAS 16 are met. A has no interests in B other than its equity stake, and is not committed to any reimbursement should B generate losses.

Of the profit of £80m made by A, 30% (£24m) would normally be eliminated as unrealised, but this exceeds the carrying amount of B (£15m). Should the excess of unrealised profit over the carrying amount of the investment in B (i.e. £9m) be eliminated in the consolidated financial statements of A?

IAS 28.22 applies to profits and losses resulting from 'upstream' and 'downstream' transactions between an investor and an associate. It requires unrealised profits and losses to be eliminated to the extent of the investor's interest in the associate, but it does not discuss the possibility that this might exceed the carrying amount of the associate. In the absence of guidance, it seems appropriate to analogise to IAS 28.30 (see **4.3.8** below), which deals with an associate that is making losses. In that scenario:

- after the investor's interest is reduced to zero, additional losses are provided for, and a liability recognised, only to the extent that the investor has incurred legal or constructive obligations or made payments on behalf of the associate; and
- if the associate subsequently reports profits, the investor resumes including its share of those profits only after its share of the profits equals the share of net losses not recognised.

Thus, applying the same logic here:

- A should reduce the profit on sale of plant and equipment by £15m, being the carrying amount of B immediately before the sale. Thus, it should report a profit of £65m on the sale.
- A should not recognise any further share of B's profits until B has made sufficient profits (£30m, of which A's share is £9m) to cover the amount of unrealised profit not eliminated at the time of the sale.

4.3.7 *Intercompany balances*

Because associates are not part of the group, intercompany balances between the group and associates are not eliminated. Unsettled normal trading transactions should generally be included as current assets or liabilities.

Where advances or loans by the group to the associate are not expected to be settled within 12 months, they should be shown as non-current assets.

It is not appropriate to offset amounts owed by the group to an associate against the carrying amount of the group's interest in its associates. Such a presentation breaches the offset rules set out in IAS 32 *Financial Instruments: Presentation*.

4.3.8 Associates with net asset deficiencies

If an investor's share of losses of an associate equals or exceeds its interest in the associate, the investor should discontinue recognising its share of further losses. [IAS 28.29]

An investor may have a variety of interests in an associate, both long-term and short-term, including ordinary or preferred shares, loans, advances, debt securities, options to acquire ordinary shares, and trade receivables. For the purposes of IAS 28.29, the investor's interest in an associate is the carrying amount of the investment in the associate under the equity method together with any long-term interests that, in substance, form part of the investor's net investment in the associate. [IAS 28.29]

For example, an item for which settlement is neither planned nor likely to occur in the foreseeable future is, in substance, an extension of the entity's investment in that associate. Such items may include preference shares and long-term receivables or loans. Items such as trade receivables, trade payables and any long-term receivables for which adequate collateral exists, such as secured loans, will not fall to be treated as part of the investor's interest in an associate for this purpose. [IAS 28.29]

Losses recognised under the equity method in excess of the investor's investment in ordinary shares are applied to the other components of the investor's interest in an associate in the reverse order of their seniority (i.e. priority in liquidation). [IAS 28.29]

After the investor's interest is reduced to zero, additional losses are provided for, and a liability recognised, only to the extent that the investor has incurred legal or constructive obligations or made payments on behalf of the associate. [IAS 28.30]

If the associate subsequently reports profits, the investor resumes including its share of those profits only after its share of the profits equals the share of net losses not recognised. [IAS 28.30]

This approach differs from that of FRS 9, under which losses and liabilities continue to be recognised for as long as significant influence exists. UK

Example 4.3.8

Associate with net asset deficiency

An investor invests £10 million in an associate – £5 million to acquire 25 per cent of the equity share capital of the associate and £5 million as an unsecured shareholder's loan. The investor has entered into no other guarantees or commitments in respect of the associate. Assume that the associate is in a start-up situation and expects to make significant losses in the first year, but will generate profits thereafter. The associate has sufficient cash resources to meet its liabilities as they fall due.

Assuming that the associate makes £50 million loss in the first year, the investor should recognise a loss of £5 million in respect of its equity stake. It will recognise a further loss of £5 million in respect of the shareholder's loan if, in substance, the loan forms part of the investor's net investment in the associate (as would appear to be the case). However, the balance of the investor's share of the net loss (i.e. 25 per cent of £50 million, less £10 million) is not recognised.

If, in the next year, the associate makes a profit of £10 million, the investor recognises no profit since its share of the profit (£2.5 million) equals the amount of the unrecognised loss in the previous period. For any profits made in excess of £10 million, the investor recognises its proportionate share.

4.3.9 *Discontinuing the use of the equity method*

The investor should discontinue the use of the equity method of accounting from the date when it ceases to have significant influence over the investee. From that date, the investment is accounted for in accordance with the requirements of IAS 39 *Financial Instruments: Recognition and Measurement*, provided that the associate has not become a subsidiary or a joint venture.

In addition, an investor should discontinue the use of the equity method of accounting from the date that its interest in an associate qualifies as held for sale in accordance with IFRS 5 *Non-current Assets Held for Sale and Discontinued Operations*. From that date, the investment is accounted for in accordance with the requirements of IFRS 5 (see **example 4.1F** in **chapter 29**).

4.3.9.1 *Loss of significant influence: entities that have adopted IFRS 3(2008)*

Upon adoption of IFRS 3(2008), the accounting required by IAS 28 on the loss of significant influence is amended, as discussed below. Entities that have not yet adopted IFRS 3(2008) will need to continue to apply the rules from the previous version of IAS 28, which are discussed in **4.3.9.2**.

For entities that have adopted IFRS 3(2008), on the loss of significant influence, any investment retained in the former associate is measured at fair value. Any difference between:

[IAS 28.18]

(a) the fair value of any retained investment and any proceeds from disposing of the part interest in the associate; and

(b) the carrying amount of the investment at the date when significant influence is lost;

is recognised in profit or loss.

Accordingly, when significant influence is lost, the amount recognised in profit or loss will typically be the same irrespective of whether all, some or none of the interest in the former associate has been sold.

When an investment ceases to be an associate and is accounted for in accordance with IAS 39, the fair value of the investment at the date when it ceases to be an associate is regarded as its fair value on initial recognition as a financial asset in accordance with IAS 39. [IAS 28.19]

When significant influence is lost, all amounts recognised in other comprehensive income in relation to the former associate are accounted for on the same basis as would be required if the former associate had directly disposed of the related assets or liabilities. Accordingly, if a gain or loss previously recognised in other comprehensive income by an associate would be reclassified to profit or loss on the disposal of the related assets or liabilities, the gain or loss is reclassified from equity to profit or loss (as a reclassification adjustment) when the investor loses significant influence over the associate. [IAS 28.19A]

Thus, for example:

- the gain or loss previously recognised in other comprehensive income in relation to the associate's available-for-sale financial assets will be reclassified to profit or loss; but
- if the revaluation model has been applied to any property, plant and equipment of the associate, revaluation gains or losses previously recognised in other comprehensive income in relation to those assets will not be reclassified.

If an investor's ownership interest in an associate is reduced, but the investment continues to be an associate, the investor reclassifies to profit or loss only a proportionate amount of the gain or loss previously recognised in other comprehensive income. [IAS 28.19A]

4.3.9.2 Loss of significant influence: entities that have not yet adopted IFRS 3(2008)

Upon adoption of IFRS 3(2008), the accounting required by IAS 28 on the loss of significant influence is amended, as discussed in **4.3.9.1**. Entities that have not yet adopted IFRS 3(2008) will need to continue to apply the rules from the previous version of IAS 28, which are discussed below.

For entities that have not yet adopted IFRS 3(2008), the carrying amount of the investment at the date that it ceases to be an associate will be its deemed cost for the purpose of the application of IAS 39. [IAS 28.18 & 19]

Accordingly, if significant influence is lost as a result of selling part of the interest in an associate, and if the shares retained are classified as available-for-sale:

- a gain or loss will typically be recognised in profit or loss in relation to the part sold, but
- the initial remeasurement to fair value of the part retained will be reflected in other comprehensive income, as the remeasurement of an available-for-sale financial asset.

4.3.10 Impairment

After application of the equity method, including recognising the associate's losses in accordance with the rules set out above, the investor should apply the requirements of IAS 39 *Financial Instruments: Recognition and Measurement* to determine whether it is necessary to recognise any additional impairment loss with respect to the investor's net investment in the associate. [IAS 28.31] The investor also applies the requirements of IAS 39 to determine whether any additional impairment loss should be recognised with respect to the investor's interest in the associate that does not constitute part of the net investment (e.g. loans) and the amount of that impairment loss. [IAS 28.32]

IAS 39 requires that financial assets be assessed at the end of each reporting period to determine whether there is any objective evidence that they are impaired. IAS 39.59 – 62 provide detailed guidance for the identification of such objective evidence, which is discussed in **section 6** of **chapter 18.**

The existence of the following indicators provides additional evidence as to whether an investment in an associate might be impaired:

- the financial condition and near-term prospects of the associate, including any specific events that may influence the operations of the associate (such as changes in technology that may impair the earnings potential of the investment, or the discontinuance of a segment of the business that may affect the future earnings potential);
- the intent and ability of the holder to retain its investment in the associate for a period of time sufficient to allow for any anticipated recovery in market value;
- the associate's financial performance and projections;
- trends in the general market;
- the associate's capital strength;
- the associate's dividend payment record;
- known liquidity crisis;
- bankruptcy proceedings; and
- going concern commentary in the auditor's report on the investee's most recent financial statements.

Whenever application of the requirements of IAS 39 indicates that the interest in an associate may be impaired, the entire carrying amount of the investment (including goodwill) is tested under IAS 36 *Impairment of Assets*. The recoverable amount of the investment is compared with its carrying amount. IAS 28 allows two methods for calculating the value in use of the investments which, under appropriate assumptions, should give the same result. The alternatives are:

[IAS 28.33]

- to estimate the investor's share of the present value of the estimated future cash flows expected to be generated by the associate, including the cash flows from the operations of the associate and the proceeds on the ultimate disposal of the investment; or
- to estimate the present value of the estimated future cash flows expected to arise from dividends to be received from the investment and from its ultimate disposal.

Where the investor has more than one associate, the recoverability of each interest should be assessed separately, unless an associate does not generate cash inflows from continuing use that are largely independent of those from other assets of the entity. [IAS 28.34]

Generally, in appropriate circumstances, impairment losses recognised in respect of equity accounted investments can be reversed. However, the question arises as to whether this is permitted in respect of goodwill included in the carrying amount of an equity accounted investment, given the general prohibition in IAS 36 on reversing impairment losses relating to goodwill.

If the equity carrying amount of an associate included £100 goodwill, and an impairment loss of £150 was recognised, the goodwill effectively has been eliminated. If the recoverable amount subsequently increases to its original value, can the entire impairment loss of £150 be reversed, or is the reversal restricted to £50?

IAS 28.33 states that because goodwill included in the carrying amount of an investment in an associate is not separately recognised, it is not tested for impairment separately under the principles of IAS 36. Instead the entire carrying amount of the investment is tested under IAS 36 for impairment by comparing its recoverable amount with its carrying amount, whenever application of the requirements in IAS 39 indicates that the investment may be impaired (see **4.3.3.5**). Although not specifically addressed in IAS 28, the treatment of reversals of impairment losses should mirror the requirements of IAS

28.33. The investment, therefore, is treated as a whole, and the goodwill is not treated separately; thus, there is no prohibition against restoring the carrying amount of the investment to its pre-impairment value, in appropriate circumstances. Therefore, in the example above, the entire impairment loss of £150 could be reversed.

Example 4.3.10

Non-recourse debt and impairment

Company A and Company B each make a £6 million investment in a real estate venture, Company C. Their investments are financed in part by each borrowing £5 million. The terms of the borrowing are such that, to the extent that they fail to recover their investments from C, A and B are not required to repay their borrowings.

If A's and B's investments in C are determined to be impaired under the principles set out in IAS 28.33, A and B must write their investments down in accordance with that paragraph. The existence of non-recourse debt is not justification for limiting the impairment loss. The borrowings are accounted for separately under IAS 39 *Financial Instruments: Recognition and Measurement*.

5 Separate financial statements

IAS 28 defines separate financial statements as those presented by a parent, an investor in an associate or a venturer in a jointly controlled entity, in which the investments are accounted for on the basis of the direct equity interest rather than on the basis of the reported results and net assets of the investees. [IAS 28.2]

It is important to understand that the term 'separate financial statements' does not simply mean 'financial statements other than consolidated financial statements'. As noted previously, where an entity has no subsidiaries, and therefore does not produce consolidated financial statements, it may nevertheless be required to use equity accounting in its financial statements.

'Separate financial statements' are best understood as financial statements presented in addition to the 'main' financial statements. They will most often occur when an entity that is required to produce consolidated financial statements also produces non-consolidated financial statements for the parent as a separate entity; the latter would be separate financial statements. But the definition is not as narrow as this, and would in principle also apply where an entity other than a parent prepares, in addition to its 'main' financial statements (which would use equity accounting), separate 'parent' financial statements (which would not use equity accounting).

The requirements as regards accounting for investments in associates in the separate financial statements of the investor are set out in IAS 27 *Consolidated and Separate Financial Statements* (see **section 6** of **chapter 33**). IAS 27 requires that when separate financial statements are prepared, investments in associates that are not classified as held for sale (or included in a disposal group that is classified as held for sale) in accordance with IFRS 5 *Non-current Assets Held for Sale and Discontinued Operations* should be accounted for either:

[IAS 27(2008).38, previously IAS 27(2003).37]

- at cost; or
- in accordance with IAS 39 *Financial Instruments: Recognition and Measurement.*

See **section 6** of **chapter 33** for discussion of the treatment of dividends received out of pre-acquisition profits where an investment is accounted for at cost.

The same accounting policy should be applied for all investments in associates, other than those held for sale (or included in a disposal group that is held for sale), which should be accounted for in accordance with IFRS 5 (see **chapter 29**). [IAS 27(2008).38, previously IAS 27(2003).37]

Where an investment in an associate is accounted for in accordance with IAS 39 in the consolidated financial statements (e.g. investments in associates held by venture capital organisations), it should be accounted for in the same way in the investor's separate financial statements. [IAS 27(2008).40, previously IAS 27(2003).39] Therefore, cost is not an allowed alternative for such investments in the investor's separate financial statements.

UK

*In May 2008, the IASB amended IAS 27 and IFRS 1 to change the treatment of dividends out of pre-acquisition profits (see **section 6** of **chapter 33**) and to allow the use of deemed cost for investments in subsidiaries, jointly controlled entities and associates when entities first adopt IFRSs (see **6.12** in **chapter 5**). The amendments remove an important difference between IFRSs and UK GAAP, and should make it easier for UK companies to adopt IFRSs in future. At the time of writing, these amendments to IAS 27 and IFRS 1 have not yet been endorsed for use in the EU. Since the requirements of the amended Standards differ in important*

> *respects from those of the previous versions, EU reporting entities will not be able to apply the revised versions in their statutory financial statements until the revised Standards are endorsed.*
>
> *As explained in* ***section 6*** *of* ***chapter*** *33, UK companies adopting IFRSs before the amendments are endorsed will need to consider whether, at any stage, associates have paid dividends out of pre-acquisition profits and, hence, whether the cost of investment needs to be adjusted for IFRS purposes. Thus, they may face practical difficulties in measuring the cost of an associate in their separate financial statements on first-time adoption of IFRSs because of the need to adjust historical information.*

6 Presentation and disclosure

6.1 Presentation

IAS 1 *Presentation of Financial Statements* requires that:

- investments accounted for under the equity method be presented as a separate line item in the statement of financial position; [IAS 1(2007).54(e), previously IAS 1(2003).68(e)] and
- share of profit or loss of associates and joint ventures accounted for using the equity method be presented as a separate line item in the statement of comprehensive income. [IAS 1(2007).82(c), previously IAS 1(2003).81(c)]

These presentation requirements mean that amounts relating to different categories of investment (i.e. associates and jointly controlled entities accounted for using the equity method) are combined. However, IAS 28.38 requires that

- the investor's share of the profit or loss of associates;
- the investor's share of any discontinued operations of associates; and
- the carrying amount of investments in associates

be separately disclosed (see **6.2.1** below).

Therefore, where the amounts are not analysed in the statement of financial position and the statement of comprehensive income, an analysis will be required in the notes to the financial statements. In any case, the nature of the investor's activities carried out via associates and joint ventures will often be very distinct, in which case analysis would be recommended in the statement of financial position and statement of comprehensive income.

UK

Under FRS 9, the investor's shares of the associate's operating profit and of each line item after operating profit are presented separately in the profit and loss account. Under IAS 1 Presentation of Financial Statements, *a single figure is required to be shown in profit or loss, being the investor's share of profits (see* ***section 5.2.7*** *in* ***chapter 3****).*

IAS 28 also requires that investments in associates accounted for under the equity method should be classified as non-current assets. [IAS 28.38]

The investor's share of changes recognised in other comprehensive income by the associate should be recognised by the investor in other comprehensive income. [IAS 28.39]

6.2 Disclosure

6.2.1 Financial statements in which associates are accounted for using equity accounting

The disclosure requirements in this section will normally apply to consolidated financial statements prepared in accordance with IAS 27. They will also apply, however, where the investor does not prepare consolidated financial statements, because it does not have subsidiaries, but accounts for associates in its financial statements using the equity method of accounting (see **4.1** above).

The following disclosures are required:

[IAS 28.37]

(a) the fair value of investments in associates for which there are published price quotations;

(b) summarised financial information of associates, including the aggregated amounts of assets, liabilities, revenues and profit or loss;

(c) the reasons why the presumption that an investor does not have significant influence is overcome if the investor holds, directly or indirectly through subsidiaries, less than 20 per cent of the voting or potential voting power of the investee but concludes that it has significant influence;

(d) the reasons why the presumption that an investor has significant influence is overcome if the investor holds, directly or indirectly through subsidiaries, 20% or more of the voting or potential voting power of the investee but concludes that it does not have significant influence;

(e) the end of the reporting period of the financial statements of an associate, when such financial statements are used in applying the equity method and are as of a date or for a period that is different from that of the investor, and the reason for using a different date or different period;

(f) the nature and extent of any significant restrictions (e.g. resulting from borrowing arrangements or regulatory requirements) on the ability of associates to transfer funds to the investor in the form of cash dividends, or repayment of loans or advances;

(g) the unrecognised share of losses of an associate, both for the period and cumulatively, if an investor has discontinued recognition of its share of losses of an associate;

(h) the fact that an associate is not accounted for using the equity method in accordance with IAS 28.13 (see **4.2** above); and

(i) summarised financial information of associates, either individually or in groups, that are not accounted for using the equity method, including the amounts of total assets, total liabilities, revenues and profit or loss.

Separate disclosure is required of:

[IAS 28.38]

- the investor's share of the profit or loss of associates accounted for under the equity method;
- the carrying amount of investments in associates accounted for under the equity method; and
- the investor's share of any discontinued operations of associates accounted for under the equity method.

In accordance with IAS 37 *Provisions, Contingent Liabilities and Contingent Assets*, the investor should disclose:

[IAS 28.40]

- its share of the contingent liabilities of an associate incurred jointly with other investors; and
- those contingent liabilities that arise because the investor is severally liable for all or part of the liabilities of the associate.

6.2.2 *Separate financial statements*

IAS 27 also requires a number of disclosures regarding investments in associates in an investor's separate financial statements. When an investor in an associate prepares separate financial statements, those separate financial statements should disclose:

[IAS 27(2008).43, previously IAS 27(2003).42]

- the fact that the statements are separate financial statements and the reasons why those statements are prepared if not required by law;
- a list of significant investments in subsidiaries, jointly controlled entities and associates, including:
  - the name;
  - country of incorporation or residence;
  - the proportion of ownership interest; and
  - if different, the proportion of voting power held; and
- a description of the method used to account for such investments.

The separate financial statements are also required to identify the financial statements prepared in accordance with IAS 28 (i.e. those financial statements referred to in **6.2.1** above) to which they relate. [IAS 27(2008).43, previously IAS 27(2003).42]

6.2.3 *Requirements of the Companies Act*

> *For UK companies, certain additional disclosures are required by the Companies Act, as set out in* ***sections 7.3*** *to* ***7.5*** *of* ***chapter 33****.* (UK)

36 Interests in joint ventures

1 Introduction

Accounting for joint ventures is dealt with in IAS 31 *Interests in Joint Ventures*. IAS 31 was last revised by the IASB in December 2003 as part of its Improvements Project, and was most recently amended when *Improvements to IFRSs* was issued in May 2008.

This chapter discusses the requirements of IAS 31 in the following sections:

Section 2	Scope
Section 3	Definitions
Section 4	Joint ventures and joint control
Section 5	Classification of joint ventures
Section 6	Accounting for jointly controlled operations
Section 7	Accounting for jointly controlled assets
Section 8	Accounting for interests in jointly controlled entities
Section 9	Separate financial statements
Section 10	Reporting interests in joint ventures in the financial statements of an investor
Section 11	Operators of joint ventures
Section 12	Presentation and disclosure
Section 13	First-time adoption of IFRSs
Section 14	Future developments

UK

The accounting for joint ventures under the UK standard, FRS 9 Associates and Joint Ventures, *is rather more prescribed than under IAS 31. The most significant differences are as follows.*

- *IAS 31 allows a choice between proportionate consolidation and equity accounting, whereas FRS 9 only allows the latter.*

- *Under IAS 31, proportionate consolidation or equity accounting can, in some circumstances, be required in financial statements other than consolidated financial statements. Under FRS 9, equity accounting is only possible in consolidated financial statements.*

- *When applying equity accounting under IAS 31, losses of a jointly controlled entity are recognised only until the point at which the investor's interest is reduced to nil. A liability in respect of an investment in a jointly controlled entity is recognised only to the extent that the investor has incurred legal or constructive obligations or made payments on behalf of the jointly controlled entity. This contrasts with the equity method in FRS 9, under which losses continue to be recognised for as long as joint control exists.*

- *An interest accounted for as a JANE (a joint arrangement that is not an entity) under FRS 9 may, in some circumstances, be treated as a jointly controlled entity under IAS 31, rather than as a jointly controlled operation or asset.*

- *Under FRS 9, the investor's share of the joint venture's operating profit and of each line item after operating profit are presented separately in the profit and loss account. When presenting results under the equity method, IAS 1 Presentation of Financial Statements requires a single figure to be shown in the statement of comprehensive income, being the investor's share of profits or losses after tax.*

- *For joint ventures, but not associates, FRS 9 requires an expanded form of equity accounting ('gross equity accounting'), under which the investor's share of the aggregate gross assets and liabilities underlying the net amount included for the investment is shown on the face of the balance sheet and, in the profit and loss account, the investor's share of the investee's turnover is noted. By contrast, where an entity elects to apply equity accounting for joint ventures under IAS 31, the equity method used is the same as that for associates under IAS 28 Investments in Associates.*

In addition, there are some other differences of presentation and disclosure.

2 Scope

IAS 31 should generally be applied in accounting for interests in joint ventures and the reporting of joint venture assets, liabilities, income and expenses in the financial statements of venturers and investors, regardless of the structures or forms under which the joint venture activities take place. [IAS 31.1]

IAS 31 excludes from its scope certain interests in jointly controlled entities held by venture capital organisations, and by mutual funds, unit trusts and similar entities (including investment-linked insurance funds). Where interests held by such entities are, at the time of their initial recognition, designated as at fair value through profit or loss or classified as held for trading and accounted for in accordance with IAS 39 *Financial Instruments: Recognition and Measurement*, these interests are excluded from the scope of IAS 31. They will be measured at fair value in accordance with IAS 39, with changes in fair value recognised in profit or loss in the period of change. [IAS 31.1]

For periods beginning on or after 1 January 2009, where an entity holds such an investment, it must provide the disclosures required by IAS 31.55 & 56 (see **6.2.1** below). This amendment to IAS 31 was made by *Improvements to IFRSs* issued in May 2008. Earlier application of the amendment is permitted, but an entity choosing to apply the amendment early must disclose that fact and must also apply the related amendments to IFRS 7.3, IAS 28.1 (see **section 2** in **chapter 35**) and IAS 32.4 (see **2.1** in **chapter 13**). The amendment may be applied prospectively.

Note that, in order to qualify for exclusion, the investments held by venture capital organisations and similar entities must be identified and appropriately designated at the time of their initial recognition. Investments held by such entities that are not at the time of their initial recognition designated as at fair value through profit or loss or classified as held for trading will fall within the scope of IAS 31. Following initial recognition, it will not be possible to change the treatment of an investment in a jointly controlled entity unless the venturer ceases to have joint control. Where a venturer increases its stake in a jointly controlled entity, but continues to have joint control, it should apply the existing treatment to the increased holding.

3 Definitions

A joint venture is defined as a contractual arrangement whereby two or more parties undertake an economic activity that is subject to joint control. [IAS 31.3]

Joint control is the contractually agreed sharing of control over an economic activity, and exists only when the strategic financial and operating decisions relating to the activity require the unanimous consent of the parties sharing control (the venturers). [IAS 31.3]

Control is the power to govern the financial and operating policies of an economic activity so as to obtain benefits from it. [IAS 31.3]

A venturer is a party to a joint venture and has joint control over that joint venture. An investor in a joint venture is a party to a joint venture and does not have joint control over that joint venture. [IAS 31.3]

4 Joint ventures and joint control

4.1 Contractual arrangement

The key distinguishing characteristic of a joint venture is that there is a contractual arrangement to share control. Without such a contractual arrangement, there is no joint control and, thus, an activity is not a joint venture. [IAS 31.9]

There are various ways in which the contractual arrangement may be evidenced, e.g. by a contract between the venturers or minutes of discussions between the venturers. Sometimes, the arrangement is incorporated in the articles or other by-laws of the joint venture. Whatever its form, the contractual arrangement is usually in writing and deals with such matters as:

[IAS 31.10]

- the activity, duration and reporting obligations of the joint venture;
- the appointment of the board of directors or equivalent governing body of the joint venture and the voting rights of the venturers;
- capital contributions by the venturers; and
- the sharing by the venturers of the output, income, expenses or results of the joint venture.

Joint control ensures that no single venturer is in a position to control unilaterally the activities of the joint venture. [IAS 31.11] It follows from the definition of joint control that each party sharing joint control (the venturers) will have the power of veto over strategic financial and operating decisions.

On the surface, the concepts of joint control and significant influence, as described in **chapter 35**, appear similar, and indeed they share some of the same characteristics. However, the existence of a contractual arrangement between a small number of venturers, which establishes joint control, differentiates a joint venture from an investment in an associate, where influence is often achieved primarily as a result of the size of the ownership interest.

4.2 Characteristics of joint control

Whether a particular arrangement will fall within the scope of IAS 31 will not be determined by how the arrangement is legally constituted, but by the agreements between the parties involved as to the mechanism for control.

In determining the impact of IAS 31, it is also important to consider entities that are not legally constituted as joint ventures, but where the interested parties have formalised arrangements for joint control. In these circumstances, the entity may fall within the scope of IAS 31 and may be a joint venture for accounting purposes.

The contractual arrangement will usually specify decisions essential to the goals of the joint venture which require the consent of all of the venturers and those decisions that may require the consent of a specified majority of the venturers. It will be important to consider the substance of these arrangements in determining whether they constitute joint control.

Under IAS 31, joint control exists only where the strategic financial and operating decisions require the unanimous consent of the venturers. If the matters specified as requiring the consent of all of the venturers are such that they will not be expected to have a significant impact on the financial and operating policies in practice, then they do not result in an effective sharing of control. For example, many joint venture agreements provide that unanimous consent is required for proposed amendments to the Memorandum and Articles of Association or for the dissolution of the joint venture. Such matters will usually be considered to be remote, and therefore to have no practical effect on financial and operating policies. On the other hand, such matters as authorisations for borrowings, or for the acquisition of property, plant and equipment at a level that can reasonably be expected to occur, are more likely to affect significantly the operations of the joint venture in practice and will generally provide part of the evidence of joint control.

In assessing whether joint control exists, it is also important to consider what mechanisms exist to deal with scenarios where unanimous consent is required but the venturers cannot reach agreement.

Often, a joint venture agreement will specify that where unanimous consent cannot be achieved the joint venture must be liquidated. But if, instead, in such circumstances, one of the parties (A) will be required to purchase the interest of the other party (B), this may indicate that A already has control; in effect, the mechanism gives B a put option over its non-controlling interest in A's subsidiary.

It is also useful to consider whether, irrespective of the legal form, there is in substance any joint control of economic activities. A joint venture structure may have been called for because of legal or other considerations. There are examples, however, where the economic activities being carried out by the two parties through the joint venture structure are actually quite distinct and they exist effectively as separate operations. In such circumstances, if each party has unilateral control over a separate economic activity, the arrangement will not fall to be treated as a joint venture.

4.3 Ability to influence benefits derived

In addition to the degree of joint activity and the level of input that the investor has into the financial and operating policies of the venture, it is essential to consider the degree to which the investor's return (whether in cash or as a share of output from the venture) is dependent on the results of the venture.

Control is the power to govern the financial and operating policies of an economic activity so as to obtain benefits from it. If the arrangements are such that the investor's input into the financial and operating policies cannot affect the level of benefits that it obtains (e.g. if the return of the investor is a fixed amount, or a variable amount not connected to the results of the venture) then the arrangements do not result in the investor having joint control. In these circumstances, the relationship may be a financing arrangement (where the substance of capital input is in effect a loan) or even simply a contract for services (e.g. professional advice given in return for a fixed fee). The accounting treatment will be determined by the substance of the arrangement, but will not fall within the scope of IAS 31.

4.4 Exercise of rights in practice

Although IAS 31 emphasises the substance of an arrangement, this does not mean that the way in which the arrangements are implemented in practice will necessarily change the classification of the investment.

If a venturer is entitled to jointly control the activities of a venture, it will be accounted for as a joint venture – irrespective of whether the venturer chooses to exercise that right in practice. Thus, if the venturer chooses to adopt the role of a sleeping partner and does not, in practice, provide any input into financial and operating policies, this will not exclude the arrangement from the scope of IAS 31, since at any time the venturer could choose to exercise its rights.

It is only when a party's ability to exercise its rights can be frustrated by the other party or by events that the ability to control jointly may be compromised. Joint control may be precluded when the venture is in legal reorganisation or in bankruptcy, or operates under severe long-term restrictions on its ability to transfer funds to the venturer. If joint control is continuing, however, these events are not enough in themselves to justify not accounting for joint ventures in accordance with IAS 31. [IAS 31.8]

4.5 Role of the operator of a joint venture

In practice, it is not uncommon for one of the venturers to be appointed as operator or manager of the day-to-day activities of the economic activity. As long as this operator does not have the power to control the financial and operating policies, but is merely carrying out the managerial tasks delegated to it by the other venturers, the operator is not exercising control, and it accounts for any managerial fees received as revenue (in accordance with IAS 18 *Revenue*) rather than as a return on its investment in the joint venture. If the operator has the power to determine the financial and operating policies of the economic activity, however, it controls the economic activity and, as such, accounts for its interest as an investment in a subsidiary rather than as a joint venture. [IAS 31.12 & 52]

5 Classification of joint ventures

Although acknowledging that joint venture arrangements take many different forms, both legally and in substance, IAS 31 recognises three broad categories of joint venture – jointly controlled operations, jointly controlled assets and jointly controlled entities.

5.1 Jointly controlled operations

This type of venture does not involve a structure or entity that is separate from the venturers. Each venturer uses its own assets and incurs its own expenses in the production of some joint product or service, e.g. a joint project for the construction of an aircraft where one venturer is responsible for the construction of the engine, and the other venturer builds the fuselage. Each venturer takes a share of the revenue from the joint product.

Since the jointly controlled operation is not purchasing assets or raising finance in its own right, the assets and liabilities used in the activities of the joint venture are those of the venturers. As such, they are accounted for in the financial statements of the venturer to which they belong. The only accounting issue that arises is that the output from the project is to be shared among the venturers and, therefore, there must be some mechanism for specifying the allocation of the proceeds and the sharing of any joint expenses. [IAS 31.13 – 14]

5.2 Jointly controlled assets

Although this type of joint venture does not involve the establishment of a financial structure or an entity separate from the venturers, it differs from the category of jointly controlled operations in that the joint venture assets will be jointly controlled, and may be jointly owned by the venturers. They will usually be contributed by the venturers, but may be acquired specifically for the purposes of the joint venture. The assets are used to obtain benefits for the venturers. Each venturer may take a share of the output from the assets, and will usually bear an agreed share of the expenses incurred by the venture. A common example of a jointly controlled asset is a property which is owned jointly by two entities that each take a share of the rents received and bear a share of the expenses. Another example is where entities in the oil production industry jointly control and operate an oil pipeline. Each venturer uses the pipeline to transport its own product, in return for which it bears an agreed proportion of the expenses of operating the pipeline. [IAS 31.18 – 20]

5.3 Jointly controlled entities

The distinguishing feature of this type of venture is that a separate legal entity is established – which can be in the form of a partnership, corporation or other entity. The entity controls the assets of the joint venture, incurs liabilities and expenses, and earns income. It maintains its own accounting records, enters into contracts in its own name and, generally, has an existence independent of the venturers, including the preparation of financial statements. The appropriate accounting treatment will reflect this independent existence.

The establishment of a separate entity effectively precludes the treatment of a joint venture as a jointly controlled asset or a jointly controlled operation. In particular, the Standard cites the example of transferring a jointly controlled asset into a separate legal entity, e.g. an oil pipeline is

accounting is suspended in accordance with IAS 28.29. Under proportionate consolidation, recognition of a share of losses and net liabilities would continue.

A number of other accounting differences can arise as a result of the choice between proportionate consolidation and the equity method:

- if the equity method is applied, the venturer's share of the results of the jointly controlled entity (including any current and deferred tax expense) will be reported as a single line item in profit or loss. If proportionate consolidation is applied, the results of the jointly controlled entity will be consolidated on a line by line basis in profit or loss, leading to different figures for operating profit, tax expense, etc.;

- similarly, under the equity method a single line item will appear in the statement of financial position, whereas the assets and liabilities of the jointly controlled entity will be consolidated on a line by line basis if proportionate consolidation is applied, leading to different figures for borrowings, net current assets, etc.;

- the elimination of transactions between the investor and investee is often limited to unrealised profits where the equity method is applied. If proportionate consolidation is applied, all transactions are eliminated (to the extent of the venturer's interest in the jointly controlled entity);

- amounts owed by a venturer to a jointly controlled entity, and vice versa, will not be eliminated if equity accounting is adopted, whereas they will be eliminated (at least to the extent of the venturer's interest in the jointly controlled entity) if proportionate consolidation is applied;

- where proportionate consolidation is applied, borrowing costs incurred by the venturer may be capitalised, as appropriate, as part of the carrying amount of qualifying assets (e.g. property, plant and equipment) of the jointly controlled entity. By contrast, such capitalisation is not possible where equity accounting is applied, because the investment in the jointly controlled entity is a financial asset, and financial assets are not qualifying assets (see also **example 3.1.2** in **chapter 27**); and

- if the equity method is applied, it is possible that an impairment loss may later be reversed. If proportionate consolidation is applied, any impairment loss allocated to goodwill cannot later be reversed.

Although the Standard itself favours proportionate consolidation, the present IASB (which inherited the Standard from its predecessor) is more in favour of equity accounting, and has published proposals to eliminate the option to use proportionate consolidation (see **section 13** below).

UK *Under UK GAAP, companies are not permitted by FRS 9* Associates and Joint Ventures *to use proportionate consolidation for joint ventures. In light of the IASB's proposal to eliminate proportionate consolidation, UK companies intending to adopt IFRSs may wish to continue equity accounting, particularly as users will be familiar with it (though continued use of equity accounting will result in profit or loss presentation as a single line, rather than the gross equity presentation used in FRS 9).*

Under IAS 8 *Accounting Policies, Changes in Accounting Estimates and Errors*, an entity is required to select and apply accounting policies consistently for similar transactions, other events and conditions, except where a Standard specifically requires or permits categorisation of items for which different policies may be appropriate. [IAS 8.13] The question therefore arises as to whether an investor is required to adopt the same method (whether equity accounting or proportionate consolidation) for all its joint ventures. Although the drafting of IAS 31 could be clearer on this point, in our view a mixture of methods is not permitted. SIC-18 *Consistency – Alternative Methods*, which was superseded when IAS 8 was amended in December 2003, gave IAS 31 as an example of a Standard which did not permit categorisation, and there seems no reason to suppose that the IASB has changed its view on this point. This interpretation is also supported by the drafting of IAS 31.57, which requires disclosure of 'the method' (singular) used to recognise interests in jointly controlled entities.

Subject to the exemptions discussed in **8.2** below, either proportionate consolidation or equity accounting is used regardless of whether the venturer prepares consolidated financial statements. Thus, an entity with no subsidiaries, which therefore does not produce consolidated financial statements, will nevertheless account for joint ventures either by equity accounting or by proportionate consolidation in its financial statements.

Where consolidated financial statements are prepared, however, the venturer does not apply these methods in any separate financial statements prepared in accordance with IAS 27 *Consolidated and Separate Financial Statements* (see **section 9** below).

> *The requirement, in certain circumstances, to apply proportionate consolidation or equity accounting other than in group accounts is different from UK GAAP, which permits equity accounting only in consolidated financial statements. UK companies with interests in joint ventures but no subsidiaries should be mindful of this difference when transitioning to IFRSs.*

UK

8.2 Exemptions from proportionate consolidation and the equity method

A venturer with an interest in a jointly controlled entity is exempted from the requirement to apply proportionate consolidation or the equity method of accounting when it meets one of the following conditions:

[IAS 31.2]

- the interest is classified as held for sale in accordance with IFRS 5 *Non-current Assets Held for Sale and Discontinued Operations*, in which case it should be accounted for under that Standard (see **chapter 29**); or
- the venturer is a parent that is exempt from preparing consolidated financial statements under IAS 27.10 (see **4.2** of **chapter 33**), and prepares separate financial statements as its primary financial statements. In those separate statements, the investment in the jointly controlled entity may be accounted for at cost or under IAS 39; or
- all of the following apply:
  - the venturer is a wholly-owned subsidiary, or is a partially-owned subsidiary of another entity, and its owners, including those not otherwise entitled to vote, have been informed about, and do not object to, the investor not applying proportionate consolidation or the equity method;
  - the venturer's debt or equity instruments are not traded in a public market;
  - the venturer did not file, nor is it in the process of filing, its financial statements with a securities commission or other regulatory organisation, for the purpose of issuing any class of instruments in a public market; and

- the ultimate or any intermediate parent of the venturer produces consolidated financial statements available for public use that comply with IFRSs.

A public market here means a domestic or foreign stock exchange or an over-the-counter market, including local and regional markets.

8.3 Proportionate consolidation

8.3.1 Application of proportionate consolidation

IAS 31 defines proportionate consolidation as a method of accounting whereby a venturer's share of each of the assets, liabilities, income and expenses of a jointly controlled entity is combined line by line with similar items in the venturer's financial statements or reported as separate line items in the venturer's financial statements. [IAS 31.3]

The application of proportionate consolidation means that the statement of financial position of the venturer includes its share of the assets that it controls jointly, and its share of the liabilities for which it is jointly responsible. The statement of comprehensive income of the venturer includes its share of the income and expenses of the jointly controlled entity. [IAS 31.33] Although IAS 31 does not refer to the statement of cash flows, paragraph 38 of IAS 7 *Statement of Cash Flows* requires a venturer which reports its interest in a jointly controlled entity using proportionate consolidation to include in its consolidated statement of cash flows its proportionate share of the jointly controlled entity's cash flows (see **section 6** of **chapter 30**).

The Standard gives no further guidance on the mechanics of proportionate consolidation, other than to say that many of the procedures appropriate for the application of proportionate consolidation are similar to the procedures for the consolidation of subsidiaries, as described in IAS 27 (see **chapter 33**). [IAS 31.33]

Such procedures include making adjustments to fair value the assets and liabilities of the jointly controlled entity at the date of acquisition, calculating goodwill arising on acquisition, and eliminating proportionately transactions between the venturer and the jointly controlled entity. However, under proportionate consolidation, since only the venturer's share of assets and liabilities is consolidated, the share of the net assets held by other venturers is not presented as non-controlling interest (nor, for entities that have not yet adopted IFRS 3(2008), as minority interest).

8.3.2 *Presentation*

IAS 31 offers a choice of presentation when an entity adopts proportionate consolidation. The effect of each on the net assets and net profit of the venturer is the same. The difference is merely one of presentation. It is not acceptable to use a mixture of the two methods. [IAS 31.31]

8.3.2.1 *Line-by-line presentation*

The first method is the line-by-line method of proportionate consolidation. This method is similar to the method used when consolidating a subsidiary. The venturer combines its share of each of the assets, liabilities, income and expenses of the jointly controlled entity with similar items in its consolidated financial statements on a line-by-line basis. For example, it may combine its share of the jointly controlled entity's inventory with its inventory and its share of the jointly controlled entity's property, plant and equipment with its property, plant and equipment. [IAS 31.34]

It is sometimes argued that the line-by-line presentation is inappropriate, because it results in financial statement line items that are comprised of some items that are controlled by the entity and a proportion of other items that are jointly controlled.

8.3.2.2 *Separate presentation*

The second method of presentation is the separate line item method of presentation. Under this method, separate line items are presented for the venturer's share of the assets, liabilities, income and expenses of the jointly controlled entity. For example, in the statement of financial position, a separate line item may be included for the venturer's proportionate share of a current asset of the jointly controlled entity or for the venturer's proportionate share of the property, plant and equipment of a jointly controlled entity. [IAS 31.34]

A venturer should not offset its proportionate share of the assets and liabilities or income and the related expenses of a jointly controlled entity unless a legal right of offset exists and the offsetting represents the expectation as to the realisation of the assets or settlement of the liability. [IAS 31.35]

8.3.3 *Discontinuing the use of proportionate consolidation*

A venturer should discontinue the use of proportionate consolidation from the date that it ceases to have joint control over a jointly controlled entity. [IAS 31.36]

The venturer could cease to have joint control, for example, when it disposes of its interest in the jointly controlled entity, or when external restrictions are placed on the jointly controlled entity such that the venturer no longer has joint control. [IAS 31.37] Similarly, it could cease to have joint control as a result of amendments to the contractual arrangements governing the jointly controlled entity.

When an investor ceases to have joint control over an entity, any remaining investment in that entity is accounted for in accordance with IAS 39 *Financial Instruments: Recognition and Measurement*, provided that the former jointly controlled entity does not become a subsidiary or associate:

[IAS 31.45]

- from the date when a former jointly controlled entity becomes a subsidiary, it is accounted for in accordance with IAS 27 *Consolidated and Separate Financial Statements* and IFRS 3 *Business Combinations*;
- from the date when a former jointly controlled entity becomes an associate, it is accounted for in accordance with IAS 28 *Investments in Associates*.

8.3.3.1 Loss of joint control: entities that have adopted IFRS 3(2008)

For entities that have adopted IFRS 3, IAS 31 is amended to provide further guidance on the appropriate accounting when joint control is lost.

When joint control is lost, any investment the investor retains in the former jointly controlled entity is measured at fair value. Any difference between:

(a) the fair value of any retained investment and any proceeds from disposing of the part interest in the jointly controlled entity, and

(b) the carrying amount of the investment at the date when joint control is lost,

is recognised in profit or loss. [IAS 31.45]

When an investment ceases to be a jointly controlled entity and is accounted for in accordance with IAS 39, the fair value of the investment when it ceases to be a jointly controlled entity is regarded as its fair value on initial recognition as a financial asset in accordance with IAS 39. [IAS 31.45A]

When an investor loses joint control of an entity, it accounts for all amounts recognised in other comprehensive income in relation to that entity on the same basis as would be required if the jointly controlled entity had directly disposed of the related assets or liabilities. Accordingly, if a gain or loss previously recognised in other comprehensive income would be reclassified to profit or loss on the disposal of the related assets or liabilities, the investor reclassifies the gain or loss from equity to profit or loss (as a reclassification adjustment) when the investor loses joint control of the entity. [IAS 31.45B]

For example, if a jointly controlled entity has available-for-sale financial assets and the investor loses joint control of the entity, the investor reclassifies to profit or loss the gain or loss previously recognised in other comprehensive income in relation to those assets. If an investor's ownership interest in a jointly controlled entity is reduced, but the investment continues to be a jointly controlled entity, the investor reclassifies to profit or loss only a proportionate amount of the gain or loss previously recognised in other comprehensive income. [IAS 31.45B]

Previously, IAS 31 did not include guidance on how to account when joint control is lost. No transitional provisions have been added to IAS 31; accordingly, where adoption of the new requirements leads to a change in accounting policy, that change should generally be applied retrospectively. But where a formerly jointly controlled entity has, in the past, become a subsidiary, it will be necessary to consider the transitional provisions of IAS 27 (2008), as discussed in **section 8** of **chapter 33**.

8.4 Equity accounting

As an alternative to proportionate consolidation, IAS 31 allows that jointly controlled entities may be accounted for using the equity method of accounting. [IAS 31.38]

IAS 31 defines the equity method as a method of accounting whereby an interest in a jointly controlled entity is initially recorded at cost and adjusted thereafter for the post-acquisition change in the venturer's share of net assets of the jointly controlled entity. The profit or loss of the venturer includes the venturer's share of the profit or loss of the jointly controlled entity. [IAS 31.3]

IAS 31 refers preparers of financial statements to IAS 28 *Investments in Associates* for a description of the general procedures for the application of the equity method. These are discussed in **chapter 35** of this book.

UK *When applying equity accounting under IAS 31, losses of a jointly controlled entity are recognised only until the point at which the investor's interest is reduced to nil. A liability in respect of an investment in a jointly controlled entity is recognised only to the extent that the investor has incurred legal or constructive obligations or made payments on behalf of the jointly controlled entity. This contrasts with FRS 9, under which losses continue to be recognised for as long as joint control exists (see* ***chapter 35****).*

8.4.1 *Profit-sharing not in proportion to share of equity*

Certain joint venture agreements specify a method of appropriation of profits that is not in proportion to the venturers' share of equity in the jointly controlled entity. In such cases, the venturer should apply the agreed profit-sharing ratio when accounting for post-acquisition changes in its share of net assets of the entity.

8.4.2 *Variable profit-share over the life of the venture*

In some joint venture arrangements, the proportion of profit to which the venturer is entitled will vary from year to year. Most commonly, a venturer will be entitled to a higher share of profit in the earlier years in order to recoup its investment more quickly.

Under the equity method of accounting, the venturer should take into account its share of the profits or losses of the entity each year. Therefore, in a variable profit-sharing situation, the proportion of profit that the venturer recognises will be based on the specified profit-sharing arrangements for the particular year, having regard to the substance of the arrangements.

8.4.3 *Discontinuing the use of the equity method*

A venturer should discontinue the use of the equity method from the date that it ceases to have joint control, or significant influence, over a jointly controlled entity. [IAS 31.41]

The venturer could cease to have joint control, for example, when it disposes of its interest in the jointly controlled entity, or as a result of amendments to the contractual arrangements governing the jointly controlled entity, or when external restrictions are placed on the jointly controlled entity such that the venturer no longer has joint control or significant influence.

8.4.3.1 Loss of joint control: entities that have adopted IFRS 3(2008)

The guidance set out at **8.3.3.1** also applies where an investor uses the equity method for jointly controlled entities and ceases to have joint control of an entity.

8.5 Transactions between a venturer and a joint venture

8.5.1 Downstream transactions

When a venturer contributes or sells assets to a joint venture, any portion of a gain or loss from the transaction that is recognised should reflect the transaction's substance. While the assets are retained by the joint venture, and provided that the venturer has transferred the significant risks and rewards of ownership, the venturer should recognise only that portion of the gain or loss that is attributable to the interests of the other venturers. [IAS 31.48]

> The balance of any gain or loss will not be recognised until the assets have been disposed of by the joint venture.

The venturer should recognise the full amount of any loss when the contribution or sale provides evidence of a reduction in the net realisable value of current assets or an impairment loss. [IAS 31.48]

8.5.2 Upstream transactions

When a venturer purchases assets from a joint venture, the venturer should not recognise its share of the profits of the joint venture from the transaction until it resells the assets to an independent party. [IAS 31.49]

A venturer should recognise its share of the losses resulting from these transactions in the same way as profits, except that losses should be recognised immediately when they represent a reduction in the net realis- of current assets or an impairment loss. [IAS 31.49]

8.5.3 *Non-monetary contributions*

SIC-13 *Jointly Controlled Entities – Non-Monetary Contributions by Venturers* provides guidance on the recognition of gains and losses resulting from contributions of non-monetary assets to jointly controlled entities.

Contributions to jointly controlled entities are transfers of assets by venturers in exchange for an equity interest in the jointly controlled entity. Such contributions, which may take various forms, may be made simultaneously by the venturers either at the time of establishment of the jointly controlled entity or subsequently. The venturer(s) may also receive additional consideration in exchange for the assets contributed, e.g. cash or other consideration that does not depend on future cash flows of the jointly controlled entity. [SIC-13.2]

The issues are:

[SIC-13.3]

- when the appropriate portion of gains or losses resulting from a contribution of a non-monetary asset to a jointly controlled entity in exchange for an equity interest in the jointly controlled entity should be recognised by the venturer in profit or loss;
- how additional consideration should be accounted for by the venturer; and
- how any unrealised gain or loss should be presented in the consolidated financial statements of the venturer.

The Interpretation concludes that, when applying IAS 31.48 (see **8.5.1** above) to non-monetary contributions to a jointly controlled entity in exchange for an equity interest in the jointly controlled entity, a venturer should recognise in profit or loss for the period the portion of a gain or loss attributable to the equity interests of the other venturers, except when:

[SIC-13.5]

- the significant risks and rewards of ownership of the contributed non-monetary asset(s) have not been transferred to the jointly controlled entity;
- the gain or loss on the non-monetary contribution cannot be measured reliably; or
- the contribution lacks 'commercial substance', as that term is described in IAS 16 *Property, Plant and Equipment* (see **section 4.3.2** of **chapter 6**).

Where any of the exceptions listed in the previous paragraph applies, the gain or loss should be considered unrealised and should therefore not generally be recognised in profit or loss. [SIC-13.5] The exception to this rule arises if, in addition to receiving an equity interest in the jointly controlled entity, the venturer receives monetary or non-monetary assets. In these circumstances, an appropriate portion of the gain or loss on the transaction should be recognised by the venturer in profit or loss. [SIC-13.6]

Unrealised gains or losses on non-monetary assets contributed to jointly controlled entities should not be presented as deferred gains or losses in the venturer's consolidated statement of financial position. Rather, they should be eliminated as follows:

[SIC-13.7]

- where the interest in the jointly controlled entity is accounted for using proportionate consolidation, against the underlying assets; and
- where the interest in the jointly controlled entity is accounted for using the equity method, against the investment.

SIC-13 does not describe the measurement of the gain or loss arising. However, it includes as a footnote the general requirement of IAS 16 to measure an item of property, plant and equipment acquired in exchange for a non-monetary asset or assets, or a combination of monetary and non-monetary assets, at fair value unless the exchange transaction lacks commercial substance. It follows that the gain or loss on exchange is calculated as follows:

Investor's share of the fair value of the assets contributed by the other party.

Less: Investor's share of the carrying amount of net assets given up (together with any related goodwill).

It also follows that no gain or loss arises on the investor's share of net assets retained as a result of the exchange transaction.

This approach is similar to that required under UK GAAP by UITF 31 Exchanges of businesses or other non-monetary assets for an interest in a subsidiary, joint venture or associate. *The two documents are drafted differently, but the UITF had regard to SIC-13 when preparing UITF 31. UITF 31 deals both with the measurement of gain or loss on exchange, and goodwill arising.* UK

One important difference relates to the presentation of gains in the financial statements. Under UK GAAP, the Companies Act does not allow unrealised gains to be included within the profit and loss account; accordingly, a gain will be reported in the Statement of Total Recognised Gains and Losses (STRGL), rather than the profit and loss account, to the extent that it is not in the form of qualifying consideration. There is no such constraint when reporting under IFRSs; accordingly, gains will be reported in profit or loss, irrespective of whether qualifying consideration has been received (see also **section 5.1** in **chapter 3**).

9 Separate financial statements

IAS 31 defines separate financial statements as those presented by a parent, an investor in an associate or a venturer in a jointly controlled entity, in which the investments are accounted for on the basis of the direct equity interest rather than on the basis of the reported results and net assets of the investees. [IAS 31.3]

It is important to understand that the term 'separate financial statements' does not simply mean 'financial statements other than consolidated financial statements'. As noted previously, where an entity has no subsidiaries, and therefore does not produce consolidated financial statements, it may nevertheless be required to use proportionate consolidation or equity accounting in its financial statements.

'Separate financial statements' are best understood as financial statements presented in addition to the 'main' financial statements. They will most often occur when an entity that is required to produce consolidated financial statements also produces non-consolidated financial statements for the parent as a separate entity; the latter would be separate financial statements. But the definition is not as narrow as this, and would in principle also apply where an entity other than a parent prepares, in addition to its 'main' financial statements (which would use proportionate consolidation or equity accounting), separate 'parent' financial statements (which would not use those methods).

The requirements as regards accounting for interests in jointly controlled entities in the separate financial statements of the investor are set out in IAS 27 *Consolidated and Separate Financial Statements*. IAS 27 requires that when separate financial statements are prepared, investments in jointly controlled entities that are not classified as held for sale (or included in a disposal group that is classified as held for sale) in accordance with IFRS 5 *Non-current Assets Held for Sale and Discontinued Operations* should be accounted for either:

[IAS 27(2008).38, previously IAS 27(2003).37]

- at cost; or
- in accordance with IAS 39 *Financial Instruments: Recognition and Measurement*.

See **section 6** of **chapter 33** for discussion of the treatment of dividends received out of pre-acquisition profits where an investment is accounted for at cost.

The same accounting policy should be applied for all interests in jointly controlled entities, other than those held for sale (or included in a disposal group that is held for sale), which should be accounted for in accordance with IFRS 5 (see **chapter 29**). [IAS 27(2008).38, previously IAS 27(2003).37]

Where an interest in a jointly controlled entity is accounted for in accordance with IAS 39 in the consolidated financial statements (e.g. interests in jointly controlled entities held by venture capital organisations), it should be accounted for in the same way in the venturer's separate financial statements. [IAS 27(2008).40, previously IAS 27(2003).39] Therefore, cost is not an allowed alternative for such interests in the venturer's separate financial statements.

UK

In May 2008, the IASB amended IAS 27 and IFRS 1 to change the treatment of dividends out of pre-acquisition profits (see ***section 6*** *of* ***chapter 33****) and to allow the use of deemed cost for investments in subsidiaries, jointly controlled entities and associates when entities first adopt IFRSs (see* ***6.12*** *in* ***chapter 5****). The amendments remove an important difference between IFRSs and UK GAAP, and should make it easier for UK companies to adopt IFRSs in future. At the time of writing, these amendments to IAS 27 and IFRS 1 have not yet been endorsed for use in the EU. Since the requirements of the amended Standards differ in important respects from those of the previous versions, EU reporting entities will not be able to apply the revised versions in their statutory financial statements until the revised Standards are endorsed.*

As explained in ***section 6*** *of* ***chapter 33****, UK companies adopting IFRSs before the amendments are endorsed will need to consider whether, at any stage, joint ventures have paid dividends out of pre-acquisition profits and, hence, whether the cost of investment needs to be adjusted for IFRS purposes. Thus, they may face practical difficulties in measuring the cost of* *a jointly controlled entity in their separate financial statements on first-time adoption of IFRSs, because of the need to adjust historical information.*

10 Reporting interests in joint ventures in the financial statements of an investor

When an investor does not have joint control over a joint venture, it reports its interest in accordance with the requirements of IAS 39 *Financial Instruments: Recognition and Measurement* or, if the investor has significant influence in the joint venture, in accordance with the requirements of IAS 28 *Investments in Associates*. [IAS 31.51]

This situation can only arise when there are at least three parties who have invested in the joint venture: at least two venturers, who share joint control, and a third investor who does not share joint control (either under the terms of the contractual agreement, or because the investor is not a party to the contractual agreement).

11 Operators of joint ventures

Operators or managers of a joint venture (see **4.5** above) should account for any fees in accordance with IAS 18 *Revenue*. These fees are accounted for by the joint venture as an expense. [IAS 31.52 & 53]

12 Presentation and disclosure

12.1 Presentation

IAS 1 *Presentation of Financial Statements* requires that:

- investments accounted for under the equity method be presented as a separate line item in the statement of financial position; [IAS 1(2007).54(e), previously IAS 1(2003).68(e)] and
- share of profit or loss of associates and joint ventures accounted for using the equity method be presented as a separate line item in the statement of comprehensive income. [IAS 1(2007).82(c), previously IAS 1(2003).81(c)]

These presentation requirements mean that amounts relating to different categories of investment (i.e. associates and jointly controlled entities accounted for using the equity method) are combined. IAS 28 *Investments in Associates* requires, however, that the investor's share of the results of associates and the carrying amount of investments in associates be separately disclosed (see **6.2.1** in **chapter 35**). Therefore, where the amounts are not separately analysed in the statement of financial position and the statement of comprehensive income, an analysis will be required in the notes to the financial statements. In any case, the nature of the investor's activities carried out via associates and joint ventures will sometimes be very distinct, in which case analysis would be recommended in the statement of financial position and statement of comprehensive income.

UK

Under the 'gross equity method' required by FRS 9, the investor's shares of the joint venture's turnover and operating profit and of each line item after operating profit are presented separately in the profit and loss account. In addition, the investor's share of the aggregate gross assets and liabilities underlying the net amount included for the investment is shown on the face of the balance sheet. Under IAS 1 Presentation of Financial Statements, *a single figure is required to be shown in the statement of comprehensive income, being the investor's share of profits (see* ***section 5.2.7*** *in* ***chapter 3****), and the statement of financial position amount is not analysed to show the underlying share of aggregate gross assets and liabilities.*

IAS 28 also requires that investments in associates accounted for under the equity method should be classified as non-current assets. [IAS 28.38] This requirement will apply equally to interests in jointly controlled entities accounted for under the equity method.

The venturer's share of changes recognised directly in equity by jointly controlled entities accounted for using the equity method should be recognised directly in equity by the venturer, and should be disclosed in the statement of changes in equity in accordance with IAS 1 *Presentation of Financial Statements*. [IAS 28.39]

12.2 Disclosure

12.2.1 *Financial statements in which jointly controlled entities are accounted for using equity accounting or proportionate consolidation*

The disclosure requirements in this section will normally apply to consolidated financial statements prepared in accordance with IAS 27. They will also apply, however, where the venturer does not prepare consolidated financial statements, because it does not have subsidiaries, but accounts for jointly controlled entities in its financial statements using proportionate consolidation or the equity method of accounting (see **8.1** above).

A venturer should disclose:

- the method it uses to recognise its interests in jointly controlled entities; [IAS 31.57]
- a listing and description of interests in significant joint ventures and the proportion of ownership interests held in jointly controlled entities; [IAS 31.56]
- the aggregate amount of the following contingent liabilities, unless the probability of loss is remote, separately from the amount of other contingent liabilities:
  [IAS 31.54]
  - any contingent liabilities that the venturer has incurred in relation to its interests in joint ventures and its share in each of the contingent liabilities which have been incurred jointly with other venturers;
  - its share of the contingent liabilities of the joint ventures themselves for which it is contingently liable; and
  - those contingent liabilities that arise because the venturer is contingently liable for the liabilities of the other venturers of a joint venture; and
- the aggregate amount of the following commitments in respect of its interests in joint ventures separately from other commitments:
  [IAS 31.55]
  - any capital commitments of the venturer in relation to its interests in joint ventures and its share in the capital commitments that have been incurred jointly with other venturers; and
  - its share of the capital commitments of the joint ventures themselves.

A venturer that recognises its interests in jointly controlled entities using the line-by-line format for proportionate consolidation, or the equity method, should disclose the aggregate amounts of each of current assets, long-term assets, current liabilities, long-term liabilities, income and expenses related to its joint ventures. [IAS 31.56]

12.2.2 *Separate financial statements*

IAS 27 also requires a number of disclosures regarding investments in jointly controlled entities in a venturer's separate financial statements (see **section 9** above). When a venturer prepares separate financial statements, those separate financial statements should disclose:

[IAS 27(2008).43, previously IAS 27(2003).42]

- the fact that the statements are separate financial statements and the reasons why those statements are prepared if not required by law;
- a list of significant investments in subsidiaries, jointly controlled entities and associates, including:
  - the name;
  - country of incorporation or residence;
  - the proportion of ownership interest; and
  - if different, the proportion of voting power held; and
- a description of the method used to account for such investments.

The separate financial statements are also required to identify the financial statements prepared in accordance with IAS 31 (i.e. those financial statements referred to in **12.2.1** above) to which they relate. [IAS 27(2008).43, previously IAS 27(2003).42]

12.2.3 *Requirements of the Companies Act*

*For UK companies, certain additional disclosures are required by the Companies Act, as set out in **sections 7.3 to 7.5 of chapter 33**.* UK

13 Future developments

In September 2007, the IASB published ED 9 *Joint Arrangements*, which sets out proposals to replace IAS 31. The Exposure Draft defines a joint arrangement as a contractual arrangement whereby two or more parties undertake an economic activity together and share decision-making relating to that activity. Joint arrangements include joint assets, joint operations, and joint ventures.

The Exposure Draft proposes that the legal form of an arrangement should not be the most significant factor in the determination of the appropriate accounting for the arrangement. This is unlike the approach taken under

IAS 31 which is closely aligned to the legal structure of joint venture arrangements, with only jointly controlled entities being singled out for equity accounting (or proportionate consolidation). The ED proposes that a party to a joint arrangement should:

- recognise its contractual rights and obligations (and the related income and expenses) in accordance with applicable IFRSs;
- recognise both the individual assets to which it has rights and the liabilities for which it is responsible, even if the joint arrangement operates in a separate legal entity; and
- recognise an interest in a joint venture (that is, an interest in a share of the outcome generated by the activities of a group of assets and liabilities subject to joint control) using the equity method. Proportionate consolidation would not be permitted.

The ED also proposes new requirements for disclosing information about joint arrangements, subsidiaries, and associates, including a description of the nature of joint arrangements and summarised financial information relating to an entity's interests in joint ventures.

At the time of writing, it is expected that a Standard may be issued in the first half of 2009.

37 Operating segments (IFRS 8)

1 Introduction

1.1 IFRS 8 and IAS 14

In November 2006, the IASB issued IFRS 8 *Operating Segments*, which is effective for annual financial statements for periods beginning on or after 1 January 2009. Prior to that date, entities may continue to apply IAS 14 *Segment Reporting*, which is discussed in **appendix 1**. Alternatively, entities may choose to apply IFRS 8 in advance of the 2009 effective date, provided that they disclose that fact.

IFRS 8 was endorsed for use in the EU in November 2007, so EU companies are now permitted to adopt it in advance of the 2009 effective date. UK

An overview of the impact for IFRS reporters of adopting IFRS 8 is set out below.

- IFRS 8 requires an entity to report financial and descriptive information about its reportable segments, which are operating segments or aggregations of operating segments that meet specified criteria. Operating segments are components of an entity about which separate financial information is available that is evaluated regularly by the chief operating decision maker in deciding how to allocate resources and in assessing performance. Upon adoption of IFRS 8, the identification of an entity's segments may or may not change. IAS 14 required an entity to identify two sets of segments (business and geographical), using a risks and rewards approach, with the entity's 'system of internal financial reporting to key management personnel' serving only as the starting point for the identification of such segments. One set of segments was regarded as primary and the other as secondary. If under IAS 14 an entity identified segments on the basis of the reports provided to the person whom IFRS 8 regards as the chief operating decision maker, those might become the 'operating segments' for the purposes of IFRS 8.

- IFRS 8 states that a component of an entity that sells primarily or exclusively to other operating segments of the entity will meet the definition of an operating segment if the entity is managed in that manner. IAS 14 limited reportable segments to those that earn a majority of their revenue from sales to external parties and did not require the different stages of a vertically-integrated entity to be identified as separate segments.

- IFRS 8 requires the amount reported for each segment item to be the measure reported to the chief operating decision maker for the purposes of allocating resources to that segment and assessing its performance. In contrast to IAS 14, IFRS 8 does not define segment revenue, segment expense, segment result, segment assets and segment liabilities, nor does it require segment information to be prepared in conformity with the accounting policies adopted for the entity's financial statements. As a consequence, entities will have more discretion in determining what is included in segment profit or loss under IFRS 8, limited only by their internal reporting practices.

- Under IFRS 8, additional entity-wide disclosures are prescribed that are required even when an entity has only one reportable segment. These include information about each product and service or groups of products and services.

- Analyses of revenues and certain non-current assets by geographical area are required – with an expanded requirement to disclose revenues/assets by individual foreign country (if material), irrespective of the identification of operating segments.

- IFRS 8 also introduces a requirement to disclose information about transactions with major customers. If revenues from transactions with a single external customer amount to 10 per cent or more of the entity's revenues, the total amount of revenue from each such customer and the segment or segments in which those revenues are reported must be disclosed.

- IFRS 8 makes a number of consequential amendments to other Standards, including:

- IAS 34 *Interim Financial Reporting* – IFRS 8 has expanded significantly the requirements for segment information in interim financial reports (see **3.5.1** in **chapter 39**);

- IAS 36 *Impairment of Assets* – IAS 36 requires goodwill to be tested for impairment as part of impairment testing the cash-generating unit to which it relates. In identifying the units (or groups of units) to which goodwill is allocated for the purpose of impairment testing, IAS 36 limits the size of such units or groups of units by reference to the entity's reported segments. As a result of IFRS 8 replacing IAS 14, that maximum limit is now determined by reference to the entity's operating segments as determined in accordance with IFRS 8 – which may differ from the limit previously arrived at in the context of IAS 14; and

- IFRS 6 *Exploration for and Evaluation of Mineral Resources* – similar to the IAS 36 amendments described above, the size of the cash-generating unit (or group of units) to which exploration and evaluation assets are allocated for the purpose of impairment testing is now limited by reference to the entity's operating segments as determined in accordance with IFRS 8, rather than the segments previously identified under IAS 14.

1.2 IFRS 8 *Operating Segments*

IFRS 8 *Operating Segments* sets out the requirements for entities whose debt or equity instruments are traded in a public market (and entities filing their financial statements with a regulator for the purpose of issuing instruments in a public market) for disclosure of information about their operating segments. Operating segments are identified based on the entity's internal system for reporting information to senior management.

This chapter discusses the requirements of IFRS 8 in the following sections:

Section 2	Core principle
Section 3	Scope
Section 4	Identification of operating segments
Section 5	Identification of reportable segments
Section 6	Measurement of segment information
Section 7	Disclosure

Section 8 Effective date and transition

Section 9 Future developments

UK

In certain respects, IFRS 8 is more prescriptive than its UK counterpart, SSAP 25 Segmental reporting. *The most significant differences between the two standards are highlighted below.*

- *IFRS 8 is strict in requiring information to be reported that has been generated for internal financial reporting. SSAP 25 has no such concept.*
- *IFRS 8 is more prescriptive in terms of how segments are identified and, in particular, how segments may be combined to create reportable segments.*
- *The disclosures required by IFRS 8 are more extensive than those of SSAP 25. For example, disclosures may include additions to non-current assets, depreciation and information about non-cash expenses.*
- *Unlike SSAP 25, IFRS 8 offers no exemption from disclosures on the grounds that they would be seriously prejudicial.*

2 Core principle

The core principle of IFRS 8 is as follows:

> 'An entity shall disclose information to enable users of its financial statements to evaluate the nature and financial effects of the business activities in which it engages and the economic environments in which it operates.' [IFRS 8.1]

3 Scope

IFRS 8 applies to the separate or individual financial statements of an entity and to the consolidated financial statements of a group with a parent:

[IFRS 8.2]

- whose debt or equity instruments are traded in a public market; or
- that files, or is in the process of filing, its (consolidated) financial statements with a securities commission or other regulatory organisation for the purpose of issuing any class of instruments in a public market.

The IASB has clarified that the scope of IFRS 8 does *not* include the consolidated financial statements of a group that includes a listed non-controlling interest or a subsidiary with listed debt, but whose parent has no listed financial instruments. [IFRS 8.BC23]

For the purposes above, a 'public market' is any domestic or foreign stock exchange, or an over-the-counter market, including local and regional markets. [IFRS 8.2]

Although worded differently, the scope of IFRS 8 is essentially the same as that of its predecessor Standard, IAS 14 (see **appendix 1**).

Other noteworthy points with regard to scope are that:

- where a single financial report includes both consolidated financial statements and the separate financial statements of a parent falling within the scope of IFRS 8, segment information need be presented on a consolidated basis only; [IFRS 8.4] and
- if an entity that is not required to comply with IFRS 8 (e.g. a private entity) chooses to disclose information about segments that does not comply with the requirements of that Standard, the entity is not permitted to describe the information as 'segment information'. [IFRS 8.3]

For entities outside the scope of IFRS 8 that choose to disclose some information about segments voluntarily, IFRS 8.3 represents a significant change. Previously, if a non-publicly traded entity presented any segment information in its IFRS financial statements, that information was required to comply fully with IAS 14. This approach was considered to be unnecessarily restrictive in that it might, for example, prevent a non-publicly traded entity from voluntarily disclosing sales information for segments, without also disclosing segment profit or loss. Under the IFRS 8 requirement, such entities are permitted to provide limited information on segments on a voluntary basis without triggering the need to comply fully with IFRS 8, so long as the disclosure is not referred to as segment information. [IFRS 8.BC22]

IFRS 8 applies only to information about segments reported in the financial statements. IAS 1 *Presentation of Financial Statements* defines a complete set of financial statements to include a statement of financial position, statement of comprehensive income, statement of cash flows, statement of changes in equity, and notes. Accordingly, where management voluntarily discloses certain information about segments outside of those financial statements (e.g. in the directors' report or chairman's statement) such disclosures are not affected by the restriction imposed under the second bullet above and may be described as 'segment information'.

3.1 Disclosures that might be seriously prejudicial

IFRS 8 does not provide an exemption for disclosures that the board or management deems to be prejudicial to the interests of the entity. Even where the directors of a publicly traded entity conclude that disclosure of certain segment information will be seriously prejudicial to the interests of the entity (e.g. because its main competitors are not publicly traded and, therefore, do not publish similar information), the segment information may not be omitted in IFRS financial statements.

UK

A 'seriously prejudicial' exemption is available to UK companies under SSAP 25, and companies that have historically taken advantage of it may find this a key difference if they are considering a transition to IFRSs.

4 Identification of operating segments

IFRS 8 takes a two-step approach to the identification of operating segments for which information is reported externally:

- identification of the entity's operating segments (as defined in IFRS 8); and
- identification of the entity's reportable segments (see **section 5** below).

4.1 The management approach to segment reporting

IFRS 8 adopts a strict management approach to segment reporting and requires that operating segments be identified on the same basis as financial information is reported internally for the purpose of allocating resources between segments and assessing their performance. In the past, IAS 14's approach had been loosely described as a management approach – but it differed fundamentally in that segments were identified based on the components of the business exposed to similar risks and generating similar rates of return, with the entity's 'system of internal financial reporting to key management personnel' serving only as the starting point for the identification of such segments. Under IAS 14, where internal reports were prepared on a basis that did not focus on the risks and returns of the entity's components (e.g. where internal reporting was organised solely by legal entity), that Standard required an alternative basis of segmentation for the external financial statements based on risks/rewards criteria. In contrast, under IFRS 8, the information reported for operating segments is always based on the information reported internally.

Note, however, that certain of the additional entity-wide disclosures required under IFRS 8 (e.g. analyses of revenue by type of product/service and of revenue by geographical area – see **7.6** below) will ensure that a limited amount of the information previously reported under IAS 14 is available, even where the operating segments are not identified along product/service or geographical lines.

The IASB has opted for the IFRS 8 approach based on the view that defining segments based on the structure of the entity's internal organisation allows users to see an entity 'through the eyes of management', which enhances a user's ability to predict actions or reactions of management that can significantly affect the entity's prospects for future cash flows. In addition, the Standard is expected to reduce the cost of reporting segment information externally because that information is already generated for management's use. The perceived disadvantage of this approach is that it may result in the reporting of segments that are not comparable between entities engaged in similar activities, and from year to year for an individual entity.

Example 4.1

Non-comparable segment disclosures between competitors

Entity A and Entity B both manufacture and distribute windows and insulation products used in the construction of residential and commercial units. Entity A is structured such that decisions are made and performance is evaluated on a regional basis (e.g. Americas, Europe), whereas Entity B makes decisions and evaluates performance on a product-line basis (e.g. windows, insulation).

Entity A and Entity B will not report similar operating segments under IFRS 8. Entity A should report operating segments based on regions and Entity B should report operating segments based on product lines. The management approach requires identification of operating segments on the basis of internal reports that are regularly reviewed by the entity's chief operating decision maker in order to allocate resources to the segment and assess its performance. Two entities in the same industry can have very different operating segments because each will determine its operating segments based on how management makes operating decisions and assesses performance.

4.2 Definition of operating segment

The Standard explains that an operating segment is a component of an entity:

[IFRS 8.5]

(a) that engages in business activities from which it may earn revenues and incur expenses (including revenues and expenses relating to transactions with other components of the same entity);

(b) whose operating results are regularly reviewed by the entity's chief operating decision maker to make decisions about resources to be allocated to the segment and assess its performance; and

(c) for which discrete financial information is available.

4.3 The chief operating decision maker

References in the Standard to the 'chief operating decision maker' are not necessarily to a manager with a specific title, but rather to a function – specifically, that of allocating resources to and assessing the performance of the operating segments of the entity. Often the chief operating decision maker of an entity is its chief executive officer or chief operating officer but, for example, it may be a group of executive directors or others. [IFRS 8.7]

The management approach relies on the structure of the organisation and the internal operating reports typically used by the chief operating decision maker, who determines the allocation of resources and assesses the performance of the operating segments. While the chief operating decision maker is usually an individual, sometimes the function is performed by a group.

Often the chief operating decision maker is the highest ranking management individual at the entity (or the consolidated entity, where consolidated financial statements are presented) who makes such decisions, although rank within the entity does not necessarily identify the chief operating decision maker. Such an individual typically would be the chief executive officer or chairman who may receive a host of management reports prepared in a variety of different ways.

Complex organisational and reporting structures often make it difficult to determine the chief operating decision maker and it may be helpful to consider the financial information that is presented to the board of directors as this information is typically indicative of how management views the entity's activities. An evaluation of such financial information will often help to distinguish the chief operating decision maker from other levels of line management, e.g. segment management.

Example 4.3A

Identification of the chief operating decision maker

Entity C is a publicly-traded manufacturer of various electronic instruments used in aerospace, medical and consumer products. Entity C has a chief operating officer for each of the aerospace, medical and consumer product units. The chief operating officers are responsible for operating, budgeting and reporting aspects of their respective units, and have senior management personnel within their units who report to them. The chief operating officers report to the chief executive officer (including making resource allocation recommendations for their respective units). The chief executive officer evaluates the performance of each unit based on a variety of different management reports and is responsible for entity-wide resource-allocation decisions.

In the circumstances described, even though the chief operating officers are responsible for the management of their respective units, the final decisions regarding the allocation of resources are made by the chief executive officer. Therefore, the chief executive officer is considered the chief operating decision maker. The chief operating decision maker is the individual or function responsible for decisions about overall resource allocation and performance assessment for each business unit of an entity. Generally, these decisions are made at the highest level of management, notwithstanding the fact that lower levels of management may be responsible for the operating, budgeting and reporting aspects of individual business units.

In the above fact pattern, Entity C is likely to have three operating segments and each of the chief operating officers is likely to be considered a segment manager. IFRS 8.9 states, in part, that a segment manager is 'directly accountable to and maintains regular contact with the chief operating decision maker to discuss operating activities, financial results, forecasts, or plans for the segment'.

Example 4.3B

Management committee as the chief operating decision maker

Entity D is a publicly-traded manufacturer of various electronic instruments used in aerospace, medical and consumer products. Entity D has a chief financial officer for each of the aerospace, medical and consumer-product units. Entity D is governed by a management committee comprised of each of the chief financial officers and the chief executive officer. The management committee makes all key operating decisions and determines the allocation of resources and makes assessments of performance. No one individual either on the management committee, or elsewhere in the entity, has the ability to override the management committee (except for the board of directors acting in their role of overseeing the management committee).

In the circumstances described, the chief operating decision maker is the management committee, and the reports used by the management committee are used to determine the operating segments of Entity D. Often the chief operating decision maker of an entity is its chief executive officer or chief operating officer, but it may be a group of executive directors or others, such as a management committee consisting of, for example, the entity's chief executive officer or chairman, chief operating officer, chief financial officer and others, all of whom have a vote on decisions made by the committee.

However, the existence of a management committee does not always mean that the management committee is the chief operating decision maker. For instance, the ability of the chief executive officer to override the decisions of the management committee would be an indicator that the chief executive officer, not the management committee, is the chief operating decision maker. This determination should be made for each individual case based on the specific facts and circumstances.

4.4 Segments and business activities

It need not be the case that every part of an entity is an operating segment or part of an operating segment. As examples, the Standard notes that a corporate headquarters or some functional departments may not earn revenues (or may earn revenues that are only incidental to the activities of the entity) and would not be operating segments. [IFRS 8.6]

For the purposes of IFRS 8, an entity's post-employment benefit plans are not operating segments. [IFRS 8.6]

4.5 Further guidance on identifying segments

For many entities, the three characteristics of operating segments described in **4.2** above clearly identify its operating segments. Where this is not the case, further guidance is provided in IFRS 8.8 – 10.

- An entity may produce reports in which its business activities are presented in a variety of ways. If the chief operating decision maker uses more than one set of segment information, other factors may identify a single set of components as constituting the entity's operating segments, including the nature of the business activities of each component, the existence of managers responsible for them, and information presented to the board of directors. [IFRS 8.8]
- Generally, an operating segment has a segment manager who is directly accountable to and maintains regular contact with the chief operating decision maker to discuss operating activities, financial results, forecasts, or plans for the segment. The term 'segment manager' identifies a function, not necessarily a manager with a specific title. The chief operating decision maker may also be the segment manager for some operating segments. A single manager may be the segment manager for more than one operating segment. If the characteristics in IFRS 8.5 (see **4.2** above) apply to more than one set of components of an organisation but there is only one set for which segment managers are held responsible, that set of components constitutes the operating segments. [IFRS 8.9]
- The characteristics in **4.2** above may apply to two or more overlapping sets of components for which managers are held responsible. That structure is sometimes referred to as a matrix form of organisation. For example, in some entities, some managers are responsible for different product and service lines worldwide, whereas other managers are responsible for specific geographical areas. The chief operating decision maker regularly reviews the operating results of both sets of components, and financial information is available for both. In that situation, the entity shall determine which set of components constitutes the operating segments by reference to the core principle of IFRS 8 (see **section 2** above). [IFRS 8.10]

Matrix organisational structures are commonly used for large complex organisations. The IASB has concluded that, where more than one set of segments can be identified, it should not simply mandate the use of components based on products and services as the entity's operating segments under IFRS 8, since to do so would be inconsistent with the management approach. Instead, the Standard refers back to the core principle – requiring that the identification of operating segments be made so as to enable users of the financial statements 'to evaluate the nature and financial effects of the business activities in which [the entity] engages and the economic environments in which it operates'. Management will, therefore, be required to exercise judgement as to which of the bases of segmentation satisfies this objective. [IFRS 8.BC27]

4.6 Vertically-integrated entities

Under the IFRS 8 approach, a component of an entity that sells primarily or exclusively to other operating segments of the entity will meet the definition of an operating segment if the entity is managed that way. This represents a change from IAS 14, which limited reportable segments to those earning a majority of their revenue from sales to external parties and did not require the different stages of a vertically-integrated entity to be identified as separate segments. This change has been made to ensure that information about the components engaged in each stage of production is reported, which is seen as particularly important in certain businesses such as oil and gas entities.

Example 4.6

Application of IFRS 8 to vertically-integrated entities

Entity E is a vertically-integrated oil entity that sells refined products to external customers. The refinery operation sells refined products internally to the marketing and distribution segment of Entity E (i.e. the refinery operation has no external customers). The financial results of the refinery operation are prepared separately and are reviewed on a regular basis by the chief operating decision maker to assess performance and make decisions regarding allocation of resources.

The refinery operation is an operating segment. A component of an entity is not required to have external customers or revenues in order to be classified as an operating segment. Some operating segments may only earn revenue relating to transactions with other components of the same entity, or may not yet earn revenues. The key factor in identifying operating segments is to understand the process the chief operating decision maker goes through in controlling the business. If the chief operating decision maker makes decisions and assesses operating performance regardless of revenue source or absence of revenue, the operating unit would be reported as an operating segment.

4.7 Operating unit not yet generating revenue

It is not necessary for a component of a business to actually earn revenues in order to meet the definition of an operating segment. The Standard specifically refers to start-up operations, which may engage in business activities for some time before they generate revenues, and allows that they may be operating segments at that pre-operating stage provided that the other criteria are met. [IFRS 8.5]

Example 4.7

Newly-formed operating unit

Entity F, a diversified pharmaceutical entity, has allocated 11 per cent of the combined assets of all operating segments to form an operating unit to pursue research on new drugs to fight the AIDS virus. Although expenses have been incurred, the operating unit has yet to earn revenues from any of its activities. Discrete financial information is available for the operating unit and that information is reviewed by the chief operating decision maker in making operating decisions and assessing operating performance.

The operating unit is an operating segment. The criteria set out in IFRS 8.5 (see above) are met. An operating segment can be such that it does not earn external or internal revenues and the chief operating decision maker makes decisions and assesses the performance of the segment based solely on expenses.

In this example, the intent of the entity is to allocate resources to the specific business purpose of AIDS research. Although there is a risk that revenues will never be earned from this pursuit, management has made a risk/reward determination that the cost of the research will be recovered through future revenues. If this level of resource allocation is performed and the information is reviewed by the chief operating decision maker, the operating unit should be considered an operating segment.

4.8 Identification of operating segments in the absence of discrete financial information

Example 4.8

Identification of operating segments in the absence of discrete financial information

Entity G has an operating unit that provides content to internet websites, and derives substantially all of its revenue from three service lines — advertising, promotions and customer service. The financial information reviewed by the chief operating decision maker includes revenue by service line, but operating expenses and assets are reported on a combined basis for the entire operating unit. The financial information does not include profit or loss information for the individual service lines.

The individual service lines are not separate operating segments. Discrete financial information is not available because there is no measure of segment profit or loss by service line supplied to the chief operating decision maker. The chief operating decision maker does not have sufficient information to assess performance and make resource allocation decisions by service line. In the circumstances described, it would be likely that the entire operating unit represents an operating segment, not the individual service lines.

> However, if the information provided to the chief operating decision maker contained revenue and gross profit by service line, sufficient financial information would be available to enable the chief operating decision maker to assess performance and make resource allocation decisions by service line. It is not necessary that assets be allocated for a component to be considered an operating segment.

5 Identification of reportable segments

Once the entity's operating segments have been identified, the entity must then determine which operating segments are reportable, i.e. those individual operating segments for which disclosure of information is required by the Standard.

Entities are required to report separately information about each operating segment that:

[IFRS 8.11]

(a) has been identified in accordance with IFRS 8.5 – 10 (as outlined in **section 4** above) or results from aggregating two or more of those segments in accordance with IFRS 8.12 (see **5.2** below); and

(b) exceeds the quantitative thresholds in IFRS 8.13 (see **5.3** below).

In addition, other situations in which separate information about an operating segment must be reported are specified in IFRS 8.14 – 18 (see **5.4** and **5.5** below).

The Implementation Guidance issued with IFRS 8 includes a decision tree that may be followed to assist with the identification of reportable segments. This decision tree is reproduced at **5.6** below.

5.1 Limit on the number of reportable segments

IFRS 8 does not set a precise limit on the number of operating segments for which information should be disclosed. However, it acknowledges that there may be a practical limit to the number of reportable segments that an entity separately discloses beyond which segment information becomes too detailed. The Standard suggests that, as the number of segments identified as reportable in accordance with the criteria set out in the following sections increases above ten, the entity should consider whether a practical limit has been reached. [IFRS 8.19]

Once the number of reportable operating segments exceeds a reasonable amount, an evaluation should be made of the criteria utilised by management for aggregation to determine if an appropriate aggregation of operating segments has been performed. Additionally, the existence of an unreasonably large number of operating segments may be an indication that the chief operating decision maker has not been properly identified.

5.2 Aggregation criteria

The Standard notes that operating segments often exhibit similar long-term financial performance (e.g. similar average gross margins) if they have similar economic characteristics. The question then arises as to when it is appropriate to combine operating segments which display such similar characteristics for the purpose of external reporting.

IFRS 8 states that two or more operating segments may be aggregated into a single operating segment if all of the following conditions are met:

[IFRS 8.12]

(a) aggregation is consistent with the core principle of IFRS 8 (see **section 2** above);

(b) the segments have similar economic characteristics; and

(c) the segments are similar in each of the following respects:

- (i) the nature of the products and services;
- (ii) the nature of the production processes;
- (iii) the type or class of customer for their products and services;
- (iv) the methods used to distribute their products or provide their services; and
- (v) if applicable, the nature of the regulatory environment, for example, banking, insurance, or public utilities.

The criteria for aggregation are strict, with the result that aggregation will only be permitted for quite homogeneous operations.

Both IFRS 8.BC30 and the flow chart included in the Implementation Guidance (see **5.6** below) clarify that the aggregation criteria set out above take precedence over the quantitative thresholds discussed in the next section. Therefore, if two or more components of a business meet the aggregation criteria set out above, they may be combined for external reporting purposes into a single operating segment, notwithstanding that they may individually exceed the quantitative thresholds.

Note that the Standard *permits* operating segments meeting the criteria outlined above to be combined for external reporting purposes. It does not require such combination, and entities are always entitled to report the operating segments separately if they wish to do so.

IFRS 8 does not define the term 'similar' or provide detailed guidance on the aggregation criteria and, therefore, the determination of whether two or more operating segments are similar is dependent on the individual facts and circumstances and is subject to a high degree of judgement. The guidance below may be a useful starting point for assessing whether operating segments are similar in each of the respects listed in IFRS 8.12.

Similar economic characteristics IFRS 8 states that segments with similar economic characteristics would be expected to have similar long-term average gross margins, but it does not provide any other examples of what may be used to evaluate economic characteristics. It may be appropriate for an entity to consider other performance measures such as sales growth, operating cash flows, return on assets, earnings before interest, taxes, depreciation, and amortisation (EBITDA), inventory turnover, or other standard industry measures. These factors should be evaluated from both a current, historical and 'expected future performance' perspective. An analysis based only on a future expectation of similar long-term economic performance (e.g. by reference to budgets), without reference to historical results, is unlikely to be sufficient. Additionally, competitive, operating and financial risks related to each business or industry type should be considered in determining whether two operating segments have similar economic characteristics. If operating segments are located in different geographical areas, entities may need to evaluate factors such as economic and political conditions, currency risks and foreign exchange control regulations.

The nature of the products and services IFRS 8 does not provide guidance as to how to interpret the 'nature' of products and services criterion. However, it can be considered that similar products or services have similar purposes or end uses. Thus, they may be expected to have similar rates of profitability, similar degrees of risk, and similar opportunities for growth. The assessment of whether products or services are similar may depend, in part, on the nature and breadth of an entity's product lines and overall operations.

The nature of the production process Although no specific guidance is provided in IFRS 8, similarities in the nature of the production process may be demonstrated by the sharing of common or interchangeable production or sales facilities, equipment, labour force or servicing and maintenance staff, or the use of the same or similar basic raw materials. Likewise, similar degrees of labour or capital intensiveness may indicate a similarity in the production process.

The type or class of customer for their products and services The similar type or class of customer criterion may be evaluated based on how management views the customer (e.g. similar marketing and promotional efforts, common or interchangeable sales forces, and customer demographics). Generally, retail and wholesale operations would not be considered to have similar types or classes of customers and, therefore, would not satisfy this criterion.

The methods used to distribute their products or provide the services The methods of distribution criterion may be evaluated based on the nature of the distribution channels (e.g. retail outlets, mail order, web site) and the nature of the products sold (e.g. component parts, finished goods).

If applicable, the nature of the regulatory environment, for example, banking, insurance or public utilities This criterion applies only if a unique regulatory environment exists with respect to a part of the entity's business. For example, in a situation where a utility holding entity has a regulated segment and a non-regulated segment, each segment is considered to operate in a different regulatory environment and, therefore, aggregation would not be appropriate even though they may produce the same product.

Example 5.2

Inconsistency of disclosure between the management report and segment disclosures

Entity H is a large retailer that operates two types of stores – clothing and home products (linens, decorative items and some clothing). For the purpose of IFRS 8, Entity H determines that it has two operating segments – 'Clothing' and 'Home Products'. Management's report to shareholders published with the financial statements discusses the results of operations of the home product stores separately in a manner different from that of the clothing stores by describing different customer demographics, products offered and sales and profit margin trends. The chairman's report also stresses important distinctions between the two operating segments. Is it appropriate for Entity B to aggregate its two operating segments into a single reportable operating segment for the purposes of reporting under IFRS 8?

It is unlikely that the home product segment should be aggregated with the clothing segment because the aggregation criteria in IFRS 8.12 are not fully satisfied. The aggregation criteria require, among other conditions, similar economic characteristics, similar products and similar type or class of customer. The management report and the chairman's report describe different economic characteristics, product types and customer demographics, and stress some important distinctions between the two segments. Therefore, it would not be appropriate to aggregate the home product segment with the clothing segment.

In general, while an entity may look to the aggregation criteria and conclude that it only has one reportable operating segment, such a situation would be expected to be unusual. The objective of IFRS 8 is to provide more useful information about the different types of business activities in which an entity engages. The operating segment information is intended to provide more meaningful information to the users of the financial statements.

The management approach prescribed in IFRS 8 facilitates consistent descriptions of an entity in the annual report and other published information. Information presented in the operating segment note of the financial statements should be consistent with the information presented throughout an entity's regulatory filings, whether in the annual report to shareholders, the entity's web sites, financial analyst reports, interviews and other public statements made by management, and other public documents.

5.3 Quantitative thresholds

Under IFRS 8, entities are required to report separately information about an operating segment that meets any of the following quantitative thresholds:

[IFRS 8.13]

(a) its reported revenue is 10 per cent or more of the combined revenue of all operating segments. For this purpose, revenue includes both sales to external customers and inter-segment sales or transfers; or

(b) the absolute amount of its reported profit or loss is 10 per cent or more of the greater, in absolute amount, of (i) the combined reported profit of all operating segments that did not report a loss and (ii) the combined reported loss of all operating segments that reported a loss; or

(c) its assets are 10 per cent or more of the combined assets of all operating segments.

Where segment information is reported to the chief operating decision maker after making adjustments, eliminations and allocations of revenue, expenses, and gains or losses, it would follow from IFRS 8.25 that, in applying the quantitative thresholds for the purposes of identifying reportable segments in IFRS 8.13, the thresholds should be applied on this basis, i.e. after adjustments, eliminations and allocations.

Example 5.3

Application of quantitative thresholds

Company I has identified the following operating segments: computer hardware, computer software and customer service. In applying the quantitative threshold tests set out above for the purpose of identifying reportable segments, Company I would perform the following analysis (based on the figures in the table below).

To determine the operating segments that exceed the 10 per cent revenue threshold, Company I should determine the combined revenue (external and internal) for all operating segments (£5,500). This amount includes £500 of inter-segment revenue. Ten per cent of this amount, or £550, would represent the threshold.

To determine the operating segments that exceed the 10 per cent profit or loss threshold, Company I should determine the greater, in absolute value, of (i) the combined reported profit of all operating segments that did not report a loss and (ii) the combined reported loss of all operating segments that reported a loss. Based on the calculation below, the absolute value of the total of all operating segments not reporting a loss, £350, is greater than the absolute value of the segment with a loss, £50. Ten per cent of £350, or £35, should then be used as the profit or loss threshold for identifying reportable segments.

To determine the segments that exceed the 10 per cent asset threshold, Company I should calculate the threshold based on 10 per cent of the combined segment assets of all operating segments identified (£800) before intragroup eliminations.

Note: * indicates a segment meeting the specific threshold.

Segment	Segment revenue	Segment result	Segments not reporting a loss	Segments reporting a loss	Segment assets
	£	£	£	£	£
Hardware	500	(50)		50*	400*
Software	2,500*	200	200*		300*
Service	2,500*	150	150*	—	100*
Total before eliminations	5,500	300	350	50	800

Eliminations	(500)	(10)	0	0	(10)
Total	5,000	290	350	50	790
Calculated threshold	550[a]		35[b]	35[b]	80[c]

(a) Total sales before elimination of inter-segment sales (£5,500) x 10%

(b) Threshold calculation is based on the greater of the absolute amount of all operating segments not reporting a loss and all operating segments with loss (£350) x 10%

(c) Total assets before considering inter-segment eliminations (£800) x 10%

Considering each of the operating segments in turn:

- the Hardware segment exceeds the result threshold (50 > 35) and the assets threshold (400 > 80);
- the Software segment exceeds the revenue threshold (2,500 > 550), the result threshold (200 > 35) and the assets threshold (300 > 80);
- the Service segment exceeds the revenue threshold (2,500 > 550), the result threshold (150 > 35) and the assets threshold (100 > 80).

Accordingly, all three segments meet at least one threshold and, therefore, all are reportable.

5.4 Operating segments below the quantitative thresholds

When an operating segment is below all of the quantitative thresholds set out above, the segment may be:

- designated as a reportable segment despite its size and separately disclosed, if management believes that information about the segment would be useful to users of the financial statements; [IFRS 8.13] or
- combined into a separately reportable segment with one or more other operating segment(s) that are also below all of the 10 per cent thresholds (but only if the operating segments so combined have similar economic characteristics and share a majority of the aggregation criteria set out in IFRS 8.12 – i.e. the criteria listed as (c)(i) to (c)(v) at **5.2** above). [IFRS 8.14]

Information about other business activities and operating segments that are not reportable shall be combined and disclosed in an 'all other segments' category separately from other reconciling items in the reconciliations required by IFRS 8.28 (see **7.4** below). The sources of the revenue included in the 'all other segments' category should be described. [IFRS 8.16]

5.4.1 *External revenue attributable to reportable segments to be at least 75 per cent of entity revenue*

IFRS 8 requires the total external revenue reported by operating segments to be at least 75 per cent of the entity's revenue. Where this is not the case, it is necessary to identify additional operating segments as reportable segments (even if they do not meet the quantitative thresholds in IFRS 8.13 – see **5.3** above) until at least 75 per cent of the entity's revenue is included in reportable segments. [IFRS 8.15]

Example 5.4.1

Identification of additional segments to reach 75 per cent revenue threshold

Company J has determined its reportable segments in accordance with IFRS 8 and has noted that the reportable segments constitute 68 per cent of consolidated revenue. All remaining operating segments are of similar size. How should Company J determine which operating segments to report separately?

IFRS 8 does not specify which of the remaining operating segments should be selected to achieve the 75 per cent threshold, and the operating segment chosen does not necessarily need to be the next largest by any of the measures. Judgement should be used, and each situation will be based on the individual facts and circumstances. Those additional operating segments included in order to achieve the 75 per cent threshold are treated no differently from any other reportable segment (i.e. the required disclosures are the same).

5.4.2 *Operating segment reported in preceding period that no longer exceeds quantitative thresholds*

Where an operating segment was identified as a reportable segment in the immediately preceding period (because it exceeded one of the 10 per cent thresholds), it should continue to be a reportable segment for the current period (notwithstanding that it no longer exceeds any of the 10 per cent thresholds), if the directors judge the segment to be of 'continuing significance'. [IFRS 8.17]

No further guidance is provided as to the meaning of 'continuing significance', but an operating segment normally would be regarded as having continuing significance for the current financial statements where, for example:

- its decline below the 10 per cent thresholds is considered temporary and likely to reverse;

- it has unrecognised intangible assets (such as internally-generated intangible assets) that, if recognised, would cause its segment assets to meet the 10 per cent threshold (this may indicate that the segment is of strategic importance); or
- it is held for sale.

While the items above are not an exhaustive list, management should ensure that the usefulness of the financial information and consistency in reporting is maintained.

Where management concludes that the segment is not of continuing significance, prior year information should be restated to conform to the current year's presentation, with appropriate disclosure describing the restatement.

An operating segment that has never met the quantitative thresholds may also be disclosed if management judges it to be of significance to the users of the financial statements.

5.5 Operating segment reportable in the current year but not in the preceding year

An operating segment may be identified as a reportable segment in the current period because it exceeds one of the relevant 10 per cent thresholds, even though it did not exceed any of the thresholds in the prior period. In such circumstances, prior period segment data that is presented for comparative purposes should be restated to reflect the newly reportable segment as a separate segment, unless the necessary information is not available and the cost to develop it would be excessive. [IFRS 8.18]

Although situations covered by the exception in IFRS 8.18 (see above) are expected to be unusual, consider the following example.

Example 5.5

Operating segment reportable in the current year but not in the prior year

In the past three years, Company K has grown from £100 million in sales annually to over £1 billion in sales annually as a result of five different acquisitions. Company K and each entity it acquired were managed differently. Due to its significant growth through acquisitions, Company K has recently restructured its management structure and operating segments. Historical records are not available for all of the entities in a manner consistent with the new management approach.

In this situation, it may be impracticable for Company K to restate prior period operating segment disclosures due to the number and size of its recent acquisitions.

5.6 Segment definition decision tree

The Implementation Guidance issued with IFRS 8 includes a decision tree, reproduced below, which illustrates how the requirements discussed in **section 5** are applied.

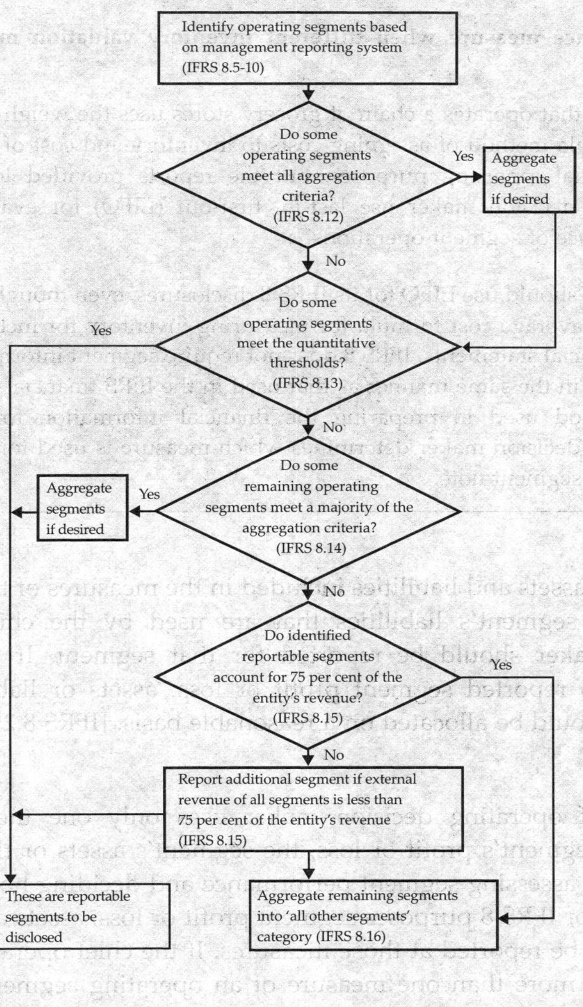

6 Measurement of segment information

Section 7 below sets out the information required to be disclosed under IFRS 8. This section summarises the guidance provided in IFRS 8 regarding the measurement of that information.

For each segment item, the amount to be reported under IFRS 8 is the measure reported to the chief operating decision maker for the purposes of making decisions about allocating resources to the segment and assessing its performance. Adjustments and eliminations made in preparing an entity's financial statements and allocations of revenues, expenses, and gains or losses should be included in determining reported segment profit or loss only if they are included in the measure of the segment's profit or loss that is used by the chief operating decision maker. [IFRS 8.25]

Example 6

Performance measure when different inventory valuation methods are used

An entity that operates a chain of grocery stores uses the weighted average cost formula method of assigning costs to inventory and cost of goods sold for financial reporting purposes, but the reports provided to the chief operating decision maker use last-in, first-out (LIFO) for evaluating the performance of segment operations.

The entity should use LIFO for its IFRS 8 disclosures, even though it uses the weighted average cost formula for measuring inventory for inclusion in its IFRS financial statements. IFRS 8 does not require segment information to be presented in the same manner as that used in the IFRS financial statements. The method used in preparing the financial information for the chief operating decision maker determines which measure is used for the IFRS 8 operating segment note.

Only those assets and liabilities included in the measures of the segment's assets and segment's liabilities that are used by the chief operating decision maker should be reported for that segment. If amounts are allocated to reported segment profit or loss, assets or liabilities, those amounts should be allocated on a reasonable basis. [IFRS 8.25]

If the chief operating decision maker uses only one measure of an operating segment's profit or loss, the segment's assets or the segment's liabilities in assessing segment performance and deciding how to allocate resources, for IFRS 8 purposes segment profit or loss, assets and liabilities should also be reported at those measures. If the chief operating decision maker uses more than one measure of an operating segment's profit or loss, the segment's assets or the segment's liabilities, the measures reported for IFRS 8 purposes should be those that management believes are determined in accordance with the measurement principles most consistent with those used in measuring the corresponding amounts in the entity's financial statements. [IFRS 8.26]

The requirements regarding measurement above signify another major change brought about by IFRS 8 in that the amount reported for each segment item is always the measure reported to the chief operating decision maker for the purposes of allocating resources to that segment and assessing its performance. IAS 14 required segment information to be prepared in conformity with the accounting policies adopted for the preparation and presentation of the external financial statements. In contrast to IAS 14, IFRS 8 does not define segment revenue, segment expense, segment result, segment assets or segment liabilities, but does require an explanation of how segment profit or loss, segment assets and segment liabilities are measured for each operating segment. As a consequence, entities will have more discretion in determining, for example, what is included in segment profit or loss under IFRS 8, limited only by their internal reporting practices.

This change resulted in two members of the Board dissenting from the Standard. Their view was that, because IFRS 8 allows the reporting of any measure of segment profit or loss as long as that measure is reviewed by the chief operating decision maker, this will result in items of revenue and expense directly attributable to a segment not being included in the reported profit or loss of that segment, and in items not directly attributable to any given segment not being allocated. They considered that proper external reporting of segment information should not permit non-GAAP measures because they mislead users. In its basis of conclusions, the majority of the Board defends the IFRS 8 approach on the basis that the reconciliations required of total segment amounts to the amounts recognised in the entity's financial statements (see **7.4** below) will enable users to understand and judge the basis on which the segment amounts were determined. The Board also noted that to define the measurement of such amounts would be a departure from the requirements of SFAS 131 (the equivalent US Standard) that would involve additional time and cost for entities and would be inconsistent with the management perspective on segment information.

7 Disclosure

The overall principle established by IFRS 8 is that entities should disclose information to enable users of their financial statements to evaluate the nature and financial effects of the business activities in which they engage and the economic environments in which they operate. [IFRS 8.20]

To give effect to this overall principle, entities are required to disclose the following:

[IFRS 8.21]

(a) general information (see **7.1**);

(b) information about reported segment profit or loss, including specified revenues and expenses included in reported segment profit or loss, segment assets, segment liabilities (see **7.2**) and the basis of measurement (see **7.3**); and

(c) reconciliations of the totals of segment revenues, reported segment profit or loss, segment assets, segment liabilities, and other material segment items to corresponding entity amounts (see **7.4**).

The information should be reported for each period for which a statement of comprehensive income is presented, with reconciliations of the amounts in the statement of financial position reported for each date at which a statement of financial position is presented. [IFRS 8.21]

Measurement principles for the amounts reported under (b) above are set out in IFRS 8.25 – 27 (see **section 6** above).

Requirements regarding the restatement of prior period segment information are set out in IFRS 8.29 & 30 (see **7.5**).

Additional entity-wide disclosures are also mandated by the Standard (see **7.6**).

The Implementation Guidance issued with IFRS 8 includes a number of illustrations of how the disclosure requirements of the Standard might be met. The illustrations are for a single hypothetical entity referred to as Diversified Company. For convenience, these illustrations are included in the relevant sections below. Note, however, that the formats in the illustrations are not requirements and that the IASB encourages entities to choose a format that provides the information in the most understandable manner in the specific circumstances. [IFRS 8.IG1]

7.1 General information

Entities are required to disclose the following general information:

[IFRS 8.22]

(a) factors used to identify the entity's reportable segments, including the basis of organisation (e.g. whether management has chosen to organise the entity around differences in products and services, geographical areas, regulatory environments, or a combination of factors, and whether operating segments have been aggregated); and

(b) types of products and services from which each reportable segment derives its revenues.

Example 7.1A

Factors that management used to identify the entity's reportable segments (IFRS 8.22(a))

[IFRS 8.IG2]

Diversified Company's reportable segments are strategic business units that offer different products and services. They are managed separately because each business requires different technology and marketing strategies. Most of the businesses were acquired as individual units, and the management at the time of the acquisition was retained.

Example 7.1B

Description of the types of products and services from which each reportable segment derives its revenues (IFRS 8.22(b))

[IFRS 8.IG2]

Diversified Company has five reportable segments: car parts, motor vessels, software, electronics and finance. The car parts segment produces replacement parts for sale to car parts retailers. The motor vessels segment produces small motor vessels to serve the offshore oil industry and similar businesses. The software segment produces application software for sale to computer manufacturers and retailers. The electronics segment produces integrated circuits and related products for sale to computer manufacturers. The finance segment is responsible for portions of the company's financial operations including financing customer purchases of products from other segments and property lending operations.

7.2 Information about profit or loss, assets and liabilities

For each reportable segment, entities are required to report a measure of:

[IFRS 8.23]

(a) profit or loss; and

(b) total assets.

Entities are required to report a measure of liabilities for each reportable segment if such an amount is regularly provided to the chief operating decision maker. [IFRS 8.23]

Entities are also required to disclose the following about each reportable segment if the specified amounts are included in the measure of segment profit or loss reviewed by the chief operating decision maker (or are otherwise regularly provided to the chief operating decision maker, even if not included in that measure of segment profit or loss):

[IFRS 8.23]

(a) revenues from external customers;

(b) revenues from transactions with other operating segments of the same entity;

(c) interest revenue;

(d) interest expense;

(e) depreciation and amortisation;

(f) material items of income and expense disclosed in accordance with IAS 1(2007).97 (previously IAS 1(2003).86 – see **5.3.1** in **chapter 3**);

(g) the entity's interest in the profit or loss of associates and joint ventures accounted for by the equity method;

(h) income tax expense or income; and

(i) material non-cash items other than depreciation and amortisation.

Interest revenue should be reported separately from interest expense for each reportable segment, unless:

[IFRS 8.23]

(a) a majority of the segment's revenues are from interest; and

(b) the chief operating decision maker relies primarily on net interest revenue to assess the performance of the segment and make decisions about resources to be allocated to the segment.

Where both conditions above are met, an entity may report that segment's interest revenue net of its interest expense and disclose that it has done so. [IFRS 8.23]

Entities are required to disclose the following about each reportable segment if the specified amounts are included in the measure of segment assets reviewed by the chief operating decision maker (or are otherwise regularly provided to the chief operating decision maker even if not included in the measure of segment assets):

[IFRS 8.24]

(a) the amount of investment in associates and joint ventures accounted for by the equity method, and

(b) the amounts of additions to non-current assets other than financial instruments, deferred tax assets, post-employment benefit assets (see **7.2.1** in **chapter 24**) and rights arising under insurance contracts.

Regarding the disclosure of additions to non-current assets, for assets classified according to a liquidity presentation, non-current assets are assets that include amounts expected to be recovered more than twelve months after the reporting period. [Footnote to IFRS 8.24]

Example 7.2

Information about reportable segment profit or loss, assets and liabilities

[IFRS 8.IG3]

The following table illustrates a suggested format for disclosing information about reportable segment profit or loss, assets and liabilities (IFRS 8.23 & 24). The same type of information is required for each year for which a statement of comprehensive income is presented. Diversified Company does not allocate tax expense (tax income) or non-recurring gains and losses to reportable segments. In addition, not all reportable segments have material non-cash items other than depreciation and amortisation in profit or loss. The amounts in this illustration, denominated as 'currency units (CU)', are assumed to be the amounts in reports used by the chief operating decision maker.

	Car parts	Motor vessels	Software	Electronics	Finance	All other	Totals
	CU	CU	CU	CU	CU	CU	CU
Revenues from external customers	3,000	5,000	9,500	12,000	5,000	1,000[a]	35,500
Inter-segment revenues	–	–	3,000	1,500	–	–	4,500
Interest revenue	450	800	1,000	1,500	–	–	3,750
Interest expense	350	600	700	1,100	–	–	2,750
Net interest revenue [b]	–	–	–	–	1,000	–	1,000
Depreciation and amortisation	200	100	50	1,500	1,100	–	2,950
Reportable segment profit	200	70	900	2,300	500	100	4,070
Other material non-cash items:							

	Car parts	Motor vessels	Software	Electronics	Finance	All other	Totals
	CU	CU	CU	CU	CU	CU	CU
Impairment of assets	–	200	–	–	–	–	200
Reportable segment assets	2,000	5,000	3,000	12,000	57,000	2,000	81,000
Expenditures for reportable segment non-current assets	300	700	500	800	600	–	2,900
Reportable segment liabilities	1,050	3,000	1,800	8,000	30,000	_	43,850

(a) Revenues from segments below the quantitative thresholds are attributable to four operating segments of Diversified Company. Those segments include a small property business, an electronics equipment rental business, a software consulting practice and a warehouse leasing operation. None of those segments has ever met any of the quantitative thresholds for determining reportable segments.

(b) The finance segment derives a majority of its revenue from interest. Management primarily relies on net interest revenue, not the gross revenue and expense amounts, in managing that segment. Therefore, as permitted by IFRS 8.23, only the net amount is disclosed.

7.3 Explanation of the measurement of segment information

Entities are required to provide an explanation of the measurements of segment profit or loss, segment assets and segment liabilities for each reportable segment. At a minimum, an entity is required to disclose the following:

[IFRS 8.27]

(a) the basis of accounting for any transactions between reportable segments;

(b) the nature of any differences between the measurements of the reportable segments' profits or losses and the entity's profit or loss before income tax expense or income and discontinued operations (if not apparent from the reconciliations required under IFRS 8.28 – see **7.4** below). Those differences could include accounting policies and policies for allocation of centrally incurred costs that are necessary for an understanding of the reported segment information;

(c) the nature of any differences between the measurements of the reportable segments' assets and the entity's assets (if not apparent from the reconciliations required under IFRS 8.28 – see **7.4** below). Those differences could include accounting policies and policies for allocation of jointly used assets that are necessary for an understanding of the reported segment information;

(d) the nature of any differences between the measurements of the reportable segments' liabilities and the entity's liabilities (if not apparent from the reconciliations required under IFRS 8.28 – see **7.4** below). Those differences could include accounting policies and policies for allocation of jointly utilised liabilities that are necessary for an understanding of the reported segment information;

(e) the nature of any changes from prior periods in the measurement methods used to determine reported segment profit or loss and the effect, if any, of those changes on the measure of segment profit or loss; and

(f) the nature and effect of any asymmetrical allocations to reportable segments. For example, an entity might allocate depreciation expense to a segment without allocating the related depreciable assets to that segment.

Example 7.3

Measurement of operating segment profit or loss, assets and liabilities (IFRS 8.27)

[IFRS 8.IG2]

The accounting policies of the operating segments are the same as those described in the summary of significant accounting policies except that pension expense for each operating segment is recognised and measured on the basis of cash payments to the pension plan. Diversified Company evaluates performance on the basis of profit or loss from operations before tax expense not including non-recurring gains and losses and foreign exchange gains and losses.

Diversified Company accounts for inter-segment sales and transfers as if the sales or transfers were to third parties, i.e. at current market prices.

7.4 Reconciliations

Entities are required to provide reconciliations of all of the following:

[IFRS 8.28]

(a) the total of the reportable segments' revenues to the entity's revenue;

(b) the total of the reportable segments' measures of profit or loss to the entity's profit or loss before tax expense (tax income) and discontinued operations. However, if an entity allocates to reportable segments items such as tax expense (tax income), the entity may reconcile the total of the segments' measures of profit or loss to the entity's profit or loss after those items;

(c) the total of the reportable segments' assets to the entity's assets;

(d) the total of the reportable segments' liabilities to the entity's liabilities (if segment liabilities are reported in accordance with IFRS 8.23); and

(e) the total of the reportable segments' amounts for every other material item of information disclosed to the corresponding amount for the entity.

For the purposes of these reconciliations, all material reconciling items should be separately identified and described. For example, the amount of each material adjustment needed to reconcile reportable segment profit or loss to the entity's profit or loss arising from different accounting policies should be separately identified and described. [IFRS 8.28]

As discussed at **5.4** above, information about other business activities and operating segments that do not meet the quantitative thresholds specified in IFRS 8.13 – 15 and, therefore, are not identified as reportable segments should be combined and disclosed in an 'all other segments' category. This should be reported separately from other reconciling items in the reconciliations of segment amounts to consolidated financial statement amounts required by IFRS 8.28.

Example 7.4

Reconciliations of reportable segment revenues, profit or loss, assets and liabilities

[IFRS 8.IG4]

The following illustrate reconciliations of reportable segment revenues, profit or loss, assets and liabilities to the entity's corresponding amounts (IFRS 8.28(a) – (d)). Reconciliations also are required to be shown for every other material item of information disclosed (IFRS 8.28(e)). The entity's financial statements are assumed not to include discontinued operations. As discussed in paragraph IG2 (reproduced above as **example 7.3**), the entity recognises and measures pension expense of its reportable segments on the basis of cash payments to the pension plan, and it does not allocate certain items to its reportable segments.

Revenues	**CU**
Total revenues for reportable segments	39,000
Other revenues	1,000
Elimination of inter-segment revenues	(4,500)
Entity's revenues	35,500

Profit or loss	CU
Total profit or loss for reportable segments	3,970
Other profit or loss	100
Elimination of inter-segment profits	(500)
Unallocated amounts:	
Litigation settlement received	500
Other corporate expenses	(750)
Adjustment to pension expense in consolidation	(250)
Income before income tax expense	3,070

Assets	CU
Total assets for reportable segments	79,000
Other assets	2,000
Elimination of receivable from corporate headquarters	(1,000)
Other unallocated amounts	1,500
Entity's assets	81,500

Liabilities	CU
Total liabilities for reportable segments	43,850
Unallocated defined benefit pension liabilities	25,000
Entity's liabilities	68,850

Other material items	Reportable segment totals	Adjustments	Entity totals
	CU	CU	CU
Interest revenue	3,750	75	3,825
Interest expense	2,750	(50)	2,700
Net interest revenue (finance segment only)	1,000	–	1,000
Expenditures for assets	2,900	1,000	3,900
Depreciation and amortisation	2,950	–	2,950
Impairment of assets	200	–	200

The reconciling item to adjust expenditures for assets is the amount incurred for the corporate headquarters building, which is not included in segment information. None of the other adjustments are material.

7.5 Restatement of previously-reported information

If an entity changes the structure of its internal organisation in a manner that causes the composition of its reportable segments to change, the corresponding information for earlier periods, including interim periods, should generally be restated. [IFRS 8.29]

IFRS 8 does not require such restatement where the information is not available and the cost to develop it would be excessive. The determination of whether the information is not available and the cost to develop it would be excessive is made for each individual item of disclosure. [IFRS 8.29]

Following a change in the composition of reportable segments, entities are required to disclose whether they have restated the corresponding items of segment information for earlier periods. [IFRS 8.29]

If an entity has changed the structure of its internal organisation in a manner that causes the composition of its reportable segments to change and if segment information for earlier periods, including interim periods, is not restated to reflect the change, the entity is required to disclose in the year in which the change occurs segment information for the current period on both the old basis and the new basis of segmentation, unless the necessary information is not available and the cost to develop it would be excessive. [IFRS 8.30]

7.6 Entity-wide disclosures

In addition to the disclosure requirements for individual segments set out above, IFRS 8 sets out a number of entity-wide disclosure requirements that apply to all entities falling within its scope, including those entities that have a single reportable segment. Some entities' business activities are not organised on the basis of differences in related products and services or differences in geographical areas of operations. Such an entity's reportable segments may report revenues from a broad range of essentially different products and services, or more than one of its reportable segments may provide essentially the same products and services. Similarly, an entity's reportable segments may hold assets in different geographical areas and report revenues from customers in different geographical areas, or more than one of its reportable segments may operate in the same geographical area. The information required by IFRS 8.32 – 34) (as outlined in **7.6.1** to **7.6.3** below) need be provided only if it is not provided as part of the reportable segment information required by IFRS 8. [IFRS 8.31]

Although the identification of operating segments and information disclosed in respect of those operating segments under IFRS 8 are based on the management approach (see **4.1** above), entity-wide disclosures standardise a portion of the segment disclosures between entities. The amounts reported for the entity-wide disclosures should be based on the financial information that is used to produce the IFRS financial statements and not the operating segment note (unless they happen to be the same basis). The result is that the entity-wide disclosures will agree with the corresponding amounts in the IFRS financial statements.

7.6.1 *Information about products and services*

Entities are required to report the revenues from external customers for each product and service or each group of similar products and services, unless the necessary information is not available and the cost to develop it would be excessive. Where these disclosures are not made because the information is not available and the cost to develop it would be excessive, that fact should be disclosed. [IFRS 8.32]

The amounts of revenues to be reported under this requirement are based on the financial information used to produce the entity's financial statements. [IFRS 8.32]

If the entity determines its reportable segments on the basis of products and services and such information is disclosed in the operating segments' disclosure, disclosure of this information need not be repeated in the entity-wide disclosures.

7.6.2 *Information about geographical areas*

Entities are required to report the following geographical information, unless the necessary information is not available and the cost to develop it would be excessive:

[IFRS 8.33]

(a) revenues from external customers:

  (i) attributed to the entity's country of domicile; and

  (ii) attributed to all foreign countries in total from which the entity derives revenues;

(b) separate disclosure of revenues from external customers attributed to an individual foreign country, where those revenues are material;

(c) the basis for attributing revenues from external customers to individual countries;

(d) non-current assets other than financial instruments, deferred tax assets, post-employment benefit assets, and rights arising under insurance contracts:

   (i) located in the entity's country of domicile; and

   (ii) located in all foreign countries in total in which the entity holds assets; and

(e) separate disclosure of assets in an individual foreign country, where those assets are material.

The amounts to be reported under IFRS 8.33 as outlined above are based on the financial information that is used to produce the entity's financial statements. [IFRS 8.33]

If the necessary information is not available and the cost to develop it would be excessive, that fact should be disclosed. [IFRS 8.33]

Note that, if they wish to do so, entities may provide, in addition to the information set out above, subtotals of geographical information about groups of countries. [IFRS 8.33]

If the entity determines its reportable segments on a geographical basis and such information is disclosed in the operating segments' disclosure, disclosure of this information need not be repeated in the entity-wide disclosures. However, if the entity manages its business based on geographical regions and determines its reportable segments accordingly, it still must provide separate disclosures required by IFRS 8.33 for each country in which revenues are material. Some entities provide this disclosure by presenting material countries separately with subtotals by region.

Example 7.6.2

Geographical information

[IFRS 8.IG5]

The following illustrates the geographical information required by IFRS 8.33. (Because Diversified Company's reportable segments are based on differences in products and services, no additional disclosures of revenue information about products and services are required (IFRS 8.32).)

Geographical information	Revenues (a)	Non-current assets
	CU	CU
United States	19,000	11,000
Canada	4,200	–
China	3,400	6,500
Japan	2,900	3,500
Other countries	6,000	3,000
Total	35,500	24,000

(a) Revenues are attributed to countries on the basis of the customer's location.

7.6.3 *Information about major customers*

Under IFRS 8, entities are required to provide information about the extent of their reliance on major customers.

If revenues from transactions with a single external customer amount to 10 per cent or more of an entity's revenues, the entity is required to disclose:

[IFRS 8.34]

(a) that fact;

(b) the total amount of revenues from each such customer; and

(c) the identity of the segment or segments reporting the revenues.

The Standard explicitly states that entities are not required to disclose the identity of a major customer, nor the amount of revenues that each segment reports from that customer. [IFRS 8.34]

For the purposes of these requirements, a group of entities known to a reporting entity to be under common control is considered a single customer and a government (national, state, provincial, territorial, local or foreign) and entities known to the reporting entity to be under the control of that government are considered a single customer. [IFRS 8.34]

Example 7.6.3

Information about major customers

[IFRS 8.IG6]

Revenues from one customer of Diversified Company's software and electronics segments represent approximately £5,000 of the Company's total revenues.

8 Effective date and transition

Entities are required to apply IFRS 8 in annual financial statements for periods beginning on or after 1 January 2009. [IFRS 8.35]

Earlier application is permitted. If an entity applies IFRS 8 in its financial statements for a period before 1 January 2009, it shall disclose that fact. [IFRS 8.35]

Segment information for prior years that is reported as comparative information for the initial year of application should be restated to conform to the requirements of IFRS 8, unless the necessary information is not available and the cost to develop it would be excessive. [IFRS 8.36]

Note that IFRS 8 results in a number of consequential amendments to other Standards (including significantly expanding the segment information to be disclosed in interim financial reports prepared in compliance with IAS 34 *Interim Financial Reporting* and potentially changing the basis for assessment of impairment losses on goodwill under IAS 36 *Impairment of Assets* and on exploration and evaluation assets under IFRS 6 *Exploration for and Evaluation of Mineral Resources*). These changes are also effective for annual periods beginning on or after 1 January 2009. If an entity applies IFRS 8 for an earlier period, the consequential amendments to other Standards should also be applied for that earlier period. [IFRS 8.Appendix B]

9 Future developments

The IASB has indicated that, at a future date, it will consider extending the scope of IFRS 8 to all entities that have public accountability rather than just entities whose securities are publicly traded. At the time of writing, no timescale has been indicated for such an extension.

38 Earnings per share

1 Introduction

IAS 33 *Earnings per Share* prescribes principles for the determination and presentation of earnings per share (EPS) information. The Standard was revised by the IASB in December 2003, and was most recently amended when the revised version of IFRS 3 *Business Combinations* was issued in January 2008.

This chapter discusses the requirements of IAS 33 in the following sections:

Section 2	Scope
Section 3	Definitions
Section 4	Calculation of basic earnings per share
Section 5	Calculation of diluted earnings per share
Section 6	Reporting additional earnings per share on an alternative basis
Section 7	Presentation and disclosure
Section 8	Future developments

> *The equivalent UK standard, FRS 22* Earnings per Share, *is based on the text of IAS 33, but with very limited amendments. Those amendments grant an exemption to companies adopting the Financial Reporting Standard for Smaller Entities (FRSSE), and add appendices giving specific guidance on the interaction with certain UK accounting standards (FRSs 3 and 6), but do not otherwise change the requirements of IAS 33 in any way.* UK

2 Scope

When the IASB issued IFRS 8 *Operating Segments*, it took the opportunity to amend IAS 33.2 so as to clarify the scope of the EPS Standard. Following that amendment, IAS 33 applies to:

[IAS 33.2 & 3]

- the separate or individual financial statements of an entity:
  - whose ordinary shares or potential ordinary shares are traded in a public market (a domestic or foreign stock exchange or an over-the-counter market, including local and regional markets) or
  - that files, or is in the process of filing, its financial statements with a securities commission or other regulatory information for the purpose of issuing ordinary shares in a public market; and
- the consolidated financial statements of a group with a parent:
  - whose ordinary shares or potential ordinary shares are traded in a public market (a domestic or foreign stock exchange or an over-the-counter market, including local and regional markets) or
  - that files, or is in the process of filing, its financial statements with a securities commission or other regulatory information for the purpose of issuing ordinary shares in a public market; and
- entities voluntarily choosing to present EPS information.

Prior to amendment by IFRS 8, IAS 33.2 referred to entities whose ordinary shares or potential ordinary shares are publicly traded and entities that are in the process of issuing ordinary shares or potential ordinary shares in public markets.

The amendment by IFRS 8 makes clear that, for a group, it is the shares of the parent that must be considered. Thus, an unlisted group which includes a listed subsidiary is not automatically within the scope of the Standard.

The scope of the Standard includes entities that are in the process of filing financial statements with a securities commission or other regulatory information for the purpose of issuing ordinary shares in a public market. This means that EPS information is required in financial statements prepared for the purpose of the issue of a prospectus.

2.1 Mutual-to-shares conversions

The definition of a financial liability in IAS 32 *Financial Instruments: Presentation* was amended in February 2008 in order for certain puttable financial instruments and obligations arising on liquidation to be presented as equity, as opposed to a financial liability. Prior to that amendment, many entities with a mutual form of ownership had no equity instruments under IFRSs (see **section 2.1.2** of **chapter 15**) as the most subordinate instrument issued by the entity had an obligation for the entity to pay cash or another financial asset. Due to the strict criteria in the amendments to IAS 32, certain entities with a mutual form of ownership may continue to have no equity. In the instances where such entities convert from a mutual form of ownership to share ownership that is classified as equity, the EPS should be based on earnings subsequent to conversion as it is only for the period subsequent to conversion that the entity had equity instruments outstanding. Reporting EPS based on earnings subsequent to conversion may result in an EPS amount that will not be comparable to EPS amounts determined in future years. Further, such an EPS amount may not reflect fully the expected relationship between earnings for the period and the amount of outstanding shares at the end of the reporting period. Therefore, the statement of comprehensive income caption should be sufficiently descriptive to inform the reader of the unique nature of EPS in the year of conversion, and the method of presentation should be described in the notes.

The amended IAS 32.11 recognises that puttable instruments and obligations arising on liquidation that are presented as equity following the amendment do meet the definition of a financial liability but are presented as equity as an exception. As IAS 33 was not amended when the amendments to IAS 32 was issued there was confusion as to whether IAS 33 would apply to an entity which previously had no equity but following the amendments presented its puttable instruments or obligations arising at liquidation as equity. In May 2008, the IASB agreed to amend IAS 32 to make clear that entities that previously had no equity that would present instruments as equity following the IAS 32 amendment should apply IAS 33 in the period when the amended IAS 32 is applied.

2.2 Entities voluntarily presenting EPS information

IAS 33 requires that any entity that presents EPS information does so in accordance with that Standard. Therefore, any entity whose ordinary shares or potentially ordinary shares are not publicly traded that voluntarily presents EPS information is bound by the requirements of IAS 33. [IAS 33.3]

2.3 Consolidated and separate financial statements

Where an entity presents both consolidated financial statements and separate financial statements in accordance with IAS 27 *Consolidated and Separate Financial Statements*:

[IAS 33.4]

- the disclosures required by IAS 33 need only be given in respect of the consolidated information;
- if the entity chooses to disclose EPS information based on its separate financial statements, it is required to prepare that information in accordance with IAS 33 and to present it only in its statement of comprehensive income; and
- EPS information based on the separate financial statements should not be presented in the consolidated financial statements (either in the statement of comprehensive income or in the notes).

If an entity presents the components of profit or loss in a separate income statement as described in IAS 1(2007).81 (see **section 5** of **chapter 3**), EPS should be presented only in that separate statement. [IAS 33.4A]

2.4 Shares listed but not intended to be traded

Example 2.4

Shares listed but not intended to be traded

The shares of Company A are listed on the Luxembourg exchange. Company A has completed a listing for marketing purposes only because its investors (which are pension funds) are restricted by their governing laws to investing in listed entities. It is not expected that these shares will be traded.

Although these shares are not expected to be traded, nevertheless the entity is within the scope of IAS 33 and EPS disclosures will be required. The notion of 'publicly traded' does not require the actual trading of shares, but the ability to trade the shares publicly.

3 Definitions

3.1 Ordinary share

IAS 33 defines an ordinary share as an equity instrument that is subordinate to all other classes of equity instruments. [IAS 33.5] An equity instrument is defined in IAS 32 *Financial Instruments: Presentation* as any contract that evidences a residual interest in the assets of an entity after deducting all of its liabilities. [IAS 32.11] The Standard explains that ordinary shares participate in profit for the period only after other types of shares (such as preference shares) have participated. Ordinary shares of the same class have the same rights to receive dividends, but it is possible for an entity to have more than one class of ordinary shares. [IAS 33.6]

3.2 Potential ordinary share

A potential ordinary share is defined as a financial instrument or other contract that may entitle its holder to ordinary shares. [IAS 33.5] Examples of potential ordinary shares include:

[IAS 33.7]

- financial liabilities or equity instruments, including preference shares, that are convertible into ordinary shares;
- options and warrants (i.e. financial instruments issued by the entity that give the holder the right to purchase ordinary shares); and
- shares that would be issued upon the satisfaction of conditions resulting from contractual arrangements, such as the purchase of a business or other assets.

The concept that an instrument may be considered the equivalent of ordinary shares has evolved to meet the reporting needs of investors in entities that have issued certain types of convertible and other complex securities. The holders of these instruments can expect to participate in the appreciation in value of the ordinary shares resulting principally from the earnings and earnings potential of the issuing entity. The attractiveness of these instruments to investors often is based on the potential right to participate in increases in the earnings potential of the entity, rather than on fixed returns or other senior security characteristics. The value of instruments that are considered potential ordinary shares is derived largely from the value of the ordinary shares to which they relate. Changes in the value of such instruments tend to reflect changes in the value of the ordinary shares.

3.2.1 *Derivatives over own equity*

If an entity enters into a derivative over its own ordinary shares that may entitle the holder to ordinary shares, that derivative is a potential ordinary share. This is the case where the settlement terms of the derivative permit or require settlement net in ordinary shares of the entity or in a fixed number of ordinary shares for a fixed amount of cash. This applies irrespective of whether the settlement terms are at the option of the holder or the issuer.

If, however, the settlement terms of the derivative permit only net settlement in cash or other financial assets, and/or settlement by the exchange of gross amounts of cash or other financial assets, the instrument does not 'entitle its holder to ordinary shares' and is not a potential ordinary share. This is true irrespective of whether the settlement terms are at the option of the holder or the issuer.

4 Calculation of basic earnings per share

The objective of basic EPS information is to provide a measure of the interests of each ordinary share of a parent entity in the performance of the entity over the reporting period. [IAS 33.11] Basic EPS amounts are required to be calculated for:

[IAS 33.9]

- profit or loss attributable to ordinary equity holders of the parent entity; and
- if presented, profit or loss from continuing operations attributable to those equity holders.

Basic EPS is calculated as:

[IAS 33.10]

$$\frac{\text{Profit (loss) attributable to ordinary equity holders of the parent entity}}{\text{Weighted average number of ordinary shares outstanding during the period}}$$

4.1 Earnings numerator

The starting point for the earnings numerator (for results both from continuing operations and for the entity as a whole) is the profit or loss after tax attributable to the equity holders of the parent entity (i.e. excluding the amount attributable to non-controlling interests). [IAS 33.12]

4.1.1 Non-controlling interests

The profit or loss attributable to equity holders of the parent will be readily available, as it is required to be presented in the statement of comprehensive income (or, where applicable, the separate income statement), under IAS 1 *Presentation of Financial Statements*, separately from the profit or loss attributable to non-controlling interests. [IAS 1(2007).83, previously IAS 1(2003).82] Where applicable, however, the profit for the period from continuing operations presented in the statement of comprehensive income (which is before the allocation to non-controlling interests) will need to be adjusted for the non-controlling interests' share of those earnings in order to arrive at the amount attributable to equity holders of the parent.

4.1.2 The impact of preference shares

The profit or loss attributable to the equity holders of the parent entity will already be after deduction of dividends and other profit or loss effects relating to preference shares *classified as liabilities*. [IAS 33.13] For the purposes of calculating basic EPS, the profit or loss attributable to the equity holders of the parent entity is further adjusted for the following after-tax amounts relating to preference shares *classified as equity*:

[IAS 33.12]

- preference dividends;
- differences arising on the settlement of such preference shares; and
- other similar effects of such preferences shares.

4.1.2.1 Preference dividends

The after-tax amount of preference dividends to be deducted in determining the profit or loss attributable to ordinary equity holders of the parent entity is:

[IAS 33.14]

- for non-cumulative preference shares classified as equity, the after-tax amount of preference dividends declared in respect of the period; and
- for cumulative preference shares classified as equity, the full after-tax amount of the required preference dividends for the period (whether or not declared). This does not include amounts paid or declared on cumulative preference shares in the current period in respect of previous periods.

For non-cumulative preference shares, dividends 'declared in respect of the period' are any dividends on the preference shares that are recognised as a liability at the end of the period, plus any dividends paid during the period that were not accrued at the end of the prior period. They do not include dividends declared after the end of the period that, in accordance with IAS 10 *Events after the Reporting Period*, are not recognised as a liability.

Example 4.1.2.1

Liquidating dividends on preference shares

Company X issued one share of Series A Non-Voting Convertible Preference Shares for £1,000,000. The liquidation preference on this preference share is £1,000,000, plus a 12 per cent cumulative dividend from the issue date. Company X also issued one share of Series B Non-Voting Convertible Preference Shares for £2,000,000. The shareholder of the Series B Preference share is entitled to a non-cumulative dividend at the rate of five per cent per annum on the liquidation preference. The liquidation preference is £2,000,000, plus a 12 per cent cumulative dividend from the issue date. All payments on both preference shares are at the discretion of Company X and, therefore, they are both presented as equity.

In calculating profit or loss attributable to ordinary shareholders, Company X should not deduct the 12 per cent cumulative liquidating dividends for either the Series A or Series B shares. Although cumulative, the liquidating dividends are intended to provide a preference to the Series A and Series B preference shareholders in the event of a liquidation of Company X and, therefore, should not be included in determining profit or loss attributable to ordinary shareholders until a liquidating event occurs.

4.1.2.2 *Differences arising on the settlement of preference shares*

Differences may arise on the settlement of preference shares in the following circumstances:

- where the preference shares are repurchased under a tender offer, and the fair value of the consideration paid to the preference shareholders differs from their carrying amount. Any excess of the fair value of the consideration over the carrying amount represents a return to the holders of the preference shares and is charged to retained earnings in the period of repurchase. This amount is deducted in calculating the earnings numerator for basic EPS. [IAS 33.16] Any excess of the carrying amount of the shares over the fair value of the consideration is added in calculating the earnings numerator for basic EPS; [IAS 33.18] and
- on early conversion of convertible preference shares, as a result of favourable changes to the original conversion terms or the payment of additional consideration. The excess of the fair value of the

ordinary shares or other consideration paid over the fair value of the ordinary shares issuable under the original conversion terms is a return to the preference shareholders, and is deducted in calculating the earnings numerator for basic EPS. [IAS 33.17]

Some entities issue classes of shares characterised as 'tracking' or 'targeted' shares to measure the performance of a specific business unit or activity of the entity. The terms of tracking shares often allow the entity, at its option, to exchange or redeem one class of tracking shares for another class of tracking shares, such that the entity would have one less class of ordinary shares outstanding. The terms of this feature generally require a premium to be paid to the class being redeemed as a result of the transaction. In the period of redemption, profit or loss attributable to ordinary shareholders (whose shares are being used for the redemption) should be reduced by the premium over market value paid to redeem the tracking shares. The holders of the tracking shares being redeemed have received a benefit that constitutes an additional contractual return to them.

Example 4.1.2.2A

Payment of premium on redemption of tracking shares

Company X has two classes of ordinary shares outstanding that separately track the results of operations of two different businesses, Company A and Company B. Company X decided to redeem all of its outstanding Company B tracking shares in exchange for Company A tracking shares. The terms of the Company B shares being redeemed provide Company X with the right to redeem the Company B tracking shares, at its discretion, by issuing its Company A tracking shares with a market value equal to a 15 per cent premium over the market price of the Company B tracking shares at the time of redemption. As such, the fair value of Company A tracking shares to be exchanged for the Company B tracking shares will exceed the fair value of the Company B tracking shares by 15 per cent on the date the redemption is announced.

The profit or loss attributable to Company A tracking shares should be reduced by the amount of the 15 per cent premium when calculating the profit or loss attributable to Company A tracking shareholders for EPS purposes of Company X for the period.

Example 4.1.2.2B

Premium paid by a parent to redeem preference shares issued by a subsidiary

Company P, a publicly traded entity, has a wholly-owned subsidiary, Company S. Company S has preference shares outstanding held by parties

> outside the group that are classified as equity. The preference shares are redeemable at the option of Company S (with Company P's consent) in whole or in part, at varying dates, at £100 per share plus accumulated and unpaid distributions to the date fixed for redemption. Consistent with the view that the subsidiary's preference shares represent a non-controlling interest in the parent's consolidated financial statements, dividends or accretions to a redemption price should be classified as income allocated to non-controlling interests in the consolidated statement of comprehensive income of the parent.
>
> Company P decides to acquire Company S's preference shares. The premium paid by Company P to the third-party preference shareholders on the acquisition of Company S's preference shares is not recognised in the statement of comprehensive income of the consolidated entity as this represents a transaction with shareholders. Accordingly, the consolidated entity does not recognise in its statement of comprehensive income any gain or loss from the acquisition.
>
> The premium paid to redeem Company S's preference shares should be deducted in computing profit or loss available to ordinary shareholders in the calculation of EPS in Company P's consolidated financial statements. The premium represents a return on investment to the holders of the preference shares and is not available to ordinary shareholders, similar to preference share dividends and accretion charges. As dividends and accretion charges on preference securities of a subsidiary are treated as income allocated to non-controlling interests, premiums paid to redeem Company S's preference shares also should be deducted in computing profit or loss attributable to ordinary shareholders in the calculation of earnings per share in Company P's consolidated financial statements.

4.1.2.3 Other effects of preference shares

The results for the period will also be adjusted for other appropriations recognised in respect of preference shares classified as equity. For example, preference shares may provide for a low initial dividend to compensate the entity for selling the shares at a discount, or an above-market dividend in later periods to compensate investors for purchasing the shares at a premium. (These are sometimes called increasing rate preference shares.) Where such shares are classified as equity, the discount or premium on issue is amortised to retained earnings using the effective interest method and treated as a preference dividend for the purposes of calculating basic earnings per share. [IAS 33.15]

The following example, reproduced from Example 1 of the Illustrative Examples accompanying IAS 33, illustrates the required adjustments in respect of increasing rate preference shares.

Example 4.1.2.3

Increasing rate preference shares

[IAS 33 Illustrative Examples (Example 1)]

Entity D issued non-convertible, non-redeemable class A cumulative preference shares of CU100 par value on 1 January 20X1. The class A preference shares are entitled to a cumulative annual dividend of CU7 per share starting in 20X4.

At the time of issue, the market rate dividend yield on the class A preference shares was 7 per cent a year. Thus, Entity D could have expected to receive proceeds of approximately CU100 per class A preference share if the dividend rate of CU7 per share had been in effect at the date of issue.

In consideration of the dividend payment terms, however, the class A preference shares were issued at CU81.63 per share, i.e. at a discount of CU18.37 per share. The issue price can be calculated by taking the present value of CU100, discounted at 7 per cent over a three-year period.

Because the shares are classified as equity, the original issue discount is amortised to retained earnings using the effective interest method and treated as a preference dividend for earnings per share purposes. To calculate basic earnings per share, the following imputed dividend per class A preference share is deducted to determine the profit or loss attributable to ordinary equity holders of the parent entity:

Year	Carrying amount of class A preference shares on 1 January	Imputed dividend[a]	Carrying amount of class A preference shares 31 December[b]	Dividend paid
	CU	CU	CU	CU
20X1	81.63	5.71	87.34	-
20X2	87.34	6.12	93.46	-
20X3	93.46	6.54	100.00	-
Thereafter	100.00	7.00	107.00	(7.00)

(a) At 7%

(b) This is before dividend payment.

4.1.2.4 Contingent dividends on preference shares

Example 4.1.2.4

Contingent dividends on preference shares

Company X, a publicly traded entity, issued to Company Y convertible preference shares that earn a seven per cent dividend per year. Conversion is at Company Y's option. Company X may elect to redeem the preference shares at any time. The terms of the preference shares state that if Company Y were to convert the preference shares into a fixed number of ordinary shares of Company X, then Company Y would not receive any preference share dividends, including any cumulative dividends in arrears. Conversion is based on the initial issue price of £1,000 per share of preference shares divided by the 30-day average market price of Company X's ordinary shares. If, however, Company X redeems the shares from Company Y, then Company Y would receive cumulative dividends, including any in arrears.

While IAS 33.12 states that preference share dividends should be subtracted from net income available to ordinary shareholders for the purposes of calculating basic EPS whether paid or earned, it does not address how to account for dividend payments contingent on future events. In Company X's situation, the future event is whether Company X redeems the preference shares or Company Y converts the preference shares.

The dividends potentially will be paid in the future unless Company Y elects to convert. If Company Y elects to convert the preference shares into ordinary shares of Company X, Company Y no longer has the right to receive the preference share dividends, including any in arrears. This is analogous to how IAS 33 treats convertible debt where interest is accrued until conversion occurs.

Based on the above, dividends on the preference shares for each period should be deducted from income available to ordinary shareholders for computing basic EPS until the conversion occurs, whether or not the dividends are declared. If conversion occurs, thus removing Company Y's right to receive the dividends, including those in arrears, the EPS calculation should be adjusted prospectively in accordance with IAS 33.18 in the period that conversion occurs. Company X should not restate prior EPS amounts.

4.1.2.5 Preference shares issued by a subsidiary to its parent

Example 4.1.2.5

Preference shares issued by a subsidiary to its parent

Company S is a majority-owned subsidiary of Company P. Company P issued £100 million five per cent preference shares to the public. In connection with the offering, Company S issued £100 million five per cent preference shares to Company P (with the same terms and features as the preference shares issued to the public) primarily as a means of funding the dividends on the preference shares issued to the public, because Company P is a holding company with no independent operations or cash flows. The preference shares issued to the public are not convertible, participating, or mandatorily redeemable, nor are any of the shares held by the non-controlling interests in Company S.

The preference shares issued to the public reduce basic and diluted EPS because the dividends on these shares are deducted to determine the numerator. The subsidiary's preference shares do not affect Company P's computation of basic and diluted EPS in the consolidated financial statements, since the preference shares issued by the subsidiary to the parent and related dividends are eliminated on consolidation.

4.1.2.6 *Dividends received on share options*

Example 4.1.2.6A

Dividends received on share options (1)

Company B grants share options to its employees, which will only vest if the employee remains employed for three years. The employees are entitled to dividends in cash on the options. If the options do not vest, the employee retains the dividends paid.

In the calculation of basic EPS, the numerator is the profit or loss attributable to ordinary equity holders of the parent. The dividends paid on the share options that are payable irrespective of whether the options vest reduce the share of profit available to ordinary equity holders. Therefore, profit or loss should also be adjusted in the basic EPS calculation.

Dividends would be added back to the calculation of diluted EPS when the share options are dilutive potential ordinary shares.

Example 4.1.2.6B

Dividends received on share options (2)

Same facts as in **example 4.1.2.6A** except that the dividends to which the employees are entitled are applied to reduce the exercise price of the options. Earnings should not be adjusted for dividends that are applied to reduce the exercise price. In this scenario, the dividends do not leave the group and, therefore, should not affect earnings attributable to ordinary shareholders.

However, when calculating dilutive potential ordinary shares and the number of shares deemed to have been issued for no consideration, the exercise price will be adjusted by dividends applied.

4.1.3 *Different classes of shares*

IAS 33 requires that EPS should be calculated and presented for each class of ordinary shares that has a different right to share in the profit for the period. [IAS 33.66]

The Application Guidance set out in Appendix A to IAS 33 discusses the circumstances where the equity of an entity includes:

[IAS 33.A13]

- instruments that participate in dividends with ordinary shares according to a predetermined formula (e.g. two for one) with, at times, an upper limit on the extent of participation (e.g. up to, but not beyond, a specified amount per share); and
- a class of ordinary shares with a different dividend rate from that of another class of ordinary shares, but without prior or senior rights.

Instruments that participate in dividends with ordinary shares according to a predetermined formula are described as 'participating equity instruments'. Where there is a class of ordinary shares classified as equity but entitled to a different dividend rate from that for another class of ordinary shares classified as equity, these are described as 'two-class ordinary shares'.

> Care is required in determining whether an instrument is a participating equity instrument. An instrument may participate in dividends with ordinary shares according to a predetermined formula, but this of itself does not mean it is a participating equity instrument. Such instruments may not meet the definition of ordinary shares as they are not subordinate to all other classes of equity instrument.

For the purposes of calculating diluted EPS, conversion is assumed for those instruments described above that are convertible into ordinary shares, if the effect is dilutive. For those instruments that are not convertible into a class of ordinary shares, profit or loss for the period is allocated to the different classes of shares and participating equity instruments in accordance with their dividend rights or other rights to participate in undistributed earnings. [IAS 33.A14]

In order to allocate the earnings of the entity between these classes of shares, the following guidance is provided:

[IAS 33.A14]

- the profit or loss attributable to ordinary equity holders of the parent entity is adjusted by the amount of dividends declared in the period for each class of shares and by the contractual amount of dividends (or interest on participating bonds) that must be paid for the period (e.g. unpaid cumulative dividends);
- the remaining profit or loss is allocated to ordinary shares and participating equity instruments to the extent that each instrument shares in earnings, as if all of the profit or loss for the period had been distributed. The total profit or loss allocated to each class of

equity instrument is determined by adding together the amount allocated for dividends and the amount allocated for a participation feature; and

- the total amount of profit or loss allocated to each class of equity instrument is divided by the number of outstanding instruments to which the earnings are allocated to determine the earnings per share for the instrument.

The following example, reproduced from Example 11 of the Illustrative Examples accompanying IAS 33, illustrates the required treatment.

Example 4.1.3

Participating equity instruments and two-class ordinary shares

[IAS 33 Illustrative Examples (Example 11)]

Profit attributable to equity holders of the parent entity	CU100,000
Ordinary shares outstanding	10,000
Non-convertible preference shares	6,000
Non-cumulative annual dividend on preference shares (before any dividend is paid on ordinary shares)	CU5.50 per share

After ordinary shares have been paid a dividend of CU2.10 per share, the preference shares participate in any additional dividends on a 20:80 ratio with ordinary shares (i.e. after preference and ordinary shares have been paid dividends of CU5.50 and CU2.10 per share, respectively, preference shares participate in any additional dividends at a rate of one-fourth of the amount paid to ordinary shares on a per-share basis).

Dividends on preference shares paid	CU33,000 (CU5.50 per share)
Dividends on ordinary shares paid	CU21,000 (CU2.10 per share)

Basic earnings per share is calculated as follows:

	CU	CU
Profit attributable to equity holders of the parent entity		100,000
Less dividends paid:		
Preference	33,000	
Ordinary	21,000	(54,000)
Undistributed earnings		46,000

Allocation of undistributed earnings:

Allocation per ordinary share = A

Allocation per preference share = B; B = ¼ A

(A x 10,000) + (1/4 x A x 6,000) = CU46,000

A = CU46,000/(10,000 + 1,500)

A = CU4.00

B = ¼ A

B = CU1.00

Basic per share amounts:

	Preference shares	Ordinary shares
Distributed earnings	CU5.50	CU2.10
Undistributed earnings	CU1.00	CU4.00
Totals	CU6.50	CU6.10

4.2 Number of shares

4.2.1 Weighted average

The number of shares used in the denominator for basic EPS should be the weighted average number of ordinary shares outstanding during the period. [IAS 33.19]

The weighted average number of ordinary shares outstanding during the period is the number of shares outstanding at the beginning of the period, adjusted by the number of ordinary shares bought back or issued during the period multiplied by a time-weighting factor. [IAS 33.20] Adjusting the number of ordinary share during the period on a time-weighted basis ensures that changes in the capital structure of the entity do not result in misleading EPS simply due to the timing in the period of the change in the capital structure. Time apportioning the number of shares ensures that an increase in resources due to a capital raising is apportioned to the period where that capital is available for generating earnings. Conversely, an outflow of resources due to a reduction in capital, e.g. a share buy-back, is apportioned to the period where the resources used for buying capital are no longer available for generating earnings.

The calculation is based on all shares outstanding during the period. Whether or not a particular class or tranche of shares ranked for dividends in respect of the period is irrelevant (except in the case of partly paid shares – see **4.2.2.3** below).

The time-weighting factor is:

[IAS 33.20]

$$\frac{\textit{Number of days the shares are outstanding}}{\textit{Number of days in the period}}$$

Although the Standard defines the time-weighting factor as being determined on a daily basis, it acknowledges that a reasonable approximation of the weighted average is adequate in many circumstances. [IAS 33.20] Depending on the relative size of share movements, this might, for example, be based on the number of months for which shares were outstanding.

The following example, reproduced from Example 2 of the Illustrative Examples accompanying IAS 33, illustrates the calculation of the weighted average number of shares. Note that it calculates outstanding shares on a monthly rather than daily basis.

Example 4.2.1

Weighted average number of ordinary shares

[IAS 33 Illustrative Examples (Example 2)]

		Shares issued	Treasury shares[a]	Shares outstanding
1 January 20X1	Balance at beginning of year	2,000	300	1,700
31 May 20X1	Issue of new shares for cash	800	–	2,500
1 December 20X1	Purchase of treasury shares for cash	–	250	2,250
31 December 20X1	Balance at year end	2,800	550	2,250

Calculation of weighted average:

(1,700 x 5/12) + (2,500 x 6/12) + (2,250 x 1/12) = 2,146 shares *or*

(1,700 x 12/12) + (800 x 7/12) – (250 x 1/12) = 2,146 shares

(a) Treasury shares are equity instruments reacquired and held by the issuing entity itself or by its subsidiaries.

4.2.2 Timing for inclusion of new shares

IAS 33 also provides guidance on determining the date from which the shares are to be considered outstanding and therefore included in the weighted average number of shares for the EPS calculation.

In general, shares are to be considered outstanding from the date that the consideration for the shares becomes receivable, which is usually the date of their issue. The specific terms and conditions attaching to the issue should be examined, however, to ensure that the substance of any contract associated with the issue prevails over its legal form. [IAS 33.21]

The following table illustrates the most common circumstances in which shares are issued, and the date from which such shares are to be considered outstanding, as required by IAS 33.21 – 23 The sections following the table examine some of these rules in greater detail.

Consideration for issue of shares	Date from which the shares are included in the weighted average computation
Cash	Date cash is receivable (see **4.2.2.1** below)
Voluntary reinvestment of dividends on ordinary or preference shares (scrip dividend)	Date when dividends are reinvested
Debt instrument converted to ordinary shares	Date interest on debt instrument ceases to accrue
Substitution for interest or principal on other financial instruments	Date interest on other financial instruments ceases to accrue
Exchange for the settlement of a liability of the entity	Settlement date of the liability
Conversion of mandatorily convertible instrument	Date the contract to issue the convertible instrument is entered into
Acquisition of an asset other than cash	Date the acquisition is recognised
Business combination (see **4.2.2.2** below)	Acquisition date
Rendering of services to the entity	As the services are rendered

4.2.2.1 Shares issued for cash

Even with the above guidance, some care may be required in determining the date from which shares issued for cash should be included. **Example 4.2.2.1** illustrates one such circumstance.

Example 4.2.2.1

Shares issued for cash

An entity is making a rights issue. Provisional allotment letters for the new shares are posted on 19 October 20X1. Shareholders wishing to take up their entitlement must return the provisional allotment letter together with a remittance for the full amount payable so as to be received not later than 3pm on 17 November 20X1. Consequently, the entity will receive cash on a number of days, up to and including 17 November 20X1.

IAS 33 requires the shares to be included in the weighted average calculation from the date the cash is receivable. In this example, 17 November 20X1 is the date the cash is receivable (since that is the date by which the entity has asked to receive the cash and if no cash was received until that date, the entity could still validly issue the shares). Accordingly, the shares should be included in the weighted average calculation from 17 November 20X1, being the end of the subscription period.

4.2.2.2 *Business combinations*

Where ordinary shares are issued as part of the consideration transferred in a business combination, they are included in the weighted average number of shares from the acquisition date (which is defined in IFRS 3 *Business Combinations* as the date on which the acquirer obtains control of the acquiree). This is because the acquirer incorporates into its statement of comprehensive income the results of the acquired entity's operations from that date. [IAS 33.22]

4.2.2.3 *Partly paid shares*

As can be seen from the table set out at **4.2.2** above, the thrust of IAS 33 is to include shares in the calculation of EPS from the date the share proceeds start to generate earnings. The Standard's treatment of partly paid shares is therefore surprising. Rather than treat partly paid shares as a fraction of a share, based on the proportion of the proceeds received, the Standard requires them to be treated as a fraction of a share to the extent that they are entitled to participate in dividends relative to a fully paid-up ordinary share during the period. [IAS 33.A15] In contrast, shares that are fully paid-up are included in the calculation from the date the consideration is receivable, irrespective of whether they rank for dividend. For example, two £1 shares, each not ranking for dividend, one £1 paid and the other £0.99 paid, will be treated differently in the computation of basic EPS. Both have contributed to earnings but, while the first is included in basic EPS, the second is excluded.

Example 4.2.2.3

Partly paid shares

At 1 January 20X2, an entity has 1,000 ordinary shares outstanding. It issued 400 new ordinary shares at 1 October 20X2. The subscription price is £2.00 per share. At the date of issue, each shareholder paid £0.50. The balance of £1.50 per share will be paid during 20X3. Each partly paid share will be entitled to dividends in proportion to the percentage of the issue price paid up on the share.

In accordance with IAS 33.A15 and IAS 33.A16, the new shares issued should be included in the calculation of the weighted average number of shares as a fraction of a share to the extent that they are entitled to participate in dividends relative to a fully paid-up ordinary share during the period. In this example, dividend rights are in proportion to the percentage of the issue price paid up on the share. Calculation of the weighted average is therefore as follows:

Date/description	Shares	Fraction of period	Weighted average shares
At 1 January 20X2	1,000	9/12	750
Issue of new shares for cash*	100		
At 1 October 20X2	1,100	3/12	275
Weighted average number of shares			1025

*£0.50/£2.00 x 400 shares = 100 shares

4.2.2.4 *Contingently issuable shares*

Contingently issuable ordinary shares are defined as ordinary shares issuable for little or no cash or other consideration upon the satisfaction of specified conditions in a contingent share agreement. [IAS 33.5] In the case where the only 'contingency' is the passage of time, the instrument is not considered a contingently issuable ordinary share as the passage of time is certain (see **4.2.2.6** on deferred shares).

For a variety of reasons, an entity may issue instruments that obligate it to issue ordinary shares in the future upon the resolution of various contingencies. Such circumstances may include (1) issuing contingent share purchase warrants to customers that become exercisable based on the attainment of a certain level of purchases, or (2) the guarantee of a minimum share price for shares issued by an acquirer in a business combination that may result in issuing additional shares if the share price is less than the guaranteed price. Contingent share agreements are usually based on the passage of time combined with other conditions (such as the market price of an entity's shares), or on a specified level of earnings. Contingently issuable ordinary shares include shares that (1) will be issued in the future upon the satisfaction of specified conditions, (2) have been placed in escrow and all, or part, must be returned if specified conditions are not met, or (3) have been issued but the holder must return all, or a portion, of the shares, if specified conditions are not met.

Contingently issuable shares are included as outstanding in basic EPS calculations from the date when all necessary conditions have been satisfied and, thus, although issuing the shares is still a future transaction, it is no longer contingent. [IAS 33.24]

The following examples illustrate four circumstances in which shares are contingently issuable.

Example 4.2.2.4A

Contingency based on an event

A Limited acquires B Limited on 1 January 20X1. A Limited agrees to issue 100,000 shares to the vendor on 1 January 20X3 if, at any point prior to that date, a new product developed by B Limited is granted a licence.

A Limited's year end is 31 December. The 20X1 financial statements are approved on 22 March 20X2. The product is granted a licence on 4 March 20X2.

The 100,000 shares are excluded from the basic EPS calculations for 20X1 and will be included in the basic EPS calculations for 20X2 as if the shares had been issued on 4 March 20X2 (the date the licence was granted).

(See **section 5.5** and **examples 5.5.3.6A** and **B** for a discussion of how such shares are dealt with in the computation of diluted EPS.)

Example 4.2.2.4B

Contingency based on profits in specified periods

Company X, a publicly traded entity reporting on a calendar year basis, purchased Subsidiary Y on 1 January for £100 million plus 20,000 X ordinary shares for each year within the next five years in which Subsidiary Y has a profit after tax of £10 million or more.

If Company Y's profit after tax for the year ended 31 December 20X1 is £12 million, the shares would be included in the denominator for basic EPS for only that portion of the year for which the contingency was resolved (i.e. nothing could happen that would cause Company X to not issue the shares). Since this could only be on 31 December, the shares would have no impact on basic EPS for the 20X1 reporting period.

As there are five separate measurement periods for the contingency, each measurement period in which a finite number of ordinary shares may be issued should be treated as a separate contingency and evaluated based on whether Company X may be required to issue the ordinary shares for each period on a stand-alone basis for basic EPS.

If the purchase agreement required Company X to issue 100,000 shares of Company X ordinary shares if Company Y achieved £50 million in cumulative profits at the end of five years, no shares would be included in basic EPS until the end of the contingency period, and then only if Y had cumulative earnings in excess of £50 million.

Example 4.2.2.4C

Contingency based on average profits

A Limited acquires B Limited on 1 January 20X1. A Limited agrees to issue 100,000 shares to the vendor on 1 January 20X4 if B's profits for the three years to 31 December 20X3 average £10 million or more.

B Limited's profits for 20X1 and 20X2 are £17 million each year.

The shares are excluded from the calculation of basic EPS for both 20X1 and 20X2. Even if profits are expected for the year 20X3, such that the earnings condition will be met, the shares are excluded from the calculation of basic EPS until the contingency period has ended. Until then, it is not known for certain whether all of the necessary conditions will be satisfied since, however unlikely, a loss could be made in the year 20X3 and thus the earnings condition not be met.

(See **section 5.5** and **example 5.5.3.2** below for a discussion of how such shares are dealt with in the diluted EPS computation.)

Example 4.2.2.4D

Contingency based on continuing employment

Company M, a publicly traded entity, has a mandatory deferred compensation plan whereby covered employees are required to defer the amount of compensation payable in one calendar year in excess of £500,000 until completion of the deferral period. The deferral period ends when the employee ceases to earn £500,000 annually or reaches the defined retirement age as an employee of Company M. If the employee is terminated or resigns, he/she is not eligible to receive any distribution under the plan. The compensation deferred under the plan is only payable to the participant in Company M's ordinary shares over a five-year period once the participant is eligible to receive the distribution.

A participant's deferred compensation is held in an escrow account until the individual is eligible to receive distributions. The escrow account does not bear interest. It receives the dividend based on the equivalent number of ordinary shares that the cash value of the account would convert to, however, based on the closing price of the ordinary shares for the trading day preceding the original deferral. Distributions from the account are based on the equivalent number of ordinary shares that the cash value of the distribution would convert to, based on the closing price of the shares for the trading day preceding the distribution.

The ordinary shares issuable under the plan are considered contingently issuable as the issuable ordinary shares will only be issued if the employee neither is terminated nor resigns, and instead either retires in the employment of Company M or has annual earnings fall below £500,000. The shares issuable under the plan should be excluded from the calculation of basic EPS because there is still the possibility that the employee will never receive the shares.

Further, the number of shares contingently issuable may depend on the market price of the shares at a future date. Because the market price may change in a future period, such contingently issuable shares should not be included in basic EPS because all necessary conditions have not been satisfied. Additionally, outstanding ordinary shares that are contingently returnable (i.e. subject to recall) should be treated in the same manner as contingently issuable shares. If shares are returnable or placed in escrow until the shares are vested or some other contingent criteria are met, the shares should be excluded from the denominator in computing basic EPS even if they have been issued legally.

The following example, reproduced from Example 7 of the Illustrative Examples accompanying IAS 33, provides another illustration.

Example 4.2.2.4E

Contingently issuable shares

[IAS 33 Illustrative Examples (Example 7)]

Ordinary shares outstanding during 20X1	1,000,000 (there were no options, warrants or convertible instruments outstanding during the period)

An agreement related to a recent business combination provides for the issue of additional ordinary shares based on the following conditions:

	5,000 additional ordinary shares for each new retail site opened during 20X1
	1,000 additional ordinary shares for each CU1,000 of consolidated profit in excess of CU2,000,000 for the year ended 31 December 20X1
Retail sites opened during the year:	one on 1 May 20X1 one on 1 September 20X1
Consolidated year-to-date profit attributable to ordinary equity holders of the parent entity:	CU1,100,000 as of 31 March 20X1 CU2,300,000 as of 30 June 20X1 CU1,900,000 as of 30 September 20X1 (including a CU 450,000 loss from a discontinued operation) CU2,900,000 as of 31 December 20X1

Basic earnings per share

	First quarter	Second quarter	Third quarter	Fourth quarter	Full year
Numerator (CU)	1,100,000	1,200,000	(400,000)	1,000,000	2,900,000
Denominator:					
Ordinary shares outstanding	1,000,000	1,000,000	1,000,000	1,000,000	1,000,000
Retail site contingency	–	3,333[a]	6,667[b]	10,000	5,000[c]
Earnings contingency[d]	–	–	–	–	–
Total shares	1,000,000	1,003,333	1,006,667	1,010,000	1,005,000
Basic earnings per share (CU)	1.10	1.20	(0.40)	0.99	2.89

(a) 5,000 shares x 2/3

(b) 5,000 shares + (5,000 shares x 1/3)

(c) (5,000 shares x 8/12) + (5,000 shares x 4/12)

(d) The earnings contingency has no effect on basic earnings per share because it is not certain that the condition is satisfied until the end of the contingency period. The effect is negligible for the fourth-quarter and full-year calculations because it is not certain that the condition is met until the last day of the period.

4.2.2.5 Contingently returnable shares

Where outstanding ordinary shares are contingently returnable (i.e. subject to recall), they are not treated as outstanding and are excluded from the calculation of basic earnings per share until the date the shares are no longer subject to recall. [IAS 33.24]

Example 4.2.2.5

Contingently returnable shares

Company X granted options to its employees. The options vest over a four-year period. However, the employees may exercise their options at any time before their vesting. If an employee initiates this early exercise provision, the employee will receive restricted ordinary shares in Company X that vest under the same schedule as the employee's original option grants.

Shares that are contingently returnable (e.g. subject to repurchase if employment is terminated or the employee resigns prior to the shares fully vesting) should not be considered outstanding for the purposes of computing basic EPS until all necessary conditions that could require return of the shares have been satisfied (i.e. the shares are vested). The contingently returnable shares issued to the employee in this case should be excluded from the denominator in calculating basic EPS.

4.2.2.6 Deferred shares

Shares that will be issued at a future date and whose issue is not subject to any conditions other than the passage of time (sometimes called deferred shares) are not contingently issuable shares, because the passage of time is a certainty. [IAS 33.24] This is consistent with the treatment of mandatorily convertible shares described in **4.2.2** above. Such shares are also included in basic EPS because the issue of shares is not contingent, as the passage of time is certain.

As discussed previously, the general rule is that shares are to be considered outstanding from the date that the consideration for the shares becomes receivable. [IAS 33.21]

Although this date will often coincide with the issue date of the shares, this will not be so in the case of deferred shares. Nevertheless, if an asset is acquired, or a service is received, and the cost is to be satisfied by shares to be issued at a future date, then the deferred shares will be included in the calculation of EPS from the date of recognition of the asset or service, which is the consideration for the shares.

Deferred shares typically arise in the context of business combinations. As discussed at **4.2.2.2** above, for a business combination, the shares issued are included in EPS calculations from the date that the acquirer accounts for the results of the acquiree. The fact that the issue of some of those shares has been deferred is irrelevant – they are included in the EPS denominator immediately, provided that their issue is not subject to any conditions. For example, A Limited might purchase B Limited, paying 500,000 shares at the date of acquisition and a further 100,000 shares one year after the date of acquisition. All 600,000 shares will be included in the calculation of basic EPS from the date that B Limited is brought into A Limited's consolidated financial statements.

An agreement for the acquisition of a business may provide for further shares to be issued, but with the number of shares being determinable rather than fixed. For example, the agreement may provide that shares valued at £50,000,000 on a specified future date will be issued, the number of shares to be determined by dividing

£50,000,000 by the share price on the specified future date. Although the number of shares to be issued is uncertain, there are no circumstances under which the shares will not be issued. Nevertheless, IAS 33.54 indicates that such shares are contingently issuable shares (see the discussion at **5.5.3.3**). Because the obligation to issue shares to a particular value is a financial liability, no equity instrument exists until the end of the contingency period.

Such shares will, however, impact on the calculation of diluted EPS (see **5.5.3.3** below).

4.2.3 *Changes in share capital with no corresponding change in the entity's resources*

An entity may issue shares, or reduce the number of ordinary shares outstanding, without a corresponding change in resources, i.e. without any change in shareholders' funds.

In such circumstances, the weighted average number of ordinary shares outstanding during the period and for all periods presented is adjusted for events, other than the conversion of potential ordinary shares, that have changed the number of ordinary shares outstanding without a corresponding change in resources. [IAS 33.26]

To illustrate why such an approach is necessary, consider the following example.

Example 4.2.3

Bonus issue of shares

An entity had the following statement of financial position as at 31 December 20X1:

	£
Net assets	900,000,000
Share capital	100,000,000
Reserves	800,000,000
	900,000,000

On 31 December 20X1, and throughout the year then ended, the share capital comprised 100,000,000 £1 ordinary shares. On 1 January 20X2, the entity made a 1:1 bonus issue. The statement of financial position immediately after the bonus issue appears as follows:

	£
Net assets	900,000,000
Share capital	200,000,000

Reserves (800,000,000 – 100,000,000)		700,000,000
		900,000,000

The entity's net assets do not alter and so the revenue generating ability of the entity is unchanged. Consequently, there is no expectation that earnings will alter as a result of the change in share capital. Assuming that the profit attributable to ordinary shareholders for each of 20X1 and 20X2 was £20,000,000, then treating the bonus issue as an issue of shares for consideration would give results as follows:

	20X2	**20X1**
Earnings per share	£0.10	£0.20

Clearly, these results are not comparable – the profits are identical in each of the years and, if no shareholders had sold their shares, the number of shareholders would be identical. Yet the above result gives the appearance that the entity was less profitable in 20X2 than in 20X1.

Consequently, IAS 33 requires that EPS be adjusted as if the proportionate change in the number of ordinary shares outstanding had taken place at the start of the earliest period for which an EPS is presented. Thus, in this example, the EPS calculated in accordance with IAS 33 is:

	20X2	**20X1**
Earnings per share	£0.10	£0.10

Bonus issues are not the only example of a change to the number of shares in issue with no corresponding change in resources. The Standard lists the following examples:

[IAS 33.27]

- a bonus or capitalisation issue (sometimes referred to as a stock dividend);
- the bonus element in any other issue (e.g. a bonus element in a rights issue to existing shareholders);
- a share split; and
- a reverse share split (share consolidation).

The list is not exhaustive.

Bonus issues, share splits and share consolidations are all adjusted for in the same way, i.e. by adjusting proportionately the number of shares outstanding as if the bonus issue, share split or share consolidation had occurred at the start of the earliest period for which EPS information is presented (see **4.2.3.1** below for details). Specific rules are set out for in-substance share buy-backs, for example where a share consolidation is combined with a special dividend (see **4.2.3.2** below).

For rights issues, and bonus elements in any other issue or buy-back, the Standard specifies a formula to be used to calculate the adjustment to the shares in issue before the rights issue (see **4.2.3.3** below).

If the number of ordinary or potential ordinary shares outstanding increases as a result of a capitalisation, bonus issue or share split, or decreases as a result of a reverse share split, the calculation of basic and diluted earnings per share for all periods presented is adjusted retrospectively. Basic and diluted earnings per share of all periods presented are also adjusted for:

[IAS 33.64]

- the effects of errors; and
- adjustments resulting from changes in accounting policies accounted for retrospectively.

4.2.3.1 Bonus issue, share split or share consolidation

The number of ordinary shares outstanding is adjusted proportionately as if the bonus issue, share split or share consolidation had taken place at the start of the earliest period for which EPS is presented. [IAS 33.28]

The following example, reproduced from Example 3 of the Illustrative Examples accompanying IAS 33, illustrates the calculation of basic EPS where there has been a bonus issue.

Example 4.2.3.1

Bonus issue

[IAS 33 Illustrative Examples (Example 3)]

Profit attributable to ordinary equity holders of the parent entity 20X0	CU180
Profit attributable to ordinary equity holders of the parent entity 20X1	CU600
Ordinary shares outstanding until 30 September 20X1	200
Bonus issue on 1 October 20X1	2 ordinary shares for each ordinary share outstanding at 30 September 20X1
	200 x 2 = 400
Basic earnings per share 20X1	CU600/(200 + 400) = CU1.00
Basic earnings per share 20X0	CU180/(200 + 400) = CU0.30

Because the bonus issue was without consideration, it is treated as if it had occurred before the beginning of 20X0, the earliest period presented.

IAS 33.27 states that a bonus issue or capitalisation is sometimes referred to as a 'stock dividend'. If a stock dividend was equivalent to a bonus issue or capitalisation then restatement of the number of shares outstanding would be required. However, care is needed in determining the substance of a stock dividend and, particularly, whether it is equivalent to a bonus issue or capitalisation, i.e. whether there is a change in share capital with no corresponding change in the entity's resources. For example, if an entity enters into an arrangement that gives the shareholders the right to a dividend in cash or shares at the shareholder's option, if the cash is forfeited for shares this can be seen as consideration for the issue of shares. If the cash option is equivalent to the fair value of the shares this is equivalent to a fresh issue of shares at fair value. In such a case this is not equivalent to a bonus issue or capitalisation and therefore restatement of the number of shares outstanding is not applicable. In some instances, the share alternative may be greater than the cash alternative and in such instances the bonus element will need to be identified which will require restatement of the number of shares just as for a bonus element in a rights issue (as described in **4.2.3.3**).

4.2.3.2 *In-substance share buy-backs*

Share consolidations (or reverse share splits) generally reduce the number of ordinary shares outstanding without a corresponding reduction in resources. When the overall effect is a share repurchase at fair value, however, the reduction in the number of ordinary shares outstanding is the result of a corresponding reduction in resources. An example is a share consolidation combined with a special dividend. The weighted average number of shares outstanding for the period in which the combined transaction takes place is adjusted for the reduction in the number of ordinary shares from the date the special dividend is recognised. [IAS 33.29]

The following example demonstrates why considering the dividend and the share consolidation separately would not reflect the substance of a share buy-back.

Example 4.2.3.2

In-substance share buy-backs

An entity has 500,000 ordinary shares in issue on 1 January 20X1. The entity wishes to effect a share consolidation, as part of which it will pay a special dividend of £0.60 per share. Accordingly, on 1 July 20X1, when its share price is £6, it pays a special dividend of £300,000 and undertakes a 10:9 share consolidation, issuing nine new shares for every ten old shares held. As a result, only 450,000 shares are in issue for the remainder of 20X1.

Earnings for 20X1 total £360,000.

Although the entity has carried out a share consolidation, the special dividend has led to a corresponding reduction in resources. Thus, the overall effect when the share consolidation is combined with the special dividend is that there has been a share repurchase at fair value. To demonstrate this, suppose the entity had instead gone into the market and purchased 50,000 shares at the market price of £6 per share. It would also have paid out £300,000 and reduced the number of shares in issue to 450,000, achieving the same overall result.

Accordingly, under the approach required by IAS 33.29, the EPS is:

20X1 EPS 360,000/[500,000 – (50,000 x 6/12)] = £ 0.76

Note that this is different from the EPS figure that would have resulted from treating the special dividend as a dividend and the share consolidation as a share consolidation. Under such an approach, which would be contrary to IAS 33.29, the result would have been:

20X1 EPS 360,000/450,000 = £0.80

Combining a special dividend with a share consolidation is not the only way of achieving an in-substance share buy-back. IAS 33 cites this as one specific example of a share consolidation resulting in the overall effect of a share repurchase at fair value. Other transactions that achieve the same effect will be treated in a similar manner.

4.2.3.3 *Rights issues at less than full market price*

A rights issue is similar to an issue of options to existing shareholders in that it gives each existing shareholder the right, but not the obligation, to purchase additional shares in the entity at a fixed price. Generally, these rights may be sold by the existing shareholders to other shareholders or potential shareholders.

When shares are offered to shareholders in a rights issue, the price at which they are offered is often less than the fair value of the shares. Consider, for example, an entity whose shares are priced at £10. The entity offers its shareholders one new share for every four held, giving 100,000 new shares, at £8 per share. Share proceeds of £800,000 will be received and 100,000 shares issued. This is equivalent to issuing 80,000 shares at fair value (of £10 per share) and making a bonus issue of 20,000 shares. This is the bonus element of the rights issue.

Where there is a bonus element in a rights issue, EPS is calculated as if the bonus element (but not the total rights issue) arose proportionately at the start of the earliest period for which an EPS is presented. If there is no bonus element in the rights issue, the new shares issued are treated as an issue for cash at fair value (since that is what they are).

In order to calculate basic EPS where there is a bonus element, however, the above transaction would not be treated as an issue of 80,000 shares at fair value and a bonus issue of 20,000 shares. Instead, the Standard specifies a formula to be used. If the fair value used to calculate the number of shares issued for no consideration ('the bonus issue') is the same as the fair value of the shares immediately before the exercise of rights, the two methods give identical answers. The formula specified in the Standard is discussed and illustrated in the paragraphs below.

The specific circumstances of the bonus element in a rights issue are discussed in the application guidance issued with IAS 33, and illustrated in Illustrative Example 4. If a rights issue is offered to all existing shareholders, the number of ordinary shares outstanding prior to the rights issue is multiplied by the following factor:

[IAS 33.A2]

$$\frac{\textit{Fair value per share immediately before the exercise of rights}}{\textit{Theoretical ex rights fair value per share}}$$

The theoretical ex-rights fair value per share is calculated as:

[IAS 33.A2]

$$\frac{\textit{Aggregate market value of the shares outstanding immediately before the exercise of rights} + \textit{proceeds from the exercise of rights}}{\textit{Number of shares outstanding after the exercise of rights}}$$

The Standard specifies that where, before the exercise date, the rights are to be publicly traded separately from the shares, the 'fair value per share immediately before the exercise of rights' for the purposes of the calculations set out above is established at the close of the last day on which the shares are traded together with the rights. [IAS 33.A2]

The following example, reproduced from Example 4 of the Illustrative Examples accompanying IAS 33, illustrates the impact of a rights issue at less than fair value on basic EPS.

Example 4.2.3.3

Rights issue

[IAS 33 Illustrative Examples (Example 4)]

	20X0	20X1	20X2
Profit attributable to ordinary equity holders of the parent entity	CU1,100	CU1,500	CU1,800
Shares outstanding before rights issue	500 shares		
Rights issue	One new share for each five outstanding shares (100 new shares total)		
	Exercise price:		CU5.00
	Date of rights issue:		1 January 20X1
	Last date to exercise rights:		1 March 20X1
Market price of one ordinary share immediately before exercise on 1 March 20X1:			CU11.00
Reporting date	31 December		

Calculation of theoretical ex-rights value per share

$$\frac{\textit{Fair value of all outstanding shares before the exercise of rights} + \textit{total amount received from exercise of rights}}{\textit{Number of shares outstanding before exercise} + \textit{number of shares issued in the exercise}}$$

$$\frac{(CU11.00 \times 500\ shares) + (CU5.00 \times 100\ shares)}{(500\ shares + 100\ shares)}$$

Theoretical ex-rights value per share = CU10.00

Calculation of adjustment factor

$$\frac{\textit{Fair value per share immediately before exercise of rights}}{\textit{Theoretical ex rights value per share}} \quad \frac{CU11.00}{CU10.00} = 1.10$$

Calculation of basic earnings per share

	20X0	20X1	20X2
20X0 basic EPS as originally reported: (CU1,100/500 shares)	CU2.20		
20X0 basic EPS restated for rights issue: CU1,100/(500 shares x 1.1)	CU2.00		
20X1 basic EPS including effects of rights issue: CU1,500/[(500 x 1.1 x 2/12) + (600 x 10/12)]		CU2.54	
20X2 basic EPS: CU1,800/600 shares			CU3.00

The calculation may be further affected where the entity has some contingently issuable shares for which all of the necessary conditions have been met.

4.2.3.4 *Changes after the reporting period*

If any change in the number of ordinary or potential ordinary shares, resulting from a capitalisation or bonus issue, a share split or a reverse share split, occurs after the reporting period but before the financial statements are authorised for issue, the per share calculations for those and any prior period financial statements presented should be based on the new number of shares. [IAS 33.64]

For this purpose, adjustments should only be made when the required approval procedures have been completed. For example, no adjustment should be made for proposed bonus issues that are subject to approval at the general meeting at which the financial statements are to be approved.

The overriding consideration in these situations is the basis on which the shares are trading at the date the financial statements are issued. EPS should not be retrospectively adjusted as a result of a share dividend or share split until the shares are trading on a post-split or dividend basis. Typically, this occurs the day after the dividend or split has been distributed for larger distributions (i.e. those greater than 20 per cent). In situations in which the share dividend or share split is declared and approved prior to, but distributed subsequent to, the date of issue of the financial statements, EPS should be calculated using the number of shares on a pre-split basis, and disclosure should be made of the post-split effects on EPS in the statement of comprehensive income, with footnote disclosure of the significant terms of the pending share dividend or share split. However, because the timing of the switch to trading on a post-split basis is actually governed by the relevant exchange, and may vary depending on the size of the distribution, it is necessary to monitor the timing of the switch and adjust the EPS reporting accordingly.

Financial statements are considered to be 'issued' as of the date they are distributed for general use in a format that complies with IFRSs.

A business combination after the reporting period is not one of the circumstances in which IAS 33 specifically permits the retrospective restatement of EPS. However, a particular issue can arise for reverse acquisitions, because the number of shares outstanding after the business combination often is significantly different from the number of shares outstanding beforehand. Accordingly, the weighted average shares outstanding for purposes of presenting EPS on a comparative basis should be restated to the earliest period presented in order to reflect the effect of the recapitalisation that occurs in a reverse acquisition. In effect, the reverse acquisition is similar to a share split for the accounting acquirer, and restating the weighted average shares outstanding is consistent with the accounting required by IAS 33 for share splits, stock dividends, and reverse share splits.

When per-share calculations have been adjusted to reflect changes in the number of shares as described in the previous paragraphs, that fact should be disclosed. [IAS 33.64]

When ordinary or potential ordinary share transactions other than capitalisation issues, share splits and reverse share splits occur after the reporting period but before the financial statements are authorised for issue, disclosure of such events may be required (see **7.2.3** below). Such transactions after the reporting period, which do not affect the amount of capital used to produce profit or loss for the period and, consequently, are excluded from the calculation of EPS, include:

[IAS 33.71]

- the issue of shares for cash;
- the issue of shares when the proceeds are used to repay debt or preference shares outstanding at the end of the reporting period;
- the redemption of ordinary shares outstanding;
- the conversion or exercise of potential ordinary shares, outstanding at the end of the reporting period, into ordinary shares;
- the issue of warrants, options or convertible securities; and
- the achievement of conditions that would result in the issue of contingently issuable shares.

4.2.4 *Preference shares with characteristics of ordinary shares*

Entities will sometimes issue preference shares with many of the characteristics of ordinary shares. For the purpose of computing basic EPS, such preference shares should be evaluated based on their substance rather than their form. If they share the characteristics of ordinary shares and have no preference attributed to them, such instruments should be considered as ordinary shares for purposes of basic EPS regardless of the legal name assigned to them.

Example 4.2.4

Preference shares with characteristics of ordinary shares

Preference shares are issued on the following terms:

- no rights to preferential or cumulative dividends;
- preference shares participate rateably with ordinary shares in the event a dividend is declared on ordinary shares;
- in addition, ordinary shareholders may participate rateably in the event a dividend is declared on the preference shares;
- not publicly traded;
- voting rights are limited to certain events including liquidation;
- nominal preference in liquidation (e.g. 1p per share);
- each share is convertible into one ordinary share at any time upon the transfer of the preference shares to a third party; and
- antidilution provisions are limited only to share splits and dividends.

There is no substantive difference between these preference shares and ordinary shares. In substance, the preference shares have the characteristics of non-voting ordinary shares, and should be included in basic EPS in the same way as ordinary shares.

The holder of the preference shares can sell these shares to a third party at any time, at which point the securities would convert into ordinary shares with all the characteristics of the current outstanding ordinary shares. The sale of the preference shares is outside of the issuer's control and there are no restrictions on the sale of the preference shares. Further, preference shares have exactly the same rights to receive dividends as ordinary shares and have no substantive preference (as the liquidation preference of 1p per share is insignificant).

Furthermore, calculating basic EPS involves determining the amount of profit or loss attributable to ordinary shareholders. If the preference shares are not included in the basic EPS calculation, the calculation will be misleading because it will exclude a group of shareholders that currently have identical rights to earnings and dividends as the ordinary shareholders.

4.2.5 *Ordinary shares issued to trusts to fund retirement benefit payments*

In order to fund retirement benefit payments, an entity may issue ordinary shares to a trust which is consolidated in the financial statements of the entity. In many instances, the trusts created do not protect the assets from creditors in the case of the entity's bankruptcy (e.g. 'rabbi trusts'). The ordinary shares of the entity are held until the rabbi trust is required to meet retirement obligations, at which time the shares are sold to the public.

The shares held by the trust should not be considered outstanding in the computation of EPS because the trust is consolidated by the entity and, therefore, the shares are considered treasury shares in the consolidated financial statements until such time as the trust sells the shares outside the group. The shares held by the trust are excluded from the definition of plan assets in IAS 19 *Employee Benefits.*

4.2.6 *Shares held in trust for equity-settled share-based payments*

Example 4.2.8

Shares held in trust for equity-settled share-based payments

Company B grants its employees share options that will vest after three years of employment. Company B provides money to a trust to purchase shares in Company B in the market. The shares are then used to satisfy the exercise of the share options on vesting. Company B controls the trust and, thus, consolidates the trust in accordance with IAS 27 *Consolidated and Separate Financial Statements.*

Basic EPS is determined with reference to the weighted average number of ordinary shares outstanding during the reporting period. In the consolidated financial statements, the shares held in trust will be recognised as treasury shares. Treasury shares are not included in the denominator for the purpose of calculating basic or diluted EPS since they do not represent ordinary shares outstanding from the date acquired.

Diluted EPS is determined by reference to the weighted average number of ordinary shares and potential ordinary shares outstanding during the reporting period. The employees' share options represent potential ordinary shares that are considered in determining diluted EPS when the potential ordinary shares are dilutive at year end, in accordance with the guidance in IAS 33.45 – 48 (see **section 5**).

5 Calculation of diluted earnings per share

IAS 33 requires entities to calculate diluted earnings per share amounts for profit or loss attributable to ordinary equity holders of the parent entity and, where presented, profit or loss from continuing operations attributable to those equity holders. [IAS 33.30]

The objective of diluted EPS is consistent with that of basic earnings per share – to provide a measure of the interest of each ordinary share in the performance of an entity – while giving effect to all dilutive potential ordinary shares outstanding during a period. Accordingly:

[IAS 33.32]

- profit or loss attributable to ordinary equity holders of the parent entity is increased by the after-tax amount of dividends and interest recognised in the period in respect of dilutive potential ordinary shares and is adjusted for any other changes in income or expense that would result from the conversion of the dilutive potential ordinary shares; and
- the weighted average number of ordinary shares outstanding is increased by the weighted average number of additional ordinary shares that would have been outstanding assuming the conversion of all dilutive potential ordinary shares.

5.1 Definition and general principles

Diluted EPS is calculated as:

[IAS 33.31]

$$\frac{\textit{Earnings per basic EPS + adjustment for dilutive potential ordinary shares}}{\textit{No. of shares per basic EPS + adjustment for dilutive potential ordinary shares}}$$

As noted previously, a potential ordinary share is a financial instrument or other contract that may entitle its holder to ordinary shares. [IAS 33.5] Examples include:

[IAS 33.7]

- financial liabilities or equity instruments, including preference shares, that are convertible into ordinary shares;
- options and warrants; and
- shares that would be issued upon the satisfaction of certain conditions resulting from contractual arrangements, such as the purchase of a business or other assets.

Dilution is defined as a reduction in earnings per share or an increase in loss per share resulting from the assumption that convertible instruments are converted, that options or warrants are exercised, or that ordinary shares are issued upon the satisfaction of specified conditions. [IAS 33.5]

Antidilution is defined as an increase in earnings per share or a reduction in loss per share resulting from the assumption that convertible instruments are converted, that options or warrants are exercised, or that ordinary shares are issued upon the satisfaction of specified conditions. [IAS 33.5]

Dilutive potential ordinary shares are included in the calculation of diluted EPS as if the potential ordinary shares had been converted to ordinary shares at the start of the period (or on the date of issue of the potential ordinary shares, if later). [IAS 33.36] Antidilutive potential ordinary shares are disregarded in the calculation of diluted EPS.

5.1.1 Earnings adjustments – general

The earnings adjustment for diluted EPS is generally the actual charge to profit or loss that would be avoided by conversion of potential ordinary shares to actual ordinary shares. Accordingly, the profit or loss attributable to ordinary equity holders of the parent entity, as used for the calculation of basic EPS, is adjusted by the after-tax effect of:

[IAS 33.33]

- any dividends or other items related to dilutive potential ordinary shares deducted in arriving at profit or loss for the purposes of basic EPS;
- any interest recognised in the period related to dilutive potential ordinary shares; and
- any other changes in income or expense that would result from the conversion of dilutive potential ordinary shares.

> In calculating the after-tax amount of dividends, interest and other income or expenses for the purposes of adjusting the earnings figure, the tax rate applied should be the effective tax rate for the entity for the period under review. For an entity that is in a tax loss position, and for which a deferred tax asset in respect of those losses has not been recognised, the tax effect may be nil.

The items listed in IAS 33.33 would no longer arise if the potential ordinary shares were converted into ordinary shares. Accordingly, the earnings figures are adjusted to remove their impact, and any related tax effect. Changes in income or expense other than dividends and interest would include transaction costs and discounts accounted for in accordance with the effective interest method (see **chapter 18**). [IAS 33.34]

In addition, the entity might operate a profit-related pay or other bonus scheme. Any adjustments to profit or loss relating to potential ordinary shares might affect the amount payable to employees under the profit-related scheme (e.g. if the profit were to increase as a result of reduced interest costs, the amount of profit payable to the employees would also increase). The earnings adjustments for diluted EPS will include the effect on the incentive/bonus payable in respect of the scheme, and the consequential tax effects. [IAS 33.35]

Some compensation plans are based on the price of the entity's shares, but do not require or permit the actual issue of shares (e.g. phantom shares and formula plans). Rather, the compensation to the employee under the plan is settled entirely in cash. For plans of this nature, the computation of EPS will not be affected by the existence of the plan (except insofar as other earnings adjustments for diluted EPS would affect the amount of bonus payable, as discussed in the previous paragraph).

5.1.2 Per share adjustments – general

The number of shares used in the computation of diluted EPS is the sum of the weighted average number of ordinary shares used as the denominator for the basic EPS calculation and the weighted average number of ordinary shares that would be issued on the conversion of all dilutive potential ordinary shares. [IAS 33.36]

In calculating the weighted average number of dilutive potential ordinary shares:

[IAS 33.36 to 38]:

- dilutive potential ordinary shares are deemed to have been converted into ordinary shares at the beginning of the period or, if later, at the date of issue of the potential ordinary shares;
- the number of dilutive potential ordinary shares is determined independently for each period presented. The number of dilutive potential ordinary shares included in the year-to-date period is not a weighted average of the dilutive potential ordinary shares included in each interim computation;

- potential ordinary shares that have lapsed or been cancelled during the period are included for the time for which they were outstanding; and

- potential ordinary shares that have been converted into ordinary shares during the period are included for the period prior to actual exercise.

The terms of the potential ordinary shares are used to determine the number of ordinary shares that would be issued on the conversion of dilutive potential ordinary shares. When more than one basis of conversion exists, the computation assumes the most advantageous conversion rate or exercise price from the standpoint of the holder of the potential ordinary shares. [IAS 33.39] This ensures that the most dilutive conversion rate or exercise price is included in determining diluted EPS.

In the case where a financial liability is forgiven as consideration for the issue of shares (as is the case for convertible debt), the number of shares to be added to the denominator is the number of shares that would be issued to the holder assuming the convertible debt was converted in full. This is often referred to as the 'if-converted method'. This method does not consider what the average share price is compared to the exercise price inherent in the convertible debt and, therefore, convertible debt may be dilutive for EPS purposes even though the conversion option is not 'in-the-money' and, therefore, the holder would have no economic incentive for converting.

A different approach is used for standalone warrants and options to deliver ordinary shares. This approach determines dilution by comparing the average share price with the exercise price of the option. The approach illustrates how many shares are issued for nil consideration and, therefore, unlike the if-converted method, does take into account the extent to which the written option is 'in-the-money'. This is referred to as the 'treasury stock method'.

The existence of two different approaches in determining the adjustment for the denominator can result in different EPS amounts for very similar arrangements. For example, an issue of a convertible bond will apply the if-converted method and will result in a larger adjustment to the denominator compared to an issue of debt plus a standalone warrant where the treasury stock method will apply.

No restatement of diluted EPS of any prior period presented should be made for changes in the assumptions used or for the conversion of potential ordinary shares. [IAS 33.65]

5.2 Identifying dilutive potential ordinary shares

As noted at **5.1** above, antidilutive potential ordinary shares are disregarded in the calculation of diluted EPS. Therefore, once the entity has identified all of the potential ordinary shares in issue, the next step is to determine which of these are dilutive, and which are antidilutive.

5.2.1 *Steps for identifying dilutive potential ordinary shares*

Potential ordinary shares are treated as dilutive if their conversion to ordinary shares would decrease earnings per share or increase loss per share *from continuing operations*. [IAS 33.41]

IAS 33 specifies the steps to be followed in determining which potential ordinary shares are dilutive, as set out below. Each different category of potential ordinary shares is tested. The order in which they are tested is not left to each entity to choose, but is set out in the Standard. [IAS 33.44]

Step 1: The entity lists each different category of potential ordinary shares that it has in issue, e.g. a 5 per cent convertible bond would be considered separately from a 7 per cent convertible bond.

Step 2: For each category of potential ordinary shares, the entity determines how the earnings would have been affected had the potential ordinary shares been converted to shares on the first day of the year (or on the date of issue of the potential ordinary shares, if later). The adjustments to earnings for this purpose will be the same as the adjustments summarised at **5.8** below. The earnings will either be increased (increased profit or reduced loss) as a result of a convertible security, or will not be affected at all.

Step 3: For each category of potential ordinary shares, the entity then determines (in accordance with the rules in the Standard) the number of shares that would be issued if the potential ordinary shares were converted to shares. Thus, if an entity has bonds convertible into 100,000 ordinary shares, the number of shares to be issued will be 100,000. If the same entity has granted 100,000 share options, however, the number of shares to be used in the calculation is not 100,000, but the number deemed to be issued for nil proceeds (see **5.4.3** below). In addition, not all options are considered at this stage (see **5.4.3.1** below for a discussion as to which options to include in this exercise).

Step 4: The adjustment to earnings is then divided by the number of shares that would be issued on conversion to give, for each category of potential ordinary shares, the 'earnings per incremental share' that would have been generated had the additional shares been issued.

Step 5: These earnings per incremental share are ranked – the lowest being ranked first and the largest increase in earnings per new share being ranked last. Options and warrants are generally included first because they have no earnings effect.

Step 6: The net profit per share from continuing operations (see **5.2.2** below) is then adjusted for the category of potential ordinary shares ranked first by increasing the continuing earnings and increasing the number of shares.

Step 7: The 'before' and 'after' are compared – if the adjusted net profit per share from continuing operations is less, the potential ordinary shares are dilutive. This is repeated for each category of potential ordinary shares in turn in accordance with its ranking, until only antidilutive potential ordinary shares remain.

Step 8: Diluted EPS is calculated by adjusting basic EPS for the effect of the dilutive potential ordinary shares identified in Step 7.

5.2.2 Net profit per share from continuing operations

In order to determine which potential ordinary shares are dilutive, IAS 33 requires an analysis of the effect of conversion to ordinary shares on profit or loss from continuing operations attributable to the parent entity. [IAS 33.42]

As discussed earlier, profit/loss per share from continuing operations is calculated as:

$$\frac{\text{Profit or loss attributable to the shareholders of the parent entity after adjustments for the effects of preference shares and after excluding items relating to discontinuing operations}}{\text{Weighted average number of shares used to calculate basic EPS}}$$

5.2.3 Illustrative example

The following example, reproduced from Example 9 of the Illustrative Examples accompanying IAS 33, illustrates the process for identifying dilutive potential ordinary shares.

Example 5.2.3

Calculation of weighted average number of shares: determining the order in which to include dilutive instruments

[IAS 33 Illustrative Examples (Example 9)]

Earnings	**CU**
Profit from continuing operations attributable to the parent entity	16,400,000
Less dividends on preference shares	(6,400,000)
Profit from continuing operations attributable to ordinary equity holders of the parent entity	10,000,000
Loss from discontinued operations attributable to the parent entity	(4,000,000)
Profit attributable to ordinary equity holders of the parent entity	6,000,000
Ordinary shares outstanding	2,000,000
Average market price of one ordinary share during year	CU75.00

Potential ordinary shares

Options	100,000 with exercise price of CU60
Convertible preference shares	800,000 shares with a par value of CU100 entitled to a cumulative dividend of CU8 per share. Each preference share is convertible to two ordinary shares.
5 per cent convertible bonds	Nominal amount CU100,000,000. Each CU1,000 bond is convertible to 20 ordinary shares. There is no amortisation of premium or discount affecting the determination of interest expense.
Tax rate	40 per cent

Increase in earnings attributable to ordinary equity holders on conversion of potential ordinary shares

	Increase in earnings	Increase in number of ordinary shares	Earnings per incremental share
	CU		CU
Options			
Increase in earnings	Nil		
Incremental shares issued for no consideration 100,000 × (CU75 – CU60) ÷ CU75		20,000	Nil
Convertible preference shares			
Increase in profit CU800,000 × 100 × 0.08	6,400,000		
Incremental shares 2 × 800,000		1,600,000	4.00
5 per cent convertible bonds			
Increase in profit CU100,000,000 × 0.05 × (1 – 0.40)	3,000,000		
Incremental shares 100,000 × 20		2,000,000	1.50

The order in which to include the dilutive instruments is therefore:

(1) Options

(2) 5% convertible bonds

(3) Convertible preference shares

Calculation of diluted earnings per share

	Profit from continuing operations attributable to ordinary equity holders of the parent entity (control number)	Ordinary shares	Per share	
	CU		CU	
As reported	10,000,000	2,000,000	5.00	
Options	–	20,000		
	10,000,000	2,020,000	4.95	Dilutive
5 per cent convertible bonds	3,000,000	2,000,000		
	13,000,000	4,020,000	3.23	Dilutive
Convertible preference shares	6,400,000	1,600,000		
	19,400,000	5,620,000	3.45	Antidilutive

Because diluted earnings per share is increased when taking the convertible preference shares into account (from CU3.23 to CU3.45), the convertible preference shares are antidilutive and are ignored in the calculation of diluted earnings per share. Therefore, diluted earnings per share for profit from continuing operations is CU3.23:

	Basic EPS	Diluted EPS
	CU	CU
Profit from continuing operations attributable to ordinary equity holders of the parent entity	5.00	3.23
Loss from discontinued operations attributable to ordinary equity holders of the parent entity	(2.00)[a]	(0.99)[b]
Profit attributable to ordinary equity holders of the parent entity	3.00[c]	2.24[d]

Notes:

(a) (CU4,000,000) ÷ 2,000,000 = (CU2.00)

(b) (CU4,000,000) ÷ 4,020,000 = (CU0.99)

(c) CU6,000,000 ÷ 2,000,000 = CU3.00

(d) (CU6,000,000 + CU3,000,000) ÷ 4,020,000 = CU2.24

5.2.4 *Can diluted EPS ever be greater than basic EPS?*

Where an entity reports discontinued operations, it is possible for diluted EPS on total earnings to be greater than basic EPS. The reason for this is that IAS 33 treats potential ordinary shares as dilutive if their conversion decreases profit per share *from continuing operations*. Both basic and diluted EPS, on the other hand, will be calculated both on profit from continuing operations and on total earnings. Thus, although diluted EPS can never exceed basic EPS for continuing operations, it is possible for diluted EPS to exceed basic EPS when calculated for total earnings.

The Application Guidance to IAS 33 cites the following example. [IAS 33.A3]

Example 5.2.4A

Control number

[IAS 33.A3]

Assume that an entity has profit from continuing operations attributable to the parent entity of CU4,800, a loss from discontinued operations attributable to the parent entity of (CU7,200), a loss attributable to the parent entity of (CU2,400), and 2,000 ordinary shares and 400 potential ordinary shares outstanding. The entity's basic earnings per share is CU2.40 for continuing operations, (CU3.60) for discontinued operations and (CU1.20) for the loss. The 400 potential ordinary shares are included in the diluted earnings per share calculation because the resulting CU2.00 earnings per share for continuing operations is dilutive, assuming no profit or loss impact of those 400 potential ordinary shares. Because profit from continuing operations attributable to the parent entity is the control number, the entity also includes those 400 potential ordinary shares in the calculation of the other earnings per share amounts, even though the resulting earnings per share amounts are antidilutive to their comparable basic earnings per share amounts, i.e. the loss per share is less [(CU3.00) per share for the loss from discontinued operations and (CU1.00) per share for the loss].

5.3 Convertible debt or equity instruments

5.3.1 Approach

Conversion to ordinary shares is assumed to occur on the first day of the period, or the later date of issue of the convertible instrument.

Mathematically, convertible instruments will be antidilutive whenever (in the case of convertible preference shares) the amount of the dividend declared in or accumulated for the current period per ordinary share obtainable on conversion, or (in the case of convertible debt instruments) the after-tax effect of interest and similar costs per ordinary share obtainable on conversion, exceeds basic EPS. [IAS 33.50]

For example, suppose that convertible debt, pursuant to its original conversion terms, converts at a rate of £10 per ordinary share. The market value of A's shares at the date the convertible debt was issued was £8 per share. By year-end, A's share price had fallen to £6 per share. Even though an economically rational person would not be expected to convert the debt to ordinary shares at that time, the convertible debt is included in the computation of diluted EPS if the interest expense (net of tax and other adjustments) per ordinary share obtainable on conversion does not exceed basic EPS.

5.3.2 *Adjustment to earnings*

The adjustment is the post-tax amount recognised in profit or loss for finance costs related to the potential ordinary shares (and any consequential adjustments, as discussed at **5.1.1**).

For a debt instrument, this will be the post-tax effect of:

- interest costs recognised;
- amortisation of issue costs;
- fair value gains/losses if the instrument is fair valued through profit or loss; and
- amortisation of redemption premium or discount.

For shares, the adjustment will be the post-tax effect of:

- dividends recognised in the period;
- amortisation of issue costs;
- fair value gains/losses if the instrument is fair valued through profit or loss; and
- amortisation of redemption premium or discount.

The calculation used for determining diluted EPS for convertible instruments is often referred to as the 'if-converted method'.

Example 5.3.2

Convertible instruments

An entity has a profit attributable to ordinary shareholders for the year ended 31 December 20X5 of £7,400,000. The entity has three different classes of potential ordinary shares, as follows:

- £1,000,000 6 per cent convertible redeemable bonds (issued in 20X2);
- £1,000,000 8 per cent convertible bonds (issued 1 July 20X5); and
- 1,000,000 £1 17 per cent convertible preference shares (issued in 20X3).

The finance costs recognised in profit or loss (and associated tax effects) for the year ended 31 December 20X5 were as follows:

	Finance costs recognised in profit or loss for the year	Associated tax credit	Net of tax cost
	£	£	£
6 per cent bonds*	70,000	21,000	49,000
8 per cent bonds**	40,000	12,000	28,000
Preference shares	170,000	–	170,000

*Including accrued redemption premium

**The bonds were only issued on 1 July 20X5 and so the finance cost is calculated from that date

The right hand column, headed 'net of tax cost' is used to adjust earnings in the diluted EPS calculation.

The redemption or induced conversion of convertible preference shares may affect only a portion of the previously outstanding convertible preference shares. In such cases, any excess consideration (as discussed at **4.1.2.2** above) is attributed to those shares that are redeemed or converted for the purpose of determining whether the remaining outstanding preference shares are dilutive. The shares redeemed or converted are considered separately from those shares that are not redeemed or converted. [IAS 33.51]

5.3.3 *Adjustment to number of shares*

The adjustment assumes (in respect of convertible instruments that are dilutive) that all convertible instrument holders exercise all rights to convert to ordinary shares. Where different conversion ratios are allowed at different dates, the ratio used should assume the most advantageous conversion rate or exercise price from the standpoint of the holder of the potential ordinary shares.

5.3.4 *Options to exchange preference shares for ordinary shares*

Example 5.3.4

Options to exchange preference shares for ordinary shares

Company A issued 1,000 options that, if exercised, require the holder to tender preference shares in Company A (each having £2,750 face value) in exchange for 500 ordinary shares in Company A per preference share. On the date the option was issued, the ordinary shares of Company A were trading at £5 per share. The preference shares pay dividends at 10 per cent of face value annually. The following year, Company A had a net profit of £15,000,000, weighted average shares outstanding of 4,000,000, and the ordinary shares of Company A had an average market price of £15 per share.

Because the terms of the options require the holder to tender a preference share, the effect of the options is to change 1,000 preference shares into convertible instruments. The impact on diluted EPS is therefore calculated as for other convertible instruments. The exercise of the option is dilutive to EPS, computed as follows:

	Basic	Adjustments	Diluted
Net profit attributable to ordinary shareholders	£15,000,000	£275,000[a]	£15,275,000
divided by			
Weighted average shares outstanding	4,000,000	500,000[b]	4,500,000
Earnings per share	£3.75		£3.39

(a) Adjustment to the numerator (£2,750 x 1,000 x 10%) = £275,000

(b) Adjustment to the denominator (1,000 options x 500 shares) = 500,000

5.4 Options, warrants and similar items

5.4.1 *Approach*

IAS 33 deals with options and warrants (and other potential ordinary shares that lead to cash proceeds) by increasing the number of shares only for the number of shares deemed to be issued for no consideration. This is commonly referred to as the 'treasury stock method'.

For simplicity, the remainder of this section refers only to options. The rules are equally applicable to warrants and other equivalent instruments.

A rights issue is similar to an issuance of options to existing shareholders (see **section 4.2.3.3**). After the issue date of the rights issue, but before the exercise of the rights, diluted EPS should consider these rights to the extent that they are dilutive, in the same way as other options.

5.4.2 *Adjustment to earnings*

There is no adjustment to earnings if the potential ordinary share meets the definition of equity in IAS 32 *Financial Instruments: Presentation*.

The non-adjustment to earnings for potential ordinary shares that meet the definition of equity is appropriate as equity instruments do not have an impact on earnings. As IAS 33 was not updated for the additional guidance on derivatives over own equity introduced in IAS 32 as part of the Improvements Project in 2004, it is questionable how options and warrants that do not meet the definition of equity should be accounted with respect to the numerator in the calculation of diluted EPS.

If the option is a potential ordinary share that is classified as at fair value through profit or loss under IAS 39 *Financial Instruments: Recognition and Measurement* because it does not meet the definition of equity in IAS 32.11 (e.g. because it is an exchange of a fixed amount of shares for a variable amount of cash or it has a cash settlement alternative), then earnings are impacted during the instrument's life. It is consistent with the non-adjustment of earnings for equity instruments to adjust earnings for those potential ordinary shares that do impact earnings. By adjusting earnings, EPS illustrates the impact on the financial statements had the potential ordinary shares been converted into ordinary shares at the start of the reporting period. Examples where earnings are adjusted when applying the treasury stock method are provided in the table at **5.8** below

5.4.3 *Adjustment to number of shares*

For the purposes of calculating diluted EPS, the exercise of all dilutive options is assumed. The assumed proceeds from these instruments are regarded as having been received from the issue of ordinary shares at the average market price of ordinary shares during the period. The difference between the number of ordinary shares issued and the number of ordinary shares that would have been issued at the average market price of ordinary shares during the period is treated as an issue of ordinary shares for no consideration. [IAS 33.45]

IAS 33 does not provide any further guidance on what is meant by the 'average market price of the ordinary shares during the period'. When options or warrants are issued during the reporting period, the Standard does not specify if the 'average market price' for this *purpose should be taken to be only the average for the period the options or warrants were outstanding, or for the entire reporting* period.

Logically, the fair value of an instrument prior to its being issued should have no bearing on whether that instrument is dilutive or anti-dilutive. Therefore, the average for the shorter of (a) the period the options or warrants were outstanding, and (b) the reporting period, should be used.

Example 5.4.3A

Consideration for acquisition to be settled in cash or in shares

Company A acquires Company B. The purchase price of £16 million is to be paid in three instalments: £3 million at the close of the transaction, £10 million in one year, and £3 million in two years. At the seller's option, the final payment will be made either in cash or 100,000 of Company A's ordinary shares.

The terms of the final instalment constitute a written call option for Company A. The seller of Company B may call for 100,000 shares at a strike price of £3 million. Prior to the exercise or expiry of the written call option, diluted EPS should be determined in accordance with IAS 33.45.

To calculate diluted EPS, potential ordinary shares are treated as consisting of both of the following:

[IAS 33.46]

- a contract to issue a certain number of ordinary shares at their average market price during the period. Such ordinary shares are assumed to be fairly priced and to be neither dilutive nor antidilutive. They are ignored in the calculation of diluted EPS; and
- a contract to issue the remaining ordinary shares for no consideration. Such ordinary shares generate no proceeds and have no effect on profit or loss attributable to ordinary shares outstanding. Therefore, such shares are dilutive (at least for a profitable entity – see **5.4.3.1** for an entity with a loss from continuing operations) and are added to the number of ordinary shares outstanding in the calculation of diluted EPS.

The following table summarises the steps involved in the diluted EPS calculation.

Step 1:	Calculate the cash proceeds that would be received if all options were exercised at the contracted exercise price.

Step 2:	Calculate the number of shares that, if issued at the average market price for the period, would generate the same proceeds, i.e.: • compute the average market price of ordinary shares for the accounting period; and • divide the cash proceeds from Step 1 by this average market price.
Step 3:	Compute the number of bonus shares implicit in the option issue, i.e.: • compute the total number of shares that would be issued if all options were exercised; and • deduct from this total the number of shares deemed to be issued at the average market price from Step 2.
Step 4:	Treat the resulting number of bonus shares as shares issued for no consideration.

The following example, reproduced from Example 5 of the Illustrative Examples accompanying IAS 33, illustrates the impact of share options on diluted EPS.

Example 5.4.3B

Effect of share options on diluted earnings per share

[IAS 33 Illustrative Examples (Example 5)]

Profit attributable to ordinary equity holders of the parent entity for year 20X1	CU1,200,000
Weighted average number of ordinary shares outstanding during year 20X1	500,000 shares
Average market price of one ordinary share during year 20X1	CU20.00
Weighted average number of shares under option during year 20X1	100,000 shares
Exercise price for shares under option during Year 20X1	CU15.00

Calculation of earnings per share

	Earnings	Shares	Per share
Profit attributable to ordinary equity holders of the parent entity for year 20X1	CU1,200,000		
Weighted average shares outstanding during year 20X1		500,000	
Basic earnings per share			CU2.40
Weighted average number of shares under option		100,000	
Weighted average number of shares that would have been issued at average market price: (100,000 x CU15.00) / CU20.00	*	(75,000)	
Diluted earnings per share	CU1,200,000	525,000	CU2.29

*Earnings have not increased because the total number of shares has increased only by the number of shares (25,000) deemed to have been issued for no consideration (see paragraph 46(b) of the Standard).

5.4.3.1 *Identifying dilutive options*

Only dilutive potential ordinary shares are included in the calculation of diluted EPS.

IAS 33.46 states that options and warrants are dilutive when they would result in the issue of ordinary shares for less than the average market price of ordinary shares during the period. For a written call option, the amount of the dilution is the average market price of ordinary shares during the period less the issue price. For a written put option, the amount of the dilution is the average market price of ordinary shares during the period less the repurchase price.

Example 5.4.3.1

Identifying dilutive options

At 1 January and 31 December 20X1, an entity had the following written call options outstanding:

Number of shares under option	Exercise price (£)	Average share price during year (£)	Dilutive (D) or antidilutive (A)	Number of shares deemed issued for no consideration
10,000	7	10	D	3,000
5,000	8	10	D	1,000
15,000	9	10	D	1,500
10,000	12	10	A	–
20,000	11	10	A	–
				5,500

Where an entity has a loss from continuing operations, the exercise of in-the-money options will increase the number of shares to which that loss is allocated, so that loss per share will decrease. Thus, in-the-money options will not be dilutive for such an entity, since dilution is defined by IAS 33.5 as a reduction in earnings per share or an increase in loss per share resulting from the assumption that options are exercised.

This raises the question of whether out-of-the-money options should be considered dilutive for an entity with a loss from continuing operations. The option holders would (irrationally) be paying too much for these shares, which is equivalent, under the approach to dilution taken by IAS 33, to the entity issuing a negative number of shares for no consideration (i.e. buying back some shares for no consideration). Accordingly, since the exercise of out-of-the-money options would, if this method is applied, result in a reduction in the number of shares, it is mathematically correct that loss per share will increase.

Although the definition of dilution in IAS 33.5 might apparently lead to out-of-the-money options being considered dilutive, IAS 33.47 states:

'Options and warrants have a dilutive effect only when the average market price of ordinary shares during the period exceeds the exercise price of the options or warrants (i.e. they are 'in the money').'

Accordingly, since it would also be economically irrational for holders to exercise out-of-the-money options, it appears that out-of-the-money options should not be treated as dilutive for an entity with a loss from continuing operations.

5.4.3.2 *Share-based payments*

When dealing with share options and other share-based payment arrangements to which IFRS 2 *Share-based Payment* applies, the issue and exercise prices for the purposes of the calculations in the previous sections should include the fair value of any goods or services to be supplied to the entity in the future under the share option or other share-based payment arrangement. [IAS 33.47A]

Employee share options with fixed or determinable terms and non-vested ordinary shares are treated as options in the calculation of diluted EPS, even though they may be contingent on vesting. They are treated as outstanding on the grant date.

The dilutive effect of employee share options with fixed or determinable terms and non-vested ordinary shares is determined using the treasury stock method. The assumed exercise price will include the amount the employee must pay on exercise of the option as well as the balance of any amounts calculated under IFRS 2 that have not yet been recognised because they relate to future services. For share based payments treated as equity-settled under IFRS 2, the numerator is not adjusted as the IFRS 2 charge to date will not be saved upon exercise; the IFRS 2 charge is part of the cost of employee services, and employees will continue to render services. For those share-based payments treated as cash-settled under IFRS 2, the numerator will be adjusted only for the amount in profit or loss that would not have been recognised in profit or loss had the arrangement been classified wholly as an equity instrument (as if the arrangement was treated as equity settled). The following example, reproduced from Example 5A of the Illustrative Examples accompanying IAS 33, illustrates the determination of the exercise price of employee share options.

Example 5.4.3.2

Determining the exercise price of employee share options

[IAS 33 Illustrative Examples (Example 5A)]

Weighted average number of unvested share options per employee	1,000
Weighted average amount per employee to be recognised over the remainder of the vesting period for employee services to be rendered as consideration for the share options, determined in accordance with IFRS 2 *Share-based Payment*	CU1,200
Cash exercise price of unvested share options	CU15
Calculation of adjusted exercise price	
Fair value of services yet to be rendered per employee:	CU1,200
Fair value of services yet to be rendered per option: (CU1,200/1,000)	CU1.20
Total exercise price of share options: (CU15.00 + CU1.20)	CU16.20

IAS 33.47A states that the *"fair value* of any goods or services to be supplied to the entity in the future" (our emphasis) should be included as an adjustment to the exercise price under a share option or share-based payment arrangement. A literal application of fair value in the diluted EPS calculation would require the re-estimation of the current value of goods or services to be supplied at each

reporting period, as opposed to the fair value determined at grant date that has yet to be recognised in profit or loss. In practice, on grounds of materiality, entities typically apply the latter approach and do not re-estimate the fair value at each reporting period. This is consistent with Example 5A in the Appendix to IAS 33 reproduced above.

IAS 33 does not provide clear guidance on whether the proceeds from the assumed exercise of employee options include the tax benefits that would be credited to equity upon exercise of the employee option. As part of the IASB's deliberations on amending IAS 33 in May 2008, the IASB stated that it did not intend IAS 33 to exclude those tax benefits and, therefore, this would be clearer in the proposed amendment to IAS 33 expected to be issued in the third quarter of 2008. This approach is consistent with the US equivalent standard, SFAS 128 *Earnings per Share*.

Performance-based employee share options are treated as contingently issuable shares because their issue is contingent upon satisfying specified conditions in addition to the passage of time. [IAS 33.48] Contingently issuable shares are discussed in more detail in **5.5** below.

5.4.3.3 *Calculating average market price during the period*

When calculating diluted EPS, the average market price of ordinary shares assumed to be issued is calculated on the basis of the average market price of ordinary shares during the period. In theory, the average could be determined by using every market transaction in the entity's shares during the period. In practice, however, a simple average of weekly or monthly closing prices will usually be adequate. [IAS 33.A4]

Where prices fluctuate widely over the period, week or month being used, an average of the high and low prices for the period will usually produce a more representative price than simply using the closing price for the period. [IAS 33.A5]

The method used to compute the average market price should be used consistently, unless it is no longer representative because of changed conditions. For example, an entity that uses closing market prices to compute the average market price for several years of relatively stable market prices might need to change to an average of high and low prices if prices start fluctuating greatly and the closing market prices no longer produce a representative average market price. [IAS 33.A5]

Example 5.4.3.3A

Computation of average market price when trading volume is limited

Company A's shares trade in the over-the-counter market. During the fourth quarter of 20X1, Company A's shares were traded on only 15 days. The frequency of trades during the fourth quarter is representative of the normal trading volume on Company A's ordinary shares. In applying the treasury shares method, should the average of the limited trading prices be used, or is another method more appropriate?

When an entity's ordinary shares trade on a very irregular basis (e.g. limited trading volume), such that an average of the closing ordinary share price is not meaningful, it would be acceptable to use the average of the bid and ask price for the ordinary shares for a period to determine the average ordinary trading price. This method should be applied until the entity's ordinary shares trade on a regular basis and an average of the closing prices would yield an effective average ordinary share price.

As with any potential ordinary share, options are included in the calculation of diluted EPS as if conversion into ordinary shares had occurred on the first day of the accounting period or, if later, on the date on which the options or other potential ordinary shares were granted. Where options are granted part way through a year, the question arises as to whether the average market price should be the average from the date the option is granted to the end of the year or the average for the entire accounting period.

Example 5.4.3.3B

Options in issue for only part of a period

An entity's share price is £3 for the four months 1 January to 30 April, £4 for the four months 1 May to 31 August and £5 for the four months 1 September to 31 December. The average price for the year is therefore £4.

On 1 July, the entity grants 100,000 options exercisable at £4 per share, the then market price.

The average price from 1 July to 31 December is £4.67.

Thus, the shares are neither dilutive nor antidilutive if compared with the average for the year, but are dilutive if compared to the average price since the date the options were granted.

In **example 5.4.3.3B**, using the average for the year results in no dilution, whereas using the average from the date of grant of the options results in dilution. Given that the latter approach reflects the substance of what has happened, it seems appropriate that the entity should use the average from the date of grant of the options, notwithstanding that a literal reading of IAS 33 could point to the former approach.

Similar considerations apply when options are exercised during the year.

5.4.3.4 Options to purchase convertible instruments

Options to purchase convertible instruments are assumed to be exercised to purchase the convertible instrument whenever the average prices of both the convertible instrument and the ordinary shares obtainable upon conversion are above the exercise price of the options. However, exercise is not assumed unless the conversion of similar outstanding convertible instruments, if any, is also assumed. [IAS 33.A6]

Example 5.4.3.4

Options to purchase convertible instruments

Company A issued 1,000 options that allow the holder to purchase convertible preference shares at £5,000 per share. The convertible preference shares are convertible to ordinary shares at £25 per ordinary share after two years. On the date the options were issued, the ordinary shares of Company A were trading at £25 per share. Three years later on 31 December, the ordinary shares of Company A had an average market price of £40 per share.

The options on the ordinary shares are 'in-the-money'. Therefore, using the treasury stock method (illustrated below), Company A would assume that the holders of the options would elect to exercise their options and receive the convertible preference shares for £5,000 per share. The treasury stock method should be applied to compute the incremental dilutive shares as follows:

Shares assumed issued (1,000 x £5,000)/£25		200,000
Total assumed proceeds (1,000 x £5,000)	£5,000,000	
Divided by the average market price	40	
Less: shares assumed to be issued at full value		125,000
Incremental shares to be included in diluted EPS		75,000

As the 1,000 options do not meet the definition of equity per IAS 32.11 (as they represent an option over an instrument that itself has an option to convert into equity), the options would be fair valued through profit or loss. If the add back of the fair value gains/losses in the period to the numerator was less in proportion to the incremental shares added to the denominator then the effect would be dilutive.

5.4.3.5 *Options to be exercised using instruments of the entity*

The terms of options may permit or require debt or other instruments of the entity (or its parent or a subsidiary) to be tendered in payment of all or a portion of the exercise price. When calculating diluted EPS, those options have a dilutive effect if:

[IAS 33.A7]

- the average market price of the related ordinary shares for the period exceeds the exercise price; or
- the selling price of the instrument to be tendered is below that at which the instrument may be tendered under the option agreement and the resulting discount establishes an effective exercise price below the market price of the ordinary shares obtainable upon exercise.

When calculating diluted EPS, those options are assumed to be exercised and the debt or other instruments are assumed to be tendered. If tendering cash is more advantageous to the option holder and is permitted by the contract, tendering of cash is assumed. Interest (net of tax) on any debt assumed to be tendered is added back as an adjustment to the numerator. [IAS 33.A7]

Similar treatment is given to preference shares that have similar provisions or to other instruments that have conversion options that permit the investor to pay cash for a more favourable conversion rate. [IAS 33.A8]

5.4.3.6 *Proceeds from options to be applied to redeem debt or other instruments*

Some options may have underlying terms that require the proceeds received from the exercise of those instruments to be applied to redeem debt or other instruments of the entity (or its parent or a subsidiary). When calculating diluted EPS, those options are assumed to be exercised and the proceeds applied to purchase the debt at its average market price rather than to purchase ordinary shares. Nevertheless, the excess proceeds received from the assumed exercise over the amount used for the assumed purchase of debt are taken into account in calculating diluted EPS (i.e. the excess is assumed to be used to buy back ordinary shares). Interest (net of tax) on any debt assumed to be purchased is added back as an adjustment to the numerator. [IAS 33.A9]

Example 5.4.3.6

Proceeds from options applied to repurchase preference shares

Company A issued 400,000 options, which allow the holder to purchase ordinary shares at £40 per share and which, if exercised, require Company A to repurchase 1,000 preference shares of £2,750 face value per share with the proceeds. The preference shares pay dividends at 10 per cent annually and had an average fair value of £2,800. The following year, Company A had net income of £15,000,000, weighted average shares outstanding of 4,000,000, and the ordinary shares of Company A had an average market price of £50 per share.

Since the exercise of the options does not require the holder to be the holder of a preference share, the dilutive effect of these options should be determined in accordance with IAS 33.45. The options on the ordinary shares are 'in-the-money'. Therefore, using the treasury stock method, Company A would assume that the holders of the options would elect to exercise their options. As the exercise of the options would dilute EPS, Company A would apply the treasury stock method to compute the incremental dilutive shares as follows:

	Basic	Adjustments	Diluted
Net profit attributable to ordinary shareholders	£15,000,000	£275,000[a]	£15,275,000
divided by			
Weighted average shares outstanding	4,000,000	136,000[b]	4,136,000
Earnings per share	3.75		3.69
(a) Adjustment to the numerator (£2,750 x 1,000 x 10%)		£275,000	
(b) Shares in issue			400,000
Total assumed proceeds (400,000 x £40)		£16,000,000	
Less: amount required to retire preference shares (£2,800 x 1,000)		£2,800,000	
Excess proceeds assumed to buy treasury shares	£13,200,000		
Divided by the average price of the ordinary shares	50		
Less: shares assumed to be issued at full value		264,000	
Adjustment to the denominator (incremental shares) (400,000 – 264,000)			136,000

5.5 Contingently issuable shares

5.5.1 Approach

Contingently issuable shares are shares that will be issued at a future date, subject to the satisfaction of conditions. The conditions can be linked to earnings, the market price of the shares or something else. Although contingently issuable shares are another example of potential ordinary shares, they are nevertheless sometimes included in the calculation of basic EPS (see **4.2.2.4** above). The following sections discuss the impact of contingently issuable shares on diluted EPS.

By virtue of their inclusion in basic EPS, ordinary shares whose issue is contingent upon the occurrence of certain events are also included in the calculation of diluted EPS if the conditions have been met (i.e. the events have occurred) at the end of the reporting period.

If all necessary conditions have not been satisfied (and, therefore, these shares have not been included in the calculation of basic EPS), the number of contingently issuable shares included in diluted EPS is to be based on the number of shares, if any, that would be issuable if the end of the reporting period were the end of the contingency period and if the result would be dilutive. [IAS 33.52]

Those contingently issuable shares will be included in the denominator of diluted EPS as of the beginning of the period (or as of the date of the contingent share agreement, if later). [IAS 33.52]

5.5.2 *Adjustment to earnings*

Contingently issuable shares have no impact on the earnings figure used to calculate diluted EPS. This applies even if the condition relates to earnings levels. The reason for this is that the number of contingently issuable shares included in the diluted EPS calculation is always based on the status of the condition at the end of the reporting period. Thus, when the condition relates to earnings levels, shares are not included in the calculation unless the required earnings level has already been achieved.

5.5.3 *Adjustment to number of shares*

As discussed at **4.2.2.4**, contingently issuable shares will be included in the calculation of basic EPS if the conditions have been satisfied at the end of the reporting period. Contingently issuable shares are included in basic EPS calculations from the date when all necessary conditions have been satisfied and, thus, although issuing the shares is still a future transaction, it is no longer contingent. [IAS 33.24]

Where the conditions have not been satisfied before the end of the reporting period, and the shares remain contingently issuable, they will be included in the calculation of diluted EPS based on the number of shares that would be issuable if the end of the reporting period were the end of the contingency period. [IAS 33.52]

Restatement of amounts previously reported for diluted EPS is not permitted if the conditions are not met when the contingency period expires. [IAS 33.52]

5.5.3.1 Condition expressed as the attainment of a specified amount of earnings

If the condition for contingent issue is the attainment or maintenance of a specified amount of earnings for a period, and if that amount has been attained at the end of the period but must be maintained beyond the end of the reporting period for an additional period, then the additional ordinary shares are taken into account, if the effect is dilutive, when calculating diluted EPS. The calculation of diluted EPS is based on the number of ordinary shares that would be issued if the amount of earnings at the end of the reporting period were the amount of earnings at the end of the contingency period. [IAS 33.53]

The calculation of basic EPS does not include such contingently issuable ordinary shares until the end of the contingency period because not all necessary conditions have been satisfied, in that earnings may change in a future period (see **example 4.2.2.4C**). [IAS 33.53]

5.5.3.2 Condition expressed as an average over a period

Where a condition is expressed as an average over a period, it has the same effect as if it were expressed as a cumulative amount over the period, i.e. the performance achieved to date is deemed to be that achieved over the whole of the contingency period. For example, if the number of shares to be issued depends on whether profits average £1,000,000 per annum over a three year period, the condition is expressed in terms of a cumulative target of £3,000,000 over the three year period. If, at the end of the first year, profits are £1,500,000, no additional shares are brought into the calculation. On the other hand, if profits of £5,000,000 have been achieved at the end of the first period, the additional shares are included in the calculation of diluted EPS because if the end of the first period were the end of the contingency period, the condition would have been achieved.

Again, this can be contrasted with the treatment for the purposes of basic EPS, as discussed at **4.2.2.4** above. Even where £5,000,000 has been earned by the end of the first period, the shares are not included for the purposes of basic EPS, because the condition has not been achieved. It cannot be achieved until the end of the contingency period – since there is a possibility (however remote) of losses for the remainder of the period, which could reduce average profits below the target level.

Example 5.5.3.2

Contingency based on average profits

A Limited acquires B Limited on 1 January 20X1. A Limited agrees to issue 100,000 shares to the vendor on 1 January 20X4 if B Limited's profits for the three years to 31 December 20X3 average £10 million or more.

B Limited's profits for 20X1 and 20X2 are £17 million each year. The requirement for average profits of £10 million over three years is treated as a requirement for total profits of £30 million over the three years.

Actual profits in 20X1 of £17 million are below the target of £30 million and, accordingly, the 100,000 shares are excluded from the diluted EPS calculation for 20X1.

Actual profits for 20X1 and 20X2 together total £34 million. This exceeds the target and, thus, the 100,000 shares would be included in diluted EPS for 20X2. The shares will be included even if B Limited expects to make a loss of £4 million or more in 20X3.

See **example 4.2.2.4C** above for a discussion of how the shares would be included in basic EPS.

5.5.3.3 Condition dependent on future market price of shares

Where the number of shares that may be issued in the future depends upon the market price of the shares of the issuing entity, the number of shares to be included in the calculation of diluted EPS, if dilutive, is based on the number that would be issued if the market price at the end of the reporting period were the market price at the end of the contingency period. [IAS 33.54]

If the condition is based on the average of market prices over some period of time that extends beyond the end of reporting period, the average for the period or time that has lapsed is used. [IAS 33.54]

The calculation of basic EPS does not include such contingently issuable ordinary shares because not all necessary conditions have been satisfied, in that the market price may change in a future period. [IAS 33.54]

Example 5.5.3.3

Contingency based on share price movements

An entity is to issue the following shares to a third party on 1 October 20X2, dependent upon the entity's share price on 30 September 20X2:

Number of shares	Share price on 30 September 20X2
Nil	£10 or less
10,000	>£10 and <£11
15,000	£11 or above

If, on 31 December 20X1, the last day of the entity's reporting period, the share price were £9, no shares would be included in the diluted EPS calculation, whereas an additional 10,000 shares would be included if the share price on 31 December 20X1 were £10.20.

If the share price had been above £10 every day between 21 November 20X1 and the date the financial statements were signed, other than on 31 December 20X1 when the price dipped to £9.98, based on the principles discussed above, none of these shares would be included in the diluted EPS calculation.

If the issue had been conditional upon the average share price for the last five business days up to and including 30 September 20X2, the diluted EPS would be computed by looking at the share price on the last five business days up to and including 31 December 20X1 and comparing this with the target average price.

5.5.3.4 Multiple conditions

When the share issue is dependent on a number of conditions being met (e.g. a product licence being granted before a certain date *and* a profit target over the same period), then the diluted EPS calculation should only include those shares when all (or both in the case of this example) the conditions have been met at the end of the reporting period.

Similarly, where the number of shares contingently issuable depends both on future earnings and future prices of the ordinary shares, the number of ordinary shares included in diluted EPS is based on both conditions (i.e. earnings to date and the current market price at the end of the reporting period). The contingently issuable shares are not included in diluted EPS unless both conditions are met. [IAS 33.55]

5.5.3.5 Number of shares to be issued not known

For deferred consideration agreements in which the value of consideration is fixed but the number of shares issuable is not known, the number of shares to be included in the calculation of diluted EPS is based on the market price at the end of the reporting period as if it were the end of the contingency period if the effect is dilutive. (See **4.2.2.6** above for the treatment of such shares in the calculation of basic EPS.) [IAS 33.54]

5.5.3.6 Other conditions

If the contingency is based on a condition other than earnings or market price, the contingently issuable shares are included in the diluted EPS calculation on the assumption that the status of the condition at the end of the reporting period will remain unchanged until the end of the contingency period. [IAS 33.56] For example, if a further issue of shares is generated on the opening of the tenth new retail outlet and, at the year end, only five have been opened, no contingently issuable shares are included in the diluted computation.

Example 5.5.3.6A

Contingency based on an event

A Limited acquires B Limited on 1 January 20X1. A Limited agrees to issue 100,000 shares to the vendor on 1 January 20X3 if, at any point prior to that date, a new product developed by B Limited is granted a licence.

A Limited's year end is 31 December. The 20X1 financial statements are approved on 22 March 20X2. The product is granted a licence on 4 March 20X2.

Even though the directors of A Limited know, at the date they approve the 20X1 financial statements, that the additional 100,000 shares will be issued to the vendor on 1 January 20X3, the shares are excluded from the calculation of diluted EPS for 20X1, because, as at the end of the reporting period, the licence had not been granted.

The 100,000 shares will be included in the calculation of diluted EPS for 20X2, as if they had been in issue throughout the entire year.

See **example 4.2.2.4A** above for a discussion of how the shares would be included in the calculation of basic EPS for 20X2.

Another example of a contingency based on an event is where shares are contingently issuable upon the favourable outcome of a lawsuit. Such shares should be excluded from the calculation of basic and diluted EPS until the outcome of the lawsuit is determined. When the outcome of the lawsuit is final, the shares should be included in basic EPS from the date of finalisation of the lawsuit and included in diluted EPS from the beginning of the period in which the lawsuit is finalised.

Similar logic should be applied for shares that will be issued in the event that the entity makes an Initial Public Offering (IPO). Since there are many factors that can affect the successful completion of an IPO, the contingency is not met until the IPO actually becomes effective. Therefore, for periods ending prior to the effective date of the IPO, the shares would not be considered in the denominator for computation of diluted EPS. For periods ending after the IPO is effective, the shares would be included in the denominator of diluted EPS under the usual method. For basic EPS, instruments that are convertible in the event of an IPO should not be included in the denominator until the actual shares are issued, and then only on a weighted average basis.

The following example, reproduced from Example 7 of the Illustrative Examples accompanying IAS 33, continues from **example 4.2.2.4E** above and provides another illustration of contingently issuable shares.

Example 5.5.3.6B

Contingently issuable shares

[IAS 33 Illustrative Examples (Example 7)]

Ordinary shares outstanding during 20X1	1,000,000 (there were no options, warrants or convertible instruments outstanding during the period)

An agreement related to a recent business combination provides for the issue of additional ordinary shares based on the following conditions:

	5,000 additional ordinary shares for each new retail site opened during 20X1
	1,000 additional ordinary shares for each CU1,000 of consolidated profit in excess of CU2,000,000 for the year ended 31 December 20X1
Retail sites opened during the year:	one on 1 May 20X1 one on 1 September 20X1
Consolidated year-to-date profit attributable to ordinary equity holders of the parent entity:	CU1,100,000 as of 31 March 20X1 CU2,300,000 as of 30 June 20X1 CU1,900,000 as of 30 September 20X1 (including a CU 450,000 loss from a discontinued operation) CU2,900,000 as of 31 December 20X1

[The calculation of basic EPS is illustrated in **example 4.2.2.4E** above.]

Diluted earnings per share

	First quarter	Second quarter	Third quarter	Fourth quarter	Full year
Numerator (CU)	1,100,000	1,200,000	(400,000)	1,000,000	2,900,000
Denominator:					
Ordinary shares outstanding	1,000,000	1,000,000	1,000,000	1,000,000	1,000,000
Retail site contingency	–	5,000	10,000	10,000	10,000
Earnings contingency	–[a]	300,000[b]	–[c]	900,000[d]	900,000[d]
Total shares	1,000,000	1,305,000	1,010,000	1,910,000	1,910,000
Diluted earnings per share (CU)	1.10	0.92	(0.40)[e]	0.52	1.52

(a) Company A does not have year-to-date profit exceeding CU2,000,000 at 31 March 20X1. The Standard does not permit projecting future earnings levels and including the related contingent shares.

(b) [(CU2,300,000 – CU2,000,000)/1,000] x 1,000 shares = 300,000 shares.

(c) Year-to-date profit is less than CU2,000,000.

(d) [(CU2,900,000 – CU2,000,000)/1,000] x 1,000 shares = 900,000 shares

(e) Because the loss during the third quarter is attributable to a loss from a discontinued operation, the antidilution rules do not apply. The control number (i.e. profit or loss from continuing operations attributable to the equity holders of the parent entity) is positive. Accordingly, the effect of potential ordinary shares is included in the calculation of diluted earnings per share.

5.5.4 *Contingently issuable potential ordinary shares*

To assess whether contingently issuable potential ordinary shares (other than those covered by a contingent share agreement, such as contingently issuable convertible instruments) should be included in the diluted EPS calculation:

[IAS 33.57]

- determine whether the potential ordinary shares may be assumed to be issuable on the basis of the conditions specified for their issue, based on the guidance outlined in the previous sections for contingently issuable shares; and

- if those potential ordinary shares should be reflected in diluted EPS, determine their impact on the calculation of diluted EPS by following the appropriate rules discussed above for the type of potential ordinary share (options and warrants, convertible instruments etc.).

Exercise or conversion is not assumed for the purpose of calculating diluted EPS, however, unless exercise or conversion of similar outstanding potential ordinary shares that are not contingently issuable is assumed. [IAS 33.57]

Thus, for example, contingently issuable options will be included in the calculation of diluted EPS if both of the following conditions are met:

- if the end of the reporting period were the end of the contingency period, the options would be issued; and
- the effect of the options is dilutive.

Example 5.5.4

Contingently issuable options

On 1 July 20X1, an entity agreed that, provided its profit over the two years to 30 June 20X3 exceeds a specified target, on 1 July 20X3 it will issue 10,000 share options exercisable at £5 per share from 1 July 20X4 to 30 June 20X9.

The average market price of the entity's ordinary shares during the year ended 31 December 20X2 was £5.50.

The treatment of the options will depend on whether the profit target has been reached at the end of the reporting period (31 December 20X2):

- If it has, the options will be included in the 20X2 diluted EPS calculation (i.e. as if they were an issue of 9,091 shares that are not dilutive and 909 shares that are dilutive).
- If it hasn't, nothing is included in the 20X2 diluted EPS calculation in respect of the options.

5.5.5 *Contracts that may be settled in cash or in shares*

5.5.5.1 *Conversion at the option of the issuer*

An entity may issue a contract that may be settled in cash or in ordinary shares at the entity's option (e.g. a debt instrument that, on maturity, gives the entity the unrestricted right to settle the principal amount in cash or in its own shares). For such contracts, the calculation of diluted EPS should be based on the assumption that the contract will be settled in ordinary shares, so that the resulting potential ordinary shares should be included in diluted EPS if the effect is dilutive. [IAS 33.58]

When such a contract is presented for accounting purposes as an asset or a liability, or has an equity component and a liability component, the numerator in the diluted EPS calculation should be adjusted for any changes in profit or loss that would have resulted during the period if the contract had been classified wholly as an equity instrument. [IAS 33.59] The adjustment is similar to those discussed at **5.1.1** above.

The following example, reproduced from Example 8 of the Illustrative Examples accompanying IAS 33, provides an illustration of convertible bonds settled in shares or cash at the issuer's option.

Example 5.5.5.1

Convertible bonds settled in shares or cash at the issuer's option

[IAS 33 Illustrative Examples (Example 8)]

An entity issues 2,000 convertible bonds at the beginning of Year 1. The bonds have a three-year term, and are issued at par with a face value of CU1,000 per bond, giving total proceeds of CU2,000,000. Interest is payable annually in arrears at a nominal annual interest rate of 6 per cent. Each bond is convertible at any time up to maturity into 250 common shares. The entity has an option to settle the principal amount of the convertible bonds in ordinary shares or in cash.

When the bonds are issued, the prevailing market interest rate for similar debt without a conversion option is 9 per cent. At the issue date, the market price of one common share is CU3. Income tax is ignored.

Profit attributable to ordinary equity holders of the parent entity Year 1	CU1,000,000
Ordinary shares outstanding	1,200,000
Convertible bonds outstanding	2,000
Allocation of proceeds of the bond issue:	
Liability component	CU1,848,122[a]
Equity component	CU151,878
	CU2,000,000

The liability and equity components would be determined in accordance with IAS 32 *Financial Instruments: Presentation*. These amounts are recognised as the initial carrying amounts of the liability and equity components. The amount assigned to the issuer conversion option equity element is an addition to equity and is not adjusted.

Basic earnings per share Year 1:

CU1,000,000/1,200,000 = CU0.83 per ordinary share

Diluted earnings per share Year 1:

It is presumed that the issuer will settle the contract by the issue of ordinary shares. The dilutive effect is therefore calculated in accordance with paragraph 59 of the Standard.

(CU1,000,000 + CU166,331[b])/(1,200,000 + 500,000[c]) = CU0.69 per share

(a) This represents the present value of the principal and interest discounted at 9% – CU2,000,000 payable at the end of three years; CU120,000 payable annually in arrears for three years.

(b) Profit is adjusted for the accretion of CU166,331 (CU1,848,122 x 9%) of the liability because of the passage of time.

(c) 500,000 ordinary shares = 250 ordinary shares x 2,000 convertible bonds.

Example 8 of the Illustrative Examples accompanying IAS 33 (reproduced above) shows a convertible bond split into its financial liability and equity components. The Example states that the issuer has the option to settle the principal amount of the convertible bond in ordinary shares or cash. The Example is not clear whether the issuer's right is to settle the principal in a fixed number of ordinary shares or a variable number of ordinary shares equal to the amount of the principal. As a financial liability is recognised for the present value of the interest and principal amount and a written call option is recognised in equity for the holder's right to convert the liability into a fixed number of shares then it is assumed that the issuer's option must be a right to settle the principal amount in either cash or a variable number of shares equal to the value of the principal amount. The issuer's option cannot be a right to settle the principal amount in a fixed number of shares or this itself would be equity, i.e. a purchased put option.

Had the issuer's option instead been a right for the issuer to settle in a fixed number of shares or cash equal to the value of the shares in the instance when the holder chose to convert then the whole instrument would be classified as a financial liability (i.e. without an equity component) as the holder's right to convert would include a cash settlement alternative which would prevent the conversion option meeting the definition of equity in IAS 32. In this case, the if-converted method would be applied and the total impact in earnings with respect to the instrument would be added to the numerator in determining earnings for diluted EPS.

5.5.5.2 Conversion at the option of the holder

Where the holder has the option to choose between settlement in ordinary shares or cash, the more dilutive of cash settlement and share settlement is used in calculating diluted EPS. [IAS 33.60]

An example of this type of instrument is a written put option that gives the holder a choice of settling in ordinary shares or in cash. [IAS 33.61]

5.6 Purchased options

Contracts such as purchased put options and purchased call options (i.e. options held by the entity on its own ordinary shares) are not included in the calculation of diluted EPS. This is because including them would be antidilutive: a put option would be exercised only if the exercise price were higher than the market price, and a call option would be exercised only if the exercise price were lower than the market price. [IAS 33.62)]

5.7 Written put options

Contracts that require the entity to repurchase its own shares, such as written put options, are reflected in the calculation of diluted EPS if the effect is dilutive. If these contracts are in-the-money during the period (i.e. the exercise or settlement price is above the average market price for that period), the potential dilutive effect on EPS is calculated as follows:

[IAS 33.63]

- it is assumed that, at the beginning of the period, sufficient ordinary shares will be issued (at the average market price during the period) to raise proceeds to satisfy the contract;
- it is assumed that the proceeds from the issue are used to satisfy the contract (i.e. to buy back the ordinary shares); and
- the incremental ordinary shares (i.e. the difference between the number of ordinary shares assumed issued and the number of ordinary shares received from satisfying the contract) are included in the calculation of diluted EPS.

This technique is commonly referred to as the 'reverse treasury stock method'.

Example 5.7A

Written put options (1)

[IAS 33.A10]

Assume that an entity has outstanding 120 written put options on its ordinary shares with an exercise price of CU35. The average market price of its ordinary shares for the period is CU28. In calculating diluted earnings per share, the entity assumes that it issued 150 shares at CU28 per share at the beginning of the period to satisfy its put obligation of CU4,200. The difference between the 150 ordinary shares issued and the 120 ordinary shares received from satisfying the put option (30 incremental ordinary shares) is added to the denominator in calculating diluted earnings per share.

Example 5.7B

Written put options (2)

Company A issued £100 million in debt instruments with detachable put options on its ordinary shares. Purchasers of each £1,000 note will receive 10 put options each, giving the holder the right to require A to purchase one share of its ordinary shares for £25 per share, the market price of the ordinary shares on the date the put options were issued. The puts are exercisable at any time during a three-year period. Assume the average market price of the ordinary shares for the period is £20 per share.

The number of incremental shares to be added to the denominator of the diluted EPS calculation is computed as follows:

Cash required to settle put option (£100 million/£1,000) x 10 options x £25	£25,000,000
Divided by the average market price per share	20
Number of shares that would need to be issued to settle put option	1,250,000
Less: Shares assumed repurchased under put option (£100 million/£1,000) x 10 options	1,000,000
Incremental shares	250,000

5.7.1 *Forward purchase of own shares*

A forward purchase of own shares is similar in substance to a written put option at the forward sale price and a purchased call option at the forward sale price.

In terms of IAS 33.62 (see **5.6** above), the purchased call option is not dilutive. The effect of the written put option on the denominator should be determined in accordance with IAS 33.63 (see **5.7**), i.e. the shares subject to forward purchase should be regarded as outstanding for the period.

The interest cost recognised in profit or loss in respect of the forward purchase liability should be added back for the purposes of determining diluted EPS.

The above treatment is consistent with IAS 33.63. Although that paragraph is headed *Written put options*, it also refers to 'forward purchase contracts'.

5.7.2 *Forward sale of own shares*

A forward sale of own shares is similar in substance to a written call option at the forward sale price and a purchased put option at the forward sale price.

In terms of IAS 33.62 (see **5.6** above), the purchased put option is not dilutive. The effect of the written call option on the denominator should be determined in accordance with IAS 33.45 (see **5.4.3**). If the forward sale contract has been recognised as a derivative, any gain or loss recognised in earnings should be adjusted for the purposes of calculating diluted EPS.

This treatment differs from that for mandatorily convertible instruments, which are included in the denominator for basic EPS. Although a mandatorily convertible instrument and a forward sale of own shares will always result in the delivery of shares, the former is a funded instrument (i.e. proceeds were received for the issue of shares when the instrument was issued but the issuer has yet to deliver the shares), whereas for the latter the arrangement is unfunded (i.e. it is a derivative, and both the cash to be received and the delivery of shares remain outstanding). The mandatorily convertible instrument is not treated as a potential ordinary share, but rather as shares that have already been delivered. This compares with the forward sale of own shares being treated as if the entity has a potential future transaction to sell shares, because of the inclusion of what is in effect, for EPS purposes, a written call option embedded within the transaction.

5.8 Summary of adjustments for potential ordinary shares in diluted EPS calculations

The following table sets out a summary of the adjustments to earnings and the number of shares in diluted EPS calculations for each of the major categories of potential ordinary shares. Each of these categories is considered in detail in the preceding sections.

Potential ordinary shares	Adjustment to earnings	Adjustment to number of shares
Convertible bonds, debentures and preference shares (classified as a compound instrument or wholly as a financial liability)	Add back interest, dividends, fair value gains/losses and other finance costs recognised in the period, net of tax.	Add number of new shares assuming full conversion.
Warrants and options, e.g. written call option for an exchange of a fixed amount of shares for a fixed amount of functional currency cash (classified as equity)	None	Add number of shares deemed to be issued for no consideration.
Contingently issuable shares (classified as equity)	None	Add number of shares that would be issued if the end of the reporting period were the end of the contingency period.
Warrants and options, e.g. written call option for an exchange of a fixed amount of shares for a variable amount of cash, or an exchange of a fixed amount of shares for a fixed amount of cash with a net cash settlement alternative (classified as a financial liability)	Add back fair value gains/losses, net of tax	Add number of shares equal to the number of shares that would have been issued for nil consideration based on the average fair value of the shares over the period.
Forward purchase contract to buy own shares or a written put option to potentially reacquire own shares (classified as a financial liability)	Add back interest and any other gains/losses, net of tax	Add number of shares equal to the number of shares that would have to be issued to satisfy the obligation based on the average fair value of the shares over the period less the number of shares that are to be acquired under the contract.

Where the numerator is adjusted for gains/losses already recognised in profit or loss this may result in the instrument being anti-dilutive. Consider an example where a written call option may result in the physical delivery of own equity and is classified as at fair value through profit or loss. Assume the option is in-the-money for the holder at the period end, i.e. the average market price of the shares is greater than the strike price under the option. It would appear superficially that the written call option is dilutive as the option is in-the-money for the holder. However, in the case where the written call option is fair valued through profit or loss and a loss has been recognised in the reporting period (because the market price of the share fell in the period), the reversal of the loss in the numerator calculation will increase earnings. Where this adjustment to earnings is smaller in proportion to the adjustment to the numerator, i.e. the number of shares that are deemed to be issued for nil consideration, the instrument will be anti-dilutive in the reporting period and, therefore, will not be included in the calculation of diluted EPS.

5.9 Potential ordinary shares issued by a subsidiary, joint venture or associate

5.9.1 Instruments that entitle holders to shares in subsidiary, joint venture or associate

Instruments issued by a subsidiary, joint venture or associate that enable their holders to obtain ordinary shares of the subsidiary, joint venture or associate are included in calculating the diluted EPS data of the subsidiary, joint venture or associate. Those earnings per share are then included in the reporting entity's EPS calculations based on the reporting entity's holding of the instruments of the subsidiary, joint venture or associate. [IAS 33.A11(a)]

For the purpose of determining the EPS effect of these instruments, they are assumed to be converted, and the numerator (profit or loss attributable to the ordinary equity holders of the parent entity) adjusted as necessary, as discussed at **5.1.1** above. In addition to those adjustments, the numerator is adjusted for any change in the profit or loss recognised by the reporting entity (such as equity method income) that is attributable to the increase in the number of ordinary shares of the subsidiary, joint venture or associate as a result of the conversion. The denominator for the diluted EPS calculation at the consolidated level is unaffected because the number of shares of the reporting entity outstanding would not change upon the assumed conversion. [IAS 33.A12]

The following example, reproduced from Example 10 of the Illustrative Examples accompanying IAS 33, provides an illustration of instruments issued by a subsidiary.

Example 5.9.1

Instruments of a subsidiary: calculation of basic and diluted earnings per share

[IAS 33 Illustrative Examples (Example 10)]

Parent:

Profit attributable to ordinary equity holders or of the parent entity	CU12,000 (excluding any earnings of, or dividends paid by, the subsidiary)
Ordinary shares outstanding	10,000
Instruments of subsidiary owned by the parent	800 ordinary shares
	30 warrants exercisable to purchase ordinary shares of subsidiary
	300 convertible preference shares
Subsidiary:	
Profit	CU5,400
Ordinary shares outstanding	1,000
Warrants	150, exercisable to purchase ordinary shares of the subsidiary
Exercise price	CU10
Average market price of one ordinary share	CU20
Convertible preference shares	400, each convertible into one ordinary share
Dividends on preference shares	CU1 per share

No inter-company eliminations or adjustments were necessary except for dividends.

For the purposes of this illustration, income taxes have been ignored.

Subsidiary's earnings per share

Basic EPS CU5.00 calculated:	(CU5,400[a] – CU400[b])/1,000[c]
Diluted EPS CU3.66 calculated:	CU5,400[d]/(1,000 + 75[e] + 400[f])

(a) Subsidiary's profit attributable to ordinary equity holders.

(b) Dividends paid by subsidiary on convertible preference shares.

(c) Subsidiary's ordinary shares outstanding.

(d) Subsidiary's profit attributable to ordinary equity holders (CU5,000) increased by CU400 preference dividends for the purpose of calculating diluted earnings per share.

(e) Incremental shares from warrants, calculated: [(CU20 – CU 10)/CU20] x 150.

(f) Subsidiary's ordinary shares assumed outstanding from conversion of convertible preference shares, calculated: 400 convertible preference shares x conversion factor of 1.

Consolidated earnings per share

Basic EPS CU1.63 calculated:	(CU12,000[g] + CU4,300[h])/10,000[i]
Diluted EPS CU1.61 calculated	(CU12,000 + CU2,298[j] + CU55[k] + CU1,098[l])/10,000

(g) Parent's profit attributable to ordinary equity holders of the parent entity.

(h) Portion of subsidiary's profit to be included in consolidated basic earnings per share, calculated: (800 x CU5.00) + (300 x CU1.00).

(i) Parent's ordinary shares outstanding.

(j) Parent's proportionate interest in subsidiary's earnings attributable to ordinary shares, calculated: (800/1,000) x (1,000 shares x CU3.66 per share).

(k) Parent's proportionate interest in subsidiary's earnings attributable to warrants, calculated: (30/150) x (75 incremental shares x CU3.66 per share).

(l) Parent's proportionate interest in subsidiary's earnings attributable to convertible preference shares, calculated: (300/400) x (400 shares from conversion x CU3.66 per share).

5.9.2 *Instruments that entitle holders to shares in the reporting entity*

Instruments of a subsidiary, joint venture or associate that are convertible into the reporting entity's ordinary shares are considered among the potential ordinary shares of the reporting entity for the purpose of calculating diluted EPS. Similarly, options or warrants issued by a subsidiary, joint venture or associate to purchase ordinary shares of the reporting entity are considered among the potential ordinary shares of the reporting entity in the calculation of consolidated diluted EPS. [IAS 33.A11(b)]

5.10 Partly paid shares

To the extent that partly paid shares are not entitled to participate in dividends during the financial period (and, therefore, are excluded from the calculation of basic EPS), they are to be regarded as the equivalent of warrants or options in the calculation of diluted EPS. The unpaid balance is assumed to represent proceeds used to purchase ordinary shares. The number of shares included in diluted EPS is the difference between the number of shares subscribed and the number of shares assumed to be purchased. [IAS 33.A16]

Together with the guidance on how to include partly paid shares in basic EPS (see **4.2.2.3** above), this implies that if a reporting entity has, say, 9,000 ordinary shares, two-thirds paid up and entitled to two-thirds of the dividend declared on fully paid shares, then, in calculating diluted EPS, the entity includes the partly paid shares as if they were two-thirds (6,000 shares) in issue and included in basic EPS, and additionally there are options over 3,000 shares (one third of 9,000) where the exercise price of the options is equal to the amount remaining to be paid on the shares.

5.11 Potential ordinary shares outstanding for part of an accounting period

Where potential ordinary shares are issued during a period (e.g. convertible bonds are issued four months before the end of the accounting period), diluted EPS is calculated as if the potential ordinary shares had been converted to ordinary shares on the date the potential ordinary shares were issued. [IAS 33.36] Thus, in the example, the convertible bonds would be included in diluted EPS as if they had been converted into ordinary shares four months before the end of the accounting period.

Similarly, where potential ordinary shares are converted into ordinary shares, are cancelled, or lapse, they are included in the calculation of diluted EPS for the period the potential ordinary shares were in existence as potential ordinary shares.

Accordingly, having no potential ordinary shares outstanding at the end of the reporting period does not automatically mean that the reporting entity's diluted EPS will be the same as basic EPS. Where an entity has no potential ordinary shares in existence at the end of the reporting period, but had potential ordinary shares outstanding at some point during the year, it should still calculate diluted EPS separately.

Example 5.11

Potential ordinary shares in issue for part of a period

An entity has 1,000,000 ordinary shares in issue at the start of its accounting period, 1 January 20X1.

In addition, on 1 January, it has £100,000 convertible bonds in issue. The bonds were converted into 100,000 ordinary shares on 1 April 20X1. The finance cost recognised in profit or loss in respect of the bonds from 1 January to 31 March was £2,500 and the associated tax relief was £750.

The profit attributable to ordinary shareholders (all from continuing operations) for 20X1 was £100,000.

The weighted average number of shares outstanding during 20X1 and used to calculate basic EPS is: (1,000,000 x 12/12) + (100,000 x 9/12) =	1,075,000
Thus, basic EPS is: £100,000/1,075,000 =	£0.093

Diluted EPS is calculated as:

(£100,000 + £2,500 – £750) /
((1,075,000 + (100,000 x 3/12)) = £101,750/1,100,000 =£0.925

The denominator is equal to the number of shares that would have been outstanding had the convertible bond been fully converted at the start of the reporting period.

6 Reporting additional earnings per share on an alternative basis

An entity is permitted to present EPS figures other than the basic and diluted EPS figures required to be presented under IAS 33. Such figures may be calculated based on a reported component of the statement of comprehensive income other than those required by IAS 33 (i.e. profit or loss from continuing operations attributable to the ordinary equity holders of the parent entity and profit or loss attributable to the ordinary equity holders of the parent entity). However, the denominator (i.e. the weighted average number of shares) should still be determined in accordance with the Standard. [IAS 33.73]

The entity is required to indicate the basis on which the numerator(s) is (are) determined, including whether amounts per share are before tax or after tax. [IAS 33.73]

In addition, if the numerator (earnings figure) used is not reported as a line item in the statement of comprehensive income, a reconciliation is required between the numerator and a line item that is reported in the statement of comprehensive income. [IAS 33.73]

Further, when such additional EPS figures are presented, both basic and diluted EPS figures are required to be presented with equal prominence and included in the notes to the financial statements. [IAS 33.73]

Paragraph 73 applies equally to an entity that discloses, in addition to basic and diluted EPS, amounts per share using a reported component of the separate income statement described in IAS 1(2007).81, other than one required by IAS 33. [IAS 33.73A]

The spirit of IAS 33.73 would seem to suggest that the additional EPS figures should be presented in the notes, rather than in the statement of comprehensive income (since otherwise the reference to the notes appears superfluous). Nevertheless, a literal reading of the words does not prohibit presentation in the notes and also in the statement of comprehensive income, although this is unlikely to be seen as best practice.

7 Presentation and disclosure

7.1 Presentation

IAS 33 requires the following amounts per share to be presented in the statement of comprehensive income (with equal prominence for basic and diluted EPS for all periods presented):

[IAS 33.66]

- profit or loss from continuing operations attributable to the ordinary equity holders of the parent entity; and
- profit or loss attributable to the ordinary equity shareholders of the parent entity.

These amounts are required to be presented for each class of ordinary shares that has a different right to share in profit for the period. [IAS 33.66] They are presented even if the amounts are negative (i.e. a loss per share). [IAS 33.69]

If an entity presents the components of profit or loss in a separate income statement as permitted by IAS 1(2007).81 (see **section 5** of **chapter 3**), the basic and diluted per share amounts should be presented in that separate statement. [IAS 33.67A]

Entities that report a discontinued operation are required to disclose the basic and diluted amounts per share for the discontinued operation either in the statement of comprehensive income, or in the notes to the financial statements. [IAS 33.68] Where a separate income statement is presented (see previous paragraph), the basic and diluted per share amounts are presented either in that separate statement or in the notes. [IAS 33.68A]

Earnings per share is presented for every period for which a statement of comprehensive income (or, where applicable, a separate income statement) is presented. If diluted EPS is reported for at least one period, it should be reported for all periods presented, even if it equals basic earnings per share. If basic and diluted earnings per share are equal, dual presentation can be accomplished in one line in the statement of comprehensive income. [IAS 33.67]

Therefore, where basic and diluted EPS are equal, the amount could be described in a one-line item in the statement of comprehensive income as 'Basic and diluted earnings per share'.

7.1.1 *EPS disclosures for tracking or targeted shares*

Some entities issue certain classes of shares characterised as 'tracking' or 'targeted' shares to measure the performance of a specific business unit or activity of the entity. The presentation of complete financial statements of the targeted business generally is discouraged, and requires clear, cautionary disclosures, because investors may get an inaccurate view that their investment in targeted shares represents a direct investment in a legal entity. However, condensed financial statements that allow investors to understand fully the computation of earnings available for dividends are preferable to complete statements.

EPS should not be shown in separate financial statements of the business unit represented by the tracking shares. EPS disclosures should only be presented in the legal issuer's financial statements. Per IAS 33.66 (see **4.1.3**), the entity should determine EPS for each class of shares using the two-class method.

7.2 Disclosure

7.2.1 *General*

The following should be disclosed:

[IAS 33.70]

- the amounts used as the numerators in calculating basic and diluted EPS and a reconciliation of those amounts to the profit or loss attributable to the parent entity for the period. The reconciliation should include the individual effect of each class of instruments that affects EPS;
- the weighted average number of ordinary shares used as the denominators in calculating basic and diluted EPS and a reconciliation of these denominators to each other. The reconciliation should include the individual effect of each class of instruments that affects EPS; and

- instruments (including contingently issuable shares) that could potentially dilute basic EPS in the future, but were not included in the calculation of diluted EPS because they are antidilutive for the period(s) presented.

7.2.2 *Restatement for bonus and similar issues*

An entity should disclose the fact that the calculations have been adjusted for a capitalisation/bonus issue, share split or reverse share split, occurring either during the period, or after the reporting period but before the financial statements are authorised for issue. [IAS 33.64]

7.2.3 *Changes in share capital after the reporting period*

A description should be provided of any other changes in ordinary shares or potential ordinary shares after the reporting period that would, had they occurred before the end of the reporting period, have changed significantly the number of ordinary shares or potential ordinary shares outstanding at the end of the period. [IAS 33.70(d)]

IAS 33 lists the following as examples of transactions that might be disclosed under this requirement:

[IAS 33.71]

- an issue of shares for cash;
- an issue of shares when the proceeds are used to repay debt or preference shares outstanding at the end of the reporting period;
- the redemption of ordinary shares;
- the conversion or exercise of potential ordinary shares, outstanding at the end of the reporting period, into ordinary shares;
- the issue of warrants, options or convertible instruments; and
- the achievement of conditions that would result in the issue of contingently issuable shares.

7.2.4 *Additional recommended disclosures*

Where the terms and conditions of an instrument that generates potential ordinary shares affect the measurement of basic and diluted EPS, disclosure of the terms and conditions is encouraged, but not required. [IAS 33.72] IAS 33 notes that the terms and conditions may determine whether any potential ordinary shares are dilutive and, if so, determine the effect on the weighted average number of shares outstanding, together with any consequential adjustments to the profit or loss attributable to ordinary equity holders.

7.2.5 *Illustrative disclosures*

Example 12 of the Illustrative Examples accompanying IAS 33 illustrates how an entity with a complex capital structure (Company A) might calculate and present EPS in accordance with IAS 33. The suggested presentation for the statement of comprehensive income from that example is reproduced below.

Example 7.2.5

Presentation of EPS in statement of comprehensive income

[Extract from IAS 33 Illustrative Examples (Example 12)]

The following illustrates how Company A might present its earnings per share data in its statement of comprehensive income. Note that the amounts per share for the loss from discontinued operations are not required to be presented in the statement of comprehensive income.

	For the year ended 20X1
	CU
Earnings per ordinary share	
Profit from continuing operations	1.93
Loss from discontinued operations	(0.33)
Profit	1.60
Diluted earnings per ordinary share	
Profit from continuing operations	1.78
Loss from discontinued operations	(0.30)
Profit	1.48

8 Future developments

The IASB has been working on a project jointly with the US FASB on amending the requirements for earnings per share. The proposed amendments are part of their wider project of convergence. One of the main proposed amendments to IAS 33 will be to clarify the impact on EPS of potential ordinary shares (whether standalone or embedded in other financial instruments) that are fair valued through profit or loss. The proposal, referred to as the 'fair value method', will result in no adjustment to basic or diluted EPS for such instruments as the dilutive effects of such instruments are already recognised in income. Additionally, the current standard requires the use of the average share price in calculating diluted EPS which will be changed to the share price at the end of the reporting period. The amendments will also clarify the dilutive effect of forward purchase contracts and written put options over own equity. An Exposure Draft is expected in the third quarter of 2008.

39 Interim financial reporting

1 Introduction

IAS 34 *Interim Financial Reporting* prescribes the minimum content for an interim financial report, and the principles for recognition and measurement in complete and condensed financial statements for an interim period. It has been effective since 1 January 1999, and was most recently amended by *Improvements to IFRSs* issued in May 2008.

IFRS 8 *Operating Segments*, which supersedes IAS 14 *Segment Reporting* and is effective for periods beginning on or after 1 January 2009, has expanded the segment information to be disclosed in interim financial reports (see **section 3.5.3** below). Earlier application of IFRS 8 is permitted. If an entity chooses to apply IFRS 8 for an earlier period, the amendments to IAS 34 should also be applied for that earlier period (i.e. the entity will need to comply with the interim disclosures based on IFRS 8, rather than those based on IAS 14).

IAS 34 has also been amended as a consequential amendment of IAS 1(2007), resulting in changes in terminology, and in the titles and layout of certain of the financial statements to be included in interim financial reports. These amendments are effective for periods beginning on or after 1 January 2009, with earlier application permitted.

This chapter discusses the requirements of IAS 34 in the following sections:

Section 2	Scope
Section 3	Content of an interim financial report
Section 4	Accounting policies
Section 5	Recognition and measurement
Section 6	Disclosure and Transparency Rules, AIM and Listing Rules requirements

In 2006, the Financial Services Authority ('FSA') implemented the EU Transparency Obligations Directive by inserting its requirements into the UK

> *Disclosure Rules handbook. These rules, called the 'Disclosure and Transparency Rules' (DTR), set out, amongst others, the requirements for half-yearly financial reports to comply with IAS 34 and additional reporting in the form of 'interim management statements' (IMS) (see* **6.1.2***). The DTR apply to companies with listed shares or debt on a regulated market. Specific exemptions for some companies exist (see* **6.1***).*

2 Scope

IAS 34 applies to interim financial reports that are described as complying with International Financial Reporting Standards. [IAS 34.3]

Interim financial reports are financial reports containing either a complete set of financial statements (as described in IAS 1 *Presentation of Financial Statements*) or a set of condensed financial statements (as described later in this chapter) for an interim period. An interim period is a financial reporting period shorter than a full financial year. [IAS 34.4]

IAS 34 does not contain any rules as to which entities should publish interim financial reports, how frequently, or how soon after the end of an interim period. The Standard notes that governments, securities regulators, stock exchanges, and accountancy bodies often require entities with publicly-traded debt or equity to publish interim financial reports, and that those regulations will generally specify the frequency and timing of such reports. However, IAS 34 *encourages* publicly-traded entities:

[IAS 34.1]

- to provide interim financial reports at least as of the end of the first half of their financial year; and
- to make their interim financial reports available no later than 60 days after the end of the interim period.

2.1 No requirement for interim reports to comply with IAS 34

Each financial report, annual or interim, is evaluated on a stand-alone basis for compliance with IFRSs. It is important to note that entities that prepare annual financial statements in accordance with IFRSs are not precluded from preparing interim financial reports that do *not* comply with IFRSs, provided that the interim report does not state that it is IFRS-compliant. The fact that an entity has not published interim financial reports during a financial year, or that it has published interim financial reports that do not comply with IAS 34, does not prevent the entity's annual financial statements from conforming to IFRSs, if they are otherwise IFRS-compliant. [IAS 34.1 & 2]

> *Some UK companies are nevertheless required to comply with IAS 34, as discussed in* ***section 6****.* (UK)

2.2 Preliminary announcements of interim results

> *Neither the Listing Rules nor the DTR make any reference to preliminary announcements for interim periods. As explained in* ***6.1.1****, the half-yearly report must be announced in full unedited text. Therefore, it is unlikely that UK companies will wish to make an additional preliminary announcement of the half-yearly results.* (UK)

IAS 34 does not address the content of preliminary interim earnings announcements (i.e. those earnings announcements issued shortly after the end of an interim period that disclose abbreviated preliminary financial information for the interim period just ended). IAS 34.3 does state, however, that if an interim financial report is described as complying with IFRSs, it must comply with all of the requirements of IAS 34. Therefore, if any reference to IFRSs is made in a preliminary interim earnings announcement that does not comply with IAS 34, the following sentences (or something substantively similar), should be included in that earnings release.

> 'While the financial figures included in this preliminary interim earnings announcement have been computed in accordance with International Financial Reporting Standards (IFRSs) applicable to interim periods, this announcement does not contain sufficient information to constitute an interim financial report as that term is defined in IFRSs. The directors expect to publish an interim financial report that complies with IAS 34 in March 20X2.'

3 Content of an interim financial report

3.1 Minimum components

Entities reporting in accordance with IAS 34 are required to include in their interim reports, at a minimum, the following components:

[IAS 34.8]

- a condensed statement of financial position;
- a condensed statement of comprehensive income, presented as either:
  - a condensed single statement; or
  - a condensed separate income statement and a condensed statement of comprehensive income;
- a condensed statement of changes in equity;
- a condensed statement of cash flows; and
- selected explanatory notes.

If, in its annual financial statements, an entity presents the components of profit or loss in a separate income statement as described in IAS 1(2007).81 (see **section 5** of **chapter 3**), it should also present interim condensed information in a separate statement. [IAS 34.8A]

Note that the titles of the financial statements listed above have been amended as a consequential amendment of IAS 1(2007) *Presentation of Financial Statements*. Entities are permitted to use titles for those statements other than those set out above. An entity would be expected to use the same titles in its interim financial report as are used in its annual financial statements.

These amendments are effective for periods beginning on or after 1 January 2009, with earlier application permitted. In the year in which an entity first adopts IAS 1(2007), it should describe the changes made in its first interim financial report for that year (see **4.2** below).

An entity that has not yet adopted IAS 1(2007) will instead present a condensed income statement, together with a condensed statement of changes in equity showing either (a) all changes in equity or (b) changes in equity other than those arising from capital transactions with owners and distributions to owners. [IAS 34.8]

The option chosen for the condensed statement of changes in equity should be the same as in the annual financial statements.

If additional information to the minimum components set out above is included in the interim report, this information should be presented in a manner that is consistent with that in the full annual financial statements.

3.2 Periods required to be presented

IAS 34.20 requires interim reports to include interim financial statements (whether condensed or complete – see **3.4**) for the periods listed in the following table.

Statement	Current	Comparative
Statement of financial position	End of current interim period	End of immediately preceding financial year
Statement of comprehensive income (and, where applicable, separate income statement)	Current interim period and cumulatively for the year-to-date	Comparable interim period and year-to-date of immediately preceding financial year
Statement of changes in equity	Cumulative for the current financial year-to-date	Comparable year-to-date of immediately preceding financial year
Statement of cash flows	Cumulatively for the current financial year-to-date	Comparable year-to-date of immediately preceding financial year

The selected explanatory notes and additional information should contain comparatives for each of the periods presented in the primary statements.

The comparable information for the statement of financial position as at the preceding financial year end and any additional voluntary comparable information covering the preceding financial year should be regarded as constituting non-statutory accounts as defined in the Companies Acts. The rules regarding the publication of such information are considered at ***9.1*** *in* ***chapter 45****. An example of a statement appropriate in such circumstances is provided below:* UK

Example 3.2

Full year comparatives in interim results

The results for the year ended (date) are not statutory accounts. A copy of the statutory accounts for that year has been delivered to the Registrar of Companies. The auditors reported on those accounts: their report was unqualified, did not draw attention to any matters by way of emphasis and did not contain a statement under [s498(2) or (3) Companies Act 2006] [s237(2) or (3) Companies Act 1985].

3.2.1 *Entities that report half-yearly*

Based on the requirements of IAS 34.20, **example 3.2.1** illustrates the statements required to be presented in the interim financial report of an entity that reports half-yearly, with a 31 December 20X9 year end.

Example 3.2.1

Statements required for entities that report half-yearly

	Current	**Comparative**
Statement of financial position at	30 June 20X9	31 December 20X8
Statement of comprehensive income (and, where applicable, separate income statement)		
– 6 months ended	30 June 20X9	30 June 20X8
Statement of changes in equity		
– 6 months ended	30 June 20X9	30 June 20X8
Statement of cash flows		
– 6 months ended	30 June 20X9	30 June 20X8

3.2.2 *Entities that report quarterly*

Based on the requirements of IAS 34.20, **example 3.2.2** illustrates the statements required to be presented in the half-year interim financial report of an entity that reports quarterly, with a 31 December 20X9 year end.

Example 3.2.2

Statements required for entities that report quarterly

	Current	**Comparative**
Statement of financial position at	30 June 20X9	31 December 20X8
Statement of comprehensive income (and, where applicable, separate income statement)		
– 6 months ended	30 June 20X9	30 June 20X8
– 3 months ended	30 June 20X9	30 June 20X8
Statement of changes in equity		
– 6 months ended	30 June 20X9	30 June 20X8
Statement of cash flows		
– 6 months ended	30 June 20X9	30 June 20X8

3.2.3 *Entities with seasonal businesses*

The requirements of IAS 34.20, as discussed above, set out the minimum periods for which interim financial statements are to be presented. However, entities may wish to provide additional information. For example, entities whose business is highly seasonal are encouraged to disclose financial information relating to the twelve-month period up to the end of the interim period, and comparative information for the equivalent twelve-month period in the prior year. [IAS 34.21]

3.2.4 *Change of financial year end*

IAS 34 does not consider the circumstances where there is a change in the financial year end of the reporting entity. IAS 34.20 requires the presentation of comparatives for the statement of comprehensive income, statement of changes in equity, and statement of cash flows, for 'comparable' periods. Accordingly, in preparing the interim financial report based on the new financial year end, the entity should ideally present comparatives for the same interim period, which may not have been the basis for the interim financial information previously reported.

Example 3.2.4

Comparative interim periods when financial year end changes

An entity with a 31 March year end, which reported half-year information to 30 September 20X1, moves to a 31 December year end. It produces 'annual' financial statements for the nine months ended 31 December 20X1. Its half-year interim report for 20X2 will be for the six months ended 30 June 20X2.

The appropriate comparative period for the June 20X2 interim financial report is the six months ended 30 June 20X1. This would enable users to compare trends over time, particularly for a seasonal business. The statements for the six months ended 30 September 20X1 are not directly comparable and therefore restatement is advisable.

If it is not practicable to restate 20X1 to the new interim period basis, the comparatives for the six months ended 30 September 20X1 as previously published should be presented, with disclosure that restatement to the new interim period basis was not practicable and that the amounts presented are not directly comparable. This is consistent with the treatment in the annual financial statements in accordance with IAS 1(2007).36 or IAS 1(2003).49.

UK *If a company changes its accounting reference date, it must notify a Regulatory Information Service of the change and of the new accounting reference date as soon as possible. [LR 9.6.20R] Where the change in accounting reference date results in the extension of the accounting period to more than 14 months, the company must prepare and publish a second interim report in accordance with DTR 4.2. [LR 9.6.21R] The second interim report should be in respect of the period either to the old accounting reference date or to an alternative date within the last six months of the new accounting period. [LR 9.6.22G]*

3.2.5 *Comparatives for first interim financial reports*

When an entity is preparing its first interim financial report under IAS 34, unless the report relates to the first period of operation, it should generally include comparatives as discussed in the previous sections. In the exceptional circumstances where the entity does not have available in its accounting records the financial information that is needed to prepare the comparative interim financial statements, the entity has no choice but to omit disclosure of prior period comparative financial statements.

In the circumstances described, however, the omission of the comparatives represents a non-compliance with IAS 34. Therefore, the interim financial report cannot be described as complying with IAS 34 without an 'except for' statement regarding the omission of prior period comparative figures. Both the fact of, and the reason for, the omission should be disclosed.

3.3 Consolidated financial statements

If the entity's most recent annual financial statements were consolidated statements, then the interim financial report should also be prepared on a consolidated basis. If the entity's annual financial report included the parent's separate financial statements in addition to consolidated financial statements, IAS 34 neither requires nor prohibits the inclusion of the parent's separate statements in the entity's interim report. [IAS 34.14]

Where the entity has disposed of all of its subsidiaries during the interim period, such that it has no subsidiaries at the end of the interim reporting period, it should prepare its interim financial report on a consolidated basis because it had subsidiaries at some point during the interim period. The statement of comprehensive income, statement of changes in equity and statement of cash flows will include the impact of the subsidiaries up to the date(s) of disposal and the effects of the disposal.

3.4 Form and content of interim financial statements

Where the minimum required information for interim financial statements prescribed by IAS 34.8 (as listed in **3.1**) is presented, the resultant financial statements are described as 'condensed'. However, entities also have the option of producing a complete set of financial statements for inclusion in their interim financial reports. Where an entity takes this alternative, the form and content of the financial statements must conform to the requirements of IAS 1 *Presentation of Financial Statements* for a complete set of financial statements, in addition to complying with the requirements of IAS 34. [IAS 34.7 & 9] Therefore, the measurement and disclosure requirements of all relevant Standards apply. These include all measurement and disclosure requirements of IAS 34 and, in particular, the selected explanatory note disclosures listed in IAS 34.16 (see **3.5**).

IAS 34 does not repeat the general principles underlying the preparation of financial information set out in IAS 1 *Presentation of Financial Statements*. However, preparers need to refer to IAS 1 itself for clarification in this regard.

IAS 1(2007).4 (previously IAS 1(2003).3) states, in part, that 'this Standard does not apply to the structure and content of condensed interim financial statements prepared in accordance with IAS 34 *Interim Financial Reporting*. However, paragraphs 15 – 35 apply to such financial statements'.

Paragraphs 15 – 35 of IAS 1(2007) (previously IAS 1(2003).13 – 41), which therefore apply when preparing condensed financial statements for interim purposes, deal with:

- fair presentation and compliance with IFRSs;
- going concern;
- accrual basis of accounting;
- consistency of presentation;
- materiality and aggregation;
- offsetting; and
- comparative information.

3.4.1 *Items to appear in condensed financial statements*

IAS 34 requires that, for each component (statement of financial position, statement of comprehensive income, statement of changes in equity, and statement of cash flows), each of the headings and sub-totals that were included in the entity's most recent annual financial statements should be disclosed. Additional line items are required if their omission would make the condensed interim financial statements misleading. [IAS 34.10]

In prescribing the minimum content, IAS 34 uses the terms 'headings' and 'sub-totals', thereby seeming to imply that not all of the line items that were presented in the most recent annual financial statements are necessarily required. Such an interpretation would do a disservice, however, to a user of the financial statements who is trying to assess trends in the interim period in relation to financial years. Accordingly, the phrase should be interpreted, in nearly all cases, to mean the line items that were included in the entity's most recent annual financial statements. The line items in most published financial statements are already highly aggregated and it would be difficult to think of a line item in the annual statement of comprehensive income, in particular, that would not also be appropriate in an interim statement of comprehensive income. For example, it would not be appropriate to begin a condensed statement of comprehensive income with the gross profit figure, omitting figures for revenue and cost of goods sold.

For the statement of financial position, a too literal interpretation of 'each of the headings and subtotals' might lead to an interim statement of financial position that presented lines only for total current assets, total non-current assets, total current liabilities, total non-current liabilities and total equity, which will generally be insufficient for trend analysis.

For the statement of changes in equity, all material movements in equity occurring in the interim period should be disclosed separately.

In the case of the statement of cash flows, some aggregation of the lines from the annual statement may be appropriate, but subtotals for 'operating', 'investing' and 'financing' only are unlikely to be sufficient.

If a particular category of asset, liability, equity, income, expense or cash flows was so material as to require separate disclosure in the financial statements in the most recent annual financial statements, such separate disclosure will generally be appropriate in the interim financial report. Further aggregation would only be anticipated where the line items in the annual statements are unusually detailed.

Under IAS 34.10, additional line items should be included if their omission would make the condensed interim financial statements misleading. Therefore, a new category of asset, liability, income, expense, equity or cash flow arising for the first time in the interim period may require presentation as an additional line item in the condensed financial statements.

Also, a category of asset, liability, income, expense, equity or cash flow may be significant in the context of the interim financial statements even though it is not significant enough in the annual financial statements to be presented separately on the face of the annual financial statements. In such cases, separate presentation on the face of the condensed interim financial statements may be required.

3.4.2 *Use of the term 'condensed'*

The requirements discussed in the previous section will result in the presentation of at least some statements that include all of the line items, headings and sub-totals that were presented in the most recent annual financial statements. The question then arises as to whether such statements should, in practice, be described as 'condensed'.

Given that the notes supplementing the interim financial statements are limited, the presentation package taken together is condensed from what would be reported in a complete set of financial statements under IAS 1 *Presentation of Financial Statements* and other Standards. In such circumstances, the information presented in the statement of financial position, statement of comprehensive income, statement of changes in equity and statement of cash flows is condensed – even if the appearance of the statements has not changed. These interim statements should therefore be described as 'condensed', since otherwise a user may infer that they constitute a complete set of financial statements under IAS 1, which they do not. A complete set of financial statements must include a full note presentation consistent with the annual presentation.

3.4.3 *Earnings per share*

When an entity is within the scope of IAS 33 *Earnings per Share* (see **section 2** of **chapter 38**), it should present basic and diluted earnings per share (EPS) for the interim period in the statement that presents the components of profit or loss for that period. [IAS 34.11]

If an entity presents the components of profit or loss in a separate income statement as described in paragraph 81 of IAS 1(2007) (see **section 5** of **chapter 3**), basic and diluted EPS should be presented in that separate statement. [IAS 34.11A]

As a consequential amendment of IAS 1(2007) *Presentation of Financial Statements*, IAS 34.11 was amended (and IAS 34.11A added) to make clear that the EPS information should be presented in the statement that presents the components of profit or loss for the interim period. As outlined at **3.1** above, this may be in a statement of comprehensive income or, where the entity has elected to present a separate income statement, in that separate income statement.

IAS 34.11 was further amended by *Improvements to IFRSs* issued in May 2008. The amendment has clarified that EPS information need be presented only when the entity is within the scope of IAS 33 *Earnings per Share*. Although this clarification is expected to have a minimal effect on accounting, the Board considered that it was necessary because, prior to amendment, IAS 34.11 could have been read as requiring the disclosure of EPS in an interim financial report even if the entity is not within the scope of IAS 33.

3.4.3.1 *Measures of EPS to be presented*

IAS 34 does not make any specific reference to the requirements of IAS 33 regarding which measures of basic and diluted EPS should be presented. Nevertheless, to enable users to compare trends, the same EPS figures should be presented in the interim financial report as in annual financial statements. Therefore, irrespective of whether the interim financial statements are described as 'condensed', the following should be presented in the interim financial report, with equal prominence for all periods presented:

- basic and diluted EPS for profit or loss attributable to the ordinary equity shareholders of the parent entity; and
- where a discontinued operation is reported, basic and diluted EPS for profit or loss from continuing operations attributable to the ordinary equity holders of the parent entity.

These should be presented for each class of ordinary shares that has a different right to share in profit for the period.

EPS figures should be provided for all periods presented in the interim financial report. Therefore, for an entity presenting information separately for the current interim period and the current year-to-date, with comparatives for each, EPS (both basic and diluted) should be presented for the same four periods.

3.4.3.2 *Interim period diluted EPS on a year-to-date basis*

Any change in assumptions for the purposes of computing diluted EPS during the interim period may result in an apparent anomaly. For example, the sum of diluted EPS for the first quarter plus diluted EPS for the second quarter may not always equal diluted EPS for the half-year period.

Diluted EPS for the first quarter is based on assumptions that were valid during and at the end of that quarter. IAS 33 states that diluted EPS should not be restated for changes in the assumptions used or for conversions of potential ordinary shares into outstanding ordinary shares. Therefore, diluted EPS for the second quarter and for the half-year period may be based on different assumptions than those used in computing diluted EPS for the first quarter. Also, certain outstanding potential ordinary shares may have been 'anti-dilutive' (their conversion to ordinary shares would increase EPS) in the first quarter and would, therefore, be excluded from first quarter diluted EPS. In the second quarter and on a six-month basis, however, they may have been dilutive, and would therefore be included in diluted EPS.

Example 3.4.3.2

Interim period diluted EPS on a year-to-date basis

The following information relates to a quarterly reporter:

	Quarter 1 (1 January to 31 March)	**Quarter 2 (1 April to 30 June)**	**Half year (1 January to 30 June)**
Net income	£1,000	£1,000	£2,000
Ordinary shares outstanding	1,000	1,000	1,000
Weighted average quoted market price of ordinary shares	£8	£20	£14

Throughout the half-year, the entity had outstanding 100 options each allowing the holder to purchase one ordinary share for £10. No options were exercised. For the second quarter interim report, IAS 34.20(b) requires a statement of comprehensive income (and, where appropriate, a separate income statement) for the second quarter and for the half-year. Calculations of basic and diluted EPS are as follows:

	Quarter 1 (1 January to 31 March)	**Quarter 2 (1 April to 30 June)**	**Half year (1 January to 30 June)**
Basic EPS	£1,000/1,000 = £1.00	£1,000/1,000 = £1.00	£2,000/1,000 = £2.00
Diluted EPS – numerator	£1,000	£1,000	£2,000
Diluted EPS – denominator	1,000*	1,050 (1,000 + 50**)	1,028.57 (1,000 + 28.57***)
Diluted EPS	£1	£0.9524	£1.9444

* The exercise price of the options is greater than the average market price of shares during the period. Therefore, the options are ignored in computing diluted EPS.

** If the share options were exercised, the proceeds of issue of £1,000 would equate to an issue of 50 shares at the average market price of £20. Therefore, the remaining 50 shares are assumed to have been issued for no consideration and are added to the number of ordinary shares outstanding for the computation of diluted EPS.

*** If the share options were exercised, the proceeds of issue of £1,000 would equate to an issue of 71.43 shares at the average market price of £14. Therefore, the remaining 28.57 shares are assumed to have been issued for no consideration and are added to the number of ordinary shares outstanding for the computation of diluted EPS.

Note that the sum of diluted EPS for the first quarter (£1.00) plus diluted EPS for the second quarter (£0.9524) does not equal diluted EPS for the first half-year (£1.9444).

3.4.3.3 *Calculation of weighted average number of ordinary shares for an interim reporting period*

Example 3.4.3.3

Calculation of weighted average number of shares for an interim reporting period

A publicly traded entity is required to prepare interim financial statements in accordance with IAS 34. Thirty days before the end of the six-month interim period, a substantial number of shares is issued by the entity.

These new shares should be weighted for inclusion in the denominator of the interim earnings per share calculation based on the number of days that the shares are outstanding as a proportion of the total number of days in the period. A reasonable approximation of the weighted average is adequate in many circumstances.

The number of shares issued should be weighted by the number of days that the shares are outstanding (i.e. 30 days) divided by the number of days in the period (i.e. 182 days).

3.4.3.4 *EPS calculation at interim reporting date for an entity with contingently issuable shares*

Example 3.4.3.4

EPS calculation at interim reporting date for an entity with contingently issuable shares

Company X, a publicly traded entity reporting on a calendar year basis, purchased Subsidiary Y on 1 January for £100 million plus 20,000 Company X ordinary shares if Subsidiary Y has a net income in the year following the acquisition of £10 million or more. By 30 June of Year 1, Subsidiary Y has net income of $15 million.

While the 20,000 shares would be issuable if the end of the contingency period were 30 June instead of 31 December, the 20,000 ordinary shares should be excluded from basic EPS for the six months ended 30 June, because events could transpire in the following six months that would cause Company X not to issue the shares (e.g. Subsidiary Y could lose £6 million in the following six months). But the contingently issuable ordinary shares should be included in diluted EPS for the six months ended 30 June because, based on the current status, the contingency is met.

See **chapter 38** for a more detailed examination of the impact of contingently issuable shares on the calculation of basic and diluted EPS.

3.5 Selected explanatory notes

IAS 34 specifies that an interim financial report should contain selected explanatory notes.

3.5.1 Required disclosures

The disclosure requirements of IAS 34 are based on the assumption that anyone reading the interim financial report will have access to the most recent annual financial statements. Therefore, not all of the supplementary notes in the annual financial statements are required for interim reporting purposes, since this would result in repetition, or the reporting of relatively insignificant changes. The explanatory notes included with the interim financial information are intended to provide an explanation of events and transactions that are significant to an understanding of the changes in financial position and performance of the entity since the end of the last annual reporting period. [IAS 34.15]

The list below sets out the minimum explanatory notes required by IAS 34. The information is generally presented on a year-to-date basis. However, the entity is also required to disclose any events or transactions that are material to an understanding of the current interim period. [IAS 34.16]

The following information should be disclosed in the notes to the interim financial statements, if material to an understanding of the interim period:

[IAS 34.16]

(a) a statement that the same accounting policies and methods of computation are followed in the interim financial statements as were followed in the most recent annual financial statements or, if those policies or methods have been changed, a description of the nature and effect of the change (see **section 4**);

(b) explanatory comments about the seasonality or cyclicality of interim operations;

(c) the nature and amount of items affecting assets, liabilities, equity, net income or cash flows, that are unusual because of their size, nature or incidence;

(d) the nature and amount of changes in estimates of amounts reported in prior interim periods of the current financial year, or changes in estimates of amounts reported in prior financial years, if those changes have a material effect in the current interim period;

(e) issuances, repurchases and repayments of debt and equity securities;

(f) dividends paid (aggregate or per share), separately for ordinary shares and other shares;

(g) for entities required by IFRS 8 *Operating Segments* (see **3.5.3**) to disclose segment information in their annual financial statements, the following segment information:

(i) revenues from external customers, if included in the measure of segment profit or loss reviewed by the chief operating decision maker or otherwise regularly provided to the chief operating decision maker;

(ii) intersegment revenues, if included in the measure of segment profit or loss reviewed by the chief operating decision maker or otherwise regularly provided to the chief operating decision maker;

(iii) a measure of segment profit or loss;

(iv) total assets for which there has been a material change from the amount disclosed in the last annual financial statements;

(v) a description of differences from the last annual financial statements in the basis of segmentation or in the basis of measurement of segment profit or loss; and

(vi) a reconciliation of the total of the reportable segments' measures of profit or loss to the entity's profit or loss before tax expense (tax income) and discontinued operations. However, if an entity allocates to reportable segments items such as tax expense (tax income), the entity may reconcile the total of the segments' measures of profit or loss to profit or loss after those items. Material reconciling items should be separately identified and described in that reconciliation;

(h) material events after the end of the interim period that have not been reflected in the interim financial statements;

(i) the effect of changes in the composition of the entity during the interim period, including business combinations (see **3.5.4**), obtaining or losing control of subsidiaries and long-term investments, restructurings and discontinued operations; and

(j) changes in contingent liabilities or contingent assets since the end of the last reporting period.

The Standard requires the entity to provide explanatory comments about the seasonality or cyclicality of interim operations under IAS 34.16(b). Discussion of changes in the business environment (such as changes in demand, market shares, prices and costs) and discussion of prospects for the full current financial year of which the interim period is a part will normally be presented as part of a management discussion and analysis or financial review, outside of the notes to the interim financial statements.

IAS 34.17 provides the following examples of the kinds of disclosures that are required:

- the write-down of inventories to net realisable value and the reversal of any such write-down;
- recognition of a loss arising from the impairment of property, plant, and equipment, intangible assets, or other assets, and the reversal of any such impairment loss;
- the reversal of any provisions for the costs of restructuring;
- acquisitions and disposals of items of property, plant, and equipment;
- commitments for the purchase of property, plant, and equipment;
- litigation settlements;
- corrections of prior period errors;
- any loan default or any breach of a loan agreement that has not been remedied on or before the end of the reporting period; and
- related party transactions.

3.5.2 *Detail required in explanatory notes*

IAS 34 does not specify the level of detail for the disclosures required by IAS 34.16 and IAS 34.17. The guiding principle is that the interim disclosures should be those that are useful in understanding the changes in financial position and performance of the entity since the end of the last annual reporting period. IAS 34.18 points out that the detailed disclosures required by other IFRSs are not required in an interim financial report that includes condensed financial statements and selected explanatory notes. Therefore, in general, the level of detail in interim note disclosures will be less than the level of detail in annual note disclosures. To illustrate:

- IAS 2.37 suggests that amounts of inventories at the end of a period and changes in inventories during the period are normally classified between merchandise, production supplies, materials, work in progress and finished goods. That level of detail would not normally be required in condensed interim financial statements unless it is significant to an understanding of the changes in financial position and performance of the entity since the end of the last annual reporting period. Therefore, the disclosure of a write-down of inventories to net realisable value and the reversal of such a write-down, as required by IAS 34.17(a), will generally be made at the entity-wide level in condensed interim financial statements, rather than analysed between different classes of inventories; and

- IAS 36.126 requires disclosure of impairment losses and reversals for each class of assets. The disclosure of impairment losses and reversals required by IAS 34.17(b) will generally be made at the entity-wide level in condensed interim financial statements, rather than by class of assets, except where a particular impairment or reversal is deemed significant to an understanding of the changes in financial position and performance of the entity since the end of the last annual reporting period.

- IAS 24.16 requires disclosure of key management personnel compensation by category. Such detailed disclosures of the remuneration of key management personnel are not generally required in interim financial reports unless there has been a significant change since the end of the last annual reporting period and disclosure of that change is necessary for an understanding of the interim period. For example, a bonus granted or share options awarded to members of key management personnel during the interim period are likely to be significant to an understanding of the interim period and therefore should be disclosed.

3.5.3 *Segment information – application of IFRS 8*

IFRS 8 supersedes IAS 14 *Segment Reporting* for periods beginning on or after 1 January 2009. The consequential amendments to IAS 34 (i.e. the expanded disclosure requirements under IAS 34.16(g) listed at **3.5.1**) are effective for annual periods beginning on or after 1 January 2009. Therefore, for calendar year entities, the expanded requirements apply for interim periods beginning on or after 1 January 2009.

Earlier application is permitted. If an entity chooses to apply IFRS 8 for an earlier period, the amendments to IAS 34 are also required to be applied for that earlier period (i.e. the entity will need to comply with the interim disclosures based on IFRS 8, rather than those based on IAS 14).

The disclosure requirements set out in IAS 34.16(g) (see **3.5.1**) are based on the premise that the full segment disclosures in the most recent annual report are available and that insignificant updates to that information are not generally required in interim periods. This premise will not be appropriate in the first year of adoption of IFRS 8, unless the segments under IFRS 8 are not materially different to those previously presented under IAS 14. Therefore, in the first interim report affected by IFRS 8, it would seem appropriate to disclose:

- a measure of total assets for each reportable segment (rather than simply explaining material changes as is required on an ongoing basis); and
- a comprehensive description of the basis of segmentation of information and the basis of measurement of segment profit or loss (rather than simply explaining any changes in those bases as is required on an ongoing basis).

If the segments identified in accordance with IFRS 8 do not materially change those previously disclosed under IAS 14, a statement to that effect should be included in the first interim report affected by IFRS 8 to meet the disclosure requirement in respect of changes in accounting policy in accordance with IAS 34.16(a). Any segmental information presented should be sufficient to ensure that the interim report includes all information that is relevant to understanding an entity's financial position and performance during that interim period.

In that first interim financial report, in line with the general transitional provisions for IFRS 8, segment information reported in comparative interim financial reports should be restated, unless the necessary information is not available and the cost to develop it would be excessive. [IFRS 8.36]

For periods beginning before 1 January 2009, entities required to disclose segment information in their annual financial statements, but that do not elect to adopt IFRS 8 in advance of its effective date, should continue to apply the requirements of IAS 14. For such entities, interim financial reports are required to disclose segment revenue and segment result for business segments or geographical segments, whichever is the entity's primary basis of segment reporting.

3.5.4 *Business combinations occurring during the interim period*

Where business combinations have occurred during the interim period, IAS 34.16(i) requires the entity to disclose all of the details prescribed for annual financial statements by IFRS 3 *Business Combinations* (see **section 13** of **chapter 34**).

3.5.5 *Comparative information required for explanatory note disclosures*

Comparative information is required for the explanatory note disclosures provided under IAS 34.16. Although there is no explicit requirement to this effect in IAS 34, reference should be made to IAS 1 *Presentation of Financial Statements* (see **3.4**).

IAS 1(2007).38 (previously IAS 1(2003).36) states:

> 'Except when IFRSs permit or require otherwise, an entity shall disclose comparative information in respect of the previous period for all amounts reported in the current period's financial statements. An entity shall include comparative information for narrative and descriptive information when it is relevant to an understanding of the current period's financial statements.'

IAS 34.16 contains no express reference to the requirement for comparative information – therefore IAS 1(2007).38 applies by default and comparative information is required for all numerical information, and for narrative and descriptive information to the extent that it is relevant to an understanding of the current interim period's financial statements.

For the purposes of interim financial statements, the 'previous period' referred to in IAS 1(2007).38 should be taken to mean the equivalent interim period. Therefore, for example, where disclosures are made under IAS 34.16 in respect of business combinations or share issues on a financial year-to-date basis, then comparative information for the equivalent year to date should be reported. While the share issue results in dilution and as such is important in understanding the changes to EPS, it may also be significant to understanding the financial position at the end of the interim period. If this is the case, additional comparative information supporting the statement of financial position may be necessary.

When an entity prepares a complete set of financial statements for interim reporting purposes, then all of the requirements of IAS 1 apply and, therefore, comparative information is required for the explanatory note disclosures under IAS 34.16.

3.5.6 *Inclusion of interim period disclosures in next annual financial statements*

If an item of information is deemed significant and, therefore, is disclosed in an entity's interim financial report, that item of information will not necessarily be disclosed in the entity's next annual financial report that includes the interim period in which the disclosure was made. Under IAS 34, interim period disclosures are determined based on materiality levels that are assessed by reference to the interim period financial data (see **3.7**). The Standard recognises that the notes to interim financial statements are intended to explain events and transactions that are significant to an understanding of the changes in financial position and performance of the entity since the end of the last annual reporting period. A disclosure that is useful for that purpose may not be useful in the annual financial statements.

To illustrate, IAS 34.16(c) requires disclosure of the nature and amount of any item that affects assets, liabilities, equity, net income or cash flows if it is unusual because of its nature, size or incidence. For example, such an item may be unusual in size in the context of a single quarter or half-year period, but not so with respect to the full financial year.

As discussed at **3.8**, IAS 34.26 does require disclosure in the notes to the annual financial statements where an estimate of an amount reported in an earlier interim period is changed significantly during the final interim period of the financial year but a separate financial report is not produced for that final interim period.

3.5.7 *Inclusion of interim period disclosures in subsequent interim periods of the same financial year*

If an item of information is deemed significant and, therefore, is disclosed in an entity's interim financial report for the first quarter, that item of information will not necessarily be disclosed in the interim financial reports for the subsequent quarters of the same financial year. Under IAS 34, materiality is assessed by reference to each interim period's financial data (see **3.7**). Therefore, an item that is considered material in the context of one interim period may not be material for subsequent interim periods of the same financial year. IAS 34.16 indicates that note disclosures are normally on a year-to-date basis.

For example, the explanatory notes in the interim financial report as of 30 June for a 31 December year-end entity that reports quarterly will cover the period 1 January to 30 June. An item of information that was deemed significant in the first quarter report and, therefore, was disclosed in the notes to the interim financial report for the three months ending 31 March, may not be significant on a 30 June six-month year-to-date basis. If that is the case, disclosure in the six-month interim financial report is not required.

By contrast, an item might be significant to understanding the performance of the entity for the current interim period (in the example above, the three months ended 30 June) but not for the year-to-date (six months ended 30 June). IAS 34.16 specifically requires disclosure of such items – in addition to reporting information on a year-to-date basis, the entity is required to disclose any events or transactions that are material to an understanding of the current interim period.

3.6 Disclosure of compliance with IFRSs

IAS 34.19 requires that, where an interim financial report has been prepared in accordance with the requirements of that Standard, that fact should be disclosed. An interim financial report should not be described as complying with International Financial Reporting Standards unless it complies with all of the requirements of IFRSs. The latter statement will be appropriate only where interim financial statements are complete rather than condensed.

As condensed interim financial reports do not include all of the disclosures required by IAS 1 *Presentation of Financial Statements* and other Standards, they do not meet this requirement. They are, therefore, more appropriately described as having been prepared 'in accordance with IAS 34 *Interim Financial Reporting*' rather than 'in accordance with IFRSs'.

UK *In particular, UK companies may wish to refer to the condensed interim financial report having been prepared 'in accordance with IAS 34* Interim Financial Reporting *as adopted for use by the European Union'.*

IAS 34 clarifies that, where other Standards call for disclosures in financial statements, in that context they mean a complete set of financial statements of the type normally included in an annual financial report. Such disclosures are not required if the interim financial report includes only condensed financial statements and selected explanatory notes. [IAS 34.18]

Therefore, when presenting condensed interim financial information, the entity needs to consider compliance with Standards at two levels:

- compliance with all of the measurement and presentation rules contained in extant Standards and Interpretations (as stated in the previous paragraph, compliance with the disclosure requirements of Standards other than IAS 34 is not required); and
- compliance with the disclosure requirements and the measurement principles for interim reporting purposes specified by IAS 34.

3.7 Materiality

IAS 34.23 states that, in deciding how to recognise, measure, classify, or disclose an item for interim financial reporting purposes, materiality should be assessed in relation to the interim period financial data. In making assessments of materiality, it should be recognised that interim measurements may rely on estimates to a greater extent than measurements of annual financial data.

While materiality judgements are always subjective, the overriding concern is to ensure that an interim financial report includes all of the information that is relevant to understanding the financial position and performance of the entity during the interim period. Therefore, it is inappropriate to base quantitative estimates of materiality on projected annual figures.

3.8 Disclosure in annual financial statements

It is quite common that entities do not prepare a separate report for the final interim period in a financial year. This will be determined on the basis of the rules of local regulators. For example, an entity with a reporting period to 31 December, which reports half-yearly, may not be required to produce a separate interim report covering the period from July to December.

In such circumstances, IAS 34 requires disclosure in the notes to the *annual* financial statements where an estimate of an amount reported in an earlier interim period is changed significantly during the final interim period. The nature and amount of that change in estimate are required to be disclosed. [IAS 34.26] This requirement is intended to provide the user of the financial statements with details of changes in estimates in the final interim period consistent with those generally required by IAS 8 *Accounting Policies, Changes in Accounting Estimates and Errors.* The Standard does state, however, that this disclosure requirement is intended to be narrow in scope, relating only to the change in estimate, and it is not intended to introduce a general requirement to include additional interim period financial information in the entity's annual financial statements. [IAS 34.27]

> IAS 34.27 makes clear that, when such a change in estimate occurs and is required to be disclosed in the annual financial statements, the disclosure represents additional interim period financial information. Consequently, although the disclosure is made in the annual financial statements, materiality will be determined by reference to interim period financial data.

4 Accounting policies

4.1 Same accounting policies as annual financial statements

The accounting policies applied in the interim financial statements should be consistent with those applied in the most recent annual financial statements, except for accounting policy changes made after the date of the most recent annual financial statements that are to be reflected in the next annual financial statements. [IAS 34.28]

Entities are required to disclose in their interim financial reports that this requirement has been met. [IAS 34.16(a)]

4.2 Changes in accounting policies

Preparers of interim financial reports in compliance with IAS 34 are required to consider any changes in accounting policies that will be applied for the next annual financial statements, and to implement the changes for interim reporting purposes. Such changes will generally encompass:

- changes required by an IFRS that will be effective for the annual financial statements; and
- changes that are proposed to be adopted for the annual financial statements, in accordance with the requirements of IAS 8 *Accounting Policies, Changes in Accounting Policies and Errors*, on the basis that they will result in the financial statements providing reliable and more relevant information.

If there has been any change in accounting policy since the most recent annual financial statements, the interim financial report is required to include a description of the nature and effect of the change. [IAS 34.16(a)]

If a new Standard that is effective in the current financial year requires disclosures in annual financial statements, these disclosures would not ordinarily be required in a condensed interim financial report, unless specifically required by IAS 34. For example, IFRS 7 *Financial Instruments: Disclosures* would not generally impact an entity's interim financial report as disclosures in accordance with IFRS 7 are not required unless their omission would make the condensed interim financial statements misleading. In contrast, IFRS 8 *Operating Segments* resulted in a consequential amendment to IAS 34, which may require more detailed segmental information in the interim financial report (see **3.5.1** above).

If a new Standard or Interpretation has been published during the first interim period but it is not effective until after the end of the annual reporting period, an entity may decide in the second interim period to adopt this Standard or Interpretation early for its annual financial statements. The fact that the new Standard or Interpretation was not early adopted in its first interim financial statements does not generally preclude the entity from adopting a new policy in the second interim period or at the end of the annual reporting period. The requirements for restating previously reported interim periods are discussed at **4.3**.

UK

Where a change of accounting policy may be expected as a result of a new or amended Standard or Interpretation, UK companies will also need to consider whether that Standard or Interpretation has been, or is likely to be, endorsed by the European Commission. This issue is discussed at ***1.2*** *in* ***chapter 1***.

If an entity adopts a change in accounting policy based on a new or amended Standard or Interpretation that has not been endorsed at the end of the interim period but is expected to be endorsed by the end of the annual reporting period, it would be advisable to include a statement to that effect in the interim financial report.

4.3 Restatement of previously reported interim periods

A change in accounting policy, other than one for which the transitional provisions are specified by a new IFRS, should be reflected by:

[IAS 34.43]

- restating the financial statements of prior interim periods of the current financial year, and the comparable interim periods of prior financial years that will be restated in annual financial statements in accordance with IAS 8; or
- when it is impracticable to determine the cumulative effect at the beginning of the financial year of applying a new accounting policy to all prior periods, adjusting the financial statements of prior interim periods of the current financial year, and comparable interim periods of prior financial years, to apply the new accounting policy prospectively from the earliest date practicable.

IAS 34.44 states that an objective of these principles is to ensure that a single accounting policy is applied to a particular class of transactions throughout an entire financial year. That is not to say that voluntary changes in accounting policy part-way through the year are prohibited. Such changes are permitted, provided that the conditions of IAS 8 are met. What IAS 34.44 requires is that, where a change in accounting policy is adopted at some point during the year, the amounts reported for earlier interim periods should be restated to reflect the new policy.

5 Recognition and measurement

5.1 General principles

As discussed at **4.1** above, in preparing their interim financial reports, entities are required to apply the same accounting policies as will be applicable for their next annual financial statements. The principles for recognising assets, liabilities, income and expenses for interim periods are the same as in annual financial statements.

It is not intended, however, that each interim period should be seen to stand alone as an independent period. The Standard states that the frequency of an entity's reporting (annual, half-yearly or quarterly) should not affect the measurement of its annual results. To achieve that objective, measurements for interim reporting purposes are made on a year-to-date basis. [IAS 34.28]

There is a degree of inconsistency in IAS 34. The requirement set out at **section 4.1** above (that the same accounting policies should be applied in the interim financial statements as are applied in annual financial statements) represents a 'discrete period' approach to interim reporting. On the other hand, IAS 34.28's requirement that measurements for interim reporting purposes should be made on a year-to-date basis so that the frequency of the entity's reporting does not affect the measurement of its annual results represents an 'integral period' approach.

This inconsistency has led to a number of areas of potential conflict between the requirements of IAS 34 and those of other Standards applied at the end of interim reporting periods. IFRIC 10 deals with one such issue (see **5.6.16.1** below).

5.2 Seasonal, cyclical or occasional revenues

Revenues that are received seasonally, cyclically or occasionally within a financial year should not be anticipated or deferred as of an interim date, if anticipation or deferral would not be appropriate at the end of the financial year. [IAS 34.37]

Thus, for example, an entity engaged in retailing does not divide forecasted revenue by two to arrive at its half-year revenue figures. Instead, it reports its actual results for the six-month period. If the retailer wishes to demonstrate the cyclicality of its revenues, it could include, as additional information, revenue for the 12 months up to the end of the interim reporting period and comparative information for the corresponding previous 12-month period.

5.3 Uneven costs

The rule on revenues also applies to costs. Costs that are incurred unevenly during an entity's financial year should be anticipated or deferred for interim reporting purposes if, and only if, it is also appropriate to anticipate or defer that type of cost at the end of the financial year. [IAS 34.39]

A cost that does not meet the definition of an asset at the end of an interim period is *not* deferred in the statement of financial position at the interim reporting date either to await future information as to whether it has met the definition of an asset, or to smooth earnings over interim periods within a financial year. [IAS 34.30(b)] Thus, when preparing interim financial statements, the entity's usual recognition and measurement practices are followed. The only costs that are capitalised are those incurred *after* the specific point in time at which the criteria for recognition of the particular class of asset are met. Deferral of costs as assets in an interim statement of financial position in the hope that the criteria will be met before the year end is prohibited (see also **5.6.6** below).

Example 5.3A

Major advertising campaign early in the financial year

An entity reports quarterly. In the first quarter of the financial year, the entity introduces new models of its products that will be sold throughout the year. At that time, it incurs a substantial cost for running a major advertising campaign (completed by the end of that quarter) that will benefit sales throughout the year. Is it appropriate to spread the advertising cost over the period in which benefits (in the form of revenues) are expected – all four quarters of the year – or is the entire cost an expense of the first quarter?

The entire cost is recognised in the first quarter. Explanatory note disclosure may be required. IAS 38.69(c) requires that all expenditure on advertising and promotional activities should be recognised as an expense when incurred (see **section 5** of **chapter 8**). As outlined above, a cost that does not meet the definition of an asset at the end of an interim period is not deferred, either to await future information as to whether it has met the definition of an asset or to smooth earnings over interim periods within a financial year.

Example 5.3B

Fixed costs of a manufacturer whose business is seasonal

A manufacturer's shipments of finished products are highly seasonal (shares of annual sales are respectively 20 per cent, 5 per cent, 10 per cent, and

65 per cent for the four quarters of the financial year). Manufacturing takes place more evenly throughout the year. The entity incurs substantial fixed costs, including fixed costs relating to manufacturing, selling and general administration, and wishes to allocate all of its fixed costs to the four quarters based on each quarter's share of estimated annual sales volume.

Such an allocation is not acceptable under IAS 34. IAS 34.39 states that costs that are incurred unevenly during an entity's financial year should be anticipated or deferred for interim reporting purposes if, and only if, it is also appropriate to anticipate or defer that type of cost at the end of the financial year.

In the circumstances described, the fixed costs should be split between manufacturing fixed costs and non-manufacturing fixed costs. IAS 2.12 requires that the cost of manufactured inventories should include a systematic allocation of fixed production overheads (i.e. fixed manufacturing costs). Because manufacturing takes place evenly throughout the year, the entity will recognise cost of goods sold expense only when sales are made and, therefore, it will achieve its objective of allocating fixed manufacturing costs to the four quarters based on sales volume.

Fixed non-manufacturing costs, however, are different. IAS 2.16 makes clear that that administrative overheads that do not contribute to bringing inventories to their present location and condition, and selling costs (whether variable or fixed), are excluded from the cost of inventories and are recognised as expenses in the periods in which they are incurred. Therefore, the entity must recognise its fixed non-manufacturing costs in profit or loss as incurred in each of the four quarters. As required by IAS 34.16, explanatory comments about the seasonality or cyclicality of interim operations should be disclosed in the notes to interim financial statements. In addition, IAS 34.21 encourages seasonal businesses to present 'rolling' 12-month financial statements in addition to interim period financial statements.

Example 5.3C

Production tooling costs incurred early in the financial year

An entity reports quarterly. In the first quarter of each financial year, the entity introduces new models of its products that will be sold throughout the year. At that time, it incurs a substantial cost for retooling its production line to manufacture the new models. Is it appropriate to spread the tooling cost over the benefit period (all four quarters of the year), or is the entire cost an expense of the first quarter?

It is appropriate to spread these costs provided that they meet the recognition criteria in IAS 16.7 *Property, Plant and Equipment* (see **section 3** of **chapter 6**). Those criteria require that an item of property, plant and equipment be recognised as an asset if, and only if:

- it is probable that future economic benefits associated with the item will flow to the entity; and

- the cost of the item can be measured reliably.

Assuming that the tooling costs meet these criteria, the costs would be capitalised and amortised over the model year, regardless of the entity's interim reporting policy. To illustrate, if the entity's financial year is the calendar year, but new products are introduced in September for a model-year from 1 September to 31 August, then at 31 December some portion of the tooling costs would be carried forward as an asset into the next financial year, whether or not the entity prepared any interim financial reports.

5.4 Use of estimates

IAS 34.41 requires that measurement procedures used in interim financial reports produce information that is reliable, with all material relevant financial information being appropriately disclosed. It nevertheless acknowledges that, while reasonable estimates are often used for both annual and interim financial reports, interim reports generally will require a greater use of estimation methods than annual financial reports.

Appendix C to the Standard provides a number of examples of the use of estimates in interim financial reports, which are reproduced below.

Examples of the use of estimates for interim reporting purposes

[Appendix C to IAS 34]

Inventories: Full stock-taking and valuation procedures may not be required for inventories at interim dates, although it may be done at financial year end. It may be sufficient to make estimates at interim dates based on sales margins.

Classifications of current and non-current assets and liabilities: Entities may do a more thorough investigation for classifying assets and liabilities as current or non-current at the end of annual reporting periods than at interim dates.

Provisions: Determination of the appropriate amount of a provision (such as a provision for warranties, environmental costs, and site restoration costs) may be complex and often costly and time-consuming. Entities sometimes engage outside experts to assist in the annual calculations. Making similar estimates at interim dates often entails updating of the prior annual provision rather than the engaging of outside experts to do a new calculation.

Pensions: IAS 19 *Employee Benefits* requires that an entity determine the present value of defined benefit obligations and the market value of plan assets at the end of each reporting period and encourages an entity to involve a professionally qualified actuary in measurement of the obligations. For interim reporting purposes, reliable measurement is often obtainable by extrapolation of the latest actuarial valuation.

Income taxes: Entities may calculate income tax expense and deferred income tax liability at annual dates by applying the tax rate for each individual jurisdiction to measures of income for each jurisdiction. IAS 34.B14 acknowledges that while that degree of precision is desirable at the end of interim reporting periods as well, it may not be achievable in all cases, and a weighted average of rates across jurisdictions or across categories of income is used if it is a reasonable approximation of the effect of using more specific rates.

Contingencies: The measurement of contingencies may involve the opinions of legal experts or other advisers. Formal reports from independent experts are sometimes obtained with respect to contingencies. Such opinions about litigation, claims, assessments, and other contingencies and uncertainties may or may not also be needed at interim dates.

Revaluations and fair value accounting: IAS 16 *Property, Plant and Equipment* allows an entity to choose as its accounting policy the revaluation model whereby items of property, plant and equipment are revalued to fair value. Similarly, IAS 40 *Investment Property* requires an entity to determine the fair value of investment property. For those measurements, an entity may rely on professionally-qualified valuers at the end of annual reporting periods, though not at the end of interim reporting periods.

Intercompany reconciliations: Some intercompany balances that are reconciled on a detailed level in preparing consolidated financial statements at financial year end might be reconciled at a less detailed level in preparing consolidated financial statements at an interim date.

Specialised industries: Because of complexity, costliness and time, interim period measurements in specialised industries might be less precise than at financial year-end. An example would be calculation of insurance reserves by insurance companies.

Financial instruments: Financial instruments that are carried at fair value should be remeasured at the interim date using the same methodology as at the end of the annual reporting period. Also, the carrying amount of financial instruments at amortised cost should be recalculated at the interim date.

Share based payments: Liabilities in respect of cash-settled share based payments will generally be based on the fair value of the share options as at the end of the previous reporting period. If changes in the fair value of the share options since the most recent annual financial statements are material to the interim period, the fair value of the cash-settled share based payment should be remeasured at the interim date.

In relation to equity-settled share based payments, an entity should consider whether, at the interim date, there is any change to the number of equity instruments expected to vest. Where the change could have a material impact on the interim period, the number of equity instruments expected to vest should be re-estimated at the interim date.

5.5 Changes in estimates

As an illustration of the impact of changes in estimates, IAS 34 considers the rules for recognising and measuring losses from inventory write-downs, restructurings or impairments. The principles to be followed in an interim period are the same as those for annual periods. If such items are recognised and measured in, say, the first quarter of a financial year and the estimate changes in the second quarter of the year, the original estimate is adjusted in the second interim period, either by recognition of an additional amount or by reversal of the previously-recognised amount. [IAS 34.30(a)]

If changes in estimates arise, the results of previous interim periods of the current year are not retrospectively adjusted. However, the nature and amount of any significant changes in estimates must be disclosed either:

[IAS 34.16(d), 26 & 35]

- in the annual report, if there has been no subsequent interim period financial report that has disclosed the change in estimate (see **3.8**); or
- in the following interim period financial report of the same year.

IFRIC 10 gives guidance on certain circumstances in which an impairment loss should not be reversed (see **5.6.16.1**).

Changes in estimates should also be disclosed in the corresponding interim report for the following year, so that the comparative figures (which are not restated) will not be misleading.

5.6 Additional examples

Appendix B to IAS 34 contains a number of detailed examples to illustrate the application of the recognition and measurement principles discussed in the previous sections. These are reproduced below, together with a number of additional examples developed to illustrate important principles.

5.6.1 *Employer payroll taxes and insurance contributions*

If employer payroll taxes or contributions to government-sponsored insurance funds are assessed on an annual basis, the employer's related expense is recognised in interim periods using an estimated average annual effective payroll tax or contribution rate, even though a large portion of the payments may be made early in the financial year. A common example is an employer payroll tax or insurance contribution that is imposed up to a certain maximum level of earnings per employee. For higher income employees, the maximum income is reached before the end of the financial year, and the employer makes no further payments through the end of the year. [IAS 34.B1]

5.6.2 *Major planned periodic maintenance or overhaul*

The cost of a planned major periodic maintenance or overhaul or other seasonal expenditure that is expected to occur late in the year is not anticipated for interim reporting purposes, unless an event has caused the entity to have a legal or constructive obligation. The mere intention or necessity to incur expenditure related to the future is not sufficient to give rise to an obligation. [IAS 34.B2]

5.6.3 *Provisions*

A provision is recognised when an entity has no realistic alternative but to make a transfer of economic benefits as a result of an event that has created a legal or constructive obligation. The amount of the obligation is adjusted upward or downward, with a corresponding loss or gain recognised in profit or loss, if the entity's best estimate of the amount of the obligation changes.

IAS 34 requires that an entity apply the same criteria for recognising and measuring a provision at an interim date as it would at the end of its financial year. The existence or non-existence of an obligation to transfer benefits is not a function of the length of the reporting period. It is a question of fact. [IAS 34.B3 & B4]

5.6.4 *Year-end bonuses*

The nature of year-end bonuses varies widely. Some are earned simply by continued employment during a time period. Some bonuses are earned based on a monthly, quarterly, or annual measure of operating result. They may be purely discretionary, contractual, or based on years of historical precedent.

A bonus is anticipated for interim reporting purposes if, and only if:

[IAS 34.B5 & B6]

- the bonus is a legal obligation, or past practice would make the bonus a constructive obligation and the entity has no realistic alternative but to make the payments; and
- a reliable estimate of the obligation can be made.

IAS 19 *Employee Benefits* provides guidance on the application of the recognition rules to year-end bonuses.

5.6.5 *Contingent lease payments*

Contingent lease payments can be an example of a legal or constructive obligation that is recognised as a liability. If a lease provides for contingent payments based on the lessee achieving a certain level of annual sales, an obligation can arise in the interim period of the financial year before the required annual level of sales has been achieved, if that required level of sales is expected to be achieved and the entity, therefore, has no realistic alternative but to make the future lease payment. [IAS 34.B7]

5.6.6 *Intangible assets*

Entities are required to apply the definition and recognition criteria for an intangible asset in the same way in an interim period as in an annual period. Costs incurred before the recognition criteria for an intangible asset are met are recognised as an expense. Costs incurred after the specific point in time at which the criteria are met are recognised as part of the cost of an intangible asset. 'Deferring' costs as assets in an interim statement of financial position in the hope that the recognition criteria will be met later in the financial year is not justified. [IAS 34.B8]

Example 5.6.6

Development costs that meet the IAS 38 capitalisation criteria midway in an interim period

An entity engaged in the pharmaceutical sector, with a December year end, reports quarterly. Throughout 20X2, its research department is engaged in a major drug development project. Development costs incurred in 20X2, by quarter, are as follows:

First quarter		£100
Second quarter		£100
Third quarter:		
	July 1 to 31 August	£80
	1 September to 30 September	£60
Fourth quarter		£150

The entity publishes its half-year report on 15 August, and the £200 development costs incurred during the first and second quarters are recognised in profit or loss. On 1 September, the research department determines that the criteria set out in IAS 38 for capitalising the development costs as an intangible asset have been met.

IAS 38 provides that asset recognition (cost capitalisation) begins at the point in time at which the recognition criteria are met, not at the start of the financial reporting period in which those criteria are met. Therefore, the following amounts are reported in the interim financial reports for the second half of the financial year, and in the annual report at 31 December 20X2:

		30 September £	**31 December** £
Asset recognised in the statement of financial position		60	210
	3 months ended 30 September £	**9 months ended 30 September** £	**12 months ended 31 December** £
Development costs recognised in profit or loss	80	280	280

5.6.7 *Pensions*

The pension cost for an interim period is calculated on a year-to-date basis by using the actuarially-determined pension cost rate at the end of the prior financial year, adjusted for significant market fluctuations since that time and for significant curtailments, settlements or other significant one-time events. [IAS 34.B9]

5.6.8 *Vacations, holidays, and other short-term compensated absences*

Accumulating compensated absences are those that are carried forward and can be used in future periods if the current period's entitlement is not used in full. IAS 19 *Employee Benefits* requires that an entity measure the expected cost of and obligation for accumulating compensated absences at the amount the entity expects to pay as a result of the unused entitlement that has accumulated at the end of the reporting period. That principle is also applied at the end of interim financial reporting periods. Conversely, an entity recognises no expense or liability for non-accumulating compensated absences at the end of an interim reporting period, just as it recognises none at the end of an annual reporting period. [IAS 34.B10]

Example 5.6.8

Vacation accruals at interim dates

An entity reports quarterly. Its financial year end is 31 December. Holiday entitlement accumulates with employment over the year, but any unused entitlement cannot be carried forward past 31 December. Most of the entity's employees take a substantial portion of their annual leave in July or August. Should an appropriate portion of employees' salaries during the July/August vacation period be accrued in the first and second quarter interim financial statements?

A portion should be accrued if the employees' vacation days are earned (accumulate) through service during the first and second quarters. Vacations are a form of short-term compensated absence as defined in IAS 19. IAS 19.11 requires that the expected cost of short-term accumulating compensated absences be recognised when the employees render service that increases their entitlement to future compensated absences. This principle is applied in both annual and interim financial statements.

5.6.9 *Other planned but irregularly occurring costs*

An entity's budget may include certain costs expected to be incurred irregularly during the financial year, such as charitable contributions and employee-training costs. Those costs generally are discretionary, even though they are planned and tend to recur from year to year. Recognising an obligation at the end of an interim financial reporting period for such costs that have not yet been incurred generally is not consistent with the definition of a liability. [IAS 34.B11]

5.6.10 *Measuring interim income tax expense*

5.6.10.1 Use of estimated annual rate

The interim period income tax expense is accrued using the tax rate that would be applicable to expected total annual earnings, i.e. the estimated average annual effective income tax rate applied to the pre-tax income of the interim period. [IAS 34.B12]

This is consistent with the basic principle set out in IAS 34.28 that the same accounting recognition and measurement principles should be applied in an interim financial report as are applied in annual financial statements. Income taxes are assessed on an annual basis. Interim period income tax expense is calculated by applying to an interim period's pre-tax income the tax rate that would be applicable to total annual earnings. [IAS 34.B13]

To the extent practicable, a separate estimated average annual effective income tax rate is determined for each tax jurisdiction and applied individually to the interim period pre-tax income of each jurisdiction. Similarly, if different income tax rates apply to different categories of income (such as capital gains or income earned in particular industries), to the extent practicable, a separate rate is applied to each individual category of interim period pre-tax income. While that degree of precision is desirable, it may not be achievable in all cases and a weighted average of rates across jurisdictions or across categories of income is used if it is a reasonable approximation of the effect of using more specific rates. [IAS 34.B14]

5.6.10.2 *Impact of progressive (graduated) tax rates*

The estimated average annual effective income tax rate will reflect a blend of the progressive tax rate structure expected to be applicable to the full year's earnings, including enacted or substantively enacted changes in the income tax rates scheduled to take effect later in the financial year. [IAS 34.B13] **Example 5.6.10.2**, which is drawn from Appendix B to IAS 34, illustrates the impact of progressive tax rates.

Example 5.6.10.2

Progressive tax rates

[IAS 34.B15]

An entity reporting quarterly expects to earn 10,000 pre-tax each quarter and operates in a jurisdiction with a tax rate of 20 per cent on the first 20,000 of annual earnings and 30 per cent on all additional earnings. Actual earnings match expectations. The following table shows the amount of income tax expense that is reported in each quarter:

	1st Quarter	2nd Quarter	3rd Quarter	4th Quarter	Annual
Tax expense	2,500	2,500	2,500	2,500	10,000

5.6.10.3 *Uneven earnings throughout the year*

Example 5.6.10.3, again drawn from Appendix B to IAS 34, illustrates the application of the IAS 34 principles when earnings are distributed unevenly throughout the year.

Example 5.6.10.3

Uneven earnings throughout the year

[IAS 34.B16]

An entity reports quarterly, earns 15,000 pre-tax profit in the first quarter but expects to incur losses of 5,000 in each of the three remaining quarters (thus having zero income for the year), and operates in a jurisdiction in which its estimated average annual income tax rate is expected to be 20 per cent. The following table shows the amount of income tax expense that is reported in each quarter:

	1st Quarter	2nd Quarter	3rd Quarter	4th Quarter	Annual
Tax expense	3,000	(1,000)	(1,000)	(1,000)	0

5.6.10.4 *Change in estimate of annual tax rate*

When preparing the tax estimate to be included in an interim period, the tax expense is based on the best estimate of the weighted average *annual* income tax rate expected for the full financial year. Therefore, as for other changes in estimates, amounts accrued for income tax expense in one interim period may have to be adjusted in a subsequent interim period if the estimate of the annual income tax rate changes. [IAS 34.30(c)] The estimated average annual income tax rate would be re-estimated on a year-to-date basis, consistent with IAS 34.28.

The nature and amount of any significant changes in the estimated tax rate should be disclosed either:

[IAS 34.16(d), 26 & 35]

- in the annual report, if there has been no subsequent interim period financial report that has disclosed the change in estimate (see **3.8**); or
- in the following interim period financial report of the same year.

5.6.10.5 *Difference in financial reporting year and tax year*

If the financial reporting year and the income tax year differ, the income tax expense for the interim periods of that financial reporting year is measured using separate weighted average estimated effective tax rates for each of the income tax years applied to the portion of pre-tax income earned in each of those income tax years. [IAS 34.B17]

Example 5.6.10.5

Difference in financial reporting year and tax year

[IAS 34.B18]

An entity's financial reporting year ends 30 June and it reports quarterly. Its taxable year ends 31 December. For the financial year that begins 1 July, Year 1 and ends 30 June, Year 2, the entity earns 10,000 pre-tax each quarter. The estimated average annual income tax rate is 30 per cent in Year 1 and 40 per cent in Year 2.

	Quarter ending 30 Sept Year 1	Quarter ending 31 Dec Year 1	Quarter ending 31 Mar Year 2	Quarter ending 30 June Year 2	Year ending 30 June Year 2
Tax expense	3,000	3,000	4,000	4,000	14,000

5.6.10.6 Tax credits

Some tax jurisdictions give taxpayers credits against the tax payable based on amounts of capital expenditure, exports, research and development expenditure, or other bases. Anticipated tax benefits of this type for the full year are generally reflected in computing the estimated annual effective income tax rate, because those credits are granted and calculated on an annual basis under most tax laws and regulations. On the other hand, tax benefits that relate to a one-time event are recognised in computing income tax expense in the interim period in which that event occurs, in the same way that special tax rates applicable to particular categories of income are not blended into a single effective annual tax rate. Moreover, in some jurisdictions, tax benefits or credits that are reported on the income tax return, including those related to capital expenditure and levels of exports, are more similar to a government grant and are recognised in the interim period in which they arise. [IAS 34.B19]

5.6.10.7 Tax loss and tax credit carrybacks and carryforwards

The benefits of a tax loss carryback are reflected in the interim period in which the related tax loss occurs. IAS 12 *Income Taxes* provides that 'the benefit relating to a tax loss that can be carried back to recover current tax of a previous period should be recognised as an asset'. A corresponding reduction of tax expense or increase of tax income is also recognised. [IAS 34.B20]

IAS 12 also provides that 'a deferred tax asset should be recognised for the carryforward of unused tax losses and unused tax credits to the extent that it is probable that future taxable profit will be available against which the unused tax losses and unused tax credits can be utilised'. Detailed criteria are specified for the purpose of assessing the availability of future taxable profit against which the unused tax losses and credits can be utilised. [IAS 34.B21]

For interim reporting purposes, the criteria for recognition of deferred tax assets are applied at the end of each interim period and, if they are met, the effect of the tax loss carryforward is reflected in the computation of the estimated average annual effective income tax rate. [IAS 34.B21]

Example 5.6.10.7A

Tax loss carryforward at the end of an interim reporting period

[IAS 34.B22]

An entity that reports quarterly, has an operating loss carryforward of 10,000 for income tax purposes at the start of the current financial year for which a deferred tax asset has not been recognised. The entity earns 10,000 in the first quarter of the current year and expects to earn 10,000 in each of the three remaining quarters. Excluding the carryforward, the estimated average annual income tax rate is expected to be 40 per cent. Tax expense is as follows:

	1st Quarter	2nd Quarter	3rd Quarter	4th Quarter	Annual
Tax expense	3,000	3,000	3,000	3,000	12,000

The tax effect of losses that arise in the early portion of a financial year should be recognised only when the tax benefits are expected to be realised either during the current year or as a deferred tax asset at the end of the year. For the purpose of applying this guidance, an established seasonal pattern of loss in the early interim periods followed by income in later interim periods is generally sufficient to support a conclusion that realisation of the tax benefit from the early losses is probable. Recognition of the tax benefit of losses incurred in early interim periods will generally not occur in those interim periods if available evidence indicates that income is not expected in later interim periods.

If the tax benefits of losses that are incurred in early interim periods of a financial year are not recognised in those interim periods, no income tax expense will be provided on income generated in later interim periods until the tax effects of the previous losses are offset.

The tax effect of a deferred tax asset expected to be recognised at the end of a financial year for deductible temporary differences and carryforwards that originate during the current financial year should be spread throughout the financial year by an adjustment to the annual effective tax rate.

Example 5.6.10.7B

Recognition of deferred tax assets at the end of an interim reporting period

Assume that during the first quarter of 20X1, an entity, operating in a tax jurisdiction with a 50 per cent tax rate, generates a tax credit of £4,000 (i.e. sufficient to cover taxable profits of £8,000) that, under tax law, will expire at the end of 20X2. At the end of the first quarter of 20X1, available evidence about the future indicates that taxable income of £2,000 and £4,000 will be generated during 20X1 and 20X2, respectively. Therefore, the entity expects to utilise £1,000 (£2,000 x 50 per cent) of the tax credit to offset tax on its 20X1 taxable income, and £2,000 (£4,000 x 50 per cent) to offset tax on its 20X2 income. It expects to recognise a deferred tax asset in its statement of financial position at the end of 20X1 of £2,000 (relating to the tax relief available in 20X2), and the balance of £1,000 will not be recognised as it is not probable that sufficient taxable profit will be available against which it can be utilised before the losses expire.

Because the tax credit is generated during the current year, the tax consequence of the £2,000 deferred tax asset expected to be recognised at the end of 20X1 is applied rateably to each of the interim periods during 20X1.

Therefore, if profits arise on a straight line basis through 20X1, a benefit for income taxes of £500 [£2,000 × 1/4)] will be recognised during the first interim period. Assuming the estimates about the future do not change during the remainder of the year, the tax benefit of the remaining £1,500 (£2,000 – £500) of net deferred tax asset will be recognised rateably over the pre-tax accounting income generated in the later interim periods of 20X1.

5.6.10.8 *Change in estimate as to recoverability of tax loss carryforward*

It is not clear whether IAS 34.B21 applies equally to all circumstances where a previously recognised deferred tax asset is no longer expected to be recoverable. There appear to be two acceptable approaches: the first is to derecognise at the interim reporting date all the amounts assessed as not recoverable and the second is to spread the derecognition via the estimated annual effective tax rate.

Example 5.6.10.8

Change in estimate as to recoverability of tax loss carryforward

An entity operates in a tax jurisdiction with a 50 per cent tax rate. In 20X1, the entity incurs tax losses of £50,000, which can be carried forward to offset against future taxable profits until 20X3. At 31 December 20X1, the entity estimates that £40,000 of the losses can be recovered against profits in 20X2 (budgeted profit £15,000) and 20X3 (budgeted profit £25,000), and therefore recognises a deferred tax asset of £20,000 (£40,000 x 50 per cent) in its annual financial statements for 20X1.

At the end of the first quarter of 20X2, actual year-to-date profits and anticipations for the remainder of the year are in line with budget. However, the budgeted profit for 20X3 is revised downward to £20,000.

If the deferred tax asset derecognition is accounted for entirely at the date at which it is assessed as not recoverable (the first approach), at the end of the first quarter of 20X2 the carrying amount of the deferred tax asset should be reduced by £2,500 (£5,000 at 50 per cent). Therefore, in quarter 1 of 20X2, assuming taxable profits of £6,000 and an estimated effective annual rate of 50%, the income tax expense for the quarter is estimated as follows:

Tax expense in quarter 1:	(£6,000 x 50%) + £2,500 = £5,500
Deferred tax asset recognised in quarter 1 (not estimated as recoverable at interim reporting date):	nil

Alternatively if the deferred tax asset derecognition is spread throughout the year as part of the computation of the annual effective tax rate (the second approach), the carrying amount of the deferred tax asset should be reduced by £2,500 (£5,000 at 50 per cent) only at the end of 20X2. Therefore, in quarter 1 of 20X2, assuming taxable profits of £6,000 out of estimated annual profits of £15,000, the income tax expense for the quarter is estimated as follows:

Estimated effective annual tax rate:	[(£15,000 x 0.50) + £2,500] /£15,000 = 66.7%
Tax expense in quarter 1:	£6,000 x 66.7% = £4,000
Deferred tax asset remaining at quarter 1 (not estimated as recoverable at interim reporting date):	£2,500 – (£6,000 x [66.7%-50%]) = £1,500

5.6.11 *Contractual or anticipated purchase price changes*

Volume rebates or discounts and other contractual changes in the prices of raw materials, labour, or other purchased goods and services are anticipated in interim periods, by both the payer and the recipient, if it is probable that they have been earned or will take effect. Thus, contractual rebates and discounts are anticipated, but discretionary rebates and discounts are not anticipated because the definitions of asset and liability (requiring *control* over resources to be received, or an *obligation* to pay out resources) would not be met. [IAS 34.B23]

5.6.12 *Depreciation and amortisation*

Depreciation and amortisation charges for an interim period are based only on assets owned during that interim period. They should not take into account asset acquisitions or disposals planned for later in the financial year. [IAS 34.B24]

It would not generally be necessary to reassess residual values for items of property, plant and equipment as at the interim date, unless there are indicators that there has been a material change in residual values since the end of the previous reporting period.

5.6.13 *Inventories*

5.6.13.1 Measurement of inventories – general

Inventories are measured for interim financial reporting using the same principles as at financial year end. IAS 2 *Inventories* establishes standards for recognising and measuring inventories. Inventories pose particular problems at the end of any financial reporting period because of the need to determine inventory quantities, costs and net realisable values. Nonetheless, the same measurement principles are applied for inventories at the end of interim reporting periods. To save cost and time, entities often use estimates to measure inventories at interim dates to a greater extent than at the end of annual reporting periods. The following sections set out examples of how to apply the net realisable value test at an interim date and how to treat manufacturing variances at interim dates. [IAS 34.B25]

5.6.13.2 Net realisable value of inventories

The net realisable value of inventories is determined by reference to selling prices and related costs to complete and dispose at interim dates. [IAS 34.B26]

An entity should reverse a write-down to net realisable value in a subsequent reporting period only if it would be appropriate to do so at the end of the financial year. [IAS 34.B26]

5.6.13.3 Interim period manufacturing cost variances

Price, efficiency, spending and volume variances of a manufacturing entity are recognised in income at the end of interim reporting periods to the same extent that those variances are recognised in income at financial year end. Deferral of variances that are expected to be absorbed by the year end is not appropriate because it could result in reporting inventory at the interim date at more or less than its portion of the actual cost of manufacture. [IAS 34.B28]

5.6.14 *Foreign currency translation gains and losses*

Foreign currency translation gains and losses are measured for interim financial reporting using the same principles as at financial year end. [IAS 34.B29]

IAS 21 *The Effects of Changes in Foreign Exchange Rates* specifies how to translate the financial statements for foreign operations into the presentation currency, including guidelines for using average or closing foreign exchange rates and guidelines for including the resulting adjustments in profit or loss or in other comprehensive income. Consistent with IAS 21, the actual average and closing rates for the interim period are used. Entities do not anticipate changes in foreign exchange rates in the remainder of the current financial year when translating foreign operations at an interim date. [IAS 34.B30]

If IAS 21 requires that translation adjustments are recognised as income or as expenses in the period in which they arise, that principle is applied during each interim period. Entities do not defer some foreign currency translation adjustments at an interim date if the adjustment is expected to reverse before the end of the financial year. [IAS 34.B31]

5.6.15 *Interim financial reporting in hyperinflationary economies*

Interim financial reports in hyperinflationary economies are prepared following the same principles as at financial year end. IAS 29 *Financial Reporting in Hyperinflationary Economies* requires that the financial statements of an entity that reports in the currency of a hyperinflationary economy be stated in terms of the measuring unit current at the end of the reporting period, and the gain or loss on the net monetary position is included in net income. Also, comparative financial data reported for prior periods is restated to the current measuring unit. [IAS 34.B32 & B33]

Entities are required to follow the same principles at interim dates, thereby presenting all interim data in the measuring unit as of the end of the interim period, with the resulting gain or loss on the net monetary position included in the interim period's net income. Entities should not annualise the recognition of the gain or loss. Nor do they use an estimated annual inflation rate in preparing an interim financial report in a hyperinflationary economy. [IAS 34.B34]

5.6.16 *Impairment of assets*

IAS 36 *Impairment of Assets* requires that an impairment loss be recognised if the recoverable amount of an asset has declined below its carrying amount. IAS 34 requires that an entity apply the same impairment testing, recognition and reversal criteria at an interim date as it would at the end of its financial year. That does not mean, however, that an entity must necessarily make a detailed impairment calculation at the end of each interim period. Rather, an entity will review for indications of significant impairment since the end of the most recent financial year to determine whether such a calculation is needed. [IAS 34.B35 & B36]

5.6.16.1 *IFRIC 10 Interim Financial Reporting and Impairment*

As discussed at **4.1** and **5.1** above, IAS 34.28 requires an entity to apply the same accounting policies in its interim financial statements as are applied in its annual financial statements. It also states that the frequency of an entity's reporting (annual, half-yearly, or quarterly) should not affect the measurement of its annual results. To achieve that objective, measurements for interim reporting purposes should be made on a year-to-date basis.

IFRIC Interpretation 10 *Interim Financial Reporting and Impairment* addresses the interaction between the requirements in IAS 34.28 and those dealing with the recognition of impairment losses on goodwill in IAS 36 and certain financial assets in IAS 39, and the effect of that interaction on subsequent interim and annual financial statements:

- IAS 36.124 states that 'an impairment loss recognised for goodwill shall not be reversed in a subsequent period';
- IAS 39.69 states that 'impairment losses recognised in profit or loss for an investment in an equity instrument classified as available-for-sale shall not be reversed through profit or loss'; and
- IAS 39.66 requires that impairment losses for financial assets carried at cost (such as an impairment loss on an unquoted equity instrument that is not carried at fair value because its fair value cannot be reliably measured) should not be reversed.

The issue addressed by IFRIC 10 is whether an entity should reverse impairment losses recognised in an interim period on goodwill and investments in equity instruments and in financial assets carried at cost if a loss would not have been recognised, or a smaller loss would have been recognised, had an impairment assessment been made only at the end of the subsequent reporting period.

The issue is best illustrated by considering the example of Entity A and Entity B, which each hold the same equity investment with the same acquisition cost. Entity A prepares quarterly interim financial statements whilst Entity B prepares half-yearly financial statements. Both entities have the same financial year-end date. If there was a significant decline in the fair value of the equity instrument below its cost in the first quarter, Entity A would recognise an impairment loss in its first quarter interim financial statements. However, if the fair value of the equity instrument subsequently recovered, so that by the half-year date there had not been a significant decline in fair value below cost, Entity B would not recognise an impairment loss in its half-yearly financial statements if it tested for impairment only at the end of the half-year reporting period. Therefore, unless Entity A reversed the impairment loss that had been recognised in an earlier interim period, the frequency of reporting would affect the measurement of its annual results when compared with Entity B's approach.

The consensus in the Interpretation is that an entity should not reverse an impairment loss recognised in a previous interim period in respect of goodwill or an investment in an equity instrument or a financial asset carried at cost. Essentially, IFRIC 10 concludes that the prohibitions on reversals of recognised impairment losses on goodwill in IAS 36 and on investments in equity instruments and financial assets carried at cost in IAS 39 should take precedence over the more general statement in IAS 34 regarding the frequency of an entity's reporting not affecting the measurement of its annual results.

IFRIC 10 emphasises that an entity should not extend the consensus of this Interpretation by analogy to other areas of potential conflict between IAS 34 and other Standards.

5.6.17 Capitalisation of borrowing costs in interim periods

Example 5.6.17

Capitalisation of borrowing costs in interim periods

An entity capitalises borrowing costs directly attributable to construction of qualifying assets under IAS 23 *Borrowing Costs*. The entity funds its asset construction with general borrowings, rather than project-specific borrowings. Further, it uses general borrowings for purposes other than construction, so that the amount of borrowings in any period is not necessarily related to the amount of construction during that period. The entity reports quarterly.

IAS 23.14 requires that the capitalisation rate for general borrowings be the weighted average of borrowing costs applicable to borrowings of the entity that are outstanding during the period. For interim reporting purposes, the reference to 'period' in IAS 23.14 should be interpreted to mean the year-to-date period, not each individual quarter so that, in accordance with IAS 34.28 and IAS 34.36, the amount of borrowing costs capitalised is 'trued-up' each quarter on a year-to-date basis.

5.6.18 Non-current assets held for sale and discontinued operations

The measurement and presentation principles of IFRS 5 *Non-current Assets Held for Sale and Discontinued Operations* should be applied in interim financial reports in the same way as at the end of the annual reporting period. Therefore, a non-current asset that meets the criteria to be classified as held-for-sale at the interim date should be presented as such. In assessing any potential impairment loss and fair value less costs to sell of the non-current asset held-for-sale, a greater use of estimation methods may be acceptable than at the end of the annual reporting period.

6 Disclosure and Transparency Rules, AIM and Listing Rules requirements

UK *This section is divided into two sections:*

- ***Section 6.1*** *discusses the requirements on periodic financial reporting of the Disclosure and Transparency Rules (DTR), which apply to companies with listed shares or debt on a regulated market.*
- ***Section 6.2*** *discusses the requirements of the AIM Rules, which apply to companies admitted to trading on the Alternative Investment Market.*

6.1 Disclosure and Transparency Rules (DTR)

UK *The DTR, which are effective for periods beginning on or after 20 January 2007, set out various requirements for annual financial reports (see* ***section 1*** *of* ***chapter 45****), half-yearly financial reports (see* **6.1.1***) and interim management statements (see* **6.1.2***).*

6.1.1 *Half-yearly financial report*

UK

A company with shares or debt listed on a regulated market (see **2.2** *in* **chapter 1***) must prepare a half-yearly report, on a group basis where relevant, covering the first six months of the financial year.*

DTR 4.4 and DTR TP 1 contain exemptions from the requirements to produce a half-yearly financial report for:

- *public sector companies (a state, a regional or local authority of a state, a public international body of which at least one European Economic Area (EEA) State is a member, the European Central Bank (ECB) and EEA States' national central bank);*
- *companies that issue exclusively debt securities admitted to trading with a denomination per unit of at least 50,000 Euros (i.e. wholesale debt);*
- *credit institutions with listed debt only, if the total nominal amount of all listed debt is less than €100m and if the credit institution has not published a prospectus in accordance with the prospectus directive;*
- *companies with debt securities where those debt securities were admitted to the official list before 1 January 2005 pursuant to chapter 23 of the previous version of the Listing Rules (see below);*
- *companies already existing on 31 December 2003 with exclusively listed debt unconditionally and irrevocably guaranteed by the company's home member state or a regional or local authority of that state;*
- *companies with listed transferable securities convertible into shares; and*
- *companies with listed depositary receipts.*

The transitional provisions of the DTR contain an exemption for companies with listed debt only, whose debt was listed prior to 1 January 2005. Under this transitional provision, qualifying companies are not required to prepare half-yearly financial reports until annual periods beginning on or after 1 January 2015. Note that a half-yearly financial report will be required prior to 2015 if there has been an issue of new debt securities since that date.

Companies should publish their half-yearly financial reports within two calendar months of the end of the six-month period to which it relates. Note that the publication deadlines under the DTR are calendar months.

Many retailing companies prepare their half-yearly financial reports for the first 26 week period of the financial year. Consistent with the year end, this practice is generally accepted as an approximation of the six month period.

The half-yearly financial report must be disseminated in unedited full text via a regulated information service (RIS). It is no longer required that companies publish their half-yearly financial report in a national newspaper or send it to their shareholders. Online communication is sufficient. Half-yearly financial reports have to remain publicly available for at least five years. The published half-yearly financial report via the RIS should contain a clear reference to the company's website where the information is made available. The FSA newsletter List! *for March 2008 further clarified that the information presented on the company's website should be consistent with and should not contain any additional information to the RIS announcement.*

Each half-yearly financial report should contain at least a condensed set of financial statements, an interim management report (IMR) and a responsibility statement. [DTR 4.2.3]

6.1.1.1 Condensed set of financial statements

UK

Companies preparing consolidated accounts in accordance with the EU Seventh Directive are required to prepare their half-yearly condensed set of financial statements in accordance with IAS 34.

This requirement raises the question whether a single listed company reporting under IFRSs is required to follow IAS 34 in its half-yearly financial report. The DTR and FSA guidance is not entirely clear in this area.

DTR 4.2.4 only mandates IAS 34 in half-yearly financial reports for companies that are required to prepare consolidated financial statements in accordance with the Seventh Directive.

DTR 4.2.10 states that the requirement to confirm a true and fair view in the responsibility statement is satisfied by 'including a statement that the condensed set of financial statements have been prepared in accordance with:

(a) IAS 34; or

(b) for UK issuers not using IFRSs, pronouncements on interim reporting issued by the Accounting Standards Board …'.

The converse of (b) is that UK companies using IFRSs should apply IAS 34 to give a true and fair view in their half-yearly reports. This is also reiterated by the FSA newsletter List! *for April 2007 which states that 'issuers using IFRS for their annual accounts … will be required to produce half-yearly reports in accordance with IAS 34 on Interim Financial Reporting'. Therefore it is strongly recommended that single companies reporting under IFRSs adopt IAS 34 in their half-yearly financial reports.*

DTR 4.2.6 sets out the general requirement that condensed half-yearly financial statements (both IAS 34 and non-IAS 34) should be based on accounting policies and presentation that are consistent with those in the latest published annual accounts. Where accounting policies and presentation are to be changed in the subsequent annual financial statements, the new accounting policies and presentation should be followed in the condensed set of financial statements. Such changes and the reason for the changes are to be disclosed in the condensed half-yearly financial statements.

Under the DTR, companies can choose whether or not to have their half-yearly report reviewed by their auditors. If the condensed set of financial statements has been audited or reviewed in line with Auditing Practices Board (APB) guidance, the audit report or review report must be included in the condensed financial statements in full. If no audit or review has been performed, the condensed set of financial statements should include a statement to this effect. This statement is often combined with the statement on non-statutory accounts dealt with in **3.2**.

6.1.1.2 Interim management report (IMR)

The DTR require that a half-yearly financial report contains an interim management report (IMR) which includes as a minimum: UK

- *an indication of important events that have occurred during the first six months of the financial year and their impact on the condensed financial statements; and*
- *a description of the principal risks and uncertainties for the remaining six months of the financial year.*

For companies with listed shares, DTR 4.2.8 requires the following additional information on related party transactions to be included in the IMR:

- *related party transactions that have taken place in the first six months of the financial year which had a material effect on the financial position or performance of the company/group; and*
- *any changes in the related party transactions described in the latest annual report which could have a material effect on the financial position or performance of the group in the first six months of the financial year.*

The FSA newsletter List! for March 2008 contains further guidance on the use of cross references to the detailed risks and uncertainties disclosures in the latest annual report. The FSA recognises that 'most companies give considerable thought to the subject of risks and uncertainties' in their annual reports and that these risks and uncertainties may continue to be valid at the half year. If this is the case, the FSA considers it acceptable for the company to:

- *'state that the principal risks and uncertainties have not changed;*
- *provide a summary of those principal risks and uncertainties; and*
- *include a cross-reference to where a detailed explanation of the principal risks and uncertainties can be found in the Annual Report.'*

In addition, if the risks and uncertainties have changed since the latest annual report, the new risks and uncertainties should be described in the interim management report.

6.1.1.3 Responsibility statement

UK *Companies are required to provide a responsibility statement in their half-yearly financial reports. Such a statement must be made by the persons responsible within the company (usually the directors). The responsibility statement should include the name and function of any person making a statement. [DTR 4.2.10]*

It is expected that only one person would be required physically to sign the responsibility statement, and sign on behalf of the board of directors. Ultimately, it is for each company to decide which person(s) is (are) considered responsible within the company. In its April 2008 newsletter List!, *the FSA confirms that the responsibility statement should 'identify those individuals responsible for the half-yearly report' and that in most cases this would be 'either the whole board of directors or one or more directors on behalf of the whole board'.*

Each person making a responsibility statement must confirm that to the best of his or her knowledge:

- *the condensed set of financial statements, which has been prepared in accordance with the applicable set of accounting standards, gives a true and fair view of the assets, liabilities, financial position and profit or loss of the company, or the undertakings included in the consolidation as a whole;*
- *the interim management report includes a fair review of the information required by DTR 4.2.7 (indication of important events and their*

impact, and description of principal risks and uncertainties for the remaining six months of the financial year); and

- *in the case of a company with listed shares, the interim management report includes a fair review of the information required on related party transactions.*

DTR 4.2.10(4) establishes that the requirement to confirm that the condensed set of financial statements gives a true and fair view will be satisfied if the responsibility statement includes a confirmation that the condensed financial statements have been prepared in accordance with:

- *IAS 34; or*
- *for UK companies not using IFRSs, pronouncements on interim reporting issued by the ASB; or*
- *for all other companies not using IFRSs, a national accounting standard relating to interim reporting.*

In all cases, the above applies provided the person making the statement has reasonable grounds to be satisfied that the condensed set of financial statements prepared in accordance with such a standard is not misleading.

The question arises as to what 'true and fair' means in relation to a condensed set of financial statements. The FSA recognises that 'true and fair' has a different meaning in the context of half-yearly financial reports and condensed financial statements compared to annual reports. Consequently, the FSA clarified in its Policy Statement PS06/11on the Implementation of the Transparency Directive (October 2006) that the requirement to provide a true and fair view in half-yearly financial reports is satisfied by a statement in accordance with DTR 4.2.10(4) (see above). A further explicit statement confirming that the condensed financial statements give a true and fair view is not necessary. The FSA further clarified in that Policy Statement that this decision has no effect on the interpretation of the true and fair view for annual accounts.

There is no specific requirement on where to present the responsibility statement within the half-yearly financial report. Responsibility statements included within the notes to the condensed financial statements may be seen to relate only to those condensed financial statements rather than the full half-yearly report and a different location with the appropriate prominence should be considered.

6.1.2 *Interim management statement* (IMS)

UK

The DTR on interim management statements only apply to companies which have shares listed on a regulated market. DTR 4.4 contains some exemptions from the requirements to produce an IMS for:

- *public sector companies (a state, a regional or local authority of a state, a public international body of which at least one EEA State is a member, the ECB and EEA States' national central bank);*
- *companies with listed transferable securities convertible into shares;*
- *companies with listed preference shares only; and*
- *companies with listed depositary receipts.*

Companies with only debt securities admitted to trading on a regulated market are outside the scope of DTR 4.3 and hence are not required to prepare an IMS.

Companies that publish quarterly reports (in accordance with national legislation, in accordance with the rules of a regulated market or voluntarily) do not have to produce a separate IMS. The quarterly report is taken to satisfy the requirements for an IMS. [DTR 4.3.6] There is no guidance on what constitutes a quarterly report. However, in practice a quarterly report would generally be expected to contain, as a minimum, the primary statements and related notes as well as a management commentary.

A company must publish one interim management statement in each six-month period of the financial year. This means one IMS during the first six months and another IMS during the second six months of the financial year.

The IMS must be made in a period between 10 weeks from the beginning, and six weeks before the end, of the relevant six-month period. For example, a company with a 31 January 2010 year end is required to publish its first IMS between 12 April 2009 and 19 June 2009. The second IMS is due between 9 October 2009 and 20 December 2009.

Each IMS must contain information covering the period from the beginning of the relevant six-month period up until the date of publication of the statement.

6.1.2.1 *Minimum content of the IMS*

UK

The IMS must provide:

- *an explanation of material events and transactions that have taken place during the relevant period and their impact on the financial position of the company/group; and*
- *a general description of the financial position and performance of the company/group during the relevant period.*

In essence, the purpose of the IMS is to give stakeholders a brief update on events since the last annual or half-yearly financial report and how the company is developing.

Other than the general requirements above, there is no detailed guidance on the content of the IMS. Items and events included in the IMS should not be generic. The content of the IMS should be entity-specific and tailored to the specific market requirements. The FSA reiterates that the content of the IMS should be market-led, based on discussions between preparers and users. Companies should use their judgement to decide whether something is important and should be reported in the IMS.

There is no explicit requirement for the IMS to contain financial information. However, the content of an IMS will depend on the facts and circumstances for each company and the markets in which it operates. The nature, scale and complexity of the transactions and events within the company will determine the content of the IMS and the manner in which they are best reported. Where the nature, scale and complexity of the issuer are such that it can provide a meaningful narrative description of the major events and transactions that have occurred, their impact on the financial position, and a general description of financial position and performance, a purely narrative statement may be sufficient.

It is not expected that, in preparing an IMS, companies need to look at requirements for quarterly reporting. The FSA confirms this in its April 2007 newsletter List!. *It reports that it is '. . . our expectation that IMS would be less demanding than producing quarterly reports. We would not expect issuers to apply the conventions currently required for annual and interim reporting'.*

6.2 Alternative Investment Market companies

AIM Rule 18 states that: UK

'An AIM company must prepare a half-yearly report in respect of the six month period from the end of the financial period for which financial information has been disclosed in its admission document

> *and at least every subsequent six months thereafter (apart from the final period of six months preceding its accounting reference date for its annual audited accounts).'*

Such reports should be notified to a Regulatory Information Service without delay and, in any case, within three months of the end of the relevant period. The guidance notes to the AIM Rules make clear that the Exchange will suspend AIM companies which are late in publishing their half-yearly statement.

AIM Rule 18 requires the information contained in a half-yearly report to include at least:

- *a balance sheet (i.e. a statement of financial position),*
- *an income statement (i.e. a statement of comprehensive income),*
- *a cash flow statement (i.e. a statement of cash flows); and*
- *comparative figures for the corresponding period in the preceding financial year.*

The half-yearly report is to be presented and prepared in a form consistent with that which will be adopted in the AIM company's annual accounts, having regard to the accounting standards applicable to such annual accounts. Where the half-yearly report has been audited, a statement to this effect should be included.

For periods beginning on or after 1 January 2007, all AIM companies are required to prepare their consolidated financial statements in accordance with International Accounting Standards. There is no requirement for AIM companies to prepare their half-yearly reports in accordance with IAS 34. However, the half-yearly report should be prepared in accordance with IFRS policies and presentation to comply with the AIM requirement about consistency with the annual accounts. If any reference to IFRSs is made in a half-yearly report that does not comply with IAS 34, the following sentences (or something substantively similar), should be included.

> *'The condensed set of financial statements has been prepared using accounting policies consistent with International Financial Reporting Standards (IFRSs). The same accounting policies, presentation and methods of computation are followed in the condensed set of financial statements as applied in the Group's latest annual audited financial statements [except for …]. While the financial figures included in this half-yearly report have been computed in accordance with IFRSs applicable to interim periods, this half-yearly report does not contain sufficient information to constitute an interim financial report as that term is defined in IAS 34.'*

6.3 PLUS companies

PLUS-listed companies are required to comply with the FSA's Disclosure and Transparency Rules in full and therefore the requirements are those set out at **6.1** *above.* UK

PLUS-quoted companies are required to comply with the PLUS Rules for Issuers. Issuers are required to announce interim results in respect of the first half of each financial year (beginning with the end of the last period for which audited accounts were published on admission) within three months of the end of the relevant period. Those results are required to be prepared on a basis consistent with the accounting policies which will be applied in the next annual accounts and must contain:

- *a statement by the board;*
- *the profit and loss account (i.e. statement of comprehensive income); and*
- *a statement of whether or not the information has been reviewed by the issuer's auditor.*

There is no requirement for such announcements to comply with IAS 34, nor to provide any primary statements other than the profit and loss account, nor any explanatory notes.

40 Construction contracts

1 Introduction

IAS 11 *Construction Contracts* prescribes the accounting treatment of revenue and costs associated with construction contracts. It has been effective since 1 January 1995, and was most recently amended when IAS 1 *Presentation of Financial Statements* was revised in September 2007.

This chapter discusses the requirements of IAS 11 in the following sections:

Section 2	Scope
Section 3	Types of construction contract
Section 4	Combining and segmenting contracts
Section 5	Contract revenue
Section 6	Contract costs
Section 7	Recognition of contract revenue and costs
Section 8	Recognition of amounts in the statement of financial position
Section 9	Disclosure
Section 10	Service concession arrangements
Section 11	Future developments

UK

The material in IAS 11 is fairly similar, albeit expressed in different terms, to that on long-term contracts set out in the UK standard SSAP 9 Stocks and long-term contracts. *Although IAS 11 is entitled 'Construction Contracts', its scope may not be significantly narrower than that of SSAP 9 since, under IAS 11, construction contracts include contracts for the rendering of services which are directly related to the construction of the asset, for example, those for the services of project managers and architects. Moreover, to the extent that long-term contracts are not within the scope of IAS 11, they are caught by IAS 18, which is based on essentially the same principles.*

There are some differences of substance between IAS 11 and SSAP 9. The most significant of these are as follows:

- *IAS 11 does not include the explicit requirement of SSAP 9 for the calculation of attributable profit to take into account any known inequalities of profitability in the various stages of a contract (though it will generally be appropriate to take account of such inequalities under IAS 11).*
- *Whereas SSAP 9 analyses balances related to long-term contracts between amounts recoverable on contracts (a debtor), work in progress (inventory) and payments on account (a creditor), the IAS 11 analysis is different and less detailed. In particular, no distinction is drawn between amounts recoverable on contracts and work in progress. This is similar to the approach of SSAP 9 prior to 1986.*

2 Scope

IAS 11 deals with the accounting for construction contracts in the financial statements of contractors. [IAS 11.1]

The term 'contractors' is not defined in IAS 11 but can be taken to refer to reporting entities engaged in contracting activities.

A construction contract is defined as a contract specifically negotiated for the construction of an asset or a combination of assets that are closely interrelated or interdependent in terms of their design, technology and function or their ultimate purpose or use. [IAS 11.3]

IAS 11 does not provide for a minimum duration (such as one year) for the construction contracts falling within its scope. Nor does it refer to 'long-term contracts'. The principles of IAS 11 will need to be applied for all construction contracts where the contract activity starts in one reporting period and ends in another, thus creating an allocation problem for contract income and expenses.

Where an entity is, for example, engaged in the construction of large machines that are individually built to customer order and unique specifications, such activity will also fall within the scope of IAS 11. IAS 11.4 cites as examples of construction contracts the construction of single assets such as a bridge, building, dam, pipeline, road, ship or tunnel. This is not, however, a complete list — and the manufacture of machines built to customer order and specifications with a negotiated price will fall within the definition of a construction contract.

Software development contracts for fully bespoke products meet the definition of a construction contract in IAS 11 and should be accounted for in accordance with IAS 11 including the full disclosure requirements. Software contracts for the supply of products already developed in-house or with minimal customisation fall into the scope of IAS 18 as the supply of goods.

In the context of IAS 11, construction contracts include:

[IAS 11.5]

- contracts for the rendering of services that are directly related to the construction of assets, e.g. those for the services of project managers and architects; and
- contracts for the destruction or restoration of assets, and the restoration of the environment following the demolition of assets.

IAS 11 does not address the accounting for other long-term contracts (e.g. long-term service contracts other than those referred to in the previous paragraph). The recognition of revenue under such contracts is dealt with under IAS 18 *Revenue* (see **chapter 23**). IAS 18 establishes a general principle that revenue should be recognised by reference to the stage of completion of a service transaction at the end of the reporting period, which is consistent with IAS 11. Therefore, although service contracts do not fall generally within the scope of IAS 11, they will be dealt with under IAS 18 using principles consistent with those established in IAS 11, and IAS 11 provides useful guidance in this regard.

In some circumstances, careful judgement may be required to determine whether a contract should be regarded as being for the supply of construction services or simply for the supply of goods. In particular, merely because a contract requires items to be supplied that have not yet been constructed, it does not necessarily follow that the contract is for construction services.

In July 2008, IFRIC 15 *Agreements for the Construction of Real Estate* was issued. It addresses whether an agreement is within the scope of IAS 11 or IAS 18, and when revenue from the construction of real estate should be recognised. [IFRIC 15.6] The Interpretation is discussed at **2.1** in **chapter 23**.

3 Types of construction contract

The compensation element of construction contracts can be negotiated in a number of ways. IAS 11 classifies contracts according to their compensation element as being either fixed price contracts or cost plus contracts.

A fixed price contract is defined as a construction contract in which the contractor agrees to a fixed contract price, or a fixed rate per unit of output, which in some cases is subject to cost escalation clauses. [IAS 11.3]

A cost plus contract is defined as a construction contract in which the contractor is reimbursed for allowable or otherwise defined costs, plus a percentage of those costs or a fixed fee. [IAS 11.3]

Some construction contracts may have characteristics of both fixed price and cost plus contracts. For example, a cost plus contract may nevertheless be subject to a maximum price. When assessing whether the outcome of such a contract can be estimated reliably, it will be necessary to consider the factors discussed both in **7.1.1** and in **7.1.2** below. [IAS 11.6]

4 Combining and segmenting contracts

The requirements of IAS 11 are usually applied to individual construction contracts. However, in some circumstances, it may be appropriate to treat several related contracts as forming one contract or, conversely, to treat one contract as comprising several separate contracts. The main factor in making such a determination is the manner in which the contract is negotiated. However, the Standard sets out several other factors that are to be considered, as discussed in **sections 4.1** to **4.3**.

The requirements of IAS 11 regarding the combining and segmenting of contracts are aimed at reflecting the substance of the transaction(s) rather than their legal or contractual form. The underlying question is whether the contractor negotiated the contract and the related profit independently of other related contracts, or the deal was negotiated as a package, albeit legally segregated into several contracts. The combination (or segregation) of contracts can have a significant impact, as can be seen from the following example.

Example 4

Effects of combining and segmenting contracts

An entity has five construction contracts in progress at the end of 20X1, as set out in the table below. Assume that the outcome of each contract can be estimated reliably.

	Contract					
	1	2	3	4	5	Total
	£'000	£'000	£'000	£'000	£'000	£'000
Total contract revenue	250	600	550	300	180	1,880
Total contract costs	210	450	450	350	210	1,670
Expected profit (loss)	40	150	100	(50)	(30)	210
Costs incurred to December 200X	84	390	450	35	42	1,001
Stage of completion at December 200X	40%	87%	100%	10%	20%	60%

If all of the contracts are combined and treated as one contract, the entity recognises 60 per cent of the total expected profit of £210,000 (i.e. a profit of £126,000).

If each contract is treated separately, the entity recognises the following profits and losses in 20X1:

	Contract					
	1	2	3	4	5	Total
Expected profit (loss) £'000	40	150	100	(50)	(30)	
Percentage complete	40%	87%	100%	10%	20%	
Percentage of profit (loss) recognised	40%	87%	100%	100%	100%	
Profit (loss) £'000	16	130	100	(50)	(30)	166

4.1 Segregating contracts

A construction contract may cover the construction of more than one asset. When this is the case, such projects are required to be treated as separate contracts when:

[IAS 11.8]

- separate proposals have been submitted for each asset;
- each asset has been subject to separate negotiation and the contractor and customer have been able to accept or reject that part of the contract relating to each asset; and
- the costs and revenues of each asset can be separately identified.

Example 4.1

Segmenting a contract covering the construction of more than one asset

A contractor submits two separate bids for the construction of a 10 mile section of motorway and a bridge included in the 10 mile stretch. The Government has structured the tender process such that the contract for the motorway construction will be awarded separately from the contract for the bridge construction.

Since separate proposals have been submitted for the motorway and the bridge, even if one contractor wins the work on both projects and the terms agreed with the Government for both projects are included in one legal contract, each project, the bridge and the motorway, will be accounted for separately under IAS 11. The contractor will need to have a cost system in place to allow segregation of costs between the two parts of the contract.

The key determinant is whether the customer is able to accept one proposal and reject the other. Segmenting contracts is not a matter of choice, but is required when the criteria in IAS 11.8 are met.

4.2 Combining contracts

A group of contracts should be treated as a single contract, notwithstanding that the contracts may be with different counter parties, when: [IAS 11.9]

- the group of contracts is negotiated as a single package;
- the contracts are so closely interrelated that they are, in effect, part of a single project with an overall profit margin; and
- the contracts are performed concurrently or in a continuous sequence.

Example 4.2

Combining contracts to be accounted for as a single contract

A contractor submits one bid for the construction of a 10 mile section of motorway and a bridge which is at one end of the 10 mile stretch. The bridge is in a different local authority district from the motorway and, therefore, although only one bid is submitted because the two local authorities have agreed to work together on the construction of the road, separate contracts exist for the bridge and the motorway because the counter party (the relevant local authority) differs in each case.

Since one proposal was submitted for the motorway and the bridge, even if two separate contracts are eventually signed, the contracts have been negotiated as a single package. The bid was submitted on the basis that one project could not be awarded without the other, and so the contractor must have worked out the expected gross margin on both projects together. Therefore, the two separate contracts will be accounted for as one contract under IAS 11.

For combination to be required, the group of contracts must be performed concurrently or in a continuous sequence. If performance is separated by a period of time long enough to result in differing economic environments in the periods of performance, then separate accounting should be applied.

Combining contracts is not a matter of choice, but is required when the criteria in IAS 11.9 are met.

4.3 Construction of additional assets

A construction contract may provide an option for the construction of an additional asset or the customer may amend the contract to include the construction of an additional asset. In such circumstances, the construction of the additional asset is required to be treated as a separate construction contract when:

[IAS 11.10]

- the asset differs significantly in design, technology or function from the asset or assets covered by the original contract; or
- the price of the asset is negotiated without regard to the original contract price.

Example 4.3

Construction of an additional asset to be treated as a separate contract?

A contractor is nearing completion of a 10 mile stretch of motorway under a contract with the Government. Under the contract, the contractor is paid £10 million per mile. If the Government and contractor amend the contract to cover 13 miles of motorway at the same rate of £10 million per mile, the amendment is considered part of the original contract since the price of the amendment is the same as originally negotiated, and the asset (motorway) does not differ significantly from the asset (motorway) covered by the original contract.

5 Contract revenue

In order to apply the accounting principles specified by IAS 11, an entity must be able to estimate contract revenue and costs. This section deals with the components of contract revenue.

The measurement of contract revenue is affected by a variety of uncertainties that depend on the outcome of future events. The estimates often need to be revised as events occur and uncertainties are resolved. Therefore, the estimate of contract revenue may increase or decrease from one period to the next, for example as a result of:

[IAS 11.12]

- variations or claims agreed between the contractor and the customer in a period subsequent to that in which the contract was initially agreed;
- in the case of a fixed price contract, cost escalation clauses;

- penalties arising from delays caused by the contractor in the completion of the contract; and
- in the case of a fixed price contract involving a fixed price per unit of output, increases or decreases in the number of units.

The Standard stipulates that the entity's estimate of contract revenue at any point in time should comprise:

[IAS 11.11]

- the initial amount of revenue agreed in the construction contract; and
- variations, claims and incentive payments to the extent that it is probable that they will result in revenue and that they are capable of being reliably measured.

> The revenue recognition criteria for variations, claims and incentive payments are the same as for other types of revenue. The additional criteria discussed in the following sections are intended to illustrate how the general revenue recognition criteria should be applied to variations, claims and incentive payments.

5.1 Variations

A variation is defined in IAS 11.13 as an instruction by the customer for a change in the scope of the work to be performed under the contract. Depending on the circumstances, variations may lead to increases or decreases in contract revenue. For example, once a project has been negotiated, a customer may finalise the design of the item to be constructed, and the changes in design may have implications for the amount of work required from the contractor.

In practice, problems arise when assessing the likelihood of recovery of variations and, thus, whether they should be included in contract revenue. IAS 11 indicates that a variation should be included in contract revenue when:

[IAS 11.14]

- it is probable that the customer will approve the variation and the amount of revenue arising from the variation; and
- the amount of revenue can be reliably measured.

In many cases, it is a matter of judgement as to whether a variation will be approved by the customer and, due to the fact that the amount recovered is often based on a negotiation process, the amount included in contract revenue relating to variations is also usually an estimate.

5.2 Claims

A claim is defined in IAS 11.14 as an amount that the contractor seeks to collect from the customer or another party as reimbursement for costs not included in the contract price. A claim in this context does not usually imply that a legal claim has been filed in a court of law. Claims may arise from customer-caused delays, errors in specifications or design, or disputed variations in contract work. Since claims are initiated by the contractor, their recoverability may be even more uncertain than that of variations. The amount included in contract revenue with respect to claims is therefore an estimate based on management's judgement. As for variations, claims are often settled at the end of the contract as a result of a negotiation. IAS 11 indicates that claims should only be included in contract revenue when:

[IAS 11.14]

- negotiations have reached an advanced stage such that it is probable that the customer will accept the claim; and
- the amount that it is probable will be accepted by the customer can be measured reliably.

5.3 Incentive payments

Incentive payments are additional amounts paid to the contractor if specified performance standards are met or exceeded. Commonly, such incentive payments relate to completion dates and, thus, the earlier the work is completed, the more contract revenue will be receivable. IAS 11 indicates that incentive payments should be included in contract revenue when:

[IAS 11.15]

- the contract is sufficiently advanced that it is probable that the specified performance standards will be met or exceeded; and
- the amount of the incentive payments can be measured reliably.

5.4 Sales revenue denominated in foreign currency

Where a construction contract is entered into with an overseas entity, and the contract revenue is denominated in the foreign currency in which that overseas entity operates, the revenue recognised incrementally over the course of the contract will be the incremental foreign currency revenue translated at the spot rate as construction activity occurs. This treatment reflects the general requirement of IAS 21 *The Effects of Changes in Foreign Exchange Rates* that foreign currency transactions should be recognised by applying to the foreign currency amount the spot exchange rate between the functional currency and the foreign currency at the date of the transaction. [IAS 21.21] In practice, if incremental revenue accrues fairly steadily over a period, it may be acceptable to translate it at an average rate for that period.

6 Contract costs

6.1 Components of contract costs

Contract costs should comprise the components listed in the following table.

Costs that relate directly to the specific contract. [IAS 11.16(a)]	Including: [IAS 11.17] • site labour costs, including supervision; • costs of materials used in construction; • depreciation of plant and equipment used on the contract; • cost of moving plant, equipment and materials to and from the contract site; • costs of hiring plant and equipment; • costs of design and technical assistance that are directly related to the contract; • the estimated costs of rectification work and guarantee work, including expected warranty costs; and • claims from third parties. These costs may be reduced by incidental income such as income from the sale of surplus materials or equipment at the end of the contract.

Costs that are attributable to contract activity in general and can be allocated to the contract. [IAS 11.16(b)] Allocation should be based on the normal level of construction activity. Methods used should be systematic and rational, and applied consistently to all costs having similar characteristics. [IAS 11.18]	Including: [IAS 11.18)] • insurance; • costs of design and technical assistance that ar not directly related to a specific contract; • construction overheads; and • borrowing costs capitalised under IAS 23 *Borrowing Costs* Any borrowing costs capitalised under IAS 23 should be reduced by any investment income arising on the temporary investment of funds borrowed specifically for the assets concerned. For example, where a contract is funded by advances from the customer, and no interest is charged on those advances, any interest income earned on the temporary investment of those advances is treated as a negative contract cost.
Other costs that are specifically chargeable to the customer under the terms of the contract. [IAS 11.16(c)]	These may include general administration costs and development costs for which reimbursement is specified in the terms of the contract. [IAS 11.19]

When costs cannot be allocated or attributed to a particular contract, they are not included in contract costs. The Standard identifies the following costs that should be excluded from contract costs:

[IAS 11.20]

- general administration costs for which reimbursement is not specified in the contract;
- selling costs;
- research and development costs for which reimbursement is not specified in the contract; and
- depreciation of idle plant and equipment that is not used on a particular contract.

6.2 Pre-contract costs

6.2.1 Costs incurred in securing a contract

Costs should generally be allocated to a contract only from the date of securing the contract. However, IAS 11.21 specifies that the direct costs associated with securing a contract should be included in the cost of the contract if they can be separately identified and measured reliably, and it is probable that the contract will be obtained. Otherwise, they should be expensed in the period in which they are incurred.

Consider the example of a software design company that develops software specifically suited for a particular customer. In order to secure a contract with a particular customer, the entity incurs costs related to determining what steps and internal costs will need to be incurred in order to bid on a project. Such costs may include labour costs, general administration costs, research and development costs, etc. Many of these costs are incurred prior to securing the contract (i.e. pre-contract costs).

The inclusion of such costs in contract costs will only be appropriate in very exceptional circumstances. Paragraph 89 of the Framework states that an asset is recognised in the statement of financial position when it is probable that the future economic benefits will flow to the entity and the asset has a cost or value that can be measured reliably. The IFRIC Agenda Committee agreed at its August 2002 meeting that guidance in IAS 11.21 and the Framework are clear, and that '. . . a great deal of care should be taken when determining whether pre-contract costs should be capitalised.' This conclusion is supported by IAS 37.33 which states that contingent assets should not be recognised and that, in order to justify recognition of an asset in this type of situation, the realisation of income must be '... virtually certain . . .'

These factors suggest that, unless it is probable that the contract will be obtained, and the realisation of income is virtually certain, pre-contract costs should be expensed when incurred.

6.2.2 *Pre-contract costs that have already been expensed*

If pre-contract costs of the nature referred to in **6.2.1** are recognised as an expense in the period in which they are incurred, and the contract is subsequently awarded to the reporting entity, the costs should not be included in contract costs. [IAS 11.21]

Example 6.2.2

Expensed pre-contract costs

An entity incurred £3 million of pre-contract costs during December 20X1, which were directly attributable to the anticipated contract and which the entity believed would be recoverable under that contract. However, due to the uncertainty of the outcome, the costs were expensed when they were incurred in 20X1. The contract was ultimately signed in 20X2 for a price of £18 million. The entity's remaining estimated costs to complete the contract were £6 million.

Since the pre-contract costs were already expensed in the 20X1 financial year, they should be excluded from contract costs. The entity should account for this contract prospectively, recognising £18 million of contract revenue and £6 million of contract costs as work on the contract is performed.

It is not appropriate to include pre-contract costs that have previously been expensed in contract costs for the purposes of determining the stage of completion of a contract, when the stage of completion is determined on a proportionate-cost basis. Such costs are excluded both from the measure of contract costs incurred to date and the estimate of total contract costs.

7 Recognition of contract revenue and costs

As a general principle, IAS 11 requires that construction contracts are accounted for using the percentage of completion method, i.e. that contract revenue and contract costs associated with a contract should be recognised as revenue and expenses respectively by reference to the stage of completion of the contract at the end of the reporting period.

Under this method, at the end of the reporting period an entity estimates the outcome, or total profit or loss, expected to be achieved on a contract. As part of this process, the entity estimates the stage or percentage of completion of the contract. When the entity is able to make a reliable estimate of the outcome of the contract, it applies the estimated percentage of completion to the total expected revenue and expenses related to the contract to determine the amount of revenue and cost to be recognised in the period. If an entity expects that a loss will be made on the contract, it is recognised immediately. [IAS 11.22]

It is not acceptable under IAS 11 to recognise all of the revenue and costs related to a contract at the end of the contract (sometimes referred to as the 'completed-contract' method).

Under UK GAAP, before the issue of Application Note G to FRS 5 and UITF 40 Revenue Recognition and Service Contracts, *some companies followed the 'completed-contract' method for short-term contracts (i.e. contracts that do not meet the definition of a long-term contract under* UK

SSAP 9) and recognised revenue and profits only on contract completion. No distinction is drawn in IAS 11 (or in IAS 18) between short and long-term contracts. Accordingly, regardless of UK historical practice, when adopting IFRSs, companies must use the percentage of completion method for all construction contracts, whether short or long.

7.1 Estimating the outcome of a contract

Initially, the entity should consider whether it is in a position to make a reliable estimate of the outcome of a contract. The conditions imposed by the Standard for both fixed price and cost plus contracts are discussed in the following sections.

7.1.1 Fixed price contracts

For fixed price contracts, IAS 11.23 specifies that the outcome of a construction contract can be estimated reliably when all of the following conditions are satisfied:

- total contract revenue can be measured reliably;
- it is probable that the economic benefits associated with the contract will flow to the entity;
- both the contract costs to complete the contract and the stage of contract completion at the end of the reporting period can be measured reliably; and
- the contract costs attributable to the contract can be clearly identified and measured reliably so that actual contract costs incurred can be compared with prior estimates.

7.1.2 Cost plus contracts

For cost plus contracts, IAS 11.24 specifies that the outcome of a construction contract can be estimated reliably when both of the following conditions are satisfied:

- it is probable that the economic benefits associated with the contract will flow to the entity; and
- the contract costs attributable to the contract, whether or not specifically reimbursable, can be clearly identified and measured reliably.

Thus, when an entity enters into a cost plus contract, in order to estimate reliably the outcome of the contract, it must be able to identify contract costs attributable to the contract, whether or not they are specifically reimbursable. Unlike a fixed price contract, the amount of revenue related to a cost plus contract is generally unknown but can be calculated based on the terms of the contract and the estimated costs of the contract. In addition, in order to use the percentage of completion method, it must be probable that the economic benefits will flow to the entity.

7.2 Estimating the stage of completion

For both fixed price and cost plus contracts, the percentage of completion of a contract at the end of the reporting period must be estimated. In practice, progress payments or advances received from a customer are not normally reliable indicators of the percentage of completion of a contract, since they are usually intended to fund the activities of the contractor rather than to reimburse him for work performed to date. IAS 11 suggests several bases for estimating the percentage of completion, including:

[IAS 11.30]

- the proportion that contract costs incurred for work performed to date bear to the estimated total contract costs;
- surveys of work performed; and
- completion of a physical proportion of the contract work.

The selection of the most appropriate method for the determination of the stage of completion of a project will be made by each entity according to its own circumstances and the nature of its business. For example, the main contractor will normally hire an architect to certify the progress of contracts and, therefore, surveys of work performed are readily available for the purpose of ascertaining the percentage of completion of a contract. On the other hand, subcontractors may be more likely to rely on estimates of the proportion that costs incurred to date bear to the estimated total contract costs or, where appropriate, on the completion of a physical proportion of the contract work.

SSAP 9, the UK equivalent of IAS 11, requires the calculation of attributable profit to take into account any known inequalities of profitability in the various stages of a contract. IAS 11 includes no such explicit requirement. Nevertheless, when identifying the most appropriate method by which to apply IAS 11, it will generally be appropriate to take account of such inequalities, since to do so will give a more accurate estimate of the extent to which a construction contract has been performed, and of the costs associated with that performance. UK

When the stage of completion is determined by reference to the contract costs incurred to date, only those contract costs that reflect work performed are included in costs incurred to date. For example, contract costs that relate to future activity on the contract, such as costs of materials that have been purchased but not yet used, or payments made to subcontractors in advance of work being performed, would be excluded from costs incurred to date. However, if materials have been made specifically for the contract, they are included in contract costs even if they have not yet been used, on the basis that it is unlikely that they would be suitable for use on other contracts. [IAS 11.31]

Example 7.2A

Treatment of prepaid costs in estimating the percentage of completion (1)

A contractor undertakes a 3 year contract. At the end of Year 1, management estimates are as follows:

	£
Revenue	1,000
Costs incurred to date	(300)
Estimated costs to complete	(600)
Estimated gross profit	100

During Year 1, however, the contractor purchased materials for £50 to be used in Year 2. Therefore, when calculating the percentage of completion of this contract, based on the proportion of costs incurred to date to total costs of the contract, an adjustment is made in respect of those purchases:

	£
Costs incurred to date	300
Less: materials purchased for future years	(50)
Costs incurred related to work performed to date	250
Total estimated costs	900
Percentage of completion at end of Year 1	28%

Therefore, in Year 1, contract revenue of £280 and contract costs of £250 are recognised in profit or loss.

At a minimum, at the end of each reporting period, an entity reviews its estimates relating to the outcome of a contract and makes revisions as appropriate. Since the percentage of completion method is applied to each contract on a cumulative basis, revisions are treated as changes in estimates and are used in estimating the percentage of completion and the outcome of the contract in the period of change and in future periods. As such, prior periods are not adjusted. [IAS 11.38] In practice, most contractors review progress and expected outcomes much more frequently than at the end of each reporting period in order to maintain control over the project.

Example 7.2B

Treatment of prepaid costs in estimating the percentage of completion (2)

The facts are the same as in **example 7.2A**. In Year 2, costs of £300 are incurred. Management estimates that costs of £350 will be incurred in Year 3.

	£
Costs incurred in Year 1 relating to work performed to date	250
Costs incurred in Year 1 relating to materials used in Year 2	50
Other costs incurred in Year 2	300
Costs incurred to date	600
Estimated costs to complete	350
Total estimated costs	950
Estimated revenue	1,000
Estimated gross profit	50
Percentage of completion at end of Year 2	63%

No adjustment is made to the revenue or expenses recognised in Year 1 due to the change in estimate in Year 2. The change will be reflected in Year 2 and Year 3.

Therefore, in Year 2, contract revenue of £350 (i.e. £1,000 x 63% – £280) and contract costs of £350 (i.e. £600 – £250) are recognised in profit or loss.

For a discussion of the accounting treatment in the circumstances where a reliable estimate of the outcome of a contract cannot be made, see **7.6** below.

7.3 Recognition of contract losses

When an entity estimates that the outcome of a contract will be a loss, the expected loss is recognised as an expense immediately. [IAS 11.36] The amount of the loss is the expected loss on the entire contract, and thus is determined without reference to:

[IAS 11.37]

- whether or not work has commenced on the contract;
- the stage of completion of contract activity; or
- the amount of profits expected to arise on other contracts which are not treated as the same contract under the rules of IAS 11 (see **section 4** above).

Example 7.3

Recognition of contract losses

The facts are the same as in **example 7.2B**, except that in Year 2 the estimated costs to complete the contract in Year 3 are £500.

	£
Costs incurred to date	600
Estimated costs to complete	500
Total estimated costs	1,100
Estimated revenue	1,000
Estimated loss	(100)
Percentage of completion at end of Year 2	54.5%

Since management now estimates a loss on the contract, the £100 loss is recognised immediately as an expense in Year 2 when the estimate is made. In addition, any profit recognised in Year 1 is reversed in Year 2, with the result that the total loss reported in Year 2 is £130.

Accordingly, in Year 2, contract revenue of £265 (i.e. £1,000 x 54.5% – £280) is recognised in profit or loss. The loss relating to work already performed is £55 (cumulative revenue of £545 less cumulative costs of £600, or 54.5% of total losses of £100), so a provision is required for future losses of £45. Thus, in Year 2, total contract costs (including the provision for future losses) of £395 (£600 – £250 + £45) are recognised in profit or loss.

7.4 Recognition of contract revenue

In order to recognise the revenue earned to date on a contract, it must be probable that the associated future economic benefits will flow to the entity and that their amount can be estimated reliably. In general, the amount of future economic benefits can be estimated reliably when it is possible to estimate reliably the outcome of a contract as described above. If it becomes apparent subsequent to recognition as income that the revenue related to a contract will not be collectable, the uncollectable amount is recognised as an expense rather than as an adjustment to contract revenue. [IAS 11.28]

The amount of revenue recognised in a period is determined by applying the estimated percentage of completion at the end of the reporting period to total contract revenue.

7.5 Recognition of contract costs

When the proportion of contract costs incurred for work performed to date to total contract costs is used to estimate the percentage of completion, this generally results in contract costs being expensed in the period incurred. If costs have been incurred which relate to future activity on the contract, they may be carried forward provided that it is probable that they will be recovered under the contract. [IAS 11.27] Such costs may relate to, but are not limited to, materials purchased for future use or advance payments to subcontractors.

If other methods are used to estimate the percentage of completion on a contract, this may result in contract costs being recognised in the statement of financial position and charged to profit or loss in later periods.

When contract costs are not probable of being recovered, they are recognised as an expense immediately. IAS 11 gives the following examples of circumstances where the recoverability of contract costs incurred may not be probable, and where contract costs may need to be recognised as an expense immediately:

[IAS 11.34]

- contracts that are not fully enforceable, i.e. their validity is seriously in question;
- contracts whose completion is subject to the outcome of pending litigation or legislation;
- contracts relating to properties that are likely to be condemned or expropriated;
- contracts where the customer is unable to meet its obligations; and
- contracts where the contractor is unable to complete the contract or otherwise meet its obligations under the contract.

7.6 When the outcome of a contract cannot be estimated reliably

When the outcome of a contract cannot be estimated reliably, IAS 11.32 specifies that:

- revenue should be recognised only to the extent of contract costs incurred that it is probable will be recoverable; and
- contract costs should be recognised as an expense in the period in which they are incurred.

When the outcome of a contract cannot be estimated, it is inappropriate to recognise any profit on that contract. This is achieved by limiting the revenue recognised to the extent of costs incurred that are expected to be recoverable, with all costs being recognised as expenses as incurred. This method is often referred to as the zero profit method.

Even where the outcome of a contract cannot be estimated reliably, it may be possible to foresee that total contract costs will exceed total contract revenues, i.e. that not all contract costs will be recoverable. In such circumstances, the expected excess of total contract costs over total contract revenue should be recognised as an expense immediately.

Example 7.6

Outcome of contract cannot be estimated reliably

The facts are the same as in **example 7.2A**, except that management is unable to estimate reliably the costs that will be incurred in order to complete the contract.

Therefore, revenue is only recognised to the extent of costs incurred. Thus £250 of revenue is recognised and £250 of expenses are recognised, resulting in no gross profit being recognised in the period.

When the uncertainties that prevented reliable estimation of the outcome of a construction contract no longer exist, contract revenue and expenses are recognised using the percentage of completion method. [IAS 11.35]

IAS 11 does not address the disclosure in the period in which the outcome of a contract becomes capable of reliable estimation. In the first period in which the percentage of completion method is applied, the profit on the contract that has not been recognised in previous periods will be recognised. This recognition would lead to a distortion of the profit figure included in the financial statements related to a particular contract. Although not specifically required by IAS 11, it would be good practice to disclose the reason for such distortion, if significant. Such disclosure might also fall to be required under IAS 1(2007).97 (previously IAS 1(2003).86) (see **section 5.3.1** of **chapter 3**).

8 Recognition of amounts in the statement of financial position

At the end of each reporting period, for all contracts in progress for which costs incurred plus recognised profits (less recognised losses) exceed progress billings, a gross amount due from customers for contract work is recognised as an asset in the statement of financial position. The amount is disclosed separately from inventories to which IAS 2 applies.

Similarly, at the end of each reporting period, for all contracts in progress for which progress billings exceed costs incurred plus recognised profits (less recognised losses), a gross amount due to customers for contract work is recognised as a liability in the statement of financial position.

Progress billings are amounts billed for work performed on a contract whether or not they have been paid by the customer. [IAS 11.41]

The wording used in IAS 11 of 'gross amount due from customers' may be misleading in that actual trade amounts receivable from customers (i.e. amounts already billed) are not part of this figure. These are recognised as separate assets in the statement of financial position.

UK

IAS 11 differs from SSAP 9 in that the amounts included in the statement of financial position are more aggregated under the former. SSAP 9 analyses balances related to long-term contracts between amounts recoverable on contracts (a debtor), work in progress (inventory) and payments on account (deducted from items above, or a creditor). This follows from the UK practice of including work in progress on contracts within the heading for 'stocks and work in progress'. IAS 11 draws no distinction between amounts recoverable on contracts and work in progress, but presents contract balances to which IAS 11 applies separately from inventory to which IAS 2 applies.

Example 8A

Presentation of amounts in the statement of financial position

A contractor enters into a 3 year contract. At the outset, estimated revenue is £10,000 and estimated total costs are £8,000.

During Year 2, however, management revises its estimate of total costs to be incurred and, thus, the outcome of the contract. As a result, during Year 2, a loss for the year is recognised on the contract, even though the contract will still be profitable overall.

	Year 1	Year 2	Year 3
	£	£	£
Estimated revenue	10,000	10,000	10,000
Estimated total costs	8,000	9,000	9,000
Estimated total profit	2,000	1,000	1,000
Costs incurred to date	4,000	6,750	9,000
Percentage of completion	50%	75%	100%
Cumulative recognised profit	1,000	750	1,000
Recognised profit (loss) in year	1,000	(250)	250

Progress billings of £4,000, £4,000 and £1,000 are made on the last day of each year and are received in the first month of the following year.

The asset or liability at the end of each year is:

Costs incurred	4,000	6,750	9,000
Recognised profits	1,000	1,000	1,250
Recognised losses	-	(250)	(250)
Progress billings	(4,000)	(8,000)	(9,000)
Amount recognised as an asset / (liability)	1,000	(500)	1,000

In addition, at each year-end, the entity recognises a trade receivable for the progress billings outstanding at the end of the year of £4,000, £4,000 and £1,000 respectively.

Gross amounts due from customers will generally be considered monetary items. Monetary items are defined in IAS 21.8 as 'units of currency held and assets and liabilities to be received or paid in a fixed or determinable number of units of currency'. IAS 11.43 and IAS 11.44 provide guidance on how the gross amounts due from and due to customers are determined. Depending on the level of progress billings, the amount may change from a liability to an asset, and that amount would then be settled or recovered by additional work performed subsequently, profits or losses recognised, or any additional work performed in completing the contract.

In the absence of any other factors, the amount due from customers is a recognised asset that is probable of being recovered from the customer in cash (provided those are the terms of the arrangement) once the amount has been billed. While the right to cash may not have been established contractually through the billing (see **2.7** in **chapter 13**), the nature of the asset is monetary nonetheless.

However, gross amounts due to customers will generally be considered non-monetary items where the contractor is expected to fulfil its obligations through work performed. Amounts due to customers may arise due to high progress billings in the early parts of the construction project that are in excess of the costs incurred plus recognised profits and less recognised losses. Such an obligation is generally offset by work performed at a later stage of the project, not through settlement by units of currency. It may occur, depending on the circumstances, that an amount due to a customer becomes payable in units of currency. In that case those amounts should be classified as monetary items.

9 Disclosure

9.1 Accounting policies

The methods used to determine the contract revenue recognised in the period and the methods used to determine the stage of completion of contracts in progress should be disclosed. [IAS 11.39 (b) & (c)]

9.2 Contract revenue

The amount of contract revenue recognised as revenue in the period should be disclosed. [IAS 11.39(a)]

9.3 Statement of financial position

The following should be disclosed for contracts in progress at the end of the reporting period:

[IAS 11.40]

- the aggregate amount of costs incurred and recognised profits (less recognised losses) to date;
- the amount of advances received; and
- the amount of retentions.

Advances are amounts received by the contractor before the related work is performed. [IAS 11.41] Advances are commonly made in order to fund the purchase of materials by a contractor before the related work on a contract begins. Advances are recognised as liabilities until the related revenue is earned.

Retentions are amounts of progress billings that are not paid until the satisfaction of conditions specified in the contract for the payment of such amounts or until defects have been rectified. [IAS 11.41] Retentions are recognised as receivables in the statement of financial position of the contractor.

An entity should present:

[IAS 11.42]

- the gross amount due from customers for contract work as an asset; and
- the gross amount due to customers for contract work as a liability.

These terms are explained in **section 8**.

10 Service concession arrangements

10.1 Background

In November 2006, the IASB published IFRIC 12 *Service Concession Arrangements*. Service concession arrangements are arrangements whereby a government or other body ('the grantor') grants contracts for the supply of public services, such as roads, energy distribution, prisons, or hospitals, to a private sector entity ('the operator'). This is often referred to as a 'public-to-private' arrangement.

A typical arrangement that falls within the scope of the Interpretation is a 'build-operate-transfer' arrangement. An operator constructs the infrastructure to be used to provide the public service and operates and maintains that infrastructure for a specified period of time. The operator is paid for its services over the period of the arrangement. The arrangement is governed by a contract that sets out performance standards, pricing mechanisms, and arrangements for arbitrating disputes. [IFRIC 12.2] Alternatively the operator may upgrade existing infrastructure and maintain and operate the upgraded infrastructure. This second type of arrangement is sometimes referred to as a 'rehabilitate-operate-transfer' arrangement.

Outsourcing the operation of an entity's internal services (e.g. employee restaurant, building maintenance, accounting or IT functions) does not constitute a service concession arrangement. [SIC-29.1]

Some common features of service concession arrangements are described below.

[IFRIC 12.3]

- The grantor is a public sector entity, including a governmental body, or a private sector entity to which the responsibility for the service has been devolved.

- The operator is responsible for at least some of the management of the infrastructure and related services and does not merely act as an agent on behalf of the grantor.

- The contract sets the initial prices to be levied by the operator and regulates price revisions over the period of the service arrangement.

- The operator is obliged to hand over the infrastructure to the grantor in a specified condition at the end of the period of the arrangement, for little or no incremental consideration irrespective of which party initially financed it.

It is important to note that for a public service obligation to exist, the services offered do not have to be made available to all members of the public. Rather, the services need to be available to benefit members of the public. For example, prisons are only open to those required to stay there by law, and cannot be accessed by members of the public seeking accommodation. However, prisons would still be considered to provide services to the public.

UK

Private Finance Initiative arrangements (PFI), which are a common example of service concession arrangements in the UK, are considered in Application Note F to FRS 5 Reporting the Substance of Transactions. *Application Note F takes a different approach to accounting for such arrangements than that used in IFRIC 12 and as such it is not possible to list all the differences.*

Application note F requires the application of the following approach:

(1) *Consider whether the contract can be separated into property and service elements. If the elements can be separated then, once any service elements have been disregarded, apply SSAP 21 Accounting for leases and hire purchase contracts to the payments for property. This treatment is required where the residual element does not include any service, i.e. the resulting residual payment is only in respect of the provision of an asset.*

(2) *Apply FRS 5 to assess which party has the risks and benefits of the property where the residual element of the payment includes both payment for the provision of an asset and payment for non-separable services. FRS 5 describes seven risks that must be considered in determining which party has the asset of the property.*

(3) *Recognise the property as an asset of the party that has the risks associated with the property. Where the grantor recognises the asset, the grantor also recognises a liability to the operator for construction services provided to date and the operator recognises a debtor (financial asset).*

The scope of Application Note F is wider than IFRIC 12. Application Note F provides guidance on the circumstances where it is appropriate for the operator to recognise the property as an asset. IFRIC 12 does not include such arrangements within its scope. Further, Application Note F provides guidance for grantors in contrast to IFRIC 12 which specifically excludes such guidance.

10.2 Scope of IFRIC 12

A public-to-private arrangement will not automatically fall within IFRIC 12; specified scope criteria need to be satisfied. The following flow chart summarises the scope criteria of IFRIC 12.

[Extract from IFRIC 12 (Information Note 1)]

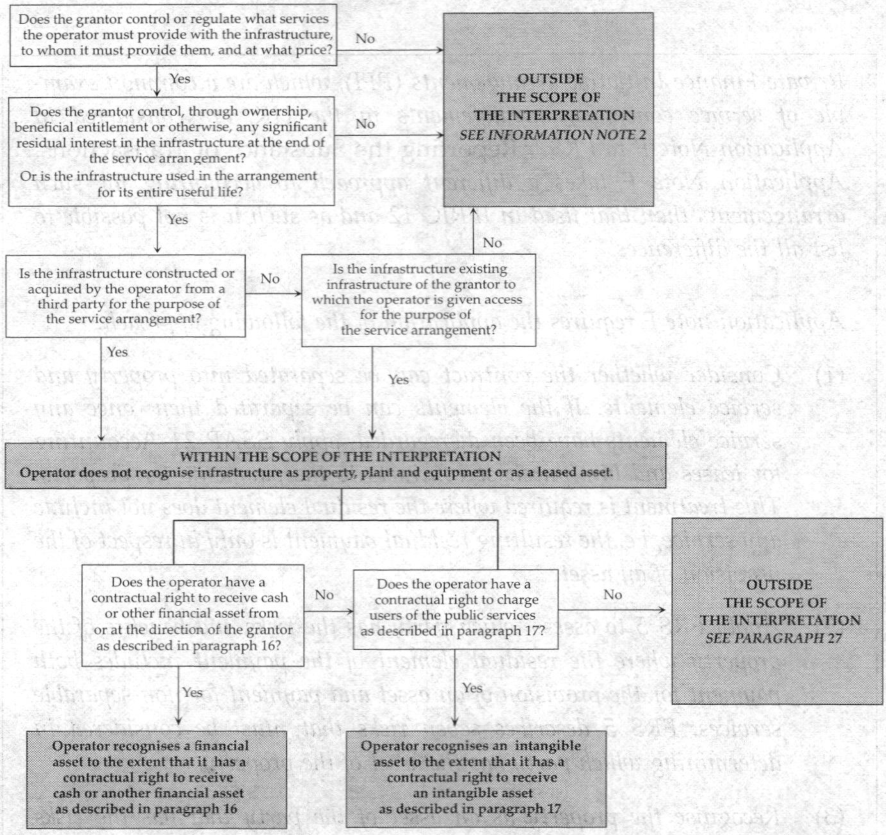

The Interpretation applies to public-to-private service concession arrangements if:

[IFRIC 12.5]

(a) the grantor controls or regulates what services the operator must provide with the infrastructure, to whom it must provide them, and at what price; and

(b) the grantor controls – through ownership, beneficial entitlement or otherwise – any significant residual interest in the infrastructure at the end of the term of the arrangement.

This means that IFRIC 12 applies to a public-to-private service concession arrangement where the infrastructure is used for its entire useful life ('whole of life assets') provided condition (a) above is met. This applies irrespective of which party controls any remaining insignificant residual interest. [IFRIC 12.6]

A grantor does not need to have complete control over price but would need to have an element of control. If a cap is set that would only ever take effect in very remote circumstances then the grantor is not considered to have control over the price, e.g. stating in the contract that a road toll must not exceed £1000, when the anticipated toll is £2. Such a price capping mechanism would be considered non-substantive and the arrangement would be outside the scope of IFRIC 12.

When considering whether a significant residual interest exists, the residual value should be estimated as the infrastructure's current value as if it was of the age and condition expected as at the end of the contract. An asset which will only be able to be sold for scrap value is unlikely to have a significant residual value at the end of the contract. Conversely, a building with a 50 year useful life that is only used in a service concession arrangement for 20 years is likely to have a significant residual value at the end of the arrangement, and if the building is retained by the operator the arrangement would be outside the scope of IFRIC 12.

IFRIC 12 does not address the circumstance in which the grantor provides an indemnification to the operator in respect of the residual value of the assets at the end of the arrangement. Where such an indemnification is provided the facts and circumstances relating to the arrangement will need to be analysed to determine whether the arrangement is within the scope of the Interpretation.

The Interpretation applies to both:

[IFRIC 12.7]

(a) infrastructure that the operator constructs or acquires from a third party for the purpose of the service arrangement; and

(b) existing infrastructure to which the grantor gives the operator access for the purpose of the service arrangement.

The requirements may apply to previously recognised property, plant and equipment of the operator where the derecognition criteria of IFRSs are met. If the operator is considered to have disposed of the asset by passing the significant risks and rewards of that asset to the grantor, then the operator should derecognise that asset in accordance with IAS 16.67. For further guidance relating to the derecognition of property, plant and equipment see **section 9** of **chapter 6**. Having disposed of its previously held asset the operator would need to determine whether the arrangement was within the scope of IFRIC 12.

IFRIC 12 does not scope in private-to-private arrangements but it could be applied to such arrangements by analogy under the hierarchy set out in paragraphs 7–12 of IAS 8 *Accounting Policies, Changes in Accounting Estimates and Errors*. [IFRIC 12.BC14]

The Interpretation specifically excludes the accounting by grantors, i.e. public sector accounting. [IFRIC 12.9]

Where an arrangement does not fall within the scope of IFRIC 12 it may fall within the scope of other IFRS pronouncements. The following table, extracted from Information Note 2 to IFRIC 12, indicates which Standards may be applicable:

Category	Lessee	Service provider			Owner	
Typical arrangement types	Lease (e.g. Operator leases asset from grantor)	Service and/or maintenance contract (specific tasks e.g. debt collection)	Rehabilitate-operate-transfer	Build-operate-transfer	Build-own-operate	100% Divestment/ Privatisation/ Corporation
Asset ownership	Grantor				Operator	
Capital investment	Grantor		Operator			
Demand risk	Shared	Grantor	Operator and/or Grantor		Operator	
Typical duration	8–20 years	1–5 years	25–30 years			Indefinite (or may be limited by licence)
Residual interest	Grantor				Operator	
Relevant IFRSs	IAS 17	IAS 18	IFRIC 12		IAS 16	

When assessing the contractual terms of some arrangements it is possible that they could fall within the scope of both IFRIC 4 *Determining whether an Arrangement contains a Lease* and IFRIC 12. To eliminate any inconsistencies between the accounting treatment for contracts which have similar economic effects, the IFRIC amended IFRIC 4 to specify that if a contract appears to fall within the scope of both Interpretations then the requirements of IFRIC 12 prevail.

10.3 The accounting models

10.3.1 Revenue

An operator provides services under the terms of the contractual arrangements and receives payment for its services over the period of the arrangement. This typically involves the operator constructing or upgrading infrastructure which is used to provide a public service and then being responsible for operating and maintaining that infrastructure for a specified period of time. [IFRIC 12.12]

Revenues and costs of the operator relating to the construction or upgrade services phase of the contract are accounted for in accordance with IAS 11 *Construction Contracts* [IFRIC 12.14] and the revenue and costs relating to the operating phase are accounted for in accordance with IAS 18 *Revenue.* Where the operator performs more than one service under a single contract or arrangement the consideration received or receivable is allocated by reference to the fair value of services delivered when the amounts are separately identifiable. [IFRIC 12.13]

The nature of the consideration determines its subsequent accounting treatment (see **10.3.2** below).

10.3.2 Determining the nature of the operator's asset

The infrastructure within the scope of IFRIC 12 is not recognised as property, plant and equipment of the operator. This is because the operator does not have the right to control the asset, but merely has access to the infrastructure in order to provide the public service in accordance with the terms specified in the contract. [IFRIC 12.11] It is also not treated as a lease as the operator does not have the right to control the use of the asset. [IFRIC 12.BC 23] Instead, the operator's right to consideration is recorded as a financial asset, an intangible asset or a combination of the two.

The requirements of IFRIC 12 regarding the nature of the asset to be recognised can be summarised as follows

Operator's rights	Classification	Examples
Unconditional, contractual right to receive cash or other financial asset from the grantor.	Financial asset [IFRIC 12.16]	• Operator receives a fixed amount from the grantor over term of arrangement.
		• Operator has a right to charge users over term of arrangement, but any shortfall will be reimbursed by the grantor.
Amounts to be received are contingent on the extent that the public uses the service.	Intangible asset [IFRIC 12.17]	• Operator has a right to charge users over the term of the arrangement.
		• Operator has a right to charge the grantor based on usage of the services over the term of the arrangement.
Consideration received partly in the form of a financial asset and partly in the form of an intangible asset	Bifurcated model [IFRIC 12.18]	• Operator receives a fixed amount from the grantor and a right to charge users over the term of the arrangement

Where an operator is given infrastructure items by the grantor as part of the consideration payable by the grantor for the services, to keep or deal with as the operator wishes (i.e. they are not for the purposes of the service arrangement) then these assets are recognised as assets of the operator and measured at fair value on initial recognition. The assets would not be viewed as government grants as defined in IAS 20. [IFRIC 12.27]

Example 10.3.2

Determining the nature of the operator's asset

Company A enters into a service concession arrangement in which it will build and operate a new hospital for a period of 30 years. In exchange, the government provides Company A with a fixed annual cash payment, and title to a substantial plot of land surrounding the hospital. Company A is free to use the land as it wishes. Company A should recognise the land as its own property at fair value at the date of initial recognition.

10.4 Financial asset model

As outlined above, the financial asset model applies if the operator has a contractual right to receive cash from or at the direction of the grantor and the grantor has little, if any, discretion to avoid payment. This will be the case if the grantor contractually guarantees to pay the operator:

[IFRIC 12.16]

- specified or determinable amounts; or
- the shortfall, if any, between amounts received from users of the public service and specified or determinable amounts.

A financial asset exists in these circumstances even if the payments are contingent on the operator ensuring that the infrastructure meets specified quality or efficiency requirements.

The financial asset model cannot apply if the grantor only pays when users use the service or if the grantor only grants a right to charge users for the service.

The financial asset is accounted for in accordance with IAS 39 *Financial Instruments: Recognition and Measurement*. The requirements of IAS 32 *Financial Instruments: Presentation* and IFRS 7 *Financial Instruments: Disclosures* also apply. The financial asset will, depending on the circumstances, be required to be classified:

- as at fair value through profit or loss, if so designated upon initial recognition (and providing the conditions for that classification are met); or
- as a loan or receivable; or
- as 'available-for-sale'.

The asset can only be classified as a loan or receivable if payments are fixed or determinable and the only substantial risk of non-recovery of the initial investment is credit deterioration of the counter-party. (For further guidance on the classification of financial assets, see **section 3** in **chapter 14**). IFRIC 12 assumes that the financial asset will not be classified as held to maturity. [IFRIC 12.BC61]

Revenues and costs relating to the construction or upgrade phase of the contract are accounted for in accordance with IAS 11. Revenues from the operational phase are recognised in accordance with IAS 18. The financial asset is reduced when amounts are received.

Example 10.4

Financial asset model

An operator enters into a contract to provide construction services costing £100. It has been determined that the fair value of the construction services provided is £110. The total cash inflows over the entire life of the contract are fixed by the grantor at £200. The appropriate finance revenue to be recognised derived from applying the effective interest rate method in accordance with IAS 39 is in total £10 over the entire life of the service concession arrangement, and the balance of £80 (£200 – £110 – £10) relates to services provided during the operational phase. The following journal entries are made in this scenario.

During construction

		£	£
Dr	Financial asset	110	
Cr	Construction revenue		110

to recognise revenue relating to construction services, to be settled in cash.

Dr	Cost of construction	100	
Cr	Cash		100

to recognise costs relating to construction services.

During the operational phase

Dr	Financial asset	10	
Cr	Finance revenue		10

to recognise finance revenues.

Dr	Financial asset	80	
Cr	Revenue		80

to recognise revenues relating to the operational phase.

Dr	Cash	200	
Cr	Financial asset		200

to recognise cash received from the grantor.

Total revenue over the life of the contract	£200
Total cash inflows over the life of the contract	£200

A more detailed example of the financial asset model is included as Example 1 in the Illustrative Examples to IFRIC 12.

10.5 Intangible asset model

As outlined above, the intangible asset model applies if the operator receives a right (a licence) to charge users, or the Government, based on usage of the public service. There is no unconditional right to receive cash as the amounts are contingent on the extent that the public uses the service. [IFRIC 12.17]

During the construction phase the operator recognises revenue in respect of construction activities with the corresponding entry increasing the amount recognised for the intangible asset. This is because the operator exchanges construction services in return for a licence. The grantor makes a non-cash payment for the construction services by giving the operator an intangible asset in exchange for the construction services. As this is an exchange of dissimilar goods and services, in accordance with IAS 18.12, revenue must be recognised on the transaction.

The intangible asset generates a second stream of revenue when the operator receives cash from users or from the grantor based on usage. This contrasts with the financial asset model in which monies received are treated as partial repayment of the financial asset. In the intangible asset model the intangible is reduced by amortisation rather than repayment.

This results in revenue being recognised twice – once on the provision of construction services (in exchange for the intangible asset) and a second time on the receipt of payments for usage.

As an intangible asset is being recognised it must be accounted for in accordance with IAS 38 *Intangible Assets* (see **chapter 8**). The intangible asset should be amortised over the period of the concession. The annuity method of amortisation is specifically prohibited. [IFRIC 12.BC65] The most appropriate method of amortisation of the intangible is usually the straight-line method. However, in some circumstances, where the licence expires based on usage, it may be appropriate to use an alternative method of amortisation.

Example 10.5A

Amortisation under intangible asset model

Company B enters into an arrangement under which it will build and operate a toll bridge. Company B is entitled to charge users for driving over the toll bridge for the period from the completion of construction until 1 million cars have driven across the bridge, at which point the concession arrangement will end. It would be appropriate for Company B to amortise its intangible asset based on usage, as Company B's licence to operate the bridge expires on the basis of usage rather than with the passage of time.

Example 10.5B

Intangible asset model

As in **example 10.4**, an operator enters into a contract to provide construction services costing £100. It has been determined that the fair value of the construction services provided is £110. The total cash inflows over the entire life of the contract are expected to be £200, however this amount is not guaranteed by the grantor. The following entries are made in this scenario:

During construction

		£	£
Dr	Cost of construction	100	
Cr	Cash		100

to recognise costs relating to construction services.

Dr	Intangible asset	110	
Cr	Revenue		110

to recognise revenue relating to construction services provided for non-cash consideration.

During the operational phase

Dr	Amortisation expense	110	
Cr	Intangible asset		110

to recognise amortisation expense relating to the operational phase.

Dr	Cash	220	
Cr	Revenue		200

to recognise revenues received from users in the operational phase.

Total revenue over the life of the contract	£310
Total cash inflows over the life of the contract	£200

A more detailed example of the intangible asset model is included as Example 2 in the Illustrative Examples to IFRIC 12.

10.6 Bifurcated model

Where an operator receives a financial asset and an intangible asset as consideration, it is necessary to account separately for the component parts. At initial recognition, both components are recognised at the fair value of the consideration received or receivable in respect of work carried out up until that date. [IFRIC 12.18] A 'residual approach' is taken in arriving at a value for both components. To the extent that the operator receives a contractual right to receive cash from or at the direction of the grantor, a financial asset is recognised. Any excess of the fair value of the construction services provided over the fair value of the financial asset recognised will be recognised as an intangible asset.

Example 10.6

Bifurcated model

As in **example 10.4**, an operator enters into a contract to provide construction services costing £100. It has been determined that the fair value of the construction services provided is £110. The total cash inflows over the entire life of the contract are expected to be £200. Of these, £60 are guaranteed by the grantor. The appropriate finance revenue to be recognised derived from applying the effective interest rate method in accordance with IAS 39 is in total £6 over the entire life of the service concession arrangement. The following entries are made in this scenario:

During construction

		£	£
Dr	Financial asset	60	
Cr	Revenue		60

to recognise revenue relating to construction services, to be settled in cash.

Dr	Cost of construction	100	
Cr	Cash		100

to recognise costs relating to construction services.

Dr	Intangible asset	50	
Cr	Revenue		50

to recognise revenue relating to construction services provided for non-cash consideration.

During the operational phase

Dr	Financial asset	6	
Cr	Finance revenue		6

to recognise finance revenues.

Dr	Amortisation expense	50	
Cr	Intangible asset		50

to recognise amortisation expense relating to the operational phase.

Dr	Cash	200	
Cr	Revenue		134
Cr	Financial asset		66

to recognise revenues relating to the operational phase and cash received from the grantor and users.

Total revenue over the life of the contract	£250
Total cash inflows over the life of the contract	£200

A more detailed example of the bifurcated model is included as Example 3 in the Illustrative Examples to IFRIC 12.

10.7 Maintenance obligations

A service concession arrangement contract may require an operator to:

1. maintain the infrastructure to a specified level of serviceability; or
2. restore the infrastructure to a specified condition at the end of the arrangement before it is handed over to the grantor.

For example, an operator of a toll road may be required to resurface a road to ensure that it does not deteriorate below a specified condition. IFRIC 12.21 states that such contractual obligations to maintain or restore the infrastructure shall be recognised and measured in accordance with IAS 37 *Provisions, Contingent Liabilities and Contingent Assets*. Therefore, an estimate of the expenditure that would be required to settle the present obligation at the end of the reporting period needs to be made and recorded as a provision. In the case of resurfacing a road, it is likely that the amount required to settle the obligation at any point in time is linked to the number of vehicles that have travelled over the road.

IFRIC 12 envisages that maintenance obligations could alternatively be a revenue earning activity, in particular under the financial asset model as illustrated in IFRIC 12 (Example 1). If the grantor reimburses the operator for maintenance, such as resurfacing the road, then the operator would not record the obligation in the statement of financial position but recognise the revenue and expense in profit or loss when the resurfacing work is performed.

10.8 Borrowing costs

The requirements of IAS 23 *Borrowing Costs* in respect of the capitalisation of eligible borrowing costs are discussed in **chapter 27**. Where an entity's accounting policy is to capitalise eligible borrowing costs (as required by the revised version of IAS 23 issued in 2007), borrowing costs attributable to an arrangement may be capitalised during the construction phase, in accordance with IAS 23, if the operator has a contractual right to receive an intangible asset. A financial asset is not a qualifying asset and so borrowing costs are recognised as an expense in the period in which they are incurred. [IFRIC 12.22] Under the financial asset model interest is imputed on the financial asset using the effective interest method. This income goes some way in offsetting the borrowing cost expensed.

10.9 Disclosures about service concession arrangements

SIC-29 *Service Concession Arrangements: Disclosures* specifies certain disclosures that are required for such service concession arrangements to meet the requirements of paragraph 112(c) of IAS 1(2007) (previously IAS 1(2003).103(c)). The disclosure requirements apply to all service concession arrangements, not just those within the scope of IFRIC 12. The requirements are discussed at **7.4.3** in **chapter 3**.

10.10 Effective date and transition

IFRIC 12 applies for annual periods beginning on or after 1 January 2008, with earlier application permitted. If an entity applies the Interpretation for a period beginning before 1 January 2008 that fact must be disclosed.

The Interpretation should be applied retrospectively, in accordance with IAS 8. However, if it is not practicable for an operator to apply the Interpretation retrospectively at the start of the earliest period presented it shall:

[IFRIC 12.30]

- recognise financial assets and intangible assets that existed at the start of the earliest period presented;
- use the previous carrying amounts of those financial and intangible assets (however previously classified) as their carrying amounts as at that date; and
- test financial and intangible assets recognised at that date for impairment, unless this is not practicable, in which case the amounts shall be tested for impairment as at the start of the current period.

At the time of writing, IFRIC 12 has not yet been endorsed by the European Commission for adoption in Europe. Where an entity within the scope of the IAS Regulation (see **1.2** *in* **chapter 1***) has an arrangement to which IFRIC 12 would apply, and for which the entity has considered that IFRIC 4 currently applies, it will not be possible to adopt the requirements of IFRIC 12 for reporting in the EU until the Interpretation has been endorsed.* UK

11 Future developments

11.1 Revenue recognition project

IAS 18 and IAS 11 are currently under review in a project entitled *Revenue Recognition*. The IASB is working with the US Financial Accounting

Standards Board on a joint project to develop concepts for revenue recognition and a general standard based on those concepts.

At the time of writing, a discussion paper outlining the approaches discussed by the boards is expected to be published towards the end of 2008.

41 Government grants

1 Introduction

IAS 20 *Accounting for Government Grants and Disclosure of Government Assistance* prescribes the accounting for, and disclosure of, government grants and other forms of government assistance.

IAS 20 was amended by *Improvements to IFRSs* issued in May 2008. A substantive change was made regarding the accounting for government loans at below-market rates of interest (see **section 4.3**). In addition, a number of changes were made to the terminology in the Standard to be consistent with other IFRSs. These terminology changes, which are not expected to have any effect on accounting, have been reflected throughout this chapter.

> *At the time of writing, the amended version of IAS 20 has not yet been endorsed for use in the EU. Since the requirements in respect of government loans at below-market rates of interest differ from those of the previous version of IAS 20, EU reporting entities will not be able to apply the revised version in their statutory financial statements until it is endorsed.* UK

In fact, there are currently two Standards that address government grants – IAS 20, and IAS 41 *Agriculture* (see **chapter 43**). IAS 20 sets out the accounting and disclosure requirements for government grants and other forms of government assistance, apart from certain government grants relating to agricultural activity, which are dealt with under IAS 41. In addition, SIC-10 *Government Assistance – No Specific Relation to Operating Activities* deals with government assistance granted subject to conditions that may not be specifically related to the operating activities of the entity (see **section 3.2**).

This chapter discusses the requirements of IAS 20 in the following sections:

Section 2 Scope

Section 3 Definitions

Section 4 Recognition of government grants

UK

The accounting for government grants under IAS 20 is very similar to that required under UK GAAP by SSAP 4 Accounting for government grants. *The most significant difference relates to the presentation of grants related to assets. Under UK GAAP, companies are not permitted to deduct the grant from the asset's carrying amount, because of restrictions within the Companies Act 1985, though this option is available under SSAP 4 to entities other than companies.*

2 Scope

IAS 20 should be applied in accounting for government grants (as defined in **section 3**), and in the disclosure of government grants and other forms of government assistance. [IAS 20.1]

The Standard does not deal with:

[IAS 20.2]

- the special problems arising in accounting for government grants in financial statements reflecting the effects of changing prices or in supplementary information of a similar nature;
- government assistance that is provided for an entity in the form of benefits that are available in determining taxable profit or loss or that are determined or limited on the basis of income tax liability (such as income tax holidays, investment tax credits, accelerated depreciation allowances and reduced income tax rates);
- government participation in the ownership of the entity; or
- government grants covered by IAS 41 *Agriculture*.

3 Definitions

For the purposes of IAS 20, the term 'government' refers to government, government agencies and similar bodies, whether local, national or international. [IAS 20.3]

3.1 Government assistance

Government assistance is action by government designed to provide an economic benefit specific to an entity or range of entities qualifying under certain criteria. [IAS 20.3]

Government assistance excludes benefits provided only indirectly through action affecting general trading conditions, such as the provision of infrastructure in development areas or the imposition of trading constraints on competitors. [IAS 20.3]

3.2 Government grants

Government grants represent a particular form of government assistance involving awards given in return for the fulfilment of conditions. Such grants (which may sometimes be called by other names such as subsidies, subventions or premiums) are defined in IAS 20.3 as assistance by government in the form of transfers of resources to an entity in return for past or future compliance with certain conditions relating to the operating activities of the entity.

Forms of government assistance that are not classified as government grants are:

[IAS 20.3]

- those that cannot reasonably have a value placed upon them (e.g. free technical or marketing advice or export credit guarantees); and
- transactions with government that are indistinguishable from the normal trading transactions of the entity (such as a government procurement policy that is responsible for a significant part of the entity's sales).

SIC-10 *Government Assistance – No Specific Relation to Operating Activities* addresses the classification of government assistance that is not specifically related to the operating activities of the entity (e.g. transfers of resources by governments to entities that operate in a particular industry). The Interpretation concludes that government assistance to an entity will meet the definition of government grants even if there are no conditions specifically relating to the operating activities of the entity other than the requirement to operate in certain regions or industry sectors. Such grants should therefore be accounted for under IAS 20. [SIC-10.3]

Government grants fall into two categories.

[IAS 20.3]

1. Grants related to assets – i.e. government grants whose primary condition is that the entity qualifying for them should purchase, construct or otherwise acquire long-term assets. There may also be subsidiary conditions restricting the type or location of the assets, or the periods during which they are to be acquired or held.

2. Grants related to income – i.e. government grants other than those related to assets.

4 Recognition of government grants

4.1 General principles

A government grant is not recognised until there is reasonable assurance that:

[IAS 20.7]

- the entity will comply with the conditions attaching to it; and
- the grant will be received. Receipt of a grant is not of itself conclusive evidence that the conditions attaching to the grant have been or will be fulfilled.

IAS 20 does not define 'reasonable assurance'. One of the recognition criteria included in the Framework, however, is that it must be probable that any future economic benefit associated with an item will flow to or from an entity. Therefore, 'reasonable assurance' can be appropriately interpreted in this context as meaning that both compliance with the conditions attaching to a grant, and the receipt of the grant, are probable.

The manner in which a grant is received does not affect the accounting treatment adopted. Thus, a grant is accounted for in the same manner whether it is received in cash or as a reduction of a liability to the government, or in the form of non-monetary assets. [IAS 20.9]

A forgivable loan from government, where the government has undertaken to waive repayment under certain prescribed conditions, is treated as a government grant when there is reasonable assurance that the entity will meet the terms for forgiveness of the loan. [IAS 20.10] Specific rules apply for government loans at below-market rates of interest (see **4.3**).

Once a government grant is recognised, any related contingent liability or contingent asset is dealt with in accordance with IAS 37 *Provisions, Contingent Liabilities and Contingent Assets*. [IAS 20.11]

4.2 Recognition in profit or loss

Government grants are recognised in profit or loss on a systematic basis over the periods in which the entity recognises as expenses the related costs for which the grants are intended to compensate. [IAS 20.12]

IAS 20 clearly rules out what is referred to as the 'capital approach' to the accounting treatment of government grants (under which grants are recognised outside profit or loss), in favour of the 'income approach'. The arguments in support of the income approach are as follows:

[IAS 20.15]

- government grants are receipts from a source other than shareholders, and therefore they should not be recognised directly in equity but should be recognised in profit or loss in appropriate periods;
- government grants are rarely given free of obligations, but are earned by the entity through compliance with the conditions attached and, therefore, ought to be recognised in profit or loss over the periods in which the entity recognises as expenses the related costs for which the grant is intended to compensate; and
- just as income and other taxes are expenses, it is logical to deal with government grants, which are an extension of fiscal policies, in profit or loss.

Consistent with IAS 1 *Presentation of Financial Statements*, the income approach requires application of the accruals concept by recognising government grants in profit or loss on a systematic basis over the periods in which the entity recognises as expenses the related costs. In other words, grants are not recognised on receipt unless no rational basis exists for allocating the grant to a period other than the one in which it was received. [IAS 20.16]

In most cases, it is not difficult to identify the periods over which expenditure relating to a government grant is recognised. For example, grants related to depreciable assets are usually recognised in profit or loss over the periods in which depreciation expense on those assets is recognised, corresponding to the useful lives of the assets. [IAS 20.17]

Grants related to non-depreciable assets may have certain conditions attached, and thus are recognised in profit or loss over the periods in which the costs of meeting those conditions are incurred. For example, a grant of freehold land may be conditional upon the erection of a building on the site and it may be appropriate to recognise the grant in profit or loss over the life of the building. [IAS 20.18]

In some instances, a government grant may be receivable as compensation for expenses or losses already incurred in a previous accounting period. Alternatively, a grant may be receivable for the purpose of giving immediate financial support to the entity with no future related costs. In such cases, the grant is recognised in profit or loss in the period in which it becomes receivable, with disclosures provided to ensure the effect is understood. [IAS 20.20]

Grants are sometimes received as part of a package of financial or fiscal aids to which a number of conditions are attached. In such cases, care is needed in identifying which of the conditions give rise to costs and expenses, since those are the conditions that determine the period over which the grant is earned. It may be appropriate to allocate part of a grant on one basis and part on another. [IAS 20.21]

An issue on which the Standard is silent relates to depreciable assets whose residual value increases over time. Such an asset will initially be depreciated, but often depreciation will cease before the end of the asset's useful life, because residual value has increased so as to exceed carrying amount. In such circumstances, how should any associated grant be recognised in profit or loss? At least three possibilities might be envisaged:

- to recognise the whole of the grant over the asset's useful life, regardless of how much depreciation expense is recognised. For example, if an asset has a useful life of 40 years, 2.5 per cent of the grant would be released each year irrespective of whether and how the depreciation expense continues to be recognised;

- to match the grant to the initial cost of the asset, so that it is in part recognised with the depreciation expense but with the balance being recognised only on disposal. For example, if an asset initially cost £1,000, and ceased to be depreciated when its carrying amount was £860 (because residual value had risen to exceed this), 14 per cent of the grant would by then have been recognised in profit or loss, with 86 per cent being held in the statement of financial position and released only on disposal; or

- each year to release a proportion of the remaining grant, so that the remaining balance reflects the amount of the asset yet to be amortised (i.e. the excess of carrying amount over updated residual value) as a proportion of expected total depreciation on the asset (see **example 4.2** below).

IAS 20.12 indicates that government grants should be recognised 'on a systematic basis over the periods in which the entity recognises as expenses the related costs for which the grants are intended to compensate'. The first approach above does not focus at all on when costs are recognised, and is therefore arguably the least appropriate of the three. The second approach may be judged closest to the requirements of IAS 20.12 if in fact the grant is intended to compensate both the use of the asset and its subsequent disposal; it may also be the most appropriate approach if there are any arrangements under which a proportion of the grant must be repaid by reference to sale proceeds received.

It may be judged, however, that the grant is intended only to compensate for the costs of using the asset, not disposing of it; if so, the third approach perhaps best approximates this. The third approach is, arguably, also closest to the requirement of IAS 20.17 that grants for depreciable assets be recognised in profit or loss 'over the periods and in the proportions in which depreciation expense on those assets is recognised'. The application of the third approach is illustrated in the example below.

Example 4.2

Grant relates to a depreciable asset with increasing residual value

A film library is purchased on 1 January 20X1 for £1,000, and a grant of £200 is received in relation to it. There are no obligations to repay the grant if the library is subsequently sold. The estimated useful life of the film library to the entity is five years, and the pattern of depreciation for the first four years is as follows:

	Opening carrying amount £	Opening remaining life (years)	Estimated residual value £	Depreciation charged £
Year to Dec 20X1	1,000	5	600	80
Year to Dec 20X2	920	4	720	50
Year to Dec 20X3	870	3	840	10
Year to Dec 20X4	860	2	900	-
Year to Dec 20X5	860	1	920	-

The release of the grant would be calculated as follows:

	Cumulative depreciation recognised	Estimated total depreciation	Proportion not yet recognised	Closing grant balance	Grant recognised in profit or loss
	£	£	%	£	£
Year to Dec 20X1	80	400	80.0	160	40
Year to Dec 20X2	130	280	53.6	107	53
Year to Dec 20X3	140	160	12.5	25	82
Year to Dec 20X4	140	140	-	-	25
Year to Dec 20X5	140	140	-	-	-

4.3 Government loans at below-market rate of interest

Improvements to IFRSs issued in May 2008 amended the requirements of IAS 20 in respect of government loans at below-market rates of interest.

Following the amendment, the benefit of a government loan at a below-market rate of interest is treated as a government grant. The loan is recognised and measured in accordance with IAS 39 *Financial Instruments: Recognition and Measurement*. The benefit of the below-market rate of interest is measured as the difference between the initial carrying value of the loan determined in accordance with IAS 39 and the proceeds received. [IAS 20.10A]

The benefit so calculated is accounted for in accordance with the general principles discussed in earlier sections. The entity is required to consider the conditions and obligations that have been, or must be, met when identifying the costs for which the benefit of the loan is intended to compensate. [IAS 20.10A]

Paragraph 10A is effective for government loans received in periods beginning on or after 1 January 2009. Earlier application is permitted, provided that fact is disclosed. [IAS 20.43]

The requirements of paragraph 10A are to be applied prospectively to government loans received after the amendments to the Standard are adopted. [IAS 20.43] The requirement for prospective application is intended to avoid the necessity to measure the fair value of loans at a past date.

Prior to the amendments in May 2008, paragraph 37 of IAS 20 stated that: 'Loans at nil or low interest rates are a form of government assistance, but the benefit is not quantified by the imputation of interest.' Therefore, prior to the implementation of the May 2008 amendments, entities did not quantify the benefit inherent in government-subsidised loans, and the only requirement was that the nature, extent and duration of such loans be disclosed if necessary in order that the financial statements not be misleading. The introduction of paragraph 10A, therefore, represents quite a significant change. This change has been made to address an apparent inconsistency between the guidance in IAS 20 and in IAS 39. IAS 20 previously stated that no interest should be imputed for such a loan, whereas IAS 39 requires all loans to be recognised at fair value, thus requiring interest to be imputed on loans with a below-market rate of interest. The Board considered that the imputation of interest provides more relevant information to a user of the financial statements, and amended IAS 20 accordingly.

At the time of writing, the amended version of IAS 20 has not yet been endorsed for use in the EU. Since the requirements in respect of government loans at below-market rates of interest differ from those of the previous version of IAS 20, EU reporting entities will not be able to apply the revised version in their statutory financial statements until it is endorsed. UK

Example 4.3

Government loans received at below-market rates of interest

Entity Q received a loan of £3 million from the government. The loan is at 2% interest and is repayable in 5 years. Using prevailing market interest rates of 5%, the fair value of the loan is calculated at £2,610,347.

Under IAS 39.43, the loan is recognised at £2,610,347. The difference between this amount and proceeds received (£389,653) is the benefit derived from the below-market interest and is recognised as deferred income. Therefore, on the date that the loan is received, the following entries are recognised:

		£	£
Dr	Cash	3,000,000	
Cr	Government loan		2,610,347
Cr	Deferred income (government grant)		389,653

The interest expense is recognised in profit or loss at 5% in accordance with IAS 39.

	Opening balance on loan	**Interest calculated at 5%**	**Interest paid (at 2%) plus capital repayment in Year 5**	**Closing balance on loan**
	£	£	£	£
Year 1	2,610,347	130,517	(60,000)	2,680,864
Year 2	2,680,864	134,044	(60,000)	2,754,908
Year 3	2,754,908	137,745	(60,000)	2,832,653
Year 4	2,832,653	141,633	(60,000)	2,914,286
Year 5	2,914,286	145,714	(3,060,000)	nil

In accordance with IAS 20.12, the amount of the government grant (£389,653) is recognised in profit or loss on a systematic basis over the periods in which Entity Q recognises as expenses the related costs for which the grant is intended to compensate.

The costs for which the below-market interest rate is intended to compensate are assessed on the basis of the particular circumstances. For example:

- the loan may be intended to subsidise training costs over a 3-year period. The costs may be incurred on a straight-line basis, in which case the government grant will be released to income on a straight-line basis – i.e. £129,884 (£389,653/3) each year for 3 years;
- the loan may be intended as a rescue measure for the purpose of giving immediate financial support. In such circumstances, under IAS 20.21 (see above), it may be appropriate to recognise the benefit in profit or loss immediately; or
- the loan may be intended to finance a depreciable asset. In this case, the benefit would be recognised on the same basis as depreciation.

5 Measurement of non-monetary grants

If a government grant takes the form of a non-monetary asset, such as land or other resources, it is usual to account for the grant and the asset at fair value. [IAS 20.23] This is consistent with the requirement in IAS 18 *Revenue* that revenue be measured at the fair value of the consideration received or receivable. Fair value is defined in IAS 20 as the amount for which an asset could be exchanged between a knowledgeable, willing buyer and a knowledgeable, willing seller in an arm's length transaction. [IAS 20.3]

Note, however, that the recognition of non-monetary grants at fair value is not mandatory. The Standard allows as an alternative treatment that the grant and the asset be recorded at a nominal amount. [IAS 20.23]

6 Presentation

6.1 Grants related to assets

IAS 20 permits two methods of presentation of government grants related to assets in the statement of financial position, namely either:

[IAS 20.24]

- recognising the grant as deferred income, which is recognised in profit or loss on a systematic basis over the useful life of the asset; or

- deducting the grant in calculating the carrying amount of the asset, in which case the grant is recognised in profit or loss over the life of a depreciable asset by way of a reduced depreciation expense.

Although SSAP 4 also allows both these options, the latter is not available to companies reporting under UK GAAP where they are subject to the restrictions within the Companies Act. The second option is nevertheless available under UK GAAP to entities other than companies. UK

While IAS 20 permits netting off government grants against the carrying amount of related assets, it goes on to note that such transactions can have a significant impact on the cash flows of an entity. For this reason, and also to show the gross investment in assets, the statement of cash flows often discloses as separate items the purchase of assets and the receipt of related grants, regardless of whether the grant is deducted from the asset for presentation purposes in the statement of financial position. [IAS 20.28]

Example 6.1

Presentation of grants related to assets

At the beginning of 20X1, an entity invests £1,000,000 in an item of equipment, which has an anticipated useful life of five years. Depreciation is recognised on a straight-line basis. In the year of acquisition, the entity receives a government grant of £250,000 towards purchase of the equipment, which is conditional on certain employment targets being achieved within the next three years, i.e. to the end of 20X3. Under the alternative methods of presentation allowed for under IAS 20, the disclosure is as follows:

Method A: Grant shown as deferred income

	£
20X1:	
Credit to deferred income – grant received	250,000
Less: recognised in profit or loss (£250,000 / 5 years)	(50,000)
Deferred income balance at year end	200,000
Cost of equipment	1,000,000
Depreciation expense (£1,000,000 / 5 years)	(200,000)
Carrying amount of equipment at year end	800,000
Years 20X2 to 20X5:	
Deferred income recognised in profit or loss	50,000
Depreciation expense	(200,000)
Net expense in profit or loss (£750,000 / 5 years)	(150,000)

Note that the condition requiring certain employment targets to be met within three years is not relevant for determining the period over which deferred income is recognised in profit or loss. The condition requires disclosure, however, as a contingency.

Method B: Grant deducted from cost of asset

	£
20X1:	
Cost of equipment	1,000,000
Less: grant received	(250,000)
Net cost of equipment	750,000
Depreciation expense (£750,000/ 5 years)	(150,000)
Carrying amount of equipment at year end	600,000
Years 20X2 to 20X5:	
Depreciation expense	(150,000)

It is evident from **example 6.1** that, while the net impact of the two methods on the reported result for each year is identical, the presentation in each case is very different. Method A clearly separates the asset from the deferred income, and also shows the crediting of the grant separately as income, while recognising the depreciation expense in full. Method B nets off the grant against the asset, while showing only the depreciation expense, reduced by the amount of the grant that would otherwise have been recognised in profit or loss.

6.2 Grants related to income

IAS 20 permits two methods of presentation in the financial statements of grants related to income:

[IAS 20.29]

- directly as a credit in the statement of comprehensive income, either separately or under a general heading such as 'other income'; or
- as a deduction in reporting the related expense.

If an entity presents the components of profit or loss in a separate income statement as described in IAS 1(2007).81 (see **section 5** of **chapter 3**), it presents grants related to income as required in IAS 20.29 (see above) in that separate statement. [IAS 20.29A]

Again, the Standard demonstrates its flexibility in permitting, as equally acceptable, alternative methods of presentation of government grants. Essentially, IAS 20 has sought to accommodate two rather differing views on the treatment of income-related grants, namely those who oppose netting off income and expense items and prefer to keep disclosure of the grant separate for the purposes of comparison, and those who argue that, since the entity might not have incurred the expense if the grant had not been available, it might be misleading to show the expense without offsetting the grant.

7 Grants related to agricultural activities

IAS 41 *Agriculture* prescribes a different treatment for government grants related to agricultural activities. The relevant rules are discussed in **chapter 43**.

8 Repayment of government grants

IAS 20 requires that a government grant that becomes repayable should be accounted for as a change in accounting estimate in accordance with IAS 8 *Accounting Policies, Changes in Accounting Estimates and Errors*. [IAS 20.32] As described in **chapter 4**, a change in estimate is accounted for in the period of change if the change affects that period only, or in the period of change and in future periods, if the change affects both.

The accounting treatment for the repayment of a government grant is as follows:

[IAS 20.32]

- repayment of a grant related to income should be applied first against any unamortised deferred credit recognised in respect of the grant. To the extent that repayment exceeds any such deferred credit, or when no deferred credit exists, the repayment should be recognised immediately as an expense; and
- repayment of a grant related to an asset should be recognised by increasing the carrying amount of the asset or reducing the deferred income balance by the amount repayable. The cumulative additional depreciation that would have been recognised in profit or loss to date in the absence of the grant should be recognised immediately in profit or loss.

Example 8

Repayment of a government grant

The facts are the same as in **example 6.1**. At the end of 20X3, it is evident that the entity has failed to fulfil the employment conditions attached to the receipt of the asset-related grant. The grant therefore becomes repayable. Under the two methods of presentation of the grant, the treatment of the repayment is as follows:

Method A: Grant shown as deferred income

	£
Grant received, credited in 20X1 to deferred income	250,000
Recognised in profit or loss 20X1 to 20X3 (3 x £50,000)	(150,000)
Deferred income balance at end of 20X3, before repayment of grant	100,000
Total repayment of grant	250,000
Repayment debited to deferred income balance	(100,000)
Balance of repayment recognised in profit or loss	150,000

Note that, under this method, the repayment of the grant has no effect on the carrying amount of the equipment or on the depreciation charge.

Method B: Grant deducted from cost of asset

	£
Cost of equipment	1,000,000
Less: grant received in 20X1	(250,000)
Net cost of equipment	750,000
Depreciation expense recognised 20X1 to 20X3 (3 x £150,000)	(450,000)
Carrying amount of equipment at end of 20X3, before repayment of grant	300,000
Add back grant repayable	250,000
	550,000
Cumulative additional depreciation recognised in profit or loss for 20X1 to 20X3 (3 x £50,000)	(150,000)
Carrying amount of plant at end of 20X3, after repayment of grant	400,000

The circumstances surrounding the repayment of a government grant may require consideration to be given to the possible impairment of the new carrying amount of the asset. [IAS 20.33] This could occur, for example, if the repayment of the grant resulted from a failure to comply with government regulations or conditions attached to receipt of the grant, which, in turn, reflected adverse changes in the operating environment of the entity.

9 Disclosure

IAS 20 requires the following disclosures in respect of government grants:

[IAS 20.39]

- the accounting policy adopted for government grants, including the methods of presentation adopted in the financial statements;
- the nature and extent of government grants recognised in the financial statements; and

- unfulfilled conditions and other contingencies attaching to government assistance that has been recognised.

Where grants relate to income, the Standard suggests that:

[IAS 20.31]

- separate disclosure of a grant may be necessary for a proper understanding of the financial statements; and
- disclosure of the effect of the grant on any item of income or expenditure that is required to be shown separately is usually appropriate.

Separate disclosure should, in particular, be considered where a grant has been netted against the related expense in the statement of comprehensive income.

The Standard also requires an indication of forms of government assistance other than government grants from which the entity has directly benefited. [IAS 20.39] Although the benefit resulting from such forms of assistance may not be measurable, the impact of items such as free technical or marketing advice, or guarantees should be disclosed where it is significant. Even though such assistance is not recognised as income in the financial statements, it may benefit the entity to such an extent that disclosure of the nature, extent and duration of the assistance is necessary for the financial statements not to be misleading. [IAS 20.34 – 37]

10 Future developments

The IASB believes that IAS 20 is out of date, contains too many options to provide relevant information to users of financial statements, and is inconsistent with the Framework. A project was started to amend the Standard, but work has been deferred. The Board believes that there are important interactions between this project and other projects (particularly the projects on amendments to IAS 37, revenue recognition and emission trading schemes) and the IAS 20 project has been suspended pending further progress on those other projects.

42 Financial reporting in hyperinflationary economies

1 Introduction

IAS 29 *Financial Reporting in Hyperinflationary Economies* applies to the financial statements of entities whose functional currency is the currency of a hyperinflationary economy. The Standard has been effective since 1 January 1990, and was most recently amended by *Improvements to IFRSs* issued in May 2008, primarily to make its terminology consistent with other IFRSs.

This chapter discusses the requirements of IAS 29 in the following sections:

Section 2	Scope
Section 3	Definition of hyperinflation
Section 4	Restatement of financial statements – general principles
Section 5	Historical cost financial statements
Section 6	Current cost financial statements
Section 7	Economies ceasing to be hyperinflationary
Section 8	Disclosure

The premise underlying IAS 29 is that, since money rapidly loses its purchasing power in a hyperinflationary economy, to report an entity's operating results and financial position in the currency of that economy without restatement would be meaningless to a user of the accounts. Comparative information would have no value, and even the profits of a single financial period would be distorted. For example, the difference between the cost at which inventory is acquired and the price at which it is sold would not only reflect a normal trading profit margin, but also include the impact of a price change that is beyond the control of the entity.

Under UK GAAP, FRS 24 Financial Reporting in Hyperinflationary Economies *embodies IAS 29, but makes amendments for UK entities,* UK *primarily to exempt FRSSE companies and to adjust references to other accounting standards. FRS 24 is mandatory for some entities and optional for others, but may only be adopted as part of a package of standards that also includes FRSs 24 to 26 and 29.*

UK companies not adopting FRS 24 continue to follow UITF Abstract 9 Accounting for operations in hyper-inflationary economies. *In addition to dealing with the inclusion in consolidated accounts of an operation in a hyperinflationary economy, IAS 29 deals with the accounting to be adopted in individual financial statements when the functional currency of the entity is the currency of a hyperinflationary economy. UITF Abstract 9 offers a choice of methods for eliminating the distortions caused by hyperinflation, whereas IAS 29 allows only one method.*

2 Scope

IAS 29 addresses the issues associated with financial reporting when the functional currency of an entity (i.e. the currency of the primary economic environment in which the entity operates) is that of a hyperinflationary economy, and applies equally to the financial statements of individual entities and consolidated financial statements. [IAS 29.1]

The Standard also applies equally to financial statements based on historical cost accounting and those based on current cost accounting (i.e. those reflecting the effects of changes in the specific prices of assets held). In either case, the financial statements should be stated in terms of the measuring unit current at the end of the reporting period.

All entities that report in the currency of a hyperinflationary economy should, ideally, apply IAS 29 from the same date in order to achieve consistency in financial reporting between entities. However, this objective will not always be achieved. The Standard places responsibility on individual entities to consider the potential impact of hyperinflation and to apply IAS 29 from the beginning of the reporting period in which they identify the existence of hyperinflation in the country in whose currency they report. [IAS 29.4]

In practice, very few countries fall within the scope of the Standard. Whether or not a country is considered to be experiencing hyperinflation for the purposes of the Standard will generally be determined by a consensus of the accounting profession, rather than by each entity individually.

financial statements to determine when restatement of financial statements *in accordance with IAS 29 becomes necessary. [IAS 29.3]*

Characteristics of the economic environment of a country which indicate the existence of hyperinflation include:

[IAS 29.3]

- the general population prefers to keep its wealth in non-monetary assets or in a relatively stable foreign currency. Amounts of local currency held are immediately invested to maintain purchasing power;
- the general population regards monetary amounts not in terms of the local currency but in terms of a relatively stable foreign currency. Prices may be quoted in that currency;
- sales and purchases on credit take place at prices that compensate for the expected loss of purchasing power during the credit period, even if the period is short;
- interest rates, wages and prices are linked to a price index; and
- the cumulative inflation rate over three years approaches, or exceeds, 100 per cent.

4 Restatement of financial statements – general principles

The financial statements of an entity whose functional currency is the currency of a hyperinflationary economy should be stated in terms of the measuring unit current at the end of the reporting period. [IAS 29.8]

The Standard notes that one of the most important factors in restating financial statements will be consistency from period to period in applying

4.2 Required adjustments

IAS 29 requires the following adjustments to amounts reported in the currency of a hyperinflationary economy:

[IAS 29.8 & 9]

- the current period's financial statements should be stated in terms of the measuring unit current at the end of the reporting period;
- the corresponding figures for the previous period, and any information in respect of earlier periods, should also be stated in terms of the measuring unit current at the end of the reporting period; and
- the gain or loss on the net monetary position (see **4.4**) should be included in profit or loss, and separately disclosed.

Restatements are made by applying a general price index. Monetary items, which are already stated at the measuring unit current at the end of the reporting period, are not restated. Other items are restated based on the change in the general price index between the date those items were acquired, incurred or revalued and the end of the reporting period.

4.3 General price index

In order to express financial statements in terms of the measuring unit current at the end of the reporting period, amounts are restated by applying a general price index. The general price index to be used is one that reflects changes in general purchasing power. [IAS 29.37] No further guidance is given by the Standard in this area.

The Standard states that it is desirable for all entities reporting in the currency of any particular hyperinflationary economy to use the same index, in order to achieve comparability between the financial statements of different entities. [IAS 29.37]

> Any reporting entity implementing the principles of IAS 29 should therefore first consider which price index is used by other local reporting entities, particularly those in the same industry, and apply that index, provided that it is believed to be an indicator of changes in general purchasing power.

A general price index may not be available, particularly for the restatement of the historical cost of property, plant and equipment acquired over an extended period (see **5.1.1.2** below). In such circumstances, the inflation rate may be estimated by considering the depreciation of the exchange rate of the hyperinflationary currency against a relatively stable foreign currency. [IAS 29.17]

> In the absence of a reliable, independently determined index (either by the Government or the private sector), the difference between the exchange rate at the beginning of the period between a stable currency (e.g. the US dollar) and the local currency and the same exchange rate differential at the end of the period may be used as a guideline to determine the index. In making this estimate, it is important that the impact of inflation in the stable currency is excluded.

Example 4.3

Imputing a general price index

Assume that the exchange rate at 1 January 20X5 for Local Currency and Stable Currency was 200:1. At 31 December 20X5, the exchange rate was

350:1. There has been a 75 per cent depreciation in Local Currency in relation to Stable Currency. Assuming that inflation in the Stable Currency economy for the 20X5 calendar year was three per cent, the index should be an increase of 80.25 per cent (1.75 x 1.03).

4.4 Gain or loss on net monetary position

An entity's net monetary position is the difference between its monetary assets and monetary liabilities. Monetary items are defined as money held and items to be received or paid in money. All other items are non-monetary.

The following table lists a number of the most common monetary and non-monetary items.

Monetary items	**Non-monetary items**
Cash	Property, plant and equipment
Bank balances and loans	Intangible assets
Deposits	Goodwill
Employee benefit liability	Shareholders' equity
Accrued expenses	Prepaid expenses
Trade payables	Investments in associates
Taxation	Advances received on sales or paid on purchases provided that they are linked to specific sales or purchases
Debt securities	Inventories
Trade receivables	Allowance for inventory obsolescence (because inventories are non-monetary)
Allowance for doubtful debts (because trade receivables are monetary)	Deferred income
Notes and other receivables	Equity securities
Notes and other payables	
Holiday pay provision	
Deferred tax assets/liabilities*	
Payables under finance leases	

* Although deferred tax assets and liabilities are monetary items, they are restated at the end of the reporting period because they are affected by movements in non-monetary items.

In a period of inflation, an entity holding an excess of monetary assets over monetary liabilities loses purchasing power, and an entity with an excess of monetary liabilities over monetary assets gains purchasing power to the extent that the assets and liabilities are not linked to a price level. [IAS 29.27] The detailed calculation of the gain or loss on net monetary position is dealt with in **5.3** below.

4.5 Deferred taxes

The restatement of financial statements in accordance with IAS 29 may give rise to differences between the carrying amount of individual assets and liabilities and their tax bases. These differences are accounted for in accordance with IAS 12 *Income Taxes*. [IAS 29.32]

For financial statements restated under IAS 29, deferred tax is not calculated by simply indexing the historical cost deferred tax amount. Instead, a revised closing deferred tax calculation should be performed using the carrying amounts and tax bases that exist after the restatement for hyperinflationary purposes. Generally, there is no tax relief for hyperinflation and, as such, the tax base will remain unchanged. The difference between the opening restated deferred tax balance, and the revised closing deferred tax balance, is the deferred tax expense or credit for the period.

Example 4.5

Restatement of deferred taxation

At 31 December 20X1, an entity recognised a deferred tax liability related to a non-current asset with a carrying amount of 1,600 and a tax base of 750. The resulting temporary difference of 850 gave rise to a deferred tax liability of 255 (tax rate 30 per cent).

At 31 December 20X2, assuming an index rate of 1.5 and no other movements in the carrying amount or the tax base of the asset, the deferred tax liability is calculated as follows:

Carrying amount (1,600 x 1.5)	2,400
Tax base	750
Temporary difference	1,650
Deferred tax at 30%	495

The opening deferred tax balance of 255 should be indexed by 1.5. The effect of this is that the comparative information in respect of deferred tax is restated to 382.50. However, in performing a revised deferred tax computation at the end of the current year, the closing deferred tax balance should be 495. The difference between the closing deferred tax amount of 495 and the restated opening deferred tax amount of 382.50 (i.e. 112.50) is the current year deferred tax charge.

4.6 Statement of cash flows

IAS 29 requires that all items in the statement of cash flows are expressed in terms of the measuring unit current at the end of the reporting period. [IAS 29.33]

4.7 Consolidated financial statements

A parent that reports in the currency of a hyperinflationary economy may have subsidiaries that also report in the currencies of hyperinflationary economies. The financial statements of any such subsidiary need to be restated by applying the general price index of the country in whose currency it reports before they are included in the consolidated financial statements issued by the parent. Where such a subsidiary is a foreign subsidiary, its restated financial statements are translated at closing rates. The financial statements of subsidiaries that do not report in the currencies of hyperinflationary economies are dealt with in accordance with IAS 21 *The Effects of Changes in Foreign Exchange Rates* (see **chapter 28**). [IAS 29.35]

If financial statements with different ends of the reporting periods are consolidated, all items, whether non-monetary or monetary, need to be restated into the measuring unit current at the date of the consolidated financial statements. [IAS 29.36]

4.8 IFRIC 7 *Applying the Restatement Approach under IAS 29 Financial Reporting in Hyperinflationary Economies*

In November 2005, the IFRIC issued IFRIC 7 *Applying the Restatement Approach under IAS 29 Financial Reporting in Hyperinflationary Economies*. The Interpretation contains guidance on how an entity would restate its financial statements in the first year in which it identifies the existence of hyperinflation in the economy of its functional currency.

In the first year in which an entity identifies the existence of hyperinflation, it must start applying IAS 29 as if the economy had always been hyperinflationary. Therefore, an entity recreates an opening statement of financial position at the beginning of the earliest annual accounting period presented in the restated financial statements so that:

[IFRIC 7.3]

- non-monetary items measured at historical cost are restated to reflect the effect of inflation from the date the assets were acquired and the liabilities were incurred or assumed until the end of the reporting period; and

- non-monetary items carried at amounts current at dates other than those of acquisition or incurrence are restated to reflect the effect of inflation from the dates those carrying amounts were determined until the end of the reporting period.

Deferred tax figures in the opening statement of financial position for the reporting period are determined in the following way:

[IFRIC 7.4]

- deferred tax items are remeasured in accordance with IAS 12 after the entity has restated the nominal carrying amounts of its non-monetary items at the date of the opening statement of financial position of the reporting period by applying the measuring unit at that date; and
- those deferred tax items are restated for the change in the measuring unit from the date of the opening statement of financial position of the reporting period to the end of that reporting period.

The approach above is applied in the opening statement of financial position of any comparative periods presented in the restated financial statements for the reporting period in which the entity applies IAS 29.

All corresponding figures (including deferred tax items) in subsequent financial statements are restated by applying the change in the measuring unit for the subsequent reporting period only to the restated financial statements for the previous reporting period. [IFRIC 7.5]

The Interpretation is accompanied by an Illustrative Example, which shows the mechanics of the restatement approach for deferred tax items. Entities are required to apply IFRIC 7 for annual periods beginning on or after 1 March 2006, but earlier application is encouraged.

5 Historical cost financial statements

5.1 Statement of financial position

The treatment required by IAS 29 for the components of a historical cost statement of financial position is summarised in the table below. Specific categories are considered in the sections following.

Item in the statement of financial position	Treatment	Examples
Assets and liabilities having a pre-defined link to price changes	Adjust in accordance with the particular agreements in place	Index-linked bonds and loans

Other monetary items	These do not require restatement, since they are already expressed in terms of the measuring unit current at the end of the reporting period	Cash, receivables and payables
Non-monetary assets carried at a valuation that is current at the end of the reporting period	These do not require restatement, since they are already expressed in terms of the measuring unit current at the end of the reporting period	Inventory carried at net realisable value. Investment property carried at fair value
Non-monetary assets carried at a valuation that is not current at the end of the reporting period	Restatement is required from the date of the valuation to the end of the reporting period	Property revalued at a date other than the end of the reporting period
Other items in the statement of financial position, i.e. items carried at cost, or cost less depreciation and impairment losses	These are restated in terms of the measuring unit current at the end of the reporting period by applying a general price index	When carried at cost: property, plant and equipment, investments, inventories, goodwill and intangible assets. Also prepaid expenses and deferred income

5.1.1 Property, plant and equipment

5.1.1.1 Property, plant and equipment carried at valuation

Property, plant and equipment carried at a valuation that is current at the end of the reporting period need not be restated, since the assets are already expressed in terms of the measuring unit current at the end of the reporting period. [IAS 29.14]

For property, plant and equipment carried at a valuation that is not current at the end of the reporting period, the change in the general price index from the date of the last valuation of the item to the end of the reporting period is applied to the revalued amount. [IAS 29.18]

5.1.1.2 *Property, plant and equipment carried at cost less accumulated depreciation and accumulated impairment losses*

For property, plant and equipment stated at cost less depreciation and impairment losses, the change in the general price index from the date of acquisition of the item to the end of the reporting period is applied to the historical cost and, where relevant, accumulated depreciation and accumulated impairment losses. [IAS 29.15]

The treatment of items of property, plant and equipment that have been depreciated can often be complex. Cost is restated by adjusting the purchase price by the change in the index between the date of acquisition and the end of the reporting period. Depreciation arises over time, and hence the balance of accumulated depreciation brought forward at the start of each period must be adjusted by the change in the index between the start and end of the period, while the depreciation charge for each period is calculated based on the index-adjusted cost at the end of the period. Another way to arrive at the same answer is to apply the depreciation rate to the historical cost and apply the index from the date of acquisition of the asset to the end of the reporting period.

Example 5.1.1.2

Restatement of property, plant and equipment

An entity acquires an item of property, plant and equipment on 31 December 20X1 for 1,000, when the general price index is 100. At 31 December 20X2, the index is 140 and the asset has been depreciated by 10 per cent. At 31 December 20X3, the index is 190 and the asset has been depreciated at 10 per cent for a second year.

	Balance brought forward	Indexing adjustment	Calculation of accumulated depreciation	Adjusted balance
Cost	1,000	140/100		1,400
Accumulated depreciation	-		(1,400 x 10%)	(140)
At 31 December 20X2				1,260
Cost	1,400	190/140		1,900
Accumulated depreciation	(140)		(140 x 190/140) + (1,900 x 10%)*	(380)
At 31 December 20X3				1,520

* The depreciation charge for the period 1 January 20X3 to 31 December 20X3 can also be expressed as 1,000 x 10% x 190/100.

In the first period of application of IAS 29, it may be difficult to establish the basis for restatement of information due to the absence of detailed records of the acquisition dates of items of property, plant and equipment. In the rare circumstances where it is not practicable to make a reliable estimate, the Standard suggests that it may be appropriate to use an independent professional assessment of the value of the items as the basis for their restatement. [IAS 29.16]

5.1.2 *Inventories*

In the restatement of a historical cost statement of financial position:

[IAS 29.15]

- inventories of raw materials and merchandise are to be restated by applying the change in the general price index from the date of acquisition to the end of the reporting period; and
- work-in-progress and finished goods are restated from the dates on which the costs of purchase and of conversion were incurred. This may prove to be a complex exercise, particularly where products take a long period to manufacture, as illustrated in **example 5.1.2**.

Example 5.1.2

Restatement of inventories

An entity, operating in a hyperinflationary economy, is preparing financial statements at its period end, 31 December. Assume labour and overheads are utilised evenly over a period, and the following changes in the general price index apply:

31 August	100
30 September	105
31 October	110
30 November	115
31 December	120

		Historical cost at end of the reporting period	Indexing adjustment	31 December adjusted balance
Raw materials	Purchased 31 October	250	120/110	273
	Purchased 30 November	250	120/115	261

		Historical cost at end of the reporting period	Indexing adjustment	31 December adjusted balance
Work-in-progress	Use of raw materials purchased 30 September	500	120/105	571
	Labour / overheads incurred from 31 October to 31 December	500	120/115 *	522
Finished goods	Use of raw materials purchased 31 August	500	120/100	600
	Labour / overheads incurred from 30 September to 31 December	500	120/112.5 **	533
Total		2,500		2,760

* 115 is the average for October to December

** 112.5 is the average for September to December

5.1.3 *Investments accounted for under the equity method*

Where the entity holds an investment that is accounted for under the equity method, and the investee reports in the currency of a hyperinflationary economy, the following steps are followed:

[IAS 29.20]

- the statement of financial position and statement of comprehensive income of the investee are restated in accordance with IAS 29 in order to calculate the investor's share of its net assets and profit or loss; and
- when the restated financial statements of the investee are expressed in a foreign currency, they are translated at closing rates.

5.1.4 *Borrowing costs*

In a hyperinflationary economy, the impact of inflation is usually recognised in borrowing costs. A loan agreement may provide for repayment of capital adjusted by a pre-defined index, with interest being charged at a 'normal' rate. Alternatively, loans may be negotiated at an interest rate in excess of the 'normal' rate that compensates for the loss in purchasing power of the money being loaned. Where an entity operates in a hyperinflationary economy, only the 'normal' element of the borrowing costs may be capitalised (see **chapter 27**). It is inappropriate to capitalise that part of the borrowing costs that compensates for inflation. This portion should be expensed as incurred. [IAS 29.21]

Where assets are acquired on deferred payment terms with no explicit interest charge, and it is impracticable to impute an amount of interest, the Standard allows that such assets are restated from the payment date and not the date of purchase. [IAS 29.22]

The logic for the treatment outlined in the previous paragraph is as follows. Normally, if resources flow out of the entity at the later date without any additional cost, the net monetary position can only be affected from that date. However, in practice, in a hyperinflationary economy, credit is only likely to be given if the cost of the asset is increased to compensate the seller for the loss in purchasing power of the cash during the credit period. Hence, it should be possible to impute an interest rate to the transaction and therefore capitalise the asset at a lower amount. The interest itself will be charged against income and the asset will be restated from the date of purchase. If no amount of interest can be imputed, then a reasonable approximation to this technically 'correct' position may be achieved by putting the asset in the accounts at the value actually paid and applying the index from the payment date.

5.1.5 *Impairment*

Where a balance has been restated, the restated amount is compared with the item's recoverable amount. When the restated amount exceeds the recoverable amount, an impairment loss is recognised with the effect that:

[IAS 29.19]

- inventories will be written down to net realisable value in line with IAS 2 *Inventories* (see **chapter 10**); and
- items of property, plant and equipment, and intangible assets, will be reduced to their recoverable amount in accordance with IAS 36 *Impairment of Assets* (see **chapter 9**).

5.1.6 *Equity*

When IAS 29 is first applied, the components of owners' equity at the *beginning* of the period will be adjusted as follows:

[IAS 29.24]

- any revaluation surplus that arose in previous periods is eliminated (i.e. it is absorbed in adjusted retained earnings);
- with the exception of retained earnings, other components (equity, share premium, and any other existing reserves) are restated by applying a general price index from the dates the components were contributed or otherwise arose; and
- restated retained earnings are calculated as the balancing figure after all adjustments have been made to all other components of the statement of financial position.

At the end of the first period, and in subsequent periods, all components of equity are again restated, this time by applying a general price index from the beginning of the period or the date of contribution, whichever is the later. These movements should be disclosed in the statement of changes in equity in accordance with IAS 1 *Presentation of Financial Statements*. [IAS 29.25]

Note that the elimination of a revaluation surplus is required only when IAS 29 is first applied. IAS 29 does not include a requirement that subsequent revaluations of property, plant and equipment or intangible assets, to the extent that they exceed the remeasurement arising from inflation, should be recognised in retained earnings. Such revaluations should be recognised in a revaluation surplus.

Example 5.1.6

Restatement of components of equity

An entity acquires an item of property, plant and equipment on 31 December 20X1 for 1,000, when the general price index is 100. At 31 December 20X2, the index is 140. The entity's policy is to revalue its property, plant and equipment. At 31 December 20X2, the item of property, plant and equipment has a fair value of 1,500.

	Historic cost	Indexing adjustment	Adjusted balance
Cost	1,000	140/100	1,400
Revaluation surplus (1,500 – 1,400)			100

5.2 Statement of comprehensive income

As for the statement of financial position, all items in the statement of comprehensive income should be expressed in terms of the measuring unit current at the end of the reporting period. Again, this is achieved by applying the change in a general price index from the dates when the income and expenses were first recorded. [IAS 29.26]

Since there may be a large number of transactions in the statement of comprehensive income, some estimation may be necessary. Furthermore, the general price index selected may not be published daily. Clearly, if prices are rising at a reasonably steady rate, and if the transactions being adjusted arise evenly, it might be an adequate approximation to use an average movement in the general price index over a period. However, judgement is required as to whether an average will result in a fair approximation. For example, if there are large, irregular transactions, an average rate will be unsuitable and actual rates should be used.

5.2.1 *Depreciation*

The method of calculating the charge for depreciation is illustrated in **example 5.1.1.2**.

5.2.2 *Cost of goods sold*

Another potentially complex area is the calculation of the cost of goods sold for inclusion in the statement of comprehensive income.

Example 5.2.2

Restatement of cost of goods sold

An entity has inventory of 200 at the beginning of the period, when the general price index is at 100. Purchases of 1,200 are made at an even rate throughout the year and closing inventory is 200. The closing inventory was acquired in two instalments in the last two months of the year, when the index was 120 and 122 respectively. At the end of the reporting period, the general price index is 124, and inflation rose steadily all year, giving an average rate of 112.

		Unadjusted balances	**Indexing adjustment**		**Adjusted balances**
Opening inventory		200	124/100		248
Purchases		1,200	124/112		1,329
Closing inventory	(100)		124/120	(103)	
	(100)		124/122	(102)	
		(200)			(205)
Cost of goods sold		1,200			1,372

5.2.3 *Current taxation*

The current taxation charge accrues over the period. Therefore, the restated current taxation charge is calculated by restating monthly tax expenses for each month in terms of balance-sheet-date purchasing power, using the increase in the general price index from the related month until the end of the reporting period. Where the movement in the index is not material, the current tax at year end may be indexed using average rates (i.e. as for other expenses). The difference between the opening restated deferred tax balance, and the revised closing deferred tax balance (as discussed at **4.5**) should be added to the above amount. (In **example 4.5** this amount will be 112.50).

5.3 Gain or loss arising on net monetary position

The gain or loss arising on the net monetary position as a result of all of the adjustments to items in the statement of financial position is included in profit or loss and separately disclosed. The Standard suggests that the gain or loss may be estimated by applying the change in the general price index to the weighted average for the period of the difference between monetary assets and monetary liabilities. However, it is more accurately calculated as the difference arising from:

[IAS 29.27]

- the restatement of non-monetary assets, owners' equity and items in the statement of comprehensive income; and
- the adjustment of index-linked assets and liabilities (where these exist), such as index-linked bonds and loans.

The Standard indicates that separate, but linked, disclosure may be appropriate in the statement of comprehensive income of:

[IAS 29.28]

- the net effect of restating non-monetary assets, owners' equity and items in the statement of comprehensive income;
- the net effect of adjusting any index-linked assets and/or liabilities;
- interest income and expense; and
- foreign exchange differences relating to invested and/or borrowed funds.

Example 5.3

Gain or loss arising on net monetary position

An entity has a loan linked to an index which was 100 at the start of the period and at the period end is 125. In preparing its financial statements, the entity uses a different index, which at the start of the period was 100 and at the end of the period is 120. Inflation is assumed to have occurred at an even rate throughout the period. The unadjusted depreciation charge for the period relates to assets acquired (on average) when the index stood at 80. (Note that for ease of use the example ignores the effects of taxation.)

	Unadjusted balances	Indexing adjustment	Adjusted balances	Gain/ (Loss)
Non-monetary assets	1,000	120/100	1,200	200
Monetary assets	500		500	
Index-linked loan	(100)	125/100	(125)	(25)
Monetary liabilities	(100)		(100)	
	1,300		1,475	
Capital	500	120/100	600	(100)
Retained earnings b/f	600	120/100	720	(120)
Profit for the period:				
-before depreciation	250	120/110 *	273	(23)
-less depreciation	(50)	120/80	(75)	25
Profit after depreciation	200		198	
Net monetary and index loss			(43) **	(43)
Retained earnings c/f	800		875	
	1,300		1,475	

* average rate

** calculated as demonstrated in the column on the right

Note that the loss of 25 on the index-linked loan has been shown separately in the column on the right as separate disclosure is suggested by IAS 29.

6 Current cost financial statements

6.1 Statement of financial position

As is clear from the previous discussion, items in the statement of financial position already carried at a current valuation do not require restatement, since they are already expressed in terms of the measuring unit current at the end of the reporting period. Therefore, in current cost financial statements, items of property, plant and equipment, investments and inventories, which will have been restated to current cost, do not require further adjustment. Items linked to changes in prices will be adjusted in accordance with the relevant agreements and other monetary items will again require no adjustment. [IAS 29.29]

Other items in the statement of financial position will, however, need to be restated. This includes goodwill, deferred credits and components of owners' equity. The guidance outlined above for items in a historical cost statement of financial position should be applied. [IAS 29.29]

6.2 Statement of comprehensive income

The current cost statement of comprehensive income, before restatement, generally reports costs current at the time at which the underlying transactions or events occurred. Cost of sales and depreciation are recorded at current costs at the time of consumption; sales and other expenses are recorded at their monetary amounts when they occurred. All of these amounts in the statement of comprehensive income should be restated in the measuring unit current at the end of the reporting period by applying a general price index. [IAS 29.30]

6.3 Gain or loss on net monetary position

The gain or loss on the net monetary position is accounted for as set out above for historical cost financial statements (see **5.3**). [IAS 29.31]

In current cost financial statements, there may already be an adjustment taking items from a historical cost basis to a current cost basis. Such adjustments are treated as part of the gain or loss on the net monetary position, and the two amounts will be treated as one for the purpose of disclosure.

7 Economies ceasing to be hyperinflationary

There are two simple rules to be applied when the economy ceases to be hyperinflationary: [IAS 29.38]

- the entity will cease to prepare its financial statements in accordance with IAS 29; and
- the carrying amounts of assets and liabilities in the entity's previous set of financial statements, which are the opening balances for the period in which the economy ceases to be hyperinflationary, will be treated as the basis for the carrying amounts in its subsequent financial statements. No adjustment is required to any balances in the financial statements.

8 Disclosure

The following disclosures are required:

[IAS 29.39]

- the fact that the financial statements and the corresponding figures have been restated for changes in the general purchasing power of the functional currency and, consequently, are stated in terms of the measuring unit current at the end of the reporting period;
- whether the financial statements are based on a historical cost approach or a current cost approach; and
- the price index that has been used, its level at the end of the reporting period and the movement in the index during the current and previous reporting periods.

The Standard does not further specify what is meant by the 'movement in the index' during the current and prior periods. Simple disclosure of the level of the index at the start of the current and previous periods may not, however, be sufficient. An indication should also be given of the extent of fluctuations during the period where these are material.

43 Agriculture

1 Introduction

IAS 41 *Agriculture* establishes standards of accounting for agricultural activity – the management of the biological transformation and harvest of biological assets (living plants and animals) into agricultural produce (harvested product of the entity's biological assets). As can be seen from the definitions set out in **section 3**, agricultural activity is not restricted to traditional farming operations, but will also apply to some entities operating in the bio-technology sector.

The Standard has been effective since 1 January 2003, and was most recently amended by *Improvements to IFRSs* issued in May 2008.

This chapter discusses the requirements of IAS 41 in the following sections:

Section 2	The fair value model for agricultural activity
Section 3	Scope
Section 4	Recognition of assets
Section 5	Measurement
Section 6	Reporting of gains and losses
Section 7	Government grants
Section 8	Presentation and disclosure

UK

Under UK GAAP, biological assets and agricultural produce are measured at historical cost in accordance with SSAP 9 Stocks and long-term contracts. *The fair value approach required by IAS 41 is significantly different, and may be expected to result in earlier profit recognition for many companies.*

2 The fair value model for agricultural activity

IAS 41 has introduced a fair value model for agricultural activity, which is a major shift away from the historical cost model widely applied in the initial recognition and measurement of assets. Under IAS 41, the measurement of all biological assets and agricultural produce is based on their fair value at the end of the reporting period and the point of harvest respectively. This fair value model has been introduced with the objective of providing more relevant information about the performance and future prospects of agricultural entities.

Some agricultural activity, such as the raising of livestock and the growing of timber, may take several years to give rise to produce for sale. Under the historical cost model, a sales transaction is generally required before the recognition of any gain is triggered. However, in the context of agricultural activity, the event giving rise to such gains is the progress of development of the biological assets, e.g. growth, procreation, harvest. The fair value model is intended to capture these gains as they occur.

3 Scope

IAS 41 should be applied when accounting for biological assets, agricultural produce at the point of harvest, and government grants, when they relate to agricultural activity. [IAS 41.1] The definitions set out in the following paragraphs clarify this statement of scope.

3.1 Definitions

The following are the key definitions for the purposes of IAS 41:

[IAS 41.5]

- agricultural activity refers to the management by an entity of the biological transformation and harvest of biological assets for sale of for conversion into agricultural produce or into additional biological assets;
- a biological asset is defined as a living animal or plant;
- biological transformation comprises the processes of growth, degeneration, production and procreation that cause qualitative or quantitative changes in a biological asset;
- agricultural produce is defined as the harvested product of the entity's biological assets;
- harvest is the detachment of produce from a biological asset or the cessation of a biological asset's life processes; and
- costs to sell are the incremental costs directly attributable to the disposal of an asset, excluding finance costs and income taxes.

The definition of costs to sell was introduced by *Improvements to IFRSs* issued in May 2008, which also deleted previous references to 'point-of-sale costs'. The IASB decided that 'point-of-sale costs' and 'costs to sell' meant the same thing in the context of IAS 41 and, therefore, decided to replace the terms 'point-of-sale costs' and 'estimated point-of-sale costs' with 'costs to sell' to make IAS 41 consistent with IFRS 5 and IAS 36. As there is no intended change of substance, this chapter refers only to the new terminology.

Agricultural activity covers a diverse range of activities such as raising livestock, forestry, cropping, cultivating orchards and plantations, floriculture, and aquaculture (including fish farming). The key feature that often differentiates agricultural activities from other related activities is the entity's management of the biological transformation. For example, the entity may manage biological transformation by enhancing, or at least stabilising, conditions necessary for the process to take place (e.g. nutrient levels, moisture, temperature, fertility and light). Harvesting from unmanaged sources (such as open ocean fishing and deforestation) is not agricultural activity since it does not involve management of the resource. [IAS 41.6]

Example 3.1

Plant breeding: seed multiplication

Following on the development of new plant breeds, a plant-breeding entity uses the developed breeding seed to multiply the seed into basic seed which will then be sold.

The multiplication of seeds to be harvested for sale is an agricultural activity as it represents a biological transformation process of biological assets managed by the entity for sale – that is, the entity transforms the breeding seeds into seeds for sale using biological processes, and this activity is, therefore, within the scope of IAS 41.

A resource may be 'managed' by government, through the use of mechanisms such as licensing and quotas, but this does not of itself result in the activity being classified as an agricultural activity under IAS 41. What matters is whether the entity itself manages the resource.

Agricultural activities do not include:

- holding investments in a forest as a carbon sink, which gives rise to carbon credits that can either be sold or used to offset pollution caused by the entity;

- using animals such as greyhounds, horses, pigeons or whippets for racing;
- exhibiting performing animals, for example in a theme park; or
- managing living assets that are not animals and plants, such as viruses and blood cells used in research.

3.2 Accounting after the point of harvest

IAS 41 deals only with the treatment of biological assets up to the point of harvest, and not with any further transformations that they may undergo thereafter. After the harvest is completed, the assets are generally accounted for under IAS 2 *Inventories* (see **chapter 10**). [IAS 41.3] In more limited circumstances, they may be accounted for under another Standard. For example, if an entity harvests logs and decides to use them for constructing its own building, IAS 16 *Property, Plant and Equipment* is applied in accounting for the logs. [IAS 41.B8]

The following table, reproduced from IAS 41.4, sets out a number of examples of biological assets, agricultural produce, and products that are the result of processing after harvest.

Biological assets	Agricultural produce	Products that are the result of processing after harvest
Sheep	Wool	Yarn, carpet
Trees in a plantation forest	Felled trees	Logs, lumber
Plants	Cotton	Thread, clothing
	Harvested cane	Sugar
Dairy cattle	Milk	Cheese
Pigs	Carcass	Sausages, cured hams
Bushes	Leaf	Tea, cured tobacco
Vines	Grapes	Wine
Fruit trees	Picked fruit	Processed fruit

Specifically excluded from the scope of IAS 41 are ageing or maturation processes that occur after harvest (e.g. wine production from grapes and cheese production from milk). [IAS 41.3] Some had argued for the inclusion of such processing within the scope of IAS 41 because it is a logical and natural extension of agricultural activity, and the events taking place are similar to biological transformation. The IASB decided, however, not to include such processes in the scope of the Standard because of concerns about difficulties in differentiating them from other manufacturing processes. [IAS 41.B11)]

3.3 Other assets used in agricultural activity

The Standard does not address the accounting treatment for land on which agricultural activity is conducted, nor intangible assets (e.g. milk quotas) related to agricultural activity. These are covered by IAS 16 *Property, Plant and Equipment* (see **chapter 6**), IAS 40 *Investment Property* (see **chapter 7**) and IAS 38 *Intangible Assets* (see **chapter 8**). [IAS 41.2)]

Example 3.3

Plant breeding: new seed development

An entity's activity is plant breeding. In the initial stages of the plant-breeding process, the entity must develop new varieties by selection of seeds and cross-breeding in a laboratory, as well as performing field tests. This process can take up to twelve years.

The development of new breeds of seed is not within the scope of IAS 41 but is accounted for in accordance with the requirements of IAS 38 *Intangible Assets* that relate to research and development costs. IAS 41.2(b) states that the Standard does not apply to intangible assets related to agricultural activity.

4 Recognition of assets

Entities are required to recognise biological assets or agricultural produce when, and only when, all of the following conditions are met:

[IAS 41.10]

- the entity controls the asset as a result of past events;
- it is probable that future economic benefits associated with the asset will flow to the entity; and
- the fair value or cost of the asset can be measured reliably.

Where future agricultural produce (fruit, wool, etc.) is attached to biological assets (trees, vines, animals, etc.), it should not be recognised separately before harvest. Until harvest, that future agricultural produce forms part of the total biological asset and this asset should be measured as a whole. For example, all else being equal, trees with fruit have a higher fair value immediately before harvest than immediately after harvest, and unshorn sheep have a higher fair value than those that are shorn.

Example 4

Separate recognition of produce before harvest

An entity owns an apple orchard. The trees are mature and their fair value (excluding fruit) has not increased during the reporting period. The fair value (less costs to sell) of the apples on the trees is £100,000 immediately before harvest.

The following journal entries would be recorded to reflect the recognition and harvesting of the apples:

	Debit	Credit
	£	£
Apple trees	100,000	
Gain on biological assets		100,000
being the recognition of the increase in fair value of apple trees due to apples growing on them (up to the point of harvest).		
Inventory	100,000	
Gain on harvest of apples		100,000
being the recognition of the apples at harvest at fair value (less costs to sell).		
Loss on biological assets	100,000	
Apple trees		100,000
being the recognition of the decrease in the fair value of apple trees due to apples being harvested.		

Control over biological assets or agricultural produce may be evidenced by, for example, legal ownership of cattle and the branding or otherwise marking of the cattle on acquisition, birth, or weaning. The future benefits are normally assessed by measuring the significant physical attributes. [IAS 41.11]

5 Measurement

5.1 Biological assets

IAS 41 requires that biological assets be measured on initial recognition and at the end of each reporting period at fair value less costs to sell, unless fair value cannot be measured reliably (see **5.1.4**). [IAS 41.12)]

5.1.1 Measuring fair value

Fair value is defined as the amount for which an asset could be exchanged, or a liability settled, between knowledgeable, willing parties in an arm's length transaction. [IAS 41.8]

The following guidance is provided on the measurement of fair value.

[IAS 41.17 – 20]

- A quoted market price in an active market for a biological asset in its present location and condition is the most reliable basis for determining the fair value of that asset. If the entity has access to more than one active market, then the entity should use the most relevant market, generally the market expected to be used.
- If an active market does not exist, IAS 41 suggests that reference be made to the following market-based measures, considering the reasons for any differences between them in order to arrive at the most reliable estimate:
    - the most recent market price for that type of asset, provided that there has not been a significant change in economic circumstances between the date of that transaction and the end of the reporting period;
    - market prices for similar assets appropriately adjusted to reflect differences; and
    - sector benchmarks such as the value of an orchard expressed per export tray, bushel or hectare, and the value of cattle expressed per kilogram of meat.
- If reliable market-based prices are not available for the biological asset in its present condition, the present value of expected net cash flows from the asset should be used in determining fair value.

Where the present value of expected future net cash flows from the asset is to be used as the basis for measuring fair value, the Standard sets out the following rules:

[IAS 41.20 – 23]

- the cash flows should be discounted using a current market-determined rate;
- in order to determine the fair value of the asset in its present location and condition, an entity includes the net cash flows that market participants would expect the asset to generate in its most relevant market.;
- the possibility of variations in cash flows should be reflected either in the cash flows or in the discount rate, taking care to avoid assumptions being double-counted or ignored;
- financing and taxation cash flows should be excluded; and

- cash flows related to re-establishing biological assets after harvest (e.g. the cost of planting replacement crops) should be excluded.

The words in the first two bullets above are as amended by *Improvements to IFRSs* issued in May 2008, and apply prospectively for annual periods beginning on or after 1 January 2009. Earlier application is permitted, but if an entity applies the amendments for an earlier period it should disclose that fact.

Improvements to IFRSs deleted from IAS 41.20 a requirement to use a pre-tax discount rate. It also deleted from IAS 41.21 a requirement that the present condition of a biological asset should exclude any increases in value from additional biological transformation and future activities of the entity, such as those related to enhancing the future biological transformation, harvesting, and selling.

Diversity in practice had developed from different interpretations of the latter requirement, because it could be read to exclude from such calculations increases in cash flows arising from 'additional biological transformation'. The IASB decided that not including these cash flows resulted in a carrying amount that is not representative of an asset's fair value, and noted that an entity should consider the risks associated with cash flows from 'additional biological transformation' in determining the expected cash flows, the discount rate, or some combination of the two. Because applying the changes to this requirement and that relating to pre-tax discount rates retrospectively might require some entities to remeasure the fair value of biological assets at a past date, the IASB decided that these amendments should be applied prospectively. [IAS 41.BC8 – BC10]

The Standard recognises that, in limited circumstances, cost is an appropriate indicator of fair value. This will be particularly so where little biological transformation has taken place since the cost was incurred (e.g. seedlings planted immediately prior to the end of the reporting period), or where the impact of biological transformation on price is not expected to be material (e.g. in the very early stages of a 30-year plantation growth cycle). [IAS 41.24]

Although agricultural land is excluded from the scope of IAS 41, as discussed at **3.3** above, biological assets that are physically attached to land (e.g. trees in a plantation forest) are accounted for under the Standard. There may be no separate market for biological assets that are attached to land, but an active market may exist for the combined assets, i.e. for the biological assets, raw land and land improvements as a package. The Standard allows the entity to use information regarding the combined assets to determine fair value for the biological assets. For example, the fair value of raw land and land improvements may be deducted from the fair value of the combined assets to arrive at the fair value of the biological assets. [IAS 41.25]

5.1.2 *Transport and other costs to sell*

The fair value of an asset is based on its present location and condition, and therefore it reflects a market price less transport and other costs necessary to get an asset to market. As a result, for example, the fair value of cattle at a farm is the price for the cattle in the relevant market less the transport and other costs of getting the cattle to that market. [IAS 41.9]

Other costs to sell, which are deducted from fair value in the measurement of biological assets, include the following:

- brokers' and dealers' commissions;
- levies by regulatory agencies and commodity exchanges; and
- transfer taxes and other duties.

Because costs to sell are deducted from fair value when biological assets are first recognised, they can give rise to an immediate loss. For example, if an asset is purchased for its fair value of £100, and it is estimated that a 10 per cent commission would be payable if the asset were ever sold, then the asset is recognised in the balance sheet at £90, and a £10 loss recognised in profit or loss. This is irrespective of whether the entity expects to make a profit on the ultimate realisation of the asset or, indeed, whether it has any intention of ever selling the asset (e.g. a bearer biological asset that will not be sold).

5.1.3 *Assets subject to sale contracts*

The Standard highlights that, where the reporting entity has entered into sales contracts for the disposal of the biological assets at a future date, those contract prices are not necessarily taken into account in determining fair value. Fair value is not an entity-specific measure, and it is required to reflect the current market in which a willing buyer and seller would enter into a transaction. Sales contracts entered into in the past may not reflect the price that a willing buyer and seller would otherwise have agreed at the date of measurement. Therefore, the fair value at any point in time is not adjusted because of the existence of guaranteed sales contracts. [IAS 41.16]

In certain cases, a contract for the sale of biological assets may be an onerous contract within the meaning of IAS 37 *Provisions, Contingent Liabilities and Contingent Assets* (see **chapter 11**).

5.1.4 *Inability to measure fair value reliably*

IAS 41 presumes that fair value can be measured reliably for most biological assets. That presumption can be rebutted, however, where the following conditions are met at the time the biological asset is initially recognised in the financial statements:

[IAS 41.30]

- market-determined prices or values are not available for the biological asset; and
- other methods of reasonably estimating fair value are determined to be clearly unreliable.

Where these conditions are met, the biological asset is measured at cost less accumulated depreciation and any accumulated impairment losses. [IAS 41.30] IAS 41 directs preparers to IAS 2 *Inventories*, IAS 16 *Property, Plant and Equipment*, and IAS 36 *Impairment of Assets* for guidance in these circumstances.

If circumstances change, and fair value becomes reliably measurable, a switch to fair value less costs to sell is required. [IAS 41.30] This is likely to occur as biological transformation progresses.

Once a non-current biological asset meets the criteria to be classified as held for sale (or is included in a disposal group that is classified as held for sale) in accordance with IFRS 5 *Non-current Assets Held for Sale and Discontinued Operations* (see **chapter 29**), it is presumed that fair value can be measured reliably. [IAS 41.30]

The presumption that fair value can be measured reliably can be rebutted only on initial recognition. An entity that has previously measured a biological asset at its fair value less costs to sell continues to measure that biological asset at its fair value less costs to sell until disposal. [IAS 41.31] Therefore, the Standard does not permit use of the measurement reliability exception in circumstances where an entity has previously measured a particular biological asset at fair value, and market transactions become less frequent or market prices become less readily available, so that it becomes more difficult to determine the fair value of the asset. This prohibition on changing the measurement basis from fair value to cost is designed to prevent entities using the reliability exception as an excuse to discontinue fair value accounting in a falling market.

5.1.5 *Leased assets*

Biological assets held by lessees under finance leases and biological assets provided by lessors under operating leases should be measured in accordance with the requirements of IAS 41. These assets are specifically excluded from the measurement requirements of IAS 17 *Leases*. [IAS 17.2]

Therefore, biological assets acquired under a finance lease should be initially recognised and subsequently measured in accordance with the measurement requirements of IAS 41 – i.e. at fair value less costs to sell, except where the fair value cannot be measured reliably. Due to their nature, it is unlikely that fair value could not be measured reliably for leased assets.

The disclosure requirements of both IAS 41 and IAS 17 should be followed when preparing financial reports in such circumstances.

5.2 Agricultural produce

IAS 41 requires that agricultural produce be measured at fair value less costs to sell at the point that it is harvested from the entity's biological assets. [IAS 41.13] The guidance outlined in **section 5.1** above as regards the measurement of fair value less costs to sell applies equally to agricultural produce.

However, there is no measurement reliability exception (as discussed in **5.1.4**) for agricultural produce. Because harvested produce is a marketable commodity, the Standard reflects the view that the fair value of agricultural produce at the point of harvest can always be measured reliably. Therefore, in all cases, such produce is required to be measured at fair value less costs to sell. [IAS 41.32]

The fair value measurement of agricultural produce at the point of harvest is the cost of that produce for subsequent accounting under IAS 2 *Inventories*, or another applicable International Accounting Standard. [IAS 41.13]

Thus, for example, corn that has not yet been harvested will be remeasured at the end of each reporting period, reflecting changes in market prices, because it will meet the definition of a biological asset. Once it has been harvested, however, that remeasurement will generally cease, and it will be carried under IAS 2 at the lower of cost (defined as fair value less costs to sell at the point of harvest) and net realisable value.

6 Reporting of gains and losses

When a biological asset is first recognised at fair value less costs to sell, any gain or loss arising is reported in the profit or loss for the period. A loss on initial recognition can arise in relation to an asset purchased at fair value, due to the requirement to deduct costs to sell. A gain can arise, for example, when a biological asset is first recognised following the birth of a calf.

Gains and losses will also arise over the life of the biological asset to reflect changes in fair value less costs to sell. These gains and losses are also reported in profit or loss in the period in which they arise. [IAS 41.26] Thus, for example, changes in fair value as a calf grows are also recognised in profit or loss.

The gain or loss arising on initial recognition of agricultural produce at fair value less costs to sell is included in profit or loss for the period in which it arises. [IAS 41.28] Agricultural produce is first recognised at the time of harvest (up to that point the asset has been classified as a biological asset). As a result of harvesting, a gain or loss may arise, and that is recognised in profit or loss.

7 Government grants

IAS 41 sets out specific rules for accounting for government grants related to agricultural activity, which are discussed in this section. The treatment prescribed may give a different result than would arise if IAS 20 *Accounting for Government Grants and Disclosure of Government Assistance* were applied. This divergence may be eliminated in the medium term as the IASB intends in due course to revise IAS 20 (see **chapter 41** for further details). For the present, however, two different sets of rules apply. The only time that IAS 20 should be applied in relation to biological assets is where those assets are carried on a cost basis (i.e. the measurement reliability exception is applied), as described below.

7.1 Biological assets measured on a fair value basis

IAS 41 requires that unconditional grants related to biological assets measured at fair value less costs to sell should be recognised in profit or loss when, and only when, the grant becomes receivable. [IAS 41.34]

If the grant is conditional, it should be recognised in profit or loss when, and only when, the conditions attached to the grant are met. This includes grants under the conditions of which entities are required not to engage in specified agricultural activity. [IAS 41.35]

Government grants related to agricultural activity will frequently be subject to conditions such as the requirement to continue to engage in a specified activity (or to refrain from engaging in a specified activity) for an extended period of time. If the condition is breached, then all of the grant may be refundable. In such circumstances, no part of the grant is recognised in profit or loss until the specified period has elapsed. However, where the terms of the government grant allow part of the funds to be retained according to the time that has elapsed, then the entity should recognise that part of the grant in profit or loss as time passes. [IAS 41.36]

7.2 Biological assets measured on a cost basis

The rules set out above relate to biological assets that are measured at fair value less costs to sell. As discussed at **5.1.4**, there will be occasions where it is not possible to measure reliably the fair value of a biological asset, in which case it is recorded at cost less accumulated depreciation and impairment losses. Government grants relating to biological assets accounted for on a historical cost basis are dealt with under IAS 20 (see **chapter 41**). [IAS 41.37]

8 Presentation and disclosure

8.1 Presentation

IAS 1 *Presentation of Financial Statements* requires an entity to present the carrying amount of its biological assets (other than those included in disposal groups – see **chapter 29**) separately in its statement of financial position. [IAS 1(2007).54(f), previously IAS 1(2003).68(f)]

8.2 Disclosure

IAS 41's disclosure requirements, which are set out below, are illustrated in detail in Example 1 of the Illustrative Examples published as Appendix A to the Standard.

8.2.1 Description of biological assets and activities

The entity is required to provide a description of each group of biological assets (defined as an aggregation of similar living animals or plants), which may take the form of a narrative or quantified description. Entities are encouraged to provide a quantified description of each group, distinguishing between consumable biological assets (i.e. those to be harvested, such as crops) and bearer biological assets (e.g. orchards), or between mature and immature biological assets, as appropriate. The basis for any such analysis should be disclosed. [IAS 41.41 – 44]

If not disclosed elsewhere in information published with the financial statements, the following should also be described:

[IAS 41.46]

- the nature of the entity's activities involving each group of biological assets; and
- non-financial measures or estimates of the physical quantities of:
  - each group of the entity's biological assets at the end of the period; and
  - the output of agricultural produce during the period.

8.2.2 Gains and losses recognised during the period

The entity is required to disclose the aggregate gain or loss arising during the current period on the initial recognition of biological assets and agricultural produce, and from the change in fair value less costs to sell of biological assets. [IAS 41.40]

Note that there is no requirement to disclose separately the gain or loss related to biological assets and the gain or loss related to agricultural produce.

Occasionally, events may cause material gains or losses that should be disclosed separately in accordance with IAS 1(2007).97 (previously IAS

1(2003).86) (see **section 5.3.1** of **chapter 3**). In the context of agricultural activity, such events may include, for example, disease, flood, drought, frost or plague. [IAS 41.53]

8.2.3 Reconciliation of changes in biological assets

A detailed reconciliation is required of changes in the carrying amount of biological assets between the beginning and the end of the accounting period, which includes:

[IAS 41.50]

- the gain or loss arising from changes in fair values less costs to sell;
- increases arising from purchases;
- decreases attributable to sales and biological assets classified as held for sale (or included in a disposal group that is classified as held for sale) in accordance with IFRS 5 (see **chapter 29**);
- decreases due to harvest;
- increases arising from business combinations;
- net exchange differences arising from the translation of financial statements into a different presentation currency, and on the translation of a foreign operation into the presentation currency of the reporting entity; and
- any other changes.

8.2.4 Basis for measurement of fair value

The entity is required to disclose the methods and significant assumptions used in determining the fair value of each group of agricultural produce at the point of harvest, and each group of biological assets. [IAS 41.47]

8.2.5 Produce harvested during the year

The fair value less costs to sell of agricultural produce harvested during the year, determined at the point of harvest, should be disclosed. [IAS 41.48]

8.2.6 Restricted assets, commitments and risk management strategies

The entity should disclose:

[IAS 41.49]

- the existence and carrying amounts of biological assets whose title is restricted, and the carrying amounts of biological assets pledged as security for liabilities;
- the amount of commitments for the development or acquisition of biological assets; and
- financial risk management strategies in relation to its agricultural activities.

8.2.7 Additional disclosures where fair value cannot be measured reliably

If biological assets are measured at cost less accumulated depreciation and impairment losses (see **5.1.4**), the following disclosures are required:

[IAS 41.54]

- a description of the biological assets;
- an explanation as to why fair value cannot be determined reliably;
- the range of estimates within which fair value is highly likely to lie, if possible;
- the depreciation method used;
- the useful lives or depreciation rates used; and
- the gross carrying amount and the accumulated depreciation and impairment losses at the beginning and end of the period.

Any gain or loss arising on the disposal of biological assets held at cost less accumulated depreciation and accumulated impairment losses should be disclosed. In addition, the amounts for biological assets held on a cost basis should be disclosed separately in the detailed reconciliation for biological assets set out at **8.2.3**, and the reconciliation should disclose impairment losses, reversals of impairment losses and depreciation charged during the period. [IAS 41.55]

Where an entity moves from a cost basis to a fair value basis during the year, it is required to provide a description of the affected biological assets, an explanation as to why the fair value can now be measured reliably, and the effect of the change. [IAS 41.56]

8.2.8 Government grants

The following disclosures are required for government grants relating to agricultural activity:

[IAS 41.57]

- the nature and extent of government grants recognised;
- unfulfilled conditions and other contingencies attaching to grants; and
- significant decreases expected in the level of government grants.

8.2.9 *Additional recommended disclosures*

The Standard encourages, but does not require, separate disclosure of the effects of physical change and price change resulting in changes to the carrying amount of biological assets, particularly when there is a production cycle of more than one year. [IAS 41.51] Growth, degeneration, production, procreation and harvest are each types of physical change that are observable and measurable. Example 2 of the Illustrative Examples published as Appendix A to IAS 41 illustrates how to separate physical change and price change. [IAS 41.52]

44 Insurance contracts

1 Introduction

Specific accounting requirements for insurance entities are, for the most part, outside the scope of this book. Nevertheless, this chapter provides an overview of IFRS 4 *Insurance Contracts*, in part as a general introduction and in part because the interaction of its requirements with those of other Standards (in particular, IAS 18 *Revenue* and IAS 39 *Financial Instruments: Recognition and Measurement*) is important to entities other than insurance entities.

IFRS 4 *Insurance Contracts* was issued by the IASB in March 2004, completing the first phase of the Board's insurance project. The Standard is seen only as a stepping stone to the second phase (see **section 6**) and its objectives are quite restricted. IFRS 4 requires:

[IFRS 4.1]

- limited improvements to accounting for insurance contracts by those who accept obligations under such contracts; and
- disclosures that identify and explain the amounts in an insurer's financial statements arising from insurance contracts and help users of those financial statements understand the amount, timing and uncertainty of future cash flows from insurance contracts.

The IASB recognises that accounting practices for insurance contracts have been diverse and have often differed from practices in other sectors. The Board is committed to completing the second phase of its insurance project without delay once it has investigated all relevant conceptual and practical questions and completed its full due process.

This chapter discusses the requirements of IFRS 4 in the following sections:

Section 2	When is a contract an insurance contract?
Section 3	Scope of IFRS 4
Section 4	Recognition and measurement

Section 5 Disclosure

Section 6 Future developments

UK

> *Despite its limited scope, IFRS 4 may have a significant impact on UK insurers, not least in that it requires some contracts, which previously may have been treated as insurance contracts under UK GAAP, to be accounted for in accordance with IAS 39* Financial Instruments: Recognition and Measurement.

2 When is a contract an insurance contract?

2.1 Definition of an insurance contract

The definition of an insurance contract determines whether a contract is within the scope of IFRS 4 or another Standard. An insurance contract is defined as a contract under which one party (the insurer) accepts significant insurance risk from another party (the policyholder) by agreeing to compensate the policyholder if a specified uncertain future event (the insured event) adversely affects the policyholder. [IFRS 4(Appendix A)]

Section 2.2 below discusses certain key aspects of this definition, namely:

- the requirement for a specified uncertain future event;
- the meaning of insurance risk;
- whether insurance risk is significant; and
- whether the insured event adversely affects the policyholder.

2.2 Key elements of the definition

2.2.1 Specified uncertain future event

The definition in **2.1** requires the identification of an insured event, which is defined as an uncertain future event that is covered by an insurance contract and creates insurance risk. [IFRS 4(Appendix A)] The element of uncertainty (or risk) is essential for a contract to be considered an insurance contract, and at least one of the following must be uncertain at the inception of an insurance contract:

[IFRS 4.B2]

- whether an insured event will occur;
- when it will occur; or

- how much the insurer will need to pay if it occurs.

Depending on the nature of the insurance contract, the insured event could be:

[IFRS 4.B3 & B4]

- the discovery of a loss during the term of the contract (even if the loss arises from an event that occurred before the inception of the contract);
- an event that occurs during the term of the contract (even if the resulting loss is discovered after the end of the contract term); or
- where an insurance contract covers an event that has already occurred, but whose financial effect is still uncertain, the discovery of the ultimate cost. As an example, where a reinsurance contract covers the direct insurer against adverse development of claims already reported by policyholders, the insured event is the discovery of the ultimate cost of those claims.

2.2.2 *Insurance risk vs financial risk*

IFRS 4 distinguishes 'insurance risk' from 'financial risk'. A contract is not an insurance contract unless the insurer accepts significant insurance risk.

[IFRS 4(Appendix A)]

- Financial risk is defined as the risk of a possible future change in one or more of a specified interest rate, financial instrument price, commodity price, foreign exchange rate, index of prices or rates, credit rating or credit index or other variable, provided in the case of a non-financial variable that the variable is not specific to a party to the contract.
- Insurance risk is defined as risk, other than financial risk, transferred from the holder of a contract to the issuer.

The presence of significant financial risk does not prevent a contract from being an insurance contract. What matters is that there is significant insurance risk, irrespective of the level of financial risk. For example, many life insurance contracts both guarantee a minimum rate of return to policyholders (creating financial risk) and promise death benefits that can significantly exceed the policyholder's account balance (creating insurance risk in the form of mortality risk). Such contracts are insurance contracts under IFRS 4. [IFRS 4.B10]

UK

> *Nevertheless, it is likely that some financial contracts, which have historically been regarded as insurance contracts under UK GAAP, will not be treated as insurance contracts under IFRS 4. This will be the case, for example, where those contracts include no insurance risk or the amount of insurance risk accepted by the insurer is not significant. Such contracts will not be within the scope of IFRS 4 and are likely instead to fall within the scope of IAS 18* Revenue *(see* ***chapter*** **23***) and/or IAS 39* Financial Instruments: Recognition and Measurement *(see* ***chapters*** **13** *to* **22**).

Under some contracts, an insured event triggers the payment of an amount linked to a price index. Provided that the payment that is contingent on the insured event can be significant, such contracts are insurance contracts. IFRS 4.B11 gives the example of a life-contingent annuity linked to a cost-of-living index. The contract transfers insurance risk because payment is triggered by an uncertain event, namely the survival of the annuitant. The link to the price index is an embedded derivative, but it also transfers insurance risk. If the resulting transfer of insurance risk is significant, the embedded derivative meets the definition of an insurance contract, in which case it need not be separated and measured at fair value (see **3.4**). [IFRS 4.B11]

2.2.2.1 *Is a non-financial variable specific to a party to the contract?*

The definition of financial risk in **2.2.2** above lists both financial and non-financial variables, but the latter are included in financial risk only if they are not specific to a party to the contract. IFRS 4.B9 gives the example of an index of earthquake losses in a particular region or an index of temperatures in a particular city.

Financial risk excludes non-financial variables that are specific to a party to the contract, such as the occurrence or non-occurrence of a fire that damages or destroys an asset of that party. In addition, the risk of changes in the fair value of a non-financial asset is not a financial risk if the fair value reflects not only changes in market prices for such assets (a financial variable) but also the condition of a specific non-financial asset held by a party to a contract (a non-financial variable). If, for example, a guarantee of the residual value of a specific car exposes the guarantor to the risk of changes in the car's physical condition, that risk is insurance risk, not financial risk. [IFRS 4.B9]

2.2.2.2 *Is insurance risk accepted from another party?*

The definition of insurance risk in **2.2.2** refers to risk that is transferred to the insurer from the policyholder. Accordingly, insurance risk can only be a pre-existing risk of the policyholder – a new risk created by the contract is not insurance risk. [IFRS 4.B12]

An insurer can accept significant insurance risk from the policyholder only if the insurer is an entity separate from the policyholder. In the case of a mutual insurer, the mutual accepts risk from each policyholder and pools that risk. Although policyholders bear that pooled risk collectively in their capacity as owners, the mutual has still accepted the risk that is the essence of an insurance contract. [IFRS 4.B17]

2.2.3 *Is insurance risk significant?*

The definition of an insurance contract (see **2.1**) requires the transfer of 'significant' insurance risk. IFRS 4.B23 indicates that insurance risk is significant if, and only if, an insured event could cause an insurer to pay significant additional benefits in some scenario, excluding scenarios that lack commercial substance (i.e. scenarios that have no discernible effect on the economics of the transaction). If significant additional benefits would be payable in scenarios that have commercial substance, this condition may be met even if the insured event is extremely unlikely or even if the expected (i.e. probability-weighted) present value of contingent cash flows is a small proportion of the expected present value of all the remaining contractual cash flows. [IFRS 4.B23]

> Thus, where a future event is very unlikely, but would be catastrophic if it occurred, a contract paying out a large sum on the occurrence of that event may well be an insurance contract. However, a contract relating to a future event which is very unlikely and would not be particularly damaging may be less likely to have commercial substance. Accordingly, insurance risk for the latter may not be significant.

Appendix B to IFRS 4 includes further guidance as to how to determine whether insurance risk is significant, as discussed below.

2.2.3.1 *Additional benefits*

When considering whether significant additional benefits (as described in **2.2.3**) would be payable on the occurrence of an insured event, it is necessary to identify the amounts in excess of those that would be payable if no insured event occurred (excluding scenarios that lack commercial substance). Those additional amounts include claims handling and claims assessment costs, but exclude:

[IFRS 4.B24]

(a) the loss of the ability to charge the policyholder for future services. In an investment-linked life insurance contract, for example, the death of the policyholder means that the insurer can no longer provide investment management services for a fee. This economic loss for the insurer does not reflect insurance risk, just as a mutual fund manager does not take on insurance risk relating to the possible death of the client. Accordingly, the potential loss of future investment management fees is not relevant in assessing how much insurance risk is transferred by a contract;

(b) waiver on death of charges that would be made on cancellation or surrender. Because the contract brought those charges into existence, the waiver of these charges does not compensate the policyholder for a pre-existing risk. Hence, they are not relevant in assessing how much insurance risk is transferred by a contract;

(c) a payment conditional on an event that does not cause a significant loss to the holder of the contract. Suppose, for example, that an issuer is required to pay £1,000,000 if an asset suffers physical damage causing an insignificant economic loss of £500 to the holder. In such a contract, the holder transfers to the insurer the insignificant risk of losing £500, but the contract creates non-insurance risk that the issuer will need to pay £999,500 if the specified event occurs. Because the issuer does not accept significant insurance risk from the holder, such a contract is not an insurance contract; and

(d) possible reinsurance recoveries. The insurer accounts separately for these.

2.2.3.2 *Contract-by-contract assessment*

The significance of insurance risk is assessed on a contract-by-contract basis, rather than by reference to materiality to the financial statements, but treating contracts entered into simultaneously with a single counterparty (or contracts that are otherwise interdependent) as a single contract. Accordingly, even if there is a minimal probability of material losses for a whole book of contracts, insurance risk may be significant. A contract-by-contract assessment makes it easier to classify a contract as an insurance contract. The Standard allows, however, that if a relatively homogeneous book of small contracts is known to consist of contracts that all transfer insurance risk, it is not necessary for the insurer to examine each contract within that book to identify a few non-derivative contracts that transfer insignificant insurance risk. [IFRS 4.B25]

2.2.3.3 *Death benefit*

If a contract pays a death benefit exceeding the amount payable on survival, the contract is an insurance contract unless the additional death benefit is insignificant (judged by reference to the contract rather than to an entire book of contracts). As noted at **2.2.3.1**, the waiver on death of cancellation or surrender charges is not included in this assessment if this waiver does not compensate the policyholder for a pre-existing risk. Similarly, an annuity contract that pays out regular sums for the rest of a policyholder's life is an insurance contract, unless the aggregate life-contingent payments are insignificant. [IFRS 4.B26]

2.2.3.4 *Timing of payment*

The reference to additional benefits in **2.2.3** could include a requirement to pay benefits earlier if the insured event occurs earlier and the payment is not adjusted for the time value of money. The Standard gives the example of whole life insurance for a fixed amount (i.e. insurance that provides a fixed death benefit whenever the policyholder dies, with no expiry date for the cover). Although it is certain that the policyholder will die, the date of death is uncertain. The insurer will suffer a loss on those individual contracts for which policyholders die early, even if there is no overall loss on the whole book of contracts. [IFRS 4.B27]

2.2.3.5 *Deposit and insurance components*

A deposit component is a contractual component that is not accounted for as a derivative under IAS 39 and would be within the scope of IAS 39 if it were a separate instrument. [IFRS 4(Appendix A)] Where an insurance contract is unbundled into a deposit component and an insurance component, the significance of insurance risk transferred is assessed by reference to the insurance component. The significance of insurance risk transferred by an embedded derivative is assessed by reference to that embedded derivative. [IFRS 4.B28]

2.2.4 *Does the insured event adversely affect the policyholder?*

Under some contracts, payment is required if a specified uncertain event occurs, regardless of whether there is an adverse effect on the policyholder. Such contracts are not insurance contracts, even if the holders use them to mitigate underlying risk exposures. The definition of an insurance contract (see **2.1**) requires an adverse effect on the policyholder, arising from a specified uncertain future event, to be a contractual precondition for payment. Although this contractual precondition does not require the insurer to investigate whether the event actually caused an adverse effect, it permits the insurer to deny payment if it is not satisfied that the event caused an adverse effect. [IFRS 4.B14]

Accordingly, where a holder uses a derivative to hedge an underlying non-financial variable that is correlated with cash flows from an asset of the entity, the derivative is not an insurance contract, because payment is not conditional on whether the holder is adversely affected by a reduction in the cash flows from the asset. [IFRS 4.B14]

Although the definition of an insurance contract requires an adverse effect on the policyholder, it does not limit the payment by the insurer to an amount equal to the financial impact of the adverse event. Thus, 'new-for-old' coverage, which pays the policyholder an amount sufficient to replace a damaged old asset with a new asset, is not excluded. Similarly, payments under a term life insurance contract are not limited to the financial loss suffered by the dependants, and the payment of predetermined amounts to quantify the loss caused by death or an accident is not precluded. [IFRS 4.B13]

2.2.4.1 *Lapse, persistency and expense risk*

Lapse risk is the risk that the counterparty will cancel the contract earlier than the issuer had expected in pricing the contract. Persistency risk is the risk that the counterparty will cancel the contract later than the issuer had expected in pricing the contract. Finally, expense risk is the risk of unexpected increases in the administrative costs associated with the servicing of a contract (rather than in costs associated with insured events). [IFRS 4.B15]

None of these risks is an insurance risk, because the payment to the counterparty is not contingent on an uncertain future event that adversely affects the counterparty. For example, an unexpected increase in the insurer's expenses does not adversely affect the counterparty. [IFRS 4.B15]

Accordingly, a contract that exposes the issuer to lapse risk, persistency risk or expense risk is not an insurance contract unless it also exposes the issuer to insurance risk. If the issuer of that contract mitigates that risk, however, by using a second contract to transfer part of that risk to another party, the second contract will expose that other party to insurance risk. [IFRS 4.B16]

2.3 Payments in kind

Under some insurance contracts, payments are permitted or required to be made in kind. For example, an insurer may replace a stolen item directly, instead of reimbursing the policyholder, or may use its own hospitals and medical staff to provide medical services covered by the contracts. [IFRS 4.B5]

Some fixed-fee service contracts, in which the level of service depends on an uncertain event, will meet the definition of an insurance contract in IFRS 4, even though they are not regulated as insurance contracts in some countries. For example:

[IFRS 4.B6]

- a service provider may agree, under a maintenance contract, to repair specified equipment after a malfunction. The fixed service fee is based on the expected number of malfunctions, but it is uncertain whether a particular machine will break down. The malfunction of the equipment adversely affects the owner and the contract compensates the owner (in kind, rather than cash); and
- under a contract for car breakdown services, the provider may agree, for a fixed annual fee, to provide roadside assistance or to tow the car to a nearby garage. The contract could meet the definition of an insurance contract even if the provider does not agree to carry out repairs or replace parts.

The IASB's view is that applying IFRS 4 to such contracts is likely to be no more of a burden than applying the IFRSs that would be applicable if such contracts were outside the scope of IFRS 4. In particular:

[IFRS 4.B7]

- there are unlikely to be material liabilities for malfunctions and breakdowns that have already occurred;
- if IAS 18 *Revenue* applied, the service provider would recognise revenue by reference to the stage of completion (and subject to other specified criteria). That approach is also acceptable under IFRS 4, which permits the service provider:
  - to continue its existing accounting policies for such contracts unless they involve practices prohibited by IFRS 4.14 (see **4.2**); and
  - to improve its accounting policies if so permitted by IFRS 4.22 – 30 (see **4.3**);

- the service provider considers whether the cost of meeting its contractual obligation to provide services exceeds the revenue received in advance. To do this, it applies the liability adequacy test described at **4.2.1**. If IFRS 4 did not apply to these contracts, the service provider would apply IAS 37 *Provisions, Contingent Liabilities and Contingent Assets* to determine whether the contracts are onerous; and

- for such contracts, the disclosure requirements in IFRS 4 are unlikely to add significantly to disclosures required by other IFRSs.

2.4 Changes in the level of insurance risk

Once a contract qualifies as an insurance contract, it remains an insurance contract until all rights and obligations are extinguished or expire. [IFRS 4.B30]

Some contracts do not transfer any insurance risk to the issuer at inception, although they do transfer insurance risk at a later time. IFRS 4 gives the example of a contract that provides a specified investment return and includes an option for the policyholder to use the proceeds of the investment on maturity to buy a life-contingent annuity at then current annuity rates. No insurance risk is transferred to the issuer until the option is exercised, because the insurer is free to price the annuity on a basis that reflects the insurance risk transferred to the insurer at that time. If the contract specifies the annuity rates (or a basis for setting the annuity rates), however, the contract transfers insurance risk to the issuer at inception. [IFRS 4.B29]

2.5 Examples of insurance contracts

Appendix B to IFRS 4 lists the following examples of contracts that will be insurance contracts, provided that the transfer of insurance risk is significant:

[IFRS 4.B18]

(a) insurance against theft or damage to property;

(b) insurance against product liability, professional liability, civil liability or legal expenses;

(c) life insurance and prepaid funeral plans (since, although death is certain, it is uncertain when death will occur or, for some types of life insurance, whether death will occur within the period covered by the insurance);

(d) life-contingent annuities and pensions (i.e. contracts that provide compensation for the uncertain future event – the survival of the annuitant or pensioner – to assist the annuitant or pensioner in maintaining a given standard of living, which would otherwise be adversely affected by his or her survival);

(e) disability and medical cover;

(f) surety bonds, fidelity bonds, performance bonds and bid bonds (i.e. contracts that provide compensation if another party fails to perform a contractual obligation, e.g. an obligation to construct a building);

(g) credit insurance that provides for specified payments to be made to reimburse the holder for a loss it incurs because a specified debtor fails to make payment when due under the original or modified terms of a debt instrument. Such contracts could have various legal forms, e.g. a guarantee, some types of letter of credit, a credit derivative default contract or an insurance contract. Although these contracts meet the definition of an insurance contract, they also meet the definition of a financial guarantee contract in IAS 39, and are within the scope of IAS 32, IAS 39 and IFRS 7 rather than IFRS 4. See **3.3.1** for guidance on the very limited circumstances in which they may be accounted for under IFRS 4;

(h) product warranties. Product warranties issued by another party for goods sold by a manufacturer, dealer or retailer are within the scope of IFRS 4. Product warranties issued directly by a manufacturer, dealer or retailer are outside its scope, however, because they are within the scope of IAS 18 *Revenue* (see **chapter 23**) and IAS 37 *Provisions, Contingent Liabilities and Contingent Assets* (see **chapter 11**);

(i) title insurance, i.e. insurance against the discovery of defects in title to land that were not apparent when the insurance contract was written. In this case, the insured event is the discovery of a defect in the title, not the defect itself;

(j) travel assistance, i.e. compensation in cash or in kind to policyholders for losses suffered while they are travelling. (Some contracts of this kind are discussed at **2.3** above);

(k) catastrophe bonds that provide for reduced payments of principal, interest or both if a specified event adversely affects the issuer of the bond (unless the specified event does not create significant insurance risk, for example if the event is a change in an interest rate or foreign exchange rate);

(l) insurance swaps and other contracts that require a payment based on changes in climatic, geological or other physical variables that are specific to a party to the contract; and

(m) reinsurance contracts.

2.6 Examples of contracts that are not insurance contracts

Appendix B to IFRS 4 lists the following examples of contracts that are not insurance contracts:

[IFRS 4.B19]

(a) investment contracts that have the legal form of an insurance contract but do not expose the insurer to significant insurance risk. An example is a life insurance contract in which the insurer bears no significant mortality risk (such contracts are non-insurance financial instruments or service contracts – see **2.6.1**);

(b) contracts that have the legal form of insurance, but pass all significant insurance risk back to the policyholder through non-cancellable and enforceable mechanisms that adjust future payments by the policyholder as a direct result of insured losses. Examples are some financial reinsurance contracts and some group contracts (such contracts are normally non-insurance financial instruments or service contracts – see **2.6.1**);

(c) self-insurance (i.e. retaining a risk that could have been covered by insurance; there is no insurance contract because there is no agreement with another party);

(d) contracts (such as gambling contracts) that require a payment if a specified uncertain future event occurs, but do not require, as a contractual precondition for payment, that the event adversely affects the policyholder. This does not, however, preclude the specification of a predetermined payout to quantify the loss caused by a specified event such as death or an accident (see also **2.2.4**);

(e) derivatives that expose one party to financial risk but not insurance risk, because they require that party to make payment based solely on changes in one or more of a specified interest rate, financial instrument price, commodity price, foreign exchange rate, index of prices or rates, credit rating or credit index or other variable, provided in the case of a non-financial variable that the variable is not specific to a party to the contract (see **section 2** of **chapter 16**);

(f) a credit-related guarantee (or letter of credit, credit derivative default contract or credit insurance contract) that requires payments even if the holder has not incurred a loss on the failure of the debtor to make payments when due (see **section 2** of **chapter 16**);

(g) contracts that require a payment based on a climatic, geological or other physical variable that is not specific to a party to the contract (commonly described as weather derivatives); and

(h) catastrophe bonds that provide for reduced payments of principal, interest or both, based on a climatic, geological or other physical variable that is not specific to a party to the contract.

2.6.1 *Accounting for contracts other than insurance contracts*

The appropriate accounting for the contracts described at **2.6** above will depend on whether they create financial assets and liabilities:

- if the contracts create financial assets or financial liabilities, they are within the scope of IAS 39 (see **chapters 13** to **22**). Among other things, this means that the parties to the contract use what is sometimes called 'deposit accounting', which involves: [IFRS 4.B20 & B21]
    - one party recognising the consideration received as a financial liability, rather than as revenue; and
    - the other party recognising the consideration paid as a financial asset, rather than as an expense; and
- if the contracts do not create financial assets or financial liabilities, IAS 18 applies (see **chapter 23**). Under IAS 18, revenue associated with a transaction involving the rendering of services is recognised by reference to the stage of completion of the transaction if the outcome of the transaction can be estimated reliably.

Example 2.6.1

Accounting for the 'laying-off' of bets by a gaming operator

A gaming operator may wish to 'lay off' some of the risk it has taken on from gamblers in addition to managing the odds on any additional bets relating to the particular outcome or event. This may happen when the operator has accepted too many bets for a particular outcome. This lay-off is achieved by the operator buying wagers (as opposed to selling wagers).

In the circumstances described, the acquisition of wagers used to transfer a portion of the operator's risk of its sold wagers to other operators does not constitute an insurance contract within the scope of IFRS 4. IFRS 4.2 states that the Standard applies only to contracts that are either insurance contracts issued by the entity or reinsurance contracts held by the entity (or to financial instruments issued by an entity that have a discretionary participation feature – not relevant in this example). The contract to lay off some of the risk held by the gaming operator is, therefore, only within the scope of

IFRS 4 if it meets the definition of a reinsurance contract. A reinsurance contract is defined as 'an insurance contract issued by one insurer (the reinsurer) to compensate another insurer (the cedant) for losses on one or more contracts issued by the cedant'. The contracts between the gaming operator and the gamblers are not considered insurance contracts in accordance with IFRS 4.B19(d) (see **2.6** above) and, therefore, the lay-off contract cannot be a reinsurance contract.

In the circumstances described, the operator has purchased a derivative financial asset that should be recorded in its financial statements at fair value with subsequent changes in fair value recognised in profit or loss.

Because the gaming operator does not have a legally enforceable right to set off the financial asset arising from the lay-off transaction against the underlying risk exposure arising on the wagers accepted, offset in the financial statements is not permitted as per IAS 32.42.

The accounting treatment for an operator who accepts and lays-off bets is also described in **section 4** of **chapter 16**.

3 Scope of IFRS 4

IFRS 4 applies to certain contracts and instruments, as defined in the Standard, rather than to entities that are involved with such contracts and instruments. Thus, the Standard applies to insurance contracts rather than to insurers per se. This approach has important consequences. It means, in particular, that:

- some entities that are not regarded as insurers for legal or supervisory purposes may nevertheless have contracts or instruments that fall within the scope of the Standard; and
- some contracts and instruments with which an insurer is involved will be outside the scope of IFRS 4 and will not therefore be entitled to the exemptions offered by the Standard.

IFRS 4 describes any entity that issues an insurance contract as an insurer, whether or not the issuer is regarded as an insurer for legal or supervisory purposes. [IFRS 4.5]

3.1 Direct insurance contracts and reinsurance contracts

In certain respects, IFRS 4 applies differently to direct insurance contracts and to reinsurance contracts, so it is important to distinguish between them.

The definition of an insurance contract is discussed above in **section 2**. The parties to an insurance contract are:

[IFRS 4(Appendix A)]

- the policyholder, defined as a party that has a right to compensation under an insurance contract if an insured event occurs; and
- the insurer, defined as the party that has an obligation under an insurance contract to compensate a policyholder if an insured event occurs.

A reinsurance contract is a particular type of insurance contract, entered into between parties that are both insurers (though in respect of different contracts). The Standard provides the following definitions:

[IFRS 4(Appendix A)]

- a cedant is the policyholder under a reinsurance contract;
- a reinsurer is the party that has an obligation under a reinsurance contract to compensate a cedant if an insured event occurs; and
- a reinsurance contract is an insurance contract issued by one insurer (the reinsurer) to compensate another insurer (the cedant) for losses on one or more contracts issued by the cedant.

A direct insurance contract is then defined as an insurance contract that is not a reinsurance contract. [IFRS 4(Appendix A)]

References in IFRS 4 (and in this chapter) to insurance contracts apply equally to direct insurance contracts and to reinsurance contracts. [IFRS 4.6]

3.2 Items to which IFRS 4 applies

IFRS 4 applies to:

[IFRS 4.2]

- insurance contracts (including reinsurance contracts) issued by an entity;
- reinsurance contracts (but not direct insurance contracts) held by an entity; and
- financial instruments issued by an entity that have a discretionary participation feature (see **4.5**).

IFRS 4 does not address other aspects of accounting by insurers, such as accounting for financial assets held by insurers and financial liabilities issued by insurers (covered by IAS 32 *Financial Instruments: Presentation*, IAS 39 *Financial Instruments: Recognition and Measurement* and IFRS 7 *Financial Instruments: Disclosures* – see **chapters 13 to 22**). [IFRS 4.3]

3.3 Items to which IFRS 4 does not apply

IFRS 4 does not apply to:

[IFRS 4.4]

- product warranties issued directly by a manufacturer, dealer or retailer. These are dealt with by IAS 18 *Revenue* (see **chapter 23**) and IAS 37 *Provisions, Contingent Liabilities and Contingent Assets* (see **chapter 11**);
- employers' assets and liabilities under employee benefit plans. These are dealt with by IAS 19 *Employee Benefits* (see **chapter 24**) and IFRS 2 *Share-based Payment* (see **chapter 25**);
- retirement benefit obligations reported by defined benefit retirement plans. These are dealt with by IAS 26 *Accounting and Reporting by Retirement Benefit Plans*;
- contractual rights or contractual obligations that are contingent on the future use of, or right to use, a non-financial item (e.g. some licence fees, royalties, contingent lease payments and similar items), as well as a lessee's residual value guarantee embedded in a finance lease. These are dealt with by IAS 17 *Leases* (see **chapter 26**), IAS 18 *Revenue* (see **chapter 23**) and IAS 38 *Intangible Assets* (see **chapter 8**); and
- contingent consideration payable or receivable in a business combination. This is dealt with by IFRS 3 *Business Combinations* (see **chapter 34**).

In addition, IFRS 4 does not apply to:

- financial guarantee contracts (see **2.3.2** in **chapter 13** for definition and further guidance) unless the issuer has previously asserted explicitly that it regards such contracts as insurance contracts and has used accounting applicable to insurance contracts, in which case the issuer may elect to apply either IAS 39 and IAS 32 or IFRS 4 to such financial guarantee contracts. This election is available on a contract-by-contract basis, but is irrevocable once made; [IFRS 4.4(d)] and

- direct insurance contracts in which the entity is the policyholder (but note that IFRS 4 does apply to reinsurance contracts in which the entity is the cedant). [IFRS 4.4(f)]

3.4 Embedded derivatives

As explained in **chapter 17**, IAS 39 requires some embedded derivatives to be separated from their host contracts and measured at fair value, with changes in fair value recognised in profit or loss. Apart from the two exceptions described below, those requirements of IAS 39 apply irrespective of whether the host contracts are within the scope of IFRS 4. In other words, unless one of the exceptions below applies, where an entity has derivatives embedded in insurance contracts or in financial instruments issued with a discretionary participation feature, they will be separated out (or not) in accordance with IAS 39. [IFRS 4.7]

The two exceptions to this are as follows;

- IAS 39 does not apply to a derivative embedded in an insurance contract if that embedded derivative is itself an insurance contract; [IFRS 4.7] and
- an insurer need not separate, and measure at fair value, a policyholder's option to surrender an insurance contract (or a financial instrument issued with a discretionary participation feature) for a fixed amount (or for an amount based on a fixed amount and an interest rate), even if the exercise price differs from the carrying amount of the host insurance liability. [IFRS 4.8 & 9]

However, IAS 39 applies to a put option or cash surrender option embedded in an insurance contract (or a financial instrument issued with a discretionary participation feature) if the surrender value varies in response to the change in a financial variable (such as an equity or commodity price or index), or a non-financial variable that is not specific to a party to the contract. Furthermore, IAS 39 also applies if the holder's ability to exercise a put option or cash surrender option is triggered by a change in such a variable (e.g. a put option that can be exercised if a stock market index reaches a specified level). [IFRS 4.8 & 9]

3.5 Unbundling of deposit components

Some insurance contracts contain both an insurance component and a deposit component (see **2.2.3.5**). Depending on whether certain conditions are met, as set out in the diagram below, IFRS 4 either requires, permits or prohibits the unbundling of those components (i.e. accounting for them as if they were separate contracts). [IFRS 4.10]

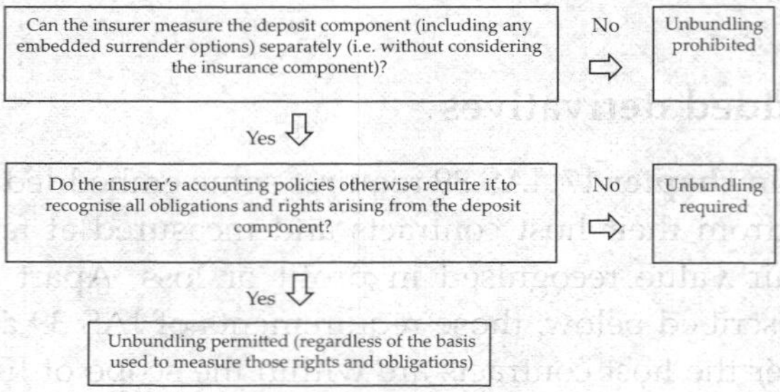

Where a deposit component is unbundled:

[IFRS 4.12]

- IFRS 4 is applied to the insurance component; and
- IAS 39 is applied to the deposit component.

The following example is based on paragraph 11 of IFRS 4.

Example 3.5

Insurer's accounting policies do not require it to recognise all obligations arising from a deposit component

[IFRS 4.11]

A cedant receives compensation for losses from a reinsurer, but the contract obliges the cedant to repay the compensation in future years. That obligation arises from a deposit component. If the cedant's accounting policies would otherwise permit it to recognise the compensation as income without recognising the resulting obligation, unbundling is required.

4 Recognition and measurement

As explained in **section 1**, the objectives of IFRS 4 are quite limited, because the IASB is still working on the major issues in its insurance project. On recognition and measurement, therefore, when IFRS 4 was first introduced, the Board tried to steer a path between, on the one hand, being too prescriptive when it had not yet finalised its thinking and, on the other hand, being too permissive in allowing practices to continue that, based on its deliberations to date, the Board did not favour.

Against this background, IFRS 4's approach to recognition and measurement may be summarised as follows:

- when the Standard was first introduced, as a default, insurers were permitted to retain the accounting policies they had previously adopted for insurance contracts (and other contracts within the scope of IFRS 4), whether under IFRSs or under another GAAP; but
- IFRS 4 introduced certain minimum requirements that must nevertheless be met;
- where an insurer seeks to change its accounting policies for insurance contracts (and other contracts within the scope of IFRS 4), additional constraints apply; and
- in addition, IFRS 4 specifies the approach to be taken to:
  - insurance contracts acquired in a business combination or portfolio transfer; and
  - discretionary participation features.

Each of these aspects is considered in the sub-sections that follow.

4.1 Retention of existing accounting policies

Under IAS 8 *Accounting Policies, Changes in Accounting Estimates and Errors*, the general principle is that, where no IFRS applies specifically to an item, an entity looks to the criteria set out in IAS 8.10 – 12 in developing an accounting policy for that item (see **chapter 4**). To allow insurers to continue with their existing practices (subject to the constraints discussed in the following sections), IFRS 4 exempts an insurer from applying those criteria to its accounting policies for:

[IFRS 4.13]

- insurance contracts that it issues, including related acquisition costs and related intangible assets, such as those described in IFRS 4.31 & 32 (see **4.4**); and
- reinsurance contracts that it holds.

4.2 Minimum requirements for accounting policies

The IASB believes that certain implications of the IAS 8 criteria for developing accounting policies nevertheless remain relevant for contracts within the scope of IFRS 4. Accordingly, the Standard requires an insurer:

[IFRS 4.14]

- not to recognise as a liability any provisions for possible future claims, if those claims arise under insurance contracts that are not in existence at the end of the reporting period (such as catastrophe provisions and equalisation provisions);
- to carry out a liability adequacy test (see **4.2.1**);
- to remove an insurance liability (i.e. the insurer's net contractual obligations under an insurance contract), or a part of an insurance liability, from its statement of financial position when, and only when, it is extinguished (i.e. when the obligation specified in the contract is discharged or cancelled or expires);
- not to offset:
  - reinsurance assets (being a cedant's net contractual rights under a reinsurance contract) against the related insurance liabilities; or
  - income or expense from reinsurance contracts against the expense or income from the related insurance contracts; and
- to consider whether its reinsurance assets are impaired (see **4.2.2**).

4.2.1 Liability adequacy test

IFRS 4 defines a liability adequacy test as an assessment of whether the carrying amount of an insurance liability needs to be increased (or the carrying amount of related deferred acquisition costs or related intangible assets decreased), based on a review of future cash flows. [IFRS 4(Appendix A)]

An insurer must carry out a liability adequacy test at the end of each reporting period, using current estimates of future cash flows under its insurance contracts. If that assessment shows that the carrying amount of its insurance liabilities (less related deferred acquisition costs and related intangible assets, such as those discussed in IFRS 4.31 & 32 – see **4.4**) is inadequate in the light of the estimated future cash flows, the entire deficiency is to be recognised in profit or loss. [IFRS 4.15]

The Standard acknowledges that some insurers will already apply liability adequacy tests. If these meet the specified minimum requirements set out in **4.2.1.1**, they will be acceptable under IFRS 4. Where this is not the case, IFRS 4 requires the approach set out in **4.2.1.2** to be followed.

4.2.1.1 Minimum requirements for a liability adequacy test

The minimum requirements for a liability adequacy test are that:

[IFRS 4.16]

- the test considers current estimates of all contractual cash flows, and of related cash flows such as claims handling costs, as well as cash flows resulting from embedded options and guarantees; and
- if the test shows that the liability is inadequate, the entire deficiency is recognised in profit or loss.

Where an insurer applies a liability adequacy test that meets these minimum requirements, the further requirements discussed at **4.2.1.2** do not apply. [IFRS 4.16] In particular, providing the insurer's liability adequacy test meets these minimum requirements, there are no constraints over the level of aggregation. [IFRS 4.18]

4.2.1.2 Approach where minimum requirements not met

The approach described below must be applied for 'relevant insurance liabilities', i.e. those insurance liabilities (and related deferred acquisition costs and related intangible assets) for which the insurer's accounting policies do not require a liability adequacy test that meets the minimum requirements in **4.2.1.1**. [IFRS 4.17] The comparison is made at the level of a portfolio of contracts that are subject to broadly similar risks and managed together as a single portfolio. [IFRS 4.18]

The insurer is required to:

[IFRS 4.17]

(a) determine the carrying amount of the relevant insurance liabilities less the carrying amount of:

  (i) any related deferred acquisition costs; and

  (ii) any related intangible assets, such as those acquired in a business combination or portfolio transfer (see **4.4**). Related reinsurance assets are not considered, however, because an insurer accounts for them separately (see **4.2.2**); and

(b) determine whether the amount described in (a) is less than the carrying amount that would be required if the relevant insurance liabilities were within the scope of IAS 37 *Provisions, Contingent Liabilities and Contingent Assets* (see **chapter 11**). If it is less, the insurer must recognise the entire difference in profit or loss and decrease the carrying amount of the related deferred acquisition costs or related intangible assets or increase the carrying amount of the relevant insurance liabilities.

The amount described in (b) above (i.e. the result of applying IAS 37) is to reflect future investment margins (see **4.3.4**) if, and only if, the amount described in (a) also reflects those margins. [IFRS 4.19]

4.2.2 Impairment of reinsurance assets

If a cedant's reinsurance asset is impaired, its carrying amount should be reduced accordingly and the impairment loss recognised in profit or loss. A reinsurance asset is impaired if, and only if:

[IFRS 4.20]

- there is objective evidence, as a result of an event that occurred after initial recognition of the reinsurance asset, that the cedant may not receive all amounts due to it under the terms of the contract; and
- that event has a reliably measurable impact on the amounts that the cedant will receive from the reinsurer.

4.3 Changes in accounting policies

The requirements discussed in this section apply both to changes made by an insurer that already applies IFRSs and to changes made by an insurer adopting IFRSs for the first time. [IFRS 4.21]

An insurer may change its accounting policies for insurance contracts if, and only if, the change makes the financial statements:

[IFRS 4.22]

- more relevant to the economic decision-making needs of users and no less reliable; or
- more reliable and no less relevant to those needs.

Relevance and reliability are judged by the criteria in IAS 8. [IFRS 4.22] A change in accounting policies for insurance contracts should bring an insurer's financial statements closer to meeting the criteria in IAS 8, but the change need not achieve full compliance with those criteria. [IFRS 4.23] Additional requirements are discussed in **sections 4.3.1** to **4.3.5**.

4.3.1 *Current market interest rates*

An insurer is permitted, but not required, to change its accounting policies so that it:

[IFRS 4.24]

- remeasures designated insurance liabilities (which, for this purpose, include related deferred acquisition costs and related intangible assets, such as those discussed in **4.4**) to reflect current market interest rates; and
- recognises changes in those liabilities in profit or loss.

At that time, the insurer may also introduce accounting policies that require other current estimates and assumptions for the designated liabilities. This election permits an insurer to change its accounting policies for designated liabilities, without applying those policies consistently to all similar liabilities (as IAS 8 would otherwise require). Where an insurer designates liabilities for this election, it must continue to apply current market interest rates (and, if applicable, the other current estimates and assumptions) consistently in all periods to all these liabilities until they are extinguished. [IFRS 4.24]

4.3.2 *Continuation of existing practices*

The following practices may be continued where they form part of an existing accounting policy, but an insurer may not introduce any of them as part of a change of accounting policy:

[IFRS 4.25]

(a) measuring insurance liabilities on an undiscounted basis;

(b) measuring contractual rights to future investment management fees at an amount that exceeds their fair value as implied by a comparison with current fees charged by other market participants for similar services. (IFRS 4 indicates that the fair value at inception of those contractual rights is likely to equal the origination costs paid, unless future investment management fees and related costs are out of line with market comparables); and

(c) using non-uniform accounting policies for the insurance contracts (and related deferred acquisition costs and related intangible assets, if any) of subsidiaries, except as permitted in **4.3.1**. If those accounting policies are not uniform, an insurer may change them if the change does not make the accounting policies more diverse and also satisfies the other requirements in IFRS 4.

4.3.3 *Prudence*

An insurer need not change its accounting policies for insurance contracts to eliminate excessive prudence. If an insurer already measures its insurance contracts with sufficient prudence, however, it should not introduce additional prudence. [IFRS 4.26]

4.3.4 *Future investment margins*

An insurer need not change its accounting policies for insurance contracts to eliminate future investment margins. There is a rebuttable presumption, however, that an insurer's financial statements will become less relevant and reliable if it introduces an accounting policy that reflects future investment margins in the measurement of insurance contracts, unless those margins affect the contractual payments. Two examples of accounting policies that reflect those margins are:

[IFRS 4.27]

(a) using a discount rate that reflects the estimated return on the insurer's assets; or

(b) projecting the returns on those assets at an estimated rate of return, discounting those projected returns at a different rate and including the result in the measurement of the liability.

The rebuttable presumption described above may be overcome if, and only if, the other components of a change in accounting policies increase the relevance and reliability of an insurer's financial statements sufficiently to outweigh the decrease in relevance and reliability caused by the inclusion of future investment margins. [IFRS 4.28]

The Standard gives the following example.

Example 4.3.4

Change in accounting policy

[IFRS 4.28]

Suppose that an insurer's existing accounting policies for insurance contracts involve excessively prudent assumptions set at inception and a discount rate

> prescribed by a regulator without direct reference to market conditions, and ignore some embedded options and guarantees. The insurer might make its financial statements more relevant and no less reliable by switching to a comprehensive investor-oriented basis of accounting that is widely used and involves:
>
> (a) current estimates and assumptions;
>
> (b) a reasonable (but not excessively prudent) adjustment to reflect risk and uncertainty;
>
> (c) measurements that reflect both the intrinsic value and time value of embedded options and guarantees; and
>
> (d) a current market discount rate, even if that discount rate reflects the estimated return on the insurer's assets.

In some measurement approaches, the discount rate is used to determine the present value of a future profit margin and that profit margin is then attributed to different periods using a formula. In those approaches, the discount rate affects the measurement of the liability only indirectly. In particular, the use of a less appropriate discount rate has a limited or no effect on the measurement of the liability at inception. In other approaches, however, the discount rate determines directly the measurement of the liability. In the latter case, because the introduction of an asset-based discount rate has a more significant effect, the Standard indicates that it is highly unlikely that an insurer could overcome the rebuttable presumption described in IFRS 4.27. [IFRS 4.29]

4.3.5 *Shadow accounting*

In some accounting models, realised gains or losses on an insurer's assets have a direct effect on the measurement of some or all of:

[IFRS 4.30]

- its insurance liabilities;
- related deferred acquisition costs; and
- related intangible assets, such as those described in **4.4**.

An insurer is permitted, but not required, to change its accounting policies so that a recognised but unrealised gain or loss on an asset affects those measurements in the same way as does a realised gain or loss. The related adjustment to the insurance liability (or deferred acquisition costs or intangible assets) is recognised in other comprehensive income if, and only if, the unrealised gains or losses are recognised in other comprehensive income. This practice is sometimes known as 'shadow accounting'. [IFRS 4.30]

4.4 Insurance contracts acquired in a business combination or portfolio transfer

When insurance liabilities are assumed and insurance assets (i.e. an insurer's net contractual rights under an insurance contract) are acquired by an insurer in a business combination, they should be measured at fair value at the acquisition date, in accordance with IFRS 3 *Business Combinations* (see **chapter 34**). IFRS 4 permits but does not require the use of an expanded presentation that splits the fair value of acquired insurance contracts into two components:

[IFRS 4.31]

(a) a liability measured in accordance with the insurer's accounting policies for insurance contracts that it issues; and

(b) an intangible asset, representing the difference between:

  (i) the fair value of the contractual insurance rights acquired and insurance obligations assumed; and

  (ii) the amount described in (a).

The subsequent measurement of this asset should be consistent with the measurement of the related insurance liability.

An insurer acquiring a portfolio of insurance contracts may also use the expanded presentation described above. [IFRS 4.32]

Where such intangible assets are recognised, they are excluded from the scope of IAS 36 *Impairment of Assets* (see **chapter 9**) and IAS 38 *Intangible Assets* (see **chapter 8**). It must be emphasised, however, that IAS 36 and IAS 38 apply to customer lists and customer relationships reflecting the expectation of future contracts that are not part of the contractual insurance rights and contractual insurance obligations that existed at the date of a business combination or portfolio transfer. [IFRS 4.33]

> In other words, the approach described above applies only to an intangible asset whose value, on acquisition, is part of the fair value of insurance contracts. It does not apply to any intangible that would be required, under IAS 38, to be recognised separately from insurance contracts.

4.5 Discretionary participation features

Some contracts provide for a policyholder or investor to receive only 'guaranteed benefits', which IFRS 4 defines as payments or other benefits to which a particular policyholder or investor has an unconditional right that is not subject to the contractual discretion of the issuer. [IFRS 4(Appendix A)] Others may include discretionary participation features.

IFRS 4 defines a discretionary participation feature as a contractual right to receive, as a supplement to guaranteed benefits, additional benefits:

[IFRS 4(Appendix A)]

- that are likely to be a significant portion of the total contractual benefits;
- whose amount or timing is contractually at the discretion of the issuer; and
- that are contractually based on:
  - the performance of a specified pool of contracts or a specified type of contract;
  - realised and/or unrealised investment returns on a specified pool of assets held by the issuer; or
  - the profit or loss of the company, fund or other entity that issues the contract.

Where a contract contains a discretionary participation feature, an obligation to pay guaranteed benefits is referred to as the 'guaranteed element'.

IFRS 7 *Financial Instruments: Disclosures* requires disclosure about financial instruments, including financial instruments that contain discretionary participation features (see **chapter 21**).

In November 2005, the IFRIC declined a request to give further guidance on:

- the definition of a discretionary participation feature; and
- the interaction of the liability adequacy test (see **4.2.1**) with the minimum measurement of the guaranteed element of a financial liability containing a discretionary participation feature.

The IFRIC was informed of concerns that key disclosures regarding these features are required only in respect of items regarded as discretionary participation features. Consequently, a narrow interpretation of the definition would fail to ensure clear and comprehensive disclosure about contracts that include these features. The IFRIC noted that disclosure is particularly important in this area, given the potential for a wide range of treatments until the IASB completes phase II of the project on insurance contracts. The IFRIC noted that IFRS 4 requires an insurer to disclose information that identifies and explains the amounts in its financial statements arising from insurance contracts (see **5.1**) and information that helps users to understand the amount, timing and uncertainty of future cash flows from insurance contracts (see **5.2**).

The IFRIC also noted that the Implementation Guidance attached to IFRS 4 was designed to help entities to develop disclosures about insurance contracts that contain a discretionary participation feature. The IFRIC decided not to add this topic to its agenda, because it involves some of the most difficult questions that the IASB will need to resolve in phase II of its project on insurance contracts. The fact that, in developing IFRS 4, the IASB chose to defer such questions to phase II limits the scope for reducing diversity through an Interpretation.

4.5.1 Discretionary participation features in insurance contracts

Where an insurance contract contains a discretionary participation feature as well as a guaranteed element, IFRS 4 specifies the following requirements.

[IFRS 4.34]

(a) The issuer is permitted, but not required, to recognise the guaranteed element separately from the discretionary participation feature. If the issuer does not recognise them separately, the whole contract should be classified as a liability. If the issuer classifies them separately, the guaranteed element should be classified as a liability.

(b) If the issuer recognises the discretionary participation feature separately from the guaranteed element, that feature should be classified as either a liability or a separate component of equity. IFRS 4 does not specify how to determine whether a discretionary participation feature is a liability or equity. The issuer may split that feature into liability and equity components and use a consistent accounting policy for that split, but it must not classify that feature as an intermediate category that is neither liability nor equity.

(c) The issuer may recognise all premiums received as revenue without separating any portion that relates to the equity component. The resulting changes in the guaranteed element and in the portion of the discretionary participation feature classified as a liability are recognised in profit or loss. If part or all of the discretionary participation feature is classified in equity, a portion of profit or loss may be attributable to that feature (in the same way that a portion may be attributable to non-controlling interests). The portion of profit or loss attributable to any equity component of a discretionary participation feature is recognised as an allocation of profit or loss, not as expense or income (see the discussion of IAS 1 *Presentation of Financial Statements* in **chapter 3**).

(d) If the contract contains an embedded derivative within the scope of IAS 39, IAS 39 is applied to that embedded derivative.

(e) Except to the extent that changes are necessary to comply with the requirements discussed in **section 4.2** and in (a) to (d) above, the issuer should continue its existing accounting policies for such contracts, unless it changes those accounting policies in a way that complies with the requirements discussed in **section 4.3**.

4.5.2 *Discretionary participation features in financial instruments*

The requirements discussed in **4.5.1** also apply to a financial instrument that contains a discretionary participation feature. In addition:

[IFRS 4.35]

(a) if the entire discretionary participation feature is classified as a liability, the liability adequacy test in **4.2.1** is applied to the whole contract (i.e. both the guaranteed element and the discretionary participation feature). It is not necessary to determine the amount that would result from applying IAS 39 to the guaranteed element;

(b) if part or all of the discretionary participation feature is classified as a separate component of equity, the liability recognised for the whole contract must not be less than the amount that would result from applying IAS 39 to the guaranteed element. That amount includes the intrinsic value of an option to surrender the contract, but need not include its time value if that option is exempt from measurement at fair value as discussed at **3.4**. The issuer need not disclose the amount that would result from applying IAS 39 to the guaranteed element, nor need it present that amount separately. Furthermore, the issuer need not determine that amount if the total liability recognised is clearly higher; and

(c) although these contracts are financial instruments, the issuer may continue to recognise the premiums for those contracts as revenue and recognise as an expense the resulting increase in the carrying amount of the liability.

5 Disclosure

5.1 Explanation of recognised amounts

As an overall principle, IFRS 4 requires that an insurer should disclose information that identifies and explains the amounts in its financial statements arising from insurance contracts. [IFRS 4.36] To that end, the following disclosures are specifically required:

[IFRS 4.37]

(a) the insurer's accounting policies for insurance contracts and related assets, liabilities, income and expense;

(b) the recognised assets, liabilities, income and expense (and, if the insurer presents its statement of cash flows using the direct method, cash flows) arising from insurance contracts. In addition, if the insurer is a cedant, it should disclose:

  (i) gains and losses recognised in profit or loss on buying reinsurance; and

  (ii) if the cedant defers and amortises gains and losses arising on buying reinsurance, the amortisation for the period and the amounts remaining unamortised at the beginning and end of the period;

(c) the process used to determine the assumptions that have the greatest effect on the measurement of the recognised amounts described in (b). When practicable, an insurer should also give quantified disclosure of those assumptions;

(d) the effect of changes in assumptions used to measure insurance assets and insurance liabilities, showing separately the effect of each change that has a material effect on the financial statements; and

(e) reconciliations of changes in insurance liabilities, reinsurance assets and, if any, related deferred acquisition costs.

5.2 Amount, timing and uncertainty of cash flows

As an overall principle, IFRS 4 requires that an insurer should disclose information that helps users to understand the amount, timing and uncertainty of future cash flows from insurance contracts. [IFRS 4.38] To that end, the following disclosures are specifically required:

[IFRS 4.39]

(a) the insurer's objectives in managing risks arising from insurance contracts and its policies for mitigating those risks;

(b) [deleted by IFRS 7];

(c) information about insurance risk (both before and after risk mitigation by reinsurance), including information about:

  (i) the sensitivity of profit or loss and equity to changes in variables that have a material effect on them;

  (ii) concentrations of insurance risk; and

  (iii) actual claims compared with previous estimates (i.e. claims development). The disclosure about claims development should go back to the period when the earliest material claim arose for which there is still uncertainty about the amount and timing of the claims payments, but need not go back more than ten years. An insurer need not disclose this information for claims for which uncertainty about the amount and timing of claims payments is typically resolved within one year;

(d) the information about interest rate risk and credit risk that paragraphs 31 – 42 of IFRS 7 would require if the insurance contracts were within the scope of IFRS 7 (see **chapter 21**); and

(e) information about exposures to interest rate risk or market risk under embedded derivatives contained in a host insurance contract if the insurer is not required to, and does not, measure the embedded derivatives at fair value.

6 Future developments

The Board issued a Discussion Paper titled *Preliminary Views on Insurance Contracts* in May 2007 and has been considering comments since November 2007. It does not expect to issue an Exposure Draft on this subject before 2009, with the final Standard predicted for 2011. That final Standard will replace the temporary dispensations and interim accounting Standard developed in IFRS 4.

The Discussion Paper outlined the Board's preliminary views on the main components of the Phase II accounting model for all insurance contracts, including life, non-life, direct insurance and reinsurance. It focused on the measurement of insurance liabilities and the need for an approach that will provide more relevant information on the amount, timing and uncertainty of future cash flows, a consistent approach to changes in estimates, consistency of approach to all types of insurance and reinsurance for both life and non-life contracts, and consistency with other IFRSs.

The Discussion Paper did not redefine 'insurance' as set out in IFRS 4 (see **section 2.1** above), but stated that the proposed Exposure Draft would expose the current definition to further comment.

The Discussion Paper also briefly touched on the recognition and derecognition criteria for insurance liabilities, i.e. recognition of the rights and obligations when the insurer becomes a party to the contract and derecognition when any specified obligation is discharged, cancelled or expired.

45 Preparation, filing and publishing of financial statements

1 Preparation of financial statements

Every UK company registered under the Companies Acts is required to prepare accounts for each financial year (individual accounts). [CA 2006 s394, previously CA 1985 s226(1)] Subject to the requirements and constraints discussed in **chapter 1**, the accounts may be 'Companies Act individual accounts' (prepared in accordance with UK accounting standards) or 'IAS individual accounts' (prepared in accordance with IFRSs). However, this manual is concerned only with the latter. If the company is a parent company, consolidated financial statements (group financial statements) must also be prepared unless an exemption is available (see **4.2** in **chapter 33**). [CA 2006 s399(1), previously CA 1985 s227(1)]

For periods commencing on or after 20 January 2007, listed companies have to comply with the requirements on periodic financial reporting in the Disclosure and Transparency Rules (DTR) issued by the Financial Services Authority. The DTR require the annual report to include the audited financial statements, a management report and a responsibility statement. The DTR do not impose any new requirements on the content of the financial statements although they require publication within four months rather than six months under the previous listing rules. The requirements for a management report do not extend the existing requirement for a business review in the directors' report except in one very minor respect (see **chapter 46**). The requirement for a responsibility statement is new (see **chapter 46**).

1.1 Presentation of company name

Although there are no statutory or other requirements in this respect, it is good practice to state clearly the name of the company at the head or foot of each page of the financial statements.

A change in the company's name during the period or since the end of the period may be disclosed by mentioning the former name in the heading on each page of the financial statements. However, as there is no legal requirement to do so, companies often choose instead to note this only on the contents page and in the directors' report.

Example 1.1

Presentation of company name

Delto Plastics Limited

(formerly Delto Plastics (Birmingham) Limited)

2 Approval and signing of financial statements

The annual financial statements must be approved by the board of directors and signed on their behalf by a director on the face of the company's balance sheet. [CA 2006 s414, previously CA 1985 s233] Any copies of the balance sheet which are laid before the company in general meeting or otherwise issued, including those delivered to the Registrar of Companies must state the name of the signatory. [CA 2006 s433, s444, s445, s446, s447, previously CA 1985 s233]

When group financial statements are prepared, it is normal practice for the consolidated balance sheet to be signed as well as the company balance sheet although there is no requirement to do so.

Only one director is required by law to sign the balance sheet on behalf of the board but, in the case of quoted companies, it is quite common to see the balance sheet signed by two directors, for example, the Chairman and the Finance Director. To some extent this is probably a hangover from the days, prior to the Companies Act 1989, when the balance sheet had to be signed by two directors.

The date on which the financial statements are approved by the board of directors (or authorised for issue by the board of management, or equivalent, of an organisation which does not have directors) should be disclosed in the financial statements. [IAS 10.17] This date is important in establishing the date to which the directors are responsible for adjusting for or disclosing material events after the end of the reporting period (see **chapter 31**).

It is recommended that this date be shown either on the face of the statement of financial position above the signature of the directors or as the first item in the notes to the financial statements. Any other position within the financial statements is acceptable, but the date should not be disclosed only in the directors' report as this does not form part of the financial statements.

Example 2

Approval and signing of financial statements

Approved by the Board of Directors on 24 July 20X1.

3 Persons entitled to receive copies of financial statements and reports

A copy of the financial statements, together with the auditors' report and directors' report, must be sent to:

[CA 2006 s423, previously CA 1985 s238]

(a) every member of the company;

(b) every holder of the company's debentures; and

(c) every person who is entitled to receive notice of general meetings (e.g. the company's Articles may provide for other categories of entitled persons such as directors).

The time limits are considered in **section 7** below. Copies do not need to be sent to people for whom the company does not have a current address. Dormant companies and certain categories of small company are not required to appoint auditors or to obtain an auditors' report. Quoted companies (as defined in the legislation) are also required to send copies of their directors' remuneration report (see **chapter 48**).

Normally the financial statements and reports sent to members and debenture holders will be the same as those filed at Companies House. However, differences may arise:

(a) small and medium-sized companies are entitled to different levels of exemption in the financial statements and directors' reports sent to members, etc., and those filed at Companies House. These exemptions are outside of the scope of this manual but a brief summary is given at **3.4** in **chapter 1**; and

(b) companies need not, in certain circumstances, send copies of annual financial statements to those members who do not wish to receive them, but may instead send to them a summary financial statement. [CA 2006 s426, previously CA 1985 s251] The form and content of such statements are dealt with in **chapter 50**.

4 Laying of financial statements and reports at the annual general meeting

The directors of a public company must lay copies of the annual financial statements, together with the auditors' report and directors' report, and for a quoted company the directors' remuneration report, before the company in general meeting (normally the AGM). The time period allowed for the laying of accounts under the Companies Act 2006 is no later than 6 months after the last day of the relevant accounting reference period. [CA 2006 s437] This is a change from the Companies Act 1985 whereby the period allowed was 7 months. [CA 1985 s241] As from 1 October 2007 private companies are no longer required to lay their annual accounts and reports before a general meeting. Again, dormant companies and certain categories of small company are not required to appoint auditors or to obtain an auditors' report.

Such reports and financial statements should be sent to members and debenture holders not less than 21 days before the date of the meeting. [CA 2006 s424, previously CA 1985 s238]

Electronic communication with members is considered in **section 12** below.

At least 21 days' notice of the AGM must be given. [CA 2006 s307, previously CA 1985 s369] In addition the Combined Code (which applies to certain listed companies – see **chapter 47**) requires the notice of the AGM and related papers to be sent to shareholders at least 20 working days prior to the AGM.

5 Delivery of financial statements and reports to the Registrar

The directors of every company (including overseas companies having a place of business in the UK, but excluding an unlimited company which is not a qualifying company or a subsidiary undertaking or parent company of a limited company) must deliver a copy of the annual financial statements, auditors' report and directors' report, and where applicable the directors' remuneration report to the Registrar of Companies (see **section 7** below for time limits). [CA 2006 s444, s444A, s445, s446, s447, previously CA 1985 s242] Small and medium-sized companies are entitled to exemptions from some filing requirements. These exemptions are outside of the scope of this manual but a brief summary is given at **3.4** in

chapter 1. As noted previously, dormant companies and certain categories of small company are not required to appoint auditors or to obtain an auditors' report.

A company that is a member of a qualifying partnership at the end of that partnership's financial year should, unless an exemption applies, append a copy of the partnership's financial statements to the copy of its own annual financial statements, which is next delivered to the Registrar of Companies in accordance with s444, s444A, s445, s446 and s447 of the 2006 Act, previously s242 of the 1985 Act. [CA 2006 SI 2008/569 Reg 5(1), previously CA 1985 SI 1993/1820 Reg 5(1)]

5.1 Quality of documents filed with the Registrar

Annual financial statements and other documents filed with the Registrar of Companies were for many years microfilmed. The Registrar now scans documents to produce electronic images that can be viewed on-line. This development has prompted a sharp increase in the number of documents rejected by the Registrar on the grounds that they are of unacceptable quality, in that they do not produce an adequate scanned image. This issue is particularly likely to affect glossy financial statements of listed companies.

Every document delivered to the Registrar must comply with requirements specified by the Registrar relating to the legibility of that document. Guidance issued by the Registrar requires that documents should:

(a) be on A4 size, plain white paper between 80gsm and 100gsm in weight with a matt finish;

(b) have good margins;

(c) use black ink or black type;

(d) use bold lettering (some elegant thin typefaces and pens give poor quality copies);

(e) not be carbon copies;

(f) not be printed on a dot matrix printer; and

(g) avoid photocopies which can result in grey shades that will not scan well.

The guidance goes on to note that companies which produce colour-printed glossy financial statements should save them for shareholders and others who will appreciate them. Companies House require a black and white copy on matt finish paper. A typed unbound version or printers proof is ideal, provided it has the necessary signatures.

All statutory documents submitted to the Registrar, including financial statements and reports, are required to show in a prominent position, the registered number of the company to which they relate. This is normally shown on the front page in the top right hand corner with the company's name and the accounting period.

The guidance can be accessed on the Companies House web site http://www.companieshouse.gov.uk and it is also available in printed booklets from Companies House.

6 Companies in liquidation, subject to other insolvency procedures or to be struck off the register

Where a liquidator has been appointed, the directors no longer have any powers and so do not have the authority to prepare and approve financial statements. For this reason, once the relevant notification of appointment has been filed with Companies House, the Registrar does not expect to see a set of financial statements filed by the directors. However, where a liquidator has yet to be appointed a company may still wish to file audited financial statements, for example, to meet a filing deadline and avoid penalties or because a regulator needs to see audited financial statements. Also, financial statements may still be required by HM Revenue & Customs or for other purposes even if they are not required to be filed with the Registrar. But, depending on the circumstances, such financial statements may not have to comply with all statutory requirements or to be audited.

There are three types of liquidation.

1. *Members' voluntary liquidation (MVL):* This can only take place when the directors believe that the company is solvent. It is initiated by the directors and involves a statutory declaration of solvency by them and a resolution of the members to wind up the company;

2. *Creditors' voluntary liquidation (CVL):* This is appropriate when the company cannot pay its debts. It is initiated by the company passing a special resolution that it be wound up voluntarily (see s84 of the Insolvency Act 1986 as amended by the 2006 Act). A meeting with the creditors is then held and a liquidator appointed. An MVL may be converted into a CVL if the liquidator decides that the company will not be able to pay its debts in full in the period stated in the directors' statutory declaration; and

3. *Compulsory liquidation:* This is when a court orders the company to be wound up. This may be as a result of a petition by one or more of the

company's creditors, the company itself, the company's directors or one or more members, a liquidator, a temporary administrator, or justice's chief executive, the Secretary of State or the Official Receiver.

Once proceedings have been initiated and initial liquidation documents have been filed under any of these forms of liquidation, audited financial statements will no longer be expected by the Registrar. Insolvency legislation includes requirements in relation to the preparation of accounts by liquidators but these are outside of the scope of this publication. Such accounts will be prepared by a licensed insolvency practitioner familiar with the relevant legislation.

There are other forms of insolvency procedure such as voluntary arrangements, administration orders and receiverships. These procedures do not generally have any effect on the obligation of the company to file audited financial statements because they assume that the company will continue in existence. But it is always possible that the company will subsequently be placed in one of the forms of liquidation described above. The Companies House website (*http://www.companieshouse.gov.uk*) contains useful guidance booklets on liquidation and insolvency.

It is also possible in some circumstances for a company to be 'struck off' the register without recourse to one of the formal liquidation procedures described above. The striking-off of a company can be initiated by the directors or the Registrar of Companies and financial statements will not generally be expected by the Registrar once the formal strike-off action has been initiated. Although this strike-off procedure is cheap and simple, it is not an alternative to a formal liquidation where this is appropriate. In particular, any unpaid creditors are likely to object to the striking-off. Even if a company is struck off and dissolved, creditors and others could apply to have it restored to the register. Another consideration is that if the company has any assets representing the share capital and other non-distributable reserves, these cannot be lawfully distributed without some form of capital reduction or share repurchase. When a company is dissolved, all its assets are deemed to be 'bona vacantia' and accordingly belong to the Crown, the Duchy of Lancaster or the Duchy of Cornwall. [CA 2006 s1012, previously CA 1985 s654]

A private company can apply to be struck off if, in the previous three months, it has not traded or otherwise carried on business, subject to certain conditions. If it is anticipated that a company will be dissolved before the filing deadline for its statutory financial statements, the Registrar will not expect to receive them and they need not be prepared.

7 Time limits for delivering financial statements and reports

7.1 Financial periods beginning before 6 April 2008

For financial periods beginning before 6 April 2008, the time periods from the end of the accounting reference period in which the annual financial statements and reports must be delivered to the Registrar of Companies are:

[CA 1985 s244(1)]

- public company – 7 months; and
- private company – 10 months.

Special provisions apply to:

(a) a company's first accounting period exceeding 12 months; [CA 1985 s244(2)] and

(b) an accounting period shortened by virtue of a notice given under CA 1985 s225. [CA 1985 s244(4)]

If the relevant accounting reference period is the company's first and is a period of more than 12 months, the period allowed is whichever is the longer of:

[CA 1985 s244(2)]

(a) 10 months or 7 months, as the case may be, from the first anniversary of the incorporation of the company; or

(b) 3 months from the end of the accounting reference period.

Where the accounting reference period is shortened by a change of accounting reference date, the period allowed is whichever is the longer of:

[CA 1985 s244(4)]

(a) 10 months or 7 months, as the case may be, from the end of the new accounting reference period; or

(b) 3 months after the notice has been given to change the accounting reference date.

Companies can apply for an extension of the period allowed for delivering reports and accounts on a discretionary basis under CA 1985 s244(5) which provides that the period may be extended 'if for any special reason the Secretary of State thinks fit'. It is likely that such an extension would be granted only in rare circumstances.

7.2 Financial periods beginning on or after 6 April 2008

For financial periods beginning on or after 6 April 2008, the time periods from the end of the accounting reference period in which the annual financial statements and reports must be delivered to the Registrar of Companies are:

[CA 2006 s442(1), (2)]

- public company – 6 months; and
- private company – 9 months.

Special provisions apply to:

(a) a company's first accounting period exceeding 12 months; [CA 2006 s442(3)] and

(b) an accounting period shortened by virtue of a notice given under s392 of the 2006 Act. [CA 2006 s442(4)]

If the relevant accounting reference period is the company's first and is a period of more than 12 months, the period allowed is whichever is the longer of:

[CA 2006 s442(3)]

(a) 9 months or 6 months, as the case may be, from the first anniversary of the incorporation of the company; or

(b) 3 months from the end of the accounting reference period.

Where the accounting reference period is shortened by a change of accounting reference date, the period allowed is whichever is the longer of:

[CA 2006 s442(4)]

(a) 9 months or 6 months, as the case may be, from the end of the new accounting reference period; or

(b) 3 months after the notice has been given to change the accounting reference date.

Companies can apply for an extension of the period allowed for delivering accounts and reports on a discretionary basis under s442(5) of the 2006 Act which provides that the period may be extended 'if for any special reason the Secretary of State thinks fit'. It is likely that such an extension would be granted only in rare circumstances.

7.3 Penalties for late filing

Companies are liable to a civil penalty if they fail to deliver to the Registrar of Companies a copy of the annual financial statements and reports within the prescribed period from the financial year end. The amount of the penalty is determined by reference to whether the company is public or private and the length of the period between the end of the period allowed for delivering financial statements and the day on which the financial statements are actually delivered to the Registrar. [CA 2006 s453, previously CA 1985 s242A]

Companies filing financial statements and reports with the Registrar prior to 1 February 2009 will be subject the existing penalty levels under the 1985 Act:

Length of period	**Public company**	**Private company**
Not more than 3 months	£500	£100
More than 3 months but not more than 6 months	£1,000	£250
More than 6 months but not more than 12 months	£2,000	£500
More than 12 months	£5,000	£1,000

Where filing takes place after 1 February 2009 the following table of penalties applies:

Length of period	**Public company**	**Private company**
Not more than 1 month	£750	£150
More than 1 month but not more than 3 months	£1,500	£375
More than 3 months but not more than 6 months	£3,000	£750
More than 6 months	£7,500	£1,500

In addition if a company failed to comply with the filing requirements in the previous year, the penalty will be double that shown above.

The penalties in the table above apply to any accounts prepared under the 2006 Act or the 1985 Act delivered late on or after 1 February 2009.

The penalties above are in addition to, not in place of, the penalties payable by directors under s451 of the 2006 Act (previously CA 1985 s242).

Companies may be liable to penalties even if they attempt to file their financial statements before the relevant deadline but the financial statements are rejected for some reason by the Registrar. A company, Livepine Limited, attempted to file its annual report and financial statements six days before the deadline. Although the statement of financial position and auditors' report were properly signed, the directors' report was not and so the document was returned to the company. By the time the directors' report had been signed and returned to Companies House, the deadline had passed and the late filing penalty was automatically imposed. On appeal the penalty was reversed in the County Court, but reimposed by the High Court.

7.4 Calculation of time period allowed

The Registrar of Companies has previously stated that periods allowed for the filing of financial statements under CA 1985 actually expire at midnight on the date in the last month for filing which corresponds to the last day of the company's accounting reference period. For example, in the case of a private company which has 10 months to file its financial statements and which has an accounting reference date of 30 September, its financial statements must be filed on 30 July at the latest and not on 31 July. This follows the judgment in *Dodds v Walker* 1981. So in the case of a private company the filing deadlines would be as follows:

Example 7.4A

Illustrative filing deadlines for a private company

End of relevant accounting reference period	Deadline for delivery to Companies House
31.1.X1	30.11.X1
28.2.X1	28.12.X1
31.3.X1	31.1.X2
30.4.X1	28.2.X2
31.5.X1	31.3.X2
30.6.X1	30.4.X2

For financial periods beginning on or after 6 April 2008 the method of calculating the period for filing a company's accounts and reports has been altered under s443 of the 2006 Act. Under the new rules the filing period expires on the date in the appropriate month corresponding to the last day of the company's accounting reference period. However if the last day of the company's accounting period is the last day of a month then the filing period expires on the last day of the appropriate month (irrespective of whether this corresponds with the accounting reference date). For example, in the case of a private company which has 9 months to file its financial statements and which has an accounting reference date of 30 November, its financial statements must be filed by 31 August at the latest. So in the case of a private company preparing financial statements for a financial period beginning on or after 6 April 2008 the filing deadlines would be as follows:

Example 7.4B

Illustrative filing deadlines for a private company

End of relevant accounting reference period	Deadline for delivery to Companies House
31.1.X1	31.10.X1
28.2.X1	30.11.X1
31.3.X1	31.12.X1
30.4.X1	31.1.X2
31.5.X1	28.2.X2
30.6.X1	31.3.X2

7.5 Listing Rules and AIM rules

The Listing Rules required listed companies to publish their annual reports and financial statements as soon as possible after they have been approved, and in any event within six months following the date of the end of the financial period. [LR 9.8.1R]

For periods commencing on or after 20 January 2007, these requirements of the Listing Rules are superseded by the Disclosure and Transparency Rules. These rules have a slightly broader application than listed companies but do not extend to AIM companies. They require that an issuer must publish its annual report, at the latest, four months after the end of the financial year.

AIM companies are, by the AIM rules of the London Stock Exchange, required to issue their annual reports and financial statements within six months following the date of the end of the financial period.

8 Requirements for subsidiary companies

Subsidiary companies incorporated in the UK are subject to the same general requirements to prepare, publish and file annual financial statements and reports as companies generally. However, there are special rules applying to the disclosures required of subsidiaries. These both add disclosures and provide relief from certain disclosure requirements. These exemptions and requirements are dealt with in the relevant chapters.

9 Publication of financial statements

9.1 Statutory and non-statutory accounts

The Act requires that where a company or group:

(a) publishes any of its 'statutory accounts' (i.e. its individual or group financial statements for a financial year as required to be delivered to the Registrar of Companies under s441 of the 2006 Act (previously s242 of the 1985 Act)), they must be accompanied by the auditors' report on those accounts (unless the company is exempt from audit and has taken advantage of that exemption). If the company is a parent company, it may not publish its own statutory accounts without also publishing its group statutory accounts; [CA 2006 s434, previously CA 1985 s240] and

(b) publishes 'non-statutory accounts' (i.e. any balance sheet or profit and loss account relating to any financial year of the company otherwise than as part of the company's statutory accounts, such as a preliminary announcement of annual results or employee reports which contain information which can be regarded as a balance sheet or profit and loss account), it must publish with them a statement indicating:

   (i) that the accounts are not the company's statutory accounts;

   (ii) whether statutory accounts dealing with any financial year with which the non-statutory accounts purport to deal have been delivered to the Registrar of Companies; and

   (iii) whether an auditors' report has been made on the statutory accounts and, if so, whether the report was qualified or unqualified, or included a reference to any matters to which the auditor drew attention by way of emphasis without qualifying the report, or contained a statement under subsections (2) or (3) of s498 of the 2006 Act (previously subsections (2) or (3) of s237 of the 1985 Act) (i.e. accounting records or returns inadequate, accounts or the auditable part of the directors' remuneration report not agreeing with records and returns or failure to obtain necessary information and explanations). [CA 2006 s435, previously CA 1985 s240]

The company must not publish the auditors' report on the company's statutory accounts with non-statutory accounts. However, the directors may wish to include an explanation of the nature of the qualification to assist users of the non-statutory accounts in understanding its significance.

The term 'publishes' in this context means that the company publishes, issues or circulates the document or otherwise makes it available for public inspection in a manner calculated to invite any member of the public to read it. [CA 2006 s436, previously CA 1985 s240(4)] This includes publication on the internet.

The Act exempts summary financial statements (see **chapter 50**) from the publication requirements of s434 and s435 of the 2006 Act (previously s240 of the 1985 Act) in relation to the provision of such statements to entitled persons. Entitled persons are those normally entitled to receive copies of a company's report and financial statements, being: every member of the company, every debenture holder of the company, and every person entitled to receive notice of general meetings. [CA 2006 s434(6),s435(7), previously CA 1985 s251(7)] However, in Bulletin 2001/1 the Auditing Practices Board advises that the inclusion of summary financial statements on a company's web site may render them accessible to an audience wider than entitled persons. In these circumstances the requirements of s434 and s435 of the 2006 Act (previously s240 of the 1985 Act) concerning the publication of a statement indicating the status of the financial statements become applicable.

9.2 Preliminary announcements and interim reports

A preliminary announcement made by a listed company will amount to the publication of non-statutory accounts. The announcement should therefore contain the statement required by s435 of the 2006 Act (previously CA 1985 s240). Guidance on the form of the appropriate statement in these circumstances is set out at **example 3.3.1** and **example 3.3.2** in **chapter 51**.

An interim report made by a listed company will not necessarily amount to publication of non-statutory accounts. This is because non-statutory accounts are defined as relating to a financial year and an interim report will relate only to part of a year. However, many listed companies provide comparative figures for the previous full financial year in their interim reports. This brings the interim report within the scope of s435 of the 2006 Act (previously s240 of the 1985 Act) and an appropriate statement must be made. Guidance on the form of the appropriate statement in these circumstances is set out at **example 3.2** in **chapter 39**.

10 Rules regarding company year ends and accounting periods

10.1 Introduction

The Act requires the directors to prepare for each financial year accounts comprising a balance sheet as at the last day of the year and a profit and loss account. [CA 2006 s394, previously CA 1985 s226] The following sections summarise the rules regarding accounting periods and give guidance on the procedures for varying the statutorily determined length of accounting reference periods.

The Act requires that the directors of a parent company should secure that, except where in their opinion there are good reasons against it, the financial year of each of its subsidiary undertakings coincides with the company's own financial year. [CA 2006 s390, previously CA 1985 s223(5)] It is therefore possible, although unusual, for subsidiaries to prepare their financial statements to a different date from their parent. However, as discussed in **chapter 33**, the Act and IAS 27 restrict the extent to which such financial statements may be used to prepare the consolidated financial statements of the group.

10.2 Definitions

Accounting reference date (*ARD*): the date on which the accounting reference period ends in each calendar year (see **10.2.1** below). [CA 2006 s391, previously CA 1985 s224]

Accounting reference period (*ARP*): the period by reference to which financial statements have to be prepared and presented to members (see **10.2.2** and **10.3** below). [CA 2006 s391, previously CA 1985 s224]

Financial year: the period covered by the statutory profit and loss account, whether this is a year or not (see **10.2.3** below). [CA 2006 s390, previously CA 1985 s223]

10.2.1 Accounting reference date

The ARD of a company incorporated on or after 1 April 1996 is the last day of the month in which the anniversary of its incorporation falls. [CA 2006 s391(4), previously CA 1985 s224(3A)] Thus, a company incorporated on 15 April 20X1 would have an ARD of 30 April 20X2. If the directors wish to change this ARD, they may do so – see **10.3** below.

10.2.2 *Accounting reference periods*

The first ARP begins on the date of incorporation and ends on the ARD and is a period of more than six months and not more than 18 months (but the period can be shortened to one of less than six months as described at **10.3** below). [CA 2006 s391(5), previously CA 1985 s224(4)]

Succeeding ARPs will be for 12 months, unless valid notice is given of an alteration in ARD. They start on the day after that on which the preceding ARP ends. [CA 2006 s391(6), previously CA 1985 s224(5)]

10.2.3 *Financial year*

The financial year of a company will normally be the same as its ARP. However, to accommodate 52-week accounting, the financial year may begin or end on dates which are not more than seven days before or after the ARD. [CA 2006 s390(3), previously CA 1985 s223(3)]

Many retailing companies take advantage of the ability to 'flex' the end of the financial year by 7 days to prepare their financial statements for a 52 week or 53 week period ending on a Saturday. Where this is done the profit and loss account should be appropriately described, e.g. 52 weeks ending 27 September and the length of the corresponding period given. The statement of financial position should also be appropriately described, e.g. as at 27 September and not 30 September.

10.3 Changes in accounting reference periods

To change an ARP [CA 2006 s392, previously CA 1985 s225], notice must be given in the prescribed form to the Registrar of Companies specifying a new ARD having effect in relation to:

(a) the company's current ARP and subsequent periods; or

(b) the company's previous ARP and subsequent periods.

A notice may be given for a previous accounting period if the period allowed for laying and delivering financial statements and reports for that previous period has not already expired. [CA 2006 s392(4), previously CA 1985 s225(5)] The notice should state whether the current or previous ARP is to be treated as being shortened or lengthened. [CA 2006 s392(2), previously CA 1985 s225(3)]

In addition, a company that is regulated by the Financial Services Authority must notify the FSA if it changes its accounting reference date (Supervision Handbook 16.3.17). Notification must be made before:

- the original date, if it is lengthening the period; or
- the new date, if it is shortening the period.

This is stricter than the Companies Act requirement.

If a listed company changes its accounting reference date, it must notify a Regulatory Information Service without delay. [LR 9.6.20R] Where the change in accounting reference date results in the extension of the accounting period to more than 14 months, the company must prepare and publish a second interim report (see **chapter 39**). [LR 9.6.21R]

Accounting periods may be lengthened only if:

(a) at least five years have passed from the end of any earlier ARP which itself had been extended; or

(b) the new ARD is that of its parent company or its subsidiary undertaking and that parent or subsidiary undertaking is established under the law of any part of the UK or the law of any other European Economic Area (EEA) State. [CA 2006 s392(3), previously CA 1985 s225(4)] The EEA includes Norway, Iceland and Liechtenstein as well as the EU Member States.

The ARP must not exceed 18 months. [CA 2006 s392(5), previously CA 1985 s225(6)]

There are no restrictions on making changes that shorten the ARP.

Whilst ARPs are not normally shorter than six months, as s391 of the 2006 Act (previously s224(4) of the 1985 Act) does not allow this, s392 of the 2006 Act (previously s225 of the 1985 Act) does allow a shorter period so in practice a newly incorporated company could produce its first set of financial statements for a period less than six months as follows:

(a) on incorporation a company is assigned an ARD of the last day of the month of the anniversary of incorporation – therefore, every company other than one incorporated on the last day of any given month will initially have a first accounting period of 12 or more but less than 13 months; and

(b) the first ARP can be altered (either shortened or extended) by notice under s392 of the 2006 Act (previously s225 of the 1985 Act) (see above). This is not precluded by s391 of the 2006 Act (previously s224 of the 1985 Act) which notes that: 'This section has effect subject to the provisions of section 392 relating to the alteration of accounting reference dates and the consequences of such alteration.' [CA 2006 s391(7), previously CA 1985 s224(6)]

Example 10.3

Changes in accounting reference periods

A company is incorporated on 16 March 20X1. Its automatic ARD is therefore 31 March.

First financial statements are required for the period 16 March 20X1 to 31 March 20X2.

Period ending/ended 31 March 20X2 can be altered (either shortened or extended) by notice s392 of the 2006 Act (previously s225 of the 1985 Act) filed and accepted any time up to the deadline for filing financial statements for the period ended 31 March 20X2.

It will be noticed that certain changes can be made only if the new ARD is that of the parent company or subsidiary undertaking. There appears to be nothing to prevent the acquisition of a subsidiary company for this purpose, even if the new company is formed after the end of the ARP which is to be changed.

11 Accounting records

11.1 Introduction

11.1.1 Scope

This section summarises the requirements concerning the maintenance by companies of accounting records as it:

(a) provides guidance on the meaning of 'proper accounting records' and 'adequate accounting records' (see **11.2** below);

(b) discusses indications and consequences of failure to keep proper or adequate accounting records (see **11.3** below); and

(c) discusses issues relating to retention of and access to accounting records (see **11.4** below).

It does not consider the special requirements concerning records that apply to building societies, banks and other entities in the financial services sector.

11.1.2 *Requirements to keep accounting records*

Every company must keep accounting records that are adequate to show and explain the company's transactions and to enable the directors to prepare annual financial statements. The accounting records must enable the company's financial position to be disclosed, with reasonable accuracy, at any time. [CA 2006 s386, previously CA 1985 s221] The records must also enable the directors to ensure that financial statements produced from them comply with the Act's requirements concerning content, valuation of assets and liabilities, presentation, and giving a true and fair view of the company's financial position and profit or loss for the year.

The specific requirements of s386 of the 2006 Act (which are similar to those in s221 of the 1985 Act with one exception explained below) are as follows:

> '(1) Every company must keep adequate accounting records.
>
> (2) Adequate accounting records means records that are sufficient -
>
> (a) to show and explain the company's transactions,
>
> (b) to disclose with reasonable accuracy, at any time, the financial position of the company at that time, and
>
> (c) to enable the directors to ensure that any accounts required to be prepared comply with the requirements of this Act (and, where applicable, of Article 4 of the IAS Regulations).
>
> (2) Accounting records must, in particular, contain -
>
> (a) entries from day to day of all sums of money received and expended by the company, and the matters in respect of which the receipt and expenditure takes place; and
>
> (b) a record of the assets and liabilities of the company.'

Section 221 of the 1985 Act did not use the word 'adequate' when referring to the accounting records that a company must keep. However, with the exception of the word "adequate", the specific requirements with regard to such accounting records were identical to those contained within s386 of the 2006 Act as detailed above. Further discussion of the meaning of accounting records and 'adequate accounting records' is provided below in **11.2**.

The words 'and, where applicable, of Article 4 of the IAS Regulation' were added as part of the amendments to the 1985 Act permitting companies to prepare accounts under IFRSs. However, the implications of these words in this section are not entirely clear.

Section 386 of the 2006 Act (previously s221 of the 1985 Act) is concerned with the accounting records for an individual company rather than a group. Article 4 of the IAS Regulation imposes a requirement on certain companies to prepare their consolidated accounts in accordance with IFRSs. It is therefore concerned only with consolidated accounts. A possible explanation for this drafting is that a parent company should keep sufficient records of its own transactions to enable those transactions to be reflected in the group accounts in accordance with IFRSs. For example, information about the fair value of certain assets and liabilities may be required to comply with Article 4 of the IAS Regulation in relation to the consolidated accounts even though the information is not necessary for the preparation of the individual accounts of the parent company under UK GAAP.

Subsection (4) of s386 of the 2006 Act (previously subsection (3) of s221 of the 1985 Act) supplements the above requirements for companies which deal in goods. Subsection (5) of s386 of the 2006 Act (previously subsection (4) of s221 of the 1985 Act) obliges a parent company which has a subsidiary undertaking to which the requirements of subsections (1), (2) (3) and (4) do not apply (e.g. because it is incorporated outside the UK) to take reasonable steps to secure that the undertaking keeps such accounting records as to enable the directors of the parent company to ensure that any accounts prepared under Part VII of the Act comply with the requirements of the Act (and, where applicable, of Article 4 of the IAS Regulations).

In this context the reference to Article 4 of the IAS Regulation is more logical because it is concerned with obtaining the information that is necessary to prepare the consolidated accounts.

Section 387 of the 2006 Act (previously subsections (5) and (6) of s221 of the 1985 Act) imposes penalties on directors who fail to comply with these requirements unless they can show that they acted honestly and that, in the circumstances in which the company's business was carried on, the default was excusable.

11.1.3 *Auditors and accounting records*

The auditors' responsibilities are stated in s498 of the 2006 Act (previously s237 of the 1985 Act) and include forming an opinion on the following matters:

(1) whether adequate accounting records have been kept;

(2) whether proper returns adequate for audit purposes have been received from branches not visited by them; and

(3) whether the financial statements are in agreement with the accounting records and returns.

If the auditors are not satisfied with regard to these matters, they must state this fact in the audit report. [CA 2006 s498(2), previously CA 1985 s237(2)] In certain cases, a failure to maintain adequate accounting records may also mean that the auditors have not received all the information they required for the purposes of the audit. When auditors have not received all the information they required for the purpose of the audit, they may be unable to conclude whether adequate accounting records have been kept. Where either of these circumstances occur, auditors have a statutory duty to state that fact in their report. Further consideration of auditors' responsibilities and auditors' reports in relation to the maintenance of adequate accounting records is outside the scope of this publication.

Section 237 of the 1985 Act referred to 'proper accounting records' rather than 'adequate accounting records'. The introduction of the word 'adequate' in both s386 of the 2006 Act, as discussed in **11.1.2** above, and s498 of the 2006 Act bring the directors and auditors responsibilities into line. Further discussion of the meaning of accounting records and the use of 'adequate' or 'proper' in the context of such is provided below in **11.2**.

11.2 Keeping proper or adequate accounting records

11.2.1 *Meaning of 'accounting records'*

A company's normal accounting records would include cash books, sales and purchase day books, sales and purchase returns books, debtors and creditors ledgers, transfer journal and general ledger. These records may be retained in book form or on computer or in any other suitable readable form. Other accounting records may be used to assist the directors in preparing management accounts. These may include stock books to record continuous stock records used in a company's costing systems.

Both the 1985 Act and 2006 Act require certain accounting records to be set up, safeguarded and retained. The auditors are now required under the

2006 Act to carry out such investigations as will enable them to form an opinion as to whether adequate accounting records have been kept by the company. Under the 1985 Act this requirement related to the preparation of 'proper accounting records'. The term 'adequate accounting records' is not defined in the Act and the wording change from 'proper' to 'adequate' is not expected to be interpreted as a significant change. Guidance on this subject is expected to be issued by the Financial Reporting Council (FRC), which is giving consideration to the implications for both management and auditors.

Guidance on the contents, form and organisation of accounting records as required by the 1985 Act was issued by the Institute of Chartered Accountants in England and Wales (ICAEW) in Technical Release FRAG 5/92. Although FRAG 5/92 will be superseded by the guidance from the FRC mentioned above, that guidance is not expected to reach significantly different conclusions from FRAG 5/92, which states that:

> 'The accounting records should comprise an orderly, classified collection of information capable of timely retrieval, containing details of the company's transactions, assets and liabilities. An unorganised collection of vouchers and documents will not suffice: whatever the physical form of the records, the information should be so organised as to enable a trial balance to be constructed. If, for example, the information is held in a computer database as a subset of a set of wider information, the software should be capable of retrieving the appropriate data.'

Guidance is also contained in paragraphs 62 – 74 of Section 8.1 of the ICAEW Members' Handbook 'Financial and accounting responsibilities of directors'. Paragraph 65 states that 'the directors have an overriding responsibility to ensure that they have adequate information to enable them to discharge their duty to manage the company's business' and paragraph 66 expands on what that responsibility entails:

> 'The duty to manage the company's business will involve ensuring that adequate control is kept over its records and transactions, for example:
>
> (a) cash;
>
> (b) debtors and creditors;
>
> (c) stock and work in progress;
>
> (d) capital expenditure; and
>
> (e) major contracts.'

In addition to records of transactions, the guidance states:

> '68 To restrict the possibility of actions for wrongful trading, directors will need constantly to be aware of the company's financial position and progress, and the accounting records should be sufficient to enable

them to be provided with the information required for drawing conclusions on these matters. The directors should also be satisfied that proper systems to provide them with regular and prompt information are in place.

69 Directors must also be aware of a company's prospects. It may therefore be prudent to prepare a plan against which the subsequent performance of the business can be measured. Periodic management accounts assist in enabling the actual operating results and the cash position to be compared with the plan. Once again, the need for, extent and frequency of such accounts will depend on the size, scope and nature of the business. However, the directors' report on the financial statements must also contain an indication of the likely future developments in the business of the company and its subsidiary undertakings (Companies Act 1985, Schedule 7), and a plan is likely to be helpful in this context'

In the absence of the proposed guidance from the FRC on the meaning of 'adequate accounting records' reference instead is made to FRAG 5/92 in the following sections to assist in the understanding of the meaning of accounting records.

11.2.2 Content of accounting records

Section 386(3)(b) of the 2006 Act (previously s221(2)(a) of 1985 Act) requires the accounting records to contain entries from day to day of all sums of money received and expended. The accounting records must therefore contain the dates of transactions, the sums received and expended and the matters in respect of which the receipts and expenditure took place. Transactions may be grouped (e.g. a record of individual receipts is not necessary to explain the records of daily cash takings in a shop).

Section 386(3)(b) of the 2006 Act (previously s221(2)(b) of the 1985 Act) requires that assets and liabilities be recorded. Therefore details, including dates of transactions, of all the company's assets and liabilities such as debtors, creditors, properties and plant must be included.

Section 386(4) of the 2006 Act (previously s221(3) of the 1985 Act) requires that where a company's business involves dealing in goods, statements of stock are to be part of the accounting records. FRAG 5/92 states that a statement of stock 'is taken to mean a summary supporting the amount included in the annual financial statements in respect of stock'. Any statements of stocktakings (e.g. continuous stock records or original stock sheets) supporting the year-end stock summary also form part of the accounting records.

11.2.3 *Disclosure of the financial position at any time*

Difficulties have arisen concerning the meaning of the legal requirement to 'disclose with reasonable accuracy at any time the financial position of the company at that time'. FRAG 5/92 provides clarification concerning the correct interpretation of this expression, as it explains that:

(1) 'at any time' emphasises the obligation to keep accounting records up to date and does not impose an obligation to keep accounting records capable of disclosing the financial position at any time in the past;

(2) transactions and events need not be recorded instantaneously – it is sufficient they are recorded within a reasonable time, depending on the nature of the business and other circumstances;

(3) 'reasonable accuracy' recognises that it is not practicable to keep accounting records in such a way as to enable financial statements to be prepared giving a true and fair view at every moment during the year – the concept of true and fair is extremely wide and embraces information not necessarily contained within the accounting records themselves;

(4) the accounting records should contain the primary material on which a set of financial statements would be based. The financial position is not limited to the cash position, but includes assets and liabilities and provisions for such matters as depreciation, bad debts and other losses which are often made only at the end of an accounting year. The requirement to disclose the financial position will normally be satisfied if a procedure exists to ensure that an adequate record is made and retained, for example by way of a memorandum, of any expected loss, liability or contingency material to the assessment of the current position; and

(5) a sufficient record of stocks within the total picture will depend on the circumstances, including materiality of stock and extent of stock movements.

11.2.4 *Format of records*

The form, content and arrangement of the underlying accounting records is driven by the format of the accounts and the mandatory disclosure requirements of the Act and accounting standards. This includes, for example, the analysis of turnover and profit by activity or geographical segment, the breakdown of staff costs and the historical cost equivalent of revalued fixed assets. Other statutes and any requirements to make specific information available to regulatory and fiscal authorities (e.g. VAT and PAYE records), overseas parents, banks and other external bodies will also influence the format of the accounting records.

Voluntary choices relating to the form and extent of disclosure may also require the format of the accounting records to be adapted to provide the necessary information. For example, if any item in the financial statements is to be shown in more detail than required by Standards, the underlying records have to be capable of producing the necessary information.

Another area which may influence the format of accounting records concerns directors' loans and other transactions with directors, where the Act provides limits and reliefs for different purposes and different types of transaction and where IAS 24 *Related Party Disclosures* requires disclosure of transactions and balances with related parties. Adequate underlying records will again be helpful in avoiding unintended breaches of the requirements.

The legislation ss1134–1138 of the 2006 Act (previously SI 1985 No 724 – The Companies (Registers and other records) Regulations 1985 and ss722–723 of the 2006 Act) permits records to be kept in hard copy or electronic form. Section 1138 of the 2006 Act (previously s722 of the 1985 Act) requires the directors to take adequate precautions for guarding against falsification. This requirement strictly only applies where the records are 'kept otherwise than in bound books' but directors clearly also need to take adequate precautions concerning any records in bound book format to meet their broader responsibilities under the Act. The requirement for a reasonable system of internal control is therefore implicit in the Act.

11.2.5 *Complying with the Act*

Complying with the requirements imposed by the Act regarding accounting records should normally present no difficulties to a company that is being run efficiently, because the statutory standards are close to those required by normal commercial prudence. However, if accounting records fall short of reasonable commercial standards, the company may be in breach of the statutory requirements. There are no hard and fast rules. Whether proper accounting records have been kept is a matter of judgement based on the facts and to some extent on the nature and size of the company concerned.

What constitutes an adequate accounting system will depend on the size, nature and complexity of the enterprise. In its simplest form, for a small business dealing primarily with cash sales and with only a few suppliers, the accounting system may only need to consist of an analysed cash book and a list of unpaid invoices. In contrast, a company manufacturing several different products and operating through a number of dispersed locations may need a complex accounting system to enable information required for financial statements to be assembled. The failure of commodity dealers to maintain records of purchase and sales orders would almost certainly constitute a failure to maintain adequate accounting records, because the liability for any losses that might result from orders could not be established. On the other hand, a failure to record purchase orders for office supplies by another type of company, for example a property company, might not be commercially prudent but would not constitute a failure to maintain adequate accounting records because the likelihood of losses arising would be small.

11.3 Failure to maintain proper or adequate accounting records

11.3.1 Matters to consider

Failure to maintain proper or adequate accounting records may result from inadequate internal control or the ignorance or inexperience of management or staff.

The questions that normally should be considered in determining whether accounting records have been properly maintained during a financial year include the following.

(1) Did the records required by the legislation exist?

(2) Were the records in a format permitted by the law?

(3) Were the records safeguarded as required?

(4) Were the records kept up to date?

(5) Were the records accurate and complete?

(6) Were the records free of fictitious or significantly incorrect items?

(7) Did the records provide the information required in the manner required?

(8) Were the records such as to disclose the financial position of the company at any time and to enable the directors to prepare financial statements complying with the Act and showing a true and fair view of the company's profit or loss and state of affairs?

In addition, a fraud may indicate that proper or adequate accounting records have not been kept, as the Act requires that the directors maintain adequate precautions for guarding against falsification. As noted earlier, the Act only makes this specific requirement where the records are 'not kept by making entries in a bound book' but directors clearly also need to take adequate precautions concerning any records in bound book format to meet their broader responsibilities under the law.

11.3.2 *Consequence of failure to maintain proper or adequate accounting records*

Under the penalty provisions of s387 of the 2006 Act (previously s221(5) and (6) of the 1985 Act), every officer of a company which fails to comply with s386 of the 2006 Act (previously s221 of the 1985 Act) is guilty of a criminal offence unless he/she shows that he/she acted honestly and that in the circumstances in which the company's business was carried on the default was excusable. Companies and all directors found to be in default of their statutory obligations regarding proper accounting records are each liable to default fines and additional fines for each day of default. Directors may also be liable to imprisonment and disqualification from acting as directors in cases of persistent default (under the terms of the Act and the Company Directors Disqualification Act 1986).

A significant failure to maintain proper or adequate accounting records may entail a qualified auditors' report as discussed at **11.1.3** above. Such a report may result in a more detailed examination than usual by HMRC and regulatory bodies such as the Review Panel.

11.4 Retention and access

11.4.1 *Retention of accounting records*

Directors are required to retain accounting records for at least six years (for public companies) or three years (for private companies). [CA 2006 s388(4), previously CA 1985 s222(5)] These requirements are subject (in the case of a company in liquidation) to any provision contained in rules made under the Insolvency Act 1986 and may be overridden by other statutory regulations. The guidance provided by FRAG 5/92 'Accounting records' indicates that 'where programmed instructions and any supporting documentation are needed for retrieval of information in usable form, for example, from a computer database, they must be available for the same period, as must any necessary hardware.'

In addition to the Act, there are numerous other sources of requirements regarding record keeping that are outside of the scope of this publication. For example, taxation law and contract law will need to be considered. Records should generally be retained only as long as they are really needed for commercial or legal purposes. Company policy on this matter may be dictated by:

(a) economic considerations (e.g. the cost of staff, equipment, space and supplies);

(b) legal and related requirements (e.g. specific retention periods required by law, audit considerations and enforceability of contracts); and

(c) actual or potential demand for copies and historical value (e.g. policy decisions, precedents, and technical or scientific archives).

Important documents may need to be kept indefinitely or for long periods, possibly in their original form, whereas it may be possible to dispose of others as soon as permitted by the law. It is usually helpful to discuss policy on the retention of records (especially microfilming or optical scanning) with the auditors before originals are destroyed.

11.4.2 Access to accounting records

The Act requires a company's directors to keep its accounting records either at its registered office or at such other places as they may think appropriate. [CA 2006 s388, previously CA 1985 s222] In any event, they must be open to inspection by the company's officers (defined as including its directors, secretary and managers) at all times. [CA 2006 s1173, previously CA 1985 s744] The auditors also have a right of access at all times to the company's accounting records but not directly to the accounting records of any subsidiary undertakings, unless they are also the auditors of those subsidiaries. [CA 2006 s499, previously CA 1985 s389A] They have rights, however, to obtain information regarding subsidiary undertakings, either from the subsidiary directly, if it is incorporated in the UK, or via the parent company if the subsidiary is unincorporated or incorporated elsewhere.

If the accounting records are kept outside the United Kingdom, the Act requires accounts and returns concerning business dealt with in those records to be sent to, and retained in, the United Kingdom, where they must be open to inspection by the company's officers and auditors at all times. [CA 2006 s388(2), previously CA 1985 s222(2)] These returns must at least be adequate to disclose with reasonable accuracy, at six-monthly intervals, the financial position of the relevant business. [CA 2006 s388(3), previously s222(3)] They must also allow the directors to prepare true and fair annual financial statements. There is no requirement to maintain them in the English language or to denominate them in Sterling.

12 Electronic communications for companies

Companies have been permitted to communicate with their shareholders (e.g. sending them annual reports and notices of meetings) by electronic means since 2000. However, this facility has been little used due to the need to obtain the explicit agreement of shareholders to this means of communication. Those companies that have offered this facility have received a very low take up ranging from 0.5 per cent to 10 per cent according to the Institute of Chartered Secretaries & Administrators. As a result, millions of hard copy documents are printed by companies each year and never read.

The Companies Act 2006 makes significant changes in this respect. Going forward, it will be assumed that shareholders want electronic communications and they will have to opt out if they still want to receive printed copies. These provisions of the 2006 Act came into effect on 20 January 2007 although companies will first have to pass the necessary resolutions and communicate with their shareholders in hard copy to ascertain whether they want to opt out of electronic communications. The new procedures apply to all companies although in practice it is likely to be quoted companies that make significant use of electronic communications.

Companies will have to write to each shareholder to see if they accept electronic communications (i.e. email) or website communications (i.e. making the document available on a website) and give them the option to continue to receive printed copies. In the case of website communications, there is a requirement to notify the shareholder about the presence of the document on the website. This can be done either by post or, where the shareholder has supplied an email address, by email.

Companies can deem that shareholders have agreed to website communications if there is no response within 28 days. However, as explained above, it will still be necessary to send a paper notification each time a document is made available on the website unless an email address has been supplied. Nevertheless, this will still achieve considerable cost savings compared with sending, for example, the full annual report.

The provisions are drafted generally to encourage more electronic communications with shareholders. So this goes wider than just annual reports.

It is necessary to ensure that the appropriate administrative resolutions have been passed to allow communications with shareholders via email and/or the internet. If this was done when the earlier provisions were introduced in 2000, then it may not be necessary to pass any further resolutions.

Further useful guidance about this subject has been issued by the Institute of Chartered Secretaries & Administrators and can be found on their website at:

http://www.icsa.org.uk/

Companies House also provide for certain documents to be filed electronically although this does not currently extend to annual reports except for dormant companies and the abbreviated accounts of audit exempt companies.

46 Documents accompanying UK financial statements

1 Introduction

All financial statements are required by the 2006 Act and 1985 Act to be accompanied by a directors' report including information specified by the Acts. This chapter considers the requirements for directors' reports and other statements that may accompany the financial statements according to the circumstances. The structure of the chapter is set out below.

Section 2 Statements of directors' responsibilities	Auditing standards require that, where the annual report does not include an adequate statement of directors' responsibilities, the auditors should include a description in their report. As a result, the directors themselves will normally include the required statement in the annual report, removing the need for the auditors to do so. This is discussed in **section 2.1** below. In addition, for periods beginning on or after 20 January 2007, the Disclosure and Transparency Rules of the Financial Services Authority require the annual report of a listed company to be accompanied by a responsibility statement. This is discussed in **section 2.2** below.
Section 3 Directors' report	The requirements of the Acts in relation to directors' reports, including the business review, are discussed in **section 3** below. This section also covers those requirements of the Listing Rules which are conventionally dealt with in the directors' report.
Section 4 Five-year record	Most listed companies provide a comparative table of results covering a five-year period, although there is no requirement in the Listing Rules to do so. Such five-year records are considered in **section 4**.
Section 5 Operating and Financial Review	Companies may voluntarily prepare an Operating and Financial Review (OFR). The latest guidance as to the content is provided in the Reporting Statement *Operating and Financial Review* published by the Accounting Standards Board (ASB). These recommendations are considered in **section 5**.

The requirements relating to corporate governance statements and directors' remuneration reports are discussed in **chapter 47** and **chapter 48** respectively.

Most listed companies also publish a Chairman's statement. There are no formal requirements for this although it was recommended by the London Stock Exchange in 1964. Although the original purpose of the Chairman's statement may have been overtaken by the requirement to publish a business review and the recommendation to publish an OFR, it is likely that most listed companies will continue to include a personal statement from the Chairman.

The sections of the 2006 Act relating to the directors' report are effective for periods commencing on or after 6 April 2008. Throughout this chapter appropriate references have been inserted for the 2006 and 1985 Acts. Many of the detailed requirements of the 2006 Act are now included within the Accounting Regulations.

2 Statements of directors' responsibilities

For many years there has been a requirement for a statement of directors' responsibilities imposed, in effect, by auditing standards. The statement explains the responsibilities of the directors for the preparation of the financial statements with the aim of distinguishing those responsibilities from the responsibilities of the auditors. This is considered at **2.1** below.

Under the Combined Code, Code Provision C.1.1 also requires the directors to explain their responsibility for preparing the financial statements.

In addition, for periods beginning on or after 20 January 2007, there is a requirement for those companies that are within the scope of the Disclosure and Transparency Rules (DTR) of the Financial Services Authority to include a 'responsibility statement' in their annual report. The statement is an acknowledgement by those responsible for the annual report of their responsibilities. This is considered at **2.2** below.

2.1 Statement to meet the requirements of auditing standards

International Standard on Auditing (ISA) (UK and Ireland) 700 requires that 'where the financial statements or accompanying information do not include an adequate description of the relevant responsibilities of those charged with governance, the auditors' report should include a description of those responsibilities'. This repeats the substance of the previous requirement in SAS 600. However, ISA (UK and Ireland) 700 contains merely this high level requirement and does not specify the minimum contents for such a statement to be 'adequate' in the way that SAS 600 did (see below).

In September 2006 the APB issued Bulletin 2006/6 *Auditor's Reports on Financial Statements in the United Kingdom*. This contains an illustrative example of a statement of directors' responsibilities for a non-publicly traded company preparing its financial statements under UK GAAP. No illustrative examples are given for companies reporting under IFRSs. The Bulletin comments that 'the APB has not prepared an illustrative example of a statement of directors' responsibilities for a publicly traded company as the directors' responsibilities which are in part dependent on the particular regulatory environment, will vary dependent on the rules of the market on which its securities are admitted to trading'.

The guidance in this section is, therefore, based on SAS 600.

In most cases, the directors will include an adequate statement themselves, avoiding the need for the auditors to do so. SAS 600(4) indicated that it will aid communication with the reader if the statement of directors' responsibilities is included immediately before the auditors' report.

What normally constitutes an adequate description of company directors' responsibilities in the context of a company's statutory financial statements was given in the explanatory material to SAS 600. This should be followed in the absence of any guidance in ISA 700 (UK and Ireland). According to that explanatory material, such a description will normally be considered adequate when it includes directors' responsibilities to:

- prepare, in accordance with company law, financial statements for each financial year which give a true and fair view of the company's (or group's) state of affairs at the end of the year and profit or loss for the year then ended;
- select suitable accounting policies and then apply them on a consistent basis, making judgements and estimates that are prudent and reasonable;
- state whether applicable accounting standards have been followed, subject to any material departures disclosed and explained in the financial statements (this applies only to large companies, i.e. companies which are not small or medium-sized companies as defined by the Act);
- apply the going concern basis, unless it is not appropriate to presume that the company will continue in business (this is only necessary where no separate statement on going concern is made by the directors);

- keep proper accounting records; and
- safeguard the assets of the company (or group) and take reasonable steps for the prevention and detection of fraud and other irregularities.

In addition, it is important that the financial reporting framework which the directors are using is described (e.g. 'International Financial Reporting Standards').

These responsibilities apply to most corporate entities, but will need to be adapted for different legal requirements applicable to entities not subject to the Act. For reporting entities other than companies, the adequacy of the description should be assessed by reference to statutory or other specific requirements with which the principals or management of those entities are required to comply.

As noted above, the APB has not issued any guidance on the form and content of a statement of directors' responsibilities for a company reporting under IFRSs. The form of the statement will depend on whether the separate financial statements of the parent company are prepared under IFRSs or UK GAAP.

The example statement of directors' responsibilities illustrated below is suitable for a listed company that is required to prepare consolidated financial statements under IFRSs and also elects to prepare its separate financial statements under IFRSs. Modifications will be required in other cases. The statement meets the relevant requirements but other approaches are acceptable.

Example 2.1

Directors' responsibilities statement where the consolidated and separate financial statements are prepared under IFRSs

The directors are responsible for preparing the Report and the financial statements in accordance with applicable law and regulations. Company law requires the directors to prepare financial statements for each financial year. The directors are required by the IAS Regulation to prepare the group financial statements under International Financial Reporting Standards (IFRSs) as adopted by the European Union and have also elected to prepare the parent company financial statements in accordance with IFRSs as adopted by the European Union. The financial statements are also required by law to be properly prepared in accordance with the Companies Act [1985] [2006] and Article 4 of the IAS Regulation.

International Accounting Standard 1 requires that financial statements present fairly for each financial year the company's financial position, financial performance and cash flows. This requires the faithful representation of the effects of transactions, other events and conditions in accordance with the definitions and recognition criteria for assets, liabilities, income and expenses set out in the International Accounting Standards Board's 'Framework for the preparation and Presentation of Financial Statements'. In virtually all circumstances, a fair presentation will be achieved by compliance with all applicable International Financial Reporting Standards. Directors are also required to:

- properly select and apply accounting policies;
- present information, including accounting policies, in a manner that provides relevant, reliable, comparable and understandable information; and
- provide additional disclosures when compliance with the specific requirements in IFRSs is insufficient to enable users to understand the impact of particular transactions, other events and conditions on the entity's financial position and financial performance.

The directors are responsible for keeping proper accounting records which disclose with reasonable accuracy at any time the financial position of the company, for safeguarding the assets, for taking reasonable steps for the prevention and detection of fraud and other irregularities and for the preparation of a directors' report and directors' remuneration report which comply with the requirements of the Companies Act [1985] [2006].

The directors are responsible for the maintenance and integrity of the company website. Legislation in the United Kingdom governing the preparation and dissemination of financial statements differs from legislation in other jurisdictions.

[No reference is made to the going concern basis in this example on the assumption that a separate going concern statement by the directors is provided in accordance with the Listing Rules elsewhere in the annual report.]

Directors are required to give a description rather than a statement of their responsibilities and therefore it is acceptable to have, as an alternative to a separate statement, a section of the directors' report headed up as 'Directors' responsibilities'. In such circumstances, it is recommended that the section is included in the final part of the directors' report, so as to be next to the auditors' report which follows it.

No specific reference is made to the group in the paragraph about accounting records because the directors are responsible for the accounting records and assets of the company. Responsibility for the accounting records and assets of subsidiaries rests with the directors of the subsidiaries.

The electronic publication of annual reports and accounts is increasingly becoming the norm for listed companies. APB Bulletin 2001/1 *The electronic publication of auditors' reports* recommends that auditors encourage the directors to state clearly their responsibility for the preparation and dissemination of financial statements (particularly in relation to potential differences between the relevant legislation in the UK and that in other jurisdictions) and for the maintenance and integrity of the website. This could be included in the statement of directors' responsibilities, as in **example 2.1** above, or a more generic website disclaimer notice. If these statements are not sufficiently clear, or if the auditors otherwise consider it appropriate, the APB recommends that the auditors add a note at the end of the electronic version of the auditors' report.

2.2 Statement to meet the requirements of the DTR

For periods beginning on or after 20 January 2007, companies admitted to trading on a regulated market have to comply with the requirements on periodic financial reporting in chapter 4 of the Disclosure and Transparency Rules (DTR) issued by the Financial Services Authority. These rules replace some of the Listing Rules for such periods. They are derived from the EU Transparency Obligations Directive and apply to companies whose transferable securities, whether shares or debt, are admitted to trading on a regulated market and whose home state is the United Kingdom. The periodic financial reporting rules in the DTR do not apply to AIM companies, nor those with only debt securities listed on the Professional Securities Market, and there are certain exemptions available to companies with only wholesale debt admitted to trading or in the public sector.

The requirements of the DTR for the annual financial report include a 'responsibility statement'. Such a statement must be made by the persons responsible within the company (usually the directors). The responsibility statement should include the name and function of any person making a statement. [DTR 4.1.12]

It is expected that only one person would be required physically to sign the responsibility statement, and sign on behalf of the board of directors. Ultimately, it is for each company to decide which person(s) are considered responsible within the company.

Each person making a responsibility statement must confirm that to the best of his or her knowledge:

[DTR 4.1.12]

- the financial statements, prepared in accordance with the applicable set of accounting standards, give a true and fair view of the assets, liabilities, financial position and profit or loss of the company and the undertakings included in the consolidation taken as a whole; and

- the management report (i.e. in practice, the directors' report) includes a fair review of the development and performance of the business and the position of the company and the undertakings included in the consolidation taken as a whole, together with a description of the principal risks and uncertainties that they face.

A possible form of responsibility statement meeting the requirements of the DTR is set out in the example below.

Example 2.2

Responsibility statement

We confirm that to the best of our knowledge:

- the financial statements, prepared in accordance with International Financial Reporting Standards, give a true and fair view of the assets, liabilities, financial position and profit or loss of the company and the undertakings included in the consolidation taken as a whole; and

- the management report, which is incorporated into the directors' report, includes a fair review of the development and performance of the business and the position of the company and the undertakings included in the consolidation taken as a whole, together with a description of the principal risks and uncertainties that they face.

By order of the Board

[Signature]	[Signature]
Chief Executive Officer	Chief Financial Officer
[Name of signatory]	[Name of signatory]
[Date]	[Date]

It is for the company to decide who and how many of those responsible should sign the responsibility statement. The name and function of whoever signs the statement must be clearly indicated in the responsibility statement.

The DTR do not specify where the responsibility statement should be included in the annual report. Companies may choose to combine the responsibility statement with their description of responsibilities.

3 Directors' report

3.1 General requirements

The requirement to produce a directors' report is contained in s415 of the 2006 Act and s234 of the 1985 Act. The information required to be disclosed is detailed in s416–419 of the 2006 Act, Sch. 7 of the Accounting Regulations and s234 and Sch. 7 of the 1985 Act.

The Disclosure and Transparency Rules (DTR) of the Financial Services Authority require most listed companies to prepare an annual 'management report' to accompany their financial statements. However, with one exception, these requirements duplicate existing requirements within the law concerning the content of the directors' report. The exception relates to the disclosure of branches. The DTR require information about the existence of branches which goes further than the equivalent requirement in the Acts, which is restricted to branches outside the UK.

The directors' report should be approved by the board of directors and signed on behalf of the board by a director or the secretary of the company. [CA 2006 s419(1), previously CA 1985 s234A]

Under s234A of the 1985 Act, the copy of the report which is sent to the Registrar of Companies should be physically signed by a director or the company secretary. This is also a requirement of the 2006 Act as amended by the transitional provisions of the 5th Commencement Order (for example s447 in the case of a quoted company). It is expected that these transitional provisions will be in due course be replaced with authentication requirements imposed by the Registrar of Companies which will also deal with the authentication of documents which are filed electronically. Other copies of the report, for example those circulated to members, may just state the name of the signatory.

Difficulties of interpretation and application of the relevant disclosure provisions of the Act arise particularly where disclosure is required only if an item is 'material', 'significant' or 'substantial', as no definitions of these terms are given. It should be emphasised that, except where the Act gives an exemption on the grounds of materiality or significance, the information should be given even if it is considered unimportant or immaterial by the directors.

In general, comparative figures are not required in the directors' report. In practice many companies include comparative figures so that the reader can better appreciate changes in performance. For this reason it is recommended that comparative information be given in the review of developments section of the report (see **3.3** below).

Section 234 of the 1985 Act and section 415 of the 2006 Act specify that for a financial year in which the company is a parent company, and the directors prepare group accounts, the directors' report must be a consolidated report (a 'group directors' report') relating, to the extent specified in the Act, to the company and its subsidiary undertakings included in the consolidation. [CA 2006 s415(2), previously CA 1985 s234(2)] A group directors' report may, where appropriate, give greater emphasis to the matters that are significant to the company and its subsidiary undertakings included in the consolidation, taken as a whole. [CA 2006 s415(3), previously CA 1985 s234(3)]

If a directors' report does not comply with the provisions of the Act, every director who knew that it did not comply or was reckless as to whether it complied, and failed to take all reasonable steps to secure compliance with the provisions in question, is guilty of an offence and liable to a fine. [CA 2006 s419(3), previously CA 1985 s234(5)]

3.1.1 Directors' liability for disclosures in the report

Section 463 of the Companies Act 2006 is effective for reports first sent to members from 20 January 2007 onwards. The section gives protection from civil liability in respect of statements or omissions made in directors' reports and directors' remuneration reports (and any summary financial statements derived from those reports).

Directors are only liable if they make a statement that is untrue or misleading and know that the statement is untrue or misleading or are reckless as to whether it is untrue or misleading. Dishonest concealment of material facts also causes a director to be liable.

Directors are only liable to the company and not to shareholders and third parties. Any shareholder who suffers a loss has to demonstrate that the company has suffered a loss to bring a claim.

Similar protection is provided for statements prepared to meet the requirements of the Transparency Obligations Directive.

The protection extends only to the stated reports. Statements made in, for example, a voluntary OFR would not be protected. This may lead to more OFRs being cross-referred into the directors' report to bring the OFR contents within the scope of the protection.

This clarifies for the first time a director's position in terms of statements included in the directors' report. The provision is designed to encourage directors to provide more meaningful disclosures, particularly relating to the future, in the knowledge that, in the absence of bad faith, they will not be liable for statements not borne out by future events.

3.2 Principal activities of the company

The directors' report should state the principal activities of the company in the course of the year. [CA 2006 s416(1)(b), previously CA 1985 s234ZZA(1)(b)]

In relation to a group directors' report, this requirement has effect as if the reference to the company was a reference to the company and its subsidiary undertakings included in the consolidation. [CA 2006 s416(2), previously s234ZZA(2)]

The section makes no explicit reference to significant changes in activities in the financial year. In practice, such information would usually be necessary to meet the requirement to state the principal activities 'in the course of the year'.

Principal activities disclosed are usually taken to mean categories of important horizontal diversification representing distinct classes of industry and commerce (e.g. textiles, oil, publishing, electrical equipment). Vertical analysis (e.g. wholesale, retail, manufacturing, factored, domestic, export) may be made for internal management and other reporting purposes, but is usually less meaningful for the reader of the financial statements.

Example 3.2

Principal activities

The company and its subsidiaries are engaged principally in the manufacture, distribution and sale of food products, in hotel and catering operations and in property development.

3.3 The business review

3.3.1 *Requirements for the review*

The requirements for a 'review of the development of the business' in s234ZZB of the 1985 Act are repeated in s417 of the 2006 Act. This is sometimes referred to as the 'enhanced business review'. Additional requirements are imposed on quoted companies by the 2006 Act for periods beginning on or after 1 October 2007.

The 2006 Act also includes a 'purpose' for the business review which does not appear in the 1985 Act. The business review is to inform members of the company and help them assess how the directors have performed their duty under s172 of the 2006 Act (i.e. duty to promote the success of the company). It may be helpful to bear this in mind when the business review is being drafted or reviewed.

3.3.1.1 *Requirements of business review for all companies excluding small companies*

The directors' report must contain:

[CA 2006 s417(3), previously CA 1985 s234ZZB(1)]

- a fair review of the business of the company; and
- a description of the principal risks and uncertainties facing the company.

The Act specifies that the review should be a balanced and comprehensive analysis of:

- the development and performance of the business of the company during the financial year; and
- the position of the company at the end of that year,

consistent with the size and complexity of the business. [CA 2006 s417(4), previously CA 1985 s234ZZB(2)]

The review must, to the extent necessary for an understanding of the development, performance or position of the business of the company, include:

[CA 2006 s417(6), previously s234ZZB(3)]

- an analysis using financial key performance indicators; and

- where appropriate, analysis using other key performance indicators, including information relating to environmental matters and employee matters.

The review must, where appropriate, include references to, and additional explanations of, amounts included in the financial statements. [CA 2006 s417(8), previously CA 1985 s234ZZB(4)]

'Key performance indicators' are defined, for this purpose, to mean 'factors by reference to which the development, performance or position of the business of the company can be measured effectively'. [CA 2006 s417(6), previously CA 1985 s234ZZB(5)]

The recommendations relating to the Operating and Financial Review (OFR) (see **section 5** below) may provide a helpful source of reference.

The DTI (now BERR) issued a document "Guidance on the changes to the Directors' Report requirements in the Companies Act 1985- April and December 2005" which compared the business review requirements in the 1985 Act with the requirements in the Reporting Statement issued by the ASB for OFRs. The document indicates that the Reporting Statement highlights additional areas where disclosures are required including trends and factors likely to affect the future development, performance and position of the business, and information about environmental, employee, social and community issues and policies. Companies producing a business review are not specifically required to make disclosures in as many of these additional areas, but will need to consider doing so where information is material to the understanding the development, performance and position of the company, their principal risks and uncertainties or to provide an indication of likely future developments. As noted in **3.3.1.2**, the disclosure requirements for business reviews have been enhanced for quoted companies in the 2006 Act.

In relation to a group directors' report, references to a company should be taken as references to the company and its subsidiary undertakings included in the consolidation. [CA 2006 s417(9), previously CA 1985 s234ZZB(6)]

Small companies that are entitled to the exemptions under s246 of the 1985 Act and s382 of the 2006 Act are exempt from the requirements of s234ZZB of the 1985 Act and s417 of the 2006 Act respectively . [CA 2006 s417(1), previously CA 1985 s246(4)]

Medium-sized companies that qualify for the exemptions in s246A of the 1985 Act and s465 of the 2006 Act are exempt from the requirement of s234ZZB(3) of the 1985 Act and s417(6) of the 2006 Act (business review to include analysis using key performance indicators) so far as they relate to non-financial information. [CA 2006 s417(7), previously CA 1985 s246A(2A)]

Under both the 2006 and 1985 Acts, being a member of an "ineligible" group does not prevent these exemptions for the directors' report being used. [CA 2006 s415A(1), previously CA 1985 s247A]

> Therefore small and medium-sized entities that are part of groups can take advantage of the relevant exemptions for the directors' report as if they are stand-alone companies. They are allowed to take full advantage of exemptions under EU Accounting Directives for the directors' report, even if they form part of a group. However, a small or medium-sized company cannot use the exemptions if it is a public company, a company that is an authorised insurance company, a banking company, an e-money issuer, an ISD investment firm or a UCITS management company, or carries on an insurance market activity.

3.3.1.2 *Additional business review requirements for quoted companies*

The 2006 Act imposes additional disclosure requirements in the business review for quoted companies for periods beginning on or after 1 October 2007. The business review must, to the extent necessary for an understanding of the development, performance or position of the company's business, include

- the main trends and factors likely to affect the future development, performance and position of the company's business; [s417(5)(a)]
- information about:
  - environmental matters (including the impact of the company's business on the environment):
  - the company's employees, and
  - social and community issues,

including information about any policies of the company in relation to those matters and the effectiveness of those policies; [s417(5)(b) (i)(ii)(iii)] and

- subject to the exception explained below, information about persons with whom the company has contractual or other arrangements which are essential to the business of the company. [s417(5)(c)]

If the review does not contain information of each kind mentioned in the second bullet point above, it must state which of those kinds of information it does not contain. [s417(5)]

The exception referred to in s417(5)(c) is that the section does not require the disclosure of information about a person if the disclosure would, in the opinion of the directors, be seriously prejudicial to that person and contrary to the public interest. It is important to note that the exemption is available only where the disclosure would be seriously prejudicial to the person concerned and contrary to the public interest. Therefore, it is likely to apply only in very rare cases.

> The ASB published additional narrative reporting guidance in January 2008 This illustrates the linkage between the enhanced business review requirements in the 2006 Act and the ASB's Reporting Statement on the OFR. The guidance indicates that the ASB believes that all the enhanced business review requirements found in the 2006 Act are already included in the Reporting Statement. Therefore a company which prepares an OFR in compliance with the Reporting Statement and cross refers this information into the Directors' Report will meet the requirements of the Act.

3.3.2 *Published forecasts*

Listed companies are required to give an explanation if the results for the period under review differ from any published forecast or estimate by the company.

The Listing Rules require disclosure in the annual report and accounts of 'any information required by LR 9.2.18R'. [LR 9.8.4R(2)]

LR 9.2.18R applies to any unaudited information in a class 1 circular or a prospectus or to any profit forecast or profit estimate (all as defined in the Listing Rules). [LR 9.2.18R(1)]

> This requirement could refer not only to the obvious example of a forecast given in an offer or rebuttal document, but also any forecast given in an earlier chairman's statement or directors' report. However, it does not apply to forecasts made by third parties such as investment analysts and the press.

The first time a listed company publishes financial information as required by LR 9.7 to LR 9.9 (i.e. a preliminary announcement, annual report and accounts or half-yearly report) after the publication of the unaudited financial information, profit forecast or profit estimate, it must:

[LR 9.2.18R(2)]

(a) reproduce that financial information, profit forecast or profit estimate in its next annual report and accounts;

(b) produce and disclose in the annual report and accounts the actual figures for the same period covered by the information reproduced under (a); and

(c) provide an explanation of the difference, if there is a difference of 10 per cent or more between the figures required by (b) and those reproduced under (a).

The requirement does not apply to:

[LR 9.2.19G]

(a) pro forma financial information prepared in accordance with Annex 1 and Annex 2 of the Prospectus Directive Regulations; or

(b) any preliminary statement of annual results or half-yearly or quarterly reports that are reproduced with the unaudited financial information.

3.4 Future developments in the business

The report should contain an indication of the likely future developments in the business of the company and its subsidiaries. [Acc Regs Sch. 7: 7(1)(b), previously CA 1985 Sch. 7: 6(b)]

This seems to require:

(a) a statement, in general terms, of the expectation of the directors regarding the trend of earnings in the forthcoming year;

(b) details of decisions made which will have a significant impact on earnings or on the course of the business (e.g. new products, plans for expansion/rationalisation, proposed disposals/acquisitions); and

(c) the effect of significant events beyond the control of the company which have occurred or are expected to occur (e.g. restrictive legislation, technological changes, loss of markets or shortage of supplies, political or economic disturbances in the company's markets, interest rate changes).

This is an area of overlap with the OFR. Those companies preparing an OFR (see **section 5** below) will, in practice, give this information in the OFR rather than in the directors' report, in which case a cross reference from the directors' report to those specific sections of the OFR should be included.

There is a danger that, in complying with this requirement, directors might inadvertently make a profit forecast (in the context of **3.3.2** above) which may, in some circumstances, have onerous consequences under the Listing Rules and the City Code on Take-overs and Mergers.

3.5 Dividends

The directors' report should state the amount, if any, recommended to be paid as dividend. [CA 2006 s416(3), previously CA 1985 s234(1)(b)] Where the directors do not propose a dividend, it is customary to state this.

Listed companies should give details of any arrangement under which a shareholder has waived or has agreed to waive any dividends. [LR 9.8.4R(12)]

Where a shareholder has agreed to waive future dividends, details of such waiver should be given together with those relating to dividends which are payable during the period under review. [LR 9.8.4R(13)]

The annual report need not include details of waivers of dividends of less than 1% of the total value of any dividend provided that some payment has been made on each share of the relevant class during the relevant calendar year. [LR 9.8.5R]

3.6 Post balance sheet events

The directors' report should contain particulars of any important events affecting the company or any of its subsidiaries which have occurred since the end of the financial year. [Acc Regs Sch. 7: 7(1)(a), previously CA 1985 Sch. 7: 6(a)]

There is a similar requirement in IAS 10 for disclosure in the notes to the accounts of 'non-adjusting events' after the end of the reporting period which are of such materiality that their non-disclosure might influence the economic decisions of users taken on the basis of the financial statements. It could be argued that certain events might be thought sufficiently important to require disclosure in the directors' report, but not be necessary for a proper understanding of the financial position and therefore not need to be disclosed under IAS 10. However, such an approach would be open to challenge and should be viewed with caution. Conversely, any event which needs to be disclosed in the notes to the accounts under IAS 10 should certainly be viewed as an important event to be disclosed in the directors' report to comply with the Act. It is suggested that, in these circumstances, it is sometimes appropriate to make only a brief mention of the matter in the directors' report, with a reference to the relevant note in the financial statements.

3.7 Fixed assets

The directors' report should contain particulars of any substantial difference between the market value and balance sheet value of interests in land held by the company or any of its subsidiary undertakings if the directors decide that this is significant to shareholders or debenture holders. [Acc Regs Sch. 7: 2(1), previously CA 1985 Sch. 7: 1(2)]

'Land' should be taken to include buildings and other capitalised building improvements such as car parks and drainage. Schedule 1 of the Interpretation Act 1978 states that 'land includes buildings and other structures, land covered with water, and any estate, interest, easement, servitude or right in or over land'.

No guidance is provided by the Act as to what is 'substantial' and as to the circumstances in which the information should be regarded as 'significant'. A substantial difference between book and market value is usually significant to shareholders or debenture holders where land and buildings are suitable for alternative uses or redevelopment so that their current value greatly exceeds book value. Since the realisation of such a difference could often be achieved only by the company selling the property in question, a fair presentation would also disclose any tax liabilities which would arise as a result of such a sale.

It is not generally expected that the directors will have to obtain a professional valuation to make this disclosure, given the requirement to disclose the difference between market value and book value 'with such degree of precision as practicable'. There is no requirement to make a negative statement where the directors do not consider the difference to be material but this should be viewed as good practice where the company has significant interests in land and buildings.

3.8 Research and development

The directors' report should contain an indication of the activities (if any) of the company and its subsidiaries in the field of research and development. [Acc Regs Sch. 7: 7(1)(c), previously 1985 Act Sch. 7: 6(c)] This appears to require a description of the progress of projects which are expected to result in new or improved products, services, or production techniques.

Directors should take care to avoid a situation in which this disclosure appears inconsistent with the financial statements. For example, if the directors' report discusses significant research and development activities, the financial statements should also include the disclosures required by IAS 38.126 (see **13.2.9** in **chapter 8**).

3.9 Acquisition of own shares

3.9.1 Disclosure

Where a company purchases its own shares during the year, the following information should be given in the directors' report:

[Acc Regs Sch. 7: Part II, previously CA 1985 Sch. 7: Part II]

(a) the number and nominal value of shares purchased and the percentage of the called-up share capital which those shares represent;

(b) the consideration paid; and

(c) the reasons for the purchases.

Other dealings in own shares, which should also be disclosed under both Schedule 7 of the Accounting Regulations and the 1985 Act include own shares which are:

(a) acquired by the company through forfeiture or gift; or

(b) acquired by the company's nominee or by others with company financial assistance, where the company has a beneficial interest; or

(c) made subject to a lien or charge by the company.

The disclosures required in these circumstances are contained in Sch. 7: 9 of the Accounting Regulations and Sch. 7: 8 of the 1985 Act.

3.9.2 *Listed companies*

Listed companies incorporated in the UK are required to disclose the following additional information regarding arrangements for the acquisition of their own shares:

[LR 9.8.6R(4)]

(a) details of any shareholders' authority for the company to purchase its own shares that is still valid at the end of the period under review;

(b) in the case of purchases made otherwise than through the market or by tender to all shareholders, the names of the sellers of the shares being purchased, or proposed to be purchased, during the period under review;

(c) in the case of any purchases made otherwise than through the market or by tender to all shareholders, or options or contracts to make such purchases, entered into since the end of the period covered by the report, information equivalent to that required by the Act in respect of purchases during the year (see **3.9.1** above); and

(d) in the case of sales of treasury shares for cash made otherwise than through the market, or in connection with an employee share scheme, or otherwise than pursuant to an opportunity which (so far as practicable) was made available to all holders of the listed company's securities (or to all holders of a relevant class of its securities) on the same terms, particulars of names of purchasers of such shares sold by the company during the period under review.

The circumstances under which a company may legally purchase or redeem its own shares, including provisions to allow companies to hold their own shares 'in treasury', and the requirements to ensure maintenance of capital, are discussed in **chapter 49**.

3.10 Directors

Disclosure is required of the names of the persons who were directors of the company at any time during the financial year. [CA 2006 s416(1)(a), previously CA 1985 s234(2)] This can be achieved either by listing the names of the directors in the directors' report itself or referring the reader to the page where this information may be found.

The following information, which is not required by either of the Acts, or any other regulation, is also often given in either the directors' report or the board's remuneration report to shareholders (see **chapter 48**):

(a) the dates of appointments or resignations occurring during the period;

(b) changes in the directors since the end of the financial year; and

(c) the directors who retire at the annual general meeting and whether they offer themselves for re-election.

Listed companies are subject to further disclosure requirements about directors and membership of board committees to achieve compliance with the Combined Code. These requirements are addressed in **chapter 47**.

3.11 Directors' interests in shares or debentures

The requirement for companies to maintain registers of directors' interests and for those interests to be disclosed in the directors' report or financial statements were repealed by provisions of the 2006Act which came into effect on 6 April 2007. Reports approved after that date are not required to make any disclosures about directors' share interests under company law. However, a listed company incorporated in the UK is required to include, in its annual report, a statement setting out all interests of each director of the company that are notifiable to the company under section 3.1.2R of the Disclosure and Transparency Rules as at the end of the period under review, including:

[LR 9.8.6R(1)]

(a) all changes in the interests of each director that have occurred between the end of the period under review and one month prior to the date of the notice of the annual general meeting; or

(b) if there have been no changes during that period, a statement that there have been no changes in the interests of each director.

DTR 3.1.2R requires that 'persons discharging managerial responsibilities and their connected persons must notify the issuer in writing of the occurrence of all transactions conducted on their own account in the shares of the issuer, or derivatives or any other financial instruments relating to those shares within four business days on which the transaction occurred.'

3.12 Employees

3.12.1 Employee involvement

Schedule 7. 11 of the Accounting Regulations and Schedule 7. 11 of the 1985 Act require the directors' report to contain a statement describing the action that has been taken during the financial year to introduce, maintain or develop arrangements aimed at:

(a) providing employees systematically with information on matters of concern to them as employees;

(b) consulting employees or their representatives on a regular basis, so that the views of employees can be taken into account in making decisions which are likely to affect their interests;

(c) encouraging the involvement of employees in the company's performance through an employees' share scheme or by some other means; and

(d) achieving a common awareness on the part of all employees of the financial and economic factors affecting the performance of the company.

This requirement applies only where the average number of persons employed during the financial year exceeds 250. The number of employees for this purpose is determined by dividing the sum of the number of employees employed under contracts of service in each week (whether throughout the week or not, but excluding those persons who worked wholly or mainly outside the UK) by the number of weeks in the financial year.

As explained at **3.1** above, s234 of the 1985 Act and s415 of the 2006 Act specify that for a financial year in which the company is a parent company, and the directors prepare group accounts, the directors' report must be a consolidated report (a 'group directors' report') relating, to the extent specified in the Act, to the company and its subsidiary undertakings included in the consolidation. The above disclosures will therefore depend on the number of employees in the group.

3.12.2 *Disabled persons*

Schedule 7. 10 of the Accounting Regulations and Schedule 7. 9 of the 1985 Act require the directors' report to contain a statement describing the company's policy in respect of employment of disabled persons as it has been applied during the financial year:

(a) for giving full and fair consideration to applications for employment by the company made by disabled persons, having regard to their particular aptitudes and abilities;

(b) for continuing the employment of, and for arranging appropriate training for, employees of the company who have become disabled persons during the period when they were employed by the company; and

(c) otherwise for the training, career development and promotion of disabled persons employed by the company.

This requirement applies to a company which employs more than 250 persons for each week of the financial year. The calculation of the number of employees for this purpose and the treatment of groups is the same as for the disclosures applicable to employee involvement (see **3.12.1** above).

3.13 Related party transactions

The Listing Rules include several requirements for disclosure of related party transactions:

- details of certain small related party transactions as required by LR 11.1.10R(2); [LR 9.8.4R(3)]
- details of certain 'contracts of significance'; and [LR 9.8.4R(10)]
- details of certain contracts for the provision of services to the listed company or any of its subsidiary undertakings by a controlling shareholder. [LR 9.8.4R(11)]

These requirements are discussed in detail at **6.4** in **chapter 32**.

3.14 Major holdings

Sections 198 to 208 of the Companies Act 1985 were repealed with effect from 20 January 2007 through the First Commencement Order under the Companies Act 2006. These sections required certain major share interests to be notified to public companies and for those companies to maintain a register of such interests. Listed companies (but not unlisted public companies) are now instead subject to the requirements of the Disclosure and Transparency Rules of the FSA which impose similar, but different, requirements on them.

A listed company incorporated in the UK is required by the Listing Rules to include in its annual report a statement showing, as at a date not more than one month prior to the date of the notice of the annual general meeting:

[LR 9.8.6R(2)]

- all information disclosed to the company in accordance with DTR 5; or
- if no disclosures have been made, a statement to that effect.

The detailed requirements of DTR 5 Vote Holder and Issuer Notification Rules are outside the scope of this publication. In summary, acquisition and disposal of major shareholdings and voting rights are required to be notified to the company

3.15 Charitable donations

If a company and its subsidiaries have given money for charitable purposes, which in aggregate total more than £2,000 in the financial year, then it is necessary to state, in the case of each of the purposes for which money has been given, the amount of money given for that purpose. [Acc Regs Sch. 7: 5] This requirement is the same as in Schedule 7 of the 1985 Act, except that the de minimis level for reporting charitable donations has been increased from £200.

The reference to 'each of the purposes' appears to be a drafting error in the legislation carried forward from the 1985 Act into the 2006 Act. It is advisable to give an indication of the nature of the charitable purpose or purposes for which money has been given to ensure compliance with the law.

Money given for charitable purposes to persons not ordinarily resident in the UK is excluded for the purposes of this requirement. Wholly owned subsidiaries of companies incorporated in the United Kingdom are exempt from this requirement. [Acc Regs Sch. 7: 5] Under the 1985 Act, only wholly owned subsidiaries of companies incorporated in Great Britain are exempt from this requirement and therefore wholly owned subsidiaries of companies incorporated in Northern Ireland are not able to claim this exemption.

3.16 Political donations and expenditure

The disclosure requirements in the 2006 Act are consistent with those in Schedule 7 of the 1985 Act with the exception that the de minimis level for reporting political donations in the EU area has been increased from £200 and the scope has been extended to include donations to independent election candidates.

For political donations and expenditure in the EU area, including donations to independent election candidates, the following disclosures are required where the amounts, individually or in aggregate, exceed £2000 (separately identified by reference to each subsidiary):

[Acc Regs Sch. 7: 3]

(a) the name of each registered political party , other EU political organisation or independent election candidate which has been the recipient of a donation;

(b) the total amount given to that party or organisation in the financial year; and

(c) the total amount of EU political expenditure incurred by the company in the financial year.

Disclosure is also required for contributions to non-EU political parties as a single aggregate figure for the financial year. [Acc Regs Sch. 7: 4]

These disclosures are not required to be given by wholly owned subsidiaries of companies incorporated in United Kingdom. [Acc Regs Sch. 7: 3(3)(b)] Under the 1985 Act, only wholly owned subsidiaries of companies incorporated in Great Britain are exempt from this requirement and therefore wholly owned subsidiaries of companies incorporated in Northern Ireland are not able to claim this exemption.

Reference should be made to sections 363–365 of the 2006 Act and sections 347A-347K of the 1985 Act, which deal with the control of political donations and contain definitions that are relevant for the interpretation of these disclosure requirements.

3.17 Existence of branches

Where a limited company has branches outside the UK, the directors' report is required to give an indication of the existence of those branches. [Acc Regs Sch. 7: 7(1)(d), previously 1985 Act Sch. 7: 6(d)]

> This is the one respect in which the requirements of the Disclosure and Transparency Rules in relation to the 'management report' go beyond the requirements of the Acts. Under these rules, listed companies should disclose information about the existence of branches generally, rather than just those outside the UK.

Schedule 7 of each of the 1985 Act and Accounting Regulations cross refers to the definition of a branch contained in s698(2) of the 1985 Act and s1046(3) of the 2006 Act respectively. However, these definitions merely refer to a branch within the meaning of the Eleventh Company Law Directive although the Directive does not itself define a branch.

There is a body of law and guidance concerning the definition of a branch for the purposes of applying the law which requires certain overseas companies with branches or places of business in the UK to register with Companies House and file accounts. These requirements are outside the scope of this manual but the following is a summary with respect to the definition of a branch for this purpose.

Guidance Notes issued by Companies House in February 2008 are very brief on the point, merely stating that:

> 'A branch is part of an overseas limited company organised to conduct business through local representatives in Great Britain rather than referring it abroad.'

More detailed guidance issued by Companies House in July 1996 is more expansive stating that:

> 'A branch will be organised so as to conduct business on behalf of a company. This means that a person resident here will be able to deal direct with the branch, instead of the company in its home country.
>
> It should be noted that the term "branch" is not used in the commonly understood sense of a local bank branch or an office branch at a single locality. Rather, it is used more in a sense closer to the concept of a subsidiary, although it will not be a separate corporate body. It may, however, operate from a number of locations within a common management structure.'

The 1996 guidance also states that when an overseas company performs functions in Great Britain that are only ancillary or incidental to the company's business as a whole (e.g. warehousing facilities, administrative offices, internal data processing and share transfer or registration offices) then the company should register under the place of business regime (rather than the branch regime).

The Guidance Notes issued by Companies House take the meaning of a branch from the judgements given in the European Court of Justice in *Etablissements Somafer SA v Saar-Ferngas AG* and in *Blanckaert and Willems v Trost*. At a meeting in 1994 of the EC Accounts Contact Committee, all delegations confirmed that the definition given by the European Court of Justice in *Somafer v Saar-Ferngas AG* was essentially the same as that in Article 1 of the Directive.

> Using this definition, a branch will be a part of a company which is organised so as to conduct business on behalf of the company. Any activity which is an integral part of the company's business as a whole (and not just its principal activity) is included. For example, an airline selling tickets through its own outlet in Great Britain is likely to have established a branch and will thus need to register under the branch regime. The Companies House Guidance Notes explain that if such a company set up its main advertising and promotional operations in Great Britain, this similarly is likely to constitute a branch. A place of business will not, however, amount to a branch if the business carried on at that place is only ancillary or incidental to the company's business as a whole.

3.18 Policy on the payment of creditors

3.18.1 Introduction

The directors' report of a company which at any time during the year was:

(a) a public company; or

(b) a member of a group of which the parent was a public company, and the company did not qualify as small or medium-sized under s382 and s465 of the 2006 Act or s247 of the 1985 Act,

should include a statement setting out the company's policy for the next financial year in respect of the payment of trade creditors and should disclose 'creditor days' in respect of amounts due at the year end. [Acc Regs Sch. 7: Part V, previously CA 1985 Sch. 7: Part VI]

The term 'public company' is used in the sense in which it is defined in s4(2) of the 2006 Act and s1(3) of the 1985 Act. To fall within this definition a company must be incorporated under a UK Companies Act. Therefore even a very large subsidiary of an overseas listed company is not subject to the disclosure requirement unless it is itself incorporated as a public company rather than a private company.

3.18.2 *Disclosure of policy*

The statement of policy should disclose:

(a) whether, in respect of some or all of its suppliers, it is the company's policy to follow a code or standard payment practice and, if so, the name of the code or standard and where information about, and copies of, it can be obtained;

(b) whether, in respect of some or all of its suppliers, it is the company's policy to:

  (i) agree the terms of payment when agreeing the terms of the transaction;

  (ii) ensure that the supplier is aware of the terms of payment; and

  (iii) abide by those terms; and

(c) the policy in respect of those suppliers that do not fall within (a) or (b) above.

The statement should identify the suppliers or classes of suppliers to which the various policies apply. [Acc Regs Sch. 7: 12(2), previously CA 1985 Sch. 7: 12(2)]

Example 3.18.2

Disclosure of policy

The company's policy is to settle terms of payment with suppliers when agreeing the terms of each transaction, ensure that suppliers are made aware of the terms of payment and abide by the terms of payment.

3.18.3 *Disclosure of creditor days*

In calculating 'creditor days':

(a) creditor days is defined by the regulations as:

X/Y multiplied by the number of days in the financial year;

where

X = the aggregate of the amounts which were owed to trade creditors at the end of the year; and

Y = the aggregate of the amounts which the company was invoiced by suppliers during the year; and

(b) the amounts which were owed to trade creditors are taken to be the amounts shown under the heading 'Trade creditors' (amounts falling due within one year) within the various balance sheet formats set out in the Act.

The 'amount invoiced by suppliers' will, where relevant, include VAT. This will ensure comparability with the figure for trade creditors. However, it means that the figure for 'amounts invoiced by suppliers' may not be immediately ascertainable from the accounts or accounting records without some work.

Companies reporting under IFRSs will not follow the Companies Act formats, but they will still need to identify the amount that would have been included as trade creditors for the purpose of this calculation. [Acc Regs Sch. 7: 12(5)(c), previously CA 1985 Sch. 7: 12(5)(c)]

Example 3.18.3

Disclosure of creditor days

Trade creditor days of the company at 31 March 20X1, calculated in accordance with the requirements of the Companies Act 1985, were 29.5 days. This represents the ratio, expressed in days, between the amounts invoiced to the company in the year by its suppliers and the amounts due, at the year end, to trade creditors falling due for payment within one year.

A person is a supplier of a company at any time if:

[Acc Regs Sch. 7: 12(4), previously CA 1985 Sch. 7: 12(4)]

(a) at that time, it is owed an amount in respect of goods and services supplied; and

(b) that amount would be included under the heading corresponding to trade creditors falling due within one year if accounts were prepared in accordance with the Act at that time.

The fixed formula for calculating creditor days can produce a strange result in certain circumstances, e.g. in a seasonal business with particularly high activity before the year end. In such circumstances, although the figure given by applying the formula should not be adjusted, it is acceptable to include a sentence stating why the figure does not appear to reflect the payment policy.

3.18.4 Groups

As explained at **3.1** above, s415 of the 2006 Act and s234 of the 1985 Act specify that for a financial year in which the company is a parent company, and the directors prepare group accounts, the directors' report must be a consolidated report (a 'group directors' report') relating, to the extent specified in the Act, to the company and its subsidiary undertakings included in the consolidation. The above disclosures are, therefore, made for the group rather than for the parent company.

3.19 Reappointment of auditors

Although there is no statutory requirement for the directors' report to refer to the reappointment of the auditor, it is normal for it to do this. For financial years beginning on or after 1 October 2007 the 2006 Act introduces new arrangements for the reappointment of auditors of private companies to avoid the need for an annual general meeting. Sections 384–388A of the 1985Act continue to operate in respect of periods beginning before that date. The transitional arrangements for the 2006 Act allow an elective resolution passed pursuant to s386 1985 Act, and in force immediately before 1 October 2007, to continue to operate until it is revoked or superseded by a further resolution, the auditors to which it applies cease to hold office or it ceases to have effect in accordance with its terms.

Under sections 485–488 of the 2006 Act the auditors of a private company are generally deemed to be reappointed, subject to certain specified circumstances, for example, if the Articles of Association require actual reappointment or at least five per cent of the members (or any lesser percentage specified in the Articles) give notice to the company excluding deemed reappointment.

Example 3.19A below addresses the situation where the auditors are to be re-appointed at a general meeting. **Example 3.19B** addresses the situation where a private company has dispensed with the annual appointment of auditors under s386 of the 1985 Act and the election is in force immediately before 1 October 2007. **Example 3.19C** addresses reappointment for financial years beginning on or after 1 October 2007 pursuant to sections 485–488 of the 2006 Act.

Example 3.19A

Reappointment at general meeting

A resolution to reappoint [*Name of auditors*] as auditors will be proposed at the forthcoming Annual General Meeting.

Example 3.19B

Election in force immediately before 1 October 2007

Pursuant to s386 Companies Act 1985, an elective resolution was passed on 7 April 2002 dispensing with the requirement to appoint auditors annually. This election was in force immediately before 1 October 2007. Therefore, [*Name of auditors*] are deemed to continue as auditors..

Example 3.19C

Reappointment for financial years beginning on or after 1 October 2007

[*Name of auditors*] have indicated their willingness to be reappointed for another term and appropriate arrangements have been put in place [are being made] for them to be deemed reappointed as auditors in the absence of an AGM..

3.20 The use of financial instruments

In relation to the use of financial instruments by a company and its subsidiary undertakings, the directors' report must contain an indication of:

[Acc Regs Sch. 7: 6(1), previously CA 1985 Sch. 7: 5A(1)]

(a) the financial risk management objectives and policies of the company and its subsidiary undertakings included in the consolidation, including the policy for hedging each major type of forecasted transaction for which hedge accounting is used; and

(b) the exposure of the company and its subsidiary undertakings included in the consolidation to price risk, credit risk, liquidity risk and cash flow risk.

This is not required if the information is not material for the assessment of the assets, liabilities, financial position and profit or loss of the company and its subsidiary undertakings included in the consolidation.

These disclosures requirements do not apply to small companies as these requirements are not included in Schedule 5 to The Small Companies and Groups (Accounting and Directors' Report) Regulations 2008 and a specific exemption from making these disclosures was included in s246(4)(ba) of 1985 Act.

The disclosure requirement applies to all companies other than those that qualify as small companies for the purposes of s382 of the 2006 Act and s246 of the 1985 Act. However, being a member of an 'ineligible group' does not prevent the exemptions for the directors' report being used. Therefore, a subsidiary within a listed group which falls within the relevant size criteria will be able to use the exemption provided that it is not itself a public company, a company that is an authorised insurance company, a banking company, an e-money issuer, an ISD investment firm or a UCITS management company, or carries on an insurance market activity.

The requirement is not restricted to companies that use fair value accounting for financial instruments or those that make use of derivative financial instruments in their business. Most companies will therefore be expected to provide some disclosures about the use of financial instruments unless the information is clearly immaterial or they are exempt as described above. For businesses with only trade debtors, trade creditors and equity shares the disclosures are likely to be brief. Where no information is to be given, good practice is to explain that no disclosure is being made on the grounds of materiality. This will prevent readers, including regulators, from reaching the conclusion that information has been omitted inadvertently.

Schedule 7 states that the expressions 'hedge accounting', 'price risk', 'credit risk', 'liquidity risk' and 'cash flow risk' have the same meaning as they have in the Fourth and Seventh Directives (as amended by the Fair Value Directive). However, these Directives do not actually define the expressions. This was explained as follows in a DTI Consultation Document on the implementation of the Fair Value Directive's requirements in the UK.

> 'The Fair Value Directive uses many technical accounting terms (e.g. financial instruments, hedge accounting) that are not defined in the Directive. The European Commission made clear in its Explanatory Memorandum to the Directive that this was deliberate, and entirely consistent with the principles that have underpinned the Accounting Directives since their adoption.: 'As framework rules, they have not contained generic definitions of accounting terms which are well defined elsewhere in accounting standards and the accounting literature. Any definitions of financial instruments that were

included would become outdated very quickly in the light of the constantly growing variations of complex derivative financial instruments."

The Consultation Document explained that not all of the terms were currently defined in UK GAAP but noted the ASB's proposals to issue standards that would include such definitions, in line with the definitions in IFRSs. The ASB has subsequently published FRS 26 *Financial instruments: Recognition and Measurement.*

3.21 Disclosure of relevant information to auditors

This disclosure requirement was introduced by the Companies (Audit, Investigations and Community Enterprise) Act 2004. It does not apply to any company that has taken advantage of the exemption from audit under Part 16 of the 2006 Act or s249A(1) or s249AA(1) of the 1985 Act. [CA 2006 s418(1), previously CA 1985 s234ZA(1)]

The directors' report must contain a statement to the effect that, in the case of each of the persons who are directors at the time when the directors' report is approved, the following applies:

[CA 2006 s418(2), previously CA 1985 s234ZA(2)]

(a) so far as the director is aware, there is no relevant audit information of which the company's auditors are unaware, and

(b) he/she has taken all the steps that he/she ought to have taken as a director to make himself/herself aware of any relevant audit information and to establish that the company's auditors are aware of that information.

Relevant audit information is defined as information needed by the company's auditors in connection with preparing their report. [CA 2006 s418(3), previously CA 1985 s234ZA(3)]

A director has taken all the steps that he/she ought to have taken as a director in order to do the things mentioned in paragraph (b) above if he/she has:

(a) made such enquiries of his/her fellow directors and of the company's auditors for that purpose, and

(b) taken such other steps (if any) for that purpose,

as were required by his/her duty as a director of the company to exercise due care, skill and diligence. [CA 2006 s418(4), previously CA 1985 s234ZA(4)]

In determining for the purposes of this requirement, the extent of the duty in the case of a particular director, the 1985 Act indicates that the following considerations are, in particular, relevant:

[CA 1985 s234ZA(5)]

(a) the knowledge, skill and experience that may reasonably be expected of a person carrying out the same functions as are carried out by the directors in relation to the company; and

(b) so far as they exceed what may reasonably be so expected, the knowledge, skill and experience that the director in fact has.

Section 418 of the 2006 Act does not include a similar guidance. However, s171–177 of the 2006 Act codify directors' duties for the first time and s174(2) of the 2006 Act is consistent with s234ZA(5) of the 1985 Act.

Where a directors' report containing a statement required by s234ZA(2) of the 1985 Act or s418(2) of the 2006 Act is approved but the statement is false, every director of the company who knew that the statement was false, or was reckless as to whether it was false, and failed to take reasonable steps to prevent the report from being approved, is guilty of an offence and liable to imprisonment or a fine or both. [CA 2006 s418(5) &(6), previously CA 1985 s234ZA(6)]

This is a complex area of the law on which directors may wish to take legal advice. This manual is concerned only with the disclosure requirement in the directors' report and does not provide guidance on the interpretation of the law more generally.

The following example illustrates the possible wording of such a statement.

Example 3.21

Disclosure of information to auditors

Each of the persons who is a director at the date of approval of this annual report confirms that:

- so far as the director is aware, there is no relevant audit information of which the company's auditors are unaware; and
- the director has taken all the steps that he/she ought to have taken as a director in order to make himself/herself aware of any relevant audit information and to establish that the company's auditors are aware of that information.

> This confirmation is given and should be interpreted in accordance with the provisions of [s234ZA of the Companies Act 1985] [s418 of the Companies Act 2006].

3.22 Qualifying third party indemnity provisions

This disclosure requirement, which was introduced by the Companies (Audit, Investigations and Community Enterprise) Act 2004, came into effect on 6 April 2005 and applies to any directors' report issued after that date.

Qualifying third party indemnity provisions are defined in s234 of the 2006 Act and s309B of the 1985 Act as amended by the Companies (Audit, Investigations and Community Enterprise) Act 2004. 'Associated company' is defined for this purpose in s256 of the 2006 Act and s309A of the 1985 Act and is broadly any parent, subsidiary or fellow subsidiary.

There are two separate disclosure requirements although they look similar. The first focuses on provisions for the benefit of one or more directors of the company, whether made by the company or not. The second focuses on provisions made by the company for the benefit of one or more directors of an associated company.

If:

(a) at the time when the directors' report is approved any qualifying third party indemnity provision (whether made by the company or otherwise) is in force for the benefit of one or more directors of the company, or

(b) at any time during the financial year, any such provision was in force for the benefit of one or more persons who were then directors of the company,

the directors' report must state that any such provision is or (as the case may be) was so in force. [CA 2006 s236(2)&(3), previously CA 1985 s309C(2)]

If the company has made a qualifying third party indemnity provision and

(a) at the time when the directors' report is approved any qualifying third party indemnity provision made by the company is in force for the benefit of one or more directors of an associated company, or

(b) at any time during the financial year, any such provision was in force for the benefit of one or more persons who were then directors of an associated company, the directors' report must state that any such provision is or (as the case may be) was so in force. [CA 2006 s236(4)&(5), previously CA 1985 s309C(3)]

3.23 Capital structure

Companies with securities carrying voting rights traded on a regulated market at the year end are required to include disclosures in their directors' reports about the control and structure of their shares. These requirements came into effect for periods commencing on or after 20 May 2006 and implement the EU Takeovers Directive (Directive 2004/25/EC). They were originally introduced through Regulations but were subsequently inserted as paragraph 13 in Schedule 7 to the 1985 Act. There are equivalent provisions in Schedule 7 Part 6 of the 2008 Accounting Regulations.

These requirements apply to the directors' report for a financial year if the company had securities carrying voting rights admitted to trading on a regulated market at the end of that year. [Acc Regs Sch. 7: 13(1), previously CA 1985 Sch. 7: 13 (1)]

The report should contain detailed information, by reference to the end of that year, on the following matters:

[Acc Regs Sch. 7: 13(2), previously CA 1985 Sch. 7: 13(2)]

(a) the structure of the company's capital, including in particular

  (i) the rights and obligations attaching to the shares or, as the case may be, to each class of shares in the company; and

  (ii) where there are two or more such classes, the percentage of the total share capital represented by each class;

(b) any restrictions on the transfer of securities in the company, including in particular:

  (i) limitations on the holding of securities; and

  (ii) requirements to obtain the approval of the company, or of other holders of securities in the company, for a transfer of securities;

(c) in the case of each person with a significant direct or indirect holding of securities in the company, such details as are known to the company of:

  (i) the identity of the person;

  (ii) the size of the holding; and

(iii) the nature of the holding;

(d) in the case of each person who holds securities carrying special rights with regard to control of the company:

(i) the identity of the person; and

(ii) the nature of the rights;

(e) where the company has an employees' share scheme, and shares to which the scheme relates have rights with regard to control of the company that are not exercisable directly by the employees, how those rights are exercisable;

(f) any restrictions on voting rights, including in particular:

(i) limitations on voting rights of holders of a given percentage or number of votes;

(ii) deadlines for exercising voting rights; and

(iii) arrangements by which, with the company's cooperation, financial rights carried by securities are held by a person other than the holder of the securities;

(g) any agreements between holders of securities that are known to the company and may result in restrictions on the transfer of securities or on voting rights;

(h) any rules that the company has about:

(i) appointment and replacement of directors; or

(ii) amendment of the company's articles of association;

(i) the powers of the company's directors, including in particular any powers in relation to the issuing or buying back by the company of its shares;

(j) any significant agreements to which the company is a party that take effect, alter or terminate upon a change of control of the company following a takeover bid, and the effects of any such agreements; and

(k) any agreements between the company and its directors or employees providing for compensation for loss of office or employment (whether through resignation, purported redundancy or otherwise) that occurs because of a takeover bid.

For the purposes of (a), a company's capital includes any securities in the company that are not admitted to trading on a regulated market. [Acc Regs Sch. 7: 13(3), previously CA 1985 Sch. 7: 13(3)]

For the purposes of (c), a person has an indirect holding of securities if:

[Acc Regs Sch. 7: 13(4), previously CA 1985 Sch. 7: 13(4)]

(a) they are held on his behalf; or

(b) he is able to secure that rights carried by the securities are exercised in accordance with his wishes.

Paragraph (j) does not apply to an agreement if:

[Acc Regs Sch. 7: 13(5), previously CA 1985 Sch. 7: 13(5)]

(a) disclosure of the agreement would be seriously prejudicial to the company; and

(b) the company is not under any other obligation to disclose it.

For the purposes of these disclosure requirements, 'securities' means shares or debentures and 'takeover bid' has the same meaning as in the Takeovers Directive. 'Voting rights' means rights to vote at general meetings of the company in question, including rights that arise only in certain circumstances. [Acc Regs Sch. 7: 13(6), previously CA 1985 Sch. 7: 13(6)]

The directors' report must also contain any necessary explanatory material with regard to the information described above. [Acc Regs Sch.7: 14, previously CA 1985 s234ZZA(5)]

There is no guidance on what type of explanatory material should be disclosed under this requirement. However, it is presumably intended to cover material that is required to set the prescribed disclosures in context or to ensure that those disclosures are not misleading due to a lack of completeness.

3.24 Closed-ended investment funds

In September 2007, the Listing Rules were restructured to replace the chapters dealing with investment companies and venture capital trusts with new chapters dealing with closed-ended investment funds and open-ended investment companies. Open-ended-investment companies incorporated in the UK are not likely to be encountered in practice and are not considered further in this publication. However, the definition of a closed-ended investment fund is broader than just investment companies (as defined in s833 of the 2006 Act and s266 of the 1985 Act) and venture capital trusts. There are many such entities with listed securities.

A closed-ended investment fund is defined as an entity:

[LR Glossary]

- which is an undertaking with limited liability, including a company, limited partnership, or limited liability partnership; and
- whose primary object is investing and managing its assets (including pooled funds contributed by holders of its listed securities) in property of any description and with a view to spreading investment risk.

The definition therefore covers property investment companies (including but not limited to Real Estate Investment Trusts) as well as companies that invest in securities.

Chapter 15 of the Listing Rules applies to closed-ended investment funds with a primary listing of equity securities. [LR 15.1.1R] It imposes additional requirements on such entities. They must comply with all of the requirements of LR 9 (continuing obligations) including those related to financial reporting, subject to the modifications and additional requirements set out in LR 15. [LR 15.4.1R]

In addition to the requirements of LR 9.8 (dealt with elsewhere in this chapter), a closed-ended investment fund must include in its annual report:

[LR 15.6.2R]

- a statement (including a quantitative analysis) explaining how it has invested its assets with a view to spreading investment risk in accordance with its published investment policy);
- a statement, set out in a prominent position, as to whether in the opinion of the directors, the continuing appointment of the investment manager on the terms agreed is in the interests of its shareholders as a whole, together with a statement of the reasons for this view;
- the names of the fund's investment managers and a summary of the principal contents of any agreements between the fund and each of its investment managers, including but not limited to:
  - an indication of the terms and duration of their appointment;
  - the basis for their remuneration; and
  - any arrangement relating to the termination of their appointment including compensation payable in the event of termination; and
- the full text of its current published investment policy; and
- a comprehensive and meaningful analysis of its portfolio.

Additional requirements apply to a fund that, as at the end of its financial year, has invested more than 20% of its assets in property (defined for this purpose as freehold, heritable or leasehold property). It must include in its annual financial report, a summary of the valuation of its portfolio carried out in accordance with prescribed rules. [LR 15.6.3R]

The valuation required for this purpose must be carried out by an external valuer as defined in the Appraisal and Valuation Standards (5th edition) issued by the Royal Institution of Chartered Surveyors and either:

[LR 15.6.4R]

- be made in accordance with those Standards; or
- where the valuation does not comply in all applicable respects with those Standards, include a statement which sets out a full explanation of such non-compliance.

The summary of the valuation of the portfolio must include:

- the total value of properties held at the year end;
- totals of the cost of properties acquired;
- the net book value of properties disposed of during the year; and
- an indication of the geographical location and type of properties held at the year end.

Most of these disclosures will be made in the financial statements to comply with IAS 40 but attention should be paid to the additional requirements of the Listing Rules.

4 Five-year record

Most listed companies provide a comparative table of results covering a five-year period. There is no requirement in the Listing Rules to do so but the practice is widespread and has its origins in a recommendation from the London Stock Exchange in 1964. Originally such comparative tables covered a ten year period but current practice is generally to cover the latest five years.

The figures disclosed have in the past tended to be key profit and loss account numbers such as:

- turnover;

- operating profit;
- pre-tax profit;
- post-tax profit;
- dividends; and
- retained earnings.

Many companies also provide balance sheet and, in some cases, cash flow information.

A significant issue is that it will often be impracticable to restate the periods prior to the date of transition to IFRSs. Where this is the case, a clear explanation should be given that the earlier periods are not comparable. One approach to this problem is to use a 'bridge' presentation where one year is given both under IFRSs (to be comparable with later periods) and under UK GAAP (to be comparable with earlier periods).

5 Operating and Financial Review

5.1 Background

For many years there has been recognition that financial statements do not meet all of the information needs of users. One of the earliest pronouncements on this was the 1964 recommendation from the London Stock Exchange that listed companies should present a Chairman's statement. In 1992 the Cadbury Committee (see **chapter 47**) recommended that directors should pay particular attention to their duty to present a balanced and understandable assessment of their company's position.

This was followed in July 1993 by publication of the ASB's Statement *Operating and financial review*. The statement built on the foundations of existing best practice by providing a framework within which directors could discuss the main factors underlying the company's performance and financial position. It made clear that while the OFR was not a forecast of future results, it should nevertheless draw on those aspects of the year under review that were relevant to an assessment of future prospects. An updated version of the statement was issued in January 2003.

The final report of the Company Law Review Steering Group, published in 2001, recommended that both public and large private companies should be required by law to prepare an OFR. In July 2003 the Government announced that it intended to implement this recommendation through secondary legislation. Detailed proposals were published by the DTI in May 2004 in a Consultation Document *Draft Regulations on the Operating and Financial Review and Directors' Report*. One significant change from the original recommendation of the Company Law Review was that the scope of the requirement would be restricted to quoted companies.

On 21 March 2005 the Companies Act 1985 (Operating and Financial Review and Directors' Report etc.) Regulations 2005 were made. They were intended to have effect, in relation to the requirement to prepare an OFR, for financial years which began on or after 1 April 2005. But in November 2005 the Government reversed its decision to introduce a statutory OFR and the Regulations were repealed before they ever had to be applied in practice. Some of the requirements of an OFR, for example key performance indicators, are now part of the business review which applies to all companies (unless they are small) as described at **3.2** above. In addition, quoted companies will have to comply with some additional requirements in their business review when the relevant provisions of the Companies Act 2006 come into effect (see **3.3.1.2** above).

The statutory regime (now repealed) provided for the law to be supplemented by a reporting standard issued by a body specified for that purpose. In May 2005, the ASB issued Reporting Standard 1 *Operating and Financial Review* (RS 1) having been specified by the Government as the body authorised to issue such standards. Following the repeal of the statutory regime, RS 1 was revised and reissued as the Reporting Statement *Operating and Financial Review* (see **5.2** below).

5.2 The Reporting Statement

In January 2006 the ASB published the Reporting Statement *Operating and Financial Review*. This had previously been issued in May 2005 as Reporting Standard 1, but following the decision not to proceed with a statutory OFR, was reissued to include recommendations rather than requirements. This section describes the background to the Statement and explains its content and structure. The section does not seek to reproduce all of the recommendations of the Statement and, accordingly, those preparing an OFR should consult the Statement itself or an appropriate disclosure checklist.

5.2.1 Scope

The Reporting Statement was written with quoted companies in mind, but is also applicable to any other entities that purport to prepare an OFR.

If a narrative report is called 'Operating and Financial Review', shareholders will expect directors to have followed the ASB's best practice guidance, and if this is not the case it would be useful to give the narrative report a different name, such as 'Management Review.'

5.2.2 *Effective date*

The Statement did not include an effective date, and hence became effective when it was issued in January 2006.

5.2.3 *Content and structure*

The Statement defines an OFR as follows:

> 'An OFR is a narrative explanation, provided in the annual report, of the main trends and factors underlying the development, performance and position of an entity during the financial year covered by the financial statements, and those which are likely to affect the entity's future development, performance and position.'

The Statement is divided into three main sections. The first is entitled 'Principles'. The key principles are that the OFR should:

(a) set out an analysis of the business through the eyes of the board of directors;

(b) focus on matters that are relevant to the interests of members;

(c) have a forward-looking orientation, identifying those trends and factors relevant to the members' assessment of the current and future performance of the business and the progress towards the achievement of long-term business objectives;

(d) complement as well as supplement the financial statements, to enhance the overall corporate disclosure;

(e) be comprehensive and understandable;

(f) be balanced and neutral, dealing even-handedly with both good and bad aspects; and

(g) be comparable over time.

Each of these principles is explained further in the Statement.

The second section of the Statement is the 'Disclosure framework'. This is essentially a list of disclosure requirements. The Reporting Statement states that its purpose is to set out the key content elements that have to be addressed within the OFR. However, it is not a template and does not specify the headings to be used in the OFR. It is for the directors to consider how best to use the framework to structure the OFR and the precise content, including the level of detail to be disclosed. These will be affected by the particular circumstances, including the industries in which the entity operates, the range of products, services or processes it offers and the number of markets it serves.

The third main section of the Statement deals with key performance indicators (KPIs) and other performance indicators. The Statement does not specify which KPIs must be disclosed but specifies disclosure requirements for those KPIs that are disclosed.

The Statement includes a 'seriously prejudicial' exemption which means that no disclosure is required about impending developments or about matters in the course of negotiation if the disclosure would, in the opinion of the directors, be seriously prejudicial to the interests of the entity.

The Statement is accompanied by Implementation Guidance which:

(a) outlines some suggestions and illustrations of the content required to be covered in the OFR with regard to the disclosure framework and related KPIs; and

(b) provides some further 'signposting' guidance as to the areas directors will need to consider with regard to the 'particular matters' identified.

The ASB published additional narrative reporting guidance in January 2008 This illustrates the linkage between the enhanced business review requirements in the 2006 Act and the ASB's Reporting Statement on the OFR. The guidance indicates that the ASB believes that all the enhanced business review requirements found in the Companies Act 2006 are already included in its Reporting Statement. Therefore a company which prepares an OFR in compliance with the Reporting Statement and cross refers this information into the Directors' Report will meet the requirements of the Act.

5.3 Going concern statement

'Going Concern and Financial Reporting – Guidance for Directors of Listed Companies Registered in the UK' was issued by the ICAEW in November 1994. It indicates that the going concern statement should be included in the OFR even though there was (and still is) no mandatory requirement to prepare an OFR. The Reporting Statement does not comment on this issue but there appears to be no reason why the going concern statement required by the Listing Rules should not continue to be made in the OFR. Further discussion of this topic is included in **section 8** in **chapter 47**.

5.4 Regulatory scrutiny

The Financial Reporting Review Panel's powers were extended to include directors' reports for accounting periods commencing on or after 1 April 2006. This will include the OFR and other narrative reports, for example a chief executive's statement or finance review, to the extent that they form part of the directors' report, that is, there are cross references from the directors' report to the OFR and other narrative reports.

6 Future developments

6.1 International Financial Reporting Standards

There is, at present, no international accounting or reporting standard dealing with the matters discussed in this chapter.

The IASB published in October 2005 a discussion paper, 'Management Commentary'. The discussion paper assesses the role the IASB could play in improving the quality of the management commentary that accompanies financial statements. The paper reviews existing national requirements or principles on management commentary and offers recommendations on how the IASB might promote the wider adoption of best practice in the interests of investors and others who use financial reports. The Board sought comments on whether developing requirements for such a commentary should be a priority for the Board and, if so, whether any guidance should be mandatory or not. The IASB discussed the responses to the discussion paper at its meeting in January 2007 and noted that the overall response was positive. At the IASB meeting in December 2007, it was agreed that the Board would not undertake management commentary as a standards-level project. Instead, a project would be undertaken to produce best practice, non mandatory guidance. The timing of the Exposure Draft for this guidance is uncertain.

47 Corporate governance disclosures

1 Introduction

Listed companies are required by the listing rules to make certain disclosures concerning corporate governance matters in their annual reports. This chapter is concerned primarily with those disclosure requirements rather than providing guidance on good corporate governance practice. Companies which are not subject to these disclosure requirements, such as AIM companies, may wish to consider making them on a voluntary basis.

A brief history of corporate governance requirements in the UK is provided at **1.1** below. At the heart of these requirements is the Combined Code and the related 'comply or explain' regime. This is sometimes contrasted with the 'comply or go to jail' approach that exists in the US for SEC registrants.

The most recent version of the Combined Code applies to periods commencing on or after 29 June 2008 although there are only a few changes from the previous 2006 Code. References to the Combined Code in this chapter are to the 2006 Code unless otherwise stated.

The remainder of this chapter is divided into the following sections:

- the Listing Rules (**section 2**);
- the Alternative Investment Market (**section 3**);
- the Combined Code (**section 4**);
- the Statement of Compliance with the Code (**section 5**);
- the Narrative Statement on how the principles of good governance have been applied (**section 6**);
- internal control statements (**section 7**);
- going concern statements (**section 8**);
- other governance disclosures (**section 9**); and
- future developments (**section 10**).

This chapter does not deal with disclosures relating to directors' remuneration, which are considered in **chapter 48**.

1.1 Brief history

The corporate governance path has been a busy one. As a result of major companies failing in the late 1980s, the Cadbury Committee published 'The Financial Aspects of Corporate Governance' in 1992 that gave directors guidance on what was expected of them. This was followed in 1994 by the Rutteman guidance on internal financial control and guidance on going concern. In 1995, following media interest about the amount of remuneration that directors of large companies were earning, the Greenbury Committee published a report recommending various additional disclosures to be made in listed company accounts. These 'remuneration' requirements have been incorporated into the Listing Rules and the law. They are discussed in **chapter 48**. Subsequently the Hampel Committee hoped to reduce the box-ticking approach to governance which had emerged, and so produced a report in 1998 which, following discussions with the London Stock Exchange, was tailored to form the Combined Code.

January 2003 saw the publication of two reports dealing with corporate governance matters. The first was a review of the role and effectiveness of non-executive directors by the late Sir Derek Higgs ('the Higgs report'). The second report contained guidance on audit committees developed by a Financial Reporting Council appointed working group chaired by Sir Robert Smith ('the Smith report'). The Higgs report contained a proposed revised Combined Code incorporating its own recommendations and some of the key recommendations in the Smith report. There was then a twelve-week consultation period for a 'fatal flaw review' although the Financial Reporting Council stated that it did not intend to re-open the substance of the recommendations. The proposals, some of which were seen as controversial, were subject to extensive debate and modified in the light of comments received. A revised Code was published in July 2003 for reporting years beginning on or after 1 November 2003.

In June 2004 the FRC announced that it intended to undertake regular reviews of the Combined Code to ensure that it is working effectively and to identify whether any amendments are needed. The first formal review took place in 2005.

That FRC review concluded that 'good progress has been made in implementing the revised Combined Code on Corporate Governance following its introduction in 2003. The Code is bedding down well and having a positive impact. There is no appetite for major change and only two suggested amendments carried strong support'. As a result, in June 2006, an updated Code was issued. The 2006 Code contained the following changes:

- to relax the existing provisions to allow the chairman to sit on the remuneration committee;
- to add a new provision regarding companies including a 'vote withheld' box on AGM proxy forms; and
- to allow companies to make the terms of reference of their committees available on a website only as opposed to on a website and on request.

The 2006 Code is applicable for financial periods commencing on or after 1 November 2006.

The second review took place in 2007 and concluded that the Code was working reasonably well and that, again, there was no need for major changes. The FRC proposed two amendments to the 2006 Code.

- To remove the restriction on an individual chairing more than one FTSE 100 company; and
- To allow the chairman of a smaller listed company (outside the FTSE 350) to be a member of (but not chair) the audit committee where he or she was considered independent on appointment.

When announcing the findings the chairman of the FRC, Sir Christopher Hogg, provided a stark warning to companies:

"There is no room for complacency. While respondents strongly endorsed the flexible "comply or explain" approach, it is clear that it is not always applied as intended. All parties share responsibility for ensuring it remains an effective alternative to regulation – companies by providing robust explanations when they choose not to follow the Code, and investors and their advisors by assessing each explanation on its merits rather than applying a rigid set of rules."

The proposed amendments were accepted and have been included in a 2008 version of the Code. The 2008 Code is applicable for periods commencing on or after 29 June 2008. Also applicable from this date are the new Disclosure and Transparency Rules on corporate governance statements and audit committees. These are considered in **section 9.5** below.

It is hoped that having a regular review of the Combined Code will help to ensure that there is a regular dialogue with companies, investors and other stakeholders.

2 The Listing Rules

The main disclosure requirements on corporate governance are set out in the Listing Rules. The requirements for disclosure of directors' remuneration are considered in **chapter 48**.

A listed company incorporated in the UK is required to make a statement about how it has applied the principles in the Combined Code and a statement of compliance with the Code. The exact requirements are as follows:

> 'A statement of how the listed company has applied the principles set out in Section 1 of the Combined Code, in a manner that would enable shareholders to evaluate how the principles have been applied.' [LR 9.8.6R(5)]
>
> 'A statement as to whether the listed company has:
>
> (a) complied throughout the accounting period with all relevant provisions set out in Section 1 of the Combined Code; or
>
> (b) not complied throughout the accounting period with all relevant provisions set out in Section 1 of the Combined Code and if so, setting out:
>
> (i) those provisions, if any it has not complied with;
>
> (ii) in the case of provisions whose requirements are of a continuing nature, the period within which, if any, it did not comply with some or all of those provisions; and
>
> (iii) the company's reasons for non-compliance.' [LR 9.8.6R(6)]

In addition, LR 9.8.6R(3) states that, for a company incorporated in the UK, there should be a statement by the directors that the business is a going concern with supporting assumptions or qualifications as necessary (see **section 8** below).

For periods commencing on or after 29 June 2008 the Financial Services Authority's Disclosure and Transparency Rules set out certain mandatory disclosures in addition to the Listing Rules disclosure requirements. These are discussed further in **section 9** below.

The background to the Combined Code is considered in **1.1** above. The contents of the Code are discussed in **section 4** below. The Code can be downloaded from the Financial Reporting Council website at:

www.frc.org.uk/corporate/combinedcode.cfm

For periods commencing before 29 June 2008 it is the 2006 Code that the Listing Rules require compliance with. Any company that implements the relaxations allowed by the 2008 Code early would need to disclose a breach of the 2006 Code. Example wording is as follows.

Example 2

Disclosure of breach

> 'Apart from the matters detailed below, the Company has complied throughout the financial year ended 31 December 2008 with all the Code provisions set out in Section 1 of the 2006 Combined Code. During the year, the Company decided to take advantage of the relaxation to the 2006 Code that will be permitted by the updated version of the Code issued by the Financial Reporting Council in June 2008 for reporting years starting on or after 29 June 2008. Accordingly, the Chairman now holds the role of Chairman in another FTSE 100 company. Further details of this appointment can be found in the directors' biographies on page [ ].'

Where a company has acquired listed status during the year, it seems reasonable to disclose compliance for the period since listing only, provided a clear explanation is given.

2.1 Exemptions for certain listed companies

Exemptions from disclosures relating to corporate governance are available for various categories of companies. The exemptions available vary for each of the categories of companies and are described in **2.1.1** to **2.1.6** below. The extent of the exemption should be considered carefully, as in certain cases some governance disclosures are still required. It is worth the company secretary checking the position with the Financial Services Authority if a company wishes to avail itself of an exemption to ensure a further amendment has not been made.

If a company avails itself of one of the exemptions, the directors should ideally disclose which exemption the company has availed itself of and the grounds for doing so. Such a disclosure would assist readers of annual reports and accounts who otherwise may mistakenly believe that the directors have omitted information on aspects of the company's corporate governance. Suggested wording, which could be included in the directors' report, is given in **example 2.1A** below. Such an indication would normally be given in the directors' report and not within the audited financial statements. Companies that can avail themselves of an exemption from some or all corporate governance disclosures but are choosing to provide them voluntarily may wish to include a sentence explaining that they are eligible for an exemption, but have decided not to take it. Suggested wording is given in **example 2.1B** below.

Example 2.1A

Overseas company taking advantage of exemption

As the company is not incorporated/trust is not constituted* within the UK, it has availed itself of an exemption from the Financial Services Authority's requirements to make corporate governance disclosures and for auditor review thereof.

* Delete as appropriate

Example 2.1B

Company entitled to exemption choosing to make voluntary disclosure

The company is eligible for exemption from the Financial Services Authority's requirements relating to corporate governance disclosures but the directors have decided to provide such disclosures which are set out on page x below.

2.1.1 *Debt securities*

Companies with only listed debt securities do not have to comply with the requirements of LR 9 and instead comply with LR 17 which does not include any of the corporate governance disclosure requirements.

2.1.2 *Preference shares*

A company that has a primary listing of preference shares must comply with LR 9.8 with certain exceptions as set out in LR 9.1.2R. These exceptions include LR 9.8.6R(5) which is the requirement for a statement about how the Code Principles have been applied and LR 9.8.6R(6) which is the requirement for a statement of compliance with the Code.

Such companies are not exempt from the requirement to make a going concern statement.

2.1.3 *Overseas companies with a primary listing*

An overseas company with a primary listing of equity shares is generally required to comply with LR 9. However, the requirements of LR 9.8.6R apply only to a listed company incorporated in the UK. Overseas companies with a primary listing are therefore exempt from LR 9.8.6R(3) (going concern statement), LR 9.8.6R(5) (statement about how the Code Principles have been applied) and LR 9.8.6R(6) (statement of compliance with the Code).

An overseas company with a primary listing must disclose in its annual report and accounts:

[LR 9.8.7R]

(1) whether or not it complies with the corporate governance regime of its country of incorporation;

(2) the significant ways in which its actual corporate governance practices differ from those set out in the Combined Code; and

(3) the unexpired term of the service contract of any director proposed for election or re-election at the forthcoming annual general meeting and, if any director proposed for election or re-election does not have a service contract, a statement to that effect.

2.1.4 *Overseas companies with a secondary listing*

Overseas companies with a secondary listing are not required to comply with LR 9 and instead comply with LR 14 which does not include any corporate governance disclosure requirements.

2.1.5 *Closed-ended investment funds*

The requirements for closed-ended investment companies are set out in LR 15. As explained at **3.24** in **chapter 46**, these include, but are not limited to, investment companies and venture capital trusts.

A closed-ended investment fund must comply with LR 9, with certain additions and amendments. LR 15.6.6.R states that, for a closed-ended investment fund that has no executive directors, LR 9.8.6R(6) (i.e. statement of compliance with the Combined Code) need not include details about principles B.1 to B.2 and provisions B.1.1 to B.1.6 and B.2.1 to B.2.4 of the Combined Code except to the extent that they relate specifically to non-executive directors.

2.1.6 *Convertible securities*

A company that has a primary listing of securities that are convertible into equity shares must comply with LR 9.8 with certain exceptions as set out in LR 9.1.3R. The exceptions are the same as for a company that has a primary listing of preference shares (see **2.1.2** above).

3 Alternative Investment Market (AIM) companies

Companies that have securities traded on AIM are required to prepare annual reports and accounts in accordance with 'The AIM Rules' issued by the London Stock Exchange. These rules do not require AIM companies to disclose the extent of their compliance with the Combined Code or to make any other corporate governance disclosures.

In February 2007 the Quoted Companies Alliance issued 'Corporate Governance Guidelines for AIM Companies'. The guide helps AIM companies to develop their corporate governance culture by using a simpler and less time consuming framework.

Some AIM companies may wish to make a statement on the degree of compliance with the Code and discuss how they have applied the principles within the Code. Similarly, although there is no requirement for the annual report and accounts of AIM companies to include additional disclosures on directors' remuneration, AIM companies might wish to give the disclosures required by the Listing Rules.

It is recommended that the directors disclose that they are volunteering the information.

Example 3

Explanation of voluntary disclosures

Although not required to, the directors have decided to provide corporate governance and directors' remuneration* disclosures similar to those that would be required of a listed company.

* Delete as appropriate

Where the directors of an AIM company choose not to give any disclosures in respect of corporate governance they should consider stating that AIM companies are not required to provide corporate governance disclosures. Where they have chosen to provide a limited number of disclosures, they should consider stating that, whilst not required to comply with the Code, they have chosen to give selected disclosures that they believe are necessary or valuable for readers.

4 The Combined Code

As explained at **1.1** above, the Combined Code first came into existence in 1998 and has been revised in 2003, 2006 and 2008. It is not the purpose of this chapter to reproduce the requirements of the Code or to discuss their merits. The requirements of the Listing Rules for various statements related to the Code are described in **sections 5 to 8** below. The disclosure requirements to be found in the Code are summarised at **9.1** below.

The text of the Code can be found on the FRC website at:

www.frc.org.uk/corporate/combinedcode.cfm

The following material is also available from that website:

- Guidance on Internal Controls (the 'Turnbull guidance');
- Guidance on Audit Committees (the 'Smith guidance'); and
- Suggestions for Good Practice from the Higgs Report.

5 Statements of compliance

5.1 Form of statement

The company must make a statement as to whether or not it has complied throughout the financial year with the Code provisions set out in section 1 of the Combined Code. A company that has not complied with the Code provisions, or complied with only some of them or complied for only part of the year, must specify the Code provisions with which it has not complied, for what part of the period such non-compliance continued, and give reasons for any non-compliance. [LR 9.8.6R(6)] The exact wording of the Code in this respect is reproduced in **section 2** above.

Where there is compliance with all of the Code provisions for all of the year, the statement of compliance might be worded along the following lines:

Example 5.1A

Full compliance

Throughout the year ended 31 December 2008, the company has been in compliance with the Code provisions set out in section 1 of the 2006 FRC Combined Code.

During the period of transition from the 2006 Code to the 2008 Code, it is important for the statement of compliance to be specific as to which Code had been complied with.

A company may not have complied with the version of the Code in force for its financial year but instead complied with a different version. For example, it may have complied fully with a previous version of the Code or one that does not come into force until a future date. In this case, it is important that the statement of compliance refers to any non-compliance with the applicable code. Example wording is included in **section 2** above for the situation where a company has taken advantage of the relaxations in the 2008 Code for a period when it is still required to report on compliance with the 2006 Code.

Where there are one or more areas of non-compliance with the Code provisions, the statement of compliance might be worded along the following lines:

Example 5.1B

Compliance but with some exceptions

Throughout the year ended 31 December 2008, the company has been in compliance with the Code provisions set out in section 1 of the 2006 FRC Combined Code, except for the following matters:

[Specify the relevant provisions of the Code, the period affected and the reason for non-compliance.]

Any disclosure of non-compliance should be clear and specific so as to leave the reader in no doubt that there has been a departure from the Code, the nature of that departure and the reason for it. This will usually be best achieved by providing a concise list of areas of non-compliance rather than dealing with them under separate headings spread throughout the corporate governance statement. In particular, references to compliance 'except as described below' should be avoided unless the list of non-compliances follows immediately and is easily identified. It is not generally thought to be necessary to refer to the Code provisions by their numbers. It is more helpful for readers if the Code provisions that have not been complied with are described.

5.2 Location of statement

No official guidance has been issued on the location of the statement of compliance or the narrative statement about how the Code Principles have been applied (see **section 6** below). Most companies include them in a separate corporate governance section of the annual report although they could alternatively be included in the directors' report. As for the relative positioning of the two statements, it is sometimes suggested that it is useful for the narrative statement to precede the statement of compliance to enable the directors to explain their approach to governance before they deal with how it reconciles with the Code provisions. However, an alternative view is that there should be a clear 'up front' statement about compliance (or otherwise) in order to set the scene for the narrative statement. Where there is non-compliance with the Code, this approach also avoids potential criticism that the disclosures have been given insufficient prominence. Both approaches are acceptable and widely encountered in practice.

5.3 Independent non-executive directors

A number of Code provisions refer to independent non-executive directors. For example, Code provision A.3.2 requires that at least half the board, excluding the chairman, should comprise non-executive directors determined by the board to be independent. Code provision A.3.1 requires boards to identify in their annual reports each non-executive director the board considers to be independent. Therefore issues may arise about the independence of non-executive directors for the purposes of deciding whether there has been any non-compliance with the Code.

The Combined Code contains the following requirements in respect of the independence of non-executive directors which were added when the Code was revised in 2003:

> 'The board should identify in the annual report each non-executive director it considers to be independent. The board should determine whether the director is independent in character and judgement and whether there are relationships or circumstances which are likely to affect, or could appear to affect, the director's judgement. The board should state its reasons if it determines that a director is independent notwithstanding the existence of relationships or circumstances which may appear relevant to its determination, including if the director:
>
> - has been an employee of the company or group within the last five years;
> - has, or has had within the last three years, a material business relationship with the company either directly, or as a partner, shareholder, director or senior employee of a body that has such a relationship with the company;

- has received or receives additional remuneration from the company apart from a director's fee, participates in the company's share option or performance-related pay scheme, or is a member of the company's pension scheme;
- has close family ties with any of the company's advisers, directors or senior employees;
- holds cross-directorships or has significant links with other directors through involvement in other companies or bodies;
- represents a significant shareholder; or
- has served on the board for more than nine years from the date of their first election.' [Code A.3.1]

APB Bulletin 2006/5 makes clear that it is not the auditors' responsibility to satisfy themselves whether the directors are properly described as being 'independent' non-executives. Nor should auditors lay down more precise criteria with respect to the meaning of the term 'independent' than those set out in the Combined Code.

6 Narrative statements

The Company must provide a statement of how it has applied the Principles of Good Governance set out in section 1 of the Combined Code, in a manner that would enable shareholders to evaluate how the Principles have been applied. The exact wording of the Code in this respect is reproduced in **section 2** above. [LR 9.8.6R(5)]

This statement is generally referred to as the 'narrative statement' which was the term used in earlier versions of the Listing Rules. Following the revision of the Listing Rules at 1 July 2005, the word 'narrative' does not appear in LR 9.8.6R(5) but this accepted terminology is used in this chapter for convenience.

The Preamble to the Combined Code notes that the statement should cover both the main and supporting Principles. It also states that the form and content of this statement is not prescribed and indicates that companies should have a free hand to explain their governance policies in the light of the Principles, including any special circumstances applying to them which have led to a particular approach.

A brief bland statement will not suffice. Directors should satisfy themselves that all the Principles and supporting Principles are sufficiently covered in the narrative. But they should avoid 'boilerplate' recitals of Code provisions which have been complied with.

The focus should be on how those provisions have been applied to the company's particular circumstances and any areas of non-compliance should be properly disclosed.

No official guidance has been issued on the location of the narrative statement. Companies are including it either in a separate 'corporate governance statement' or within the directors' report. The relative positioning of the statement of compliance with the Code and the narrative statement is considered in **section 5** above.

Numerous types of disclosures have been published, ranging from brief statements to those giving detailed information on every principle and provision. Given that directors have to use their judgement as to whether certain provisions have been complied with or not, the more information given about the reason behind a decision the more helpful this is to investors and the fewer questions are likely to be asked at the AGM.

When drafting a narrative statement, it is useful to consider whether:

- it should be either in one continuous statement or in different places but cross-referenced;
- to include the internal control statement in (or cross-refer it to) the narrative statement, as one of the principles (C.2) is on internal control;
- the board wishes to describe the steps which it has carried out in the year to improve its governance arrangements;
- to organise the statement under the headings for the principles set out in the Combined Code, although directors may find such an approach difficult or too mechanistic; and
- there are key issues relating to the size of the business, the nature of the risks faced, the type of management information which the board uses, the identity of the providers of external advice and the organisation of the board and its subcommittees which require explanation.

There are numerous ways the narrative statement can be presented.

For periods commencing on or after 29 June 2008 the FSA has modified LR 9.8.6R(5) to reduce the amount of boiler-plate disclosures, so that a company to which the rule applies will need to include in its annual report 'a statement of how it has applied the Main Principles set out in Section 1 of the Combined Code, in a manner that would enable shareholders to evaluate how the principles have been applied'. The purpose of this change is to clarify that the focus should be on the Main Principles and that it is not necessary to describe, in the narrative statement, how each of the Code Provisions has been applied.

7 Internal control statements

7.1 The Combined Code and internal control

Combined Code principle C.2 states that 'The board should maintain a sound system of internal control to safeguard shareholders' investment and the company's assets'. In addition, provision C.2.1 of the Code states that 'the board should, at least annually, conduct a review of the effectiveness of the group's system of internal controls and should report to shareholders that they have done so. The review should cover all material controls including financial, operational and compliance controls and risk management systems'.

Following publication of the original Combined Code, the Institute of Chartered Accountants in England and Wales (ICAEW) convened a working party chaired by Nigel Turnbull to produce guidance for directors on the scope, extent, nature and review of the internal controls to which (what are now) Code Principle C.2 and Code Provision C.2.1 refer. This was necessary because the requirements in the Combined Code went further than the requirements under the previous Cadbury Code for which purpose the review could (and usually was) limited to internal *financial* controls. The guidance was published in September 1999 as Internal Control: Guidance for Directors on the Combined Code. It was updated and re-issued in October 2005. The guidance is generally referred to as the 'Turnbull guidance' and is available separately in the corporate governance section of the FRC website.

7.2 The Turnbull guidance

This section considers the revised Turnbull guidance which took effect for periods commencing on or after 1 January 2006. The guidance helps boards of directors to:

(a) assess how the company has applied Code principle C.2 (see **7.1** above);

(b) implement the requirements of Code provisions C.2.1 (see **7.1** above); and

(c) report on these matters to shareholders in the annual report and accounts.

A key feature is that a company's system of internal control should aim to manage risks that are significant to the fulfilment of the company's business objectives, with a view to safeguarding the company's assets and enhancing over time the value of the shareholders' investment. Application of the guidance is therefore not limited to financial reporting controls.

The preface to the guidance emphasises that the directors should review their application of the guidance on a continuing basis. There should be evidence of more than a one-off discussion on internal control and Turnbull in board papers and of a continuing process of review for periods to which the guidance applies.

The disclosures recommended by the Turnbull guidance for full compliance are as follows:

(a) As a minimum, in the company's narrative statement of how it has applied Code principle C.2, disclosure that there is an ongoing process for identifying, evaluating and managing the significant risks faced by the company that:

(i) has been in place for the year under review and up to the date of the approval of the annual report and accounts;

(ii) is regularly reviewed by the board; and

(iii) accords with the Turnbull guidance.

(b) In relation to the application of principle C.2, an acknowledgement by the board that it is responsible for the company's system of internal control and for reviewing its effectiveness.

(c) An explanation that the system of internal control is designed to manage rather than eliminate the risk of failure to achieve business objectives, and can only provide reasonable and not absolute assurance against material misstatement or loss.

(d) In relation to Code provision C.2.1, a summary of the process the board (where applicable, through its committees) has applied in reviewing the effectiveness of the system of internal control.

(e) Confirmation that necessary actions have been or are being taken to remedy any significant failings or weaknesses identified from that review.

(f) The process applied by the board to deal with material internal control aspects of any significant problems disclosed in the annual report and accounts.

(g) Where material joint ventures and associates have not been dealt with as part of the group for the purposes of applying the Turnbull guidance, this should be stated.

The annual report should include such meaningful, high level information as the board considers necessary to assist shareholders' understanding of the main features of the company's risk management processes and system of internal control, and should not give a misleading impression. Where a company cannot make one or more of the disclosures in (a), (d), (e) or (f) above, the guidance explicitly requires that this fact should be stated and an explanation provided. But failure to meet the other disclosure requirements of the Turnbull guidance (i.e. (b), (c) and (g) above) might be viewed as non-compliance with the Code and therefore such disclosures should always be made.

The Listing Rules require companies to state whether or not they have complied with the Code's provisions during the year. Therefore, this rule would require the board to disclose if it has failed to conduct a review of the effectiveness of the group's system of internal control (as required by Code provision C.2.1). This non-compliance disclosure would fall within the compliance statement (see **section 5** above).

Neither the Financial Services Authority nor the guidance encourages disclosure of any opinions on the effectiveness of the system of internal control. SEC registrants are now required to report on the effectiveness of their system of internal controls as a result of the Sarbanes-Oxley Act and related SEC rules. These requirements are outside of the scope of this publication.

Some companies will wish to adopt a minimalist approach to disclosure. Others will wish to go further.

Disclosure is expected in relation to the process the board has applied to deal with material internal control aspects of any significant problems disclosed in the annual report and accounts. The board should preferably minute the rationale for their decisions where there is any possibility that a reported problem deemed to be insignificant could be construed as significant by other parties. It may need to be able to justify such decisions later.

The full annual report and accounts, the interims and other statements made during the year should be read to ensure that there are no references to significant problems (which arise from material internal control issues) which are not responded to in the statement of internal control under the full compliance regime. Otherwise, criticisms could be made of the directors.

When disclosing significant problems with internal control aspects, directors should focus on the processes that they have applied to deal with internal control aspects and steps being taken to remedy the problems.

The guidance stresses that there should be appropriate documentation to support the statement on internal control. The guidance for auditors, APB Bulletin 2006/5, states that the objective of the auditor's review is to assess whether the company's summary of the process the board (and where applicable its committees) has adopted in reviewing the effectiveness of the system of internal control, is both supported by the documentation prepared by or for the directors and appropriately reflects that process.

The requirement to confirm necessary actions referred to in (e) above requires full consideration by the Board before the related disclosures are included in the internal control statement.

Where the company is the parent of a group, the statement on internal control should be from the perspective of the group as a whole.

The following are some areas for particular consideration:

(a) maintaining key risk indicators which allow management to monitor risks and identify developments which require interventions;

(b) ensuring that the system is actually 'ongoing';

(c) ensuring that all employees collectively possess the necessary skills, technical knowledge, objectivity and understanding of the organisation and the industries and markets in which the company operates;

(d) maintaining an environment that promotes learning within the company on risk and control issues, including the provision of relevant training;

(e) improving internal reporting on risk and control, especially where currently there is only reporting by exception;

(f) making risk management and control more explicit across the organisation; and

(g) strengthening and repositioning internal audit.

Key questions for a board to consider include the following:

(a) Is the process for identifying, evaluating and managing the key risks ongoing?

(b) Does this process accord with the guidance?

(c) What work needs to be done to ensure that the directors have established the necessary procedures to implement the guidance?

(d) Is sufficient resource being applied to create the level of control environment specified by the guidance?

(e) Does the group have key risk indicators which enable immediate reporting of major control weaknesses?

(f) Is there an environment that promotes learning within the company on risk and control issues, including the provision of relevant training as now expected by the guidance?

Pitfalls for directors to avoid include:

(a) treating Turnbull only as a disclosure issue;

(b) continuing with too narrow a definition of risk;

(c) concentrating only on comfort areas (e.g. internal financial controls);

(d) identifying too many risks;

(e) not creating a top down process. Such a process would usefully involve members of the board participating at the outset and taking into account the views of the executive committee on the key business risks;

(f) not putting in place procedures to find out from all levels of the organisation other significant risks or risk which they perceive as poorly controlled;

(g) not addressing cultural issues;

(h) not creating a process which is embedded and ongoing;

(i) creating a situation where one person/department (i.e. the Financial Director, the Head of Risk Assessment, the Head of Internal Audit or the Audit Committee) is accountable for management of all risks; accountability for managing risk should be allocated across the organisation to relevant people and there should be a collective sense of concern to ensure that key risks are kept under control;

(j) a lack of linkage between the strategy review and risk management processes;

(k) 'throwing the baby out with the bathwater', i.e. not keeping the key elements of the system of control that are already successful.

7.3 Location of statement on internal control

The positioning of the internal control statement is not prescribed but it is possible that it will appear in:

(a) a separate statement;

(b) the narrative corporate governance statement; or

(c) the directors' report.

It is preferable that the statement on internal control should be included in, or cross-referred to in, the narrative statement required by the Listing Rules (see **section 2** above). The reason for this is that the maintenance of the system of internal control is expected under principle C.2 and there is a need to describe how the principles are applied in the narrative statement.

7.4 Interaction with the business review and any OFR

This section considers the relationship between the disclosures required in the business review in the directors' report, those recommended to be included in any Operating and Financial Review (OFR) (see **9.3** below) and those required to comply with the Turnbull guidance.

There is a requirement to report in the business review (and a recommendation to report in the OFR) on 'principal risks and uncertainties' with a commentary of the directors' approach to them. In particular, the directors' policy for managing principal risks should be disclosed.

As explained at **7.2** above, the Turnbull guidance sets out a framework for maintaining a sound system of internal control and reviewing its effectiveness. It recommends that, as a minimum, companies should disclose that there is an ongoing process for identifying, evaluating and managing significant risks faced by the company and that this process is regularly reviewed by the board. In addition, it requires the board to summarise the process it has applied in reviewing the effectiveness of the system of internal control.

Despite the significant similarities in the two disclosures, companies should note that the Turnbull guidance requires disclosures on the process directors have applied in reviewing the effectiveness of the system of internal control whereas the business review and OFR disclosures are in respect of the policy directors have adopted for managing principal risks. Thus the requirements should not overlap although some references can be made from the corporate governance section of the annual report to the business review and OFR.

See **9.5** below for information on the new requirements for companies, whose securities (equity or debt) are traded on a regulated market in the EU, to include a corporate governance statement in their directors' report. This corporate governance statement is required to include a description of the main features of the company's internal control and risk management systems in relation to the financial reporting process.

8 Going concern statements

8.1 The Combined Code and the Listing Rules

The requirement for a statement that the business is a going concern, with supporting assumptions or qualifications as necessary, was first introduced in 1992 as one of the provisions of the Cadbury Code (see **1.1** above). The requirement was subsequently incorporated into the Listing Rules although certain categories of companies are exempt from this requirement (see **2.1** above). The requirement is also currently to be found in code Provision C.1.2 of the Combined Code. A company failing to make such a statement (unless exempt) would be in breach of both the Listing Rules and the Code.

The requirement for a going concern statement is now set out in LR 9.8.6R(3) which requires:

> 'A statement made by the directors that the business is a going concern, together with supporting assumptions or qualifications as necessary, that has been prepared in accordance with "Going Concern and Financial Reporting: Guidance for Directors of listed companies registered in the United Kingdom", published in November 1994.'

Following the introduction of the original requirement, a Joint Working Group comprising members of the accountancy profession and representatives of preparers of accounts was established to provide guidance on the application of the requirement. The Group published its final guidance, entitled *Going Concern and Financial Reporting*, in November 1994. The purpose of the guidance is to:

(a) explain the significance of going concern in relation to the financial statements;

(b) describe the procedures that an explicit statement on going concern may entail; and

(c) recommend appropriate disclosure.

The Listing Rules make explicit reference to the fact that the going concern statement should be 'prepared in accordance with' the 1994 guidance.

8.2 The 1994 guidance

This section contains a summary of the requirements of *Going Concern and Financial Reporting* as described at **8.1** above. However, reference should be made to the complete text of the guidance when preparing the statement required by the Code and the Listing Rules.

> Curiously, the 1994 guidance on going concern is not available separately on the FRC website. However, the 1994 guidance can be downloaded from the ICAEW website (*www.icaew.co.uk*) under Technical and business topics / Corporate governance / Guides and other publications / Publications.

Although the 1994 guidance is intended principally for directors of listed companies incorporated in the UK, the Joint Working Group noted that it may also be of assistance to directors of other companies and, in particular, large private companies and 'public interest' companies.

The 1994 guidance specifies that directors should carry out an assessment of their company's financial position, to determine whether the company will continue in operational existence for the foreseeable future and hence is a going concern, and make disclosures in the financial statements based on that assessment. The guidance does not define 'foreseeable future' as a specific period. It states that the foreseeable future depends on the specific circumstances at a point in time, including the nature of the company's business, associated risks and external influences.

However, where the foreseeable future considered by the directors has been limited to a period of less than one year from the date of approval of the financial statements, the guidance states that the directors should determine whether the financial statements require any additional disclosures to explain adequately the assumptions that underlie the use of the going concern basis.

Since the introduction of FRS 18 *Accounting Policies*, directors have been required, under UK GAAP, to disclose the fact where they have considered a period of less than one year from the date of approval of the financial statements. IAS 1 *Presentation of Financial Statements* includes requirements on going concern that are broadly similar to UK GAAP but with some differences. In particular, when assessing whether the going concern assumption is appropriate, IAS 1 requires management to take into account all available information about the future 'which is at least, but is not limited to, twelve months from the end of the reporting period'. The minimum period to be considered under IAS 1 (i.e. twelve months from the end of the reporting period) is potentially shorter than that under UK GAAP (i.e. twelve months from the date of approval of the financial statements). The implications of this are discussed at **2.4** in **chapter 3**.

The directors' statement on going concern should be made based on what is known at the date on which they approve the financial statements; in practice, most of their work will be performed before the date of approval and updated as appropriate.

The following areas are identified in the 1994 guidance as ones which directors will need to consider to determine whether they are or could become significant:

- forecasts and budgets;

- borrowing requirements;
- liability management;
- contingent liabilities;
- products and markets;
- financial risk management; and
- financial adaptability.

The appendix to the 1994 guidance includes detailed procedures that may need to be performed under each of the above headings. The list of procedures is not intended to be used as a checklist, since there may be other procedures which are relevant and not all the procedures listed will be appropriate for every company.

However, directors are best placed to know which factors are likely to be of greater significance in relation to their company. The relative importance of the factors will vary by industry and from company to company within a particular industry. The relative significance of the factors can also vary over time.

The 1994 guidance identifies three conclusions which the directors can reach when considering the results of their procedures:

(a) they have a reasonable expectation that the company will continue in operational existence for the foreseeable future and have therefore used the going concern basis in preparing the financial statements;

(b) they have identified factors that cast doubt on the ability of the company to continue in operational existence for the foreseeable future, but they consider that it is appropriate to use the going concern basis in preparing the financial statements;

(c) they consider that the company is unlikely to continue in operational existence for the foreseeable future and therefore the going concern basis is not an appropriate one on which to draw up the financial statements.

The 1994 guidance includes example wording of the directors' statement for the first two situations, but suggests that legal advice be sought if directors find themselves in the third situation, i.e. they consider that the company is unlikely to continue in operational existence. Example wording for a statement is given at **8.4** below.

The suggested conclusion in the third situation is potentially inconsistent with IAS 1(2003).23 and IAS 1(2007).25 which require financial statements to be prepared on a going concern basis 'unless management either intends to liquidate the entity or to cease trading, or has no realistic alternative but to do so'. Such situations should, however, be very rare and will require careful consideration based on the particular facts.

8.3 The location of the statement

The 1994 guidance indicates that the going concern statement should be included in the Operating and Financial Review (OFR). The guidance explains that the OFR will contain a significant amount of discussion and analysis which will help to put the statement on going concern in context. However, there is and was, at the time the guidance was written, no requirement for any company to prepare an OFR. Many companies have included the going concern statement in the corporate governance section of the annual report and this practice has become accepted.

As described in **section 5** of **chapter 46**, the ASB issued a Reporting Statement on the OFR in January 2006. That statement makes no mention of the going concern statement.

8.4 Form of the statement

Where the directors are satisfied that the company will continue in operational existence, they should make a statement to that effect.

The example wording included in the 1994 guidance does not indicate that the judgement is formed at a point in time. However, it is important that readers of a statement on going concern understand that this is the case and thus the example set out below differs from the example wording set out in the guidance, by making specific reference to this.

Example 8.4

Going concern statement

After making enquiries, the directors have formed a judgement, at the time of approving the financial statements, that there is a reasonable expectation that the company has adequate resources to continue in operational existence for the foreseeable future. For this reason, the directors continue to adopt the going concern basis in preparing the financial statements.

Where the directors have identified factors which cast doubt on the appropriateness of the going concern assumption, the directors should explain the circumstances so as to identify the factors which give rise to the problem (including any external factors outside their control which may affect the outcome) and an explanation of how they intend to deal with the problem so as to resolve it.

In accordance with IAS 1 *Presentation of Financial Statements* (see **chapter 3**) and auditing standards, the financial statements will refer to any material uncertainties of which the directors are aware in making their assessment of events or conditions that may cast significant doubt upon the entity's ability to continue as a going concern. Such disclosures are typically made in a separate going concern note. The 1994 guidance draws attention to the possible need for a cross reference from the going concern statement to such a note within the audited financial statements. APB Bulletin 2006/5 also stresses that the statement by the directors should not be inconsistent with the disclosures regarding going concern in the financial statements or the auditors' report. One method of ensuring consistency is for the directors' statement to be limited to a cross reference to the relevant note in the financial statements. International Standard on Auditing (UK and Ireland) 570 'Going Concern' includes guidance on matters that need to be included in the note to the financial statements where there is significant uncertainty.

Even in straightforward situations, directors should take care not to extend their responsibilities unnecessarily by making gratuitous statements that go beyond those set out in the guidance. To limit any additional responsibility, directors are likely to wish to consult with their auditors and, in some circumstances, their legal advisers, regarding the form of disclosure that they should make.

While doubts about the ability of a company to remain as a going concern do not necessarily mean that the company is or is likely to become insolvent, directors are rightly concerned that disclosure of such doubts may have an adverse effect on the public's perception of the company's position which, in turn, might exacerbate the company's future operations. They nevertheless have a responsibility to make a reasonable judgement based on all available information at the time the financial statements are approved by them and report accordingly.

As noted at **8.2** above, there is a potential conflict between the guidance (which was written on the basis of UK GAAP in 1994) and the requirements of IAS 1 regarding the circumstances in which the financial statements should be prepared on a basis other than going concern. Such situations will be very rare and will require careful consideration based on the particular facts.

The fact that the company is not a going concern does not necessarily mean that the company is insolvent. However, the directors will need to consider whether the company may be or become insolvent. Specialist advice should be sought when the directors know or suspect that there is no reasonable prospect that the company can avoid going into insolvent liquidation (i.e. there may be a possibility of action for wrongful trading).

8.5 Groups

In respect of groups, the 1994 guidance states that the directors of the parent company should make their statement regarding going concern in respect of both the parent company and the group as a whole. A statement regarding the going concern status of the group does not mean that each of the companies within the group is a going concern. It is possible that the directors may have doubts about the going concern status of a member of the group (other than the parent) and still conclude that the group will remain a going concern for the foreseeable future.

8.6 Interim reporting

Although the primary purpose of the 1994 guidance is to outline procedures and disclosures for year end reporting, it also includes a paragraph on interim reporting. At the half-year stage, the guidance suggests that directors review the work performed at the previous year end to determine whether any of the significant factors which they had identified at that time have changed to such an extent as to affect the appropriateness of the going concern presumption. However, no guidance is given on reporting at the interim stage.

Where there are doubts about the appropriateness of the going concern presumption at the interim stage, directors are likely to increase the extent of their procedures in the going concern area. They should also consider including wording on the appropriateness of the going concern basis in the management report required by the Disclosure and Transparency Rules to be contained in the half-yearly report.

8.7 Preliminary announcements

Where a listed company produces a preliminary announcement, the Listing Rules require it to include details of the nature of any likely modification to the auditors' report. The requirement would include, for example, an emphasis of matter referring to going concern issues. Whether or not the auditors' report is 'likely to be modified' should be assessed in the light of conditions at the date of the preliminary announcement, and not on those that may prevail when the audit report is actually signed (see the discussion at **2.1** in **chapter 51**).

9 Other governance disclosures

9.1 The Combined Code

In addition to the statements on compliance with the Code, internal control and going concern, the Code requires the following other disclosures to be made:

- a statement of how the board operates, including a high level statement of which types of decisions are to be taken by the board and which are to be delegated to management (A.1.1);
- the names of the chairman, the deputy chairman (where there is one), the chief executive, the senior independent director and the chairmen and members of the nomination, audit and remuneration committees (A.1.2);
- the number of meetings of the board and those committees and individual attendance by directors (A.1.2);
- if, exceptionally, a board decides that the chief executive should become chairman, the board should consult major shareholders in advance and should set out its reasons to shareholders at the time of the appointment and in the next annual report (A.2.2)
- the names of the non-executive directors whom the board determines to be independent. The board should state its reasons if it determines that a director is independent notwithstanding the existence of relationships or circumstances which may appear relevant to its determination (see **5.3** above) (A.3.1);
- the other significant commitments of the chairman and any changes to them during the year (A.4.3);
- how performance evaluation of the board, its committees and its directors has been conducted (A.6.1);

- a separate section describing the work of the nomination committee, including the process it has used in relation to board appointments and an explanation if neither external search consultancy nor open advertising has been used in the appointment of a chairman or a non-executive director (A.4.6);
- a description of the work of the remuneration committee as required by Schedule 7A of the 1985 Act (or s421 of the 2006 Act), including, where an executive director serves as a non-executive director elsewhere, whether or not the director will retain such earnings and, if so, what the remuneration is (B.1.4);
- an explanation from the directors of their responsibility for preparing the financial statements (see **section 2** in **chapter 46**) and a statement by the auditors about their reporting responsibilities (C.1.1);
- a separate section describing the work of the audit committee in discharging its responsibilities (see **9.2** below) (C.3.3);
- where there is no internal audit function, the reasons for the absence of such a function (C.3.5);
- where the board does not accept the audit committee's recommendation on the appointment, reappointment or removal of an external auditor, a statement from the audit committee explaining the recommendation and the reasons why the board has taken a different position (C.3.6);
- an explanation of how, if the auditor provides non-audit services, auditor objectivity and independence is safeguarded (see **9.2** and **9.4** below) (C.3.7); and
- the steps the board has taken to ensure that members of the board and in particular the non-executive directors, develop an understanding of the views of major shareholders about their company (D.1.2).

In addition, the Combined Code requires the following to be 'made available':

- the terms of reference of the nomination committee, explaining its role and the authority delegated to it by the board (A.4.1);
- the terms of reference of the remuneration committee, explaining its role and the authority delegated to it by the board (B.2.1);
- where remuneration consultants are appointed, a statement of whether they have any other connection with the company (B.2.1);

The reference to 'other' connections with the company appears to refer to connections other than as advisers to the remuneration committee. There are statutory disclosure requirements concerning the identity of persons who have provided advice or services to the remuneration committee, that materially assisted the committee in the consideration of directors' remuneration.

- the terms of reference of the audit committee, including its role and the authority delegated to it by the board (C.3.3).

As a minimum, the 2006 Code requires companies to make the terms of reference available on a website. Companies may wish to include this information in their annual reports or at least consider making reference to the fact that it is available on the company's website.

Code provision A.4.4 requires that the terms and conditions of appointment of non-executive directors should be made available for inspection. The information has to be made available for inspection by any person at the company's registered office during normal business hours and at the AGM (for 15 minutes prior to and during the meeting).

Although it is unlikely to be appropriate to include these details in full in the annual report, it may be appropriate to provide some key terms or at least refer to the fact that the terms and conditions are available for inspection.

The Code also requires the following information to be set out in the papers accompanying a resolution to elect or re-elect directors:

- the names of directors submitted for election or re-election, accompanied by sufficient biographical details and other relevant information to enable shareholders to take an informed decision on their election or re-election (A.7.1);
- in the case of the election of a non-executive director, the board should set out to shareholders why it believes that an individual should be elected (A.7.2); and
- when proposing the re-election of a non-executive director, the chairman should confirm to shareholders that, following formal performance evaluation, the individual's performance continues to be effective and to demonstrate commitment to the role (A.7.2).

In practice, these details will often be provided within the annual report which will either include, or be distributed with, the notice of the annual general meeting.

Most listed companies provide biographical details of all of their directors rather than just those proposed for election or re-election.

9.2 The audit committee report

Code Provision C.3.3 requires that a separate section of the annual report should describe the work of the audit committee in discharging its responsibilities.

The reference to a 'separate section' of the annual report is presumably to ensure that the description is clearly identifiable. A sub-section within a larger corporate governance report would appear to meet the letter of the requirement. However, it is preferable that the audit committee report should be in the form of a separate report, written by the audit committee and signed by the chairman of the committee.

The Smith Guidance for audit committees recommends that the section dealing with the work of the audit committee should include:

- a summary of the role of the audit committee:
- the names and qualifications of all members of the audit committee during the period;
- the number of audit committee meetings; and
- a report on the way the audit committee has discharged its responsibilities.

The guidance states that the section should also include the explanation of how auditors objectivity and independence is safeguarded if the auditor provides non-audit services.

Although the Smith Guidance does not impose mandatory requirements, the recommendations contained within it should be adopted as best practice.

Appendix II of the Smith Report, the pre-cursor to the Smith Guidance published in 2003, gives more detailed guidance on the information to include in the report on the activities of the audit committee. This is reproduced below for ease of reference.

Extract 9.2

Outline report on the activities of the audit committee

(Appendix II to the Smith Report)

1. Role of the audit committee

- Main responsibilities of the audit committee

2. Composition of the audit committee

- Members and secretary – names and appointment/resignation dates
- Appointment process
- The relevant qualifications, expertise and experience of each member

3. Resources

- Any dedicated resources available to the committee, internal or bought-in

4. Meetings

- Number of meetings, and attendance

5. Remuneration of the members of the audit committee

- Describe the specific policies in relation to members of the audit committee (or cross refer to the Directors' Remuneration Report)

Main activities of the Committee in the year to xxxx

6. Financial statements

- Describe the activities carried out in order to monitor the integrity of the financial statements

7. Internal financial control and risk management systems

- Describe the activities carried out in order to review the integrity of the company's internal financial control and risk management systems

8. External auditors

- Describe the procedures adopted to review the independence of the external auditors, including disclosure of the policy on the provision of non audit services and an explanation of how the policy protects auditor independence
- Describe the oversight of the external audit process and confirm that an assessment of the effectiveness of the external audit was made
- Explain the recommendation to the board on the appointment of the auditors and, if appropriate, the process adopted to select the new auditor.

9. Internal audit function

- Confirm that a review of the plans and work of the department was carried out. If there is no function explain the committee's consideration of whether there is a need for an internal audit function in accordance with the recommendations of the Turnbull report

9.3 Operating and Financial Review (OFR)

Code Principle C.1 requires a balanced and understandable assessment of the company's position and prospects. This requirement has, in the past, been met in a variety of ways. One way of meeting the requirement is to provide an Operating and Financial Review as described in **section 5** of **chapter 46.**

The interaction between disclosure requirements on internal control in the Turnbull guidance and any OFR is considered at **7.4** above.

9.4 Disclosures of auditors' remuneration

Code Provision C.3.7 requires an explanation of how, if the auditor provides non-audit services, auditor objectivity and independence is preserved. The requirements for disclosure of auditors' remuneration are more fully considered at **8.2 in chapter 3**.

9.5 The Disclosure and Transparency Rules

Following amendments to the EU Fourth and Seventh Directives, the Financial Services Authority has introduced some new rules into the Disclosure and Transparency Rules relating to corporate governance statements and audit committees. These rules are applicable for periods commencing on or after 29 June 2008.

The requirements apply to all companies incorporated in an EU Member State and whose securities (equity or debt) are traded on a regulated market in the EU. Such companies will have to include a corporate governance statement in their directors' reports referring to:

- the corporate governance code that the company has decided to apply or is subject to under the law of the Member State in which it is incorporated; [DTR 7.2.2R (1) & (2)]
- all relevant information about the corporate governance practices applied beyond the requirements under national law and where this information and/or the relevant corporate governance code is publicly available; [DTR 7.2.2R (3) & 7.2.3R (1)(a) & (2)]
- an explanation as to whether, and to what extent, the company complies with that code or those practices. To the extent that a company departs from the code or practices, the company should explain from which parts of the code or practices it departs and the reasons for doing so; [DTR 7.2.3R(1)(b) & (3)]

- a description of the main features of the company's internal control and risk management systems in relation to the financial reporting process; [DTR 7.2.5R]
- major shareholdings and related matters already required by the Takeover Directive (see **3.23** in **chapter 46**); [DTR 7.2.6R] and
- a description of the composition and operation of the company's administrative, management and supervisory bodies and their committees. [DTR 7.2.7R]

Companies already complying in full with the Combined Code, the Turnbull Guidance and the relevant parts of the Takeover Directive will not need to make any additional disclosures to meet these new requirements.

A company may elect that, instead of including its corporate governance statement in its directors' report, the information required may be set out:

- in a separate report published together with and in the same manner as its annual report. In the event of a separate report, the corporate governance statement must contain either the information required by DTR 7.2.6R or a reference to the directors' report where that information is made available; or
- by means of a reference in its directors' report to where such document is publicly available on the company's website.

Companies preparing a group directors' report must include in that report a description of the main features of the group's internal control and risk management systems in relation to the process for preparing consolidated accounts.

Under the new rules, companies whose securities are traded on a regulated market in the EU are also required to have a body which is responsible for performing the functions detailed below. At least one member of that body must be independent and at least one member must have competence in accounting and/or auditing. The requirements for independence and competence in accounting and/or auditing may be satisfied by the same member or by different members of the relevant body. [DTR 7.1.1R and DTR 7.1.2G]

The company must ensure that, as a minimum, the relevant body must:

[DTR 7.1.3R]

- monitor the financial reporting process;

- monitor the effectiveness of the company's internal control, internal audit where applicable, and risk management systems;
- monitor the statutory audit of the annual and consolidated accounts; and
- review and monitor the independence of the statutory auditor, and in particular the provision of additional services to the company.

A company is required to base any proposal to appoint a statutory auditor on a recommendation made by the relevant body. [DTR 7.1.4R] The company must make a statement available to the public disclosing which body carries out the functions required by DTR 7.1.3R and how it is composed. [DTR 7.1.5R] This statement can be included in any corporate governance statement.

DTR 7.1.7G states that 'in the FSA's view, compliance with provisions A.1.2, C.3.1, C.3.2 and C.3.3 of the Combined Code will result in compliance with DTR 7.1.1R to 7.1.5R.

9.6 ABI guidelines on responsible investment disclosure

In February 2007 the Association of British Insurers (ABI) issued a revised version of their Responsible Investment Disclosure Guidelines which can be obtained from the ABI's website at *www.abi.org.uk*. These replaced the guidelines issued in 2001. The revisions were modest and the guidelines continue to encourage boards to confirm that they have assessed significant environmental, social and governance risks and that these are being monitored and managed appropriately. The guidelines serve as a good indication of what investors regard as valuable in the business review.

> Companies should note that an OFR should not be seen as a replacement for reporting to a wider stakeholder group, for example on corporate social responsibility or environmental issues. The ASB Reporting Statement *Operating and Financial Review* makes this clear. Companies should consider whether it is more appropriate to report separately on these issues elsewhere in the annual report rather than in an OFR.
>
> Companies should bear in mind that if a separate corporate social responsibility report or another report discusses some crucial issues, these should be summarised and included in any OFR as well. The Reporting Statement specifically recommends disclosure of the policies of the entity and the extent to which these policies have been successfully implemented in relation to environmental matters, employees and social and community issues. If separate reports are

presented, companies should ensure that the contents are consistent with the disclosures made in any OFR.

For companies that do not prepare an OFR, similar considerations apply to disclosures made in the business review in the directors' report.

10 Future developments

10.1 Review of the Smith Guidance for audit committees

The Financial Reporting Council is currently considering the responses to its consultation on proposed changes to the Smith Guidance as part of the implementation phase of its Choice in the UK Audit Market project. This follows the recommendations of the Market Participants Group (MPG), which was established in October 2006 to provide advice to the Financial Reporting Council on market-led actions to mitigate the risk that could arise in the event of one of more of the Big Four audit firms leaving the market. The Group's final report, containing 15 recommendations to enhance the efficiency of the UK audit market, was published in October 2007.

A number of the MPG's recommendations were targeted at companies. Four of these have particular relevance to audit committees. The recommendations called for:

- company boards to provide information to shareholders relevant to their auditor selection decision;
- company boards to disclose any contractual obligations (such as loan agreements) to appoint certain types of audit firm;
- large companies to consider the need to include the risk of the withdrawal of their auditor from the market in their risk evaluation and planning; and
- sections of the Smith Guidance dealing with auditor independence to be reviewed for consistency with the relevant ethical standards for auditors.

The proposed changes to the Smith Guidance reflect these recommendations and place new requirements on the audit committee. In addition to the proposed changes based on the MPG recommendations, the draft revised guidance also contains further changes needed following the publication of the 2008 Code.

48 Directors' remuneration

1 Introduction

Directors' remuneration is an area of financial reporting which attracts a great deal of scrutiny. Unfortunately there are several overlapping sets of rules which makes for a great deal of complexity. The disclosure requirements in the 2006 Act and the Accounting Regulations are largely unchanged from those in the 1985 Companies Act. Throughout this chapter appropriate references have been inserted for the 2006 Act and accompanying Accounting Regulations and the 1985 Act.

Schedule 5 to the Accounting Regulations and Schedule 6 to the 1985 Act set out the basic disclosure requirements for directors' remuneration that apply to all companies. These requirements were last revised significantly in 1997. A quoted company that has to prepare a directors' remuneration report, as described below, is exempt from all but paragraph 1 of Schedule 5 to the Accounting Regulations and paragraph 1 of Schedule 6 to the 1985 Act.

In 1995, following media interest about the amount of remuneration directors of large companies were earning, the Greenbury Committee published a report recommending various additional disclosures to be made in listed company accounts. Most of these recommendations were subsequently incorporated into the Combined Code and the Listing Rules. In 2002, the Directors' Remuneration Report Regulations introduced a statutory requirement for quoted companies (as defined) to prepare a directors' remuneration report. The requirements for this report are now in Schedule 8 to the Accounting Regulations and Schedule 7A to the 1985 Act and provide for extensive disclosures about the remuneration of individual directors.

There is a great deal of duplication between the Companies Act requirements and the Listing Rules. It was hoped that the requirements of the Listing Rules would be removed following the introduction of similar statutory requirements. This has not yet happened although the Financial Services Authority (FSA) has indicated its intention to do so in due course. It is understood that the FSA is liaising with BERR with a view to some aspects of the Listing Rules being incorporated into the statutory requirements although the opportunity has been missed to do this in the Accounting Regulations under the 2006 Act. The Listing Rules will then be amended to delete the duplicated requirements. Although there is a great deal of duplication between the Companies Acts and the Listing Rules, there are some important differences and care must be taken to ensure that all disclosures are given. The differences are highlighted in the section of this chapter dealing with the requirements of the Listing Rules.

This chapter is divided into the following sections:

- **Section 2** deals with the requirements which apply to unquoted companies including, for this purpose, AIM companies;
- **Section 3** covers the basic requirements that apply to quoted companies including the definition of such companies;
- **Section 4** sets out the requirements for a directors' remuneration report as required by Schedule 8 to the Accounting Regulations and Schedule 7A to the 1985 Act for a quoted company;
- **Section 5** covers the requirements of Schedule 5 to the Accounting Regulations and Schedule 6 to the 1985 Act that apply to quoted companies;
- **Section 6** deals with matters of interpretation which are generally common to the Companies Act requirements;
- **Section 7** deals with the requirements of the Listing Rules;
- **Section 8** deals with the requirements of the Combined Code although most of these were removed from the Code when it was revised in 2003;
- **Section 9** refers to additional sources of disclosure requirements that may be relevant in some cases; and
- **Section 10** deals with future developments.

The compensation of key management personnel (including, but not restricted to, directors) must also be disclosed under IAS 24 *Related Party Disclosures* (see **chapter 32**).

2 Unquoted companies (including AIM companies)

2.1 Disclosure requirements of Schedule 5 to the Accounting Regulations and Schedule 6 to the 1985 Act

Schedule 5 to the Accounting Regulations and Schedule 6 to the 1985 Act require disclosure of various amounts which fall under four general headings: remuneration; increases to pensions and other retirement benefits; compensation payments; and payments to third parties. The disclosures are required to be in the notes to the accounts and, in the main, are required for the directors in aggregate. Additionally, in certain instances specified details have to be disclosed for the highest paid director (see **2.2** below). The disclosures in respect of the directors in aggregate are as follows:

(a) *Remuneration*: disclosure is required of the aggregate for each of the following (see **6.2** to **6.6** for interpretation):

<table>
<tr><th>Companies whose securities are traded on AIM</th><th>Companies whose securities are not traded on AIM</th></tr>
<tr><td colspan="2">Emoluments paid to or receivable by directors in respect of qualifying services including salary, fees and bonuses, sums paid by way of expenses allowance so far as chargeable to UK income tax and the estimated money value of non-cash benefits but excluding:
• share options granted to a director;
• gains made on the exercise of share options;
• Contributions paid, or treated as paid, to a pension scheme by a person other than the director in respect of whom the contributions are made;
• any benefits to which a director is entitled under a pension scheme;
• any money or other assets paid to or received or receivable by the director under a long-term incentive scheme. [Acc Regs Sch. 5: 9(1)(2), previously CA 1985 Sch. 6: 1(1) and (3)]</td></tr>
<tr><td>Gains made by directors on the exercise of share options (being the difference between the market price of the shares on the date of exercise and the price paid for the shares). [Acc Regs Sch. 5: 1(1), previously CA 1985 Sch. 6: 1(1) and (5)]</td><td>The number of directors who exercised share options. [Acc Regs Sch. 5: 1(3)(a), previously CA 1985 Sch. 6: 1(2)]</td></tr>
<tr><td>Money paid to or receivable by directors, together with the net value of other assets (other than share options) received or receivable by directors under long-term incentive schemes in respect of qualifying services. [Acc Regs Sch. 5: 1(1)(c), previously CA 1985 Sch. 6: 1(1)]</td><td>Money paid to or receivable by directors, together with the net value of other assets (other than shares and share options) received or receivable by directors under long-term incentive schemes in respect of qualifying services. [Acc Regs Sch. 5: 1(1)(c), previously CA 1985 Sch. 6: 1(1) and (2)]</td></tr>
</table>

<table>
<tr><th>Companies whose securities are traded on AIM</th><th>Companies whose securities are not traded on AIM</th></tr>
<tr><td></td><td>The number of directors in respect of whose qualifying services shares were received or receivable under long-term incentive schemes. [Acc Regs Sch. 5: 1(3)(b), previously CA 1985 Sch. 6: 1(2)]</td></tr>
<tr><td colspan="2">The value of contributions paid, or treated as paid, to a pension scheme by a person other than the director to whom retirement benefits are accruing in respect of directors' qualifying services to the extent that the contributions might lead to money purchase benefits being payable [Acc Regs Sch. 5: 1(1)(d), previously CA 1985 Sch. 6: 1(1)] (see 6.6).</td></tr>
<tr><td colspan="2">The number of directors, if any, to whom retirement benefits are accruing in respect of qualifying services in respect of each of:
• money purchase schemes; and
• defined benefit schemes. [Acc Regs Sch. 5: 1(2), previously CA 1985 Sch. 6: 1(1)]</td></tr>
</table>

(b) *Increases to pensions and other retirement benefits*: the aggregate of directors' and past directors' pensions and other retirement benefits payable under pension schemes in excess of the pensions and other benefits to which they were entitled on the later of the date the pensions and other benefits first became payable and 31 March 1997. The nature of any non-cash benefit must also be disclosed; [Acc Regs Sch. 5: 3(1), previously CA 1985 Sch. 6: 7]

(c) *Compensation for loss of office*: aggregate compensation, including non-cash benefits, to directors or past directors in respect of loss of office. The nature of any non-cash benefit must also be disclosed [Acc Regs Sch. 5: 4, previously CA 1985 Sch. 6: 8] (see **6.7** below); and

(d) *Consideration paid to third parties*: aggregate consideration, including non-cash consideration, paid to or receivable by third parties for making available the services of any person as a director of the company or, while director of the company, as director of any of its subsidiaries or otherwise in connection with the management of the affairs of the company or any of its subsidiaries. The nature of any non-cash consideration must also be disclosed [Acc Regs Sch. 5: 5, previously CA 1985 Sch. 6: 9] (see **6.8** below).

Awards under annual bonus schemes are included in emoluments whether payable to directors in cash, shares or some other assets. The inclusion of shares applies for all companies, irrespective of whether their securities are traded on AIM. This contrasts with awards in the form of shares under long-term incentive schemes where there is one treatment for companies whose securities are traded on AIM and another treatment for all other companies.

The 1985 Act specifically states that (other than for the aggregate of gains made on the exercise of options, for increases in pensions and other retirement benefits (see **4.2.6**) and for sums paid to third parties) information shall be treated as shown if it is capable of being readily ascertained from other information which is shown. [Sch. 6: 1(6)(a), 2(6) and 8(5)] In the Accounting Regulations, this exemption has been extended to cover all information which is required to be disclosed under Schedule 6. [Acc Regs Sch. 5: 6(2)]

2.2 Highest paid director

2.2.1 *Threshold for disclosures*

Certain details about the highest paid director have to be disclosed for any company (other than a quoted company) where the total of the following three elements of aggregate directors' remuneration is £200,000 or more in any accounting period (regardless of its length). [Acc Regs Sch. 5: 2(1), previously CA 1985 Sch. 6: 2(1)]

Companies whose securities are traded on AIM	**Companies whose securities are not traded on AIM**
Emoluments paid to or receivable by directors in respect of qualifying services.	
Gains made by directors on the exercise of share options.	N/a.
Money and the net value of other assets (other than share options) paid to or receivable by directors under long-term incentive schemes in respect of qualifying services.	Money and the net value of other assets (other than shares and share options) paid to or receivable by directors under long-term incentive schemes in respect of qualifying services.

2.2.2 *Required disclosures*

The highest paid director is the one to whom is attributable the greatest part of the total of the three items listed in **2.2.1** above. [Acc Regs Sch. 5: 10, previously CA 1985 Sch. 6: 2(5)]

The details that have to be disclosed about the highest paid director, who need not be named, are:

(a) the total of the three items in **2.2.1** above that is attributable to the highest paid director; [Acc Regs Sch. 5: 2(1)(a), previously CA 1985 Sch. 6: 2(1)]

(b) the amount of contributions to pension schemes attributable to the highest paid director's qualifying services in respect of which money purchase benefits may be payable; [Acc Regs Sch. 5: 2(1)(b), previously CA 1985 Sch. 6: 2(1)]

(c) for companies whose securities are not traded on AIM, if the highest paid director exercised any share options, that fact should be disclosed and, if any shares were received or receivable by that director in respect of qualifying services under a long-term incentive scheme, that fact should be disclosed; [Acc Regs Sch. 5: 2(3)(a)(b), previously CA 1985 Sch. 6: 2(3)(a)(b)] and

This disclosure is not required for companies whose securities are traded on AIM because the amounts disclosed will include amounts for gains on share options and the value of any shares received or receivable under LTIPs.

(d) where the pension accruing to the highest paid director as a result of his or her qualifying services is either of the defined benefit type or is under a hybrid scheme that might make defined benefit payments, the following has to be disclosed:
[Acc Regs Sch.5: 2(2), previously CA 1985 Sch. 6: 2(2)]

   (i) the amount at the end of the year of the accrued pension; and

   (ii) the amount, if any, of the accrued lump sum.

In disclosing the accrued pension and the accrued lump sum, no account shall be taken of the possible effect of commutation of the pension or inverse commutation of the lump sum. [Acc Regs Sch. 5: 13(2), previously CA 1985 Sch. 6: 2(5)] An example of the calculation of the amount of accrued pension is included at **4.2.5.4** below.

For UK pension schemes, there will not usually be a lump sum to disclose because a person's entitlement will be to a pension on retirement. The scheme rules may provide for an employee to take a lump sum on retirement in exchange for accepting a reduced pension. This is known as a 'commutation' and the law specifies that this should be ignored when disclosing the accrued pension. The reference to 'inverse commutation' is to circumstances where a person has a basic entitlement to a lump sum but elects to take a pension in exchange for a reduced lump sum. This is unlikely to arise with a UK pension scheme.

In determining which director is the highest paid director, companies whose securities are traded on AIM have to include gains made on the exercise of options. This could result in the person meeting the definition of highest paid director changing from one year to the next. Comparatives are required to all the directors' remuneration disclosures. Accordingly, where one director is the highest paid in the current year and a different director was the highest paid in the previous year, the comparative to the current disclosure will be in respect of the person who was the highest paid director in that previous year (rather than giving last year's remuneration for the director who is the highest paid in the current year).

Where a company has to give disclosure of the highest paid director's remuneration in 20X1, but not in 20X2 (because the threshold triggering the disclosure is not met in 20X2), what disclosure, if any, is required in the 20X2 accounts? It is normal practice, where a disclosure is required one year but not the next, for the subsequent year's accounts (for 20X2 in this case) to contain the information for the comparative period and this approach should be applied here. Thus, although there will be no information about the highest paid director's remuneration for 20X2, the information about 20X1 should again be given. It may be appropriate to provide a narrative explanation of why no disclosure is required for 20X2 to avoid confusion.

Conversely, where a company did not have to give disclosure of the highest paid director's remuneration one year, say 20X1, but is required to give the disclosure the following year (because the threshold triggering the disclosure is met), is a comparative required in the 20X2 accounts? IAS 1.36 requires comparative information to be given for the previous period for all amounts reported in the financial statements, except when a Standard or Interpretation permits or requires otherwise. Accordingly, in the 20X2 accounts, as well as giving the information required about the highest paid director in 20X2, there should be stated, by way of comparative, the information about the highest paid director in 20X1 (even though this was not disclosed in the 20X1 accounts themselves).

3 Quoted companies

3.1 Introduction

This section explains the requirement for a quoted company to prepare a directors' remuneration report and considers the definition of 'quoted company' for this purpose. **Section 4** sets out the requirements for a directors' remuneration report in accordance with Schedule 8 to the Accounting Regulations and Schedule 7A to the 1985 Act. **Section 5** covers the requirements of Schedule 6 that apply to quoted companies. **Section 6** deals with matters of interpretation and **section 7** deals with the requirements of the Listing Rules.

3.2 Scope

The disclosures on directors' remuneration dealt with in this section apply only to quoted companies. A 'quoted company' for this purpose means a company whose equity share capital:

[CA 2006 s385; previously 1985 CA s262]

(a) has been included in the official list in accordance with the provisions of Part 6 of the Financial Services and Markets Act 2000; or

(b) is officially listed in an EEA State; or

(c) is admitted to dealing on either the New York Stock Exchange or the exchange known as Nasdaq.

In paragraph (a) above, the 'official list' has the meaning given in section 103(1) of the Financial Services and Markets Act 2000. EEA is the European Economic Area and an EEA state is one in the EU, Norway, Iceland or Liechtenstein.

Under s241A of the 1985 Act, any company that is a quoted company immediately before the end of its financial year is required to obtain shareholder approval of its remuneration report. As a result of this requirement, a company that ceases to be quoted after its year-end will still need to produce a remuneration report in accordance with Schedule 7A to the 1985 Act. The position is the same under the 2006 Act. Section 420 requires the directors of a quoted company to prepare a directors' remuneration report for each financial year of the company. Section 385 defines a quoted company (see above) and also clarifies that, for the purposes of Part 15 of the Act, a company is a quoted company, in relation to a financial year, if it is a quoted company immediately before the end of the accounting reference period by reference to which that financial year was determined.

AIM companies and companies which have only debt or non-equity share capital listed do not fall within the scope of the requirements set out in this section. Some AIM companies voluntarily give additional information about the remuneration of individual directors and some comply in full with the requirements for a directors' remuneration report under the law and the Listing Rules. However, it is important that a misleading impression of full compliance is not given where full compliance has not in fact been achieved.

The definition of 'equity share capital' for this purpose is a matter of law and is unconnected with whether the share capital is accounted for as equity or as a liability in accordance with IAS 32. Where a company has only preference shares listed, it *may* be within the scope of the requirements set out in this section. Under the Acts, a share which carries an uncapped right to participate in either a revenue or capital distribution is an equity share.[CA 2006 s548; previously CA 1985 s744] For example, a preference share carrying fixed dividend rights but which carries unrestricted rights on a winding-up would meet the Companies Acts definition of an equity share. Thus, where such shares are listed, the company is required to apply Schedule 8 to the Accounting Regulations or Schedule 7A to the 1985 Act, even if no other shares are listed.

3.3 Requirements

3.3.1 Directors' remuneration report by the board

In addition to the disclosures required by paragraph 1 of Schedule 5 to the Accounting Regulations and Schedule 6 to the 1985 Act, which are set out in **section 5** below, the directors of a quoted company (see **3.2** above) are required by the Act to include a directors' remuneration report in the annual report. The report should contain the information specified in Schedule 8 to the Accounting Regulations and Schedule 7A to the 1985 Act. [CA 2006 s420, previously CA 1985 s234B] The form and content of this report, as required by Schedule 8 to the Accounting Regulations and Schedule 7A to the 1985 Act, is dealt with in **section 4**. Supplementary information and interpretation of the terms are in **section 6.**

When information is required to be included in the report in respect of a particular person, it should be linked to that person by their name. [Acc Regs Sch. 8: 1(2), previously CA 1985 Sch. 7A: 1(2)]

As a result of the requirement above, the Act does not require details of the highest paid director to be disclosed separately as details are given for all directors by name.

The 'relevant financial year' is the financial year for which the financial statements and directors' remuneration report are being produced. [CA 2006 s420(1), Sch. 8: 1(1), previously CA 1985 s234B(1), Sch. 7A: 1(1)]

3.3.2 Shareholder vote

The Act requires the directors' remuneration report to be put to a shareholder vote as an ordinary resolution. [CA 2006 s439(1), previously CA 1985 s241A(3)] No entitlement of a person to remuneration is made conditional on the resolution being passed. [CA 2006 s439(5), previously CA 1985 s241A(8)]

Although, under the Regulations, companies are required to put their directors' remuneration report to a shareholder vote, the inclusion of subsection (5) in s439 of the 2006 Act and (8) in s241A of the 1985 Act makes the vote advisory only. Therefore, the vote cannot alter the amount that the company has contracted to pay to the directors.

4 Content of directors' remuneration report

The Act specifies that some of the disclosures in the directors' remuneration report are subject to audit but that some are not. The report should distinguish between the audited and unaudited disclosures as explained at **4.2.1** below. This is usually achieved by dividing the report into audited and unaudited sections.

4.1 Information not subject to audit

4.1.1 Consideration by the directors of matters relating to directors' remuneration

If a committee of the company's directors has considered matters relating to the directors' remuneration for the relevant financial year, the directors' remuneration report should:

[Acc Regs Sch. 8: 2, previously CA 1985 Sch. 7A: 2]

(a) name each director who was a member of the committee at any time when the committee was considering any such matter;

(b) name any person (including directors not named under (a)) who provided to the committee advice or services that materially assisted the committee in its consideration of any such matter; and

Supporting principles B.2 in the Combined Code states that remuneration committees should consult the chairman and/or CEO. This is not a code provision in the 2006 or 2008 Code although it was a provision in the original Code. Nevertheless, most companies would be expected to follow this principle. Accordingly, companies stating that they comply with the provisions in the Combined Code will probably name the chairman and/or CEO to meet the requirement described in (b) above.

A person must be named in (b) if he or she materially assisted the committee in its consideration of the directors' remuneration for the relevant financial year. A person therefore does not need to be named if he or she only assisted in drafting the report or in determining remuneration for subsequent years. Similarly, if a person provides factual information, e.g. salary or Total Shareholder Return (TSR) details for comparator companies, this on its own would not amount to material assistance.

The disclosure required under (b) is the name of the 'person'. In the case of a remuneration consultancy, the required disclosure is the name of the consultancy rather than the name of the individual consultant within the consultancy.

(c) in the case of any person named under (b), who is not a director of the company, state the nature of any other services that they provided to the company during the relevant financial year and whether they were appointed by the committee.

The Act does not require a list of names of the committee members during the year or at the date the remuneration report is signed. Instead, it requires the names of those persons who were members *at any time* when the committee considered *matters relating to the directors' remuneration for the relevant financial year.*

4.1.1.1 *Services provided to the remuneration committee*

Some companies have chosen to give a brief summary of the services provided to the committee by those giving it material assistance.

4.1.2 *Policy on directors' remuneration*

The directors' remuneration report should contain a statement of the company's policy on directors' remuneration for the following financial year and for financial years subsequent to that. [Acc Regs Sch. 8: 3(1), previously CA 1985 Sch. 7A: 3(1)]

The policy statement is required to include the following:

[Acc Regs Sch. 8: 3(2)(3) and (4), previously CA 1985 Sch. 7A: 3(2), (3) and (4)]

(a) for each director (see next paragraph for definition), a detailed summary of any performance conditions to which any entitlement of the director to share options, or under a long-term incentive scheme, is subject;

(b) an explanation as to why any such performance conditions were chosen;

(c) a summary of the methods to be used in assessing whether any such performance conditions are met and an explanation as to why those methods were chosen;

(d) if any such performance condition involves any comparison with factors external to the company:

  (i) a summary of the factors to be used in making each such comparison, and

  (ii) if any of the factors relates to the performance of another company, of two or more other companies or of an index on which the securities of a company or companies are listed, the identity of that company, of each of those companies or of the index;

(e) a description of, and an explanation for, any significant amendment proposed to be made to the terms and conditions of any entitlement of a director to share options or under a long-term incentive scheme;

(f) if any entitlement of a director to share options, or under a long-term incentive scheme, is not subject to performance conditions, an explanation as to why that is the case;

(g) in respect of each director's terms and conditions relating to remuneration, an explanation of the relative importance of those elements which are, and those which are not, related to performance; and

(h) a summary and explanation of the company's policy on the duration of contracts with directors, and the notice periods, and termination payments, under such contracts.

In the preceding paragraph, where information is required to be shown for a director, it must be given for any person who serves as a director of the company at any time during the period which starts at the end of the relevant financial year and finishes on the date when the directors' remuneration report is laid before the company in general meeting. [Acc Regs Sch. 8: 3(5), previously CA 1985 Sch. 7A: 3(5)]

Under the Listing Rules, companies have to give a statement of the company's policy on executive directors' remuneration (for which there is no specified minimum disclosure) and a statement on the company's policy on the granting of options or awards under its employee share schemes and other long-term incentive schemes together with details of any departure from policy or changes in policy during the period. The statutory requirements considerably expand on these.

There is no exemption from the disclosure of performance criteria on the grounds of commercial sensitivity. However, performance criteria for annual bonuses, where the conditions are more likely to be commercially sensitive, do not have to be disclosed.

For a remuneration report relating to the year to 31 December 20X1, Schedule 8 to the Accounting Regulations and Schedule 7A to the 1985 Act will require disclosure about policy for 20X2 and beyond. Since LTIPs and most share options have conditions which must be met over a number of years, typically, at least three, the question arises as to whether the disclosure is required in respect of a scheme which is part way through the performance period at 31 December 20X1 (e.g. is two years through a three year performance period). The argument against disclosure is that the performance criteria were determined, and the scheme set up, in earlier years. The argument for disclosure is that performance in the following year(s) affects the amount of remuneration received in future years. It is suggested that in such instances disclosure should be given.

Disclosure on general policy could usefully cover those matters set out in paragraph 5.5 of the Greenbury Report that are relevant to the company. Most of the points in paragraph 5.5 are covered in Schedule 8 to the Accounting Regulations and Schedule 7A to the 1985 Act as set out above. Four points which are not covered and could be considered are:

(a) the total level of remuneration;

(b) the main parameters and rationale for annual bonus schemes, including caps;

(c) the policy on allowing executives to accept outside appointments and retain payments from sources outside the company; and

(d) the pension and retirement benefit schemes for directors, including the type of scheme, the main terms and parameters, what elements of remuneration are pensionable, how the HMRC pensions' cap has been accommodated and whether the scheme is part of, or separate from, the main company scheme.

Although the statement on policy called for by the Listing Rules relates only to executive directors, the statement on policy required by Schedule 8 to the Accounting Regulations and Schedule 7A to the 1985 Act simply refers to directors' remuneration and thus includes both executive and non-executive directors. The policy in respect of non-executive directors will generally be best dealt with in a free-standing paragraph.

4.1.3 Performance graph

The report should contain a line graph that shows for each of:

(a) a holding of shares of that class of the company's equity share capital which have resulted in the company meeting the definition of 'quoted company', i.e. the class of shares that are listed, and

(b) a hypothetical holding of shares made up of shares of the same kinds and number as those underlying a broad equity market index (e.g. a company in the FTSE-100 may choose the FTSE-100),

a line drawn by joining up points plotted to represent, for each of the five financial years ending with the relevant financial year, the total shareholder return on that holding. [Acc Regs Sch. 8: 5(1) and (2), previously CA 1985 Sch. 7A: 4(1) and (2)] Thus a company in the FTSE-100 may choose to plot the Total Shareholder Return (TSR) for itself and, in aggregate, for the companies in the FTSE-100. Where the company has been in existence for less than five financial years, the period shown by the graph is shortened to the number of years for which the company has been in existence (ending with the relevant financial year). [Acc Regs Sch. 8: 5(3), previously CA 1985 Sch. 7A: 4(3)]

If a company was formed over five years ago, but has only satisfied the definition of quoted for the last three years, the letter of the legislation would require the graph to be plotted for five years. However, it would appear reasonable if such a company were to plot the graph just for the three years since it became quoted and to explain this.

The name of the index chosen for the purposes of the graph must be stated along with the reasons for selecting it. [Acc Regs Sch. 8: 5(1)(b), previously CA 1985 Sch. 7A: 4(1)]

The index to be plotted is not prescribed. The Act refers simply to a 'broad equity market index'. Indices that companies can choose from are: FTSE 100; FTSE 250; FTSE 350; mid 250; and All-cap. Although the reference to 'broad' should permit established sector indices to be used providing they comprise a reasonable number of companies, the use of 'bespoke' indices is not permitted. An index comprising ten or fewer companies is unlikely to be acceptable.

It is, however, acceptable for companies to include more than one performance graph in their report, so long as at least one complies with Schedule 8 to the Accounting Regulations or Schedule 7A to the 1985 Act. This approach gives companies the flexibility to provide what they believe to be most relevant information. For example, they may wish to illustrate their performance against a bespoke comparator group used in their long term incentive plan, or to show performance over the three year period over which a plan vested.

For the purposes of plotting the graph referred to above:

(a) 'total shareholder return' for the relevant period on a holding of shares must be calculated using a fair method that:

(i) takes as its starting point the percentage change over the period in the market price of the holding;

(ii) involves making the assumptions specified in (b) and (c) below for reinvestment of income and the funding of liabilities; and

(iii) makes provision for any replacement of shares in the holding by shares of a different description.

The same method must be used for the company's shares and for the shares underlying the chosen index; [Acc Regs Sch. 8: 5(4), previously CA 1985 Sch. 7A: 4(4)]

(b) the assumptions as to reinvestment of income are that any benefit (which is any benefit, including, in particular, any dividend, receivable in respect of any shares in the holding by the holder from the company of whose share capital the shares form part):

(i) in the form of shares of the same kind as those in the holding is added to the holding at the time the benefit becomes receivable, thus if a scrip, rather than cash, dividend were paid by a company, the number of shares paid out by dividend would be added to the holding from the dividend payment date; and

(ii) in cash, and an amount equal to the value of any non-cash benefit (excluding shares falling within (i)), is used at the time the benefit becomes receivable, to purchase the same kind of shares as those in the holding, at their market price. The shares purchased are added to the holding at that time; [Acc Regs Sch. 8: 5(5) and (6), previously CA 1985 Sch. 7A: 4(5) and (6)] and

(c) the assumption as to the funding of liabilities is that, where holders have a liability to the company, in which they have their holding of shares (being a liability arising in respect of any shares in the holding or from the exercise of a right attached to any of those shares), shares are sold from the holding:

(i) immediately before the time by which the liability is due to be satisfied, and

(ii) in such numbers that, at the time of the sale, the market price of the shares sold equals the amount of the liability in respect of the shares in the holding that are not being sold.[Acc Regs Sch. 8: 5(7) and (8), previously CA 1985 Sch. 7A: 4(7) and (8)]

It is unclear whether the index line required by Schedule 8 to the Accounting Regulations and Schedule 7A to the 1985 Act is intended to be weighted or unweighted. The Act requires the TSR of the notional investment to be calculated using 'shares of the same kinds and number as those by reference to which a broad equity market index is calculated'. One argument is that the reference to 'number' implies that a weighted TSR should be calculated whereas the counter argument is that it means the same number of constituent companies as is in the index should be used.

Another issue is that the companies in the index will change over the five years. Taking the FTSE 100 as an example, the 100 companies comprising the FTSE 100 on day 1 of the five year period are unlikely to be the same 100 companies making up the index on the last day. One option is to take the companies that make up the index at the start of the five-year period and plot the TSR for those companies over the five years, notwithstanding that some of them will not be in the FTSE 100 by the end. Another option would be to assume the investment in a company is sold at the point it leaves the FTSE 100 and the hypothetical proceeds are invested in shares in whichever company replaces it. The first option would appear to be preferable. Under the second option, the TSR for the index is likely to be skewed upwards as it rejects companies whose share price is performing badly. A further issue to address if weighted TSR is calculated is what to do if the weightings of the companies alter over the five-year period. Again, it would appear appropriate to calculate using the initial weightings only. In the absence of further guidance, it is suggested that companies choose one of the options (e.g. plot an unweighted index for the companies in the index at the start of the five year period), use this consistently and explain in the remuneration report the approach adopted.

Schedule 8 to the Accounting Regulations and Schedule 7A to the 1985 Act require points to be plotted for each of the five years ending with the relevant financial year and for a line to join up these points. Two issues arise from this phraseology. The first is should the TSR each year be the TSR for the year only or should it be the cumulative TSR from the start of the five year period? It is understood that BERR intended the graph to be cumulative not annual. The second issue is whether a straight line should join up the points or whether it can be a fluctuating line? Although the legislation might lead a reader to assume that a straight line is required, a fluctuating line does not appear to be ruled out. The legislation simply requires a 'line' (not a 'straight line'). If a straight line joins up the points, then the only points on the line which represent TSR will be the points at each year end, whereas if a fluctuating line is plotted any point on it will represent the TSR at that time.

Additional graphs

Companies should consider whether they wish additionally to plot the performance of the criteria used in the operation of their LTIP or option scheme, which might be, for example, the TSR of ten named comparator companies. Some companies have chosen to plot additional graphs whilst others have put additional lines on to the graph required by Schedule 8 to the Accounting Regulations and Schedule 7A to the 1985 Act.

Averaging period

Either spot or average TSR values can be used, provided that the same basis is used for both lines. Where average values are used, a 30 day average is common. A longer period such as three months may be acceptable. But one year averaging is unacceptable because it would smooth out any trends in the data. The basis of averaging should be disclosed.

Mean or median

The requirement to illustrate performance against a broad market index suggests that it is the mean that should be plotted. An alternative approach would be to track the median company of the index which would remove the influence of the outliers in the group. But this approach is not generally regarded as acceptable because only one company's performance would be shown (i.e. the median performer).

Reinvestment of dividends

Schedule 8 to the Accounting Regulations and Schedule 7A to 1985 Act stipulate that income should be reinvested when receivable. Reinvesting gross would remove the need to make any assumptions about the individual's marginal tax rate. Reinvesting net would reflect the actual income received. Reinvesting on the ex-dividend date would reflect the last day at which shareholders would be entitled to the dividend and is also the point at which the share price adjusts. Reinvesting on the payment date would reflect the actual date on which income is received. The most common approach appears to be to assume that dividends are reinvested gross on the ex-dividend date.

Indices which have existed for less than five years

If the index did not exist five years previous to the year end, the TSR graph could be compiled using the median for five years of the companies in the index at the year end. Alternatively, it would be possible to use the companies in the index for the period during which it existed and compile information for the period prior to this using the companies in the index on day one. It would not be acceptable to plot a graph for less than five years.

4.1.4 Service contracts

The directors' remuneration report should contain, for the contract of service or contract for services of each person who has served as a director of the company at any time during the relevant financial year, the following information:

[Acc Regs Sch. 8: 6(1), previously CA 1985 Sch. 7A: 5(1)]

(a) the date of the contract, the unexpired term and the details of any notice periods;

(b) any provision for compensation payable upon early termination of the contract; and

(c) such details of other provisions in the contract as are necessary to enable members of the company to estimate the liability of the company in the event of early termination of the contract.

The directors' remuneration report should also contain an explanation for any significant award made to a person in the circumstances described in **4.2.7**. [Acc Regs Sch. 8: 6(2), previously CA 1985 Sch. 7A: 5(2)]

Large compensation payments to directors on loss of office, particularly those on two or more years rolling contracts, have given rise to much high-profile criticism. The Combined Code recommends, therefore, that directors' service contracts should normally have notice periods of no more than one year.

Schedule 8 to the Accounting Regulations and Schedule 7A to the 1985 Act require a number of disclosures that are additional to those required by the Listing Rules. Details of all notice periods and all provisions for compensation payable on early termination must be disclosed. The Listing Rules only require disclosure of notice periods in excess of one year and provisions which exceed one year's salary. However, the Listing Rules additionally require disclosure of the reason for a notice period that is in excess of one year.

4.2 Information subject to audit

4.2.1 General

Bulletin 2002/2 'The United Kingdom Directors' Remuneration Report Regulations 2002', issued by the Auditing Practices Board, recommends that directors indicate in the remuneration report which disclosures have been audited.

4.2.2 Amount of each director's emoluments and compensation in the relevant financial year

For each person who has served as a director of the company at any time during the relevant financial year, disclosure should be made, in tabular form, of the total amount of each of the following paid to or receivable by that person in respect of qualifying services (see **6.2** below) for the relevant financial year:

[Acc Regs Sch. 8: 7(1), (2) and (4), previously CA 1985 Sch. 7A: 6(1), (2) and (4)]

(a) salary and fees;

(b) bonuses;

(c) sums paid by way of expenses allowance that are chargeable to UK income tax (or would be if the person were an individual);

(d) compensation for loss of office and other payments in connection with the termination of qualifying services (see **6.7**);

(e) estimated value of any benefits received by the person otherwise than in cash, not disclosed within any of sub-paragraphs (a) – (d) above or within **4.2.3** and **4.2.4** (i.e. share options and LTIPs);

(f) the amount that is the total of the sums disclosed above under (a) to (e); and

(g) the total of the amounts in paragraphs (a) to (e) for the financial year preceding the relevant financial year.

The directors' remuneration report should state the nature of any element of a remuneration package, which is not cash. [Acc Regs Sch. 8: 7(3), previously CA 1985 Sch. 7A: 6(3)]

The totals of (a) to (e) for the previous financial year must be shown for each person. This is required only for persons who were directors during the current year but it is usual to show amounts in respect of former directors in the comparative period. In some cases it may be appropriate to show former directors in aggregate.

4.2.3 *Information on share options*

The following information on share options, including SAYE options, should be given for each person who has served as a director of the company at any time in the relevant financial year ((a) to (c) must be given in tabular form):

[Acc Regs Sch. 8: 8, previously CA 1985 Sch. 7A: 8]

(a) the number of shares that are subject to a share option:

  (i) at the beginning of the relevant financial year (or date of appointment if later); and

  (ii) at the end of the relevant financial year (or on the cessation of appointment if earlier);

  (iii) in each case differentiating between share options having different terms and conditions;

(b) the information identifying those share options which, during the relevant financial year:

(i) were awarded;

(ii) were exercised;

(iii) expired unexercised; and

(iv) had their terms and conditions varied;

(c) for each share option that is unexpired at any time in the relevant financial year:

(i) price paid, if any, for its award;

(ii) exercise price;

(iii) date from which the option may be exercised; and

(iv) the expiry date of the option;

(d) a description of any variation made in the relevant financial year in the terms and conditions of a share option;

(e) a summary of any performance criteria upon which the award or exercise of a share option is conditional, including a description of any variation made in such performance criteria during the relevant financial year;

(f) for each share option that has been exercised during the relevant financial year, the market price of the shares at the date of exercise; and

(g) for each share option that is unexpired at the end of the relevant financial year, the following details of each share that is subject to the option:

(i) the market price at the end of that year; and

(ii) the highest and lowest market prices during that year.

The table required by Schedule 8 to the Accounting Regulations and Schedule 7A to the 1985 Act should deal only with options granted to a person for 'qualifying services' whereas the aggregate disclosure required by paragraph 1 of Schedule 5 to the Accounting Regulations and Schedule 6 to the 1985 Act makes no such distinction (i.e. it includes options granted to or acquired by the director prior to appointment). There is therefore a potential inconsistency between the amounts which should be disclosed. This should be explained if relevant.

Given users' expectations, companies are likely to wish to give disclosure about all options. In this case those granted since a person became a director should be identified, say, by marking those granted before or after appointment as a director (whichever is easier) with an asterisk and including an appropriate explanation in a footnote. In the absence of any disclosure to the contrary it should be presumed that all options have been granted in respect of qualifying services.

Schedule 8 to the Accounting Regulations and Schedule 7A to the 1985 Act require that information on share options, including SAYE options, should be given for each person who has served as a director of the company at any time in the relevant financial year. Accordingly, a person must be included in the table even if he or she ceased to be a director part way through the accounting period.

The equivalent requirements of the Listing Rules refer to 'any share options, including 'Save-as-you earn' options, for each director, by name, in accordance with the requirements of the Directors' Remuneration Report Regulations'. Therefore meeting the statutory requirements in this respect will ensure compliance with the Listing Rules.

Schedule 8 to the Accounting Regulations and Schedule 7A to the 1985 Act do not require the gain on exercise of options in the period to be quantified for each director but ensures that sufficient information is made available for the gains to be calculated. Paragraphs 1 of Schedule 8 and Schedule 6 require the aggregate gains on exercise of options for all directors to be disclosed, but not individual amounts. It is, however, regarded as good practice to disclose the gains for each director.

The following example illustrates how the disclosures required by Schedule 8 to the Accounting Regulations and Schedule 7A to the 1985 Act could be presented.

Example 4.2.3

Example illustration of A plc
Year ended 31 December 20X5

	Scheme	Number of options during the year					Exercise price	Market price at date of exercise	Date from which exercisable	Expiry date
		At 01.01.X5	Granted	Lapsed	Exercised	At 31.12.X5				
Sam Smith	ESOS	100	–	–	(100)	–	50p	130p	31.12.X4	31.12.X9
Janet Jones	ESOS	100	–	–	–	100	50p	–	31.12.X4	31.12.X9
	ESOS	–	50	–	–	50	120p	–	31.12.X8	31.12.Y3
	SAYE	300	–	–	–	300	100p	–	31.12.X5	31.12.X7
Rob Right	ESOS	200	–	–	(100)	100	50p	120p	31.12.X4	31.12.X9
	SAYE	300	–	–	–	300	100p	–	31.12.X5	31.12.X7
Chris Clark	ESOS	100	–	–	–	100	150p	–	31.12.X6	31.12.Y1
	ESOS	–	50	–	–	50	120p	–	31.12.X8	31.12.13

Exercise of options under the Executive Share Option Scheme is subject to meeting the performance criteria that earnings per share growth over the first three years of an options life would place the Company in the upper quartile of the FTSE 100 companies.

The market price of the ordinary shares at 31.12.X5 was 140p and the range during the year was 106p to 142p.

Key

ESOS – A plc Executive Share Option Scheme

SAYE – A plc SAYE Share Option Scheme

4.2.3.1 *More concise disclosures allowed for share options*

If, in the opinion of the directors of the company, disclosure in accordance with **4.2.3** would result in a disclosure of excessive length then:

[Acc Regs Sch. 8: 10(1), previously CA 1985 Sch. 7A: 9(1)]

(a) information disclosed for a person under (a) in **4.2.3** need not differentiate between share options having different terms and conditions;

(b) for the purposes of disclosure in respect of a person under (c)(i), (c)(ii) and (g) in **4.2.3**, share options may be aggregated and (instead of disclosing prices for each share option) disclosure may be made of weighted average prices of aggregations of share options; and

(c) for the purposes of disclosure in respect of a person under (c)(iii) and (c)(iv) in **4.2.3**, share options may be aggregated and (instead of disclosing dates for each share option) disclosure may be made of ranges of dates for aggregation of share options.

In the preceding paragraph, (b) and (c) do not permit the aggregation of share options in respect of shares whose market price at the end of the relevant financial year is below the option exercise price ('out of the money'), with those where it is equal to, or exceeds, the option exercise price ('in the money'). [Acc Regs Sch. 8: 10(2), previously CA 1985 Sch. 7A: 9(2)]

The preceding paragraphs do not apply (and accordingly, full disclosure must be made in accordance with **4.2.3**) for share options that during the relevant financial year have been awarded or exercised or had their terms and conditions varied. [Acc Regs Sch. 8: 10(3), previously CA 1985 Sch. 7A: 9(3)]

The disclosures required under the more concise method are laid out below in an easy to follow fashion. The following information must be given:

(a) the number of shares that are subject to a share option: -

(i) at the beginning of the relevant financial year (or date of appointment if later); and

(ii) at the end of the relevant financial year (or on the cessation of appointment if earlier);

(b) the information identifying those share options which, during the relevant financial year:

(i) were awarded;

(ii) were exercised;

(iii) expired unexercised; and

(iv) had their terms and conditions varied;

(c) for each share option that is unexpired at any time in the relevant financial year (excluding those that were granted, exercised or had their terms or conditions varied during the relevant financial year):

(i) the weighted average* price paid, if any, for its award;

(ii) the weighted average* exercise price;

(iii) the range of dates from which the options may be exercised; and

(iv) the range of dates on which the options expire;

(* the weighted average of options out of the money must be shown separately from the weighted average of options whose exercise price is equal to, or below the market price)

(d) a description of any variation made in the relevant financial year in the terms and conditions of a share option;

(e) a summary of any performance criteria upon which the award or exercise of a share option is conditional, including a description of any variation made in such performance criteria during the relevant financial year;

(f) for each share option that has been exercised during the relevant financial year, the market price of the shares at the date of exercise;

(g) for each share option that is unexpired at the end of the relevant financial year, the following details of each share that is subject to the option:

(i) the market price at the end of that year; and

(ii) the highest and lowest market prices during that year; and

(h) for each of the share options that were granted, exercised and/or had their terms or conditions varied during the financial year:-

(i) the number of share options;

(ii) the price paid, if any, for its award;

(iii) exercise price, if applicable;

(iv) date from which the option may be exercised; and

(v) date on which the option expires.

The Act states that (g)(i) and (g)(ii) can be weighted averages, but it is difficult to see how any summarisation can be made.

Where concise rather than full disclosure is adopted, it has previously been regarded as good practice for a reference to be made to the fact that the company's Register of Directors' Interests contains full details of directors' shareholdings and options to subscribe. However, the requirement to maintain such a register was repealed with effect from 6 April 2006 on implementation of the relevant sections of the Companies Act 2006.

The example below illustrates how the disclosure under the more concise approach could be presented.

Example 4.2.3.1

A plc

Year ended 31 December 20X5

Remuneration report (extract)

Share options

A performance condition has to be met before options can be exercised. The performance condition is set each year by the Remuneration Committee, having regard to recommendations of the Investment Protection Committees of the major investing institutions. For options granted in 20X5, the Company's adjusted earnings per share must increase by six percentage points more than the increase in the RPI in a three year period, before the options become exercisable. For all other options, the company's adjusted earnings per share must increase by five percentage points more than RPI in a three year period.

	Ordinary shares under option					Price		Dates	
DIRECTORS' OPTIONS	01/01/ X5	Granted	Exercised	31/12/ X5	Weighted average option price	Option price	Market price on date of exercise	First date from which exercisable	Date option expires
Steve Smith	-	50,000		50,000		550p		01/05/X8	30/04/ Y5
A	30,000			30,000	450p			01/05/X2 – 01/05/X4	30/04/ X9 – 30/04/ Y1
B	60,000			60,000	800p			01/05/X3 – 01/05/X5	30/04/ Y2 – 30/04/ Y6
C	60,000			60,000	700p			01/05/X6 – 01/05/X9	30/04/ Y3 – 30/04/ Y9
Total	150,000	50,000	–	200,000	690p				

DIRECTORS' OPTIONS	Ordinary shares under option					Price		Dates	
	01/01/X5	Granted	Exercised	31/12/X5	Weighted average option price	Option price	Market price on date of exercise	First date from which exercisable	Date option expires
Jenny Jones	-	100,000		100,000		550p		01/05/X8	30/04/Y5
A	80,000			80,000	540p			01/05/X2 – 01/05/X4	30/04/X9 – 30/04/Y1
B	90,000			90,000	700p			01/05/X3 – 01/05/X5	30/04/Y2 – 30/04/Y6
C	130,000			130,000	660p			01/05/X6 – 01/05/X9	30/04/Y3 – 30/04/Y9
Total	300,000	100,000	–	400,000	640p				
Richard Right	-	80,000		80,000		550p		01/05/X8	30/04/Y5
B	140,000			140,000	870p			01/05/X3 – 01/05/X5	30/04/Y2 – 30/04/Y6
C	140,000			140,000	680p			01/05/X6 – 01/05/X9	30/04/Y3 – 30/04/Y9
Total	280,000	80,000	–	360,000	775p				
Wendy White	-	180,000		180,000		550p		01/05/X8	30/04/Y5
	10,000		10,000	-		420p	740p	01/05/X0	30/04/X7
A	30,000			30,000	450p			01/05/X2 – 01/05/X4	30/04/X9 – 30/04/Y1
B	220,000			220,000	880p			01/05/X3 – 01/05/X5	30/04/Y2 – 30/04/Y6
C	250,000			250,000	670p			01/05/05 – 01/05/09	30/04/Y3 – 30/04/Y9
Total	510,000	180,000	10,000	680,000	749p				

Shares under option at 31 December 20X5 are designated as:

A where the options are exercisable and the market price per share at 31 December 20X5 was above the option price;

B where the options are exercisable but the market price at 31 December 20X5 was below the option price; and

C where the options are not yet exercisable.

The market price on 31 December 20X5 was 650p per share and the range during the year was 500p to 850p per share.

4.2.4 *Long-term incentive schemes*

The Act requires specific details to be given of any long-term incentive schemes, other than share option schemes included under the requirements of the previous section (see **4.2.3** above).

Long-term incentive schemes are defined as any agreement or arrangement under which money or other assets may become receivable by a person and which includes one or more qualifying conditions with respect to service or performance that cannot be fulfilled within a single financial year, and for this purpose the following shall be disregarded, namely:

[Acc Regs Sch. 8: 11(5), previously CA 1985 Sch. 7A: 10(5)]

(a) any bonus the amount of which falls to be determined by reference to service or performance within a single financial year;

(b) compensation in respect of loss of office, payments for breach of contract and other termination payments; and

(c) retirement benefits.

In respect of each person who has served as a director of the company at any time in the relevant financial year, disclosure of the following information, linked to that person by their name, in tabular form, is required:

[Acc Regs Sch. 8: 12, previously CA 1985 Sch. 7A: 11]

(a) details of the scheme interests:

   (i) held by the person at the beginning of the relevant financial year (or on the date of appointment if later);

   (ii) awarded to the person during the relevant financial year (if shares may become receivable in respect of the interest the details must include the following:

      – the number of those shares,

      – the market price of each of those shares when the scheme interest was awarded, and

      – details of qualifying conditions that are conditions with respect to performance);

   (iii) held by the person at the end of the relevant financial year (or on cessation of appointment if earlier);

(b) for each scheme interest within paragraph (a)(i)–(iii):

   (i) the end of the period over which the qualifying conditions for that interest have to be fulfilled (or if there are different periods for different conditions, the end of whichever period ends the latest); and

   (ii) a description of any variation made in the terms and conditions of the scheme interests during the relevant financial year; and

(c) for each scheme interest that has vested in the relevant financial year give details of any of the following which have become receivable in respect of the interest:

  (i) the following details for any shares:

    – the number of those shares,

    – the date on which the scheme interest was awarded,

    – the market price per share both when the scheme interest was awarded and when it vested, and

    – details of qualifying conditions that were conditions with respect to performance;

  (ii) the amount of any money; and

  (iii) the value of any other assets.

In the preceding paragraph:

[Acc Regs Sch. 8: 11(4), previously CA 1985 Sch. 7A: 10(4)]

(a) 'scheme interest', in relation to a person, means an interest under a long-term incentive scheme in respect of which assets may become receivable under the scheme in respect of qualifying services of the person; and

(b) such an interest 'vests' at the earliest time when it has been ascertained that the qualifying conditions have been fulfilled, and the nature and quantity of the assets receivable under the scheme in respect of the interest have been ascertained.

Example 4.2.4A

Long term incentive scheme

A plc has a 31 December year end. Mr X was appointed as a director on 1 February 20X5 having worked in the group for 10 years prior to this. In March 20X5, he received £10,000 cash under an LTIP with a performance period running from 1 January 20X2 to 31 December 20X4. The cash was only payable in March 20X5 to Mr X, and the other participating employees, if they were still employed on that date. Under the rules in Schedule 8 to the Accounting Regulations and Schedule 7A to the 1985 Act the interest under the LTIP vests in March 20X5.

The differences between the statutory disclosures and the Listing Rules disclosures on long-term incentive schemes are set out in **7.3.5**.

The following example illustrates how the Acts' disclosure requirements could be presented.

Example 4.2.4B

Another plc

Year ended 31 December 20X5

Directors' remuneration (extract)

Long Term Incentive Plan

	Award date	Share price at date of award	Awards held at 1/1/X5	Awards granted during the year*	Vested during the year (when share price was £10.50)**	Lapsed during the year	Awards held at 31/12/X5	End of period when qualifying conditions must be met	Any variation in terms and conditions during the year
			Number of shares						
S.Sharp	30/3/X2	£6.10	100,000		75,000	25,000	-	30/6/X5	
	30/3/X3	£7.00	50,000		-		50,000	30/6/X7	The Remuneration Committee agreed to extend the performance period for the 20X3 award by one year to 30/6/X7.
	30/3/X4	£8.30	80,000				80,000	30/6/X7	
	30/3/X5	£9.20		150,000			150,000	30/6/X8	
B.Bate	30/3/X2	£6.10	130,000		97,500	32,500	-	30/6/X5	
	30/3/X3	£7.00	60,000				60,000	30/6/X7	The Remuneration Committee agreed to extend the performance period for the 20X3 award by one year to 30/6/X7.
	30/3/X4	£8.30	90,000				90,000	30/6/X7	
	30/3/X5	£9.20		200,000			200,000	30/6/X8	
G.Good	30/3/X2	£6.10	90,000		67,500	22,500	-	30/6/X5	
	30/3/03	£7.00	40,000				40,000	30/6/X7	The Remuneration Committee agreed to extend the performance period for the 20X3 award by one year to 30/6/X7.
	30/3/X4	£8.30	70,000				70,000	30/6/X7	

	Award date	Share price at date of award	Awards held at 1/1/X5	Awards granted during the year*	Vested during the year (when share price was £10.50)**	Lapsed during the year	Awards held at 31/12/X5	End of period when qualifying conditions must be met	Any variation in terms and conditions during the year
			Number of shares						
	30/3/X5	£9.20		150,000			150,000	30/6/X8	
J.James	30/3/X4	£8.30	30,000				30,000	30/6/X7	
	30/3/X5	£9.20		100,000			100,000	30/6/X8	

* All awards granted during the year were subject to the condition that the total shareholder return in relation to the Company's shares (i.e. growth in share price plus reinvested dividends) is ranked in the top 20 per cent of the FTSE 100 index at the end of the three years ended March 20X8. The maximum number of shares will be paid to the directors if the TSR is in the top 10 per cent and only half will be paid if the company is ranked in the top 20 per cent but below the top 10 per cent. The shares only vest with the directors if they are still employed in the group on 30 June 20X8.

**All awards which vested during the year were subject to the condition that the total shareholder return in relation to the Company's shares is ranked in the top 40 per cent of the FTSE 100 index at the end of the three years ended March 20X5 and only vested on 30 June 20X5 if the director was still employed in the group on that date. The maximum number of shares would have vested in the directors if the TSR had finished in the top 10 per cent, 75 per cent if the TSR finished in the second 10 per cent, 50 per cent if the TSR finished in the third 10 per cent and only 25 per cent if the TSR finished in the fourth 10 per cent. The company's TSR was ranked 19th and so 75 per cent of the maximum number of shares vested.

4.2.5 *Pensions*

For each person who has served as a director of the company at any time during the relevant financial year, the Acts require disclosure of the pension information linked to that person by their name in **4.2.5.1** (defined benefit scheme) and **4.2.5.2** (money purchase scheme). [Acc Regs Sch. 8: 13(1), previously CA 1985 Sch. 7A: 12(1)]

4.2.5.1 *Defined benefit scheme*

Where a person has rights under a pension scheme any of which are due to qualifying services and the scheme is a defined benefit scheme in relation to that person, disclosure is required of:

[Acc Regs Sch. 8: 13(2), previously CA 1985 Sch. 7A: 12(2)]

(a) the increase or decrease during the relevant financial year in the person's accrued benefits under the scheme;

(b) the person's accrued benefits under the scheme as at the end of that year;

(c) the transfer value (see **4.2.5.3**) of the person's accrued benefits under the scheme at the end of the relevant financial year;

(d) the transfer value (see **4.2.5.3**) of the person's accrued benefits under the scheme as at the end of the previous financial year; and

(e) the amount obtained by subtracting:

   (i) the transfer value of the person's accrued benefits required by paragraph (d); from

   (ii) the transfer value of those benefits required by paragraph (c);

   (iii) and then subtracting from the result of that calculation the amount of any contributions made to the scheme by the person in the relevant financial year.

The disclosures required by the Listing Rules are similar but not the same (see **4.2.5.4** below).

> There is no requirement to show contributions made to a defined benefit scheme. Some companies show this for completeness so that the table of transfer values will add across.

4.2.5.2 Money purchase scheme

Where the person has rights under a pension scheme, any of which are due to qualifying services and the scheme is a money purchase scheme in relation to the person, details of any contribution to the scheme in respect of the person that is paid or payable by the company for the relevant financial year or paid by the company in that year for another financial year should be disclosed. [Acc Regs Sch. 8: 13(3), previously CA 1985 Sch. 7A: 12(3)]

> The wording of paragraph 13(3) of Schedule 8 and 12(3) of Schedule 7A could be read as requiring disclosure of contributions to a money purchase scheme both in the year in which they accrue and the year in which they are paid. This does not appear to be the intention, however, and it would be reasonable to ignore a payment of amounts that have already been disclosed on an accruals basis in a previous year.
>
> Disclosure on an accruals basis would be consistent with paragraph 20 of Schedule 8 and paragraph 19 of Schedule 7A which states

that the amounts to be shown for any financial year are 'the sums receivable in respect of that year (whenever paid) or, in the case of sums not receivable in respect of a period, the sums paid during that year'. Therefore the reference in paragraph 13(3) and 12(3) to contributions 'paid by the company in that year for another financial year' would pick up amounts paid in respect of a prior year which had not been disclosed in that earlier year (perhaps because they were only decided retrospectively) but would not be interpreted as picking up amounts that had already been disclosed as accruing in the earlier year.

4.2.5.3 *Transfer values*

Transfer values in **4.2.5.1** (c) and (d) must be calculated in a manner consistent with 'Retirement Benefit Schemes – Transfer Values (GN 11)' published by the Institute of Actuaries and the Faculty of Actuaries and dated 6 April 2001. [Acc Regs Sch. 8: 13(2)(b), previously CA 1985 Sch. 7A: 12(2)]

The Act requires disclosure of the transfer value at the beginning and end of the year, in addition to the movement in transfer value. The accrued benefit is the annual pension that a director would receive at retirement age if he or she stopped working for the company at the balance sheet date. The transfer value, on the other hand, is the capital cost of securing the specified annual pension.

Disclosure of the increase in transfer value in the year, as required by Schedule 8 and Schedule 7A, may be confusing because transfer values are discounted amounts which depend on market conditions, so are likely to change materially from year to year, even if no additional benefits are promised in relation to services during the year. The original 1998 Combined Code stated that 'companies may wish to make clear that the transfer value of the increase in directors' accrued pension benefits represents a liability of the company, not a sum paid or due to the individual'. However, in some cases this wording may not be correct and the following alternative wording is recommended.

'The transfer values disclosed above do not represent a sum paid or payable to the individual director. Instead they represent a potential liability of the pension scheme.'

The following example illustrates the disclosure required by the Regulations.

Example 4.2.5.3

The A Group plc

Year ended 31 December 20X2

Directors' remuneration report (extract)

Four directors are members of the company's defined benefit pension scheme. The following directors had accrued entitlements under the scheme as follows:

	Accrued pension 31 December 20X1	Increase in accrued pension in the year	Accrued pension 31 December 20X2
	£'000	£'000	£'000
Mr A	63	8	71
Mr B	19	6	25
Ms C	9	3	12
Ms D	35	5	40

The following table sets out the transfer value of the directors' accrued benefits under the scheme calculated in a manner consistent with 'Retirement Benefit Schemes – Transfer Values (GN11)' published by the Institute of Actuaries and the Faculty of Actuaries.

	Transfer value 31 December 20X1	Contributions made by the director	Increase in transfer value in the year net of contributions	Transfer value 31 December 20X2
	£'000	£'000	£'000	£'000
Mr A	720	3	197	920
Mr B	200	3	97	300
Ms C	80	3	37	120
Ms D	200	3	57	260

As explained at **4.2.5.4** below, additional disclosures are required to meet the requirements of the Listing Rules.

An issue arises where a person, already accruing benefits under the company pension scheme, is appointed a director part way through the year. Schedule 8 and Schedule 7A specify that the disclosure required is:

(a) the transfer value at the end of the year; and

(b) either (i) the transfer value disclosed in the previous year's remuneration report (i.e. the transfer value at the end of the previous year), or (ii) if there was no remuneration report under Schedule 8 or Schedule 7A, or there was such a report but there was no transfer value disclosed in it for a particular director, the transfer value as at the first day of the accounting period; and

(c) the difference between (a) and (b) less members' contributions.

Where a person, who has been working for a group for a number of years and thus accruing benefits under the group defined benefit scheme, is appointed as a director part way through the accounting period, say, on 1 August 20X1 (for a calendar year end company), the letter of the legislation requires the transfer values as at 31 December 20X1 and 1 January 20X1 to be disclosed together with the change for the entire twelve month period. The spirit of the legislation would suggest also disclosing the transfer values at 1 August 20X1 together with the change for this five month period to 31 December 20X1.

4.2.5.4 *Transfer values: Regulations v Listing Rules*

Although the Listing Rules contain broadly similar requirements for defined benefit pension schemes to those in Schedule 8 and Schedule 7A, two additional disclosures are required to meet in full the requirements of the Listing Rules:

(a) the increase in accrued pension in the year must be stated net of inflation rather than as the absolute amount of the increase; and

(b) the Listing Rules require the transfer value of that increase whereas Schedule 8 and Schedule 7A require the actual increase in transfer value (in both cases net of directors' contributions).

The difference referred to in (b) may be significant because of the effect of changes in discount rates.

Schedule 8 and Schedule 7A require the change in transfer value, from beginning to end of the year, less members' contributions to be disclosed. Thus, if market conditions change in a particular way, the disclosure may be negative, because the transfer value has gone down, even though the accrued pension has increased. The Listing Rules, on the other hand, require disclosure (unless a narrative alternative is given) of the transfer value of the increase in accrued pension, which will always be positive.

The following example illustrates how the amounts should be calculated under Schedule 8 and Schedule 7A and under the Listing Rules. The exact calculation will be determined by the particular scheme rules.

Example 4.2.5.4A

Transfer values

Director A had 15 years of pensionable service at 31 December 20X2, 12 of which were as an employee of the company prior to his appointment as a director and his basic salary for the year ended 31 December 20X2 was £140,000 (20X1 – £125,000). His pension accrues at the rate of one-thirtieth per annum, with the maximum pension payable being equal to two-thirds of basic salary in the final year before retirement.

The calculation of the amount of the accrued pension at 31 December 20X2 for A is as follows.

What annual pension (excluding any attributable to voluntary contributions paid by the director) would A be entitled to if he left the group's service at the end of the year and there was no increase in the general level of prices between the year end and A reaching normal pension age?

i.e. Number of years' service (whether as a director or not)

divided by

Rate of accrual of pension

multiplied by

Remuneration on which pension would be calculated if A left the group's service on the balance sheet date.

i.e. 15/30 × £140,000 per annum

i.e. £70,000 per annum

Similarly, the calculation of the amount of the accrued pension at 31 December 20X1 is as follows:

14/30 × £125,000 per annum = £58,333 per annum

The difference between the two figures is £11,667 per annum. This is the figure that is required to be disclosed under the Regulations.

However, the disclosure required by the Listing Rules is of the increase in accrued benefit less inflation.

The relevant rate of inflation for 20X2 is 1.7 per cent therefore the increase in accrued pension attributable to inflation is:

Rate of inflation multiplied by accrued pension entitlement for the previous year

i.e. 0.017 × £58,333 = £992

Accordingly, the increase for the year excluding inflation is £10,675. This is the figure that is required to be disclosed under the Listing Rules.

The inflation rate to be used should be that rate published by the Secretary of State for Social Security each year in accordance with Sch. 3 Pension Schemes

Act 1993; the published rate is updated annually by Statutory Instrument, titled 'The Occupational Pensions (Revaluation) Order [20XX]'. This is not specified in the Listing Rules but was indicated in an example that was published with the amendment to the Listing Rules that introduced the requirement.

The following example illustrates the additional disclosures required by the Listing Rules which should be made in addition to those illustrated at **4.2.5.3** above which meet the requirements of Schedule 8 and Schedule 7A.

Example 4.2.5.4B

The A Group plc

Year ended 31 December 20X1

Directors' remuneration report (extract)

The following additional information is given to comply with the requirements of the Listing Rules which differ in some respects from the equivalent statutory requirements.

	Increase in accrued pension in the year in excess of inflation	Transfer value of increase in year less directors' contributions
	£'000	£'000
Mr A	5	150
Mr B	5	82
Ms C	2	30
Ms D	3	45

4.2.6 *Excess retirement benefits of directors and past directors*

Subject to **4.2.6.1**, the directors' remuneration report shall show in respect of each person who has served as a director of the company at any time during the relevant financial year, or at any time before the beginning of that year (i.e. directors and past directors), the amount of retirement benefits paid to or receivable by the person under pension schemes (for definition see **6.6**) that is in excess of the retirement benefits to which he or she was entitled on the later of the date the benefits first became payable and 31st March 1997. [Acc Regs Sch. 8: 14(1), previously CA 1985 Sch. 7A: 13(1)] The definition of 'retirement benefit' is given in **6.6.**

This is a sort of 'anti-avoidance' disclosure, calling for the disclosure of any discretionary increases to the retirement benefits being paid to directors and former directors.

Once a director or former director who is receiving retirement benefits is awarded an increase in those benefits, disclosure will be required in each subsequent set of accounts until the increased payments cease.

The definition of pension scheme encompasses unfunded, as well as funded, schemes.

The disclosure is of any pension, lump sum, gratuity or other benefit, whether payable in cash or otherwise. The nature of any benefits in kind must be disclosed in the notes to the financial statements. [Acc Regs Sch. 8:14(4), previously CA 1985 Sch. 7A: 13(4)]

4.2.6.1 Excluded excess retirement benefits

Amounts paid or receivable under a pension scheme need not be included in an amount required to be shown under **4.2.6** if:

[Acc Regs Sch. 8: 14(3), previously CA 1985 Sch. 7A: 13(3)]

(a) the funding of the scheme was such that the amounts were, or could have been, paid without recourse to additional contributions; and

(b) amounts were paid to or receivable by all pensioner members (defined as any person who is entitled to the present payment of retirement benefits under the scheme) of the scheme on the same basis.

4.2.7 Compensation for past directors and other 'significant awards'

The directors' remuneration report is required to contain details of any significant award made in the relevant financial year to any past director of the company who was not a director of the company at the time the award was made. This includes (in particular) compensation in respect of loss of office and pensions but excludes any sums that have already been shown under paragraph **4.2.2**(d). [Acc Regs Sch. 8: 15, previously CA 1985 Sch. 7A: 14]

What has to be disclosed is open to interpretation as 'award' and 'significant' are not defined. No explanation is given other than 'award' includes compensation for loss of office and pensions. The Listing Rules have a slightly different requirement that 'any significant payments made to former directors during the period under review' be disclosed. An 'award made' is not the same as a 'payment made'. 'Award' is defined in the dictionary to include 'a grant made by a court of law, especially of damages in a civil action'. This, together with the references in Schedule 7A and Schedule 8 to an award including compensation for loss of office and pensions and that the exclusion is for amounts already disclosed under paragraphs 7(1)(d) and 6(1)(d) (compensation for loss of office) of Schedules 8 and 7A respectively rather than amounts already disclosed under paragraphs 7(1) and 6(1) (emoluments including compensation for loss of office), suggests that 'award' should be interpreted as meaning something other than payment for services rendered (which is encapsulated by the Listing Rules' requirement).

Compensation for loss of office is disclosed under both Schedule 7A paragraph 6 or Schedule 8 paragraph 7 (see **4.2.2**(d)) and Schedule 7A paragraph 14 or Schedule 8 paragraph 15 (discussed above). As a result of the interaction of the disclosures it would appear that disclosure is under the latter (i.e. paragraph 15 of Schedule 8 and paragraph 14 of Schedule 7A) where it has been determined in a year after the year the person ceases to be a director. It is these amounts that have to be explained under service contracts (see **4.1.4**).

4.2.8 *Sums paid to third parties in respect of a director's services*

In respect of each person who served as a director of the company at any time during the relevant financial year, disclosure is required of the aggregate amount of any consideration paid to or receivable by third parties for making available the services of the person as a director of the company, or while director of the company:

[Acc Regs Sch. 8: 16(1), previously CA 1985 Sch. 7A: 15(1)]

(a) as director of any of its subsidiary undertakings; or

(b) as director of any other undertaking of which he or she was (while director of the company) a director by virtue of the company's nomination (direct or indirect); or

(c) otherwise in connection with the management of the affairs of the company or any such other undertaking.

The nature of any consideration otherwise than in cash must be in the report. [Acc Regs Sch. 8: 16(2), previously CA 1985 Sch. 7A: 15(2)]

For a definition of third parties, see **6.8.**

5 Disclosure requirements for quoted companies under Schedule 5 Part 1 to the Accounting Regulations and Schedule 6 part I to the 1985 Act.

Quoted companies are exempt from giving the information specified in paragraphs 2 to 15 of Schedule 5 to the Accounting Regulations and paragraphs 2 to 14 in Part I of Schedule 6 to the 1985 Act. They only have to disclose the information required by paragraph 1 of Schedule 5 and paragraph 1 of Schedule 6. The disclosures required (summarised below for ease of reference) are the same as those in **2.1** (a) and they should be shown in the notes to the financial statements.

> These disclosures are required to be included in the notes to the financial statements. However, it is common practice to include them in the Directors' Remuneration Report and to include a specific cross reference to their location in the notes to the financial statements. This is regarded as meeting the requirement.

The disclosures are as follows:

(a) total emoluments paid to or receivable by directors in respect of qualifying services (see **6.2**), including salary, fees and bonuses, sums paid by way of expenses allowance so far as chargeable to UK income tax and the estimated money value of non-cash benefits but excluding:

[Acc Regs Sch. 5: 1(1) and 9, previously CA 1985 Sch. 6: 1(1) and (3)]

- share options granted to a director;
- gains made on the exercise of share options;
- contributions paid, or treated as paid, to a pension scheme by a person other than the director in respect of whom the contributions are made;
- any benefits to which a director is entitled under a pension scheme; and
- any money or other assets paid to or received or receivable by the director under a long-term incentive scheme;

(b) gains made by directors on the exercise of share options (being the difference between the market price of the shares on the date of exercise less the price paid for the shares); [Acc Regs Sch. 5: 1(1) and 9, previously CA 1985 Sch. 6: 1(1) and (5)]

(c) money paid to or receivable by directors, together with the net value of other assets (other than share options) received or receivable by directors under long-term incentive schemes in respect of qualifying services; [Acc Regs Sch. 5: 1(1), previously CA 1985 Sch. 6: 1(1)]

(d) the value of contributions paid, or treated as paid, to a pension scheme by a person other than the director to whom retirement benefits are accruing in respect of directors' qualifying services to the extent that the contributions might lead to money purchase benefits being payable [Acc Regs Sch. 5: 1(1), previously CA 1985 Sch. 6: 1(1)] (see **6.6**); and

(e) the number of directors, if any, to whom retirement benefits are accruing in respect of qualifying services in respect of each of:

[Acc Regs Sch. 5: 1(2), previously CA 1985 Sch. 6: 1(1)]

- money purchase schemes; and
- defined benefit schemes.

The 1985 Act specifically states that (other than in respect of the aggregate of gains made on the exercise of options) information shall be treated as shown if it is capable of being readily ascertained from other information which is shown. [CA 1985 Sch. 6: 1(6)(a)] This is repeated in the Accounting Regulations except that the concession is broader as it does not exclude gains made on the exercise of options. [Acc Regs Sch. 5: 6(2)]

Thus if by complying with Schedule 7A and Schedule 8 the company discloses sufficient information about each individual director to enable the aggregate emoluments paid to or receivable by the directors to be derived, it need not also disclose the aggregate figure. However, care should be taken to ensure that information in respect of comparative figures is also readily ascertainable. For example, as explained previously, Schedule 6 and Schedule 5 require remuneration to be disclosed separately from compensation for loss of office, whereas under Schedule 7A, Schedule 8 and the Listing Rules these figures are combined for comparative purposes (see **4.2.2** and **7.3.3**). In addition, as the Schedule 6 and Schedule 5 information is required to be presented in the notes to the financial statements, a cross-reference in the financial statements to the information disclosed under Schedule 7A and Schedule 8 will be required.

6 Interpretation and Supplementary Information for Schedules 5 and 8 to the Accounting Regulations and Schedules 6 and 7A to the 1985 Act

Schedules 5 and 8 to the Accounting Regulations and Schedules 6 and 7A to the 1985 Act include provisions dealing with interpretation and supplementary requirements. These provisions are largely consistent although there are some differences which are explained, where relevant, in this section.

6.1 Supplementary information on amounts to be disclosed

The amounts to be disclosed under Schedule 5 Part 1 and Schedule 8 to the Accounting Regulations and Schedule 6 Part I and Schedule 7A to the 1985 Act include all relevant sums paid by or receivable from:

(a) the company;

(b) the company's subsidiary undertakings; and

(c) any other person.

But they exclude sums to be accounted for by the director to the company or any of its subsidiary undertakings or any other undertaking of which any person has been a director while director of the company (for Schedule 5 and Schedule 6, by virtue of the company's nomination, direct or indirect), by virtue of section 219 of the 2006 Act and sections 314 and 315 of the 1985 Act, to past or present members of the company or any of its subsidiaries or any class of those members (see also **6.7** below). [Acc Regs Sch. 5: 8(1) and 14(1)(2), previously CA 1985 Sch. 6: 10(2) and 13(2)] [Acc Regs Sch. 8: 19(2), previously CA 1985 Sch. 7A: 18(2)] However, if the director's liability is subsequently released or is not enforced within two years, then the amount involved must be disclosed separately in the first accounts in which it is practicable to disclose it. [Acc Regs Sch. 5: 8(2), previously CA 1985 Sch. 6: 11(2)] [Acc Regs Sch. 8: 20(2), previously CA 1985 Sch. 7A: 19(2)]

Schedule 5 paragraph 8 and Schedule 6 paragraph 10, unlike Schedule 7A paragraph 18, does not specifically state 'other undertakings of which any person has been a director while director of the company by virtue of the company's nomination direct or indirect' as an exclusion (see above). However, the interpretation in paragraph 14 of Schedule 5 to the 1985 Act and paragraph 13 of Schedule 6 to the 1985 Act is that this is included in any reference to a subsidiary undertaking in relation to a director.

The amounts to be shown for any financial year are the sums receivable in respect of that year, even if not actually paid during it or, in the case of sums not receivable in respect of a period, the sums paid during that year. [Acc Regs Sch. 5: 7(4), previously CA 1985 Sch. 6: 11(1)] [Acc Regs Sch. 8: 20(1), previously CA 1985 Sch. 7A: 19 (1)]

For example, directors' fees paid in respect of the financial year should be included at their proposed amount, even if they do not become due until approved by the shareholders in general meeting. However, a one-off discretionary bonus that is not in respect of any particular period(s) should be included in the period in which it is paid.

Where the financial statements cover a financial year which is shorter or longer than 12 months, the remuneration will be that for the financial year and thus will not be for a 12-month period. To avoid misinterpretation of comparative information, the periods covered by the information should be described clearly.

Amounts paid to or receivable by a director include amounts paid to or receivable by a person connected with him or her or a body corporate controlled by him or her (but not to require an amount to be counted twice). [Acc Regs Sch. 5: 7(3), previously CA 1985 Sch. 6: 10(4)] [Acc Regs Sch. 8: 19(3), previously CA 1985 Sch. 7A: 18 (3)]

It should be noted that the information to be given concerns directors of the reporting company. Thus, in the notes to the financial statements and remuneration report for a group, it is only the payments to the directors of the parent company that should be disclosed. Payments made to a person who is a director of a subsidiary company, but not of the parent, should be excluded from the disclosures even if he or she receives some or all of his or her remuneration from the parent company.

Information in Schedule 5 Part 1 and Schedule 8 to the 2006 Act and Schedule 6 Part I and Schedule 7A to the 1985 Act is to be given only so far as it is contained in the company's books and papers, available to members of the public or the company has the right to obtain it. [Acc Regs Sch. 5: 6(1), previously CA 1985 Sch. 6: 14] [Acc Regs Sch. 8: 22, previously CA 1985 Sch. 7A: 21]

6.2 Qualifying services

Qualifying services means a person's services as a director of the company and his or her services at any time while he or she is a director of the company:

[Acc Regs Sch. 5: 15(1) and Acc Regs Sch. 8: 17(1), previously CA 1985 Sch. 6: 1(5) and Sch. 7A: 16(1)]

(a) as a director of an undertaking that is a subsidiary undertaking of the company at that time;

(b) as a director of any other undertaking of which he or she is a director by virtue of the company's nomination (direct or indirect); or

(c) otherwise in connection with the management of the affairs of the company or any such subsidiary undertaking or any such other undertaking.

Schedule 5 paragraph 15 to the Accounting Regulations and Schedule 6 paragraph 1 to the 1985 Act appear to give a different definition to that given above in Schedule 8 of the Accounting Regulations and Schedule 7A to the 1985 Act, as the former include only the conditions in (a) and (c) above. However, paragraph 14 of Schedule 5 to the Accounting Regulations and paragraph 13 of Schedule 6 to the 1985 Act state that the condition in (b) above would be included in any reference to a subsidiary undertaking. This means that the definition in Schedule 5 to the Accounting Regulations and Schedule 6 to the 1985 Act will lead to the same outcome as above.

Whether the director is receiving remuneration for services as a director of a company or otherwise in connection with the management of its affairs is a question of fact. The presumption must be that any payments he or she receives from the company (which are not reimbursements of expenses) are for one of these purposes unless it can be demonstrated clearly that they do not. One exception could be payments made to a director in a professional capacity (e.g. as a solicitor) as payment for professional services performed for the company. Here, it is usually a question of degree. For example, if a solicitor is a director and occasionally performs (or his or her firm performs) intermittent conveyancing work for which the normal scale fees are paid, it could be accepted that these payments were not caught by the above paragraphs in the Accounting Regulations and 1985 Act, particularly if the director was non-executive. However, if his or her main work for the company was conveyancing (e.g. as director of a property company), it would be difficult to accept this view.

The position is less obvious if a non-executive director is a management consultant. It can be argued that intermittent advice given by the director to the chief executive for which the director's firm charges professional fees on its normal basis does not involve services in connection with the management of the company and therefore such fees should not be included as directors' emoluments. Obviously, the facts must be considered closely.

Sometimes, the details of a service agreement between the company and the director confirm that certain payments are part of his or her remuneration and the minutes also may give confirmation. Absence of such confirmation is, of course, not conclusive nor would a negative agreement (e.g. confirming that the payments made to a director were not in respect of his or her services as a director) provide irrefutable evidence.

Where it is concluded that a payment to a director does not form part of his or her remuneration, it may nevertheless have to be disclosed to meet other requirements including those of IAS 24 and s413 of the 2006 Act (previously Part II of Schedule 6 to the 1985 Act) relating to other transactions with directors.

6.2.1 *Appointment during an accounting period*

Where a person is appointed as a director of the company part way through an accounting period, only his or her emoluments since he or she became a director of the company are disclosed.

Example 6.2.1

Appointment during an accounting period

A Limited's accounting period ends on 31 December each year. On 1 September 20X1, Mr X was appointed as a director of A Limited. Mr X received emoluments of £35,000 from 1 January to 31 August 20X1 and £25,000 for the remainder of 20X1. In A Limited's financial statements for 20X1, the amount in respect of Mr X included in the aggregate emoluments will be the £25,000 payable to him since his appointment as a director.

6.2.2 *Parent company not producing group accounts*

Where a parent company is not preparing group accounts (e.g. because it is an intermediate holding company) the remuneration disclosed will still be the remuneration its directors receive for their services to its subsidiaries as well as to the company.

Example 6.2.2

Parent company not producing group accounts

A Limited has three subsidiaries, B Limited, C Limited and D Limited. Mr X is a director of all four companies and receives emoluments of £25,000 for his services to each of the four companies. In A Limited's financial statements, the amount in respect of Mr X included in the aggregate emoluments will be £100,000, irrespective of whether group financial statements are prepared.

6.2.3 *Disclosure by subsidiaries*

Where a company is a member of a group other than as the parent, care is necessary to identify the appropriate directors' remuneration disclosures. The following should be noted:

(a) only remuneration of directors of the company should be included;

(b) all of the remuneration disclosures other than, under Schedule 5 to the Accounting Regulations and Schedule 6 to the 1985 Act, the gains made on the exercise of options (or, for companies with securities neither admitted to the Official List nor traded on AIM, the number of directors who exercised options) are for remuneration in respect of qualifying services, i.e. are in respect of services to the company and its subsidiaries (if any); and

(c) remuneration in respect of services to its parent company or any fellow subsidiaries should be excluded, whether or not the director concerned is also a director of these companies.

6.2.3.1 *Director accruing pension benefits from parent*

Example 6.2.3.1

Director accruing pension benefits from parent

Mr X is a director of ABC Ltd and receives emoluments of £8,000 in respect of his services to ABC Ltd plus £10,000 in respect of his services to its subsidiary A Ltd. The emoluments to be included in the financial statements of ABC Ltd are £18,000. The emoluments to be included in the financial statements of A Ltd are £10,000 if Mr X is a director of A Ltd and nil if he is not. Pension benefits are accruing, under the group defined benefit pension scheme, in respect of his services to both ABC Ltd and A Ltd. In the financial statements of ABC Ltd, Mr X will be included in the number of directors disclosed as accruing benefits under the defined benefit scheme. If Mr X is also a director of A Ltd, he will also be included in the number of directors disclosed as accruing benefits under the defined benefit scheme in its financial statements.

6.2.3.2 *Parent employee is director of subsidiary*

Example 6.2.3.2

Parent employee is director of subsidiary

Mr Y is employed as a manager of ABC Ltd at a salary of £9,000 per year. He also acts as a director of its subsidiary B Ltd at a fee of £5,000. No disclosure is required in the financial statements of ABC Ltd, since Mr Y is not a director of that company. The emoluments to be disclosed in the financial statements of B Ltd are £5,000. The group operates a pension scheme under which Mr Y is accruing benefits in respect of his services to ABC Ltd and is not accruing benefits in respect of his role as a director of B Ltd. Since Mr Y is not a director of ABC Ltd, there is nothing to disclose in respect of his pension entitlements in its financial statements. Similarly, there is nothing to disclose in respect of his pension entitlements in the financial statements of B Ltd, since pension benefits do not accrue to him in respect of his role as director of B Ltd.

6.2.3.3 *Exercise of options*

Example 6.2.3.3

Exercise of options

Mr Z is a director of ABC plc, a listed company. He also acts as a director of its subsidiary C Ltd. During the year ended 31 December 20X1, Mr Z exercised options over 3,000 shares at £2.50 per share. At the date of exercise, the market price of the shares was £3.50 per share. In the financial statements of ABC plc, £3,000 (being 3,000 × (£3.50 – £2.50)) is included in respect of this transaction within the aggregate of gains made on the exercise of options. In addition, in the financial statements of C Ltd, Mr Z will be included in the disclosure of the number of directors who exercised options (see **6.5** below).

6.2.3.4 *Remuneration not allocated among subsidiaries*

A situation which can cause difficulty is when directors of subsidiary companies are paid a single salary in respect of their services to the whole group and no allocation is made between the separate companies.

Schedule 5 paragraph 7(6) and Schedule 8 paragraph 21 to the Accounting Regulations and Schedule 6 paragraph 12 and Schedule 7A paragraph 20 to the 1985 Act state that the directors may apportion any payments in such manner, as they think appropriate. However, directors do not always feel able to make an appropriate apportionment. In such cases, it is necessary to give adequate disclosure, including the total amount receivable by the directors.

Example 6.2.3.4

Remuneration not allocated among subsidiaries

ABC Ltd has three subsidiaries: A Ltd, B Ltd and C Ltd.

X, Y and Z are directors of each of the subsidiary undertakings and executives of ABC Ltd, the holding company. ABC Ltd pays X, Y and Z £20,000 per annum each, but no allocation between their services, as executives of ABC Ltd and directors of each of the subsidiary undertakings, is made nor is ABC Ltd prepared to attempt such allocation. The directors accrue benefits under the group pension scheme, which pays a pension based on final salary and the total £20,000 is pensionable.

The best disclosure in the financial statements of each of the subsidiary undertakings would be a recital of the facts, for example:

The directors are executives of the holding company, ABC Ltd, and are also directors of A Ltd, B Ltd and C Ltd. The directors received total emoluments of £60,000 from ABC Ltd during the year, but it is not practicable to allocate this between their services as executives of ABC Ltd and their services as directors of A Ltd, B Ltd and C Ltd. In addition, the three directors are each accruing benefits under the ABC Ltd group pension scheme, which is a defined benefit scheme, in respect of their services to the four group companies.

However, it is important to distinguish the circumstances illustrated in the example above from the case where the amount to be allocated to a subsidiary is nil. For example, an individual may be a full time executive of the parent company and paid for his services as such. His duties may include attending the Board meetings of subsidiary companies. It may be acceptable to regard him as being an unpaid non-executive director in relation to those subsidiaries where the facts support the conclusion. In that case, the amount disclosed in the subsidiary will be nil because that is the amount receivable by the director in respect of qualifying services to that company.

6.3 Golden hellos

Emoluments paid or receivable or share options granted in respect of a person's accepting office as a director are to be treated as emoluments paid or receivable or share options granted in respect of his or her services as a director. [Acc Regs Sch. 5: 15(3), previously CA 1985 Sch. 6: 1(6)(b) and Acc Regs Sch. 8: 18(1), previously 1985 Act Sch. 7A: 17(1)]

The above references to share options in Schedule 8 paragraph 18(1) and Schedule 7A paragraph 17(1) are needed to ensure that any such options are included in the disclosures required in the remuneration report. However, the inclusion of share options granted is puzzling with respect to the Schedule 5 and Schedule 6 disclosures. Share options granted during a year are not disclosed as directors' remuneration under the Schedule 5 and Schedule 6 disclosure requirements. Schedules 5 and 6 only require options to be disclosed as part of directors' remuneration when they are exercised. Accordingly, share options granted as part of a 'golden hello' will not be disclosed under the Schedule 5 and 6 directors' remuneration requirements when they are granted but will be disclosed, as for other share options, when they are exercised.

6.4 Emoluments

Emoluments include any sums paid by way of expense allowance which are chargeable to UK income tax. Under Schedule 8 to the Accounting Regulations and Schedule 7A to the 1985 Act this is specifically extended to add 'or would be if the person were an individual'. Such emoluments might arise if a director was granted a round sum allowance for expenses which he or she could not justify to the tax authorities, for example, a living allowance paid to an employee on secondment from a different geographic region. If any payments of this nature are not disclosed in the appropriate year (on the grounds that they are not expected to be charged to tax), but they are charged to tax subsequently, then they should be shown separately in the first accounts in which it is practicable to do so. [Acc Regs Sch. 5: 7(5), previously CA 1985 Sch. 6: 11(2) and Acc Regs Sch.8: 17(1), previously CA 1985Sch. 7A: 16(1)]

Emoluments include the estimated value of benefits received otherwise than in cash (other than share options and benefits under a pension scheme and under long-term incentive schemes). A common example is the private use by a director of a company car. As benefits in kind enjoyed by a director are assessable to income tax, this requirement is often interpreted as requiring disclosure of the amounts on which the income tax assessment is based. While, in many cases, the amount will be similar, it is emphasised that the disclosure requirement is not directly related to assessment to income tax and that the estimated value of all benefits in kind, even if they are not so assessed, should be included.

6.5 Share options

A share option means a right to acquire shares. This includes shares (whether allotted or not) in the company, or any undertaking which is a group undertaking in relation to the company, and includes a share warrant as defined by section 779(2) of the 2006 Act and section 188(1) of the 1985 Act. [Acc Regs Sch. 5: 12, previously CA 1985 Sch. 6: 1(5)] [Acc Regs Sch. 8: 17(1), previously CA 1985 Sch. 7A: 16(1)]

The gain on the exercise of an option is the difference between the market price on the date of exercise and the price actually paid for the shares. The value for shares received or receivable on any day by a director means the market price of the shares on that day. [Acc Regs Sch. 5: 12, previously CA 1985 Sch. 6: 1(5)] [Acc Regs Sch. 8: 17(1), previously CA 1985 Sch. 7A: 16(1)]

Usually, the director has to remain with the company for a set period of time (e.g. three years) before he or she is able to exercise the options. Executive options are often exercisable at a price equal to the market price of the shares on the date the option was granted. The Acts specifically state that the grant of an option is excluded from the definition of emoluments. Instead under Schedule 5 Part 1 to the Accounting Regulations and Schedule 6 part I to the 1985 Act, companies with securities admitted to the Official List and companies whose securities are traded on AIM are required to disclose the gains made on the exercise of options. Other companies have the less demanding requirement to disclose the number of directors who exercised options. Additional information, including the number of shares under option, summary of performance conditions and the exercise price, has to be disclosed only by quoted companies under Schedule 8 to the Accounting Regulations and Schedule 7A to the 1985 Act.

In many cases, directors do not pay anything to acquire the options, with the options being granted to them for nil consideration as part of their remuneration package. Where, however, a director has paid to acquire the option (perhaps because it was not granted as part of a remuneration package, but instead he or she purchased it on the open market), the question arises as to whether the Act's phrase 'price actually paid for the shares' includes the cost of the option itself. It might at first be thought that the phrase refers only to the exercise price of the option. However, in substance, the total 'price' paid by the director for the shares will include the cost of acquiring the option. Accordingly, it is suggested that the cost of acquiring the option is included in the calculation of the gain on exercise and the fact that it has been included is clearly explained. If a director had acquired an option other than as part of his or her remuneration, disclosure would only be relevant under Schedule 5 to the Accounting Regulations and Schedule 6 to the 1985 Act and would not be required under Schedule 8 to the Accounting Regulations and Schedule 7A to the 1985 Act.

In Schedule 5 to the Accounting Regulations and Schedule 6 to the 1985 Act, the disclosure requirements for options for both listed and unlisted companies are not linked in any way to qualifying services. Therefore, disclosure is not limited to options granted for qualifying services and exercised now, i.e. granted and exercised since the person had been appointed as a director of the company. Indeed, as highlighted in the preceding paragraph, disclosure will be required under Schedule 5 to the Accounting Regulations and Schedule 6 to the 1985 Act even where a director exercises options bought on the open market, and even if those options were acquired before he or she became a director or was in any way connected with the company. In such circumstances, the company might wish to provide a brief explanation, since readers may otherwise assume that the options arose in connection with the director's remuneration package. In Schedule 8 to the Accounting Regulations and Schedule 7A to the 1985 Act the disclosures required are for share options granted in respect of qualifying services of the person [Acc Regs Sch. 8: 9, previously CA 1985 Sch. 7A: 8], although, as explained in **4.2.3** above, listed companies have generally given disclosure of all options and are likely to wish to continue doing so.

6.5.1 Options granted prior to appointment

Example 6.5.1

Options granted prior to appointment

The accounting period of ABC plc, a listed company, ends on 31 December each year. Mr X was appointed as a director of ABC plc on 1 July 20X5 having worked for the group for ten years. On 1 October 20X5, he exercised 2,000 options granted to him (at nil cost) in 20X0 at an exercise price of £4 per share. The market price on the date of exercise was £5 per share.

In ABC plc's financial statements for 20X5, the amount in respect of Mr X included in the aggregate gains on the exercise of options, disclosable under

Schedule 5 to the Accounting Regulations and Schedule 6 to the 1985 Act, will be £2,000, irrespective of whether Mr X retains or sells the shares. However, the options are not required by Schedule 8 to the Accounting Regulations and Schedule 7A to the 1985 Act to be detailed in the remuneration report, although, given the Schedule 5 and 6 disclosures and users' expectations, ABC plc is likely to wish to include details of such options in its remuneration report.

6.5.2 *Options exercised prior to appointment*

The requirement for companies with securities admitted to the Official List and companies whose securities are traded on AIM under Schedule 5 to the Accounting Regulations and Schedule 6 to the 1985 Act is to disclose the aggregate of the amount of gains made by directors on the exercise of share options and, for unlisted companies, is to disclose the number of directors who exercised share options. Although there is no reference to 'qualifying services', the reference to 'directors' does mean that it is only options exercised after becoming a director that are disclosed.

Example 6.5.2

Options exercised prior to appointment

Assume the same facts as in **example 6.5.1** except that Mr X exercised the options on 1 March 20X5 and not on 1 October 20X5.

In ABC plc's financial statements for 20X5, no amount will be included in the aggregate gains on the exercise of options disclosable under Schedule 5 to the Accounting Regulations and Schedule 6 to the 1985 Act in respect of Mr X. The options are also excluded from the Schedule 8 and Schedule 7A disclosures required to be in the remuneration report.

6.6 Pension schemes

The following sets out the Acts' rules on disclosure of pension scheme information. The definitions in Schedules 5 and 8 to the Accounting Regulations and Schedules 7A and Schedule 6 Part I to the 1985 Act are the same.

Schedule 5 and Schedule 6 disclosures are shown in **2.1** and in **section 5** and Schedule 8 and 7A disclosures are shown in **4.2.5.**

A pension scheme means a retirement benefits scheme within the meaning given by section 611 of the Income and Corporation Taxes Act 1988 (i.e. 'a scheme for the provision of benefits consisting of or including relevant benefits, but not including any national scheme providing such benefits'). Retirement benefits means relevant benefits within the meaning given by section 612(1) of the Income and Corporation Taxes Act 1988 which is as follows: [Acc Regs Sch. 5: 13(1), previously CA 1985 Sch. 6: 13(3)] [Acc Regs Sch. 8: 17(1), previously CA 1985 Sch. 7A: 16(1)]

> 'any pension, lump sum, gratuity or other like benefit given or to be given on retirement or on death, or by virtue of a pension sharing order or provision, or in anticipation of retirement, or in connection with past service, after retirement or death, or to be given on or in anticipation of or in connection with any change in the nature of the service of the employee in question, except that it does not include any benefit which is to be afforded solely by reason of the disablement by accident of a person occurring during his service or of his death by accident so occurring and for no other reason.'

The definition of 'pension scheme' within the Act is generally interpreted as extending to unfunded arrangements.

Company contributions, in relation to a pension scheme and a director, means any payments (including insurance premiums) made, or treated as made, to the scheme in respect of the director by a person other than the director. [Acc Regs Sch. 5: 13(3), previously CA 1985 Sch. 6: 1(5)] [Acc Regs Sch. 8: 17(1), previously CA 1985 Sch. 7A: 16(1)]

A money purchase scheme, in relation to a director, is a pension scheme under which all of the benefits that may become payable to or in respect of the director are money purchase benefits.

> '"Money purchase benefits", in relation to a director, means retirement benefits payable under a pension scheme the rate or amount of which is calculated by reference to payments made, or treated as made, by the director or by any other person in respect of the director and which are not average salary benefits.' [Acc Regs Sch. 5: 13(4), previously CA 1985 Sch. 6: 1(5)] [Acc Regs Sch. 8: 17(1), previously CA 1985 Sch. 7A: 16(1)]

A defined benefit scheme, in relation to a director, is a pension scheme other than a money purchase scheme. [Acc Regs Sch. 5: 13(4), previously CA 1985 Sch. 6: 1(5)] [Acc Regs Sch. 8: 17(1), previously CA 1985 Sch. 7A: 16(1)]

Hybrid schemes which pay either money purchase benefits or defined benefits, whichever is the higher, will therefore meet the definition of a 'defined benefit scheme'.

For the purposes of the disclosures on remuneration, companies operating such a hybrid scheme in respect of a director can classify the scheme by reference to the type of benefits which appear more likely in respect of the director at the end of the company's financial year. [Acc Regs Sch. 5: 13(6), previously CA 1985 Sch. 6: 1(7)] [Acc Regs Sch. 8: 18(2), previously CA 1985 Sch. 7A: 17(2)] For the purposes of determining whether a pension scheme is a money purchase scheme or a defined benefit scheme in relation to a person, any death in service benefits provided for by the scheme are disregarded.

Where a company takes advantage of this option, it may be helpful to users for the facts to be explained briefly, particularly where the judgement as to which type of benefits appears more likely changes from one year to the next.

The following example illustrates the disclosures required under Schedule 5 paragraph 1 to the Accounting Regulations and Schedule 6 paragraph 1 to the 1985 Act which apply to all companies. The example includes the amounts required for the highest paid director which need to be given by all companies excluding quoted companies applying Schedule 8 to the Accounting Regulations and Schedule 7A to the 1985 Act.

Example 6.6

Pension schemes

ABC plc has four directors, all of whom are members of the company's pension scheme. The scheme is funded as if it were a defined benefit scheme paying out a maximum pension of two-thirds of basic salary after 20 years' service. However, the actual pension payable will be the higher of the defined benefits calculated in this way and the pension that would have accrued had the company instead paid contributions, equal to six per cent of basic salary, into a money purchase scheme that invested these contributions in FTSE 100 tracker funds.

In preparing the company's financial statements for its year ended 31 December 20X1, the company considers the scheme to determine which benefits appear to be the higher. If it concludes that the money purchase benefits would be the higher, it will disclose:

1(a) the amount of contributions for the directors in aggregate upon which the money purchase benefits are calculated, i.e. six per cent of basic salary;

1(b) all four directors as being members of a money purchase scheme (though it may choose to add a further explanation that the scheme is in fact a hybrid scheme and that the directors have been classified in this way on the basis that the money purchase benefits appear higher); and

1(c) the amount of contributions in respect of the highest paid director upon which the money purchase benefits are calculated, i.e. six per cent of basic salary (see **2.2**).

If, instead, it had concluded that the defined benefits would be the higher, it would disclose:

2(a) all four directors as being members of a defined benefit scheme (though, again, it may choose to add a further explanation that the scheme is in fact a hybrid scheme and that the directors have been classified in this way on the basis that the defined benefits appear higher); and

2(b) the amount of the accrued benefit for the highest paid director (see **2.2**).

(NB 1(c) and 2(b) are not required for quoted companies although under Schedule 8 to the Accounting Regulations and Schedule 7A to the 1985 Act the amount of the contributions (scenario 1) or the accrued benefits (scenario 2) together with other disclosures (for scenario 2) would be disclosed for each of the four directors by name).

In the above example, the company could choose not to estimate which of the benefits it thinks will be the higher. If so, it would disclose:

(a) the amount of contributions for the directors in aggregate upon which the money purchase benefits are calculated, i.e. six per cent of basic salary (even if it is defined benefits that might be payable);

(b) all four directors as being members of a defined benefit scheme (though, once again, it may choose to add a further explanation that the scheme is in fact a hybrid scheme);

(c) the amount of contributions in respect of the highest paid director upon which the money purchase benefits are calculated, i.e. six per cent of basic salary (see **2.2**); and

(d) the amount of the accrued benefit for the highest paid director (see **2.2**).

Disclosures (c) and (d) are for the highest paid director and are not required for quoted companies although similar disclosures are required by Schedule 8 to the Accounting Regulations and Schedule 7A to the 1985 Act in respect of each named director.

6.7 Compensation to directors or past directors in respect of loss of office

The amount disclosed must include any sums (including the money value of any benefits otherwise than in cash) received or receivable by a director or past director by way of compensation for:

[Acc Regs Sch. 5: 4(2)(3) and (4), previously CA 1985 Sch. 6: 8(2), (3) and (4)]

(a) loss of office as director of the company; or

(b) loss, while director of the company or on or in connection with his ceasing to be a director of it; of:

    (i) any other office in connection with the management of the company's affairs; or

    (ii) any office as director or otherwise in connection with the management of the affairs of any undertaking that, immediately before the loss, is a subsidiary undertaking of the company or an undertaking of which he or she is a director by virtue of the company's nomination (direct or indirect); and

(c) compensation in consideration for, or in connection with, a person's retirement from office.

The Act clarifies that where retirement from the office of director is because of a breach of contract, any damages or settlements in respect of the breach shall be disclosed as compensation for loss of office. [Acc Regs Sch. 5: 8(3), previously CA 1985 Sch. 6: 8(4)] [Acc Regs Sch. 8: 17(2), previously CA 1985 Sch. 7A: 16(2)]

Sections 215 to 226 of the 2006 Act, which came into effect on 1 October 2007, set out requirements for the approval of payments to directors for loss of office. These requirements replace similar, but not identical, requirements under the 1985 Act. Under s217, a company may not make a payment for loss of office to a director of the company unless the payment has been approved by a resolution of the members of the company. Also, a company may not make a payment for loss of office to a director of its holding company unless the payment has been approved by a resolution of the members of each of those companies. Payments for loss of office are defined in s215.

However, there is an important exception to the requirement for approval in s220. Approval is not required for a payment made in good faith in discharge of an existing legal obligation (as defined); by way of damages for breach of such an obligation; by way of settlement or compromise of any claim arising in connection with the termination of a person's office or employment; or by way of pension in respect of past services. In practice, most compensation payments to directors are under the terms of their service contracts and therefore do not require approval by the members. It is not the purpose of this publication to provide guidance on the requirements for approval of compensation payments. Legal advice should be sought where appropriate.

As noted above, the requirements for disclosure in the accounts apply irrespective of whether the compensation is for breach of contract or otherwise.

When, in connection with an offer for a company's shares (for example, on a takeover), a payment is to be made to a director by way of compensation for loss of office, or in connection with retirement from office, the director must comply with the provisions of section 219 of the 2006 Act or section 314 of the 1985 Act.

Under section 219 of the 2006 Act, no payment for loss of office may be made to a director of a company in connection with a transfer of shares in the company, or in a subsidiary of the company resulting from a takeover bid unless the payment has been approved by a resolution of the relevant shareholders. No approval is required on the part of the shareholders in a body corporate that either is not a UK- registered company, or is a wholly-owned subsidiary of another body corporate. If a payment is made in contravention of section 219, any sums received by the director will be excluded from compensation for loss of office, because the director is required to account for those sums to past or present members of the company. [Acc Regs Sch. 5: 8(1) and Acc Regs Sch. 8: 19(2)]

Section 314 of the 1985 Act requires the director to take all reasonable steps to ensure that particulars of the payment are disclosed to shareholders in the offer document. If he or she fails to do so, or if shareholders' approval for the payment is not obtained in accordance with s315, any payments received by the director are deemed to be held on trust for the relevant shareholders. [s315] In these circumstances, any sums received by the director will be excluded from compensation for loss of office, because the director is required to account for those sums to past or present members of the company. [CA 1985 Sch. 6: 10(2) and Sch. 7A: 18(2)]

However, if the director's liability is subsequently released or is not enforced within two years, then the amount involved must be disclosed separately in the first accounts in which it is practicable to disclose it. [Acc Regs Sch. 5: 8(2), previously CA 1985 Sch. 6: 11(2)] [Acc Regs Sch. 8: 19(2), previously CA 1985 Sch. 7A: 18(2)]

When a director's pension entitlements are increased as part of his or her ceasing to be a director, the question arises as to whether this should be disclosed as part of compensation for loss of office or pensions to directors and former directors. Where the increase is made as part of his or her ceasing to be a director, the capital cost of the increase should be disclosed as part of compensation for loss of office, irrespective of whether the employer directly pays additional contributions (to cover the increase) into the pension scheme or whether the increase is funded by an existing surplus in the scheme. Any increase in pension entitlements after a person has ceased to be a director may require disclosure as excess retirement benefits to directors and past directors (see **4.2.6**).

6.8 Consideration paid to third parties

Disclosure is required of the aggregate consideration paid to or receivable by third parties for making available the services of a person as a director. Third parties are persons other than:

(a) the director;

(b) persons connected with the director;

(c) a body corporate controlled by the director;

(d) the company;

(e) any of the company's subsidiary undertakings (see below if disclosure is under Schedule 8 or Schedule 7A); and

(f) any other undertaking of which he or she was (while director of the company) a director by virtue of the company's nomination (direct or indirect). [Acc Regs Sch. 5: 5(3), previously CA 1985 Sch. 6: 9(3)] [Acc Regs Sch. 8: 16(3), previously CA 1985 Sch. 7A: 15(3)]

The references to a person being 'connected' with a director and to a director 'controlling' a body corporate should be construed in accordance with s252 to 255 of the 2006 Act and s346 of the 1985 Act (see **6.3.1.1** in **chapter 32**). [Acc Regs Sch. 5: 15(2), previously CA 1985 Sch. 6: 13(4)] [Acc Regs Sch. 8: 17(4), previously CA 1985 Sch. 7A: 16(4)]

This requirement would typically be relevant where a bank has a non-executive director on the board and invoices the company for the director's fees which are never receivable by the director personally. However, payments made to a director's own private company (i.e. one controlled by him) would not be 'payments to third parties' and would be disclosable as directors' emoluments in the normal way.

Schedule 5 paragraph 5(3) and Schedule 6 paragraph 9(3), unlike Schedule 8 paragraph 16(3) and Schedule 7A paragraph 15(3), do not specifically state 'any other undertaking of which he or she was (while director of the company) a director by virtue of the company's nomination (direct or indirect)' as an exclusion (see above). However, the interpretation in paragraph 15 of Schedule 5 and paragraph 13 of Schedule 6 show that such undertakings are included in any reference to a subsidiary in relation to a director. This means the definitions in Schedules 5 and 6 and Schedules 8 and 7A will lead to the same outcome.

Item (e) 'any of the company's subsidiary undertakings', is not one of the exclusions listed in Schedule 8 paragraph 16 and Schedule 7A paragraph 15, whereas it is listed as an exclusion in Schedule 5 paragraph 5 and Schedule 6 paragraph 9. However, it seems absurd for a subsidiary undertaking to be considered as a third party, so for disclosure purposes, for both Schedules 5 and 6 and Schedules 8 and 7A, subsidiary undertakings should not be included as a third party.

7 Requirements of the Listing Rules

7.1 Introduction

There is a great deal of duplication between the Companies Act requirements and the Listing Rules. It was hoped that the requirements of the Listing Rules would be removed following the introduction of similar statutory requirements. This has not yet happened although the Financial Services Authority (FSA) has indicated its intention to do so in due course. It is understood that the FSA is liaising with BERR with a view to some aspects of the Listing Rules being incorporated into the statutory requirements although the opportunity has been missed to do this in the Accounting Regulations under the 2006 Act. The Listing Rules will then be amended to delete the duplicated requirements. Although there is a great deal of duplication between the statutory requirements and the Listing Rules, there are some important differences and care must be taken to ensure that all disclosures are given.

7.2 Scope

The disclosure requirements dealt with in this section are those in section 8 of chapter 9 of the Listing Rules and apply to companies with a primary listing of equity shares (including investment companies and venture capital trusts). However, with the exception of the disclosures about waiver of emoluments (see **7.3.11** below) they apply only to companies incorporated in the UK. Overseas companies, whether they have a primary listing or a secondary listing are not required to prepare a report on directors' remuneration.

Companies that have a primary listing of preference shares (and not of equity shares) are required to comply with section 8 of chapter 9 of the Listing Rules but are exempt from certain requirements including those regarding waivers of directors' emoluments and the preparation of a report on directors' remuneration. Therefore the requirements set out in this section of this chapter are not relevant to such companies.

Companies with a primary listing of preference shares would also usually be exempt from the requirements of Schedule 8 and Schedule 7A which apply only to companies with quoted equity securities. However, care should be taken to look at the specific terms of the shares in question against the relevant definitions in the Act and the Listing Rules.

Companies with quoted debt securities are outside the scope of chapter 9 of the Listing Rules and are dealt with separately in chapter 17 of the Listing Rules. They are not required to make the disclosures about directors' remuneration set out in this section of this chapter.

7.3 Requirements

7.3.1 Remuneration report by the board

A company that has a primary listing of equity shares and is incorporated in the UK must include in its annual report and accounts a report to shareholders by the Board which contains the matters specified in LR 9.8.8R relating to directors' remuneration. [LR 9.8.6R(7)]

The equivalent statutory requirement to prepare a directors' remuneration report is considered in **section 3** and **section 4** above.

7.3.2 Policy on executive directors' remuneration

The directors' remuneration report should contain a statement setting out the company's policy on executive directors' remuneration. [LR 9.8.8R(1)]

The equivalent requirements of Schedules 8 and 7A are set out at **4.1.2** above. They are more extensive and apply to all directors rather than just executive directors. Therefore, compliance with the requirements of Schedules 8 and 7A will be sufficient to ensure compliance with this aspect of the Listing Rules.

7.3.3 *The amount of each element of remuneration for the period*

The directors' remuneration report should contain the following information presented in tabular form, unless inappropriate, together with explanatory notes where necessary. The report should state the amount of each element in the remuneration package for the period under review for each director, by name, including but not restricted to:

[LR 9.8.8R(2)(a)]

- basic salary and fees;
- the estimated money value of benefits in kind;
- annual bonuses;
- deferred bonuses; and
- compensation for loss of office and payments for breach of contract or other termination payments.

The total remuneration for each director for the period under review and for the corresponding prior period should also be shown. [LR 9.8.8R(2)(b)]

Schedules 8 and 7A also require an emoluments table (see **4.2.2** above) and do not permit presentation in anything other than tabular form (the Listing Rules 'unless inappropriate' is not in the Act). Presentation of an emoluments table under Schedules 8 and 7A should satisfy the requirement in the Listing Rules, although some 'deferred bonuses' under the Listing Rules may be long-term incentive plans under Schedules 8 and 7A.

Any significant payments made to former directors during the period under review should also be disclosed. [LR 9.8.8R(2)(c)]

As with most of the Listing Rules' requirements on directors' remuneration, the requirement to disclose significant payments made to former directors during the period under review was originally introduced in response to the Greenbury report. The wording in the Greenbury report is, 'Also disclosed should be any payments and benefits not previously disclosed, including any additional pension provisions, receivable by Directors who have retired during the accounting period or the previous accounting period'.

Clearly, what is included in the Listing Rules is much wider. It would require disclosure, for example, of payments made to a former director for consultancy services in the current year.

Schedule 7A contains requirements for the disclosure of compensation for past directors and 'other significant awards' as described at **4.2.7** above.

7.3.4 *Information on share options*

The directors' remuneration report should include information in tabular form, unless inappropriate, together with explanatory notes as necessary on any share options, including 'Save-as-you-earn' options, for each director, by name 'in accordance with the requirements of the Directors' Remuneration Report Regulations'. [LR 9.8.8R(2)(d)]

The Directors' Remuneration Report Regulations 2002 introduced the requirements that are now in Schedules 8 and 7A. Therefore, provided that the report meets the relevant statutory requirements (see **4.2.3** above), it will also meet the requirements of the Listing Rules.

7.3.5 *Long-term incentive schemes*

The Listing Rules require that details should be given of any long-term incentive schemes, other than share options for which separate requirements apply (see **7.3.4** above).

A long-term incentive scheme is defined in the Listing Rules as any arrangement (other than a retirement benefit plan, a deferred bonus or any other arrangement that is an element of an executive director's remuneration package) which may involve the receipt of any asset (including cash or any security) by a director or employee of the group:

(a) which includes one or more conditions in respect of service and/or performance to be satisfied over more than one financial year; and

(b) pursuant to which the group must incur (other than in relation to the establishment and administration of the arrangement) either a cost or a liability, whether actual or contingent.

This is similar to the definition for the purposes of the statutory disclosure requirements (see **4.2.4** above) although not identical.

The Listing Rules requirement is to disclose details of:

(a) any long-term incentive schemes, other than share options, including the interests of each director, by name, in the scheme at the start of the period under review; [LR 9.8.8R(3)]

(b) any entitlements or awards granted and commitments made to each director under any long-term incentive scheme during the period, showing which crystallise either in the same year or subsequent years; [LR 9.8.8R(4)]

(c) the monetary value and number of shares, cash payments or other benefits received by each director under any long-term incentive schemes during the period; and [LR 9.8.8R(5)]

(d) the interests of each director in the long-term incentive schemes at the end of the period. [LR 9.8.8R(6)]

An extra column can be added, showing awards lapsed during the year. This disclosure is not required by the Listing Rules, but it is helpful because it enables the figures to 'add across'. Although the Listing Rules do not use the words 'maximum potential', the interpretation of (a), (b) and (d) above is that the maximum potential awards have to be disclosed. The disclosure under (c) is of the actual award.

If the disclosures under LTIPs required by paragraph 12 of Schedule 8 and paragraph 11 of Schedule 7A are given there will only be one additional disclosure required by the Listing Rules. This arises because the Listing Rules require disclosure of the money value (as well as number) of shares received by each director during the year, i.e. the money value of the shares in aggregate, whereas Schedules 8 and 7A require, inter alia, disclosure of the number of shares and market price per share. Two further possible differences, however, are that:

(a) some schemes may be classified as a deferred bonus under the Listing Rules that would meet the definition of an LTIP under Schedules 8 and 7A; and

(b) traditionally, all LTIPs have been disclosed under the Listing Rules whereas Schedules 8 and 7A only require interests in respect of qualifying services to be disclosed. Given users' expectations, companies are likely to wish to continue to give details of all LTIP interests if there are any differences.

7.3.5.1 LTIPs where the only participant is a director

The Listing Rules require that any long-term incentive scheme in which one or more directors is entitled to participate must be approved by an ordinary resolution of shareholders in general meeting. [LR 9.4.1R] There are two exceptions to this general rule, one of which is where the only participant is a director (or an individual whose appointment as a director is being contemplated) and the arrangement is established specifically to facilitate, in unusual circumstances, the recruitment or retention of the relevant individual. [LR 9.4.2R(2)] Where this exemption is used, the following disclosures should be made in the first annual report published after the individual becomes eligible to participate in the scheme:

[LR 9.4.3R and LR 9.8.4R(4)]

(a) the name of the sole participant;

(b) the date on which the individual first became eligible to participate in the arrangement;

(c) explanation of why the circumstances in which the arrangement was established were unusual;

(d) the conditions to be satisfied under the terms of the arrangement;

(e) the maximum award(s) under the terms of the arrangement or, if there is no maximum, the basis on which awards will be determined; and [LR 9.4.3R]

(f) the information set out in LR 13.8.11R, namely:

  (i) either the full text of the scheme or a description of its principal terms;

  (ii) where directors of the company are trustees of the scheme, or have a direct or indirect interest in the trustees, details of such trusteeship or interest;

  (iii) a statement that the provisions (if any) relating to:

   – the persons to whom, or for whom, securities, cash or other benefits are provided under the scheme (the 'participants');

   – limitations on the number or amount of the securities, cash or other benefits subject to the scheme;

   – the maximum entitlement for any one participant;

   – the basis for determining a participant's entitlement to, and the terms of, securities, cash or other benefit to be provided and for the adjustment thereof (if any) in the event of a capitalisation issue, rights issue or open offer, sub-division or consolidation of shares or reduction of capital or any other variation of capital;

cannot be altered to the advantage of participants without the prior approval of shareholders in general meeting (except for minor amendments to benefit the administration of the scheme, to take account of a change in legislation or to obtain or maintain favourable tax, exchange control or regulatory treatment for participants in the scheme or for the company operating the scheme or for members of its group); and

(iv) a statement of whether benefits under the scheme will be pensionable and, if so, the reasons for this.

7.3.6 *Explanation of pensionable remuneration*

It is normally the case that only basic salary is pensionable. The Listing Rules therefore require that if any element of remuneration, other than basic salary, is pensionable then the directors' remuneration report should give an explanation and justification of why this is the case. [LR 9.8.8R(7)]] This is additional to the disclosures required by Schedules 8 and 7A (i.e. there is no similar requirement in the Act).

7.3.7 *Directors' service contracts*

Details should be disclosed of any directors' service contracts with a notice period in excess of one year or with provision for pre-determined compensation on termination which exceeds one year's salary and benefits in kind, giving the reasons for such notice periods. [LR 9.8.8R(8)]

Large compensation payments to directors on loss of office, particularly those on three-year rolling contracts, have, in the past, given rise to much high-profile criticism. The Combined Code states that notice or contract periods should be set at one year or less. The Code also states that, if it is necessary to offer longer notice or contract periods to new directors recruited from outside, such periods should reduce to one year or less after the initial period. Most listed companies now follow this recommendation.

Although Schedules 8 and 7A require disclosure of the length of directors' service contracts (see **4.1.4** above) they do not require disclosure of the reason for a period of greater than one year. Therefore this requirement of the Listing Rules goes beyond the requirements of Schedules 8 and 7A.

7.3.8 *Unexpired service periods*

The unexpired period of any service contract of any director proposed for election or re-election at the AGM should be given in the directors' remuneration report. Where any such director does not have a service contract, a statement to that effect in the remuneration report is required. [LR 9.8.8R(9)]

> If the Schedule 8 and 7A disclosures are given (see **4.1.4** above) this disclosure requirement should be met.

7.3.9 *Pension entitlements*

For money purchase pension schemes (as defined in the Act), details of the contribution or allowance payable or made by the company in respect of each director during the period should be disclosed. [LR 9.8.8R(11)]

> This is also required by Schedules 8 and 7A and so does not impose any additional requirement (see **4.2.5.2** above).

For defined benefit pension schemes (as defined in the Act), the following information should be given for each individual director who served during the accounting period:

(a) details of the amount of the increase during the period (excluding inflation) and of the accumulated total amount at the end of the period in respect of the accrued benefit to which the director would be entitled on leaving service or is entitled having left service during the period; [LR 9.8.8R(12)(a)] and

(b) either the transfer value (less director's contributions) of the relevant increase in accrued benefit (to be calculated in accordance with Actuarial Guidance Note GN11, but making no deduction for underfunding) as at the end of the period or, alternatively, so much of the following information as is necessary to make a reasonable assessment of the transfer value:
[LR 9.8.8R(12)(b)]

  (i) age;

  (ii) normal retirement age;

  (iii) the amount of any contributions paid or payable by the director under the terms of the scheme during the period;

  (iv) details of spouse's and dependants' benefits;

(v) early retirement rights and options;

(vi) expectations of pension increases after retirement (whether guaranteed or discretionary);

(vii) discretionary benefits for which allowance is made in transfer values on leaving; and

(viii) any other relevant information which will significantly affect the value of the benefits.

The Listing Rules state that contributions made by the directors voluntarily and the benefits accrued in respect of such voluntary contributions should not be disclosed. [LR 9.8.8R(12)(c)]

This is an area where there are some important differences between the Listing Rules and Schedules 8 and 7A. These are described at **4.2.5.4** above where an illustration is included of the additional disclosures required to comply with the Listing Rules.

The Listing Rules permit narrative information to be given instead of the transfer value of the increase in accrued benefits. This dispensation was given when the requirement was first introduced to recognise sensitivities about the cost of calculating the transfer values and also concerns that users of financial statements might misinterpret the very large numbers that can arise. However, when the equivalent statutory requirements were introduced in 2002, no similar dispensation was given. Therefore companies have to obtain and publish information about transfer values to comply with Schedules 8 and 7A. The alternative narrative disclosures can therefore only be given to meet the additional requirements of the Listing Rules (see **4.2.5.4** above) and are now rarely seen in practice.

When the London Stock Exchange first issued its Listing Rule requiring disclosure of pension entitlements, it also issued a summary of the comments received on its earlier consultation. In this, the London Stock Exchange explained that a number of commentators asked whether death in service benefits should be included in pension entitlements. The London Stock Exchange's view was that these benefits should be included in 'benefits in kind' in the detailed analysis of individual director's remuneration. However, as explained above, benefits under pension schemes should be excluded from the 'emoluments' disclosure under the Act. Accordingly, where a company is combining the disclosures under both the Act and the Listing Rules, it should disclose separately the value of the death in service benefit, so that the Act's information can be derived.

The Listing Rules are silent on the issue of comparatives except that the requirement for the detailed analysis of remuneration (see **7.3.3** above) does explicitly require a comparative. Accordingly, this would suggest that the Listing Rules do not require comparatives to the pension entitlements disclosure. Except to the extent that a Standard or Interpretation permits or requires otherwise, IAS 1(2003).36 and IAS 1(2007).38 require comparative information to be given for the previous period for all amounts reported in the financial statements. Where the board's remuneration report is located outside the financial statements (as is normally the case), comparatives may not be required to the pension disclosure. However, where the information is located within the financial statements (and included in the remuneration report by cross reference), comparatives should be given.

7.3.10 *Policy on granting of options or awards under employee share and other long-term incentive schemes*

The directors' remuneration report should include a statement of the company's policy on the granting of options or awards under employee share schemes and other long-term incentive schemes. The statement should include explanation and justification of any departure from that policy in the period under review and any change in policy from the preceding year. [LR 9.8.8R(10)]

This is additional to the disclosures required by Schedules 8 and 7A. As with most of the disclosure requirements on directors' remuneration, this requirement was introduced in response to the Greenbury report. The recommendations in the Greenbury report that led to the requirement were:

(a) a recommendation that grants under executive share option and other long-term incentive schemes should normally be phased rather than awarded in one large block; and

(b) the recommendation that if such awards were in one large block rather than phased, the remuneration report should contain an explanation and justification.

The London Stock Exchange consulted extensively and no consensus emerged on the definition of 'one large block'. Consequently the Listing Rules instead called for disclosure of the company's policy on the granting of options or awards. The original Combined Code included a requirement for the remuneration report to explain and justify if grants under executive share option or other long-term incentive schemes were awarded in one large block rather than being phased. However, this requirement was removed when the Code was revised in 2003.

7.3.11 *Waiver of emoluments*

Companies are required to disclose details of any arrangement under which a director of the company has waived or agreed to waive any emoluments from the company or any subsidiary undertaking. [LR 9.8.4R(5)] Companies are also required, where a director has agreed to waive future emoluments, to disclose details of such waiver together with those relating to emoluments which were waived during the period under review. [LR 9.8.4R(6)]

This disclosure requirement uses the term 'emoluments' and not 'remuneration'. The term 'emoluments' is not defined in the Listing Rules. In the past, the term 'emoluments' was used to refer to the total remuneration package. More recently, however, it has been used to refer to just a part of the total remuneration package. This disclosure requirement was introduced before the change in the meaning of emoluments. It is therefore suggested that its requirements are followed in respect of the waiver of any element in the remuneration package.

7.3.12 *Period covered by remuneration disclosures*

The Listing Rules do not specify the period to be covered by the directors' remuneration disclosures, although there are several references to the 'period under review'. This is generally interpreted as the company's statutory reporting period. This interpretation is supported by the Companies Act disclosures which have to be given for the statutory reporting period.

It can happen that a new company is formed, say, on a merger or demerger, whose first statutory accounting period is shorter or longer than 12 months and for which the underlying business has existed for many years. In these instances companies often present pro forma financial results for 12 months (together with comparatives for 12 months) in addition to giving the financial results for the statutory period, say, seven months. The question therefore arises as to the period for which the directors' remuneration disclosures should be given in the Board's remuneration report. As noted above, the legal requirement is to disclose information for the financial year of the company, so there is little to be achieved by seeking a dispensation from the requirements of the Listing Rules to give the disclosures for twelve months instead. However, in these circumstances, companies often give information for a twelve month period with comparatives for the previous twelve month period in addition to the information required by law and the Listing Rules.

8 The Combined Code

The Combined Code is considered more fully in **chapter 47**. The original 1998 Combined Code included significant disclosure requirements on directors' remuneration. However, most of these were subsequently incorporated into the Listing Rules and Schedules 8 and 7A. Therefore, when the Code was revised in 2003, these requirements were deleted. The following requirements that are relevant to disclosure of directors' remuneration are derived from the 2006 Code (and are unchanged in the 2008 Code).

Provision B.1.4 requires that, where a company releases an executive director to serve as a non-executive director elsewhere, the remuneration report should include a statement as to whether or not the director will retain such earnings and, if so, what the remuneration is.

Under provision B.2.1, the following should be 'made available':

(a) the remuneration committee's terms of reference, explaining its role and the authority delegated to it by the board; and

(b) where remuneration consultants are appointed, a statement of whether they have any other connection with the company.

The 2006 Code states that the requirement to make this information available may be met by making it available on the company's website. However, companies may wish to give the information in their directors' remuneration report or at least to include a cross reference to where it may be obtained.

In addition, paragraph 1 of Schedule A to the Code indicates that upper limits on directors' annual bonuses should be set and disclosed.

While this is not a formal Code provision from which any departure would have to be explained, such disclosure would usually be made in the context of the discussion of remuneration policies required by the Listing Rules and Schedules 8 and 7A.

9 Other disclosures

The Greenbury Report included a number of recommendations for disclosures that were not included in the Listing Rules. One such disclosure that companies might wish to make is of the extent to which performance criteria have been met, together with any particular performance criteria on which individual directors' entitlements depend. For quoted companies, performance criteria for share options schemes and other LTIPs have to be disclosed under Schedules 8 and 7A. Such companies may wish to disclose the extent to which the performance criteria were met where the performance period has ended.

The Association of British Insurers (ABI) issues guidelines on policies and practices for executive remuneration. These were revised and reissued in December 2007 in their report 'Executive Remuneration-Guidelines on Policies and Practices'. The guidelines primarily make recommendations about remuneration policies although they also make some recommendations for disclosures that in some cases go beyond the Listing Rules and Schedules 8 and 7A. A potential source of confusion is that some of the recommended disclosures are aimed at documents seeking approval of employee share schemes by shareholders and would not necessarily be repeated in full in the remuneration report each year. The ABI and the National Association of Pension Funds (NAPF) have also produced a joint statement on 'Executive Contracts and Severance' which was updated in February 2008. The guidelines can be downloaded from the ABI website at: *http://www.abi.org.uk*

IAS 24 *Related Party Disclosures* requires disclosures about the compensation of key management personnel in total and for each of the following categories:

(a) short-term employee benefits;

(b) post-employment benefits;

(c) other long-term benefits;

(d) termination benefits; and

(e) share-based payment.

These requirements are addressed in **chapter 32**.

Although the disclosures required by IAS 24 are only in aggregate for all key management personnel, it is important to remember that this term is potentially broader than 'directors' and may include other senior executives of the company and its subsidiaries. It should also be noted that the extensive disclosures required by the law and the Listing Rules will not necessarily provide all of the information required to meet the requirement of IAS 24. For example, the requirement to disclose an amount for 'share-based payment' is interpreted to mean a figure calculated on a basis that is consistent with IFRS 2 *Share-based payment*.

10 Future developments

As discussed at **7.1** above the requirements of the Listing Rules on directors' remuneration may be removed as there is a lot of duplication between them and the Act. The timing of any such amendment remains unclear.

Paragraph 4 of Schedule 8 to the Accounting Regulations includes a new requirement for the content of the directors' remuneration report for a quoted company. This new requirement is not subject to audit and concerns a statement of consideration of conditions elsewhere in the company and group when setting remuneration policy. It is effective for periods commencing on or after 6 April 2009.

The directors' remuneration report must contain a statement of how pay and employment conditions of employees of the company and of other undertakings within the same group as the company were taken into account when determining directors' remuneration for the relevant financial year. [Acc Regs Sch. 8: 4]

49 Dividends, share purchases and capital maintenance

1 Introduction

This chapter summarises the main aspects of the Acts relating to:

(a) the issue of share capital (see **section 2** below);

(b) the repurchase or redemption of share capital (see **section 3** below);

(c) the granting of financial assistance by a company for acquisition of its own shares (see **section 4** below);

(d) distributions (see **section 5** below); and

(e) reduction of share capital (see **section 6** below).

The requirements of IAS 1 relating to the presentation and disclosure of share capital and reserves in financial statements, together with the accounting for that purpose under IAS 32 *Financial Instruments: Presentation*, are not covered in this chapter (see **4.5.2** in **chapter 3** and **chapters 13** to **22**.

1.1 IFRSs and distributable profits

Reporting under IFRSs, or under UK standards such as FRS 25 *Financial Instruments: Presentation* and FRS 26 *Financial Instruments: Recognition and Measurement* that have been converged with IFRSs, does not directly impact on the legal requirements concerning capital maintenance. However, there may be significant implications for distributions as a result of the adoption of these standards because of their effect on profits and net assets. Also, a number of complex legal issues arise concerning the interpretation of the law and earlier guidance on distributable profits when companies report under these standards.

A number of Technical Releases have been issued jointly by the ICAEW and ICAS providing guidance on realised and distributable profits. In February 2008 TECH 01/08 was published which consolidates and supersedes all of the previous these Technical Releases on distributable profits including:

- TECH 7/03 *Guidance on the determination of realised profits and losses in the context of distributions under the Companies Act 1985;*
- TECH 50/04 *Guidance on the effect of FRS 17 'Retirement benefits' and IAS 19 'Employee benefits' on realised profits and losses;*
- TECH 64/04 *Guidance on the effect on realised and distributable profits of accounting for employee share schemes in accordance with UITF Abstract 38 and revised UITF Abstract 17*; and
- TECH 02/07 Distributable profits: Implications of recent accounting changes (which consolidated the draft guidance in TECH 21/05 *Distributable profits: Implications of IFRS* and TECH 57/05 *Distributable profits: Implications of IAS 10 and FRS 21 for dividends*).

TECH 01/08 is a consolidation of existing guidance under the Companies Act 1985. The equivalent provisions of the 2006 Act come into effect on 6 April 2008 but do not make substantive changes to the law in this area. Some related changes to the law on capital reductions, including the new procedure for private companies to reduce their capital by solvency statement, come into effect from 1 October 2008. An updated version of TECH 01/08 which takes account of the 2006 Act is expected to be published by the end of 2008.

Reference to this guidance is made in **section 5** below.

1.2 Companies Act 2006

The Companies Act 2006 received Royal Assent on 8 November 2006 (see **1.3.1** in **chapter 1**). In the area of capital maintenance it makes some limited changes to the existing requirements including:

- a new procedure whereby a private company can reduce its capital by way of a 'solvency statement' by the directors (see **section 6** below) from 1 October 2008;
- the abolition, for private companies, of the statutory prohibition on giving financial assistance for the purchase of their own shares (see **4.2** below) from 1 October 2008;
- statutory provisions for the redenomination of share capital from one currency to another currency from 1 October 2009; and
- a new section to remove doubt about the implications of the Aveling Barford case for transfers of assets to members of the company (see **5.9** below) from 6 April 2008.

The Government did not use the opportunity, as some had hoped, to make a more radical simplification to the law on distributable profits for private companies. For public companies, the Government's ability to change the law in this area is constrained by the need to comply with the EU Second Company Law Directive. However, it has become apparent that the UK has implemented the Directive in a much more restrictive way than some other EU Member States. For example, some do not impose any 'realisation' test on profits that may be distributed. Private companies are not within the scope of the Second Directive and so it would be possible to break the link with profits for financial reporting purposes and move to some form of solvency basis for distributions. Any such move would, however, require primary legislation because the 2006 Act does not include any power to make changes of this type through secondary legislation (i.e. a statutory instrument).

In addition, as part of the consultation on implementation of the 2006 Act, BERR (previously the DTI) is considering whether to implement some changes to the law on capital maintenance that would be permitted by amendments that have been made to the EU Second Company Law Directive. The UK is not required to implement these changes which introduce some additional Member State options. The changes would introduce some limited relaxations of the existing requirements in some circumstances but would make the law more complex and benefit very few companies. BERR is expected to publish proposals to implement these changes to the law during 2008.

Within this chapter, where reference is made to a section of the 2006 Act, the date that the provision of the 2006 Act is applicable from is 1 October 2009 unless otherwise stated. In particular, the provisions of the 2006 Act on distributions (see **section 5** below) came into effect on 6 April 2008.

1.3 IFRSs and capital maintenance

Those aspects of the Acts that deal with matters outside of the scope of IFRSs continue to apply when accounts are prepared under IFRSs. All of the rules on capital maintenance in the Acts therefore continue to apply. For example, the requirement to establish a share premium account, and the uses to which that account may be put, still apply irrespective of the fact that the balance on the account might be included in liabilities, and not disclosed separately, in IFRS financial statements. Similarly, the ability to pay dividends on preference shares is still determined by reference to the availability of distributable profits even if those dividends are reported as an expense in accordance with IFRSs.

This is illustrated in the following example.

Example 1.3

Capital maintenance

A company issues redeemable preference shares with a nominal value of £100 for £1,000. They are redeemable at their issue price of £1,000. They are presented as a liability for financial reporting purposes in accordance with IAS 32. However, this does not mean that the share capital and share premium cease to exist. They are merely presented in the balance sheet within liabilities. The shares can still be redeemed only out of distributable profits (or a fresh issue of shares) in accordance with the Act. Similarly, dividends can only be paid out of distributable profits even though they may be presented as an expense in the income statement.

On issue of the shares, the following entries will be required.

Dr	Cash	1,000	
Cr	Share capital (presented as a liability)		100
Cr	Share premium (presented as a liability)		900

Being proceeds of issue

If the shares are redeemed out of distributable profits, the following entries will be required.

Dr	Share capital (presented as a liability)	100	
Dr	Distributable profits	900	
Cr	Cash		1,000

Being payment on redemption

Dr	Distributable profits	100	
Cr	Capital redemption reserve		100

Being transfer equal to nominal value of shares required by section 733 of the 2006 Act (previously s170 of the 1985 Act)

Dr	Share premium (presented as a liability)	900	
Cr	Share premium (presented within equity)		900

Being reclassification of share premium because there is no liability to record

The above entries follow the legal form. If instead it is assumed that the cash payment settles the liability in accordance with the substance of the arrangements, the following entries achieve the same end result.

Dr	Liability	1,000	
Cr	Cash		1,000

Being payment on redemption

Dr	Distributable profits	1,000	
Cr	Share premium		900
Cr	Capital redemption reserve		100

Being adjustment to correct legal analysis of reserves on redemption

This is a simple example. The analysis will become more complicated where compound financial instruments are involved, where instruments are redeemed early or where instruments are converted. However, the underlying legal principle is that reporting under IFRSs does not affect the existence of legal reserves such as the share premium and capital redemption reserve or the uses to which they may be put.

2 Issue of share capital

The Acts contain regulations regarding the issue of share capital. [CA 2006 s549–609, previously CA 1985 s80–116] A summary of the major provisions follows below. Several of the provisions are complex and, where necessary, reference should be made to the relevant Act.

Shares may not be allotted at a discount. [CA 2006 s580, previously CA 1985 s100] This means that shares cannot be issued, as fully paid, for consideration less than their nominal value.

The board of directors may not allot 'relevant securities' (see below) in the company unless it is given authority to do so by the company's Articles or by an ordinary resolution of the company. [CA 2006 s549 and s551, previously CA 1985 s80] Normally, such authority may not exceed five years.

Under the 1985 Act, the board of directors of a private company may be given authority for an indefinite period, or a period in excess of five years, by an elective resolution of the company. [CA 1985 s80A] (An elective resolution requires 21 days' notice and unanimous approval.)

A new provision was inserted into the 2006 Act to allow the directors of a private company which has only one class of shares to exercise any power of the company to allot shares of that class or to grant rights to subscribe for or to convert any security into such shares unless they are prohibited from doing so by the company's articles. [CA 2006 s550] This section of the 2006 Act comes into force from 1 October 2009.

The 1985 Act uses the term 'relevant securities' which are:

(a) shares in the company other than shares shown in the Memorandum to have been taken by the subscribers to it or shares allotted in pursuance of an employees' share scheme; and

(b) any right to subscribe for, or to convert any security into, shares in the company (other than shares so allotted).

Although the 2006 Act does not use this term, the requirement of the 2006 Act remains the same as s549(2) clarifies that subsection 1 of section 549 does not apply to:

(a) the allotment of shares in pursuance of an employees' share scheme; or

(b) the grant of a right to subscribe for, or to convert any security into, shares so allotted.

An allotment of relevant securities includes the grant of a right to subscribe, convert, etc. but does not then include the subsequent allotment of shares pursuant to such a right.

Ordinary shares or securities convertible into ordinary shares (other than those to be allotted in pursuance of an employees' share scheme) to be allotted for cash must first be offered pro rata to existing holders of shares or securities of the same class on terms similar to or more favourable than those on which they are to be offered to others (pre-emption rights). [CA 2006 s561, previously CA 1985 s89] A number of other shares are also affected. [CA 2006 s560 and s561, previously CA 1985 s89 and s94] Private companies can exclude pre-emption rights altogether by means of a provision in their Memorandum or Articles. [CA 2006 s567, previously CA 1985 s91] Where directors are authorised to issue shares (see above), a company can, by special resolution , permit the directors to issue shares under that authority without regard to pre-emption rights. [CA 2006 s569–570, previously CA 1985 s95]

No share of a public company can be allotted unless one quarter of its nominal value and the whole of any premium is paid up. [CA 2006 s586, previously CA 1985 s101]

A public company cannot allot shares otherwise than for cash (except in connection with a takeover or merger) unless the consideration has been valued within the previous six months. The valuation report required for this purpose will usually be given by the auditor, who may rely on the valuation of an expert. [CA 2006 s593, previously CA 1985 s103]

The purchase of a company's own shares by an ESOP trust does not amount to a purchase of own shares for the purposes of the Act. ESOP trusts are considered in **section 9** of **chapter 25**. Where a company makes a loan or gift to an ESOP trust to enable it to purchase the company's own shares, the provisions of the Act in respect of financial assistance for the purchase of own shares will be relevant. This is considered at **4.1** below.

3 Purchase or redemption of own shares

This part of the chapter discusses the following aspects of share redemptions and purchases. Part 18 (s658–737) of the 2006 Act relating to 'acquisition by limited company of its own shares' comes into effect from

1 October 2009 (with the exception of the repeal of the restrictions under the 1985 Act on financial assistance for acquisition of shares in private companies, see **section 4** below).

(a) **General requirements** An overview of the rules governing the purchase or redemption of shares out of distributable reserves or out of a fresh issue, and the limited circumstances in which accounting entries will then affect the share premium account (see **3.1** below).

(b) **Capital redemption reserve** A discussion of the accounting entries affecting the capital redemption reserve (see **3.2** below).

(c) **Private companies and permissible capital payments** Guidance on the requirements for private companies which, having insufficient distributable reserves, purchase or redeem shares out of capital (see **3.3** below).

(d) **Purchasing or redeeming share capital denominated in a foreign currency** A discussion of some specific issues that can arise where share capital is denominated in a foreign currency (see **3.4** below).

(e) **Expenses of purchasing ordinary shares** The accounting treatment of such expenses (see **3.5** below).

(f) **Treasury shares** A brief overview of the law which permits certain companies to hold their own shares in treasury rather than cancelling them (see **3.6** below).

The rules governing share redemption can be both complex and confusing. In addition, a number of misconceptions are relatively widespread, particularly in relation to the accounting entries affecting the share premium account and the capital redemption reserve. Care should therefore be taken to apply all the relevant material when dealing with a specific case.

As well as being able to redeem or purchase their own shares subject to certain safeguards, limited companies are also able to reduce their share capital. Under the 1985 Act, this action required court approval. This route is still available under the 2006 Act but, in addition, private companies may also reduce their share capital by means of a special resolution of shareholders and a solvency statement signed by all directors. This is considered in **section 6** below.

3.1 General requirements

The Act contains provisions which permit limited companies to redeem or purchase their own shares in strictly limited circumstances. [CA 2006 s690–723, previously CA 1985 s159–181] The relevant sections are summarised below. Although sections 159 to 160 of the 1985 Act (CA 2006 684–689) refer to redemption of shares they apply to a purchase of own shares under s162 of the 1985 Act (CA 2006 s690).

Section 159(1) and s162(1) of the 1985 Act states that a company may redeem or purchase its own shares only if so authorised by its Articles. The 2006 Act removes, for private companies only, the requirement for prior authorisation in the company's articles for a proposed allotment of redeemable shares. However, the articles of a private limited company may exclude or restrict the issue of redeemable shares. [CA 2006 s684 and s690]

Section 685 of the 2006 Act enables the directors of both private and public companies to determine the terms, conditions and manner of redemption of redeemable shares if they are authorised to do so by the company's articles or by special resolution of the company.

Shareholder approval is required for the purchase as follows:

(a) **off-market purchase**: the terms of the proposed contract must be authorised by a special resolution. Under the 1985 Act the authorisation must take place before the contract is entered into. For companies under the 2006 Act a company may enter into a contract for an off-market purchase of its own shares conditional on the contract being approved by the shareholders. If, however, the shareholders do not subsequently pass a special resolution approving the contract, the company may not purchase the shares in question and the contract will lapse; for a public company, this resolution must specify the date on which the authority expires, which must not be more than 18 months from the date of the resolution; [CA 2006 s694, previously CA 1985 s164] and

(b) **market purchase**: authority must be obtained from the company in general meeting. The authority:

   (i) may be restricted to a specific class of share capital or may be a general authority to purchase its own shares;

   (ii) may be conditional or unconditional;

   (iii) must state the maximum number of shares to be acquired;

   (iv) must state the maximum and minimum prices to be paid; and

   (v) must specify the date on which it expires, which must not be more than 18 months from the date of the resolution. [CA 2006 s701, previously CA 1985 s166]

A purchase is 'off-market' if a company purchases its own shares otherwise than on a recognised investment exchange (RIE) or if they are purchased on an RIE but are not subject to a marketing arrangement on that exchange. A purchase that is not off-market is called a 'market purchase'. [CA 2006 s693, previously CA 1985 s163]

The power to issue redeemable shares or to purchase a company's own shares is limited by the requirement that there must always be a member of the company who holds non-redeemable shares. [CA 2006 s684(4) and 690(2), previously CA 1985 ss159(2) and 162(3)]

Under the 1985 Act, shares may not be redeemed or purchased unless they are fully paid. The terms of purchase or redemption must provide for payment on purchase or redemption. [CA 2006 s686 and s691, previously CA 1985 s159(3)] Legal advice on the meaning of this under the 1985 Act suggests that the consideration must be cash and cannot be deferred.

The 2006 Act has amended the provision for payment for redeemable shares slightly in that the terms of redemption of shares in a limited company may provide that the amount payable on redemption may, by agreement between the company and the holder of the shares, be paid on a date later that the redemption date. [CA 2006 s686(2)] Unless the redeemable shares have been redeemed in accordance with a provision authorised by 686(2) the shares must be paid for on redemption. [CA 2006 s686] No equivalent amendment has been made to the provision for payment for purchase of own shares. [CA 2006 s691]

Shares redeemed or purchased must be cancelled and for companies under the 1985 Act such cancellation does not reduce the authorised share capital (companies subject to the 2006 Act no longer need to have an authorised share capital). [CA 2006 s688 and s706, previously CA 1985 s160(4)] This is subject to an exception in the case of 'treasury shares' which, subject to some restrictions, may be held by a company without being cancelled (i.e. so that they can be sold or used for an employee share scheme at a later date). Treasury shares are dealt with at **3.6** below.

Except in the case of private companies (see **3.3** below), shares may only be redeemed or purchased out of distributable profits or out of the proceeds of a new issue made for that purpose. [CA 2006 s687(2) and s692(2)(a), previously CA 1985 160(1)(a)] To the extent that the redemption or purchase of the nominal value of the shares is made out of distributable profits or exceeds the proceeds of a new issue of shares, a transfer must be made to the capital redemption reserve (see **3.2** below). [CA 2006 s733, previously CA 1985 s170] See **5.2** below as regards distributable profits for this purpose for investment companies.

With the exceptions given below, any premium payable on the redemption or purchase of shares (i.e. the difference between the redemption (purchase) consideration and the nominal value of the shares) must be paid out of the distributable profits of the company, and not out of the share premium account. [CA 2006 s687(3) and 692(2)(b), previously CA 1985 s160(1)(b)]

3.1.1 The share premium account

Where shares which have been redeemed or purchased were issued at a premium, any premium payable on their redemption or purchase may be paid out of the proceeds of a fresh issue of shares made for the purpose up to the lesser of:

[CA 2006 s687(4–5) and s692 (3–4), previously CA 1985 s160(2)]

(a) the amount of the premium originally received by the company on the issue of the shares redeemed or purchased; and

(b) the current balance on share premium account (including any premium on the new shares).

The effect is that the amount which can be charged against share premium is the lower of:

(a) the original premium received;

(b) the balance on share premium account; and

(c) the proceeds of a fresh issue.

Thus where there is no fresh issue, no amount may be charged to share premium.

This rule is a source of frequent misunderstandings. It is possible for the share premium account to be reduced where a redemption or repurchase of shares is paid out of the proceeds of a fresh issue of shares. It is also possible that the share premium account may be reduced where a company makes a permissible capital payment (see **3.3**) or reduces capital (see **section 6**). But where shares are redeemed wholly out of distributable profits and there is no fresh issue, there can be no reduction in the share premium account, irrespective of whether the shares were originally issued at a premium.

Having the proceeds of the new issue of the shares equal to the redemption (or purchase) amount is not sufficient on its own to avoid the need to make a transfer out of distributable profits.

Consider the following four examples: in the first three examples, the transfer out of distributable profits represents the difference between the amount by which the redemption proceeds exceeds the nominal value of the shares redeemed and the share premium which arose when the shares were issued. This will not always be the case, however, since the balance on the share premium account, including that arising on the new issue of shares, may be lower than the share premium which arose when the shares were first issued. In this scenario, the transfer out of distributable profits will be even greater; consider the fourth example for an illustration of this.

Example 3.1.1A

Effects of share redemption (1)

New shares with a nominal value of £10,000 were issued for £40,000. Shares having a nominal value of £10,000, which were originally issued for £40,000, are redeemed or purchased for £40,000. The capital and reserves section of the balance sheet before the transactions was as follows:

	£
Issued share capital	50,000
Share premium	30,000
Distributable profits	60,000
	140,000

The relevant journal entries are as follows:

	Debit	**Credit**
	£	£
Called up share capital	10,000	
Share premium account	30,000	
Cash		40,000
Cash	40,000	
Called up share capital		10,000
Share premium		30,000

To record the redemption (purchase) of 10,000 £1 shares at £4.00 per share and the issue of 10,000 new £1 shares for £4.00 per share to fund the redemption (purchase).

The capital and reserves section of the balance sheet after the transactions is as follows:

	£
Issued share capital	50,000
Share premium	30,000
Distributable profits	60,000
	140,000

In this example, the balance on the share premium account at the date of redemption, including the premium that arose on the new issue of shares, totals £60,000 (£30,000 + £30,000) and the share premium that originally arose on the issue of the shares now redeemed totals £30,000. The lower of the two is £30,000. Therefore, the premium on redemption can be funded out of the share premium account rather than out of distributable profits up to a maximum of £30,000. The premium on redemption is £30,000 (i.e. redemption proceeds of £40,000 less the nominal value of the shares redeemed of £10,000) and so the whole redemption premium is funded out of share premium account.

Example 3.1.1B

Effects of share redemption (2)

New shares with a nominal value of £10,000 were issued for £40,000. Shares having a nominal value of £10,000, which were originally issued at par, are redeemed or purchased for £40,000. The capital and reserves section of the balance sheet before the transactions was as follows:

	£
Issued share capital	50,000
Share premium	30,000
Distributable profits	60,000
	140,000

The relevant journal entries are as follows:

	Debit £	Credit £
Called up share capital	10,000	
Distributable profits	30,000	
Cash		40,000
Cash	40,000	
Called up share capital		10,000
Share premium		30,000

To record the redemption (purchase) of 10,000 £1 shares at £4.00 per share, including the transfer out of distributable profits to fund the premium payable on redemption (purchase), and the issue of 10,000 new £1 shares for £4.00 per share.

The capital and reserves section of the balance sheet after the transactions is as follows:

	£
Issued share capital	50,000
Share premium	60,000
Distributable profits	30,000
	140,000

In this example, the balance on the share premium account at the date of redemption, including the premium that arose on the new issue of shares, totals £60,000 (consisting of the £30,000 premium on the new issue of shares, together with the £30,000 balance on the share premium account immediately before the new issue; this latter amount is included in the calculation even though it arose on an issue of shares other than those to be redeemed).

The share premium that originally arose on the issue of the shares now redeemed, however, is nil. The lower of the two is nil. Therefore, none of the premium on redemption can be funded out of the share premium account and it must all be funded out of distributable profits (even though the company had a balance on its share premium account). The premium on redemption is £30,000 (i.e. redemption proceeds of £40,000 less the nominal value of the shares redeemed of £10,000) and this must come out of distributable profits.

Example 3.1.1C

Effects of share redemption (3)

New shares with a nominal value of £10,000 were issued for £40,000. Shares having a nominal value of £5,000, which were originally issued for £20,000, are redeemed or purchased for £40,000. The capital and reserves section of the balance sheet before the transactions was as follows:

	£
Issued share capital	65,000
Share premium	15,000
Distributable profits	60,000
	140,000

The relevant journal entries are as follows:

	Debit	Credit
	£	£
Called up share capital	5,000	
Share premium account	15,000	
Distributable profits	20,000	
Cash		40,000
Cash	40,000	
Called up share capital		10,000
Share premium		30,000

To record the redemption (purchase) of 10,000 £0.50 shares at £4.00 per share, including the transfer out of distributable profits of £20,000 to fund the premium payable on redemption (purchase) in excess of the premium received on the issue of the shares, and the issue of 10,000 new £1 shares for £4.00 per share.

The capital and reserves section of the balance sheet after the transactions is as follows:

	£
Issued share capital	70,000
Share premium	30,000
Distributable profits	40,000
	140,000

In this example, the balance on the share premium account at the date of redemption, including the premium that arose on the new issue of shares, totals £45,000 and the share premium that originally arose on the issue of the shares now redeemed totals £15,000. The lower of the two is £15,000. Therefore, the premium on redemption can be funded out of the share premium account rather than out of distributable profits up to a maximum of £15,000. The premium on redemption is £35,000 (i.e. redemption proceeds of £40,000 less the nominal value of the shares redeemed of £5,000) and so £15,000 of the redemption premium is funded out of share premium account and the balance of £20,000 is funded out of distributable profits.

Example 3.1.1D

Effects of share redemption (4)

New shares with a nominal value of £30,000 were issued for £40,000. Shares having a nominal value of £5,000, which were originally issued for £20,000, are redeemed or purchased for £40,000. The capital and reserves section of the balance sheet before the transactions was as follows:

	£
Issued share capital	80,000
Share premium	–
Distributable profits	60,000
	140,000

Although share premium arose on the issue of the shares now being redeemed, there is no balance in the share premium account, because it was all used to fund a bonus issue of shares two years ago.

The relevant journal entries are as follows:

	Debit	Credit
	£	£
Called up share capital	5,000	
Share premium account	10,000	
Distributable profits	25,000	
Cash		40,000
Cash	40,000	
Called up share capital		30,000
Share premium		10,000

To record the redemption (purchase) of 10,000 £0.50 shares at £4.00 per share, including the transfer out of distributable profits of £25,000 to fund the premium payable on redemption (purchase) in excess of the balance on the share premium account, and the issue of 30,000 new £1 shares for £1.33 per share.

The capital and reserves section of the balance sheet after the transactions is as follows:

	£
Issued share capital	105,000
Share premium	–
Distributable profits	35,000
	140,000

In this example, the balance on the share premium account at the date of redemption, including the premium that arose on the new issue of shares (£10,000), totals £10,000 and the share premium that originally arose on the issue of the shares now redeemed totals £15,000. The lower of the two is £10,000. Therefore, the premium on redemption can be funded out of the share premium account rather than out of distributable profits up to a maximum of £10,000. The premium on redemption is £35,000 (i.e. redemption proceeds of £40,000 less the nominal value of the shares redeemed of £5,000) and so £10,000 of the redemption premium is funded out of share premium account and the balance of £25,000 is funded out of distributable profits.

3.2 Capital redemption reserve

Where shares are redeemed or purchased wholly out of distributable profits, the Act requires a transfer to be made to the capital redemption reserve. [CA 2006 s733, previously CA 1985 s170] In such a case, the amount of the required transfer is the amount by which the company's share capital is diminished on cancellation of the shares, i.e. the nominal value of the shares.

Example 3.2A

Capital redemption reserve (1)

Shares having a nominal value of £100,000 (and which were originally issued for £120,000) are redeemed or purchased for £130,000. The relevant journal entries are as follows:

	Debit	**Credit**
	£	**£**
Profit and loss account (distributable reserves)	30,000	
Called up share capital	100,000	
Cash		130,000
Profit and loss account (distributable reserves)	100,000	
Capital redemption reserve		100,000

To record the redemption (purchase) of 100,000 £1 shares at £1.30 per share and to transfer the nominal value of such shares to the capital redemption reserve.

The above journal entries have been set out to follow the legal requirement for a transfer from distributable profits to capital redemption reserve. However, it may be noted that the combined effect of these entries is to charge the cash payment to distributable reserves and reclassify the amount previously shown as share capital as capital redemption reserve.

The transfer to capital redemption reserve would be the same even if the shares were purchased at a discount to nominal value.

Where the redemption or purchase is financed wholly or partly by a new issue of shares, the transfer required is reduced by the proceeds of the new issue. [CA 2006 s733, previously CA 1985 s170] The transfer required should be further reduced to the extent that the company can make a permissible capital payment (see **3.3** below).

In summary, the transfer from distributable profits to capital redemption reserve is:

	£
Nominal value of shares purchased/redeemed	X
Less: Proceeds of fresh issue	(X)
Less: Permissible capital payment (if any, for a private company)	(X)
Amount of transfer	X

Note: In addition to this reduction in distributable profits, any premium payable must also be dealt with as explained in **3.1** above.

A strict reading of the Act could lead to a reduction in capital if the maximum amount of a new issue is used to fund the premium on the redemption of shares and the residual amount of the proceeds of the new issue is less than the nominal value of the shares being redeemed. [s170] (See **3.1** above) This shortfall occurs because the Act requires a transfer to the capital redemption reserve of the amount by which the proceeds of the fresh issue is less than the nominal value of the shares redeemed or purchased. [CA 2006 s733, previously CA 1985 s170] This requirement ignores the extent to which the premium on redemption is funded by the fresh issue. If capital levels are to be maintained, then the reference to 'aggregate amount of proceeds' should be taken as being reduced to the extent that the fresh issue finances the premium on redemption. [CA 2006 s733, previously CA 1985 s170]

Example 3.2B

Capital redemption reserve (2)

Shares with a nominal value of £50,000 were issued for £100,000. The shares were issued to finance the redemption of shares with a nominal value of £100,000. The shares, which were originally issued at a premium of £5,000, were redeemed for £120,000.

Balance sheet prior to redemption

	£
Issued share capital	300,000
Share premium (includes £5,000 arising on the issue of shares to be redeemed)	20,000
	320,000
Distributable profits	130,000
	450,000

Redemption of shares

	Nominal £	Premium £
Redemption costs to be financed	100,000	20,000
Maximum amount that can finance the premium on redemption is the lower of the premium originally received on the shares being redeemed (£5,000) and the balance on the share premium account after the new issue (£70,000)		5,000
Balance of premium financed from distributable profits		15,000
Redemption of nominal value financed by the balance of fresh issue proceeds (£100,000 – £5,000)	95,000	
Balance of nominal value not financed by fresh issue proceeds	5,000	

Balance sheet after redemption – following the strict reading of s733 of the 2006 Act (previously CA 1985 s170)

The aggregate proceeds of £100,000 are not less than the £100,000 nominal value of the shares redeemed, therefore no transfer is required to the capital redemption reserve. This results in the 'creditors' buffer', the aggregate of share capital and share premium, being reduced by £5,000.

	£
Issued share capital (£300,000 – £100,000 + £50,000)	250,000
Share premium (£20,000 – £5,000 + £50,000)	65,000
	315,000
Distributable profits (£130,000 – £15,000)	115,000
	430,000

Balance sheet after redemption – reading s733 of the 2006 Act (previously CA 1985 s170) to require a transfer of £5,000 to the capital redemption reserve

The excess of the nominal value of the redeemed shares over the proceeds of the fresh issue, net of the portion used to finance the share premium, is £5,000.

	£
Issued share capital (£300,000 – £100,000 + £50,000)	250,000
Share premium (£20,000 – £5,000 + £50,000)	65,000
Capital redemption reserve	5,000
	320,000
Distributable profits (£130,000 – £15,000 – £5,000)	110,000
	430,000

The Acts state that redeemable shares may only be redeemed out of distributable profits of the company or out of the proceeds of a fresh issue of shares made for the purposes of the redemption. [CA 2006 s687(2) and 692(2), previously CA 1985 s160(1)] Accordingly, this would suggest that the transfer of £5,000 to the capital redemption reserve in the above example is required (since the proceeds of the fresh issue fall short of the redemption proceeds by £20,000, thus requiring £20,000 of the redemption proceeds to be funded by distributable profits). A company not wishing to make a transfer in these circumstances should take legal advice.

3.3 Private companies and permissible capital payments

A private company may redeem or purchase its shares out of capital. The 2006 Act removes the requirement under the 1985 Act for prior authorisation in the articles. Members can restrict or prohibit a payment out of capital is they wish by including a provision to this effect in the company's articles. [CA 2006 s709, previously CA 1985 s171] The capital portion, referred to as the permissible capital payment, is defined as the price of redemption or purchase less the sum of any distributable profits and the proceeds of any new issue of shares made for the purpose of the redemption or purchase. [CA 2006 s710, previously CA 1985 s171(3)] Where the aggregate of the permissible capital payment plus the proceeds of a new issue is greater than the nominal amount of the shares redeemed or purchased, the excess may be applied to reduce the amount of any capital redemption reserve, share premium account, fully paid share capital of the company or revaluation reserve. If the permissible capital payment is less than the nominal value of the shares redeemed or purchased, the difference must be transferred to the capital redemption reserve. [CA 2006 s734(2–3), previously CA 1985 s171(4–5)]

Where the excess is deducted from fully paid share capital it is necessary to consider how this should be presented in the balance sheet. The Act refers to the fully paid share capital being reduced and it is therefore generally appropriate to reduce the amount shown as share capital in the balance sheet rather than to show the deduction as a separate negative reserve on the face of the balance sheet. However, it does not appear that the number or nominal value of the shares will be affected by this deduction so it may be best to show the deduction as a separate item within the share capital note (i.e. reconciling the nominal value of the shares in issue with the amount included in the balance sheet as called-up share capital).

A further complication is that the share capital from which the excess is deducted might be presented as a liability in the balance sheet. In this case it would be wrong to reduce the liability by the excess because this would result in a misstatement of the liability. Therefore the excess would have to be included as a separate negative reserve within equity. This might be explained as follows:

> 'The other reserve arose from the repurchase of shares out of capital in the year and represents the amount of the permissible capital payment deducted from share capital in accordance with section [734(3) of the Companies Act 2006/171(5) of the Companies Act 1985]. The share capital from which this amount is deducted as a matter of law is presented as a liability in the balance sheet in accordance with applicable financial reporting requirements.'

In summary:

	£
Price of redemption/purchase	X
Less: Balance of distributable profits	(X)
Less: Proceeds of fresh issue	(X)
Permissible capital payment (if positive)	X

These rules are illustrated in the examples below. The effect of these requirements is that any balance of distributable profits is first utilised to pay the cost of redemption or purchase. Once distributable profits are exhausted, a private company may (with the appropriate authority, and after going through the steps explained later in this section) reduce its capital.

To the extent that the aggregate of the permissible capital payment plus the proceeds of a new issue is less than the nominal amount of the shares redeemed or purchased, a transfer must be made to the capital redemption reserve (see **3.2** above for a full discussion of journals affecting that reserve). If this rule did not exist, a repurchase of shares at a discount to nominal value would create a distributable profit. This is demonstrated in **example 3.3A** below.

Example 3.3A

Permissible capital payments (1)

Shares having a nominal value of £100,000 are redeemed or purchased for £80,000. The company has no distributable profits. Therefore, the relevant figures are calculated as follows:

	£
Cost of purchase	80,000
Less: Distributable profits	NIL
Proceeds of fresh issue	NIL
Permissible capital payment	80,000

	£
Nominal value of purchase	100,000
Less: Proceeds of fresh issue	NIL
Less: Permissible capital payment	80,000
Transfer to capital redemption reserve	20,000

The relevant journal entries are as follows:

	Debit £	Credit £
Called up share capital	100,000	
Cash		80,000
Capital redemption reserve		20,000

To record the redemption (purchase) of 100,000 £1 shares at £0.80 per share out of capital and to transfer the excess nominal value of such shares to the capital redemption reserve.

Example 3.3B

Permissible capital payments (2)

New shares with a nominal value of £100,000 were issued for £250,000. Shares having a nominal value of £500,000 are redeemed or purchased for £700,000. The capital and reserves section of the balance sheet before the transactions was as follows:

	£
Issued share capital	1,000,000
Share premium (none of this arose on the shares now redeemed)	1,000,000
Distributable profits	300,000
	2,300,000

The relevant figures are calculated as follows:

	£
Price paid for redemption	700,000
Less: distributable profits	(300,000)
Less: proceeds of new issue	(250,000)
Permissible capital payment	150,000

Nominal value of shares redeemed	500,000
Less: permissible capital payment	(150,000)
Less: proceeds of new issue	(250,000)
Transfer to capital redemption reserve	100,000

The relevant journal entries are as follows:

	Debit £	Credit £
Profit and loss account (distributable reserves)	200,000	
Called up share capital	500,000	
Cash		700,000
Cash	250,000	
Called up share capital		100,000
Share premium		150,000
Profit and loss account (distributable reserves)	100,000	
Capital redemption reserve		100,000

To record the redemption (purchase) of 500,000 £1 shares at £1.40 per share, the issue of 100,000 new £1 shares for £2.50 per share and to transfer an amount equal to the difference between the nominal value of the shares redeemed (purchased) and the aggregate of the proceeds of the fresh issue and the permissible capital payment to the capital redemption reserve.

The following safeguards must be met before a payment out of capital can lawfully be made:

[CA 2006 s713, previously CA 1985 ss173–176]:

(a) the payment must be approved by a special resolution; [CA 2006 s716(1), previously CA 1985 s173(2)]

(b) the directors must make a statement (see below); [CA 2006 s714(1–3), previously CA 1985 s173(3)]

(c) a report by the company's auditors must be annexed to the directors' declaration (see below); [CA 2006 s714(6), previously CA 1985 s173(5)] and

(d) a notice of the proposed capital payment, giving the information specified in s719 of the 2006 Act (previously CA 1985 s175), must be published in the Gazette and either published in a national newspaper or given by written notice to each creditor within a week of the date of the resolution. [CA 2006 s719, previously CA 1985 s175] 'The Gazette' means, for companies registered in England and Wales, the *London Gazette* and, for companies registered in Scotland the *Edinburgh Gazette*. [CA 2006 s1173, previously CA 1985 s744] Creditors and members may apply to the court within five weeks of the date of the resolution for the resolution to be cancelled. The payment must not be made less than five weeks or more than seven weeks after the date of the resolution. [CA 2006 s723, previously CA 1985 s174(1)]

As a consequence of the 2006 Act, the directors' statutory declaration has been renamed 'the directors' statement'. The requirements have not changed but for the purposes of this manual the term directors' statement is used. The directors' statement must have annexed to it a report by the company's auditors addressed to the directors, stating that the auditors have inquired into the company's state of affairs, that the amount specified as the permissible capital payment has, in the auditors' opinion, been properly determined and that the auditors are not aware of anything to indicate that the opinion expressed by the directors in their declaration is unreasonable in all the circumstances. [CA 2006 s714(6), previously CA 1985 s173(2);s173(5)] If the auditors are unable to issue such a report without qualification, the company cannot legally purchase or redeem any of its shares out of capital.

The directors' statement must state the amount of the 'permissible capital payment' and that, in their opinion, there are no grounds on which the company could be found unable to pay its debts immediately following the date of the payment and that the company will be able to carry on business as a going concern (and accordingly pay its debts as they fall due) throughout the following year. [CA 2006 s714(2–3), previously CA 1985 s173(3)] The auditors' report on the directors' statement is certainly no formality and may often involve a substantial amount of work. Companies proposing to redeem or repurchase their own shares out of capital should therefore consult their auditors at an early stage to avoid any misunderstandings about what will be involved.

From 1 October 2008, private companies are able to reduce their capital by solvency statement (see **section 6** below). This procedure does not require a report by the auditor and may therefore be an attractive alternative for private companies which intend to redeem or purchase shares.

3.4 Purchasing or redeeming share capital denominated in a foreign currency

Companies may issue share capital denominated in a currency that is not their functional currency. Under previous UK GAAP (i.e. before FRS 25), non-equity share capital was sometimes retranslated at each balance sheet date and there were arguments for and against this depending on the circumstances. Under IAS 32 (and FRS 25), the position is different because, in most cases, shares for which retranslation would have been considered appropriate will now be presented as liabilities.

When foreign currency share capital is presented as a liability in the balance sheet, for example because the holder can require redemption, the liability will be retranslated at each balance sheet date in accordance with IAS 21.

By contrast, because it represents a residual interest and is not a liability to shareholders, equity share capital is recorded initially at the exchange rate ruling at the date of issue and is not retranslated subsequently under IAS 21.

A difficulty is encountered where a company that has previously issued foreign currency share capital wishes to redeem, cancel or purchase some or all of those shares. This can be illustrated by the following example.

Example 3.4

Shares denominated in foreign currency

A company issues 1,000 equity shares for $1 each. The shares each have a nominal value of $1. The company's functional (or local) currency is Sterling. The exchange rate ruling when the shares were issued was $2:£1.

Several years later, the company purchases those shares for $1 each and then cancels the shares. Assume at this date the exchange rate is (i) $1.50:£1 and (ii) $2.50:£1.

On issue, the share capital of $1,000 would be translated to £500.

The company does not retranslate the share capital in subsequent years' accounts. Therefore, at the date of purchase and cancellation, the share capital is still recorded at £500.

However, the $1,000 paid to purchase the shares translates to either (i) £667 or (ii) £400.

Two questions arise as highlighted by the double-entry, which is:

	$1.50:£1		**$2.50:£1**	
	Debit	**Credit**	**Debit**	**Credit**
	£	**£**	**£**	**£**
Called up share capital	500		500	
?	167			100
Cash		667		400
Distributable profits	?		?	
Capital redemption reserve		?		?

The first question is which account is debited with £167 or credited with £100?

The second question is how much should be transferred out of distributable profits to capital redemption reserve: £500 or £667/£400?

On the first question, it is necessary to consider whether the share premium account might be available for any debit. Assuming the shares were not originally issued at a premium, the share premium account is not available to fund the debit and it would, therefore, seem logical for the entry to be to distributable profits. In the case of the credit entry, again it seems logical for the entry to be to distributable profits, provided that the shares were originally issued for cash or near cash.

This tends to suggest that the transfer to the capital redemption reserve ought to be the $ amount of share capital translated at the historic exchange rate (i.e. a transfer of £500). However, some legal advice has apparently suggested that, under the Act's capital maintenance rules, the transfer to the capital redemption reserve should be the nominal value of the shares translated at the exchange rate ruling at the date of the redemption or purchase, i.e. £667/£400.

Therefore, if a company has foreign currency share capital and wishes to redeem or purchase the shares, it should take legal advice.

TECH 01/08 specifically excludes this issue from its scope. However, it is understood that the ICAEW and ICAS are seeking legal advice on this matter and may issue guidance in due course.

3.5 Expenses of purchasing equity shares

The expenses of repurchasing shares that are accounted for as equity instruments are charged direct to equity together with the purchase price. This follows from IAS 32(35) which states that transaction costs of an equity transaction, other than costs of issuing an equity instrument that are directly attributable to the acquisition of a business, are accounted for as a deduction from equity, net of any related income tax benefit.

When shares are presented as a liability, any costs of repurchase or redemption are accounted for as the costs of settlement of that liability and are therefore charged in profit or loss.

3.6 Treasury shares

Regulations which came into force on 1 December 2003 relaxed, in some circumstances, the requirement that a company that purchases its own shares must subsequently cancel them.

The Regulations allow companies that purchase their own shares out of distributable profits the option of holding them 'in treasury' for sale at a later date or transferring them for the purposes of, or pursuant to, an employee share scheme. The Regulations also allow the shares to be subsequently cancelled. The objective is to give companies greater flexibility to adjust their capital and could consequently lead to an overall reduction in their cost of capital. The 2006 Act does not amend the existing law in this area.

Only 'qualifying shares' may be held in treasury. Qualifying shares are shares which:

[CA 2006 s724(2), previously CA 1985 s162(4)]

(a) are included in the official list in accordance with the provisions of Part 6 of the Financial Services and Markets Act 2000 (e.g. listed on the London Stock Exchange);

(b) are traded on the market known as the Alternative Investment Market established under the rules of the London Stock Exchange;

(c) are officially listed in an EEA State; or

(d) are traded on a regulated market in an EEA State.

Private companies, and public companies with shares which are not listed or traded on one of the above markets, continue to be required to cancel immediately any of their own shares which they purchase.

Where qualifying shares are purchased by a company out of distributable profits, the company may:

(a) hold the shares (or any of them); [CA 2006 s724(3), previously CA 1985 s162A(1)] or

(b) sell the shares (or any of them) for cash; [CA 2006 s727(1), previously CA 1985 162D(1)] or

(c) transfer the shares (or any of them) for the purposes of or pursuant to an employee share scheme; [CA 2006 s727(1), previously CA 1985 162D(1)] or

(d) cancel the shares (or any of them). [CA 2006 s729(1), previously CA 1985 s162D(1)]

For this purpose 'cash' is defined more restrictively than in connection with share issues. [CA 2006 s583(3), previously CA 1985 s738(2)] Here 'cash' means:

[CA 2006 s727(2), previously CA 1985 s162D(2)]

(a) cash (including foreign currency) received by the company; or

(b) a cheque received by the company in good faith which the directors have no reason for suspecting will not be paid; or

(c) a release of a liability of the company for a liquidated sum; or

(d) an undertaking to pay cash to the company on or before a date not more than 90 days after the date on which the company agrees to sell the shares; or

for companies under the 2006 Act:

(e) payment by any other means giving rise to a present or future entitlement (of the company or a person acting on the company's behalf) to a payment, or credit equivalent to payment, in cash. [CA 2006 s727(2)(e)]

If the company cancels shares held as treasury shares, the company must diminish the amount of the issued share capital by the nominal value of the shares cancelled. [CA 2006 s729(4), previously CA 1985 s162D(4)] If shares held as treasury shares cease to be qualifying shares (e.g. because they cease to be listed), the company is required to cancel them forthwith. But this does not apply in respect of shares which are only suspended from listing. [CA 2006 s729(2–3), previously CA 1985 s162E] When treasury shares are cancelled, section 733 of the 2006 Act (previously s170 of the 1985 Act) applies and the amount by which the company's issued share capital is diminished is transferred to the capital redemption reserve (see **3.2** above).

The aggregate nominal value of the shares held as treasury shares must not at any time exceed 10 per cent of the nominal value of the issued share capital of the shares in that class at that time. Where a company contravenes this requirement, it must dispose of or cancel the excess shares in accordance with the requirements of the Act within twelve months of when the contravention occurs. [CA 2006 s725, previously CA 1985 s162B]

The company must not exercise any rights (including those to attend and vote at meetings) in respect of the treasury shares. Any purported exercise of such a right is void. No dividend may be paid, and no other distribution (in cash or otherwise) may be made, to the company in respect of treasury shares. But this should not be taken as preventing an allotment of shares as fully paid bonus shares in respect of the treasury shares or the payment of any amount payable on the redemption of the treasury shares (if they are redeemable shares). [CA 2006 s726, previously CA 1985 s162C]

As noted above, any purchase of shares to be held as treasury shares will have been made out of distributable profits. The distributable profits of the company will have therefore been reduced by the amount of the purchase price. The Act specifies how the proceeds of sale of any treasury shares should affect distributable profits.

Where the proceeds of sale are equal to or less than the purchase price paid by the company for the shares, the proceeds should be treated as a realised profit. Where the proceeds of sale exceed the purchase price paid by the company for the shares, that part of the proceeds that is equal to the purchase price paid should be treated as a realised profit of the company (i.e. to restore the original reduction in realised profits). A sum equal to the excess should be transferred to the share premium account (i.e. so that the purchase and sale of shares cannot create a realised profit). For these purposes, the purchase price paid by the company for the shares should be determined by the application of a weighted average price method. Where the shares were allotted to the company as fully paid bonus shares, the purchase price paid for them should, for the purpose of calculating the weighted average, be treated as nil. [CA 2006 s731, previously CA 1985 s162F]

The FSA effected changes to the Listing Rules to take account of the introduction of treasury shares. The new rules were designed to maintain investor protection and to reduce any perceived scope for market manipulation. The principal changes to the Listing Rules were:

(a) a prohibition on the sale or transfer of shares out of treasury when a company is in a close period or in possession of unpublished price-sensitive information;

(b) a requirement to disclose all transfers of shares into and out of treasury (and cancellations of shares held in treasury) together with the resultant number of shares held in treasury following each transaction; and

(c) a limit on the discount to market price at which shares can be sold for cash out of treasury non pre-emptively (this limit does not apply to 'all employee' share option schemes).

In accordance with IAS 32.33 the amount paid to purchase the treasury shares is recognised directly in equity. IAS 32.34 requires the amount of treasury shares held to be disclosed separately, either on the face of the balance sheet or in the notes. The accounting treatment for treasury shares is considered further in **section 5** of **chapter 15**.

If the amount of treasury shares held is shown as a separate line on the face of the balance sheet, it should clearly be a component of equity rather than a deduction from a sub-total described as equity.

There are arguments for and against the presentation of treasury shares as a separate line on the face of the balance sheet but either treatment is acceptable under IAS 32. Given that the consideration paid for the shares must be treated as reducing profits available for distribution, however, perhaps the simplest treatment is to reduce the balance on retained earnings. Where treasury shares are shown as a separate item, this amount will have to be taken into account together with the balance on retained earnings when considering whether a dividend may lawfully be paid.

4 Financial assistance for acquisition of own shares

4.1 General prohibition

From 1 October 2008, the 2006 Act brings in changes to the provisions applying to companies regarding financial assistance by a company for acquisition of its own shares. Under the 1985 Act there was, subject to certain exceptions, a general prohibition on companies giving financial assistance for the purpose of an acquisition of shares in its own shares. The law surrounding financial assistance for the purpose of acquisition of shares for private companies has been relaxed under the 2006 Act. See **4.2** below.

The provisions covered in s151 to 154 of the 1985 Act which applied to all companies are similar to s678 to 682 of the 2006 Act except that the provisions in the 2006 Act apply only to public companies (and subsidiaries of public companies).

This general prohibition states that, with certain exceptions, including those outlined below, it is unlawful for a company to give financial assistance directly or indirectly (i.e. loan, gift, guarantee, indemnity or security, etc.) for the purpose of the acquisition of its shares or those of its holding company or for the purpose of reducing or discharging any liability incurred in the acquisition of such shares. [CA 2006 s678–679, previously CA 1985 s151] The Act defines 'reducing or discharging a liability' as wholly or partly restoring the person's financial position to what it was before the acquisition took place. [CA 2006 s683(2), previously CA 1985 s152(3)]

In respect of the 2006 Act, where a person is acquiring or proposing to acquire shares in a public company, it is not lawful for that company, or a company that is a subsidiary of that company, to give financial assistance directly or indirectly for the purpose of the acquisition before or at the same time as the acquisition takes place. [CA 2006 678(1)]

Under the 2006 Act there is also a restriction over assistance by public company for acquisition of shares in its private holding company. Where a person is acquiring or proposing to acquire shares in a private company, it is not lawful for a public company that is a subsidiary of that company to give financial assistance directly or indirectly for the purpose of the acquisition before or at the same time as the acquisition takes place. [CA 2006 s679(1)]

This prohibition is wide and would include, for example, giving the person acquiring shares a gift of cash or granting the person a loan specifically to replace the cash of its own that it had used to buy the shares. The law in this area is complex and may have unexpected consequences. For example, there is no time limit on when financial assistance after an acquisition ceases to be unlawful. Accordingly many transactions between holding companies and subsidiaries after the acquisition are capable of being challenged as breaches of section 678(3) or 679(3) of the 2006 Act (previously CA 1985 s151(2)). If in doubt, legal advice should be obtained.

This prohibition does not apply where:

[CA 2006 s682(2), previously CA 1985 s153(4)]

(a) the lending of money is part of the ordinary business of the company and the money is lent in the ordinary course of business; or

(b) the provision of financial assistance is made for the purpose of an employees' share scheme; or

(c) the provision of financial assistance by the company or its subsidiaries is to enable or facilitate transactions in the company's shares between (and involving the acquisition of beneficial ownership of those shares by) employees or former employees or their spouses, widow(er)s or infant children or stepchildren; or

(d) the loan is made to bona fide employees (not directors) to enable them to purchase shares in the company or its holding company to be held by them by way of beneficial ownership

And also where:

[CA 2006 678(2) and 679(2), previously CA 1985 s153(1)

(e) the principal purpose of the transaction is not to give financial assistance for the purpose of the acquisition of shares, or is incidental to some larger purpose, and the assistance is given in good faith in the interests of the company.

However, a public company may only give financial assistance under (a) to (d) above if its net assets are not thereby reduced or, to the extent that net assets are reduced, the assistance is provided out of distributable profits. [CA 2006 682, previously CA 1985 s154] For this purpose, net assets means the book value of the company's net assets, as opposed to their actual value, immediately before the financial assistance is given.

This requirement will be relevant where a public company makes use of the exemption to provide financial assistance for the purposes of an employee share scheme. An example of this would be where a company makes a loan or gift to an ESOP trust to enable it to buy shares in the company.

Guidance on this issue under UK GAAP and IFRSs is provided in TECH 01/8 *Guidance on the determination of realised profits and losses in the context of distributions under the Companies Act 1985* (see **section 5.7** below). UITF Abstract 38 is consistent with IAS 32 in requiring 'own shares' to be deducted within equity rather than presented as an asset. However, as more fully explained in **section 9** of **chapter 25**, UITF Abstract 38 requires the deduction to be made in the individual financial statements of the sponsoring company of the trust whereas IFRSs will not necessarily require this treatment. Under IFRSs the sponsoring company might instead record a gift or loan to the trust so that the deduction in equity would arise only in the consolidated financial statements, with the trust being treated as a subsidiary under SIC-12. TECH 01/08 explains that the deduction for own shares does not reduce net assets for the purposes of applying s682 of the 2006 Act or s154 of the 1985 Act because, for that purpose, net assets should be determined for the company as a legal person using 'narrow entity accounting' (i.e. ignoring the accounting required by Abstract 38). Therefore the position is broadly the same regardless of whether a company is reporting under UK GAAP or IFRSs. If the assistance is in the form of a loan and the loan is regarded as fully recoverable, there is no reduction in net assets for the purposes of s678 of the 2006 Act (previously CA 1985 s154). Nevertheless, financial assistance is a complex legal subject and appropriate legal advice should be sought where necessary.

4.2 Private companies

The restriction under the 1985 Act on financial assistance for acquisition of shares in private companies is repealed in relation to financial assistance given on or after 1 October 2008. The 2006 Act abolishes the prohibition on private companies giving financial assistance for the purpose of the acquisition of their own shares, or shares of their private holding company (although if the company has a subsidiary which is a public company, the public company may not assist the acquisition of shares in its private holding company). [CA 2006 s679(1)] As a consequence, the 'whitewash' procedure (see **4.2.1** below) will no longer be required.

Concern was expressed about whether financial assistance given by private companies for the purchase of their own shares might continue to be unlawful under common law despite the repeal of the statutory provisions with effect from 1 October 2008. In response to these concerns, a savings provision was included in paragraph 52 of Schedule 4 to The Companies Act (Commencement No.5, Transitional Provisions and Savings) Order 2007 (SI 2007/3495). Although the wording of paragraph 52 is difficult to understand, its practical effect is explained quite clearly in the BERR Explanatory Memorandum to the Order. The relevant paragraphs are reproduced below.

"7.4 Abolition of the prohibition in section 151 renders redundant for private companies the exceptions contained in section 153 and the relaxation from the prohibition contained in sections 155 to 158 (known as the "whitewash" procedure).

7.5 In the Department's view, abolition of the prohibition will mean that a transaction which is currently prohibited by section 151 (but would otherwise be lawful) will not be prohibited by any statutory provision, or by reason of any rule of law relating to the giving of financial assistance by a private company for the purpose of the acquisition of shares in itself or another private company, irrespective of whether or not the transaction falls within section 153 or is capable of being subject to "whitewash".

7.6 In particular, the repeal will not lead to the revival, or the renewed application, of case law (or any rule of law derived from case law), so far as it relates to financial assistance for purchase of own shares, in any case to which the prohibition in section 151 would have applied, whether "whitewash" would have been available in that case or not. The enactment of the predecessors of sections 151 to 158 caused any previously applicable rule of law derived from case law to the effect that financial assistance by a company for acquisition of its own shares was unlawful to cease to have effect in respect of such assistance. This was in accordance with the general principle under which case law ceases to apply (unless Parliament decides otherwise) in cases falling within the scope of application of a statutory provision; and in accordance with section 16(1)(a) of the Interpretation Act 1978, the repeal of those statutory provisions does not revive that case law.

7.7 The rule of law in question is said to have been derived from cases not directly concerned with financial assistance for purchase of own shares, such as *Trevor v Whitworth*, in which the House of Lords decided that a company might not (as the law then stood) purchase its own shares, on the ground that "neither the paid-up nor the nominal capital of the company shall be reduced otherwise than in the manner permitted by [Act of Parliament]".

7.8 The rule in *Trevor v Whitworth* is wider than the prohibition contained in section 151 and therefore may still, in some cases, be relevant to a transaction which would also previously have been prohibited by section 151. An example is where a company which has no (or insufficient) distributable reserves makes a gift of money to a shareholder with which to purchase further shares in the company. This transaction would still be prohibited, notwithstanding the repeal of section 151, because it would result in an unlawful reduction of capital by the company. Similarly, if a company with no (or insufficient) distributable reserves made a loan to a shareholder with a view to the shareholder purchasing further shares in the company and the company was aware when the loan was made that there was no reasonable prospect of the borrower being able to repay it, so that the company would be required to make an immediate provision in respect of the loan, this would similarly continue to be prohibited because it would give rise to an unlawful reduction of capital."

In summary, this appears to mean that a private company can give financial assistance for the purchase of its won shares, irrespective of whether the arrangements could have been 'whitewashed' under the 1985 Act, provided that it does not result in a unlawful reduction of capital.

4.2.1 Financial assistance given before 1 October 2008

Where financial assistance is given before 1 October 2008 the provisions of the 1985 Act continue to apply.

The prohibition on the giving of financial assistance imposed by s151 of the 1985 Act does not apply to a private company, provided the company fulfils certain requirements for safeguarding the interests of creditors and shareholders. [CA 1985 ss156–158] This is sometimes referred to as the 'whitewash' procedure.

The principal limitation imposed on any financial assistance given which does not fall into the exemptions given by s153 of the 1985 Act (see **4.1** above) is that the company has net assets which are not reduced by the financial assistance or, to the extent that the net assets are reduced, the assistance shall be made out of distributable profits. [CA 1985 s155] The safeguards which must be met before the financial assistance can lawfully be given include:

(a) approval of the assistance by special resolution in general meeting (unless the company is a wholly owned subsidiary);

(b) a statutory declaration by the directors; and

(c) a report by the company's auditors on the directors' statutory declaration.

The financial assistance must not be given before the expiry of four weeks from the date on which the special resolution was passed (unless all the members of the company entitled to attend and vote on the special resolution voted in favour of it) nor must it be given later than eight weeks after the date on which the statutory declaration was given. [CA 1985 s157–158] Thus, where financial assistance is to be given at regular intervals (e.g. payments of interest and principal over a prolonged period), a statutory declaration supported by an auditors' report will have to be given at the appropriate regular intervals to enable repeated financial assistance to be given in compliance with the Act.

Loans and other financial assistance which may be given by a company under the above rules must not include any loans, etc. to directors which are prohibited by CA 1985 s330 (see **6.3.2** in **chapter 32**).

Where a private company taking advantage of the relaxations for private companies is doing so to give assistance for the acquisition of shares in its parent, there are additional conditions that must be met. [CA 1985 s155–158] These additional conditions include:

(a) the parent whose shares are being or have been acquired must also be a private company;

(b) a private company cannot give assistance for the acquisition of shares in its private parent if that parent has a subsidiary which is a public company and that public company is a parent to the company giving the assistance; and

(c) special resolutions and statutory declarations have to be given by the company giving the assistance, by the company whose shares are being or have been acquired and by any other company which is an intermediate holding company of the company giving the assistance (except, with respect to the special resolution, any company which is a wholly owned subsidiary).

5 Profits available for distribution

5.1 Introduction

There may be significant implications for distributions as a result of the adoption of IFRSs because of the effect on profits and net assets. Also, a number of complex legal issues arise concerning the interpretation of the law and earlier guidance on distributable profits when companies report under IFRSs. The ICAEW and ICAS have published guidance on these issues in TECH 01/08 *Guidance on the determination of realised profits and losses in the context of distributions under the Companies Act 1985* (see **1.1** above). The guidance contained in TECH 01/08 (excluding the appendices) has been reproduced in this section, updated to reflect the requirements of, and references to, the 2006 Act. The guidance has been written for use by companies preparing accounts in accordance with IFRSs and UK GAAP. As explained in 1.1 above, TECH 01/08 consolidates a number of Technical Releases issued previously.

The structure of this section, which follows the structure set out in TECH 01/08, is as follows:

Section 5.2 The legal framework [TECH 01/08 section 2]

Section 5.3 Realised profits [TECH 01/08 section 3]

Section 5.4 Fair value accounting [TECH 01/08 section 4]

Section 5.5 Hedge accounting [TECH 01/08 section 5]

Section 5.6 Issues arising from IAS 32 [TECH 01/08 section 6]

Section 5.7 Employee share schemes [TECH 01/08 section 7]

Section 5.8 Retirement benefit schemes [TECH 01/08 section 8]

Section 5.9 Intragroup transactions [TECH 01/08 section 9]

Section 5.10 Other issues [TECH 01/08 section 10]

In addition, **section 5.11** deals with unlawful distributions.

5.2 The legal framework

The legal requirements concerning distributions are set out in sections 263 to 281 of the 1985 Act. Part 23 (s829–853) of the 2006 Act, which deals with distributions, came into effect on 6 April 2008 and applies to distributions made on or after 6 April 2008. It did not make any significant changes to the law on distributions although there are some minor changes of drafting.

All references to sections of the Act below refer to the 2006 Act. For distributions made before 6 April 2008 refer to TECH 01/08 which can be downloaded from the ICAEW website (*www.icaew.co.uk*).

5.2.1 The common law

The legal framework relating to the determination of realised profits and losses and of profits available for distribution consists of two elements: common law and statutory provisions. Under sections 851 and 852, any restrictions in common law or imposed by the company's memorandum or articles on the sums available for distribution or the cases in which a distribution may be made, take precedence over the statutory provisions. [TECH 01/08 2.1]

Section 851(2) makes an exception to this rule. It provides that the lawfulness and amount of any distribution in kind are established by the statutory rules in sections 845 and 846 (see **5.2.4** below) and not by the applicable common law rules.

The 2006 Act partly codifies the general duties of directors under common law. However, this does not extend to the duties in relation to capital maintenance or duties in relation to creditors of the company which remain governed by common law.

Under common law, a company cannot lawfully make a distribution out of capital. Thus, the directors must consider, both at the time of proposing the distribution and at the time it is made (see **section 5.2.5** below), whether the company, subsequent to the balance sheet date to which the 'relevant accounts' were prepared, has incurred losses that have eroded its profits available for distribution (the 'capital maintenance rule'). Guidance on the application of the capital maintenance rule to the introduction of a new accounting standard is given in **section 5.3.5.2** below. [TECH 01/08 2.2]

5.2.2 *Fiduciary duties and volatility*

In addition, directors are subject to fiduciary duties in the exercise of the powers conferred on them. Examples of fiduciary duties include the obligation on directors to safeguard the company's assets and to ensure that the company is in a position to settle its debts as they fall due. Directors must therefore specifically consider whether the company will still be solvent following a proposed distribution. Thus, directors should consider both the immediate cash flow implications of a distribution and the continuing ability of the company to pay its debts as they fall due. In reaching their decision they must take into account any change in the financial position of the company after the balance sheet date of the relevant accounts and the future cash needs of the company. [TECH 01/08 2.3]

In the context of fair value accounting, volatility is an aspect where directors will need to consider their fiduciary duties. The fair value of financial instruments may be volatile even though such fair value is properly determined in accordance with IAS 39 *Financial Instruments: Recognition and Measurement*. Directors should consider, as a result of their fiduciary duties, whether it is prudent to distribute profits arising from changes in the fair values of financial instruments considered to be volatile, even though they may otherwise be realised profits in accordance with this guidance. [TECH 01/08 2.4]

Similarly, IAS 39 is based on a 'mixed measurement model' whereby some financial instruments may be included at fair value while others may be included on an amortised cost basis. This may, in some cases, lead to volatility in the profit or loss for the period. For example, an asset and a liability may provide an economic hedge but if the asset is measured at fair value and the liability is not, a profit may be reported on one but a loss not reported on the other. Although such profits may be realised profits in accordance with this guidance, directors should consider, as a result of their fiduciary duties, whether it would be prudent to distribute them. [TECH 01/08 2.5]

5.2.3 *Definition of a distribution for Part 23 of the 2006 Act*

A 'distribution' is defined by section 829 as every description of distribution of a company's assets to its members, whether in cash or otherwise, subject to the following exceptions:

[TECH 01/08 2.6]

(a) an issue of shares as fully or partly paid bonus shares;

(b) the reduction of share capital;

  (i) by extinguishing or reducing the liability of any of the members on any of the company's shares in respect of share capital not paid up or,

  (ii) by repaying paid-up share capital;

(c) the redemption or purchase of any of the company's own shares out of capital (including the proceeds of any fresh issue of shares) or out of unrealised profits in accordance with Chapter 3, 4 or 5 of Part 18; and

(d) a distribution of assets to members of the company on its winding-up.

5.2.4 *Profits available for distribution*

A company may make a distribution only out of profits available for that purpose (section 830(1)) (the common law position is set out in **5.21** above). A company's profits available for distribution are its accumulated, realised profits (so far as not previously distributed or capitalised) less its accumulated, realised losses (so far as not previously written off in a reduction or reorganisation of its share capital) (section 830(2)). Thus realised losses may not be offset against unrealised profits. Section 831 imposes a further restriction on public companies (see **5.2.10** below). [TECH 01/08 2.7]

Section 853(4) of the Act states that "references to realised profits and realised losses . . . are to such profits or losses as fall to be treated as realised in accordance with principles generally accepted at the time when the accounts are prepared, with respect to the determination for accounting purposes of realised profits or losses". [TECH 01/08 2.8]

Section 846 provides that where a company makes a distribution consisting of, or including, or treated as arising in consequence of, the sale, transfer or other disposition by the company of a non-cash asset and any part of the amount at which the asset is stated in the accounts relevant to the distribution represents an unrealised profit, that profit is to be treated as realised for the purposes of the distribution. There is nothing in section 846 to require a company to revalue a non-cash asset prior to distributing it in specie or to require the distribution to be recorded at anything other than the book value of the asset. Thus if a company wishes to distribute in specie an asset with a historical cost of £100 and which is in the books at £130 (with the surplus in the revaluation reserve), the surplus of £30 is treated as realised for this purpose and only £100 of other realised profits are needed. However, if the surplus has been capitalised, it is no longer available for this purpose and other realised profits of £130 would be needed to cover the proposed distribution. [TECH 01/08 2.9]

Section 846 applies not only where the company makes a distribution consisting of, or including, a non-cash asset, but also where a company makes a distribution arising from the sale, transfer or other disposition by it of a non-cash asset. This refers to the circumstances dealt with in section 845 of the Act.

Section 845 is a new provision (not in the 1985 Act) which removes doubts arising from the decision in *Aveling Barford Ltd v Perion Ltd* [1989] BCLC 626. Following that decision, it was unclear whether intragroup transfers of assets can be conducted by reference to the asset's book value rather than its market value (which will frequently be higher than book value). In BERR's view the new section does not disturb the position in the *Aveling Barford* case such that where a company which does not have distributable profits makes a distribution by way of a transfer of assets at an undervalue, this will be an unlawful distribution.

However, it clarifies the position where a company does have distributable profits and could make a distribution without contravening any of the provisions of Part 23. It provides that the amount of any distribution consisting of or arising from the sale, transfer or other disposition by the company of a non-cash asset to a member of the company should be calculated by reference to the value at which that asset is included in the company's accounts (i.e. its book value). If an asset is transferred for a consideration not less than its book value, the amount of the distribution is zero. But if the asset is transferred for a consideration less than its book value, the amount of the distribution is equal to that shortfall, which will therefore need to be covered by distributable profits.

In determining whether a company has profits available for distribution for the purposes of section 845, the company's profits available for distribution are treated as increased by the amount (if any) by which the amount or value of any consideration for the disposition exceeds the book value of the asset.

It appears that this provision in s835(3) can be applied only to increase a zero or positive balance on distributable reserves. It cannot be applied when the balance is negative. Therefore, a company that has a shortfall of distributable reserves cannot rely on section 845 to make a transfer of an asset at undervalue even if the profit on disposal would eliminate the shortfall and leave the company with a positive balance of distributable reserves. However, it would be possible to make the transfer lawfully in these circumstances by revaluing the asset to the sale price and applying the provisions of section 846 to treat the resulting surplus as a realised profit for the purposes of the distribution. The ICAEW and ICAS are seeking legal advice on this point and regard should be had to any guidance issued.

The reference to the amount or value of consideration in section 845 is not restricted to consideration that would meet the definition of 'qualifying consideration' in this guidance.

5.2.5 *Date of distribution*

A distribution is made either when a dividend is declared by the company in general meeting and thereby becomes a liability of the company regardless of the date on which it is to be paid; or, in the case of an interim dividend authorised under common form articles of association (for example, Table A), when the dividend is paid. See **5.9.4** below regarding the meaning of "payment" in the context of intragroup transactions. [TECH 01/08 2.10]

5.2.6 *Merger relief and group reconstruction relief*

Where the company has entered into a transaction which gives rise to group reconstruction relief or merger relief under sections 611 or 612, it may choose under section 615 to disregard any amount that would otherwise have been included in the share premium account in determining the amount at which the acquired asset is stated in the company's balance sheet (note that s611, 612 and 615 come into effect on 1 October 2009 but do not change in substance the existing requirements under s131, 132 and 133 of the 1985 Act). The asset may therefore be stated at the nominal value of the shares issued together with any minimum premium value recognised when applying group reconstruction relief. However, it is also possible to record the asset acquired at fair value and to credit the amount of that relief to an other reserve (often called a merger reserve). In such a case, that reserve is in law a profit and is initially treated as unrealised but becomes realised in a manner similar to a revaluation reserve. Thus, provided the merger reserve is not capitalised (by way of a bonus issue of shares), the decision as to whether or not to record the merger reserve should not overall have any effect on the level of the company's realised profits. The accounting choice referred to in this paragraph may be restricted by the application of accounting standards. This is considered further at **5.9.10** below. [TECH 01/08 2.11]

5.2.7 *Relevant accounts*

5.2.7.1 *General*

Under both the Act and common law, distributions are made by individual companies and not by groups. The group accounts are therefore not relevant for the purpose of determining a company's profits available for distribution (see **5.10.1** below). The status of accounts prepared in accordance with IAS 28 *Investments in Associates* or IAS 31 *Interests in Joint Ventures* (i.e. using equity accounting) where a company has an associate or jointly controlled entity but has no subsidiaries is considered at **5.10.1** below. [TECH 01/08 2.12]

Whether or not a distribution may be made within the terms of the Act is determined by reference to a company's 'relevant accounts'. Where it is proposed to make a distribution during the company's first accounting reference period or before any accounts have been circulated, initial accounts must be prepared. In all other cases the relevant accounts are its last annual accounts that were circulated to members or interim accounts if the proposed distribution cannot be justified by reference to those accounts [s836] [TECH 01/08 2.13]

The items in these accounts to which reference is made in determining the amount of a distribution which may be made are listed in section 836(1) as profits, losses, assets, liabilities, provisions, share capital and reserves (including undistributable reserves). Thus, valuations or contingencies referred to in notes to the financial statements, but not incorporated in the balance sheet, do not affect the amount of realised profit calculated by reference to the relevant accounts. For example, if the relevant accounts record an unrealised profit but state in a note that, as a consequence of an event subsequent to the balance sheet date, the profit has become realised, interim accounts must nevertheless be prepared before a distribution can be made out of these profits. Provisions are defined for this purpose in section 836(1) as, in the case of Companies Act accounts, provisions of any kind specified for this purpose by regulations under section 396 and, in the case of IAS accounts, provisions of any kind. [TECH 01/08 2.14]

Similarly, disclosures about the impact of future changes of accounting policy, such as those required by IAS 8.30, do not affect the amount of realised profit calculated by reference to the relevant accounts. However, they may be relevant to the application of the common law on capital maintenance where a distribution is to be made in the period in relation to which the change of policy will be implemented (see **5.3.5** below). [TECH 01/08 2.15]

In practice it may not be sufficient to determine the amount of realised profits simply by examining the relevant accounts as further enquiries may be necessary as to the composition of the various reserves included in the balance sheet. For example, certain reserves may include both realised and unrealised profits. As there is no legal requirement for a company to distinguish in its accounts between distributable and non distributable profits as such (see **5.2.8** below), companies should keep sufficient records to enable them to distinguish between those profits which are available for distribution and those which are not. [TECH 01/08 2.16]

Under section 395, a company's individual accounts must be prepared either as "Companies Act individual accounts" or as "IAS individual accounts". Thus, the relevant accounts will be either its "Companies Act individual accounts" or "IAS individual accounts", depending on the choice made by the company. It follows that when a company elects to prepare its statutory individual accounts in accordance with EU-adopted IFRSs, it is the amounts stated in those accounts that are relevant for the purposes of justifying a distribution. [TECH 01/08 2.17]

The detailed requirements for relevant accounts (annual, interim or initial) are summarised in the following paragraphs. [TECH 01/08 2.18]

5.2.7.2 Annual accounts – all companies

If the company's last annual accounts constitute the relevant accounts they must be prepared under Part 15 of the Act (Accounts and Reports) and comply with the requirements of section 837. Such accounts may be either "Companies Act individual accounts" or "IAS individual accounts" (see **5.2.7.1** above). The requirements of section 837 are that:

(a) the accounts must have been properly prepared in accordance with the Act (including the requirement in section 393 to give a true and fair view of the assets, liabilities, financial position and profit or loss of the company), subject only to matters not material for determining the lawfulness of a distribution;

(b) the accounts must have been circulated to members in accordance with section 423. Where a company circulates to members a summary financial statement, the relevant accounts are the full accounts from which the summary financial statement was derived;

(c) the accounts must be accompanied, where applicable, by the report of the auditor under section 495; and

(d) if the report of the auditor is qualified, the auditor must state in writing whether in his opinion the matter in respect of which his report is qualified is material for determining the lawfulness of the distribution. The statement by the auditor, which can be subsequent to the report, must be laid before the company in general meeting in the case of a public company, or be circulated to members in accordance with section 423 in the case of a private company.

The last two sub-paragraphs do not apply where the directors of the company have taken advantage of the audit exemption conferred by sections 477(1) or 480(1). [TECH 01/08 2.19]

Where the group prepares accounts using IFRSs whilst the parent's individual accounts continue to be prepared using UK GAAP, two audit reports are required, one for each reporting framework. The auditors' statement under s837(4) relates exclusively to the parent's accounts, as this is the legal entity which has proposed the distribution. Accordingly, qualifications in the parent's audit report rather than the group's need to be considered for the purposes of the statement. If the auditors' statement is to be included with the accounts it should be in the parent's rather than group's accounts.

An 'emphasis of matter' paragraph in the auditors' report does not constitute a qualification. Directors should, nevertheless, consider the possible consequences on their dividend policy of any uncertainty referred to in such a paragraph if they are contemplating making a distribution.

5.2.7.3 Initial and interim accounts – public companies

Sections 838 and 839 respectively provide that interim and initial accounts of a public company must have been 'properly prepared', or have been properly prepared subject only to matters that are not material for determining, by reference to those accounts, whether the proposed distribution would contravene sections 830 or 831. A copy of the interim and initial accounts must have been delivered to the Registrar of Companies. [TECH 01/08 2.20]

'Properly prepared' means that the accounts must comply with sections 395 to 397 which includes the true and fair requirement in relation to Companies Act accounts and the requirement to apply IFRSs in relation to IAS accounts. These requirements are to be applied with such modifications as are necessary because the accounts are prepared otherwise than in respect of an accounting reference period. In the case of interim accounts the balance sheet must be signed in accordance with section 414. There is no equivalent statutory requirement for initial accounts to be signed in accordance with section 414 but, in practice, the auditors will require the accounts to be approved by the directors before the report of the auditors can be signed. [TECH 01/08 2.21]

In requiring the interim and initial accounts to be 'properly prepared', or to be properly prepared except for matters which are not relevant in determining whether a proposed dividend would be lawful under the Act, the legislation permits a public company to choose between preparing interim or initial accounts which give a true and fair view and accounts which give such a view subject only to the exclusion of information which is not relevant in determining whether a distribution would be lawful under the Act. In practice, therefore, interim or initial accounts will consist of a balance sheet and profit and loss account (in the format required by the Accounting Regulations when reporting under UK GAAP or in accordance with IAS 1 when reporting under IFRSs) but the notes may be restricted to those matters that are relevant to a distribution. Corresponding amounts for the previous financial year would not be relevant. [TECH 01/08 2.22]

Many of the additional disclosures required by the Act and accounting standards would not be required as a result of the exemption in sections 838 and 839. For example the disclosure of such items as fixed asset movements, directors' remuneration, cash flow statement, analysis of stocks, particulars of the tax charge, segmental analysis, which would be required in the annual accounts, would not be necessary.

Interim accounts are not required to be audited. However, initial accounts of a public company must be accompanied by a report by the auditors stating whether, in their opinion, the accounts have been 'properly prepared'. If their report is qualified (which would be the case if the company chooses to prepare initial accounts which do not give a true and fair view, as described above), the auditors must make an additional statement which states whether, in their opinion, the matters in respect of which their report is qualified is material for determining, by reference to the initial accounts, whether the distribution would contravene sections 830 or 831.

A copy of the auditors' statement must also have been delivered to the Registrar of Companies and laid before the company in general meeting. [TECH 01/08 2.23]

Due to an anomaly in the law, which also existed under the 1985 Act, where a company omits disclosures which are not material for the purposes of determining whether the proposed distribution is lawful, the auditors will have to qualify their report even though the omission of these disclosures is expressly permitted by the law. This is because s839(5–6) requires auditors to report on whether the financial statements have been 'properly prepared' as defined in s839(4). It makes no mention of the dispensation granted in s839(2) concerning matters which are not material to the proposed distribution.

Where the auditors' report is qualified (as may well be the case for the reasons just explained), the auditors are required to state in writing whether, in their opinion, the matter in respect of which their report is qualified is material for determining whether the distribution would contravene the relevant sections. [s839(6)] However, a qualification solely because the initial accounts have been properly prepared except for matters which are not relevant in determining whether a proposed dividend would be lawful under the Act must by definition not be material for determining whether the distribution is permitted.

Where it appears that a 'technical' qualification, as described above, will be needed because the initial accounts are deficient only in respect of non-relevant matters, companies should consider the cost implications of the steps necessary to remove it (i.e. the additional preparation effort and the cost implications for the audit). Most companies will be prepared to accept a technical qualification. However, others (particularly publicly quoted companies) may prefer to incur the additional effort and expense of preparing, and having audited, the additional disclosures to enable an unqualified opinion to be given.

5.2.7.4 Initial and interim accounts – private companies

The requirements of sections 838 and 839 regarding the form and content of interim and initial accounts of public companies do not apply to private companies. Instead, the only requirement for private companies flows from the general definition at the start of those sections of interim or initial accounts as those necessary to enable a reasonable judgement to be made as to profits, losses, assets and liabilities, provisions, and share capital and reserves. Reliable management accounts which deal with these matters will satisfy this requirement. However, management accounts will often not deal with all relevant matters. For example, they may exclude tax. In these cases, appropriate adjustments need to be made to the management accounts. [TECH 01/08 2.24]

5.2.8 *Disclosure of distributable profits*

There is no requirement under law or accounting standards for financial statements to distinguish between realised profits and unrealised profits or between distributable profits and non-distributable profits. **Section 5.2.7.1** above draws attention to the need for companies to maintain sufficient records to enable them to distinguish between those profits that are available for distribution and those which are not. [TECH 01/08 2.25]

The guidance at **5.2.7.1** above is likely to be of greater significance when reporting under IFRSs or using the fair value accounting rules under UK GAAP than has previously been the case. One reason for this is that the restriction in the Accounting Regulations that only profits realised at the balance sheet date may be included in the profit and loss account does not apply in these cases. [TECH 01/08 2.26]

It may be thought helpful to users of financial statements if there is an indication of which reserves are distributable but, as noted above, there is no legal requirement to do so. In some cases, there may be practical difficulties with providing such an analysis. For example, there may be uncertainties about whether certain profits are realised or unrealised. There is generally no need for directors to form a view on whether profits are realised unless they intend to utilise them to make a distribution. [TECH 01/08 2.27]

5.2.9 *Subsequent events*

Under common law, a company cannot lawfully make a distribution out of capital. Therefore it may be necessary to take into account losses incurred after the balance sheet date (see **5.2.1** above). [TECH 01/08 2.28]

One or more distributions may already have been made by reference to a particular set of accounts; for example, an interim dividend or a purchase of own shares. In determining the lawfulness of any proposed further distribution by reference to the same accounts, the directors must take account of any such distributions (s840(1)). [TECH 01/08 2.29]

5.2.10 *Public companies*

A further restriction is placed on distributions by public companies (s831). A public company may make a distribution only if, after giving effect to such distribution, the amount of its net assets (as defined in section 831(2)) is not less than the aggregate of its called up share capital and undistributable reserves as shown in the relevant accounts. [TECH 01/08 2.30]

Under section 831(4) the following are undistributable reserves:

(a) share premium account (see also section 610);

(b) capital redemption reserve (see also section 733);

(c) the excess of accumulated unrealised profits, so far as not previously utilised by capitalisation, over the accumulated unrealised losses, so far as not previously written off in a reduction or reorganisation of its share capital; and

(d) any other reserve which the company is prohibited from distributing by any enactment (e.g. a redenomination reserve arising under section 628), or by its articles of association (or equivalent).

This means that, in calculating the amount available for distributions, a public company must reduce the amount of its net realised profits available for distribution by the amount of its net unrealised losses. The effects of this rule in relation to holdings of own shares through an ESOP trust and in relation to the presentation of shares as liabilities in the balance sheet are addressed at **5.7.1.6** and **5.6.3** respectively. [TECH 01/08 2.31]

5.2.11 *Provisions and asset revaluations*

The general rule is that any provision (including one for depreciation or diminution in value as well as provisions for liabilities, charges or losses) is treated as a realised loss. [TECH 01/08 2.32]

As an exception to the general rule, a provision for diminution in value of a fixed asset appearing on a revaluation of all the fixed assets (other than goodwill) is not treated as a realised loss (s841(3)). However, this exception would not apply where the fixed asset has been sold or scrapped, because in these circumstances any loss would need to be reclassified as realised. Furthermore, unrealised losses which exceed unrealised profits are relevant to a public company in determining the amount available for distribution as the requirements of section 831 (Restrictions on the distribution of assets) referred to at **5.2.10** above must be satisfied. These issues are considered further at **5.10.2** below, including their continued application under IFRSs. [TECH 01/08 2.33]

For this exception to apply, it is not necessary for a revaluation of all the fixed assets to be recorded in the accounts. Section 841(4) provides that a revaluation of all the fixed assets is treated as having taken place if:

(1) the directors consider the value of any assets that have not actually been revalued;

(2) they are satisfied that the aggregate value of those assets is not less than that stated in the company's accounts; and

(3) the notes to the accounts include a statement to that effect.

The notes to the accounts should also state that amounts are stated in the accounts on the basis that a revaluation of fixed assets is treated as having taken place. [TECH 01/08 2.34]

Special considerations apply where a fixed asset has been revalued and an unrealised profit is recorded. Where a sum written off or retained for depreciation on or after the revaluation exceeds that which would have been charged if the unrealised profit had not been made, the excess does not give rise overall to a realised loss as there is a corresponding realisation of the related revaluation surplus, to the extent that that surplus has not previously been capitalised (s841(5)). This means that the loss arising on the depreciation of revalued fixed assets is, in effect, calculated for distribution purposes by using historical cost principles, except to the extent that the surplus has previously been capitalised. [TECH 01/08 2.35]

If an asset is revalued downwards below its recoverable amount, as defined in FRS 11 or IAS 36, then the difference between that revalued amount and recoverable amount is treated as an unrealised loss as it reflects a revaluation adjustment rather than a provision as defined in section 841. [TECH 01/08 2.36]

Under IAS 16, any revaluation loss that exceeds an existing revaluation surplus will be recognised as an expense in the income statement. Under FRS 15, such a loss would be recognised in the Statement of Total Recognised Gains and Losses to the extent that the asset's recoverable amount was greater than its revalued amount. Also, under FRS 15, where an impairment loss on a revalued asset is caused by a clear consumption of economic benefits, the loss will be taken to the profit and loss account. Under IAS 16, it will be taken to equity to the extent that there is a revaluation surplus relating to the asset. Consequently, losses may be reported differently under IFRSs and UK GAAP but the effect on accumulated realised profits will be the same. [TECH 01/08 2.37]

5.2.12 *Development costs*

Section 844 requires that development costs shown as an asset should be treated as a realised loss, except where the directors justify the costs carried forward being treated as an asset. This would be the case if the costs are carried forward in accordance with applicable accounting standards. The justification must be included in a note to the accounts (s844(3)). [TECH 01/08 2.38]

5.2.13 *Continued application of capital maintenance law under IFRSs*

Those aspects of the Act that deal with matters other than those relating to the form and content of accounts will continue to apply when accounts are prepared under EU-adopted IFRSs. All of the rules on capital maintenance in the Act therefore continue to apply. That is to say, the legal rules regarding shares (and the share premium account) continue to control, for example, payments in respect of those shares even though the shares (and related share premium) may be presented as liabilities in the accounts. For example, the ability to pay dividends on preference shares is still determined by reference to the availability of distributable profits even if those dividends are reported as an expense in accordance with EU-adopted IFRSs. [TECH 01/08 2.39] This is illustrated in **example 1.3** above.

5.2.14 *Treasury shares*

Sections 724 to 732 of the Act relax, in some circumstances, the requirement that when a company purchases its own shares they are automatically cancelled. They allow certain public companies that purchase their own "qualifying shares" out of distributable profits the option of holding them "in treasury" (i.e. un-cancelled) for sale at a later date (which must be for cash) or transferring them for the purposes of, or pursuant to, an employee share scheme. The treasury shares may also be cancelled at a later date. Only "qualifying shares" may be held in treasury. Qualifying shares are shares which are included in the Official List, traded on AIM, officially listed in another EEA state or traded on a regulated market established in an EEA state. In all other cases, shares purchased are cancelled by the automatic operation of the law in accordance with section 688 and section 706. [TECH 01/08 2.40]

Any purchase of shares to be held in treasury has to be made out of distributable profits which will be reduced by the amount of the purchase price. [TECH 01/08 2.41]

The Act specifies how the proceeds of sale of any treasury shares for cash affects distributable profits. Where the proceeds of sale are equal to or less than the purchase price paid by the company for the shares, the proceeds should be treated as realised profits (i.e. to reverse the original reduction in realised profits up to the purchase price paid). Where the proceeds of sale exceed the purchase price paid by the company for the shares, that part of the proceeds that is equal to the purchase price paid should be treated as a realised profit of the company. A sum equal to the excess should be transferred to the share premium account (i.e. so that the purchase and sale of shares cannot create an overall increase in realised profits). For these purposes, section 731(4) provides that the purchase price paid by the company for the shares should be determined by the application of a weighted average price method. [TECH 01/08 2.42]

Investments in own shares through an ESOP trust are not treasury shares as a matter of law. The distributable profit implications of shares held by an ESOP trust are considered in **section 5.7**. The purchase by an ESOP trust of shares held as treasury shares is considered at **5.7.1.9**. [TECH 01/08 2.43] Further details of the legal requirements concerning treasury shares are set out at **3.6** above.

5.2.15 *Section 832 – Investment companies*

Investment companies are defined in section 833. Under section 832 they are permitted, subject to meeting certain requirements in section 832(5), to make distributions in circumstances, described in the following paragraph, which would not be permitted for other public companies under section 831. However, section 832 is an alternative rather than an additional test for investment companies. An investment company may be able to make a distribution in accordance with section 831 even if it fails the test in section 832 that its assets are at least equal to one and a half times the aggregate of its liabilities to creditors.

An investment company may make distributions at any time out of its accumulated realised revenue profits, so far as not previously utilised by a distribution or capitalisation, less its accumulated revenue losses (whether realised or unrealised), so far as not previously written off in a reduction or reorganisation of capital duly made:

[TECH 01/08 2.44]

- if at that time the amount of its assets is at least equal to one and a half times the aggregate of its liabilities to creditors;
- if, and to the extent that, the distribution does not reduce that amount to less than one and a half times that aggregate; and

- the conditions set out in section 832(5) are met.

In most circumstances, these rules allow an investment company to ignore capital losses, whether realised or unrealised, when making a distribution. [TECH 01/08 2.45]

As noted at **5.6.3** in relation to section 831, the presentation of financial instruments in accordance with the substance of their contractual terms under IFRSs may affect the amount of a company's liabilities as stated in its relevant accounts. In particular, where all or part of the amount attributable to preference shares is presented as a liability, total liabilities will be increased by that amount. The amount of a company's assets is unaffected by the reclassification of shares as liabilities. [TECH 01/08 2.46]

However, section 832 refers to "liabilities to creditors". Although "creditors" is not defined for this purpose in the Act, it is the clear intention that this amount should exclude amounts in respect of shares. "Liabilities to creditors" therefore excludes amounts in respect of share capital and share premium that have been presented as liabilities. It also excludes other amounts due to shareholders in their capacity as such including accruals for dividends and redemption premiums that have been presented as expenses in the income statement and liabilities in the balance sheet. It would not, however, as explained by the DTI (now BERR) in their guidance, exclude general accruals, deferred income or deferred tax. [TECH 01/08 2.47]

5.3 Realised profits

5.3.1 General

Section 830(2) of the Act defines a company's profits available for distribution as 'its accumulated, realised profits, so far as not previously utilised by distribution or capitalisation, less its accumulated, realised losses, so far as not previously written off in a reduction or reorganisation of capital duly made'. Realised profits and realised losses are defined as 'such profits or losses of the company as fall to be treated as realised in accordance with principles generally accepted at the time when the accounts are prepared, with respect to the determination for accounting purposes of realised profits or losses' (s853(4)). It is apparent from the use of the words 'fall to be treated as realised' (rather than, simply, 'realised') that the concept of a realised profit is intended to be dynamic, changing with the development of generally accepted accounting principles, as well as bringing within the definition profits which might not in ordinary language be called realised. [TECH 01/08 3.1]

The determination of a company's profits available for distribution is derived from what is recorded in its accounts which are relevant for this purpose (see **5.2.7** above). It is fundamental for this purpose that the company's accounts have been properly prepared in accordance with the law and generally accepted accounting principles. Profits available for distribution may include amounts reported outside the profit and loss account (i.e. in the Statement of Total Recognised Gains and Losses or Reconciliation of Movements in Shareholders' Funds and their equivalents under IFRSs). [TECH 01/08 3.2]

5.3.2 *Principles of realisation*

It is generally accepted that profits shall be treated as realised for the purpose of applying the definition of realised profits in companies legislation only when realised in the form of cash or of other assets the ultimate cash realisation of which can be assessed with reasonable certainty. In this context, "realised" may also encompass profits relating to assets that are readily realisable. This would embrace profits and losses resulting from the recognition of changes in fair values, in accordance with relevant accounting standards, to the extent that they are readily convertible to cash. [TECH 01/08 3.3]

The principles of realisation set out in this guidance are consistent with the notion of realisation as expressed in FRS 18. They are, however, relevant irrespective of whether the relevant accounts are prepared under UK GAAP or under IFRSs. The guidance also recognises that certain amounts may, as a matter of law, be profits (see **5.3.3.1** below). [TECH 01/08 3.4]

In assessing whether a company has a realised profit, transactions and arrangements should not be looked at in isolation. A realised profit will arise only where the overall commercial effect on the company satisfies the definition of realised profit set out in this guidance. Thus a group or series of transactions or arrangements should be viewed as a whole, particularly if they are artificial, linked (whether legally or otherwise) or circular. This principle is likely to be of particular relevance for intragroup transactions which are considered in **section 5.9**. [TECH 01/08 3.5]

A profit previously regarded as unrealised becomes realised when the relevant criteria set out in this guidance are met (for example, a revaluation surplus becomes realised when the related asset is sold for 'qualifying consideration'). Similarly, a profit previously regarded as realised becomes unrealised when the criteria set out in this guidance cease to be met. [TECH 01/08 3.6]

5.3.3 *Definitions*

The definitions which follow should be read in conjunction with the principles of realisation as well as the guidance on their interpretation set out in TECH 01/08 and reproduced below. [TECH 01/08 3.7]

5.3.3.1 *Profit*

'Profit' for the purpose of section 853(4) comprises:

[TECH 01/08 3.8]

(a) 'gains', as defined in the Accounting Standards Board's *Statement of Principles for Financial Reporting* and 'income' as defined in the International Accounting Standards Board's *Framework* which both convey (with different wording) increases in ownership interest not resulting from contributions from owners; and

(b) other amounts which are profits as a matter of law, or which are treated as profits, including:

   (i) gratuitous contributions of assets from owners in their capacity as such; and

   (ii) an amount taken to a so-called 'merger reserve' reflecting the extent that relief is obtained under sections 611 or 612 of the Act from the requirement to recognise a share premium account.

5.3.3.2 *Realised profit*

A profit is realised, as a matter of generally accepted accounting practice, where it arises from:

[TECH 01/08 3.9]

(a) a transaction where the consideration received by the company is 'qualifying consideration'; or

(b) an event which results in 'qualifying consideration' being received by the company in circumstances where no consideration is given by the company; or

(c) the recognition in the financial statements of a change in fair value, in those cases where fair value has been determined in accordance with the fair value measurement guidance in the relevant accounting standards, and to the extent that the change recognised is readily convertible to cash; or

(d) the translation of:

(i) a monetary asset which comprises qualifying consideration; or

(ii) a liability,

denominated in a foreign currency; or

(e) the reversal of a loss previously regarded as realised; or

(f) a profit (which has not been capitalised) previously regarded as unrealised (such as amounts taken to a revaluation reserve, merger reserve or other similar reserve,) becoming realised as a result of:

(i) consideration previously received by the company becoming 'qualifying consideration'; or

(ii) the related asset being disposed of in a transaction where the consideration received by the company is 'qualifying consideration'; or

(iii) a realised loss being recognised on the scrapping or disposal of the related asset; or

(iv) a realised loss being recognised on the write-down for depreciation, amortisation, diminution in value or impairment of the related asset;

(v) the distribution in specie of the asset to which the unrealised profit relates; or

(vi) the receipt of a dividend in the form of qualifying consideration when no profit is recognised because the dividend is deducted from the book value of the investment to which the unrealised profit relates (e.g. as required by IAS 27 prior to its amendment in May 2008 in the case of dividends out of pre-acquisition profits of subsidiaries) (see **5.9.3.4** below),

in which case the appropriate proportion of the related unrealised profit becomes a realised profit. In the case of (f)(iii) and (iv), the loss is treated as a realised loss under paragraph **5.3.4.2** (TECH 01/08 3.15). However, part of this realised loss is compensated by a reclassification from unrealised to realised profit.

In addition, The Companies (Reduction of Share Capital) Order 2008 SI 2008/1915 (which comes into force on 1 October 2008) specifies the cases in which a reserve arising from a reduction in a company's share capital is to be treated as a realised profit as a matter of law. They are as follows:

(a) if an unlimited company reduces its share capital, a reserve arising from the reduction is treated a realised profit;

(b) if a private company limited by shares reduces its share capital and the reduction is supported by a solvency statement but has not been subject to an application to the court for an order confirming it, the reserve arising from the reduction is treated as a realised profit; and

(c) if a limited company having a share capital reduces its share capital and the reduction is confirmed by order of court, the reserve arising from the reduction is treated as a realised profit unless the court orders otherwise.

These provisions are without prejudice to any contrary provisions of an order or undertaking given to the court, the resolution for, or any other resolution relevant to, the reduction of capital, or the company's memorandum or articles of association. They come into effect on 1 October 2008 but apply irrespective of when the reduction in capital occurred or when the reserve arose. They therefore apply to capital reductions made under the 1985 Act.

5.3.3.3 *Realised loss*

Losses should be regarded as realised losses except to the extent that the law, accounting standards or this guidance provide otherwise. The statutory position is set out in **5.1** above.[TECH 01/08 3.10]

5.3.3.4 *Qualifying consideration*

Qualifying consideration comprises:

[TECH 01/08 3.11]

(a) cash; or

(b) an asset that is readily convertible to cash; or

(c) the release, or the settlement or assumption by another party, of all or part of a liability of the company, unless:

(i) the liability arose from the purchase of an asset that does not meet the definition of qualifying consideration and has not been disposed of for qualifying consideration; and

(ii) the purchase and release are part of a group or series of transactions or arrangements that fall within paragraph 3.5 of TECH 01/08 (see **5.3.2** above); or

(d) an amount receivable in any of the above forms of consideration where:

(i) the debtor is capable of settling the receivable within a reasonable period of time; and

(ii) there is a reasonable certainty that the debtor will be capable of settling when called upon to do so; and

(iii) there is an expectation that the receivable will be settled.

In practice it will usually be straightforward to determine whether the criteria in (a), (b) or (c) have been met. The exception in (c) is in the nature of an anti-avoidance provision to prevent certain artificial arrangements and is unlikely to be relevant except in rare cases.

For example, consider the situation where a company acquires property and the consideration is initially left outstanding as a creditor. If that creditor is then almost immediately waived, the substance of the transaction is that the company has acquired the property for no consideration. Even if the property is recorded at fair value on acquisition, any profit recognised will not be a realised profit. The position will be less clear cut if the creditor is waived at a later date and this was not envisaged at the date of the original transfer of the property.

More difficulty is likely to be encountered when applying criterion (d). TECH 01/08 does not provide any further clarification of the meaning of 'a reasonable period of time'. Judgement will be required in assessing whether there is 'reasonable certainty' that the debtor will be capable of settling when called upon to do so and whether there is an 'expectation' that the receivable will be settled.

Although TECH 01/08 does not say so, criterion (d) was written primarily to deal with intragroup transactions in which balances may arise where there is no intention that they will ever be settled. Criterion (d) will not usually be an issue for arm's length transactions between independent parties.

5.3.3.5 *Readily convertible to cash*

An asset, or change in the fair value of an asset or liability, is considered to be "readily convertible to cash" if:

[TECH 01/08 3.12]

(a) a value can be determined at which a transaction in the asset or liability could occur, at the date of determination (see **5.4.2.9** for a limited exception to this rule for the determination of the effect that any block discounts on securities traded in an active market has on realised profits) , in its state at that date, without negotiation and/or marketing, to either convert the asset, liability or change in fair value into cash, or to close out the asset, liability or change in fair value; and

(b) in determining the value, information such as prices, rates or other factors that market participants would consider in setting a price is observable; and

(c) the company's circumstances must not prevent immediate conversion to cash or close out of the asset, liability or change in fair value; for example, the company must be able to dispose of, or close out the asset, liability or the change in fair value, without any intention or need to liquidate or curtail materially the scale of its operations, or to undertake a transaction on adverse terms.

Further guidance on the application of "readily convertible to cash" is provided in **section 5.4**. The position regarding fair value losses is dealt with at **5.4.5** below. [TECH 01/08 3.13]

5.3.4 Application

5.3.4.1 Instances of realised profit

In addition to those instances which are readily apparent from the definition of realised profit, in applying the principles of realisation and the definitions set out above the following would constitute a realised profit:

[TECH 01/08 3.14]

(a) the receipt or accrual of investment or other income receivable in the form of qualifying consideration; or

(b) a gain arising on a return of capital on an investment where the return is in the form of qualifying consideration; or

(c) a gift (such as a 'capital contribution') received in the form of qualifying consideration; or

(d) the release of a provision for a liability or loss which was treated as a realised loss; or

(e) the reversal of a write-down or provision for diminution in value or impairment of an asset which was treated as a realised loss.

5.3.4.2 Instances of realised loss

Realised losses will include:

[TECH 01/08 3.15]

(a) a cost or expense (other than one charged to the share premium account) which results in a reduction in recorded net assets;

(b) a loss arising on the sale or other disposal or scrapping of an asset;

(c) the writing down, or providing for the depreciation, amortisation, diminution in value or impairment, of an asset (see **5.3.3.2** for additional considerations where the asset has been revalued or is otherwise represented to any extent by an unrealised profit), except as noted at **5.2.11** above and as described in paragraph 3.16 of TECH 01/08;

(d) the creation of, or increase in, a provision for a liability or loss (other than deferred tax in the circumstances described below) which results in an overall reduction in recorded net assets;

(e) a gift made by the company (or the release of all or part of a debt due to the company or the assumption of a liability by the company) to the extent that it results in an overall reduction in recorded net assets; and

(f) a loss arising from fair value accounting where profits on remeasurement of the same asset or liability would be treated as realised profits.

Where a fixed asset is revalued to an amount which is below its 'recoverable amount' as defined in FRS 11 or IAS 36, the resulting loss below recoverable amount is not an impairment (as stated in FRS 15(70)) and is therefore treated as an unrealised loss (see **5.2.11** above). Such a loss would become realised in the event of a subsequent scrapping, disposal or impairment of the asset. [TECH 01/08 3.16]

A provision for deferred tax should generally be regarded as a realised loss. However, when assets are revalued to their fair value and the gain is regarded as unrealised, the deferred tax on that gain should be treated as a reduction in that unrealised gain rather than as a realised loss. [TECH 01/08 3.17]

Deferred tax is discussed further at **5.10.8** below.

5.3.4.3 Exchange of assets ('top-slicing')

Where an asset is sold partly for qualifying consideration and partly for other consideration (for example, a mixed consideration of cash and a freehold property), any profit arising is a realised profit to the extent that the fair value of the consideration received is in the form of qualifying consideration. This approach is sometimes referred to as 'top-slicing'. [TECH 01/08 3.18]

Example 5.3.4.3

Top-slicing

An investment with a book value of £50,000 is sold for consideration with a fair value of £100,000 comprising cash of £40,000 and a freehold property worth £60,000.

	£
Fair value of consideration	100,000
Book value of asset sold	50,000
Gain on disposal	50,000
Realised profit (limited to cash consideration)	40,000

5.3.4.4 Hedging

Where hedge accounting is obtained in accordance with the relevant accounting standards, it is necessary to consider the combined effect of both sides of the hedging relationship to determine whether there is a realised profit or loss in accordance with the criteria in this guidance. [TECH 01/08 3.19]

Application of this principle is considered in **section 5.5** below. [TECH 01/08 3.20]

5.3.4.5 Foreign exchange profits and losses

Paragraph 65 of SSAP 20 *Foreign currency translation*, which was issued in 1983, states that 'the application of paragraph 50 of this statement may result in unrealised exchange gains on unsettled long-term monetary items being taken to the profit and loss account'. Since then, however, the currency markets have become more sophisticated and companies have significantly more flexibility to crystallise exchange profits on long-term monetary items. Consequently, unless there are doubts as to the convertibility or marketability of the currency in question, foreign exchange profits arising on the retranslation of monetary items are realised, irrespective of the maturity date of the monetary item. The position regarding certain exchange differences reported in a separate component of equity (i.e. not in the income statement) is considered at **5.5.3** below in relation to cash flow hedge accounting and at **5.10.12** in relation to foreign operations and the use of a reporting currency which is different from the company's functional currency. [TECH 01/08 3.21]

5.3.4.6 Goodwill in an individual company

Where goodwill arises in a company's individual accounts (which would be the case, for example, where the company has purchased an unincorporated business) the goodwill will become a realised loss as the goodwill is amortised or written down for impairment in accordance with relevant accounting standards. [TECH 01/08 3.22]

Where such purchased goodwill was accounted for under SSAP 22 *Accounting for goodwill* by way of immediate elimination against reserves and, under the transitional arrangements in FRS 10, that goodwill remains eliminated against reserves, FRS 10 continues the application of the guidance in Appendix 2 to SSAP 22 (which is reproduced, almost verbatim, as Appendix V of FRS 10). This states that where goodwill is written off on acquisition as a matter of accounting policy (i.e. under the immediate write-off method) rather than because of an actual diminution in value, the write-off does not constitute an immediate realised loss but becomes a realised loss over its useful economic life at the same time and to the same extent as would be the case if the company had adopted a policy of capitalisation and amortisation of the goodwill. Realised profits and losses are therefore calculated after notional amortisation of goodwill which has been written off against reserves.[TECH 01/08 3.23]

5.3.4.7 Negative goodwill in an individual company

The following guidance on negative goodwill applies under UK GAAP and IFRSs unless otherwise stated. IFRS 3 does not use the term 'negative goodwill' but instead refers to an 'excess of the acquirer's interest in the net fair value of the identifiable assets, liabilities and contingent liabilities over cost'. For simplicity, such an amount is described in this guidance as negative goodwill. [TECH 01/08 3.24]

Negative goodwill up to the fair values of the non-monetary assets acquired should be treated as being realised in the periods in which the non-monetary assets are recovered, whether through depreciation or sale. Where the negative goodwill exceeds the value of the non-monetary assets, this excess should be treated as being realised in the periods expected to benefit. However, negative goodwill should not be treated as a realised profit in the case of a sale of the non-monetary assets where the consideration received is not qualifying consideration. [TECH 01/08 3.25]

Under UK GAAP, negative goodwill recognised in the profit and loss account in accordance with FRS 10 therefore represents a realised profit except in the case of a sale of the non-monetary assets where the consideration received is not qualifying consideration. Where negative goodwill was accounted for under SSAP 22 in the accounts of an individual company, it would have been regarded initially as an unrealised profit. It will become a realised profit on the same basis as if it had been negative goodwill accounted for under FRS 10. [TECH 01/08 3.26]

IFRS 3 requires the immediate recognition of negative goodwill as a profit for financial reporting purposes but this does not accelerate the realisation of negative goodwill which is as set out above irrespective of the accounting framework adopted. [TECH 01/08 3.27]

5.3.5 *Changes in circumstances including changes in accounting policies and on the adoption of IFRSs*

5.3.5.1 *Introduction*

The treatment of a retained profit or loss as realised (or unrealised), or the recognition of an item as a profit or loss or an asset or liability, may change subsequent to its original recognition as a result of:

[TECH 01/08 3.28]

(a) a change in the principles of realisation; or

(b) a change in the law or in accounting standards or interpretations, either through an express reference to the realisation or otherwise of the profit or loss or, more commonly, through the derecognition of the profit (or the recognition of a loss). A company adopting IFRSs for the first time will, in effect, be making a number of changes in accounting policies; or

(c) some other change in circumstance (for example, where a receivable was initially regarded as qualifying consideration but circumstances change such that there is now no expectation that the receivable will be settled in the form of qualifying consideration).

Although the effect of these changes may be to reduce or even eliminate a company's net realised profits, that would not render unlawful a distribution already made out of realised profits determined by reference to 'relevant accounts' which had been prepared in accordance with generally accepted accounting principles applicable to those accounts (this is subject to **5.3.5.2** below). This is because the Act defines realised profits and losses for determining the lawfulness of a distribution as 'such profits and losses of the company as fall to be treated as realised in accordance with principles generally accepted at the time when the accounts are prepared, with respect to the determination for accounting purposes of realised profits or losses' (s853(4), emphasis added). [TECH 01/08 3.29]

5.3.5.2 Changes in accounting policies

The effects of the introduction of a new accounting standard or on the adoption of IFRSs become relevant to the application of the common law capital maintenance rule only in relation to distributions accounted for in periods in which the change will first be recognised in the accounts. Where items will fall to be treated as liabilities under a new standard in a period after the period in which the dividend is accounted for, directors do not have to pay regard to such future liabilities merely because they are disclosed in the notes to the accounts. [TECH 01/08 3.30]

Where the directors are considering the payment of an interim dividend in respect of a financial year, and a new accounting standard may, for example, lead to items being recognised as liabilities in the accounts for that year, the directors must, under common law, have regard to the effect of these liabilities on the expected level of profits available for distribution at the end of the financial year when determining the lawfulness of the interim dividend. [TECH 01/08 3.31]

For example, for a company adopting IFRSs for its individual accounts in 2009 the position is as follows:

[TECH 01/08 3.32]

- any final dividend for 2008 will not be provided in the 2008 UK GAAP accounts and will first be accounted for in the 2009 accounts. Such a dividend would therefore have to have regard to the effect of adoption of IFRSs even though the 'relevant accounts' may still be those for 2008 prepared under UK GAAP;

- any interim dividend paid during 2009 would have to have regard to the effect of adoption of IFRSs even though the "relevant accounts" may still be those for 2008 prepared under UK GAAP; and

- the 2009 accounts prepared under IFRSs would be the relevant accounts for the purposes of the final dividend approved by the shareholders in 2010. The effect of a change in accounting policy known to be adopted in 2010 needs to be taken into account in determining the dividend to be approved by the shareholders in 2010. The dividend will be recognised in the 2010 accounts.

The considerations set out above apply to all dividends whether in respect of shares classified as equity or shares classified as debt (or partly shares and partly debt as a compound instrument) under either IFRSs or UK GAAP. [TECH 01/08 3.33]

If the effect of a new accounting standard or guidance on profits which fall to be treated as realised is to increase the company's accumulated profits and the company wishes to distribute an amount in excess of that which could be determined by reference to what would otherwise constitute the company's 'relevant accounts', the company is required to prepare interim accounts complying with the new accounting standard or guidance. Where a public company is in this position, those interim accounts are required to be delivered to the Registrar under section 838. [TECH 01/08 3.34]

For the purposes of a dividend made by reference, under statute, to UK GAAP relevant accounts, but at a time when the foregoing guidance requires the effect of a current year changeover to IFRSs to be considered, the directors will need to understand the consequences of adopting IFRSs for the company's profits available for distribution. There is no statutory requirement to prepare interim accounts under section 836 (and section 838 in the case of a public company) if a proposed distribution can be justified by reference to the relevant accounts. However, under common law, a company cannot lawfully make a distribution out of capital. The directors may, for example, by reason of their duties to exercise appropriate skill and care, consider preparing interim accounts under IFRSs, as of the date shortly before the time of paying the proposed dividend, to satisfy themselves that the accumulated realised profits shown in the last statutory individual accounts have not been eliminated, or reduced to such an extent that the proposed distribution would be unlawful. (It should be noted that these 'interim accounts' would not be interim accounts within the meaning of section 836(2) of the Act and section 838 would not therefore apply to them.) For a public company, the directors will also have to consider the impact of the restriction on distributions arising from section 831 (see **5.6.3**). It may not always be necessary to prepare interim accounts, for example, in very straightforward cases where the directors are satisfied that no material adjustments arise from the transition to IFRSs. [TECH 01/08 3.35]

The directors of a company may not yet have decided whether to adopt IFRSs for the current financial year. Similarly, they may not have decided whether to adopt early a new accounting standard that has been issued but is not mandatory for the financial year. In these cases, the company's accounting policies are those that it has previously applied until a decision is made to change them. Therefore, in applying the foregoing guidance, it is not necessary to have regard to possible changes of policy that are being considered but have not yet been agreed. [TECH 01/08 3.36]

Where a company believes that the implementation of IFRSs will increase its balance of distributable profits, and it wishes to distribute those profits as increased, the guidance above will be relevant. [TECH 01/08 3.37]

5.3.5.3 *Realised profits that have been distributed and are subsequently eliminated by a change of circumstances*

Where the effect of a change in circumstance is that a profit previously recognised as realised can no longer be regarded as being realised, the amount of that profit should either be eliminated through a prior year adjustment or be reclassified as unrealised (as appropriate) in the relevant accounts in which the change in circumstance is first recognised. However, as profits are fungible, unless there is evidence that the profit affected by the change in circumstances has been distributed, it should be assumed that the first distribution made after the recognition of the profit was made pro rata out of all available profits shown in the relevant accounts. Accordingly, the balance remaining after that distribution would include a proportionate amount of the affected profit. Similarly each subsequent distribution would reduce proportionately the amount of the affected profit. [TECH 01/08 3.38]

The following example set out in paragraph 3.39 of TECH 01/08 illustrates this:

Example 5.3.5.3

Change in circumstances

[TECH 01/08 3.39]

A company has accumulated realised profits of 40 brought forward at the beginning of Year 1. During that year it makes realised profits of 60 of which 40 arose from a specific transaction in that period, and distributes 70, leaving a balance of 30. In Year 2 it generates a further 170 of realised profits and distributes 150. A change in circumstances in year 3 leads to the 40 recognised in Year 1 becoming treated as unrealised. The amount of the original profit of 40 that would be regarded as having been distributed in Year 1 would be 28 (70% [i.e. 70/100] of 40), leaving 12 of the original profit to be carried forward in the closing balance of 30 at the end of Year 1. In Year 2 the amount of this 12 that would be regarded as having been distributed in Year 2 would be 9 (75% [i.e. 150/200] of 12), leaving 3 of the original profit to be carried forward in the closing balance of 50 at the end of Year 2. Thus the amount of profit to be reclassified as unrealised in Year 3 as a result of the change in circumstance would be 3.

		Total	Affected profit
YEAR 1:	Brought forward	40	-
	Profit for year	60	40
	Available for distribution	100	40
	Distributed	(70)	(28)
YEAR 2:	Brought forward	30	12
	Profit for year	170	-
	Available for distribution	200	12
	Distributed	(150)	(9)
YEAR 3:	Brought forward	50	3

Where after making all reasonable enquiries it proves impracticable to trace a profit in this way, it would be appropriate to assume that the profit has been distributed (to the extent that there have been distributions). [TECH 01/08 3.40]

5.3.6 *Effect of errors*

Under UK GAAP, only changes in accounting policies and correction of *fundamental* errors are accounted for by restatement of comparatives. This means that errors that are material but not "fundamental" are accounted for in the year in which they are detected without any restatement. In contrast, IAS 8 requires all *material* errors to be corrected retrospectively through a restatement of comparatives. Consequently, it is likely that correction of errors by restatement will be more common when reporting under IFRSs. A distribution may have been made by reference to the original accounts which would not have been justified if the error had not occurred. The question arises of whether such a distribution would be rendered unlawful. [TECH 01/08 3.41]

It is the error, rather than its correction, that may have the effect of making a previous distribution unlawful. The effect of reporting under IFRSs will be to make such errors more visible because of the requirement for retrospective restatement for all material errors. But whether or not an error is corrected in this way does not, of itself, govern the lawfulness of a previous distribution. The effect of an error on the lawfulness of a distribution raises complex legal issues that are beyond the scope of this guidance. [TECH 01/08 3.42]

5.4 Fair value accounting

5.4.1 *Introduction*

The directors of any particular company need to consider their own company's facts and circumstances in determining whether an accounting profit arising through changes in fair value is readily convertible to cash in accordance with the definition and can therefore be considered as realised for distribution purposes. Consideration should also be given to **5.2.2** above regarding volatility and fiduciary duties. This sub-section provides guidance on:

[TECH 01/08 4.1]

(a) the application of the definition of 'readily convertible to cash' to particular situations (see **5.4.2**);

(b) available-for-sale investments and the fair value reserve (see **5.4.3**);

(c) the fair value option (see **5.4.4**); and

(d) losses arising from fair value accounting (see **5.4.5**).

5.4.2 *Guidance on the application of 'readily convertible to cash'*

5.4.2.1 Financial instruments

The definition of "readily convertible to cash" in paragraph 12 of TECH 01/08 (see **5.3.3.5**) is closely but not completely aligned with the measurement guidance in IAS 39. Necessary differences remain. [TECH 01/08 4.2]

In situations where:

(a) the financial instrument is traded in an active market; or

(b) the financial instrument is valued using a valuation technique whose variables include only data from observable markets,

it will generally be possible to enter into a transaction to convert the change in value to cash at short notice without any period of marketing and/or negotiation. Even when the instrument is not traded in an active market, there may be many institutions which will be prepared to quote a price based on observable market data at which a transaction could take place immediately. Such a change in value that is a profit would therefore, subject also to the test in TECH 01/08 3.12(c) (see **5.3.3.5** above), be regarded as realised. [TECH 01/08 4.3]

However, a change in the fair value of a financial instrument that is a profit which is determined using a valuation technique where not all of the variables include data from observable markets would be regarded as unrealised. This would not be so where part of the profit can be closed out independently of the rest and that part may be realised pursuant to the guidance on close out in **5.4.2.2** below. [TECH 01/08 4.4]

5.4.2.2 Close out

A financial asset, financial liability or change in the fair value of a financial asset or financial liability may be capable of being readily convertible to cash for the purposes of applying condition (a) of the readily convertible to cash test at **5.3.3.5** above if it could be immediately closed out, meaning the relevant contract or underlying market risk position is capable of being immediately offset in the market and the normal market practice would be to close out the position in this way. For example, risks inherent in a derivative may be eliminated by taking out other financial instruments, including derivative contracts, with an offsetting risk profile. When it is possible under normal market practice to enter into such arrangements to "lock in" any profit on the original contract, the profit that could be "locked in" could be regarded as readily convertible to cash. It is not necessary for an actual transaction to have occurred. [TECH 01/08 4.5]

Whilst the previous paragraph addresses the ability to close out in the context of condition (a) of paragraph 3.12 of TECH 01/08 (see **5.3.3.5** above), conditions (b) and (c) of that paragraph must also be considered. In the context of condition (b), consideration should be given to whether the valuation of the close-out instrument is based on observable market data. In addition, in relation to condition (a), consideration should be given to whether the cash flows from the close-out instrument meet the definition of qualifying consideration, in particular the criteria set out in paragraph 3.11 of TECH 01/08. [TECH 01/08 4.6]

The position regarding fair value losses is dealt with at **5.4.5** below. [TECH 01/08 4.7]

5.4.2.3 Embedded derivatives

Unless the whole contract has been designated at fair value through profit or loss, an embedded derivative that is determined not to be closely related to the economic characteristics and risks of the host contract is required to be separated from its host for accounting purposes (bifurcation) and fair valued, as if it were a standalone derivative with the same terms. Changes in fair value of the embedded derivative are recognised in profit or loss. However, where a change in fair value is a profit it does not constitute a realised profit unless the embedded derivative can be closed out in the manner described above in "Close out" or the host contract and embedded derivative together meet the "readily convertible to cash" test (including by reference to close-out if appropriate). [TECH 01/08 4.8]

5.4.2.4 Top-slicing

Fair value accounting under the relevant accounting standards involves the valuation of the whole item or, in the case of fair value hedge accounting, a particular risk and the recognition of the change in fair value in the financial statements. Where the change is a profit, it is not necessary to have completed a transaction to determine whether the whole of the increase in fair value is to be treated as realised. The criteria for determining whether an increase in fair value that is a profit could be readily converted to cash and thus be treated as realised are set out in paragraph 3.12 of TECH 01/08 (see **5.3.3.5** above). The concept of top-slicing a gain into realised and unrealised parts as envisaged by paragraph 3.18 of TECH 01/08 (see **5.3.4.3**) arises when there has been a transaction involving qualifying and other consideration. On remeasurement there is no transaction involved in the recognition of a fair value profit, hence the question of top-slicing (i.e. determining, by reference to mixed consideration receivable, whether part of the profit should be treated as realised as opposed to the whole of such profit) does not occur. [TECH 01/08 4.9]

5.4.2.5 *Unquoted equity investments*

Although increases in the fair value of many financial assets will meet the test of being "readily convertible to cash" in paragraph 3.12 of TECH 01/08 (see **5.3.3.5**), this will not generally be true of unquoted equity investments. The measurement of such investments at fair value may be precluded because the range of reasonable fair value estimates is significant and the probabilities of the various estimates cannot reasonably be assessed. Even where the value can be estimated sufficiently reliably to meet the requirements of IAS 39 and an increase in fair value is recognised, it is unlikely that the amount would be readily convertible to cash at the date of determination. This is because, for example, a period of marketing and/or negotiation would generally be required to dispose of such an investment. [TECH 01/08 4.10]

5.4.2.6 *Strategic investments*

Under a company's business strategy it may hold investments for strategic purposes. Such investments are not readily disposable in the sense required to meet condition (c) of the readily convertible to cash test in paragraph 3.12 of TECH 01/08 (see **5.3.3.5**), as a company's strategy cannot be readily changed so as to allow the investment to be realised immediately at the date of determination. For example, the company might have a strategic investment in a listed company that qualifies to be accounted for as an associate under IAS 28. It is possible for the company to elect under IAS 28 to account for its associates (in its separate financial statements) at fair value under IAS 39 (e.g. as an available-for-sale asset, with fair value changes reported in equity). Increases in fair value of such a strategic investment might be regarded as realised but for condition (c) of the test for readily convertible to cash. Thus the fair value increases are, consequently, unrealised. [TECH 01/08 4.11]

A similar analysis may be made for a company's holding of other financial assets, such as government bonds, that are classified as available-for-sale and are thus remeasured at fair value but nevertheless are held to meet the company's business strategy or regulatory requirements. Any fair value increases of such assets are unrealised as the company cannot readily change its business strategy or regulatory compliance to allow the financial assets to be realised immediately at the date of determination. [TECH 01/08 4.12]

5.4.2.7 *Investment **properties***

None of an increase in fair value of investment property is readily convertible to cash and is not therefore treated as a realised profit. This is because a period of marketing and/or negotiation would be required to dispose of such an investment and therefore it could not be converted to cash at the date of determination. This is not intended to preclude a profit being regarded as realised at the date of determination in those cases when the process of marketing and/or negotiation is complete at that date and legal completion occurs shortly after the date of determination. [TECH 01/08 4.13]

5.4.2.8 *Own credit*

When liabilities (e.g. bank debt or bond issues) and over-the-counter derivative contracts are measured at fair value, their value may be affected by the reporting company's own creditworthiness. Consequently, a profit may arise in circumstances where the company's creditworthiness is deteriorating, that is, the fair value of the liability is decreasing. In such cases, it is necessary to consider whether the company would be able to realise the profit by settling the liability at its fair value. This may not be possible, particularly if the company is experiencing financial difficulties, and the relevant profit will therefore not be a realised profit. However, in most circumstances where a company is not in financial difficulties and it would be able to settle the debt at fair value, there will be no need to analyse the fair value changes between the amount attributable to marginal changes in the creditworthiness of the liability and changes due to movements in interest rates and other market factors. [TECH 01/08 4.14]

It should be noted, however, that the tests set out in paragraph 3.12 of TECH 01/08 (see **5.3.3.5**) are wider than solely the ability to settle at fair value and must all be met. For example, the company must be able to settle on the date of determination without negotiation or marketing. Thus where a large volume of debt is under consideration, this is akin to a question of whether the company could refinance that large volume of debt on that date without negotiation, which would often not be the case. [TECH 01/08 4.15]

5.4.2.9 Block discounts for securities traded in an active market

IAS 39 requires certain financial instruments to be valued on a basis that does not take account of the size of the holding. That is to say that the valuation included in the accounts uses the published price quotation in an active market as the best estimate of fair value and does not reflect any "block discount" that might apply if the entire holding was disposed of at the date of determination. In the case of assets (e.g. investments) that are traded on an active market, it may be possible to dispose of the entire holding at the date of determination but it is necessary to recognise that the proceeds may be less than the value recognised in the balance sheet in accordance with IAS 39. [TECH 01/08 4.16]

Holdings in financial assets traded in an active market that might be regarded as relatively small (e.g. less than 1% of a company's share capital) may nevertheless be large in relation to the volume of business done in that company's shares on a typical day in the market. For example, some such investments held by investment companies and other financial institutions fall into this category. Such investments are rarely, if ever, disposed of in a single block but are instead disposed of in a number of smaller blocks either all on the same day or over a short period of time, in accordance with normal market practice, to reduce or eliminate the effect of any block discount. In these limited circumstances, the effect of any block discount on realised profits may be calculated on the basis set out in the following paragraphs rather than on the basis that the entire holding is disposed of in a single block on the date of determination. This is a limited departure from the principle established in paragraph 3.12(a) of TECH 01/08 (see **5.3.3.5** above). [TECH 01/08 4.17]

Part 4 of the Statement of Recommended Practice *Accounting for Securities by Banks* (the SORP) issued by the British Bankers' Association contained the following guidance:

> "Where a holding of a quoted security (other than one to which paragraph [62][which dealt with instruments held for hedging] or [63][which dealt with investment securities stated at cost] applies) is so large that it could be disposed of only at an unfavourable price or over an extended period, it should be valued at an appropriate discount to the market price. The discount should be sufficient to reflect the reduction in price resulting from the size of the holding or all future costs likely to be incurred in disposing of the interest over time in the ordinary course of business."

The SORP has been withdrawn because it is not applicable to banks reporting under IFRSs or applying FRS 26 under UK GAAP. It nevertheless provides an indication of generally accepted practice for the valuation of large holdings. Although this approach no longer applies for financial reporting purposes for companies applying IFRSs or FRS 26, it continues to be relevant to the determination of realised profits. [TECH 01/08 4.18]

Where it is determined that a block discount exists in relation to a holding of securities traded in an active market, only the part of the profit that may not be realisable over a short period of time in the ordinary course of business should be treated as unrealised. This would not necessarily be the same as the block discount that may apply if the entity disposed of the entire holding in a single block at the date of determination (e.g. in a forced sale), and which applies to situations other than those covered by the previous sentence for the purposes of determining the part of the profit that is unrealised. A similar adjustment is not required when an overall (i.e. cumulative) loss is recognised on the remeasurement of a financial instrument in accordance with IAS 39. The potential additional loss, equivalent to the block discount, that would arise on disposal of the entire holding at the date of determination is not recorded as a loss in the financial statements. Consequently, the realised loss will equal the loss reported in the financial statements, which will exclude the effect of any block discount. [TECH 01/08 4.19]

Estimation of the unrealised profit referred to above will require the exercise of judgement. Directors of companies frequently have to exercise judgement in making accounting estimates. The position concerning block discounts is no different. Directors do not have to be able to quantify this unrealised profit precisely; an estimate is all that is required. It will often be clear that there is a sufficient margin of profit available for distribution (over and above the proposed distribution) to absorb a prudent assessment of the effect of any unrealised profit attributable to block discounts. [TECH 01/08 4.20]

Directors should consider their common law duty to avoid an unlawful distribution of capital. If an investment is sold after the date of determination to finance a distribution, the impact of any resulting loss (whether due to the unrealised component of a block discount or otherwise) on profits available for distribution should be considered. [TECH 01/08 4.21]

The case of a block discount can be distinguished from that of investment property and most unquoted equity investments when none of the profit is treated as realised due to the period of marketing and/or negotiation required to dispose of such investments, such that the profit could not be readily converted to cash at the date of determination. [TECH 01/08 4.22]

5.4.3 *Available-for-sale financial assets and the fair value reserve*

Under IAS 39, profits and losses on "available-for-sale" financial assets are recognised directly in equity through the statement of changes in equity or statement of recognised income and expense (except for dividends, interest, impairment losses and foreign exchange profits and losses on monetary items). This applies until the assets are derecognised (e.g. sold) at which time the cumulative profit or loss previously recognised in equity is recognised in profit or loss (i.e. "recycled"). A similar rule applies for companies using FRS 26, with profits and losses being taken through the STRGL. [TECH 01/08 4.23]

Profits and losses arising on the remeasurement of available-for-sale financial assets will be realised or unrealised according to the same principles that would apply if the same assets had been accounted for at fair value through profit or loss (see above). For example, it would be illogical if the question of whether a profit was realised or unrealised depended on whether the directors designated the particular assets "at fair value through profit or loss" on initial recognition, when using the fair value option in the circumstances permitted by the relevant accounting standards (see **5.4.4** below). Profits on remeasurement of available-for-sale financial assets will be realised or unrealised in accordance with the principles described above, irrespective of whether they meet the requirements to be accounted for at fair value through profit or loss. [TECH 01/08 4.24]

For companies reporting under IFRSs (i.e. directly under the IAS Regulation), there is no requirement to credit profits taken direct to equity on available-for-sale investments to any particular reserve. For companies reporting under UK GAAP (FRS 26), such profits will be taken to the fair value reserve in accordance with the requirements of the Accounting Regulations. There is no specific legal restriction on the distribution of profits included in the fair value reserve in either the Act or the EU Fair Value Directive (2001/65/EC) from which the provisions on fair value accounting in UK legislation are drawn. Therefore, there is no constraint on treating profits on remeasurement of available-for-sale financial assets as available for distribution if they are in all other respects realised profits in accordance with this guidance. [TECH 01/08 4.25]

5.4.4 *Fair value option*

IAS 39, the EU adopted version of IAS 39 and FRS 26 now contain the same conditions regarding when it is permitted to use the fair value option to designate financial instruments "at fair value through profit or loss" on initial recognition. The conditions for using the fair value option are set out in paragraph 9 *et seq* of IAS 39. [TECH 01/08 4.26]

Where the fair value option is used it is necessary to consider whether the changes in fair value of the relevant financial instruments that are recognised in the profit and loss account meet the conditions to be treated as realised. In this respect, the guidance above on "Financial instruments", "Embedded derivatives", "Own credit" and "Block discounts" will be most relevant in interpreting the "readily convertible to cash" criterion as defined in 3.12 of TECH 01/08 (see **5.3.3.5**) above. [TECH 01/08 4.27]

In addition, it is recognised that the use of the fair value option to eliminate or significantly reduce an accounting mismatch may validly be used in place of hedge accounting for hedges of fair value exposures. Consequently, where this is the case, although the designated financial instrument that is fair valued under the fair value option and the derivative that would otherwise give rise to the accounting mismatch are not in a formal IAS 39 hedge relationship, consideration of the guidance in 5.2 to 5.6 "Fair value hedge accounting" in TECH 01/08 (which contains further guidance on the principle set out in paragraph 3.19 of TECH 01/08 (see **5.3.4.4** above)) would be relevant in determining the effect on realised profits of the combined effect of the designated financial instruments and the derivatives concerned (see **5.5.2** below). [TECH 01/08 4.28]

5.4.5 Losses

Losses arising from fair value accounting should be treated as realised losses where profits on remeasurement of the same asset or liability would be treated as realised profits in accordance with paragraph 3.15(f) of TECH 01/08 (see **5.3.4.2** above). [TECH 01/08 4.29]

A loss that represents the reversal of an unrealised profit will not reduce cumulative realised profits. Even if the loss is treated as a realised loss, for example because it represents an impairment, the unrealised profit will become realised in accordance with 3.9(f) of TECH 01/08 (see **5.3.3.2**). [TECH 01/08 4.30]

Cumulative net losses arising on fair value accounting will be unrealised only if both:

[TECH 01/08 4.31]

(a) profits on remeasurement of the same asset or liability would be unrealised; and

(b) the losses would not have been recorded otherwise than pursuant to fair value accounting.

With reference to paragraph (b) above, absent fair value accounting a loss may need to be recorded for example, in relation to an asset, on the basis of historical/ amortised costs less impairment provisions; and in relation to a liability, under either an amortised cost basis of financial instrument accounting or as an onerous contract liability. [TECH 01/08 4.32]

It is well established that the recoverable amount of tangible fixed assets (e.g. properties used in a business) may exceed their fair value (see paragraph 65 of FRS 15). In the case of other assets (including investment property), it may be more difficult to justify a recoverable amount that is greater than fair value. Each case should be considered on its merits and, where there is doubt, losses should be treated as realised. [TECH 01/08 4.33]

5.5 Hedge accounting

5.5.1 Introduction

As stated in paragraph 3.19 of TECH 01/08 (see **5.3.4.4** above), the principle to be applied to the determination of realised profits and losses when hedge accounting is used is as follows:

> "Where hedge accounting is obtained in accordance with the relevant accounting standards, it is necessary to consider the combined effect of both sides of the hedging relationship to determine whether there is a realised profit or loss in accordance with the criteria in this guidance."

The application of this principle to different types of hedge accounting permitted by IAS 39 is described below. [TECH 01/08 5.1]

5.5.2 Fair value hedge accounting

In the case of fair value hedges under IAS 39, the gross profits and losses on remeasuring the hedging instrument and the hedged item for the hedged risk are both recognised in profit or loss. In many instances both the profit on one and the loss on the other will be realised by reference to the readily convertible to cash and other criteria. In such cases, no special consideration of hedging aspects is required (including hedge effectiveness or ineffectiveness). [TECH 01/08 5.2]

In some cases, however, the profit on either the hedged item or the hedging instrument may, absent consideration of the hedging aspect, be unrealised (e.g. if a fair value movement is not readily convertible to cash).

The following paragraphs explain how the principle set out at **5.5.1** above should be applied in circumstances where the profit is not realised. [TECH 01/08 5.3]

Where the hedge accounting relationship results in a net loss, this amount will generally be treated as a realised loss. For example, consider the situation where there is an unrealised profit on the hedged item of £90 and a realised loss on the hedging instrument of £100. The net loss of £10, which arises from hedge ineffectiveness, is recognised in the profit and loss account and is treated as a realised loss. Due to the hedge accounting relationship, the remaining £90 of the gross loss on the hedging instrument is not treated as a realised loss and is set off against the unrealised profit on the hedged item. [TECH 01/08 5.4]

Where there is a net profit, it will be necessary to consider whether that profit is a realised profit. This will depend on the relationship between the gross components. For example, if there is an unrealised profit of £100 and a realised loss of £90, only the net profit of £10 will be treated as unrealised. [TECH 01/08 5.5]

This approach applies irrespective of whether the profits or losses in question arise from changes in fair value of open contracts or from settled transactions. For example, the hedge accounting policy may designate a series of rolling derivatives as the hedging instrument, some of which have already been settled in cash, whereas there have been no past settlements in respect of the hedged item. [TECH 01/08 5.6]

5.5.3 *Cash flow hedge accounting*

In the case of cash flow hedges under IAS 39, the portion of the profit or loss on the hedging instrument that is determined to be an effective hedge is recognised directly in equity through the statement of changes in equity. Such profits and losses are unrealised and become realised only when the hedged transaction affects profit or loss (or IAS 39 otherwise requires the gain or loss to be recycled through profit or loss). This is based on the principle (set out in **5.5.1** above) that it is necessary to have regard to the combined effect of both sides of the hedge accounting relationship to determine whether there is a realised profit or loss. To the extent that the profit or loss is recognised directly in equity (or, later on, added to the cost of a non-financial asset) in accordance with IAS 39, it must arise in connection with a valid hedge accounting relationship. It would therefore be inappropriate to consider this profit or loss in isolation from the hedged item. To the extent that any ineffective element of the profit or loss on the hedging instrument is recognised in profit or loss, that element should be assessed as to whether it is realised in accordance with normal principles (e.g. the "readily convertible to cash" test). [TECH 01/08 5.7]

The hedging principle in **5.5.1** above applies irrespective of whether the profits or losses in question arise from changes in fair value of open contracts or from settled transactions. The amounts taken direct to equity may, for example, include profits or losses on short-term derivative contracts that form part of a rolling-hedge strategy but which have matured. Such profits and losses should be treated as unrealised provided that IAS 39 requires them still to be deferred in equity as part of a cash flow hedge accounting relationship. [TECH 01/08 5.8]

Accounting for a cash flow hedge in accordance with IAS 39 will affect net assets although the profit or loss is regarded as unrealised. Where the cumulative net amount on the cash flow hedge component of equity (cash flow hedge reserve) is an overall unrealised loss, this may additionally restrict the ability of a public company to make distributions because of the application of section 831 (see **5.6.3** below). [TECH 01/08 5.9]

5.5.4 *Net investment hedge accounting*

Under IAS 39, net investment hedge accounting policies will generally arise only in the context of consolidated financial statements. Those financial statements are not relevant for the purposes of justifying distributions. However, it is possible that in some instances, in accordance with IAS 21, a branch may be treated as a foreign operation in the individual accounts of a company. In this case, net investment hedge accounting may be relevant to the individual accounts of a company. A net investment hedge under IAS 39 is accounted for similarly to a cash flow hedge. So far as the hedge accounting is concerned, the question of whether the hedged item gives rise to realised profits is dealt with at **5.10.12** below. [TECH 01/08 5.10]

The circumstances where a company previously adopted hedge accounting for a foreign equity investment (i.e. shares) in accordance with paragraph 51 of SSAP 20 is considered below. [TECH 01/08 5.11]

5.5.5 *Transition from SSAP 20 – hedge accounting for foreign equity investments*

Under UK GAAP, SSAP 20 permits a form of hedge accounting for foreign equity investments, subject to certain conditions. Where a company has used foreign currency borrowings to finance, or provide a hedge against, its foreign equity investments, it may denominate those investments in the appropriate foreign currencies and translate the amounts at the balance sheet date at closing rate. Where this policy is adopted, the resulting exchange differences are taken to reserves. The exchange differences on the related foreign currency borrowings are, subject to certain conditions, also taken to reserves. In some cases hedge accounting may be possible for such arrangements under IAS 39 but as a fair value hedge through profit or loss. This is subject to more stringent conditions which do not apply under UK GAAP. Therefore companies may not be able to obtain hedge accounting for such financing arrangements under IFRSs. [TECH 01/08 5.12]

The hedge accounting for foreign equity investments under SSAP 20 described above is not restricted to investments in subsidiaries but this is its most common application. TECH 01/08 assumes, for simplicity, that the equity investment is in a subsidiary. [TECH 01/08 5.13]

Where hedge accounting is not available under IAS 39, the exchange differences on the borrowings will be included in profit or loss. Unless the equity investment is held at fair value under IAS 39, there will be no offsetting difference on the investment and it is usually, in effect, frozen at its historical cost in the functional currency of the investor. It is then necessary to determine whether the exchange difference on the borrowings is realised or unrealised. [TECH 01/08 5.14]

The exchange difference on the borrowings should be treated as realised in accordance with the general principles in **section 5.3** where hedge accounting is not applied. This is irrespective of whether the purpose of the loan is for hedging an investment and of whether hedge accounting would have been permitted in the circumstances. This is the same as the position under SSAP 20 when the use of hedge accounting was optional. [TECH 01/08 5.15]

It should be noted that even though hedge accounting is not available, the purpose of the loan may still be to provide an "economic hedge" against the related equity investment. As stated at **5.2.2**, although profits on the borrowings will be realised profits, directors should consider, as a result of their fiduciary duties, whether it would be prudent to distribute them. [TECH 01/08 5.16]

Where hedge accounting was used under SSAP 20 and is not possible (or is otherwise not used) under IFRSs, it will be necessary, subject to IFRS 1, to restate the investment to either cost or fair value in accordance with IAS 27. On first-time adoption of IFRSs, paragraphs 29 and 30 of IFRS 1 will be relevant in these circumstances. They state that "if, before the date of transition to IFRSs, an entity had designated a transaction as a hedge but the hedge does not meet the conditions for hedge accounting in IAS 39 the entity shall apply paragraphs 91 and 101 of IAS 39 (as revised in 2003) to discontinue hedge accounting". Those paragraphs require hedge accounting to be discontinued prospectively. The practical effect of this is that, if a policy of stating the investment at cost is adopted, the cumulative translation differences from applying SSAP 20 remain adjusted against the carrying value of the investment (i.e. the investment in the subsidiary is frozen at the amount determined by translating the historic foreign currency cost of the investment at the spot rate prevailing at the date of transition). [TECH 01/08 5.17]

When this treatment is applicable, the profits and losses taken to reserves under SSAP 20 will remain within equity under IAS 39. In this case the assessment of whether those profits and losses are realised should continue to be made by reference to the net amount included within equity. [TECH 01/08 5.18]

5.6 Issues arising from IAS 32 (and its equivalent, FRS 25)

5.6.1 Introduction

Under IFRSs, financial instruments are presented according to the substance of the contractual arrangement, determined by the rules in IAS 32. This may differ from their legal form. For example, redeemable preference shares bearing mandatory dividends are presented as liabilities in the balance sheet and their corresponding distributions as interest charges in the income statement because the issuer has no ability to avoid payment in cash of either the principal or distributions. The substance of the contractual arrangement is therefore debt. Also, compound financial instruments are accounted for under the relevant standards using "split accounting", whereby the proceeds of issue are split between a liability component and an equity component. Examples of compound financial instruments are convertible redeemable preference shares and convertible debt (assuming that the conversion feature itself meets the definition of equity in IAS 32). [TECH 01/08 6.1]

Prior to 1 January 2005, under UK GAAP, such instruments were previously accounted for according to their legal form and without splitting so that preference shares were presented as share capital and convertible debt was presented wholly as a liability. For accounting periods beginning on or after 1 January 2005, FRS 25's requirements on debt and equity presentation (equivalent to IAS 32's) supersede those of FRS 4, and the Schedules to the Act dealing with accounts' formats have been amended to facilitate presentation in accordance with the new accounting standard. [TECH 01/08 6.12]

The following guidance considers the implications for distributable profits of companies, for example, entering into contracts involving their own shares that may require classification in whole, or in part, as liabilities. [TECH 01/08 6.3]

The guidance in TECH 01/08 summarises the ten key principles in relation to determining distributable profits when dealing with such contracts. The guidance then applies the principles to scenarios based on examples 1, 2, 4, 6 and 9 set out in the Illustrative Examples appendices to IAS 32 and FRS 25 involving contracts on own equity instruments. In addition, other scenarios are considered involving preference shares presented as liabilities, mandatorily redeemable preference shares and convertible preference shares. [TECH 01/08 6.4]

Appendix 1 to TECH 01/08 provides illustrations of the accounting and capital maintenance book-keeping entries for the eight scenarios referred to above. The appendices have not been reproduced in this manual. [TECH 01/08 6.5]

The ten principles underpinning the guidance in this section are set out below. The principles are split between those applying to all companies and those specific to public companies resulting from the application of the net assets test of section 831 of the Act. The principles are those underlying statute and common law in respect of distributions and capital maintenance. [TECH 01/08 6.6]

5.6.2 Principles – General

Principle 1 – A distribution or a capital repayment is not as a matter of law a loss, notwithstanding that it may be presented for accounting purposes as an interest charge in the income statement [TECH 01/08 6.7]

Section 830(2) of the Act provides that, "a company's profits available for distribution are its accumulated, realised profits, so far as not previously utilised by distribution or capitalisation, less its accumulated, realised losses, so far as not previously written off in a reduction or reorganisation of capital duly made." This is based on the premise that distributions are not losses. If distributions were losses they would be dealt with by the words "less its accumulated, realised losses," and thus the words "so far as not previously utilised by distribution" would be superfluous. [TECH 01/08 6.8]

A distribution or capital repayment may on occasion be presented as an accounting loss. For example, in some cases dividends on a preference share are presented as interest charges in the profit and loss account.

Notwithstanding the accounting presentation, such distributions or capital repayments remain, as a matter of law, distributions or capital repayments for the purposes of Part 23 of the Act. Accordingly, they are not counted as losses – and thus not as realised or unrealised losses – for the purposes of Part 23 of the Act. [TECH 01/08 6.9]

Principle 2 – An advance recognition of a future distribution or capital repayment is not a loss notwithstanding that it may be presented for accounting purposes as an interest charge in the income statement [TECH 01/08 6.10]

A distribution or capital repayment is not, as a matter of law, a loss. Thus the advance recognition of a future distribution or capital repayment is not a loss either. Hence, the accrual, as an interest charge, of a dividend in respect of a preference share presented as debt is an advance recognition of a future distribution but it is not a loss for distribution purposes even though the accrual is charged as interest the profit and loss account. [TECH 01/08 6.11]

Principle 3 – A distribution or a capital repayment consumes distributable profits when paid or when a dividend is declared by a company in general meeting [TECH 01/08 6.12]

An accounting liability recognised for accrued unpaid dividends or a capital repayment is an advance recognition of a future distribution or capital repayment and is not, as a matter of law, a loss. [TECH 01/08 6.13]

A distribution does not consume distributable profits until such time as, as a matter of law, the distribution occurs, e.g. when paid under the authority of the directors, under common form articles of association, or when declared by members in general meeting. [TECH 01/08 6.14]

The repurchase price for shares does not consume distributable profits until such time as, as a matter of law, the distribution and/or capital repayment comprised in the price occurs. In particular, notwithstanding that there are arrangements in place that will lead to repurchase, the company is not liable to pay the purchase price, and thus distributable profits are not consumed, until the shares are actually repurchased. For example, the holder of the shares cannot sue for damages in the event of failure by the company to repurchase those shares (see section 735 of the Act). [TECH 01/08 6.15]

Principle 4 – Premiums received by the issuer on written options to issue or repurchase own equity shares are profits when received [TECH 01/08 6.16]

A premium received by the writer of an option over its own equity shares is regarded as a profit at law. This is because it is value received by the company otherwise than in payment up of a share and otherwise than for taking on a liability. In particular, a written put option is not, as a matter of law, a liability of the company; for example, the holder of the option cannot sue for damages in the event of failure by the company to repurchase the shares (see section 735 of the Act). [TECH 01/08 6.17]

Thus to the extent that the premium is received in the form of qualifying consideration, it is a realised profit at the outset. [TECH 01/08 6.18]

Principle 5 – When a company issues a compound financial instrument that is legally a debt, the original credit to equity determined using split accounting is not, as a matter of law, a profit; the original credit to equity is eliminated as accounting charges, which are not as a matter of law losses, accrue upwards the amount recorded as a liability [TECH 01/08 6.19]

The initial credit to equity is not an accounting profit because in accounting terms it is the equivalent of the issue of an equity instrument. As a matter of law there is not a profit either, because the proceeds received are in consideration for taking on a liability (in which respect it is distinctly different from a legally separate option contract addressed in Principle 4) albeit a liability that is not fully reflected as such in the accounts. The liability becomes fully reflected in the accounts through an additional interest charge that is not, as a matter of law, a loss because the full instrument that is legally a debt is reflected in the balance sheet at issue albeit in different places. Thus the cumulative debit in equity arising from these additional charges is available to eliminate the initial credit. [TECH 01/08 6.20]

Principle 6 – When a company issues a compound financial instrument that is legally a share, the original credit to equity determined using split accounting is share capital, and if applicable share premium; accounting charges made to accrue upwards the amount recorded for accounting purposes as a liability component, are not, as a matter of law, losses [TECH 01/08 6.21]

The initial credit to equity as a result of split accounting is share capital, and if applicable share premium, and is reflected as such. Subsequent accounting charges, to accrue upwards the amount recorded for accounting purposes as a liability component, are not, as a matter of law, losses because they are advance recognition of a future distribution or capital repayment. [TECH 01/08 6.22]

In some circumstances, there may be a debit to be recognised in equity on an issue of shares to a parent company or fellow subsidiary, where the shares do not qualify to be classified in the accounts as equity of the issuer. The shares are recognised initially by the issuer as a liability at their fair value. However, the fair value may be greater than the proceeds received for their issue because the terms are off-market and, for example, involve redemption for significant amounts above the original proceeds and/or bear coupons that are substantial. In such circumstances, this difference between fair value and proceeds, a debit, is in effect advance recognition of future distributions and/or a future capital repayment and is recognised in equity. Consequently, this debit is not a loss at initial recognition. [Principle 2] The debit will consume distributable profits either as dividends on the shares are made, which are distributions as a matter of law, or at the date of redemption (i.e. when the payments are set against the liability over time or at the end). [Principle 3] [TECH 01/08 6.23]

5.6.3 *Principles – Impact of section 831 for public companies*

Principle 7 – The treatment of certain shares wholly as liabilities under IFRSs does not in itself affect the application of the section 831 of the Act net assets test for public companies and thus does not restrict distributable profits [TECH 01/08 6.24]

Section 831 states that a public company may only make a distribution at any time:

[TECH 01/08 6.25]

- if at that time the amount of its net assets is not less than the aggregate of its called-up share capital and undistributable reserves (as defined); and
- if, and to the extent that, the distribution does not reduce the amount of those assets to less than that aggregate.

Section 831 defines "net assets" for this purpose to mean the aggregate of the company's assets less the aggregate of its liabilities. By virtue of section 836, net assets for the purposes of section 831 are those shown in the "relevant accounts" prepared in accordance with applicable accounting standards; that is, its "IAS individual accounts", or its "Companies Act individual accounts". Therefore in the case of the issue of a financial instrument that is presented as debt in accordance with the substance of its contractual arrangements rather than their strict legal form, the company's net assets are unaffected for the purposes of section 831. This is because a liability is recorded (being in respect of the nominal value plus related share premium attributable to the shares) equal to the cash received as issue proceeds. [TECH 01/08 6.26]

It is less clear from the drafting of section 831 whether there is any effect on the amount of a company's "share capital and undistributable reserves" arising from the issue of shares for which the presentation of share capital and related share premium is as a liability. In legal form there will have been an increase in share capital and related share premium. However, in accordance with section 836, the amount of share capital and undistributable reserves is determined by reference to the amount as stated in the company's relevant accounts. Accordingly, it appears that any amount of share capital and related share premium that has been presented as a liability should be excluded from the amount of share capital and undistributable reserves for the purposes of applying section 831. This is because the amount of share capital and undistributable reserves as stated in the relevant accounts excludes this amount. [TECH 01/08 6.27]

This interpretation of section 831 is consistent with the "*Guidance for British companies on changes to reporting and accounting provisions of the Companies Act 1985*" (originally issued by the DTI (now BERR) in November 2004 and updated in August 2005). The DTI's guidance states that "the interaction of section 264 and section 270(2) [of the 1985 Act, now sections 831 and 836(1) of the 2006 Act] is such that, where preference shares are classified as liabilities, they should be treated as such for the purposes of the net asset test, and should not be treated as part of called-up share capital and undistributable reserves for that purpose". [TECH 01/08 6.28]

Consequently the issue of shares with their nominal value and related share premium presented as debt does not result in an immediate restriction in the amount of profits available for distribution by a public company under section 831, because the issue leaves both net assets and share capital and undistributable reserves (as defined) unaffected. [TECH 01/08 6.29]

When the section 831 test comes to be applied to the repurchase or redemption of the shares, it should be borne in mind that whilst the repayment of the nominal value and issue premium on the shares will leave net assets unaffected, "share capital and undistributable reserves" will increase due to the recording of the capital redemption reserve and the inclusion in the share premium account within equity of the issue premium which has always existed and which is no longer required to be presented as a liability. Under section 831(1) the net assets must be at least equal to the "share capital and undistributable reserves" both before (sub-section (1)(a)) and after (sub-section (1)(b)) the repayment for it to be lawful. [TECH 01/08 6.30]

Principle 8 – A debit to equity arising from an advance recognition of a future distribution or capital repayment does not form part of share capital and undistributable reserves (as defined) for the purposes of section 831 and thus restricts distributable profits for public companies under that section [TECH 01/08 6.31]

Despite not representing a realised loss or a consumption of distributable profits, nevertheless an advance recognition of a future distribution or capital repayment restricts distributable profits for public companies. This is due to the advanced recognition of the distribution as a liability, reducing net assets, but the corresponding debit to equity (via the income statement/profit and loss account) not reducing "share capital and undistributable reserves" as defined by section 831. [TECH 01/08 6.32]

The above contrasts with Principle 1 because in the context of section 831, the Act gives precedence to the accounting presentation and this restricts the amount of the profits available for distribution. [TECH 01/08 6.33]

The question may arise as to whether this restriction might operate to prevent the distribution or capital repayment in question when it comes to be made, e.g. because the effect might be that the surplus of net assets over "share capital and undistributable reserves" might be reduced to an amount less than the distribution or capital repayment to be made. However, there will be no restricting effect on the making of such amount of a distribution or capital repayment as has been recognised in advance, provided that immediately beforehand the net assets are not less than "share capital and undistributable reserves". This is because, accordingly, the company will meet the test in section 831(1)(a); and on the actual making of the distribution or capital repayment, which has previously been recognised as a liability, net assets are unaffected and thus remain no less than "share capital and undistributable reserves", thereby meeting section 831(1)(b). If the shares in question were originally classified as debt, then the operation of section 831 in relation to the original issue price is as described in principle 7 above. [TECH 01/08 6.34]

Principle 9 – On initial recognition, split accounting for compound financial instruments does not restrict distributable profits for public companies under section 831 [TECH 01/08 6.35]

If the compound financial instrument is legally a share (for example, a redeemable preference share with discretionary dividends) and is split into its debt and equity components, at the outset there is no effect on distributable profits. The initial liability is matched by an equal amount of cash proceeds and there is no effect on net assets. In respect of the equity component, the initial credit to equity is, at law, share capital (and share premium) and is included in "share capital and undistributable reserves" for the purposes of the section 831 net assets test. This increase on one side of the net assets equation is balanced by the corresponding amount of cash proceeds which increases the company's net assets. Thus, "share capital and undistributable reserves" do not exceed net assets and therefore there is no restriction on distributable profits at the outset. [TECH 01/08 6.36]

If the compound financial instrument is legally a debt (for example, a convertible debt) and it is split into its debt and equity components, the initial liability is exceeded by the amount of cash proceeds, equal in amount to that of the initial credit to equity, and accordingly there is an increase in net assets. However, in respect of the initial credit to equity itself, this does not form part of "share capital and undistributable reserves". As a result, an increase in net assets is recorded (being the difference between the consideration received and the liability recognised) with no corresponding increase in "share capital and undistributable reserves". Thus the issue of this instrument contributes an excess of net assets over "share capital and undistributable reserves". This has the effect of reducing any pre-existing restriction on distributable profits under section 831. However, where there is no pre-existing restriction, or such a restriction is more than eliminated by the issue of this instrument, distributable profits are not created; this is because section 831 has effect only to reduce the ability to distribute realised profits. [TECH 01/08 6.37]

Principle 10 – The accretion of the liability component of compound financial instruments reduces distributable profits for public companies under section 831 unless the instrument is legally a debt [TECH 01/08 6.38]

Where the compound financial instrument is legally a share, the "interest charge" for the accretion of the liability component is not a loss as a matter of law [Principle 6] and has no effect on the amount shown as "share capital and undistributable reserves" in the relevant accounts. That is, the initial credit to equity (being share capital (and share premium)) cannot be used to absorb the accumulating "interest charge" debited to retained earnings (via the profit and loss account) due to the accretion of the liability. Hence, under the section 831 net assets test, the amount that a public company can distribute is restricted by the accumulated amount of the "interest charge" debit, which ultimately will be equal to the initial credit to equity. In other words, net assets are reduced but there is no corresponding reduction of 'share capital and undistributable reserves' and thus over time the cumulative restriction of distributable profits will equal the initial credit to equity. [TECH 01/08 6.39]

Where a compound financial instrument is legally a debt, the accretion of the liability is an accounting loss (although not a loss as a matter of law

[Principle 5]) that reduces net assets for the purposes of the section 831 net assets test (see principle 8). However this eliminates the initial increase to net assets recorded as a result of the split accounting and thus of itself does not restrict distributable profits. [TECH 01/08 6.40]

5.6.4 *Examples*

The following examples set out in TECH 01/08 illustrate the application of the ten principles described above. The first five examples addressed below are based on examples 1, 2, 4, 6 and 9 involving contracts on own equity instruments set out in the Illustrative Examples appendices to IAS 32 and FRS 25. Three further examples address preference shares presented as liabilities, mandatorily redeemable preference shares and convertible preference shares. [TECH 01/08 6.41]

Appendix 1 to TECH 01/08 provides illustrations of the accounting and statutory capital maintenance book-keeping entries for the eight examples. This appendix has not been reproduced in the manual. [TECH 01/08 6.42]

5.6.4.1 *Assumptions*

The contracts described below do not contain a cash settlement option. [TECH 01/08 6.43]

Any redemption of the relevant shares will be made out of profits available for distribution and not out of the proceeds of a fresh issue of shares for the purpose of the redemption unless the text below otherwise indicates. Payment of any dividends and redemption amounts are contingent upon such payments/redemption being lawful under the Act at the time of payment/redemption, with, where appropriate, the relevant amount being deferred until such time as the Act's restrictions fall away. [TECH 01/08 6.44]

The shares, contracts and convertible instruments described below are denominated in the issuer's functional currency, pay dividends and are redeemed in that currency, and, where convertible are convertible into shares denominated in that currency. It is also assumed that there are no contingent settlement provisions (see paragraph 25 of IAS 32 and FRS 25) or alternate settlement options (see paragraph 26 of IAS 32 and FRS 25). The effect of foreign currency, contingent settlement provisions and/or alternate settlement options can have an impact on the accounting to deny equity treatment in certain cases. [TECH 01/08 6.45]

5.6.4.2 Forward contract to repurchase own equity shares

Example 5.6.4.2

Forward contract to repurchase own equity shares

[TECH 01/08 6.46–6.50]

Where a company enters into a forward contract to repurchase its own shares that are equity shares under the relevant standard, the standards require the company to set up a liability, at the outset, for the present value of the payment to be made (i.e. a discounted amount), with a corresponding debit taken directly to equity. The accounting effect is as if the equity shares had been repurchased immediately.

The initial debit to equity, for the present value of the consideration payable, is not a realised loss. This is because the eventual payment is not a loss, but is in fact a distribution (or a capital repayment to the extent not out of distributable profits). [Principle 2]

Over time the (discounted) liability is accreted up to the eventual repayment amount, with a corresponding charge to finance expense (interest) in the profit and loss account (income statement). The accretion of the liability over time up to full value of the eventual redemption amount is presented as an accounting loss – it is shown as part of the interest charge. Again, however, the ultimate payment of the full amount is either a distribution or a capital repayment and is not therefore, as a matter of law, a loss nor, therefore, a realised loss. [Principle 2]

The effect on a public company

For a public company the effect is to restrict distributable profits. [Principle 8]

Combining the accounting and statutory capital maintenance entries to complete the repurchase of non-equity shares:

When payment is made to repurchase the shares, it is, for accounting purposes, set against the liability. To the extent that the payment must, in law, come out of distributable profits, the debit in reserves (i.e. the initial debit to equity, together with the interest charge for the accretion) is set against and consumes distributable profits. To the extent that the payment must in law be charged to capital (e.g. funded by a fresh issue), then this debit is set against called-up share capital (and share premium as the case may be). Any necessary transfer from called-up share capital to capital redemption reserve is made in the usual way.

5.6.4.3 Written option to repurchase own equity shares

Example 5.6.4.3

Written option to repurchase own equity shares

[TECH 01/08 6.51–6.53]

The accounting standards require the same accounting for a written option to repurchase equity shares as for a forward to repurchase equity shares (**example 5.6.4.2**), save that in the case of the written option, any premium received at the outset is required to be taken directly to equity. So far as accounting for the repurchase price itself is concerned, the distributable profits considerations are the same as for the forward (see **5.6.4.2** above).

The option premium is regarded as a profit at law and, to the extent that the premium is received in the form of qualifying consideration, is a realised profit. [Principle 4] As a matter of law, the repurchase price for the shares is a future distribution or capital repayment. [Principle 3]

The effect on a public company

For a public company the effect of the recognition of the liability for the present value of the payment to be made and the subsequent accretion of the liability to the payment amount, is to restrict distributable profits. [Principle 8]

5.6.4.4 *Forward contract to issue own equity shares*

Example 5.6.4.4

Forward contract to issue own equity shares

[TECH 01/08 6.54–6.56]

A forward contract to deliver, through a fresh issue of shares, a fixed number of the company's own equity shares in exchange for a fixed amount of cash meets the definition of an equity instrument in the relevant standard because it cannot be settled otherwise than through the delivery of shares in exchange for cash (see assumptions in **5.6.4.1** above). Consequently, the right to receive the cash in a future accounting period is not recognised by the company, and the standards do not require accounting entries to be made until the forward contract matures, when the company receives cash and issues shares to the contract's counterparty.

Assuming the fair value of the forward contract at inception is zero, no cash is paid or received at that date, and thus no accounting entries are required on inception. Therefore, where a company enters into a forward contract to issue equity shares, the required accounting for such an arrangement raises no issues of distributable profits.

The effect on a public company

There are no additional considerations for a public company.

5.6.4.5 Written option to issue own equity shares

Example 5.6.4.5

Written option to issue own equity shares

[TECH 01/08 6.57–6.58]

The relevant standards require the premium received on the writing of an option to issue own shares, that are presented as equity, to be credited directly to equity. The premium stays in equity regardless of whether the option ultimately is exercised or lapses, although it may be transferred between components of equity (i.e. between reserves). The premium, to the extent that it is received in the form of qualifying consideration, is, in law, a realised profit at the outset. [Principle 4]

The effect on a public company

There are no additional considerations for a public company.

5.6.4.6 Convertible debt

Example 5.6.4.6

Convertible debt

[TECH 01/08 6.59–6.61]

Under the relevant standards, an issuer of debt convertible into the issuer's own equity shares will use split accounting (see assumptions in **5.6.4.1** above). That is, part of the issue proceeds are recognised as a liability, with the balance recognised directly in equity at the date the convertible debt is issued, being the component deemed to relate to the written option to issue own equity shares (the equity conversion option). There is a correspondingly higher interest charge over the life of the debt because of the need also to charge the increase in the recorded amount of the liability as interest. That additional interest is an accounting loss but is not, as a matter of law, a loss. [Principle 5]

The initial credit to equity is not a profit but as the liability component is fully reflected in the accounts, it offsets the additional interest charge. [Principle 5]

The effect on a public company

There are no additional considerations for a public company. [Principle 10]

5.6.4.7 *Preference shares presented as liabilities*

Example 5.6.4.7

Preference shares presented as liabilities

[TECH 01/08 6.62–6.70]

Where a company issues a class of preference shares that are redeemable at a specified date, or at the holders' option, and the dividends on the shares are non-discretionary and cumulative, IAS 32/FRS 25 requires that the company classifies this class of shares as a liability (i.e. debt). Under IAS 39/FRS 26, the liability has to be carried at inception at its fair value, which will be the sum of the nominal value of the shares and any associated share premium where the shares have been issued at fair value. Over the life of the shares the non-discretionary dividend is accrued between each payment date and is presented in profit or loss as an 'interest charge'. A dividend when paid is set against the accrued liability.

To the extent that the preference shares are to be redeemed contractually at a premium, the liability will need to be accreted over time such that by redemption the carrying amount of the liability is equal to the redemption price. The accretion of the redemption premium attributable to an accounting period will be presented together with the accrued dividend as the 'interest charge' for that period in profit or loss.

The presentation of the nominal value of, and any share premium associated with, the preference shares as debt has no effect on the determination of the company's realised profits and losses.

The accrued preference dividend (and any accrued redemption premium) that is presented as an "interest charge", and thus an accounting loss, is, as a matter of law, a distribution at the time of its making and not a loss. Thus such accruals do not affect the company's realised profits. [Principles 1, 2 and 3]

The effect on a public company

For a public company, the presentation of preference shares (i.e. the nominal value and any associated share premium) as debt does not result in an immediate restriction in the amount of profits available for distribution by a public company under section 831. [Principle 7]

Nevertheless, the effect of the accounting for the dividends (and any redemption premium) on the preference shares should be considered. The accounting liability recognised for the accrued unpaid preference dividend (and any redemption premium) is an advance recognition for accounting purposes of the eventual distribution (and/or capital repayment) and thus does not consume distributable profits until it is actually made as a distribution (or capital repayment). [Principle 3] However, profits available for distribution by a public company under section 831 will be restricted due to the reduction in net assets. [Principle 8]

Combining the accounting and statutory capital maintenance entries to complete the redemption

When payment is made to redeem the preference shares, it is for accounting purposes, set against the debt.

However, at redemption the law requires the following, where the redemption is made out of distributable profits:

(1) the nominal value of the redeemed shares is added to the capital redemption reserve; and

(2) the redemption price consumes distributable profits equal to its amount.

Therefore to reconcile these positions, the nominal value of the redeemed shares should be credited to the capital redemption reserve. Any share premium on the original issue of the shares now being redeemed should be credited to share premium account in equity at the date of redemption. The sum of the amounts added to the capital redemption reserve and added to share premium account is applied against retained earnings; this sum combined with the accumulated "interest charge" in respect of any redemption premium (which has built up in retained earnings over time) is equal to the amount of the redemption price that the law recognises as consuming distributable profits. As established earlier, the debit that builds up over time in retained earnings in respect of the redemption premium is the advance recognition of part of the redemption price and is disregarded as to its effect on distributable profits until the actual redemption takes place. [Principle 3]

5.6.4.8 *Mandatorily redeemable preference shares*

Example 5.6.4.8

Mandatorily redeemable preference shares

[TECH 01/08 6.71–6.77]

Under IAS 32/FRS 25, an issuer of mandatorily redeemable preference shares, which bear non-cumulative discretionary dividends, has a compound instrument and has to use split accounting (see assumptions in **5.6.4.1** above). That is, the standards require the company to set up a liability, at the outset, for the present value of the payment to be made on redemption of the shares. This will take into account any contractual premium to be paid on redemption. The difference between the proceeds received on issue of the shares and the net present value of the redemption amount is credited (or debited) directly to equity at the outset. Over time the (discounted) liability is accreted up to the contracted redemption price, with a corresponding 'interest charge' being expensed in profit or loss.

As a matter of law, all of the nominal value and any associated share premium of the preference shares are share capital and share premium irrespective of where they may now be presented in the balance sheet. Consequently, the initial credit to equity is share capital/share premium, albeit that it is the only part that is allowed by the relevant accounting standard to be shown as such, and is not a profit. The presentation of shares partly within liabilities and partly within equity has no effect on the determination of the company's realised profits and losses.

The interest expense from the accretion up to the full amount of the redemption price is, however, presented as an accounting loss – it is shown as an "interest charge". Since the ultimate payment is either a distribution or a capital repayment, the interest charge is, as a matter of law, not a loss even though it is accounted for as if it were a loss. [Principle 2]

The effect on a public company

For a public company, the effect of this IAS 32/FRS 25 accounting is to restrict the maximum amount of profits available for distribution over time by the amount of the cumulative accruals for the redemption price. [Principle 10]

Combining the accounting and statutory capital maintenance entries to complete the redemption

For IAS 32/FRS 25 purposes, the payment to redeem the shares is set against the fully accreted liability.

However, at redemption the law requires the following, where the redemption is made out of distributable profits:

(1) no amount remains recorded in called-up share capital for the redeemed shares;

(2) the nominal value of the redeemed shares is added to the capital redemption reserve; and

(3) the redemption price consumes distributable profits equal to its amount.

Therefore to reconcile these positions, the nominal value of the redeemed shares should be credited to the capital redemption reserve in equity and the corresponding amount for this entry is used to eliminate the original credit to equity to the extent recorded as share capital (which is now cancelled share capital). Any share premium on the original issue of the shares now being redeemed, if hitherto presented as part of the liability, should be credited to share premium account in equity at the date of redemption. The sum of the amount added to the capital redemption reserve, but not used to make a corresponding elimination of the original credit to share capital, and that added to share premium account is applied against retained earnings; this sum, combined with the accumulated "interest charge" in respect of any redemption premium (which has built up in retained earnings over time) is equal to the amount of the redemption price that the law recognises as consuming distributable profits. As established earlier, the 'interest charge' debit in retained earnings is the advance recognition of part of the redemption price and has no effect on cumulative realised profits until the actual redemption takes place.

5.6.4.9 Convertible redeemable preference shares

Example 5.6.4.9

Convertible redeemable preference shares

[TECH 01/08 6.78–6.87]

Under IAS 32/FRS 25, convertible redeemable preference shares are a compound instrument and an issuer of such instruments will use split accounting (see assumptions in **5.6.4.1** above). This is similar to debt convertible into an issuer's own equity instruments as described in **example 5.6.4.6** above. That is, a liability is recognised for the debt component and a credit is recognised in equity for the equity component (the equity conversion option). However, the analysis for distributable profits purposes is more akin to that for the mandatorily redeemable shares with discretionary dividends described in **example 5.6.4.7** above. This is because the initial credit to equity is share capital (and share premium).

It is assumed that the preference shares are convertible at any time by the holder into ordinary shares of the issuer and are mandatorily redeemed at the end of their term if not converted. The conversion feature cannot be settled other than by an exchange of the preference shares for a fixed number of the issuer's ordinary shares.

The presentation of the shares (inclusive of their share premium) as partly debt and partly as a credit in equity has no effect on the determination of realised profits and losses.

Any accrued unpaid preference dividends and the accretion up to the full amount of the redemption price, although presented as accounting losses through the profit and loss account, are disregarded in determining whether distributable profits have been consumed until their actual payment. [Principle 6]

The effect on a public company

At the outset there is no effect on distributable profits. [Principle 9] There will be a restriction for a public company on the maximum amount of profits available for distribution over time by the amount of the cumulative accruals for the redemption price. [Principle 10]

Combining the accounting and statutory capital maintenance entries where the shares are redeemed

The same analysis applies as given in **example 5.6.4.7** in respect of the mandatorily redeemable preference shares with discretionary dividends.

Combining the accounting and statutory capital maintenance entries where the shares are converted

Under IAS 32/FRS 25, when the holders exercise their option to convert the preference shares into the issuer's ordinary shares, the amount of the liability at conversion is transferred to equity.

However, to establish the impact on profits available for distribution it is necessary to re-analyse the aggregate entries in equity to establish the amounts that represent:

(1) the nominal value of the ordinary shares issued on conversion;

(2) the relevant amount of share premium to be included in the share premium account; and

(3) the elimination of the "interest charge" debit in retained earnings.

This is achieved at conversion by crediting to retained earnings an amount equal to the accumulated "interest charge" in respect of accrued unpaid dividends and accretion to the issue price of the shares from the amount transferred from liabilities to equity. The aggregate of the balance of the transfer to equity and the initial credit to equity is equal to the total of the nominal value and share premium attributable to the ordinary shares issued on conversion.

The allocation of part of the transfer from liabilities equal to the accrued "interest charge" effectively reverses the "interest charge" accounting entries. At law the debit accounting entries had not consumed distributable profits and therefore the effective reversal of these entries has no effect on the quantum of distributable profits. However, for public companies, the effective reversal of the "interest charge" debit at conversion removes the restriction under the section 831 net assets test.

5.7 Employee share schemes

5.7.1 ESOP trusts

5.7.1.1 Introduction

Paragraphs 7.4 to 7.45 of TECH 01/08 are concerned with the effect of a company's sponsorship of a trust (ESOP trust) that holds shares in the company, which may be delivered to the company's employees under an employee share scheme. This differs from the case of the direct holding of a company's own shares (treasury shares) which are addressed at paragraphs 2.40 to 2.43 of TECH 01/08 (see **5.2.14** above). [TECH 01/08 7.1]

The practice of employing ESOP trusts evolved party because of restrictions on a company acquiring its own shares (s658) or acquiring shares in its parent company (s136). These restrictions were eased from 1 December

2003 when certain companies were permitted, subject to some restrictions, to hold their own shares as treasury shares. The use of ESOP trusts has, however, remained widespread.

The provision of funds by a company to an ESOP trust to enable it to buy shares in the company or its parent company will generally fall within the definition of financial assistance for the acquisition of own shares (s677). Such assistance is generally prohibited, subject to certain exceptions, for a public company or a subsidiary of a public company (s678). Under the 1985 Act, similar restrictions applied to all companies. However, one of the exceptions to the general rules in s682(2)(b) is 'the provision by the company, in good faith in the interests of the company or its holding company, of financial assistance for the purposes of an employee share scheme'.

In the case of a public company, that exception is subject to a restriction in s682(1) that the financial assistance may only be given if the company has net assets which are not thereby reduced, or to the extent that those assets are thereby reduced, the financial assistance is provided out of distributable profits. Although paragraphs 7.25 to 7.32 of TECH 01/08 (see **5.7.1.8**) address the interaction of this restriction with the accounting for ESOP trusts, the general question of the lawfulness of financial assistance is not within the scope of TECH 01/08 and accordingly directors may wish to consider seeking legal advice. [TECH 01/08 7.3]

5.7.1.2 ESOP trusts under UK GAAP

Under UK GAAP, UITF Abstract 38 *Accounting for ESOP trusts* requires the sponsoring company of an ESOP trust to recognise the assets and liabilities of the trust in its own accounts whenever it had de facto control of those assets and liabilities. Where the trust purchases the company's own shares, the consideration paid for those shares should be deducted in equity until such time as the shares vest unconditionally in the company's employees. The effect of this deduction, which occurs in the individual accounts of the sponsoring company and not merely on consolidation, is considered below. [TECH 01/08 7.4]

The sponsoring company of an ESOP trust may be a company other than the one whose shares are held by the trust. For example, a subsidiary may be the sponsoring company of an ESOP trust that holds shares in its parent. In this case the shares will not be 'own shares' from the perspective of the subsidiary's financial statements. The shares would be recognised as an asset in the subsidiary's balance sheet and the issues addressed in this guidance would not arise. [TECH 01/08 7.5]

5.7.1.3 *ESOP trusts under IFRSs*

The guidance set out below in relation to investments in own shares held through an ESOP trust will be relevant to companies reporting under IFRSs if they account for investments in own shares in their individual balance sheets in a manner similar to that required by UITF Abstract 38. However, published literature suggests that a different accounting treatment may be permitted in individual accounts under IFRSs. Whereas UITF Abstract 38 requires the assets and liabilities of the trust to be included in the individual balance sheet of the sponsoring company, under IFRSs it may be acceptable to account for the ESOP trust as an investment in a subsidiary. The IFRIC was asked to address the question of which of these treatments is appropriate but declined to do so on the basis that it would be unable to reach a consensus on a timely basis given the different types of trusts and arrangements that exist in practice (see IFRIC Update, November 2006, for further details which can be found at http://www.iasb.org/Updates/Updates.htm). [TECH 01/08 7.6]

Where the ESOP trust is accounted for as a subsidiary, any loans to the trust by the sponsoring company, to the extent that they are regarded as recoverable, may therefore be recognised as assets in the individual balance sheet of the sponsoring company even though they have been used to finance an investment in own shares by the trust. The guidance set out below concerning the effects of a deduction within equity is not relevant when this accounting treatment is adopted because the deduction will arise only in the consolidated financial statements. [TECH 01/08 7.7]

5.7.1.4 *Note of legal considerations attached to Abstract 38*

A note of legal considerations attached to Abstract 38 sets out legal advice that the UITF received on the implications for distributable profits when the accounting treatment required by the Abstract is followed. The note of legal considerations is reproduced in Appendix 3 to TECH 01/08 but not reproduced in this manual. This guidance is consistent with that note of legal considerations but additionally addresses some issues that were not covered in that note as well as considering some issues in greater depth. [TECH 01/08 7.8]

5.7.1.5 *Effect of deduction within equity on realised profits*

A purchase of a company's own shares though an ESOP trust is not a distribution at law. This is because, at law, the shares have been purchased by the trust, notwithstanding that assistance may have been given by the company (by way of gift or loan, some or all of which may be ultimately irrecoverable, or by guarantee of the trust's borrowings that may ultimately be called upon to some extent). See **5.7.1.8** below for regulation of the transaction for a public company as financial assistance. [TECH 01/08 7.9]

Neither does such a purchase, of itself, give rise to an immediate realised loss. Therefore, such an acquisition does not reduce the amount of profits available for distribution under section 830. [TECH 01/08 7.10]

In addition, whilst the acquisition of shares will not, of itself, give rise to an immediate realised loss, the impact of other factors such as the granting of rights over those shares should be considered (see **5.7.1.12** below). [TECH 01/08 7.11]

5.7.1.6 Effect on section 831 restriction on purchase of own shares for a public company

The consideration paid on the purchase of shares by an ESOP trust sponsored by a public company will immediately restrict the profits available for distribution by virtue of section 831 by the amount of the consideration paid. As more fully explained below, there will be an immediate reduction in net assets but no change in share capital or undistributable reserves. [TECH 01/08 7.12]

A public company may only make a distribution at any time:

[TECH 01/08 7.13]

(a) if at that time the amount of its net assets is not less than the aggregate of its called-up share capital and undistributable reserves; and

(b) if, and to the extent that, the distribution does not reduce the amount of those assets to less than that aggregate.

Change in net assets

Section 831 states that "net assets" means the aggregate of the company's assets less the aggregate of its liabilities. Under section 836, net assets are those as shown in the company's "relevant accounts" which are normally the last annual accounts under Part 15 of the Act, properly prepared under the Act; in certain circumstances, the relevant accounts are initial accounts or interim accounts, which are prepared to a similar standard. Net assets for the purposes of section 831 should therefore be determined in accordance with accounting standards and UITF Abstracts. Accordingly, the relevant accounts and the net assets should include the assets and liabilities of the ESOP trust as reported under Abstract 38 ("extended entity accounting") rather than, for example, any loan between the company and the ESOP trust ("narrow entity accounting"). [TECH 01/08 7.14]

The effect of the accounting treatment required by Abstract 38 is that, in drawing up the relevant accounts, any own shares held by an ESOP would be recorded as a deduction in arriving at shareholders' funds rather than as an asset. Therefore, it follows that the relevant aggregate net asset amount for the purposes of the definition in section 831(2) would be reduced by the own shares held (being the consideration paid for the shares). [TECH 01/08 7.15]

Disclosure by way of note that the company also has an "asset" of own shares held through an ESOP trust would not restore the net assets for the purposes of section 831 (see **5.2.7.1** above). If the shares are not an asset for accounting purposes they cannot be an asset for the purposes of calculating net assets when applying section 831. [TECH 01/08 7.16]

Change in share capital or undistributable reserves

A company's undistributable reserves are defined in section 831. In short, they include the company's unrealised profits less its unrealised losses, except that this amount is never less than zero (i.e. net unrealised losses are not within the definition). [TECH 01/08 7.17]

The correct characterisation, as a matter of law, of the deduction in equity is not straightforward. On the one hand the deduction should not be characterised as a loss at all (thereby rendering redundant questions of realisation) because from the point of view of the company's individual accounts (which are on an extended entity basis) the company has not lost control of the shares nor have these shares suffered any objectively measurable diminution in value. On the other hand, given that the applicable accounting treatment does not permit the company to treat the shares as an asset, some might argue that the deduction should be categorised as a loss, although the nearest equivalent could be said to be a return of capital. The characterisation which gives primacy to the substance rather than presentation is the view to be preferred and accordingly the deduction should not be characterised as a loss. [TECH 01/08 7.18]

Accordingly, the deduction for own shares in equity is neither a realised loss nor an unrealised loss and does not affect the balance of undistributable reserves. [TECH 01/08 7.19]

The effect on profits available for distribution under section 831

Thus with net assets reduced but share capital and undistributable reserves unaffected, the purchase of ESOP shares affects the maximum distribution permissible by virtue of the application of section 831 (the "maximum distribution permissible"). In other words, the effect of the section is such that the profits available for distribution are restricted by a reduction in net assets that is neither a realised nor an unrealised loss. [TECH 01/08 7.20]

Furthermore, the existence of any unrealised profits does not alter this situation (e.g. such unrealised profits cannot be applied to offset the deduction, because the deduction is not an unrealised loss). [TECH 01/08 7.21]

5.7.1.7 *Effect on section 831 restriction on subscription for own shares for a public company*

A subscription for new shares in a public company by its own sponsored ESOP trust will immediately restrict the maximum distribution permissible. [TECH 01/08 7.22]

The application of section 831 is considered above. In the case of a subscription for new shares, there is no change in net assets. This is because the cash subscribed for the shares by the ESOP trust is recorded in the balance sheet of the sponsoring company both before and after the subscription in accordance with Abstract 38. [TECH 01/08 7.23]

However, the amount of the company's called-up share capital is increased by the nominal value of the shares issued to the trust. The amount of the company's undistributable reserves is also increased to the extent of any share premium arising on the issue, for example where the ESOP trusts subscribes for the shares at market value which is at a premium to nominal value. There is no other effect of the subscription on undistributable reserves as defined in section 831. Consequently, any excess of the company's net assets over the aggregate amount of the company's called-up share capital and undistributable reserves is reduced and hence the amount of the company's maximum distribution permissible is restricted by the amount attributable to the share issue (i.e. the proceeds of subscription for the shares by the trust). [TECH 01/08 7.24]

5.7.1.8 *The effect of the financial assistance rules in relation to a public company*

Assuming that the relevant assistance is permitted by virtue of section 682(2), in the case of a public company the assistance can only be given if the company has net assets which are not thereby reduced or, to the extent that those assets are thereby reduced, if the assistance is provided out of distributable profits. [TECH 01/08 7.25]

Net assets

For the purposes of section 682, "net assets" are defined as the amount by which the aggregate of the company's assets exceeds the aggregate of its liabilities, taking the amount of both its assets and liabilities to be as stated in the company's accounting records immediately before the financial assistance is given. This is in contrast to section 831 where, by reason of section 836, net assets are the aggregate of the company's assets less the aggregate of its liabilities as shown in the company's relevant accounts. [TECH 01/08 7.26]

Section 386 imposes a duty to keep accounting records which are sufficient to show and explain the company's transactions and to enable the directors to ensure that any balance sheet and profit and loss account prepared under Part 15 of the Act complies with the requirements of the Act. Thus the records must at least be consistent with accounting standards and interpretations by the UITF or the IFRIC as the case may be. However, this does not impose an obligation to maintain the entries in the accounting records fully in accordance with accounting standards and interpretations provided that it is evident from those records how to make suitable adjustments to prepare accounts in accordance with the requirements of the Act. Accordingly, section 386 does not require net assets for the purposes of section 682 to be determined by reference to "extended entity accounting" (as described at **5.7.1.6** above). [TECH 01/08 7.27]

Thus, in the absence of any such requirement, the company's assets and liabilities should be given their natural meaning, namely the assets and liabilities of the company as a legal person. In other words, the "narrow entity accounting" basis is used for determining the net asset position of the company concerned and whether the financial assistance has reduced the company's net assets. There is thus in this respect no change to the assessment of a company's net asset position as a result of applying Abstract 38. [TECH 01/08 7.28]

The effect of section 831 where financial assistance is provided out of distributable profits.

Where a company has provided financial assistance out of distributable profits which has reduced its net assets and shares have been acquired by an ESOP trust, section 831 does not require a further restriction in the maximum distribution permissible equal to the amount of the reduction in net assets calculated under section 682. [TECH 01/08 7.29]

Section 682 and section 831 are directed to different objectives. Section 682 determines the legality of the provision of financial assistance tested on a narrow entity basis. Section 831 determines the maximum distribution permissible tested on an extended entity basis. On the extended entity basis the assistance provided to the ESOP trust will not be treated as having been paid away until the shares are purchased at which point the net assets are reduced by the consideration paid for the shares (as described at **5.7.1.6** above). [TECH 01/08 7.30]

Section 840 contains accumulation rules where distributions are proposed by reference to particular accounts and prior distributions have taken place. Section 840(2) makes it clear that financial assistance which is given out of distributable profits is taken into account in the accumulation rules. These rules continue to apply. [TECH 01/08 7.31]

As explained at **5.3.5.1** above, a change in accounting policy that has the effect of reducing net assets (whether related to the financial assistance or otherwise) does not affect the lawfulness of earlier financial assistance at the time it was given. It may, however, have the effect of restricting the maximum distribution permissible if the shares are still held by the ESOP trust at the balance sheet date because of the effect of section 831. [TECH 01/08 7.32]

5.7.1.9 Purchase by an ESOP trust of shares held as treasury shares by a listed public company

A purchase of treasury shares by an ESOP trust for cash will be a sale of treasury shares for cash for the purposes of section 731 (see next paragraph). The proceeds will therefore increase distributable profits up to an amount equal to the original purchase price of the shares (i.e. reversing the decrease that would have occurred at the time of purchase of the treasury shares). Any excess will be credited to share premium. At the same time, the former treasury shares, now shares held by the ESOP trust, will be accounted for and treated for distributable profit purposes just as if they had been purchased at the same price from a third party, i.e. the entire consideration paid by the ESOP trust restricts the amount of profits available for distribution (see 7.12 to 7.32 of TECH 01/08 discussed in sections **5.7.1.6** to **5.7.1.8** above). [TECH 01/08 7.33]

Section 727(1) states that where shares are held as treasury shares, a company may at any time "(a) sell the shares . . . for a cash consideration or (b) transfer the shares . . . for the purposes of or pursuant to an employees' shares scheme". Section 729(1) states that where shares are held as treasury shares the company may at any time "cancel the shares". Section 731 deals with the treatment of the proceeds when shares "are sold" and requires any excess over the purchase price to be credited to share premium, with the remainder to replenish distributable profits. No treatment is otherwise specified for the proceeds when shares are 'transferred' to an employee share scheme in accordance with section 727(1)(b). A sale of treasury shares to an ESOP trust for cash consideration falls within section 731. That is, section 731 does not apply exclusively to sales falling solely within section 727(1)(a) but applies to any sale of treasury shares to an ESOP trust notwithstanding that the sale might also be a transfer under section 727(1)(b). [TECH 01/08 7.34]

The requirement in section 731 to transfer an amount to share premium when shares are sold for more than their purchase price applies only to treasury shares. Such a transfer is not required, or permitted, when shares held by an ESOP trust are sold in comparable circumstances. Whether or not the resulting surplus in the trust is a distributable profit from the perspective of the company is addressed in paragraphs 7.42 to 7.45 of TECH 01/08 (see **5.7.1.14** below). [TECH 01/08 7.35]

5.7.1.10 Effect on distributable profits for a public company when proceeds are received for sale of shares by an ESOP trust

In the case of a public company, the initial acquisition of the ESOP shares would have an immediate effect on distributable profits under section 831 because net assets were reduced without a corresponding reduction in share capital and undistributable reserves (see **5.7.1.6** above). However, if option holders then subscribe for the shares or the shares are sold in the market, the receipt of proceeds gives rise to an accounting entry (debit cash, credit shareholders' funds) that reverses the situation and restores distributable profits to the extent of those proceeds. That is, net assets are increased for the purposes of section 831 but there is no corresponding increase in share capital and undistributable reserves. [TECH 01/08 7.36]

5.7.1.11 Realised loss when shares held by an ESOP trust are transferred to employees – where shares originally acquired externally

The purchase of shares by an ESOP trust does not, of itself, give rise to a realised loss (see **5.7.1.5** above) and, other than in the case of a public company, does not otherwise immediately affect the distribution of available profits. However, it is clear that if the shares are to be transferred to employees for less than their purchase price, the shortfall will at some time fall to be treated as a realised loss. In some cases options may be granted with an exercise price that is lower than the price at which the shares were purchased. In other cases shares may be transferred to employees for no consideration on the achievement of specified performance or service conditions. In all such cases, the difference between the purchase price of the shares and the proceeds received from the employee should be regarded as becoming a realised loss over the relevant amortisation or charging period. This will achieve the same effect, in terms of realised profits and losses, as the accounting treatment formerly required under UITF Abstract 13, which required investments in own shares to be recognised as assets. This has become generally accepted in determining profits available for distribution. [TECH 01/08 7.37]

There is a precedent for calculating realised profits and losses on a basis that is different from the accounting. This concerns the treatment of goodwill eliminated immediately against reserves under a previous UK accounting standard as described in paragraph 3.23 TECH 01/08 (see **5.3.4.6** above). [TECH 01/08 7.38]

Where options have been granted over the shares in question but those options are "out-of-the-money" or where there are "surplus" shares that have not been allocated to any particular share scheme, a realised loss may also arise if the market value of the shares falls below their purchase price. Under the previous requirements of UITF Abstract 13, shares would have been written down for impairment in certain circumstances (i.e. as required by paragraph 19(2) of Schedule 1 to the Accounting Regulations for a 'permanent diminution in value'). The considerations involved in deciding whether such a provision for impairment would have been required (and the interaction of this with the amortisation of any difference between the purchase price and the proceeds to be received from the employees) are complex and beyond the scope of this guidance. But if a provision would have been required had the ESOP shares been recorded as an asset at historical cost under Abstract 13, an equal amount should be regarded as a realised loss under UITF Abstract 38. This applies irrespective of what the accounting treatment for financial assets might be under current accounting standards. [TECH 01/08 7.39]

The note of legal considerations attached to UITF Abstract 38 states that although the acquisition of shares by an ESOP trust will not, of itself, result in a realised profit or loss for the company concerned "a company will still need to consider other transactions with the ESOP, for example a loan to the ESOP to fund acquisitions of shares, and these may affect the company's realised profits and losses". The reference to a loan to the ESOP might be read as implying that realised profits and losses should be determined by reference to "narrow entity accounting" (see **5.7.1.6** above). This is not the case and the UITF Abstract 38 note refers to the existence of a loan as only one of a number of factors that might be relevant. If a purchase of shares by an ESOP trust is funded by a loan from the company and those shares are put under option at a lower price, the shortfall would affect the recoverability of the loan. It might appear that this approach would lead to realised profits being reduced by the full amount of the shortfall immediately on the granting of the rights over the shares rather than the effect being spread over the performance period as described above. This is not the case (but see **5.7.1.8** regarding financial assistance by a public company) because the loan (or alternatively a gift) to an ESOP trust could be regarded as a prepayment and, absent any impairment (see above), effectively amortised over the performance period as would be the case with a cash bonus that was contingent on future service. [TECH 01/08 7.40]

5.7.1.12 *Realised loss when shares held by an ESOP trust are transferred to employees – where shares originally subscribed*

The subscription for shares by an ESOP trust does not, of itself, give rise to a realised loss (see **5.7.1.5** above) and, other than in the case of a public company, does not otherwise immediately affect the distribution of available profits. However, as in the case of a purchase of shares described at 7.37 to 7.40 of TECH 01/08 (see **5.7.1.11** above), a realised loss may arise if the shares are subsequently transferred to employees for less than their subscription price. In all such cases, the difference between the subscription price of the shares and the proceeds received from the employee should be regarded as becoming a realised loss over the relevant amortisation or charging period. [TECH 01/08 7.41]

5.7.1.13 *Whether a surplus on disposal of shares by an ESOP trust is a realised and distributable profit from the perspective of the sponsoring company*

As explained below, a surplus on disposal of shares held by an ESOP trust is a realised profit. However, in respect of it being distributable, the directors should have regard to their wider common law duties as required by sections 851 and 852 (see **5.2.1** above). As explained below, the profit therefore may not become distributable until some time in the future. [TECH 01/08 7.42]

Under Abstract 38, a sponsoring company includes the assets, liabilities and transactions of its ESOP trust in its accounts as if the trust were a division or branch of the company. This is therefore not just a matter of including the trust in consolidated accounts. The assets, liabilities and transactions of the trust are included in the company's individual accounts. These are the "relevant accounts" for the purposes of determining profits available for distribution. Where the trust has a surplus in the equivalent of its profit and loss account, the question arises of whether this should be reflected in the calculation of the company's realised profits. [TECH 01/08 7.43]

Where the trust has a surplus (e.g. from the sale of shares at more than their purchase price), it is arguable that, just as a parent would not treat a surplus in a subsidiary as a realised profit in its own individual accounts, the parent should not regard the surplus in the trust as increasing its realised profits. But there is a clear difference in that Abstract 13 required the assets and liabilities of the trust to be included in the company's own individual accounts and made no mention of any legal difficulties about including any "profits" of the trust in the company's profit and loss account. Under Abstract 38, no such profits arise to be included in the company's profit and loss account but the issue is still relevant to the determination of the company's realised profits. Where the consideration received by the trust for the sale of the shares is in the form of cash (or other "qualifying consideration") that will be included in the company's balance sheet in accordance with the requirements of Abstract 38, the profit will be a realised profit from the company's perspective. [TECH 01/08 7.44]

However, the directors should have regard to their wider common law duties as required by sections 851 and 852 (see **5.2.1** above). It would not be regarded as prudent to distribute an amount that represents assets that are retained in the ESOP trust and therefore not available for the general purposes of the company. If the assets of the trust are used in future to meet an expense, an equivalent amount of the gain should at that time be treated as distributable. Therefore to the extent that the realised loss arising from the expense does not exceed the previously recognised gain that was treated as undistributable, there will be no reduction in distributable profits. [TECH 01/08 7.45]

5.7.2 *Expenses for share based payments required by IFRS 2 and FRS 20*

IFRS 2 (and FRS 20) require expenses to be recognised in profit or loss for cash-settled share-based payment arrangements. The credit entry will be either a cash payment or a provision. The expense recognised will therefore be a realised loss. The paragraphs which follow are concerned with equity-settled arrangements. [TECH 01/08 7.46]

IFRS 2 (and FRS 20) require expenses to be recognised in profit or loss for equity-settled share-based payment arrangements. The standard requires the credit entry arising from recognition of this expense to be credited within equity but does not specify any particular component of equity. [TECH 01/08 7.47]

Any expense recognised in accordance with IFRS 2 will be a realised loss. This follows from the principle that all losses should be regarded as realised losses except to the extent that the law, accounting standards or TECH 01/08 provide otherwise (see **5.3.3.3** above). However, the overall impact of the IFRS 2 expense on distributable profits will depend on the status of the credit entry in equity. [TECH 01/08 7.48]

If the consideration for an issue of shares is, as a matter of law, the provision of goods or services to the company, it will be necessary to credit share capital and share premium with the fair value of those goods or services. Similarly, if shares are, as a matter of law, issued in settlement of a monetary liability, it will be necessary to credit share capital and share premium with the amount of the liability discharged. Where this is so, the credit entry to equity required by IFRS 2 cannot be a realised profit. [TECH 01/08 7.49]

In the case of share options, the note of legal considerations appended to UITF Abstract 17 (now superseded by FRS 20) provided the following guidance.

> "The UITF has received legal advice on the implications for share premium account when the accounting treatment required by this Abstract is followed. It has been advised that where new shares are issued in connection with an employee share scheme the share premium account will normally have to reflect only the cash subscribed for the shares (e.g. by the employee or by an ESOP). In such cases, any difference between the cash subscribed for the shares (which must be at least as much as the nominal value, as shares cannot be issued at a discount) and the fair value at the date of grant of rights should be credited to reserves other than the share premium account. This is on the basis that the services of the employee do not, as a matter of law, form part of the consideration received for the shares issued, and the UITF has been advised that this would be the usual legal interpretation of such transactions. Exceptionally, however, the terms of a transaction might be such as to lead to the opposite interpretation, and companies may need to take legal advice on this point. In such a case, the operation of section 99(2) of the Companies Act 1985 [prohibition of public company accepting undertaking to perform services in payment up of its shares] and section 103 [non-cash consideration to be valued before allotment of shares] would also have to be considered."

However, the arrangements referred to in the last two sentences of the quoted paragraph are not typical. Instead, for example, in the case of share options, the credit to equity required by IFRS 2 will usually be a credit to reserves other than share premium account. [TECH 01/08 7.50]

The note of legal considerations does not, however, address whether the credit to equity in the case of options to subscribe for shares is a realised profit. However, an unrealised reserve will be treated as having become realised by the amortisation or writing down of the related asset (see 3.9(f) of TECH 01/08 at **5.3.3.3** above). Therefore, assuming that the IFRS 2 expense has been included in profit or loss (which would be the case except where the charge had been capitalised as part of the cost of production of an asset) the credit entry in equity will be a realised profit. The IFRS 2 expense will therefore have no net effect on distributable profits. [TECH 01/08 7.51]

The manner of settlement (e.g. subscription for new shares or purchase of shares in the market by an ESOP trust) does not affect the expense recognised under IFRS 2 or whether this is a realised loss. However, it will be necessary to consider the effect on realised profits arising from any shares held by an ESOP trust (see **5.7.1.11** and **5.7.1.12** above). [TECH 01/08 7.52]

5.7.3 *Intragroup recharges for share-based payments*

In November 2006, the International Financial Reporting Interpretations Committee (IFRIC) issued IFRIC 11 "IFRS 2 – Group and Treasury Share Transactions". The Exposure Draft upon which this was based (IFRIC D17) included some material on the treatment of inter-company recharges made within groups in connection with share-based payment arrangements. The IFRIC decided not to address these issues in IFRIC 11 because it did not wish to widen the scope of the Interpretation to an issue that relates to accounting for intragroup payments generally. The appropriate accounting for such recharges is thus a matter of currently developing practice, including that in some cases the treatment that was set out in the draft guidance in IFRIC D17, described below, may be appropriate. [TECH 01/08 7.53]

The situation in question is one in which the company, being a subsidiary, makes a cash payment to its parent in relation to a share-based payment in favour of the company's own employees and where IFRS 2 and IFRIC 11 require an equity-settled share-based payment charge in the company's accounts. The proposals in IFRIC D17 envisaged that where a charge is made by the parent to the subsidiary which exceeds the expense that the subsidiary is required to recognise under IFRS 2, the excess is accounted for by the subsidiary as a distribution. For example, this may arise if a charge is made on the basis of intrinsic value at exercise date which will generally be higher than the grant date fair value recognised as an expense in accordance with IFRS 2. The accounting treatment of any such charge does not affect whether or not it is a distribution as a matter of law. In particular, if there is a commercial basis for such a charge, it will not be a distribution as a matter of law. An example of a commercial basis would be the expense that the subsidiary would have incurred if it had purchased shares in the market to satisfy the options. Consequently, it will not be unlawful for the subsidiary to make the reimbursement payment, even in the absence of distributable profits, provided that the payment is not a distribution as a matter of law. [TECH 01/08 7.54]

However, the entire reimbursement payment will have the effect of reducing accumulated realised profits or increasing accumulated realised losses of the subsidiary. The debit to equity arising from the payment will first reduce the credit in equity arising from IFRS 2 which will no longer be available to offset the realised loss recognised as a result of the IFRS 2 expense. Any debit to equity in excess of this amount will be a realised loss even though it will not have been accounted for as a loss in the financial statements. [TECH 01/08 7.55]

A liability may be recognised by the subsidiary where the parent has a contractual right to reimbursement at a future date. The amount of the realised loss at any date will generally be based on the amount of the liability recognised at that date but the particular facts of each case should be considered. [TECH 01/08 7.56]

5.8 Retirement benefit schemes

5.8.1 Introduction

The guidance in this section is written in terms of compliance with FRS 17 but is equally applicable when the equivalent international standard IAS 19 *Employee benefits* is being applied. When IAS 19 is being applied, the guidance should be applied to the amounts reported under that standard. For simplicity, this guidance refers throughout to the relevant requirements of FRS 17. [TECH 01/08 8.1]

The guidance set out below applies both to pension schemes acquired in a business combination and those that are started by the reporting company. [TECH 01/08 8.2]

5.8.2 Defined contribution schemes

For defined contribution retirement benefit schemes, the cost charged to the profit and loss account under FRS 17 is equal to the contributions payable to the scheme for the accounting period. The charge to the profit and loss account for the contributions payable is a realised loss. [TECH 01/08 8.3]

5.8.3 Multi-employer schemes

Under FRS 17, some companies account for their participation in certain multi-employer defined benefit retirement benefit schemes as if they were defined contribution schemes. Where a scheme meets the criteria for this treatment in FRS 17, the position as regards realised profits and losses will be the same as for any other defined contribution scheme. [TECH 01/08 8.4]

5.8.4 Defined benefit schemes

5.8.4.1 Summary

In summary, what is required in relation to a defined benefit scheme is to identify whether any adjustment is required to reserves, to exclude unrealised profits, in arriving at the amount of distributable profits. To do so, it is first necessary to ascertain the cumulative amounts charged or credited in relation to the pension scheme, whether through the profit and loss account or through the statement of total recognised gains and losses (i.e. the total amounts taken to reserves). Paragraphs 8.11 to 8.13 of TECH 01/08 (see **5.8.4.2** below) determine whether that cumulative amount is realised or unrealised, with the test being different for cumulative net debits as against cumulative net credits. The cumulative net debit or credit will not be readily apparent from the accounts and so paragraphs 8.14 to 8.15 of TECH 01/08 (see **5.8.4.2** below) provide that it is determined from the movement in the pension scheme asset or liability on the balance sheet since inception of the scheme (i.e. when it is started by the company or when it was acquired in a business combination) and the cumulative net cash paid to the scheme. The cumulative cash flows may themselves be difficult to obtain and so paragraphs 8.16 to 8.17 of TECH 01/08 (see **5.8.4.2** below) provide a method of estimating the amounts. Paragraph 8.18 (see **5.8.4.2** below) then describes some circumstances when it is possible to deduce easily, without working through these procedures, that all amounts accumulated in reserves are realised. [TECH 01/08 8.5]

This calculation is unaffected by the date of adoption of FRS 17 and the accounting adopted previously (i.e. SSAP 24). A company may have established the cumulative amount in reserves for the pension scheme on adoption of FRS 17 in which case the amount can be rolled forward from year to year. However, the approach set out below will enable the position to be established at a particular date if no such calculation was performed.

5.8.4.2 *General principles*

It is the cumulative gain or loss credited or debited to reserves in respect of a pension scheme, rather than the existence of a surplus or deficit, that affects the realised profits and losses of a company. Appendix 3 to TECH 01/08 provides an illustration of this principle and is reproduced below as **example 5.8.4.2**.

The effect of FRS 17 on reserves must be calculated to identify whether any adjustment in respect of pensions is needed to reported reserves to arrive at realised reserves. No adjustment is required if a net cumulative loss has been taken to reserves. If a net cumulative gain has been taken to reserves, and under the guidance set out at 8.12 in TECH 01/08 that gain is in part or in full unrealised, a deduction equivalent to the unrealised element must be made to reserves in assessing the level of realised reserves. [TECH 01/08 8.7]

In establishing the impact that a surplus or deficit under FRS 17 has on a company's realised profits, it is therefore necessary to:

[TECH 01/08 8.8]

(a) identify the cumulative net gain or loss taken to reserves in respect of the pension surplus or deficit; and

(b) establish the extent to which that gain or loss is realised.

Although the various elements making up the changes in the defined benefit asset or liability are disclosed separately in the performance statements (see paragraph 50 of FRS 17), it is the net amount that represents the cost to the company of the pension promise. Thus it is the cumulative net gain or loss taken to reserves that falls to be categorised as realised or unrealised. There is no need to distinguish that cumulative balance between amounts charged or credited in the profit and loss account and those recognised in the statement of total recognised gains and losses (STRGL). The entries in the STRGL are considered for this purpose as revisions of past estimates of the net pension cost and are not precluded from being treated as realised simply because they have passed through the STRGL rather than the profit and loss account. [TECH 01/08 8.9]

The impact on reserves is not usually the same as the pension asset or liability recognised in the balance sheet. It will be different due to the net contributions paid to the scheme (see 8.15 *et seq* of TECH 01/08 discussed below) and any asset or liability introduced as the result of a business combination (see 8.19 *et seq* of TECH 01/08 at **5.8.4.3**). [TECH 01/08 8.10]

A cumulative net debit in reserves in respect of the pension scheme constitutes a realised loss as it results from the creation of, or an increase in, a provision for a liability or loss resulting in an overall reduction in net assets. This follows from 2.32, 3.10 and 3.15(d) of TECH 01/08 at **5.2.11**, **5.3.3.3** and **5.3.4.2** respectively. [TECH 01/08 8.11]

A cumulative net credit in reserves in respect of the pension scheme constitutes a realised profit only to the extent that it is represented by an asset to be recovered by refunds that have been agreed by the pension scheme trustees at the balance sheet date of the relevant accounts and the refunds will take the form of qualifying consideration. This follows from 3.9(a) of TECH 01/08 (**5.3.3.2** above) which refers to "a transaction where the consideration received by the company is 'qualifying consideration'". An asset that is recognised based on a reduction in future contributions or on expected refunds that are not agreed at the balance sheet date will not meet the definition of 'qualifying consideration'. [TECH 01/08 8.12]

To the extent that a cumulative net credit in reserves exceeds any such agreed refunds it is unrealised, but it becomes realised in subsequent periods to the extent that it offsets subsequent net debits to reserves being recognised as realised losses in respect of the pension scheme (i.e. as the cumulative net credit reduces). This follows from 3.9(f)(iii) and (iv) of TECH 01/08 (see **5.3.3.2** above). [TECH 01/08 8.13]

To establish the effect on realised profits at a particular date, a company must therefore establish the cumulative net credit or debit in reserves for the pension scheme at that date. This equals the amount of the surplus or deficit recognised before taking account of deferred tax, adjusted for:

(a) cumulative net contributions less refunds made in respect of the pension scheme; and

(b) in the rare cases in which the company has recognised a pension asset or liability in its individual accounts on the acquisition of an unincorporated business (in respect of the pension scheme of that business), the amount initially recognised (see **5.8.4.3** below).

Example 5.8.4.2

Distinguishing the cumulative gain or loss in reserves from the pension surplus or deficit

[Tech 01/08 Appendix 3]

It is the cumulative gain or loss credited or debited to reserves in respect of a pension scheme, rather than the existence of a surplus or deficit, that affects the realised profits and losses of a company. Consider the example below of a scheme set up at the start of the year. For simplicity, current and deferred tax is ignored. The scheme has a surplus of 4 at the end of the year that would be reported on the company's balance sheet as an asset. Contributions have been paid which are equal to the expense recognised in the profit and loss account of 20. An actuarial gain of 4 has also been recognised in the STRGL.

	Increase/ (decrease) in pension asset	(Reduction) in cash balance	Amount debited/ (credited) in reserves
Brought forward	0		
Debited to profit and loss	(20)		20
Credited in STRGL	4		(4)
Contributions paid	20	(20)	—
Carried forward	4	(20)	16

The net effect on the balance sheet in the above example is:

Dr	Pension asset	4	
Dr	Reserves	16	
Cr	Cash		20

It is the cumulative loss of 16 in the above example that has been debited to reserves in respect of the pension scheme that falls to be treated as realised, rather than any notional "credit" relating to the asset of 4. [50/04 A3]

Establishing the effect on realised profits at a particular date

This example illustrates the application of paragraph 8.14 of the guidance in the case where the company has recognised a pension asset on acquisition of an unincorporated business.

In 2005, a company acquired an unincorporated business and the fair values of the net assets recognised included a pension asset of 20. At 31 December 2007, cumulative post-acquisition contributions of 4 have been made and the asset has reduced to 18. The cumulative amount included in reserves is calculated as follows:

Surplus recognised in balance sheet	18
Cumulative net contributions	(4)
Surplus recognised on acquisition	(20)
Amount included in reserves (debit)	(6)

Another way of expressing the same calculation is as follows:

Cumulative net contributions		(4)
Surplus recognised in balance sheet	18	
Less: Surplus recognised on acquisition	(20)	
Decrease in surplus recognised		(2)
Amount included in reserves (debit)		(6)

It can be seen from this example that there must be a cumulative debit in reserves if the asset recognised in the balance sheet is less than the amount

> recognised on acquisition provided that the cumulative net post-acquisition contributions are not negative and the scheme has not been combined with any other scheme.

As explained in paragraph 8.18 of TECH 01/08 it will often be obvious, without any calculations, that all of the amounts included in reserves arising from pension scheme accounting are realised. [TECH 01/08 8.14]

Companies that are able to establish the precise amount of the cumulative net credit or debit in reserves in respect of the pension scheme will treat it as realised or unrealised in accordance with 8.11 to 8.13 of TECH 01/08 as explained above. [TECH 01/08 8.15]

It may not be practicable for companies with long-established schemes to ascertain the total cumulative net contributions less refunds made since the scheme commenced, to perform with precision the analysis in 8.13 of TECH 01/08 (although, in view of their rarity, it is likely that the company would be able to identify all refunds made and these should be included in the calculation). For such schemes the estimated approach set out in this paragraph may be taken:

[TECH 01/08 8.16]

(a) the calculation set out in paragraph 8.14 of TECH 01/08 may be performed initially using the amount of those cumulative net contributions the company has been able to identify; and

(b) that calculation may be revisited subsequently, as set out in paragraph 8.17 of TECH 01/08, if further contributions are identified that were made prior to the date of the assessment.

A company adopting the estimated approach set out at 8.16 of TECH 01/08 might be able to revise that estimate subsequently by identifying additional contributions that have been made since the scheme was established or acquired. If so, it may be able to revise upwards the amount of a net cumulative realised loss in reserves and therefore treat as realised net credits arising in subsequent periods that would otherwise be treated as unrealised. [TECH 01/08 8.17]

It will often be obvious, without any calculations, that all of the amounts included in reserves arising from pension scheme accounting are realised. Therefore, no adjustments will be required to the amounts stated in the accounts when determining the cumulative amount of realised profits available for distribution. Other than sometimes in those rare cases where a pension asset or liability has been recognised in the company's individual accounts on a past acquisition, no adjustment is necessary if a liability is recognised in the balance sheet (i.e. because the net cumulative contributions cannot be negative). Where a pension asset is recognised in the balance sheet, it is only necessary to determine that the cumulative net contributions exceed this amount to be able to confirm that no adjustment is necessary. The calculations are more complex when a past acquisition is involved. [TECH 01/08 8.18]

5.8.4.3 *Acquisition of an unincorporated business*

Where part of a company's pension asset or liability arose on the acquisition of an unincorporated business, it will have been recorded initially at fair value as required by FRS 7. That initial asset or liability will not have affected the company's reserves directly and must therefore be taken into account as part of the adjustment in arriving at the impact of FRS 17 on reserves. [TECH 01/08 8.19]

FRS 17 did not change the requirement of FRS 7 to record the pension asset or liability at fair value, although it may have required fair value to be measured using a different method from that used when the acquisition was first recorded. FRS 17 paragraph 97 notes that any difference between the FRS 17 measure of fair value and that originally used "should be treated as a change in assumptions (i.e. an actuarial gain or loss) arising since acquisition". Such a difference will therefore have given rise to a gain or loss that falls to be categorised as realised or unrealised in accordance with the general approach noted above. As a result, it is the asset or liability recognised initially as part of the acquisition accounting that is taken into account (together with the net contributions paid since acquisition) in assessing the reserves position under FRS 17. [TECH 01/08 8.20]

5.8.4.4 *Deferred tax*

The deferred tax asset or liability arising from different treatments of pension costs for accounting and tax purposes generally relates to the pension asset or liability in the balance sheet and is not necessarily associated with the cumulative net debit or credit in reserves. [TECH 01/08 8.21]

The cumulative debit in reserves in respect of a deferred tax liability relating to a pension asset should be treated as a realised loss. However, to the extent that there is an unrealised cumulative net credit in reserves in respect of the pension asset, then the amount of the debit in respect of deferred tax should be treated as a reduction in that unrealised profit rather than as a realised loss. It is not necessary to restrict the offset by applying the tax rate to the amount of the unrealised profit. [TECH 01/08 8.22]

The cumulative credit in reserves in respect of a deferred tax asset relating to a pension liability should be treated as an unrealised profit. However, to the extent that there is a realised cumulative net debit in reserves in respect of the pension liability, then the amount of the credit in respect of deferred tax should be treated as a reduction in that realised loss rather than as an unrealised profit. It is not necessary to restrict the offset by applying the tax rate to the amount of the realised loss. [TECH 01/08 8.23]

The approach set out above is consistent with paragraph 3.17 of TECH 01/08 set out above. [TECH 01/08 8.24]

5.8.4.5 Companies with more than one scheme

The guidance in TECH 01/08 assumes the company has only one scheme. A company that operates more than one defined benefit scheme should assess separately for each scheme the impact of an FRS 17 asset or liability on its realised profits and losses. However, there may be situations where two schemes are to merge. In such situations a company may treat any net credit to reserves that has been recorded in respect of one scheme as a reduction in the realised loss caused by a net debit in respect of the other scheme from the point at which the trustees of the schemes have irrevocably agreed that they will merge and to extent that the surplus and deficit are permitted to be offset for funding purposes. A similar argument applies in cases where a transfer has been irrevocably agreed between different schemes. [TECH 01/08 8.25]

A company that operates more than one defined benefit scheme may find that it can follow 8.11 to 8.13 of TECH 01/08 set out above for schemes formed or acquired in an acquisition of an unincorporated business relatively recently but may need to follow paragraph 8.16 of TECH 01/08 above for schemes operated by the company for a longer time. TECH 01/08 does not preclude such a mixed approach. [TECH 01/08 8.26]

5.9 Intragroup transactions

5.9.1 Introduction

Under both common law and statute, distributions are made by companies and not by groups. The group accounts are therefore not relevant for the purpose of determining realisation or distributability; for example, realised profits which are reflected in a parent's own accounts may be eliminated in the group accounts, and profits retained by subsidiaries are not distributable by the parent. [TECH 01/08 9.1]

The ability of a parent to control the actions of its subsidiary must also be borne in mind when considering the substance of an intragroup transaction carried out by or with that subsidiary. [TECH 01/08 9.2]

It is not practicable to attempt to illustrate every circumstance in which difficulties may arise in determining whether a profit is realised. The principles set out in TECH 01/08 should be applied in relation to the group company seeking to establish a realised profit; in particular, those provisions of paragraph 3.5 (see **5.3.2**) which relate to artificial, linked (whether legally or otherwise) or circular transactions or arrangements should be applied. The examples which follow are intended to illustrate the factors to be considered in determining whether intragroup transactions give rise to realised profits. [TECH 01/08 9.3]

5.9.2 *Cash pooling arrangements and group treasury functions*

In a group, where there is a cash pooling arrangement or a similar group treasury function, from the perspective of the company seeking to establish a realised profit an increase in debt due from, and/or a decrease in debt due to, the group finance/treasury company will constitute qualifying consideration, provided it:

(a) is not a transaction or arrangement that falls within paragraph 3.5 of TECH 01/08; and

(b) meets the criteria in paragraph 3.11 of TECH 01/08 (i.e. the definition of qualifying consideration).

An example of a cash pooling arrangement is where a group finance/treasury company effectively acts as a banker by accepting funds and settling debts on behalf of the group company seeking to establish a realised profit. [TECH 01/08 9.4]

5.9.3 *Dividends*

5.9.3.1 *Dividend received or receivable on an investment in a subsidiary*

For a dividend received or receivable from a subsidiary to be treated as a realised profit, the consideration must be in the form of qualifying consideration. Accounting for dividends receivable and payable, including payment of intragroup dividends through inter-company accounts, is considered at paragraphs 9.6 *et seq* of TECH 01/08 (see **5.9.3.2**). It will also be necessary to consider the effect any dividend has on the value of the investment in the subsidiary and, where its recoverable amount has fallen below its book value, to take account of the effect of any such impairment (and, where appropriate, any consequential release from revaluation, merger or other similar reserve). [TECH 01/08 9.5]

5.9.3.2 Accrual of intragroup dividends payable and receivable

The following paragraphs deal with income that is dividend income or appropriation for legal purposes and which for accounting purposes is dealt with as a dividend by the paying and receiving companies (rather than as interest under IAS 32 or FRS 25). [TECH 01/08 9.6]

Adoption of IAS 10 (and its UK GAAP equivalent FRS 21) had the effect of changing the timing of recognition of dividends payable and receivable. For dividends payable this did not raise any particular concerns except where there is a change of accounting policy as discussed at **5.3.5.2**. Although a proposed final dividend no longer accrues as a liability in the accounts of the year in question, those accounts are still the relevant accounts by which its payment will be justified. [TECH 01/08 9.7]

However, the change in the timing of recognition of dividends receivable had significant implications for some companies for their profits available for distribution. Previously, under SSAP 17, companies were permitted to accrue dividends receivable from subsidiaries and associates that were declared after the balance sheet date if they related to periods prior to the balance sheet date of the parent company. This is no longer possible under IAS 10 (and FRS 21). Therefore, companies may have to consider paying up interim dividends before the balance sheet date to ensure that the parent company has adequate distributable reserves to support the expected level of the proposed final dividend. [TECH 01/08 9.8]

IAS 10 refers to dividends "declared" after the balance sheet date with the implication that those "declared" before the balance sheet date would be accrued (by both the subsidiary and the parent). However, IAS 10 refers to dividends that are declared as those that are "appropriately authorised and no longer at the discretion of the entity". In the UK, interim dividends do not become a legally binding liability until they are paid and final dividends do not become a legally binding liability until they are approved by a general meeting or, for private companies, by the members passing a written resolution (see **5.2.5** above). [TECH 01/08 9.9]

As explained in paragraph 9.8 of TECH 01/08, it may be necessary for subsidiary companies to pay up interim dividends before the parent company's balance sheet date to ensure that the parent company has adequate distributable reserves to support the expected level of its proposed final dividend. [TECH 01/08 9.10]

As explained in paragraph 2.10 (see **5.2.5**), under common form articles of association (for example, Table A), a distribution by way of interim dividend is made when it is paid. This therefore raises the question as to what constitutes payment of an interim dividend and, consequently, the timing of its recognition as a distribution by the paying company and as a profit by the recipient company. The question of whether a profit recorded by the recipient company is a realised profit falls to be determined under the general principles in this guidance, for example, whether it is qualifying consideration. [TECH 01/08 9.11]

Where there is a transfer of cash the answer will be clear as payment has been received. This conclusion would not be affected by the cash being immediately or closely afterwards reinvested in the paying company either by way of loan or by way of capital investment, although the fact of such reinvestment will require consideration of the guidance in paragraph 9.19 of TECH 01/08 (see **5.9.3.3**) as to whether the profit is realised or unrealised in the parent company's hands. [TECH 01/08 9.12]

Where the dividend is recorded on inter-company account and the effect of such an entry reduces the amount recorded as receivable from the parent to the dividend paying subsidiary, this would constitute settlement by way of set-off and would be equivalent to a payment in cash taking place at the date that the book entries were made by both companies (or later if these should be different) to the extent that this does not reduce the amount recorded as receivable from the parent to the dividend-paying subsidiary below nil. [TECH 01/08 9.13]

Where the dividend is recorded on inter-company account and the book entry creates or increases a liability of the paying subsidiary, the question arises as to whether the dividend falls to be treated as paid and received. [TECH 01/08 9.14]

Effecting the dividend via a group treasury function (see **5.9.2** above) where the subsidiary company instructs the group treasury function to debit the subsidiary's account and credit the parent's account, would constitute payment. [TECH 01/08 9.15]

In other circumstances, more than just entries into the accounting records of the paying and receiving company are likely to be required. If there were no doubt as to the paying subsidiary's ability to pay the dividend, payment in respect of individual dividends could be effected by the execution as a Deed of an acknowledgment of liability to pay the amount entered in the accounting records as a payable by the subsidiary and a receivable by the parent company or the constitution of such liability pursuant to an enforceable contract under Scots Law. [TECH 01/08 9.16]

Any doubts as to the payment of an interim dividend recorded by book entry can be removed by the conversion of the interim dividend into a final dividend before the year end. Under common form articles of association, this will require a recommendation by the directors and the declaration of the dividend either by approval by the members in a general meeting or, for private companies, by the members passing a written resolution. [TECH 01/08 9.17]

In scenarios other than those discussed above, the position is more complex and dependent on the specific facts and circumstances and companies in doubt as to the position may wish to seek legal advice. [TECH 01/08 9.18]

5.9.3.3 *Dividend by a subsidiary to a parent which provides or reinvests the funds in the subsidiary*

Investment by a parent in a subsidiary which has paid a dividend in the form of qualifying consideration does not in itself preclude that dividend from continuing to be treated as a realised profit by the parent. However, if a subsidiary pays a dividend to a parent which directly or indirectly provides the funds for the dividend or reinvests the proceeds in the subsidiary in circumstances where the transactions or arrangements fall within paragraph 3.5 of TECH 01/08 (see **5.3.2**), the dividend will not represent a realised profit for the parent if it does not receive in return for the provision of funds or their reinvestment an asset which is in the form of qualifying consideration. Thus, in such a case, the profit will be unrealised if, for example:

[TECH 01/08 9.19]

(a) the provision or reinvestment of funds is in the form of:

  (i) a subscription for shares, as the subsidiary is in effect capitalising its realised profits; or

  (ii) a capital contribution (i.e. a gift); or

  (iii) a loan which does not meet the definition of qualifying consideration; or

  (iv) a guarantee of borrowings used to fund the dividend (unless the likelihood that the guarantee will be called upon is remote); or

(b) the subsidiary is unlikely to be able to meet its obligations under any borrowings used to fund the dividend without recourse directly or indirectly to the parent.

5.9.3.4 *Dividends received out of pre-acquisition profits*

The Act does not deal specifically with the onward distribution by a parent of dividends out of the pre-acquisition profits of its subsidiaries. Under UK GAAP such dividends should be treated by a parent in the same way as any other dividend which it receives from a subsidiary, including taking account of any impairment in accordance with paragraph 9.5 of TECH 01/08 as explained in the following paragraph. The position under IFRSs is considered below. [TECH 01/08 9.20]

Under UK GAAP, it has for many years been accepted that dividends received out of pre-acquisition profits of subsidiaries are treated as giving rise to a profit unless the dividend causes a diminution in the value of the investment below its book amount. This is separate from the question of whether or not such dividends are realised profits which will depend on whether they have been received in the form of qualifying consideration. [TECH 01/08 9.21]

Under IAS 27, when investments in subsidiaries are stated using the cost model, any dividends received out of their pre-acquisition profits will be credited against the cost of investment. This is explained as follows in IAS 27:

> "The cost method is a method of accounting for an investment whereby the investment is recognised at cost. The investor recognises income from the investment only to the extent that the investor receives distributions from accumulated profits of the investee arising after the date of acquisition. Distributions received in excess of such profits are regarded as a recovery of investment and are recognised as a reduction of the cost of the investment." [IAS 27 paragraph 4]

In May 2008, the IASB issued an amendment to IAS 27 which removes this requirement. At the same time, it also issued an amendment to IFRS 1 which permits the use of the previous GAAP carrying amount of subsidiaries as their deemed cost on transition to IFRSs. However, these amendments have not yet been adopted by the EU and so the unamended Standards continue to apply to UK companies applying IFRSs in their individual accounts. The guidance which follows is relevant when applying the unamended IAS 27 and IFRS 1. When applying the amended Standards there will generally be no adjustment to the carrying amount of the investment in subsidiaries on transition to IFRSs so there is no effect on accumulated realised profits.

On transition to IFRSs, when applying the unamended IAS 27, companies have to determine the extent to which any dividends have been received out of the pre-acquisition profits of their subsidiaries. This may be difficult when investments were acquired many years ago but there is no exemption from the requirement in the unamended IAS 27 or the unamended IFRS 1. [TECH 01/08 9.23]

The position may be further complicated by the effect of group reorganisations. For example, if a new intermediate holding company is inserted between a parent company and its subsidiary, the retained profits of the subsidiary at the date of the restructuring appear to be pre-acquisition from the perspective of the intermediate holding company even though they may be post-acquisition from the perspective of the group. This is a financial reporting issue which is outside the scope of this guidance on distributable profits. The guidance in the next paragraph will be relevant when dividends received are accounted for as a reduction in the cost of investment, which may include circumstances where the investment arose on a group reconstruction. [TECH 01/08 9.24]

To the extent that dividends received are accounted for as a reduction in the cost of investment, they are not treated as accounting profits at all. Accumulated realised profits available for distribution will therefore be reduced compared with what they were under UK GAAP. However, to the extent that the acquisition of the subsidiary benefited from merger relief or group reconstruction relief, the receipt of such a dividend in the form of qualifying consideration will result in the realisation of an equivalent amount of the related merger reserve (see **5.9.10** below). [TECH 01/08 9.25]

Most companies will record investments in subsidiaries in accordance with the cost model. IAS 27 also permits such investments to be accounted for at fair value in accordance with IAS 39. The requirement in IAS 27 for the treatment of dividends out of pre-acquisition profits appears in the definition of the cost method. A similar, more general, requirement appears in paragraph 32 of IAS 18. Therefore, the requirement applies even when the investments are recorded at fair value in accordance with IAS 39, although it assumes much less importance in such a case since the company's income (in its income statement and directly in equity – e.g. on an available-for-sale classification) comprises the totality of the change in fair value of the investment. In relation to that total income, any dividend could be seen as merely a conversion of part of that income into another form of asset (e.g. cash or a receivable) with a corresponding reduction in the investment carrying value. [TECH 01/08 9.26]

When IAS 39 is used, profits on remeasurement will generally be treated as unrealised (see **5.4.2.5** above, dealing with unquoted equity investment carried at fair value). As explained above, when this treatment is adopted, it is still a requirement that any dividends received out of pre-acquisition profits are credited against the carrying value of the investment. To the extent that the profit arising on remeasurement of the investment has been received as a dividend in the form of qualifying consideration, the profit will be a realised profit. Therefore the overall effect is that dividends received out of pre-acquisition profits will increase accumulated realised profits when a policy of remeasuring investments in subsidiaries at fair value is adopted. [TECH 01/08 9.27]

5.9.4 *Sale of an asset by a parent to its subsidiary*

If a parent sells an asset to a subsidiary in circumstances where the transactions or arrangements fall within paragraph 3.5 of TECH 01/08 (see **5.3.2**), any profit on the sale of the asset will not represent a realised profit for the parent if it does not receive an asset which is in the form of qualifying consideration. Thus, in such a case, the profit will be unrealised if, for example:

[TECH 01/08 9.28]

(a) there is an agreement or understanding regarding the repurchase of the asset by the parent; or

(b) the parent directly or indirectly provides the funds for the purchase or reinvests the proceeds in the subsidiary where the provision or reinvestment of funds is in the form of:

  (i) a subscription for shares; or

  (ii) a capital contribution (i.e. a gift); or

  (iii) a loan which does not meet the definition of qualifying consideration; or

  (iv) a guarantee of borrowings used to fund the purchase (unless the likelihood that the guarantee will be called upon is remote); or

(c) the subsidiary is unlikely to be able to meet its obligations under any borrowings used to fund the purchase without recourse directly or indirectly to the parent.

5.9.5 *Sale of an asset by a subsidiary to a parent followed by a dividend to the parent of the resulting profit*

The subsidiary should apply factors similar to those in paragraph 9.28 of TECH 01/08 (see **5.9.4**) in determining whether it has made a realised profit on the sale of an asset to its parent. [TECH 01/08 9.29]

If a subsidiary sells an asset to its parent and pays a dividend out of the resulting profit in circumstances where the transactions or arrangements, from the parent's perspective, fall within paragraph 3.5 of TECH 01/08, the dividend will not give rise to a realised profit for the parent unless the asset which the parent purchased meets the definition of qualifying consideration. This is because the overall commercial effect of such an arrangement for the parent is similar to a dividend in specie (see **5.9.7**). [TECH 01/08 9.30]

5.9.6 *Sale of an asset by a subsidiary to a fellow subsidiary followed by a dividend to the parent of the resulting profit*

The subsidiary should apply factors similar to those in paragraph 9.28 of TECH 01/08 (see **5.9.4**) in determining whether it has made a realised profit on the sale of an asset to its fellow subsidiary. [TECH 01/08 9.31]

If a subsidiary sells an asset to a fellow subsidiary and pays a dividend to the parent out of the resulting profit in circumstances where the transactions or arrangements, from the parent's perspective, fall within paragraph 3.5 of TECH 01/08 (see **5.3.2**), the dividend will not give rise to a realised profit for the parent if, for example:

[TECH 01/08 9.32]

(a) the parent directly or indirectly provides the funds for the purchase where the provision of funds is in the form of:

   (i) a subscription for shares; or

   (ii) a capital contribution (i.e., a gift); or

   (iii) a loan which does not meet the definition of qualifying consideration; or

(b) the parent directly or indirectly reinvests the dividend (or equivalent consideration) in the subsidiary which paid the dividend or the fellow subsidiary to which the asset was sold and the asset which the parent receives from this reinvestment is not in the form of qualifying consideration; or

(c) the parent directly or indirectly guarantees any borrowings used to provide either the fellow subsidiary with the consideration for its purchase of the asset or the vendor subsidiary with funds for its dividend (in either case unless the likelihood that the guarantee will be called upon is remote) or the subsidiary in question is unlikely to be able to meet its obligations under the borrowings without recourse directly or indirectly to the parent.

5.9.7 *Dividend in specie*

A dividend in specie from a subsidiary is an unrealised profit in the hands of the parent (even where there is a cash alternative) unless the asset distributed meets the definition of qualifying consideration. However, if the non-cash asset is distributed by the parent then, following section 846, that unrealised profit would be treated by the parent as a realised profit for the purpose of that onward distribution, provided that the profit was recorded in the relevant accounts. [TECH 01/08 9.33]

5.9.8 *Return of capital contribution*

Where a capital contribution is returned directly or indirectly to the donor company in circumstances where the transactions or arrangements fall within paragraph 3.5 of TECH 01/08 (see **5.3.2**), it will not give rise to a realised profit in the hands of the donor. [TECH 01/08 9.34]

5.9.9 *Debits within equity arising on group reconstructions*

Business combinations involving entities or businesses under common control are excluded from the scope of IFRS 3, "Business combinations". Typical examples include a group reorganisation involving either a transfer of a company within a group or the transfer of a business from one group member to another. [TECH 01/08 9.35]

When a company carries out a transaction under common control (as defined in IFRS 3) such as acquiring the business of another company within the same group, the directors may determine that it is not appropriate to recognise the net assets acquired at their fair values and that it is not appropriate to recognise goodwill. For example, a company may purchase the trade and assets of a division from its parent company, the consideration being a combination of cash and shares. The directors may determine that the appropriate accounting is to recognise the net assets acquired at the transferor's book amounts. The consideration paid, say, measured at the nominal value of the shares issued plus the value of the cash element, may exceed the book amount of the net assets acquired and this will leave a debit difference to be recognised. It is not goodwill. The debit is sometimes referred to as a "merger difference" and is recorded in equity. [TECH 01/08 9.36]

A business combination involving members of the same group is completed under the direction of the controlling party, the common parent. Consequently, any excess paid by the acquirer over the book amount of the vendor's net assets is accounted for in a similar manner to a distribution or return of capital to the common parent. Distributions and returns of capital are dealt with through equity, and therefore it is logical also to recognise the debit in equity. [TECH 01/08 9.37]

Such a debit directly to equity is not necessarily, however, a distribution as a matter of law. This is because the debit described above is determined on a book basis, whereas the question as to whether there would be an actual distribution is determined by whether the company gives consideration other than an issue of its shares, to its parent or a fellow subsidiary, with a fair value in excess of the fair value of the net assets and business acquired. Accordingly the debit may form part of an actual distribution or may not. [TECH 01/08 9.38]

In a case where the debit in equity does not form part of an actual distribution, then at the date of acquisition the debit does not represent a loss; the acquiring company has purchased net assets worth at least the book value of the consideration given but, under the appropriate accounting, has recognised these at a lower amount. The difference between the two is the amount of the debit. As the debit is not a loss at all, it is neither realised nor unrealised. [TECH 01/08 9.39]

To the extent that the assets, if they had been recognised at the higher amount, would have been written down, say, by depreciation or impairment, an equivalent amount of the debit becomes a realised loss. It is a realised, rather than unrealised, loss because, had the debit been carried as an asset, any write down for depreciation or impairment would be required, by section 841 and the principles of realisation (see **section 5.3**), to be regarded as realised. [TECH 01/08 9.40]

The above guidance is written in the context of IFRS 3 but is equally applicable to a group reconstruction accounted for under FRS 6. [TECH 01/08 9.41]

5.9.9.1 Additional consideration for a public company

For a public company, the initial recognition of the debit will restrict the maximum amount of profits available for distribution to the extent the cash paid out (or the book value of other non-equity consideration given) is greater than the book value of the net assets acquired. This is because the acquirer's net assets as shown in the company's relevant accounts for section 836 purposes would be reduced as a result of paying out cash consideration but increased by a smaller amount by recognising the acquired net assets at a lower amount. Since the debit is neither a realised loss nor an unrealised loss it has no effect on the "share capital and undistributable reserves" part of the section 831 net assets test. Consequently, the maximum permissible distribution would be restricted. [TECH 01/08 9.42]

5.9.10 Merger relief and group reconstruction relief

As explained in paragraph 2.11 of TECH 01/08 (see **5.2.6** above), when shares were issued as consideration for the acquisition of a subsidiary, the issuing company may have benefited from merger relief (s612) or group reconstruction relief (s611). In accordance with section 615 of the Act, under UK GAAP, such companies may have stated the cost of investment at the nominal value of the shares issued (for merger relief) or based on the minimum premium value (for group reconstruction relief). This accounting treatment may not be permitted when reporting under IFRSs but this is affected by the amendments made to IFRS 1 and IAS 27 in May 2008.

This accounting treatment may not be permitted when reporting under IFRSs but this is affected by the amendments made to IFRS 1 and IAS 27 in May 2008. [TECH 01/08 9.43]

In May 2008, the IASB issued an amendment to IFRS 1 which permits the use of the previous GAAP carrying amount of subsidiaries as their deemed cost on transition to IFRSs. This amendment has not yet been adopted by the EU and so the unamended Standard continues to apply to UK companies applying IFRSs in their individual accounts. However, if the exemption in the amended IFRS 1 is used (once adopted), there will be no adjustment to the carrying amount of the investment on transition to IFRSs and consequently no effect on accumulated realised profits.

In May 2008, the IASB also amended IAS 27 to insert a new requirement for the accounting treatment to be adopted by a new parent company (including an intermediate parent company) established as a result of a group reorganisation when certain criteria are met. When these criteria are met, the new parent accounts for the cost of its investment in the original parent at the carrying amount of its share of the equity items shown in the separate financial statements of the original parent at the date of the reorganisation. This amendment has not yet been adopted by the EU and so the unamended Standard continues to apply to UK companies applying IFRSs in their individual accounts. The amendment requires only prospective application to reorganisations occurring in annual periods beginning on or after 1 January 2009. No restatement is required for past reorganisations. However, for future reorganisations, the application of the new requirement may have the effect of restricting the ability of a public company to make distributions because the net assets of the new parent company may (depending on the circumstances) be stated at an amount which is less than its share capital and undistributable reserves.

Before the amendment described above, IAS 27 is generally considered to require the acquired asset to be booked at fair value in some or all cases. Therefore, on transition to IFRSs, it may be necessary to gross up the cost of investment to the fair value at the date of acquisition and to recognise a corresponding 'merger reserve'. Although different views have been expressed on this financial reporting issue, the following paragraph deals with the treatment for distributable profit purposes when the merger reserve is recorded. [TECH 01/08 9.43]

The adjustment to establish the merger reserve will have no direct impact on accumulated realised profits because the reserve will represent an unrealised profit. However, the reserve may become realised at a later date. This may, for example, occur on disposal of the investment for qualifying consideration or if the investment is written down for impairment. Similarly, it may also occur to the extent that dividends are received from the subsidiary out of pre-acquisition profits in the form of qualifying consideration and those dividends are recognised as a reduction in the cost of investment (see **5.3.3.2** and **5.9.3.4**). [TECH 01/08 9.44]

5.10 Other issues

5.10.1 IAS 27, IAS 28 and IAS 31 – Separate financial statements

The balance of profits available for distribution is that available to the company, not to its group. The availability of such profits is to be judged by reference to accounts, which must therefore be the company's individual accounts. Except when initial or interim accounts are required, the "relevant accounts" for this purpose are the individual accounts forming part of the annual accounts, whether they are "Companies Act individual accounts" or "IAS individual accounts" (see **section 5.2** above). [TECH 01/08 10.1]

IFRSs do not use the term "individual accounts" but uses the term "separate financial statements" which are defined in IAS 27 as follows:

> "Separate financial statements are those presented by a parent, an investor in an associate or a venturer in a jointly controlled entity, in which the investments are accounted for on the basis of the direct equity interests rather than on the basis of the reported results and net assets of the investee." [TECH 01/08 10.2]

Where a company prepares consolidated financial statements, these 'separate financial statements' will be the company's "IAS individual accounts" for the purposes of section 395 and therefore the relevant accounts under section 836 for the purposes of justifying any distribution. [TECH 01/08 10.3]

However, where a company has an associate or jointly controlled entity but has no subsidiaries, in some circumstances IAS 28 and/or IAS 31, when considered outside the EU legal framework, require the preparation of financial statements that are neither separate financial statements nor consolidated financial statements. In such financial statements, the investments in associates and jointly controlled entities are accounted for using the equity method or proportional consolidation as appropriate (see IAS 28.4 and IAS 31.5). In these circumstances, the company is not required by IFRSs (when considered outside of the EU legal framework) to prepare separate financial statements. One point of view is that the financial statements including investments on the basis of equity accounting and/or proportional consolidation are not relevant for the purposes of justifying distributions and that the "separate financial statements" are the "IAS individual accounts". [TECH 01/08 10.4]

Within the EU legal framework, an alternative point of view is that the financial statements required by IAS 28 and IAS 31 (i.e. those including investments on the basis of equity accounting and/or proportional consolidation) are a company's "IAS individual accounts". The Institutes have to date not been able to establish which view is the correct interpretation of the law and of EU-adopted IFRSs. The European Commission's Accounting Regulatory Committee has considered some related issues but has so far not provided clear guidance on this specific point. [TECH 01/08 10.5]

Were the accounts including the equity accounting to be the "IAS individual accounts", the share of results of associates/jointly-controlled-entities is not realised save to the extent that it is received as distributions in the form of qualifying consideration. Therefore the amount of a company's accumulated realised profits will be the same irrespective of which interpretation of the law is correct. [TECH 01/08 10.6]

5.10.2 Section 841

Section 841(1), (2) states that for the purposes of Part 23, the following are treated as realised losses:

[TECH 01/08 10.7]

- in the case of Companies Act accounts, provisions of a kind specified for the purposes of this paragraph by regulations under section 396 (except revaluation provisions); and
- in the case of IAS accounts, provisions of any kind (except revaluation provisions).

Due to changes in accounting methods and choices as between cost and valuation, effected by the implementation of IFRSs, the question might arise as to whether the exception provided for by section 841(1), (2) continues to be capable of use under IFRSs. The following paragraphs explain the exception, the questions that might arise, and the conclusion that the exception does continue to be capable of use under IFRSs. [TECH 01/08 10.8]

Section 841(3) defines a "revaluation provision" to mean a provision in respect of a diminution in value of a fixed asset appearing on a revaluation of all the fixed assets of a company, or of all of its fixed assets other than goodwill. This preserves, for companies applying IFRSs, an exception to the normal rule that all provisions are treated as realised losses. [TECH 01/08 10.9]

For example, using section 841, an impairment write down of one subsidiary may be offset by an increase in value of another subsidiary for the purposes of determining profits available for distribution (although the impairment would still have to be recorded in the profit and loss account for financial reporting purposes). Similarly where financial assets are regarded as fixed assets, such as in the case of investment companies, any decrease in the fair value of investments may be offset by any increase in the fair value of other investments for the purposes of determining profits available for distribution (even though certain increases in fair value might be treated as unrealised for the purposes of this guidance). [TECH 01/08 10.10]

5.10.2.1 Definition of "fixed assets"

The definition of a "revaluation provision" uses the term "fixed assets" which are defined in section 853(6) as meaning assets of a company which are intended for use on a continuing basis in the company's activities. This term is not used in IFRSs. "Non-current assets" as defined in IAS 1 will not correspond with "fixed assets" as defined in section 853(6), for example because the former may include long term debtors. [TECH 01/08 10.11]

For the purposes of applying section 841, fixed assets are those assets that meet the section 853(6) definition of "fixed assets". As noted above, in "IAS individual accounts", these will not necessarily correspond with those presented as non-current assets in the relevant accounts. However, there is nothing in section 841 that requires the fixed assets to be shown in the balance sheet as such for the section to be applied. [TECH 01/08 10.12]

5.10.2.2 Ability to revalue assets

Investments in subsidiaries present a particular issue in the context of section 841 and IFRSs. Under IFRSs, only two accounting policies are available for investments in subsidiaries that are not classified as held for sale:

(a) cost as determined under paragraph 4 of IAS 27 (see **5.9.3.4** above); or

(b) in accordance with IAS 39, which requires such investments to be maintained at fair value.

In practice, fair value under (b) above may be precluded because the range of reasonable fair value estimates is significant and the probabilities of the various estimates cannot reasonably be assessed (see IAS 39, AG 80–81). IAS 39 requires such investments to be carried at cost. Even where a fair value policy is possible, it will require valuations to be obtained each time a balance sheet is drawn up. This is likely to be unattractive to most companies. The expectation, therefore, is that most companies will hold subsidiaries at cost. The issue that arises is whether it is possible to apply the exception for "revaluation provisions" in section 841 in circumstances where the accounting policy is cost (either through choice or because IAS 39 does not permit the assets to be revalued). [TECH 01/08 10.13]

Any assessment of the value of an asset can be described, for the purpose of the exception in section 841, as a revaluation, even if it is not in accordance with relevant accounting standards. In particular, the consideration of the value of an asset for the purposes of an impairment review could be described as a revaluation in this broad sense. Accordingly, section 841 does not use the term "revaluation" as meaning a revaluation in accordance with relevant accounting standards. However, depreciation of an asset is not consideration of the value of an asset for the purposes of section 841. [TECH 01/08 10.14]

It is also relevant that, for the purposes of a revaluation of all the fixed assets (or all other than goodwill) under section 841, the assets do not have to be included in the balance sheet at their revalued amounts nor do they have to be permitted to be included in the balance sheet at a valuation. In accordance with section 841(4), "for the purposes of sub-sections (2) and (3) any consideration by the directors of the value at a particular time of a fixed asset is treated as a revaluation" (subject to the requirements of sub-section (4)). Section 841(4) refers to "any consideration by the directors of the value ...." without any explicit requirement for that value to be determined on a basis that would be permitted for inclusion in the balance sheet. [TECH 01/08 10.15]

In conclusion, it is possible to apply the exception for "revaluation provisions" in section 841 in circumstances where the accounting policy is cost (either through choice or because IAS 39 does not permit the assets to be revalued). Thus, for example, an impairment write down of one subsidiary recognised in the financial statements may be offset by an increase in value of another subsidiary for the purposes of determining profits available for distribution even though the accounting policy is to carry investments in subsidiaries at cost and thus the increase in value is not recognised in the balance sheet. [TECH 01/08 10.16]

5.10.3 IFRS 1 – Fair value or revaluation as deemed cost

Under IFRS 1, a first-time adopter may elect to measure an item of property, plant and equipment at the date of transition to IFRSs at its fair value and to use that fair value as deemed cost. A first-time adopter may also elect to use a previous GAAP valuation of an item of property, plant and equipment subject to various conditions. For example, it would be possible for a company that was carrying a property at a "frozen valuation" under the transitional provisions of FRS 15 to deem that valuation as cost on transition to IFRSs. These elections are also available for investment property when a company elects to use the cost model under IAS 40 and also, in certain limited circumstances, for intangible assets. [TECH 01/08 10.17]

IFRS 1 does not specify the treatment of any revaluation reserve existing under previous GAAP or of any excess of fair value over cost when the election is used to measure the asset at fair value at the date of transition. However, it is clear that this should not be presented as a revaluation surplus because the asset is regarded as held at cost (and, for example, any subsequent fall in value would have to be charged in the income statement rather than treated as a reversal of a revaluation surplus). In the absence of any other requirement in IFRS 1, the adjustment on transition may be reflected in retained earnings. [TECH 01/08 10.18]

Nevertheless, the treatment of a revaluation as deemed cost for the purposes of IFRSs does not alter the nature of the revaluation surplus which will usually be unrealised. Therefore, companies that elect for this treatment will have to keep an analysis of the balance of retained earnings to ensure that they can identify the amount of unrealised profit included. The unrealised profit will become realised as the asset is depreciated or written down for impairment, or is sold for qualifying consideration. This is consistent with the application of section 841(5) which is summarised at **5.2.11** above. [TECH 01/08 10.19]

The assets that are included on the basis of fair value or revaluation as deemed cost may have been depreciated under UK GAAP. Consider a tangible fixed asset that cost £100 and, at the date of transition to IFRSs, had a net book value of £50. Suppose that the fair value at the date of transition is £120 and the company elects to use this as deemed cost. The excess above original cost of £20 is clearly unrealised. It might be argued that the other £50 of the adjustment is a realised profit because it reverses the depreciation that had previously been charged as a realised loss. However, this analysis is not appropriate because the restatement to fair value is in the nature of a revaluation and it is generally accepted that depreciation is not written back to the profit and loss account on a revaluation. This is implicit in paragraph 63 of FRS 15. Similarly, when a previous valuation is treated as deemed cost, nothing of substance has occurred to cause the previously unrealised profit to become realised. This situation may be contrasted with an adjustment to depreciation that arises from a change in accounting policy for depreciation to comply with IAS 16 (see *Changes to depreciation policies* at **5.10.4** below). It may be possible to argue that some component of the restatement to deemed cost relates to a reconsideration of residual values and is therefore a realised profit (see **5.10.4**). But, in practice, it would not usually be practicable to distinguish this component. [TECH 01/08 10.20]

5.10.4 IFRS 1 and IAS 16 – Changes to depreciation policies

Under IFRS 1, any change in estimated useful life or depreciation pattern is accounted for prospectively from the date that the change of estimate is made provided that the depreciation methods and rates under previous GAAP are acceptable under IFRSs. However, in some cases, a company's depreciation methods and rates under previous GAAP may not be acceptable under IFRSs. If those differences have a material effect on the financial statements, the company adjusts the accumulated depreciation in its opening IFRS balance sheet retrospectively so that it complies with IFRSs (see IFRS 1.IG7). [TECH 01/08 10.21]

The requirements of IAS 16 are, in general, similar to those of FRS 15 and so the depreciation methods and rates used for UK GAAP will usually be acceptable under IFRSs. However, a difference may arise because of the different way in which residual value is measured in the standards. Under FRS 15, residual values are based on the prices prevailing at the date of acquisition or revaluation of the asset. Under IAS 16, they are based on prices prevailing at the balance sheet date. Therefore, in general, cumulative depreciation will be lower under IFRSs assuming that prices are rising with inflation. Where such an effect is material, and an adjustment is made to reduce accumulated depreciation, the adjustment will be regarded as a realised profit because it represents the reversal of a previous realised loss. [TECH 01/08 10.22]

5.10.5 IFRS 1 – Deferred tax on business combinations

The requirements of IFRS 1 and IFRS 3 for business combinations will generally be relevant only to the consolidated financial statements and therefore have no effect on distributable profits. However, in some cases it is necessary to account for a business combination in the individual accounts of a company, for example where it acquires an unincorporated business. [TECH 01/08 10.23]

In some circumstances, IFRS 1 may require deferred tax to be provided in respect of assets or liabilities acquired through a previous business combination. For example, in many instances no deferred tax would have been provided on the revaluation of tangible fixed assets to fair value under UK GAAP but such a provision would be required under IFRSs. When the company is not required to restate the business combination in accordance with IFRS 3 and uses this exemption, the deferred tax provision still has to be recognised but is adjusted against retained earnings rather than against goodwill. [TECH 01/08 10.24]

The tax provision will reduce accumulated realised profits available for distribution where the transaction involved the acquisition of an unincorporated business by an individual company. It does not matter that the tax provision would not have been treated in this way had IFRS 3 been applied. It is the accounting that has actually been applied in the relevant accounts, in accordance with applicable accounting standards, which affects the amount of profits available for distribution. [TECH 01/08 10.25]

5.10.6 IFRS 1 – Past capitalisation of revaluation reserve

Under UK GAAP, some companies have revalued assets, in particular properties and investments in subsidiaries, and subsequently capitalised all or part of the resulting revaluation reserve through a bonus issue of shares. The issue that arises on transition to IFRSs is the status of the debit entry in reserves if revalued assets are restated to a cost basis. [TECH 01/08 10.26]

5.10.6.1 *Investment properties and property, plant and equipment*

Under SSAP 19, investment properties are required to be included in the balance sheet at their open market value. Under FRS 15, companies that chose to adopt a policy of revaluation for classes of tangible fixed assets (property, plant and equipment) have to ensure that those assets are carried at their current value at the balance sheet date. On transition to IFRSs, companies are not required to continue to apply a revaluation policy for their investment properties or property, plant and equipment. In effect, IFRS 1 allows companies on transition to IFRSs to state their investment properties or property, plant and equipment at depreciated historical cost, or, in the case of property, plant and equipment, at a "deemed cost" that could be a previous valuation or fair value at the date of transition. This guidance addresses the position where a company chooses to restate to depreciated historical cost. In the case of a transition using a "deemed cost" the revaluation survives transition and there is no restatement to consider. [TECH 01/08 10.27]

Where the revaluation surplus has not been used at all for a bonus issue of shares and is still recorded in the balance sheet at the date of transition to IFRSs, the adjustment required will be simply to eliminate the revaluation reserve and reduce the revalued assets by the same amount to restate them to their depreciated historical cost. However, if the revaluation surplus has been capitalised, in full or in part, through a past bonus issue of shares, it will not be possible to reduce the reserve in this way. Neither is it possible to apply the debit to reduce share capital by the amount of the bonus shares. The question therefore arises as to the status of the debit entry in reserves arising from reversal of the past revaluation. [TECH 01/08 10.28]

Paragraph 3.15(c) of TECH 01/08 (see **5.3.4.2**) states that, with two exceptions explained at 2.33 (see **5.2.11**) and 3.16 (see **5.3.4.2**), realised losses will include the writing down, or providing for depreciation, amortisation, diminution in value or impairment of an asset. However, the entry to reverse the previous revaluation surplus is not depreciation or amortisation. It also does not relate to the diminution in the value of the assets or impairment but instead relates to a reduction in the amount at which those assets are recorded in the balance sheet. The actual value of the assets remains unchanged. [TECH 01/08 10.29]

The exception described in paragraph 3.16 of TECH 01/08 is as follows:

> Where a fixed asset is revalued to an amount which is below its "recoverable amount", paragraph 65(b) of FRS 15 requires the loss below recoverable amount to be reflected in the Statement of Total Recognised Gains and Losses (rather than the profit and loss account for the year). Paragraph 70 of

> FRS 15 states that where the recoverable amount is greater than the revalued amount, the resulting difference is clearly not an impairment; in these circumstances the difference is treated as an unrealised loss (see paragraph [2.28]). Such a loss would become realised in the event of a subsequent scrapping, disposal or impairment of the asset." [TECH 01/08 10.30]

This principle may be applied to the restatement of a revalued asset to its depreciated historical cost. Therefore the debit entry to reserves arising from such a restatement (which equates to the revaluation element of the carrying value that is not yet depreciated) will be an unrealised loss provided that the recoverable amount of the asset is equal to or greater than the book amount prior to the restatement. To the extent that the revaluation surplus still exists as an unrealised reserve, the unrealised loss will simply eliminate that unrealised reserve. To the extent that the revaluation surplus has been utilised, in part or in full, for a bonus issue of shares, the resulting net debit entry will represent an unrealised loss. [TECH 01/08 10.31]

The entry to reverse the previous revaluation surplus is not a provision for the purposes of applying section 841(2). In the case of Companies Act individual accounts, "provisions of a kind specified for the purposes of this paragraph by regulations under section 396 (except revaluation provisions)" are treated as realised losses. In the case of "IAS individual accounts", "provisions of any kind (except revaluation provisions)" are treated as realised losses. The entry to reverse the previous revaluation surplus is not a provision of the kind specified by the regulations under section 396 and is not a provision at all in the sense that the term is used for accounting purposes. On the restatement to historical cost there will be no provision deducted from the asset. [TECH 01/08 10.32]

5.10.6.2 Investments in subsidiaries

Under the alternative accounting rules in Schedule 1 to the Accounting regulations, investments in subsidiaries may be stated "at a market value determined as at the date of their last valuation" or "at a value determined on any basis which appears to the directors to be appropriate in the circumstances of the company". There is no obligation under the law or UK accounting standards to keep such valuations up to date although it is necessary to consider whether the assets have become impaired. Under IFRSs, two accounting policies are available for investments in subsidiaries. The first policy is that of cost, using the IAS 27-cost method. The second is to account for such investments in accordance with IAS 39. This would require such investments to be maintained at fair value. In practice, the measurement of such equity investments at fair value may be precluded because the range of reasonable fair value estimates is significant and the probabilities of the various estimates cannot reasonably be assessed (see IAS 39, AG 80–81). Even where such a policy is possible, it will require valuations to be obtained each time a balance sheet is drawn up. This is likely to be unattractive to most companies. The expectation is that most companies will hold subsidiaries at cost, as determined under IAS 27. [TECH 01/08 10.33]

Hence the guidance on the effect of a restatement to depreciated historical cost of a previously revalued investment property or tangible fixed asset is equally applicable to a restatement of previously revalued investments in subsidiaries on to an IAS 27-cost basis. [TECH 01/08 10.34]

Effect of restatements for a public company

For a public company, the restatement of a revalued asset (whether investment property, other property, plant and equipment or investment in subsidiaries) to a cost basis will restrict its profits available for distribution under section 831 to the extent that the revaluation surplus was capitalised. The effect of the unrealised loss on the restriction imposed by section 831 may be mitigated by the existence of recognised unrealised profits. [TECH 01/08 10.35]

5.10.7 IAS 11 – Accounting for construction contracts

Under UK GAAP (SSAP 9), accounting for profit on long-term contracts results in debtor balances described as "Amounts recoverable on contracts". This treatment was adopted when the standard was revised in 1988 because legal advice suggested that it was not possible to include the profit element in work-in-progress because of the requirement to state work-in-progress at cost. [TECH 01/08 10.36]

The accounting required for construction contracts under IAS 11 is broadly similar to that required by SSAP 9 (although the scope of the standards is different). However, IAS 11 is not specific as to the nature of the asset to be recognised. In practice the item may simply be disclosed as "construction contracts" although it may also be included within debtors or within work-in-progress. [TECH 01/08 10.37]

Under UK GAAP it would usually have been clear that the debtor balance for "Amounts recoverable on contracts" would have met the definition of "qualifying consideration" (see **5.3.3.4** above). Therefore profit recognised on such contracts would have been regarded as a realised profit. On the basis that this treatment has been generally accepted under UK GAAP, any profits recognised in accordance with IAS 11 should be regarded as realised profits, irrespective of how the asset is described in the balance sheet. [TECH 01/08 10.38]

5.10.8 IAS 12 – Income taxes – Deferred tax

As stated in paragraph 3.17 of TECH 01/08 (see **5.3.4.2** above), a provision for deferred tax should generally be regarded as a realised loss. However, when assets are revalued to their fair value, with any gain being recorded in the profit and loss account even though regarded as unrealised, the deferred tax on that gain should be treated as a reduction in that unrealised gain rather than as a realised loss (paragraph 14 of Appendix III to FRS 19 *Deferred tax*). [TECH 01/08 10.39]

This principle is also applicable to deferred tax provisions recognised under IAS 12, irrespective of whether profits are recognised in profit or loss, or direct in equity. For many financial instruments, profits arising from fair value accounting are realised profits (see **section 5.4** above). Any attributable deferred tax provision will be a realised loss. [TECH 01/08 10.40]

It is likely that deferred tax will more often be recognised on unrealised profits under IFRSs than under UK GAAP. For example, the remeasurement of investment property at fair value will result in unrealised profits (see **section 5.4** above) on which deferred tax will have to be provided. Such a deferred tax provision is treated as a reduction in the unrealised profit rather than as a realised loss. [TECH 01/08 10.41]

When a convertible debt instrument is accounted for using "split accounting" (see **example 5.6.4.6** above), a deferred tax provision is established and debited against the initial carrying amount of the equity component in accordance with paragraph 23 of IAS 12. This occurs if the tax base of the debt is its full amount but the book amount is lower by the amount of the equity component. The deferred tax provision reverses through profit or loss over the life of the instrument as illustrated in Example 4 in Appendix B to IAS 12. It does not represent a future cash outflow for payment of tax. The deferred tax provision should be treated as a reduction in the credit to equity rather than as a realised loss. The equity component of the financial instrument is not a profit at all and therefore does not fall to be classified as realised or unrealised (see **example 5.6.4.6** above). An adjustment to such an item does not affect realised profits. [TECH 01/08 10.42]

In some cases it may be necessary to provide for current tax on an unrealised profit. A current tax provision should be treated as a realised loss even if it arises from the taxation of an unrealised profit. This is because a provision for current tax represents a specific cash outflow that will arise irrespective of whether the related profit is realised or not. [TECH 01/08 10.43]

5.10.9 Property, plant and equipment – asset swaps

One or more items of property, plant and equipment may be acquired in exchange for a non-monetary asset or assets, or a combination of monetary and non-monetary assets. IAS 16 requires the cost of such an item of property, plant and equipment to be measured at fair value unless the transaction lacks commercial substance or the fair value of neither the asset received nor the asset given up is reliably measurable. IAS 16 provides guidance on the circumstances in which the fair value of an asset is reliably measurable for this purpose. [TECH 01/08 10.44]

A profit may therefore be recognised on such an exchange transaction in accordance with IFRSs. This profit is likely to be unrealised because an item of property, plant and equipment is unlikely to meet the definition of "qualifying consideration" (see paragraph 3.11 at **5.3.3.5** above). [TECH 01/08 10.45]

When a combination of property, plant and equipment and qualifying consideration (e.g. cash) is received, the guidance in paragraph 3.18 (see **5.3.4.3** above) on "top-slicing" will be relevant. [TECH 01/08 10.46]

Any profit treated as unrealised, will become realised as the related asset is depreciated, written down for impairment or sold for qualifying consideration. [TECH 01/08 10.47]

A loss arising on such a transaction will usually be a realised loss. However, in some cases the loss may be similar in substance to an unrealised revaluation deficit (see 2.28 of TECH 01/08 above). [TECH 01/08 10.48]

For example, if a factory used in a business was exchanged for a similar factory and a loss recognised under IAS 16 by reference to the market value of the factories, the loss will be unrealised if there would have been no need to write down the original factory for impairment because its value in use was higher than its market value. It will also be necessary to consider the value in use of the new factory which might be different from the value in use of the old factory, even though their market value is the same (e.g. because one is larger than the other). [TECH 01/08 10.49]

IAS 38 provides for the same accounting treatment for swaps of intangibles as that under IAS 16 in respect of property, plant and equipment, and therefore the foregoing analysis also applies to intangibles under IAS 38. [TECH 01/08 10.50]

There are no specific requirements in UK accounting standards dealing with such asset swaps. The above guidance will be relevant to any profit recognised under UK GAAP although it should be noted that only profits realised at the balance sheet date may be included in the profit and loss account (Acc Regs Sch. 1: 13). [TECH 01/08 10.51]

5.10.10 Revenue – Barter transactions

When goods are sold or services rendered in exchange for dissimilar goods or services, the exchange is regarded as a transaction that generates revenue in accordance with IAS 18. The revenue is measured at the fair value of the goods or services received, adjusted by the amount of any cash or cash equivalents transferred. When the fair value cannot be measured reliably, the revenue is measured at the fair value of the goods or services given up, adjusted by the amount of any cash or cash equivalents transferred. [TECH 01/08 10.52]

When an asset is received, in determining whether any profit on such an exchange is realised or unrealised, it is necessary to determine whether such asset meets the definition of qualifying consideration. For example, when a property is received, it will be straightforward to assess whether or not it meets the definition of qualifying consideration. Any profit will not become realised until that property is depreciated, written down for impairment or sold for qualifying consideration. [TECH 01/08 10.53]

Where services are exchanged, the effect of the accounting entries is to gross up the revenue and the costs by the same amount. Accordingly, there will be no effect on profit. When services are receivable but have not yet been received at the balance sheet date, a prepayment will be recognised. A prepayment does not meet the definition of qualifying consideration. [TECH 01/08 10.54]

Where an exchange of services straddles the end of an accounting reference period, such that services are provided but not received before the balance sheet date, any profit at the year end would not be realised. Any such profit initially recognised will not become realised until the service has been received in exchange. That is, the profit will be realised by the prepayment being expensed to profit or loss when the service has been received. [TECH 01/08 10.55]

There are no specific requirements in UK accounting standards dealing with barter transactions other than UITF Abstract 26 which is concerned with barter transactions for advertising. The above guidance will be relevant to any profit recognised under UK GAAP although it should be noted that only profits realised at the balance sheet date may be included in the profit and loss account (Acc Regs Sch. 1: 13). [TECH 01/08 10.56]

5.10.11 *Currency in which distributable profits are determined*

IAS 21 (and FRS 23) requires foreign currency assets, liabilities and transactions to be measured using a company's functional currency. This is defined as the currency of the primary economic environment in which the entity operates. Functional currency is a matter of fact and is not an accounting policy choice. However, IAS 21 (and FRS 23) also permits a company to present its financial statements in a currency other than its functional currency. Such a currency is referred to as a presentation currency. [TECH 01/08 10.57]

The "relevant accounts" for the purposes of justifying a distribution are determined in accordance with section 836 but will generally be the company's most recent statutory individual accounts. The currency in which those accounts are presented will determine the currency by which the amount of profits available for distribution is measured, but see **5.10.12** below where the presentation currency is not the functional currency. [TECH 01/08 10.58]

5.10.12 *Exchange differences taken directly to equity*

Under IAS 21, certain exchange differences are reported directly in a separate component of equity (i.e. not in the income statement). This can arise when the legal entity has a foreign operation (i.e. a branch) which has a functional currency which is different from that of the legal entity. This issue can also arise under UK GAAP because SSAP 20 and FRS 23 contain similar requirements. In addition, companies reporting under IFRSs (and UK GAAP under FRS 23) may freely adopt a presentation currency that is different from their functional currency. The exchange differences arising on translation to the presentation currency are similarly taken direct to equity. The issue that arises is whether these exchange differences that are taken direct to equity are realised or unrealised. [TECH 01/08 10.59]

In the case of a foreign operation (branch) with a functional currency that is different from the functional currency of the legal entity, the exchange differences taken to equity should be analysed according to the nature of the assets and liabilities on which they arise. A profit that arises on retranslation of an asset which comprises qualifying consideration, or a liability, is a realised profit in accordance with paragraph 3.9(d) of TECH 01/08 (see **5.3.3.2** above). A profit arising on the retranslation of assets which do not comprise qualifying consideration (e.g. property, plant and equipment) is an unrealised profit. A loss arising on retranslation is a realised loss unless it is the reversal of an unrealised profit. The gross profits and losses on retranslation (rather than the net amount taken direct to equity) should be assessed separately. It is therefore possible, for example, that there is a realised loss to be taken into account when determining profits available for distribution, even though the net amount taken direct to equity is a profit. [TECH 01/08 10.60]

The analysis in the previous paragraph will apply only in straightforward situations where the composition of the company's assets has not changed significantly during the period. For example, it would not be appropriate to regard the exchange difference related to the amount of the opening cash balance (i.e. the beginning to the end of year exchange difference computed in relation to that part of the opening net assets equal to the opening cash balance) as realised if that cash balance did not exist throughout the period (e.g. because it was invested in assets such as property, plant and equipment which would not comprise qualifying consideration). [TECH 01/08 10.61]

The exchange difference taken to equity will also include the difference between the profit or loss for the period translated at actual (or average) rate and that profit or loss translated at closing rate. The profit or loss for the period arises on changes in the amounts and/or composition of the company's assets and liabilities (e.g. on an exchange of stocks for cash). [TECH 01/08 10.62]

Thus taking together the exchange differences on retranslation of the profit or loss for the period and on the opening net assets, the total amount arises in relation to an asset base that changes throughout the year. To establish whether this exchange difference is realised, partly realised or unrealised will require careful analysis of the facts. Ultimately, it would be necessary to compute and assess exchange differences continually. In conducting the analysis, reasonable approximations may be made. [TECH 01/08 10.63]

If a company's share capital is denominated in a currency that is not its functional currency, complex issues may arise regarding the nature of exchange differences on share capital. Complex issues also arise concerning the nature of the exchange differences that arise when a legal entity uses a presentation currency that is different from its functional currency. The analysis above does not necessarily apply in these cases although the accounting treatment is similar. These issues are not addressed in TECH 01/08. [TECH 01/08 10.64]

5.11 Unlawful distributions

The Act makes shareholders liable to repay a distribution if, at the time of the distribution, they knew, or had reasonable grounds for believing, that the distribution was in contravention of the Act. [CA 2006 s847] Where the directors of a company believe that the company may have made a distribution in contravention of the Act, they should consider seeking legal advice. One matter for consideration will be whether or not the shareholders are liable to repay the distribution. This will depend on the facts but, as a general rule, it appears unlikely that a private shareholder would be held to have known or had reasonable grounds for believing that the distribution had been made in contravention of the Act. The position of a holding company receiving a dividend from its subsidiary raises different issues and it is perhaps more likely that it would be held to be liable to repay the distribution. However, it may also be the case, particularly for a dividend from a subsidiary to a parent, that the shareholder will be prepared to repay the dividend to regularise the position irrespective of whether or not it is legally liable to do so. There is also the possibility that the directors may be held to be liable to repay the dividend if it was paid in breach of their fiduciary duties. In these circumstances companies sometimes arrange for a resolution to be passed by the shareholders in general meeting to confirm that recovery from the directors should not be pursued. But it is stressed that appropriate legal advice should be sought where appropriate.

Where the shareholder has agreed to repay the distribution, a debtor should be recognised for the amount recoverable. However, in many instances the possibility of repayment will be uncertain and the company will have a contingent asset which cannot be recognised in the balance sheet because its recovery is not 'virtually certain'. In this scenario it is sometimes suggested that the irrecoverable amount should be charged in the profit and loss account as a bad debt expense in arriving at the profit for the financial year. This view is to some extent supported by comments made in the 1994 DTI (now BERR) Inspectors' Report into the affairs of The Bestwood plc (see below). However, this treatment is not generally adopted in practice and the more common treatment appears to be to continue to show the unlawful distribution as an appropriation. This view is based on the premise that a distribution is still a distribution even if it is made in contravention of the Act.

The further question then arises as to whether any additional disclosure is required concerning a dividend which has been, or may have been, paid in contravention of the Act. The 1994 DTI (now BERR) Inspectors' Report mentioned above commented on this issue in the following terms:

> 'We were disturbed by the suggestion by [the auditors] that auditors had no duty under the Companies Act 1985 to qualify their audit opinion in respect

> of illegal payments such as the payment of an unlawful dividend. Given that this suggestion was made by a reputable firm of chartered accountants, we consider that there may be some uncertainty in this regard. Accordingly, we consider that the requirement should clearly be set out by way of an amendment to the existing legislation.'

Although there has been no change in the law since this was written, ISA 250 (UK and Ireland) *Consideration of laws and regulations in the audit of financial statements* includes the following requirement in paragraph 35:

> 'If the auditor concludes that the non-compliance has a material effect on the financial statements, and has not been properly reflected in the financial statements, the auditor should express a qualified or an adverse opinion.'

ISA 250 does not provide any specific guidance on whether an unlawful dividend should be regarded as having a material effect on the financial statements but some auditors are likely to take this view. This is more likely to be so following the findings of the Review Panel in respect of QA Services (No 2) Limited. The Review Panel's Press Notice PN 72 issued in November 2001 commented on the issue as follows:

> 'Secondly, the period to 31 May was the company's first accounting period. Therefore, as a public company, initial accounts should have been prepared in advance of payment of the interim dividend in accordance with section 273 of the Companies Act 1985. No such accounts were prepared and the directors relied on management accounts to show that sufficient profits had been earned to support the proposed level of distribution. As the statutory procedures in respect of a distribution were not complied with, the amount distributed is potentially recoverable under the Companies Act 1985. This fact should, in the opinion of the Panel, have been disclosed as additional information in the financial statements in order to show a true and fair view.'

It may be appropriate to seek legal advice on the form of such a disclosure. The nature of the disclosure will be influenced by the action proposed by the directors to deal with the matter. In addition, to comply with IAS 37, it will be necessary to consider whether the unlawful dividend has given rise to an asset or to a contingent asset and, if the latter, whether an inflow of economic benefits is 'probable'. IAS 37 only requires disclosure of contingent assets for which an inflow of economic benefits is probable. If such inflows are not probable, any disclosures in respect of the unlawful dividend must be drafted with care to avoid giving misleading indications of the likelihood of income arising. [IAS 37.89 & 90]

The extract from the Review Panel's findings quoted above also draws attention to one of the more common reasons why a dividend may be paid unlawfully. In the case of QA Services this arose from the failure to file 'initial accounts' with the Registrar of Companies in respect of a newly incorporated company. However, a similar situation may arise when a public company proposes to pay an interim dividend which is in excess of the distributable reserves shown by the last annual accounts laid before the company in general meeting (see **5.2.7** above). In this case the company should prepare and file 'interim accounts' (see **5.2.7** above) before the distribution is made.

6 Reduction of capital

The Acts are founded on the capital maintenance principle that once a limited company issues shares, then the capital base is increased permanently. Where part of this capital base is repaid, then it must be replaced at that time from new capital or from distributable profits. By comparison, unlimited companies may freely distribute capital to members. There are two exceptions for limited companies. The first is that a private company may redeem or purchase its own shares out of capital subject to certain safeguards. This is considered at **3.3** above. The second exception is a capital reduction.

Under the 1985 Act a capital reduction set out in s135 of the 1985 Act required court approval.

The 2006 Act introduces an additional means by which a private company can reduce its share capital. The new procedure in s641 of the 2006 Act allows a private company to reduce its capital by means of a special resolution of shareholders and a solvency statement signed by all directors. This is a cheaper and quicker alternative to a court approved capital reduction. Public companies will continue to need to seek court approval.

This section of the chapter deals with the following:

1. Reduction of capital by special resolution confirmed by the court (see **6.1**)
2. Reduction of capital by a solvency statement (only available on or after 1 October 2008) (see **6.2**).

6.1 Reduction of capital by special resolution confirmed by the court

A company limited by shares may reduce its share capital by special resolution confirmed by the court. This option is available under both the 1985 and 2006 Companies Acts.

The requirements for a capital reduction are:

(a) authority in the company's articles;

(b) passing of a special resolution; and

(c) confirmation by the Court.

Subject to these requirements, s641 of the 2006 Act (previously s135 of the 1985 Act) gives a company the power to reduce its share capital in any way and, without prejudice to that general power, goes on to mention three particular circumstances in which this might be done:

(a) where the company wishes to reduce the liability on any of its shares in respect of share capital not paid up;

(b) where the company is over-capitalised; and

(c) where the company has suffered a loss of capital (i.e. cancelling share capital which is lost or unrepresented by available assets).

Although s641 of the 2006 Act (previously s135 of the 1985 Act) specifically refers to share capital, the procedures in that section also apply to a reduction in those reserves which are akin to share capital, i.e. the share premium account and the capital redemption reserve. It does not apply to any merger reserve but of course it would be possible to capitalise the merger reserve and then to apply to the court in respect of the enlarged share capital.

An application to the court for a reduction in capital on the grounds of a serious loss of capital is relatively common so that companies with large debit balances on the profit and loss account can in effect write off the loss and resume the payment of dividends. Such an application would need to demonstrate evidence of a permanent (i.e. so far as presently foreseeable) loss of capital.

> One possible use of such a capital reduction is to eliminate a deficit on the profit and loss account arising from the recognition of a pension deficit under FRS 17 or IAS 19.

Where the reduction does not involve the diminution of liability or the repayment of any paid up capital (e.g. there has been a permanent loss of capital) then the procedures are relatively straightforward:

(a) check the articles for the power to reduce share capital;

(b) a special resolution will be required approving the reduction;

(c) following the passing of the necessary resolutions, petitions are presented in Chambers. The petition sets out, inter alia, the capital structure of the company, its main object, any relevant provisions in the Articles, the financial position of the company and details of the scheme of reduction passed by the special resolution. Where it is alleged that the capital is unrepresented by available assets an affidavit of a valuer confirming this point may be required;

(d) issue of a summons for directions (generally at the same time the petition is presented in Chambers). On the hearing of the summons, the evidence is considered and orders are generally made as to the publication of notices and advertisements in the *London Gazette* and other papers;

(e) the petition is heard. Before the order can take effect, it must be registered at the Companies Registration Office, along with a minute setting out the revised details of share capital; and

(f) notice of the registration must be advertised.

Where the rights of creditors are potentially threatened, the procedure is more complicated.

Where the application is made on the basis of a permanent loss of capital, the position of creditors is not prejudiced by a reduction in capital. But in other cases the court is likely to look for an undertaking as to the treatment of any loss that is subsequently recovered.

This is often achieved by the court accepting an undertaking that the amount of the proposed reduction (to the extent that it is not eliminating a deficit on the profit and loss account) be transferred to a special reserve that shall not be treated as distributable 'so long as there shall remain outstanding any liabilities of the company which would be admissible to proof in the winding up of the company commencing on the day on which the reduction of capital and cancellation of share premium account takes effect'. For this purpose, liabilities include not just actual liabilities but also contingent liabilities such as guarantees and warranties. Such an undertaking thus protects existing creditors, including contingent creditors, at the date of the capital reduction (but not future creditors).

A relatively common procedure in the past was to apply to the Court, under section 641 of the 2006 Act (previously s135 of the 1985 Act), for a balance on the share premium account to be transferred to a newly created special reserve which could then be used to write off goodwill arising on consolidation (or in some instances goodwill arising at the level of the individual company) prior to FRS 10. Although writing off goodwill to reserves is no longer permitted (subject to the transitional provisions of FRS 10), such 'special reserves' may still be found in financial statements. For example, there may be a 'special reserve' in the parent company that is eliminated on consolidation because it has been used to write off pre-FRS 10 goodwill arising on consolidation.

The accounting is dictated by the terms of the scheme of reduction which the Court has approved but the following general guidance may be helpful:

(a) the capital reduction only becomes effective when approved by the Court. Therefore it can only be reflected in the balance sheet when Court approval has been granted before the balance sheet date (i.e. Court approval is a *non*-adjusting post balance sheet event);

(b) if Court approval has been granted between the balance sheet date and the date of approval of the accounts, that fact should be disclosed as a post balance sheet event either as part of the share capital note or as a separate post balance sheet event note;

(c) it is possible to highlight the effect of a capital reduction that has been confirmed after the balance sheet date by including a pro-forma balance sheet. This could be in the form of a separate statement outside of the audited financial statements or by inclusion of an extra column on the face of the audited balance sheet. When the latter approach is adopted the pro-forma column should be clearly labeled as such and cross referred to an appropriate note explaining the adjustments that have been made; and

(d) there is no requirement to disclose a capital reduction which is merely planned at the balance sheet date although the directors may wish to make reference to this fact. In such cases the note should state that the capital reduction is subject to Court approval.

A reduction or cancellation of capital which results in a credit to reserves where the reduction or cancellation is confirmed by the Court is a realised profit except to the extent that, and for so long as, the company has undertaken that it will not treat the reserve as a realised profit, or where the Court has directed that it shall not be treated as a realised profit. This is confirmed in paragraph 3.9(g) of TECH 01/08 (as drafted for the 1985 Act). The treatment of a reserve arising from a reduction in a company's share capital explained at **5.3.3.2** above is written in the context of the 2006 Act but the conclusion is consistent.

6.2 Reduction of capital by special resolution and solvency statement (effective 1 October 2008)

From 1 October 2008, the 2006 Act allows a limited company having share capital to reduce its share capital by special resolution supported by a solvency statement. [CA 2006 s641(1)(b)] This new procedure is a quicker and cheaper alternative for private companies to the court approved procedure explained at **6.1** above. In addition, no auditors' report is required.

This method of capital reduction cannot be used if as a result of the reduction there would no longer be any member of the company holding shares other than redeemable shares or if its articles do not allow it. [CA 2006 s641(2)]

Under this new procedure, directors must make a solvency statement confirming that each director:

[CA 2006 s643]

(a) has formed the opinion , as regards the company's situation at the date of the statement, that there is no ground on which the company could then be found to be unable to pay (or otherwise discharge) its debts; and

(b) has also formed the opinion

(i) if it is intended to commence the winding up of the company within twelve months of that date, that the company will be able to pay (or otherwise discharge) its debts in full within twelve months of the commencement of the winding up; or

(ii) in any other case, that the company will be able to pay (or otherwise discharge) its debts as they fall due during the year immediately following that date.

In practice the solvency statement confirms that the company is a going concern and will be able to pay its debts in the following year. It is essentially a two part test. First there is a snapshot 'assets exceed liabilities' test calculated on the basis of fair values not book values. Secondly, there is a one year 'cash flow' test i.e. can the company pay its debts as they fall due?

The statement must also state the date on which it is made and the name of each director of the company.

Further requirements for the solvency statement were added by a statutory instrument 'The Companies (Reduction of Share Capital) Order 2008' (SI 2008/1915) which was made in July 2008 and comes into force on 1 October 2008.

The statutory instrument confirms that the solvency statement

- must be in writing;
- must indicate that it is a solvency statement for the purposes of s642 of the 2006 Act; and

- be signed by each of the directors.

The shareholders must then pass a special resolution reducing the share capital no later than 15 days after the directors have made the solvency statement. [CA 2006 s642]

Within 15 days of the shareholders passing the resolution the company has to file with the Registrar of Companies:

[CA 2006 s644]

- the solvency statement;
- the special resolution;
- a statement of capital setting out the details of the share capital as reduced; and
- a further statement by the directors confirming that the solvency statement was made not more than 15 days before the date on which the resolution was passed and that it was provided to members in accordance with the requirements of the Act.

The resolution takes effect on registration by the registrar.

Unlike for a reduction of capital confirmed by the court, creditors have no right to object to a reduction of capital supported by a solvency statement.

A credit to reserves arising from a reduction or cancellation of capital supported by solvency statement is a realised profit (see **5.3.3.2** above). Section 654(1) of the 2006 Act prohibits a reserve arising from the reduction of a company's share capital from being distributable unless an order has been made under that section. Statutory instrument 2008/1915 (see above) states that the prohibition in s654(1) of the 2006 Act does not apply and that a reserve arising from the reduction is to be treated as a realised profit. The statutory instrument also confirms that the same applies to an unlimited company reducing its share capital. The provisions of SI 2008/1915 are without prejudice to any contrary provisions of an order or undertaking given to the court, the resolution for, or any other resolution relevant to, the reduction of capital, or the company's memorandum or articles of association.

50 Summary financial statements

1 Introduction

All companies that have had their accounts audited may choose to issue summary financial statements under s426 of the 2006 Act (previously s251 of the 1985 Act). While the full financial statements still need to be sent to the Registrar of Companies, a company may send copies of a summary financial statement to shareholders, debenture holders and other persons entitled to receive notice of general meetings ('entitled persons') if it has obtained the entitled person's consent and provided the company's Articles or debenture trust deed or governing instrument do not require the full financial statements to be sent to entitled persons. [CA 2006 s426 and SI 2008 No 374 The Companies (Summary Financial Statement) Regulations 2008, previously CA 1985 s251 and SI 1995 No 2092 The Companies (Summary Financial Statement) Regulations 1995 (as amended)]

When the option of summary financial statements was first introduced these documents were often very brief. There has subsequently been an increase in the number of companies using summary financial statements in a different way, binding them in a 'glossy' annual review of the company (see **section 5** below).

These provisions were originally restricted to listed companies but changes made with effect from 1 October 2005 widened the scope. The changes made at that time also ensure that companies preparing their financial statements in accordance with IFRSs can prepare summary financial statements.

2 Conditions for sending out summary financial statements

The detailed conditions for consent are set out in paragraphs 5–8 of SI 2008 No 374 (previously paragraphs 4–6 of SI 1995 No 2092). An entitled person gives its consent:

(a) if it notifies the company in writing that it wishes to receive a summary financial statement instead of the full financial statements and does not subsequently countermand the instruction; or

(b) if it fails to reply to a 'relevant consultation' or 'consultation by notice' carried out in accordance with the detailed rules in SI 2008 No 374 (previously SI 1995 No 2092).

Listed companies will normally take advice on the form of consultation from their registrars.

Communications for this purpose to a company may also be transmitted electronically to an address specified by it for this purpose and may be made electronically by a company to the shareholder who has consented to this. Written communications to persons within an EEA state must be accompanied by a card or form on which the company has paid or will pay the postage.

3 Content of a summary financial statement

The content of a summary financial statement is specified by SI 2008 No 374 (previously SI 1995 No 2092). The statement should:

(a) include a profit and loss account and balance sheet and, for a company required to produce a directors' remuneration report, a summary of that report. Comparative figures are required in the summary profit and loss account and balance sheet;

(b) state that it is only a summary of information in the company's annual financial statements;

(c) state the name of the director who signed the statement following its approval by the board;

(d) include a statement in a prominent position, to the effect that the summary financial statement does not contain sufficient information to allow a full understanding of the results and state of affairs of the company/group, and of its policies and arrangements concerning directors' remuneration, as would be provided by the full annual financial statements and reports, and that members and debenture holders requiring more detailed information have the right to obtain, free of charge, a copy of the company's last full financial statements and reports (see **example 3A** below);

(e) contain a clear, conspicuous statement of how members and debenture holders can obtain, free of charge, a copy of the company's last full financial statements and reports and of how members and debenture holders can elect to receive the full financial statements and reports instead of the summary financial statements in all future years (see **example 3B** below);

(f) contain the auditors' opinion as to whether:

 (i) the summary financial statement is consistent with the company's annual accounts and, in the case of a quoted company, directors' remuneration report, and where information derived from the directors' report is included in the statement, with that report or review; and

 (ii) the summary financial statement complies with the requirements of section 428 (quoted companies) / section 427 (unquoted companies) of the 2006 Act (previously section 251 of the 1985 Act) and the Regulations;

(g) state whether the auditors' report on the company's annual accounts, and where relevant the auditable part of the directors' remuneration report, was qualified or unqualified;

(h) state whether the auditors' statement with regard to whether the directors' report is consistent with the accounts was qualified or unqualified;

(i) contain any other information necessary to ensure that the statement is consistent with the full accounts and reports for the financial year in question.

An example of a statement to the effect that the summary financial statements do not contain sufficient information to allow a full understanding of the results and state of affairs is set out below. It should be noted that, while this statement was once prescribed and could not be amended, this is no longer the case. SI 2008 No 374 (previously SI 1995 No 2092) sets out what is to be covered by the statement, but does not prescribe the words to be used. The statement should appear in a prominent position.

Example 3A

Illustrative statement regarding summary financial statement

This summary financial statement does not contain sufficient information to allow as full an understanding of the results of the group and state of affairs of the company or of the group, [and of their policies and arrangements concerning directors' remuneration], as would be provided by the full annual financial statements and reports. Members and debenture holders requiring more detailed information have the right to obtain, free of charge, a copy of the company's last full financial statements and reports.

The statement, of how members and debenture holders can obtain, free of charge, a copy of the company's last full financial statements and reports and of how they may elect in writing to receive full financial statements and reports in place of the summary financial statements for all future years, should be clear and conspicuous. An example of such a statement is set out below.

Example 3B

Illustrative statement regarding full financial statements

Members and debenture holders who wish to receive, free of charge, a copy of the full annual financial statements and reports for the year ended [date] or who wish to receive full financial statements and reports in place of the summary financial statements for all future years should write to the company's registrars at [address of registrars].

4 Form of a summary financial statement

4.1 Basic principles

The summary financial statement of a company that is required to prepare group accounts and prepares IAS group accounts or, in the case of a company that is not required to prepare group accounts, prepares IAS individual accounts, must be in the form and contain the information required by Schedule 7 (individual accounts) or Schedule 8 (group accounts) to the 2008 Regulations (previously Schedule 3A to the 1995 Regulations), so far as applicable to such a company. The contents of the summary financial statement of a company that prepares financial statements in accordance with International Accounting Standards are discussed in **4.2** to **4.6** below. Special provisions relate to banking and insurance companies and groups. These are set out in Schedules 2, 3, 5 and 6 to SI 2008 No 374 (previously Schedules 2 and 3 to SI 1995 No 2092 as amended by SI 2005 No 2281).

The rules under UK GAAP are different and are not dealt with in this manual.

The Act and the regulations set a minimum level of information. They require the summary financial statement to contain any other information necessary to ensure that the statement is consistent with the full accounts and reports for the year in question. They do not prevent additional information being added. Listing Rule 9.8.13 requires that the earnings per share figure should also be given in the summary financial statement.

Summary financial statements are normally exempt, by virtue of s435(7) of the 2006 Act (previously s251(7) of the 1985 Act), from the requirement of s435(1) of the 2006 Act (previously s240 of the 1985 Act) to indicate that they are non-statutory financial statements. However, where summary financial statements are included on a company's website, this exemption may no longer apply, since publication on the website may render them accessible to an audience wider than those persons normally entitled to receive copies of a company's report and financial statements. Consequently where summary financial statements are published on a website, they should include a statement that they are not the company's statutory financial statements and other information as required by s435(1) of the 2006 Act (previously s240(3) of the 1985 Act) (see **section 9** of **chapter 45**).

4.2 Summary directors' report

There was previously a requirement for a summary directors' report but this was repealed with effect for periods commencing on or after 1 April 2005.

Where a company chooses to publish a summary directors' report, the auditors' statement on the summary financial statements must include their opinion as to whether the information derived from the directors' report is consistent with the directors' report which forms part of the company's annual accounts (see **section 3.1** above). SI 2008 No 374 (previously SI 1995 No 2092) requires that the explanatory material required by paragraph 14 of Schedule 7 to the Accounting Regulations (previously s234ZZA(5) of the 1985 Act) regarding the structure of the company's capital should be included in the summary financial statement or sent to those receiving the summary financial statement at the same time as that statement is sent. Where this information is included in the summary financial statement, the auditors' will be required to report on the consistency of that information.

4.3 Directors' remuneration

The summary statements of all companies, whether or not they are required to prepare a directors' remuneration report, should contain the whole, or a summary, of that portion of the notes to the financial statements which sets out the information on aggregate directors' emoluments (paragraph 1 of Sch. 3 to the Small Companies Accounts Regulations and paragraph 1 of Sch. 5 to the Accounting Regulations; previously Part I of Sch. 6). If a company is also required to prepare a directors' remuneration report (see **chapter 48**), the summary financial statements should include the whole, or a summary, of those portions of the directors' remuneration report relating to the company's policy on remuneration and the performance graph (paragraphs 3 and 5 of Schedule 8 to the Accounting Regulations, previously paragraphs 3 and 4 of Sch. 7A to the 1985 Act).

There is a great degree of flexibility in this area of the legislation and companies have been taking widely differing approaches. In particular, directors will need to determine the extent of the material on remuneration policy that should be included. However, as a minimum, it is suggested that the following should be included:

(a) the whole, or a summary of, the disclosures required by sub-paragraphs 2,3 and 4 in paragraph 3 of Sch. 8 of the Accounting Regulations (previously 2, 3 and 4 in paragraph 3 of Sch. 7A to the 1985 Act);

(b) any issues from the full report that are likely to be of particular interest to the reader (although it may be preferable to reproduce the whole policy statement if there are issues that could be regarded as controversial); and

(c) the performance graph required by paragraph 5 of Sch. 8 to the Accounting Regulations (previously paragraph 4 of Sch. 7A to the 1985 Act).

4.4 Summary profit and loss account

The summary financial statement should contain a summary profit and loss account showing either:

(a) each of the headings and sub-totals included in the full profit and loss account in accordance with international accounting standards (see **section 5** of **chapter 3**);or

(b) where the directors consider it appropriate, a combination of such headings and sub-totals where they are of a similar nature.

The summary financial statement should also contain the information concerning recognised and proposed dividends included in the full accounts and reports.

Where group accounts are prepared, it is the consolidated profit and loss account which is summarised.

4.5 Summary balance sheet

The summary financial statement should contain a summary balance sheet showing either —

(a) each of the headings and sub-totals included in the full balance sheet in accordance with international accounting standards (see **section 4** of **chapter 3**); or

(b) where the directors consider it appropriate, a combination of such headings and sub-totals where they are of a similar nature.

When group accounts are prepared, it is the consolidated balance sheet which is summarised.

4.6 Corresponding amounts

Corresponding amounts are required for every item shown in the summary profit and loss account and summary balance sheet.

5 Other information

As described in **section 1** above, companies often include summary financial statements in a booklet with additional 'annual review' material such as the OFR. In some cases this material may legally form part of the summary financial statement. However, another approach taken by some companies is for only certain pages of the document to form the summary financial statement. These will be the pages within the scope of the auditors' report on the summary financial statement. The other material, typically the OFR and corporate governance statement, legally forms part of the full annual report which comprises two documents taken together, the 'Annual review' and the 'Financial statements'. The two documents may then be placed together in a folder for those receiving the full annual report. There are variations on this approach in practice. If a company's auditors become aware of any inconsistencies or apparently misleading statements in such material they will consider the impact for their report.

The Regulations do not explicitly require a cash flow statement or a statement of changes in equity or statement of comprehensive income. However, companies should consider whether to include these statements to meet the expectations of users.

51 Preliminary announcements

1 Introduction

For periods beginning on or after 20 January 2007 there is no regulatory requirement for listed companies to issue a preliminary announcement. However, preliminary announcements are optional for all companies with listed shares. The Listing Rules set requirements where a company chooses to produce a preliminary announcement (see **section 2** below).

The Auditing Practices Board (APB) has issued a Bulletin for auditors on the Listing Rules requirement that the announcement should have been 'agreed' with the auditors prior to publication. The implications of the APB Bulletin for the preparation of the preliminary announcement are considered in **section 3** below.

Companies with securities traded on the Alternative Investment Market (AIM) often make a preliminary announcement although they are not required to do so by the AIM Rules (see **section 4** below).

The Accounting Standards Board (ASB) has published a non-mandatory Statement of best practice for preliminary announcements. The ASB Statement is considered in **section 5** below.

Future developments which may affect preliminary announcements are considered in **section 6** below.

The Listing Rules use the expression 'preliminary statement of annual results' although the statement is required to include a balance sheet and cash flow statement as well as details about the results for the period. This chapter uses the expression 'preliminary announcement' which is in common use.

2 Listing Rules requirements

Preliminary announcements are optional for periods beginning on or after 20 January 2007. The previous requirements to publish the preliminary announcement within 120 days, were deleted and replaced with a new rule LR 9.7A. For periods beginning on or after 20 January 2007, listed companies (with some limited exceptions, e.g. companies with debt securities listed on the Professional Securities Market) are required to comply with the Disclosure and Transparency Rules (DTR). The DTR require companies to publish their annual reports within four calendar months of the year end. As a consequence of the shortening of this deadline (compared with six months previously) the FSA decided to remove the requirement for a preliminary announcement, which is not mandated by EU law. But if a company chooses to produce a preliminary announcement, LR 9.7A sets out the requirements and these are largely unchanged. In practice, many companies are continuing to issue a preliminary announcement as it is still a requirement to notify the market when a decision has been taken to pay a dividend (see **2.4** below).

The Financial Services Authority (FSA) published guidance in June 2008 confirming that where a company publishes a preliminary announcement, this does not fulfil their obligations under DTR 4.1 to publish the Annual Report within four months of the year end. However, where a preliminary announcement is issued based on audited financial information, it may well also serve to satisfy the requirement to disseminate the annual report under DTR 6.3 provided that it also contains a reference to the website where a full copy of the annual financial statement may be found.

2.1 Requirements in respect of preliminary announcements

For periods beginning on or after 20 January 2007, a listed company is not required to produce a preliminary announcement. Where a listed company chooses to produce such an announcement:

[LR 9.7A.1R]

- the preliminary announcement must be published as soon as possible after it has been approved by the board;
- the preliminary announcement must be agreed with the company's auditors prior to publication (see **section 3** below);
- the preliminary announcement must show the figures in the form of a table, including the items required for a half-yearly report, consistent with the presentation to be adopted in the annual accounts for that financial year;

- the preliminary announcement must give details of the nature of any likely modification that may be contained in the auditors report required to be included with the annual financial report; and
- the preliminary announcement must include any significant additional information necessary for the purpose of assessing the results being announced.

The requirements in relation to announcement of dividends are set out at **2.4** below.

For periods beginning on or after 20 January 2007, the requirements for a half-yearly report for a company preparing consolidated financial statements are a condensed set of financial statements prepared in accordance with IAS 34, an interim management report and a responsibility statement (see **chapter 39**). It is not entirely clear how the requirement for 'figures in the form of a table, including the items required for a half-yearly report' should be interpreted in the light of this. However, it would be reasonable to assume that this means the primary statements should be presented in the level of detail that would be required in the half-yearly report. In issue 18 of the newsletter List! (March 2008), the Financial Services Authority has clarified that the reference to the half-yearly report does not require that preliminary announcements should be prepared in accordance with IAS 34.

The FSA may authorise the omission of information required by LR 9.7A.1R or LR 9.7A.2R (see above and **2.4** below) if it considers that disclosure of such information would be contrary to the public interest or seriously detrimental to the listed company, provided that such omission would not be likely to mislead the public with regards to facts and circumstances, knowledge of which is essential for the assessment of the shares. [LR 9.7A.3G]

2.2 Compliance with IFRSs

The question arises as to whether the limited financial information disclosed in preliminary announcements can be described as having been prepared in conformity with IFRSs. Because such preliminary announcements will not generally comply with the full requirements of IFRSs, if any reference to IFRSs is made in the announcement, the following sentences (or something similar) should be included in the announcement.

Example 2.2

Words to be included with preliminary announcement of results

'While the financial information included in this preliminary announcement has been prepared in accordance with the recognition and measurement criteria of International Financial Reporting Standards (IFRSs), this announcement does not itself contain sufficient information to comply with IFRSs. The Company [published / expects to publish] full financial statements that comply with IFRSs in March 20X1.'

2.3 Pro forma or non-statutory information

Issues surrounding the presentation of non-statutory information in preliminary announcements and in annual and interim reports have gained increasing prominence, largely because of US related requirements.

In issue 12 of the newsletter List! (February 2006), the FSA made clear that it would not expect non-GAAP numbers to be given greater prominence than GAAP numbers. The FSA also referred to CESR's guidance of November 2005 (Recommendation on the use of alternative performance measures), which indicated that comparatives should be given for non-GAAP numbers, that such information should be calculated consistently over time, and that GAAP numbers should be included and the differences between the two explained. Although the newsletter's guidance was written in the context of interims, it is equally valid for preliminary announcements.

APB Bulletin 2008/2 provides guidance to the auditors of listed companies on how they should consider the presentation of 'Alternative Performance Measures (APM's)' in preliminary announcements (see **section 3** below). Although the pronouncements mentioned above from the FSA and the APB were issued in the context of interim reports and preliminary announcements respectively, they have a wider application. In effect, the guidance should be considered in relation to all narrative reports associated with financial statements, preliminary announcements, interim reports and in the press release which may be issued with any of the foregoing. The extension to press releases is a difficult area. Some companies' press releases are in substance, for example, the preliminary announcement. Where auditors are referred to in the press release (with their agreement) as having audited or reviewed the related financial information, they are likely to expect companies to handle pro formas therein in the same way as in documents from which they are derived.

The following are some pointers to be considered by companies regarding the inclusion of pro formas in such documents:

(a) all numbers should be accurately and fully described. For example, if a company refers to a 25 per cent increase in operating profit but that percentage is based on operating profit before goodwill impairment, then it should be described as operating profit before goodwill impairment;

(b) it is acceptable to use descriptions such as 'operating profit*' if the asterisk is then explained on that page as operating profit before goodwill impairment of £x. The asterisk should be explained on the page or the page should contain a cross reference to where the asterisk is explained;

(c) some companies may use a particular description such as 'headline profit' or 'headline EPS' throughout their narrative reporting. A reconciliation from these headline numbers to the statutory numbers should be given. It is not necessary to repeat the reconciliation or reference thereto on every occasion these headline numbers are used within a report. But, to assist the user, a reconciliation or reference thereto may be appropriate within each of the major sections in a report;

(d) at the front of any of the reports, companies may disclose four or five key financial highlights. In the past, these key statistics may have been based entirely on pro forma numbers. The trend presented by these numbers can be different from the percentage changes in the statutory numbers. Therefore, in the light of the FSA and APB guidance, such numbers may now be regarded as misleading or, at best, failing to give sufficient prominence to the statutory numbers. Companies should therefore insert some statutory numbers into these highlights; and

(e) as noted in (c), reconciliations should be given. If the difference is only one number, e.g. goodwill impairment, then it will suffice to say that operating profit is before goodwill impairment of £x. In other words, a tabular reconciliation would not be required. However, in practice some pro forma numbers take

guidance in APB Bulletin 2008/2 and in the ASB's Statement *Preliminary announcements* (see **section 5** below) notes that the audit must be at an 'advanced stage' for this to happen. The following guidance in APB Bulletin 2008/2 will be applied by auditors when deciding if the audit is at an advanced stage:

'20 The auditor will need to be satisfied that any matters outstanding with respect to the audit will be unlikely to result in changes to the information contained in the preliminary announcement. This means that the audit of the financial statements must be at an advanced stage and that, subject only to unforeseen events, the auditor expects to be in a position to issue the auditor's report on the financial statements incorporating the amounts upon which the preliminary announcement is based, and know what that auditor's report will say.

21 This means completing the audit, including the engagement quality control review as described in paragraphs 38 to 40 of ISA (UK and Ireland) 220 *Quality control for audits of historical financial information*, subject only to the following:

(a) clearing outstanding audit matters which the auditors are satisfied are unlikely to have a material impact on the financial statements or disclosures in the preliminary announcement;

(b) completing audit procedures on the detail of note disclosures to the financial statements that will not have a material impact on the primary financial statements and completing the auditor's reading of the "other information" in the annual report in accordance with ISA (UK and Ireland) 720 *Other information in documents containing audited financial statements*)

(c) updating the subsequent events review to cover the period between the issue of the preliminary announcement and the date of the auditor's report on the financial statements; and

(d) obtaining final signed written representations from management and establishing that the financial statements have been reviewed and approved by the directors.'

3.2.2 *Considerations relating to Alternative Performance Measures (APMs)*

Paragraph 26 of the Bulletin states that, among other things, when the announcement includes Alternative Performance Measures (APMs), auditors consider whether:

a) appropriate prominence is given to statutory financial information and related narrative explanations compared to the prominence given to APMs and their related narrative explanations;

b) APMs are reconciled, where appropriate, to the statutory financial information and sufficient prominence is given to that reconciliation;

c) APMs are clearly and accurately described; and

d) APMs are not otherwise misleading in the form and context in which they appear.

The Bulletin states that APMs include adjustments of statutory information to exclude certain items to give alternative earnings numbers (e.g. EBITDA), exclude certain business segments or activities or reflect significant non-adjusting post balance sheet events (e.g. disposals and acquisitions). Such information is also often referred to as 'pro forma' information and is considered further at **2.3** above.

If auditors consider that a preliminary announcement does not satisfy these conditions then they should seek to resolve the issues arising with the directors. If they are unable to resolve the issues, then the auditors consider whether to withhold their consent to the release of the preliminary announcement.

3.2.3 Modifications

As explained at **2.1** above, the Listing Rules require details of the nature of any likely 'modification' of the auditors' report. APB Bulletin 2008/2 also requires details of the matters giving rise to the modification (whether a qualified opinion or emphasis of matter paragraph) of the auditors' report to be disclosed. The Bulletin emphasises that directors should give adequate prominence to this information in the announcement, and auditors will consider whether the disclosures are sufficiently prominent before giving their consent. When giving details about a modification of the auditors' report, care needs to be taken to check compliance with the Act, which states that an auditors' report on the statutory accounts may not be published with non-statutory accounts (see **3.6** below). [CA 2006 s435, previously CA 1985 s240]

In addition to considering modifications to the audit report, auditors need to consider whether any significant additional information necessary for the purposes of assessing the results being announced has also been disclosed as required by Listing Rule 9.7A.1R.

Whether or not the auditors' report is 'likely to be modified' should be assessed in the light of circumstances at the time of the preliminary announcement rather than those which may prevail when the audit report is actually signed. For example, if refinancing is being negotiated when the preliminary announcement is made the auditors would consider the disclosures around going concern on the basis that the new funds are not available, even though the additional resources may have been obtained by the time the audit report is signed. However, there may be certain aspects of audit work that have not been completed at the date of the preliminary announcement but will be by the time the audit report is signed. Examples of this type of outstanding work are described at paragraph 21 of the Bulletin and in the context of a preliminary announcement they would not normally give rise to a qualified limitation of scope opinion.

3.3 Company law requirements for non-statutory accounts

Preliminary announcements contain information covering both the current and preceding financial year and these figures should be regarded as constituting non-statutory accounts. The Act requires that where a company or group publishes non-statutory accounts (i.e. any balance sheet or profit and loss account relating to any financial year of the company otherwise than as part of the company's statutory accounts, such as a preliminary announcement of annual results which contains information which can be regarded as a balance sheet or profit and loss account), it should publish with them a statement indicating:
[CA 2006 s435, previously CA 1985 s240]

(a) that the accounts are not the company's statutory accounts;

(b) whether statutory accounts dealing with any financial year with which the non-statutory accounts purport to deal have been delivered to the Registrar of Companies;

(c) whether the auditor has made a report in respect of the statutory accounts and,

(d) if so, whether the auditor's report:

  (i) was qualified or unqualified or included a reference to any matters to which the auditor drew attention by was of emphasis without qualifying its report; or

  (ii) contained a statement under s498(2) of the 2006 Act (previously s237(2) of the 1985 Act) (accounting records or returns inadequate or accounts or directors' remuneration report not agreeing with records and returns), or s498(3) of the 2006 Act (previously s237(3) of the 1985 Act) (failure to obtain necessary information and explanations).

The company must not publish the auditors' report on the company's statutory accounts with non-statutory accounts.

The term 'publishes' in this context means that the company publishes, issues or circulates the document or otherwise makes it available for public inspection in a manner calculated to invite members of the public generally, or any class of members of the public to read it. [CA 2006 s436, previously CA 1985 s240(4)]

The examples below suggest forms of words which satisfy the requirements, in the case of unqualified audit reports, and make clear the status of the numbers.

3.3.1 *Example: announcement based on audited accounts*

Example 3.3.1

Announcement based on audited accounts (unqualified audit reports)

The financial information set out above does not constitute the company's statutory accounts for the years ended 31 December 20X2 or 20X1, but is derived from those accounts. Statutory accounts for 20X1 have been delivered to the Registrar of Companies and those for 20X2 will be delivered following the company's annual general meeting. The auditors have reported on those accounts: their reports were unqualified, did not draw attention to any matters by way of emphasis and did not contain statements under [s498 (2) or (3) Companies Act 2006] [s237(2) or (3) Companies Act 1985].

3.3.2 *Example: announcement based on draft accounts*

Example 3.3.2

Announcement based on draft accounts (unqualified audit report)

The financial information set out in the announcement does not constitute the company's statutory accounts for the years ended 31 December 20X2 or 20X1. The financial information for the year ended 31 December 20X1 is derived from the statutory accounts for that year which have been delivered to the Registrar of Companies. The auditors reported on those accounts: their report was unqualified, did not draw attention to any matters by way of emphasis and did not contain a statement under [s498 (2) or (3) Companies Act 2006] [s237(2) or (3) Companies Act 1985]. The audit of the statutory accounts for the year ended 31 December 20X2 is not yet complete. These accounts will be finalised on the basis of the financial information presented by the directors in this preliminary announcement and will be delivered to the Registrar of Companies following the company's annual general meeting.

Note: In this example 'draft accounts' should be interpreted as 'audit is at an advanced stage'

The statement required in the period of first-time adoption of IFRSs may require further explanation that the information for the comparative period has been restated from that which was contained in the statutory financial statements for the period. A similar explanation may be useful where the prior year figures have been restated on grounds of error or change of accounting policy.

4 Alternative Investment Market and PLUS companies

Companies with securities which have been admitted to AIM are not required under the AIM Rules to issue a preliminary announcement. In practice, many AIM companies choose to make a preliminary announcement. In the absence of specific rules for AIM companies, companies and auditors will normally use the Listing Rules and APB Bulletin discussed above as guidance.

AIM Companies must notify a Regulatory Information Service about declaration of dividends. Details about the timing of such notifications are contained in the 'Dividend procedure timetable' on the London Stock Exchange website (*www.londonstockexchange.com*).

Companies with securities traded on the PLUS-listed market are required to comply with the requirements applicable to listed companies. Companies with securities traded on the PLUS-quoted market are required by rule 31 of the 'Rules for issuers' to announce final results as soon as possible and, in any event, not later than five months after the period end. The announcement must contain the information specified in Appendix 5 to the rules which is:

- a statement by the board;
- a profit and loss account;
- a balance sheet;
- a statement of earnings or loss per share;
- any decision to pay a dividend together with the dividend timetable;

- comparative information for the above items for the corresponding period of the previous financial year;
- a summary of any change of accounting policy likely to affect the validity of the comparison;
- if there is likely to be a qualification or statement of uncertainty contained in the audit opinion, confirmation of that fact; and
- a statement of whether the information contained in the announcement has been extracted from audited information or agreed with the auditors, or an appropriate negative statement.

5 ASB Statement of best practice

Historically, many companies expanded the disclosures in their preliminary announcements beyond the requirements of the Listing Rules. To improve the timeliness, quality and relevance of these communications and aid comparability with previous published accounts, the ASB issued a Statement *Preliminary announcements* in July 1998. It is commended to companies as a statement of best practice and thus compliance with it is voluntary.

The Statement has not been updated since 1998 and has consequently does not take account of more recent developments. Its recommendations are therefore not considered in this publication.

The Statement makes reference to various UK accounting standards and other reporting requirements that will not be applicable for companies reporting under IFRSs. Where such companies wish to follow the Statement as a guide to best practice, they will need to read such references in the light of any different requirements of IFRSs.

52 Revised financial statements

1 Introduction

IAS 8 *Accounting Policies, Changes in Accounting Estimates and Errors* discusses the accounting that should be adopted when an error is discovered (see **chapter 4**), but does not give any guidance on the revision of financial statements.

Revision of the annual financial statements, the directors' report or the directors' remuneration report and any associated summary or abbreviated financial statements may be appropriate when information becomes available which suggests that the original financial statements or report did not comply with the requirements of the Companies Act or, where applicable, of Article 4 of the IAS Regulation. The following paragraphs provide guidance on the revision of 'defective' financial statements under s454 to 457 of the 2006 Act (previously s245 to 245C of the 1985 Act). A special auditors' report is required in such cases.

Annual financial statements, the directors' report and the directors' remuneration report are referred to collectively as 'financial statements or reports' in this chapter.

The Companies Act 1989 introduced procedures for:

(a) voluntary revision of defective financial statements by the directors; and

(b) mandatory revisions of defective financial statements by court order.

These provisions are now contained in s454 to 457 of the 2006 Act (previously s245 to 245C of the 1985 Act). The basic provisions are supplemented, in the case of voluntary revision, by SI 2008 No 373 The Companies (Revision of Defective Accounts and Report) Regulations 2008 (previously SI 1990 No 2570 The Companies (Revision of Defective Accounts and Report) Regulations 1990).

In common with the other financial reporting requirements of the 2006 Act, the requirements for the revision of defective accounts apply to financial years beginning on or after 6 April 2008. Consequently, the revision will be made under the Act which applied to the original accounts, even if it is made several years later. For example if revised accounts for the year ended 31 December 2008 are issued in June 2010, they will be prepared in accordance with the applicable provisions of the 1985 Act and the revision will be made in accordance with the 1990 Regulations. The main practical effect of this is that the statement about the revision (see **examples 4.1 and 4.2** below) will continue to refer to the 1985 Act and the 1990 Regulations when the period in question began before 6 April 2008.

There is no authoritative financial reporting guidance on the preparation of revised financial statements. For periods commencing prior to 6 April 2008, Practice Note 8 'Reports by auditors under company legislation in the United Kingdom', issued by the Auditing Practices Board, includes limited guidance on the audit of revised financial statements with the form of auditors' report set out in APB Bulletin 2007/1. For periods commencing on or after 6 April 2008, the guidance and form of report are set out in APB Bulletin 2008/5. More extensive draft guidance on revised financial statements was issued in 1991 by the Auditing Practices Committee in the form of an Exposure Draft of an Auditing Guideline. However, the guidance was never issued in final form and was effectively superseded by Practice Note 8. The following paragraphs draw on some of the 1991 guidance to the extent that it is still relevant.

International Standard on Auditing (UK and Ireland) 560 'Subsequent events' also refers to revised financial statements. It notes that when, after the financial statements have been issued, the auditors become aware of a fact which existed at the date of the auditors' report and which, if known at that date, may have caused the auditors to modify their report, the auditors should consider whether the financial statements need revision, should discuss the matter with management, and take the action appropriate in the circumstances.

2 Alternatives to voluntary revisions

Before explaining the detailed requirements relating to voluntary revision in accordance with s454 of the 2006 Act (previously s245 of the 1985 Act), it is worth pausing to consider the alternatives which may be available. Not every error which comes to light in previously approved financial statements will result in the need to prepare formal revised financial statements. It is for the directors to decide in each case on the appropriate action to take although difficult issues may arise if the directors decide not to issue revised financial statements in circumstances where the auditors believe that this would be appropriate. Alternatives to the preparation of revised financial statements may include:

(a) doing nothing, for example in the case of a minor typographical error;

(b) issuing an 'erratum slip' to explain the error;

(c) destroying all copies of the original financial statements where it is clear that no copies have been distributed; and

(d) dealing with the matter by way of explanation or restatement in the financial statements for the following year. This may be particularly relevant where the error comes to light during the preparation of those subsequent financial statements.

These alternatives are discussed below.

In the case of minor errors and inconsistencies, it may be acceptable to do nothing because there is little danger of anyone being misled and the cost of preparing revised financial statements would not be justified. If the error comes to light after the financial statements have been printed but before they have been distributed, it may be possible to make the correction by means of an 'erratum slip'. However, it is unlikely that the Registrar of Companies would agree to file such a correction and the only way to amend the financial statements on the public record after they have been filed is through the formal procedure under s454 of the 2006 Act (previously s245 of the 1985 Act).

In some cases an error may come to light before the financial statements have been filed at Companies House and before any copies have been distributed to other interested parties. For example, in a group situation, the financial statements of all of the subsidiaries may be approved on the same day as the group financial statements but these may then 'sit in a drawer' because they are not due to be filed for many months. In such circumstances, it would appear to be possible for the financial statements to be destroyed and for a new set of financial statements to be prepared and approved by the directors and auditors. However, this approach can only be adopted when it is certain that no other copies have been made of the originally signed copies.

The significance of an error may diminish with the passage of time. If the financial statements for the succeeding year are about to be issued, it will often be preferable to deal with the error in those financial statements rather than through the preparation of revised financial statements for the earlier period. In accordance with IAS 8, a material error will be dealt with by means of a prior year adjustment.

In some cases the directors will have no choice but to prepare revised financial statements. For example, BERR or the Financial Reporting

Review Panel (FRRP) may request a company to prepare revised financial statements. They cannot force the directors to prepare such revised financial statements but the threat of invoking the procedure for mandatory revision by court order will usually be sufficient to persuade the directors to prepare revised financial statements. One feature of revision by court order is that the directors who were party to the approval of the defective financial statements may be required to pay the costs of the application to the court and any reasonable expenses incurred by the company in connection with or in consequence of the preparation of the revised financial statements.

In other cases the directors will decide to prepare revised financial statements because they do not believe any of the above alternatives to be appropriate in the particular circumstances. However, as explained below, this procedure cannot be used to correct immaterial errors that would not have amounted to non-compliance with the Act or the IAS Regulation. The following paragraphs deal with the procedures for voluntary revision under s454 of the 2006 Act (previously s245 of the 1985 Act). However, these procedures would also be generally relevant in the rare case of a mandatory revision by court order, subject to any specific directions by the court.

3 Voluntary revision under section 454 of the 2006 Act (previously section 245 of the 1985 Act)

Section 454(1) of the 2006 Act (previously s245(1) of the 1985 Act) provides that the directors may prepare revised financial statements or a revised report if it appears to them that 'the company's annual accounts, the directors' report, the directors' remuneration report, or the summary financial statement of the company did not comply with the requirements of the Act (or, where applicable, of Article 4 of the IAS Regulation)'. Section 454(2) of the 2006 Act (previously s245(2) of the 1985 Act) then provides that where copies of those financial statements or that report have been laid before the company in general meeting or delivered to the registrar, the revisions shall be confined to 'the correction of those respects in which the previous accounts or report did not comply with the requirements of this Act (or, where applicable, of Article 4 of the IAS Regulation) and the making of any necessary consequential alterations'. The Act therefore permits some flexibility to make additional changes but only where the financial statements or report have been neither laid before the company in general meeting nor delivered to the registrar. This flexibility will therefore only rarely be available in practice.

However, no revision is possible at all unless the original financial statements or report did not comply with the requirements of the Act or the IAS Regulation. It is not therefore possible to revise financial statements or reports merely to 'improve' them, for example applying an alternative accounting policy or adopting a clearer presentation where the original one complied with the requirements of the Act (including the requirement to give a true and fair view for the financial statements). This is confirmed by APB Practice Note 8 which states that 'the only revisions which may be made are those necessary to correct errors in the original financial statements and the directors' reports'. Similarly, Bulletin 2008/5 notes that revisions must be confined to the correction of those respects in which the previous accounts or report did not comply with the requirements of the Act (or, where applicable, of Article 4 of the IAS Regulation), and the making of any necessary consequential alterations. This view is also reflected in the form of the auditors' report on the revised financial statements under which the auditors state that in their opinion 'the original financial statements failed to comply with the requirements of the Act in the respects identified by the directors'. Auditors are therefore unlikely to be prepared to issue an unqualified report on the revised financial statements if, for example, they regard the errors as trivial. It may be useful in such situations to consider whether it is likely that the auditors would have been prepared to issue an unqualified report on the original financial statements if they had been aware of the error at that time. But even where it is thought that they would not have done so, this does not necessarily mean that the preparation of revised financial statements is the most appropriate action.

In determining whether the original financial statements or report did comply with the requirements of the Acts, regulation 3 of the Regulations limits the use of hindsight by providing that financial statements or report should only reflect events which took place, or knowledge that was available, before the original financial statements or report were approved, and not at some subsequent date. Moreover, the fact that certain estimates can be seen at a later date to have been inaccurate does not mean that the original financial statements did not comply with the Act unless it can be demonstrated that the facts on which the initial estimates were reached were incomplete or incorrect at the time.

One issue which arises from time to time is whether a simple clerical error could amount to non-compliance with the Act. It is unlikely that a simple typographical error in narrative would meet this test unless the effect was to change the meaning in a material way (e.g. the omission of 'not' from a sentence). Similarly, an immaterial error in a disclosed amount (e.g. a transposition error whereby the disclosure of operating lease rentals was shown as £55,600 instead of £56,500) would not usually amount to non-compliance with the Act. However, it would usually be thought acceptable to issue revised financial statements where there are 'visible' errors, for example, where a note does not agree with the amount shown in the primary statement or totals have been incorrectly calculated.

4 Form of revised financial statements or report

When a revision of financial statements or a directors' report or directors' remuneration report is undertaken under s454 of the 2006 Act (previously s245 of the 1985 Act) (i.e. because the original financial statements or report did not comply with the Act or the IAS Regulation) it can be effected by either:

(a) replacement of the original with a corrected set of financial statements or report; or

(b) the issue of a supplementary note.

The directors are free to choose which method to use. In both instances, the financial statements or report should be prepared 'as if … prepared and approved by the directors as at the date of the original annual financial statements [or directors' report or directors' remuneration report]'.

Where the directors have prepared revised financial statements or a revised report under s454 of the 2006 Act (previously s245 of the 1985 Act) and copies of the original financial statements or report have been sent to any person under s423 of the 2006 Act (previously s238 of the 1985 Act), the directors are required to send to such person:

(a) in the case of revision by replacement, a copy of the revised financial statements or revised report together with the auditors' report thereon; or

(b) in the case of revision by supplementary note, a copy of that note together with the auditors' report thereon,

no more than 28 days after revision. In addition, the directors must also send the revised financial statements or report together with the auditors' report thereon to any other person who at the time of the revision is a member, a holder of the company's debentures or a person entitled to receive notice of general meetings.

Where the original financial statements or report have been laid before the company in general meeting, then any revised financial statements or report together with the auditors' report thereon must also be laid before the next general meeting of the company after the date of revision at which any financial statements or report for a financial year are laid. Where the original financial statements or report have been delivered to the Registrar, then any revised financial statements or report together with the auditors' report thereon must also be delivered to the Registrar within 28 days of the revision.

4.1 Revision by replacement

Where the original financial statements or report have been sent to the members, laid before the company in general meeting or delivered to the Registrar of Companies, the directors must include a statement concerning the revision in the revised financial statements or report. The statement must be in a 'prominent position' and include:

(a) confirmation that the revised financial statements or report replace the original financial statements or report for the financial year (specifying it) and, in the case of financial statements, confirmation that they are now the statutory financial statements;

(b) confirmation that the financial statements or report have been revised as at the date of the originals and not as at the date of the revision, and accordingly do not deal with events between those dates;

(c) the respects in which the original financial statements or report did not comply with the requirements of the 2006 Act (previously 1985 Act); and

(d) details of any significant amendments made consequential upon the remedying of those defects.

Guidance on the form, content and positioning of such a statement is set out in **example 4.1** below. The date of approval of the revised financial statements, and related auditors' report, should be the actual date on which they were approved and not the date of approval of the original financial statements or report.

Example 4.1

Illustrative disclosures for revision by replacement

These revised financial statements replace the original financial statements for the year ended 31 December 20X1 which were approved by the board on 15 March 20X2. They are now the statutory financial statements of the company for that financial year. In accordance with the Companies Act [2006] [1985] ('the Act'), the financial statements have been revised as at the date of the original financial statements and not as at the date of this revision. Accordingly they do not deal with events between those dates.

The original financial statements did not comply with the Act in the following respect. [The share capital and share premium were incorrectly stated in the balance sheet and related notes. This arose due to a misclassification between share capital and share premium relating to the issue of ordinary shares during the year. The effect of the revision is to reduce the issued share capital by £x and to increase the share premium by the same amount. There is no effect on the profit for the year or the net assets of the company.] [*If the adjustments are complex it may be preferable to give a brief description here and cross refer to more details in a note to the financial statements.*]

The Act requires that where revised financial statements are issued, a revised auditors' report is issued and this is attached.

Under [section 454] [section 245] of the Act the directors have authority to revise annual financial statements, the directors' report or directors' remuneration report if they do not comply with the Act. The revised financial statements or report must be amended in accordance with [the Companies (Revision of Defective Accounts and Report) Regulations 2008] [the Companies (Revision of Defective Accounts and Report) Regulations 1990] and in accordance therewith do not take account of events which have taken place after the date on which the original financial statements were approved. The Regulations require that the revised financial statements show a true and fair view as if they were prepared and approved by the directors as at the date of the original financial statements. [*Alternatively this paragraph can be added to the Statement of directors' responsibilities.*]

Note: The Regulations require this statement to be made in a 'prominent position' in the revised financial statements. It is recommended that this statement should appear as the first page of the document (after the front cover). It is also recommended that the front cover should use the term 'Revised financial statements' or refer to the revision in some other way so that the revised financial statements may be easily distinguished from the original version. It is also permissible to include the text of the statement in the directors' report. When this is done, it will be necessary to remember that the directors' report will have been revised and therefore to refer to the revised directors' report as well as the revised financial statements where necessary.

4.2 Revision by supplementary note

Where the revision is by way of a supplementary note, the note itself should provide adequate information concerning the defect in the original financial statements or report and any consequential amendments and is required by the Regulations to include a statement that:

(a) the note revises the original financial statements or report in certain respects and is to be treated as forming part of those financial statements or report; and

(b) the annual financial statements or report have been revised as at the date of the originals and not as at the date of revision and accordingly do not deal with events between those dates.

Guidance on the form and content of such a statement is set out in **example 4.2** below. The date of approval of the supplementary note, and related auditors' report, should be the actual date on which they were approved and not the date of approval of the original financial statements.

Example 4.2

Illustrative disclosures for revision by supplementary note

Delto plc

To the members

Supplementary note to the 31 December 20X1 financial statements

This supplementary note revises, in certain respects, the original financial statements of the company approved on 15 March 20X2 and is to be treated as forming part of those financial statements. The original financial statements did not comply with the Companies Act [2006] [1985] ('the Act') by virtue of not disclosing details of a material contingent liability. In accordance with the Act, the financial statements have been revised as at the date of the original financial statements and not as at the date of this revision. Accordingly they do not deal with events between those dates.

The Act requires that where a supplementary note is issued, a revised auditors' report is issued and this is attached.

Directors' responsibilities

In addition to the directors' responsibilities described in the original financial statements, under [section 454] [section 245] of the Act the directors have authority to revise annual financial statements, the directors' report or directors' remuneration report if they do not comply with the Act. The revised financial statements or report must be amended in accordance with [the Companies (Revision of Defective Accounts and Report) Regulations 2008] [the Companies (Revision of Defective Accounts and Report) Regulations 1990] and in accordance therewith do not take account of events which have taken place after the date on which the original financial statements were approved. The Regulations require that the revised financial statements show a true and fair view as if they were prepared and approved by the directors as at the date of the original financial statements.

Statement of revision

The effect of the revision is to include the following additional note at the end of the original financial statements.

'37 Contingent liabilities

A claim has been lodged by a customer against the group in respect of a major contract. The claim calls for rectification and for compensation for alleged damage to the customer's business. It has been estimated that the maximum liability should the action be successful is of the order of £______ . The group has taken legal advice to the effect that the action is unlikely to succeed and accordingly no provision has been made in the financial statements. In the event that the claim were to succeed, the first £______ would be covered by insurance.'

This supplementary note was approved by the board of directors on 30 June 20X2 and signed on its behalf by:

[Signature]

[Name of signatory to be stated]

Director

[Address of registered office]

Note: In this example the effect of the revision is evident from the additional note to the financial statements. Where changes are made to an existing primary statement or note it will be appropriate to explain the nature of the amendments made. This may be followed by a statement to the effect that 'A revised note x is attached which replaces note x contained in the original financial statements' but in some straightforward cases this may not be necessary.

5 Summary Financial Statements (SFS)

If an SFS has been sent to shareholders prior to revision of the financial statements, the directors should consider whether the statement, had it been prepared by reference to the revised financial statements or report, would comply with section 426 of the 2006 Act (previously section 251 of the 1985 Act) and the Companies (Summary Financial Statement) Regulations 2008 (previously the Companies (Summary Financial Statement) Regulations 1995) (see below). If the SFS requires revision, a revised statement should be sent to members and any person who received a copy of the original SFS. Where no amendment is required, a note should be sent to members and recipients of the SFS indicating that the directors' report and/or the financial statements for the financial year (specifying it) have been revised in a respect which has no bearing on the SFS for that year. If the auditors' report on the revised financial statements or directors' report is qualified, a copy of that report should be attached to the note.

Regulation 17 of the 2008 Regulations (previously regulation 14 of the 1990 Regulations, as amended in 2005), requires that where the summary financial statement does not comply with section 426 of the 2006 Act (previously section 251 of the 1985 Act) or the Companies (Summary Financial Statement) Regulations 2008 (previously the Companies (Summary Financial Statement) Regulations 1995), or if it had been prepared by reference to revised accounts or a revised report or review would not have complied with those requirements, the directors should prepare a further summary financial statement under section 454 of the 2006 Act (previously section 251 of the 1985 Act) and to send that statement to:

(a) any person who received a copy of the original summary financial statement; and

(b) any person to whom the company would be entitled, as at the date the revised summary financial statement is prepared, to send a summary financial statement for the current financial year.

The effect is that a revised SFS will be required where the contents of the SFS are affected by the amendment to the full financial statements or report and therefore the original SFS would no longer comply with the Act (e.g. because it would not be consistent with the revised full financial statements or report).

6 Qualified reports on revised financial statements and distributions

Where the auditors' report on the revised financial statements is qualified, the company may not proceed to make a distribution by reference to those financial statements until the auditors' statement required in such circumstances by s837 of the 2006 Act (previously s271 of the 1985 Act) of the Act has been made.

7 Abbreviated accounts

The Regulations also deal with the revision of abbreviated accounts. This may become necessary either as a consequence of a revision of the full financial statements or because of an error in the abbreviated accounts themselves. Abbreviated accounts are outside the scope of this publication.

Appendix 1 Segment reporting (IAS 14)

1 Introduction

1.1 IFRS 8 and IAS 14

In November 2006, the IASB issued IFRS 8 *Operating Segments* (see **chapter 37**), which is effective for annual financial statements for periods beginning on or after 1 January 2009. Prior to that date, entities may continue to apply IAS 14 *Segment Reporting*, which is discussed in this appendix. Alternatively, entities may choose to apply IFRS 8 in advance of the 2009 effective date, provided that they disclose that fact.

> *IFRS 8 was endorsed for use in the EU in November 2007, so EU companies are now permitted to adopt it in advance of the 2009 effective date.* (UK)

An overview of the impact for IFRS reporters of adopting IFRS 8 is set out below.

- IFRS 8 requires an entity to report financial and descriptive information about its reportable segments, which are operating segments or aggregations of operating segments that meet specified criteria. Operating segments are components of an entity about which separate financial information is available that is evaluated regularly by the chief operating decision maker in deciding how to allocate resources and in assessing performance. Upon adoption of IFRS 8, the identification of an entity's segments may or may not change. IAS 14 required an entity to identify two sets of segments (business and geographical), using a risks and rewards approach, with the entity's 'system of internal financial reporting to key management personnel' serving only as the starting point for the identification of such segments. One set of segments was regarded as primary and the other as secondary. If under IAS 14 an entity identified segments on the basis of the reports provided to the person whom IFRS 8 regards as the chief operating decision maker, those might become the 'operating segments' for the purposes of IFRS 8.

- IFRS 8 states that a component of an entity that sells primarily or exclusively to other operating segments of the entity will meet the definition of an operating segment if the entity is managed in that manner. IAS 14 limited reportable segments to those that earn a majority of their revenue from sales to external parties and did not require the different stages of a vertically-integrated entity to be identified as separate segments.

- IFRS 8 requires the amount reported for each segment item to be the measure reported to the chief operating decision maker for the purposes of allocating resources to that segment and assessing its performance. In contrast to IAS 14, IFRS 8 does not define segment revenue, segment expense, segment result, segment assets and segment liabilities, nor does it require segment information to be prepared in conformity with the accounting policies adopted for the entity's financial statements. As a consequence, entities will have more discretion in determining what is included in segment profit or loss under IFRS 8, limited only by their internal reporting practices.

- Under IFRS 8, additional entity-wide disclosures are prescribed that are required even when an entity has only one reportable segment. These include information about each product and service or groups of products and services.

- Analyses of revenues and certain non-current assets by geographical area are required – with an expanded requirement to disclose revenues/assets by individual foreign country (if material), irrespective of the identification of operating segments.

- IFRS 8 also introduces a requirement to disclose information about transactions with major customers. If revenues from transactions with a single external customer amount to 10 per cent or more of the entity's revenues, the total amount of revenue from each such customer and the segment or segments in which those revenues are reported must be disclosed.

- IFRS 8 makes a number of consequential amendments to other Standards, including the following.

- IAS 34 *Interim Financial Reporting* – IFRS 8 has expanded significantly the requirements for segment information in interim financial reports (see **3.5.1** in **chapter 39**).

- IAS 36 *Impairment of Assets* – IAS 36 requires goodwill to be tested for impairment as part of impairment testing the cash-generating unit to which it relates. In identifying the units (or groups of units) to which goodwill is allocated for the purpose of impairment testing, IAS 36 limits the size of such units or groups of units by reference to the entity's reported segments. As a result of IFRS 8 replacing IAS 14, that maximum limit is now determined by reference to the entity's operating segments as determined in accordance with IFRS 8 – which may differ from the limit previously arrived at in the context of IAS 14.

- IFRS 6 *Exploration for and Evaluation of Mineral Resources* – similar to the IAS 36 amendments described above, the size of the cash-generating unit (or group of units) to which exploration and evaluation assets are allocated for the purpose of impairment testing is now limited by reference to the entity's operating segments as determined in accordance with IFRS 8, rather than the segments previously identified under IAS 14.

1.2 IAS 14 *Segment Reporting*

IAS 14 *Segment Reporting* requires entities with publicly traded equity or debt securities (and entities in the process of issuing such securities) to report data for business segments (groups of related products or services) and geographical segments. Based on the structure of its internal reporting system, management identifies one of those bases of segmentation as primary and the other as secondary, with fewer disclosures required for the secondary basis.

This appendix discusses the requirements of IAS 14 in the following sections:

Section 2	Scope
Section 3	IAS 14's 'management approach' to segment identification
Section 4	Identification of segments
Section 5	Segment revenue, expense, result, assets and liabilities
Section 6	Segment accounting policies

Section 7 Disclosure requirements

UK *IAS 14 is rather more prescriptive than its UK counterpart, SSAP 25* Segmental reporting, *leaving less to the judgement of directors. The most significant differences between the two standards are highlighted below.*

- *IAS 14 requires an entity to determine whether its primary segment reporting format will be business segments or geographical segments. In most cases, this will reflect the structure of internal financial reporting, i.e. if internal reporting is primarily by type of business, business segments will be the primary segment reporting format, and geographical segments will be the secondary segment reporting format. Disclosures are required in respect of both business and geographical segments regardless, but they are more extensive for whichever is the primary segmentation.*
- *The rules of IAS 14 are relatively prescriptive in terms of how a segment is identified and, in particular, how segments may be combined to create reportable segments.*
- *The disclosures required by IAS 14 are more extensive than those of SSAP 25. For example, under the primary segment reporting format, disclosures will include additions to fixed assets, depreciation and information about non-cash expenses.*
- *Unlike SSAP 25, IAS 14 offers no exemption from disclosures on the grounds that they would be seriously prejudicial.*

2 Scope

IAS 14 applies to the published financial statements of all entities whose equity or debt securities are publicly traded and entities that are in the process of issuing equity or debt securities in public securities markets. [IAS 14.1 & 3]

The notion of 'publicly traded' does not require the actual trading of securities, but the *ability* to trade the securities publicly. In some circumstances, securities are listed but it is not expected that the securities will be traded. For example, the shares of an entity may be listed for marketing purposes only, with a restricted number of investors. That entity will fall within the scope of IAS 14.

Other noteworthy points with regard to scope are that:

- reporting of segment information by non-publicly traded entities is encouraged; [IAS 14.4]

- if a non-publicly traded entity chooses to present segment information in its published IFRS financial statements, that information is required to comply fully with the requirements of IAS 14; [IAS 14.5]
- where a single annual report includes both consolidated financial statements and the separate financial statements of the parent or one or more of its subsidiaries, segment information need be presented on a consolidated basis only. If a subsidiary is itself an entity whose securities are publicly traded, it will present segment information in its own separate financial report; [IAS 14.6] and
- where a single annual report includes both the financial statements of a publicly traded entity and the separate financial statements of an equity-method associate or joint venture in which the entity has an interest, segment information need be presented only on the basis of the entity's financial statements. If the equity-method associate or joint venture is itself a publicly traded entity, it will present segment information in its own separate financial report. [IAS 14.7]

Note that IAS 14 applies to segment information included in 'complete sets of published financial statements that comply with International Financial Reporting Standards'. [IAS 14.1] IAS 14.2 explains that such a complete set includes a statement of financial position, a statement of comprehensive income (and, where applicable, a separate income statement), a statement of cash flows, a statement of changes in equity, and notes, in accordance with IAS 1 *Presentation of Financial Statements* (see **chapter 3**).

Therefore, where management voluntarily discloses certain segment information outside of those financial statements (e.g. in the directors' report or chairman's statement) this does not in itself trigger a requirement to comply with IAS 14 under the second bullet above.

2.1 Disclosures that might be seriously prejudicial

Note that IAS 14 does not provide an exemption for disclosures that the board or management deems to be prejudicial to the interests of the entity. Even where the directors of a publicly traded entity conclude that disclosure of certain segment information will be seriously prejudicial to the interests of the entity (e.g. because its main competitors are not publicly traded and, therefore, do not publish similar information), the segment information may not be omitted in IFRS financial statements.

UK

> *A 'seriously prejudicial' exemption is available to UK companies under SSAP 25, and companies that have historically taken advantage of it may find this a key difference on transition to IFRSs.*

3 IAS 14's 'management approach' to segment identification

IAS 14 requires disclosure of segment information based on components of the business that are exposed to similar risks and that generate similar rates of return. Because variations in risks and returns will determine how most entities are organised and managed, the organisational/management structure of the entity and its internal reporting system will normally be the starting point for the purposes of segment reporting. Accordingly, segment information should generally be reported on the same basis that financial information is reported internally to top management. This method is often referred to as the 'management approach'. (Note that IFRS 8 adopts a more stringent 'management approach' to segment reporting because information reported under that Standard is always based on information reported to the chief operating decision maker, whereas IAS 14 uses the internal reporting system only as the starting point for identifying segments.)

Under IAS 14, the management approach will not be appropriate where internal reports to top management are prepared on a basis that does not focus on the risks and returns of the entity's components. For example, internal reporting may be organised solely by legal entity, so that internal segments are composed of groups of unrelated products and services. In these circumstances, an alternative basis of presentation will need to be developed by the entity for the purposes of reporting segment information externally (see **4.1.2**).

4 Identification of segments

IAS 14 takes a three-step approach to the identification of segments for external reporting purposes:

- identification of the entity's distinct business and geographical segments;
- determination of primary and secondary reporting formats; and
- identification of reportable segments.

4.1 Step 1: Identification of business and geographical segments

4.1.1 *Definitions*

A business segment is a distinguishable component of an entity that is engaged in providing an individual product or service or a group of related products or services and that is subject to risks and returns that are different from those of other business segments. [IAS 14.9]

A geographical segment is a distinguishable component of an entity that is engaged in providing products or services within a particular economic environment and that is subject to risks and returns that are different from those of components operating in other economic environments. [IAS 14.9]

4.1.2 *Segment identification where internal reporting system is based neither on products nor on geography*

Using the management approach to the identification of segments (as discussed in **section 3** above), the business and geographical segments identified for reporting externally will generally be based on those components for which information is already reported internally to top management. However, if the internal reporting system is based neither on products/services nor on geography, the business and geographical segments of the entity for the purposes of external reporting will need to be determined based on the factors discussed below.

For the purposes of identifying business segments, the Standard lists the following factors (not in any particular order) that should be considered in determining whether products and services are related:

[IAS 14.9]

- the nature of the products or services;
- the nature of the production processes;
- the type or class of customer for the products or services;
- the methods used to distribute the products or provide the services; and
- if applicable, the nature of the regulatory environment (e.g. banking, insurance, or public utilities).

Although there may be differences between some of these factors for different products or services within a single business segment, the majority of the factors should be similar. Where this is not the case, it indicates that more than one segment exists. A single business segment does not include products and services with significantly differing risks and rates of return.

Example 4.1.2

Identification of business segments

Company A has an operating unit that provides content to internet websites and derives substantially all of its revenue from three service lines — advertising, promotions and customer service. The financial information reported to the chief executive officer and the board of directors includes revenue by service line, but operating expenses and assets are reported on a combined basis only for the entire entity, and no measure of result is reported internally by service line. Does each of the service lines represent a business segment?

Whether the service lines represent separate business segments depends on whether they are subject to risks and returns that are different. The criteria for making this determination are listed above.

If it is determined that the risks and returns of the three service lines are different, all of the required items of financial information (as detailed in **section 7**) must be disclosed for each segment (including segment result and segment assets), even if those items of information are not reported to the chief executive officer and the board.

The Standard lists the following factors (not in any particular order) that should be considered in identifying geographical segments:

[IAS 14.9]

- similarity of economic and political conditions;
- relationships between operations in different geographical areas;
- proximity of operations;
- special risks associated with operations in a particular area;
- exchange control regulations; and
- the underlying currency risks.

Depending on the circumstances, a geographical segment may be a country, a group of countries or a region within a country. A geographical segment does not include operations in economic environments with significantly differing risks and rates of return.

In order to identify its geographical segments, each entity must assess how it is affected by the different economic environments in which it operates. Economic environments are affected by political conditions, which can differ from country to country, as well as by other factors that are peculiar to the way an entity operates. Therefore, for example, it is not necessarily appropriate to group all of the countries that are members of a regional economic community (such as NAFTA, the EU or APEC) as a single economic environment.

4.1.2.1 *Additional guidance where the internal reporting system is based neither on products nor on geography*

IAS 14 includes additional detailed guidance on how segments should be identified in circumstances where the internal reporting system is based neither on business segments nor on geographical segments. As discussed under **4.1.2** above, IAS 14.9 identifies certain factors that must be considered when identifying business and geographical segments, but the Standard also states that:

[IAS 14.32]

- if one or more of the segments reported internally to the directors and management is a business segment or a geographical segment based on the factors in the definitions in IAS 14.9 but others are not, those internally-reported segments that meet the definition should not be further segmented;

- for those internally-reported segments that do not satisfy the definitions in IAS 14.9, management should look to the next lower level of internal segmentation that reports information along product and service lines or geographical lines (as appropriate under the definitions in IAS 14.9) and, if such an internally-reported lower-level segment meets the definition of a business segment or geographical segment based on the factors in IAS 14.9, the criteria in IAS 14.34 and IAS 14.35 for identifying reportable segments should be applied to that segment (see **4.3.1** and **4.3.2** below).

Summing up the overall approach:

- where internal segmental reporting is already along business or geographical lines, this will be the starting point for external segment reporting (although it may occasionally be necessary to subdivide further a particular segment, or to reassess how certain items are, or are not, allocated between segments); and

- where internal segmental reporting is not along business or geographical lines:
  - those segments that nevertheless meet the IAS 14 criteria are not further amended; and
  - those that do not meet the IAS 14 criteria are subdivided to the next level and, provided that at that level the criteria are met, are then recombined by following the rules on combining segments to create reportable segments (see **4.3** below).

Appendix A to IAS 14 sets out a decision tree that may be followed to enable reportable segments to be identified. This decision tree is reproduced at **4.4** below.

4.1.3 Choice of location of production or markets in identifying geographical segments

The definition of a geographical segment allows geographical segmentation to be based on either:

[IAS 14.13]

- the location of the entity's production or service facilities and other assets; or
- the location of its markets and customers.

When identifying geographical segments, the Standard requires that management should consider whether the risks and returns of the entity are more greatly influenced by where its products are produced (or its service activities are based), or by where its products are sold (or services are rendered). In practice, risks and returns arise from each. An entity's organisation and internal reporting structure will, however, normally provide evidence as to whether its dominant source of geographical risks results from the location of its assets (the origin of its sales) or the location of its customers (the destination of its sales). [IAS 14.14]

The choice for the identification of geographical segments between the location of an entity's production/service facilities and the location of its markets and customers is not a free choice. The choice should be based on which approach better differentiates the risks and rates of return facing the entity. Whichever analysis is chosen as the entity's main approach to geographical segments, IAS 14.71 and

IAS 14.72 may require some additional disclosures using the other approach to geographical segments (see **7.2** below).

4.2 Step 2: Determination of primary and secondary reporting formats

IAS 14 specifies differing levels of disclosure for an entity's 'primary' and 'secondary' segment reporting formats. The entity therefore needs to determine which basis of segmentation (business or geographical) is to be used for its primary reporting format.

If the risks and rates of return of an entity are affected predominantly by differences in the products or services it produces, its primary format for reporting segment information is business segments, with secondary information reported geographically. [IAS 14.26]

Alternatively, if the risks and rates of return of an entity are affected predominantly by the fact that it operates in different countries or other geographical areas, its primary format for reporting segment information is geographical segments, with secondary information reported for business segments. [IAS 14.26]

The predominant influence on the nature of the risks faced by an entity, and the differing rates of return it achieves, can usually be identified from the entity's internal organisational and management structure and its system of internal financial reporting to senior management. There are two exceptions to this general rule, which are expected to occur only infrequently.

Firstly, the entity may report internally to senior management using both business segment information and geographical segment information (the 'matrix approach') because its risks and rates of return are strongly affected both by differences in the products and services it supplies and by differences in the geographical areas in which it operates. In such circumstances, IAS 14 specifies that the entity should use business segments as its primary segment reporting format and geographical segments as its secondary reporting format. [IAS 14.27(a)] Alternatively, the entity may choose to present full segment disclosures both for business segments and for geographical segments (i.e. to report as though both were primary reporting formats). Such additional information is neither required nor prohibited by the Standard. [IAS 14.29]

Secondly, the entity's reports to senior management may be based neither on business segments nor on geographical segments (e.g. internal reporting may be based solely on legal entities, which results in internal segments composed of groups of unrelated products and services). In these circumstances, the directors and management are required to determine whether the entity's risks and rates of return are more product/service driven or geographically driven, and to choose either business segments or geographical segments as the entity's primary basis of segment reporting. [IAS 14.27(b)]

Where an entity has a single geographical segment but several business segments, it will not be possible to designate that geographical segment as primary and the business segments as secondary (with a consequent reduction in the disclosures for business segments). In such cases, the business segments would constitute the primary segments. This follows necessarily from IAS 14's approach to identifying the primary format, which focuses on where the most significant variations in risks and returns arise between segments.

The same logic would apply where an entity has a single business segment but several geographical segments – the latter would be the primary segments.

4.3 Step 3: Identification of reportable segments

Once the business segments and geographical segments have been identified, and the primary and secondary reporting formats have been determined, the entity must then determine which segments are reportable, i.e. those individual segments for which disclosure of information is required by the Standard.

IAS 14 does not limit the number of business segments or geographical segments for which segment information should be disclosed. While IFRS 8 suggests that ten is a practical limit to the number of segments, there is no comparable suggestion in IAS 14. In practice, however, the quantitative threshold tests set out in **4.3.2** are likely to lead to no more than ten segments in most cases.

4.3.1 Segments that can be combined

For reporting purposes, it is possible to combine two or more internally-reported business segments or geographical segments as a single business segment or geographical segment, but only if they are substantially similar. Two or more business segments or geographical segments are substantially similar only if:

[IAS 14.34]

- they exhibit similar long-term financial performance; and
- they are similar in all of the factors for the identification of business or geographical segments, as appropriate (see **4.1.2** above).

As regards the first requirement of IAS 14.34, 'similar long-term financial performance' should be assessed by considering measures such as the following (using actual historical amounts rather than forecasted amounts):

- long-term average gross margin;
- sales growth;
- operating cash flows;
- return on assets;
- earnings before interest, taxes, depreciation, and amortisation (EBITDA);
- inventory turnover; and
- other performance measures that are standard in the industry in which the segments operate.

This list is not exhaustive. The facts and circumstances should determine the result of this assessment. By analogy to IAS 14.45, it is appropriate in particular to consider the measures used by management to evaluate long-term financial performance.

As regards the second requirement of IAS 14.34, it may be noted that the condition for combining segments is, in effect, more onerous than that required to identify segments in the first place. As discussed at **4.1.2** above, it is not essential that all of the listed factors are similar for all products and services within a business segment. This is essential, however, if separate segments are to be combined for reporting purposes.

4.3.2 *Quantitative thresholds*

Under IAS 14, a business or geographical segment should be identified as a reportable segment if a majority of its revenue is earned from sales to external customers and:

[IAS 14.35]

- its revenue from sales to external customers and from transactions with other segments is 10 per cent or more of the total revenue, external and internal, of all segments; or
- its segment result, whether profit or loss, is 10 per cent or more of the combined result of all segments in profit or the combined result of all segments in loss, whichever is the greater in absolute amount; or
- its assets are 10 per cent or more of the total assets of all segments.

Example 4.3.2

Application of quantitative thresholds

Company A has identified the following business segments: computer hardware, computer software and customer service. Each business segment earns a majority of its revenue from external customers. In applying the quantitative threshold tests set out above for the purpose of identifying reportable segments, Company A would perform the following analysis (based on the figures in the table below).

To determine the segments that exceed the 10 per cent revenue threshold, Company A should determine the combined revenue (external and internal) for all business segments (£5,500). This amount includes £500 of inter-segment revenue. Ten per cent of this amount, or £550, would represent the threshold.

To determine the segments that exceed the 10 per cent profit or loss threshold, Company A should determine the greater, in absolute value, of the total of all segments that reported a profit and the total of all segments that reported a loss. Based on the calculation below, the absolute value of the total of all segments with profits, £350, is greater than the absolute value of the segment with a loss, £50. Ten per cent of £350, or £35, should then be used as the profit or loss threshold for identifying reportable segments.

To determine the segments that exceed the 10 per cent asset threshold, Company A should calculate the threshold based on 10 per cent of the segment assets identified (£800) before intragroup eliminations.

Note: * indicates a segment meeting the specific threshold.

Segment	Segment revenue	Segment result	Segments with profit	Segments with loss	Segment assets
	£	£	£	£	£
Hardware	500	(50)		50*	400*
Software	2,500*	200	200*		300*
Service	2,500*	150	150*	—	100*
Total before eliminations	5,500	300	350	50	800

Eliminations	(500)	(10)	0	0	(10)
Total	5,000	290	350	50	790
Calculated threshold	550[a]		35[b]	35[b]	80[c]

(a) Total sales before elimination of inter-segment sales (£5,500 x 10%)

(b) Threshold calculation is based on the greater of the absolute amount of all operating segments with profit or all operating segments with loss (£350 x 10%)

(c) Total assets before considering inter-segment eliminations (£800 x 10%)

Considering each of the segments in turn:

- the Hardware segment exceeds the result threshold (50 > 35) and the assets threshold (400 > 80);
- the Software segment exceeds the revenue threshold (2,500 > 550), the result threshold (200 > 35) and the assets threshold (300 > 80);
- the Service segment exceeds the revenue threshold (2,500 > 550), the result threshold (150 > 35) and the assets threshold (100 > 80).

Accordingly, all three segments meet at least one threshold and, therefore, all are reportable.

4.3.3 *Segments below the quantitative thresholds*

When an internally-reported segment is below all of the thresholds set out above, management has three options. The segment may be:

[IAS 14.36]

- designated as a reportable segment despite its size; or
- combined into a separately reportable segment with one or more other similar internally-reported segment(s) that are also below all of the 10 per cent thresholds (but only if the segments so defined are substantially similar – see **4.3.1** above); or
- included as an unallocated reconciling item.

4.3.4 *Revenue attributable to reportable segments to be at least 75 per cent of entity revenue*

If, after an entity has identified its reportable segments, total external revenue attributable to those reportable segments constitutes less than 75 per cent of the total consolidated or entity revenue, additional segments must be identified as reportable segments, even if they do not exceed any of the 10 per cent thresholds, until at least 75 per cent of total consolidated or entity revenue is included in reportable segments. [IAS 14.37]

Example 4.3.4

Identification of additional segments to reach 75 per cent revenue threshold

Company A has determined its reportable segments in accordance with IAS 14 and has noted that the reportable segments constitute 68 per cent of consolidated revenue. All remaining business segments (or geographical segments) are of similar size. How should Company A determine which business segments (or geographical segments) to report separately?

IAS 14 does not specify which of the remaining segments should be selected to achieve the 75 per cent threshold, and the segment chosen does not necessarily need to be the next largest by any of the measures. Judgement should be used, and each situation will be based on the individual facts and circumstances. Those additional segments included in order to achieve the 75 per cent threshold are treated no differently from any other reportable segment (i.e. the required disclosures are the same).

4.3.5 *Segment reported in preceding period that no longer exceeds quantitative thresholds*

Where a segment was identified as a reportable segment in the immediately preceding period (because it exceeded one of the 10 per cent thresholds), it should continue to be a reportable segment for the current period (notwithstanding that it no longer exceeds any of the 10 per cent thresholds), if the directors judge the segment to be of 'continuing significance'. [IAS 14.42]

No further guidance is provided as to the meaning of 'continuing significance', but a segment normally would be regarded as having continuing significance for the current financial statements where, for example:

- its decline below the 10 per cent thresholds is considered temporary and likely to reverse;
- it has unrecognised intangible assets (such as internally generated intangible assets) that, if recognised, would cause its segment assets to meet the 10 per cent threshold (this may indicate that the segment is of strategic importance); or
- it is held for sale.

While the items above are not an exhaustive list, management should ensure that the usefulness of the financial information and consistency in reporting is maintained.

4.3.6 *Restatement when part of a segment has been disposed of*

Example 4.3.6

Restatement when part of a segment has been disposed of

Company A has identified the following business segments: computer hardware, computer software and customer service. In the current year, Company A sold a portion of its computer hardware segment. In preparing the current year's business segment disclosures, should Company A restate prior year segment information to remove the portion of the computer hardware segment disposed of in the current year?

The answer will depend on whether the operation that has been disposed of meets the definition of a discontinued operation under IFRS 5 *Non-current Assets Held for Sale and Discontinued Operations*.

- If it doesn't (so that it continues to be presented as part of continuing operations), the comparative information will not be restated.
- If it does, IFRS 5.34 requires restatement of comparative prior period information to segregate the results from discontinued operations. Segment revenue, expenses, result and cash flows (if disclosed) should include those of a discontinued operation, but separately disclosed (see **7.1** below). In accordance with IFRS 5, segment assets and liabilities for the comparative period will not be restated where an operation becomes discontinued during the current year.

4.3.7 *Segment reportable in the current year but not in the preceding year*

A segment may be identified as a reportable segment in the current period because it exceeds one of the relevant 10 per cent thresholds, even though it did not exceed any of the relevant 10 per cent thresholds in the prior period. In such circumstances, prior period segment data that is presented for comparative purposes should be restated to reflect the newly reportable segment as a separate segment, unless it is impracticable to do so. [IAS 14.43]

Although situations in which it is impracticable to restate prior period operating segment disclosures are expected to be unusual, consider the following example.

Example 4.3.7

Segment reportable in the current year but not in the prior year

In the past three years, Company B has grown from £100 million in sales annually to over £1 billion in sales annually as a result of five different acquisitions. Company B and each entity it acquired were managed differently. Due to its significant growth through acquisition, Company B has recently restructured its management structure and segments. Historical records are not available for all of the entities in a manner consistent with the new management approach. In this situation, it may be impracticable for Company B to restate prior period segment disclosures due to the number and size of its recent acquisitions.

If an entity has changed the identification of its segments and has concluded that restatement of prior period segment information is impracticable, IAS 14.76 requires the entity to provide current period segment information under both the old and new bases of segmentation for the year in which the change occurs (see **7.3.5.1**).

4.3.8 Vertically-integrated operations

As noted at **4.3.2**, the Standard requires that a majority of a segment's revenue must be earned from external sales in order for it to qualify as a reportable segment. Accordingly, vertically-integrated operations that report internally as separate segments will not necessarily be required to be reported externally as separate segments. This situation is acknowledged in IAS 14.40 which encourages, but does not require, the voluntary reporting of vertically-integrated activities as separate segments. An appropriate description should be provided, including disclosure of the basis of pricing inter-segment transfers (as discussed at **7.3.4**).

The Standard goes on to require that, where vertically-integrated activities are not reported as separate segments, the selling segment should be combined with the buying segment for the purpose of identifying externally-reportable business segments. In circumstances where there is no reasonable basis for combining the selling and buying segments, and the selling segment on its own does not qualify for separate reporting, the selling segment should be included as an unallocated reconciling item. [IAS 14.41]

Example 4.3.8

Vertically-integrated operations

An oil company has two subsidiaries which concentrate on each of the following:

- exploration and production; and
- refining and marketing.

In the normal course of business, the only operating revenue of the exploration and production subsidiary is from intragroup sales of crude oil to the refining and marketing subsidiary. Therefore, the exploration and production subsidiary does not meet the definition of a reportable segment and its revenue and expenses are combined with those of the refining and marketing subsidiary for the purposes of segment disclosure. However, IAS 14 encourages disclosure as if the exploration and production subsidiary were a reportable segment with appropriate description of the basis of pricing inter-segment transfers.

4.3.9 *Start-up activity with no external revenue*

An entity may make a substantial investment in a new facility or operation whose risks and potential for returns are quite different from the entity's existing business segments. The investment in the facility and equipment may be more than 10 per cent of the entity's combined assets. In the start-up period, while the facility may incur expenditure, it may earn no external revenue.

Even where financial information for the facility is reported to senior management, it is not required to be treated as a reportable segment under IAS 14. Although the Standard does not require that an activity actually earns revenue to qualify as a business segment, IAS 14.35 will not require a segment to be treated as reportable unless it has a 'majority of its revenue . . .from sales to external customers'.

Although the entity is not required to report segment information in respect of the start-up activity, it can choose to do so in accordance with IAS 14.36 (see **4.3.3**).

4.4 Segment definition decision tree

Appendix A to IAS 14 sets out a decision tree, reproduced below, which illustrates how the requirements discussed in **section 4** are applied.

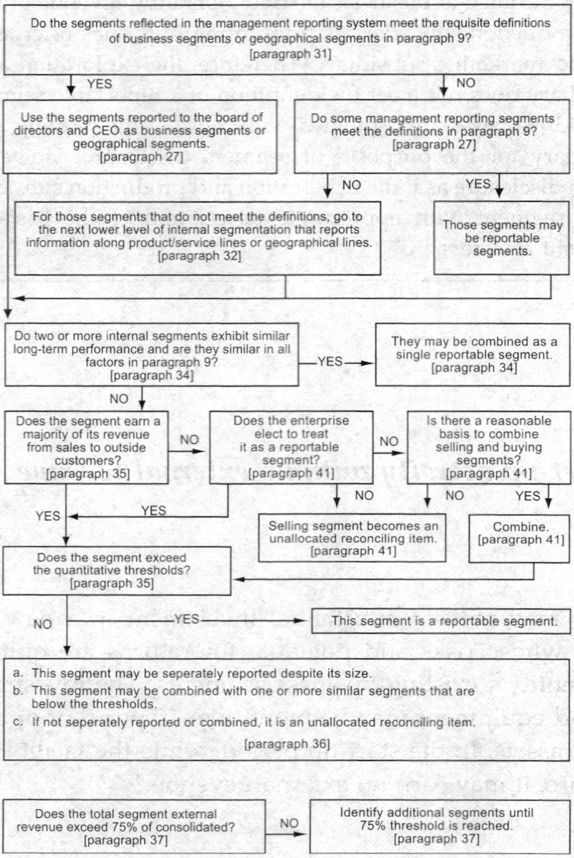

5 Segment revenue, expense, result, assets and liabilities

The definitions for segment revenue, expense, result, assets and liabilities are set out below, and are discussed in the following paragraphs. These definitions encompass amounts that are directly attributable to a segment and amounts that can be allocated to a segment on a reasonable basis.

Segment revenue is revenue reported in the entity's statement of comprehensive income that is directly attributable to a segment and the relevant portion of entity revenue that can be allocated on a reasonable basis to a segment, whether from sales to external customers or from transactions with other segments of the same entity. [IAS 14.16]

Segment expense is expense resulting from the operating activities of a segment that is directly attributable to the segment and the relevant portion of any expense that can be allocated on a reasonable basis to the segment, including expenses relating to external customers and expenses relating to transactions with other segments of the same entity. [IAS 14.16]

Segment result is segment revenue less segment expense, determined before any adjustments for non-controlling interest. [IAS 14.16]

Segment assets are those operating assets that are employed by a segment in its operating activities and that either are directly attributable to the segment or can be allocated to the segment on a reasonable basis. [IAS 14.16]

Segment liabilities are those operating liabilities that result from the operating activities of a segment and that either are directly attributable to the segment or can be allocated to the segment on a reasonable basis. [IAS 14.16]

The starting point for identifying items that are directly attributable, or that can reasonably be allocated, to segments is the internal financial reporting system of the entity. It is presumed that amounts that have been identified with segments for internal financial reporting purposes are directly attributable or can reasonably be allocated to those segments. [IAS 14.17]

An entity may, however, as a matter of policy, use a system of allocation for management purposes that results in an inappropriate allocation of assets, liabilities, revenue and expenses to segments for the purposes of the Standard. This will be the case, for example, if the basis of allocation, notwithstanding that it is understood by entity management, 'could be deemed subjective, arbitrary, or difficult to understand by external users'. [IAS 14.18] Similarly, certain items may not be allocated for management purposes, even though a reasonable basis for allocation exists. In both such circumstances, the definitions and guidance provided in the Standard should be considered in order to ensure that any required adjustments are identified and properly reflected for external segment reporting.

Segment revenue, segment expense, segment assets and segment liabilities are determined before intragroup balances and intragroup transactions are eliminated as part of the consolidation process, except to the extent that such intragroup balances and transactions are between group entities within a single segment. [IAS 14.24]

5.1 Segment revenue

Segment revenue does not include:

[IAS 14.16]

- interest or dividend income, including interest earned on advances or loans to other segments, unless the operations of the segment are primarily of a financial nature;
- gains on sales of investments or gains on extinguishment of debt unless the operations of the segment are primarily of a financial nature; or
- an entity's share of profits or losses of associates, joint ventures, or other investments accounted for under the equity method, unless those items are included in consolidated or total entity revenue.

Segment revenue includes a joint venturer's share of the revenue of a jointly controlled entity that is accounted for by proportionate consolidation in accordance with IAS 31 *Interests in Joint Ventures* (see **chapter 36**). [IAS 14.16]

5.2 Segment expense

Segment expense does not include:

[IAS 14.16]

- interest, including interest incurred on advances or loans from other segments, unless the operations of the segment are primarily of a financial nature;
- losses on sales of investments or losses on extinguishment of debt unless the operations of the segment are primarily of a financial nature;
- an entity's share of losses of associates, joint ventures, or other investments accounted for under the equity method;
- income tax expense; or
- general administrative expenses, head office expenses, and other expenses that arise at the entity level and relate to the entity as a whole. However, costs are sometimes incurred at the entity level on behalf of a segment, and such costs are segment expenses if they relate to the operating activities of the segment and they can be directly attributed or allocated to the segment on a reasonable basis.

Segment expense includes a joint venturer's share of the expenses of a jointly controlled entity that is accounted for by proportionate consolidation in accordance with IAS 31 *Interests in Joint Ventures* (see **chapter 36**). [IAS 14.16]

For a segment with operations that are primarily of a financial nature, interest income and interest expense may be reported as a single net amount for segment reporting purposes only if those amounts are netted in the consolidated or entity financial statements. [IAS 14.16]

5.3 Segment result

As a result of the parameters set for segment revenue and segment expense, as described in **5.1** and **5.2**, segment result is normally a measure of operating profit before:

- corporate head office expenses;
- interest income or expense (except for financial segments);
- income taxes;
- investment gains and losses (except for financial segments);
- income and expenses of equity method associates and joint ventures; and
- non-controlling interests.

5.4 Segment assets

Segment assets include, but are not limited to:

[IAS 14.19]

- goodwill that is directly attributable to a segment or that can be allocated on a reasonable basis; and
- property, plant and equipment, assets held under finance leases, intangible assets and current assets that are used in the operating activities of the segment.

The Standard requires 'symmetry' in the inclusion of items in segment result and in segment assets. For example:

- if the results of a segment include interest or dividend income, its segment assets include the related receivables, loans, investments or other income-producing assets; [IAS 14.16]
- if the results of a segment include the depreciation expense for a particular item of property, plant and equipment, that item of property, plant and equipment is included in its segment assets; [IAS 14.19] and
- if the results of a segment include any impairment loss recognised for a particular amount of goodwill, that amount of goodwill is included in its segment assets. [IAS 14.19]

Segment assets do not include income tax assets or assets used for general entity or head office purposes. Operating assets shared by two or more segments will be allocated to segments, but only if a reasonable basis for allocation exists and their related revenues and expenses are also allocated to those segments. [IAS 14.16, 19 & 47]

Investments accounted for under the equity method are included in segment assets only if the profit or loss from such investments is included in segment revenue. A joint venturer's share of the operating assets of a jointly controlled entity that is accounted for by proportionate consolidation under IAS 31 *Interests in Joint Ventures* (see **chapter 36**) is included in segment assets. [IAS 14.16]

Segment assets are determined after deducting related allowances that are reported as direct offsets in the entity's statement of financial position, such as allowances for bad debts or inventory obsolescence. [IAS 14.16]

Measurements of segment assets include fair value adjustments to the prior carrying amounts of assets acquired in a business combination, even if those adjustments are made only for the purpose of preparing consolidated financial statements and are not recognised in either the parent's or the subsidiary's separate financial statements. Similarly, if property, plant and equipment has been revalued subsequent to acquisition, then measurements of segment assets reflect those revaluations. [IAS 14.21]

5.5 Segment liabilities

Segment liabilities include, but are not limited to:

[IAS 14.20]

- trade and other payables;
- accrued liabilities;

- customer advances; and
- product warranty provisions and other claims relating to the provision of goods and services.

Segment liabilities do not generally include:

[IAS 14.20]

- borrowings;
- liabilities related to assets held under finance leases; or
- other liabilities that are incurred for financing rather than operating purposes.

Such borrowings and similar liabilities are excluded from the liabilities of segments whose operations are not primarily of a financial nature, because segment result represents an operating, rather than a net-of-financing, profit or loss. In addition, because debt is often issued at the head-office level on an entity-wide basis, it is often not possible to directly attribute, or reasonably allocate, the interest-bearing liability to the segment. [IAS 14.20]

Application of the symmetry principle discussed in **5.4** above means that, if the result of a segment includes interest expense, its segment liabilities should include the related interest-bearing liabilities. [IAS 14.16]

Segment liabilities do not include income tax liabilities. [IAS 14.16]

A joint venturer's share of the liabilities of a jointly controlled entity that is accounted for by proportionate consolidation in accordance with IAS 31 *Interests in Joint Ventures* (see **chapter 36**) should be included in segment liabilities. [IAS 14.16]

Measurements of segment liabilities include fair value adjustments to the prior carrying amounts of liabilities acquired in a business combination, even if those adjustments are made only for the purpose of preparing consolidated financial statements and are not recognised in either the parent's or the subsidiary's separate financial statements. [IAS 14.21]

6 Segment accounting policies

IAS 14 requires that segment information be prepared in conformity with the accounting policies adopted for preparing and presenting the financial statements of the consolidated group or entity. [IAS 14.44] This rule does not imply, however, that the accounting policies are applied to each segment as if it were a stand-alone entity. Some accounting policies may be applied on an entity basis and allocated to the appropriate segments on a consistent and reasonable basis. For example, pension costs may be determined for an entity as a whole and allocated to each segment based on salary and demographic data.

IAS 14 does not prohibit the presentation of additional segment information prepared using accounting policies that differ from those used for presenting the consolidated group or entity financial statements, provided that:

[IAS 14.46]

- the information is reported internally to the board of directors and the chief executive officer for the purposes of making decisions about allocating resources to the segment and assessing its performance; and
- the basis of measurement for the additional information is clearly described.

In other words, information that is not reported internally will probably not be useful to external users of financial statements and, therefore, would be superfluous and potentially misleading. If information is reported internally to help senior management manage the business and the risks of the entity, however, it is probably useful and relevant information for external financial statement users and, therefore, the Standard allows such information to be presented in addition to the normal segment disclosures.

7 Disclosure requirements

The following sections set out the disclosures required by the Standard for the entity's primary and secondary reporting formats. These disclosures are illustrated in Appendix B to the Standard.

The requirement in IAS 14.1 to apply the Standard in complete sets of published financial statements that comply with International Financial Reporting Standards, results in the same level of disclosure for current and comparative periods.

7.1 Primary reporting format

The following disclosures are required for each reportable segment based on an entity's primary reporting format:

- segment revenue from sales to external customers; [IAS 14.51]
- segment revenue from transactions with other segments; [IAS 14.51]
- total segment revenue; [IAS 14.51]
- segment result, presenting the result from continuing operations separately from the result of discontinued operations. [IAS 14.52] The analysis of segment result disclosed for prior periods is restated to reflect operations that have been classified as discontinued at the end of the latest reporting period presented; [IAS 14.52A]
- the total carrying amount of segment assets; [IAS 14.55]
- segment liabilities; [IAS 14.56]
- the total cost incurred during the period (on an accruals rather than a cash basis) to acquire segment assets that are expected to be used during more than one period (property, plant and equipment, and intangible assets); [IAS 14.57]

> The phrase 'property, plant, equipment, and intangible assets' in IAS 14.57 should be read as indicative only. This disclosure should include expenditures for all non-current operating assets but not financial assets (unless the operations of the entity are primarily of a financial nature). Examples of these additional assets include investment property, land use rights, biological assets, construction in progress and assets leased to others under operating leases.

- the total amount of expense included in segment result for depreciation and amortisation of segment assets for the period; [IAS 14.58]
- the total amount of significant non-cash expenses, other than depreciation and amortisation, included in segment expense; [IAS 14.61]
- the aggregate of the entity's share of the profit or loss of associates, joint ventures, and other investments accounted for under the equity method, if substantially all of the operations of the associate, joint venture or other investment are within that single segment (while this disclosure is a single amount, the determination of whether substantially all the operations of an associate, joint venture or other investment are within a single segment is made on an individual basis); [IAS 14.64 & 65] and
- when the aggregate share of profit or loss of equity-accounted associates, joint ventures and investments is disclosed, the aggregate investments in those associates and joint ventures should also be disclosed by reportable segment. [IAS 14.66]

The information disclosed should be reconciled to the aggregated information in the consolidated or entity financial statements. In particular:

[IAS 14.67]

- segment revenue should be reconciled to entity revenue from external customers (including disclosure of the amount of entity revenue from external customers not included in any segment's revenue);
- segment result from continuing operation should be reconciled to a comparable measure of entity operating profit or loss from continuing operations as well as to entity net profit or loss from continuing operations;
- segment result from discontinued operations should be reconciled to entity profit or loss from discontinued operations;
- segment assets should be reconciled to entity assets; and
- segment liabilities should be reconciled to entity liabilities.

7.2 Secondary reporting format

7.2.1 Where primary format is business segments

If an entity's primary format is business segments, then the secondary format will be geographical segments, and the entity should disclose:

[IAS 14.69]

- segment revenue from external customers by geographical area, based on the geographical location of its customers, for each geographical segment whose revenue from sales to external customers is 10 per cent or more of total entity revenue from sales to all external customers;
- the total carrying amount of segment assets by geographical location of assets, for each geographical segment whose segment assets are 10 per cent or more of the total assets of all geographical segments; and
- the total cost incurred during the period to acquire segment assets that are expected to be used during more than one period (property, plant and equipment, and intangible assets) by geographical location of assets, for each geographical segment whose segment assets are 10 per cent or more of the total assets of all geographical segments.

7.2.2 *Where primary format is geographical segments*

If an entity's primary format is geographical segments, the secondary format will be business segments, and the entity should disclose the following for each business segment whose revenue from sales to external customers is 10 per cent or more of total entity revenue from sales to all external customers, or whose segment assets are 10 per cent or more of the total assets of all business segments:

[IAS 14.70]

- segment revenue from external customers;
- the total carrying amount of segment assets; and
- the total cost incurred during the period to acquire segment assets that are expected to be used during more than one period (property, plant and equipment, and intangible assets).

In addition, when the primary reporting format of an entity is geographical segments based on the location of its assets, and the location of its customers is different from the location of its assets, then the entity should disclose revenue from sales to external customers for each customer-based geographical segment whose revenue from sales to external customers is 10 per cent or more of total entity revenue from sales to all external customers. [IAS 14.71]

When the primary reporting format of an entity is geographical segments based on the location of its customers, and the assets of the entity are located in different geographical areas from its customers, then the entity should disclose the following for each asset-based geographical segment whose revenue from sales to external customers or segment assets are 10 per cent or more of the equivalent consolidated or total entity amounts:

[IAS 14.72]

- the total carrying amount of segment assets by geographical location of the assets; and
- the total cost incurred during the period to acquire segment assets that are expected to be used during more than one period (property, plant and equipment, and intangible assets) by location of the assets.

7.3 Other disclosure requirements

A number of additional disclosures are required, each of which is discussed in the following paragraphs:

- segments that are not reportable, but for which revenue from sales to external customers is 10 per cent or more of total entity revenue;
- the types of products and services included in each segment;
- the composition of geographical segments;
- inter-segment transfer pricing policy; and
- changes in accounting policies.

7.3.1 *Non-reportable segments representing 10% or more of external revenue*

A business segment or geographical segment for which information is reported to the board of directors and chief executive officer may not be a reportable segment because it earns a majority of its revenue from sales to other segments, and the entity may not elect to voluntarily disclose it as a reportable segment (despite the encouragement in IAS 14.40) – see **4.3.8**). In such circumstances, if the segment's revenue from sales to external customers is 10 per cent or more of total entity revenue from sales to all external customers, the entity is required to disclose:

[IAS 14.74]

- that fact;
- the amount of revenue from sales to external customers; and
- the amount of revenue from internal sales to other segments.

7.3.2 *Types of products and services*

If not otherwise disclosed in the financial statements or elsewhere in the annual report, an entity is required to disclose the types of products and services included in each reported business segment, both primary and secondary. [IAS 14.81]

7.3.3 *Composition of geographical segments*

If not otherwise disclosed in the financial statements or elsewhere in the annual report, an entity is required to indicate the composition of each reported geographical segment, both primary and secondary. [IAS 14.81]

7.3.4 *Inter-segment transfer pricing*

When measuring and reporting segment revenue from transactions with other segments, inter-segment transfers are required to be measured on the basis that the entity actually used to price those transfers. The basis of pricing inter-segment transfers and any change therein is required to be disclosed. [IAS 14.75]

When an entity changes the method that it uses to price inter-segment transfers, it is not a change in accounting policy for which comparative segment data is required to be restated (as discussed at **7.3.5**), but the nature of the change is required to be disclosed. [IAS 14.80]

7.3.5 Changes in accounting policies

Two types of change in accounting policy may affect segment reporting:

- changes in accounting policies adopted for segment reporting; and
- changes in accounting policies at the entity level.

7.3.5.1 Changes in accounting policies adopted for segment reporting

Some changes in accounting policies relate specifically to segment reporting, e.g. changes in the identification of segments and changes in the basis for allocating revenues and expenses to segments. However, such changes will not affect the information reported at the aggregate consolidated or entity level.

When an entity changes an accounting policy adopted for segment reporting, and the change has a material effect on segment information, the comparative segment information is required to be restated in line with the new policy, unless it is impracticable to do so, and the following information should be disclosed:

[IAS 14.76]

- the nature of the change;
- the reasons for the change;
- the fact that comparative information has been restated or that is impracticable to do so; and
- the financial effect of the change, if it is reasonably determinable.

If an entity changes the identification of its segments and it does not restate comparative segment information on the grounds of impracticality, then the entity is required to report segment data for both the old and the new bases of segmentation in the year in which it changes the identification of its segments. [IAS 14.76]

7.3.5.2 *Changes in accounting policies at the entity level*

Changes in accounting policies at the entity level will be accounted for in accordance with IAS 8 *Accounting Policies, Changes in Accounting Estimates and Errors* (see **chapter 4**). Unless another Standard or Interpretation requires otherwise, a change in accounting policy is applied retrospectively, and prior period comparative information, including the segment information, is restated (unless it is impracticable to do so and that fact is disclosed).

7.4 Additional primary reporting format disclosures encouraged by IAS 14

The Standard encourages, but does not require, the following additional disclosures for each reportable segment based on the primary reporting format.

- In addition to segment result (as defined in **section 5** above), segment net profit or loss or some other measure of segment profitability, such as gross profit or profit or loss from ordinary activities, if it can be computed without arbitrary allocations and is appropriately described. A clear description of the basis of measurement should be given if this is other than the accounting policies for the consolidated or entity financial statements. [IAS 14.53 & 54]
- The nature and amount of any items of segment revenue or segment expense that are of such size, nature, or incidence that their disclosure is relevant to explain the performance of each reportable segment for the period. [IAS 14.59]
- The amount of the cash flows arising from the operating, investing and financing activities of each reported business segment and geographical segment. Entities which disclose this information do not need to disclose segment depreciation and amortisation expense and segment non-cash expenses (as discussed at **7.1**). [IAS 14.62 & 63]
- Significant non-cash revenues that were included in segment revenue and, therefore, included in the measurement of segment result. [IAS 14.62]

Segments reported in the immediately preceding period that no longer exceed the quantitative thresholds established in the Standard are not generally reported separately (but see **4.3.5** where such segments are of continuing significance). The Standard notes, however, that it may be helpful to financial statement users for an entity to explain the reasons why a previously-reported segment is no longer reported. To be useful, such an explanation would not simply state that the quantitative thresholds are no longer being breached, but would provide an explanation of the factors that contributed to the situation, such as a decline in demand or a change in management strategy or because a part of the operations of the segment has been sold or combined with other segments. [IAS 14.83]

Appendix 2 Business combinations (IFRS 3(2004))

1 Introduction

1.1 IFRS 3(2008) and IFRS 3(2004)

In January 2008, the IASB issued a revised version of IFRS 3 *Business Combinations* (see **chapter 34**), which is effective for business combinations for which the acquisition date is on or after the beginning of the first annual reporting period after 1 July 2009. For business combinations with earlier acquisition dates, entities may continue to apply the previous version of IFRS 3 (as issued in 2004), which is discussed in this appendix. Alternatively, subject to certain rules on transition, entities may choose to apply the revised version of IFRS 3 in advance of the 2009 effective date, provided that they disclose that fact.

At the same time as IFRS 3(2008), the IASB also issued a revised version of IAS 27 *Consolidated and Separate Financial Statements*. The changes to IAS 27 are discussed in **chapter 33**, but the most significant impacts are listed below.

UK

At the time of writing, the revised versions of IFRS 3 and IAS 27 have not yet been endorsed for use in the EU. Since the requirements of the revised Standards differ in important respects from those of the previous versions, EU reporting entities will not be able to apply the revised versions of IFRS 3 and IAS 27 in their statutory financial statements until the revised Standards are endorsed.

Some key drivers behind the changes to IFRS 3 and IAS 27 are:

- a greater emphasis on the use of fair value, potentially increasing the judgement and subjectivity around business combination accounting and requiring greater input by valuation experts;

- a focus on change in control as a significant economic event – introducing requirements to re-measure interests to fair value at the time control is achieved or lost, and recognising the impact of all transactions between controlling and non-controlling shareholders, not involving a loss of control, directly in equity; and

- a focus on what is given to the vendor as consideration, rather than what is spent to achieve the acquisition. Transaction costs, changes in the value of contingent consideration, settlement of pre-existing contracts, share-based payments and similar items will generally be accounted for separately from the business combination and affect profit or loss.

An overview of the most significant impacts for IFRS reporters of adopting IFRS 3(2008) and IAS 27(2008) is set out below.

- Costs incurred to effect a business combination (e.g. finder's fees, advisory, legal, accounting, valuation, and other professional or consulting fees) are expensed in the period incurred. (Costs incurred to issue debt or equity securities continue to be recognised in accordance with IAS 39 *Financial Instruments: Recognition and Measurement*.)

- Where the acquirer has a pre-existing equity interest in the entity acquired, it remeasures that previously-held interest to fair value as at the date of obtaining control, and recognises any resulting gain or loss in profit or loss.

- The term 'non-controlling interest' (NCI) replaces minority interest. At an acquisition date, the acquirer may choose, on a transaction by transaction basis, whether to measure NCI at:

  - fair value; or

  - the NCI's proportionate share of the net identifiable assets of the entity acquired.

  In order to measure NCI at fair value it may be possible to use market prices for the equity shares not held by the acquirer. When a market price is not available, because the shares are not publicly traded, an alternative valuation technique will need to be used to measure the NCI's fair value.

- Goodwill is measured at the acquisition date as the difference between:

- the aggregate of:
  - o the acquisition-date fair value of the consideration transferred;
  - o the amount of any non-controlling interests (NCI) in the entity acquired; and
  - o the acquisition-date fair value of any previously-held equity interest in the entity acquired (in a business combination achieved in stages); and
- the net of the acquisition-date fair value of the identifiable assets acquired and the liabilities assumed.

Accordingly, where an acquirer chooses to measure NCI at fair value at the acquisition date, the goodwill reported will typically be higher, reflecting goodwill attributable to the NCI.

- Once control is obtained, all subsequent increases and decreases in ownership interests that do not involve the loss of that control are treated as transactions among equity holders. Goodwill is not remeasured or adjusted. Instead, any difference between the change in the NCI and the fair value of the consideration paid or received is recognised directly in equity and attributed to the owners of the parent.

- Consideration for an acquisition, including contingent consideration, is measured at fair value at the acquisition date. Changes resulting from events after the acquisition date, such as the acquiree meeting an earnings target or reaching a specified share price, are recognised in profit or loss.

- The revised IAS 27 requires an entity to attribute their share of profit or loss to the NCI even if this results in the NCI having a deficit balance.

- When a parent ceases to have control of a subsidiary, the parent derecognises all assets, liabilities and NCI at their carrying amount. Any interest retained in the former subsidiary is recognised at its fair value at the date control is lost. Any gain or loss arising on loss of control is recognised in profit or loss. Note that a parent can lose control of a subsidiary through a sale or distribution, or through some other transaction or event in which it takes no part (e.g.

expropriation or the subsidiary being placed in administration or bankruptcy). If the loss of control of a former subsidiary involves the distribution of equity interests to owners of the parent acting in their capacity as owners, that distribution is recognised at the date control is lost.

- Other important changes include the following:

  - The scope of the revised IFRS 3 has been widened to include business combinations between mutual entities and business combinations achieved by contract alone.

  - The revised IFRS 3 includes specific guidance on whether replacement share based payment awards are part of the consideration transferred, and measurement of reacquired rights on initial recognition.

  - The revised Standard clarifies that an entity needs to reassess the classification of contractual arrangements on acquisition with the exception of insurance contracts and leases (for which the original classification as finance or operating stands). This is particularly relevant when looking at financial instruments, embedded derivatives and hedging relationships.

1.2 IFRS 3 *Business Combinations* (2004)

This appendix discusses the requirements of IFRS 3(2004) in the following sections:

Section 2	Scope
Section 3	Method of accounting
Section 4	Application of the acquisition method – identifying the acquirer
Section 5	Application of the acquisition method – measuring the cost of a business combination
Section 6	Application of the acquisition method – allocating the cost of a business combination to the net assets acquired
Section 7	Initial accounting determined provisionally
Section 8	Disclosure

This appendix includes consideration of issues in IAS 38 *Intangibles Assets* and IAS 36 *Impairment of Assets* (see **section 6**) which are specific to IFRS 3. More detailed guidance on these Standards is included in **chapter 8** and **chapter 9** respectively.

The term 'acquisition method' is used in this appendix. Although the term 'purchase method' is used in IFRS 3(2004), IASB reverted to 'acquisition method' in subsequent literature.

UK

Prior to the adoption of IFRS 3(2008), the most significant differences between IFRSs and UK GAAP in respect of business combinations are that, under IFRSs:

- *merger accounting is not permitted for business combinations which are not group reorganisations;*
- *there may be identification and recognition of more acquired intangible assets, and consequent reduction in the residual balance of goodwill; and*
- *there is no amortisation of goodwill.*

2 Scope

IFRS 3 applies to 'business combinations' [IFRS 3(2004).2], which are defined in IFRS 3 Appendix A, and explained in **2.1** below. IFRS 3(2004) does not apply in four cases, which are:

[IFRS 3(2004).3]

- business combinations which result in a joint venture (see **2.5** below);
- common control transactions (see **2.4** below);
- business combinations involving mutual entities (see **2.2** below); and
- business combinations achieved through a contract alone, such as a dual-listed structure, rather than by a purchase or exchange of equity (see **2.3** below).

2.1 Definition of a business combination

2.1.1 IFRS 3 definitions

A business combination is defined as:

[IFRS 3(2004)(Appendix A)]

> 'The bringing together of separate entities or businesses into one reporting entity.'

A business is then defined as:

[IFRS 3(2004)(Appendix A)]

> 'An integrated set of activities and assets conducted and managed for the purpose of providing:
>
> (a) a return to investors; or
>
> (b) lower costs or other economic benefits directly and proportionately to policyholders or participants.
>
> A business generally consists of inputs, processes applied to those inputs, and resulting outputs that are, or will be, used to generate revenues. If goodwill is present in a transferred set of activities and assets, the transferred set shall be presumed to be a business.'

2.1.2 *In-substance business combinations*

The IASB has indicated its desire to include transactions or events that are, in substance, business combinations regardless of their form which may reflect legal or taxation considerations. [IFRS 3(2004).5] Therefore, a business combination could include:

- the purchase by an entity of another entity's equity, where IFRS 3 is applied in consolidated financial statements;
- the purchase of some or all of another entity's net assets, or the assumption of its liabilities, where IFRS 3 is applied in the acquiring entity's financial statements;
- a transaction between shareholders, between entities, or between an entity and shareholders of another entity; and
- the creation of a new controlling entity or the restructuring of an existing entity whereby, for example, control changes by virtue of a buy-back of shares with some, but not all, shareholders.

2.1.3 *Presence of goodwill*

A distinguishing feature of a business which is apparent from the above definition is the presence of goodwill, that is, the possibility that the fair value of the acquired trade may be different from the sum of the fair values of the underlying net assets. The definition of goodwill in IFRS 3 is 'future economic benefits arising from assets that are not capable of being individually identified and separately recognised.' [IFRS 3(2004).A]

The presence of customers generating a separate revenue stream is an indicator that goodwill, and hence a business, exists. However, the presence of a workforce is not, of itself, a clear indicator of a business.

Where it is determined that an acquired group of assets or net assets does not constitute a business, then the entire purchase cost is allocated to identified assets and liabilities in proportion to their relative fair values at acquisition. [IFRS 3(2004).4]

2.1.4 *Identified assets as a balancing figure*

In certain industries, such as the extractive industries or regulated industries, it was common accepted practice to attribute any residual balance of consideration to, for example, mineral reserves or a licence such that goodwill was never recognised. Where such practice represents the reduction of an uncertain estimate of fair value, in order to avoid negative goodwill, it may continue to be acceptable (and indeed may be required by IFRS 3(2004).56). However, in other cases where goodwill is likely to be positive, it is unlikely to be an acceptable practice since IFRS 3 presumes fair value of identified assets is determinable. This is considered further in **section 6** below.

Under UK GAAP, the reduction of fair value to avoid negative goodwill would, in accordance with FRS 19, exclude deferred tax from identified liabilities. Application of IAS 12 results in the recognition of deferred tax such that the balancing asset under IFRSs is higher than under UK GAAP. UK

2.1.5 *Outsourcing contracts*

Example 2.1.5

Outsourcing contracts

An outsourcing service provider signs a contract with a client that may comprise a service contract for a specified period for which the client will pay a fixed price per unit (of data delivered, data processed, and machine time used); the takeover of certain assets, liabilities, and employees of the client; and the payment of an up-front sum by the service provider to the client (see **example 5.2B** in **chapter 23**).

The contract may be structured as a combination of a straight-forward service contract together with an asset (or rather net asset) purchase by the service provider. Alternatively, the service provider, who has entered into a service contract with the client (seller), may purchase a legal structure that houses certain assets, liabilities, and employees of the client.

Does the transfer of assets, liabilities, and employees from a client to a service provider in the context of signing an outsourcing contract constitute a business combination under IFRS 3?

The assessment of whether the transfer of assets, liabilities, and employees from a client to a service provider (whether in the form of the purchase of a legal entity or a purchase of net assets), occurring simultaneously with the signing of an outsourcing contract, is a business combination depends on a careful analysis of the facts and circumstances.

If the service provider is not able to use the assets purchased for any purpose other than to provide services to the client (e.g. because the assets are too specific or there are contractual restrictions on their use), the transaction is unlikely to be a purchase of a business. The purchase of a business normally involves the ability to provide services (or goods) to several clients so that further revenues can be generated.

Accordingly, a careful analysis of the substance of the transaction must be performed. In particular, this analysis must take into consideration:

- whether the transaction is concluded with a view to enter a new market or service line or to improve the market share of the service provider in a market or service line; and
- whether the elements taken over comprise a portfolio of clients to service (other than the seller).

Furthermore, if it is possible to determine the value of the service contract separately, it is probably possible to determine whether an element of goodwill has been paid for. In accordance with IFRS 3(2004), when goodwill is present in a transferred set of activities and assets, the transferred set should be presumed to be a business. When there is no goodwill present, it is likely that there is a combination of an asset purchase, a service contract, and an up-front payment from the service provider to the client.

2.2 Mutual entities

A mutual entity is:

[IFRS 3(2004)(Appendix A)]

> 'An entity other than an investor-owned entity, such as a mutual insurance company or a mutual cooperative entity, that provides lower costs or other economic benefits directly and proportionately to its policyholders or participants.'

IFRS 3(2004) indicates that business combinations involving two or more mutual entities are outside the scope of the Standard.

Subsequent to the issue of IFRS 3, in April 2004, the IASB issued a further Exposure Draft which proposed an amendment to IFRS 3 to remove this scope exclusion and require application of the acquisition method using a 'modified' approach which limited goodwill arising. However, in June 2004, the Board decided not to proceed with this amendment. Instead, the Board decided to consider issues discussed by the United States' FASB, and bring forward new proposals as part of its business combinations phase 2 project. Nevertheless, the Board observed that it had previously tentatively decided in this project that the objective of accounting for a business combination is to determine and recognise the fair value of the business acquired. Also, in the basis of conclusions to IFRS 3(2004), the Board stated that no exception to its general rule, that the acquisition method provides superior information to the pooling of interests method, would be entertained. [IFRS 3(2004).BC54 – BC55]

The Board noted that one of the implications of this decision was that business combinations involving mutual entities could no longer be accounted for under IAS 22 (IFRS 3's predecessor) since that Standard had been superseded. Instead, entities would need to determine an appropriate accounting policy by applying the hierarchy of IAS 8 *Accounting Policies, Changes in Accounting Estimates and Errors*, and this may include looking to IFRS 3 for guidance.

Business combinations involving two or more mutual entities are within the scope of IFRS 3(2008), as discussed in **chapter 34**.

2.2.1 *Not-for-profit sector entities*

UK

Certain types of entity in the UK, especially those in the not-for-profit sector, do not have shareholder investors, and it has, therefore, not been possible to apply the criteria for merger accounting. In such cases, it has been common practice in the UK to apply merger accounting criteria 'in substance' to test whether an acquirer can be identified. For example, it has been argued that in a combination of two housing associations, where protected tenants continue to enjoy benefits as before the combination, no acquirer can be identified and hence merger accounting may be used.

Under IFRSs, such combinations would appear to be comparable to a combination of mutual entities, and the acquisition method would be required. In the case of a combination of two housing associations, the acquiree entity would be fair valued.

2.3 Combinations achieved by contract (dual-listed entities)

The most common example of a contractual combination is where separate entities are brought together to form a dual listed corporation.

The combining entities, or groups, remain legally separate, but agree to operate as a combined group and share in combined results through an equalisation agreement. The agreement provides for common control of the combined businesses, and an equalisation payment such that shareholders receive dividends in an agreed ratio.

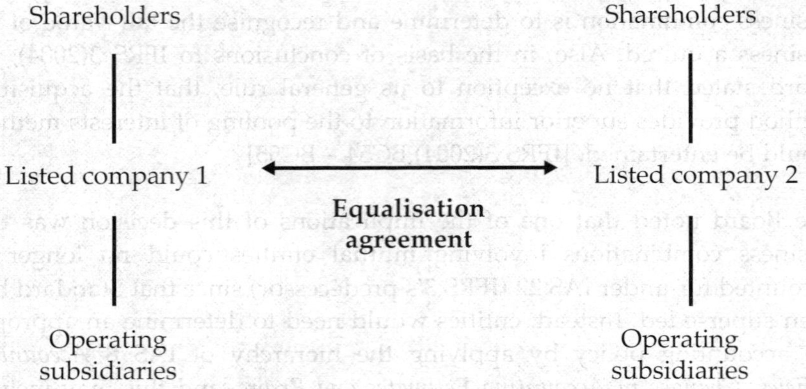

Examples of dual listed corporations are Rio Tinto, Brambles Industries and BHP Billiton.

Extract from BHP Billiton website:

> 'Our Structure
>
> BHP Billiton is a Dual Listed Company (DLC) comprising BHP Billiton Limited and BHP Billiton Plc. The two entities continue to exist as separate companies, but operate as a combined group known as BHP Billiton.
>
> BHP Billiton was created through the DLC merger of BHP Limited (now BHP Billiton Limited) and Billiton Plc (now BHP Billiton Plc), which was concluded on 29 June 2001.
>
> The headquarters of BHP Billiton Limited, and the global headquarters of the combined BHP Billiton Group, are located in Melbourne, Australia. BHP Billiton Plc is located in London, United Kingdom. Both companies have identical boards of directors and are run by a unified management team. Shareholders in each company have equivalent economic and voting rights in the BHP Billiton Group as a whole.
>
> The DLC structure maintains pre-existing primary listings on the Australian Stock Exchange (through BHP Billiton Limited) and

> London Stock Exchange (through BHP Billiton Plc), along with a secondary listing on the Johannesburg Stock Exchange (through BHP Billiton Plc) and American Depositary Receipts listings on the New York Stock Exchange.'

Business combinations involving two or more mutual entities are outside the scope of IFRS 3(2004). The further discussion of business combinations of mutual entities (see above) also applies to business combinations achieved by contract.

Business combinations achieved by contract are within the scope of IFRS 3(2008), as discussed in **chapter 34**.

2.4 Exclusion for common control transactions

IFRS 3 excludes from its scope a business combination involving entities or businesses under common control. [IFRS 3(2004).3(b)] This is defined as:

[IFRS 3(2004)(Appendix A)]

> 'A business combination in which all of the combining entities or businesses ultimately are controlled by the same party or parties both before and after the combination, and that control is not transitory.'

The exclusion from the scope of IFRS 3 of common control transactions has wide effect since it only requires the combining entities to be under control from the same source before and after the transaction. It does not require the relative interests and rights of the controlling parties to be the same before and after the combination.

The exclusion would, therefore, apply to:

- group reorganisations where subsidiaries or businesses are transferred within a group having the same parent, regardless of whether the interest of any minority interest is changed by the combination; [IFRS 3(2004).13] and
- combinations of entities owned by the same individual, or group of individuals acting together under a contractual arrangement, regardless of whether the controlling parties are subject to any financial reporting requirements or the combining entities are included within the same consolidated financial statements. [IFRS 3(2004).12]

The requirement that 'control is not transitory' is intended to prevent the use of the common control scope exclusion when business combinations between parties acting at arm's length are structured through the use of 'grooming' transactions so that, for a brief period immediately before the combination, the combining entities or businesses are under common control. In this way, it might be possible for combinations that would otherwise be accounted for in accordance with the IFRS using the acquisition method to be accounted for using some other method. [IFRS 3(2004).BC28]

UK

The common control scope exclusion of IFRS 3 is wider than a group reorganisation described in FRS 6. For a group reorganisation to be dealt with under the merger basis of accounting, FRS 6 requires that the ultimate shareholders, and their relative rights, remain the same before and after the combination. This would preclude any change to the rights attaching to a minority shareholding.

2.4.1 *Use of newly formed entities to restructure part of an entity before sale*

A new entity may be formed by a parent to issue equity instruments to acquire one or more subsidiaries that are part of the parent's existing group. A reorganisation involving the formation of such a new entity to facilitate the sale of part of an organisation is not a business combination within the scope of IFRS 3. This is because the combining entities that existed before the combination were entities under common control that was not transitory.

Under IFRS 3(2004).22, when an entity is formed to issue equity instruments to effect a business combination, one of the combining entities that existed before the combination is identified as the acquirer on the basis of the evidence available. To be consistent with the principle in IFRS 3(2004).22, the test of whether the entities or businesses are under common control should be applied to the combining entities that existed before the combination, excluding the newly formed entity. Therefore, where an existing parent forms a new entity to undertake a pre-sale restructuring, the transaction is excluded from the scope of IFRS 3 as a 'business combination involving entities or businesses under common control'.

This was confirmed by an IFRIC agenda rejection published in the March 2006 *IFRIC Update*.

2.4.2 *Required accounting for common control transactions*

IFRS 3 excludes from its scope business combinations involving entities or businesses under common control. In the absence of any specific IASB literature, IAS 8.10 requires management to use its judgement in developing and applying an accounting policy that results in information that is relevant and reliable. IAS 8.10 & 11 provide additional guidance, including (in descending order) IFRSs on similar issues, IASB Framework, pronouncements of other standard setters with a similar conceptual framework, and accepted industry practices. Where acquisition accounting is adopted, IFRS 3 provides relevant guidance.

Where no acquirer is identified, common features of accounting approaches to common control transactions are:

- recording of assets and liabilities at previous carrying amounts;
- recognition of the difference between purchase consideration and net assets transferred as an adjustment to equity; and
- in consolidated financial statements, the restatement of comparative figures to a combined basis.

Since there is no IFRS dealing with this topic, care should be taken to provide a detailed description of the accounting policy used.

2.5 Exclusion for businesses contributed to a joint venture

IFRS 3 excludes from its scope 'business combinations in which separate entities or businesses are brought together to form a joint venture.' [IFRS 3(2004).3(a)]

The definition of joint venture is consistent with IAS 31 *Interests in Joint Ventures* and guidance is contained in that Standard, and in SIC-13 *Jointly Controlled Entities – Non-monetary Contributions by Venturers*. Guidance is included in **chapter 36**.

2.6 Deemed acquisitions

IFRS 3 includes within its scope business combinations where one entity obtains control over another without an exchange transaction. [IFRS 3(2004).8] This could occur when:

- an entity buys-back shares from some investors such that control passes to a remaining shareholder;

- an entity issues shares to existing shareholders (a rights issue) but some shareholders do not take up their entitlement such that control passes to a shareholder that does take up its entitlement.

In such cases, the interest of the new parent entity in the net assets of its new subsidiary will have changed. The requirements of IFRS 3 in respect of business combinations achieved in stages will be relevant (see **section 6.8** below).[IFRS 3(2004).58 – 60)]

3 Method of accounting

IFRS 3 requires all business combinations falling within its scope to be accounted for by applying the acquisition method. [IFRS 3(2004).14)] It will not be acceptable to use either the pooling of interests method, or any other version of the acquisition method other than that set out in IFRS 3.

IFRS 3 deals with the application of the acquisition method in three stages:

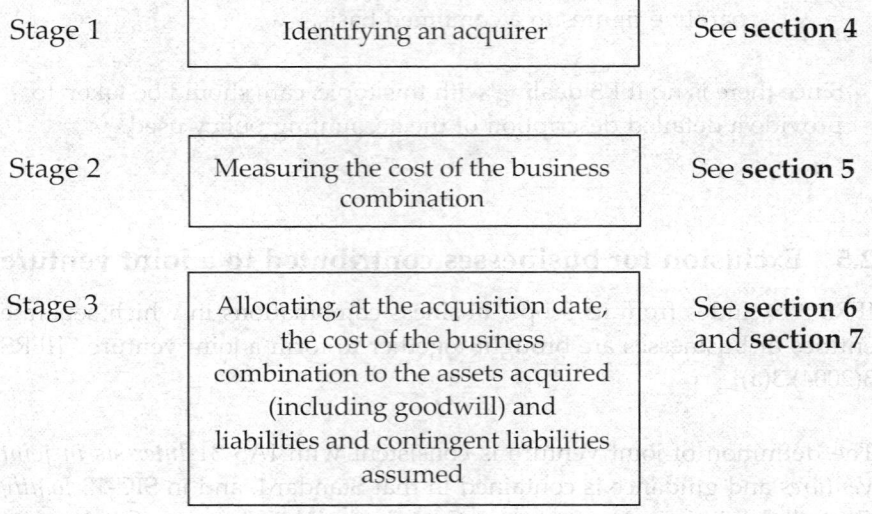

Stage 1	Identifying an acquirer	See **section 4**
Stage 2	Measuring the cost of the business combination	See **section 5**
Stage 3	Allocating, at the acquisition date, the cost of the business combination to the assets acquired (including goodwill) and liabilities and contingent liabilities assumed	See **section 6** and **section 7**

3.1 Business combinations in which one entity obtains control

The acquisition method faithfully represents the underlying economics of business combinations in which one entity obtains control of another entity or business, and which is presumed to result from an exchange transaction negotiated at arm's length between independent parties. [IFRS 3(2004).BC44] The acquisition method views the combination as a purchase by the acquirer, that is, the entity obtaining control. The acquirer allocates purchase consideration, in whatever form it takes, to the acquired assets, liabilities and contingent liabilities based on their fair values including those that may not have been recognised by the acquiree. [IFRS 3(2004).15] The resulting net assets of the acquiree recognised by the acquirer are described as being 'at cost' to the acquirer. Assets and liabilities of the acquirer which are not the subject of the purchase are not affected.

The acquisition method deals only with the financial statements of the acquirer. It does not impact the financial statements of the acquiree.

Where an acquiree wishes to restate its net assets to amounts recognised by an acquirer on acquisition, it will be necessary to follow other Standards to determine whether such remeasurement is possible and, if so, the consequent accounting entries. This process is termed 'push-down accounting' in some countries. Restrictions on remeasurement in a number of IFRSs mean that, generally, full 'push-down accounting' is unlikely to be possible.

3.2 Business combinations in which none of the combining entities obtains control

The Board recognises that 'true mergers' or 'mergers of equals', where none of the combining entities obtains control, may exist. It concluded that there were no satisfactory criteria which would distinguish a true merger from an acquisition and, in any event, would not accept the pooling of interests method as appropriate in the event that such criteria could be developed. [IFRS 3(2004).BC48]

Therefore, the Board has stated that, while there may be some rare circumstances where it will be difficult to identify an acquirer, it will not permit any exceptions to the use of the acquisition method to business combinations falling within the scope of IFRS 3. [IFRS 3(2004).BC55]

4 Application of the acquisition method – identifying the acquirer

IFRS 3 requires an acquirer to be identified for all business combinations falling within its scope. The acquirer is the combining entity that obtains control of the other combining entities or businesses. [IFRS 3(2004).17]

4.1 Meaning of control

The definition of control, and added guidance, in IFRS 3 is consistent with IAS 27 *Consolidated and Separate Financial Statements* – see **chapter 33**. Thus, control is defined as:

[IFRS 3(2004)(Appendix A)]

> 'The power to govern the financial and operating policies of an entity or business so as to obtain benefits from its activities'

A combining entity is presumed to have control when it acquires more than one-half of another entity's voting rights, unless it can be demonstrated that such ownership does not constitute control. Other indicators of control are:

[IFRS 3(2004).19]

- power over a majority of voting rights through a shareholder agreement;
- power to govern the financial and operating policies under statute or an agreement;
- power to appoint or remove the majority of the members of the board of directors or equivalent governing body; or
- power to cast the majority of votes at meetings of the board of directors or equivalent governing body.

Consideration should also be given to the guidance on control in SIC-12 *Consolidation – Special Purpose Entities* which includes:

[SIC-12.10]

- the activities of the acquiree are conducted on behalf of the entity according to its specific business needs so that the entity obtains benefits from the acquiree's operations;
- the entity has the decision-making powers to obtain the majority of benefits or has delegated those powers through an 'autopilot' mechanism;
- the entity has rights to obtain the majority of benefits and, therefore, may be exposed to risks from the acquiree's activities; or
- the entity retains the majority of residual or ownership risks related to the acquiree or its assets in order to obtain benefits from its activities.

The definition and guidance on control is intended to identify whether one entity has sole control over one or more other entities. Where two entities have joint control, that is they are able to exercise control by cooperating but neither can exercise control without the agreement of the other, then the arrangement will not fall within the scope of either IAS 27 or IFRS 3, but will fall within the scope of IAS 31 *Interests in Joint Ventures*.

4.2 Indicators of an acquirer

IFRS 3 includes three indicators of an acquirer:

[IFRS 3(2004).20]

- the fair value of one combining entity (the acquirer) is significantly greater than the other;
- where consideration for voting ordinary shares includes cash or other assets, the entity paying cash or other assets is likely to be the acquirer; and
- the management of one entity (the acquirer) is able to dominate the selection of the management team of the combined entity.

In addition, where a combination involves two or more existing entities, consideration should be given to:

[IFRS 3(2004).23]

- which entity initiated the combination; and
- whether the assets or revenues of one entity significantly exceed those of the others.

4.3 New entity

Where a new entity is formed to effect a business combination between two or more existing entities, one of the combining entities that existed before the combination shall be identified as the acquirer. [IFRS 3(2004).22] It follows that the new entity cannot be the acquirer, and therefore cannot apply the acquisition method to each of the combining entities. [IFRS 3(2004).BC66]

Example 4.3

New entity formed to effect business combination

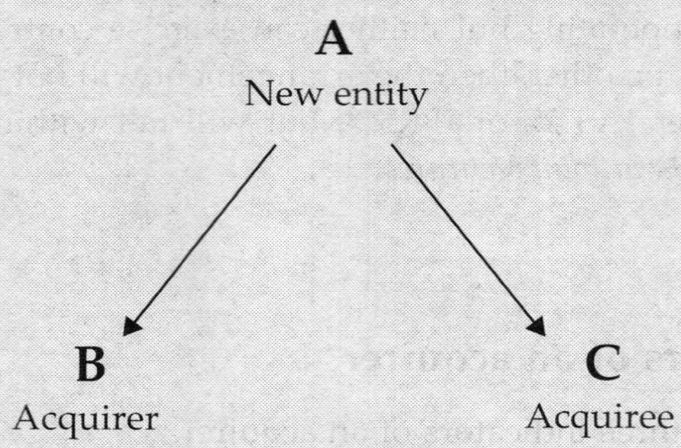

B and C are existing entities. B effects a business combination with C by creating a new entity, A, which issued shares to the existing shareholders of both B and C. Applying the principles of IFRS 3, B is identified as the acquirer, and C is identified as the acquiree.

Since A is a new entity without substance, IFRS 3 prohibits A from applying the acquisition method to both B and C. Instead, the consolidated financial statements of A will be prepared on the following basis:

- share capital will be that of A;
- the remainder of B's statement of financial position will be aggregated at existing carrying amounts;
- any difference between A and B's share capital will be adjusted against shareholders' funds;
- the historical record will be that of B; and
- C will be included under the acquisition method.

The method of combining A and B together may be described as an application of reverse acquisition accounting. However, since A is a shell, the effect in this case is the same as that achieved under the pooling of interests method.

4.4 Reverse acquisition

Application of IFRS 3 may lead to the conclusion that an entity whose shares have been acquired (legally the subsidiary) is the acquirer, and the entity issuing shares (legally the parent) is the acquiree. This is termed a reverse acquisition. This may occur, for example, when a private entity arranges to have itself 'acquired' by a smaller public entity in order to obtain a stock exchange listing.

IFRS 3 does not provide detailed guidance as to when a combination is a reverse acquisition. It is suggested that the two primary factors which may lead to a reverse acquisition conclusion are:

- the former shareholders of the entity whose shares are acquired own the majority of shares, and control the majority of votes, in the combined entity; and
- the management of the combined entity is drawn predominantly from the entity whose shares are acquired.

UK

IFRS 3 leads to the conclusion that a reverse acquisition occurs where the previous owners of the legal subsidiary have control through a simple majority interest in shares carrying votes. This differs from the view generally applied in the UK in the past which assumed that the legal parent had little or no business of its own, or its business was discontinued, and hence it was very clear that the legal subsidiary was the acquirer.

4.4.1 *Accounting for a reverse acquisition*

IFRS 3 Appendix B contains detailed guidance on the preparation of financial statements for a reverse acquisition. For understanding, this guidance is set out below as a comparison with a conventional acquisition. The terminology used for a reverse acquisition is that the acquirer is the legal subsidiary, and the acquiree is the legal parent.

	Conventional acquisition	**Reverse acquisition [IFRS 3(2004).B1-B15]**
Consolidated financial statements issued	In the name of the legal parent.	In the name of the legal parent (with disclosure in the notes as a continuation of the legal subsidiary).

	Conventional acquisition	Reverse acquisition [IFRS 3(2004).B1-B15]
Cost of combination	Fair value of consideration given by legal parent. Fair value of equity instruments may be estimated by reference to fair value of the acquirer or acquiree, whichever is more clearly evident.	Fair value of the notional number of equity instruments which would have been issued by the legal subsidiary to the legal parent to provide the resulting percentage ownership in the combined entity. If the fair value of the legal subsidiary's equity instruments is not clearly evident, then the cost of combination may be estimated from the pre-combination fair value of all the issued equity of the legal parent.
Net assets of legal parent (NALP)	Not restated from pre-combination carrying amounts.	Restated to fair value in the consolidated financial statements.
Net assets of legal subsidiary (NALS)	Restated to fair value in the consolidated financial statements.	Not restated from pre-combination carrying amounts.
Goodwill / 'negative goodwill'	Cost of combination less NALS at fair value.	Cost of combination less NALP at fair value.
Consolidated issued equity instruments.	Actual issued equity instruments of legal parent.	Issued equity of the legal subsidiary pre-combination plus the cost of combination. However, the actual equity structure of the legal parent shall be shown. An adjustment will be required for the difference between legal parent and legal subsidiary issued equity.

	Conventional acquisition	Reverse acquisition [IFRS 3(2004).B1-B15]
Consolidated retained earnings at date of combination.	Legal parent only.	Legal subsidiary only.
Minority interests in legal subsidiary	Minority share of legal subsidiary net assets at fair value.	Minority share of legal subsidiary net assets at pre-combination carrying amounts.
Comparative information	Legal parent only.	Legal subsidiary only.
Earnings per share	Earnings based on consolidated earnings. Weighted average number of shares reflects actual shares issued for legal subsidiary from date of acquisition.	Earnings based on consolidated earnings. Weighted average number of shares reflects actual shares issued by the legal parent for legal subsidiary to the date of combination, and total actual shares of the legal parent in issue after the date of acquisition.
Separate financial statements of legal parent.	Legal parent.	Legal parent.

4.4.2 *Worked example of a reverse acquisition*

Example 4.4.2

Reverse acquisition

The statements of financial position of A and B are summarised as follows:

	A	B
	£	£
Share capital – £1 shares	100	300
Retained earnings	200	500
Net assets at carrying amount	300	800
Net assets at fair value	500	2,000
Fair value of whole business	5,000	25,000

On the date that the statements of financial position were drawn up, A issued 500 new shares in exchange for the entire share capital of B.

On a normal acquisition basis:

A would be deemed the acquirer.

Cost of the combination is £25,000.

B's net assets are stated to fair value of £2,000. A's net assets remain at pre-combination amount of £300.

Goodwill is £23,000 being the cost of combination of £25,000 less the fair value of B's net assets of £2,000.

Retained earnings at the date of combination are those of A being £200.

The consolidated statement of financial position would be determined as follows:

	A	B	Adjustments	Consolidated
	£	£	£	£
Investment in B	+25,000	–	-25,000	–
Goodwill	–	–	+23,000	+23,000
Other net assets	+300	+800	+1,200	+2,300
Share capital	-600	-300	+300	-600
Other reserve	-24,500	–	–	-24,500
Retained earnings	-200	-500	+500	-200
	0	0	0	0

On a reverse acquisition basis:

B would be deemed the acquirer.

The cost of the combination would be £5,000. This equals the fair value of 60 new shares in B, being the notional number that B would issue to give the shareholders of A 1/6th of the combined entity.

A's net assets are stated to fair value of £500. B's net assets remain at pre-combination amount of £800.

Goodwill is £4,500 being the cost of the combination of £5,000 less the fair value of A's net assets of £500.

Retained earnings at the date of combination are those of B being £500.

The consolidated statement of financial position would be determined as follows:

	A	B	Adjustments	Consolidated
	£	£	£	£
Investment in B	+25,000	–	-25,000	–
Goodwill	–	–	+4,500	+4,500

	A	B	Adjust-ments	Consoli-dated
	£	£	£	£
Other net assets	+300	+800	+200	+1,300
Share capital (see note * below)	-600	-300	+300	-600
Other reserve (see note * below)	-24,500	–	+19,800	-4,700
Retained earnings	-200	-500	+200	-500
	0	0	0	0

Note * Following the requirement of IFRS 3(2004).B7, the amount recognised as issued equity instruments of £5,300, being the aggregate of share capital and other reserve, equals the pre-combination issued share capital of B plus the cost of the combination. In the table above, this is allocated between share capital and other reserve so that the disclosed share capital equals that of the legal parent, A.

Earnings per share would be based on the consolidated earnings (pre-combination earnings of B, and post-combination earnings of A + B). The weighted average number of shares would be based on 500 shares pre-combination (being the number of shares in A issued to shareholders of B) and 600 shares post-combination. [IFRS 3(2004).B13]

Goodwill arising would be subject to impairment testing under IAS 36 *Impairment of Assets*. Where the legal parent has little or no business of its own, or that business is discontinued following the reverse acquisition, any goodwill on the acquisition of A is likely to be impaired.

5 Application of the acquisition method – measuring the cost of a business combination

IFRS 3(2004) requires the acquirer to measure the cost of a business combination as the aggregate of:

[IFRS 3(2004).24]

- the fair values, at the date of exchange, of assets given, liabilities incurred or assumed, and equity instruments issued by the acquirer, in exchange for control of the acquiree; plus
- any costs directly attributable to the business combination.

The reference in the definition to 'in exchange for control' indicates that this requirement for measurement of cost is set in the context of an entity becoming a subsidiary. Although many of the principles will be the same, it does not include:

- exchange transactions which result in an investment falling under IAS 28 *Investments in Associates* (see **chapter 35**), IAS 31 *Interests in Joint Ventures* (see **chapter 36**), or IAS 39 *Financial Instruments: Recognition and Measurement* (see **chapters 13** to **22**); or
- exchange transactions which increase the percentage interest in an entity which is already a subsidiary (see **6.8** below).

5.1 Acquisition date and date of exchange

The acquisition date is defined as:

[IFRS 3(2004)(Appendix A)]

> 'The date on which the acquirer effectively obtains control of the acquiree.'

The date of exchange is defined as:

[IFRS 3(2004)(Appendix A)]

> 'When a business combination is achieved in a single exchange transaction, the date of exchange is the acquisition date. When a business combination involves more than one exchange transaction, for example when it is achieved in stages by successive share purchases, the date of exchange is the date that each individual investment is recognised in the financial statements of the acquirer.'

5.1.1 Successive share purchases

As indicated above, when control is achieved through a single purchase, the date of acquisition and the date of exchange will be the same. However, when control is achieved in stages:

[IFRS 3(2004).25]

- the cost of the combination is the aggregate cost of the individual exchange transactions; and
- the date of acquisition is the date on which the acquirer obtains control; and
- there is more than one date of exchange, being the dates that each exchange was recognised by the acquirer.

Example 5.1.1

Successive share purchases

A acquired 25 per cent of the issued share capital of B in a market transaction on 1 April. 25,000 shares were purchased for £1 per share.

Subsequently on 1 July, A made an offer for the remaining 75,000 shares of B. Following unconditional acceptance on 1 September, A paid £1.20 in cash for each of the additional shares on 1 October.

The date of acquisition, being the date that control is achieved, is 1 September.

The dates of exchange, being the dates on which A recognises its investment, are 1 April and 1 September.

The cost of the combination is £115,000 being the aggregate cash paid on 1 April of £25,000 and on 1 October of £90,000.

5.1.2 *Further guidance on the date of exchange*

IFRS 3 does not contain detailed guidance on the determination of the date of acquisition and the date of exchange. The following guidance, based on UK accounting literature, would often represent best practice.

Public offer of shares

Where a public offer of shares is made, the date of exchange is the date when the offer becomes unconditional. This is usually the date that the number of acceptances passes a predetermined threshold. In the absence of such a threshold, it is the date the offer is declared unconditional.

Private treaty

For a private treaty, the date of exchange will be the date that an unconditional offer is accepted.

Other share transactions

Where purchase is by virtue of some other form of share transaction, e.g. new shares issued to minority shareholders or existing shares repurchased from a majority shareholder, the date of exchange will be the date of share issue or cancellation. For an issue of shares, this is generally the date that shares are allotted and, thus, qualify to be recorded as called up share capital in the issuer's statement of financial position.

Other scenarios

A number of indicators may be relevant, including:

(a) the date that the acquirer commences direction of operating and financial policies;

(b) the date from which the flow of economic benefits changes; or

(c) the date that consideration passes (although this is not conclusive, since it is capable of being adjusted either forwards or backwards or settled in instalments).

In practice, the date adopted should reflect all the various circumstances surrounding the transfer of control.

UK *The above guidance is based on FRS 2.85.*

5.1.3 *Use of contractual dates*

Application of the acquisition method starts from the acquisition date, which is the date on which the acquirer obtains control over the acquiree. Because control is the power to govern the financial and operating policies of an entity or business so as to obtain benefits from its activities, it is not necessary for a transaction to be closed or finalised at law before the acquirer obtains control. All pertinent facts and circumstances shall be considered in assessing when the acquirer has obtained control. [IFRS 3(2004).39]

The date of acquisition and the date of exchange will be a matter of fact. They cannot be artificially altered, for example, by indicating in the purchase agreement that control is deemed to exist from an earlier date, or that profits accrue to the purchaser from some earlier or later date. This latter feature may represent a mechanism to adjust the amount of purchase consideration.

5.2 Deferred consideration and use of present values

The cost of a business combination includes assets given and liabilities incurred or assumed. This will include both consideration given at the time of the business combination and an estimate of deferred consideration based on payments that are expected to be made.

5.2.1 *Measurement of deferred consideration*

IFRS 3 states that where settlement of all or part of the cost of a business combination is deferred, the fair value of that deferred component shall be determined by discounting the amounts payable to their present value at the date of exchange, taking into account any premium or discount likely to be incurred in settlement. [IFRS 3(2004).26]

IFRS 3 does not provide guidance on the appropriate discount rate to be used. It is suggested that, since the discount rate is applied to a liability for future payment, it would be appropriate to use that rate at which the acquirer would obtain a similar borrowing.

Unwinding of the discount is an expense, which would be classified as a financing expense. No adjustment should be made to goodwill for the unwinding of the discount.

5.2.2 *Classification of deferred consideration*

Deferred consideration is classified in accordance with IAS 32 *Financial Instruments: Presentation*. This results in:

- deferred consideration which is payable in cash or by the issue of debt instruments (or an obligation to deliver a variable number of equity shares to a fixed value) being disclosed as a liability; and
- deferred consideration which does not meet the definition of a liability (e.g. an obligation to deliver a fixed number of equity shares) being disclosed within shareholders' funds.

It is not clear where in the statement of financial position the liability should be shown, in particular whether it is classified as a provision under IAS 37, or as a creditor. IFRS literature is not prescriptive. A point to consider when deciding where to disclose the liability is whether, in situations where an estimate has been used to calculate the liability, it may give a misleading impression to users to include it within creditors. The key principle for determining classification is transparency.

Where either the acquirer or the acquiree's former shareholders have the option to receive shares or cash consideration, reference should be made to IAS 32 to classify the obligation as debt or equity (see **chapter 15**).

5.3 Measurement of equity instruments

IFRS 3 includes guidance on the measurement of equity instruments given as consideration in a business combination. [IFRS 3(2004).27] One general consideration is that all aspects of the combination, including significant factors influencing the negotiations, should be considered.

5.3.1 *Quoted equity instruments*

The published price at the date of exchange of a quoted equity instrument provides the best evidence of the instrument's fair value and shall be used, except in rare circumstances. Other evidence and valuation methods should be considered only in the rare circumstances when the acquirer can demonstrate that the published price at the date of exchange is an unreliable indicator of fair value, and that the other evidence and valuation methods provide a more reliable measure of the equity instrument's fair value. The published price at the date of exchange is an unreliable indicator only when it has been affected by the thinness of the market. If the published price at the date of exchange is an unreliable indicator or if a published price does not exist for equity instruments issued by the acquirer, the fair value of those instruments could, for example, be estimated by reference to their proportional interest in the fair value of the acquirer or by reference to the proportional interest in the fair value of the acquiree obtained, whichever is the more clearly evident. [IFRS 3(2004).27]

5.3.2 *Other equity instruments*

IFRS 3 does not include specific guidance, but directs preparers to guidance in IAS 39 *Financial Instruments: Recognition and Measurement* (see **chapters 13** to **22**).

5.3.3 *Cash alternatives*

The fair value at the date of exchange of monetary assets given to owners of the acquiree as an alternative to equity instruments may also provide evidence of the total fair value given by the acquirer in exchange for control of the acquiree. [IFRS 3(2004).27]

5.3.4 *Merger relief and group reconstruction relief*

UK

Merger relief and group reconstruction relief are reliefs offered by the Companies Act, in certain restricted circumstances discussed below, from recognising the full share premium that would otherwise have resulted on certain share issues. Despite their names, the reliefs are not restricted to situations in which merger accounting or group reconstruction accounting are adopted.

For companies reporting under UK GAAP, the Act offers a related option to record shares acquired at an amount less than the fair value of shares issued. As explained at **5.3.4.4**, *this option is not available to UK companies choosing to report under IFRSs.*

5.3.4.1 *Merger relief – CA 2006 section 612 (previously CA 1985 section 131)*

UK

Merger relief, or relief from recording a share premium, was originally written into company law as a foundation for merger accounting. However, the conditions of section 612 and 613 of the Companies Act 2006 (previously section 131 of the Companies Act 1985) mean that it applies in a wider set of circumstances.

The conditions for merger relief are:

[CA 2006 s612 & 613, previously CA 1985 s131]

- *equity shares are issued as part of an acquisition 'arrangement';*
- *in consideration, the issuer takes its interest in another body corporate from below 90 per cent equity holding to a 90 per cent or above equity holding (excluding any treasury shares held by that body corporate);*
- *for this purpose, holdings of the issuing company, its holding company, subsidiaries and fellow subsidiaries, and nominees of any of those entities, are aggregated;*
- *where the acquired body corporate has more than one class of equity shares, the 90 per cent condition must be met in respect of each separate class of equity share (i.e. must exceed 90 per cent on all classes to achieve merger relief on any); and*
- *the conditions for group reconstruction relief are not met (see* **5.3.4.2** *below).*

The implications of the relief are:

- *it applies to the entity that issues shares;*
- *it applies only to equity shares issued to acquire equity shares, including a part payment in equity shares; if company A acquires 100 per cent of the equity share capital of company B, paying £80,000 in cash and £20,000 in shares, being 1,000 shares of £1 nominal value each, the merger relief will apply to the issue of 1,000 shares provided all the conditions in section 612 and 613 of the Companies Act 2006 (previously section 131 of the Companies Act 1985) are met;*

- *where the arrangement includes the acquisition of non-equity shares in another body corporate, then merger relief extends to any shares issued, both equity and non-equity; [CA 2006 s612(3), previously CA 1985 s131(3)]*
- *where the conditions are met, the wording of section 612(2) of the Companies Act 2006 (previously section 131(2) of the Companies Act 1985) '. . . section 610 [130] does not apply to the premiums ...' means that the relief is mandatory; consequently any premium which is voluntarily recorded should not be classified as a share premium but as an 'other reserve' such as 'merger reserve';*
- *the term 'arrangement' is widely defined in section 616(1) of the Companies Act 2006 (previously section 131(7) of the Companies Act 1985) and would include an acquisition which is consummated through a series of stages (provided it can be demonstrated that there was an ultimate plan to acquire in excess of 90 per cent), a scheme of arrangement under Part 26 of the Companies Act 2006 (previously an arrangement under section 425 of the Companies Act 1985), and an arrangement with a liquidator;*
- *in a partial acquisition which is not part of an 'arrangement', the relief is available on the transaction which results in the holding passing the 90 per cent threshold. Thus, if company A acquired 15 per cent of company B 10 years ago and now acquires a further 80 per cent, the relief will be available on the acquisition of the 80 per cent.*

5.3.4.2 *Group reconstruction relief – CA 2006 section 611 (previously CA 1985 section 132)*

UK

Group reconstruction relief is founded on the presumption that assets will sometimes be transferred within a wholly-owned group at book value, that is avoiding the recognition of any unrealised gain or loss. Consequently, it does not totally exempt intragroup transactions from recording a share premium, but restricts the amount of share premium by reference to previous carrying value.

The conditions for group reconstruction relief are:

[CA 2006 s611, previously CA 1985 s132]

- *the issuing company is a wholly-owned subsidiary;*
- *the issuing company allots shares, equity or non-equity, to another member of the wholly-owned group (i.e. any holding company of*

which the issuer is a wholly-owned subsidiary, and any other wholly-owned subsidiaries of that holding company);

- *consideration for the issue is the transfer of non-cash assets from another member of the wholly-owned group.*

The issuing company is required to record share premium on the issue of shares equal to the 'minimum premium value'. This is calculated as:

	£
Lower of cost and carrying value of assets transferred	x
Less: Carrying value of liabilities transferred	(x)
Base value of consideration	x
Less: Nominal value of shares issued	(x)
Minimum premium value	x

The implications of the relief are:

- *share premium is not avoided, but is restricted to avoid unrealised gains or losses arising;*
- *where base value of consideration is less than the nominal value of shares issued, shares are recorded at nominal value to avoid an issue at a discount (N.B fair value must exceed nominal value to avoid an illegal issue at a discount);*
- *where the conditions are met, the wording of section 611(2) of the Companies Act 2006 (previously section 132(2) of the Companies Act 1985) '. . . is not required by section 610 [130]...' means that the relief is voluntary; consequently any premium in excess of the required minimum which is voluntarily recorded may either be classified as a share premium or alternatively as an 'other reserve'.*

5.3.4.3 *Deciding which relief applies*

UK

Merger relief is not available for any issue of shares that qualifies for group reconstruction relief. Therefore, in particular, merger relief is not available where the issuing company is a wholly-owned subsidiary and it acquires shares in a body corporate from another member of the wholly-owned group (i.e. any holding company of which the issuer is a wholly-owned subsidiary, and any other wholly-owned subsidiaries of that holding company).

Where a new intermediate holding company is being inserted within an existing group, it can be structured to achieve either merger relief or group reconstruction relief as follows:

- *merger relief is applicable where the issuing company is first formed, or an off-the-shelf company acquired, independently (for example, any arrangement that avoids a group company being the founder shareholder for a newly formed company or the shareholder in the off-the-shelf purchase) and, as a result of the share exchange, it becomes a subsidiary;*
- *group reconstruction relief is applicable where the issuing company is first formed, or an off-the-shelf company acquired, as a wholly-owned subsidiary, and then issues further shares in exchange for another body corporate.*

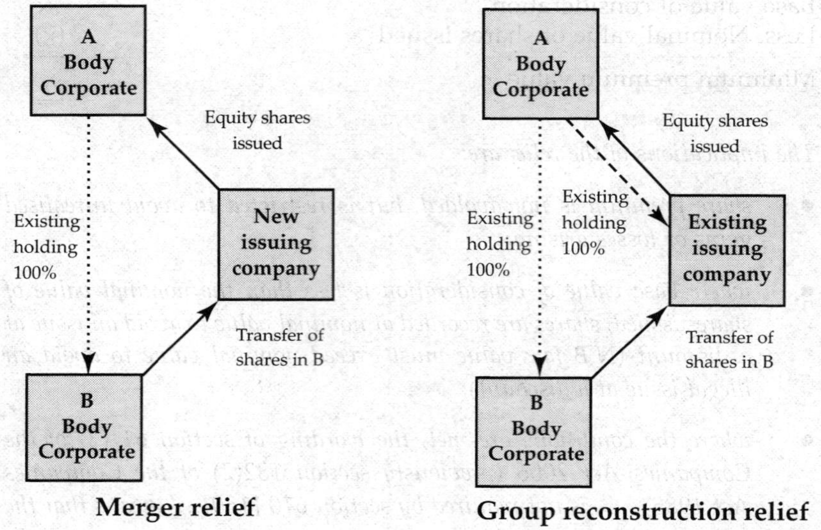

If the merger relief route is taken, the initial shares, say, two £1 shares, in the new issuing company could be owned by, say, the directors or lawyers of A. Once the new shares have been issued to A in exchange for the shares in B, the initial shares could be sold to A for their original cost or they could be purchased by Newco for cost and cancelled.

5.3.4.4 *Carrying value of investments – CA 2006 section 615 (previously CA 1985 section 133)*

UK

Where an interest in another body corporate is acquired by issuing shares, to the extent that relief from recording share premium is available (whether merger relief or group reconstruction relief), section 615 of the Companies Act 2006 (previously section 133(1) of the Companies Act 1985) allows an option to reduce the carrying value of the related investment by a similar amount. For example, if shares with a fair value of £1,000 are acquired through the issue of shares with an aggregate nominal value of £200, and merger relief applies, then this section allows the option of recording the cost of investment as £200 rather than £1,000.

However, this option is not available to UK companies that report under IFRSs, because it conflicts with the requirement in IAS 27 to record an investment in a subsidiary either at cost or at fair value. The IASB Glossary definition of 'cost' includes '... the fair value of the other consideration given'.

5.3.4.5 *Uses of a merger reserve*

UK

Once established, a merger reserve (group reconstruction reserve, capital reserve or whatever it is called) has an economic relationship with the related investment in the same way that a revaluation reserve is related to a revalued asset. The uses of a merger reserve should, therefore, be considered to be similar to those of a revaluation reserve under the Companies Act. This would suggest that the merger reserve can be used to:

(*a*) *make a bonus (or capitalisation) issue of fully paid shares, providing this is permitted by the company's articles;*

(*b*) *transfer to the profit and loss account reserve an amount equal to the amount that has become realised by virtue of either:*

  (*i*) *the disposal of the related investment; or*

  (*ii*) *an amount being written off the related investment and charged against the profit and loss account, for example, as the result of an impairment.*

5.4 Liabilities incurred or assumed

The cost of a business combination includes liabilities incurred or assumed by the acquirer in exchange for control of the acquiree. Future losses or other costs expected to be incurred as a result of a combination are not liabilities incurred or assumed by the acquirer in exchange for control of the acquiree, and are not, therefore, included as part of the cost of the combination. [IFRS 3(2004).28]

5.5 Acquisition costs

The cost of a business combination includes any costs which are directly attributable to the combination. [IFRS 3(2004).29]

5.5.1 *Included costs*

IFRS 3 specifically includes 'professional fees paid to accountants, legal advisers, valuers and other consultants'.

The principle supporting these costs is that they are both direct and incremental to the combination, that is, they would not have been incurred if the combination had not occurred. On this basis, it is suggested that the cost of a due diligence report prepared by an external party on the acquiree can be capitalised as part of the cost of the combination. This will be acceptable even where the report relates to a management buy-out (MBO) provided that a new entity is formed to hold the shares of the existing business. Similarly, travel and other direct costs incurred by the acquirer's own employees in connection with the acquisition could be capitalised, although the salary of those employees could not be capitalised (being a cost that would have been incurred had the acquisition not taken place). However, if the acquirer employed some temporary staff to carry out various investigations into the target acquiree, the cost of the staff could be capitalised if the acquisition goes ahead, being a direct cost incurred.

Example 5.5.1

Bonus payments related to a business combination

Bonus payments may be made to the acquirer's employees as a reward for completing a business combination. These payments may be conditional on completing a particular business combination, a number of unspecified business combinations in a particular period, or some other criteria. Such 'bonuses' may extend to the directors and other key management personnel of the acquirer to compensate them for due diligence services provided. Can bonus payments paid to the employees of an acquirer as a reward for completing a business combination be included in the cost of the business combination?

In general, bonus payments should be expensed as incurred. However, bonus payments can be included in the cost of a business combination to the extent that they are directly attributable to a specific business combination and are incremental. To be included in the cost of a business combination, the bonus scheme or plan must be established prior to the business combination being negotiated, and there must be a direct link between the bonus payment and the specific business combination. To be incremental, the bonus relating to the business combination would need to be an amount paid over and above any normal annual bonus payments.

Therefore:

- a bonus payment that is conditional on completing a particular combination with an identified acquirer, and paid in addition to the normal annual bonus, may be included in the cost of the combination, as it is directly attributable and incremental;
- a general bonus payment, even if conditional on completing a specified number of business combinations with unspecified entities, would not be included in the cost of a combination, as the payments are not directly attributable to a specific combination; and
- bonus payments that represent additional compensation for due diligence-type activities for a particular business combination would be capitalised into the cost of that combination, as they are directly attributable to the combination and are incremental. However, general due diligence costs that are incurred (e.g. assessing possible acquisition targets, etc.) would be expensed.

5.5.2 *Excluded costs*

IFRS 3 specifically excludes 'general administrative costs, including the costs of maintaining an acquisitions department, and other costs that cannot be directly attributed to the particular combination'. Such costs are recognised as an expense.

The principle preventing capitalisation of such costs is that they would have been incurred whether or not a specific business combination occurred. The exclusion would, therefore, extend to any allocation of management time. Post-combination reorganisation costs are not direct costs of the acquisition, and are expensed.

Costs of arranging and issuing financial liabilities are an integral part of the liability issue transaction rather than costs directly attributable to the combination. Therefore, they are not included in the cost of the business combination. In accordance with IAS 39, such costs are included in the initial measurement of the liability. [IFRS 3(2004).30]

Similarly, costs of issuing equity instruments are an integral part of the equity issue transaction rather than costs directly attributable to the combination. Therefore, they are not included in the cost of the business combination. In accordance with IAS 32, such costs reduce the proceeds from the equity issue. [IFRS 3(2004).31]

Costs such as arrangement fees for bridging finance, participation fees and costs of researching alternative financing arrangements for a takeover are not incremental costs incurred directly in making an acquisition and, therefore, should not be included as part of the cost of the acquisition, but should be expensed immediately.

UK

This latter guidance was issued in the UK by UITF in Information Sheet 35.

Example 5.5.2

Determining the costs of a business combination

Entity F acquires Entity G. The outflows of economic benefits from Entity F in respect of this transaction are as follows:

(a) Entity F issues 1,000,000 new shares to the shareholders of Entity G with terms equivalent to those traded on the market, and the market price of Entity F's shares is £4. The costs associated with the issue of the shares total £25,000.

(b) Entity F pays £1,000,000 in cash to the previous shareholders of Entity G.

(c) Entity F incurs liability of £500,000 to a customer of Entity G in respect of termination of a supply agreement that was necessitated by the business combination.

(d) Entity F pays accounting fees in relation to the transaction of £225,000 and legal fees of £200,000.

(e) Entity F extends the terms of its finance arrangements in order to obtain the cash required for the transaction. The cost of the extension is £50,000.

(f) Entity F has an acquisitions department, which incurred £200,000 in running costs over the period of completing the business combination. Staff in the department estimate they have spent 25 per cent of their time on the acquisition of Entity G over this period.

(g) Entity F will incur expenditure of £200,000 on updating Entity G's accounting systems to be consistent with those used by Entity F.

The following items would be included in the cost of acquisition:

	£
Equity instruments issued (a)	4,000,000
Cash (b)	1,000,000
Liability (c)	500,000
Accounting Fees (d)	225,000
Legal Fees (d)	200,000
Total cost of acquisition	5,925,000

Notes:

1. Equity issue costs of £25,000 are taken directly to equity, but do not reduce the value of instruments issued when determining the cost of acquisition.

2. The liability extension costs (item (e)) would be included in the measurement of the liability that Entity F takes out to finance the acquisition.
3. The £50,000 share of the acquisition department expenses (item (f)) and the future systems expenditure of £200,000 (item (g)) are expensed when incurred.

5.5.3 *Costs related to uncertain business combination*

Where a business combination is in process but is not complete, the question arises whether costs incurred can be deferred as part of the eventual cost of combination, or should be expensed on the basis that the combination is not certain to occur. The criteria for deferring costs will depend on whether the criteria for recognition as an asset are met. This will involve an assessment of the probability of the business combination being consummated. If an entity is in the initial stages of researching the viability of the transaction, or considering a number of alternatives, the probability criterion may not be met. If the entity has made a tentative decision to proceed with the business combination, has discontinued exploration of other alternatives and is in the final stages of due diligence type activities the probability criterion may be met. If the transaction is considered probable, directly attributable costs should be deferred until the outcome of the negotiations is certain. If a decision is made not to proceed, the costs should be expensed immediately following this decision.

5.5.4 *Hedging the cost of a business combination*

The following example should be read in conjunction with the more extensive guidance on hedge accounting set out in **chapter 20**.

Example 5.5.4

Foreign exchange hedging of a business combination

Company A (with Euro functional currency) enters into a firm commitment with Company C to acquire 100 per cent of Company B (with US dollar functional currency) for US$150 million in one month's time. (No contingent liabilities or intangible assets are being acquired. In the consolidated financial statements of A, B will be considered to be one cash-generating unit and A will perform an impairment test at this level.)

Concurrently, A enters into a USD/EUR foreign exchange option (premium equals US$20 million) with a third party to hedge the foreign exchange risk arising from the acquisition of B. This option has a one-month maturity and is only exercisable at maturity date. Company A wants to designate the foreign exchange option as a hedge of the foreign currency risk of the firm commitment to acquire 100 per cent of B. (All criteria required by IAS 39 for documenting a hedge relationship are met.) The hedging documentation contemplated is as follows:

- documented hedged risk is the foreign currency risk; and
- hedge effectiveness is assessed based on the intrinsic value of the option only.

In its accounting policies, A has chosen to apply a basis adjustment to cash flow hedge relationships of non financial assets in accordance with IAS 39.98(b). The fair value of the option, split between its intrinsic value and its time value, is as follows:

USD (in millions)	**Fair value**	**Intrinsic value**	**Time value**
At inception	20	0	20
At maturity date	22	22	0

The statement of financial position of Company B at the date of the acquisition is as follows:

USD (in millions)	**Carrying amount**	**Fair value**
Financial assets	80	90
Non-financial assets	50	50
Financial liabilities	60	60
Net assets	70	80

Is the foreign exchange derivative included in the scope of IAS 39 or IFRS 3?

The foreign exchange derivative is a financial instrument in the scope of IAS 39 which A has decided to enter into to hedge the foreign exchange risk on its firm commitment to acquire B at a fixed US dollar price in one-month's time. Consequently, the premium paid for the option cannot be included in the cost of the business combination. The option premium is not a directly attributable cost of the business combination but a cost incurred by A as a consequence of its hedging strategy.

Can the foreign exchange derivative be designated as a hedge of the foreign exchange risk arising from the firm commitment to acquire B?

The foreign exchange derivative can be designated in a fair value hedge of the foreign exchange risk arising from the firm commitment to acquire B. IAS 39.AG98 explicitly states that a firm commitment to acquire a business in a business combination can be a hedged item for foreign exchange risk.

If A chooses to apply cash flow hedge accounting, as allowed by IAS 39.87, assuming the hedge is 100 per cent effective, how is the hedging relationship accounted for before the date of acquisition? What is the treatment on and after the date of acquisition?

Prior to the date of acquisition, the changes in intrinsic value of the hedging derivative are recognised in a separate component of equity. Changes in fair value, resulting from changes in time value, are recognised directly in profit or loss as they are not designated as part of the hedging relationship in accordance with IAS 39.74.

On the date of acquisition, the changes in intrinsic value, recognised in a separate component of equity, are treated as a basis adjustment of the acquisition of a non-financial asset, i.e. a basis adjustment of the purchase price, and, therefore, of goodwill. Without basis adjustment, the amount of goodwill would be US$70 million, i.e. acquisition price of US$150 million less US$80 million, which is the fair value of the acquired net assets and liabilities.

With the basis adjustment, goodwill will amount to US$48 million, i.e. US$70 million less US$22 million, being the changes in intrinsic value of the option that have been recognised in the separate component of equity up to the date of acquisition.

Additionally, at year-end, if A performs an impairment test and determines that the recoverable amount of goodwill is less than US$48 million, then A must recognise an impairment loss on goodwill. (If the entity has a policy of not basis-adjusting non-financial items, US$22 million would remain in equity and would be partly/fully released to profit or loss in the instance when the recoverable amount of goodwill fell below US$48 million. The amount of impairment loss is not affected by the entity's accounting policy choice over whether to basis-adjust.)

A consequence of applying basis adjustment is that goodwill may be reduced or eliminated, or may result in negative goodwill being recognised immediately in profit or loss in accordance with IFRS 3(2004).56.

If A chooses to apply fair value hedge accounting as allowed by IAS 39.87, how is the hedge relationship accounted for, assuming the hedge is 100 per cent effective? In particular, how are the cumulative changes in fair value of the hedged firm commitment derecognised from the statement of financial position, i.e. how is the initial carrying amount of the hedged item adjusted?

Prior to the date of acquisition, the changes in intrinsic value of the hedging derivative are recognised in profit or loss and offset the changes in fair value of the hedged foreign currency risk of the firm commitment. Changes resulting from time value of the option are recognised directly in profit or loss, as they are not designated as part of the hedge relationship in accordance with IAS 39.74.

The firm commitment will be derecognised on the date of acquisition and recognised as part of the carrying amount of the goodwill, similar to the treatment above. The accounting policy of basis-adjusting non-financial items is irrelevant, as it applies to cash flow hedges only.

5.5.5 *Business acquired through exercise of a put option*

Example 5.5.5

Business acquired through exercise of a put option

Company A has written a put to Company C over 100 per cent of the ordinary share capital of Company B at a fixed price of €150 million that is exercisable only at the date of maturity. The put option is considered to be neither deeply in nor deeply out of the money at inception; thus, the exercise of the put will result in A gaining control over B. (Company A does not control Company B until the put is exercised. Company A holds neither shares nor presently exercisable potential voting rights.) Company A receives a premium from C of €10 million for the put.

Company C exercises the put. Company A acquires 100 per cent of the ordinary share capital of B and, in accordance with IFRS 3, applies the purchase accounting method. On the exercise date of the written put, the fair value of B's ordinary shares is €120 million and the fair value of the written put is a €30 million liability for A.

The written put option is within the scope of IAS 39. IAS 39.2(g) excludes from the scope of IAS 39 'contracts between an acquirer and a vendor in a business combination to buy or sell an acquiree at a future date'. However, at the date when A enters into the derivative contract, it is not possible to conclude a business combination will occur since the derivative is a written option that is not deeply in the money at inception. The written put option is accounted for under IAS 39 as a derivative liability with changes in fair value recognised through profit or loss until exercise or maturity of the option.

At the date of initial recognition of the written put option, A records the following entries:

Journal entry	Debit	Credit
Cash	€ 10	
Written put liability		€ 10

At acquisition date, the gains/losses due to changes in fair value of the written put recognised previously through profit or loss are not reversed. When the put is exercised by C, the payment of the purchase price by A is treated as settlement of the written put liability of €30 million and acquisition of B at a cost equal to the fair value of B's shares, i.e. €120 million. The accounting entries in the consolidated accounts of Company A at the date of acquisition are as follows:

Journal entry	Debit	Credit
Profit or loss	€ 20	
Written put liability		€ 20

To record the increase in fair value of the written put since initial recognition to the date of exercise in the statement of comprehensive income.

Journal entry	Debit	Credit
Written put liability	€ 30	
Cost of the business combination	€ 120	
Cash		€ 150

To recognise the cash paid to settle the put option and the cost of the acquisition of B.

(These accounting entries assume that there is no end of a reporting period between the date the put is entered into and the date the put is exercised.)

Goodwill on the acquisition of B is determined by comparing the cost of the business combination of €120 million (instead of the cash amount paid of €150 million) with the fair value of the identifiable assets, liabilities and contingent liabilities acquired.

If the put had not been exercised by C, the following entry in the consolidated accounts for A at the date of maturity of the option would have been required (instead of the two journal entries shown above):

Journal entry	Debit	Credit
Written put liability	€ 10	
Profit or loss		€ 10

(This accounting entry assumes that there is no end of a reporting period between the date the put is entered into and the date the put matures.)

5.6 Contingent consideration

Business combination agreements may allow for adjustments to the cost of the combination that are contingent on one or more future events. Examples are the level of profits generated by the acquiree post-combination or the market price of instruments issued. In most cases, it is possible to estimate adjustments reliably at the date of initial accounting. Where estimates are revised, the cost of the combination is adjusted. [IFRS 3(2004).33]

5.6.1 Subsequent adjustment to cost of combination

IFRS 3(2004) further requires:

- the acquirer shall include the adjustment in the cost of the combination at the acquisition date if the adjustment is probable and can be measured reliably; [IFRS 3(2004).32] and

- the adjustment is not included in the cost of the combination at the time of initial accounting for the combination if it is either not probable or cannot be measured reliably. However, if that adjustment subsequently becomes probable and can be measured reliably, the additional consideration shall be treated as an adjustment to the cost of the combination. [IFRS 3(2004).34]

There is no time limit to adjustments to the cost of the combination, and consequently no time limit to any resulting changes to goodwill.

Example 5.6.1A

Contingent cost of acquisition

Entity G acquires Entity H. If the average profitability of Entity H exceeds £1m per year for the next three years then an additional payment of £300,000 will be made to the previous owners of Entity H. Entity H has historically made profits between £900,000 and £1,200,000. Unless there is evidence to the contrary (such as an intended significant change in the business model employed by Entity H), it would seem probable that the payment will be made, the amount of £300,000 is reliably measurable, and therefore the £300,000 is included in the cost of acquisition.

Subsequent to acquisition if Entity H makes profits of only £500,000 in the first year, it is likely that the payment will no longer be considered probable (as in each of the remaining two years of the agreement a profit of £1,250,000 which exceeds the historical profit range would be needed for the payment to be required). Accordingly, the cost of acquisition will be adjusted for the £300,000 contingent payment no longer expected to be made, resulting in a £300,000 decrease in recognised goodwill.

Example 5.6.1B

Interest on contingent consideration

Company A enters into a business combination in 20X1. A portion of the consideration is contingent on Company B meeting a specified profit target by 20X6. At the date of acquisition, it is considered probable that B will meet the profit target. Therefore, additional consideration is recognised at the date of acquisition. Should the contingent consideration be discounted and, if so, should the subsequent unwinding of that discount be recognised in profit or loss, or as an adjustment to the cost of the combination and, hence, goodwill?

In accordance with IFRS 3(2004).32, contingent consideration should be recognised at the date it becomes probable and can be reliably measured. Company A considers that the consideration is probable at the date of acquisition. Therefore, the corresponding liability should be recorded at the date of acquisition in accordance with IFRS 3(2004).24. Contingent consideration is excluded from the scope of IAS 32 *Financial Instruments: Presentation*, and IAS 39 *Financial Instruments: Recognition and Measurement*, and, therefore, falls within the scope of IAS 37 *Provisions, Contingent Liabilities and Contingent Assets*. IAS 37.45 requires the amount of a provision to be discounted where the effect of the time value of money is material. Therefore, the contingent consideration should be recognised at its present value at the date of acquisition.

The interest expense that arises on subsequently unwinding the discount is not a directly attributable cost of the business combination. Therefore, it should not be included in the cost of the combination. The unwinding of the discount represents the increase in the carrying amount of the liability for the passage of time; therefore, it is recognised as an interest expense in profit or loss for the period.

Example 5.6.1C

Contingent consideration not initially probable

Company A enters into a business combination in 20X1. A portion of the consideration is contingent on Company B meeting a specified profit target by 20X6. At the date of acquisition it is not considered probable that B will meet the profit target. The probability of meeting the profit target is reassessed regularly. At 30 September 20X2, it becomes probable that B will meet the profit target.

In accordance with IFRS 3(2004).34, contingent consideration should be recognised at the date it becomes probable and can be reliably measured. Company A only considers that the consideration is probable from 30 September 20X2. Therefore, the cost of the acquisition (and therefore goodwill) should be adjusted for additional consideration at 30 September 20X2 based on A's best estimate of the expenditure that will be required to settle the obligation. As in **example 5.6.1B**, the necessary provision shall be discounted, and any subsequent unwinding of that discount does not form part of the cost of the business combination.

Example 5.6.1D

Classification of contingent consideration in a business combination involving settlement in shares

Company A acquires 100 per cent of Company B from Company Z. In addition to up-front cash consideration, A agrees to pay consideration by issuing its own shares to Z if B meets a specified profit target two years after the business combination. On the business combination date, it is probable that B will meet the profit target (i.e. it is probable that the contingent consideration will become payable).

If the profit target is met, the number of shares given will be determined as follows, on the basis of the share price of B two years after the business combination:

- If B's share price is below a certain level (the 'trigger share price'), A will issue a fixed number of shares.
- If B's share price is at or above the trigger share price, A will issue a variable number of shares equivalent to a fixed monetary amount.

On the business combination date, the current share price of B is much lower than the trigger share price, but the trigger share price is still achievable and therefore is considered genuine. How should the contingent consideration be accounted for?

Contracts for contingent consideration are outside the scope of IAS 32 *Financial Instruments: Presentation*, and IAS 39 *Financial Instruments: Recognition and Measurement* for the acquirer. [IAS 32.4(c), IAS 39.2(f)] Instead, they are within the scope of IFRS 3(2004).32–35. On the business combination date, the requirements of IAS 37 *Provisions, Contingent Liabilities and Contingent Assets* relating to uncertain future outflows must be applied. Because the contingency (i.e. the specified profit target) is expected to be met, a credit balance is set up by reference to the share price on the date of the business combination (with a corresponding adjustment to the cost of the business combination) and will be reassessed at the end of each reporting period.

- When the share price is below the trigger share price, the company is committed to the issue of a fixed number of shares and, therefore, recognises the credit balance in equity as 'shares to be issued'.
- When the share price exceeds the trigger share price, there will be a reclassification from 'shares to be issued' to recognition of a liability. If, after a liability is recognised, the share price falls below the 'trigger' share price, a reclassification will be required to equity. Any resulting adjustments will be recognised against goodwill as necessary.

Note that when a provision exists, the provision recognised will be the present value of the expected expenditure, if the time value of money is material.

5.6.2 *Subsequent payment which is a guarantee*

The acquirer may be required to make a subsequent payment to the seller to compensate for a reduction in the value of consideration paid, for example, the acquirer has guaranteed the market price of equity or debt instruments and is required to make a payment to restore the value of such instruments to the originally determined cost. Such payments shall not increase the cost of the business combination.

Where contingent consideration is equity instruments, the fair value of the additional payment is offset by an equal reduction in the cost of the combination and equity such that there is no net effect on the statement of financial position, that is, cost of the combination and equity are both reduced, and then increased, by the same amount.

Where contingent consideration is a debt instrument, the fair value of the additional payment is debited against the carrying amount of the original issue as a reduction in the premium or an increase in the discount on the initial issue. [IFRS 3(2004).35]

Example 5.6.2

Guaranteed value of consideration

Entity H a listed entity acquires Entity I. The combination is effected by Entity H issuing the previous owners of Entity I with 1,000,000 shares, with a value of £5 each. The acquisition agreement has a clause that if the market price of Entity H's shares has fallen below £5 six months after the date of acquisition, Entity H will issue further shares such that the market value of shares in Entity H held by the previous owners of Entity I six months after the acquisition cannot fall below £5,000,000.

Six months after the date of acquisition, the market price of shares in Entity H has fallen to £4. In accordance with the agreement, Entity J issues a further 250,000 shares ((5,000,000 – 1,000,000*4)/4). The entity may record a journal entry as follows:

Dr	Equity (shares issued at date of acquisition)	£1,000,000	
Cr	Equity (new instruments issued)		1,000,000

As a result no change in the recognised cost of the business combination is recorded.

5.6.3 *Accounting for indemnities in a business combination*

When a purchaser acquires an entity that has a significant contingent liability, the seller may, as part of the arrangement, indemnify the purchaser so that, if the contingent liability crystallises, the seller will pay the purchaser whatever amount crystallises in the acquiree. In other words, the seller may agree to reimburse some of the acquisition cost paid by the purchaser in the event that the contingent liability crystallises.

Such an indemnity must be considered in determining the cost of acquisition for the purchaser. The cost of acquisition on the acquisition date should only be reduced by an amount equal to the expected payment if it is probable that the payment will be made in accordance with IFRS 3(2004).32.

Since the indemnity payment is contingent on the crystallisation of the liability and is, therefore, not probable on the acquisition date, no adjustment is made to the cost of acquisition when the combination is initially accounted for. If, subsequently, it becomes probable that the seller will pay the indemnity, this payment should be recognised as an adjustment to the cost of acquisition in accordance with IFRS 3(2004).34.

The fair value of the contingent liability is recognised at the date of acquisition when allocating the cost of the business combination to the acquiree's identifiable assets, liabilities, and contingent liabilities. The fair value of the contingent liability takes into account the probability of the payment being made and is, therefore, lower than the amount of indemnity payment.

This may result in a mismatch in profit or loss in the future because the final indemnity payment will adjust the cost of acquisition, whereas any changes to the contingent liability beyond the 12-month-hindsight period for adjustment of acquisition date fair values will be recognised in profit or loss.

Example 5.6.3

Accounting for an indemnity against a contingent liability

Purchaser A acquires Entity B from Seller X for consideration of £150m. On the acquisition date, B has a significant contingent liability. If the liability crystallises, B will be required to pay £50m. Seller X indemnifies A against the contingent liability of £50m crystallising. On the acquisition date, the fair value of the contingent liability is £20m and the fair value of the identifiable assets and liabilities of B (excluding the contingent liability) is £110m.

On the acquisition date, A records the following entries in its consolidated financial statements:

		£m	£m
Dr	Net assets	110	
Dr	Goodwill	60	
Cr	Contingent liability		20
Cr	Cash		150

If the contingent liability does not subsequently crystallise, but expires, the following entries are required (assume the 12-months period for adjustment of acquisition date fair values has passed):

		£m	£m
Dr	Contingent liability	20	
Cr	Profit or loss		20

If the contingent liability subsequently crystallises, the following entries are required (assume the 12-months period for adjustment of acquisition date fair values has passed):

		£m	£m
Dr	Contingent liability	20	
Dr	Profit or loss	30	
Cr	Liability		50
Dr	Receivable	50	
Cr	Goodwill (cost of acquisition) *		50

* The adjustment of the cost of acquisition is first applied to reduce any goodwill that arose on that business combination. Any adjustments required in excess of goodwill should be recognised in profit or loss.

5.7 Relationship with IFRS 2 *Share-based payment*

Acquisition agreements may require payments to be made in various forms, e.g. as non-competition payments or as bonuses to the vendors who continue to work for the acquired entity. In such circumstances, it is necessary to determine which elements of payment are part of the cost of the combination and which are remuneration for services or profit-sharing to be expensed in the period to which they relate or which may fall within the scope of IFRS 2 *Share-based Payment*.

In determining whether a payment, dependent upon future performance, say, a profit or sales target, is part of the purchase consideration or is employee remuneration, consideration should be given to all relevant factors:

- **Linkage of continued employment and contingent consideration** — arrangements in which the contingent payments are not affected by employment termination may be a strong indicator that the contingent payments are additional purchase price rather than remuneration.

- **Duration of continued employment required** — if the length of time of required employment coincides with or is longer than the contingent payment period, that fact may indicate that the contingent payments are, in substance, remuneration.

- **Level of remuneration** — situations in which employee remuneration other than the contingent payments is at a reasonable level in comparison to that of other key employees in the combined entity may indicate that the contingent payments are additional purchase price rather than remuneration.

- **Contingent payout is different for former shareholders based on whether they are employees** — the fact that selling shareholders who do not become employees receive lower contingent payments on a per share basis from what the previous owners who become employees of the combined entity receive, may indicate that the incremental amount of contingent payments to the selling shareholders who become employees is remuneration.

- **Level of consideration** — consistent with the point above on level of remuneration, the total consideration paid (including contingent consideration) should equate to the fair value of the exchange transaction. Where contingent consideration results in a total consideration which is in excess of fair value, this may indicate the contingent consideration is remuneration. Conversely, where the total consideration is reasonable in the context of fair value, this may indicate the contingent consideration is indeed part of consideration and not remuneration.

Understanding why the acquisition agreement includes provision for contingent payments may be helpful in assessing the substance of the arrangement. For example, if the initial consideration paid at the acquisition date is based on the low end of a range established in the valuation of the acquired entity and the contingent formula relates to that valuation approach, that fact may suggest that the contingent payments are additional purchase price. Alternatively, if the contingent payment formula is consistent with prior profit-sharing arrangements, that fact may suggest that the substance of the arrangement is to provide remuneration.

The formula used to determine the contingent payment might be helpful in assessing the substance of the arrangement. For example, a contingent payment of five times earnings may suggest that the formula is intended to establish or verify the fair value of the acquired entity, while a contingent payment of 10 per cent of earnings may suggest a profit-sharing arrangement.

The determination of whether equity instruments issued for contingent consideration in a purchase combination are remuneration to current employees or part of the purchase price to the former owners is a matter that requires a full assessment of the facts and careful judgement.

6 Application of the acquisition method – allocating the cost of a business combination to the net assets acquired

IFRS 3(2004) requires, at the acquisition date, an allocation of the cost of a business combination to:

- Identifiable assets, liabilities and contingent liabilities except non-current assets classified as held for sale at their fair values as follows:
  - Intangible assets, if fair value can be measured reliably (see **6.2** below).
  - Other assets, if it is probable that any associated future economic benefits will flow to the acquirer, and their fair value can be measured reliably (see **6.3** below).
  - Contingent liabilities, if fair value can be measured reliably (see **6.4** below).
  - Other liabilities, if it is probable that an outflow of resources embodying economic benefits will be required to settle the obligation, and the fair value of the liabilities can be measured reliably (see **6.3** below).
- Non-current assets (or disposal groups) that are classified as held for sale in accordance with IFRS 5 *Non-current Assets Held for Sale and Discontinued Operations* at fair value less costs to sell (see **6.5** below).

Any positive balance is recognised as goodwill (see **6.6** below). Any negative balance is recognised in profit or loss after reassessing the identification and measurement of all fair values involved in the calculation (see **6.7** below). [IFRS 3(2004).36 – 37]

Any minority interest in the acquiree is initially stated at the minority's proportion of the net fair value, at the acquisition date, of recognised identifiable assets, liabilities and contingent liabilities. [IFRS 3(2004).40]

Subsequent to the acquisition, the acquirer's statement of comprehensive income reflects the acquiree's income and expenses based on the cost of the business combination to the acquirer, and hence the allocation of that cost based on fair values. For example, depreciation expense will be based on the fair values of the acquiree's assets rather than their carrying amount in the acquiree's separate financial statements. [IFRS 3(2004).38]

When determining minority interest on the acquisition of a subsidiary, an entity should not take into account any goodwill recognised in the subsidiary's own financial statements. The minority interest on acquisition is calculated as the minority's proportion of the net fair value of the acquiree's identifiable assets, liabilities, and contingent liabilities that satisfy the recognition criteria at the acquisition date. [IFRS 3(2004).40, IAS 27(2003).22] Any pre-existing goodwill recognised in the acquiree's separate financial statements is ignored, as goodwill is the residual arising from the difference between the acquired assets and liabilities at fair value and the consideration paid for the acquisition.

6.1 General principles

In allocating the cost of the business combination, the acquirer recognises only assets, liabilities and contingent liabilities of the acquiree that existed at the acquisition date, and which satisfy recognition criteria. As a result:

- liabilities for terminating or reducing the activities of the acquiree are recognised only when the acquiree has, at the acquisition date, an existing liability for restructuring in accordance with IAS 37 *Provisions, Contingent Liabilities and Contingent Assets*; [IFRS 3(2004).41(a)]
- future losses or other costs expected to be incurred as a result of the business combination are not recognised; [IFRS 3(2004).41(b)]
- payments which the acquiree is contractually required to make in the event that it is acquired, for example, to employees, suppliers or financiers, are recognised; [IFRS 3(2004).42]
- costs of restructuring plans of the acquiree whose execution is conditional upon its being acquired are not recognised since there is no present obligation of the acquiree to proceed with the plan immediately before the business combination; [IFRS 3(2004).43] and
- identifiable assets and liabilities may include assets and liabilities not previously recognised in the acquiree's financial statements, for example, the acquirer may recognise an asset for the future tax benefit of the acquiree's unrecognised tax losses on the basis of their probable recovery by the acquirer. [IFRS 3(2004).44]

Amounts for acquired assets and liabilities stated within purchase agreements are often affected by tax considerations. Accordingly, these amounts should be treated with scepticism and subjected to a separate verification of their fair value.

Example 6.1

Recognition of contractual provisions under IFRS 3(2004).42 – 43

Entity F acquires Entity G. Prior to the date of acquisition, Entity G has entered into a retrenchment package for directors, such that if the entity is acquired by another party the directors will become entitled to a one-off aggregate payment of £50,000. In addition, a restructuring plan with a total cost of £115,000 would be implemented.

In allocating the cost of the business combination, Entity F recognises the liability of £50,000 to the directors, because this represents a contractual obligation of Entity G that has become probable by virtue of the consummation of the business combination, but does not recognise the liability for the restructuring of £115,000 – this amount would be recognised as an expense when the recognition criteria in IAS 37 are met.

6.2 Intangible assets

6.2.1 *Identification of intangible assets*

The acquirer recognises separately an intangible asset of the acquiree at the acquisition date if it meets the definition of an intangible asset in IAS 38 *Intangible Assets* and its fair value can be measured reliably. [IFRS 3(2004).45]

The definition of an intangible asset in IAS 38 is:

[IAS 38.8]

> 'an identifiable non-monetary asset without physical substance.'

An asset meets the identifiability criterion in the definition only if it:

[IFRS 3(2004).46]

(a) is separable, i.e. capable of being separated or divided from the entity and sold, transferred, licensed, rented or exchanged, either individually or together with a related contract, asset or liability; or

(b) arises from contractual or other legal rights, regardless of whether those rights are transferable or separable from the entity or from other rights and obligations.

UK

This differs from FRS 10 which recognises only items in (a), that is, separable intangible assets. FRS 10 was designed to make the allocation of the cost of a combination between identified intangible assets and residual goodwill neutral since both were subsequently dealt with on the same basis. In each case they were amortised if their estimated useful life was finite, but were carried unamortised (subject to impairment testing) if their life was indefinite. By comparison, IFRS 3 has differing requirements for the subsequent treatment of identified intangible assets and residual goodwill. This has a consequent impact on the importance of identifying intangible assets.

The inclusion of (b) above results in the inclusion of intangible assets which may not be separable, provided they are identifiable and legally protected.

IAS 38.33 – 34 give further guidance on the identification of an intangible asset in a business combination. Two points arising are:

- the usual requirement regarding the probability of future economic benefits flowing to the entity, which is required for the recognition of any asset, is considered always to be satisfied for intangible assets acquired in business combinations; and
- in-process research and development is recognised (see below).

6.2.2 *In-process research and development*

IAS 38 generally requires research expenditure and development expenditure not meeting certain criteria to be expensed. However, in allocating the cost of a business combination, it is likely that in-process research and development (IPR&D) projects will have a fair value, and this is recognised if the requirements of IFRS 3(2004).45 are met, that is, it meets the definition of an intangible asset and fair value can be measured reliably. [IFRS 3(2004).45]

Neither IFRS 3 nor IAS 38 includes any guidance on the subsequent accounting for the fair value recognised at the date of acquisition. Therefore, the general requirements of IAS 38 regarding measurement after recognition, and amortisation, will apply. This is confirmed in the IAS 38 Basis for Conclusions. [IAS 38.BC84] The subsequent basis of accounting is thus:

(a) cost less any accumulated amortisation and any accumulated impairment losses; or

(b) revalued amount, being the asset's fair value, determined by reference to an active market, at the date of revaluation less any subsequent accumulated amortisation and any subsequent accumulated impairment losses.

Amortisation would be based on the useful life of the IPR&D. [IAS 38.88]

It is unlikely that the conditions for revaluation will exist, since it is unlikely that an active market will exist for IPR&D and, consequently, the cost method will be used. In the event that a research project does not lead to future economic benefits, the amount carried would be subject to impairment testing. Where future economic benefits are forecast, amortisation would be based on the useful life assessed by number of production, or similar, units representing that useful life.

Subsequent to the business combination, capitalisation of further expenditure is subject to the usual requirements of IAS 38. [IAS 38.42]

Example 6.2.2

In-process research and development

Entity N acquires a research laboratory. The lab is involved in the development of medical research techniques. At the date of acquisition, the entity has two projects in process. One is the development of a proven cure for a common disease into a commercially viable drug, and the second is research into the curative characteristics of a particular chemical compound.

On initial acquisition the intangible assets arising from these projects are measured at their fair value and recognised as assets acquired in the business combination.

In subsequent years, providing the IAS 38 recognition criteria are met, development expenditure directly attributable to the first project is capitalised, and the asset tested for impairment if any indicators of impairment are considered to exist. All subsequent expenditure attributable to the second project is expensed when incurred, until such time as the project meets all the criteria in the standard for recognition as a development asset. Once the criteria are satisfied, expenditure that has been previously expensed cannot be reinstated into the development asset.

6.2.3 *Examples of identified intangible assets*

The IASB has issued illustrative examples which 'accompany, but are not part of, IFRS 3'. These include 'Examples of items acquired in a business combination that meet the definition of an intangible asset'. [IFRS 3(2004)(Illustrative Examples)]

The following is a summary of the list, which is not intended to be an exhaustive list of items that would qualify for recognition. Reference should be made to the text of the illustrative examples for further explanation on the items listed.

'A Marketing-related intangible assets

1 Trademarks, trade names, service marks, collective marks and certification marks

2 Internet domain names

3 Trade dress (unique colour, shape or package design)

4 Newspaper mastheads

5 Non-competition agreements

B Customer-related intangible assets

1 Customer lists

2 Order or production backlog

3 Customer contracts and the related customer relationships

4 Non-contractual customer relationships

C Artistic-related intangible assets

1 Plays, operas and ballets

2 Books, magazines, newspapers and other literary works

3 Musical works such as compositions, song lyrics and advertising jingles

4 Pictures and photographs

5 Video and audiovisual material, including films, music videos and television programmes

D Contract-based intangible assets

1 Licensing, royalty and standstill agreements

2 Advertising, construction, management, service or supply contracts

3 Lease agreements

4 Construction permits

5 Franchise agreements

6 Operating and broadcasting rights

7 Use rights such as drilling, water, air, mineral, timber-cutting and route authorities

8 Servicing contracts such as mortgage servicing contracts

9 Employment contracts that are beneficial contracts from the perspective of the employer because the pricing of those contracts is below their current market value

E Technology-based intangible assets

1 Patented technology

2 Computer software and mask works

3 Unpatented technology

4 Databases

5 Trade secrets such as secret formulas, processes or recipes.'

6.2.4 *Measurement of identified intangible assets*

IFRS 3(2004).B16(g) states that:

> 'for intangible assets the acquirer shall determine fair value:
>
> (i) by reference to an active market as defined in IAS 38 *Intangible Assets*; or
>
> (ii) if no active market exists, on a basis that reflects the amounts the acquirer would have paid for the assets in arm's length transactions between knowledgeable willing parties, based on the best information available (see IAS 38 for further guidance on determining the fair values of intangible assets acquired in business combinations).'

The further guidance referred to in IAS 38 is summarised as follows:

- uncertainty, evidenced by a range of possible estimates, enters into the measurement of fair value, rather than demonstrating an inability to measure fair value reliably; [IAS 38.35]
- if an intangible asset acquired in a business combination has a finite useful life, there is a rebuttable presumption that its fair value can be measured reliably; [IAS 38.35]
- an intangible asset which is separable but only together with related assets, for example, a publishing title may only be sold together with a subscriber database, is valued together with those other assets as a single asset if individual fair values are not reliably measurable; [IAS 38.36]
- the only circumstance in which it might not be possible to measure reliably a separable intangible asset is when there is no history or evidence of exchange transactions for the same or similar assets; [IAS 38.38]
- quoted market bid prices in an active market provide the most reliable estimate of fair value; [IAS 38.39]

- if no active market exists, an entity estimates what that market price would have been based on recent transactions for similar assets; [IAS 38.40] and
- entities involved in the purchase and sale of unique intangible assets may use valuation models which reflect current transactions and practices in the industry to which the asset belongs. [IAS 38.41]

IFRS 3 Illustrative Examples include four examples to illustrate the application of IFRS 3 to customer relationships: example 1 deals with a supply agreement, example 2 deals with customer contracts, example 3 deals with purchase orders, and example 4 deals with insurance contracts.

6.2.5 *Acquisition of an intangible which will not be used*

An acquirer may acquire an intangible asset as part of a business acquisition which it has no intention to use. For example, an acquiree's identified net assets may include a trademark being the logo previously used by the acquiree as a direct competitor to the acquirer. When acquired, the acquirer has no intention to use this logo anymore. The question arises whether the intangible should be recognised and, if so, on what basis it is measured.

It is suggested that the logo is separable by itself as it can be, for example, licensed and arises from legal rights. In acquiring the logo, the entity makes sure that future economic benefits will flow to itself, and increase, as the entity stops or reduces the business of its competitor. The criteria of IAS 38.12 and IAS 38.21 are met; therefore, an intangible asset should be recognised.

However, if the entity has no intention to use the logo after the acquisition it will not be possible to allocate the logo to existing cash-generating units. Consequently, it should be identified as a cash-generating unit by itself as the management intends to exclude the logo from the operating process. The cash inflows related to the logo are nil. However, immediately after acquisition it would appear reasonable that the fair value less costs to sell are not significantly different from the amount recognised, and accordingly an impairment loss is not recognised. The asset must be amortised over its useful life. The useful life to the entity is the length of time for which holding the logo will be effective in discouraging competition, which would be likely to be a fairly short period, as an unexploited logo loses value very quickly. As the entity acquired the asset with the express intention of denying others the opportunity to use the asset, it appears unlikely that the asset will be sold in the future, and accordingly the residual value is zero. As a result, an amortisation charge for the full carrying amount of the asset is recognised over the useful life (which may be as short as a single accounting period).

6.2.6 Non-competition agreements

Non-competition agreements are discussed at **3.2.3** in **chapter 8**.

6.2.7 Operating leases at below or above market rates

In a business combination, the acquiree may be party to operating lease arrangements that involve future lease payments at below or above market rates. IFRS 3(2004).B16 gives no guidance on leasehold interests.

If an acquiree is a lessee in an operating lease that involves future rentals at below (or above) market rates, the shortfall (or excess) of rentals, compared to market rates, should be recognised as an asset (or liability) in the allocation of the cost of the business combination. This is confirmed by the inclusion of lease agreements within the illustrative examples of contract-based intangible assets accompanying IFRS 3 (see **6.2.3** above). The existence of an operating lease at below or above market rates will inflate or depress the purchase price that an acquirer is willing to pay for the acquiree.

6.3 Net assets other than intangible assets and assets held for sale

IFRS 3 requires assets, other than intangible assets and non-current assets (or disposal groups) that are classified as held for sale in accordance with IFRS 5, to be recognised at fair value provided it is probable that any associated future economic benefits will flow to the acquirer, and their fair value can be measured reliably. It requires liabilities, other than contingent liabilities, to be recognised at fair value if it is probable that an outflow of resources embodying economic benefits will be required to settle the obligation, and their fair value can be measured reliably. [IFRS 3(2004).37(a)]

IFRS 3(2004).B16 provides further guidance on the measurement of fair value of specific assets and liabilities, on which the following paragraphs are based.

6.3.1 *Land and buildings*

The acquirer shall use market value. [IFRS 3(2004).B16(e)]

Example 6.3.1

Acquisition of investment property with existing operating lease in place

Company A acquires Company B which is acting as a lessor over an investment property with an operating lease that is not at current market rates.

The fair value of an operating lease over an investment property should not be recognised separately from the fair value of the investment property. Where an acquiree is acting as a lessor over an investment property with operating leases at above or below current market rates, the fair value of the operating lease should be incorporated as part of the value of the investment property.

Example 5.2.2 in **chapter 7** deals with the acquisition, outside a business combination, of an investment property where an operating lease is not at current market rates.

6.3.2 *Plant and equipment*

The acquirer shall use market values, normally determined by appraisal. If there is no market-based evidence of fair value because of the specialised nature of the item of plant and equipment and the item is rarely sold, except as part of a continuing business, an acquirer may need to estimate fair value using an income or a depreciated replacement cost approach. [IFRS 3(2004).B16(f)]

6.3.3 *Inventories*

The IFRS distinguishes raw materials, work in progress, and finished goods. For inventories of:

[IFRS 3(2004).B16(d)]

- raw materials the acquirer shall use current replacement costs;
- work in progress the acquirer shall use selling prices of finished goods less the sum of (1) costs to complete, (2) costs of disposal and (3) a reasonable profit allowance for the completing and selling effort based on profit for similar finished goods; and

- finished goods and merchandise the acquirer shall use selling prices less the sum of (1) the costs of disposal and (2) a reasonable profit allowance for the selling effort of the acquirer based on profit for similar finished goods and merchandise.

The deduction for 'a reasonable profit allowance for the completing and selling effort' does not extend to the entire profit. Fair value at the point of acquisition (i.e. the date of combination) includes profit attributed to past production effort, i.e. in bringing the goods or services to their current condition. Generally, it is not appropriate to assign the acquiree's carrying amount to the cost of acquired inventories, because the acquiree's cost does not reflect the manufacturing profit that is recognised by the acquiree through the normal selling process. This manufacturing profit should be considered as part of the fair value assigned to the inventory.

In determining a reasonable profit allowance, the following factors should be considered:

- the historical turnover rate for inventories of the acquiree and for the acquiree's industry;
- industry statistics for normal profit allowances and turnover rates; and
- nature of the selling network and marketing techniques employed by the acquiree or that will be employed by the acquirer, if significantly different.

In the case of retail operations, costs to dispose may include inventory stocking costs and warehousing and distribution costs for the acquired inventory. However, it is inappropriate to allocate general and administrative overhead costs to finished goods inventory in the acquisition.

6.3.4 *Receivables and beneficial contracts*

The acquirer shall use the present values of the amounts to be received, determined at appropriate current interest rates, less allowances for uncollectibility and collection costs, if necessary. However, discounting is not required for short-term receivables, beneficial contracts and other identifiable assets when the difference between the nominal and discounted amounts is not material. [IFRS 3(2004).B16(c)]

6.3.5 *Financial instruments*

The IFRS distinguishes financial instruments traded on an active market from those not traded:

- For financial instruments traded in an active market the acquirer shall use current market values. [IFRS 3(2004).B16(a)]
- For financial instruments not traded in an active market the acquirer shall use estimated values that take into consideration features such as price-earnings ratios, dividend yields and expected growth rates of comparable instruments of entities with similar characteristics. [IFRS 3(2004).B16(b)]

6.3.6 *Accounts and notes payable, long-term debt, liabilities, accruals and other claims payable*

The acquirer shall use the present values of amounts to be disbursed in settling the liabilities determined at appropriate current interest rates. However, discounting is not required for short-term liabilities when the difference between the nominal and discounted amounts is not material. [IFRS 3(2004).B16(j)]

6.3.7 *Onerous contracts and other identifiable liabilities of the acquiree*

The acquirer shall use the present values of amounts to be disbursed in settling the obligations determined at appropriate current interest rates. [IFRS 3(2004).B16(k)]

Operating leases at above or below market rates are discussed at **6.2.7** above.

6.3.8 *Net employee benefit assets and liabilities for defined benefit plans*

The acquirer shall use the present value of the defined benefit obligation less the fair value of any plan assets. However, an asset is recognised only to the extent that it is probable it will be available to the acquirer in the form of refunds from the plan or a reduction in future contributions. [IFRS 3(2004).B16(h)]

It follows that any unamortised actuarial gains and losses carried in the statement of financial position of the acquiree are excluded from fair value on acquisition.

6.3.9 *Tax assets and liabilities*

The acquirer shall use the amount of the tax benefit arising from tax losses or the taxes payable in respect of profit or loss in accordance with IAS 12 *Income Taxes*, assessed from the perspective of the combined entity. The tax asset or liability is determined after allowing for the tax effect of restating identifiable assets, liabilities and contingent liabilities to their fair values and is not discounted. [IFRS 3(2004).B16(i)]

Temporary differences arise when the tax bases of the identifiable assets acquired and liabilities assumed are not affected by the business combination or are affected differently. For example:

- When the carrying amount of an asset is increased to fair value but the tax base of the asset remains at cost to the previous owner, a taxable temporary difference arises which results in a deferred tax liability that affects goodwill. [IAS 12.19]
- Similarly, when a liability assumed is recognised at the acquisition date but the related costs are not deducted in determining taxable profits until a later period, a deductible temporary difference arises which results in a deferred tax asset. A deferred tax asset also arises when the fair value of an identifiable asset acquired is less than its tax base. In both cases, the resulting deferred tax asset affects goodwill. [IAS 12.26(c)]

Deferred tax on temporary differences which arise from the inclusion of the acquiree's net assets at fair value is recognised as an identifiable asset (subject to recognition criteria of IAS 12.24) or liability and, consequently, affects goodwill. However, any temporary difference which arises from goodwill itself, for example from a difference between the carrying amount and tax base of goodwill, is not recognised in accordance with IAS 12.15(a), since this would involve the grossing-up of goodwill. [IAS 12.66]

Where the business combination results in an acquirer being able to recover its own unrecognised deferred tax asset, for example due to the ability to relieve its tax losses against the acquiree's profits, it may record the resulting deferred tax asset but does not include it as part of the accounting for the business combination. Consequently, it will not affect goodwill. [IAS 12.67]

Where fair values are assessed on a provisional basis and at the date of initial accounting no deferred tax asset is recognised, but subsequently a tax asset is realised, then:

[IAS 12.68 and IFRS 3(2004).65]

- the resulting tax income is included in profit or loss;
- the carrying amount of goodwill is reduced by the amount that would have been recognised if the tax asset had been recognised on acquisition; and
- the reduction in goodwill is included as an expense.

Example 6.3.9

Tax losses

A acquired B in 20X1. At that time, B had unrelieved tax losses which, if relieved, would give rise to a reduction of £100,000 of tax liabilities. Nevertheless, A assessed that only £20,000 met recognition criteria and were included as a fair value asset. Consequently, a balance of £200,000 was recognised as goodwill.

Subsequently, in 20X5, the group obtained relief for tax losses giving rise to a tax saving of £60,000.

Applying the requirements of IFRS 3(2004).65 above, the tax saving is reported in profit or loss as a component of income tax expense, and an equal amount is written off the carrying amount of goodwill and reported in profit or loss as an operating expense.

6.3.10 Emission rights acquired in a business combination

Example 6.3.10

Emission rights

Entity A acquires Entity B. Entity B's accounting policy is to adopt the net liability approach for recognition of emission rights (see **9.1.3** in **chapter 11**). It has been granted emission rights by the government for no charge and, at acquisition date, it holds emission rights in excess of actual emissions made. Accordingly, no asset or provision is recognised in the financial statements of B in respect of emissions.

On acquisition, A's consolidated financial statements will include the emission rights held by B as an asset and will include a separate provision for the actual emissions made as at that date. Both the asset and the provision will need to be recognised at fair value, in accordance with IFRS 3. Accordingly, the net liability approach may not be applied in the consolidated financial statements; instead, the consolidated financial statements will thereafter reflect an expense for actual emissions made.

Fair value at acquisition date will be determined by reference to an active market for emission rights or, if no active market exists, on a basis that reflects the amount the acquirer would have paid for the rights in an arm's length transaction between knowledgeable willing parties, based on the best information available.

6.3.11 *Treatment of performance obligations in a business combination*

Example 6.3.11

Treatment of performance obligations

Company A acquires Company B in a business combination. As of the acquisition date, B has recognised deferred income related to a customer contract. The deferred income represents a prepayment received by B for future services.

IFRS 3(2004).41 requires the acquirer to recognise 'the identifiable assets, liabilities and contingent liabilities of the acquiree that existed at the acquisition date and satisfy the recognition criteria in paragraph 37'. As of the acquisition date, A should recognise a liability in its consolidated financial statements to the extent that the deferred income represents an obligation to provide future services that will be the combined entity's responsibility after the acquisition date. That is, a liability should be recognised because A has a performance obligation to provide future services for which payment has already been received. This liability should be measured at fair value as of the acquisition date and consideration should be given to whether any intangible assets should be recognised as part of the business combination with respect to B's customer contracts (see **6.2.1**).

6.4 Contingent liabilities

IFRS 3 requires contingent liabilities of the acquiree to be recognised separately at their fair value only if fair value can be reliably determined. [IFRS 3(2004).37(c)]

6.4.1 *Measurement of contingent liabilities at acquisition*

In measuring fair value, IFRS 3 requires that the acquirer shall use the amounts that a third party would charge to assume those contingent liabilities. Such an amount shall reflect all expectations about possible cash flows and not the single most likely or the expected maximum or minimum cash flow. [IFRS 3(2004).B16(l)]

If fair value cannot be measured reliably, no amount is recognised. However, information about the contingent liability required by IAS 37 shall be disclosed. [IFRS 3(2004).47]

Example 6.4.1

Recognition of contingent liabilities

Entity F acquires Entity G. In completing the transaction, two legal proceedings against Entity G are identified. The first is a personal injury claim, notice of which has only just been given to Entity G. Entity G's lawyers are considering the merits of the claim, and the most appropriate means of dealing with the claim. The second is a warranty claim, for which negotiations are in advanced stages. Entity G's lawyers have indicated that there is a 60 per cent chance that G will have to pay nothing, a 15 per cent chance they will have to pay £90,000 and a 25 per cent chance they will have to pay £150,000.

No contingent liability is recognised on the personal injury claim because the fair value of such a liability could not be measured reliably. A contingent liability of £51,000 [(60% * 0) + (15%*90,000) + (25%*150,000)] is discounted to its present value and recognised in respect of the warranty claim, taking account of the range of probable outcomes.

UK *FRS 7.15 requires a fair value to be attributed both to contingent assets and contingent liabilities. In practice, there are few instances where such a fair value is deemed to be reliably measurable.*

6.4.2 *Subsequent accounting for contingent liabilities recognised in a business combination*

Contingent liabilities recognised separately as part of allocating the cost of a business combination are:

- excluded from the scope of IAS 37, but are subject to the disclosures of IAS 37; [IFRS 3(2004).50] and
- after initial recognition, measured by the acquirer at the higher of:

  [IFRS 3(2004).48]

  - the amount that would be recognised in accordance with IAS 37; and
  - the amount initially recognised less, when appropriate, cumulative amortisation recognised in accordance with IAS 18 *Revenue*.

This requirement does not apply to contracts accounted for in accordance with IAS 39. However, loan commitments excluded from the scope of IAS 39 are accounted for as contingent liabilities. [IFRS 3(2004).49]

6.5 Non-current assets held for sale

IFRS 3 requires that non-current assets (or disposal groups) of the acquiree that are classified as held for sale in accordance with IFRS 5 *Non-current Assets Held for Sale and Discontinued Operations* are recognised at fair value less costs to sell. [IFRS 3(2004).36] Further guidance on such assets is in IFRS 5 and not IFRS 3.

A disposal group is defined as:

[IFRS 5(Appendix A)]

> 'A group of assets to be disposed of, by sale or otherwise, together as a group in a single transaction, and liabilities directly associated with those assets that will be transferred in the transaction. The group includes goodwill acquired in a business combination if the group is a cash generating unit to which goodwill has been allocated in accordance with the requirements of paragraphs 80–87 of IAS 36 *Impairment of Assets* (as revised in 2004) or if it is an operation within such a cash-generating unit.'

IFRS 5 supersedes the provisions previously included in IAS 27 which allowed the exclusion from consolidation of subsidiaries when control was intended to be temporary. The provisions of IFRS 5 are wider, in that they apply to individual assets and disposal groups rather than just the consolidation of subsidiaries, and more robust, in that the requirements for measurement as held for sale are more extensive.

A summary of the key requirements of IFRS 5 is set out below, with further detail included in **chapter 29**.

6.5.1 Conditions for classification as held for sale

In order to be classified as held for sale, an asset (or disposal group) must satisfy the following conditions:

- carrying amount will be recovered principally through a sale transaction;
- the asset (or disposal group) must be available for immediate sale in its present condition and its sale must be highly probable;
- an active programme to locate a buyer and complete the sale plan must have been initiated;
- the advertised sale price must be reasonable in relation to current fair value; and

- the sale should be expected to qualify for recognition as a completed sale within one year from the date of classification.

The requirement for sale within one year must be met at the date of acquisition, and the other conditions must be met within 3 months of the date of acquisition. [IFRS 5.6 – 12]

6.5.2 *Measurement and presentation of an asset (or disposal group) held for sale*

A subsidiary which is acquired exclusively with a view to resale also falls within the scope of a discontinued operation. [IFRS 5.32] Accordingly:

- the disposal group is first measured at fair value less costs to sell;
- in the statement of financial position, this amount is allocated between the aggregate liabilities of the disposal group held for sale measured at fair value, with the balance allocated to aggregate assets held for sale. The total assets held for sale, and liabilities held for sale, are disclosed separately from other assets and liabilities and may not be netted off; [IFRS 5.38] and
- in the statement of comprehensive income, a single amount is presented in profit or loss comprising the total of:
  - the post-tax profit or loss of discontinued operations; and
  - the post-tax gain or loss recognised on the measurement to fair value less costs to sell or on the disposal of the assets or disposal group.

Further analysis of the single amount disclosed in profit or loss is required, and analysis of amounts included in the statement of cash flows is required. [IFRS 5.33]

Prior to IFRS 5, the results of businesses held for sale would have been excluded from the statement of comprehensive income. The effect of IFRS 5 is to require the results to be reported as a single line, potentially with a consequential adjustment to bring the statement of financial position carrying amount back to the amount calculated above.

UK *Under UK GAAP, where a subsidiary is acquired exclusively with a view to subsequent resale, it is excluded from consolidation in accordance with FRS 7.16. There is no similar exemption under IFRS 5, and accordingly such a subsidiary will be consolidated. However, providing the criteria in IFRS 5 are met, the subsidiary's assets and liabilities will be presented as held for sale in the statement of financial position, and its results will be presented as part of discontinued operations in the statement of comprehensive income.*

If a subsidiary held for sale ceases to qualify as held for sale, the results of operations of that subsidiary previously presented in discontinued operations shall be reclassified and included in income from continuing operations for all periods presented. [IFRS 5.36]

Example 6.5.2

Measuring and presenting subsidiaries acquired with a view to resale and classified as held for sale

[Guidance on Implementing IFRS 5 (Example 13)]

Entity A acquires an entity H, which is a holding company with two subsidiaries, S1 and S2. S2 is acquired exclusively with a view to sale and meets the criteria to be classified as held for sale. In accordance with IFRS 5.32(c), S2 is also a discontinued operation.

The estimated fair value less costs to sell of S2 is CU135. A accounts for S2 as follows:

- initially, A measures the identifiable liabilities of S2 at fair value, say at CU40
- initially, A measures the acquired assets as the fair value less costs to sell of S2 (CU135) plus the fair value of the identifiable liabilities (CU40), i.e. at £175
- at the end of the reporting period, A remeasures the disposal group at the lower of its cost and fair value less costs to sell, say at CU130. The liabilities are remeasured in accordance with applicable IFRSs, say at CU35. The total assets are measured at CU130 + CU35, i.e. at CU165
- at the end of the reporting period, A presents the assets and liabilities separately from other assets and liabilities in its consolidated financial statements as illustrated in the Guidance on Implementing IFRS 5(Example 12) (reproduced as **example 7.2** in **chapter 29**), and
- in the statement of comprehensive income, A presents the total of the post-tax profit or loss of S2 and the post-tax gain or loss recognised on the subsequent remeasurement of S2, which equals the remeasurement of the disposal group from CU135 to CU130.

Further analysis of the assets and liabilities or of the change in value of the disposal group is not required.

6.6 Treatment of goodwill

Where the cost of a business combination exceeds the net fair value of the recognised net assets of the acquiree, the excess is goodwill.

6.6.1 *Requirement for goodwill arising in a business combination*

At acquisition, IFRS 3 requires:

[IFRS 3(2004).51 – 55]

- goodwill acquired in a business combination to be recognised as an asset;
- initial measurement shall be cost;
- subsequently, the goodwill shall not be amortised, but carried at cost less any accumulated impairment losses; and
- impairment testing shall be carried out annually, or more frequently if events or changes in circumstances indicate it might be impaired, in accordance with IAS 36 *Impairment of Assets* (see **chapter 9**).

6.6.2 *Goodwill related to equity method investments*

An investment in an associate is accounted for using the equity method from the date on which it becomes an associate. On acquisition of the investment any difference between the cost of the investment and the investor's share of the net fair value of the associate's identifiable assets, liabilities and contingent liabilities is accounted for in accordance with IFRS 3. Therefore:

[IAS 28.23]

(a) goodwill relating to an associate is included in the carrying amount of the investment. However, amortisation of that goodwill is not permitted and is, therefore, not included in the determination of the investor's share of the associate's profits or losses; and

(b) any excess of the investor's share of the net fair value of the associate's identifiable assets, liabilities and contingent liabilities over the cost of the investment is excluded from the carrying amount of the investment and is instead included as income in the determination of the investor's share of the associate's profit or loss in the period in which the investment is acquired.

Because goodwill included in the carrying amount of an equity-accounted investment is not separately recognised, it is not tested for impairment separately by applying the requirements for impairment testing of goodwill in IAS 36. Instead, the entire carrying amount of the investment is tested under IAS 36 for impairment, by comparing its recoverable amount with its carrying amount whenever application of the requirements in IAS 39 indicates that the investment may be impaired. [IAS 28.33]

6.7 Net assets in excess of cost ('negative goodwill')

Where the cost of a business combination is less than the net fair value of the recognised net assets of the acquiree, IFRS 3 does not use the term 'negative goodwill', but uses the rather more lengthy term 'excess of acquirer's interest in the net fair value of acquiree's identifiable assets, liabilities and contingent liabilities over cost'. In such cases, IFRS 3 requires:

[IFRS 3(2004).56]

- a reassessment of the fair value of both cost of the combination and acquiree's net assets; and
- any excess remaining after this reassessment is recognised immediately in profit or loss.

The IFRS explains that any gain recognised immediately in profit or loss could be the result of:

[IFRS 3(2004).57]

- possible future costs which have not been included in fair values correctly; and/or
- measurement of assets and liabilities in accordance with accounting standards at other than fair value, for example, tax assets and liabilities not discounted in accordance with IAS 12; and/or
- a bargain purchase.

In view of the requirement to reassess fair values before taking any excess as an immediate gain, it is unlikely that any gain will remain in two circumstances:

- initial allocation of cost identifies significant intangible assets which are inherently subjective to fair value; and

- a high proportion of cost is allocated to tangible fixed assets for which there is significant uncertainty over fair value demonstrated by a wide possible range of values. An example would be the extractive industries where the valuation of mineral or oil and gas reserves is inherently subjective.

In both of these circumstances, it is likely that the asset whose fair value is uncertain will be reduced so as to eliminate the excess which would otherwise be reported as a gain. It follows that circumstances where an immediate gain is reported will occur only where fair values can be reliably determined through, for example, observable market values.

6.8 Business combination achieved in stages

6.8.1 Control achieved in two or more exchange transactions

A business combination may be achieved by more than one exchange transaction. For example, an acquirer may purchase two or more tranches of shares in an acquiree before the aggregate interest amounts to a controlling interest.

In such cases:

[IFRS 3(2004).58 – 60]

- IFRS 3 requires goodwill to be calculated separately for each exchange transaction, based on the cost of each exchange transaction, and the appropriate share of the acquiree's net assets based on net fair values at the time of each exchange transaction;
- when control is achieved, the acquiree's net assets are stated at net fair value at the date of acquisition;
- any adjustment to fair values related to previously held interests (including but not limited to interests which were equity accounted under IAS 28 *Investments in Associates*) is a revaluation, which is accounted for as an adjustment directly in equity;
- such a revaluation does not indicate that a policy of revaluation within the meaning of IAS 16 has been adopted.

IFRS 3 Illustrative Example 6 is a full worked example of a business combination achieved in two stages, the first being 20 per cent, and the second an additional 60 per cent. The example considers two scenarios, firstly where the initial 20 per cent is accounted for at fair value with changes in fair value included in profit or loss, and secondly where the initial 20 per cent was an associate which was equity accounted. [IFRS 3(2004).IE Example 6]

6.8.2 *Purchases and sales of shares in a controlled entity*

Changes in percentage of interests (increases and decreases) of a controlled entity that do not result in a change in control do not fall within the definition of business combinations in IFRS 3. The accounting for such transactions was not covered by any authoritative IASB guidance, until the issue of IFRS 3(2008), and the associated revision of IAS 27. Prior to those revised Standards being applied, practices vary widely and, consequently, management is required to develop and apply an accounting policy in accordance with IAS 8.10 – 12.

Six methods currently used are explained below using the following example.

Example 6.8.2

Increasing a stake in a subsidiary

Company A holds 80 per cent of Company B, which was purchased for 1,000 at 1 January 20X5. In accordance with IAS 27, Company A consolidates Company B. Company A decides to acquire the residual 20 per cent of Company B at 31 December 20X6 for cash consideration of 400. The following are the assets and liabilities of Company B

	Recognised amounts		
	As recognised by Company A on acquisition	**As recognised by Company A at 31 December 20X6**	**Fair value at 31 December 20X6 (excluding goodwill)**
Goodwill	200	200	n/a
Other intangible	250	150	300
Property, plant & equipment	1,400	1,120	1,340
Receivables	250	550	550
Cash	200	500	500
Total assets	**2,300**	**2,520**	**2,690**
Payables	500	400	400
Other liabilities	600	500	500

Total liabilities	**1,100**	**900**	**900**
Net assets	**1,200**	**1,620**	**1,790**
Equity	1,000	1,000	
Post acquisition parent entity profits	–	336	
Outside equity interest	200	200	
Post acquisition profits – minority	–	84	
Total equity	**1,200**	**1,620**	

(NB: for the purposes of simplicity deferred tax impacts have been excluded from this example)

Method 1

Calculate goodwill as the difference between the consideration paid for the additional interest and the carrying amount of the net assets of the subsidiary.

Goodwill calculation

Consideration paid	400
Carrying amount of interest acquired	284
Goodwill recognised	116

Journal entry on acquisition

Dr	Minority interest (initial equity)	200	
Dr	Minority interest (retained profits)	84	
Dr	Goodwill	116	
Cr	Cash (cost of acquisition)		400

Advantages

- Ease of availability of information.
- Reflects fact that there is no change to assets and liabilities consolidated – 100 per cent was already consolidated and it appears reasonable that there should be no change in the values consolidated arising from this transaction.

Disadvantages

- Increases in asset values that would be considered by Company A in making the purchase decision over the extra 20 per cent are not separately recognised and are effectively subsumed in goodwill.
- This may in turn affect the recognition of impairment losses in future years as losses that should have been attributed to particular assets will be attributed to goodwill.

Method 2

Calculate goodwill by revaluing all of the identifiable assets and liabilities of the subsidiary to fair value. This is effected by completing the following steps:

- in the consolidated financial statements revalue the net identifiable assets and liabilities of the subsidiary to their fair value.
- allocate the revaluation difference arising between the revaluation reserve and the minority interest.
- calculate goodwill arising as the difference between the additional cost of the interest acquired and the increase in the group's interest, based on the fair value of net intangible assets.

Step 1: All identifiable assets and liabilities are revalued to their fair value at 31 December 20X6

Journal entry

Dr	P, P & E	220	
Dr	Intangible	150	
Cr	Revaluation		370

Step 2: Allocate the revaluation difference between the revaluation reserve and the minority interest

Revaluation entry above is split as follows

Cr	Revaluation – parent entity interest	296
Cr	Revaluation – minority interest	74

Step 3 :Calculate goodwill arising as difference between additional cost of shares acquired and increase in the group's interest (based on new fair values)

Goodwill calculation

Cost of additional interest	400
20% * net assets (1790*0.2)	358
Goodwill arising	42

Journal entry on acquisition

Dr	Minority interest – initial	200	
Dr	Minority interest – retained profits	84	
Dr	Minority interest – revaluation reserve	74	
Dr	Goodwill	42	
Cr	Cash (Cost of acquisition)		400

Advantages

- Reflects the fair value of the business at the date of the latest acquisition transaction.
- Attributes the fair value of the business to the appropriate assets and liabilities.
- Is directly analogous to a treatment allowed by IFRSs (that is step acquisitions prior to obtaining control in accordance with IFRS 3).

Disadvantages

- Enables entities to recognise revaluations that would otherwise be prohibited (i.e. the revaluation of the intangible above, revaluations of inventory).
- Would require entities to identify and measure intangibles and contingent liabilities subsequent to obtaining control – e.g. recognition of an internally generated intangible.
- Is a treatment that is like a business combination but does not meet the definition of business combinations as such, which may pose a problem in interacting with other standards that have special requirements relating to business combinations (e.g. IAS 12).
- A question could be raised as to whether this treatment triggers the need for an ongoing policy of revaluations (e.g. for P,P&E) as it could be considered that the exemption in IFRS 3 (that is, that revaluation accounting is not triggered by step acquisitions prior to obtaining control) cannot be applied.

Method 3

Calculate goodwill on the same basis as under method 2, but recognise only the proportion of the values attributable to the additional interest acquired.

Step 1: Revalue net identifiable assets and liabilities of the entity

In this example the P, P & E and intangibles had a different fair value than carrying amount.

	Carrying amount	Fair value	20% uplift
P,P & E	1,120	1,340	44
Intangible	150	300	30

Dr	P,P & E	44	
Dr	Intangible	30	
Cr	Revaluation reserve – minority interest		74

Step 2: Not required

Step 3: Calculate goodwill arising as difference between additional cost of shares acquired and increase in the group's interest (based on new fair values)

Goodwill calculation

Cost of additional interest	400
20% of net assets (1,420*0.2) +74	358
Goodwill	42

Journal entry on acquisition

Dr	Minority interest – initial	200
Dr	Minority interest – retained profits	84
Dr	Minority interest – revaluation reserve	74

Dr	Goodwill	42	
Cr	Cash – cost of acquisition		400

Advantages

- Does not recognise fair value adjustments on the previously held share of assets that would otherwise not be revalued.
- Reflects the fair value of what is being acquired.

Disadvantages

- Creates a mixed measurement model – the carrying amount of assets is neither original cost nor fair value at the later date.

Method 4

Calculate goodwill arising on the same basis as method 2, but not to recognise any of the revaluation surplus in the consolidated statement of financial position, instead debiting the variance to a reserve (for the purposes of illustration this is shown as a separate reserve, although it could be included in any relevant existing reserve balance, including potentially retained profits).

Calculation of goodwill

Cost of additional interest	400
20% * net assets (1790*0.2)	358
Goodwill arising	42

Journal entry on acquisition

Dr	Minority interest – initial	200	
Dr	Minority interest – retained profits	84	
Dr	Goodwill	42	
Dr	Reserve	74	
Cr	Cash – cost of acquisition		400

Advantages

- Assets carried at a single measurement model – that is the cost originally recognised when first consolidated.
- Minority interest share of uplift in value is reflected in the resulting net assets.

Disadvantages

- Creation of a reserve which does not have any apparent basis, and being a contra-equity item is not easily understood (if included in an existing reserve an explanation of the transaction would still be required as part of the equity reconciliation requirements).
- Increases in asset values that would be considered by Company A in making the purchase decision over the extra 20 per cent are not separately recognised and are effectively subsumed in a debit to equity. It is unclear how the debit balance in equity is carried forward, particularly considering issues of impairment – this is a debit to the

statement of financial position arising on an acquisition which is apparently never subjected to impairment testing.

Method 5

Goodwill should be based on the initial purchased goodwill, with changes in ownership interest recognised as an equity transaction. Therefore, goodwill should be adjusted on an increase in ownership to reflect that portion of goodwill attributable to the minority interest at the acquisition date that is now attributable to the parent. (Again, for illustrative purposes, the debit to equity is shown as a separate reserve, albeit that it may be feasible to include it within any relevant existing equity balance).

Calculation of goodwill

Initial acquisition goodwill (80%)	200
Therefore, 100% goodwill	250
Difference (Attributable to minority previously not recognised)	50

Journal entry on acquisition

Dr	Minority interest – initial	200	
Dr	Minority interest – retained profits	84	
Dr	Goodwill	50	
Dr	Reserve	66	
Cr	Cash – cost of acquisition		400

Advantages

- Goodwill is based on the value paid when the transaction was first considered a business combination.
- Assets carried at a single measurement model – that is the cost originally recognised when first consolidated.
- Ease of availability of information.

Disadvantages

- Creation of a reserve which does not have any apparent basis, and being a contra-equity item is not easily understood.
- Increases in asset values that would be considered by Company A in making the purchase decision over the extra 20 per cent are not separately recognised and are effectively subsumed in a debit to equity. It is unclear how the debit balance in equity is carried forward, particularly considering issues of impairment – this is a debit to the statement of financial position arising on an acquisition which is apparently never subjected to impairment testing.

Method 6

By reference to IFRS 3(2008), the increase in stake is treated as a transaction with equity holders and no adjustment is made to goodwill. Instead, the difference between the amount paid (£400) and the book value of the minority interest eliminated (£284), i.e. £116, is taken directly to equity.

Advantages

- Consistent with most recent IASB thinking on such transactions (see **5.6.1** in **chapter 33**).

Disadvantages

- An entity adopting this policy will never be able to recognise the 'full' amount of goodwill if, on obtaining control, it has less than 100% of a subsidiary, because IFRS 3(2004) does not allow minority interest to be recognised at fair value at the acquisition date.

Resulting statements of financial position of Company B recognised by Company A on consolidation

	Method 1	Method 2	Method 3	Method 4	Method 5	Method 6
Goodwill	316	242	242	242	250	200
Other intangible	150	300	180	150	150	150
Property, plant & equipment	1,120	1,340	1,164	1,120	1,120	1,120
Receivables	550	550	550	550	550	550
Cash	500	500	500	500	500	500
Total assets	2,636	2,932	2,636	2,562	2,570	2,520
Payables	400	400	400	400	400	400
Other liabilities	500	500	500	500	500	500
Total liabilities	900	900	900	900	900	900
Net assets	1,736	2,032	1,736	1,662	1,670	1,620
Equity	1,400	1,400	1,400	1,400	1,400	1,400
Post-acquisition parent entity profits	336	336	336	336	336	336
Revaluation/Other reserve	–	296	–	(74)	(66)	(116)
Outside equity interest	–	–	–			
Post acquisition profits – minority	–	–	–			
Total equity	1,736	2,032	1,736	1,662	1,670	1,620

Similarly, for decreases in the parent's ownership interest that do not result in a change in control, an entity will need to adopt a policy that is compatible with the approach it has taken to account for increases (e.g. if it capitalises additional goodwill for an increased interest, it will derecognise an appropriate proportion of goodwill on a decrease). Any difference between consideration received and the adjustments made to minority interests and goodwill will either be recognised in profit or loss as a gain or loss on partial disposal, or treated as a transaction with owners of equity (providing that whichever policy is chosen is compatible with that taken to account for increases.)

6.8.3 *Statutory obligation to launch a takeover bid*

Example 6.8.3

Statutory obligation to launch a takeover bid

Entity A has an agreement with the shareholders of Entity B to acquire a 60 per cent interest in B, a listed company. Under local law, an investor purchasing at least 30 per cent of a listed company is obliged to launch a takeover bid on the remaining shares. All conditions for the acquisition of the 60 per cent interest have been satisfied. Should the obligation to launch a takeover bid for the remaining interest in the listed company result in the recognition of a liability?

Entity A is obliged under local law to offer to acquire the remaining shares of B. A financial instrument is any contract that gives rise to a financial asset of one entity and a financial liability or equity instrument of another entity. In addition, IAS 32.AG12 clarifies that liabilities or assets that are not contractual (such as income taxes that are created as a result of statutory requirements imposed by governments) are not financial liabilities or financial assets.

For the holders of the remaining 40 percent of the shares in B, this statutory offer is not a contractual right to receive cash evidenced by a financial instrument and is not a financial asset. For A, the statutory offer is not a contractual obligation evidenced by a financial instrument and no financial liability should be recognised.

The acquisition of the minority interest is accounted for when it occurs. Therefore, when A acquires all or some of the minority interest after the 60 per cent interest acquisition, the minority interest acquisition will be accounted for separately. Entity A's selected accounting policy for the acquisition of minority interests will apply (see **example 6.8.2**).

Entity A should consider whether a provision for an onerous contract should be recognised in accordance with IAS 37 as a result of the statutory obligation to launch a takeover bid.

7 Initial accounting determined provisionally

IFRS 3 specifies accounting and disclosure requirements for initial accounting which can only be determined provisionally, subsequent adjustments to provisional fair values, subsequent correction of errors, and subsequent revisions of estimates.

Initial accounting involves identifying and measuring fair values of the cost of the combination, and the acquiree's net assets. Where, at the end of the acquirer's first accounting period following the combination, this can only be done on a provisional basis, then the following steps apply:

- In the first period, the acquirer accounts using provisional fair values. [IFRS 3(2004).62]
- The fact that provisional values have been used shall be disclosed together with an explanation of why this is the case. [IFRS 3(2004).69]
- Adjustments to provisional values may be made within twelve months of the acquisition date, and accounted for as if they were made at the acquisition date. [IFRS 3(2004).62] Therefore:
    - acquiree's net assets are calculated as if the adjusted fair value was recognised at the acquisition date, for example, depreciation is restated based on the revised fair value from the acquisition date;
    - goodwill or 'negative goodwill' taken as immediate income is restated as at the acquisition date;
    - comparative figures are restated accordingly; [IFRS 3(2004).62] and
    - disclosure is required of the amounts and explanations of adjustments recognised in the current period; [IFRS 3(2004).73(b)]
- Revisions of estimates identified after the twelve month period are not adjusted retrospectively, but accounted for in the period in which they are identified. [IFRS 3(2004).63]
- Two exceptions to the twelve month limit on adjustment to provisional fair values are:
    - adjustments arising from re-estimating contingent consideration; [IFRS 3(2004).33 – 34] and
    - recovery of the acquiree's tax loss carry-forwards and other deferred tax assets which did not qualify for recognition at acquisition – see **6.3.9** above. [IFRS 3(2004).65]

There appears to be little logic in the IASB's decision to limit the hindsight period for adjustment of provisional fair values to twelve months from the acquisition date rather than to the end of the accounting period in which that anniversary falls. In practice, the time limit will have most impact where there is some reporting requirement, such as interim financial statements, occurring between the anniversary and the end of that same accounting period.

IFRS 3's Illustrative Examples include three relevant examples: example 7 provides an example of the use and adjustment of provisional fair value of land, example 8 illustrates an error in the fair value of property, plant and equipment, and example 9 illustrates an error in the fair value of property, plant and equipment with a consequent impact on goodwill impairment.

8 Disclosure

IFRS 3 contains extensive disclosure requirements which cover:

- business combinations which occurred in the period (see **8.1**);
- gains and losses and adjustments in the current period which relate to business combinations in the current or previous periods (see **8.2**);
- changes to the carrying amount of goodwill (see **8.3**); and
- business combinations occurring after the reporting period but before the financial statements are authorised for issue (see **8.4**).

8.1 Business combinations occurring during the period

8.1.1 Disclosures required

The overall objective is to disclose information that will enable users of financial statements to evaluate the nature and financial effect of business combinations. [IFRS 3(2004).66] If the information listed in the following sections is insufficient to meet this objective, whatever additional information is necessary should also be provided. [IFRS 3(2004).77]

The following should be disclosed for each business combination that was effected during the period:

[IFRS 3(2004).67]

(a) the names and descriptions of the combining entities or businesses;

(b) the acquisition date;

(c) the percentage of voting equity instruments acquired;

(d) the cost of the combination and a description of the components of that cost, including any costs directly attributable to the combination. When equity instruments are issued or issuable as part of the cost, the following should also be disclosed:

   (i) the number of equity instruments issued or issuable; and

   (ii) the fair value of those instruments and the basis for determining that fair value.

If no published price exists for the instruments at the date of exchange, the significant assumptions used to determine fair value should be disclosed.

If a published price exists at the date of exchange but was not used as the basis for determining the cost of the combination, that fact should be disclosed together with:

- the reasons the published price was not used;
- the method and significant assumptions used to attribute a value to the equity instruments; and
- the aggregate amount of the difference between the value attributed to, and the published price of, the equity instruments;

(e) details of any operations the entity has decided to dispose of as a result of the combination;

(f) the amounts recognised at the acquisition date for each class of the acquiree's assets, liabilities and contingent liabilities, and, unless disclosure would be impracticable, the carrying amounts of each of those classes, determined in accordance with IFRSs, immediately before the combination. If such disclosure would be impracticable, that fact should be disclosed, together with an explanation of why this is the case;

(g) the amount of any excess recognised in profit or loss in accordance with IFRS 3(2004).56 (see **6.7**), and the line item in the statement of comprehensive income in which the excess is recognised;

(h) a description of the factors that contributed to a cost that results in the recognition of goodwill — a description of each intangible asset that was not recognised separately from goodwill and an explanation of why the intangible asset's fair value could not be measured reliably—or a description of the nature of any excess recognised in profit or loss in accordance with IFRS 3(2004).56 (see **6.7**); and

(i) the amount of the acquiree's profit or loss since the acquisition date included in the acquirer's profit or loss for the period, unless disclosure would be impracticable. If such disclosure would be impracticable, that fact should be disclosed, together with an explanation of why this is the case.

8.1.2 *Business combinations that are individually immaterial*

The information listed at **8.1.1** should be disclosed in aggregate for business combinations effected during the reporting period that are individually immaterial. [IFRS 3(2004).68]

8.1.3 *Initial accounting determined provisionally*

If the initial accounting for a business combination effected during the period was determined only provisionally (see **section 7**), that fact should be disclosed together with an explanation of why this is the case. [IFRS 3(2004).69]

8.1.4 *Other disclosures*

Unless disclosure would be impracticable, the following information should also be given:

[IFRS 3(2004).70]

(a) the revenue of the combined entity for the period as though the acquisition date for all business combinations effected during the period had been the beginning of that period; and

(b) the profit or loss of the combined entity for the period as though the acquisition date for all business combinations effected during the period had been the beginning of the period.

If disclosure of this information would be impracticable, that fact should be disclosed, together with an explanation of why this is the case.

8.2 Gains, losses, error corrections and other adjustments

Information should be disclosed so as to enable users of financial statements to evaluate the financial effects of gains, losses, error corrections and other adjustments recognised in the current period that relate to business combinations that were effected in the current or in previous periods. [IFRS 3(2004).72] If the detailed information listed below is insufficient to meet this objective, whatever additional information is necessary should also be provided. [IFRS 3(2004).77]

The following information should be given:

[IFRS 3(2004).73]

(a) the amount and an explanation of any gain or loss recognised in the current period that:

(i) relates to the identifiable assets acquired or liabilities or contingent liabilities assumed in a business combination that was effected in the current or a previous period; and

(ii) is of such size, nature or incidence that disclosure is relevant to an understanding of the combined entity's financial performance;

(b) if the initial accounting for a business combination that was effected in the immediately preceding period was determined only provisionally at the end of that period, the amounts and explanations of the adjustments to the provisional values recognised during the current period;

(c) the information about error corrections required to be disclosed by IAS 8 for any of the acquiree's identifiable assets, liabilities or contingent liabilities, or changes in the values assigned to those items, that the acquirer recognises during the current period in accordance with IFRS 3(2004).63 & 64 (see **section 7**).

8.3 Changes to goodwill

Information should be disclosed so as to enable users of financial statements to evaluate changes in the carrying amount of goodwill during the period. [IFRS 3(2004).74] If the detailed information listed below is insufficient to meet this objective, whatever additional information is necessary should also be provided. [IFRS 3(2004).77]

A reconciliation of the carrying amount of goodwill at the beginning and end of the period should be provided, showing separately:

[IFRS 3(2004).75]

(a) the gross amount and accumulated impairment losses at the beginning of the period;

(b) additional goodwill recognised during the period except goodwill included in a disposal group that, on acquisition, meets the criteria to be classified as held for sale in accordance with IFRS 5 (see **chapter 29**);

(c) adjustments resulting from the subsequent recognition of deferred tax assets during the period in accordance with IFRS 3(2004).65 (see **section 6.3.9**);

(d) goodwill included in a disposal group classified as held for sale in accordance with IFRS 5 (see **chapter 29**) and goodwill derecognised during the period without having previously been included in a disposal group classified as held for sale;

(e) impairment losses recognised during the period in accordance with IAS 36 (see **chapter 9**);

(f) net exchange differences arising during the period in accordance with IAS 21 (see **chapter 28**);

(g) any other changes in the carrying amount during the period; and

(h) the gross amount and accumulated impairment losses at the end of the period.

In addition to requirement (e) above, any disclosures required by IAS 36 in respect of the recoverable amount and impairment of goodwill should also be provided (see **chapter 9**). [IFRS 3(2004).76]

8.4 Business combinations occurring after the reporting period

Unless such disclosure would be impracticable, the information listed at **8.1.1** should also be disclosed for each business combination effected after the reporting period but before the financial statements are authorised for issue. If disclosure of any of that information would be impracticable, that fact should be disclosed, together with an explanation of why this is the case. [IFRS 3(2004).71]

Index